The Holy Qur'an

Text, Translation and Commentary

by

Abdullah Yusuf Ali

Published by

Tahrike Tarsile Qur'an, Inc.

Publishers and Distributers of Holy Qur'an

P.O. Box 731115

Elmhurst, New York 11373-0115

Published by

Tahrike Tarsile Qur'an, Inc.

P.O. Box 731115

Elmhurst, New York 11373-0115

E-mail: ttq@koranusa.org

http://www.koranusa.org

U.S. Edition 2001

Library of Congress Catalog Number: 87-051218

British Library Cataloging in Publication Data

ISBN: Paperback 0-940368-31-5

ISBN: Hardback 0-940368-32-3

Printed in Great Britain

PREFACE TO FIRST EDITION, 1934

I DO not wish to write a long Preface. I wish merely to explain the history of my Project, the scope and plan of this work, and the objects I have held in view.

In separate introductory Notes I have mentioned the useful books to which I have referred, under the headings: Commentaries on the Qur-ān; Translations of the Qur-ān; and Useful Works of Reference. I have similarly explained the system which I have followed in the transliteration of Arabic words and names; the Abbreviations I have used; and the principal divisions of the Qur-ān.

It may be asked: Is there any need for a fresh English Translation? To those who ask this question I commend a careful consideration of the facts which I have set out in my Note on Translations. After they have read it, I would invite them to take any particular passage in Part I, say ii. 74 or ii. 102, or ii. 164 in the second Part and compare it with any previous version they choose. If they find that I have helped them even the least bit further in understanding its meaning, or appreciating its beauty, or catching something of the grandeur of the original, I would claim that my humble attempt is justified.

It is the duty of every Muslim, man, woman, or child, to read the Qur-ān and understand it according to his own capacity. If any one of us attains to some knowledge or understanding of it by study, contemplation, and the test of life, both outward and inward, it is his duty, according to his capacity, to instruct others, and share with them the joy and peace which result from contact with the spiritual world. The Qur-ān—indeed every religious book—has to be read, not only with the tongue and voice and eyes, but with the best light that our intellect can supply, and even more, with the truest and purest light which our heart and conscience can give us. It is in this spirit that I would have my readers approach the Qur-ān.

It was between the ages of four and five that I first learned to read its Arabic words, to revel in its rhythm and music, and wonder at its meaning. I have a dim recollection of the *Khatm* ceremony which closed that stage. It was called "completion": it really just *began* a spiritual awakening that has gone on ever since. My revered father taught me Arabic, but I must have imbibed from him into my innermost being something more,—something which told me that all the world's thoughts, all the world's most beautiful languages and literatures, are but vehicles for that ineffable message which comes to the heart in rare moments of ecstasy. The soul of mysticism and ecstasy is in the Qur-ān, as well as that plain guidance for the plain man which a world in a hurry affects to consider as sufficient. It is good to make this personal confession, to an age in which it is in the highest degree unfashionable to speak of religion or spiritual peace or consolation, an age in which words like these draw forth only derision, pity, or contempt.

I have explored Western lands, Western manners, and the depths of Western thought and Western learning, to an extent which has rarely fallen to the lot of an Eastern mortal. But I have never lost touch with my Eastern heritage. Through all my successes and failures I have learned to rely more and more upon the one true thing in all life—the voice that speaks in a tongue above that of mortal man. For me the embodiment of that voice has been in the noble words of the Arabic Qur-ān, which I have tried to translate for myself and apply to my experience again and again. The service of the Qur-ān has been the pride and the privilege of many Muslims. I felt that with such life-experience as has fallen to my lot, my service to the Qur-ān should be to present it in a fitting garb in English. That ambition I have cherished in my mind for more than forty years. I have collected books and materials for it. I have visited places, undertaken journeys, taken notes, sought the society of men, and tried to explore their thoughts and hearts, in order to equip

myself for the task. Sometimes I have considered it too stupendous for me,—the double task of understanding the original, and reproducing its nobility, its beauty, its poetry, its grandeur, and its sweet practical reasonable application to everyday experience. Then I have blamed myself for lack of courage,—the spiritual courage of men who dared all in the Cause which was so dear to them.

Two sets of apparently accidental circumstances at last decided me. A man's life is subject to inner storms far more devastating than those in the physical world around him. In such a storm, in the bitter anguish of a personal sorrow which nearly unseated my reason and made life seem meaningless, a new hope was born out of a systematic pursuit of my long-cherished project. Watered by tears, my manuscript began to grow in depth and earnestness if not in bulk. I guarded it like a secret treasure. Wanderer that I am, I carried it about, thousands of miles, to all sorts of countries and among all sorts of people. At length, in the city of Lahore, I happened to mention the matter to some young people who held me in respect and affection. They showed an enthusiasm and an eagerness which surprised me. They almost took the matter out of my hands. They asked for immediate publication. I had various bits ready, but not even one complete *Sīpāra*. They made me promise to complete at least one *Sīpāra* before I left Lahore. As if by magic, a publisher, a *kātib* (calligraphist to write the Arabic Text), an engraver of blocks for such text, and a printer were found, all equally anxious to push forward the scheme. Blessed be youth, for its energy and determination. "Where others flinch, rash youth will dare!"

Gentle and discerning reader! what I wish to present to you is an English Interpretation, side by side with the Arabic Text. The English shall be, not a mere substitution of one word for another, but the best expression I can give to the fullest meaning which I can understand from the Arabic Text. The rhythm, music, and exalted tone of the original should be reflected in the English Interpretation. It may be but a faint reflection, but such beauty and power as my pen can command shall be brought to its service. I want to make English itself an Islamic language, if such a person as I can do it. And I must give you all the accessory aid which I can. In rhythmic prose, or free verse (whichever you like to call it), I prepare the atmosphere for you in a running Commentary. Introducing the subject generally, I come to the actual *Sūras*. Where they are short, I give you one or two paragraphs of my rhythmic Commentary to prepare you for the Text. Where the *Sūra* is long, I introduce the subject-matter in short appropriate paragraphs of the Commentary from time to time, each indicating the particular verses to which it refers. The paragraphs of the running Commentary are numbered consecutively, with some regard to the connection with the preceding and the following paragraphs. It is possible to read this running rhythmic Commentary by itself to get a general bird's-eye view of the contents of the Holy Book before you proceed to the study of the Book itself.

The text in English is printed in larger type than the running Commentary, in order to distinguish, at a glance, the substance from the shadow. It is also displayed differently, in parallel columns with the Arabic Text. Each *Sūra* and the verse of each *Sūra* is separately numbered, and the numbers are shown page by page. The system of numbering the verses has not been uniform in previous translations. European editors and translators have allowed their numbering to diverge considerably from that accepted in the East. This causes confusion in giving and verifying references. The different *Qirāats* sometimes differ as to the punctuation stops and the numbering of the verses. This is not a vital matter, but it causes confusion in references. It is important that at least in Islamic countries one system of numbering should be adopted. I have adopted mainly that of the Egyptian edition published under the authority of the King of Egypt. This will probably be accepted in Egypt and in Arabic-speaking countries, as those countries generally look up to Egypt in matters of literature. I am glad to see that the text shortly to be published by the Anjuman-i-Ḥimāyat-i-Islām of Lahore is following the same

system of numbering. I recommend to other publishers in India the same good example. If once this is done we shall have a uniform system of numbering. I have retained the numbering of Sections, as it is universally used in the Arabic copies, and marks a logical division of the *Sūras*. I have supplied a further aid to the reader in indicating sub-divisions of the Sections into paragraphs. They are not numbered, but are distinguished by the use of a flowery initial letter.

In translating the Text I have aired no views of my own, but followed the received Commentators. Where they differ among themselves, I have had to choose what appeared to me to be the most reasonable opinion from all points of view. Where it is a question merely of words, I have not considered the question important enough to discuss in the Notes, but where it is a question of substance, I hope adequate explanations will be found in the Notes. Where I have departed from the literal translation in order to express the spirit of the original better in English, I have explained the literal meaning in the Notes. For example, see ii. 104 n. and ii. 26 n. In choosing an English word for an Arabic word a translator necessarily exercises his own judgment and may be unconsciously expressing a point of view, but that is inevitable.

Let me explain the scope of the Notes. I have made them as short as possible consistently with the object I have in view, *viz.*, to give to the English reader, scholar as well as general reader, a fairly complete but concise view of what I understand to be the meaning of the Text. To discuss theological controversies or enter into polemical arguments I have considered outside my scope. Such discussions and arguments may be necessary and valuable, but they should find a place in separate treatises, if only out of respect to the Holy Book. Besides, such discussions leave no room for more important matters on which present-day readers desire information. In this respect our Commentators have not always been discreet. On questions of law, the Qur-ān lays down general principles, and these I have explained. I have avoided technical details: these will be found discussed in their proper place in my book on "Anglo-Muhammadan Law." Nor have I devoted much space to grammatical or philological Notes. On these points I consider that the labours of the vast body of our learned men in the past have left little new to say now. There is usually not much controversy, and I have accepted their conclusions without setting out the reasons for them. Where it has been necessary for the understanding of the Text to refer to the particular occasion for the revelation of a particular verse, I have done so briefly, but have not allowed it to absorb a disproportionate amount of space. It will be found that every verse revealed for a particular occasion has also a general meaning. The particular occasion and the particular people concerned have passed away, but the general meaning and its application remain true for all time. What we are concerned about now, in the fourteenth century of the Hijra, is: what guidance can we draw for ourselves from the message of God?

I spoke of the general meaning of the verses. Every earnest and reverent student of the Qur-ān, as he proceeds with his study, will find, with an inward joy difficult to describe, how this general meaning also enlarges as his own capacity for understanding increases. It is like a traveller climbing a mountain: the higher he goes, the farther he sees. From a literary point of view the poet Keats has described his feeling when he discovered Chapman's Homer:—

Then felt I like some watcher of the skies
When a new planet swims into his ken,
Or like stout Cortez when with eagle eyes
He stared at the Pacific,—and all his men
Looked at each other with a wild surmise,—
Silent, upon a peak in Darien.

How much greater is the joy and sense of wonder and miracle when the Qur-ān opens our spiritual eyes! The meaning which we thought we had grasped expands. New worlds are opened out. As we progress, still newer, and again newer worlds "swim into our ken." The miracle deepens and deepens, and almost com-

pletely absorbs us. And yet we know that the "face of God"—our final goal—has not yet been reached. We are in the *mulk* of Sulaiman (Q. ii. 102), which the evil ones denied, belied, and even turned into blasphemy. But we can ignore blasphemy, ridicule and contempt, for we are on the threshold of Realities, and a little perfume from the garden of the Holy One has already gladdened our nostrils.

Such meaning it is most difficult to express. But where I can, I have indicated it in the Notes, in the Commentary, and with the help of the rhythm and the elevated language of the Text.

The Arabic Text I have had printed from photographic blocks made for me by Master Muḥammad Sharīf. The calligraphy is from the pen of Pīr 'Abdul Hamīd, with whom I have been in touch and who has complied with my desire for a bold round hand, with the words clearly separated, the vowel points accurately placed over or under the letters to which they relate, and the verses duly numbered and placed in juxtaposition with their English equivalents. Calligraphy occupies an important place in Muslim Art, and it is my desire that my version should not in any way be deficient in this respect.

I have been fortunate in securing the co-operation of Professor Ẕafar Iqbál in looking over the proofs of the Arabic Text. In connection with the Anjuman's edition of the Arabic Qur-ān he has devoted much time and thought to the correct punctuation of the Text, and he has also investigated its history and problems. I hope he will some day publish these valuable notes. I have been privileged to see the Anjuman's Text before its formal publication. I consider it the most carefully prepared Text of any produced in India, and I have generally followed it in punctuation and the numbering of verses,—the only points on which any difficulties are likely to arise on the Quranic Text.

It has been my desire to have the printing done in the best style possible, with new type, on good glazed paper, and with the best ink procurable. I hope the result will please those who are good enough to approve of the more essential features of the work. The proprietors of the Ripon Press and all their staff, but especially Mr. Badruddīn Badr, their Proof Examiner, have taken a keen interest in their work. The somewhat unusual demands made on their time and attention they have met cheerfully, and I am obliged to them. The publisher, Shaikh Muḥammad Ashraf, has thrown himself heart and soul into his work, and I hope the public will appreciate his efforts.

My plan is to issue each *Sīpāra* as it is ready, at intervals of not more than three months. As the work proceeds, I hope it will be possible to accelerate the pace. The paging will be continuous in the subsequent volumes. The final binding will be in either three or two volumes. It is my intention to provide a complete analytical Index to the whole. I hope all interested will sign the publisher's subscription order in advance.

One final word to my readers. Read, study, and digest the Holy Book. Read slowly, and let it sink into your heart and soul. Such study will, like virtue, be its own reward. If you find anything in this volume to criticise, please let it not spoil your enjoyment of the rest. If you write to me, quoting chapter and verse, I shall be glad to consider your criticism, but let it not vex you if I exercise my own judgment in deciding for myself. Any corrections accepted will be gratefully acknowledged. On the other hand, if there is something that specially pleases you or helps you, please do not hesitate to write to me. I have given up other interests to help you. It will be a pleasure to know that my labour has not been in vain. If you address me care of my Publisher at his Lahore address, he will always forward the letters to me.

A. YŪSUF 'ALĪ.

LAHORE
4th April, 1934
=18th of the month
of Pilgrimage, 1352 H.

PREFACE TO THIRD EDITION, 1938

Besides the names which I mentioned in my Preface of 1934, of those who have assisted me in various ways, I have much pleasure in adding a few more at this stage. Khān Ṣāḥib Khwāja Laṭīf Aḥmad, of the Central Provinces Educational Service, has been a diligent and critical reader of the Parts as issued, and his friendly correspondence has enabled me to correct misprints and elucidate some points. Mr. Fadhl Muḥammad Khān, I.F.S., of Lahore, as well as Mian Muhammad 'Abdullāh, B.A., LL.B., of Lahore, have also been helpful in pointing out misprints. Maulvi Muhammad Shafī', Principal of the Oriental College, Lahore, has been good enough to answer most readily my queries on questions of scholarship referred to him. To these and other gentlemen, who have favoured me with correspondence, I have much pleasure in expressing my obligation.

The zeal and energy which my publisher, Shaikh Muḥammad Ashraf, has thrown into the work, require renewed acknowledgement. For four years he and I have co-operated in a great undertaking, and all processes connected with it have been carried out by loving Muslim hands.

Since I last greeted my readers collectively I have been able to perform the Pilgrimage to the holy city of Mecca and the sacred territory around it and seen with my own eyes the city and territory of Medina, with all the country around and between the holy Cities. I have realised for myself the scenes in which the revelations came which I have humbly sought to interpret. I hope that some glimpses of this experience will have been conveyed to my dear readers. Will they pray that God may give me strength to complete this work and to serve Islam in other ways ?

A. YŪSUF 'ALĪ.

PREFACE TO THIRD EDITION, 1938

Besides the ladies which I mentioned in my Preface of 1934, as those who have assisted me in various ways, I have much pleasure in adding a few more at this stage. Khan Sahib Khwaja Laqir Ahmad, of the Central Provinces Educational Service, has been a diligent and critical reader of the parts as issued and his friendly correspondence has enabled me to correct misprints and elucidate some points. Mr. Kazim Muhammad Khan, I.C.S. of Lahore, as well as Mian Muhammad Abdullah, B.A., LL.B., of Lahore, have also been helpful in pointing out omissions. Maulvi Muhammad Shafi, Principal of the Oriental College, Lahore, has been good enough to answer most readily my queries on questions of scholarship referred to him. To these and other gentlemen, who have favoured me with correspondence, I have much pleasure in expressing my obligation.

The zeal and energy which my publisher, Shaikh Muhammad Ashraf, has thrown into the work require renewed acknowledgement. For four years he and I have co-operated in a great undertaking, and all processes connected with it have been carried out by loving Muslim hands.

Since I last greeted my readers collectively I have been able to perform the Pilgrimage to the holy city of Mecca and the sacred territory around it and seen with my own eyes the city and territory of Madinah, with all the country around and between the holy Cities. I have realised for myself the scenes in which the revelations came which I have humbly sought to interpret. I hope that some glimpses of this experience will have been conveyed to my dear readers. Will they pray that God may give me strength to complete this work and to serve Islam in other ways?

A. YUSUF ALI

COMMENTARIES ON THE QUR-ĀN

QURANIC literature is so voluminous that no single man can compass a perusal of the whole. Besides the extant works there were innumerable works written for special groups of people or from special points of view or for special purposes, which have perished. And more works are being added every day. The activity in this line has never been greater than it is now.

There is no Book in the world in whose service so much talent, so much labour, so much time and money have been expended as has been the case with the Qur-ān. A mere glance at Imām Suyūṭī's (d. 911 H.) *Itqān* or Ḥājī Khalīfa's (d. 1059 H.) *Kashf-uẓ-ẓunūn* will show the encyclopædic volume of the Quranic sciences in their day.

Since then the volume has continued to go on increasing, although it must be admitted that the quality of the later literature on the subject leaves much to be desired. With the retrogression of the Islamic nations in original work in science, art, and philosophy, and the concomitant limitation in their outlook and experience in various phases of intellectual and spiritual life, has come a certain limitation in the free spirit of research and enquiry. The new Renaissance of Islam which is just beginning will, it is hoped, sweep away cobwebs and let in the full light of reason and understanding.

The need for an explanation of the verses of the Qur-ān arose quite early. Even before the whole of the Qur-ān was revealed, people used to ask the Apostle all sorts of questions as to the meaning of certain words in the verses revealed, or of their bearing on problems as they arose, or details of certain historical or spiritual matters on which they sought more light. The Apostle's answers were carefully stored in the memory of the Companions (*aṣ-ḥāb*) and were afterwards written down. In the next generation, the *Tābi'īn*, were those who had not personally conversed with the Apostle, like the Companions, but had conversed with the Companions and learned from them. Subsequent generations always went back to establish a chain of evidence through the *Tābi'īn* and the Companions. Through them grew up the science of *Hadīth* or Traditions. As this literature grew, it became necessary to establish strict rules by which the evidence could be examined and tested, so as to separate that which was considered to be established from that which was doubtful or weak, and that which was to be rejected as unproved. In the evolution of the science of *Ḥadīth*, it became clear that even among the Companions certain persons had better memories than others, or better opportunities of becoming really acquainted with the Apostle's true meaning, or in other ways, a better title to be called true expositors, and the number of such persons came to be limited to ten only. Similarly the claims of the *Tābi'īn* came to be examined and graded, and so on. Thus arose a new science, in which the names and positions of persons in *Ḥadīth* literature were examined biographically and in other ways.

The *Ḥadīth* literature dealt with all sorts of matters, including Theology, Ethics, and Exegesis (explanation of the Qur-ān). Exegesis soon became an independent science by itself and was called *Tafsīr*, and the sphere of *Tafsīr* itself began to widen as the experience and knowledge of the Arabs and Arabic writers began to increase. Besides the examination of correct traditions from various kinds and grades of authorities, it began to examine the meaning of words philologically, collecting a vast amount of learning as to root meanings, the usage of the Quraish tribe of Arabs, to which the Apostle belonged, the usage and meaning of words in the purest original Arabic before it became mixed up with foreign idioms and usages by the use of the Arabic language by non-Arabs in Islam, and by the influence of the enormous geographical expansion of the Arab race in the first few centuries of Islam. The increasing knowledge of history and of Jewish and Christian legends enabled

the Commentators to illustrate the Text of the Holy Book with reference to these. Sometimes the amount of Jewish stuff (some of it absurd), which found its way into the Commentaries, was out of all proportion to its importance and relevance, and gave rise to the legend, which has been exploited by polemical Christian and Jewish writers, that Islam was built up on an imperfect knowledge of Christianity and Judaism, or that it accepts as true the illustrative legends from the Talmud or the Midrash or various fantastic schools of Christianity. Then came philosophy and the mystic doctrine of the *Ṣūfī* schools. The development of the science of *kalām* (built on formal logic), and its further offshoot the *'Ilm-ul-'Aqāid* (the philosophical exposition of the grounds of our belief) introduced further elements on the intellectual side, while *Tāawīl* (esoteric exposition of the hidden or inner meaning) introduced elements on the spiritual side, based on a sort of transcendental intuition of the expositor. The Sūfī mystics at least adhered to the rules of their own Orders, which were very strict. But many of the non-Ṣūfī writers on *Tāawīl* indulged in an amount of licence in interpretation which has rightly called forth a protest on the part of the more sober 'Ulamā.

For my part I agree with this protest. While freely reserving the right of individual judgment on the part of every earnest writer, I think the art of interpretation must stick as closely as possible to the text which it seeks to interpret. Every serious writer and thinker has a right to use all the knowledge and experience he possesses in the service of the Qur-ān. But he must not mix up his own theories and conclusions, however reasonable, with the interpretation of the Text itself, which is usually perfectly perspicuous, as it claims it to be. Our difficulties in interpretation often arise from various causes, of which I will mention just a few:

(1) Arabic words in the Text have acquired other meanings than those which were understood by the Apostle and his Companions. All living languages undergo such transformations. The early Commentators and Philologists went into these matters with a very comprehensive grasp, and we must accept their conclusions. Where they are not unanimous, we must use our judgment and historic sense in adopting the interpretation of that authority which appeals to us most. We must not devise new verbal meanings.

(2) Even since the early Commentators wrote, the Arabic language has further developed, and later Commentators often abandon the interpretations of earlier Commentators without sufficient reason. In exercising our selective judgment in such cases it would be a good rule to prefer the earlier to the later interpretation, though, where a later writer has reviewed the earlier interpretations and given good reasons for his own view, he has an advantage which we must freely concede to him.

(3) Classical Arabic has a vocabulary in which the meaning of each root-word is so comprehensive that it is difficult to interpret it in a modern analytical language word for word, or by the use of the same word in all places where the original word occurs in the Text. A striking example is furnished by the word *Ṣabr*, about which see my notes on ii. 45 and ii. 153. Even though one particular shade of meaning may be predominant in any particular passage, the others are latent. So in a ray of light, when a prism analyses it, we may look at a portion of the field where a particular colour predominates, but other colours do not escape our glance. An Arabic word is often a full ray of light; when a translator looks at it through the prism of a modern analytical language, he misses a great deal of its meaning by confining his attention to one particular colour. European translators have often failed in this respect and sometimes even been landed in absurdities because these delicate rich tones are not studied in their languages or literatures, and they do not look for them or appreciate them in the best examples of Oriental style. If they despise them or think them fantastic, they had best leave the interpretation of Oriental literatures alone. This is all the more so in religious or spiritual literature. No human language can possibly be adequate for the expression of the highest spiritual thought. Such thought must be expressed symbolically in terse and comprehensive words, out of which people will

perceive just as much light and colour as their spiritual eyes are capable of perceiving. It is possible that their prism will only show them a dark blue while a whole glorious symphony of colours is hidden from their eyes. And so it comes about that through the prism of a clever English translation, poor 'Umar (Omar) Khayyām emerges as a sensualist and cynic who sees no higher purpose in life than drinking wine, dallying with women, and holding up his hands in despair at "this sorry scheme of things entire." And so the parables of stern morality in the Qur-ān, its mystic earnestness, and its pictures of future beatitude are distorted into idle fables, incoherent effusions, and a sensual paradise!

(4) An opposite error sometimes arises because in certain matters the rich vocabulary of the Qur-ān distinguishes between things and ideas of a certain kind by special words, for which there is only a general word in English. Instances are: *Raḥmān* and *Raḥīm* (Most Merciful); see i. 1. n.; *afā*, *ṣafaḥa*, *gafara* (to forgive); see ii. 109 n.; and the various words for Creation; see ii. 117 n. The fact is that it gives us a very limited idea of God's Mercy, when we only use the English word "mercy": the Quranic idea implies not only pity and forgiveness but the Grace which protects us and keeps us from sin, and indeed guides us to the light of His "Countenance." So the "forgiveness" of God is a thing totally different in quality from the forgiveness which a man can give to his brother man: the equation implied in "Forgive us our trespasses as we forgive those that trespass against us" is a misleading fallacy. So, again, "Creation" is not just a simple process done by God at some remote time and finished with: the Quranic idea implies various processes and the continuous presence and activity of God in His Creation.

(5) God's purpose is eternal, and His plan is perfect, but man's intelligence is limited at its very best. In the same individual it grows and declines according to the strength of his powers and the width of his experience. If we take mankind collectively the variations are even greater from age to age and from people to people. There is thus no finality in human interpretation. And in the thing interpreted—God's Creation—there is constant flux and change. So that the impact of the one on the other must yield diverse results. The view of Kunchinjunga must vary infinitely according to the position of the observer, even if Kunchinjunga remained the same. But if Kunchinjunga itself varies, there is a double cause of variation in the view. So I believe in progressive interpretation, in the need for understanding and explaining spiritual matters from different angles. The difficulties that confront me may not be the same as those that confront you. The problems which our age has to meet may not be the same as the problems which puzzled earnest minds of the fourth or sixth or later centuries of the Hijra. Therefore it is no merit to hug the solutions offered in the fourth or sixth centuries when our souls cry out in hunger for solace in the fourteenth century of the Hijra.

The distinction drawn by Commentators between matters of report (*manqūlāt*) and matters of judgment (*ma'qūlāt*) is a sound one, and I heartily accept it. But I would extend the scope of the *ma'qūlāt* far beyond questions of idiom and meaning. In the former the issues are: what actually happened, or what was actually said, or how were certain things done? Here the closer we go back to contemporary authority, the better. In the latter, the issues are: what is the bearing of this truth on our lives, or what illustration helps us best to grasp this, or what is the wisdom we can extract from this? In such matters, the closer we come to our own circumstances and experiences, the better. It is not only our right but our duty to seek honestly our own solutions, and while we respect authority, we must not neglect or despise the gifts which God has accumulated for us through the ages.

The principles on which I have worked may be briefly stated. In matters of philology and language I accept the best authority among those who were competent to deal with these questions: the older the better. In matters of narration, contemporary authorities are best, subject to such corrections as have to be applied for their points of view. As to the particular occasions on which particular verses

were revealed, the information is interesting and valuable from a historical point of view, and our older writers have collected ample material for it. But to lay too much stress on it to-day puts the picture out of all perspective. The Qur-ān was not revealed for a particular occasion only, but for all time. The particular occasion is now past. Our chief interest now is to see how it can guide us in our present lives. Its meaning is so manifold, and when tested, it is so true, that we should be wise to concentrate on the matters that immediately help us. So in nature plants seek out of the soil just that food which gives them nourishment. There is plenty of other food left in the soil, which other plants take, which can digest it. In matters of remote history or folk lore, we must take the results of the latest researches. In interpreting Jewish or Christian legends or beliefs we must go to Jewish or Christian sources, but by way of illustration only, not in the direction of incorporating such beliefs or systems. Though they were true in their original purity, we are not sure of the form which they subsequently took, and in any case the fuller light of the sun obscures the lesser light of the stars.

In the application of spiritual truths to our own times and our own lives, we must use every kind of knowledge, science, and experience which we possess, but we must not obtrude irrelevant matter into our discussions. Let us take simple examples. When we speak of the rising of sun in the east, we do not go on to reconcile the expression with the Copernican system of astronomy. What we *mean* is as true under the Copernican system as it was under the Ptolemæic system. When we speak of the endless plains of India, we are not put on our defence because the earth is round. Nor will such poetic expressions as the seven firmaments raise questions as to the nature of space in modern astronomy. Man's intellect is given to him to investigate the nature of the physical world around him. He forms different conceptions of it at different times. Spiritual truths are quite independent of the question which of these conceptions are true. They deal with matters which are beyond the ken of physical science. In explaining or illustrating them we shall use such language as is current among the people to whom we speak.

Let me set out the names of the most important *Tafsīrs*, especially those to which I have from time to time referred. They are not, however, in any sense my authorities. They belong to widely different schools of thought, and some of them express extreme views with which I do not agree. I only adopt the general sense of accepted Commentaries.

(1) The monumental work of Abū Ja'far Muhammad Ibn Jarīr *Ṭabarī*, d. 310 H A perfect mine of historical information, as the author was both a historian and a Traditionist. Copies are not easily accessible.

(2) The *Mufradāt*, a dictionary of difficult words and phrases in the Qur-ān, by Abul-Qāsim Ḥusain Rāgib, of Ispahān, d. 503 H. Also explains allusions.

(3) The *Kashshāf*, by Abul-Qāsim Maḥmūd *Zamakhshari*, of Khwārism, d. 538 H. Very full in the explanation of words and idioms; takes a decidedly rational and ethical view of doctrine. Numerous Commentaries have been written on this Commentary.

(4) *Tafsīr Kabīr*, by Fakhr-ud-dīn Muḥammad *Rāzī*, d. 606 H. Very comprehensive. Strong in interpretations from a Ṣūfī or spiritual point of view.

(5) *Anwār-ut-Tanzīl*, by Qādhī Naṣir-ud-dīn Abū Ṣa'id *Baidhāwī*, d. 685 H. Has drawn largely from the *Mufradāt*, the *Kashshāf*, and the *Tafsīr Kabīr*, but incorporates a good deal of original matter. A very popular Commentary, on which again numerous Commentaries have been written.

(6) The Tafsīr of Abul-Fidā Ismā'īl *Ibn Kathīr*, d. 774 H. Voluminous, but has great authority among the 'Ulamā.

(7) *Itqān fī 'ulūm-il-Qur-ān*, by Jalāl-ud-dīn Suyūṭī, d. 911 H. A comprehensive review of the sciences of the Qur-ān, being an introduction to his *Majma'-ul-Bahrain*.

(8) *Tafsīr Jalālain.*—Written by the two Jalāl-ud-dīns, one of whom was the author of the *Itqān*, mentioned above, d. 911 H. A concise and meritorious Commentary, on which again a number of Commentaries have been written.

(9) Our country has produced some notable scholars in the realm of *Tafsīr*. They wrote in Arabic and Persian, and the latter ones have written in Urdu.

The earliest I can trace is Shaikh 'Alī Ibn Aḥmad Mahāimī (of Māhim, near Bombay), d. 835 H. = 1432 A.D., author of the *Tafsīr Raḥmānī*. Almost contemporary with him was 'Allāma Shams-ud-dīn, of Daulatābād and Delhi, who lived during the brilliant reign of Ibrāhīm Sharqī of Jaunpur (1400—1440 A.D.). He wrote in Persian. During the nineteenth century, the famous Muhaddith of Delhi, Shāh Walī-ullāh, and his two sons Shāh 'Abdul 'Azīz (d. 1824) and Shāh 'Abdul Qādir (d. 1826) wrote both translations and Commentaries. Shāh 'Abdul 'Azīz wrote in Persian and Shāh 'Abdul Qādir in Urdu. The Urdu Commentary of Sir Sayyid Aḥmad Khān of 'Alīgarh (d. 1898) has not met the approval of the 'Ulamā. On the other hand the more recent Urdu Commentary of Maulvi 'Abdul Haqq, the *Tafsīr Haqqānī*, has passed through several editions, is quite modern in tone and manageable in bulk, and is widely circulated in India. I have derived much instruction from it and have used it constantly. The Commentary of Maulvi Abul Kalām Āzād has been planned on a spacious scale and has not yet been finished.

(10) The Modernist school in Egypt got a wise lead from the late Shaikh Muhammad 'Abduh (d. 1323 H. = 1905 A.D.), whose unfinished Commentary is being completed by Muḥammad Rashīd Ridhā, the talented editor of the *Manār* newspaper. The work of Shaikh Tantāwī, Jauharī, a pupil of 'Abduh, finds the "jewels" of the Qur-ān and of the sciences mutually illuminative, and suggests many new lines of thought. 'Allāma Farīd Wajdī is also spoken of as a good modern Commentator: I have not yet been able to get a copy of his work.

(11) It has been said that the Qur-ān is its own best Commentary. As we proceed with the study of the Book, we find how true this is. A careful comparison and collation of passages from the Qur-ān removes many difficulties. Use a good Concordance, such as the one I have named among the Works of Reference, and you will find that one passage throws light on another.

ALMOST all languages spoken by Muslims have translations of the Qur-ān in them. Usually the Text is printed with the Translation. If the language is undeveloped, many of the Arabic words of the Qur-ān are taken over bodily into it for want of corresponding words in the language. Even in cultivated languages like Persian or Turkish, the introduction of religious terms from Arabic gave a body of words which were common to the whole Islamic world, and thus cemented that unity of the Muslim Brotherhood which is typified by the Qibla. Where the notion itself is new to the speakers of polished languages, they are glad to borrow the Arabic word expressing that notion and all the associations connected with it. Such a word is *Qibla*. Where the language is undeveloped, the translation is nothing more than a rough explanation of the Arabic Text. The translation has neither grammatical finish nor a form which can stand independently by itself. That is what happened with the earlier Urdu translations. They were really rough explanations. The ambition of every learned Muslim is to read the Qur-ān in Arabic. The ambition of every Muslim is to read the *sounds* of the Arabic Text. I wish that his or her ambition were also to *understand* the Qur-ān, either in Arabic or in the mother tongue or some well-developed tongue which he or she understands. Hence the need for good and accurate translations.

The translations into non-European languages known to me are: Persian, Turkish, Urdu, Tamil (used by Moplas), Pashto (for Afghans), Bengali, Malay, some of the languages of the Eastern Archipelago, and some of the African languages. I believe there is also a Chinese (dialectical) translation.

The earliest Urdu translation was by Shāh 'Abdul Qādir of Delhi (d 1826). He has already been mentioned among the Indian Commentators. Since then numerous Urdu translations have followed, some of which have been left incomplete. Among the complete ones, much used at the present day, may be mentioned those of Shāh Rafī'-ud-dīn of Delhi, Shāh Ashraf 'Alī Thānawī, and Maulvi Nazīr Ahmad (d. 1912). Personally I prefer the last. The projected Urdu translation by Hakīm Ahmad Shujā' has not yet been published.

Before the development of the modern European vernaculars, the cultivated language of Europe was Latin. A Latin translation was made for the Monastery of Clugny about 1143 (in the sixth century of the Hijra) but not published till 1543. The place of publication was Basle and the publisher Bibliander. This was translated into Italian, German, and Dutch. Schweigger's German translation was published at Nurenburg (Bavaria) in 1616. A French translation by Du Ryer was published at Paris in 1647, and a Russian one at St. Petersburg in 1776. Savary's French translation appeared in 1783, and Kasimirski's French translation (which has passed through several editions) first appeared in 1840, the French interest in Islam having been stimulated by French conquests in Algeria and North Africa. The Germans have followed up Schweigger with Boysen's translation in 1773, Wahl's in 1828, and Ullmann's (first edition in 1840). I believe the Aḥmadīya Association of Lahore have in hand a fresh translation into German and Dutch.

Meanwhile Maracci had produced in 1689 a Latin version of the Qur-ān with the Arabic Text and quotations from various Arabic Commentaries, carefully selected and garbled, so as to give the worst possible impression of Islam to Europe. Maracci was a learned man, and there is no pretence about the object he had in view, *viz.*, to discredit Islam by an elaborate show of quotations from Muslim authorities themselves. Maracci was himself a Confessor to Pope Innocent XI; his work is dedicated to the holy Roman Emperor Leopold I; and he introduces it by an introductory volume containing what he calls a "Refutation of the Qur-ān."

The first English translation by A. Ross was but a translation of the first French translation of Du Ryer of 1647, and was published a few years after Du Ryer's. George Sale's translation (1734) was based on Maracci's Latin version, and even his notes and his Preliminary Discourse are based mainly on Maracci. Considering that Maracci's object was to discredit Islam in the eyes of Europe, it is remarkable that Sale's translation should be looked upon as a standard translation in the English-speaking world, and should pass through edition after edition, being even included in the series called the

Chandos Classics and receiving the benediction of Sir E. Denison Ross. The Rev. J. M. Rodwell arranged the Sūras in a rough chronological order. His translation was first published in 1861. Though he tries to render the idiom fairly, his notes show the mind of a Christian clergyman, who was more concerned to "show up" the Book than to appreciate or expound its beauties. Prof. E. H. Palmer's translation (first published in 1876) suffers from the idea that the Qur-ān ought to be translated into colloquial language. He failed to realise the beauty and grandeur of style in the original Arabic. To him that style was "rude and rugged": we may more justifiably call his translation careless and slipshod.

The amount of mischief done by these versions of non-Muslim and anti-Muslim writers has led Muslim writers to venture into the field of English translation. The first Muslim to undertake an English translation was Dr. Muḥammad 'Abdul Ḥakim Khān, of Patiala, 1905. Mīrzā Hairat of Delhi also published a translation, (Delhi 1919): the Commentary which he intended to publish in a separate volume of Introduction was, as far as I know, never published. My dear friend, the late Nawwāb 'Imād-ul-Mulk Saiyid Husain Bilgrāmī of Hyderabad, Deccan, translated a portion, but he did not live to complete his work. The Aḥmadīya Sect has also been active in the field Its Qādiyān Anjuman published a version of the first Sīpāra in 1915. Apparently no more was published. Its Lahore Anjuman has published Maulvi Muḥammad 'Alī's translation (first edition in 1917), which has passed through more than one edition. It is a scholarly work, and is equipped with adequate explanatory matter in the notes and the Preface, and a fairly full Index. But the English of the Text is decidedly weak, and is not likely to appeal to those who know no Arabic. There are two other Muslim translations of great merit. But they have been published without the Arabic Text. Ḥāfiẕ Gulām Sarwar's translation (published in 1930 or 1929 deserves to be better known than it is. He has provided fairly full summaries of the Sūras, section by section, but he has practically no notes to his Text. I think such notes are necessary for a full understanding of the Text. In many cases the Arabic words and phrases are so pregnant of meaning that a Translator would be in despair unless he were allowed to explain all that he understands by them. Mr. Marmaduke Pickthall's translation was published in 1930. He is an English Muslim, a literary man of standing, and an Arabic scholar. But he has added very few notes to elucidate the Text. His rendering is "almost literal": it can hardly be expected that it can give an adequate idea of a Book which (in his own words) can be described as "that inimitable symphony the very sounds of which move men to tears and ecstasy." Perhaps the attempt to catch something of that symphony in another language is impossible. Greatly daring, I have made that attempt. We do not blame an artist who tries to catch in his picture something of the glorious light of a spring landscape.

The English language being widely spread over the world, many people interested in Islam will get their ideas of the Qur-ān from English translations. It is good that qualified Muslims should make the attempt to present the picture which their own mental and spiritual vision presents to themselves. The Indian educational system has enthroned English as the common language of culture for a population of 350 millions. The most educated of its 80 millions of Muslims—unless they know Arabic—look to English as the most cultivated medium of expression. Their non-Muslim fellow countrymen judge—usually misjudge—their religion by the material which is available to them in English. We should improve and increase this material as much as we can and from as many points of view as we can. Some Muslim nations—like the Turks—have now determined to provide their religious literature (including the Holy Book) in their own national language. In order to keep them in touch with the thought and points of view of their brethren in faith, the English language would under present conditions be the most convenient medium. These are the considerations which have moved me to undertake the stupendous task of providing an English Interpretation of the Qur-ān. I pray for strength and light, so that I may be enabled to succeed in this service to Islam.

USEFUL WORKS OF REFERENCE

The wide compass of the Qur-ān makes it necessary to consult works of reference on almost every conceivable subject, to enable us to elucidate the various points that arise. To deal adequately with such a Book, the widest reading is necessary as well as the most varied experience in life. But the interests of readers require that a handy Commentary should not roam too far afield. Bearing this in view the three essential kinds of books would be: (*a*) Previous Commentaries; (*b*) previous Translations; (*c*) Dictionaries and General Works of Reference, easily accessible. I have set out (*a*) and (*b*) in the previous two Notes. I note a few under (*c*):—

1. Imām Abul-Qāsim Ḥusain Rāgib's *Mufradāt*: a concise Arabic dictionary of words and phrases in the Qur-ān. Already mentioned under Commentaries.

2. The well-known Arabic Dictionary, *Qāmūs*.

3. The well-known Arabic Dictionary, *Lisān-ul-'Arab*.

4. The concise Arabic-Perisan Dictionary, *Ṣurāḥ*.

5. J. Penrice's *Dictionary & Glossary of the Koran*.

6. E. W. Lane: *English-Arabic Lexicon*.

7. Imām Jalāl-ud-dīn Suyūṭī's *Itqān fī 'ulūm-il-Qur-ān*: a veritable encyclopædia of Quranic sciences.

8. Nöldeke und Schwally: *Geschichte des Qorans*. A German Essay on the Chronology of the Qur-ān. Its criticisms and conclusions are from a non-Muslim point of view and to us not always acceptable, though it is practically the last word of European scholarship on the subject.

9. *Encyclopædia of Islam*. Nearly completed. Very unequal in its various parts.

10. *Encyclopædia Britannica*, 14th edition. A great advance on previous editions, as regards the attention it devotes to Arabic learning.

11. Hughes's *Dictionary of Islam*. Out of date, but still useful.

12. Ibn Hishām: *Sīrat-ur-Rasūl*. A fairly detailed Life of the Apostle.

13. Maulvi Shiblī Nu'māni (d. 1914=1334 H.): *Sīrat-un-Nabī* (an Urdu Life of the Apostle).

14. *Fatḥ-ur-Rahmān*, an Arabic Concordance to the Qur-ān, by Faidh-ullāh Bik Hasanī, printed in Cairo in 1346 H. Full and well arranged, and easy to use.

TRANSLITERATION OF ARABIC WORDS AND NAMES

THE following table shows the system which I have followed in transliterating the letters of the Arabic alphabet :—

ا ء	{Consonantal sound}	a	ط	....	ṭ
			ظ	....	z̲
ا	Long vowel *	a	ع	....	' (Inverted apostrophe)
ب	....	b	غ	....	g̲h
ت	....	t	ف	....	f
ث	....	t̲h̲	ق	....	q
ج	....	j	ك	....	k
ح	....	ḥ	ل	....	l
خ	....	k̲h̲	م	....	m
د	....	d	ن	....	n
ذ	....	z	ه ة	....	h
ر	....	r	و	consonant	w
ز	....	z	و	long vowel *	ū
س	....	s	و	diphthong	au
ش	....	sh	ي	consonant	y
ص	....	ṣ	ي	long vowel *	ī
ض	....	d̲h̲	ي	diphthong	ai

Short vowels: ـَـ (*fatḥa*) a
ـِـ (*kasra*) i
ـُـ (*d̲hamma*) u

1. For the *hamzā* (ء) I have used no distinctive sign. An apostrophe for it and an inverted apostrophe for the *'ain* (ع), or *vice versa*, is confusing to English readers. As a moved consonant, it is sufficiently shown in English by the long or short vowel which moves it, *e.g., ab, Raūf.* Where it is a hiatus preceded by a *fatḥa,* I have shown it by a second *a* : thus, *Iqraa,* the cave of *Hiraa.* In other cases it has not been possible to show it without using a distinctive sign. The name of the Holy Book is usually written Qurān ; but I prefer to write *Qur-ān.*

2. The final *h* preceded by the short *a* is scarcely pronounced, and I have left it out. Hence Sūra, Fātiḥa, Hijra, etc., where the Arabic spelling would require Sūrah, Fātihah, Hijrah, etc.

3. In internationalised words and names I have used the spelling ordinarily current in English ; *e.g.,* Mecca, Medina, Maulvi, Urdu, Islam, Israel, Abraham, Jacob. Here the boundary is thin and rather ill-defined, and possibly my practice and that of my proof-readers have not been absolutely uniform.

4. Some names, *e.g.,* Ishmael, Hagar, etc., have acquired a contemptuous association in their European forms, while the persons they represent are sacred personages held in great honour in Islam. I have, therefore, avoided the European forms and used the Arabic forms, Ismā'il, Hājar, etc.

* Where it is really *pronounced* long. Hence, *k̲h̲alaqnā-kum* but *k̲h̲alaqnal-insān* ; *Abū Sufyān* but *Abul-Qāsim* ; *fin-nār* but *fī-hi.*

ABBREVIATIONS USED

I have not used many abbreviations. Those I have used are shown below :—

A.D. = Anno Domini = year of the Christian Calendar.

A.H. = Anno Hegiræ = year of the Hijra.

Bk. = Book.

C. = The running Commentary, in rhythmic prose.

Cf. = compare.

d. = date of death of an author (to show the age in which he lived).

Deut. = The Book of Deuteronomy in the Old Testament.

E. B. = *Encyclopædia Britannica*, 14th edition.

e.g. = *exempli gratia* = for example.

Exod. = The Book of Exodus, Old Testament.

Gen. = The Book of Genesis, Old Testament.

H. = year of the Hijra.

H. G. S. = Ḥāfiẓ Gulām Sarwar's Translation of the Qur-ān.

i.e. = *id est* = that is.

Josh. = Book of Joshua, Old Testament.

Matt. = Gospel of St. Matthew, New Testament.

M. M. A. = Maulvi Muḥammad 'Alī's Translation of the Qur-ān.

M. P. = Mr. M. Pickthall's ***The Meaning of the Glorious Koran.***

n. = note.

nn. = notes.

Num. = The Book of Numbers, Old Testament.

p. = page.

pp. = pages.

Q. = Qur-ān.

xx. 25 = Qur-ān, Sūra 20, verse 25.

Rev. = Revelation of St. John, New Testament.

S. = sūra.

v. = verse.

vv. = verses.

viz. = *videlicet* = namely.

$\frac{1}{30}$, $\frac{2}{30}$, **etc.** = the end of one Sīpāra, two Sīpāras, etc. A Sīpāra is arithmetically the 30th part of the Qur-ān.

PUNCTUATION MARKS IN THE ARABIC TEXT

THE punctuation marks in the Arabic Text have been worked out by our 'Ulamā with great care and minute attention to details. The earliest manuscripts had few or no punctuation marks. Their growth and development furnish an interesting history, on which I hope Professor Ẕafar Iqbāl, who has gone into the question, will publish his notes. In classical Europe, Greek had practically no punctuation marks. Later Latin had one or two rudimentary ones. In modern Europe they developed with printing. Aldus Manutius (16th century) was the first to work out a regular system. The Muslims were much earlier in the field for Quranic purposes, although in current Urdu, Persian, or Arabic, punctuation is not a strong point.

Quranic punctuation is an elaborate system, in which three kinds of marks are used. First, there are marks to show the variations in the systems of Qirāat. The most important of these is what is known as the Mu'ānaqa معانقه. This literally means the action of two persons embracing each other shoulder to shoulder, as in the ceremonious salute at the celebration of 'Īd. The technical meaning in connection with the Quranic text is that a certain word or expression so marked can be construed as going either with the words or expressions preceding it or with those following it. The word or expression in question is indicated by three dots ∴ placed before and after it, above other punctuation marks if any. An example will be found in ii. 2, where the word *fī-hi* may be construed either as referring to the word *raib* in the preceding clause, or to the word *hudan* in the succeeding clause. Either or both constructions are admissible. Passages where such constructions occur are indicated in the margin of the Arabic Text: by the abbreviation مع, where this was worked out by the earlier Commentators (*Mutaqaddimīn*), or by the word معانقه in full, where it was worked out by the later Commentators (*Mutaakhkhirīn*). The numeral above it shows the serial number of the *Mu'ānaqa* of each series.

Secondly, there are marginal marks showing division into sections or paragraphs. These are denoted by the letter *'ain* (ع) in the margin, and are explained under the heading "Divisions of the Qur ān."

Thirdly, there are the ordinary punctuation marks in the Text. A knowledge of the most important of these is necessary for an intelligent reading of the Text. Most important of all is a big circle ◯ to denote the end of one Āyat and the beginning of another. If the end of the Āyat is not also the end of a sentence, the mark of a smaller stop is put above it. Where one mark is put on the top of another, the former governs the latter. A warning not to stop is denoted by لا. The letter م (*lāzim*) shows that a stop is absolutely necessary; otherwise the sense is spoilt. This is so important that it is also shown prominently in the margin as وقف لازم. ج (*jāiz*) shows that a stop is optional, but if you do not stop, the sense is not spoiled. There are other marks to show the extent to which a stop is permissible, *e.g.*, for taking breath, etc., or where option is allowed, whether it is better to stop or not to stop. The letter ط (*muṭlaq*) denotes a full stop, *i.e.*, the end of a sentence, but not the end of an argument, as in the case of a paragraph or section (ع).

DIVISIONS OF THE QUR-ĀN

THE reading of the Qur-ān is considered a pious duty by every Muslim and is actually performed in practice by every literate person, man, woman, and child. For the convenience of those who wish to complete the whole reading in a given time, the whole Text is divided into thirty equal parts, or seven equal parts. The thirtieth Part is called *juz-un* in Arabic, and *Sīpāra* or simply *Pāra* in Persian and Urdu. If you read a *Sīpāra* every day, you complete the whole reading in a month of thirty days. The seventh part is called a *Manzil*. If one is read every day, the whole is completed in a week. Usually the arithmetical quarters of a ***Sīpāra*** (one-fourth, one-half, three quarters) are also marked in the Arabic copies as ***Ar-rub'***, ***An-nisf***, and ***Ath-thalātha***.

According to subject-matter, the division is different. The whole of the Qur-ān is arranged in 114 Sūras of very unequal size. The Sūras are numbered and the consecutive number is shown just before the title of the Sūra, both in Arabic and English. In Arabic, the figure just after the title shows the chronological order as usually accepted by Muslim writers. Each Sūra consists of a number of ***Āyats.*** Sūra I contains 7 Āyats and Sūra II contains 286. For the meaning of ***Sūra*** and ***Āyat*** see C. 42 nn. 15-17. The most convenient form of quotation is to name the Sūra and the Āyat : thus ii. 120 means the 120th Āyat of the second Sūra. A Sūra is usually spoken of as a Chapter in English, but that translation is hardly satisfactory. If you examine the order you will find that each Sūra is a step in a gradation. I have left the word untranslated, as a technical term in our religious literature. The Āyat or verse division is usually determined by the rhythm and cadence in the Arabic Text. Sometimes an Āyat contains many sentences. Sometimes a sentence is divided by a break in an Āyat. But usually there is a pause in meaning at the end of an Āyat.

A division of the Sūra into Sections is shown in all Arabic Texts. These are logical divisions according to meaning. The word translated " Section " is in Arabic ***Rukū'***, a " bowing of the head " The end of a ***Rukū'*** is shown in Arabic by ع. Usually three figures are written with ع. The top figure shows the number of Rukū's completed in that Sūra. The middle figure shows the number of Āyats in the Rukū' just completed. The bottom figure shows the number of Rukū's completed in that ***Sīpāra***, irrespective of Sūras. For example, the first ع in Sīpāra II which continues Sūra II from Sīpāra I is usually marked ١٧ ع ٦ ١ . It means that at that point 17 Rukū's of Sūra II have been completed, that the Rukū' of which it marks the close contains 6 Āyats, and that it is the first Rukū' that falls in Sīpāra II. I have further marked the sub-division of Rukū's into shorter paragraphs where necessary, by using in the English text a bold flowery Initial: *e.g.*, see the initial **A** in ii. 6 or the initial **W** in ii. 35.

DIVISIONS OF THE QUR-AN

The reading of the Qur-an is considered a pious duty by every Muslim and is actually performed in practice by every literate person, man, woman and child. For the convenience of those who wish to complete the whole reading in a given time, the whole Text is divided into thirty equal parts, or seven equal parts. The thirtieth part is called *juz'* in Arabic, and *Sipara* or simply *Para* in Persian and Urdu. If you read a *Sipara* every day, you complete the whole reading in a month of thirty days. The seventh part is called a *Manzil*. If one is read every day, the whole is completed in a week. Usually the arithmetical quarters of a *Sipara* (one fourth, one half, three quarters) are also marked in the Arabic copies as *Al-rub'*, *Al-nisf*, and *Al-thalatha*.

According to subject-matter the division is different. The whole of the Qur-an is arranged in 114 *Suras* of very unequal size. The *Suras* are numbered and the consecutive number is shown just before the title of the *Sura* both in Arabic and English. In Arabic the figure just after the title shows the chronological order as usually accepted by Muslim writers. Each *Sura* consists of a number of *Ayats*. Sura I contains 7 *Ayats* and Sura II contains 286. For the meaning of *Sura* and *Ayat* see C. 2 n. 15-17. The most convenient form of quotation is to name the *Sura* and the *Ayat*: thus ii. 120 means the 120th *Ayat* of the second *Sura*. A *Sura* is usually spoken of as a Chapter in English, but that translation is hardly satisfactory. If you examine the order you will find that each *Sura* is a step in a gradation. I have left the word untranslated, as a technical term in our religious literature. The *Ayat* or verse division is greatly determined by the rhythm and cadence in the Arabic Text. Sometimes an *Ayat* contains many sentences. Sometimes a sentence is divided by a break in an *Ayat*. But usually there is a pause in meaning at the end of an *Ayat*.

A division of the *Suras* into Sections is shown in all Arabic Texts. These are logical divisions according to meaning. The word translated "Section" is in Arabic *Ruku'*, a "bowing of the head." The end of a *Ruku'* is shown in Arabic by ع. Usually three figures are written with ع. The top figure shows the number of *Ruku's* completed in that *Sura*. The middle figure shows the number of *Ayats* in the *Ruku'* just completed. The bottom figure shows the number of *Ruku's* completed in that *Sipara*, irrespective of *Suras*. For example, the first ع in *Sipara* II which continues *Sura* II from *Sipara* I, is usually marked ع. It means that at that point 17 *Ruku's* of *Sura* II have been completed, that the *Ruku'* of which it marks the close contains 8 *Ayats*, and that it is the first *Ruku'* that falls in *Sipara* II. I have further marked the subdivision of *Ruku's* into shorter paragraphs where necessary, by using in the English text a bold flowery initial: e.g., see the initial [illegible] in i. 6 or the initial [illegible] in i. 15.

CONTENTS

Sūra VI : *An'ām—(Contd.).* **PAGES.**

Sūra VII : *A'rāf.*

Sūra IX : *Tauba* or *Barāat*—(*Contd.*). PAGES.

Sūra X : *Yūnus.*

Sūra X : *Yūnus*—(*Contd.*).

Sūra XI : *Hūd*.

Sūra XI : *Hūd*—(*Contd.*).

Sūra XXI : *Anbiyāa*—(*Contd.*). PAGES.

Sūra XXII : *Hajj*.

Sūra XXIII : *Mū-minūn*.

Sūra XXX : *Rūm*—(*Contd.*). PAGES.

Sūra L : *Qāf*—(*Contd.*). PAGES.

Sūra LI : *Ẓāriyāt*.

Sūra LII : *Ṭūr*.

Sūra LIII : *Najm*.

Sūra LIV : *Qamar*.

INTRODUCTION

C. 1.—Glory to God Most High, full of Grace and Mercy;
He created All, including Man.
To Man He gave a special place in His Creation.
He honoured man to be His Agent,
And to that end, endued him with understanding,
Purified his affections, and gave him spiritual insight;
So that man should understand Nature,
Understand himself,
And know God through His wondrous Signs,
And glorify Him in Truth, reverence, and unity.

C. 2.—For the fulfilment of this great trust
Man was further given a Will,
So that his acts should reflect God's universal Will and Law,
And his mind, freely choosing,
Should experience the sublime joy
Of being in harmony with the Infinite,
And with the great drama of the world around him,
And with his own spiritual growth.

C. 3.—But, created though he was in the best of moulds,
Man fell from Unity when his Will was warped,
And he chose the crooked path of Discord.
And sorrow and pain, selfishness and degradation,
Ignorance and hatred, despair and unbelief
Poisoned his life, and he saw shapes of evil
In the physical, moral, and spiritual world,
And in himself.

C. 4.—Then did his soul rise against himself,
And his self-discord made discord between kith and kin:
Men began to fear the strong and oppress the weak,
To boast in prosperity, and curse in adversity,
And to flee each other, pursuing phantoms,
For the truth and reality of Unity
Was gone from their minds.

C. 5.—When men spread themselves over the earth,
And became many nations,
Speaking diverse languages,
And observing diverse customs and laws;

The evils became multiplied,
As one race or nation
Became alienated from another.
The Brotherhood of Man was now doubly forgotten,—
First, between individuals, and secondly, between nations.
Arrogance, selfishness, and untruth
Were sown and reaped in larger fields;
And Peace, Faith, Love and Justice
Were obscured over masses of men,
As large tracts of land are starved
Of sunshine by clouds floating far on high.

C. 6.—But God, in His infinite mercy and love,
Who Forgives and guides individuals and nations,
And turns to good even what seems to us evil,
Never forsakes the struggling soul that turns to Him,
Nor the groups of men and women
Who join together to obey His Will and Law
And strengthen each other in unity and truth,
Nor the Nations that dwell
In mountain or valley, heat or cold,
In regions fertile or arid,
In societies that roam over land or seas,
Or hunt, or tend flocks, or till the soil,
Or seek the seas for food or oil or fat or gems,
Or dig out from the bowels of the earth
Precious stones or metals or stored-up heat and energy,
Or practise arts and crafts, or produce abundant wealth
By machines of ingenious workmanship,
Or live a frugal life of contemplation :
For all are children of One God,
And share His loving care
And must be brought within the pale
Of His eternal unity and harmony.

C. 7.—And so this light of eternal Unity
Has shone in all ages and among all nations,
Through chosen Apostles of God, who came
As men to dwell among men,
To share their joys and sorrows,
To suffer for them and with them,—
Aye, and to suffer more than falls
To ordinary mortal lot,—
That so their message and their life

Might fulfil the eternal
And unchanging purpose of the Most High,—
To lead man to his noblest destiny.

C. 8.—Ever this eternal light of Unity,
This mystic light of God's own Will,
Has shone and shines with undiminished splendour.
The names of many Messengers are inscribed
In the records of many nations and many tongues,
And many were the forms in which their message was delivered,
According to the needs of the times and the understanding of the people;
And manifold were the lives of the Messengers,
And manifold also was the response of their people;
But they all witnessed to the One Truth :
Of God's unity, might, grace and love.

C. 9.—As the records of man are imperfect,
And the memory of man unstable :
The names of many of these messengers
Are known in one place and not in another,
Or among one people and not among others;
And some of their names may have perished utterly;
But their message stands one and indivisible,
Even though it may have been forgotten,
Or twisted by ignorance, error, superstition or perversity;
Or misunderstood in the blinding light
Of time or tortuous Circumstance.

C. 10.—Many were the faiths in the composite world
Of Western Asia, Northern Africa, and Europe,
And many were the fragments of ancient wisdom,
Saved, transformed, renewed, or mingled;
And many new streams of wisdom were poured through the crucibles
Of noble minds,—prophets, poets, preachers,
Philosophers, and thinking men of action;
And many were the conflicts, and many
The noble attempts reaching out towards Unity,
And many were the subtle influences
Interchanged with the other worlds
Of further and Eastern Asia,—
Aye, and perchance with the scattered Isles
Of the Pacific and the world between
The Atlantic and the Pacific.

C. 11.—At length came the time when the Voice of Unity

Should speak and declare to the People,
Without the need of Priests or Priest-craft,
Without miracles save those that happen
Now and always in the spiritual world,
Without mystery, save those mysteries
Which unfold themselves in the growing
Inner experience of man and his vision of God,—
To declare with unfaltering voice
The Unity of God, the Brotherhood of Man,
And Grace and Mercy, Bounty and Love,
Poured out in unstinted measure for ever and ever.

C. 12.—And this great healing light shone
Among a people steeped in ignorance,
Brave and free, but without cohesion or union,
Simple and rude, but with an easy familiarity with Nature,
Accustomed to Nature's hardships and her rugged resistance to man,
But dreaming of the delights of gardens and fruitful fields,
Cruel, yet with a rough sense of equality,
And wielding a tongue, flexible, beautiful,
And able to respond, with brevity and eloquence,
To the sublimest thoughts which man could conceive.

C. 13.—Who were fit to be vehicles of this light?—
Not men intoxicated with words and mysteries,
Men whom politics had debauched or tyranny had subdued,
Men whose refinement had ended in vices,
Who saw Nature only through books or artificial conceits,
Or in moods which bred softness, indolence, or luxury,
Who spoke of love and justice, but practised
Gross selfishness between class and class,
Sex and sex, condition and condition;
And had perverted their language, once beautiful,
Into jargons of empty elegance and unmeaning futility.

C. 14.—For the glory of Hellas, and her freedom and wisdom had departed;
Rome's great systems of law, organisation, and universal citizenship
Had sunk into the mire of ecclesiastical formalism,
And dogmatism, and exclusive arrogance;
The living fire of Persia's Prophet scarce smouldered
In her votaries of luxury;
In India, countless castes and kingdoms
Cancelled the unity of Buddha's teaching;
The wounds of China had not yet been healed by T'ang culture;
And Japan was still a disciple of China.

C. 15.—Then, in the sacred city of pagan Arabia,
Shone a light that spread in all directions.
It was centrally placed for the bounds of the world
Of men's habitations in Asia, Europe, and Africa.
It made the Arabs the leading nation of culture and science,
Of organised enterprise, law, and arts,
With a zeal for the conquest of Nature and her mysteries.

C. 16.—Behold! There was born into the world of sense
The unlettered Apostle, the comely child,
Noble of birth, but nobler still
In the grace and wisdom of human love
And human understanding; dowered with the key
Which opened to him the enchanted palace
Of nature; marked out to receive—
To receive and preach in burning words
The spiritual truth and message of the Most High.

C. 17.—Others before him had been born
In darkness, beyond the reach
Of history; others again it pleased God
To send as Messengers, preaching, working
In the dim twilight of history,
Wherein men fashion legends
After their own hearts and dimly seek
A light afar, remote from the lives
Mean and sordid, such as they knew.

C. 18.—But Muḥammad came in the fullest blaze
Of history; with no learning he put to shame
The wisdom of the learned; with pasture folk
He lived and worked, and won their love; in hills
And valleys, caves and deserts, he wandered,
But never lost his way to truth and righteousness;
From his pure and spotless heart the Angels washed
Off the dust that flew around him; through the ways
Of crooked city folk, he walked upright and straight,
And won from them the ungrudging name
Of the Man of Faith [1] who never broke his word.

C. 19.—To the Praiseworthy [2] indeed be praise:
Born in the Sacred City [3] he destroyed
Its superstition; loyal to his people to the core,

1. Al-Amin. 2. Muḥammad. 3. Mecca.

He stood for all humanity; orphan-born
And poor, he envied not the rich,
And made his special care all those
Whom the world neglected or oppressed,—
Orphans, women, slaves, and those in need
Of food or comforts, mental solace, spiritual strength,
Or virtues downtrodden in the haunts of men.

C. 20.—His mother[4] and his foster-mother[5]
Loved and wondered at the child;
His grandfather, 'Abdul Muṭṭalib,
Of all his twice-eight children and their offspring,
Loved him best and all his sweet and gentle ways;
His uncle Abū Ṭālib, loth though he was
To give up the cult of his fathers,
Knew well the purity of Muḥammad's
Mind and soul, and was his stoutest champion
When the other chiefs of Mecca sought to kill
The man who challenged in his person
Their narrow Pagan selfish lives.

C. 21.—To his cousin 'Alī, the well-beloved,[6]
Born when he was thirty, he appeared
As the very pattern of a perfect man,
As gentle as he was wise and true and strong,
The one in whose defence and aid
He spent his utmost strength and skill,
Holding life cheap in support of a cause so high,
And placing without reserve his chivalry,
His prowess, his wit and learning, and his sword
At the service of this mighty Messenger of God.

C. 22.—Not till the age of forty[7] did he receive
The Commission to stand forth and proclaim
The Bounty of God, and His gift, to lowly Man,
Of knowledge by Word and Pen; but all through
His years of preparation he did search
The Truth: he sought it in Nature's forms and laws,
Her beauty and her stern unflinching ways;
He sought it in the inner world
Of human lives, men's joys and sorrows,
Their kindly virtues and their sins

4. Amina. 5. Ḥalīma. 6. Murtaḏhā. 7. The Arabian year before H. 10 was roughly luni-solar: See Appendix XI, p. 1077.

Of pride, injustice, cruel wrong,
And greed of gain, scarce checked by the inner voice
That spoke of duty, moral law, and higher still,
The Will Supreme of God, to which the will
Of man must tune itself to find its highest bliss.

C. 23.—But he grew steadfastly in virtue and purity;
Untaught by men, he learnt from them, and learned
To teach them; even as a boy of nine,
When he went in a trade caravan with Abū Ṭālib
To Syria,[8] his tender soul marked inwardly
How God did speak in the wide expanse
Of deserts, in the stern grandeur of rocks,
In the refreshing flow of streams, in the smiling
Bloom of gardens, in the art and skill with which
Men and birds and all life sought for light
From the Life of Lives, even as every plant
Seeks through devious ways the light of the Sun.

C. 24.—Nor less was he grieved at Man's ingratitude
When he rebelled and held as naught the Signs
Of God, and turned His gifts to baser uses,
Driving rarer souls to hermit life,
Clouding the heavenly mirror of pure affections
With selfish passions, mad unseemly wrangles,
And hard unhallowed loathsome tortures of themselves.

C. 25—He worked, and joyed in honest labour;
He traded with integrity to himself and to others;
He joined the throngs of cities and their busy life,
But saw its good and evil as types
Of an inner and more lasting life hereafter;
People gladly sought his help as umpire
And peacemaker because they knew his soul
Was just and righteous: he loved the society
Of old and young, but oft withdrew to solitude
For Prayer and inward spiritual strength;
He despised not wealth but used it for others;
He was happy in poverty and used it as his badge

---

8. It was on such visits that he met and conversed with Nestorian Christian monks like Babīrā who were quick to recognise his spiritual worth. Perhaps the meeting was in Busrā بُصرىٰ in the Jabal Druze district of Syria, some 80 miles south of Damascus. There was another Busrā in Edom, north of Petra in Transjordania. Busrā was famous for trade in costly red dyes, and is referred to as Bozrah in Isaiah, lxiii. l. Neither of these towns is to be confounded with the modern Basra.

and his pride[9] when wealth was within his reach
But not within his grasp, as a man among men.

C. 26.—At twenty-five he was united in the holy bonds
Of wedlock with Khadīja the Great, the noble lady
Who befriended him when he had no worldly resources,
Trusted him when his worth was little known,
Encouraged and understood him in his spiritual struggles,
Believed in him when with trembling steps
He took up the Call and withstood obloquy,
Persecution, insults, threats, and tortures,
And was a life-long helpmate till she was gathered
To the saints in his fifty-first year,—
A perfect woman, the mother of those that believe.

C. 27.—There is a cave in the side of Mount Hiraa
Some three miles north of the City of Mecca,
In a valley which turns left from the road to 'Arafāt.
To which Muḥammad used to retire for peaceful contemplation:
Often alone, but sometimes with Khadīja.
Days and nights he spent there with his Lord.
Hard were the problems he revolved in his mind,—
Harder and more cross-grained than the red granite
Of the rock around him,—problems not his own,
But his people's, yea, and of human destiny,
Of the mercy of God, and the age-long conflict
Of evil and righteousness, sin and abounding Grace.

C. 28.—Not till forty years of earthly life had passed
That the veil was lifted from the Preserved Tablet
And its contents began to be transferred to the tablet of his mind,
To be proclaimed to the world, and read and studied
For all time,—a fountain of mercy and wisdom,
A warning to the heedless, a guide to the erring,
An assurance to those in doubt, a solace to the suffering,
A hope to those in despair,—to complete the chain
Of Revelation through the mouths
Of divinely inspired Apostles.

C. 29.—The Chosen One[10] was in the Cave of Ḥiraa.
For two years and more he had prayed there and adored
His Creator and wondered at the mystery
Of man with his corruptible flesh, just growing

9. *Alfaqru fakhrī*: "Poverty is my pride." 10. Muṣṭafā.

Out of a clot,[10-A] and the soul in him
Reaching out to knowledge sublime, new
And ever new, taught by the bounty
Of God, and leading to that which man himself
Knoweth not. And now, behold! a dazzling
Vision of beauty and light overpowered his senses,
And he heard the word "*Iqraa!*"

C. 30.—"*Iqraa!*"—which being interpreted may mean
"Read!" or "Proclaim!" or "Recite!"
The unlettered Apostle was puzzled;
He could not read. The Angel seemed
To press him to his breast in a close embrace,
And the cry rang clear "Iqraa!"
And so it happened three times; until
The first overpowering sensation yielded
To a collected grasp of the words which made clear
His Mission; its Author, God the Creator,
Its subject, Man, God's wondrous handiwork,
Capable, by Grace, of rising to heights sublime;
And the instrument of that mission, the sanctified Pen,
And the sanctified Book, the Gift of God,
Which men might read, or write, or study, or treasure in their souls

C. 31.—The veil was lifted from the Chosen One's eyes,
And his soul for a moment was filled with divine
Ecstasy...When this passed,
And he returned to the world of Time
And Circumstance and this world of Sense,
He felt like one whose eyes had seen
A light of dazzling beauty, and felt dazed
On his return to common sights.
The darkness now seemed tenfold dark;
The solitude seemed tenfold empty;
The mount of Ḥiraa, henceforth known
As the Mountain of Light,[11] the mere shell
Of an intense memory. Was it a dream?
Terror seized his limbs and he straightway sought
Her who shared his inmost life,
And told her of his sense of exaltation,
And the awful void when the curtain closed.

C. 32.—She understood, rejoiced, and comforted him;
Gave strength to his shaken senses;

10-A. See xcvi. 2, and n. 6205.

11. Jabal-un-Nūr

Wrapped up in warmth his shivering body,
Unused as yet to bear the strain and stress
Of an experience rare to mortal men.
She knew it was no dream or delusion.
She went and consulted her cousin Waraqa,
A devout worshipper of God in the Faith of Christ,
Learned in spiritual lore. He listened
And with her rejoiced that he, Muhammad,
Was God's Chosen One to renew the Faith.

C. 33.—She said : Blessed be thou, Chosen One!
Do we not see thy inner life,—true and pure?
Do not all see thy outer life,—kind and gentle?—
Loyal to kin, hospitable to strangers?
No thought of harm or mischief ever stained thy mind
Nor word ever passed thy lips that was not true
Or stilled not the passions of narrower men.
Ever ready in the service of God, thou art he
Of whom I bear witness : there's no God but He,
And thou art His chosen Apostle.

C. 34.—Khadīja believed, exalted in faith
Above all women; 'Alī, the well-beloved,
Then a child of ten, but lion hearted,
Plighted his faith, and became from that moment
The right hand of Islam; Abū Bakr, the Sincere,[12]
The True-hearted, the man of wealth and influence,
Who used both without stint for the Cause,
The sober Counsellor, the inseparable friend,
Never hesitated to declare his faith;
And Zaid, the freedman of Muḥammad,
Counted his freedom as naught compared
With the service of Muḥammad and Islam.
These were the first fruits of the mission :
A woman, a child, a man of affairs, and a freedman,
All banded together in the equality of Islam.

C. 35.—The revelation had come, the mission
And the inspiration. But what was it leading to?
It was a miracle, but not in the sense
Of a reversing of Nature; Muṣṭafā's vision
Was linked with Eternity, but he was no soothsayer
Foretelling passing events; the mysteries

12. Ṣadīq or Ṣiddīq, the title of Abū Bakr.

Of knowledge were being opened out, but his message
Was no mere esoteric doctrine, to be grasped
By a few in contemplation, fleeing from action ;
Nor was it the practice of single or social monasticism,
Undisturbed by the whims or passions of life.
He was asked to stand forth, to preach, to declare
The One Universal God, the Gracious, the Merciful,
And to lead men to the Right and forbid the Wrong.

C. 36.—The wrong ?—The selfish pride of birth,
The massing of power and wealth in the hands
Of a few, the slaughter of female infants,
The orgies of gambling and drunkenness,
The frauds of temples and idols and priests,
The feuds and arrogance of tribes and races,
The separation of Sacred and Profane,
As if the unity of All Life and All Truth
Did not flow from the unity of God Most High.

C. 37.—He was loyal to his family, but could he support
Their monopoly of power ?—To his tribe,
But were the Quraish the only creatures
Of God ?—To the temple of Mecca, but
Could he wink at Lāt and 'Uzzā, and the other monsters,
Whose worship killed the spiritual growth of Man ?—
To the earlier Revelations, but could he hold
With the superstitions and falsehoods, the dogmas and creeds
Which went against reason and nature, and the inner light
Which was now fanned into flame by the Will of God ?

C. 38.—And so his very virtues and loyalties pointed
To offence and conflict, mockery and misrepresentation,
Hatred and persecution, threats, tortures, and exile
For him and his, and martydoms, wars, revolutions,
And the shaking of the foundations of history
And the social order. But Islam meant
The willing submission of his will to God,
The active attainment of Peace through Conflict.

C. 39.—And he gave that submission, not without effort,
Even as Moses[13] did before him,
And Jesus[14] in the agony of the garden of Gethsemane.

* * *

13. Qur-ān xx. 25-32.

14. Matt. xxvi.

C. 40.—For three and twenty years, in patience,
Conflict, hope, and final triumph,
Did this man of God receive
And teach the Message of the Most High.
It came, like the fruit of the soul's own yearning,
To teach profound spiritual truths,
Answer questions, appeal to men
In their doubts and fears, help and put heart
In them in moments of trial, and ordain
For them laws by which they could live
In society lives of purity, goodness and peace.

C. 41.—These messages came as inspiration
To Muḥammad as the need arose,
On different occasions and in different places:
He recited them, and they were recorded
By the Pen: they were imprinted on his heart
And mind, and on the memory
Of his loving disciples: as the body
Of sacred Scripture grew, it was arranged
For purposes of public prayer and reading:
This is the Book, or the Reading, or the Qur-ān.

INTRODUCTION TO SŪRA I (*Fātiḥa*)

C. 42.—First comes that beautiful Sūra,[15]
The Opening Chapter[16] of Seven Verses,[17]
Rightly called the Essence of the Book.
It teaches us the perfect Prayer.
For if we can pray aright, it means
That we have some knowledge of God
And His attributes, of His relations
To us and His creation, which includes
Ourselves; that we glimpse the source
From which we come, and that final goal
Which is our spiritual destiny
Under God's true judgment: then
We offer ourselves to God and seek His light.

C. 43.—Prayer is the heart of Religion and Faith
But how shall we pray? What words shall convey
The yearnings of our miserable ignorant hearts
To the Knower of all? Is it worthy of Him
Or of our spiritual nature to ask
For vanities, or even for such physical needs
As our daily bread? The Inspired One
Taught us a Prayer that sums up our faith,
Our hope, and our aspiration in things that matter.
We think in devotion of God's name and His Nature;
We praise Him for His creation and His Cherishing care;
We call to mind the Realities, seen and unseen;
We offer Him worship and ask for His guidance;
And we know the straight from the crooked path
By the light of His grace that illumines the righteous.

---

15. Each chapter or portion of the Qur-ān is called a Sūra, which means a Degree or Step, by which we mount up. Sometimes whole Sūras were revealed, and sometimes portions, which were arranged together according to subject-matter under the Apostle's directions. Some Sūras are long, and some are short, but a logical thread runs through them all. Each verse of the Sūra is called an *Āyat* (plural, *Āyāt*), which means also a sign. A verse of revelation is a Sign of God's wisdom and goodness just as much as God's beautiful handiwork in the material creation or His dealings in history are signs to us, if we would understand. Some *Āyāts* are long, and some are short. The *Āyat* is the true unit of the Qur-ān.

16. *Fātiḥa*=Opening Chapter.

17. These seven verses form a complete unit by themselves, and are recited in every prayer and on many other occasions. *Cf.* xv. 87.

Sūra I.

Fātiḥa, or the Opening Chapter.[18]

1. *In the name of God, Most Gracious, Most Merciful.*[19]

2. Praise be to God,
The Cherisher and Sustainer[20] of the Worlds;

3. Most Gracious, Most Merciful;

4. Master of the Day of Judgment.

5. Thee do we worship,[21]
And Thine aid we seek.

18. By universal consent it is rightly placed at the beginning of the Qur-ān, as summing up, in marvellously terse and comprehensive words, man's relation to God in contemplation and prayer. In our spiritual contemplation the first words should be those of praise. If the praise is from our inmost being, it brings us into union with God's will. Then our eyes see all good, peace, and harmony. Evil, rebellion, and conflict are purged out. They do not exist for us, for our eyes are lifted up above them in praise. Then we see God's attributes better (verses 2-4). This leads us to the attitude of worship and acknowledgment (verse 5). And finally comes prayer for guidance, and a contemplation of what guidance means (verses 6-7).

• God needs no praise, for He is above all praise; He needs no petition, for He knows our needs better than we do ourselves; and His bounties are open without asking, to the righteous and the sinner alike. The prayer is for our own spiritual education, consolation, and confirmation.

That is why the words in this Sūra are given to us in the form in which we should utter them. When we reach enlightenment, they flow spontaneously from us.

19. The Arabic words "*Raḥmān*" and "*Raḥīm*," translated "Most Gracious" and "Most Merciful" are both intensive forms referring to different aspects of God's attribute of Mercy. The Arabic intensive is more suited to express God's attributes than the superlative degree in English. The latter implies a comparison with other beings, or with other times or places, while there is no being like unto God, and He is independent of Time and Place. Mercy may imply pity, long-suffering, patience, and forgiveness, all of which the sinner needs and God Most Merciful bestows in abundant measure. But there is a Mercy that goes before even the need arises, the Grace which is ever watchful, and flows from God Most Gracious to all His creatures, protecting them, preserving them, guiding them, and leading them to clearer light and higher life. For this reason the attribute *Raḥmān* (Most Gracious) is not applied to any but God, but the attribute *Raḥīm* (Merciful), is a general term, and may also be applied to Men. To make us contemplate these boundless gifts of God, the formula: "In the name of God Most Gracious, Most Merciful": is placed before every Sūra of the Qur-ān (except the ninth), and repeated at the beginning of every act by the Muslim who dedicates his life to God, and whose hope is in His Mercy.

Opinion is divided whether the *Bismillāh* should be numbered as a separate verse or not. It is unanimously agreed that it is a part of the Qur-ān. Therefore it is better to give it an independent number in the first Sūra. For subsequent Sūras it is treated as an introduction or head-line, and therefore not numbered.

20. The Arabic word *Rabb*, usually translated Lord, has also the meaning of cherishing, sustaining, bringing to maturity. God cares for all the worlds He has created.

There are many worlds,—astronomical and physical worlds, worlds of thought, spiritual worlds, and so on. In every one of them, God is all in all. We express only one aspect of it when we say: "In Him we live, and move, and have our being." The mystical division between (1) *Nāsūt*, the human world knowable by the senses, (2) *Malakūt*, the invisible world of angels, and (3) *Lāhūt*, the divine world of Reality, requires a whole volume to explain it.

21. On realizing in our souls God's love and care, His grace and mercy, and His power and justice (as Ruler of the Day of Judgment), the immediate result is that we bend in the act of worship, and see both our shortcomings and His all-sufficient power. The emphatic form means that not only do we reach the position of worshipping God and asking for His help, but we worship Him alone and ask for His aid only. For there is none other than He worthy of our devotion and able to help us. The plural "we" indicates that we associate ourselves with all who seek God, thus strengthening ourselves and strengthening them in a fellowship of faith.

6. Show[22] us the straight way,	٦- اِهْدِنَا الصِّرَاطَ الْمُسْتَقِيمَ ۝
7. The way of those on whom Thou hast bestowed Thy Grace, Those whose (portion) Is not wrath,[23] And who go not astray.[24]	٧- صِرَاطَ الَّذِينَ أَنْعَمْتَ عَلَيْهِمْ ۥ غَيْرِ ع الْمَغْضُوبِ عَلَيْهِمْ وَلَا الضَّآلِّينَ ۝

22. If we translate by the English word "guide," we shall have to say: Guide us to and in the straight Way." For we may be wandering aimlessly, and the first step is to find the Way; and the second need is to keep in the Way: our own wisdom may fail in either case. The straight Way is often the narrow Way, or the steep Way, which many people shun (xc. 11). By the world's perversity the straight Way is sometimes stigmatized and the crooked Way praised. How are we to judge? We must ask for God's guidance. With a little spiritual insight we shall see which are the people who walk in the light of God's grace, and which are those that walk in the darkness of Wrath. This also would help our judgment.

23. Note that the words relating to Grace are connected actively with God; those relating to Wrath are impersonal. In the one case God's Mercy encompasses us beyond our deserts. In the other case our own actions are responsible for the Wrath,—the negative of Grace, Peace, or Harmony.

24. Are there two categories?—those who are in the darkness of Wrath and those who stray? The first are those who deliberately break God's law; the second those who stray out of carelessness or negligence. Both are responsible for their own acts or omissions. In opposition to both are the people who are in the light of God's Grace: for His Grace not only protects them from active wrong (if they will only submit their will to Him) but also from straying into paths of temptation or carelessness. The negative *gair* should be construed as applying not to the way, but as describing men protected from two dangers by God's Grace.

INTRODUCTION TO SŪRA II (*Baqara*)

As the Opening Sūra sums up in seven beautiful verses the essence of the Qur-ān, so this Sūra sums up in 286 verses the whole teaching of the Qur-ān. It is a closely reasoned argument.

Summary.—It begins (verses 1-29) with mystic doctrine as to the three kinds of men and how they receive God's message.

This leads to the story of the creation of man, the high destiny intended for him, his fall, and the hope held out to him (ii. 30-39).

Israel's story is then told according to their own records and traditions—what privileges they received and how they abused them (ii. 40-86), thus illustrating again as by a parable the general story of man.

In particular, reference is made to Moses and Jesus and their struggles with an unruly people: how the people of the Book played false with their own lights and in their pride rejected Muhammad, who came in the true line of apostolic succession (ii. 87-121).

They falsely laid claim to the virtues of Father Abraham: he was indeed a righteous Imām, but he was the progenitor of Ismā'īl's line (Arabs) as well as of Israel's line, and he with Ismā'īl built the Ka'ba (Temple of Mecca) and purified it, thus establishing a common religion, of which Islam is the universal exponent (ii. 122-141).

The Ka'ba was now to be the centre of universal worship and the symbol of Islamic unity (ii. 142-167).

The Islamic *Ummat* (brotherhood) having thus been established with its definite centre and symbol, ordinances are laid down for the social life of the community, with the proviso (ii. 177) that righteousness does not consist in formalities, but in faith, kindness, prayer, charity, probity, and patience under suffering. The ordinances relate to food and drink, bequests, fasts, *jihād*, wine and gambling, treatment of orphans and women, etc. (ii. 168-242).

Lest the subject of *jihād* should be misunderstood, it is taken up again in the story of Saul, Goliath and David, in contrast to the story of Jesus (ii. 243-253).

And so the lesson is enforced that true virtue lies in practical deeds of manliness, kindness, and good faith (ii. 254-283), and God's nature is called to mind in the sublime *Ayat-ul-Kursī*, the Verse of the Throne (ii. 255).

The Sūra ends with an exhortation to Faith, Obedience, a sense of Personal Responsibility, and Prayer (ii. 284-286).

This is the longest Sūra of the Qur-ān, and in it occurs the longest verse (ii. 282). The name of the Sūra is from the Parable of the Heifer in ii. 67-71, which illustrates the insufficiency of carping obedience. When faith is lost, people put off obedience with various excuses: even when at last they obey in the letter, they fail in the spirit, which means that they get fossilized, and their self-sufficiency prevents them from seeing that spiritually they are not alive but dead. For life is movement, activity, striving, fighting against baser things. And this is the burden of the Sūra.

This is in the main an early Medina Sūra.

C. 44.—The Message of God is a guide that is sure
(ii. 1-29) To those who seek His light. But those
Who reject faith are blind: their hearts
Are sealed. Woe to the hypocrites,
Self-deceived and deceiving others,
With mockery on their lips, and mischief
In their hearts, and fear; the clouds
That bring fertilizing rain to others,
To them bring but deafening thunder-peals
And lightning flashes blinding to their eyes.

Sūra II.

Baqara, or the Heifer.

In the name of God, Most Gracious,
Most Merciful.

1. A. L. M.[25]

2. This is the Book;
In it is guidance sure, without doubt,
To those who fear[26] God;

3. Who believe in the Unseen,
Are steadfast in prayer,
And spend out of what We
Have provided for them;[27]

4. And who believe in the Revelation
Sent to thee,

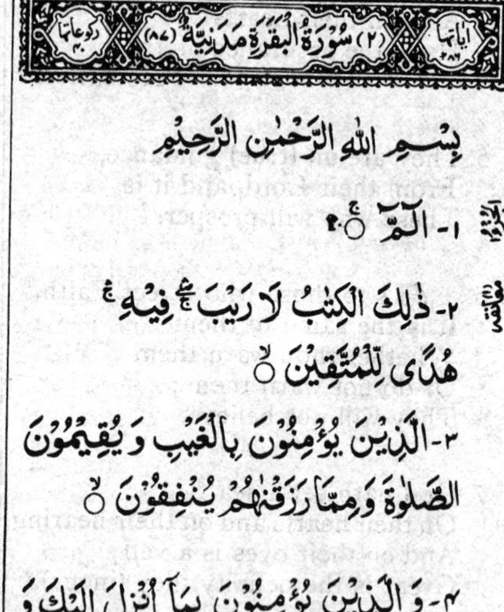

25. These are abbreviated letters, the *Muqaṭṭa'āt*, on which a general discussion will be found in Appendix I (to be printed at the end of this Sūra).

The particular letters, A. L. M., are found prefixed to this Sūra, and Sūras iii, xxix, xxx, xxxi and xxxii (six in all). In ii and iii the argument is about the rise and fall of nations, their past, and their future in history, with ordinances for the new universal People of Islam. In xxix a similar argument about nations leads off to the mystery of Life and Death, Failure and Triumph, Past and Future, in the history of individual souls. The burden of xxx is that God is the source of all things and all things return to Him. In xxxi and xxxii the same lesson is enforced: God is the Creator and He will be the judge on the Last Day. There is therefore a common thread, the mystery of Life and Death, Beginning and End.

Much has been written about the meaning of these letters, but most of it is pure conjecture. Some commentators are content to recognize them as some mystic symbols, of which it is unprofitable to discuss the meaning by mere verbal logic. In mysticism we accept symbols as such for the time being: their esoteric meaning comes from the inner light when we are ready for it.

Among the conjectures there are two plausible theories. One is that each initial represents an attribute of God. Among the attributes it is not difficult to select three which will fit in with these letters. Another theory, favoured by Baidhāwī, is that these letters are the initial, the final and the middle (or again the initial) letter of three names: Allāh, Jibrīl, and Muḥammad,—the source of revelation, the heavenly Messenger who brought it, and the human Messenger through whom it was promulgated in human speech. This might be appropriate to the first *Sūra* (which *Baqara* really is if we treat *Fātiḥa* as a preface): but if it was prefixed to others, why to these six only?

If we look to the nature of the sounds which the letters represent, A is a breathing and comes from the throat, L is a lingual-palatal-dental sound from the middle of the mouth, and M is a labial or lip-sound. Can we not take them as symbolical of the Beginning, Middle and End? If so, are they not appropriate to the Sūras which treat specifically of Life, Growth, and Death—the Beginning and the End? In the New Testament Greek scripture, the first and the last letters of the Greek alphabet, Alpha and Omega, are symbolical of the Beginning and the End, and give one of the titles of God: "I am Alpha and Omega, the beginning and the ending, saith the Lord, which is, and which was, and which is to come, the Almighty." (Rev. i. 8.) The symbolism of the three things is better with three letters.

26. *Taqwā*, and the verbs and nouns connected with the root, signify: (1) the fear of God, which, according to the writer of Proverbs (i. 7) in the Old Testament, is the beginning of Wisdom; (2) restraint, or guarding one's tongue, hand, and heart from evil; (3) hence righteousness, piety, good conduct. All these ideas are implied: in the translation, only one or other of these ideas can be indicated, according to the context. See also xlvii. 17; and lxxiv. 56, n. 5808.

27. All bounties proceed from God. They may be physical gifts, *e.g.*, food, clothing, houses, gardens, wealth, etc., or intangible gifts, *e.g.*, influence, power, birth and the opportunities flowing from it, health, talents, etc., or spiritual gifts, *e.g.*, insight into good and evil, understanding of men, the capacity for love, etc. We are to use all in humility and moderation. But we are also to give out of every one of them something that contributes to the well-being of others. We are to be neither ascetics nor luxurious sybarites, neither selfish misers nor thoughtless prodigals.

And sent before thy time,
And (in their hearts)
Have the assurance of the
Hereafter.[28]

مَآ أُنزِلَ مِن قَبْلِكَ وَبِالْآخِرَةِ هُمْ
يُوقِنُونَ ۝

5. They are on (true) guidance,
From their Lord, and it is
These who will prosper.[29]

٥- أُولَٰٓئِكَ عَلَىٰ هُدًى مِّن رَّبِّهِمْ وَأُولَٰٓئِكَ
هُمُ الْمُفْلِحُونَ ۝

6. As to those who reject Faith,[30]
It is the same to them
Whether thou warn them
Or do not warn them;
They will not believe.

٦- إِنَّ الَّذِينَ كَفَرُوا سَوَآءٌ عَلَيْهِمْ
ءَأَنذَرْتَهُمْ أَمْ لَمْ تُنذِرْهُمْ لَا يُؤْمِنُونَ ۝

7. God hath set a seal[31]
On their hearts and on their hearing,
And on their eyes is a veil;
Great is the penalty they (incur).[32]

٧- خَتَمَ اللَّهُ عَلَىٰ قُلُوبِهِمْ وَعَلَىٰ سَمْعِهِمْ وَ
عَلَىٰٓ أَبْصَٰرِهِمْ غِشَٰوَةٌ وَلَهُمْ عَذَابٌ عَظِيمٌ ۝

SECTION 2.

8. Of the people there are some
who say:[33]
"We believe in God and the Last
Day;"
But they do not (really) believe.

٨- وَمِنَ النَّاسِ مَن يَقُولُ ءَامَنَّا بِاللَّهِ وَ
بِالْيَوْمِ الْآخِرِ وَمَا هُم بِمُؤْمِنِينَ ۝

9. Fain would they deceive
God and those who believe,
But they only deceive themselves,
And realize (it) not!

٩- يُخَٰدِعُونَ اللَّهَ وَالَّذِينَ ءَامَنُوا وَمَا
يَخْدَعُونَ إِلَّآ أَنفُسَهُمْ وَمَا يَشْعُرُونَ ۝

10. In their hearts is a disease;

١٠- فِي قُلُوبِهِم مَّرَضٌ فَزَادَهُمُ اللَّهُ مَرَضًا

28. Righteousness comes from a secure faith, from sincere devotion to God, and from unselfish service to Man.

29. Prosperity must be taken as referring to all the kinds of bounty which we discussed in the note to ii. 3 above. The right use of one kind leads to an increase in that and other kinds, and that is prosperity.

30. *Kafara, kufr, kāfir,* and derivative forms of the word, imply a deliberate rejection of Faith as opposed to a mistaken idea of God or faith, which is not inconsistent with an earnest desire to see the truth. Where there is such desire, the grace and mercy of God gives guidance. But that guidance is not efficacious when it is deliberately rejected, and the possibility of rejection follows from the grant of free will. The consequence of the rejection is that the spiritual faculties become dead or impervious to better influences. See also n. 93 to ii. 88.

31. All actions are referred to God. Therefore when we get the penalty of our deliberate sin, and our senses become impervious to good, the penalty is referred to the justice of God.

32. The penalty here is the opposite of the prosperity referred to in ii. 5. As we go down the path of sin, our penalty gathers momentum, just as goodness brings its own capacity for greater goodness.

33. We now come to a third class of people, the hypocrites. They are untrue to themselves, and therefore their hearts are diseased (ii. 10). The disease tends to spread, like all evil. They are curable, but if they harden their hearts, they soon pass into the category of those who deliberately reject light.

And God has increased their
disease:[34]
And grievous is the penalty they
(incur),
Because they are false
(to themselves).

وَلَهُمْ عَذَابٌ أَلِيمٌ ۙ بِمَا كَانُوا
يَكْذِبُونَ ○

11. When it is said to them:
"Make not mischief on the earth,"
They say: "Why, we only
Want to make peace!"

١١- وَإِذَا قِيلَ لَهُمْ لَا تُفْسِدُوا فِي الْأَرْضِ
قَالُوا إِنَّمَا نَحْنُ مُصْلِحُونَ ○

12. Of a surety, they are the ones
Who make mischief,
But they realize (it) not.[35]

١٢- أَلَا إِنَّهُمْ هُمُ الْمُفْسِدُونَ وَلَٰكِنْ لَا
يَشْعُرُونَ ○

13. When it is said to them:
"Believe as the others believe:"
They say: "Shall we believe
As the fools believe?"—
Nay, of a surety they are the fools,
But they do not know.[36]

١٣- وَإِذَا قِيلَ لَهُمْ آمِنُوا كَمَا آمَنَ النَّاسُ
قَالُوا أَنُؤْمِنُ كَمَا آمَنَ السُّفَهَاءُ ۗ أَلَا إِنَّهُمْ
هُمُ السُّفَهَاءُ وَلَٰكِنْ لَا يَعْلَمُونَ ○

14. When they meet those who believe,[37]
They say: "We believe;"
But when they are alone
With their evil ones,
They say: "We are really with you:
We (were) only jesting."

١٤- وَإِذَا لَقُوا الَّذِينَ آمَنُوا قَالُوا آمَنَّا ۚ وَإِذَا
خَلَوْا إِلَىٰ شَيَاطِينِهِمْ ۙ قَالُوا إِنَّا مَعَكُمْ ۙ إِنَّمَا
نَحْنُ مُسْتَهْزِئُونَ ○

15. God will throw back
Their mockery on them,
And give them rope in their
trespasses;
So they will wander like blind ones
(To and fro).

١٥- اللَّهُ يَسْتَهْزِئُ بِهِمْ وَيَمُدُّهُمْ فِي طُغْيَانِهِمْ
يَعْمَهُونَ ○

16. These are they who have bartered
Guidance for error:

١٦- أُولَٰئِكَ الَّذِينَ اشْتَرَوُا الضَّلَالَةَ بِالْهُدَىٰ

34. The insincere man who thinks he can get the best of both worlds by compromising with good and evil only increases the disease of his heart, because he is not true to himself. Even the good which comes to him he can pervert to evil. So the rain which fills out the ear of corn or lends fragrance to the rose also lends strength to the thorn or adds strength to the poison of the deadly night-shade.

35. Much mischief is caused (sometimes unwittingly) by people who think that they have a mission of peace, when they have not even a true perception of right and wrong. By their blind arrogance they depress the good and encourage the evil.

36. This is another phase of the hypocrite and the cynic. "Faith," he says, "is good enough to fools." But his cynicism may be the greatest folly in the eyes of God.

37. A deeper phase of insincerity is actual duplicity. But it never pays in the end. If we compare such a man to a trader, he loses in the bargain.

But their traffic is profitless,
And they have lost true direction,

فَمَا رَبِحَتْ تِّجَارَتُهُمْ وَمَا كَانُوا مُهْتَدِينَ ○

17. Their similitude is that of a man[38]
Who kindled a fire;
When it lighted all around him,
God took away their light
And left them in utter darkness.
So they could not see.

١٧- مَثَلُهُمْ كَمَثَلِ الَّذِي اسْتَوْقَدَ نَارًا فَلَمَّا
أَضَاءَتْ مَا حَوْلَهُ ذَهَبَ اللَّهُ بِنُورِهِمْ وَتَرَكَهُمْ
فِي ظُلُمَٰتٍ لَّا يُبْصِرُونَ ○

18. Deaf, dumb, and blind,
They will not return (to the path).

١٨- صُمٌّ بُكْمٌ عُمْيٌ فَهُمْ لَا يَرْجِعُونَ ○

19. Or (another similitude)[39]
Is that of a rain-laden cloud
From the sky: in it are zones
Of darkness, and thunder and lightning:
They press their fingers in their ears
To keep out the stunning thunder-clap,
The while they are in terror of death.
But God is ever round
The rejecters of Faith!

١٩- أَوْ كَصَيِّبٍ مِّنَ السَّمَاءِ فِيهِ ظُلُمَٰتٌ وَ
رَعْدٌ وَبَرْقٌ
يَجْعَلُونَ أَصَٰبِعَهُمْ فِي ءَاذَانِهِم مِّنَ الصَّوَٰعِقِ
حَذَرَ الْمَوْتِ
وَاللَّهُ مُحِيطٌ بِالْكَٰفِرِينَ ○

20. The lightning all but snatches away
Their sight; every time the light
(Helps) them, they walk therein,
And when the darkness grows on them,
They stand still.
And if God willed, He could take away
Their faculty of hearing and seeing;
For God hath power over all things.

٢٠- يَكَادُ الْبَرْقُ يَخْطَفُ أَبْصَٰرَهُمْ كُلَّمَا
أَضَاءَ لَهُم مَّشَوْا فِيهِ وَإِذَا أَظْلَمَ عَلَيْهِمْ
قَامُوا وَلَوْ شَاءَ اللَّهُ لَذَهَبَ بِسَمْعِهِمْ وَ
أَبْصَٰرِهِمْ
إِنَّ اللَّهَ عَلَىٰ كُلِّ شَيْءٍ قَدِيرٌ ○

---

38. The man wanted light; he only kindled a fire. It produced a blaze, and won the applause of all around. But it did not last long. When the flame went out as was inevitable, the darkness was worse than before. And they all lost their way. So hypocrisy, deception, arrogant compromise with evil, cynicism, or duplicity may win temporary applause. But the true light of faith and sincerity is wanting, and therefore it must mislead and ruin all concerned. In the consternation they cannot speak or hear each other, and of course they cannot see; so they end like the deliberate rejecters of Faith (ii. 7), wildly groping about, dumb, deaf and blind.

39. A wonderfully graphic and powerful simile applying to those who reject Faith. In their self-sufficiency they are undisturbed normally. But what happens when a great storm breaks over them? They cover their ears against thunder-claps, and the lightning nearly blinds them. They are in mortal fear, but God encompasses them around—even them, for He at all times encompasses all. He gives them rope. In the intervals of deafening noise and blinding flashes, there are moments of steady light, and these creatures take advantage of them, but again they are plunged into darkness. Perhaps they curse; perhaps they think that the few moments of effective light are due to their own intelligence! How much wiser would they be if they humbled themselves and sought the light of God!

Section 3.

21. O ye people!
Adore your Guardian-Lord,
Who created you
And those who came before you,
That ye may have the chance
To learn righteousness;[40]

٢١- يَٰٓأَيُّهَا ٱلنَّاسُ ٱعْبُدُوا۟ رَبَّكُمُ ٱلَّذِى
خَلَقَكُمْ وَٱلَّذِينَ مِن قَبْلِكُمْ لَعَلَّكُمْ
تَتَّقُونَ ○

22. Who has made the earth your couch,
And the heavens your canopy;
And sent down rain from the heavens;
And brought forth therewith
Fruits for your sustenance;
Then set not up rivals[41] unto God
When ye know (the truth).

٢٢- ٱلَّذِى جَعَلَ لَكُمُ ٱلْأَرْضَ فِرَٰشًا وَٱلسَّمَآءَ
بِنَآءً وَأَنزَلَ مِنَ ٱلسَّمَآءِ مَآءً فَأَخْرَجَ
بِهِۦ مِنَ ٱلثَّمَرَٰتِ رِزْقًا لَّكُمْ فَلَا تَجْعَلُوا۟
لِلَّهِ أَندَادًا وَأَنتُمْ تَعْلَمُونَ ○

23. And if ye are in doubt
As to what We have revealed
From time to time to Our servant,
Then produce a Sūra
Like thereunto;
And call your witnesses or helpers
(If there are any) besides God,
If your (doubts) are true.[42]

٢٣- وَإِن كُنتُمْ فِى رَيْبٍ مِّمَّا نَزَّلْنَا عَلَىٰ
عَبْدِنَا فَأْتُوا۟ بِسُورَةٍ مِّن مِّثْلِهِۦ وَٱدْعُوا۟
شُهَدَآءَكُم مِّن دُونِ ٱللَّهِ إِن كُنتُمْ
صَٰدِقِينَ ○

24. But if ye cannot—
And of a surety ye cannot—
Then fear the Fire
Whose fuel is Men and Stones,—
Which is prepared for those

٢٤- فَإِن لَّمْ تَفْعَلُوا۟ وَلَن تَفْعَلُوا۟ فَٱتَّقُوا۟ ٱلنَّارَ
ٱلَّتِى وَقُودُهَا ٱلنَّاسُ وَٱلْحِجَارَةُ أُعِدَّتْ
لِلْكَٰفِرِينَ ○

40. For Taqwā see ii. 2 n. 26. I connect this dependent clause with "adore, etc." above, though it could be connected with "created." According to my construction the argument will be as follows. Adoration is the act of the highest and humblest reverence and worship. When you get into that relationship with God, Who is your Creator and Guardian, your faith produces works of righteousness. It is a chance given you: will you exercise your free will and take it? If you do, your whole nature will be transformed.

41. Further proofs of God's goodness to you are given in this verse. Your whole life, physical and spiritual, depends upon Him. The spiritual is figured by the Canopy of Heaven. The truth has been brought plainly before you. Will you still resist it and go after false gods, the creation of your own fancy? The false gods may be idols, superstitions, Self, or even great or glorious things like Poetry, Art, or Science, when set up as rivals to God. They may be pride of race, pride of birth, pride of wealth or position, pride of power, pride of learning, or even spiritual pride.

42. How do we know that there is revelation, and that it is from God? Here is a concrete test. The Teacher of God's Truth has placed before you many Sūras. Can you produce one like it? If there is any one besides God, who can inspire spiritual truth in such noble language, produce your evidence. Or is it that your doubts are merely argumentative, refractory, against your own inner light, or conscience? All true revelation is itself a miracle, and stands on its own merits.

Who reject Faith.[43]

25. But give glad tidings
To those who believe
And work righteousness,
That their portion is Gardens,
Beneath which rivers flow.
Every time they are fed
With fruits therefrom,
They say: "Why, this is
What we were fed with before,"
For they are given things in
similitude;
And they have therein
Companions pure (and holy);[44]
And they abide therein (for ever).

٢٥- وَبَشِّرِ الَّذِينَ اٰمَنُوا وَعَمِلُوا الصّٰلِحٰتِ
أَنَّ لَهُمْ جَنّٰتٍ تَجْرِي مِنْ تَحْتِهَا الْأَنْهٰرُ ۖ
كُلَّمَا رُزِقُوا مِنْهَا مِنْ ثَمَرَةٍ رِّزْقًا ۙ قَالُوا
هٰذَا الَّذِي رُزِقْنَا مِنْ قَبْلُ ۙ وَأُتُوا بِهٖ
مُتَشٰبِهًا ۖ
وَلَهُمْ فِيهَا أَزْوَاجٌ مُّطَهَّرَةٌ ۙ وَهُمْ
فِيهَا خٰلِدُونَ ۝

26. God disdains not to use
The similitude of things,
Lowest[45] as well as highest.

٢٦- إِنَّ اللّٰهَ لَا يَسْتَحْيٖٓ أَنْ يَضْرِبَ مَثَلًا

43. If by your own efforts you cannot match the spiritual light, and yet contumaciously reject spiritual Faith, then there will be a fire in your souls, the Punishment that burns up all your cherished idols. Perhaps you will at least fear this penalty, which your self-loving souls can understand. This fire consumes both the worshippers of the False and the Idols which they falsely worship. Can this bring them to their senses? Its power is not only over the feeling, palpitating heart of man (heart in a spiritual sense, as it persists long after the physical heart), but he cannot escape from it even if he imagines himself reduced to inertness like stocks or stones; for it is all-devouring.

44. This is the antithesis to the last verse. If fire is the symbol of Punishment, the Garden is the symbol of felicity. And what can be more delightful than a Garden where you observe from a picturesque height a beautiful landscape round you,—rivers flowing with crystal water, and fruit trees of which the choicest fruit is before you. The fruit of goodness is goodness, similar, but choicer in every degree of ascent. You think it is the same, but it is because of your past experiences and associations of memory. Then there is companionship. If sex is suggested, its physical associations are at once negatived by the addition of the word *Muṭahharatun* "pure and holy." The Arabic epithet is in the intensive form, and must be translated by two adjectives denoting purity in the highest degree. The Companionship is that of souls and applies to both sexes in the physical world of men and women. And this felicity is not a mere passing phase but will abide beyond the realms of Time.

45. The word for "the lowest" in the original Arabic means a gnat, a byword in the Arabic language for the weakest of creatures. In xxix. 41, which was revealed before this Sūra, the similitude of the Spider was used, and similarly in xxii. 73, there is the similitude of the Fly. For similitudes taken from magnificent forces of nature, expressed in exalted language, see ii. 19 above. To God all His creation has some special meaning appropriate to itself, and some of what we consider the lowest creatures have wonderful aptitudes, *e.g.*, the spider or the fly. Parables like these may be an occasion of stumbling to those "who forsake the path"; in other words those who deliberately shut their eyes to God's Signs, and their Penalty is attributed to God, the Cause of all causes. But lest there should be misunderstanding, it is immediately added that the stumbling and offence only occur as the result of the sinner's own choice of the wrong course. Verses 26 and 27 form one sentence and should be read together. "Forsaking the path" is defined in ii. 27; *viz.*, breaking solemn covenants which the sinner's own soul had ratified, causing division among mankind, who were meant to be one brotherhood, and doing as much mischief as possible in the life on this earth, for the life beyond will be on another plane, where no rope will be given to evil.

The mention of the Covenant (ii. 27) has a particular and a general signification. The particular one has reference to the Jewish tradition that a Covenant was entered into with "Father Abraham" that in return for God's favours the seed of Abraham would serve God faithfully. But as a matter of fact a great part of Abraham's progeny were in constant spiritual rebellion against God, as is testified by their own Prophets and Preachers and by Muḥammad Muṣṭafā. The general signification is that a similar Covenant is metaphorically entered into by every creature of God: for God's loving care, we at least owe Him the fullest gratitude and willing obedience. The Sinner, before he darkens his own conscience, knows this, and yet he not only "forsakes the path" but resists the Grace of God which comes to save him. That is why his case becomes hopeless. But the loss is his own. He cannot spoil God's design. The good man is glad to retrace his steps from any lapses of which he may have been guilty, and in his case God's Message reclaims him with complete understanding.

Those who believe know
That it is truth from their Lord;
But those who reject Faith say:
"What means God by this
similitude?"
By it He causes many to stray,
And many He leads into the right
path;
But He causes not to stray,
Except those who forsake
(the path),—

مَّا بَعُوضَةً فَمَا فَوْقَهَا ۚ فَأَمَّا الَّذِينَ آمَنُوا
فَيَعْلَمُونَ أَنَّهُ الْحَقُّ مِن رَّبِّهِمْ ۖ وَأَمَّا
الَّذِينَ كَفَرُوا فَيَقُولُونَ مَاذَا أَرَادَ اللَّهُ
بِهَٰذَا مَثَلًا ۘ يُضِلُّ بِهِ كَثِيرًا وَيَهْدِي
بِهِ كَثِيرًا ۚ
وَمَا يُضِلُّ بِهِ إِلَّا الْفَاسِقِينَ ۝

27. Those who break God's Covenant
After it is ratified,
And who sunder what God
Has ordered to be joined,
And do mischief on earth:
These cause loss (only) to
themselves.

٢٧- الَّذِينَ يَنقُضُونَ عَهْدَ اللَّهِ مِن بَعْدِ
مِيثَاقِهِ وَيَقْطَعُونَ مَا أَمَرَ اللَّهُ بِهِ أَن
يُوصَلَ وَيُفْسِدُونَ فِي الْأَرْضِ ۚ أُولَٰئِكَ
هُمُ الْخَاسِرُونَ ۝

28. How can ye reject[46]
The faith in God?—
Seeing that ye were without life,
And He gave you life;
Then will He cause you to die,
And will again bring you to life;
And again to Him will ye return.

٢٨- كَيْفَ تَكْفُرُونَ بِاللَّهِ وَكُنتُمْ أَمْوَاتًا
فَأَحْيَاكُمْ ۖ ثُمَّ يُمِيتُكُمْ ثُمَّ يُحْيِيكُمْ ثُمَّ
إِلَيْهِ تُرْجَعُونَ ۝

29. It is He Who hath created for you
All things that are on earth;
Moreover His design comprehended
the heavens,
For He gave order and perfection
To the seven firmaments;
And of all things
He hath perfect knowledge.

٢٩- هُوَ الَّذِي خَلَقَ لَكُم مَّا فِي الْأَرْضِ
جَمِيعًا ثُمَّ اسْتَوَىٰ إِلَى السَّمَاءِ فَسَوَّاهُنَّ
سَبْعَ سَمَاوَاتٍ ۚ
وَهُوَ بِكُلِّ شَيْءٍ عَلِيمٌ ۝

C. 45.—Yet man! What wonderful destiny
(ii. 30-39.) Is Thine! Created to be
God's vicegerent on earth!
A little higher than angels!

46. In the preceding verses God has used various arguments. He has recalled His goodness (ii. 21-22); resolved doubts (ii. 23); plainly set forth the penalty of wrong-doing (ii. 24); given glad tidings (ii. 25); shown how misunderstandings arise from a deliberate rejection of the light and breach of the Covenant (ii. 26-27). Now (ii. 28-29) He pleads with His creatures and appeals to their own subjective feelings. He brought you into being. The mysteries of life and death are in His hands. When you die on this earth, that is not the end. You were of Him, and you must return to Him. Look around you and realize your own dignity: it is from Him. The immeasurable depths of space above and around you may stagger you. They are part of His plan. What you have imagined as the seven firmaments (and any other scheme you may construct) bears witness to His design of order and perfection, for His knowledge (unlike yours) is all-comprehending. And yet will you deliberately reject or obscure or deaden the faculty of Faith which has been put into you?

Yet beguiled by evil! Set for a season
On this earth on probation
To purge thy stain, with the promise
Of guidance and hope from on high,
From the Oft-Returning, Merciful!
Wilt thou choose right and regain
Thy spiritual home with God?

SECTION 4.

30. Behold, thy Lord said to the angels: "I will create
A vicegerent on earth." They said:
"Wilt Thou place therein one who will make
Mischief therein and shed blood?—
Whilst we do celebrate Thy praises
And glorify Thy holy (name)?"
He said: "I know what ye know not."[47]

٣٠- وَإِذْ قَالَ رَبُّكَ لِلْمَلٰٓئِكَةِ إِنِّي جَاعِلٌ
فِي الْأَرْضِ خَلِيفَةً ۖ قَالُوٓا أَتَجْعَلُ فِيهَا
مَن يُفْسِدُ فِيهَا وَيَسْفِكُ الدِّمَآءَ ۚ وَ
نَحْنُ نُسَبِّحُ بِحَمْدِكَ وَنُقَدِّسُ لَكَ ۖ قَالَ
إِنِّيٓ أَعْلَمُ مَا لَا تَعْلَمُونَ ○

31. And He taught Adam the nature[48]
Of all things; then He placed them
Before the angels, and said: "Tell Me
The nature of these if ye are right."

٣١- وَعَلَّمَ ءَادَمَ الْأَسْمَآءَ كُلَّهَا ثُمَّ عَرَضَهُمْ
عَلَى الْمَلٰٓئِكَةِ فَقَالَ أَنۢبِـُٔونِي بِأَسْمَآءِ هٰٓؤُلَآءِ
إِن كُنتُمْ صٰدِقِينَ ○

32. They said: "Glory to Thee: of knowledge

٣٢- قَالُوا سُبْحٰنَكَ لَا عِلْمَ لَنَآ إِلَّا مَا عَلَّمْتَنَآ

47. It would seem that the angels, though holy and pure, and endued with power from God, yet represented only one side of Creation. We may imagine them without passion or emotion, of which the highest flower is love. If man was to be endued with emotions, those emotions could lead him to the highest and drag him to the lowest. The power of will or choosing would have to go with them, in order that man might steer his own bark. This power of will (when used aright) gave him to some extent a mastery over his own fortunes and over nature, thus bringing him nearer to the God-like nature, which has supreme mastery and will. We may suppose the angels had no independent wills of their own: their perfection in other ways reflected God's perfection but could not raise them to the dignity of vicegerency. The perfect vicegerent is he who has the power of initiative himself, but whose independent action always reflects perfectly the will of his Principal. The distinction is expressed by Shakespeare (Sonnet 94) in those fine lines: "They are the lords and owners of their faces, Others but stewards of their excellence." The angels in their one-sidedness saw only the mischief consequent on the misuse of the emotional nature by man; perhaps they also, being without emotions, did not understand the whole of God's nature, which gives and asks for love. In humility and true devotion to God, they remonstrate: we must not imagine the least tinge of jealousy, as they are without emotion. This mystery of love being above them, they are told that they do not know, and they acknowledge (in ii. 32 below) not their fault (for there is no question of fault) but their imperfection of knowledge. At the same time, the matter is brought home to them when the actual capacities of man are shown to them (ii. 31, 33).

48. The literal words in Arabic throughout this passage are: "The names of things:" which commentators take to mean the inner nature and qualities of things, and things here would include feelings. The whole passage is charged with mystic meaning. The particular qualities or feelings which were outside the nature of angels were put by God into the nature of man. Man was thus able to love and understand love, and thus plan and initiate, as becomes the office of vicegerent. The angels acknowledged this. These things they could only know from the outside, but they had faith, or belief in the Unseen. And they knew that God saw all—what others see, what others do not see, what others may even wish to conceal. Man has many qualities which are latent or which he may wish to suppress or conceal, to his own detriment.

We have none, save what Thou
Hast taught us: in truth it is Thou
Who art perfect in knowledge and wisdom."

إِنَّكَ أَنْتَ الْعَلِيمُ الْحَكِيمُ ○

33. He said: "O Adam! tell them
Their natures." When he had told them,
God said: "Did I not tell you
That I know the secrets of heaven
And earth, and I know what ye reveal
And what ye conceal?"

٣٣- قَالَ يٰٓاٰدَمُ اَنْۢبِئْهُمْ بِاَسْمَآئِهِمْ فَلَمَّا
اَنْۢبَاَهُمْ بِاَسْمَآئِهِمْ قَالَ اَلَمْ اَقُلْ لَّكُمْ اِنِّيٓ
اَعْلَمُ غَيْبَ السَّمٰوٰتِ وَالْاَرْضِ وَاَعْلَمُ مَا
تُبْدُوْنَ وَمَا كُنْتُمْ تَكْتُمُوْنَ ○

34. And behold, We said to the angels:
"Bow down to Adam:" and they bowed down:
Not so Iblīs:[49] he refused and was haughty:
He was of those who reject Faith.

٣٤- وَاِذْ قُلْنَا لِلْمَلٰٓئِكَةِ اسْجُدُوْا لِاٰدَمَ
فَسَجَدُوْٓا اِلَّآ اِبْلِيْسَ اَبٰى وَاسْتَكْبَرَ وَكَانَ
مِنَ الْكٰفِرِيْنَ ○

35. We said: "O Adam! dwell thou
And thy wife in the Garden;[50]
And eat of the bountiful things therein
As (where and when) ye will; but approach not this tree,
Or ye run into harm and transgression."[51]

٣٥- وَقُلْنَا يٰٓاٰدَمُ اسْكُنْ اَنْتَ وَزَوْجُكَ
الْجَنَّةَ وَكُلَا مِنْهَا رَغَدًا حَيْثُ شِئْتُمَا
وَلَا تَقْرَبَا هٰذِهِ الشَّجَرَةَ فَتَكُوْنَا مِنَ
الظّٰلِمِيْنَ ○

36. Then did Satan[52] make them slip
From the (Garden), and get them out

٣٦- فَاَزَلَّهُمَا الشَّيْطٰنُ عَنْهَا فَاَخْرَجَهُمَا

49. The Arabic may also be translated: "They bowed down, except Iblīs." In that case Iblīs (Satan) would be one of the angels. But the theory of fallen angels is not usually accepted in Muslim theology. In xviii. 50, Iblīs is spoken of as a Jinn. We shall discuss later the meaning of this word.

50. Was the Garden of Eden a place on this earth? Obviously not. For, in verse 36 below, it was after the Fall that the sentence was pronounced: "On earth will be your dwelling-place." Before the Fall, we must suppose Man to be on another plane altogether—of felicity, innocence, trust, a spiritual existence, with the negation of enmity, want of faith, and all evil. Perhaps Time and Space also did not exist, and the Garden is allegorical as well as the tree. The forbidden tree was not the tree of knowledge, for man was given in that perfect state fuller knowledge than he has now (ii. 31): it was the tree of Evil, which he was forbidden not only to eat of, but even to approach.

51. "*Ẓulm*" in Arabic implies harm, wrong, injustice, or transgression, and may have reference to oneself; when the wrong is done to others it implies tyranny and oppression; the idea of wrong naturally connects itself with darkness, which is another shade of meaning carried with the root word.

52. "Iblīs" in ii. 34 is apparently the Power of Evil, with the root idea of desperateness or rebellion. "Satan" in this verse is the Power of Evil, with the root idea of perversity or enmity. Note the appropriateness of the term on each occasion. Also, "slipping" from the Garden denotes the idea of Evil gradually tempting man from a higher to a lower state.

Of the state (of felicity) in which
They had been. We said:
"Get ye down, all (ye people[53]),
With enmity between yourselves.
On earth will be your dwelling-
place
And your means of livelihood[54]—
For a time."

مِمَّا كَانَا فِيْهِ ۪
وَقُلْنَا اهْبِطُوْا بَعْضُكُمْ لِبَعْضٍ عَدُوٌّ ۚ
وَلَكُمْ فِى الْاَرْضِ مُسْتَقَرٌّ وَّمَتَاعٌ اِلٰى
حِيْنٍ ○

37. Then learnt Adam from his Lord
Words of inspiration,[55] and his
Lord
Turned towards him; for He
Is Oft-Returning, Most Merciful.

۳۷- فَتَلَقّٰٓى اٰدَمُ مِنْ رَّبِّهٖ كَلِمٰتٍ فَتَابَ
عَلَيْهِ ؕ اِنَّهٗ هُوَ التَّوَّابُ الرَّحِيْمُ ○

38. We said: "Get ye down all from
here;
And if, as is sure, there comes to you
Guidance from Me,[56] whosoever
Follows My guidance, on them
Shall be no fear, nor shall they
grieve.

۳۸- قُلْنَا اهْبِطُوْا مِنْهَا جَمِيْعًا ۚ
فَاِمَّا يَاْتِيَنَّكُمْ مِّنِّىْ هُدًى فَمَنْ تَبِعَ
هُدَاىَ فَلَا خَوْفٌ عَلَيْهِمْ وَلَا هُمْ
يَحْزَنُوْنَ ○

39. "But those who reject Faith
And belie Our Signs,
They shall be Companions of the
Fire;
They shall abide therein."[57]

۳۹- وَالَّذِيْنَ كَفَرُوْا وَكَذَّبُوْا بِاٰيٰتِنَآ اُولٰٓئِكَ
اَصْحٰبُ النَّارِ ۚ هُمْ فِيْهَا خٰلِدُوْنَ ○ ع

C. 46.—Amongst men what nation had higher chances
(ii. 40-86.) In the realm of the Spirit than the Children of Israel?
But again and again did they fail in the Spirit.

---

53. God's decree is the result of man's action. Note the transition in Arabic from the singular number in ii. 33, to the dual in ii. 35, and the plural here, which I have indicated in English by "All ye people." Evidently Adam is the type of all mankind, and the sexes go together in all spiritual matters. Moreover, the expulsion applied to Adam, Eve, and Satan, and the Arabic plural is appropriate for any number greater than two.

54 Man's sojourn in this lower state, where he is partly an animal of this earth, is for a time. But he must fulfil his lower duties also, for they too are a part of his spiritual training.

55. As "names" in verse 31 above is used for the "nature of things," so "words" here mean "inspiration," "spiritual knowledge." The Arabic word used for "learn" here implies some effort on his part, to which God's Grace responded.

The Arabic word for "Repentance" (*tauba*) means "turning," and the intensive word (*tauwāb*) for God's forgiveness ("Oft-Returning" or "Ever-Returning") is from the same root. For repentance, three things are necessary: the sinner must acknowledge his wrong; he must give it up; and he must resolve to eschew it for the future. Man's nature is weak, and he may have to return again and again for mercy. So long as he does it sincerely, God is Oft-Returning, Most Merciful. For His grace helps out the sinner's shortcomings.

56. Note the transition from the plural "We" at the beginning of the verse to the singular "Me" later in the same verse. God speaks of Himself usually in the first person plural "We": it is the plural of respect and honour, and is used in human language in Royal proclamations and decrees. But where a special personal relationship is expressed the singular, "I" or "Me" is used *Cf.* xxvi 52. etc.

In spite of Man's fall, and in consequence of it, assurance of guidance is given. In case man follows the guidance, he is free from any fear for the present or the future, and any grief or sorrow for the past. The soul thus freed grows nearer to God.

57. But if the soul, in spite of the Oft-Returning Mercy of God, rejects the higher light and goes on sinning against that light, the inevitable consequence must be the spiritual Fire. It is not merely a fortuitous incident. As his rejection was deliberate and definite, so the consequences must be of an abiding character.

They rebelled against Moses and murmured
In the wilderness; the Prophets they slew
And the Signs they rejected; they falsified
Scripture and turned their backs on righteousness.

SECTION 5.

40. Children of Israel! call to mind
The (special) favour which I bestowed
Upon you, and fulfil your Covenant[58]
With Me as I fulfil My Covenant
With you, and fear none but Me.

۴۰- يٰبَنِيٓ إِسۡرَآءِيلَ اذۡكُرُوا نِعۡمَتِيَ الَّتِيٓ
أَنۡعَمۡتُ عَلَيۡكُمۡ وَأَوۡفُوا بِعَهۡدِيٓ أُوفِ
بِعَهۡدِكُمۡ
وَإِيَّايَ فَارۡهَبُونِ ○

41. And believe in what I reveal,[59]
Confirming the revelation
Which is with you,
And be not the first to reject
Faith therein, nor sell My Signs
For a small price; and fear Me,
And Me alone.

۴۱- وَاٰمِنُوا بِمَآ أَنۡزَلۡتُ مُصَدِّقًا لِّمَا مَعَكُمۡ
وَلَا تَكُونُوٓا أَوَّلَ كَافِرٍۭ بِهٖ وَلَا تَشۡتَرُوا
بِاٰيٰتِي ثَمَنًا قَلِيلًا
وَإِيَّايَ فَاتَّقُونِ ○

42. And cover not Truth
With falsehood, nor conceal
The Truth when ye know
(what it is).

۴۲- وَلَا تَلۡبِسُوا الۡحَقَّ بِالۡبَاطِلِ وَتَكۡتُمُوا
الۡحَقَّ وَأَنۡتُمۡ تَعۡلَمُونَ ○

43. And be steadfast in prayer;
Practise regular charity;
And bow down your heads[60]
With those who bow down
(in worship).

۴۳- وَأَقِيمُوا الصَّلٰوةَ وَاٰتُوا الزَّكٰوةَ وَارۡكَعُوا
مَعَ الرّٰكِعِينَ ○

44. Do ye enjoin right conduct
On the people, and forget
(To practise it) yourselves,
And yet ye study the Scripture?
Will ye not understand?

۴۴- أَتَأۡمُرُونَ النَّاسَ بِالۡبِرِّ وَتَنۡسَوۡنَ
أَنۡفُسَكُمۡ وَأَنۡتُمۡ تَتۡلُونَ الۡكِتٰبَ
أَفَلَا تَعۡقِلُونَ ○

---

58 The appeal is made to Israel subjectively in terms of their own tradition. You claim to be a favoured nation: have you forgotten My favours? You claim a special Covenant with Me: I have fulfilled My part of the Covenant by bringing you out of the land of bondage and giving you Canaan, the land "flowing with milk and honey": how have you fulfilled your part of the Covenant? Do you fear for your national existence? If you fear Me, nothing else will matter.

59 You received revelations before: now comes one confirming it: its first appeal should be to you: are you to be the first to reject it? And reject it for what? God's Signs are worth more than all your paltry considerations. And the standard of duty and righteousness is to be taken from God, and not from priests and customs.

60. The argument is still primarily addressed to the Jews, but is of universal application, as in all the teachings of the Qur-ān. The chief feature of Jewish worship was and is the bowing of the head.

45. Nay, seek (God's) help
With patient perseverance[61]
And prayer:
It is indeed hard, except
To those who bring a lowly spirit,—

٤٥- وَاسْتَعِينُوا بِالصَّبْرِ وَالصَّلٰوةِ ۚ وَإِنَّهَا
لَكَبِيرَةٌ إِلَّا عَلَى الْخٰشِعِينَ ۝

46. Who bear in mind the certainty
That they are to meet their Lord,
And that they are to return to Him.

٤٦- الَّذِينَ يَظُنُّونَ أَنَّهُم مُّلٰقُوا رَبِّهِمْ وَ
أَنَّهُمْ إِلَيْهِ رٰجِعُونَ ۝

SECTION 6.

47. Children of Israel! call to mind
The (special) favour which I bestowed
Upon you,[62] and that I preferred you
To all others (for My Message).

٤٧- يٰبَنِي إِسْرٰٓءِيلَ اذْكُرُوا نِعْمَتِيَ الَّتِي
أَنْعَمْتُ عَلَيْكُمْ وَأَنِّي فَضَّلْتُكُمْ عَلَى
الْعٰلَمِينَ ۝

48. Then guard yourselves against a day
When one soul shall not avail another
Nor shall intercession be accepted for her,
Nor shall compensation be taken from her,
Nor shall anyone be helped (from outside).[63]

٤٨- وَاتَّقُوا يَوْمًا لَّا تَجْزِي نَفْسٌ عَن
نَّفْسٍ شَيْـًٔا
وَلَا يُقْبَلُ مِنْهَا شَفٰعَةٌ
وَلَا يُؤْخَذُ مِنْهَا عَدْلٌ
وَلَا هُمْ يُنصَرُونَ ۝

49. And remember, We delivered you
From the people of Pharaoh: they set you
Hard tasks and punishments, slaughtered

٤٩- وَإِذْ نَجَّيْنٰكُم مِّنْ آلِ فِرْعَوْنَ يَسُومُونَكُمْ
سُوٓءَ الْعَذَابِ يُذَبِّحُونَ أَبْنَآءَكُمْ وَ
يَسْتَحْيُونَ نِسَآءَكُمْ ۚ

---

61. The Arabic word *Ṣabr* implies many shades of meaning, which it is impossible to comprehend in one English word. It implies (1) patience in the sense of being thorough, not hasty; (2) patient perseverance, constancy, steadfastness, firmness of purpose; (3) systematic as opposed to spasmodic or chance action; (4) a cheerful attitude of resignation and understanding in sorrow, defeat, or suffering, as opposed to murmuring or rebellion, but saved from mere passivity or listlessness, by the element of constancy or steadfastness.

62. These words are recapitulated from ii. 40, which introduced a general account of God's favours to Israel; now we are introduced to a particular account of incidents in Israel's history. Each incident is introduced by the Arabic word "*Iẕ*," which is indicated in the translation by "Remember."

63. Before passing to particular incidents, the conclusion is stated. Be on your guard; do not think that special favours exempt you from the personal responsibility of each soul.

Your sons and let your women-folk live;[64] Therein was a tremendous trial from your Lord.	وَ فِيْ ذٰلِكُمْ بَلَآءٌ مِّنْ رَّبِّكُمْ عَظِيْمٌ ○
50. And remember We divided The Sea for you and saved you And drowned Pharaoh's people Within your very sight.[65]	٥٠- وَاِذْ فَرَقْنَا بِكُمُ الْبَحْرَ فَاَنْجَيْنٰكُمْ وَ اَغْرَقْنَآ اٰلَ فِرْعَوْنَ وَاَنْتُمْ تَنْظُرُوْنَ ○
51. And remember We appointed Forty nights for Moses,[66] And in his absence ye took The calf (for worship), And ye did grievous wrong.	٥١- وَاِذْ وٰعَدْنَا مُوْسٰىٓ اَرْبَعِيْنَ لَيْلَةً ثُمَّ اتَّخَذْتُمُ الْعِجْلَ مِنْۢ بَعْدِهٖ وَاَنْتُمْ ظٰلِمُوْنَ ○
52. Even then We did forgive you;[67] There was a chance for you To be grateful.	٥٢- ثُمَّ عَفَوْنَا عَنْكُمْ مِّنْۢ بَعْدِ ذٰلِكَ لَعَلَّكُمْ تَشْكُرُوْنَ ○
53. And remember We gave Moses the Scripture and the Criterion[68]	٥٣- وَاِذْ اٰتَيْنَا مُوْسَى الْكِتٰبَ وَ الْفُرْقَانَ

64. The bondage of Egypt was indeed a tremendous trial. Even the Egyptians' wish to spare the lives of Israel's females when the males were slaughtered, added to the bitterness of Israel. Their hatred was cruel, but their "love" was still more cruel. About the hard tasks, see Exod. i. 14: "They made their lives bitter with hard bondage, in mortar and in brick, and in all manner of service in the field: all their service, wherein they made them serve, was with rigour." Pharaoh's taskmasters gave no straw, yet ordered the Israelites to make bricks without straw: Exod. v. 5-19. Pharaoh's decree was: "Every son that is born ye shall cast into the river, and every daughter ye shall save alive": Exod. i. 22. It was in consequence of this decree that Moses was hidden three months after he was born, and when he could be hidden no longer, he was put into an ark of bulrushes and cast into the Nile, where he was found by Pharaoh's daughter and wife (xxviii. 9), and adopted into the family: Exod. ii. 2-10. *Cf.* xx. 37-40. Thus Moses was brought up by the enemies of his people. He was chosen by God to deliver his people, and God's wisdom made the learning and experience and even cruelties of the Egyptian enemies themselves to contribute to the salvation of his people.

65. When the Israelites at last escaped from Egypt, they were pursued by Pharaoh and his host. By a miracle the Israelites crossed the Red Sea, but the host of Pharaoh was drowned: Exod. xiv. 5-31.

66. This was after the Ten Commandments and the Laws and Ordinances had been given on Mount Sinai: Moses was asked up into the Mount, and he was there forty days and forty nights: Exod. xxiv. 18. But the people got impatient of the delay, made a calf of melted gold, and offered worship and sacrifice to it: Exod. xxxii. 1-8.

67. Moses prayed for his people, and God forgave them. This is the language of the Qur-ān. The Old Testament version is rougher: "The Lord repented of the evil which He thought to do unto His people"; Exod. xxxii. 14. The Muslim position has always been that the Jewish (and Christian) scriptures as they stand cannot be traced direct to Moses or Jesus, but are later compilations. Modern scholarship and Higher Criticism has left no doubt on the subject. But the stories in these traditional books may be used in an appeal to those who use them: only they should be spiritualized, as they are here, and especially in ii. 54 below.

68. God's revelation, the expression of God's Will, is the true standard of right and wrong. It may be in a Book or in God's dealings in history. All these may be called His Signs or Miracles. In this passage some commentators take the Scripture and the Criterion (Furqān) to be identical. Others take them to be two distinct things: Scripture being the written Book and the Criterion being other Signs. I agree with the latter view. The word Furqān also occurs in xxi. 48 in connection with Moses and Aaron and in the first verse of Sūra xxv. as well as in its title, in connection with Muḥammad. As Aaron received no Book, Furqān must mean the other Signs. Muṣṭafā had both the Book and the other Signs: perhaps here too we take the other Signs as supplementing the Book. *Cf.* Wordsworth's "Arbiter undisturbed of right and wrong." (Prelude, Book 4.)

(Between right and wrong) : there was A chance for you to be guided aright.	لَعَلَّكُمْ تَهْتَدُوْنَ ○
54. And remember Moses said To his people : "O my people! Ye have indeed wronged Yourselves by your worship of the calf : So turn (in repentance) to your Maker, And slay yourselves (the wrong-doers) ;[69] That will be better for you In the sight of your Maker." Then He turned towards you (in forgiveness) : For He is Oft-Returning, Most Merciful.	٥٤- وَاِذْ قَالَ مُوْسٰى لِقَوْمِهٖ يٰقَوْمِ اِنَّكُمْ ظَلَمْتُمْ اَنْفُسَكُمْ بِاتِّخَاذِكُمُ الْعِجْلَ فَتُوْبُوْآ اِلٰى بَارِىِٕكُمْ فَاقْتُلُوْٓا اَنْفُسَكُمْ ۭ ذٰلِكُمْ خَيْرٌ لَّكُمْ عِنْدَ بَارِىِٕكُمْ ۭ فَتَابَ عَلَيْكُمْ ۭ اِنَّهٗ هُوَ التَّوَّابُ الرَّحِيْمُ ○
55. And remember ye said :[70] "O Moses! We shall never believe in thee Until we see God manifestly," But ye were dazed With thunder and lightning Even as ye looked on.	٥٥- وَاِذْ قُلْتُمْ يٰمُوْسٰى لَنْ نُّؤْمِنَ لَكَ حَتّٰى نَرَى اللّٰهَ جَهْرَةً فَاَخَذَتْكُمُ الصّٰعِقَةُ وَاَنْتُمْ تَنْظُرُوْنَ ○
56. Then We raised you up After your death : Ye had the chance To be grateful.	٥٦- ثُمَّ بَعَثْنٰكُمْ مِّنْۢ بَعْدِ مَوْتِكُمْ لَعَلَّكُمْ تَشْكُرُوْنَ ○
57. And We gave you the shade of clouds	٥٧- وَظَلَّلْنَا عَلَيْكُمُ الْغَمَامَ وَاَنْزَلْنَا عَلَيْكُمُ

69. Moses's speech may be construed literally, as translated, in which case it reproduces Euod. xxxii. 27-28 but in a much softened form, for the Old Testament says : "Go in and out from gate to gate throughout the camp, and slay every man his brother, and every man his companion, and every man his neighbour . . . and there fell of the people that day 3,000 men." A more spiritualized version would be that the order for slaying was given by way of trial, but was withdrawn, for God turned to them in forgiveness. A still more spiritualized way of construing it would be to take "*anfusakum*" as meaning "souls," not "selves." Then the sense of Moses's speech (abbreviated) would be : "By the worship of the calf you have wronged your own souls ; repent : mortify (=slay) your souls now ; it will be better in the sight of God."

The word here translated Maker [*Bāri*] has also in it a touch of the root-meaning of "liberator,"—an apt word as referring to the Israelites, who had just been liberated from bondage in Egypt.

70. We have hitherto had instances from the Jewish traditional *Taurāt* (or Pentateuch). Now we have some instances from Jewish traditions in the Talmud, or body of exposition in the Jewish theological schools. They are based on the Jewish scriptures, but add many marvellous details and homilies. As to seeing God, we have in Exod. xxxiii. 20 : "And He said, 'Thou canst not see My face : for there shall no man see Me and live'." The punishment for insisting on seeing God was therefore death : but those who rejected faith were forgiven, and yet they were ungrateful.

And sent down to you
Manna[71] and quails, saying:
"Eat of the good things
We have provided for you:"
(But they rebelled);
To Us they did no harm,
But they harmed their own souls.

الْمَنَّ وَالسَّلْوٰى ط
كُلُوْا مِنْ طَيِّبٰتِ مَا رَزَقْنٰكُمْ ط
وَمَا ظَلَمُوْنَا وَلٰكِنْ كَانُوْٓا اَنْفُسَهُمْ يَظْلِمُوْنَ ۝

58. And remember We said:
"Enter this town,[72] and eat
Of the plenty therein
As ye wish; but enter
The gate with humility,
In posture and in words,
And We shall forgive you your faults
And increase (the portion of)
Those who do good."

٥٨- وَاِذْ قُلْنَا ادْخُلُوْا هٰذِهِ الْقَرْيَةَ
فَكُلُوْا مِنْهَا حَيْثُ شِئْتُمْ رَغَدًا وَّادْخُلُوا
الْبَابَ سُجَّدًا وَّقُوْلُوْا حِطَّةٌ نَّغْفِرْ لَكُمْ
خَطٰيٰكُمْ ط
وَسَنَزِيْدُ الْمُحْسِنِيْنَ ۝

59. But the transgressors
Changed the word from that
Which had been given them;
So We sent on the transgressors
A plague from heaven,
For that they infringed
(Our command) repeatedly.

٥٩- فَبَدَّلَ الَّذِيْنَ ظَلَمُوْا قَوْلًا غَيْرَ الَّذِيْ
قِيْلَ لَهُمْ فَاَنْزَلْنَا عَلَى الَّذِيْنَ ظَلَمُوْا رِجْزًا
مِّنَ السَّمَآءِ بِمَا كَانُوْا يَفْسُقُوْنَ ۝ ع

SECTION 7.

60. And remember Moses prayed
For water for his people;
We said: "Strike the rock
With thy staff." Then gushed forth

٦٠- وَاِذِ اسْتَسْقٰى مُوْسٰى لِقَوْمِهٖ فَقُلْنَا
اضْرِبْ بِّعَصَاكَ الْحَجَرَ ط فَانْفَجَرَتْ مِنْهُ

71. Manna=Hebrew, *Man-hu*: Arabic *Mā-huwa?*=What is it? In Exod. xvi. 14 it is described as "a small round thing, as small as the hoar frost on the ground." It usually rotted if left over till next day; it melted in the hot sun; the amount necessary for each man was about an Omer, a Hebrew measure of capacity equal to about 2½ quarts. This is the Hebrew account, probably distorted by traditional exaggeration. The actual Manna found to this day in the Sinai region is a gummy saccharine secretion found on a species of Tamarisk. It is produced by the puncture of a species of insect like the cochineal, just as lac is produced by the puncture of the lac insect on certain trees in India. As to quails, large flights of them are driven by winds in the Eastern Mediterranean in certain seasons of the year, as was witnessed during the Great War of 1914-1918 by many Indian officers who campaigned between Egypt and Palestine.

72. This probably refers to Shittim. It was the "town of acacias," just east of the Jordan, where the Israelites were guilty of debauchery and the worship of and sacrifices to false gods (Num. xxv. 1-2, also 8-9); a terrible punishment ensued, including the plague, of which 24,000 died. The word which the transgressors changed may have been a pass-word. In the Arabic text it is "*Hiṭṭatun*" which implies humility and a prayer of forgiveness, a fitting emblem to distinguish them from their enemies. From this particular incident a more general lesson may be drawn: in the hour of triumph we are to behave humbly as in God's sight, and our conduct should be exemplary according to God's word: otherwise our arrogance will draw its own punishment.

These verses, 58-59, may be compared with vii. 161-162. There are two verbal differences. Here (ii. 58) we have "*enter* the town" and in vii. 161 we have "dwell in this town." Again in ii. 59 here we have "infringed (Our command)," and in vii. 162, we have "transgressed." The verbal differences make no difference to the sense.

Therefrom twelve springs.
Each group[73] knew its own place
For water. So eat and drink
Of the sustenance provided by God,
And do no evil nor mischief
On the (face of the) earth.

اثْنَتَا عَشْرَةَ عَيْنًا ۖ قَدْ عَلِمَ كُلُّ أُنَاسٍ
مَّشْرَبَهُمْ ۖ كُلُوا وَاشْرَبُوا مِنْ رِّزْقِ اللهِ وَ
لَا تَعْثَوْا فِي الْأَرْضِ مُفْسِدِيْنَ ○

61. And remember ye said:
"O Moses! we cannot endure
One kind of food (always);
So beseech thy Lord for us
To produce for us of what the earth
Groweth,—its pot-herbs, and cucumbers,
Its garlic, lentils, and onions."
He said: "Will ye exchange
The better for the worse?
Go ye down to any town,[74]
And ye shall find what ye want!"

٦١- وَإِذْ قُلْتُمْ يٰمُوسٰى لَنْ نَّصْبِرَ عَلٰى
طَعَامٍ وَّاحِدٍ فَادْعُ لَنَا رَبَّكَ يُخْرِجْ لَنَا
مِمَّا تُنْبِتُ الْأَرْضُ مِنْ بَقْلِهَا وَقِثَّآئِهَا
وَفُوْمِهَا وَعَدَسِهَا وَبَصَلِهَا ۖ قَالَ أَتَسْتَبْدِلُوْنَ
الَّذِيْ هُوَ أَدْنٰى بِالَّذِيْ هُوَ خَيْرٌ ۚ
اهْبِطُوْا مِصْرًا فَإِنَّ لَكُمْ مَّا سَأَلْتُمْ

73. Here we have a reference to the tribal organization of the Jews, which played a great part in their forty years' march through the Arabian deserts (Num. i. and ii.) and their subsequent settlement in the land of Canaan (Josh. xiii. and xiv.). The twelve tribes were derived from the sons of Jacob, whose name was changed to Israel (soldier of God) after he had wrestled, says Jewish tradition, with God (Genesis xxxii. 28). Israel had twelve sons (Gen. xxxv. 22-26), including Levi and Joseph. The descendants of these twelve sons were the "Children of Israel." Levi's family got the priesthood and the care of the Tabernacle; they were exempted from military duties, for which the census was taken (Num. i. 47-53), and therefore from the distribution of Land in Canaan (Josh. xiv. 3); they were distributed among all the Tribes, and were really a privileged caste and not numbered among the Tribes; Moses and Aaron belonged to the house of Levi. On the other hand Joseph, on account of the high position to which he rose in Egypt as the Pharaoh's minister, was the progenitor of two tribes, one in the name of each of his two sons Ephraim and Manasseh. Thus there were twelve Tribes in all, as Levi was cut out and Joseph represented two tribes. Their having fixed stations and watering places in camp and fixed territorial areas later in the Promised Land prevented confusion and mutual jealousies and is pointed to as an evidence of the Providence of God acting through His prophet Moses. *Cf.* also vii. 160.

The gushing of twelve springs from a rock evidently refers to a local tradition well known to Jews and Arabs in Muṣṭafā's time. Near Horeb close to Mount Sinai, where the Law was given to Moses, is a huge mass of red granite, twelve feet high and about fifty feet in circumference, where European travellers (*e.g.*, Breydenbach in the 15th Century after Christ) saw abundant springs of water twelve in number (see Sale's notes on this passage). It existed in Muṣṭafā's time and may still exist to the present day, for anything we know to the contrary. The Jewish tradition would be based on Exod. xvii. 6: "Thou shalt smite the rock, and there shall come water out of it that the people may drink."

The story is used as a parable, as is clear from the latter part of the verse. In the desolation and among the rocks of this life people grumble. But they will not be left starving or thirsty of spiritual life. God's Messenger can provide abundant spiritual sustenance even from such unpromising things as the hard rocks of life. And all the nations can be grouped round it, each different, yet each in perfect order and discipline. We are to use with gratitude all spiritual food and drink provided by God, and He sometimes provides from unexpected places. We must restrain ourselves from mischief, pride, and every kind of evil, for our higher life is based on our probation on this very earth.

74. The declension of the word *Miṣr* in the Arabic text here shows that it is treated as a common noun meaning any town, but this is not conclusive, and the reference may be to the Egypt of Pharaoh. The *Tanwīn* expressing indefiniteness may mean "any Egypt", *i.e.*, any country as fertile as Egypt. There is here a subtle reminiscence as well as a severe reproach. The rebellious children of Israel murmured at the sameness of the food they got in the desert. They were evidently hankering after the delicacies of the Egypt which they had left, although they should have known that the only thing certain for them in Egypt was their bondage and harsh treatment. Moses's reproach to them was twofold: (1) Such variety of foods you can get in any town: would you, for their sake, sell your freedom? Is not freedom better than delicate food? (2) In front is the rich Promised Land, which you are reluctant to march to; behind is Egypt, the land of bondage. Which is better? Would you exchange the better for the worse?

They were covered with humiliation[75] And misery; they drew On themselves the wrath of God. This because they went on Rejecting the Signs of God And slaying His Messengers Without just cause. This because they rebelled And went on transgressing.	وَضُرِبَتْ عَلَيْهِمُ الذِّلَّةُ وَالْمَسْكَنَةُ وَبَآءُو بِغَضَبٍ مِّنَ اللّٰهِ ذٰلِكَ بِاَنَّهُمْ كَانُوْا يَكْفُرُوْنَ بِاٰيٰتِ اللّٰهِ وَيَقْتُلُوْنَ النَّبِيّٖنَ بِغَيْرِ الْحَقِّ ذٰلِكَ بِمَا عَصَوْا وَّكَانُوْا يَعْتَدُوْنَ ۝ ع

SECTION 8.

62. Those who believe (in the Qur-ān), And those who follow the Jewish (scriptures), And the Christians and the Sabians,[76] — Any who believe in God And the Last Day, And work righteousness, Shall have their reward	٦٢- اِنَّ الَّذِيْنَ اٰمَنُوْا وَالَّذِيْنَ هَادُوْا وَالنَّصٰرٰى وَالصّٰبِـِٕيْنَ مَنْ اٰمَنَ بِاللّٰهِ وَالْيَوْمِ الْاٰخِرِ وَعَمِلَ صَالِحًا فَلَهُمْ اَجْرُهُمْ عِنْدَ رَبِّهِمْ

75. From here the argument becomes more general. They got the Promised Land. But they continued to rebel against God. And their humiliation and misery became a national disaster. They were carried in captivity to Assyria. They were restored under the Persians, but still remained under the Persian yoke, and they were under the yoke of the Greeks, the Romans, and Arabs. They were scattered all over the earth, and have been a wandering people ever since, because they rejected faith, slew God's messengers, and went on transgressing.

The slaying of the Prophets begins with the murder of Abel, who was in the ancestry of Israel. The elder sons of Jacob attempted the murder of Joseph when they dropped him into the well, and if he was afterwards rescued by strangers, their blood-guilt was none the less. In later history they attempted to slay Jesus, inasmuch as they got the Roman Governor to crucify one in his likeness, and they attempted to take the life of Muṣṭafā.

But the moral goes wider than the Children of Israel. It applies to all nations and all individuals. If they are stiff-necked, if they set a greater value on perishable goods than on freedom and eternal salvation, if they break the law of God and resist His grace, their portion must be humiliation and misery in the spiritual world and probably even on this earth if a long view is taken.

76. Latest researches have revealed a small remnant of a religious community numbering about 2,000 souls in Lower Irāq, near Baṣra. In Arabic they are called Ṣubbī (plural, Ṣubbā). They are also called Sabians and Nasoræans; or Mandæans, or Christians of St. John. They claim to be Gnostics, or Knowers of the Great Life. They dress in white, and believe in frequent immersions in water. Their Book Ginza is in a dialect of Aramaic. They have theories of Darkness and Light as in Zoroastrianism. They use the name *Yardan* (Jordan) for any river. They live in peace and harmony among their Muslim neighbours. They resemble the Ṣābi-ūn mentioned in the Qur-ān, but are not probably identical with them.

The pseudo-Sabians of Ḥarrān, who attracted the attention of Khalifa Mamūn-al-Rashīd in 830 A.D. by their long hair and peculiar dress probably adopted the name as it was mentioned in the Qur-ān, in order to claim the privileges of the People of the Book. They were Syrian Star-worshippers with Hellenistic tendencies, like the Jews contemporary with Jesus. It is doubtful whether they had any right to be called People of the Book in the technical sense of the term. But I think that in this matter (though many authorities would dissent) the term can be extended by analogy to cover earnest followers of Zoroaster, the Vedas, Buddha, Confucius and other Teachers of the moral law.

There was another people called the Sabæans, who played an important part in the history of early Arabia, and are known through their inscriptions in an alphabet allied to the Phœnician and the Babylonian. They had a flourishing kingdom in the Yemen tract in South Arabia about 800-700 B.C., though their origin may have been in North Arabia. They worshipped the planets and stars (Moon, Sun, Venus). Probably the Queen of Sheba is connected with them. They succumbed to Abyssinia about 350 A.D. and to Persia about 579 A.D. Their capital was near Ṣan'ā. They had beautiful stone buildings, in which the pointed arch is noticeable. (See E. B. on Sabæans.)

With their Lord : on them
Shall be no fear, nor shall they
grieve.[77]

وَلَا خَوْفٌ عَلَيْهِمْ وَلَا هُمْ يَحْزَنُونَ ○

63. And remember We took
Your Covenant
And We raised above you
(The towering height)
Of Mount (Sinai)[78] :
(Saying) : "Hold firmly
To what We have given you
And bring (ever) to remembrance
What is therein :
Perchance ye may fear God."

٦٣- وَإِذْ أَخَذْنَا مِيثَاقَكُمْ وَرَفَعْنَا فَوْقَكُمُ الطُّورَ
خُذُوا مَا آتَيْنَاكُمْ بِقُوَّةٍ
وَاذْكُرُوا مَا فِيهِ لَعَلَّكُمْ تَتَّقُونَ ○

64. But ye turned back thereafter :
Had it not been for the Grace
And Mercy of God to you,
Ye had surely been
Among the lost.

٦٤- ثُمَّ تَوَلَّيْتُمْ مِنْ بَعْدِ ذَٰلِكَ فَلَوْلَا
فَضْلُ اللَّهِ عَلَيْكُمْ وَرَحْمَتُهُ لَكُنْتُمْ
مِنَ الْخَاسِرِينَ ○

65. And well ye knew
Those amongst you
Who transgressed
In the matter of the Sabbath :
We said to them :
"Be ye apes,
Despised and rejected."[79]

٦٥- وَلَقَدْ عَلِمْتُمُ الَّذِينَ اعْتَدَوْا مِنْكُمْ
فِي السَّبْتِ فَقُلْنَا لَهُمْ
كُونُوا قِرَدَةً خَاسِئِينَ ○

66. So We made it an example
To their own time

٦٦- فَجَعَلْنَاهَا نَكَالًا لِمَا بَيْنَ يَدَيْهَا وَمَا

77. *Cf.* ii. 38, where the same phrase occurs. And it recurs again and again afterwards.

The point of the verse is that Islam does not teach an exclusive doctrine, and is not meant exclusively for one people. The Jews claimed this for themselves, and the Christians in their origin were a sect of the Jews. Even the modern organized Christian churches, though they have been, consciously or unconsciously, influenced by the Time-spirit, including the historical fact of Islam, yet cling to the idea of Vicarious Atonement, which means that all who do not believe in it or who lived previously to the death of Christ are at a disadvantage spiritually before the Throne of God. The attitude of Islam is entirely different. Islam existed before the preaching of Muḥammad on this earth : the Qur-ān expressly calls Abraham a Muslim (iii. 67). Its teaching (submission to God's will) has been and will be the teaching of Religion for all time and for all peoples.

78. The Mountain of Sinai (*Ṭūr-u-Sīnīn*), a prominent mountain in the Arabian desert, in the peninsula between the two arms of the Red Sea. Here the Ten Commandments and the Law were given to Moses. Hence it is now called the Mountain of Moses (*Jabal Mūsa*). The Israelites encamped at the foot of it for nearly a year. The Covenant was taken from them under many portents (Exod. xix. 5, 8, 16, 18), which are described in Jewish tradition in great detail. Under thunder and lightning the mountain must indeed have appeared an awe-inspiring sight above to the Camp at its foot. And the people solemnly entered into the Covenant : all the people answered together and said, "All that the Lord hath spoken we will do."

79. The punishment for breach of the Sabbath under the Mosaic law was death. "Every one that defileth it (the Sabbath) shall surely be put to death : for whosoever doeth any work therein, that soul shall be cut off from among his people" : (Exod. xxxi. 14). There must have been a Jewish tradition about a whole fishing community in a seaside town, which persisted in breaking the Sabbath and were turned into apes : *cf.* vii. 163-166. Or should we translate in both these passages, "Be *as* apes", instead of "Be apes"? This is the suggestion of Maulvi Muḥammad 'Ali on this passage, on the authority of Mujāhid and Ibn Jarīr Ṭabarī. The punishment would be, not for the breach of the Sabbath in itself, but for their contumacious defiance of the Law.

And to their posterity,
And a lesson
To those who fear God.

خَلْفَهَا وَمَوْعِظَةً لِّلْمُتَّقِيْنَ ○

67. And remember Moses said
To his people: "God commands
That ye sacrifice a heifer."[80]
They said: "Makest thou
A laughing-stock of us?"
He said: "God save me
From being an ignorant (fool)!"

٦٧- وَ اِذْ قَالَ مُوْسٰى لِقَوْمِهٖٓ اِنَّ اللّٰهَ
يَاْمُرُكُمْ اَنْ تَذْبَحُوْا بَقَرَةً ۭ قَالُوْٓا اَتَتَّخِذُنَا
هُزُوًا ۭ قَالَ اَعُوْذُ بِاللّٰهِ اَنْ اَكُوْنَ مِنَ
الْجٰهِلِيْنَ ○

68. They said: "Beseech on our behalf
Thy Lord to make plain to us
What (heifer) it is!"
He said: "He says: the heifer
Should be neither too old
Nor too young, but of middling
Age: now do what ye are commanded!"

٦٨- قَالُوا ادْعُ لَنَا رَبَّكَ يُبَيِّنْ لَّنَا مَا هِيَ ۭ
قَالَ اِنَّهٗ يَقُوْلُ اِنَّهَا بَقَرَةٌ لَّا فَارِضٌ وَّ
لَا بِكْرٌ ۭ
عَوَانٌۢ بَيْنَ ذٰلِكَ ۭ
فَافْعَلُوْا مَا تُؤْمَرُوْنَ ○

69. They said: "Beseech on our behalf
Thy Lord to make plain to us
Her colour." He said: "He says:
A fawn-coloured heifer,
Pure and rich in tone,
The admiration of beholders!"

٦٩- قَالُوا ادْعُ لَنَا رَبَّكَ يُبَيِّنْ لَّنَا مَا لَوْنُهَا ۭ
قَالَ اِنَّهٗ يَقُوْلُ اِنَّهَا بَقَرَةٌ صَفْرَاۗءُ ۙ فَاقِعٌ
لَّوْنُهَا تَسُرُّ النّٰظِرِيْنَ ○

70. They said: "Beseech on our behalf
Thy Lord to make plain to us
What she is: to us are all heifers
Alike: we wish indeed for guidance,
If God wills."

٧٠- قَالُوا ادْعُ لَنَا رَبَّكَ يُبَيِّنْ لَّنَا مَا هِيَ ۙ
اِنَّ الْبَقَرَ تَشٰبَهَ عَلَيْنَا ۭ
وَاِنَّآ اِنْ شَاۗءَ اللّٰهُ لَمُهْتَدُوْنَ ○

---

80. This story or parable of the heifer in ii. 67-71 should be read with the parable of the dead man brought to life in ii. 72-73. The stories were accepted in Jewish traditions, which are themselves based on certain sacrificial directions in the Old Testament. The heifer story of Jewish tradition is based on Num. xix. 1-10, in which Moses and Aaron ordered the Israelites to sacrifice a red heifer without spot or blemish; her body was to be burnt and the ashes were to be kept for the purification of the congregation from sin. The parable of the dead man we shall refer to later.

The lesson of the heifer parable is plain. Moses announced the sacrifice to the Israelites, and they treated it as a jest. When Moses continued solemnly to ask for the sacrifice, they put him off on one pretext and another, asking a number of questions which they could have answered themselves if they had listened to Moses's directions. Their questions were carping criticisms rather than the result of a desire for information. It was a mere thin pretence that they were genuinely seeking for guidance. When at last they were driven into a corner, they made the sacrifice, but the will was wanting, which would have made the sacrifice efficacious for purification from sin. The real reason for their prevarications was their guilty conscience, as we see in the parable of the dead man (ii. 72-73).

71. He said: "He says: a heifer
Not trained to till the soil
Or water the fields; sound
And without blemish." They said:
"Now hast thou brought
The truth." Then they offered
Her in sacrifice,
But not with good-will.

٧١- قَالَ إِنَّهُ يَقُولُ إِنَّهَا بَقَرَةٌ لَّا ذَلُولٌ تُثِيرُ
الْأَرْضَ وَلَا تَسْقِي الْحَرْثَ مُسَلَّمَةٌ لَّا
شِيَةَ فِيهَا قَالُوا الْآنَ جِئْتَ بِالْحَقِّ فَذَبَحُوهَا
وَمَا كَادُوا يَفْعَلُونَ ۝ ع

Section 9.

72. Remember ye slew a man[81]
And fell into a dispute
Among yourselves as to the crime:
But God was to bring forth
What ye did hide.

٧٢- وَإِذْ قَتَلْتُمْ نَفْسًا فَادَّارَأْتُمْ فِيهَا
وَاللَّهُ مُخْرِجٌ مَّا كُنتُمْ تَكْتُمُونَ ۝

73. So We said: "Strike the (body)
With a piece of the (heifer)."
Thus God bringeth the dead
To life and showeth you His
Signs:
Perchance ye may understand.

٧٣- فَقُلْنَا اضْرِبُوهُ بِبَعْضِهَا
كَذَٰلِكَ يُحْيِي اللَّهُ الْمَوْتَىٰ
وَيُرِيكُمْ آيَاتِهِ لَعَلَّكُمْ تَعْقِلُونَ ۝

74. Thenceforth were your hearts
Hardened: they became
Like a rock and even worse
In hardness. For among rocks
There are some from which
Rivers gush forth; others
There are which when split
Asunder send forth water;
And others which sink

٧٤- ثُمَّ قَسَتْ قُلُوبُكُم مِّن بَعْدِ ذَٰلِكَ
فَهِيَ كَالْحِجَارَةِ أَوْ أَشَدُّ قَسْوَةً وَإِنَّ مِنَ
الْحِجَارَةِ لَمَا يَتَفَجَّرُ مِنْهُ الْأَنْهَارُ وَإِنَّ
مِنْهَا لَمَا يَشَّقَّقُ فَيَخْرُجُ مِنْهُ الْمَاءُ وَ
إِنَّ مِنْهَا لَمَا يَهْبِطُ مِنْ خَشْيَةِ اللَّهِ وَ

---

81. In Deut. xxi. 1-9 it is ordained that if the body of a slain man be found in a field and the slayer is not known, a heifer shall be beheaded, and the elders of the city next to the slain man's domicile shall wash their hands over the heifer and say that they neither did the deed nor saw it done, thus clearing themselves from the blood-guilt.

The Jewish story based on this was that in a certain case of this kind, every one tried to clear himself of guilt and lay the blame at the door of others. In the first place they tried to prevaricate and prevent a heifer being slain as in the last parable. When she was slain, God by a miracle disclosed the really guilty person. A portion of the sacrificed heifer was ordered to be placed on the corpse, which came to life and disclosed the whole story of the crime.

The lesson of this parable is that men may try to hide their crimes individually or collectively, but God will bring them to light in unexpected ways. Applying this further to Jewish national history, the argument is developed in the following verses that the Children of Israel played fast and loose with their own rites and traditions, but they could not thus evade the consequences of their own sin.

For fear of God. And God is
Not unmindful of what ye do.[82]

مَا اللّٰهُ بِغَافِلٍ عَمَّا تَعْمَلُوْنَ ○

75. Can ye (O ye men of Faith)
Entertain the hope that they
Will believe in you?—
Seeing that a party of them
Heard the Word of God,
And perverted it knowingly
After they understood it.

٧٥- اَفَتَطْمَعُوْنَ اَنْ يُّؤْمِنُوْا لَكُمْ وَقَدْ كَانَ
فَرِيْقٌ مِّنْهُمْ يَسْمَعُوْنَ كَلٰمَ اللّٰهِ ثُمَّ
يُحَرِّفُوْنَهٗ مِنْۢ بَعْدِ مَا عَقَلُوْهُ وَهُمْ
يَعْلَمُوْنَ ○

76. Behold! when they meet[83]
The men of Faith, they say:
"We believe": but when
They meet each other in private,
They say: "Shall you tell them
What God hath revealed to you,
That they may engage you
In argument about it
Before your Lord?"—
Do ye not understand (their aim)?

٧٦- وَاِذَا لَقُوا الَّذِيْنَ اٰمَنُوْا قَالُوْٓا اٰمَنَّا ۚ وَ
اِذَا خَلَا بَعْضُهُمْ اِلٰى بَعْضٍ قَالُوْٓا اَتُحَدِّثُوْنَهُمْ
بِمَا فَتَحَ اللّٰهُ عَلَيْكُمْ لِيُحَآجُّوْكُمْ بِهٖ عِنْدَ
رَبِّكُمْ ۭ
اَفَلَا تَعْقِلُوْنَ ○

77. Know they not that God
Knoweth what they conceal
And what they reveal?.

٧٧- اَوَلَا يَعْلَمُوْنَ اَنَّ اللّٰهَ يَعْلَمُ مَا يُسِرُّوْنَ
وَمَا يُعْلِنُوْنَ ○

---

82. The sinner's heart gets harder and harder. It is even harder than rocks, of which a beautiful poetical allegory is placed before us. In nature we think there is nothing harder than rocks. But there are rocks that weep voluntarily, like repentant hearts that come to God of their own accord: such are the rocks from which rivers and springs flow spontaneously, sometimes in small trickles, sometimes in big volumes. Then there are rocks which have to be split or dug into or blown up with dynamite, and underneath we find abundant waters, as in wells beneath rocky soil. Such are the hearts of a less degree of fineness, which yet melt into tears when some great blow or calamity calls the mind to higher things. And lastly, there are the rocks which slip or sink by geological pressure or in an earthquake, and send forth large spouts of water, as happened, for example, in the Bihar earthquake of 1934: such sinking or quaking may be poetically ascribed to fear. So there are hearts which will come to God by no higher motive than fear, but yet fear will melt them into tears of repentance. But the hardened sinner is worse than all these. His case is worse than that of rocks, for nothing will melt him.

83. The immediate argument applies to the Jews of Medina, but the more general argument applies to the people of Faith and the people without Faith, as we shall see below. If the Muslims of Medina ever entertained the hope that the Jews in their city would as a body welcome Muḥammad Muṣṭafā as the Prophet prophesied in their own books, they were mistaken. In Deut. xviii. 18, they read: "I will raise them up a Prophet from among their brethren, like unto thee," (*i.e.*, like unto Moses): which was interpreted by some of their doctors as referring to Muḥammad, and they came into Islam. The Arabs are a kindred branch of the Semitic family, and are correctly described in relation to the Jews as, "their brethren"; and there is no question that there was not another Prophet "like unto Moses" until Muḥammad came; in fact the postscript of Deuteronomy, which was written many centuries after Moses, says: "There arose not a prophet since in Israel like unto Moses, whom the Lord knew face to face." But the Jews as a body were jealous of Muḥammad, and played a double part. When the Muslim community began to grow stronger they pretended to be of them, but really tried to keep back any knowledge of their own Scriptures from them, lest they should be beaten by their own arguments.

The more general interpretation holds good in all ages. Faith and Unfaith are pitted against each other. Faith has to struggle against power, position, organization, and privilege. When it gains ground, Unfaith comes forward insincerely and claims fellowship. But in its own mind it is jealous of the armoury of science and knowledge which Faith brings into the service of God. But God knows all, and if the people of Faith will only seek knowledge sincerely wherever they can find it,—even as far afield as China, as Muhammad said they can defeat Unfaith on its own ground.

78. And there are among them[84]
Illiterates, who know not the Book,
But (see therein their own) desires,
And they do nothing but
conjecture.

٧٨- وَمِنْهُمْ أُمِّيُّونَ لَا يَعْلَمُونَ الْكِتٰبَ
إِلَّآ أَمَانِيَّ وَإِنْ هُمْ إِلَّا يَظُنُّونَ ○

النصف

79. Then woe to those who write
The Book with their own hands,
And then say: "This is from God,"
To traffic with it
For a miserable price!—
Woe to them for what their hands
Do write, and for the gain
They make thereby.

٧٩- فَوَيْلٌ لِّلَّذِينَ يَكْتُبُونَ الْكِتٰبَ بِأَيْدِيهِمْ
ثُمَّ يَقُولُونَ هٰذَا مِنْ عِنْدِ اللّٰهِ لِيَشْتَرُوا بِهِ
ثَمَنًا قَلِيلًا ۖ فَوَيْلٌ لَّهُمْ مِّمَّا كَتَبَتْ أَيْدِيهِمْ
وَوَيْلٌ لَّهُمْ مِّمَّا يَكْسِبُونَ ○

80. And they say: "The Fire[85]
Shall not touch us
But for a few numbered days:"
Say: "Have ye taken a promise
From God, for He never
Breaks His promise?
Or is it that ye say of God
What ye do not know?"

٨٠- وَقَالُوا لَنْ تَمَسَّنَا النَّارُ إِلَّآ أَيَّامًا مَّعْدُودَةً ۚ
قُلْ أَتَّخَذْتُمْ عِنْدَ اللّٰهِ عَهْدًا فَلَنْ يُّخْلِفَ
اللّٰهُ عَهْدَهٗٓ أَمْ تَقُولُونَ عَلَى اللّٰهِ مَا لَا
تَعْلَمُونَ ○

81. Nay, those who seek gain[86]
In Evil, and are girt round
By their sins,—
They are Companions of the Fire:
Therein shall they abide
(For ever).

٨١- بَلٰى مَنْ كَسَبَ سَيِّئَةً وَّأَحَاطَتْ بِهٖ
خَطِيٓـَٔتُهٗ فَأُولٰٓئِكَ أَصْحٰبُ النَّارِ ۚ
هُمْ فِيهَا خٰلِدُونَ ○

82. But those who have faith
And work righteousness,

٨٢- وَالَّذِينَ اٰمَنُوا وَعَمِلُوا الصّٰلِحٰتِ

---

84. The argument of i. 76 is continued. The Jews wanted to keep back knowledge, but what knowledge had they? Many of them, even if they could read, were no better than illiterates, for they knew not their own true Scriptures, but read into them what they wanted, or at best their own conjectures. They palmed off their own writings for the Message of God. Perhaps it brought them profit for the time being: but it was a miserable profit if they "gained the whole world and lost their own souls" (Matt. xvi. 26). "Writing with their own hands" means inventing books themselves, which had no divine authority.

The general argument is similar. Unfaith erects its own false gods. It attributes things to causes which only exist in its own imagination. Sometimes it even indulges in actual dishonest traffic in the ignorance of the multitude. It may pay for a time, but the bubble always bursts.

85. The Jews in their arrogance might say: Whatever the terror of Hell may be for other people, our sins will be forgiven, because we are the children of Abraham: at worst, we shall suffer a short definite punishment and then be restored to the "bosom of Abraham." This bubble is pricked here. Read this verse with ii. 81-82.

The general application is also clear. If Unfaith claims some special prerogative, such as race, "civilization," political power, historical experience, and so on, these will not avail in God's sight. His promise is sure, but His promise is for those who seek God in Faith, and show it in their conduct.

86. This is many degrees worse than merely falling into evil: it is going out to "earn evil," as the Arabic text has it, *i.e.*, to seek gain in evil. Such a perverse attitude means that the moral and spiritual fortress erected around us by the Grace of God is voluntarily surrendered by us and demolished by Evil, which erects its own fortress, so that access to Good may be more and more difficult.

They are Companions of the
Garden :
Therein shall they abide
(For ever).

أُولٰٓئِكَ اَصۡحٰبُ الۡجَنَّةِ ۚ هُمۡ فِيۡهَا خٰلِدُوۡنَ ؏

SECTION 10.

83. And remember We took[87]
A Covenant from the Children
Of Israel (to this effect):
Worship none but God;
Treat with kindness
Your parents and kindred,
And orphans and those in need;
Speak fair to the people;
Be steadfast in prayer;
And practise regular charity.
Then did ye turn back,
Except a few among you,
And ye backslide (even now).

٨٣- وَاِذۡ اَخَذۡنَا مِيۡثَاقَ بَنِيۡۤ اِسۡرَآءِيۡلَ لَا
تَعۡبُدُوۡنَ اِلَّا اللّٰهَ ۟ وَبِالۡوَالِدَيۡنِ اِحۡسَانًا
وَّذِى الۡقُرۡبٰى وَالۡيَتٰمٰى وَالۡمَسٰكِيۡنِ وَ
قُوۡلُوۡا لِلنَّاسِ حُسۡنًا وَّاَقِيۡمُوا الصَّلٰوةَ وَ
اٰتُوا الزَّكٰوةَ ؕ ثُمَّ تَوَلَّيۡتُمۡ اِلَّا قَلِيۡلًا مِّنۡكُمۡ
وَاَنۡتُمۡ مُّعۡرِضُوۡنَ

84. And remember We took[88]
Your Covenant (to this effect):
Shed no blood amongst you,
Nor turn out your own people
From your homes: and this
Ye solemnly ratified,
And to this ye can bear witness.

٨٤- وَاِذۡ اَخَذۡنَا مِيۡثَاقَكُمۡ لَا تَسۡفِكُوۡنَ
دِمَآءَكُمۡ وَلَا تُخۡرِجُوۡنَ اَنۡفُسَكُمۡ مِّنۡ
دِيَارِكُمۡ ثُمَّ اَقۡرَرۡتُمۡ وَاَنۡتُمۡ تَشۡهَدُوۡنَ

85. After this it is ye, the same people,
Who slay among yourselves,
And banish a party of you
From their homes; assist
(Their enemies) against them,
In guilt and rancour;
And if they come to you
As captives, ye ransom[89] them,

٨٥- ثُمَّ اَنۡتُمۡ هٰٓؤُلَآءِ تَقۡتُلُوۡنَ اَنۡفُسَكُمۡ وَ
تُخۡرِجُوۡنَ فَرِيۡقًا مِّنۡكُمۡ مِّنۡ دِيَارِهِمۡ تَظٰهَرُوۡنَ
عَلَيۡهِمۡ بِالۡاِثۡمِ وَالۡعُدۡوَانِ ؕ وَاِنۡ
يَّاۡتُوۡكُمۡ اُسٰرٰى تُفٰدُوۡهُمۡ

87. So far from the Covenant being of the kind you suggest in ii. 80, the real Covenant is about the moral law, which is set out in ii. 83. This moral law is universal, and if you break it, no privileges will lighten your punishment or help you in any way (ii. 86). "Speak fair to the people" not only means outward courtesy from the leaders to the meanest among the people, but the protection of the people from being exploited, deceived, defrauded, or doped with things to lull their intelligence.

88. Verse 83 referred to the universal moral law. This verse 84 refers to its application under a special Covenant entered into with the Jews of Medina by the new-born Muslim Commonwealth under its Guide and teacher Muhammad. This Covenant is given in Ibn Hishām's *Sīrat-ur-Rasūl*, and comments on it will be found in Ameer 'Ali's *Spirit of Islam* (London. 1922), pp. 57-61. It was entered into in the second year of the Hijra, and was treacherously broken by the Jews almost immediately afterwards.

89. I understand "ransom them" here to mean "take ransom for them," though most of the Commentators take it to mean "give ransom for them." Muṣṭafā had made a Pact which, if it had been faithfully observed by all parties, would have brought a reign of law and order for Medina. But some of the treacherous Jews never intended to observe its terms. They fought and slew each other and not only banished those who were obnoxious to them but intrigued with their enemies. If by any chance they came back into their hands as captives, they demanded ransom for them to return to their homes although they had no right to banish them at all. If we understand by "ransom them" pay "ransom for them to release them from the hands of their enemies," it would mean that they did this pious act for show, although they were themselves the authors of their unlawful banishment. I think the former makes better sense.

Though it was not lawful
For you to banish them.
Then is it only a part of the Book
That ye believe in,
And do ye reject the rest?
But what is the reward for those
Among you who behave like this
But disgrace in this life?—
And on the Day of Judgment
They shall be consigned
To the most grievous penalty.
For God is not unmindful
Of what ye do.

وَهُوَ مُحَرَّمٌ عَلَيْكُمْ إِخْرَاجُهُمْ
أَفَتُؤْمِنُونَ بِبَعْضِ الْكِتٰبِ وَتَكْفُرُونَ
بِبَعْضٍ فَمَا جَزَآءُ مَنْ يَّفْعَلُ ذٰلِكَ مِنْكُمْ
إِلَّا خِزْيٌ فِي الْحَيٰوةِ الدُّنْيَا وَيَوْمَ الْقِيٰمَةِ
يُرَدُّونَ إِلٰى أَشَدِّ الْعَذَابِ
وَمَا اللّٰهُ بِغَافِلٍ عَمَّا تَعْمَلُونَ ○

86. These are the people who buy
The life of this world at the price
Of the Hereafter: their penalty
Shall not be lightened
Nor shall they be helped.

٨٦- أُولٰٓئِكَ الَّذِينَ اشْتَرَوُا الْحَيٰوةَ الدُّنْيَا
بِالْأٰخِرَةِ فَلَا يُخَفَّفُ عَنْهُمُ الْعَذَابُ
وَلَا هُمْ يُنْصَرُونَ ○

C. 47.—The people of Moses and the people of Jesus
(ii 87-121.) Were given revelations, but alas!
They played false with their own lights,
And, in their selfishness, made narrow
God's universal message. To them
It seemed incredible that His light
Should illumine Arabia and reform
The world. But His ways are wondrous,
And they are clear to those who have Faith.

Section 11.

87. We gave Moses the Book
And followed him up
With a succession of Apostles;[89-A]
We gave Jesus the son of Mary[90]
Clear (Signs) and strengthened him
With the holy spirit. Is it
That whenever there comes to you
An Apostle with what ye
Yourselves desire not, ye are
Puffed up with pride?—
Some ye called impostors,
And others ye slay![91]

٨٧- وَلَقَدْ اٰتَيْنَا مُوسَى الْكِتٰبَ وَقَفَّيْنَا مِنْ
بَعْدِهٖ بِالرُّسُلِ وَاٰتَيْنَا عِيسَى ابْنَ مَرْيَمَ
الْبَيِّنٰتِ وَأَيَّدْنٰهُ بِرُوحِ الْقُدُسِ
أَفَكُلَّمَا جَآءَكُمْ رَسُولٌ بِمَا لَا تَهْوٰى
أَنْفُسُكُمُ اسْتَكْبَرْتُمْ
فَفَرِيقًا كَذَّبْتُمْ وَفَرِيقًا تَقْتُلُونَ ○

89-A. The word "apostle" is used here and throughout the Translation in the literal sense of "One Sent," and not in a specialized sense.

90. As to the birth of Jesus, *cf.* xix. 16-34. Why is he called the "Son of Mary"? W t are his "clear signs"? What is the "holy spirit" by which he was strengthened? We reserve a later stage a discussion of the Quranic teaching on these questions. See iii 62 n. 401.

91. Notice the sudden transition from the past tense in "some ye *called* impostors" to the present tense in "others ye slay." There is a double significance. First, reviewing the long course of Jewish history, we have come to the time of Jesus: they have often given the lie to God's Apostles, and even now they are trying to slay Jesus. Secondly, extending the review of that history to the time of Muḥammad, they are even now trying to take the life of that holy Apostle. This would be literally true at the time the words were promulgated to the people. And this transition leads on naturally to the next verse, which refers to the actual conditions before Muḥammad in Medina in the second year of the Hijra.

Sections 11-13 (ii. 87-121) refer to the People of the Book generally, Jews and Christians. Even where Moses and the Law of Sinai are referred to, those traditions are common to both Jews and Christians. The argument is about the people who ought to have learnt from previous Revelations and welcomed Muḥammad's teaching, and yet they both took up an attitude of arrogant rejection.

88. They say, "Our hearts
Are the wrappings[92] (which
preserve
God's Word: we need no more)."
Nay, God's curse is on them
For their blasphemy:[93]
Little is it they believe.

٨٨- وَقَالُوا قُلُوبُنَا غُلْفٌ ۚ
بَلْ لَعَنَهُمُ اللَّهُ بِكُفْرِهِمْ
فَقَلِيلًا مَا يُؤْمِنُونَ ○

89. And when there comes to them
A Book[94] from God, confirming
What is with them,—although
From of old they had prayed
For victory against those
Without Faith,—when there comes
To them that which they
(Should) have recognized,
They refuse to believe in it
But the curse of God
Is on those without Faith.

٨٩- وَلَمَّا جَاءَهُمْ كِتٰبٌ مِنْ عِنْدِ اللَّهِ
مُصَدِّقٌ لِمَا مَعَهُمْ ۙ
وَكَانُوا مِنْ قَبْلُ يَسْتَفْتِحُونَ
عَلَى الَّذِينَ كَفَرُوا ۚ فَلَمَّا جَاءَهُمْ
مَا عَرَفُوا كَفَرُوا بِهِ ۚ
فَلَعْنَةُ اللَّهِ عَلَى الْكٰفِرِينَ ○

90. Miserable is the price
For which they have sold
Their souls, in that they
Deny (the revelation)
Which God has sent down,
In insolent envy that God
Of His Grace should send it
To any of His servants He
pleases:[95]

٩٠- بِئْسَمَا اشْتَرَوْا بِهِ أَنْفُسَهُمْ
أَنْ يَكْفُرُوا بِمَا أَنْزَلَ اللَّهُ بَغْيًا
أَنْ يُنَزِّلَ اللَّهُ مِنْ فَضْلِهِ عَلَىٰ مَنْ يَشَاءُ
مِنْ عِبَادِهِ ۚ

92. The Jews in their arrogance claimed that all wisdom and all knowledge of God were enclosed in their hearts. But there were more things in heaven and earth than were dreamt of in their philosophy. Their claim was not only arrogance but blasphemy. In reality they were men without Faith. (I take *Gulfān* here to be the plural of *Gilāfun* the wrapping or cover of a book, in which the book is preserved.)

As usual, there is a much wider meaning. How many people at all times and among all nations close their hearts to any extension of knowledge or spiritual influence because of some little fragment which they have got and which they think is the whole of God's Truth? Such an attitude shows really want of faith and is a blasphemous limitation of God's unlimited spiritual gifts to His creatures.

93. The root *kafara* has many shades of meaning: (1) to deny God's goodness, to be ungrateful, (2) to reject Faith, deny His revelation, (3) to blaspheme, to ascribe some limitation or attribute to God which is derogatory to His nature. In a translation, one shade or another must be put forward according to the context, but all are implied.

94. The Jews, who pretended to be so superior to the people without Faith—the Gentiles—should have been the first to recognize the new Truth—or the Truth renewed—which it was Muḥammad's mission to bring, because it was so similar in form and language to what they had already received. But they had more arrogance than faith. It is this want of faith that brings on the curse, *i.e.*, deprives us (if we adopt such an attitude) of the blessings of God.

Again the lesson applies to a much wider circle than the Jews. We are all apt, in our perverseness, to reject an appeal from our brother even more summarily than one from an outsider. If we have a glimmering of the truth, we are apt to make ourselves impervious to further truth, and thus lose the benefit of God's Grace.

95. Racial arrogance made the Jews averse to the reception of Truth when it came through a servant of God, not of their own race. Again the lesson is wider. Is that averseness unknown in our own times, and among other races? Yet how can a race or a people set bounds to God's choice? God is the Creator and Cherisher of all races and all worlds.

Thus have they drawn
On themselves Wrath upon Wrath.
And humiliating is the punishment
Of those who reject Faith.

فَبَآءُو بِغَضَبٍ عَلٰى غَضَبٍ ؕ
وَلِلْكٰفِرِيْنَ عَذَابٌ مُّهِيْنٌ ○

91. When it is said to them,
"Believe in what God
Hath sent down," they say,
"We believe in what was sent down
To us": yet they reject
All besides, even if it be Truth
Confirming what is with them.
Say: "Why then have ye slain
The prophets of God in times
Gone by, if ye did indeed
Believe?"[96]

٩١- وَإِذَا قِيْلَ لَهُمْ اٰمِنُوْا بِمَآ أَنْزَلَ اللهُ
قَالُوْا نُؤْمِنُ بِمَآ أُنْزِلَ عَلَيْنَا
وَيَكْفُرُوْنَ بِمَا وَرَآءَهٗ ق وَهُوَ الْحَقُّ
مُصَدِّقًا لِّمَا مَعَهُمْ ؕ
قُلْ فَلِمَ تَقْتُلُوْنَ أَنْۢبِيَآءَ اللهِ
مِنْ قَبْلُ إِنْ كُنْتُمْ مُّؤْمِنِيْنَ ○

92. There came to you Moses
With clear (Signs); yet
Ye worshipped the Calf
(Even) after that, and ye
Did behave wrongfully.

٩٢- وَلَقَدْ جَآءَكُمْ مُّوْسٰى بِالْبَيِّنٰتِ
ثُمَّ اتَّخَذْتُمُ الْعِجْلَ
مِنْۢ بَعْدِهٖ وَأَنْتُمْ ظٰلِمُوْنَ ○

93. And remember We took
Your Covenant and We raised
Above you (the towering height)
Of Mount (Sinai):
(Saying): "Hold firmly
To what We have given you,
And hearken (to the Law)":[97]
They said: "We hear,
And we disobey":[98]
And they had to drink[99]

٩٣- وَإِذْ أَخَذْنَا مِيْثَاقَكُمْ
وَرَفَعْنَا فَوْقَكُمُ الطُّوْرَ ؕ
خُذُوْا مَآ اٰتَيْنٰكُمْ بِقُوَّةٍ
وَّاسْمَعُوْا ؕ قَالُوْا سَمِعْنَا وَعَصَيْنَا ق
وَأُشْرِبُوْا

96. Even the race argument is often a flimsy and hollow pretext. Did not the Jews reject Prophets of their own race who told them unpleasant truths? And do not other nations do likewise? The real trouble is selfishness, narrowness, a mean dislike of anything which runs counter to habits, customs or inclinations.

97. *Cf.* the introductory words of ii. 63. which are the same as the introductory words here, but the argument is developed in a different direction in the two places. In ii. 63, after they are reminded of the solemn Covenant under the towering height of Mount Sinai they are told how they broke the Covenant in after ages. Here, after they are reminded of the same solemn Covenant, they are told that even then they never meant to observe it. Their thought is expressed in biting words of sarcasm. They said in words: "All that the Lord hath spoken, we will do." But they said in their hearts: "We shall disobey."

98. What they should have said was: "We hear and we obey": this is the attitude of the true men of Faith (ii. 285).

99. After the Commandments and the Law had been given at Mount Sinai, and the people had solemnly given their Covenant, Moses went up to the Mount, and in his absence, the people made the golden calf. When Moses returned, his anger waxed hot. "He took the Calf which they had made, and burnt it in the fire, and ground it to powder, and strewed it upon the water, and *made the children of Israel drink of it.*" (Exod. xxxii. 20). This incident is interpreted in the Qur-ān allegorically. The Calf is the symbol of disobedience, rebellion, want of faith. It was like a taint of poison. Their punishment was to swallow the taint of poison which they had themselves produced. They swallowed it not into their stomachs, but into their hearts, their very being. They had to mortify and humble themselves in the sight of God, as was shown in another allegory based on the Jewish narrative (see ii. 54 and note, above).

Into their hearts
(Of the taint) of the Calf
Because of their Faithlessness.
Say: "Vile indeed
Are the behests of your Faith
If ye have any faith!"

فِي قُلُوبِهِمُ الْعِجْلَ بِكُفْرِهِمْ ۚ
قُلْ بِئْسَمَا يَأْمُرُكُم بِهِۦٓ إِيمَانُكُمْ إِن كُنتُم
مُّؤْمِنِينَ ۝

94. Say: "If the last Home,
With God, be for you specially,
And not for anyone else,
Then seek ye for death,
If ye are sincere."

٩٤- قُلْ إِن كَانَتْ لَكُمُ الدَّارُ الْآخِرَةُ عِندَ
اللَّهِ خَالِصَةً مِّن دُونِ النَّاسِ
فَتَمَنَّوُا الْمَوْتَ إِن كُنتُمْ صَٰدِقِينَ ۝

95. But they will never seek
For death, on account of the (sins)
Which their hands have sent
On before them.[100]
And God is well-acquainted
With the wrong-doers.

٩٥- وَلَن يَتَمَنَّوْهُ أَبَدًۢا
بِمَا قَدَّمَتْ أَيْدِيهِمْ ۗ
وَاللَّهُ عَلِيمٌۢ بِالظَّٰلِمِينَ ۝

96. Thou wilt indeed find them,
Of all people, most greedy
Of life,—even more
Than the idolaters:
Each one of them wishes
He could be given a life
Of a thousand years:
But the grant of such life
Will not save him
From (due) punishment.
For God sees well
All that they do.

٩٦- وَلَتَجِدَنَّهُمْ أَحْرَصَ النَّاسِ عَلَىٰ حَيَوٰةٍ
وَمِنَ الَّذِينَ أَشْرَكُوا ۚ
يَوَدُّ أَحَدُهُمْ لَوْ يُعَمَّرُ أَلْفَ سَنَةٍ
وَمَا هُوَ بِمُزَحْزِحِهِۦ مِنَ الْعَذَابِ أَن
يُعَمَّرَ ۗ
وَاللَّهُ بَصِيرٌۢ بِمَا يَعْمَلُونَ ۝

SECTION 12.

97. Say: Whoever is an enemy[101]
To Gabriel—for he brings down

٩٧- قُلْ مَن كَانَ عَدُوًّا لِّجِبْرِيلَ فَإِنَّهُۥ

100. The phrase "What their hands have sent on before them" frequently occurs in the Qur-ān. Here, and in many places, it refers to sins. In such passages as lxxviii. 40. or lxxxi 14, it is implied that both good and bad deeds go before us to the judgment-seat of God before we do ourselves. In ii. 110, it is the good that goes before us. Our deeds are personified. They are witnesses for or against us, and they always go before us. Their good or bad influence begins to operate before we even know it. This is more general than the New Testament idea in the First Epistle of St. Paul to Timothy, v. 24: "Some men's sins are open beforehand, going before to judgment; and some men they follow after."

101. A party of the Jews in the time of Muḥammad ridiculed the Muslim belief that Gabriel brought down revelations to Muḥammad Muṣṭafā. Michael was called in their books "the great prince which standeth for the children of thy people": (Daniel, xii. 1). The vision of Gabriel inspired fear (Daniel, viii. 16-17). But this pretence—that Michael was their friend and Gabriel their enemy—was merely a manifestation of their unbelief in angels, apostles, and God Himself; and such unbelief could not win the love of God. In any case it was disingenuous to say that they believed in one angel and not in another. Muḥammad's inspiration was through visions of Gabriel. Muḥammad had been helped to the highest spiritual light, and the message which he delivered and his spotless integrity and exemplary life were manifest Signs which every one could understand except those who were obstinate and perverse. Besides, the verses of the Qur-ān were in themselves reasonable and clear.

The (revelation) to thy heart
By God's will, a confirmation
Of what went before,
And guidance and glad tidings
For those who believe,—

نَزَّلَهٗ عَلٰى قَلْبِكَ بِاِذْنِ اللّٰهِ مُصَدِّقًا
لِّمَا بَيْنَ يَدَيْهِ وَهُدًى وَّ بُشْرٰى
لِلْمُؤْمِنِيْنَ ○

98. Whoever is an enemy to God
And His angels and apostles,
To Gabriel and Michael,—
Lo! God is an enemy to those
Who reject Faith.

٩٨- مَنْ كَانَ عَدُوًّا لِّلّٰهِ وَمَلٰٓئِكَتِهٖ وَرُسُلِهٖ
وَجِبْرِيْلَ وَمِيْكٰلَ فَاِنَّ اللّٰهَ عَدُوٌّ
لِّلْكٰفِرِيْنَ ○

99. We have sent down to thee
Manifest Signs (*āyāt*);
And none reject them
But those who are perverse.

٩٩- وَلَقَدْ اَنْزَلْنَآ اِلَيْكَ اٰيٰتٍۢ بَيِّنٰتٍ
وَمَا يَكْفُرُ بِهَآ اِلَّا الْفٰسِقُوْنَ ○

100. Is it not (the case) that
Every time they make a Covenant,
Some party among them
Throw it aside?—Nay,
Most of them are faithless.

١٠٠- اَوَكُلَّمَا عٰهَدُوْا عَهْدًا
نَّبَذَهٗ فَرِيْقٌ مِّنْهُمْ
بَلْ اَكْثَرُهُمْ لَا يُؤْمِنُوْنَ ○

101. And when there came to them
An Apostle from God,
Confirming what was with them,
A party of the People of the Book
Threw away the Book of God [102]
Behind their backs,
As if (it had been something)
They did not know!

١٠١- وَلَمَّا جَآءَهُمْ رَسُوْلٌ مِّنْ عِنْدِ اللّٰهِ
مُصَدِّقٌ لِّمَا مَعَهُمْ
نَبَذَ فَرِيْقٌ مِّنَ الَّذِيْنَ اُوْتُوا الْكِتٰبَ كِتٰبَ
اللّٰهِ وَرَآءَ ظُهُوْرِهِمْ كَاَنَّهُمْ لَا يَعْلَمُوْنَ ○

102. They followed what the evil ones [103]
Gave out (falsely)
Against the power
Of Solomon: the blasphemers
Were, not Solomon, but
The evil ones, teaching men

١٠٢- وَاتَّبَعُوْا مَا تَتْلُوا الشَّيٰطِيْنُ عَلٰى
مُلْكِ سُلَيْمٰنَ وَمَا كَفَرَ سُلَيْمٰنُ وَلٰكِنَّ
الشَّيٰطِيْنَ كَفَرُوْا يُعَلِّمُوْنَ النَّاسَ السِّحْرَ

---

102. I think that by "the Book of God" here is meant, not the Qur-ān, but the Book which the People of the Book had been given, *viz.*, the previous Revelations. The argument is that Muhammad's Message was similar to Revelations which they had already received, and if they had looked into their own Books honestly and sincerely, they would have found proofs in them to show that the new Message was true and from God. But they ignored their own Books or twisted or distorted them according to their own fancies. Worse, they followed something which was actually false and mischievous and inspired by the evil one. Such was the belief in magic and sorcery. These are described in the next verse in terms referring to the beliefs and practices of the "People of the Book."

103. This is a continuation of the argument in ii. 101. The People of the Book, instead of sticking to the plain Books of Revelations, and seeking to do the will of God, ran after all sorts of occult knowledge, most of which was false and evil. Many wonderful tales of occult power attributed the power of Solomon to magic. But Solomon dealt in no arts of evil. It was the powers of evil that pretended to force the laws of nature and the will of God; such a pretence is plainly blasphemy.

Magic, and such things
As came down at Babylon
To the angels Hārūt and
Mārūt.[104]
But neither of these taught anyone
(Such things) without saying:
"We are only for trial;
So do not blaspheme."
They learned from them[105]
The means to sow discord
Between man and wife.
But they could not thus
Harm anyone except
By God's permission.
And they learned what harmed
them,
Not what profited them.
And they knew that the buyers
Of (magic) would have
No share in the happiness
Of the Hereafter. And vile
Was the price for which
They did sell their souls,
If they but knew!

وَمَآ أُنزِلَ عَلَى ٱلْمَلَكَيْنِ بِبَابِلَ هَٰرُوتَ
وَمَٰرُوتَ
وَمَا يُعَلِّمَانِ مِنْ أَحَدٍ
حَتَّىٰ يَقُولَآ إِنَّمَا نَحْنُ فِتْنَةٌ فَلَا تَكْفُرْ
فَيَتَعَلَّمُونَ مِنْهُمَا مَا يُفَرِّقُونَ بِهِۦ بَيْنَ
ٱلْمَرْءِ وَزَوْجِهِۦ
وَمَا هُم بِضَآرِّينَ بِهِۦ مِنْ أَحَدٍ إِلَّا بِإِذْنِ ٱللَّهِ
وَيَتَعَلَّمُونَ مَا يَضُرُّهُمْ وَلَا يَنفَعُهُمْ
وَلَقَدْ عَلِمُوا۟ لَمَنِ ٱشْتَرَىٰهُ مَا لَهُۥ فِى
ٱلْءَاخِرَةِ مِنْ خَلَٰقٍ
وَلَبِئْسَ مَا شَرَوْا۟ بِهِۦٓ أَنفُسَهُمْ
لَوْ كَانُوا۟ يَعْلَمُونَ ○

103. If they had kept their Faith
And guarded themselves from evil,

١٠٣- وَلَوْ أَنَّهُمْ ءَامَنُوا۟ وَٱتَّقَوْا۟ لَمَثُوبَةٌ

104. This verse has been interpreted variously. Who were Hārūt and Mārūt? What did they teach? Why did they teach it? The view which commends itself to me is that of the *Tafsīr Ḥaqqānī*, following Baidhāwī and the *Tafsīr Kabīr*. The word "angels" as applied to Hārūt and Mārūt is figurative. It means "good men, of knowledge, science (or wisdom), and power." In modern languages the word "angel" is applied to a good and beautiful woman. The earlier tradition made angels masculine, and applied to them the attributes which I have mentioned, along with the attribute of beauty, which was implied in goodness, knowledge, wisdom, and power.

Hārūt and Mārūt lived in Babylon, a very ancient seat of science, especially the science of astronomy. The period may be supposed to be anywhere about the time when the ancient Eastern Monarchies were strong and enlightened: probably even earlier, as Mā-rū-tu or Marduk was a deified hero afterwards worshipped as a god of magic in Babylon. Being good men, Hārūt and Mārūt of course dabbled in nothing evil, and their hands were certainly clean of fraud. But knowledge and the arts, if learned by evil men, can be applied to evil uses. The evil ones, besides their fraudulent magic, also learnt a little of this true science and applied it to evil uses. Hārūt and Mārūt did not withhold knowledge, yet never taught anyone without plainly warning them of the trial and temptation of knowledge in the hands of evil men. Being men of insight, they also saw the blasphemy that might rise to the lips of the evil ones puffed up with science and warned them against it. Knowledge is indeed a trial or temptation: if we are warned, we know its dangers: if God has endowed us with free will, we must be free to choose between the benefit and the danger.

Among the Jewish traditions in the Midrash (Jewish *Tafsīrs*) was a story of two angels who asked God's permission to come down to earth but succumbed to temptation, and were hung up by their feet at Babylon for punishment. Such stories about sinning angels who were cast down to punishment were believed in by the early Christians also. (See the Second Epistle of Peter, ii. 4, and the Epistle of Jude, verse 6). There may be an allusion to such legends here, but much spiritualized and we are expressly warned against dabbling in magic or believing that anything can hurt us except by God's will, and God is just and righteous.

105. What the evil ones learnt from Hārūt and Mārūt (see last note) they turned to evil. When mixed with fraud and deception, it appeared as charms and spells and love potions. They did nothing but cause discord between the sexes. But of course their power was limited to the extent to which God permitted the evil to work, for His grace protected all who sought His guidance and repented and returned to Him. But apart from the harm that these false pretenders might do to others, the chief harm which they did was to their own souls. They sold themselves into slavery to the Evil One, as is shown in the allegory of Goethe's *Faust*. That allegory dealt with the individual soul. Here the tragedy is shown to occur not only to individuals but to whole groups of people, for example, the People of the Book. Indeed the story might be extended indefinitely.

Far better had been
The reward from their Lord,
If they but knew!

مِّنْ عِنْدِ اللّٰهِ خَيْرٌ
لَوْ كَانُوْا يَعْلَمُوْنَ ع

SECTION 13.

104. O ye of Faith!
Say not (to the Apostle)
Words of ambiguous import,[106]
But words of respect;
And hearken (to him):
To those without Faith
Is a grievous punishment.

١٠٤- يٰٓاَيُّهَا الَّذِيْنَ اٰمَنُوْا
لَا تَقُوْلُوْا رَاعِنَا
وَ قُوْلُوا انْظُرْنَا وَ اسْمَعُوْا
وَ لِلْكٰفِرِيْنَ عَذَابٌ اَلِيْمٌ

105. It is never the wish
Of those without Faith
Among the People of the Book,
Nor of the Pagans,
That anything good
Should come down to you
From your Lord.
But God will choose
For His special Mercy
Whom He will—for God is
Lord of grace abounding.

١٠٥- مَا يَوَدُّ الَّذِيْنَ كَفَرُوْا
مِنْ اَهْلِ الْكِتٰبِ
وَلَا الْمُشْرِكِيْنَ
اَنْ يُّنَزَّلَ عَلَيْكُمْ مِّنْ خَيْرٍ مِّنْ رَّبِّكُمْ
وَاللّٰهُ يَخْتَصُّ بِرَحْمَتِهٖ مَنْ يَّشَآءُ
وَاللّٰهُ ذُو الْفَضْلِ الْعَظِيْمِ

106. None of Our revelations[107]
Do We abrogate
Or cause to be forgotten,
But We substitute

١٠٦- مَا نَنْسَخْ مِنْ اٰيَةٍ
اَوْ نُنْسِهَا نَاْتِ

---

106. The word disapproved is *Rāʻinā*, which as used by the Muslims meant "Please look at us, attend to us." But it was ridiculed by enemies by a little twist to suggest some insulting meaning. So an unambiguous word "Unẓurnā," with the same meaning is suggested. The general lesson is that we must guard ourselves against the cynical trick of using words which sound complimentary to the ear but have a hidden barb in them. Not only must we be plain and honest in our words. We must respectfully hearken to the words of a Teacher whom we have addressed. Thoughtless people use vain words or put foolish questions, and straightway turn their minds to something else.

107. The word which I have translated by the word "revelations" is Āyat. See C. 41 and n. 15. It is not only used for verses of the Qur-ān, but in a general sense for God's revelations, as in ii. 39 and for other Signs of God in history or nature, or miracles, as in ii. 61. It has even been used for human signs and tokens of wonder, as, for example, monuments or landmarks built by the ancient people of 'Ād (xxvi. 128). What is the meaning here? If we take it in a general sense, it means that God's Message from age to age is always the same, but that its form may differ according to the needs and exigencies of the time. That form was different as given to Moses and then to Jesus and then to Muḥammad. Some commentators apply it also to the Āyāt of the Qur-ān. There is nothing derogatory in this if we believe in progressive revelation. In iii, 7 we are told distinctly about the Qur-ān, that some of its verses are basic or fundamental, and others are allegorical, and it is mischievous to treat the allegorical verses and follow them (literally). On the other hand, it is absurd to treat such a verse as ii. 115 as if it were abrogated by ii. 144 about the Qibla. We turn to the Qibla, but we do not believe that God is only in one place. He is everywhere. See second note to ii. 144.

There may be express abrogation, or there may be "causing or permitting to forget." How many good and wise institutions gradually become obsolete by afflux of time? Then there is the gradual process of disuse or forgetting in evolution. This does not mean that eternal principles change. It is only a sign of God's infinite Power that His creation should take so many forms and shapes not only in the material world but in the world of man's thought and expression.

Something better or similar :
Knowest thou not that God
Hath power over all things ?

107. Knowest thou not
That to God belongeth
The dominion of the heavens
And the earth ?
And besides Him ye have
Neither patron nor helper.

108. Would ye question
Your Apostle as Moses[108]
Was questioned of old ?
But whoever changeth
From Faith to Unbelief,
Hath strayed without doubt
From the even way.[109]

109. Quite a number of the People
Of the Book wish they could
Turn you (people) back
To infidelity after ye have believed,
From selfish envy,
After the Truth hath become
Manifest unto them :
But forgive and overlook,[110]
Till God accomplish
His purpose ;[111] for God
Hath power over all things.[112]

بِخَيْرٍ مِّنْهَآ اَوْ مِثْلِهَا ؕ
اَلَمْ تَعْلَمْ اَنَّ اللّٰهَ عَلٰى كُلِّ شَىْءٍ قَدِيْرٌ ○

١٠٧- اَلَمْ تَعْلَمْ اَنَّ اللّٰهَ لَهٗ مُلْكُ السَّمٰوٰتِ
وَالْاَرْضِ ؕ وَمَا لَكُمْ مِّنْ دُوْنِ اللّٰهِ مِنْ
وَّلِىٍّ وَّلَا نَصِيْرٍ ○

١٠٨- اَمْ تُرِيْدُوْنَ اَنْ تَسْـَٔلُوْا رَسُوْلَكُمْ
كَمَا سُئِلَ مُوْسٰى مِنْ قَبْلُ ؕ
وَمَنْ يَّتَبَدَّلِ الْكُفْرَ بِالْاِيْمَانِ
فَقَدْ ضَلَّ سَوَآءَ السَّبِيْلِ ○

١٠٩- وَدَّ كَثِيْرٌ مِّنْ اَهْلِ الْكِتٰبِ
لَوْ يَرُدُّوْنَكُمْ مِّنْ بَعْدِ اِيْمَانِكُمْ كُفَّارًا ۚۖ
حَسَدًا مِّنْ عِنْدِ اَنْفُسِهِمْ مِّنْ بَعْدِ مَا
تَبَيَّنَ لَهُمُ الْحَقُّ ۚ
فَاعْفُوْا وَاصْفَحُوْا حَتّٰى يَاْتِىَ اللّٰهُ بِاَمْرِهٖ ؕ
اِنَّ اللّٰهَ عَلٰى كُلِّ شَىْءٍ قَدِيْرٌ ○

---

108. Moses was constantly harassed with foolish, impertinent, or disingenuous questions by his own people. We must not follow that bad example. In spiritual matters, posers do no good: questions should be asked only for real instruction.

109. "Even way": the Arabic word *sawāa* signifies smoothness as opposed to roughness; symmetry as opposed to want of plan; equality or proportion as opposed to want of design; rectitude as opposed to crookedness; a mean as opposed to extremes; and fitness for the object held in view as opposed to faultiness.

110. Three words are used in the Qur-ān, with a meaning akin to "forgive", but each with a different shade of meaning. *'Afā* (here translated "forgive") means to forget, to obliterate from one's mind. *Ṣafaḥa* (here translated "overlook") means to turn away from, to ignore, to treat a matter as if it did not affect one. *Gafara* (which does not occur in this verse) means to cover up something, as God does to our sins with His grace: this word is particularly appropriate in God's attribute of *Gaffār*, the One who forgives again and again.

111. The word *Amr* is comprehensive, and includes (1) an order or command as in xcvi. 12; or (2) a purpose, design, will, as in xviii. 82; or (3) affairs, working, doing, carrying out or execution of a design, as in lxxxix. 5. In many cases some of these meanings run together.

112. Note how this phrase, seemingly repeated from ii. 106, and occurring in many other places, has an appropriate signification in each place. In ii. 106 we were told about progressive revelation, how the same thing may take different forms, and seeming human infirmity contribute to the fulfilment of God's design, for God's power is unlimited. Here we are told to be patient and forgiving against envy and injustice: this too may be fulfilling God's purpose, for His power is infinite.

110. And be steadfast in prayer
And regular in charity:
And whatever good
Ye send forth for your souls[113]
Before you, ye shall find it
With God: for God sees
Well all that ye do.

١١٠- وَاَقِيْمُوا الصَّلٰوةَ وَاٰتُوا الزَّكٰوةَ ط
وَمَا تُقَدِّمُوْا لِاَنْفُسِكُمْ مِّنْ خَيْرٍ تَجِدُوْهُ
عِنْدَ اللّٰهِ ط
اِنَّ اللّٰهَ بِمَا تَعْمَلُوْنَ بَصِيْرٌ ۝

111. And they say: "None
Shall enter Paradise unless
He be a Jew or a Christian."
Those are their (vain) desires.
Say: "Produce your proof
If ye are truthful."

١١١- وَقَالُوْا لَنْ يَّدْخُلَ الْجَنَّةَ اِلَّا مَنْ
كَانَ هُوْدًا اَوْ نَصٰرٰى ط تِلْكَ اَمَانِيُّهُمْ ط قُلْ
هَاتُوْا بُرْهَانَكُمْ اِنْ كُنْتُمْ صٰدِقِيْنَ ۝

112. Nay,—whoever submits
His whole self[114] to God
And is a doer of good,—
He will get his reward
With his Lord;
On such shall be no fear,
Nor shall they grieve.[115]

١١٢- بَلٰى ق مَنْ اَسْلَمَ وَجْهَهٗ لِلّٰهِ
وَهُوَ مُحْسِنٌ فَلَهٗۤ اَجْرُهٗ عِنْدَ رَبِّهٖ ص
وَلَا خَوْفٌ عَلَيْهِمْ وَلَا هُمْ يَحْزَنُوْنَ ۝ ع

SECTION 14.

113. The Jews say: "The Christians
Have naught (to stand) upon;
And the Christians say:
"The Jews have naught
(To stand) upon." Yet they
(Profess to) study the (same) Book.
Like unto their word
Is what those say who know
not;[116]

١١٣- وَقَالَتِ الْيَهُوْدُ لَيْسَتِ النَّصٰرٰى عَلٰى
شَيْءٍ ص وَّقَالَتِ النَّصٰرٰى لَيْسَتِ الْيَهُوْدُ
عَلٰى شَيْءٍ لا وَّهُمْ يَتْلُوْنَ الْكِتٰبَ ط
كَذٰلِكَ قَالَ الَّذِيْنَ لَا يَعْلَمُوْنَ مِثْلَ قَوْلِهِمْ ج

113. *Cf.* ii. 95 n.

114. The word translated "self" is *Wajh*, a comprehensive Arabic word. It means (1) literally "face": but it may imply (2) countenance or favour, as in xcii. 20; (3) honour, glory, Presence as applied to God, as in ii. 115, and perhaps also in lv. 27; (4) cause, sake ("for the sake of") as in lxxvi. 8; (5) the first part, the beginning, as in iii. 71; (6) nature, inner being, essence, self, as in v. 111, xxviii. 88, and perhaps also in lv. 27. Here I understand meaning 6; the face expresses the personality or the whole inner self of man.

115. This phrase comes in aptly in its own context many times. In this Sūra it occurs in ii. 38, 62, 112, 262, 274, and 277. It serves the same purpose as a refrain in a very well-arranged Song, or a *motif* in Wagner's powerful music.

116. It is a sure sign of ignorance and prejudice when you study the same book as another or a similar one and yet are absolutely intolerant of the meaning which the other draws from it. You should know better, but you speak like the ignorant. In this case the primary reference in the word "ignorant" may be to the Pagan Arabs.

But God will judge
Between them in their quarrel
On the Day of Judgment.

فَاللّٰهُ يَحْكُمُ بَيْنَهُمْ يَوْمَ الْقِيٰمَةِ فِيْمَا كَانُوْا
فِيْهِ يَخْتَلِفُوْنَ ○

114. And who is more unjust
Than he who forbids [117]
That in places for the worship
Of God, God's name should be
Celebrated ?—whose zeal
Is (in fact) to ruin them ?
It was not fitting that such
Should themselves enter them
Except in fear. For them
There is nothing but disgrace
In this world, and in the world
To come, an exceeding torment.

١١٤- وَمَنْ اَظْلَمُ مِمَّنْ مَّنَعَ مَسٰجِدَ اللّٰهِ
اَنْ يُّذْكَرَ فِيْهَا اسْمُهٗ وَسَعٰى فِيْ خَرَابِهَا ؕ
اُولٰٓئِكَ مَا كَانَ لَهُمْ اَنْ يَّدْخُلُوْهَا اِلَّا
خَآئِفِيْنَ ؕ
لَهُمْ فِي الدُّنْيَا خِزْيٌ وَّلَهُمْ فِي الْاٰخِرَةِ
عَذَابٌ عَظِيْمٌ ○

115. To God belong the East
And the West : whithersoever
Ye turn, there is the Presence [118]
Of God. For God is
All-Pervading,
All-Knowing.

١١٥- وَلِلّٰهِ الْمَشْرِقُ وَالْمَغْرِبُ ق
فَاَيْنَمَا تُوَلُّوْا فَثَمَّ وَجْهُ اللّٰهِ ؕ
اِنَّ اللّٰهَ وَاسِعٌ عَلِيْمٌ ○

116. They say : " God hath begotten
A son " : Glory be to Him.—Nay,
To Him belongs all
That is in the heavens
And on earth : everything
Renders worship to Him. [119]

١١٦- وَقَالُوا اتَّخَذَ اللّٰهُ وَلَدًا ۙ
سُبْحٰنَهٗ ؕ بَلْ لَّهٗ مَا فِي السَّمٰوٰتِ وَالْاَرْضِ ؕ
كُلٌّ لَّهٗ قٰنِتُوْنَ ○

117. To Him is due
The primal origin

١١٧- بَدِيْعُ السَّمٰوٰتِ وَالْاَرْضِ ؕ

---

117. There were actually Pagans in Mecca who tried to shut out the Muslim Arabs from the Ka'ba, the universal place of Arab worship. The Pagans themselves called it the House of God. With what face could they exclude the Muslims, who wanted to worship the true God instead of worshipping idols ? If these Pagans had succeeded, they would only have caused violent divisions among the Arabs and destroyed the sanctity and the very existence of the Ka'ba.

This verse, taken in a general sense, establishes the principle of freedom of worship in a public mosque or place dedicated to the worship of God. This is recognized in Muslim law. There may be differences of opinion between one individual and another, or between one group and another as to the nature of God or the proper mode of worship, but no tests can be laid down, nor can one individual or sect exclude another. So long as a person enters reverently and does nothing outwardly to cause offence to the other worshippers, he has a right to go and worship in a public place set apart for God's worship.

118. The word translated " Presence " is *Wajh*, literally " face. " See note to ii. 112 above.

119. It is a derogation from the glory of God—in fact it is blasphemy—to say that God begets sons, like a man or an animal. The Christian doctrine is here emphatically repudiated. If words have any meaning, it would mean an attribution to God of a material nature, and of the lower animal functions of sex. In a spiritual sense, we are all children of God. And all Creation celebrates His glory. Verse 117 should be read with this to complete the argument.

Of the heavens and the earth:[120]
When He decreeth a matter,
He saith to it: "Be,"
And it is.

وَإِذَا قَضَىٰٓ أَمْرًا فَإِنَّمَا يَقُولُ لَهُۥ كُن
فَيَكُونُ ○

118. Say those without knowledge:
" Why speaketh not God
Unto us? Or why cometh not
Unto us a Sign?"
So said the people before them
Words of similar import.
Their hearts are alike.
We have indeed made clear
The Signs unto any people
Who hold firmly
To Faith (in their hearts).

۱۱۸- وَقَالَ ٱلَّذِينَ لَا يَعْلَمُونَ لَوْلَا
يُكَلِّمُنَا ٱللَّهُ أَوْ تَأْتِينَآ ءَايَةٌ ۗ
كَذَٰلِكَ قَالَ ٱلَّذِينَ مِن قَبْلِهِم مِّثْلَ
قَوْلِهِمْ ۘ
تَشَٰبَهَتْ قُلُوبُهُمْ ۗ
قَدْ بَيَّنَّا ٱلْءَايَٰتِ لِقَوْمٍ يُوقِنُونَ ○

119. Verily We have sent thee
In truth as a bearer
Of glad tidings and a warner:
But of thee no question
Shall be asked of the Companions
Of the Blazing Fire.

۱۱۹- إِنَّآ أَرْسَلْنَٰكَ بِٱلْحَقِّ بَشِيرًا وَ
نَذِيرًا ۙ
وَلَا تُسْـَٔلُ عَنْ أَصْحَٰبِ ٱلْجَحِيمِ ○

120. Never will the Jews
Or the Christians be satisfied
With thee unless thou follow
Their form of religion. Say:

۱۲۰- وَلَن تَرْضَىٰ عَنكَ ٱلْيَهُودُ وَلَا ٱلنَّصَٰرَىٰ
حَتَّىٰ تَتَّبِعَ مِلَّتَهُمْ ۗ قُلْ

---

120. The previous verse told us that everything in heaven and earth celebrates the glory of God. Lest anyone should think that the heavens and the earth were themselves primeval and eternal, we are now told that they themselves are creatures of God's will and design. *Cf.* vi. 102, where the word *bada'a* is used as here for the creation of the heavens and the earth, and *khalaqa* is used for the creation of all things. *Bada'a* goes back to the very primal beginning, as far as we can conceive it. The materialists might say that primeval matter was eternal: other things, *i.e.*, the forms and shapes as we see them now, were called into being at some time or other, and will perish. When they perish, they dissolve into primeval matter again, which stands as the base of all existence. We go further back. We say that if we postulate such primeval matter, it owes its origin itself to God, Who is the final basis of existence, the Cause of all Causes. If this is conceded, we proceed to argue that the process of Creation is not then completed. "All things in the heavens and on the earth" are created by gradual processes. In "things" we include abstract as well as material things. We see the abstract things and ideas actually growing before us. But that also is God's creation, to which we can apply the word *khalaqa*, for in it is involved the idea of measuring, fitting it into a scheme of other things. *Cf.* liv. 49; also xxv. 59. Here comes in what we know as the process of evolution. On the other hand, the "*amr*" (=Command, Direction, Design) is a single thing, unrelated to Time, "like the twinkling of an eye" (liv. 50). Another word to note in this connection is *ja'ala* "making" which seems to imply new shapes and forms, new dispositions, as the making of the Signs of the Zodiac in the heavens, or the setting out of the sun and moon for light, or the establishment of the succession of day and night (xxv. 61-62). A further process with regard to the soul is described in the word *sawwā*, bringing it to perfection (xci. 7) but this we shall discuss in its place. *Faṭara* (xlii. 11) implies, like *bada'a*, the creating of a thing out of nothing and after no pre-existing similitude, but perhaps *faṭara* implies the creation of primeval matter to which further processes have to be applied later, as when one prepares dough but leaves the leavening to be done after. *Badaa* (without the '*ain*), xxx. 27, implies beginning the process of creation: this is made further clear in xxxii. 7 where the beginning of the creation of pristine man from clay refers to his physical body, leaving the further processes of reproduction and the breathing in of the soul to be described in subsequent verses. Lastly, *baraa* is creation implying liberation from pre-existing matter or circumstance, *e.g.*, man's body from clay (lix. 24) or a calamity from previously existing circumstances (lvii. 22). See also vi. 94, n. 916; vi. 98, n. 923; lix. 24, nn. 5405-6.

"The Guidance of God,—that
Is the (only) Guidance."
Wert thou to follow their desires
After the knowledge
Which hath reached thee,
Then wouldst thou find
Neither Protector nor Helper
Against God.

إِنَّ هُدَى اللّٰهِ هُوَ الْهُدٰى ۗ
وَلَئِنِ اتَّبَعْتَ أَهْوَاءَهُمْ بَعْدَ الَّذِي
جَاءَكَ مِنَ الْعِلْمِ ۙ
مَا لَكَ مِنَ اللّٰهِ مِنْ وَّلِيٍّ وَّلَا نَصِيْرٍ ○

121. Those to whom We have sent
The Book study it as it
Should be studied: they are
The ones that believe therein:
Those who reject faith therein,—
The loss is their own.

١٢١- الَّذِيْنَ اٰتَيْنٰهُمُ الْكِتٰبَ يَتْلُوْنَهٗ حَقَّ
تِلَاوَتِهٖ ۗ اُولٰٓئِكَ يُؤْمِنُوْنَ بِهٖ ۗ وَمَنْ
يَّكْفُرْ بِهٖ فَاُولٰٓئِكَ هُمُ الْخٰسِرُوْنَ ○

C. 48.—If the People of the Book rely
(ii. 122-141.) Upon Abraham, let them study
His history. His posterity included
Both Israel and Ismā'īl. Abraham
Was a righteous man of God,
A Muslim, and so were his children.
Abraham and Ismā'īl built
The Ka'ba as the house of God,
And purified it, to be a centre
Of worship for all the world:
For God is the God of all Peoples.[121]

SECTION 15.

122. Children of Israel! call to mind
The special favour which I bestowed
Upon you, and that I preferred you
To all others (for My Message).

١٢٢- يٰبَنِيْٓ اِسْرَآءِيْلَ اذْكُرُوْا نِعْمَتِيَ الَّتِيْٓ
اَنْعَمْتُ عَلَيْكُمْ
وَاَنِّيْ فَضَّلْتُكُمْ عَلَى الْعٰلَمِيْنَ ○

123. Then guard yourselves against a Day

١٢٣- وَاتَّقُوْا يَوْمًا

121. The argument now proceeds on another line. Ye People of the Book who go back to Abraham! not only is your claim to exclusive knowledge of God false and derogatory to the Lord of All the Worlds. If you must appeal to Abraham, he was also the progenitor of the Arab race through Ismā'īl. Indeed Abraham and Ismā'īl together built the House of God in Mecca (long before the Temple of Jerusalem was built). They purified it and laid the foundations of the universal religion, which is summed up in the word Islam, or complete submission to the Will of God. Abraham and Ismā'īl were thus true Muslims. Whence then your rancour against Islam?

Historically the Temple at Mecca must have been a far more ancient place of worship than the Temple at Jerusalem. Arab tradition connects various places in and around Mecca with the name of Abraham and identifies the well of *Zam-zam* with the well in the story of the child Ismā'īl. Arab tradition also refers the story of the Sacrifice to Ismā'īl and not to Isaac, therein differing from the Jewish tradition in Gen. xxii. 1-19.

When one soul shall not avail
another,
Nor shall compensation be
accepted from her
Nor shall intercession profit her
Nor shall anyone be helped
(from outside).[122]

لَا تَجْزِي نَفْسٌ عَنْ نَفْسٍ شَيْئًا
وَلَا يُقْبَلُ مِنْهَا عَدْلٌ
وَلَا تَنْفَعُهَا شَفَاعَةٌ
وَلَا هُمْ يُنْصَرُونَ ○

124. And remember that Abraham
Was tried by his Lord
With certain Commands,[123]
Which he fulfilled:
He said: "I will make thee
An Imām[124] to the Nations."
He pleaded: "And also
(Imāms) from my offspring!"
He answered: "But My Promise
Is not within the reach
Of evil-doers."

١٢٤- وَإِذِ ابْتَلَىٰ إِبْرٰهِمَ رَبُّهُ
بِكَلِمٰتٍ فَأَتَمَّهُنَّ
قَالَ إِنِّي جَاعِلُكَ
لِلنَّاسِ إِمَامًا
قَالَ وَمِنْ ذُرِّيَّتِي
قَالَ لَا يَنَالُ عَهْدِي الظّٰلِمِينَ ○

125. Remember We made the House[125]
A place of assembly for men
And a place of safety;
And take ye the Station
Of Abraham as a place
Of prayer; and We covenanted
With Abraham and Ismā'īl,
That they should sanctify
My House for those who
Compass it round, or use it

١٢٥- وَإِذْ جَعَلْنَا الْبَيْتَ مَثَابَةً لِلنَّاسِ
وَأَمْنًا
وَاتَّخِذُوا مِنْ مَقَامِ إِبْرٰهِمَ مُصَلًّى
وَعَهِدْنَا إِلَىٰ إِبْرٰهِمَ وَإِسْمٰعِيلَ
أَنْ طَهِّرَا بَيْتِيَ

122. Verses 122-123 repeat verses 47-48 (except for a slight verbal variation in ii. 123. which does not affect the sense). The argument about the favours to Israel is thus beautifully rounded off, and we now proceed to the argument in favour of the Arabs as succeeding to the spiritual inheritance of Abraham.

123. *Kalimāt*: literally "words": here used in the mystic sense of God's Will or Decree or Purpose. This verse may be taken to be the sum of the verses following. In everything Abraham fulfilled God's wish: he purified God's house; he built the sacred refuge of the Ka'ba; he submitted his will to God's, and thus became the type of Islam. He was promised the leadership of the world; he pleaded for his progeny, and his prayer was granted, with the limitation that if his progeny was false to God, God's promise did not reach the people who proved themselves false.

124. *Imām*: the primary sense is that of being foremost: hence it may mean: (1) leader in religion: (2) leader in congregational prayer; (3) model, pattern, example; (4) a book of guidance and instruction (xi. 17): (5) a book of evidence or record (xxxvi. 12). Here, meanings 1 and 3 are implied. In ix. 12 the word is applied to leaders of Unbelief or Blasphemy.

125. The Ka'ba, the House of God. Its foundation goes back by Arab tradition to Abraham. Its fourfold character is here referred to (1) It was the centre to which all the Arab tribes resorted for trade, for poetic contests, and for worship. (2) It was sacred territory, and was respected by friend and foe alike. At certain seasons, all fighting was and is forbidden within its limits, and even arms are not allowed to be carried, and no game or other thing is allowed to be killed. Like the Cities of Refuge under the Mosaic Dispensation, to which manslayers could flee (Num. xxxv. 6), or the Sanctuaries in Mediæval Europe, to which criminals could not be pursued, Mecca was recognized by Arab custom as inviolable for the pursuit of revenge or violence. (3) It was a place of prayer: even to-day there is a Station of Abraham within the enclosure, where Abraham was supposed to have prayed. (4) It must be held pure and sacred for all purposes.

Though the verse as a whole is expressed in the First Person Plural, the House is called "My House," to emphasize the personal relation of the One True God to it, and repudiate the Polytheism which defiled it before it was purified again by Muḥammad.

As a retreat, or bow, or
Prostrate themselves (therein[126]
In prayer).

لِلطَّآئِفِينَ وَالْعٰكِفِينَ وَالرُّكَّعِ
السُّجُودِ ○

126. And remember Abraham said:
"My Lord, make this a City
Of Peace,[127] and feed its People
With fruits,[128]—such of them
As believe in God and the Last
Day."
He said: "(Yea), and such as
Reject Faith,—for a while
Will I grant them their pleasure,
But will soon drive them
To the torment of Fire,—
An evil destination (indeed)!"

١٢٦- وَإِذْ قَالَ إِبْرٰهِمُ رَبِّ اجْعَلْ هٰذَا بَلَدًا
اٰمِنًا وَّارْزُقْ اَهْلَهُ مِنَ الثَّمَرٰتِ
مَنْ اٰمَنَ مِنْهُمْ بِاللّٰهِ وَالْيَوْمِ الْاٰخِرِ ط
قَالَ وَمَنْ كَفَرَ فَاُمَتِّعُهُ قَلِيلًا
ثُمَّ اَضْطَرُّهُ اِلٰى عَذَابِ النَّارِ ط
وَبِئْسَ الْمَصِيرُ ○

127. And remember Abraham
And Isma'il raised
The foundations of the House
(With this prayer): "Our Lord!
Accept (this service) from us:
For Thou art the All-Hearing,
The All-Knowing.

١٢٧- وَإِذْ يَرْفَعُ إِبْرٰهِمُ الْقَوَاعِدَ مِنَ
الْبَيْتِ وَإِسْمٰعِيلُ ط
رَبَّنَا تَقَبَّلْ مِنَّا ط
اِنَّكَ اَنْتَ السَّمِيعُ الْعَلِيمُ ○

128. "Our Lord! make of us
Muslims, bowing to Thy (Will),
And of our progeny a people
Muslim, bowing to Thy (Will);
And show us our places for
The celebration of (due) rites;
And turn unto us (in Mercy);
For Thou art the Oft-Returning,
Most Merciful.

١٢٨- رَبَّنَا وَاجْعَلْنَا مُسْلِمَيْنِ لَكَ
وَمِنْ ذُرِّيَّتِنَآ اُمَّةً مُّسْلِمَةً لَّكَ ص
وَاَرِنَا مَنَاسِكَنَا وَتُبْ عَلَيْنَا ج
اِنَّكَ اَنْتَ التَّوَّابُ الرَّحِيمُ ○

129. "Our Lord! send amongst them
An Apostle of their own,
Who shall rehearse Thy Signs
To them and instruct them

١٢٩- رَبَّنَا وَابْعَثْ فِيهِمْ رَسُولًا مِّنْهُمْ
يَتْلُوا عَلَيْهِمْ اٰيٰتِكَ

126. Four rites are here enumerated, which have now acquired a technical meaning. (1) Compassing the sacred territory, or going round the Ka'ba: *Ṭawāf*. There are special guides who take pilgrims and visitors round. (2) Retiring to the place as a spiritual retreat, for contemplation and prayer: *I'tikāf*. (3) The posture of bending the back in prayer: *Rukū'*. (4) The posture of prostrating oneself on the ground in prayer: *Sujūd*. The protection of the holy territory is for all, but special cleanliness and purity is required for the sake of the devotees who undertake these rites.

127. The root *salama* in the word Islam implies (among other ideas) the idea of Peace, and therefore when Mecca is the city of Islam, it is also the City of Peace. The same root occurs in the latter part of the name Jerusalem, the Jewish City of Peace. When the day of Jerusalem passed (see verse 134 or 141 below), Mecca became the "New Jerusalem"—or rather the old and original "City of Peace" restored and made universal

128. The territory of Mecca is barren and rocky, compared with, say, Ṭaif, a city 70-75 miles east of Mecca. A prayer for the prosperity of Mecca therefore includes a prayer for the good things of material life. This is the literal meaning. But note that the opposition in this verse is between the fruits of the Garden for the righteous and the torments of the Fire for the evil ones—a spiritual allegory of great force and aptness.

In Scripture and Wisdom,
And sanctify them:
For Thou art the Exalted in Might,
The Wise."[129]

وَيُعَلِّمُهُمُ الْكِتٰبَ وَالْحِكْمَةَ وَيُزَكِّيْهِمْ ؕ
اِنَّكَ اَنْتَ الْعَزِيْزُ الْحَكِيْمُ ۝ ع

SECTION 16.

130. And who turns away
From the religion of Abraham
But such as debase their souls
With folly? Him We chose[130]
And rendered pure in this world:
And he will be in the Hereafter
In the ranks of the Righteous.

١٣٠- وَمَنْ يَّرْغَبُ عَنْ مِّلَّةِ اِبْرٰهٖمَ
اِلَّا مَنْ سَفِهَ نَفْسَهٗ ؕ وَلَقَدِ اصْطَفَيْنٰهُ
فِي الدُّنْيَا ۚ وَاِنَّهٗ فِي الْاٰخِرَةِ لَمِنَ
الصّٰلِحِيْنَ ۝

131. Behold! his Lord said
To him: "Bow (thy will to Me):"
He said: "I bow (my will)
To the Lord and Cherisher
Of the Universe."

١٣١- اِذْ قَالَ لَهٗ رَبُّهٗٓ
اَسْلِمْ ۙ
قَالَ اَسْلَمْتُ لِرَبِّ الْعٰلَمِيْنَ ۝

132. And this was the legacy
That Abraham left to his sons,
And so did Jacob;
"Oh my sons! God hath chosen
The Faith for you; then die not
Except in the Faith of Islam."

١٣٢- وَوَصّٰى بِهَآ اِبْرٰهٖمُ بَنِيْهِ وَيَعْقُوْبُ ؕ
يٰبَنِيَّ اِنَّ اللّٰهَ اصْطَفٰى لَكُمُ الدِّيْنَ
فَلَا تَمُوْتُنَّ اِلَّا وَاَنْتُمْ مُّسْلِمُوْنَ ۝ؕ

133. Were ye witnesses[131]
When Death appeared before Jacob?
Behold, he said to his sons:
"What will ye worship after me?"
They said: "We shall worship

١٣٣- اَمْ كُنْتُمْ شُهَدَآءَ اِذْ حَضَرَ يَعْقُوْبَ
الْمَوْتُ ۙ اِذْ قَالَ لِبَنِيْهِ مَا تَعْبُدُوْنَ
مِنْۢ بَعْدِيْ ؕ قَالُوْا نَعْبُدُ اِلٰهَكَ وَ

---

129. How beautiful this prayer is, and how aptly it comes in here in the argument! Such Paganism or star-worship or planet-worship as there was in Abraham's time was first cleared out of Mecca by Abraham. This is the chief meaning of "sanctification" or purification in ii. 125, although of course physical cleanliness is (in physical conditions) a necessary element of purification in the higher sense. Abraham and his elder son Ismā'īl then built the Ka'ba and established the rites and usages of the sacred city. He was thus the founder of the original Islam (which is as old as mankind) in Arabia. As becomes a devout man, he offers and dedicates the work to God in humble supplication, addressing Him as the All-Hearing and the All-Knowing. He then asks for a blessing on himself and his progeny generally, both the children of his eldest-born Ismā'īl and his younger son Isaac. With prophetic vision he foresees that there will be corruption and backsliding in both branches of his family: Mecca will house 360 idols, and Jerusalem will become a harlot city (Ezekiel xvi. 15), a city of abomination. But the light of Islam will shine, and reclaim the lost people in both branches and indeed in all the world. So he prays for God's mercy, addressing Him as the Oft-Returning, Most Merciful. And finally he foresees in Mecca an Apostle teaching the people as one "of their own," and in their own beautiful Arabic language: he asks for a blessing on Muḥammad's ministry, appealing to the Power and Wisdom of God.

130. *Iṣṭafā*: chose; chose because of purity; chose and purified. It is the same root from which *Muṣṭafā* is derived, one of the titles of Muḥammad.

131. The whole of the Children of Israel are called to witness one of their slogans, that they worshipped "the God of their fathers." The idea in their minds got narrowed down to that of a tribal God. But they are reminded that their ancestors had the principle of Islam in them,—the worship of the One True and Universal God. The death-bed scene is described in Jewish tradition.

Thy God and the God of thy
fathers,[132]—
Of Abraham, Ismā'īl, and Isaac,—
The One (True) God :
To Him we bow (in Islam)."

الٰهَ اٰبَآئِكَ اِبْرٰهٖمَ وَاِسْمٰعِيْلَ وَاِسْحٰقَ
اِلٰهًا وَّاحِدًا ۚۖ
وَّنَحْنُ لَهٗ مُسْلِمُوْنَ ○

134. That was a People that hath
Passed away. They shall reap
The fruit of what they did,
And ye of what ye do !
Of their merits
There is no question in your case![133]

١٣٤- تِلْكَ اُمَّةٌ قَدْ خَلَتْ ۚ لَهَا مَا
كَسَبَتْ وَلَكُمْ مَّا كَسَبْتُمْ ۚ وَلَا تُسْـَٔلُوْنَ
عَمَّا كَانُوْا يَعْمَلُوْنَ ○

135. They say : "Become Jews
Or Christians if ye would be guided
(To salvation)." Say thou :
"Nay ! (I would rather) the
Religion
Of Abraham the True,[134]
And he joined not gods with God."

١٣٥- وَقَالُوْا كُوْنُوْا هُوْدًا اَوْ نَصٰرٰى
تَهْتَدُوْا ؕ قُلْ
بَلْ مِلَّةَ اِبْرٰهٖمَ حَنِيْفًا ؕ
وَمَا كَانَ مِنَ الْمُشْرِكِيْنَ ○

136. Say ye : "We believe
In God, and the revelation
Given to us, and to Abraham,
Ismā'īl, Isaac, Jacob,
And the Tribes, and that given
To Moses and Jesus, and that given
To (all) Prophets from their Lord :
We make no difference
Between one and another of them :
And we bow to God (in Islam)."[135]

١٣٦- قُوْلُوْٓا اٰمَنَّا بِاللّٰهِ وَمَآ اُنْزِلَ اِلَيْنَا وَمَآ
اُنْزِلَ اِلٰٓى اِبْرٰهٖمَ وَاِسْمٰعِيْلَ وَاِسْحٰقَ وَ
يَعْقُوْبَ وَالْاَسْبَاطِ وَمَآ اُوْتِيَ مُوْسٰى وَ
عِيْسٰى وَمَآ اُوْتِيَ النَّبِيُّوْنَ مِنْ رَّبِّهِمْ ۚ لَا نُفَرِّقُ
بَيْنَ اَحَدٍ مِّنْهُمْ ۖ وَنَحْنُ لَهٗ مُسْلِمُوْنَ ○

137. So if they believe
As ye believe, they are indeed
On the right path ; but if
They turn back, it is they

١٣٧- فَاِنْ اٰمَنُوْا بِمِثْلِ مَآ اٰمَنْتُمْ بِهٖ
فَقَدِ اهْتَدَوْا ۚ وَاِنْ تَوَلَّوْا فَاِنَّمَا

132. "Fathers" means ancestors, and includes uncles, grand-uncles, as well as direct ascendants.

133. I have made a free paraphrase of what would read literally : "Ye shall not be asked about what they used to do." On the Day of Judgment each soul would have to answer for its own deeds : it cannot claim merit from others, nor be answerable for the crimes or sins of others. Here the argument is : if the Jews or Christians claim the merits of Father Abraham and the Patriarchs or of Jesus, we cannot follow them. Because there were righteous men in the past, it cannot help us unless we are ourselves righteous. The doctrine of personal responsibility is a cardinal feature of Islam.

134. *Ḥanīf* : inclined to right opinion, orthodox (in the literal meaning of the Greek words), firm in faith, sound and well-balanced, true. Perhaps the last word, True, sums up most of the other shades.

The Jews, though taught Unity, went after false gods, and the Christians invented the Trinity or borrowed it from Paganism. We go back to the pure, *ḥanīf* doctrine of Abraham, to live and die in faith in the One True God.

135. Here we have the Creed of Islam : to believe in (1) the One Universal God, (2) the Message to us through Muḥammad and the Signs (*āyāt*) as interpreted on the basis of personal responsibility, (3) the Message delivered by other Teachers in the past. These are mentioned in three groups : (1) Abraham, Ismā'īl, Isaac, Jacob, and the Tribes : of these Abraham had apparently a Book (lxxxvii. 19) and the others followed his tradition ; (2) Moses and Jesus, who each left a scripture ; these scriptures are still extant, though not in their pristine form ; and (3) other scriptures, Prophets, or Messengers of God, not specifically mentioned in the Qur-ān (xl. 78). We make no difference between any of these. Their Message (in essentials) was one, and that is the basis of Islam.

Who are in schism; but God will
Suffice thee as against them,[136]
And He is the All-Hearing,
The All-Knowing.

هُمْ فِي شِقَاقٍ ۚ فَسَيَكْفِيكَهُمُ اللّٰهُ ۚ
وَهُوَ السَّمِيعُ الْعَلِيمُ ۝

138. (Our religion is)
The Baptism of God: [137]
And who can baptize better
Than God? And it is He
Whom we worship.

١٣٨- صِبْغَةَ اللّٰهِ ۚ وَمَنْ أَحْسَنُ مِنَ اللّٰهِ
صِبْغَةً ۫ وَنَحْنُ لَهُ عٰبِدُونَ ۝

139. Say: Will ye dispute
With us about God, seeing
That He is our Lord
And your Lord; that we
Are responsible for our doings
And ye for yours; and that
We are sincere (in our faith)
In him?

١٣٩- قُلْ أَتُحَآجُّونَنَا فِي اللّٰهِ
وَهُوَ رَبُّنَا وَرَبُّكُمْ ۚ
وَلَنَآ أَعْمَالُنَا وَلَكُمْ أَعْمَالُكُمْ ۚ
وَنَحْنُ لَهُ مُخْلِصُونَ ۝

140. Or [138] do ye say that
Abraham, Ismā'īl, Isaac,
Jacob and the Tribes were
Jews or Christians?
Say: Do ye know better
Than God? Ah! who
Is more unjust than those
Who conceal the testimony
They have from God?
But God is not unmindful
Of what ye do!

١٤٠- أَمْ تَقُولُونَ إِنَّ إِبْرٰهِيمَ وَإِسْمٰعِيلَ
وَإِسْحٰقَ وَيَعْقُوبَ وَالْأَسْبَاطَ كَانُوا هُودًا
أَوْ نَصٰرٰى ۗ قُلْ ءَأَنْتُمْ أَعْلَمُ أَمِ اللّٰهُ ۗ
وَمَنْ أَظْلَمُ مِمَّنْ كَتَمَ شَهٰدَةً عِنْدَهُ
مِنَ اللّٰهِ ۗ
وَمَا اللّٰهُ بِغٰفِلٍ عَمَّا تَعْمَلُونَ ۝

141. That was a people that hath
Passed away. They shall reap
The fruit of what they did,
And ye of what ye do!
1 Of their merits
30 There is no question in your case: [139]

١٤١- تِلْكَ أُمَّةٌ قَدْ خَلَتْ ۚ
لَهَا مَا كَسَبَتْ وَلَكُمْ مَا كَسَبْتُمْ ۚ
وَلَا تُسْـَٔلُونَ عَمَّا كَانُوا يَعْمَلُونَ ۝

136. We are thus in the true line of those who follow the one and indivisible Message of the One God, wherever delivered. If others narrow it or corrupt it, it is they who have left the faith and created a division or schism. But God sees and knows all. And He will protect His own, and His support will be infinitely more precious than the support which men can give.

137. *Ṣibgat*: baptism: the root-meaning implies a dye or colour; apparently the Arab Christians mixed a dye or colour in the baptismal water, signifying that the baptized person got a new colour in life. We do not believe that it is necessary to be baptized to be saved. Our higher baptism is the "Baptism" of God, by which we take on a colour (symbolically) of God, and absorb His goodness in us.

The accusative case of *Ṣibgat* puts it in opposition to *millat* ("religion") in ii. 135.

138. The alternative is with the question in the last verse. Do you dispute with us although we worship the same God as you and claim that ours is the same religion as that of your ancestors? Or do you really assert that Abraham and his son and his sons' sons, who founded the Tribes long before Moses, followed your Jewish religion as you know it? History of course proves that claim absurd. If the Christians claim that these Patriarchs knew of and followed the teaching of Jesus, the claim is still more absurd,—except in the sense of Islam that God's teaching is one in all ages.

139. Verse 134 began a certain argument, which is now rounded off in the same words in this verse. To use a musical term, the *motif* is now completed. The argument is that it is wrong to claim a monopoly for God's Message: it is the same for all peoples and in all ages: if it undergoes local variations or variations according to times and seasons those variations pass away. This leads to the argument in the remainder of the Sūra that with the renewal of the Message and the birth of a new People, a new symbolism and new ordinances become appropriate, and they are now expounded.

C. 49.—But those people have passed away,
(ii. 142-167.) Who promised to uphold the Law of God.
Their progeny having been found
Unworthy, their place was taken
By a new people looking towards Mecca,—
A new people, with a new Messenger,
To bear witness to God's Law,
To proclaim the truth, maintain
His Symbols, and strive and fight
For Unity in God's Way.

SECTION 17.

142. The Fools among the people[140]
Will say: "What hath turned
Them from the Qibla[141] to which
They were used?" Say:
To God belong both East and West:
He guideth whom He will
To a Way that is straight.

١٤٢- سَيَقُولُ السُّفَهَآءُ مِنَ النَّاسِ
مَا وَلّٰىهُمْ عَنْ قِبْلَتِهِمُ الَّتِىْ كَانُوْا عَلَيْهَا ؕ
قُلْ لِّلّٰهِ الْمَشْرِقُ وَالْمَغْرِبُ ؕ
يَهْدِىْ مَنْ يَّشَآءُ اِلٰى صِرَاطٍ مُّسْتَقِيْمٍ ۝

143. Thus[142] have We made of you
An *Ummat* justly balanced,[143]
That ye might be witnesses[144]
Over the nations,

١٤٣- وَكَذٰلِكَ جَعَلْنٰكُمْ اُمَّةً وَّسَطًا
لِّتَكُوْنُوْا شُهَدَآءَ عَلَى النَّاسِ

---

140. *Nās*=People, the unthinking multitude that sway to and fro, instead of being firm in God's Way. The reference here is to the idolaters, the Hypocrites, and the party of Jews who were constantly seeking to "entangle in their talk" Muṣṭafā and his disciples in Medina even as the Pharisees and the Sadducees of Jesus's day tried to entangle Jesus (Matt. xxii, 15, 23).

141. *Qibla*=the direction to which Muslims turn in prayer. Islam lays great stress on social prayer in order to emphasise our universal Brotherhood and mutual co-operation. For such prayer, order, punctuality, precision, symbolical postures, and a common direction are essential, so that the Imām (leader) and all his congregation may face one way and offer their supplications to God. In the early days, before they were organised as a people, they followed as a symbol for their Qibla the sacred city of Jerusalem, sacred both to the Jews and the Christians, the people of the Book. This symbolised their allegiance to the continuity of God's revelation. When, despised and persecuted, they were turned out of Mecca and arrived in Medina, Muṣṭafā under divine direction began to organise his people as an *Ummat*, an independent people, with laws and rituals of their own. At that stage the Ka'ba was established as a Qibla, thus going back to the earliest centre, with which the name of Abraham was connected, and traditionally also the name of Adam. Jerusalem still remained (and remains) sacred in the eyes of Islam on account of its past, but Islam is a progressive religion, and its new symbolism enabled it to shake off the tradition of a dead past and usher in the era of untrammelled freedom dear to the spirit of Arabia. The change took place about 16½ months after Hijrat.

142. *Thus*: By giving you a Qibla of your own, most ancient in history, and most modern as a symbol of your organisation as a new nation (*Ummat*).

143. *Justly balanced*: The essence of Islam is to avoid all extravagances on either side. It is a sober, practical religion. But the Arabic word (*wasat*) also implies a touch of the literal meaning of Intermediacy. Geographically Arabia is in an intermediate position in the Old World, as was proved in history by the rapid expansion of Islam, north, south, west and east.

144. *Witnesses*: When two persons dispute, they advance extravagant claims. A just witness comes between them, and brings the light of reason to bear on them, pruning all their selfish extravagances. So the mission of Islam is to curb, for instance, the extreme formalism of the Mosaic law and the extreme "other-worldliness" professed by Christianity. The witness must be unselfish, equipped with first-hand knowledge, and ready to intervene in the cause of justice. Such is the position claimed by Islam among rival systems. Similarly, within Islam itself, the position of witness to whom disputants can appeal is held by Muḥammad Muṣṭafā.

And the Apostle a witness
Over yourselves;
And We appointed the Qibla
To which thou wast used,
Only to test those who followed
The Apostle from those
Who would turn on their heels[145]
(From the Faith). Indeed it was
(A change) momentous, except
To those guided by God.
And never would God
Make your faith of no effect.[146]
For God is to all people
Most surely full of kindness,
Most Merciful.

وَيَكُوْنَ الرَّسُوْلُ عَلَيْكُمْ شَهِيْدًا ؕ
وَمَا جَعَلْنَا الْقِبْلَةَ الَّتِىْ كُنْتَ عَلَيْهَآ
اِلَّا لِنَعْلَمَ مَنْ يَّتَّبِعُ الرَّسُوْلَ
مِمَّنْ يَّنْقَلِبُ عَلٰى عَقِبَيْهِ ؕ
وَاِنْ كَانَتْ لَكَبِيْرَةً اِلَّا عَلَى الَّذِيْنَ هَدَى
اللّٰهُ ؕ
وَمَا كَانَ اللّٰهُ لِيُضِيْعَ اِيْمَانَكُمْ ؕ
اِنَّ اللّٰهَ بِالنَّاسِ لَرَءُوْفٌ رَّحِيْمٌ ○

144. We see the turning
Of thy face (for guidance)
To the heavens:[147] now
Shall We turn thee
To a Qibla that shall
Please thee. Turn then
Thy face in the direction
Of the sacred Mosque:[148]
Wherever ye are, turn
Your faces in that direction.

١٤٤- قَدْ نَرٰى تَقَلُّبَ وَجْهِكَ فِى السَّمَآءِ ۚ
فَلَنُوَلِّيَنَّكَ قِبْلَةً تَرْضٰىهَا ص
فَوَلِّ وَجْهَكَ شَطْرَ الْمَسْجِدِ الْحَرَامِ ؕ
وَحَيْثُ مَا كُنْتُمْ فَوَلُّوْا وُجُوْهَكُمْ شَطْرَهٗ ؕ
وَاِنَّ الَّذِيْنَ اُوْتُوا الْكِتٰبَ لَيَعْلَمُوْنَ اَنَّهُ

---

145. The Qibla of Jerusalem might itself have seemed strange to the Arabs, and the change from it to the Ka'ba might have seemed strange after they had become used to the other. In reality one direction or another, or east or west, in itself did not matter, as God is in all places, and is independent of Time and Place. What mattered was the sense of discipline, on which Islam lays so much stress: which of us is willing to follow the directions of the chosen Apostle of God? Mere quibblers about non-essential matters are tested by this.

146. What became of prayer with the Jerusalem Qibla? It was equally efficacious before the new Qibla was ordained. God regards our faith: every act of true and genuine faith is efficacious with Him, even if formalists pick holes in such acts.

147. This shows the sincere desire of Muṣṭafā to seek light from above in the matter of the Qibla. Until the organisation of his own People into a well-knit community, with its distinctive laws and ordinances, he followed a practice based on the fact that the Jews and Christians looked upon Jerusalem as a sacred city. But there was no universal Qibla among them. Some Jews turned towards Jerusalem, especially during the Captivity, as we shall see later. At the time of our Prophet, Jerusalem was in the hands of the Byzantine Empire, which was Christian. But the Christians oriented their churches to the East (hence the word "orientation"), which is a point of the compass, and not the direction of any sacred place. The fact of the altar being in the East does not mean that every worshipper has his face to the east; for, according at least to modern practice, the seats in a church are so placed that different worshippers may face in different directions. The Preacher of Unity naturally wanted, in this as in other matters, a symbol of complete unity, and his heart was naturally delighted when the Qibla towards the Ka'ba was settled. Its connection with Abraham gave it great antiquity: its character of being an Arab centre made it appropriate when the Message came in Arabic, and was preached through the union of the Arabs; at the time it was adopted, the little Muslim community was shut out of it, being exiles in Medina, but it became a symbol of hope and eventual triumph, of which Muḥammad lived to see the fulfilment; and it also became the centre and gathering ground of all peoples in the universal pilgrimage, which was instituted with it.

148. *The Sacred Mosque*: The Ka'ba in the sacred city of Mecca. It is not correct to suggest that the command making the Ka'ba the Qibla abrogates ii. 115, where it is stated that East and West belong to God, and He is everywhere. This is perfectly true at all times, before and after the institution of the Qibla. As if to emphasise this, the same words about East and West are repeated in this very passage; see ii. 142 above. Where the *Itqān* mentions *mansūkh* in this connection, I am sorry I cannot follow that opinion, unless *mansukh* is defined in a special way, as some of the commentators do.

The people of the Book [149]
Know well that that is
The truth from their Lord.
Nor is God unmindful
Of what they do.

الْحَقُّ مِنْ رَّبِّهِمْ ۗ
وَمَا اللّٰهُ بِغَافِلٍ عَمَّا يَعْمَلُوْنَ ○

145. Even if thou wert to bring
To the people of the Book
All the Signs (together),
They would not follow
Thy Qibla ; nor art thou
Going to follow their Qibla ;
Nor indeed will they follow [150]
Each other's Qibla. If thou
After the knowledge hath reached thee,
Wert to follow their (vain)
Desires,—then wert thou
Indeed (clearly) in the wrong.

١٤٥- وَلَئِنْ اَتَيْتَ الَّذِيْنَ اُوْتُوا الْكِتٰبَ
بِكُلِّ اٰيَةٍ مَّا تَبِعُوْا قِبْلَتَكَ ۚ
وَمَآ اَنْتَ بِتَابِعٍ قِبْلَتَهُمْ ۚ
وَمَا بَعْضُهُمْ بِتَابِعٍ قِبْلَةَ بَعْضٍ ۗ
وَلَئِنِ اتَّبَعْتَ اَهْوَآءَهُمْ
مِّنْ بَعْدِ مَا جَآءَكَ مِنَ الْعِلْمِ ۙ
اِنَّكَ اِذًا لَّمِنَ الظّٰلِمِيْنَ ○

146. The people of the Book
Know this as they know
Their own sons ; [151] but some
Of them conceal the truth
Which they themselves know.

١٤٦- اَلَّذِيْنَ اٰتَيْنٰهُمُ الْكِتٰبَ يَعْرِفُوْنَهٗ كَمَا
يَعْرِفُوْنَ اَبْنَآءَهُمْ ۗ وَاِنَّ فَرِيْقًا مِّنْهُمْ
لَيَكْتُمُوْنَ الْحَقَّ وَهُمْ يَعْلَمُوْنَ ○

147. The Truth is from thy Lord ; [152]
So be not at all in doubt.

١٤٧- اَلْحَقُّ مِنْ رَّبِّكَ فَلَا تَكُوْنَنَّ مِنَ الْمُمْتَرِيْنَ ○

---

149. Glimmerings of such a Qibla were already foreshadowed in Jewish and Christian practice but its universality was only perfected in Islam.

150. See n. 147 to ii. 144 above.

The Jews and Christians had a glimmering of the Qibla idea, but in their attitude of self-sufficiency they were not likely to welcome the Qibla idea as perfected in Islam. Nor is Islam, after the fuller knowledge which it has received, likely to revert to the uncertain, imperfect, and varying ideas of orientation held previously.

A very clear glimpse of the old Jewish practice in the matter of the Qibla and the importance attached to it is found in the book of Daniel, vi. 10. Daniel was a righteous man of princely lineage and lived about 606-538 B.C. He was carried off to Babylon by Nebuchadnezzar, the Assyrian, but was still living when Assyria was overthrown by the Medes and Persians. In spite of the "captivity" of the Jews, Daniel enjoyed the highest offices of state at Babylon, but he was ever true to Jerusalem. His enemies (under the Persian monarch) got a penal law passed against any one who "asked a petition of any god or man for 30 days" except the Persian King. But Daniel continued true to Jerusalem. "His windows being open in his chamber towards Jerusalem, he kneeled upon his knees three times a day, and prayed, and gave thanks before his God, as he did aforetime."

151. The People of the Book should have known all this as well as "they knew their own sons", as their past traditions and teaching should have made them receptive of the new Message. Some commentators construe the demonstrative pronoun "this" to refer to the Apostle. In that case the interpretation would be: The People of the Book know Muhammad as well as they know their own sons; they know him to be true and upright; they know him to be in the line of Abraham; they know him to correspond to the description of the prophet foretold among themselves; but selfishness induces some of them to act against their own knowledge and conceal the truth.

152. Truth only comes from God, and it remains truth, however men might try to conceal it or throw doubts on it.

SECTION 18.

148. To each is a goal
To which God[153] turns him;
Then strive together (as in a race)
Towards all that is good.
Wheresoever ye are,
God will bring you
Together. For God
Hath power over all things.

١٤٨- وَلِكُلٍّ وِّجْهَةٌ هُوَ مُوَلِّيهَا فَاسْتَبِقُوا
الْخَيْرٰتِ
اَيْنَ مَا تَكُوْنُوْا يَاْتِ بِكُمُ اللّٰهُ جَمِيْعًا
اِنَّ اللّٰهَ عَلٰى كُلِّ شَيْءٍ قَدِيْرٌ ○

149. From whencesoever
Thou startest forth,[154] turn
Thy face in the direction
Of the Sacred Mosque;
That is indeed the truth
From thy Lord. And God
Is not unmindful
Of what ye do.

١٤٩- وَمِنْ حَيْثُ خَرَجْتَ فَوَلِّ
وَجْهَكَ شَطْرَ الْمَسْجِدِ الْحَرَامِ
وَاِنَّهٗ لَلْحَقُّ مِنْ رَّبِّكَ
وَمَا اللّٰهُ بِغَافِلٍ عَمَّا تَعْمَلُوْنَ ○

150. So from whencesoever
Thou startest forth, turn
Thy face in the direction
Of the Sacred Mosque;
And wheresoever ye are,
Turn your face thither:
That there be no ground
Of dispute against you
Among the people,
Except those of them that are
Bent on wickedness; so fear
Them not, but fear Me;
And that I may complete
My favours on you, and ye
May (consent to) be guided;

١٥٠- وَمِنْ حَيْثُ خَرَجْتَ فَوَلِّ
وَجْهَكَ شَطْرَ الْمَسْجِدِ الْحَرَامِ
وَحَيْثُ مَا كُنْتُمْ
فَوَلُّوْا وُجُوْهَكُمْ شَطْرَهٗ
لِئَلَّا يَكُوْنَ لِلنَّاسِ عَلَيْكُمْ حُجَّةٌ
اِلَّا الَّذِيْنَ ظَلَمُوْا مِنْهُمْ
فَلَا تَخْشَوْهُمْ وَاخْشَوْنِيْ
وَلِاُتِمَّ نِعْمَتِيْ عَلَيْكُمْ وَلَعَلَّكُمْ تَهْتَدُوْنَ ○

---

153. The question is how we are to construe the pronoun *huwa* in the original. The alternative translation would be: "To each is a goal to which he turns."

The simile of life being a race in which we all zealously run forward to the one goal, *viz.*, the goal of good, may be applied individually and nationally. This supplies another argument of the Ka'ba Qibla, *viz.*, the unity of goal, with diversity of races, traditions and temperaments.

154. The simile of a race is continued, and so the Qibla command is repeated from that point of view. In ii. 144 it was mentioned as the new symbol of the new nation (Muslim): now it is shown as the symbol of Good, at which we should all aim, from whichever point we started, *e.g.*, as Jews or Christians, or our individual point of view; the Qibla will unite us as a symbol of the Goal of the Future. In ii. 150 below, it is repeated: first for the individual, on the ground of uniformity and the removal of all occasions of dispute and argument; and secondly for the Muslim people, on the same ground, as a matter of discipline. There is another little harmony in the matter of the repetitions. Note that the race and starting point argument begins at ii. 149 and is rounded off in the first part of ii. 150; while the national and general argument beginning at ii. 144 is rounded off in the latter part of ii. 150. The latter argument includes the former, and is more widely worded: "wheresoever ye are": which in the Arabic expression would imply three things; in whatever circumstances ye are, or at whatever time ye are, or in whatever place ye are. I have spoken before of a sort of musical harmony in verbal repetitions: here there is a sort of pictorial harmony, as of a larger circle symmetrically including a smaller concentric circle.

151. A similar (favour
Have ye already received)[155]
In that We have sent
Among you an Apostle
Of your own, rehearsing to you
Our Signs, and sanctifying
You, and instructing you
In Scripture and Wisdom,
And in new Knowledge.

١٥١- كَمَآ أَرْسَلْنَا فِيكُمْ رَسُولًا مِّنكُمْ
يَتْلُوا عَلَيْكُمْ ءَايَٰتِنَا
وَيُزَكِّيكُمْ وَيُعَلِّمُكُمُ الْكِتَٰبَ وَالْحِكْمَةَ
وَيُعَلِّمُكُم مَّا لَمْ تَكُونُوا تَعْلَمُونَ ۝

152. Then do ye remember[156]
Me; I will remember
You. Be grateful to Me,
And reject not Faith.

١٥٢- فَاذْكُرُونِىٓ أَذْكُرْكُمْ
وَاشْكُرُوا لِى وَلَا تَكْفُرُونِ ۝

SECTION 19.

153. O ye who believe! seek help
With patient Perseverance[157]
And Prayer: for God is with those
Who patiently persevere.

١٥٣- يَٰٓأَيُّهَا الَّذِينَ ءَامَنُوا اسْتَعِينُوا
بِالصَّبْرِ وَالصَّلَوٰةِ ۚ
إِنَّ اللَّهَ مَعَ الصَّٰبِرِينَ ۝

154. And say not of those
Who are slain in the way[158]

١٥٤- وَلَا تَقُولُوا لِمَن يُقْتَلُ فِى سَبِيلِ اللَّهِ

---

155. This verse should be read with ii. 150, of which the sentence is here completed. The argument is that in the grant of the Ka'ba Qibla, God was perfecting religion and fulfilling the prayer for the future made by Abraham. That prayer was threefold: (1) That Mecca should be made a sacred Sanctuary (ii. 126); (2) that a truly believing (Muslim) nation should be raised, with places of devotion there (ii. 128); and (3) that an Apostle should be sent among the Arabs with certain qualities (ii. 129), which are set out there and again repeated here to complete the argument.

156. The word "remember" is too pale a word for *ẓikr*, which has now acquired a large number of associations in our religious literature, especially Ṣūfī literature. In its verbal signification it implies: to remember; to praise by frequently mentioning; to rehearse; to celebrate or commemorate; to make much of; to cherish the memory of as a precious possession. In Ṣūfī devotions ẓikr represents both a solemn ritual and a spiritual state of mind or heart, in which the devotee seeks to realise the presence of God. Thus there is ẓikr of the mind and ẓikr of the heart. For beginners the one may lead to the other, but in many cases the two may be simultaneous. There is a subtler distinction, between the ẓikr that is open, and the ẓikr that is secret, corresponding to the two doors of the heart, the fleshly and the spiritual. In English some account (very imperfect) of ẓikr will be found in Hughes's Dictionary of Islam, covering over 14 columns.

From here on to ii. 167 there is a great deal of mystic doctrine. That it is linked with the institution of the Qibla shows that the Qibla is itself connected with a great many root-ideas of the mystical interpretation of Unity.

157 See ii. 45 and n. An additional meaning implied in *ṣabr* is self-restraint. Ḥaqqāni defines it in his *Tafsīr* as following Reason and restraining Fear, Anger, and Desire. What can be a higher reward for patience, perseverance, self-restraint and constancy than that God should be with us? For this promise opens the door to every kind of spiritual well-being.

158. The "patient perseverance and prayer" mentioned in the last verse is not mere passivity. It is active striving in the way of Truth, which is the way of God. Such striving is the spending of one's self in God's way, either through our property or through our own lives, or the lives of those nearest and dearest to us, or it may be the loss of all the fruits of a lifetime's labour not only in material goods but in some intellectual or moral gain, some position which seemed in our eyes to be eminently desirable in itself, but which we must cheerfully sacrifice if necessary for the Cause. With such sacrifice, our apparent loss may be our real gain: he that loses his life may really gain it; and the rewards or "fruits" that seem lost were mere impediments on our path to real inward progress.

These extreme sacrifices must be made under the orders and instructions of a righteous Imām, who can see the whole field of spiritual and physical warfare and judge justly of their necessity. Otherwise there is no inherent virtue in mere sacrifice as such or when exercised at the whim of an individual. Courage (the resistance to the test of Fear) and Self-denial (the resistance to the test of Hunger or Desire), are also, if they are to be virtues, subject to similar conditions.

Of God: "They are dead."
Nay, they are living,
Though ye perceive (it) not.

أَمْوَاتٌ ؕ
بَلْ أَحْيَاءٌ وَّلٰكِنْ لَّا تَشْعُرُوْنَ ۝

155. Be sure we shall test you
With something of fear
And hunger, some loss
In goods or lives or the fruits
(Of your toil), but give
Glad tidings[159] to those
Who patiently persevere,—

١٥٥- وَلَنَبْلُوَنَّكُمْ بِشَيْءٍ
مِّنَ الْخَوْفِ وَالْجُوْعِ وَنَقْصٍ مِّنَ الْاَمْوَالِ
وَالْاَنْفُسِ وَالثَّمَرٰتِ ؕ
وَبَشِّرِ الصّٰبِرِيْنَ ۝ ۙ

156. Who say, when afflicted
With calamity: "To God
We belong, and to Him
Is our return":—

١٥٦- الَّذِيْنَ اِذَآ اَصَابَتْهُمْ مُّصِيْبَةٌ ۙ
قَالُوْٓا اِنَّا لِلّٰهِ وَاِنَّآ اِلَيْهِ رٰجِعُوْنَ ۝ ؕ

157. They are those on whom
(Descend) blessings from God,
And Mercy,
And they are the ones
That receive guidance.

١٥٧- اُولٰٓئِكَ عَلَيْهِمْ صَلَوٰتٌ مِّنْ رَّبِّهِمْ
وَرَحْمَةٌ قف
وَاُولٰٓئِكَ هُمُ الْمُهْتَدُوْنَ ۝

158. Behold! Ṣafā and Marwa
Are among the Symbols[160]
Of God. So if those who visit
The House[161] in the Season
Or at other times,
Should compass them round,
It is no sin in them.
And if any one obeyeth his own

١٥٨- اِنَّ الصَّفَا وَالْمَرْوَةَ مِنْ شَعَآئِرِ اللّٰهِ ۚ
فَمَنْ حَجَّ الْبَيْتَ اَوِ اعْتَمَرَ
فَلَا جُنَاحَ عَلَيْهِ اَنْ يَّطَّوَّفَ بِهِمَا ؕ
وَمَنْ تَطَوَّعَ خَيْرًا ۙ

159. The glad tidings are the blessings of God in ii. 157 or (which is the same thing) the promise in ii. 153 that God will be with them.

160. The virtue of patient perseverance in faith leads to the mention of two symbolic monuments of that virtue. These are the two little hills of Ṣafā and Marwa now absorbed in the city of Mecca, and close to the well of Zam-zam. Here, according to tradition, the lady Hājar, mother of the infant Ismā'īl, prayed for water in the parched desert, and in her eager quest round these hills, she found her prayer answered and saw the Zam-zam spring. Unfortunately the Pagan Arabs had placed a male and a female idol here, and their gross and superstitious rites caused offence to the early Muslims. They felt some hesitation in going round these places during the Pilgrimage. As a matter of fact they should have known that the Ka'ba (the House of God) had been itself defiled with idols, and was sanctified again by the purity of Muḥammad's life and teaching. The lesson is that the most sacred things may be turned to the basest uses; that we are not therefore necessarily to ban a thing misused; that if our intentions and life are pure, God will recognise them even if the world cast stones at us because of some evil associations which they join with what we do, or with the people we associate with, or with the places which claim our reverence.

161. *The House*=the Sacred Mosque, the Ka'ba. *The Season* of regular Hajj culminates in the visit to 'Arafāt on the ninth day of the month of Zul-ḥajj, followed by the circumambulation of the Ka'ba. A visit to the Sacred Mosque and the performance of the rites of pilgrimage at any other time is called an *'Umra*. The symbolic rites are the same in either case, except that the 'Arafāt rites are omitted in the *'Umra*. The Ṣafā and Marwa are included among the Monuments, as pointing to one of the highest of Muslim virtues.

Impulse to Good,—[162]
Be sure that God
Is He Who recogniseth
And knoweth.

فَإِنَّ اللَّهَ شَاكِرٌ عَلِيمٌ ○

159. Those who conceal
The clear (Signs) We have
Sent down, and the Guidance,
After We have made it
Clear for the People
In the Book,—on them
Shall be God's curse,
And the curse of those
Entitled to curse,—[163]

١٥٩- إِنَّ الَّذِينَ يَكْتُمُونَ
مَا أَنزَلْنَا مِنَ الْبَيِّنَٰتِ وَالْهُدَىٰ
مِنۢ بَعْدِ مَا بَيَّنَّٰهُ لِلنَّاسِ فِي الْكِتَٰبِ ۙ
أُولَٰٓئِكَ يَلْعَنُهُمُ اللَّهُ
وَيَلْعَنُهُمُ اللَّٰعِنُونَ ○

160. Except those who repent
And make amends
And openly declare (the Truth):
To them I turn;
For I am Oft-returning,
Most Merciful.

١٦٠- إِلَّا الَّذِينَ تَابُوا وَأَصْلَحُوا وَبَيَّنُوا
فَأُولَٰٓئِكَ أَتُوبُ عَلَيْهِمْ ۚ
وَأَنَا التَّوَّابُ الرَّحِيمُ ○

161. Those who reject Faith,
And die rejecting,—
On them is God's curse,
And the curse of angels,
And of all mankind;

١٦١- إِنَّ الَّذِينَ كَفَرُوا وَمَاتُوا وَهُمْ كُفَّارٌ
أُولَٰٓئِكَ عَلَيْهِمْ لَعْنَةُ اللَّهِ
وَالْمَلَٰٓئِكَةِ وَالنَّاسِ أَجْمَعِينَ ○

162. They will abide therein:[164]
Their penalty will not
Be lightened, nor will
Respite be their (lot).

١٦٢- خَٰلِدِينَ فِيهَا ۖ لَا يُخَفَّفُ عَنْهُمُ الْعَذَابُ
وَلَا هُمْ يُنظَرُونَ ○

163. And your God
Is One God:
There is no god
But He,

١٦٣- وَإِلَٰهُكُمْ إِلَٰهٌ وَٰحِدٌ ۖ
لَّا إِلَٰهَ إِلَّا هُوَ

---

162. The impulse should be to Good; if once we are sure of this, we must obey it without hesitation, whatever people may say.

163. *Those entitled to curse*: *i.e.*, angels and mankind (see ii. 161 below): the cursed ones will deprive themselves of the protection of God and of the angels, who are the Powers of God, and of the good wishes of mankind, because by contumaciously rejecting Faith, they not only sin against God but are false to their own manhood, which God created in the "best of moulds" (Q. xcv. 4). The terrible curses denounced in the Old Testament are set out in Deut. xxviii. 15-68. There is one difference. Here it is for the deliberate rejection of Faith, a theological term for the denying of our higher nature. There it is for a breach of the least part of the ceremonial Law.

164. *Therein*=in the curse. A curse is not a matter of words: it is a terrible spiritual state, opposite to the state of Grace. Can man curse? Not of course in the same sense in which we speak of the curse of God. A mere verbal curse is of no effect. Hence the English saying: "A causeless curse will not come." But if men are oppressed or unjustly treated, their cries can ascend to God in prayer, and then it becomes God's "wrath" or curse, the deprivation of God's Grace as regards the wrong-doer.

Most Gracious,
Most Merciful.[165]

الرَّحْمٰنُ الرَّحِيْمُ ۝ ع

SECTION 20.

164. Behold! In the creation
Of the heavens and the earth;
In the alternation
Of the Night and the Day;
In the sailing of the ships
Through the Ocean
For the profit of mankind;
In the rain which God
Sends down from the skies,
And the life which He gives
therewith
To an earth that is dead;
In the beasts of all kinds
That He scatters
Through the earth;
In the change of the winds,
And the clouds which they
Trail like their slaves
Between the sky and the earth;—
(Here) indeed are Signs
For a people that are wise.[166]

١٦٤- اِنَّ فِیْ خَلْقِ السَّمٰوٰتِ وَ الْاَرْضِ
وَ اخْتِلَافِ الَّیْلِ وَ النَّهَارِ
وَ الْفُلْكِ الَّتِیْ تَجْرِیْ فِی الْبَحْرِ
بِمَا یَنْفَعُ النَّاسَ وَ مَاۤ اَنْزَلَ اللّٰهُ مِنَ السَّمَآءِ
مِنْ مَّآءٍ
فَاَحْیَا بِهِ الْاَرْضَ بَعْدَ مَوْتِهَا
وَ بَثَّ فِیْهَا مِنْ كُلِّ دَآبَّةٍ
وَّ تَصْرِیْفِ الرِّیٰحِ وَ السَّحَابِ
الْمُسَخَّرِ بَیْنَ السَّمَآءِ وَ الْاَرْضِ
لَاٰیٰتٍ لِّقَوْمٍ یَّعْقِلُوْنَ ۝

165. Yet there are men
Who take (for worship)
Others besides God,
As equal (with God):

١٦٥- وَ مِنَ النَّاسِ مَنْ یَّتَّخِذُ مِنْ دُوْنِ
اللّٰهِ اَنْدَادًا

165. Where the terrible consequences of Evil, *i.e.*, the rejection of God, are mentioned, there is always stress laid on God's attributes of Grace and Mercy. In this case Unity is also stressed, because we have just been told about the Qibla symbol of unity and are about to pass the theme of unity in diversity, in Nature and in the social laws of human society.

166. This magnificent Nature passage stands out like a hill in a landscape, enhancing the beauty of our view, and preparing us for the every-day laws and ordinances which follow.

Note its literary architecture. God is one: and among His wondrous Signs is the unity of design in the widest diversity of Nature. The Signs are taken from the features of beauty, power, and utility to man himself, and lead up to an appeal to Man's own intelligence and wisdom. We begin with the glory of the heavens and the earth, the wide spaces covered by man's imagination, remote and yet so near to his own life. The most striking every-day phenomenon resulting from the interrelations of the heavens and the earth is the alternation of day and night, regular and yet changing in duration with the Seasons and the latitudes of our globe. The night for rest, and the day for work; and we can think of the work in terms of nature's beauty; the stately ships "flowing" (as the original text has it) across the seas, for communications and merchandise as between men and men. The seas thus serve us no less than land, and the give-and-take as between sea, sky, and land, is further exemplified by the rain. The rain leads to the fertility of land, and here we are reminded of the contrast between the Winter's death of Nature and her revivification in the Spring. Here we are reminded of agriculture and the use we make of cattle and all kinds of living creatures. The word translated "beasts" has a wide meaning, including crawling creatures, insects, etc.—all contributing to the round of Nature's operations. This leads us on to the wonderful winds, the region of the air, which man is just beginning to explore and navigate. The personified winds drive the clouds in the sky like "slaves". Here is another aspect of clouds besides that of giving rain. The fleecy clouds are things of sunset beauty; at mid-day they temper the glare of the sun; at all times they affect radiation and other processes going on in the sky. So we come back to the sky, rounding off the argument, and correlating our human life with the Will and Power of God, if we had the wisdom to see!

They love them
As they should love God.
But those of Faith are
Overflowing in their love
For God. If only
The unrighteous could see,
Behold, they would see
The Penalty: that to God
Belongs all power, and God
Will strongly enforce
The Penalty.[167]

يُحِبُّوْنَهُمْ كَحُبِّ اللّٰهِ ۭ
وَالَّذِيْنَ اٰمَنُوْٓا اَشَدُّ حُبًّا لِّلّٰهِ ۭ
وَلَوْ يَرَى الَّذِيْنَ ظَلَمُوْٓا اِذْ يَرَوْنَ الْعَذَابَ ۙ
اَنَّ الْقُوَّةَ لِلّٰهِ جَمِيْعًا ۙ
وَّاَنَّ اللّٰهَ شَدِيْدُ الْعَذَابِ ○

166 Then would those
Who are followed
Clear themselves of those
Who follow (them):
They would see the Penalty,
And all relations
Between them would be cut off.

١٦٦- اِذْ تَبَرَّاَ الَّذِيْنَ اتُّبِعُوْا مِنَ الَّذِيْنَ
اتَّبَعُوْا وَرَاَوُا الْعَذَابَ
وَتَقَطَّعَتْ بِهِمُ الْاَسْبَابُ ○

167. And those who followed
Would say: "If only
We had one more chance,
We would clear ourselves
Of them, as they have
Cleared themselves of us."
Thus will God show them
(The fruits of) their deeds
As (nothing but) regrets.
Nor will there be a way
For them out of the Fire.[168]

١٦٧- وَقَالَ الَّذِيْنَ اتَّبَعُوْا
لَوْ اَنَّ لَنَا كَرَّةً فَنَتَبَرَّاَ مِنْهُمْ كَمَا تَبَرَّءُوْا
مِنَّا ۭ
كَذٰلِكَ يُرِيْهِمُ اللّٰهُ اَعْمَالَهُمْ حَسَرٰتٍ
عَلَيْهِمْ ۭ
وَمَا هُمْ بِخٰرِجِيْنَ مِنَ النَّارِ ○

C. 50.—The Society thus organised
(ii. 168-242.) Must live under laws
That would guide their every-day life,—
Based on eternal principles
Of righteousness and fair dealing.

---

167. Everything around and within us points to unity of purpose and design,—points to God. Yet there are foolish persons (unrighteous=those who deliberately use the choice given them to go wrong). They think something else is equal to God. Perhaps they even do lip service to God, but their heart is in their fetish,—unlike the heart of the righteous, who are wholly devoted and absorbed in the love of God. If only the unrighteous could see the consequences, they would see the terrible Penalty, and that all Power is in God's hands, not in that of any one else. Who are these others who are used as fetishes by the misguided? It may be: (1) creatures of their own imagination, or of their faculties misused; the idea lying behind Idols is akin to this, for no intelligent idol-worshipper owns to worshipping stocks and stones; or (2) good leaders whose names have been misused out of perversity to erect them to a position of equality with God; or (3) Powers of evil that deliberately mislead. When it comes to the inevitable consequences of blasphemy and the rejection of God, the eyes of all are opened and these false and artificial relations dissolve. The idea which was created into a fetish disowns its follower, *i.e.*, is seen to have no reasonable basis in the life of the follower, and the follower is forced to renounce it as false. The good leaders whose names were misused would of course disown the misuse of their names, and he tevil ones would take an unholy delight in exposing the facts. The Reality is now irresistible, but alas! at what cost?

168. Our deeds are irrevocable and we must pass through the Fire of repentance and regrets.

Cleanliness and sobriety,
Honesty and helpfulness,
One to another,—yet shaped
Into concrete forms, to suit
Times and circumstances,
And the varying needs
Of average men and women :
The food to be clean and wholesome ;
Blood-feuds to be abolished ;
The rights and duties of heirs
To be recognised after death,
Not in a spirit of Formalism,
But to help the weak and the needy
And check all selfish wrong-doing ;
Self-denial to be learnt by fasting ;
The courage to fight in defence
Of right, to be defined ;
The Pilgrimage to be sanctified
As a symbol of unity ;
Charity and help to the poor
To be organised ; unseemly riot
And drink and gambling
To be banished ; orphans to be protected ;
Marriage, divorce, and widowhood
To be regulated ; and the rights of women,
Apt to be trampled under foot,
Now clearly affirmed.

SECTION 21.

168. O ye people !
Eat of what is on earth,
Lawful and good ; [169]
And do not follow
The footsteps of the Evil One,
For he is to you
An avowed enemy.

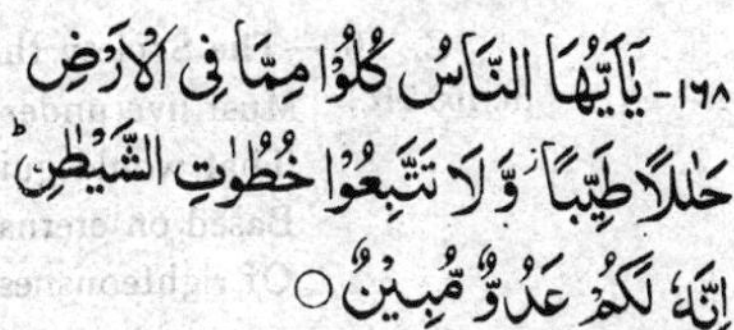

169. We now come to the regulations about food. First (ii. 168-71) we have an appeal to all people, Muslims, Pagans, as well as the People of the Book ; then (ii. 172-73) to the Muslims specially ; then (ii 174-76) to the sort of men who then (as some do now) either believe in too much formalism or believe in no restrictions at all. Islam follows the Golden Mean. All well-regulated societies lay down reasonable limitations. These become incumbent on all loyal members of any given society, and show what is "lawful" in that society. But if the limitations are reasonable, as they should be, the "lawful" will also coincide more and more with what is "good".

Good : *Ṭaiyib*=Pure, clean, wholesome, nourishing, pleasing to the taste.

The general principle then would be: what is lawful and what is good, should be followed, not what is evil, or shameful, or foisted on by false ascription to divine injunctions, or what rests merely on the usage of ancestors, even though the ancestors were ignorant or foolish. An example of a shameful custom would be that among the Pagan Arabs of taking congealed blood and eating it fried.

169. For he commands you
What is evil
And shameful,
And that ye should say
Of God that of which
Ye have no knowledge.

١٦٩- اِنَّمَا يَاْمُرُكُمْ
بِالسُّوْٓءِ وَالْفَحْشَآءِ
وَاَنْ تَقُوْلُوْا عَلَى اللّٰهِ مَا لَا تَعْلَمُوْنَ ○

170. When it is said to them:
"Follow what God hath revealed:"
They say: "Nay! we shall follow
The ways of our fathers."
What! even though their fathers
Were void of wisdom and
guidance?

١٧٠- وَاِذَا قِيْلَ لَهُمُ اتَّبِعُوْا مَآ اَنْزَلَ اللّٰهُ
قَالُوْا بَلْ نَتَّبِعُ مَآ اَلْفَيْنَا عَلَيْهِ اٰبَآءَنَا
اَوَلَوْ كَانَ اٰبَآؤُهُمْ
لَا يَعْقِلُوْنَ شَيْـًٔا وَّلَا يَهْتَدُوْنَ ○

171. The parable of those
Who reject Faith is
As if one were to shout
Like a goat-herd, to things
That listen to nothing
But calls and cries:[170]
Deaf, dumb, and blind,[171]
They are void of wisdom.

١٧١- وَمَثَلُ الَّذِيْنَ
كَفَرُوْا كَمَثَلِ الَّذِيْ
يَنْعِقُ بِمَا لَا يَسْمَعُ اِلَّا دُعَآءً وَّنِدَآءً
صُمٌّۢ بُكْمٌ عُمْيٌ فَهُمْ لَا يَعْقِلُوْنَ ○

172. O ye who believe!
Eat of the good things
That We have provided for you,
And be grateful to God,
If it is Him ye worship.[172]

١٧٢- يٰٓاَيُّهَا الَّذِيْنَ اٰمَنُوْا كُلُوْا مِنْ طَيِّبٰتِ مَا
رَزَقْنٰكُمْ وَاشْكُرُوْا لِلّٰهِ
اِنْ كُنْتُمْ اِيَّاهُ تَعْبُدُوْنَ ○

173. He hath only forbidden you
Dead meat,[173] and blood,
And the flesh of swine,
And that on which

١٧٣- اِنَّمَا حَرَّمَ عَلَيْكُمُ
الْمَيْتَةَ وَالدَّمَ وَلَحْمَ الْخِنْزِيْرِ

170. If you reject all faith, the highest wisdom and the most salutary regulations are lost on you. You are like "dumb driven cattle" who can merely hear calls, but cannot distinguish intelligently between shades of meaning or subtle differences of values.

171. *Cf.* ii. 18, where we are told that the rejectors of faith are "deaf, dumb and blind: they will not return to the path." Here the consequence of their not using their senses is that they have no wisdom. In each context there is just the appropriate deduction.

172. Gratitude for God's gifts is one form of worship.

173. Dead meat: *maitat*: carrion; animal that dies of itself: the original Arabic has a slightly wider meaning given to it in *Fiqah* (Religious Law): anything that dies of itself and is not expressly killed for food with the *Takbīr* duly pronounced on it. But there are exceptions, *e.g.*, fish and locusts are lawful, though they have not been made specially *ḥalāl* with the *Takbīr*. But even fish or locusts as carrion would be obviously ruled out.

Any other name hath been invoked
Besides that of God.[174]
But if one is forced by necessity,
Without wilful disobedience,
Nor transgressing due limits,—
Then is he guiltless.
For God is Oft-forgiving
Most Merciful.

وَمَآ اُهِلَّ بِهٖ لِغَيْرِ اللّٰهِ ۚ
فَمَنِ اضْطُرَّ غَيْرَ بَاغٍ وَّلَا عَادٍ
فَلَآ اِثْمَ عَلَيْهِ ۚ
اِنَّ اللّٰهَ غَفُوْرٌ رَّحِيْمٌ ۝

174. Those who conceal
God's revelations in the Book,
And purchase for them
A miserable profit,—
They swallow into themselves[175]
Naught but Fire;
God will not address them
On the Day of Resurrection,
Nor purify them:
Grievous will be
Their Penalty.

۱۷۴- اِنَّ الَّذِيْنَ يَكْتُمُوْنَ
مَآ اَنْزَلَ اللّٰهُ مِنَ الْكِتٰبِ
وَيَشْتَرُوْنَ بِهٖ ثَمَنًا قَلِيْلًا ۙ
اُولٰٓئِكَ مَا يَاْكُلُوْنَ فِيْ بُطُوْنِهِمْ اِلَّا النَّارَ
وَلَا يُكَلِّمُهُمُ اللّٰهُ يَوْمَ الْقِيٰمَةِ
وَلَا يُزَكِّيْهِمْ ۚ وَلَهُمْ عَذَابٌ اَلِيْمٌ ۝

175. They are the ones
Who buy Error
In place of Guidance
And Torment in place
Of Forgiveness.
Ah! what boldness
(They show) for the Fire!

۱۷۵- اُولٰٓئِكَ الَّذِيْنَ اشْتَرَوُا الضَّلٰلَةَ
بِالْهُدٰى
وَالْعَذَابَ بِالْمَغْفِرَةِ ۚ
فَمَآ اَصْبَرَهُمْ عَلَى النَّارِ ۝

176. (Their doom is) because
God sent down the Book
In truth but those who seek
Causes of dispute in the Book

۱۷۶- ذٰلِكَ بِاَنَّ اللّٰهَ نَزَّلَ الْكِتٰبَ بِالْحَقِّ ۗ
وَاِنَّ الَّذِيْنَ اخْتَلَفُوْا فِي الْكِتٰبِ

---

174. For prohibited foods, *cf.* also Q. v. 4-5; vi. 121, 138-146; etc. The teachers of *Fiqah* (Religious Law) work out the details with great elaboration. My purpose is to present general principles, not technical details. Carrion or dead meat and blood as articles of food would obviously cause disgust to any refined person. So would swine's flesh where the swine live on offal. Where swine are fed artificially on clean food, the objections remain: (1) that they are filthy animals in other respects, and the flesh of filthy animals taken as food affects the eater; (2) that swine's flesh has more fat than muscle-building material; and (3) that it is more liable to disease than other kinds of meat; *e.g.*, trichinosis, characterised by hair-like worms in the muscular tissue. As to food dedicated to idols or false gods, it is obviously unseemly for the Children of Unity to partake of it.

175. "They eat nothing but fire into their bellies" is a literal translation that produces an effect of rude inelegance which is not in the Arabic words. Even in the matter of food and drinks, the mission of Islam is to avoid the extremes of lawlessness on the one hand and extreme formalism on the other. It has laid down a few simple and very reasonable rules. Their infraction causes loss of health or physical powers in any case. But if there is further a spirit of subjective rebellion or fraud—passing off in the name of religion something which is far from the purpose,—the consequences become also moral and spiritual. Then it becomes a sin against Faith and Spirit. Continuing the physical simile, we actually swallow fire into ourselves. Imagine the torments which we should have if we swallowed fire into our physical body! They would be infinitely worse in our spiritual state, and they would go on to the Day of Resurrection, when we shall be deprived even of the words which the Judge speaks to a reasonable culprit, and we shall certainly not win His Grace and Mercy.

Are in a schism[176]
Far (from the purpose).

SECTION 22.

177. It is not righteousness
That ye turn your faces
Towards East or West;
But it is righteousness—[177]
To believe in God[178]
And the Last Day,
And the Angels,
And the Book,
And the Messengers;
To spend of your substance,[179]
Out of love for Him,
For your kin,
For orphans,
For the needy,
For the wayfarer,
For those who ask,
And for the ransom of slaves;
To be steadfast in prayer,[180]
And practice regular charity;
To fulfil the contracts
Which ye have made;

لَفِىْ شِقَاقٍۢ بَعِيْدٍ ۝

١٧٧- لَيْسَ الْبِرَّ اَنْ تُوَلُّوْا وُجُوْهَكُمْ
قِبَلَ الْمَشْرِقِ وَالْمَغْرِبِ
وَلٰكِنَّ الْبِرَّ مَنْ اٰمَنَ بِاللّٰهِ
وَالْيَوْمِ الْاٰخِرِ وَالْمَلٰٓئِكَةِ وَالْكِتٰبِ
وَالنَّبِيّٖنَ ۚ
وَاٰتَى الْمَالَ عَلٰى حُبِّهٖ ذَوِى الْقُرْبٰى
وَالْيَتٰمٰى وَالْمَسٰكِيْنَ
وَابْنَ السَّبِيْلِ ۙ وَالسَّآئِلِيْنَ وَفِى الرِّقَابِ ۚ
وَاَقَامَ الصَّلٰوةَ وَاٰتَى الزَّكٰوةَ ۚ
وَالْمُوْفُوْنَ بِعَهْدِهِمْ اِذَا عٰهَدُوْا ۚ

---

176. From the mere physical regulation we are at once lifted up into the sphere of morals and faith. For the one acts and reacts on the other. If we are constantly carping at wholesome regulations, we shall do nothing but cause division and schisms among the people, and ordered society would tend to break up.

177. As if to emphasise again a warning against deadening formalism, we are given a beautiful description of the righteous and God-fearing man. He should obey salutary regulations, but he should fix his gaze on the love of God and the love of his fellow-men. We are given four heads: (1) our faith should be true and sincere; (2) we must be prepared to show it in deeds of charity to our fellow-men; (3) we must be good citizens, supporting social organisation; and (4) our own individual soul must be firm and unshaken in all circumstances. They are interconnected, and yet can be viewed separately.

178. Faith is not merely a matter of words. We must realise the presence and goodness of God. When we do so, the scales fall from our eyes: all the falsities and fleeting nature of the Present cease to enslave us, for we see the Last Day as if it were to-day. We also see God's working in His world and in us: His Powers (angels), His Messengers and His Message are no longer remote from us, but come within our experience.

179. Practical deeds of charity are of value when they proceed from love, and from no other motive. In this respect, also, our duties take various forms, which are shown in reasonable gradation: our kith and kin; orphans (including any persons who are without support or help); people who are in real need but who never ask (it is our duty to find them out, and they come before those who ask); the stranger, who is entitled to laws of hospitality; the people who ask and are entitled to ask, *i.e.*, not merely lazy beggars, but those who seek our assistance in some form or another (it is our duty to respond to them); and the slaves (we must do all we can to give or buy their freedom). Slavery has many insidious forms, and all are included.

180. Charity and piety in individual cases do not complete our duties. In prayer and charity, we must also look to our organised efforts: where there is a Muslim State, these are made through the State, in facilities for public prayer, and public assistance, and for the maintenance of contracts and fair dealing in all matters.

And to be firm and patient,[181]
In pain (or suffering)
And adversity,
And throughout
All periods of panic.
Such are the people
Of truth, the God-fearing.

178. O ye who believe!
The law of equality[182]
Is prescribed to you
In cases of murder:[183]
The free for the free,
The slave for the slave,
The woman for the woman.
But if any remission
Is made by the brother[184]
Of the slain, then grant
Any reasonable demand,[185]
And compensate him

وَالصّٰبِرِيْنَ فِي الْبَاْسَآءِ وَالضَّرَّآءِ وَحِيْنَ
الْبَاْسِ ؕ
اُولٰٓئِكَ الَّذِيْنَ صَدَقُوْا ؕ
وَاُولٰٓئِكَ هُمُ الْمُتَّقُوْنَ ۝
١٧٨- يٰٓاَيُّهَا الَّذِيْنَ اٰمَنُوْا
كُتِبَ عَلَيْكُمُ الْقِصَاصُ فِي الْقَتْلٰى ؕ
اَلْحُرُّ بِالْحُرِّ
وَالْعَبْدُ بِالْعَبْدِ
وَالْاُنْثٰى بِالْاُنْثٰى ؕ
فَمَنْ عُفِيَ لَهٗ مِنْ اَخِيْهِ شَيْءٌ

181. Then come the Muslim virtues of firmness and patience. They are to "preserve the dignity of man, with soul erect" (Burns). Three sets of circumstances are specially mentioned for the exercise of this virtue: (1) bodily pain or suffering, (2) adversities or injuries of all kinds, deserved and underserved, and (3) periods of public panic, such as war, violence, pestilence, etc.

182. Note first that this verse and the next make it clear that Islam has much mitigated the horrors of the pre-Islamic custom of retaliation. In order to meet the strict claims of justice, equality is prescribed, with a strong recommendation for mercy and forgiveness. To translate *qiṣāṣ*, therefore, by retaliation, is I think incorrect. The Latin legal term *Lex Talionis* may come near it, but even that is modified here. In any case it is best to avoid technical terms for things that are very different. "Retaliation" in English has a wider meaning, equivalent almost to returning evil for evil, and would more fitly apply to the blood-feuds of the Days of Ignorance. Islam says: if you *must* take a life for a life, at least there should be some measure of equality in it; the killing of the slave of a tribe should not involve a blood feud where many free men would be killed; but the law of mercy, where it can be obtained by consent, with reasonable compensation, would be better.

Our law of equality only takes account of three conditions in civil society; free for free, slave for slave, woman for woman. Among free men or women, all are equal: you cannot ask that because a wealthy, or high-born, or influential man is killed, his life is equal to two or three lives among the poor or the lowly. Nor, in cases of murder, can you go into the value or abilities of a slave. A woman is mentioned separately because her position as a mother or an economic worker is different. She does not form a third class, but a division in the other two classes. One life having been lost, do not waste many lives in retaliation: at most, let the Law take one life under strictly prescribed conditions, and shut the door to private vengeance or tribal retaliation. But if the aggrieved party consents (and this condition of consent is laid down to prevent worse evils), forgiveness and brotherly love is better, and the door of Mercy is kept open. In Western law, no felony can be compounded.

183. The jurists have carefully laid down that the law of *qiṣāṣ* refers to murder only. *Qiṣāṣ* is not applicable to manslaughter, due to a mistake or an accident. There, there would be no capital punishment.

184. *The brother*: the term is perfectly general; all men are brothers in Islam. In this, and in all questions of inheritance, females have similar rights to males, and therefore the masculine gender imports both sexes. Here we are considering the rights of the heirs in the light of the larger brotherhood. In ii. 178-79 we have the rights of the heirs to life (as it were): in ii. 180-82 we proceed to the heirs to property.

185. The demand should be such as can be met by the party concerned, *i.e.*, within his means, and reasonable according to justice and good conscience. For example, a demand could not be made affecting the honour of a woman or a man. The whole penalty can be remitted if the aggrieved party agrees, out of brotherly love. In meeting that demand the culprit or his friends should equally be generous and recognise the good-will of the other side. There should be no subterfuges, no bribes, no unseemly bye-play: otherwise the whole intention of mercy and peace is lost.

With handsome gratitude.
This is a concession
And a Mercy
From your Lord.
After this whoever
Exceeds the limits
Shall be in grave penalty.

فَاتِّبَاعٌۢ بِالْمَعْرُوْفِ وَاَدَاۤءٌ اِلَيْهِ بِاِحْسَانٍ ؕ
ذٰلِكَ تَخْفِيْفٌ مِّنْ رَّبِّكُمْ وَرَحْمَةٌ ؕ
فَمَنِ اعْتَدٰى بَعْدَ ذٰلِكَ
فَلَهٗ عَذَابٌ اَلِيْمٌ ۝

179. In the Law of Equality
There is (saving of) Life
To you, O ye men of understanding;
That ye may
Restrain yourselves.

١٧٩- وَلَكُمْ فِى الْقِصَاصِ حَيٰوةٌ
يّٰۤاُولِى الْاَلْبَابِ
لَعَلَّكُمْ تَتَّقُوْنَ ۝

180. It is prescribed,
When death approaches
Any of you, if he leave
Any goods, that he make a bequest
To parents and next of kin,[186]
According to reasonable usage;
This is due
From the God-fearing.

١٨٠- كُتِبَ عَلَيْكُمْ اِذَا حَضَرَ اَحَدَكُمُ الْمَوْتُ
اِنْ تَرَكَ خَيْرًا ۖۚ الْوَصِيَّةُ لِلْوَالِدَيْنِ
وَالْاَقْرَبِيْنَ بِالْمَعْرُوْفِ ۚ
حَقًّا عَلَى الْمُتَّقِيْنَ ؕ ۝

181. If anyone changes the bequest
After hearing it,
The guilt shall be on those
Who make the change.
For God hears and knows
(All things).

١٨١- فَمَنْۢ بَدَّلَهٗ بَعْدَمَا سَمِعَهٗ
فَاِنَّمَاۤ اِثْمُهٗ عَلَى الَّذِيْنَ يُبَدِّلُوْنَهٗ ؕ
اِنَّ اللّٰهَ سَمِيْعٌ عَلِيْمٌ ۝

182. But if anyone fears
Partiality or wrong-doing[187]
On the part of the testator,
And makes peace between

١٨٢- فَمَنْ خَافَ مِنْ مُّوْصٍ جَنَفًا اَوْ اِثْمًا
فَاَصْلَحَ بَيْنَهُمْ

186. There are rules of course for the disposal of intestate property. But it is a good thing that a dying man or woman should, of his own free-will, think of his parents and his next of kin, not in a spirit of injustice to others, but in a spirit of love and reverence for those who have cherished him. He must, however, do it "according to reasonable usage": the limitations will be seen further on.

187. A verbal will is allowed, but it is expected that the testator will be just to his heirs and not depart from what is considered equitable. For this reason definite shares were laid down for heirs later (see Q. iv. 11, etc.). These define or limit the testamentary power, but do not abrogate it. For example, amongst kin there are persons (*e.g.*, an orphan grandson in the presence of surviving sons) who would not inherit under the intestate scheme, and the testator might like to provide for them. Again, there may be outsiders for whom he may wish to provide, and jurists have held that he has powers of disposition up to one-third of his property. But he must not be partial to one heir at the expense of another, or attempt to defeat lawful creditors. If he tries to do this, those who are witnesses to his oral disposition may interfere in two ways. One way would be to persuade the testator to change his bequest before he dies. The other way would be, after death, to get the interested parties together and ask them to agree to a more equitable arrangement. In such a case they are acting in good faith, and there is no fraud. They are doing nothing wrong. Islam approves of every lawful device for keeping brethren at peace, without litigation and quarrels. Except for this, the changing of the provisions of a Will is a crime, as it is under all Law.

(The parties concerned),
There is no wrong in him:
For God is Oft-forgiving,
Most Merciful.

فَلَآ إِثْمَ عَلَيْهِ ؕ
ع إِنَّ اللّٰهَ غَفُورٌ رَّحِيمٌ ۟

SECTION 23.

183. O ye who believe!
Fasting is prescribed to you
As it was prescribed[188]
To those before you,
That ye may (learn)
Self-restraint,—

١٨٣- يٰٓأَيُّهَا الَّذِينَ اٰمَنُوا كُتِبَ عَلَيْكُمُ الصِّيَامُ
كَمَا كُتِبَ عَلَى الَّذِينَ مِنْ قَبْلِكُمْ
لَعَلَّكُمْ تَتَّقُونَ ۟

184. (Fasting) for a fixed[189]
Number of days;
But if any of you is ill,
Or on a journey,[190]
The prescribed number
(Should be made up)
From days later.
For those who can do it[191]
(With hardship), is a ransom,
The feeding of one
That is indigent.
But he that will give
More, of his own free will,—
It is better for him.
And it is better for you
That ye fast,
If ye only knew.

١٨٤- أَيَّامًا مَّعْدُودٰتٍ ؕ
فَمَنْ كَانَ مِنْكُمْ مَّرِيضًا
أَوْ عَلٰى سَفَرٍ
فَعِدَّةٌ مِّنْ أَيَّامٍ أُخَرَ ؕ
وَعَلَى الَّذِينَ يُطِيقُونَهُ فِدْيَةٌ طَعَامُ
مِسْكِينٍ ؕ فَمَنْ تَطَوَّعَ خَيْرًا فَهُوَ خَيْرٌ لَّهُ ؕ
وَأَنْ تَصُومُوا خَيْرٌ لَّكُمْ
إِنْ كُنْتُمْ تَعْلَمُونَ ۟

---

188. *As it was prescribed*: this does not mean that the Muslim fast is like the other fasts previously observed, in the number of days, in the time or manner of the fast, or in other incidents; it only means that the principle of self-denial by fasting is not a new one.

189. This verse should be read with the following verses, 185-88, in order that the incidents of the physical fast may be fully understood with reference to its spiritual meaning.

The Muslim fast is not meant for self-torture. Although it is stricter than other fasts, it also provides alleviations for special circumstances. If it were merely a temporary abstention from food and drink, it would be salutary to many people, who habitually eat and drink to excess. The instincts for food, drink, and sex are strong in the animal nature, and temporary restraint from all these enables the attention to be directed to higher things. This is necessary through prayer, contemplation and acts of charity, not of the showy kind, but by seeking out those really in need. Certain standards are prescribed, but much higher standards are recommended.

190. Illness and journey must not be interpreted in an elastic sense: they must be such as to cause real pain or suffering if the fast were observed. For journeys, a minimum standard of three marches is prescribed by some Commentators; others make it more precise by naming a distance of 16 farsakhs, equivalent to 48 miles. A journey of 8 or 9 miles on foot is more tiring than a similar one by bullock cart. There are various degrees of fatigue in riding a given distance on horseback or by camel or in a comfortable train or by motor car or by steamer, aeroplane, or airship. In my opinion the standard must depend on the means of locomotion and on the relative resources of the traveller. It is better to determine it in each case according to circumstances.

191. Those who can do it with hardship: such as aged people, or persons specially circumstanced. The Shāfi'is would include a woman expecting a child, or one who is nursing a baby, but on this point opinion is not unanimous, some holding that they ought to put in the fasts later, when they can.

185. Ramadhan is the (month)
In which was sent down
The Qur-ān, as a guide
To mankind, also clear (Signs)
For guidance and judgment[192]
(Between right and wrong).
So every one of you
Who is present (at his home)
During that month
Should spend it in fasting,
But if any one is ill,
Or on a journey,
The prescribed period
(Should be made up)
By days later.
God intends every facility
For you; He does not want
To put you to difficulties.
(He wants you) to complete
The prescribed period,
And to glorify Him[193]
In that He has guided you;
And perchance ye shall be
grateful.

١٨٥- شَهْرُ رَمَضَانَ الَّذِىٓ اُنْزِلَ فِيْهِ الْقُرْاٰنُ
هُدًى لِّلنَّاسِ
وَبَيِّنٰتٍ مِّنَ الْهُدٰى وَالْفُرْقَانِ ۚ
فَمَنْ شَهِدَ مِنْكُمُ الشَّهْرَ فَلْيَصُمْهُ ۖ
وَمَنْ كَانَ مَرِيْضًا
اَوْ عَلٰى سَفَرٍ
فَعِدَّةٌ مِّنْ اَيَّامٍ اُخَرَ ۖ
يُرِيْدُ اللّٰهُ بِكُمُ الْيُسْرَ
وَلَا يُرِيْدُ بِكُمُ الْعُسْرَ
وَلِتُكْمِلُوا الْعِدَّةَ
وَلِتُكَبِّرُوا اللّٰهَ عَلٰى مَا هَدٰىكُمْ
وَلَعَلَّكُمْ تَشْكُرُوْنَ ○

186. When My servants
Ask thee concerning Me,
I am indeed
Close (to them): I listen
To the prayer of every
Suppliant when he calleth on Me:
Let them also, with a will,
Listen to My call,
And believe in Me:
That they may walk
In the right way.[194]

١٨٦- وَاِذَا سَاَلَكَ عِبَادِىْ
عَنِّىْ فَاِنِّىْ قَرِيْبٌ ۖ
اُجِيْبُ دَعْوَةَ الدَّاعِ
اِذَا دَعَانِ ۙ
فَلْيَسْتَجِيْبُوْا لِىْ
وَلْيُؤْمِنُوْا بِىْ لَعَلَّهُمْ يَرْشُدُوْنَ ○

187. Permitted to you,
On the night of the fasts,
Is the approach to your wives.
They are your garments

١٨٧- اُحِلَّ لَكُمْ لَيْلَةَ الصِّيَامِ الرَّفَثُ اِلٰى
نِسَآئِكُمْ ۚ هُنَّ لِبَاسٌ لَّكُمْ

---

192. Judgment (between right and wrong): *Furqān*=the criterion or standard by which we judge between right and wrong. See ii. 53 n.

193. The regulations are again and again coupled with an insistence on two things: (*a*) the facilities and concessions given, and (*b*) the spiritual significance of the fast, without which it is like an empty shell without a kernel. If we realise this, we shall look upon Ramadhān, not as a burden, but as a blessing, and shall be duly grateful for the lead given to us in this matter.

194. These verses 186 and 188 are not foreign to the subject of Ramadhān, but emphasise its spiritual aspect. Here we are told of Prayer and the nearness of God, and in 188 we are asked not to "eat up" other people's substance.

And ye are their garments.[195]
God knoweth what ye
Used to do secretly among
yourselves;
But He turned to you
And forgave you;
So now associate with them,
And seek what God
Hath ordained for you,[196]
And eat and drink,
Until the white thread
Of dawn appear to you
Distinct from its black thread;[197]
Then complete your fast
Till the night appears;[198]
But do not associate
With your wives
While ye are in retreat[199]
In the mosques. Those are[200]
Limits (set by) God:
Approach not nigh thereto.
Thus doth God make clear
His Signs to men: that
They may learn self-restraint.

وَأَنتُمْ لِبَاسٌ لَّهُنَّ عَلِمَ اللَّهُ أَنَّكُمْ كُنتُمْ
تَخْتَانُونَ أَنفُسَكُمْ فَتَابَ عَلَيْكُمْ
وَعَفَا عَنكُمْ
فَالْـَٔنَ بَاشِرُوهُنَّ
وَابْتَغُوا مَا كَتَبَ اللَّهُ لَكُمْ وَكُلُوا وَاشْرَبُوا
حَتَّى يَتَبَيَّنَ لَكُمُ الْخَيْطُ الْأَبْيَضُ مِنَ الْخَيْطِ
الْأَسْوَدِ مِنَ الْفَجْرِ
ثُمَّ أَتِمُّوا الصِّيَامَ إِلَى الَّيْلِ
وَلَا تُبَاشِرُوهُنَّ وَأَنتُمْ عَاكِفُونَ فِي الْمَسَاجِدِ
تِلْكَ حُدُودُ اللَّهِ فَلَا تَقْرَبُوهَا
كَذَلِكَ يُبَيِّنُ اللَّهُ آيَاتِهِ لِلنَّاسِ
لَعَلَّهُمْ يَتَّقُونَ ○

188. And do not eat up
Your property among yourselves
For vanities, nor use it
As bait for the judges,
With intent that ye may
Eat up wrongfully and knowingly

١٨٨- وَلَا تَأْكُلُوا أَمْوَالَكُمْ بَيْنَكُمْ بِالْبَاطِلِ
وَتُدْلُوا بِهَا إِلَى الْحُكَّامِ
لِتَأْكُلُوا فَرِيقًا مِّنْ أَمْوَالِ النَّاسِ بِالْإِثْمِ

---

195. Men and women are each other's garments: *i.e.*, they are for mutual support, mutual comfort, and mutual protection, fitting into each other as a garment fits the body. A garment also is both for show and concealment. The question of sex is always delicate to handle: here we are told that even in such matters a clear, open, and honest course is better than fraud or self-deception. The sex instinct is classed with eating and drinking, an animal thing to be restrained, but not to be ashamed of. The three things are prohibited during the fast by day, but permitted after the fast is broken at night till the next fast commences.

196. There is difference of opinion as to the exact meaning of this. I would connect this as a parallel clause with the clause "eat and drink", which follows, all three being governed by "until the white thread", etc. That is, all three things must stop when the fast begins again in the early morning. Or it may mean: What is permitted is well enough, but seek the higher things ordained for you.

197. Those in touch with Nature know the beautiful effects of early dawn. First appear thin white indefinable streaks of light in the east; then a dark zone supervenes; followed by a beautiful pinkish white zone clearly defined from the dark. This is the true dawn; after that the fast begins.

198. *Till the night appears*: From the actual practice of the Holy Apostle, this is rightly interpreted to mean: "Till sunset."

199. Retreat to the Mosques by night after the fast is broken is specially recommended towards the end of Ramadhân, so that all carnal temptations may be avoided.

200. I construe these limits as applying to the whole of the regulations about fasts.

A little of (other) people's
property.[201]

عٌ وَاَنۡتُمۡ تَعۡلَمُوۡنَ ۝

SECTION 24.

189. They ask thee
Concerning the New Moons.[202]
Say: They are but signs
To mark fixed periods of time
In (the affairs of) men,
And for Pilgrimage.
It is no virtue if ye enter
Your houses from the back:
It is virtue if ye fear God.
Enter houses
Through the proper doors:[203]
And fear God:
That ye may prosper.

١٨٩ - يَسۡـَٔلُوۡنَكَ عَنِ الۡاَهِلَّةِ ؕ
قُلۡ هِىَ مَوَاقِيۡتُ لِلنَّاسِ وَالۡحَجِّ ؕ
وَلَيۡسَ الۡبِرُّ بِاَنۡ تَاۡتُوا الۡبُيُوۡتَ مِنۡ
ظُهُوۡرِهَا
وَلٰكِنَّ الۡبِرَّ مَنِ اتَّقٰى ۚ
وَاۡتُوا الۡبُيُوۡتَ مِنۡ اَبۡوَابِهَا ۚ
وَاتَّقُوا اللّٰهَ لَعَلَّكُمۡ تُفۡلِحُوۡنَ ۝

190. Fight in the cause of God
Those who fight you,[204]
But do not transgress limits;
For God loveth not transgressors.

١٩٠ - وَقَاتِلُوۡا فِىۡ سَبِيۡلِ اللّٰهِ الَّذِيۡنَ يُقَاتِلُوۡنَكُمۡ
وَلَا تَعۡتَدُوۡا ؕ اِنَّ اللّٰهَ لَا يُحِبُّ الۡمُعۡتَدِيۡنَ ۝

191. And slay them
Wherever ye catch them,
And turn them out
From where they have

١٩١ - وَاقۡتُلُوۡهُمۡ حَيۡثُ ثَقِفۡتُمُوۡهُمۡ
وَاَخۡرِجُوۡهُمۡ مِّنۡ حَيۡثُ اَخۡرَجُوۡكُمۡ

---

201. Besides the three primal physical needs of man, which are apt to make him greedy, there is a fourth greed in society, the greed of wealth and property. The purpose of fasts is not completed until this fourth greed is also restrained. Ordinarily honest men are content if they refrain from robbery, theft, or embezzlement. Two more subtle forms of the greed are mentioned here. One is where one uses one's own property for corrupting others—judges or those in authority—so as to obtain some material gain even under the cover and protection of the law. The words translated "other people's property" may also mean "public property". A still more subtle form is where we use our own property or property under our own control—"among yourselves" in the Text—for vain or frivolous uses. Under the Islamic standard this is also greed. Property carries with it its own responsibilities. If we fail to understand or fulfil them, we have not learnt the full lesson of self-denial by fasts.

202. There were many superstitions connected with the New Moon, as there are to the present day. We are told to disregard such superstitions. As a measure of time, where the lunar calendar is used, the New Moon is one great sign, for which people watch with eagerness. Muslim festivals, including the Pilgrimage, are fixed by the appearance of the New Moon. The Arabs, among other superstitions, had one which made them enter their houses by the back door during or after the Pilgrimage. This is disapproved, for there is no virtue in any such artificial restrictions. All virtue proceeds from the love and fear of God.

203. This is a Muslim proverb now, and much might be written about its manifold meanings. A few may be noted here. (1) If you enter a society, respect its manners and customs. (2) If you want to achieve an object honourably, go about it openly and not "by a backdoor". (3) Do not beat about the bush. (4) If you wish success in an undertaking, provide all the necessary instruments for it.

The subject of the New Moon provides a good transition between the Ramadhān fast, which begins and ends with the New Moon, the Pilgrimage, whose ten days commence with the New Moon, and the Wars which Islam had to wage in self-defence against the Pagans, who wanted to exclude them from the Pilgrimage after they had driven them out of house and home.

204. War is only permissible in self-defence, and under well-defined limits. When undertaken, it must be pushed with vigour, but not relentlessly, but only to restore peace and freedom for the worship of God. In any case strict limits must not be transgressed: women, children, old and infirm men should not be molested, nor trees and crops cut down, nor peace withheld when the enemy comes to terms.

Turned you out;
For tumult and oppression
Are worse than slaughter;
But fight them not[205]
At the Sacred Mosque,
Unless they (first)
Fight you there;
But if they fight you,
Slay them.
Such is the reward
Of those who suppress faith.[206]

وَالْفِتْنَةُ اَشَدُّ مِنَ الْقَتْلِ ۚ
وَلَا تُقٰتِلُوْهُمْ عِنْدَ الْمَسْجِدِ الْحَرَامِ
حَتّٰى يُقٰتِلُوْكُمْ فِيْهِ ۚ
فَاِنْ قٰتَلُوْكُمْ فَاقْتُلُوْهُمْ ؕ
كَذٰلِكَ جَزَآءُ الْكٰفِرِيْنَ ○

192. But if they cease,
God is Oft-forgiving,
Most Merciful.

١٩٢- فَاِنِ انْتَهَوْا
فَاِنَّ اللّٰهَ غَفُوْرٌ رَّحِيْمٌ ○

193. And fight them on
Until there is no more
Tumult or oppression,
And there prevail
Justice and faith in God;[207]
But if they cease,[208]
Let there be no hostility
Except to those
Who practise oppression.

١٩٣- وَقٰتِلُوْهُمْ حَتّٰى لَا تَكُوْنَ فِتْنَةٌ
وَّيَكُوْنَ الدِّيْنُ لِلّٰهِ ؕ
فَاِنِ انْتَهَوْا فَلَا عُدْوَانَ اِلَّا عَلَى
الظّٰلِمِيْنَ ○

205. This passage is illustrated by the events that happened at Ḥudaibiya in the sixth year of the Hijra, though it is not clear that it was revealed on that occasion. The Muslims were by this time a strong and influential community. Many of them were exiles from Mecca, where the Pagans had established an intolerant autocracy, persecuting Muslims, preventing them from visiting their homes, and even keeping them out by force from performing the Pilgrimage during the universally recognised period of truce. This was intolerance, oppression, and autocracy to the last degree, and the mere readiness of the Muslims to enforce their rights as Arab citizens resulted without bloodshed in an agreement which the Muslims faithfully observed. The Pagans, however, had no scruples in breaking faith, and it is unnecessary here to go into subsequent events.

In general, it may be said that Islam is the religion of peace, goodwill, mutual understanding, and good faith. But it will not acquiesce in wrong-doing, and its men will hold their lives cheap in defence of honour, justice, and the religion which they hold sacred. Their ideal is that of heroic virtue combined with unselfish gentleness and tenderness, such as is exemplified in the life of the Apostle. They believe in courage, obedience, discipline, duty, and a constant striving, by all the means in their power, physical, moral, intellectual, and spiritual, for the establishment of truth and righteousness. They know that war is an evil, but they will not flinch from it if their honour demands it and (*a most important condition*) a righteous *Imām* (such as Muḥammad was *par excellence*) commands it, for then they know they are not serving carnal ends. In other cases, war has nothing to do with their faith, except that it will always be regulated by its humane precepts.

206. *Suppress faith*: in the narrower as well as the larger sense. If they want forcibly to prevent you from exercising your sacred rites, they have declared war on your religion, and it would be cowardice to ignore the challenge or to fail in rooting out the tyranny.

207. *Justice and faith.* The Arabic word is *Dīn*, which is comprehensive. It implies the ideas of indebtedness, duty, obedience, judgment, justice, faith, religion, customary rites, etc. The clause means: "until there is *Dīn* for God."

208. If the opposite party cease to persecute you, your hostility ends with them as a party, but it does not mean that you become friends to oppression. Your fight is against wrong; there should be no rancour against men.

194. The prohibited month[209]
For the prohibited month,—
And so for all things prohibited,—
There is the law of equality.
If then any one transgresses
The prohibition against you,
Transgress ye likewise
Against him.
But fear God, and know[210]
That God is with those
Who restrain themselves.

١٩٤- اَلشَّهْرُ الْحَرَامُ بِالشَّهْرِ الْحَرَامِ
وَالْحُرُمٰتُ قِصَاصٌ ؕ
فَمَنِ اعْتَدٰى عَلَيْكُمْ
فَاعْتَدُوْا عَلَيْهِ بِمِثْلِ مَا اعْتَدٰى
عَلَيْكُمْ ص
وَاتَّقُوا اللّٰهَ وَاعْلَمُوْٓا اَنَّ اللّٰهَ مَعَ الْمُتَّقِيْنَ ○

195. And spend of your substance
In the cause of God,
And make not your own hands
Contribute to (your) destruction;[211]
But do good;
For God loveth those
Who do good.

١٩٥- وَاَنْفِقُوْا فِىْ سَبِيْلِ اللّٰهِ وَلَا تُلْقُوْا
بِاَيْدِيْكُمْ اِلَى التَّهْلُكَةِ ۛ
وَاَحْسِنُوْا ۛ اِنَّ اللّٰهَ يُحِبُّ الْمُحْسِنِيْنَ ○

196. And complete
The *Hajj* or *'umra*[212]

١٩٦- وَاَتِمُّوا الْحَجَّ وَالْعُمْرَةَ لِلّٰهِ ؕ

---

209. *Ḥarām*—prohibited, sacred. The month of Pilgrimage (*Ẓul-ḥajj*) was a sacred month, in which warfare was prohibited by Arab custom. The month preceding (*Ẓul-qa'd*) and the month following (*Muḥarram*) were included in the prohibition, and *Muḥarram* was specially called *al-Ḥarām*. Possibly *Muḥarram* is meant in the first line, and the other months and other prohibited things in "all things prohibited". In Rajab, also, war was prohibited. If the pagan enemies of Islam broke that custom and made war in the prohibited months, the Muslims were free also to break that custom but only to the same extent as the others broke it. Similarly the territory of Mecca was sacred, in which war was prohibited. If the enemies of Islam broke that custom, the Muslims were free to do so to that extent. Any convention is useless if one party does not respect it. There must be a law of equality. Or perhaps the word reciprocity may express it better.

210. At the same time the Muslims are commanded to exercise self-restraint as much as possible. Force is a dangerous weapon. It may have to be used for self-defence or self-preservation, but we must always remember that self-restraint is pleasing in the eyes of God. Even when we are fighting, it should be for a principle, not out of passion.

211. Every fight requires the wherewithals for the fight, the "sinews of war". If the war is just, and in the cause of God, all who have wealth must spend it freely. That may be their contribution to the Cause, in addition to their personal effort, or if for any reason they are unable to fight. If they hug their wealth, perhaps their own hands are helping in their own self destruction. Or if their wealth is being spent, not in the Cause of God, but in something which pleases their fancy, it may be that the advantage goes to the enemy, and they are by their action helping their own destruction. In all things, their standard should be, not selfishness, but the good of their brethren, for such good is pleasing to God.

212. See ii. 158, n. 161. The Ḥajj is the complete pilgrimage, of which the chief rites are during the first ten days of the month of *Ẓul-ḥajj*. The '*umra* is a less formal pilgrimage at any time of the year. In either case, the intending pilgrim commences by putting on a simple garment of unsewn cloth in two pieces when he is some distance yet from Mecca. The putting on of the pilgrim garb (*iḥrām*) is symbolical of his renouncing the vanities of the world. After this and until the end of the pilgrimage he must not wear other clothes, or ornaments, anoint his hair, use perfumes, hunt, or do other prohibited acts. The completion of the pilgrimage is symbolised by the shaving of the head for men, and the cutting off of a few locks of the hair of the head for women, the putting off of the *iḥrām* and the resumption of the ordinary dress.

Here we are told: (1) that having once undertaken the pilgrimage, we must complete it; (2) that we must do it not for worldly ends, but as a symbol of our service and worship to God; (3) that if we are prevented, for any reason, from completing the rites, a symbolical completion can be made by sending an offering for sacrifice; sacrifice would have been offered if we had been present personally: here we would send the sacrifice vicariously, and when it is likely to reach the place of sacrifice, we could then shave our heads and resume our ordinary dress and avocations.

In the service of God.
But if ye are prevented
(From completing it),
Send an offering
For sacrifice,
Such as ye may find,
And do not shave your heads
Until the offering reaches
The place of sacrifice.
And if any of you is ill,[213]
Or has an ailment in his scalp,
(Necessitating shaving),
(He should) in compensation
Either fast, or feed the poor,
Or offer sacrifice ;
And when ye are
In peaceful conditions (again),[214]
If any one wishes
To continue the *'umra*
On to the *ḥajj*,
He must make an offering,
Such as he can afford,
But if he cannot afford it,
He should fast
Three days during the *ḥajj*
And seven days on his return,
Making ten days in all.
This is for those
Whose household
Is not in (the precincts[215]
Of) the Sacred Mosque.
And fear God,
And know that God.
Is strict in punishment.[216]

فَإِنْ أُحْصِرْتُمْ فَمَا اسْتَيْسَرَ مِنَ الْهَدْيِ ۚ
وَلَا تَحْلِقُوا رُءُوسَكُمْ
حَتَّىٰ يَبْلُغَ الْهَدْيُ مَحِلَّهُ ۚ
فَمَنْ كَانَ مِنْكُمْ مَرِيضًا
أَوْ بِهِ أَذًى مِنْ رَأْسِهِ فَفِدْيَةٌ مِنْ صِيَامٍ
أَوْ صَدَقَةٍ أَوْ نُسُكٍ ۚ
فَإِذَا أَمِنْتُمْ
فَمَنْ تَمَتَّعَ بِالْعُمْرَةِ إِلَى الْحَجِّ
فَمَا اسْتَيْسَرَ مِنَ الْهَدْيِ ۚ
فَمَنْ لَمْ يَجِدْ فَصِيَامُ ثَلَاثَةِ أَيَّامٍ فِي الْحَجِّ
وَسَبْعَةٍ إِذَا رَجَعْتُمْ ۗ
تِلْكَ عَشَرَةٌ كَامِلَةٌ ۗ
ذَٰلِكَ لِمَنْ لَمْ يَكُنْ أَهْلُهُ حَاضِرِي الْمَسْجِدِ
الْحَرَامِ ۚ
وَاتَّقُوا اللَّهَ
وَاعْلَمُوا أَنَّ اللَّهَ شَدِيدُ الْعِقَابِ ○

213. If any one is taken ill after putting on the *iḥrām*, so that he has to put on other clothes, or if he has trouble or skin disease in his head or insects in his hair, and he has to shave his head before completion, he should fast (three days, say the Commentators), or feed the poor, or offer sacrifice.

214. When this was revealed, the city of Mecca was in the hands of the enemies of Islam, and the regulations about the fighting and the pilgrimage came together and were interconnected. But the revelation provides, as always, for the particular occasion, and also for normal conditions. Mecca soon passed out of the hands of the enemies of Islam. People sometimes came long distances to Mecca before the Pilgrimage season began. Having performed the *'umra*, they stayed on for the formal *Hajj*. In case the pilgrim had spent his money, he is shown what he can do, rich or poor, and yet hold his head high among his fellows, as having performed all rites as prescribed.

215. For residents in Mecca the question does not arise. They are there every day, and there is no question of *'umra* for them.

216. This closes the section about the duties of fighting and introduces the connected question of pilgrimage in a sort of transition. Fighting is connected with fear, and while it is meritorious to obey God, we are warned that we must not allow our selfish passions to carry us away, because it is in such times of stress that our spirit is tested. Verse 195 ended with a benediction for those who do good. This verse ends with a warning to those who take advantage of God's cause to transgress the limits, for the punishment is equally sure. The next verse shows us the pitfalls we must avoid in a large concourse of people.

Section 25.

197. For *Ḥajj*
Are the months well known.[217]
If any one undertakes
That duty therein,
Let there be no obscenity,
Nor wickedness,
Nor wrangling
In the *Ḥajj*.
And whatever good
Ye do, (be sure)
God knoweth it.
And take a provision[218]
(With you) for the journey,
But the best of provisions
Is right conduct.
So fear Me,
O ye that are wise.

١٩٧- الحج اشهر معلومات ج
فمن فرض فيهن الحج فلا رفث
ولا فسوق لا
ولا جدال في الحج ط
وما تفعلوا من خير يعلمه الله ط
وتزودوا فان خير الزاد التقوى ز
واتقون يأولي الالباب ○

198. It is no crime in you
If ye seek of the bounty
Of your Lord (during
pilgrimage).[219]
Then when ye pour down
From (Mount) 'Arafāt,
Celebrate the praises of God
At the Sacred Monument,[220]

١٩٨- ليس عليكم جناح
ان تبتغوا فضلا من ربكم ط
فاذا افضتم من عرفت
فاذكروا الله عند المشعر الحرام

217. *The months well known*: the months of *Shawwāl*, *Zul-qa'd*, and *Zul-ḥajj* (up to the 10th or the 13th) are set apart for the rites of *Ḥajj*. That is to say, the first rites may begin as early as the beginning of Shawwāl, with a definite approach to Mecca, but the chief rites are concentrated on the first ten days of *Zul-ḥajj*, and specially on the 8th, 9th and 10th of that month, when the concourse of pilgrims reaches its height. The chief rites may be briefly enumerated: (1) The wearing of the pilgrim garment (*iḥrām*) from certain points definitely fixed on all the roads to Mecca; after this the pilgrimage prohibitions come into operation and the pilgrim is dedicated to worship and prayer and the denial of vanities; (2) the going round the Ka'ba seven times (*ṭawāf*), typifying activity, with the kissing of the little Black Stone built into the wall, the symbol of concentration in the love of God; (3) after a short prayer at the Station of Abraham (Q. ii. 125), the pilgrim goes to the hills Ṣafā and Marwa (Q. ii. 158), the symbols of patience and perseverance; (4) the great Sermon (*Khuṭba*) on the 7th of *Zul-ḥajj*, when the whole assembly listens to an exposition of the meaning of *Ḥajj*; (5) the visit on the eighth, of the whole body of pilgrims to the Valley of Minā (about six miles north of Mecca), where the pilgrims halt and stay the night, proceeding on the ninth to the plain and hill of 'Arafāt, about five miles further north, which commemorates the reunion of Adam and Eve after their wanderings, and is also called the Mount of Mercy; (6) the tenth day, the 'Id Day, the day of Sacrifice, when the sacrifice is offered in the Valley of Minā, and the symbolic ceremony of casting seven stones at the Evil One is performed on the first occasion; it is continued on subsequent days; both rites are connected with the story of Abraham: this is the Id-ul-Adhḥā; note that the ceremony is symbolically connected with the rejection of evil in thought, word, and deed. This closes the Pilgrimage, but a stay of two or three days after this is recommended, and this is called *Tashrīq*.

218. It is recommended that pilgrims should come with provisions, so that they should not be compelled to resort to begging. But, as usual, our thought is directed at once from the physical to the spiritual. If provisions are required for a journey on earth, how much more important to provide for the final journey into the future world? The best of such provisions is right conduct, which is the same as the fear of God.

219. Legitimate trade is allowed, in the interests both of the honest trader, who can thus meet his own expenses, and of the generality of pilgrims, who would otherwise be greatly inconvenienced for the necessaries of life. But the profit must be sought as from the "bounty of God". There should be no profiteering, or trade "tricks". Good honest trade is a form of service to the community, and therefore to God.

220. About midway between 'Arafāt and Minā (see n. 217 to ii. 197) is a place called Muzdalifa where the Holy Apostle offered up a long prayer. It has thus become a Sacred Monument and pilgrims are directed to follow that example on their return. A special reason for this is given in the note following.

And celebrate His praises
As He has directed you,
Even though, before this,
Ye went astray.[221]

وَاذْكُرُوهُ كَمَا هَدَاكُمْ
وَإِنْ كُنْتُمْ مِنْ قَبْلِهِ لَمِنَ الضَّالِّينَ ○

199. Then pass on
At a quick pace from the place
Whence it is usual
For the multitude[222]
So to do, and ask
For God's forgiveness.
For God is Oft-forgiving,
Most Merciful.

١٩٩- ثُمَّ أَفِيضُوا مِنْ حَيْثُ أَفَاضَ
النَّاسُ
وَاسْتَغْفِرُوا اللَّهَ
إِنَّ اللَّهَ غَفُورٌ رَحِيمٌ ○

200. So when ye have
Accomplished your holy rites,
Celebrate the praises of God,
As ye used to celebrate
The praises of your fathers,—[223]
Yea, with far more
Heart and soul.
There are men who say:
"Our Lod! Give us
(Thy bounties) in this world!"
But they will have
No portion in the Hereafter.[224]

٢٠٠- فَإِذَا قَضَيْتُمْ مَنَاسِكَكُمْ
فَاذْكُرُوا اللَّهَ
كَذِكْرِكُمْ آبَاءَكُمْ أَوْ أَشَدَّ ذِكْرًا
فَمِنَ النَّاسِ مَنْ يَقُولُ رَبَّنَا آتِنَا فِي
الدُّنْيَا
وَمَا لَهُ فِي الْآخِرَةِ مِنْ خَلَاقٍ ○

201. And there are men who say:
"Our Lord! Give us
Good in this world
And good in the Hereafter,
And defend us
From the torment
Of the Fire!"

٢٠١- وَمِنْهُمْ مَنْ يَقُولُ رَبَّنَا آتِنَا
فِي الدُّنْيَا حَسَنَةً وَفِي الْآخِرَةِ حَسَنَةً
وَقِنَا عَذَابَ النَّارِ ○

221. Certain arrogant tribes living in Mecca used not to go to 'Arafāt with the crowd but to stop short at Muzdalifa. They are rebuked for their arrogance and told that they must perform all the rites like the rest of the pilgrims. There is equality in Islam.

222. See the last note. Towards the end of the Pilgrimagé the crowd is very great, and if any people loitered after Arafāt, it would cause great confusion and inconvenience. The pace has therefore to be quick for every one, a very salutary regulation. Every member of the crowd must think of the comfort and convenience of the whole mass.

223. After the Pilgrimage, in Pagan times, the pilgrims used to gather in assemblies in which the praises of ancestors were sung. As the whole of the pilgrimage rites were spiritualised in Islam, so this aftermath of the Pilgrimage was also spiritualised. It was recommended for pilgrims to stay on two or three days after the pilgrimage, but they must use them in prayer and praise to God. See ii. 203 below.

224. If you hasten to get all the good things of the world, and only think of them and pray for them, you would lose the higher things of the future. The proper Muslim attitude is neither to renounce this world nor to be so engrossed in it as to forget the spiritual future.

202. To these will be allotted[225]
What they have earned;
And God is quick in account.

٢٠٢- أُولٰٓئِكَ لَهُمْ نَصِيبٌ مِّمَّا كَسَبُوْا ۚ
وَاللّٰهُ سَرِيْعُ الْحِسَابِ ○

203. Celebrate the praises of God
During the Appointed Days.[226]
But if any one hastens
To leave in two days,
There is no blame on him,
And if any one stays on,
There is no blame on him,
If his aim is to do right.
Then fear God, and know
That ye will surely
Be gathered unto Him.

٢٠٣- وَاذْكُرُوا اللّٰهَ فِيْٓ اَيَّامٍ مَّعْدُوْدٰتٍ ۚ
فَمَنْ تَعَجَّلَ فِيْ يَوْمَيْنِ
فَلَآ اِثْمَ عَلَيْهِ ۚ
وَمَنْ تَاَخَّرَ فَلَآ اِثْمَ عَلَيْهِ ۙ لِمَنِ اتَّقٰى ۗ
وَاتَّقُوا اللّٰهَ
وَاعْلَمُوْٓا اَنَّكُمْ اِلَيْهِ تُحْشَرُوْنَ ○

204. There is the type of man[227]
Whose speech
About this world's life
May dazzle thee,
And he calls God to witness
About what is in his heart;
Yet is he the most contentious
Of enemies.

٢٠٤- وَمِنَ النَّاسِ مَنْ يُّعْجِبُكَ
قَوْلُهٗ فِي الْحَيٰوةِ الدُّنْيَا
وَيُشْهِدُ اللّٰهَ عَلٰى مَا فِيْ قَلْبِهٖ ۙ
وَهُوَ اَلَدُّ الْخِصَامِ ○

205. When he turns his back,
His aim everywhere
Is to spread mischief
Through the earth and destroy
Crops and cattle.
But God loveth not mischief.

٢٠٥- وَاِذَا تَوَلّٰى سَعٰى فِي الْاَرْضِ
لِيُفْسِدَ فِيْهَا وَيُهْلِكَ الْحَرْثَ وَالنَّسْلَ ۗ
وَاللّٰهُ لَا يُحِبُّ الْفَسَادَ ○

206. When it is said to him,
"Fear God,"
He is led by arrogance
To (more) crime.

٢٠٦- وَاِذَا قِيْلَ لَهُ اتَّقِ اللّٰهَ
اَخَذَتْهُ الْعِزَّةُ بِالْاِثْمِ

225. Our spiritual account is mounting up, both on the debit and credit side. In worldly accounts, both our profits and our losses may be delayed. But in God's books there is no delay. Our actions go before us. (See ii. 95. n.)

226. *The Appointed Days*: the three days after the tenth, when the Pilgrims stay on in the Valley of Minā for prayer and praise. They are the days of *Tashrīq* (see ii. 200, n. 223). It is optional for pilgrims to leave on the second or third day.

227. The two contrasted types of men mentioned in ii. 200 and 201 are here further particularised: the glib hypocrite who appears worldly-wise but plans harm, contrasted with the sincere believer who is prepared to suffer martyrdom for his faith. The Commentators give names of people who exemplified these types. The mischief-maker has a smooth tongue and indulges in plausible talk with many oaths. He appears to be worldly-wise, and though you may despise him for his worldliness, you may not realise his frauds. Behind your back he is an implacable enemy. He stirs up quarrels, and causes all sorts of mischief to you or your friends. He can never win God's love, and we are warned against his tricks.

Enough for him is Hell;—
An evil bed indeed
(To lie on)![228]

فَحَسْبُهٗ جَهَنَّمُ ؕ وَلَبِئْسَ الْمِهَادُ ○

207. And there is the type of man
Who gives his life
To earn the pleasure of God;
And God is full of kindness
To (His) devotees.[229]

٢٠٧- وَمِنَ النَّاسِ مَنْ يَّشْرِيْ نَفْسَهُ
ابْتِغَآءَ مَرْضَاتِ اللّٰهِ ؕ
وَاللّٰهُ رَءُوْفٌ بِالْعِبَادِ ○

208. O ye who believe!
Enter into Islam
Whole-heartedly;
And follow not
The footsteps
Of the Evil One;
For he is to you
An avowed enemy.

٢٠٨- يٰٓاَيُّهَا الَّذِيْنَ اٰمَنُوا
ادْخُلُوْا فِی السِّلْمِ كَآفَّةً
وَلَا تَتَّبِعُوْا خُطُوٰتِ الشَّيْطٰنِ ؕ
اِنَّهٗ لَكُمْ عَدُوٌّ مُّبِيْنٌ ○

209. If ye backslide
After the clear (Signs)
Have come to you,
Then know that God
Is Exalted in Power, Wise.[230]

٢٠٩- فَاِنْ زَلَلْتُمْ مِّنْۢ بَعْدِ مَا جَآءَتْكُمُ
الْبَيِّنٰتُ
فَاعْلَمُوْٓا اَنَّ اللّٰهَ عَزِيْزٌ حَكِيْمٌ ○

210. Will they wait
Until God comes to them
In canopies of clouds,
With angels (in His train)
And the question
Is (thus) settled?
But to God
Do all questions
Go back (for decision).[231]

٢١٠- هَلْ يَنْظُرُوْنَ اِلَّآ اَنْ يَّاْتِيَهُمُ اللّٰهُ
فِیْ ظُلَلٍ مِّنَ الْغَمَامِ
وَالْمَلٰٓئِكَةُ وَقُضِیَ الْاَمْرُ ؕ
ع وَاِلَى اللّٰهِ تُرْجَعُ الْاُمُوْرُ ○

SECTION 26.

211. Ask the Children of Israel[232]
How many Clear (Signs)

٢١١- سَلْ بَنِیْٓ اِسْرَآءِيْلَ كَمْ اٰتَيْنٰهُمْ مِّنْ

---

228. According to the English saying, "As you have made your bed, so you must lie in it."

229 This second type of man,—firm, sincere, devoted, willing to give his life for the faith that is in him—was common in early Islam. Such men were its pillars. Through persecution, obloquy, torture, threat to their own lives or the lives of those dear to them, they stood by their leader, and many of them gave their lives. That is what established Islam. We are asked in the next verse to follow this type and shun the other or evil type. If we do that, our Cause is safe.

230. If you backslide after the conviction has been brought home to you, you may cause some inconvenience to the Cause, or to those who counted upon you, but do not be so arrogant as to suppose that you will defeat God's Power and Wisdom. The loss will be your own.

231. If faith is wanting, all sorts of excuses are made to resist the appeal of God. They might and do say: "Oh yes! we shall believe if God appears to us with His angels in His glory!" In other words they want to settle the question in their way, and not in God's way. That will not do. The decision in all questions belongs to God. If we are true to Him, we wait for His times and seasons, and do not expect Him to wait on ours.

232. The Israelites under Moses were shown God's glory and many clear Signs and yet they went after their own ways and preferred their own whims and fancies. So do people in all ages. But let them not deceive themselves God's justice is sure, and when it comes, it will be strict and unmistakable to those who reject His grace.

We have sent them.
But if any one,
After God's favour
Has come to him,
Substitutes (something else),
God is strict in punishment.[233]

آيَةٍ بَيِّنَةٍ ؕ وَمَنْ يُّبَدِّلْ نِعْمَةَ اللّٰهِ
مِنْۢ بَعْدِ مَا جَآءَتْهُ
فَاِنَّ اللّٰهَ شَدِيْدُ الْعِقَابِ ○

212. The life of this world
Is alluring to those
Who reject faith,
And they scoff at those
Who believe.
But the righteous
Will be above them
On the Day of Resurrection;
For God bestows His abundance
Without measure
On whom He will.[234]

٢١٢- زُيِّنَ لِلَّذِيْنَ كَفَرُوا الْحَيٰوةُ الدُّنْيَا
وَيَسْخَرُوْنَ مِنَ الَّذِيْنَ اٰمَنُوْا ۘ (وقف لازم)
وَالَّذِيْنَ اتَّقَوْا فَوْقَهُمْ يَوْمَ الْقِيٰمَةِ ؕ
وَاللّٰهُ يَرْزُقُ مَنْ يَّشَآءُ
بِغَيْرِ حِسَابٍ ○

213. Mankind was one single nation,
And God sent Messengers
With glad tidings and warnings;
And with them He sent
The Book in truth,
To judge between people
In matters wherein
They differed;
But the People of the Book,
After the clear Signs
Came to them, did not differ
Among themselves,
Except through selfish contumacy.
God by His Grace
Guided the Believers
To the Truth,
Concerning that
Wherein they differed.
For God guides
Whom He will
To a path
That is straight.

٢١٣- كَانَ النَّاسُ اُمَّةً وَّاحِدَةً قف
فَبَعَثَ اللّٰهُ النَّبِيّٖنَ مُبَشِّرِيْنَ وَمُنْذِرِيْنَ
وَاَنْزَلَ مَعَهُمُ الْكِتٰبَ بِالْحَقِّ
لِيَحْكُمَ بَيْنَ النَّاسِ
فِيْمَا اخْتَلَفُوْا فِيْهِ ؕ وَمَا اخْتَلَفَ فِيْهِ
اِلَّا الَّذِيْنَ اُوْتُوْهُ مِنْۢ بَعْدِ
مَا جَآءَتْهُمُ الْبَيِّنٰتُ بَغْيًا بَيْنَهُمْ ج
فَهَدَى اللّٰهُ الَّذِيْنَ اٰمَنُوْا
لِمَا اخْتَلَفُوْا فِيْهِ
مِنَ الْحَقِّ بِاِذْنِهٖ ؕ وَاللّٰهُ يَهْدِيْ مَنْ
يَّشَآءُ اِلٰى صِرَاطٍ مُّسْتَقِيْمٍ ○

214. Or do ye think
That ye shall enter

٢١٤- اَمْ حَسِبْتُمْ اَنْ تَدْخُلُوا الْجَنَّةَ

233. *Cf.* ii 196 (end) where the question was of those who do not fear God. Here the question is of those who reject God's Signs.

234. God's gifts in this world seem unequal, and sometimes those get them who seem to deserve them least. God's bounty is unlimited to the just as well as the unjust. In His wisdom He may give to whomsoever He pleases. The account is not taken now, but will be taken in the end, when the balance will be redressed.

The Garden (of Bliss)
Without such (trials)
As came to those
Who passed away
Before you?
They encountered
Suffering and adversity,
And were so shaken in spirit
That even the Apostle
And those of faith
Who were with him
Cried: " When (will come)
The help of God?"
Ah! Verily, the help of God
Is (always) near!

وَلَمَّا يَأْتِكُم مَّثَلُ الَّذِينَ خَلَوْا مِن
قَبْلِكُم ۖ
مَّسَّتْهُمُ الْبَأْسَاءُ وَالضَّرَّاءُ وَزُلْزِلُوا
حَتَّىٰ يَقُولَ الرَّسُولُ وَالَّذِينَ آمَنُوا
مَعَهُ
مَتَىٰ نَصْرُ اللَّهِ ۗ
أَلَا إِنَّ نَصْرَ اللَّهِ قَرِيبٌ ○

215. They ask thee
What they should spend
(In charity). Say: Whatever
Ye spend that is good,[235]
Is for parents and kindred
And orphans
And those in want
And for wayfarers.
And whatever ye do
That is good,—God
Knoweth it well.

٢١٥- يَسْأَلُونَكَ مَاذَا يُنفِقُونَ ۖ
قُلْ مَا أَنفَقْتُم مِّنْ خَيْرٍ
فَلِلْوَالِدَيْنِ وَالْأَقْرَبِينَ
وَالْيَتَامَىٰ وَالْمَسَاكِينِ وَابْنِ السَّبِيلِ ۗ
وَمَا تَفْعَلُوا مِنْ خَيْرٍ
فَإِنَّ اللَّهَ بِهِ عَلِيمٌ ○

216. Fighting is prescribed
For you, and ye dislike it.[236]
But it is possible
That ye dislike a thing
Which is good for you,
And that ye love a thing
Which is bad for you.
But God knoweth,
And ye know not.

٢١٦- كُتِبَ عَلَيْكُمُ الْقِتَالُ وَهُوَ كُرْهٌ لَّكُمْ ۖ
وَعَسَىٰ أَن تَكْرَهُوا شَيْئًا وَهُوَ خَيْرٌ لَّكُمْ ۖ
وَعَسَىٰ أَن تُحِبُّوا شَيْئًا
وَهُوَ شَرٌّ لَّكُمْ ۗ
وَاللَّهُ يَعْلَمُ وَأَنتُمْ لَا تَعْلَمُونَ ○

235. Three questions arise in charity: (1) What shall we give? (2) to whom shall we give? and (3) how shall we give? The answer is here. Give anything that is good, useful, helpful, valuable. It may be property or money; it may be a helping hand; it may be advice; it may be a kind word; "whatever ye do that is good" is charity. On the other hand, if you throw away what is useless, there is no charity in it. Or if you give something with a harmful intent, *e.g.*, a sword to a madman, or a drug or sweets or even money to some one whom you want to entrap or corrupt, it is no charity but a gift of damnation. To whom should you give? It may be tempting to earn the world's praise by a gift that will be talked about, but are you meeting the needs of those who have the first claim on you? If you are not, you are like a person who defrauds creditors: it is no charity. Every gift is judged by its unselfish character: the degree of need or claim is a factor which you should consider; if you disregard it, there is something selfish behind it. How should it be given? As in the sight of God; this shuts out all pretence, show, and insincerity.

236 To fight in the cause of Truth is one of the highest forms of charity. What can you offer that is more precious than your own life? But here again the limitations come in. If you are a mere brawler, or a selfish aggressive person, or a vainglorious bully, you deserve the highest censure. If you offer your life to the righteous Imâm, who is only guided by God, you are an unselfish hero. God knows the value of things better than you do.

SECTION 27.

217. They ask thee
Concerning fighting
In the Prohibited Month.[237]
Say: "Fighting therein
Is a grave (offence);
But graver is it
In the sight of God
To prevent access
To the path of God,
To deny Him,
To prevent access
To the Sacred Mosque,
And drive out its members."[238]
Tumult and oppression[239]
Are worse than slaughter.
Nor will they cease
Fighting you until
They turn you back
From your faith
If they can.
And if any of you
Turn back from their faith
And die in unbelief,
Their works will bear no fruit
In this life
And in the Hereafter;
They will be
Companions of the Fire
And will abide therein.

218. Those who believed
And those who suffered exile
And fought (and strove and
struggled)
In the path of God,—
They have the hope
Of the Mercy of God:
And God is Oft-forgiving,
Most Merciful.

٢١٧- يَسْـَٔلُونَكَ عَنِ الشَّهْرِ الْحَرَامِ قِتَالٍ فِيهِ
قُلْ قِتَالٌ فِيهِ كَبِيرٌ
وَصَدٌّ عَن سَبِيلِ اللَّهِ وَكُفْرٌ بِهِ
وَالْمَسْجِدِ الْحَرَامِ
وَإِخْرَاجُ أَهْلِهِ مِنْهُ أَكْبَرُ عِندَ اللَّهِ
وَالْفِتْنَةُ أَكْبَرُ مِنَ الْقَتْلِ
وَلَا يَزَالُونَ يُقَاتِلُونَكُمْ حَتَّىٰ يَرُدُّوكُمْ
عَن دِينِكُمْ إِنِ اسْتَطَاعُوا
وَمَن يَرْتَدِدْ مِنكُمْ
عَن دِينِهِ فَيَمُتْ
وَهُوَ كَافِرٌ
فَأُولَٰئِكَ حَبِطَتْ أَعْمَالُهُمْ
فِي الدُّنْيَا وَالْآخِرَةِ
وَأُولَٰئِكَ أَصْحَابُ النَّارِ
هُمْ فِيهَا خَالِدُونَ ○

٢١٨- إِنَّ الَّذِينَ آمَنُوا وَالَّذِينَ هَاجَرُوا
وَجَاهَدُوا فِي سَبِيلِ اللَّهِ
أُولَٰئِكَ يَرْجُونَ رَحْمَتَ اللَّهِ
وَاللَّهُ غَفُورٌ رَّحِيمٌ ○

237. *Prohibited Month*: See ii. 194, n. 209.

238. The intolerance and persecution of the Pagan clique at Mecca caused untold hardships to the holy Messenger of Islam and his early disciples. They bore all with meekness and long-suffering patience until the holy one permitted them to take up arms in self-defence. Then they were twitted with breach of the custom about Prohibited Months, though they were driven to fight during that period against their own feeling in self defence. But their enemies not only forced them to engage in actual warfare, but interfered with their conscience, persecuted them and their families, openly insulted and denied God, kept out the Muslim Arabs from the Sacred Mosque, and exiled them. Such violence and intolerance are deservedly called worse than slaughter.

239. *Cf.* ii. 191, 193, where a similar phrase occurs. *Fitna*=trial, temptation, as in ii. 102; or tumult, sedition, oppression, as here; M. M. A., H. G. S., and M. P. translate "persecution" in this passage, which is also legitimate, seeing that persecution is the suppression of some opinion by violence, force, or threats.

219. They ask thee
Concerning wine[240] and
gambling.[241]
Say : " In them is great sin,
And some profit, for men ;
But the sin is greater
Than the profit."
They ask thee how much
They are to spend ;
Say : " What is beyond[242]
Your needs."
Thus doth God
Make clear to you
His Signs : in order that
Ye may consider—

٢١٩- يَسْـَٔلُونَكَ عَنِ الْخَمْرِ وَالْمَيْسِرِ ط
قُلْ فِيهِمَآ إِثْمٌ كَبِيرٌ
وَّمَنَافِعُ لِلنَّاسِ ز
وَإِثْمُهُمَآ أَكْبَرُ مِن نَّفْعِهِمَا ط
وَيَسْـَٔلُونَكَ مَاذَا يُنفِقُونَ ۵
قُلِ الْعَفْوَ ط كَذٰلِكَ يُبَيِّنُ اللّٰهُ لَكُمُ الْاٰيٰتِ
لَعَلَّكُمْ تَتَفَكَّرُونَ لا

220. (Their bearings) on
This life and the Hereafter.[243]

They ask thee
Concerning orphans.[244]
Say : " The best thing to do
Is what is for their good ;
If ye mix
Their affairs with yours,
They are your brethren ;
But God knows

٢٢٠- فِى الدُّنْيَا وَالْاٰخِرَةِ ط
وَيَسْـَٔلُونَكَ عَنِ الْيَتٰمٰى ط
قُلْ إِصْلَاحٌ لَّهُمْ خَيْرٌ ط
وَإِن تُخَالِطُوهُمْ فَإِخْوَانُكُمْ ط
وَاللّٰهُ يَعْلَمُ

---

240. *Wine* : *Khamr* : literally understood to mean the fermented juice of the grape ; applied by analogy to all fermented liquor, and by further analogy to any intoxicating liquor or drug. There may possibly be some benefit in it, but the harm is greater than the benefit, especially if we look at it from a social as well as an individual point of view.

241. *Gambling* : *maisir* : literally, a means of getting something too easily, getting a profit without working for it; hence gambling. That is the principle on which gambling is prohibited. The form most familiar to the Arabs was gambling by casting lots by means of arrows, on the principle of a lottery : the arrows were marked, and served the same purpose as a modern lottery ticket. Something, *e.g.*, the carcase of a slaughtered animal, was divided into unequal parts. The marked arrows were drawn from a bag. Some were blank and those who drew them got nothing. Others indicated prizes, which were big or small. Whether you got a big share or a small share, or nothing, depended on pure luck, unless there was fraud also on the part of some persons concerned. The principle on which the objection is based is : that, even if there is no fraud, you gain what you have not earned, or lose on a mere chance. Dice and wagering are rightly held to be within the definition of gambling. But insurance is not gambling, when conducted on business principles. Here the basis for calculation is statistics on a large scale, from which mere chance is eliminated. The insurers themselves pay premia in proportion to risks, exactly and statistically calculated.

242. Hoarding is no use either to ourselves, or to any one else. We should use the wealth we need ; any superfluities we must spend in good works or in charity.

243 Gambling and intemperance are social as well as individual sins. They may ruin us in our ordinary every-day worldly life, as well as our spiritual future. In case it is suggested that there is no harm in a little indulgence, we are asked to think over all its aspects, social and individual,—worldly and spiritual.

244. For orphans the best rule is to keep their property, household, and accounts separate, lest there should be any temptation to get a personal advantage to their guardian by mixing them with the guardian's property, household or accounts.—also to keep clear of any ideas of marriage, where this fiduciary relation exists. Q. vi. 152 may possibly suggest complete separation. But it may be an economy and an advantage to the orphan to have his property and accounts administered with the guardian's property and accounts and to have him live in the guardian's household, or to marry into the guardian's family, especially where the orphan's property is small and he or she has no other friend. The test is : what is best in the orphan's interests ? If the guardian does fall into temptation, even if human law does not detect him, he is told he is sinning in God's sight and that should keep him straight.

The man who means mischief
From the man who means good.
And if God had wished,
He could have put you
Into difficulties : He is indeed
Exalted in Power, Wise." [245]

المُفْسِدَ مِنَ الْمُصْلِحِ ط
وَلَوْ شَاءَ اللّٰهُ لَاَعْنَتَكُمْ ط
اِنَّ اللّٰهَ عَزِيْزٌ حَكِيْمٌ ○

221. Do not marry
Unbelieving women (idolaters),
Until they believe :
A slave woman who believes
Is better than an unbelieving
woman,
Even though she allure you.
Nor marry (your girls)
To unbelievers until
They believe :
A man slave who believes
Is better than an unbeliever,
Even though he allure you. [246]
Unbelievers do (but)
Beckon you to the Fire.
But God beckons by His Grace
To the Garden (of Bliss)
And forgiveness,
And makes His Signs
Clear to mankind :
That they may
Celebrate His praise.

٢٢١- وَلَا تَنْكِحُوا الْمُشْرِكٰتِ حَتّٰى يُؤْمِنَّ ط
وَلَاَمَةٌ مُّؤْمِنَةٌ خَيْرٌ مِّنْ مُّشْرِكَةٍ
وَّلَوْ اَعْجَبَتْكُمْ ج
وَلَا تُنْكِحُوا الْمُشْرِكِيْنَ حَتّٰى يُؤْمِنُوْا ط
وَلَعَبْدٌ مُّؤْمِنٌ
خَيْرٌ مِّنْ مُّشْرِكٍ وَّلَوْ اَعْجَبَكُمْ ط
اُولٰٓئِكَ يَدْعُوْنَ اِلَى النَّارِ ۚ
وَاللّٰهُ يَدْعُوْٓا اِلَى الْجَنَّةِ
وَالْمَغْفِرَةِ بِاِذْنِهٖ ۚ
وَيُبَيِّنُ اٰيٰتِهٖ لِلنَّاسِ
ع لَعَلَّهُمْ يَتَذَكَّرُوْنَ ○

Section 28.

222. They ask thee
Concerning women's courses.
Say : They are
A hurt and a pollution : [247]

٢٢٢- وَيَسْـَٔلُوْنَكَ عَنِ الْمَحِيْضِ ط
قُلْ هُوَ اَذًى لا

245. The idea in Islam is not to make God's Law a burdensome fetter, but to ease a man's path in all kinds of difficult situations by putting him on his honour and trusting him. The strictest probity is demanded of him, but if he falls short of it, he is told that he cannot escape God's punishment even though he may evade human punishment.

246. Marriage is a most intimate communion, and the mystery of sex finds its highest fulfilment when intimate spiritual harmony is combined with the physical link. If religion is at all a real influence in life to both parties or to either party, a difference in this vital matter must affect the lives of both more profoundly than differences of birth, race, language, or position in life. It is therefore only right that the parties to be married should have the same spiritual outlook. If two persons love each other, their outlook in the highest things of life must be the same. Note that religion is not here a mere label or a matter of custom or birth. The two persons may have been born in different religions, but if, by their mutual influence, they come to see the truth in the same way, they must openly accept the same rites and the same social brotherhood. Otherwise the position will become impossible individually and socially.

247. *Azan* : hurt, pollution. Both aspects must be remembered. Physical cleanliness and purity make for health, bodily and spiritual. But the matter should be looked at from the woman's point of view as well as the man's. To her there is danger of hurt, and she should have every consideration. In the animal world, instinct is a guide which is obeyed. Man should in this respect be better: he is often worse.

So keep away from women
In their courses, and do not
Approach them until
They are clean.
But when they have
Purified themselves,
Ye may approach them
In any manner, time, or place [248]
Ordained for you by God.
For God loves those
Who turn to Him constantly
And He loves those
Who keep themselves pure and
clean.

فَاعْتَزِلُوا النِّسَاءَ فِي الْمَحِيضِ
وَلَا تَقْرَبُوهُنَّ حَتَّىٰ يَطْهُرْنَ
فَإِذَا تَطَهَّرْنَ
فَأْتُوهُنَّ مِنْ حَيْثُ أَمَرَكُمُ اللَّهُ
إِنَّ اللَّهَ يُحِبُّ التَّوَّابِينَ
وَيُحِبُّ الْمُتَطَهِّرِينَ ○

223. Your wives are
As a tilth [249] unto you;
So approach your tilth
When or how ye will;
But do some good act
For your souls beforehand;
And fear God,
And know that ye are
To meet Him (in the Hereafter),
And give (these) good tidings [250]
To those who believe.

٢٢٣- نِسَآؤُكُمْ حَرْثٌ لَّكُمْ
فَأْتُوا حَرْثَكُمْ أَنَّىٰ شِئْتُمْ
وَقَدِّمُوا لِأَنفُسِكُمْ
وَاتَّقُوا اللَّهَ
وَاعْلَمُوا أَنَّكُم مُّلَاقُوهُ
وَبَشِّرِ الْمُؤْمِنِينَ ○

224. And make not
God's (name) an excuse
In your oaths against
Doing good, or acting rightly,
Or making peace
Between persons;

٢٢٤- وَلَا تَجْعَلُوا اللَّهَ عُرْضَةً
لِّأَيْمَانِكُمْ أَن تَبَرُّوا
وَتَتَّقُوا وَتُصْلِحُوا بَيْنَ النَّاسِ

248. *Haithu*: A comprehensive word referring to manner, time, or place. The most delicate matters are here referred to in the most discreet and yet helpful terms. In sex morality, manner, time, and place are all important: and the highest standards are set by social laws, by our own refined instinct of mutual consideration, and above all, by the light shed by the highest Teachers from the wisdom which they receive from our Maker, Who loves purity and cleanliness in all things.

249. Sex is not a thing to be ashamed of, or to be treated lightly, or to be indulged to excess. It is as solemn a fact as any in life. It is compared to a husbandman's tilth; it is a serious affair to him: he sows the seed in order to reap the harvest. But he chooses his own time and mode of cultivation. He does not sow out of season nor cultivate in a manner which will injure or exhaust the soil. He is wise and considerate and does not run riot. Coming from the simile to human beings, every kind of mutual consideration is required, but above all, we must remember that even in these matters there is a spiritual aspect. We must never forget our souls, and that we are responsible to God.

It was carnal-minded men who invented the doctrine of original sin: "Behold," says the Psalmist, "I was shapen in iniquity, and in sin did my mother conceive me" (Psalms li. 5). This is entirely repudiated by Islam, in which the office of father and mother is held in the highest veneration. Every child of pure love is born pure. Celibacy is not necessarily a virtue, and may be a vice.

250. Our highest spiritual ambition should be the hope of meeting God. To uphold such a hope is to give glad tidings to people of faith. It would only be unrepentant sinners who would fear the meeting. Note how the most sensuous matters are discussed frankly, and immediately taken up into the loftiest regions of spiritual upliftment.

For God is One
Who heareth and knoweth[251]
All things.

وَاللّٰهُ سَمِيْعٌ عَلِيْمٌ ○

225. God will not
Call you to account
For thoughtlessness
In your oaths,
But for the intention
In your hearts;[252]
And He is
Oft-forgiving
Most Forbearing.

٢٢٥- لَا يُؤَاخِذُكُمُ اللّٰهُ
بِاللَّغْوِ فِيْٓ اَيْمَانِكُمْ
وَلٰكِنْ يُّؤَاخِذُكُمْ بِمَا كَسَبَتْ قُلُوْبُكُمْ ط
وَاللّٰهُ غَفُوْرٌ حَلِيْمٌ ○

226. For those who take
An oath for abstention
From their wives,
A waiting for four months
Is ordained;
If then they return,
God is Oft-forgiving,
Most Merciful.

٢٢٦- لِلَّذِيْنَ يُؤْلُوْنَ مِنْ نِّسَآئِهِمْ
تَرَبُّصُ اَرْبَعَةِ اَشْهُرٍ ج
فَاِنْ فَآءُوْ
فَاِنَّ اللّٰهَ غَفُوْرٌ رَّحِيْمٌ ○

227. But if their intention
Is firm for divorce,
God heareth
And knoweth all things.[253]

٢٢٧- وَاِنْ عَزَمُوا الطَّلَاقَ
فَاِنَّ اللّٰهَ سَمِيْعٌ عَلِيْمٌ ○

228. Divorced women
Shall wait concerning themselves

٢٢٨- وَالْمُطَلَّقٰتُ يَتَرَبَّصْنَ

---

251. The Arabs had many special kinds of oaths, for each of which they had a special name in their language. Some of them related to sex matters, and caused misunderstanding, alienation, division, or separation between husband and wife. This and the following three verses refer to them. In ii. 224 we are first of all told in perfectly general terms that we are not to make an oath in the name of God an excuse for not doing the right thing when it is pointed out to us, or for refraining from doing something which will bring people together. If we were swayed by anger or passion or mere caprice, God knows our inmost hearts, and right conduct and not obstinacy or quibbling is what He demands from us.

252. It has been held that thoughtless oaths, if there is no intention behind them, can be expiated by an act of charity.

253. Verses 225-27 should be read together with verse 224. The latter, though it is perfectly general, leads up to the other three.

The Pagan Arabs had a custom very unfair to women in wedlock, and this was suppressed by Islam. Sometimes, in a fit of anger or caprice, a husband would take an oath by God not to approach his wife. This deprived her of conjugal rights, but at the same time kept her tied to him indefinitely, so that she could not marry again. If the husband was remonstrated with, he would say that his oath by God bound him. Islam in the first place disapproved of thoughtless oaths, but insisted on proper solemn intentional oaths being scrupulously observed. In a serious matter like that affecting a wife, if the oath was put forward as an excuse, the man is told that it is no excuse at all. God looks to intention, not mere thoughtless words. The parties are allowed a period of four months to make up their minds and see if an adjustment is possible. Reconciliation is recommended, but if they are really determined against reconciliation, it is unfair to keep them tied indefinitely. Divorce is the only fair and equitable course, though, as the Apostle has declared, of all things permitted, divorce is the most hateful in the sight of God. In the circumstances, God will forgive, for He knows the real grievances of each of the parties, and will hear the cry of all who suffer.

For three monthly periods.
Nor is it lawful for them
To hide what God
Hath created in their wombs,
If they have faith
In God and the Last Day.
And their husbands
Have the better right
To take them back
In that period, if
They wish for reconciliation.[254]
And women shall have rights
Similar to the rights
Against them, according
To what is equitable;
But men have a degree
(Of advantage) over them.[255]
And God is Exalted in Power,
Wise.

بِاَنْفُسِهِنَّ ثَلٰثَةَ قُرُوْٓءٍ ؕ
وَلَا يَحِلُّ لَهُنَّ
اَنْ يَّكْتُمْنَ مَا خَلَقَ اللّٰهُ فِىْٓ اَرْحَامِهِنَّ
اِنْ كُنَّ يُؤْمِنَّ بِاللّٰهِ وَالْيَوْمِ الْاٰخِرِ ؕ
وَبُعُوْلَتُهُنَّ اَحَقُّ بِرَدِّهِنَّ فِىْ ذٰلِكَ اِنْ
اَرَادُوْٓا اِصْلَاحًا ؕ
وَلَهُنَّ مِثْلُ الَّذِىْ عَلَيْهِنَّ بِالْمَعْرُوْفِ ص
وَلِلرِّجَالِ عَلَيْهِنَّ دَرَجَةٌ ؕ
وَاللّٰهُ عَزِيْزٌ حَكِيْمٌ ۝

SECTION 29.

229. A divorce is only[256]
Permissible twice: after that,
The parties should either hold
Together on equitable terms,
Or separate with kindness.[257]
It is not lawful for you,
(Men), to take back
Any of your gifts (from your wives),
Except when both parties
Fear that they would be
Unable to keep the limits

۲۲۹- اَلطَّلَاقُ مَرَّتٰنِ ص
فَاِمْسَاكٌۢ بِمَعْرُوْفٍ اَوْ تَسْرِيْحٌۢ
بِاِحْسَانٍ ؕ
وَلَا يَحِلُّ لَكُمْ اَنْ تَاْخُذُوْا مِمَّآ
اٰتَيْتُمُوْهُنَّ شَيْـًٔا
اِلَّآ اَنْ يَّخَافَآ اَلَّا يُقِيْمَا حُدُوْدَ اللّٰهِ ؕ

254. Islam tries to maintain the married state as far as possible, especially where children are concerned, but it is against the restriction of the liberty of men and women in such vitally important matters as love and family life. It will check hasty action as far as possible, and leave the door to reconciliation open at many stages. Even after divorce a suggestion of reconciliation is made, subject to certain precautions (mentioned in the following verses) against thoughtless action. A period of waiting (*'iddat*) for three monthly courses is prescribed, in order to see if the marriage conditionally dissolved is likely to result in issue. But this is not necessary where the divorced woman is a virgin: Q. xxxiii. 49. It is definitely declared that women and men shall have similar rights against each other.

255. The difference in economic position between the sexes makes the man's rights and liabilities a little greater than the woman's. Q. iv. 34 refers to the duty of the man to maintain the woman, and to a certain difference in nature between the sexes. Subject to this, the sexes are on terms of equality in law, and in certain matters the weaker sex is entitled to special protection.

256. Where divorce for mutual incompatibility is allowed, there is danger that the parties might act hastily, then repent, and again wish to separate. To prevent such capricious action repeatedly, a limit is prescribed. Two divorces (with a reconciliation between) are allowed. After that the parties must definitely make up their minds, either to dissolve their union permanently, or to live honourable lives together in mutual love and forbearance—to "hold together on equitable terms," neither party worrying the other nor grumbling nor evading the duties and responsibilities of marriage.

257. If a separation is inevitable, the parties should not throw mud at each other, but recognise what is right and honourable on a consideration of all the circumstances. In any case a man is not allowed to ask back for any gifts or property he may have given to the wife. This is for the protection of the economically weaker sex. Lest that protective provision itself work agiainst the woman's freedom, an exception is made in the next clause.

Ordained by God.[258]
If ye (judges) do indeed
Fear that they would be
Unable to keep the limits
Ordained by God,
There is no blame on either
Of them if she give
Something for her freedom.
These are the limits
Ordained by God;
So do not transgress them
If any do transgress
The limits ordained by God,
Such persons wrong
(Themselves as well as others).[259]

230. So if a husband
Divorces his wife (irrevocably),[260]
He cannot, after that,
Re-marry her until
After she has married
Another husband and
He has divorced her.
In that case there is
No blame on either of them
If they re-unite, provided
They feel that they
Can keep the limits
Ordained by God.
Such are the limits
Ordained by God,
Which He makes plain
To those who understand.

231. When ye divorce[261]
Women, and they fulfil

فَإِنْ خِفْتُمْ أَلَّا يُقِيمَا حُدُودَ اللَّهِ ۙ
فَلَا جُنَاحَ عَلَيْهِمَا فِيمَا افْتَدَتْ
بِهِ ۗ
تِلْكَ حُدُودُ اللَّهِ
فَلَا تَعْتَدُوهَا ۚ
وَمَن يَتَعَدَّ حُدُودَ اللَّهِ
فَأُولَٰئِكَ هُمُ الظَّالِمُونَ ○

٢٣٠- فَإِن طَلَّقَهَا
فَلَا تَحِلُّ لَهُ
مِن بَعْدُ حَتَّىٰ تَنكِحَ زَوْجًا غَيْرَهُ ۗ
فَإِن طَلَّقَهَا
فَلَا جُنَاحَ عَلَيْهِمَا
أَن يَتَرَاجَعَا إِن ظَنَّا أَن يُقِيمَا حُدُودَ
اللَّهِ ۗ
وَتِلْكَ حُدُودُ اللَّهِ
يُبَيِّنُهَا لِقَوْمٍ يَعْلَمُونَ ○

٢٣١- وَإِذَا طَلَّقْتُمُ النِّسَاءَ فَبَلَغْنَ

258. All the prohibitions and limits prescribed here are in the interests of good and honourable lives for both sides, and in the interests of a clean and honourable social life, without public or private scandals. If there is any fear that in safeguarding her economic rights, her very freedom of person may suffer, the husband refusing the dissolution of marriage, and perhaps treating her with cruelty, then, in such exceptional cases, it is permissible to give some material consideration to the husband, but the need and equity of this should be submitted to the judgment of impartial judges, *i.e.*, properly constituted courts. A divorce of this kind is called *khul'a*.

259. *Wrong (themselves as well as others)*: *Ẓālimūn*: for the root meaning of *ẓulm* see n. 51. ii. 35.

260. This is in continuation of the first sentence of ii. 229. Two divorces followed by re-union are permissible; the third time the divorce becomes irrevocable, until the woman marries some other man and he divorces her. This is to set an almost impossible condition. The lesson is: if a man loves a woman he should not allow a sudden gust of temper or anger to induce him to take hasty action. What happens after two divorces, if the man takes her back? See n. 261 to ii. 231.

261. If the man takes back his wife after two divorces, he must do so only on equitable terms, *i.e.*, he must not put pressure on the woman to prejudice her rights in any way, and they must live clean and honourable lives, respecting each other's personalities. There are here two conditional clauses: (1) when ye divorce women, and (2) when they fulfil their *'Iddat*; followed by two consequential clauses, (3) take them back on equitable terms, or (4) set them free with kindness. The first is connected with the third and the second with the fourth. Therefore if the husband wishes to resume the marital relations, he need not wait for *'Iddat*. But if he does not so wish, she is free to marry some one else after *'Iddat*. For the meaning of *'Iddat* see n. 254 above.

The term of their (*'Iddat*),
Either take them back
On equitable terms
Or set them free
On equitable terms;
But do not take them back
To injure them, (or) to take
Undue advantage;[262]
If any one does that,
He wrongs his own soul.
Do not treat God's Signs
As a jest,[263]
But solemnly rehearse[264]
God's favours on you,
And the fact that He
Sent down to you
The Book
And Wisdom,
For your instruction.
And fear God,
And know that God
Is well acquainted
With all things.

أَجَلَهُنَّ فَأَمْسِكُوهُنَّ بِمَعْرُوفٍ
أَوْ سَرِّحُوهُنَّ بِمَعْرُوفٍ ۚ
وَلَا تُمْسِكُوهُنَّ ضِرَارًا لِّتَعْتَدُوا ۚ
وَمَن يَفْعَلْ ذَٰلِكَ
فَقَدْ ظَلَمَ نَفْسَهُ ۚ
وَلَا تَتَّخِذُوا آيَاتِ اللَّهِ هُزُوًا ۚ
وَاذْكُرُوا نِعْمَتَ اللَّهِ عَلَيْكُمْ
وَمَا أَنزَلَ عَلَيْكُم
مِّنَ الْكِتَابِ وَالْحِكْمَةِ
يَعِظُكُم بِهِ ۚ وَاتَّقُوا اللَّهَ
وَاعْلَمُوا
أَنَّ اللَّهَ بِكُلِّ شَيْءٍ عَلِيمٌ ۝

SECTION 30.

232. When ye divorce
Women, and they fulfil
The term of their (*'Iddat*),
Do not prevent them[265]
From marrying
Their (former) husbands,
If they mutually agree
On equitable terms.
This instruction
Is for all amongst you,
Who believe in God
And the Last Day.
That is (the course

٢٣٢- وَإِذَا طَلَّقْتُمُ النِّسَاءَ فَبَلَغْنَ أَجَلَهُنَّ
فَلَا تَعْضُلُوهُنَّ أَن يَنكِحْنَ أَزْوَاجَهُنَّ
إِذَا تَرَاضَوْا بَيْنَهُم بِالْمَعْرُوفِ ۗ
ذَٰلِكَ يُوعَظُ بِهِ
مَن كَانَ مِنكُمْ
يُؤْمِنُ بِاللَّهِ وَالْيَوْمِ الْآخِرِ ۗ

262. Let no one think that the liberty given to him can be used for his own selfish ends. If he uses the law for the injury of the weaker party, his own moral and spiritual nature suffers.

263. These difficult questions of sex relations are often treated as a joke. But they profoundly affect our individual lives, the lives of our children, and the purity and well-being of the society in which we live. This aspect of the question is reiterated again and again.

264. *Rehearse*: *zikr*. *Cf.* ii. 151 and n. 156. We are asked to remember in our own minds, and to proclaim and praise, and be proud of God's favours on us. His favours are immeasurable: not the least are His Revelations, and the wisdom which He has given to us to enable us to judge and act up to His guidance.

265. The termination of a marriage bond is a most serious matter for family and social life. And every lawful device is approved which can equitably bring back those who have lived together, provided only there is mutual love and they can live on honourable terms with each other. If these conditions are fulfilled, it is not right for outsiders to prevent or hinder re-union. They may be swayed by property or other considerations. This verse was occasioned by an actual case that was referred to the holy Apostle in his life-time.

Making for) most virtue
And purity amongst you.
And God knows,
And ye know not.

ذٰلِكُمْ أَزْكٰى لَكُمْ وَأَطْهَرُ
وَاللّٰهُ يَعْلَمُ وَأَنْتُمْ لَا تَعْلَمُونَ ○

233. The mothers shall give suck [266]
To their offspring
For two whole years,
If the father desires
To complete the term.
But he shall bear the cost
Of their food and clothing
On equitable terms.
No soul shall have
A burden laid on it
Greater than it can bear.
No mother shall be
Treated unfairly
On account of her child.
Nor father
On account of his child,
An heir shall be chargeable
In the same way.
If they both decide
On weaning,
By mutual consent,
And after due consultation,
There is no blame on them.
If ye decide
On a foster-mother
For your offspring,
There is no blame on you,
Provided ye pay (the mother)
What ye offered,
On equitable terms.
But fear God and know
That God sees well
What ye do.

٢٣٣- وَالْوَالِدٰتُ يُرْضِعْنَ أَوْلَادَهُنَّ
حَوْلَيْنِ كَامِلَيْنِ
لِمَنْ أَرَادَ أَنْ يُتِمَّ الرَّضَاعَةَ
وَعَلَى الْمَوْلُودِ لَهُ رِزْقُهُنَّ
وَكِسْوَتُهُنَّ بِالْمَعْرُوفِ
لَا تُكَلَّفُ نَفْسٌ إِلَّا وُسْعَهَا
لَا تُضَآرَّ وَالِدَةٌ بِوَلَدِهَا
وَلَا مَوْلُودٌ لَّهُ بِوَلَدِهِ
وَعَلَى الْوَارِثِ مِثْلُ ذٰلِكَ
فَإِنْ أَرَادَا فِصَالًا عَنْ تَرَاضٍ مِّنْهُمَا
وَتَشَاوُرٍ فَلَا جُنَاحَ عَلَيْهِمَا
وَإِنْ أَرَدْتُّمْ
أَنْ تَسْتَرْضِعُوٓا أَوْلَادَكُمْ
فَلَا جُنَاحَ عَلَيْكُمْ
إِذَا سَلَّمْتُمْ مَّآ آتَيْتُمْ بِالْمَعْرُوفِ
وَاتَّقُوا اللّٰهَ
وَاعْلَمُوٓا أَنَّ اللّٰهَ بِمَا تَعْمَلُونَ بَصِيرٌ ○

234. If any of you die
And leave widows behind,

٢٣٤- وَالَّذِينَ يُتَوَفَّوْنَ مِنْكُمْ وَيَذَرُونَ

266. As this comes in the midst of the regulations on divorce, it applies primarily to cases of divorce, where some definite rule is necessary, as the father and mother would not, on account of the divorce, probably be on good terms, and the interests of the children must be safeguarded. As, however, the wording is perfectly general, it has been held that the principle applies equally to the father and mother in wedlock: each must fulfil his or her part in the fostering of the child. On the other hand, it is provided that the child shall not be used as an excuse for driving a hard bargain on either side. By mutual consent they can agree to some course that is reasonable and equitable, both as regards the period before weaning (the maximum being two years) and the engagement of a wet-nurse, or (by analogy) for artificial feeding. But the mother's privileges must not be curtailed simply because by mutual consent she does not nurse the baby. In a matter of this kind the ultimate appeal must be to godliness, for all legal remedies are imperfect and may be misused.

They shall wait concerning
themselves
Four months and ten days:[267]
When they have fulfilled
Their term, there is no blame
On you if they dispose
Of themselves in a just
And reasonable manner.
And God is well acquainted
With what ye do.

أزواجا يتربصن بأنفسهن أربعة أشهر
وعشرا ۚ فإذا بلغن أجلهن
فلا جناح عليكم فيما
فعلن في أنفسهن بالمعروف ۗ
والله بما تعملون خبير ۝

235. There is no blame
On you if ye make
An offer of betrothal
Or hold it in your hearts.[268]
God knows that ye
Cherish them in your hearts:
But do not make a secret contract
With them except in terms
Honourable, nor resolve on the tie
Of marriage till the term
Prescribed is fulfilled.
And know that God
Knoweth what is in your hearts,
And take heed of Him;
And know that God is
Oft-forgiving, Most Forbearing.

٢٣٥- ولا جناح عليكم فيما عرضتم به
من خطبة النساء أو أكننتم في أنفسكم ۚ
علم الله أنكم ستذكرونهن
ولكن لا تواعدوهن سرا إلا أن تقولوا
قولا معروفا ۚ ولا تعزموا عقدة النكاح
حتى يبلغ الكتاب أجله ۚ
واعلموا أن الله يعلم ما في أنفسكم
فاحذروه ۚ واعلموا أن الله غفور حليم ۝

SECTION 31.

236. There is no blame on you
If ye divorce women
Before consummation
Or the fixation of their dower;
But bestow on them
(A suitable gift),
The wealthy
According to his means,
And the poor
According to his means;—

٢٣٦- لا جناح عليكم
إن طلقتم النساء
ما لم تمسوهن
أو تفرضوا لهن فريضة ۚ ومتعوهن
على الموسع قدره وعلى المقتر قدره

267. The *'Iddat* of widowhood (four months and ten days) is longer than the *'Iddat* of divorce (three monthly courses. ii 228). In the latter the only consideration is to ascertain if there is any unborn issue of the marriage dissolved. This is clear from xxxiii. 49. where it is laid down that there is no *'Iddat* for virgin divorcees. In the former there is in addition the consideration of mourning and respect for the deceased husband. In either case, if it is proved that there is unborn issue, there is of course no question of remarriage for the woman until it is born and for a reasonable time afterwards. Meanwhile her maintenance on a reasonable scale is chargeable to the late husband or his estate.

268. A definite contract of remarriage for the woman during her period of *'Iddat* of widowhood is forbidden as obviously unseemly, as also any secrecy in such matters. It would bind the woman at a time when she is not fitted to exercise her fullest judgment. But circumstances may arise when an *offer* (open for future consideration but not immediately decided) may be to her interests, and this is permissible. In mystic interpretation the cherishing of love in one's heart without outward show or reward is the true test of sincerity and devotion.

A gift of a reasonable amount
Is due from those
Who wish to do the right thing.

مَتَاعًا بِالْمَعْرُوفِ حَقًّا عَلَى الْمُحْسِنِينَ ○

237. And if ye divorce them
Before consummation,
But after the fixation
Of a dower for them,
Then the half of the dower
(Is due to them), unless
They remit it
Or (the man's half) is remitted[269]
By him in whose hands
Is the marriage tie;[270]
And the remission
(Of the man's half)
Is the nearest to righteousness.
And do not forget
Liberality between yourselves.
For God sees well
All that ye do.

٢٣٧- وَإِنْ طَلَّقْتُمُوهُنَّ
مِنْ قَبْلِ أَنْ تَمَسُّوهُنَّ وَقَدْ فَرَضْتُمْ
لَهُنَّ فَرِيضَةً فَنِصْفُ مَا فَرَضْتُمْ
إِلَّا أَنْ يَعْفُونَ
أَوْ يَعْفُوَا الَّذِي
بِيَدِهِ عُقْدَةُ النِّكَاحِ
وَأَنْ تَعْفُوا أَقْرَبُ لِلتَّقْوَى
وَلَا تَنْسَوُا الْفَضْلَ بَيْنَكُمْ
إِنَّ اللَّهَ بِمَا تَعْمَلُونَ بَصِيرٌ ○

238. Guard strictly
Your (habit of) prayers,
Especially the Middle Prayer;[271]
And stand before God
In a devout (frame of mind).

٢٣٨- حَافِظُوا عَلَى الصَّلَوَاتِ
وَالصَّلَاةِ الْوُسْطَى
وَقُومُوا لِلَّهِ قَانِتِينَ ○

239. If ye fear (an enemy),[272]
Pray on foot, or riding,
(As may be most convenient),
But when ye are
In security, celebrate
God's praises in the manner
He has taught you,
Which ye knew not (before).

٢٣٩- فَإِنْ خِفْتُمْ فَرِجَالًا أَوْ رُكْبَانًا
فَإِذَا أَمِنْتُمْ فَاذْكُرُوا اللَّهَ
كَمَا عَلَّمَكُمْ
مَا لَمْ تَكُونُوا تَعْلَمُونَ ○

269. The law declares that in such a case half the dower fixed shall be paid by the man to the woman. But it is open to the woman to remit the half due to her or to the man to remit the half which he is entitled to deduct, and thus pay the whole.

270. *Him in whose hands is the marriage tie*: According to Ḥanafi doctrine this is the husband himself, who can ordinarily by his act dissolve the marriage. It therefore behoves him to be all the more liberal to the woman and pay her the full dower even if the marriage was not consummated.

271. *The Middle Prayer*: *Ṣalātul-wusṭā*: may be translated "the best or the most excellent prayer." Authorities differ as to the exact meaning of this phrase. The weight of authorities seems to be in favour of interpreting this as the *'Aṣr* prayer (in the middle of the afternoon). This is apt to be most neglected, and yet this is the most necessary, to remind us of God in the midst of our worldly affairs. There is a special Sūra (S. ciii.) entitled 'Aṣr, of which the mystic meaning is appropriately dealt with under that Sūra.

272. *Verses* 238-39 are parenthetical, introducing the subject of prayer in danger. This is more fully dealt with in iv. 101-03.

240. Those of you
Who die and leave widows
Should bequeath
For their widows
A year's maintenance
And residence;[273]
But if they leave
(The residence),
There is no blame on you
For what they do
With themselves,
Provided it is reasonable.
And God is Exalted in Power,
Wise.

٢٤٠- وَالَّذِينَ يُتَوَفَّوْنَ مِنكُمْ وَيَذَرُونَ
أَزْوَاجًا ۖ وَصِيَّةً لِّأَزْوَاجِهِم
مَّتَاعًا إِلَى الْحَوْلِ غَيْرَ إِخْرَاجٍ ۚ
فَإِنْ خَرَجْنَ فَلَا جُنَاحَ عَلَيْكُمْ
فِي مَا فَعَلْنَ فِي أَنفُسِهِنَّ مِن مَّعْرُوفٍ ۗ
وَاللَّهُ عَزِيزٌ حَكِيمٌ ○

241. For divorced women
Maintenance (should be provided)
On a reasonable (scale).
This is a duty
On the righteous.

٢٤١- وَلِلْمُطَلَّقَاتِ مَتَاعٌ بِالْمَعْرُوفِ ۖ
حَقًّا عَلَى الْمُتَّقِينَ ○

242. Thus doth God
Make clear His Signs
To you: in order that
Ye may understand.

٢٤٢- كَذَٰلِكَ يُبَيِّنُ اللَّهُ لَكُمْ آيَاتِهِ
ع لَعَلَّكُمْ تَعْقِلُونَ ○

C. 51.—Fighting in defence of Truth and Right
(ii. 243-253.) **Is not to be undertaken light-heartedly,**
Nor to be evaded as a duty.
Life and Death are in the hands of God.
Not all can be chosen to fight
For God. It requires constancy,
Firmness, and faith. Given these,
Large armies can be routed
By those who battle for God,
As shown by the courage of David,
Whose prowess single-handed
Disposed of the Philistines.
The mission of some of the apostles,
Like Jesus, was different,—
Less wide in scope than that
Of Muṣṭafā. God's plan
Is universal, and He carries it out
As He wills.

---

273. Opinions differ whether the provision (of a year's maintenance, with residence), for a widow is abrogated by the share which the widow gets (one-eighth or one-fourth) as an heir (Q. iv. 12). I do not think it is. The bequest (where made) takes effect as a charge on the property, but the widow can leave the house before the year is out, and presumably the maintenance then ceases.

Section 32.

243. Didst thou not
Turn by vision to those
Who abandoned their homes,
Though they were thousands
(In number), for fear of death ?
God said to them : " Die " :
Then He restored them to life.[274]
For God is full of bounty
To mankind, but
Most of them are ungrateful.

٢٤٣- أَلَمْ تَرَ إِلَى الَّذِينَ خَرَجُوا مِن دِيَارِهِمْ
وَهُمْ أُلُوفٌ حَذَرَ الْمَوْتِ
فَقَالَ لَهُمُ اللَّهُ مُوتُوا ثُمَّ أَحْيَاهُمْ
إِنَّ اللَّهَ لَذُو فَضْلٍ عَلَى النَّاسِ
وَلَٰكِنَّ أَكْثَرَ النَّاسِ لَا يَشْكُرُونَ ○

244. Then fight in the cause
Of God, and know that God
Heareth and knoweth all things.[275]

٢٤٤- وَقَاتِلُوا فِي سَبِيلِ اللَّهِ
وَاعْلَمُوا أَنَّ اللَّهَ سَمِيعٌ عَلِيمٌ ○

245. Who is he
That will loan to God
A beautiful loan,[276] which God
Will double unto his credit
And multiply many times ?
It is God that giveth (you)
Want or Plenty,
And to Him shall be
Your return.

٢٤٥- مَّن ذَا الَّذِي
يُقْرِضُ اللَّهَ قَرْضًا حَسَنًا
فَيُضَاعِفَهُ لَهُ أَضْعَافًا كَثِيرَةً
وَاللَّهُ يَقْبِضُ وَيَبْسُطُ
وَإِلَيْهِ تُرْجَعُونَ ○

246. Hast thou not
Turned thy vision to the Chiefs
Of the Children of Israel
After (the time of) Moses ?[277]

٢٤٦- أَلَمْ تَرَ إِلَى الْمَلَإِ
مِن بَنِي إِسْرَائِيلَ مِن بَعْدِ مُوسَىٰ

274. We now return to the subject of *Jihād*, which we left at ii 214-216. We are to be under no illusion about it. If we are not prepared to fight for our faith, with our lives and all our resources, both our lives and our resources will be wiped out by our enemies. As to life, God gave it, and a coward is not likely to save it. It has happened again and again in history that men who tamely submitted to be driven from their homes although they were more numerous than their enemies, had the sentence of death pronounced on them for their cowardice, and they deserved it. But God gives further and further chances in His mercy. This is a lesson to every generation. The Commentators differ as to the exact episode referred to, but the wording is perfectly general, and so is the lesson to be learnt from it.

275. For God's cause we must fight, but never to satisfy our own selfish passions or greed, for the warning is repeated : " God heareth and knoweth all things " : all deeds, words, and motives are perfectly open before Him, however we might conceal them from men or even from ourselves. See ii. 216, n. 236.

276. Spending in the cause of God is called metaphorically " a beautiful loan ". It is excellent in many ways : (1) it shows a beautiful spirit of self-denial ; (2) in other loans there may be a doubt as to the safety of your capital or any return thereon ; here you give to the Lord of All, in Whose hands are the keys of want or plenty ; giving, you may have manifold blessings, and withholding, you may even lose what you have. If we remember that our goal is God, can we turn away from His cause ?

277. The next generation after Moses and Aaron was ruled by Joshua, who crossed the Jordan and settled the tribes in Palestine. His rule lasted for 25 years, after which there was a period of 320 years when the Israelites had a chequered history. They were not united among themselves, and suffered many reverses at the hands of the Midianites, Amalekites, and other tribes of Palestine. They frequently lapsed into idolatry and deserted the worship of the true God. From time to time a leader appeared among them who assumed dictatorial powers. Acting under a sort of theocratic commission from God, he pointed out their backslidings, re-united them under His banner, and restored, from time to time and place to place, the power of Israel. These dictators are called Judges in the English translation of the Old Testament. The last of their line was Samuel, who marks the transition towards the line of Kings on the one hand and of the later Prophets on the other. He may be dated approximately about the 11th century B.C.

They said to a Prophet[278]
(That was) among them:
" Appoint for us a King, that we
May fight in the cause of God."
He said: " Is it not possible,[279]
If ye were commanded
To fight, that that ye
Will not fight?" They said:
" How could we refuse
To fight in the cause of God,
Seeing that we were turned out
Of our homes and our families?"
But when they were commanded
To fight, they turned back,
Except a small band
Among them. But God
Has full knowledge of those
Who do wrong.

إذ قالوا لنبي
لهم ابعث لنا ملكا نقاتل في سبيل
الله ۖ قال هل عسيتم إن كتب عليكم
القتال ألا تقاتلوا ۖ
قالوا وما لنا ألا نقاتل في سبيل الله
وقد أخرجنا من ديارنا وأبنائنا ۖ
فلما كتب عليهم القتال
تولوا إلا قليلا منهم ۗ
والله عليم بالظالمين ○

247. Their Prophet said to them:
" God hath appointed
Ṭālūt[280] as king over you."
They said: " How can he
Exercise authority over us
When we are better fitted
Than he to exercise authority,
And he is not even gifted,
With wealth in abundance?"
He said: " God hath
Chosen him above you,
And hath gifted him
Abundantly with knowledge
And bodily prowess: God

٢٤٧- وقال لهم نبيهم
إن الله قد بعث لكم طالوت ملكا ۚ
قالوا أنى يكون له الملك علينا
ونحن أحق بالملك منه
ولم يؤت سعة من المال ۚ
قال إن الله اصطفاه عليكم
وزاده بسطة في العلم والجسم

278. This was Samuel. In his time Israel had suffered from much corruption within and many reverses without. The Philistines had made a great attack and defeated Israel with great slaughter. The Israelites, instead of relying on Faith and their own valour and cohesion, brought out their most sacred possession, the Ark of the Covenant, to help them in the fight. But the enemy captured it, carried it away, and retained it for seven months. The Israelites forgot that wickedness cannot screen itself behind a sacred relic. Nor can a sacred relic help the enemies of faith. The enemy found that the Ark brought nothing but misfortune for themselves, and were glad to abandon it. It apparently remained twenty years in the village (*qarya*) of Ya'ārim (Kirjath-jearim): I. Samuel, vii. 2. Meanwhile the people pressed Samuel to appoint them a king. They thought that a king would cure all their ills, whereas what was wanting was a spirit of union and discipline and a readiness on their part to fight in the cause of God.

279. Samuel knew as a Prophet that the people were fickle and only wanted to cover their own want of union and true spirit by asking for a king. They replied with spirit in words, but when it came to action, they failed. They hid themselves in caves and rocks, or ran away, and even those who remained " followed him trembling": I. Samuel, xiii. 6-7.

280. Ṭālūt is the Arabic name for Saul, who was tall and handsome, but belonged to the tribe of Benjamin, the smallest tribe in Israel. His worldly belongings were slender, and it was when he went out to search for some asses which had been lost from his father's house that he met Samuel and was anointed king by him. The people's fickleness appeared immediately he was named. They raised all sorts of petty objections to him. The chief consideration in their minds was selfishness: each one wanted to be leader and king himself, instead of desiring sincerely the good of the people as a whole, as a leader should do.

Granteth His authority to whom
He pleaseth. God careth
For all, and He knoweth
All things."

وَاللّٰهُ يُؤْتِيْ مُلْكَهٗ مَنْ يَّشَآءُ ؕ
وَاللّٰهُ وَاسِعٌ عَلِيْمٌ ○

248. And (further) their Prophet
Said to them: "A Sign
Of his authority
Is that there shall come
To you the Ark of the Covenant,[281]
With (an assurance) therein
Of security[282] from your Lord,
And the relics left
By the family of Moses
And the family of Aaron,
Carried by angels.[283]
In this is a Symbol
For you if ye indeed
Have faith."

٢٤٨- وَقَالَ لَهُمْ نَبِيُّهُمْ
اِنَّ اٰيَةَ مُلْكِهٖٓ
اَنْ يَّاْتِيَكُمُ التَّابُوْتُ فِيْهِ سَكِيْنَةٌ
مِّنْ رَّبِّكُمْ وَبَقِيَّةٌ مِّمَّا تَرَكَ اٰلُ مُوْسٰى
وَاٰلُ هٰرُوْنَ تَحْمِلُهُ الْمَلٰٓئِكَةُ ؕ
اِنَّ فِيْ ذٰلِكَ لَاٰيَةً لَّكُمْ
اِنْ كُنْتُمْ مُّؤْمِنِيْنَ ع

SECTION 33.

249. When Talūt set forth
With the armies, he said:[284]
"God will test you
At the stream: if any
Drinks of its water,
He goes not with my army:
Only those who taste not
Of it go with me:
A mere sip out of the hand
Is excused." But they all
Drank of it, except a few.
When they crossed the river,—
He and the faithful ones with him,—
They said: "This day[285]
We cannot cope
With Goliath and his forces."

٢٤٩- فَلَمَّا فَصَلَ طَالُوْتُ بِالْجُنُوْدِ ۙ
قَالَ اِنَّ اللّٰهَ مُبْتَلِيْكُمْ بِنَهَرٍ ۚ
فَمَنْ شَرِبَ مِنْهُ فَلَيْسَ مِنِّيْ ۚ
وَمَنْ لَّمْ يَطْعَمْهُ فَاِنَّهٗ مِنِّيْٓ
اِلَّا مَنِ اغْتَرَفَ غُرْفَةًۢ بِيَدِهٖ ۚ
فَشَرِبُوْا مِنْهُ اِلَّا قَلِيْلًا مِّنْهُمْ ؕ فَلَمَّا جَاوَزَهٗ
هُوَ وَالَّذِيْنَ اٰمَنُوْا مَعَهٗ ۙ
قَالُوْا لَا طَاقَةَ لَنَا الْيَوْمَ بِجَالُوْتَ وَجُنُوْدِهٖ ؕ

---

281. *Ark of the Covenant*: *Tābūt*: a chest of acacia wood covered and lined with pure gold, about 5ft. × 3ft. × 3ft. See Exod. xxv. 10-22. It was to contain the "testimony of God", or the Ten Commandments engraved on stone, with relics of Moses and Aaron. Its Gold lid was to be the "Mercy Seat", with two cherubims of beaten gold, with wings outstretched. This was a sacred possession to Israel. It was lost to the enemy in the early part of Samuel's ministry: see n. 278 to ii. 246: when it came back, it remained in a village for twenty years, and was apparently taken to the capital when kingship was instituted. It thus became a symbol of unity and authority.

282. *Security*: *sakīna* = safety, tranquillity, peace. Later Jewish writings use the same word for a symbol of God's Glory in the Tabernacle or tent in which the Ark was kept, or in the Temple when it was built by Solomon.

283. *Carried by angels*: these words refer to the Tābūt or Ark: the cherubims with outstretched wings on the lid may well be supposed to carry the security or peace which the Ark symbolised.

284. A Commander is hampered by a large force if it is not in perfect discipline and does not whole-heartedly believe in its Commander. He must get rid of all the doubtful ones, as did Gideon before Saul, and Henry V. in Shakespeare's story long afterwards. Saul used the same test as Gideon: he gave a certain order when crossing a stream: the greater part disobeyed, and were sent back. Gideon's story will be found in Judges. vii. 2-7.

285. Even in the small band that remained faithful, there were some who were appalled by the number of the enemy when they met him face to face, and saw the size and strength of the enemy Commander, the giant Goliath (Jālūt). But there was a very small band who were determined to face all odds because they had perfect confidence in God and in the cause for which they were fighting. They were for making a firm stand and seeking God's help. Of that number was David: see next note.

But those who were convinced
That they must meet God,
Said: "How oft, by God's will,
Hath a small force
Vanquished a big one?
God is with those
Who steadfastly persevere."

قَالَ الَّذِيْنَ يَظُنُّوْنَ اَنَّهُمْ مُّلٰقُوا اللّٰهِ ۙ
كَمْ مِّنْ فِئَةٍ قَلِيْلَةٍ
غَلَبَتْ فِئَةً كَثِيْرَةً ۢ بِاِذْنِ اللّٰهِ ۗ
وَاللّٰهُ مَعَ الصّٰبِرِيْنَ ○

250. When they advanced
To meet Goliath and his forces,
They prayed: "Our Lord!
Pour out constancy on us
And make our steps firm:
Help us against those
That reject faith."

٢٥٠- وَلَمَّا بَرَزُوْا لِجَالُوْتَ وَجُنُوْدِهٖ
قَالُوْا رَبَّنَآ اَفْرِغْ عَلَيْنَا صَبْرًا
وَّثَبِّتْ اَقْدَامَنَا
وَانْصُرْنَا عَلَى الْقَوْمِ الْكٰفِرِيْنَ ○

251. By God's will,
They routed them;
And David[286] slew Goliath;
And God gave him
Power and wisdom
And taught him
Whatever (else) He willed.[287]
And did not God
Check one set of people
By means of another,
The earth would indeed
Be full of mischief:
But God is full of bounty
To all the worlds.[288]

٢٥١- فَهَزَمُوْهُمْ بِاِذْنِ اللّٰهِ
وَقَتَلَ دَاوٗدُ جَالُوْتَ
وَاٰتٰىهُ اللّٰهُ الْمُلْكَ
وَالْحِكْمَةَ وَعَلَّمَهٗ مِمَّا يَشَآءُ ۗ
وَلَوْلَا دَفْعُ اللّٰهِ النَّاسَ بَعْضَهُمْ بِبَعْضٍ ۙ
لَّفَسَدَتِ الْاَرْضُ
وَلٰكِنَّ اللّٰهَ ذُوْ فَضْلٍ عَلَى الْعٰلَمِيْنَ ○

252. These are the Signs
Of God: we rehearse them
2 To thee in truth: verily
30 Thou art one of the Apostles.

٢٥٢- تِلْكَ اٰيٰتُ اللّٰهِ نَتْلُوْهَا عَلَيْكَ بِالْحَقِّ ۗ
وَاِنَّكَ لَمِنَ الْمُرْسَلِيْنَ ○

---

286. Note how the whole story is compressed into a few words as regards narration, but its spiritual lessons are dwelt upon from many points of view. The Old Testament is mainly interested in the narrative, which is full of detail, but says little about the universal truths of which every true story is a parable. The Qur-ān assumes the story, but tells the parable.

David was a raw youth, with no arms or armour. He was not known even in the Israelite camp, and the giant Goliath mocked him. Even David's own elder brother chid him for deserting his sheep, for he was a poor shepherd lad to outward appearance, but his faith had made him more than a match for the Philistine hosts. When Saul offered his own armour and arms to David, the young hero declined, as he had not tried them, while his shepherd's sling and staff were his well-tried implements. He picked up five smooth pebbles on the spot from the stream, and used his sling to such effect that he knocked down Goliath. He then used Goliath's own sword to slay him. There was consternation in the Philistine army: they broke and fled, and were pursued and cut to pieces.

Apart from the main lesson that if we would preserve our national existence and our faith it is our duty to fight with courage and firmness, there are other lessons in David's story: (1) numbers do not count, but faith, determination and the blessing of God; (2) size and strength are of no avail against truth, courage, and careful planning; (3) the hero tries his own weapons, and those that are available to him at the time and place, even though people may laugh at him; (4) if God is with us, the enemy's weapon may become an instrument of his own destruction; (5) personality conquers all dangers, and puts heart into our own wavering friends; (6) pure faith brings God's reward, which may take many forms; in David's case it was Power, Wisdom, and other gifts; see next note.

287. David was not only a shepherd, a warrior, a king, a wise man, and a prophet, but was also endowed with the gifts of poetry and music. His Psalms (*zabūr*) are still extant.

288. God's plan is universal. He loves and protects *all* His creatures and His bounties are for all worlds (i. 2.n.). To protect one He may have to check another, but we must never lose faith that His love is for all in boundless measure.

253. Those apostles
We endowed with gifts,
Some above others:[289]
To one of them God spoke;[290]
Others He raised
To degrees (of honour);[291]
To Jesus the son of Mary
We gave Clear (Signs),[292]
And strengthened him
With the holy spirit.
If God had so willed,
Succeeding generations
Would not have fought
Among each other, after
Clear (Signs) had come to them,
But they (chose) to wrangle,
Some believing and others
Rejecting. If God had so willed,
They would not have fought
Each other; but God
Fulfilleth His plan.[293]

٢٥٣- تِلْكَ الرُّسُلُ
فَضَّلْنَا بَعْضَهُمْ عَلٰى بَعْضٍ مِنْهُمْ مَّنْ
كَلَّمَ اللّٰهُ وَرَفَعَ بَعْضَهُمْ دَرَجٰتٍ
وَاٰتَيْنَا عِيْسَى ابْنَ مَرْيَمَ الْبَيِّنٰتِ
وَاَيَّدْنٰهُ بِرُوْحِ الْقُدُسِ وَلَوْ شَآءَ اللّٰهُ
مَا اقْتَتَلَ الَّذِيْنَ مِنْ بَعْدِهِمْ
مِّنْ بَعْدِ مَا جَآءَتْهُمُ الْبَيِّنٰتُ وَلٰكِنِ
اخْتَلَفُوْا فَمِنْهُمْ مَّنْ اٰمَنَ وَمِنْهُمْ مَّنْ
كَفَرَ وَلَوْ شَآءَ اللّٰهُ مَا اقْتَتَلُوْا
وَلٰكِنَّ اللّٰهَ يَفْعَلُ مَا يُرِيْدُ ۝

C. 52.—Who can describe the nature of God?

(ii. 254-283.) The Living, the Eternal: His Throne
Extends over worlds and worlds
That no imagination can compass.
His truth is clear as daylight: how
Can compulsion advance religion?
The keys of Life and Death, and the mysteries
Of everything around us, are in His hands.
Our duty then is to seek the path
Of goodness, kindness, upright
Conduct and Charity,—to grasp

---

289. Different gifts and different modes of procedure are prescribed to God's Apostles in different ages, and perhaps their degrees are different though it is not for us mortals, with our imperfect knowledge, to make any difference between one and another of God's Apostles (ii. 136). As this winds up the argument about fighting, three illustrations are given from the past, how it affected God's Messengers. To Moses God spoke in clouds of glory: he led his men for forty years through the wilderness, mainly fighting against the unbelief of his own people; he organised them to fight with the sword for Palestine, but was raised to God's mercy before his enterprise ripened, and it fell to Joshua to carry out his plan. David, though a mere shepherd boy, was chosen by God. He overthrew the greatest warrior of his time, became a king, and waged successful wars, being also a prophet, a poet, and a musician. Jesus was "strengthened with the holy spirit": he was given no weapons to fight, and his mission was of a more limited character. In Muḥammad's mission these and other characters were combined. Gentler than Jesus, he organised on a vaster scale than Moses, and from Medina he ruled and gave laws, and the Qur-ān has a vaster scope than the Psalms of David.

290. Moses: see note above.

291. There is a two-fold sense: they were raised to high posts of honour, and they rose by degrees. I take the reference to be to David.

292. *Cf.* ii. 87. See n. 401 to iii. 62.

293. If some power of choice was to be given to man, his selfishness inevitably caused divisions. It must not be supposed that it frustrates God's Plan. He carries it out as He will.

At no advantage from a brother's need,
To stand by the word that is pledged,
To bear true witness, and remove all cause
Of misunderstandings in our dealings
As between man and man.

SECTION 34.

254. O ye who believe!
Spend out of (the bounties)[294]
We have provided for you,
Before the Day comes
When no bargaining
(Will avail), nor friendship
Nor intercession.[295]
Those who reject Faith—they
Are the wrong-doers.

255. God! There is no god
But He,—the Living,
The Self-subsisting, Eternal.[296]
No slumber can seize Him
Nor sleep. His are all things
In the heavens and on earth.
Who is there can intercede
In His presence except
As He permitteth? He knoweth
What (appeareth to His creatures

۲۵۴- يَاَيُّهَا الَّذِيْنَ اٰمَنُوْٓا
اَنْفِقُوْا مِمَّا رَزَقْنٰكُمْ
مِّنْ قَبْلِ اَنْ يَّاْتِيَ يَوْمٌ لَّا بَيْعٌ فِيْهِ
وَلَا خُلَّةٌ وَّلَا شَفَاعَةٌ ؕ
وَالْكٰفِرُوْنَ هُمُ الظّٰلِمُوْنَ ○

۲۵۵- اَللّٰهُ لَآ اِلٰهَ اِلَّا هُوَ ۚ
اَلْحَيُّ الْقَيُّوْمُ ۚ
لَا تَاْخُذُهٗ سِنَةٌ وَّلَا نَوْمٌ ؕ
لَهٗ مَا فِي السَّمٰوٰتِ وَمَا فِي الْاَرْضِ ؕ مَنْ
ذَا الَّذِيْ يَشْفَعُ عِنْدَهٗٓ اِلَّا بِاِذْنِهٖ ؕ

---

294. *Spend, i.e.*, give away in charity, or employ in good works, but do not hoard. Good works would in Islam include everything that advances the good of one that is in need whether a neighbour or a stranger, or that advances the good of the community, or even the good of the person himself to whom God has given the bounty. But it must be real good and there should be no admixture of baser motives, such as vainglory, or false indulgence, or encouragement of idleness, or playing off one person against another. The bounties include mental and spiritual gifts as well as wealth and material gifts.

295. *Cf.* ii. 123 and ii. 48.

296. This is the *Āyat-ul-Kursi*, the "Verse of the Throne". Who can translate its glorious meaning, or reproduce the rhythm of its well-chosen and comprehensive words? Even in the original Arabic the meaning seems to be greater than can be expressed in words.

The attributes of God are so different from anything we know in our present world that we have to be content with understanding that the only fit word by which we can name Him is "He,"—the pronoun standing for His name. His name—God or Allāh—is sometimes misused and applied to other beings or things; and we must emphatically repudiate any idea or suggestion that there can be any compeer of God, the one true living God. He lives, but His life is self-subsisting and eternal: it does not depend upon other beings and is not limited to time and space. Perhaps the attribute of *Qaiyūm* includes not only the idea of "Self-subsisting" but also the idea of "Keeping up and maintaining all life," His life being the source and constant support of all derived forms of life. Perfect life is perfect activity, in contrast to the imperfect life which we see around us, which is not only subject to death but to the need for rest or slowed-down activity, (something which is between activity and sleep, for which I in common with other translators have used the word "slumber") and the need for full sleep itself. But God has no need for rest or sleep. His activity, like His life, is perfect and self-subsisting. Contrast with this the expression used in Psalms lxxviii. 65: "Then the Lord awaked as one out of sleep, and like a mighty man that shouteth by reason of wine."

As) Before or After
Or Behind them.[297]
Nor shall they compass
Aught of His knowledge
Except as He willeth.
His Throne doth extend[298]
Over the heavens
And the earth, and He feeleth
No fatigue in guarding
And preserving them[299]
For He is the Most High,
The Supreme (in glory).

يَعْلَمُ مَا بَيْنَ أَيْدِيهِمْ وَمَا خَلْفَهُمْ
وَلَا يُحِيطُونَ بِشَيْءٍ مِّنْ عِلْمِهِ
إِلَّا بِمَا شَاءَ
وَسِعَ كُرْسِيُّهُ السَّمٰوٰتِ وَالْأَرْضَ
وَلَا يَئُودُهُ حِفْظُهُمَا
وَهُوَ الْعَلِيُّ الْعَظِيمُ

256. Let there be no compulsion[300]
In religion: Truth stands out
Clear from Error: whoever
Rejects Evil and believes
In God hath grasped
The most trustworthy
Hand-hold, that never breaks.[301]
And God heareth
And knoweth all things.

٢٥٦- لَا إِكْرَاهَ فِي الدِّينِ
قَدْ تَبَيَّنَ الرُّشْدُ مِنَ الْغَيِّ
فَمَنْ يَكْفُرْ بِالطَّاغُوتِ وَيُؤْمِنْ بِاللَّهِ
فَقَدِ اسْتَمْسَكَ بِالْعُرْوَةِ الْوُثْقَىٰ لَا انْفِصَامَ
لَهَا وَاللَّهُ سَمِيعٌ عَلِيمٌ

257. God is the Protector
Of those who have faith:

٢٥٧- اللَّهُ وَلِيُّ الَّذِينَ آمَنُوا

297. After we realise that His Life is absolute Life, His Being is absolute Being, while others are contingent and evanescent, our ideas of heaven and earth vanish like shadows. What is behind that shadow is He. Such reality as our heavens and our earth possess is a reflection of His absolute Reality. The pantheist places the wrong accent when he says that everything is He. The truth is better expressed when we say that everything is His. How then can any creatures stand before Him as of right, and claim to intercede for a fellow-creature? In the first place both are His, and He cares as much for one as for the other. In the second place, they are both dependent on His will and command. But He in His Wisdom and Plan may grade his creatures and give one superiority over another. Then by His will and permission such a one may intercede or help according to the laws and duties laid on him. God's knowledge is absolute, and is not conditioned by Time or Space. To us, His creatures, these conditions always apply. His knowledge and our knowledge are therefore in different categories, and our knowledge only gets some reflection of Reality when it accords with His Will and Plan.

298. *Throne*: seat, power, knowledge, symbol of authority. In our thoughts we exhaust everything when we say "the heavens and the earth". Well, then, in everything is the working of God's power, and will, and authority. Everything of course includes spiritual things as well as things of sense *Cf.* Wordsworth's fine outburst in "Tintern Abbey": "Whose dwelling is the light of setting suns, And the round ocean and the living air, And in the blue sky, and in the mind of man: A motion and a spirit that impels all thinking things, all objects of all thought, And rolls through all things."

299. A life of activity that is imperfect or relative would not only need rest for carrying on its own activities, but would be in need of double rest when it has to look after and guard, or cherish, or help other activities. In contrast with this is the Absolute Life, which is free from any such need or contingency. For it is supreme above anything that we can conceive.

300. Compulsion is incompatible with religion: because (1) religion depends upon faith and will, and these would be meaningless if induced by force; (2) Truth and Error have been so clearly shown up by the mercy of God that there should be no doubt in the minds of any persons of good-will as to the fundamentals of faith; (3) God's protection is continuous, and His Plan is always to lead us from the depths of darkness into the clearest light.

301. *Hand-hold*: something which the hands can grasp for safety in a moment of danger. It may be a loop or a handle, or anchor. If it is without flaw, so that there is no danger of breaking, our safety is absolutely assured so long as we hold fast to it. Our safety then depends on our own will and faith: God's help and protection will always be unfailing if we hold firmly to God and trust in Him.

From the depths of darkness
He will lead them forth
Into light. Of those
Who reject faith the patrons
Are the Evil Ones: from light
They will lead them forth
Into the depths of darkness.
They will be Companions
Of the fire, to dwell therein
(For ever).

يُخْرِجُهُم مِّنَ الظُّلُمٰتِ إِلَى النُّورِ ۖ
وَالَّذِينَ كَفَرُوٓا أَوْلِيَآؤُهُمُ الطّٰغُوتُ
يُخْرِجُونَهُم مِّنَ النُّورِ إِلَى الظُّلُمٰتِ ۗ
أُولٰٓئِكَ أَصْحٰبُ النَّارِ ۖ
هُمْ فِيهَا خٰلِدُونَ ○

SECTION 35.

258. Hast thou not
Turned thy vision to one
Who disputed with Abraham[302]
About his Lord, because
God had granted him
Power? Abraham said:
"My Lord is He Who
Giveth life and death."
He said: "I give life and death."
Said Abraham: "But it is God
That causeth the sun
To rise from the East:
Do thou then cause him
To rise from the West."
Thus was he confounded
Who (in arrogance) rejected
Faith. Nor doth God
Give guidance
To a people unjust.[303]

٢٥٨- أَلَمْ تَرَ إِلَى الَّذِى حَآجَّ إِبْرٰهِـۧمَ فِى
رَبِّهِۦٓ أَنْ ءَاتٰىهُ اللَّهُ الْمُلْكَ ۘ
إِذْ قَالَ إِبْرٰهِـۧمُ رَبِّىَ الَّذِى يُحْىِۦ وَيُمِيتُ
قَالَ أَنَا۠ أُحْىِۦ وَأُمِيتُ ۖ
قَالَ إِبْرٰهِـۧمُ فَإِنَّ اللَّهَ
يَأْتِى بِالشَّمْسِ مِنَ الْمَشْرِقِ
فَأْتِ بِهَا مِنَ الْمَغْرِبِ
فَبُهِتَ الَّذِى كَفَرَ ۗ
وَاللَّهُ لَا يَهْدِى الْقَوْمَ الظّٰلِمِينَ ○

259. Or (take) the similitude
Of one who passed

٢٥٩- أَوْ كَالَّذِى مَرَّ عَلٰى قَرْيَةٍ

302. The three verses 258-260 have been the subject of much controversy as to the exact meaning to be attached to the incidents and the precise persons alluded to, whose names are not mentioned. M. M. A's learned notes give some indication of the points at issue. In such matters, where the Qur-ān has given no names and the Holy Apostle has himself given no indication, it seems to me useless to speculate, and still worse to put forward positive opinions. In questions of learning, speculations are often interesting. But it seems to me that the meaning of the Qur-ān is so wide and universal that we are in danger of missing the real and eternal meaning if we go on disputing about minor points. All three incidents are such as may happen again and again in any prophet's lifetime, and be seen in impersonal vision at any time. Here they are connected with Muṣṭafā's vision as shown by the opening words of verse 258.

303. The first point illustrated is the pride of power, and the impotence of human power as against God's power. The person who disputed with Abraham may have been Nimrod or some ruler in Babylonia, or indeed elsewhere. I name Babylonia as it was the original home of Abraham (Ur of the Chaldees), and Babylon prided herself on her arts and sciences in the ancient world. Science can do many wonderful things: it could then; it can now. But the mystery of Life baffled science then, as it continues to baffle science now, after many centuries of progress. Abraham had faith, and referred back everything to the true Cause of Causes. A sceptical ruler might jestingly say: "I have the power of life and death." A man of science might say: "We have investigated the laws of life and death." Different kinds of powers lie in the hands of kings and men of knowledge. The claim in both cases is true in a very limited sense. But Abraham confounded the claimer by going back to fundamentals. "If you had the ultimate power, why could you not make the sun rise from the West?'

By a hamlet, all in ruins[304]
To its roofs. He said:
"Oh! how shall God
Bring it (ever) to life,
After (this) its death?"
But God caused him
To die for a hundred years,
Then raised him up (again).
He said: "How long
Didst thou tarry (thus)?"
He said: "(Perhaps) a day
Or part of a day." He said:
"Nay, thou hast tarried
Thus a hundred years;
But look at thy food
And thy drink; they show
No signs of age; and look
At thy donkey: and that
We may make of thee
A Sign unto the people,
Look further at the bones,
How We bring them together
And clothe them with flesh."[305]
When this was shown clearly
To him, he said: "I know
That God hath power
Over all things."

وَّهِيَ خَاوِيَةٌ عَلٰى عُرُوْشِهَا ۚ
قَالَ اَنّٰى يُحْيٖ هٰذِهِ اللّٰهُ بَعْدَ مَوْتِهَا ۚ
فَاَمَاتَهُ اللّٰهُ مِائَةَ عَامٍ
ثُمَّ بَعَثَهٗ ۗ قَالَ كَمْ لَبِثْتَ ۗ
قَالَ لَبِثْتُ يَوْمًا اَوْ بَعْضَ يَوْمٍ ۗ
قَالَ بَلْ لَّبِثْتَ مِائَةَ عَامٍ
فَانْظُرْ اِلٰى طَعَامِكَ
وَشَرَابِكَ لَمْ يَتَسَنَّهْ ۚ
وَانْظُرْ اِلٰى حِمَارِكَ
وَلِنَجْعَلَكَ اٰيَةً لِّلنَّاسِ
وَانْظُرْ اِلَى الْعِظَامِ كَيْفَ نُنْشِزُهَا
ثُمَّ نَكْسُوْهَا لَحْمًا ۗ
فَلَمَّا تَبَيَّنَ لَهٗ ۙ قَالَ اَعْلَمُ
اَنَّ اللّٰهَ عَلٰى كُلِّ شَيْءٍ قَدِيْرٌ ○

260. Behold! Abraham said:
"My Lord! Show me how
Thou givest life to the dead."[306]
He said: "Dost thou not
Then believe?" He said:
"Yea! but to satisfy

٢٦٠- وَاِذْ قَالَ اِبْرٰهٖمُ رَبِّ اَرِنِيْ كَيْفَ
تُحْيِ الْمَوْتٰى ۗ قَالَ اَوَلَمْ تُؤْمِنْ ۗ
قَالَ بَلٰى وَلٰكِنْ لِّيَطْمَئِنَّ قَلْبِيْ ۗ

---

304. This incident is referred variously (1) to Ezekiel's vision of dry bones (Ezekiel, xxxvii. 1-10); (2) to Nehemiah's visit to Jerusalem in ruins after the Captivity, and to its re-building (Nehemiah, i. 12-20): and (3) to 'Uzair, or Ezra, or Esdras, the scribe, priest, and reformer, who was sent by the Persian King after the Captivity to Jerusalem, and about whom there are many Jewish legends. As to (1), there are only four words in this verse about bones. As to (2) and (3), there is nothing specific to connect this verse with either. The wording is perfectly general, and we must understand it as general. I think it does refer not only to individual, but to national, death and resurrection.

305. A man is in despair when he sees the destruction of a whole people, city, or civilisation. But God can cause resurrection, as He has done many times in history, and as He will do at the final Resurrection. Time is nothing before God. The doubter thinks that he has been dead or "tarried thus" a day or less when the period has been a century. On the other hand, the food and drink which he left behind is intact, and as fresh as it was when he left it. But the donkey is not only dead, but nothing but bones is left of it. And before the man's eyes, the bones are reunited, clothed with flesh and blood, and restored to life. Moral: (1) Time is nothing to God; (2) It affects different things in different ways; (3) The keys of life and death are in God's hands; (4) Man's power is nothing; his faith should be in God.

306. Verse 258, we saw, illustrated God's power over Life and Death, contrasted with man's vain boasts or imaginings. Verse 259 illustrated how Time is immaterial to God's working; things, individuals and nations are subject to laws of life and death, which are under God's complete control, however much we may be misled by appearances. Now in Verse 200 we are shown the power of wisdom and love: if man can tame birds so that they know him and fly to him, how much more will God's creatures obey His call at the Resurrection?

My own understanding." [307]
He said: "Take four birds;
Tame them to turn to thee;
Put a portion [308] of them
On every hill, and call to them:
They will come to thee
(Flying) with speed.
Then know that God
Is Exalted in Power, Wise."

قَالَ فَخُذْ اَرْبَعَةً مِّنَ الطَّيْرِ
فَصُرْهُنَّ اِلَيْكَ
ثُمَّ اجْعَلْ عَلٰى كُلِّ جَبَلٍ مِّنْهُنَّ جُزْءًا
ثُمَّ ادْعُهُنَّ يَأْتِيْنَكَ سَعْيًا ۭ
وَاعْلَمْ اَنَّ اللّٰهَ عَزِيْزٌ حَكِيْمٌ ۝ ع

SECTION 36.

261. The parable of those
Who spend their substance
In the way of God is that
Of a grain of corn: it groweth
Seven ears, and each ear
Hath a hundred grains.
God giveth manifold increase
To whom He pleaseth:
And God careth for all
And He knoweth all things

٢٦١- مَثَلُ الَّذِيْنَ يُنْفِقُوْنَ اَمْوَالَهُمْ
فِيْ سَبِيْلِ اللّٰهِ كَمَثَلِ حَبَّةٍ اَنْۢبَتَتْ سَبْعَ
سَنَابِلَ فِيْ كُلِّ سُنْۢبُلَةٍ
مِّائَةُ حَبَّةٍ ۭ وَاللّٰهُ يُضٰعِفُ لِمَنْ يَّشَاۗءُ ۭ
وَاللّٰهُ وَاسِعٌ عَلِيْمٌ ۝

262. Those who spend
Their substance in the cause
Of God, and follow not up
Their gifts with reminders
Of their generosity
Or with injury,—for them
Their reward is with their Lord:
On them shall be no fear,
Nor shall they grieve.

٢٦٢- اَلَّذِيْنَ يُنْفِقُوْنَ اَمْوَالَهُمْ فِيْ سَبِيْلِ
اللّٰهِ ثُمَّ لَا يُتْبِعُوْنَ مَآ اَنْفَقُوْا
مَنًّا وَّلَآ اَذًى ۙ
لَّهُمْ اَجْرُهُمْ عِنْدَ رَبِّهِمْ ۚ
وَلَا خَوْفٌ عَلَيْهِمْ وَلَا هُمْ يَحْزَنُوْنَ ۝

263. Kind words [309]
And the covering of faults

٢٦٣- قَوْلٌ مَّعْرُوْفٌ وَّمَغْفِرَةٌ

307 Abraham had complete faith in God's power, but he wanted, with God's permission, to give an explanation of that faith to his own heart and mind. Where I have translated "satisfy my own understanding," the literal translation would be "satisfy my own heart."

308. A *portion* of them: *Juz-an.* The received Commentators understand this to mean that the birds were to be cut up and pieces of them were to be put on the hills. The cutting up or killing is not mentioned, but they say that it is implied by an ellipsis, as the question is how God gives life to the dead. Of the modern Muslim Commentators, M.P. is non-committal, but H.G.S. and M.M.A. understand that the birds were not killed, but that a "portion" here means a unit, single birds were placed on hills, and they flew to the one who tamed them. This last view commends itself to me, as the cutting up of the birds to pieces is nowhere mentioned, unless we understand the word for "taming" in an unusual and almost impossible sense.

309. A very high standard is set for charity. (1) It must be in the way of God. (2) It must expect no reward in this world. (3) It must not be followed by references or reminders to the act of charity. (4) Still less should any annoyance or injury be caused to the recipient, *e.g.*, by boasting that the giver relieved the person in the hour of need. Indeed, the kindness and the spirit which turns a blind eye to other people's faults or short-comings is the essence of charity: these things are better than charity if charity is spoilt by tricks that do harm. At the same time, while no reward is to be *expected*, there is abundant reward from God—material, moral, and spiritual—according to His own good pleasure and plan. If we spend in the way of God, it is not as if God was in need of our charity. On the contrary our short-comings are so great that we require His utmost forbearance before any good that we can do can merit His praise or reward. Our motives are so mixed that our best may really be very poor if judged by a very strict standard.

Are better than charity
Followed by injury.
God is Free of all wants,
And He is most Forbearing.

خَيْرٌ مِّنْ صَدَقَةٍ يَّتْبَعُهَآ أَذًى ۭ
وَاللّٰهُ غَنِيٌّ حَلِيْمٌ ○

264. O ye who believe!
Cancel not your charity
By reminders of your generosity
Or by injury,—like those
Who spend their substance
To be seen of men,
But believe neither
In God nor in the Last Day.[310]
They are in Parable like a hard,
Barren rock, on which
Is a little soil: on it
Falls heavy rain,
Which leaves it
(Just) a bare stone.
They will be able to do nothing
With aught they have earned.
And God guideth not
Those who reject faith.

٢٦٤- يٰٓأَيُّهَا الَّذِيْنَ اٰمَنُوْا
لَا تُبْطِلُوْا صَدَقٰتِكُمْ بِالْمَنِّ وَالْاَذٰى ۙ
كَالَّذِيْ يُنْفِقُ مَالَهٗ رِئَآءَ النَّاسِ
وَلَا يُؤْمِنُ بِاللّٰهِ وَالْيَوْمِ الْاٰخِرِ ۭ
فَمَثَلُهٗ كَمَثَلِ صَفْوَانٍ
عَلَيْهِ تُرَابٌ فَاَصَابَهٗ وَابِلٌ فَتَرَكَهٗ صَلْدًا ۭ
لَا يَقْدِرُوْنَ عَلٰى شَيْءٍ
مِّمَّا كَسَبُوْا ۭ
وَاللّٰهُ لَا يَهْدِي الْقَوْمَ الْكٰفِرِيْنَ ○

265. And the likeness of those
Who spend their substance,
Seeking to please God
And to strengthen their souls,
Is as a garden, high
And fertile: heavy rain[311]
Falls on it but makes it yield
A double increase
Of harvest, and if it receives not
Heavy rain, light moisture
Sufficeth it. God seeth well
Whatever ye do.

٢٦٥- وَمَثَلُ الَّذِيْنَ يُنْفِقُوْنَ اَمْوَالَهُمُ
ابْتِغَآءَ مَرْضَاتِ اللّٰهِ
وَتَثْبِيْتًا مِّنْ اَنْفُسِهِمْ كَمَثَلِ جَنَّةٍ بِرَبْوَةٍ
اَصَابَهَا وَابِلٌ فَاٰتَتْ اُكُلَهَا ضِعْفَيْنِ ۚ
فَاِنْ لَّمْ يُصِبْهَا وَابِلٌ فَطَلٌّ ۭ
وَاللّٰهُ بِمَا تَعْمَلُوْنَ بَصِيْرٌ ○

310. False charity, "to be seen of men," is really no charity. It is worse, for it betokens a disbelief in God and the Hereafter. "God seeth well whatever ye do" (ii. 265). It is compared to a hard barren rock on which by chance has fallen a little soil. Good rain, which renders fertile soil more fruitful, washes away the little soil which this rock had, and exposes its nakedness. What good can hypocrites derive even from the little wealth they may have amassed?

311. True charity is like a field with good soil on a high situation. It catches good showers of rain, the moisture penetrates the soil, and yet its elevated situation keeps it well-drained, and healthy favourable conditions increase its output enormously. But supposing even that the rain is not abundant, it catches dew and makes the most of any little moisture it can get, and that is sufficient for it. So a man of true charity is spiritually healthy; he is best situated to attract the bounties of God, which he does not hoard selfishly but circulates freely. In lean times he still produces good works, and is content with what he has. He looks to God's pleasure and the strengthening of his own soul.

266. Does any of you wish
That he should have a garden[312]
With date-palms and vines
And streams flowing
Underneath, and all kinds
Of fruit, while he is stricken
With old age, and his children
Are not strong (enough[313]
To look after themselves)—
That it should be caught
In a whirlwind,
With fire therein,
And be burnt up?
Thus doth God make clear
To you (His) Signs;
That ye may consider.

٢٦٦ - أَيَوَدُّ أَحَدُكُمْ أَن تَكُونَ لَهُ جَنَّةٌ
مِّن نَّخِيلٍ وَأَعْنَابٍ
تَجْرِي مِن تَحْتِهَا الْأَنْهَارُ
لَهُ فِيهَا مِن كُلِّ الثَّمَرَاتِ
وَأَصَابَهُ الْكِبَرُ وَلَهُ ذُرِّيَّةٌ ضُعَفَاءُ
فَأَصَابَهَا إِعْصَارٌ فِيهِ نَارٌ فَاحْتَرَقَتْ
كَذَٰلِكَ يُبَيِّنُ اللَّهُ
لَكُمُ الْآيَاتِ لَعَلَّكُمْ تَتَفَكَّرُونَ ۝ ع

SECTION 37.

267. O ye who believe!
Give of the good things
Which ye have (honourably)
earned,[314]
And of the fruits of the earth
Which We have produced

٢٦٧ - يَا أَيُّهَا الَّذِينَ آمَنُوا
أَنفِقُوا مِن طَيِّبَاتِ مَا كَسَبْتُمْ
وَمِمَّا أَخْرَجْنَا لَكُم مِّنَ الْأَرْضِ

312. The truly spiritual nature of charity having been explained in three parables (ii. 261, 264, 265) a fourth parable is now added, explaining its bearing on the whole of our life. Suppose we had a beautiful garden well-watered and fertile, with delightful views of streams, and a haven of rest for mind and body; suppose old age were creeping in on us, and our children were either too young to look after themselves or too feeble in health; how should we feel if a sudden whirlwind came with lightning or fire in its train, and burnt it up, thus blasting the whole of our hopes for the present and for the future, and destroying the result of all our labour and savings in the past? Well, this life of ours is a probation. We may work hard, we may save, we may have good luck. We may make ourselves a goodly pleasance, and have ample means of support for ourselves and our children. A great whirlwind charged with lightning and fire comes and burns up the whole show. We are too old to begin again: our children are too young or feeble to help us to repair the mischief. Our chance is lost, because we did not provide against such a contingency. The whirlwind is the "wrath to come": the provision against it is a life of true charity and righteousness, which is the only source of true and lasting happiness in this world and the next. Without it we are subject to all the vicissitudes of this uncertain life. We may even spoil our so-called "charity" by insisting on the obligation which others owe to us or by doing some harm, because our motives are not pure.

313. *Not strong (enough)*: *ḍhu'afā-u*: literally weak, decrepit, infirm, possibly referring to both health and will or character.

314. According to the English proverb "Charity covers a multitude of sins". Such a sentiment is strongly disapproved in Islam. Charity has value only if (1) something good and valuable is given, (2) which has been honourably earned or acquired by the giver, or (3) which is produced in nature and can be referred to as a bounty of God. (1) may include such things as are of use and value to others though they may be of less use to us or superfluous to us on account of our having acquired something more suitable for our station in life; for example, discarded clothes, or an old horse or a used motor car; but if the horse is vicious, or the car engine so far gone that it is dangerous to use, then the gift is worse than useless; it is positively harmful, and the giver is a wrong-doer. (2) applies to fraudulent company-promoters, who earn great credit by giving away in charity some of their ill-gotten gains, or to robbers (even if they call themselves by high-sounding names) who "rob Peter to pay Paul". Islam will have nothing to do with tainted property. Its economic code requires that every gain should be honest and honourable. Even "charity" would not cover or destroy the taint. (3) lays down a test in cases of a doubtful gain. Can we refer to it as a gift of God? Obviously the produce of honest labour or agriculture can be so referred to. In modern commerce and speculation there is much of quite the contrary character, and charity will not cover the taint. Some kind of art, skill, or talent are God-given: it is the highest kind of charity to teach them or share their product. Others are the contrary: they are bad or tainted. In the same way some professions or services may be tainted, if these tend to moral harm.

For you, and do not even aim[315]
At getting anything
Which is bad, in order that
Out of it ye may give away
Something, when ye yourselves
Would not receive it
Except with closed eyes.[316]
And know that God
Is Free of all wants,
And Worthy of all praise.[317]

وَلَا تَيَمَّمُوا الْخَبِيْثَ
مِنْهُ تُنْفِقُوْنَ
وَلَسْتُمْ بِاٰخِذِيْهِ
اِلَّآ اَنْ تُغْمِضُوْا فِيْهِ ؕ
وَاعْلَمُوْٓا اَنَّ اللّٰهَ غَنِيٌّ حَمِيْدٌ ○

268. The Evil One threatens
You with poverty
And bids you to conduct
Unseemly. God promiseth
You His forgiveness
And bounties.[318]
And God careth for all
And He knoweth all things.

٢٦٨- اَلشَّيْطٰنُ يَعِدُكُمُ الْفَقْرَ
وَيَاْمُرُكُمْ بِالْفَحْشَآءِ ۚ
وَاللّٰهُ يَعِدُكُمْ مَّغْفِرَةً مِّنْهُ وَفَضْلًا ؕ
وَاللّٰهُ وَاسِعٌ عَلِيْمٌ ۖ ○

269. He granteth wisdom
To whom He pleaseth ;
And he to whom wisdom
Is granted receiveth
Indeed a benefit overflowing ;
But none will grasp the Message
But men of understanding.

٢٦٩- يُّؤْتِي الْحِكْمَةَ مَنْ يَّشَآءُ ۚ
وَمَنْ يُّؤْتَ الْحِكْمَةَ
فَقَدْ اُوْتِيَ خَيْرًا كَثِيْرًا ؕ
وَمَا يَذَّكَّرُ اِلَّآ اُولُوا الْاَلْبَابِ ○

270. And whatever ye spend
In charity or devotion,
Be sure God knows it all.
But the wrong-doers
Have no helpers.

٢٧٠- وَمَآ اَنْفَقْتُمْ مِّنْ نَّفَقَةٍ
اَوْ نَذَرْتُمْ مِّنْ نَّذْرٍ فَاِنَّ اللّٰهَ يَعْلَمُهٗ ؕ
وَمَا لِلظّٰلِمِيْنَ مِنْ اَنْصَارٍ ○

315. The preceding note tries to indicate some of the things which are bad or tainted. We should not even think of acquiring them for ourselves, soothing our conscience by the salve that we shall practise charity out of them.

316. *Closed eyes* imply disgust or connivance because of some feature which we would not openly acknowledge.

317. To dedicate tainted things to God is a dishonour to God, Who is independent of all wants, and Who is worthy of all honour and praise.

318. Good and evil draw us opposite ways and by opposite motives, and the contrast is well marked out in charity. When we think of doing some real act of kindness or charity, we are assailed with doubts and fear of impoverishment ; but Evil supports any tendency to selfishness, greed, or even to extravagant expenditure for show, or self-indulgence, or unseemly appetites. On the other hand, God draws us on to all that is kind and good, for that way lies the forgiveness of our sins, and greater real prosperity and satisfaction. No kind or generous act ever ruined any one. It is false generosity that is sometimes shown as leading to ruin. As God knows all our motives and cares for all, and has everything in His power, it is obvious which course a wise man will choose. But wisdom is rare, and it is only wisdom that can appreciate true well-being and distinguish it from the false appearance of well-being.

271. If ye disclose (acts[319]
Of) charity, even so
It is well,
But if ye conceal them,
And make them reach
Those (really) in need,
That is best for you:
It will remove from you
Some of your (stains
Of) evil. And God
Is well acquainted
With what ye do.

٢٧١- إِنْ تُبْدُوا الصَّدَقَٰتِ
فَنِعِمَّا هِيَ ۚ وَإِنْ تُخْفُوهَا
وَتُؤْتُوهَا الْفُقَرَآءَ
فَهُوَ خَيْرٌ لَّكُمْ ۚ
وَيُكَفِّرُ عَنكُم مِّن سَيِّـَٔاتِكُمْ ۗ
وَاللَّهُ بِمَا تَعْمَلُونَ خَبِيرٌ ○

272. It is not required
Of thee (O Apostle),
To set them on the right path,[320]
But God sets on the right path
Whom He pleaseth.
Whatever of good ye give
Benefits your own souls,
And ye shall only do so
Seeking the "Face"[321]
Of God. Whatever good
Ye give, shall be
Rendered back to you,
And ye shall not
Be dealt with unjustly.

٢٧٢- لَّيْسَ عَلَيْكَ هُدَٰهُمْ
وَلَٰكِنَّ اللَّهَ يَهْدِي مَن يَشَآءُ ۗ
وَمَا تُنفِقُوا مِنْ خَيْرٍ فَلِأَنفُسِكُمْ ۚ
وَمَا تُنفِقُونَ
إِلَّا ابْتِغَآءَ وَجْهِ اللَّهِ ۚ
وَمَا تُنفِقُوا مِنْ خَيْرٍ
يُوَفَّ إِلَيْكُمْ وَأَنتُمْ لَا تُظْلَمُونَ ○

273. (Charity is) for those
In need, who, in God's cause[322]
Are restricted (from travel),
And cannot move about

٢٧٣- لِلْفُقَرَآءِ الَّذِينَ
أُحْصِرُوا فِي سَبِيلِ اللَّهِ لَا يَسْتَطِيعُونَ

319. It is better to seek no publicity in charity. But if it is known there is no harm. If it is for public purposes, it must necessarily be known, and a pedantic show of concealment may itself be a fault. The harm of publicity lies in motives of ostentation. We can better reach the really deserving poor by quietly seeking for them. The spiritual benefit enures to our own souls, provided our motives are pure, and we are really seeking the good pleasure of God.

320. In connection with charity this means that we must relieve those really in need, whether they are good or bad, on the right path or not, Muslims or otherwise. It is not for us to judge in these matters. God will give light according to His wisdom. Incidentally it adds a further meaning to the command, "Let there be no compulsion in religion" (ii. 256). For compulsion may not only be by force, but by economic necessity. In matters of religion we must not even compel by a bribe of charity. The chief motive in charity should be God's pleasure and our own spiritual good. This was addressed in the first instance to Muṣṭafā in Medina, but it is of universal application.

321. See note to ii. 112. *Wajh* means literally: face, countenance; hence, favour, glory, Self, Presence.

322 Indiscriminate acts of so-called charity are condemned as they may do more harm than good (see ii. 262). The real beneficiaries of charity are here indicated. They must be in want. And the want must be due to some honourable cause. For example, they may be doing some unpaid service, such as teaching, or acquiring knowledge or skill, or be in exile for their faith, or in other ways be prevented from seeking employment or doing strenuous work. "God's cause" must not be narrowly interpreted. All sincere and real service to humanity comes within the definition, as well as actual devotion to religion or to the righteous Imām. Such men do not beg from door to door. It is the duty of those who are well-to-do, or of the Public Purse, to find them out.

In the land, seeking
(For trade or work):
The ignorant man thinks,
Because of their modesty,
That they are free from want.
Thou shalt know them
By their (unfailing) mark:
They beg not importunately
From all and sundry.
And whatever of good
Ye give, be assured
God knoweth it well.

ضَرْبًا فِي الْأَرْضِ
يَحْسَبُهُمُ الْجَاهِلُ أَغْنِيَاءَ مِنَ التَّعَفُّفِ
تَعْرِفُهُمْ بِسِيمَاهُمْ
لَا يَسْئَلُونَ النَّاسَ إِلْحَافًا
وَمَا تُنْفِقُوا مِنْ خَيْرٍ
فَإِنَّ اللّٰهَ بِهٖ عَلِيمٌ ○

SECTION 38.

274. Those who (in charity)[323]
Spend of their goods
By night and by day,
In secret and in public,
Have their reward
With their Lord:
On them shall be no fear,
Nor shall they grieve.

٢٧٤- اَلَّذِينَ يُنْفِقُونَ أَمْوَالَهُمْ بِالَّيْلِ
وَالنَّهَارِ سِرًّا وَّعَلَانِيَةً
فَلَهُمْ أَجْرُهُمْ عِنْدَ رَبِّهِمْ
وَلَا خَوْفٌ عَلَيْهِمْ وَلَا هُمْ يَحْزَنُونَ ○

275. Those who devour usury[324]
Will not stand except
As stands one whom
The Evil One by his touch
Hath driven to madness.[325]
That is because they say:
"Trade is like usury,"[326]
But God hath permitted trade

٢٧٥- اَلَّذِينَ يَأْكُلُونَ الرِّبٰوا لَا يَقُومُونَ
إِلَّا كَمَا يَقُومُ الَّذِي يَتَخَبَّطُهُ الشَّيْطٰنُ
مِنَ الْمَسِّ ذٰلِكَ بِأَنَّهُمْ قَالُوا إِنَّمَا الْبَيْعُ
مِثْلُ الرِّبٰوا وَأَحَلَّ اللّٰهُ الْبَيْعَ وَحَرَّمَ

---

323. We recapitulate the beauty of charity (*i.e.*, unselfish giving of one's self or one's goods) before we come to its opposite, *i.e.*, the selfish grasping greed of usury against those in need or distress. Charity instead of impoverishing you will enrich you; you will have more happiness and less fear. Contrast it with what follows,—the degradation of the grasping usurer.

324. Usury is condemned and prohibited in the strongest possible terms. There can be no question about the prohibition. When we come to the definition of Usury there is room for difference of opinion. Hadhrat 'Umar, according to Ibn Kathir, felt some difficulty in the matter, as the Apostle left this world before the details of the question were settled. This was one of the three questions on which he wished he had had more light from the Apostle, the other two being Khilāfat and Kalālat (see iv. 12. n. 518). Our 'Ulamā, ancient and modern, have worked out a great body of literature on Usury, based mainly on economic conditions as they existed at the rise of Islam. I agree with them on the main principles, but respectfully differ from them on the definition of Usury. As this subject is highly controversial, I shall discuss it, not in this Commentary but on a suitable occasion elsewhere. The definition I would accept would be: undue profit made, not in the way of legitimate trade, out of loans of gold and silver, and necessary articles of food, such as wheat, barley, dates, and salt (according to the list mentioned by the Holy Apostle himself). My definition would include profiteering of all kinds, but exclude economic credit, the creature of modern banking and finance.

325. An apt simile: whereas legitimate trade or industry increases the prosperity and stability of men and nations, a dependence on Usury would merely encourage a race of idlers, cruel blood-suckers, and worthless fellows who do not know their own good and are therefore akin to madmen.

326. The sharp opposition between legitimate trade and usury supports my definition in the last note but one. *Bai'* (literary, Sale or Barter) is also used more generally for trade and commerce, and various kinds of transactions.

And forbidden usury.
Those who after receiving
Direction from their Lord,
Desist, shall be pardoned
For the past; their case
Is for God (to judge);
But those who repeat
(The offence) are Companions
Of the Fire: they will
Abide therein (for ever).

الرِّبٰوا ۚ فَمَنْ جَآءَهٗ مَوْعِظَةٌ مِّنْ رَّبِّهٖ
فَانْتَهٰى فَلَهٗ مَا سَلَفَ ؕ
وَاَمْرُهٗۤ اِلَى اللّٰهِ ؕ
وَمَنْ عَادَ فَاُولٰٓئِكَ اَصْحٰبُ النَّارِ ۚ
هُمْ فِيْهَا خٰلِدُوْنَ ○

276. God will deprive
Usury of all blessing,
But will give increase
For deeds of charity:
For He loveth not
Creatures ungrateful
And wicked.

٢٧٦- يَمْحَقُ اللّٰهُ الرِّبٰوا
وَيُرْبِى الصَّدَقٰتِ ؕ
وَاللّٰهُ لَا يُحِبُّ
كُلَّ كَفَّارٍ اَثِيْمٍ ○

277. Those who believe,
And do deeds of righteousness,
And establish regular prayers
And regular charity,
Will have their reward
With their Lord:
On them shall be no fear,
Nor shall they grieve.[327]

٢٧٧- اِنَّ الَّذِيْنَ اٰمَنُوْا وَعَمِلُوا الصّٰلِحٰتِ
وَاَقَامُوا الصَّلٰوةَ وَاٰتَوُا الزَّكٰوةَ
لَهُمْ اَجْرُهُمْ عِنْدَ رَبِّهِمْ ۚ
وَلَا خَوْفٌ عَلَيْهِمْ وَلَا هُمْ يَحْزَنُوْنَ ○

278. O ye who believe!
Fear God, and give up
What remains of your demand
For usury, if ye are
Indeed believers.

٢٧٨- يٰۤاَيُّهَا الَّذِيْنَ اٰمَنُوا اتَّقُوا اللّٰهَ
وَذَرُوْا مَا بَقِىَ مِنَ الرِّبٰوٓا
اِنْ كُنْتُمْ مُّؤْمِنِيْنَ ○

279. If ye do it not,
Take notice of war[328]
From God and His Apostle:
But if ye turn back,
Ye shall have
Your capital sums:
Deal not unjustly,
And ye shall not
Be dealt with unjustly.

٢٧٩- فَاِنْ لَّمْ تَفْعَلُوْا فَاْذَنُوْا بِحَرْبٍ
مِّنَ اللّٰهِ وَرَسُوْلِهٖ ۚ وَاِنْ تُبْتُمْ
فَلَكُمْ رُءُوْسُ اَمْوَالِكُمْ ۚ
لَا تَظْلِمُوْنَ وَلَا تُظْلَمُوْنَ ○

327. The contrast between charity and unlawful grasping of wealth began at ii 274, where this phrase occurs as a theme. Here the theme finishes with the same phrase. The following four verses refer to further concessions on behalf of debtors, as creditors are asked to (a) give up even claims arising out of the past on account of usury, and (b) to give time for payment of capital if necessary, or (c) to write off the debt altogether as an act of charity.

328. This is not war for opinions, but an ultimatum of war for the liberation of debtors unjustly dealt with and oppressed.

280. If the debtor is
In a difficulty,
Grant him time
Till it is easy
For him to repay.
But if ye remit it
By way of charity,
That is best for you
If ye only knew.

٢٨٠- وَإِنْ كَانَ ذُو عُسْرَةٍ
فَنَظِرَةٌ إِلَىٰ مَيْسَرَةٍ ۚ
وَأَنْ تَصَدَّقُوا خَيْرٌ لَكُمْ
إِنْ كُنْتُمْ تَعْلَمُونَ ○

281. And fear the Day
When ye shall be
Brought back to God.
Then shall every soul
Be paid what it earned,
And none shall be
Dealt with unjustly.

٢٨١- وَاتَّقُوا يَوْمًا
تُرْجَعُونَ فِيهِ إِلَى اللَّهِ ۖ
ثُمَّ تُوَفَّىٰ كُلُّ نَفْسٍ مَا كَسَبَتْ
وَهُمْ لَا يُظْلَمُونَ ○ ع

SECTION 39.

282. O ye who believe!
When ye deal with each other,
In transactions involving
Future obligations
In a fixed period of time,
Reduce them to writing[329]
Let a scribe write down
Faithfully as between
The parties : let not the scribe
Refuse to write : as God[330]
Has taught him,
So let him write.
Let him who incurs
The liability dictate,
But let him fear
His Lord God,
And not diminish
Aught of what he owes.
If the party liable
Is mentally deficient,

٢٨٢- يَا أَيُّهَا الَّذِينَ آمَنُوا
إِذَا تَدَايَنْتُمْ بِدَيْنٍ
إِلَىٰ أَجَلٍ مُسَمًّى فَاكْتُبُوهُ ۚ
وَلْيَكْتُبْ بَيْنَكُمْ كَاتِبٌ بِالْعَدْلِ ۚ
وَلَا يَأْبَ كَاتِبٌ
أَنْ يَكْتُبَ كَمَا عَلَّمَهُ اللَّهُ ۚ فَلْيَكْتُبْ
وَلْيُمْلِلِ الَّذِي عَلَيْهِ الْحَقُّ
وَلْيَتَّقِ اللَّهَ رَبَّهُ
وَلَا يَبْخَسْ مِنْهُ شَيْئًا ۚ
فَإِنْ كَانَ الَّذِي عَلَيْهِ الْحَقُّ سَفِيهًا

329. The first part of the verse deals with transactions involving future payment or future consideration, and the second part with transactions in which payment and delivery are made on the spot. Examples of the former are if goods are bought now and payment is promised at a fixed time and place in the future, or if cash is paid now and delivery is contracted for at a fixed time and place in the future. In such cases a written document is recommended, but it is held that the words later on in this verse, that it is "juster...more suitable as evidence, and more convenient to prevent doubts,' etc., imply that it is not obligatory in law. Examples of the latter kind—cash payment and delivery on the spot—require no evidence in writing, but apparently oral witnesses to such transactions are recommended.

330. The scribe in such matters assumes a fiduciary capacity : he should therefore remember to act as in the presence of God, with full justice to both parties. The art of writing he should look upon as a gift from God, and he should use it as in His service. In an illiterate population the scribe's position is still more responsible.

Or weak, or unable
Himself to dictate,[331]
Let his guardian
Dictate faithfully.
And get two witnesses,
Out of your own men,[332]
And if there are not two men,
Then a man and two women,
Such as ye choose,
For witnesses,
So that if one of them errs,
The other can remind her.
The witnesses
Should not refuse
When they are called on
(For evidence).
Disdain not to reduce
To writing (your contract)
For a future period,
Whether it be small
Or big: it is juster
In the sight of God,
More suitable as evidence,
And more convenient
To prevent doubts
Among yourselves
But if it be a transaction
Which ye carry out
On the spot among yourselves,
There is no blame on you
If ye reduce it not
To writing.
But take witnesses
Whenever ye make
A commercial contract;
And let neither scribe
Nor witness suffer harm.
If ye do (such harm),
It would be wickedness
In you. So fear God;
For it is God
That teaches you.
And God is well acquainted
With all things.[333]

أَوْ ضَعِيفًا أَوْ لَا يَسْتَطِيعُ
أَنْ يُمِلَّ هُوَ فَلْيُمْلِلْ وَلِيُّهُ بِالْعَدْلِ ۚ
وَاسْتَشْهِدُوا شَهِيدَيْنِ
مِنْ رِجَالِكُمْ ۖ فَإِنْ لَمْ يَكُونَا رَجُلَيْنِ
فَرَجُلٌ وَامْرَأَتَانِ
مِمَّنْ تَرْضَوْنَ مِنَ الشُّهَدَاءِ
أَنْ تَضِلَّ إِحْدَاهُمَا
فَتُذَكِّرَ إِحْدَاهُمَا الْأُخْرَىٰ ۚ
وَلَا يَأْبَ الشُّهَدَاءُ إِذَا مَا دُعُوا ۚ
وَلَا تَسْأَمُوا أَنْ تَكْتُبُوهُ
صَغِيرًا أَوْ كَبِيرًا إِلَىٰ أَجَلِهِ ۚ
ذَٰلِكُمْ أَقْسَطُ عِنْدَ اللَّهِ
وَأَقْوَمُ لِلشَّهَادَةِ وَأَدْنَىٰ أَلَّا تَرْتَابُوا
إِلَّا أَنْ تَكُونَ تِجَارَةً
حَاضِرَةً
تُدِيرُونَهَا بَيْنَكُمْ
فَلَيْسَ عَلَيْكُمْ جُنَاحٌ أَلَّا تَكْتُبُوهَا ۗ
وَأَشْهِدُوا إِذَا تَبَايَعْتُمْ ۚ
وَلَا يُضَارَّ كَاتِبٌ وَلَا شَهِيدٌ ۚ
وَإِنْ تَفْعَلُوا فَإِنَّهُ فُسُوقٌ بِكُمْ ۗ
وَاتَّقُوا اللَّهَ ۖ وَيُعَلِّمُكُمُ اللَّهُ ۗ
وَاللَّهُ بِكُلِّ شَيْءٍ عَلِيمٌ ○

331. Possibly the person "mentally deficient, or weak, or unable to dictate," may also be incapable of making a valid contract, and the whole duty would be on his guardian, who again must act in perfect good faith, not only protecting but vigilantly promoting the interests of his ward.

332. It is desirable that the men (or women) who are chosen as witness should be from the circle to which the parties belong, as they would best be able to understand the transaction, and be most easily available if their evidence is required in future.

333. Commercial morality is here taught on the highest plane and yet in the most practical manner, both as regards the bargains to be made, the evidence to be provided, the doubts to be avoided, and the duties and rights of scribes and witnesses. Probity even in worldly matters is to be, not a mere matter of convenience or policy, but a matter of conscience and religious duty. Even our every-day transactions are to be carried out as in the presence of God.

283. If ye are on a journey,
And cannot find
A scribe, a pledge
With possession (may serve
The purpose).[334]
And if one of you
Deposits a thing
On trust with another,[335]
Let the trustee
(Faithfully) discharge
His trust, and let him
Fear his Lord.
Conceal not evidence;
For whoever conceals it,—
His heart is tainted[336]
With sin. And God
Knoweth all that ye do.

٢٨٣- وَإِنْ كُنْتُمْ عَلَىٰ سَفَرٍ
وَلَمْ تَجِدُوا كَاتِبًا
فَرِهَٰنٌ مَقْبُوضَةٌ ۖ
فَإِنْ أَمِنَ بَعْضُكُمْ بَعْضًا
فَلْيُؤَدِّ الَّذِي اؤْتُمِنَ أَمَانَتَهُ
وَلْيَتَّقِ اللَّهَ رَبَّهُ ۗ
وَلَا تَكْتُمُوا الشَّهَادَةَ ۚ
وَمَنْ يَكْتُمْهَا فَإِنَّهُ آثِمٌ قَلْبُهُ ۗ
وَاللَّهُ بِمَا تَعْمَلُونَ عَلِيمٌ ۝ ع

C. 53. – Our honesty and upright conduct
(ii. 284-286.) Are not mere matters of policy
Or convenience: all our life in this world
Must be lived as in the presence of God.
The finest example of Faith we have
In the Apostle's life: full of faith,
Let us render willing obedience
To God's Will. Our responsibility,
Though great, is not a burden
Greater than we can bear: let us
Pray for God's assistance, and He will help.

SECTION 40.

284. To God belongeth all
That is in the heavens
And on earth. Whether
Ye show what is in your minds
Or conceal it, God
Calleth you to account for it.

٢٨٤- لِلَّهِ مَا فِي السَّمَاوَاتِ وَمَا فِي الْأَرْضِ ۗ
وَإِنْ تُبْدُوا مَا فِي أَنْفُسِكُمْ
أَوْ تُخْفُوهُ يُحَاسِبْكُمْ بِهِ اللَّهُ ۖ

334. A pledge or security stands on its own independent footing, though it is a very convenient form of closing the bargain where the parties cannot trust each other, and cannot get a written agreement with proper witnesses.

335. The law of Deposit implies great trust in the Depositary on the part of the Depositor. The Depositary becomes a trustee, and the doctrine of Trust can be further developed on that basis. The trustee's duty is to guard the interests of the person on whose behalf he holds the trust and to render back the property and accounts when required according to the terms of the trust. This duty again is linked to the sanction of Religion, which requires a higher standard than Law.

336. It sometimes happens that if some inconvenient piece of evidence is destroyed or concealed, we gain a great advantage materially. We are warned not to yield to such a temptation. The concealment of evidence has a serious effect on our own moral and spiritual life, for it taints the very source of higher life, as typified by the heart. The heart is also the seat of our secrets. We are told that the sin will reach our most secret being, though the sin may not be visible or open to the world. Further, the heart is the seat of our affections, and false dealing taints all our affections.

He forgiveth whom He pleaseth,
And punisheth whom He pleaseth.
For God hath power
Over all things.

285. The Apostle believeth
In what hath been revealed
To him from his Lord,
As do the men of faith.
Each one (of them) believeth
In God, His angels,
His books, and His apostles.[337]
" We make no distinction (they say)
Between one and another[338]
Of His apostles." And they say:
" We hear, and we obey:
(We seek) Thy forgiveness,[339]
Our Lord, and to Thee
Is the end of all journeys."

286. On no soul doth God
Place a burden greater
Than it can bear.[340]
It gets every good that it earns,
And it suffers every ill that it earns.
(Pray:) " Our Lord!
Condemn us not
If we forget or fall
Into error; our Lord!
Lay not on us a burden
Like that which Thou
Didst lay on those before us;[341]

فَيَغْفِرُ لِمَنْ يَّشَآءُ وَيُعَذِّبُ مَنْ يَّشَآءُ ؕ
وَاللّٰهُ عَلٰى كُلِّ شَىْءٍ قَدِيْرٌ ۝
٢٨٥- اٰمَنَ الرَّسُوْلُ بِمَآ اُنْزِلَ اِلَيْهِ
مِنْ رَّبِّهٖ وَالْمُؤْمِنُوْنَ ؕ
كُلٌّ اٰمَنَ بِاللّٰهِ وَمَلٰٓئِكَتِهٖ
وَكُتُبِهٖ وَرُسُلِهٖ ۚ
لَا نُفَرِّقُ بَيْنَ اَحَدٍ مِّنْ رُّسُلِهٖ ۚ
وَقَالُوْا سَمِعْنَا وَاَطَعْنَا ۚ
غُفْرَانَكَ رَبَّنَا وَاِلَيْكَ الْمَصِيْرُ ۝
٢٨٦- لَا يُكَلِّفُ اللّٰهُ نَفْسًا اِلَّا وُسْعَهَا ؕ
لَهَا مَا كَسَبَتْ وَعَلَيْهَا مَا اكْتَسَبَتْ ؕ
رَبَّنَا لَا تُؤَاخِذْنَآ اِنْ نَّسِيْنَآ
اَوْ اَخْطَاْنَا ۚ
رَبَّنَا وَلَا تَحْمِلْ عَلَيْنَآ
اِصْرًا كَمَا حَمَلْتَهٗ
عَلَى الَّذِيْنَ مِنْ قَبْلِنَا ۚ

---

337. This Sūra started with the question of Faith (ii. 3-4), showed us various aspects of Faith and the denial of Faith, gave us ordinances for the new People of Islam as a community, and now rounds off the argument again with a confession of Faith and of its practical manifestation in conduct (" we hear and we obey "), and closes on a note of humility, so that we may confess our sins, ask for forgiveness, and pray for God's help and guidance.

338. *Cf.* ii. 136 and ii. 253, n. 289. It is not for *us* to make any distinction between one and another of God's apostles: we must honour them all equally, though we know that God in His wisdom sent them with different kinds of mission and gave them different degrees of rank.

339. When our faith and conduct are sincere, we realise how far from perfection we are, and we humbly pray to God for the forgiveness of our sins. We feel that God imposes no burden on us that we cannot bear, and with this realisation in our hearts and in the confession of our lips, we go to Him and ask for His help and guidance.

340. *Cf.* ii. 233. In that verse the burden was in terms of material wealth: here it is in terms of spiritual duty. Assured by God that He will accept from each soul just such duty as it has the ability to offer, we pray further on for the fulfilment of that promise.

341. We must not be arrogant, and think that because God has granted us His favour and mercy we have no need to exert ourselves, or that we are ourselves superior to those before us. On the contrary, knowing how much they failed, we pray that our burdens should be lightened, and we confess our realisation that we have all the greater need for God's mercy and forgiveness.

And so we end the whole argument of the Sūra with a prayer for God's help, not in our own selfish ends, but in our resolve to uphold God's truth against all Unbelief.

Our Lord ! lay not on us
A burden greater than we
Have strength to bear.
Blot out our sins,
And grant us forgiveness.
Have mercy on us.
Thou art our Protector ;
Help us against those
Who stand against Faith "

رَبَّنَا وَلَا تُحَمِّلْنَا مَا لَا طَاقَةَ لَنَا بِهٖ
وَاعْفُ عَنَّا
وَاغْفِرْ لَنَا
وَارْحَمْنَا أَنْتَ مَوْلٰىنَا
فَانْصُرْنَا عَلَى الْقَوْمِ الْكٰفِرِينَ

APPENDIX I.

The Abbreviated Letters (*Al-Muqaṭṭa'āt*)

Certain Sūras have certain initials prefixed to them, which are called the "Abbreviated Letters". A number of conjectures have been made as to their meaning. Opinions are divided as to the exact meaning of each particular letter or combination of letters, but it is agreed that they have a mystic meaning.

Mystic meaning, not intelligible at first sight, is not inconsistent with the character of the Qur-ān as a "plain book". The book of nature is also a plain book, but how few can fully understand it? Every one can get out of the Qur-ān plain guidance for his life according to his capacity for spiritual understanding. As his capacity grows, so will his understanding grow. The whole Book is a Record for all time. It must necessarily contain truths that only gradually unfold themselves to humanity. Even parables and tales of mystic meaning employ symbolism. The plain man may find the symbolism helpful, as a soldier finds his National Flag helpful. But what proportion of British soldiers or citizens understands the full symbolism of the British Union Jack?

This is not a mystery of the same class as "mysteries" by which we are asked to believe against the dictates of reason. If we are asked to believe that one is three and three is one, we can give no intelligible meaning to the words. If we are asked to believe that certain initials have a meaning which will be understood in the fullness of time or of spiritual development, we are asked to draw upon Faith, but we are not asked to do any violence to our reason.

I shall try to discuss some of the probable meanings of any particular abbreviated letter or set of abbreviated letters on the first occasion on which it appears in the Qur-ān. But it may be desirable here to take a general view of the facts of their occurrence to help us in appreciating the various views which are held about them.

There are 29 letters in the Arabic alphabet (counting *hamza* and *alif* as two letters), and there are 29 Sūras which have abbreviated letters prefixed to them. One of these Sūras (S. xlii.) has two sets of abbreviated letters, but we need not count this Sūra twice. If we take the half of the alphabet, omitting the fraction, we get 14, and this is the number of letters which actually occur in the Muqaṭṭa'āt.

The 14 letters, which occur in various combinations, are :—

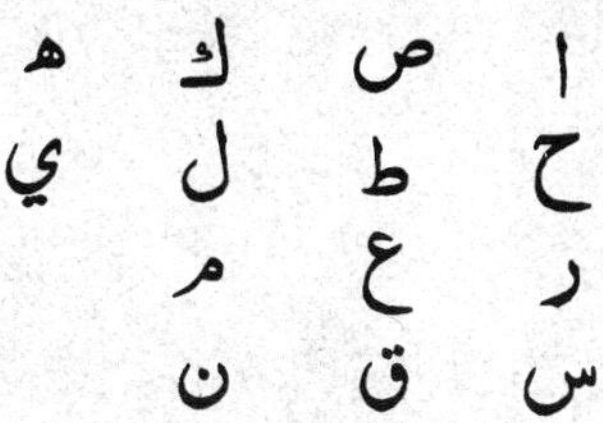

The science of phonetics tells us that our vocal sounds arise from the expulsion of the air from the lungs, and the sounds are determined by the way in which the breath passes through the various organs of speech, *e.g.*, the throat (guttural), or the various positions of the tongue to the middle or front of the palate or to the teeth, or the play of the lips. Everyone of these kinds of sounds is represented in these letters.

Let us now examine the combinations.

Three of these letters occur alone, prefixed each to only one Sūra. The letters and Sūras are:—

S. xxxviii. ص

S. l. ق

S. lxviii. ن

The combinations of two letters occur in ten Sūras as shown below. Three of them occur only once each, but the fourth (حم) occurs in seven consecutive Sūras.

S. xx. طه

S. xxvii. طس

S. xxxvi. يس

S. xl.
S. xli.
S. xlii.
S. xliii. } حم
S. xliv.
S. xlv.
S. xlvi.

Note that S. xlii. has a double combination of abbreviated letters, one of two followed by one of three. See under combinations of five.

There are three combinations of three letters each, occurring as follows in 13 Sūras:—

S. ii.
S. iii.
S. xxix.
S. xxx. } الم
S. xxxi.
S. xxxii.

S. x.
S. xi.
S. xii. } الر
S. xiv.
S. xv.

S. xxvi.
S. xxviii. } طسم

Combinations of four lettres occur twice, each only once:—

S. vii. المص

S. xiii.* المر

* Note that the three preceding and the two following Sūras have the triple letters الر .

Finally there remain the combinations of five letters, each of which occurs once only, as follows:—

S. xix. كهيعص

S. xlii. حم عسق

In S. xlii. the حم and عسق are put in separate verses. From that point of view they may be considered two separate combinations. The first combination has already been listed under the group of two-letter combinations.

This arithmetical analysis brings certain facts into prominence. I do not know how far they have a bearing on the inner meaning of the *Muqaṭṭa'āt*.

The combinations of abbreviated letters that run in a series in consecutive Sūras is noticeable. For example, حم occurs in seven consecutive Sūras from xl. to xlvi. The combination الر occurs in six consecutive Sūras x. to xv., but in one of them (S. xiii.) it is modified to المر, connecting it with the الم series. The الم series covers 6 Sūras. It begins with S. ii. and S. iii., which are practically the beginning of the Qur-ān, and ends with the four consecutive Sūras xxix. to xxxii. I call S. ii. and S. iii. practically the beginning of the Qur-ān, because S. i. is considered a general introduction to the Qur-ān, and the first Sīpāra is commonly known as الم, the first verse of S. ii. The combination طسم is prefixed to S. xxvi. and S. xxviii., but the intervening S. xxvii. has the combination طس, which may be considered a syncopated form, or the three-letter combination طسم may be considered an extended form of طس. Again the question arises: Does the م in الم, حم, and طسم, stand for the same signification, or does it mean a different thing in each case? We may generalise and say that there are three series of six, and one series of three, and the others occur all singly.

We should logically look for a common factor in the Sūras bearing the same initials, and this factor should be different for Sūras bearing other initials. In all cases where the abbreviated letters occur, there is some mention of the Qur-ān or the Book. The *Itqān* makes an exception in the case of three Sūras, *'Ankabūt* (S. xxix), *Rūm* (S. xxx), and *Nūn* (S. lxviii). But a close perusal will show that these Sūras are no exceptions. In xxix. 27 we have a reference to the Book remaining in the family of Abraham, and later on we have a whole Section, (Rukū' No. 5), devoted to the Book, with special reference to the continuity of revelation in the previous Books and the Qur-ān (xxix. 45-51). In xxx. 58 there is express mention of the Qur-ān, and the whole argument of the Sūra leads up to the intimate relation between God's "Signs" in nature (xxx. 20-27) and His revelation in the Qur-ān. In S. lxviii. the very first verse begins the theme with the Pen as the instrument of writing, exhorts Muṣṭafā to stand forth boldly to proclaim the Message, and ends (lxviii. 52) with the declaration that it is a Message for all the worlds.

These are general considerations, which I have thought it most convenient to present in the form of an Appendix.

INTRODUCTION TO SŪRA III (*Āl-i-'Imrān*).

This Sūra is cognate to Sūra II, but the matter is here treated from a different point of view. The references to Badr (Ramadhān, H. 2) and Uḥud (Shawwāl, H. 3.) give a clue to the dates of those passages.

Like Sūra II, it takes a general view of the religious history of mankind, with special reference to the People of the Book, proceeds to explain the birth of the new People of Islam and their ordinances, insists on the need of struggle and fighting in the cause of Truth, and exhorts those who have been blessed with Islam to remain constant in Faith, pray for guidance, and maintain their spiritual hope for the Future.

The new points of view developed are: (1) The emphasis is here laid on the [illegible] of the Christians to accept the new light; the Christians are here specially appealed to, as the Jews were specially appealed to in the last Sūra; (2) the lessons of the battles of Badr and Uḥud are set out for the Muslim community; and (3) the responsibilities of that community are insisted on both internally and in their relations to those outside.

Summary.—God having revealed His Book, confirming previous revelations, we must accept it in all reverence, try to understand its meaning, and reject the base motives which make Truth unacceptable to those who reject Faith. (iii. 1-20, and C. 54.)

The People of the Book had only a portion of the Book, and if they reject the complete Book, the People of Faith must part company with them, and their day is done. (iii. 21-30, and C. 55.)

The story of the family of 'Imrān (the father of Moses) leads us from the Mosaic Dispensation to the miracles connected with the birth of Jesus and his ministry. (iii. 31-63, and C. 56.)

God's revelation being continuous, all people are invited to accept its completion in Islam, and controversies are deprecated. The Muslims are asked to hold together in union and harmony, and are promised security from harm from their enemies, and enjoined to seek friendship among their own people. (iii. 64-120, and C. 57.)

The battle of Badr showed how God helps and upholds the virtuous, and how patience, perseverance, and discipline find their reward; on the other hand, the lessons of Uḥud must be learnt, not in despair, but in the exercise of the higher virtues and in contempt of pain and death. (iii. 121-148, and C. 58.)

The misfortunes at Uḥud are shown to be due to the indiscipline of some, the indecision and selfishness of others, and cowardice on the part of the Hypocrites, but no enemy can hurt God's Cause. (iii. 149-180, and C. 59.)

The taunts of the enemy should be disregarded, and sincere prayer offered to God, Who would grant His servants success and prosperity. (iii. 181-200, and C. 60.)

C. 54.—The Qur-ān revelation has, step by step,
(iii. 1-20.) Confirmed the Law of Moses and the Gospel
Of Jesus. It is a guide from God,
And appeals to reason and understanding.
Let us understand it rightly, in reverence
And truth, unswayed by those who reject
Faith, and seeking ever the reward
Of the pleasure of God, through firmness,
Patience, discipline, and charity, and offering others
The light which we have ourselves received.

Sūra III.
Āl-i-'Imrān, or The Family of 'Imrān.

In the name of God, Most Gracious, Most Merciful.

بِسۡمِ اللّٰهِ الرَّحۡمٰنِ الرَّحِيۡمِ

1. A. L. M.[342]

١-الٓمّٓ ۚ

2. God! There is no god
But He,—the Living,
The Self-Subsisting, Eternal.[343]

٢-اللّٰهُ لَآ اِلٰهَ اِلَّا هُوَ الۡحَىُّ الۡقَيُّوۡمُ ؕ

3. It is He Who sent down
To thee (step by step),
In truth, the Book,
Confirming what went before it;
And He sent down the Law
(Of Moses) and the Gospel[344]
(Of Jesus) before this,
As a guide to mankind,
And He sent down the Criterion[345]
(Of judgment between right and wrong).

٣-نَزَّلَ عَلَيۡكَ الۡكِتٰبَ بِالۡحَقِّ
مُصَدِّقًا لِّمَا بَيۡنَ يَدَيۡهِ
وَاَنۡزَلَ التَّوۡرٰىةَ وَالۡاِنۡجِيۡلَ
مِنۡ قَبۡلُ هُدًى لِّلنَّاسِ
وَاَنۡزَلَ الۡفُرۡقَانَ ؕ

4. Then those who reject
Faith in the Signs of God
Will suffer the severest
Penalty, and God
Is Exalted in Might,
Lord of Retribution.

٤-اِنَّ الَّذِيۡنَ كَفَرُوۡا بِاٰيٰتِ اللّٰهِ
لَهُمۡ عَذَابٌ شَدِيۡدٌ ؕ
وَاللّٰهُ عَزِيۡزٌ ذُو انۡتِقَامٍ

5. From God, verily
Nothing is hidden
On earth or in the heavens.

٥-اِنَّ اللّٰهَ لَا يَخۡفٰى عَلَيۡهِ شَىۡءٌ
فِى الۡاَرۡضِ وَلَا فِى السَّمَآءِ ؕ

6. He it is Who shapes you
In the wombs as He pleases.[346]

٦-هُوَ الَّذِىۡ يُصَوِّرُكُمۡ فِى الۡاَرۡحَامِ كَيۡفَ

---

342. See note to ii. 1.

343. *Cf.* ii. 255.

344. In some editions the break between verses 3 and 4 occurs here in the middle of the sentence, but in the edition of *Hāfiz* 'Uthmān, followed by the Egyptian Concordance *Fatḥ-ur-Raḥmān*, the break occurs at the word *Furqān*. In verse-divisions our classicists have mainly followed rhythm. As the word *Furqān* from this point of view is parallel to the word *Intiqām*, which ends the next verse, I have accepted the verse-division at *Furqān* as more in consonance with Quranic rhythm. It makes no real difference to the numbering of the verses, as there is only a question of whether one line should go into verse 3 or verse 4.

From this point onwards in this Sūra, M. M. A., followed by H. G. S., numbers the verses so that there is a deficiency of one compared with the accepted numbering in the most approved Texts, which I have followed, including that of the Egyptian Royal Edition and that of our Anjuman-i-Himāyat-i-Islām.

345. *Criterion* : *Furqān* : for meaning see ii. 53, n. 68.

346. Who can penetrate the mystery of life when a new life is just being born, except God? The reference to the mystery of birth prepares us for the mystery of the birth of Jesus mentioned in iii. 41 and the following verses.

There is no god but He,
The Exalted in Might,
The Wise.

7. He it is Who has sent down
To thee the Book:
In it are verses
Basic or fundamental
(Of established meaning);
They are the foundation[347]
Of the Book: others
Are allegorical. But those
In whose hearts is perversity follow
The part thereof that is allegorical,
Seeking discord, and searching
For its hidden meanings,
But no one knows
Its hidden meanings except God.
And those who are firmly grounded[348]
In knowledge say: "We believe
In the Book; the whole of it
Is from our Lord:" and none
Will grasp the Message
Except men of understanding.

8. "Our Lord!" (they say),
"Let not our hearts deviate
Now after Thou hast guided us,
But grant us mercy
From Thine own Presence;
For Thou art the Grantor
Of bounties without measure.

يَشَآءُ ۚ لَآ إِلٰهَ إِلَّا
هُوَ الْعَزِيزُ الْحَكِيمُ ○

٧- هُوَ الَّذِىٓ أَنزَلَ عَلَيْكَ الْكِتٰبَ
مِنْهُ ءَايٰتٌ مُّحْكَمٰتٌ
هُنَّ أُمُّ الْكِتٰبِ وَأُخَرُ مُتَشٰبِهٰتٌ ۖ
فَأَمَّا الَّذِينَ فِى قُلُوبِهِمْ زَيْغٌ
فَيَتَّبِعُونَ مَا تَشٰبَهَ
مِنْهُ ابْتِغَآءَ الْفِتْنَةِ وَابْتِغَآءَ تَأْوِيلِهِ ۗ
وَمَا يَعْلَمُ تَأْوِيلَهُۥٓ إِلَّا اللَّهُ ۘ
وَالرّٰسِخُونَ فِى الْعِلْمِ
يَقُولُونَ ءَامَنَّا بِهِۦ
كُلٌّ مِّنْ عِندِ رَبِّنَا ۗ
وَمَا يَذَّكَّرُ إِلَّآ أُو۟لُوا الْأَلْبٰبِ ○

٨- رَبَّنَا لَا تُزِغْ قُلُوبَنَا بَعْدَ إِذْ هَدَيْتَنَا
وَهَبْ لَنَا مِن لَّدُنكَ رَحْمَةً ۚ
إِنَّكَ أَنتَ الْوَهَّابُ ○

وقف النبى صلعم وقف لازم

347. This passage gives us an important clue to the interpretation of the Holy Qur-ān. Broadly speaking it may be divided into two portions, not given separately, but intermingled; *viz.* (1) the nucleus or foundation of the Book, literally "the mother of the Book", and (2) the part which is figurative, metaphorical, or allegorical. It is very fascinating to take up the latter, and exercise our ingenuity about its inner meaning, but it refers to such profound spiritual matters that human language is inadequate to it, and though people of wisdom may get some light from it, no one should be dogmatic, as the final meaning is known to God alone. The Commentators usually understand the verses "of established meaning" (*muḥkam*) to refer to the categorical orders of the *Sharī'at* (or the Law), which are plain to everyone's understanding. But perhaps the meaning is wider: the "mother of the Book" must include the very foundation on which all Law rests, the essence of God's Message, as distinguished from the various illustrative parables, allegories, and ordinances.

If we refer to xi. 1 and xxxix. 23, we shall find that in a sense the whole of the Qur-ān has both "established meaning" and allegorical meaning. The division is not between the verses, but between the meanings to be attached to them. Each verse is but a Sign or Symbol: what it represents is something immediately applicable, and something eternal and independent of time and space,—the "Forms of Ideas" in Plato's Philosophy. The wise man will understand that there is an "essence" and an illustrative clothing given to the essence, throughout the Book. We must try to understand it as best we can, but not waste our energies in disputing about matters beyond our depth.

348. One reading, rejected by the majority of Commentators, but accepted by Mujāhid and others, would not make a break at the point here marked *Waqfa Lāzim*, but would run the two sentences together. In that case the construction would run: "No one knows its hidden meanings except God and those who are firm in knowledge. They say", etc.

9. " Our Lord! Thou art He
That will gather mankind
Together against a Day about which
There is no doubt ; for God
Never fails in His promise." [349]

٩- رَبَّنَآ اِنَّكَ جَامِعُ النَّاسِ
لِيَوْمٍ لَّا رَيْبَ فِيْهِ ط
اِنَّ اللّٰهَ لَا يُخْلِفُ الْمِيْعَادَ ○

SECTION 2.

10. Those who reject Faith,—
Neither their possessions
Nor their (numerous) progeny
Will avail them aught
Against God : they are themselves
But fuel for the Fire.

١٠- اِنَّ الَّذِيْنَ كَفَرُوْا لَنْ تُغْنِيَ عَنْهُمْ
اَمْوَالُهُمْ وَلَآ اَوْلَادُهُمْ مِّنَ اللّٰهِ شَيْـًٔا ط
وَاُولٰٓئِكَ هُمْ وَقُوْدُ النَّارِ ○

11. (Their plight will be)
No better than that
Of the people of Pharaoh, [350]
And their predecessors :
They denied our Signs,
And God called them to account
For their sins.
For God is strict
In punishment.

١١- كَدَاْبِ اٰلِ فِرْعَوْنَ لا
وَالَّذِيْنَ مِنْ قَبْلِهِمْ ط
كَذَّبُوْا بِاٰيٰتِنَا ۚ فَاَخَذَهُمُ اللّٰهُ بِذُنُوْبِهِمْ ط
وَاللّٰهُ شَدِيْدُ الْعِقَابِ ○

12. Say to those who reject Faith:
" Soon will ye be vanquished [351]
And gathered together
To Hell,—an evil bed
Indeed (to lie on)!

١٢- قُلْ لِّلَّذِيْنَ كَفَرُوْا سَتُغْلَبُوْنَ
وَتُحْشَرُوْنَ اِلٰى جَهَنَّمَ ط
وَبِئْسَ الْمِهَادُ ○

13. " There has already been
For you a Sign

١٣- قَدْ كَانَ لَكُمْ اٰيَةٌ

349. This is the prayer of those who are firmly grounded in knowledge. The more they know, the more they realise how little they know of all the depths of Truth in the spiritual world. But they have Faith. The glimpses they get of Truth they wish to hold fast in their hearts, and they pray to God to preserve them from deviating even from what light they have got. They are sure of their eventual return to God, when all doubts will be solved.

350. From the beginning of the world, sin, oppression, arrogance, and want of Faith have gone together. The Pharaoh of the time of Moses relied upon his power, his territory, his armies, and his resources to mock at Moses the man of God and to oppress the people of Moses. God saved the Israelites and punished their oppressors through many plagues and calamities.

351. As Moses warned the Egyptians, so the warning is here sounded to the Pagan Arabs, the Jews and the Christians, and all who resisted Faith, that their resistance would be in vain. Already the battle of Badr (referred to in the next verse) had been a warning how Faith must conquer with the help of God. The next few decades saw the Byzantine and the Persian Empires overthrown because of their arrogance and their resistance to the Law of God.

In the two armies
That met (in combat) : [352]
One was fighting in the Cause
Of God, the other
Resisting God ; these saw
With their own eyes
Twice their number. [353]
But God doth support
With His aid whom He pleaseth.
In this is a warning
For such as have eyes to see."

14. Fair in the eyes of men
Is the love of things they covet : [354]
Women and sons ;
Heaped-up hoards
Of gold and silver ; horses
Branded (for blood and excellence) ;
And (wealth of) cattle
And well-tilled land.
Such are the possessions
Of this world's life ;
But in nearness to God
Is the best of the goals
(To return to).

15. Say : Shall I give you
Glad tidings of things
Far better than those ?
For the righteous are Gardens

فِىْ فِئَتَيْنِ الْتَقَتَا ۖ فِئَةٌ تُقَاتِلُ فِىْ سَبِيْلِ
اللّٰهِ وَاُخْرٰى كَافِرَةٌ
يَّرَوْنَهُمْ مِّثْلَيْهِمْ رَاْىَ الْعَيْنِ ۚ
وَاللّٰهُ يُؤَيِّدُ بِنَصْرِهٖ مَنْ يَّشَآءُ ۚ
اِنَّ فِىْ ذٰلِكَ لَعِبْرَةً لِّاُولِى الْاَبْصَارِ ۝

١٤- زُيِّنَ لِلنَّاسِ حُبُّ الشَّهَوٰتِ مِنَ
النِّسَآءِ وَالْبَنِيْنَ وَالْقَنَاطِيْرِ الْمُقَنْطَرَةِ
مِنَ الذَّهَبِ وَالْفِضَّةِ
وَالْخَيْلِ الْمُسَوَّمَةِ
وَالْاَنْعَامِ وَالْحَرْثِ ۗ
ذٰلِكَ مَتَاعُ الْحَيٰوةِ الدُّنْيَا ۚ
وَاللّٰهُ عِنْدَهٗ حُسْنُ الْمَاٰبِ ۝

١٥- قُلْ اَؤُنَبِّئُكُمْ بِخَيْرٍ مِّنْ ذٰلِكُمْ ۗ
لِلَّذِيْنَ اتَّقَوْا عِنْدَ رَبِّهِمْ جَنّٰتٌ

352. This refers to the battle of Badr in Ramadhān in the second year of the Hijra. The little exiled community of Meccan Muslims, with their friends in Medina, had organised themselves into a God-fearing community, but were constantly in danger of being attacked by their Pagan enemies of Mecca, in alliance with some of the disaffected elements (Jews and Hypocrites) in or near Medina itself. The design of the Meccans was to gather all the resources they could, and with an overwhelming force, to crush and annihilate Muḥammad and his party. To this end Abū Sufyān was leading a richly-laden caravan from Syria to Mecca. He called for armed aid from Mecca. The battle was fought in the plain of Badr, about 50 miles south-west of Medina. The Muslim force consisted of only about 313 men, mostly unarmed, but they were led by Muḥammad, and they were fighting for their Faith. The Meccan army, well-armed and well-equipped, numbered over a thousand and had among its leaders some of the most experienced warriors of Arabia, including Abū Jahl, the inveterate foe and persecutor of Islam. Against all odds the Muslims won a brilliant victory, and many of the enemy leaders, including Abū Jahl, were killed.

353. It was impossible, without the miraculous aid of God, for such a small and ill-equipped force as was the Muslim band, to defeat the large and well-found force of the enemy. But their firmness, zeal, and discipline won them divine aid. Enemy prisoners stated that the enemy ranks saw the Muslim force to be many times larger than it was.

354. The pleasures of this world are first enumerated : women for love ; sons for strength and pride ; hoarded riches, which procure all luxuries ; the best and finest pedigree horses ; cattle, the measure of wealth in the ancient world, as well as the means and symbols of good farming in the modern world ; and broad acres of well-tilled land. By analogy, we may include, for our mechanized age, machines of all kinds,—tractors, motor-cars, aeroplanes, the best internal-combustion engines, etc., etc. In "heaped-up hoards of gold and silver," the Arabic word translated *hoards* is *qanāṭīr* plural of *quintār*, which literally means a Talent of 1,200 ounces of gold. That quantity of pure gold would coin into 5,097 sterling gold sovereigns, each containing 123·274 grains of gold 22 carats fine. These at present prices (say, Rs. 20 to the sovereign) would be worth more than a lakh of rupees. Heaped hoards of *qanāṭīr* would therefore be boundless wealth "as wish can claim".

In nearness to their Lord,
With rivers flowing beneath;
Therein is their eternal home;
With Companions pure (and holy);[355]
And the good pleasure of God.
For in God's sight
Are (all) His servants,—

تَجْرِي مِن تَحْتِهَا الْأَنْهَارُ
خَالِدِينَ فِيهَا وَأَزْوَاجٌ مُّطَهَّرَةٌ
وَرِضْوَانٌ مِّنَ اللَّهِ ۗ
وَاللَّهُ بَصِيرٌ بِالْعِبَادِ ۝

16. (Namely), those who say:
"Our Lord! we have indeed
Believed: forgive us, then,
Our sins, and save us
From the agony of the Fire;"—

١٦- الَّذِينَ يَقُولُونَ رَبَّنَا
إِنَّنَا آمَنَّا فَاغْفِرْ لَنَا ذُنُوبَنَا
وَقِنَا عَذَابَ النَّارِ ۝

17. Those who show patience,
Firmness and self-control;[356]
Who are true (in word and deed);
Who worship devoutly;
Who spend (in the way of God);
And who pray for forgiveness
In the early hours of the morning.[357]

١٧- الصَّابِرِينَ وَالصَّادِقِينَ
وَالْقَانِتِينَ وَالْمُنفِقِينَ
وَالْمُسْتَغْفِرِينَ بِالْأَسْحَارِ ۝

18. There is no god but He:
That is the witness of God,
His angels, and those endued
With knowledge, standing firm[358]
On justice. There is no god but He,
The Exalted in Power,
The Wise.

١٨- شَهِدَ اللَّهُ أَنَّهُ لَا إِلَٰهَ إِلَّا هُوَ
وَالْمَلَائِكَةُ وَأُولُو الْعِلْمِ قَائِمًا بِالْقِسْطِ ۚ
لَا إِلَٰهَ إِلَّا هُوَ الْعَزِيزُ الْحَكِيمُ ۝

19. The Religion before God
Is Islam (submission to His Will):
Nor did the People of the Book
Dissent therefrom except

١٩- إِنَّ الدِّينَ عِندَ اللَّهِ الْإِسْلَامُ ۗ
وَمَا اخْتَلَفَ الَّذِينَ أُوتُوا الْكِتَابَ

355. *Cf.* ii. 25 and n. 44.

356. *Ṣabr* (Ṣābirīn) includes many shades of meaning: I have specified three here, *viz.*, patience, firmness, and self-control. See ii. 45 and ii. 153 and notes thereon.

357. True servants of God are described in iii. 16 and 17. They have faith, humility, and hope (iii. 16); and they have certain virtues (iii. 17) *viz.*, (1) patience, steadfastness, self-restraint, and all that goes under the full definition of Ṣabr; this shows a certain attitude of mind; (2) in all their dealings they are true and sincere as they are also in their promises and words; this marks them out in social conduct: (3) further, their spiritual worship is earnest and deep, an inner counterpart of their outward conduct; (4) their worship of God shows itself in their love of their fellow-men, for they are ready and liberal in charity; and (5) their self-discipline is so great that the first thing they do every morning is humbly to approach their God.

358. God Himself speaks to us through His revelations (through angels) and through His Creation, for all Nature glorifies God. No thinking mind, if it only judges the matter fairly, can fail to find the same witness in his own heart and conscience. All this points to the Unity of God, His exalted nature, and His wisdom.

Through envy of each other,[359]
After knowledge had come to them.
But if any deny the Signs of God,
God is swift in calling to account.

الَّا مِنْ بَعْدِ مَا جَاۗءَهُمُ الْعِلْمُ بَغْيًا بَيْنَهُمْ ۭ وَمَنْ يَّكْفُرْ بِاٰيٰتِ اللّٰهِ فَاِنَّ اللّٰهَ سَرِيْعُ الْحِسَابِ ۝

20. So if they dispute with thee,
Say: "I have submitted
My whole self[360] to God
And so have those
Who follow me."
And say to the People of the Book
And to those who are unlearned:[361]
"Do ye (also) submit yourselves?"
If they do, they are in right guidance,
But if they turn back,
Thy duty is to convey the Message;
And in God's sight
Are (all) His servants.[362]

٢٠- فَاِنْ حَاۗجُّوْكَ فَقُلْ اَسْلَمْتُ وَجْهِيَ لِلّٰهِ وَمَنِ اتَّبَعَنِ ۭ
وَقُلْ لِّلَّذِيْنَ اُوْتُوا الْكِتٰبَ وَالْاُمِّيّٖنَ ءَاَسْلَمْتُمْ ۭ
فَاِنْ اَسْلَمُوْا فَقَدِ اھْتَدَوْا ۚ
وَاِنْ تَوَلَّوْا فَاِنَّمَا عَلَيْكَ الْبَلٰغُ ۭ
وَاللّٰهُ بَصِيْرٌۢ بِالْعِبَادِ ۝ ع

C. 55.—If the People who received
(iii. 21-30.) Earlier revelations confine themselves
To partial truths, and in their pride
Shut their eyes to the whole of the Book
Of God, their day is done:
Let the Muslims seek the society
And friendship of their own, and trust
In God, who knows all, and holds
Every soul responsible for its own deeds.

SECTION 3.

21. As to those who deny
The Signs of God, and in defiance

٢١- اِنَّ الَّذِيْنَ يَكْفُرُوْنَ بِاٰيٰتِ اللّٰهِ

359. *Bagyan*: through envy, through selfish contumacy or obstinacy, through sheer contrary-mindedness, or desire to resist or rebel. *Cf.* ii. 90, and ii. 213.

360. *Wajh*: whole self. See n. 114 to ii. 112.

361. The People of the Book may be supposed to know something about the previous religious history of mankind. To them the appeal should be easy and intelligible, as all Religion is one, and it is only being renewed in Islam. But the appeal is also made to the Pagan Arabs, who are unlearned, and who can well be expected to follow the example of one of their own, who received divine enlightenment, and was able to bring new knowledge to them. A great many of both these classes did so. But the few who resisted God's grace, and actually threatened and persecuted those who believed, are told that God will look after His own.

362. Note the literary skill in the argument as it proceeds. The mystery of birth faintly suggests that we are coming to the story of Jesus. The exposition of the Book suggests that Islam is the same religion as that of the People of the Book. Next we are told that the People of the Book made their religion one-sided, and through the priesthood of the family of 'Imrān, we are brought to the story of Jesus, who was rejected by a body of the Jews as Muḥammad was rejected by a body of both Jews and Christians.

Of right,[363] slay the prophets,
And slay those who teach
Just dealing whith mankind,[364]
Announce to them a grievous
penalty.

وَيَقْتُلُوْنَ النَّبِيّٖنَ بِغَيْرِ حَقٍّ ۙ وَّيَقْتُلُوْنَ
الَّذِيْنَ يَاْمُرُوْنَ بِالْقِسْطِ مِنَ النَّاسِ ۙ
فَبَشِّرْهُمْ بِعَذَابٍ اَلِيْمٍ ○

22. They are those whose works
Will bear no fruit[365]
In this world
And in the Hereafter,
Nor will they have
Anyone to help.

٢٢- اُولٰٓئِكَ الَّذِيْنَ حَبِطَتْ اَعْمَالُهُمْ
فِى الدُّنْيَا وَالْاٰخِرَةِ
وَمَا لَهُمْ مِّنْ نّٰصِرِيْنَ ○

23. Hast thou not turned
Thy vision to those
Who have been given a portion[366]
Of the Book ? They are
Invited to the Book of God,
To settle their dispute,
But a party of them
Turn back and decline
(The arbitration).[367]

٢٣- اَلَمْ تَرَ اِلَى الَّذِيْنَ اُوْتُوْا نَصِيْبًا مِّنَ
الْكِتٰبِ يُدْعَوْنَ اِلٰى كِتٰبِ اللّٰهِ
لِيَحْكُمَ بَيْنَهُمْ ثُمَّ يَتَوَلّٰى فَرِيْقٌ مِّنْهُمْ
وَهُمْ مُّعْرِضُوْنَ ○

24. This because they say:
" The Fire shall not touch us
But for a few numbered days ":[368]
For their forgeries deceive them
As to their own religion.

٢٤- ذٰلِكَ بِاَنَّهُمْ قَالُوْا لَنْ تَمَسَّنَا النَّارُ
اِلَّآ اَيَّامًا مَّعْدُوْدٰتٍ
وَغَرَّهُمْ فِىْ دِيْنِهِمْ مَّا كَانُوْا يَفْتَرُوْنَ ○

25. But how (will they fare)
When We gather them together

٢٥- فَكَيْفَ اِذَا جَمَعْنٰهُمْ

---

363. *Right* : *ḥaqq* has many shades of meaning : (1) right, in the sense of having a right to something ; (2) right, in the sense of straight conduct, as opposed to wrong ; (3) truth ; (4) justice. All these shades are implied here.

364. Examples of the Prophets slain were : "the righteous blood shed upon the earth, from the blood of righteous Abel unto the blood of Zacharias, son of Barachias, whom ye slew between the temple and the altar": Matt. xxiii. 35. *Cf.* Q. ii. 61, n. 75. Again, John the Baptist (Yaḥyā, noble, chaste, a prophet, of the goodly company of the righteous, Q. iii. 39), was bound, imprisoned, and beheaded, and his head presented to a dancing harlot : Matt. xiv. 1-11. An example of a just man in another nation, who taught righteousness and was put to death, was Socrates, the Greek philosopher.

365. *Cf.* ii. 217, end.

366. *A portion of the Book.* I conceive that God's revelation as a whole throughout the ages is "The Book". The Law of Moses, and the Gospel of Jesus were portions of the Book. The Qur-ān completes the revelation and is *par excellence* the Book of God.

367. The Commentators mention a particular incident when a dispute was submitted by the Jews for arbitration to the Holy Apostle. He appealed to the authority of their own books, but they tried to conceal and prevaricate. The general lesson is that the People of the Book should have been the first to welcome in Muḥammad the living exponent of the Message of God as a whole, and some of them did so ; but others turned away from guilty arrogance, relying on corrupted texts and doctrines forged out of their own fancies, though they were not conformable to reason and good sense.

368. *Cf.* Q. ii. 80.

Against a Day about which
There is no doubt,
And each soul will be paid out
Just what it has earned,
Without (favour or) injustice?

لِيَوْمٍ لَّا رَيْبَ فِيهِ
وَوُفِّيَتْ كُلُّ نَفْسٍ مَّا كَسَبَتْ
وَهُمْ لَا يُظْلَمُونَ ○

26. Say: "O God!
Lord of Power (and Rule),
Thou givest Power
To whom Thou pleasest,
And Thou strippest off Power
From whom Thou pleasest:
Thou enduest with honour
Whom Thou pleasest,
And Thou bringest low
Whom Thou pleasest:
In Thy hand is all Good.[369]
Verily, over all things
Thou hast power.

٢٦- قُلِ اللّٰهُمَّ مٰلِكَ الْمُلْكِ
تُؤْتِي الْمُلْكَ مَنْ تَشَآءُ
وَتَنْزِعُ الْمُلْكَ مِمَّنْ تَشَآءُ
وَتُعِزُّ مَنْ تَشَآءُ
وَتُذِلُّ مَنْ تَشَآءُ
بِيَدِكَ الْخَيْرُ
إِنَّكَ عَلٰى كُلِّ شَيْءٍ قَدِيرٌ ○

27. "Thou causest the Night
To gain on the Day,
And Thou causest the Day
To gain on the Night;[370]
Thou bringest the Living
Out of the Dead,
And Thou bringest the Dead
Out of the Living;[371]
And Thou givest sustenance
To whom Thou pleasest,
Without measure."[372]

٢٧- تُولِجُ الَّيْلَ فِي النَّهَارِ
وَتُولِجُ النَّهَارَ فِي الَّيْلِ
وَتُخْرِجُ الْحَيَّ مِنَ الْمَيِّتِ
وَتُخْرِجُ الْمَيِّتَ مِنَ الْحَيِّ
وَتَرْزُقُ مَنْ تَشَآءُ بِغَيْرِ حِسَابٍ ○

28. Let not the Believers
Take for friends or helpers

٢٨- لَا يَتَّخِذِ الْمُؤْمِنُونَ الْكٰفِرِينَ أَوْلِيَآءَ

369. Another glorious passage, full of meaning, both obvious and mystic. The governing phrase in it all is: "In Thy hand is all Good." What is the standard by which we may judge Good? It is God's Will. Therefore when we submit to God's Will, and real Islam illuminates us, we see the highest Good. There has been and is much controversy as to what is the Highest Good. To the Muslim there is no difficulty: it is the Will of God. He must ever strive to learn and understand that Will. But once in that fortress, he is secure. He is not troubled with the nature of Evil. Evil is the negation of God's Will. Good is conformity to God's Will. He does not cry with impatience against many things which give him pain and sorrow. He knows that "God is in His world", and that God is Good. God's Will is another name for God's Plan. There is nothing arbitrary or haphazard. We do not see the whole Plan or Will. But we have Faith. All is, will be, must be, right in the end.

370. True in many senses. In every twenty-four hours, night merges into day, and day into night, and there is no clear boundary between them. In every solar year, the night gains on the day after the summer solstice, and the day gains on the night after the winter solstice. But further, if light and darkness are viewed as symbols of (*a*) knowledge and ignorance, (*b*) happiness and misery, (*c*) spiritual insight and spiritual blindness, God's Plan or Will works here too as in the physical world, and in His hand is all Good.

371. We can interpret Dead and Living in even more senses than Day and Night: death physical, intellectual, emotional, spiritual. Life and Death may also apply to collective, group, or national life. And who has ever solved the mystery of Life? But Faith refers it to God's Will and Plan.

372. Again true in all the senses suggested in the two previous notes. The only true Reality is God. All else has its basis and sustenance in Him. Lest our little minds create fear out of "nicely calculated less or more", we are told at once that God's bounty is without measure or account.

Unbelievers rather than
Believers: if any do that,
In nothing will there be help
From God: except by way
Of precaution, that ye may
Guard yourselves from them.[373]
But God cautions you
(To remember) Himself;
For the final goal
Is to God.

مِنْ دُوْنِ الْمُؤْمِنِيْنَ ۚ
وَمَنْ يَّفْعَلْ ذٰلِكَ فَلَيْسَ مِنَ اللّٰهِ فِيْ
شَيْءٍ اِلَّآ اَنْ تَتَّقُوْا مِنْهُمْ تُقٰىةً ۗ
وَيُحَذِّرُكُمُ اللّٰهُ نَفْسَهٗ ۗ
وَاِلَى اللّٰهِ الْمَصِيْرُ ○

29. Say: "Whether ye hide
What is in your hearts
Or reveal it,
God knows it all:
He knows what is
In the heavens,
And what is on earth.
And God has power
Over all things.

٢٩- قُلْ اِنْ تُخْفُوْا مَا فِيْ صُدُوْرِكُمْ
اَوْ تُبْدُوْهُ يَعْلَمْهُ اللّٰهُ ۗ
وَيَعْلَمُ مَا فِي السَّمٰوٰتِ وَمَا فِي الْاَرْضِ ۗ
وَاللّٰهُ عَلٰى كُلِّ شَيْءٍ قَدِيْرٌ ○

30. "On the Day when every soul
Will be confronted
With all the good it has done,
And all the evil it has done,
It will wish there were
A great distance
Between it and its evil.
But God cautions you
(To remember) Himself.
And God is full of kindness
To those that serve Him."

٣٠- يَوْمَ تَجِدُ كُلُّ نَفْسٍ
مَّا عَمِلَتْ مِنْ خَيْرٍ مُّحْضَرًا ۚ
وَمَا عَمِلَتْ مِنْ سُوْٓءٍ ۚ
تَوَدُّ لَوْ اَنَّ بَيْنَهَا وَبَيْنَهٗٓ اَمَدًا بَعِيْدًا ۗ
وَيُحَذِّرُكُمُ اللّٰهُ نَفْسَهٗ ۗ
وَاللّٰهُ رَءُوْفٌ بِالْعِبَادِ ○

معانقة عند المتأخرين

C. 56.—God's truth is continuous, and His Apostles
(iii. 31-63.) From Adam, through Noah and Abraham,
Down to the last of the Prophets, Muḥammad,
Form one brotherhood. Of the progeny
Of 'Imrān, father of Moses and Aaron,
Sprang a woman, who devoted
Her unborn offspring to God.
The child was Mary the mother of Jesus.
Her cousin was the wife of the priest
Zakarīya, who took charge of Mary.

373. If Faith is a fundamental matter in our lives our associations and friendships will naturally be with those who share our Faith. "Evil communications corrupt good manners": and evil company may corrupt Faith. In our ordinary every-day affairs of business, we are asked to seek the help of Believers rather than Unbelievers. Only in this way can our community be strong in organisation and unity. But where there is no question of preference, or where in self-defence we have to take the assistance of those not belonging to our Faith, that is permissible. In any case we must not weaken our Brotherhood: we must try to make it stronger if possible.

To Zakarīya, in his old age, was born
A son Yaḥyā, amid prodigies :
Yahyā was the herald of Jesus
The son of Mary, and was known
As John the Baptist. Jesus
Was of virgin birth,
And performed many miracles.
But those to whom he came as Prophet
Rejected him, and plotted for his death.
Their plots failed, for God's Plan
Is above man's plots. So will it be
With Islam, the Truth from all eternity.

SECTION 4.

31. Say : " If ye do love God, Follow me : God will love you And forgive you your sins : For God is Oft-Forgiving, Most Merciful. "	٣١- قُلْ إِنْ كُنْتُمْ تُحِبُّونَ اللّٰهَ فَاتَّبِعُونِي يُحْبِبْكُمُ اللّٰهُ وَيَغْفِرْ لَكُمْ ذُنُوبَكُمْ وَاللّٰهُ غَفُورٌ رَّحِيمٌ ۝
32. Say : " Obey God And His Apostle " : But if they turn back, God loveth not those Who reject Faith.	٣٢- قُلْ أَطِيعُوا اللّٰهَ وَالرَّسُولَ ۚ فَإِنْ تَوَلَّوْا فَإِنَّ اللّٰهَ لَا يُحِبُّ الْكٰفِرِينَ ۝
33. God did choose Adam and Noah, the family Of Abraham, and the family Of 'Imrān above all people,—	٣٣- إِنَّ اللّٰهَ اصْطَفٰى اٰدَمَ وَنُوحًا وَاٰلَ إِبْرٰهِيمَ وَاٰلَ عِمْرٰنَ عَلَى الْعٰلَمِينَ ۝
34. Offspring, one of the other : [374] And God heareth And knoweth all things.	٣٤- ذُرِّيَّةً بَعْضُهَا مِنْ بَعْضٍ ۗ وَاللّٰهُ سَمِيعٌ عَلِيمٌ ۝
35. Behold ! a woman of 'Imrān [375] Said : " O my Lord ! I do	٣٥- إِذْ قَالَتِ امْرَاَتُ عِمْرٰنَ رَبِّ إِنِّي

374. The Prophets in the Jewish-Christian-Muslim Dispensation form one family literally. But the argument is wider. All men of God form spiritually one family. If you love and obey God, love and obey His Messenger who is actually present with you (in the flesh or in his teaching). Your love, obedience, and discipline will be the test of your Faith.

375. Now we begin the story of Jesus. As a prelude we have the birth of Mary and the parallel story of John the Baptist, Yaḥyā the son of Zakarīya. Yaḥyā's mother Elisabeth was a cousin of Mary the mother of Jesus (Luke i. 36), and therefore John and Jesus were cousins by blood, and there was a spiritual cousinhood in their birth and career. Elisabeth was of the daughters of Aaron (Luke i. 5), of a priestly family which went back to Aaron the brother of Moses and son of 'Imrān. Her husband Zakarīya was actually a priest, and her cousin Mary was presumably also of a priestly family. By tradition Mary's mother was called Hannah (in Latin, Anna, and in English, Anne), and her father was called 'Imrān. Hannah is therefore both a descendant of the priestly house of 'Imrān and the wife of 'Imrān,—" a woman of 'Imrān " in a double sense.

Dedicate unto Thee
What is in my womb
For Thy special service:[376]
So accept this of me:
For Thou hearest
And knowest all things."

نَذَرْتُ لَكَ مَا فِي بَطْنِي مُحَرَّرًا
فَتَقَبَّلْ مِنِّي
إِنَّكَ أَنتَ السَّمِيعُ الْعَلِيمُ ○

36. When she was delivered,
She said: "O my Lord!
Behold! I am delivered
Of a female child!"—
And God knew best
What she brought forth—[377]
"And nowise is the male
Like the female.[378]
I have named her Mary,
And I commend her
And her offspring
To Thy protection
From the Evil One,
The Rejected."

٣٦- فَلَمَّا وَضَعَتْهَا قَالَتْ رَبِّ إِنِّي وَضَعْتُهَا
أُنثَىٰ
وَاللَّهُ أَعْلَمُ بِمَا وَضَعَتْ
وَلَيْسَ الذَّكَرُ كَالْأُنثَىٰ
وَإِنِّي سَمَّيْتُهَا مَرْيَمَ
وَإِنِّي أُعِيذُهَا بِكَ
وَذُرِّيَّتَهَا مِنَ الشَّيْطَانِ الرَّجِيمِ ○

37. Right graciously
Did her Lord accept her:
He made her grow
In purity and beauty:
To the care of Zakariya
Was she assigned.
Every time that he entered
(Her) chamber to see her,
He found her supplied
With sustenance. He said:
"O Mary! Whence (comes) this
To you?" She said:
"From God: for God
Provides sustenance
To whom He pleases,
Without measure."[379]

٣٧- فَتَقَبَّلَهَا رَبُّهَا بِقَبُولٍ حَسَنٍ
وَأَنبَتَهَا نَبَاتًا حَسَنًا وَكَفَّلَهَا زَكَرِيَّا
كُلَّمَا دَخَلَ عَلَيْهَا زَكَرِيَّا الْمِحْرَابَ
وَجَدَ عِندَهَا رِزْقًا
قَالَ يَا مَرْيَمُ أَنَّىٰ لَكِ هَٰذَا
قَالَتْ هُوَ مِنْ عِندِ اللَّهِ
إِنَّ اللَّهَ يَرْزُقُ مَن يَشَاءُ
بِغَيْرِ حِسَابٍ ○

---

376. *Muḥarrar*=freed from all worldly affairs and specially dedicated to God's service. She expected a son, who was to be a special devotee, a miraculous son of the old age of his parents, but God gave her instead a daughter. But that daughter was Mary the mother of Jesus, the chosen one among the women: iii. 42.

377. The mother of Mary expected a male child. Was she disappointed that it was a female child? No, for she had Faith, and she knew that God's Plan was better than any wishes of hers. Mary was no ordinary girl: only God knew what it was that her mother brought forth.

378. The female child could not be devoted to Temple service under the Mosaic law, as she intended. But she was marked out for a special destiny as a miracle-child, to be the mother of the miracle-child Jesus. She was content to seek God's protection for her against all evil. There is a certain sense of pride in the girl on the part of the mother.

379. Mary grew under God's special protection. Her sustenance, under which we may include both her physical needs and her spiritual food, came from God, and her growth was indeed a "goodly growth" which I have tried to express in the Text by the words "purity and beauty". Some apocryphal Christian writings say that she was brought up in the Temple to the age of twelve like a dove, and that she was fed by angels.

38. There did Zakarīya
Pray to his Lord, saying:
" O my Lord! Grant unto me
From Thee a progeny
That is pure: for Thou
Art He that heareth prayer![380]

٣٨- هُنَالِكَ دَعَا زَكَرِيَّا رَبَّهُ ۚ قَالَ رَبِّ هَبْ
لِي مِن لَّدُنكَ ذُرِّيَّةً طَيِّبَةً ۚ
إِنَّكَ سَمِيعُ الدُّعَاءِ ○

39. While he was standing
In prayer in the chamber,
The angels called unto him:
" God doth give thee
Glad tidings of Yaḥya,
Witnessing the truth
Of a Word from God,[381] and (be
Besides) noble, chaste,
And a Prophet,—
Of the (goodly) company
Of the righteous."

٣٩- فَنَادَتْهُ الْمَلَٰٓئِكَةُ
وَهُوَ قَآئِمٌ يُصَلِّي فِي الْمِحْرَابِ ۙ
أَنَّ اللَّهَ يُبَشِّرُكَ بِيَحْيَىٰ
مُصَدِّقًا بِكَلِمَةٍ مِّنَ اللَّهِ
وَسَيِّدًا وَّحَصُورًا
وَّنَبِيًّا مِّنَ الصَّٰلِحِينَ ○

40. He said: "O my Lord!
How shall I have a son,
Seeing I am very old,
And my wife is barren?"
"Thus," was the answer,
" Doth God accomplish
What He willeth."

٤٠- قَالَ رَبِّ أَنَّىٰ يَكُونُ لِي غُلَٰمٌ
وَّقَدْ بَلَغَنِيَ الْكِبَرُ
وَامْرَأَتِي عَاقِرٌ ۖ
قَالَ كَذَٰلِكَ اللَّهُ يَفْعَلُ مَا يَشَآءُ ○

41. He said: " O my Lord!
Give me a Sign!"
" Thy Sign," was the answer,
" Shall be that thou
Shalt speak to no man
For three days
But with signals.
Then celebrate
The praises of thy Lord
Again and again,
And glorify Him
In the evening
And in the morning."

٤١- قَالَ رَبِّ اجْعَل لِّي ءَايَةً ۖ
قَالَ ءَايَتُكَ أَلَّا تُكَلِّمَ النَّاسَ
ثَلَٰثَةَ أَيَّامٍ
إِلَّا رَمْزًا ۗ
وَاذْكُر رَّبَّكَ كَثِيرًا
ع وَسَبِّحْ بِالْعَشِيِّ وَالْإِبْكَٰرِ ○

380. The birth of Mary, the mystic mother of Jesus, of John the Baptist, the precursor of Jesus, and of Jesus, the mystic prophet of Israel, whom Israel rejected, occurred in that order chronologically, and are told in that order. They are all inter-connected. *Zakarīya* prayed for no ordinary son. He and his wife were past the age of parenthood. Seeing the growth of the mystic girl Mary, he prayed for some mystic child from God,—"from Thee, a progeny that is pure". Perhaps he had adoption in his mind. Did he want to adopt Mary? To his surprise, he is given a son in the flesh, ushered in by a mystic Sign.

381. Notice: "*a* Word from God", not "*the* Word of God", the epithet that mystical Christianity uses for Jesus. As stated in iii. 59 below, Jesus was created by a miracle, by God's word "Be", and he was.

SECTION 5.

42. Behold! the angels said:
" O Mary ! God hath chosen thee
And purified thee—chosen thee
Above the women of all nations.[382]

۴۲- وَإِذْ قَالَتِ الْمَلٰٓئِكَةُ يٰمَرْيَمُ إِنَّ اللهَ
اصْطَفٰكِ وَطَهَّرَكِ وَاصْطَفٰكِ عَلٰى نِسَآءِ
الْعٰلَمِينَ ○

43. " O Mary! worship
Thy Lord devoutly:
Prostrate thyself,
And bow down (in prayer)
With those who bow down."

۴۳- يٰمَرْيَمُ اقْنُتِي لِرَبِّكِ وَاسْجُدِي
وَارْكَعِي مَعَ الرّٰكِعِينَ ○

44. This is part of the tidings
Of the things unseen,[383]
Which We reveal unto thee
(O Apostle!) by inspiration:
Thou wast not with them
When they cast lots
With arrows,[384] as to which
Of them should be charged
With the care of Mary:
Nor wast thou with them
When they disputed (the point).[385]

۴۴- ذٰلِكَ مِنْ أَنۢبَآءِ الْغَيْبِ
نُوحِيهِ إِلَيْكَ ۚ وَمَا كُنتَ لَدَيْهِمْ
إِذْ يُلْقُونَ أَقْلٰمَهُمْ
أَيُّهُمْ يَكْفُلُ مَرْيَمَ
وَمَا كُنتَ لَدَيْهِمْ
إِذْ يَخْتَصِمُونَ ○

45. Behold! the angels said:
" O Mary! God giveth thee
Glad tidings of a Word
From Him: his name
Will be Christ Jesus,[386]
The son of Mary, held in honour
In this world and the Hereafter
And of (the company of) those
Nearest to God;[387]

۴۵- إِذْ قَالَتِ الْمَلٰٓئِكَةُ يٰمَرْيَمُ إِنَّ اللهَ
يُبَشِّرُكِ بِكَلِمَةٍ مِّنْهُ ۖ
اسْمُهُ الْمَسِيحُ عِيسَى ابْنُ مَرْيَمَ
وَجِيهًا فِي الدُّنْيَا وَالْأٰخِرَةِ
وَمِنَ الْمُقَرَّبِينَ ○

382. Mary the mother of Jesus was unique, in that she gave birth to a son by a special miracle, without the intervention of the customary physical means. This of course does not mean that she was more than human, any more than that her son was more than human. She had as much need to pray to God as anyone else. The Christian dogma, in all sects except the Unitarian, holds that Jesus was God and the son of God. The worship of Mary became the practice in the Roman Catholic Church, which calls Mary the Mother of God. This seems to have been endorsed by the Council of Ephesus in 431, in the century before Muḥammad was born to sweep away the corruptions of the Church of Christ. For *'ālamīn* as meaning all nations, see iii. 96, n. 423.

383. *Things unseen*: mystic, spiritual. The whole story has a mystic meaning, and it would be unseemly to dispute or speculate about it.

384. Literally, *reeds*: *aqlām*. For the Arab custom of casting lots with arrows, see ii. 219, n. 241.

385. Christian apocryphal writings mention the contention between the priests as to the honour of taking charge of Mary, and how it was decided by means of rods or reeds in favour of Zakariya.

386. *Christ*: Greek, *Christos*=anointed: kings and priests were anointed to symbolise consecration to their office. The Hebrew and Arabic form is Masīh.

387. Nearest to God: *Muqarrabīn*, *Cf.* Q. lvi. 11.

46. "He shall speak to the people
In childhood and in maturity.[388]
And he shall be (of the company)
Of the righteous."

٤٦- وَيُكَلِّمُ النَّاسَ فِي الْمَهْدِ وَكَهْلًا
وَّمِنَ الصّٰلِحِيْنَ ○

47. She said: "O my Lord![389]
How shall I have a son
When no man hath touched me?"
He said: "Even so:
God createth
What He willeth:
When He hath decreed
A Plan, He but saith
To it, 'Be,' and it is!

٤٧- قَالَتْ رَبِّ اَنّٰى يَكُوْنُ لِيْ وَلَدٌ
وَّلَمْ يَمْسَسْنِيْ بَشَرٌ ؕ
قَالَ كَذٰلِكِ اللّٰهُ يَخْلُقُ مَا يَشَآءُ ؕ
اِذَا قَضٰۤى اَمْرًا
فَاِنَّمَا يَقُوْلُ لَهٗ كُنْ فَيَكُوْنُ ○

48. "And God will teach him
The Book and Wisdom,
The Law and the Gospel,

٤٨- وَيُعَلِّمُهُ الْكِتٰبَ وَالْحِكْمَةَ
وَالتَّوْرٰىةَ وَالْاِنْجِيْلَ ○ۚ

49. "And (appoint him)
An apostle to the Children
Of Israel, (with this message):
"'I have come to you,
With a Sign from your Lord,
In that I make for you
Out of clay, as it were,
The figure of a bird,
And breathe into it,
And it becomes a bird
By God's leave:[390]
And I heal those
Born blind, and the lepers,
And I quicken the dead,
By God's leave;
And I declare to you
What ye eat, and what ye store[391]
In your houses. Surely
Therein is a Sign for you
If ye did believe;

٤٩- وَرَسُوْلًا اِلٰى بَنِيْۤ اِسْرَآءِيْلَ ۙ
اَنِّيْ قَدْ جِئْتُكُمْ بِاٰيَةٍ مِّنْ رَّبِّكُمْ ۙ
اَنِّيْۤ اَخْلُقُ لَكُمْ مِّنَ الطِّيْنِ كَهَيْـَٔةِ الطَّيْرِ
فَاَنْفُخُ فِيْهِ فَيَكُوْنُ طَيْرًا
بِاِذْنِ اللّٰهِ ۚ
وَاُبْرِئُ الْاَكْمَهَ وَالْاَبْرَصَ
وَاُحْيِ الْمَوْتٰى بِاِذْنِ اللّٰهِ ۚ
وَاُنَبِّئُكُمْ بِمَا تَاْكُلُوْنَ وَمَا تَدَّخِرُوْنَ ۙ
فِيْ بُيُوْتِكُمْ ؕ اِنَّ فِيْ ذٰلِكَ لَاٰيَةً لَّكُمْ اِنْ
كُنْتُمْ مُّؤْمِنِيْنَ ○

388. The ministry of Jesus lasted only about three years, from 30 to 33 years of his age, when in the eyes of his enemies he was crucified. But the Gospel of Luke (ii. 46) describes him as disputing with the doctors in the Temple at the age of 12, and even earlier, as a child, he was "strong in spirit, filled with wisdom" (Luke ii. 40). Some apocryphal Gospels describe him as preaching from infancy.

389. She was addressed by angels, who gave her God's message. In reply she speaks as to God. In reply, apparently an angel again gives God's message.

390. This miracle of the clay birds is found in some of the apocryphal Gospels; those of curing the blind and the lepers and raising the dead are in the canonical Gospels. The original Gospel (see iii. 48) was not the various stories written afterwards by disciples, but the real Message taught direct by Jesus.

391. I do not know whether this clause refers to a particular incident, or generally to a prophetic knowledge of what is not known to ordinary people.

50. "'(I have come to you),
To attest the Law
Which was before me.
And to make lawful
To you part of what was
(Before) forbidden to you;
I have come to you
With a Sign from your Lord.
So fear God,
And obey me.

٥٠- وَمُصَدِّقًا لِّمَا
بَيْنَ يَدَيَّ مِنَ التَّوْرٰىةِ
وَلِأُحِلَّ لَكُمْ بَعْضَ الَّذِي
حُرِّمَ عَلَيْكُمْ وَجِئْتُكُمْ بِاٰيَةٍ مِّنْ رَّبِّكُمْ
فَاتَّقُوا اللّٰهَ وَاَطِيْعُوْنِ ○

51. "'It is God
Who is my Lord
And your Lord;
Then worship Him.
This is a Way
That is straight.'"

٥١- إِنَّ اللّٰهَ رَبِّي
وَرَبُّكُمْ فَاعْبُدُوْهُ ؕ
هٰذَا صِرَاطٌ مُّسْتَقِيْمٌ ○

52. When Jesus found
Unbelief on their part
He said: "Who will be
My helpers to (the work
Of) God?" Said the Disciples:
"We are God's helpers:
We believe in God,
And do thou bear witness
That we are Muslims.[392]

٥٢- فَلَمَّآ اَحَسَّ عِيْسٰى مِنْهُمُ الْكُفْرَ
قَالَ مَنْ اَنْصَارِيْٓ اِلَى اللّٰهِ ؕ
قَالَ الْحَوَارِيُّوْنَ نَحْنُ اَنْصَارُ اللّٰهِ ۚ
اٰمَنَّا بِاللّٰهِ ۚ
وَاشْهَدْ بِاَنَّا مُسْلِمُوْنَ ○

53. "Our Lord! we believe
In what Thou hast revealed,
And we follow the Apostle;
Then write us down
Among those who bear witness."

٥٣- رَبَّنَآ اٰمَنَّا بِمَآ اَنْزَلْتَ
وَاتَّبَعْنَا الرَّسُوْلَ
فَاكْتُبْنَا مَعَ الشّٰهِدِيْنَ ○

54. And (the unbelievers)
Plotted and planned,
And God too planned,[393]
And the best of planners
Is God.

٥٤- وَمَكَرُوْا وَمَكَرَ اللّٰهُ ؕ
وَاللّٰهُ خَيْرُ الْمٰكِرِيْنَ ع

392. The story of Jesus is told with special application to the time of the Apostle Muḥammad. Note the word helpers (Anṣār) in this connection, and the reference to plotters in iii. 54. It was the one Religion—the Religion of God, which was in essence the religion of Abraham, Moses, and Jesus. The argument runs: why do ye then now make divisions and reject the living Teacher? Islam is: bowing to the Will of God. All who have faith should bow to the Will of God and be Muslims.

393. The Arabic *makara* has both a bad and a good meaning, that of making an intricate plan to carry out some secret purpose. The enemies of God are constantly doing that. But God—in whose hands is all good—has His plans also, against which the evil ones will have no chance whatever.

Section 6.

55. Behold! God said:
"O Jesus! I will take thee[394]
And raise thee to Myself
And clear thee (of the falsehoods)[395]
Of those who blaspheme;
I will make those
Who follow thee superior[396]
To those who reject faith,
To the Day of Resurrection:
Then shall ye all
Return unto me,
And I will judge
Between you of the matters
Wherein ye dispute.[397]

٥٥- إِذْ قَالَ اللّٰهُ يٰعِيسٰٓى إِنِّي مُتَوَفِّيكَ
وَرَافِعُكَ إِلَيَّ وَمُطَهِّرُكَ
مِنَ الَّذِينَ كَفَرُوا
وَجَاعِلُ الَّذِينَ اتَّبَعُوكَ فَوْقَ
الَّذِينَ كَفَرُوٓا إِلٰى يَوْمِ الْقِيٰمَةِ
ثُمَّ إِلَيَّ مَرْجِعُكُمْ
فَأَحْكُمُ بَيْنَكُمْ
فِيمَا كُنْتُمْ فِيهِ تَخْتَلِفُونَ ○

56. "As to those who reject faith,
I will punish them
With terrible agony
In this world and in the Hereafter,
Nor will they have
Anyone to help.

٥٦- فَأَمَّا الَّذِينَ كَفَرُوا فَأُعَذِّبُهُمْ عَذَابًا
شَدِيدًا فِي الدُّنْيَا وَالْآخِرَةِ
وَمَا لَهُمْ مِنْ نّٰصِرِينَ ○

57. "As to those who believe
And work righteousness,
God will pay them (in full)
Their reward;
But God loveth not
Those who do wrong.

٥٧- وَأَمَّا الَّذِينَ اٰمَنُوا وَعَمِلُوا الصّٰلِحٰتِ
فَيُوَفِّيهِمْ أُجُورَهُمْ
وَاللّٰهُ لَا يُحِبُّ الظّٰلِمِينَ ○

58. "This is what we rehearse
Unto thee of the Signs
And the Message
Of Wisdom."

٥٨- ذٰلِكَ نَتْلُوهُ عَلَيْكَ مِنَ الْاٰيٰتِ
وَالذِّكْرِ الْحَكِيمِ ○

---

394. Read this with iv. 157, where it is said that the Jews neither crucified nor killed Jesus, but that another was killed in his likeness. The guilt of the Jews remained, but Jesus was eventually taken up to God.

395. Jesus was charged by the Jews with blasphemy as claiming to be God or the son of God. The Christians (except a few early sects which were annihilated by persecution, and the modern sect of Unitarians, who are almost Muslims) adopted the substance of the claim, and made it the cornerstone of their faith. God clears Jesus of such a charge or claim.

396. *Those who follow thee*: The Muslims are the true Christians, for they follow (or should follow the true teaching of Christ, which did not include the blasphemy that he was God or the Son of God in the literal sense. But there is a large body of men, who by birth inherit such teaching nominally, but their hearts do not consent to it. Their real Muslim virtues (which from their point of view they call Christian virtues) entitle them to be called Christians, and to receive the leading position which they at present occupy in the world of men.

397. All the controversies about dogma and faith will disappear when we appear before God. He will judge not by what we profess but by what we are.

59. The similitude of Jesus
Before God is as that of Adam;[398]
He created him from dust,
Then said to him: "Be":
And he was.

٥٩- إِنَّ مَثَلَ عِيسَىٰ عِندَ اللَّهِ كَمَثَلِ آدَمَ ۖ
خَلَقَهُ مِن تُرَابٍ
ثُمَّ قَالَ لَهُ كُن فَيَكُونُ ○

60. The Truth (comes)
From God alone;
So be not of those
Who doubt.[399]

٦٠- الْحَقُّ مِن رَّبِّكَ
فَلَا تَكُن مِّنَ الْمُمْتَرِينَ ○

61. If any one disputes
In this matter with thee,
Now after (full) knowledge
Hath come to thee,
Say: "Come! let us
Gather together,—
Our sons and your sons,
Our women and your women,
Ourselves and yourselves:
Then let us earnestly pray,
And invoke the curse
Of God on those who lie!"[400]

٦١- فَمَنْ حَاجَّكَ فِيهِ
مِن بَعْدِ مَا جَاءَكَ مِنَ الْعِلْمِ فَقُلْ تَعَالَوْا
نَدْعُ أَبْنَاءَنَا وَأَبْنَاءَكُمْ
وَنِسَاءَنَا وَنِسَاءَكُمْ وَأَنفُسَنَا وَأَنفُسَكُمْ
ثُمَّ نَبْتَهِلْ فَنَجْعَل
لَّعْنَتَ اللَّهِ عَلَى الْكَاذِبِينَ ○

62. This is the true account:[401]
There is no god
Except God;
And God—He is indeed

٦٢- إِنَّ هَٰذَا لَهُوَ الْقَصَصُ الْحَقُّ ۚ
وَمَا مِنْ إِلَٰهٍ إِلَّا اللَّهُ ۚ وَإِنَّ اللَّهَ لَهُوَ

---

398. After a description of the high position which Jesus occupies as a prophet, we have a repudiation of the dogma that he was God, or the son of God, or anything more than a man. If it is said that he was born without a human father, Adam was also so born. Indeed Adam was born without either a human father or mother. As far as our physical bodies are concerned they are mere dust. In God's sight Jesus was as dust just as Adam was or humanity is. The greatness of Jesus arose from the divine command "Be": for after that he was—more than dust—a great spiritual leader and teacher.

399. The truth does not necessarily come from priests, or from the superstitions of whole peoples. It comes from God, and where there is a direct revelation, there is no room for doubt.

400. In the year of Deputations, 10th of the Hijra, came a Christian embassy from Najrān (towards Yaman, about 150 miles north of Ṣana'ā). They were much impressed on hearing this passage of the Qur-ān explaining the true position of Christ, and they entered into tributary relations with the new Muslim State. But ingrained habits and customs prevented them from accepting Islam as a body. The Holy Apostle, firm in his faith, proposed a *Mubāhala, i.e.*, a solemn meeting, in which both sides should summon not only their men, but their women and children, earnestly pray to God, and invoke the curse of God on those who should lie. Those who had a pure and sincere faith would not hesitate. The Christians declined, and they were dismissed in a spirit of tolerance, with a promise of protection from the State in return for tribute, "the wages of rule," as it is called in the *Āīn-i-Akbārī*.

401. We are now in a position to deal with the questions which we left over at ii. 87. Jesus is no more than a man. It is against reason and revelation to call him God or the son of God. He is called the son of Mary to emphasize this. He had no known human father, as his birth was miraculous. But it is not this which raises him to his high spiritual position as a prophet, but because God called him to his office. The praise is due to God, Who by His word gave him spiritual strength—"strengthened him with the holy spirit". The miracles which surround his story relate not only to his birth and his life and death, but also to his mother Mary and his precursor Yaḥyā. These were the "Clear Signs" which he brought. It was those who misunderstood him who obscured his clear Signs and surrounded him with mysteries of their own invention.

The Exalted in Power,
The Wise.

الْعَزِيزُ الْحَكِيمُ ○

63. But if they turn back,
God hath full knowledge
Of those who do mischief.

٦٣- فَإِنْ تَوَلَّوْا
فَإِنَّ اللَّهَ عَلِيمٌ بِالْمُفْسِدِينَ ○ ع

C. 57. (iii. 64-120.) Islam doth invite all people
To the Truth : there is no cause
For dissembling or disputing.
False are the people who corrupt
God's truth, or hinder men
From coming to God. Let the Muslims
Hold together in unity and discipline,
Knowing that they have a mission
Of righteousness for humanity.
No harm can come to them.
Though there are good men and true
In other Faiths, Muslims must
Be true to their own Brotherhood.
They should seek help and friendship
From their own, and stand firm
In constancy and patient perseverance.

SECTION 7.

64. Say: "O People
Of the Book! come
To common terms
As between us and you:
That we worship
None but God;
That we associate
No partners with Him;
That we erect not,
From among ourselves,
Lords and patrons
Other than God."[402]
If then they turn back,
Say ye: "Bear witness
That we (at least)
Are Muslims (bowing
To God's Will)."

٦٤- قُلْ يَاأَهْلَ الْكِتٰبِ تَعَالَوْا إِلٰى كَلِمَةٍ
سَوَاءٍ بَيْنَنَا وَبَيْنَكُمْ
أَلَّا نَعْبُدَ إِلَّا اللَّهَ
وَلَا نُشْرِكَ بِهٖ شَيْئًا وَلَا يَتَّخِذَ
بَعْضُنَا بَعْضًا أَرْبَابًا
مِّنْ دُونِ اللَّهِ فَإِنْ تَوَلَّوْا
فَقُولُوا اشْهَدُوا
بِأَنَّا مُسْلِمُونَ ○

402. In the abstract the People of the Book would agree to all three propositions. In practice they fail. Apart from doctrinal lapses from the unity of the One True God, there is the question of a consecrated Priesthood (among the Jews it was hereditary also), as if a mere human being—Cohen, or Pope, or Priest, or Brahman,—could claim superiority apart from his learning and the purity of his life, or could stand between man and God in some special sense. The same remarks apply to the worship of saints. They may be pure and holy, but no one can protect us or claim Lordship over us except God. For *Rabb*, see i. 2. n. Abraham was a true man of God, but he could not be called a Jew or a Christian as he lived long before the Law of Moses or the Gospel of Jesus was revealed.

65. Ye People of the Book!
Why dispute ye
About Abraham,
When the Law and the Gospel
Were not revealed
Till after him?
Have ye no understanding?

٦٥- يٰٓاَهْلَ الْكِتٰبِ
لِمَ تُحَآجُّوْنَ فِيْٓ اِبْرٰهِيْمَ
وَمَآ اُنْزِلَتِ التَّوْرٰىةُ وَالْاِنْجِيْلُ
اِلَّا مِنْۢ بَعْدِهٖ ؕ اَفَلَا تَعْقِلُوْنَ ○

66. Ah! Ye are those
Who fell to disputing
(Even) in matters of which
Ye had some knowledge![403]
But why dispute ye
In matters of which
Ye have no knowledge?
It is God Who knows,
And ye who know not!

٦٦- هٰٓاَنْتُمْ هٰٓؤُلَآءِ حَاجَجْتُمْ
فِيْمَا لَكُمْ بِهٖ عِلْمٌ
فَلِمَ تُحَآجُّوْنَ فِيْمَا
لَيْسَ لَكُمْ بِهٖ عِلْمٌ ؕ
وَاللّٰهُ يَعْلَمُ وَاَنْتُمْ لَا تَعْلَمُوْنَ ○

67. Abraham was not a Jew
Nor yet a Christian;
But he was true in Faith,
And bowed his will to God's,
(Which is Islam),
And he joined not gods with God.[404]

٦٧- مَا كَانَ اِبْرٰهِيْمُ يَهُوْدِيًّا
وَّلَا نَصْرَانِيًّا
وَّلٰكِنْ كَانَ حَنِيْفًا مُّسْلِمًا ؕ
وَمَا كَانَ مِنَ الْمُشْرِكِيْنَ ○

68. Without doubt, among men,
The nearest of kin to Abraham,
Are those who follow him,
As are also this Apostle
And those who believe:
And God is the Protector
Of those who have faith.

٦٨- اِنَّ اَوْلَى النَّاسِ بِاِبْرٰهِيْمَ
لَلَّذِيْنَ اتَّبَعُوْهُ وَهٰذَا النَّبِيُّ
وَالَّذِيْنَ اٰمَنُوْا ؕ
وَاللّٰهُ وَلِيُّ الْمُؤْمِنِيْنَ ○

69. It is the wish of a section
Of the People of the Book
To lead you astray.
But they shall lead astray
(Not you), but themselves,
And they do not perceive!

٦٩- وَدَّتْ طَّآئِفَةٌ مِّنْ اَهْلِ الْكِتٰبِ
لَوْ يُضِلُّوْنَكُمْ ؕ وَمَا يُضِلُّوْنَ اِلَّآ اَنْفُسَهُمْ
وَمَا يَشْعُرُوْنَ ○

70. Ye People of the Book!
Why reject ye

٧٠- يٰٓاَهْلَ الْكِتٰبِ لِمَ تَكْفُرُوْنَ

403. The number of sects among the Jews and Christians shows that they wrangled and disputed even about some of the matters of their own religion, of which they should have had some knowledge. But when they talk of Father Abraham, they are entirely out of court, as he lived before their peculiar systems were evolved.

404. *Cf.* ii. 135 and the whole argument in that passage.

The Signs of God,
Of which ye are
(Yourselves) witnesses?

بِاٰيٰتِ اللّٰهِ
وَاَنْتُمْ تَشْهَدُوْنَ ○

71. Ye People of the Book!
Why do ye clothe
Truth with falsehood,
And conceal the Truth,
While ye have knowledge?[405]

٧١- يٰاَهْلَ الْكِتٰبِ لِمَ تَلْبِسُوْنَ
الْحَقَّ بِالْبَاطِلِ
وَتَكْتُمُوْنَ الْحَقَّ وَاَنْتُمْ تَعْلَمُوْنَ ○

Section 8.

72. A section of the People
Of the Book say:
"Believe in the morning[406]
What is revealed
To the Believers,
But reject it at the end
Of the day; perchance
They may (themselves)
Turn back;

٧٢- وَقَالَتْ طَّآئِفَةٌ مِّنْ اَهْلِ الْكِتٰبِ
اٰمِنُوْا بِالَّذِيْٓ
اُنْزِلَ عَلَى الَّذِيْنَ
اٰمَنُوْا وَجْهَ النَّهَارِ
وَاكْفُرُوْٓا اٰخِرَهٗ لَعَلَّهُمْ يَرْجِعُوْنَ ○

73. "And believe no one
Unless he follows
Your religion."
Say: "True guidance
Is the guidance of God:
(Fear ye) lest a revelation[407]
Be sent to someone (else)
Like unto that which was sent
Unto you? Or that those
(Receiving such revelation)
Should engage you in argument
Before your Lord?"[408]
Say: "All bounties
Are in the hand of God:
He granteth them
To whom He pleaseth:

٧٣- وَلَا تُؤْمِنُوْٓا
اِلَّا لِمَنْ تَبِعَ دِيْنَكُمْ
قُلْ اِنَّ الْهُدٰى هُدَى اللّٰهِ
اَنْ يُّؤْتٰٓى اَحَدٌ
مِّثْلَ مَآ اُوْتِيْتُمْ
اَوْ يُحَآجُّوْكُمْ عِنْدَ رَبِّكُمْ
قُلْ اِنَّ الْفَضْلَ بِيَدِ اللّٰهِ
يُؤْتِيْهِ مَنْ يَّشَآءُ

---

405. There are many ways of preventing the access of people to the truth. One is to tamper with it, or trick it out in colours of falsehood: half-truths are often more dangerous than obvious falsehoods. Another is to conceal it altogether. Those who are jealous of a man of God, whom they actually see before them, do not allow his credentials or virtues to be known, or vilify him, or conceal facts which would attract people to him. When people do this of set purpose, against their own light ("of which ye are yourselves witnesses"), they are descending to the lowest depths of degradation, and they are doing more harm to themselves than to anyone else.

406. *Wajh* here has the sense of "beginning", "early part". The cynics who plotted against Islam actually asked their accomplices to join the Believers and then repudiate them.

407. The two clauses following have been variously construed, and some translations leave the sense ambiguous. I have construed the conjunction "*an*" to mean "lest", as it undoubtedly does in vii. 172, "*an taqūlū*", etc.

408. *Cf.* ii 76. The People of the Book were doubly annoyed at the Muslims: (1) that they should (being outside their ranks) receive God's revelations, and (2) that having received such revelations, they should be able to convict them out of their own scriptures before their Lord!

And God careth for all,
And He knoweth all things."

وَاللّٰهُ وَاسِعٌ عَلِيْمٌ ۚ

74. For His Mercy He specially chooseth
Whom He pleaseth;
For God is the Lord
Of bounties unbounded.

٧٤- يَخْتَصُّ بِرَحْمَتِهٖ مَنْ يَّشَآءُ ۗ
وَاللّٰهُ ذُو الْفَضْلِ الْعَظِيْمِ ○

75. Among the People of the Book
Are some who, if entrusted
With a hoard of gold,[409]
Will (readily) pay it back;
Others, who, if entrusted
With a single silver coin,[410]
Will not repay it unless
Thou constantly stoodest
Demanding, because,
They say, "there is no call
On us (to keep faith)
With these ignorant (Pagans)."[411]
But they tell a lie against God,
And (well) they know it.

٧٥- وَمِنْ اَهْلِ الْكِتٰبِ مَنْ اِنْ تَاْمَنْهُ
بِقِنْطَارٍ يُّؤَدِّهٖۤ اِلَيْكَ ۚ
وَمِنْهُمْ مَّنْ اِنْ تَاْمَنْهُ بِدِيْنَارٍ لَّا يُؤَدِّهٖۤ
اِلَيْكَ اِلَّا مَا دُمْتَ عَلَيْهِ قَآئِمًا ۗ
ذٰلِكَ بِاَنَّهُمْ قَالُوْا لَيْسَ عَلَيْنَا
فِى الْاُمِّيّٖنَ سَبِيْلٌ ۚ
وَيَقُوْلُوْنَ عَلَى اللّٰهِ الْكَذِبَ وَهُمْ يَعْلَمُوْنَ ○

76. Nay.—Those that keep
Their plighted faith
And act aright,—verily
God loves those
Who act aright.

٧٦- بَلٰى مَنْ اَوْفٰى بِعَهْدِهٖ
وَاتَّقٰى
فَاِنَّ اللّٰهَ يُحِبُّ الْمُتَّقِيْنَ ○

77. As for those who sell
The faith they owe to God
And their own plighted word
For a small price,[412]
They shall have no portion
In the Hereafter:

٧٧- اِنَّ الَّذِيْنَ يَشْتَرُوْنَ بِعَهْدِ اللّٰهِ
وَاَيْمَانِهِمْ ثَمَنًا قَلِيْلًا
اُولٰٓئِكَ لَا خَلَاقَ لَهُمْ فِى الْاٰخِرَةِ

---

409. *Hoard of gold*: qinṭār: a talent of 1,200 ounces of gold, more than a lakh of rupees. See iii. 14, n. 354.

410. *Silver coin*: *dīnār*. In the later Roman Empire, the denarius was a small silver coin, about the size of a four-anna piece. It must have been current in Syria and the markets of Arabia in the time of our Apostle. It was the coin whose name is translated in the English Bible by the word penny, Matt. xxii. 19: hence the abbreviation of penny is *d* (=denarius). The later Arabian coin *dīnār* coined by the Umaivads, was a gold coin after the pattern of the Byzantine (Roman) *denarius aureus* and weighed about 66.349 grains troy, just a little more than a half-sovereign.

411. Every race imbued with race arrogance resorts to this kind of moral or religious subterfuge. Even if its members are usually honest or just among themselves, they are contemptuous of those outside their circle, and cheat and deceive them without any qualms of conscience. This is a "lie against God".

412. All our duties to our fellow creatures are referred to the service and faith we owe to God. But in the matter of truth an appeal is made to our own self-respect as responsible beings: is it becoming that we should be false to our own word, to ourselves? And then we are reminded that the utmost we can gain by falsifying God's word or being untrue to ourselves is but a miserable price. We get at best something very paltry as the price for selling our very souls.

Nor will God
(Deign to) speak to them
Or look at them
On the Day of Judgment,
Nor will He cleanse them[413]
(Of sin) : they shall have
A grievous Penalty.

وَلَا يُكَلِّمُهُمُ اللّٰهُ
وَلَا يَنْظُرُ اِلَيْهِمْ يَوْمَ الْقِيٰمَةِ
وَلَا يُزَكِّيْهِمْ
وَلَهُمْ عَذَابٌ اَلِيْمٌ ○

78. There is among them
A section who distort
The Book with their tongues :
(As they read) you would think
It is a part of the Book,
But it is no part
Of the Book ; and they say,
" That is from God,"
But it is not from God :
It is they who tell
A lie against God,
And (well) they know it !

٧٨ - وَاِنَّ مِنْهُمْ لَفَرِيْقًا يَّلْوٗنَ اَلْسِنَتَهُمْ
بِالْكِتٰبِ لِتَحْسَبُوْهُ مِنَ الْكِتٰبِ
وَمَا هُوَ مِنَ الْكِتٰبِ ۚ وَيَقُوْلُوْنَ هُوَ مِنْ
عِنْدِ اللّٰهِ وَمَا هُوَ مِنْ عِنْدِ اللّٰهِ ۚ
وَيَقُوْلُوْنَ عَلَى اللّٰهِ الْكَذِبَ
وَهُمْ يَعْلَمُوْنَ ○

79. It is not (possible)
That a man, to whom
Is given the Book,
And Wisdom,
And the Prophetic Office,
Should say to people :
" Be ye my worshippers
Rather than God's " :[414]
On the contrary
(He would say) :
" Be ye worshippers
Of Him Who is truly
The Cherisher of all :
For ye have taught
The Book and ye
Have studied it earnestly."

٧٩ - مَا كَانَ لِبَشَرٍ اَنْ يُّؤْتِيَهُ اللّٰهُ
الْكِتٰبَ وَالْحُكْمَ وَالنُّبُوَّةَ
ثُمَّ يَقُوْلَ لِلنَّاسِ
كُوْنُوْا عِبَادًا لِّيْ
مِنْ دُوْنِ اللّٰهِ
وَلٰكِنْ كُوْنُوْا رَبّٰنِيّٖنَ
بِمَا كُنْتُمْ تُعَلِّمُوْنَ الْكِتٰبَ
وَبِمَا كُنْتُمْ تَدْرُسُوْنَ ○

80. Nor would he instruct you
To take angels and prophets[415]
For Lords and Patrons.
What ! would he bid you

٨٠ - وَلَا يَاْمُرَكُمْ اَنْ تَتَّخِذُوا الْمَلٰٓئِكَةَ
وَالنَّبِيّٖنَ اَرْبَابًا ۗ اَيَاْمُرُكُمْ بِالْكُفْرِ

413. Even on sinners—ordinary sinners—God will look with compassion and mercy ; He will speak words of kindness and cleanse them of their sins. But those who are in active rebellion against God and sin against their own light,—what mercy can they expect ?

414. It is not in reason or in the nature of things that God's messenger should preach against God. Jesus came to preach the true God.

415. Jesus was a prophet, and the Holy Spirit " with which he was strengthened " was the Angel who brought the revelations to him.

To unbelief after ye have
Bowed your will
(To God in Islam)?

بعد اذ انتم مسلمون ع

SECTION 9.

81. Behold! God took
The Covenant of the Prophets,[416]
Saying: "I give you
A Book and Wisdom;
Then comes to you
An Apostle, confirming
What is with you;
Do ye believe in him
And render him help."
God said: "Do ye agree,
And take this my Covenant
As binding on you?"
They said: "We agree."
He said: "Then bear witness,
And I am with you
Among the witnesses."

٨١- و اذ اخذ الله ميثاق النبين
لما اتيتكم من كتب وحكمة
ثم جاءكم رسول مصدق لما معكم
لتؤمنن به و لتنصرنه
قال ءاقررتم و اخذتم على ذلكم
اصري ط قالوا اقررنا
قال فاشهدوا
و انا معكم من الشهدين ○

82. If any turn back
After this, they are
Perverted transgressors.

٨٢- فمن تولى بعد ذلك
فاولئك هم الفسقون ○

83. Do they seek
For other than the Religion
Of God?—while all creatures
In the heavens and on earth
Have, willing or unwilling,[417]
Bowed to His Will
(Accepted Islam),
And to Him shall they
All be brought back.

٨٣- افغير دين الله يبغون و له اسلم
من في السموت و الارض
طوعا و كرها
و اليه يرجعون ○

---

416. *Cf.* ii. 63, n. 78. The argument is: You (People of the Book) are bound by your own oaths, sworn solemnly in the presence of your own Prophets. In the Old Testament as it now exists, Muḥammad is foretold in Deut. xviii. 18; and the rise of the Arab nation in Isaiah, xlii. 11, for Kedar was a son of Ismā'īl and the name is used for the Arab nation: in the New Testament as it now exists, Muḥammad is foretold in the Gospel of St. John, xiv. 16, xv. 26, and xvi. 7: the *future* Comforter cannot be the Holy Spirit as understood by Christians, because the Holy Spirit already was present, helping and guiding Jesus. The Greek word translated "Comforter" is "Paracletos", which is an easy corruption from "Periclytos", which is almost a literal translation of "Muḥammad" or "Aḥmad": see Q. lxi. 6. Further, there were other Gospels that have perished, but of which traces still remain, which were even more specific in their reference to Muḥammad; *e.g.*, the Gospel of St. Barnabas, of which an Italian translation is extant in the State Library at Vienna. It was edited in 1907 with an English translation by Mr. Lonsdale and Laura Ragg.

417. God's Truth is manifest, and all that is good and true and sane and normal accepts it with joy. But even where there is "disease in the heart" (Q. ii. 10), or judgment is obscured by perversity, every creature must eventually see and acknowledge God and His power (ii. 167). *Cf.* R. Bridges: "Testament of Beauty": iv. 1419-22:—"For God's love is unescapable as nature's environment, which if a man ignore or think to thrust it off, he is the ill-natured fool that runneth blindly on death." All Nature adores God, and Islam asks for nothing peculiar or sectarian; it but asks that we follow our nature and make our will conformable to God's Will as seen in Nature, history, and revelation. Its message is universal.

84. Say: "We believe
In God, and in what
Has been revealed to us
And what was revealed
To Abraham, Ismā'īl;
Isaac, Jacob, and the Tribes,
And in (the Books)
Given to Moses, Jesus,
And the Prophets,
From their Lord:
We make no distinction
Between one and another
Among them, and to God do we
Bow our will (in Islam)."

٨٤- قُلْ اٰمَنَّا بِاللّٰهِ وَمَآ اُنْزِلَ عَلَيْنَا
وَمَآ اُنْزِلَ عَلٰٓى اِبْرٰهِيْمَ وَاِسْمٰعِيْلَ
وَاِسْحٰقَ وَيَعْقُوْبَ وَالْاَسْبَاطِ
وَمَآ اُوْتِيَ مُوْسٰى وَعِيْسٰى
وَالنَّبِيُّوْنَ
مِنْ رَّبِّهِمْ لَا نُفَرِّقُ
بَيْنَ اَحَدٍ مِّنْهُمْ
وَنَحْنُ لَهٗ مُسْلِمُوْنَ ○

85. If anyone desires
A religion other than
Islam (submission to God),[418]
Never will it be accepted
Of him; and in the Hereafter
He will be in the ranks
Of those who have lost
(All spiritual good).

٨٥- وَمَنْ يَّبْتَغِ
غَيْرَ الْاِسْلَامِ دِيْنًا
فَلَنْ يُّقْبَلَ مِنْهُ
وَهُوَ فِي الْاٰخِرَةِ
مِنَ الْخٰسِرِيْنَ ○

86. How shall God
Guide those who reject
Faith after they accepted it
And bore witness
That the Apostle was true
And that Clear Signs
Had come unto them?
But God guides not
A people unjust.

٨٦- كَيْفَ يَهْدِي اللّٰهُ قَوْمًا
كَفَرُوْا بَعْدَ اِيْمَانِهِمْ
وَشَهِدُوْٓا
اَنَّ الرَّسُوْلَ حَقٌّ
وَّجَآءَهُمُ الْبَيِّنٰتُ
وَاللّٰهُ لَا يَهْدِي الْقَوْمَ الظّٰلِمِيْنَ ○

87. Of such the reward
Is that on them (rests)

٨٧- اُولٰٓئِكَ جَزَآؤُهُمْ

---

418. The Muslim position is clear. The Muslim does not claim to have a religion peculiar to himself. Islam is not a sect or an ethnic religion. In its view all Religion is one, for the Truth is one. It was the religion preached by all the earlier Prophets. It was the truth taught by all the inspired Books. In essence it amounts to a consciousness of the Will and Plan of God and a joyful submission to that Will and Plan. If any one wants a religion other than that, he is false to his own nature, as he is false to God's Will and Plan. Such a one cannot expect guidance, for he has deliberately renounced guidance.

The curse of God,
Of His angels,
And of all mankind;—

أَنَّ عَلَيْهِمْ لَعْنَةَ اللّٰهِ
وَالْمَلٰٓئِكَةِ وَالنَّاسِ أَجْمَعِيْنَ ۝

88. In that will they dwell;
Nor will their penalty
Be lightened, nor respite
Be their (lot);—[418-A]

٨٨- خٰلِدِيْنَ فِيْهَا ۚ لَا يُخَفَّفُ
عَنْهُمُ الْعَذَابُ وَلَا هُمْ يُنْظَرُوْنَ ۝

89. Except for those that repent
(Even) after that,
And make amends;
For verily God
Is Oft-Forgiving,
Most Merciful.

٨٩- إِلَّا الَّذِيْنَ تَابُوْا
مِنْ بَعْدِ ذٰلِكَ
وَأَصْلَحُوْا ۖ
فَإِنَّ اللّٰهَ غَفُوْرٌ رَّحِيْمٌ ۝

90. But those who reject
Faith after they accepted it,
And then go on adding
To their defiance of Faith,—
Never will their repentance
Be accepted; for they
Are those who have
(Of set purpose) gone astray.

٩٠- إِنَّ الَّذِيْنَ كَفَرُوْا
بَعْدَ إِيْمَانِهِمْ
ثُمَّ ازْدَادُوْا كُفْرًا
لَّنْ تُقْبَلَ تَوْبَتُهُمْ ۚ
وَأُولٰٓئِكَ هُمُ الضَّآلُّوْنَ ۝

91. As to those who reject
Faith, and die rejecting,—
Never would be accepted
From any such as much
Gold as the earth contains,
Though they should offer it
For ransom. For such
3 Is (in store) a penalty grievous,
30 And they will find no helpers.

٩١- إِنَّ الَّذِيْنَ كَفَرُوْا وَمَاتُوْا وَهُمْ كُفَّارٌ
فَلَنْ يُّقْبَلَ مِنْ أَحَدِهِمْ
مِّلْءُ الْأَرْضِ ذَهَبًا وَّلَوِ افْتَدٰى بِهٖ ۗ
أُولٰٓئِكَ لَهُمْ عَذَابٌ أَلِيْمٌ
وَّمَا لَهُمْ مِّنْ نّٰصِرِيْنَ ۝ ع

418-A. *Cf.* ii. 161-62.

SECTION 10.

92. By no means shall ye
Attain righteousness unless
Ye give (freely) of that[419]
Which ye love; and whatever
Ye give, of a truth
God knoweth it well.

93. All food was lawful
To the Children of Israel,
Except what Israel[420]
Made unlawful for itself,
Before the Law (of Moses)
Was revealed. Say:
"Bring ye the Law
And study it,
If ye be men of truth."

94. If any, after this, invent
A lie and attribute it
To God, they are indeed
Unjust wrong-doers.

95. Say: "God speaketh
The Truth: follow
The religion of Abraham,
The sane in faith; he
Was not of the Pagans."[421]

96. The first House (of worship)
Appointed for men
Was that at Bakka:[422]
Full of blessing

٩٢- لَنْ تَنَالُوا الْبِرَّ حَتّٰى تُنْفِقُوْا مِمَّا تُحِبُّوْنَ ۬ۚ
وَمَا تُنْفِقُوْا مِنْ شَىْءٍ
فَإِنَّ اللّٰهَ بِهٖ عَلِيْمٌ ○

٩٣- كُلُّ الطَّعَامِ كَانَ حِلًّا لِّبَنِىٓ إِسْرَآءِيْلَ
إِلَّا مَا حَرَّمَ إِسْرَآءِيْلُ عَلٰى نَفْسِهٖ
مِنْ قَبْلِ أَنْ تُنَزَّلَ التَّوْرٰىةُ ؕ
قُلْ فَأْتُوْا بِالتَّوْرٰىةِ فَاتْلُوْهَآ
إِنْ كُنْتُمْ صٰدِقِيْنَ ○

٩٤- فَمَنِ افْتَرٰى عَلَى اللّٰهِ الْكَذِبَ مِنْ بَعْدِ
ذٰلِكَ فَأُولٰٓئِكَ هُمُ الظّٰلِمُوْنَ ○

٩٥- قُلْ صَدَقَ اللّٰهُ ۗ
فَاتَّبِعُوْا مِلَّةَ إِبْرٰهِيْمَ حَنِيْفًا ؕ
وَمَا كَانَ مِنَ الْمُشْرِكِيْنَ ○

٩٦- إِنَّ أَوَّلَ بَيْتٍ وُّضِعَ لِلنَّاسِ
لَلَّذِىْ بِبَكَّةَ مُبٰرَكًا

419. The test of charity is: do you give something that you value greatly, something that you love? If you give your life in a Cause, that is the greatest gift you can give. If you give yourself, that is, your personal efforts, your talents, your skill, your learning, that comes next in degree. If you give your earnings, your property, your possessions, that is also a great gift; for many people love them even more than other things. And there are less tangible things, such as position, reputation, the well-being of those we love, the regard of those who can help us, etc. It is unselfishness that God demands, and there is no act of unselfishness, however small or intangible, but is well within the knowledge of God.

420. The Arabs ate the flesh of the camel, which is lawful in Islam, but it was prohibited by the Jewish Law of Moses (Leviticus xi. 4). But that Law was very strict because of the "hardness of heart" of Israel, because of Israel's insolence and iniquity (Q.vi. 146). Before it was promulgated Israel was free to choose its own food. I take "Israel" here to stand for the people of Israel.

421. The greater freedom of Islam in the matter of the ceremonial law, compared with the Mosaic Law, is not a reproach but a recommendation. We go back to an older source than Judaism,—the institutions of Abraham. By common consent his Faith was sound, and he was certainly not a Pagan, a term contemptuously applied to the Arabs by the Jews.

422. *Bakka*: same as Mecca; perhaps an older name. The foundation of the Ka'ba goes back to Abraham, but there are place associations in the sacred territory with the names of Adam and Eve, *e.g.*, at 'Arafāt, the Mount of Mercy (see n. 217 to ii. 197).

And of guidance
For all kinds of beings:[423]

وَهُدًى لِّلْعٰلَمِيْنَ ۝

97. In it are Signs
Manifest; (for example),
The Station of Abraham;[424]
Whoever enters it
Attains security;[425]
Pilgrimage thereto is a duty
Men owe to God,—
Those who can afford
The journey; but if any
Deny faith, God stands not
In need of any of His creatures.

٩٧- فِيْهِ اٰيٰتٌۢ بَيِّنٰتٌ مَّقَامُ اِبْرٰهِيْمَ ۚ
وَمَنْ دَخَلَهٗ كَانَ اٰمِنًا ؕ
وَلِلّٰهِ عَلَى النَّاسِ حِجُّ الْبَيْتِ
مَنِ اسْتَطَاعَ اِلَيْهِ سَبِيْلًا ؕ
وَمَنْ كَفَرَ
فَاِنَّ اللّٰهَ غَنِيٌّ عَنِ الْعٰلَمِيْنَ ۝

98. Say: "O People of the Book!
Why reject ye the Signs
Of God, when God
Is Himself witness
To all ye do?"

٩٨- قُلْ يٰۤاَهْلَ الْكِتٰبِ
لِمَ تَكْفُرُوْنَ بِاٰيٰتِ اللّٰهِ ۖ
وَاللّٰهُ شَهِيْدٌ عَلٰى مَا تَعْمَلُوْنَ ۝

99. Say: "O ye People of the Book!
Why obstruct ye
Those who believe,
From the Path of God,
Seeking to make it crooked,
While ye were yourselves
Witnesses (to God's Covenant)?[426]
But God is not unmindful
Of all that ye do."

٩٩- قُلْ يٰۤاَهْلَ الْكِتٰبِ
لِمَ تَصُدُّوْنَ عَنْ سَبِيْلِ اللّٰهِ
مَنْ اٰمَنَ تَبْغُوْنَهَا عِوَجًا
وَّاَنْتُمْ شُهَدَآءُ ؕ
وَمَا اللّٰهُ بِغَافِلٍ عَمَّا تَعْمَلُوْنَ ۝

100. O ye who believe!
If ye listen
To a faction
Among the People of the Book,
They would (indeed)
Render you apostates
After ye have believed!

١٠٠- يٰۤاَيُّهَا الَّذِيْنَ اٰمَنُوْۤا
اِنْ تُطِيْعُوْا فَرِيْقًا
مِّنَ الَّذِيْنَ اُوْتُوا الْكِتٰبَ
يَرُدُّوْكُمْ بَعْدَ اِيْمَانِكُمْ كٰفِرِيْنَ ۝

101. And how would ye
Deny Faith while unto you
Are rehearsed the Signs
Of God, and among you

١٠١- وَكَيْفَ تَكْفُرُوْنَ
وَاَنْتُمْ تُتْلٰى عَلَيْكُمْ اٰيٰتُ اللّٰهِ وَفِيْكُمْ

423. 'Alamin: all the worlds (i. 2. n.); all kinds of beings; all nations (iii. 42); all creatures (iii. 97).

424. *Station of Abraham*: see ii. 125 and n. 125.

425. See reference in last note.

426. *Cf.* iii 81.

Lives the Apostle?
Whoever holds
Firmly to God
Will be shown
A Way that is straight.

SECTION 11.

102. O ye who believe!
Fear God as He should be[427]
Feared, and die not
Except in a state[428]
Of Islam.

103. And hold fast,
All together, by the Rope[429]
Which God (stretches out
For you), and be not divided
Among yourselves;
And remember with gratitude
God's favour on you;
For ye were enemies[430]
And He joined your hearts
In love, so that by His Grace,
Ye became brethren;
And ye were on the brink
Of the Pit of Fire,
And He saved you from it.
Thus doth God make
His Signs clear to you:
That ye may be guided.

104. Let there arise out of you
A band of people
Inviting to all that is good,
Enjoining what is right,

رَسُوْلُهٗ ؕ وَمَنْ يَّعْتَصِمْ بِاللّٰهِ
فَقَدْ هُدِيَ اِلٰى صِرَاطٍ مُّسْتَقِيْمٍ ۝ ع

۱۰۲- يٰۤاَيُّهَا الَّذِيْنَ اٰمَنُوا
اتَّقُوا اللّٰهَ حَقَّ تُقٰتِهٖ وَلَا تَمُوْتُنَّ
اِلَّا وَاَنْتُمْ مُّسْلِمُوْنَ ۝

۱۰۳- وَاعْتَصِمُوْا بِحَبْلِ اللّٰهِ جَمِيْعًا
وَّلَا تَفَرَّقُوْا ۠ وَاذْكُرُوْا نِعْمَتَ اللّٰهِ عَلَيْكُمْ
اِذْ كُنْتُمْ اَعْدَآءً فَاَلَّفَ بَيْنَ قُلُوْبِكُمْ
فَاَصْبَحْتُمْ بِنِعْمَتِهٖۤ اِخْوَانًا ۚ
وَكُنْتُمْ عَلٰى شَفَا حُفْرَةٍ مِّنَ النَّارِ
فَاَنْقَذَكُمْ مِّنْهَا ؕ
كَذٰلِكَ يُبَيِّنُ اللّٰهُ
لَكُمْ اٰيٰتِهٖ
لَعَلَّكُمْ تَهْتَدُوْنَ ۝

۱۰۴- وَلْتَكُنْ مِّنْكُمْ اُمَّةٌ يَّدْعُوْنَ اِلَى الْخَيْرِ
وَيَاْمُرُوْنَ بِالْمَعْرُوْفِ

427. Fear is of many kinds: (1) the abject fear of the coward; (2) the fear of a child or an inexperienced person in the face of an unknown danger; (3) the fear of a reasonable man who wishes to avoid harm to himself or to people whom he wishes to protect; (4) the reverence which is akin to love, for it fears to do anything which is not pleasing to the object of love. The first is unworthy of man; the second is necessary for one spiritually immature; the third is a manly precaution against evil as long as it is unconquered; and the fourth is the seed-bed of righteousness Those mature in faith cultivate the fourth; at earlier stages, the third or the second may be necessary; they are fear, but not the fear of God. The first is a feeling of which anyone should be ashamed.

428. Our whole being should be permeated with Islam; it is not a mere veneer or outward show.

429. The simile is that of people struggling in deep water, to whom a benevolent Providence stretches out a strong and unbreakable rope of rescue. If all hold fast to it together, their mutual support adds to the chance of their safety.

430. Yathrib was torn with civil and tribal feuds and dissensions before the Apostle of God set his sacred feet on its soil. After that, it became the City of the Prophet, Medina, an unmatched Brotherhood, and the pivot of Islam. This poor quarrelsome world is a larger Yathrib: can we establish the sacred feet on its soil, and make it a new and larger Medina?

And forbidding what is wrong:
They are the ones
To attain felicity.[431]

وَيَنْهَوْنَ عَنِ الْمُنْكَرِ ۚ
وَأُولَٰٓئِكَ هُمُ الْمُفْلِحُونَ ○

105. Be not like those
Who are divided
Amongst themselves
And fall into disputations
After receiving
Clear Signs:
For them
Is a dreadful Penalty,—

١٠٥- وَلَا تَكُونُوا كَالَّذِينَ تَفَرَّقُوا
وَاخْتَلَفُوا
مِنْ بَعْدِ مَا جَآءَهُمُ الْبَيِّنٰتُ ۚ
وَأُولَٰٓئِكَ لَهُمْ عَذَابٌ عَظِيمٌ ○

106. On the Day when
Some faces will be (lit up
With) white, and some faces
Will be (in the gloom of) black:[432]
To those whose faces
Will be black, (will be said):
"Did ye reject Faith
After accepting it?
Taste then the Penalty
For rejecting Faith."

١٠٦- يَوْمَ تَبْيَضُّ وُجُوهٌ وَتَسْوَدُّ وُجُوهٌ ۚ
فَأَمَّا الَّذِينَ اسْوَدَّتْ وُجُوهُهُمْ
أَكَفَرْتُمْ بَعْدَ إِيمَانِكُمْ
فَذُوقُوا الْعَذَابَ
بِمَا كُنْتُمْ تَكْفُرُونَ ○

107. But those whose faces
Will be (lit with) white,—
They will be in (the light
Of) God's mercy: therein
To dwell (for ever).

١٠٧- وَأَمَّا الَّذِينَ ابْيَضَّتْ وُجُوهُهُمْ
فَفِي رَحْمَةِ اللَّهِ ۖ
هُمْ فِيهَا خٰلِدُونَ ○

108. These are the Signs
Of God: We rehearse them
To thee in Truth:
And God means
No injustice to any
Of His creatures.

١٠٨- تِلْكَ آيٰتُ اللَّهِ
نَتْلُوهَا عَلَيْكَ بِالْحَقِّ ۗ
وَمَا اللَّهُ يُرِيدُ ظُلْمًا لِلْعٰلَمِينَ ○

109. To God belongs all
That is in the heavens

١٠٩- وَلِلَّهِ مَا فِي السَّمٰوٰتِ

---

431. *Mufliḥ, aflaḥa, falāḥ*: the root idea is attainment of desires; happiness, in this world and the next; success; prosperity; freedom from anxiety, care, or a disturbed state of mind;—the opposite of *'aẓāb* in the next verse, which includes: failure; misery; punishment or penalty; agony or anguish.

The ideal Muslim community is happy, untroubled by conflicts or doubts, sure of itself, strong, united, and prosperous: because it invites to all that is good; enjoins the right; and forbids the wrong,—a master-stroke of description in three clauses.

432. The "face" (*wajh*) expresses our Personality, our inmost being. White is the colour of Light; to become white is to be illumined with Light, which stands for felicity, the rays of the glorious light of God. Black is the colour of darkness, sin, rebellion, misery; removal from the grace and light of God. These are the Signs of heaven and hell. The standard of decision in all questions is the justice of God.

And on earth: to Him Do all questions Go back (for decision).[433]	وَمَا فِي الْأَرْضِ ۚ وَإِلَى اللَّهِ تُرْجَعُ الْأُمُورُ ۝ ع

SECTION 12.

110. Ye are the best Of Peoples, evolved For mankind, Enjoining what is right, Forbidding what is wrong, And believing in God.[434] If only the People of the Book Had faith, it were best For them: among them Are some who have faith, But most of them Are perverted transgressors.	١١٠- كُنتُمْ خَيْرَ أُمَّةٍ أُخْرِجَتْ لِلنَّاسِ تَأْمُرُونَ بِالْمَعْرُوفِ وَتَنْهَوْنَ عَنِ الْمُنكَرِ وَتُؤْمِنُونَ بِاللَّهِ ۗ وَلَوْ آمَنَ أَهْلُ الْكِتَابِ لَكَانَ خَيْرًا لَّهُم ۚ مِّنْهُمُ الْمُؤْمِنُونَ وَأَكْثَرُهُمُ الْفَاسِقُونَ ۝
111. They will do you no harm, Barring a trifling annoyance; If they come out to fight you, They will show you their backs, And no help shall they get.	١١١- لَن يَضُرُّوكُمْ إِلَّا أَذًى ۖ وَإِن يُقَاتِلُوكُمْ يُوَلُّوكُمُ الْأَدْبَارَ ثُمَّ لَا يُنصَرُونَ ۝
112. Shame is pitched over them[435] (Like a tent) wherever They are found, Except when under a covenant (Of protection) from God And from men; they draw On themselves wrath from God, And pitched over them Is (the tent of) destitution. This because they rejected The Signs of God, and slew The Prophets in defiance of right;[436]	١١٢- ضُرِبَتْ عَلَيْهِمُ الذِّلَّةُ أَيْنَ مَا ثُقِفُوا إِلَّا بِحَبْلٍ مِّنَ اللَّهِ وَحَبْلٍ مِّنَ النَّاسِ وَبَاءُو بِغَضَبٍ مِّنَ اللَّهِ وَضُرِبَتْ عَلَيْهِمُ الْمَسْكَنَةُ ۚ ذَٰلِكَ بِأَنَّهُمْ كَانُوا يَكْفُرُونَ بِآيَاتِ اللَّهِ وَيَقْتُلُونَ الْأَنبِيَاءَ بِغَيْرِ حَقٍّ ۚ

433. *Cf.* ii 210.

434. The logical conclusion to the evolution of religious history is a non-sectarian, non-racial, non-doctrinal, universal religion, which Islam claims to be. For Islam is just submission to the Will of God. This implies (1) Faith, (2) doing right, being an example to others to do right, and having the power to see that the right prevails, (3) eschewing wrong, being an example to others to eschew wrong, and having the power to see that wrong and injustice are defeated. Islam therefore lives, not for itself, but for mankind. The People of the Book, if only they had faith, would be Muslims, for they have been prepared for Islam. Unfortunately there is Unfaith, but it can never harm those who carry the banner of Faith and Right, which must always be victorious.

435. *Ḍhuribat*: I think there is a simile from the pitching of a tent. Ordinarily a man's tent is a place of tranquillity and honour for him. The tent of the wicked wherever they are found is ignominy, shame, and humiliation. It is pity from God or from men that gives them protection when their pride has a fall. Using the same simile of a tent in another way, their home will be destitution and misery.

436. *Cf.* iii. 21, n. 363.

This because they rebelled
And transgressed beyond bounds.

ذٰلِكَ بِمَا عَصَوْا وَّكَانُوْا يَعْتَدُوْنَ ○

113. Not all of them are alike:
Of the People of the Book
Are a portion that stand
(For the right); they rehearse
The Signs of God all night long,
And they prostrate themselves[437]
In adoration.

١١٣- لَيْسُوْا سَوَآءً ۭ مِنْ اَهْلِ الْكِتٰبِ
اُمَّةٌ قَآىِٕمَةٌ
يَّتْلُوْنَ اٰيٰتِ اللّٰهِ
اٰنَآءَ الَّيْلِ وَهُمْ يَسْجُدُوْنَ ○

114. They believe in God
And the Last Day;
They enjoin what is right,
And forbid what is wrong;
And they hasten (in emulation)
In (all) good works:
They are in the ranks
Of the righteous.

١١٤- يُؤْمِنُوْنَ بِاللّٰهِ وَالْيَوْمِ الْاٰخِرِ
وَيَاْمُرُوْنَ بِالْمَعْرُوْفِ وَيَنْهَوْنَ عَنِ الْمُنْكَرِ
وَيُسَارِعُوْنَ فِى الْخَيْرٰتِ ۭ
وَاُولٰۗىِٕكَ مِنَ الصّٰلِحِيْنَ ○

115. Of the good that they do,
Nothing will be rejected
Of them; for God knoweth well
Those that do right.

١١٥- وَمَا يَفْعَلُوْا مِنْ خَيْرٍ فَلَنْ يُّكْفَرُوْهُ ۭ
وَاللّٰهُ عَلِيْمٌۢ بِالْمُتَّقِيْنَ ○

116. Those who reject Faith,—
Neither their possessions
Nor their (numerous) progeny
Will avail them aught against
God:
They will be Companions
Of the Fire,—dwelling
Therein (for ever).[438]

١١٦- اِنَّ الَّذِيْنَ كَفَرُوْا لَنْ تُغْنِىَ عَنْهُمْ
اَمْوَالُهُمْ وَلَآ اَوْلَادُهُمْ
مِّنَ اللّٰهِ شَيْـًٔا ۭ وَاُولٰۗىِٕكَ اَصْحٰبُ النَّارِ ۚ
هُمْ فِيْهَا خٰلِدُوْنَ ○

117. What they spend
In the life
Of this (material) world
May be likened to a Wind
Which brings a nipping frost:
It strikes and destroys the harvest
Of men who have wronged

١١٧- مَثَلُ مَا يُنْفِقُوْنَ فِىْ هٰذِهِ الْحَيٰوةِ الدُّنْيَا
كَمَثَلِ رِيْحٍ فِيْهَا صِرٌّ
اَصَابَتْ حَرْثَ
قَوْمٍ ظَلَمُوْٓا اَنْفُسَهُمْ فَاَهْلَكَتْهُ ۭ

437. In Islam we respect sincere faith and true righteousness in whatever form they appear.

438. *Cf.* iii. 10.

Their own souls : it is not God
That hath wronged them, but
They wrong themselves.[439]

وَمَا ظَلَمَهُمُ اللّٰهُ
وَلٰكِنْ اَنْفُسَهُمْ يَظْلِمُوْنَ ○

118. O ye who believe!
Take not into your intimacy
Those outside your ranks :
They will not fail
To corrupt you. They
Only desire your ruin :
Rank hatred has already
Appeared from their mouths :
What their hearts conceal
Is far worse.
We have made plain
To you the Signs,
If ye have wisdom.

١١٨- يٰۤاَيُّهَا الَّذِيْنَ اٰمَنُوْا
لَا تَتَّخِذُوْا بِطَانَةً مِّنْ دُوْنِكُمْ
لَا يَاْلُوْنَكُمْ خَبَالًا ۭ وَدُّوْا مَا عَنِتُّمْ ۚ
قَدْ بَدَتِ الْبَغْضَاۗءُ مِنْ اَفْوَاهِهِمْ ښ
وَمَا تُخْفِيْ صُدُوْرُهُمْ اَكْبَرُ ۭ
قَدْ بَيَّنَّا لَكُمُ الْاٰيٰتِ
اِنْ كُنْتُمْ تَعْقِلُوْنَ ○

119. Ah! ye are those
Who love them,
But they love you not,—
Though ye believe
In the whole of the Book.[440]
When they meet you,
They say, "We believe" :[441]
But when they are alone,
They bite off the very tips
Of their fingers at you
In their rage. Say :
"Perish in your rage ;
God knoweth well
All the secrets of the heart."

١١٩- هٰۤاَنْتُمْ اُولَاۗءِ تُحِبُّوْنَهُمْ وَلَا يُحِبُّوْنَكُمْ
وَتُؤْمِنُوْنَ بِالْكِتٰبِ كُلِّهٖ ۚ
وَاِذَا لَقُوْكُمْ قَالُوْٓا اٰمَنَّا ڌ
وَاِذَا خَلَوْا
عَضُّوْا عَلَيْكُمُ الْاَنَامِلَ
مِنَ الْغَيْظِ ۭ قُلْ مُوْتُوْا بِغَيْظِكُمْ ۭ
اِنَّ اللّٰهَ عَلِيْمٌۢ بِذَاتِ الصُّدُوْرِ ○

120. If aught that is good
Befalls you, it grieves them ;
But if some misfortune
Overtakes you, they rejoice

١٢٠- اِنْ تَمْسَسْكُمْ حَسَنَةٌ تَسُؤْهُمْ ۡ
وَاِنْ تُصِبْكُمْ سَيِّئَةٌ يَّفْرَحُوْا بِهَا ۭ

---

439. False "spending" may be either in false "charity" or in having a "good time". For the man who resists God's purpose, neither of them is any good. The essence of charity is faith and love. Where these are wanting, charity is no charity. Some baser motive is there : ostentation, or even worse, getting a person into the giver's power by a pretence of charity : something that is connected with the life of this grasping, material world. What happens? You expect a good harvest. But "while you think, good easy man, full surely your greatness is a-ripening," there comes a nipping frost, and destroys all your hopes. The frost is some calamity, or the fact that you are found out! Or perhaps it is "High blown pride," as in Shakespeare's *Henry VIII*, ii. 3. In your despair you may blame blind Fate or you may blame God! Blind Fate does not exist, for there is God's Providence, which is just and good. The harm or injustice has come, not from God, but from your own soul. You wronged your soul, and it suffered the frost. Your base motive brought you no good : it may have reduced you to poverty, shame, and disgrace. All the brave show of the wicked in this life is but a wind charged with evil to themselves.

440. Islam gives you the complete revelation, "the whole of the Book," though partial revelations have come in all ages. (*Cf.* iii. 23, and n. 366.)

441. *Cf.* ii. 14.

At it. But if ye are constant
And do right,
Not the least harm
Will their cunning
Do to you; for God
Compasseth round about
All that they do.

وَإِنْ تَصْبِرُوا وَتَتَّقُوا
لَا يَضُرُّكُمْ كَيْدُهُمْ شَيْئًا
ع إِنَّ اللَّهَ بِمَا يَعْمَلُونَ مُحِيطٌ

C. 58.—God's help comes to those who strive
(iii. 121-148.) With firmness, as it did at Badr.
Much can be learnt from the misfortunes
At Uḥud. It is not for us
To question God's Plan, which is full
Of wisdom and mercy for all. Our duty
Is to stand firm and unswerving,
To obey, and in steadfast courage
To persevere, to retrieve our mistakes,
Not in grief and despair, but in firm hope
In God and in contempt of pain and death.

SECTION 13.

121. Remember that morning
Thou didst leave
Thy household (early)
To post the Faithful
At their stations for battle:[442]
And God heareth
And knoweth all things:

١٢١- وَإِذْ غَدَوْتَ مِنْ أَهْلِكَ
تُبَوِّئُ الْمُؤْمِنِينَ
مَقَاعِدَ لِلْقِتَالِ
وَاللَّهُ سَمِيعٌ عَلِيمٌ

442. The battle of Uḥud was a great testing time for the young Muslim community. Their mettle and the wisdom and strength of their Leader were shown in the battle of Badr (iii. 13 and note), in which the Meccan Pagans suffered a crushing defeat. The Meccans were determined to wipe off their disgrace and to annihilate the Muslims in Medina. To this end they collected a large force and marched to Medina. They numbered some 3,000 fighting men under Abū Sufyān, and they were so confident of victory that their women-folk came with them, and showed the most shameful savagery after the battle. To meet the threatened danger the Muslim Leader, Muḥammad Muṣṭafā, with his usual foresight, courage, and initiative, resolved to take his station at the foot of Mount Uḥud, which dominates the city of Medina some three miles to the north. Early in the morning, on the 7th of Shawwāl, A.H. 3 (January, 625), he made his dispositions for battle. Medina winters are notoriously rigorous, but the warriors of Islam (700 to 1000 in number) were up early. A torrent bed (*Nullah*) was to their south, and the passes in the hills at their back were filled with 50 archers to prevent the enemy attack from the rear. The enemy were set the task of attacking the walls of Medina, with the Muslims at their rear. In the beginning the battle went well for the Muslims. The enemy wavered, but the Muslim archers, in disobedience of their orders, left their posts to join in the pursuit and share in the booty. There was also treachery on the part of the 300 "Hypocrites" led by 'Abdullāh ibn Ubai, who deserted. The enemy took advantage of the opening left by the archers, and there was severe hand-to-hand fighting, in which numbers told in favour of the enemy. Many of the Companions and Helpers were killed. But there was no rout. Among the Muslim martyrs was the gallant Ḥamza, a brother of the Apostle's father. The graves of the martyrs are still shown at Uḥud. The Apostle himself was wounded in his head and face, and one of his front teeth was knocked off. Had it not been for his firmness, courage, and coolness, all would have been lost. As it was, the Apostle, in spite of his wound, and many of the wounded Muslims, inspired by his example, returned to the field next day, and Abū Sufyān and his Meccan army thought it most prudent to withdraw. Medina was saved, but a lesson in faith, constancy, firmness, and steadfastness was learnt by the Muslims.

122. Remember two of your parties[443]
Meditated cowardice;
But God was their protector,
And in God should the Faithful
(Ever) put their trust.

١٢٢- إِذْ هَمَّتْ طَّآئِفَتَانِ مِنكُمْ
أَن تَفْشَلَا وَاللَّهُ وَلِيُّهُمَا
وَعَلَى اللَّهِ فَلْيَتَوَكَّلِ الْمُؤْمِنُونَ ○

123. God had helped you
At Badr, when ye were
A contemptible little force;
Then fear God; thus
May ye show your gratitude.[444]

١٢٣- وَلَقَدْ نَصَرَكُمُ اللَّهُ بِبَدْرٍ
وَأَنتُمْ أَذِلَّةٌ
فَاتَّقُوا اللَّهَ لَعَلَّكُمْ تَشْكُرُونَ ○

124. Remember thou saidst
To the Faithful: "Is it not enough
For you that God should help you
With three thousand angels
(Specially) sent down?[445]

١٢٤- إِذْ تَقُولُ لِلْمُؤْمِنِينَ أَلَن يَكْفِيَكُمْ
أَن يُمِدَّكُمْ رَبُّكُم
بِثَلَاثَةِ آلَافٍ مِّنَ الْمَلَآئِكَةِ مُنزَلِينَ ○

125. "Yea,—if ye remain firm,
And act aright, even if
The enemy should rush here
On you in hot haste,
Your Lord would help you
With five thousand angels
Making a terrific onslaught."[446]

١٢٥- بَلَىٰ إِن تَصْبِرُوا وَتَتَّقُوا
وَيَأْتُوكُم مِّن فَوْرِهِمْ هَٰذَا يُمْدِدْكُمْ
رَبُّكُم بِخَمْسَةِ آلَافٍ
مِّنَ الْمَلَآئِكَةِ مُسَوِّمِينَ ○

126. God made it but a message
Of hope for you, and an assurance
To your hearts: (in any case)
There is no help
Except from God,
The Exalted, the Wise:[447]

١٢٦- وَمَا جَعَلَهُ اللَّهُ إِلَّا بُشْرَىٰ لَكُمْ
وَلِتَطْمَئِنَّ قُلُوبُكُم بِهِ
وَمَا النَّصْرُ إِلَّا مِنْ عِندِ اللَّهِ
الْعَزِيزِ الْحَكِيمِ ○

443. The two parties wavering in their minds were probably the Banū Salma Khazrajī and the Banū Ḥāritha, but they rallied under the Apostle's inspiration. That incident shows that man may be weak, but if he allows his weak will to be governed by the example of men of God, he may yet retrieve his weakness.

444. Gratitude to God is not to be measured by words. It should show itself in conduct and life. If all the Muslims had learnt the true lesson from the victory at Badr, their archers would not have left the posts appointed for them, nor the two tribes mentioned in the last note ever wavered in their faith.

445. Read verse 124 with the following five verses, to get its full signification.

446. *Musawwim*: this is the active voice of the verb, not to be confused with the passive voice in iii. 14, which has a different signification.

447. Whatever happens, whether there is a miracle or not, all help proceeds from God. Man should not be so arrogant as to suppose that his own resources will change the current of the world plan. God helps those who show constancy, courage, and discipline, and use all the human means at their disposal, not those who fold their hands and have no faith. But God's help is determined on considerations exalted far above our petty human motive, and by perfect wisdoms, of which we can have only faint glimpses.

127. That He might cut off
A fringe of the Unbelievers[448]
Or expose them to infamy,
And they should then
Be turned back,
Frustrated of their purpose.

١٢٧- لِيَقْطَعَ طَرَفًا
مِّنَ الَّذِينَ كَفَرُوٓا
أَوْ يَكْبِتَهُمْ فَيَنقَلِبُوا خَآئِبِينَ ○

128. Not for thee, (but for God),
Is the decision:
Whether He turn in mercy
To them, or punish them;
For they are indeed wrong-
doers.[449]

١٢٨- لَيْسَ لَكَ مِنَ الْأَمْرِ شَيْءٌ
أَوْ يَتُوبَ عَلَيْهِمْ
أَوْ يُعَذِّبَهُمْ فَإِنَّهُمْ ظَٰلِمُونَ ○

129. To God belongeth all
That is in the heavens
And on earth.
He forgiveth whom He pleaseth
And punisheth whom He pleaseth;
But God is Oft-Forgiving,
Most Merciful.

١٢٩- وَلِلَّهِ مَا فِي السَّمَٰوَٰتِ وَمَا فِي الْأَرْضِ
يَغْفِرُ لِمَن يَشَآءُ
وَيُعَذِّبُ مَن يَشَآءُ
وَاللَّهُ غَفُورٌ رَّحِيمٌ ○

SECTION 14.

130. O ye who believe!
Devour not Usury,[450]
Doubled and multiplied;
But fear God; that
Ye may (really) prosper.[451]

١٣٠- يَٰٓأَيُّهَا الَّذِينَ آمَنُوا لَا تَأْكُلُوا الرِّبَوٰٓا
أَضْعَٰفًا مُّضَٰعَفَةً
وَاتَّقُوا اللَّهَ لَعَلَّكُمْ تُفْلِحُونَ ○

131. Fear the Fire, which is prepared
For those who reject Faith:

١٣١- وَاتَّقُوا النَّارَ
الَّتِيٓ أُعِدَّتْ لِلْكَٰفِرِينَ ○

---

448. ***A fringe of the Unbelievers***: an extremity, an end, either upper or lower. Here it may mean that the chiefs of the Meccan Pagans, who had come to exterminate the Muslims with such confidence, went back frustrated in their purpose. The shameless cruelty with which they and their women mutilated the Muslim corpses on the battle-field will stand recorded to their eternal infamy. Perhaps it also exposed their real nature to some of those who fought for them, *e.g.*, Khālid ibn Walīd, who not only accepted Islam afterwards, but became one of the most notable champions of Islam. He was with the Muslims in the conquest of Mecca, and later on, won distinguished honours in Syria and 'Irāq.

449 Uḥud is as much a sign-post for Islam as Badr. For us in these latter days it carries an ever greater lesson. God's help will come if we have faith, obedience, discipline, unity, and the spirit of acting in righteousness and justice. If we fail, His mercy is always open to us. But it is also open to our enemies, and those who seem to us His enemies. His Plan may be to bring sinners to repentance, and to teach us righteousness and wisdom through those who seem in our eyes to be rebellious or even defiant. There may be good in them that He sees and we do not,—a humbling thought that must lead to our own self-examination and self-improvement.

450. *Cf.* ii. 275 and note. The last verse spoke of forgiveness, even to enemies. If such mercy is granted by God to erring sinners, how much more is it incumbent on us, poor sinners to refrain from oppressing our fellow-beings in need, in matters of mere material and ephemeral wealth? Usury is the opposite extreme of charity, unselfishness, striving, and giving of ourselves in the service of God and of our fellow-men.

451. Real prosperity consists, not in greed, but in giving,—the giving of ourselves and of our substance in the cause of God and God's truth and in the service of God's creatures.

132. And obey God
And the Apostle;
That ye may obtain mercy.

١٣٢- وَأَطِيعُوا اللّٰهَ وَالرَّسُولَ
لَعَلَّكُمْ تُرْحَمُونَ ۝

133. Be quick in the race
For forgiveness from your Lord,
And for a Garden whose width
Is that (of the whole)
Of the heavens
And of the earth,[452]
Prepared for the righteous,—

١٣٣- وَسَارِعُوٓا إِلَىٰ مَغْفِرَةٍ مِّن رَّبِّكُمْ
وَجَنَّةٍ
عَرْضُهَا السَّمٰوٰتُ وَالْأَرْضُ
أُعِدَّتْ لِلْمُتَّقِينَ ۝

134. Those who spend (freely),[453]
Whether in prosperity,
Or in adversity;
Who restrain anger,
And pardon (all) men;—
For God loves those
Who do good;—

١٣٤- الَّذِينَ يُنفِقُونَ فِي السَّرَّآءِ وَالضَّرَّآءِ
وَالْكٰظِمِينَ الْغَيْظَ
وَالْعَافِينَ عَنِ النَّاسِ ط
وَاللّٰهُ يُحِبُّ الْمُحْسِنِينَ ۝

135. And those who,[454]
Having done something
To be ashamed of,
Or wronged their own souls,[455]
Earnestly bring God to mind,
And ask for forgiveness
For their sins,—
And who can forgive
Sins except God?—
And are never obstinate
In persisting knowingly
In (the wrong) they have done

١٣٥- وَالَّذِينَ إِذَا فَعَلُوا فَاحِشَةً
أَوْ ظَلَمُوٓا أَنفُسَهُمْ ذَكَرُوا اللّٰهَ
فَاسْتَغْفَرُوا لِذُنُوبِهِمْ
وَمَن يَغْفِرُ الذُّنُوبَ إِلَّا اللّٰهُ
وَلَمْ يُصِرُّوا عَلَىٰ مَا فَعَلُوا
وَهُمْ يَعْلَمُونَ ۝

452. The Fire (iii. 131) is, as always, contrasted with the Garden in a spiritual sense,—in other words, Hell contrasted with Heaven. Lest we should think that heaven is a sort of enclosed material Garden somewhere in the skies, we are told that its width alone is that of the whole of the heavens and the earth,—all the creation we can imagine. In other words our spiritual felicity covers not merely this or that part of our being, but all life and all existence. Who can measure its width, or length, or depth?

453. Another definition of the righteous (*vv.* 134-35). So far from grasping material wealth, they give freely, of themselves and their substance, not only when they are well-off and it is easy for them to do so, but also when they are in difficulties, for other people may be in difficulties at the same time. They do not get ruffled in adversity, or get angry when other people behave badly, or their own good plans fail. On the contrary they redouble their efforts. For the charity—or good deed—is all the more necessary in adversity. And they do not throw the blame on others. Even where such blame is due and correction is necessary, their own mind is free from a sense of grievance, for they forgive and cover other men's faults. This as far as other people are concerned. But we may be ourselves at fault, and perhaps we brought some calamity on ourselves. The righteous man is not necessarily perfect. In such circumstances his behaviour is described in the next verse.

454. The righteous man, when he finds he has fallen into sin or error, does not whine or despair, but asks for God's forgiveness, and his faith gives him hope. If he is sincere, that means that he abandons his wrong conduct and makes amends.

455. Sin is a sort of oppression of ourselves by ourselves. This follows from the doctrine of personal responsibility, as opposed to that of blind fate or of an angry God or gods lying in wait for revenge or injury on mankind.

136. For such the reward
Is forgiveness from their Lord,
And Gardens with rivers
Flowing underneath,—
An eternal dwelling:
How excellent a recompense
For those who work (and strive)!

١٣٦- أُولَٰئِكَ جَزَآؤُهُم
مَّغْفِرَةٌ مِّن رَّبِّهِمْ وَجَنَّٰتٌ تَجْرِى مِن
تَحْتِهَا ٱلْأَنْهَٰرُ خَٰلِدِينَ فِيهَا ۚ
وَنِعْمَ أَجْرُ ٱلْعَٰمِلِينَ ○

137. Many were the Ways of Life[456]
That have passed away
Before you: travel through
The earth, and see what was
The end of those
Who rejected Truth.

١٣٧- قَدْ خَلَتْ مِن قَبْلِكُمْ سُنَنٌ
فَسِيرُوا فِى ٱلْأَرْضِ
فَٱنظُرُوا
كَيْفَ كَانَ عَٰقِبَةُ ٱلْمُكَذِّبِينَ ○

138. Here is a plain statement
To men, a guidance
And instruction to those
Who fear God!

١٣٨- هَٰذَا بَيَانٌ لِّلنَّاسِ
وَهُدًى وَمَوْعِظَةٌ لِّلْمُتَّقِينَ ○

139. So lose not heart,
Nor fall into despair:
For ye must gain mastery
If ye are true in Faith.

١٣٩- وَلَا تَهِنُوا وَلَا تَحْزَنُوا
وَأَنتُمُ ٱلْأَعْلَوْنَ إِن كُنتُم مُّؤْمِنِينَ ○

140. If a wound hath touched you,[457]
Be sure a similar wound
Hath touched the others.
Such days (of varying fortunes)
We give to men and men
By turns: that God may know
Those that believe,
And that He may take
To Himself from your ranks
Martyr-witnesses (to Truth).
And God loveth not
Those that do wrong.

١٤٠- إِن يَمْسَسْكُمْ قَرْحٌ
فَقَدْ مَسَّ ٱلْقَوْمَ قَرْحٌ مِّثْلُهُۥ ۚ
وَتِلْكَ ٱلْأَيَّامُ نُدَاوِلُهَا بَيْنَ ٱلنَّاسِ
وَلِيَعْلَمَ ٱللَّهُ ٱلَّذِينَ ءَامَنُوا
وَيَتَّخِذَ مِنكُمْ شُهَدَآءَ ۗ
وَٱللَّهُ لَا يُحِبُّ ٱلظَّٰلِمِينَ ○

456. *Cf.* Tennyson (In Memoriam): "Our little systems have their day, They have their day and cease to be: They are but broken lights of Thee, And Thou, O Lord! art more than they." Only God's Truth will last, and it will gain the mastery in the end. If there is defeat, we must not be dejected, lose heart, or give up the struggle. Faith means hope, activity, striving steadfastly on to the goal.

457. These general considerations apply in particular to the disaster at Uhud. (1) In a fight for truth, if you are hurt, be sure the adversary has suffered hurt also, the more so as he has no faith to sustain him. (2) Success or failure in this world comes to all at varying times: we must not grumble, as we do not see the whole of God's Plan. (3) Men's true mettle is known in adversity as gold is assayed in fire; *Cf.* also iii 154, n. 467. (4) Martyrdom is in itself an honour and a privilege: how glorious is the fame of Ḥamza the Martyr, and in later times, of Ḥasan and Ḥusain? (5) If there is any dross in us, it will be purified by resistance and struggle. (6) When evil is given rope a little, it works out its own destruction: the orgies of cruelty indulged in by the Pagans after what they supposed to be their victory at Uhud filled up their cup of iniquity; it lost them the support and adherence of the best in their own ranks, and hastened the destruction of Paganism from Arabia. *Cf.* iii. 127 and n. 448.

141. God's object also is to purge[458]
Those that are true in Faith
And to deprive of blessing
Those that resist Faith.

١٤١- وَلِيُمَحِّصَ اللّٰهُ الَّذِيْنَ اٰمَنُوْا
وَيَمْحَقَ الْكٰفِرِيْنَ ۝

142. Did ye think that ye
Would enter Heaven[459]
Without God testing
Those of you who fought hard
(In His Cause) and
Remained steadfast?

١٤٢- اَمْ حَسِبْتُمْ اَنْ تَدْخُلُوا الْجَنَّةَ
وَلَمَّا يَعْلَمِ اللّٰهُ الَّذِيْنَ جٰهَدُوْا مِنْكُمْ
وَيَعْلَمَ الصّٰبِرِيْنَ ۝

143. Ye did indeed
Wish for Death
Before ye met him:
Now ye have seen him
With your own eyes,
(And ye flinch!)

١٤٣- وَلَقَدْ كُنْتُمْ تَمَنَّوْنَ الْمَوْتَ
مِنْ قَبْلِ اَنْ تَلْقَوْهُ
ع فَقَدْ رَاَيْتُمُوْهُ وَاَنْتُمْ تَنْظُرُوْنَ ۝

SECTION 15.

144. Muḥammad is no more[460]
Than an Apostle: many
Were the Apostles that passed away
Before him. If he died
Or were slain, will ye then
Turn back on your heels?
If any did turn back
On his heels, not the least
Harm will he do to God;
But God (on the other hand)
Will swiftly reward those
Who (serve him) with gratitude.

١٤٤- وَمَا مُحَمَّدٌ اِلَّا رَسُوْلٌ
قَدْ خَلَتْ مِنْ قَبْلِهِ الرُّسُلُ اَفَا۟ئِنْ مَّاتَ
اَوْ قُتِلَ
انْقَلَبْتُمْ عَلٰٓى اَعْقَابِكُمْ
وَمَنْ يَّنْقَلِبْ عَلٰى عَقِبَيْهِ
فَلَنْ يَّضُرَّ اللّٰهَ شَيْئًا
وَسَيَجْزِى اللّٰهُ الشّٰكِرِيْنَ ۝

145. Nor can a soul die
Except by God's leave,

١٤٥- وَمَا كَانَ لِنَفْسٍ اَنْ تَمُوْتَ اِلَّا بِاِذْنِ اللّٰهِ

458. The purge or purification was in two senses. (1) It cleared out the Hypocrites from the ranks of the Muslim warriors. (2) The testing-time strengthened the faith of the weak and wavering: for suffering has its own mission in life. The Apostle's example—wounded but staunch, and firmer than ever—put new life into the Community.

459. *Cf.* ii. 214.

460. This verse primarily applies to the battle of Uḥud, in the course of which a cry was raised that the Apostle was slain He had indeed been severely wounded, but Ṭalḥa, Abū Bakr, and 'Alī were at his side, and his own unexampled bravery saved the Muslim army from a rout. This verse was recalled again by Abū Bakr when the Apostle actually died a natural death eight years later, to remind people that God, Whose Message he brought, lives for ever. And we have need to remember this now and often for two reasons: (1) when we feel inclined to pay more than human honour to one who was the truest, the purest, and the greatest of men, and thus in a sense to compound for our forgetting the spirit of his teaching, and (2) when we feel depressed at the chances and changes of time, and forget that the eternal God lives and watches over us and over all His creatures now as in all history in the past and in the future.

The term being fixed
As by writing. If any
Do desire a reward
In this life, We shall give it[461]
To him; and if any
Do desire a reward
In the Hereafter, We shall
Give it to him.
And swiftly shall We reward
Those that (serve us with)
gratitude.

كِتٰبًا مُّؤَجَّلًا ۗ
وَمَنْ يُّرِدْ
ثَوَابَ الدُّنْيَا نُؤْتِهٖ مِنْهَا ۚ
وَمَنْ يُّرِدْ ثَوَابَ الْاٰخِرَةِ
نُؤْتِهٖ مِنْهَا ۗ
وَسَنَجْزِي الشّٰكِرِيْنَ ○

146. How many of the Prophets
Fought (in God's way),
And with them (fought)
Large bands of godly men?
But they never lost heart
If they met with disaster
In God's way, nor did
They weaken (in will)
Nor give in. And God
Loves those who are
Firm and steadfast.

١٤٦- وَكَاَيِّنْ مِّنْ نَّبِيٍّ قٰتَلَ ۙ مَعَهٗ
رِبِّيُّوْنَ كَثِيْرٌ ۚ فَمَا وَهَنُوْا
لِمَآ اَصَابَهُمْ فِيْ سَبِيْلِ اللّٰهِ
وَمَا ضَعُفُوْا
وَمَا اسْتَكَانُوْا ۗ
وَاللّٰهُ يُحِبُّ الصّٰبِرِيْنَ ○

147. All that they said was:
"Our Lord! forgive us
Our sins and anything
We may have done
That transgressed our duty:
Establish our feet firmly,
And help us against
Those that resist
Faith."

١٤٧- وَمَا كَانَ قَوْلَهُمْ اِلَّآ اَنْ قَالُوْا
رَبَّنَا اغْفِرْ لَنَا
ذُنُوْبَنَا وَاِسْرَافَنَا فِيْٓ اَمْرِنَا
وَثَبِّتْ اَقْدَامَنَا
وَانْصُرْنَا عَلَى الْقَوْمِ الْكٰفِرِيْنَ ○

148. And God gave them
A reward in this world,
And the excellent reward
Of the Hereafter. For God
Loveth those who do good.

١٤٨- فَاٰتٰىهُمُ اللّٰهُ ثَوَابَ الدُّنْيَا وَحُسْنَ
ثَوَابِ الْاٰخِرَةِ ۗ وَاللّٰهُ يُحِبُّ الْمُحْسِنِيْنَ ○

C. 59.—Uhud showed how dangerous it was
(iii. 149-180.) To lend ear to enemy suggestions,
To disobey orders, dispute, lose courage,
Or seek selfish ends; some even followed

---

461. There is a slight touch of irony in this. As applied to the archers at Uhud, who deserted their posts for the sake of plunder, they might have got some plunder, but they put themselves and the whole of their army into jeopardy. For a little worldly gain, they nearly lost their souls. On the other hand, those who took the long view and fought with staunchness and discipline,—their reward was swift and sure. If they died, they got the crown of martyrdom. If they lived, they were heroes honoured in this life and the next.

The evil course of turning back.
But great is God's mercy: where He helps,
No harm can come. Trust your Leader.
The Hypocrites, in withdrawing from battle,
Were really helping the Unbelievers,
But glorious were those who knew
No fear: those killed in the Cause of God
Yet live and thrive and do rejoice;
And never can those who fight against Faitl
Hurt in the least the Cause of God.

SECTION 16.

149. O ye who believe!
If ye obey the Unbelievers,
They will drive you back
On your heels, and ye
Will turn back (from Faith)
To your own loss.

١٤٩- يَأَيُّهَا الَّذِينَ آمَنُوا إِن تُطِيعُوا الَّذِينَ
كَفَرُوا يَرُدُّوكُمْ عَلَىٰ أَعْقَابِكُمْ
فَتَنقَلِبُوا خَاسِرِينَ ○

150. Nay, God is your Protector,
And He is the best of helpers.

١٥٠- بَلِ اللَّهُ مَوْلَاكُمْ ۚ وَهُوَ خَيْرُ النَّاصِرِينَ ○

151. Soon shall We cast terror
Into the hearts of the Unbelievers,
For that they joined companions
With God, for which He had sent
No authority: their abode
Will be the Fire: and evil
Is the home of the wrong-doers!

١٥١- سَنُلْقِي فِي قُلُوبِ الَّذِينَ كَفَرُوا الرُّعْبَ
بِمَا أَشْرَكُوا بِاللَّهِ
مَا لَمْ يُنَزِّلْ بِهِ سُلْطَانًا ۚ وَمَأْوَاهُمُ النَّارُ ۖ
وَبِئْسَ مَثْوَى الظَّالِمِينَ ○

152. God did indeed fulfil
His promise to you
When ye with His permission
Were about to annihilate
Your enemy,—until ye flinched
And fell to disputing
About the order,[462]
And disobeyed it
After He brought you in sight
(Of the Booty) which ye covet.
Among you are some
That hanker after this world
And some that desire
The Hereafter. Then did He

١٥٢- وَلَقَدْ صَدَقَكُمُ اللَّهُ وَعْدَهُ إِذْ
تَحُسُّونَهُم بِإِذْنِهِ ۖ حَتَّىٰ إِذَا فَشِلْتُمْ
وَتَنَازَعْتُمْ فِي الْأَمْرِ
وَعَصَيْتُم مِّن بَعْدِ مَا أَرَاكُم مَّا
تُحِبُّونَ ۚ
مِنكُم مَّن يُرِيدُ الدُّنْيَا
وَمِنكُم مَّن يُرِيدُ الْآخِرَةَ ۚ

462. The order was: not to run after booty, but strictly to maintain discipline. Uhud was in the beginning a victory for the Muslims. Many of the enemy were slain, and they were retiring when a part of the Muslims, against orders, ran in pursuit, attracted by the prospects of booty. See note to iii. 121.

Divert you from your foes
In order to test you.[463]
But He forgave you:
For God is full of grace
To those who believe.

ثُمَّ صَرَفَكُمْ
عَنْهُمْ لِيَبْتَلِيَكُمْ ۚ وَلَقَدْ عَفَا عَنكُمْ ۗ
وَاللَّهُ ذُو فَضْلٍ عَلَى الْمُؤْمِنِينَ ○

153. Behold! ye were climbing up
The high ground, without even
Casting a side glance
At any one, and the Apostle
In your rear was calling you
Back. There did God give you
One distress after another
By way of requital,[464]
To teach you not to grieve
For (the booty) that had escaped you
And for (the ill) that had befallen you.
For God is well aware
Of all that ye do.

١٥٣- إِذْ تُصْعِدُونَ
وَلَا تَلْوُونَ عَلَىٰ أَحَدٍ وَالرَّسُولُ
يَدْعُوكُمْ فِي أُخْرَاكُمْ
فَأَثَابَكُمْ غَمًّا بِغَمٍّ
لِّكَيْلَا تَحْزَنُوا
عَلَىٰ مَا فَاتَكُمْ
وَلَا مَا أَصَابَكُمْ ۗ
وَاللَّهُ خَبِيرٌ بِمَا تَعْمَلُونَ ○

154. After (the excitement)
Of the distress, He sent down
Calm on a band of you
Overcome with slumber,[465]
While another band
Was stirred to anxiety
By their own feelings,
Moved by wrong suspicions
Of God—suspicions due
To Ignorance. They said:
"What affair is this of ours?"[466]
Say thou: "Indeed, this affair

١٥٤- ثُمَّ أَنزَلَ عَلَيْكُم مِّن بَعْدِ الْغَمِّ
أَمَنَةً نُّعَاسًا يَغْشَىٰ طَائِفَةً مِّنكُمْ ۖ
وَطَائِفَةٌ قَدْ أَهَمَّتْهُمْ أَنفُسُهُمْ
يَظُنُّونَ بِاللَّهِ غَيْرَ الْحَقِّ ظَنَّ الْجَاهِلِيَّةِ ۖ
يَقُولُونَ هَل لَّنَا مِنَ الْأَمْرِ مِن شَيْءٍ ۗ
قُلْ إِنَّ الْأَمْرَ

463. The disobedience seemed at first pleasant: they were chasing the enemy, and there was the prospect of booty. But when the gap was noticed by the enemy, they turned the flank round the hill and nearly overwhelmed the Muslims. Had it not been for God's grace, and the firmness of their Leader and his immediate Companions, they would have been finished.

464. It would seem that a party of horsemen led by the dashing Khālid ibn Walīd came through the gap in the passes where the Muslim archers should have been, and in the confusion that arose, the retreating foe rallied and turned back on the Muslims. From the low ground on the bank of the Nullah the Muslims retreated in their turn and tried to gain the hill. They had a double loss: (1) they were baulked of the booty they had run after, and (2) their own lives and the lives of their whole army were in danger, and many lives were actually lost from their ranks. Their own lives being in danger, they had hardly time to grieve for the loss of booty or the general calamity. But it steadied them, and some of them stood the test.

465. After the first surprise, when the enemy turned on them, a great part of the Muslims did their best, and seeing their mettle, the enemy withdrew to his camp. There was a lull; the wounded had rest; those who had fought the hard fight were visited by kindly Sleep, sweet Nature's nurse. In contrast to them was the band of Hypocrites, whose behaviour is described in the next note.

466. The Hypocrites withdrew from the fighting. Apparently they had been among those who had been counselling the defence of Medina within the walls instead of boldly coming out to meet the enemy. Their distress was caused by their own mental state: the sleep of the just was denied them: and they continued to murmur of what might have been. Only fools do so: wise men face actualities.

Is wholly God's." They hide
In their minds what they
Dare not reveal to thee.
They say (to themselves):
"If we had had anything
To do with this affair,
We should not have been
In the slaughter here."
Say: "Even if you had remained
In your homes, those
For whom death was decreed
Would certainly have gone forth
To the place of their death";
But (all this was)[467]
That God might test
What is in your breasts
And purge what is
In your hearts.
For God knoweth well
The secrets of your hearts.

كُلَّهٗ لِلّٰهِ ۗ يُخْفُوْنَ فِيْٓ اَنْفُسِهِمْ
مَّا لَا يُبْدُوْنَ لَكَ ۭ يَقُوْلُوْنَ
لَوْ كَانَ لَنَا مِنَ الْاَمْرِ شَيْءٌ
مَّا قُتِلْنَا هٰهُنَا ۭ قُلْ لَّوْ كُنْتُمْ
فِيْ بُيُوْتِكُمْ
لَبَرَزَ الَّذِيْنَ كُتِبَ عَلَيْهِمُ
الْقَتْلُ اِلٰى مَضَاجِعِهِمْ ۚ
وَلِيَبْتَلِيَ اللّٰهُ مَا فِيْ صُدُوْرِكُمْ
وَلِيُمَحِّصَ مَا فِيْ قُلُوْبِكُمْ ۭ
وَاللّٰهُ عَلِيْمٌۢ بِذَاتِ الصُّدُوْرِ ○

155. Those of you[468]
Who turned back
On the day the two hosts
Met,—it was Satan
Who caused them to fail,
Because of some (evil)
They had done. But God
Has blotted out (their fault):
For God is Oft-forgiving,
Most Forbearing.

١٥٥- اِنَّ الَّذِيْنَ تَوَلَّوْا مِنْكُمْ يَوْمَ الْتَقَى
الْجَمْعٰنِ ۙ اِنَّمَا اسْتَزَلَّهُمُ الشَّيْطٰنُ
بِبَعْضِ مَا كَسَبُوْا ۚ
وَلَقَدْ عَفَا اللّٰهُ عَنْهُمْ ۭ
اِنَّ اللّٰهَ غَفُوْرٌ حَلِيْمٌ ○ ع

SECTION 17.

156. O ye who believe!
Be not like the Unbelievers,
Who say of their brethren,
When they are travelling
Through the earth or engaged
In fighting: "If they had stayed
With us, they would not
Have died, or been slain."

١٥٦- يٰٓاَيُّهَا الَّذِيْنَ اٰمَنُوْا لَا تَكُوْنُوْا كَالَّذِيْنَ
كَفَرُوْا وَقَالُوْا لِاِخْوَانِهِمْ
اِذَا ضَرَبُوْا فِي الْاَرْضِ اَوْ كَانُوْا غُزًّى
لَّوْ كَانُوْا عِنْدَنَا مَا مَاتُوْا وَمَا قُتِلُوْا ۚ

467. That testing by God is not in order that it may add to His knowledge, for He knows all. It is in order to help us subjectively, to mould our will, and purge us of any grosser motives, that will be searched out by calamity. If it is a hardened sinner, the test brings conviction out of his own self *Cf.* also iii. 140.

468. It was the duty of all who were able to fight, to fight in the sacred cause at Uhud. But a small section were timid: they were not quite as bad as those who railed against God, or those who thoughtlessly disobeyed orders. But they still failed in their duty. It is our inner motives that God regards. These timorous people were forgiven by God. Perhaps they were given another chance: perhaps they rose to it and did their duty then.

This that God may make it
A cause of sighs and regrets
In their hearts. It is God
That gives Life and Death,[469]
And God sees well
All that ye do.

لِيَجْعَلَ اللّٰهُ ذٰلِكَ حَسْرَةً فِىْ قُلُوْبِهِمْ ۗ
وَاللّٰهُ يُحْىٖ وَيُمِيْتُ ۗ
وَاللّٰهُ بِمَا تَعْمَلُوْنَ بَصِيْرٌ ○

157. And if ye are slain, or die,
In the way of God,
Forgiveness and mercy
From God are far better
Than all they could amass.[470]

١٥٧- وَلَئِنْ قُتِلْتُمْ فِىْ سَبِيْلِ اللّٰهِ
اَوْ مُتُّمْ لَمَغْفِرَةٌ مِّنَ اللّٰهِ
وَرَحْمَةٌ خَيْرٌ مِّمَّا يَجْمَعُوْنَ ○

158. And if ye die, or are slain,
Lo! it is unto God
That ye are brought together.

١٥٨- وَلَئِنْ مُّتُّمْ اَوْ قُتِلْتُمْ
لَاِلَى اللّٰهِ تُحْشَرُوْنَ ○

159. It is part of the Mercy
Of God that thou dost deal
Gently with them.[471]
Wert thou severe
Or harsh-hearted,
They would have broken away
From about thee: so pass over
(Their faults), and ask
For (God's) forgiveness
For them; and consult
Them in affairs (of moment).
Then, when thou hast
Taken a decision,
Put thy trust in God.

١٥٩- فَبِمَا رَحْمَةٍ مِّنَ اللّٰهِ لِنْتَ لَهُمْ ۚ
وَلَوْ كُنْتَ فَظًّا غَلِيْظَ الْقَلْبِ
لَانْفَضُّوْا مِنْ حَوْلِكَ ۖ
فَاعْفُ عَنْهُمْ
وَاسْتَغْفِرْ لَهُمْ
وَشَاوِرْهُمْ فِى الْاَمْرِ ۚ
فَاِذَا عَزَمْتَ فَتَوَكَّلْ عَلَى اللّٰهِ ۗ

469. It is want of faith that makes people afraid (1) of meeting death, (2) of doing their duty when it involves danger, as in travelling in order to earn an honest living, or fighting in a sacred cause. Such fear is part of the punishment for want of faith. If you have faith, there is no fear in meeting death, for it brings you nearer to your goal, nor in meeting danger for a sufficient cause, because you know that the keys of life and death are in God's hands. Nothing can happen without God's Will. If it is God's Will that you should die, your staying at home will not save you. If it is His Will that you should live, the danger you incur in a just cause brings you glory. Supposing it is His Will that you should lose your life in the danger, there are three considerations that would make you eager to meet it: (1) dying in doing your duty is the best means of reaching God's Mercy; (2) the man of faith knows that he is not going to an unknown country of which he has no news; he is going nearer to God; and (3) he is being "brought together" unto God; *i.e.*, he will meet all his dear ones in faith: instead of the separation which the souls without faith fear, he looks forward to a surer reunion than is possible in this life.

470. Notice a beautiful little literary touch here. At first sight you would expect the second person here ("*you* could amass"), to match the second person in the earlier clause. But remember that the second person in earlier clause refers to the man of faith, and the third person in the last line refers to the Unbelievers; as if it said: "Of course you as a man of faith would not be for hoarding riches: your wealth,—duty and the mercy of God,—is far more precious than anything the Unbelievers can amass in their selfish lives."

471. The extremely gentle nature of Muhammad endeared him to all, and it is reckoned as one of the Mercies of God. One of the Apostle's titles is "A Mercy to all Creation." At no time was this gentleness, this mercy, this long-suffering with human weaknesses, more valuable than after a disaster like that at Uhud. It is a God-like quality, which then, as always, bound and binds the souls of countless men to him.

For God loves those
Who put their trust (in Him).

إِنَّ اللّٰهَ يُحِبُّ الْمُتَوَكِّلِينَ ○

160. If God helps you,
Non can overcome you:
If He forsakes you,
Who is there, after that,
That can help you?
In God, then,
Let Believers put their trust.

١٦٠- إِن يَنصُرْكُمُ اللّٰهُ فَلَا غَالِبَ لَكُمْ
وَإِن يَخْذُلْكُمْ
فَمَن ذَا الَّذِي يَنصُرُكُم مِّن بَعْدِهِ
وَعَلَى اللّٰهِ فَلْيَتَوَكَّلِ الْمُؤْمِنُونَ ○

161. No prophet could (ever)[472]
Be false to his trust.
If any person is so false,
He shall, on the Day
Of Judgment, restore
What he misappropriated;
Then shall every soul
Receive its due,—
Whatever it earned,—
And none shall be
Dealt with unjustly.

١٦١- وَمَا كَانَ لِنَبِيٍّ أَن يَغُلَّ
وَمَن يَغْلُلْ
يَأْتِ بِمَا غَلَّ يَوْمَ الْقِيٰمَةِ
ثُمَّ تُوَفّٰى
كُلُّ نَفْسٍ مَّا كَسَبَتْ
وَهُمْ لَا يُظْلَمُونَ ○

162. Is the man who follows
The good pleasure of God
Like the man who draws
On himself the wrath
Of God, and whose abode
Is in Hell?—
A woeful refuge!

١٦٢- أَفَمَنِ اتَّبَعَ رِضْوَانَ اللّٰهِ
كَمَنۢ بَآءَ بِسَخَطٍ مِّنَ اللّٰهِ
وَمَأْوٰىهُ جَهَنَّمُ
وَبِئْسَ الْمَصِيرُ ○

163. They are in varying grades
In the sight of God,
And God sees well
All that they do.

١٦٣- هُمْ دَرَجٰتٌ عِندَ اللّٰهِ
وَاللّٰهُ بَصِيرٌۢ بِمَا يَعْمَلُونَ ○

164. God did confer
A great favour

١٦٤- لَقَدْ مَنَّ اللّٰهُ

472. Besides the gentleness of his nature, Muṣṭafā was known from his earliest life for his trustworthiness. Hence his title of *Al-Amīn*. Unscrupulous people often read their own low motives into other men, and their accusation, which is meant to injure, fastens on the various virtues for which the man they attack is well known. Some of the Hypocrites after Uḥud raised some doubts about the division of the spoils, thinking to sow the seeds of poison in the hearts of the men who had deserted their posts in their craving for booty. Those low suspicions were never believed in by any sensible people, and they have no interest for us now. But tne general principles here declared are of eternal value. (1) Men of God do not act from unworthy motives. (2) Those who act from such motives are spiritually the lowest of creatures, and they will make no profit. (3) A man of God is not to be judged by the same standard as a greedy creature. (4) In God's eyes there are various grades of men, and we must try to understand and appreciate such grades. If we trust our Leader, we shall not question his honesty without cause. If he is dishonest, he is not fit to be a leader.

On the Believers[473]
When He sent among them
An Apostle from among
Themselves, rehearsing
Unto them the Signs
Of God, sanctifying them,
And instructing them
In Scripture and Wisdom,
While, before that,
They had been
In manifest error.

عَلَى الْمُؤْمِنِيْنَ إِذْ بَعَثَ فِيْهِمْ
رَسُوْلًا مِّنْ أَنْفُسِهِمْ
يَتْلُوْا عَلَيْهِمْ اٰيٰتِهٖ
وَيُزَكِّيْهِمْ وَيُعَلِّمُهُمُ الْكِتٰبَ وَالْحِكْمَةَ
وَإِنْ كَانُوْا مِنْ قَبْلُ
لَفِيْ ضَلٰلٍ مُّبِيْنٍ ○ النصف

165. What! When a single
Disaster smites you,
Although ye smote (your enemies)
With one twice as great,
Do ye say?—
"Whence is this?"
Say (to them):
"It is from yourselves:
For God hath power
Over all things."[474]

١٦٥- أَوَلَمَّآ أَصَابَتْكُمْ مُّصِيْبَةٌ
قَدْ أَصَبْتُمْ مِّثْلَيْهَا
قُلْتُمْ أَنّٰى هٰذَا
قُلْ هُوَ مِنْ عِنْدِ أَنْفُسِكُمْ
إِنَّ اللّٰهَ عَلٰى كُلِّ شَيْءٍ قَدِيْرٌ ○

166. What ye suffered
On the day the two armies
Met, was with the leave
Of God, in order that
He might test[475] the Believers,—

١٦٦- وَمَآ أَصَابَكُمْ يَوْمَ الْتَقَى الْجَمْعٰنِ
فَبِإِذْنِ اللّٰهِ
وَلِيَعْلَمَ الْمُؤْمِنِيْنَ ○

167. And the Hypocrites also.[476]
These were told: "Come,
Fight in the way of God,
Or (at least) drive
(The foe from your city)."
They said: "Had we known
How to fight, we should
Certainly have followed you."

١٦٧- وَلِيَعْلَمَ الَّذِيْنَ نَافَقُوْا وَقِيْلَ لَهُمْ
تَعَالَوْا قَاتِلُوْا فِيْ سَبِيْلِ اللّٰهِ
أَوِ ادْفَعُوْا
قَالُوْا لَوْ نَعْلَمُ قِتَالًا لَّاتَّبَعْنٰكُمْ

473. *Cf.* ii. 151.

474. If Uḥud was a reverse to the Muslims, they had inflicted a reverse twice as great on the Meccans at Badr. This reverse was not without God's permission, for He wanted to test and purify the faith of those who followed Islam, and to show them that they must strive and do all in their power to deserve God s help. If they disobeyed orders and neglected discipline, they must attribute the disaster to themselves and not to God.

475. *Test*: literally *know*. See n. 467 to iii. 154.

476. The testing of the Hypocrites was the searching out of their motives and exposing them to the sight of their brethren, who might otherwise have been taken in. In the first place they gave counsels of caution: in their minds it was nothing but cowardice. In the second place, what they wished was not the good of the community but its being placed in a contemptible position. When others were for self-sacrifice, they were for ease and fair words. Pretending to be Muslims, they were nearer to Unbelief. Ironically they pretended to know nothing of fighting, and left their devout brethren to defend their faith and ideals. If that devout spirit did not appeal to them, they might at least have defended their city of Medina when it was threatened,—defended their hearths and homes as good citizens.

They were that day
Nearer to Unbelief
Than to Faith,
Saying with their lips
What was not in their hearts.
But God hath full knowledge
Of all they conceal.

هُمْ لِلْكُفْرِ يَوْمَئِذٍ أَقْرَبُ مِنْهُمْ لِلْإِيمَانِ ۚ
يَقُولُونَ بِأَفْوَاهِهِم
مَّا لَيْسَ فِي قُلُوبِهِمْ ۗ
وَاللَّهُ أَعْلَمُ بِمَا يَكْتُمُونَ ○

168. (They are) the ones that say,
(Of their brethren slain),
While they themselves
Sit (at ease): "If only
They had listened to us,
They would not have been slain."
Say: "Avert death
From your own selves,
If ye speak the truth."

١٦٨- الَّذِينَ قَالُوا لِإِخْوَانِهِمْ
وَقَعَدُوا لَوْ أَطَاعُونَا مَا قُتِلُوا ۗ
قُلْ فَادْرَءُوا عَنْ أَنفُسِكُمُ الْمَوْتَ
إِن كُنتُمْ صَادِقِينَ ○

169. Think not of those
Who are slain in God's way
As dead. Nay, they live,[477]
Finding their sustenance
In the Presence of their Lord;

١٦٩- وَلَا تَحْسَبَنَّ الَّذِينَ قُتِلُوا فِي سَبِيلِ
اللَّهِ أَمْوَاتًا ۚ
بَلْ أَحْيَاءٌ عِندَ رَبِّهِمْ يُرْزَقُونَ ○

170. They rejoice in the Bounty
Provided by God:
And with regard to those
Left behind, who have not
Yet joined them (in their bliss),
The (Martyrs) glory in the fact
That on them is no fear,
Nor have they (cause to) grieve.[478]

١٧٠- فَرِحِينَ بِمَا آتَاهُمُ اللَّهُ مِن فَضْلِهِ
وَيَسْتَبْشِرُونَ
بِالَّذِينَ لَمْ يَلْحَقُوا بِهِم مِّنْ خَلْفِهِمْ
أَلَّا خَوْفٌ عَلَيْهِمْ وَلَا هُمْ يَحْزَنُونَ ○

171. They glory in the Grace
And the Bounty from God,
And in the fact that
God suffereth not

١٧١- يَسْتَبْشِرُونَ بِنِعْمَةٍ مِّنَ اللَّهِ وَفَضْلٍ
وَأَنَّ اللَّهَ

477. A beautiful passage about the Martyrs in the cause of Truth. They are not dead: they live,—and in a far higher and deeper sense than in the life they have left. Even those who have no faith in the Hereafter honour those that die in their cause, with the crown of immortality in the minds and memories of generations unborn. But in Faith we see a higher, truer, and less relative immortality. Perhaps "immortality" is not the right word in this connection, as it implies a continuation of this life. In their case, through the gateway of death, they enter, the true real Life, as opposed to its shadow here. Our carnal life is sustained with carnal food, and its joys and pleasures at their best are those which are projected on the screen of this material world. Their real Life is sustained from the ineffable Presence and Nearness of God. *Cf.* ii. 154, and see how the idea is further developed here.

478. The Martyrs not only rejoice at the bliss they have themselves attained The dear ones left behind are in their thoughts: it is part of their glory that they have saved their dear ones from fear, sorrow, humiliation, and grief, in this life, even before they come to share in the glories of the Hereafter.

Note how the refrain: "on them shall be no fear, nor shall they grieve": comes in here with a new and appropriate meaning. Besides other things, it means that the dear ones have no cause to grieve at the death of the Martyrs; rather have they cause to rejoice.

The reward of the Faithful
To be lost (in the least).

لَا يُضِيعُ أَجْرَ الْمُؤْمِنِينَ ۝

SECTION 18.

172. Of those who answered
The call of God
And the Apostle,
Even after being wounded,
Those who do right
And refrain from wrong
Have a great reward;—

١٧٢- الَّذِينَ اسْتَجَابُوا لِلَّهِ وَالرَّسُولِ
مِنْ بَعْدِ مَا أَصَابَهُمُ الْقَرْحُ ۚ
لِلَّذِينَ أَحْسَنُوا مِنْهُمْ وَاتَّقَوْا
أَجْرٌ عَظِيمٌ ۝

173. Men said to them:
"A great army is gathering
Against you":
And frightened them:
But it (only) increased
Their Faith: they said:
"For us God sufficeth,
And He is the best
Disposer of affairs."

١٧٣- الَّذِينَ قَالَ لَهُمُ النَّاسُ
إِنَّ النَّاسَ قَدْ جَمَعُوا لَكُمْ
فَاخْشَوْهُمْ
فَزَادَهُمْ إِيمَانًا ۖ
وَقَالُوا حَسْبُنَا اللَّهُ وَنِعْمَ الْوَكِيلُ ۝

174. And they returned
With Grace and Bounty
From God: no harm
Ever touched them:
For they followed
The good pleasure of God:
And God is the Lord
Of bounties unbounded.

١٧٤- فَانْقَلَبُوا بِنِعْمَةٍ مِنَ اللَّهِ وَفَضْلٍ
لَمْ يَمْسَسْهُمْ سُوءٌ
وَاتَّبَعُوا رِضْوَانَ اللَّهِ ۗ
وَاللَّهُ ذُو فَضْلٍ عَظِيمٍ ۝

175. It is only the Evil One
That suggests to you
The fear of his votaries:
Be ye not afraid
Of them, but fear Me,
If ye have Faith.

١٧٥- إِنَّمَا ذَٰلِكُمُ الشَّيْطَانُ يُخَوِّفُ أَوْلِيَاءَهُ
فَلَا تَخَافُوهُمْ
وَخَافُونِ إِنْ كُنْتُمْ مُؤْمِنِينَ ۝

176. Let not those grieve thee
Who rush headlong
Into Unbelief:
Not the least harm
Will they do to God:
God's Plan is that He

١٧٦- وَلَا يَحْزُنْكَ الَّذِينَ يُسَارِعُونَ فِي
الْكُفْرِ ۚ إِنَّهُمْ لَنْ يَضُرُّوا اللَّهَ شَيْئًا ۗ
يُرِيدُ اللَّهُ

479. After the confusion at Uḥud, men rallied round the Apostle. He was wounded, and they were wounded, but they were all ready to fight again. Abū Sufyān with his Meccans withdrew, but left a challenge with them to meet him and his army again at the fair of Badr Ṣugrā next year. The challenge was accepted, and a picked band of Muslims under their intrepid Leader kept the tryst, but the enemy did not come. They returned, not only unharmed, but enriched by the trade at the fair, and (it may be presumed) strengthened by the accession of new adherents to their cause.

Will give them no portion
In the Hereafter,
But a severe punishment.

أَلَّا يَجْعَلَ لَهُمْ حَظًّا فِي الْآخِرَةِ ۚ
وَلَهُمْ عَذَابٌ عَظِيمٌ ○

177. Those who purchase
Unbelief at the price
Of faith,—
Not the least harm
Will they do to God,
But they will have
A grievous punishment.

١٧٧- إِنَّ الَّذِينَ اشْتَرَوُا
الْكُفْرَ بِالْإِيمَانِ
لَنْ يَضُرُّوا اللَّهَ شَيْئًا ۚ
وَلَهُمْ عَذَابٌ أَلِيمٌ ○

178. Let not the Unbelievers
Think that Our respite
To them is good for themselves:
We grant them respite
That they may grow[480]
In their iniquity:
But they will have
A shameful punishment.

١٧٨- وَلَا يَحْسَبَنَّ الَّذِينَ كَفَرُوا
أَنَّمَا نُمْلِي لَهُمْ خَيْرٌ لِأَنْفُسِهِمْ ۚ
إِنَّمَا نُمْلِي لَهُمْ لِيَزْدَادُوا إِثْمًا ۚ
وَلَهُمْ عَذَابٌ مُهِينٌ ○

179. God will not leave
The Believers in the state
In which ye are now,
Until He separates
What is evil
From what is good.[481]
Nor will He disclose
To you the secrets
Of the Unseen.[482]
But He chooses
Of His Apostles
(For the purpose)
Whom He pleases.
So believe in God
And His Apostles:
And if ye believe
And do right,
Ye have a reward
Without measure.

١٧٩- مَا كَانَ اللَّهُ لِيَذَرَ الْمُؤْمِنِينَ
عَلَىٰ مَا أَنْتُمْ عَلَيْهِ
حَتَّىٰ يَمِيزَ الْخَبِيثَ مِنَ الطَّيِّبِ ۗ
وَمَا كَانَ اللَّهُ
لِيُطْلِعَكُمْ عَلَى الْغَيْبِ وَلَٰكِنَّ اللَّهَ
يَجْتَبِي مِنْ رُسُلِهِ مَنْ يَشَاءُ ۖ
فَآمِنُوا بِاللَّهِ وَرُسُلِهِ ۚ
وَإِنْ تُؤْمِنُوا
وَتَتَّقُوا فَلَكُمْ أَجْرٌ عَظِيمٌ ○

---

480. That the cup of their iniquity may be full. The appetite for sin grows with what it feeds on. The natural result is that the sinner sinks deeper into sin. If there is any freedom of will, this naturally follows, though God's Grace is always ready for the repentant. If the Grace is rejected, the increase of iniquity makes the nature of iniquity plainer to those who might otherwise be attracted by its glitter. The working of God's Law is therefore both just and merciful. See also the next verse.

481. The testing of good men by calamities and evil men by leaving them in the enjoyment of good things is part of the Universal Plan, in which some freedom of choice is left to man. The psychological and subjective test is unfailing, and the separation is effected partly by the operation of the human wills, to which some freedom is allowed. But it must be effected, if only in the interests of the good.

482. Man in his weak state would be most miserable if he could see the secrets of the Future or the secrets of the Unseen. But things are revealed to him from time to time as may be expedient for him, by Apostles chosen for the purpose. Our duty is to hold fast by faith and lead a good life.

180. And let not those
Who covetously withhold
Of the gifts which God
Hath given them of His Grace,[483]
Think that it is good for them :
Nay, it will be the worse
For them : soon shall the things
Which they covetously withheld
Be tied to their necks
Like a twisted collar,[484]
On the Day of Judgment.
To God belongs the heritage[485]
Of the heavens and the earth ;
And God is well-acquainted
With all that ye do.

١٨٠- وَلَا يَحْسَبَنَّ الَّذِينَ
يَبْخَلُونَ بِمَآ اٰتٰىهُمُ اللّٰهُ مِنْ فَضْلِهٖ
هُوَ خَيْرًا لَّهُمْ ؕ
بَلْ هُوَ شَرٌّ لَّهُمْ ؕ سَيُطَوَّقُوْنَ
مَا بَخِلُوْا بِهٖ يَوْمَ الْقِيٰمَةِ ؕ
وَلِلّٰهِ مِيْرَاثُ السَّمٰوٰتِ وَالْاَرْضِ ؕ
وَاللّٰهُ بِمَا تَعْمَلُوْنَ خَبِيْرٌ ۝

C. 60.—Regard, unmoved, the taunts of those
(iii. 181-200.) Who laugh at faith ; nor let their falsehood
Nor their seeming prosperity, raise
Questions in your minds. All
Who can read the Signs of God in Nature
Know His wisdom, goodness, power,
And justice. They know His promise
Is sure, and in humble prayer,
Wholly put their trust in Him.

SECTION 19.

181. God hath heard
The taunt of those
Who say : " Truly, God[486]
Is indigent and we
Are rich !"—We shall
Certainly record their word

١٨١- لَقَدْ سَمِعَ اللّٰهُ قَوْلَ الَّذِيْنَ
قَالُوْٓا اِنَّ اللّٰهَ فَقِيْرٌ
وَّنَحْنُ اَغْنِيَآءُ ۘ سَنَكْتُبُ مَا قَالُوْا

483. The gifts are of all kinds : material gifts, such as wealth, property, strength of limbs, etc., or intangible gifts, such as influence, birth in a given set, intellect, skill, insight, etc., or spiritual gifts of the highest kind. The spending of all these things (apart from what is necessary for ourselves) for those who need them, is charity, and purifies our own character. The withholding of them (apart from our needs) is similarly greed and selfishness, and is strongly condemned.

484. By an apt metaphor the miser is told that his wealth or the other gifts which he hoarded will cling round his neck and do him no good. He will wish he could get rid of them, but he will not be able to do so. According to the Biblical phrase in another connection they will hang like a millstone round his neck (Matt. xviii. 6). The metaphor here is fuller. He hugged his wealth or his gifts about him. They will become like a heavy collar, the badge of slavery, round his neck. They will be tied tight and twisted, and they will give him pain and anguish instead of pleasure. *Cf.* also xvii. 13.

485. Another metaphor is now introduced. Material wealth or property is only called ours during our short life here : it then descends to heirs and heirs until it goes to the ultimate heir, the State So all gifts are ours in trust only ; they ultimately revert to God, to Whom belongs all that is in the heavens or on earth.

486. In ii. 245 we read : " Who is he that will loan to God a beautiful loan ?" In other places charity or spending in the way of God is metaphorically described as giving to God. The holy Apostle often used that expression in appealing for funds to be spent in the way of God. The scoffers mocked and said : " So God is indigent and we are rich !" This blasphemy was of a piece with all their conduct in history, in slaying the Prophets and men of God.

And (their act) of slaying
The Prophets in defiance[487]
Of right, and We shall say:
"Taste ye the Penalty
Of the Scorching Fire!

وَقَتْلَهُمُ الْأَنْبِيَاءَ
بِغَيْرِ حَقٍّ
وَنَقُولُ ذُوقُوا عَذَابَ الْحَرِيقِ ○

182. "This is because
Of the (unrighteous deeds)
Which your hands
Sent on before ye:[488]
For God never harms
Those who serve Him."

١٨٢- ذٰلِكَ بِمَا قَدَّمَتْ أَيْدِيكُمْ
وَأَنَّ اللّٰهَ
لَيْسَ بِظَلَّامٍ لِّلْعَبِيدِ ○

183. They (also) said: "God took
Our promise not to believe
In an apostle unless
He showed us a sacrifice
Consumed by fire[489]
(From heaven)." Say:
"There came to you
Apostles before me,
With Clear Signs
And even with what
Ye ask for: why then
Did ye slay them,
If ye speak the truth?"

١٨٣- اَلَّذِينَ قَالُوا إِنَّ اللّٰهَ عَهِدَ إِلَيْنَا
أَلَّا نُؤْمِنَ لِرَسُولٍ
حَتّٰى يَأْتِيَنَا بِقُرْبَانٍ تَأْكُلُهُ النَّارُ
قُلْ قَدْ جَاءَكُمْ رُسُلٌ مِّنْ قَبْلِي
بِالْبَيِّنٰتِ وَبِالَّذِي قُلْتُمْ
فَلِمَ قَتَلْتُمُوهُمْ
إِنْ كُنْتُمْ صٰدِقِينَ ○

184. Then if they reject thee,
So were rejected apostles
Before thee, who came
With Clear Signs,
Books of dark prophecies,
And the Book of Enlightenment.[490]

١٨٤- فَإِنْ كَذَّبُوكَ فَقَدْ كُذِّبَ رُسُلٌ
مِّنْ قَبْلِكَ جَاءُو بِالْبَيِّنٰتِ
وَالزُّبُرِ وَالْكِتٰبِ الْمُنِيرِ ○

487. For the expression "slaying in defiance of right," *Cf.* iii. 21. and iii. 112.

488. *Cf.* ii 95 and note.

489. Burnt sacrifices figured in the Mosaic Law, and in the religious ceremonies long before Moses, but it is not true that the Mosaic Law laid down a fire from heaven on a burnt sacrifice as a test of the credentials of Prophets. Even if it had been so, did the Jews obey the Prophets who showed this Sign? In Leviticus ix. 23-24, we are told of a burnt offering prepared by Moses and Aaron: "and there came a fire out from before the Lord, and consumed upon the altar the burnt offering and the fat." Yet the people rebelled frequently against Moses, and rebellion against a Prophet is spiritually an attempt to kill him. Abel's offering (sacrifice) was probably a burnt offering: it was accepted by God, and he was killed by Cain out of jealousy: Gen. iv. 3-8. Mosaic sacrifices were no longer needed by the people of Jesus or the people of Muḥammad.

490. The three things mentioned in the Text are: (1) Clear Signs (*baiyināt*); (2) *zubūr*, and (3) *kitāb-il-Munīr*. The signification of (1) I have explained in the note to iii. 62, as far as they relate to Jesus. In a more general sense, it means the clear evidence which God's dealings furnish about a man of God having a true mission: *e.g.*, Moses in relation to Pharaoh. I have translated (2) as Books of Dark Prophecies, as the root *zabara* implies something hard. The Commentators are not agreed, but the Prophetic writings which seemed to contemporaries difficult to understand may well come under this description. David's Psalms (*Zubūr*, iv. 163) may also come under this description. As to (3), there is no doubt about the literal meaning of the words, "the Book of Enlightenment". But what does it precisely refer to? I take it to mean the fundamental guide to conduct,—the clear rules laid down in all Dispensations to help men to lead good lives.

185. Every soul shall have
A taste of death:[491]
And only on the Day
Of Judgment shall you
Be paid your full recompense.
Only he who is saved
Far from the Fire
And admitted to the Garden
Will have attained
The object (of Life):
For the life of this world
Is but goods and chattels
Of deception.[492]

١٨٥- كُلُّ نَفْسٍ ذَآئِقَةُ الْمَوْتِ
وَإِنَّمَا تُوَفَّوْنَ أُجُورَكُمْ يَوْمَ الْقِيٰمَةِ
فَمَنْ زُحْزِحَ عَنِ النَّارِ
وَأُدْخِلَ الْجَنَّةَ فَقَدْ فَازَ
وَمَا الْحَيٰوةُ الدُّنْيَآ
إِلَّا مَتَاعُ الْغُرُورِ ۝

186. Ye shall certainly
Be tried and tested
In your possessions
And in your personal selves;[493]
And ye shall certainly
Hear much that will grieve you,
From those who received
The Book before you
And from those who
Worship many gods.
But if ye persevere
Patiently, and guard
Against evil,—then
That will be
A determining factor
In all affairs.

١٨٦- لَتُبْلَوُنَّ فِيٓ أَمْوَالِكُمْ وَأَنْفُسِكُمْ
وَلَتَسْمَعُنَّ مِنَ الَّذِينَ
أُوتُوا الْكِتٰبَ مِنْ قَبْلِكُمْ
وَمِنَ الَّذِينَ
أَشْرَكُوٓا أَذًى كَثِيرًا
وَإِنْ تَصْبِرُوا
وَتَتَّقُوا
فَإِنَّ ذٰلِكَ مِنْ عَزْمِ الْأُمُورِ ۝

187. And remember
God took a Covenant
From the People of the Book,[494]
To make it known
And clear to mankind,
And not to hide it;

١٨٧- وَإِذْ أَخَذَ اللّٰهُ مِيثَاقَ
الَّذِينَ أُوتُوا الْكِتٰبَ
لَتُبَيِّنُنَّهُ لِلنَّاسِ وَلَا تَكْتُمُونَهُ

---

491. The soul will not die; but the death of the body will give a taste of death to the soul when the soul separates from the body. The soul will then know that this life was but a probation. And seeming inequalities will be adjusted finally on the Day of Judgment.

492. *Cf.* Longfellow's Psalm of Life: "All this world's a fleeting show, For man's illusion given. The only Reality will be when we have attained our final goal.

493. Not wealth and possessions only (or want of them), are the means of our trial. All our personal talents, knowledge, opportunities, and their opposites,—in fact everything that happens to us and makes up our personality is a means of our testing. So is our Faith: we shall have to put up for it many insults from those who do not share it.

494. Truth—God's Message—comes to any man or nation as a matter of sacred trust. It should be broadcast and published and taught and made clear to all within reach. Privileged priesthood at once erects a barrier. But worse,—when such priesthood tampers with the truth, taking what suits it and ignoring the rest, it has sold God's gift for a miserable ephemeral profit; how miserable, it will learn when Nemesis comes.

But they threw it away
Behind their backs,[495]
And purchased with it
Some miserable gain!
And vile was the bargain
They made!

فَنَبَذُوهُ وَرَآءَ ظُهُورِهِمْ
وَاشْتَرَوْا بِهِ ثَمَنًا قَلِيلًا
فَبِئْسَ مَا يَشْتَرُونَ ○

188. Think not that those
Who exult in what they
Have brought about, and love
To be praised for what
They have not done,—[496]
Think not that they
Can escape the Penalty.
For them is a Penalty
Grievous indeed.

١٨٨- لَا تَحْسَبَنَّ الَّذِينَ يَفْرَحُونَ بِمَآ أَتَوْا
وَّيُحِبُّونَ أَنْ يُّحْمَدُوا
بِمَا لَمْ يَفْعَلُوا فَلَا تَحْسَبَنَّهُمْ
بِمَفَازَةٍ مِّنَ الْعَذَابِ
وَلَهُمْ عَذَابٌ أَلِيمٌ ○

189. To God belongeth
The dominion
Of the heavens
And the earth;
And God hath power
Over all things.

١٨٩- وَلِلّٰهِ
مُلْكُ السَّمٰوٰتِ وَالْأَرْضِ
ع وَاللّٰهُ عَلٰى كُلِّ شَىْءٍ قَدِيرٌ ○

SECTION 20.

190. Behold! In the creation
Of the heavens and the earth,
And the alternation
Of Night and Day,—[497]
There are indeed Signs
For men of understanding,—

١٩٠- إِنَّ فِى خَلْقِ السَّمٰوٰتِ وَالْأَرْضِ
وَاخْتِلَافِ الَّيْلِ وَالنَّهَارِ
لَاٰيٰتٍ لِّأُولِى الْأَلْبَابِ ○

191. Men who celebrate
The praises of God,
Standing, sitting,
And lying down on their sides,[498]
And contemplate
The (wonders of) creation

١٩١- الَّذِينَ يَذْكُرُونَ اللّٰهَ قِيٰمًا
وَّقُعُودًا وَّعَلٰى جُنُوبِهِمْ
وَيَتَفَكَّرُونَ فِى خَلْقِ

495. *Cf.* ii. 101.

496. A searching picture of the worldly wise! They may cause mischief and misery to others, but gloat over any glory it may bring them! They may trample down God's truths, and enthrone false standards of worship. They may take credit for virtues they do not possess and seeming successes that come in spite of their despicable deceptions.

497. See ii. 164. The two items mentioned here are just brief symbols recalling the six or seven mentioned in the other passage. And those too are but brief symbols and reminders of the glorious majesty of God and His goodness to man.

498. That is, in all postures, which again is symbolical of all circumstances, personal, social, economic, historical and other.

In the heavens and the earth,
(With the thought):
"Our Lord! not for naught
Hast Thou created (all) this!
Glory to Thee! Give us[499]
Salvation from the Penalty
Of the Fire.

السَّمٰوٰتِ وَالْاَرْضِ ۚ
رَبَّنَا مَا خَلَقْتَ هٰذَا بَاطِلًا ۚ
سُبْحٰنَكَ
فَقِنَا عَذَابَ النَّارِ ○

192. "Our Lord! any whom Thou
Dost admit to the Fire,
Truly Thou coverest with shame,
And never will wrong-doers
Find any helpers!

۱۹۲- رَبَّنَآ اِنَّكَ مَنْ تُدْخِلِ النَّارَ
فَقَدْ اَخْزَيْتَهٗ ؕ
وَمَا لِلظّٰلِمِيْنَ مِنْ اَنْصَارٍ ○

193. "Our Lord! we have heard
The call of one calling
(Us) to Faith, 'Believe ye
In the Lord,' and we
Have believed. Our Lord!
Forgive us our sins,
Blot out from us
Our iniquities, and take
To Thyself our souls
In the company of the righteous.

۱۹۳- رَبَّنَآ اِنَّنَا سَمِعْنَا
مُنَادِيًا يُّنَادِيْ لِلْاِيْمَانِ
اَنْ اٰمِنُوْا بِرَبِّكُمْ فَاٰمَنَّا ۖ
رَبَّنَا فَاغْفِرْ لَنَا ذُنُوْبَنَا
وَكَفِّرْ عَنَّا سَيِّاٰتِنَا
وَتَوَفَّنَا مَعَ الْاَبْرَارِ ○

194. "Our Lord! Grant us
What Thou didst promise
Unto us through Thine Apostles,
And save us from shame
On the Day of Judgment:
For Thou never breakest
Thy promise."

۱۹۴- رَبَّنَا وَاٰتِنَا مَا وَعَدْتَّنَا
عَلٰى رُسُلِكَ
وَلَا تُخْزِنَا يَوْمَ الْقِيٰمَةِ ؕ
اِنَّكَ لَا تُخْلِفُ الْمِيْعَادَ ○

195. And their Lord hath accepted
Of them, and answered them:
"Never will I suffer to be lost
The work of any of you,

۱۹۵- فَاسْتَجَابَ لَهُمْ رَبُّهُمْ اَنِّيْ لَآ اُضِيْعُ
عَمَلَ عَامِلٍ

499. It is the thought of Salvation that connects all these glories with man. Otherwise man would be a miserable, contemptible creature in these beauties and wonders of Nature. With his high destiny of Salvation he can be lifted even higher than these glories! The Fire is a symbol of penalty. We pray for salvation from the penalty.

Be he male or female :
Ye are members, one of
another :[500]
Those who have left their homes,
Or been driven out therefrom,
Or suffered harm in My Cause,
Or fought or been slain,—
Verily, I will blot out
From them their iniquities,
And admit them into Gardens
With rivers flowing beneath ;—
A reward from the Presence[501]
Of God, and from His Presence
Is the best of rewards."

مِّنكُم مِّن ذَكَرٍ أَوْ أُنثَىٰ
بَعْضُكُم مِّن بَعْضٍ فَالَّذِينَ هَاجَرُوا
وَأُخْرِجُوا مِن دِيَارِهِمْ
وَأُوذُوا فِي سَبِيلِي
وَقَاتَلُوا وَقُتِلُوا
لَأُكَفِّرَنَّ عَنْهُمْ سَيِّئَاتِهِمْ وَلَأُدْخِلَنَّهُمْ
جَنَّاتٍ تَجْرِي مِن تَحْتِهَا الْأَنْهَارُ
ثَوَابًا مِّنْ عِندِ اللَّهِ
وَاللَّهُ عِندَهُ حُسْنُ الثَّوَابِ ○

196. Let not the strutting about
Of the Unbelievers
Through the land
Deceive thee :

١٩٦- لَا يَغُرَّنَّكَ تَقَلُّبُ الَّذِينَ
كَفَرُوا فِي الْبِلَادِ ○

197. Little is it for enjoyment :
Their ultimate abode
Is Hell : what an evil bed
(To lie on) !

١٩٧- مَتَاعٌ قَلِيلٌ ثُمَّ مَأْوَاهُمْ جَهَنَّمُ
وَبِئْسَ الْمِهَادُ ○

198. On the other hand, for those
Who fear their Lord,
Are Gardens, with rivers
Flowing beneath ; therein
Are they to dwell (for ever),—
A gift from the Presence
Of God ; and that which is
In the Presence of God
Is the best (bliss)
For the righteous.

١٩٨- لَٰكِنِ الَّذِينَ اتَّقَوْا رَبَّهُمْ
لَهُمْ جَنَّاتٌ تَجْرِي مِن تَحْتِهَا الْأَنْهَارُ
خَالِدِينَ فِيهَا
نُزُلًا مِّنْ عِندِ اللَّهِ
وَمَا عِندَ اللَّهِ خَيْرٌ لِّلْأَبْرَارِ ○

199. And there are, certainly,
Among the People of the Book,

١٩٩- وَإِنَّ مِنْ أَهْلِ الْكِتَابِ

500. In Islam the equal status of the sexes is not only recognised but insisted on. If sex distinction, which is a distinction in nature, does not count in spiritual matters, still less of course would count artificial distinctions, such as rank, wealth, position, race, colour, birth, etc.

501. Here, and in iii. 198 below, and in many places elsewhere, stress is laid on the fact that whatever gift, or reward, or bliss will come to the righteous, its chief merit will be that it proceeds from the Presence of God Himself. "Nearness to God" expresses it better than any other symbol.

Those who believe in God,
In the revelation to you,
And in the revelation to them,
Bowing in humility to God:
They will not sell
The Signs of God
For a miserable gain!
For them is a reward
With their Lord,
And God is swift in account.

200. O ye who believe!
Persevere in patience[502]
And constancy; vie
In such perseverance;
Strengthen each other;
And fear God;
That ye may prosper.[503]

لَمَنْ يُّؤْمِنُ بِاللّٰهِ وَمَآ اُنْزِلَ اِلَيْكُمْ
وَمَآ اُنْزِلَ اِلَيْهِمْ
خٰشِعِيْنَ لِلّٰهِ ۙ لَا يَشْتَرُوْنَ بِاٰيٰتِ اللّٰهِ
ثَمَنًا قَلِيْلًا ۗ اُولٰٓئِكَ لَهُمْ
اَجْرُهُمْ عِنْدَ رَبِّهِمْ ۗ
اِنَّ اللّٰهَ سَرِيْعُ الْحِسَابِ ○

٢٠٠- يٰٓاَيُّهَا الَّذِيْنَ اٰمَنُوا اصْبِرُوْا
وَصَابِرُوْا
وَرَابِطُوْا قف
وَاتَّقُوا اللّٰهَ لَعَلَّكُمْ تُفْلِحُوْنَ ○ ع

502. The full meaning of *Ṣabr* is to be understood here, *viz.*: Patience, perseverance, constancy, self-restraint, refusing to be cowed down. These virtues we are to exercise for ourselves and in relation to others; we are to set an example, so that others may vie with us, and we are to vie with them, lest we fall short; in this way we strengthen each other and bind our mutual relations closer, in our common service to God.

503. Prosperity (*falāḥ*) here and in other passages is to be understood in a wide sense, including prosperity in our mundane affairs as well as in spiritual progress. In both cases it implies happiness and the attainment of our wishes, purified by the love of God.

INTRODUCTION TO SŪRA IV (*Nisāa*)

This Sūra is closely connected chronologically with Sūra III. Its subject-matter deals with the social problems which the Muslim community had to face immediately after Uḥud. While the particular occasion made the necessity urgent, the principles laid down have permanently governed Muslim Law and social practice

Broadly speaking, the Sūra consists of two parts: (1) that dealing with women, orphans, inheritance, marriage, and family rights generally, and (2) that dealing with the recalcitrants in the larger family, the community at Medina, *viz.*, the Hypocrites and their accomplices.

Summary.—It begins with an appeal to the solidarity of mankind, the rights of women and orphans, and the implications of family relationship, including an equitable distribution of property after death. (iv. 1-14 and C. 61.)

While the decencies of family life should be enforced, women should be held in honour and their rights recognized, in marriage, property, and inheritance; and this principle of goodness should be extended to all beings, great and small. (iv. 15-42, and C. 62.)

The sections in Medina, not yet in the Muslim community, should not go after false gods, but should accept the authority of the Apostle, and obey him. Then it will be their privilege to be admitted to a great and glorious Fellowship. (iv. 43-70, and C. 63.)

The Believers should organize in self-defence against their enemies, and beware of the secret plots and mischiefs of the Hypocrites; how deserters should be treated. (iv. 71-91, and C. 64).

Caution about the taking of life; recommendations for leaving places inimical to Islam; religious duties in the midst of war. (iv. 92-104, and C. 65.)

Treachery and the lure of evil. (iv. 105-126, and C. 66.)

Women and orphans to be justly dealt with; Faith must go with justice, sincerity, and moderation in speech. (iv. 127-152, and C. 67.)

Where People of the Book went wrong, with honourable exceptions. (iv. 153-176, and C. 68).

C. 61.—All mankind are one, and mutual rights
(iv. 1-14.) Must be respected: the sexes
Must honour, each the other;
Sacred are family relationships
That rise through marriage
And women bearing children;
Orphans need especial loving care;
In trust is held all property;
With duties well-defined;
And after death, due distribution
Should be made in equitable shares
To all whose affection, duty,
And trust shed light and joy
On this our life below.

Sūra IV.

Nisāa, or The Women.

In the name of God, Most Gracious
Most Merciful.

1. O mankind! reverence
Your Guardian-Lord,
Who created you
From a single Person,[504]
Created, of like nature,
His mate, and from them twain
Scattered (like seeds)
Countless men and women;—
Reverence God, through Whom[505]
Ye demand your mutual (rights),
And (reverence) the wombs[506]
(That bore you): for God
Ever watches over you.

2. To orphans restore their property
(When they reach their age),
Nor substitute (your) worthless things
For (their) good ones; and devour not
Their substance (by mixing it up)[507]

بِسْمِ اللّٰهِ الرَّحْمٰنِ الرَّحِيْمِ ○

١- يٰٓاَيُّهَا النَّاسُ اتَّقُوْا رَبَّكُمُ
الَّذِىْ خَلَقَكُمْ مِّنْ نَّفْسٍ وَّاحِدَةٍ
وَّخَلَقَ مِنْهَا زَوْجَهَا وَبَثَّ مِنْهُمَا
رِجَالًا كَثِيْرًا وَّنِسَآءً
وَاتَّقُوا اللّٰهَ الَّذِىْ تَسَآءَلُوْنَ بِهٖ
وَالْاَرْحَامَ
اِنَّ اللّٰهَ كَانَ عَلَيْكُمْ رَقِيْبًا ○

٢- وَاٰتُوا الْيَتٰمٰٓى اَمْوَالَهُمْ
وَلَا تَتَبَدَّلُوا الْخَبِيْثَ بِالطَّيِّبِ
وَلَا تَاْكُلُوْٓا اَمْوَالَهُمْ

---

504. *Nafs* may mean: (1) soul; (2) self; (3) person, living person; (4) will, good pleasure, as in iv. 4 below. *Minhā*: I follow the construction suggested by Imām Rāzī. The particle *min* would then suggest here not a portion or a source of something else, but a species, a nature, a similarity. The pronoun *hā* refers of course to *Nafs*. The Biblical story of the creation of Eve from a rib of Adam may be allegorical, but we need not assume it in Quranic teaching.

505. All our mutual rights and duties are referred to God. We are his creatures; His Will is the standard and measure of Good; and our duties are measured by our conformity with His Will. "Our wills are ours, to make them Thine," says Tennyson (*In Memoriam*). Among ourselves (human beings) our mutual rights and duties arise out of God's Law, the sense of Right that is implanted in us by him.

506. Among the most wonderful mysteries of our nature is that of sex. The unregenerate male is apt, in the pride of his physical strength, to forget the all-important part which the female plays in his very existence, and in all the social relationships that arise in our collective human lives. The mother that bore us must ever have our reverence. The wife, through whom we enter parentage, must have our reverence. Sex, which governs so much of our physical life, and has so much influence on our emotional and higher nature, deserves—not our fear, or our contempt, or our amused indulgence, but—our reverence in the highest sense of the term. With this fitting introduction we enter on a discussion of women, orphans, and family relationships.

507. Justice to orphans is enjoined, and three things are particularly mentioned as temptations in the way of a guardian: (1) He must not postpone restoring all his ward's property when the time comes; subject to iv. 5 below. (2) If there is a list of property, it is not enough that that list should be technically followed: the property restored must be of equal value to the property received: the same principle applies where there is no list. (3) If property is managed together, or where perishable goods must necessarily be consumed, the strictest probity is necessary when the separation takes place, and this is insisted on. See also ii. 220 and note.

With your own. For this is
Indeed a great sin.

إِلَىٰٓ أَمْوَٰلِكُمْ ۚ إِنَّهُۥ كَانَ حُوبًا كَبِيرًا ○

3. If ye fear that ye shall not
Be able to deal justly
With the orphans,[508]
Marry women of your choice,
Two, or three, or four;
But if ye fear that ye shall not
Be able to deal justly (with them),
Then only one, or (a captive)
That your right hands possess.
That will be more suitable,
To prevent you
From doing injustice.[509]

٣- وَإِنْ خِفْتُمْ أَلَّا تُقْسِطُوا۟ فِى ٱلْيَتَٰمَىٰ
فَٱنكِحُوا۟ مَا طَابَ لَكُم مِّنَ ٱلنِّسَآءِ
مَثْنَىٰ وَثُلَٰثَ وَرُبَٰعَ ۖ
فَإِنْ خِفْتُمْ أَلَّا تَعْدِلُوا۟ فَوَٰحِدَةً
أَوْ مَا مَلَكَتْ أَيْمَٰنُكُمْ ۚ
ذَٰلِكَ أَدْنَىٰٓ أَلَّا تَعُولُوا۟ ○

4. And give the women
(On marriage) their dower
As a free gift; but if they,
Of their own good pleasure,
Remit any part of it to you,
Take it and enjoy it
With right good cheer.

٤- وَءَاتُوا۟ ٱلنِّسَآءَ صَدُقَٰتِهِنَّ نِحْلَةً ۚ
فَإِن طِبْنَ لَكُمْ عَن شَىْءٍ
مِّنْهُ نَفْسًا
فَكُلُوهُ هَنِيٓـًٔا مَّرِيٓـًٔا ○

5. To those weak of
understanding[510]
Make not over your property,[511]
Which God hath made
A means of support for you,
But feed and clothe them
Therewith, and speak to them
Words of kindness and justice.

٥- وَلَا تُؤْتُوا۟ ٱلسُّفَهَآءَ
أَمْوَٰلَكُمُ ٱلَّتِى جَعَلَ ٱللَّهُ لَكُمْ قِيَٰمًا
وَٱرْزُقُوهُمْ فِيهَا وَٱكْسُوهُمْ
وَقُولُوا۟ لَهُمْ قَوْلًا مَّعْرُوفًا

---

508. Notice the conditional clause about orphans, introducing the rules about marriage. This reminds us of the immediate occasion of the promulgation of this verse. It was after Uhud, when the Muslim community was left with many orphans and widows, and some captives of war. Their treatment was to be governed by principles of the greatest humanity and equity. The occasion is past, but the principles remain. Marry the orphans if you are quite sure that you will in that way protect their interests and their property, with perfect justice to them and to your own dependants if you have any. If not, make other arrangements for the orphans.

509. The unrestricted number of wives of the "Times of Ignorance" was now strictly limited to a maximum of four, provided you could treat them with perfect equality, in material things as well as in affection and immaterial things. As this condition is most difficult to fulfil, I understand the recommendation to be towards monogamy.

510. This applies to orphans, but the wording is perfectly general, and defines principles like those of Chancery in English Law and the Court of Wards in Indian Law. Property has not only its rights but also its responsibilities. The owner may not do just what he likes absolutely; his right is limited by the good of the community of which he is a member, and if he is incapable of understanding it, his control should be removed. This does not mean that he is harshly dealt with. On the contrary his interests must be protected, and he must be treated with special kindness because of his incapacity.

511. *Your* property: Ultimately all property belongs to the Community, and is intended for the support of *you, i.e.*, the community. It is held in trust by a particular individual. If he is incapable, he is put aside but gently and with kindness. While his incapacity remains, the duties and responsibilities devolve on his guardian even more strictly than in the case of the original owner: for he may not take any of the profits for himself unless he is poor, and in that case his remuneration for his trouble must be on a scale that is no more than just and reasonable.

6. Make trial of orphans
Until they reach the age[512]
Of marriage; if then ye find
Sound judgment in them,
Release their property to them;
But consume it not wastefully,
Nor in haste against their growing up.
If the guardian is well-off,
Let him claim no remuneration,
But if he is poor, let him
Have for himself what is
Just and reasonable.
When ye release their property
To them, take witnesses
In their presence:
But all-sufficient
Is God in taking account.[513]

٦- وَابْتَلُوا الْيَتٰمٰى حَتّٰى إِذَا بَلَغُوا النِّكَاحَ ۚ
فَإِنْ اٰنَسْتُمْ مِّنْهُمْ رُشْدًا
فَادْفَعُوا إِلَيْهِمْ أَمْوَالَهُمْ ۚ
وَلَا تَأْكُلُوهَا إِسْرَافًا وَّبِدَارًا أَنْ يَّكْبَرُوا ۚ
وَمَنْ كَانَ غَنِيًّا فَلْيَسْتَعْفِفْ ۚ
وَمَنْ كَانَ فَقِيرًا فَلْيَأْكُلْ بِالْمَعْرُوفِ ۚ
فَإِذَا دَفَعْتُمْ إِلَيْهِمْ أَمْوَالَهُمْ
فَأَشْهِدُوا عَلَيْهِمْ ۚ
وَكَفٰى بِاللّٰهِ حَسِيبًا ○

7. From what is left by parents
And those nearest related[514]
There is a share for men
And a share for women,
Whether the property be small
Or large,—a determinate share.

٧- لِلرِّجَالِ نَصِيبٌ مِّمَّا تَرَكَ الْوَالِدٰنِ
وَالْأَقْرَبُونَ وَلِلنِّسَاءِ نَصِيبٌ مِّمَّا تَرَكَ
الْوَالِدٰنِ وَالْأَقْرَبُونَ
مِمَّا قَلَّ مِنْهُ أَوْ كَثُرَ ۚ نَصِيبًا مَّفْرُوضًا ○

8. But if at the time of division
Other relatives, or orphans,
Or poor, are present,
Feed them out of the (property),
And speak to them
Words of kindness and justice.

٨- وَإِذَا حَضَرَ الْقِسْمَةَ أُولُوا الْقُرْبٰى وَ
الْيَتٰمٰى وَالْمَسٰكِينُ فَارْزُقُوهُمْ مِّنْهُ
وَقُولُوا لَهُمْ قَوْلًا مَّعْرُوفًا ○

9. Let those (disposing of an estate)
Have the same fear in their minds
As they would have for their own
If they had left a helpless family behind:
Let them fear God, and speak
Words of appropriate (comfort).[515]

٩- وَلْيَخْشَ الَّذِينَ لَوْ تَرَكُوا مِنْ خَلْفِهِمْ
ذُرِّيَّةً ضِعٰفًا خَافُوا عَلَيْهِمْ ۖ
فَلْيَتَّقُوا اللّٰهَ وَلْيَقُولُوا قَوْلًا سَدِيدًا ○

---

512. The age of marriage is the age when they reach their majority.

513. It is good to take human witnesses when you faithfully discharge your trust; but remember that, however fully you satisfy your fellow-men when you give your account to them, there is a stricter account due from you to God. If you are righteous in God's eyes, you must follow these stricter standards.

514. I have resisted the temptation to translate "next of kin," as this phrase has a technical meaning in Indian Law, referring to certain kinds of heirs, whereas here the people meant are those whose inheritance is to be divided. The shares are specified. Here the genereral principles are laid down that females inherit as well as males, and that relatives who have no legal shares, orphans, and indigent people are not to be treated harshly, if present at the division. Their "feed" may be charged to the property as part of the funeral expenses.

515. It is a touching argument addressed to those who have to divide an estate. 'How anxious would you be if you had left a helpless family behind? If others do so, help and be kind.

10. Those who unjustly
Eat up the property
Of orphans, eat up
A Fire into their own
Bodies: they will soon
Be enduring a blazing Fire!

١٠- إِنَّ الَّذِينَ يَأْكُلُونَ أَمْوَالَ الْيَتٰمٰى ظُلْمًا
إِنَّمَا يَأْكُلُونَ فِي بُطُونِهِمْ نَارًا ۖ
وَسَيَصْلَوْنَ سَعِيرًا ۝

SECTION 2.

11. God (thus) directs you
As regards your children's[516]
(Inheritance): to the male,
A portion equal to that
Of two females: if only
Daughters, two or more,[517]
Their share is two-thirds
Of the inheritance;
If only one, her share
Is a half.

For parents, a sixth share
Of the inheritance to each,
If the deceased left children;
If no children, and the parents
Are the (only) heirs, the mother
Has a third; if the deceased
Left brothers (or sisters)
The mother has a sixth.
(The distribution in all cases
Is) after the payment
Of legacies and debts.
Ye know not whether
Your parents or your children
Are nearest to you
In benefit. These are
Settled portions ordained[518]

١١- يُوصِيكُمُ اللّٰهُ فِي أَوْلَادِكُمْ ۖ
لِلذَّكَرِ مِثْلُ حَظِّ الْأُنْثَيَيْنِ ۚ
فَإِنْ كُنَّ نِسَاءً فَوْقَ اثْنَتَيْنِ
فَلَهُنَّ ثُلُثَا مَا تَرَكَ ۖ وَإِنْ كَانَتْ وَاحِدَةً
فَلَهَا النِّصْفُ ۚ وَلِأَبَوَيْهِ
لِكُلِّ وَاحِدٍ مِنْهُمَا السُّدُسُ
مِمَّا تَرَكَ إِنْ كَانَ لَهُ وَلَدٌ ۚ فَإِنْ لَمْ يَكُنْ لَهُ
وَلَدٌ وَوَرِثَهُ أَبَوَاهُ فَلِأُمِّهِ الثُّلُثُ ۚ
فَإِنْ كَانَ لَهُ إِخْوَةٌ
فَلِأُمِّهِ السُّدُسُ مِنْ بَعْدِ وَصِيَّةٍ
يُوصِي بِهَا أَوْ دَيْنٍ ۗ
آبَاؤُكُمْ وَأَبْنَاؤُكُمْ لَا تَدْرُونَ
أَيُّهُمْ أَقْرَبُ لَكُمْ نَفْعًا ۚ فَرِيضَةً

516. The principles of inheritance law are laid down in broad outline in the Qur-ān; the precise details have been worked out on the basis of the Apostle's practice and that of his Companions, and by interpretation and analogy. Muslim jurists have collected a vast amount of learning on this subject, and this body of law is enough by itself to form the subject of life-long study. Here we shall deal only with the broad principles to be gathered from the Text, as interpreted by the Jurists.

(1) The power of testamentary disposition extends over only one-third of the Property; the remaining two-thirds are distributed among heirs as laid down. (2) All distribution takes place after the legacies and debts (including funeral expenses) have first been paid. (3) Legacies cannot be left to any of the heirs included in the scheme of distribution; or it will amount to upsetting the shares and undue preference of one heir to another. (4) Generally, but not always, the male takes a share double that of a female in his own category.

517. At first sight, the Arabic words seem to mean: "if more than two daughters." But the alternative in the next clause is: "if only one daughter." Logically, therefore, the first clause must mean: "if daughters, two or more." This is the general interpretation, and is confirmed by the supplementary provision in iv. 176 at the end of the Sūra, which should be read along with this.

518. This verse deals with the portions allotted to (*a*) children, and (*b*) parents. The next verse deals with the portions allotted to (*c*) husband or wife of the deceased, and (*d*) collaterals. The children's shares are fixed, but their amount will depend upon what goes to the parents. If both parents are living, and there are also children, both father and mother take a sixth each; if only one parent is living, he or she takes his or her sixth; and the rest goes to the children. If the parents are living, and there is no child or other heir, the mother gets a third (and the father the remaining two-thirds); if there are no children, but there are brothers or sisters (this is interpreted strictly in the plural), the mother has a sixth, and the father apparently the residue, as the father excludes collaterals. This is far from being an exhaustive statement, but it establishes the proposition that children and parents have always some share if they survive, but their shares are affected by the existence and number of the heirs in these categories.

By God; and God is
All-knowing, All-wise.

12. In what your wives leave,
Your share is a half,
If they leave no child;
But if they leave a child,
Ye get a fourth; after payment
Of legacies and debts.
In what ye leave,
Their share is a fourth,[519]
If ye leave no child;
But if ye leave a child,
They get an eighth; after payment
Of legacies and debts.

If the man or woman
Whose inheritance is in question,
Has left neither ascendants nor
descendants,[520]
But has left a brother[521]
Or a sister, each one of the two
Gets a sixth; but if more
Than two, they share in a third;
After payment of legacies
And debts; so that no loss[522]
Is caused (to any one).
Thus is it ordained by God;
And God is All-knowing,
Most Forbearing.

مِّنَ اللّٰهِ ۭ اِنَّ اللّٰهَ كَانَ عَلِيْمًا حَكِيْمًا ○

١٢- وَلَكُمْ نِصْفُ مَا تَرَكَ اَزْوَاجُكُمْ
اِنْ لَّمْ يَكُنْ لَّهُنَّ وَلَدٌ ۚ فَاِنْ كَانَ لَهُنَّ
وَلَدٌ فَلَكُمُ الرُّبُعُ مِمَّا تَرَكْنَ مِنْۢ بَعْدِ
وَصِيَّةٍ يُّوْصِيْنَ بِهَآ اَوْ دَيْنٍ ۭ
وَلَهُنَّ الرُّبُعُ مِمَّا تَرَكْتُمْ اِنْ لَّمْ يَكُنْ لَّكُمْ
وَلَدٌ ۚ فَاِنْ كَانَ لَكُمْ وَلَدٌ فَلَهُنَّ
الثُّمُنُ مِمَّا تَرَكْتُمْ مِّنْۢ بَعْدِ وَصِيَّةٍ
تُوْصُوْنَ بِهَآ اَوْ دَيْنٍ ۭ وَاِنْ كَانَ رَجُلٌ
يُّوْرَثُ كَلٰلَةً اَوِ امْرَاَةٌ وَّلَهٗٓ اَخٌ
اَوْ اُخْتٌ فَلِكُلِّ وَاحِدٍ مِّنْهُمَا السُّدُسُ ۚ
فَاِنْ كَانُوْٓا اَكْثَرَ مِنْ ذٰلِكَ فَهُمْ شُرَكَاۗءُ فِي
الثُّلُثِ مِنْۢ بَعْدِ وَصِيَّةٍ يُّوْصٰى بِهَآ اَوْ دَيْنٍ ۙ
غَيْرَ مُضَاۗرٍّ ۚ وَصِيَّةً مِّنَ اللّٰهِ ۭ وَاللّٰهُ عَلِيْمٌ حَلِيْمٌ ۭ

---

519. The husband takes a half of his deceased wife's property if she leaves no child, the rest going to residuaries; if she leaves a child, the husband gets only a fourth. Following the rule that the female share is generally half the male share, the widow gets a fourth of her deceased husband's property, if he leaves no children, and an eighth if he leaves children. If there are more widows than one, their collective share is a fourth or an eighth as the case may be; *inter se* they divide equally.

520. The word in Arabic is *kalālat*, which is so construed usually. But it was nowhere defined authoritatively in the lifetime of the Apostle. This was one of the three terms about which *Hadhrat* Umar wished that the Apostle had defined them in his lifetime, the other two being *Khilāfat*, and *ribā* (usury). On the accepted definition, we are concerned with the inheritance of a person who has left no descendant or ascendant (however distant), but only collaterals, with or without a widow or widower. If there is a widow or widower surviving, she or he takes the share as already defined, before the collaterals come in.

521. A "brother or sister" is here interpreted to mean a uterine brother or sister, *i.e.*, a brother or sister by the same mother but not by the same father, as the case of full brothers and sisters or brothers and sisters by the same father but different mothers is understood to be dealt with later, in the last verse of this Sūra. The uterine brother or sister, if only one survives, takes a sixth; if more than one survive, they take a third collectively, and divide among themselves; this on the supposition that there are no descendants or ascendants, however remote. There may, however, be a widow or widower surviving: she or he takes her or his share, as already specified.

The shares of collaterals generally are calculated on a complicated system which cannot be described in a brief note. For these, and the rules about Residuaries (*'Aṣaba*) reference should be made to special legal treatises.

522. Debts (in which funeral expenses take first rank) and legacies are the first charge on the estate of a deceased person, before distribution takes place. But equity and fair dealing should be observed in all matters, so that no one's interests are prejudiced. Thus funeral expenses should be reasonable; debts must be genuine and not reckless debts; and the shares must be calculated with fairness.

13. Those are limits
Set by God : those who
Obey God and His Apostle
Will be admitted to Gardens
With rivers flowing beneath,
To abide therein (for ever)
And that will be
The Supreme achievement.[522-A]

١٣- تِلْكَ حُدُودُ اللّٰهِ ۚ وَمَنْ يُطِعِ اللّٰهَ
وَرَسُولَهُ يُدْخِلْهُ جَنّٰتٍ
تَجْرِي مِنْ تَحْتِهَا الْأَنْهٰرُ خٰلِدِينَ فِيهَا ۚ
وَذٰلِكَ الْفَوْزُ الْعَظِيمُ ○

14. But those who disobey
God and His Apostle
And transgress His limits
Will be admitted
To a Fire, to abide therein :
And they shall have
A humiliating punishment.

١٤- وَمَنْ يَعْصِ اللّٰهَ وَرَسُولَهُ
وَيَتَعَدَّ حُدُودَهُ يُدْخِلْهُ نَارًا
خٰلِدًا فِيهَا ۖ
وَلَهُ عَذَابٌ مُهِينٌ ○ ع

C. 62.—What can be a holier cement to Society
(iv. 15—42) Than that women should be chaste and pure,
And crimes against sex rooted out ?
Let decency, kindness, and justice
Prevail in all sex relationships ;
Let marriage be cherished and carefully guarded ;
Women's rights secured ; family jars
Adjusted ; and all life lived
In faith, charity, and kindness sincere
To all our fellow-creatures.

Section 3.

15. If any of your women
Are guilty of lewdness,[523]
Take the evidence of four[524]
(Reliable) witnesses from amongst
you
Against them ; and if they testify,
Confine them to houses until
Death do claim them,

١٥- وَالّٰتِي يَأْتِينَ الْفٰحِشَةَ مِنْ نِسَآئِكُمْ
فَاسْتَشْهِدُوا عَلَيْهِنَّ أَرْبَعَةً مِنْكُمْ ۚ
فَإِنْ شَهِدُوا فَأَمْسِكُوهُنَّ فِي الْبُيُوتِ
حَتّٰى يَتَوَفّٰهُنَّ الْمَوْتُ

522-A. *Cf.* xliv. 57, n. 4733 ; also App. XII, 15, p. 1469.

523. Most commentators understand this to refer to adultery or fornication ; in that case they consider that the punishment was altered to 100 stripes by the later verse, xxiv. 2. But I think it refers to unnatural crime between women, analogous to unnatural crime between men in iv. 16 below ; because (1) no punishment is specified here for the man, as would be the case where a man was involved in the crime ; (2) the word *al-lātī*, the purely feminine plural of *al-latī*, is used for the parties to the crime ; (3) the punishment is indefinite ; see the next note but one.

524. To protect the honour of women, stricter evidence is required, *i.e.*, the evidence of four instead of the usual two witnesses. It is the same for adultery (see xxiv. 4).

Or God ordain for them
Some (other) way.[525]

أَوْ يَجْعَلَ اللَّهُ لَهُنَّ سَبِيلًا ○

16. If two men among you
Are guilty of lewdness,
Punish them both.
If they repent and amend,
Leave them alone; for God
Is Oft-returning, Most Merciful.

١٦- وَالَّذَانِ يَأْتِيَانِهَا مِنكُمْ فَآذُوهُمَا
فَإِن تَابَا وَأَصْلَحَا
فَأَعْرِضُوا عَنْهُمَا
إِنَّ اللَّهَ كَانَ تَوَّابًا رَّحِيمًا ○

17. God accepts the repentance
Of those who do evil
In ignorance and repent
Soon afterwards; to them
Will God turn in mercy:
For God is full of knowledge
And wisdom.

١٧- إِنَّمَا التَّوْبَةُ عَلَى اللَّهِ
لِلَّذِينَ يَعْمَلُونَ السُّوٓءَ بِجَهَالَةٍ
ثُمَّ يَتُوبُونَ مِن قَرِيبٍ
فَأُولَٰٓئِكَ يَتُوبُ اللَّهُ عَلَيْهِمْ
وَكَانَ اللَّهُ عَلِيمًا حَكِيمًا ○

18. Of no effect is the repentance
Of those who continue[526]
To do evil, until Death
Faces one of them, and he says,
"Now have I repented indeed;"
Nor of those who die
Rejecting Faith: for them
Have we prepared
A punishment most grievous.

١٨- وَلَيْسَتِ التَّوْبَةُ لِلَّذِينَ يَعْمَلُونَ السَّيِّئَاتِ
حَتَّىٰٓ إِذَا حَضَرَ أَحَدَهُمُ الْمَوْتُ
قَالَ إِنِّي تُبْتُ الْـَٔـٰنَ
وَلَا الَّذِينَ يَمُوتُونَ وَهُمْ كُفَّارٌ
أُولَٰٓئِكَ أَعْتَدْنَا لَهُمْ عَذَابًا أَلِيمًا ○

19. O ye who believe!
Ye are forbidden to inherit
Women against their will.[527]
Nor should ye treat them

١٩- يَٰٓأَيُّهَا الَّذِينَ آمَنُوا
لَا يَحِلُّ لَكُمْ أَن تَرِثُوا النِّسَاءَ كَرْهًا
وَلَا تَعْضُلُوهُنَّ

525. Keep them in prison until some definite order is received. Those who take the crime to be adultery or fornication construe this definite order ("some other way") to mean some definite pronouncement by the Prophet under inspiration; this was the punishment of flogging under xxiv. 2. If we understand the crime to be unnatural crime, we might presume, in the absence of any definite order ("some other way") that the punishment would be similar to that for men in the next verse. That is itself indefinite, and perhaps intentionally so, as the crime is most shameful, and should be unknown in a well-regulated society. The maximum punishment would of course be imprisonment for life.

526. Note the fine touch. A sin may be fashionable, and people may sin together without compunction. When one of them is faced with Death, he repents, but that sort of repentance is no good.

527. Among many nations, including Arabs in the Days of Ignorance, a step-son or brother took possession of a dead man's widow or widows along with his goods and chattels. This shameful custom is forbidden. See also iv. 22 below.

With harshness, that ye may
Take away part of the dower[528]
Ye have given them,—except
Where they have been guilty
Of open lewdness;
On the contrary live with them
On a footing of kindness and
equity.
If ye take a dislike to them
It may be that ye dislike
A thing, and God brings about
Through it a great deal of good.

لِتَذْهَبُوْا بِبَعْضِ
مَآ اٰتَيْتُمُوْهُنَّ
اِلَّآ اَنْ يَّاْتِيْنَ بِفَاحِشَةٍ مُّبَيِّنَةٍ ۚ
وَعَاشِرُوْهُنَّ بِالْمَعْرُوْفِ ۚ
فَاِنْ كَرِهْتُمُوْهُنَّ
فَعَسٰٓى اَنْ تَكْرَهُوْا شَيْئًا
وَّيَجْعَلَ اللّٰهُ فِيْهِ خَيْرًا كَثِيْرًا ○

20. But if ye decide to take
One wife in place of another,
Even if ye had given the latter
A whole treasure[529] for dower,
Take not the least bit of it back:
Would ye take it by slander
And a manifest wrong?

٢٠- وَاِنْ اَرَدْتُّمُ اسْتِبْدَالَ زَوْجٍ مَّكَانَ
زَوْجٍ ۙ وَّاٰتَيْتُمْ اِحْدٰىهُنَّ قِنْطَارًا
فَلَا تَاْخُذُوْا مِنْهُ شَيْئًا ۭ
اَتَاْخُذُوْنَهٗ بُهْتَانًا وَّاِثْمًا مُّبِيْنًا ○

21. And how could ye take it
When ye have gone in
Unto each other, and they have
Taken from you a solemn
covenant?

٢١- وَكَيْفَ تَاْخُذُوْنَهٗ
وَقَدْ اَفْضٰى بَعْضُكُمْ اِلٰى بَعْضٍ
وَّاَخَذْنَ مِنْكُمْ مِّيْثَاقًا غَلِيْظًا ○

22. And marry not women
Whom your fathers married,—
Except what is past:
It was shameful and odious,—
An abominable custom indeed.[530]

٢٢- وَلَا تَنْكِحُوْا مَا نَكَحَ اٰبَآؤُكُمْ مِّنَ
النِّسَآءِ اِلَّا مَا قَدْ سَلَفَ ۭ
اِنَّهٗ كَانَ فَاحِشَةً وَّمَقْتًا ۭ وَسَآءَ سَبِيْلًا ○ ع

528 Another trick to detract from the freedom of married women was to treat them badly and force them to sue for a *Khul'a* divorce (see ii. 229, n. 258) or its equivalent in pre-Islamic custom, when the dower could be claimed back. This is also forbidden. Or the harshness may be exercised in another way: a divorced woman may be prevented by those who have control of her, from re-marrying unless she remits her dower. All kinds of harshness are forbidden.

529. Treasure: *Qinṭār*=a Talent of gold: see iii. 14, first note.

530. See above: iv. 19, n. 527.

SECTION 4.

23. Prohibited to you
(For marriage) are :—[531]
Your mothers, daughters,[532]
Sisters ; father's sisters,
Mother's sisters ; brother's
daughters,
Sister's daugters ; foster-mothers [533]
(Who gave you suck), foster-sisters ;
Your wives' mothers ;
Your step-daughters under your[534]
Guardianship, born of your wives
To whom ye have gone in,—
No prohibition if ye have not gone
in ;—
(Those who have been)
Wives of your sons [535] proceeding
From your loins ;
And two sisters in wedlock
At one and the same time,[536]
Except for what is past ;
For God is Oft-forgiving,
4/30 Most Merciful ;—

٢٣- حُرِّمَتْ عَلَيْكُمْ أُمَّهٰتُكُمْ وَبَنٰتُكُمْ
وَأَخَوٰتُكُمْ وَعَمّٰتُكُمْ وَخٰلٰتُكُمْ وَبَنٰتُ
الْأَخِ وَبَنٰتُ الْأُخْتِ
وَأُمَّهٰتُكُمُ الّٰتِىٓ أَرْضَعْنَكُمْ
وَأَخَوٰتُكُم مِّنَ الرَّضٰعَةِ
وَأُمَّهٰتُ نِسَآئِكُمْ وَرَبٰٓئِبُكُمُ الّٰتِى
فِى حُجُورِكُم مِّن نِّسَآئِكُمُ الّٰتِى
دَخَلْتُم بِهِنَّ فَإِن لَّمْ تَكُونُوا
دَخَلْتُم بِهِنَّ فَلَا جُنَاحَ عَلَيْكُمْ
وَحَلٰٓئِلُ أَبْنَآئِكُمُ الَّذِينَ مِنْ أَصْلٰبِكُمْ
وَأَن تَجْمَعُوا بَيْنَ الْأُخْتَيْنِ
إِلَّا مَا قَدْ سَلَفَ
إِنَّ اللّٰهَ كَانَ غَفُورًا رَّحِيمًا ○

531. This Table of Prohibited Degrees agrees in the main with what is usually accepted among all nations, except in minor details. It begins in the last verse (with father's widows or divorcees). The scheme is drawn up on the assumption that the person who proposes to marry is a man : if it is a woman, the same scheme will apply, *mutatis mutandis* : it will read : "your fathers, sons, brothers," etc.; or you can always read it from the husband's view of relationship, as there must always be a husband in a marriage.

532. "Mother" includes grandmother (through the father or mother), great-grandmother, etc ; "daughter" includes grand-daughter (through son or daughter), great-grand-daughter, etc ; "sister" includes full-sister and half-sister. "Father's sister" includes grandfather's sister, etc., and "mother's sister" includes grandmother's sister, etc.

533. "Fosterage" or milk-relationships play an important part in Muslim Law, and count like blood-relationships : it would therefore seem that not only foster-mothers and foster-sisters, but foster-mother's sister, etc., all come within the prohibited degrees.

534. It is generally (but not unanimously) held that "under your guardianship" is a description, not a condition. Therefore a step-daughter not "under your guardianship" is still within the prohibition if the other condition (about her mother) is fulfilled.

535. "Sons" includes grandsons, but excludes adopted sons, or persons treated as such, on account of the words "proceeding from your loins."

536. The bar against two sisters in marriage together applies to aunt and niece together, but not to deceased wife's sister after the wife dies.

24. Also (prohibited are)
Women already married,
Except those
Whom your right hands possess:[537]
Thus hath God ordained
(Prohibitions) against you:
Except for these, all others
Are lawful, provided
Ye seek (them in marriage)
With gifts from your property,—
Desiring chastity, not lust.[538]
Seeing that ye derive
Benefit from them, give them
Their dowers (at least)[539]
As prescribed; but if,
After a dower is prescribed, ye agree
Mutually (to vary it),
There is no blame on you,
And God is All-knowing
All-wise.

٢٤- وَّالْمُحْصَنٰتُ مِنَ النِّسَآءِ
اِلَّا مَا مَلَكَتْ اَيْمَانُكُمْ ۚ
كِتٰبَ اللّٰهِ عَلَيْكُمْ ۚ
وَاُحِلَّ لَكُمْ مَّا وَرَآءَ ذٰلِكُمْ
اَنْ تَبْتَغُوْا بِاَمْوَالِكُمْ
مُّحْصِنِيْنَ غَيْرَ مُسٰفِحِيْنَ ۗ
فَمَا اسْتَمْتَعْتُمْ بِهٖ مِنْهُنَّ
فَاٰتُوْهُنَّ اُجُوْرَهُنَّ فَرِيْضَةً ۗ
وَلَا جُنَاحَ عَلَيْكُمْ
فِيْمَا تَرٰضَيْتُمْ بِهٖ مِنْۢ بَعْدِ الْفَرِيْضَةِ ۗ
اِنَّ اللّٰهَ كَانَ عَلِيْمًا حَكِيْمًا ۝

25. If any of you have not
The means wherewith
To wed free believing women,
They may wed believing
Girls from among those
Whom your right hands possess:[540]
And God hath full knowledge
About your Faith.
Ye are one from another:
Wed them with the leave
Of their owners, and give them
Their dowers, according to what

٢٥- وَمَنْ لَّمْ يَسْتَطِعْ مِنْكُمْ
طَوْلًا اَنْ يَّنْكِحَ الْمُحْصَنٰتِ الْمُؤْمِنٰتِ
فَمِنْ مَّا مَلَكَتْ اَيْمَانُكُمْ
مِّنْ فَتَيٰتِكُمُ الْمُؤْمِنٰتِ ۗ
وَاللّٰهُ اَعْلَمُ بِاِيْمَانِكُمْ ۗ بَعْضُكُمْ مِّنْۢ بَعْضٍ ۚ
فَانْكِحُوْهُنَّ بِاِذْنِ اَهْلِهِنَّ
وَاٰتُوْهُنَّ اُجُوْرَهُنَّ بِالْمَعْرُوْفِ

537. *Whom your right hands possess*: i.e. captives in a Jihād, or war under the orders of the righteous Imām against those who persecute Faith. In such cases formal hostility dissolves civil ties.

538. After defining the prohibited degrees, the verse proceeds to say that women other than those specified may be sought in marriage, but even so, not from motives of lust, but in order to promote chastity between the sexes. Marriage in the original Arabic is here described by a word which suggests a fortress (ḥiṣn): marriage is, therefore, the fortress of chastity.

539. As the woman in marriage surrenders her person, so the man also must surrender (besides some part of his independence) at least some of his property according to his means. And this gives rise to the law of Dower. A minimum dower is prescribed, but it is not necessary to stick to the minimum, and in the new relationship created, the parties are recommended to act towards each other with the greatest confidence and liberality.

540. That is, captives taken in a *Jihād*: see note 537 above. "*Your* right hands" does not mean necessarily that she has been assigned to you, or is your property. All captures in war belong to the community, they are "yours" in that sense. If you seek such a person in marriage, do it from no base motives. Safeguard your faith, and see that she too does believe. In that case, after all, she is of the human brotherhood, and her condition is accidental and redeemable. If the slave bore a child to her master, she would become free. The slave condition is now out of date, in the true spirit of Islam. But there are other conditions in which a woman's (or man's) freedom is restricted, and the principle would apply there also.

Is reasonable: they should be
Chaste, not lustful, nor taking
Paramours: when they
Are taken in wedlock,
If they fall into shame,
Their punishment is half
That for free women.
This (permission) is for those
Among you who fear sin;
But it is better for you
That ye practise self-restraint.
And God is Oft-forgiving,
Most Merciful.

مُحْصَنٰتٍ غَيْرَ مُسٰفِحٰتٍ
وَّلَا مُتَّخِذٰتِ اَخْدَانٍ ۚ
فَاِذَآ اُحْصِنَّ فَاِنْ اَتَيْنَ بِفَاحِشَةٍ
فَعَلَيْهِنَّ نِصْفُ مَا عَلَى الْمُحْصَنٰتِ مِنَ
الْعَذَابِ ۚ ذٰلِكَ لِمَنْ خَشِيَ الْعَنَتَ مِنْكُمْ ۚ
وَاَنْ تَصْبِرُوْا خَيْرٌ لَّكُمْ ۚ
وَاللّٰهُ غَفُوْرٌ رَّحِيْمٌ ۝ ع

SECTION 5.

26. God doth wish
To make clear to you
And to show you
The ordinances of those
Before you; and (He
Doth wish to) turn to you
(In Mercy): and God
Is All-knowing, All-wise.

٢٦- يُرِيْدُ اللّٰهُ لِيُبَيِّنَ لَكُمْ
وَيَهْدِيَكُمْ سُنَنَ الَّذِيْنَ مِنْ قَبْلِكُمْ
وَيَتُوْبَ عَلَيْكُمْ ۚ
وَاللّٰهُ عَلِيْمٌ حَكِيْمٌ ۝

27. God doth wish
To turn to you,
But the wish of those
Who follow their lusts
Is that ye should turn
Away (from Him),—
Far, far away.

٢٧- وَاللّٰهُ يُرِيْدُ اَنْ يَّتُوْبَ عَلَيْكُمْ قف
وَيُرِيْدُ الَّذِيْنَ
يَتَّبِعُوْنَ الشَّهَوٰتِ
اَنْ تَمِيْلُوْا مَيْلًا عَظِيْمًا ۝

28. God doth wish
To lighten your (difficulties):
For man was created
Weak (in flesh).

٢٨- يُرِيْدُ اللّٰهُ اَنْ يُّخَفِّفَ عَنْكُمْ ۚ
وَخُلِقَ الْاِنْسَانُ ضَعِيْفًا ۝

29. O ye who believe![541]
Eat not up your property

٢٩- يٰٓاَيُّهَا الَّذِيْنَ اٰمَنُوْا لَا تَاْكُلُوْٓا اَمْوَالَكُمْ

---

541. Let me paraphrase this verse, for there is profound meaning in it. (1) All your property you hold in trust, whether it is in your name, or belongs to the community, or to people over whom you have control. To waste is wrong. (2) In ii. 188 the same phrase occurred, to caution us against greed. Here it occurs, to encourage us to increase property by economic use (traffic and trade), recalling Christ's parable of the Talents (Matt. xxv. 14-30), where the servants who had increased their master's wealth were promoted and the servant who had hoarded was cast into darkness. (3) We are warned that our waste may mean our own destruction ("nor kill or destroy yourselves.") But there is a more general meaning also: we must be careful of our own and other people's lives. We must commit no violence. This is the opposite of "trade and traffic by mutual good-will." (4) Our violence to our own brethren is particularly preposterous, seeing that God has loved and showered His mercies on us and all His creatures.

Among yourselves in vanities:
But let there be amongst you
Traffic and trade
By mutual good-will:
Nor kill (or destroy)
Yourselves: for verily
God hath been to you
Most Merciful!

بَيْنَكُمْ بِالْبَاطِلِ
إِلَّا أَنْ تَكُونَ تِجَارَةً عَنْ تَرَاضٍ مِّنْكُمْ
وَلَا تَقْتُلُوا أَنْفُسَكُمْ
إِنَّ اللهَ كَانَ بِكُمْ رَحِيمًا ○

30. If any do that
In rancour and injustice,—
Soon shall We cast them
Into the Fire: and easy
It is for God.

٣٠ - وَمَنْ يَّفْعَلْ ذٰلِكَ عُدْوَانًا وَّظُلْمًا
فَسَوْفَ نُصْلِيهِ نَارًا
وَكَانَ ذٰلِكَ عَلَى اللهِ يَسِيرًا ○

31. If ye (but) eschew
The most heinous
Of the things
Which ye are forbidden to do,
We shall expel
Out of you
All the evil in you,
And admit you to a Gate
Of great honour.

٣١ - إِنْ تَجْتَنِبُوا كَبَآئِرَ
مَا تُنْهَوْنَ عَنْهُ
نُكَفِّرْ عَنْكُمْ سَيِّاٰتِكُمْ
وَنُدْخِلْكُمْ مُّدْخَلًا كَرِيمًا ○

32. And in no wise covet[542]
Those things in which God
Hath bestowed His gifts
More freely on some of you
Than on others: to men
Is allotted what they earn,
And to women what they earn:
But ask God of His bounty.
For God hath full knowledge
Of all things.

٣٢ - وَلَا تَتَمَنَّوْا مَا فَضَّلَ اللهُ بِهٖ بَعْضَكُمْ
عَلٰى بَعْضٍ لِلرِّجَالِ نَصِيبٌ مِّمَّا اكْتَسَبُوا
وَلِلنِّسَآءِ نَصِيبٌ مِّمَّا اكْتَسَبْنَ
وَسْئَلُوا اللهَ مِنْ فَضْلِهٖ
إِنَّ اللهَ كَانَ بِكُلِّ شَيْءٍ عَلِيمًا ○

33. To (benefit) every one,
We have appointed
Sharers and heirs[543]
To property left

٣٣ - وَلِكُلٍّ جَعَلْنَا مَوَالِيَ مِمَّا تَرَكَ
الْوَالِدٰنِ وَالْأَقْرَبُونَ

542. Men and women have gifts from God—some greater than others. They seem unequal, but we are assured that Providence has allotted them by a scheme by which people receive what they earn. If this does not appear clear in our sight, let us remember that we have no full knowledge but God has. We must not be jealous if other people have more than we have—in wealth or position or strength or honour or talent or happiness. Probably things are equalized in the aggregate or in the long run, or equated to needs and merits on a scale which we cannot appraise. If we want more, instead of being jealous or covetous, we should pray to God and place before Him our needs. Though He knows all, and has no need of our prayer, our prayer may reveal to ourselves our shortcomings and enable us to deserve more of God's bounty or make ourselves fit for it.

543. *Mawālī*, plural of *Maulā*; from the root *walā*, to be near in place or relationship, to follow. *Maulā* may therefore mean: (1) nearly related, (2) heir, (3) sharer or partner; these three meanings are implied here; (4) neighbour, or friend, or protector, or client (xliv. 44); (5) lord, or master (xvi. 76)

By parents and relatives.
To those, also, to whom
Your right hand was pledged,[544]
Give their due portion.
For truly God is witness
To all things.

وَالَّذِيْنَ عَقَدَتْ اَيْمَانُكُمْ
فَاٰتُوْهُمْ نَصِيْبَهُمْ ؕ
اِنَّ اللّٰهَ كَانَ عَلٰى كُلِّ شَىْءٍ شَهِيْدًا ۝

SECTION 6.

34. Men are the protectors[545]
And maintainers of women,
Because God has given
The one more (strength)
Than the other, and because
They support them
From their means.
Therefore the righteous women
Are devoutly obedient, and guard
In (the husband's) absence
What God would have them
guard.[546]
As to those women
On whose part ye fear
Disloyalty and ill-conduct,
Admonish them (first),[547]
(Next), refuse to share their beds,
(And last) beat them (lightly);
But if they return to obedience,
Seek not against them[548]
Means (of annoyance):

٣٤- اَلرِّجَالُ قَوّٰمُوْنَ عَلَى النِّسَآءِ
بِمَا فَضَّلَ اللّٰهُ بَعْضَهُمْ عَلٰى بَعْضٍ
وَّبِمَآ اَنْفَقُوْا مِنْ اَمْوَالِهِمْ ؕ
فَالصّٰلِحٰتُ قٰنِتٰتٌ حٰفِظٰتٌ لِّلْغَيْبِ
بِمَا حَفِظَ اللّٰهُ ؕ
وَالّٰتِىْ تَخَافُوْنَ نُشُوْزَهُنَّ فَعِظُوْهُنَّ
وَاهْجُرُوْهُنَّ فِى الْمَضَاجِعِ
وَاضْرِبُوْهُنَّ ۚ
فَاِنْ اَطَعْنَكُمْ
فَلَا تَبْغُوْا عَلَيْهِنَّ سَبِيْلًا ؕ

---

544. When the emigration took place from Mecca to Medina, bonds and links of brotherhood were established between the Emigrants and the Helpers, and they shared in each other's inheritance. Later, when the Community was solidly established, and relations with those left behind in Mecca were resumed, the rights of blood-relations in Mecca, and the Helper-brethren in Medina were both safeguarded. This is the particular meaning. The more general meaning is similar: respect your ties of blood, of neighbourhood, and of friendly compacts and understandings. Be just to all.

545. *Qawwām*: one who stands firm in another's business, protects his interests, and looks after his affairs; or it may be, standing firm in his own business, managing affairs with a steady purpose. *Cf.* iv. 135.

546. Or the sentence may be rendered: "and protect (the husband's interests) in his absence, as God has protected them." If we take the rendering as in the text, the meaning is: the good wife is obedient and harmonious in her husband's presence, and in his absence guards his reputation and property and her own virtue, as ordained by God. If we take the rendering as in the note, we reach the same result in a different way: the good wife, in her husband's absence, remembering how God has given her a sheltered position, does everything to justify that position by guarding her own virtue and his reputation and property.

547. In case of family jars four steps are mentioned, to be taken in that order: (1) perhaps verbal advice or admonition may be sufficient; (2) if not, sex relations may be suspended; (3) if this is not sufficient, some slight physical correction may be administered; but Imām Shafi'ī considers this inadvisable, though permissible, and all authorities are unanimous in deprecating any sort of cruelty, even of the nagging kind, as mentioned in the next clause; (4) if all this fails, a family council is recommended in iv. 35 below.

548. Temper, nagging, sarcasm, speaking at each other in other people's presence, reverting to past faults which should be forgiven and forgotten,—all this is forbidden. And the reason given is characteristic of Islam. You must live all your life as in the presence of God, Who is high above us, but Who watches over us. How petty and contemptible will our little squabbles appear in His presence!

For God is Most High,
Great (above you all).

إِنَّ اللَّهَ كَانَ عَلِيًّا كَبِيرًا ○

35. If ye fear a breach
Between them twain,
Appoint (two) arbiters,
One from his family,
And the other from hers ;[549]
If they wish for peace,
God will cause
Their reconciliation :
For God hath full knowledge,
And is acquainted
With all things.

٣٥- وَإِنْ خِفْتُمْ شِقَاقَ بَيْنِهِمَا
فَابْعَثُوا حَكَمًا مِّنْ أَهْلِهِ
وَحَكَمًا مِّنْ أَهْلِهَا ج
إِن يُرِيدَا إِصْلَاحًا
يُوَفِّقِ اللَّهُ بَيْنَهُمَا ط
إِنَّ اللَّهَ كَانَ عَلِيمًا خَبِيرًا ○

36. Serve God, and join not[550]
Any partners with Him ;
And do good—
To parents, kinsfolk,
Orphans, those in need,
Neighbours who are near,[551]
Neighbours who are strangers,
The Companion by your side,[552]
The way-farer (ye meet),
And what your right hands
possess :[553]
For God loveth not
The arrogant, the vainglorious ;—[554]

٣٦- وَاعْبُدُوا اللَّهَ وَلَا تُشْرِكُوا بِهِ شَيْئًا
وَبِالْوَالِدَيْنِ إِحْسَانًا
وَبِذِي الْقُرْبَىٰ وَالْيَتَامَىٰ وَالْمَسَاكِينِ
وَالْجَارِ ذِي الْقُرْبَىٰ وَالْجَارِ الْجُنُبِ
وَالصَّاحِبِ بِالْجَنبِ وَابْنِ السَّبِيلِ
وَمَا مَلَكَتْ أَيْمَانُكُمْ ط
إِنَّ اللَّهَ لَا يُحِبُّ مَن كَانَ مُخْتَالًا فَخُورًا ○

---

549 An excellent plan for settling family disputes, without too much publicity or mud-throwing, or resort to the chicaneries of the law. The Latin countries recognise this plan in their legal systems. It is a pity that Muslims do not resort to it universally, as they should. The arbiters from each family would know the idiosyncracies of both parties, and would be able, with God's help to effect a real reconciliation.

550. The essence of Islam is to serve God and do good to your fellow-creatures. This is wider and more comprehensive than "Love God and love your neighbour" For it includes duties to animals as our fellow-creatures, and emphasises practical service rather than sentiment.

551. *Neighbours who are near*: that is, in local situation as well as intimate relationships, just as *neighbours who are strangers* includes those whom we do not know or who live away from us or in a different sphere altogether.

552. The *Companion by your side* may be your intimate friends and associates, just as the *way-farer you meet* may be a casual acquaintance on your travels. This last is much wider than the "stranger within your gate."

553. *What your right hands possess*: anything that has no civil rights. It includes captives or slaves (where they exist in any form whatever), people in your power, or dumb animals with whom you have to deal. They are all God's creatures and deserve our sympathy and our *practical service. Cf.* Coleridge's "Rime of the Ancient Mariner": "He prayeth best who loveth best All things both great and small, For the dear God who loveth us, He made and loveth all."

554. Real deeds of service and kindness proceed, not from showing off or from a superior sort of condescension (*Cf.* "White Man's Burden"), but from a frank recognition of our own humility and the real claims, before God, of all our fellow-creatures. For in our mutual needs we are equal before God, or perhaps the best of us (as the world sees us) may be worse than the worst of us (from the same point of view).

37. (Nor) those who are niggardly
Or enjoin niggardliness on others,
Or hide the bounties
Which God hath bestowed[555]
On them ; for We have prepared,
For those who resist Faith,
A Punishment that steeps[556]
Them in contempt ;—

٣٧- الَّذِينَ يَبْخَلُونَ
وَيَأْمُرُونَ النَّاسَ بِالْبُخْلِ
وَيَكْتُمُونَ مَا آتَاهُمُ اللَّهُ مِنْ فَضْلِهِ ۗ
وَأَعْتَدْنَا لِلْكَافِرِينَ عَذَابًا مُهِينًا ۝

38. Nor those who spend
Of their substance, to be seen[557]
Of men, but have no faith
In God and the Last Day :
If any take the Evil One
For their intimate,
What a dreadful intimate he is !

٣٨- وَالَّذِينَ يُنْفِقُونَ أَمْوَالَهُمْ رِئَاءَ النَّاسِ
وَلَا يُؤْمِنُونَ بِاللَّهِ وَلَا بِالْيَوْمِ الْآخِرِ ۗ
وَمَنْ يَكُنِ الشَّيْطَانُ لَهُ قَرِينًا فَسَاءَ
قَرِينًا ۝

39. And what burden
Were it on them if they
Had faith in God
And in the Last Day,
And they spent
Out of what God hath
Given them for sustenance ?[558]
For God hath full
Knowledge of them.

٣٩- وَمَاذَا عَلَيْهِمْ لَوْ آمَنُوا بِاللَّهِ
وَالْيَوْمِ الْآخِرِ
وَأَنْفَقُوا مِمَّا رَزَقَهُمُ اللَّهُ
وَكَانَ اللَّهُ بِهِمْ عَلِيمًا ۝

40. God is never unjust
In the least degree :
If there is any good (done),
He doubleth it,
And giveth from His own
Presence a great reward.[559]

٤٠- إِنَّ اللَّهَ لَا يَظْلِمُ مِثْقَالَ ذَرَّةٍ ۚ
وَإِنْ تَكُ حَسَنَةً يُضَاعِفْهَا
وَيُؤْتِ مِنْ لَدُنْهُ أَجْرًا عَظِيمًا ۝

41. How then if We brought
From each People a witness,

٤١- فَكَيْفَ إِذَا جِئْنَا مِنْ كُلِّ أُمَّةٍ بِشَهِيدٍ

555 Arrogance is one reason why our deeds of love and kindness do not thrive. Another is niggardliness or selfishness. God does not love either the one or the other, for they both proceed from want of love of God, or faith in God. Niggardly is the worldly wise man who not only refuses to spend himself in service, but by example and precept prevents others from doing so, as otherwise he would be made odious by comparison, before his fellow-creatures. So he either makes a virtue of his caution, or hides the gifts which have been given him—wealth, position, talent, etc.

556. Note how the punishment fits the crime. The niggard holds other people in contempt, and in doing so, becomes himself contemptible.

557. A fault opposed to niggardliness, and equally opposed to true Charity, is to spend lavishly to be seen of men. It is mere hypocrisy ; there is no love in it, either for God or for man.

558. *Sustenance*: physical, intellectual, spiritual—everything pertaining to life and growth. Our being is from God, and we must therefore spend ourselves freely for God. How can it be a burden ? It is merely a response to the demand of our own healthy nature.

559. Any little good of our own comes from the purity of our heart. Its results in the world are doubled and multiplied by God's grace and mercy ; but an even greater reward comes from His own Presence, His good pleasure, which brings us nearer to Him.

And We brought thee
As a witness against
These People ![560]

وَجِئْنَا بِكَ عَلَىٰ هَٰؤُلَاءِ شَهِيدًا ۞

وقف النبي عليه السلام

42. On that day
Those who reject Faith
And disobey the Apostle
Will wish that the earth
Were made one with them :[561]
But never will they hide
A single fact from God !

۴۲- يَوْمَئِذٍ يَوَدُّ الَّذِينَ كَفَرُوا
وَعَصَوُا الرَّسُولَ
لَوْ تُسَوَّىٰ بِهِمُ الْأَرْضُ
وَلَا يَكْتُمُونَ اللَّهَ حَدِيثًا ۞ ٦ع

C. 63.—Be clean and pure, and seek not occasions
(iv. 43-70) For quibbles, nor go after sorcery
Or false gods. Be faithful
In your trusts, learn obedience,
And settle your quarrels under the guidance
Of God's Apostle. Ever keep away
From hypocrisy and every kind of falsehood.
Then will you be admitted to a glorious Fellowship
With the highest and noblest in the spiritual world.

SECTION 7.

43. O ye who believe !
Approach not prayers
With a mind befogged,[562]
Until ye can understand
All that ye say,—
Nor in a state
Of ceremonial impurity
(Except when travelling on the road),
Until after washing
Your whole body.
If ye are ill,
Or on a journey,
Or one of you cometh
From offices of nature,

۴۳- يَا أَيُّهَا الَّذِينَ آمَنُوا لَا تَقْرَبُوا الصَّلَوٰةَ
وَأَنْتُمْ سُكَارَىٰ
حَتَّىٰ تَعْلَمُوا مَا تَقُولُونَ
وَلَا جُنُبًا إِلَّا عَابِرِي سَبِيلٍ
حَتَّىٰ تَغْتَسِلُوا وَإِنْ كُنْتُمْ مَرْضَىٰ
أَوْ عَلَىٰ سَفَرٍ
أَوْ جَاءَ أَحَدٌ مِنْكُمْ مِنَ الْغَائِطِ

560. Each Prophet and Leader is a witness for his People and his contemporaries—for those who accept God, and against those who reject Him.

561. Those who reject God's message will wish, when their eyes are opened, that they were reduced to dust, for existence itself will be agony to them. They might like to hide in the dust, but nothing is hidden from God. All their past will stand out clear before Him.

562. The reference is either to a state of intoxication or to a dazed state of mind on account of drowsiness or some other cause. Or perhaps both are implied. Before the prohibition of intoxicants altogether was promulgated, it was at least unbecoming that people should come to prayers in such a state. For prayers it is only right that we should collect our whole minds and approach God in a spirit of reverence. "Prayers" (*Ṣalāt*) here may mean "a place of prayers," a Mosque: the resulting meaning would be the same.

Or ye have been
In contact with women,
And ye find no water,[563]
Then take for yourselves
Clean sand or earth,
And rub therewith
Your faces and hands.
For God doth blot out sins
And forgive again and again.

أَوْ لٰمَسْتُمُ النِّسَآءَ
فَلَمْ تَجِدُوْا مَآءً
فَتَيَمَّمُوْا صَعِيْدًا طَيِّبًا
فَامْسَحُوْا بِوُجُوْهِكُمْ وَ اَيْدِيْكُمْ ؕ
اِنَّ اللّٰهَ كَانَ عَفُوًّا غَفُوْرًا ۝

44. Hast thou not turned
Thy vision to those
Who were given a portion[564]
Of the Book? They traffic
In error, and wish that ye
Should lose the right path.

۴۴- اَلَمْ تَرَ اِلَى الَّذِيْنَ اُوْتُوْا نَصِيْبًا مِّنَ
الْكِتٰبِ يَشْتَرُوْنَ الضَّلٰلَةَ
وَيُرِيْدُوْنَ اَنْ تَضِلُّوا السَّبِيْلَ ۝ؕ

45. But God hath full knowledge
Of your enemies:
God is enough for a Protector,
And God is enough for a Helper.

۴۵- وَاللّٰهُ اَعْلَمُ بِاَعْدَآئِكُمْ
وَكَفٰى بِاللّٰهِ وَلِيًّا ۙ وَّكَفٰى بِاللّٰهِ نَصِيْرًا ۝

46. Of the Jews there are those
Who displace words
From their (right) places,
And say: "We hear
And we disobey";[565]
And "Hear what is not
Heard"; and "*Rā'ina*";[566]
With a twist of their tongues
And a slander to Faith.
If only they had said:
"We hear and we obey";
And "Do hear";

۴۶- مِنَ الَّذِيْنَ هَادُوْا يُحَرِّفُوْنَ الْكَلِمَ
عَنْ مَّوَاضِعِهٖ
وَيَقُوْلُوْنَ سَمِعْنَا وَعَصَيْنَا
وَاسْمَعْ غَيْرَ مُسْمَعٍ وَّرَاعِنَا لَيًّا بِاَلْسِنَتِهِمْ
وَطَعْنًا فِى الدِّيْنِ ؕ وَلَوْ اَنَّهُمْ قَالُوْا سَمِعْنَا
وَاَطَعْنَا وَاسْمَعْ

---

563. The strictest cleanliness and purity of mind and body are required, especially at the time of prayer. But there are circumstances when water for ablutions is not easily obtainable, especially in the dry conditions of Arabia, and then washing with dry sand or clean earth is recommended. Four such circumstances are mentioned: the two last when washing is specially required; the two first when washing may be necessary, but it may not be easy to get water. For a man, when he is ill, cannot walk out far to get water, and a man on a journey has no full control over his supplies. In all four cases, where water cannot be got, cleaning with dry sand or dry earth is recommended. This is called *Tayammum.*

564. *Cf.* iii. 23 and n. 366.

565. See ii. 93, n. 98. A trick of the Jews was to twist words and expressions, so as to ridicule the most solemn teachings of Faith. Where they should have said, "We hear and we obey," they said aloud, "We hear," and whispered, "We disobey." Where they should have said respectfully, "We hear," thea added in a whisper, "What is not heard," by way of ridicule. Where they claimed the attention of the Teacher, they used an ambiguous word apparently harmless, but in their intention disrespectful.

566. See ii. 104, n. 106. "*Rā'ina*" if used respectfully in the Arabic way, would have meant "Please attend to us." With a twist of their tongue, they suggested an insulting meaning, such as "O thou that takest us to pasture!", or in Hebrew, "Our bad one!"

And " Do look at us ":
It would have been better
For them, and more proper;
But God hath cursed them
For their Unbelief; and but few
Of them will believe.

وَانْظُرْنَا لَكَانَ خَيْرًا لَّهُمْ وَاَقْوَمَ ۙ
وَلٰكِنْ لَّعَنَهُمُ اللّٰهُ
بِكُفْرِهِمْ فَلَا يُؤْمِنُوْنَ اِلَّا قَلِيْلًا ○

47. O ye People of the Book!
Believe in what We
Have (now) revealed, confirming
What was (already) with you,
Before We change the face and fame[567]
Of some (of you) beyond all recognition,
And turn them hindwards,
Or curse them as We cursed
The Sabbath-breakers,[568]
For the decision of God
Must be carried out.

۴۷- يٰۤاَيُّهَا الَّذِيْنَ اُوْتُوا الْكِتٰبَ اٰمِنُوْا
بِمَا نَزَّلْنَا مُصَدِّقًا لِّمَا مَعَكُمْ
مِّنْ قَبْلِ اَنْ نَّطْمِسَ وُجُوْهًا
فَنَرُدَّهَا عَلٰۤى اَدْبَارِهَاۤ
اَوْ نَلْعَنَهُمْ كَمَا لَعَنَّاۤ اَصْحٰبَ السَّبْتِ ؕ
وَكَانَ اَمْرُ اللّٰهِ مَفْعُوْلًا ○

48. God forgiveth not
That partners should be set up
With Him; but He forgiveth
Anything else, to whom
He pleaseth; to set up
Partners with God
Is to devise a sin[569]
Most heinous indeed.

۴۸ اِنَّ اللّٰهَ لَا يَغْفِرُ اَنْ يُّشْرَكَ بِهٖ
وَيَغْفِرُ مَا دُوْنَ ذٰلِكَ لِمَنْ يَّشَآءُ ۚ
وَمَنْ يُّشْرِكْ بِاللّٰهِ
فَقَدِ افْتَرٰۤى اِثْمًا عَظِيْمًا ○

49. Hast thou not turned
Thy vision to those
Who claim sanctity
For themselves?[570]

۴۹- اَلَمْ تَرَ اِلَى الَّذِيْنَ
يُزَكُّوْنَ اَنْفُسَهُمْ ؕ

---

567. Literally, "before We obliterate some features (or faces) and turn them front to back (or back to front)": an Arabic idiom, which must be translated freely to yield its proper meaning in English. The face is the chief expression of a man's own real essence; it is also the index of his fame and estimation. The People of the Book had been specially favoured by God with spiritual revelations. If they proved themselves unworthy, they lost their "face." Their eminence would, owing to their own conduct, be turned into degradation. Others would take their place. The first shall be last and the last shall be first: Matt. xix. 30.

568. *Cf.* ii. 65 and n. 79.

569. Just as in an earthly kingdom the worst crime is that of treason, as it cuts at the very existence of the State, so in the spiritual kingdom, the unforgivable sin is that of contumacious treason against God by putting up God's creatures in rivalry against Him. This is rebellion against the essence and source of spiritual Life. It is what Plato would call the "lie in the soul." But even here, if the rebellion is through ignorance, and is followed by sincere repentance and amendment, God's Mercy is always open (iv. 17).

570. The sanctimonious or self-sanctified people are the farthest from sanctity or purity, which can only proceed from God. They cannot play with God's Truth and yet go on claiming to be guided and purified or justified by God. Their falsehood in itself condemns them: no further proof is needed of their selfishness and evil.

Nay—but God
Doth sanctify
Whom He pleaseth.
But never will they
Fail to receive justice
In the least little thing.[571]

بَلِ اللّٰهُ يُزَكِّيْ مَنْ يَّشَآءُ
وَلَا يُظْلَمُوْنَ فَتِيْلًا ○

50. Behold! how they invent
A lie against God!
But that by itself
Is a manifest sin!

٥٠- اُنْظُرْ كَيْفَ يَفْتَرُوْنَ عَلَى اللّٰهِ الْكَذِبَ ط
وَكَفٰى بِهٖٓ اِثْمًا مُّبِيْنًا ○ ع

Section 8.

51. Hast thou not turned
Thy vision to those
Who were given a portion[572]
Of the Book? They believe
In Sorcery and Evil,[573]
And say to the Unbelievers
That they are better guided
In the (right) way
Than the Believers!

٥١- اَلَمْ تَرَ اِلَى الَّذِيْنَ اُوْتُوْا نَصِيْبًا مِّنَ
الْكِتٰبِ
يُؤْمِنُوْنَ بِالْجِبْتِ وَالطَّاغُوْتِ
وَيَقُوْلُوْنَ لِلَّذِيْنَ كَفَرُوْا هٰٓؤُلَآءِ
اَهْدٰى مِنَ الَّذِيْنَ اٰمَنُوْا سَبِيْلًا ○

52. They are (men) whom
God hath cursed:
And those whom God
Hath cursed, thou wilt find,
Have no one to help.[574]

٥٢- اُولٰٓئِكَ الَّذِيْنَ لَعَنَهُمُ اللّٰهُ ط
وَمَنْ يَّلْعَنِ اللّٰهُ
فَلَنْ تَجِدَ لَهٗ نَصِيْرًا ○

53. Have they a share
In dominion or power?
Behold, they give not a farthing[575]
To their fellow-men?

٥٣- اَمْ لَهُمْ نَصِيْبٌ مِّنَ الْمُلْكِ
فَاِذًا لَّا يُؤْتُوْنَ النَّاسَ نَقِيْرًا ○

571. Literally, the small skin in the groove of a date stone, a thing of no value: *qatīl*.

572. *Cf.* iii. 23 and n. 366. The phrase also occurs in iv. 44.

573. The word I have translated *Sorcery* is *jibt*, which may mean divination, sorcery, magic, or any false object of belief or worship, such as an idol. The word I have translated *Evil* (here and in ii. 256) is *Tāgūt*, which means the evil one, the one who exceeds all bounds, Satan; or it may refer to some idol worshipped by the Pagan Arabs, with whom the Jews of Medina were intriguing against the Holy Apostle. The Jews had taken much to sorcery, magic, divination, and such superstitions.

574. The Jews were then seeking the aid of the Meccan Pagans against Muḥammad, but so far from getting any help from them, they and the Pagans were both overthrown. That was the immediate occasion, but the words have a perfectly general—a universal—meaning.

575. The word I have translated *farthing* is *naqīr*, the groove in a date stone, a thing of no value whatever. Close-fistedness and envy are among the worst forms of selfishness, and appear specially incongruous in people of power, authority, or influence, from whom is expected generosity in giving and generosity in seeing other people's prosperity or happiness.

54. Or do they envy mankind
For what God hath given them
Of his bounty? But We
Had already given the people
Of Abraham the Book
And Wisdom, and conferred
Upon them a great kingdom.[576]

٥٤- أَمْ يَحْسُدُونَ النَّاسَ
عَلَىٰ مَا آتَاهُمُ اللَّهُ مِنْ فَضْلِهِ ۖ
فَقَدْ آتَيْنَا آلَ إِبْرَاهِيمَ الْكِتَابَ
وَالْحِكْمَةَ وَآتَيْنَاهُمْ مُلْكًا عَظِيمًا ○

55. Some of them believed,
And some of them averted
Their faces from him: and enough
Is Hell for a burning fire.[577]

٥٥- فَمِنْهُمْ مَنْ آمَنَ بِهِ وَمِنْهُمْ مَنْ
صَدَّ عَنْهُ ۚ وَكَفَىٰ بِجَهَنَّمَ سَعِيرًا ○

56. Those who reject
Our Signs, We shall soon
Cast into the Fire:
As often as their skins
Are roasted through,
We shall change them
For fresh skins,
That they may taste
The Penalty: for God
Is Exalted in Power, Wise.

٥٦- إِنَّ الَّذِينَ كَفَرُوا بِآيَاتِنَا
سَوْفَ نُصْلِيهِمْ نَارًا ۖ
كُلَّمَا نَضِجَتْ جُلُودُهُمْ بَدَّلْنَاهُمْ جُلُودًا
غَيْرَهَا لِيَذُوقُوا الْعَذَابَ ۗ
إِنَّ اللَّهَ كَانَ عَزِيزًا حَكِيمًا ○

57. But those who believe
And do deeds of righteousness,
We shall soon admit to Gardens,
With rivers flowing beneath,—
Their eternal home:
Therein shall they have
Companions pure and holy:[578]
We shall admit them
To shades, cool and ever
deepening.[579]

٥٧- وَالَّذِينَ آمَنُوا وَعَمِلُوا الصَّالِحَاتِ
سَنُدْخِلُهُمْ جَنَّاتٍ تَجْرِي
مِنْ تَحْتِهَا الْأَنْهَارُ خَالِدِينَ فِيهَا أَبَدًا ۖ
لَهُمْ فِيهَا أَزْوَاجٌ مُطَهَّرَةٌ ۖ
وَنُدْخِلُهُمْ ظِلًّا ظَلِيلًا ○

58. God doth command you
To render back your Trusts
To those to whom they are due;
And when ye judge

٥٨- إِنَّ اللَّهَ يَأْمُرُكُمْ أَنْ تُؤَدُّوا الْأَمَانَاتِ
إِلَىٰ أَهْلِهَا وَإِذَا حَكَمْتُمْ

576. Such as the kingdoms of David and Solomon, for they had international fame.

577. Envy is like an internal fire, which is in itself a hell.

578. *Cf.* ii 25 and n. 44.

579. The Garden is contrasted with the Fire: the shade is contrasted with the roasting. Evil grows with what it feeds on. So goodness and felicity grow with their practice. The good may be alone to start with, but (unlike evil ones) they get holy Companions. Just as spiritual agony increases with what it suffers (typified by fresh skins growing as the old ones burn out), so spiritual felicity finds deeper and deeper meaning (typified by the shades in a Garden, which grow deeper and cooler as you proceed into the interior).

Between man and man,
That ye judge with justice :
Verily how excellent
Is the teaching which He giveth
you !
For God is He Who heareth
And seeth all things.

بَيْنَ النَّاسِ
أَنْ تَحْكُمُوا بِالْعَدْلِ ۚ
إِنَّ اللَّهَ نِعِمَّا يَعِظُكُمْ بِهِ ۗ
إِنَّ اللَّهَ كَانَ سَمِيعًا بَصِيرًا ○

59. O ye who believe !
Obey God, and obey the Apostle,
And those charged
With authority among you.[580]
If ye differ in anything
Among yourselves, refer it
To God and His Apostle,
If ye do believe in God
And the Last Day :
That is best, and most suitable
For final determination.

٥٩- يَا أَيُّهَا الَّذِينَ آمَنُوا
أَطِيعُوا اللَّهَ وَأَطِيعُوا الرَّسُولَ وَأُولِي الْأَمْرِ
مِنْكُمْ ۖ فَإِنْ تَنَازَعْتُمْ فِي شَيْءٍ
فَرُدُّوهُ إِلَى اللَّهِ وَالرَّسُولِ
إِنْ كُنْتُمْ تُؤْمِنُونَ بِاللَّهِ وَالْيَوْمِ الْآخِرِ ۚ
ذَٰلِكَ خَيْرٌ وَأَحْسَنُ تَأْوِيلًا ○ ع

SECTION 9.

60. Hast thou not turned
Thy vision to those[581]
Who declare that they believe
In the revelations
That have come to thee
And to those before thee ?
Their (real) wish is
To resort together for judgment
(In their disputes)
To the Evil One,
Though they were ordered
To reject him.
But Satan's wish
Is to lead them astray
Far away (from the Right).

٦٠- أَلَمْ تَرَ إِلَى الَّذِينَ
يَزْعُمُونَ أَنَّهُمْ آمَنُوا بِمَا أُنْزِلَ إِلَيْكَ
وَمَا أُنْزِلَ مِنْ قَبْلِكَ
يُرِيدُونَ أَنْ يَتَحَاكَمُوا
إِلَى الطَّاغُوتِ
وَقَدْ أُمِرُوا أَنْ يَكْفُرُوا بِهِ ۚ
وَيُرِيدُ الشَّيْطَانُ أَنْ يُضِلَّهُمْ ضَلَالًا
بَعِيدًا ○

61. When it is said to them :
" Come to what God hath revealed,

٦١- وَإِذَا قِيلَ لَهُمْ تَعَالَوْا إِلَىٰ مَا أَنْزَلَ اللَّهُ

580. *Ulū-l-amr*=those charged with authority or responsibility or decision, or the settlement of affairs. All ultimate authority rests in God. Men of God derive their authority from Him. As Islam makes no sharp division between sacred and secular affairs, it expects ordinary governments to be imbued with righteousness, and stand in the place of the righteous Imām, and we must respect and obey such authority ; otherwise there will be no order or discipline. Where, in actual fact, there is a sharp division between law and morality, between secular and religious affairs, as is the case in most countries at the present day, Islam still expects secular authority to be exercised in righteousness, and on that condition, enjoins obedience to such authority.

581. The immediate reference was to the Hypocrites (*Munāfiqīn*) of Medina, but the words are general, and the evil of hypocrisy has to be dealt with in all ages. The type of these men is what is called Mr. Facing-both-ways in Bunyan's "Pilgrim's Progress." Such men declare that they are always with the Right, but calmly intrigue with Evil and Injustice, and even make Injustice their judge if their personal interests are served in that way.

And to the Apostle":
Thou seest the Hypocrites avert
Their faces from thee in disgust.

والى الرسول رايت المنفقين يصدون
عنك صدودا ○

62. How then, when they are
Seized by misfortune,
Because of the deeds
Which their hands have sent forth?
Then they come to thee,
Swearing by God:
"We meant no more
Than good-will and conciliation!"

٦٢- فكيف اذا اصابتهم مصيبة
بما قدمت ايديهم
ثم جاءوك يحلفون
بالله ان اردنا الا احسانا وتوفيقا ○

63. Those men,—God knows
What is in their hearts;
So keep clear of them,[582]
But admonish them,
And speak to them a word
To reach their very souls.

٦٣- اولئك الذين يعلم الله ما في قلوبهم
فاعرض عنهم وعظهم
وقل لهم في انفسهم قولا بليغا ○

64. We sent not an Apostle,
But to be obeyed, in accordance
With the Will of God.
If they had only,
When they were unjust
To themselves,
Come unto thee
And asked God's forgiveness,
And the Apostle had asked
Forgiveness for them,
They would have found
God indeed Oft-returning,
Most Merciful.

٦٤- وما ارسلنا من رسول
الا ليطاع باذن الله
ولو انهم اذ ظلموا انفسهم
جاءوك فاستغفروا الله
واستغفر لهم الرسول
لوجدوا الله توابا رحيما ○

65. But no, by thy Lord,
They can have
No (real) Faith,
Until they make thee judge
In all disputes between them,
And find in their souls
No resistance against
Thy decisions, but accept
Them with the fullest conviction.[583]

٦٥- فلا وربك لا يؤمنون
حتى يحكموك فيما شجر بينهم
ثم لا يجدوا في انفسهم
حرجا مما قضيت ويسلموا تسليما ○

582. How should hypocrites be treated? To take them into your confidence would of course be foolish. To wage unrelenting war against them may destroy the hope of reforming them and purging them of their hypocrisy. The man of God keeps clear of their wiles, but at the same time, does not hesitate to show them the error of their ways, nor to put in a word in season, to penetrate their hearts and win them back to God.

583. The test of true Faith is not mere lip profession, but bringing all our doubts and disputes to the one in whom we profess faith. Further, when a decision is given we are not only to accept it, but find in our inmost souls no difficulty and no resistance, but on the contrary a joyful acceptance springing from the conviction of our own faith.

66. If We had ordered them
To sacrifice their lives
Or to leave their homes,
Very few of them
Would have done it:[584]
But if they had done
What they were (actually) told,
It would have been best
For them, and would have gone
Farthest to strengthen their (faith);

٦٦- وَلَوْ أَنَّا كَتَبْنَا عَلَيْهِمْ أَنِ اقْتُلُوْا أَنْفُسَكُمْ
أَوِ اخْرُجُوْا مِنْ دِيَارِكُمْ
مَّا فَعَلُوْهُ إِلَّا قَلِيْلٌ مِّنْهُمْ
وَلَوْ أَنَّهُمْ فَعَلُوْا مَا يُوْعَظُوْنَ بِهِ
لَكَانَ خَيْرًا لَّهُمْ وَأَشَدَّ تَثْبِيْتًا ۝

67. And We should then have
Given them from Our Presence
A great reward;

٦٧- وَّإِذًا لَّآتَيْنٰهُمْ
مِّنْ لَّدُنَّا أَجْرًا عَظِيْمًا ۝

68. And We should have
Shown them the Straight Way.[585]

٦٨- وَّلَهَدَيْنٰهُمْ صِرَاطًا مُّسْتَقِيْمًا ۝

69. All who obey God
And the Apostle
Are in the company
Of those on whom
Is the Grace of God,—
Of the Prophets (who teach),
The Sincere (lovers of Truth),
The Witnesses (who testify),
And the Righteous (who do good):
Ah! what a beautiful Fellowship![586]

٦٩- وَمَنْ يُّطِعِ اللّٰهَ وَالرَّسُوْلَ
فَأُولٰٓئِكَ مَعَ الَّذِيْنَ أَنْعَمَ اللّٰهُ عَلَيْهِمْ
مِّنَ النَّبِيّٖنَ وَالصِّدِّيْقِيْنَ
وَالشُّهَدَآءِ وَالصّٰلِحِيْنَ
وَحَسُنَ أُولٰٓئِكَ رَفِيْقًا ۝

---

584. The highest in faith willingly sacrifice their lives, their homes, and all that they hold dearest, in the cause of God. Those whose faith is not so strong are expected at least to do what a loyal member of any society does, submit his doubts and disputes to the head of the society and cheerfully accept his decision and submit to it. The contrast is between the Hypocrites who will not even do this, and the really devoted men and women who would voluntarily sacrifice their lives.

585. Four advantages of obedience to God are mentioned, in the order in which they will appeal to the beginner in faith: (1) his own benefit ("best for them"); (2) strengthening of his faith, as he becomes more and more at home in the spiritual world; (3) reward from God's own Presence, such intense conviction that no further arguments are needed; (4) the Straight Way, in which there is no doubt or difficulty whatever in our practical conduct.

586. A passage of the deepest spiritual meaning. Even the humblest man who accepts Faith and does good becomes at once an accepted member of a great and beautiful spiritual Fellowship. It is a company which lives perpetually in the sunshine of God's Grace. (This passage partly illustrates Q. i. 5.) It is a glorious hierarchy, of which four grades are specified: (1) The highest is that of the Prophets or Apostles, who get plenary inspiration from God, and who teach mankind by example and precept. That rank in Islam is held by Muḥammad Muṣṭafā. (2) The next are those whose badge is sincerity and truth; they love and support the truth with their person, their means, their influence, and all that is theirs. That rank was held by the special Companions of Muḥammad, among whom the type was that of Ḥaḍhrat Abū Bakr Ṣiddīq. (3) The next are the noble army of Witnesses, who testify to the truth. The testimony may be by martyrdom, as in the case of Imāms Ḥasan and Ḥusain. Or it may be by the tongue of the true Preacher or the pen of the devoted scholar, or the life of the man devoted to service. (4) Lastly, there is the large company of Righteous people, the ordinary folk who do their ordinary business, but always in a righteous way. They are the rank and file of the beautiful Fellowship, in which each has his place and yet all feel that they derive glory from the common association.

70. Such is the Bounty
From God: and sufficient
Is it that God knoweth all.[587]

٧٠- ذٰلِكَ الْفَضْلُ مِنَ اللّٰهِ ۚ وَكَفٰى بِاللّٰهِ عَلِيْمًا ۝

C. 64.—Keep together in your noble Brotherhood:
(iv. 71-91.) Share its joys and sorrows: strive
And fight the good fight, and never fear:
For this life is short, and the Hereafter
Eternal. Allow not yourselves to be drawn
Into unbelief and cowardice:
Maintain the Right. Protect yourselves
Against Hypocrites and Deserters,
But pursue them not unrelentingly.

SECTION 10.

71. O ye who believe!
Take your precautions,
And either go forth in parties
Or go forth all together.[588]

٧١- يٰٓاَيُّهَا الَّذِيْنَ اٰمَنُوْا خُذُوْا حِذْرَكُمْ
فَانْفِرُوْا ثُبَاتٍ اَوِ انْفِرُوْا جَمِيْعًا ۝

72. There are certainly among you
Men who would tarry behind:[589]
If a misfortune befalls you,
They say: "God did favour us
In that we were not
Present among them."

٧٢- وَاِنَّ مِنْكُمْ لَمَنْ لَّيُبَطِّئَنَّ ۚ
فَاِنْ اَصَابَتْكُمْ مُّصِيْبَةٌ قَالَ قَدْ اَنْعَمَ
اللّٰهُ عَلَيَّ اِذْ لَمْ اَكُنْ مَّعَهُمْ شَهِيْدًا ۝

73. But if good fortune comes to you
From God, they would be sure
To say—as if there had never been
Ties of affection between you
and them—
"Oh! I wish I had been with them;
A fine thing should I then
Have made of it!"[590]

٧٣- وَلَئِنْ اَصَابَكُمْ فَضْلٌ مِّنَ اللّٰهِ
لَيَقُوْلَنَّ كَاَنْ لَّمْ تَكُنْۢ بَيْنَكُمْ وَبَيْنَهٗ
مَوَدَّةٌ يّٰلَيْتَنِيْ كُنْتُ مَعَهُمْ
فَاَفُوْزَ فَوْزًا عَظِيْمًا ۝

---

587. If a generous General gives the private soldier the privilege of sitting with his comrades and officers, high and low, in one common Brotherhood, people may perhaps wonder: how may this be? If we are admitted to that Fellowship, we want to know no more. It is enough to us that God knows our humility and our unworthiness, and with His full knowledge admits us to that glorious Fellowship!

588. No fight should be undertaken without due preparations and precautions. When these are taken, we must go boldly forward. "Go forth" is therefore repeated for emphasis. But we must go forth in a collective spirit, and not in a selfish spirit—either in small parties or all together, as our Leader determines. We must not tarry like the doubter in the next two verses.

589. The doubter detaches himself in thought and action from the community. If the general body has a reverse, he blesses God that he was not among them, instead of being ashamed of himself for desertion. If the general body wins a success, he does not rejoice for the common cause, but only regrets for himself that he was not there to share in the glory and the gains!

590. Just a selfish man's thought. Such men are far from being a source of strength to their community. They are no use in a fight, and the next verse by implication discards them.

74. Let those fight
In the cause of God
Who sell the life of this world
For the Hereafter.[591]
To him who fighteth
In the cause of God,—
Whether he is slain
Or gets victory—
Soon shall We give him
A reward of great (value).

٧٤- فَلْيُقَاتِلْ فِي سَبِيْلِ اللهِ
الَّذِيْنَ يَشْرُوْنَ الْحَيٰوةَ الدُّنْيَا بِالْاٰخِرَةِ ؕ
وَمَنْ يُّقَاتِلْ فِيْ سَبِيْلِ اللهِ
فَيُقْتَلْ اَوْ يَغْلِبْ
فَسَوْفَ نُؤْتِيْهِ اَجْرًا عَظِيْمًا ۝

75. And why should ye not
Fight in the cause of God
And of those who, being weak,[592]
Are ill-treated (and oppressed)?—
Men, women, and children,
Whose cry is: "Our Lord!
Rescue us from this town,
Whose people are oppressors;
And raise for us from Thee
One who will protect;
And raise for us from Thee
One who will help!"[593]

٧٥- وَمَا لَكُمْ لَا تُقَاتِلُوْنَ فِيْ سَبِيْلِ اللهِ
وَالْمُسْتَضْعَفِيْنَ مِنَ الرِّجَالِ وَالنِّسَآءِ وَ
الْوِلْدَانِ الَّذِيْنَ يَقُوْلُوْنَ رَبَّنَآ اَخْرِجْنَا مِنْ
هٰذِهِ الْقَرْيَةِ الظَّالِمِ اَهْلُهَا ۚ
وَاجْعَلْ لَّنَا مِنْ لَّدُنْكَ وَلِيًّا ۚ
وَّاجْعَلْ لَّنَا مِنْ لَّدُنْكَ نَصِيْرًا ۝

76. Those who believe
Fight in the cause of God,
And those who reject Faith
Fight in the cause of Evil:
So fight ye against the
Friends[594] of Satan: feeble indeed
Is the cunning of Satan.

٧٦- اَلَّذِيْنَ اٰمَنُوْا يُقَاتِلُوْنَ فِيْ سَبِيْلِ اللهِ ۚ
وَالَّذِيْنَ كَفَرُوْا يُقَاتِلُوْنَ فِيْ سَبِيْلِ
الطَّاغُوْتِ فَقَاتِلُوْٓا اَوْلِيَآءَ الشَّيْطٰنِ ۚ
اِنَّ كَيْدَ الشَّيْطٰنِ كَانَ ضَعِيْفًا ۝ ع

SECTION 11.

77. Hast thou not turned
Thy vision to those

٧٧- اَلَمْ تَرَ اِلَى الَّذِيْنَ

591. It is not every one,—least of all, poltroons and faint-hearted persons—who is fit to fight in the cause of God. To do so is a privilege, and those who understand the privilege are prepared to sacrifice all their interests in this life, and this life itself; for they know that it is the sacrifice of something fleeting and of little value, for the sake of something everlasting, and of immense value. Whether (in appearance) they win or lose, in reality they win the prize for which they are fighting,—*viz.*, honour and glory in the sight of God. Note that the only alternatives here are Death or Victory! The true fighter knows no defeat.

592. *Mustaḍh'af*=one reckoned weak, and therefore ill-treated and oppressed. *Cf.* iv. 98, and vii. 150.

593. Even from the human point of view the cause of God is the cause of justice, the cause of the oppressed. In the great persecution, before Mecca was won again, what sorrows, threats, tortures, and oppressions were suffered by those whose faith was unshaken? Muḥammad's life and that of his adherents was threatened: they were mocked, assaulted, insulted and beaten; those within the power of the enemy were put into chains and cast into prison; others were boycotted, and shut out of trade, business, and social intercourse; they could not even buy the food they wanted, or perform their religious duties. The persecution was redoubled for the believing slaves, women, and children after the Hijrat. Their cry for a protector and helper from God was answered when Muḥammad the Chosen One brought freedom and peace to Mecca again.

594. *Auliyāa*, plural of *wali*, friend, supporter, protector, patron; from the same root as *maulā*, for which see iv. 33, n. 543.

Who were told to hold back[595]
Their hands (from fight)
But establish regular prayers
And spend in regular Charity?
When (at length) the order
For fighting was issued to them,
Behold! a section of them
Feared men as—
Or even more than—
They should have feared God:
They said: "Our Lord!
Why hast Thou ordered us
To fight? Wouldst Thou not
Grant us respite
To our (natural) term,[596]
Near (enough)?" Say: "Short
Is the enjoyment of this world:
The Hereafter is the best
For those who do right:
Never will ye be
Dealt with unjustly
In the very least!

قِيلَ لَهُمْ كُفُّوٓا أَيْدِيَكُمْ
وَأَقِيمُوا الصَّلٰوةَ وَءَاتُوا الزَّكٰوةَ
فَلَمَّا كُتِبَ عَلَيْهِمُ الْقِتَالُ إِذَا فَرِيقٌ مِّنْهُمْ
يَخْشَوْنَ النَّاسَ كَخَشْيَةِ اللّٰهِ
أَوْ أَشَدَّ خَشْيَةً
وَقَالُوا رَبَّنَا لِمَ كَتَبْتَ
عَلَيْنَا الْقِتَالَ
لَوْلَآ أَخَّرْتَنَآ إِلَىٰٓ أَجَلٍ قَرِيبٍ
قُلْ مَتَاعُ الدُّنْيَا قَلِيلٌ
وَالْءَاخِرَةُ خَيْرٌ لِّمَنِ اتَّقَىٰ
وَلَا تُظْلَمُونَ فَتِيلًا ۝

78. "Wherever ye are,
Death will find you out,
Even if ye are in towers
Built up strong and high!"

If some good befalls them,
They say, "This is from God";
But if evil, they say,
"This is from thee" (O Prophet).[597]

٧٨- أَيْنَمَا تَكُونُوا يُدْرِككُّمُ الْمَوْتُ وَلَوْ كُنتُمْ
فِي بُرُوجٍ مُّشَيَّدَةٍ وَإِن تُصِبْهُمْ حَسَنَةٌ
يَقُولُوا هٰذِهِ مِنْ عِندِ اللّٰهِ
وَإِن تُصِبْهُمْ سَيِّئَةٌ
يَقُولُوا هٰذِهِ مِنْ عِندِكَ

595. Before the command for fighting was issued there were some who were impatient, and could scarcely be held back. They wanted fighting from human motives,—pugnacity, the love of plunder, hatred against their enemies, the gaining of personal ends. Fighting from such motives is wrong at all times. When the testing time came, and they had to fight, not for their own hand, but for a Sacred Cause, in which there was much suffering and little personal gain, the Hypocrites held back and were afraid.

596. "Our natural term of life," they would say, "is short enough; why should we jeopardize it by fighting in which there is no personal gain?" The answer is begun in this verse and continued in the next.

Briefly, the answer is: (1) in any case the pleasures of this world are short; this life is fleeting; the first thing for a righteous man to do is to emancipate himself from its obsessions; (2) to do your duty is to do right; therefore turn your attention mainly to duty; (3) when duty calls for self-sacrifice, be sure that God's call is never unjust, and never such as to exceed your capacity; and (4) if you fear death, you will not by fear escape death; it will find you out wherever you are; why not face it boldly when duty calls?

597. The Hypocrites were inconsistent, and in this reflect unregenerate mankind. If a disaster happens, due to their own folly, they blame somebody else; but if they are fortunate, they claim reflected credit by pretending that Heaven has favoured them because of their own superior merits. The modern critic discards even this pretence, eliminates Heaven altogether, and claims all credit direct to himself, unless he brings in blind Chance, but that he does mostly to "explain" misfortune. If we look to the ultimate Cause of all things, all things come from God. But if we look to the proximate cause of things, our own merit is so small, that we can hardly claim credit for good ourselves with any fairness. In God's hand is all good: iii. 26. On the other hand, the proximate cause of our evil is due to some wrong in our own inner selves; for never are we dealt with unjustly in the very least: iv. 77.

Say : "All things are from God."
But what hath come
To these people,
That they fail
To understand
A single fact ?

قُلْ كُلٌّ مِّنْ عِنْدِ اللّٰهِ ۭ
فَمَالِ هٰٓؤُلَاۗءِ الْقَوْمِ
لَا يَكَادُوْنَ يَفْقَهُوْنَ حَدِيْثًا ○

79. Whatever good, (O man !)
Happens to thee, is from God;
But whatever evil happens
To thee, is from thy (own) soul.
And We have sent thee
As an Apostle [598]
To (instruct) mankind.
And enough is God
For a witness.

٧٩- مَآ اَصَابَكَ مِنْ حَسَنَةٍ فَمِنَ اللّٰهِ ۡ
وَمَآ اَصَابَكَ مِنْ سَيِّئَةٍ فَمِنْ نَّفْسِكَ ۭ
وَ اَرْسَلْنٰكَ لِلنَّاسِ رَسُوْلًا ۭ
وَكَفٰى بِاللّٰهِ شَهِيْدًا ○

80. He who obeys
The Apostle, obeys God :
But if any turn away,
We have not sent thee
To watch over
Their (evil deeds).[599]

٨٠- مَنْ يُّطِعِ الرَّسُوْلَ فَقَدْ اَطَاعَ اللّٰهَ ۚ
وَمَنْ تَوَلّٰى
فَمَآ اَرْسَلْنٰكَ عَلَيْهِمْ حَفِيْظًا ○

81. They have "Obedience"
On their lips; but
When they leave thee,
A section of them
Meditate all night
On things very different
From what thou tellest them.
But God records
Their nightly (plots) :
So keep clear of them,
And put thy trust in God,
And enough is God

٨١- وَيَقُوْلُوْنَ طَاعَةٌ ۡ
فَاِذَا بَرَزُوْا مِنْ عِنْدِكَ بَيَّتَ طَاۗىِٕفَةٌ مِّنْهُمْ
غَيْرَ الَّذِيْ تَقُوْلُ ۭ
وَاللّٰهُ يَكْتُبُ مَا يُبَيِّتُوْنَ ۚ
فَاَعْرِضْ عَنْهُمْ
وَتَوَكَّلْ عَلَى اللّٰهِ ۭ

598. To blame a man of God for our misfortunes is doubly unjust. For he comes to save us from misfortune, and it is because we flout him or pay no heed to him, that our own rebellion brings its own punishment. If we realise this truth we shall be saved from two sins: (1) the sin of injustice to God's Messengers, who come for our good, and not for our harm; (2) the sin of not realising our own shortcomings or rebellion, and thus living in spiritual darkness. If the Message is from God, that carries its own authority: "enough is God for a witness."

599. The Apostle was sent to preach, guide, instruct, and show the Way,—not to drive people to good, or to detect all that was evil. That is not God's Plan, which trains the human Will. The Apostle's duty is therefore to convey the Message of God, in all the ways of persuasion that are open to him. If men perversely disobey that Message, they are not disobeying him but they are disobeying God. In the same way those who obey the Message are obeying God. They are not obliging the Messenger: they are merely doing their duty.

As a disposer of affairs.[600] وَكَفٰى بِاللّٰهِ وَكِيْلًا ○

82. Do they not consider
The Qur-ān (with care)?
Had it been from other
Than God, they would surely
Have found therein
Much discrepancy.[601]

٨٢- اَفَلَا يَتَدَبَّرُوْنَ الْقُرْاٰنَ ؕ
وَلَوْ كَانَ مِنْ عِنْدِ غَيْرِ اللّٰهِ
لَوَجَدُوْا فِيْهِ اخْتِلَافًا كَثِيْرًا ○

83. When there comes to them
Some matter touching
(Public) safety or fear,
They divulge it.
If they had only referred it
To the Apostle, or to those
Charged with authority
Among them, the proper
Investigators would have
Tested it from them (direct).
Were it not for the Grace
And Mercy of God unto you,
All but a few of you
Would have fallen
Into the clutches of Satan.[602]

٨٣- وَاِذَا جَآءَهُمْ
اَمْرٌ مِّنَ الْاَمْنِ اَوِ الْخَوْفِ اَذَاعُوْا بِهٖ ؕ
وَلَوْ رَدُّوْهُ اِلَى الرَّسُوْلِ
وَاِلٰٓى اُولِى الْاَمْرِ مِنْهُمْ
لَعَلِمَهُ الَّذِيْنَ يَسْتَنْۢبِطُوْنَهٗ مِنْهُمْ ؕ
وَلَوْلَا فَضْلُ اللّٰهِ عَلَيْكُمْ وَرَحْمَتُهٗ
لَاتَّبَعْتُمُ الشَّيْطٰنَ اِلَّا قَلِيْلًا ○

84. Then fight in God's cause—
Thou art held responsible
Only for thyself—
And rouse the Believers.
It may be that God
Will restrain the fury

٨٤- فَقَاتِلْ فِيْ سَبِيْلِ اللّٰهِ ۚ
لَا تُكَلَّفُ اِلَّا نَفْسَكَ وَحَرِّضِ الْمُؤْمِنِيْنَ ۚ
عَسَى اللّٰهُ اَنْ يَّكُفَّ بَاْسَ

600. If we trust to people who are not true, they are more likely to hinder than to help. But God is All-good as well as All-powerful, and all our affairs are best entrusted to His care. He is the best Guardian of all interests.

Therefore we should not trust the lip professions of Hypocrites, but trust in God. Nor should our confidence in God be shaken by any secret plots that enemies hatch against us. We should take all human precautions against them, but having done so, we should put our trust in God, Who knows the inner working of events better than any human mind can conceive.

601. The unity of the Qur-ān is admittedly greater than that of any other sacred book. And yet how can we account for it except through the unity of God's purpose and design? From a mere human point of view, we should have expected much discrepancy, because (1) the Messenger who promulgated it was not a learned man or philosopher, (2) it was promulgated at various times and in various circumstances, and (3) it is addressed to all grades of mankind. Yet, when properly understood, its various pieces fit together better than a jig-saw puzzle even when arranged without any regard to chronological order. There was just the One Inspirer and the One Inspired.

602. In times of war or public panic, thoughtless repetition of gossip is rightly restrained by all effective States. If false, such news may cause needless alarm: if true, it may frighten the timid and cause some misgivings even to the bravest, because the counterpart of it—the preparations made to meet the danger—is not known. Thoughtless news, true or false, may also encourage the enemy. The proper course is quietly to hand all news direct to those who are in a position to investigate it. They can then sift it and take suitable measures to checkmate the enemy. Not to do so, but to deal with news either thoughtlessly or maliciously, is to fall directly into the snares of Evil.

Of the Unbelievers;
For God is the strongest
In might and in punishment.[603]

الَّذِينَ كَفَرُوا ۗ
وَاللّٰهُ أَشَدُّ بَأْسًا وَّأَشَدُّ تَنْكِيلًا ○

85. Whoever recommends
And helps a good cause
Becomes a partner therein:
And whoever recommends
And helps an evil cause,
Shares in its burden:
And God hath power[604]
Over all things.

٨٥- مَنْ يَّشْفَعْ شَفَاعَةً حَسَنَةً يَّكُنْ لَّهُ
نَصِيبٌ مِّنْهَا ۚ وَمَنْ يَّشْفَعْ شَفَاعَةً سَيِّئَةً
يَّكُنْ لَّهُ كِفْلٌ مِّنْهَا ۗ
وَكَانَ اللّٰهُ عَلَىٰ كُلِّ شَيْءٍ مُّقِيتًا ○

86. When a (courteous) greeting
Is offered you, meet it
With a greeting still more
Courteous, or (at least)
Of equal courtesy.
God takes careful account[605]
Of all things.

٨٦- وَإِذَا حُيِّيتُمْ بِتَحِيَّةٍ
فَحَيُّوا بِأَحْسَنَ مِنْهَا
أَوْ رُدُّوهَا ۗ
إِنَّ اللّٰهَ كَانَ عَلَىٰ كُلِّ شَيْءٍ حَسِيبًا ○

87. God! There is no god
But He: of a surety
He will gather you together
Against the Day of Judgment,
About which there is no doubt.
And whose word can be
Truer than God's?

٨٧- اللّٰهُ لَا إِلٰهَ إِلَّا هُوَ ۗ
لَيَجْمَعَنَّكُمْ إِلَىٰ يَوْمِ الْقِيٰمَةِ
لَا رَيْبَ فِيهِ ۗ
وَمَنْ أَصْدَقُ مِنَ اللّٰهِ حَدِيثًا ○ ع

SECTION 12.

88. Why should ye be
Divided into two parties

٨٨- فَمَا لَكُمْ فِي الْمُنٰفِقِينَ فِئَتَيْنِ

603. The courage of Muhammad was as notable as his wisdom, his gentleness, and his trust in God. Facing fearful odds, he often stood alone, and took the whole responsibility on himself. But his example and visible trust in God inspired and roused the Muslims, and also—speaking purely from a human point of view—restrained the fury of his enemies. When we consider that he was God's inspired Messenger, to carry out His Plan, we can see that nothing can resist that Plan. If the enemy happens to have strength, power, or resources, God's strength, power, and resources are infinitely greater. If the enemy is meditating punishment on the righteous for their righteousness, God's punishment for such wickedness will be infinitely greater and more effective.

604. In this fleeting world's chances God's providence and justice may not always appear plain to our eyes. But we are asked to believe that if we help and support a good cause, we share in all its credit and in its eventual victory. And conversely, we cannot support a bad cause without sharing in all its evil consequences. If appearances seem against this faith, let us not be deceived by appearances. For God has power over all things.

605 The necessary correlative to the command to fight in a good cause is the command to cultivate sweetness and cordiality in our manners at all times. For fighting is an exceptional necessity while the sweetness of daily human intercourse is a normal need. Further, we give kindness and courtesy without asking, and return it if possible in even better terms than we received, or at least in equally courteous terms. For we are all creatures of One God, and shall be brought together before Him.

About the Hypocrites?[606]
God hath upset them
For their (evil) deeds.
Would ye guide those
Whom God hath thrown
Out of the Way? For those
Whom God hath thrown
Out of the Way, never
Shalt thou find the Way.

وَاللّٰهُ اَرْكَسَهُمْ بِمَا كَسَبُوْا ۭ
اَتُرِيْدُوْنَ اَنْ تَهْدُوْا مَنْ اَضَلَّ اللّٰهُ ۭ
وَمَنْ يُّضْلِلِ اللّٰهُ
فَلَنْ تَجِدَ لَهٗ سَبِيْلًا ۝

89. They but wish that ye
Should reject Faith,
As they do, and thus be
On the same footing (as they):
But take not friends
From their ranks
Until they flee[607]
In the way of God
(From what is forbidden).
But if they turn renegades,
Seize them and slay them
Wherever ye find them;
And (in any case) take
No friends or helpers
From their ranks;—

٨٩- وَدُّوْا لَوْ تَكْفُرُوْنَ كَمَا كَفَرُوْا
فَتَكُوْنُوْنَ سَوَاۗءً
فَلَا تَتَّخِذُوْا مِنْهُمْ اَوْلِيَاۗءَ
حَتّٰى يُهَاجِرُوْا فِيْ سَبِيْلِ اللّٰهِ ۭ
فَاِنْ تَوَلَّوْا
فَخُذُوْهُمْ وَاقْتُلُوْهُمْ حَيْثُ وَجَدْتُّمُوْهُمْ
وَلَا تَتَّخِذُوْا مِنْهُمْ وَلِيًّا وَّلَا نَصِيْرًا ۝

90. Except those who join
A group between whom
And you there is a treaty[608]

٩٠- اِلَّا الَّذِيْنَ يَصِلُوْنَ اِلٰى قَوْمٍۢ بَيْنَكُمْ
وَبَيْنَهُمْ مِّيْثَاقٌ

606. When the desertion of the Hypocrites at Uhud nearly caused a disaster to the Muslim cause there was great feeling among the Muslims of Medina against them. One party wanted to put them to the sword: another to leave them alone. The actual policy pursued avoided both extremes, and was determined by these verses. It was clear that they were a danger to the Muslim community if they were admitted into its counsels, and in any case they were a source of demoralisation. But while every caution was used, no extreme measures were taken against them. On the contrary, they were given a chance of making good. If they made a sacrifice for the cause ("flee from what is forbidden," see next verse), their conduct purged their previous cowardice, and their sincerity entitled them to be taken back. But if they deserted the Muslim community again, they were treated as enemies, with the additional penalty of desertion which is enforced by all nations actually at war. Even so, a humane exception was made in the two cases specified in iv. 90.

607. *Flee*: the verbal form from which the noun *hijrat* is derived. Bukhari interprets this rightly as fleeing from all that is forbidden. This would include hijrat in the technical sense of leaving a place in which the practice of religion is not allowed. But it is more general. In time of war, if a man is willing to submit to discipline and refrain from infringing orders issued, he has proved his fidelity and may be treated as a member of the community at war.

On the other hand if he by false pretences comes into the inner counsels merely to betray them, he may rightly be treated as a traitor or deserter and be punished for his treason or desertion; or if he escapes, he can be treated as an enemy and is entitled to no mercy. He is worse than an enemy: he has claimed to be of you in order to spy on you, and been all the time helping the enemy.

608. *Except*: the exception refers to "seize them and slay them", the death penalty for repeated desertion. Even after such desertion, exemption is granted in two cases. One is where the deserter took asylum with a tribe with whom there was a treaty of peace and amity. Presumably such a tribe (even though outside the pale of Islam) might be trusted to keep the man from fighting against the forces of Islam—in the modern phrase, to disarm him and render him harmless. The second case for exemption is where the man from his own heart desires never to take up arms against Islam, though he does not wish to join the forces of Islam, to fight against a hostile tribe (perhaps his own) fighting against Islam. But he must make a real approach, giving guarantees of his sincerity. In the modern phrase he would be "on parole". But this provision is much milder than that in modern military codes, which grant the privilege only to enemy prisoners, not to those who have deserted from the army granting them parole. The Hypocrites were in that position, but humanity as well as policy treated them with great leniency.

(Of peace), or those who approach[609]
You with hearts restraining
Them from fighting you
As well as fighting their own
People. If God had pleased,
He could have given them
Power over you, and they
Would have fought you:
Therefore if they withdraw
From you but fight you not,
And (instead) send you
(Guarantees of) peace, then God
Hath opened no way
For you (to war against them).

أَوْ جَآءُوكُمْ حَصِرَتْ صُدُورُهُمْ
أَن يُقَٰتِلُوكُمْ أَوْ يُقَٰتِلُوا۟ قَوْمَهُمْ ۚ
وَلَوْ شَآءَ ٱللَّهُ لَسَلَّطَهُمْ عَلَيْكُمْ فَلَقَٰتَلُوكُمْ ۚ
فَإِنِ ٱعْتَزَلُوكُمْ
فَلَمْ يُقَٰتِلُوكُمْ
وَأَلْقَوْا۟ إِلَيْكُمُ ٱلسَّلَمَ
فَمَا جَعَلَ ٱللَّهُ لَكُمْ عَلَيْهِمْ سَبِيلًا ۝

91. Others you will find
That wish to gain
Your confidence as well
As that of their people:
Every time they are sent back[610]
To temptation, they succumb
Thereto: if they withdraw not
From you nor give you (guarantees)
Of peace besides
Restraining their hands,
Seize them and slay them
Wherever ye get them:
In their case
We have provided you
With a clear argument
Against them.

٩١- سَتَجِدُونَ ءَاخَرِينَ
يُرِيدُونَ أَن يَأْمَنُوكُمْ وَيَأْمَنُوا۟ قَوْمَهُمْ ۚ
كُلَّمَا رُدُّوٓا۟ إِلَى ٱلْفِتْنَةِ أُرْكِسُوا۟ فِيهَا ۚ
فَإِن لَّمْ يَعْتَزِلُوكُمْ
وَيُلْقُوٓا۟ إِلَيْكُمُ ٱلسَّلَمَ وَيَكُفُّوٓا۟ أَيْدِيَهُمْ
فَخُذُوهُمْ وَٱقْتُلُوهُمْ حَيْثُ ثَقِفْتُمُوهُمْ ۚ
وَأُو۟لَٰٓئِكُمْ جَعَلْنَا لَكُمْ عَلَيْهِمْ سُلْطَٰنًا
مُّبِينًا ۝

C. 65.—The lives of those who believe
(iv. 92-104.) Are sacred: if one is slain
By mistake, full compensation
Should be made. Nor should
A stranger, even in time of war,
Be treated as an enemy, without

609. *Approach* or come: refers not to the physical act of coming, but to the mental attitude: the heart is mentioned for sincerity. When they sincerely promise not to fight against you, do not pursue them. Remember that if they had fought against you, your difficulties would have been increased. Their neutrality itself may be a great advantage to you. So long as you are satisfied that they are sincere and their acts support their declarations of peace with you, you should not consider yourself justified in pursuing them and warring against them.

610. As opposed to the two classes of deserters to whom clemency may be shown, there is a class which is treacherous and dangerous and cannot be left alone. They try to win your confidence, and are all the time in the confidence of the enemy. Every time they get a chance, they succumb to the temptation of double-dealing. The best way of dealing with them is to treat them as open enemies. Keep them not in your midst. If they give you guarantees of peace and do not actually fight against you, well and good. If not, they are deserters actively fighting in the ranks of the enemy. They have openly given you proof, and you can fairly seize and slay them in war as deserters and enemies.

The fullest investigation. Live not
In places hostile to Islam,
If ye are able to migrate,—
And spacious is God's earth.
Devotion and prayer may be
Shortened in times of danger.
Take every precaution for safety,
But be bold and undaunted in fight.

Section 13.

92. Never should a Believer
Kill a Believer; but
(If it so happens) by mistake,[611]
(Compensation is due):
If one (so) kills a Believer,
It is ordained that he
Should free a believing slave,
And pay compensation
To the deceased's family,
Unless they remit it freely.
If the deceased belonged
To a people at war with you,
And he was a Believer,
The freeing of a believing slave
(Is enough). If he belonged
To a people with whom
Ye have a treaty of mutual
Alliance, compensation should
Be paid to his family,
And a believing slave be freed.
For those who find this
Beyond their means, (is prescribed)
A fast for two months
Running: by way of repentance
To God: for God hath
All knowledge and all wisdom.

٩٢- وَمَا كَانَ لِمُؤْمِنٍ اَنْ يَّقْتُلَ مُؤْمِنًا
اِلَّا خَطَـًٔا ۚ وَمَنْ قَتَلَ مُؤْمِنًا
خَطَـًٔا فَتَحْرِيْرُ رَقَبَةٍ مُّؤْمِنَةٍ
وَّدِيَةٌ مُّسَلَّمَةٌ اِلٰٓى اَهْلِهٖٓ
اِلَّآ اَنْ يَّصَّدَّقُوْا ۭ
فَاِنْ كَانَ مِنْ قَوْمٍ عَدُوٍّ لَّكُمْ
وَهُوَ مُؤْمِنٌ فَتَحْرِيْرُ رَقَبَةٍ مُّؤْمِنَةٍ ۭ
وَاِنْ كَانَ مِنْ قَوْمٍۢ بَيْنَكُمْ وَبَيْنَهُمْ
مِّيْثَاقٌ فَدِيَةٌ مُّسَلَّمَةٌ اِلٰٓى اَهْلِهٖ
وَتَحْرِيْرُ رَقَبَةٍ مُّؤْمِنَةٍ ۚ
فَمَنْ لَّمْ يَجِدْ
فَصِيَامُ شَهْرَيْنِ مُتَتَابِعَيْنِ تَوْبَةً مِّنَ اللّٰهِ
وَكَانَ اللّٰهُ عَلِيْمًا حَكِيْمًا ۝

611. Life is absolutely sacred in the Islamic Brotherhood. But mistakes will sometimes happen, as did happen in the *mêlée* at Uhud, when some Muslims were killed (being mistaken for the enemy) by Muslims. There was no guilty intention: therefore there was no murder. But all the same, the family of the deceased was entitled to compensation unless they freely remitted it, and in addition it was provided that the unfortunate man who made the mistake should free a believing slave. Thus a deplorable mistake was made the occasion for winning the liberty of a slave who was a Believer, for Islam discountenances slavery. The compensation could only be paid if the deceased belonged to a Muslim society or to some people at peace with the Muslim society. Obviously it could not be paid if, though the deceased was a Believer, his people were at war with the Muslim society; even if his people could be reached, it is not fair to increase the resources of the enemy. If the deceased was himself an enemy at war, obviously the laws of war justify his being killed in warfare unless he surrendered. If the man who took life unintentionally has no means from which to free a believing slave or to give compensation, he must still by an act of strict self-denial (fasting for two whole months running) show that he is cognizant of the grave nature of the deed he has done and sincerely repentant. I take this to apply to all three cases mentioned: that is, where a Believer killed a Believer unintentionally and the deceased (1) belonged to the same community as you, or (2) belonged to a community at war with you, or (3) belonged to a community in alliance with you.

93. If a man kills a Believer
Intentionally, his recompense[612]
Is Hell, to abide therein
(For ever): and the wrath
And the curse of God
Are upon him, and
A dreadful penalty
Is prepared for him.

٩٣- وَمَنْ يَّقْتُلْ مُؤْمِنًا مُّتَعَمِّدًا
فَجَزَآؤُهٗ جَهَنَّمُ خٰلِدًا فِيْهَا
وَغَضِبَ اللّٰهُ عَلَيْهِ وَلَعَنَهٗ
وَاَعَدَّ لَهٗ عَذَابًا عَظِيْمًا ○

94. O ye who believe!
When ye go abroad[613]
In the cause of God,
Investigate carefully,
And say not to any one
Who offers you a salutation:
"Thou art none of a Believer!"
Coveting the perishable goods
Of this life: with God
Are profits and spoils abundant.
Even thus were ye yourselves
Before, till God conferred
On you His favours: therefore
Carefully investigate.
For God is well aware
Of all that ye do.

٩٤- يٰٓاَيُّهَا الَّذِيْنَ اٰمَنُوْٓا اِذَا ضَرَبْتُمْ فِيْ
سَبِيْلِ اللّٰهِ فَتَبَيَّنُوْا وَلَا تَقُوْلُوْا
لِمَنْ اَلْقٰٓى اِلَيْكُمُ السَّلٰمَ لَسْتَ مُؤْمِنًا ۚ
تَبْتَغُوْنَ عَرَضَ الْحَيٰوةِ الدُّنْيَا ۫
فَعِنْدَ اللّٰهِ مَغَانِمُ كَثِيْرَةٌ ۭ
كَذٰلِكَ كُنْتُمْ مِّنْ قَبْلُ
فَمَنَّ اللّٰهُ عَلَيْكُمْ فَتَبَيَّنُوْا ۭ
اِنَّ اللّٰهَ كَانَ بِمَا تَعْمَلُوْنَ خَبِيْرًا ○

95. Not equal are those
Believers who sit (at home)
And receive no hurt,
And those who strive
And fight in the cause
Of God with their goods
And their persons.
God hath granted
A grade higher to those
Who strive and fight

٩٥- لَا يَسْتَوِي الْقٰعِدُوْنَ مِنَ الْمُؤْمِنِيْنَ
غَيْرُ اُولِي الضَّرَرِ وَالْمُجٰهِدُوْنَ فِيْ سَبِيْلِ
اللّٰهِ بِاَمْوَالِهِمْ وَاَنْفُسِهِمْ
فَضَّلَ اللّٰهُ الْمُجٰهِدِيْنَ
بِاَمْوَالِهِمْ وَاَنْفُسِهِمْ

612. What is mentioned here is the punishment in the Hereafter, the spiritual consequences. The legal consequences, enforceable by human society, are mentioned in ii. 178, under the rules of *Qiṣāṣ*. That is, a life should be taken for a life destroyed, but this should be on a scale of equality: a single murder should not commit a whole tribe to a perpetual blood-feud, as in the days of ignorance. But if the heirs of the man slain accept reasonable compensation, this should be accepted, and the taking of a life for a life should be put a stop to. This course leads to the saving of life, and is commanded to men of understanding.

613. *Go abroad: ḍharaba* = to travel, to go abroad, either for *jihād*, or for honest trade or other service, which if done with pure motives, counts as service in the cause of God. The immediate occasion was in connection with *jihād*, but the words are general, and can be applied to all circumstances in which a man falls through spiritual pride: he thinks he is not as other men are, but forgets that, but for the grace of God, he is himself a sinner! In war (or in peace) we are apt to catch some worldly advantage by pluming ourselves on our superiority in Faith. In war perhaps we want to gain glory or booty by killing a supposed enemy! In peace we make light of other people in order to steal some advantage or material gain! This is wrong. The righteous man, if he is really out in God's service, has more abundant and richer gifts to think of in the spiritual world.

With their goods and persons
Than to those who sit (at home).
Unto all (in Faith)[614]
Hath God promised good:
But those who strive and fight
Hath He distinguished
Above those who sit (at home)
By a special reward,—

عَلَى الْقٰعِدِيْنَ دَرَجَةً ۭ
وَكُلًّا وَّعَدَ اللّٰهُ الْحُسْنٰى ۭ
وَفَضَّلَ اللّٰهُ الْمُجٰهِدِيْنَ
عَلَى الْقٰعِدِيْنَ اَجْرًا عَظِيْمًا ۝

96. Ranks specially bestowed
By Him, and Forgiveness
And Mercy. For God is
Oft-forgiving, Most Merciful.

٩٦- دَرَجٰتٍ مِّنْهُ وَمَغْفِرَةً وَّرَحْمَةً ۭ
وَكَانَ اللّٰهُ غَفُوْرًا رَّحِيْمًا ۝ ع

Section 14.

97. When angels take
The souls of those
Who die in sin
Against their souls,[615]
They say: "In what (plight)
Were ye?" They reply:
"Weak and oppressed
Were we in the earth."
They say: "Was not
The earth of God
Spacious enough for you
To move yourselves away
(From evil)?" Such men
Will find their abode
In Hell,—What an evil
Refuge!—

٩٧- اِنَّ الَّذِيْنَ تَوَفّٰىهُمُ الْمَلٰۗىِٕكَةُ
ظَالِمِيْٓ اَنْفُسِهِمْ
قَالُوْا فِيْمَ كُنْتُمْ ۭ
قَالُوْا كُنَّا مُسْتَضْعَفِيْنَ فِي الْاَرْضِ ۭ
قَالُوْٓا اَلَمْ تَكُنْ اَرْضُ اللّٰهِ وَاسِعَةً
فَتُهَاجِرُوْا فِيْهَا ۭ
فَاُولٰۗىِٕكَ مَاْوٰىهُمْ جَهَنَّمُ ۭ
وَسَاۗءَتْ مَصِيْرًا ۝

614. God's goodness is promised to all people of Faith. But there are degrees among men and women of Faith. There are people with natural inertia: they do the minimum that is required of them, but no more. There are people who are weak in will: they are easily frightened. There are people who are so strong in will and so firm in faith that they are determined to conquer every obstacle, whether in their own physical or other infirmities or in the external world around them. In a time of jihād, when people give their all, and even their lives, for the common cause, they must be accounted more glorious than those who sit at home, even though they have good-will to the cause and carry out minor duties in aid. The special reward of such self-sacrifice is high spiritual rank, and special forgiveness and mercy, as proceeding from the direct approbation and love of God.

615. The immediate occasion for this passage was the question of migration (*hijrat*) from places where Islam was being persecuted and suppressed. Obviously the duty of Muslims was to leave such places, even if it involved forsaking their homes, and join and strengthen the Muslim community among whom they could live in peace and with whom they could help in fighting the evils around them. But the meaning is wider. Islam does not say: "Resist not evil." On the contrary it requires a constant, unceasing struggle against evil. For such struggle it may be necessary to forsake home and unite and organise and join our brethren in assaulting and overthrowing the fortress of evil. For the Muslim's duty is not only to enjoin good but to prohibit evil. To make our assault we must be prepared to put ourselves in a position from which such assault would be possible, and God's earth is spacious enough for the purpose. "Position" includes not only local position, but moral and material position. For example, we must shun evil company where we cannot put it down, but organise a position from which we can put it down.

98. Except those who are
(Really) weak and oppressed—
Men, women, and children—
Who have no means
In their power, nor (a guide-post)[616]
To direct their way.

٩٨- إلا المستضعفين من الرجال و
النساء والولدان لا يستطيعون حيلة
ولا يهتدون سبيلا ○

99. For these, there is hope
That God will forgive:
For God doth blot out (sins)
And forgive again and again.

٩٩- فأولئك عسى الله أن يعفو عنهم
وكان الله عفوا غفورا ○

100. He who forsakes his home
In the cause of God,
Finds in the earth
Many a refuge,
Wide and spacious:
Should he die
As a refugee from home
For God and His Apostle,
His reward becomes due
And sure with God:
And God is Oft-forgiving,
Most Merciful.

١٠٠- ومن يهاجر في سبيل الله
يجد في الأرض مراغما كثيرا وسعة
ومن يخرج من بيته مهاجرا إلى الله
ورسوله ثم يدركه الموت
فقد وقع أجره على الله
وكان الله غفورا رحيما ○ ع

SECTION 15.

101. When ye travel
Through the earth,
There is no blame on you
If ye shorten your prayers,[617]
For fear the Unbelievers
May attack you:
For the Unbelievers are
Unto you open enemies.

١٠١- وإذا ضربتم في الأرض
فليس عليكم جناح أن تقصروا من
الصلوة إن خفتم أن يفتنكم الذين كفروا
إن الكافرين كانوا لكم عدوا مبينا ○

616. If through physical, mental, or moral incapacity, we are unable to fight the good fight, we must rest content with putting up with evil and just guarding ourselves from it. God's gracious Mercy will recognise and forgive our weakness if it is real weakness, and not merely an excuse.

617. Verse 101 gives permission to shorten congregational prayers when people are on a journey: verses 102 104 deal with cases when they are in danger at war, in face of the enemy. The shortening of congregational prayers in both cases is further governed as to details by the practice of the Apostle and his Companions. As to journeys, two questions arise: (1) what constitutes a journey for this purpose? (2) is the fear of an attack an essential condition for the shortening of congregational prayers? As to (1), it is best to leave the matter to discretion, having regard to all the circumstances of the journey, as in the case of the journeys which excuse a fast: see ii. 184, n. 190. The text leaves it to discretion. As to (2), the practice of the Apostle shows that danger is not an essential condition: it is merely mentioned as a possible incident. The Apostle usually shortened the prayers from four Rak'ats to two Rak'ats in *Zuhr* (midday prayer), *'Aṣr* (afternoon prayer) and *'Ishāa* (night prayer): the other two are in any case short, *Fajr* (morning prayer) having two Rak'ats and *Magrib* (evening prayer) having three.

102. When thou (O Apostle)
Art with them, and standest
To lead them in prayer,
Let one party of them
Stand up (in prayer) with thee,
Taking their arms with them:
When they finish
Their prostrations, let them
Take their position in the rear.
And let the other party come up
Which hath not yet prayed—
And let them pray with thee,
Taking all precautions,
And bearing arms:
The Unbelievers wish,
If ye were negligent
Of your arms and your baggage,
To assault you in a single rush.[618]
But there is no blame on you
If ye put away your arms
Because of the inconvenience
Of rain or because ye are ill;
But take (every) precaution
For yourselves. For the
Unbelievers
God hath prepared
A humiliating punishment.

١٠٢- وَإِذَا كُنتَ فِيهِمْ فَأَقَمْتَ لَهُمُ الصَّلٰوةَ
فَلْتَقُمْ طَآئِفَةٌ مِّنْهُم مَّعَكَ
وَلْيَأْخُذُوٓا أَسْلِحَتَهُمْ فَإِذَا سَجَدُوا
فَلْيَكُونُوا مِن وَرَآئِكُمْ وَلْتَأْتِ طَآئِفَةٌ
أُخْرٰى لَمْ يُصَلُّوا فَلْيُصَلُّوا مَعَكَ
وَلْيَأْخُذُوا حِذْرَهُمْ وَأَسْلِحَتَهُمْ
وَدَّ الَّذِينَ كَفَرُوا لَوْ تَغْفُلُونَ عَنْ أَسْلِحَتِكُمْ
وَأَمْتِعَتِكُمْ فَيَمِيلُونَ عَلَيْكُم
مَّيْلَةً وَاحِدَةً وَلَا جُنَاحَ عَلَيْكُمْ
إِن كَانَ بِكُمْ أَذًى مِّن مَّطَرٍ
أَوْ كُنتُم مَّرْضٰى
أَن تَضَعُوٓا أَسْلِحَتَكُمْ
وَخُذُوا حِذْرَكُمْ
إِنَّ اللّٰهَ أَعَدَّ لِلْكٰفِرِينَ عَذَابًا مُّهِينًا ○

103. When ye pass[619]
(Congregational) prayers,
Celebrate God's praises,
Standing, sitting down,
Or lying down on your sides;
But when ye are free
From danger, set up
Regular Prayers:
For such prayers
Are enjoined on Believers
At stated times.

١٠٣- فَإِذَا قَضَيْتُمُ الصَّلٰوةَ
فَاذْكُرُوا اللّٰهَ قِيٰمًا
وَّقُعُودًا وَّعَلٰى جُنُوبِكُمْ
فَإِذَا اطْمَأْنَنتُمْ فَأَقِيمُوا الصَّلٰوةَ
إِنَّ الصَّلٰوةَ كَانَتْ عَلَى الْمُؤْمِنِينَ كِتٰبًا
مَّوْقُوتًا ○

618. The congregational prayer in danger in face of the enemy rests on the principle that the congregation should be divided into two parties; one party prays while the other watches the enemy, and then the second party comes up to prayers while the first falls back to face the enemy; either party does only one or two Rak'ats, or about half the cogregational prayer; every precaution is taken to prevent a rush by the enemy; even while at prayers armour and arms need not be put off except when rain is likely to cause inconvenience to the wearer and damage to the arms, or when illness or fatigue causes the wearer's strength to fail. Details can be varied according to circumstances, as was actually done by the Apostle at different times.

619. Two interpretations are possible: (1) "when ye have finished congregational prayers", or (2) "when (on account of extreme danger) ye have to pass over congregational prayers altogether,—even the shorter form indicated for times of danger". I prefer the latter, as it accords better with the following sentence, which allows you to remember God individually in any posture possible during the danger. But when the danger is past, the full prayers should be offered at the stated times.

104. And slacken not
In following up the enemy:
If ye are suffering hardships,
They are suffering similar
Hardships; but ye have
Hope from God, while they[620]
Have none. And God
Is full of knowledge and wisdom.

١٠٤- وَلَا تَهِنُوا فِي ابْتِغَاءِ الْقَوْمِ ۖ
إِن تَكُونُوا تَأْلَمُونَ فَإِنَّهُمْ يَأْلَمُونَ كَمَا
تَأْلَمُونَ ۖ وَتَرْجُونَ مِنَ اللَّهِ مَا لَا يَرْجُونَ ۗ
وَكَانَ اللَّهُ عَلِيمًا حَكِيمًا ۝

C. 66.—Beware of treachery, that would use
(IV. 105—126.) The good and pious for its wicked
Ends: its plots will but recoil
On its own head. The righteous
Have no cause for secrecy, except
In doing good. 'Tis evil that
Misleads, deceives, and even dares
Deface fair Nature, as by God
Created. Shun all evil, and be firm
In righteousness and faith in God.

SECTION 16.

105. We have sent down
To thee the Book in truth,
That thou mightest judge
Between men, as guided
By God: so be not (used)
As an advocate by those
Who betray their trust;[621]

١٠٥- إِنَّا أَنزَلْنَا إِلَيْكَ الْكِتَابَ بِالْحَقِّ
لِتَحْكُمَ بَيْنَ النَّاسِ
بِمَا أَرَاكَ اللَّهُ ۚ
وَلَا تَكُن لِّلْخَائِنِينَ خَصِيمًا ۝

106. But seek the forgiveness
Of God; for God is
Oft-forgiving, Most Merciful.

١٠٦- وَاسْتَغْفِرِ اللَّهَ ۖ
إِنَّ اللَّهَ كَانَ غَفُورًا رَّحِيمًا ۝

620. Religion should be a source of strength and not of weakness in all our affairs. If we have to struggle hard and suffer hardships, those without faith have to do the same, with this difference, that the man of Faith is full of hope in God, whereas the man without Faith has nothing to sustain him.

621. The Commentators explain this passage with reference to the case of Ta ima ibn Ubairaq, who was nominally a Muslim but really a Hypocrite, and given to all sorts of wicked deeds. He was suspected of having stolen a set of armour, and when the trail was hot, he planted the stolen property into the house of a Jew, where it was found. The Jew denied the charge and accused Ṭa'ima, but the sympathies of the Muslim community were with Ṭa'ima on account of his nominal profession of Islam. The case was brought to the Apostle, who acquitted the Jew according to the strict principle of justice, as "guided by God". Attempts were made to prejudice him and deceive him into using his authority to favour Ṭa'ima.

The general lesson is that the righteous man is faced with all sorts of subtle wiles: the wicked will try to appeal to his highest sympathies and most honourable motives to deceive him and use him as an instrument for defeating justice. He should be careful and cautious, and seek the help of God for protection against deception and for firmness in dealing the strictest justice without fear or favour. To do otherwise is to betray a sacred trust: the trustee must defeat all attempts made to mislead him.

107. Contend not on behalf
Of such as betray
Their own souls;[622]
For God loveth not
One given to perfidy
And crime;

۱۰۷- وَلَا تُجَادِلْ عَنِ الَّذِينَ يَخْتَانُونَ
أَنْفُسَهُمْ ۚ إِنَّ اللّٰهَ لَا يُحِبُّ
مَنْ كَانَ خَوَّانًا أَثِيمًا ۝

108. They may hide
(Their crimes) from men,
But they cannot hide
(Them) from God, seeing that
He is in their midst
When they plot by night,
In words that He cannot
Approve: and God
Doth compass round[623]
All that they do.

۱۰۸- يَسْتَخْفُونَ مِنَ النَّاسِ
وَلَا يَسْتَخْفُونَ مِنَ اللّٰهِ
وَهُوَ مَعَهُمْ إِذْ يُبَيِّتُونَ مَا لَا يَرْضَىٰ
مِنَ الْقَوْلِ ۚ
وَكَانَ اللّٰهُ بِمَا يَعْمَلُونَ مُحِيطًا ۝

109. Ah! these are the sort
Of men on whose behalf
Ye may contend in this world;
But who will contend with God
On their behalf on the Day
Of Judgment, or who
Will carry their affairs through?

۱۰۹- هَٰأَنْتُمْ هٰٓؤُلَآءِ
جَٰدَلْتُمْ عَنْهُمْ فِي الْحَيٰوةِ الدُّنْيَا
فَمَنْ يُجَٰدِلُ اللّٰهَ عَنْهُمْ يَوْمَ الْقِيٰمَةِ
أَمْ مَنْ يَكُونُ عَلَيْهِمْ وَكِيلًا ۝

110. If any one does evil
Or wrongs his own soul
But afterwards seeks
God's forgiveness, he will find
God Oft-forgiving,
Most Merciful.

۱۱۰- وَمَنْ يَعْمَلْ سُوٓءًا أَوْ يَظْلِمْ نَفْسَهُ
ثُمَّ يَسْتَغْفِرِ اللّٰهَ
يَجِدِ اللّٰهَ غَفُورًا رَحِيمًا ۝

111. And if any one earns[624]
Sin, he earns it against

۱۱۱- وَمَنْ يَكْسِبْ إِثْمًا فَإِنَّمَا يَكْسِبُهُ

---

622. Our souls are a sort of trust with us. We have to guard them against all temptation. Those who surrender to crime or evil betray that trust. We are warned against being deceived into taking their part, induced either by plausible appearances, or by such incentives to partiality as that they belong to our own people or that some link connects them with us, whereas when we are out to do justice, we must not allow any irrelevant considerations to sway us.

623. The plots of sinners are known fully to God, and He can fully circumvent them if necessary, according to the fulness of His wisdom. The word used is: *Compass them round*: *muhīṭ*: not only does God know all about it, but He is all round it: if in His wisdom He allows it, it is not because He has not complete control over it, but because, having it as it were enclosed in a complete circle, He can use it to further His own Plan. Even out of evil He can bring good.

624. *Kasaba* = to earn, to gain, to work for something valuable, to lay up a provision for the future life. We do a day's labour to earn our livelihood: so in a spiritual sense, whatever good or evil we do in this life, earns us good or evil in the life to come. In verses 110-112 three cases are considered: (1) if we do ill and repent, God will forgive; (2 if we do ill and do not repent, thinking that we can hide it, we are wrong; nothing is hidden from God, and we shall suffer the full consequences in the life to come, for we can never evade our personal responsibility: (3) if we do ill, great or small, and impute it to another, our original responsibility for the ill remains, but we add to it something else; for we tie round our necks the guilt of falsehood, which converts even our minor fault into a great sin, and in any case brands us even in this life with shame and ignominy.

His own soul: for God
Is full of knowledge and wisdom.

عَلٰى نَفْسِهٖ ۭ وَكَانَ اللّٰهُ عَلِيْمًا حَكِيْمًا ○

112. But if any one earns
A fault or a sin
And throws it on to one
That is innocent,
He carries (on himself)
(Both) a falsehood
And a flagrant sin.

١١٢- وَمَنْ يَّكْسِبْ خَطِيْۗـــَٔةً اَوْ اِثْمًا
ثُمَّ يَرْمِ بِهٖ بَرِيْۗـــــًٔا
فَقَدِ احْتَمَلَ بُهْتَانًا
وَّاِثْمًا مُّبِيْنًا ○

SECTION 17.

113. But for the Grace of God
To thee and His Mercy,
A party of them would
Certainly have plotted
To lead thee astray.
But (in fact) they will only
Lead their own souls astray,
And to thee they can do
No harm in the least.
For God hath sent down
To thee the Book and Wisdom
And taught thee what thou
Knewest not (before):
And great is the Grace
Of God unto thee.

١١٣- وَلَوْلَا فَضْلُ اللّٰهِ عَلَيْكَ
وَرَحْمَتُهٗ
لَهَمَّتْ طَّاۗىِٕفَةٌ مِّنْهُمْ اَنْ يُّضِلُّوْكَ ۭ
وَمَا يُضِلُّوْنَ اِلَّآ اَنْفُسَهُمْ
وَمَا يَضُرُّوْنَكَ مِنْ شَيْءٍ ۭ
وَاَنْزَلَ اللّٰهُ عَلَيْكَ الْكِتٰبَ وَالْحِكْمَةَ
وَعَلَّمَكَ مَا لَمْ تَكُنْ تَعْلَمُ ۭ
وَكَانَ فَضْلُ اللّٰهِ عَلَيْكَ عَظِيْمًا ○

114. In most of their secret talks
There is no good: but if
One exhorts to a deed
Of charity or justice
Or conciliation between men,[625]
(Secrecy is permissible):
To him who does this,
Seeking the good pleasure
Of God, We shall soon give
A reward of the highest (value).

١١٤- لَا خَيْرَ فِيْ كَثِيْرٍ مِّنْ نَّجْوٰىهُمْ
اِلَّا مَنْ اَمَرَ بِصَدَقَةٍ اَوْ مَعْرُوْفٍ
اَوْ اِصْلَاحٍۢ بَيْنَ النَّاسِ ۭ
وَمَنْ يَّفْعَلْ ذٰلِكَ ابْتِغَاۗءَ مَرْضَاتِ اللّٰهِ
فَسَوْفَ نُؤْتِيْهِ اَجْرًا عَظِيْمًا ○

625. Usually secrecy is for evil ends, or from questionable motives, or because the person seeking secrecy is ashamed of himself and knows that if his acts or motives became known, he would make himself odious. Islam therefore disapproves of secrecy and loves and enjoins openness in all consultations and doings. But there are three things in which secrecy is permissible, and indeed laudable, provided the motive be purely unselfish, to earn "the good pleasure of God": (1) if you are doing a deed of charity or beneficence, whether in giving material things or in helping in moral, intellectual, or spiritual matters; here publicity may not be agreeable to the recipient of your beneficence, and you have to think of his feelings; (2) where an unpleasant act of justice or correction has to be done; this should be done, but there is no virtue in publishing it abroad and causing humiliation to some parties or adding to their humiliation by publicity; (3) where there is a delicate question of conciliating parties to a quarrel; they may be very touchy about publicity but quite amenable to the influence of a man acting in private.

115. If anyone contends with
The Apostle even after
Guidance has been plainly
Conveyed to him, and follows
A path other than that
Becoming to men of Faith,
We shall leave him
In the path he has chosen,
And land him in Hell,—
What an evil refuge!

١١٥- وَمَنْ يُشَاقِقِ الرَّسُولَ
مِنْ بَعْدِ مَا تَبَيَّنَ لَهُ الْهُدَىٰ
وَيَتَّبِعْ غَيْرَ سَبِيلِ الْمُؤْمِنِينَ نُوَلِّهِ
مَا تَوَلَّىٰ وَنُصْلِهِ جَهَنَّمَ
وَسَاءَتْ مَصِيرًا ۝

SECTION 18.

116. God forgiveth not
(The sin of) joining other gods[626]
With Him; but He forgiveth
Whom He pleaseth other sins
Than this: one who joins
Other gods with God,
Hath strayed far, far away
(From the Right).

١١٦- إِنَّ اللَّهَ لَا يَغْفِرُ أَنْ يُشْرَكَ بِهِ
وَيَغْفِرُ مَا دُونَ ذَٰلِكَ لِمَنْ يَشَاءُ
وَمَنْ يُشْرِكْ بِاللَّهِ
فَقَدْ ضَلَّ ضَلَالًا بَعِيدًا ۝

117. (The Pagans), leaving Him,
Call but upon female deities:[627]
They call but upon Satan
The persistent rebel!

١١٧- إِنْ يَدْعُونَ مِنْ دُونِهِ إِلَّا إِنَاثًا
وَإِنْ يَدْعُونَ إِلَّا شَيْطَانًا مَرِيدًا ۝

118. God did curse him,
But he said: "I will take
Of Thy servants a portion[628]
Marked off;

١١٨- لَعَنَهُ اللَّهُ وَقَالَ لَأَتَّخِذَنَّ مِنْ
عِبَادِكَ نَصِيبًا مَفْرُوضًا ۝

119. "I will mislead them,[629]
And I will create

١١٩- وَلَأُضِلَّنَّهُمْ وَلَأُمَنِّيَنَّهُمْ

626. *Cf.* iv. 48 and n. 569. Blasphemy in the spiritual kingdom is like treason in the political kingdom.

627. The unity, power, and goodness of God are so manifest in nature and in the human mind when it is in accord with the universal spirit, that only the most abject perversion can account for the sin of spiritual treason. That sin arises from perverted ideas of sex or perverted ideas of self. The perversion of sex is to suppose that sex rules in spiritual matters. From it arise such horrible creations of the imagination as Kāli, the blood-thirsty goddess of India, or Hecate, the goddess of revenge and hate in Greek mythology. Even in beautiful forms like Saraswatī (the goddess of learning) or Minerva (the virgin goddess of sport and arts), to say nothing of Venus (the goddess of carnal pleasures), the emphasis laid on sex destroys a right view of spiritual nature. Perverted ideas of self are typified in the story of Satan, who was so puffed up with arrogance that he disobeyed God, and God cursed him. Both these perversions, if allowed lodgment, completely ruin our spiritual nature and deface God's handiwork. Hence it is not merely an outer sin but one that corrupts us through and through.

628. Satan obtained God's permission to tempt man, and this was implied in such free-will as was granted to man by God. Satan's boast is that the portion of mankind seduced by him will be so corrupted in their nature that they will bear a sort of brand that will mark them off as his own; or that they will be like a portion assigned to himself.

629. Satan's deceptions are with false desires, false superstitions, and false fears.

In them false desires; I will
Order them to slit the ears[630]
Of cattle, and to deface
The (fair) nature created[631]
By God." Whoever,
Forsaking God, takes Satan
For a friend, hath
Of a surety suffered
A loss that is manifest.

وَلَاٰمُرَنَّهُمْ فَلَيُبَتِّكُنَّ اٰذَانَ الْاَنْعَامِ
وَلَاٰمُرَنَّهُمْ فَلَيُغَيِّرُنَّ خَلْقَ اللّٰهِ ؕ
وَمَنْ يَّتَّخِذِ الشَّيْطٰنَ وَلِيًّا
مِّنْ دُوْنِ اللّٰهِ
فَقَدْ خَسِرَ خُسْرَانًا مُّبِيْنًا ۝

120. Satan makes them promises,
And creates in them false desires;
But Satan's promises
Are nothing but deception.

١٢٠- يَعِدُهُمْ وَيُمَنِّيْهِمْ ؕ
وَمَا يَعِدُهُمُ الشَّيْطٰنُ اِلَّا غُرُوْرًا ۝

121. They (his dupes)
Will have their dwelling
In Hell, and from it
They will find no way
Of escape.

١٢١- اُولٰٓئِكَ مَاْوٰىهُمْ جَهَنَّمُ ؗ
وَلَا يَجِدُوْنَ عَنْهَا مَحِيْصًا ۝

122. But those who believe
And do deeds of righteousness,—
We shall soon admit them
To Gardens, with rivers
Flowing beneath,—to dwell
Therein for ever.
God's promise is the truth,
And whose word can be
Truer than God's?

١٢٢- وَالَّذِيْنَ اٰمَنُوْا وَعَمِلُوا الصّٰلِحٰتِ
سَنُدْخِلُهُمْ جَنّٰتٍ تَجْرِيْ مِنْ تَحْتِهَا
الْاَنْهٰرُ
خٰلِدِيْنَ فِيْهَآ اَبَدًا ؕ وَعْدَ اللّٰهِ حَقًّا ؕ
وَمَنْ اَصْدَقُ مِنَ اللّٰهِ قِيْلًا ۝

123. Not your desires, nor those[632]
Of the People of the Book

١٢٣- لَيْسَ بِاَمَانِيِّكُمْ وَلَآ اَمَانِيِّ اَهْلِ

630. Slitting the ears of cattle is just one instance of the superstitions to which men become slaves when they run after false gods. Astrology, magic, and vain beliefs in things that do not exist lead men away from the one true God.

631. To deface the (fair) nature created by God: there is both a physical and a spiritual meaning. We see many kinds of defacements practised on men and animals, against their true nature as created by God, partly on account of superstition, partly on account of selfishness. Spiritually the case is even worse. How many natures are dwarfed or starved and turned from their original instincts by cruel superstitions or customs? God created man pure: the Evil One defaces the image.

632. Personal responsibility is again and again insisted on as the key-note of Islam. In this are implied faith and right conduct. Faith is not an external thing: it begins with an act of will, but if true and sincere, it affects the whole being, and leads to right conduct. In this it is distinguished from the kind of faith which promises salvation because some one else in whom you are asked to believe has borne away the sins of men, or the kind of faith which says that because you are born of a certain race ("Children of Abraham") or a certain caste, you are privileged, and your conduct will be judged by a different standard from that of other men. Whatever you are, if you do evil, you must suffer the consequences, unless God's Mercy comes to your help.

(Can prevail): whoever
Works evil, will be
Requited accordingly.
Nor will he find, besides God,
Any protector or helper.

الْكِتٰبِ مَنْ يَّعْمَلْ سُوْٓءًا يُّجْزَ بِهٖ ۙ
وَلَا يَجِدْ لَهٗ مِنْ دُوْنِ اللّٰهِ وَلِيًّا وَّلَا نَصِيْرًا ۝

124. If any do deeds
Of righteousness,—
Be they male or female –
And have faith,
They will enter Heaven,
And not the least injustice[633]
Will be done to them.

١٢٤- وَمَنْ يَّعْمَلْ مِنَ الصّٰلِحٰتِ
مِنْ ذَكَرٍ اَوْ اُنْثٰى وَهُوَ مُؤْمِنٌ
فَاُولٰٓئِكَ يَدْخُلُوْنَ الْجَنَّةَ
وَلَا يُظْلَمُوْنَ نَقِيْرًا ۝

125. Who can be better
In religion than one
Who submits his whole self
To God, does good,
And follows the way
Of Abraham the true in faith?
For God did take
Abraham for a friend.[634]

١٢٥- وَمَنْ اَحْسَنُ دِيْنًا
مِّمَّنْ اَسْلَمَ وَجْهَهٗ لِلّٰهِ وَهُوَ مُحْسِنٌ
وَّاتَّبَعَ مِلَّةَ اِبْرٰهِيْمَ حَنِيْفًا ؕ
وَاتَّخَذَ اللّٰهُ اِبْرٰهِيْمَ خَلِيْلًا ۝

126. But to God belong all things
In the heavens and on earth:
And He it is that
Encompasseth all things.[635]

١٢٦- وَلِلّٰهِ مَا فِي السَّمٰوٰتِ وَمَا فِي الْاَرْضِ ؕ
وَكَانَ اللّٰهُ بِكُلِّ شَيْءٍ مُّحِيْطًا ۝ ع

C. 67.—Justice to women and orphans
(iv. 127-152.) **Is part of religion and the fear**
Of God. Stand out firmly
For justice to all, even against
Yourselves or your nearest of kin.
Remain firm in faith, and consort not
With evil or hypocrisy. Be true
In speech, and wound not others:
Nor distinguish between Teachers of Truth,
For God's Truth is one and should be believed.

---

633. *Naqīr*=the groove in a date-stone, a thing of no value whatever. *Cf.* n. 575 to iv. 53.

634. Abraham is distinguished in Muslim theology with the title of "Friend of God". This does not of course mean that he was anything more than a mortal. But his faith was pure and true, and his conduct was firm and righteous in all circumstances. He was the fountain and origin of the three streams of religious thought, which were afterwards crystallised in the institutions of Moses, Jesus, and Muhammad the Chosen One.

635. *Muḥīṭ*. *Cf.* iv. 108, and n. 623.

SECTION 19.

127. They ask thy instruction
Concerning the Women
Say: God doth
Instruct you about them:
And (remember) what hath
Been rehearsed unto you[636]
In the Book, concerning
The orphans of women to whom
Ye give not the portions
Prescribed, and yet whom ye
Desire to marry, as also
Concerning the children
Who are weak and oppressed:[637]
That ye stand firm
For justice to orphans.
There is not a good deed
Which ye do, but God
Is well-acquainted therewith.

١٢٧- وَيَسْتَفْتُونَكَ فِي النِّسَاءِ ط
قُلِ اللّٰهُ يُفْتِيكُمْ فِيهِنَّ لا
وَمَا يُتْلٰى عَلَيْكُمْ فِي الْكِتٰبِ
فِي يَتٰمَى النِّسَاءِ الّٰتِي
لَا تُؤْتُونَهُنَّ مَا كُتِبَ لَهُنَّ
وَتَرْغَبُونَ أَنْ تَنْكِحُوهُنَّ
وَالْمُسْتَضْعَفِينَ مِنَ الْوِلْدَانِ لا
وَأَنْ تَقُومُوا لِلْيَتٰمٰى بِالْقِسْطِ ط
وَمَا تَفْعَلُوا مِنْ خَيْرٍ
فَإِنَّ اللّٰهَ كَانَ بِهِ عَلِيمًا ۝

128. If a wife fears
Cruelty or desertion
On her husband's part,
There is no blame on them
If they arrange
An amicable settlement
Between themselves;
And such settlement is best;

١٢٨- وَإِنِ امْرَأَةٌ خَافَتْ
مِنْ بَعْلِهَا نُشُوزًا أَوْ إِعْرَاضًا
فَلَا جُنَاحَ عَلَيْهِمَا
أَنْ يُصْلِحَا بَيْنَهُمَا صُلْحًا ط
وَالصُّلْحُ خَيْرٌ ط

---

636. Again and again is it impressed on the community of Islam to be just in their dealings with women, orphans, children, and all whose weakness requires special consideration. The law about widows and orphans, inheritance, dower, and marriage had already been declared in iv. 2-35, and further instructions are now given on a further reference. The words translated *orphans of women* mean I think the orphaned children of widows, of whom there were several after the battle of Uḥud, and whom it was the duty of the community to provide for. But some Commentators take them to mean "female orphans". In any case, because women were orphans or widows, it was not right that anyone should take advantage of their helpless position to deprive them of dower or of their portion in inheritance.

637. *Cf.* iv. 75, n. 592.

Both widows and orphans are to be helped because they are ordinarily weak, ill-treated, and oppressed. In communities which base their civil rights on brute strength, the weaker go to the wall, and public opinion expects nothing else. In Nietzsche's philosophy of the Superman that doctrine is stressed strongly, and some of the militarist nations in our own time seem inclined to support this reversion to our primitive instincts. Even in modern democracies of the saner sort, we are often told that it is the fate of minorities to suffer: strength of numbers here becomes the passport to power and privilege. Islam, while upholding sane manly views in general, enjoins the most solicitous care for the weak and oppressed in every way—in rights of property, in social rights, and in the right to opportunities of development. Spiritual strength or weakness does not necessarily go with physical or numerical strength.

Even though men's souls
Are swayed by greed.[638]
But if ye do good
And practise self-restraint,
God is well-acquainted
With all that ye do.

وَأُحْضِرَتِ الْأَنْفُسُ الشُّحَّ ۚ
وَإِنْ تُحْسِنُوا وَتَتَّقُوا
فَإِنَّ اللَّهَ كَانَ بِمَا تَعْمَلُونَ خَبِيرًا ○

129. Ye are never able
To be fair and just
As between women,
Even if it is
Your ardent desire :
But turn not away
(From a woman) altogether,
So as to leave her (as it were)
Hanging (in the air).[639]
If ye come to a friendly
Understanding, and practise
Self-restraint, God is
Oft-forgiving, Most Merciful.

١٢٩- وَلَنْ تَسْتَطِيعُوا
أَنْ تَعْدِلُوا بَيْنَ النِّسَاءِ
وَلَوْ حَرَصْتُمْ
فَلَا تَمِيلُوا كُلَّ الْمَيْلِ
فَتَذَرُوهَا كَالْمُعَلَّقَةِ ۚ
وَإِنْ تُصْلِحُوا وَتَتَّقُوا
فَإِنَّ اللَّهَ كَانَ غَفُورًا رَحِيمًا ○

130. But if they disagree
(And must part), God
Will provide abundance
For all from His
All-reaching bounty :
For God is He
That careth for all
And is Wise.

١٣٠- وَإِنْ يَتَفَرَّقَا
يُغْنِ اللَّهُ كُلًّا مِنْ سَعَتِهِ ۚ
وَكَانَ اللَّهُ وَاسِعًا حَكِيمًا ○

131. To God belong all things
In the heavens and on earth.[640]

١٣١- وَلِلَّهِ مَا فِي السَّمٰوٰتِ وَمَا فِي الْأَرْضِ ۗ

638. To protect the woman's economic interests, various rules are prescribed for dower in marriage. But the sanctity of marriage itself is greater than any economic interests. Divorce is, of all things permitted, most hateful to God. Therefore if a breach between husband and wife can be prevented by some economic consideration, it is better to make that concession than to imperil the future of the wife, the children, and probably the husband also. Such concessions are permissible, in view of the love of wealth ingrained in unregenerate man, but a recommendation is made that we should practise self-restraint, and do what we can to come to an amicable settlement without any economic sacrifice on the part of the woman.

639. In this material world there are two principal causes of division between man and wife, money and "the other woman" or "the other man". Money was dealt with in the last verse. Here is the case of "the other woman". Legally more than one wife (up to four) are permissible on the condition that the man can be perfectly fair and just to all. But this is a condition almost impossible to fulfil. If, in the hope that he might be able to fulfil it, a man puts himself in that impossible position, it is only right to insist that he should not discard one but at least fulfil all the outward duties that are incumbent on him in respect of her.

640. Notice the refrain: "To God belong all things in the heavens and on earth": repeated three times, each time with a new application. In the first instance it follows the statement of God's universal providence and love. If two persons, in spite of every sincere desire to love and comfort each other, fail to achieve that end, and have to separate, God's all-reaching bounty never fails, for He is the Lord of all things. In the second instance it is connected with God's Self-existence, Self-excellence, and independence of all creatures: all His commands are for our good, and they are given to all His creatures, according to their capacities. In the third instance, it is connected with His universal power; for He could destroy any individual or nation and create a new one without any loss to Himself; but He gives a chance to all again and again, and even rewards them beyond their own ambitions.

Verily We have directed
The People of the Book
Before you, and you (O Muslims)
To fear God. But if ye
Deny Him, lo! unto God
Belong all things
In the heavens and on earth,
And God is free
Of all wants, worthy[641]
Of all praise.

وَلَقَدْ وَصَّيْنَا الَّذِينَ أُوتُوا الْكِتٰبَ
مِنْ قَبْلِكُمْ
وَإِيَّاكُمْ أَنِ اتَّقُوا اللّٰهَ ؕ
وَإِنْ تَكْفُرُوا
فَإِنَّ لِلّٰهِ مَا فِي السَّمٰوٰتِ وَمَا فِي الْأَرْضِ ؕ
وَكَانَ اللّٰهُ غَنِيًّا حَمِيدًا ۝

132. Yea, unto God belong
All things in the heavens
And on earth, and enough
Is God to carry through[642]
All affairs.

۱۳۲- وَلِلّٰهِ مَا فِي السَّمٰوٰتِ
وَمَا فِي الْأَرْضِ ؕ
وَكَفٰى بِاللّٰهِ وَكِيلًا ۝

133. If it were His Will,
He could destroy you,
O mankind, and create
Another race; for He
Hath power this to do.

۱۳۳- إِنْ يَشَأْ يُذْهِبْكُمْ أَيُّهَا النَّاسُ
وَيَأْتِ بِآخَرِينَ ؕ
وَكَانَ اللّٰهُ عَلٰى ذٰلِكَ قَدِيرًا ۝

134. If any one desires
A reward in this life,
In God's (gift) is the reward
(Both) of this life
And of the Hereafter:[643]
For God is He that heareth
And seeth (all things).

۱۳۴- مَنْ كَانَ يُرِيدُ ثَوَابَ الدُّنْيَا
فَعِنْدَ اللّٰهِ ثَوَابُ الدُّنْيَا وَالْآخِرَةِ ؕ
وَكَانَ اللّٰهُ سَمِيعًا بَصِيرًا ۝ ع

641. God's existence is absolute existence. It does not depend on any other person or any other thing. And it is worthy of all praise, for it is all-good and comprises every possible excellence. It is necessary to stress this point in order to show that the moral law for man is not a mere matter of transcendental commands, but really rests on the essential needs of mankind itself. If therefore such schools of thought as Behaviourism proved their theories up to the hilt, they do not affect the position of Islam in the least. The highest ethical standards are enjoined by Islam, not as dogmatic imperatives, but because they can be shown to follow from the needs of man's nature and the results of man's experience.

642. This refers to the next verse. He does not need us, but we need Him. Our hopes, our happiness, our success centre in Him; but He is Self-sufficient. He has the power to supersede us, but His goodness is ever seeking to give us every chance in this world as well as in the Hereafter.

643. Man in this life can only see up to the horizon of this life. The highest rewards which his wishes or ambitions can conceive of are conceived in the terms of this life. But God can give him not only these but something infinitely higher,—the rewards of the Hereafter,—which it did not even enter his heart to ask for or his imagination to conceive.

SECTION 20.

135. O ye who believe !
Stand out firmly
For justice, as witnesses[644]
To God, even as against
Yourselves, or your parents,
Or your kin, and whether
It be (against) rich or poor :[645]
For God can best protect both.
Follow not the lusts
(Of your hearts), lest ye
Swerve, and if ye
Distort (justice) or decline
To do justice, verily
God is well-acquainted
With all that ye do.

١٣٥- يَاَيُّهَا الَّذِيْنَ اٰمَنُوْا كُوْنُوْا قَوّٰمِيْنَ
بِالْقِسْطِ شُهَدَآءَ لِلّٰهِ
وَلَوْ عَلٰٓى اَنْفُسِكُمْ اَوِ الْوَالِدَيْنِ
وَالْاَقْرَبِيْنَ ۚ اِنْ يَّكُنْ غَنِيًّا اَوْ فَقِيْرًا
فَاللّٰهُ اَوْلٰى بِهِمَا ۫
فَلَا تَتَّبِعُوا الْهَوٰٓى
اَنْ تَعْدِلُوْا ۚ
وَاِنْ تَلْوٗٓا اَوْ تُعْرِضُوْا
فَاِنَّ اللّٰهَ كَانَ بِمَا تَعْمَلُوْنَ خَبِيْرًا ○

136. O ye who believe !
Believe in God
And His Apostle,
And the scripture which He
Hath sent to His Apostle
And the scripture which He sent
To those before (him).[646]
Any who denieth God,
His angels, His Books,
His Apostles, and the Day
Of Judgment, hath gone
Far, far astray.

١٣٦- يَاَيُّهَا الَّذِيْنَ اٰمَنُوْٓا
اٰمِنُوْا بِاللّٰهِ وَرَسُوْلِهٖ
وَالْكِتٰبِ الَّذِيْ نَزَّلَ عَلٰى رَسُوْلِهٖ
وَالْكِتٰبِ الَّذِيْٓ اَنْزَلَ مِنْ قَبْلُ ۭ
وَمَنْ يَّكْفُرْ بِاللّٰهِ
وَمَلٰٓئِكَتِهٖ وَكُتُبِهٖ وَرُسُلِهٖ وَالْيَوْمِ الْاٰخِرِ
فَقَدْ ضَلَّ ضَلٰلًا بَعِيْدًا ○

---

644 Justice is God's attribute, and to stand firm for justice is to be a witness to God, even if it is detrimental to our own interests (as we conceive them) or the interests of those who are near and dear to us. According to the Latin saying, "Let justice be done though heaven should fall."

But Islamic justice is something higher than the formal justice of Roman Law or any other human Law. It is even more penetrative than the subtler justice in the speculations of the Greek philosophers. It searches out the innermost motives, because we are to act as in the presence of God, to whom all things, acts, and motives are known.

645. Some people may be inclined to favour the rich, because they expect something from them. Some people may be inclined to favour the poor because they are generally helpless. Partiality in either case is wrong. Be just, without fear or favour. Both the rich and the poor are under God's protection as far as their legitimate interests are concerned, but they cannot expect to be favoured at the expense of others. And He can protect their interests far better than any man.

646. If your belief is by habit or birth or the example of those you love or respect or admire, make that belief more specific and personal to yourself. We must not only have faith, but realise that faith in our inmost being. The chief objects of our Faith are God, His Apostle, and His Revelations. To all these we must give a home in our hearts. The angels we do not see and realise as we realise God, who is nearer to us than the vehicle of our life-blood, and the Day of Judgment is for our future experience, but we must not deny them, or we cut off a part of our spiritual view.

137. Those who believe,
Then reject Faith,
Then believe (again)
And (again) reject Faith,
And go on increasing
In Unbelief,—God
Will not forgive them
Nor guide them on the Way.[647]

١٣٧- إِنَّ الَّذِينَ آمَنُوا ثُمَّ كَفَرُوا
ثُمَّ آمَنُوا ثُمَّ كَفَرُوا
ثُمَّ ازْدَادُوا كُفْرًا
لَّمْ يَكُنِ اللَّهُ لِيَغْفِرَ لَهُمْ
وَلَا لِيَهْدِيَهُمْ سَبِيلًا ۝

138. To the Hypocrites give
The glad tidings that
There is for them
(But) a grievous Penalty;—

١٣٨- بَشِّرِ الْمُنَافِقِينَ
بِأَنَّ لَهُمْ عَذَابًا أَلِيمًا ۝

139. Yea, to those who take
For friends Unbelievers
Rather than Believers:
Is it honour they seek
Among them? Nay,—
All honour is with God.[648]

١٣٩- الَّذِينَ يَتَّخِذُونَ الْكَافِرِينَ أَوْلِيَاءَ
مِن دُونِ الْمُؤْمِنِينَ ۚ
أَيَبْتَغُونَ عِندَهُمُ الْعِزَّةَ
فَإِنَّ الْعِزَّةَ لِلَّهِ جَمِيعًا ۝

140. Already has He sent you[649]
Word in the Book, that when
Ye hear the Signs of God
Held in defiance and ridicule,
Ye are not to sit with them
Unless they turn to a different
Theme: if ye did, ye would be
Like them. For God will
Collect the Hypocrites and those
Who defy Faith—all in Hell;—

١٤٠- وَقَدْ نَزَّلَ عَلَيْكُمْ فِي الْكِتَابِ أَنْ إِذَا
سَمِعْتُمْ آيَاتِ اللَّهِ يُكْفَرُ بِهَا وَيُسْتَهْزَأُ بِهَا
فَلَا تَقْعُدُوا مَعَهُمْ
حَتَّىٰ يَخُوضُوا فِي حَدِيثٍ غَيْرِهِ ۚ
إِنَّكُمْ إِذًا مِّثْلُهُمْ ۗ إِنَّ اللَّهَ جَامِعُ الْمُنَافِقِينَ
وَالْكَافِرِينَ فِي جَهَنَّمَ جَمِيعًا ۝

---

647. Those who go on changing sides again and again can have no real Faith at any time. Their motives are mere worldly double-dealing. How can they expect God's grace or forgiveness?

Here is a clear warning against those who make their religion a mere matter of worldly convenience. True religion goes far deeper. It transforms the very nature of man. After that transformation it is as impossible for him to change as it is for light to become darkness.

648. If the motive is some advantage, some honour,—the fountain of all good is God. How can it really be expected from those who deny Faith? And if there is some show of worldly honour, what is it worth against the contempt they earn in the spiritual world?

649. *Cf.* vi. 68, an earlier and Meccan verse.

Where we see or hear Truth held in light esteem, we ought to make our protest and withdraw from such company, not out of arrogance, as if we thought ourselves superior to other people, but out of real humility, lest our own nature be corrupted in such society. But it is possible that our protest or our sincere remonstrance may change the theme of discourse. In that case we have done good to those who were inclined to hold Truth in light esteem, for we have saved them for ridiculing Truth.

141. (These are) the ones who
Wait and watch about you:
If ye do gain
A victory from God,
They say: "Were we not
With you?"—but if
The Unbelievers gain
A success, they say
(To them): "Did we not
Gain an advantage over you,
And did we not guard
You from the Believers?"
But God will judge
Betwixt you on the Day
Of Judgment. And never
Will God grant
To the Unbelievers
A way (to triumph)
Over the Believers.[650]

١٤١- الَّذِينَ يَتَرَبَّصُونَ بِكُمْ
فَإِنْ كَانَ لَكُمْ فَتْحٌ مِّنَ اللّٰهِ
قَالُوٓا أَلَمْ نَكُنْ مَّعَكُمْ
وَإِنْ كَانَ لِلْكٰفِرِينَ نَصِيبٌ
قَالُوٓا أَلَمْ نَسْتَحْوِذْ عَلَيْكُمْ
وَنَمْنَعْكُمْ مِّنَ الْمُؤْمِنِينَ
فَاللّٰهُ يَحْكُمُ بَيْنَكُمْ
يَوْمَ الْقِيٰمَةِ
وَلَنْ يَّجْعَلَ اللّٰهُ
لِلْكٰفِرِينَ عَلَى الْمُؤْمِنِينَ سَبِيلًا ۝

Section 21.

142. The Hypocrites—they think
They are over-reaching God,
But He will over-reach them:
When they stand up to prayer,
They stand without earnestness,
To be seen of men,
But little do they hold
God in remembrance;

١٤٢- إِنَّ الْمُنٰفِقِينَ يُخٰدِعُونَ اللّٰهَ
وَهُوَ خٰدِعُهُمْ
وَإِذَا قَامُوٓا إِلَى الصَّلٰوةِ قَامُوا كُسَالٰى
يُرَآءُونَ النَّاسَ
وَلَا يَذْكُرُونَ اللّٰهَ إِلَّا قَلِيلًا ۝

143. (They are) distracted in mind
Even in the midst of it,—
Being (sincerely) for neither
One group nor for another.
Whom God leaves straying,—
Never wilt thou find

١٤٣- مُّذَبْذَبِينَ بَيْنَ ذٰلِكَ
لَآ إِلٰى هٰٓؤُلَآءِ وَلَآ إِلٰى هٰٓؤُلَآءِ
وَمَنْ يُّضْلِلِ اللّٰهُ فَلَنْ تَجِدَ

650. The methods and motives of Hypocrisy are thoroughly unmasked here. It has no principles, but watches for an opportunity to turn any event to its own advantage. If battle is joined between two inconsistent principles, it has no belief in either, but watches the result. There is unceasing fight between Good and Evil in this world. If the Good seems to win, the hypocrites range themselves on its side with unctuous words, taking a great part of the credit to themselves. Perhaps the balance tips the other way later, and they have to make their peace with Evil. "Oh!" they say airily, "we were in the ranks of your enemy before, on purpose to protect you when they were too strong for you!" This may suit the ways of the world. But the day of their account will come eventually. For the Good must ultimately triumph.

For him the Way.[651]

لَهٗ سَبِيْلًا ۝

144. O ye who believe!
Take not for friends
Unbelievers rather than
Believers: do ye wish
To offer God an open
Proof against yourselves?

١٤٤- يٰۤاَيُّهَا الَّذِيْنَ اٰمَنُوْا لَا تَتَّخِذُوا الْكٰفِرِيْنَ
اَوْلِيَآءَ مِنْ دُوْنِ الْمُؤْمِنِيْنَ ؕ اَتُرِيْدُوْنَ
اَنْ تَجْعَلُوْا لِلّٰهِ عَلَيْكُمْ سُلْطٰنًا مُّبِيْنًا ۝

145. The Hypocrites will be
In the lowest depths
Of the Fire: no helper
Wilt thou find for them;—

١٤٥- اِنَّ الْمُنٰفِقِيْنَ فِي الدَّرْكِ الْاَسْفَلِ
مِنَ النَّارِ ۚ وَلَنْ تَجِدَ لَهُمْ نَصِيْرًا ۝

146. Except for those who repent,
Mend (their life), hold fast
To God, and purify their religion
As in God's sight: if so
They will be (numbered)[652]
With the Believers.
And soon will God
Grant to the Believers
A reward of immense value.

١٤٦- اِلَّا الَّذِيْنَ تَابُوْا
وَاَصْلَحُوْا وَاعْتَصَمُوْا بِاللّٰهِ
وَاَخْلَصُوْا دِيْنَهُمْ لِلّٰهِ
فَاُولٰٓئِكَ مَعَ الْمُؤْمِنِيْنَ ؕ وَسَوْفَ يُؤْتِ
اللّٰهُ الْمُؤْمِنِيْنَ اَجْرًا عَظِيْمًا ۝

147. What can God gain
By your punishment,
If ye are grateful
And ye believe?
Nay, it is God
That recogniseth[653]
5 (All good), and knoweth
30 All things.

١٤٧- مَا يَفْعَلُ اللّٰهُ بِعَذَابِكُمْ
اِنْ شَكَرْتُمْ وَاٰمَنْتُمْ ؕ
وَكَانَ اللّٰهُ شَاكِرًا عَلِيْمًا ۝

651. If we choose evil deliberately and double our guilt by fraud and deception, we do not deceive God, but we deceive ourselves. We deprive ourselves of the Grace of God, and are left straying away from the Path. In that condition who can guide us or show us the Way? Our true and right instincts become blunted; our fraud makes us unstable in character; when our fellow-men find out our fraud, any advantages we may have gained by the fraud are lost; and we become truly distracted in mind.

652. Even Hypocrites can obtain forgiveness, on four conditions: (1) sincere repentance, which purifies their mind; (2) amendment of their conduct, which purifies their outer life; (3) steadfastness and devotion to God, which strengthens their faith and protects them from the assaults of evil; and (4) sincerity in their religion, or their whole inner being, which brings them as full members into the goodly Fellowship of Faith.

653. There is no pleasure nor advantage to God in punishing His own creatures, over whom He watches with loving care. On the contrary He recognises any good—however little—which He finds in us, and delights to give us a reward beyond all measure. His recognition of us is compared by a bold metaphor to our gratitude to Him for His favours. The epithet *Shākir* is applied to God, as here, in ii. 158, and other passages. In xvi. 121 it is applied to Abraham: "he showed his gratitude for the favours of God, who chose him and guided him to a Straight Way."

148. God loveth not that evil
Should be noised abroad[654]
In public speech, except
Where injustice hath been
Done; for God
Is He who heareth
And knoweth all things.

١٤٨- لَا يُحِبُّ اللّٰهُ الْجَهْرَ بِالسُّوْٓءِ مِنَ الْقَوْلِ
إِلَّا مَنْ ظُلِمَ ؕ
وَكَانَ اللّٰهُ سَمِيْعًا عَلِيْمًا ۝

149. Whether ye publish
A good deed or conceal it
Or cover evil with pardon,
Verily God doth blot out
(Sins) and hath power
(In the judgment of values).[655]

١٤٩- إِنْ تُبْدُوْا خَيْرًا أَوْ تُخْفُوْهُ
أَوْ تَعْفُوْا عَنْ سُوْٓءٍ
فَإِنَّ اللّٰهَ كَانَ عَفُوًّا قَدِيْرًا ۝

150. Those who deny God
And His apostles, and (those
Who) wish to separate
God from His apostles,
Saying: "We believe in some
But reject others":
And (those who) wish
To take a course midway,—[656]

١٥٠- إِنَّ الَّذِيْنَ يَكْفُرُوْنَ بِاللّٰهِ وَرُسُلِهٖ
وَيُرِيْدُوْنَ أَنْ يُّفَرِّقُوْا بَيْنَ اللّٰهِ وَرُسُلِهٖ
وَيَقُوْلُوْنَ نُؤْمِنُ بِبَعْضٍ وَّنَكْفُرُ بِبَعْضٍ ۙ
وَّيُرِيْدُوْنَ أَنْ يَّتَّخِذُوْا بَيْنَ ذٰلِكَ سَبِيْلًا ۙ

151. They are in truth
(Equally) Unbelievers;

١٥١- أُولٰٓئِكَ هُمُ الْكٰفِرُوْنَ حَقًّا ۚ

654. We can make a public scandal of evil in many ways. (1) It may be idle sensation-mongering: it often leads to more evil by imitation, as where criminal deeds are glorified in a cinema, or talked about shamelessly in a novel or drama. (2) It may be malicious gossip of a foolish, personal kind: it does no good, but it hurts people's feelings. (3) It may be malevolent slander or libel: it is intended deliberately to cause harm to people's reputation or injure them in other ways, and is rightly punishable under all laws. (4) It may be a public rebuke or correction or remonstrance, without malice. (1), (2), and (3) are absolutely forbidden. (4) may be by a person in authority; in which case the exception applies, for all wrong or injustice must be corrected openly, to prevent its recurrence. Or (4) may be by a person not vested with authority, but acting either from motives of public spirit, or in order to help some one who has been wronged; here again the exception will apply. But if the motive is different, the exception does not apply. (4) would also include a public complaint by a person who has suffered a wrong; he has every right to seek public redress.

655. *Qadīr*: I have translated it more fully than most translators. The root *qadara* not only implies power, ability, strength, but two other ideas which it is difficult to convey in a single word, *viz*, the act and power of estimating the true value of a thing or persons, as in vi. 91; and the act and power of regulating something so as to bring it into correspondence with something. "Judgment of values" I think sums up these finer shades of meaning. God forgives what is wrong and is able fully to appreciate and judge of the value of our good deeds whether we publish them or conceal them.

656. Unbelief takes various forms. Three are mentioned here: (1) denial of God and His revelation to mankind through inspired men; (2) a sort of nominal belief in God and His apostles, but one which is partial, and mixed up with racial pride, which does not allow of the recognition of any apostles beyond those of a particular race; and (3) a nominal belief in universal revelation, but so hedged round with peculiar doctrines of exclusive salvation, that it practically approaches to a denial of God's universal love for all mankind and all Creation. All three amount to Unbelief, for they really deny God's universal love and care.

And We have prepared
For Unbelievers a humiliating
Punishment.

وَ اَعْتَدْنَا لِلْكٰفِرِيْنَ عَذَابًا مُّهِيْنًا ○

152. To those who believe
In God and His apostles
And make no distinction
Between any of the apostles,
We shall soon give
Their (due) rewards:
For God is Oft-forgiving,
Most Merciful.

١٥٢- وَ الَّذِيْنَ اٰمَنُوْا بِاللّٰهِ وَ رُسُلِهٖ
وَ لَمْ يُفَرِّقُوْا بَيْنَ اَحَدٍ مِّنْهُمْ
اُولٰٓئِكَ سَوْفَ يُؤْتِيْهِمْ اُجُوْرَهُمْ ط
وَ كَانَ اللّٰهُ غَفُوْرًا رَّحِيْمًا ○ ع

C. 68.—The People of the Book went wrong:
(iv. 153-176.) The Jews in breaking their Covenant,
And slandering Mary and Jesus,
And in their usury and injustice;
And the Christians in raising
Jesus the Apostle to equality
With God. God's revelation
Is continued in the Qur-ān,
Which comes with manifest proof
And a clear light to those who understand.

SECTION 22.

153. The People of the Book
Ask thee to cause
A book to descend to them
From heaven: indeed
They asked Moses
For an even greater
(Miracle), for they said:
"Show us God in public,"[657]
But they were dazed
For their presumption,
With thunder and lightning.
Yet they worshipped the calf
Even after Clear Signs
Had come to them;
Even so We forgave them;
And gave Moses manifest
Proofs of authority.

١٥٣- يَسْـَٔلُكَ اَهْلُ الْكِتٰبِ اَنْ تُنَزِّلَ عَلَيْهِمْ
كِتٰبًا مِّنَ السَّمَآءِ
فَقَدْ سَاَلُوْا مُوْسٰٓى اَكْبَرَ مِنْ ذٰلِكَ
فَقَالُوْٓا اَرِنَا اللّٰهَ جَهْرَةً
فَاَخَذَتْهُمُ الصّٰعِقَةُ بِظُلْمِهِمْ ج
ثُمَّ اتَّخَذُوا الْعِجْلَ مِنْۢ بَعْدِ مَا جَآءَتْهُمُ
الْبَيِّنٰتُ فَعَفَوْنَا عَنْ ذٰلِكَ ج
وَ اٰتَيْنَا مُوْسٰى سُلْطٰنًا مُّبِيْنًا ○

657. *Cf.* ii. 55, for the thunder and lightning which dazed those who were presumptuous enough to ask that they should see God face to face, and ii. 51 and n. 66, for the worship of the golden calf.

The lesson is that it is presumptuous on the part of man to judge of spiritual things in terms of material things, or to ask to see God with their material eyes when God is above material forms and is independent of time and space.

154. And for their Covenant
We raised over them
(The towering height)
Of Mount (Sinai);[658]
And (on another occasion)
We said: "Enter the gate
With humility"; and (once again)
We commanded them:
"Transgress not in the matter
Of the Sabbath."
And We took from them
A solemn Covenant.

١٥٤- وَرَفَعْنَا فَوْقَهُمُ الطُّوْرَ
بِمِيْثَاقِهِمْ
وَقُلْنَا لَهُمُ ادْخُلُوا الْبَابَ
سُجَّدًا
وَقُلْنَا لَهُمْ لَا تَعْدُوْا فِي السَّبْتِ
وَاَخَذْنَا مِنْهُمْ مِّيْثَاقًا غَلِيْظًا ○

155. (They have incurred divine[659]
Displeasure): in that they
Broke their Covenant;
That they rejected the Signs
Of God; that they slew
The Messengers in defiance[660]
Of right; that they said,
"Our hearts are the wrappings[661]
(Which preserve God's Word;
We need no more)";—nay,
God hath set the seal on their hearts
For their blasphemy,
And little is it they believe;—

١٥٥- فَبِمَا نَقْضِهِمْ مِّيْثَاقَهُمْ
وَكُفْرِهِمْ بِاٰيٰتِ اللّٰهِ
وَقَتْلِهِمُ الْاَنْۢبِيَآءَ بِغَيْرِ حَقٍّ
وَّقَوْلِهِمْ قُلُوْبُنَا غُلْفٌ
بَلْ طَبَعَ اللّٰهُ عَلَيْهَا بِكُفْرِهِمْ
فَلَا يُؤْمِنُوْنَ اِلَّا قَلِيْلًا ○

156. That they rejected Faith;
That they uttered against Mary

١٥٦- وَّبِكُفْرِهِمْ وَقَوْلِهِمْ عَلٰى مَرْيَمَ

658. In this verse there is a recapitulation of three salient incidents of Jewish refractoriness already referred to in the second Sūra: *viz*, (1) the Covenant under the towering height of Sinai, ii. 63; (2) their arrogance where they were commanded humility in entering a town, ii. 58; and (3) their transgression of the Sabbath, ii. 65.

659. In verses 155, 156, 157, 160 (latter half), and 161 with parenthetical clauses including those in verses 158-159, and 160 (first half), there is a catalogue of the iniquities of which the Jews were guilty, and for these iniquities we must understand some such words as: "They are under divine displeasure." Each clause of the indictment I have indicated by prefixing the word "that."

660. *Cf.* iii. 21, and nn. 363 and 364.

661. *Cf.* ii 88, and n. 92, where the full meaning is explained.
Note the crescendo (heightening effect) in the argument. Their iniquities were: (1) that they broke their Covenant; (2) that they rejected God's guidance as conveyed in His Signs; (3) that they killed God's Messengers and incurred a double guilt, *viz.*, that of murder and that of a deliberate defiance of God's law; and (4) that they imagined themselves arrogantly self-sufficient, which means a blasphemous closing of their hearts for ever against the admission of God's grace. Then begins another series of iniquities from a different point of view: (1) that they rejected Faith; (2) that they made false charges against a saintly woman like Mary, who was chosen by God to be the mother of Jesus; (3) that they boasted of having killed Jesus when they were victims of their own self-hallucination; (4) that they hindered people from God's way; and (5) that by means of usury and fraud they oppressed their fellow-men.

A grave false charge ;[662]

بُهْتَانًا عَظِيمًا ۝

157. That they said (in boast),
" We killed Christ Jesus
The son of Mary,
The Apostle of God " ;—
But they killed him not,
Nor crucified him,[663]
But so it was made
To appear to them,
And those who differ
Therein are full of doubts,
With no (certain) knowledge,
But only conjecture to follow,
For of a surety
They killed him not :—

١٥٧- وَّقَوْلِهِمْ اِنَّا قَتَلْنَا الْمَسِيْحَ عِيْسَى
ابْنَ مَرْيَمَ رَسُوْلَ اللّٰهِ ۚ
وَمَا قَتَلُوْهُ وَمَا صَلَبُوْهُ وَلٰكِنْ شُبِّهَ لَهُمْ ۗ
وَاِنَّ الَّذِيْنَ اخْتَلَفُوْا فِيْهِ
لَفِيْ شَكٍّ مِّنْهُ ۗ مَا لَهُمْ بِهٖ مِنْ عِلْمٍ
اِلَّا اتِّبَاعَ الظَّنِّ ۚ
وَمَا قَتَلُوْهُ يَقِيْنًا ۝

158. Nay, God raised him up[664]
Unto Himself ; and God
Is Exalted in Power, Wise ;—

١٥٨- بَلْ رَّفَعَهُ اللّٰهُ اِلَيْهِ ۗ
وَكَانَ اللّٰهُ عَزِيْزًا حَكِيْمًا ۝

159. And there is none
Of the People of the Book

١٥٩- وَاِنْ مِّنْ اَهْلِ الْكِتٰبِ

---

662. The false charge against Mary was that she was unchaste. *Cf.* xix. 27-28. Such a charge is bad enough to make against any woman, but to make it against Mary, the mother of Jesus, was to bring into ridicule God's power itself. Islam is specially strong in guarding the reputation of women. Slanderers of women are bound to bring four witnesses in support of their accusations, and if they fail to produce four witnesses, they are to be flogged with eighty stripes and debarred for ever from being competent witnesses : xxiv. 4.

663. The end of the life of Jesus on earth is as much involved in mystery as his birth, and indeed the greater part of his private life, except the three main years of his ministry. It is not profitable to discuss the many doubts and conjectures among the early Christian sects and among Muslim theologians. The Orthodox Christian Churches make it a cardinal point of their doctrine that his life was taken on the Cross, that he died and was buried, that on the third day he rose in the body with his wounds intact, and walked about and conversed, and ate with his disciples, and was afterwards taken up bodily to heaven. This is necessary for the theological doctrine of blood sacrifice and vicarious atonement for sins, which is rejected by Islam. But some of the early Christian sects did not believe that Christ was killed on the Cross. The Basilidans believed that some one else was substituted for him. The Docetæ held that Christ never had a real physical or natural body, but only an apparent or phantom body, and that his Crucifixion was only apparent, not real. The Marcionite Gospel (about A.D. 138) denied that Jesus was born, and merely said that he appeared in human form. The Gospel of St. Barnabas supported the theory of substitution on the Cross. The Quranic teaching is that Christ was not crucified nor killed by the Jews, notwithstanding certain apparent circumstances which produced that illusion in the minds of some of his enemies ; that disputations, doubts, and conjectures on such matters are vain ; and that he was taken up to God (see next verse and note).

664. There is difference of opinion as to the exact interpretation of this verse. The words are : The Jews did not kill Jesus, but God raised him up (*rafa'a*) to Himself. One school holds that Jesus did not die the usual human death, but still lives in the body in heaven ; another holds that he did die (v. 120) but not when he was supposed to be crucified, and that his being " raised up " unto God means that instead of being disgraced as a malefactor, as the Jews intended, he was on the contrary honoured by God as His Apostle : see also next verse. The same word *rafa'a* is used in association with honour in connection with Muṣṭafā in xciv. 4.

But must believe in him
Before his death;[665]
And on the Day of Judgment
He will be a witness[666]
Against them;—

إِلَّا لَيُؤْمِنَنَّ بِهِ قَبْلَ مَوْتِهِ ۚ
وَيَوْمَ الْقِيٰمَةِ
يَكُونُ عَلَيْهِمْ شَهِيدًا ۝

160. For the iniquity of the Jews
We made unlawful for them[667]
Certain (foods) good and wholesome
Which had been lawful for them;—
In that they hindered many
From God's Way;—

١٦٠- فَبِظُلْمٍ مِّنَ الَّذِينَ هَادُوا
حَرَّمْنَا عَلَيْهِمْ طَيِّبٰتٍ
أُحِلَّتْ لَهُمْ
وَبِصَدِّهِمْ عَنْ سَبِيلِ اللّٰهِ كَثِيرًا ۝

161. That they took usury,
Though they were forbidden;
And that they devoured
Men's substance wrongfully;—
We have prepared for those
Among them who reject Faith
A grievous punishment.

١٦١- وَّأَخْذِهِمُ الرِّبٰوا وَقَدْ نُهُوا عَنْهُ
وَأَكْلِهِمْ أَمْوَالَ النَّاسِ بِالْبٰطِلِ ۚ
وَأَعْتَدْنَا لِلْكٰفِرِينَ مِنْهُمْ
عَذَابًا أَلِيمًا ۝

162. But those among them
Who are well-grounded in knowledge,
And the Believers,
Believe in what hath been
Revealed to thee and what was
Revealed before thee:
And (especially) those
Who establish regular prayer
And practise regular charity
And believe in God
And in the Last Day:
To them shall We soon
Give a great reward.

١٦٢- لٰكِنِ الرّٰسِخُونَ فِي الْعِلْمِ مِنْهُمْ
وَالْمُؤْمِنُونَ يُؤْمِنُونَ بِمَا أُنْزِلَ إِلَيْكَ
وَمَا أُنْزِلَ مِنْ قَبْلِكَ
وَالْمُقِيمِينَ الصَّلٰوةَ
وَالْمُؤْتُونَ الزَّكٰوةَ
وَالْمُؤْمِنُونَ بِاللّٰهِ وَالْيَوْمِ الْآخِرِ ۗ
أُولٰئِكَ سَنُؤْتِيهِمْ أَجْرًا عَظِيمًا ۝

665. *Before his death.* Interpreters are not agreed as to the exact meaning. Those who hold that Jesus did not die (see last note) refer the pronoun "his" to Jesus. They say that Jesus is still living in the body and that he will appear just before the Final Day in preparation for the coming of Imām Mahdī, when the world will be purified of sin and unbelief. There will be a final death before the final Resurrection, but all will have believed before that final death. Others think that "his" is better referred to "none of the People of the Book", and that the emphatic form "must believe" (***lā-yū-minanna***) denotes more a question of duty than of fact.

666. *Cf.* iv. 41.

667. *Cf.* vi. 146. The ceremonial law of the Jews forbade the eating of the flesh of the camel, rabbit and hare (Leviticus xi. 4-6), and the fat of oxen, sheep, and goats (Leviticus vii. 23), and was in other respects very strict.

Section 23.

163. We have sent thee
Inspiration, as We sent it
To Noah and the Messengers[668]
After him: We sent
Inspiration to Abraham,[669]
Ismā'īl, Isaac, Jacob
And the Tribes, to Jesus,
Job, Jonah, Aaron, and Solomon,
And to David We gave
The Psalms.

١٦٣- إِنَّآ أَوْحَيْنَآ إِلَيْكَ
كَمَآ أَوْحَيْنَآ إِلَىٰ نُوحٍ وَّالنَّبِيّٖنَ مِنۢ بَعْدِهٖ ۚ
وَأَوْحَيْنَآ إِلَىٰٓ إِبْرٰهِيمَ وَإِسْمٰعِيلَ وَإِسْحٰقَ
وَيَعْقُوبَ وَالْأَسْبَاطِ وَعِيسٰى وَأَيُّوبَ وَ
يُونُسَ وَهٰرُونَ وَسُلَيْمٰنَ ۚ وَءَاتَيْنَا دَاوُدَ زَبُورًا ۝

164. Of some apostles We have
Already told thee the story;
Of others we have not;—
And to Moses God spoke
direct;—[670]

١٦٤- وَرُسُلًا قَدْ قَصَصْنٰهُمْ عَلَيْكَ مِن
قَبْلُ وَرُسُلًا لَّمْ نَقْصُصْهُمْ عَلَيْكَ ۚ
وَكَلَّمَ اللّٰهُ مُوسٰى تَكْلِيمًا ۝

165. Apostles who gave good news[671]
As well as warning,
That mankind, after (the coming)
Of the apostles, should have
No plea against God:
For God is Exalted in Power,
Wise.

١٦٥- رُسُلًا مُّبَشِّرِينَ وَمُنذِرِينَ لِئَلَّا
يَكُونَ لِلنَّاسِ عَلَى اللّٰهِ حُجَّةٌۢ
بَعْدَ الرُّسُلِ ۚ وَكَانَ اللّٰهُ عَزِيزًا حَكِيمًا ۝

166. But God beareth witness
That what He hath sent
Unto thee He hath sent
From His (own) knowledge,[672]

١٦٦- لٰكِنِ اللّٰهُ يَشْهَدُ بِمَآ أَنزَلَ إِلَيْكَ
أَنزَلَهُ بِعِلْمِهٖ ۖ وَالْمَلٰٓئِكَةُ يَشْهَدُونَ ۚ

668. First we have a general statement: that inspiration was sent to many Messengers, and the inspiration was of the same kind as that sent to the Apostle Muḥammad, for God's Message is one. Note that what is spoken of here is Inspiration, not necessarily a Book. Every nation or group of people had an apostle: x. 47. Some of these apostles have been mentioned by name in the Qur-ān, and some not: iv. 164.

669. *Cf.* ii. 136 and iii. 84. The list here given is in three groups. (1) The first group, Abraham's family, is the same as in ii. 136 (where see the note) and in iii. 84. (2) Then we have the tragic figures of Jesus, Job and Jonah, whose mission was from a worldly point of view unsuccessful. (3) Then we have Aaron the priest and Solomon the King, both great figures, but each subordinate to another primary figure, *viz.*, Moses (mentioned in the next verse) and David (mentioned at the end of this verse), David's distinction was the Psalms, which are still extant. Though their present form may possibly be different from the original, and they do undoubtedly include Psalms not written by David, the collection contains much devotional poetry of a high order.

670. God spoke to Moses on Mount Sinai through a cloud: Exod. xxxiv. 5. Hence the title of Moses in Muslim theology: *Kalīm-ullāh*: the one to whom God spoke.

671. Every apostle proclaims God's goodness to the righteous and forgiveness to those who repent, (good news), and the Wrath to come for those who reject Faith and live in iniquity (warning). Their mission of warning is a prelude and complement to their mission of good news. No one can then say that he or she did not know.

672. Inspiration, though it is clothed in human language, and shaped to the personality of the inspired one, proceeds from the knowledge of God, and therefore often contains more meaning than the inspired one himself realises.

And the angels bear witness:
But enough is God for a witness.

وَكَفَىٰ بِاللَّهِ شَهِيدًا ۝

167. Those who reject Faith
And keep off (men)
From the Way of God,
Have verily strayed far,
Far away from the Path.

١٦٧- إِنَّ الَّذِينَ كَفَرُوا وَصَدُّوا عَن سَبِيلِ اللَّهِ
قَدْ ضَلُّوا ضَلَالًا بَعِيدًا ۝

168. Those who reject Faith
And do wrong,—God
Will not forgive them
Nor guide them
To any way—

١٦٨- إِنَّ الَّذِينَ كَفَرُوا وَظَلَمُوا
لَمْ يَكُنِ اللَّهُ لِيَغْفِرَ لَهُمْ
وَلَا لِيَهْدِيَهُمْ طَرِيقًا ۝

169. Except the way of Hell,
To dwell therein for ever.
And this to God is easy.[673]

١٦٩- إِلَّا طَرِيقَ جَهَنَّمَ خَالِدِينَ فِيهَا أَبَدًا
وَكَانَ ذَٰلِكَ عَلَى اللَّهِ يَسِيرًا ۝

170. O mankind! the Apostle
Hath come to you in truth
From God: believe in him:
It is best for you.[674] But if
Ye reject Faith, to God
Belong all things in the heavens
And on earth: and God
Is All-knowing, All-wise.

١٧٠- يَا أَيُّهَا النَّاسُ قَدْ جَاءَكُمُ الرَّسُولُ
بِالْحَقِّ مِن رَّبِّكُمْ فَآمِنُوا خَيْرًا لَّكُمْ وَإِن
تَكْفُرُوا فَإِنَّ لِلَّهِ مَا فِي السَّمَاوَاتِ وَالْأَرْضِ
وَكَانَ اللَّهُ عَلِيمًا حَكِيمًا ۝

171. O People of the Book!
Commit no excesses[675]
In your religion: nor say
Of God aught but the truth.

١٧١- يَا أَهْلَ الْكِتَابِ لَا تَغْلُوا فِي دِينِكُمْ
وَلَا تَقُولُوا عَلَى اللَّهِ إِلَّا الْحَقَّ

---

673. *Easy*—not in the sense that God takes any pleasure in any of His creatures going astray. The contrary is the case: for God's Grace recognises all good in us to such an extent that it is compared to gratitude in iv. 147; see n. 653. We must understand *easy* in the sense that God is Supreme in knowledge and power; if any forces of rebellion foolishly think that they can evade punishment, they are mistaken. Punishment comes as a matter of course. It is not a matter of difficulty or exertion on the part of God.

674. God's solicitude for us is for our own good, not because He gets any advantage from it. For He is independent of all things, and everything declares His glory and praise.

675. Just as a foolish servant may go wrong by excess of zeal for his master, so in religion people's excesses may lead them to blasphemy or a spirit the very opposite of religion. The Jewish excesses in the direction of formalism, racialism, exclusiveness, and rejection of Christ Jesus have been denounced in many places. Here the Christian attitude is condemned, which raises Jesus to an equality with God; in some cases venerates Mary almost to idolatry; attributes a physical son to God; and invents the doctrine of the Trinity, opposed to all reason, which according to the Athanasian Creed, unless a man believes, he is doomed to hell for ever. Let our Muslims also beware lest they fall into excesses either in doctrine or in formalism.

Christ Jesus the son of Mary
Was (no more than)
An apostle of God,
And His Word,
Which He bestowed on Mary,
And a Spirit proceeding
From Him: so believe
In God and His apostles.
Say not "Trinity": desist:[676]
It will be better for you:
For God is One God:
Glory be to Him:
(Far Exalted is He) above
Having a son. To Him
Belong all things in the heavens
And on earth. And enough
Is God as a Disposer of affairs.

إِنَّمَا الْمَسِيحُ عِيسَى ابْنُ مَرْيَمَ
رَسُولُ اللَّهِ وَكَلِمَتُهُ ۚ
أَلْقَاهَا إِلَىٰ مَرْيَمَ وَرُوحٌ مِّنْهُ
فَآمِنُوا بِاللَّهِ وَرُسُلِهِ ۖ وَلَا تَقُولُوا ثَلَاثَةٌ ۚ
انتَهُوا خَيْرًا لَّكُمْ ۚ
إِنَّمَا اللَّهُ إِلَٰهٌ وَاحِدٌ ۚ
سُبْحَانَهُ أَن يَكُونَ لَهُ وَلَدٌ
لَّهُ مَا فِي السَّمَاوَاتِ وَمَا فِي الْأَرْضِ ۗ
وَكَفَىٰ بِاللَّهِ وَكِيلًا ۝

Section 24.

172. Christ disdaineth not
To serve and worship God,[677]
Nor do the angels, those
Nearest (to God):
Those who disdain
His worship and are arrogant,—
He will gather them all
Together unto Himself[678]
To (answer).

١٧٢- لَّن يَسْتَنكِفَ الْمَسِيحُ
أَن يَكُونَ عَبْدًا لِّلَّهِ
وَلَا الْمَلَائِكَةُ الْمُقَرَّبُونَ ۚ
وَمَن يَسْتَنكِفْ عَنْ عِبَادَتِهِ وَيَسْتَكْبِرْ
فَسَيَحْشُرُهُمْ إِلَيْهِ جَمِيعًا ۝

173. But to those who believe
And do deeds of righteousness,
He will give their (due)
Rewards,—and more,
Out of His bounty:
But those who are
Disdainful and arrogant,
He will punish

١٧٣- فَأَمَّا الَّذِينَ آمَنُوا وَعَمِلُوا الصَّالِحَاتِ
فَيُوَفِّيهِمْ أُجُورَهُمْ
وَيَزِيدُهُم مِّن فَضْلِهِ ۖ
وَأَمَّا الَّذِينَ اسْتَنكَفُوا وَاسْتَكْبَرُوا

676. Christ's attributes are mentioned: (1) that he was the son of a woman, Mary, and therefore a man; (2) but an apostle, a man with a mission from God, and therefore entitled to honour; (3) a Word bestowed on Mary, for he was created by God's word "Be" (*kun*), and he was; iii. 59; (4) a spirit proceeding from God, but not God: his life and his mission were more limited than in the case of some other apostles, though we must pay equal honour to him as a man of God. The doctrines of Trinity, equality with God, and sonship, are repudiated as blasphemies. God is independent of all needs and has no need of a son to manage His affairs. The Gospel of John (whoever wrote it) has put in a great deal of Alexandrian and Gnostic mysticism round the doctrine of the Word (Greek, Logos), but it is simply explained here, and our Ṣūfis work on this explanation.

677. Christ often watched and prayed, as a humble worshipper of God; and his agony in the Garden of Gethsemane was full of human dignity, suffering, and self-humiliation (see Matt. xxvi. 36-45).

678. The disdainful and the arrogant are the crew of Satan, who will be gathered together before the Supreme Throne for punishment.

With a grievous penalty;
Nor will they find,
Besides God, any
To protect or help them.

فَيُعَذِّبُهُمْ عَذَابًا أَلِيمًا ۙ وَلَا يَجِدُونَ
لَهُم مِّن دُونِ اللَّهِ وَلِيًّا وَلَا نَصِيرًا ○

174. O mankind! Verily
There hath come to you
A convincing proof
From your Lord:
For We have sent unto you
A light (that is) manifest.[679]

۱۷۴- يَا أَيُّهَا النَّاسُ قَدْ جَاءَكُم بُرْهَانٌ
مِّن رَّبِّكُمْ
وَأَنزَلْنَا إِلَيْكُمْ نُورًا مُّبِينًا ○

175. Then those who believe
In God, and hold fast
To Him,—soon will He
Admit them to Mercy
And Grace from Himself,[680]
And guide them to Himself
By a straight Way.

۱۷۵- فَأَمَّا الَّذِينَ آمَنُوا بِاللَّهِ
وَاعْتَصَمُوا بِهِ
فَسَيُدْخِلُهُمْ فِي رَحْمَةٍ مِّنْهُ وَفَضْلٍ
وَيَهْدِيهِمْ إِلَيْهِ صِرَاطًا مُّسْتَقِيمًا ○

176. They ask thee
For a legal decision.
Say: God directs (thus)
About those who leave
No descendants or ascendants
As heirs. If it is a man[681]
That dies, leaving a sister
But no child, she shall

۱۷۶- يَسْتَفْتُونَكَ ۚ
قُلِ اللَّهُ يُفْتِيكُمْ فِي الْكَلَالَةِ ۚ
إِنِ امْرُؤٌ هَلَكَ لَيْسَ لَهُ وَلَدٌ
وَلَهُ أُخْتٌ فَلَهَا

---

679. The Proof and the Light are the Qur-ān and the Personality, Life, and Teaching of Muḥammad Muṣṭafā.

680. *From Himself*=From His Presence: see iii. 195 and n. 501. The Mercy and Grace are expressed here as specially flowing from Him.

681. This verse supplements the rule of inheritance to the estate of a deceased person who has left as heir neither a descendant nor an ascendant. We shall call such a person *A*, who may be either a male or a female. In iv. 12 (second half), *A*'s case was considered where he had left uterine brothers or sisters. Here *A*'s case is considered where he has left brothers and/or sisters by the father's side, whether the mother was the same or not "Brothers" and "sisters" in this verse must be construed to be such brothers and sisters

For the sake of clearness I have expanded the terse language of the original in the translation. Let me explain it more concretely in this note. *A*, and "brother" and "sister" being strictly defined as above, we proceed to consider how *A*'s inheritance would be divided. If *A* left a widow or widower, the widow's or widower's share would first be calculated as in the first half of iv. 12; if *A* left no spouse, this calculation would not be necessary. Then if *A* left a single "sister," she would have a half share, the remaining half (in so far as it, or a part of it, does not fall to a spouse, if any) going to remoter heirs; if a single "brother," he would have the whole (subject to the spouse's right if there is a spouse); if more than one "brother," they divide the whole (subject to, etc). If *A* left two or more "sisters," they get between them two-thirds, subject to the spouse's right, if any. If *A* left a "brother" and "sister," or "brothers" and "sisters," they divide on the basis that each "brother's" share is twice that of the "sister" (subject to, etc.). In all cases debts, funeral expenses, and legacies (to the amount allowed) have priority as in n. 522.

Have half the inheritance:
If (such a deceased was)
A woman, who left no child,
Her brother takes her inheritance:
If there are two sisters,
They shall have two-thirds
Of the inheritance
(Between them): if there are
Brothers and sisters, (they share),
The male having twice
The share of the female.
Thus doth God make clear
To you (His law), lest
Ye err. And God
Hath knowledge of all things.

نِصۡفُ مَا تَرَكَ ۚ
وَهُوَ يَرِثُهَآ
إِن لَّمۡ يَكُن لَّهَا وَلَدٌ ۚ
فَإِن كَانَتَا ٱثۡنَتَيۡنِ
فَلَهُمَا ٱلثُّلُثَانِ مِمَّا تَرَكَ ۚ وَإِن كَانُوٓاْ إِخۡوَةً
رِّجَالًا وَنِسَآءً فَلِلذَّكَرِ مِثۡلُ حَظِّ ٱلۡأُنثَيَيۡنِ ۗ
يُبَيِّنُ ٱللَّهُ لَكُمۡ أَن تَضِلُّواْ ۗ
وَٱللَّهُ بِكُلِّ شَيۡءٍ عَلِيمٌۢ ۝

INTRODUCTION TO SŪRA V (*Māida*).

This Sūra deals, by way of recapitulation, with the backsliding of the Jews and Christians from their pure religions, to which the coping stone was placed by Islam. It refers particularly to the Christians, and to their solemn Sacrament of the Last Supper, to whose mystic meaning they are declared to have been false.

As a logical corollary to the corruption of the earlier religions of God, the practical precepts of Islam, about food, cleanliness, justice, and fidelity are recapitulated.

The fourth verse contains the memorable declaration: "This day have I perfected your religion for you": which was promulgated in 10 H., during the Apostle's last Pilgrimage to Mecca. Chronologically it was the last verse to be revealed.

Summary.—Beginning with an appeal to fulfil, as sacred, all obligations, human and divine, it points to certain regulations about food, as conducive to a sober and social life, without superstition and without bias or hatred (v. 1-6, and C. 69).

Cleanliness of body, and justice and uprightness of dealing are nearest to Piety (v. 7-12, and C. 70).

If the Jews and the Christians turned back from the Truth and violated their Covenants, they have had their warning (v. 13-29, and C. 71).

The murder of Abel by Cain is the type of the treatment which the just man suffers from the envious. There is punishment from God. The just man must not grieve (v. 30-46, and C. 72).

Muslims must do impartial justice, but must protect their own Brotherhood and their Faith from insult and scorn: they must appreciate piety, humility, and other good points among the Christians (v. 47-89, and C. 73).

They must enjoy with gratitude all that is good and lawful, but guard themselves against excess. Swearing, intoxication, gambling, violation of the Sanctuary, superstitions of all kinds, and false evidence are condemned (v. 90-111, and C. 74).

The miracles of Jesus, and how they were misused by those who bore his name (v. 112-123, and C. 75).

C. 69.—All obligations are sacred, human
(v. 1-6.) Or divine. In the spiritual world
We owe duties to God, which must
Be fulfilled. But whilst we are
In this world of sense, those duties
Are by no means isolated
From what we owe to ourselves
And our fellows in the world
Of men. We must respect the laws
And customs of the Sacred Mosque
And the Sacred Sanctuary.
In food our laws are simple:
All things good and pure are lawful.
We refuse not social intercourse
With men and women,—
People of the Book.

Sūra V.

Maïda, or The Table Spread.

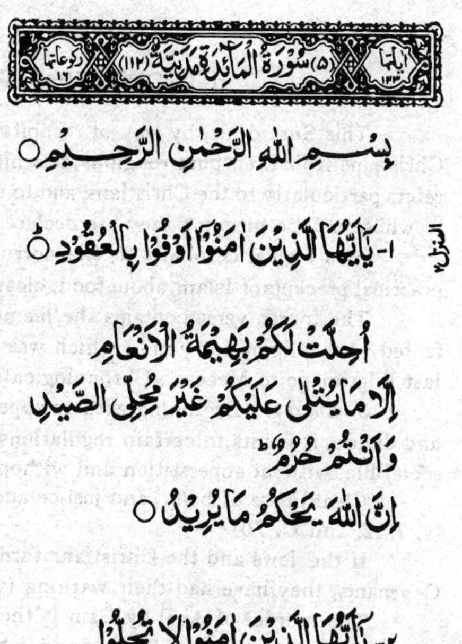

In the name of God, Most Gracious, Most Merciful.

1. O ye who believe!
Fulfil (all) obligations.[682]

Lawful unto you (for food)
Are all four-footed animals,
With the exceptions named:[683]
But animals of the chase
Are forbidden while ye
Are in the Sacred Precincts
Or in pilgrim garb:[684]
For God doth command
According to His Will and Plan.[685]

2. O ye who believe!
Violate not the sanctity

682. This line has been justly admired for its terseness and comprehensiveness. Obligations: *'uqūd*: the Arabic word implies so many things that a whole chapter of Commentary can be written on it. First, there are the divine obligations that arise from our spiritual nature and our relation to God. He created us and implanted in us the faculty of knowledge and foresight; besides the intuition and reason which He gave us, He made Nature responsive to our needs, and His Signs in Nature are so many lessons to us in our own inner life; He further sent Messengers and Teachers, for the guidance of our conduct in individual, social, and public life. All these gifts create corresponding obligations which we must fulfil. But in our own human and material life we undertake mutual obligations, express and implied. We make a promise; we enter into a commercial or social contract; we enter into a contract of marriage: we must faithfully fulfil all obligations in all these relationships. Our group or our State enters into a treaty: every individual in that group or State is bound to see that as far as lies in his power, such obligations are faithfully discharged. There are tacit obligations: living in civil society, we must respect its tacit conventions unless they are morally wrong, and in that case we must get out of such society. There are tacit obligations in the characters of host and guest, wayfarer or companion, employer or employed, etc., etc., which every man of Faith must discharge conscientiously. The man who deserts those who need him and goes to pray in a desert is a coward who disregards his obligations. All these obligations are inter-connected. Truth and fidelity are parts of religion in all relations of life.

This verse is numbered separately from the succeeding verses by Ḥafiẓ 'Uthmān and the Fatḥ-ur-Raḥmān. As it forms a paragraph or chapter by itself, I have followed that numbering throughout this Sūra, thus reluctantly diverging from the numbering in the edition of the *Anjuman-i-Ḥimāyat-i-Islām* throughout this chapter.

683. See v. 4 below.

684. *Cf*. v. 97-99. Hunting and the use of game are forbidden "while ye are *ḥurumun*," *i.e.*, while ye are (1) in the Sacred Precincts, or (2) in the special pilgrim garb (iḥrām), as to which see n. 212, ii. 196. In most cases the two amount to the same thing. The Sacred Precincts are sanctuary both for man and beast.

685. God's commands are not arbitrary. His Will is the perfect Archetype or Plan of the world. Everything He wills has regard to His Plan, in which are reflected His perfect wisdom and goodness.

Of the Symbols of God,[686]
Nor of the Sacred Month,[687]
Nor of the animals brought
For sacrifice, nor the garlands
That mark out such animals,
Nor the people resorting
To the Sacred House,[688]
Seeking of the bounty
And good pleasure
Of their Lord.
But when ye are clear
Of the Sacred Precincts[689]
And of pilgrim garb,
Ye may hunt
And let not the hatred
Of some people
In (once) shutting you out
Of the Sacred Mosque
Lead you to transgression
(And hostility on your part).[690]
Help ye one another
In righteousness and piety,
But help ye not one another
In sin and rancour:
Fear God: for God
Is strict in punishment.

شَعَآئِرَ اللّٰهِ وَلَا الشَّهْرَ الْحَرَامَ
وَلَا الْهَدْيَ وَلَا الْقَلَآئِدَ
وَلَآ آٰمِّيْنَ الْبَيْتَ الْحَرَامَ
يَبْتَغُوْنَ فَضْلًا مِّنْ رَّبِّهِمْ وَرِضْوَانًا ط
وَإِذَا حَلَلْتُمْ فَاصْطَادُوْا ط
وَلَا يَجْرِمَنَّكُمْ شَنَاٰنُ قَوْمٍ
أَنْ صَدُّوْكُمْ
عَنِ الْمَسْجِدِ الْحَرَامِ
أَنْ تَعْتَدُوْا م
وَتَعَاوَنُوْا عَلَى الْبِرِّ وَالتَّقْوٰى ص
وَلَا تَعَاوَنُوْا عَلَى الْإِثْمِ وَالْعُدْوَانِ ص
وَاتَّقُوا اللّٰهَ ط
إِنَّ اللّٰهَ شَدِيْدُ الْعِقَابِ ○

3. Forbidden to you (for food)
Are: dead meat, blood,

٣- حُرِّمَتْ عَلَيْكُمُ الْمَيْتَةُ وَالدَّمُ

686. *Cf.* ii 158, where Ṣafā and Marwa are called "Symbols (*sha'āir*) of God". Here the Symbols are everything connected with the Pilgrimage, *viz.*, (1) the places (like Safā and Marwa, or the Ka'ba or 'Arafāt, etc.); (2) the rites and ceremonies prescribed; (3) prohibitions (such as that of hunting, etc.); (4) the times and seasons prescribed. There is spiritual and moral symbolism in all these. See notes on ii. 158, ii. 194-200.

687. The month of pilgrimage, or else, collectively, the four sacred months (ix. 36), *viz.*, Rajab (7th), Ẕul-qa'd (11th), Ẕul-hajj (12th, the month of Pilgrimage), and Muḥarram (the first of the year). In all these months War was prohibited. Excepting Rajab the other three months are consecutive.

688. The immunity from attack or interference extended to the animals brought as offerings for sacrifice and the garlands or fillets or distinguishing marks which gave them immunity. They were treated as sacred symbols. And of course every protection or immunity was enjoyed by the Pilgrims.

689. This is the state opposite to that described in n. 684, *i.e.*, when ye have left the Sacred Precincts, and have doffed the special pilgrim garb, showing your return to ordinary life.

690. See n. 205 to ii. 191. In the sixth year of the Hijra the Pagans, by way of hatred and persecution of the Muslims, had prevented them from access to the Sacred Mosque. When the Muslims were re-established in Mecca, some of them wanted to retaliate and exclude the Pagans or in some way to interfere with them in the Pilgrimage. This is condemned. Passing from the immediate event to the general principle, we must not retaliate or return evil for evil. The hatred of the wicked does not justify hostility on our part. We have to help each other in righteousness and piety, not in perpetuating feuds of hatred and enmity. We may have to fight and put down evil, but never in a spirit of malice or hatred, but always in a spirit of justice and righteousness.

The flesh of swine, and that
On which hath been invoked
The name of other than God;[691]
That which hath been
Killed by strangling,
Or by a violent blow,
Or by a headlong fall,
Or by being gored to death;
That which hath been (partly)
Eaten by a wild animal;
Unless ye are able
To slaughter it (in due form);[692]
That which is sacrificed[693]
On stone (altars);
(Forbidden) also is the division[694]
(Of meat) by raffling
With arrows: that is impiety.

This day have those who
Reject Faith given up
All hope of your religion:[695]
Yet fear them not
But fear Me.
This day have I
Perfected your religion[696]
For you, completed
My favour upon you,
And have chosen for you
Islam as your religion.

But if any is forced
By hunger, with no inclination
To transgression, God is
Indeed Oft-forgiving,
Most Merciful.

وَلَحْمُ الْخِنْزِيرِ وَمَآ أُهِلَّ لِغَيْرِ اللّٰهِ بِهٖ
وَالْمُنْخَنِقَةُ
وَالْمَوْقُوذَةُ
وَالْمُتَرَدِّيَةُ
وَالنَّطِيحَةُ
وَمَآ أَكَلَ السَّبُعُ إِلَّا مَا ذَكَّيْتُمْ ۖ
وَمَا ذُبِحَ عَلَى النُّصُبِ
وَأَنْ تَسْتَقْسِمُوا بِالْأَزْلَامِ ۚ
ذٰلِكُمْ فِسْقٌ ۗ
الْيَوْمَ يَئِسَ الَّذِينَ كَفَرُوا مِنْ دِينِكُمْ
فَلَا تَخْشَوْهُمْ وَاخْشَوْنِ ۚ
الْيَوْمَ أَكْمَلْتُ لَكُمْ دِينَكُمْ
وَأَتْمَمْتُ عَلَيْكُمْ نِعْمَتِي
وَرَضِيتُ لَكُمُ الْإِسْلَامَ دِينًا ۚ
فَمَنِ اضْطُرَّ فِي مَخْمَصَةٍ غَيْرَ مُتَجَانِفٍ
لِإِثْمٍ ۙ
فَإِنَّ اللّٰهَ غَفُورٌ رَحِيمٌ ○

691. *Cf.* ii. 173 and nn. 173 and 174. The prohibition of dead meat, blood, the flesh of swine, and that on which other names than that of God has been invoked, has been there explained.

692. If an animal dies by strangling, or by a violent blow, or a headlong fall, or by being gored to death, or by being attacked by a wild animal, the presumption is that it becomes carrion, as the life-blood is congealed before being taken out of the body. But the presumption can be rebutted. If the life-blood still flows and the solemn mode of slaughter (*ẓabḥ*) in the name of God as a sacrifice is carried out, it becomes lawful as food.

693. This was also an idolatrous rite, different from that in which a sacrifice was devoted to a particular idol or a false god.

694. Gambling of all kinds is forbidden: ii. 291. A sort of lottery or raffle practised by Pagan Arabs has been described in n. 241. Division of meat in this way is here forbidden, as it is a form of gambling.

695. So long as Islam was not organised, with its own community and its own laws, the Unbelievers had hoped to wean the Believers from the new Teaching. Now that hope was gone, with the complete organisation of Islam.

696. The last verse revealed chronologically, marking the approaching end of Muṣṭafā's ministry in his earthly life.

4. They ask thee what is
Lawful to them (as food).[697]
Say: Lawful unto you
Are (all) things good and pure:
And what ye have taught
Your trained hunting animals
(To catch) in the manner
Directed to you by God:
Eat what they catch for you,[698]
But pronounce the name
Of God over it: and fear
God; for God is swift
In taking account.

٤- يَسْـَٔلُونَكَ مَاذَآ أُحِلَّ لَهُمْ ۖ
قُلْ أُحِلَّ لَكُمُ ٱلطَّيِّبَٰتُ ۙ
وَمَا عَلَّمْتُم مِّنَ ٱلْجَوَارِحِ مُكَلِّبِينَ
تُعَلِّمُونَهُنَّ مِمَّا عَلَّمَكُمُ ٱللَّهُ
فَكُلُوا۟ مِمَّآ أَمْسَكْنَ عَلَيْكُمْ
وَٱذْكُرُوا۟ ٱسْمَ ٱللَّهِ عَلَيْهِ ۖ وَٱتَّقُوا۟ ٱللَّهَ ۚ
إِنَّ ٱللَّهَ سَرِيعُ ٱلْحِسَابِ ۝

5. This day are (all) things
Good and pure made lawful
Unto you. The food
Of the People of the Book[699]
Is lawful unto you
And yours is lawful
Unto them.
(Lawful unto you in marriage)
Are (not only) chaste women
Who are believers, but
Chaste women among
The People of the Book,[700]

٥- ٱلْيَوْمَ أُحِلَّ لَكُمُ ٱلطَّيِّبَٰتُ ۖ
وَطَعَامُ ٱلَّذِينَ أُوتُوا۟ ٱلْكِتَٰبَ حِلٌّ
لَّكُمْ ۖ
وَطَعَامُكُمْ حِلٌّ لَّهُمْ ۖ
وَٱلْمُحْصَنَٰتُ مِنَ ٱلْمُؤْمِنَٰتِ
وَٱلْمُحْصَنَٰتُ مِنَ ٱلَّذِينَ أُوتُوا۟ ٱلْكِتَٰبَ

697. The previous verse was negative; it defined what was not lawful for food, *viz.*, things gross, or disgusting, or dedicated to superstition. This verse is positive: it defines what *is* lawful, *viz.*, all things that are good and pure.

698. In the matter of the killing for meat, the general rule is that the name of the true God should be pronounced as a rite in order to call our attention to the fact that we do not take life thoughtlessly but solemnly for food, with the permission of God, to whom we render the life back. The question of hunting is then raised. How can this solemn rite be performed when we send forth trained hawks, trained hounds, or trained cheetahs or other animals trained for the chase? They must necessarily kill at some distance from their masters. Their game is legalised on these conditions: (1) that they are trained to kill, not merely for their own appetite, or out of mere wantonness, but for their master's food; the training implies that something of the solemnity which God has taught us in this matter goes into their action; and (2) we are to pronounce the name of God over the quarry; this is interpreted to mean that the *Takbīr* should be pronounced when the hawk or dog, etc., is released to the quarry.

699. The question is for food generally, such as is ordinarily "good and pure": in the matter of meat it should be killed with some sort of solemnity analogous to that of the *Takbīr*. The rules of Islam in this respect being analogous to those of the People of the Book, there is no objection to mutual recognition, as opposed to meat killed by Pagans with superstitious rites. In this respect the Christian rule is the same: "That ye abstain from meats offered to idols, and from blood, and from things strangled, and from fornication." (Acts, xv. 29.). Notice the bracketing of fornication with things unlawful to eat.

700. Islam is not exclusive. Social intercourse, including inter-marriage, is permitted with the People of the Book. A Muslim man may marry a woman from their ranks on the same terms as he would marry a Muslim woman, *i.e.*, he must give her an economic and moral status, and must not be actuated merely by motives of lust or physical desire. A Muslim woman may not marry a non-Muslim man, because her Muslim status would be affected: the wife ordinarily takes the nationality and status given by her husband's law. A non-Muslim woman marrying a Muslim husband would be expected eventually to accept Islam. Any man or woman, of any race or faith, may, on accepting Islam, freely marry any Muslim woman or man, provided it be from motives of purity and chastity and not of lewdness.

Revealed before your time,—
When ye give them
Their due dowers, and desire
Chastity, not lewdness,
Nor secret intrigues.
If any one rejects faith,[701]
Fruitless is his work,
And in the Hereafter
He will be in the ranks
Of those who have lost
(All spiritual good).

مِنْ قَبْلِكُمْ إِذَآ ءَاتَيْتُمُوهُنَّ
أُجُورَهُنَّ مُحْصِنِينَ
غَيْرَ مُسَٰفِحِينَ وَلَا مُتَّخِذِىٓ أَخْدَانٍ
وَمَن يَكْفُرْ بِٱلْإِيمَٰنِ فَقَدْ حَبِطَ عَمَلُهُۥ
وَهُوَ فِى ٱلْءَاخِرَةِ مِنَ ٱلْخَٰسِرِينَ ۝

C. 70.—God wishes us to be clean and pure,
(v. 7-12.) At prayer and at other times.
But justice and right conduct,
Even in the face of spite and hatred,
Are nearest to Piety and the love
Of God: in Him we put our trust.

SECTION 2.

6. O ye who believe!
When ye prepare
For prayer, wash[702]
Your faces, and your hands
(And arms) to the elbows;
Rub your heads (with water);
And (wash) your feet
To the ankles.
If ye are in a state
Of ceremonial impurity,[703]
Bathe your whole body.
But if ye are ill,
Or on a journey,
Or one of you cometh
From offices of nature,
Or ye have been
In contact with women,
And ye find no water,
Then take for yourselves
Clean sand or earth,[704]

٦- يَٰٓأَيُّهَا ٱلَّذِينَ ءَامَنُوٓا۟ إِذَا قُمْتُمْ إِلَى ٱلصَّلَوٰةِ
فَٱغْسِلُوا۟ وُجُوهَكُمْ وَأَيْدِيَكُمْ
إِلَى ٱلْمَرَافِقِ
وَٱمْسَحُوا۟ بِرُءُوسِكُمْ وَأَرْجُلَكُمْ إِلَى ٱلْكَعْبَيْنِ
وَإِن كُنتُمْ جُنُبًا فَٱطَّهَّرُوا۟
وَإِن كُنتُم مَّرْضَىٰٓ
أَوْ عَلَىٰ سَفَرٍ
أَوْ جَآءَ أَحَدٌ مِّنكُم مِّنَ ٱلْغَآئِطِ
أَوْ لَٰمَسْتُمُ ٱلنِّسَآءَ فَلَمْ تَجِدُوا۟ مَآءً
فَتَيَمَّمُوا۟ صَعِيدًا طَيِّبًا

701. As always, food, cleanliness, social intercourse, marriage and other interests in life, are linked with our duty to God and faith in Him. Duty and faith are for our own benefit, here and in the Hereafter

702. These are the essentials of Wuḍhū, or ablutions preparatory to prayers, *viz.* (1) to bathe the whole face in water, and (2) both hands and arms to the elbows, with (3) a little rubbing of the head with water (as the head is usually protected and comparatively clean), and (4) the bathing of the feet to the ankles. In addition, following the practice of the Apostle, it is usual first to wash the mouth, the throat, and the nose, before proceeding with the face, etc.

703. *Cf.* iv. 43 and n. 563. Ceremonial impurity arises from sex pollution.

704. This is *Tayammum*, or washing with clean sand or earth where water is not available. I take it that this substitute is permissible both for Wuḍhū and for a full bath, in the circumstances mentioned.

And rub therewith
Your faces and hands.
God doth not wish
To place you in a difficulty,
But to make you clean,
And to complete
His favour to you,
That ye may be grateful.

فَامْسَحُوا بِوُجُوهِكُمْ وَأَيْدِيكُمْ مِّنْهُ ۚ
مَا يُرِيدُ اللَّهُ لِيَجْعَلَ عَلَيْكُم مِّنْ حَرَجٍ
وَلَٰكِن يُرِيدُ لِيُطَهِّرَكُمْ
وَلِيُتِمَّ نِعْمَتَهُ عَلَيْكُمْ لَعَلَّكُمْ تَشْكُرُونَ ○

7. And call in remembrance
The favour of God
Unto you, and His Covenant,[705]
Which He ratified
With you, when ye said:
"We hear and we obey":
And fear God, for God
Knoweth well
The secrets of your hearts.

٧- وَاذْكُرُوا نِعْمَةَ اللَّهِ عَلَيْكُمْ
وَمِيثَاقَهُ الَّذِي وَاثَقَكُم بِهِ
إِذْ قُلْتُمْ سَمِعْنَا وَأَطَعْنَا
وَاتَّقُوا اللَّهَ ۚ
إِنَّ اللَّهَ عَلِيمٌ بِذَاتِ الصُّدُورِ ○

8. O ye who believe!
Stand out firmly
For God, as witnesses[706]
To fair dealing, and let not
The hatred of others
To you make you swerve[707]
To wrong and depart from
Justice. Be just: that is
Next to Piety: and fear God.
For God is well-acquainted
With all that ye do.

٨- يَا أَيُّهَا الَّذِينَ آمَنُوا كُونُوا قَوَّامِينَ
لِلَّهِ شُهَدَاءَ بِالْقِسْطِ ۖ
وَلَا يَجْرِمَنَّكُمْ شَنَآنُ قَوْمٍ عَلَىٰ أَلَّا
تَعْدِلُوا ۚ اعْدِلُوا هُوَ أَقْرَبُ لِلتَّقْوَىٰ ۖ
وَاتَّقُوا اللَّهَ ۚ
إِنَّ اللَّهَ خَبِيرٌ بِمَا تَعْمَلُونَ ○

9. To those who believe
And do deeds of righteousness
Hath God promised forgiveness
And a great reward.

٩- وَعَدَ اللَّهُ الَّذِينَ آمَنُوا وَعَمِلُوا الصَّالِحَاتِ ۙ
لَهُم مَّغْفِرَةٌ وَأَجْرٌ عَظِيمٌ ○

---

705. There is a particular and a general meaning. The particular meaning refers to the solemn Pledge and Covenant taken by two groups of people at 'Aqaba, a valley near Minā, the first about fourteen months before the Hijra, and the second a little later. These were Pledges of fealty to the Apostle of God, comparable to the Covenant under Mount Sinai taken in the time of Moses (See Q. ii. 63 and n 78.) The general meaning has been explained in n. 682 to v. 1: man is under a spiritual obligation under an implied Covenant with God: God has given man reason, judgment, the higher faculties of the soul, and even the position of God's vicegerent on earth (ii. 30), and man is bound to serve God faithfully and obey His Will. That obedience begins with cleanliness in bodily functions, food, etc. It goes on to cleanliness of mind and thought, and culminates in purity of motives in the inmost recesses of his heart and soul.

706. *Cf.* iv. 135.

707. To do justice and act righteously in a favourable or neutral atmosphere is meritorious enough, but the real test comes when you have to do justice to people who hate you or to whom you have an aversion. But no less is required of you by the higher moral law.

10. Those who reject faith
And deny Our Signs
Will be Companions
Of Hell-fire.

١١- وَالَّذِينَ كَفَرُوا وَكَذَّبُوا بِآيَاتِنَا
أُولَٰئِكَ أَصْحَابُ الْجَحِيمِ ۝

11. O ye who believe!
Call in remembrance
The favour of God
Unto you when
Certain men formed the design
To stretch out
Their hands against you,
But (God) held back
Their hands from you:[708]
So fear God. And on God
Let Believers put
(All) their trust.

١١- يَا أَيُّهَا الَّذِينَ آمَنُوا اذْكُرُوا
نِعْمَتَ اللَّهِ عَلَيْكُمْ
إِذْ هَمَّ قَوْمٌ أَنْ يَبْسُطُوا إِلَيْكُمْ
أَيْدِيَهُمْ فَكَفَّ أَيْدِيَهُمْ عَنْكُمْ ۖ
وَاتَّقُوا اللَّهَ ۚ
وَعَلَى اللَّهِ فَلْيَتَوَكَّلِ الْمُؤْمِنُونَ ۝

C. 71.—If the men who received revelations
(v. 13-29.) Before were false to their trust,
If they broke their agreements
And twisted God's Message from its aim,
If they rebelled against Truth and followed
Their fancies, God's grace was withdrawn
From them and they wandered in the wilderness.

Section 3.

12. God did aforetime
Take a Covenant from
The Children of Israel,[709]
And We appointed twelve
Captains among them.
And God said: "I am
With you: if ye (but)
Establish regular Prayers,

١٢- وَلَقَدْ أَخَذَ اللَّهُ مِيثَاقَ بَنِي إِسْرَائِيلَ
وَبَعَثْنَا مِنْهُمُ اثْنَيْ عَشَرَ نَقِيبًا ۖ
وَقَالَ اللَّهُ إِنِّي مَعَكُمْ ۖ
لَئِنْ أَقَمْتُمُ الصَّلَاةَ

708. In the life-time of the Apostle it happened again and again that the enemies of Islam stretched out their hands against the Apostle, his people, and his teaching. The odds were, from a worldly point of view, in their favour, but their hands were rendered inert and powerless because they were fighting against the truth of God. So does it happen always, now as it did then. True faith must take heart, and at the same time humbly recognise God's favour and mercy, and be grateful.

709. *Cf.* ii. 63 and n. 78. "Moses...called for the elders of the people....and all the people answered together and said, 'All that the Lord hath spoken we will do'." (Exod. xix. 7-8.) This was under the towering height of Mount Sinai.

The captains or elders or leaders of the people were selected, one from each of the twelve tribes (see ii. 60 and n. 73). For census purposes the names of the elders of the tribes are given in Num. i. 4-16: they are called "every one the head of the house of his fathers". Later, twelve other "heads of the Children of Israel" were selected to spy out the land of Canaan: their names are mentioned in Num. xiii. 1-16. See also, below, v. 22-29 and notes.

Practise regular Charity,
Believe in My apostles,
Honour and assist them,
And loan to God
A beautiful loan,[710]
Verily I will wipe out
From you your evils,
And admit you to Gardens
With rivers flowing beneath;
But if any of you, after this,
Resisteth faith, he hath truly
Wandered from the path
Of rectitude."[711]

13. But because of their breach
Of their Covenant, We
Cursed them,[712] and made
Their hearts grow hard:
They change the words
From their (right) places
And forget a good part
Of the Message that was
Sent them, nor wilt thou
Cease to find them—
Barring a few—ever
Bent on (new) deceits:[713]
But forgive them, and overlook[714]
(Their misdeeds): for God
Loveth those who are kind.

14. From those, too, who call
Themselves Christians,

وَاٰتَيْتُمُ الزَّكٰوةَ وَاٰمَنْتُمْ بِرُسُلِيْ
وَعَزَّرْتُمُوْهُمْ وَاَقْرَضْتُمُ اللّٰهَ قَرْضًا حَسَنًا
لَّاُكَفِّرَنَّ عَنْكُمْ سَيِّاٰتِكُمْ
وَلَاُدْخِلَنَّكُمْ جَنّٰتٍ تَجْرِيْ
مِنْ تَحْتِهَا الْاَنْهٰرُ ۚ
فَمَنْ كَفَرَ بَعْدَ ذٰلِكَ مِنْكُمْ
فَقَدْ ضَلَّ سَوَآءَ السَّبِيْلِ ○
١٣- فَبِمَا نَقْضِهِمْ مِّيْثَاقَهُمْ لَعَنّٰهُمْ
وَجَعَلْنَا قُلُوْبَهُمْ قٰسِيَةً ۚ
يُحَرِّفُوْنَ الْكَلِمَ عَنْ مَّوَاضِعِهٖ ۙ
وَنَسُوْا حَظًّا مِّمَّا ذُكِّرُوْا بِهٖ ۚ
وَلَا تَزَالُ تَطَّلِعُ عَلٰى خَآئِنَةٍ مِّنْهُمْ
اِلَّا قَلِيْلًا مِّنْهُمْ
فَاعْفُ عَنْهُمْ وَاصْفَحْ ۭ
اِنَّ اللّٰهَ يُحِبُّ الْمُحْسِنِيْنَ ○
١٤- وَمِنَ الَّذِيْنَ قَالُوْٓا اِنَّا نَصٰرٰٓى

710. *Cf.* ii. 245, n. 276. The phrase means "spending in the cause of God." God in His infinite grace looks upon this as a loan, for which He gives a recompense manifold.

711. *The path of rectitude*: or the even way: see ii. 108, n. 109.

712. *Cursed them*: that means that because of the breach of their Covenant. God withdrew His overflowing Grace from them. The withdrawal of Grace made their hearts grow hard in two ways: (1) they were no longer protected from the assaults of evil, and (2) they became impervious even to the message of forgiveness and mercy which is open to all God's creatures.

713. Israel, when it lost God's grace as above, began to sin against truth and religion in three ways: (1) they began to misuse Scripture itself, by either taking words out of their right meaning, or applying them to things for which they were never meant; (2) in doing so, they conveniently forgot a part of the Message and purpose of God; and (3) they invented new deceits to support the old ones.

714. *Cf.* ii. 109 and n. 110, where I have explained the different shades of meaning in the words for "forgiveness."

We did take a Covenant,[715]
But they forgot a good part
Of the Message that was
Sent them: so We estranged
Them, with enmity and hatred
Between the one and the other,
To the Day of Judgment.
And soon will God[715A] show
Them what it is
They have done.

أَخَذْنَا مِيثَاقَهُمْ
فَنَسُوا حَظًّا مِّمَّا ذُكِّرُوا بِهِ
فَأَغْرَيْنَا بَيْنَهُمُ الْعَدَاوَةَ وَالْبَغْضَاءَ
إِلَىٰ يَوْمِ الْقِيٰمَةِ
وَسَوْفَ يُنَبِّئُهُمُ اللّٰهُ بِمَا كَانُوا يَصْنَعُونَ ۝

15. O People of the Book!
There hath come to you
Our Apostle, revealing
To you much that ye
Used to hide in the Book,
And passing over much
(That is now unnecessary):

١٥- يٰأَهْلَ الْكِتٰبِ قَدْ جَاءَكُمْ رَسُولُنَا
يُبَيِّنُ لَكُمْ كَثِيرًا مِّمَّا كُنتُمْ تُخْفُونَ مِنَ
الْكِتٰبِ
وَيَعْفُوا عَن كَثِيرٍ ۝

There hath come to you
From God a (new) light
And a perspicuous Book,—[716]

قَدْ جَاءَكُم مِّنَ اللّٰهِ نُورٌ
وَكِتٰبٌ مُّبِينٌ ۝

16. Wherewith God guideth all
Who seek His good pleasure
To ways of peace and safety,
And leadeth them out
Of darkness, by His Will,
Unto the light,—guideth them
To a Path that is Straight.

١٦- يَهْدِي بِهِ اللّٰهُ مَنِ اتَّبَعَ رِضْوَانَهُ سُبُلَ
السَّلٰمِ
وَيُخْرِجُهُم مِّنَ الظُّلُمٰتِ إِلَى النُّورِ بِإِذْنِهِ
وَيَهْدِيهِمْ إِلَىٰ صِرٰطٍ مُّسْتَقِيمٍ ۝

17. In blasphemy indeed
Are those that say
That God is Christ
The son of Mary.
Say: "Who then
Hath the least power

١٧- لَقَدْ كَفَرَ الَّذِينَ
قَالُوا إِنَّ اللّٰهَ هُوَ الْمَسِيحُ ابْنُ مَرْيَمَ
قُلْ فَمَن يَمْلِكُ

715. The Christian Covenant may be taken to be the charge which Jesus gave to his disciples, and which the disciples accepted, to welcome Aḥmad (Q. lxi. 6). Glimpses of this are to be found in the Gospel of St. John even as it exists now (John xv. 26, xvi. 7). It is those who call themselves "Christians" who reject this. True Christians have accepted it. The enmity between those who call themselves Christians and the Jews will continue till the Last Day.

715-A. The change from the First Person in the beginning of the verse to the Third Person here illustrates the change from the personal relationship of the Covenant, to the impersonal operation of Justice at Judgment. *Cf.* xxxv. 9.

716. *Mubīn*: I wish I could translate by a simpler word than "perspicuous". But "plain" may mean unadorned, the opposite of beautiful, and this Book is among the most beautiful that it is the privilege of mankind to read. "Clear" would be right as far as it means "unambiguous, self-evident, not involved in mysteries of origin, history, or meaning, one which every one can understand as to the essentials necessary for him, without the intervention of priests or privileged persons". *Mubīn* has all these meanings, but it suggests, besides, some quality of a shining light, by which we are able to *make* things clear, to distinguish the true from the false. This I think is suggested better by "perspicuous" than by the word "clear". Besides it is hardly good idiom to speak of "a clear Book".

Against God, if His Will
Were to destroy Christ
The son of Mary, his mother,
And all—every one
That is on the earth?
For to God belongeth
The dominion of the heavens
And the earth, and all
That is between. He createth[717]
What He pleaseth. For God
Hath power over all things."

مِنَ اللّٰهِ شَيْـًٔا اِنْ اَرَادَ اَنْ يُّهْلِكَ الْمَسِيْحَ
ابْنَ مَرْيَمَ وَاُمَّهٗ
وَمَنْ فِي الْاَرْضِ جَمِيْعًا ؕ
وَلِلّٰهِ مُلْكُ السَّمٰوٰتِ وَالْاَرْضِ
وَمَا بَيْنَهُمَا ؕ يَخْلُقُ مَا يَشَآءُ ؕ
وَاللّٰهُ عَلٰى كُلِّ شَيْءٍ قَدِيْرٌ ۝

18. (Both) the Jews and the Christians
Say: "We are sons
Of God, and His beloved."[718]
Say: "Why then doth He
Punish you for your sins?
Nay, ye are but men,—
Of the men He hath created:
He forgiveth whom He pleaseth,
And He punisheth whom He pleaseth:
And to God belongeth[719]
The dominion of the heavens
And the earth, and all
That is between:
And unto Him
Is the final goal (of all)"

١٨- وَقَالَتِ الْيَهُوْدُ وَالنَّصٰرٰى
نَحْنُ اَبْنٰٓؤُا اللّٰهِ وَاَحِبَّآؤُهٗ ؕ
قُلْ فَلِمَ يُعَذِّبُكُمْ بِذُنُوْبِكُمْ ؕ
بَلْ اَنْتُمْ بَشَرٌ مِّمَّنْ خَلَقَ ؕ
يَغْفِرُ لِمَنْ يَّشَآءُ
وَيُعَذِّبُ مَنْ يَّشَآءُ ؕ
وَلِلّٰهِ مُلْكُ السَّمٰوٰتِ وَالْاَرْضِ
وَمَا بَيْنَهُمَا ؕ
وَاِلَيْهِ الْمَصِيْرُ ۝

19. O People of the Book!
Now hath come unto you,
Making (things) clear unto you,
Our Apostle, after the break[720]

١٩- يٰٓاَهْلَ الْكِتٰبِ قَدْ جَآءَكُمْ رَسُوْلُنَا
يُبَيِّنُ لَكُمْ عَلٰى فَتْرَةٍ مِّنَ الرُّسُلِ

---

717. The most honoured of the apostles of God are but men. All power belongs to God, and not to any man. God's creation may take many forms, but because in any particular form it is different from what we see daily around us, it does not cease to be Creation, or to be subject to the power of God. No creature can be God.

718. *Sons of God*: *Cf.* Job, xxxviii. 7: "When the morning stars sang together, and all the sons of God shouted for joy." In the 29th Psalm, 1st verse, the authorised Translation "O ye mighty" should apparently be "O ye sons of Elim", El being a name of God. *Cf.* also Genesis, vi. 2: "The sons of God saw the daughters of men."

Beloved: *Cf.* Psalms, cxxvii. 2: "He giveth his beloved sleep."

If used figuratively, these and like words refer to the love of God. Unfortunately, "son" used in a physical sense, or "beloved" in an exclusive sense as if God loved only the Jews, make a mockery of religion.

719. This refrain in the last verse negatives the idea of sonship, and in this verse negatives the idea of an exclusive "Beloved". In both cases it means that God is independent of physical relationships or exclusive partiality.

720. The six hundred years (in round figures) between Christ and Muḥammad were truly the dark ages of the world. Religion was corrupted; the standard of morals fell low; many false systems and heresies arose; and there was a break in the succession of apostles until the advent of Muḥammad.

In (the series of) our apostles,
Lest ye should say:
"There came unto us
No bringer of glad tidings
And no warner (from evil)":
But now hath come
Unto you a bringer
Of glad tidings
And a warner (from evil).
And God hath power
Over all things.

أَنْ تَقُولُوا مَا جَآءَنَا مِنْ بَشِيرٍ
وَّلَا نَذِيرٍ
فَقَدْ جَآءَكُمْ بَشِيرٌ وَّنَذِيرٌ
وَاللّٰهُ عَلٰى كُلِّ شَيْءٍ قَدِيرٌ ○

SECTION 4.

20. Remember Moses said
To his people: "O my People!
Call in remembrance the favour
Of God unto you, when He
Produced prophets among you,[721]
Made you kings,[722] and gave
You what He had not given
To any other among the peoples.[723]

٢٠- وَإِذْ قَالَ مُوسٰى لِقَوْمِهِ
يٰقَوْمِ اذْكُرُوا نِعْمَةَ اللّٰهِ عَلَيْكُمْ
إِذْ جَعَلَ فِيكُمْ أَنْبِيَآءَ وَجَعَلَكُمْ مُّلُوكًا
وَّاٰتٰكُمْ مَّا لَمْ يُؤْتِ أَحَدًا مِّنَ الْعٰلَمِينَ ○

21. "O my people! enter[724]
The holy land which
God hath assigned unto you,
And turn not back
Ignominiously, for then
Will ye be overthrown,
To your own ruin."

٢١- يٰقَوْمِ ادْخُلُوا الْأَرْضَ الْمُقَدَّسَةَ
الَّتِي كَتَبَ اللّٰهُ لَكُمْ
وَلَا تَرْتَدُّوا عَلٰى أَدْبَارِكُمْ
فَتَنْقَلِبُوا خٰسِرِينَ ○

721. There was a long line of patriarchs and prophets before Moses, *e.g.*, Abraham, Isaac, Ismā'īl, Jacob, etc.

722. From the slavery of Egypt the Children of Israel were made free and independent, and thus each man became as it were a king, if only he had obeyed God and followed the lead of Moses.

723. *Cf.* Exod. xix. 5: "Now, therefore, if ye will obey my voice indeed, and keep my covenant, then ye shall be a peculiar treasure unto me above all people." Israel was chosen to be the vehicle of God's message, the highest honour which any nation can receive.

724. We now come to the events detailed in the 13th and 14th chapters of the Book of Numbers in the Old Testament. Read these as a Commentary, and examine a good map of the Sinai Peninsula, showing its connections with Egypt on the west, North-West Arabia on the east, and Palestine on the north-east. We may suppose that Israel crossed from Egypt into the Peninsula somewhere near the northern extremity of the Gulf of Suez. Moses organised and numbered the people, and instituted the Priesthood. They went south about 200 miles to Mount Sinai where the Law was received. Then, perhaps a hundred and fifty miles north, was the desert of Paran, close to the southern borders of Canaan. From the camp there twelve men were sent to spy out the land, and they penetrated as far as Hebron, say about 150 miles north of their camp, about 20 miles south of the future Jerusalem. They saw a rich country, and brought from it pomegranates and figs and a bunch of grapes so heavy that it had to be carried by two men on a staff. They came back and reported that the land was rich, but the men there were too strong for them. The people of Israel had no courage and no faith, and Moses remonstrated with them.

22. They said : " O Moses !
In this land are a people
Of exceeding strength :[725]
Never shall we enter it
Until they leave it :
If (once) they leave,
Then shall we enter."

٢٢- قَالُوا يٰمُوسٰٓى إِنَّ فِيهَا قَوْمًا جَبَّارِينَ ۖ
وَإِنَّا لَن نَّدْخُلَهَا
حَتّٰى يَخْرُجُوا مِنْهَا ۚ
فَإِن يَخْرُجُوا مِنْهَا فَإِنَّا دٰخِلُونَ ○

23. (But) among (their) God-fearing men
Were two on whom
God had bestowed His grace :[726]
They said : "Assault them
At the (proper) Gate :
When once ye are in,
Victory will be yours ;

But on God put your trust
If ye have faith."

٢٣- قَالَ رَجُلَانِ مِنَ الَّذِينَ يَخَافُونَ
أَنْعَمَ اللّٰهُ
عَلَيْهِمَا ادْخُلُوا عَلَيْهِمُ الْبَابَ ۚ
فَإِذَا دَخَلْتُمُوهُ فَإِنَّكُمْ غٰلِبُونَ ۚ
وَعَلَى اللّٰهِ فَتَوَكَّلُوٓا إِن كُنتُم مُّؤْمِنِينَ ○

24. They said : " O Moses !
While they remain there,
Never shall we be able
To enter, to the end of time.
Go thou, and thy Lord,
And fight ye two,
While we sit here[727]
(And watch)."

٢٤- قَالُوا يٰمُوسٰٓى إِنَّا لَن نَّدْخُلَهَآ أَبَدًا
مَّا دَامُوا فِيهَا
فَاذْهَبْ أَنتَ وَرَبُّكَ فَقٰتِلَآ
إِنَّا هٰهُنَا قٰعِدُونَ ○

25. He said : " O my Lord !
I have power only

٢٥- قَالَ رَبِّ إِنِّي لَآ أَمْلِكُ

725. The people were not willing to follow the lead of Moses, and were not willing to fight for their "inheritance" In effect they said: "Turn out the enemy first, and then we shall enter into possession." In God's Law we must work and strive for what we wish to enjoy.

726. Among those who returned after spying out the land were two men who had faith and courage. They were Joshua and Caleb. Joshua afterwards succeeded Moses in the leadership after 40 years. These two men pleaded for an immediate entry through the proper Gate, which I understand to mean, "after taking all due precautions and making all due preparations". *Cf.* ii. 189 and n. 203. But of course, they said, they must put their trust in God for victory.

727. The advice of Joshua and Caleb, and the proposals of Moses under divine instructions were unpalatable to the crowd. whose prejudices were further inflamed by the other ten men who had gone with Joshua and Caleb. They made an "evil report," and were frightened by the great stature of the Canaanites. The crowd was in open rebellion, was prepared to stone Moses, Aaron, Joshua, and Caleb, and return to Egypt. Their reply to Moses was full of irony, insolence. blasphemy. and cowardice. In effect they said: "You talk of your God and all that: go with your God and fight there if you like: we shall sit here and watch."

Over myself and my brother:[728]
So separate us from this
Rebellious people!"

إِلَّا نَفْسِي وَأَخِي
فَافْرُقْ بَيْنَنَا وَبَيْنَ الْقَوْمِ الْفٰسِقِينَ ۝

26. God said: "Therefore
Will the land be out
Of their reach for forty years:[729]
In distraction will they
Wander through the land:
But sorrow thou not
Over these rebellious people.

٢٦- قَالَ فَإِنَّهَا مُحَرَّمَةٌ عَلَيْهِمْ أَرْبَعِينَ
سَنَةً ۚ يَتِيهُونَ فِي الْأَرْضِ ۚ
فَلَا تَأْسَ عَلَى الْقَوْمِ الْفٰسِقِينَ ۝ ع

C. 72.—The jealousy of Cain against Abel,
(v. 30-46.) Which led to the murder
Of innocent Abel, is the type
Of the jealousy between the People
Of the Book and their younger brethren
In Islam. Jealousy leads to envy
And murder. Such crimes against
Individuals are often crimes
Against whole peoples. There are
Men who are ready to catch up
Every lie told against a just man.
The just man should not grieve,
For that is their way.

SECTION 5.

27. Recite to them the truth[730]
Of the story of the two sons[731]

٢٧- وَاتْلُ عَلَيْهِمْ نَبَأَ ابْنَيْ

728. "Moses and Aaron fell on their faces before all the assembly of the congregation." (Num. xiv. 5). According to the words in the Old Testament story, God said: "I will smite them with the pestilence, and disinherit them." (Num. xiv. 12). Moses prayed and interceded. But as we are told here, (a spiritual touch not found in the Jewish story), Moses was careful to separate himself and his brother from the rebellion.

729. The punishment of the rebellion of these stiff-necked people, rebellion that was repeated "these ten times" (Num. xiv. 22) and more, was that they were left to wander distractedly hither and thither through the wilderness for forty years. That generation was not to see the Holy Land. All those that were twenty years old and upwards were to die in the wilderness: "your carcasses shall fall in this wilderness." (Num. xiv. 29). Only those who were then children would reach the promised land. And so it happened. From the desert of Paran they wandered south, north, and east for forty years. From the head of what is now the Gulf of 'Aqaba, they travelled north, keeping to the east side of the depression of which the Dead Sea and the river Jordan are portions. Forty years afterwards they crossed the Jordan opposite what is now Jericho, but by that time Moses, Aaron, and the whole of the elder generation had died.

730. Literally, "recite to them in truth the story", etc. The point is that the story in Gen. iv. 1-15 is a bare narrative, not including the lessons now to be enforced. The apostle is told now to supply the truth of the matter, the details that will enforce the lessons.

731. The two sons of Adam were Hābīl (in the English Bible, Abel) and Qābīl (in English, Cain). Cain was the elder, and Abel the younger,—the righteous and innocent one. Presuming on the right of the elder, Cain was puffed up with arrogance and jealousy, which led him to commit the crime of murder. Among the Christians, Cain was the type of the Jew as against Abel the Christian. The Jew tried to kill Jesus and exterminate the Christian. In the same way, as against Muḥammad, the younger brother of the Semitic family, Cain was the type of the Old Testament and New Testament people, who tried to resist and kill Muḥammad and put down his people.

Of Adam. Behold! they each
Presented a sacrifice (to God):
It was accepted from one,
But not from the other.
Said the latter: "Be sure
I will slay thee." "Surely,"
Said the former, "God
Doth accept of the sacrifice
Of those who are righteous.

وقف لازم
اٰدَمَ بِالْحَقِّ ۘ اِذْ قَرَّبَا قُرْبَانًا
فَتُقُبِّلَ مِنْ اَحَدِهِمَا
وَلَمْ يُتَقَبَّلْ مِنَ الْاٰخَرِ ؕ
قَالَ لَاَقْتُلَنَّكَ ؕ
النصف
قَالَ اِنَّمَا يَتَقَبَّلُ اللّٰهُ مِنَ الْمُتَّقِيْنَ ۝

28. "If thou dost stretch thy hand
Against me, to slay me,
It is not for me to stretch
My hand against thee
To slay thee: for I do fear
God, the Cherisher of the Worlds.

٢٨- لَئِنْۢ بَسَطْتَّ اِلَيَّ يَدَكَ لِتَقْتُلَنِيْ
مَاۤ اَنَا بِبَاسِطٍ يَّدِيَ اِلَيْكَ لِاَقْتُلَكَ ۚ
اِنِّيْۤ اَخَافُ اللّٰهَ رَبَّ الْعٰلَمِيْنَ ۝

29. "For me, I intend to let
Thee draw on thyself
My sin as well as thine,[732]
For thou wilt be among
The Companions of the Fire,
And that is the reward
Of those who do wrong."[733]

٢٩- اِنِّيْۤ اُرِيْدُ اَنْ تَبُوْٓاَ بِاِثْمِيْ وَاِثْمِكَ
فَتَكُوْنَ مِنْ اَصْحٰبِ النَّارِ ۚ
وَذٰلِكَ جَزٰٓؤُا الظّٰلِمِيْنَ ۝

30. The (selfish) soul of the other
Led him to the murder
Of his brother: he murdered
Him, and became (himself)
One of the lost ones.[734]

٣٠- فَطَوَّعَتْ لَهٗ نَفْسُهٗ قَتْلَ اَخِيْهِ
فَقَتَلَهٗ
فَاَصْبَحَ مِنَ الْخٰسِرِيْنَ ۝

31. Then God sent a raven,
Who scratched the ground,

٣١- فَبَعَثَ اللّٰهُ غُرَابًا يَّبْحَثُ فِى الْاَرْضِ

---

732. *My sin as well as thine.* There are two possible interpretations: (1) The obvious one is that the unjust murderer not only carried on himself the burden of his own sin, but also the burden of his victim's sins. The victim, in suffering a wrong or injustice, is forgiven his own sins, and the wrong-doer, having been warned, aggravates his own sin. (2) "My sin" has also been interpreted as "the sin against me, in that thou slayest me": in that case "thy sin" may mean either "thy crime in committing a murder," or "thy sin against thyself, for the crime causes real loss to thyself in the Hereafter." See the last clause of the next verse.

733. Abel's speech is full of meaning. He is innocent and God-fearing. To the threat of death held out by the other, he returns a calm reply, aimed at reforming the other. "Surely," he pleads, "if your sacrifice was not accepted, there was something wrong in you, for God is just and accepts the sacrifice of the righteous. If this does not deter you, I am not going to retaliate, though there is as much power in me against you as you have against me. I fear my Maker, for I know He cherishes all His Creation. Let me warn you that you are doing wrong. I do not intend even to resist, but do you know what the consequences will be to you? You will be in spiritual torment."

734. The innocent unselfish pleading of the younger brother had no effect, for the soul of the other was full of pride, selfishness, and jealousy. He committed the murder, but in doing so, ruined his own self.

To show him how to hide
The shame of his brother.[735]
"Woe is me!" said he;
"Was I not even able
To be as this raven,
And to hide the shame
Of my brother?" Then he became
Full of regrets—[736]

32. On that account: We ordained
For the Children of Israel
That if any one slew
A person—unless it be
For murder or for spreading
Mischief in the land—
It would be as if
He slew the whole people:[737]
And if any one saved a life,
It would be as if he saved
The life of the whole people.
Then although there came
To them Our Apostles
With Clear Signs, yet,
Even after that, many
Of them continued to commit
Excesses in the land.

33. The punishment of those
Who wage war against God
And His Apostle, and strive
With might and main
For mischief through the land[738]
Is: execution, or crucifixion,

لِيُرِيَهُۥ كَيْفَ يُوَٰرِى سَوْءَةَ أَخِيهِ ۚ
قَالَ يَٰوَيْلَتَىٰٓ أَعَجَزْتُ أَنْ أَكُونَ مِثْلَ
هَٰذَا ٱلْغُرَابِ فَأُوَٰرِىَ سَوْءَةَ أَخِى ۖ
فَأَصْبَحَ مِنَ ٱلنَّٰدِمِينَ ۝

٣٢- مِنْ أَجْلِ ذَٰلِكَ ۚ
كَتَبْنَا عَلَىٰ بَنِىٓ إِسْرَٰٓءِيلَ
أَنَّهُۥ مَن قَتَلَ نَفْسًۢا
بِغَيْرِ نَفْسٍ أَوْ فَسَادٍ فِى ٱلْأَرْضِ
فَكَأَنَّمَا قَتَلَ ٱلنَّاسَ جَمِيعًا ۖ
وَمَنْ أَحْيَاهَا فَكَأَنَّمَآ أَحْيَا ٱلنَّاسَ جَمِيعًا ۚ
وَلَقَدْ جَآءَتْهُمْ رُسُلُنَا بِٱلْبَيِّنَٰتِ
ثُمَّ إِنَّ كَثِيرًا مِّنْهُم
بَعْدَ ذَٰلِكَ فِى ٱلْأَرْضِ لَمُسْرِفُونَ ۝

٣٣- إِنَّمَا جَزَٰٓؤُا۟ ٱلَّذِينَ يُحَارِبُونَ ٱللَّهَ
وَرَسُولَهُۥ وَيَسْعَوْنَ فِى ٱلْأَرْضِ فَسَادًا
أَن يُقَتَّلُوٓا۟ أَوْ يُصَلَّبُوٓا۟

735. *Sau-at* may mean "corpse", with a suggestion of nakedness and shame in two senses: (1) the sense of being exposed without burial, and (2) the sense of being insulted by being violently deprived by the unwarranted murder, of the soul which inhabited it,—the soul, too, of a brother.

736. The thought at last came home to the murderer. It was dreadful indeed to slay any one—the more so as he was a brother, and an innocent righteous brother! But worse still, the murderer had not even the decency to bury the corpse, and of this simple duty he was reminded by a raven—a black bird usually held in contempt! His regret was on that account. That was not true repentance.

737. The story of Cain is referred to in a few graphic details in order to tell the story of Israel. Israel rebelled against God, slew and insulted righteous men who did them no harm but on the contrary came in all humility. When God withdrew His favour from Israel because of its sins and bestowed it on a brother nation, the jealousy of Israel plunged it deeper into sin. To kill or seek to kill an individual because he represents an ideal is to kill all who uphold the ideal. On the other hand, to save an individual life in the same circumstances is to save a whole community. What could be stronger condemnation of individual assassination and revenge?

738. For the double crime of treason against the State, combined with treason against God, as shown by overt crimes, four alternative punishments are mentioned, any one of which is to be applied according to circumstances, *viz.*, execution (cutting off of the head), crucifixion, maiming, or exile. These were features of the Criminal Law then and for centuries afterwards, except that tortures such as "hanging, drawing, and quartering" in English Law, and piercing of eyes and leaving the unfortunate victim exposed to a tropical sun, which was practised in Arabia, and all such tortures were abolished. In any case sincere repentance before it was too late was recognised as a ground for mercy.

Or the cutting off of hands
And feet from opposite sides,[739]
Or exile from the land:
That is their disgrace
In this world, and
A heavy punishment is theirs
In the Hereafter;

أَوْ تُقَطَّعَ أَيْدِيهِمْ وَأَرْجُلُهُم مِّنْ خِلَافٍ
أَوْ يُنفَوْا مِنَ الْأَرْضِ
ذَٰلِكَ لَهُمْ خِزْيٌ فِي الدُّنْيَا
وَلَهُمْ فِي الْآخِرَةِ عَذَابٌ عَظِيمٌ ○

34. Except for those who repent
Before they fall
Into your power:
In that case, know
That God is Oft-forgiving,
Most Merciful.

٣٤- إِلَّا الَّذِينَ تَابُوا
مِن قَبْلِ أَن تَقْدِرُوا عَلَيْهِمْ
فَاعْلَمُوا أَنَّ اللَّهَ غَفُورٌ رَّحِيمٌ ○ ع

SECTION 6.

35. O ye who believe!
Do your duty to God,[740]
Seek the means
Of approach unto Him,
And strive with might
And main in His cause:
That ye may prosper.[741]

٣٥- يَا أَيُّهَا الَّذِينَ آمَنُوا اتَّقُوا اللَّهَ
وَابْتَغُوا إِلَيْهِ الْوَسِيلَةَ
وَجَاهِدُوا فِي سَبِيلِهِ
لَعَلَّكُمْ تُفْلِحُونَ ○

36. As to those who reject
Faith,—if they had
Everything on earth,
And twice repeated,
To give as ransom
For the penalty of the Day
Of Judgment, it would
Never be accepted of them.
Theirs would be
A grievous Penalty.

٣٦- إِنَّ الَّذِينَ كَفَرُوا
لَوْ أَنَّ لَهُم مَّا فِي الْأَرْضِ جَمِيعًا
وَمِثْلَهُ مَعَهُ
لِيَفْتَدُوا بِهِ مِنْ عَذَابِ يَوْمِ الْقِيَامَةِ
مَا تُقُبِّلَ مِنْهُمْ وَلَهُمْ عَذَابٌ أَلِيمٌ ○

37. Their wish will be
To get out of the Fire,
But never will they
Get out therefrom:

٣٧- يُرِيدُونَ أَن يَخْرُجُوا مِنَ النَّارِ
وَمَا هُم بِخَارِجِينَ مِنْهَا

---

739. Understood to mean the right hand and the left foot.

740. *Taqwā* here too might be translated "fear of God", but the very next clause shows that "fear of God" does not mean "fear" in the ordinary sense, which would make you avoid the object of fear. On the contrary the "fear of God" is the intense desire to avoid everything that is against His Will and Law. It is in fact duty to God, for we are told to seek ardently the means by which we may approach Him, and that can only be done by striving with might and main for His cause.

741. "Prosper" in the spiritual sense, for that is all that matters, as the life of this world is brief and fleeting, and of small account as against Eternity.

Their Penalty will be
One that endures.

وَلَهُمْ عَذَابٌ مُّقِيمٌ ○

38. As to the thief,[742]
Male or female,
Cut off his or her hands:
A punishment by way
Of example, from God,
For their crime:
And God is Exalted in Power.

٣٨- وَالسَّارِقُ وَالسَّارِقَةُ
فَاقْطَعُوٓا أَيْدِيَهُمَا جَزَآءً
بِمَا كَسَبَا نَكَالًا مِّنَ اللّٰهِ ؕ
وَاللّٰهُ عَزِيزٌ حَكِيمٌ ○

39. But if the thief repent
After his crime,
And amend his conduct,
God turneth to him
In forgiveness; for God
Is Oft-forgiving, Most Merciful.

٣٩- فَمَنْ تَابَ مِنْ بَعْدِ ظُلْمِهِ وَأَصْلَحَ
فَإِنَّ اللّٰهَ يَتُوبُ عَلَيْهِ ؕ
إِنَّ اللّٰهَ غَفُورٌ رَّحِيمٌ ○

40. Knowest thou not[743]
That to God (alone)
Belongeth the dominion
Of the heavens and the earth?
He punisheth whom He pleaseth,
And He forgiveth whom He pleaseth:
And God hath power
Over all things.

٤٠- أَلَمْ تَعْلَمْ
أَنَّ اللّٰهَ لَهُ مُلْكُ السَّمٰوٰتِ وَالْأَرْضِ ؕ
يُعَذِّبُ مَنْ يَّشَآءُ
وَيَغْفِرُ لِمَنْ يَّشَآءُ ؕ
وَاللّٰهُ عَلٰى كُلِّ شَيْءٍ قَدِيرٌ ○

41. O Apostle! let not
Those grieve thee, who race
Each other into Unbelief:[744]
(Whether it be) among those
Who say "We believe"
With their lips but
Whose hearts have no faith;

٤١- يٰٓأَيُّهَا الرَّسُولُ لَا يَحْزُنْكَ الَّذِينَ
يُسَارِعُونَ فِي الْكُفْرِ مِنَ الَّذِينَ
قَالُوٓا اٰمَنَّا بِأَفْوَاهِهِمْ وَلَمْ تُؤْمِنْ قُلُوبُهُمْ ۛ

742. Here we touch upon jurisprudence. The Canon Law jurists are not unanimous as to the value of the property stolen, which would involve the penalty of the cutting off of the hand. The majority hold that petty thefts are exempt from this punishment. The general opinion is that only one hand should be cut off for the first theft, on the principle that "if thy hand or thy foot offend thee, cut them off, and cast them from thee" (Matt. xviii. 8). Apparently in the age of Jesus thieves were crucified (Matt. xxvii. 38).

743. Punishment really does not belong to mortals, but to God alone. Only, in order to keep civil society together, and protect innocent people from crime, certain principles are laid down on which people can build up their criminal law. But we must always remember that God not only punishes but forgives, and forgiveness is the attribute which is more prominently placed before us. It is not our wisdom that can really define the bounds of forgiveness or punishment, but His Will or Plan, which is the true standard of righteousness and justice.

744. Two classes of men are meant, *viz.*, the Hypocrites and the Jews. For both of them Mustafā laboured earnestly and assiduously, and it must have been a cause of great grief and disappointment to him that some among them showed so much insincerity, cunning, and hardness of heart. These are types not yet extinct.

Or it be among the Jews,—
Men who will listen
To any lie,—will listen
Even to others who have
Never so much as come[745]
To thee. They change the words
From their (right) times[746]
And places: they say,
"If ye are given this,
Take it, but if not,
Beware!" If any one's trial
Is intended by God, thou hast
No authority in the least
For him against God.
For such—it is not
God's will to purify
Their hearts. For them
There is disgrace
In this world, and
In the Hereafter
A heavy punishment.

وَمِنَ الَّذِينَ هَادُوا ۛ سَمّٰعُونَ لِلْكَذِبِ
سَمّٰعُونَ لِقَوْمٍ ءَاخَرِينَ ۙ لَمْ يَأْتُوكَ ۖ
يُحَرِّفُونَ الْكَلِمَ مِنْ بَعْدِ مَوَاضِعِهِ ۖ
يَقُولُونَ إِنْ أُوتِيتُمْ هٰذَا فَخُذُوهُ
وَإِنْ لَمْ تُؤْتَوْهُ فَاحْذَرُوا ۚ
وَمَنْ يُرِدِ اللّٰهُ فِتْنَتَهُ
فَلَنْ تَمْلِكَ لَهُ مِنَ اللّٰهِ شَيْئًا ۚ
أُولٰٓئِكَ الَّذِينَ لَمْ يُرِدِ اللّٰهُ
أَنْ يُطَهِّرَ قُلُوبَهُمْ ۚ لَهُمْ فِي الدُّنْيَا خِزْيٌ ۖ
وَلَهُمْ فِي الْءَاخِرَةِ عَذَابٌ عَظِيمٌ ○

42. (They are fond of) listening
To falsehood, of devouring[747]
Anything forbidden.
If they do come to thee,
Either judge between them,
Or decline to interfere.[748]
If thou decline, they cannot
Hurt thee in the least.
If thou judge, judge
In equity between them.
For God loveth those
Who judge in equity.

٤٢- سَمّٰعُونَ لِلْكَذِبِ أَكّٰلُونَ لِلسُّحْتِ ۚ
فَإِنْ جَاءُوكَ فَاحْكُمْ بَيْنَهُمْ أَوْ أَعْرِضْ
عَنْهُمْ ۖ وَإِنْ تُعْرِضْ عَنْهُمْ
فَلَنْ يَضُرُّوكَ شَيْئًا ۖ
وَإِنْ حَكَمْتَ فَاحْكُمْ بَيْنَهُمْ بِالْقِسْطِ ۚ
إِنَّ اللّٰهَ يُحِبُّ الْمُقْسِطِينَ ○

---

745. There were men among the Jews who were eager to catch up any lie against the Apostle. They had their ears open even to tales from people who had never so much as come near to the Apostle. If we understand "for" instead of "to" before "others" (for the Arabic word would bear both meanings), the sense will be: They are keen listeners or spies for any lies they can catch; and they will act as spies for others (their Rabbis, etc.) who are in the background but to whom they carry false tales.

746. *Cf.* v. 14. The addition of the words *min ba'di* here suggests the change of words from their right *times* as well as places. They did not deal honestly with their Law, and misapplied it, by distorting the meaning. Or it may be that as tale-bearers they distorted the meaning by misrepresenting the context.

747. *Devouring anything forbidden*: both in a literal and in a figurative sense. In the figurative sense, it would be: the taking of usury or bribes, or taking undue advantage of people's weak position or their own fiduciary powers to add to their own wealth.

748. Where it is merely a trick to catch out the unwary, a just man may honourably decline to interfere in a cause submitted to him, as also in a case where the parties are not honestly desirous of justice, but each hopes that some partiality will be shown to it.

43. But why do they come[749]
To thee for decision,
When they have (their own)
Law before them?—
Therein is the (plain)
Command of God; yet
Even after that, they would
Turn away. For they
Are not (really)
People of Faith.

٤٣- وَكَيْفَ يُحَكِّمُونَكَ
وَعِنْدَهُمُ التَّوْرٰىةُ
فِيهَا حُكْمُ اللّٰهِ
ثُمَّ يَتَوَلَّوْنَ مِنْ بَعْدِ ذٰلِكَ ط
وَمَآ أُولٰٓئِكَ بِالْمُؤْمِنِينَ ۝ ع

C. 73.—True justice accords with God's Law.
(v. 47-89.) Follow not men's selfish desires,
But God's Will, which was revealed
To Moses and Jesus, and now to Muḥammad.
Take not for friends and protectors
Those in whose hearts is a disease,—
To whom religion is a mockery
Or a plaything,—who worship evil.
Proclaim the Truth of God, and be
Not afraid. Eschew their iniquities,
Which were denounced by David
And Jesus. But recognise with justice
Those who are sincere and humble,
Though they may be themselves
Not of your flock, if they witness to Truth.

Section 7.

44. It was We who revealed
The Law (to Moses): therein
Was guidance and light.[750]
By its standard have been judged
The Jews, by the Prophets
Who bowed (as in Islam)
To God's Will, by the Rabbis[751]
And the Doctors of Law:

٤٤- إِنَّآ أَنْزَلْنَا التَّوْرٰىةَ فِيهَا هُدًى وَّنُورٌ ج
يَحْكُمُ بِهَا النَّبِيُّونَ الَّذِينَ أَسْلَمُوا
لِلَّذِينَ هَادُوا
وَالرَّبّٰنِيُّونَ وَالْأَحْبَارُ

749. This is a searching question as to the motive of the Jews in bringing their cases for decision to the Apostle. They came either (1) to ridicule whatever he said, or (2) to deceive him as to facts and snatch a favourable decision which was against equity. If their own Law did not suit their selfish interests, they sometimes twisted it. But Muḥammad was always inflexible in his justice.

750. *Guidance*, with reference to conduct; *light*, with reference to insight into the higher realms of the spirit.

751. *Rabbānī* may, I think, be rightly translated by the Jewish title of *Rabbi* for their learned men. Jewish learning is identified with Rabbinical literature. Aḥbār is the plural of ḥibr or ḥabr, by which we may understand Jewish Doctors of Law. Later the term was applied to those of other religions. Query: Is the word connected with the same root as "Hebrew", or "Eber" (Gen. x. 21), the ancestor of the Hebrew race? This seems negatived by the fact that the Arabic root connected with the word "Hebrew" is *'Abar*, not *Ḥabar*.

For to them was entrusted
The protection of God's Book,
And they were witnesses thereto:[752]
Therefore fear not men,
But fear Me, and sell not
My Signs for a miserable price.[753]
If any do fail to judge
By (the light of) what God
Hath revealed, they are
(No better than) Unbelievers.

بِمَا اسْتُحْفِظُوْا مِنْ كِتٰبِ اللّٰهِ وَكَانُوْا عَلَيْهِ
شُهَدَآءَ ۚ فَلَا تَخْشَوُا النَّاسَ وَاخْشَوْنِ
وَلَا تَشْتَرُوْا بِاٰيٰتِيْ ثَمَنًا قَلِيْلًا ۗ
وَمَنْ لَّمْ يَحْكُمْ بِمَآ اَنْزَلَ اللّٰهُ
فَاُولٰٓئِكَ هُمُ الْكٰفِرُوْنَ ○

45. We ordained therein for them:[754]
"Life for life, eye for eye,
Nose for nose, ear for ear,
Tooth for tooth, and wounds
Equal for equal." But if
Any one remits the retaliation
By way of charity, it is
An act of atonement for himself.[755]
And if any fail to judge
By (the light of) what God
Hath revealed, they are
(No better than) wrong-doers.[756]

۴۵- وَكَتَبْنَا عَلَيْهِمْ فِيْهَآ
اَنَّ النَّفْسَ بِالنَّفْسِ ۙ وَالْعَيْنَ بِالْعَيْنِ
وَالْاَنْفَ بِالْاَنْفِ وَالْاُذُنَ بِالْاُذُنِ
وَالسِّنَّ بِالسِّنِّ ۙ وَالْجُرُوْحَ قِصَاصٌ ۗ
فَمَنْ تَصَدَّقَ بِهٖ فَهُوَ كَفَّارَةٌ لَّهٗ ۗ وَمَنْ لَّمْ
يَحْكُمْ بِمَآ اَنْزَلَ اللّٰهُ فَاُولٰٓئِكَ هُمُ الظّٰلِمُوْنَ ○

46. And in their footsteps
We sent Jesus the son

۴۶- وَقَفَّيْنَا عَلٰٓى اٰثَارِهِمْ بِعِيْسَى ابْنِ

---

752. They were living witnesses to the truth of Scripture, and could testify that they had made it known to the people: *Cf.* ii. 143, and iv. 135.

753. Two charges are made against the Jews: (1) that even the books which they had, they twisted in meaning, to suit their own purposes, because they feared men rather than God: (2) that what they had was but fragments of the original Law given to Moses, mixed up with a lot of semi-historical and legendary matter, and some fine poetry. The *Taurāt* mentioned in the Qur-ān is not the Old Testament as we have it; nor is it even the Pentateuch (the first five books of the Old Testament, containing the Law embedded in a great deal of semi-historical and legendary narrative). See Appendix II, on the *Taurāt* (printed at the end of this Sūra).

754. The retaliation is prescribed in three places in the Pentateuch, *viz.*, Exod. xxi 23-25; Leviticus xxiv. 18-21, and Deut. xix. 21. The wording in the three quotations is different, but in none of them is found the additional rider for mercy, as here. Note that in Matt. v. 38, Jesus quotes the Old Law "eye for eye," etc., and modifies it in the direction of forgiveness, but the Quranic injunction is more practical. This appeal for mercy is as between man and man in the spiritual world. Even where the injured one forgives, the State or Ruler is competent to take such action as is necessary for the preservation of law and order in Society. For crime has a bearing that goes beyond the interests of the person injured: the Community is affected: see Q. v. 35.

755. This is not part of the Mosaic Law, but the teaching of Jesus and of Muḥammad. Notice how the teaching of Jesus is gradually introduced as leading up to the Qur-ān.

756. The seeming repetitions at the end of verses 47, 48, and 50 are not real repetitions. The significant words in the three cases are: Unbelievers, wrong-doers, and rebellious: and each fits the context. If the Jews tamper with their books they are Unbelievers; if they give false judgments, they are wrong-doers. If the Christians follow not their light, they are rebellious.

Of Mary, confirming
The Law that had come
Before him: We sent him
The Gospel: therein
Was guidance and light,[757]
And confirmation of the Law
That had come before him:
A guidance and an admonition
To those who fear God.

مَرْيَمَ مُصَدِّقًا لِّمَا بَيْنَ يَدَيْهِ مِنَ التَّوْرٰىةِ
وَاٰتَيْنٰهُ الْاِنْجِيْلَ فِيْهِ هُدًى وَّنُوْرٌ
وَّمُصَدِّقًا لِّمَا بَيْنَ يَدَيْهِ مِنَ التَّوْرٰىةِ
وَهُدًى
وَّمَوْعِظَةً لِّلْمُتَّقِيْنَ ۝

47. Let the People of the Gospel
Judge by what God hath revealed
Therein. If any do fail
To judge by (the light of)
What God hath revealed,
They are (no better than)
Those who rebel.[758]

٤٧- وَلْيَحْكُمْ اَهْلُ الْاِنْجِيْلِ بِمَآ اَنْزَلَ
اللّٰهُ فِيْهِ
وَمَنْ لَّمْ يَحْكُمْ بِمَآ اَنْزَلَ اللّٰهُ
فَاُولٰٓئِكَ هُمُ الْفٰسِقُوْنَ ۝

48. To thee We sent the Scripture
In truth, confirming
The scripture that came
Before it, and guarding it[759]
In safety: so judge
Between them by what
God hath revealed,
And follow not their vain
Desires, diverging
From the Truth that hath come
To thee. To each among you
Have We prescribed a Law
And an Open Way.[760]
If God had so willed,
He would have made you[761]
A single People, but (His

٤٨- وَاَنْزَلْنَآ اِلَيْكَ الْكِتٰبَ
بِالْحَقِّ مُصَدِّقًا لِّمَا بَيْنَ يَدَيْهِ مِنَ
الْكِتٰبِ وَمُهَيْمِنًا عَلَيْهِ
فَاحْكُمْ بَيْنَهُمْ بِمَآ اَنْزَلَ اللّٰهُ
وَلَا تَتَّبِعْ اَهْوَآءَهُمْ
عَمَّا جَآءَكَ مِنَ الْحَقِّ
لِكُلٍّ جَعَلْنَا مِنْكُمْ شِرْعَةً وَّمِنْهَاجًا
وَلَوْ شَآءَ اللّٰهُ لَجَعَلَكُمْ اُمَّةً وَّاحِدَةً

---

757. *Guidance and light*: see n. 750 above. For the meaning of the Gospel (Injīl), see Appendix III, "On the *Injīl*", (printed at the end of this Sūra).

758. See n. 756 above.

759. After the corruption of the older revelations, the Qur-ān comes with a twofold purpose: (1) to confirm the true and original Message, and (2) to guard it, or act as a check to its interpretation. For example, if people seek retaliation in a spirit of revenge, it holds forth mercy. If they glibly mask their cowardice or sentimentalism by empty talk of "turning the other cheek," it tests them by the practical test of forgiveness and mercy.

760. *Law*: *shir'at*=rules of practical conduct. *Open Way*: *Minhāj*=the finer things which are above the law, but which are yet available to every one, like a sort of open highway. The *light* in verses 47 and 49 above, I understand to be something in the still higher regions of the spirit, which is common to mankind, though laws and rules may take different forms among different Peoples.

761. By origin mankind were a single people or nation: iv. 1, and ii. 213. That being so, God could have kept us all alike, with one language, one kind of disposition, and one set of physical conditions (including climate) to live in. But in His wisdom, He gives us diversity in these things, not only at any given time, but in different periods and ages. This tests our capacity for Unity (Wahdāniyat) still more, and accentuates the need of Unity and Islam.

Plan is) to test you in what
He hath given you : so strive
As in a race in all virtues.
The goal of you all is to God ;
It is He that will show you
The truth of the matters
In which ye dispute ;[762]

وَّلٰكِنْ لِّيَبْلُوَكُمْ فِيْ مَآ اٰتٰكُمْ
فَاسْتَبِقُوا الْخَيْرٰتِ ؕ
اِلَى اللّٰهِ مَرْجِعُكُمْ جَمِيْعًا
فَيُنَبِّئُكُمْ بِمَا كُنْتُمْ فِيْهِ تَخْتَلِفُوْنَ ۙ

49. And this (He commands) :
Judge thou between them
By what God hath revealed,
And follow not their vain
Desires, but beware of them
Lest they beguile thee
From any of that (teaching)
Which God hath sent down
To thee. And if they turn
Away, be assured that
For some of their crimes
It is God's purpose to punish
Them. And truly most men
Are rebellious.

۴۹- وَاَنِ احْكُمْ بَيْنَهُمْ بِمَآ اَنْزَلَ اللّٰهُ
وَلَا تَتَّبِعْ اَهْوَآءَهُمْ
وَاحْذَرْهُمْ اَنْ يَّفْتِنُوْكَ عَنْۢ بَعْضِ مَآ
اَنْزَلَ اللّٰهُ اِلَيْكَ ؕ فَاِنْ تَوَلَّوْا
فَاعْلَمْ اَنَّمَا يُرِيْدُ اللّٰهُ اَنْ يُّصِيْبَهُمْ
بِبَعْضِ ذُنُوْبِهِمْ ؕ
وَاِنَّ كَثِيْرًا مِّنَ النَّاسِ لَفٰسِقُوْنَ ○

50. Do they then seek after
A judgment of (the Days[763]
Of) Ignorance ? But who,
For a people whose faith
Is assured, can give
Better judgment than God ?

۵۰- اَفَحُكْمَ الْجَاهِلِيَّةِ يَبْغُوْنَ ؕ
وَمَنْ اَحْسَنُ مِنَ اللّٰهِ حُكْمًا لِّقَوْمٍ
يُّوْقِنُوْنَ ○ ع

SECTION 8.

51. O ye who believe !
Take not the Jews
And the Christians
For your friends and protectors :[764]
They are but friends and protectors
To each other. And he

۵۱- يٰۤاَيُّهَا الَّذِيْنَ اٰمَنُوْا
لَا تَتَّخِذُوا الْيَهُوْدَ وَالنَّصٰرٰۤى اَوْلِيَآءَ ۘ وقف لازم
بَعْضُهُمْ اَوْلِيَآءُ بَعْضٍ ؕ وَمَنْ

---

762. As our true goal is God, the things that seem different to us from different points of view, will ultimately be reconciled in Him. Einstein is right in plumbing the depths of Relativity in the world of physical science. It points more and more to the need of Unity in God in the spiritual world.

763. The Days of Ignorance were the days of tribalism, feuds, and selfish accentuation of differences in man. Those days are really not yet over. It is the mission of Islam to take us away from that false mental attitude, towards the true attitude of Unity. If our Faith is certain (and not merely a matter of words), God will guide us to that Unity.

764. That is, look not to them for help and comfort. They are more likely to combine against you than to help you. And this happened more than once in the lifetime of the Apostle, and in after-ages again and again. He who associates with them and shares their counsels must be counted as of them. The trimmer loses whichever way the wheel of fortune turns.

Amongst you that turns to them
(For friendship) is of them.
Verily God guideth not
A people unjust.

يتولهم منكم فإنه منهم
إن الله لا يهدي القوم الظلمين ○

52. Those in whose hearts[765]
Is a disease—thou seest
How eagerly they run about
Amongst them, saying:
"We do fear lest a change
Of fortune bring us disaster."
Ah! perhaps God will give
(Thee) victory, or a decision
According to His Will.
Then will they repent
Of the thoughts which they secretly
Harboured in their hearts.

٥٢- فترى الذين في قلوبهم مرض
يسارعون فيهم
يقولون نخشى أن تصيبنا دائرة
فعسى الله أن يأتي بالفتح أو أمر من
عنده فيصبحوا
على ما أسروا في أنفسهم ندمين ○

53. And those who believe
Will say: "Are these
The men who swore
Their strongest oaths by God,
That they were with you?"[766]
All that they do
Will be in vain,
And they will fall
Into (nothing but) ruin.

٥٣- ويقول الذين آمنوا أهؤلاء الذين
أقسموا بالله جهد أيمانهم
إنهم لمعكم
حبطت أعمالهم
فأصبحوا خسرين ○

54. O ye who believe!
If any from among you
Turn back from his Faith,
Soon will God produce
A people whom He will love
As they will love Him,—
Lowly with the Believers,
Mighty against the Rejecters,
Fighting in the Way of God,
And never afraid
Of the reproaches

٥٤- يأيها الذين آمنوا
من يرتد منكم عن دينه
فسوف يأتي الله بقوم يحبهم ويحبونه
أذلة على المؤمنين أعزة على الكفرين
يجاهدون في سبيل الله
ولا يخافون لومة لائم

---

765. *Cf.* ii. 10.

766. The Hypocrites, while matters were doubtful, pretended to be with Muslims, but were in league with their enemies. When matters came to a decision and God granted victory to Islam, their position was awkward. They were not only disowned by the Muslims, but the Muslims could well say in reproach to their enemies: "Are these the men who swore friendship for you? What was their friendship worth to you? Where are they now?"

Of such as find fault.[767]
That is the Grace of God,
Which He will bestow
On whom He pleaseth.
And God encompasseth all,
And He knoweth all things.

ذٰلِكَ فَضْلُ اللّٰهِ
يُؤْتِيْهِ مَنْ يَّشَآءُ ؕ
وَاللّٰهُ وَاسِعٌ عَلِيْمٌ ۝

55. Your (real) friends are
(No less than) God,
His Apostle, and the (Fellowship
Of) Believers,—those who
Establish regular prayers
And regular charity,
And they bow
Down humbly (in worship).

٥٥- اِنَّمَا وَلِيُّكُمُ اللّٰهُ وَرَسُوْلُهٗ وَالَّذِيْنَ
اٰمَنُوا
الَّذِيْنَ يُقِيْمُوْنَ الصَّلٰوةَ
وَيُؤْتُوْنَ الزَّكٰوةَ وَهُمْ رٰكِعُوْنَ ۝

56. As to those who turn
(For friendship) to God,
His Apostle, and the (Fellowship
Of) Believers,—it is
The Fellowship of God
That must certainly triumph.

٥٦- وَمَنْ يَّتَوَلَّ اللّٰهَ وَرَسُوْلَهٗ
وَالَّذِيْنَ اٰمَنُوْا
فَاِنَّ حِزْبَ اللّٰهِ هُمُ الْغٰلِبُوْنَ ۝ ع

SECTION 9.

57. O ye who believe!
Take not for friends
And protectors those
Who take your religion
For a mockery or sport,—[768]
Whether among those
Who received the Scripture
Before you, or among those

٥٧- يٰۤاَيُّهَا الَّذِيْنَ اٰمَنُوْا
لَا تَتَّخِذُوا الَّذِيْنَ اتَّخَذُوْا دِيْنَكُمْ هُزُوًا
وَّلَعِبًا
مِّنَ الَّذِيْنَ اُوْتُوا الْكِتٰبَ مِنْ قَبْلِكُمْ

767. As "most men are rebellious" (v. 52), it is inevitable that there should be apostates even from such a religion of reason and common-sense as Islam. But here is a warning to the Muslim body that they should not repeat the history of the Jews, and become so self-satisfied or arrogant as to depart from the spirit of God's teaching. If they do, the loss will be their own. God's bounty is not confined to one group or section of humanity. He can always raise up people who will follow the true spirit of Islam. That spirit is defined in two ways: first in general terms; they will love God and God will love them; and secondly, by specific signs; amongst the Brethren, their attitude will be that of humility, but to wrong-doers they will offer no mealy-mouthed compromises; they will always strive and fight for truth and right; they will know no fear, either physical, or that more insidious form, which says: "What will people say if we act thus?" They are too great in mind to be haunted by any such thought. For, as the next verse says, their friends are God, His Apostle, and His people, the people who judge rightly, without fear or favour.

768. It is not right that we should be in intimate association with those to whom religion is either a subject of mockery or at best is nothing but a plaything. They may be amused, or they may have other motives for encouraging you. But your association with them will sap the earnestness of your Faith, and make you cynical and insincere

Who reject Faith;
But fear ye God,
If ye have Faith (indeed).

وَالْكُفَّارَ أَوْلِيَآءَ ج
وَاتَّقُوا اللّٰهَ إِنْ كُنْتُمْ مُّؤْمِنِيْنَ ○

58. When ye proclaim
Your call to prayer,
They take it (but)
As mockery and sport;
That is because they are
A people without understanding.

٥٨- وَإِذَا نَادَيْتُمْ إِلَى الصَّلٰوةِ
اتَّخَذُوهَا هُزُوًا وَّلَعِبًا ط
ذٰلِكَ بِأَنَّهُمْ قَوْمٌ لَّا يَعْقِلُوْنَ ○

59. Say: "O People of the Book!
Do ye disapprove of us
For no other reason than
That we believe in God,
And the revelation
That hath come to us
And that which came
Before (us), and (perhaps)
That most of you
Are rebellious and disobedient?"[769]

٥٩- قُلْ يٰٓأَهْلَ الْكِتٰبِ
هَلْ تَنْقِمُوْنَ مِنَّآ إِلَّآ أَنْ اٰمَنَّا بِاللّٰهِ
وَمَآ أُنْزِلَ إِلَيْنَا
وَمَآ أُنْزِلَ مِنْ قَبْلُ لا
وَأَنَّ أَكْثَرَكُمْ فٰسِقُوْنَ ○

60. Say: "Shall I point out
To you something much worse
Than this, (as judged)
By the treatment it received
From God? Those who
Incurred the curse of God
And His wrath, those of whom some
He transformed into apes and swine,[770]
Those who worshipped Evil;—
These are (many times) worse
In rank, and far more astray
From the even Path!"

٦٠- قُلْ هَلْ أُنَبِّئُكُمْ بِشَرٍّ مِّنْ ذٰلِكَ
مَثُوْبَةً عِنْدَ اللّٰهِ ط
مَنْ لَّعَنَهُ اللّٰهُ وَغَضِبَ عَلَيْهِ
وَجَعَلَ مِنْهُمُ الْقِرَدَةَ وَالْخَنَازِيْرَ وَعَبَدَ
الطَّاغُوْتَ ط
أُولٰٓئِكَ شَرٌّ مَّكَانًا
وَّأَضَلُّ عَنْ سَوَآءِ السَّبِيْلِ ○

61. When they come to thee,
They say: "We believe":

٦١- وَإِذَا جَآءُوْكُمْ قَالُوْٓا اٰمَنَّا

---

769. There is the most biting irony in this and the next verse. 'You People of the Book! Do you hate us because we believe in God and not only our scripture, but yours also? Perhaps you hate us because we obey and you are in rebellion against God! Why hate us? There are worse things than our obedience and our Faith. Shall I tell you some of them? Our test will be: what treatment God meted out to the things I mention. Who were the people who incurred the curse of God? (See Deut. xi. 28, and xxviii. 15-68; and numerous passages like Hosea viii. 14, and ix 1.). Who provoked God's wrath? (See numerous passages like Deut. i. 34; Matt. iii. 7.) Who forsook God, and worshipped evil? (See Jeremiah, xvi. 11-13.) That is your record. Is that why you hate us?'

770. For apes see Q. ii. 65. For men possessed by devils, and the devils being sent into swine, see Matt. viii. 28-32. Or perhaps both apes and swine are allegorical: those who falsified God's scriptures became lawless like apes, and those who succumbed to filth, gluttony, or gross living became like swine.

But in fact they enter
With a mind against Faith,
And they go out
With the same.
But God knoweth fully
All that they hide.

وَقَد دَّخَلُوا بِالْكُفْرِ
وَهُمْ قَدْ خَرَجُوا بِهِ
وَاللَّهُ أَعْلَمُ بِمَا كَانُوا يَكْتُمُونَ ○

62. Many of them dost thou
See, racing each other
In sin and rancour,
And their eating of things[771]
Forbidden. Evil indeed
Are the things that they do.

٦٢- وَتَرَىٰ كَثِيرًا مِّنْهُمْ يُسَارِعُونَ فِي
الْإِثْمِ وَالْعُدْوَانِ وَأَكْلِهِمُ السُّحْتَ
لَبِئْسَ مَا كَانُوا يَعْمَلُونَ ○

63. Why do not the Rabbis
And the doctors of law forbid
Them from their (habit
Of) uttering sinful words
And eating things forbidden?
Evil indeed are their works.

٦٣- لَوْلَا يَنْهَاهُمُ الرَّبَّانِيُّونَ وَالْأَحْبَارُ
عَن قَوْلِهِمُ الْإِثْمَ وَأَكْلِهِمُ السُّحْتَ
لَبِئْسَ مَا كَانُوا يَصْنَعُونَ ○

64. The Jews say: "God's hand[772]
Is tied up." Be *their* hands
Tied up and be they accursed
For the (blasphemy) they utter.
Nay, both His hands
Are widely outstretched:
He giveth and spendeth
(Of His bounty) as He pleaseth.
But the revelation that
Cometh to thee from God
Increaseth in most of them
Their obstinate rebellion[773]
And blasphemy. Amongst them
We have placed enmity[774]

٦٤- وَقَالَتِ الْيَهُودُ يَدُ اللَّهِ مَغْلُولَةٌ
غُلَّتْ أَيْدِيهِمْ وَلُعِنُوا بِمَا قَالُوا
بَلْ يَدَاهُ مَبْسُوطَتَانِ
يُنفِقُ كَيْفَ يَشَاءُ
وَلَيَزِيدَنَّ كَثِيرًا مِّنْهُم
مَّا أُنزِلَ إِلَيْكَ مِن رَّبِّكَ طُغْيَانًا وَكُفْرًا
وَأَلْقَيْنَا بَيْنَهُمُ الْعَدَاوَةَ

771. *Eating of things forbidden*: may be construed in a literal or a figurative sense. From its juxtaposition with sin and hatred, it is better to construe it in a figurative sense, as referring to their fraudulent misappropriations of other people's property or trust property. "Eating" is used in v. 69 below in the general sense of enjoyment and happiness.

772. *Cf.* v. 13, and ii. 245, for a "beautiful loan to God", and iii. 181, for the blasphemous taunt, "Then God is poor!" It is another form of the taunt to say, "Then God's hands are tied up, He is close-fisted, He does not give!" This blasphemy is repudiated. On the contrary, boundless is God's bounty, and He gives, as it were, with both hands outstretched,—a figure of speech for unbounded liberality.

773. Their jealousy—because Muṣtafā is chosen for God's Message—is so great that it only confirms and strengthens their rebellion and blasphemy.

774. *Cf.* v. 15, where the eternal warring of the Christian sects, among themselves and against the Jews, is referred to. The reference is to the whole of the People of the Book, Jews and Christians,—their internal squabbles and their external disputes, quarrels, and wars.

And hatred till the Day
Of Judgment. Every time
They kindle the fire of war,
God doth extinguish it;
But they (ever) strive
To do mischief on earth.
And God loveth not
Those who do mischief.[775]

وَالْبَغْضَاءَ إِلَىٰ يَوْمِ الْقِيَامَةِ ۚ
كُلَّمَا أَوْقَدُوا نَارًا لِّلْحَرْبِ أَطْفَأَهَا اللَّهُ ۚ
وَيَسْعَوْنَ فِي الْأَرْضِ فَسَادًا ۚ
وَاللَّهُ لَا يُحِبُّ الْمُفْسِدِينَ ○

65. If only the People of the Book
Had believed and been righteous,
We should indeed have
Blotted out their iniquities
And admitted them
To Gardens of Bliss.

٦٥- وَلَوْ أَنَّ أَهْلَ الْكِتَابِ آمَنُوا وَاتَّقَوْا
لَكَفَّرْنَا عَنْهُمْ سَيِّئَاتِهِمْ
وَلَأَدْخَلْنَاهُمْ جَنَّاتِ النَّعِيمِ ○

66. If only they had stood fast
By the Law, the Gospel,
And all the revelation that was sent
To them from their Lord,
They would have enjoyed
Happiness from every side.[776]
There is from among them
A party on the right course:
But many of them
Follow a course that is evil.

٦٦- وَلَوْ أَنَّهُمْ أَقَامُوا التَّوْرَاةَ وَالْإِنجِيلَ
وَمَا أُنزِلَ إِلَيْهِم مِّن رَّبِّهِمْ
لَأَكَلُوا مِن فَوْقِهِمْ
وَمِن تَحْتِ أَرْجُلِهِم ۚ مِّنْهُمْ أُمَّةٌ مُّقْتَصِدَةٌ ۖ
وَكَثِيرٌ مِّنْهُمْ سَاءَ مَا يَعْمَلُونَ ○ ع

Section 10.

67. O Apostle! proclaim
The (Message) which hath been
Sent to thee from thy Lord.[777]
If thou didst not, thou

٦٧- يَا أَيُّهَا الرَّسُولُ بَلِّغْ مَا أُنزِلَ إِلَيْكَ
مِن رَّبِّكَ ۖ وَإِن لَّمْ تَفْعَلْ

775. The argument of the whole verse may be thus stated. The Jews blaspheme and mock, and because of their jealousy, the more they are taught, the more obstinate they become in their rebellion. But what good will it do to them? Their selfishness and spite sow quarrels among themselves, which will not be healed till the Day of Judgment. When they stir up wars, especially against the innocent, God's Mercy is poured down like a flood of water to extinguish them. But their wickedness continues to devise ever new mischief. And God loves not mischief or those who do mischief.

776. The literal translation of the two lines would be: "They would have eaten from above them and from below their feet." To eat (*akala*) is a very comprehensive word, and denotes enjoyment generally, physical, social, mental and moral, and spiritual. "To eat what is forbidden" in verses 65 and 66 referred to taking unlawful profit, from usury or trust funds or in other ways. Here "eating" would seem to mean receiving satisfaction or happiness in ordinary life as well as in the spiritual world. "From above them" may refer to heavenly or spiritual satisfaction, and "from below their feet" to earthly satisfaction. But it is better to take the words as a general idiom, and understand "satisfaction or happiness from every side."

777. Muḥammad had many difficulties to contend with, many enemies and dangers to avoid. This is to assure him that his Message was true and from God. His mission must be fulfilled. And he must—as he did—go forward and proclaim that Message and fulfil his mission, trusting to God for protection, and unconcerned if people who had lost all sense of right rejected it or threatened him.

Wouldst not have fulfilled
And proclaimed His Mission.
And God will defend thee
From men (who mean mischief).
For God guideth not
Those who reject Faith.

فَمَا بَلَّغْتَ رِسَالَتَهُ ۚ
وَاللّٰهُ يَعْصِمُكَ مِنَ النَّاسِ ۗ
إِنَّ اللّٰهَ لَا يَهْدِى الْقَوْمَ الْكٰفِرِينَ ○

68. Say: "O People of the Book!
Ye have no ground
To stand upon unless
Ye stand fast by the Law,
The Gospel, and all the revelation
That has come to you from
Your Lord." It is the revelation
That cometh to thee from
Thy Lord, that increaseth in most
Of them their obstinate
Rebellion and blasphemy.
But sorrow thou not
Over (these) people without Faith.[778]

٦٨- قُلْ يٰٓأَهْلَ الْكِتٰبِ لَسْتُمْ عَلٰى شَىْءٍ
حَتّٰى تُقِيمُوا التَّوْرٰىةَ وَالْإِنْجِيلَ
وَمَآ أُنْزِلَ إِلَيْكُمْ مِّنْ رَّبِّكُمْ ۗ
وَلَيَزِيدَنَّ كَثِيرًا مِّنْهُمْ مَّآ أُنْزِلَ إِلَيْكَ
مِنْ رَّبِّكَ
طُغْيٰنًا وَّكُفْرًا ۚ
فَلَا تَأْسَ عَلَى الْقَوْمِ الْكٰفِرِينَ ○

69. Those who believe (in the Qur-ān),
Those who follow the Jewish
(scriptures),
And the Sabians and the
Christians,—
Any who believe in God
And the Last Day,
And work righteousness,—[779]
On them shall be no fear,
Nor shall they grieve.

٦٩- إِنَّ الَّذِينَ اٰمَنُوا
وَالَّذِينَ هَادُوا وَالصّٰبِئُونَ وَالنَّصٰرٰى
مَنْ اٰمَنَ بِاللّٰهِ وَالْيَوْمِ الْاٰخِرِ
وَعَمِلَ صٰلِحًا
فَلَا خَوْفٌ عَلَيْهِمْ وَلَا هُمْ يَحْزَنُونَ ○

70. We took the Covenant
Of the Children of Israel
And sent them apostles.
Every time there came
To them an apostle
With what they themselves
Desired not—some
(Of these) they called

٧٠- لَقَدْ أَخَذْنَا مِيثَاقَ بَنِىٓ إِسْرَآءِيلَ
وَأَرْسَلْنَآ إِلَيْهِمْ رُسُلًا ۗ
كُلَّمَا جَآءَهُمْ رَسُولٌۢ
بِمَا لَا تَهْوٰىٓ أَنْفُسُهُمْ ۙ فَرِيقًا

778. In v. 29 Moses was told not to sorrow over a rebellious people. Here Muḥammad is told not to sorrow over people without Faith. The second situation is even more trying than the first. Rebellion may be a passing phase. Want of faith is an attitude of mind that is well-nigh hopeless. Yet the Apostle patiently reasoned with them and bore their taunts and insults. If, the argument runs, you do not believe in anything, even in the things that you may be expected to believe in, how can you receive in Faith God's Message that has come in another form? In fact your jealousy adds to your obstinacy and unbelief.

779. *Cf.* ii. 62. As God's Message is one, Islam recognises true faith in other forms, provided that it be sincere, supported by reason, and backed up by righteous conduct. Note 76 explains who the Sabians were.

Impostors, and some they
(Go so far as to) slay.[780]

كَذَّبُوا وَفَرِيقًا يَقْتُلُونَ ○

71. They thought there would be
No trial (or punishment);
So they became blind and deaf;[781]
Yet God (in mercy) turned
To them; yet again many
Of them became blind and deaf.
But God sees well
All that they do.

٧١- وَحَسِبُوٓا أَلَّا تَكُونَ فِتْنَةٌ فَعَمُوا وَ
صَمُّوا ثُمَّ تَابَ اللّٰهُ عَلَيْهِمْ
ثُمَّ عَمُوا وَصَمُّوا كَثِيرٌ مِّنْهُمْ
وَاللّٰهُ بَصِيرٌۢ بِمَا يَعْمَلُونَ ○

72. They do blaspheme who say:
"God is Christ the son
Of Mary." But said Christ:[782]
"O Children of Israel!
Worship God, my Lord
And your Lord." Whoever
Joins other gods with God,—
God will forbid him
The Garden, and the Fire
Will be his abode. There will
For the wrong-doers
Be no one to help.

٧٢- لَقَدْ كَفَرَ الَّذِينَ قَالُوٓا إِنَّ اللّٰهَ هُوَ
الْمَسِيحُ ابْنُ مَرْيَمَ ط
وَقَالَ الْمَسِيحُ يٰبَنِيٓ إِسْرَآءِيلَ اعْبُدُوا
اللّٰهَ رَبِّي وَرَبَّكُمْ ط إِنَّهُ مَنْ يُّشْرِكْ بِاللّٰهِ
فَقَدْ حَرَّمَ اللّٰهُ عَلَيْهِ الْجَنَّةَ
وَمَأْوٰىهُ النَّارُ ط وَمَا لِلظّٰلِمِينَ مِنْ أَنْصَارٍ ○

73. They do blaspheme who say:
God is one of three
In a Trinity: for there is
No god except One God.
If they desist not
From their word (of blasphemy),
Verily a grievous penalty
Will befall the blasphemers
Among them.

٧٣- لَقَدْ كَفَرَ الَّذِينَ قَالُوٓا إِنَّ اللّٰهَ ثَالِثُ
ثَلٰثَةٍ م وَمَا مِنْ إِلٰهٍ إِلَّآ إِلٰهٌ وَّاحِدٌ ط
وَإِنْ لَّمْ يَنْتَهُوا
عَمَّا يَقُولُونَ لَيَمَسَّنَّ الَّذِينَ كَفَرُوا
مِنْهُمْ عَذَابٌ أَلِيمٌ ○

وقف لازم

74. Why turn they not to God,
And seek His forgiveness?
For God is Oft-forgiving,
Most Merciful.

٧٤- أَفَلَا يَتُوبُونَ إِلَى اللّٰهِ وَيَسْتَغْفِرُونَهُ ط
وَاللّٰهُ غَفُورٌ رَّحِيمٌ ○

75. Christ the son of Mary
Was no more than
An Apostle; many were
The apostles that passed away

٧٥- مَا الْمَسِيحُ ابْنُ مَرْيَمَ إِلَّا رَسُولٌ ج
قَدْ خَلَتْ مِنْ قَبْلِهِ الرُّسُلُ ط

780. *Cf.* ii. 87, and n. 91.

781. That is, they turned away their eyes from God's Signs and they turned a deaf ear to God's Message.

782. *Cf.* Matt. iv. 10, where Christ rebukes Satan for desiring the worship of other than God; John xx. 17, where Christ says to Mary Magdalene, "Go unto my brethren, and say unto them, I ascend unto my Father and your Father; and to my God and your God." *Cf.* also Luke xviii. 19, where Christ rebukes a certain ruler for calling him Good Master: "Why callest thou me good? None is good, save One, that is, God." In Mark xii. 25 Jesus says: "The first of all the commandments is, Hear, O Israel; the Lord our God is One Lord."

Before him. His mother
Was a woman of truth.[783]
They had both to eat
Their (daily) food.
See how God doth make
His Signs clear to them;[784]
Yet see in what ways
They are deluded
Away from the truth!

وَاُمُّهٗ صِدِّيْقَةٌ ۭ
كَانَا يَاْكُلٰنِ الطَّعَامَ ۭ
اُنْظُرْ كَيْفَ نُبَيِّنُ لَهُمُ الْاٰيٰتِ
ثُمَّ انْظُرْ اَنّٰى يُؤْفَكُوْنَ ۝

76. Say: "Will ye worship,
Besides God, something
Which hath no power either
To harm or benefit you?
But God,—He it is
That heareth and knoweth
All things."

٧٦- قُلْ اَتَعْبُدُوْنَ مِنْ دُوْنِ اللّٰهِ
مَا لَا يَمْلِكُ لَكُمْ ضَرًّا وَّلَا نَفْعًا ۭ
وَاللّٰهُ هُوَ السَّمِيْعُ الْعَلِيْمُ ۝

77. Say: "O People of the Book!
Exceed not in your religion[785]
The bounds (of what is proper),
Trespassing beyond the truth,
Nor follow the vain desires
Of people who went wrong
In times gone by,—who misled
Many, and strayed (themselves)
From the even Way.

٧٧- قُلْ يٰٓاَهْلَ الْكِتٰبِ
لَا تَغْلُوْا فِيْ دِيْنِكُمْ غَيْرَ الْحَقِّ
وَلَا تَتَّبِعُوْٓا اَهْوَاۗءَ قَوْمٍ قَدْ ضَلُّوْا مِنْ قَبْلُ
وَاَضَلُّوْا كَثِيْرًا
وَّضَلُّوْا عَنْ سَوَاۗءِ السَّبِيْلِ ۝ ع

SECTION 11.

78. Curses were pronounced
On those among the Children
Of Israel who rejected Faith,
By the tongue of David[786]
And of Jesus the son of Mary:[787]
Because they disobeyed
And persisted in Excesses.

٧٨- لُعِنَ الَّذِيْنَ كَفَرُوْا مِنْۢ بَنِيْٓ اِسْرَاۗءِيْلَ
عَلٰي لِسَانِ دَاوٗدَ وَعِيْسَى ابْنِ مَرْيَمَ ۭ
ذٰلِكَ بِمَا عَصَوْا وَّكَانُوْا يَعْتَدُوْنَ ۝

783. She never claimed that she was a mother of God, or that her son was God. She was a pious virtuous woman.

784. Note how logically the argument has led up from Jewish back-slidings and want of faith, to blasphemies associated with the names of Jesus and Mary, and in the following verses to the worship of senseless stocks and stones. God is One; His Message is one; yet how people's perversity transforms truth into falsehood, religion into superstition!

785. Excess, as opposed to moderation and reason, is the simplest test by which a hypocrite or a selfish man who "trades" on religion, is known from a sincere, pious, and truly religious man. Excess means that truth is sometimes concealed or trampled upon, that the fashions of ancestors or contemporaries are copied or overdone, and God's name is dishonoured by blasphemies or the setting up of false gods or fetishes, or that good (or even bad) men are deified and worshipped. The true path is the even path, the path of rectitude. (*Cf.* ii. 108, and v. 13).

786. The Psalms of David have several passages of imprecations against the wicked. *Cf.* Psalms cix. 17-18; lxxviii. 21-22 ("Therefore the Lord heard this and was wroth: so a fire was kindled against Jacob, and anger also came up against Israel; because they believed not in God, and trusted not in His salvation"); Psalms lxix. 22-28, and Psalms v. 10.

787. *Cf.* Matt. xxiii. 33 ("Ye serpents, ye generation of vipers, how can ye escape the damnation of Hell?); also Matt. xii. 34.

79. Nor did they (usually)
Forbid one another[788]
The iniquities which they
Committed: evil indeed
Were the deeds which they did.

٧٩- كَانُوا لَا يَتَنَاهَوْنَ عَن مُّنكَرٍ فَعَلُوهُ ۚ
لَبِئْسَ مَا كَانُوا يَفْعَلُونَ ○

80. Thou seest many of them
Turning in friendship
To the Unbelievers.
Evil indeed are (the works) which
Their souls have sent forward
Before them (with the result),
That God's wrath
Is on them,
And in torment
Will they abide.

٨٠- تَرَىٰ كَثِيرًا مِّنْهُمْ
يَتَوَلَّوْنَ الَّذِينَ كَفَرُوا ۚ
لَبِئْسَ مَا قَدَّمَتْ لَهُمْ أَنفُسُهُمْ
أَن سَخِطَ اللَّهُ عَلَيْهِمْ
وَفِي الْعَذَابِ هُمْ خَالِدُونَ ○

81. If only they had believed
In God, in the Apostle,
And in what hath been
Revealed to him, never
Would they have taken
Them for friends and protectors,
But most of them are
Rebellious wrong-doers.

٨١- وَلَوْ كَانُوا يُؤْمِنُونَ بِاللَّهِ وَالنَّبِيِّ
وَمَا أُنزِلَ إِلَيْهِ
مَا اتَّخَذُوهُمْ أَوْلِيَاءَ
وَلَٰكِنَّ كَثِيرًا مِّنْهُمْ فَاسِقُونَ ○

82. Strongest among men in enmity
To the Believers wilt thou
Find the Jews and Pagans;
And nearest among them in love
To the Believers wilt thou
Find those who say,[789]
" We are Christians":
Because amongst these are
Men devoted to learning[790]
And men who have renounced
6 The world, and they
30 Are not arrogant.

٨٢- لَتَجِدَنَّ أَشَدَّ النَّاسِ عَدَاوَةً لِّلَّذِينَ
آمَنُوا الْيَهُودَ وَالَّذِينَ أَشْرَكُوا ۖ
وَلَتَجِدَنَّ أَقْرَبَهُم مَّوَدَّةً لِّلَّذِينَ آمَنُوا
الَّذِينَ قَالُوا إِنَّا نَصَارَىٰ ۚ ذَٰلِكَ بِأَنَّ مِنْهُمْ
قِسِّيسِينَ وَرُهْبَانًا
وَأَنَّهُمْ لَا يَسْتَكْبِرُونَ ○

---

788. There are bad men in every community, but if leaders connive at the misdeeds of the commonalty,—and even worse, if leaders themselves share in the misdeeds, as happened with the Pharisees and Scribes against whom Jesus spoke out, then that community is doomed.

789. The meaning is not that they merely call themselves Christians, but that they are such sincere Christians that they appreciate Muslim virtues, as did the Abyssinians to whom Muslim refugees went during the persecution in Mecca. They would say: "It is true we are Christians, but we understand your point of view, and we know you are good men." They are Muslims at heart, whatever their label may be.

790. *Qissis*: I have translated as "devoted to learning," following the Commentators. It seems to be a foreign word, possibly Abyssinian rather than Syriac, as the reference seems to be to the Abyssinian Christians. Their real devotion to learning and the renunciation of the world by the Monastic Orders are contrasted with the hypocrisy and arrogance of the Pharisees and Scribes.

الجزء السابع

83. And when they listen
To the revelation received
By the Apostle, thou wilt
See their eyes overflowing
With tears, for they
Recognise the truth:
They pray: "Our Lord!
We believe; write us
Down among the witnesses.

٨٣- وَإِذَا سَمِعُوا مَا أُنْزِلَ إِلَى الرَّسُولِ
تَرَى أَعْيُنَهُمْ تَفِيضُ مِنَ الدَّمْعِ
مِمَّا عَرَفُوا مِنَ الْحَقِّ
يَقُولُونَ رَبَّنَا آمَنَّا
فَاكْتُبْنَا مَعَ الشّٰهِدِينَ ○

84. "What cause can we have
Not to believe in God
And the truth which has
Come to us, seeing that
We long for our Lord
To admit us to the company
Of the righteous?"

٨٤- وَمَا لَنَا لَا نُؤْمِنُ بِاللّٰهِ
وَمَا جَاءَنَا مِنَ الْحَقِّ
وَنَطْمَعُ أَنْ يُدْخِلَنَا رَبُّنَا
مَعَ الْقَوْمِ الصّٰلِحِينَ ○

85. And for this their prayer
Hath God rewarded them
With Gardens, with rivers
Flowing underneath,—their eternal
Home. Such is the recompense
Of those who do good.

٨٥- فَأَثَابَهُمُ اللّٰهُ بِمَا قَالُوا
جَنّٰتٍ تَجْرِي مِنْ تَحْتِهَا الْأَنْهٰرُ
خٰلِدِينَ فِيهَا وَذٰلِكَ جَزَاءُ الْمُحْسِنِينَ ○

86. But those who reject Faith
And belie Our Signs,—
They shall be Companions
Of Hell-fire.

٨٦- وَالَّذِينَ كَفَرُوا وَكَذَّبُوا بِآيٰتِنَا
أُولٰئِكَ أَصْحٰبُ الْجَحِيمِ ○

ع

C. 74.—In the physical pleasures of life
(v. 90—111.) The crime is excess: there is no merit
In abstention from things that are good
And lawful.. Take no rash vows,
But to solemn oaths be faithful. Shun
As abominations drinking and gambling,
And superstitions of all kinds.
But be reverent to what is sacred
In rites and associations. Not the same
Are things good and things evil.
Learn to distinguish, but pry not
Into questions beyond your ken.
Guard your own souls in truth
And justice, and no harm can befall you.

SECTION 12.

87. O ye who believe!
Make not unlawful

٨٧- يٰأَيُّهَا الَّذِينَ آمَنُوا لَا تُحَرِّمُوا

The good things which God
Hath made lawful for you,
But commit no excess:[791]
For God loveth not
Those given to excess.

طَيِّبٰتِ مَآ اَحَلَّ اللّٰهُ لَكُمْ
وَلَا تَعْتَدُوْا ؕ
اِنَّ اللّٰهَ لَا يُحِبُّ الْمُعْتَدِيْنَ ۝

88. Eat of the things which
God hath provided for you,
Lawful and good; but fear
God, in Whom ye believe.

٨٨- وَكُلُوْا مِمَّا رَزَقَكُمُ اللّٰهُ حَلٰلًا طَيِّبًا
وَّاتَّقُوا اللّٰهَ الَّذِیْٓ اَنْتُمْ بِهٖ مُؤْمِنُوْنَ ۝

89. God will not call you
To account for what is
Futile in your oaths,[792]
But He will call you
To account for your deliberate
Oaths: for expiation, feed
Ten indigent persons,
On a scale of the average
For the food of your families;
Or clothe them; or give
A slave his freedom.
If that is beyond your means,
Fast for three days.
That is the expiation
For the oaths ye have sworn.
But keep to your oaths.
Thus doth God make clear
To you His Signs, that ye
May be grateful.

٨٩- لَا يُؤَاخِذُكُمُ اللّٰهُ بِاللَّغْوِ فِیْٓ اَيْمَانِكُمْ
وَلٰكِنْ يُّؤَاخِذُكُمْ بِمَا عَقَّدْتُّمُ الْاَيْمَانَ ۚ
فَكَفَّارَتُهٗٓ اِطْعَامُ عَشَرَةِ مَسٰكِيْنَ
مِنْ اَوْسَطِ مَا تُطْعِمُوْنَ اَهْلِيْكُمْ
اَوْ كِسْوَتُهُمْ اَوْ تَحْرِيْرُ رَقَبَةٍ ؕ
فَمَنْ لَّمْ يَجِدْ فَصِيَامُ ثَلٰثَةِ اَيَّامٍ ؕ ذٰلِكَ
كَفَّارَةُ اَيْمَانِكُمْ اِذَا حَلَفْتُمْ ؕ
وَاحْفَظُوْٓا اَيْمَانَكُمْ ؕ
كَذٰلِكَ يُبَيِّنُ اللّٰهُ لَكُمْ اٰيٰتِهٖ
لَعَلَّكُمْ تَشْكُرُوْنَ ۝

90. O ye who believe!
Intoxicants and gambling,[793]

٩٠- يٰٓاَيُّهَا الَّذِيْنَ اٰمَنُوْٓا اِنَّمَا الْخَمْرُ وَالْمَيْسِرُ

---

791. In pleasures that are good and lawful the crime is excess. There is no merit merely in abstention or asceticism, though the humility or unselfishness that may go with asceticism may have its value. In v. 85 Christian monks are praised for particular virtues, though here and elsewhere monasticism is disapproved of. Use God's gifts of all kinds with gratitude, but excess is not approved of by God.

792. Vows of penance or abstention may sometimes be futile, or even stand in the way of a really good or virtuous act. See ii. 224-226, and notes. The general principles established are: (1) take no futile oaths; (2) use not God's name, literally or in intention, to fetter yourself against doing a lawful or good act; (3) keep to your solemn oaths to the utmost of your ability; (4) where you are unable to do so, expiate your failure by feeding or clothing the poor, or obtaining some one's freedom, or if you have not the means, by fasting. This is from a spiritual aspect. If any party suffers damage from your failure, compensation will be due to him, but that would be a question of law or equity.

793. *Cf.* ii. 219, and notes 240 and 241.

(Dedication of) stones,[794]
And (divination by) arrows,[795]
Are an abomination,—
Of Satan's handiwork:
Eschew such (abomination),
That ye may prosper.

وَالْاَنْصَابُ وَالْاَزْلَامُ
رِجْسٌ مِّنْ عَمَلِ الشَّيْطٰنِ
فَاجْتَنِبُوْهُ لَعَلَّكُمْ تُفْلِحُوْنَ ○

91. Satan's plan is (but)
To excite enmity and hatred
Between you, with intoxicants
And gambling, and hinder you
From the remembrance
Of God, and from prayer:
Will ye not then abstain?

٩١- اِنَّمَا يُرِيْدُ الشَّيْطٰنُ
اَنْ يُّوْقِعَ بَيْنَكُمُ الْعَدَاوَةَ وَالْبَغْضَآءَ فِي
الْخَمْرِ وَالْمَيْسِرِ وَيَصُدَّكُمْ عَنْ ذِكْرِ اللّٰهِ
وَعَنِ الصَّلٰوةِ ۚ فَهَلْ اَنْتُمْ مُّنْتَهُوْنَ ○

92. Obey God, and obey the Apostle,[796]
And beware (of evil):
If ye do turn back,
Know ye that it is
Our Apostle's duty
To proclaim (the Message)[797]
In the clearest manner.

٩٢- وَاَطِيْعُوا اللّٰهَ وَاَطِيْعُوا الرَّسُوْلَ
وَاحْذَرُوْا ۚ
فَاِنْ تَوَلَّيْتُمْ فَاعْلَمُوْٓا اَنَّمَا عَلٰى رَسُوْلِنَا
الْبَلٰغُ الْمُبِيْنُ ○

93. On those who believe
And do deeds of righteousness
There is no blame
For what they ate (in the past),
When they guard themselves
From evil, and believe,
And do deeds of righteousness,—
(Or) again, guard themselves
From evil and believe,—
(Or) again, guard themselves
From evil and do good.

٩٣- لَيْسَ عَلَى الَّذِيْنَ اٰمَنُوْا وَعَمِلُوا
الصّٰلِحٰتِ
جُنَاحٌ فِيْمَا طَعِمُوْٓا اِذَا مَا اتَّقَوْا
وَّاٰمَنُوْا وَعَمِلُوا الصّٰلِحٰتِ
ثُمَّ اتَّقَوْا وَّاٰمَنُوْا
ثُمَّ اتَّقَوْا وَّاَحْسَنُوْا ۭ

794. *Cf.* v. 4. The stones there referred to were stone altars or stone columns on which oil was poured for consecration, or slabs on which meat was sacrificed to idols. Any idolatrous or superstitious practices are here condemned. The anṣāb were objects of worship, and were common in Arabia before Islam. See Renan, "History of Israel", Chapter IV. and *Corpus Inscriptionum Semiticarum*, Part I. p. 154: Illustrations Nos. 123 and 123 *bis* are Phœnician columns of that kind, found in Malta.

795. *Cf.* v. 4. The arrows there referred to were used for the division of meat by a sort of lottery or raffle. But arrows were also used for divination, *i.e.*, for ascertaining lucky or unlucky moments, or learning the wishes of the heathen gods, as to whether men should undertake certain actions or not. All superstitions are condemned.

796. We are asked to obey the commands of God (which are always reasonable), instead of following superstitions (which are irrational), or seeking undue stimulation in intoxicants or undue advantage in gambling. To some there may be temporary excitement or pleasure in these, but that is not the way either of prosperity or piety.

797. *Cf.* v. 70. Both the worldly and the spiritual aspects of loss are pointed out. Can God's Message do more?

For God loveth those
Who do good.[798]

SECTION 13.

94. O ye who believe!
God doth but make a trial of you
In a little matter
Of game well within reach
Of your hands and your lances,
That He may test[799]
Who feareth Him unseen:
Any who transgress
Thereafter, will have
A grievous penalty.

95. O ye who believe!
Kill not game
While in the Sacred
Precincts or in pilgrim garb.[800]
If any of you doth so
Intentionally, the compensation
Is an offering, brought
To the Ka'ba, of a domestic animal
Equivalent to the one he killed,[801]

ع وَاللّٰهُ يُحِبُّ الْمُحْسِنِيْنَ ۝

٩٤- يٰۤاَيُّهَا الَّذِيْنَ اٰمَنُوْا لَيَبْلُوَنَّكُمُ اللّٰهُ
بِشَيْءٍ مِّنَ الصَّيْدِ تَنَالُهٗۤ اَيْدِيْكُمْ وَ
رِمَاحُكُمْ لِيَعْلَمَ اللّٰهُ مَنْ يَّخَافُهٗ بِالْغَيْبِ ۚ
فَمَنِ اعْتَدٰى بَعْدَ ذٰلِكَ
فَلَهٗ عَذَابٌ اَلِيْمٌ ۝

٩٥- يٰۤاَيُّهَا الَّذِيْنَ اٰمَنُوْا لَا تَقْتُلُوا الصَّيْدَ
وَاَنْتُمْ حُرُمٌ ۗ
وَمَنْ قَتَلَهٗ مِنْكُمْ مُّتَعَمِّدًا
فَجَزَآءٌ مِّثْلُ مَا قَتَلَ مِنَ النَّعَمِ

---

798. There is a subtle symphony in what appears at first sight to be a triple repetition. The relation of such simple regulations as those of food, or game, or the reverence due to a sacred place or sacred institution, has to be explained *vis-a-vis* man's higher duties. Baidhāwi is right in classifying such duties under three heads: those due to God, those due from a man to himself (his self-respect), and those due to other creatures of God. Or perhaps all duties have this threefold aspect. The first may be called Believing or Faith; the second, Guarding ourselves from evil, or Conscience; and the third, doing good or Righteousness. But the simplest physical rules, *e.g.*, those about eating, cleanliness, etc., if they are good, refer also to the higher aspects. If we eat bad food, we hurt ourselves, we cause offence to our neighbours, and we disobey God. If we have faith and righteousness, are we likely to be wanting in conscience? If we have conscience and faith, are we likely to fail in righteousness? If we have conscience and righteousness, what can be their foundation but faith? All three manifest themselves in a willing obedience to God, and love for Him. We realise His love in loving and doing good to His creatures, and our love for Him is meaningless without such good.

799. Literally, "know". *Cf.* iii. 166, and iii. 154, n. 467. Game is forbidden in the Sacred Precincts. If we deliberately break that injunction, we have no faith and reverence.

800. See v. 2, and n. 684. The pilgrim garb, Iḥrām, has been explained in n. 212, ii. 196.

801. For an inadvertent breach of the game rule there is apparently no penalty. Intentional breach will be prevented, if possible, by previous action. If in some case the preventive action is not effective, the penalty is prescribed. The penalty is in three alternatives: an equivalent animal should be brought to the Ka'ba for sacrifice; if so, the meat would be distributed to the poor; *or* the poor must be fed, with grain or money, according to the value of the animal if one had been sacrificed; *or* the offender must fast as many days as the number of the poor who would have been fed under the second alternative. Probably the last alternative would only be open if the offender is too poor to afford the first or second, but on this point Commentators are not agreed. The "equivalent animal" in the first alternative would be a domestic animal of similar value or weight in meat or of similar shape (*e.g.*, goat to antelope), as adjudged by two just men on the spot.

The alternatives about the penalty and its remission ("God forgives what is past") or exaction explain the last two lines of the verse: being "Exalted and Lord of Retribution", God can remit or regulate according to His just laws.

As adjudged by two just men
Among you; or by way
Of atonement, the feeding
Of the indigent; or its
Equivalent in fasts: that he
May taste of the penalty
Of his deed. God
Forgives what is past:
For repetition God will
Exact from him the penalty.
For God is Exalted,
And Lord of Retribution.

يَحْكُمُ بِهٖ ذَوَا عَدْلٍ مِّنْكُمْ هَدْيًا بٰلِغَ
الْكَعْبَةِ اَوْ كَفَّارَةٌ طَعَامُ مَسٰكِيْنَ
اَوْ عَدْلُ ذٰلِكَ صِيَامًا لِّيَذُوْقَ وَبَالَ
اَمْرِهٖ ؕ عَفَا اللّٰهُ عَمَّا سَلَفَ ؕ
وَمَنْ عَادَ فَيَنْتَقِمُ اللّٰهُ مِنْهُ ؕ
وَاللّٰهُ عَزِيْزٌ ذُو انْتِقَامٍ ○

96. Lawful to you is the pursuit[802]
Of water-game and its use
For food,—for the benefit
Of yourselves and those who
Travel; but forbidden
Is the pursuit of land-game;—
As long as ye are
In the Sacred Precincts
Or in pilgrim garb.
And fear God, to Whom
Ye shall be gathered back.

٩٦- اُحِلَّ لَكُمْ صَيْدُ الْبَحْرِ وَطَعَامُهٗ
مَتَاعًا لَّكُمْ وَلِلسَّيَّارَةِ ۚ
وَحُرِّمَ عَلَيْكُمْ صَيْدُ الْبَرِّ
مَا دُمْتُمْ حُرُمًا ؕ
وَاتَّقُوا اللّٰهَ الَّذِيْۤ اِلَيْهِ تُحْشَرُوْنَ ○

97. God made the Ka'ba,
The Sacred House, an asylum
Of security for men, as
Also the Sacred Months,[803]
The animals for offerings,
And the garlands that mark them:[804]
That ye may know
That God hath knowledge
Of what is in the heavens
And on earth and that God
Is well acquainted
With all things.[805]

٩٧- جَعَلَ اللّٰهُ الْكَعْبَةَ
الْبَيْتَ الْحَرَامَ قِيٰمًا لِّلنَّاسِ
وَالشَّهْرَ الْحَرَامَ
وَالْهَدْيَ وَالْقَلَآئِدَ ؕ
ذٰلِكَ لِتَعْلَمُوْۤا اَنَّ اللّٰهَ
يَعْلَمُ مَا فِي السَّمٰوٰتِ وَمَا فِي الْاَرْضِ
وَاَنَّ اللّٰهَ بِكُلِّ شَيْءٍ عَلِيْمٌ ○

98. Know ye that God
Is strict in punishment

٩٨- اِعْلَمُوْۤا اَنَّ اللّٰهَ شَدِيْدُ الْعِقَابِ

---

802. *Water-game*: *i.e.*, game found in water, *e.g.*, water-fowl, fish, etc. "Water" includes sea, river, lake, pond, etc.

803. The Sacred or Prohibited Months are explained in n. 209, ii. 194, and n. 687, v. 3.

804. See v. 3 and n. 688.

805 All sorts of people from all parts of the earth gather during the Pilgrimage. They must not think that they are strangers, that nobody knows them, and that they may behave as they like. It is the House of God, and He has supreme knowledge of all things, of all thoughts, and all motives. As the next verse says, while He is Oft-forgiving, Most Merciful, He is also strict in enforcing respect for His ordinances.

And that God is
Oft-forgiving, Most Merciful.

وَاَنَّ اللّٰهَ غَفُوْرٌ رَّحِيْمٌ ۝

99. The Apostle's duty is
But to proclaim (the Message).
But God knoweth all
That ye reveal and ye conceal.

٩٩- مَا عَلَى الرَّسُوْلِ اِلَّا الْبَلٰغُ ۭ
وَاللّٰهُ يَعْلَمُ مَا تُبْدُوْنَ وَمَا تَكْتُمُوْنَ ۝

100. Say: "Not equal are things
That are bad and things
That are good, even though
The abundance of the bad
May dazzle thee;[806]
So fear God, O ye
That understand;
That (so) ye may prosper."

١٠٠- قُلْ لَّا يَسْتَوِي الْخَبِيْثُ
وَالطَّيِّبُ وَلَوْ اَعْجَبَكَ كَثْرَةُ الْخَبِيْثِ ۚ
فَاتَّقُوا اللّٰهَ يٰٓاُولِي الْاَلْبَابِ
لَعَلَّكُمْ تُفْلِحُوْنَ ۝ ربع

SECTION 14.

101. O ye who believe!
Ask not questions
About things which,
If made plain to you,
May cause you trouble.
But if ye ask about things
When the Qur-ān is being
Revealed, they will be
Made plain to you,[807]
God will forgive those:
For God is Oft-forgiving,
Most Forbearing.

١٠١- يٰٓاَيُّهَا الَّذِيْنَ اٰمَنُوْا لَا تَسْـَٔلُوْا
عَنْ اَشْيَاۗءَ اِنْ تُبْدَ لَكُمْ تَسُؤْكُمْ ۚ
وَاِنْ تَسْـَٔلُوْا
عَنْهَا حِيْنَ يُنَزَّلُ الْقُرْاٰنُ تُبْدَ لَكُمْ ۭ
عَفَا اللّٰهُ عَنْهَا ۭ
وَاللّٰهُ غَفُوْرٌ حَلِيْمٌ ۝

102. Some people before you
Did ask such questions,[808]

١٠٢- قَدْ سَاَلَهَا قَوْمٌ مِّنْ قَبْلِكُمْ

---

806. *Cf.* ii. 204. People often judge by quantity rather than quality. They are dazzled by numbers: their hearts are captured by what they see everywhere around them. But the man of understanding and discrimination judges by a different standard. He knows that good and bad things are not to be lumped together, and carefully chooses the best, which may be the scarcest, and avoids the bad, though evil may meet him at every step.

807. Many secrets are wisely hidden from us. If the future were known to us, we need not necessarily be happy. In many cases we should be miserable. If the inner meaning of some of the things we see before our eyes were disclosed to us, it might cause a lot of mischief. God's Message, in so far as it is necessary for shaping our conduct, is plain and open to us. But there are many things too deep for us to understand, either individually or collectively. It would be foolish to pry into them, as some foolish people tried to do in the time of the Apostle. Where a matter is mentioned in the Qur-ān, we can reverently ask for its meaning. That is not forbidden. But we should never pass the bounds of (1) our own capacity to understand, (2) the time and occasion when we ask questions, and (3) the part of the Universal Plan which it is God's purpose to reveal to us.

808. For example, the merely fractious questions asked of Moses by the Jews: ii. 68-71. They showed that they had no faith. When foolish questions are asked, and there is no answer, it also shakes the faith of the foolish ones.

And on that account
Lost their faith.

ثُمَّ أَصْبَحُوا بِهَا كٰفِرِينَ ○

103. It was not God
Who instituted (superstitions[809]
Like those of) a slit-ear
She-camel, or a she-camel
Let loose for free pasture,
Or idol sacrifices for
Twin-births in animals,
Or stallion-camels
Freed from w k
It is blasphemers
Who Invent a lie
Against God; but most
Of them lack wisdom.

١٠٣- مَا جَعَلَ اللّٰهُ مِنْ بَحِيرَةٍ
وَّلَا سَآئِبَةٍ
وَّلَا وَصِيلَةٍ
وَّلَا حَامٍ
وَّلٰكِنَّ الَّذِينَ كَفَرُوا
يَفْتَرُونَ عَلَى اللّٰهِ الْكَذِبَ
وَأَكْثَرُهُمْ لَا يَعْقِلُونَ ○

104. When it is said to them:
"Come to what God
Hath revealed; come
To the Apostle":
They say: "Enough for us[810]
Are the ways we found
Our fathers following."
What! even though their fathers
Were void of knowledge
And guidance?

١٠٤- وَإِذَا قِيلَ لَهُمْ تَعَالَوْا إِلٰى مَآ أَنْزَلَ
اللّٰهُ وَإِلَى الرَّسُولِ
قَالُوا حَسْبُنَا مَا وَجَدْنَا عَلَيْهِ آبَآءَنَا
أَوَلَوْ كَانَ آبَآؤُهُمْ لَا يَعْلَمُونَ شَيْئًا
وَّلَا يَهْتَدُونَ ○

105. O ye who believe!
Guard your own souls:
If ye follow (right) guidance,
No hurt can come to you
From those who stray.
The goal of you all
Is to God: it is He
That will show you
The truth of all
That ye do.[811]

١٠٥- يٰٓأَيُّهَا الَّذِينَ آمَنُوا عَلَيْكُمْ
أَنْفُسَكُمْ
لَا يَضُرُّكُمْ مَّنْ ضَلَّ إِذَا اهْتَدَيْتُمْ
إِلَى اللّٰهِ مَرْجِعُكُمْ جَمِيعًا
فَيُنَبِّئُكُمْ بِمَا كُنْتُمْ تَعْمَلُونَ ○

809. A number of Arab Pagan superstitions are referred to. The Pagan mind, not understanding the hidden secrets of nature, attributed certain phenomena to divine anger and were assailed by superstitious fears which haunted their lives. If a she-camel or other female domestic animal had a large number of young, she (or one of her offspring) had her ear slit and she was dedicated to a god: such an animal was a *baḥīra*. On return in safety from a journey, or on recovery from an illness a she-camel was similarly dedicated and let loose for free pasture: she was called a *sāiba*. Where an animal bore twins, certain sacrifices or dedications were made to idols: an animal so dedicated was a *waṣīla*. A stallion-camel dedicated to the gods by certain rites was a *ḥām*. The particular examples lead to the general truth: that superstition is due to ignorance, and is degrading to men and dishonouring to God.

810 *Cf.* ii. 170. Where an apostle of Truth comes to teach us the better way, it is foolish to say: "What our ancestors did is good enough for us."

811. *Cf.* v. 51. There the unity of God will reconcile different views. The unity of the one Judge will do perfect justice to each one's conduct, however different in form it may have appeared in this world.

106. O ye who believe!
When death approaches
Any of you, (take) witnesses
Among yourselves when making
Bequests,—two just men
Of your own (brotherhood)
Or others from outside
If ye are journeying
Through the earth,
And the chance of death
Befalls you (thus).
If ye doubt (their truth),
Detain them both
After prayer, and let them both
Swear by God:
"We wish not in this
For any worldly gain,
Even though the (beneficiary)
Be our near relation:
We shall hide not
The evidence before God:
If we do, then behold!
The sin be upon us!"[812]

١٠٦- يَاَيُّهَا الَّذِيْنَ اٰمَنُوْا شَهَادَةُ بَيْنِكُمْ
اِذَا حَضَرَ اَحَدَكُمُ الْمَوْتُ
حِيْنَ الْوَصِيَّةِ اثْنٰنِ ذَوَا عَدْلٍ مِّنْكُمْ
اَوْ اٰخَرٰنِ مِنْ غَيْرِكُمْ
اِنْ اَنْتُمْ ضَرَبْتُمْ فِي الْاَرْضِ
فَاَصَابَتْكُمْ مُّصِيْبَةُ الْمَوْتِ
تَحْبِسُوْنَهُمَا مِنْۢ بَعْدِ الصَّلٰوةِ
فَيُقْسِمٰنِ بِاللّٰهِ
اِنِ ارْتَبْتُمْ لَا نَشْتَرِيْ بِهٖ ثَمَنًا
وَّلَوْ كَانَ ذَا قُرْبٰى
وَلَا نَكْتُمُ شَهَادَةَ اللّٰهِ
اِنَّآ اِذًا لَّمِنَ الْاٰثِمِيْنَ ○

107. But if it gets known
That these two were guilty
Of the sin (of perjury),
Let two others stand forth
In their places,—nearest
In kin from among those
Who claim a lawful right:[813]
Let them swear by God:
"We affirm that our witness
Is truer than that
Of those two, and that we
Have not trespassed (beyond
The truth): if we did,
Behold! the wrong be
Upon us!"

١٠٧- فَاِنْ عُثِرَ عَلٰٓى اَنَّهُمَا اسْتَحَقَّآ اِثْمًا
فَاٰخَرٰنِ يَقُوْمٰنِ مَقَامَهُمَا
مِنَ الَّذِيْنَ اسْتَحَقَّ عَلَيْهِمُ الْاَوْلَيٰنِ
فَيُقْسِمٰنِ بِاللّٰهِ
لَشَهَادَتُنَآ اَحَقُّ مِنْ شَهَادَتِهِمَا
وَمَا اعْتَدَيْنَآ
اِنَّآ اِذًا لَّمِنَ الظّٰلِمِيْنَ ○

108. That is most suitable:
That they may give the evidence

١٠٨- ذٰلِكَ اَدْنٰٓى اَنْ يَّاْتُوْا بِالشَّهَادَةِ

812. Ordinarily this oath should be decisive, and the matter must rest here. But if it gets known that the oath was false, other evidence may be taken as in the next verse.

813. *Istaḥaqqa* = Deserved having something (good or evil) attributed to one; hence the alternative meanings: (1) committed or was guilty (of a sin); (2) had or claimed a lawful right (to property). The procedure was followed in an actual case in the Apostle's life-time. A man from Medina died abroad, having made over his goods to two friends, to be delivered to his designated heirs in Medina. They, however, kept back a valuable silver cup. When this was found out, oaths were taken from those who knew, and justice was done.

In its true nature and shape,
Or else they would fear
That other oaths would be
Taken after their oaths.
But fear God, and listen
(To His counsel): for God
Guideth not a rebellious people:

عَلٰى وَجْهِهَآ اَوْ يَخَافُوْٓا اَنْ تُرَدَّ اَيْمَانٌۢ
بَعْدَ اَيْمَانِهِمْ ۗ وَاتَّقُوا اللّٰهَ وَاسْمَعُوْا ۗ
وَاللّٰهُ لَا يَهْدِى الْقَوْمَ الْفٰسِقِيْنَ ۝ ع

C. 75.—Jesus did feed his disciples by miracle,
(v. 112-123.) But he claimed not divinity: he was
A true servant of God, to Whom doth belong
The dominion of the heavens and the earth:
Glory and power are His, and His alone.

SECTION 15.

109. One day will God
Gather the apostles together,
And ask: "What was
The response ye received
(From men to your teaching)?"
They will say: "We
Have no knowledge: it is Thou
Who knowest in full
All that is hidden."[814]

١٠٩- يَوْمَ يَجْمَعُ اللّٰهُ الرُّسُلَ
فَيَقُوْلُ مَاذَآ اُجِبْتُمْ ۗ
قَالُوْا لَا عِلْمَ لَنَا ۗ
اِنَّكَ اَنْتَ عَلَّامُ الْغُيُوْبِ ۝

110. Then will God say:
"O Jesus the son of Mary!
Recount My favour[815]
To thee and to thy mother.
Behold! I strengthened thee[816]
With the holy spirit,
So that thou didst speak
To the people in childhood
And in maturity.[817]
Behold! I taught thee
The Book and Wisdom,[818]
The Law and the Gospel.
And behold! thou makest[819]
Out of clay, as it were,

١١٠- اِذْ قَالَ اللّٰهُ يٰعِيْسَى ابْنَ مَرْيَمَ
اذْكُرْ نِعْمَتِيْ عَلَيْكَ وَعَلٰى وَالِدَتِكَ ۘ
اِذْ اَيَّدْتُّكَ بِرُوْحِ الْقُدُسِ ۗ
تُكَلِّمُ النَّاسَ فِى الْمَهْدِ وَكَهْلًا ۚ
وَاِذْ عَلَّمْتُكَ الْكِتٰبَ وَالْحِكْمَةَ
وَالتَّوْرٰىةَ وَالْاِنْجِيْلَ ۚ
وَاِذْ تَخْلُقُ مِنَ الطِّيْنِ

---

814. A scene of the Day of Reckoning is put before us in graphic words, showing the responsibility and the limitations of the men of God, sent to preach God's Message to men. with special reference to the Message of Jesus. The Messengers are sent to preach the Truth. What fantastic forms the Message takes in men's reactions to it was beyond their knowledge at the time, and beyond their responsibility.

815. In a solemn scene before the Court of Judgment, Jesus is asked to recount all the mercies and favours shown to him, so that his followers should become ashamed of their ingratitude in corrupting that Message, when they could have done so much in profiting by its purity and spiritual truth. This argument continues to the end of the Sūra.

816. *Cf.* ii. 87, and iii. 62, n. 401.

817. *Cf.* iii. 46, and n. 388.

818. *Cf.* iii 48.

819. *Cf.* iii. 49, and n. 390.

The figure of a bird,
By My leave,
And thou breathest into it,
And it becometh a bird
By My leave,
And thou healest those
Born blind, and the lepers,
By My leave.
And behold! thou
Bringest forth the dead
By My leave.[820]
And behold! I did
Restrain the Children of Israel
From (violence to) thee[821]
When thou didst show them
The Clear Signs,
And the unbelievers among them
Said: 'This is nothing
But evident magic.'[822]

كَهَيْـَٔةِ الطَّيْرِ بِإِذْنِى
فَتَنْفُخُ فِيهَا
فَتَكُونُ طَيْرًا بِإِذْنِى
وَتُبْرِئُ الْأَكْمَهَ وَالْأَبْرَصَ بِإِذْنِى
وَإِذْ تُخْرِجُ الْمَوْتَى بِإِذْنِى
وَإِذْ كَفَفْتُ بَنِىٓ إِسْرَٰٓءِيلَ عَنْكَ
إِذْ جِئْتَهُمْ بِالْبَيِّنَٰتِ
فَقَالَ الَّذِينَ كَفَرُوا مِنْهُمْ
إِنْ هَٰذَآ إِلَّا سِحْرٌ مُّبِينٌ ○

111. "And behold! I inspired
The Disciples to have faith
In Me and Mine Apostle:
They said, 'We have faith,
And do thou[823] bear witness
That we bow to God
As Muslims'."[824]

١١١- وَإِذْ أَوْحَيْتُ إِلَى الْحَوَارِيِّـۧنَ
أَنْ ءَامِنُوا بِى وَبِرَسُولِى
قَالُوٓا ءَامَنَّا
وَاشْهَدْ بِأَنَّنَا مُسْلِمُونَ ○

112. Behold! the Disciples said:
"O Jesus the son of Mary!
Can thy Lord send down to us
A Table set (with viands)

١١٢- إِذْ قَالَ الْحَوَارِيُّونَ يَٰعِيسَى ابْنَ مَرْيَمَ
هَلْ يَسْتَطِيعُ رَبُّكَ أَنْ يُنَزِّلَ عَلَيْنَا مَآئِدَةً

820. Note how the words "by My leave" are repeated with each miracle to emphasize the fact that they arose, not out of the power or will of Jesus, but by the leave and will and power of God, who is supreme over Jesus as He is over all other mortals.

821. The Jews were seeking to take the life of Jesus long before their final attempt to crucify him: see Luke iv. 28-29. Their attempt to crucify him was also foiled, according to the teaching we have received: Q. iv. 157.

822. According to Luke (xi. 15), when Christ performed the miracle of casting out devils, the Jews said he did it through the chief of the devils, *i.e.*, they accused him of black magic. No such miracle of casting out devils is mentioned in the Qur-ān, nor are we asked to believe in demoniacal possession of that kind. But Moses, Jesus, and Muḥammad were all accused of magic and sorcery, by those who could find no other explanation of God's power.

823. "Thou" refers to Jesus, who is being addressed by his Disciples. *Cf.* iii. 52.

824. Before or after Muḥammad's life on this earth, all who bowed to God's Will were Muslims, and their religion is Islam. *Cf.* iii. 52, and n. 392.

From heaven?" Said Jesus:
"Fear God, if ye have faith."[825]

مِنَ السَّمَآءِ ۚ قَالَ اتَّقُوا اللّٰهَ اِنْ كُنْتُمْ مُّؤْمِنِيْنَ ○

113. They said: "We only wish
To eat thereof and satisfy
Our hearts, and to know
That thou hast indeed
Told us the truth; and
That we ourselves may be
Witnesses to the miracle."

١١٣- قَالُوْا نُرِيْدُ اَنْ نَّاْكُلَ مِنْهَا وَ
تَطْمَئِنَّ قُلُوْبُنَا
وَنَعْلَمَ اَنْ قَدْ صَدَقْتَنَا
وَنَكُوْنَ عَلَيْهَا مِنَ الشّٰهِدِيْنَ ○

114. Said Jesus the son of Mary:
"O God our Lord!
Send us from heaven
A Table set (with viands),[826]
That there may be for us—
For the first and the last of us—
A solemn festival
And a Sign from Thee;
And provide for our sustenance,[827]
For Thou art the best
Sustainer (of our needs)."

١١٤- قَالَ عِيْسَى ابْنُ مَرْيَمَ اللّٰهُمَّ رَبَّنَآ
اَنْزِلْ عَلَيْنَا مَآئِدَةً مِّنَ السَّمَآءِ
تَكُوْنُ لَنَا عِيْدًا لِّاَوَّلِنَا وَاٰخِرِنَا
وَاٰيَةً مِّنْكَ ۚ
وَارْزُقْنَا وَاَنْتَ خَيْرُ الرّٰزِقِيْنَ ○

115. God said: "I will
Send it down unto you:
But if any of you
After that resisteth faith,
I will punish him
With a penalty such
As I have not inflicted
On any one among

١١٥- قَالَ اللّٰهُ اِنِّيْ مُنَزِّلُهَا عَلَيْكُمْ ۚ
فَمَنْ يَّكْفُرْ بَعْدُ مِنْكُمْ
فَاِنِّيْٓ اُعَذِّبُهٗ عَذَابًا
لَّآ اُعَذِّبُهٗٓ اَحَدًا مِّنَ

825. The request of the Disciples savours a little of (1) want of faith, (2) too much attention to physical food, and (3) a childish desire for miracles or Signs. All these three can be proved from the Canonical Gospels. (1) Simon Peter, quite early in the story, asked Jesus to depart from him, as he (Simon) was a sinful man (Luke v. 8). The same Peter afterwards denied his Master three several times shamelessly when the Master was in the power of his enemies. And one of the Disciples (Judas) actually betrayed Jesus. (2) Even in the Canonical Gospels, so many of the miracles are concerned with food and drink; *e.g.*, the turning of the water into wine (John, ii. 1-11); the conversion of five loaves and two small fishes into food for 5,000 men (John vi. 5 13), this being the *only* miracle recorded in all the four Gospels; the miraculous number of fishes caught for food (Luke v. 4-11); the cursing of the fig tree because it had no fruit (Matt. xxi. 18-19); the allegory of eating Christ's flesh and drinking his blood (John vi. 53-57). (3) Because the Samaritans would not receive Jesus into their village, the Disciples James and John wanted a fire to come down from heaven and consume them (Luke ix. 54).

826. The words of the Prayer seem to suggest the Last Supper. *Cf.* also the vision of Peter in "The Acts of the Apostles", x. 9-16.

827. As in Islam, so in Christ's Prayer, sustenance should be taken for both physical and spiritual strength, especially the latter. "Give us this day our daily bread" seems the rendering of a literalist whose attention was fixed too much on bread.

All the peoples."[828]

الْعٰلَمِيْنَ ۝ ع ١٥

SECTION 16.

116. And behold! God will say:
"O Jesus the son of Mary!
Didst thou say unto men,
Worship me and my mother
As gods in derogation of God'?"
He will say: "Glory to Thee!
Never could I say
What I had no right
(To say). Had I said
Such a thing, Thou wouldst
Indeed have known it.
Thou knowest what is
In my heart, though I
Know not what is
In Thine. For Thou
Knowest in full
All that is hidden."[829]

١١٦- وَإِذْ قَالَ اللّٰهُ يٰعِيْسَى ابْنَ مَرْيَمَ
ءَأَنْتَ قُلْتَ لِلنَّاسِ اتَّخِذُوْنِيْ وَأُمِّيَ
إِلٰهَيْنِ مِنْ دُوْنِ اللّٰهِ
قَالَ سُبْحٰنَكَ
مَا يَكُوْنُ لِيْٓ أَنْ أَقُوْلَ مَا لَيْسَ لِيْ بِحَقٍّ
إِنْ كُنْتُ قُلْتُهٗ فَقَدْ عَلِمْتَهٗ
تَعْلَمُ مَا فِيْ نَفْسِيْ
وَلَآ أَعْلَمُ مَا فِيْ نَفْسِكَ
إِنَّكَ أَنْتَ عَلَّامُ الْغُيُوْبِ ۝

وقف النبي صلى الله عليه وسلم

117. "Never said I to them
Aught except what Thou
Didst command me
To say, to wit, 'Worship
God, my Lord and your Lord';[830]
And I was a witness
Over them whilst I dwelt
Amongst them; when thou
Didst take me up
Thou wast the Watcher
Over them, and Thou
Art a witness to all things.[831]

١١٧- مَا قُلْتُ لَهُمْ إِلَّا مَآ أَمَرْتَنِيْ بِهٖٓ
أَنِ اعْبُدُوا اللّٰهَ رَبِّيْ وَرَبَّكُمْ
وَكُنْتُ عَلَيْهِمْ شَهِيْدًا
مَّا دُمْتُ فِيْهِمْ فَلَمَّا تَوَفَّيْتَنِيْ
كُنْتَ أَنْتَ الرَّقِيْبَ عَلَيْهِمْ
وَأَنْتَ عَلٰى كُلِّ شَيْءٍ شَهِيْدٌ ۝

118. "If Thou dost punish them,
They are Thy servants:

١١٨- إِنْ تُعَذِّبْهُمْ فَإِنَّهُمْ عِبَادُكَ

828. A forceful allegory. It is a wicked generation that asks for Signs and Miracles. Usually they are not vouchsafed. But where they are, the responsibility of those who ask for them is increased. If, after that, they reject faith, invent lies, and go after false gods or false ideals, their penalty wili be worse than that of other people. How this works out practically among those who call themselves Christians is exemplified in such books as the late Mr. W. T. Stead's "If Christ Came to Chicago?."

829. Jesus disclaims here any knowledge of the sort of things that are attributed to him by those who take his name. The worship of Mary, though repudiated by the Protestants, was widely spread in the earlier Churches, both in the East and the West.

830. *Cf.* v. 75, and n. 782.

831. Jesus here acknowledges that he was mortal, and that his knowledge was limited like that of a mortal.

If Thou dost forgive them,
Thou art the Exalted in power,
The Wise."[832]

وَإِنْ تَغْفِرْ لَهُمْ
فَإِنَّكَ أَنْتَ الْعَزِيزُ الْحَكِيمُ ○

119. God will say: "This is
A day on which
The truthful will profit
From their truth: theirs
Are Gardens, with rivers
Flowing beneath,—their eternal
Home: God well-pleased
With them, and they with God:
That is the great Salvation,[833]
(The fulfilment of all desires).

١١٩- قَالَ اللّٰهُ هٰذَا يَوْمُ يَنْفَعُ الصّٰدِقِيْنَ
صِدْقُهُمْ ۭ لَهُمْ جَنّٰتٌ تَجْرِيْ مِنْ تَحْتِهَا
الْاَنْهٰرُ خٰلِدِيْنَ فِيْهَآ اَبَدًا ۭ
رَضِيَ اللّٰهُ عَنْهُمْ وَرَضُوْا عَنْهُ ۭ
ذٰلِكَ الْفَوْزُ الْعَظِيْمُ ○

120. To God doth belong the dominion
Of the heavens and the earth,
And all that is therein,
And it is He who hath power
Over all things.

١٢٠- لِلّٰهِ مُلْكُ السَّمٰوٰتِ وَالْاَرْضِ
وَمَا فِيْهِنَّ ۭ
وَهُوَ عَلٰى كُلِّ شَيْءٍ قَدِيْرٌ ○

832 A Master can justly punish His servants for disobedience: no one can say Him nay, for He is high above all. But if He chooses to forgive, He in His wisdom sees things that we mortals cannot see. This is the limit of intercession that men of God can make on behalf of sinners.

833. *Fauz*=Felicity, happiness, achievement, salvation, the attainment or fulfilment of desires. What a beautiful definition of salvation or the end of life!—that we should win God's good pleasure and that we should reach the stage at which His good pleasure is all-in-all to us.

APPENDIX II.

On the *Taurāt* (see v. 47, n. 753)

The *Taurāt* is frequently referred to in the Qur-ān. It is well to have clear ideas as to what it exactly means. Vaguely we may say that it was the Jewish Scripture. It is mentioned with honour as having been, in its purity, a true revelation from God.

To translate it by the words "The Old Testament" is obviously wrong. The "Old Testament" is a Christian term, applied to a body of old Jewish records. The Protestants and the Roman Catholics are not agreed precisely as to the number of records to be included in the canon of the "Old Testament." They use the term in contradistinction to the "New Testament," whose composition we shall discuss in Appendix III.

Nor is it correct to translate *Taurāt* as the "Pentateuch," a Greek term meaning the "Five Books." These are the first five books of the Old Testament, known as Genesis, Exodus, Leviticus, Numbers, and Deuteronomy. They contain a semi-historical and legendary narrative of the history of the world from the Creation to the time of the arrival of the Jews in the Promised Land. There are in them some beautiful idylls but there are also stories of incest, fraud, cruelty, and treachery, not always disapproved. A great part of the Mosaic Law is embodied in this narrative. The books are traditionally ascribed to Moses, but it is certain that they were not written by Moses or in an age either contemporary with Moses or within an appreciable distance of time from Moses. They were in their present form probably compiled some time after the return of the Jews from the Babylonian Captivity. The decree of Cyrus permitting such return was in 536 B.C. Some books now included in the Old Testament, such as Haggai, Zechariah, and Malachi were admittedly written after the return from the captivity, Malachi being as late as 420-397 B.C. The compilers of the Pentateuch of course used some ancient material: some of that material is actually named. Egyptian and Chaldæan terms are relics of local colour and contemporary documents.

But there are some ludicrous slips, which show that the compilers did not always understand their material. Modern criticism distinguishes two distinct sources among the documents of different dates used by the editors. For the sake of brevity and convenience they may be called (*a*) Jehovistic, and (*b*) Elohistic. Then there are later miscellaneous interpolations. They sometimes overlap and sometimes contradict each other.

Logically speaking, the Book of Joshua, which describes the entry into the Promised Land, should be bracketed with the Pentateuch, and many writers speak of the six books together as the Hexateuch (Greek term for Six Books).

The Apocrypha contain certain Books which are not admitted as Canonical in the English Bible. But the early Christians received them as part of the Jewish Scriptures, and the Council of Trent (A.D. 1545-1563) seems to have recognised the

greater part of them as Canonical. The statement in 2 Esdras (about the first century A.D.) that the law was burnt and Ezra (say, about 458-457 B.C.) was inspired to rewrite it, is probably true as to the historical fact that the law was lost, and that what we have now is no earlier than the time of Ezra, and some of it a good deal later.

So far we have spoken of the Christian view of the Old Testament. What is the Jewish view? The Jews divide their Scripture into three parts: (1) the Law (*Torah*), (2) the Prophets (*Nebiim*), and (3) the Writings (*Kethubim*). The corresponding Arabic words would be: (1) *Taurāt*, (2) *Nabīyīn*, and (3) *Kutub*. This division was probably current in the time of Jesus. In Luke xxiv. 44 Jesus refers to the Law, the Prophets and the Psalms. In other places (*e.g.*, Matt. vii. 12) Jesus refers to the Law and the Prophets as summing up the whole Scripture. In the Old Testament Book, II. Chronicles xxxiv. 30, the reference to the Book of the Covenant must be to the *Torah* or the original Law. This is interesting, as the Qur-ān frequently refers to the Covenant with reference to the Jews. The modern Christian terms "Old Testament" and "New Testament" are substitutes for the older terms "Old Covenant" and "New Covenant." The Samaritans, who claim to be the real Children of Israel and disavow the Jews as schismatics from their Law of Moses, only recognise the Pentateuch, of which they have their own version slightly different from that in the Old Testament.

The view of the school of Higher Criticism is radically destructive. According to Renan it is doubtful whether Moses was not a myth. Two versions of Sacred History existed, different in language, style, and spirit, and they were combined together into a narrative in the reign of Hezekiah (B.C. 727-697). This forms the greater part of the Pentateuch as it exists to-day, excluding the greater part of Deuteronomy and Leviticus. In the reign of Josiah about 622 B.C., certain priests and scribes (with Jeremiah the prophet) promulgated a new code, pretending that they had found it in the Temple (II. Kings, xxii. 8). This Law (*Torah*=*Taurāt*) was the basis of Judaism, the new religion then founded in Palestine. This was further completed by the sacerdotal and Levitical *Torah*, compiled under the inspiration of Ezekiel, say, about 575 B.C., and contained mainly in the Book of Leviticus, with scattered fragments in Exodus, Numbers, and Joshua. We are entitled to accept the general results of a scientific examination of documents, probabilities, and dates, even though we reject the premise which we believe to be false, *viz.*, that God does not send inspired Books through inspired Prophets. We believe that Moses existed; that he was an inspired man of God; that he gave a message which was afterwards distorted or lost; that attempts were made by Israel at various times to reconstruct that message; and that the *Taurāt* as we have it is (in view of the statement in 2 Esdras) no earlier than the middle of the fifth century B.C.

The primitive *Torah* must have been in old Hebrew, but there is no Hebrew manuscript of the Old Testament which can be dated with certainty earlier than 916 A.D. Hebrew ceased to be a spoken language with the Jews during or after the Captivity, and by the time we come to the period of Jesus, most cultivated Hebrews used the Greek language, and others used Aramaic (including Syriac and Chaldee), Latin, or local dialects. There were also Arabic versions. For historical purposes

the most important versions were the Greek version, known as the Septuagint, and the Latin version, known as the Vulgate. The Septuagint was supposed to have been prepared by 70 or 72 Jews (Latin, septuaginta=seventy) working independently and at different times, the earliest portion dating from about 284 B.C. This version was used by the Jews of Alexandria and the Hellenized Jews who were spread over all parts of the Roman Empire. The Vulgate was a Latin translation made by the celebrated Father of the Christian Church, St. Jerome, from Hebrew, early in the fifth century A.D., superseding the older Latin versions. Neither the Septuagint nor the Vulgate have an absolutely fixed or certain text. The present standard text of the Vulgate as accepted by the Roman Catholic Church was issued by Pope Clement VIII (A.D. 1592-1605).

It will be seen therefore that there is no standard text of the Old Testament in its Hebrew form. The versions differ from each other frequently in minor particulars and sometimes in important particulars. The Pentateuch itself is only a small portion of the Old Testament. It is in narrative form, and includes the laws and regulations associated with the name of Moses, but probably compiled and edited from older sources by Ezra (or Esdras Arabic, 'Uzair) in the 5th century B.C. As Renan remarks in the preface to his *History of the People of Israel*, the "definite constitution of Judaism" may be dated only from the time of Ezra. The very early Christians were divided into two parties. One was a Judaizing party, which wished to remain in adherence to the Jewish laws and customs while recognising the mission of Jesus. The other, led by Paul, broke away from Jewish customs and traditions. Ultimately Pauline Christianity won. But both parties recognised the Old Testament in its present form (in one or another of its varying versions) as Scripture. It was the merit of Islam that it pointed out that as scripture it was of no value, although it recognised Moses as an inspired apostle and his original Law as having validity in his period until it was superseded. In its criticism of the Jewish position it said in effect: "You have lost your original Law; even what you have now as its substitute, you do not honestly follow; is it not better, now that an inspired Teacher is living among you, that you should follow him rather than quibble over uncertain texts?"

But the Jews in the Apostle's time (and since) went a great deal by the Talmud, or a body of oral exposition, reduced to writing in different Schools of doctors and learned men. "Talmud" in Hebrew is connected with the Arabic root in *Talmīẓ*, "disciple" or "student." The Talmudists took the divergent texts of the Old Testament and in interpreting them by a mass of traditional commentary and legendary lore, evolved a standard body of teaching. The Talmudists are of special interest to us, as, in the sixth century A.D., just before the preaching of Islam, they evolved the Massorah, which may be regarded as the body of authoritative Jewish Hadīth, to which references are to be found in passages addressed to the Jews in the Qur-ān.

The first part of the Talmud is called the *Mishna*,—a collection of traditions and decisions prepared by the Rabbi Judah about 150 A.D. He summed up the results of a great mass of previous rabbinical writings. The *Mishna* is the "Second Law":

Cf. the Arabic *Thān-in*=second. "It bound heavy burdens, grievous to be borne, and laid them on men's shoulders" : Matt. xxiii. 4.

There were also many Targums or paraphrases of the Law among the Jews. "Targum" is connected in root with the Arabic word *Tarjama*, "he translated." There were many Targums, mostly in Aramaic, and they constituted the teaching of the Law to the masses of the Jewish people.

The correct translation of the *Taurāt* is therefore "The Law." In its original form it was promulgated by Moses, and is recognised in Islam as having been an inspired Book. But it was lost before Islam was preached. What passed as "The Law" with the Jews in the Apostle's time was the mass of traditional writing which I have tried to review in this Appendix.

Authorities: *Encyclopœdia Britannica*, "Bible"; *Helps to the Study of the Bible*, Oxford University Press; A. F. Kirkpatrick, *Divine Library of the Old Testament*; C. E. Hammond, *Outlines of Textual Criticism*; E. Renan, *History of Israel*; G. F. Moore, *Literature of the Old Testament*, and the bibliography therein (Home University Library); Sir Frederic Kenyon, *The Story of the Bible*, 1936.

* * * * *

APPENDIX III.

On the *Injīl* (see v. 49, n. 757)

Just as the *Taurāt* is not the Old Testament, or the Pentateuch, as now received by the Jews and Christians, so the *Injīl* mentioned in the Qur-ān is certainly not the New Testament, and it is not the four Gospels as now received by the Christian Church, but an original Gospel which was promulgated by Jesus, as the Taurāt was promulgated by Moses and the Qur-ān by Muḥammad Muṣṭafā.

The New Testament as now received consists of (*a*) four Gospels with varying contents (Matthew, Mark, Luke, and John); and other miscellaneous matter; *viz.*, (*b*) the Acts of the Apostles (probably written by Luke and purporting to describe the progress of the Christian Church under St. Peter and St. Paul from the supposed Crucifixion of Jesus to about 61 A.D.); (*c*) twenty-one Letters or Epistles (the majority written by St. Paul to various churches or individuals, but a few written by other Disciples, and of a general nature); and (*d*) the Book of Revelation or Apocalypse (ascribed to St. John, and containing mystic visions and prophecies, of which it is difficult to understand the meaning).

As Prof. F. C. Burkitt remarks (*Canon of the New Testament*), it is an odd miscellany. "The four biographies of Jesus Christ .... are not all independent of each other, and neither of them was intended by its writer to form one of a quartette. But they are all put side by side, unharmonised, one of them being actually imperfect at the end, and one being only the first volume of a larger work." All this body of unmethodical literature was casual in its nature. No wonder, because the early Christians expected the end of the world very soon. The four canonical Gospels were only four out of many, and some others besides the four have survived. Each writer just wrote down some odd sayings of the Master that he recollected. Among the miracles described there is only one which is described in all the four Gospels, and others were described and believed in in other Gospels, which are not mentioned in any of the four canonical Gospels. Some of the Epistles contain expositions of doctrine, but this has been interpreted differently by different Churches. There must have been hundreds of such Epistles, and not all the Epistles now received as canonical were always so received or intended to be so received. The Apocalypse also was not the only one in the field. There were others. They were prophecies of "things which must shortly come to pass"; they could not have been meant for long preservation, "for the time is at hand."

When were these four Gospels written? By the end of the second century A.D. they were in existence, but it does not follow that they had been selected by that date to form a canon. They were merely pious productions comparable to Dean Farrar's *Life of Christ*. There were other Gospels besides. And further, the writers of two of them, Mark and Luke, were not among the Twelve Disciples "called" by Jesus. About the Gospel of St. John there is much controversy as to authorship, date, and even as to whether it was all written by one person. Clement of Rome (about 97 A.D.) and Polycarp (about 112 A.D.) quote sayings of Jesus in a form

different from those found in the present canonical Gospels. Polycarp (Epistle, vii) inveighs much against men " who pervert the sayings of the Lord to their own lusts," and he wants to turn " to the Word handed down to us from the beginning," thus referring to a Book (or a Tradition) much earlier than the four orthodox Gospels. An Epistle of St. Barnabas and an Apocalypse of St. Peter were recognised by Presbyter Clement of Alexandria (flourished about 180 A.D.). The Apocalypse of St. John, which is a part of the present Canon in the West, forms no part of the Peshitta (Syriac) version of the Eastern Christians, which was produced about 411-433 A.D. and which was used by the Nestorian Christians. It is probable that the Peshitta was the version (or an Arabic form of it) used by the Christians in Arabia in the time of the Apostle. The final form of the New Testament canon for the West was fixed in the fourth century A.D. (say, about 367 A.D.) by Athanasius and the Nicene creed. The beautiful Codex Sinaiticus which was acquired for the British Museum in 1934, and is one of the earliest complete manuscripts of the Bible, may be dated about the fourth century. It is written in the Greek language. Fragments of unknown Gospels have also been discovered, which do not agree with the received canonical Gospels.

The *Injīl* (Greek, Evangel=Gospel) spoken of by the Qur-ān is not the New Testament. It is not the four Gospels now received as canonical. It is the single Gospel which, Islam teaches, was revealed to Jesus, and which he taught. Fragments of it survive in the received canonical Gospels and in some others, of which traces survive (*e.g.*, the Gospel of Childhood or the Nativity, the Gospel of St. Barnabas, etc.). Muslims are therefore right in respecting the present Bible (New Testament and Old Testament), though they reject the peculiar doctrines taught by orthodox Christianity or Judaism. They claim to be in the true tradition of Abraham, and therefore all that is of value in the older revelations, it is claimed, is incorporated in the teaching of the Last of the Prophets.

In v. 85 we are told that nearest in love to the Believers among the People of the Book are the Christians. I do not agree that this does not apply to modern Christians " because they are practically atheists or freethinkers. " I think that Christian thought like the world's thought) has learnt a great deal from the protest of Islam against priest domination, class domination, and sectarianism, and its insistence on making this life pure and beautiful while we are in it. We must stretch a friendly hand to all who are sincere and in sympathy with our ideals.

Authorities: The first two mentioned for Appendix II, and in addition: Prof. F. C. Burkitt. on the Cannon of the New Testament, in *Religion*, June 1934, the Journal of Transactions of the Society for Promoting the Study of Religions; R. W. Mackay, *Rise and Progress of Christianity*; G. R. S. Mead, *The Gospel and the Gospels*; B. W. Bacon, *Making of the New Testament*, with its Bibliography; Sir Frederic Kenyon, *The Story of the Bible*; R. Hone, *The Apocryphal New Testament*, London 1820; H. I Bell and T. C. Skeat, *Fragments of an Unknown Gospel and other Christian Papyri*, published by the British Museum, 1935. See also chapter 15 of Gibbon's *Decline and Fall of the Roman Empire*, where the genesis of the early churches and sects in the Roman Empire is briefly reviewed.

INTRODUCTION TO SŪRA VI (*An'ām*)

This is a Sūra of the late Meccan period. The greater part of it was revealed entire. Its place in the traditional order of arrangement is justified by logical considerations. We have already had the spiritual history of mankind, a discussion of the earlier revelations and how they were lost or corrupted, the regulations for the outer life of the new Community, and the points in which the Jews and Christians failed to maintain the central doctrine of Islam—the unity of God. The next step now taken is to expound this doctrine in relation to Pagan Arabia.

Summary.—The nature of God and the method by which he reveals Himself are first expounded, and the weakness of Paganism is exposed (vi. 1-30, and C. 76).

The emptiness of this world's life is contrasted with the evidences of God's wonderful handiwork in all Creation. It is He who holds the keys of the Unseen and the secrets of all that we see (vi. 31-60, and C. 77).

God's working in His world and His constant care and guidance should give a clue to His unity, as it did to Abraham when he argued with those who worshipped false gods (vi. 61-82, and C. 78).

The succession of prophets after Abraham kept God's truth alive, and led up to the Qur-ān. How can man fail to understand the majesty and goodness of God, when he contemplates God's nature and His Messages tomankind ? (vi. 83-110, and C. 79).

The obstinate and the rebellious are deceived : they should be avoided. Though they turn for assistance to each other, they will receive due punishment (vi. 111-129, and C. 80).

God's decrees will come to pass, in spite of all the crimes and superstitions of the ungodly (vi. 130-150, and C. 81).

The better course is to follow the straight Way, the Way of God, as directed in the Qur-ān, with unity and the full dedication of our lives (vi. 151-165, and C. 82).

C. 76.—God did separate Light from Darkness ;
(vi. 1-30.) He reigns not only in heaven but also
On earth ; Mercy is His Law ;
To Him shall we all return
At the end of all things. How can we
Then depart from truth and forge lies
Against Him ? It is folly to say that there is
Nothing beyond this our present life.

Sūra VI.

An'ām, or Cattle.

اٰياتها ١٦٥ (٦) سُوْرَةُ الْاَنْعَامِ مَكِّيَّةٌ (٥٥) ركوعاتها ٢٠

In the name of God, Most Gracious,
Most Merciful.

بِسْمِ اللّٰهِ الرَّحْمٰنِ الرَّحِيْمِ ○

1. Praise be to God,
Who created the heavens
And the earth,
And made the Darkness
And the Light.
Yet those who reject Faith
Hold (others) as equal.[834]
With their Guardian-Lord.[835]

١- اَلْحَمْدُ لِلّٰهِ الَّذِيْ خَلَقَ السَّمٰوٰتِ وَ
الْاَرْضَ
وَجَعَلَ الظُّلُمٰتِ وَالنُّوْرَ ۬
ثُمَّ الَّذِيْنَ كَفَرُوْا بِرَبِّهِمْ يَعْدِلُوْنَ ○

2. He it is Who created[836]
You from clay, and then
Decreed a stated term[837]
(For you). And there is
In His Presence another
Determined term; yet
Ye doubt within yourselves!

٢- هُوَ الَّذِيْ خَلَقَكُمْ مِّنْ طِيْنٍ
ثُمَّ قَضٰٓى اَجَلًا ؕ
وَاَجَلٌ مُّسَمًّى عِنْدَهٗ
ثُمَّ اَنْتُمْ تَمْتَرُوْنَ ○

3. And He is God
In the heavens
And on earth.
He knoweth what ye
Hide, and what ye reveal,
And He knoweth
The (recompense) which
Ye earn (by your deeds).[838]

٣- وَهُوَ اللّٰهُ فِي السَّمٰوٰتِ وَفِي الْاَرْضِ ؕ
يَعْلَمُ سِرَّكُمْ
وَجَهْرَكُمْ
وَيَعْلَمُ مَا تَكْسِبُوْنَ ○

---

834. *'Adala* has various meanings: (1) to hold something as equal to something else, as here; to balance nicely; (2) to deal justly, as between one party and another, xlii. 15; (3) to give compensation or reparation, or something as equivalent to something else, vi. 70; (4) to turn the balance the right way, to give a right disposition, to give a just bias or proportion, lxxxii. 7; (5) to turn the balance the wrong way, to swerve, to show bias, iv. 135.

835. The argument is threefold: (1) God created everything you see and know: how can you then set up any of His own creatures as equal to Him? (2) He is your own Guardian-Lord; He cherishes and loves you; how can you be so ungrateful as to run after something else? (3) Darkness and Light are to help you to distinguish between the true from the false: how then can you confound the true God with your false ideas and superstitions? There may also be a repudiation of the Duality of old Persian theology; Light and Darkness are not conflicting Powers; they are both creatures of the one true God.

836. After the general argument, the argument comes to man personally. Can such a miserable creature, created from clay, put himself in opposition to his Creator? And can man forget or doubt that he is here only for a short term of probation? And then, after a period, comes the Day of Account before God.

837. This life is a period of probation. The other term leads up to Judgment.

838. It is folly to suppose that God only reigns in the heavens. He also reigns on earth. He knows all our secret thoughts and motives, and the real worth of all that is behind what we care to show. It is by our deeds that He judges us; for our deeds, whether good or evil, we shall get due recompense in due time.

4. But never did a single
One of the Signs
Of their Lord reach them,
But they turned
Away therefrom.

۴- وما تاتيهم من اية من ايت
ربهم
الا كانوا عنها معرضين ○

5. And now they reject
The truth when it reaches
Them: but soon shall they
Learn the reality of what
They used to mock at.

۵- فقد كذبوا بالحق لما جاءهم
فسوف ياتيهم انبؤا
ما كانوا به يستهزءون ○

6. See they not how many
Of those before them
We did destroy?—[839]
Generations We had established
On the earth, in strength
Such as We have not given
To you—for whom
We poured out rain
From the skies in abundance,
And gave (fertile) streams
Flowing beneath their (feet):
Yet for their sins
We destroyed them,
And raised in their wake
Fresh generations
(To succeed them).

۶- الم يروا كم اهلكنا من قبلهم
من قرن مكنهم في الارض
ما لم نمكن لكم
وارسلنا السماء عليهم مدرارا
وجعلنا الانهر تجري من تحتهم
فاهلكنهم
بذنوبهم
وانشانا من بعدهم قرنا اخرين ○

7. If We had sent
Unto thee a written
(Message) on parchment,[839 A]
So that they could
Touch it with their hands,
The Unbelievers would
Have been sure to say:
"This is nothing but

۷- ولو نزلنا عليك كتبا في قرطاس
فلمسوه بايديهم
لقال الذين كفروا
ان هذا الا

839. Now comes the argument from history, looking backwards and forwards. If we are so short-sighted or arrogant as to suppose that we are firmly established on this earth, secure in our privileges, we are reminded of much greater nations in the past, who failed in their duty and were wiped out. In their fate we must read our own fate, if we fail likewise! But those without faith, instead of facing facts squarely "turn away therefrom."

839-A. *Qirṭās*, in the Apostle's life, could only mean "parchment," which was commonly used as writing material in Western Asia from the 2nd century B.C. The word was derived from the Greek, *Charles* (*Cf.* Latin, "*Charta*"). Paper, as we know it, made from rags, was first used by the Arabs after the conquest of Samarqand in 751 A.D. The Chinese had used it by the 2nd century B.C. The Arabs introduced it into Europe it was; used in Greece in the 11th or 12th century, and in Spain through Sicily in the 12th century. The Papyrus, made from an Egyptian reed, was used in Egypt as early as 2500 B.C. It gave place to paper in Egypt in the 10th century.

Obvious magic ! "[840]

سِحْرٌ مُّبِينٌ ○

8. They say : " Why is not
An angel sent down to him ? "
If We did send down
An angel, the matter
Would be settled at once,
And no respite
Would be granted them.[841]

٨- وَقَالُوا لَوْلَآ أُنزِلَ عَلَيْهِ مَلَكٌ
وَلَوْ أَنزَلْنَا مَلَكًا
لَّقُضِيَ الْأَمْرُ
ثُمَّ لَا يُنظَرُونَ ○

9. If We had made it
An angel, We should
Have sent him as a man,
And We should certainly
Have caused them confusion
In a matter which they have
Already covered with confusion.[842]

٩- وَلَوْ جَعَلْنَٰهُ مَلَكًا
لَّجَعَلْنَٰهُ رَجُلًا
وَلَلَبَسْنَا عَلَيْهِم
مَّا يَلْبِسُونَ ○

10. Mocked were (many)
Apostles before thee ;
But their scoffers
Were hemmed in
By the thing that they mocked.[843]

١٠- وَلَقَدِ اسْتُهْزِئَ بِرُسُلٍ مِّن قَبْلِكَ
فَحَاقَ بِالَّذِينَ سَخِرُوا مِنْهُم
مَّا كَانُوا بِهِ يَسْتَهْزِءُونَ ○ ع

SECTION 2.

11. Say : " Travel through the earth
And see what was the end
Of those who rejected Truth".

١١- قُلْ سِيرُوا فِي الْأَرْضِ ثُمَّ انظُرُوا
كَيْفَ كَانَ عَاقِبَةُ الْمُكَذِّبِينَ ○

12. Say : " To whom belongeth
All that is in the heavens

١٢- قُل لِّمَن مَّا فِي السَّمَٰوَٰتِ

---

840. The materialists want to see actual physical material things before them, but if such a thing came from an unusual source or expressed things they cannot understand, they give it some name like magic, or superstition, or whatever name is in fashion, and they are not helped at all in attaining faith, because their " hearts are diseased " (ii. 10).

841. *Cf.* ii. 210. An angel is a heavenly being, a manifestation of God's glory, invisible to men who live gross material lives. Such men are given plenty of respite in which to turn in repentance to God and make themselves worthy of His light. But if their prayer to see an angel were granted, it would do them no good, for they would be destroyed as darkness is destroyed by light.

842. Supposing an angel should appear to their grosser senses, he could only do it in human form. In that case their present confused notions about spiritual life would be still more confounded. They would say : " We wanted to see an angel, and we have only seen a man ! "

843. " The scoffers were mocked by the thing that they mocked " would express epigrammatically part of the sense, but not the whole. " Hemmed in " implies that the logic of events turned the tables, and as a man might be besieged and surrounded by an enemy in war, and would be forced to surrender, so these mockers will find that events would justify Truth, not them. The mockers of Jesus,—where were they when Titus destroyed Jerusalem ? The mockers who drove out Muḥammad from Mecca,—what was their plight when Muḥammad came back in triumph and they sued for mercy,—*and he gave it to them* ! According to the Latin proverb, Great is Truth, and must prevail.

And on earth ?" Say :
" To God. He hath inscribed
For Himself (the rule of) Mercy.[844]
That He will gather you
Together for the Day of Judgment,
There is no doubt whatever.
It is they who have lost
Their own souls, that will
Not believe.

وَالْاَرْضِ ۖ قُلْ لِّلّٰهِ ۖ كَتَبَ
عَلٰى نَفْسِهِ الرَّحْمَةَ ۖ
لَيَجْمَعَنَّكُمْ اِلٰى يَوْمِ الْقِيٰمَةِ لَا رَيْبَ
فِيْهِ ۖ اَلَّذِيْنَ خَسِرُوْٓا اَنْفُسَهُمْ
فَهُمْ لَا يُؤْمِنُوْنَ ○

13. To him belongeth all
That dwelleth (or lurketh)[845]
In the Night and the Day.
For He is the One
Who heareth and knoweth
All things." [846]

١٣- وَلَهٗ مَا سَكَنَ
فِى الَّيْلِ وَالنَّهَارِ ۖ
وَهُوَ السَّمِيْعُ الْعَلِيْمُ ○

14. Say : " Shall I take
For my protector
Any other than God,
The Maker of the heavens
And the earth ?
And He it is that
Feedeth but is not fed." [847]
Say : " Nay ! but I am
Commanded to be the first
Of those who bow
To God (in Islam),
And be not thou
Of the company of those
Who join gods with God."

١٤- قُلْ اَغَيْرَ اللّٰهِ اَتَّخِذُ وَلِيًّا
فَاطِرِ السَّمٰوٰتِ وَالْاَرْضِ
وَهُوَ يُطْعِمُ وَلَا يُطْعَمُ ۖ
قُلْ اِنِّيْٓ اُمِرْتُ اَنْ اَكُوْنَ اَوَّلَ
مَنْ اَسْلَمَ
وَلَا تَكُوْنَنَّ مِنَ الْمُشْرِكِيْنَ ○

---

844. History, travel, human experience, all prove the Mercy of God and the law that without it those who reject Truth tend to lose their own souls and destroy themselves.

845. *Sakana*=(1) to dwell ; (2) to rest, to be still, to stop (moving), to lurk ; (3) to be quiescent, as a letter which is not moved with a vowel.

If we imagine Night and Day to be places, and each to have (dwelling in them) things that are open and things that are concealed, things that move and things that are still, things that are sounded and things that are quiescent, we get some idea of the imagery implied. The mystery of Time (which seems more abstract than Space) is thus explained and illustrated by the idea of Place or Space, which also is a notion and not a concrete thing. But He Who has control of all these things is the one true God.

846. Throughout this section we have a sort of implied dialogue, of which one part is understood from the other part, which is expressed. In verse 11. we might have an imaginary objector saying : "Why go back to the past ?" The answer is : "Well, travel through the world, and see whether it is not true that virtue and godliness exalt a nation, and the opposite are causes of ruin. Both the past and the present prove this." In verse 12 the objector may say : " But you speak of God's power ?" The man of God replies : "Yes, but Mercy is God's own attribute, and knowledge and wisdom beyond what man can conceive."

847. *Feedeth but is not fed* : true both literally and figuratively. To God we owe the satisfaction of all needs, but He is independent of all needs.

15. Say: "I would, if I
Disobeyed my Lord,
Indeed have fear
Of the Penalty
Of a Mighty Day.

١٥- قُلْ إِنِّىٓ أَخَافُ
إِنْ عَصَيْتُ
رَبِّى عَذَابَ يَوْمٍ عَظِيمٍ ○

16. "On that day, if the Penalty
Is averted from any,
It is due to God's Mercy;
And that would be (Salvation),
The obvious fulfilment
Of all desire.[848]

١٦- مَنْ يُصْرَفْ عَنْهُ يَوْمَئِذٍ
فَقَدْ رَحِمَهُ ۚ
وَذٰلِكَ الْفَوْزُ الْمُبِينُ ○

17. "If God touch thee
With affliction, none
Can remove it but He;
If He touch thee with happiness,
He hath power over all things.[849]

١٧- وَإِنْ يَّمْسَسْكَ اللّٰهُ بِضُرٍّ فَلَا كَاشِفَ
لَهٗٓ إِلَّا هُوَ ۚ وَإِنْ يَّمْسَسْكَ بِخَيْرٍ
فَهُوَ عَلٰى كُلِّ شَىْءٍ قَدِيرٌ ○

18. "He is the Irresistible, (watching)
From above over His worshippers;
And He is the Wise,
Acquainted with all things."

١٨- وَهُوَ الْقَاهِرُ فَوْقَ عِبَادِهٖ ۚ
وَهُوَ الْحَكِيمُ الْخَبِيرُ ○

19. Say: "What thing is most
Weighty in evidence?"
Say: "God is witness
Between me and you;
This Qur-ān hath been
Revealed to me by inspiration,
That I may warn you
And all whom it reaches.
Can ye possibly bear witness
That besides God there is
Another God?" Say:
"Nay! I cannot bear witness!"
Say: "But in truth
He is the One God,

١٩- قُلْ اَىُّ شَىْءٍ اَكْبَرُ شَهَادَةً ۚ
قُلِ اللّٰهُ شَهِيدٌۢ بَيْنِى وَبَيْنَكُمْ
وَاُوحِىَ إِلَىَّ هٰذَا الْقُرْاٰنُ
لِاُنْذِرَكُمْ بِهٖ وَمَنْۢ بَلَغَ ۚ اَئِنَّكُمْ
لَتَشْهَدُوْنَ اَنَّ مَعَ اللّٰهِ اٰلِهَةً اُخْرٰى ۚ
قُلْ لَّآ اَشْهَدُ ۚ
قُلْ إِنَّمَا هُوَ إِلٰهٌ وَّاحِدٌ

848 We continue the implied dialogue suggested in n. 846. In verse 14, the objector might say: "But we have other interests in life than religion and God." "No," says the man of God, "My Creator is the one and only Power whose protection I seek; and I strive to be first in the race." In verse 15, the objector suggests: "Enjoy the good things of this life; it is short." The answer is: "The Hereafter is more real to me, and promises the true fulfilment of all desire; happiness or affliction comes not from the fleeting pettinesses or illusions of this life, but from the power and wisdom of God." In verse 19. the objector makes his final splash: "What evidence is there for all this?" The reply is: "I know it is true. for God's voice is within me, and my living Teacher awakens that voice; and there is the Book of Inspiration. God is one, and there is none other besides."

849. The vulgar worship false gods out of fear that they would harm them or hope that they would confer some benefit on them. These false gods can do neither. All power, all goodness is in the hands of the One True God. All else is pretence or illusion.

And I truly am innocent
Of (your blasphemy of) joining
Others with Him."

وَإِنَّنِي بَرِيٓءٌ مِّمَّا تُشْرِكُونَ ۝

وقف لازم باختلاف

20. Those to whom
We have given the Book
Know this as they know[850]
Their own sons.
Those who have lost
Their own souls
Refuse therefore to believe.

٢٠- اَلَّذِينَ اٰتَيْنٰهُمُ الْكِتٰبَ يَعْرِفُونَهٗ
كَمَا يَعْرِفُونَ اَبْنَآءَهُمْ اَلَّذِينَ خَسِرُوٓا
اَنْفُسَهُمْ فَهُمْ لَا يُؤْمِنُونَ ۝

وقف لازم

SECTION 3.

21. Who doth more wrong
Than he who inventeth
A lie against God
Or rejecteth His Signs?
But verily the wrong-doers
Never shall prosper.

٢١- وَمَنْ اَظْلَمُ مِمَّنِ افْتَرٰى عَلَى اللّٰهِ
كَذِبًا اَوْ كَذَّبَ بِاٰيٰتِهٖ
اِنَّهٗ لَا يُفْلِحُ الظّٰلِمُونَ ۝

22. One day shall We gather
Them all together: We
Shall say to those
Who ascribed partners (to Us):
"Where are the partners
Whom ye (invented
And) talked about?"

٢٢- وَيَوْمَ نَحْشُرُهُمْ جَمِيعًا
ثُمَّ نَقُولُ لِلَّذِينَ اَشْرَكُوٓا
اَيْنَ شُرَكَآؤُكُمُ
الَّذِينَ كُنْتُمْ تَزْعُمُونَ ۝

23. There will then be (left)
No subterfuge for them[851]
But to say: "By God
Our Lord, we were not
Those who joined gods
With God."

٢٣- ثُمَّ لَمْ تَكُنْ فِتْنَتُهُمْ
اِلَّآ اَنْ قَالُوا وَاللّٰهِ رَبِّنَا
مَا كُنَّا مُشْرِكِينَ ۝

24. Behold! how they lie
Against their own souls!

٢٤- اُنْظُرْ كَيْفَ كَذَبُوا عَلٰٓى اَنْفُسِهِمْ

---

850. *Cf.* ii. 146 and n. 151. In both passages the pronoun translated "this" may mean "him" and refer to Muḥammad the Apostle of God, as some Commentators think.

851. *Fitnat* has various meanings, from the root idea of "to try, to test, to tempt;" *e.g.*, (1) a trial or temptation, as in ii. 102; (2) trouble, tumult, oppression, persecution, as in ii. 191, 193, 217; (3) discord, as in iii. 7, (4) subterfuge, an answer that amounts to a sedition, and excuse founded on a falsehood, as here. Other shades of meaning will be noticed as they occur.

Those who blasphemed God in imagining false gods will now see the vanity of their imaginations for themselves. What answer can they give now? In their perversity they will deny that they *ever* entertained the notion of false gods.

But the (lie) which they
Invented will leave them[852]
In the lurch.

وَضَلَّ عَنْهُم مَّا كَانُوا يَفْتَرُونَ ۝

25. Of them there are some
Who (pretend to) listen to thee;
But We have thrown
Veils on their hearts,
So they understand it not,[852-A]
And deafness in their ears;
If they saw every one
Of the Signs, not they
Will believe in them;
In so much that
When they come to thee,
They (but) dispute with thee;
The Unbelievers say:
"These are nothing
But tales of the ancients."

٢٥- وَمِنْهُم مَّن يَسْتَمِعُ إِلَيْكَ ۚ
وَجَعَلْنَا عَلَىٰ قُلُوبِهِمْ أَكِنَّةً
أَن يَفْقَهُوهُ وَفِي آذَانِهِمْ وَقْرًا ۚ
وَإِن يَرَوْا كُلَّ آيَةٍ
لَّا يُؤْمِنُوا بِهَا ۚ
حَتَّىٰ إِذَا جَاءُوكَ يُجَادِلُونَكَ
يَقُولُ الَّذِينَ كَفَرُوا
إِنْ هَٰذَا إِلَّا أَسَاطِيرُ الْأَوَّلِينَ ۝

26. Others they keep away from it,
And themselves they keep away;
But they only destroy
Their own souls,
And they perceive it not.

٢٦- وَهُمْ يَنْهَوْنَ عَنْهُ وَيَنْأَوْنَ عَنْهُ ۖ
وَإِن يُهْلِكُونَ
إِلَّا أَنفُسَهُمْ وَمَا يَشْعُرُونَ ۝

27. If thou couldst but see
When they are confronted
With the Fire!
They will say:
"Would that we were
But sent back!
Then would we not reject
The Signs of our Lord,
But would be amongst those
Who believe!"

٢٧- وَلَوْ تَرَىٰ إِذْ وُقِفُوا عَلَى النَّارِ
فَقَالُوا يَا لَيْتَنَا نُرَدُّ
وَلَا نُكَذِّبَ
بِآيَاتِ رَبِّنَا
وَنَكُونَ مِنَ الْمُؤْمِنِينَ ۝

28. Yea, in their own (eyes)
Will become manifest
What before they concealed.
But if they were returned,
They would certainly relapse
To the things they were forbidden,

٢٨- بَلْ بَدَا لَهُم مَّا كَانُوا يُخْفُونَ مِن
قَبْلُ ۖ
وَلَوْ رُدُّوا لَعَادُوا لِمَا نُهُوا عَنْهُ

852. The lies which they used to tell have now "wandered" from the channels which they use to occupy, and left the liars in the lurch. In denying the indubitable fact that they took false gods, they admit the falsity of their notions and thus are practically convicted out of their own mouths.

852-A. *It*=The Qur-ān.

For they are indeed liars.[853]

وَاِنَّهُمْ لَكٰذِبُوْنَ ○

29. And they (sometimes) say:
"There is nothing except
Our life on this earth,
And never shall we be
Raised up again."

٢٩- وَقَالُوْٓا اِنْ هِيَ اِلَّا حَيَاتُنَا الدُّنْيَا
وَمَا نَحْنُ بِمَبْعُوْثِيْنَ ○

30. If thou couldst but see
When they are confronted
With their Lord!
He will say:
"Is not this the truth?"
They will say:
"Yea, by our Lord!"
He will say:
"Taste ye then the Penalty,
Because ye rejected Faith."

٣٠- وَلَوْ تَرٰٓى اِذْ وُقِفُوْا عَلٰى رَبِّهِمْ ط
قَالَ اَلَيْسَ هٰذَا بِالْحَقِّ ط
قَالُوْا بَلٰى وَرَبِّنَا ط
قَالَ فَذُوْقُوا الْعَذَابَ
بِمَا كُنْتُمْ تَكْفُرُوْنَ ○ ع

C. 77.—The life of this world is but empty:
(vi. 31-60.) What is serious is the life hereafter.
The teacher of God's truth is not baulked
By frivolous objections or insults
Or persecution. The wicked will be
Cut off to the last remnant. God's wisdom
Pervades the whole of His Creation,
And in His hands are the keys of the Unseen,
And the secrets of all that we see.

SECTION 4.

31. Lost indeed are they
Who treat it as a falsehood
That they must meet God,—
Until on a sudden
The hour is on them,
And they say: "Ah! woe
Unto us that we took
No thought of it";
For they bear their burdens[854]
On their backs,

٣١- قَدْ خَسِرَ الَّذِيْنَ كَذَّبُوْا بِلِقَآءِ اللّٰهِ ط
حَتّٰىٓ اِذَا جَآءَتْهُمُ السَّاعَةُ بَغْتَةً
قَالُوْا يٰحَسْرَتَنَا عَلٰى مَا فَرَّطْنَا فِيْهَا لا
وَهُمْ يَحْمِلُوْنَ اَوْزَارَهُمْ عَلٰى
ظُهُوْرِهِمْ ط

853. Their falsity was not due to want of knowledge, but to perversity and selfishness. In their heart was a disease (ii. 10): therefore neither their understanding, nor their ears, nor their eyes do their proper work. They twist what they see, hear, or are taught, and go deeper and deeper into the mire. The deceptions which they used to practise on other people will, before the Seat of Judgment, become clear in their own eyes.

854. Grievous is the burden of sins which the wicked will bear on their backs when they become conscious of them. Some Commentators personify Sins as ugly Demons riding on the backs of men, while the men's Good Deeds become the strong and patient mounts which will carry the men on their backs. If the Good Deeds are few and the Sins many, the man and his Good Deeds will be crushed under the load of the Evil which they carry.

And evil indeed are
The burdens that they bear?

أَلَا سَآءَ مَا يَزِرُونَ

32. What is the life of this world
But play and amusement?[855]
But best is the Home
In the Hereafter, for those
Who are righteous.
Will ye not then understand?

۳۲- وَمَا الْحَيٰوةُ الدُّنْيَآ إِلَّا لَعِبٌ وَّلَهْوٌ
وَلَلدَّارُ الْاٰخِرَةُ خَيْرٌ
لِّلَّذِينَ يَتَّقُونَ ۗ أَفَلَا تَعْقِلُونَ

33. We know indeed the grief
Which their words do cause thee:
It is not thee they reject:
It is the Signs of God,
Which the wicked contemn.

۳۳- قَدْ نَعْلَمُ إِنَّهُ لَيَحْزُنُكَ الَّذِي يَقُولُونَ
فَإِنَّهُمْ لَا يُكَذِّبُونَكَ
وَلٰكِنَّ الظّٰلِمِينَ بِاٰيٰتِ اللّٰهِ يَجْحَدُونَ

34. Rejected were the Apostles
Before thee: with patience
And constancy they bore
Their rejection and their wrongs,
Until Our aid did reach
Them: there is none
That can alter the Words
(And Decrees) of God.
Already hast thou received
Some account of those Apostles.

۳۴- وَلَقَدْ كُذِّبَتْ رُسُلٌ مِّنْ قَبْلِكَ
فَصَبَرُوا عَلٰى مَا كُذِّبُوا
وَأُوذُوا حَتّٰى أَتٰهُمْ نَصْرُنَا ۚ
وَلَا مُبَدِّلَ لِكَلِمٰتِ اللّٰهِ ۚ
وَلَقَدْ جَآءَكَ مِنْ نَّبَإِي الْمُرْسَلِينَ

35. If their spurning is hard
On thy mind, yet if
Thou wert able to seek
A tunnel in the ground
Or a ladder to the skies
And bring them a Sign,—[856]
(What good?). If it were
God's Will, He could
Gather them together
Unto true guidance:

۳۵- وَإِنْ كَانَ كَبُرَ عَلَيْكَ إِعْرَاضُهُمْ
فَإِنِ اسْتَطَعْتَ أَنْ تَبْتَغِيَ نَفَقًا فِي
الْأَرْضِ أَوْ سُلَّمًا فِي السَّمَآءِ
فَتَأْتِيَهُمْ بِاٰيَةٍ ۚ
وَلَوْ شَآءَ اللّٰهُ لَجَمَعَهُمْ عَلَى الْهُدٰى

---

855. Play and amusement are for preparing our minds for the serious things of life: in themselves they are not serious. So this life is a preparation for the Eternal Home to which we are going, which is far more important than the ephemeral pleasures which may possibly seduce us in this life.

856. There were many Signs of a divine mission in the Apostle's life and in the Message which he delivered. If these did not convince the Unbelievers, was it not vain to seek a miraculous Sign from the bowels of the earth or by a visible ascent to the skies? If in the Apostle's eagerness to get all to accept his Message he was hurt at their callousness, active opposition, and persecution of him, he is told that a full knowledge of the working of God's Plan would convince him that impatience was misplaced. This was in the days of persecution before the Hijrat. The history in Medina and after shows how God's truth was ultimately and triumphantly vindicated. Who among the sincere devotees of Muḥammad can fail to read vi. 33-35 without tears in his eyes?

So be not thou
Amongst those who are swayed
By ignorance (and impatience)!

فَلَا تَكُونَنَّ مِنَ الْجٰهِلِينَ ۝

نصف

36. Those who listen (in truth),[857]
Be sure, will accept:
As to the dead, God will
Raise them up; then will they
Be turned unto Him.

٣٦- إِنَّمَا يَسْتَجِيبُ الَّذِينَ يَسْمَعُونَ ؕ
وَالْمَوْتٰى يَبْعَثُهُمُ اللّٰهُ
ثُمَّ إِلَيْهِ يُرْجَعُونَ ۝

۱- وقف غفران
۲- وقف منزل

37. They say: "Why is not
A Sign sent down
To him from his Lord?"
Say: "God hath certainly
Power to send down a Sign:
But most of them
Understand not."[858]

٣٧- وَقَالُوا لَوْلَا نُزِّلَ عَلَيْهِ آيَةٌ
مِنْ رَبِّهِ ؕ
قُلْ إِنَّ اللّٰهَ قَادِرٌ عَلٰى أَنْ يُنَزِّلَ آيَةً
وَلٰكِنَّ أَكْثَرَهُمْ لَا يَعْلَمُونَ ۝

38. There is not an animal
(That lives) on the earth,
Nor a being that flies
On its wings, but (forms
Part of) communities like you.[859]
Nothing have we omitted
From the Book, and they (all)
Shall be gathered to their Lord
In the end.

٣٨- وَمَا مِنْ دَآبَّةٍ فِي الْأَرْضِ
وَلَا طٰٓئِرٍ يَطِيرُ بِجَنَاحَيْهِ
إِلَّآ أُمَمٌ أَمْثَالُكُمْ ؕ
مَا فَرَّطْنَا فِي الْكِتٰبِ مِنْ شَيْءٍ
ثُمَّ إِلٰى رَبِّهِمْ يُحْشَرُونَ ۝

39. Those who reject our Signs
Are deaf and dumb,—[860]

٣٩- وَالَّذِينَ كَذَّبُوا بِآيٰتِنَا صُمٌّ وَبُكْمٌ

857. There is a double meaning here. (1) If people listen to truth sincerely and earnestly, they must believe; even if the spiritual faculty is dead, God will by His grace revive it and they will come to Him, if they really try earnestly to understand. (2) The sincere will believe; but those whose hearts are dead will not listen, yet they cannot escape being brought to the Judgment Seat before him.

858. Signs are all around them, but they do not understand. If they want a particular Sign to suit their gross ignorance, they will not be humoured, for they can always pick holes in anything that descends to their level.

859. "Animals living on the earth" include those living in the water,—fishes, reptiles, crustaceans, insects, as well as four-footed beasts. Life on the wing is separately mentioned. "Tāir," which is ordinarily translated as "bird," is anything that flies, including mammals like bats. In our pride we may exclude animals from our purview, but they all live a life, social and individual, like ourselves, and all life is subject to the Plan and Will of God. In vi. 59 we are told that not a leaf falls but by His Will, and things dry and green are recorded in His Book. In other words they all obey His archetypal Plan, the Book which is also mentioned here. They are all answerable in their several degrees to His Plan ("shall be gathered to their Lord in the end"). This is not Pantheism: it is ascribing all life, activity, and existence to the Will and Plan of God.

860. The limited free-will of man makes a little difference. If he sees the Signs but shuts his ears to the true Message, and refuses (like a dumb thing) to speak out the Message which all Nature proclaims, then according to the Plan (of his limited free-will) he must suffer and wander, just as, in the opposite case, he will receive grace and salvation.

In the midst of darkness
Profound: whom God willeth,
He leaveth to wander:
Whom He willeth, He placeth
On the Way that is Straight.

فِي الظُّلُمٰتِ
مَنْ يَّشَاِ اللّٰهُ يُضْلِلْهُ ؕ وَمَنْ يَّشَاْ
يَجْعَلْهُ عَلٰى صِرَاطٍ مُّسْتَقِيْمٍ ○

40. Say: "Think ye to yourselves,
If there come upon you
The Wrath of God,
Or the Hour (that ye dread),
Would ye then call upon
Other than God?—
(Reply) if ye are truthful!

۴۰- قُلْ اَرَءَيْتَكُمْ
اِنْ اَتٰىكُمْ عَذَابُ اللّٰهِ
اَوْ اَتَتْكُمُ السَّاعَةُ اَغَيْرَ اللّٰهِ تَدْعُوْنَ ۚ
اِنْ كُنْتُمْ صٰدِقِيْنَ ○

41. "Nay,—On Him would ye
Call, and if it be
His Will, He would remove
(The distress) which occasioned
Your call upon Him,
And ye would forget
(The false gods) which ye
Join with Him!"

۴۱- بَلْ اِيَّاهُ تَدْعُوْنَ
فَيَكْشِفُ مَا تَدْعُوْنَ اِلَيْهِ
اِنْ شَآءَ
وَتَنْسَوْنَ مَا تُشْرِكُوْنَ ○ ع

SECTION 5.

42. Before thee We sent
(Apostles) to many nations,
And We afflicted the nations
With suffering and adversity,
That they might learn humility.

۴۲- وَلَقَدْ اَرْسَلْنَآ اِلٰٓى اُمَمٍ مِّنْ قَبْلِكَ
فَاَخَذْنٰهُمْ بِالْبَاْسَآءِ وَالضَّرَّآءِ
لَعَلَّهُمْ يَتَضَرَّعُوْنَ ○

43. When the suffering reached
Them from Us, why then
Did they not learn humility?[861]
On the contrary their hearts
Became hardened, and Satan
Made their (sinful) acts
Seem alluring to them.

۴۳- فَلَوْلَآ اِذْ جَآءَهُمْ بَاْسُنَا
تَضَرَّعُوْا وَلٰكِنْ قَسَتْ قُلُوْبُهُمْ
وَزَيَّنَ لَهُمُ الشَّيْطٰنُ
مَا كَانُوْا يَعْمَلُوْنَ ○

44. But when they forgot
The warning they had received,

۴۴- فَلَمَّا نَسُوْا مَا ذُكِّرُوْا بِهٖ

861. Sorrow and suffering may (if we take them rightly) turn out to be the best gifts of God to us. According to the Psalms (xciv. 12). "Blessed is the man whom Thou chastenest, O Lord!" Through suffering we learn humility, the antidote to many vices and the fountain of many virtues. But if we take them the wrong way, we grumble and complain, we become faint hearted; and Satan gets his opportunity to exploit us by putting forward the alluring pleasures of his Vanity Fair.

We opened to them the gates
Of all (good) things,[862]
Until, in the midst
Of their enjoyment
Of our gifts,
On a sudden, We called
Them to account, when lo!
They were plunged in despair!

فَتَحْنَا عَلَيْهِمْ أَبْوَابَ كُلِّ شَيْءٍ ط
حَتّٰى إِذَا فَرِحُوا بِمَا أُوتُوا
أَخَذْنٰهُمْ بَغْتَةً
فَإِذَا هُمْ مُبْلِسُونَ ○

45. Of the wrong-doers the last
Remnant was cut off.
Praise be to God,
The Cherisher of the Worlds.[863]

٤٥- فَقُطِعَ دَابِرُ الْقَوْمِ الَّذِينَ ظَلَمُوا ط
وَالْحَمْدُ لِلّٰهِ رَبِّ الْعٰلَمِينَ ○

46. Say: "Think ye, if God
Took away your hearing
And your sight, and sealed up[864]
Your hearts, who—a god
Other than God—could
Restore them to you?"
See how We explain
The Signs by various (symbols);
Yet they turn aside.

٤٦- قُلْ أَرَءَيْتُمْ إِنْ أَخَذَ اللّٰهُ سَمْعَكُمْ
وَأَبْصَارَكُمْ وَخَتَمَ عَلٰى قُلُوبِكُمْ
مَنْ إِلٰهٌ غَيْرُ اللّٰهِ يَأْتِيكُمْ بِهِ ط
اُنْظُرْ كَيْفَ نُصَرِّفُ الْاٰيٰتِ
ثُمَّ هُمْ يَصْدِفُونَ ○

47. Say: "Think ye, if
The Punishment of God
Comes to you,
Whether suddenly or openly,[865]
Will any be destroyed
Except those who do wrong?

٤٧- قُلْ أَرَءَيْتَكُمْ إِنْ أَتٰكُمْ عَذَابُ اللّٰهِ
بَغْتَةً أَوْ جَهْرَةً
هَلْ يُهْلَكُ إِلَّا الْقَوْمُ الظّٰلِمُونَ ○

48. We send the apostles
Only to give good news[866]

٤٨- وَمَا نُرْسِلُ الْمُرْسَلِينَ إِلَّا مُبَشِّرِينَ

---

862. Learning the inner truth of ourselves and the world presupposes a certain advanced stage of sensitiveness and spiritual development. There is a shallower stage, at which prosperity and the good things of life may teach us sympathy and goodness and cheerfulness like that of Mr. Cheeribyles in Dickens. In such cases the Message takes root. But there is another type of character which is puffed up in prosperity. For them prosperity is a trial or even a punishment from the higher point of view. They go deeper and deeper into sin, until they are pulled up of a sudden, and then instead of being contrite they merely become desperate.

863. God's punishment of wrong-doers is a measure of justice, to protect the true and righteous from their depredations and maintain His righteous decrees. It is an aspect of His character which is emphasised by the epithet "Cherisher of the Worlds."

864. *Cf.* ii. 7 and n.

865. *Suddenly*=without warning. *Openly*=with many warnings, even to the sinners, though they heed them not. As to those who understand and read the signs of God, they could always tell that all wrong-doing must eventually have its punishment. But it will affect the wrong-doers, not the righteous. It is justice, not revenge.

866. The Apostles are not sent to cancel man's limited free-will. They are sent to preach and teach,—to preach hope to the repentant ("good news"), and to warn the rebellious of the Wrath to come.

And to warn: so those
Who believe and mend
(Their lives),—upon them
Shall be no fear,
Nor shall they grieve.

وَمُنْذِرِيْنَ ۚ فَمَنْ اٰمَنَ وَاَصْلَحَ
فَلَا خَوْفٌ عَلَيْهِمْ
وَلَا هُمْ يَحْزَنُوْنَ ○

49. But those who reject
Our Signs,—them
Shall punishment touch,
For that they ceased not
From transgressing.

٤٩- وَالَّذِيْنَ كَذَّبُوْا بِاٰيٰتِنَا
يَمَسُّهُمُ الْعَذَابُ
بِمَا كَانُوْا يَفْسُقُوْنَ ○

50. Say: "I tell you not
That with me
Are the Treasures of God,[867]
Nor do I know
What is hidden,
Nor do I tell you I am
An angel. I but follow
What is revealed to me."
Say: "Can the blind
Be held equal to the seeing?"[868]
Will ye then consider not?

٥٠- قُلْ لَّآ اَقُوْلُ لَكُمْ عِنْدِيْ خَزَآئِنُ
اللّٰهِ وَلَآ اَعْلَمُ الْغَيْبَ
وَلَآ اَقُوْلُ لَكُمْ اِنِّيْ مَلَكٌ ۚ
اِنْ اَتَّبِعُ اِلَّا مَا يُوْحٰٓى اِلَيَّ ۚ
قُلْ هَلْ يَسْتَوِى الْاَعْمٰى وَالْبَصِيْرُ ۚ
ع اَفَلَا تَتَفَكَّرُوْنَ ○

Section 6.

51. Give this warning to those[869]
In whose (hearts) is the fear
That they will be brought
(To Judgment) before their Lord:
Except for Him
They will have no protector
Nor intercessor:
That they may guard
(Against evil).

٥١- وَاَنْذِرْ بِهِ الَّذِيْنَ يَخَافُوْنَ
اَنْ يُّحْشَرُوْٓا اِلٰى رَبِّهِمْ
لَيْسَ لَهُمْ مِّنْ دُوْنِهٖ
وَلِيٌّ وَّلَا شَفِيْعٌ
لَّعَلَّهُمْ يَتَّقُوْنَ ○

867. Literally, it might mean that the men of God are not like vulgar soothsayers, who pretend to reveal hidden treasures, or peer into future, or claim to be something of a different nature from men. But the meaning is wider: they deal out God's great treasures of truth, but the treasures are not theirs, but God's; they have greater insight into the higher things, but that insight is not due to their own wisdom, but to God's inspiration; they are of the same flesh and blood with us, and the sublimity of their words and teaching arises through God's grace—to them and to those who hear them.

868. Therefore compare not the men of God ("the seeing") with ordinary men ("the blind"). The men of God, although they be but men, have the higher light with them; therefore do not exact of them petty ephemeral services. Though they are men, they are not as other men, and are entitled to reverence.

869. There are some men—sinners—who yet believe in Judgment; let them be warned of their personal responsibility to guard against evil; let them not rely upon protectors or intercessors before God; their sins can only be forgiven by God's own Mercy.

52. Send not away those
Who call on their Lord
Morning and evening,
Seeking His Face.[870]
In naught art thou accountable
For them, and in naught are they
Accountable for thee,[871]
That thou shouldst turn
Them away, and thus be
(One) of the unjust.

٥٢- وَلَا تَطْرُدِ الَّذِينَ يَدْعُونَ رَبَّهُمْ
بِالْغَدٰوةِ وَالْعَشِيِّ يُرِيدُونَ وَجْهَهٗ
مَا عَلَيْكَ مِنْ حِسَابِهِمْ مِّنْ شَيْءٍ
وَّمَا مِنْ حِسَابِكَ عَلَيْهِمْ مِّنْ شَيْءٍ
فَتَطْرُدَهُمْ فَتَكُونَ مِنَ الظّٰلِمِينَ ○

53. Thus did We try
Some of them by comparison[872]
With others, that they
Should say: "Is it these
Then that God hath
Favoured from amongst us?"
Doth not God know best
Those who are grateful?

٥٣- وَكَذٰلِكَ فَتَنَّا بَعْضَهُمْ بِبَعْضٍ
لِّيَقُولُوٓا أَهٰٓؤُلَآءِ مَنَّ اللّٰهُ عَلَيْهِمْ
مِّنْۢ بَيْنِنَا ؕ
أَلَيْسَ اللّٰهُ بِأَعْلَمَ بِالشّٰكِرِينَ ○

54. When those come to thee
Who believe in Our Signs,
Say: "Peace be on you:[873]
Your Lord hath inscribed
For Himself (the rule[874]
Of) Mercy: verily,
If any of you did evil
In ignorance, and thereafter

٥٤- وَإِذَا جَآءَكَ الَّذِينَ يُؤْمِنُونَ بِاٰيٰتِنَا
فَقُلْ سَلٰمٌ عَلَيْكُمْ
كَتَبَ رَبُّكُمْ عَلٰى نَفْسِهِ الرَّحْمَةَ ۙ
أَنَّهٗ مَنْ عَمِلَ مِنْكُمْ سُوٓءًۢا بِجَهَالَةٍ ثُمَّ

870. *Face*: *wajh*: see ii. 112 and n. 114. "Face" is used for God's Grace or Presence, the highest aim of spiritual aspiration.

871. Some of the rich and influential Quraish thought it beneath their dignity to listen to Muḥammad's teaching in company with the lowly disciples, who were gathered round him. But he refused to send away these lowly disciples, who were sincere seekers after God. From a worldly point of view they had nothing to gain from Muḥammad as he was himself poor, and he had nothing to gain from them as they had no influence. But that was no reason for turning them away; indeed their true sincerity entitled them to precedence over wordly men in the kingdom of God, whose justice was vindicated in Muhammad's daily life in this as in other things. If their sincerity was in any way doubtful, it involved no responsibility for the Preacher.

872. Pursue the argument of the last note. The influential people who were not given precedence over the poor and humble but sincere disciples, were on their trial as to their spiritual insight. Their temptation was to say (and they said it in scorn): "We are much greater than they: has God then selected these lowly people for His teaching?" But that was so. And God knew best those who were grateful to Him for His guidance.

873. The humble who had sincere faith, were not only not sent away to humour the wealthy: they were honoured and were given a special salutation, which has become the characteristic salutation in Islam: "Peace be on you,"—the word peace, "*salām*" having special affinity with the word "*Islām*." In words they are given the salutation; in life they are promised Mercy by the special grace of God.

874. *Cf.* vi. 12.

Repented, and amended
(His conduct), lo! He is
Oft-forgiving, Most Merciful.

تَابَ مِنْۢ بَعْدِهٖ وَاَصْلَحَ
فَاَنَّهٗ غَفُوْرٌ رَّحِيْمٌ ۝

55. Thus do We explain
The Signs in detail:
That the way of the sinners
May be shown up.[875]

٥٥- وَكَذٰلِكَ نُفَصِّلُ الْاٰيٰتِ
وَلِتَسْتَبِيْنَ سَبِيْلُ الْمُجْرِمِيْنَ ۝ ع

Section 7.

56. Say:[876] "I am forbidden
To worship those—others
Than God—whom ye
Call upon." Say: "I will
Not follow your vain desires:
If I did, I would stray
From the path, and be not
Of the company of those
Who receive guidance."

٥٦- قُلْ اِنِّيْ نُهِيْتُ اَنْ اَعْبُدَ
الَّذِيْنَ تَدْعُوْنَ مِنْ دُوْنِ اللّٰهِ ؕ
قُلْ لَّآ اَتَّبِعُ اَهْوَآءَكُمْ ۙ
قَدْ ضَلَلْتُ اِذًا
وَّمَآ اَنَا مِنَ الْمُهْتَدِيْنَ ۝

57. Say: "For me, I (work)
On a clear Sign from my Lord,
But ye reject Him. What ye[877]
Would see hastened, is not
In my power. The Command
Rests with none but God:
He declares the Truth,
And He is the best of judges."

٥٧- قُلْ اِنِّيْ عَلٰى بَيِّنَةٍ مِّنْ رَّبِّيْ
وَكَذَّبْتُمْ بِهٖ ؕ مَا عِنْدِيْ مَا تَسْتَعْجِلُوْنَ
بِهٖ ؕ اِنِ الْحُكْمُ اِلَّا لِلّٰهِ ؕ
يَقُصُّ الْحَقَّ وَهُوَ خَيْرُ الْفٰصِلِيْنَ ۝

58. Say: "If what ye would see
Hastened were in my power,
The matter would be settled
At once between you and me.[878]

٥٨- قُلْ لَّوْ اَنَّ عِنْدِيْ مَا تَسْتَعْجِلُوْنَ
بِهٖ لَقُضِيَ الْاَمْرُ بَيْنِيْ وَبَيْنَكُمْ ؕ

---

875. If the way of the sinners (in jealousy and worldly pride) is shown up, and details are given how to honour the truly sincere, it forms the best illustration of the teaching of God.

876. There are a number of arguments now put forward against the Meccans who refused to believe in God's Message. Each argument is introduced with the word "Say." Here are the first four: (1) I have received Light and will follow it; (2) I prefer my Light to your vain desires (3) your challenge—"if there is a God, why does He not finish the blasphemers at once?"—it is not for me to take up; punishment rests with God; (4) if it rested with me, it would be for me to take up your challenge; all I know is that God is not unacquainted with the existence of folly and wickedness, and many other things besides, that no mortal can know; you can see little glimpses of His Plan, and you can be sure that He will not be tardy in calling you to account.

877. *What ye would see hastened*: what ye, deniers of God, are so impatient about; the punishment which ye mockingly say does not come to you. *Cf.* xiii. 6.

878. The Messenger of God is not here to settle scores with the wicked. It is not a matter between them and him. It is a matter between them and God; he is only a warner against sin, and a declarer of the gospel of salvation.

But God knoweth best
Those who do wrong."

وَاللّٰهُ اَعْلَمُ بِالظّٰلِمِيْنَ ۝

59. With Him are the keys[879]
Of the Unseen, the treasures
That none knoweth but He.
He knoweth whatever there is
On the earth and in the sea.
Not a leaf doth fall
But with His knowledge:
There is not a grain
In the darkness (or depths)
Of the earth, nor anything
Fresh or dry (green or withered),
But is (inscribed) in a Record[880]
Clear (to those who can read).

۵۹- وَعِنْدَهٗ مَفَاتِحُ الْغَيْبِ
لَا يَعْلَمُهَآ اِلَّا هُوَ ؕ
وَيَعْلَمُ مَا فِى الْبَرِّ وَالْبَحْرِ ؕ
وَمَا تَسْقُطُ مِنْ وَّرَقَةٍ اِلَّا يَعْلَمُهَا
وَلَا حَبَّةٍ فِىْ ظُلُمٰتِ الْاَرْضِ
وَلَا رَطْبٍ وَّلَا يَابِسٍ
اِلَّا فِىْ كِتٰبٍ مُّبِيْنٍ ۝

60. It is He Who doth take
Your souls by night,
And hath knowledge of all
That ye have done by day:
By day doth He raise
You up again; that a term
Appointed be fulfilled;
In the end unto Him
Will be your return;[881]
Then will He show you
The truth of all
That ye did.

۶۰- وَهُوَ الَّذِىْ يَتَوَفّٰىكُمْ بِالَّيْلِ
وَيَعْلَمُ مَا جَرَحْتُمْ بِالنَّهَارِ
ثُمَّ يَبْعَثُكُمْ فِيْهِ لِيُقْضٰٓى اَجَلٌ مُّسَمًّى ۚ
ثُمَّ اِلَيْهِ مَرْجِعُكُمْ
ثُمَّ يُنَبِّئُكُمْ
ع بِمَا كُنْتُمْ تَعْمَلُوْنَ ۝

C. 78.—God's loving care doth encompass
(vi. 61-82.) Us round throughout life,
And deliver us from dangers
By land and sea. He is the only
Protector: how can we then

---

879. *Mafātiḥ*: Plural of either *miftaḥ*=a key, or *maftaḥ*=a treasure. Both meanings are implied, and I have accordingly put both in my translation.

880. This is the mystic Record, the archetypal Plan, the Eternal Law, according to which everything seen and unseen is ordered and regulated. There is much mystic doctrine here, explained by beautiful metaphors and illustrations. The simplest things in Nature are subject to His Law. The fresh and the withered, the living and the lifeless—nothing is outside the Plan of His Creation.

881. As the rest of His Creation is subject to His Law and Plan, so is man's life in every particular and at every moment, awake or asleep. The mystery of Sleep—"the twin brother of death"—is called the taking of our soul by Him, with the record of all we have done in our waking moments, and this record sometimes appears to us in confused glimpses in dreams. By day we awaken again to our activities, and so it goes on until we fulfil the term of our life appointed for this earth. Then comes the other Sleep (death), with the longer record of our Day (Life); and then, in the end comes the Resurrection and Judgment, at which we see everything clearly and not as in dreams, for that is the final Reality.

Forget Him or run after things
That are mere creatures of His,
And shall perish,—while He
Is the Eternal God, adored
By Abraham and all the prophets?

Section 8.

61. He is the Irresistible, (watching)
From above over His worshippers,
And He sets guardians[882]
Over you. At length,
When death approaches
One of you, Our angels[883]
Take his soul, and they
Never fail in their duty.

٦١- وَهُوَ الْقَاهِرُ فَوْقَ عِبَادِهِ
وَيُرْسِلُ عَلَيْكُمْ حَفَظَةً
حَتَّىٰٓ إِذَا جَآءَ أَحَدَكُمُ الْمَوْتُ
تَوَفَّتْهُ رُسُلُنَا وَهُمْ لَا يُفَرِّطُونَ ○

62. Then are men returned
Unto God, their Protector,
The (only) Reality:[884]
Is not His the Command?
And He is the Swiftest
In taking account.

٦٢- ثُمَّ رُدُّوٓا إِلَى اللّٰهِ مَوْلٰىهُمُ الْحَقِّ
أَلَا لَهُ الْحُكْمُ
وَهُوَ أَسْرَعُ الْحٰسِبِينَ ○

63. Say:[885] "Who is it
That delivereth you
From the dark recesses[886]
Of land and sea,
When ye call upon Him
In humility

٦٣- قُلْ مَنْ يُنَجِّيكُمْ
مِّنْ ظُلُمٰتِ الْبَرِّ وَالْبَحْرِ
تَدْعُونَهُ تَضَرُّعًا

---

882. *Guardians*: most Commentators understand this to mean guardian angels. The idea of guardianship is expressed in a general term. God watches over us and guards us, and provides all kinds of agencies, material, moral, and spiritual, to help our growth and development, keep us from harm, and bring us nearer to our Destiny.

883. *Angels*: the word used is ***rusul***, the Sent Ones,—the same word as for human Apostles and Messengers sent by God to teach mankind. The agents who come to take our souls at death are accurate in the performance of their duty. They come neither before nor after their appointed time, nor do they do it in any manner other than that fixed by the Command of God.

884. *The only Reality*: *al-haqq*, the Truth, the only True One. The point is that our illusions of the life of this lower world now vanish, when we are rendered back to God, from Whom we came. And now we find that so far from the results of our actions being delayed, they follow more swiftly than we can express in terms of Time. Here is the answer to the taunt of those who were impatient of the working of God's Plans (vi. 57-58).

885. In continuation of the four heads of argument referred to in n. 876, we have three more heads here in vi. 63 65: (5) your calling upon Him in times of danger shows that in the depths of your hearts you feel His need; (6) God's Providence saves you, and yet you ungratefully run after false gods; (7) it is not only physical calamities that you have to fear; your mutual discords and vengeances are even more destructive, and only faith in God can save you from them.

886. ***Ẕulumāt***: dark recesses, terrible lurking dangers, as in deserts or mountains, or forests, or seas.

And silent terror:[887]
'If He only delivers us
From these (dangers),
(We vow) we shall truly
Show our gratitude'.?"

وَّ خُفْيَةً ۚ
لَئِنْ اَنْجٰنَا مِنْ هٰذِهٖ
لَنَكُوْنَنَّ مِنَ الشّٰكِرِيْنَ ○

64. Say: "It is God
That delivereth you
From these and all (other)
Distresses: and yet
Ye worship false gods!"

٦٤- قُلِ اللّٰهُ يُنَجِّيْكُمْ
مِّنْهَا وَمِنْ كُلِّ كَرْبٍ
ثُمَّ اَنْتُمْ تُشْرِكُوْنَ ○

65. Say: "He hath power
To send calamities[888]
On you, from above
And below, or to cover
You with confusion
In party strife,
Giving you a taste
Of mutual vengeance—
Each from the other."
See how We explain
The Signs by various (symbols);[889]
That they may understand.

٦٥- قُلْ هُوَ الْقَادِرُ عَلٰٓى اَنْ يَّبْعَثَ
عَلَيْكُمْ عَذَابًا مِّنْ فَوْقِكُمْ
اَوْ مِنْ تَحْتِ اَرْجُلِكُمْ
اَوْ يَلْبِسَكُمْ شِيَعًا وَّيُذِيْقَ بَعْضَكُمْ
بَاْسَ بَعْضٍ ۗ اُنْظُرْ كَيْفَ نُصَرِّفُ
الْاٰيٰتِ لَعَلَّهُمْ يَفْقَهُوْنَ ○

66. But thy people reject
This, though it is
The Truth. Say: "Not mine
Is the responsibility
For arranging your affairs;[890]

٦٦- وَكَذَّبَ بِهٖ قَوْمُكَ وَهُوَ الْحَقُّ ۗ
قُلْ لَّسْتُ عَلَيْكُمْ بِوَكِيْلٍ ○

67. For every Message
Is a limit of time,
And soon shall ye
Know it."

٦٧- لِكُلِّ نَبَاٍ مُّسْتَقَرٌّ
وَّسَوْفَ تَعْلَمُوْنَ ○

887. There are two readings, but they both ultimately yield the same meaning. (1) *Khufyatan*, silently, secretly, from the depth of your inner heart, suggesting unspeakable terror. (2) *Khifatan*, out of terror or fear or reverence, as in vii. 205.

888. *Calamities from above and below*: such as storms and blizzards, torrential rain, etc., or earthquakes, floods, landslides, etc.

889. *Cf.* vi. 46, where this refrain commences the argument now drawing to a close.

890. At the date of this revelation, the Apostle's people had as a body not only rejected God's truth, but were persecuting it. The Aspotle's duty was to deliver his Message, which he did. He was not responsible for their conduct. But he told them plainly that all warnings from God had their time limit, as they would soon find out. And they did find out within a very few years. For the leaders of the resistance came to an evil end, and their whole system of fraud and selfishness was destroyed, to make room for the purer Faith of Islam. Apart from that particular application, there is the more general application, for the present time and for all time.

68. When thou seest men
Engaged in vain discourse
About Our Signs, turn
Away from them unless
They turn to a different[891]
Theme. If Satan ever
Makes thee forget, then
After recollection, sit not
Thou in the company
Of those who do wrong.

٦٨- وَإِذَا رَأَيْتَ الَّذِينَ يَخُوضُونَ
فِيٓ ءَايٰتِنَا فَأَعْرِضْ عَنْهُمْ حَتّٰى يَخُوضُوا
فِي حَدِيثٍ غَيْرِهِۦ ۚ وَإِمَّا يُنسِيَنَّكَ
الشَّيْطٰنُ فَلَا تَقْعُدْ بَعْدَ الذِّكْرٰى
مَعَ الْقَوْمِ الظّٰلِمِينَ ۝

69. On their account
No responsibility
Falls on the righteous,[892]
But (their duty)
Is to remind them,
That they may (learn
To) fear God.

٦٩- وَمَا عَلَى الَّذِينَ يَتَّقُونَ مِنْ
حِسَابِهِم مِّن شَيْءٍ
وَلٰكِن ذِكْرٰى
لَعَلَّهُمْ يَتَّقُونَ ۝

70. Leave alone those
Who take their religion
To be mere play
And amusement,[893]
And are deceived
By the life of this world.
But proclaim (to them)
This (truth): that every soul
Delivers itself to ruin
By its own acts:[894]
It will find for itself
No protector or intercessor
Except God: if it offered
Every ransom, (or
Reparation), none
Will be accepted: such is
(The end of) those who
Deliver themselves to ruin
By their own acts:
They will have for drink
(Only) boiling water,

٧٠- وَذَرِ الَّذِينَ
اتَّخَذُوا دِينَهُمْ لَعِبًا وَلَهْوًا
وَغَرَّتْهُمُ الْحَيٰوةُ الدُّنْيَا
وَذَكِّرْ بِهِۦٓ أَن تُبْسَلَ نَفْسٌۢ بِمَا
كَسَبَتْ ۖ
لَيْسَ لَهَا مِن دُونِ اللَّهِ
وَلِيٌّ وَلَا شَفِيعٌ ۚ
وَإِن تَعْدِلْ كُلَّ عَدْلٍ لَّا يُؤْخَذْ
مِنْهَآ ۗ أُولٰٓئِكَ الَّذِينَ أُبْسِلُوا بِمَا كَسَبُوا ۖ
لَهُمْ شَرَابٌ مِّنْ حَمِيمٍ

891. *Cf.* iv. 140. If in any gathering truth is ridiculed, we must not sit in such company. If we find ourselves in it, as soon as we realise it, we must show our disapproval by leaving.

892. "Evil to him who evil thinks," or evil does. Every man is responsible for his own conduct. But the righteous have two duties: (1) to protect themselves from infection, and (2) to proclaim God's truth, for even in the most unlikely circumstances, it is possible that it may have some effect.

893. *Cf.* vi. 32, where we are told that the life of this world is mere play and amusement, and Religion and the Hereafter are the serious things that require our attention. Worldly people reverse this, because they are deceived by the allurements of this life. But their own acts will find them out.

894. We must never forget our own personal responsibility for al we do, or deceive ourselves by the illusion of vicarious atonement.

And for punishment,
One most grievous:
For they persisted
In rejecting God.

وَعَذَابٌ أَلِيمٌ
بِمَا كَانُوا يَكْفُرُونَ ۝ ع

SECTION 9.

71. Say:[895] "Shall we indeed
Call on others besides God,—
Things that can do us
Neither good nor harm,—
And turn on our heels
After receiving guidance
From God?—like one
Whom the evil ones
Have made into a fool,
Wandering bewildered
Through the earth, his friends
Calling 'Come to us',
(Vainly) guiding him to the Path."

Say: "God's guidance
Is the (only) guidance,
And we have been directed
To submit ourselves
To the Lord of the worlds;—

٧١- قُلْ أَنَدْعُوا مِنْ دُونِ اللَّهِ
مَا لَا يَنْفَعُنَا
وَلَا يَضُرُّنَا
وَنُرَدُّ عَلَىٰ أَعْقَابِنَا بَعْدَ إِذْ هَدَانَا اللَّهُ
كَالَّذِي اسْتَهْوَتْهُ الشَّيَاطِينُ فِي
الْأَرْضِ حَيْرَانَ
لَهُ أَصْحَابٌ يَدْعُونَهُ إِلَى الْهُدَى ائْتِنَا
قُلْ إِنَّ هُدَى اللَّهِ
هُوَ الْهُدَىٰ
وَأُمِرْنَا لِنُسْلِمَ لِرَبِّ الْعَالَمِينَ ۝

72. "To establish regular prayers
And to fear God:
For it is to Him
That we shall be
Gathered together."

٧٢- وَأَنْ أَقِيمُوا الصَّلَاةَ
وَاتَّقُوهُ
وَهُوَ الَّذِي إِلَيْهِ تُحْشَرُونَ ۝

73. It is He Who created
The heavens and the earth
In true (proportions):[896]
The day He saith, "Be,"

٧٣- وَهُوَ الَّذِي خَلَقَ السَّمَاوَاتِ وَالْأَرْضَ
بِالْحَقِّ وَيَوْمَ يَقُولُ كُنْ فَيَكُونُ

---

895. In continuation of the seven heads of argument referred to in nn. 876 and 885, we have here the final two heads: (8) who would, after receiving guidance from the living, eternal God, turn to lifeless idols? To do so would indeed show that we were made into fools, wandering to a precipice; (9) therefore accept the only true guidance, the guidance of God, and obey His Law, for we shall have to answer before His judgment-seat.

896. The argument mounts up here, leading to the great insight of Abraham the true in faith, who did not stop short at the wonders of nature, but penetrated "from nature up to nature's God." God not only created the heavens and the earth: with every increase of knowledge we see in what true and perfect proportions all Creation is held together. Creatures are subject to Time, but the Creator is not: His word is the key that opens the door of existence. It is not only the starting point of existence, but the whole measure and standard of Truth and Right. There may possibly be, to our sight in this great world, aberrations of human or other wills, but the moment the trumpet sounds for the last day, His judgment-seat will, with perfect justice, restore the dominion of Right and Reality. For His knowledge and wisdom cover all reality.

Behold! it is. His Word
Is the Truth. His will be
The dominion the day
The trumpet will be blown.
He knoweth the Unseen
As well as that which is
Open. For He
Is the Wise, well acquainted
(With all things).

قَوْلُهُ الْحَقُّ ۚ
وَلَهُ الْمُلْكُ
يَوْمَ يُنْفَخُ فِي الصُّوْرِ ۚ
عٰلِمُ الْغَيْبِ وَالشَّهَادَةِ ۚ
وَهُوَ الْحَكِيْمُ الْخَبِيْرُ ○

74. Lo! Abraham said
To his father Āzar:
"Takest thou idols for gods?
For I see thee
And thy people
In manifest error."

٧٤- وَإِذْ قَالَ إِبْرٰهِيْمُ لِأَبِيْهِ آزَرَ
أَتَتَّخِذُ أَصْنَامًا آلِهَةً ۚ
إِنِّيْ أَرٰىكَ وَقَوْمَكَ فِيْ ضَلٰلٍ مُّبِيْنٍ ○

75. So also did We show[897]
Abraham the power
And the laws of the heavens
And the earth, that he
Might (with understanding)
Have certitude.

٧٥- وَكَذٰلِكَ نُرِيْ
إِبْرٰهِيْمَ مَلَكُوْتَ السَّمٰوٰتِ وَالْأَرْضِ
وَلِيَكُوْنَ مِنَ الْمُوْقِنِيْنَ ○

76. When the night
Covered him over,
He saw a star:
He said: "This is my Lord."
But when it set,
He said: "I love not
Those that set."[898]

٧٦- فَلَمَّا جَنَّ عَلَيْهِ الَّيْلُ
رَاٰ كَوْكَبًا ۚ
قَالَ هٰذَا رَبِّيْ ۚ
فَلَمَّآ أَفَلَ قَالَ لَآ أُحِبُّ الْاٰفِلِيْنَ ○

77. When he saw the moon
Rising in splendour,
He said: "This is my Lord."
But when the moon set,

٧٧- فَلَمَّا رَاَ الْقَمَرَ بَازِغًا
قَالَ هٰذَا رَبِّيْ ۚ فَلَمَّآ أَفَلَ

---

897. Now comes the story of Abraham. He lived among the Chaldeans, who had great knowledge of the stars and heavenly bodies. But he got beyond that physical world and saw the spiritual world behind. His ancestral idols meant nothing to him. That was the first step. But God took him many degrees higher. God showed him with certitude the spiritual glories behind the magnificent powers and laws of the physical universe.

898. This allegory shows the stages of Abraham's spiritual enlightenment. It should not be supposed that he literally worshipped stars or heavenly bodies. Having seen through the folly of ancestral idol worship, he began to see the futility of worshipping distant beautiful things that shine, which the vulgar endue with a power which does not reside in them. A type of such is a star shining in the darkness of the night. Superstition might read fortunes in it, but truer knowledge shows that it rises and sets according to laws whose author is God. And its light is extinguished in the broader light of day. Its worship is therefore futile. It is not a Power, much less the Supreme Power.

He said: "Unless my Lord
Guide me, I shall surely
Be among those
Who go astray."[899]

قَالَ لَئِنْ لَّمْ يَهْدِنِيْ رَبِّيْ
لَاَكُوْنَنَّ مِنَ الْقَوْمِ الضَّآلِّيْنَ ○

78. When he saw the sun
Rising in splendour,
He said: "This is my Lord;
This is the greatest (of all)."
But when the sun set,
He said: "O my people!
I am indeed free
From your (guilt)
Of giving partners to God.[900]

٧٨- فَلَمَّا رَاَ الشَّمْسَ بَازِغَةً
قَالَ هٰذَا رَبِّيْ
هٰذَآ اَكْبَرُ ج
فَلَمَّآ اَفَلَتْ
قَالَ يٰقَوْمِ اِنِّيْ بَرِيْٓءٌ مِّمَّا تُشْرِكُوْنَ ○

79. "For me, I have set
My face, firmly and truly,
Towards Him Who created
The heavens and the earth,
And never shall I give
Partners to God."

٧٩- اِنِّيْ وَجَّهْتُ وَجْهِيَ لِلَّذِيْ
فَطَرَ السَّمٰوٰتِ وَالْاَرْضَ حَنِيْفًا
وَّمَآ اَنَا مِنَ الْمُشْرِكِيْنَ ○

80. His people disputed[901]
With him. He said:
"(Come) ye to dispute
With me, about God,
When He (Himself)
Hath guided me?
I fear not (the beings)
Ye associate with God:

٨٠- وَحَآجَّهٗ قَوْمُهٗ ط
قَالَ اَتُحَآجُّوْٓنِّيْ فِي اللّٰهِ
وَقَدْ هَدٰىنِ ط
وَلَآ اَخَافُ مَا تُشْرِكُوْنَ بِهٖٓ

---

899. Continuing the allegory, the moon, though she looks bigger and brighter than the star, turns out on closer knowledge, not only to set like the star, but to change her shape from hour to hour, and even to depend for her light on some other body! How deceptive are appearances! That is not God! At that stage you begin to search for something more reliable than appearances to the eye in the darkness of the night. You ask for guidance from God.

900. The next stage in the allegory is the sun. You are in the open light of Day. Now you have the right clue. You see the biggest object in the heavens. But is it the biggest? There are thousands of stars in the universe bigger than the sun. And every day the sun appears and disappears from your sight. Such is not the God who created you and all these wonderful works of His. What folly to worship creatures, when we might turn to the true God? Let us abjure all these follies and proclaim the one true God.

901. To continue Abraham's allegory: if spiritual enlightenment go so far as to take a man beyond his ancestral worship, people will come to dispute with him. They will frighten him with the dire consequences of his dissent. What does he care? He has found the truth. He is free from superstitious fears, for has he not found the true God, without Whose Will nothing can happen? On the contrary he knows that it is the godless who have just grounds for fear. And he offers admonition to them, and arguments that should bring them the clearness of truth instead of the vagueness and mystery of superstition,—the security of Faith instead of the haunting fear of those who have no clear guidance.

Unless my Lord willeth,
(Nothing can happen).
My Lord comprehendeth
In His knowledge all things.
Will ye not (yourselves)
Be admonished?

إِلَّآ أَن يَشَآءَ رَبِّي شَيْـًٔا
وَسِعَ رَبِّي كُلَّ شَيْءٍ عِلْمًا
أَفَلَا تَتَذَكَّرُونَ ۝

81. "How should I fear
(The beings) ye associate
With God, when ye
Fear not to give partners
To God without any warrant
Having been given to you?
Which of (us) two parties
Hath more right to security?
(Tell me) if ye know.

٨١- وَكَيْفَ أَخَافُ مَآ أَشْرَكْتُمْ
وَلَا تَخَافُونَ أَنَّكُمْ أَشْرَكْتُم بِاللَّهِ
مَا لَمْ يُنَزِّلْ بِهِ عَلَيْكُمْ سُلْطَانًا
فَأَيُّ الْفَرِيقَيْنِ أَحَقُّ بِالْأَمْنِ
إِن كُنتُمْ تَعْلَمُونَ ۝

82. "It is those who believe
And confuse not their beliefs
With wrong—that are
(Truly) in security, for they
Are on (right) guidance."

٨٢- الَّذِينَ آمَنُوا وَلَمْ يَلْبِسُوٓا إِيمَانَهُم
بِظُلْمٍ أُولَٰٓئِكَ لَهُمُ الْأَمْنُ وَهُم مُّهْتَدُونَ ۝

C. 79.—The good men and true, who succeeded
(vi. 83-110.) Abraham, received the gifts
Of revelation and guidance, and kept
Alive God's Message, which now
Is proclaimed in the Qur-ān,
In which is blessing and confirmation
Of all that went before. In the daily
Pageants of Nature,—the dawn
And the restful night, the sun,
The moon, the stars that guide
The mariner in distant seas,
The rain-clouds pouring abundance,
And the fruits that delight the heart
Of man—can ye not read
Signs of God? No vision can
Comprehend Him, yet He
Knoweth and comprehendeth all.

Section 10.

83. That was the reasoning
About Us, which
We gave to Abraham
(To use) against his people:[902]

٨٣- وَتِلْكَ حُجَّتُنَآ آتَيْنَاهَآ إِبْرَاهِيمَ عَلَىٰ
قَوْمِهِ نَرْفَعُ دَرَجَاتٍ مَّن نَّشَآءُ

902. The spiritual education of Abraham raised him many degrees above his contemporaries, and he was expected to use that knowledge and dignity for preaching the truth among his own people.

We raise whom We will,
Degree after degree:
For thy Lord is full
Of wisdom and knowledge.

إِنَّ رَبَّكَ حَكِيمٌ عَلِيمٌ ○

84. We gave him Isaac
And Jacob: all (three)
We guided:[903]
And before him,
We guided Noah,[904]
And among his progeny,
David, Solomon, Job,
Joseph, Moses, and Aaron:
Thus do We reward
Those who do good:

٨٤- وَوَهَبْنَا لَهُ إِسْحٰقَ وَيَعْقُوبَ ط
كُلًّا هَدَيْنَا وَنُوحًا هَدَيْنَا مِنْ قَبْلُ
وَمِنْ ذُرِّيَّتِهِ دَاوُدَ وَسُلَيْمٰنَ وَأَيُّوبَ
وَيُوسُفَ وَمُوسٰى وَهٰرُونَ ط
وَكَذٰلِكَ نَجْزِي الْمُحْسِنِينَ ○

85. And Zakarīya and John,[905]
And Jesus and Elias:
All in the ranks
Of the Righteous:

٨٥- وَزَكَرِيَّا وَيَحْيٰى وَعِيسٰى وَإِلْيَاسَ ط
كُلٌّ مِنَ الصّٰلِحِينَ ○

86. And Isma'īl and Elisha,[906]
And Jonas, and Lot:

٨٦- وَإِسْمٰعِيلَ وَالْيَسَعَ وَيُونُسَ وَلُوطًا ط

---

903. We have now a list of eighteen Apostles in four groups, covering the great Teachers accepted among the three great religions based on Moses, Jesus, and Muḥammad. The first group to be mentioned is that of Abraham, his son Isaac, and Isaac's son Jacob. Abraham was the first to have a Book. His Book is mentioned in Q. lxxxvii. 19, though it is now lost. They were therefore the first to receive Guidance in the sense of a Book.

904. In the second group, we have the great founders of families, apart from Abraham, *viz.*, Noah, of the time of the Flood; David and Solomon, the real establishers of the Jewish monarchy; Job, who lived 140 years, saw four generations of descendants, and was blessed at the end of his life with large pastoral wealth (Job xlii. 16, 12); Joseph, who as Minister of State did great things in Egypt and was the progenitor of two Tribes; and Moses and Aaron, the leaders of the Exodus from Egypt. They led active lives and are called "doers of good."

905. The third group consists not of men of action, but Preachers of Truth, who led solitary lives. Their epithet is: "the Righteous." They were mystic prophets and form a connected group round Jesus. Zakarīya was the father of John the Baptist, the precursor of Jesus (iii. 37-41); and Jesus referred to John the Baptist as Elias: "this is Elias, which was for to come" (Matt. xi. 14); and Elias is said to have been present and talked to Jesus at the Transfiguration on the Mount (Matt. xvii. 3). Elias is the same as Elijah.

906. This is the last group, described as those "favoured above the nations." It consists of four men who had all great misfortunes to contend with, and were concerned in the clash of nations, but they kept in the path of God, and came through above the clash of nations. Ismā'īl was the eldest son of Abraham; when he was a baby, he and his mother had nearly died of thirst in the desert round Mecca; but they were saved by the well of Zamzam, and he became the founder of the new Arab nation. Elisha (Al-Yasa') succeeded to the mantle of the Prophet Elijah (same as Elias, see last note); he lived in troublous times for both the Jewish kingdoms (of Judah and Israel); there were wicked kings, and other nations were pressing in on them; but he performed many miracles, and some check was given to the enemies under his advice. The story of Jonas (Yūnus) is well-known: he was swallowed by a fish or whale, but was saved by God's mercy: through his preaching, his city (Nineveh) was saved (x. 98). Lot was a contemporary and nephew of Abraham: when the city of Sodom was destroyed for its wickedness, he was saved as a just man (vii. 80-84).

And to all We gave
Favour above the nations :

وَكُلًّا فَضَّلْنَا عَلَى الْعٰلَمِيْنَ ۝

87. (To them) and to their fathers,[907]
And progeny and brethren :
We chose them,
And We guided them
To a straight Way.

٨٧- وَمِنْ اٰبَآئِهِمْ وَذُرِّيّٰتِهِمْ وَاِخْوَانِهِمْ
وَاجْتَبَيْنٰهُمْ وَهَدَيْنٰهُمْ
اِلٰى صِرَاطٍ مُّسْتَقِيْمٍ ۝

88. This is the Guidance
Of God : He giveth
That guidance to whom
He pleaseth, of His worshippers.
If they were to join
Other gods with Him,
All that they did
Would be vain for them.

٨٨- ذٰلِكَ هُدَى اللّٰهِ يَهْدِيْ بِهٖ مَنْ
يَّشَآءُ مِنْ عِبَادِهٖ
وَلَوْ اَشْرَكُوْا لَحَبِطَ عَنْهُمْ
مَّا كَانُوْا يَعْمَلُوْنَ ۝

89. These were the men
To whom We gave
The Book, and Authority,
And Prophethood : if these
(Their descendants) reject them,[908]
Behold ! We shall entrust
Their charge to a new People
Who reject them not.

٨٩- اُولٰٓئِكَ الَّذِيْنَ اٰتَيْنٰهُمُ الْكِتٰبَ وَ
الْحُكْمَ وَالنُّبُوَّةَ
فَاِنْ يَّكْفُرْ بِهَا هٰٓؤُلَآءِ فَقَدْ وَكَّلْنَا بِهَا
قَوْمًا لَّيْسُوْا بِهَا بِكٰفِرِيْنَ ۝

90. Those were the (prophets)
Who received God's guidance :
Copy the guidance they received ;
Say : "No reward for this
Do I ask of you :
This is no less than
A Message for the nations."

٩٠- اُولٰٓئِكَ الَّذِيْنَ هَدَى اللّٰهُ
فَبِهُدٰىهُمُ اقْتَدِهْ
قُلْ لَّآ اَسْئَلُكُمْ عَلَيْهِ اَجْرًا
اِنْ هُوَ اِلَّا ذِكْرٰى لِلْعٰلَمِيْنَ ۝

SECTION 11.

91. No just estimate of God[909]
Do they make when they say :

٩١- وَمَا قَدَرُوا اللّٰهَ حَقَّ قَدْرِهٖٓ اِذْ قَالُوْا

907. I take verse 87 to refer back to all the four groups just mentioned.

908. *Them, i.e.*, the Book, and Authority and Prophethood. They were taken away from the other People of the Book and entrusted to the holy Apostle Muḥammad and his People.

909. *Qadara* : to weigh, judge, or estimate the value or capacity of anything ; to have power so to do. *Cf. Qadīr* in iv. 149 and n. 655. The Jews who denied the inspiration of Muḥammad had a good answer in their own books about the inspiration of Moses. To those who do not believe in Moses, the answer is more general : is it a just estimate of God to think either that He has not the power or the will to guide mankind, seeing that He is Omnipotent and the Source of all good ? If you say that guidance comes, not through an inspired book or man, but through our general intelligence, we point to the spiritual ignorance of "you and your ancestors" the sad spiritual darkness of men and nations high in the intellectual scale.

"Nothing doth God send down
To man (by way of revelation)":
Say: "Who then sent down
The Book which Moses brought?—
A light and guidance to man:[910]
But ye make it into
(Separate) sheets for show,[911]
While ye conceal much
(Of its contents): therein
Were ye taught that
Which ye knew not—
Neither ye nor your fathers."
Say: "God (sent it down)":
Then leave them to plunge
In vain discourse and trifling.

مَآ أَنْزَلَ اللّٰهُ عَلٰى بَشَرٍ مِّنْ شَىْءٍ ؕ
قُلْ مَنْ أَنْزَلَ الْكِتٰبَ الَّذِىْ جَآءَ بِهٖ
مُوْسٰى نُوْرًا وَّهُدًى لِّلنَّاسِ
تَجْعَلُوْنَهٗ قَرَاطِيْسَ تُبْدُوْنَهَا
وَتُخْفُوْنَ كَثِيْرًا ۚ
وَعُلِّمْتُمْ مَّا لَمْ تَعْلَمُوْٓا أَنْتُمْ وَلَآ
اٰبَآؤُكُمْ ؕ قُلِ اللّٰهُ ۙ
ثُمَّ ذَرْهُمْ فِىْ خَوْضِهِمْ يَلْعَبُوْنَ ○

92. And this is a Book
Which We have sent down,
Bringing blessings,[912] and confirming
(The revelations) which came
Before it: that thou
Mayest warn the Mother[913]
Of Cities and all around her.
Those who believe
In the Hereafter
Believe in this (Book),
And they are constant
In guarding their Prayers.[914]

٩٢- وَهٰذَا كِتٰبٌ أَنْزَلْنٰهُ مُبٰرَكٌ مُّصَدِّقُ
الَّذِىْ بَيْنَ يَدَيْهِ وَلِتُنْذِرَ أُمَّ الْقُرٰى
وَمَنْ حَوْلَهَا ؕ
وَالَّذِيْنَ يُؤْمِنُوْنَ بِالْاٰخِرَةِ
يُؤْمِنُوْنَ بِهٖ
وَهُمْ عَلٰى صَلَاتِهِمْ يُحَافِظُوْنَ ○

93. Who can be more wicked
Than one who inventeth

٩٣- وَمَنْ أَظْلَمُ مِمَّنِ

910. *Cf.* v. 47 and n. 750, and v. 49. In those passages Guidance (in practical conduct) is put before Light (or spiritual insight), as they refer to ordinary or average men. Here Light (or spiritual insight) is put first as the question is: does God send inspiration?

911. The Message to Moses had unity: it was one Book. The present Old Testament is a collection of odd books ("sheets") of various kinds: see Appendix II. end of S. v. In this way you can make a show, but there is no unity, and much of the spirit of the original is lost or concealed or overlaid. The same applies to the New Testament: see Appendix III., after Appendix II.

912. *Mubārak*: blessed, as having received God's blessing; bringer of blessings to others, as having been blessed by God. God's highest blessing is the Guidance and Light which the Book brings to us, and which brings us nearer to Him.

913. *Mother of Cities*: Mecca, now the Qibla and Centre of Islam. If this verse was (like the greater part of the Chapter) revealed in Mecca before the Hijrat, and before Mecca was made the Qibla of Islam, Mecca was nonetheless the Mother of Cities, being traditionally associated with Abraham and with Adam and Eve (see ii. 125, and n. 217 to ii. 197).

All round Mecca: would mean, the whole world if we look upon Mecca as the Centre.

914. An earnest study of the Qur-ān is true worship; so is Prayer, and so are all deeds of goodness and charity.

A lie against God,
Or saith, "I have
Received inspiration,"
When he hath received
None, or (again) who saith,
"I can reveal the like
Of what God hath revealed"?
If thou couldst but see
How the wicked (do fare)
In the flood of confusion
At death!—the angels
Stretch forth their hands,
(Saying), "Yield up your souls:[915]
This day shall ye receive
Your reward,—a penalty
Of shame, for that ye used
To tell lies against God,
And scornfully to reject
Of His Signs!"

94. "And behold! ye come
To Us bare and alone
As We created you
For the first time:[916]
Ye have left behind you
All (the favours) which
We bestowed on you:
We see not with you
Your intercessors
Whom ye thought to be
Partners in your affairs:
So now all relations
Between you have been
Cut off, and your (pet) fancies
Have left you in the lurch!"[917]

افْتَرٰى عَلَى اللّٰهِ كَذِبًا اَوْ قَالَ اُوْحِيَ اِلَيَّ
وَلَمْ يُوْحَ اِلَيْهِ شَيْءٌ
وَّمَنْ قَالَ سَاُنْزِلُ مِثْلَ مَآ اَنْزَلَ اللّٰهُ
وَلَوْ تَرٰٓى اِذِ الظّٰلِمُوْنَ
فِيْ غَمَرٰتِ الْمَوْتِ
وَالْمَلٰٓئِكَةُ بَاسِطُوْٓا اَيْدِيْهِمْ
اَخْرِجُوْٓا اَنْفُسَكُمْ
اَلْيَوْمَ تُجْزَوْنَ عَذَابَ الْهُوْنِ
بِمَا كُنْتُمْ تَقُوْلُوْنَ عَلَى اللّٰهِ غَيْرَ الْحَقِّ
وَكُنْتُمْ عَنْ اٰيٰتِهٖ تَسْتَكْبِرُوْنَ ○

٩٤- وَلَقَدْ جِئْتُمُوْنَا فُرَادٰى
كَمَا خَلَقْنٰكُمْ اَوَّلَ مَرَّةٍ
وَّتَرَكْتُمْ مَّا خَوَّلْنٰكُمْ وَرَآءَ ظُهُوْرِكُمْ
وَمَا نَرٰى مَعَكُمْ شُفَعَآءَكُمُ الَّذِيْنَ
زَعَمْتُمْ اَنَّهُمْ فِيْكُمْ شُرَكٰٓؤُا
لَقَدْ تَّقَطَّعَ بَيْنَكُمْ
وَضَلَّ عَنْكُمْ مَّا كُنْتُمْ تَزْعُمُوْنَ ○

915. *Yield up your souls*: or "get your souls to come out of your bodies" The wicked, we may suppose, are not anxious to part with the material existence in their bodies for the "reward" which in irony is stated to be there to welcome them.

916. Some of the various ideas connected with "creation" are noted in n. 120 to ii. 117. In the creation of man there are various processes. If his body was created out of clay, *i.e.*, earthy matter, there was an earlier process of the creation of such earthy matter. Here the body is left behind, and the soul is being addressed. The soul underwent various processes of fashioning and adapting to its various functions in its various surroundings (xxxii. 7-9). But each individual soul, after release from the body, comes back as it was created, with nothing more than its history, "the deeds which it has earned," which are really a part of it. Any exterior things given to help in its development, "the favours which we bestowed on you," it must necessarily leave behind, however it may have been proud of them. These exterior things may be material things, *e.g.*, wealth, property, signs of power, influence and pride such as sons, relatives, and friends, etc., or they may be intangible things, like talents, intellect, social gifts, etc.

917. The false ideas of intercessors, demi-gods, gods, saviours, etc., now vanish like unsubstantial visions, "leaving not a wrack behind." Now the soul is face to face with reality. Its personal responsibility is brought home to it.

SECTION 12.

95. It is God Who causeth[918] The seed-grain And the date-stone To split and sprout.[919] He causeth the living To issue from the dead, And He is the One To cause the dead To issue from the living.[920] That is God: then how Are ye deluded Away from the truth ?	٩٥-إِنَّ اللّٰهَ فَالِقُ الْحَبِّ وَالنَّوٰى ؕ يُخْرِجُ الْحَيَّ مِنَ الْمَيِّتِ وَمُخْرِجُ الْمَيِّتِ مِنَ الْحَيِّ ؕ ذٰلِكُمُ اللّٰهُ فَاَنّٰى تُؤْفَكُوْنَ ○

918. Another beautiful nature passage, referring to God's wonderful artistry in His Creation. In how few and how simple words, the whole pageant of Creation is placed before us! Beginning from our humble animal needs and dependence on the vegetable world, we are asked to contemplate the interaction of the living and the dead. Here is mystic teaching, referring not only to physical life but to the higher life above the physical plane,—not only to individual life but to the collective life of nations. Then we take a peep into the daily miracle of morning, noon, and night, and pass on to the stars that guide the distant mariner. We rise still higher to the mystery of the countless individuals from the one human soul,—their sojourn and their destiny. So we get back to the heavens: the description of the luscious fruits which the "gentle rain from heaven" produces, leaves us to contemplate the spiritual fruits which faith will provide for us, with the aid of the showers of God's mercy.

919. The seed-grain and the date-stone are selected as types in the vegetable kingdom, showing how our physical life depends on it. The fruits mentioned later (in vi. 99) start another allegory which we shall notice later. Botanists will notice that the seed-grain includes the cereals (such as wheat, barley, rice, millet, etc.) which are monocotyledons, as well as the pulses (such as beans, peas, gram, etc.) and other seeds which are dicotyledons. These two represent the most important classes of food-grains, while the date-palm, a monocotyledon, represents for Arabia both food, fruit, confectionery thatch and pillars for houses, shady groves in oases. and a standard measure of wealth and well being. "*Split and sprout*": both ideas are included in the root *falaqa*, and a third is expressed by the word "cleave" in the next verse, for the action of evolving day-break from the dark. I might almost have used the word "churn," familiar to students of Hindu lore in the Hindu allegory of the "churning of the ocean." For vegetables, "split and sprout" represents a double process: (1) the seed divides. and (2) one part shoots up, seeking the light, and forming leaves and the visible parts of the future tree, and the other part digs down into the dark, forming the roots and seeking just that sustenance from the soil, which is adapted for the particular plant. This is just one small instance of the "judgment and ordering" of God, referred to in the next verse.

920. This does not mean that in physical nature there are no limits between life and non-life, between the organic and the non-organic. In fact physicists are baffled at the barrier between them and frankly confess that they cannot solve the mystery of Life. If there is such a barrier in physical nature, is it not all the more wonderful that God can create Life out of nothing? He has but to say, "Be," and it is. He can bring Life from non-Life and annihilate Life. But there are two other senses in which we can contemplate the contrast between the living and the dead. (1) We have just been speaking of the botanical world. Take it as a whole, and see the contrast between the winter of death, the spring of revivification, the summer of growth, and the autumn of decay, leading back to the death of winter. Here is a cycle of living from dead, and dead from living. (2) Take our spiritual life, individual or collective. We rise from the darkness of spiritual nothingness to the light of spiritual life. And if we do not follow the spiritual laws, God will take away that life and we shall be again as dead. We may die many deaths. The keys of life and death are in God's hands. Neither Life nor Death are fortuitous things. Behind them both is the Cause of Causes,—and only He.

96. He it is that cleaveth
The day-break (from the dark):
He makes the night
For rest and tranquillity,
And the sun and moon
For the reckoning (of time):
Such is the judgment[921]
And ordering of (Him),
The Exalted in Power,
The Omniscient.

٩٦- فَالِقُ الْإِصْبَاحِ ۚ
وَجَعَلَ الَّيْلَ سَكَنًا
وَّالشَّمْسَ
وَالْقَمَرَ حُسْبَانًا ۚ
ذٰلِكَ تَقْدِيْرُ
الْعَزِيْزِ الْعَلِيْمِ ○

97. It is He Who maketh
The stars (as beacons) for you,
That ye may guide yourselves,
With their help,
Through the dark spaces
Of land and sea:[922]
We detail Our Signs
For people who know.

٩٧- وَهُوَ الَّذِيْ جَعَلَ لَكُمُ النُّجُوْمَ
لِتَهْتَدُوْا بِهَا
فِيْ ظُلُمٰتِ الْبَرِّ وَالْبَحْرِ ۚ
قَدْ فَصَّلْنَا الْاٰيٰتِ
لِقَوْمٍ يَّعْلَمُوْنَ ○

98. It is He Who hath
Produced you[923]
From a single person:
Here is a place of sojourn
And a place of departure:[924]
We detail Our signs
For people who understand.

٩٨- وَهُوَ الَّذِيْٓ اَنْشَاَكُمْ
مِّنْ نَّفْسٍ وَّاحِدَةٍ
فَمُسْتَقَرٌّ وَّمُسْتَوْدَعٌ ۚ
قَدْ فَصَّلْنَا الْاٰيٰتِ لِقَوْمٍ يَّفْقَهُوْنَ ○

---

921. The night, the day, the sun, the moon,—the great astronomical universe of God. How far, and yet how near to us! God's universe is boundless, and we can barely comprehend even its relations to us. But this last we must try to do if we want to be numbered with "the people who know". *Taqdīr*: *Cf.* vi. 91 and n. 909, and iv. 149 and n. 655.

922. See the last note. At sea, or in deserts or forests, or "in fairy scenes forlorn,"—whenever we sweep over wide spaces, it is the stars that act as our guides, just as the sun and moon have already been mentioned as our measures of time.

923. *Produced*: *ansha-a* = made you grow, increase, develop, reach maturity: another of the processes of creation. This supplements n. 120 to ii. 117 and n. 916 to vi. 94. It is one of the wonders of God's Creation, that from one person we have grown to be so many, and each individual has so many faculties and capacities, and yet we are all one. In the next verse we have the allegory of grapes and other fruits: all grapes may be similar to look at, yet each variety has a distinctive flavour and other distinctive qualities, and each individual grape may have its own special qualities. So for man.

924. In the sojourn of this life we must respond to God's hand in fashioning us, by making full use of all our faculties, and we must get ready for our departure into the Life that will be eternal.

99. It is He Who sendeth down
Rain from the skies:[925]
With it We produce
Vegetation of all kinds:
From some We produce
Green (crops), out of which
We produce grain,
Heaped up (at harvest);
Out of the date-palm
And its sheaths (or spathes)
(Come) clusters of dates
Hanging low and near:
And (then there are) gardens
Of grapes, and olives,
And pomegranates,
Each similar (in kind)
Yet different (in variety):[926]
When they begin to bear fruit,
Feast your eyes with the fruit
And the ripeness thereof.[927]
Behold! in these things
There are Signs for people
Who believe.[928]

٩٩- وَهُوَ الَّذِيٓ أَنزَلَ مِنَ السَّمَآءِ مَآءً
فَأَخْرَجْنَا بِهِۦ نَبَاتَ كُلِّ شَيْءٍ
فَأَخْرَجْنَا مِنْهُ خَضِرًا
نُّخْرِجُ مِنْهُ حَبًّا مُّتَرَاكِبًا
وَمِنَ النَّخْلِ مِن طَلْعِهَا
قِنْوَانٌ دَانِيَةٌ
وَجَنَّٰتٍ مِّنْ أَعْنَابٍ
وَالزَّيْتُونَ وَالرُّمَّانَ مُشْتَبِهًا
وَغَيْرَ مُتَشَٰبِهٍ
انظُرُوٓا إِلَىٰ ثَمَرِهِۦٓ
إِذَآ أَثْمَرَ وَيَنْعِهِۦٓ
إِنَّ فِي ذَٰلِكُمْ
لَأٓيَٰتٍ لِّقَوْمٍ يُؤْمِنُونَ ○

---

925. Our allegory now brings us to maturity, the fruit, the harvest, the vintage. Through the seed we came up from nothingness to life; we lived our daily life of rest and work and passed the mile-stones of time; we had the spiritual experience of traversing through vast spaces in the spiritual world, guiding our course through the star of Faith; we grew; and now for the harvest or the vintage! How satisfied the grower must be when the golden grain is harvested in heaps or the vintage gathered! So will man if he has produced the fruits of Faith!

926. Each fruit—whether it is grapes, or olives, or pomegranates,—looks alike in its species, and yet each variety may be different in flavour, consistency, shape, size, colour, juice or oil contents, proportion of seed to fruit, etc In each variety individuals may be different. Apply the allegory to man, whose varied spiritual fruit may be equally different and yet equally valuable!

927. And so we finish this wonderful allegory. Search through the world's literature, and see if you can find another such song or hymn,—so fruity in its literary flavour, so profound in its spiritual meaning!

928. There is a refrain in this song, which is subtly varied. In verse 97 it is: "We detail our Signs for people who *know*." So far we were speaking of the things we see around us every day. Knowledge is the appropriate instrument for these things. In verse 98 we read: "We detail Our Signs for people who *understand*." Understanding is a higher faculty than knowledge, and is necessary for seeing the mystery and meaning of this life. At the end of verse 99 we have: "In these things there are Signs for people who *believe*." Here we are speaking of the real fruits of spiritual Life. For them Faith is necessary, as bringing us nearer to God.

100. Yet they make
The Jinns equals[929]
With God, though God
Did create the Jinns;
And they falsely,
Having no knowledge,
Attribute to Him
Sons and daughters.
Praise and glory be
To Him! (for He is) above
What they attribute to Him!

١٠٠- وَجَعَلُوا لِلّٰهِ شُرَكَآءَ الْجِنَّ
وَخَلَقَهُمْ
وَخَرَقُوا لَهٗ بَنِيْنَ
وَبَنٰتٍۢ بِغَيْرِ عِلْمٍ ؕ
سُبْحٰنَهٗ
وَتَعٰلٰى عَمَّا يَصِفُوْنَ ۝

Section 13.

101. To Him is due
The primal origin
Of the heavens and the earth:[930]
How can He have a son
When He hath no consort?
He created all things,
And He hath full knowledge
Of all things.

١٠١- بَدِيْعُ السَّمٰوٰتِ وَالْاَرْضِ ؕ
اَنّٰى يَكُوْنُ لَهٗ وَلَدٌ
وَّلَمْ تَكُنْ لَّهٗ صَاحِبَةٌ ؕ
وَخَلَقَ كُلَّ شَيْءٍ ۚ
وَهُوَ بِكُلِّ شَيْءٍ عَلِيْمٌ ۝

102. That is God, your Lord!
There is no god but He,
The Creator of all things:
Then worship ye Him:
And He hath power
To dispose of all affairs.

١٠٢- ذٰلِكُمُ اللّٰهُ رَبُّكُمْ ۚ
لَآ اِلٰهَ اِلَّا هُوَ ۚ
خَالِقُ كُلِّ شَيْءٍ فَاعْبُدُوْهُ ۚ
وَهُوَ عَلٰى كُلِّ شَيْءٍ وَّكِيْلٌ ۝

103. No vision can grasp Him,
But His grasp is over

١٠٣- لَا تُدْرِكُهُ الْاَبْصَارُ ۡ وَهُوَ يُدْرِكُ

929. *Jinns*: who are they? In xviii. 50 we are told that Iblis was one of the Jinns, and it is suggested that that was why he disobeyed the Command of God. But in that passage and other similar passages, we are told that God commanded the angels to bow down to Adam, and they obeyed except Iblis. That implies that Iblis had been of the company of angels. In many passages Jinns and men are spoken of together. In lv. 14-15, man is stated to have been created from clay, while Jinns from a flame of fire. The root meaning of *janna, yajinnu*, is "to be covered or hidden," and *janna yajunnu*, in the active voice, "to cover or hide," as in vi. 76. Some people say that *jinn* therefore means the hidden qualities or capacities in man; others that it means wild or jungle folk hidden in the hills or forests. I do not wish to be dogmatic, but I think, from a collation and study of the Quranic passages, that the meaning is simply "a spirit," or an invisible or hidden force. In folk-lore stories and romances like the Arabian Nights they become personified into fantastic forms, but with them we are not concerned here.

930. *Cf.* ii. 117, and n. 120.

All vision: He is
Above all comprehension,[931]
Yet is acquainted with all things.

الْأَبْصَارَ ۚ
وَهُوَ اللَّطِيفُ الْخَبِيرُ ○

104. "Now have come to you,
From your Lord, proofs
(To open your eyes):
If any will see,
It will be for (the good
Of) his own soul;
If any will be blind,
It will be to his own
(Harm): I am not (here)
To watch over your doings."[932]

١٠٤- قَدْ جَاءَكُمْ
بَصَائِرُ مِنْ رَبِّكُمْ ۖ
فَمَنْ أَبْصَرَ
فَلِنَفْسِهِ ۖ
وَمَنْ عَمِيَ فَعَلَيْهَا ۚ
وَمَا أَنَا عَلَيْكُمْ بِحَفِيظٍ ○

105. Thus do We explain
The Signs by various (symbols):[933]
That they may say,
"Thou hast taught (us) diligently,"
And that We may make
The matter clear
To those who know.[934]

١٠٥- وَكَذَٰلِكَ نُصَرِّفُ الْآيَاتِ
وَلِيَقُولُوا دَرَسْتَ
وَلِنُبَيِّنَهُ
لِقَوْمٍ يَعْلَمُونَ ○

106. Follow what thou art taught
By inspiration from thy Lord:
There is no god but He:
And turn aside from those
Who join gods with God.

١٠٦- اتَّبِعْ مَا أُوحِيَ إِلَيْكَ مِنْ رَبِّكَ ۖ
لَا إِلَٰهَ إِلَّا هُوَ ۖ
وَأَعْرِضْ عَنِ الْمُشْرِكِينَ ○

---

931. *Laṭīf*: fine, subtle, so fine and subtle as to be invisible to the physical eye; so fine as to be imperceptible to the senses; figuratively, so pure as to be above the mental or spiritual vision of ordinary men. The active meaning should also be understood: 'One who understands the finest mysteries': *Cf.* xxii. 63, and n. 2844.

932. I understand "Say" to be understood in the beginning of this verse. The words would then be the words of the Apostle, as in fact is suggested in verse 107 below. That is why I have enclosed them in inverted commas.

933. *Cf.* vi. 65, and n. 889.

934. The teaching in the Qur-ān explains things by various symbols, parables, narratives, and appeals to nature. Each time, a new phase of the question is presented to our minds. This is what a diligent and earnest teacher would do, such as was Muḥammad Muṣṭafā. Those who were in search of knowledge and had thus acquired some knowledge of spiritual things were greatly helped to understand more clearly the things of which, before the varied explanations, they had only one-sided knowledge.

107. If it had been God's Plan,[935]
They would not have taken
False gods: but We
Made thee not one
To watch over their doings,
Nor art thou set
Over them to dispose
Of their affairs.

١٠٧- وَلَوْ شَآءَ اللّٰهُ
مَآ اَشْرَكُوْا ؕ
وَمَا جَعَلْنٰكَ
عَلَيْهِمْ حَفِيْظًا ۚ
وَمَآ اَنْتَ عَلَيْهِمْ بِوَكِيْلٍ ○

108. Revile not ye
Those whom they call upon
Besides God, lest
They out of spite
Revile God
In their ignorance.
Thus have We made
Alluring to each people[936]
Its own doings.
In the end will they
Return to their Lord,
And We shall then

١٠٨- وَلَا تَسُبُّوا الَّذِيْنَ
يَدْعُوْنَ مِنْ دُوْنِ اللّٰهِ
فَيَسُبُّوا اللّٰهَ عَدْوًا
بِغَيْرِ عِلْمٍ ؕ
كَذٰلِكَ زَيَّنَّا
لِكُلِّ اُمَّةٍ عَمَلَهُمْ ۠
ثُمَّ اِلٰى رَبِّهِمْ مَّرْجِعُهُمْ

---

935. God's Plan is to use the human will to co-operate in understanding Him and His relations to us. This is the answer to an objector who might say: "If He is All-powerful, why does sin or evil exist in the world? Can He not destroy it?" He can, but His Plan is different, and in any case it is not for a Teacher to force any one to accept the truths which he is inspired to preach and proclaim.

936. A man's actual personal religion depends upon many things,—his personal psychology, the background of his life, his hidden or repressed feelings, tendencies, or history (which psycho-analysis tries to unravel), his hereditary dispositions or antipathies, and all the subtle influences of his education and his environment. The task before the man of God is: (1) to use any of these which can subserve the higher ends, (2) to purify such as have been misused, (3) to introduce new ideas and modes of looking at things, and (4) to combat what is wrong and cannot be mended: all for the purpose of leading to the truth and gradually letting in spiritual light where there was darkness before. If that is not done with discretion and the skill of a spiritual Teacher, there may be not only a reaction of obstinacy, but an unseemly show of dishonour to the true God and His Truth, and doubts would spread among the weaker brethren whose faith is shallow and infirm. What happens to individuals is true collectively of nations or groups of people. They think in their self-obsession that their own ideas are right. God in His infinite compassion bears with them, and asks those who have purer ideas of faith not to vilify the weaknesses of their neighbours, lest the neighbours in their turn vilify the real truth and make matters even worse than before. In so far as there are mistakes, God will forgive and send His grace for helping ignorance and folly. In so far as there is active evil, He will deal with it in His own way. Of course the righteous man must not hide his light under a bushel, or compromise with evil, or refuse to establish right living where he has the power to do so.

Tell them the truth
Of all that they did.

فَيُنَبِّئُهُمْ بِمَا كَانُوا يَعْمَلُونَ ○

109. They swear their strongest
Oaths by God, that if
A (special) Sign came
To them, by it they would
Believe. Say: "Certainly
(All) Signs are in the power
Of God: but what will
Make you (Muslims) realise
That (even) if (special) Signs
Came, they will not believe."? [937]

١٠٩- وَأَقْسَمُوا
بِاللَّهِ جَهْدَ أَيْمَانِهِمْ
لَئِن جَاءَتْهُمْ آيَةٌ
لَّيُؤْمِنُنَّ بِهَا
قُلْ إِنَّمَا الْآيَاتُ عِندَ اللَّهِ
وَمَا يُشْعِرُكُمْ
أَنَّهَا إِذَا جَاءَتْ
لَا يُؤْمِنُونَ ○

110. We (too) shall turn
To (confusion) their hearts [938]
And their eyes, even as they
Refused to believe in this
In the first instance:
We shall leave them
7 In their trespasses,
30 To wander in distraction. [939]

١١٠- وَنُقَلِّبُ أَفْئِدَتَهُمْ
وَأَبْصَارَهُمْ كَمَا لَمْ يُؤْمِنُوا بِهِ
أَوَّلَ مَرَّةٍ
وَنَذَرُهُمْ فِي طُغْيَانِهِمْ يَعْمَهُونَ ○ ع ١٩

937. If the Unbelievers are merely obstinate, nothing will convince them. There is no story more full of miracles than the story of Jesus. Yet in that same story we are told that Jesus said: "A wicked adulterous generation seeketh after a sign; and there shall no sign be given unto it, but the sign of the Prophet Jonas": Matt. xvi. 4. There are Signs given by God every day—understood by those who believe. A mere insistence upon some particular or special Sign means mere contumacy and misunderstanding of the spiritual world.

938. Where there is sheer obstinacy and ridicule of faith, the result will be that such a sinner's heart will be hardened and his eyes will be sealed, so that he cannot even see the things visible to ordinary mortals. The sinner gathers impetus in his descent towards wrong.

939. *Cf.* ii. 15. God's grace is always ready to help human weakness or ignorance, and to accept repentance and give forgiveness. But where the sinner is in actual rebellion, he will be given rope, and it will be his own fault if he wanders about distractedly, without any certain hope or refuge.

C. 80.—Those in obstinate rebellion
(vi. 111-129.) Against God are merely deceived
And deceive each other. Leave them
Alone, but trust and obey God
Openly and in the inmost recesses
Of your heart. The plots of the wicked
Are but plots against their own souls.

SECTION 14.

111. Even if We did send
Unto them angels,
And the dead did speak
Unto them, and We gathered
Together all things before[940]
Their very eyes, they are not
The ones to believe,
Unless it is in God's Plan.
But most of them
Ignore (the truth).

الجزء الثامن

١١١- وَلَوْ أَنَّنَا نَزَّلْنَآ إِلَيْهِمُ الْمَلٰٓئِكَةَ
وَكَلَّمَهُمُ الْمَوْتٰى
وَحَشَرْنَا عَلَيْهِمْ كُلَّ شَىْءٍ قُبُلًا
مَّا كَانُوا لِيُؤْمِنُوٓا إِلَّآ أَنْ يَّشَآءَ اللّٰهُ
وَلٰكِنَّ أَكْثَرَهُمْ يَجْهَلُونَ ○

112. Likewise did We make
For every Messenger
An enemy,—evil ones[941]
Among men and Jinns,
Inspiring each other
With flowery discourses
By way of deception.
If thy Lord had so planned,
They would not have
Done it: so leave them
And their inventions alone.

١١٢- وَكَذٰلِكَ جَعَلْنَا لِكُلِّ نَبِيٍّ
عَدُوًّا شَيٰطِيْنَ الْإِنْسِ وَالْجِنِّ
يُوْحِيْ بَعْضُهُمْ إِلٰى بَعْضٍ
زُخْرُفَ الْقَوْلِ غُرُوْرًا
وَلَوْ شَآءَ رَبُّكَ مَا فَعَلُوْهُ
فَذَرْهُمْ وَمَا يَفْتَرُوْنَ ○

113. To such (deceit)
Let the hearts of those
Incline, who have no faith
In the Hereafter: let them
Delight in it, and let them
Earn from it what they may.[942]

١١٣- وَلِتَصْغٰٓى إِلَيْهِ أَفْئِدَةُ الَّذِيْنَ
لَا يُؤْمِنُوْنَ بِالْاٰخِرَةِ وَلِيَرْضَوْهُ
وَلِيَقْتَرِفُوْا مَا هُمْ مُّقْتَرِفُوْنَ ○

940. The most stupendous miracles even according to their ideas would not have convinced them. If the whole pageant of the spiritual world were brought before them, they would not have believed, because they—of their own choice and will—refuse knowledge and faith.

941. What happened in the history of the Holy Prophet happens in the history of all righteous men who have a Message from God. The spirit of evil is ever active and uses men to practise deception by means of highly embellished words and plausible excuses and objections. God permits these things in His Plan. It is not for us to complain. Our faith is tested, and we must stand the test steadfastly.

942. People who have no faith in the future destiny of man may listen to and be taken in by the deceit of evil. If they take a delight in it, let them. See what they gain by it. Their gains will be as deceitful as their delight. For the end of evil must be evil.

114. Say: "Shall I seek
For judge other than God?—
When He it is
Who hath sent unto you
The Book, explained in detail."[943]
They know full well,
To whom We have given
The Book, that it hath been
Sent down from thy Lord
In truth. Never be then
Of those who doubt.

١١٤- أَفَغَيْرَ اللّٰهِ أَبْتَغِي حَكَمًا
وَهُوَ الَّذِي أَنْزَلَ إِلَيْكُمُ
الْكِتٰبَ مُفَصَّلًا
وَالَّذِينَ آتَيْنٰهُمُ الْكِتٰبَ
يَعْلَمُونَ أَنَّهُ مُنَزَّلٌ مِنْ رَبِّكَ بِالْحَقِّ
فَلَا تَكُونَنَّ مِنَ الْمُمْتَرِينَ ○

115. The Word of thy Lord
Doth find its fulfilment
In truth and in justice:
None can change His Words:
For He is the one Who
Heareth and knoweth all.

١١٥- وَتَمَّتْ كَلِمَتُ رَبِّكَ
صِدْقًا وَعَدْلًا لَا مُبَدِّلَ لِكَلِمٰتِهِ
وَهُوَ السَّمِيعُ الْعَلِيمُ ○

116. Wert thou to follow
The common run of those
On earth, they will lead
Thee away from the Way
Of God. They follow
Nothing but conjecture: they
Do nothing but lie.

١١٦- وَإِنْ تُطِعْ أَكْثَرَ مَنْ فِي الْأَرْضِ
يُضِلُّوكَ عَنْ سَبِيلِ اللّٰهِ
إِنْ يَتَّبِعُونَ إِلَّا الظَّنَّ
وَإِنْ هُمْ إِلَّا يَخْرُصُونَ ○

117. Thy Lord knoweth best
Who strayeth from His Way:
He knoweth best
Who they are that receive
His guidance.

١١٧- إِنَّ رَبَّكَ هُوَ أَعْلَمُ
مَنْ يَضِلُّ عَنْ سَبِيلِهِ
وَهُوَ أَعْلَمُ بِالْمُهْتَدِينَ ○

118. So eat of (meats)
On which God's name
Hath been pronounced,
If ye have faith
In His Signs.

١١٨- فَكُلُوا مِمَّا ذُكِرَ اسْمُ اللّٰهِ عَلَيْهِ
إِنْ كُنْتُمْ بِآيٰتِهِ مُؤْمِنِينَ ○

119. Why should ye not
Eat of (meats) on which
God's name hath been
Pronounced, when He hath
Explained to you in detail
What is forbidden to you—

١١٩- وَمَا لَكُمْ أَلَّا تَأْكُلُوا مِمَّا ذُكِرَ اسْمُ
اللّٰهِ عَلَيْهِ
وَقَدْ فَصَّلَ لَكُمْ مَا حَرَّمَ عَلَيْكُمْ

943. The righteous man seeks no other standard of judgment but God's Will. How can he, when God in His grace has explained His Will in the Qur-ān, with details which men of every capacity can understand? The humblest can learn lessons of right conduct in daily life, and the most advanced can find the highest wisdom in its spiritual teaching, enriched as it is with all kinds of beautiful illustrations from nature and the story of man.

Except under compulsion[944]
Of necessity?
But many do mislead (men)
By their appetites unchecked
By knowledge. Thy Lord
Knoweth best those who
transgress

إِلَّا مَا اضْطُرِرْتُمْ إِلَيْهِ ۗ
وَإِنَّ كَثِيرًا لَّيُضِلُّونَ بِأَهْوَائِهِم
بِغَيْرِ عِلْمٍ ۗ
إِنَّ رَبَّكَ هُوَ أَعْلَمُ بِالْمُعْتَدِينَ ○

120. Eschew all sin,
Open or secret:
Those who earn sin
Will get due recompense
For their "earnings."

١٢٠- وَذَرُوا ظَاهِرَ الْإِثْمِ وَبَاطِنَهُ ۚ
إِنَّ الَّذِينَ يَكْسِبُونَ الْإِثْمَ
سَيُجْزَوْنَ بِمَا كَانُوا يَقْتَرِفُونَ ○

121. Eat not of (meats)
On which God's name
Hath not been pronounced:
That would be impiety.
But the evil ones
Ever inspire their friends
To contend with you
If ye were to obey them,
Ye would indeed be Pagans.

١٢١- وَلَا تَأْكُلُوا
مِمَّا لَمْ يُذْكَرِ اسْمُ اللَّهِ عَلَيْهِ
وَإِنَّهُ لَفِسْقٌ ۗ وَإِنَّ الشَّيَاطِينَ
لَيُوحُونَ إِلَىٰ أَوْلِيَائِهِمْ لِيُجَادِلُوكُمْ ۖ
وَإِنْ أَطَعْتُمُوهُمْ إِنَّكُمْ لَمُشْرِكُونَ ○ ع

SECTION 15.

122. Can he who was dead,[945]
To whom We gave life,
And a Light whereby
He can walk amongst men,
Be like him who is
In the depths of darkness,
From which he can
Never come out?
Thus to those without Faith
Their own deeds seem pleasing.

١٢٢- أَوَمَن كَانَ مَيْتًا فَأَحْيَيْنَاهُ
وَجَعَلْنَا لَهُ نُورًا يَمْشِي بِهِ فِي النَّاسِ
كَمَن مَّثَلُهُ فِي الظُّلُمَاتِ
لَيْسَ بِخَارِجٍ مِّنْهَا ۚ
كَذَٰلِكَ زُيِّنَ لِلْكَافِرِينَ مَا كَانُوا يَعْمَلُونَ ○

123. Thus have We placed
Leaders in every town,

١٢٣- وَكَذَٰلِكَ جَعَلْنَا فِي كُلِّ قَرْيَةٍ أَكَابِرَ

944. *Cf.* v. 4. When a clear law has explained what is lawful and unlawful in food, it is wrong to raise fresh scruples and mislead the ignorant.

945. Here is an allegory of the good man with his divine mission and the evil man with his mission of evil. The former, before he got his spiritual life, was like one dead. It was God's grace that gave him spiritual life, with a Light by which he could walk and guide his own footsteps as well as the footsteps of those who are willing to follow God's light. The opposite type is that which hates God's light, which lives in the depths of darkness, and which plots and burrows against all that is good. But the plots of evil recoil on itself, although it thinks that they will hurt the good. Can these two types be for a moment compared with each other? Perhaps the lead in every centre of population is taken by the men of evil. But the good men should not be discouraged. They should work in righteousness and fulfil their mission.

Its wicked men, to plot
(And burrow) therein:
But they only plot
Against their own souls,
And they perceive it not.

مُجْرِمِيهَا لِيَمْكُرُوا فِيهَا ۖ
وَمَا يَمْكُرُونَ إِلَّا بِأَنْفُسِهِمْ
وَمَا يَشْعُرُونَ ○

124. When there comes to them
A Sign (from God),
They say: "We shall not
Believe until we receive
One (exactly) like those
Received by God's apostles."[946]
God knoweth best where
(And how) to carry out
His mission. Soon
Will the wicked
Be overtaken by
Humiliation before God,
And a severe punishment,
For all their plots.

١٢٤- وَإِذَا جَاءَتْهُمْ آيَةٌ
قَالُوا لَنْ نُؤْمِنَ حَتَّىٰ نُؤْتَىٰ
مِثْلَ مَا أُوتِيَ رُسُلُ اللَّهِ ۘ
اللَّهُ أَعْلَمُ حَيْثُ يَجْعَلُ رِسَالَتَهُ ۗ
سَيُصِيبُ الَّذِينَ أَجْرَمُوا صَغَارٌ عِنْدَ
اللَّهِ
وَعَذَابٌ شَدِيدٌ بِمَا كَانُوا يَمْكُرُونَ ○

125. Those whom God (in His Plan)
Willeth to guide,—He openeth[947]
Their breast to Islam;
Those whom He willeth
To leave straying,—He maketh
Their breast close and constricted,
As if they had to climb
Up to the skies: thus
Doth God (heap) the penalty
On those who refuse to believe.

١٢٥- فَمَنْ يُرِدِ اللَّهُ أَنْ يَهْدِيَهُ
يَشْرَحْ صَدْرَهُ لِلْإِسْلَامِ ۖ وَمَنْ يُرِدْ أَنْ
يُضِلَّهُ يَجْعَلْ صَدْرَهُ ضَيِّقًا حَرَجًا
كَأَنَّمَا يَصَّعَّدُ فِي السَّمَاءِ ۚ
كَذَٰلِكَ يَجْعَلُ اللَّهُ الرِّجْسَ
عَلَى الَّذِينَ لَا يُؤْمِنُونَ ○

126. This is the Way
Of thy Lord, leading straight:

١٢٦- وَهَٰذَا صِرَاطُ رَبِّكَ مُسْتَقِيمًا ۗ

946. Besides the teaching in God's Word, and the teaching in God's world, of nature and history and human contacts, many Signs come to the men of God, which they humbly receive and try to understand; and many Signs also come to the ungodly, in the shape of warnings or otherwise, which the ungodly either do not heed, or deliberately reject. The Signs in the two cases are not the same, and that becomes one of their perverse arguments against Faith. But God's working will be according to His own Will and Plan, and not according to the wishes or whims of the ungodly.

947. God's Universal Plan is the *Qadhā wa Qadr*, which is so much misunderstood. That Plan is unalterable, and that is His Will. It means that in the spiritual world, as in the physical world, there are laws of justice, mercy, grace, penalty, etc., which work as surely as anything we know. If, then, a man refuses Faith, becomes a rebel, with each step he goes further and further down, and his pace will be accelerated; he will scarcely be able to take spiritual breath, and his recovery,—in spite of God's mercy which he has rejected,—will be as difficult as if he had to climb up to the skies On the other hand, the godly will find, with each step, the next step easier. Jesus expressed this truth paradoxically: "He that hath, to him shall be given; but he that hath not, from him shall be taken away even that which he hath": Mark. iv. 25. John (vi. 65) makes Jesus say: "No man can come unto me, except it were given unto him of my Father."

We have detailed the Signs
For those who
Receive admonition.

قَدْ فَصَّلْنَا الْاٰيٰتِ لِقَوْمٍ يَّذَّكَّرُوْنَ ○

127. For them will be a Home
Of Peace in the presence
Of their Lord: He will be
Their Friend, because
They practised (righteousness).

١٢٧- لَهُمْ دَارُ السَّلٰمِ عِنْدَ رَبِّهِمْ
وَهُوَ وَلِيُّهُمْ
بِمَا كَانُوْا يَعْمَلُوْنَ ○

128. One day will He gather
Them all together, (and say):
"O ye assembly of Jinns![949]
Much (toll) did ye take
Of men." Their friends
Amongst men will say:
"Our Lord! we made profit[950]
From each other: but (alas!)
We reached our term—
Which Thou didst appoint
For us." He will say:
"The Fire be your dwelling-place:
You will dwell therein for ever,
Except as God willeth."[951]
For thy Lord is full
Of wisdom and knowledge.

١٢٨- وَيَوْمَ يَحْشُرُهُمْ جَمِيْعًا
يٰمَعْشَرَ الْجِنِّ
قَدِ اسْتَكْثَرْتُمْ مِّنَ الْاِنْسِ
وَقَالَ اَوْلِيٰٓؤُهُمْ مِّنَ الْاِنْسِ
رَبَّنَا اسْتَمْتَعَ بَعْضُنَا بِبَعْضٍ
وَّبَلَغْنَآ اَجَلَنَا الَّذِيْٓ اَجَّلْتَ لَنَا
قَالَ النَّارُ مَثْوٰىكُمْ خٰلِدِيْنَ فِيْهَآ
اِلَّا مَا شَآءَ اللّٰهُ اِنَّ رَبَّكَ حَكِيْمٌ عَلِيْمٌ ○

129. Thus do We make
The wrong-doers turn
To each other, because
Of what they earn.[952]

١٢٩- وَكَذٰلِكَ نُوَلِّيْ بَعْضَ الظّٰلِمِيْنَ
بَعْضًا بِمَا كَانُوْا يَكْسِبُوْنَ ○ ع

C. 81.—God punishes not mere shortcoming:
(vi. 130-150.) There are degrees in good and evil
Deeds. God is Merciful, but
His Plan is sure, and none
Can stand in its way. We must
Avoid all superstition, and all excess,
And humbly ask for His guidance.

---

949. Jinns are spirits—here evil spirits. See vi. 100, n. 929.

950. It is common experience that the forces of evil make an alliance with each other, and seem thus to make a profit by their mutual log-rolling. But this is only in this material world. When the limited term expires, their unholy bargains will be exposed, and there will be nothing but regrets.

951. Eternity and infinity are abstract terms. They have no precise meaning in our human experience. The qualification, "except as God willeth," makes it more intelligible, as we can form some idea—however inadequate—of a Will and Plan, and we know God by His attribute of Mercy as well as of Justice.

952. See n. 950 above. Evil consorts with evil because of their mutual bargains. But in doing so they save the righteous from further temptation.

Section 16.

130. "O ye assembly of Jinns
And men! came there not
Unto you apostles from
amongst you,[953]
Setting forth unto you
My Signs, and warning you
Of the meeting of this Day
Of yours?" They will say:
"We bear witness against
Ourselves." It was
The life of this world
That deceived them. So
Against themselves will they
Bear witness that they
Rejected Faith.

١٣٠- يٰمَعْشَرَ الْجِنِّ وَالْإِنْسِ
أَلَمْ يَأْتِكُمْ رُسُلٌ مِّنْكُمْ
يَقُصُّوْنَ عَلَيْكُمْ اٰيٰتِيْ
وَيُنْذِرُوْنَكُمْ لِقَآءَ يَوْمِكُمْ هٰذَا
قَالُوْا شَهِدْنَا عَلٰٓى اَنْفُسِنَا
وَغَرَّتْهُمُ الْحَيٰوةُ الدُّنْيَا
وَشَهِدُوْا عَلٰٓى اَنْفُسِهِمْ
اَنَّهُمْ كَانُوْا كٰفِرِيْنَ ○

131. (The apostles were sent) thus,
For thy Lord would not
Destroy for their wrong-doing
Men's habitations whilst
Their occupants were unwarned.

١٣١- ذٰلِكَ اَنْ لَّمْ يَكُنْ رَّبُّكَ مُهْلِكَ
الْقُرٰى بِظُلْمٍ
وَّاَهْلُهَا غٰفِلُوْنَ ○

132. To all are degrees (or ranks)[954]
According to their deeds:
For thy Lord
Is not unmindful
Of anything that they do.

١٣٢- وَلِكُلٍّ دَرَجٰتٌ مِّمَّا عَمِلُوْا
وَمَا رَبُّكَ بِغَافِلٍ
عَمَّا يَعْمَلُوْنَ ○

133. Thy Lord is Self-sufficient,[955]
Full of Mercy: if it were
His Will, He could destroy
You, and in your place
Appoint whom He will
As your successors, even as
He raised you up
From the posterity
Of other people.

١٣٣- وَرَبُّكَ الْغَنِيُّ ذُو الرَّحْمَةِ
اِنْ يَّشَاْ يُذْهِبْكُمْ
وَيَسْتَخْلِفْ مِنْۢ بَعْدِكُمْ
مَّا يَشَآءُ كَمَآ اَنْشَاَكُمْ
مِّنْ ذُرِّيَّةِ قَوْمٍ اٰخَرِيْنَ ○

953. "*Apostles from amongst you.*" This is addressed to the whole gathering of men and Jinns. Are the Jinns but disembodied spirits of evil men?

954. On good and evil there are infinite degrees, in our deeds and motives: so will there be degrees in our spiritual position. For everything is known to God, better than it is to ourselves.

955. God is not dependent on our prayer or service. It is out of His Mercy that He desires our own good. Any race or people to whom He gives chances should understand that its failure does not affect God. He could create others in their place, as He did in times past, and is doing in our own day, if only we had the wit to see it.

134. All that hath been[956]
Promised unto you
Will come to pass:
Nor can ye frustrate it
(In the least bit).

١٣٤- إِنَّ مَا تُوعَدُونَ لَآتٍ ۖ
وَمَآ أَنتُم بِمُعْجِزِينَ ○

135. Say: "O my people!
Do whatever ye can:[957]
I will do (my part):
Soon will ye know
Who it is whose end
Will be (best) in the Hereafter:
Certain it is that
The wrong-doers will not prosper."

١٣٥- قُلْ يَٰقَوْمِ ٱعْمَلُوا۟ عَلَىٰ مَكَانَتِكُمْ
إِنِّى عَامِلٌ ۖ فَسَوْفَ تَعْلَمُونَ ۙ
مَن تَكُونُ لَهُۥ عَٰقِبَةُ ٱلدَّارِ ۗ
إِنَّهُۥ لَا يُفْلِحُ ٱلظَّٰلِمُونَ ○

136. Out of what God
Hath produced in abundance
In tilth and in cattle,
They assigned Him a share:
They say, according to their
fancies:[958]
"This is for God, and this"—
For Our "partners"!
But the share of their "partners"
Reacheth not God, whilst
The share of God reacheth
Their "partners"! Evil
(And unjust) is their assignment!

١٣٦- وَجَعَلُوا۟ لِلَّهِ مِمَّا ذَرَأَ مِنَ ٱلْحَرْثِ وَ
ٱلْأَنْعَٰمِ
نَصِيبًا فَقَالُوا۟ هَٰذَا لِلَّهِ بِزَعْمِهِمْ
وَهَٰذَا لِشُرَكَآئِنَا ۖ
فَمَا كَانَ لِشُرَكَآئِهِمْ فَلَا يَصِلُ إِلَى ٱللَّهِ ۖ
وَمَا كَانَ لِلَّهِ فَهُوَ يَصِلُ إِلَىٰ شُرَكَآئِهِمْ ۗ
سَآءَ مَا يَحْكُمُونَ ○

---

956. Both the good news and the warning which God's apostles came to give will be fulfilled. Nothing can stop God's Universal Plan. See n. 947 to vi. 125.

957. In so far as this is addressed to the Unbelievers it is a challenge: "Do your utmost; nothing will deter me from my duty: we shall see who wins in the end." Passing from the particular occasion, we can understand it in a more general sense, which is true for all time. Let the evil ones do their worst. Let those who believe do all they can, according to their opportunities and abilities. The individual must do the straight duty that lies before him. In the end God will judge, and His judgment is always true and just.

958. There is scathing sarcasm here, which some of the Commentators have missed. The Pagans have generally a big Pantheon, though above it they have a vague idea of a Supreme God. But the material benefits go to the godlings, the fancied "partners" of God; for they have temples, priests, dedications, etc., while the true and supreme God has only lip-worship, or at best a share with numerous "partners". This was so in Arabia also. The shares assigned to the "partners" went to the priests and hangers-on of the "partners", who were many and clamorous for their rights. The share assigned to God possibly went to the poor, but more probably went to the priests who had the cult of the "partners", for the Supreme God had no separate priests of His own. It is also said that when heaps were thus laid out, if any portion of God's heap fell into the heaps of the "partners", the priests greedily and promptly appropriated it, while in the contrary case, the "partners'," priests were careful to reclaim any portion from what they called "God's heap". The absurdity of the whole thing is ridiculed. God created everything: how can He have a *share*?

137. Even so, in the eyes
Of most of the Pagans,[959]
Their "partners" made alluring
The slaughter of their children,
In order to lead them
To their own destruction,
And cause confusion
In their religion.
If God had willed,
They would not have done so:
But leave alone
Them and their inventions.

١٣٧- وَكَذَٰلِكَ زَيَّنَ لِكَثِيرٍ مِّنَ الْمُشْرِكِينَ
قَتْلَ أَوْلَادِهِمْ شُرَكَاؤُهُمْ لِيُرْدُوهُمْ
وَلِيَلْبِسُوا عَلَيْهِمْ دِينَهُمْ ۖ
وَلَوْ شَاءَ اللَّهُ
مَا فَعَلُوهُ ۖ
فَذَرْهُمْ وَمَا يَفْتَرُونَ ○

138. And they say that
Such and such cattle and crops[960]
Are taboo, and none should
Eat of them except those
Whom—so they say—We
Wish; further, there are
Cattle forbidden to yoke[961]
Or burden, and cattle
On which, (at slaughter),
The name of God is not[962]
Pronounced;—inventions
Against God's name: soon
Will He requite them
For their inventions.

١٣٨- وَقَالُوا هَٰذِهِ أَنْعَامٌ وَحَرْثٌ حِجْرٌ
لَّا يَطْعَمُهَا إِلَّا مَن نَّشَاءُ
بِزَعْمِهِمْ وَأَنْعَامٌ حُرِّمَتْ ظُهُورُهَا وَ
أَنْعَامٌ
لَّا يَذْكُرُونَ اسْمَ اللَّهِ عَلَيْهَا
افْتِرَاءً عَلَيْهِ ۚ
سَيَجْزِيهِم بِمَا كَانُوا يَفْتَرُونَ ○

139. They say: "What is
In the wombs of
Such and such cattle
Is specially reserved
(For food) for our men,
And forbidden to our women;
But if it is still-born,
Then all have shares therein.[953]

١٣٩- وَقَالُوا مَا فِي بُطُونِ هَٰذِهِ الْأَنْعَامِ
خَالِصَةٌ لِّذُكُورِنَا
وَمُحَرَّمٌ عَلَىٰ أَزْوَاجِنَا ۖ
وَإِن يَكُن مَّيْتَةً فَهُمْ فِيهِ شُرَكَاءُ ۚ

959 The false gods and idols—among many nations, including the Arabs—were supposed to require human sacrifices. Ordinarily such sacrifices are revolting to man, but they are made "alluring"—a sacred rite—by Pagan custom, which falsely arrogates to itself the name of religion. Such customs, if allowed, would do nothing but destroy the people who practise them, and make their religion but a confused bundle of revolting superstitions.

960 A taboo of certain foods is sometimes a device of the priesthood to get special things for itself. It has to be enforced by pretending that the prohibition for others is by the Will of God. It is a lie or invention against God. Most superstitions are.

961. Cattle dedicated to heathen gods may be reserved from all useful work; in that case they are a dead loss to the community, and they may, besides, do a great deal of damage to fields and crops.

962. If meat is killed in the name of heathen gods, it would naturally not be killed by the solemn rite in God's name, by which alone the killing can be justified for food. See n. 698 to v. 5.

963. These are further Pagan superstitions about cattle. Some have already been noted in v. 106, which may be consulted with the notes.

For their (false) attribution
(Of superstitions to God),
He will soon punish them:
For He is full
Of wisdom and knowledge.

سَيَجْزِيهِمْ وَصْفَهُمْ
إِنَّهُ حَكِيمٌ عَلِيمٌ ○

140. Lost are those who slay
Their children, from folly,
Without knowledge, and forbid
Food which God hath provided
For them, inventing (lies)
Against God. They have
Indeed gone astray
And heeded no guidance.

١٤٠- قَدْ خَسِرَ الَّذِينَ قَتَلُوا أَوْلَادَهُمْ سَفَهًا
بِغَيْرِ عِلْمٍ وَحَرَّمُوا مَا رَزَقَهُمُ اللَّهُ
افْتِرَاءً عَلَى اللَّهِ
قَدْ ضَلُّوا وَمَا كَانُوا مُهْتَدِينَ ○

Section 17.

141. It is He who produceth[964]
Gardens, with trellises
And without, and dates,
And tilth with produce
Of all kinds, and olives
And pomegranates,
Similar (in kind)
And different (in variety):[965]
Eat of their fruit
In their season, but render
The dues that are proper
On the day that the harvest
Is gathered. But waste not[966]
By excess: for God
Loveth not the wasters.

١٤١- وَهُوَ الَّذِي أَنْشَأَ جَنَّاتٍ مَعْرُوشَاتٍ
وَغَيْرَ مَعْرُوشَاتٍ وَالنَّخْلَ
وَالزَّرْعَ مُخْتَلِفًا أُكُلُهُ وَالزَّيْتُونَ
وَالرُّمَّانَ مُتَشَابِهًا وَغَيْرَ مُتَشَابِهٍ
كُلُوا مِنْ ثَمَرِهِ إِذَا أَثْمَرَ
وَآتُوا حَقَّهُ يَوْمَ حَصَادِهِ
وَلَا تُسْرِفُوا
إِنَّهُ لَا يُحِبُّ الْمُسْرِفِينَ ○

142. Of the cattle are some
For burden and some for meat:[967]

١٤٢- وَمِنَ الْأَنْعَامِ حَمُولَةً وَفَرْشًا

---

964. *Ansha-a*: see vi. 98, n. 923.

965. A beautiful passage, with music to match the meaning. *Cf.* vi. 99 and notes.

966. "Waste not, want not," says the English proverb. Here the same wisdom is preached from a higher motive. See what magnificent means God provides in nature for the sustenance of all His creatures, because He loves them all. Enjoy them in moderation and be grateful. But commit no excess, and commit no waste: the two things are the same from different angles of vision. If you do, you take away something from other creatures and God would not like your selfishness.

967. Superstition kills true religion. We come back to the Arab Pagan superstitions about cattle for food. The horse is not mentioned, because horse flesh was not an article of diet and there were no superstitions about it. Sheep and goats, camels and oxen were the usual sources of meat. Sheep and goats were not used as beasts of burden, but camels (of both sexes) were used for carrying burdens, and oxen for the plough, though cows were mainly used for milk and meat. The words "some for burden and some for meat" do not differentiate whole species, except that they give you the first two and the last two as categories.

Eat what God hath provided
For you, and follow not
The footsteps of Satan :
For he is to you
An avowed enemy.

كُلُوْا مِمَّا رَزَقَكُمُ اللّٰهُ
وَلَا تَتَّبِعُوْا خُطُوٰتِ الشَّيْطٰنِ ؕ
اِنَّهٗ لَكُمْ عَدُوٌّ مُّبِيْنٌ ۙ

143. (Take) eight (head of cattle)[968]
In (four) pairs:
Of sheep a pair,
And of goats a pair;
Say, hath He forbidden
The two males,
Or the two females,
Or (the young) which the wombs
Of the two females enclose?
Tell me with knowledge
If ye are truthful:

۱۴۳- ثَمٰنِيَةَ اَزْوَاجٍ ۚ مِنَ الضَّاْنِ اثْنَيْنِ
وَمِنَ الْمَعْزِ اثْنَيْنِ ؕ
قُلْ ءٰٓالذَّكَرَيْنِ حَرَّمَ
اَمِ الْاُنْثَيَيْنِ
اَمَّا اشْتَمَلَتْ عَلَيْهِ اَرْحَامُ الْاُنْثَيَيْنِ ؕ
نَبِّـُٔوْنِيْ بِعِلْمٍ اِنْ كُنْتُمْ صٰدِقِيْنَ ۙ

144. Of camels a pair,
And of oxen a pair;
Say, hath He forbidden
The two males,
Or the two females,
Or (the young) which the wombs
Of the two females enclose?—
Were ye present when God
Ordered you such a thing?
But who doth more wrong
Than one who invents
A lie against God,
To lead astray men
Without knowledge?
For God guideth not
People who do wrong

۱۴۴- وَمِنَ الْاِبِلِ اثْنَيْنِ
وَمِنَ الْبَقَرِ اثْنَيْنِ ؕ
قُلْ ءٰٓالذَّكَرَيْنِ حَرَّمَ اَمِ الْاُنْثَيَيْنِ
اَمَّا اشْتَمَلَتْ عَلَيْهِ اَرْحَامُ الْاُنْثَيَيْنِ ؕ
اَمْ كُنْتُمْ شُهَدَآءَ اِذْ وَصّٰىكُمُ اللّٰهُ بِهٰذَا ۚ
فَمَنْ اَظْلَمُ مِمَّنِ افْتَرٰى عَلَى اللّٰهِ كَذِبًا
لِّيُضِلَّ النَّاسَ بِغَيْرِ عِلْمٍ ؕ
اِنَّ اللّٰهَ لَا يَهْدِى الْقَوْمَ الظّٰلِمِيْنَ ۙ ع

SECTION 18.

145. Say: "I find not
In the Message received
By me by inspiration
Any (meat) forbidden
To be eaten by one
Who wishes to eat it,
Unless it be dead meat,
Or blood poured forth,[969]

۱۴۵- قُلْ لَّآ اَجِدُ فِيْ مَآ اُوْحِيَ اِلَيَّ
مُحَرَّمًا عَلٰى طَاعِمٍ
يَّطْعَمُهٗٓ اِلَّآ اَنْ يَّكُوْنَ مَيْتَةً اَوْ دَمًا
مَّسْفُوْحًا

---

968. The superstitions referred to in vi. 139 and v. 106 are further ridiculed in this verse and the next.

969. *Blood poured forth*: as distinguished from blood adhering to flesh, or the liver, or such other internal organs purifying the blood.

Or the flesh of swine,—
For it is an abomination—
Or, what is impious, (meat)
On which a name has been
Invoked, other than God's."
But (even so), if a person
Is forced by necessity,
Without wilful disobedience,
Nor transgressing due limits,—
Thy Lord is Oft-forgiving,
Most Merciful.

أَوْ لَحْمَ خِنْزِيرٍ
فَإِنَّهُ رِجْسٌ أَوْ فِسْقًا
أُهِلَّ لِغَيْرِ اللَّهِ بِهِ
فَمَنِ اضْطُرَّ غَيْرَ بَاغٍ وَلَا عَادٍ
فَإِنَّ رَبَّكَ غَفُورٌ رَّحِيمٌ ○

146. For those who followed
The Jewish Law, We forbade
Every (animal) with
Undivided hoof,[970]
And We forbade them
The fat of the ox[971]
And the sheep, except
What adheres to their backs
Or their entrails,
Or is mixed up
With a bone:
This in recompense
For their wilful disobedience:
For We are True
(In Our ordinances).

١٤٦- وَعَلَى الَّذِينَ هَادُوا
حَرَّمْنَا كُلَّ ذِي ظُفُرٍ
وَمِنَ الْبَقَرِ وَالْغَنَمِ
حَرَّمْنَا عَلَيْهِمْ شُحُومَهُمَا
إِلَّا مَا حَمَلَتْ ظُهُورُهُمَا
أَوِ الْحَوَايَا أَوْ مَا اخْتَلَطَ بِعَظْمٍ
ذَٰلِكَ جَزَيْنَاهُمْ بِبَغْيِهِمْ
وَإِنَّا لَصَادِقُونَ ○

147. If they accuse thee
Of falsehood, say:
"Your Lord is full
Of mercy all-embracing;
But from people in guilt
Never will His wrath
Be turned back.

١٤٧- فَإِنْ كَذَّبُوكَ فَقُلْ رَّبُّكُمْ
ذُو رَحْمَةٍ وَاسِعَةٍ
وَلَا يُرَدُّ بَأْسُهُ عَنِ الْقَوْمِ الْمُجْرِمِينَ ○

148. Those who give partners
(To God) will say:

١٤٨- سَيَقُولُ الَّذِينَ أَشْرَكُوا

970. *Zufur* may mean claw or hoof; it is in the singular number; but as no animal has a single claw, and there is no point in a division of claws, we must look to a hoof for the correct interpretation. In the Jewish Law (Leviticus, xi. 3-6), "whatsoever parteth the hoof, and is cloven-footed, and cheweth the cud, among the beasts" was lawful as food, but the camel, the coney (rabbit), and the hare were not lawful, because they do not "divide the hoof". "Undivided hoof" therefore is the correct interpretation. These three animals, unlawful to the Jews, are lawful in Islam. *Cf.* iv. 160.

971. In Leviticus (vii. 23) it is laid down that "ye shall eat no manner of fat, of ox, or of sheep, or of goat." As regards the exceptions, it is to be noticed that priests were enjoined (Leviticus, vii. 6) to eat of the fat in the trespass offering, which was considered holy, *viz.*, "the rump" (back and bone) "and the fat that covereth the inwards" (entrails), (Leviticus, vii. 3).

"If God had wished,
We should not have
Given partners to Him,
Nor would our fathers;
Nor should we have had[972]
Any taboos." So did
Their ancestors argue
Falsely, until they tasted
Of Our wrath. Say:
"Have ye any (certain)
Knowledge? If so, produce
It before us. Ye follow
Nothing but conjecture:
Ye do nothing but lie."

لَوْ شَآءَ اللّٰهُ مَآ اَشْرَكْنَا وَلَآ اٰبَآؤُنَا
وَلَا حَرَّمْنَا مِنْ شَيْءٍ ۭ
كَذٰلِكَ كَذَّبَ الَّذِيْنَ مِنْ قَبْلِهِمْ
حَتّٰى ذَاقُوْا بَاْسَنَا ۭ
قُلْ هَلْ عِنْدَكُمْ مِّنْ عِلْمٍ فَتُخْرِجُوْهُ لَنَا ۭ
اِنْ تَتَّبِعُوْنَ اِلَّا الظَّنَّ
وَاِنْ اَنْتُمْ اِلَّا تَخْرُصُوْنَ ○

149. Say: "With God is the argument[973]
That reaches home: if it had
Been His Will, He could
Indeed have guided you all."

١٤٩- قُلْ فَلِلّٰهِ الْحُجَّةُ الْبَالِغَةُ ۚ
فَلَوْ شَآءَ لَهَدٰىكُمْ اَجْمَعِيْنَ ○

150. Say: "Bring forward your witnesses
To prove that God did
Forbid so and so." If they
Bring such witnesses,
Be not thou amongst them:[974]
Nor follow thou the vain
Desires of such as treat
Our Signs as falsehoods,
And such as believe not
In the Hereafter: for they
Hold others as equal
With their Guardian-Lord."[975]

١٥٠- قُلْ هَلُمَّ شُهَدَآءَكُمُ
الَّذِيْنَ يَشْهَدُوْنَ اَنَّ اللّٰهَ حَرَّمَ هٰذَا ۚ
فَاِنْ شَهِدُوْا فَلَا تَشْهَدْ مَعَهُمْ ۚ
وَلَا تَتَّبِعْ اَهْوَآءَ الَّذِيْنَ كَذَّبُوْا بِاٰيٰتِنَا
وَالَّذِيْنَ لَا يُؤْمِنُوْنَ بِالْاٰخِرَةِ
وَهُمْ بِرَبِّهِمْ يَعْدِلُوْنَ ○

C. 82.—God's commands are not irrational
(vi. 151-165.) Taboos, but based on the moral law,
And conformable to reason. His Way

---

972. As used by the Pagans, the argument is false, for it implies (*a*) that men have no personal responsibility, (*b*) that they are the victims of a Determinism against which they are helpless, and (*c*) that they might therefore go on doing just what they liked. It is also inconsistent, for if (*b*) is true, (*c*) cannot be true. Nor is it meant to be taken seriously.

973. On the other hand, the argument cuts true and deep, as from God to His creatures. God is Omnipotent, and can do all that we can conceive. But He, in His Plan, has given man some responsibility, and some choice in order to train man's will. If man fails, he is helped in various ways by God's mercy and grace. But man cannot go on sinning, and in a state of sin, expect God to be pleased with him (vi. 147).

974. The Pagan superstitions were of course baseless, and in many cases harmful and debasing. If God's name was taken as supporting them, no true man of God could be taken in, or join in support simply because God's name was taken in vain.

975. *Cf.* vi. 1. God, who created and who cherishes and cares for all, should have the first claim on our attention. Those who set up false gods fail to understand God's true governance or their own true destiny.

Is the straight Way, of justice and truth.
In unity and faith must we dedicate
All our life to His service, and His
Alone, to Whom we shall return.

SECTION 19.

151. Say: "Come, I will rehearse
What God hath (really)[976]
Prohibited you from": join not
Anything as equal with Him;
Be good to your parents;
Kill not your children
On a plea of want;—We
Provide sustenance for you
And for them;—come not
Nigh to shameful deeds,
Whether open or secret;
Take not life, which God
Hath made sacred, except
By way of justice and law:[977]
Thus doth He command you,
That ye may learn wisdom.

١٥١- قُلْ تَعَالَوْا أَتْلُ مَا حَرَّمَ رَبُّكُمْ عَلَيْكُمْ
أَلَّا تُشْرِكُوا بِهِ شَيْئًا
وَبِالْوَالِدَيْنِ إِحْسَانًا
وَلَا تَقْتُلُوا أَوْلَادَكُم مِّنْ إِمْلَاقٍ
نَّحْنُ نَرْزُقُكُمْ وَإِيَّاهُمْ وَلَا تَقْرَبُوا
الْفَوَاحِشَ مَا ظَهَرَ مِنْهَا وَمَا بَطَنَ
وَلَا تَقْتُلُوا النَّفْسَ الَّتِي حَرَّمَ اللَّهُ إِلَّا بِالْحَقِّ
ذَٰلِكُمْ وَصَّاكُم بِهِ لَعَلَّكُمْ تَعْقِلُونَ ○

152. And come not nigh
To the orphan's property,
Except to improve it,
Until he attain the age
Of full strength; give measure
And weight with (full) justice;—
No burden do We place
On any soul, but that
Which it can bear;—
Whenever ye speak, speak justly,

١٥٢- وَلَا تَقْرَبُوا مَالَ الْيَتِيمِ
إِلَّا بِالَّتِي هِيَ أَحْسَنُ حَتَّىٰ يَبْلُغَ أَشُدَّهُ
وَأَوْفُوا الْكَيْلَ وَالْمِيزَانَ بِالْقِسْطِ
لَا نُكَلِّفُ نَفْسًا إِلَّا وُسْعَهَا
وَإِذَا قُلْتُمْ فَاعْدِلُوا

976. Instead of following Pagan superstitions, and being in constant terror of imaginary taboos and prohibitions, we should study the true moral law, whose sanction is God's Law. The first step is that we should recognise that He is the One and Only Lord and Cherisher. The mention of goodness to parents immediately afterwards suggests: (1) that God's love of us and care for us may—on an infinitely higher plane—be understood by our ideal of parental love, which is purely unselfish; (2) that our first duty among our fellow creatures is to our father and mother, whose love leads us to the conception of divine love. Arising from that is the conception of our converse duties to our children. God provides sustenance (material and spiritual) not only for us, but for them; hence any custom like the Pagan custom of sacrificing children to Moloch stands condemned. Then come the moral prohibitions against lewdness and all unseemly acts, relating to sex or otherwise, open or secret. This is followed by the prohibition of killing or fighting. All these things are conformable to our own interests, and therefore true wisdom from our own point of view.

977. For the comprehensive word *ḥaqq* I have used the two words "justice and law": other significations implied are: right, truth, what is becoming, etc. It is not only that human life is sacred, but all life is sacred. Even in killing animals for food, a dedicatory formula "in the name of God" has to be employed, to make it lawful: see n. 698 to v. 5, and n. 962 to vi. 138.

Even if a near relative
Is concerned; and fulfil
The Covenant of God:[978]
Thus doth He command you,
That ye may remember.

وَلَوْ كَانَ ذَا قُرْبَىٰ
وَبِعَهْدِ اللّٰهِ اَوْفُوْا
ذٰلِكُمْ وَصّٰكُمْ بِهٖ لَعَلَّكُمْ تَذَكَّرُوْنَ ۝

153. Verily, this is My Way,
Leading straight: follow it:
Follow not (other) paths:
They will scatter you about
From His (great) Path:
Thus doth He command you,
That ye may be righteous.[979]

١٥٣- وَاَنَّ هٰذَا صِرَاطِىْ مُسْتَقِيْمًا فَاتَّبِعُوْهُ
وَلَا تَتَّبِعُوا السُّبُلَ فَتَفَرَّقَ بِكُمْ عَنْ
سَبِيْلِهٖ
ذٰلِكُمْ وَصّٰكُمْ بِهٖ لَعَلَّكُمْ تَتَّقُوْنَ ۝

154. Moreover, We gave Moses
The Book, completing
(Our favour) to those
Who would do right,
And explaining all things[980]
In detail,—and a guide
And a mercy, that they
Might believe in the meeting
With their Lord.

١٥٤- ثُمَّ اٰتَيْنَا مُوْسَى الْكِتٰبَ تَمَامًا
عَلَى الَّذِىْٓ اَحْسَنَ
وَتَفْصِيْلًا لِّكُلِّ شَيْءٍ
وَّهُدًى وَّرَحْمَةً
لَّعَلَّهُمْ بِلِقَآءِ رَبِّهِمْ يُؤْمِنُوْنَ ۝

SECTION 20.

155. And this is a Book
Which We have revealed
As a blessing: so follow it
And be righteous, that ye
May receive mercy:

١٥٥- وَهٰذَا كِتٰبٌ اَنْزَلْنٰهُ مُبٰرَكٌ فَاتَّبِعُوْهُ
وَاتَّقُوْا لَعَلَّكُمْ تُرْحَمُوْنَ ۝

156. Lest ye should say:
"The Book was sent down
To two Peoples before us,
And for our part, we
Remained unacquainted[981]

١٥٦- اَنْ تَقُوْلُوْٓا اِنَّمَآ اُنْزِلَ الْكِتٰبُ عَلٰى
طَآئِفَتَيْنِ مِنْ قَبْلِنَا وَاِنْ كُنَّا عَنْ

978. *Cf.* v. 1, and n. 682.

979. Note again the triple refrain with variations, in vi. 151, 152, and 153. In verse 151, we have the moral law, which it is for our own good to follow: "Thus doth He command you, that ye may learn wisdom." In verse 152, we have to deal justly and rightly with others; we are apt to think too much of ourselves and forget others: "Thus doth He command you, that ye may remember." In verse 153 our attention is called to the Straight Way, the Way of God, the only Way that leads to righteousness: "Thus doth He command you, that ye may be righteous."

980. The revelation to Moses went into the details of people's lives, and thus served as a practical guide to the Jews and after them to the Christians. Admittedly the Message delivered by Christ dealt with general principles only and in no way with details. The message of Islam as in the Qur-ān is the next complete guide in point of time after that of Moses.

981. Because the diligent studies of the earlier People of the Book were in languages foreign to the new People of Islam, or because they were meant for circumstances different from those of the new world after Islam.

With all that they learned
By assiduous study ; "

دِرَاسَتِهِمْ لَغٰفِلِيْنَ ۝

157. Or lest ye should say :
" If the Book had only
Been sent down to us,
We should have followed
Its guidance better than they."
Now then hath come
Unto you a Clear (Sign)[982]
From your Lord,—and a guide
And a mercy : then who
Could do more wrong
Than one who rejecteth
God's Signs, and turneth
Away therefrom ? In good time
Shall We requite those
Who turn away from Our Signs,
With a dreadful penalty,
For their turning away.

١٥٧- أَوْ تَقُوْلُوْا لَوْ أَنَّآ أُنْزِلَ عَلَيْنَا الْكِتٰبُ
لَكُنَّآ أَهْدٰى مِنْهُمْ ۚ
فَقَدْ جَآءَكُمْ بَيِّنَةٌ مِّنْ رَّبِّكُمْ
وَهُدًى وَّرَحْمَةٌ ۚ
فَمَنْ أَظْلَمُ مِمَّنْ كَذَّبَ بِاٰيٰتِ اللّٰهِ
وَصَدَفَ عَنْهَا ۗ
سَنَجْزِي الَّذِيْنَ يَصْدِفُوْنَ عَنْ اٰيٰتِنَا
سُوْٓءَ الْعَذَابِ بِمَا كَانُوْا يَصْدِفُوْنَ ۝

158. Are they waiting to see
If the angels come to them,
Or thy Lord (Himself),
Or certain of the Signs
Of thy Lord !
The day that certain
Of the Signs of thy Lord
Do come, no good
Will it do to a soul[983]
To believe in them then,
If it believed not before
Nor earned righteousness
Through its Faith. Say :
" Wait ye : we too
Are waiting."[984]

١٥٨- هَلْ يَنْظُرُوْنَ إِلَّآ أَنْ تَأْتِيَهُمُ
الْمَلٰٓئِكَةُ أَوْ يَأْتِيَ رَبُّكَ
أَوْ يَأْتِيَ بَعْضُ اٰيٰتِ رَبِّكَ ۗ
يَوْمَ يَأْتِيْ بَعْضُ اٰيٰتِ رَبِّكَ
لَا يَنْفَعُ نَفْسًا إِيْمَانُهَا
لَمْ تَكُنْ اٰمَنَتْ مِنْ قَبْلُ
أَوْ كَسَبَتْ فِيْٓ إِيْمَانِهَا خَيْرًا ۗ
قُلِ انْتَظِرُوْٓا إِنَّا مُنْتَظِرُوْنَ ۝

---

982. The Qur-ân and the life and the teaching of Muḥammad the Apostle of God.

983. There is no merit in faith in things that you are compelled to acknowledge when they actually happen. Faith is belief in things which you do not see with your eyes but you understand with your spiritual sense : if your whole will consents to it, it results in deeds of righteousness, which are the evidence of your faith.

984. The waiting in the two cases is in quite different senses : the foolish man without faith is waiting for things which will not happen, and is surprised by the real things which do happen ; the righteous man of faith is waiting for the fruits of righteousness, of which he has an assured hope ; in a higher state of spiritual elevation, even the fruits have no personal meaning to him, for God is to him all-in-all ; vi. 162.

159. As for those who divide[985]
Their religion and break up
Into sects, thou hast
No part in them in the least:
Their affair is with God:
He will in the end
Tell them the truth
Of all that they did.

١٥٩- إن الذين فرقوا دينهم وكانوا شيعا
لست منهم في شيء
إنما أمرهم إلى الله
ثم ينبئهم بما كانوا يفعلون ○

160. He that doeth good
Shall have ten times
As much to his credit:
He that doeth evil
Shall only be recompensed
According to his evil:[986]
No wrong shall be done
Unto (any of) them.

١٦٠- من جاء بالحسنة فله عشر أمثالها
ومن جاء بالسيئة
فلا يجزى إلا مثلها
وهم لا يظلمون ○

161. Say: "Verily, my Lord
Hath guided me to
A Way that is straight,—
A religion of right,—
The Path (trod) by Abraham
The true in faith,
And he (certainly)
Joined not gods with God."

١٦١- قل إنني هداني ربي إلى صراط
مستقيم دينا قيما
ملة إبراهيم حنيفا
وما كان من المشركين ○

162. Say: "Truly, my prayer
And my service of sacrifice,
My life and my death,
Are (all) for God,
The Cherisher of the Worlds:

١٦٢- قل إن صلاتي ونسكي
ومحياي ومماتي
لله رب العلمين ○

163. No partner hath He:
This am I commanded,
And I am the first
Of those who bow
To His Will.

١٦٣- لا شريك له
وبذلك أمرت
وأنا أول المسلمين ○

164. Say: "Shall I seek
For (my) Cherisher

١٦٤- قل أغير الله أبغي ربا

985. *Divide their religion*: *farraqū*: *i.e.*, (1) make a distinction between one part of it and another, take the part which suits them and reject the rest; or (2) have religion one day of the week and the world the rest of the six days; or (3) keep "religion in its right place," as if it did not claim to govern the whole life; make a sharp distinction between the secular and the religious; or (4) show a sectarian bias, seek differences in views, so as to break up the unity of Islam.

986. God is just as well as generous. To the good the reward is multiplied ten times (*i.e.*, far above merits) on account of His generosity. To the evil, the punishment is no more than commensurate with their sin, and even so the door of mercy is always open to those who sincerely repent and show it by their conduct.

Other than God, When He is the Cherisher Of all things (that exist)? Every soul draws the meed Of its acts on none[987] But itself: no bearer Of burdens can bear The burden of another. Your goal in the end Is towards God: He will tell You the truth of the things Wherein ye disputed."	وَهُوَ رَبُّ كُلِّ شَيْءٍ ۚ وَلَا تَكْسِبُ كُلُّ نَفْسٍ إِلَّا عَلَيْهَا ۚ وَلَا تَزِرُ وَازِرَةٌ وِزْرَ أُخْرَىٰ ۚ ثُمَّ إِلَىٰ رَبِّكُم مَّرْجِعُكُمْ فَيُنَبِّئُكُم بِمَا كُنتُمْ فِيهِ تَخْتَلِفُونَ ۝
165. It is He Who hath made You (His) agents, inheritors[988] Of the earth: He hath raised You in ranks, some above Others: that He may try you In the gifts He hath given you: For thy Lord is quick In punishment: yet He Is indeed Oft-forgiving, Most Merciful.	١٦٥- وَهُوَ الَّذِي جَعَلَكُمْ خَلَائِفَ الْأَرْضِ وَرَفَعَ بَعْضَكُمْ فَوْقَ بَعْضٍ دَرَجَاتٍ لِّيَبْلُوَكُمْ فِي مَا آتَاكُمْ ۗ إِنَّ رَبَّكَ سَرِيعُ الْعِقَابِ وَإِنَّهُ لَغَفُورٌ رَّحِيمٌ ۝

987. The doctrine of personal responsibility again. We are fully responsible for our acts ourselves: we cannot transfer the consequences to someone else. Nor can any one vicariously atone for our sins. If people have honest doubts or differences about important questions of religion, they should not start futile disputes. All will be clear in the end. Our duty here is to maintain unity and discipline, and do the duty that comes to us.

988. *Cf.* ii. 30 and n., where I have translated "Khalifa" as "Vicegerent", it being God's Plan to make Adam (as representing mankind) His vicegerent on earth. In C. 1 I have construed the same word by the word "Agent." Another idea implied in "Khalifa" is that of "successor, heir, or inheritor," *i.e.*, one who has the ultimate ownership after the present possessors, to whom a life-tenancy has been given by the owner, have passed away. In xv. 23 occurs the striking word "heirs" (*wārithūn*) as applied to God: "We give life and death, and We are the Heirs (or Inheritors)." The same idea occurs in iii. 180, where see n. 485. The translation here attempts to express both the ideas which I understand from the original.

INTRODUCTION TO SŪRA VII (*A'rāf*)

This Sūra is closely connected, both chronologically and in respect of the argument, with the previous Sūra. But it expounds the doctrine of revelation and man's spiritual history by illustrations from Adam onwards, through various Prophets, and the details of Moses's struggles, to the time of the Apostle Muḥammad, in whom God's revelation is completed.

Summary.—The note, "learn from the past," is struck from the very beginning. The opposition of Evil to Good is illustrated by the story of Adam and Iblīs. Arrogance leads to rebellion; the rebel is jealous and tempts the natural man, who is warned against deceit and all excess (vii. 1-31, and C. 83).

If the warning is not heeded, the future penalties are indicated, while the privileges and the bliss and peace of the righteous are shown in a picture of the Hereafter, as well as in the power and goodness of God in the world that we see around us (vii. 32-58, and C. 84).

The story of Noah and the Flood, and the stories of Hūd, Ṣāliḥ, Lot, and Shu'aib, all point to the lesson that the Prophets were resisted and rejected, but truth triumphed in the end, and evil was humbled, for God's Plan never fails (vii. 59-99, and C. 85).

The story of Moses is told in greater detail, not only in his struggles with Pharaoh, but in his preparation for his mission, and his struggles with his own rebellious people. Even from the time of Moses the coming of the unlettered Apostle was foreshadowed (vii. 100-157, and C. 86).

But the people of Moses frequently lapsed from God's Law as promulgated to them, and transgressed God's Covenant, and they were scattered through the earth in sections (vii. 158-171, and C. 87).

The children of Adam have multiplied, but many of them have rejected truth and go by degrees to destruction in ways that they do not realise. The righteous listen to the Message of God, and serve Him in humility (vii. 172-206, and C. 88).

C. 83.—Revelation should ease the difficulties
(vii. 1-31.) Of heart and mind, for it tells
The story of man's spiritual past,
And teaches the end of good and evil.
Iblīs fell from jealousy and arrogance,
And Adam fell because he listened
To his deceit. But God did grant
In His Mercy gifts and guidance
To men, warned them against excess,
And taught them moderation and justice.

Sūra VII.

A'rāf, or The Heights.

*In the name of God, Most Gracious,
Most Merciful.*

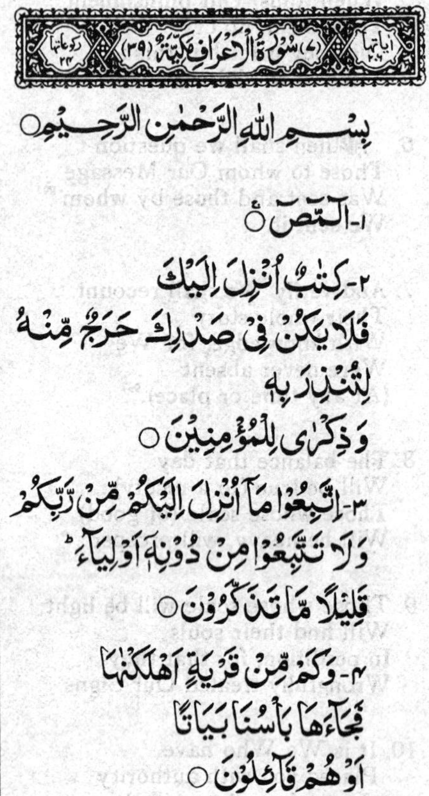

1. Alif, Lām, Mīm, Ṣād.[989]

2. A Book revealed unto thee,—
So let thy heart be oppressed[990]
No more by any difficulty
On that account,—
That with it thou mightest
Warn (the erring) and teach
The Believers.

3. Follow (O men!) the revelation
Given unto you from your Lord,
And follow not, as friends
Or protectors, other than Him.
Little it is ye remember
Of admonition.[991]

4. How many towns have We
Destroyed (for their sins)?
Our punishment took them
On a sudden by night
Or while they slept
For their afternoon rest.

---

989. This is a combination of four Abbreviated Letters. For Abbreviated Letters generally, see Appendix I (at the end of Sūra II). The combination here includes the three letters A. L. M., which occurred at the beginning of Sūra II, and are discussed in n. 25 to ii. 1.

The additional letter Ṣād occurs in combination here and in Sūra xix, and by itself at the beginning of S. xxxviii, and nowhere else. The factor common to S. vii, S. xix, and S. xxxviii, is that in each case the core of the Sūra consists in the stories (qiṣaṣ) of the Prophets. In this Sūra we have the stories of Noah, Hūd, Ṣāliḥ, Lot, Shu'aib, and Moses, leading up to Muḥammad, and in S. xxxviii. the stories of David Solomon, and Job similarly lead up to Muḥammad, occupying three out of the five sections. Sūra xix consists almost entirely of such stories. Can we understand Ṣād to stand for qiṣaṣ, of which it is the most characteristic letter? In this Sūra vii. we have also the spiritual history of mankind traced,—the Beginning, the Middle, and the End, which, as explained in n. 25, might be represented symbolically by A. L. M. If so, this Sūra, dealing with the Beginning, Middle, and End of man's spiritual story, and illustrating it by the stories of the Prophets, might well be represented symbolically by the letters *Alif, Lām, Mīm, Ṣād*. But no one can be dogmatic about these symbols. We must accept them as symbols with a mystic meaning.

990. *Heart*: in the original, *breast*. I have used the word most appropriate to the English idiom. The meaning is that Muṣṭafā is consoled for all the difficulties which he encountered in his mission, with the fact that he had clear guidance in the Book for his preaching.

991. This is added in order that men might not be puffed up with such little knowledge as they possessed, for there are great heights to be scaled in the spiritual kingdom.

5. When (thus) Our punishment
Took them, no cry
Did they utter but this:
"Indeed we did wrong."[992]

٥- فَمَا كَانَ دَعْوٰىهُمْ إِذْ جَآءَهُمْ بَأْسُنَآ
إِلَّآ أَنْ قَالُوٓا إِنَّا كُنَّا ظٰلِمِينَ ○

6. Then shall we question
Those to whom Our Message
Was sent and those by whom[993]
We sent it.

٦- فَلَنَسْـَٔلَنَّ الَّذِينَ أُرْسِلَ إِلَيْهِمْ
وَلَنَسْـَٔلَنَّ الْمُرْسَلِينَ ○

7. And verily We shall recount
Their whole story
With knowledge, for We
Were never absent
(At any time or place).[994]

٧- فَلَنَقُصَّنَّ عَلَيْهِمْ بِعِلْمٍ
وَمَا كُنَّا غَآئِبِينَ ○

8. The balance that day
Will be true (to a nicety):
Those whose scale (of good)
Will be heavy, will prosper:

٨- وَالْوَزْنُ يَوْمَئِذٍ الْحَقُّ فَمَنْ ثَقُلَتْ
مَوٰزِينُهُۥ فَأُولٰٓئِكَ هُمُ الْمُفْلِحُونَ ○

9. Those whose scale will be light,
Will find their souls
In perdition, for that they
Wrongfully treated Our Signs.

٩- وَمَنْ خَفَّتْ مَوٰزِينُهُۥ فَأُولٰٓئِكَ الَّذِينَ
خَسِرُوٓا أَنْفُسَهُمْ بِمَا كَانُوا بِـَٔايٰتِنَا يَظْلِمُونَ ○

10. It is We Who have
Placed you with authority
On earth, and provided
You therein with means
For the fulfilment of your life:[995]
Small are the thanks
That ye give!

١٠- وَلَقَدْ مَكَّنّٰكُمْ فِى الْأَرْضِ
وَجَعَلْنَا لَكُمْ فِيهَا مَعٰيِشَ
قَلِيلًا مَّا تَشْكُرُونَ ○ ع

992. The spiritual story of man begins with a prelude. Think of the towns and nations ruined by their iniquity. God gave them many opportunities, and sent them warners and teachers. But they arrogantly went on in their evil ways, till some dreadful calamity came like a thief in the night and wiped out their traces. In a warm climate the disturbance in the heat of the midday rest is even more than the disturbance at night. It was when the catastrophe came that the people realised their sins, but it was too late

993. In the final reckoning, the warners and teachers will give evidence of their preaching the truth, and the wicked will themselves have to acknowledge the truth. We picture it like a court scene, when the story is related, but the Judge knows all, even more than the parties can tell.

994. God is never absent from any place or at any time, for Time and Place are relative conceptions for our limited natures, while He is the Absolute, independent of such relative conceptions.

995. That is, all the material things which are necessary to sustain, beautify, and refine life, as well as all those powers, faculties, and opportunities which are instrumental in bringing up life to a higher plane and preparing man for his high spiritual destiny.

SECTION 2.

11. It is We Who created you
And gave you shape;[996]
Then We bade the angels
Bow down to Adam, and they
Bowed down; not so Iblīs;
He refused to be of those[997]
Who bow down.

١١- وَلَقَدْ خَلَقْنٰكُمْ ثُمَّ صَوَّرْنٰكُمْ
ثُمَّ قُلْنَا لِلْمَلٰٓئِكَةِ اسْجُدُوْا لِاٰدَمَ ۖ
فَسَجَدُوْٓا اِلَّآ اِبْلِيْسَ ۭ
لَمْ يَكُنْ مِّنَ السّٰجِدِيْنَ ○

12. (God) said: "What prevented
Thee from bowing down
When I commanded thee?"
He said: "I am better
Than he: Thou didst create
Me from fire, and him from clay."[998]

١٢- قَالَ مَا مَنَعَكَ اَلَّا تَسْجُدَ اِذْ اَمَرْتُكَ ۭ
قَالَ اَنَا خَيْرٌ مِّنْهُ ۚ
خَلَقْتَنِيْ مِنْ نَّارٍ وَّخَلَقْتَهٗ مِنْ طِيْنٍ ○

13. (God) said: "Get thee down
From this:[999] it is not
For thee to be arrogant
Here: get out, for thou
Art of the meanest (of creatures)."

١٣- قَالَ فَاهْبِطْ مِنْهَا
فَمَا يَكُوْنُ لَكَ اَنْ تَتَكَبَّرَ فِيْهَا
فَاخْرُجْ اِنَّكَ مِنَ الصّٰغِرِيْنَ ○

14. He said: "Give me respite
Till the day they are
Raised up."

١٤- قَالَ اَنْظِرْنِيْٓ
اِلٰى يَوْمِ يُبْعَثُوْنَ ○

15. (God) said: "Be thou
Among those who have respite."[1000]

١٥- قَالَ اِنَّكَ مِنَ الْمُنْظَرِيْنَ ○

---

996. *Shape* or form must be interpreted not only to refer to the physical form, which changes day by day, but also the various forms or shapes which our ideal and spiritual existence may take from time to time according to our inner experiences: *Cf.* lxxxii. 8. The original Form or Idea or Pattern, according to Plato's mystic doctrine as developed in his "Republic," may also be compared with the "names" or nature and quality of things, which God taught Adam: Q. ii. 31 and n. 48; and vi. 94, n. 916. It was after Adam (as standing for all mankind) had been so taught that the angels were asked to bow down to him, for, by God's grace, his status had actually been raised higher. Note the transition from "you" (plural) in the first clause to "Adam" in the second clause: Adam and mankind are synonymous: the plural is reverted to in vii. 14, 16-18.

997. Iblīs not only refused to bow down: he refused to be of those who bowed down. In other words he arrogantly despised the angels who bowed down, as well as man to whom they bowed down; and he was in rebellion against God for not obeying His order. Arrogance, jealousy, and rebellion were his triple crime.

998. Notice the subtle wiles of Iblīs: his egotism in putting himself above man, and his falsehood in ignoring the fact that God had not merely made man's body from clay, but had given him spiritual form,—in other words, had taught him the nature of things and raised him above the angels.

999. "*This*": the situation as it was then,—a rebellious creature impertinent to His Creator. At every step Iblīs falls lower: arrogance, jealousy, disobedience, egotism and untruth.

1000. Are there others under respite? Yes, Iblīs has a large army of wicked seducers, and those men who are their dupes. For though degradation takes effect at once, its appearance may be long delayed.

16. He said: "Because thou
Hast thrown me out [1001]
Of the Way, lo! I will
Lie in wait for them
On Thy Straight Way:

١٦- قَالَ فَبِمَآ أَغْوَيْتَنِى
لَأَقْعُدَنَّ لَهُمْ صِرَٰطَكَ ٱلْمُسْتَقِيمَ ○

17. "Then will I assault them
From before them and behind them,
From their right and their left:
Nor wilt Thou find,
In most of them,
Gratitude (for Thy mercies)." [1002]

١٧- ثُمَّ لَءَاتِيَنَّهُم مِّنۢ بَيْنِ أَيْدِيهِمْ وَ
مِنْ خَلْفِهِمْ وَعَنْ أَيْمَٰنِهِمْ وَعَن
شَمَآئِلِهِمْ وَلَا تَجِدُ أَكْثَرَهُمْ شَٰكِرِينَ ○

18. (God) said: "Get out
From this, disgraced
And expelled. If any
Of them follow thee,—
Hell will I fill
With you all.

١٨- قَالَ ٱخْرُجْ مِنْهَا مَذْءُومًا مَّدْحُورًا
لَّمَن تَبِعَكَ مِنْهُمْ
لَأَمْلَأَنَّ جَهَنَّمَ مِنكُمْ أَجْمَعِينَ ○

19. "O Adam! dwell thou [1003]
And thy wife in the Garden,
And enjoy [1004] (its good things)
As ye wish: but approach not
This tree, or ye run
Into harm and transgression."

١٩- وَيَٰٓـَٔادَمُ ٱسْكُنْ أَنتَ وَزَوْجُكَ ٱلْجَنَّةَ
فَكُلَا مِنْ حَيْثُ شِئْتُمَا وَلَا تَقْرَبَا هَٰذِهِ
ٱلشَّجَرَةَ فَتَكُونَا مِنَ ٱلظَّٰلِمِينَ ○

20. Then began Satan [1005] to whisper
Suggestions to them, bringing
Openly before their minds
All their shame [1006]

٢٠- فَوَسْوَسَ لَهُمَا ٱلشَّيْطَٰنُ لِيُبْدِىَ
لَهُمَا مَا وُۥرِىَ عَنْهُمَا مِن سَوْءَٰتِهِمَا

1001. Another instance of Iblis's subtlety and falsehood. He waits till he gets the respite. Then he breaks out into a lie and impertinent defiance. The lie is in suggesting that God had thrown him out of the Way, in other words misled him; whereas his own conduct was responsible for his degradation. The defiance is in his setting snares on the Straight Way to which God directs men. Iblis now falls a step lower than the five steps mentioned in n. 999. His sixth step is defiance.

1002. The assault of evil is from all sides. It takes advantage of every weak point, and sometimes even our good and generous sympathies are used to decoy us into the snares of evil. Man has every reason to be grateful to God for all His loving care and yet man in his folly forgets his gratitude and does the very opposite of what he should do.

1003. Now the story turns to man. He was placed in a spiritual Garden of innocence and bliss, but it was God's Plan to give him a limited faculty of choice. All that he was forbidden to do was to approach the Tree of Evil, but he succumbed to Satan's suggestions.

1004. *Enjoy*: literally, "eat." *Cf.* the meaning of *ṭa'ama* in vi. 14, n. 847 and *akala* in v. 69, n. 776.

1005. The transition from the name "Iblis" to the name "Satan" is similar to that in ii. 36, where it is explained in n. 52.

1006. Our first parents as created by God (and this applies to all of us) were innocent in matters material as well as spiritual. They knew no evil. But the faculty of choice, which was given to them and which raised them above the angels, also implied that they had the capacity of evil, which by the training of their own will, they were to reject. They were warned of the danger. When they fell, they realised the evil. They were (and we are) still given the chance, in this life on a lower plane, to make good and recover the lost status of innocence and bliss.

That was hidden from them
(Before): he said: "Your Lord
Only forbade you this tree,
Lest ye should become angels
Or such beings as live for ever."

وَقَالَ مَا نَهٰىكُمَا رَبُّكُمَا عَنْ هٰذِهِ
الشَّجَرَةِ اِلَّآ اَنْ تَكُوْنَا مَلَكَيْنِ اَوْ تَكُوْنَا
مِنَ الْخٰلِدِيْنَ ○

21. And he swore to them
Both, that he was
Their sincere adviser.

٢١- وَقَاسَمَهُمَآ اِنِّيْ لَكُمَا لَمِنَ
النّٰصِحِيْنَ ○

22. So by deceit he brought about
Their fall: when they
Tasted of the tree,
Their shame became manifest
To them, and they began
To sew together the leaves
Of the Garden over their bodies.
And their Lord called
Unto them: "Did I not
Forbid you that tree,
And tell you that Satan
Was an avowed
Enemy unto you?"

٢٢- فَدَلّٰىهُمَا بِغُرُوْرٍ فَلَمَّا ذَاقَا الشَّجَرَةَ
بَدَتْ لَهُمَا سَوْاٰتُهُمَا
وَطَفِقَا يَخْصِفٰنِ عَلَيْهِمَا مِنْ وَّرَقِ
الْجَنَّةِ
وَنَادٰىهُمَا رَبُّهُمَآ
اَلَمْ اَنْهَكُمَا عَنْ تِلْكُمَا الشَّجَرَةِ وَاَقُلْ
لَّكُمَآ اِنَّ الشَّيْطٰنَ لَكُمَا عَدُوٌّ مُّبِيْنٌ ○

23. They said: "Our Lord!
We have wronged our own souls:
If Thou forgive us not
And bestow not upon us
Thy Mercy, we shall
Certainly be lost."

٢٣- قَالَا رَبَّنَا ظَلَمْنَآ اَنْفُسَنَا
وَاِنْ لَّمْ تَغْفِرْ لَنَا وَتَرْحَمْنَا
لَنَكُوْنَنَّ مِنَ الْخٰسِرِيْنَ ○

24. (God) said: "Get ye down,
With enmity between yourselves.
On earth will be your dwelling-place
And your means of livelihood,—
For a time."

٢٤- قَالَ اهْبِطُوْا بَعْضُكُمْ لِبَعْضٍ عَدُوٌّ
وَلَكُمْ فِي الْاَرْضِ مُسْتَقَرٌّ
وَّمَتَاعٌ اِلٰى حِيْنٍ ○

25. He said: "Therein shall ye
Live, and therein shall ye
Die; but from it shall ye
Be taken out (at last)."[1007]

٢٥- قَالَ فِيْهَا تَحْيَوْنَ وَفِيْهَا تَمُوْتُوْنَ
وَمِنْهَا تُخْرَجُوْنَ ○

1007. *Cf.* this whole passage about Adam with the passage in ii. 30-39, and with other passages in subsequent Sūras. In places the words are precisely the same, and yet the whole argument is different. In each case it exactly fits the context. In S. ii, the argument was about the origin of man. Here the argument is a prelude to his history on earth, and so it continues logically in the next section to address the Children of Adam, and goes on afterwards with the story of the various apostles that came to guide mankind. Truth is one, but its apt presentment in human words shows a different facet in different contexts.

SECTION 3.

26. O ye Children of Adam!
We have bestowed raiment[1008]
Upon you to cover
Your shame, as well as
To be an adornment to you.
But the raiment of righteousness,—
That is the best.
Such are among the Signs
Of God, that they
May receive admonition!

٢٦-يٰبَنِيْٓ اٰدَمَ قَدْ اَنْزَلْنَا عَلَيْكُمْ لِبَاسًا
يُّوَارِيْ سَوْاٰتِكُمْ وَرِيْشًا ۭ
وَلِبَاسُ التَّقْوٰى ۙ
ذٰلِكَ خَيْرٌ ۭ
ذٰلِكَ مِنْ اٰيٰتِ اللّٰهِ
لَعَلَّهُمْ يَذَّكَّرُوْنَ ○

27. O ye Children of Adam!
Let not Satan seduce you,
In the same manner as[1009]
He got your parents out
Of the Garden, stripping them
Of their raiment, to expose
Their shame: for he
And his tribe watch you
From a position where ye
Cannot see them: We made
The Evil Ones friends
(Only) to those without Faith.

٢٧-يٰبَنِيْٓ اٰدَمَ لَا يَفْتِنَنَّكُمُ الشَّيْطٰنُ
كَمَآ اَخْرَجَ اَبَوَيْكُمْ مِّنَ الْجَنَّةِ
يَنْزِعُ عَنْهُمَا لِبَاسَهُمَا لِيُرِيَهُمَا سَوْاٰتِهِمَا ۭ
اِنَّهٗ يَرٰىكُمْ هُوَ وَقَبِيْلُهٗ مِنْ حَيْثُ لَا
تَرَوْنَهُمْ ۭ اِنَّا جَعَلْنَا الشَّيٰطِيْنَ اَوْلِيَاۗءَ
لِلَّذِيْنَ لَا يُؤْمِنُوْنَ ○

28. When they do aught
That is shameful, they say:
"We found our fathers
Doing so"; and "God
Commanded us thus":
Say: "Nay, God never

٢٨-وَاِذَا فَعَلُوْا فَاحِشَةً
قَالُوْا وَجَدْنَا عَلَيْهَآ اٰبَاۗءَنَا
وَاللّٰهُ اَمَرَنَا بِهَا ۭ قُلْ اِنَّ اللّٰهَ لَا يَاْمُرُ

1008. There is a double philosophy of clothes here, to correspond with the double signification of verse 20 above, as explained in n. 1006. Spiritually, God created man "bare and alone" (vi. 94): the soul in its naked purity and beauty knew no shame because it knew no guilt: after it was touched by guilt and soiled by evil, its thoughts and deeds became its clothing and adornments, good or bad, honest or meretricious, according to the inner motives which gave them colour. So in the case of the body: it is pure and beautiful, as long as it is not defiled by misuse: its clothing and ornaments may be good or meretricious, according to the motives in the mind and character: if good, they are the symbols of purity and beauty: but the best clothing and ornament we could have comes from righteousness, which covers the nakedness of sin, and adorns us with virtues. In secular literature, the philosophy of clothes is the theme of Carlyle's "*Sartor Resartus*," but it is strong meat to the novice in literature.

1009. That is, by fraud and deceit,—by putting you off your guard and telling lies. Adam's story here becomes an introduction to the later spiritual history of mankind: vii. 20-22. In the Garden Satan's deceit stripped off their raiment of honour and innocence. In this life on a lower plane he seeks to strip us of the raiment of righteousness. And he can take up positions on a vantage ground of worldly power or influence or riches, in which he and his confederates are not seen in their true colours. They may assume a fair-seeming disguise of disinterested friendship or high motives of patriotism or public spirit, or loyalty to ancestors, when beneath it there is nothing but spite and selfishness.

Commands what is shameful:
Do ye say of God
What ye know not?"

بِالْفَحْشَآءِ ۚ
أَتَقُولُونَ عَلَى اللَّهِ مَا لَا تَعْلَمُونَ ○

29. Say: "My Lord hath commanded
Justice; and that ye set
Your whole selves (to Him)[1010]
At every time and place
Of prayer, and call upon Him,
Making your devotion sincere
As in His sight:
Such as He created you[1011]
In the beginning, so
Shall ye return."

۲۹- قُلْ أَمَرَ رَبِّي بِالْقِسْطِ ۖ
وَأَقِيمُوا وُجُوهَكُمْ
عِنْدَ كُلِّ مَسْجِدٍ
وَادْعُوهُ مُخْلِصِينَ لَهُ الدِّينَ ۚ
كَمَا بَدَأَكُمْ تَعُودُونَ ○

30. Some He hath guided:
Others have (by their choice)
Deserved the loss of their way;[1012]
In that they took
The Evil Ones, in preference
To God, for their friends
And protectors, and think
That they receive guidance.

۳۰- فَرِيقًا هَدَىٰ وَفَرِيقًا حَقَّ عَلَيْهِمُ
الضَّلَالَةُ ۗ إِنَّهُمُ اتَّخَذُوا الشَّيَاطِينَ
أَوْلِيَاءَ مِنْ دُونِ اللَّهِ
وَيَحْسَبُونَ أَنَّهُمْ مُهْتَدُونَ ○

31. O Children of Adam!
Wear your beautiful apparel[1013]
At every time and place
Of prayer: eat and drink:
But waste not by excess,
For God loveth not the wasters.

۳۱- يَا بَنِي آدَمَ خُذُوا زِينَتَكُمْ عِنْدَ
كُلِّ مَسْجِدٍ وَكُلُوا وَاشْرَبُوا وَلَا تُسْرِفُوا ۚ
إِنَّهُ لَا يُحِبُّ الْمُسْرِفِينَ ○ ع

1010. For *wajh*, see ii. 112 and n. 114 Our devotion should be sincere, not as in other men's sight, but by presenting our whole selves, heart and soul, to God. Even so, it may not be enough; for the sight of our heart and soul may be faulty. We should call upon God to give us the light, by which our sincerity may commend itself to Him as true sincerity "as in His sight".

1011. *Cf.* vi. 94. Our sincerity should be real sincerity, as in God's sight; for when we return to Him, we shall be stripped of all pretence, even such self-deception as may satisfy us in this life.

1012. Guidance is for all. But in some it takes effect; in others the doors are closed against it, because they have taken Evil for their friend. If they have lost their way, they have richly deserved it; for they deliberately took their choice, even though, in their self-righteousness, they may think that their sin is their virtue, and that their Evil is their Good.

1013. *Beautiful apparel*: *zinat*: adornments or apparel for beautiful living: construed to mean not only clothes that add grace to the wearer, but toilet and cleanliness, attention to hair, and other small personal details which no self-respecting man or woman ought to neglect when going solemnly even before a great human dignitary, if only out of respect for the dignity of the occasion. How much more important it is to attend to these details when we solemnly apply our minds to the Presence of God, though He is always present everywhere! But the caution against excess applies: men must not go to prayer in silks or ornaments appropriate to women. Similarly sober food, good and wholesome, is not to be divorced from offices of religion; only the caution against excess applies strictly. A dirty, unkempt, slovenly Faqīr could not claim sanctity in Islam.

C. 84.—God has forbidden the things
(VII. 32-58.) That are evil, not those that are good,
For these were created for man's
Enjoyment. The transgressors
Are those who reject God's Signs.
They will have no share in the Bliss
Of the Hereafter. But the righteous
Will dwell in Peace, and the Hope
That was promised will be theirs.

SECTION 4.

32. Say: Who hath forbidden
The beautiful (gifts) of God,[1014]
Which He hath produced
For His servants,
And the things, clean and pure,
(Which He hath provided)
For sustenance?
Say: They are, in the life
Of this world, for those
Who believe, (and) purely[1015]
For them on the Day
Of Judgment. Thus do We
Explain the Signs in detail
For those who understand.

٣٢- قُلْ مَنْ حَرَّمَ زِيْنَةَ اللّٰهِ
الَّتِيْٓ اَخْرَجَ لِعِبَادِهٖ
وَالطَّيِّبٰتِ مِنَ الرِّزْقِ ۭ
قُلْ هِيَ لِلَّذِيْنَ اٰمَنُوْا فِي الْحَيٰوةِ
الدُّنْيَا
خَالِصَةً يَّوْمَ الْقِيٰمَةِ ۭ
كَذٰلِكَ نُفَصِّلُ الْاٰيٰتِ لِقَوْمٍ يَّعْلَمُوْنَ ○

33. Say: The things that my Lord
Hath indeed forbidden are:[1016]
Shameful deeds, whether open
Or secret; sins and trespasses
Against truth or reason; assigning
Of partners to God, for which
He hath given no authority;
And saying things about God
Of which ye have no knowledge.

٣٣- قُلْ اِنَّمَا حَرَّمَ رَبِّيَ الْفَوَاحِشَ مَا ظَهَرَ
مِنْهَا وَمَا بَطَنَ وَالْاِثْمَ وَالْبَغْيَ
بِغَيْرِ الْحَقِّ وَاَنْ تُشْرِكُوْا بِاللّٰهِ
مَا لَمْ يُنَزِّلْ بِهٖ سُلْطٰنًا
وَّاَنْ تَقُوْلُوْا عَلَى اللّٰهِ مَا لَا تَعْلَمُوْنَ ○

1014. Asceticism often means the negation of art and beauty. It has no necessary sanctity attached to it.

1015. The beautiful and good things of life are really meant for, and should be the privilege of, those with faith in God. If they do not always have them in this life, and if there is sometimes the semblance of others having them who do not deserve them, let us at least consider the matter in another light. Our Faith in God's wisdom is unshaken and we know that these are but fleeting and mixed types of the things in the spiritual world. Their pure counterparts in the spiritual world will be only for those who proved, in all the trials of this world, that they had faith.

1016. The forbidden things are described in four categories: (1) what is shameful or unbecoming; the sort of things which have also legal and social sanctions, not of a local but of a universal kind; they may be called offences against society; (2) sins against self and trespasses or excesses of every sort; these are against truth and reason; here would come in indiscipline, failure in doing intangible duties not clearly defined by law; selfishness or self-aggrandisement, which may be condoned by custom and not punished by law, etc.; (3) erecting fetishes or false gods; this is treason against the true God; and (4) corrupting religion by debasing superstitions, etc.

34. To every People is a term.[1017]
Appointed: when their term
Is reached, not an hour
Can they cause delay,
Nor (an hour) can they
Advance (it in anticipation).

٣٤- وَلِكُلِّ اُمَّةٍ اَجَلٌ فَاِذَا جَآءَ اَجَلُهُمْ
لَا يَسْتَاْخِرُوْنَ سَاعَةً
وَّلَا يَسْتَقْدِمُوْنَ ○

35. O ye Children of Adam!
Whenever there come to you
Apostles from amongst you,
Rehearsing My Signs unto you,—
Those who are righteous
And mend (their lives),—
On them shall be no fear
Nor shall they grieve.

٣٥- يٰبَنِيْۤ اٰدَمَ اِمَّا يَاْتِيَنَّكُمْ رُسُلٌ مِّنْكُمْ
يَقُصُّوْنَ عَلَيْكُمْ اٰيٰتِيْ فَمَنِ اتَّقٰى وَاَصْلَحَ
فَلَا خَوْفٌ عَلَيْهِمْ
وَلَا هُمْ يَحْزَنُوْنَ ○

36. But those who reject
Our Signs and treat them
With arrogance,—they
Are Companions of the Fire,
To dwell therein (for ever).

٣٦- وَالَّذِيْنَ كَذَّبُوْا بِاٰيٰتِنَا
وَاسْتَكْبَرُوْا عَنْهَاۤ اُولٰٓئِكَ اَصْحٰبُ النَّارِ
هُمْ فِيْهَا خٰلِدُوْنَ ○

37. Who is more unjust
Than one who invents
A lie against God
Or rejects His Signs?
For such, their portion[1018]
Appointed must reach them
From the Book (of Decrees):
Until, when Our messengers
(Of death) arrive and take
Their souls, they say:
"Where are the things
That ye used to invoke
Besides God?"
They will reply, "They

٣٧- فَمَنْ اَظْلَمُ مِمَّنِ افْتَرٰى عَلَى اللّٰهِ
كَذِبًا اَوْ كَذَّبَ بِاٰيٰتِهٖ
اُولٰٓئِكَ يَنَالُهُمْ نَصِيْبُهُمْ مِّنَ الْكِتٰبِ
حَتّٰۤى اِذَا جَآءَتْهُمْ رُسُلُنَا يَتَوَفَّوْنَهُمْ
قَالُوْۤا اَيْنَ مَا كُنْتُمْ تَدْعُوْنَ مِنْ
دُوْنِ اللّٰهِ
قَالُوْا

1017. People: *ummat.* I do not know whether "generation" would not be more appropriate here. If so, it would refer to the Time-Spirit, for it affects a whole number of people living contemporaneously, and while we deal grammatically with a group, we really have in mind the individuals composing the group. Anyway, the lesson is what is suggested in the following verses. There is only a limited time for an individual or for a group of people. If they do not make good during that time of probation, the chance is lost, and it cannot come again. We cannot retard or advance the march of time by a single hour or minute. ("Hour" in the text expresses an indefinite but short period of time.)

1018. It must not be supposed that the rebels against God would at once be cut off in this life for their sins. They will get the portion allotted to them, including the good things of life and the chance of repentance and reformation, during their probationary period on this earth. During that period they will have a full run. After that period expires, they will be called to account. They will themselves see that the false things in which they put their trust, were false, and they will confess their sin, but it will be too late.

Have left us in the lurch,"
And they will bear witness
Against themselves, that they
Had rejected God.

ضَلُّوْا عَنَّا وَ شَهِدُوْا عَلٰٓى اَنْفُسِهِمْ
اَنَّهُمْ كَانُوْا كٰفِرِيْنَ ○

38. He will say: "Enter ye
In the company of
The Peoples who passed away
Before you—men and Jinns,—
Into the Fire. Every time
A new People enters,
It curses its sister-People
(That went before), until
They follow each other, all
Into the Fire. Saith the last
About the first: "Our Lord!
It is these that misled us:
So give them a double
Penalty in the Fire."
He will say: "Doubled[1019]
For all": but this
Ye do not understand.

٣٨- قَالَ ادْخُلُوْا فِيْٓ اُمَمٍ قَدْ خَلَتْ مِنْ
قَبْلِكُمْ مِّنَ الْجِنِّ وَ الْاِنْسِ
فِي النَّارِ
كُلَّمَا دَخَلَتْ اُمَّةٌ لَّعَنَتْ اُخْتَهَا
حَتّٰٓى اِذَا ادَّارَكُوْا فِيْهَا جَمِيْعًا
قَالَتْ اُخْرٰىهُمْ لِاُوْلٰىهُمْ
رَبَّنَا هٰٓؤُلَآءِ اَضَلُّوْنَا
فَاٰتِهِمْ عَذَابًا ضِعْفًا مِّنَ النَّارِ
قَالَ لِكُلٍّ ضِعْفٌ وَّلٰكِنْ لَّا تَعْلَمُوْنَ ○

39. Then the first will say
To the last: "See then!
No advantage have ye
Over us; so taste ye
Of the Penalty for all
That ye did!"[1020]

٣٩- وَ قَالَتْ اُوْلٰىهُمْ لِاُخْرٰىهُمْ
فَمَا كَانَ لَكُمْ عَلَيْنَا مِنْ فَضْلٍ
فَذُوْقُوا الْعَذَابَ بِمَا كُنْتُمْ تَكْسِبُوْنَ ○ ع

SECTION 5.

40. To those who reject
Our Signs and treat them
With arrogance, no opening
Will there be of the gates

٤٠- اِنَّ الَّذِيْنَ كَذَّبُوْا بِاٰيٰتِنَا وَ اسْتَكْبَرُوْا
عَنْهَا لَا تُفَتَّحُ لَهُمْ اَبْوَابُ

1019 The earlier generations committed a double crime: (1) their own sins, (2) the bad example they set for those that followed. We are responsible not only for our own misdeeds, but for those which our example and our teaching to our juniors may induce them to commit. But it does not lie in the mouth of the juniors to ask for a double punishment for seniors: the motive is not justice, but pure spite, which is itself a sin. Farther, the later generations have to answer for two things: (1) their own sins, and (2) their failure to learn from the past, from the experiences of those who preceded them. They should have an advantage in this respect, being "in the foremost files of Time," but they did not learn. Thus there was nothing to choose between the earlier and later generations in the matter of guilt. But how few people understand this!

In vi. 160, we were told that good was rewarded tenfold, but evil was punished according to its guilt, in perfect justice. This verse is in no way inconsistent with it. Two crimes must have a double penalty. But we must understand "ten times" and "double" figuratively and not quantitatively.

1020. Wrong-doers have really no sense of honour towards each other. "Honour among thieves" is an exceptional, not an ordinary, experience. In real life, guilt and crime are apt to indulge in mean spite and bitter recriminations against accomplices.

Of heaven, nor will they
Enter the Garden, until
The camel can pass
Through the eye of the needle:
Such is Our reward
For those in sin.

السَّمَاۤءِ وَلَا يَدْخُلُوْنَ الْجَنَّةَ
حَتّٰى يَلِجَ الْجَمَلُ فِيْ سَمِّ الْخِيَاطِ ۭ
وَكَذٰلِكَ نَجْزِي الْمُجْرِمِيْنَ ○

41. For them there is
Hell, as a couch
(Below) and folds and folds
Of covering above: such
Is Our requital of those
Who do wrong.

٤١- لَهُمْ مِّنْ جَهَنَّمَ مِهَادٌ
وَّمِنْ فَوْقِهِمْ غَوَاشٍ ۭ
وَكَذٰلِكَ نَجْزِي الظّٰلِمِيْنَ ○

42. But those who believe
And work righteousness,—
No burden do We place
On any soul, but that
Which it can bear,—
They will be Companions
Of the Garden, therein
To dwell (for ever).

٤٢- وَالَّذِيْنَ اٰمَنُوْا وَعَمِلُوا الصّٰلِحٰتِ
لَا نُكَلِّفُ نَفْسًا اِلَّا وُسْعَهَآ
اُولٰۤىِٕكَ اَصْحٰبُ الْجَنَّةِ ۚ
هُمْ فِيْهَا خٰلِدُوْنَ ○

43. And We shall remove
From their hearts any
Lurking sense of injury;—[1021]
Beneath them will be
Rivers flowing;—and they
Shall say: "Praise be to God,
Who hath guided us
To this (felicity): never
Could we have found
Guidance, had it not been
For the guidance of God:
Indeed it was the truth.
That the Apostles of our Lord
Brought unto us." And they
Shall hear the cry:
"Behold! the Garden before you!

٤٣- وَنَزَعْنَا مَا فِيْ صُدُوْرِهِمْ مِّنْ غِلٍّ
تَجْرِيْ مِنْ تَحْتِهِمُ الْاَنْهٰرُ ۚ
وَقَالُوا الْحَمْدُ لِلّٰهِ
الَّذِيْ هَدٰىنَا لِهٰذَا
وَمَا كُنَّا لِنَهْتَدِيَ
لَوْلَآ اَنْ هَدٰىنَا اللّٰهُ ۚ
لَقَدْ جَاۤءَتْ رُسُلُ رَبِّنَا بِالْحَقِّ ۭ
وَنُوْدُوْٓا اَنْ تِلْكُمُ الْجَنَّةُ

1021. A man who may have suffered or been disappointed may have a lurking sense of injury at the back of his mind, which may spoil his enjoyment on account of past memory intruding in the midst of felicity. In such cases memory itself is pain. Even sorrow is intensified by memory: as Tennyson says, "A sorrow's crown of sorrows is remembering happier things." But that is in this our imperfect life. In the perfect felicity of the righteous, all such feelings will be blotted out. No "heartaches" then and no memories of them! The clouds of the past will have dissolved in glorious light, and no past happiness will be comparable with the perfect happiness which will have then been attained. Nor will any sense of envy or shortcoming be possible in that perfect bliss.

Ye have been made [1022]
Its inheritors, for your
Deeds (of righteousness)."

أُورِثْتُمُوهَا بِمَا كُنتُمْ تَعْمَلُونَ ۝

44. The Companions of the Garden
Will call out to the Companions
Of the Fire: "We have
Indeed found the promises
Of our Lord to us true:
Have you also found
Your Lord's promises true?"
They shall say, "Yes"; but [1023]
A Crier shall proclaim
Between them: "The curse
Of God is on the wrong-doers;—

٤٤- وَنَادَىٰ أَصْحَٰبُ ٱلْجَنَّةِ أَصْحَٰبَ ٱلنَّارِ
أَن قَدْ وَجَدْنَا مَا وَعَدَنَا رَبُّنَا حَقًّا
فَهَلْ وَجَدتُّم مَّا وَعَدَ رَبُّكُمْ حَقًّا
قَالُوا نَعَمْ
فَأَذَّنَ مُؤَذِّنٌ
بَيْنَهُمْ أَن لَّعْنَةُ ٱللَّهِ عَلَى ٱلظَّٰلِمِينَ ۝

45. "Those who would hinder (men)
From the path of God
And would seek in it
Something crooked: [1024]
They were those who
Denied the Hereafter."

٤٥- ٱلَّذِينَ يَصُدُّونَ عَن سَبِيلِ ٱللَّهِ
وَيَبْغُونَهَا عِوَجًا
وَهُم بِٱلْآخِرَةِ كَٰفِرُونَ ۝

46. Between them shall be
A veil, and on the Heights [1025]

٤٦- وَبَيْنَهُمَا حِجَابٌ وَعَلَى ٱلْأَعْرَافِ

1022. Jesus said: "Blessed are the meek, for they shall inherit the earth": Matt. v. 5. Here we are told: blessed are the righteous, for they shall inherit the kingdom of heaven. The stress here is on actual practical deeds of righteousness: whether they find their rewards on earth or not is immaterial: their attention is directed to an infinitely greater reward, the kingdom of heaven. In the Sermon on the Mount this is promised to the "poor in spirit": Matt. v. 3.

1023. The Companions of the Fire can only answer a single word, "Yes," such is their state of misery. Even so, their voice is drowned in the voice of the Crier, who explains their state: they are in a state of curse, that is, deprivation of the grace and mercy of God. Such deprivation is the highest misery that souls can suffer.

1024. The unrighteous reflect their own crooked minds when the path of God is before them. Instead of going straight, they try to find something in it that suits their own crooked ideas. Frankly they have no faith in the final Goal, the Hereafter.

1025. This is a difficult passage, and Commentators have interpreted it in different ways. Three distinct schools of thought may be discerned in the interpretation. (1) One school thinks that the men on the Heights are angels, or such men of exalted spiritual dignity (*e.g.*, the great apostles), as will be able to know the souls at sight as regards their spiritual worth: the Heights will be their exalted stations, from which they will welcome the righteous with a salutation of peace, even before the righteous have entered heaven; the salutation of peace being itself an assurance of salvation to those whom they salute. (2) Another school of thought thinks that the men on the Heights are such souls as are not decidedly on the side of merit or decidedly on the side of sin, but evenly balanced on a partition between heaven and hell. Their case is yet to be decided, but their salutation to the righteous is a wistful salutation, because they hope for God's Mercy. (3) The third line of interpretation, with which I agree, is close to the first, with this exception, that the partition and the Heights are figurative. The higher souls will rejoice at the approaching salvation of the righteous

Will be men
Who would know every one
By his marks : they will call
Out to the Companions
Of the Garden, " Peace on you " :
They will not have entered,
But they will have
An assurance (thereof.)

رِجَالٌ يَّعْرِفُوْنَ كُلًّا بِسِيْمٰهُمْ ج
وَنَادَوْا اَصْحٰبَ الْجَنَّةِ
اَنْ سَلٰمٌ عَلَيْكُمْ لَمْ يَدْخُلُوْهَا
وَهُمْ يَطْمَعُوْنَ ○

47. When their eyes[1026] shall be turned
Towards the Companions
Of the Fire, they will say :
" Our Lord ! send us not
To the company
Of the wrong-doers. "

٤٧- وَاِذَا صُرِفَتْ اَبْصَارُهُمْ
تِلْقَآءَ اَصْحٰبِ النَّارِ قَالُوْا رَبَّنَا لَا تَجْعَلْنَا
مَعَ الْقَوْمِ الظّٰلِمِيْنَ ○

Section 6.

48. The men on the Heights
Will call to certain men
Whom they will know
From their marks, saying :[1027]
" Of what profit to you
Were your hoards and your
Arrogant ways ?

٤٨- وَنَادٰۤى اَصْحٰبُ الْاَعْرَافِ رِجَالًا
يَّعْرِفُوْنَهُمْ بِسِيْمٰهُمْ
قَالُوْا مَآ اَغْنٰى عَنْكُمْ جَمْعُكُمْ
وَمَا كُنْتُمْ تَسْتَكْبِرُوْنَ ○

49. " Behold ! are these not
The men whom you swore
That God with His Mercy
Would never bless ?
Enter ye the Garden :
No fear shall be on you,
Nor shall ye grieve. "

٤٩- اَهٰٓؤُلَآءِ الَّذِيْنَ اَقْسَمْتُمْ
لَا يَنَالُهُمُ اللّٰهُ بِرَحْمَةٍ
اُدْخُلُوا الْجَنَّةَ
لَا خَوْفٌ عَلَيْكُمْ وَلَآ اَنْتُمْ تَحْزَنُوْنَ ○

50. The Companions of the Fire
Will call to the Companions
Of the Garden : " Pour down
To us water or anything

٥٠- وَنَادٰۤى اَصْحٰبُ النَّارِ اَصْحٰبَ الْجَنَّةِ
اَنْ اَفِيْضُوْا عَلَيْنَا مِنَ الْمَآءِ اَوْ مِمَّا

1026. *Their eyes* : according to interpretation (2) of the last note, " *their* " would refer to the people whose fate has not yet been decided, and the speech would be theirs ; accoding to interpretations (1) and (3) in that note, " their " would refer to the Companions of the Garden, who would realise the terrible nature of hell, and express their horror of it. I prefer the latter. Then the mention of the " men on the Heights " and their speech in verse 48 comes in naturally as a different kind of speech from a different kind of men.

1027. This speech is in three parts : (1) the last lines of this verse are addressed to the Companions of the Fire, reminding them (as a bench of judges might speak to a prisoner) of the futility of their wealth and riches and arrogance in their earthly life ; (2) the second part, in the first half of verse 49, recalls to their minds how false was their contempt of the good but lowly men who are now to be the inheritors of heaven ; and (3) the latter part of verse 49, " enter ye the Garden " is addressed to the Blessed, to give them a welcome to their state of felicity.

That God doth provide
For your sustenance."
They will say: "Both
These things hath God forbidden
To those who rejected Him;—[1028]

رِزَقَكُمُ اللّٰهُ ؕ قَالُوْٓا اِنَّ اللّٰهَ حَرَّمَهُمَا
عَلَى الْكٰفِرِيْنَ ۝

51. "Such as took their religion
To be mere amusement
And play, and were deceived
By the life of the world."
That day shall We forget them[1029]
As they forgot the meeting
Of this day of theirs,
And as they were wont
To reject Our Signs.

٥١- الَّذِيْنَ اتَّخَذُوْا دِيْنَهُمْ لَهْوًا
وَّلَعِبًا وَّغَرَّتْهُمُ الْحَيٰوةُ الدُّنْيَا ۚ
فَالْيَوْمَ نَنْسٰىهُمْ
كَمَا نَسُوْا لِقَآءَ يَوْمِهِمْ هٰذَا ۙ
وَمَا كَانُوْا بِاٰيٰتِنَا يَجْحَدُوْنَ ۝

52. For We had certainly
Sent unto them a Book,
Based on knowledge,
Which We explained
In detail,—a guide
And a mercy
To all who believe.

٥٢- وَلَقَدْ جِئْنٰهُمْ بِكِتٰبٍ
فَصَّلْنٰهُ عَلٰى عِلْمٍ هُدًى
وَّرَحْمَةً لِّقَوْمٍ يُّؤْمِنُوْنَ ۝

53. Do they just wait
For the final fulfilment
Of the event? On the day
The event is finally fulfilled,[1030]
Those who disregarded it
Before will say: "The apostles
Of our Lord did indeed
Bring true (tidings). Have we
No intercessors now to intercede
On our behalf? Or could we

٥٣- هَلْ يَنْظُرُوْنَ اِلَّا تَاْوِيْلَهٗ ؕ
يَوْمَ يَاْتِيْ تَاْوِيْلُهٗ
يَقُوْلُ الَّذِيْنَ نَسُوْهُ مِنْ قَبْلُ
قَدْ جَآءَتْ رُسُلُ رَبِّنَا بِالْحَقِّ ۚ فَهَلْ لَّنَا
مِنْ شُفَعَآءَ فَيَشْفَعُوْا لَنَآ اَوْ

1028. The Companions of the Fire will thirst for water and not get it, and for sustenance which will not be theirs, while the Companions of the Garden will have the refreshing rain of God's Mercy and the crystal waters of the springs and rivers of God's pleasure, and they will enjoy the bliss of God's Countenance, which will be their supreme nourishment and the fruit of their life of probation and seeking. These things will not be transferable. *Cf.* also xxxvii. 41-47, 62-67.

1029. "Forgetfulness" may be involuntary, from a defect of memory, or figuratively, a deliberate turning away from, or ignoring of, something we do not want, as when we say in an argument, "you conveniently forget that so-and-so is so-and-so." Here the latter kind is meant. If men deliberately ignored the Hereafter in spite of warnings, can they expect to be received by God, Whom they themselves rejected?

1030. If those without Faith want to wait and see what happens in the Hereafter, they will indeed learn the truth, but it will be too late for them to profit by it then. All the false ideals and false gods which they put their trust upon will leave them in the lurch. If they thought that the goodness or greatness of others would help them, they will be undeceived on the day when their personal responsibility will be enforced. There will be no salvation except on their own record. How they will then wish that they had another chance! But their chance will be gone.

Be sent back? Then should we
Behave differently from our
Behaviour in the past."
In fact they will have lost
Their souls, and the things
They invented will leave
Them in the lurch.

تُرَدُّ فَنَعْمَلَ غَيْرَ الَّذِي كُنَّا نَعْمَلُ
قَدْ خَسِرُوٓا أَنفُسَهُمْ
وَضَلَّ عَنْهُم
مَّا كَانُوا يَفْتَرُونَ ○

SECTION 7.

54. Your Guardian-Lord
Is God, Who created
The heavens and the earth [1031]
In six Days, and is firmly
Established on the Throne [1032]
(Of authority): He draweth
The night as a veil
O'er the day, each seeking
The other in rapid succession:
He created the sun,
The moon, and the stars,
(All) governed by laws
Under His Command.
Is it not His to create
And to govern? Blessed
Be God, the Cherisher
And Sustainer of the Worlds!

٥٤- إِنَّ رَبَّكُمُ اللَّهُ الَّذِي خَلَقَ
السَّمٰوٰتِ وَالْأَرْضَ
فِي سِتَّةِ أَيَّامٍ
ثُمَّ اسْتَوٰى عَلَى الْعَرْشِ
يُغْشِي الَّيْلَ النَّهَارَ يَطْلُبُهُ حَثِيثًا
وَالشَّمْسَ وَالْقَمَرَ وَالنُّجُومَ
مُسَخَّرٰتٍ بِأَمْرِهِ
أَلَا لَهُ الْخَلْقُ وَالْأَمْرُ
تَبَارَكَ اللَّهُ رَبُّ الْعٰلَمِينَ ○

55. Call on your Lord
With humility and in private: [1033]

٥٥- ادْعُوا رَبَّكُمْ تَضَرُّعًا وَخُفْيَةً

1031. A sublime verse, comparable to the Throne Verse, ii. 255. The Creation in *six Days* is of course metaphorical. In xlv. 14, the "Days of God" refer not so much to time as to the growth in us of a spiritual sense, a sense of sin and a sense of God's Mercy. In xxii. 47, we are told that a Day in the sight of God is *like* a thousand years of our reckoning, and in lxx. 4, the comparison is with 50,000 of our years. In the history of our material earth, we may reckon six great epochs of evolution. The significance of the figure *six* will be discussed in connection with xli. 9-12, where the matter is referred to in more detail.

1032. Throne (*'arsh*) is of course metaphorical, a symbol of authority, power, and vigilance, as *Kursī* (seat, throne), was in ii. 255. *Kursi* perhaps refers to majesty, while *'arsh* refers to power; and the slightly different shades of meaning throw light on the two passages. Here, we are told of the creation of the heavens and the earth in six days. But lest we should be obsessed with the Jewish idea that God *rested* on the seventh day, we are told that the Creation was but a prelude to God's work: for His authority is exercised constantly by the laws which He establishes and enforces in all parts of His Creation. The beautiful imagery of night and day seeking out each other in rapid succession is still further enforced in the Arabic by the double accusative of the verb *yugshī*, showing the *mutual* interactions of the day and the night, each covering the other in turn. The heavenly bodies show an order which is evidence of His *constant* care and government. Not only that, but it is only He Who creates, maintains, and governs, and no one else.

1033. In prayer, we must avoid any arrogance or show or loudness, or vanity of requests or words. If excess is condemned in all things, it is specially worthy of condemnation when we go humbly before our Lord,—we poor creatures before the Omnipotent Who knoweth all.

For God loveth not
Those who trespass beyond bounds.

إِنَّهُ لَا يُحِبُّ الْمُعْتَدِينَ ۝

56. Do no mischief on the earth,
After it hath been[1034]
Set in order, but call
On Him with fear[1035]
And longing (in your hearts):
For the Mercy of God
Is (always) near
To those who do good.

٥٦- وَلَا تُفْسِدُوا فِي الْأَرْضِ
بَعْدَ إِصْلَاحِهَا
وَادْعُوهُ خَوْفًا وَطَمَعًا ۚ إِنَّ رَحْمَتَ اللَّهِ
قَرِيبٌ مِّنَ الْمُحْسِنِينَ ۝

57. It is He Who sendeth
The Winds like heralds
Of glad tidings, going before[1036]
His Mercy: when they have
Carried the heavy-laden
Clouds, We drive them
To a land that is dead,
Make rain to descend thereon,
And produce every kind
Of harvest therewith: thus
Shall We raise up the dead:
Perchance ye may remember.

٥٧- وَهُوَ الَّذِي يُرْسِلُ الرِّيٰحَ
بُشْرًا بَيْنَ يَدَيْ رَحْمَتِهِ ۖ
حَتَّىٰ إِذَا أَقَلَّتْ سَحَابًا ثِقَالًا سُقْنَاهُ
لِبَلَدٍ مَّيِّتٍ فَأَنزَلْنَا بِهِ الْمَاءَ فَأَخْرَجْنَا
بِهِ مِن كُلِّ الثَّمَرَاتِ ۚ
كَذَٰلِكَ نُخْرِجُ الْمَوْتَىٰ لَعَلَّكُمْ تَذَكَّرُونَ ۝

58. From the land that is clean
And good, by the Will
Of its Cherisher, springs up
Produce, (rich) after its kind:[1037]

٥٨- وَالْبَلَدُ الطَّيِّبُ
يَخْرُجُ نَبَاتُهُ بِإِذْنِ رَبِّهِ ۖ

1034. The man who prays with humility and earnestness finds the ground prepared by God for his spiritual advancement. It is all set in order, and cleared of weeds. He does not, like the wicked, upset that order, to introduce evil or mischief into it.

1035. *Fear and longing*: the fear of God is really a fear lest we should diverge from His Will, or do anything which would not be pleasing to Him: unlike ordinary fear, it therefore brings us nearer to God, and in fact nourishes our longing and desire for Him.

1036. The Parable is complete in its triple significance. (1) In the physical world the winds go like heralds of glad tidings; they are the advance guard, behind which is coming a great army of winds driving heavily laden clouds before it; the wise Providence of God is their General, who directs them towards a parched land, on which the clouds deliver their gladdening showers of mercy, which convert the dead land into a living, fertile, and beautiful land bearing a rich harvest. (2) In the spiritual world, the winds are the great motive forces in the mind of man, or in the world around him, that bring the clouds or instruments of God's Mercy, which descend and fertilise souls hitherto spiritually dead. (3) If we can see or experience such things in our life here below, can we doubt the resurrection of our souls after we die here?

1037. The triple parable explained in the last note is here continued. (1) In the physical world, the fertilising showers of rain yield a rich harvest on good soil, but bad soil yields little or nothing, (2) In the spiritual world, also, God's Mercies evoke no response in some souls which have chosen evil. (3) In the final reckoning, though all will be raised, not all will achieve the fulfilment of their lives.

But from the land that is
Bad, springs up nothing
But that which is niggardly:
Thus do we explain the Signs
By various (symbols) to those
Who are grateful.[1038]

وَالَّذِيْ خَبُثَ لَا يَخْرُجُ اِلَّا نَكِدًا ؕ
كَذٰلِكَ نُصَرِّفُ الْاٰيٰتِ لِقَوْمٍ
يَّشْكُرُوْنَ ۟

C. 85.—Noah's warning was rejected by his
(vii. 59-99.) Generation, and they were destroyed
In the Flood. Hūd was defied
By his own people 'Ād, but they were
Swept away by a terrible blast.
Their successors, the Thamūd, were puffed up
With pride and injustice, but behold!
An earthquake buried them for their sins
After Ṣāliḥ had warned them from God.
With a rain of brimstone and fire
Were overwhelmed the Cities of the Plain
For their unexampled lusts, against which
Lot did warn them. The people of Midian
Were given to mischief and fraud: Shu'aib
Did warn them, but they heeded not,
And perished in an earthquake.
God's punishment is sure for wickedness and sin.

Section 8.

59. We sent Noah to his people.[1039]
He said: "O my people!
Worship God! ye have
No other god but Him.
I fear for you the Punishment
Of a dreadful Day!

٥٩- لَقَدْ اَرْسَلْنَا نُوْحًا اِلٰى قَوْمِهٖ
فَقَالَ يٰقَوْمِ اعْبُدُوا اللّٰهَ
مَا لَكُمْ مِّنْ اِلٰهٍ غَيْرُهٗ ؕ اِنِّيْۤ اَخَافُ
عَلَيْكُمْ عَذَابَ يَوْمٍ عَظِيْمٍ ۟

60. The leaders of his people
Said: "Ah! we see thee
Evidently wandering (in mind)."

٦٠- قَالَ الْمَلَاُ مِنْ قَوْمِهٖۤ
اِنَّا لَنَرٰىكَ فِيْ ضَلٰلٍ مُّبِيْنٍ ۟

1038. *Those who are grateful* are those who joyfully receive God's Message, and respond to it by deeds of holiness and righteousness.

1039. The story of Noah in greater detail will be found in xi. 25-49. Here the scheme is to tell briefly the stories of some of the Prophets between Noah and Moses, and lead up thus to a lesson for the contemporaries of the Apostle Muḥammad himself. When Noah attacked the wickedness of his generation, he was laughed at for a madman, for he mentioned the Great Day to come in the Hereafter. God's retribution came soon afterwards—the great Flood, in which his unbelieving people were drowned, but he and those who believed in him and came into the Ark were saved.

61. He said: "O my people!
No wandering is there
In my (mind): on the contrary
I am an apostle from
The Lord and Cherisher
Of the Worlds!

٦١- قَالَ يٰقَوْمِ لَيْسَ بِيْ ضَلٰلَةٌ
وَّلٰكِنِّيْ رَسُوْلٌ
مِّنْ رَّبِّ الْعٰلَمِيْنَ ○

62. "I but fulfil towards you
The duties of my Lord's mission:
Sincere is my advice to you,
And I know from God
Something that ye know not.

٦٢- أُبَلِّغُكُمْ رِسٰلٰتِ رَبِّيْ
وَأَنْصَحُ لَكُمْ
وَأَعْلَمُ مِنَ اللّٰهِ مَا لَا تَعْلَمُوْنَ ○

63. "Do ye wonder that
There hath come to you
A message from your Lord,
Through a man of your own
People, to warn you,—
So that ye may fear God
And haply receive His Mercy?"

٦٣- أَوَعَجِبْتُمْ أَنْ جَآءَكُمْ
ذِكْرٌ مِّنْ رَّبِّكُمْ
عَلٰى رَجُلٍ مِّنْكُمْ لِيُنْذِرَكُمْ
وَلِتَتَّقُوْا وَلَعَلَّكُمْ تُرْحَمُوْنَ ○

64 But they rejected him,
And We delivered him,
And those with him,
In the Ark:
But We overwhelmed
In the Flood those
Who rejected Our Signs.
They were indeed
A blind people!

٦٤- فَكَذَّبُوْهُ فَأَنْجَيْنٰهُ
وَالَّذِيْنَ مَعَهٗ فِي الْفُلْكِ
وَأَغْرَقْنَا الَّذِيْنَ كَذَّبُوْا بِاٰيٰتِنَا
إِنَّهُمْ كَانُوْا قَوْمًا عَمِيْنَ ○ ع

SECTION 9.

65. To the 'Ād people,[1040]
(We sent) Hūd, one

٦٥- وَإِلٰى عَادٍ أَخَاهُمْ هُوْدًا

1040. The 'Ād people, with their prophet Hūd, are mentioned in many places. See especially xxvi. 123-140, and xlvi. 21-26. Their story belongs to Arabian tradition. Their eponymous ancestor 'Ād was fourth in generation from Noah, having been a son of 'Aus, the son of Aram, the son of Sām, the son of Noah. They occupied a large tract of country in Southern Arabia, extending from 'Ummān at the mouth of the Persian Gulf to Ḥadhramaut and Yemen at the southern end of the Red Sea. The people were tall in stature and were great builders. Probably the long, winding tracts of sands (aḥqāf) in their dominions (xlvi. 21) were irrigated with canals. They forsook the true God, and oppressed their people. A three years' famine visited them, but yet they took no warning. At length a terrible blast of wind destroyed them and their land, but a remnant, known as the second 'Ad or the Thamūd (see below) were saved, and afterwards suffered a similar fate for their sins.

The tomb of the Prophet Hūd (*qabr Nabī Hūd*) is still traditionally shown in Ḥadhramaut, latitude 16° N. and longitude 49½ E., about 90 miles north of Mukalla. There are ruins and inscriptions in the neighbourhood. There is an annual pilgrimage to it in the month of Rajab. See "Ḥadhramaut, Some of its Mysteries Unveiled," by D. van der Meulen and H. von Wissmann, Leyden, 1932.

Of their (own) brethren :
He said : " O my people !
Worship God ! ye have
No other god but Him.
Will ye not fear (God) ? "

قَالَ يٰقَوْمِ اعْبُدُوا اللّٰهَ
مَا لَكُمْ مِّنْ اِلٰهٍ غَيْرُهٗ ؕ
اَفَلَا تَتَّقُوْنَ ○

66. The leaders of the unbelievers
Among his people said :
" Ah ! we see thou art
An imbecile ! " and " We think
Thou art a liar ! "

٦٦- قَالَ الْمَلَاُ الَّذِيْنَ كَفَرُوْا مِنْ قَوْمِهٖۤ
اِنَّا لَنَرٰىكَ فِيْ سَفَاهَةٍ
وَّاِنَّا لَنَظُنُّكَ مِنَ الْكٰذِبِيْنَ ○

67. He said : " O my people !
I am no imbecile, but
(I am) an apostle from
The Lord and Cherisher
Of the Worlds !

٦٧- قَالَ يٰقَوْمِ لَيْسَ بِيْ سَفَاهَةٌ
وَّلٰكِنِّيْ رَسُوْلٌ
مِّنْ رَّبِّ الْعٰلَمِيْنَ ○

68. " I but fulfil towards you
The duties of my Lord's mission :
I am to you a sincere
And trustworthy adviser.

٦٨- اُبَلِّغُكُمْ رِسٰلٰتِ رَبِّيْ
وَاَنَا لَكُمْ نَاصِحٌ اَمِيْنٌ ○

69. " Do ye wonder that
There hath come to you
A message from your Lord
Through a man of your own
People, to warn you ?
Call in remembrance
That He made you
Inheritors after the people
Of Noah, and gave you
A stature tall among the nations.
Call in remembrance
The benefits (ye have received)
From God : that so
Ye may prosper. "

٦٩- اَوَعَجِبْتُمْ اَنْ جَآءَكُمْ
ذِكْرٌ مِّنْ رَّبِّكُمْ عَلٰى رَجُلٍ مِّنْكُمْ
لِيُنْذِرَكُمْ ؕ
وَاذْكُرُوْۤا اِذْ جَعَلَكُمْ
خُلَفَآءَ مِنْۢ بَعْدِ قَوْمِ نُوْحٍ
وَّزَادَكُمْ فِي الْخَلْقِ بَصْۜطَةً ۚ
فَاذْكُرُوْۤا اٰلَآءَ اللّٰهِ لَعَلَّكُمْ تُفْلِحُوْنَ ○

70. They said : " Comest thou
To us, that we may worship
God alone, and give up
The cult of our fathers ?
Bring us what thou
Threatenest us with,
If so be that thou
Tellest the truth ! "

٧٠- قَالُوْۤا اَجِئْتَنَا لِنَعْبُدَ اللّٰهَ وَحْدَهٗ
وَنَذَرَ مَا كَانَ يَعْبُدُ اٰبَآؤُنَا ۚ
فَاْتِنَا بِمَا تَعِدُنَآ
اِنْ كُنْتَ مِنَ الصّٰدِقِيْنَ ○

71. He said: " Punishment
And wrath have already [1041]
Come upon you from your Lord:
Dispute ye with me
Over names which ye [1042]
Have devised—ye
And your fathers,—
Without authority from God?
Then wait: I am
Amongst you, also waiting."

٧١- قَالَ قَدْ وَقَعَ عَلَيْكُم مِّن رَّبِّكُمْ رِجْسٌ
وَّغَضَبٌ ۚ أَتُجَادِلُونَنِي فِي أَسْمَاءٍ سَمَّيْتُمُوهَا
أَنتُمْ وَآبَاؤُكُم
مَّا نَزَّلَ اللَّهُ بِهَا مِن سُلْطَانٍ ۚ فَانتَظِرُوا
إِنِّي مَعَكُم مِّنَ الْمُنتَظِرِينَ ○

72. We saved him and those
Who adhered to him,
By Our Mercy, and We
Cut off the roots of those
Who rejected Our Signs
And did not believe.

٧٢- فَأَنجَيْنَاهُ وَالَّذِينَ مَعَهُ بِرَحْمَةٍ مِّنَّا
وَقَطَعْنَا دَابِرَ الَّذِينَ كَذَّبُوا بِآيَاتِنَا
وَمَا كَانُوا مُؤْمِنِينَ ○

SECTION 10.

73. To the Thamūd people [1043]
(We sent) Ṣāliḥ, one

٧٣- وَإِلَىٰ ثَمُودَ أَخَاهُمْ صَالِحًا

1041. The past tense may be understood in three ways. (1) A terrible famine had already afflicted the 'Ād as a warning before they were overwhelmed in the final blast of hot wind (see the last note). (2) The terrible insolence and sin into which they had fallen was itself a punishment. (3) The prophetic past is used, as much as to say: " Behold! I see a dreadful calamity: it is already on you!"

1042. Why dispute over names and imaginary gods, the inventions of your minds? Come to realities. If you ask for the punishment and are waiting in insolent defiance, what can I do but also wait?—in fear and trembling for you, for I know that God's punishment is sure!

1043. The Thamūd people were the successors to the culture and civilisation of the 'Ād people, for whom see n. 1040 and vii. 65 above. They were cousins to the 'Ād, apparently a younger branch of the same race. Their story also belongs to Arabian tradition, according to which their eponymous ancestor Thamūd was a son of 'Ābir (a brother of Aram), the son of Sām, the son of Noah. Their seat was in the north-west corner of Arabia (Arabia Petræa), between Medina and Syria. It included both rocky country (*ḥijr*, xv. 80), and the spacious fertile valley (Wādī) and plains country of Qurā, which begins just north of the City of Medina and is traversed by the Ḥijāz Railway. When the holy Apostle in the 9th year of the Hijra led his expedition to Tabūk (about 400 miles north of Medina) against the Roman forces, on a reported Roman invasion from Syria, he and his men came across the archæological remains of the Thamūd. The recently excavated rock city of Petra, near Ma'ān, may go back to the Thamūd, though its architecture has many features connecting it with Egyptian and Græco-Roman culture overlaying what is called by European writers Nabatæan culture. Who were the Nabatæans? They were an old Arab tribe which played a considerable part in history after they came into conflict with Antigonus I in 312 B.C. Their capital was Petra, but they extended their territory right up to the Euphrates. In 85 B.C. they were lords of Damascus under their king Ḥāritha (Aretas of Roman history). For some time they were allies of the Roman Empire and held the Red Sea littoral. The Emperor Trajan reduced them and annexed their territory in A.D. 105. The Nabatæans succeeded the Thamūd of Arabian tradition. The Thamūd are mentioned by name in an inscription of the Assyrian King Sargon, dated 715 B.C., as a people of Eastern and Central Arabia (*Encyclopædia of Islam*). See also Appendix IX to S. xxvi.

With the advance of material civilisation, the Thamūd people became godless and arrogant, and were destroyed by an earthquake. Their prophet and warner was Ṣāliḥ, and the crisis in their history is connected with the story of a wonderful she-camel: see next note.

Of their own brethren :
He said : " O my people !
Worship God ; ye have
No other god but Him.
Now hath come unto you
A clear (Sign) from your Lord !
This she-camel of God
Is a Sign unto you :
So leave her to graze
In God's earth, and let her
Come to no harm,
Or ye shall be seized
With a grievous punishment.[1044]

قَالَ يٰقَوْمِ اعْبُدُوا اللّٰهَ
مَا لَكُمْ مِّنْ اِلٰهٍ غَيْرُهٗ
قَدْ جَآءَتْكُمْ بَيِّنَةٌ
مِّنْ رَّبِّكُمْ
هٰذِهٖ نَاقَةُ اللّٰهِ لَكُمْ اٰيَةً
فَذَرُوْهَا تَاْكُلْ فِيْٓ اَرْضِ اللّٰهِ
وَلَا تَمَسُّوْهَا بِسُوْٓءٍ
فَيَاْخُذَكُمْ عَذَابٌ اَلِيْمٌ ○

74. " And remember how He
Made you inheritors
After the 'Ād people
And gave you habitations
In the land : ye build
For yourselves palaces and castles
In (open) plains, and carve out
Homes in the mountains ;
So bring to remembrance
The benefits (ye have received)
From God, and refrain
From evil and mischief
On the earth. "

٧٤- وَاذْكُرُوْٓا اِذْ جَعَلَكُمْ خُلَفَآءَ
مِنْۢ بَعْدِ عَادٍ
وَّبَوَّاَكُمْ فِي الْاَرْضِ
تَتَّخِذُوْنَ مِنْ سُهُوْلِهَا قُصُوْرًا
وَّتَنْحِتُوْنَ الْجِبَالَ بُيُوْتًا
فَاذْكُرُوْٓا اٰلَآءَ اللّٰهِ
وَلَا تَعْثَوْا فِي الْاَرْضِ مُفْسِدِيْنَ ○

75. The leaders of the arrogant
Party among his people said

٧٥- قَالَ الْمَلَاُ الَّذِيْنَ اسْتَكْبَرُوْا

1044. The story of this wonderful she-camel, that was a Sign to the Thamūd, is variously told in tradition. We need not follow the various versions in the traditional story. What we are told in the Qur-ān is: that (1) she was a Sign or Symbol, which the prophet Ṣāliḥ used for a warning to the haughty oppressors of the poor; (2) there was scarcity of water, and the arrogant or privileged classes tried to prevent the access of the poor or their cattle to the springs, while Ṣāliḥ intervened on their behalf (**xxvi**. 155, liv. 28); (3) like water, pasture was considered a free gift of nature, in this spacious earth of God (vii. 73), but the arrogant ones tried to monopolise the pasture also; (4) this particular she-camel was made a test case (liv. 27) to see if the arrogant ones would come to reason; (5) the arrogant ones, instead of yielding to the reasonable rights of the people, ham-strung the poor she-camel and slew her, probably secretly (**x**ci. 14, liv. 29); the cup of their iniquities was full, and the Thamūd people were destroyed by a dreadful earthquake, which threw them prone on the ground and buried them with their houses and their fine buildings.

To those who were reckoned
Powerless—those among them[1045]
Who believed: "Know ye
Indeed that Ṣāliḥ is
An apostle from his Lord?"
They said: "We do indeed
Believe in the revelation[1046]
Which hath been sent
Through him."

مِنْ قَوْمِهِ
لِلَّذِينَ اسْتُضْعِفُوا
لِمَنْ آمَنَ مِنْهُمْ
أَتَعْلَمُونَ أَنَّ صَالِحًا مُرْسَلٌ مِنْ رَبِّهِ
قَالُوا إِنَّا بِمَا أُرْسِلَ بِهِ مُؤْمِنُونَ ۝

76. The arrogant party said:
"For our part, we reject
What ye believe in."

٧٦- قَالَ الَّذِينَ اسْتَكْبَرُوا
إِنَّا بِالَّذِي آمَنْتُمْ بِهِ كَافِرُونَ ۝

77. Then they ham-strung
The she-camel, and insolently
Defied the order of their Lord,
Saying: "O Ṣāliḥ! bring about
Thy threats, if thou art
An apostle (of God)!"

٧٧- فَعَقَرُوا النَّاقَةَ وَعَتَوْا عَنْ أَمْرِ رَبِّهِمْ
وَقَالُوا يَا صَالِحُ ائْتِنَا بِمَا تَعِدُنَا
إِنْ كُنْتَ مِنَ الْمُرْسَلِينَ ۝

78. So the earthquake took them[1047]
Unawares, and they lay
Prostrate in their homes
In the morning!

٧٨- فَأَخَذَتْهُمُ الرَّجْفَةُ
فَأَصْبَحُوا فِي دَارِهِمْ جَاثِمِينَ ۝

1045. As usually happens in such cases, the Believers were the lowly and the humble, and the oppressors were the arrogant, who in selfishly keeping back nature's gifts (which are God's gifts) from the people, were deaf to the dictates of justice and kindness. Ṣālih took the side of the unprivileged, and was therefore himself attacked.

1046. Notice the relation between the question and the answer. The godless chiefs wanted to discredit Ṣāliḥ, and put a personal question, as much as to say, "Is he not a liar?" The Believers took back the issue to the higher plane, as much as to say, "We know he is a man of God, but look at the justice for which he is making a stand: to resist it is to resist God". The answer of the godless was to reject God in words, and in action to commit a further act of cruelty and injustice in ham-stringing and killing the she-camel, at the same time hurling defiance at Ṣāliḥ and his God.

1047. The retribution was not long delayed. A terrible earthquake came and buried the people and destroyed their boasted civilisation. The calamity must have been fairly extensive in area and intense in the terror it inspired, for it is described (liv. 31) as a "single mighty blast" (*ṣaiḥtan wāḥidatan*), the sort of terror-inspiring noise which accompanies all big earthquakes.

79. So Ṣāliḥ left them,[1048]
Saying: "O my people!
I did indeed convey to you
The message for which
I was sent by my Lord:
I gave you good counsel,
But ye love not good counsellors!"

٧٩- فَتَوَلّٰى عَنْهُمْ وَ قَالَ يٰقَوْمِ
لَقَدْ أَبْلَغْتُكُمْ رِسَالَةَ رَبِّي
وَنَصَحْتُ لَكُمْ
وَلٰكِنْ لَّا تُحِبُّوْنَ النّٰصِحِيْنَ ۝

80. We also (sent) Lūṭ:[1049]
He said to his people:
"Do ye commit lewdness
Such as no people
In creation (ever) committed
Before you?

٨٠- وَلُوْطًا إِذْ قَالَ لِقَوْمِهٖ
أَتَأْتُوْنَ الْفَاحِشَةَ مَا سَبَقَكُمْ بِهَا مِنْ
أَحَدٍ مِّنَ الْعٰلَمِيْنَ ۝

81. "For ye practise your lusts
On men in preference
To women: ye are indeed
A people transgressing
Beyond bounds."

٨١- إِنَّكُمْ لَتَأْتُوْنَ الرِّجَالَ شَهْوَةً مِّنْ
دُوْنِ النِّسَآءِ
بَلْ أَنْتُمْ قَوْمٌ مُّسْرِفُوْنَ ۝

82. And his people gave
No answer but this:
They said, "Drive them out
Of your city: these are

٨٢- وَمَا كَانَ جَوَابَ قَوْمِهٖ إِلَّا
أَنْ قَالُوْا أَخْرِجُوْهُمْ مِّنْ قَرْيَتِكُمْ

1048. Ṣāliḥ was saved by God's mercy as a just and righteous man. His speech here may be either a parting warning, or it may be a soliloquy lamenting the destruction of his people for their sin and folly.

1049. Lūṭ is the Lot of the English Bible. His story is biblical, but freed from some shameful features which are a blot on the biblical narrative, (*e.g.*, see Gen. **xix**. 30-36). He was a nephew of Abraham, and was sent as an apostle and warner to the people of Sodom and Gomorrah, cities utterly destroyed for their unspeakable sins. They cannot be exactly located, but it may be supposed that they were somewhere in the plain east of the Dead Sea. The story of their destruction is told in the 19th chapter of Genesis. Two angels in the shape of handsome young men came to Lot in the evening and became his guests by night. The inhabitants of Sodom in their lust for unnatural crime invaded Lot's house but were repulsed. In the morning, the angels warned Lot to escape with his family. "Then the Lord rained upon Sodom and upon Gomorrah brimstone and fire from the Lord out of heaven; and He overthrew those cities, and all the plain, and all the inhabitants of the cities, and that which grew upon the ground. But his wife looked back from behind him, and she became a pillar of salt." (Gen. **xix**. 24-26.)

Note that Lot's people are the people to whom he is sent on a mission. He was not one of their own brethren, as was Ṣāliḥ or Shu'aib. But he looked upon his people as his brethren (*l.* 13), as a man of God always does.

Indeed men who want
To be clean and pure !" [1050]

إِنَّهُمْ أُنَاسٌ يَتَطَهَّرُونَ ۝

83. But we saved him
And his family, except
His wife : she was
Of those who lagged behind [1051]

٨٣- فَأَنجَيْنَاهُ وَأَهْلَهُ إِلَّا امْرَأَتَهُ
كَانَتْ مِنَ الْغَابِرِينَ ۝

84. And we rained down on them
A shower (of brimstone) : [1052]
Then see what was the end
Of those who indulged
In sin and crime !

٨٤- وَأَمْطَرْنَا عَلَيْهِم مَّطَرًا
فَانظُرْ كَيْفَ كَانَ عَاقِبَةُ الْمُجْرِمِينَ ۝ ع

SECTION 11.

85. To the Madyan people [1053]

٨٥- وَإِلَىٰ مَدْيَنَ

1050. An instance of the withering sarcasm that hardened sinners use against the righteous. They wound with words, and follow up the insult with deeds of injustice, thinking that they would bring the righteous into disgrace. But God looks after His own, and in the end, the wicked themselves are overthrown when the cup of their iniquity is full.

1051. In the biblical narrative she looks back, a physical act (see n. 1049) : here she is a type of those who lag behind, *i.e.* whose mental and moral attitude, in spite of their association with the righteous, is to hark back to the glitter of wickedness and sin. The righteous should have one sole objective, the Way of God. They should not look behind, nor yet to the right or the left.

1052. The shower is expressly stated in Q. xi. 82 to have been of stones. In xv. 73-74, we are told that there was a terrible blast or noise (*ṣaiḥat*) in addition to the shower of stones. Taking these passages into consideration along with Gen. xix. 24. (see n. 1049 above), I think it is legitimate to translate : " a shower of brimstone."

1053. "Madyan" may be identified with "Midian." Midian and the Midianites are frequently mentioned in the Old Testament, though the particular incident here mentioned belongs to Arab rather than to Jewish tradition. The Midianites were of Arab race, though, as neighbours of the Canaanites, they probably intermixed with them. They were a wandering tribe; it was Midianite merchants to whom Joseph was sold into slavery, and who took him to Egypt. Their principal territory in the time of Moses was in the north-east of the Sinai Peninsula, and east of the Amalekites. Under Moses the Israelites waged a war of extermination against them : they slew the kings of Midian, slaughtered all the males, burnt their cities and castles, and captured their cattle (Num. xxxi. 7-11). This sounds like total extermination. Yet a few generations afterwards, they were so powerful that the Israelites for their sins were delivered into the captivity of the Midianites for seven years : both the Midianites and their camels were without number : and the Israelites hid from them in "dens....caves, and strongholds" (Judges vii. 1-6). Gideon destroyed them again, (Judges vii. 1-25), say about two centuries after Moses. As the decisive battle was near the hill of Moreh, not far south of Mount Tabor, we may localise the Midianites on this occasion in the northern parts of the Jordan valley, at least 200 miles north of the Sinai Peninsula.

This and the previous destruction under Moses were local, and mention no *town* of Midian. In later times there was a town of Madyan on the east side of the Gulf of 'Aqaba. It is mentioned in Josephus, Eusebius, and Ptolemy : (*Encyclopædia of Islam*). Then it disappears from geography. In Muslim times it was a revived town with quite a different kind of population, but it never flourished. The Midianites disappeared from history.

We sent Shu'aib,[1054] one
Of their own brethren : he said :
" O my people ! worship God ;
Ye have no other god
But Him. Now hath come
Unto you a clear (Sign)
From your Lord ! Give just
Measure and weight, nor withhold
From the people the things
That are their due ; and do
No mischief on the earth
After it has been set
In order : that will be best
For you, if ye have Faith.

86. " And squat not on every road,
Breathing threats, hindering
From the path of God
Those who believe in Him,
And seeking in it
Something crooked ;
But remember how ye were
Little, and He gave you increase.
And hold in your mind's eye
What was the end

أَخَاهُمْ شُعَيْبًا
قَالَ يَٰقَوْمِ اعْبُدُوا اللَّهَ
مَا لَكُم مِّنْ إِلَٰهٍ غَيْرُهُ
قَدْ جَاءَتْكُم بَيِّنَةٌ مِّن رَّبِّكُمْ
فَأَوْفُوا الْكَيْلَ وَالْمِيزَانَ
وَلَا تَبْخَسُوا النَّاسَ أَشْيَاءَهُمْ وَلَا تُفْسِدُوا
فِي الْأَرْضِ بَعْدَ إِصْلَاحِهَا
ذَٰلِكُمْ خَيْرٌ لَّكُمْ إِن كُنتُم مُّؤْمِنِينَ

٨٦- وَلَا تَقْعُدُوا بِكُلِّ صِرَاطٍ تُوعِدُونَ
وَتَصُدُّونَ عَن سَبِيلِ اللَّهِ
مَنْ آمَنَ بِهِ وَتَبْغُونَهَا عِوَجًا
وَاذْكُرُوا إِذْ كُنتُمْ قَلِيلًا فَكَثَّرَكُمْ
وَانظُرُوا كَيْفَ كَانَ عَاقِبَةُ

1054. Shu'aib belongs to Arab rather than to Jewish tradition, to which he is unknown. His identification with Jethro, the father-in-law of Moses, has no warrant, and I reject it. There is no similarity either in names or incidents, and there are chronological difficulties (see n. 1064 below). If, as the Commentators tell us, Shu'aib was in the fourth generation from Abraham, being a great-grandson of Madyan (a son of Abraham), he would be only about a century from the time of Abraham, whereas the Hebrew Bible would give us a period of four to six centuries between Abraham and Moses. The mere fact that Jethro was a Midianite and that another name, Hobab, is mentioned for a father-in-law of Moses in Num. x. 29, is slender ground for identification. As the Midianites were mainly a nomad tribe, we need not be surprised that their destruction in one or two settlements did not affect their life in wandering sections of the tribe in other geographical regions. Shu'aib's mission was apparently in one of the settled towns of the Midianites, which was completely destroyed by an earthquake (vii. 91). If this happened in the century after Abraham, their is no difficulty in supposing that they were again a numerous tribe three or five centuries later, in the time of Moses (see last note). As they were a mixed wandering tribe, both their resilience and their eventual absorption can be easily understood. But the destruction of the settlement or settlements (if the Wood or Aika was a separate settlement, see n. 2000 to xv. 78) to which Shu'aib was sent to preach was complete, and no traces of it now remain.

The name of the highest mountain of Yemen, Nabi Shu'aib (11,000 ft.) has probably no connection with the geographical territory of the nomad Midianites, unless we suppose that their wanderings extended so far south from the territories mentioned in the last note.

Of those who did mischief.[1055]

87. "And if there is a party
Among you who believes
In the Message with which
I have been sent, and a party
Which does not believe,[1056]
Hold yourselves in patience
Until God doth decide
8 Between us: for He
30 Is the best to decide."[1057]

الْمُفْسِدِيْنَ ○

٨٧- وَإِنْ كَانَ طَآئِفَةٌ مِّنْكُمْ اٰمَنُوْا
بِالَّذِيْٓ أُرْسِلْتُ بِهٖ
وَطَآئِفَةٌ لَّمْ يُؤْمِنُوْا
فَاصْبِرُوْا حَتّٰى يَحْكُمَ اللّٰهُ بَيْنَنَا ۚ
وَهُوَ خَيْرُ الْحٰكِمِيْنَ ○

1055. The Midianites were in the path of a commercial highway of Asia, *viz.*, that between two such opulent and highly organised nations as Egypt and the Mesopotamian group comprising Assyria and Babylonia. Their besetting sins are thus characterised here: (1) giving short measure or weight, whereas the strictest commercial probity is necessary for success, (2) a more general form of such fraud, depriving people of rightful dues, (3) producing mischief and disorder, where peace and order had been established (again in a literal as well as a metaphorical sense); (4) not content with upsetting settled life, taking to highway robbery, literally as well as (5) metaphorically, in two ways, *viz.*, cutting off people from access to the worship of God, and abusing religion and piety for crooked purposes, *i.e.*, exploiting religion itself for their crooked ends, as when a man builds houses of prayer out of unlawful gains or ostentatiously gives charity out of money which he has obtained by force or fraud, etc. After setting out this catalogue of besetting sins Shu'aib makes two appeals to the past: (1) You began as an insignificant tribe, and by God's favour you increased and multiplied in numbers and resources; do you not then owe a duty to God to fulfil His Law? (2) What was the result in the case of those who fell into sin? Will you not take warning by their example?

So Shu'aib began his argument with faith in God as the source of all virtue, and ended it with destruction as the result of all sin. In the next verse he pleads with them to end their controversies and come to God.

1056. Madyan is torn by internal conflict. Shu'aib comes as a peace-maker, not in virtue of his own wisdom, but by an appeal to the truth, righteousness and justice of God. As we see later, the real motives of his opponents were selfishness, arrogance, violence, lawlessness, and injustice. But he appeals to their better nature, and is prepared to argue on the basis that the party which wants to suppress those who believe in God's Message and in righteousness, has some sincere mental difficulty in accepting Shu'aib's mission. "If," he says to them, "that is the case, do you think it justifies your intolerance, your violence, or your persecution? On the contrary, events will prove by themselves who is right and who is wrong." To the small band who believe in his mission and follow his teaching, he would preach patience and perseverance. His argument to them would be: "You have faith; surely your faith is strong enough to sustain you in the hope that God's truth will triumph in the end; there is no cause for despair or dejection."

How exactly these past experiences fit the times of our holy guide Muḥammad! And it is for that analogy and that lesson that the stories of Noah, Hūd, Sāliḥ, Lūṭ, and Shu'aib are related to us,—all different, and yet all pointing to the great lessons in Muhammad's life.

1057. See the argument in the last note. God's decision may come partly in this very life, either for the same generation or for succeeding generations, by the logic of external events. But in any case it is bound to come spiritually on a higher plane eventually, when the righteous will be comforted and the sinners will be convinced of sin from their own inner conviction.

88. The leaders, the arrogant
Party among his people, said :[1058]
" O Shu'aib ! we shall
Certainly drive thee out
Of our city—(thee) and those
Who believe with thee ;
Or else ye (thou and they)
Shall have to return
To our ways and religion."
He said : " What ! even
Though we do detest (them) ?

٨٨- قَالَ الْمَلَأُ الَّذِينَ اسْتَكْبَرُوا
مِن قَوْمِهِ لَنُخْرِجَنَّكَ يَٰشُعَيْبُ
وَالَّذِينَ آمَنُوا مَعَكَ
مِن قَرْيَتِنَا
أَوْ لَتَعُودُنَّ فِي مِلَّتِنَا ۚ
قَالَ أَوَلَوْ كُنَّا كَارِهِينَ ۝

89. " We should indeed invent[1059]
A lie against God,
If we returned to your ways
After God hath rescued
Us therefrom ; nor could we
By any manner of means
Return thereto unless it be
As in the will and plan of God,[1060]
Our Lord. Our Lord
Can reach out to the utmost
Recesses of things by His
knowledge.
In God is our trust.
Our Lord ! Decide thou[1061]
Between us and our people

٨٩- قَدِ افْتَرَيْنَا عَلَى اللَّهِ كَذِبًا
إِنْ عُدْنَا فِي مِلَّتِكُم
بَعْدَ إِذْ نَجَّانَا اللَّهُ مِنْهَا ۚ
وَمَا يَكُونُ لَنَا أَن نَّعُودَ فِيهَا
إِلَّا أَن يَشَاءَ اللَّهُ رَبُّنَا ۚ
وَسِعَ رَبُّنَا كُلَّ شَيْءٍ عِلْمًا ۚ
عَلَى اللَّهِ تَوَكَّلْنَا ۚ
رَبَّنَا افْتَحْ بَيْنَنَا وَبَيْنَ قَوْمِنَا

1058. The gentle, all-persuasive arguments of Shu'aib fell on hard hearts. Their only reply was : " Turn him out!—him and his people." When courtesy and a plea for toleration are pitted against bigotry, what room is there for logic ? But bigotry and unrighteousness have their own crooked ways of pretending to be tolerant. " O yes ! " they said, " we are very tolerant and long-suffering ! But we are for our country and religion. Come back to the ways of our fathers, and we shall graciously forgive you ! " " Ways of their fathers ! "—they meant injustice and oppression, high-handedness to the poor and the weak, fraud under cover of religion, and so on ! Perhaps the righteous were the poor and the weak. Were they likely to love such ways ? Perhaps there was implied a bribe as well as a threat. " If you come back and wink at our iniquities, you shall have scraps of prosperity thrown at you. If not, out you go in disgrace ! "

1059. The answer of the righteous is threefold. (1) " Coming back is all very well. But do you mean that we should practise the vices we detest ? " (2) " You want us to lie against our conscience and our God, after we have seen the evil of your ways." (3) " Neither bribes nor threats, nor specious appeals to patriotism or ancestral religion can move us : the matter rests with God, Whose will and pleasure we obey, and on Whom alone we rely. His knowledge will search out all your specious pretences."

1060. This, of course, does not mean that any one can ever return to evil ways with God's consent. Shu'aib has already emphatically repudiated the idea of returning " to your ways after God hath rescued us therefrom." But even if their ways had been good, the human will, he goes on to say, has no data to rely upon, and he and his followers would only be guided by God's Will and Plan.

1061. Having answered the insincere quibblers among the godless, the righteous turn to God in earnest prayer. The endless controversies in this world about abstract or speculative things never end even where both sides are sincere in their beliefs. The decision must be taken to God, Who sits on the throne of Truth, and Whose decisions will, therefore, be free from the errors and imperfections of all human judgment. The sincere have nothing to fear in the appeal to Him, as their motives are pure.

In truth, for thou
Art the best to decide."

بِالْحَقِّ وَأَنتَ خَيْرُ الْفَاتِحِينَ ○

90. The leaders, the Unbelievers
Among his people, said :
" If ye follow Shu'aib,
Be sure then ye are ruined ! "[1062]

٩٠- وَقَالَ الْمَلَأُ الَّذِينَ كَفَرُوا مِن قَوْمِهِ
لَئِنِ اتَّبَعْتُمْ شُعَيْبًا إِنَّكُمْ إِذًا لَّخَاسِرُونَ ○

91. But the earthquake took them
Unawares, and they lay
Prostrate in their homes
Before the morning ![1063]

٩١- فَأَخَذَتْهُمُ الرَّجْفَةُ
فَأَصْبَحُوا فِي دَارِهِمْ جَاثِمِينَ ○ ع

92. The men who rejected
Shu'aib became as if
They had never been
In the homes where they
Had flourished : the men
Who rejected Shu'aib—
It was they who were ruined !

٩٢- الَّذِينَ كَذَّبُوا شُعَيْبًا
كَأَن لَّمْ يَغْنَوْا فِيهَا
الَّذِينَ كَذَّبُوا شُعَيْبًا
كَانُوا هُمُ الْخَاسِرِينَ ○

93. So Shu'aib left them,
Saying : " O my people !
I did indeed convey to you
The Messages for which
I was sent by my Lord :
I gave you good counsel,
But how shall I lament

٩٣- فَتَوَلَّىٰ عَنْهُمْ
وَقَالَ يَا قَوْمِ لَقَدْ أَبْلَغْتُكُمْ
رِسَالَاتِ رَبِّي وَنَصَحْتُ لَكُمْ
فَكَيْفَ آسَىٰ

1062. The answer of the Unbelievers is characteristic. As all their bribes and subtleties have failed, they resort to threats, which are worse than the argument of the stick. "All right," they say, "there is nothing but ruin before you !" That means that the Believers will be persecuted, held up to obloquy, ostracised, and prevented from access to all means of honourable livelihood ; their families and dependants will be insulted, reviled, and tortured, if they could but be got into the enemy's power ; their homes destroyed, and their names held up to ridicule and contempt even when they are gone. But, as verse 92 says, their wicked designs recoiled on themselves : it was the wicked who were ruined and blotted out.

1063. The fate of the Madyan people is described in the same terms as that of the Thamūd in verse 78 above. An earthquake seized them by night, and they were buried in their own homes, no longer to vex God's earth. But a supplementary detail is mentioned in xxvi. 189, "the punishment of a day of overshadowing gloom," which may be understood to mean a shower of ashes and cinders accompanying a volcanic eruption. Thus a day of terror drove them into their homes, and the earthquake finished them. The lament of Shu'aib in verse 93 is almost the same as that of Ṣāliḥ in verse 79, with two differences : (1) Shu'aib's messages attacked the many sins of his people (see n. 1055) and are, therefore, expressed in the plural, while Ṣāliḥ's fight was chiefly against selfish arrogance, and his message is expressed in the singular ; (2) the Thamūd were the more cultured people of the two, and perished in their own pride ; as Ṣāliḥ said, "ye love not good counsellors" ; the Midianites were a rougher people, and their minds were less receptive of argument or faith ; as Shu'aib said, they were a people who " refused to believe."

Over a people who refuse
To believe !" [1064]

عَلٰى قَوْمٍ كٰفِرِيْنَ ۝ ع

SECTION 12.

94. Whenever We sent a prophet
To a town, We took up
Its people in suffering
And adversity, in order
That they might learn humility. [1065]

٩٤- وَمَآ اَرْسَلْنَا فِيْ قَرْيَةٍ مِّنْ نَّبِيٍّ
اِلَّآ اَخَذْنَآ اَهْلَهَا بِالْبَاْسَآءِ
وَالضَّرَّآءِ لَعَلَّهُمْ يَضَّرَّعُوْنَ ۝

95. Then We changed their suffering
Into prosperity, until they grew [1066]
And multiplied, and began
To say: "Our fathers (too)
Were touched by suffering
And affluence ".... Behold !
We called them to account
Of a sudden, while they
Realised not (their peril).

٩٥- ثُمَّ بَدَّلْنَا مَكَانَ السَّيِّئَةِ الْحَسَنَةَ
حَتّٰى عَفَوْا
وَّ قَالُوْا قَدْ مَسَّ اٰبَآءَنَا الضَّرَّآءُ
وَالسَّرَّآءُ فَاَخَذْنٰهُمْ بَغْتَةً
وَّهُمْ لَا يَشْعُرُوْنَ ۝

96. If the people of the towns
Had but believed and feared
God, We should indeed
Have opened out to them

٩٦- وَلَوْ اَنَّ اَهْلَ الْقُرٰٓى اٰمَنُوْا وَاتَّقَوْا
لَفَتَحْنَا عَلَيْهِمْ

1064. Can we get any idea of the chronological place of the destruction of the Midianites? In n. 1053 (vii. 85) we have discussed the geographical aspects. The following considerations will help us in getting some idea of their period. (1) The stories of Noah, Hūd, Ṣāliḥ Lūṭ, and Shu'aib seem to be in chronological order. Therefore Shu'aib came after Abraham, whose nephew Lūṭ was. (2) If Shu'aib was in the fourth generation from Abraham, (see n. 1590 to xi. 89), it would be impossible for him to have been a contemporary of Moses, who came many centuries later. This difficulty is recognised by Ibn Kat͟hīr and other classical commentators. (3) The identification of Shu'aib with Jethro the father-in-law of Moses is without warrant; see n. 1054 (vii. 85). (4) Shu'aib must have been before Moses; see vii. 103. (5) The Midianites who were destroyed by Moses and by Gideon after him (n. 1053) were local remnants, as we may speak of the Jews at the present day; but their existence as a nation in their original home-lands seems to have ended before Moses: "they became as if they had never been in the homes where they had flourished" (vii. 92). (6) Josephus, Eusebius, and Ptolemy mention a town of Madyan, but it was not of any importance (n. 1053). (7) After the first centuries of the Christian era Madyan as a town appears as an unimportant place resting on its past.

1065. Man was originally created pure. The need of a prophet arises when there is some corruption and iniquity, which he is sent to combat. His coming means much trial and suffering, especially to those who join him in his protest against wrong. Even so peaceful a prophet as Jesus said: "I came not to send peace but a sword" (Matt. x. 34). But it is all in God's Plan, for we must learn humility if we would be worthy of Him.

1066. God gives enough rope to the sinful. They grow and multiply, and become scornful. Neither suffering nor affluence teaches them the lessons which they are meant to learn, *viz.* patience and humility, gratitude and kindness to others. They take adversity and prosperity alike as a matter of chance. "O yes!" they say, "such things have happened in all ages! Our fathers had such experience before us, and our sons will have them after us. Thus goes on the world for all time!" But does it? What about the Plan of the Architect? They are found napping when Nemesis overtakes them in the midst of their impious tomfoolery!

(All kinds of) blessings
From heaven and earth;
But they rejected (the truth),
And We brought them
To book for their misdeeds.

بَرَكٰتٍ مِّنَ السَّمَآءِ وَالْاَرْضِ
وَلٰكِنْ كَذَّبُوْا
فَاَخَذْنٰهُمْ بِمَا كَانُوْا يَكْسِبُوْنَ ○

97. Did the people of the towns
Feel secure against the coming [1067]
Of Our wrath by night
While they were asleep?

٩٧- اَفَاَمِنَ اَهْلُ الْقُرٰٓى اَنْ يَّاْتِيَهُمْ
بَاْسُنَا بَيَاتًا وَّهُمْ نَآئِمُوْنَ ○

98. Or else did they feel
Secure against its coming
In broad daylight while they
Played about (care-free)?

٩٨- اَوَاَمِنَ اَهْلُ الْقُرٰٓى اَنْ يَّاْتِيَهُمْ
بَاْسُنَا ضُحًى وَّهُمْ يَلْعَبُوْنَ ○

99. Did they then feel secure
Against the Plan of God?—
But no one can feel
Secure from the Plan
Of God, except those
(Doomed) to ruin! [1068]

٩٩- اَفَاَمِنُوْا مَكْرَ اللّٰهِ ج
فَلَا يَاْمَنُ مَكْرَ اللّٰهِ
اِلَّا الْقَوْمُ الْخٰسِرُوْنَ ○ ع

C. 86.—While the story of the prophets who preached
(vii. 100-157.) In vain to their people pre-figures
The struggles in the early careers
Of all apostles, the story of Moses,—
His struggles, with an alien and arrogant
People, his final deliverance
Of his people from foreign domination,
And his leading them within sight
Of the Promised Land, in spite
Of the forces that resisted,—pre-figures
The early struggles and eventual triumph
Of Muḥammad the Holy Apostle of God.

1067. This and the two following verses should be read together. They furnish a commentary on the story of the five prophets that has already been related. God's wrath may come by night or by day, whether people are arrogantly defying God's laws or are sunk in lethargy or vain dreams of unreality. Who can escape God's Plan, and who can feel themselves outside it except those who are seeking their own ruin?

1068. This closes that chapter of the narrative which deals with apostles who were rejected by their own people, but who stood firm on God's message and were able to rescue a remnant who believed. In each case there were special circumstances and special besetting sins, which have been explained in the notes. The nations which as a body could not be won over to God's Law perished. So far we have been dealing with the corruptions and iniquities within each nation. In the story of Moses we have first a struggle against the bondage of Egypt, one of the foremost powers then in the world, the rescue of the Israelites and their wanderings, and their proving themselves unworthy and being left to wander in a new sense when they rejected the new Prophet (Muḥammad) who came to renew God's Message.

Section 13.

100. To those who inherit
The earth in succession
To its (previous) possessors,
Is it not a guiding (lesson)
That, if We so willed,
We could punish them (too)
For their sins, and seal up
Their hearts so that they
Could not hear? [1069]

١٠٠- أَوَلَمْ يَهْدِ لِلَّذِينَ يَرِثُونَ الْأَرْضَ
مِنْ بَعْدِ أَهْلِهَا
أَنْ لَوْ نَشَاءُ أَصَبْنَاهُمْ بِذُنُوبِهِمْ ۚ
وَنَطْبَعُ عَلَىٰ قُلُوبِهِمْ
فَهُمْ لَا يَسْمَعُونَ ○

101. Such were the towns
Whose story We (thus)
Relate unto thee:
There came indeed to them
Their apostles with clear (Signs):
But they would not believe
What they had rejected before.[1070]
Thus doth God seal up
The hearts of those
Who reject Faith.

١٠١- تِلْكَ الْقُرَىٰ
نَقُصُّ عَلَيْكَ مِنْ أَنْبَائِهَا ۚ
وَلَقَدْ جَاءَتْهُمْ رُسُلُهُمْ بِالْبَيِّنَاتِ ۚ
فَمَا كَانُوا لِيُؤْمِنُوا بِمَا كَذَّبُوا مِنْ قَبْلُ ۚ
كَذَٰلِكَ يَطْبَعُ اللَّهُ
عَلَىٰ قُلُوبِ الْكَافِرِينَ ○

102. Most of them We found not
Men (true) to their covenant:
But most of them We found
Rebellious and disobedient.

١٠٢- وَمَا وَجَدْنَا لِأَكْثَرِهِمْ مِنْ عَهْدٍ ۚ
وَإِنْ وَجَدْنَا أَكْثَرَهُمْ لَفَاسِقِينَ ○

103. Then after them We sent
Moses with Our Signs
To Pharaoh and his chiefs,
But they wrongfully rejected
them:
So see what was the end
Of those who made mischief.

١٠٣- ثُمَّ بَعَثْنَا مِنْ بَعْدِهِمْ مُوسَىٰ بِآيَاتِنَا
إِلَىٰ فِرْعَوْنَ وَمَلَئِهِ
فَظَلَمُوا بِهَا ۚ
فَانْظُرْ كَيْفَ كَانَ عَاقِبَةُ الْمُفْسِدِينَ ○

1069. The stories which have been related should give a warning to present and future generations which have inherited the land, the power, or the experience of the past. They should know that if they fall into the same sins they will meet with the same fate: when through their contumacy their hearts are hardened, they do not listen to the advice that falls on their ears.

1070. Those who have heard the Message and rejected it find it more difficult afterwards to retrace their steps. Evil has blocked the channels of God's grace to them. It begins with their breaking their Covenant with God; with each step afterwards they fall deeper and deeper into the mire.

104. Moses [1071] said: "O Pharaoh! [1072] I am an apostle from The Lord of the Worlds,—	١٠٤- وَقَالَ مُوسَىٰ يَٰفِرْعَوْنُ إِنِّي رَسُولٌ مِّن رَّبِّ الْعَٰلَمِينَ ۝
105. One for whom it is right To say nothing but truth About God. Now have I Come unto you (people), from [1073] Your Lord, with a clear (Sign): So let the Children of Israel Depart along with me."	١٠٥- حَقِيقٌ عَلَىٰٓ أَن لَّآ أَقُولَ عَلَى اللَّهِ إِلَّا الْحَقَّ ۚ قَدْ جِئْتُكُم بِبَيِّنَةٍ مِّن رَّبِّكُمْ فَأَرْسِلْ مَعِيَ بَنِيٓ إِسْرَٰٓءِيلَ ۝
106. (Pharaoh) said: "If indeed Thou hast come with a Sign,	١٠٦- قَالَ إِن كُنتَ جِئْتَ بِـَٔايَةٍ

1071. The story of Moses is told in many places in the Holy Qur-ān, with a special lesson in each context. In ii. 49-71, the story is an appeal to the Jews from their own scripture and traditions, to show their true place in the religious history of mankind, and how they forfeited it. Here we have an instructive parallelism in that story to the story of Muḥammad's mission,—how both these men of God had to fight against (1) a foreign foe, arrogant, unjust, faithless, and superstitious, and (2) against the same class of internal foe among their own people. Both of them won through In the case of Moses, the foreign foe was Pharaoh and his Egyptians, who boasted of their earlier and superior civilisation; in the case of the Prophet Muḥammad the foreign foes were the Jews themselves and the Christians of his day. Moses led his people nearly to the Land of promise in spite of rebellions among his own people; Muḥammad succeeded completely in overcoming the resistance of his own people by his own virtues and firmness of character, and by the guidance of God. What was a hope when these Meccan verses were revealed became an accomplishment before the end of his life and mission on earth.

1072. "Pharaoh" (Arabic, *Fir'aun*) is a dynastic title, not the name of any particular king in Egypt. It has been traced to the ancient Hieroglyphic words, *Per-āa*, which mean "Great House." The *nūn* is an "infirm" letter added in the process of Arabisation. Who was the Pharaoh in the story of Moses? If the Inscriptions had helped us, we could have answered with some confidence, but unfortunately the Inscriptions fail us. It is probable that it was an early Pharaoh of the XVIIIth Dynasty, say Thothmes I, about 1540 B.C. See appendix IV, on Egyptian Chronology and Israel, printed at the end of this Sūra.

1073. Notice that Moses, in addressing Pharaoh and the Egyptians, claims his mission to be not from *his* God, or *his people's* God but from "*your* Lord," from "the Lord of the Worlds." And his mission is not to *his* people only: "I come unto *you* (Egyptian people) from *your* Lord." The spirit of our version is entirely different from the spirit of the same story as told in the Old Testament (Exod. chapters i. to xv.). In Exod. iii. 18, the mission of Moses is expressed to be as from "the Lord God of the Hebrews."

The essence of the whole Islamic story is this. Joseph's sufferings and good fortune were not merely a story in a romance Joseph was a prophet; his sufferings and his subsequent rise to power and position in Egypt were to be a lesson (*a*) to his wicked brothers who sold him into slavery, (*b*) to his people who were stricken with famine and found a welcome in Egypt, and (*c*) to the Egyptians, who were arrogant over their high material civilisation, but had yet to be taught the pure faith of Abraham. Israel prospered in Egypt, and stayed there perhaps two to four centuries. (Renan allows only one century.) Times changed, and the racial bigotry of the Egyptians showed its head again, and Israel was oppressed. Moses was raised up with a threefold mission again (*a*) to learn all the learning of the Egyptians and preach God's Truth to them as one who had been brought up among themselves, (*b*) to unite and reclaim his own people, and (*c*) to rescue them and lead them to a new world, which was to open out their spiritual horizon and lead them to the Psalms of David and the glories of Solomon.

Show it forth,—
If thou tellest the truth." [1074]

فَأْتِ بِهَآ إِن كُنتَ مِنَ ٱلصَّٰدِقِينَ

107. Then (Moses) threw his rod,
And behold! it was
A serpent, plain (for all to see)! [1075]

١٠٧- فَأَلْقَىٰ عَصَاهُ
فَإِذَا هِىَ ثُعْبَانٌ مُّبِينٌ

108. And he drew out his hand,
And behold! it was white
To all beholders! [1076]

١٠٨- وَنَزَعَ يَدَهُۥ
فَإِذَا هِىَ بَيْضَآءُ لِلنَّٰظِرِينَ

SECTION 14.

109. Said the Chiefs of the people
Of Pharaoh: "This is indeed
A sorcerer well-versed.

١٠٩- قَالَ ٱلْمَلَأُ مِن قَوْمِ فِرْعَوْنَ
إِنَّ هَٰذَا لَسَٰحِرٌ عَلِيمٌ

110. "His plan is to get you out
Of your land: then
What is it ye counsel?" [1077]

١١٠- يُرِيدُ أَن يُخْرِجَكُم مِّنْ أَرْضِكُمْ
فَمَاذَا تَأْمُرُونَ

1074. The ensuing dialogue shows the psychology on the two sides. Pharaoh is sitting in his Darbar, with his ministers and chiefs around him. In their arrogance they are only amused at the effrontery and apparent revolt of the Israelite leaders, and they rely upon their own superior worldly power, aided by the magic which was a part of the Egyptian religion. Confronting them stand two men, Moses with his mission from God, and his brother Aaron who was his lieutenant. They are confident, not in their own powers, but in the mission they had received. The first thing they have to do is to act on the subjective mind of the Egyptians, and by methods which by God's miracle show that Egyptian magic was nothing before the true power of God.

1075. The serpent played a large part in Egyptian mythology. The great sun-god Ra won a great victory over the serpent Apophis, typifying the victory of light over darkness. Many of their gods and goddesses took the forms of snakes to impress their foes with terror. Moses's rod as a type of a serpent at once appealed to the Egyptian mentality. The contempt which the Egyptians had entertained in their minds before was converted into terror. Here was some one who could control the reptile which their great god Ra himself had such difficulty in overcoming!

1076. But the second Sign displayed by Moses was even more puzzling to the Egyptians. Moses drew out his hand from the folds of the garments on his breast, and it was white and shining as with divine light! This was to counter any suggestions of evil, which the serpent might have created. This was no work of evil,—of black magic, or a trick or illusion. His hand was transfigured—with a light which no Egyptian sorcerers could produce. In Islam the "white hand" of Moses has passed into a proverb, for a symbol of divine glory dazzling to the beholders.

1077. The two Signs had the desired effect on the Egyptians. They were impressed, but they judged them by their own standards. They thought to themselves, "These are ordinary sorcerers: let us search out our best sorcerers and show them that they have superior power." But like all worldly people, they began to fear for their own power and possessions. It was far from Moses's intention to drive out the Egyptians from their own land. He merely wanted to end the Egyptian oppression. But the Egyptians had a guilty conscience, and they judged other people's motives by their own. They discussed the matter in Council on quite wrong premises.

111. They said: "Keep him
And his brother in suspense
(For a while); and send
To the cities men to collect—

١١١- قَالُوٓا أَرْجِهْ وَأَخَاهُ
وَأَرْسِلْ فِي الْمَدَآئِنِ حٰشِرِينَ ○

112. And bring up to thee
All (our) sorcerers well-versed." [1078]

١١٢- يَأْتُوكَ بِكُلِّ سٰحِرٍ عَلِيمٍ ○

113. So there came
The sorcerers to Pharaoh:
They said, "Of course
We shall have a (suitable)
Reward if we win!" [1079]

١١٣- وَجَآءَ السَّحَرَةُ فِرْعَوْنَ
قَالُوٓا إِنَّ لَنَا لَأَجْرًا
إِنْ كُنَّا نَحْنُ الْغٰلِبِينَ ○

114. He said: "Yea, (and more),—
For ye shall in that case
Be (raised to posts)
Nearest (to my person)."

١١٤- قَالَ نَعَمْ
وَإِنَّكُمْ لَمِنَ الْمُقَرَّبِينَ ○

115. They said: "O Moses!
Wilt thou throw (first),
Or shall we have
The (first) throw?"

١١٥- قَالُوا يٰمُوسٰىٓ إِمَّآ أَنْ تُلْقِيَ
وَإِمَّآ أَنْ نَّكُونَ نَحْنُ الْمُلْقِينَ ○

116. Said Moses: "Throw ye (first)."
So when they threw,
They bewitched the eyes
Of the people, and struck
Terror into them: for they
Showed a great (feat of) magic. [1080]

١١٦- قَالَ أَلْقُوا
فَلَمَّآ أَلْقَوْا سَحَرُوٓا أَعْيُنَ النَّاسِ
وَاسْتَرْهَبُوهُمْ وَجَآءُو بِسِحْرٍ عَظِيمٍ ○

1078. The advice of the Council to Pharaoh shows a misreading of the situation. They were in a panic about what the magic of this evidently powerful sorcerer could do against them. So they advised the Pharaoh to summon their most powerful sorcerers from all over the country, and in the meantime to hold Moses and Aaron in suspense, —neither to yield to them nor definitely to oppose them. The men of God could well afford to wait. Time is always in favour of Truth.

1079. The most noted sorcerers of Pharaoh came. Their art was built up on trickery and imposture, and the first thing they could think of was to make a selfish bargain for themselves. The Pharaoh and his Council would in their present state of panic agree to anything. And so they did. Pharaoh not only promised them any rewards they desired if they foiled the strange power of these men, but he also promised them the highest dignities round his own person. And so the contest begins, with due observance of the amenities observed by combatants before they come to close grips.

1080. Moses and his brother Aaron were pitted against the most skilful magic-men of Egypt, but they were calm and confident and let the magic-men have their innings first. As is usual in this world, the magicians' trickery made a great impression on the people, but when Moses threw his rod, the illusion was broken, and the falsehood was all shown up. In the Old Testament story (Exod. vii. 10-12) it was Aaron that threw the rod, and he threw it before the magicians. Aaron's rod became a serpent. Then the magicians threw their rods, and they became serpents, but Aaron's rod swallowed up their rods. The story given to us is more dramatic and less literal. We are told in general terms that Moses first allowed the magic-men to play their tricks. The rod of Moses was the symbol of his authority. It must have been a simple shepherd's crook with which he used to feed his flocks. With God's grace behind him, he was able to expose all false trickery and establish the Truth.

117. We put it into Moses's mind
By inspiration : " Throw (now)
Thy rod " : and behold !
It swallows up straightway
All the falsehoods
Which they fake !

١١٧- وَأَوْحَيْنَآ إِلَىٰ مُوسَىٰٓ
أَنْ أَلْقِ عَصَاكَ
فَإِذَا هِىَ تَلْقَفُ مَا يَأْفِكُونَ ۝

118. Thus truth was confirmed,
And all that they did
Was made of no effect.

١١٨- فَوَقَعَ الْحَقُّ
وَبَطَلَ مَا كَانُوا يَعْمَلُونَ ۝

119. So the (great ones) were vanquished
There and then, and were
Made to look small.[1081]

١١٩- فَغُلِبُوا هُنَالِكَ
وَانْقَلَبُوا صٰغِرِينَ ۝

120. But the sorcerers fell down
Prostrate in adoration.

١٢٠- وَأُلْقِىَ السَّحَرَةُ سٰجِدِينَ ۝

121. Saying : " We believe
In the Lord of the Worlds, –

١٢١- قَالُوٓا ءَامَنَّا بِرَبِّ الْعٰلَمِينَ ۝

122. " The Lord of Moses and Aaron."

١٢٢- رَبِّ مُوسَىٰ وَهٰرُونَ ۝

123. Said Pharaoh : " Believe ye
In Him before I give
You permission ? Surely
This is a trick which ye
Have planned in the City
To drive out its people :
But soon shall ye know
(The consequences).[1082]

١٢٣- قَالَ فِرْعَوْنُ ءَامَنتُم بِهِۦ
قَبْلَ أَنْ ءَاذَنَ لَكُمْ إِنَّ هٰذَا لَمَكْرٌ
مَّكَرْتُمُوهُ فِى الْمَدِينَةِ
لِتُخْرِجُوا مِنْهَآ أَهْلَهَا فَسَوْفَ تَعْلَمُونَ ۝

1081. The proud ones of the Court—Pharaoh and his chiefs—were hard-hearted, and the exposure of the imposture only made them wreak their rage on those whom they could reach. On the other hand the effect on the humbler ones—those who had been made the dupes and instruments of the imposture—was quite different. Their conscience was awakened. They fell down to the ground in adoration of the Lord of the Worlds, and confessed their faith.

1082. Pharaoh and his Court were doubly angry : first because they were made to look small when confronted by the power of God, and secondly, because their dupes and instruments were snatched away from them. These men, the sorcerers, at once recognised the Signs of God, and in their case the mission of Moses and Aaron was fulfilled. They turned back on their past life of imposture, make-believe, false worship, and oppression of the weak, and confessed the One true God. As usually happens, hardened sinners resent all the more the saving of any of their companions from sin and error. Judging other people's motives by their own, they accuse them of duplicity, and if they have the power, they take cruel revenge. Here the Pharaoh threatens the repentant sinners with the extreme punishment for treason and apostasy (cutting off of hands and feet, combined with an ignominious death on the cross, as in the case of the worst malefactors). But they remained firm, and prayed to God for patience and constancy. Probably their influence spread quietly in the commonalty. Ultimately it appeared on the Throne itself, in the person of Amenophis IV about five or six generations afterwards. See Appendix V, on Egyptian Religion, printed at the end of this Sūra.

124. "Be sure I will cut off
Your hands and your feet
On opposite sides, and I
Will cause you all
To die on the cross."

١٢٤- لَاُقَطِّعَنَّ اَيْدِيَكُمْ وَاَرْجُلَكُمْ
مِّنْ خِلَافٍ
ثُمَّ لَاُصَلِّبَنَّكُمْ اَجْمَعِيْنَ ○

125. They said: "For us,
We are but sent back
Unto our Lord:

١٢٥- قَالُوْٓا
اِنَّآ اِلٰى رَبِّنَا مُنْقَلِبُوْنَ ○

126. "But thou dost wreak
Thy vengeance on us
Simply because we believed
In the Signs of our Lord
When they reached us!
Our Lord! pour out on us
Patience and constancy, and take
Our souls unto Thee
As Muslims (who bow
To Thy Will)![1083]

١٢٦- وَمَا تَنْقِمُ مِنَّآ
اِلَّآ اَنْ اٰمَنَّا بِاٰيٰتِ رَبِّنَا
لَمَّا جَآءَتْنَا ؕ
رَبَّنَآ اَفْرِغْ عَلَيْنَا صَبْرًا
وَّتَوَفَّنَا مُسْلِمِيْنَ ○

SECTION 15.

127. Said the chiefs of Pharaoh's
People: "Wilt thou leave
Moses and his people,
To spread mischief in the land,
And to abandon thee
And thy gods?" He said:
"Their male children will we
Slay; (only) their females
Will we save alive;
And we have over them

١٢٧- وَقَالَ الْمَلَاُ مِنْ قَوْمِ فِرْعَوْنَ
اَتَذَرُ مُوْسٰى وَقَوْمَهٗ لِيُفْسِدُوْا فِى الْاَرْضِ
وَيَذَرَكَ وَاٰلِهَتَكَ ؕ
قَالَ سَنُقَتِّلُ اَبْنَآءَهُمْ
وَنَسْتَحْىٖ نِسَآءَهُمْ ۚ وَاِنَّا فَوْقَهُمْ

1083. These Egyptians, by their patience and constancy, show that their repentance was true. Thus in their case the mission of Moses was fulfilled directly, and their number must have amounted to a considerable figure. They were martyrs to their faith, and their martyrdom affected their nation in two ways. In the first place, as they were the pick of those who practised the false superstition in Egypt, their conversion and disappearance dealt a staggering blow to the whole system. Secondly, the indirect effect of their martyrdom on the commonalty of Egypt must have been far greater than can be measured by numbers. The banner of God was planted, and the silent spiritual fight must have gone on ever since, though history, in recording outward events, is silent on the slow and gradual processes of transformation undergone by Egyptian religion. From a chaotic pantheon of animals and animal gods, the worship of the sun and the heavenly bodies, and the worship of the Pharaoh as the embodiment of power, they gradually came to realise the oneness and mercy of the true God. After many glimpses of Monotheism on Egyptian soil itself, the Gospel of Jesus reached them, and eventually Islam.

(Power) irresistible."[1084]

128. Said Moses to his people :
" Pray for help from God,.
And (wait) in patience and
constancy :
For the earth is God's,
To give as a heritage
To such of His servants
As He pleaseth ; and the end
Is (best) for the righteous.[1085]

129. They said : " We have had
(Nothing but) trouble, both before
And after thou camest[1086]
To us." He said :
" It may be that your Lord
Will destroy your enemy
And make you inheritors[1087]
In the earth ; that so
He may try you
By your deeds."

قَاهِرُوْنَ ○

١٢٨- قَالَ مُوْسٰى لِقَوْمِهِ
اسْتَعِيْنُوْا بِاللّٰهِ
وَاصْبِرُوْا ۚ اِنَّ الْاَرْضَ لِلّٰهِ ۙ
يُوْرِثُهَا مَنْ يَّشَآءُ مِنْ عِبَادِهٖ ۭ
وَالْعَاقِبَةُ لِلْمُتَّقِيْنَ ○

١٢٩- قَالُوْٓا اُوْذِيْنَا مِنْ قَبْلِ اَنْ تَاْتِيَنَا
وَمِنْۢ بَعْدِ مَا جِئْتَنَا ۭ
قَالَ عَسٰى رَبُّكُمْ اَنْ يُّهْلِكَ عَدُوَّكُمْ
وَيَسْتَخْلِفَكُمْ فِى الْاَرْضِ
فَيَنْظُرَ كَيْفَ تَعْمَلُوْنَ ○ ع

SECTION 16.

130. We punished the people
Of Pharaoh with years

١٣٠- وَلَقَدْ اَخَذْنَآ اٰلَ فِرْعَوْنَ بِالسِّنِيْنَ

1084. Pharaoh's order against the sorcerers was drastic enough. But his Council is not satisfied. What about Moses and the Israelites ? They had a seeming victory, and will now be more mischievous than ever. They appeal to Pharaoh's vanity and his superstition and sense of power. "If you leave them alone," they say, "where will be your authority ? You and your gods will be defied !" Pharaoh has a ready answer. He was really inwardly cowed by the apparent power of Moses. He dared not openly act against him. But he had already, before the birth of Moses, passed a cunning order to destroy the whole people of Israel. Through the instrumentality of midwives (Exod. i. 15) all the male children were to be destroyed, and the females would then be for the Egyptians : the race of Israel would thus be at an end. This order was still in force, and would remain in force until the despised race was absorbed. But Egyptian cunning and wickedness had no power against God's Plan for those who had faith. See verse 129 below.

1085. Notice the contrast between the arrogant tone of Pharaoh and the humility and faith taught by Moses. In the end the arrogance was humbled, and humility and faith were protected and advanced.

1086. There is a slight note of querulousness in the people's answer. But Moses allays it by his own example and courage, and his vision of the future : which was amply fulfilled in time. See verse 137 below

1087. The Israelites, despised and enslaved, were to be rescued and made rulers in Palestine. David and Solomon were great kings and played a notable part in history. But the greatness of Israel was conditional ; they were to be judged by their deeds. When they fell from grace, other people were given honour and power. And so it came to be the turn of the Arab race, and so on. God gives His gifts to those who are righteous and obey His Law.

(Of drought) and shortness
Of crops ; that they might
Receive admonition.

وَ نَقْصٍ مِّنَ الثَّمَرٰتِ
لَعَلَّهُمْ يَذَّكَّرُوْنَ ○

131. But when good (times) came,
They said, " This is due
To us ; " when gripped
By calamity, they ascribed it
To evil omens connected
With Moses and those with him !
Behold ! in truth the omens
Of evil are theirs [1088]
In God's sight, but most
Of them do not understand !

١٣١- فَإِذَا جَآءَتْهُمُ الْحَسَنَةُ
قَالُوْا لَنَا هٰذِهٖ ۚ وَإِنْ تُصِبْهُمْ سَيِّئَةٌ
يَّطَّيَّرُوْا بِمُوْسٰى وَمَنْ مَّعَهٗ ۗ
اَلَآ إِنَّمَا طٰٓئِرُهُمْ عِنْدَ اللّٰهِ
وَلٰكِنَّ اَكْثَرَهُمْ لَا يَعْلَمُوْنَ ○

132. They said (to Moses) :
" Whatever be the Signs
Thou bringest, to work
Therewith thy sorcery on us,[1089]
We shall never believe
In thee."

١٣٢- وَقَالُوْا مَهْمَا تَأْتِنَا بِهٖ مِنْ اٰيَةٍ
لِّتَسْحَرَنَا بِهَا ۙ
فَمَا نَحْنُ لَكَ بِمُؤْمِنِيْنَ ○

133. So We sent (plagues) on them :
Wholesale Death,[1090]
Locusts, Lice, Frogs,
And Blood : Signs openly [1091]
Self-explained : but they
Were steeped in arrogance,—
A people given to sin.

١٣٣- فَأَرْسَلْنَا عَلَيْهِمُ الطُّوْفَانَ
وَالْجَرَادَ وَالْقُمَّلَ وَالضَّفَادِعَ
وَالدَّمَ اٰيٰتٍ مُّفَصَّلٰتٍ ۫
فَاسْتَكْبَرُوْا وَكَانُوْا قَوْمًا مُّجْرِمِيْنَ ○

134. Every time the Penalty
Fell on them, they said :

١٣٤- وَلَمَّا وَقَعَ عَلَيْهِمُ الرِّجْزُ قَالُوْا

1088. Their superstition ascribed the punishment of their own wickedness to some evil omen. They thought Moses and his people brought them ill-luck. They did not look within themselves to see the root of evil, and the cause of their punishment ! So it happens in all ages. People blame the righteous for something which they do, different from other men, instead of searching out their own lapses from rectitude, which are punished by God.

1089. A type of obstinacy and resistance to God's message. As they believed in sorcery and magic, they thought anything unusual was but sorcery and magic, and hardened their hearts against Truth.

1090 *Ṭūfān*=a widespread calamity, causing wholesale death and destruction. It may be a flood, or a typhoon, or an epidemic, among men or cattle. Perhaps the last is meant, if we may interpret by the Old Testament story (Exod. ix. 3, 9, 15 ; xii. 29).

1091. In xvii. 101, the reference is to nine Clear Signs. These are : (1) the Rod (vii. 107), (2) the Radiant Hand (vii. 108), (3) the years of drought or shortage of water (vii. 130), (4) short crops (vii 130), and the five mentioned in this verse, *viz.*, (5) epidemics among men and beasts, (6) locusts, (7) lice, (8) frogs, and (9) the water turning to blood.

"O Moses! on our behalf
Call on thy Lord in virtue
Of his promise to thee:
If thou wilt remove
The Penalty from us,
We shall truly believe in thee,
And we shall send away
The Children of Israel
With thee."[1092]

يٰمُوسَى ادْعُ لَنَا رَبَّكَ
بِمَا عَهِدَ عِنْدَكَ
لَئِنْ كَشَفْتَ عَنَّا الرِّجْزَ
لَنُؤْمِنَنَّ لَكَ
وَلَنُرْسِلَنَّ مَعَكَ بَنِيٓ إِسْرَآءِيلَ ۝

135. But every time We removed
The Penalty from them
According to a fixed term
Which they had to fulfil,—[1093]
Behold! they broke their word!

١٣٥- فَلَمَّا كَشَفْنَا عَنْهُمُ الرِّجْزَ
إِلَىٰٓ أَجَلٍ
هُمْ بٰلِغُوهُ إِذَا هُمْ يَنْكُثُونَ ۝

136. So We exacted retribution
From them: We drowned them[1094]
In the sea, because they
Rejected Our Signs, and failed
To take warning from them.[1095]

١٣٦- فَانْتَقَمْنَا مِنْهُمْ فَأَغْرَقْنٰهُمْ فِي الْيَمِّ
بِأَنَّهُمْ كَذَّبُوا بِاٰيٰتِنَا
وَكَانُوا عَنْهَا غٰفِلِينَ ۝

137. And We made a people,
Considered weak (and of no
account),
Inheritors of lands
In both East and West,—

١٣٧- وَأَوْرَثْنَا الْقَوْمَ الَّذِينَ كَانُوا
يُسْتَضْعَفُونَ مَشٰرِقَ الْأَرْضِ

1092. The demand of Moses was two-fold: (1) come to God and cease from oppression, and (2) let me take Israel out of Egypt. At first it was laughed at and rejected with scorn. When the Plagues came for punishment, each time the Egyptians suffered, they promised amendment and begged Moses to intercede and cause the plague to cease. But every time it ceased, they went back to their evil attitude, until the final retribution came. This is a type of the sinner's attitude for all times.

1093. The intercession of Moses was limited to prayer. Each plague or penalty had its appointed term in God's decree. That term was duly fulfilled before the plague ceased. God's law is firm: it does not vacillate like the human will. The intercession only meant two things: (1) that God's name was invoked and His presence duly brought home to the mind and heart of the sinner who promised repentance, and (2) that the sinner was given a further chance if the prayer was accepted. This again is a universal truth.

1094. When at last Pharaoh let Israel go, they selected, not the highway to Canaan, along the Mediterranean and by Gaza, because they were unarmed and would have encountered immediate opposition there, but by way of the wilderness of Sinai. They had to cross the marshy end of the Red Sea, which they did, while Pharaoh's host which came in pursuit was drowned. *Cf.* ii. 50.

1095. Where was the Council of Pharaoh held in which Moses addressed Pharaoh? Egypt's primary capital in the XVIIIth Dynasty was Thebes (=No-Ammon), but that was more than 400 miles to the south of the Delta, in whose corner Israel dwelt. Memphis, on the apex of the Delta, a little south of where Cairo is now, was also over 100 miles from Israel's habitations. The interview must have been either in a Palace near Goshen, where the Israelites dwelt, or in Zoan (=Tanis), the Deltaic capital built by a former dynasty, which was of course still available for the reigning dynasty, and which was not far from the Israelite settlement.

Lands whereon We sent
Down Our blessings.
The fair promise of thy Lord
Was fulfilled for the Children
Of Israel, because they had
Patience and constancy,
And We levelled to the ground
The great Works and fine
Buildings
Which Pharaoh and his people
Erected (with such pride).[1096]

138. We took the Children of Israel
(With safety) across the sea.
They came upon a people
Devoted entirely to some idols[1097]
They had. They said:
"O Moses! fashion for us
A god like unto the gods
They have." He said:

وَمَغَارِبَهَا الَّتِي بٰرَكْنَا فِيهَا
وَتَمَّتْ كَلِمَتُ رَبِّكَ الْحُسْنٰى
عَلٰى بَنِيٓ إِسْرَآءِيلَ ۵
بِمَا صَبَرُوا
وَدَمَّرْنَا مَا كَانَ يَصْنَعُ فِرْعَوْنُ وَ
قَوْمُهٗ وَمَا كَانُوا يَعْرِشُونَ ○

١٣٨- وَجٰوَزْنَا بِبَنِيٓ إِسْرَآءِيلَ الْبَحْرَ
فَأَتَوْا عَلٰى قَوْمٍ يَّعْكُفُونَ عَلٰٓى أَصْنَامٍ
لَّهُمْ ۚ قَالُوا يٰمُوسَى اجْعَلْ لَّنَآ
إِلٰهًا كَمَا لَهُمْ اٰلِهَةٌ ۚ قَالَ

1096. Israel, which was despised, became a great and glorious nation under Solomon. He had goodly territory, and was doubly blest. His land and people were prosperous, and he was blessed with wisdom from God. His sway and his fame spread east and west. And thus God's promise to Israel was fulfilled. Note that Syria and Palestine had once been under the sway of Egypt. At the same time the proud and rebellious Pharaoh and his people were brought low. The splendid monuments which they had erected with so much skill and pride were mingled with the dust. Their great cities—Thebes (or No-Ammon), Memphis (or Noph, sacred to the Bull of Osiris), and the other splendid cities, became as if they had not existed, and archæologists have had to dig up their ruins from the sands. The splendid monuments—temples, palaces, tombs, statues, columns, and stately structures of all kinds—were buried in the sands. Even monuments like the Great Sphinx, which seem to defy the ages, were partly buried in the sands, and owe their rescue to the comparatively recent researches of archæologists. As late as 1743 Richard Pococke in his *Travels in Egypt* (p. 41), remarked: "Most of those pyramids are very much ruined."

The contrast between Egypt and Israel is one part of the story in the march of time. Israel also was found unworthy, and in course of time the Arabs, whom they despised as Ishmaelites, became their masters. The Jews in their Ghettos in Europe suffered much persecution. Nor are they out of the wood yet. If the Pogroms of the Slavs against them have ceased, their fate in Nazi Germany is the talk of the world. Nor had the Arabs or Turks or any nation a perpetual lease of power from God. The test is righteousness and the Muslim virtues taught in the Universal Religion of faith and right conduct.

1097. Who were these people? We are now in the Sinai Peninsula. Two conjectures are possible. (1) The Amalekites of the Sinai Peninsula were at perpetual war with the Israelites. They were probably an idolatrous nation, but we have very little knowledge of their cult. (2) From Egyptian history we know that Egypt had worked from very ancient times some copper mines in Sinai. An Egyptian settlement may have been here. Like all mining camps it contained from the beginning the dregs of the population. When the mines ceased to be worked, the settlement, or what remained of it, must have degenerated further. Cut off from civilisation, its cult must have become still narrower, without the refining influences which a progressive nation applies even to its idolatry. Perhaps Apis, the sacred bull of Memphis, lost all its allegorical meaning for them, and only gross and superstitious rites remained among them. The text speaks of "*some idols they had,*" implying that they had merely a detached fragment of a completer religion. This was a snare in the path of the Israelites, whom many generations of slavery in Egypt had debased into ignorance and superstition.

"Surely ye are a people
Without knowledge.

إِنَّكُمْ قَوْمٌ تَجْهَلُونَ ○

139. "As to these folk,—
The cult they are in
Is (but) a fragment of a ruin,[1098]
And vain is the (worship)
Which they practise."

١٣٩- إِنَّ هَٰٓؤُلَآءِ مُتَبَّرٌ
مَّا هُمْ فِيهِ
وَبَٰطِلٌ مَّا كَانُوا يَعْمَلُونَ ○

140. He said: "Shall I seek for you
A god other than the (true)
God, when it is God
Who hath endowed you
With gifts above the nations?"

١٤٠- قَالَ أَغَيْرَ اللَّهِ
أَبْغِيكُمْ إِلَٰهًا
وَهُوَ فَضَّلَكُمْ عَلَى الْعَٰلَمِينَ ○

141. And remember We rescued you
From Pharaoh's people,
Who afflicted you with
The worst of penalties,
Who slew your male children
And saved alive your females:
In that was a momentous
Trial from your Lord.[1099]

١٤١- وَإِذْ أَنجَيْنَٰكُم مِّنْ ءَالِ فِرْعَوْنَ
يَسُومُونَكُمْ سُوٓءَ الْعَذَابِ
يُقَتِّلُونَ أَبْنَآءَكُمْ وَيَسْتَحْيُونَ نِسَآءَكُمْ
وَفِي ذَٰلِكُم بَلَآءٌ مِّن رَّبِّكُمْ عَظِيمٌ ○ ع

Section 17.

142. We appointed for Moses
Thirty nights, and completed
(The period) with ten (more):
Thus was completed the term
(Of communion) with his Lord,[1100]
Forty nights. And Moses
Had charged his brother Aaron
(Before he went up):

١٤٢- وَوَٰعَدْنَا مُوسَىٰ ثَلَٰثِينَ لَيْلَةً
وَأَتْمَمْنَٰهَا بِعَشْرٍ
فَتَمَّ مِيقَٰتُ رَبِّهِۦٓ أَرْبَعِينَ لَيْلَةً
وَقَالَ مُوسَىٰ لِأَخِيهِ هَٰرُونَ

1098. If conjecture 2 in the last note is correct, this idolatrous worship was but the fragment of a ruin from Egypt, and Moses's reproach is biting: "You, who have been rescued from the bondage of living Egypt,—do you hanker after the bondage of a dead cult debased even from that from which you have been rescued?"

Mutabbar=broken in pieces, smashed into fragments, destroyed.

1099. This is God's reminder to Israel through the mouth of Moses. There was a double trial: (1) while the bondage lasted, the people were to learn patience and constancy in the midst of affliction; (2) when they were rescued, they were to learn humility, justice, and righteous deeds of prosperity.

1100. There is much mystic doctrine in this section, and the parallel between Israel and Islam continues throughout. The forty nights' communion of Moses with God on the Mount may be compared with the forty days' fast of Jesus in the wilderness before he took up his ministry (Matt. iv. 2), and with the forty years of Muṣṭafā's preparation in life before he took up his Ministry. In each case the Apostles lived alone apart from their people, before they came into the full blaze of the events of their Ministry. The forty is divided into thirty and ten, pre-figuring the thirty days of the Ramadhān fast, and the ten days of the Ẕul-Ḥajj pilgrimage in Islam.

"Act for me amongst my people:
Do right, and follow not
The way of those
Who do mischief."[1101]

اخْلُفْنِي فِي قَوْمِي وَأَصْلِحْ
وَلَا تَتَّبِعْ سَبِيلَ الْمُفْسِدِينَ ○

143. When Moses came
To the place appointed by Us,
And his Lord addressed him,
He said: "O my Lord!
Show (Thyself) to me,
That I may look upon Thee."[1102]
God said: "By no means
Canst thou see Me (direct);
But look upon the mount;
If it abide
In its place, then
Shalt thou see Me."[1103]
When his Lord manifested
His glory on the Mount,
He made it as dust,
And Moses fell down
In a swoon. When he
Recovered his senses he said:
"Glory be to Thee! To Thee
I turn in repentance, and I
Am the first to believe."[1104]

١٤٣- وَلَمَّا جَاءَ مُوسَى لِمِيقَاتِنَا
وَكَلَّمَهُ رَبُّهُ قَالَ رَبِّ
أَرِنِي أَنْظُرْ إِلَيْكَ قَالَ لَنْ تَرَانِي
وَلَكِنِ انْظُرْ إِلَى الْجَبَلِ
فَإِنِ اسْتَقَرَّ مَكَانَهُ فَسَوْفَ تَرَانِي
فَلَمَّا تَجَلَّى رَبُّهُ لِلْجَبَلِ
جَعَلَهُ دَكًّا
وَخَرَّ مُوسَى صَعِقًا
فَلَمَّا أَفَاقَ
قَالَ سُبْحَانَكَ تُبْتُ إِلَيْكَ
وَأَنَا أَوَّلُ الْمُؤْمِنِينَ ○

1101. When for any reason the man of God is absent from his people, his duty of leadership (*khilāfat*) should be taken up by his brother,—not necessarily a blood-brother, but one of his society or brotherhood. The deputy should discharge it in all humility, remembering three things: (1) that he is only a deputy, and bound to follow the directions of his Principal, (2) that right and justice are of the essence of power, and (3) that mischief gets its best chance to raise its head in the absence of the Principal, and that the deputy should always guard against the traps laid for him in the Principal's absence.

1102. Even the best of us may be betrayed into overweening confidence or spiritual ambition not yet justified by the stage we have reached. Moses had already seen part of the glory of God in his Radiant White Hand, that shone with the glory of Divine light (vii. 108, n. 1076). But he was still in the flesh, and the mission to his people was to begin after the Covenant of Sinai. It was premature of him to ask to see God.

1103. But God—the Cherisher of all His creatures—treats even our foolish requests with mercy, compassion, and understanding. Even the reflected glory of God is too great for the grosser substance of matter. The peak on which it shone became as powder before the ineffable glory, and Moses could only live by being taken out of his bodily senses. When he recovered from his swoon, he saw the true position, and the distance between our grosser bodily senses and the true splendour of God's glory. He at once turned in penitence to God, and confessed his faith. Having been blinded by the excessive Glory, he could not see with the physical eye. But he could get a glimpse of the reality through faith, and he hastened to proclaim his faith.

1104. "*First to believe.*" *Cf.* the expression "first of those who bow to God in Islam" in vi. 14 and vi. 163. "First" means here not the first in time, but most zealous in faith. It has the intensive and not the comparative meaning.

144. (God) said: "O Moses!
I have chosen thee
Above (other) men, [1105]
By the mission I (have
Given thee) and the words
I (have spoken to thee):
Take then the (revelation)
Which I give thee,
And be of those
Who give thanks." [1106]

١٤٤- قَالَ يٰمُوسٰٓى
إِنِّي اصْطَفَيْتُكَ عَلَى النَّاسِ
بِرِسٰلٰتِي وَبِكَلٰمِي
فَخُذْ مَآ ءَاتَيْتُكَ
وَكُن مِّنَ الشّٰكِرِينَ ○

145. And We ordained laws
For him in the Tablets
In all matters, both
Commanding and explaining
All things, (and said):
"Take and hold these
With firmness, and enjoin
Thy people to hold fast
By the best in the precepts: [1107]
Soon shall I show you [1108]
The homes of the wicked,— [1109]
(How they lie desolate)."

١٤٥- وَكَتَبْنَا لَهُۥ فِي الْأَلْوَاحِ
مِن كُلِّ شَيْءٍ مَّوْعِظَةً
وَتَفْصِيلًا لِّكُلِّ شَيْءٍ
فَخُذْهَا بِقُوَّةٍ
وَأْمُرْ قَوْمَكَ يَأْخُذُوا بِأَحْسَنِهَا
سَأُورِيكُمْ دَارَ الْفٰسِقِينَ ○

146. Those who behave arrogantly
On the earth in defiance

١٤٦- سَأَصْرِفُ عَنْ ءَايٰتِيَ الَّذِينَ يَتَكَبَّرُونَ

1105 "*Above (other) men*": *i.e.*, among his contemporaries. He had a high mission, and he had the honour of speaking to God.

1106. God's revelation is for the benefit of His creatures, who should receive it with reverence and gratitude While Moses was having these great spiritual experiences on the Mount, his people below were ungrateful enough to forget God and make a golden calf for worship (vii.1 47).

1107. The Tablets of the Law contained the essential spiritual Truth, from which were derived the positive injunctions and prohibitions, explanations and interpretations, which it was the function of the prophetic office to hold up for the people to follow. The precepts would contain, as the Sharī'at does, matters absolutely prohibited, matters not prohibited but disapproved, matters about which there was no prohibition or injunction, but in which conduct was to be regulated by circumstances; matters of positive and universal duty, matters recommended for those whose zeal was sufficient to enable them to work on higher than minimum standards, and matters which were sought by persons of the highest spiritual eminence. No soul is burdened beyond its capacity; but we are asked to seek the best and highest possible for us in conduct.

1108. Notice the transition from the "We" of authority and honour and impersonal dignity, to the "I" of personal concern in specially guiding the righteous.

1109. There are two meanings, one literal and the other figurative. Literally, the homes of the wicked, both individuals and nations, lie desolate, as in the case of the ancient Egyptians, the 'Ad, and the Thamūd. Figuratively, the "home" shows the inner and more intimate condition of people. If you are dazzled by the outward prosperity of the ungodly, examine their inner anguish and fear and insecurity, and you will thank God for His gracious guidance.

Of right—them will I
Turn away from My Signs:[1110]
Even if they see all the Signs,
They will not believe in them;
And if they see the way
Of right conduct, they will
Not adopt it as the Way;
But if they see the way
Of error, that is
The Way they will adopt.
For they have rejected[1111]
Our Signs, and failed
To take warning from them.

فِي الْأَرْضِ بِغَيْرِ الْحَقِّ ط
وَإِنْ يَرَوْا كُلَّ آيَةٍ لَّا يُؤْمِنُوا بِهَا ج
وَإِنْ يَرَوْا سَبِيلَ الرُّشْدِ
لَا يَتَّخِذُوهُ سَبِيلًا ج
وَإِنْ يَرَوْا سَبِيلَ الْغَيِّ يَتَّخِذُوهُ سَبِيلًا ط
ذٰلِكَ بِأَنَّهُمْ كَذَّبُوا بِآيٰتِنَا
وَكَانُوا عَنْهَا غٰفِلِينَ ○

147. Those who reject Our Signs
And the Meeting in the Hereafter,—
Vain are their deeds:
Can they expect to be rewarded
Except as they have wrought?

١٤٧- وَالَّذِينَ كَذَّبُوا بِآيٰتِنَا وَلِقَاءِ الْآخِرَةِ
حَبِطَتْ أَعْمَالُهُمْ ط هَلْ يُجْزَوْنَ
إِلَّا مَا كَانُوا يَعْمَلُونَ ○ ع

SECTION 18.

148. The people of Moses made,
In his absence, out of their
ornaments,[1112]

١٤٨- وَاتَّخَذَ قَوْمُ مُوسٰى
مِنْ بَعْدِهِ مِنْ حُلِيِّهِمْ

1110. The argument may be simplified thus in paraphrase. The right is established on the earth as God created it: Nature recognises and obeys God's law as fixed for each portion of Creation. But man, because of the gift of Will, sometimes upsets this balance. The root-cause is his arrogance, as it was in the case of Iblis. God's Signs are everywhere, but if they are rejected with scorn and blasphemy, God will withdraw His grace, for sin hardens the heart and makes it impervious to the truth. Want of faith produces a kind of blindness to spiritual facts, a kind of deafness to the warnings of a Day of Account, when the best of us will need His Mercy for our Salvation, which may be described spiritually as our "Seeing God." If we had contumaciously rejected faith, can we hope for anything but justice,—the just punishment of our sins?

1111. *Rejected Our Signs*: again a return to the Plural of impersonal Dignity and Authority, from the singular of personal concern in granting grace and guidance to the righteous.

1112. The making of the golden calf and its worship by the Israelites during the absence of Moses on the Mount were referred to in ii. 51 and some further details are given in xx. 85-97. Notice how in each case only those points are referred to which are necessary to the argument in hand. A narrator, whose object is mere narration, tells the story in all its details, and is done with it. A consummate artist, whose object is to enforce lessons, brings out each point in its proper place. Master of all details, he does not ramble, but with supreme literary skill, just adds the touch that is necessary in each place to complete the spiritual picture. His object is not a story but a lesson. Here notice the contrast between the intense spiritual communion of Moses on the Mount and the simultaneous corruption of his people in his absence. We can understand his righteous indignation and bitter grief (vii. 150). The people had melted all their gold ornaments, and made the image of a calf like the bull of Osiris in the city of Memphis in the wicked Egypt that they had turned their backs upon.

The image of a calf,
(for worship):[1113]
It seemed to low: did they[1114]
Not see that it could
Neither speak to them, nor
Show them the Way?
They took it for worship
And they did wrong.

عِجْلًا جَسَدًا لَّهُ خُوَارٌ ۚ
أَلَمْ يَرَوْا أَنَّهُ لَا يُكَلِّمُهُمْ
وَلَا يَهْدِيهِمْ سَبِيلًا ۘ
اتَّخَذُوهُ وَكَانُوا ظَالِمِينَ ۝ وقف لازم

149. When they repented, and saw
That they had erred,
They said: "If our Lord
Have not mercy upon us
And forgive us, we shall
Indeed be of those who perish."

١٤٩- وَلَمَّا سُقِطَ فِي أَيْدِيهِمْ وَرَأَوْا أَنَّهُمْ
قَدْ ضَلُّوا ۙ قَالُوا لَئِن لَّمْ يَرْحَمْنَا رَبُّنَا
وَيَغْفِرْ لَنَا لَنَكُونَنَّ مِنَ الْخَاسِرِينَ ۝

150. When Moses came back
To his people, angry and grieved,
He said: "Evil it is that ye
Have done in my place
In my absence: did ye[1115]
Make haste to bring on
The judgment of your Lord?"
He put down the Tablets,[1116]

١٥٠- وَلَمَّا رَجَعَ مُوسَىٰ إِلَىٰ قَوْمِهِ غَضْبَانَ
أَسِفًا ۙ قَالَ بِئْسَمَا خَلَفْتُمُونِي مِن بَعْدِي ۖ
أَعَجِلْتُمْ أَمْرَ رَبِّكُمْ ۖ
وَأَلْقَى الْأَلْوَاحَ

1113. *Image of a Calf*: *Jasad* is literally a body, especially the body of a man according to Khalil quoted by Rāgib. In xxi. 8 it is used obviously for the human body, as also in xxxviii. 34; but in the latter case, the idea of an image, without any real life or soul, is also suggested. In the present passage I understand many suggestions: (1) that it was a mere image, without life; (2) as such, it could not low; therefore the appearance of lowing, mentioned immediately afterwards, was a fraud; (3) unlike its prototype, the bull of Osiris, it had not even the symbolism of Osiris behind it; the Osiris myth, in the living religion of Egypt, had at least some ethical principles behind it.

1114. The lowing of the golden calf was obviously a deception practised by the Egyptian promoters of the cult. Lytton in his "Last Days of Pompeii" exposes the deception practised by the priests of Isis. Men hidden behind images imposed on the credulity of the commonalty.

1115. *Did ye make haste...?* 'In your impatience, could you not wait for me? Your lapse into idolatry has only hastened God's wrath. If you had only waited, I was bringing to you in the Tablets the most excellent teaching in the commands of God.' There is subtle irony in the speech of Moses. There is also a play upon words: *'ijl*=calf; and *'ajila*=to make haste: no translation can bring out these niceties.

1116. *Put down the Tablets*: we are not told that the Tablets were broken; in fact vii. 154 (below) shows that they were whole. They contained God's Message. There is a touch of disrespect (if not blasphemy) in supposing that God's Messenger broke the Tablets in his incontinent rage, as is stated in the Old Testament: "Moses's anger waxed hot, and he cast the tablets out of his hands, and brake them beneath the Mount." (Exod. xxxii. 10.) On this point and also on the point that Aaron (in the Old Testament story) ordered the gold to be brought, made a molten calf, fashioned it with a graving tool, and built an altar before the calf (Exod. xxxii. 2-5), our version differs from that of the Old Testament. We cannot believe that Aaron, who was appointed by God to assist Moses as God's Messenger, could descend so low as to seduce the people into idolatry, whatever his human weaknesses might be.

Seized his brother by (the hair
Of) his head, and dragged him[1117]
To him. Aaron said:
"Son of my mother! The people
Did indeed reckon me
As naught, and went near
To slaying me! Make not
The enemies rejoice over
My misfortune, nor count thou
Me amongst the people
Of sin." [1118]

وَاَخَذَ بِرَاْسِ اَخِيْهِ يَجُرُّهٗٓ اِلَيْهِ ؕ
قَالَ ابْنَ اُمَّ
اِنَّ الْقَوْمَ اسْتَضْعَفُوْنِىْ
وَكَادُوْا يَقْتُلُوْنَنِىْ ۖ
فَلَا تُشْمِتْ بِىَ الْاَعْدَآءَ
وَلَا تَجْعَلْنِىْ مَعَ الْقَوْمِ الظّٰلِمِيْنَ ○

151. Moses prayed: "O my Lord!
Forgive me and my brother! [1119]
Admit us to Thy mercy!
For Thou art the Most Merciful
Of those who show mercy!"

١٥١- قَالَ رَبِّ اغْفِرْ لِىْ وَلِاَخِىْ
وَاَدْخِلْنَا فِىْ رَحْمَتِكَ ۖ
وَاَنْتَ اَرْحَمُ الرّٰحِمِيْنَ ○ ع

SECTION 19.

152. Those who took the calf
(For worship) will indeed
Be overwhelmed with wrath
From their Lord, and with
Shame in this life: [1120]
Thus do We recompense
Those who invent (falsehoods).

١٥٢- اِنَّ الَّذِيْنَ اتَّخَذُوا الْعِجْلَ
سَيَنَالُهُمْ غَضَبٌ مِّنْ رَّبِّهِمْ
وَذِلَّةٌ فِى الْحَيٰوةِ الدُّنْيَا ؕ
وَكَذٰلِكَ نَجْزِى الْمُفْتَرِيْنَ ○

153. But those who do wrong
But repent thereafter and
(Truly) believe,—verily
Thy Lord is thereafter
Oft-forgiving, Most Merciful.

١٥٣- وَالَّذِيْنَ عَمِلُوا السَّيِّاٰتِ
ثُمَّ تَابُوْا مِنْۢ بَعْدِهَا وَاٰمَنُوْٓا اِنَّ رَبَّكَ
مِنْۢ بَعْدِهَا لَغَفُوْرٌ رَّحِيْمٌ ○

1117. Moses was but human Remembering the charge he had given to Aaron (vii. 142) he had a just grievance at the turn events had taken. But he did not wreak his vengeance on the Tablets of God's law by breaking them. He laid hands on his brother, and his brother at once explained.

1118 Aaron's speech is full of tenderness and regret. He addresses Moses as "son of my mother," —an affectionate term. He explains how the turbulent people nearly killed him for resisting them. And he states in the clearest terms that the idolatry neither originated with him nor had his consent. In xx. 85 we are told that a fellow described as the Sāmiri had led them astray. We shall discuss this when we come to that passage.

1119. As Moses was convinced that his brother was guiltless, his wrath was turned to gentleness. He prayed for forgiveness—for himself and his brother: for himself because of his wrath and for his brother because he had been unable to suppress idolatry among his people. And like a true leader that he is, he identifies himself with his lieutenant for all that has happened. Even more, he identifies himself with his whole people in his prayer in verse 155 below. Herein, again, is a type of what the Holy Prophet Muḥammad did for his people.

1120. The consequences were twofold: (1) spiritual, in that God's grace is withdrawn, and (2) even in the present life of this world, in that godly men also shun the sinner's company, and he is isolated.

154. When the anger of Moses
Was appeased, he took up
The Tablets: in the writing
Thereon was Guidance and Mercy
For such as fear their Lord.

١٥٤- وَلَمَّا سَكَتَ عَنْ مُّوسَى الْغَضَبُ
أَخَذَ الْأَلْوَاحَ ۖ وَفِي نُسْخَتِهَا هُدًى وَّ
رَحْمَةٌ لِّلَّذِينَ هُمْ لِرَبِّهِمْ يَرْهَبُونَ ○

155. And Moses chose seventy[1121]
Of his people for Our place
Of meeting: when they
Were seized with violent
quaking,[1122]
He prayed: "O my Lord!
If it had been Thy Will
Thou couldst have destroyed,
Long before, both them
And me: wouldst Thou
Destroy us for the deeds
Of the foolish ones among us?
This is no more than[1123]
Thy trial: by it Thou causest
Whom Thou wilt to stray,[1124]
And Thou leadest whom
Thou wilt into the right path.
Thou art our Protector:
So forgive us and give us
Thy mercy; for Thou art
The Best of those who forgive.

١٥٥- وَاخْتَارَ مُوسَى قَوْمَهُ سَبْعِينَ رَجُلًا
لِّمِيقَاتِنَا ۚ فَلَمَّا أَخَذَتْهُمُ الرَّجْفَةُ
قَالَ رَبِّ
لَوْ شِئْتَ أَهْلَكْتَهُم مِّن قَبْلُ وَإِيَّايَ ۖ
أَتُهْلِكُنَا بِمَا فَعَلَ السُّفَهَاءُ مِنَّا ۖ
إِنْ هِيَ إِلَّا فِتْنَتُكَ ۖ
تُضِلُّ بِهَا مَن تَشَاءُ
وَتَهْدِي مَن تَشَاءُ ۖ
أَنتَ وَلِيُّنَا
فَاغْفِرْ لَنَا وَارْحَمْنَا
وَأَنتَ خَيْرُ الْغَافِرِينَ ○

156. "And ordain for us
That which is good,
In this life
And in the Hereafter:
For we have turned unto Thee."
He said: "With My Punishment

١٥٦- وَاكْتُبْ لَنَا فِي هَٰذِهِ الدُّنْيَا حَسَنَةً
وَفِي الْآخِرَةِ
إِنَّا هُدْنَا إِلَيْكَ ۚ قَالَ عَذَابِي

1121. Seventy of the elders were taken up to the Mount, but left at some distance from the place where God spoke to Moses. They were to be silent witnesses, but their faith was not yet complete, and they dared to say to Moses: "We shall never believe in thee until we see God in public" (ii. 55). They were dazed with thunder and lightning, and might have been destroyed but for God's mercy on the intercession of Moses

1122. *Rajfat*: violent quaking, earthquake. I take it to refer to the same event as is described by the word *Sā'iqat* in ii. 55, the thunder and lightning that shook the mountain-side.

1123 Moses was guiltless, but he identifies himself with his whole people, and intercedes with God on their behalf. He recognises that it was a trial, in which some of his people failed to stand the test. Such failure was worthy of punishment. But he pleads for mercy for such as erred from weakness and not from contumacy, and were truly repentant, although all who erred were in their several degrees worthy of punishment.

1124. *Cf.* ii. 26.

I visit whom I will;
But My Mercy extendeth [1125]
To all things. That (Mercy)
I shall ordain for those
Who do right, and practise
Regular charity, and those
Who believe in Our Signs;—[1126]

157. "Those who follow the Apostle,
The unlettered Prophet,
Whom they find mentioned
In their own (Scriptures),—[1127]
In the Law and the Gospel;—
For he commands them
What is just and forbids them
What is evil; he allows
Them as lawful what is good
(And pure) and prohibits them
From what is bad (and impure);
He releases them
From their heavy burdens
And from the yokes [1128]
That are upon them.
So it is those who believe
In him, honour him,
Help him, and follow the Light
Which is sent down with him,—[1129]

أُصِيبُ بِهِ مَنْ أَشَاءُ وَرَحْمَتِي وَسِعَتْ
كُلَّ شَيْءٍ فَسَأَكْتُبُهَا لِلَّذِينَ يَتَّقُونَ
وَيُؤْتُونَ الزَّكٰوةَ
وَالَّذِينَ هُمْ بِآيٰتِنَا يُؤْمِنُونَ ۝

١٥٧- الَّذِينَ يَتَّبِعُونَ الرَّسُولَ
النَّبِيَّ الْأُمِّيَّ الَّذِي يَجِدُونَهُ مَكْتُوبًا
عِنْدَهُمْ فِي التَّوْرٰىةِ وَالْإِنْجِيلِ
يَأْمُرُهُمْ بِالْمَعْرُوفِ وَيَنْهٰىهُمْ عَنِ الْمُنْكَرِ
وَيُحِلُّ لَهُمُ الطَّيِّبٰتِ
وَيُحَرِّمُ عَلَيْهِمُ الْخَبٰٓئِثَ وَيَضَعُ عَنْهُمْ
إِصْرَهُمْ وَالْأَغْلٰلَ الَّتِي كَانَتْ عَلَيْهِمْ
فَالَّذِينَ آمَنُوا بِهِ وَعَزَّرُوهُ وَنَصَرُوهُ
وَاتَّبَعُوا النُّورَ الَّذِي أُنْزِلَ مَعَهُ

1125. God's mercy is in and for all things. All nature subserves a common purpose, which is for the good of all His creatures. Our faculties and our understandings are all instances of His grace and mercy. Each unit or factor among his creatures benefits from the others and receives them as God's mercy to itself; and in its turn, each contributes to the benefit of the others and is thus an instance of God's mercy to them. His mercy is universal and all-pervasive; while His justice and punishment are reserved for those who swerve from His plan and (to use a mediæval juridical formula) go out of His Peace.

1126. The personal grace and mercy—and their opposite—are referred to the singular pronoun "I", while the impersonal Law, by which God's Signs operate in His universe, is referred to the plural pronoun of authority and dignity, "We".

1127. In this verse is a pre-figuring, to Moses, of the Arabian Apostle, the last and greatest of the apostles of God. Prophecies about him will be found in the Taurāt and the Injīl. In the reflex of the Taurāt as now accepted by the Jews, Moses says: "The Lord thy God will raise up unto thee a Prophet from the midst of thee, of thy brethren, like unto me" (Deut. xviii. 15): the only Prophet who brought a Sharī'at like that of Moses was Muḥammad Muṣṭafā, and he came of the house of Ismā'īl the brother of Isaac the father of Israel. In the reflex of the Gospel as now accepted by the Christians, Christ promised another Comforter (John xiv. 16): the Greek word *Paraclete* which the Christians interpret as referring to the Holy Spirit is by our Doctors taken to be *Periclyte*, which would be the Greek form of Aḥmad. See Q. lxi. 6.

1128. *Aglāl*: plural of *gullun*, a yoke, an iron collar. In the formalism and exclusiveness of the Jews there were many restrictions which were removed by Islam, a religion of freedom in the faith of God, of universality in the variety of races, languages, manners and customs.

1129. *Light which is sent down with him*: the words are "with him", not "to him", emphasizing the fact that the Light which he brought illumines every one who has the privilege of joining his great and universal Fellowship.

It is they who will prosper."[1130] | ع أُولَٰئِكَ هُمُ الْمُفْلِحُونَ ۝

C. 87.—With the advent of the Holy Apostle,
(vii. 158-171.) The light and guidance which he brought
For all mankind from God
Superseded the earlier Law for the Jews.
The good and the upright among them
Followed the new Light, but
The rest were scattered through the earth.

SECTION 20.

158. Say: "O men! I am sent[1131]
Unto you all, as the Apostle
Of God, to Whom belongeth
The dominion of the heavens
And the earth: there is no god
But He: it is He that giveth
Both life and death. So believe
In God and His Apostle,
The unlettered Prophet,[1132]
Who believeth in God
And His Words: follow him
That (so) ye may be guided."

١٥٨- قُلْ يَٰٓأَيُّهَا النَّاسُ إِنِّى رَسُولُ اللَّهِ
إِلَيْكُمْ جَمِيعًا الَّذِى لَهُۥ مُلْكُ السَّمَٰوَٰتِ وَ
الْأَرْضِ ۖ لَآ إِلَٰهَ إِلَّا هُوَ يُحْىِۦ وَيُمِيتُ ۖ
فَـَٔامِنُوا بِاللَّهِ وَرَسُولِهِ النَّبِىِّ الْأُمِّىِّ
الَّذِى يُؤْمِنُ بِاللَّهِ وَكَلِمَٰتِهِۦ
وَاتَّبِعُوهُ لَعَلَّكُمْ تَهْتَدُونَ ۝

159. Of the people of Moses
There is a section
Who guide and do justice
In the light of truth.

١٥٩- وَمِن قَوْمِ مُوسَىٰٓ
أُمَّةٌ يَهْدُونَ بِالْحَقِّ وَبِهِۦ يَعْدِلُونَ ۝

1130. Falāḥ=prosperity in its general sense as well as in its spiritual sense. In the general sense it means that right conduct is the only door to happiness and well-being. In the spiritual sense it means that Faith and its fruits (right conduct) are the only gates to salvation.

1131. Our attention having been directed to various apostles, who were sent with missions to their several peoples, and in each of whose careers there is some pre-figurement of the life of the last and greatest of them, we are now asked to listen to the proclamation of Muḥammad's universal mission. We contemplate no longer, after this, partial truths. It is not now a question of saving Israel from the bondage of Egypt, nor teaching Midian the ethics of business, nor reclaiming the people of Lot from sexual sin or Thamūd from the sin of oppression in power, or Ad from arrogance and ancestor-worship. Now are set forth plainly the issues of Life and Death, the Message of the One Universal God to all mankind.

1132. "Unlettered," as applied to the Prophet here and in verse 157 above, has three special significations. (1) He was not versed in human learning; yet he was full of the highest wisdom, and had a most wonderful knowledge of the previous Scriptures. This was a proof of his inspiration. It was a miracle of the highest kind, a "Sign", which every one could test then, and every one can test now. (2) All organised human knowledge tends to be crystallized, to acquire a partial bias or flavour of some "school" of thought. The highest Teacher had to be free from any such taint, just as a clean slate is necessary if a perfectly clear and bold message has to be written on it. (3) In iii. 20 and lxii. 2, the epithet is applied to the Pagan Arabs, because, before the advent of Islam, they were unlearned. That the last and greatest of the Prophets should arise among them, and they and their language be made the vehicle of the new, full, and universal light, has also a meaning, which is explained in C. 12-15.

160. We divided them into twelve
Tribes[1133]
Or nations. We directed
Moses by inspiration,
When his (thirsty) people asked
Him for water: "Strike the rock
With thy staff": out of it
There gushed forth twelve springs:
Each group knew its own place
For water. We gave them
The shade of clouds, and sent
Down to them manna and quails,
(Saying): "Eat of the good things
We have provided for you":
(But they rebelled); to Us
They did no harm, but
They harmed their own souls.[1134]

١٦٠- وَقَطَّعْنٰهُمُ اثْنَتَيْ عَشْرَةَ اَسْبَاطًا
اُمَمًا ۗ وَاَوْحَيْنَآ اِلٰى مُوْسٰٓى اِذِ اسْتَسْقٰىهُ
قَوْمُهٗٓ اَنِ اضْرِبْ بِّعَصَاكَ الْحَجَرَ ۚ
فَانْۢبَجَسَتْ مِنْهُ اثْنَتَا عَشْرَةَ عَيْنًا ۗ
قَدْ عَلِمَ كُلُّ اُنَاسٍ مَّشْرَبَهُمْ ۗ
وَظَلَّلْنَا عَلَيْهِمُ الْغَمَامَ
وَاَنْزَلْنَا عَلَيْهِمُ الْمَنَّ وَالسَّلْوٰى ۗ
كُلُوْا مِنْ طَيِّبٰتِ مَا رَزَقْنٰكُمْ ۗ وَمَا ظَلَمُوْنَا
وَلٰكِنْ كَانُوْٓا اَنْفُسَهُمْ يَظْلِمُوْنَ ○

161. And remember it was
Said to them:
"Dwell in this town
And eat[1135] therein as ye wish,
But say the word of humility
And enter the gate
In a posture of humility:
We shall forgive you
Your faults; We shall increase
(The portion of) those who do
good."

١٦١- وَاِذْ قِيْلَ لَهُمُ اسْكُنُوْا هٰذِهِ الْقَرْيَةَ
وَكُلُوْا مِنْهَا حَيْثُ شِئْتُمْ
وَقُوْلُوْا حِطَّةٌ
وَّادْخُلُوا الْبَابَ سُجَّدًا
نَّغْفِرْ لَكُمْ خَطِيْٓـٰٔتِكُمْ ۗ
سَنَزِيْدُ الْمُحْسِنِيْنَ ○

162. But the transgressors among them
Changed the word from that
Which had been given them
So we sent on them
A plague from heaven.
For that they repeatedly
transgressed.[1136]

١٦٢- فَبَدَّلَ الَّذِيْنَ ظَلَمُوْا مِنْهُمْ
قَوْلًا غَيْرَ الَّذِيْ
قِيْلَ لَهُمْ فَاَرْسَلْنَا عَلَيْهِمْ رِجْزًا مِّنَ
السَّمَآءِ بِمَا كَانُوْا يَظْلِمُوْنَ ○ ع

SECTION 21.

163. Ask them concerning the town
Standing close by the sea.
Behold! they transgressed

١٦٣- وَسْـَٔلْهُمْ عَنِ الْقَرْيَةِ الَّتِيْ كَانَتْ
حَاضِرَةَ الْبَحْرِ ۘ اِذْ يَعْدُوْنَ

1133. We now come to some incidents in Jewish history, which have been referred to in ii. 57-60. Here they have special reference to their bearing on the times when early Islam was preached. The Twelve Tribes and the parable drawn from them have been explained in n. 73 to ii. 60.

1134. *Cf.* ii. 57 and n. 71.

1135. As in vii. 19, we may construe "eat" here to mean not only eating literally, but enjoying the good things of life.

1136. *Cf.* ii. 58-59, and n. 72. The story is here told by way of parable for the times of Islam. Hence we have a few verbal changes: *e.g.*, "dwell in this town" instead of "enter this town," etc.

In the matter of the Sabbath.[1137]
For on the day of their Sabbath
Their fish did come to them,
Openly holding up their heads,
But on the day they had
No Sabbath, they came not:
Thus did We make a trial
Of them, for they were
Given to transgression.

فِي السَّبْتِ إِذْ تَأْتِيهِمْ حِيتَانُهُمْ يَوْمَ
سَبْتِهِمْ شُرَّعًا
وَيَوْمَ لَا يَسْبِتُونَ ۙ لَا تَأْتِيهِمْ ۚ
كَذَٰلِكَ ۚ نَبْلُوهُم
بِمَا كَانُوا يَفْسُقُونَ ○

معانقة
النصف

164. When some of them said:
"Why do ye preach
To a people whom God
Will destroy or visit
With a terrible punishment?"—[1138]
Said the preachers: "To discharge
Our duty to your Lord,
And perchance they may fear
Him."

١٦٤- وَإِذْ قَالَتْ أُمَّةٌ مِّنْهُمْ
لِمَ تَعِظُونَ قَوْمًا ۙ اللَّهُ مُهْلِكُهُمْ
أَوْ مُعَذِّبُهُمْ عَذَابًا شَدِيدًا ۖ
قَالُوا مَعْذِرَةً إِلَىٰ رَبِّكُمْ
وَلَعَلَّهُمْ يَتَّقُونَ ○

165. When they disregarded the
warnings
That had been given them,
We rescued those who forbade
Evil; but We visited
The wrong-doers with a
Grievous punishment, because
They were given to transgression.

١٦٥- فَلَمَّا نَسُوا مَا ذُكِّرُوا بِهِ
أَنجَيْنَا الَّذِينَ يَنْهَوْنَ عَنِ السُّوءِ
وَأَخَذْنَا الَّذِينَ ظَلَمُوا
بِعَذَابٍ بَئِيسٍ بِمَا كَانُوا يَفْسُقُونَ ○

166. When in their insolence
They transgressed (all) prohibitions,
We said to them:
"Be ye apes,
Despised and rejected."[1139]

١٦٦- فَلَمَّا عَتَوْا عَن مَّا نُهُوا عَنْهُ
قُلْنَا لَهُمْ
كُونُوا قِرَدَةً خَاسِئِينَ ○

1137. *Cf.* ii. 65 and n. 79. Fishing, like every other activity, was prohibited to Israel on the Sabbath day. As this practice was usually observed, the fish used to come up with a sense of security to their water channels or pools openly on the Sabbath day, but not on other days when fishing was open. This was a great temptation to the law-breakers, which they could not resist. Some of their men of piety protested, but it had no effect. When their transgressions, which, we may suppose, extended to other commandments, passed beyond bounds, the punishment came. They were despised among their own people, and became like apes, without law and without order or decency

1138. There are always people who wonder, no doubt sincerely, what good it is to preach to the wicked. The answer is given to them here: (1) every man who sees evil must speak out against it; it is his duty and responsibility to God; (2) there is always a chance that the warning may have effect and save a precious soul. This passage has a special meaning for the times when our Holy Prophet was preaching in Mecca, apparently without results. But it applies to all times.

1139. *Cf.* ii. 65, n. 79.

167. Behold! thy Lord did declare[1140]
That He would send
Against them, to the Day
Of Judgment, those who would
Afflict them with grievous
Penalty. Thy Lord is quick
In retribution, but He is also
Oft-forgiving, Most Merciful.

١٦٧- وَإِذْ تَأَذَّنَ رَبُّكَ لَيَبْعَثَنَّ عَلَيْهِمْ
إِلَىٰ يَوْمِ الْقِيٰمَةِ
مَنْ يَّسُومُهُمْ سُوْٓءَ الْعَذَابِ ۗ
إِنَّ رَبَّكَ لَسَرِيْعُ الْعِقَابِ ۖ
وَإِنَّهٗ لَغَفُوْرٌ رَّحِيْمٌ ○

168. We broke them up
Into sections on this earth.[1141]
There are among them some
That are the righteous, and some
That are the opposite.
We have tried them
With both prosperity and adversity:
In order that they
Might turn (to Us).

١٦٨- وَقَطَّعْنٰهُمْ فِي الْأَرْضِ أُمَمًا ۚ
مِنْهُمُ الصّٰلِحُوْنَ
وَمِنْهُمْ دُوْنَ ذٰلِكَ ۫
وَبَلَوْنٰهُمْ بِالْحَسَنٰتِ
وَالسَّيِّاٰتِ لَعَلَّهُمْ يَرْجِعُوْنَ ○

169. After them succeeded
An (evil) generation: they
Inherited the Book, but
They chose (for themselves)[1142]
The vanities of this world,
Saying (for excuse): "(Everything)
Will be forgiven us."
(Even so), if similar vanities
Came their way, they would
(Again) seize them.
Was not the Covenant[1143]
Of the Book taken from them,
That they would not
Ascribe to God anything

١٦٩- فَخَلَفَ مِنْ بَعْدِهِمْ خَلْفٌ
وَّرِثُوا الْكِتٰبَ
يَأْخُذُوْنَ عَرَضَ هٰذَا الْأَدْنٰى
وَيَقُوْلُوْنَ سَيُغْفَرُ لَنَا ۚ
وَإِنْ يَّأْتِهِمْ عَرَضٌ مِّثْلُهٗ
يَأْخُذُوْهُ ۭ
أَلَمْ يُؤْخَذْ عَلَيْهِمْ مِّيْثَاقُ الْكِتٰبِ
أَنْ لَّا يَقُوْلُوْا عَلَى اللّٰهِ

1140. See Deut. xi. 28: "A curse if ye will not obey the commandments of the Lord your God but turn aside out of the way which I command you this day"; also Deut. xxviii. 49; "The Lord shall bring a nation against thee from afar, from the end of the earth, as swift as the eagle flieth; a nation whose tongue thou shalt not understand"; and many other passages.

1141. The dispersal of the Jews is a great fact in the world's history. Nor has their persecution ended yet, nor is it likely to end as far as we can foresee.

1142. Merely inheriting a Book, or doing lip service to it, does not make a nation righteous. If they succumb to the temptations of the world, their hypocrisy becomes all the more glaring. "High finance" is one of these temptations. *Cf.* also ii. 80: "the Fire shall not touch us except for a few numbered days": and ii. 88, about their blasphemous self-sufficiency.

1143. *Cf.* Exod. xix. 5-8; xxiv. 3; xxxiv. 27; and many other passages.

But the truth? And they
Study what is in the Book.
But best for the righteous
Is the Home in the Hereafter.
Will ye not understand?

إِلَّا الْحَقَّ وَدَرَسُوا مَا فِيهِ ۗ
وَالدَّارُ الْآخِرَةُ خَيْرٌ لِّلَّذِينَ يَتَّقُونَ ۗ
أَفَلَا تَعْقِلُونَ ۝

170. As to those who hold fast
By the Book and establish
Regular Prayer,—never
Shall we suffer the reward
Of the righteous to perish.

١٧٠- وَالَّذِينَ يُمَسِّكُونَ بِالْكِتَابِ
وَأَقَامُوا الصَّلَاةَ ۗ
إِنَّا لَا نُضِيعُ أَجْرَ الْمُصْلِحِينَ ۝

171. When We shook the Mount
Over them, as if it had been
A canopy, and they thought
It was going to fall on them
(We said): "Hold firmly[1144]
To what We have given you,
And bring (ever) to remembrance
What is therein;[1145]
Perchance ye may fear God."

١٧١- وَإِذْ نَتَقْنَا الْجَبَلَ فَوْقَهُمْ
كَأَنَّهُ ظُلَّةٌ وَظَنُّوا أَنَّهُ وَاقِعٌ بِهِمْ
خُذُوا مَا آتَيْنَاكُم بِقُوَّةٍ
وَاذْكُرُوا مَا فِيهِ
لَعَلَّكُمْ تَتَّقُونَ ۝ ع

C. 88.—Mankind have the nature of good
(vii. 172-206.) Created within them: yet doth God
By His Signs keep up a constant
Reminder to men of His holy Names.
Those who err scarce realise
How gradually they fall into sin.
Their respite has a term; the doom
Must come, and it may be on a sudden.
So humbly draw nigh to the Lord,
Declare His glory, and rejoice in His service.

SECTION 22.

172. When thy Lord drew forth[1146]
From the Children of Adam—

١٧٢- وَإِذْ أَخَذَ رَبُّكَ مِن بَنِي آدَمَ

1144. *Cf.* ii. 63 and n.

1145. *Therein*=in the Book or Revelation, in "what We have given you".

1146. This passage has led to differences of opinion in interpretation. Does it mean that each individual in the posterity of Adam had a separate existence from the time of Adam, and that a Covenant was taken from all of them, which is binding accordingly on each individual? That question really does not arise. The words in the text refer to the descendants of the Children of Adam, *i.e.*, to all humanity, born or unborn, without any limit of time. Adam's seed carries on the existence of Adam, and succeeds to his spiritual heritage. Humanity as such has a corporate aspect. Humanity has been given by God certain powers and faculties, whose possession creates on our side special spiritual obligations which we must faithfully discharge; see v. 1, and n. 682. These obligations may from a legal point of view be considered as arising from implied Covenants. In the preceding verse vii 171) a reference was made to the implied Covenant of the Jewish nation. Now we consider the implied Covenant of the whole of humanity, for the Holy Apostle's mission was world-wide.

From their loins—
Their descendants, and made them
Testify concerning themselves, (saying):
"Am I not your Lord
(Who cherishes and sustains you)?"—
They said: "Yea!
We do testify!"[1147] (This), lest
Ye should say on the Day
Of Judgment: "Of this we
Were never mindful":

مِنْ ظُهُورِهِمْ ذُرِّيَّتَهُمْ
وَأَشْهَدَهُمْ عَلَىٰ أَنْفُسِهِمْ ۚ
أَلَسْتُ بِرَبِّكُمْ ۖ
قَالُوا بَلَىٰ ۛ
شَهِدْنَا ۛ
أَنْ تَقُولُوا يَوْمَ الْقِيَامَةِ
إِنَّا كُنَّا عَنْ هَٰذَا غَافِلِينَ ۝

173. Or lest ye should say:
"Our fathers before us
May have taken false gods,
But we are (their) descendants
After them: wilt Thou then
Destroy us because of the deeds
Of men who were futile?"[1148]

١٧٣- أَوْ تَقُولُوا
إِنَّمَا أَشْرَكَ آبَاؤُنَا مِنْ قَبْلُ
وَكُنَّا ذُرِّيَّةً مِنْ بَعْدِهِمْ ۖ
أَفَتُهْلِكُنَا بِمَا فَعَلَ الْمُبْطِلُونَ ۝

174. Thus do We explain
The Signs in detail;
And perchance they may turn
(Unto Us).

١٧٤- وَكَذَٰلِكَ نُفَصِّلُ الْآيَاتِ
وَلَعَلَّهُمْ يَرْجِعُونَ ۝

175. Relate to them the story[1149]
Of the man to whom
We sent Our Signs,
But he passed them by:

١٧٥- وَاتْلُ عَلَيْهِمْ نَبَأَ الَّذِي آتَيْنَاهُ
آيَاتِنَا فَانْسَلَخَ مِنْهَا

1147. The Covenant is completed in this way. We acknowledge that God is our Creator, Cherisher, and Sustainer: therefore we acknowledge our duty to Him: when we so testify concerning ourselves, the obligation is as it were assumed by us; for it follows from our very nature when it is pure and uncorrupted.

1148. The latent faculties in man are enough to teach him the distinction between good and evil, to warn him of the dangers that beset his life. But to awaken and stimulate them, a personal appeal is made to each individual through the "still small voice" within him. This in its uncorrupted state acknowledges the truth and metaphorically swears its Covenant with God. There is, therefore, no excuse for any individual to say, either (1) that he was unmindful, or (2) that he should not be punished for the sins of his fathers, because his punishment (if any) comes from his personal responsibility and is for his own rejection of faith and the higher spiritual influences.

1149. Commentators differ whether this story or parable refers to a particular individual, and if so, to whom. The story of Balaam the seer, who was called out by Israel's enemies to curse Israel, but who blessed Israel instead, (Num. xxii., xxiii. xxiv.) is quite different. It is better to take the parable in a general sense. There are men, of talents and position, to whom great opportunities of spiritual insight come, but they perversely pass them by. Satan sees his opportunity and catches them up. Instead of rising higher in the spiritual world, their selfish and worldly desires and ambitions pull them down, and they are lost.

So Satan followed him up,
And he went astray.

فَأَتْبَعَهُ الشَّيْطٰنُ فَكَانَ مِنَ الْغٰوِينَ ○

176. If it had been Our Will,
We should have elevated him
With Our Signs; but he
Inclined to the earth,
And followed his own vain
desires.[1150]
His similitude is that
Of a dog: if you attack
Him, he lolls out his tongue,
Or if you leave him alone,
He (still) lolls out his tongue.[1151]
That is the similitude
Of those who reject Our Signs;
So relate the story;
Perchance they may reflect.

١٧٦- وَلَوْ شِئْنَا لَرَفَعْنٰهُ بِهَا
وَلٰكِنَّهُ أَخْلَدَ إِلَى الْأَرْضِ
وَاتَّبَعَ هَوٰىهُ ۚ
فَمَثَلُهُ كَمَثَلِ الْكَلْبِ ۚ
إِنْ تَحْمِلْ عَلَيْهِ يَلْهَثْ
أَوْ تَتْرُكْهُ يَلْهَثْ ۚ ذٰلِكَ مَثَلُ الْقَوْمِ
الَّذِينَ كَذَّبُوا بِاٰيٰتِنَا ۚ
فَاقْصُصِ الْقَصَصَ لَعَلَّهُمْ يَتَفَكَّرُونَ ○

177. Evil as an example are
People who reject Our Signs
And wrong their own souls.

١٧٧- سَآءَ مَثَلًا الْقَوْمُ الَّذِينَ كَذَّبُوا
بِاٰيٰتِنَا وَأَنْفُسَهُمْ كَانُوا يَظْلِمُونَ ○

178. Whom God doth guide,—
He is on the right path:
Whom He rejects from His
guidance,—
Such are the persons who perish.[1152]

١٧٨- مَنْ يَهْدِ اللّٰهُ فَهُوَ الْمُهْتَدِي ۚ
وَمَنْ يُضْلِلْ
فَأُولٰٓئِكَ هُمُ الْخٰسِرُونَ ○

179. Many are the Jinns and men
We have made for Hell:
They have hearts wherewith they
Understand not, eyes
wherewith[1153]

١٧٩- وَلَقَدْ ذَرَأْنَا لِجَهَنَّمَ كَثِيرًا
مِنَ الْجِنِّ وَالْإِنْسِ ۖ لَهُمْ قُلُوبٌ لَا
يَفْقَهُونَ بِهَا ۫ وَلَهُمْ أَعْيُنٌ

1150. Notice the contrast between the exalted spiritual honours which they would have received from God if they had followed His Will, and the earthly desires which eventually bring them low to the position of beasts and worse.

1151. The dog, especially in the hot weather, lolls out his tongue, whether he is attacked and pursued and is tired, or he is left alone. It is part of his nature to slobber. So with the man who rejects God. Whether he is warned or left alone, he continues to throw out his dirty saliva. The injury he will do will be to his own soul. But there may be infection in his evil example. So we must protect others. And we must never give up hope of his own amendment. So we must continue to warn him and make him think.

1152. Those who reject God will be deprived of God's grace and guidance. His Mercy is always open for sincere repentance. But with each step downwards, they go lower and lower, until they perish.

1153. *Cf.* ii. 18. Though they have apparently all the faculties of reason and perception, they have so deadened them that those faculties do not work, and they go headlong into Hell. They are, as it were, made for Hell.

They see not, and ears wherewith
They hear not. They are
Like cattle,—nay more
Misguided: for they
Are heedless (of warning).

لَا يُبْصِرُونَ بِهَا وَلَهُمْ آذَانٌ لَّا يَسْمَعُونَ
بِهَا ۚ أُولَٰئِكَ كَالْأَنْعَامِ
بَلْ هُمْ أَضَلُّ ۚ أُولَٰئِكَ هُمُ الْغَافِلُونَ ○

180. The most beautiful names [1154]
Belong to God:
So call on him by them;
But shun such men as
Use profanity in His names:
For what they do, they will
Soon be requited.

١٨٠- وَلِلَّهِ الْأَسْمَاءُ الْحُسْنَىٰ
فَادْعُوهُ بِهَا ۖ وَذَرُوا الَّذِينَ
يُلْحِدُونَ فِي أَسْمَائِهِ ۚ
سَيُجْزَوْنَ مَا كَانُوا يَعْمَلُونَ ○

181. Of those We have created
Are people who direct
(Others) with truth.
And dispense justice therewith.

١٨١- وَمِمَّنْ خَلَقْنَا أُمَّةٌ يَهْدُونَ
بِالْحَقِّ وَبِهِ يَعْدِلُونَ ○

Section 23.

182. Those who reject Our Signs,
We shall gradually visit
With punishment, in ways
They perceive not;

١٨٢- وَالَّذِينَ كَذَّبُوا بِآيَاتِنَا
سَنَسْتَدْرِجُهُمْ مِنْ حَيْثُ لَا يَعْلَمُونَ ○

183. Respite will I grant
Unto them: for My scheme
Is strong (and unfailing).

١٨٣- وَأُمْلِي لَهُمْ ۚ
إِنَّ كَيْدِي مَتِينٌ ○

184. Do they not reflect?
Their Companion is not seized [1155]

١٨٤- أَوَلَمْ يَتَفَكَّرُوا ۗ مَا بِصَاحِبِهِمْ

1154. As we contemplate God's nature, we can use the most beautiful names we can think of, to express His attributes. There are hundreds of such attributes. In the opening Sūra, we have these indicated in a few comprehensive words, such as *Raḥmān* (most Gracious), *Raḥīm* (most Merciful), *Rabb-ul-'ālamīn* (Cherisher and Sustainer of the worlds). Our bringing such names to remembrance is part of our Prayer and Praise. But we must not associate with people who use God's names profanely, or so as to suggest anything derogatory to His dignity or His unity. *Cf.* xvii. 110.

1155. *Their companion, i.e.*, the Holy Apostle, who lived with and amongst them. He was accused of madness because he behaved differently from them. He had no selfish ambitions; he was always true, in thought, word, and deed: he was kind and considerate to the weak, and was not dazzled by worldly power or wealth or position: he was undeterred by fear of the strong, the mockery of the cynics, the bitterness of the evil, or the indifference of the heedless. That is why he stood out boldly against wrong: he did not mince his words, and his warnings were not mealy-mouthed.

With madness: he is but
A perspicuous warner.[1156]

مِنْ جِنَّةٍ ؕ اِنْ هُوَ اِلَّا نَذِيْرٌ مُّبِيْنٌ ○

185. Do they see nothing
In the government of the heavens
And the earth and all
That God hath created?[1157]
(Do they not see) that
It may well be that
Their term is nigh
Drawing to an end?
In what Message after this
Will they then believe?

١٨٥- اَوَ لَمْ يَنْظُرُوْا فِيْ مَلَكُوْتِ السَّمٰوٰتِ
وَالْاَرْضِ وَمَا خَلَقَ اللّٰهُ مِنْ شَيْءٍ ۙ
وَّاَنْ عَسٰٓى اَنْ يَّكُوْنَ قَدِ اقْتَرَبَ اَجَلُهُمْ ۚ
فَبِاَيِّ حَدِيْثٍۢ
بَعْدَهٗ يُؤْمِنُوْنَ ○

186. To such as God rejects
From His guidance, there can be
No guide: He will
Leave them in their trespasses,
Wandering in distraction.[1158]

١٨٦- مَنْ يُّضْلِلِ اللّٰهُ
فَلَا هَادِيَ لَهٗ ؕ
وَيَذَرُهُمْ فِيْ طُغْيَانِهِمْ يَعْمَهُوْنَ ○

187. They ask thee about
The (final) Hour—when
Will be its appointed time?
Say: "The knowledge thereof
Is with my Lord (alone):
None but He can reveal
As to when it will occur.[1159]
Heavy were its burden through
The heavens and the earth.
Only, all of a sudden
Will it come to you."
They ask thee as if thou

١٨٧- يَسْـَٔلُوْنَكَ عَنِ السَّاعَةِ
اَيَّانَ مُرْسٰىهَا ؕ قُلْ اِنَّمَا عِلْمُهَا
عِنْدَ رَبِّيْ ۚ لَا يُجَلِّيْهَا لِوَقْتِهَاۤ
اِلَّا هُوَ ؔ ثَقُلَتْ فِي السَّمٰوٰتِ وَالْاَرْضِ ؕ
لَا تَاْتِيْكُمْ اِلَّا بَغْتَةً ؕ
يَسْـَٔلُوْنَكَ كَاَنَّكَ

1156. *Mubīn*; perspicuous. The reason why I have not used a simpler word, such as "plain" or "clear" is explained in n. 716 to v. 17. Muṣṭafā's sermons were not polite reminders, with an eye to the flattery of weaknesses in high places or national vanities or crowd passions. They brought out every foible into the glare of light, by a fiery eloquence fed by inspiration from God.

1157. An appeal to God's most wonderful universe should at once convince a thinking mind of man's nothingness, and God's power, glory, and goodness. Man's term here is fleeting. If he is not warned by the great Signs, and the Messages which call his attention to them, is he capable of any faith at all?

1158. *Cf.* ii. 15. If God's light is removed, the best of them can only wander hither and thither, like blind men, in distraction.

1159. The fact of its coming is a certainty: the exact time appointed for it is not revealed by God. If it were, it would be so momentous as to disturb our thoughts and life. It would be a heavy burden to us. Our duty is to be prepared for it at all times. It will come when we least expect it. In the present Gospels Jesus says the same thing: he does not know the Hour, but it will come suddenly. "But of that day and that Hour knoweth no man, no, not the angels which are in heaven, neither the Son, but the Father. Take ye heed, watch and pray: for ye know not when the time is." (Mark. xiii. 32-33.)

Wert eager in search thereof :[1160]
Say : "The knowledge thereof
Is with God (alone),
But most men know not."

حَفِيٌّ عَنْهَا ۖ قُلْ إِنَّمَا عِلْمُهَا عِنْدَ اللَّهِ
وَلَٰكِنَّ أَكْثَرَ النَّاسِ لَا يَعْلَمُونَ ○

188. Say : "I have no power
Over any good or harm
To myself except as God
Willeth. If I had knowledge
Of the unseen, I should have
Multiplied all good, and no evil
Should have touched me :
I am but a warner,
And a bringer of glad tidings
To those who have faith."[1161]

١٨٨- قُلْ لَا أَمْلِكُ لِنَفْسِي نَفْعًا وَلَا
ضَرًّا إِلَّا مَا شَاءَ اللَّهُ ۚ وَلَوْ كُنْتُ أَعْلَمُ الْغَيْبَ
لَاسْتَكْثَرْتُ مِنَ الْخَيْرِ ۚ
وَمَا مَسَّنِيَ السُّوءُ ۚ إِنْ أَنَا إِلَّا نَذِيرٌ
وَبَشِيرٌ لِقَوْمٍ يُؤْمِنُونَ ○ ع

SECTION 24.

189. It is He Who created
You from a single person,
And made his mate
Of like nature,[1162] in order
That he might dwell with her
(In love). When they are
United, she bears a light
Burden and carries it about
(Unnoticed). When she grows
Heavy, they both pray[1163]
To God their Lord, (saying) :
"If Thou givest us
A goodly child,[1164]

١٨٩- هُوَ الَّذِي خَلَقَكُمْ مِنْ نَفْسٍ وَاحِدَةٍ
وَجَعَلَ مِنْهَا زَوْجَهَا لِيَسْكُنَ إِلَيْهَا ۚ
فَلَمَّا تَغَشَّاهَا
حَمَلَتْ حَمْلًا خَفِيفًا
فَمَرَّتْ بِهِ ۚ
فَلَمَّا أَثْقَلَتْ
دَعَوَا اللَّهَ رَبَّهُمَا لَئِنْ آتَيْتَنَا صَالِحًا

1160. *Ḥafi* is usually construed to mean : "eager or anxious in search of" : the preposition following here is *'an* =concerning, about. Some commentators (including Rāġib) understand it in this passage to mean "well-acquainted." In xix. 47, with the preposition *bi* following it, it signifies "well-disposed to", "favourable to, good to, kind to."

1161. A warner to all, and a bringer of glad tidings to those who have faith, because they will profit by the glad tidings. As every one is invited to faith, the glad tidings are *offered* to all, but they are not necessarily accepted by all.

1162. *Cf.* iv. 1, and n. 504, where the construction is explained.

1163 The mystery of the physical birth of man, as it affects the father and the mother, only touches the imagination of the parents in the later stages when the child is yet unborn and yet the life stirs within the body of the expectant mother. The coming of the new life is a solemn thing, and is fraught with much hope as well as much unknown risk to the mother herself. The parents in their anxiety turn to God. If this feeling of solemnity, hope, and looking towards God were maintained after birth, all would be well for the parents as well as for the rising generation. But the attitude changes, as the verses following show.

1164. *Goodly* : *ṣāliḥ* : includes the following ideas : sound in body and mind ; healthy ; righteous of good moral disposition.

We vow we shall
(Ever) be grateful."

لَنَكُونَنَّ مِنَ الشّٰكِرِينَ ○

190. But when He giveth them
A goodly child, they ascribe [1165]
To others a share in the gift
They have received :
But God is exalted
High above the partners
They ascribe to Him.

١٩٠- فَلَمَّآ اٰتٰهُمَا صَالِحًا
جَعَلَا لَهٗ شُرَكَآءَ
فِيمَآ اٰتٰهُمَا ۚ
فَتَعٰلَى اللّٰهُ عَمَّا يُشْرِكُونَ ○

191. Do they indeed ascribe
To Him as partners things
That can create nothing,
But are themselves created ?

١٩١- اَيُشْرِكُونَ مَا لَا يَخْلُقُ شَيْئًا
وَّهُمْ يُخْلَقُونَ ○

192. No aid can they give them,
Nor can they aid themselves !

١٩٢- وَلَا يَسْتَطِيعُونَ لَهُمْ نَصْرًا وَّ
لَآ اَنْفُسَهُمْ يَنْصُرُونَ ○

193. If ye call them to guidance,
They will not obey :
For you it is the same
Whether ye call them
Or ye hold your peace ! [1166]

١٩٣- وَاِنْ تَدْعُوهُمْ اِلَى الْهُدٰى
لَا يَتَّبِعُوكُمْ ۭ سَوَآءٌ عَلَيْكُمْ
اَدَعَوْتُمُوهُمْ اَمْ اَنْتُمْ صَامِتُونَ ○

194. Verily those whom ye
Call upon besides God
Are servants like unto you : [1167]
Call upon them, and let them
Listen to your prayer,
If ye are (indeed) truthful !

١٩٤- اِنَّ الَّذِينَ تَدْعُونَ مِنْ دُونِ اللّٰهِ
عِبَادٌ اَمْثَالُكُمْ فَادْعُوهُمْ
فَلْيَسْتَجِيبُوا لَكُمْ اِنْ كُنْتُمْ صٰدِقِينَ ○

195. Have they feet to walk with ?
Or hands to lay hold with ?

١٩٥- اَلَهُمْ اَرْجُلٌ يَّمْشُونَ بِهَآ
اَمْ لَهُمْ اَيْدٍ يَّبْطِشُونَ بِهَآ

1165. When the child is born, the parents forget that it is a precious gift of God,—a miracle of Creation, which should lift their minds up to the higher things of God. Instead, their gradual familiarity with the new life makes them connect it with many superstitious ideas or rites and ceremonies, or they take it as a matter of course, as a little plaything of the material world. This leads to idolatory or false worship, or the setting up of false standards, in derogation of the dignity of God.

1166. When false worship takes root, the teacher of Truth finds much to discourage him. As far as *he* is concerned, it seems as if he has produced no effect. Yet his duty is to continue his work, in the spirit of verse 199 below, forgiving all opposition, teaching what is right, and not joining the ignorant in their attitude of doubt and indecision.

1167. False gods, whether idols or deified men, or ideas and superstitions, have no existence of their own, independent of God's creation. They are God's creatures, and like servants are subject to His authority. Deified men are not real men, but false ideas of men. They cannot help themselves : how can they help others ?

Or eyes to see with ?
Or ears to hear with ?
Say: "Call your 'god-partners',[1168]
Scheme (your worst) against me,
And give me no respite !

أَمْ لَهُمْ أَعْيُنٌ يُبْصِرُونَ بِهَا أَمْ لَهُمْ
آذَانٌ يَسْمَعُونَ بِهَا قُلِ ادْعُوا شُرَكَاءَكُمْ
ثُمَّ كِيدُونِ فَلَا تُنْظِرُونِ ○

196. "For my Protector is God,
Who revealed the Book
(From time to time),
And He will choose
And befriend the righteous.

١٩٦- إِنَّ وَلِيِّيَ اللَّهُ
الَّذِي نَزَّلَ الْكِتَابَ
وَهُوَ يَتَوَلَّى الصَّالِحِينَ ○

197. "But those ye call upon
Besides Him, are unable
To help you, and indeed
To help themselves."

١٩٧- وَالَّذِينَ تَدْعُونَ مِنْ دُونِهِ لَا
يَسْتَطِيعُونَ نَصْرَكُمْ وَلَا أَنْفُسَهُمْ يَنْصُرُونَ ○

198. If thou callest them
To guidance, they hear not.
Thou wilt see them
Looking at thee, but
They see not.[1169]

١٩٨- وَإِنْ تَدْعُوهُمْ إِلَى الْهُدَى
لَا يَسْمَعُوا وَتَرَاهُمْ يَنْظُرُونَ إِلَيْكَ
وَهُمْ لَا يُبْصِرُونَ ○

199. Hold to forgiveness ;
Command what is right ;
But turn away from the ignorant.[1170]

١٩٩- خُذِ الْعَفْوَ وَأْمُرْ بِالْعُرْفِ
وَأَعْرِضْ عَنِ الْجَاهِلِينَ ○

200. If a suggestion from Satan
Assail thy (mind),[1171]

٢٠٠- وَإِمَّا يَنْزَغَنَّكَ مِنَ الشَّيْطَانِ نَزْغٌ

1168. Here is a test and a challenge. If the false gods had any power or even existence, collect them all together, and, says the man of God, "Let them do their worst against me." They cannot; because the whole thing is based on a superstition and a chimæra.

1169. The beauty and righteousness of Muṣṭafā's life were acknowledged on all hands, until he received the mission to preach and to fight against evil. What happened then? Evil erected barricades for itself. It had eyes, but it refused to see. It had ears, but it refused to hear. It had intelligence, but it blocked up its channels of understanding. Even now, after thirteen centuries and a half, a life of unexampled purity, probity, justice, and righteousness is seen in false lights by blind detractors !

1170. God comforts the Apostle and directs his mind to three precepts: (1) to forgive injuries, insults, and persecution; (2) to continue to declare the faith that was in him, and not only to declare it, but to act up to it in all his dealings with friends and foes; (3) to pay no attention to ignorant fools, who raised doubts or difficulties, hurled taunts or reproaches, or devised plots to defeat the truth: they were to be ignored and passed by, not to be engaged in fights and fruitless controversies, or conciliated by compromises.

1171. Even a man of God is but human. He might think that revenge or retaliation, or a little tactful silence when evil stalks abroad, or some compromise with ignorance, might be best for the cause. He is to reject such suggestions.

Seek refuge with God;
For He heareth and knoweth
(All things).

201. Those who fear God,
When a thought of evil
From Satan assaults them,
Bring God to remembrance,
When lo! they see (aright)! [1172]

202. But their brethren (the evil ones)[1173]
Plunge them deeper into error,
And never relax (their efforts).

203. If thou bring them not
A revelation,[1174] they say:
"Why hast thou not
Got it together?"
Say: "I but follow
What is revealed to me
From my Lord:
This is (nothing but)
Lights from your Lord,[1175]
And Guidance, and Mercy,
For any who have Faith."

204. When the Qur-ān is read,
Listen to it with attention,

فَاسْتَعِذْ بِاللّٰهِ ۚ
إِنَّهُ سَمِيعٌ عَلِيمٌ ۝

٢٠١- إِنَّ الَّذِينَ اتَّقَوْا
إِذَا مَسَّهُمْ طَٰئِفٌ مِّنَ الشَّيْطَٰنِ
تَذَكَّرُوا فَإِذَا هُم مُّبْصِرُونَ ۝

٢٠٢- وَإِخْوَٰنُهُمْ يَمُدُّونَهُمْ فِي الْغَيِّ
ثُمَّ لَا يُقْصِرُونَ ۝

٢٠٣- وَإِذَا لَمْ تَأْتِهِم بِـَٔايَةٍ
قَالُوا لَوْلَا اجْتَبَيْتَهَا ۚ
قُلْ إِنَّمَآ أَتَّبِعُ مَا يُوحَىٰٓ إِلَيَّ مِن رَّبِّي ۚ
هَٰذَا بَصَآئِرُ مِن رَّبِّكُمْ
وَهُدًى وَرَحْمَةٌ
لِّقَوْمٍ يُؤْمِنُونَ ۝

٢٠٤- وَإِذَا قُرِئَ الْقُرْءَانُ فَاسْتَمِعُوا لَهُ

1172. God protects His own, as no one else can. He is the sure refuge—and the only one—for men of faith. If we are confused or angry, being blinded by this world, He will open our eyes.

1173. We go back to consider the ungodly, whom we left at verse 198, in order to be taught our behaviour towards evil. The forces of evil never relax their efforts to draw their "brethren" (those who go into their family) deeper and deeper into the mire of sin and destruction.

1174. "Āyat" here, I think, means specially an Āyat of the Holy Qur-ān. The infidels did not believe in revelation, and used to taunt the Holy Apostle, as much as to say that he used to put together words and promulgate them as revelation. The answer is contained in the sentence that follows. No human composition could contain the beauty, power, and spiritual insight of the Qur-ān. Without inspiration it is impossible to suppose that a man, with or without literary and philosophic training, could produce such a book as the Qur-ān.

1175. "*Lights*": eyes, faculty of spiritual insight. The revelation is for us (1) spiritual eyes, (2) guidance, and (3) mercy. (1) is the highest in degree: just as a blind man, if he is given eyes and the faculty of sight, is at once removed into an entirely new world, so those who can reach the stage of spiritual insight pass into and become citizens of a wholly new spiritual World. (2) is next in degree; the man of the world can act up to the teaching about right conduct, and prepare for the Hereafter. (3) is the Mercy of God, free to every one, saint and sinner, who sincerely believes and puts his trust in God.

And hold your peace :
That ye may receive Mercy.

وَأَنْصِتُوا لَعَلَّكُمْ تُرْحَمُونَ ۝

205. And do thou (O reader!)
Bring thy Lord to remembrance
In thy (very) soul,
With humility and in reverence,
Without loudness in words,
In the mornings and evenings;
And be not thou
Of those who are unheedful.

٢٠٥- وَاذْكُرْ رَّبَّكَ فِي نَفْسِكَ تَضَرُّعًا وَّ
خِيفَةً وَّدُونَ الْجَهْرِ مِنَ الْقَوْلِ
بِالْغُدُوِّ وَالْآصَالِ
وَلَا تَكُنْ مِّنَ الْغٰفِلِيْنَ ۝

206. Those who are near[1176]
To thy Lord, disdain not
To do Him worship:
They celebrate His praises,
And bow down before Him.[1177]

٢٠٦- إِنَّ الَّذِيْنَ عِنْدَ رَبِّكَ
لَا يَسْتَكْبِرُوْنَ عَنْ عِبَادَتِهٖ
وَيُسَبِّحُوْنَهٗ وَلَهٗ يَسْجُدُوْنَ ۝

1176. The higher you are in spiritual attainment, the more is your desire and your opportunity to serve and worship your Lord and Cherisher and the Lord and Cherisher of all the worlds; and the greater is your pride in that service and that worship.

1177. At this stage a *Sijda* or prostration is indicated, as symbolical of our humble acceptance of the privilege of serving and worshipping God,—a fitting close to a Sūra in which we are led, through a contemplation of the stories of the Messengers of God, to the meaning of revelation and its relation to our moral and spiritual progress.

APPENDIX IV.

Egypytian Chronology and Israel (see vii. 104, n. 1072)

In order to get some idea of the comparative chronology of Egypt and Israel, we must first consider what data we have for Egyptian chronology. Israel's surviving records date from a time many centuries later than Israel's contact with Egypt. On the other hand Egypt's records in monuments, inscriptions, tombs, etc., are rich and absolutely reliable as far as they go.

Of the surviving old civilizations, Egypt and China go back furthest in time with historical material. Egypt has the more interest for us, because geographically she was centrally situated, and she influenced and was influenced by almost every important cultural movement in Asia, Europe, and Africa. Nothing happened in Mediterranean history that had not some points of contact with Egypt.

The first broad division in Egyptian chronology is between the pre-Dynastic and the Dynastic periods. The pre-Dynastic period is all pre-history. But recent researches have thrown a great deal of light on the culture of that period, and we know many more details about the arts and tools of that period in Egypt than we do for the corresponding periods of pre-history in other countries.

With the first Egyptian Dynasty of rulers begins the Dynastic period. What were the Egyptian Dynasties, and why is so much prominence given to them in Egyptian chronology? The reason is that though we can form a graphic idea of the sequence of events and in many cases of the details of events, arts and crafts, manners and customs, cults and ceremonies, and social and economic conditions in the Dynastic period, we are not yet able, except for occasional and isolated glimpses, to give any accurate figures of early dates to connect them with our chronology B.C. On the other hand we have abundant materials to justify us in placing certain events or personages or ideas in some division of the Dynastic scheme. We can say that such and such ideas held sway under the 18th Dynasty or that such and such invasion, outwards or inwards, took place at the close of the 14th Dynasty.

The Dynastic scheme rests mainly on the lists and fragments preserved from the writings of one Manetho, an Egyptian priest and annalist, who lived under Ptolemy I and Ptolemy II (B.C. 313-246), the inheritors of the Egyptian portion of Alexander's Empire. For his Egyptian history in Greek he had access to Egyptian records. His scheme of Dynasties therefore supplies a rough chronological frame-work into which can be fitted our ever-increasing detailed knowledge derived from Egyptian monuments, tombs, and excavations. His first Dynasty begins with the unification of Upper and Lower Egypt, but its actual date B.C. has been placed at between such wide margins as 5500 B.C. and 3300 B.C.

The two Egypts may be considered distinct ethnical and perhaps geographical divisions, which tend to assimilate when they are united politically, but whose physical

characteristics are different, as also their outlook when there is political division. Lower Egypt looks to the Mediterranean, and its population is mixed, containing almost all the Mediterranean and Arab elements, while Upper Egypt looks to interior Africa (Nubia, Sudan, Abyssinia, etc.), and its population tends to have more and more African characteristics. The whole of Egypt has had a ribbon development, the population and cultivation being confined to the banks of the Nile. Without the Nile Egypt would be just a desert forming a link in the long chain of tropical and sub-tropical deserts stretching from the Sahara, the Libyan desert, the Arabian deserts, through the Persian, Baluchistan, Sindh, and Rajputana deserts, to the Turki and Gobi deserts in Central Asia. But Upper Egypt is purely a long irregular line along the banks of the Nile, while Lower Egypt has the broad fan-like delta in which the many mouths of the Nile run into a very irregular coast-line extending over about 200 miles. Lower Egypt had (and has) much marsh-land, and its low-lying configuration was subject to many physical changes, in the same way as invasions and foreign immigrations gave its population a less stable character. Its cities, such as Sais and Tanis (Zoan), were also less stable in character, and Memphis (near the site of modern Cairo) had to be just above the Delta. On the other hand the Capitals in Upper Egypt, such as Thebes (or No), with their magnificent temples and tombs were safe above Nile waters in the highest inundations until the modern dam of Asuān was built many miles above them. Even after the union of the two Egypts, the King wore a double crown. The boundary between Upper and Lower Egypt was never clearly defined, because in spite of frequent interruptions in the unity of the country, the identification of Egypt with the Nile made the unity of Egypt a political and economic necessity. The present boundary of Lower Egypt is just south of Cairo, making Lower Egypt include just the Delta. The tract between Cairo and Assiut is sometimes called Middle Egypt and is distinguished from the rest of Upper Egypt, which is higher up the river.

There being such wide variations in the estimate of ancient dates by competent authorities, the only practicable course is to refer ancient events to Dynasties according to Manetho's scheme. In the later dates it is sometimes possible to express a date in approximate figures B.C., but such figures are uncertain, whereas the sequence of Dynasties may be taken to be a stable fact in Egyptian history, although some of Manetho's material, when it can be tested, has proved to be inaccurate. But we have only Manetho second-hand. The inaccuracies may be due not to Manetho but to his transmitters. Thirty-one such Dynasties are reckoned, and they may be grouped into Periods as follows:—

I. The Old Kingdom, Dynasties I to VIII, including (*a*) the first three Dynasties, with a new orientation in Egyptian Art, and (*b*) Dynasties IV to VI, the Pyramid Period, during which the Great Pyramid and the second and third Pyramids of Ghizeh were built. The capital now came to Lower Egypt, to the site of Memphis, near modern Cairo.

II. The Middle Kingdom, Dynasties IX to XVII. In Dynasties IX and X the centre of gravity moved from Memphis in Lower Egypt to Middle Egypt. In the XIIth Dynasty many of the great monuments of and near Thebes (Karnak, Luxor, etc.), were constructed. Perhaps the movement higher up the river was necessitated by

foreign invasions in Lower Egypt. Dynasties XV to XVII are called the Hyksos Period, when a Syrian Dynasty was established in Lower Egypt, with a sort of lordship over the native Dynasties of Upper Egypt, and international connections in other Mediterranean countries. We shall presently speak of the Hyksos Pharaohs, who have been placed in the 17th, 18th, and even 26th century B.C.

III. The New Empire, Dynasties XVIII to XX, crowded with events. The dates now begin to be more definite: the period may be placed between about 1580 B.C. and about 1200 B.C. The foreign Hyksos were driven out; the empire was extended to Syria and Nubia; perhaps even the Euphrates was reached. Some of the most wonderful works of Egyptian art date from this period.

IV. The Dynasties of the Delta, Dynasties XXI to XXXI, including a Dynasty at Sais (on one of the western branches of the Deltaic Nile). But Assyrian and Persian invasions were now weakening the power of Egypt. The dates now became more certain. The XXIst Dynasty was roughly about 1100 B.C. The XXVIIth Dynasty was ended by the invasion of the Persians under Cambyses in 525 B.C. The Persians held sway (with Egyptian local dynasties under them) until the XXXIst Dynasty, when the last Pharaoh fled to Ethiopia about 340 B.C.

V. The Egyptian Dynasties have now ended, and we are in firm history: the Macedonian Period after Alexander's conquest, 332 B.C., and the Dynasty of the Ptolemies, 323 B.C. to 30 B.C.; and the Roman Period 30 B.C., to 639 A.D., after which the Arab and Turkish conquests evolved modern Egypt and Muslim Egyptian civilization.

Having cleared the chronological background, we are now in a position to examine the data about Israel's stay in Egypt in order to see if we can get some idea of the time in Egyptian history when the contact took place. We saw that Dynasties XV to XVII were concerned with the Hyksos (or Shepherd) kings. They were foreigners from Asia, but it is not quite clear exactly what race they belonged to. Josephus supposed that they were Israelites, but that theory is untenable. It has been conjectured that they were Phœnicians, or Amalekites, or Hittites. In any case they were Semites. They founded a city called *Zoan* (Tanis) on one of the eastern branches of the Deltaic Nile, and were in close communication with the Hittite city of Hebron in the south of Palestine. That would be their own city, but their capital would probably be the same as the old Egyptian capital at Memphis when they were well-established. They are credited with having invented the Semitic alphabet of 22 letters, which (through the Phœnician) is the parent of all modern alphabets. Their invention probably helped in the process of converting old Egyptian Hieroglyphics from picture-writing to phonetic writing. As the Hyksos had close relations with Hebron in Palestine, and Abraham and Israel had settled in the Palestine country, a nexus would be established, by which the first Israelites would be attracted to *Zoan* in Egypt. It must also be remembered that southern Palestine was a poor country and subject to frequent famines, while Deltaic Egypt was well-watered by the Nile, and suffered from famines only on the rare occasions when the Nile failed to inundate. The attraction of Egypt for the famine-stricken lands of the neighbourhood would therefore be strong. And this is proved in the story of Joseph and his brethren.

Can we form even a rough idea of the dates of the Hyksos occupation? At the latest the Hyksos period ended about 1600 B.C. Renan is therefore probably not far wrong when he places the Hyksos occupation about 2000 B.C. Possibly a date between 2000 B.C. and 1600 B.C. may be nearer the mark. If we suppose Joseph to have been the Wazīr of one of the Hyksos Pharaohs in the Delta, there is no great violence of probabilities in the suggestion, as Joseph and the Hyksos would be of kindred races. In that case Joseph's date would fall somewhere between the 19th and the 17th century B.C.

No reference to Joseph or Moses has been found in Egyptian records. The solitary reference to Israel (*Ysraer*, r = l) in a stele of Mer-en-Ptah or Mineptah (about 1225 B.C.) seems to refer to Israel in Palestine rather than to Israel in Egypt. At this we need not wonder, as the Pharaoh who honoured Joseph was strictly speaking only a foreigner. When the reaction against the Hyksos took place and the Hyksos were overthrown, the Egyptians would not probably be anxious to remember the interrupted period or to preserve its memory. The Pharaoh who "knew not Joseph" looked upon the Israelites as contemptible slaves, not worthy of a thought except when they revolted, and then only as a despised race fit to be punished and kept in its place. It may be noticed, however, that the land of Goshen in which Israel dwelt and multiplied between the time of Joseph and the time of the Exodus, was a frontier tract of Egypt in the neighbourhood of the Hyksos city of Zoan in the Delta.

In seeking the approximate date of Moses, we must again look to the probabilities of Egyptian history. It was formerly the received opinion that Rameses II (say about 1250 B.C.) was the Pharaoh who oppressed Israel in Egypt, and that the exodus may have taken place under his immediate successor Mineptah (say about 1225 B.C.). The vigorous policy of Rameses II and the spirit of his time would be consistent with this view. But this date is almost certainly too late. There are indications pointing to the Israelites having already been settled in Canaan by this time. The Hyksos were turned out by the XVIIIth Dynasty, which established the New Empire in the 16th century B.C. Thothmes I (Tethmosis I, about 1540 B.C.) is more likely, in the first flush of his nationalist campaign, to have oppressed the Israelites and led to the exodus. His date fits in better. And his character also accords with the description in sacred history. He centralised the monarchy and made it a military autocracy. Militarism went with the lust of war and foreign conquest. He carried his arms as far as the Euphrates. Slaves, plunder, and foreign tribute made Egypt opulent and arrogant, and he added many monuments to Thebes. We can imagine him in his splendid Court, scarcely paying any attention to Moses, and viewing all his complaints with amusement mingled with contempt and impatience. But retribution was to come in God's good time. The men who followed God's message—Israel in the time of Solomon (a little after 1000 B.C.), and more completely, the Muslims in the time of Hadhrat 'Umar and his successors—became lords of the East and the West (Q. vii. 137), and ancient Egypt's glories were eventually buried in the sands.

It was this same Pharaoh, Thothmes I, who took for his partner on the Throne his daughter Hatshepshut. If Thothmes was the Pharaoh in Moses's story, we may

suppose that it was this same celebrated strong-minded lady, Pharaoh's daughter, who found the child Moses (Exod. ii. 10), and brought him to her mother to be adopted into the family (Q. xxviii. 9). Like her father, she was a great supporter of the national cults. Moses was nurtured in the palace, and learned all the wisdom of the Egyptians, then reputed to be the wisest of the nations. With their own wisdom he foiled them. Thus in God's Plan the enemies of God and the enemies of Israel (Q. xx. 39) were the very ones who were used as instruments for the purposes of God and the salvation of Israel.

References : E.B., *Egypt* ; D.A. Mackenzie, *Egyptian Myth and Legend* ; Renan, *History of the People of Israel*, 3 vols. ; Joseph Cattani Pasha, *Coup d'oeil sur la chronologie de la nation Egyptienne*, Paris 1931 ; Sir W. M. Flinders Petrie, *History of Egypt*, 3 vols. ; *Cambridge Ancient History*, vol. I. Chapter IV. (iii).

APPENDIX V.

Egyptian Religion and its Steps Towards Islam (see vii. 123, n. 1082)

This should be read along with Appendix IV in which a discussion on Egyptian chronology will be found.

God's Plan works silently but surely among all nations and at all times. In the most fantastic forms of religion appear gleams of His Light of Unity, calls to Islam, *i.e.*, man's submission of his will to the Universal Will (see C. 7-10). From that point of view the religious history of Egypt from the most ancient times to the present day is most interesting, as is indeed the religious history of any country for which we have records of thought and development. That of India touches us dearly, but it is not directly relevant in a translation and exposition of the Qur-ān. The religious history of Israel is just an earlier chapter of the history of Islam, and our doctors and commentators have written in great detail about it. Sometimes, I think, they have attached exaggerated importance to it. But none of them has paid much attention to Egypt from this point of view. Our people know very little of ancient Egypt and have shown little interest in it. It is a healthy sign that modern Egypt is showing much interest in it, and I hope that it will in time recognise in it a valuable unfoldment of religious ideas leading up to Islam.

The field of Egyptology is vast and is being extended every day by the diligent researches of archæologists and scholars. I do not propose to write an essay on Egyptian religion. But I wish to put forward a few considerations to show how God's Plan and Will worked steadily, in Egypt as elsewhere, towards a greater and greater appreciation, on the part of the people, of God's true nature and the real purpose of religion. The eternal light of Unity and Islam shines in many ways, and its rays give light to the spiritual aspirations of mankind in the darkest periods. With a gifted and artistic people like the Egyptians, their religious sense was led, in spite of many rebuffs, gradually to a purer and purer conception of man's eternal destiny, until Muḥammad's Message was preached to them in the very language in which it was originally preached in Arabia. And that language, Arabic, became and is now the language of the Egyptian people themselves.

In the pre-Dynastic Egypt there must already have been a great deal of development in the religious conceptions which afterwards showed such vitality in Dynastic Egypt. The Old Kingdom, including the Pyramid Period, shows that the Egyptian mind was obsessed with the certainty of life after death. It was also impressed with ideas of grandeur, order, and precision in the universe,—ideas which found eloquent expression in the grand conceptions and mathematical symmetry and simplicity of its architecture. Its massive dignity and repose are also reflected in the faces and poses of the figures in Egyptian statuary and painting. The unending expanse and the mystery of the desert seem to have acted on the Egyptian mind like a soporific and made it less active in mundane affairs and less practical in speculation

than that of some other races of similar gifts. What mysteries are typified in the proportions of the Pyramids and their internal galleries and mysterious chambers, we shall probably never know with certainty. But a haunting sense of death and of the other world seems to oppress us in its atmosphere, as it does in the grim scenes of the "Book of the Dead". As Prof. T. E. Peet remarks (*Cambridge Ancient History*, vol. I, p. 354), "the Egyptian mind closely associated together men, gods, and the dead as merely three species of a single genus." Each of these it considered was subject to an irresistible force called *Hīke* or *Heka* : hence the force of Magic, Incantations to the Dead, and Rites and Formularies in daily life.

The Middle Kingdom brings us face to face with fresh ideas. We have no data with which to appraise the influence of foreign cults and foreign ideas during the period. But knowing, as we do, how Egypt acted as a magnet to the world at large and how many points of contact the Euphrates valley civilisations and the Nile valley civilisations had with each other, we may well suppose a broadening of Egyptian culture and civilisation in consequence. The Hyksos may have been Egyptianised in Egypt, but they could not have failed in their turn to contribute Syrian and Semitic ideas to Egypt. Among these were Monotheism, a patriarchal organisation of society, and an impatience of priestly or caste domination. These must have contrasted strangely with the chaotic Pantheon of countless deities, the lash-driven slaves living huddled in the cities, and the dedicated priests and richly endowed temples which catered for the privileged few, but lived by the sweat of the brow of the unprivileged many.

The New Empire was the flowering period of Egyptian genius and requires special consideration. The crudities of the old pre-Dynastic chaotic Pantheon had been in process of attrition through the centuries. Local gods tended to be absorbed in general gods. Some sort of rationalisation and spiritualisation had been going on throughout the Dynastic period. A process of systematisation and unification was now consciously undertaken. The primitive worship of animals had gradually been transformed into a system of animal-gods, with human bodies and animal heads. The human bodies represented the anthropomorphic tendencies, while the animal heads became types of qualities. For example, Anubis, with the dog emblem, was the door-keeper, the messenger, the custodian of the dead. Apis, or Hapis, the sacred bull of Memphis, symbolised the renewal of life ; he was identified with Osiris; there were great rejoicings when a new Apis (a black bull calf) was found, and great mourning and costly burial when one died. Thoth, the god of wisdom and magic, was symbolised by an ibis, that stately, mute, mysterious bird of passage in the Nile valley.

In addition to the symbolism of animals, there was the worship of the great phenomena of nature, the Nile, the giver of agricultural bounties to Egypt, and the sun, which, as the god Ra, became the supreme god in Egypt. Then there was the myth of Osiris the good, who came to the earth for the benefit of mankind, was killed by the malice of Set, the power of evil, and reigns as the judge of the dead in the lower world. His faithful wife Isis and his falcon-eyed son Horus figure in the mysteries. It is possible that the Osiris myth itself arose from a myth of the Nile or the sun.

There was a gradual perception of Monotheism, a realisation that God is One and above names. But the picturesque forms, festivals, and representations remained, and as the priests of all grades enjoyed special privileges and monopolised knowledge and learning, the people remained ignorant. They were exploited and practically enslaved. It was in the midst of such conditions that Moses came. He came to rescue his own people from the bondage of Egypt, a task which he performed. But it must not be forgotten that his mission was also addressed to the king of Egypt and to the people of Egypt. Here also he sowed the seed, although he did not reap the fruit. The king, the Pharaoh, was almost looked upon as a god, and looked upon himself as a god. He had to be humbled, and he was humbled. But God's purpose is not merely to humble. It is also to lead from darkness to light. If the particular Pharaoh was too hard-hearted to respond, his descendant in the fifth or sixth generation made a public confession of the One True God, as we shall see presently. What of the people ? The wise men of Egypt, who were confronted with Moses, repented of their deceit, and saw the light by the grace of God, according to the Quranic narrative. Though they were threatened and perhaps martyred, their fate must have opened the eyes of the people and prepared them for the remarkable religious revolution which we shall now proceed to describe.

The Pharaoh of the Exodus was probably Thothmes I (about 1540 B.C.). The Pharaoh Amenophis IV (about 1350 B.C.) adopted the worship of the One Supreme God as the State religion. He had been a high priest of the Sungod at Heliopolis, but had begun to look upon the multiplicity of gods in the Egyptian Pantheon as a blot on Egyptian religion. His original name had been Amen-hotep (" Ammon is satisfied") as being devoted to Ammon the great god of the State religion at Thebes. He changed his name to Akhen-Aton (" Pious to Aton ") and worshipped the Supreme God under the name of Aton. He abandoned the city of Thebes as being devoted to Ammon and founded a new city near the site of what is now Tel-al-Amarna, between Thebes and Memphis, and dedicated it to Aton the Supreme God. The clay tablets discovered at Tel-al-Amarna in 1887 throw much light on the relations of Egypt with her tributaries in Syria. The alphabet on the tablets is the Cuneiform of Assyria : the language is Semitic, and closely akin to Hebrew. Unfortunately the religious revolution of Amenophis IV did not last. The city was only inhabited twenty years. His second son-in-law and successor, Tutenkh-Aton, carried out a counter-revolution. He went back from Aton to Ammon, changed his own name to Tutenkh-Amen, and restored the temples at Karnak and the cult of Ammon. The recent finds from his tombs show what exquisite skill the artists and artisans of Egypt had then attained. The pure religion remained established on the throne only for two generations, but we need not suppose that it was rooted out of the minds of the people.

The later Dynasties, XXI to XXXI, saw the decay of Egypt as a Power. The Assyrian and Persian invasions ultimately extinguished the freedom of Egypt. With the coming of Alexander the Great (332 B.C.) and the foundation of the city of Alexandria, a new era dawned on the culture of Egypt. It mingled with Greek and other thought, and became cosmopolitan in nature. Already, in the time of Herodotus, the sensitive Greek mind had been impressed with the mystery and wisdom of Egypt. It now made the soil of Egypt cosmopolitan in religion, culture, and philosophy. The

Ptolemaic dynasty held a broadly tolerant attitude, and even imported the rites of Serapis from the Black Sea and assimilated him to Apis the Bull of Memphis. The new cult of Serapis spread widely over the East, and later, when Egypt came under the Roman Empire (30 B.C.), into the very heart of that Empire. The Serapion in Alexandria, with its famous library, became for a few centuries the true intellectual centre of the world. The very untavourable picture drawn of Egyptian religion in Lytton's *Last Days of Pompeii* must be referred to the somewhat hybrid cult of Isis as practised in foreign lands rather than to Egyptian religion generally. What course real Egyptian religion took in this period we have no means of judging accurately. In the light of earlier and later events we may suppose that the steady honest industrious Egyptian peasantry and people went on pursuing the even tenor of their career with the same mystic longing for a practical religion which was preparing them for purer forms of worship and a juster distribution of the fruits of labour.

Alexandria in the first centuries of the Christian era was resounding with the shouts of every kind of philosophy and the teaching of every kind of religious sect, from East and West, North and South, but mainly from the East, which has ever been a nursery of religious ideas. A special quarter was assigned to the Jews in the city. It became the true centre of Hellenised Judaism, and may claim Josephus among its disciples. Neo-Pythagoreanism, Neo-Platonism, Gnosticism, and Manichæism found a home there. Mithraism, which was so widely spread in theRoman Empire, especially in the army, in the first three centuries A.D., was probably represented on its philosophic side in Alexandria. Its intermixture of races, creeds, philosophies, and religions, produced an atmosphere of chaos, which was not cleared until the advent of Islam.

But from a religious point of view our greatest interest in Egypt in the first seven centuries of the Christian era is in the development of Christianity itself. It is difficult to say when exactly Christianity began to displace the older Egyptian cults. But when Christianity was well-established, we find Egypt one of its most important centres. But the new Christianity which was evolved out of the ruins of Christ's simple teaching had four distinct attitudes towards organisation, speculative doctrine, ascеticism and mysticism. (1) The native Egyptian or Coptic Church was contemplative, ascetic, and mystical. Monasticism became so rampant that it seriously affected the growth of population and degraded the position of women. (2) The Alexandrian school developed on Greek lines,—political, ambitious, speculative, philosophical, and liable to break up into numerous sects and heresies, each party trying to dominate and put down the others as heretical by the strong arm of the law. (3) The Bishop of Rome, when the seat of the Empire was transferred to Constantinople in 330, gradually developed political power in Italy. He inherited the Roman genius for organisation, and the invasion of the Germanic tribes gave him an opportunity not only of extending the Roman Catholic Church over the whole of Central and Western Europe, but of establishing the Church as superior to the state when the Papacy became an established political power. (4) The Orthodox Eastern Church, and all the sects which it fought in the East, tended ultimately to vanish before the advance of Islam. Had it not been for the vast Slav territories over which it obtained sway, in and around Russia and afterwards in Siberia, the Orthodox Eastern Church would have been reduced to a negligible position like the Coptic Church in Egypt. With pretensions to rule the State, it had yet become, in Kingsley's words in "Hypatia", the "stipendiary slave-official" of the Empire, sharing in all its effete corruption.

But we are anticipating. Before the Roman Catholic Church parted from the Orthodox Eastern Church, the united Church fought with and suppressed many so-called "heresies", some of which represented the views of primitive Christianity, and the scence of many of these doctrinal fights was in Egypt. The one that interests us most is Arianism. Arius was an Alexandrian Presbyter early in the fourth century A.D. and fought hard for the doctrine of Unity, the simple conception of the Eternal God, as against all the hair splitting and irrational distinctions in the nature and persons of the Godhead, which finally crystallised in the doctrine of the Trinity, propounded and maintained with much personal acrimony by Athanasius. Athanasius himself was born in Alexandria and became Bishop of Alexandria. He may be counted as the father of Orthodoxy (as now understood in Christianity) and the real systematiser of the doctrine of the Trinity—"three in one and one in three." Up to the third century A.D. the Unitarians had been in the majority in the Christian Church, though subtle metaphysicians had started disputes as to the meaning of "God becoming man," the Logos or the Word, the Power of God, whether the Father and the Son were of the same substance or of similar substance, whether the Son could be said to have been created by the Father, and numerous questions of that kind. They do not interest us now, but they rent the Christian world into many jarring sects until the mission of our Holy Apostle dissipated the mists and re-established the doctrine of Unity on a firm and rational basis.

As I have said, the Christian Churches in the East, as well as the Germanic nations which came later into the fold, adhered to Unity although not in the pure form which was made clear in the Holy Qur-ān. The issue was joined between Arius and Athanasius, and the first General Council of the Christian Church, that of Nicæa (in Bithynia) in 325, decided against Arius and unitarianism. The controversy, however, still continued to rage until 381, when the Council of Constantinople, called by the Emperor Theodosius the Great, confirmed the Nicene doctrine of the Trinity and declared it to be the only Orthodox one. Though controversies, protests, and persecutions continued long afterwards, we may take that date as the date of the fall of Christianity. Even in Western Christianity, as late as 496, Clovis the Frankish king was the only Christian sovereign sophisticated enough to follow the subtle doctrine of the Trinity. The others were brought into line by political power later.

The Christian creed became narrower and narrower, less and less rational, more and more inclined to use earthly weapons to suppress the eternal truth of God. In 415 the Jews were expelled from Alexandria. In the same year and in the same city the beautiful, modest, eloquent philosopher and mathematician, Hypatia, was murdered,—an outrage against both rationalism and the intellectual and religious position of woman in human society. The murder was a particularly brutal one. She was dragged from her chariot in the streets, stripped naked, and suffered a lingering death in a Christian Church. Her body was then cut to pieces and burned. The worst feature of the crime was the complicity of the Patriarch of Alexandria, who was not only the chief religious dignitary of the Orthodox Church in Egypt but the *de facto* repository of political power. Meanwhile the native Christian community—the Coptic Church,—which had all along clung to the Monophysite doctrine, a corrupt form of Unitarianism, was out of the pale, and its members were held down as a depressed class by their Orthodox brethren. The latter also, basking in official sunshine, collected

power and property into their own hands. As Kingsley remarks in ***Hypatia***, the Egyptian Church "ended as a mere chaos of idolatrous sects, persecuting each other for metaphysical propositions, which, true or false, were equally heretical in their mouths because they used them as watchwords for division." The social conditions produced an amount of discontent, for which the redress came only with the advent of Islam.

It was for this reason that the Copts and the inhabitants of Egypt generally welcomed the forces of Islam under 'Amr as deliverers in 639 A.D. The power was taken over by the victorious army of Islam from Cyrus (called Muqauqas in Arabic through the Coptic), the Patriarch of Alexandria, but it was used by the army of deliverance to enlarge the liberties of the Egyptians, to admit them into the universal brotherhood of Islam, and to improve the resources of the country for the benefit of the people. Except a negligible remnant of conservatives the Egyptians as a nation accepted the religion, the language, and the institutions of the Arabs and embarked on a new course of history, which it is unnecessary to follow further in this note.

It should be remarked, however, that what happened in Egypt happened generally in western Asia. The jarring sectarian irrational religions gave place before the triumphant religion of Unity and Brotherhood, and the Byzantine Empire receded and receded until it was swept out of existence. The feeble efforts made by the Emperor Leo the Isaurian in 726-731 to restrict the use of images were a reflection of the puritanical zeal of Islam. But they did not succeed in the area of his authority, and they completely alienated the Papacy from the Eastern Orthodox Church. The Bishop of Rome had been consolidating his power, and in the person of Gregory I (590-604) had already assumed the control of Italy and was seeking the aid and support of the Barbarian invaders who eventually became the pillars of the Papacy. The final and open rupture between the Orthodox Eastern Church and the Roman Catholic Church took place in 1054. But the earlier dates are remarkable. After the birth of the Holy Apostle of Islam the disruption of the Orthodox Christian Church (which had now become an anachronism) began. When Islam was making its triumphant march in the 8th century after Christ, the original (Greek) Church began to take some steps to put its own house in order. But it had lost its mission, and the new Islamic people took its place. The Western Church has since worked on definitely new lines, and its offshoots among the Protestant Churches have, consciously or unconsciously, been influenced by the broad principles of Islam. What the course of future religion may be and how God will unfold His All-Wise Plan it is not given to us mortals to know. In the Islamic Brotherhood many changes have taken place and are taking place. Egypt, in spite of her many vicissitudes in the Islamic period, is in the intellectual forefront among the Arabic-speaking nations of Islam. We pray that her people may be guided, through their educational, cultural, and religious channels, to work with a new spirit for the progress of Islam and the glory of God.

References: Those given for Appendix IV; and in addition: Sir E. A. Wallis Budge, *Gods of the Egyptians*; and his latest book *From Fetish to God in Ancient Egypt* (Oxford 1934); Budge, *Book of the Dead*; A. W. Shorter, *Introduction to Egyptian Religion* (1931); Adolf von Harnack, *History of Dogma*, 7 vols., is an elaborate detailed German account of how Christian Dogma grew up and may be read in an English translation; a handier book is R.W. Mackay, *Rise and Progress of Christianity* (1854); C. Kingsley's novel *Hypatia* gives a good picture of social and religious conditions in Christian Egypt in the fifth century. On the identity of al-Muqauqas (Pkauchios) with Cyrus, see Dr. A. J. Bulter's "Arab Conquest of Egypt." (Oxford 1902), pp. 508 562.

INTRODUCTION TO SŪRA VIII (*Anfāl*)

In the previous Introductions to the Sūras we have shown how each Sūra is a step or gradation in the teaching of the Qur-ān. The first seven Sūras, comprising a little less than one-third of the Qur-ān, form a gradation, sketching the early spiritual history of man and leading up to the formation of the new Ummat or Community of the Holy Apostle. Now we begin another gradation, consolidating that Ummat and directing us as to various phases in our new collective life.

In this chapter we have the lessons of the Battle of Badr enforced in their larger aspects: (1) the question of war booty ; (2) the true virtues necessary for fighting the good fight; (3) victory against odds; (4) clemency and consideration for one's own and for others in the hour of victory.

As regards booty taken in battle, the first point to note is that that should never be our aim in war. It is only an adventitious circumstance, a sort of windfall. Secondly, no soldier or troop has any inherent right to it. A righteous war is a community affair, and any accessions resulting from it belong to God, or the community or Cause. Thirdly, certain equitable principles of division should be laid down to check human greed and selfishness. A fifth share goes to the Commander, and he can use it at his discretion; for his own expenses, and for the relief of the poor and suffering, and the orphans and widows (viii. 41). The remainder was divided, according to the Prophet's practice, not only among those who were actually in the fight physically, but all who were in the enterprise, young and old, provided they loyally did some duty assigned to them. Fourthly, there should be no disputes, as they interfere with internal discipline and harmony.

These principles are followed in the best modern practice of civilised nations. All acquisitions of war belong absolutely to the Sovereign as representing the commonwealth. In the distribution of booty not only the actual captors but also the "joint captors" and the "constructive captors" share. See Sir R. Phillimore's ***International Law*** (1885), vol. 3, pp. 209 10. 221 24.

As regards the military virtues, which are the types of virtues throughout life, we are shown by an analysis of the incidents of Badr how against the greatest odds, God's help will give the victory if men are fighting not for themselves but for the sacred Cause of God. And directions are given for the treatment of prisoners and for maintaining the solidarity of the Muslim community.

The date of this Sūra is shortly after the battle of Badr, which was fought on Friday, the 17th of Ramadhān in the second year of the Hijra. A short account of the battle is given in n. 352 to iii. 13.

Summary.—All booty is really at the disposal of God's Apostle under directions from God. Men of faith accept and obey these directions with cheerfulness. Victory and the prize of victory come from God, as was proved at Badr (viii. 1-19, and C. 89).

Obedience and intelligent discipline, zeal, faith, and gratitude to God, are the true passports to success and protection from the assaults of evil. Evil will be piled up with evil and destroyed (viii. 20-37, and C. 90).

The battle of Badr was a testing time, and showed how virtue and valour can conquer against odds. Steadfastness and obedience; faith, courage, and fearlessness ; due preparation and free expenditure of resources and energy ;—these are expected from you by God, and His help is all-sufficient (viii. 38-64, and C. 91).

Even tenfold odds against you do not count if you are fighting for truth and faith against enemies of truth and faith ; but remember clemency and consideration in the hour of victory (viii. 65-75, and C. 92).

C. 89.—Fight the good fight, but dispute not
(viii. 1-19.) About the prize : that is for God
To give. Men of faith act and obey.
'Tis nobler to fight for Truth
Than to seek worldly gain.
To the pure in faith God will give
The mind and the resources to conquer.
They but fight, with no thought
Of ever turning back : the victory
Should be ascribed to God, **not men.**

Sūra VIII.

Anfāl, or the Spoils of War.

In the name of God, Most Gracious, Most Merciful.

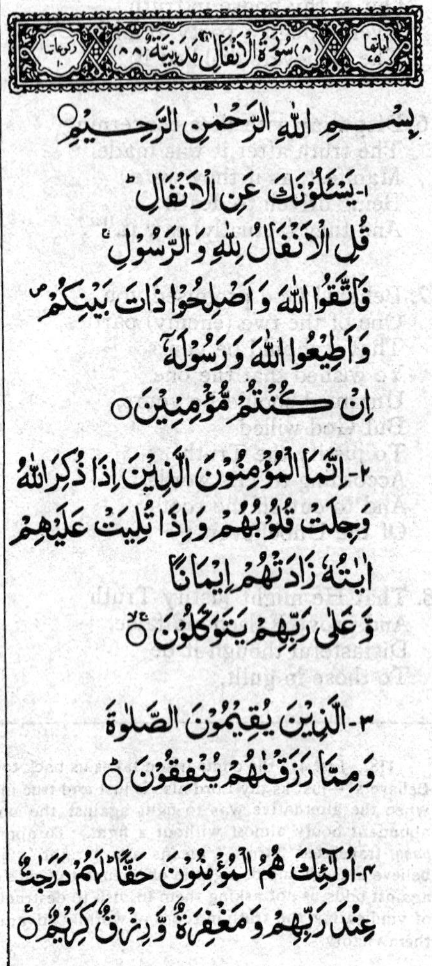

1. They ask thee [1178] concerning
(Things taken as) spoils of war.
Say: "(Such) spoils are
At the disposal of God [1179]
And the Apostle: so fear
God, and keep straight
The relations between yourselves:
Obey God and His Apostle,
If ye do believe."

2. For, Believers are those
Who, when God is mentioned,
Feel a tremor in their hearts,
And when they hear
His Signs rehearsed, find
Their faith strengthened,
And put (all) their trust
In their Lord;

3. Who establish regular prayers
And spend (freely) out of
The gifts We have given
Them for sustenance: [1180]

4. Such in truth are the Believers:
They have grades of dignity
With their Lord, and forgiveness,
And generous sustenance:

1178. The occasion was the question of the division of the booty after the battle of Badr. See Introduction to this Sūra.

1179. Booty taken in a lawful and just war does not belong to any individual. If he fought for such accessory rewards, he fought from wrong motives. It belongs to the Cause, in this case the Cause of God, as administered by His Apostle. Any portion given out to individuals are accessory gifts, windfalls from the bounty of the Commander. The chief thing is to remain staunch to the Cause of God, and have no differences among those who stand for the Cause. Our internal relations must be kept straight: they must not be disturbed by cupidity or worldly considerations of gain, for any windfalls of this kind should be outside our calculations.

1180. *Sustenance*: again in both the literal and the metaphorical sense. The object is to warn off from the love of booty and worldly wealth. Why do we want these? To all true Believers God gives generous sustenance in any case, in both senses, but especially in the spiritual sense, for it is coupled with forgiveness and grades of dignity before God, in the next verse.

5. Just as [1181] thy Lord ordered thee
Out of thy house in truth,
Even though a party among
The Believers disliked it,

٥-كَمَآ أَخْرَجَكَ رَبُّكَ مِنْۢ بَيْتِكَ بِالْحَقِّ
وَإِنَّ فَرِيقًا مِّنَ الْمُؤْمِنِينَ لَكَٰرِهُونَ ۝

6. Disputing with thee concerning
The truth after it was made
Manifest, as if they were
Being driven to death
And they (actually) saw it.[1182]

٦-يُجَٰدِلُونَكَ فِى الْحَقِّ بَعْدَ مَا
تَبَيَّنَ كَأَنَّمَا يُسَاقُونَ إِلَى الْمَوْتِ
وَهُمْ يَنظُرُونَ ۝

7. Behold! God promised you
One of the two (enemy) parties,[1183]
That it should be yours:
Ye wished that the one
Unarmed should be yours,
But God willed
To justify the Truth
According to His words,
And to cut off the roots
Of the Unbelievers;—

٧-وَإِذْ يَعِدُكُمُ اللَّهُ إِحْدَى الطَّآئِفَتَيْنِ
أَنَّهَا لَكُمْ وَتَوَدُّونَ أَنَّ غَيْرَ ذَاتِ
الشَّوْكَةِ تَكُونُ لَكُمْ
وَيُرِيدُ اللَّهُ أَن يُحِقَّ الْحَقَّ بِكَلِمَٰتِهِ
وَيَقْطَعَ دَابِرَ الْكَٰفِرِينَ ۝

8. That He might justify Truth
And prove Falsehood false,
Distasteful though it be
To those in guilt.

٨-لِيُحِقَّ الْحَقَّ وَيُبْطِلَ الْبَٰطِلَ
وَلَوْ كَرِهَ الْمُجْرِمُونَ ۝

1181. *Just as*: the comparison takes us back to the first clause in verse 4: "such in truth are the Believers"—just as thy Lord also is just and true in ordering thee out to fight against heavy odds, when the alternative was to fight against the unarmed caravan which would have given thee abundant booty almost without a fight. To appreciate the full meaning, remember that the word *ḥaqq*, translated "truth" means also "right," "just," "what is becoming." The true Believers believe in truth and do right in obedience to God's command. So God also, in asking them to fight against odds, is not asking them to rush to destruction, but is providing them with an opportunity of vindicating the truth in scorn of worldly advantage. And He made good His promise by giving them victory.

1182. In verse 6 we have again the word "truth": some of the Believers disputed concerning "the truth": they did not feel sure that the course recommended was the true and right course. They thought it would be certain destruction: they saw death almost staring them in the face.

1183. Just before Badr there were two alternatives before the Muslims in Medina, to save themselves from being overwhelmed by the Meccan Quraish with all their resources from the rich Syrian trade. One, which had least danger for the time being, and also promised much booty, was to fall upon the Quraish caravan returning from Syria to Mecca richly laden, and led by Abū Sufyan with only 40 men unarmed. From a worldly point of view this was the safest and most lucrative course. The other alternative, which was actually adopted on the recommendation of the Apostle by the guidance of God, was to leave the booty alone and march out boldly against the well-armed and well-equipped Quraish army of 1,000 men coming from Mecca. The Muslims had no more than 300 men, ill-armed, to oppose to this force. But if they could defeat it, it would shake the selfish autocracy which was in possession of Mecca. By God's help they won a splendid victory, and the standard of Truth was established, never to be lowered again.

9. Remember ye implored
The assistance of your Lord,
And He answered you:
"I will assist you
With a thousand of the angels,
Ranks on ranks."[1184]

٩-إِذْ تَسْتَغِيثُونَ رَبَّكُمْ
فَاسْتَجَابَ لَكُمْ أَنِّي مُمِدُّكُمْ
بِأَلْفٍ مِّنَ الْمَلٰٓئِكَةِ مُرْدِفِينَ ○

10. God made it but a message
Of hope, and an assurance
To your hearts: (in any case)[1185]
There is no help
Except from God:
And God is Exalted in Power,
Wise.

١٠-وَمَا جَعَلَهُ اللّٰهُ إِلَّا بُشْرٰى وَلِتَطْمَئِنَّ
بِهٖ قُلُوبُكُمْ ۚ وَمَا النَّصْرُ إِلَّا مِنْ عِنْدِ
ع اللّٰهِ ۚ إِنَّ اللّٰهَ عَزِيزٌ حَكِيمٌ ○

SECTION 2.

11. Remember He covered you
With a sort of drowsiness,[1186]
To give you calm as from
Himself, and he caused
Rain to descend on you[1187]
From heaven, to clean you
Therewith, to remove from you
The stain of Satan,[1188]
To strengthen your hearts,
And to plant your feet
Firmly therewith.

١١-إِذْ يُغَشِّيكُمُ النُّعَاسَ أَمَنَةً مِّنْهُ
وَيُنَزِّلُ عَلَيْكُم مِّنَ السَّمَآءِ مَآءً
لِّيُطَهِّرَكُم بِهٖ
وَيُذْهِبَ عَنكُمْ رِجْزَ الشَّيْطٰنِ
وَلِيَرْبِطَ عَلٰى قُلُوبِكُمْ
وَيُثَبِّتَ بِهِ الْأَقْدَامَ ○

12. Remember thy Lord inspired
The angels (with the message):
"I am with you: give
Firmness to the Believers:

١٢-إِذْ يُوحِي رَبُّكَ إِلَى الْمَلٰٓئِكَةِ
أَنِّي مَعَكُمْ فَثَبِّتُوا الَّذِينَ آمَنُوا ۚ

1184. *Cf.* iii. 123, 125, 126. The number of angels, a thousand at Badr and three thousand and five thousand at Uḥud, is probably not to be taken literally, but to express a strength at least equal to that of the enemy.

1185. All help comes ultimately from God. In special cases it may take special forms to put heart into us, and to fit in with our feelings and our psychology.

1186. *Cf.* iii. 154 for Uḥud. Calm (presence of mind) is essential in battle and in all posts of danger. If the mind is too much in a state of excitement, it cannot carry out a well-considered or well-concerted plan. This spirit of calm confidence on the part of the Muslims won against the blustering violence of the Quraish.

1187. The rain was welcome for many reasons. (1) Water was scarce both for drinking and ablutions; (2) the Muslim band, without baggage or equipment or comforts, found that their thirst aggravated their fatigue; (3) the sand was loose, and the rain consolidated it and enabled them "to plant their feet firmly."

1188. "*Stain of Satan*": both literally and figuratively. Dirt is physically a symbol of evil, and the Muslims were particular about ablutions before prayer. But the rain also refreshed their spirits and removed any lurking doubts in their minds (suggestions of the Evil One) that victory might be impossible in such adverse circumstances.

I will instil terror
Into the hearts of the Unbelievers:
Smite ye above their necks
And smite all their
Finger-tips off them."[1189]

سَأُلْقِي فِي قُلُوبِ الَّذِينَ كَفَرُوا الرُّعْبَ
فَاضْرِبُوا فَوْقَ الْأَعْنَاقِ
وَاضْرِبُوا مِنْهُمْ كُلَّ بَنَانٍ ۝

13. This because they contended
Against God and His Apostle:
If any contend against God
And His Apostle, God
Is strict in punishment.

١٣- ذٰلِكَ بِأَنَّهُمْ شَاقُّوا اللّٰهَ وَرَسُولَهُ
وَمَنْ يُشَاقِقِ اللّٰهَ وَرَسُولَهُ
فَإِنَّ اللّٰهَ شَدِيدُ الْعِقَابِ ۝

14. Thus (will it be said): "Taste ye
Then of the (punishment):
For those who resist God,
Is the penalty of the Fire."

١٤- ذٰلِكُمْ فَذُوقُوهُ
وَأَنَّ لِلْكٰفِرِينَ عَذَابَ النَّارِ ۝

15. O ye who believe!
When ye meet
The Unbelievers
In hostile array,[1190]
Never turn your backs
To them.

١٥- يٰأَيُّهَا الَّذِينَ اٰمَنُوا
إِذَا لَقِيتُمُ الَّذِينَ كَفَرُوا زَحْفًا
فَلَا تُوَلُّوهُمُ الْأَدْبَارَ ۝

16. If any do turn his back
To them on such a day—
Unless it be in a stratagem
Of war, or to retreat
To a troop (of his own)—
He draws on himself
The wrath of God,
And his abode is Hell,—
An evil refuge (indeed)!

١٦- وَمَنْ يُوَلِّهِمْ يَوْمَئِذٍ دُبُرَهُ
إِلَّا مُتَحَرِّفًا لِقِتَالٍ أَوْ مُتَحَيِّزًا إِلَى فِئَةٍ
فَقَدْ بَاءَ بِغَضَبٍ مِنَ اللّٰهِ
وَمَأْوٰهُ جَهَنَّمُ
وَبِئْسَ الْمَصِيرُ ۝

17. It is not ye who
Slew them; it was God:

١٧- فَلَمْ تَقْتُلُوهُمْ وَلٰكِنَّ اللّٰهَ قَتَلَهُمْ

1189. The vulnerable parts of an armed man are above the neck. A blow on the neck, face, or head, finishes him off. If he has armour it is difficult to get at his heart. But if his hands are put out of action, he is unable to wield his sword or lance or other weapon, and easily becomes a prisoner.

1190 The laws of spiritual fight are exactly similar to those enforced by military virtue and discipline. Meet your enemy fairly and squarely, not rashly, but after due preparation. *Zahfan* in the text (*meeting in hostile array*) implies a slow and well-planned proceeding towards a hostile army. When once in combat, carry it through: there is no room for second thoughts. Death or victory should be the motto of every soldier: it may be death for himself individually, but if he has faith, there is triumph in either case for his cause. Two exceptions are recognised: (1) *reculer pour mieux sauter*, to go back in order to jump forward; or to deceive the enemy by a feint; (2) if an individual or body is, by the chances of battle, isolated from his own force, he can fall back on his force in order to fight the battle. There is no virtue in mere single-handedness. Each individual must use his life and his resources to the best advantage for the common cause.

When thou threwest (a handful[1191]
Of dust), it was not
Thy act, but God's:
In order that He might
Test the Believers
By a gracious trial[1192]
From Himself: for God
Is He Who heareth
And knoweth (all things).

وَمَا رَمَيْتَ إِذْ رَمَيْتَ
وَلٰكِنَّ اللّٰهَ رَمٰى
وَلِيُبْلِيَ الْمُؤْمِنِينَ مِنْهُ بَلَآءً حَسَنًا
إِنَّ اللّٰهَ سَمِيعٌ عَلِيمٌ ○

18. That, and also because
God is He Who makes feeble
The plans and stratagems
Of the Unbelievers.

١٨- ذٰلِكُمْ وَأَنَّ اللّٰهَ
مُوهِنُ كَيْدِ الْكٰفِرِينَ ○

19. (O Unbelievers!) if ye prayed
For victory and judgment,[1193]
Now hath the judgment
Come to you: if ye desist
(From wrong), it will be
Best for you: if ye return
(To the attack), so shall We.
Not the least good
Will your forces be to you
Even if they were multiplied:
For verily God
Is with those who believe!

١٩- إِنْ تَسْتَفْتِحُوا فَقَدْ جَآءَكُمُ الْفَتْحُ
وَإِنْ تَنْتَهُوا فَهُوَ خَيْرٌ لَّكُمْ
وَإِنْ تَعُودُوا نَعُدْ
وَلَنْ تُغْنِيَ عَنْكُمْ فِئَتُكُمْ شَيْـًٔا
وَلَوْ كَثُرَتْ
وَأَنَّ اللّٰهَ مَعَ الْمُؤْمِنِينَ ○

C. 90.—Be ready to obey God's call, and to hold
(viii. 20-37.) **All else as naught: He will give you**
The light, turn away all evil from you,
And forgive you your sins and shortcomings.
Ever keep in remembrance His mercies and grace.
The godless may try to keep men
From God, but they will not thrive:
They will be hurled together to destruction.

1191. When the battle began, the Holy Apostle prayed, and threw a handful of dust or sand at the enemy, symbolical of their rushing blindly to their fate. This had a great psychological effect. Every act in the battle is ascribed to God, as it was in His cause, and it was not undertaken except by His command.

1192. Numerically the odds against the Muslims were three to one. In other ways they were at a disadvantage: of arms and equipment they had but little, while the enemy were well-found; they were inexperienced, while the Quraish had brought their foremost warriors. In all this there was a test, but the test was accompanied by gracious favours of countless value: their Commander was one in whom they had perfect faith, and for whom they were ready to lay down their lives; the rain refreshed them; their spirit was unshaken; and they were fighting in God's cause. Thus the trial or test became itself a blessing.

1193. *Fath*=victory, decision, judgment. The Quraish in Mecca had prayed for victory; they were confident that their superior numbers, equipment, and experience would be decisive. With a play on the word, they are told that the decision had come, and the victory—but not in the sense they had hoped for!

SECTION 3.

20. O ye who believe!
Obey God and His Apostle,
And turn not away from him
When ye hear (him speak).

٢٠- يٰۤاَيُّهَا الَّذِيْنَ اٰمَنُوْۤا اَطِيْعُوا اللّٰهَ وَرَسُوْلَهٗ
وَلَا تَوَلَّوْا عَنْهُ وَاَنْتُمْ تَسْمَعُوْنَ ۝

21. Nor be like those who say,
"We hear," but listen not: [1194]

٢١- وَلَا تَكُوْنُوْا كَالَّذِيْنَ قَالُوْا سَمِعْنَا وَ
هُمْ لَا يَسْمَعُوْنَ ۝

22. For the worst of beasts
In the sight of God
Are the deaf and the dumb,—[1195]
Those who understand not.

٢٢- اِنَّ شَرَّ الدَّوَآبِّ عِنْدَ اللّٰهِ الصُّمُّ
الْبُكْمُ الَّذِيْنَ لَا يَعْقِلُوْنَ ۝

23. If God had found in them
Any good, He would indeed
Have made them listen:
(As it is), if He had made them
Listen, they would but have
Turned back and declined (faith).

٢٣- وَلَوْ عَلِمَ اللّٰهُ فِيْهِمْ
خَيْرًا لَّاَسْمَعَهُمْ ۗ
وَلَوْ اَسْمَعَهُمْ لَتَوَلَّوْا وَّهُمْ مُّعْرِضُوْنَ ۝

24. O ye who believe!
Give your response to God
And His Apostle, when He
Calleth you to that which
Will give you life; [1196]
And know that God
Cometh in between a man [1197]
And his heart, and that
It is He to Whom
Ye shall (all) be gathered.

٢٤- يٰۤاَيُّهَا الَّذِيْنَ اٰمَنُوا
اسْتَجِيْبُوْا لِلّٰهِ وَ لِلرَّسُوْلِ
اِذَا دَعَاكُمْ لِمَا يُحْيِيْكُمْ ۚ
وَاعْلَمُوْۤا اَنَّ اللّٰهَ يَحُوْلُ بَيْنَ الْمَرْءِ
وَقَلْبِهٖ وَاَنَّهٗۤ اِلَيْهِ تُحْشَرُوْنَ ۝

1194. *Cf.* ii. 93.

1195 *Cf.* ii. 18.

1196. There are two points to note. (1) Note that after God and His Apostle are mentioned, the pronoun and verb in the next clause are singular: everything that God's Apostle put forward as an injunction came by inspiration from God: the Apostle made his will coincide completely with God's will. (2) We are asked actively to give our response in deed and life to the call of duty and conscience, for that call leads to real life, the life eternal, even though it may apparently mean in this world the loss of things that make life dear or the loss of life itself. If we refer this to Jihād, *i.e.*, fighting in and for the Cause, both literally and metaphorically, the meaning becomes quite clear.

1197. If the human heart is refractory and refuses to obey the call of God, that is not the end of the matter. God has to be reckoned with. The refusal may be because there was some pet human scheme which the heart of man was not willing to give up for God's Cause. Will that scheme come to fruition by refusing to serve the higher Cause? By no means. Man proposes, but God disposes. If the scheme or motive was perfectly secret from men, it was not secret from God. The heart is the innermost seat of man's affections and desires; but between this seat and man himself is the presence of the Omnipresent.

25. And fear tumult or oppression,[1198]
Which affecteth not in particular
(Only) those of you who do wrong:
And know that God
Is strict in punishment.

٢٥- وَاتَّقُوا فِتْنَةً
لَا تُصِيبَنَّ الَّذِينَ ظَلَمُوا مِنْكُمْ خَاصَّةً
وَاعْلَمُوا أَنَّ اللَّهَ شَدِيدُ الْعِقَابِ ○

26. Call to mind when ye
Were a small (band),
Despised through the land,
And afraid that men might
Despoil and kidnap you;[1199]
But He provided a safe asylum
For you, strengthened you
With His aid, and gave you
Good things for sustenance:
That ye might be grateful.

٢٦- وَاذْكُرُوا إِذْ أَنْتُمْ قَلِيلٌ
مُسْتَضْعَفُونَ فِي الْأَرْضِ
تَخَافُونَ أَنْ يَتَخَطَّفَكُمُ النَّاسُ
فَآوَاكُمْ وَأَيَّدَكُمْ بِنَصْرِهِ
وَرَزَقَكُمْ مِنَ الطَّيِّبَاتِ لَعَلَّكُمْ تَشْكُرُونَ ○

27. O ye that believe!
Betray not the trust
Of God and the Apostle,
Nor misappropriate knowingly
Things entrusted to you.[1200]

٢٧- يَا أَيُّهَا الَّذِينَ آمَنُوا لَا تَخُونُوا اللَّهَ
وَالرَّسُولَ وَتَخُونُوا أَمَانَاتِكُمْ
وَأَنْتُمْ تَعْلَمُونَ ○

28. And know ye
That your possessions

٢٨- وَاعْلَمُوا أَنَّمَا أَمْوَالُكُمْ

1198. *Fitnat* has many meanings: (1) the root meaning is trial or temptation, as in ii. 102 and viii. 28; (2) an analogous meaning is trial or punishment, as in v. 74; (3) tumult or oppression, as in ii. 193; and here; and in viii. 39; (4) there is here (viii. 25) the further shade of meaning suggested: discord, sedition, civil war.

This warning against internal discord or tumult was very necessary in the Civil Wars of early Islam, and was never more necessary than it is now. For it affects innocent and guilty alike.

1199. On the immediate occasion the Muslims were reminded that they were a small band in Mecca; despised and rejected; living in a state of insecurity for their persons, their lives, their property, and those of their dependants; persecuted and exiled and how by the grace of God they found a safe asylum in Medina, how they found friends and helpers, how their many needs were cared for, and how at length they gathered strength and numbers enough to defeat the forces of godlessness, injustice, and oppression.

But for every individual, in some form or other, the lesson applies. His spiritual life begins humbly; he is despised and laughed at, perhaps persecuted and shut out from ordinary privileges open to all; but God gives him strength; friends spring up for him; and he is sustained until his highest spiritual desires are gradually fulfilled.

1200. Trusts may be of various kinds: (1) property, goods, credit, etc.; (2) plans, confidences, secrets, etc.; (3) knowledge, talents, opportunities, etc., which we are expected to use for our fellow-men. Men may betray the trust of God and His Apostle by misusing property, or abusing the confidence reposed in them, or the knowledge or talents given to them. On that special occasion, when the plans for the protection of God's worshippers against annihilation were of special importance, the Apostle's trust and confidence had to be guarded with special care. Occasions for scrupulously respecting the trust and confidence of our fellow-men occur every day in our life, and few of us can claim perfection in this respect. Hence the special distinction of the man of God, who earned the title of *Al-Amīn*, the one who was true to every trust reposed in him.

And your progeny
Are but a trial;[1201]
And that it is God
With whom lies
Your highest reward.

وَاَوْلَادُكُمْ فِتْنَةٌ ۙ
وَّاَنَّ اللّٰهَ عِنْدَهٗٓ اَجْرٌ عَظِيْمٌ ۝

SECTION 4

29. O ye who believe!
If ye fear God,
He will grant you a Criterion[1202]
(To judge between right and wrong),
Remove from you (all) evil
(That may afflict) you,
And forgive you:
For God is the Lord
Of grace unbounded.

۲۹- يٰٓاَيُّهَا الَّذِيْنَ اٰمَنُوْٓا اِنْ تَتَّقُوا اللّٰهَ
يَجْعَلْ لَّكُمْ فُرْقَانًا
وَّيُكَفِّرْ عَنْكُمْ سَيِّاٰتِكُمْ
وَيَغْفِرْ لَكُمْ ۭ
وَاللّٰهُ ذُو الْفَضْلِ الْعَظِيْمِ ۝

30. Remember how the Unbelievers
Plotted against thee, to keep
Thee in bonds, or slay thee,
Or get thee out (of thy home).[1203]
They plot and plan,
And God too plans,
But the best of planners[1203-A]
Is God.

۳۰- وَاِذْ يَمْكُرُ بِكَ الَّذِيْنَ كَفَرُوْا
لِيُثْبِتُوْكَ اَوْ يَقْتُلُوْكَ اَوْ يُخْرِجُوْكَ ۭ
وَيَمْكُرُوْنَ وَيَمْكُرُ اللّٰهُ ۭ
وَاللّٰهُ خَيْرُ الْمٰكِرِيْنَ ۝

31. When Our Signs are rehearsed
To them, they say: "We
Have heard this (before):
If we wished, we could
Say (words) like these:
These are nothing
But tales of the ancients."[1204]

۳۱- وَاِذَا تُتْلٰى عَلَيْهِمْ اٰيٰتُنَا قَالُوْا قَدْ
سَمِعْنَا لَوْ نَشَاۗءُ لَقُلْنَا مِثْلَ هٰذَآ ۙ
اِنْ هٰذَآ اِلَّآ اَسَاطِيْرُ الْاَوَّلِيْنَ ۝

1201. A big family—many sons—was considered a source of power and strength: iii. 10, 116. So in English, a man with many children is said to have his "quiver full": *Cf.* Psalms, cxxvii. 4-5: "As arrows are in the hands of a mighty man, so are the children of thy youth. Happy is the man that hath his quiver full of them they shall not be ashamed, but they shall speak with the enemies in the gate." So with property and possessions: they add to a man's dignity, power, and influence. But both possessions and a large family are a temptation and a trial. They may turn out to be a source of spiritual downfall, if they are mishandled, or if the love of them excludes the love of God.

1202. *Cf.* ii. 53 and ii. 185. The battle of Badr is called the *Furqān* in Muslim theology, because it was the first trial of strength by battle, in Islam, between the powers of good and evil. Evil was defeated, and those who had real faith were tested and sorted out from those who had not faith enough to follow the banner of Faith See also viii. 41 and n. 1210.

1203. The plots against Muṣṭafā in Mecca aimed at three things. They were not only foiled, but God's wonderful working turned the tables. and brought good out of evil in each case. (1) They tried to hold the Apostle in subjection in Mecca by putting pressure on his uncles, relatives, and friends. But the more they persecuted, the more the little Muslim community grew in faith and numbers. (2) They tried to injure or slay him. But the wonderful example of his humility, perseverance, and fearlessness furthered the cause of Islam. (3) They tried to get him and his out of their homes. But they found a new home in Medina, from which they eventually reconquered not only Mecca, but Arabia and the world.

1203-A. *Cf.* iii. 54.

1204. *Cf.* vi. 25.

32. Remember how they said:
"O God! if this is indeed
The Truth from Thee,
Rain down on us a shower
Of stones from the sky,
Or send us a grievous Penalty."[1205]

٣٢-وَإِذْ قَالُوا اللّٰهُمَّ إِنْ كَانَ هٰذَا هُوَ
الْحَقَّ مِنْ عِنْدِكَ فَأَمْطِرْ عَلَيْنَا حِجَارَةً
مِّنَ السَّمَاءِ أَوِ ائْتِنَا بِعَذَابٍ أَلِيمٍ ○

33. But God was not going
To send them a Penalty
Whilst thou wast amongst them;
Nor was He going to send it
Whilst they could ask for pardon

٣٣-وَمَا كَانَ اللّٰهُ لِيُعَذِّبَهُمْ
وَأَنْتَ فِيهِمْ ۚ وَمَا كَانَ اللّٰهُ مُعَذِّبَهُمْ
وَهُمْ يَسْتَغْفِرُونَ ○

34. But what plea have they
That God should not punish
Them, when they keep out
(Men) from the Sacred Mosque—
And they are not its guardians?
No men can be its guardians
Except the righteous; but most
Of them do not understand.

٣٤-وَمَا لَهُمْ أَلَّا يُعَذِّبَهُمُ اللّٰهُ وَهُمْ
يَصُدُّونَ عَنِ الْمَسْجِدِ الْحَرَامِ وَمَا
كَانُوا أَوْلِيَاءَهُ ۚ إِنْ أَوْلِيَاؤُهُ إِلَّا الْمُتَّقُونَ
وَلٰكِنَّ أَكْثَرَهُمْ لَا يَعْلَمُونَ ○

35. Their prayer at the House
(Of God) is nothing but
Whistling and clapping of hands:
(Its only answer can be),
"Taste ye the Penalty
Because ye blasphemed."

٣٥-وَمَا كَانَ صَلَاتُهُمْ عِنْدَ الْبَيْتِ
إِلَّا مُكَاءً وَتَصْدِيَةً ۚ
فَذُوقُوا الْعَذَابَ بِمَا كُنْتُمْ تَكْفُرُونَ ○

36. The Unbelievers spend their wealth
To hinder (men) from the path
Of God, and so will they
Continue to spend; but
In the end they will have
(Only) regrets and sighs;

٣٦-إِنَّ الَّذِينَ كَفَرُوا يُنْفِقُونَ أَمْوَالَهُمْ
لِيَصُدُّوا عَنْ سَبِيلِ اللّٰهِ ۚ
فَسَيُنْفِقُونَهَا ثُمَّ تَكُونُ عَلَيْهِمْ حَسْرَةً

1205. This was actually a challenge thrown out by the Infidels in Mecca, not seriously but as a taunt. The answer is in the two following verses. God punishes in His own good time, not according to the foolish and frivolous taunts of the Unbelievers. While the Holy Apostle was with them, he—the Mercy of the Worlds—conferred a certain amount of immunity to them. There were also other Muslims, just men who asked for forgiveness. And God keeps the door of repentance and forgiveness open to all as long as they make it possible. But let them not be puffed up with pride, or think that they have lasting immunity. What became of Abū Jahl? He and some of his greatest warriors were slain at Badr. The little autocratic clique that prevented Muslims from access to the Sacred Mosque had their Nemesis not long afterwards. They pretended to be its guardians. But were they? Could they be? Only the righteous could be true guardians to God's places of worship, and particularly to the Central House of the Ka'ba. It was to be a place of pure worship, while their idolatrous worship was mere mummery,—whistling and clapping of hands. All false worship advertises itself by noise and unseemly riot: it is said that the Pagans used to go naked round the Ka'ba.

At length they will be overcome:
And the Unbelievers will be
Gathered together to Hell;—

ثُمَّ يُغْلَبُونَ ۗ
وَالَّذِينَ كَفَرُوا إِلَىٰ جَهَنَّمَ يُحْشَرُونَ ۝

37. In order that God may separate[1206]
The impure from the pure,
Put the impure, one on another,
Heap them together, and cast them
Into Hell. They will be
The ones to have lost.

٣٧- لِيَمِيزَ اللَّهُ الْخَبِيثَ مِنَ الطَّيِّبِ وَيَجْعَلَ
الْخَبِيثَ بَعْضَهُ عَلَىٰ بَعْضٍ فَيَرْكُمَهُ جَمِيعًا
فَيَجْعَلَهُ فِي جَهَنَّمَ ۚ أُولَٰئِكَ هُمُ الْخَاسِرُونَ ۝ ع ١٨

C. 91.—The battle of Badr brought to an issue
(viii. 38-64.) The fight between Truth and Unbelief.
It was the Day of Differentiation.
Not for spoils was it won, nor by numbers;
But by courage and planning, union of wills,
And pooling of strength and resources,—
Above all by the help of God,
Whose help is ever all-sufficient.

SECTION 5.

38. Say to the Unbelievers,
If (now) they desist (from Unbelief),
Their past would be forgiven them;
But if they persist, the punishment
Of those before them is already
(A matter of warning for them).

٣٨- قُل لِّلَّذِينَ كَفَرُوا إِن يَنتَهُوا يُغْفَرْ
لَهُم مَّا قَدْ سَلَفَ ۚ وَإِن يَعُودُوا فَقَدْ
مَضَتْ سُنَّتُ الْأَوَّلِينَ ۝

39. And fight them on
Until there is no mor
Tumult or oppression,
And there prevail
Justice and faith in God[1207]
Altogether and everywhere;
But if they cease, verily God
Doth see all that they do.[1208]

٣٩- وَقَاتِلُوهُمْ حَتَّىٰ لَا تَكُونَ فِتْنَةٌ
وَيَكُونَ الدِّينُ كُلُّهُ لِلَّهِ ۚ
فَإِنِ انتَهَوْا
فَإِنَّ اللَّهَ بِمَا يَعْمَلُونَ بَصِيرٌ ۝

40. If they refuse, be sure
That God is your Protector—
9 The Best to protect
30 And the Best to help.

٤٠- وَإِن تَوَلَّوْا فَاعْلَمُوا أَنَّ اللَّهَ مَوْلَاكُمْ ۚ
نِعْمَ الْمَوْلَىٰ وَنِعْمَ النَّصِيرُ ۝

1206. It is only when matters are brought to an issue that evil is separated distinctly from the good. Then evil consorts with evil, and good with good. The evil will be piled into a heap. When the cup is full, the punishment will come. There will be no mistake about it. The good should not be discouraged, because in fighting against them, all forces of evil join together and pool their resources together. The more they do so, the easier is the final arbitrament. It is all in God's Plan.

1207. *Cf.* ii. 193 and n.

1208. If they cease from fighting and from the persecution of truth, God judges them by their actions and their motives, and would not wish that they should be harassed with further hostility. But if they refuse all terms, the righteous have nothing to fear: God will help and protect them.

الجزء العاشر

41. And know that out of
All the booty that ye
May acquire (in war),
A fifth share is assigned [1209]
To God,—and to the Apostle,
And to near relatives,
Orphans, the needy,
And the wayfarer,—
If ye do believe in God
And in the revelation
We sent down to Our Servant
On the Day of Testing,—[1210]
The Day of the meeting
Of the two forces.
For God hath power
Over all things. [1211]

٤١- وَاعْلَمُوٓا أَنَّمَا غَنِمْتُم مِّن شَىْءٍ
فَأَنَّ لِلَّهِ خُمُسَهُۥ وَلِلرَّسُولِ
وَلِذِى الْقُرْبَىٰ وَالْيَتَٰمَىٰ وَالْمَسَٰكِينِ
وَابْنِ السَّبِيلِ
إِن كُنتُمْ ءَامَنتُم بِاللَّهِ
وَمَآ أَنزَلْنَا عَلَىٰ عَبْدِنَا يَوْمَ الْفُرْقَانِ
يَوْمَ الْتَقَى الْجَمْعَانِ
وَاللَّهُ عَلَىٰ كُلِّ شَىْءٍ قَدِيرٌ ○

42. Remember ye were
On the hither side
Of the valley, and they
On the farther side,
And the caravan [1212]
On lower ground than ye.
Even if ye had made
A mutual appointment
To meet, ye would certainly
Have failed in the appointment : [1213]

٤٢- إِذْ أَنتُم بِالْعُدْوَةِ الدُّنْيَا
وَهُم بِالْعُدْوَةِ الْقُصْوَىٰ
وَالرَّكْبُ أَسْفَلَ مِنكُمْ
وَلَوْ تَوَاعَدتُّمْ
لَاخْتَلَفْتُمْ فِى الْمِيعَٰدِ

1209. The rule is that a fifth share is set apart for the Imām (the Commander) and the rest is divided among the forces. The fifth share reserved is expressed to be for God and the Apostle, and for charitable purposes for those to whom charity is due. Ultimately everything is at the disposal of God and His Apostle : viii. 1 : but four-fifths are divided, and only one-fifth is retained for the special purposes. The Imām has discretion as to the mode of division. In the Apostle's life-time a certain portion was assigned to the Apostle and his near relatives.

1210. *Testing* : *Furqān* : Criterion between right and wrong, decision between the forces of faith and unbelief. The battle of Badr is called by this name. See viii. 29 and n. 1202.

1211. God's power is shown in the events detailed in the three verses following (*vv.* 42-44), leading to the complete victory of the Muslims over the pagan Quraish.

1212. The little Islamic force from Medina went out to meet the big Meccan army, and they met on the two sides of a valley at Badr, while the Quraish caravan was on lower ground towards the sea, about 3 miles from Badr.

1213. They were all at cross purposes. The caravan was making for Mecca, but scarcely thought it could get there. The Quraish force was trying to save the caravan and then annihilate the Muslims. The Muslims had decided to let the caravan alone but attack the Quraish army from Mecca, which they thought was going to be small, but which turned out to be big, more than three times their number. Yet the two forces met, precisely at the spot and at the time when a decisive battle should take place and the Muslims dispose of the pretensions of the Meccans. If they had carefully planned a mutual appointment, they could not have carried it out more precisely.

On the Muslim side the few martyrs knew that the victory was theirs and those who survived the battle enjoyed the fruits of the victory. On the pagan side, both those who died and those who lived knew fully the issue joined. Even psychologically both sides went in with full determination to decide the issue.

But (thus ye met),
That God might accomplish
A matter already enacted;
That those who died might
Die after a clear Sign
(Had been given), and those who lived
Might live after a Clear Sign
(Had been given). And verily
God is He who heareth
And knoweth (all things).

وَلٰكِنْ لِّيَقْضِيَ اللّٰهُ اَمْرًا
كَانَ مَفْعُوْلًا
لِّيَهْلِكَ مَنْ هَلَكَ عَنْ بَيِّنَةٍ
وَّيَحْيٰى مَنْ حَيَّ عَنْ بَيِّنَةٍ
وَاِنَّ اللّٰهَ لَسَمِيْعٌ عَلِيْمٌ

43. Remember in thy dream
God showed them to thee
As few: if He had shown
Them to thee as many,
Ye would surely have been
Discouraged, and ye would
Surely have disputed
In (your) decision: but God
Saved (you): for He knoweth
Well the (secrets) of (all) hearts.

۴۳-اِذْ يُرِيْكَهُمُ اللّٰهُ فِيْ مَنَامِكَ قَلِيْلًا
وَلَوْ اَرٰىكَهُمْ كَثِيْرًا لَّفَشِلْتُمْ
وَلَتَنَازَعْتُمْ فِي الْاَمْرِ
وَلٰكِنَّ اللّٰهَ سَلَّمَ
اِنَّهٗ عَلِيْمٌۢ بِذَاتِ الصُّدُوْرِ

44. And remember when ye met,
He showed them to you
As few in your eyes,
And He made you appear
As contemptible in their eyes:[1214]
That God might accomplish
A matter already enacted.
For to God do all questions
Go back (for decision).

۴۴-وَاِذْ يُرِيْكُمُوْهُمْ
اِذِ الْتَقَيْتُمْ فِيْٓ اَعْيُنِكُمْ قَلِيْلًا
وَّيُقَلِّلُكُمْ فِيْٓ اَعْيُنِهِمْ
لِيَقْضِيَ اللّٰهُ اَمْرًا كَانَ مَفْعُوْلًا
وَاِلَى اللّٰهِ تُرْجَعُ الْاُمُوْرُ

SECTION 6.

45. O ye who believe!
When ye meet a force,
Be firm, and call God
In remembrance much (and often);
That ye may prosper:

۴۵-يٰٓاَيُّهَا الَّذِيْنَ اٰمَنُوْٓا اِذَا لَقِيْتُمْ فِئَةً
فَاثْبُتُوْا وَاذْكُرُوا اللّٰهَ كَثِيْرًا
لَّعَلَّكُمْ تُفْلِحُوْنَ

46. And obey God and His Apostle;
And fall into no disputes,

۴۶-وَاَطِيْعُوا اللّٰهَ وَرَسُوْلَهٗ وَلَا تَنَازَعُوْا

1214. The Muslim army, though they knew their worldly disadvantage, did not realise the full odds against them. The Meccans came exulting in any case, and they despised the contemptible little force opposed to them. Even though they thought the Muslim force was twice as great as it was (iii. 13), still that number was contemptible, when taken with its poor equipment. Both these psychological mistakes subserved the main Plan, which was to bring the matter to a decisive issue, whether the Pagans of Mecca were to continue their arrogant oppression, or the religion of God was to be established in freedom and honour.

Lest ye lose heart
And your power depart;
And be patient and persevering:
For God is with those
Who patiently persevere:[1215]

فَتَفْشَلُوْا وَتَذْهَبَ رِيْحُكُمْ وَ
اصْبِرُوْا
إِنَّ اللهَ مَعَ الصّٰبِرِيْنَ ۝

47. And be not like those
Who started from their homes
Insolently and to be seen of men,
And to hinder (men)
From the path of God:[1216]
For God compasseth round about
All that they do.

٤٧- وَلَا تَكُوْنُوْا كَالَّذِيْنَ خَرَجُوْا
مِنْ دِيَارِهِمْ بَطَرًا وَّرِئَآءَ النَّاسِ
وَيَصُدُّوْنَ عَنْ سَبِيْلِ اللهِ
وَاللهُ بِمَا يَعْمَلُوْنَ مُحِيْطٌ ۝

48. Remember Satan made
Their (sinful) acts seem
Alluring to them, and said:
"No one among men
Can overcome you this day,
While I am near to you":
But when the two forces
Came in sight of each other,
He turned on his heels,
And said: "Lo! I am clear
Of you; lo! I see
What ye see not;
Lo! I fear God; for God
Is strict in punishment."[1217]

٤٨- وَإِذْ زَيَّنَ لَهُمُ الشَّيْطٰنُ أَعْمَالَهُمْ
وَقَالَ لَا غَالِبَ لَكُمُ الْيَوْمَ مِنَ النَّاسِ
وَإِنِّيْ جَارٌ لَّكُمْ فَلَمَّا تَرَآءَتِ الْفِئَتٰنِ
نَكَصَ عَلٰى عَقِبَيْهِ وَقَالَ إِنِّيْ بَرِيْٓءٌ
مِّنْكُمْ إِنِّيْٓ أَرٰى مَا لَا تَرَوْنَ
إِنِّيْٓ أَخَافُ اللهَ
وَاللهُ شَدِيْدُ الْعِقَابِ ۝ ع

SECTION 7.

49. Lo! the Hypocrites say, and those
In whose hearts is a disease:[1218]
"These people,—their religion
Has misled them." But
If any trust in God, behold!
God is Exalted in might, Wise.

٤٩- إِذْ يَقُوْلُ الْمُنٰفِقُوْنَ
وَالَّذِيْنَ فِيْ قُلُوْبِهِمْ مَّرَضٌ
غَرَّ هٰٓؤُلَآءِ دِيْنُهُمْ وَمَنْ يَّتَوَكَّلْ عَلَى اللهِ
فَإِنَّ اللهَ عَزِيْزٌ حَكِيْمٌ ۝

1215. A fine description of the Muslim virtues which make for success and whose loss brings about humiliation and failure. "*Power*": literally, "wind,"—the favourable wind for a sailing ship.

1216 A true description of the Meccan army which met its doom.

1217. It is the way with the leaders of evil, when they find their cause lost, that they wash their hands of their followers and leave them in the lurch. They see more clearly than their dupes. The are not simpletons: they know the consequences of the wrath of God. Satan's "fear" of God is terror combined with hatred,– the very opposite of the feeling which is described in *Taqwā*, *viz.*, the desire to avoid doing anything against God's will, such desire being founded on trust in God and the love of God.

1218. *Cf.* ii. 10, for "disease in the heart."

Trust in God brings its own reward: our eyes are opened, and we see how great, good, and wise is the Cherisher of the Worlds. Others may sneer and despise. But the blessing of God keeps our minds fresh and our hearts contented.

50. If thou couldst see,
When the angels take the souls
Of the Unbelievers (at death),[1219]
(How) they smite their faces
And their backs, (saying):
"Taste the Penalty of the blazing
Fire—

٥٠- وَلَوْ تَرٰٓى اِذْ يَتَوَفَّى الَّذِيْنَ كَفَرُوا
الْمَلٰٓئِكَةُ يَضْرِبُوْنَ وُجُوْهَهُمْ
وَاَدْبَارَهُمْ
وَذُوْقُوْا عَذَابَ الْحَرِيْقِ ○

51. "Because of (the deeds) which[1220]
Your (own) hands sent forth:
For God is never unjust
To His servants:

٥١- ذٰلِكَ بِمَا قَدَّمَتْ اَيْدِيْكُمْ
وَاَنَّ اللّٰهَ لَيْسَ بِظَلَّامٍ لِّلْعَبِيْدِ ○

52. "(Deeds) after the manner
Of the People of Pharaoh
And of those before them:
They rejected the Signs of God,
And God punished them
For their crimes: for God
Is Strong, and Strict in
punishment:

٥٢- كَدَاْبِ اٰلِ فِرْعَوْنَ وَالَّذِيْنَ مِنْ
قَبْلِهِمْ كَفَرُوْا بِاٰيٰتِ اللّٰهِ
فَاَخَذَهُمُ اللّٰهُ بِذُنُوْبِهِمْ
اِنَّ اللّٰهَ قَوِيٌّ شَدِيْدُ الْعِقَابِ ○

53. "Because God will never change[1221]
The Grace which He hath bestowed
On a people until they change
What is in their (own) souls:
And verily God is He
Who heareth and knoweth (all
things)."

٥٣- ذٰلِكَ بِاَنَّ اللّٰهَ لَمْ يَكُ مُغَيِّرًا
نِّعْمَةً اَنْعَمَهَا عَلٰى قَوْمٍ حَتّٰى يُغَيِّرُوْا
مَا بِاَنْفُسِهِمْ
وَاَنَّ اللّٰهَ سَمِيْعٌ عَلِيْمٌ ○

54. "(Deeds) after the manner
Of the People of Pharaoh
And those before them":[1222]
They treated as false the Signs
Of their Lord: so We

٥٤- كَدَاْبِ اٰلِ فِرْعَوْنَ
وَالَّذِيْنَ مِنْ قَبْلِهِمْ
كَذَّبُوْا بِاٰيٰتِ رَبِّهِمْ

1219. In contrast to the taunt against those who trust in God, "that their religion has misled them," is shown the terrible punishment, after death, of those who laughed at Faith.

1220. The punishment is shown to be due to their own deeds of wrong, because God is never unjust to the least of His servants.

1221. God bestows His grace freely, but He never withdraws it arbitrarily. Before He changes their state and circumstances, an actual state of rebellion and contumacy has arisen in their own souls, which brings about its inevitable punishment.

1222. These words from the address of the angels are quoted again, in order to add the comment that follows. Note that in verse 51, the words were that they *rejected* the Signs of God and were *punished*: here the words are that they treated the Signs as false and were *destroyed*;—a higher degree of guilt deserved a severer punishment.

Destroyed them for their crimes,
And We drowned the People
Of Pharaoh: for they were all
Oppressors and wrong-doers.

فَأَهْلَكْنٰهُمْ بِذُنُوبِهِمْ وَأَغْرَقْنَآ اٰلَ فِرْعَوْنَ ۚ وَكُلٌّ كَانُوا ظٰلِمِينَ ○

55. For the worst of beasts
In the sight of God[1223]
Are those who reject Him:
They will not believe.

٥٥-إِنَّ شَرَّ الدَّوَآبِّ عِنْدَ اللّٰهِ الَّذِينَ كَفَرُوا فَهُمْ لَا يُؤْمِنُونَ ○

56. They are those with whom
Thou didst make a covenant,[1224]
But they break their covenant
Every time, and they have not
The fear (of God).

٥٦-اَلَّذِينَ عٰهَدْتَّ مِنْهُمْ ثُمَّ يَنْقُضُونَ عَهْدَهُمْ فِي كُلِّ مَرَّةٍ وَّهُمْ لَا يَتَّقُونَ ○

57. If ye gain the mastery
Over them in war,
Disperse, with them, those
Who follow them,
That they may remember.

٥٧-فَإِمَّا تَثْقَفَنَّهُمْ فِي الْحَرْبِ فَشَرِّدْ بِهِمْ مَّنْ خَلْفَهُمْ لَعَلَّهُمْ يَذَّكَّرُونَ ○

58. If thou fearest treachery
From any group, throw back
(Their Covenant) to them, (so as
To be) on equal terms:
For God loveth not the treacherous.

٥٨-وَإِمَّا تَخَافَنَّ مِنْ قَوْمٍ خِيَانَةً فَانْبِذْ إِلَيْهِمْ عَلٰى سَوَآءٍ ۗ إِنَّ اللّٰهَ لَا يُحِبُّ الْخَآئِنِينَ ○

Section 8.

59. Let not the Unbelievers
Think that they can
Get the better (of the godly):
They will never frustrate (them).

٥٩-وَلَا يَحْسَبَنَّ الَّذِينَ كَفَرُوا سَبَقُوا ۚ إِنَّهُمْ لَا يُعْجِزُونَ ○

1223. In viii. 22 we were warned against "the worst of beasts in the sight of God", who do not make use of their faculties of hearing, speaking and understanding, in the service of God, and in fact misuse their faculties to blaspheme God. The same brute creatures are shone here in another light: they are faithless both to God and man.

1224. The immediate occasion was the repeated treachery of the Banū Quraiẓa after their treaties with the Muslims. But the general lesson remains, as noted in the two following verses. Treachery in war is doubly wrong, for it endangers so many lives. Such treachery should be punished in such a way that it gets no chance again. Not only the actual perpetrators but those who follow their standard should be rendered powerless. And the broken treaty should be denounced so that the innocent party can at least fight on equal terms. From actual physical warfare we can carry the same lesson to spiritual warfare. A truce or understanding is possible with those who respect definite principles, not with those who have no principles and are merely out for oppression and wickedness.

60. Against them make ready
Your strength to the utmost
Of your power, including[1225]
Steeds of war, to strike terror
Into (the hearts of) the enemies,
Of God and your enemies,
And others besides, whom
Ye may not know, but whom[1226]
God doth know. Whatever
Ye shall spend in the Cause
Of God, shall be repaid
Unto you, and ye shall not
Be treated unjustly.[1227]

٦٠- وَأَعِدُّوا لَهُم مَّا اسْتَطَعْتُم مِّن قُوَّةٍ
وَمِن رِّبَاطِ الْخَيْلِ تُرْهِبُونَ بِهِ
عَدُوَّ اللَّهِ وَعَدُوَّكُمْ
وَآخَرِينَ مِن دُونِهِمْ
لَا تَعْلَمُونَهُمُ اللَّهُ يَعْلَمُهُمْ
وَمَا تُنفِقُوا مِن شَيْءٍ فِي سَبِيلِ اللَّهِ
يُوَفَّ إِلَيْكُمْ وَأَنتُمْ لَا تُظْلَمُونَ ○

61. But if the enemy
Incline towards peace,
Do thou (also) incline
Towards peace, and trust
In God: for He is the One
That heareth and knoweth
(All things).[1228]

٦١- وَإِن جَنَحُوا لِلسَّلْمِ
فَاجْنَحْ لَهَا
وَتَوَكَّلْ عَلَى اللَّهِ
إِنَّهُ هُوَ السَّمِيعُ الْعَلِيمُ ○

62. Should they intend
To deceive thee,—verily God
Sufficeth thee: He it is
That hath strengthened thee
With his aid and
With (the company of)
The Believers;[1229]

٦٢- وَإِن يُرِيدُوا أَن يَخْدَعُوكَ
فَإِنَّ حَسْبَكَ اللَّهُ
هُوَ الَّذِي أَيَّدَكَ بِنَصْرِهِ
وَبِالْمُؤْمِنِينَ ○

63. And (moreover) He hath put
Affection between their hearts:

٦٣- وَأَلَّفَ بَيْنَ قُلُوبِهِمْ

1225. The immediate occasion of this injunction was the weakness of cavalry and appointments of war in the early fights of Islam. But the general meaning follows. In every fight, physical, moral, or spiritual, arm yourself with the best weapons and the best arms against your enemy, so as to instil wholesome respect into him for you and the Cause you stand for.

1226. There are always lurking enemies whom you may not know, but whom God knows. It is your duty to be ready against all, for the sacred Cause under whose banner you are fighting.

1227. Be always ready and put all your resources into your Cause. You do not do so in vain. God's reward will come in various forms. He knows all, and His reward will always be more generous than you can possibly deserve.

1228. While we must always be ready for the good fight lest it be forced on us, even in the midst of the fight we must always be ready for peace if there is any inclination towards peace on the other side. There is no merit merely in a fight by itself. It should be a joyful duty not for itself, but to establish the reign of peace and righteousness and God's Law.

1229. In working for peace there may be a certain risk of treachery on the other side. We must take that risk: because the man of God has God's aid to count upon and the strength of the united body of the righteous.

Not if thou hadst spent
All that is in the earth,
Couldst thou have produced
That affection, but God
Hath done it: for He
Is Exalted in might, Wise.[1230]

لَوْ أَنفَقْتَ مَا فِي الْأَرْضِ جَمِيعًا
مَّا أَلَّفْتَ بَيْنَ قُلُوبِهِمْ وَلَٰكِنَّ اللَّهَ
أَلَّفَ بَيْنَهُمْ ۚ إِنَّهُ عَزِيزٌ حَكِيمٌ ○

64. O Apostle! Sufficient
Unto thee is God,—
(Unto thee) and unto those
Who follow thee
Among the Believers.[1231]

٦٤- يَا أَيُّهَا النَّبِيُّ حَسْبُكَ اللَّهُ
وَمَنِ اتَّبَعَكَ مِنَ الْمُؤْمِنِينَ ○ ع

C. 92.—No man of heart, spirit, or constancy
(viii. 65-75.) Can ever be cowed down by odds
Against him. We fight not for spoils
Or for captives, but for the glory
Of God, and for truth and faith.
We must be kind to all, but specially
Regard the needs of our comrades,
Linked to us by ties of duty and affection.
Our highest reward will be forgiveness
And grace from the Giver of all.

SECTION 9.

65. O Apostle! rouse the Believers
To the fight. If there are
Twenty amongst you, patient
And persevering, they will
Vanquish two hundred: if a
hundred,
They will vanquish a thousand
Of the Unbelievers: for these
Are a people without
understanding.[1232]

٦٥- يَا أَيُّهَا النَّبِيُّ حَرِّضِ الْمُؤْمِنِينَ عَلَى
الْقِتَالِ ۚ إِن يَكُن مِّنكُمْ عِشْرُونَ
صَابِرُونَ يَغْلِبُوا مِائَتَيْنِ ۚ وَإِن يَكُن مِّنكُم
مِّائَةٌ يَغْلِبُوا أَلْفًا مِّنَ الَّذِينَ كَفَرُوا
بِأَنَّهُمْ قَوْمٌ لَّا يَفْقَهُونَ ○

1230. On the immediate occasion, the greatest miracle and most wonderful working of God's grace was the union of hearts produced among the jarring, war-like, excitable elements of Arabia under the gentle, firm, and wise guidance of Muḥammad, the Apostle of God. At all times we must pray to God for this gift above all,—union, understanding, and pure and sincere affection among those who take God's name. With it there is strength and success. Without it there is humiliation, slavery, and moral degradation. There may be many causes of difference and dispute. The reconciliation can only come from the glory and wisdom of God.

1231. *The Believers*: mere lip-profession of belief, or even the kind of belief that does not result in action, is not enough. To those whose belief is so sincere that it results in complete trust in God and in fearless action in His service, the consequences on this earth do not matter. God's good pleasure is enough for them.

1232. In a fight, odds of ten to one against any one are appalling. But they do not daunt the men of faith. Whether they personally win or die, their Cause prevails. They are sure to win: because (1) they have divine aid, and (2) even humanly speaking, those who take up arms against truth and righteousness are fools, and their seeming power is but a broken reed.

66. For the present, God
Hath lightened your (task),
For He knoweth that there is
A weak spot in you :[1233]
But (even so), if there are
A hundred of you, patient
And persevering, they will
Vanquish two hundred, and if
A thousand, they will vanquish
Two thousand, with the leave
Of God : for God is with those
Who patiently persevere.

٦٦- اَلْـٰٔنَ خَفَّفَ اللّٰهُ عَنْكُمْ
وَعَلِمَ اَنَّ فِيْكُمْ ضَعْفًا ۚ
فَاِنْ يَّكُنْ مِّنْكُمْ مِّائَةٌ صَابِرَةٌ
يَّغْلِبُوْا مِائَتَيْنِ ۚ وَاِنْ يَّكُنْ مِّنْكُمْ اَلْفٌ
يَّغْلِبُوْٓا اَلْفَيْنِ بِاِذْنِ اللّٰهِ ۗ
وَاللّٰهُ مَعَ الصّٰبِرِيْنَ ○

67. It is not fitting
For an Apostle
That he should have
Prisoners of war until
He hath thoroughly subdued[1234]
The land. Ye look
For the temporal goods
Of this world ; but God
Looketh to the Hereafter :
And God is Exalted in might, Wise.

٦٧- مَا كَانَ لِنَبِيٍّ اَنْ يَّكُوْنَ لَهٗٓ اَسْرٰى
حَتّٰى يُثْخِنَ فِى الْاَرْضِ ۗ
تُرِيْدُوْنَ عَرَضَ الدُّنْيَا ۖ
وَاللّٰهُ يُرِيْدُ الْاٰخِرَةَ ۗ
وَاللّٰهُ عَزِيْزٌ حَكِيْمٌ ○

68. Had it not been for
A previous ordainment[1235]

٦٨- لَوْلَا كِتٰبٌ

1233. Given equal conditions, Muslims on account of their faith could win against odds of ten to one. But where their organisation and equipment are weak, as was the case about the time of Badr, they were set a lighter task, and asked to tackle no more than odds of two to one against them. As a matter of fact at Badr they won through against odds of more than three to one.

1234. An ordinary war may be for territory or trade, revenge or military glory,—all "temporal goods of this world." Such a war is condemned. But a Jihād is fought under strict conditions under a righteous Imām, purely for the defence of faith and God's Law. All baser motives, therefore are strictly excluded. The greed of gain in the shape of ransom from captives has no place in such warfare.

At the same time, if there has been heavy loss of life already, captives may be taken, and it would be for the Imām to exercise his discretion as to the time when it was safe to release them, and whether the release should be free or on parole or on a fine by way of punishment. Destruction and slaughter, however repugnant to a gentle soul like that of Muḥammad, were inevitable where evil tried to suppress the good. Even Jesus, whose mission was more limited, had to say : "Think not that I am come to send peace on earth : I came not to send peace but a sword" (Matt. x. 34).

Seventy captives were taken at Badr, and it was decided to take ransom for them. While the general principle of fighting for the purpose of taking captives in order to get their ransom is condemned, the particular action in this case was approved in *vv.* 68-71.

1235. Though any motive of worldly gain, which may have been in the minds of some among the victorious Muslim army, is condemned as worthy of a severe penalty, what actually happened is ascribed to the Plan of God, which was pre-ordained. Among the prisoners taken were the Prophet's uncle 'Abbās and Ḥadhrat 'Alī's brother 'Aqīl, who afterwards became Muslims. 'Abbās was an ancestor of the founder of the celebrated 'Abbāsī Dynasty which played such a notable part in Islamic history. In his case the promise made in verse 70 was amply fulfilled. In the case of all prisoners, if there was any good in their hearts, their very fight against Islam and their capture led to their being blessed with Islam. Thus does God's Plan work in a marvellous way, and evolve good out of seeming evil.

From God, a severe penalty
Would have reached you
For the (ransom) that ye took.

مِّنَ اللّٰهِ سَبَقَ لَمَسَّكُمْ
فِيْمَآ اَخَذْتُمْ عَذَابٌ عَظِيْمٌ ○

69. But (now) enjoy[1236] what ye took
In war, lawful and good:
But fear God: for God
Is Oft-forgiving, Most Merciful.

٦٩- فَكُلُوْا مِمَّا غَنِمْتُمْ حَلٰلًا طَيِّبًا ۖ
وَّاتَّقُوا اللّٰهَ ۭ اِنَّ اللّٰهَ غَفُوْرٌ رَّحِيْمٌ ○

SECTION 10.

70. O Apostle! say to those
Who are captives in your hands:
"If God findeth any good[1237]
In your hearts, He will
Give you something better
Than what has been taken
From you, and He will
Forgive you: for God
Is Oft-forgiving, Most Merciful."

٧٠- يٰٓاَيُّهَا النَّبِيُّ قُلْ لِّمَنْ فِيْٓ اَيْدِيْكُمْ مِّنَ
الْاَسْرٰٓى ۙ
اِنْ يَّعْلَمِ اللّٰهُ فِيْ قُلُوْبِكُمْ خَيْرًا
يُّؤْتِكُمْ خَيْرًا مِّمَّآ اُخِذَ مِنْكُمْ
وَيَغْفِرْ لَكُمْ ۭ وَاللّٰهُ غَفُوْرٌ رَّحِيْمٌ ○

71. But if they have
Treacherous designs against thee,
(O Apostle!), they have already
Been in treason against God,[1238]
And so hath He given
(Thee) power over them.
And God is He who hath
(Full) knowledge and wisdom.

٧١- وَاِنْ يُّرِيْدُوْا خِيَانَتَكَ
فَقَدْ خَانُوا اللّٰهَ مِنْ قَبْلُ
فَاَمْكَنَ مِنْهُمْ ۭ
وَاللّٰهُ عَلِيْمٌ حَكِيْمٌ ○

72. Those who believed,
And adopted exile,

٧٢- اِنَّ الَّذِيْنَ اٰمَنُوْا وَهَاجَرُوْا

1236. *Enjoy*: literally, *eat*. See vii. 19, n. 1004, and v. 69, n. 776.

1237. This is a consolation to the prisoners of war. In spite of their previous hostility, God will forgive them in His mercy if there was any good in their hearts, and confer upon them a far higher gift than anything they have ever lost. This gift in its highest sense would be the blessing of Islam, but even in a material sense, there was great good fortune awaiting them, *e.g.*, in the case of 'Abbās (see n. 1235).

Note how comprehensive is God's care. He encourages and strengthens the Muslims, at the same time condemning any baser motives that may have entered their minds. He consoles the prisoners of war and promises them better things if there is any good in them at all. And He offers comfort to those who have left their homes in His Cause, and knits them into closer fellowship with those who have helped them and sympathised with them.

1238. If the kindness shown to them is abused by the prisoners of war when they are released, it is not a matter for discouragement to those who showed the kindness. Such persons have in their treachery shown already their treason to God, in that they took up arms against God's Apostle, and sought to blot out the pure worship of God. The punishment of defeat, which opened the eyes of some of their comrades, evidently did not open their eyes. But God knows all, and in His wisdom will order all things for the best. The Believers have done their duty in showing such clemency as they could in the circumstances of war. For them "God sufficeth" (viii. 62).

And fought for the Faith,
With their property
And their persons,
In the cause of God,
As well as those
Who gave (them) asylum[1239]
And aid,—these are (all)
Friends and protectors,
One of another.
As to those who believed
But came not into exile,
Ye owe no duty
Of protection to them
Until they come into exile;[1240]
But if they seek
Your aid in religion,
It is your duty
To help them,
Except against a people
With whom ye have
A treaty of mutual alliance.[1241]
And (remember) God
Seeth all that ye do.

وَجٰهَدُوْا بِاَمْوَالِهِمْ
وَاَنْفُسِهِمْ فِيْ سَبِيْلِ اللّٰهِ
وَالَّذِيْنَ اٰوَوْا وَّنَصَرُوْٓا
اُولٰٓئِكَ بَعْضُهُمْ اَوْلِيَآءُ بَعْضٍ ۭ
وَالَّذِيْنَ اٰمَنُوْا وَلَمْ يُهَاجِرُوْا
مَا لَكُمْ مِّنْ وَّلَايَتِهِمْ مِّنْ شَيْءٍ
حَتّٰى يُهَاجِرُوْا ۚ
وَاِنِ اسْتَنْصَرُوْكُمْ فِي الدِّيْنِ
فَعَلَيْكُمُ النَّصْرُ
اِلَّا عَلٰى قَوْمٍۢ بَيْنَكُمْ
وَبَيْنَهُمْ مِّيْثَاقٌ ۭ
وَاللّٰهُ بِمَا تَعْمَلُوْنَ بَصِيْرٌ ۝

73. The Unbelievers are
Protectors, one of another:
Unless ye do this,
(Protect each other),
There would be
Tumult and oppression
On earth, and great mischief.[1242]

٧٣- وَالَّذِيْنَ كَفَرُوْا بَعْضُهُمْ اَوْلِيَآءُ
بَعْضٍ ۭ اِلَّا تَفْعَلُوْهُ
تَكُنْ فِتْنَةٌ فِي الْاَرْضِ وَفَسَادٌ كَبِيْرٌ ۝

1239. The reference is to the *Muhājirīn* and the *Anṣār*, the Emigrants and the Helpers, the people who forsook their homes and adopted voluntary exile from Mecca in company with their beloved Leader, and their good friends in Medina, who gave them asylum and every kind of assistance, moral and material. Under the magnetic personality of the Holy Apostle these two groups became like blood-brothers, and they were so treated in matters of inheritance during the period when they were cut off from their kith and kin.

1240. The Believers (Muslims) were entitled to all assistance in matters of religion. But if they were not strong enough to suffer voluntary exile on behalf of the Cause and make the personal sacrifices which their more ardent brethren in faith made, they could not reasonably ask for political or military assistance or protection.

1241. If a community suffers voluntary exile on account of persecution and oppression, and some of its weaker brethren stay behind, holding fast to faith but not prepared for the higher sacrifice, the exiles have still a duty to help their weaker brethren in matters of religion. The exiles, being at open war against the State which oppressed them, would be free to fight against such State. But if the weaker brethren are in a State in mutual alliance with the Community, the Community cannot in honour interfere with that State, whether it is Muslim or not. Presumably the alliance implies that the grievances of the weaker brethren will be redressed by the State itself. But it is not honourable to embarrass your own ally.

1242. Evil consorts with evil. The good have all the more reason for drawing together and not only living in mutual harmony, but being ready at all times to protect each other. Otherwise the world will be given over to aggressions by unscrupulous people, and the good will fail in their duty to establish God's Peace and to strengthen all the forces of truth and righteousness.

74. Those who believe, And adopt exile, And fight for the Faith, In the cause of God, As well as those Who give (them) asylum And aid,—these are (all) In very truth the Believers : For them is the forgiveness Of sins and a provision Most generous.[1243]	٧٤ - وَالَّذِينَ آمَنُوا وَهَاجَرُوا وَجَاهَدُوا فِي سَبِيلِ اللَّهِ وَالَّذِينَ آوَوا وَّنَصَرُوا أُولَٰئِكَ هُمُ الْمُؤْمِنُونَ حَقًّا ط لَهُم مَّغْفِرَةٌ وَرِزْقٌ كَرِيمٌ ○
75. And those who Accept Faith subsequently,[1244] And adopt exile, And fight for the Faith In your company,— They are of you. But kindred by blood Have prior rights Against each other In the Book of God.[1245] Verily God is well-acquainted With all things.	٧٥ - وَالَّذِينَ آمَنُوا مِن بَعْدُ وَهَاجَرُوا وَجَاهَدُوا مَعَكُمْ فَأُولَٰئِكَ مِنكُمْ ط وَأُولُو الْأَرْحَامِ بَعْضُهُمْ أَوْلَىٰ بِبَعْضٍ فِي كِتَابِ اللَّهِ ط إِنَّ اللَّهَ بِكُلِّ شَيْءٍ عَلِيمٌ ○ ع

1243. Believers who make all sacrifices in the cause of God have given the best possible proof of their Faith by their actions They have loved God much, and much will be forgiven them. What they sacrificed was, perhaps, judged by universal standards, of small value, but its value will be estimated by the precious love behind it, and its reward will be of no ordinary kind. It will not be a reward in the ordinary sense at all, for a reward is given once for all. It will be a provision which lasts for ever, and is on the most generous scale.

1244. Those who come into the fold last are none the less brethren in the fullest acceptation of the term. But any special provisions made in the special circumstances of the first martyrs for the Cause will not of course apply to them as the special circumstances which made them necessary have ceased to exist. See next note.

1245. *The Book of God, i.e.*, the Universal Plan, the Eternal Decree, the Preserved Tablet (lxxxv. 22). Blood-relationship and its rights and duties do not depend on special circumstances of a temporary nature. Any temporary rights of mutual inheritance established between the early Emigrants and Helpers (n. 1239) would not apply to later recruits, who would come under entirely different circumstances.

INTRODUCTION TO SŪRA IX.

Tauba (Repentance) or *Barāat* (Immunity)

Logically this Sūra follows up the argument of the last Sūra (VIII), and indeed may be considered a part of it, although chronologically the two are separated by an interval of seven years.

We saw that Sūra VIII dealt with the large questions arising at the outset of the life of a new Ummat or organised nation: questions of defence under attack, distribution of war acquisitions after victory, the virtues needed for concerted action, and clemency and consideration for one's own and for enemies in the hour of victory. We pass on in this Sūra to deal with the question: what is to be done if the enemy breaks faith and is guilty of treachery? No nation can go on with a treaty if the other party violates it at will; but it is laid down that a period of four months should be allowed by way of notice after denunciation of the treaty; that due protection should be accorded in the intervening period; that there should always be open the door to repentance and reunion with the people of God; and that if all these fail, and war must be undertaken, it must be pushed with the utmost vigour.

These are the general principles deducible from the Sūra. The immediate occasion for their promulgation may be considered in connection with the chronological place of the Sūra.

Chronologically, verses 1-29 were a notable declaration of State policy promulgated about the month of Shawwāl, A.H. 9, and read out by Ḥadhrat 'Alī at the Pilgrimage two months later in order to give the policy the widest publicity possible. The remainder of the Sūra, verses 30-129, was revealed a little earlier, say about the month of Ramadhān, A.H. 9, and sums up the lessons of the Apostle's Tabūk expedition in the late summer of A.H. 9 (say October 630).

Tabūk is a place near the frontier of Arabia, quite close to what was then Byzantine territory in the Province of Syria (which includes Palestine). It is on the Ḥijāz Railway, about 350 miles north-west of Medina, and 150 miles south of Ma'ān. It had a fort and a spring of sweet water. In consequence of strong and persistent rumours that the Byzantines (Romans) were preparing to invade Arabia and that the Byzantine Emperor himself had arrived near the frontier for the purpose, the Apostle collected as large a force as he could, and marched to Tabūk. The Byzantine invasion did not come off. But the Apostle took the opportunity of consolidating the Muslim position in that direction and making treaties of alliance with certain Christian and Jewish tribes near the Gulf of 'Aqaba. On his return to Medina he considered the situation. During his absence the Hypocrites had played, as always, a double game, and the policy hitherto followed, of free access to the sacred centre of Islam, to Muslims and Pagans alike, was now altered, as it had been abused by the enemies of Islam.

This is the only Sūra to which the usual formula of *Bismillāh* is not prefixed. It was among the last of the Sūras revealed, and though the Apostle had directed that it should follow Sūra VIII, it was not clear whether it was to form a separate Sūra or only a part of Sūra VIII. It is now treated as a separate Sūra, but the *Bismillāh* is not prefixed to it, as there is no warrant for supposing that the Apostle used the *Bismillāh* before it in his recitation of the Qur-ān. The Sūra is known

under many names: the two most commonly used are (1) *Tauba* (Repentance), with reference to ix. 104 and (2) *Barāat* (Immunity), the opening word of the Sūra.

Summary.—Treaties with those Pagans who have treacherously broken their terms are denounced, but four months' time is given for adjustments or repentance. Pagans to be excluded from the sacred Mosques. Infidelity to be fought (ix. 1-29, and C. 93).

The People of the Book have obscured the light of God, but the Truth of God must prevail over all. We must be ready to fight for the Faith that is in us; otherwise we shall be unworthy to uphold God's banner, and He will raise other people in our place (ix. 30-42, and C. 94).

The Hypocrites and their double dealing: their evil ways pointed out. Their punishment will be as sure as the blessings of the righteous (ix. 43-72, and C. 95).

All evil should be resisted, unless there is repentance: falsehood is not content with breach of faith but mocks all good: it should not be envied but shunned (ix. 73-99, and C. 96).

The good pleasure of God is with those who are sincere and make sacrifices in His cause; He will forgive those who do wrong and repent, but not those who intend mischief and foment unbelief and disunion among believers. The Believers by their self-surrender obtain eternal Felicity. God will turn in mercy even to those who, though they waver or fail in duty, turn at last to Him (ix. 100-118, and C. 97).

Those who believe should associate with the righteous and the truthful, actively doing their duty. But if the Community marches out, a part of them should remain behind for the purpose of diligently studying religion and teaching their brethren when they return. Every Sūra increases the faith of those who believe, though those diseased in heart may add doubt to doubt. Trust in God, Lord of the Throne of Glory (ix. 119-129, and C. 98).

C. 93.—If the Pagans repeatedly break
(ix. 1-29.) Their treaties, denounce the treaties,
But give them time either to repent
Or to prepare for the just punishment
Of their treachery. Punish the chiefs
Of the treacherous, and destroy them.
But if one of them seek asylum,
Give it: let him hear the Word
Of God and escort him to security.
Be true to the true, but fight those
Who are false to plighted word
And taunt you for your Faith.
No one has the right to approach
The mosques of God unless
He believes in God and follows
God's Law, the law of righteousness.

Sūra IX.

Tauba (Repentance) or *Barāat*
(Immunity).

1. A (declaration) of immunity[1246]
From God and His Apostle,
To those of the Pagans
With whom ye have contracted
Mutual alliances :—

١- بَرَآءَةٌ مِّنَ اللّٰهِ وَرَسُوْلِهٖٓ
اِلَى الَّذِيْنَ عٰهَدْتُّمْ
مِّنَ الْمُشْرِكِيْنَ ۝

2. Go ye, then, for four months,[1247]
Backwards and forwards,
(As ye will), throughout the land,
But know ye that ye cannot
Frustrate God (by your falsehood)
But that God will cover
With shame those who reject Him.

٢- فَسِيْحُوْا فِي الْاَرْضِ اَرْبَعَةَ اَشْهُرٍ
وَّاعْلَمُوْٓا اَنَّكُمْ غَيْرُ مُعْجِزِي اللّٰهِ ۙ
وَاَنَّ اللّٰهَ مُخْزِي الْكٰفِرِيْنَ ۝

3. And an announcement from God
And His Apostle, to the people
(Assembled) on the day
Of the Great Pilgrimage,—[1248]
That God and His Apostle
Dissolve (treaty) obligations
With the Pagans.
If, then, ye repent,
It were best for you ;
But if ye turn away,

٣- وَاَذَانٌ مِّنَ اللّٰهِ وَرَسُوْلِهٖٓ اِلَى النَّاسِ
يَوْمَ الْحَجِّ الْاَكْبَرِ
اَنَّ اللّٰهَ بَرِيْٓءٌ مِّنَ الْمُشْرِكِيْنَ ۙ وَ
رَسُوْلُهٗ ۭ فَاِنْ تُبْتُمْ
فَهُوَ خَيْرٌ لَّكُمْ ۚ وَاِنْ تَوَلَّيْتُمْ

1246. *Barāat*: usually translated "immunity". I do not think that word correctly represents the Arabic word in this context. I retain it as I cannot think of any single English word as an equivalent. The general sense is explained in the introduction to this Sūra. In verse 3 below I use the periphrasis "dissolve treaty obligations," which goes some way to explain the meaning. The Pagans and enemies of Islam frequently made treaties of mutual alliance with the Muslims. The Muslims scrupulously observed their part, but the Pagans violated their part again and again when it suited them. After some years' experience it became imperative to denounce such treaties altogether. This was done in due form, with four months' notice, and a chance was given to those who faithfully observed their pledges, to continue their alliance.

1247. *Four Months.* Some Commentators understand by this the four forbidden months in which warfare by ancient Arabian custom was unlawful, *viz.*, Rajab, Ẓul-qa'd, Ẓul-ḥajj, and Muḥarram: See ii. 194 n. But it is better to take the signification of the four months immediately following the Declaration. Assuming that the Sūra was promulgated early in Shawwāl (see Introduction), the four months would be Shawwāl, Ẓul-qa'd, Ẓul-ḥajj, and Muḥarram, of which the last three would also be the customary Prohibited Months.

1248. The great day of Ḥajj is either the 9th of Ẓul-ḥajj (*'Arafa*), or the 10th (the Day of Sacrifice).

Know ye that ye cannot
Frustrate God. And proclaim
A grievous penalty to those
Who reject Faith.

فَاعْلَمُوٓا اَنَّكُمْ غَيْرُ مُعْجِزِي اللّٰهِ ؕ
وَبَشِّرِ الَّذِيْنَ كَفَرُوْا بِعَذَابٍ اَلِيْمٍ ۝

4. (But the treaties are) not dissolved[1249]
With those Pagans with whom
Ye have entered into alliance
And who have not subsequently
Failed you in aught,
Nor aided any one against you.
So fulfil your engagements
With them to the end
Of their term: for God
Loveth the righteous.

٤- اِلَّا الَّذِيْنَ عٰهَدْتُّمْ مِّنَ الْمُشْرِكِيْنَ
ثُمَّ لَمْ يَنْقُصُوْكُمْ شَيْـًٔا
وَّلَمْ يُظَاهِرُوْا عَلَيْكُمْ اَحَدًا
فَاَتِمُّوْٓا اِلَيْهِمْ عَهْدَهُمْ اِلٰى مُدَّتِهِمْ ؕ
اِنَّ اللّٰهَ يُحِبُّ الْمُتَّقِيْنَ ۝

5. But when the forbidden months[1250]
Are past, then fight and slay[1251]
The Pagans wherever ye find them,
And seize them, beleaguer them,
And lie in wait for them
In every stratagem (of war);
But if they repent,[1252]
And establish regular prayers
And practise regular charity,
Then open the way for them:
For God is Oft-forgiving,
Most Merciful.

٥- فَاِذَا انْسَلَخَ الْاَشْهُرُ الْحُرُمُ
فَاقْتُلُوا الْمُشْرِكِيْنَ حَيْثُ وَجَدْتُّمُوْهُمْ
وَخُذُوْهُمْ وَاحْصُرُوْهُمْ
وَاقْعُدُوْا لَهُمْ كُلَّ مَرْصَدٍ ۚ
فَاِنْ تَابُوْا وَاَقَامُوا الصَّلٰوةَ
وَاٰتَوُا الزَّكٰوةَ فَخَلُّوْا سَبِيْلَهُمْ ؕ
اِنَّ اللّٰهَ غَفُوْرٌ رَّحِيْمٌ ۝

1249. The sacred duty of fulfilling all obligations of every kind, to Muslims and non Muslims, in public as well as private life, is a cardinal feature of Muslim ethics. The question what is to be done with those who abuse this principle by failing in their duty but expect the Muslims to do their part is not to be solved (in the case of treaties) by a general denunciation of treaties but by a careful consideration of the cases where there has been fidelity and not treachery. There we are enjoined to give the strictest fidelity, as it is a part of righteousness and our duty to God.

1250. The emphasis is on the first clause: it is only when the four months of grace are past, and the other party show no signs of desisting from their treacherous designs by right conduct, that the state of war supervenes—between Faith and Unfaith.

1251. When war becomes inevitable, it must be prosecuted with vigour. According to the English phrase, you cannot fight with kid gloves. The fighting may take the form of slaughter, or capture, or siege, or ambush and other stratagems. But even then there is room for repentance and amendment on the part of the guilty party, and if that takes place, our duty is forgiveness and the establishment of peace

1252. The repentance must be sincere, and that is shown by conduct—a religious spirit of true prayer and charity. In that case we are not to bar the gate against the repentant. On the contrary we must do all we can to make their way easy, remembering that God is Oft-forgiving, Most Merciful.

6. If one amongst the Pagans [1253]
Ask thee for asylum,
Grant it to him,
So that he may hear the Word
Of God; and then escort him
To where he can be secure.[1254]
That is because they are
Men without knowledge.

٦- وَإِنْ أَحَدٌ مِّنَ الْمُشْرِكِينَ اسْتَجَارَكَ
فَأَجِرْهُ حَتَّىٰ يَسْمَعَ كَلَٰمَ اللَّهِ
ثُمَّ أَبْلِغْهُ مَأْمَنَهُ ۚ
ذَٰلِكَ بِأَنَّهُمْ قَوْمٌ لَّا يَعْلَمُونَ ۝

SECTION 2.

7. How can there be a league,
Before God and His Apostle,
With the Pagans, except those [1255]
With whom ye made a treaty
Near the Sacred Mosque?
As long as these stand true
To you, stand ye true to them:
For God doth love the righteous.

٧- كَيْفَ يَكُونُ لِلْمُشْرِكِينَ عَهْدٌ عِندَ
اللَّهِ وَعِندَ رَسُولِهِۦٓ إِلَّا الَّذِينَ عَٰهَدتُّمْ
عِندَ الْمَسْجِدِ الْحَرَامِ ۖ فَمَا اسْتَقَٰمُوا لَكُمْ
فَاسْتَقِيمُوا لَهُمْ ۚ إِنَّ اللَّهَ يُحِبُّ الْمُتَّقِينَ ۝

8. How (can there be such a league),[1256]
Seeing that if they get an advantage
Over you, they respect not
In you the ties either of kinship [1257]

٨- كَيْفَ وَإِن يَظْهَرُوا عَلَيْكُمْ
لَا يَرْقُبُوا فِيكُمْ إِلًّا

1253. Even among the enemies of Islam, actively fighting against Islam, there may be individuals who may be in a position to require protection. Full asylum is to be given to them, and opportunities provided for hearing the Word of God. If they accept the Word, they become Muslims and brethren, and no further question arises. If they do not see their way to accept Islam, they will require double protection: (1) from the Islamic forces openly fighting against their people, and (2) from their own people, as they detached themselves from them. Both kinds of protection should be ensured for them, and they should be safely escorted to a place where they can be safe. Such persons only err through ignorance, and there may be much good in them.

1254. *Maaman*: place or opportunity of being secure from all harm

1255. In this section we have the reasons why the treaties with treacherous Pagan foes were denounced. The clause introducing the exception is a parenthetical clause. The word "Pagans" must be connected with verse 8 which follows. In that verse the word *kaifa* resumes the clause introduced by the word *kaifa* at the beginning of verse 7. The exceptional Pagan tribes which remained true to their word were the Banū Ḥamza and the Banū Kināna, who swore their treaty near the Sacred Mosque and faithfully observed it. They were to be given the full benefit of their fidelity even though their kindred tribes were treacherous.

1256. The exceptions having been stated parenthetically in verse 7, the indictment of the general mass of Pagan tribes is now set out briefly but fully and convincingly. After that kind of behaviour how can any treaty be possible with them? The counts are: (1) that whenever they got a slight advantage, they disregarded the ties both of kinship and of covenant as against the Muslims because of their Faith. thus proving doubly treacherous; (2) that they spoke fair words, but had venom in their hearts; (3) that their attitude was one of rebellion against their plighted word; (4) that they disregarded the solemn Signs of God for some miserable worldly gain: (5) that they tried to prevent other people from coming to the Way of God. The first clause is repeated again as the last clause, to emphasise their double treachery, and round off the argument.

1257. Among the Arabs the ties of kinship were so strong as to be almost unbreakable. The Pagan Arabs went out of their way to break them in the case of the Muslims, who were kith and kin to them. Besides the bond of kinship there was the further bond of their plighted oath in the Treaty. They broke that oath because the other parties were Muslims!

Or of covenant? With (fair words
From) their mouths they entice you,
But their hearts are averse
From you; and most of them
Are rebellious and wicked.

وَلَا ذِمَّةً ۚ يُرْضُونَكُم بِأَفْوَاهِهِمْ
وَتَأْبَىٰ قُلُوبُهُمْ
وَأَكْثَرُهُمْ فَاسِقُونَ ۝

9. The Signs of God have they sold
For a miserable price,
And (many) have they hindered
From His Way: evil indeed
Are the deeds they have done.

٩- اشْتَرَوْا بِآيَاتِ اللَّهِ ثَمَنًا قَلِيلًا
فَصَدُّوا عَن سَبِيلِهِ ۚ
إِنَّهُمْ سَاءَ مَا كَانُوا يَعْمَلُونَ ۝

10. In a Believer they respect not
The ties either of kinship
Or of covenant! It is they
Who have transgressed all
bounds.[1258]

١٠- لَا يَرْقُبُونَ فِي مُؤْمِنٍ إِلًّا
وَلَا ذِمَّةً ۚ
وَأُولَٰئِكَ هُمُ الْمُعْتَدُونَ ۝

11. But (even so), if they repent,[1259]
Establish regular prayers,
And practise regular charity,—
They are your brethren in Faith:
(Thus) do We explain the Signs
In detail, for those who understand.

١١- فَإِن تَابُوا وَأَقَامُوا الصَّلَاةَ
وَآتَوُا الزَّكَاةَ فَإِخْوَانُكُمْ فِي الدِّينِ ۗ
وَنُفَصِّلُ الْآيَاتِ لِقَوْمٍ يَعْلَمُونَ ۝

12. But if they violate their oaths
After their covenant,
And taunt you for your Faith,—[1260]
Fight ye the chiefs of Unfaith:
For their oaths are nothing to
them:
That thus they may be restrained.

١٢- وَإِن نَّكَثُوا أَيْمَانَهُم مِّن بَعْدِ عَهْدِهِمْ
وَطَعَنُوا فِي دِينِكُمْ
فَقَاتِلُوا أَئِمَّةَ الْكُفْرِ ۙ
إِنَّهُمْ لَا أَيْمَانَ لَهُمْ لَعَلَّهُمْ يَنتَهُونَ ۝

13. Will ye not fight people
Who violated their oaths,

١٣- أَلَا تُقَاتِلُونَ قَوْمًا نَّكَثُوا أَيْمَانَهُمْ

1258. The catalogue of their sins being set out, it is clear that they were aggressors in the worst possible ways; and war became inevitable.

1259. The chance of repentance and mercy to the worst enemies is again emphasised, in order that people with any understanding may not be misled into thinking that war was an easy or light matter. This emphasis is balanced by the emphasis in the next verse on the causes which made war inevitable for those with any self-respect.

1260. Not only did the enemies break their oaths shamelessly, but they even taunted the Muslims on their Faith and the "simple-minded" way in which they continued to respect their part of the treaty, as if they were afraid to fight!

Plotted to expel the Apostle,[1261]
And took the aggressive
By being the first (to assault) you?
Do ye fear them ? Nay,
It is God Whom ye should
More justly fear, if ye believe !

وَهَمُّوا بِإِخْرَاجِ الرَّسُولِ وَهُمْ بَدَءُوكُمْ
أَوَّلَ مَرَّةٍ ۚ أَتَخْشَوْنَهُمْ ۚ
فَاللَّهُ أَحَقُّ أَنْ تَخْشَوْهُ إِنْ كُنْتُمْ مُؤْمِنِينَ ۝

14. Fight them, and God will
Punish them by your hands,
Cover them with shame,
Help you (to victory) over them,
Heal the breasts of Believers,[1262]

١٤- قَاتِلُوهُمْ يُعَذِّبْهُمُ اللَّهُ بِأَيْدِيكُمْ
وَيُخْزِهِمْ وَيَنْصُرْكُمْ عَلَيْهِمْ
وَيَشْفِ صُدُورَ قَوْمٍ مُؤْمِنِينَ ۝

15. And still the indignation of their
hearts.[1263]
For God will turn (in mercy)[1264]
To whom He will; and God
Is All-Knowing, All-Wise.

١٥- وَيُذْهِبْ غَيْظَ قُلُوبِهِمْ ۗ
وَيَتُوبُ اللَّهُ عَلَىٰ مَنْ يَشَاءُ ۗ
وَاللَّهُ عَلِيمٌ حَكِيمٌ ۝

16. Or think ye that ye
Shall be abandoned,
As though God did not know[1265]
Those among you who strive
With might and main, and take
None for friends and protectors
Except God, His Apostle,
And the (community of) Believers ?
But God is well-acquainted
With (all) that ye do.

١٦- أَمْ حَسِبْتُمْ أَنْ تُتْرَكُوا
وَلَمَّا يَعْلَمِ اللَّهُ الَّذِينَ جَاهَدُوا مِنْكُمْ
وَلَمْ يَتَّخِذُوا مِنْ دُونِ اللَّهِ وَلَا رَسُولِهِ
وَلَا الْمُؤْمِنِينَ وَلِيجَةً ۚ
وَاللَّهُ خَبِيرٌ بِمَا تَعْمَلُونَ ۝ ع

1261. The argument now takes a new turn. An appeal is made to the Muslims on various grounds: (1) the shameless disregard of treaties by the enemy, (2) the under-hand plots to discredit the Holy Apostle, and turn him out of Medina as he had been turned out of Mecca, (3) the aggressive taken by the Quraish and their confederates in Medina after the treaty of Ḥudaibīya (A.H. 6, Ẓul-qa'd, Feb. 628), (4) the manly attitude that fears God rather than men, and (5) the need to prove our sincere faith by test and trial and struggle and sacrifice (ix. 16).

1262. *Heal the breasts of believers, i.e.*, of wounds that they may have sustained from the assaults, taunts, and cruelty of the enemy.

1263. When the victory comes and the wounds are healed, a great peace comes to the hearts of those who have suffered, striven, and struggled. The fighting was an abnormal necessity forced by injustice and oppression. When God's Law is established, the fire of indignation is quelled, and the true Peace of Islam is attained.

1264. God's mercy is unlimited. When evil is destroyed, many of those who were enticed by evil will come into the fold of truth and righteousness, and the cessation of war and conflict will bring peace, certainly to those who fought for the right, but also possibly to those whose eyes have been opened to the working of God's Law and who in healing reconciliation become members of the Brotherhood of Peace in Islam.

1265. Some translators have taken a different verbal construction of this passage, but the ultimate effect in meaning is the same: we must all be tested and tried, but God knows our inmost hearts, and He will support those who strive in His way, out of sincere love for Him, His Apostle, and the body of the true men of faith.

SECTION 3.

17. It is not for such
As join gods with God,
To visit or maintain[1266]
The mosques of God
While they witness
Against their own souls
To infidelity. The works
Of such bear no fruit:
In Fire shall they dwell.

١٧- مَا كَانَ لِلْمُشْرِكِينَ
أَنْ يَعْمُرُوا مَسٰجِدَ اللّٰهِ
شٰهِدِينَ عَلٰٓى أَنْفُسِهِمْ بِالْكُفْرِ
أُولٰٓئِكَ حَبِطَتْ أَعْمٰلُهُمْ
وَفِي النَّارِ هُمْ خٰلِدُونَ ○

18. The mosques of God
Shall be visited and maintained
By such as believe in God
And the Last Day, establish
Regular prayers, and practise
Regular charity, and fear
None (at all) except God.[1267]
It is they who are expected
To be on true guidance.[1268]

١٨- إِنَّمَا يَعْمُرُ مَسٰجِدَ اللّٰهِ
مَنْ ءَامَنَ بِاللّٰهِ وَالْيَوْمِ الْآخِرِ
وَأَقَامَ الصَّلٰوةَ وَءَاتَى الزَّكٰوةَ
وَلَمْ يَخْشَ إِلَّا اللّٰهَ فَعَسٰٓى أُولٰٓئِكَ
أَنْ يَكُونُوا مِنَ الْمُهْتَدِينَ ○

19. Do ye make the giving[1269]
Of drink to pilgrims,

١٩- أَجَعَلْتُمْ سِقَايَةَ الْحَآجِّ

1266. *'Amara* as applied to mosques implies the following ideas: (1) to build or repair; (2) to maintain in fitting dignity; (3) to visit for purposes of devotion; and (4) fill with light and life and activity,—what would be called in Urdu *Masjid ābād karnā.* For brevity I have only used the two words "visit and maintain" in the Translation.

Before the preaching of Islam the Pagans built, repaired, and maintained the Mosque, and celebrated Pagan ceremonies in it, including naked dances round the Ka'ba. They made an income out of it. Islam protested, and the Pagans ejected Muslims and their Leader from Mecca, and shut them out from the Ka'ba itself. When the Muslims were strong enough to re-take Mecca (A.H. 8), they purified the Mosque and re-established the worship of the true God. The families who previously held control could not after this be allowed *in a state of Paganism* to control the Mosque any longer. If they became Muslims, it was a different matter. The further question arose: should they be allowed to visit it and practise their unseemly Pagan rites? Obviously this would be derogatory to the dignity and honour of the Mosque, and was forbidden. This was the particular occasion to which the verse refers. The general deduction is clear. A house of God is a place of sincere devotion, not a theatre for vulgar rites nor a source of worldly income. Only sincere Believers have a right of entry. Who the sincere Believers are, is explained in the next verse.

1267. See the previous note. Sincere Believers are those who have faith in God and the future, and have a spirit of devotion and charity—a true and abiding spirit, not merely isolated acts now and again. Moreover they must not bow to worldly greed or ambition, which produces fear of worldly power.

1268. Others may call themselves by what names they like. True guidance is shown by the tests here indicated.

1269 Giving drinks of cold water to thirsty pilgrims, and doing material services to a mosque are meritorious acts, but they are only external. If they do not touch the soul, their value is slight. Far greater, in the sight of God, are Faith, Endeavour, and self-surrender to God. Men who practise these will obtain honour in the sight of God. God's light and guidance comes to them, and not to those self-sufficient beings who think that a little show of what the world considers piety is enough.

Or the maintenance of
The Sacred Mosque, equal
To (the pious service of) those
Who believe in God
And the Last Day, and strive
With might and main
In the cause of God?
They are not comparable
In the sight of God:
And God guides not
Those who do wrong.

وَعِمَارَةَ الْمَسْجِدِ الْحَرَامِ كَمَنْ آمَنَ
بِاللَّهِ
وَالْيَوْمِ الْآخِرِ وَجَاهَدَ
فِي سَبِيلِ اللَّهِ
لَا يَسْتَوُونَ عِندَ اللَّهِ
وَاللَّهُ لَا يَهْدِي الْقَوْمَ الظَّالِمِينَ ○

20. Those who believe, and suffer
Exile and strive with might
And main, in God's cause,[1270]
With their goods and their persons,
Have the highest rank
In the sight of God:
They are the people
Who will achieve (salvation).

٢٠- الَّذِينَ آمَنُوا وَهَاجَرُوا وَجَاهَدُوا فِي
سَبِيلِ اللَّهِ بِأَمْوَالِهِمْ وَأَنفُسِهِمْ
أَعْظَمُ دَرَجَةً عِندَ اللَّهِ
وَأُولَٰئِكَ هُمُ الْفَائِزُونَ ○

21. Their Lord doth give them
Glad tidings of a Mercy
From Himself, of His good pleasure,
And of Gardens for them,
Wherein are delights
That endure:

٢١- يُبَشِّرُهُمْ رَبُّهُم بِرَحْمَةٍ مِّنْهُ
وَرِضْوَانٍ
وَجَنَّاتٍ لَّهُمْ
فِيهَا نَعِيمٌ مُّقِيمٌ ○

22. They will dwell therein
For ever. Verily in God's presence
Is a reward, the greatest (of all).[1271]

٢٢- خَالِدِينَ فِيهَا أَبَدًا
إِنَّ اللَّهَ عِندَهُ أَجْرٌ عَظِيمٌ ○

23. O ye who believe! Take not
For protectors your fathers
And your brothers if they love
Infidelity above Faith:

٢٣- يَا أَيُّهَا الَّذِينَ آمَنُوا لَا تَتَّخِذُوا آبَاءَكُمْ
وَإِخْوَانَكُمْ أَوْلِيَاءَ إِنِ اسْتَحَبُّوا الْكُفْرَ عَلَى

1270. Here is a good description of *Jihād*. It *may* require fighting in God's cause, as a form of self-sacrifice. But its essence consists in (1) a true and sincere Faith, which so fixes its gaze on God, that all selfish or worldly motives seem paltry and fade away, and (2) an earnest and ceaseless activity, involving the sacrifice (if need be) of life, person, or property, in the service of God. Mere brutal fighting is opposed to the whole spirit of *Jihād*, while the sincere scholar's pen or preacher's voice or wealthy man's contributions may be the most valuable forms of *Jihād*.

1271. Those who strive and suffer in God's cause are promised (1) a mercy specially from Himself, (2) His own good pleasure, (3) gardens of perpetual delight (4) the supreme reward, God's own Presence or nearness. These are in gradation: (1) is a special mercy, higher than flows out to all creatures; (2) is a consciousness of God's good pleasure, which raises the soul above itself; (3) is that state of permanent spiritual assurance, which is typified by gardens of perpetual delight, and (4) is the final bliss, which is the Presence of God Himself, or, in Ṣufi language *didār-i-Ilāhi*, the sight of God Himself.

If any of you do so,
They do wrong.

24. Say : If it be that your fathers,
Your sons, your brothers,
Your mates, or your kindred ;
The wealth that ye have gained ;
The commerce in which ye fear
A decline ; or the dwellings
In which ye delight—[1272]
Are dearer to you than God,
Or His Apostle, or the striving
In His cause ;—then wait
Until God brings about[1273]
His Decision : and God
Guides not the rebellious.

SECTION 4.

25. Assuredly God did help you
In many battle-fields
And on the day of Ḥunain :[1274]
Behold ! your great numbers
Elated you, but they availed
You naught : the land,
For all that it is wide,
Did constrain you, and ye

الْإِيمَانِ ۚ وَمَن يَتَوَلَّهُم مِّنكُمْ فَأُولَٰئِكَ
هُمُ الظَّالِمُونَ ○
٢٤- قُلْ إِن كَانَ آبَاؤُكُمْ وَأَبْنَاؤُكُمْ وَ
إِخْوَانُكُمْ وَأَزْوَاجُكُمْ وَعَشِيرَتُكُمْ
وَأَمْوَالٌ اقْتَرَفْتُمُوهَا وَتِجَارَةٌ تَخْشَوْنَ
كَسَادَهَا وَمَسَاكِنُ تَرْضَوْنَهَا أَحَبَّ إِلَيْكُم
مِّنَ اللَّهِ وَرَسُولِهِ وَجِهَادٍ فِي سَبِيلِهِ
فَتَرَبَّصُوا حَتَّىٰ يَأْتِيَ اللَّهُ بِأَمْرِهِ ۗ
وَاللَّهُ لَا يَهْدِي الْقَوْمَ الْفَاسِقِينَ ○ ع
٢٥- لَقَدْ نَصَرَكُمُ اللَّهُ فِي مَوَاطِنَ كَثِيرَةٍ
وَيَوْمَ حُنَيْنٍ ۙ إِذْ أَعْجَبَتْكُمْ كَثْرَتُكُمْ
فَلَمْ تُغْنِ عَنكُمْ شَيْئًا
وَضَاقَتْ عَلَيْكُمُ الْأَرْضُ بِمَا رَحُبَتْ

1272. Man's heart clings to (1) his own kith and kin—parents, children, brothers and sisters, husbands or wives, or other relatives, (2) wealth and prosperity, (3) commerce or means of profit and gain, or (4) noble buildings, for dignity or comfort. If these are a hindrance in God's cause, we have to choose which we love most. We must love God even if it involves the sacrifice of all else.

1273. If we love our earthly ties and comforts, profits and pleasures, more than we love God, and therefore fail to respond to God's cause, it is not God's cause which will suffer. God's purpose will be accomplished, with or without us. But our failure to respond to His will must leave us spiritually poorer, bereft of grace and guidance : "for God guides not the rebellious".

This is of universal application. But it was strikingly illustrated in the case of those faithful ones who obeyed the Apostle's call, left the comfort of their homes in Mecca and suffered exile in Medina, gave up their trade and their possessions, strove and fought for God's cause, sometimes against their own kith and kin or their own tribesmen who were enemies of Islam. They won through. Others were not prepared for such sacrifice, but their failure did not stop the accomplishment of God's plan and purpose.

1274. Ḥunain on the road to Ṭāif from Mecca, and about fourteen miles to the east of Mecca. It is a valley in the mountainous country between Mecca and Ṭāif. Immediately after the conquest of Mecca, (A.H. 8), the Pagan idolaters, who were surprised and chagrined at the wonderful reception which Islam was receiving, organised a great gathering near Ṭāif to concert plans for attacking the Apostle. The Hawāzin and the Thaqīf tribes took the lead and prepared a great expedition for Mecca, boasting of their strength and military skill. There was on the other hand a wave of confident enthusiasm among the Muslims at Mecca, in which the new Muslims joined. The enemy forces numbered about 4,000, but the Muslim force reached a total of ten or twelve thousand, as every one wished to join. The battle was joined at Ḥunain, as described in the next note.

Turned back in retreat.[1275]

ثُمَّ وَلَّيْتُمْ مُّدْبِرِيْنَ ۝

26. But God did pour His calm[1276]
On the Apostle and on the
Believers,
And sent down forces which ye
Saw not: He punished
The Unbelievers: thus doth He
Reward those without Faith.

٢٦- ثُمَّ اَنْزَلَ اللّٰهُ سَكِيْنَتَهٗ عَلٰى رَسُوْلِهٖ
وَعَلَى الْمُؤْمِنِيْنَ وَاَنْزَلَ جُنُوْدًا لَّمْ
تَرَوْهَا ۚ وَعَذَّبَ الَّذِيْنَ كَفَرُوْا ۭ
وَذٰلِكَ جَزَاۗءُ الْكٰفِرِيْنَ ۝

27. Again will God, after this,[1277]
Turn (in mercy) to whom
He will: for God
Is Oft-forgiving, Most Merciful.

٢٧- ثُمَّ يَتُوْبُ اللّٰهُ مِنْۢ بَعْدِ ذٰلِكَ عَلٰى
مَنْ يَّشَاۗءُ ۭ وَاللّٰهُ غَفُوْرٌ رَّحِيْمٌ ۝

28. O ye who believe! Truly
The Pagans are unclean;[1278]
So let them not,
After this year of theirs,[1279]

٢٨- يٰٓاَيُّهَا الَّذِيْنَ اٰمَنُوْٓا اِنَّمَا الْمُشْرِكُوْنَ
نَجَسٌ فَلَا يَقْرَبُوا

1275. For the first time the Muslims had at Ḥunain tremendous odds in their favour. But this itself constituted a danger. Many in their ranks had more enthusiasm than wisdom, more a spirit of elation than of faith and confidence in the righteousness of their cause. The enemy had the advantage of knowing the ground thoroughly. They laid an ambush in which the advance guard of the Muslim forces was caught. The country is hilly, in which the enemy concealed himself. As soon as the Muslim vanguard entered the Ḥunain valley, the enemy fell upon them with fury and caused havoc with their arrows from their places of concealment. In such ground the numbers of the Muslims were themselves a disadvantage. Many were slain, and many turned back in confusion and retreat. But the Apostle, as ever, was calm in his wisdom and faith. He rallied his forces and inflicted the most crushing defeat on the enemy.

1276. *Sakīn*: calm, peace, security, tranquillity. *Cf.* ii. 248. The Apostle never approved of over-weening confidence, or reliance merely upon human strength, or human resources or numbers. In the hour of danger and seeming disaster, he was perfectly calm, and with cool courage relied upon the help of God, Whose standard he carried. His calmness inspired all around him, and stopped the rout of those who had turned their backs. It was with God's help that they won, and their victory was complete. They followed it up with an energetic pursuit of the enemies, capturing their camps, their flocks and herds, and their families, whom they had boastfully brought with them in expectation of an easy victory.

1277. Examples of God's mercy and grace in difficult circumstances in one case illustrate His grace and mercy at all times to those who have faith.

1278. *Unclean*: both literally and metaphorically; because Muslims are enjoined to be strict in ablutions and physical cleanliness, as well as in purity of mind and heart, so that their word can be relied upon.

1279. *This year of theirs*: there is a two-fold meaning: (1) now that you have complete control of Mecca, and are charged with the purity of worship there, shut out all impurity from this year; (2) you have seen how the Pagans have behaved this year; their year of power and misuse of that power may be called *their* year; it is over, and now you Muslims are responsible.

Approach the Sacred Mosque.
And if ye fear poverty,[1280]
Soon will God enrich you,
If He wills, out of His bounty,
For God is All-Knowing, All-Wise.

المسجد الحرام بعد عامهم هذا وإن
خفتم عيلة فسوف يغنيكم الله من
فضله إن شاء إن الله عليم حكيم ○

29. Fight those who believe not
In God nor the Last Day,
Nor hold that forbidden
Which hath been forbidden
By God and His Apostle,
Nor acknowledge the Religion
Of Truth, (even if they are)
Of the People of the Book,
Until they pay the *Jizya*[1281]
With willing submission,[1282]
And feel themselves subdued.

٢٩- قاتلوا الذين لا يؤمنون بالله ولا
باليوم الآخر ولا يحرمون ما حرم
الله ورسوله ولا يدينون دين الحق
من الذين أوتوا الكتب
حتى يعطوا الجزية عن يد
وهم صاغرون ○

C. 94.—The enemies of Faith would fain put out
(ix. 30-42.) **God's light, but God's light will shine**
More glorious than ever. Wealth
Is for use and on trust for mankind:
Hoard not, nor misuse it. Fight
A straight fight in the cause of Right:
Go forth bravely to strive and struggle,
And prove yourselves worthy of God.

1280. The concourse in Mecca added to the profits of trade and commerce. "But fear not," we are told; "the Pagans are a waning power, bound to disappear, aud you should strengthen your own community, that they may more than counter-balance the apparent loss of custom; and God has other means of improving your economic position." This actually happened. The Pagans were extinguished from Arabia, and the concourse of Pilgrims from all parts of the world increased the numbers more than a hundred-fold. Here is commonsense, wisdom, and statesmanship, even if we look at it from a purely human point of view.

1281. *Jizya*: the root meaning is compensation. The derived meaning, which became the technical meaning, was a poll-tax levied from those who did not accept Islam, but were willing to live under the protection of Islam, and were thus tacitly willing to submit to its ideals being enforced in the Muslim State, saving only their personal liberty of conscience as regarded themselves. There was no amount fixed for it, and in any case it was merely symbolical,—an acknowledgment that those whose religion was tolerated would in their turn not interfere with the preaching and progress of Islam. Imām Shāfi'ī suggests one dīnār per year, which would be the Arabian gold dīnār of the Muslim States, equivalent in value to about half a sovereign, or about 5 to 6·7 rupees. See n. 410 to iii. 75. The tax varied in amount, and there were exemptions for the poor, for females and children (according to Abū Ḥanīfa), for slaves, and for monks and hermits. Being a tax on able-bodied males of military age, it was in a sense a commutation for military service. But see the next note.

1282. *'An Yadin* (literally, from the hand) has been variously interpreted. The hand being the symbol of power and authority, I accept the interpretation "in token of willing submission." The Jizya was thus partly symbolic and partly a commutation for military service, but as the amount was insignificant and the exemptions numerous, its symbolic character predominated. See the last note.

SECTION 5.

30. The Jews call 'Uzair a son[1283]
Of God, and the Christians
Call Christ the Son of God.
That is a saying from their mouth;
(In this) they but imitate[1284]
What the Unbelievers of old
Used to say. God's curse
Be on them: how they are deluded
Away from the Truth![1285]

31. They take their priests[1286]
And their anchorites to be
Their lords in derogation of God,[1287]
And (they take as their Lord)
Christ the son of Mary;
Yet they were commanded
To worship but One God:
There is no god but He.
Praise and glory to Him:[1288]
(Far is He) from having
The partners they associate
(With Him).

٣٠- وَقَالَتِ الْيَهُودُ عُزَيْرٌ ابْنُ اللّٰهِ
وَقَالَتِ النَّصٰرَى الْمَسِيْحُ ابْنُ اللّٰهِ ۭ
ذٰلِكَ قَوْلُهُمْ بِاَفْوَاهِهِمْ ۚ
يُضَاهِــــُٔوْنَ قَوْلَ الَّذِيْنَ كَفَرُوْا مِنْ قَبْلُ ۭ
قٰتَلَهُمُ اللّٰهُ ڔ اَنّٰى يُؤْفَكُوْنَ ○

٣١- اِتَّخَذُوْٓا اَحْبَارَهُمْ وَرُهْبَانَهُمْ
اَرْبَابًا مِّنْ دُوْنِ اللّٰهِ
وَالْمَسِيْحَ ابْنَ مَرْيَمَ ۚ
وَمَآ اُمِرُوْٓا اِلَّا لِيَعْبُدُوْٓا اِلٰهًا وَّاحِدًا ۚ
لَآ اِلٰهَ اِلَّا هُوَ ۭ
سُبْحٰنَهٗ عَمَّا يُشْرِكُوْنَ ○

1283. In n. 718 to v. 20 I have quoted passages from the Old Testament, showing how freely the expression "sons of God" was used by the Jews. A sect of them called 'Uzair a son of God, according to Baidhāwī. In Appendix II (Sūra v.) I have shown that the constitution of Judaism dates from 'Uzair (Ezra). The Christians still call Christ the Son of God.

1284. Taking men for gods or sons of God was not a new thing. All ancient mythologies have fables of that kind. There was less excuse for such blasphemies after the apostles of God had clearly explained our true relation to God than in the times of primitive ignorance and superstition.

1285. *Cf.* v. 78.

1286. *Aḥbār*: doctors of law; priests; learned men. *Cf.* v. 47, where they are associated with Rabbis. *Ruhbān*: monks, ascetics, anchorites, men who have renounced the world; where there is a celibate clergy, the term can be applied to them as well as to members of monastic orders. It is also permissible to apply the term to "saints", where they are deified or credited with divine powers, or where people pray to them as they do in the Roman Catholic Church.

1287. Priest worship, and the worship of saints and ascetics is a form of superstition to which men have been prone in all ages. The growth of Jewish superstition is shown in the Talmud, and of Christian superstition in the doctrine of papal infallibility and the worship of saints. The mere idea of a separate order of priesthood to stand between God and man and be the exclusive repository of God's secrets is derogatory to the goodness and all-pervading grace of God. The worship of "lords many and gods many" was not confined only to the Pagans. The deification of the son of Mary is put here in a special clause by itself, as it held (and still holds) in its thrall a large portion of civilised humanity.

1288. *Cf.* vi. 100.

32. Fain would they extinguish
God's Light with their mouths,[1289]
But God will not allow
But that His Light should be
Perfected, even though the
Unbelievers
May detest (it).

٣٢- يُرِيدُونَ أَن يُطْفِـُٔوا نُورَ اللَّهِ
بِأَفْوَاهِهِمْ
وَيَأْبَى اللَّهُ إِلَّا أَن يُتِمَّ نُورَهُ
وَلَوْ كَرِهَ الْكَافِرُونَ ۝

33. It is He Who hath sent
His Apostle with Guidance
And the Religion of Truth,
To proclaim it[1290]
Over all religion,
Even though the Pagans
May detest (it).

٣٣- هُوَ الَّذِي أَرْسَلَ رَسُولَهُ بِالْهُدَىٰ
وَدِينِ الْحَقِّ
لِيُظْهِرَهُ عَلَى الدِّينِ كُلِّهِ
وَلَوْ كَرِهَ الْمُشْرِكُونَ ۝

34. O ye who believe! There are
Indeed many among the priests
And anchorites, who in falsehood[1291]
Devour the substance of men
And hinder (them) from the Way
Of God. And there are those
Who bury gold and silver[1292]
And spend it not in the Way
Of God: announce unto them
A most grievous penalty—

٣٤- يَا أَيُّهَا الَّذِينَ آمَنُوا إِنَّ كَثِيرًا مِّنَ
الْأَحْبَارِ وَالرُّهْبَانِ لَيَأْكُلُونَ أَمْوَالَ النَّاسِ
بِالْبَاطِلِ وَيَصُدُّونَ عَن سَبِيلِ اللَّهِ وَ
الَّذِينَ يَكْنِزُونَ الذَّهَبَ وَالْفِضَّةَ وَلَا يُنفِقُونَهَا
فِي سَبِيلِ اللَّهِ فَبَشِّرْهُم بِعَذَابٍ أَلِيمٍ ۝

1289. *With their mouths*: there is a twofold meaning: (1) the old-fashioned open oil lamps were extinguished by blowing with the mouth: the Unbelievers would like to blow out God's Light as it is a cause of offence to them; (2) false teachers and preachers distort the Message of God by the false words of their mouth. Their wish is to put out the light of Truth for they are people of darkness; but God will perfect His Light, *i.e.*, make it shine all the brighter in the eyes of men. His Light in itself is ever perfect, but it will penetrate the hearts of men more and more, and so become more and more perfect for them.

1290. Every religion which commends itself widely to human beings and lasts through some space of time has a glimpse of Truth in it. But Islam is the perfect light of Truth. As the greater Light, through its own strength, outshines all lesser lights, so will Islam outshine all else, in spite of the displeasure of those to whom light is an offence. See also xlviii. 28, n. 4912, and lxi. 9, n. 5442.

1291. *Bil-bāṭili*=in falsehood, *i.e.*, by false pretences, or in false or vain things. This was strikingly exemplified in the history of Mediæval Europe, though the disease is apt to attack all peoples and organisations at all times. Priests got rich by issuing indulgences and dispensations; they made their office a stepping stone to worldly power and possessions. Even the Monastic Orders, which took vows of poverty for individuals, grew rich with corporate property, until their wealth became a scandal, even among their own nations.

1292. Misuse of wealth, property, and resources is frequently condemned, and in three ways: (1) do not acquire anything wrongfully or on false pretences; (2) do not hoard or bury or amass wealth for its own sake but use it freely for good, whether for yourself or for your neighbours; and (3) be particularly careful not to waste it for idle purposes, but only so that it may fructify for the good of the people.

35. On the Day when heat [1293]
Will be produced out of
That (wealth) in the fire
Of Hell, and with it will be
Branded their foreheads,
Their flanks, and their backs.
—"This is the (treasure) which ye
Buried for yourselves: [1294] taste ye,
Then, the (treasures) ye buried!"

٣٥- يَوْمَ يُحْمٰى عَلَيْهَا فِي نَارِ جَهَنَّمَ
فَتُكْوٰى بِهَا جِبَاهُهُمْ وَجُنُوبُهُمْ وَ
ظُهُورُهُمْ ۖ
هٰذَا مَا كَنَزْتُمْ لِأَنْفُسِكُمْ
فَذُوقُوا مَا كُنْتُمْ تَكْنِزُونَ ۝

36. The number of months [1295]
In the sight of God
Is twelve (in a year)—
So ordained by Him
The day He created
The heavens and the earth;
Of them four are sacred:
That is the straight usage.
So wrong not yourselves [1296]
Therein, and fight the Pagans

٣٦- إِنَّ عِدَّةَ الشُّهُورِ عِنْدَ اللّٰهِ اثْنَا عَشَرَ
شَهْرًا فِي كِتٰبِ اللّٰهِ يَوْمَ خَلَقَ السَّمٰوٰتِ
وَالْأَرْضَ مِنْهَا أَرْبَعَةٌ حُرُمٌ ۚ
ذٰلِكَ الدِّينُ الْقَيِّمُ ۚ فَلَا تَظْلِمُوا فِيهِنَّ
أَنْفُسَكُمْ وَقَاتِلُوا الْمُشْرِكِينَ

1293. A very striking metaphor is here used to figure forth the penalty to be suffered by those who misuse wealth, for such misuse is as much a spiritual sin as any other kind of disobedience to God's Will. Such misused wealth will itself become evidence against us. It will be as if the gold and silver will be heated to add to the heat of Hell-fire; that it will brand our foreheads as reflecting on our intelligence in thinking that wealth was a good thing in itself instead of a mere means of doing good; it will brand our flanks (the middle part of our body, supporting the stomach, the seat of greed), as showing that the greed produced no real satisfaction; and it will brand our backs, the source of our stability and strength, as showing that wealth which might have added to our stability and strength, destroys, by its misuse, our stability and strength.

1294. The voice enforces the moral: "did you expect satisfaction or salvation from the treasures that you misused? Behold! they add to your torment!"

1295. This and the following verse must be read together. They condemn the arbitrary and selfish conduct of the Pagan Arabs, who, because there was a long-established custom of observing four months as those in which fighting was forbidden, changed the months about or added or deducted months when it suited them, to get an unfair advantage over the enemy. The four Prohibited Months were: Ẓul-qa'd, Ẓul-hajj, Muḥarram, and Rajab. If it suited them they postponed one of these months, and so a prohibited month became an ordinary month: while their opponents might hesitate to fight, they got an undue advantage. It also upset the security of the Month of Pilgrimage. This very ancient usage made for fair dealing all round, and its infraction by the Pagans is condemned.

The question of a solar astronomical year as against the lunar ecclesiastical year does not arise here. But it may be noted that the Arab year was roughly luni solar like the Hindu year, the months being lunar and the intercalation of a month every three years brought the year nearly but not accurately up to the solar reckoning. From the year of the Farewell Pilgrimage (A. H. 10) the ecclesiastical year was definitely fixed as a purely lunar year of roughly 354 days, the months being calculated by the actual appearance of the moon After that, every month of the ecclesiastical year came about 11 days earlier in the solar year, and thus the ecclesiastical months travelled all round the seasons and the solar year. The lunar year remains the ecclesiastical year.

1296. The Muslims were at a disadvantage on account of their scruples about the Prohibited Months. They are told not to wrong themselves in this. If the Pagans fought in all months on one pretence or another, they were allowed to defend themselves in all months. But self-restraint was (as always) recommended as far as possible.

All together as they
Fight you all together.
But know that God
Is with those who restrain
Themselves.

كَآفَّةً كَمَا يُقَاتِلُوْنَكُمْ كَآفَّةً ۭ
وَاعْلَمُوْٓا
اَنَّ اللّٰهَ مَعَ الْمُتَّقِيْنَ ۝

37. Verily the transposing[1297]
(Of a prohibited month)
Is an addition to Unbelief:
The Unbelievers are led
To wrong thereby: for they make
It lawful one year,
And forbidden another year,
In order to adjust the number
Of months forbidden by God
And make such forbidden ones
Lawful. The evil of their course
Seems pleasing to them.[1298]
But God guideth not
Those who reject Faith.

٣٧- اِنَّمَا النَّسِيْٓءُ زِيَادَةٌ فِي الْكُفْرِ
يُضَلُّ بِهِ الَّذِيْنَ كَفَرُوْا
يُحِلُّوْنَهٗ عَامًا وَّيُحَرِّمُوْنَهٗ عَامًا
لِّيُوَاطِـُٔوْا عِدَّةَ مَا حَرَّمَ اللّٰهُ
فَيُحِلُّوْا مَا حَرَّمَ اللّٰهُ ۭ
زُيِّنَ لَهُمْ سُوْٓءُ اَعْمَالِهِمْ ۭ
وَاللّٰهُ لَا يَهْدِي الْقَوْمَ الْكٰفِرِيْنَ ۝

SECTION 6.

38. O ye who believe! what
Is the matter with you,[1299]
That, when ye are asked
To go forth in the Cause of God,
Ye cling heavily to the earth?[1300]
Do ye prefer the life
Of this world to the Hereafter?
But little is the comfort
Of this life, as compared
With the Hereafter.

٣٨- يٰٓاَيُّهَا الَّذِيْنَ اٰمَنُوْا مَا لَكُمْ
اِذَا قِيْلَ لَكُمُ انْفِرُوْا فِيْ سَبِيْلِ اللّٰهِ
اثَّاقَلْتُمْ اِلَى الْاَرْضِ ۭ اَرَضِيْتُمْ بِالْحَيٰوةِ الدُّنْيَا
مِنَ الْاٰخِرَةِ ۚ فَمَا مَتَاعُ الْحَيٰوةِ الدُّنْيَا فِي
الْاٰخِرَةِ اِلَّا قَلِيْلٌ ۝

1297. To meddle with an old-established custom of close time for warfare during Prohibited or Sacred Months was not only a demonstration of the Unbelievers against the Muslims on account of their Faith, but was wrong and unjust in itself, as it abolished a wholesome check on unregulated warfare, and prejudiced the law-abiding side by arbitrary decisions.

1298. *Cf.* vi. 122. The lawless man thinks he is doing a great thing in getting the better of those who are careful to observe a law they believe in. But the lawless man loses the guidance of Faith, which is a symbol of his being guided by God; he will therefore lose in the end.

1299. The immediate reference is to the expedition to Tabūk (A.H 9), for which see the Introduction to this Sūra. But the lesson is perfectly general. When a call is made on behalf of a great cause, the fortunate ones are those who have the privilege of responding to the call. The unfortunate ones are those who are so engrossed in their parochial affairs that they turn a deaf ear to the appeal. They are suffering from a spiritual disease.

1300. The choice is between two courses: will you choose a noble adventure and the glorious privilege of following your spiritual leader, or grovel in the earth for some small worldly gain or for fear of worldly loss? The people who hesitated to follow the call of Tabūk were deterred by (1) the heat of the summer, in which the expedition was undertaken on account of the threat to the existence of the little community, and (2) the fear of losing the fruit harvest, which was ripe for gathering.

39. Unless ye go forth,[1301]
He will punish you
With a grievous penalty,
And put others in your place;
But Him ye would not harm
In the least. For God
Hath power over all things.

٣٩- إِلَّا تَنفِرُوا يُعَذِّبْكُمْ عَذَابًا أَلِيمًا
وَيَسْتَبْدِلْ قَوْمًا غَيْرَكُمْ
وَلَا تَضُرُّوهُ شَيْئًا
وَاللَّهُ عَلَىٰ كُلِّ شَيْءٍ قَدِيرٌ ○

40. If ye help not (your Leader),
(It is no matter): for God
Did indeed help him,[1302]
When the Unbelievers
Drove him out: he had
No more than one companion:[1303]
They two were in the Cave,
And he said to his companion,
"Have no fear, for God
Is with us": then God
Sent down His peace upon him,[1304]
And strengthened him with forces
Which ye saw not, and humbled[1305]
To the depths the word
Of the Unbelievers.
But the word of God
Is exalted to the heights:
For God is Exalted in might, Wise

٤٠- إِلَّا تَنصُرُوهُ فَقَدْ نَصَرَهُ اللَّهُ
إِذْ أَخْرَجَهُ الَّذِينَ كَفَرُوا
ثَانِيَ اثْنَيْنِ إِذْ هُمَا فِي الْغَارِ
إِذْ يَقُولُ لِصَاحِبِهِ
لَا تَحْزَنْ إِنَّ اللَّهَ مَعَنَا
فَأَنزَلَ اللَّهُ سَكِينَتَهُ عَلَيْهِ
وَأَيَّدَهُ بِجُنُودٍ لَّمْ تَرَوْهَا
وَجَعَلَ كَلِمَةَ الَّذِينَ كَفَرُوا السُّفْلَىٰ
وَكَلِمَةُ اللَّهِ هِيَ الْعُلْيَا
وَاللَّهُ عَزِيزٌ حَكِيمٌ ○

1301. *Tanfirū*=go forth, march onward, be ready to strive and suffer. For this is the condition of all progress in the spiritual and moral, as well as in the physical, world. According to the homely English proverb, God helps those who help themselves. Inactivity and lethargy are fatal. No one can rest on his oars. Man is not necessary to God, but God is necessary to man. If a nation receives favours and fails to deserve them, it will be replaced by another: as has so often happened in history. We may take this as a special warning to Islamic nations.

1302. The Tabūk expedition was not a failure Though many hesitated, many more joined in. But a more striking example was when the Apostle was hunted out of Mecca and performed his famous *Hijrat*. His enemies plotted for his life. He had already sent his followers on to Medina. Alī had volunteered to face his enemies in his house. His single companion was Abū Bakr. They two concealed themselves in the cave of Thaur, three miles from Mecca, for three nights, with the enemy prowling around in great numbers in fruitless search of them. "We are but two," said Abū Bakr. "Nay," said Muhammad, "for God is with us." Faith gave their minds peace, and God gave them safety. They reached Medina, and a glorious chapter opened for Islam. The forces that helped them were not seen, but their power was irresistible.

1303. Literally, "the second of two," which afterwards became Abū Bakr's proud title.

1304. *Cf.* ix. 26.

1305. The superlatives in the Arabic I have rendered by the periphrases, "humbled to the depths" and "exalted to the heights," as they accord better with the genius of the English language. The enemies of Islam had boasted that they would root it out: the result showed them up as ridiculous and despicable.

41. Go ye forth, (whether equipped)[1306]
Lightly or heavily, and strive
And struggle, with your goods
And your persons, in the Cause
Of God. That is best
For you, if ye (but) knew.

٤١- اِنْفِرُوْا خِفَافًا وَّثِقَالًا
وَّجَاهِدُوْا بِاَمْوَالِكُمْ وَاَنْفُسِكُمْ فِيْ سَبِيْلِ
اللّٰهِ ذٰلِكُمْ خَيْرٌ لَّكُمْ اِنْ كُنْتُمْ تَعْلَمُوْنَ ۝

42. If there had been
Immediate gain (in sight),
And the journey easy,
They would (all) without doubt
Have followed thee, but
The distance was long,
(And weighed) on them.
They would indeed swear
By God, "If we only could,
We should certainly
Have come out with you:"
They would destroy their own
souls;[1307]
For God doth know
That they are certainly lying.

٤٢- لَوْ كَانَ عَرَضًا قَرِيْبًا
وَّسَفَرًا قَاصِدًا لَّاتَّبَعُوْكَ
وَلٰكِنْۢ بَعُدَتْ
عَلَيْهِمُ الشُّقَّةُ
وَسَيَحْلِفُوْنَ بِاللّٰهِ
لَوِ اسْتَطَعْنَا لَخَرَجْنَا مَعَكُمْ
يُهْلِكُوْنَ اَنْفُسَهُمْ
وَاللّٰهُ يَعْلَمُ اِنَّهُمْ لَكٰذِبُوْنَ ۝ ع

C. 95. The Believers do their duty, and make
(ix. 43-72.) No excuses,—unlike the Hypocrites,
Who are a burden whether they join you
Or hold back. No help should be accepted
From these last, as they are false and insincere,
And have a slanderous tongue. Alms
Are for the poor and the needy, not for those
Who come in hypocrisy and mock
At things solemn. But the Hypocrites
Will be found out and receive due punishment,
While the righteous will be rewarded
With bliss and the good pleasure of God.

1306. *Whether equipped lightly or heavily*: to be taken both literally and metaphorically. All were invited, and they were to bring such resources as they had,—light-armed or heavy-armed, on foot or mounted, experienced men for posts of danger, raw men for duties for which they were fit. All would and should help. Even those who were too old or feeble to go could contribute such money or resources as they had.

1307. The arts and excuses of the Hypocrites are here exposed. If there had been booty in sight or an easy walk-over, they would have come. All their oaths are false, and in taking the false oaths they are destroying their spiritual life. Indeed the backsliders are jeopardising their own physical lives in hanging back. If the enemy succeeded, they would all suffer.

Section 7.

43. God give thee grace![1308] Why
Didst thou grant them exemption
Until those who told the truth
Were seen by thee in a clear light,
And thou hadst proved the liars?

٤٣- عَفَا اللّٰهُ عَنْكَ
لِمَ اَذِنْتَ لَهُمْ حَتّٰى يَتَبَيَّنَ لَكَ الَّذِيْنَ
صَدَقُوْا وَتَعْلَمَ الْكٰذِبِيْنَ ○

44. Those who believe in God
And the Last Day ask thee
For no exemption from fighting
With their goods and persons.
And God knoweth well
Those who do their duty.

٤٤- لَا يَسْتَاْذِنُكَ الَّذِيْنَ يُؤْمِنُوْنَ بِاللّٰهِ وَ
الْيَوْمِ الْاٰخِرِ اَنْ يُّجَاهِدُوْا بِاَمْوَالِهِمْ وَ
اَنْفُسِهِمْ ۗ وَاللّٰهُ عَلِيْمٌ بِالْمُتَّقِيْنَ ○

45. Only those ask thee for exemption
Who believe not in God
And the Last Day, and
Whose hearts are in doubt,
So that they are tossed[1309]
In their doubts to and fro.

٤٥- اِنَّمَا يَسْتَاْذِنُكَ الَّذِيْنَ لَا يُؤْمِنُوْنَ
بِاللّٰهِ وَالْيَوْمِ الْاٰخِرِ وَارْتَابَتْ قُلُوْبُهُمْ
فَهُمْ فِيْ رَيْبِهِمْ يَتَرَدَّدُوْنَ ○

46. If they had intended
To come out, they would
Certainly have made
Some preparation therefor;
But God was averse
To their being sent forth;
So He made them lag behind,
And they were told,
"Sit ye among those
Who sit (inactive)."

٤٦- وَلَوْ اَرَادُوا الْخُرُوْجَ
لَاَعَدُّوْا لَهٗ عُدَّةً
وَّلٰكِنْ كَرِهَ اللّٰهُ انْبِعَاثَهُمْ فَثَبَّطَهُمْ
وَقِيْلَ اقْعُدُوْا
مَعَ الْقٰعِدِيْنَ ○

47. If they had come out
With you, they would not

٤٧- لَوْ خَرَجُوْا فِيْكُمْ مَّا

1308. Literally, "God give thee forgiveness!" But there is no question of fault here, and Imām Rāzī understands the expression to mean an exclamation,—as one might say in English, "God bless you!" In Shakespeare "God save you!" is a simple friendly greeting, without any question of danger: *e.g.*, in "Much Ado about Nothing," iii. 2. 82. Note that in Q. iii. 152, last clause, "forgiveness" is put in juxtaposition to "grace" as having closely allied meanings. What the Holy Apostle had done in the Tabūk expedition was that he had been granting exemptions which may appear from a military point of view too liberal. He was actuated by motives of kindness as well as policy;—kindness, because, in the urgency of the moment he did not wish any one who had a real excuse to be refused exemption; and policy, because, if any one did not come with hearty good-will, he would be a burden instead of a help to the army. The policy was justified, because in fact 30.000 men or more followed him. But that did not in any way justify the slackers, and in a review of the position, the slackers and hypocrites are justly condemned.

1309. Doubt takes away all stability of conduct, while Faith makes a man firm in action and cool and collected in mind.

Have added to your (strength)
But only (made for) disorder,
Hurrying to and fro in your
midst[1310]
And sowing sedition among you,
And there would have been
Some among you
Who would have listened to them.
But God knoweth well
Those who do wrong.

زَادُوكُمْ إِلَّا خَبَالًا
وَّلَأَوْضَعُوا خِلٰلَكُمْ
يَبْغُونَكُمُ الْفِتْنَةَ ۚ
وَفِيكُمْ سَمّٰعُونَ لَهُمْ ۗ
وَاللّٰهُ عَلِيمٌ بِالظّٰلِمِينَ ○

48. Indeed they had plotted
Sedition before, and upset
Matters for thee,—until
The Truth arrived, and the Decree
Of God became manifest,
Much to their disgust.[1311]

٤٨- لَقَدِ ابْتَغَوُا الْفِتْنَةَ مِنْ قَبْلُ وَقَلَّبُوا
لَكَ الْأُمُورَ حَتّٰى جَاءَ الْحَقُّ وَظَهَرَ
أَمْرُ اللّٰهِ وَهُمْ كٰرِهُونَ ○

49. Among them is (many) a man
Who says: "Grant me exemption
And draw me not[1312]
Into trial." Have they not
Fallen into trial already?
And indeed Hell surrounds
The Unbelievers (on all sides).

٤٩- وَمِنْهُمْ مَّنْ يَّقُولُ ائْذَنْ لِّي وَ
لَا تَفْتِنِّي ۗ
أَلَا فِي الْفِتْنَةِ سَقَطُوا ۗ
وَإِنَّ جَهَنَّمَ لَمُحِيطَةٌ ۢ بِالْكٰفِرِينَ ○

50. If good befalls thee,
It grieves them; but if
A misfortune befalls thee,
They say, "We took indeed
Our precautions beforehand,"
And they turn away rejoicing.

٥٠- إِنْ تُصِبْكَ حَسَنَةٌ تَسُؤْهُمْ ۚ وَإِنْ
تُصِبْكَ مُصِيبَةٌ
يَقُولُوا قَدْ أَخَذْنَا أَمْرَنَا مِنْ قَبْلُ
وَيَتَوَلَّوْا وَّهُمْ فَرِحُونَ ○

1310. *Khilāl* has more than one meaning, but I follow the interpretation of Rāgib and the majority of accepted Commentators, who take it to mean "in your midst".

1311. Evil plotters against Truth are only too glad to get an opportunity of meddling from within with affairs which they want to spoil or upset. They plot from outside, but they like to get into the inner circle, that their chances of intrigue may be all the greater. They are, however, unwilling to incur any danger or any self-sacrifice. Their whole activities are directed to mischief. Great wisdom is required in a leader to deal with such a situation, and the best of such leaders must need divine guidance, as was forthcoming in this case.

1312. *Fitnat*, as explained in n. 1198, viii. 25, may mean either trial or temptation, or else tumult, turmoil, or sedition. The Commentators here take the former meaning, and explain that some Hypocrites claimed exemption from service in the Tabūk expedition in the direction of Syria on the plea that they could not withstand the charms of Syrian women and ought best to stay at home. The answer is: "But you have already fallen into temptation here by refusing service and disobeying the call." But perhaps the other meaning of "turmoil" may also be permissible as a secondary echo: in that case they object to be drawn into the turmoil of war, but they are told that they are already in a moral turmoil in advancing a disingenuous plea. In using the English word "trial" in the translation, I have also had in my mind the two shades of meaning associated with that word in English.

51. Say: "Nothing will happen to us
Except what God has decreed
For us: He is our Protector":
And on God let the Believers
Put their trust.

٥١-قُلْ لَّنْ يُّصِيْبَنَآ اِلَّا مَا كَتَبَ اللّٰهُ لَنَا ۚ
هُوَ مَوْلٰىنَا ۚ
وَعَلَى اللّٰهِ فَلْيَتَوَكَّلِ الْمُؤْمِنُوْنَ ○

52. Say: "Can you expect for us
(Any fate) other than one
Of two glorious things—
(Martyrdom or victory)?
But we can expect for you
Either that God will send
His punishment from Himself,
Or by our hands. So wait
(Expectant); we too
Will wait with you."[1313]

٥٢-قُلْ هَلْ تَرَبَّصُوْنَ بِنَآ اِلَّآ اِحْدَى
الْحُسْنَيَيْنِ ۭ وَنَحْنُ نَتَرَبَّصُ بِكُمْ
اَنْ يُّصِيْبَكُمُ اللّٰهُ بِعَذَابٍ مِّنْ عِنْدِهٖٓ
اَوْ بِاَيْدِيْنَا ۖ فَتَرَبَّصُوْٓا
اِنَّا مَعَكُمْ مُّتَرَبِّصُوْنَ ○

53. Say: "Spend (for the Cause)
Willingly or unwillingly:[1314]
Not from you will it be
Accepted: for ye are indeed
A people rebellious and wicked."

٥٣-قُلْ اَنْفِقُوْا طَوْعًا اَوْ كَرْهًا
لَّنْ يُّتَقَبَّلَ مِنْكُمْ ۭ
اِنَّكُمْ كُنْتُمْ قَوْمًا فٰسِقِيْنَ ○

54. The only reasons why
Their contributions are not
Accepted are: that they reject
God and His Apostle;
That they come to prayer
Without earnestness; and that
They offer contributions
unwillingly.

٥٤-وَمَا مَنَعَهُمْ اَنْ تُقْبَلَ مِنْهُمْ
نَفَقٰتُهُمْ
اِلَّآ اَنَّهُمْ كَفَرُوْا بِاللّٰهِ وَبِرَسُوْلِهٖ
وَلَا يَاْتُوْنَ الصَّلٰوةَ اِلَّا وَهُمْ كُسَالٰى
وَلَا يُنْفِقُوْنَ اِلَّا وَهُمْ كٰرِهُوْنَ ○

55. Let not their wealth
Nor their (following in) sons[1315]

٥٥-فَلَا تُعْجِبْكَ اَمْوَالُهُمْ وَلَآ اَوْلَادُهُمْ ۭ

1313. The waiting of the Unbelievers and that of the Believers are in different senses. The Unbelievers wish for disaster to the Believers, but the Believers will either conquer or die as martyrs in the Cause, in either case happy in the issue. The Believers expect punishment for the Unbelievers for their infidelity, either through their own instrumentality, or in some other way in God's Plan, and the Unbelievers would not like it in either case. *Cf.* vi. 158.

1314. The Hypocrites, who secretly plotted against Islam, might sometimes (and they did) make a show of making some contribution to the Cause in order to keep up their pretence. Their contributions were not acceptable, whether they seemed to give willingly or unwillingly, because rebellion and disobedience were in their hearts. Three reasons are specifically given for their rejection, in the next verse: (1) they did not believe; (2) their prayers were not earnest, but for mere show; and (3) in reality their hearts were not behind the contributions which they offered. Nothing is acceptable to God which does not proceed from a pure and sincere heart.

1315. If they appeared to be prosperous, with their purses and their quivers full (metaphorically), they were not to be envied. In reality their wealth and their sons might themselves be a snare: *Cf.* viii. 28. On this particular occasion this was proved to the hilt. The wealth of the Pagans filled them with pride, darkened their understanding, and led to their destruction. Their sons and followers adopted the Faith which their fathers had fought against, much to the chagrin of the fathers, whose spiritual death was even worse than their discomfiture in this world.

Dazzle thee : in reality
God's Plan is to punish them
With these things in this life,[1316]
And that their souls may perish
In their (very) denial of God.

إنما يريد الله ليعذبهم بها في الحيوة
الدنيا
وتزهق أنفسهم وهم كفرون ○

56. They swear by God
That they are indeed
Of you ; but they are not
Of you : yet they are afraid
(To appear in their true colours).

٥٦- ويحلفون بالله إنهم لمنكم
وما هم منكم
ولكنهم قوم يفرقون ○

57. If they could find
A place to flee to,
Or caves, or a place
Of concealment, they would
Turn straightway thereto,
With an obstinate rush.[1317]

٥٧- لو يجدون ملجأ أو مغرت
أو مدخلا لولوا إليه
وهم يجمحون ○

58. And among them are men
Who slander thee in the matter
Of (the distribution of) the alms :[1318]
If they are given part thereof,
They are pleased, but if not,
Behold ! they are indignant !

٥٨- ومنهم من يلمزك في الصدقت
فإن أعطوا منها رضوا وإن لم يعطوا
منها إذا هم يسخطون ○

59. If only they had been content
With what God and His Apostle
Gave them, and had said,
" Sufficient unto us is God !
God and His Apostle will soon
Give us of His bounty :
To God do we turn our hopes ! "—
(That would have been the right
course).[1319]

٥٩- ولو أنهم رضوا
ما آتهم الله ورسوله
وقالوا حسبنا الله
سيؤتينا الله من فضله ورسوله
إنا إلى الله رغبون ○

1316. *Cf.* iii. 176-178.

1317. *Jamaha*=to be ungovernable, to run like a runaway horse, to rush madly and obstinately.

1318. *Ṣadaqa*=alms, that which is given in God's name, mainly to the poor and needy, and for the cognate purposes specified in the next verse but one. *Zakāt* is the regular and obligatory charity in an organised Muslim community, usually 2½ per cent. of merchandise and 10 per cent. on the fruits of the earth. There is a vast body of literature on this subject. The main points may be studied in the *Hidāya fil furū'*, of Shaikh Burhānud-din 'Ali.

1319. Selfish men think that charitable funds are fair game for raids, but the Islamic standards on this subject are very high. The enforcement of such standards is always unpopular, and even the Holy Apostle was subjected to obloquy and slander for his strictness to principle. In doubtful cases, claimants who are disappointed should not blame the principles or those who enforce them, but put their trust in God, whose bounties are unbounded, and are given to all, whether rich or poor, according to their needs and their deserts. For every one it is excellent advice to say : deserve before you desire.

Section 8.

60. Alms are for the poor
And the needy, and those
Employed to administer the (funds);
For those whose hearts
Have been (recently) reconciled
(To Truth); for those in bondage
And in debt; in the cause
Of God; and for the wayfarer:[1320]
(Thus is it) ordained by God,
And God is full of knowledge
And wisdom.

٦٠- إِنَّمَا الصَّدَقٰتُ لِلْفُقَرَآءِ وَالْمَسٰكِيْنِ
وَالْعٰمِلِيْنَ عَلَيْهَا وَالْمُؤَلَّفَةِ قُلُوْبُهُمْ
وَفِي الرِّقَابِ وَالْغٰرِمِيْنَ
وَفِيْ سَبِيْلِ اللّٰهِ وَابْنِ السَّبِيْلِ ط
فَرِيْضَةً مِّنَ اللّٰهِ ط
وَاللّٰهُ عَلِيْمٌ حَكِيْمٌ ○

61. Among them are men
Who molest the Prophet
And say, "He is (all) ear."[1321]
Say, "He listens to what is
Best for you: he believes
In God, has faith
In the Believers, and is a Mercy
To those of you who believe."
But those who molest the Apostle
Will have a grievous penalty.

٦١- وَمِنْهُمُ الَّذِيْنَ يُؤْذُوْنَ النَّبِيَّ
وَيَقُوْلُوْنَ هُوَ اُذُنٌ ط قُلْ اُذُنُ خَيْرٍ لَّكُمْ
يُؤْمِنُ بِاللّٰهِ وَيُؤْمِنُ لِلْمُؤْمِنِيْنَ وَرَحْمَةٌ
لِّلَّذِيْنَ اٰمَنُوْا مِنْكُمْ ط وَالَّذِيْنَ يُؤْذُوْنَ
رَسُوْلَ اللّٰهِ لَهُمْ عَذَابٌ اَلِيْمٌ ○

62. To you they swear by God.
In order to please you:
But it is more fitting
That they should please
God and His Apostle,
If they are Believers.

٦٢ يَحْلِفُوْنَ بِاللّٰهِ لَكُمْ لِيُرْضُوْكُمْ ج
وَاللّٰهُ وَرَسُوْلُهٗٓ اَحَقُّ اَنْ يُّرْضُوْهُ
اِنْ كَانُوْا مُؤْمِنِيْنَ ○

1320. Alms or charitable gifts are to be given to the poor and the needy and those who are employed in their service. That is, charitable funds are not to be diverted to other uses, but the genuine expenses of administering charity are properly chargeable to such funds. Who are the needy? Besides the ordinary indigent, there are certain classes of people whose need is great and should be relieved. Those mentioned here are: (1) men who have been weaned from hostility to Truth, who would probably be persecuted by their former associates, and require assistance until they establish new connections in their new environment; (2) those in bondage, literally and figuratively; captives of war must be redeemed; slaves should be helped to freedom; those in the bondage of ignorance or superstition or unfavourable environment should be helped to freedom to develop their own gifts; (3) those who are held in the grip of debt should be helped to economic freedom; (4) those who are struggling and striving in God's Cause, by teaching or fighting or in duties assigned to them by the righteous Imām, who are thus unable to earn their ordinary living; and (5) strangers stranded on the way. All these have a claim to charity. They should be relieved by individual or organised effort, but in a responsible way.

1321. The assonance of the Arabic words "*yū-ẓūna*" and "*uẓunun*" is of course lost in the Translation. But the sense remains. Detractors of the Prophet said, "O! he listens to everybody!" "Yes," is the answer, "he listens for their good; he is a mercy and a blessing to all men of Faith, but specially to you (who are addressed)." The general statement is emphasised for the particular people addressed.

63. Know they not that for those
Who oppose God and His Apostle,
Is the Fire of Hell?—
Wherein they shall dwell.
That is the supreme disgrace.

٦٣- اَلَمْ يَعْلَمُوْٓا اَنَّهٗ مَنْ يُّحَادِدِ اللّٰهَ وَ
رَسُوْلَهٗ فَاَنَّ لَهٗ نَارَ جَهَنَّمَ خَالِدًا فِيْهَا ۭ
ذٰلِكَ الْخِزْيُ الْعَظِيْمُ ○

64. The Hypocrites are afraid [1322]
Lest a Sūra should be sent down
About them, showing them what
Is (really passing) in their hearts.
Say: "Mock ye! But verily
God will bring to light all
That ye fear (should be revealed).

٦٤- يَحْذَرُ الْمُنٰفِقُوْنَ اَنْ تُنَزَّلَ عَلَيْهِمْ
سُوْرَةٌ تُنَبِّئُهُمْ بِمَا فِيْ قُلُوْبِهِمْ ۭ
قُلِ اسْتَهْزِءُوْا ۚ اِنَّ اللّٰهَ
مُخْرِجٌ مَّا تَحْذَرُوْنَ ○

65. If thou dost question them,
They declare (with emphasis):
"We were only talking idly
And in play." Say: "Was it
At God, and His Signs,
And His Apostle, that ye
Were mocking?"

٦٥- وَلَىِٕنْ سَاَلْتَهُمْ
لَيَقُوْلُنَّ اِنَّمَا كُنَّا نَخُوْضُ وَنَلْعَبُ ۭ
قُلْ اَبِاللّٰهِ وَاٰيٰتِهٖ وَرَسُوْلِهٖ
كُنْتُمْ تَسْتَهْزِءُوْنَ ○

66. Make ye no excuses:
Ye have rejected Faith
After ye had accepted it.
If We pardon some of you,
We will punish others amongst you,
For that they are in sin. [1323]

٦٦- لَا تَعْتَذِرُوْا قَدْ كَفَرْتُمْ بَعْدَ اِيْمَانِكُمْ ۭ
اِنْ نَّعْفُ عَنْ طَاۗىِٕفَةٍ مِّنْكُمْ نُعَذِّبْ
طَاۗىِٕفَةًۢ بِاَنَّهُمْ كَانُوْا مُجْرِمِيْنَ ○ ع

SECTION 9.

67. The Hypocrites, men and women,
(Have an understanding) with each other: [1324]

٦٧- اَلْمُنٰفِقُوْنَ وَالْمُنٰفِقٰتُ بَعْضُهُمْ
مِّنْۢ بَعْضٍ ۘ

1322. The dissection of the motives of the Hypocrites alarmed them. For it meant that they would fail in their policy of having the best of both worlds and undermining the loyalty of the weaker members of the Muslim community. So they turn it off as a jest. But they are sharply rebuked: "Can you make such solemn matters subjects of playful jokes? Fie upon you! You are found out, and your guile is of no effect." In fact many of the Hypocrites turned over a new leaf and became good Believers afterwards, while a few definitely threw in their lot with the open enemies of Islam and shared their fate. This is referred to in the next verse but one.

1323. See last note. Hypocrisy is a half-way house, a state of indecision in the choice between good and evil. Those who definitely range themselves with good obtain forgiveness; those who pass definitely to evil suffer the penalties of evil.

1324. Literally, "the Hypocrites...are of each other". The forms of hypocrisy may vary, but they are all alike, and they understand each other's hypocrisy. They hold together.

They enjoin evil, and forbid
What is just, and are close[1325]
With their hands. They have
Forgotten God; so He[1326]
Hath forgotten them. Verily
The Hypocrites are rebellious
And perverse.

يَأْمُرُونَ بِالْمُنكَرِ وَيَنْهَوْنَ عَنِ الْمَعْرُوفِ
وَيَقْبِضُونَ أَيْدِيَهُمْ ۚ
نَسُوا اللَّهَ فَنَسِيَهُمْ ۗ
إِنَّ الْمُنَافِقِينَ هُمُ الْفَاسِقُونَ ○

68. God hath promised the Hypocrites
Men and women, and the rejecters,
Of Faith, the fire of Hell:
Therein shall they dwell:
Sufficient is it for them:
For them is the curse of God,[1327]
And an enduring punishment,—

٦٨- وَعَدَ اللَّهُ الْمُنَافِقِينَ وَالْمُنَافِقَاتِ وَ
الْكُفَّارَ نَارَ جَهَنَّمَ خَالِدِينَ فِيهَا ۚ
هِيَ حَسْبُهُمْ ۚ وَلَعَنَهُمُ اللَّهُ ۖ
وَلَهُمْ عَذَابٌ مُّقِيمٌ ○

69. As in the case of those
Before you: they were
Mightier than you in power,
And more flourishing in wealth
And children. They had
Their enjoyment of their portion:
And ye have of yours, as did
Those before you; and ye
Indulge in idle talk
As they did. They!—
Their works are fruitless
In this world and in the Hereafter,
And they will lose
(All spiritual good).

٦٩- كَالَّذِينَ مِن قَبْلِكُمْ كَانُوا أَشَدَّ
مِنكُمْ قُوَّةً وَأَكْثَرَ أَمْوَالًا وَأَوْلَادًا
فَاسْتَمْتَعُوا بِخَلَاقِهِمْ فَاسْتَمْتَعْتُم
بِخَلَاقِكُمْ كَمَا اسْتَمْتَعَ الَّذِينَ مِن قَبْلِكُم
بِخَلَاقِهِمْ وَخُضْتُمْ كَالَّذِي خَاضُوا ۚ
أُولَٰئِكَ حَبِطَتْ أَعْمَالُهُمْ فِي الدُّنْيَا
وَالْآخِرَةِ ۖ وَأُولَٰئِكَ هُمُ الْخَاسِرُونَ ○

70. Hath not the story reached them
Of those before them?—
The people of Noah, and 'Ād,[1328]
And Thamūd; the people

٧٠- أَلَمْ يَأْتِهِمْ نَبَأُ الَّذِينَ مِن قَبْلِهِمْ
قَوْمِ نُوحٍ وَعَادٍ وَثَمُودَ ۙ وَقَوْمِ

1325. The English phrase "close-fisted" would cover only a part of the meaning. The hand is the symbol of power, help, and assistance. This may be financial, or it may be in other ways. The Hypocrites pretend a great deal, but are of no use or real help to any one.

1326. *Cf.* vii. 51 and n. 1029. They ignore God: and God will ignore them.

1327. "Curse," here as elsewhere, is deprivation of grace and mercy, brought about by the rejection of God by the Unbelievers.

1328. The story of Noah is told in vii 59-64; of 'Ād in vii. 65-72; and of Thamūd in vii 73-79; of Abraham in numerous places, but see specially vi. 74-82; of Midianites in vii. 85-93; and of Lot and the Cities of the Plain overthrown for their wickedness, in vii. 80-84.

Of Abraham, the men[1329]
Of Midian, and the Cities
overthrown.[1330]
To them came their apostles
With Clear Signs. It is
Not God Who wrongs them,
But they wrong their own souls.

71. The Believers, men
And women, are protectors,
One of another: they enjoin
What is just, and forbid
What is evil: they observe
Regular prayers, practise
Regular charity, and obey
God and His Apostle.
On them will God pour
His mercy: for God
Is Exalted in power, Wise.

72. God hath promised to Believers,
Men and women, Gardens
Under which rivers flow,
To dwell therein,
And beautiful mansions
In Gardens of everlasting bliss.
But the greatest bliss
Is the Good Pleasure of God:
That is the supreme felicity.

إِبْرٰهِيمَ وَأَصْحٰبِ مَدْيَنَ وَالْمُؤْتَفِكٰتِ ۚ
أَتَتْهُمْ رُسُلُهُم بِالْبَيِّنٰتِ ۖ
فَمَا كَانَ اللَّهُ لِيَظْلِمَهُمْ
وَلٰكِن كَانُوا أَنفُسَهُمْ يَظْلِمُونَ ○

٧١- وَالْمُؤْمِنُونَ وَالْمُؤْمِنٰتُ بَعْضُهُمْ
أَوْلِيَاءُ بَعْضٍ ۚ يَأْمُرُونَ بِالْمَعْرُوفِ
وَيَنْهَوْنَ عَنِ الْمُنكَرِ
وَيُقِيمُونَ الصَّلٰوةَ وَيُؤْتُونَ الزَّكٰوةَ
وَيُطِيعُونَ اللَّهَ وَرَسُولَهُ ۚ أُولٰئِكَ سَيَرْحَمُهُمُ
اللَّهُ ۗ إِنَّ اللَّهَ عَزِيزٌ حَكِيمٌ ○

٧٢- وَعَدَ اللَّهُ الْمُؤْمِنِينَ وَالْمُؤْمِنٰتِ جَنّٰتٍ
تَجْرِي مِن تَحْتِهَا الْأَنْهٰرُ خٰلِدِينَ فِيهَا
وَمَسٰكِنَ طَيِّبَةً فِي جَنّٰتِ عَدْنٍ ۚ
وَرِضْوٰنٌ مِّنَ اللَّهِ أَكْبَرُ ۚ
ذٰلِكَ هُوَ الْفَوْزُ الْعَظِيمُ ○

C. 96.—The hardest striving and fighting are needed
(ix. 73-99.) **To combat evil and hypocrisy; for sin**
Can reach a stage when the doors of forgiveness
Are closed. The good must shun all evil
As unclean, and gladly welcome all chance
Of service and sacrifice, as bringing them closer
To the Presence and Mercy of God.

1329. In the case of Noah and Abraham, the word I have translated as "people of..." is *qaum*; these prophets were messengers each to his own people or nation, as was also Hūd to the 'Ād people and Ṣāliḥ to the Thamūd people. The word used for the Midianites is *Aṣ-ḥāb-i-Madyan*, which I have translated "men of Midian" for want of a better word. The Midianites were for the greater part of their history nomads, with pasture grounds but no settled territory or town. The town of Madyan on the Gulf of 'Aqaba refers to much later times when the Midianites as a people had ceased to count. See n. 1053 to vii. 85.

1330. The Cities of the Plain, Sodom and Gomorrah, to whom Lot preached in vain to desist from their abominations: vii. 80-84.

SECTION 10.

73. O Prophet! strive hard against
The Unbelievers and the
Hypocrites,
And be firm against them.
Their abode is Hell,—
An evil refuge indeed.

٧٣- يٰٓاَيُّهَا النَّبِيُّ جَاهِدِ الْكُفَّارَ وَ
الْمُنٰفِقِيْنَ وَاغْلُظْ عَلَيْهِمْ ۗ
وَمَاْوٰىهُمْ جَهَنَّمُ ۗ
وَبِئْسَ الْمَصِيْرُ ○

74. They swear by God that they
Said nothing (evil), but indeed
They uttered blasphemy,
And they did it after accepting
Islam; and they meditated[1331]
A plot which they were unable
To carry out: this revenge
Of theirs was (their) only return
For the bounty with which
God and His Apostle had enriched
Them! If they repent,
It will be best for them;
But if they turn back
(To their evil ways),
God will punish them
With a grievous penalty
In this life and in the Hereafter:
They shall have none on earth
To protect or help them.

٧٤- يَحْلِفُوْنَ بِاللّٰهِ مَا قَالُوْا ۗ
وَلَقَدْ قَالُوْا كَلِمَةَ الْكُفْرِ
وَكَفَرُوْا بَعْدَ اِسْلَامِهِمْ
وَهَمُّوْا بِمَا لَمْ يَنَالُوْا ۚ وَمَا نَقَمُوْٓا اِلَّآ
اَنْ اَغْنٰىهُمُ اللّٰهُ وَرَسُوْلُهٗ مِنْ فَضْلِهٖ ۚ
فَاِنْ يَّتُوْبُوْا يَكُ خَيْرًا لَّهُمْ ۚ
وَاِنْ يَّتَوَلَّوْا يُعَذِّبْهُمُ اللّٰهُ
عَذَابًا اَلِيْمًا
فِي الدُّنْيَا وَالْاٰخِرَةِ ۚ
وَمَا لَهُمْ فِي الْاَرْضِ
مِنْ وَّلِيٍّ وَّلَا نَصِيْرٍ ○

75. Amongst them are men
Who made a Covenant with God,
That if He bestowed on them
Of His bounty, they would give
(Largely) in charity, and be truly
Amongst those who are righteous.

٧٥- وَمِنْهُمْ مَّنْ عٰهَدَ اللّٰهَ
لَئِنْ اٰتٰىنَا مِنْ فَضْلِهٖ لَنَصَّدَّقَنَّ
وَلَنَكُوْنَنَّ مِنَ الصّٰلِحِيْنَ ○

1331. The reference is to a plot made by the Apostle's enemies to kill him when he was returning from Tabūk. The plot failed. It was all the more dastardly in that some of the conspirators were among the men of Medina, who were enriched by the general prosperity that followed the peace and good government established through Islam in Medina. Trade flourished; justice was firmly administered with an even hand. And the only return that these men could make was a return of evil for good. That was their revenge, because Islam aimed at suppressing selfishness, stood for the rights of the poorest and humblest, and judged worth by righteousness rather than by birth or position.

76. But when He did bestow
Of His bounty, they became
Covetous, and turned back
(From their Covenant), averse
(From its fulfilment).

٧٦- فَلَمَّآ اٰتٰهُمۡ مِّنۡ فَضۡلِهٖ
بَخِلُوۡا بِهٖ وَتَوَلَّوۡا
وَّهُمۡ مُّعۡرِضُوۡنَ ○

77. So He hath put as a consequence[1332]
Hypocrisy into their hearts,
(To last) till the Day whereon
They shall meet Him: because
They broke their Covenant
With God, and because they
Lied (again and again).

٧٧- فَاَعۡقَبَهُمۡ نِفَاقًا فِىۡ قُلُوۡبِهِمۡ
اِلٰى يَوۡمِ يَلۡقَوۡنَهٗ
بِمَاۤ اَخۡلَفُوا اللّٰهَ مَا وَعَدُوۡهُ
وَبِمَا كَانُوۡا يَكۡذِبُوۡنَ ○

78. Know they not that God
Doth know their secret (thoughts)
And their secret counsels,
And that God knoweth well
All things unseen?

٧٨- اَلَمۡ يَعۡلَمُوۡۤا اَنَّ اللّٰهَ يَعۡلَمُ سِرَّهُمۡ
وَنَجۡوٰىهُمۡ
وَاَنَّ اللّٰهَ عَلَّامُ الۡغُيُوۡبِ ○

79. Those who slander such
Of the Believers as give themselves
Freely to (deeds of) charity,
As well as such as can find
Nothing to give except
The fruits of their labour,—
And throw ridicule on them,—[1333]
God will throw back

٧٩- اَلَّذِيۡنَ يَلۡمِزُوۡنَ الۡمُطَّوِّعِيۡنَ مِنَ
الۡمُؤۡمِنِيۡنَ فِى الصَّدَقٰتِ
وَالَّذِيۡنَ لَا يَجِدُوۡنَ اِلَّا جُهۡدَهُمۡ
فَيَسۡخَرُوۡنَ مِنۡهُمۡ ؕ

1332. If men are false to their covenants and words, the natural consequence will be hypocrisy to cover their falsehood. All consequences of our own acts are in Quranic language ascribed to God. Such consequences will last till the Day of Judgment, when they will have to account for their deeds. They may think that they are deceiving men by their hypocrisy, but they cannot deceive God, to Whom all their most secret thoughts and plots and doings are known.

1333. When financial help is necessary for the Cause, every Muslim contributes what he can. Those who can afford large sums are proud to bring them in of their own free-will, and those who are very poor contribute their mite or their labour. Both kinds of gifts are equally precious because of the faith and good-will behind them, and only cynics will laugh at the scantiness of the one or the lavishness of the other. Sometimes they not only laugh, but attribute wrong motives to the givers. Such conduct is here reprimanded.

Their ridicule on them :
And they shall have
A grievous penalty.

سَخِرَ اللّٰهُ مِنْهُمْ
وَلَهُمْ عَذَابٌ اَلِيْمٌ ○

80. Whether thou ask
For their forgiveness,
Or not, (their sin is unforgivable) :
If thou ask seventy times [1334]
For their forgiveness, God
Will not forgive them :
Because they have rejected
God and His Apostle : and God
Guideth not those
Who are perversely rebellious.

٨٠- اِسْتَغْفِرْ لَهُمْ
اَوْ لَا تَسْتَغْفِرْ لَهُمْ ؕ
اِنْ تَسْتَغْفِرْ لَهُمْ سَبْعِيْنَ مَرَّةً
فَلَنْ يَّغْفِرَ اللّٰهُ لَهُمْ ؕ
ذٰلِكَ بِاَنَّهُمْ كَفَرُوْا بِاللّٰهِ وَرَسُوْلِهٖ ؕ
وَاللّٰهُ لَا يَهْدِى الْقَوْمَ الْفٰسِقِيْنَ ○ ع

Section 11.

81. Those who were left behind
(In the Tabūk expedition)
Rejoiced in their inaction
Behind the back of the Apostle
Of God : they hated to strive
And fight, with their goods
And their persons, in the Cause
Of God : they said,
"Go not forth in the heat." [1335]
Say, "The fire of Hell
Is fiercer in heat." If
Only they could understand !

٨١- فَرِحَ الْمُخَلَّفُوْنَ بِمَقْعَدِهِمْ خِلٰفَ
رَسُوْلِ اللّٰهِ
وَكَرِهُوْٓا اَنْ يُّجَاهِدُوْا
بِاَمْوَالِهِمْ وَاَنْفُسِهِمْ فِىْ سَبِيْلِ اللّٰهِ
وَقَالُوْا لَا تَنْفِرُوْا فِى الْحَرِّ ؕ
قُلْ نَارُ جَهَنَّمَ اَشَدُّ حَرًّا ؕ
لَوْ كَانُوْا يَفْقَهُوْنَ ○

82. Let them laugh a little :
Much will they weep : [1336]

٨٢- فَلْيَضْحَكُوْا قَلِيْلًا وَّلْيَبْكُوْا كَثِيْرًا ۚ

1334. An awful warning for those who actively oppose the Cause of God. The Holy Apostle was by nature full of mercy and forgiveness. He prayed for his enemies. But in such a case even his prayers are nullified by their attitude of rejecting God.

1335. The Tabūk expedition had to be undertaken hurriedly in the heat of summer, because of a threat or fear of Byzantine invasion. They marched from Medina about the month of September or October in the solar calendar.

1336. They may sneer or ridicule or rejoice now : that will be only for a little ; much will they have to weep for afterwards.

A recompense for the (evil)
That they do.

جَزَآءً بِمَا كَانُوا يَكْسِبُونَ ○

83. If, then, God bring thee back
To any of them, and they ask
Thy permission to come out
(With thee), say : " Never shall ye
Come out with me, nor fight
An enemy with me :
For ye preferred to sit
Inactive on the first occasion :
Then sit ye (now)
With those who lag behind."

٨٣- فَإِن رَّجَعَكَ اللّٰهُ إِلَىٰ طَآئِفَةٍ مِّنْهُمْ
فَاسْتَأْذَنُوكَ لِلْخُرُوجِ
فَقُل لَّن تَخْرُجُوا مَعِيَ أَبَدًا
وَلَن تُقَاتِلُوا مَعِيَ عَدُوًّا ؕ
إِنَّكُمْ رَضِيتُم بِالْقُعُودِ أَوَّلَ مَرَّةٍ
فَاقْعُدُوا مَعَ الْخَالِفِينَ ○

84. Nor do thou ever pray
For any of them that dies,
Nor stand at his grave ;[1337]
For they rejected God
And His Apostle, and died
In a state of perverse rebellion.

٨٤- وَلَا تُصَلِّ عَلَىٰ أَحَدٍ مِّنْهُم مَّاتَ
أَبَدًا وَلَا تَقُمْ عَلَىٰ قَبْرِهِ ؕ
إِنَّهُمْ كَفَرُوا بِاللّٰهِ وَرَسُولِهِ
وَمَاتُوا وَهُمْ فٰسِقُونَ ○

85. Nor let their wealth
Nor their (following in) sons
Dazzle thee : God's Plan
Is to punish them
With these things in this world,
And that their souls may perish
In their (very) denial of God.[1338]

٨٥- وَلَا تُعْجِبْكَ أَمْوَالُهُمْ وَأَوْلَادُهُمْ ؕ
إِنَّمَا يُرِيدُ اللّٰهُ
أَن يُعَذِّبَهُم بِهَا فِي الدُّنْيَا
وَتَزْهَقَ أَنفُسُهُمْ
وَهُمْ كٰفِرُونَ ○

1337. On the death of a Muslim, it is the pious duty of every neighbouring Muslim who can, to assist in the simple funeral ceremonies,—the prayer for mercy before the body is consigned to the grave, and the consignment of the body to the grave, by a simple, solemn, and dignified ritual, in which the near relatives or friends help with the bier while the rest stand by the grave-side. For those who have shown hostility to Islam, this would not be seemly and is forbidden.

1338. Except for the omission of a single word (" life "), this verse repeats verse 55 above. But the repetition indicates the harmonious closing of the same argument in two aspects. In ix. 55 it occurred in connection with the reasons for refusing to receive the contributions of such persons to the expenses of an enterprise which though vital to Islam's defence was secretly opposed by such persons. Here (in ix. 85) it is a question of refusing to participate in the obsequies of such persons after their death : it is natural to omit the word " life " in this case.

86. When a Sūra comes down,
Enjoining them to believe
In God and to strive and fight
Along with His Apostle,
Those with wealth and influence
Among them ask thee
For exemption, and say:
"Leave us (behind): we
Would be with those
Who sit (at home)."

٨٦- وَإِذَآ أُنْزِلَتْ سُوْرَةٌ أَنْ اٰمِنُوْا
بِاللّٰهِ وَجَاهِدُوْا
مَعَ رَسُوْلِهِ
اسْتَأْذَنَكَ أُولُوا الطَّوْلِ مِنْهُمْ
وَقَالُوْا ذَرْنَا
نَكُنْ مَّعَ الْقٰعِدِيْنَ ○

87. They prefer to be with
(the women),
Who remain behind (at home):[1339]
Their hearts are sealed
And so they understand not.

٨٧- رَضُوْا بِأَنْ يَّكُوْنُوْا مَعَ الْخَوَالِفِ
وَطُبِعَ عَلٰى قُلُوْبِهِمْ
فَهُمْ لَا يَفْقَهُوْنَ ○

88. But the Apostle, and those
Who believe with him,
Strive and fight with their wealth
And their persons: for them
Are (all) good things:[1340]
And it is they
Who will prosper.

٨٨- لٰكِنِ الرَّسُوْلُ وَالَّذِيْنَ اٰمَنُوْا
مَعَهٗ جَاهَدُوْا بِأَمْوَالِهِمْ وَأَنْفُسِهِمْ ۖ
وَأُولٰٓئِكَ لَهُمُ الْخَيْرٰتُ ۚ
وَأُولٰٓئِكَ هُمُ الْمُفْلِحُوْنَ ○

89. God hath prepared for them
Gardens under which rivers flow,

٨٩- أَعَدَّ اللّٰهُ لَهُمْ جَنّٰتٍ تَجْرِيْ مِنْ

1339. *Khawālif*, plural of *Khālifa*, those (feminine) who remain behind at home when the men go to war; women. There is a stinging taunt in this, a suggestion that such men were cowards, preferring to remain behind like women when stiff work was to be done by men in defending their homes. They were not only cowards, but fools; as they did not understand their own best interests. If the enemy got the better of their brethren, they would themselves be crushed. "Their hearts are sealed": the habits of cowardice and hypocrisy which they have adopted have become their second nature.

1340. "Good things," and "prosperity," are to be understood both in the physical and in the highest spiritual sense as the next verse makes clear.

To dwell therein :
That is the supreme felicity.[1341]

تَحْتَهَا الْأَنْهٰرُ خٰلِدِيْنَ فِيْهَا ؕ
ذٰلِكَ الْفَوْزُ الْعَظِيْمُ ۝

SECTION 12.

90. And there were, among
The desert Arabs (also),
Men who made excuses
And came to claim exemption ;
And those who were false
To God and His Apostle
(Merely) sat inactive.[1342]
Soon will a grievous penalty
Seize the Unbelievers
Among them.

٩٠-وَجَآءَ الْمُعَذِّرُوْنَ مِنَ الْأَعْرَابِ
لِيُؤْذَنَ لَهُمْ وَقَعَدَ الَّذِيْنَ
كَذَبُوا اللّٰهَ وَرَسُوْلَهٗ ؕ
سَيُصِيْبُ الَّذِيْنَ كَفَرُوْا مِنْهُمْ
عَذَابٌ أَلِيْمٌ ۝

91. There is no blame[1343]
On those who are infirm,

٩١-لَيْسَ عَلَى الضُّعَفَآءِ

1341. In this verse there is a reminiscence, but not an exact repitition, of verse 72 above. This balances the parallel repetition or reminiscence in verse 85 above. See n. 1338. The symmetry of the argument is thus completed, as regards the Hypocrites of Medina, before we pass on to consider the case of the Hypocrites among the desert Bedouins in section 12.

1342. Not only had the Hypocrites a nest in Medina, but their tactics affected some of the village or desert Bedouins, who loved war and would have followed a standard of war even if no question of Faith or a sacred Cause was involved. But some of them, though professing Islam, were frightened by the hardships of the Tabūk expedition and the prospect of meeting the trained armies of the great Roman (Byzantine) Empire. They made all sorts of lying excuses, but really their want of faith made them ineligible for being enlisted in a sacred Cause, in the terms of ix. 46-47 and ix. 53-54. Some came to make excuses ; others did not even come, but sat at home, ignoring the summons.

1343. Though active service in person or by contributing resources is expected in emergencies of every person who believes in the Cause, there are some who must necessarily be exempted without the least blame attaching to them. Such would be those who are weak in body on account of age, sex, infirmity, or illness. Personal service in their case is out of the question, but they could contribute towards expenses if they are able. But if they are too poor to afford even such assistance, they are excused. But in all cases the motive must be sincere, and there should be a desire to serve and do such duty as they can. With such motives people are doing good or right in whatever form they express their service : sometimes, in Milton's words, "they also serve who only stand and wait." In any case their purity of motive would get God's grace and forgiveness, and we must not criticise even if we thought they might have done more.

Or ill, or who find
No resources to spend
(On the Cause), if they
Are sincere (in duty) to God
And His Apostle :
No ground (of complaint)
Can there be against such
As do right: and God
Is Oft-Forgiving, Most Merciful.

وَلَا عَلَى الْمَرْضٰى وَلَا عَلَى الَّذِيْنَ لَا
يَجِدُوْنَ
مَا يُنْفِقُوْنَ حَرَجٌ اِذَا نَصَحُوْا لِلّٰهِ وَ
رَسُوْلِهٖ ؕ مَا عَلَى الْمُحْسِنِيْنَ مِنْ سَبِيْلٍ ؕ
وَاللّٰهُ غَفُوْرٌ رَّحِيْمٌ ۙ

92. Nor (is there blame)
On those who came to thee
To be provided with mounts,[1344]
And when thou saidst,
"I can find no mounts
For you," they turned back,
Their eyes streaming with tears
Of grief that they had
No resources wherewith
To provide the expenses.

٩٢- وَّلَا عَلَى الَّذِيْنَ اِذَا مَآ اَتَوْكَ
لِتَحْمِلَهُمْ قُلْتَ لَآ اَجِدُ مَآ اَحْمِلُكُمْ
عَلَيْهِ ۠
تَوَلَّوْا وَّاَعْيُنُهُمْ تَفِيْضُ مِنَ الدَّمْعِ
حَزَنًا
اَلَّا يَجِدُوْا مَا يُنْفِقُوْنَ ؕ

93. The ground (of complaint)
Is against such as claim
Exemption while they are rich.
They prefer to stay
With the (women) who remain
Behind : God hath sealed
10 Their hearts; so they know not
30 (What they miss).[1345]

٩٣- اِنَّمَا السَّبِيْلُ عَلَى الَّذِيْنَ
يَسْتَاْذِنُوْنَكَ وَهُمْ اَغْنِيَآءُ ۚ
رَضُوْا بِاَنْ يَّكُوْنُوْا مَعَ الْخَوَالِفِ ۙ
وَطَبَعَ اللّٰهُ عَلٰى قُلُوْبِهِمْ
فَهُمْ لَا يَعْلَمُوْنَ

1344. *Ḥamala, yaḥmilu,* here seems to mean : to provide means of transport, *viz.*, mounts (horses, camels, etc.) for riding, and perhaps beasts of burden for carrying equipment and baggage, suitable to the rank of those concerned. It may possibly mean other facilities for getting about, such as boots and shoes, or provisions : for an army's march depends upon all these things. Where people fight as volunteers for a cause, without an extensive war fund, those who can afford it provide such things for themselves, but those without means, yet anxious to serve, have to be left behind. Their disappointment is in proportion to their eagerness to serve.

1345. *Cf.* ix. 87, where similar phrases are used for a similar shirking of duty by towns-folk, while here we are considering the desert folk. It is not only a duty, but a precious privilege, to serve a great Cause by personal self-sacrifice. Those who shirk such an opportunity know not what they miss.

الجزء الحادي عشر

94. They will present their excuses
To you when ye return
To them. Say thou: "Present
No excuses: we shall not
Believe you: God hath already
Informed us of the true state
Of matters concerning you:
It is your actions that God
And His Apostle will observe:
In the end will ye
Be brought back to Him
Who knoweth what is hidden
And what is open:
Then will He show you
The truth of all
That ye did."

٩٤- يَعْتَذِرُونَ إِلَيْكُمْ إِذَا رَجَعْتُمْ إِلَيْهِمْ
قُل لَّا تَعْتَذِرُوا لَن نُّؤْمِنَ لَكُمْ
قَدْ نَبَّأَنَا اللَّهُ مِنْ أَخْبَارِكُمْ
وَسَيَرَى اللَّهُ عَمَلَكُمْ وَرَسُولُهُ
ثُمَّ تُرَدُّونَ
إِلَىٰ عَالِمِ الْغَيْبِ وَالشَّهَادَةِ
فَيُنَبِّئُكُم
بِمَا كُنتُمْ تَعْمَلُونَ ○

95. They will swear to you by God,
When ye return to them,
That ye may leave them alone.
So leave them alone:
For they are an abomination,
And Hell is their dwelling-place, —
A fitting recompense
For the (evil) that they did.

٩٥- سَيَحْلِفُونَ بِاللَّهِ لَكُمْ إِذَا انقَلَبْتُمْ
إِلَيْهِمْ لِتُعْرِضُوا عَنْهُمْ فَأَعْرِضُوا عَنْهُمْ
إِنَّهُمْ رِجْسٌ وَمَأْوَاهُمْ جَهَنَّمُ
جَزَاءً بِمَا كَانُوا يَكْسِبُونَ ○

96. They will swear unto you,
That ye may be pleased with them.
But if ye are pleased with them,
God is not pleased
With those who disobey.

٩٦- يَحْلِفُونَ لَكُمْ لِتَرْضَوْا عَنْهُمْ فَإِن
تَرْضَوْا عَنْهُمْ فَإِنَّ اللَّهَ لَا يَرْضَىٰ عَنِ
الْقَوْمِ الْفَاسِقِينَ ○

97. The Arabs of the desert
Are the worst in unbelief
And hypocrisy, and most fitted
To be in ignorance
Of the command which God
Hath sent down to His Apostle:
But God is All-Knowing,
All-Wise.

٩٧- الْأَعْرَابُ أَشَدُّ كُفْرًا
وَنِفَاقًا وَأَجْدَرُ أَلَّا يَعْلَمُوا حُدُودَ
مَا أَنزَلَ اللَّهُ عَلَىٰ رَسُولِهِ
وَاللَّهُ عَلِيمٌ حَكِيمٌ ○

98. Some of the desert Arabs
Look upon their payments[1346]

٩٨- وَمِنَ الْأَعْرَابِ مَن يَتَّخِذُ مَا يُنفِقُ

1346. The payments refer to the regular Charity established by Islam—the obligatory alms. If you look upon them as a fine or a burden, their virtue is lost. If you rejoice that you have there an opportunity of helping the Community to maintain its standards of public assistance and to suppress the unseemly beggary and loathsome importunity whose relief is only governed by motives of getting rid of awkward obstacles on the way, then your outlook is entirely different. You wish for organised and effective efforts to solve the problems of human poverty and misery. In doing so, you get nearer to God, and you earn the good wishes and prayers of godly men, led by our holy Leader Muṣṭafā.

As a fine, and watch
For disasters for you: on them
Be the disaster of Evil:
For God is He that heareth
And knoweth (all things).

مَغْرَمًا وَّيَتَرَبَّصُ بِكُمُ الدَّوَآئِرَ ۚ
عَلَيْهِمْ دَآئِرَةُ السَّوْءِ ۚ
وَاللّٰهُ سَمِيْعٌ عَلِيْمٌ ○

99. But some of the desert Arabs
Believe in God and the Last Day,
And look on their payments
As pious gifts bringing them
Nearer to God and obtaining
The prayers of the Apostle.
Aye, indeed they bring them
Nearer (to Him): soon will God
Admit them to His Mercy: [1347]
For God is Oft-Forgiving,
Most Merciful.

٩٩- وَمِنَ الْاَعْرَابِ مَنْ يُّؤْمِنُ بِاللّٰهِ وَ
الْيَوْمِ الْاٰخِرِ وَيَتَّخِذُ مَا يُنْفِقُ
قُرُبٰتٍ عِنْدَ اللّٰهِ وَصَلَوٰتِ الرَّسُوْلِ ۚ
اَلَآ اِنَّهَا قُرْبَةٌ لَّهُمْ ۚ سَيُدْخِلُهُمُ اللّٰهُ فِيْ
رَحْمَتِهٖ ۚ اِنَّ اللّٰهَ غَفُوْرٌ رَّحِيْمٌ ○ ع

C. 97.—The vanguard of Faith think nothing
(ix. 100-118) Of self-sacrifice. Their reward is God's
Good Pleasure. Even those who do wrong
But repent will obtain His Mercy: not so
Those who persist in Unfaith, Hypocrisy,
And Mischief. God's grace is free and abounding
For the righteous. Even if they waver
Or fail, He will turn to them in Mercy,
If only they repent and come back unto Him.

SECTION 13.

100. The vanguard (of Islam)—[1348]
The first of those who forsook
(Their homes) and of those
Who gave them aid, and (also)
Those who follow them
In (all) good deeds,—
Well-pleased is God with them,
As are they with Him:

١٠٠- وَالسّٰبِقُوْنَ الْاَوَّلُوْنَ
مِنَ الْمُهٰجِرِيْنَ وَالْاَنْصَارِ
وَالَّذِيْنَ اتَّبَعُوْهُمْ بِاِحْسَانٍ ۙ
رَّضِيَ اللّٰهُ عَنْهُمْ وَرَضُوْا عَنْهُ

1347. The Mercy of God is always present, as the sun is always shining. But when we have prepared ourselves to receive it, we come to the full enjoyment of it, as a man who was in a shade comes out by his effort into the open, and basks in sunshine.

1348. The vanguard of Islam—those in the first rank—are those who dare and suffer for the Cause and never flinch. The first historical examples are the Muhājirs and the Anṣār. The Muhājirs—those who forsook their homes in Mecca and migrated to Medina, the holy Apostle being among the last to leave the post of danger, are mentioned first. Then come the Anṣār, the Helpers, the citizens of Medina who invited them, welcomed them, and gave them aid, and who formed the pivot of the new Community. Then are mentioned all who follow them in good deeds: not only the early heroes and ordinary men and women who had been Companions of the Apostle or had seen him, but men and women in all ages who have lived noble lives. In spite of all their sacrifice and suffering they rejoice in the precious gift of the Good Pleasure of God, and their Salvation is the Supreme Felicity which such Good Pleasure gives, symbolised by the Gardens of Heaven.

For them hath He prepared
Gardens under which rivers flow,[1349]
To dwell therein for ever:
That is the supreme Felicity.

وَاَعَدَّ لَهُمْ جَنّٰتٍ تَجْرِيْ تَحْتَهَا الْاَنْهٰرُ
خٰلِدِيْنَ فِيْهَآ اَبَدًا ۭ ذٰلِكَ الْفَوْزُ الْعَظِيْمُ ○

101. Certain of the desert Arabs
Round about you are Hypocrites,
As well as (desert Arabs) among
The Medina folk: [1350] they are
Obstinate in hypocrisy: thou
Knowest them not: We know
them:
Twice shall We punish them: [1351]
And in addition shall they be
Sent to a grievous Penalty.

١٠١- وَمِمَّنْ حَوْلَكُمْ مِّنَ الْاَعْرَابِ مُنٰفِقُوْنَ ۚ
وَمِنْ اَهْلِ الْمَدِيْنَةِ ڀ مَرَدُوْا عَلَى النِّفَاقِ ۣ
لَا تَعْلَمُهُمْ ۭ نَحْنُ نَعْلَمُهُمْ ۭ
سَنُعَذِّبُهُمْ مَّرَّتَيْنِ
ثُمَّ يُرَدُّوْنَ اِلٰى عَذَابٍ عَظِيْمٍ ○

102. Others (there are who) have
Acknowledged their wrong-doings:
They have mixed an act
That was good with another [1352]
That was evil. Perhaps God
Will turn unto them (in mercy):
For God is Oft-Forgiving,
Most Merciful.

١٠٢- وَاٰخَرُوْنَ اعْتَرَفُوْا بِذُنُوْبِهِمْ
خَلَطُوْا عَمَلًا صَالِحًا وَّاٰخَرَ سَيِّئًا ۭ
عَسَى اللّٰهُ اَنْ يَّتُوْبَ عَلَيْهِمْ ۭ
اِنَّ اللّٰهَ غَفُوْرٌ رَّحِيْمٌ ○

103. Of their goods take alms,
That so thou mightest
Purify and sanctify them;
And pray on their behalf.
Verily thy prayers are a source
Of security for them:
And God is One
Who heareth and knoweth.

١٠٣- خُذْ مِنْ اَمْوَالِهِمْ صَدَقَةً
تُطَهِّرُهُمْ وَتُزَكِّيْهِمْ بِهَا وَصَلِّ عَلَيْهِمْ ۭ
اِنَّ صَلٰوتَكَ سَكَنٌ لَّهُمْ ۭ
وَاللّٰهُ سَمِيْعٌ عَلِيْمٌ ○

1349. Note how this symbolism comes in in the descriptions of the final accomplishment of the destiny of man. In mathematical science it would be like a letter or formula which would sum up a long course of reasoning. In the graphic arts it would be like a Lotus in Buddhism, which expresses a whole complex of emotional or religious experiences. In music it would be like the characteristic notes in a Rāga or Rāginī. In this very Sūra it occurs before in ix. 72 and ix. 89, where see n. 1341. We are considering the good and bad Bedouins and rounding up the argument about them.

1350. The desert Arabs were not all simple folk. There were cunning hypocrites among them: both among certain tribes encamped round about Medina and certain others in Medina itself. I understand that both groups are of the *A'rāb*, to whom the context refers, and not of the settled citizens of Medina, whose Hypocrites were already referred to in previous sections. They might look simple, but they were in their ignorance all the more obstinate and hypocritical.

1351. Their punishment in this world was double, *viz.*, not only in their discomfiture, but because in their obstinate ignorance, they failed to understand the accomplished facts, while cleverer men realised that their hostility to Islam was hopeless. In addition to their discomfiture in this life, they would have to meet the spiritual penalties to come.

1352. There were some whose will was weak and succumbed to evil, although there was much good in them. To them is held out the promise of forgiveness if they would repent and undertake all acts of Muslim charity, which would purify their souls, aided by the prayers of God's Messenger. Then would they get the Peace that comes from purity and right conduct.

104. Know they not that God
Doth accept repentance from
His votaries and receives
Their gifts of charity, and that
God is verily He,
The Oft-Returning, Most Merciful?

١٠٤- اَلَمْ يَعْلَمُوْٓا اَنَّ اللّٰهَ هُوَ يَقْبَلُ التَّوْبَةَ
عَنْ عِبَادِهٖ وَيَاْخُذُ الصَّدَقٰتِ
وَاَنَّ اللّٰهَ هُوَ التَّوَّابُ الرَّحِيْمُ ○

105. And say: "Work
(righteousness):[1353]
Soon will God observe your work,
And His Apostle, and the
Believers:
Soon will ye be brought back
To the Knower of what is
Hidden and what is open:
Then will He show you
The truth of all that ye did."

١٠٥- وَقُلِ اعْمَلُوْا فَسَيَرَى اللّٰهُ عَمَلَكُمْ
وَرَسُوْلُهٗ وَالْمُؤْمِنُوْنَ
وَسَتُرَدُّوْنَ اِلٰى عٰلِمِ الْغَيْبِ وَالشَّهَادَةِ
فَيُنَبِّئُكُمْ
بِمَا كُنْتُمْ تَعْمَلُوْنَ ○

106. There are (yet) others,
Held in suspense for the command
Of God, whether He will
Punish them, or turn in mercy[1354]
To them: and God
Is All-Knowing, Wise.

١٠٦- وَاٰخَرُوْنَ مُرْجَوْنَ لِاَمْرِ اللّٰهِ
اِمَّا يُعَذِّبُهُمْ وَاِمَّا يَتُوْبُ عَلَيْهِمْ
وَاللّٰهُ عَلِيْمٌ حَكِيْمٌ ○

107. And there are those[1355]
Who put up a mosque

١٠٧- وَالَّذِيْنَ اتَّخَذُوْا مَسْجِدًا

1353. The repentant should be encouraged, after their repentance, to amend their conduct. The kindly interest of their brethren in them will strengthen them in virtue and blot out their past. When they go back into Eternity, they will understand the healing grace which saved them, just as the evil ones will then have their eyes opened to the real truth of their spiritual degradation (ix. 94). The similar words, in verse 84 and here, clench the contrast.

1354. Three categories of men are mentioned, whose faith was tested and found wanting in the Tabūk affair, but their characteristics are perfectly general, and we may here consider them in their general aspects: (1) the deep-dyed hypocrites, who when found out make excuses because otherwise they will suffer ignominy; they are unregenerate and obstinate, and there is no hope for them (ix. 101); (2) there are those who have lapsed into evil, but are not altogether evil; they repent and amend, and are accepted (ix. 102-105); and (3) there are doubtful cases, but God will judge them (ix. 106). A fourth category is mentioned in ix. 107, which will be discussed later.

1355. Three categories of Hypocrites having already been mentioned (n. 1354), a fourth class of insidious evil-doers is now mentioned, whose type is illustrated in the story of the Qubāa "Mosque of mischief (*dhirār*)." Qubāa is a suburb of Medina, about three miles to the south-east. When the Holy Prophet arrived at Medina for Hijrat, he rested four days in Qubāa before entering the town of Medina. Here was built the first mosque, the "Mosque of Piety" (*Taqwā*), or the mosque of the power of Islam (*Qūwat-ul-Islām*), to which he frequently came during his subsequent stay in Medina. Taking advantage of these sacred associations, some Hypocrites of the Tribe of Banī Ganam built an opposition mosque in Qubāa, pretending to advance Islam. In reality they were in league with a notorious enemy of Islam, one Abū 'Āmir, who had fought against Islam at Uḥud and who was now, after the battle of Ḥunain (A.H. 9), in Syria; his confederates wanted a mosque for him to come to, but it would only be a source of mischief and division, and the scheme was disapproved.

By way of mischief and infidelity—
To disunite the Believers—
And in preparation for one[1356]
Who warred against God
And His Apostle aforetime.
They will indeed swear
That their intention is nothing
But good; but God doth declare
That they are certainly liars.

ضِرَارًا وَّكُفْرًا وَّتَفْرِيقًا بَيْنَ الْمُؤْمِنِينَ
وَإِرْصَادًا لِّمَنْ حَارَبَ اللّٰهَ وَرَسُولَهُ مِنْ
قَبْلُ ۚ وَلَيَحْلِفُنَّ إِنْ أَرَدْنَا إِلَّا الْحُسْنٰى ۖ
وَاللّٰهُ يَشْهَدُ
إِنَّهُمْ لَكٰذِبُونَ ○

108. Never stand thou forth therein.
There is a mosque whose
foundation[1357]
Was laid from the first day
On piety; it is more worthy
Of thy standing forth (for prayer)
Therein. In it are men who
Love to be purified; and God
Loveth those who make
themselves pure.[1358]

١٠٨- لَا تَقُمْ فِيهِ أَبَدًا ۚ
لَمَسْجِدٌ أُسِّسَ عَلَى التَّقْوٰى مِنْ أَوَّلِ
يَوْمٍ أَحَقُّ أَنْ تَقُومَ فِيهِ ۚ
فِيهِ رِجَالٌ يُحِبُّونَ أَنْ يَّتَطَهَّرُوا ۚ
وَاللّٰهُ يُحِبُّ الْمُطَّهِّرِينَ ○

109. Which then is best?—he that
Layeth his foundation
On piety to God
And His Good Pleasure?—or he
That layeth his foundation
On an undermined sand-cliff[1359]
Ready to crumble to pieces?
And it doth crumble to pieces
With him, into the fire
Of Hell. And God guideth not
People that do wrong.

١٠٩- أَفَمَنْ أَسَّسَ بُنْيَانَهُ عَلٰى
تَقْوٰى مِنَ اللّٰهِ وَرِضْوَانٍ
خَيْرٌ أَمْ مَّنْ أَسَّسَ بُنْيَانَهُ
عَلٰى شَفَا جُرُفٍ هَارٍ
فَانْهَارَ بِهِ فِي نَارِ جَهَنَّمَ ۗ
وَاللّٰهُ لَا يَهْدِي الْقَوْمَ الظّٰلِمِينَ ○

110. The foundation of those
Who so build is never free

١١٠- لَا يَزَالُ بُنْيَانُهُمُ الَّذِي

1356. Abū 'Āmir, surnamed the *Rāhib* (Monk), as he had been in touch with Christian monks. See last note.

1357. The original "Mosque of Piety" built by the holy Apostle himself.

1358. The true Muslim must be pure in body, mind, and heart. His motives should always be sincere, and his religion without any alloy of worldly gain.

1359. A man who builds his life on Piety (which includes sincerity and the purity of all motives) and his hopes on the Good Pleasure of God, builds on a firm foundation of rock that will never be shaken. In contrast to him is the man who builds on a shifting sand-cliff on the brink of an abyss, already undermined by forces which he does not see. The cliff and the foundations all crumble to pieces along with him, and he is plunged into the Fire of misery from which there is no escape.

From suspicion and shakiness[1360]
In their hearts, until
Their hearts are cut to pieces.
And God is All-Knowing, Wise.

بُنْوَا رِيبَةً فِي قُلُوبِهِمْ إِلَّا أَنْ تَقَطَّعَ
قُلُوبُهُمْ ۚ وَاللَّهُ عَلِيمٌ حَكِيمٌ ○ ع

SECTION 14.

111. God hath purchased of the Believers
Their persons and their goods;
For theirs (in return)
Is the Garden (of Paradise):[1361]
They fight in His Cause,
And slay and are slain:
A promise binding on Him
In Truth, through the Law,
The Gospel, and the Qur-an:[1362]
And who is more faithful
To his Covenant than God?
Then rejoice in the bargain
Which ye have concluded:
That is the achievement supreme.

١١١- إِنَّ اللَّهَ اشْتَرَىٰ مِنَ الْمُؤْمِنِينَ
أَنْفُسَهُمْ وَأَمْوَالَهُمْ بِأَنَّ لَهُمُ الْجَنَّةَ ۚ
يُقَاتِلُونَ فِي سَبِيلِ اللَّهِ فَيَقْتُلُونَ وَ
يُقْتَلُونَ ۖ وَعْدًا عَلَيْهِ حَقًّا
فِي التَّوْرَاةِ وَالْإِنْجِيلِ وَالْقُرْآنِ ۚ
وَمَنْ أَوْفَىٰ بِعَهْدِهِ مِنَ اللَّهِ
فَاسْتَبْشِرُوا بِبَيْعِكُمُ الَّذِي بَايَعْتُمْ بِهِ ۚ
وَذَٰلِكَ هُوَ الْفَوْزُ الْعَظِيمُ ○

1360. The parable is continued further. The heart of man is the seat of his hopes and fears, the foundation of his moral and spiritual life. If that foundation is on an undermined sand-cliff already crumbling to pieces, what security or stability can he have? He is being shaken by alarms and suspicions and superstitions, until like the edge of a sand-cliff they are cut clean away and fall into a heap of ruin and his spiritual life and all its land-marks are destroyed.

1361. In a human bargain both sides give something and receive some advantage. In the divine bargain of God with man, God takes man's will and soul and his wealth and goods, and gives him in return ever-lasting Felicity. Man fights in God's Cause and carries out His will, the Universal Will. All that he has to give up is the ephemeral things of this world, while he gains eternal salvation, the fulfilment of his highest spiritual hopes,—a supreme achievement indeed.

1362. We offer our whole selves and our possessions to God, and God gives us Salvation, *i.e.*, eternal freedom from the bondage of this world. This is the true doctrine of redemption; and we are taught that this is the doctrine not only of the Qur-ān but of the earlier Revelations,—the original Law of Moses and the original Gospel of Jesus. Any other view of redemption is rejected by Islam, especially that of corrupted Christianity, which thinks that some other person suffered for our sins and we are redeemed by his blood. It is our self-surrender that counts, not other people's merits. Our complete self-surrender may include fighting for the cause, both spiritual and physical. As regards actual fighting with the sword there has been some difference in theological theories at different times, but very little in the practice of those who framed those theories. The Jewish wars were ruthless wars of extermination. The Old Testament does not mince matters on this subject. In the New Testament St. Paul, in commending the worthy fruits of Faith, mentions Gideon, Barak, and other warriors of the Old Testament as his ideals, "Who through faith subdued kingdoms,...waxed valiant in fight, turned to flight the armies of the aliens..." (Hebrews, xi. 32-34.) The monkisk morality of the Gospels in their present form has never been followed by any self-respecting Christian or other nation in history. Nor is it common-sense to ignore lust of blood in unregenerate man as a form of evil which has to be combated "within the limits set by God" (Q. ix, 112).

112. Those that turn (to God)[1363]
In repentance; that serve Him,
And praise Him; that wander
In devotion to the Cause of God;
That bow down and prostrate
themselves
In prayer; that enjoin good
And forbid evil; and observe
The limits set by God;—
(These do rejoice). So proclaim
The glad tidings to the Believers.

١١٢- اَلتَّآئِبُوْنَ الْعٰبِدُوْنَ
الْحٰمِدُوْنَ السَّآئِحُوْنَ
الرّٰكِعُوْنَ السّٰجِدُوْنَ
الْاٰمِرُوْنَ بِالْمَعْرُوْفِ وَ النَّاهُوْنَ عَنِ
الْمُنْكَرِ وَ الْحٰفِظُوْنَ لِحُدُوْدِ اللّٰهِ
وَ بَشِّرِ الْمُؤْمِنِيْنَ ○

113. It is not fitting,
For the Prophet and those
Who believe, that they should
Pray for forgiveness
For Pagans, even though
They be of kin, after it is
Clear to them that they
Are companions of the Fire.[1364]

١١٣- مَا كَانَ لِلنَّبِيِّ وَ الَّذِيْنَ اٰمَنُوْٓا
اَنْ يَّسْتَغْفِرُوْا لِلْمُشْرِكِيْنَ
وَلَوْ كَانُوْٓا اُولِيْ قُرْبٰى مِنْۢ بَعْدِ مَا تَبَيَّنَ
لَهُمْ اَنَّهُمْ اَصْحٰبُ الْجَحِيْمِ ○

114. And Abraham prayed
For his father's forgiveness
Only because of a promise
He had made to him.[1365]
But when it became clear
To him that he was
An enemy to God, he
Dissociated himself from him:
For Abraham was most
Tender-hearted, forbearing.[1366]

١١٤- وَمَا كَانَ اسْتِغْفَارُ اِبْرٰهِيْمَ لِاَبِيْهِ
اِلَّا عَنْ مَّوْعِدَةٍ وَّعَدَهَآ اِيَّاهُ
فَلَمَّا تَبَيَّنَ لَهٗٓ اَنَّهٗ عَدُوٌّ لِّلّٰهِ
تَبَرَّاَ مِنْهُ
اِنَّ اِبْرٰهِيْمَ لَاَوَّاهٌ حَلِيْمٌ ○

115. And God will not mislead[1367]
A people after He hath

١١٥- وَمَا كَانَ اللّٰهُ لِيُضِلَّ قَوْمًا بَعْدَ اِذْ

1363. We are to rejoice that by giving up such small things as ourselves and our possessions we are to be rewarded with such a great thing as the eternal life of felicity. The truly righteous, whose lives in various aspects are described in this verse, do so rejoice. The good news is to be proclaimed to all Believers, including the weakest among us, so that they may profit by that example.

1364. This is usually understood to refer to the prayers for the dead, (1) if they died unrepentant after Islam was preached to them, (2) if they actively resisted or opposed the Faith *to the last*, and (3) if the person praying knows that on account of deliberate contumacy the deceased may be said to have had the doors of mercy closed to him. How is he to know? The knowledge must come from special commands as declared by the Holy Prophet in his life-time regarding individuals. Where no light is available from this source we must follow the best judgment we can.

1365. Abraham and his unbelieving father are referred to in vi. 74. Apparently when Abraham was convinced that the conditions mentioned in the last note applied to his father, he gave up praying for him, as the physical bond was cut off by the spiritual hostility. For the promise to pray for his father, see xix. 47.

1366. Abraham was loyal and tender-hearted, and bore with much that he disapproved, being in this a prototype of Muṣṭafā, and it must have gone against his grain to cut off relations in that way. But it would obviously be wrong for a human being to entreat God for mercy on people who had finally rejected God.

1367. God's clear commands are given, so that Believers may not be misled by their human frailty into unbecoming conduct.

Guided them, in order that
He may make clear to them
What to fear (and avoid)—
For God hath knowledge
Of all things.

هَدٰىهُمْ حَتّٰى يُبَيِّنَ لَهُمْ مَّا يَتَّقُوْنَ ؕ
اِنَّ اللّٰهَ بِكُلِّ شَیْءٍ عَلِیْمٌ ○

116. Unto God belongeth
The dominion of the heavens
And the earth. He giveth life
And He taketh it. Except for Him
Ye have no protector
Nor helper.

١١٦- اِنَّ اللّٰهَ لَهٗ مُلْكُ السَّمٰوٰتِ وَالْاَرْضِ ؕ
يُحْیٖ وَيُمِيْتُ ؕ وَمَا لَكُمْ مِّنْ دُوْنِ اللّٰهِ
مِنْ وَّلِیٍّ وَّلَا نَصِيْرٍ ○

117. God turned with favour
To the Prophet, the Muhājirs,[1368]
And the Anṣār,—who followed
Him in a time of distress,
After that the hearts of a part[1369]
Of them had nearly swerved
(From duty); but He turned
To them (also): for He is
Unto them Most Kind,
Most Merciful.

١١٧- لَقَدْ تَّابَ اللّٰهُ عَلَى النَّبِیِّ وَالْمُهٰجِرِيْنَ
وَالْاَنْصَارِ الَّذِيْنَ اتَّبَعُوْهُ فِیْ سَاعَةِ
الْعُسْرَةِ مِنْۢ بَعْدِ مَا كَادَ يَزِيْغُ قُلُوْبُ
فَرِيْقٍ مِّنْهُمْ ثُمَّ تَابَ عَلَيْهِمْ ؕ
اِنَّهٗ بِهِمْ رَءُوْفٌ رَّحِيْمٌ ○

118. (He turned in mercy also)
To the three who were left
Behind; (they felt guilty)[1370]
To such a degree that the earth

١١٨- وَّعَلَى الثَّلٰثَةِ الَّذِيْنَ خُلِّفُوْا ؕ
حَتّٰۤى اِذَا ضَاقَتْ عَلَيْهِمُ الْاَرْضُ

1368. *Cf.* ix. 100. The Muhājirs were the people who originally forsook their homes in Mecca and followed Muṣṭafā in exile to Medina. The Anṣār were the Medina people who received them with honour and hospitality into their city. Both these groups were staunch supporters of Islam, and proved their Faith by great sacrifices. But in the difficult days of the Tabūk expedition some of them, not perversely, but out of lethargy and human weakness, had failed to follow the standard. They were forgiven, and they afterwards acquitted themselves with zeal.

1369. Note that the "swerving from duty" was merely an inclination due to the weakness of human nature in the face of new difficulties; that it only affected a part of the men for a time; and that it was overcome even in their case by the grace of God, so that they all did their duty, and were freely forgiven their incipient weakness, which they conquered. There were three exceptions, which are referred to in the next verse.

1370. Among the Faithful, the largest number consisted of those who were perfectly staunch and ever ready to do their duty. They obtained the love and good pleasure of God. Next came a few who wavered because their will was weak and they were daunted by the dangers and difficulties that faced them; God's saving grace protected them and they conquered their weakness, and did not fail in their duty; God forgave them and accepted their repentance. Lastly, in the illustration taken from the Tabūk affair, there were some who actually failed in their duty, not from contumacy or ill-will, but from thoughtlessness, slackness, and human weakness: they actually failed to obey the Holy Prophet's summons, and were naturally called on to explain, and were excluded from the life of the Community. Their mental state is here described graphically. Though the earth is spacious, to them it was constrained. In their own souls they had a feeling of constraint. In worldly affluence they felt poor in spirit. They realised that they could not flee from God, but could only find solace and refuge in coming back to Him. They freely repented and showed it in their deeds, and God freely forgave them and took them to His grace. Though illustrated by the particular examples of the Anṣār, *viz.*, Ka'b, Marār, and Hilāl, the lesson is perfectly general and is good for all times.

Seemed constrained to them,
For all its speciousness,
And their (very) Souls seemed
Straitened to them,—
And they perceived that
There is no fleeing from God
(And no refuge) but to Himself.
Then He turned to them,
That they might repent:
For God is Oft-Returning,
Most Merciful.

بِمَا رَحُبَتْ وَضَاقَتْ عَلَيْهِمْ أَنْفُسُهُمْ
وَظَنُّوٓا أَنْ لَا مَلْجَاَ مِنَ اللّٰهِ
إِلَّآ إِلَيْهِ ط
ثُمَّ تَابَ عَلَيْهِمْ لِيَتُوبُوا ط
إِنَّ اللّٰهَ هُوَ التَّوَّابُ الرَّحِيمُ ○ ع

C. 98.—To be true in word and deed is to hold
(IX. 119-129.) Our selfish desires at bay, and follow
God's Call: in this is our fullest satisfaction
And reward. But our striving should include
Study and teaching, for the Brethren's benefit.
For God's Message increases our Faith
And leads us to love Him and trust Him,
The Lord of the Throne of Glory Supreme.

SECTION 15.

119. O ye who believe! Fear God
And be with those
Who are true (in word and deed).

١١٩- يَٰٓأَيُّهَا الَّذِينَ اٰمَنُوا اتَّقُوا اللّٰهَ
وَكُونُوا مَعَ الصّٰدِقِينَ ○

120. It was not fitting
For the people of Medina
And the Bedouin Arabs
Of the neighbourhood, to refuse
To follow God's Apostle,
Nor to prefer their own lives
To his: because nothing
Could they suffer or do,
But was reckoned to their credit
As a deed of righteousness,—
Whether they suffered thirst,
Or fatigue, or hunger, in the Cause
Of God, or trod paths
To raise the ire of the Unbelievers,
Or received any injury[1371]

١٢٠- مَا كَانَ لِأَهْلِ الْمَدِينَةِ
وَمَنْ حَوْلَهُمْ مِّنَ الْأَعْرَابِ
أَنْ يَتَخَلَّفُوا عَنْ رَّسُولِ اللّٰهِ
وَلَا يَرْغَبُوا بِأَنْفُسِهِمْ عَنْ نَّفْسِهِ ط
ذٰلِكَ بِأَنَّهُمْ لَا يُصِيبُهُمْ ظَمَاٌ
وَّلَا نَصَبٌ وَّلَا مَخْمَصَةٌ فِي سَبِيلِ اللّٰهِ
وَلَا يَطَـُٔونَ مَوْطِئًا يَّغِيظُ الْكُفَّارَ
وَلَا يَنَالُونَ مِنْ عَدُوٍّ نَّيْلًا

1371. Again, the illustration is that of Tabūk, but the lesson is general. We must not hold our own comfort or lives dearer than that of our Leader, nor desert him in the hour of danger. If we have true devotion, we shall hold our own lives or comfort cheap in comparison to his. But whatever service we render to the Cause of God, and whatever sufferings, hardships, or injuries we endure, or whatever resources we spend for the Cause,—all goes to raise our degree in the spiritual world. Nothing is lost. Our reward is far greater in worth than any little service we can render, or any little hardship we can suffer, or any little contributions we can make to the Cause. We "painfully attain to joy".

Whatever from an enemy:
For God suffereth not
The reward to be lost
Of those who do good;—

إِلَّا كُتِبَ لَهُم بِهِ عَمَلٌ صَالِحٌ
إِنَّ اللَّهَ لَا يُضِيعُ أَجْرَ الْمُحْسِنِينَ ○

121. Nor could they spend anything
(For the Cause)—small or great—
Nor cut across a valley,[1372]
But the deed is inscribed
To their credit; that God
May requite their deed
With the best (possible reward).

١٢١- وَلَا يُنفِقُونَ نَفَقَةً صَغِيرَةً وَلَا
كَبِيرَةً
وَلَا يَقْطَعُونَ وَادِيًا إِلَّا كُتِبَ لَهُمْ
لِيَجْزِيَهُمُ اللَّهُ أَحْسَنَ مَا كَانُوا يَعْمَلُونَ ○

122. Nor should the Believers
All go forth together:
If a contingent
From every expedition
Remained behind,
They could devote themselves
To studies in religion,
And admonish the people
When they return to them,—
That thus they (may learn)[1373]
To guard themselves (against evil).

١٢٢- وَمَا كَانَ الْمُؤْمِنُونَ لِيَنفِرُوا كَافَّةً
فَلَوْلَا نَفَرَ مِن كُلِّ فِرْقَةٍ مِّنْهُمْ طَائِفَةٌ
لِّيَتَفَقَّهُوا فِي الدِّينِ
وَلِيُنذِرُوا قَوْمَهُمْ إِذَا رَجَعُوا إِلَيْهِمْ
لَعَلَّهُمْ يَحْذَرُونَ ○

SECTION 16.

123. O ye who believe! Fight
The Unbelievers who gird you
about,[1374]
And let them find firmness
In you: and know that God
Is with those who fear Him.

١٢٣- يَا أَيُّهَا الَّذِينَ آمَنُوا قَاتِلُوا الَّذِينَ
يَلُونَكُم مِّنَ الْكُفَّارِ وَلْيَجِدُوا فِيكُمْ غِلْظَةً
وَاعْلَمُوا أَنَّ اللَّهَ مَعَ الْمُتَّقِينَ ○

1372. *Cut across a valley*: this is specially mentioned in a symbolical way, as denoting an individual act of heroism, dash, or bravery. To march with the troops along valleys, or, spiritually, tread paths of danger along with our Comrades, is good and praiseworthy; but one that dashes across a stream, all alone, for some special deed of bravery where the *élan* of comradeship does not sustain him, needs special mention. Notice that both the things mentioned in this verse,—the spending of resources and the dashing across a valley—are individual acts, while those mentioned in the last verse are collective acts, which are in some ways easier. The individual acts having been mentioned, the next verse follows naturally.

1373. Fighting may be inevitable, and where a call is made by the righteous Imām, it should be obeyed. But fighting is not to be glorified to the exclusion of all else. Even among those who are able to go forth, a party should remain behind—one in each township or circle—for purposes of study; so that when the fighters return home, their minds may be attuned again to the more normal interests of religious life, under properly instructed teachers. The students and teachers are soldiers of the *Jihād* in their spirit of obedience and discipline.

1374. When conflict becomes inevitable, the first thing is to clear our surroundings of all evil, for it is only evil that we can rightly fight. To evil we must put up a stout and stiff resistance. Mealy-mouthed compromises are not right for soldiers of truth and righteousness. They are often a compound of cowardice, weariness, greed, and corruptibility.

124. Whenever there cometh down[1375]
A Sūra, some of them say:
"Which of you has had
His faith increased by it?"
Yea, those who believe,—
Their faith is increased,
And they do rejoice.

١٢٤- وَإِذَا مَآ أُنزِلَتْ سُورَةٌ فَمِنْهُم مَّن
يَقُولُ أَيُّكُمْ زَادَتْهُ هَٰذِهِۦٓ إِيمَٰنًا ۚ
فَأَمَّا ٱلَّذِينَ ءَامَنُوا۟ فَزَادَتْهُمْ إِيمَٰنًا
وَهُمْ يَسْتَبْشِرُونَ ○

125. But those in whose hearts[1376]
Is a disease,—it will add doubt
To their doubt, and they will die
In a state of Unbelief

١٢٥- وَأَمَّا ٱلَّذِينَ فِى قُلُوبِهِم مَّرَضٌ فَزَادَتْهُمْ
رِجْسًا إِلَىٰ رِجْسِهِمْ وَمَاتُوا۟ وَهُمْ كَٰفِرُونَ ○

126. See they not that they
Are tried every year[1377]
Once or twice? Yet they
Turn not in repentance,
And they take no heed.

١٢٦- أَوَلَا يَرَوْنَ أَنَّهُمْ يُفْتَنُونَ فِى كُلِّ
عَامٍ مَّرَّةً أَوْ مَرَّتَيْنِ ثُمَّ لَا يَتُوبُونَ
وَلَا هُمْ يَذَّكَّرُونَ ○

127. Whenever there cometh down
A Sūra, they look at each other,
(Saying), "Doth anyone see
you?"
Then they turn aside:
God hath turned their hearts[1378]
(From the light); for they
Are a people that understand not.

١٢٧- وَإِذَا مَآ أُنزِلَتْ سُورَةٌ نَّظَرَ بَعْضُهُمْ
إِلَىٰ بَعْضٍ
هَلْ يَرَىٰكُم مِّنْ أَحَدٍ ثُمَّ ٱنصَرَفُوا۟ ۚ صَرَفَ
ٱللَّهُ قُلُوبَهُم بِأَنَّهُمْ قَوْمٌ لَّا يَفْقَهُونَ ○

128. Now hath come unto you
An Apostle from amongst

١٢٨- لَقَدْ جَآءَكُمْ رَسُولٌ مِّنْ

1375. The incompatibility of Unfaith and Faith are contrasted in this section in respect of revelation and the divine teacher. The Unbelievers laugh at revelation, and say to each other mockingly: "Does this increase your faith?" To the Believer every new aspect of God's truth as revealed increases his faith, and wonder, and gratitude. He rejoices, because he gets added strength for life and achievement.

1376. *Cf.* ii. 10 and several similar passages. Just as the light, which to healthy eyes gives enlightenment, causes pain to the diseased eye, which emits unclean matter, so to those spiritually diseased, God's grace is unwelcome, and they put forth more doubts to cover their disease. And they die in their disease, and of their disease. Note the aptness of the metaphor.

1377. Yet, in spite of their infidelity, one or two chances are given them every year. The door is not closed to them. Yet they deliberately turn away, and take no heed of all the warnings which their own nature and the teaching and example of good men should give them.

1378. Even the Unbelievers, in their heart and conscience, feel uncomfortable when they turn aside from Faith and Truth, and therefore their turning aside is figured by furtive glances, such as we may suppose literally to have been cast by the Hypocrites in the assemblies of the holy Apostle. Then they slink away, feeling superior in their minds. And yet, if they only knew it, their contumacy deprives them of God's grace and light. They are turning Grace away, and when God withdraws it altogether, they perish utterly.

Yourselves: it grieves him
That ye should perish:
Ardently anxious is he
Over you: to the Believers
Is he most kind and merciful.[1379]

أَنفُسِكُمْ عَزِيزٌ عَلَيْهِ مَا عَنِتُّمْ حَرِيصٌ
عَلَيْكُم بِالْمُؤْمِنِينَ رَءُوفٌ رَّحِيمٌ ۝

129. But if they turn away,
Say: "God sufficeth me:
There is no god but He:
On Him is my trust,—
He the Lord of the Throne
(Of Glory) Supreme!"[1380]

١٢٩- فَإِن تَوَلَّوْا فَقُلْ حَسْبِيَ اللَّهُ ۖ
لَا إِلَٰهَ إِلَّا هُوَ ۖ عَلَيْهِ تَوَكَّلْتُ ۖ وَهُوَ رَبُّ
الْعَرْشِ الْعَظِيمِ ۝

1379. The tender heart of the Teacher is grieved that any among his flock should rush headlong to ruin. He watches ardently over them, and whenever any of them show signs of Faith, his kindness and mercy surround him and rejoice over him.

1380. But if the Message is rejected, he still proclaims the burning Faith of his heart, which is unquenchable. God is all in all. To trust Him is to find the accomplishment of all spiritual desire. His grandeur is figured by a lofty Throne, supreme in glory!

Thus have we been led, through a notable incident in Mustafā's earthly career, to truths of the highest spiritual import.

INTRODUCTION TO SŪRA X (*Yūnus*).

Chronologically this Sūra and the five that follow (Sūras xi, xii, xiii, xiv, and xv) are closely connected, and were revealed in the late Meccan period, as the great event of the Hijrat was gradually approaching down the stream of Time. But their chronology has no particular significance.

On the other hand their arrangement in the gradation of Quranic teaching fits in with the subject-matter. S. viii. and S. ix. were mainly concerned with the first questions that arose on the formation of the new and organised Community of Islam in its conflict with those who wished to suppress or destroy it or use force to prevent its growth and the consolidation of its ideals. See Introductions to those Sūras. The present group leads us to the questions that face us when external hostility has been met, and our relations to God have to be considered from a higher stand-point than that of self-preservation. How does revelation work? What is the meaning of divine grace and its withdrawal? How do the Messengers of God deliver their Message? How should we receive it?

All these questions revolve round the revelation of the Qur-ān and each Sūra of this group except the 13th has the Abbreviated Letters A. L. R. attached to it. S. xiii. has the letters A.L.M.R., and we shall discuss this variation when we come to S. xiii.

As shown in Appendix I (Sīpāra 3), the Abbreviated Letters are mystic symbols, about whose meaning there is no authoritative explanation. If the theory advanced in n. 25 to ii. 1 has any validity, and the present group A.L.R. is cognate to the group A.L.M., we have to consider and form some idea in our minds as to the probable meaning of the variation. We took A.L.M. to be a symbol of those Sūras that deal with the beginning, the middle, and the end of man's spiritual history,—the origin, the present position, and the things to come in the Last Days (eschatology, to use a theological term). We took A.L. to stand as symbols of the first two, and M. of the last. In the present group of Sūras we find hardly any eschatological matter, and therefore we can understand the absence of M., the symbol standing for such matter. In its place comes R., which is phonetically allied to L. L. is produced by the impact of the tongue to the front of the palate, and R. to the middle of the palate. In many languages the letters L. and R. are interchangeable; *e.g.*, in Arabic, *al-Raḥmān* becomes ar-Raḥmān, and R. in imperfect enunciation becomes L., as in Chinese lallations. If L. is a symbol of present-day things looking to the future, we may take R. as a symbol of present-day things looking within, *i.e.*, into the interior of the organization of the Ummat. And this symbolism fits in with the subject-matter of the Sūras in question. But no one should be dogmatic in speculation about mystic Symbols.

Let us now consider Sūra x alone. The central theme is that God's wonderful Creation must not be viewed by us as a creation of material things only, once made and finished with. Most wonderful of all is how He reveals Himself to men through

Apostles and Scriptures; how apostles are rejected by men, and the Message disbelieved until it is too late for repentance; and how, as in the case of Yūnus (Jonah) and his people, even the rejection (when repentance supervenes) does not prevent God's grace and mercy from working, and how far that working is beyond man's comprehension.

Summary.—The wonderful working of the Spirit of God through man by revelation seems like magic to men; yet they could find Signs and Messages from Him in the sun and the moon and the constantly varying yet regular phenomena of nature, from which man should take a lesson of constancy and Faith (x. 1-20, and C. 99).

All the goodness or beauty that man meets in the life around him proceeds from God. Yet man is blind and will not understand (x. 21-40, and C. 100).

As all things and beings proceed from God, so will they return to Him, and He is ever true. Why then does ungrateful man make untrue phantoms for himself instead of rejoicing in the good news which He sends? (x. 41-70, and C. 101).

God revealed Himself through Noah, but Noah's people rejected him and perished. He spoke through Moses to Pharaoh, but Pharaoh was stiff-necked and arrogant, and when he repented at all, it was too late (x. 71-92, and C. 102).

Everywhere want of faith causes people to perish. But the people of Yūnus repented, and God saved them by His wonderful grace. So God will deliver the Believers. When the Truth comes from God, follow it and be patient, for God is the most righteous of Judges (x. 93-109, and C. 103).

C. 99.—Men may wonder that a man
(x. 1-20.) Like unto them should bring a Message
From God, but God's Message shines
Forth through all nature and Creation.
He guides the human spirit, if only
Man will have Faith and put his hope
In God. Wonderful are God's relations
With man, yet man is ungrateful
And runs to fancies and fanciful gods.
Glory to the One true God, Who made
Mankind as One, and holds alone
The secrets of the Unseen in His
Great and good Universal Plan.

Sūra X.

Yūnus, or Jonah.

In the name of God, Most Gracious, Most Merciful

1. A. L. R.[1381]
These are the Āyats[1382]
Of the Book of Wisdom.

2. Is it a matter
Of wonderment to men
That We have sent
Our inspiration to a man
From among themselves?—[1383]
That he should warn mankind
(Of their danger), and give
The good news to the Believers
That they have before their Lord
The lofty rank of Truth.[1384]
(But) say the Unbelievers:
"This is indeed
An evident sorcerer!"

3. Verily your Lord is God,
Who created the heavens
And the earth in six Days,[1385]

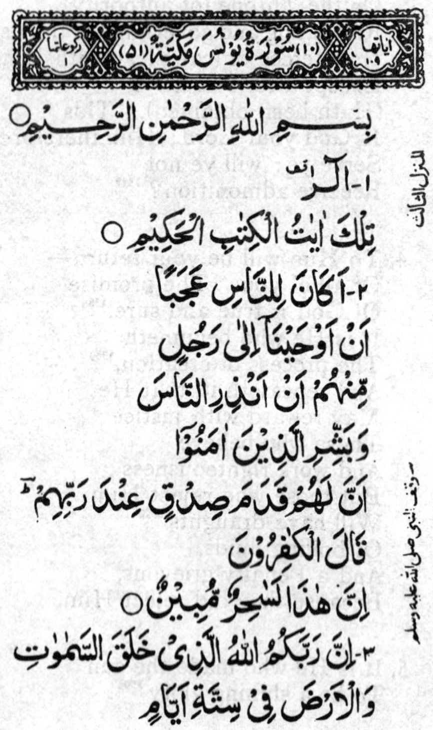

1381. For the Abbreviated Letters generally as mystic Symbols, see Appendix I. For this particular combination see the Introduction to this Sūra.

1382. *Āyāt*=Signs, or Verses of the Qur-ān. Here both meanings are to be understood. Each verse is a nugget of wisdom. And in the verses immediately following, *e.g.*, x. 3-6, examples are given of the wonders of God's material Creation. If the starry heavens impress us with their sublimity as signs of God's wisdom and power, how much more wonderful is it that He should speak to lowly man through His Messengers, in man's own language, so that he can understand?

1383. Is it not still more wonderful that the inspired man should be one of ourselves? The Arabs had known Muḥammad in other relations and conditions, and when the mighty Message came through his mouth—the message of Wisdom and Power, such as no man could speak as from himself, least of all a man not instructed in human learning,—they could only in their wonder attribute it to magic and sorcery. They failed to understand that magic and sorcery were projections of their own mind, while here was solid, enduring Truth from God!

1384. God's Message was and is not all smooth and agreeable. The first thing is to convince us of our sin and wrong-doing, and warn us of our danger. If we have Faith, we then learn what a high rank we obtain in the sight of God, through His glorious Truth, which makes us pure and free.

1385. See note 1031 to vii. 54

And is firmly established[1386] On the Throne (of authority), Regulating and governing all things. No intercessor (can plead with Him) Except after His leave (Hath been obtained). This Is God your Lord; Him therefore Serve ye: will ye not Receive admonition?[1387]	ثُمَّ اسْتَوٰى عَلَى الْعَرْشِ يُدَبِّرُ الْاَمْرَ مَا مِنْ شَفِيْعٍ اِلَّا مِنْۢ بَعْدِ اِذْنِهٖ ذٰلِكُمُ اللّٰهُ رَبُّكُمْ فَاعْبُدُوْهُ اَفَلَا تَذَكَّرُوْنَ ○
4. To Him will be your return— Of all of you. The promise Of God is true and sure.[1388] It is He who beginneth The process of creation,[1389] And repeateth it, that He May reward with justice Those who believe And work righteousness; But those who reject Him Will have draughts[1390] Of boiling fluids, And a Penalty grievous, Because they did reject Him.	٤- اِلَيْهِ مَرْجِعُكُمْ جَمِيْعًا وَعْدَ اللّٰهِ حَقًّا اِنَّهٗ يَبْدَؤُا الْخَلْقَ ثُمَّ يُعِيْدُهٗ لِيَجْزِيَ الَّذِيْنَ اٰمَنُوْا وَعَمِلُوا الصّٰلِحٰتِ بِالْقِسْطِ وَالَّذِيْنَ كَفَرُوْا لَهُمْ شَرَابٌ مِّنْ حَمِيْمٍ وَّعَذَابٌ اَلِيْمٌۢ بِمَا كَانُوْا يَكْفُرُوْنَ ○
5. It is He who made the sun To be a shining glory[1391]	٥- هُوَ الَّذِيْ جَعَلَ الشَّمْسَ ضِيَاۤءً

1386. *Istawā*, with the preposition *ilā* after it, means "to design, to set oneself to execute a design;" hence in ii. 29, I have translated, "His design comprehended the heavens," to emphasise the fact that the heavens were not eternal or co-eternal with Him, but were a part of His design, and in a sense, as they appear to man subjectively, a complement to the creation of man's Earth. With the preposition *'alā* after it, as here and in vii. 54 and elsewhere, the meaning seems to be literally, "to mount or ascend," and figuratively to be firmly established, to sit firm and unshaken, beyond question." The Throne of authority represents symbolically many ideas: *e.g.*, (1) that God is high above all His Creation; (2) that He regulates and governs it, as a king does, whose authority is unquestionably recognised; (3) that He is not, therefore, like the gods of Greece and paganism, who were imagined to be in a world apart, careless of mankind, or jealous of mankind, but on the contrary, He (4) disposes of their affairs and all affairs continuously and with justice; (4) that the authority of His prophets, ministers, and messengers is derived from Him, and such intercession as they can make is by His will and permission.

1387. *Cf.* vi. 80.

1388. *Ḥaqq*: true, right, for just ends, in right proportions, sure and certain: all these ideas are implied.

1389. *Cf.* n. 120 to ii. 117. God's creation is not a simple act, once done and finished with. It is continuous, and there are many stages, not the least important of which is the Hereafter, when the fruits of our life will be achieved.

1390. *Ḥamim*: boiling fluid; it is associated, as in xxxviii. 57, with *gassāq*, a dark, murky, or intensely cold fluid; both symbols of the grievous penalty that results from rebellion against God.

1391. The fitting epithet for the sun is *dhiāa*, "splendour and glory of brightness", and for the moon is "a light" (of beauty), the cool light that illuminates and helps in the darkness of the night. But the sun and moon also measure time. The simplest observation can keep pace with the true lunar months and lunar years, which are all that is required by a pastoral people. For agriculture solar years are required, as they indicate the changes of the seasons, but ordinary solar years are never exact; even the solar year of 365¼ days requires correction by advanced astronomical calculation.

And the moon to be a light
(Of beauty), and measured out
Stages for her; that ye might
Know the number of years
And the count (of time).
Nowise did God create this
But in truth and righteousness.[1392]
(Thus) doth He explain His Signs
In detail, for those who
understand.[1393]

وَّالْقَمَرَ نُوْرًا وَّ قَدَّرَهٗ مَنَازِلَ
لِتَعْلَمُوْا عَدَدَ السِّنِيْنَ وَالْحِسَابَ ۭ
مَا خَلَقَ اللّٰهُ
ذٰلِكَ اِلَّا بِالْحَقِّ ۚ
يُفَصِّلُ الْاٰيٰتِ لِقَوْمٍ يَّعْلَمُوْنَ ○

6. Verily, in the alternation
Of the Night and the Day,
And in all that God
Hath created, in the heavens
And the earth, are Signs
For those who fear Him.[1394]

٦- اِنَّ فِي اخْتِلَافِ الَّيْلِ وَالنَّهَارِ
وَمَا خَلَقَ اللّٰهُ فِي السَّمٰوٰتِ وَالْاَرْضِ
لَاٰيٰتٍ لِّقَوْمٍ يَّتَّقُوْنَ ○

7. Those who rest not their hope
On their meeting with Us,
But are pleased and satisfied
With the life of the Present,
And those who heed not
Our Signs,—[1395]

٧- اِنَّ الَّذِيْنَ لَا يَرْجُوْنَ لِقَاۗءَنَا
وَرَضُوْا بِالْحَيٰوةِ الدُّنْيَا وَاطْمَاَنُّوْا بِهَا
وَالَّذِيْنَ هُمْ عَنْ اٰيٰتِنَا غٰفِلُوْنَ ○

8. Their abode is the Fire,
Because of the (evil)
They earned.

٨- اُولٰۗىِٕكَ مَاْوٰىهُمُ النَّارُ
بِمَا كَانُوْا يَكْسِبُوْنَ ○

9. Those who believe,
And work righteousness,—
Their Lord will guide them
Because of their Faith:[1396]

٩- اِنَّ الَّذِيْنَ اٰمَنُوْا وَعَمِلُوا الصّٰلِحٰتِ
يَهْدِيْهِمْ رَبُّهُمْ بِاِيْمَانِهِمْ ۚ تَجْرِيْ مِنْ

1392. Everything in God's creation has use and purpose, and fits into a Design. It is true in every sense of the word and it is good and just. It is not merely a matter of sport or freak (xxi. 16). Though so varied, it proclaims God's Unity; though a limited free-will is granted to creatures, the results of evil (which is rebellion) are neutralised and harmony is restored. *Cf.* iii. 191.

1393. *Cf.* ix. 11.

1394. *Cf.* ii. 164.

1395. Those who fall from Grace are described by three epithets: (1) the meeting with God is not the object of their hope and earnest desire, but something else, *viz.* (2) the material good of this world, which not only attracts them but apparently gives them complete satisfaction, so that there is no glow of the Future in their horizon, and (3) they are deaf and dead to the resounding and living Message of God. (1) and (2) refer to the extinction of Faith in them, and (3) to their falling a prey to the evils of this world in their conduct. They are contrasted in x. 9 with the Faith and the Righteousness of those who accept Grace.

1396. Their Faith is the cause as well as the instrument of their Guidance,—the Kindly Light which leads them as well as the Joy which fills their Soul. The usual symbols of Gardens and Fire are again contrasted,—in each case the result of Good or Evil in Life.

Beneath them will flow
Rivers in Gardens of Bliss.

تَحْتِهِمُ الْأَنْهٰرُ فِي جَنّٰتِ النَّعِيمِ ۝

10. (This will be) their cry therein:
"Glory to Thee, O God!"
And "Peace" will be their greeting therein!
And the close of their cry[1397]
Will be: "Praise be to God,
The Cherisher and Sustainer
Of the Worlds!"

١٠- دَعْوٰىهُمْ فِيهَا سُبْحٰنَكَ اللّٰهُمَّ
وَ تَحِيَّتُهُمْ فِيهَا سَلٰمٌ ۚ
وَ اٰخِرُ دَعْوٰىهُمْ
اَنِ الْحَمْدُ لِلّٰهِ رَبِّ الْعٰلَمِينَ ۝

SECTION 2.

11. If God were to hasten for men
The ill (they have earned)
As they would fain hasten on
The good,—then would
Their respite be settled at once.[1398]
But We leave those
Who rest not their hope
On their meeting with Us,
In their trespasses, wandering
In distraction to and fro.

١١- وَلَوْ يُعَجِّلُ اللّٰهُ لِلنَّاسِ الشَّرَّ
اسْتِعْجَالَهُمْ بِالْخَيْرِ لَقُضِيَ اِلَيْهِمْ
اَجَلُهُمْ ۖ
فَنَذَرُ الَّذِينَ لَا يَرْجُونَ لِقَآءَنَا
فِي طُغْيَانِهِمْ يَعْمَهُونَ ۝

12. When trouble toucheth a man,
He crieth unto Us
(In all postures)—lying down[1399]
On his side, or sitting,
Or standing. But when We
Have solved his trouble,
He passeth on his way as if
He had never cried to Us
For a trouble that touched him!
Thus do the deeds of transgressors
Seem fair in their eyes![1400]

١٢- وَاِذَا مَسَّ الْاِنْسَانَ الضُّرُّ دَعَانَا
لِجَنْبِهٖۤ اَوْ قَاعِدًا اَوْ قَآئِمًا ۚ
فَلَمَّا كَشَفْنَا عَنْهُ ضُرَّهٗ
مَرَّ كَاَنْ لَّمْ يَدْعُنَاۤ اِلٰى ضُرٍّ مَّسَّهٗ ۚ
كَذٰلِكَ زُيِّنَ لِلْمُسْرِفِينَ
مَا كَانُوا يَعْمَلُونَ ۝

1397. A beautiful piece of spiritual melody! They sing and shout with joy, but their joy is in the Glory of God! The greetings they receive and the greetings they give are of Peace and Harmony! From first to last they realise that it is God Who cherished them and made them grow, and His rays are their Light.

1398. Those who have no spiritual hope for the Future grasp at any temporary advantage, and in their blindness even mockingly ask for immediate punishment for their sins (viii. 32), thus vainly challenging God, in Whom they do not believe. If the beneficent God were to take them at their word, they would have no chance at all. Their doom would be sealed. But even the respite they get they use badly. They merely wander about distractedly like blind men, to and fro. *Cf.* ii. 15.

1399. Not only do men fail to use their respite: even those who have a superficial belief in God call on Him in their trouble but forget Him when He has relieved their trouble. Their Faith is not strong enough to make them realise that all good proceeds from God. But in moments of trouble they use every position, literally and figuratively, to appeal to Him.

1400. Those without Faith are selfish, and are so wrapped up in themselves that they think every good that comes to them is due to their own merits or cleverness. That is itself a cause of their undoing. They do not see their own faults.

13. Generations before you
We destroyed when they
Did wrong: their Apostles
Came to them with Clear Signs,
But they would not believe!
Thus do We requite
Those who sin!

١٣- وَلَقَدْ أَهْلَكْنَا الْقُرُونَ مِنْ قَبْلِكُمْ
لَمَّا ظَلَمُوا ۙ وَجَاءَتْهُمْ رُسُلُهُمْ بِالْبَيِّنَٰتِ
وَمَا كَانُوا لِيُؤْمِنُوا ۚ
كَذَٰلِكَ نَجْزِي الْقَوْمَ الْمُجْرِمِينَ ○

14. Then We made you heirs
In the land after them,
To see how ye would behave![1401]

١٤- ثُمَّ جَعَلْنَٰكُمْ خَلَٰٓئِفَ فِي الْأَرْضِ
مِنْ بَعْدِهِمْ لِنَنْظُرَ كَيْفَ تَعْمَلُونَ ○

15. But when Our Clear Signs
Are rehearsed unto them,
Those who rest not their hope
On their meeting with Us,
Say: "Bring us a Reading[1402]
Other than this, or change this,"
Say: "It is not for me,
Of my own accord,
To change it: I follow
Naught but what is revealed
Unto me: if I were
To disobey my Lord,
I should myself fear the Penalty
Of a Great Day (to come)."

١٥- وَإِذَا تُتْلَىٰ عَلَيْهِمْ آيَاتُنَا بَيِّنَٰتٍ ۙ
قَالَ الَّذِينَ لَا يَرْجُونَ لِقَاءَنَا
ائْتِ بِقُرْآنٍ غَيْرِ هَٰذَا أَوْ بَدِّلْهُ ۚ
قُلْ مَا يَكُونُ لِي
أَنْ أُبَدِّلَهُ مِنْ تِلْقَاءِ نَفْسِي ۖ
إِنْ أَتَّبِعُ إِلَّا مَا يُوحَىٰ إِلَيَّ ۖ إِنِّي أَخَافُ
إِنْ عَصَيْتُ رَبِّي عَذَابَ يَوْمٍ عَظِيمٍ ○

16. Say: "If God had so willed,
I should not have rehearsed it
To you, nor whould He
Have made it known to you.[1403]
A whole life-time before this
Have I tarried amongst you:
Will ye not then understand?"[1404]

١٦- قُلْ لَوْ شَاءَ اللَّهُ مَا تَلَوْتُهُ
عَلَيْكُمْ وَلَا أَدْرَاكُمْ بِهِ ۖ
فَقَدْ لَبِثْتُ فِيكُمْ عُمُرًا مِنْ قَبْلِهِ ۚ
أَفَلَا تَعْقِلُونَ ○

1401. This is addressed to the Quraish in the first instance, for they had succeeded to the Ad and the Thamūd heritage. But the application is universal, and was true of the 'Abbāsī Empire in the time of Hārūn-ar-Rashīd, or the Muslim Empire in Spain or the Turkish Empire in its palmiest days, and indeed, apart from political power, to the Muslims and non-Muslims of our own days.

1402. *Reading*: in the Arabic, the word is "*Qur-ān*", which may mean Reading or in the special sense, the Qur-ān. The duty of God's Messenger is to deliver God's Message as it is revealed to him, whether it please or displease those who hear it. Selfish men want to read their own desires or fancies into religious precepts, and thus they are often willing to use Religion for their own ends. Most of the corruptions of Religion are due to this cause. But Religion is not to be so prostituted.

1403. It is in God's Plan that He should reveal Himself in certain ways to His creatures, and His Messengers are the instruments that carry out His Will. It is in itself His gracious Mercy that He should thus make His Will known. We should be grateful for His guidance instead of carping at it.

1404. Muḥammad Muṣṭafā had lived his whole life of purity and virtue amongst his people, and they knew and acknowledged it before he received his mission. They knew he loved his nation and was loyal to it. Why should they turn against him when he had to point out under inspiration all their sins and wrong-doing? It was for their own good. And he had to plead again and again with them: "will you not understand, and see what a glorious privilege it is for you to receive true guidance from God?"

17. Who doth more wrong
Than such as forge a lie
Against God, or deny
His Signs? But never
Will prosper those who sin.

١٧- فَمَنْ أَظْلَمُ مِمَّنِ افْتَرَىٰ
عَلَى اللَّهِ كَذِبًا أَوْ كَذَّبَ بِآيَاتِهِ ۚ
إِنَّهُ لَا يُفْلِحُ الْمُجْرِمُونَ ۝

18. They serve, besides God,
Things that hurt them not
Nor profit them, and they say:
"These are our intercessors
With God." Say: "Do ye
Indeed inform God of something
He knows not, in the heavens[1405]
Or on earth?—Glory to Him!
And far is He above the partners
They ascribe (to Him)!"

١٨- وَيَعْبُدُونَ مِنْ دُونِ اللَّهِ مَا لَا
يَضُرُّهُمْ وَلَا يَنْفَعُهُمْ وَيَقُولُونَ هَٰؤُلَاءِ
شُفَعَاؤُنَا عِنْدَ اللَّهِ ۚ قُلْ أَتُنَبِّئُونَ اللَّهَ
بِمَا لَا يَعْلَمُ فِي السَّمَاوَاتِ وَلَا فِي الْأَرْضِ ۚ
سُبْحَانَهُ وَتَعَالَىٰ عَمَّا يُشْرِكُونَ ۝

19. Mankind was but one nation,[1406]
But differed (later). Had it not
Been for a Word[1407]
That went forth before
From thy Lord, their differences
Would have been settled
Between them.

١٩- وَمَا كَانَ النَّاسُ إِلَّا أُمَّةً وَاحِدَةً
فَاخْتَلَفُوا ۚ
وَلَوْلَا كَلِمَةٌ سَبَقَتْ مِنْ رَبِّكَ
لَقُضِيَ بَيْنَهُمْ فِيمَا فِيهِ يَخْتَلِفُونَ ۝

20. They say: "Why is not
A Sign sent down to him
From his Lord?" Say:
"The Unseen is only
For God (to know).
Then wait ye: I too

٢٠- وَيَقُولُونَ لَوْلَا أُنْزِلَ عَلَيْهِ آيَةٌ مِنْ
رَبِّهِ ۖ فَقُلْ إِنَّمَا الْغَيْبُ لِلَّهِ فَانْتَظِرُوا
إِنِّي مَعَكُمْ

1405. When we shut our eyes to God's glory and goodness, and go after false gods, we give some plausible excuse to ourselves, such as that they will intercede for us. But how can stocks and stones intercede for us? And how can men intercede for us, when they themselves have need of God's Mercy? Even the best and noblest cannot intercede as of right, but only with His permission (x. 3). To pretend that there are other powers than God is to invent lies and to teach God. There is nothing in heaven or earth that He does not know, and there is no other like unto Him.

1406. *Cf.* ii. 213. All mankind was created one, and God's Message to mankind is in essence one, the Message of Unity and Truth. But as selfishness and egotism got hold of man, certain differences sprang up between individuals, races, and nations, and in His infinite Mercy He sent them messengers and messages to suit their varying mentality, to test them by His gifts, and stir them up to emulation in virtue and piety (v. 51).

1407. Here we have again the mystic doctrine of "the Word". *Cf.* vi. 115, ix. 40, and iv. 171. "Word" is the Decree of God, the expression of His Universal Will or Wisdom in a particular case. When men began to diverge from one another (see last note), God made their very differences subserve the higher ends by increasing their emulation in virtue and piety, and thus pointing back to the ultimate Unity and Reality.

Will wait with you."[1408]

ع مِنَ الْمُنْتَظِرِينَ ۝

C. 100.—The good, the beautiful, and the useful
(x. 21-40.) In man's life are derived from God ;
Yet man is ungrateful. He runs
After the ephemeral things of this life ;
Yet they are no better than the green
Of the fields, that lasts for a season
Ere it perish ! God's call is to an eternal
Home of Peace Will ye not answer it ?
Know ye not that it is He Who sustains
And cherishes ? No partner has He.
And He speaks to His creatures and guides them
Through His wonderful Book uumatched.

SECTION 3.

21. When We make mankind
Taste of some mercy after
Adversity hath touched them,
Behold ! they take to plotting
Against Our Signs ! Say :
"Swifter to plan is God !"
Verily, Our messengers record
All the plots that ye make ![1409]

٢١- وَإِذَآ أَذَقْنَا النَّاسَ رَحْمَةً مِّنۢ بَعْدِ
ضَرَّآءَ مَسَّتْهُمْ إِذَا لَهُم مَّكْرٌ فِىٓ ءَايَاتِنَا ۚ
قُلِ اللَّهُ أَسْرَعُ مَكْرًا ۚ
إِنَّ رُسُلَنَا يَكْتُبُونَ مَا تَمْكُرُونَ ۝

22. He it is who enableth you
To traverse through land
And sea ; so that ye even board
Ships ;—they sail with them
With a favourable wind,
And they rejoice thereat ;
Then comes a stormy wind
And the waves come to them
From all sides, and they think
They are being overwhelmed :
They cry unto God, sincerely
Offering (their) duty unto Him,
Saying, "If Thou dost deliver us
From this, we shall truly

٢٢- هُوَ الَّذِى يُسَيِّرُكُمْ فِى الْبَرِّ وَالْبَحْرِ ۖ
حَتَّىٰٓ إِذَا كُنتُمْ فِى الْفُلْكِ ۚ
وَجَرَيْنَ بِهِم بِرِيحٍ طَيِّبَةٍ وَفَرِحُوا بِهَا
جَآءَتْهَا رِيحٌ عَاصِفٌ وَجَآءَهُمُ الْمَوْجُ
مِن كُلِّ مَكَانٍ وَظَنُّوٓا أَنَّهُمْ أُحِيطَ
بِهِمْ ۙ دَعَوُا اللَّهَ مُخْلِصِينَ لَهُ الدِّينَ ۚ
لَئِنْ أَنجَيْتَنَا مِنْ هَٰذِهِۦ

1408. Their demand for a Sign is disingenuous. All nature and revelation furnishes them with incontestable Signs. What they want is the Book of the Unseen opened out to them like the physical leaves of a book. But they forget that a physical Book is on a wholly different plane from God's Mysteries, and that their physical natures cannot apprehend the mysteries. They must wait. Truth will also wait. But the waiting in the two cases is in quite different senses. *Cf.* vi. 158 and ix. 52.

1409. Man turns his thoughts in adversity to the spiritual forces outside his ken. But as soon as the trouble is past, he not only forgets them but actually plots against them, as if they—and not he himself—had caused his trouble. But such people are poor ignorant creatures, not realising that the Universal Plan of God is swifter to stop their petty plans, and that though they fail, the record of them remains eternally against them.

Show our gratitude!"[1410]

لَنَكُوْنَنَّ مِنَ الشّٰكِرِيْنَ ○

23. But when he delivereth them,
Behold! they transgress
Insolently through the earth
In defiance of right!
O mankind! your insolence[1411]
Is against your own souls,—
An enjoyment of the life
Of the Present: in the end,
To Us is your return,
And We shall show you
The truth of all that ye did.

٢٣- فَلَمَّآ اَنْجٰىهُمْ اِذَا هُمْ
يَبْغُوْنَ فِى الْاَرْضِ بِغَيْرِ الْحَقِّ ؕ
يٰۤاَيُّهَا النَّاسُ اِنَّمَا بَغْيُكُمْ عَلٰٓى اَنْفُسِكُمْ ۙ
مَّتَاعَ الْحَيٰوةِ الدُّنْيَا ؗ
ثُمَّ اِلَيْنَا مَرْجِعُكُمْ
فَنُنَبِّئُكُمْ بِمَا كُنْتُمْ تَعْمَلُوْنَ ○

24. The likeness of the life
Of the Present is
As the rain which We
Send down from the skies:[1412]
By its mingling arises
The produce of the earth—
Which provides food
For men and animals:
(It grows) till the earth
Is clad with its golden
Ornaments and is decked out
(In beauty): the people to whom
It belongs think they have
All powers of disposal over it:
There reaches it Our command
By night or by day,
And We make it
Like a harvest clean-mown,
As if it had not flourished

٢٤- اِنَّمَا مَثَلُ الْحَيٰوةِ الدُّنْيَا
كَمَآءٍ اَنْزَلْنٰهُ مِنَ السَّمَآءِ
فَاخْتَلَطَ بِهٖ نَبَاتُ الْاَرْضِ
مِمَّا يَاْكُلُ النَّاسُ وَالْاَنْعَامُ ؕ
حَتّٰٓى اِذَآ اَخَذَتِ الْاَرْضُ زُخْرُفَهَا
وَازَّيَّنَتْ وَظَنَّ اَهْلُهَآ
اَنَّهُمْ قٰدِرُوْنَ عَلَيْهَآ ۙ
اَتٰىهَآ اَمْرُنَا لَيْلًا اَوْ نَهَارًا
فَجَعَلْنٰهَا حَصِيْدًا كَاَنْ لَّمْ

1410. All the great inventions and discoveries on which man prides himself are the fruit of that genius and talent which God has freely given of His grace. But the spirit of man remains petty, as is illustrated by the parable from the sea. How the heart of man rejoices when the ship goes smoothly with favourable winds! How in adversity it turns, in terror and helplessness, to God, and makes vows for deliverance! and how those vows are disregarded as soon as the danger is past! *Cf.* vi. 63.

1411. In our insolence and pride we do not see how small and ephemeral is that part of us which is mortal. We shall see it at last when we appear before our Judge. In the meantime our ridiculous pretensions only hurt ourselves.

1412. Another beautiful Parable, explaining the natute of our present life. The rain comes down in drops and mingles with the earth. Through it, by God's matchless artistry, the womb of the earth is made fruitful. All kinds of good, useful, and beautiful grains, vegetables, and fruits are produced for men and animals. The earth is covered in its bravery of green and gold and all kinds of colours. Perhaps the "owner" takes all the credit to himself, and thinks that this will last eternally. A hailstorm or a blast, a frost or a volcanic eruption, comes and destroys it; or it may be, even normally, that the time of harvest comes, and the fields and orchards are stripped bare by some blight or disease. Where is the beauty and bravery of yesterday? All that is left is dust and ashes! What more can we get from this physical material life?

Only the day before!
Thus do We explain
The Signs in detail
For those who reflect.

تَغْنَ بِالْأَمْسِ ۚ كَذَٰلِكَ نُفَصِّلُ الْآيَاتِ
لِقَوْمٍ يَتَفَكَّرُونَ ○

25. But God doth call
To the Home of Peace:[1413]
He doth guide whom He pleaseth
To a Way that is straight.

٢٥- وَاللَّهُ يَدْعُوا إِلَىٰ دَارِ السَّلَامِ ۖ
وَيَهْدِي مَن يَشَاءُ إِلَىٰ صِرَاطٍ مُّسْتَقِيمٍ ○

26. To those who do right
Is a goodly (reward)—
Yea, more (than in measure)![1414]
No darkness nor shame
Shall cover their faces![1415]
They are Companions of the Garden;
They will abide therein
(For aye)!

٢٦- لِّلَّذِينَ أَحْسَنُوا الْحُسْنَىٰ وَزِيَادَةٌ ۖ
وَلَا يَرْهَقُ وُجُوهَهُمْ قَتَرٌ وَلَا ذِلَّةٌ ۚ
أُولَٰئِكَ أَصْحَابُ الْجَنَّةِ ۖ
هُمْ فِيهَا خَالِدُونَ ○

27. But those who have earned
Evil will have a reward
Of like evil:[1416] ignominy
Will cover their (faces):
No defender will they have
From (the wrath of) God:
Their faces will be covered,
As it were, with pieces
From the depth of the darkness[1417]
Of Night: they are Companions

٢٧- وَالَّذِينَ كَسَبُوا السَّيِّئَاتِ جَزَاءُ سَيِّئَةٍ
بِمِثْلِهَا وَتَرْهَقُهُمْ ذِلَّةٌ ۖ
مَّا لَهُم مِّنَ اللَّهِ مِنْ عَاصِمٍ ۖ
كَأَنَّمَا أُغْشِيَتْ وُجُوهُهُمْ قِطَعًا مِّنَ
اللَّيْلِ مُظْلِمًا ۚ أُولَٰئِكَ أَصْحَابُ النَّارِ ۖ

1413. In contrast with the ephemeral and uncertain pleasures of this material life, there is a higher life to which God is always calling. It is called the Home of Peace. For there is no fear, nor disappointment, nor sorrow there. And all are called, and those will be chosen who have sought, not material advantages, but the Good Pleasure of God. *Salām*, Peace, is from the same root as *Islām*, the Religion of Unity and Harmony.

1414. The reward of the righteous will be far more than in proportion to their merits. For they will have the supreme bliss of being near to God, and (in Ṣūfī language) "seeing His face".

1415. The face is the symbol of the Personality, the inner and real Self, which is the antithesis of the outer and ephemeral Self. It will be illuminated with God's Light, behind which is no shadow or darkness. All its old shortcomings will be blotted out, with their sense of shame, for there will be Perfection, as in God's sight.

1416. Note that the evil reward is for those who have "earned" evil, *i.e.*, brought it on themselves by the delibera e choice of evil Further, in the justice of God, they will be requited with evil similar to, and not greater in quantity or intens ty, than the evil they had done,—unlike the good, who, in God's generosity, get a reward far greater than anything they have earned or could possibly earn.

1417. Night is the negation of Light and metaphorically of joy and felicity. The intensive is indicated by "the depth of the darkness of Night."

Of the Fire: they will
Abide therein (for aye)!

هُمْ فِيهَا خٰلِدُونَ ۝

28. One Day shall We gather them
All together. Then shall We say
To those who joined gods (with Us):
"To your place! ye and those
Ye joined as 'partners'."
We shall separate them,
And their "partners" shall say:
"It was not us
That ye worshipped![1418]

٢٨- وَيَوْمَ نَحْشُرُهُمْ جَمِيعًا ثُمَّ نَقُولُ
لِلَّذِينَ
أَشْرَكُوا مَكَانَكُمْ أَنْتُمْ وَشُرَكَآؤُكُمْ
فَزَيَّلْنَا بَيْنَهُمْ وَقَالَ شُرَكَآؤُهُمْ
مَّا كُنْتُمْ إِيَّانَا تَعْبُدُونَ ۝

29. "Enough is God for a witness
Between us and you: we
Certainly knew nothing
Of your worship of us!"[1419]

٢٩- فَكَفَىٰ بِاللَّهِ شَهِيدًا بَيْنَنَا وَبَيْنَكُمْ
إِنْ كُنَّا عَنْ عِبَادَتِكُمْ لَغٰفِلِينَ ۝

30. There will every soul prove
(The fruits of) the deeds
It sent before[1420]: they will
Be brought back to God
Their rightful Lord,
And their invented falsehoods
Will leave them in the lurch.[1421]

٣٠- هُنَالِكَ تَبْلُوا كُلُّ نَفْسٍ مَّآ أَسْلَفَتْ وَ
رُدُّوٓا إِلَى اللَّهِ مَوْلٰىهُمُ الْحَقِّ
وَضَلَّ عَنْهُمْ مَّا كَانُوا يَفْتَرُونَ ۝

SECTION 4.

31. Say: "Who is it that
Sustains you (in life)
From the sky and from the
earth?[1422]

٣١- قُلْ مَنْ يَرْزُقُكُمْ مِّنَ السَّمَآءِ وَ
الْأَرْضِ

1418. The false gods are not real: they are only the figments of the imaginations of those who indulged in the false worship. But the prophets or great or good men whose names were vainly taken in competition with the name of God, and the personified Ideas or Idols treated in the same way would themselves protest against their names being used in that way, and show that the worship was paid not to them, but to the ignorance or superstition or selfish lusts of the false worshippers.

1419. See last note. They did not even know that they were being falsely worshipped in that way.

1420. *Cf.* ii. 95, where the verb used is *qaddama*. The verb *aslafa*, used here, is nearly synonymous.

1421. Instead of their false ideas helping them, they will desert them and leave them in the lurch. *Cf.* vi. 24.

1422. Sustenance may be understood in the sense of all the provision necessary for maintaining physical life as well as mental and spiritual development and well-being. Examples of the former are light and rain from heaven and the produce of the earth and facilities of movement on land and sea and in air. Examples of the latter are the mora and spiritual influences that come from our fellow-men, and from the great Teachers and Prophets.

Or who is it that
Has power over hearing[1423]
And sight? And who
Is it that brings out
The living from the dead
And the dead from the living?[1424]
And who is it that
Rules and regulates all affairs?"[1425]
They will soon say, "God".
Say, "Will ye not then
Show piety (to Him)?"

أَمَّن يَمْلِكُ السَّمْعَ وَالْأَبْصَارَ
وَمَن يُخْرِجُ الْحَيَّ مِنَ الْمَيِّتِ
وَيُخْرِجُ الْمَيِّتَ مِنَ الْحَيِّ
وَمَن يُدَبِّرُ الْأَمْرَ
فَسَيَقُولُونَ اللَّهُ
فَقُلْ أَفَلَا تَتَّقُونَ ○

32. Such is God, your real
Cherisher and Sustainer:
Apart from Truth,
What (remains) but error?[1426]
How then are ye turned away?

٣٢- فَذَٰلِكُمُ اللَّهُ رَبُّكُمُ الْحَقُّ
فَمَاذَا بَعْدَ الْحَقِّ إِلَّا الضَّلَالُ
فَأَنَّىٰ تُصْرَفُونَ ○

33. Thus is the Word
Of thy Lord proved true[1427]
Against those who rebel:
Verily they will not believe.

٣٣- كَذَٰلِكَ حَقَّتْ كَلِمَتُ رَبِّكَ عَلَى
الَّذِينَ فَسَقُوا أَنَّهُمْ لَا يُؤْمِنُونَ ○

34. Say: "Of your 'partners',[1428]
Can any originate creation
And repeat it?" Say:
"It is God Who originates
Creation and repeats it:
Then how are ye deluded
Away (from the truth)?"

٣٤- قُلْ هَلْ مِن شُرَكَائِكُم مَّن يَبْدَؤُا
الْخَلْقَ ثُمَّ يُعِيدُهُ
قُلِ اللَّهُ يَبْدَؤُا الْخَلْقَ
ثُمَّ يُعِيدُهُ فَأَنَّىٰ تُؤْفَكُونَ ○

1423. Just two of our ordinary faculties, hearing and sight, are mentioned, as examples of the rest. All the gifts of God, physical and spiritual, are enjoyed and incorporated by us by means of the faculties and capacities with which He has endowed us.

1424. *Cf.* iii. 27 and n. 371; vi. 95 and n. 920; and xxx. 19.

1425. This is the general summing-up of the argument. The government of the whole Creation and its maintenance and sustenance is in the hands of God. How futile then would it be to neglect His true worship and go after false gods?

1426. The wonderful handiwork and wisdom of God having been referred to, as the real Truth, as against the false worship and false gods that men set up, it follows that to disregard the Truth must lead us into woeful wrong, not only in our beliefs but in our conduct. We shall err and stray and be lost. How then can we turn away from the Truth?

1427. Disobedience to God brings its own terrible consequences on ourselves. The Law, the Word, the Decree, of God must be fulfilled. If we go to false gods, our Faith will be dimmed, and then extinguished. Our spiritual faculties will be dead.

1428. The argument is now turned in another direction. The false gods can neither create out of nothing nor sustain the creative energy which maintains the world. Nor can they give any guidance which can be of use for the future destiny of mankind: on the contrary they themselves (assuming they were men who were deified) stand in need of such guidance. Why then follow vain fancies, instead of going to the source of all knowledge, truth, and guidance, and worship, serve, and obey the One True God?

35. Say : "Of your 'partners'
Is there any that
Can give any guidance
Towards Truth ?" Say : "It is God
Who gives guidance
Towards Truth. Is then He
Who gives guidance to Truth
More worthy to be followed,
Or he who finds not guidance
(Himself) unless he is guided ?
What then is the matter
With you ? How judge ye ?"

۳۵- قُلْ هَلْ مِنْ شُرَكَآئِكُمْ مَّنْ
يَّهْدِيْٓ اِلَى الْحَقِّ ۗ قُلِ اللّٰهُ يَهْدِيْ لِلْحَقِّ ۗ
اَفَمَنْ يَّهْدِيْٓ اِلَى الْحَقِّ
اَحَقُّ اَنْ يُّتَّبَعَ اَمَّنْ لَّا يَهِدِّيْٓ
اِلَّآ اَنْ يُّهْدٰى ۚ
فَمَا لَكُمْ ۗ كَيْفَ تَحْكُمُوْنَ ○

36. But most of them follow
Nothing but fancy : truly
Fancy can be of no avail
Against Truth. Verily God
Is well aware of all
That they do.

۳۶- وَمَا يَتَّبِعُ اَكْثَرُهُمْ اِلَّا ظَنًّا ۭ
اِنَّ الظَّنَّ لَا يُغْنِيْ مِنَ الْحَقِّ شَيْـًٔا ۭ
اِنَّ اللّٰهَ عَلِيْمٌۢ بِمَا يَفْعَلُوْنَ ○

37. This Qur-ān is not such
As can be produced
By other than God ;
On the contrary it is
A confirmation of (revelations)
That went before it,
And a fuller explanation[1429]
Of the Book—wherein
There is no doubt—
From the Lord of the Worlds.

۳۷- وَمَا كَانَ هٰذَا الْقُرْاٰنُ
اَنْ يُّفْتَرٰى مِنْ دُوْنِ اللّٰهِ
وَلٰكِنْ تَصْدِيْقَ الَّذِيْ بَيْنَ يَدَيْهِ
وَتَفْصِيْلَ الْكِتٰبِ
لَا رَيْبَ فِيْهِ مِنْ رَّبِّ الْعٰلَمِيْنَ ○

38. Or do they say,
"He forged it" ?
Say : "Bring then
A Sūra like unto it,
And call (to your aid)
Anyone you can,
Besides God, if it be
Ye speak the truth !"[1430]

۳۸- اَمْ يَقُوْلُوْنَ افْتَرٰىهُ ۭ
قُلْ فَاْتُوْا بِسُوْرَةٍ مِّثْلِهٖ
وَادْعُوْا مَنِ اسْتَطَعْتُمْ مِّنْ دُوْنِ اللّٰهِ
اِنْ كُنْتُمْ صٰدِقِيْنَ ○

1429. *The Book* : *Cf.* iii. 23 and n. 366. God's revelation throughout the ages is one. The Qur-ān confirms, fulfils, completes, and further explains the one true revelation, which has been sent by the One True God in all ages.

1430. *Cf.* ii. 23 and n. 42.

39. Nay, they charge with falsehood
That whose knowledge they
Cannot compass, even before
The elucidation thereof[1431]
Hath reached them: thus
Did those before them
Make charges of falsehood:
But see what was the end
Of those who did wrong![1432]

٣٩-بَلْ كَذَّبُوا بِمَا لَمْ يُحِيطُوا بِعِلْمِهِ
وَلَمَّا يَأْتِهِمْ تَأْوِيلُهُ ۚ
كَذَٰلِكَ كَذَّبَ الَّذِينَ مِن قَبْلِهِمْ
فَانظُرْ كَيْفَ كَانَ عَاقِبَةُ الظَّالِمِينَ ○

40. Of them there are some
Who believe therein,
And some who do not:
And thy Lord knoweth best
Those who are out for mischief.

٤٠-وَمِنْهُم مَّن يُؤْمِنُ بِهِ
وَمِنْهُم مَّن لَّا يُؤْمِنُ بِهِ ۚ
وَرَبُّكَ أَعْلَمُ بِالْمُفْسِدِينَ ○

C. 101.—Men but wrong their own souls in shutting out
(x. 41-70.) The Truth of God. To Him will be
Their return. They have been warned
At all times and among all peoples
By chosen Apostles of God, whom they
Have flouted. The Day will come
When they will see the majesty, the glory,
The goodness, and the justice of God.
But they invent fancies and falsehoods.
Let not their blasphemies and falsehoods
Grieve the men of God: for falsehoods
And false ones will never prosper.

SECTION 5.

41. If they charge thee
With falsehood, say:
"My work to me,
And yours to you![1433]

٤١-وَإِن كَذَّبُوكَ فَقُل
لِّي عَمَلِي وَلَكُمْ عَمَلُكُمْ ۖ

1431. *Taawīl*: elucidation, explanation, final fulfilment, *Cf.* vii. 53. The Message of God not only gives us rules for our every-day conduct, but speaks of high matters of mystic significance, which require elucidation in three ways: (1) by instruction from Teachers of great spiritual experience, (2) by experience from the actual facts of life, and (3) by the final fulfilment of the hopes and warnings which we now take on trust through our Faith. The Unbelievers reject God's Message simply because they cannot understand it and without giving it even a chance of elucidation in any of these ways.

1432 Wrong-doers always came to grief ultimately. The true course of history shows it from a broad standpoint. But they are so headstrong that they prejudge issues in their ignorance before they are decided.

1433. When the man of God is rejected and charged with falsehood, he does not give up his work, but continues to teach and preach his Message. He can well say to those who interfere with him: "Mind your own business: supposing your charge against me is true, you incur no responsibility: I have to answer for it before God: and if I do my duty and deliver my Message, your rejection does not make me liable for your wrong-doing: you will have to answer before God."

Ye are free from responsibility
For what I do, and I
For what ye do!"

أَنتُم بَرِيٓـُٔونَ مِمَّآ أَعۡمَلُ
وَأَنَا۠ بَرِيٓءٌ مِّمَّا تَعۡمَلُونَ ۝

42. Among them are some who
(Pretend to) listen to thee:
But canst thou make the deaf
To hear,—even though
They are without understanding?[1434]

٤٢- وَمِنۡهُم مَّن يَسۡتَمِعُونَ إِلَيۡكَۚ
أَفَأَنتَ تُسۡمِعُ ٱلصُّمَّ
وَلَوۡ كَانُواْ لَا يَعۡقِلُونَ ۝

43. And among them are some
Who look at thee:
But canst thou guide
The blind,—even though
They will not see?

٤٣- وَمِنۡهُم مَّن يَنظُرُ إِلَيۡكَۚ
أَفَأَنتَ تَهۡدِي ٱلۡعُمۡيَ
وَلَوۡ كَانُواْ لَا يُبۡصِرُونَ ۝

44. Verily God will not deal
Unjustly with man in aught:
It is man that wrongs
His own soul.[1435]

٤٤- إِنَّ ٱللَّهَ لَا يَظۡلِمُ ٱلنَّاسَ شَيۡـٔٗا
وَلَٰكِنَّ ٱلنَّاسَ أَنفُسَهُمۡ يَظۡلِمُونَ ۝

45. One day He will
Gather them together:
(It will be) as if
They had tarried[1436]
But an hour of a day:
They will recognise each other:[1437]
Assuredly those will be lost
Who denied the meeting
With God and refused
To receive true guidance.

٤٥- وَيَوۡمَ يَحۡشُرُهُمۡ كَأَن لَّمۡ يَلۡبَثُوٓاْ
إِلَّا سَاعَةٗ مِّنَ ٱلنَّهَارِ
يَتَعَارَفُونَ بَيۡنَهُمۡۚ
قَدۡ خَسِرَ ٱلَّذِينَ كَذَّبُواْ بِلِقَآءِ ٱللَّهِ
وَمَا كَانُواْ مُهۡتَدِينَ ۝

46. Whether We show thee
(Realised in thy life-time)
Some part of what We
Promise them,—or We

٤٦- وَإِمَّا نُرِيَنَّكَ
بَعۡضَ ٱلَّذِي نَعِدُهُمۡ أَوۡ

1434. *Cf.* vi. 25, 36, 39 and notes. Hypocrites go to hear and see some great Teacher, but they get no profit out of it because they are not sincerely seeking the truth. They are like the blind, or the deaf, or the imbeciles. It is impossible to guide them, because they have not the will to be guided.

1435. God cannot be blamed for man's evil, nor will He deal unjustly with man. He has given him faculties and means of guidance. If man goes wrong, it is because he wrongs himself.

1436. In eternity our life on this earth will look as if it had been just a little part of our little day, and so also will appear any interval between our death and the call to Judgment.

1437. We shall retain some perception of our mutual relations on earth, so that the righteous judgment which will be pronounced will be intelligible to us, and we shall be convinced of its righteousness.

Take thy soul (to Our Mercy)
(Before that),—in any case,
To Us is their return :
Ultimately God is witness.[1438]
To all that they do.

نَتَوَفَّيَنَّكَ فَإِلَيْنَا مَرْجِعُهُمْ
ثُمَّ اللّٰهُ شَهِيدٌ
عَلٰى مَا يَفْعَلُونَ ○

47. To every people (was sent)
An Apostle : when their Apostle[1439]
Comes (before them), the matter
Will be judged between them
With justice, and they
Will not be wronged.

٤٧- وَلِكُلِّ أُمَّةٍ رَّسُولٌ
فَإِذَا جَآءَ رَسُولُهُمْ قُضِيَ بَيْنَهُمْ بِالْقِسْطِ
وَهُمْ لَا يُظْلَمُونَ ○

48. They say : "When
Will this promise
Come to pass,—
If ye speak the truth ?"

٤٨- وَيَقُولُونَ مَتٰى هٰذَا الْوَعْدُ
إِنْ كُنْتُمْ صٰدِقِينَ ○

49. Say : "I have no power[1440]
Over any harm or profit
To myself except as God
Willeth. To every People[1441]
Is a term appointed :
When their term is reached,
Not an hour can they cause
Delay, nor (an hour) can they
Advance (it in anticipation)."

٤٩- قُلْ لَّآ أَمْلِكُ لِنَفْسِي ضَرًّا وَّلَا نَفْعًا
إِلَّا مَا شَآءَ اللّٰهُ
لِكُلِّ أُمَّةٍ أَجَلٌ
إِذَا جَآءَ أَجَلُهُمْ فَلَا يَسْتَأْخِرُونَ سَاعَةً
وَّلَا يَسْتَقْدِمُونَ ○

1438. The Apostle is assured that the end of evil is evil, just as the end of good is good. Whether this result is made plain before his very eyes in his own life-time or afterwards, makes no difference. The wicked should not rejoice if they are given rope and seem to have the upper hand for a time, nor should the righteous lose heart : for God's promise is sure and must come to pass. And in any case, the scales can only be partially, if at all, adjusted in this life. There is the final and complete adjustment on the Day of Judgment. God is All-Knowing, and all truth will be before Him.

1439. Every people or generation or nation had its Message or Messenger : God revealed Himself to it in some way or another. If that Messenger was ignored or rejected, or his Message was twisted or misused, the Day of Reckoning will come, when perfect justice will be done and the whole Truth revealed. The Unbelievers mockingly say : "If that is true, pray tell us when that Day will come !" The answer of the Messenger is : "It will come in good time : no one can either hasten or retard it. If you want me then to save you or if you fear that I shall harm you for your treatment of me, know that this matter is in the hands of God alone, Who will do perfect justice. Even in regard to myself, any harm or good that befalls me is by the command and in the power of God."

1440. *Cf.* vii. 188.

1441. This repeats vii. 34, but the significance is different in the two contexts. Here the reply is to the Unbelievers' mocking incredulity (see n. 1439) as to whether there is such a thing as a Hereafter : they suggest to the man of God that if his claim of inspiration from God is true, he should get them punished at once for rejecting him. In vii. 34 the reference is to the punishment of iniquity as described in vii. 33 : sin is not necessarily punished at once : every People or generation gets a chance ; when their term is fulfilled, the final adjustment is made.

50. Say: "Do ye see,—
If His punishment should come
To you by night or by day,—[1442]
What portion of it
Would the Sinners
Wish to hasten?

٥٠- قُلْ أَرَءَيْتُمْ إِنْ أَتَىٰكُمْ عَذَابُهُ
بَيَاتًا أَوْ نَهَارًا
مَّاذَا يَسْتَعْجِلُ مِنْهُ الْمُجْرِمُونَ ○

51. "Would ye then believe in it
At last, when it actually cometh
To pass? (It will then be said:)
'Ah! now? and ye wanted
(Aforetime) to hasten it on!'

٥١- أَثُمَّ إِذَا مَا وَقَعَ آمَنْتُمْ بِهِ
آلْئٰنَ وَقَدْ كُنْتُمْ بِهِ تَسْتَعْجِلُونَ ○

52. "At length will be said
To the wrong-doers: 'Taste ye
The enduring punishment![1443]
Ye get but the recompense
Of what ye earned!'"

٥٢- ثُمَّ قِيلَ لِلَّذِينَ ظَلَمُوا ذُوقُوا
عَذَابَ الْخُلْدِ
هَلْ تُجْزَوْنَ إِلَّا بِمَا كُنْتُمْ تَكْسِبُونَ ○

53. They seek to be informed
By thee: "Is that true?"
Say: "Aye! by my Lord!
It is the very truth!
And ye cannot frustrate it!"

٥٣- وَيَسْتَنْبِئُونَكَ أَحَقٌّ هُوَ
قُلْ إِي وَرَبِّي إِنَّهُ لَحَقٌّ
وَمَا أَنْتُمْ بِمُعْجِزِينَ ○

SECTION 6.

54. Every soul that hath sinned,
If it possessed all
That is on earth,
Would fain give it in ransom:[1444]

٥٤- وَلَوْ أَنَّ لِكُلِّ نَفْسٍ ظَلَمَتْ
مَا فِي الْأَرْضِ لَافْتَدَتْ بِهِ

1442. The mockery of Unbelievers will be turned into panic when the wrath of God descends on them. It may do so suddenly, by night or by day, when they least expect it. Will they then say of any bit of it: "Let it be hastened"?

1443. This will be the final doom, and they will themselves have brought it on themselves!

The psychology of the Unbelievers is here analysed and exposed. This particular argument begins at x. 47 and ends at x. 53. It begins with the general statement that every People has had due warning and explanation by means of an Apostle specially sent to them; that Apostle will be a relevant witness at the final Judgment, when the matter will be judged in perfect equity. Then follows a dialogue. The Unbelievers mock and say, "Why not bring on the Punishment now?" The reply to the Unbelievers is, "It will come in God's good time". The Believers are told to watch and see how the sinners would take it if the Punishment were to come at once. Would they not think it too sudden? When it actually comes, their panic will be indescribable. "Is that true?" say the Unbelievers. "It is the very truth," is the answer, "and nothing can ward it off."

1444. *Cf.* iii. 91.

They would declare (their)
repentance[1445]
When they see the Penalty:
But the judgment between them
Will be with justice,
And no wrong will be done
Unto them.

وَأَسَرُّوا النَّدَامَةَ لَمَّا رَأَوُا الْعَذَابَ ۚ
وَقُضِيَ بَيْنَهُمْ بِالْقِسْطِ
وَهُمْ لَا يُظْلَمُونَ ۝

55. Is it not (the case) that to God
Belongeth whatever is
In the heavens and on earth?
Is it not (the case) that
God's promise is assuredly true?
Yet most of them understand not.

٥٥- أَلَا إِنَّ لِلَّهِ مَا فِي السَّمٰوٰتِ وَالْأَرْضِ
أَلَا إِنَّ وَعْدَ اللَّهِ حَقٌّ
وَلٰكِنَّ أَكْثَرَهُمْ لَا يَعْلَمُونَ ۝

56. It is He who giveth life
And who taketh it,
And to Him shall ye
All be brought back.

٥٦- هُوَ يُحْيِي وَيُمِيتُ
وَإِلَيْهِ تُرْجَعُونَ ۝

57. O mankind! there hath come
To you a direction from your Lord
And a healing for the (diseases)[1446]
In your hearts,—and for those
Who believe, a Guidance
And a Mercy.

٥٧- يٰأَيُّهَا النَّاسُ قَدْ جَاءَتْكُمْ مَوْعِظَةٌ
مِنْ رَبِّكُمْ وَشِفَاءٌ لِمَا فِي الصُّدُورِ
وَهُدًى وَرَحْمَةٌ لِلْمُؤْمِنِينَ ۝

58. Say: "In the Bounty of God.
And in His Mercy,—in that
Let them rejoice": that is better
Than the (wealth) they hoard.

٥٨- قُلْ بِفَضْلِ اللَّهِ وَبِرَحْمَتِهِ فَبِذٰلِكَ
فَلْيَفْرَحُوا هُوَ خَيْرٌ مِمَّا يَجْمَعُونَ ۝

59. Say: "See ye what things[1447]
God hath sent down to you

٥٩- قُلْ أَرَءَيْتُمْ مَا أَنْزَلَ اللَّهُ

1445. *Declare their repentance*: the verb in the original is *asarrū*, which may mean either "declare" or "reveal" or else "conceal" or "hide". The classical Commentators are divided as to the meaning to be adopted here. If the first, which I prefer, the sense would be: "When the Penalty stares the sinners in the face, they would give anything to escape it, and they would even openly declare their repentance, which would be a source of shame and ignominy to them." If the latter meaning be taken, the sense would be: "They would give anything to escape the Penalty; but the hardest thing of all for them is frankly to confess and repent, and so they conceal their sense of shame and ignominy."

1446. Those who do wrong have a disease in their hearts, which will cause their spiritual death. God in His Mercy declares His Will to them, which should direct their lives and provide a healing for their spiritual disease. If they accept Faith, the remedy acts; they find themselves in right guidance and receive God's forgiveness and mercy. Surely those are far better gifts than material advantages, wealth, or possessions.

1447. "Sustenance" is to be taken in both the literal and the metaphorical sense. In the literal sense, what fine and varied things God has provided for us on land and in sea and air, in the vegetable, animal, and mineral kingdoms? Yet narrow minds put artificial barriers against their use. In the metaphorical sense, what enchanting fields of knowledge and spiritual endeavour are provided in our individual and social lives? And who is to say that some are lawful and others forbidden? Supposing they were so in special circumstances, it is not right to attribute artificial restrictions of that kind to God and falsely erect religious sanctions against them.

For sustenance? Yet ye
Hold forbidden some things
Thereof and (some things) lawful."
Say: "Hath God indeed
Permitted you, or do ye invent
(Things) to attribute to God?"

لَكُمْ مِّنْ رِّزْقٍ فَجَعَلْتُمْ مِّنْهُ حَرَامًا وَّ
حَلٰلًا ؕ قُلْ آٰللّٰهُ اَذِنَ لَكُمْ
اَمْ عَلَى اللّٰهِ تَفْتَرُوْنَ ○

60. And what think those
Who invent lies against God,
Of the Day of Judgment?[1448]
Verily God is full of Bounty
To mankind, but most
Of them are ungrateful.[1449]

٦٠- وَمَا ظَنُّ الَّذِيْنَ يَفْتَرُوْنَ عَلَى اللّٰهِ
الْكَذِبَ يَوْمَ الْقِيٰمَةِ ؕ اِنَّ اللّٰهَ لَذُوْ فَضْلٍ
عَلَى النَّاسِ وَلٰكِنَّ اَكْثَرَهُمْ لَا يَشْكُرُوْنَ ○ ع

Section 7.

61. In whatever business thou
Mayest be, and whatever portion
Thou mayest be reciting
From the Qur-ān,—and whatever
Deed ye (mankind) may be doing,—
We are Witnesses thereof
When ye are deeply engrossed
Therein. Nor is hidden
From thy Lord (so much as)
The weight of an atom
On the earth or in heaven.
And not the least
And not the greatest
Of these things but are recorded
In a clear Record.[1450]

٦١- وَمَا تَكُوْنُ فِىْ شَاْنٍ
وَّمَا تَتْلُوْا مِنْهُ مِنْ قُرْاٰنٍ
وَّلَا تَعْمَلُوْنَ مِنْ عَمَلٍ اِلَّا كُنَّا عَلَيْكُمْ
شُهُوْدًا اِذْ تُفِيْضُوْنَ فِيْهِ ؕ
وَمَا يَعْزُبُ عَنْ رَّبِّكَ مِنْ مِّثْقَالِ ذَرَّةٍ
فِى الْاَرْضِ وَلَا فِى السَّمَآءِ
وَلَآ اَصْغَرَ مِنْ ذٰلِكَ وَلَآ اَكْبَرَ
اِلَّا فِىْ كِتٰبٍ مُّبِيْنٍ ○

62. Behold! verily on the friends
Of God there is no fear,[1451]

٦٢- اَلَآ اِنَّ اَوْلِيَآءَ اللّٰهِ لَا خَوْفٌ عَلَيْهِمْ

1448. People who lie in Religion or invent false gods, or false worship,—have they any idea of the Day of Judgment, when they will be called to account, and will have to answer for their deeds?

1449. God is most kind, and gracious, and generous with His gifts of all kinds, material and spiritual. But men do not understand, and are ungrateful in forgetting the Giver of all and setting up false objects of worship and false standards of pride.

1450. There is nothing that men can do but God is a witness to it. We may be deeply engrossed in some particular thing and for the time being be quite unconscious of other things. But God's knowledge not only comprehends all things, but has all things actively before it. Nothing is hidden from Him. And His knowledge has another quality which human knowledge has not. Human knowledge is subject to time, and is obliterated by time. God's knowledge is like a Record and endures for ever. And His Record has a further quality which human records have not. The most permanent human record may be quite intelligible to those who make it but may be ambiguous to others and may become unintelligible with the progress of time, as happens almost invariably to the most enduring inscriptions from very ancient times: but in God's "Record" or knowledge there is no ambiguity, for it is independent of time, or place, or circumstance. This is the force of *Mubīn* ("clear") here.

1451. God's all-embracing knowledge and constant watchful care over all His creatures, may be a source of fear to sinners, but there is no fear for those whom He honours with His love and friendship,—neither in this world nor in the world to come.

Nor shall they grieve ;

وَلَا هُمْ يَحْزَنُوْنَ ۝

63. Those who believe
And (constantly) guard
Against evil ;—

٦٣-الَّذِيْنَ اٰمَنُوْا وَكَانُوْا يَتَّقُوْنَ ۝

64. For them are Glad Tidings,
In the life of the Present
And in the Hereafter :
No change can there be
In the Words of God.
This is indeed
The supreme Felicity.

٦٤-لَهُمُ الْبُشْرٰى فِى الْحَيٰوةِ الدُّنْيَا
وَفِى الْاٰخِرَةِ ؕ
لَا تَبْدِيْلَ لِكَلِمٰتِ اللّٰهِ ؕ
ذٰلِكَ هُوَ الْفَوْزُ الْعَظِيْمُ ۝ؕ

65. Let not their speech[1452]
Grieve thee : for all power
And honour belong to God :
It is He Who heareth
And knoweth (all things).

٦٥-وَلَا يَحْزُنْكَ قَوْلُهُمْ ۘ
اِنَّ الْعِزَّةَ لِلّٰهِ جَمِيْعًا ؕ
هُوَ السَّمِيْعُ الْعَلِيْمُ ۝

66. Behold ! verily to God
Belong all creatures,
In the heavens and on earth.
What do they follow
Who worship as His "partners"
Other than God ? They follow
Nothing but fancy, and
They do nothing but lie.[1453]

٦٦-اَلَآ اِنَّ لِلّٰهِ مَنْ فِى السَّمٰوٰتِ وَمَنْ
فِى الْاَرْضِ ؕ وَمَا يَتَّبِعُ الَّذِيْنَ يَدْعُوْنَ
مِنْ دُوْنِ اللّٰهِ شُرَكَآءَ ؕ اِنْ يَّتَّبِعُوْنَ اِلَّا
الظَّنَّ وَاِنْ هُمْ اِلَّا يَخْرُصُوْنَ ۝

67. He it is that hath
Made you the Night
That ye may rest therein,
And the Day to make
Things visible (to you).[1454]
Verily in this are Signs
For those who listen
(To His Message).

٦٧-هُوَ الَّذِيْ جَعَلَ لَكُمُ الَّيْلَ
لِتَسْكُنُوْا فِيْهِ وَالنَّهَارَ مُبْصِرًا ؕ
اِنَّ فِيْ ذٰلِكَ لَاٰيٰتٍ
لِّقَوْمٍ يَّسْمَعُوْنَ ۝

1452. Sometimes the words of the unrighteous or their revilings hurt or grieve the righteous man, but there is no occasion for either anger or sorrow : they have no power and they can do no real dishonour, for all power and honour are from God.

1453. All creatures are subject to God. If, therefore, any false worship is set up, the false gods—so called "partners"—are merely creatures of imagination or false inventions.

1454. Our physical life—and our higher life in so far as it is linked with the physical—is sustained by the alternation of rest and activity, and the fit environment for this alternation is the succession of Nights and Days in our physical world. The Day makes the things "visible to us"—a beautiful symbol, not only of the physical work for which we go about by day, but of the higher activities which are fitly associated with seeing, perception, and enquiry. Intuition (insight) is a little out of that circle because that may come by night, when our other faculties are resting.

68. They say, "God hath begotten
A son!"—Glory be to Him!
He is Self-Sufficient! His
Are all things in the heavens
And on earth! No warrant
Have ye for this! Say ye
About God what ye know not?

٦٨- قالوا اتخذ الله ولدا سبحنه
هو الغني له ما في السموت وما في
الارض ان عندكم من سلطن بهذا
اتقولون على الله ما لا تعلمون ○

69. Say: "Those who invent
A lie against God
Will never prosper."[1455]

٦٩- قل ان الذين يفترون على الله
الكذب لا يفلحون ○

70. A little enjoyment
In this world!—
And then, to Us
Will be their return.
Then shall We make them
Taste the severest Penalty
For their blasphemies.

٧٠- متاع في الدنيا ثم الينا مرجعهم
ثم نذيقهم العذاب الشديد
بما كانوا يكفرون ○

C. 102.—God works in His world—in mercy
(x. 71-92.) For His servants, and in just punishment
For those who do wrong. Thus was it
In Noah's story, for he worked unselfishly
For his people, though rejected of them.
So was it with Moses: he preached
To Pharaoh and the Egyptians, but most
Of them preferred falsehood and pride
To the Truth of God, and perished. Even
Pharaoh's confession of God at the last
Was too late, as his life had been spent
In luxury, pride, and oppression.

SECTION 8.

71. Relate to them the story[1456]
Of Noah. Behold! he said
To his People: "O my People,
If it be hard on your (mind)

٧١- واتل عليهم نبا نوح اذ قال لقومه
يقوم ان كان كبر عليكم

1455. In Quranic language "prosperity" refers both to our every-day life and to the higher life within us,—to the Present and the Future,—health and strength, opportunities and resources, a spirit of contentment, and the power of influencing others. Here there seems to be an extra touch of meaning. A liar not only deprives himself of prosperity in all senses, but his "lie" itself against God will not succeed: it will and must be found out.

1456. The reference to Noah's story here is only incidental, to illustrate a special point. The fuller story will be found in xi. 25-48, and in many other passages, *e.g.*, vii. 59-64, xxiii. 23-32, xxvi. 105-122, and xxxvii. 75-82. At each place there is a special point in the context. The special point here is that Noah's very life and preaching among his wicked people was a cause of offence to them. But he feared nothing, trusted in God, delivered his message, and was saved from the Flood.

That I should stay (with you)
And commemorate the Signs
Of God,—yet I put
My trust in God.
Get ye then an agreement
About your plan and among
Your Partners, so your plan[1457]
Be not to you dark and dubious.
Then pass your sentence on me,
And give me no respite.

مَّقَامِي وَتَذْكِيرِي بِآيَاتِ اللَّهِ
فَعَلَى اللَّهِ تَوَكَّلْتُ
فَأَجْمِعُوا أَمْرَكُمْ وَشُرَكَاءَكُمْ
ثُمَّ لَا يَكُنْ أَمْرُكُمْ عَلَيْكُمْ غُمَّةً
ثُمَّ اقْضُوا إِلَيَّ وَلَا تُنظِرُونِ ○

72. "But if ye turn back, (consider):
No reward have I asked[1458]
Of you: my reward is only
Due from God, and I
Have been commanded to be
Of those who submit
To God's Will (in Islām)."

٧٢- فَإِن تَوَلَّيْتُمْ فَمَا سَأَلْتُكُم مِّنْ أَجْرٍ
إِنْ أَجْرِيَ إِلَّا عَلَى اللَّهِ
وَأُمِرْتُ أَنْ أَكُونَ مِنَ الْمُسْلِمِينَ ○

73. They rejected him,
But We delivered him,
And those with him,
In the Ark, and We made
Them inherit (the earth),
While We overwhelmed
In the Flood those
Who rejected Our Signs.[1459]
Then see what was the end
Of those who were warned
(But heeded not)!

٧٣- فَكَذَّبُوهُ فَنَجَّيْنَاهُ
وَمَن مَّعَهُ فِي الْفُلْكِ
وَجَعَلْنَاهُمْ خَلَائِفَ
وَأَغْرَقْنَا الَّذِينَ كَذَّبُوا بِآيَاتِنَا
فَانظُرْ كَيْفَ كَانَ عَاقِبَةُ الْمُنذَرِينَ ○

74. Then after him We sent
(Many) apostles to their Peoples:
They brought them Clear Signs,
But they would not believe
What they had already rejected[1460]

٧٤- ثُمَّ بَعَثْنَا مِن بَعْدِهِ رُسُلًا إِلَىٰ قَوْمِهِمْ
فَجَاءُوهُم بِالْبَيِّنَاتِ
فَمَا كَانُوا لِيُؤْمِنُوا بِمَا كَذَّبُوا بِهِ مِن

1457. Firm in his sense of Truth from God, Noah plainly told his people to condemn him to death if they liked, openly and in concert, so that he should at least know who would listen to his Message and who would not. He wanted them to be frank and direct, for he feared nothing.

1458. The man of God preaches for the good of his people. But he claims no reward from them, but on the contrary is reviled, persecuted, banished, and often slain.

1459. *Cf.* vii. 64.

1460. I understand the meaning to be that there is a sort of spiritual influence descending from generation to generation, among the Unbelievers as among the men of Faith. In history we find the same spiritual problems in many ages,—denial of God's grace, defiance of God's law, rejection of God's Message. These influences cause the hearts of the contumacious to be sealed and impervious to the Truth. *Cf.* ii. 7 and notes. What they do is to prejudge the issues even before the Prophet explains them.

Beforehand. Thus do We seal
The hearts of the transgressors.

قَبْلُ ۚ كَذٰلِكَ نَطْبَعُ عَلٰى قُلُوْبِ الْمُعْتَدِيْنَ ۝

75. Then after them sent We
Moses and Aaron to Pharaoh[1461]
And his chiefs with Our Signs.
But they were arrogant:
They were a people in sin.

٧٥- ثُمَّ بَعَثْنَا مِنْۢ بَعْدِهِمْ مُّوْسٰى وَ
هٰرُوْنَ اِلٰى فِرْعَوْنَ وَمَلَا۠ئِهٖ بِاٰيٰتِنَا
فَاسْتَكْبَرُوْا وَكَانُوْا قَوْمًا مُّجْرِمِيْنَ ۝

76. When the Truth did come
To them from Us, they said:
"This is indeed evident sorcery!"

٧٦- فَلَمَّا جَآءَهُمُ الْحَقُّ مِنْ عِنْدِنَا
قَالُوْٓا اِنَّ هٰذَا لَسِحْرٌ مُّبِيْنٌ ۝

77. Said Moses: "Say ye (this)
About the Truth when
It hath (actually) reached you?
Is sorcery (like) this?
But sorcerers will not prosper."[1462]

٧٧- قَالَ مُوْسٰٓى اَتَقُوْلُوْنَ لِلْحَقِّ لَمَّا جَآءَكُمْ ۭ
اَسِحْرٌ هٰذَا ۭ
وَلَا يُفْلِحُ السّٰحِرُوْنَ ۝

78. They said: "Hast thou
Come to us to turn us
Away from the ways
We found our fathers following,—
In order that thou and thy brother
May have greatness in the land?[1463]
But not we shall believe in you!"

٧٨- قَالُوْٓا اَجِئْتَنَا لِتَلْفِتَنَا عَمَّا وَجَدْنَا عَلَيْهِ
اٰبَآءَنَا وَتَكُوْنَ لَكُمَا الْكِبْرِيَآءُ فِى
الْاَرْضِ ۭ
وَمَا نَحْنُ لَكُمَا بِمُؤْمِنِيْنَ ۝

79. Said Pharaoh: "Bring me
Every sorcerer well versed."

٧٩- وَقَالَ فِرْعَوْنُ ائْتُوْنِىْ بِكُلِّ سٰحِرٍ عَلِيْمٍ ۝

80. When the sorcerers came,
Moses said to them:
"Throw ye what ye (wish)
To throw!"

٨٠- فَلَمَّا جَآءَ السَّحَرَةُ قَالَ لَهُمْ مُّوْسٰٓى
اَلْقُوْا مَآ اَنْتُمْ مُّلْقُوْنَ ۝

1461. The story of Moses, Aaron, and Pharaoh is fully told in vii. 103-137, and there are references to it in many places in the Qur-ān. The incidental reference here is to illustrate a special point, *viz.*, that the wicked are arrogant and bound up in their sin, and prefer deception to Truth: they do not hesitate to charge the men of God, who work unselfishly for them, with mean motives, such as would actuate them in similar circumstances!

1462. Sorcery is the very opposite of Truth,—being deception or plausible shows by the powers of evil. But these cannot succeed or last permanently, and Truth must ultimately prevail.

1463. Notice how they attribute evil motives to the men of God, motives of ambition and lust of power, which the men of God had been sent expressly to put down. The same device was used against Muṣṭafā.

81. When they had had their throw,[1464]
Moses said : " What ye
Have brought is sorcery :
God will surely make it
Of no effect : for God
Prospereth not the work
Of those who make mischief.

٨١- فَلَمَّآ أَلْقَوْا قَالَ مُوسٰى
مَا جِئْتُم بِهِ السِّحْرُ ط
إِنَّ اللّٰهَ سَيُبْطِلُهُ ط
إِنَّ اللّٰهَ لَا يُصْلِحُ عَمَلَ الْمُفْسِدِينَ ۝

82. " And God by His Words[1465]
Doth prove and establish
His Truth, however much
The Sinners may hate it ! "

٨٢- وَيُحِقُّ اللّٰهُ الْحَقَّ بِكَلِمٰتِهِ
وَلَوْ كَرِهَ الْمُجْرِمُونَ ۝

SECTION 9.

83. But none believed in Moses
Except some children of his
People,[1466]
Because of the fear of Pharaoh
And his chiefs, lest they
Should persecute them ; and
certainly
Pharaoh was mighty on the earth
And one who transgressed all
bounds.

٨٣- فَمَآ اٰمَنَ لِمُوسٰى إِلَّا ذُرِّيَّةٌ مِّنْ
قَوْمِهِ عَلٰى خَوْفٍ مِّنْ فِرْعَوْنَ وَمَلَا۟ئِهِمْ
أَنْ يَّفْتِنَهُمْ ط
وَإِنَّ فِرْعَوْنَ لَعَالٍ فِي الْأَرْضِ ج
وَإِنَّهُ لَمِنَ الْمُسْرِفِينَ ۝

84. Moses said : " O my People !
If ye do (really) believe
In God, then in Him
Put your trust if ye
Submit (your will to His)."

٨٤- وَقَالَ مُوسٰى يٰقَوْمِ إِنْ كُنْتُمْ اٰمَنْتُمْ
بِاللّٰهِ فَعَلَيْهِ
تَوَكَّلُوْٓا إِنْ كُنْتُمْ مُّسْلِمِينَ ۝

85. They said : " In God
Do we put our trust.

٨٥- فَقَالُوا عَلَى اللّٰهِ تَوَكَّلْنَا ج

1464. When they threw their rods, the rods became snakes by a trick of sorcery, but Moses's miracles were greater than any tricks of sorcery, and had real Truth behind them.

1465. God's Words or Commands have real power, while sorcerers' tricks only seem wonderful by deceiving the eye.

1466. The pronoun "his" in "his People" is taken by some Commentators to refer to Pharaoh. The majority of Pharaoh's people refused to believe at the time, but the sorcerers believed (vii. 120, and so did Pharaoh's wife (lxvi. 11), and ultimately Pharaoh himself, though too late (x. 90). If we took "his" to refer to Moses, it would mean that the Israelites were hard-hearted and grumbled (vii. 129) even when they were being delivered from Egypt, and only a few of them had any real faith in God's providence and the working of His Law, and they feared Pharaoh even more than they feared God.

Our Lord! make us not
A trial for those[1467]
Who practise oppression;

رَبَّنَا لَا تَجْعَلْنَا فِتْنَةً لِّلْقَوْمِ الظَّٰلِمِينَ ۝

86. "And deliver us by Thy Mercy
From those who reject (Thee)."

٨٦- وَنَجِّنَا بِرَحْمَتِكَ مِنَ الْقَوْمِ الْكَٰفِرِينَ ۝

87. We inspired Moses and his brother
With this Message: "Provide[1468]
Dwellings for your People
In Egypt, make your dwellings
Into places of worship,
And establish regular prayers:
And give Glad Tidings
To those who believe!"

٨٧- وَأَوْحَيْنَآ إِلَىٰ مُوسَىٰ وَأَخِيهِ
أَن تَبَوَّءَا لِقَوْمِكُمَا بِمِصْرَ بُيُوتًا وَاجْعَلُوا
بُيُوتَكُمْ قِبْلَةً
وَأَقِيمُوا الصَّلَوٰةَ
وَبَشِّرِ الْمُؤْمِنِينَ ۝

88. Moses prayed: "Our Lord!
Thou hast indeed bestowed
On Pharaoh and his Chiefs
Splendour and wealth in the life[1469]
Of the Present, and so,
Our Lord, they mislead (men)
From Thy Path. Deface.
Our Lord, the features of their wealth,[1470]
And send hardness to their hearts,
So they will not believe

٨٨- وَقَالَ مُوسَىٰ رَبَّنَآ إِنَّكَ ءَاتَيْتَ
فِرْعَوْنَ وَمَلَأَهُۥ زِينَةً وَأَمْوَٰلًا فِي الْحَيَوٰةِ
الدُّنْيَا
رَبَّنَا لِيُضِلُّوا عَن سَبِيلِكَ
رَبَّنَا اطْمِسْ عَلَىٰٓ أَمْوَٰلِهِمْ
وَاشْدُدْ عَلَىٰ قُلُوبِهِمْ فَلَا يُؤْمِنُوا

1467. *A trial for those who practise oppression*: the various meanings of *Fitnat* have been explained in n. 1198 to viii. 25. The prayer is that the righteous people, being weak, should be saved from being used as objects of oppression or punishment at the hands of powerful enemies. Weakness tempts Power to practise oppression, and is thus an occasion of trial for the oppressors.

1468. This instruction, we may suppose, was given when the sorcerers were brought to confusion, and some of the Egyptians believed. Moses was for a little while to remain in Egypt, so that his Message should have time to work, before the Israelites were led out of Egypt. They were to make their houses into places of prayer (*Qibla*), as Pharaoh would not probably allow them to set up public places of prayer, and they were now to be only sojourners in Egypt. The Qibla was to be symbolical of their later wanderings in Arabia, and the still later restoration of God's pure worship at the Ka'ba under Mustafā. These were the glad tidings (the Gospel) of Islam, which was preached under Noah, Abraham, Moses, and Jesus, and completed under Muḥammad.

1469. Moses's prayer, in which Aaron joined, for he was always with him, may be paraphrased thus: "O God! we understand that the glitter and the wealth of the Egyptians are not to be envied. They are but the ephemeral goods of this life. They are a disadvantage, in that in their pride of possessions the Egyptians mislead themselves and others. Let their pride be their undoing! Turn their wealth into bitterness and their hearts into hardness, for they reject Thee, and they will not believe until they actually see the Punishment of their sins!"

1470. A terrible curse! Let their wealth and splendour become so defaced in their features, that instead of being objects of desire, they become objects of loathing! The heart is the seat of affections and joy: let it be so hardened by their unbelief that it becomes the seat of hatred and grief! It is when they see the Penalty that they will believe!

Until they see
The grievous Penalty."

حَتّٰى يَرَوُا الْعَذَابَ الْاَلِيْمَ ○

89. God said: "Accepted is
Your prayer (O Moses and Aaron)!
So stand ye straight,
And follow not the path
Of those who know not."[1471]

٨٩- قَالَ قَدْ اُجِيْبَتْ دَّعْوَتُكُمَا فَاسْتَقِيْمَا
وَلَا تَتَّبِعٰٓنِّ سَبِيْلَ الَّذِيْنَ لَا يَعْلَمُوْنَ ○

90. We took the Children
Of Israel across the sea:
Pharaoh and his hosts followed them
In insolence and spite.[1472]
At length, when overwhelmed
With the flood, he said:
"I believe that there is no god
Except Him Whom the Children
Of Israel believe in:[1473]
I am of those who submit
(To God in Islām)."

٩٠- وَجٰوَزْنَا بِبَنِيْٓ اِسْرَآءِيْلَ الْبَحْرَ
فَاَتْبَعَهُمْ فِرْعَوْنُ وَجُنُوْدُهٗ بَغْيًا وَّعَدْوًا
حَتّٰٓى اِذَآ اَدْرَكَهُ الْغَرَقُ
قَالَ اٰمَنْتُ اَنَّهٗ لَآ اِلٰهَ اِلَّا
الَّذِيْٓ اٰمَنَتْ بِهٖ بَنُوْٓا اِسْرَآءِيْلَ
وَاَنَا مِنَ الْمُسْلِمِيْنَ ○

91. (It was said to him:)
"Ah now!—But a little while
Before, wast thou in rebellion!—
And thou didst mischief (and violence)!

٩١- آٰلْـٰٔنَ وَقَدْ عَصَيْتَ قَبْلُ
وَكُنْتَ مِنَ الْمُفْسِدِيْنَ ○

92. "This day shall We save thee
In thy body, that thou
Mayest be a Sign to those
Who come after thee!
But verily, many among mankind
Are heedless of Our Signs!"

٩٢- فَالْيَوْمَ نُنَجِّيْكَ بِبَدَنِكَ لِتَكُوْنَ
لِمَنْ خَلْفَكَ اٰيَةً ؕ وَاِنَّ كَثِيْرًا مِّنَ
النَّاسِ عَنْ اٰيٰتِنَا لَغٰفِلُوْنَ ○ ع

C. 103.—God's purpose of Mercy and Forgiveness
(x. 93-109.) Was shown in the mission of Jonah, when
Nineveh was pardoned on repentance, and given
A new lease of life. We must

1471. Be not dazzled by their splendour, but stand out straight for Truth, for that is your salvation! Addressed in form to Moses and Aaron, in substance it is addressed to the Israelites.

1472. Notice the swiftness of the action in the narrative. The execution of poetic justice could not have been described in fewer words.

1473. That is, in the One True God. This was death-bed repentance, and even so it was forced by the terror of the catastrophe. So it was not accepted (*cf.* iv. 18) in its entirety. Only this concession was made, that the body was saved from the sea, and presumably, according to Egyptian custom, it was embalmed and the mummy was given due rites of the dead. But the story commemorated for ever God's working, in mercy for His people, and in just punishment of oppressors.

Be patient and strive with constancy and perseverance,
For all suffering and sorrow as well as
All bounties proceed from God, Whose plan
Is righteous and for the good of His creatures.

SECTION 10.

93. We settled the Children
Of Israel in a beautiful[1474]
Dwelling-place, and provided
For them sustenance of the best:
It was after knowledge had been
Granted to them, that they
Fell into schisms. Verily
God will judge between them
As to the schisms amongst them,
On the Day of Judgment.

٩٣- وَلَقَدْ بَوَّأْنَا بَنِيٓ إِسْرَآءِيلَ مُبَوَّأَ
صِدْقٍ وَّرَزَقْنٰهُمْ مِّنَ الطَّيِّبٰتِ
فَمَا اخْتَلَفُوْا حَتّٰى جَآءَهُمُ الْعِلْمُ
إِنَّ رَبَّكَ يَقْضِيْ بَيْنَهُمْ يَوْمَ الْقِيٰمَةِ
فِيْمَا كَانُوْا فِيْهِ يَخْتَلِفُوْنَ ○

94. If thou wert in doubt
As to what We have revealed
Unto thee, then ask those
Who have been reading
The Book from before thee:[1475]
The Truth hath indeed come
To thee from thy Lord:
So be in no wise
Of those in doubt.[1476]

٩٤- فَإِنْ كُنْتَ فِيْ شَكٍّ مِّمَّآ أَنْزَلْنَآ إِلَيْكَ
فَسْئَلِ الَّذِيْنَ يَقْرَءُوْنَ الْكِتٰبَ مِنْ
قَبْلِكَ
لَقَدْ جَآءَكَ الْحَقُّ مِنْ رَّبِّكَ
فَلَا تَكُوْنَنَّ مِنَ الْمُمْتَرِيْنَ ○

95. Nor be of those who reject
The Signs of God,
Or thou shalt be of those
Who perish.

٩٥- وَلَا تَكُوْنَنَّ مِنَ الَّذِيْنَ كَذَّبُوْا بِاٰيٰتِ
اللّٰهِ فَتَكُوْنَ مِنَ الْخٰسِرِيْنَ ○

96. Those against whom the Word
Of thy Lord hath been verified[1477]

٩٦- إِنَّ الَّذِيْنَ حَقَّتْ عَلَيْهِمْ كَلِمَتُ رَبِّكَ

1474. After many wanderings the Israelites were settled in the land of Canaan, described as "a land flowing with milk and honey" (Exod. iii. 8). They had a prosperous land; and they were supplied with spiritual sustenance by men sent to deliver God's Message. They should have known better than to fall into disputes and schisms, but they did so. This was all the more inexcusable considering what bounties they had received from God. The schisms arose from selfish arrogance, and God will judge between them on the Day of Judgment.

1475. God's Truth is all one, and even in different forms men sincere in Religion recognise the oneness. So sincere Jews like 'Abdullāh ibn Salām, and sincere Christians like Waraqa or the Nestorian monk Bahīra, were ready to recognise the mission of Muḥammad Muṣṭafā. "The Book" in this connection is Revelation generally, including pre-Islamic revelations.

1476. *Cf.* iii. 60 and n. 399.

1477. God has given frequent warnings against Evil and want of Faith in all ages, through Signs and through inspiration,—the latter ("the Word") being even more direct and personal than the former. Those who did not heed the warning found to their cost that it was true, and they perished. Such contumacy in the rejection of Truth only yields when the actual penalty is in sight. Belief then is induced by irresistible facts: it is not efficacious as Faith, as was proved against Pharaoh. See x. 90 and n. 1473.

Would not believe—

لَا يُؤْمِنُونَ ۝

97. Even if every Sign was brought
Unto them,—until they see
(For themselves) the Penalty
Grievous.

٩٧- وَلَوْ جَآءَتْهُمْ كُلُّ ءَايَةٍ
حَتَّىٰ يَرَوُا الْعَذَابَ الْأَلِيمَ ۝

98. Why was there not
A single township (among those
We warned), which believed,—
So its Faith should have
Profited it,—except the People[1478]
Of Jonah? When they believed,
We removed from them
The Penalty of Ignominy
In the life of the Present,
And permitted them to enjoy
(Their life) for a while.[1479]

٩٨- فَلَوْلَا كَانَتْ قَرْيَةٌ
ءَامَنَتْ فَنَفَعَهَآ إِيمَانُهَآ إِلَّا قَوْمَ
يُونُسَ
لَمَّآ ءَامَنُوا كَشَفْنَا عَنْهُمْ عَذَابَ الْخِزْيِ
فِي الْحَيَوٰةِ الدُّنْيَا
وَمَتَّعْنَٰهُمْ إِلَىٰ حِينٍ ۝

99. If it had been thy Lord's Will,
They would all have believed,—
All who are on earth!
Wilt thou then compel mankind,

٩٩- وَلَوْ شَآءَ رَبُّكَ لَءَامَنَ مَن فِي الْأَرْضِ
كُلُّهُمْ جَمِيعًا ۚ أَفَأَنتَ تُكْرِهُ النَّاسَ

1478. God in His infinite Mercy points out the contumacy of Sin as a warning, and the exceptional case of Nineveh and its Prophet Jonah is alluded to. The story of Jonah is told in xxxvii. 139-148, which would be an appropriate place for further comments. Here it is sufficient to note that Nineveh was a very ancient town which is now no longer on the map. Its site is believed to be marked by the two mounds on the left bank of the Tigris, opposite the flourishing city of Mosul on the right bank, about 230 miles north-north-west of Bagdād. One of the mounds bears the name of "the Tomb of Nabī Yūnus." Archæologists have not yet fully explored its antiquities. But it is clear that it was a very old Sumerian town, perhaps older than 3500 B.C. It became the capital of Assyria. The first Assyrian Empire under Shalmanesser I, about 1300 B.C., became the supreme power in Western Asia. Babylon, whose tributary Assyria had formerly been, now became tributary to Assyria. The second Assyrian Empire arose about 745 B.C., and Sennacherib (705-681 B.C.) beautified the town with many Public Works. It was destroyed by the Scythians (so-called Medes) in 612 B.C. If the date of Jonah were assumed to be about 800 B.C., it would be between the First and the Second Assyrian Empire; when the City was nearly destroyed for its sins, but on account of its repentance was given a new lease of glorious life in the Second Empire.

1479. The point of the allusion here may be thus explained. Nineveh was a great and glorious City. But it became, like Babylon, a city of sin. God sent the prophet Yūnus (Jonah) to warn it. Full of iniquities though it was, it listened to the warning, perhaps in the person of a few just men. For their sakes, the All-Merciful God spared it, and gave it a new lease of glorious life. According to the chronology in the last note the new lease would be for about two centuries, after which it perished completely for its sins and abominations. Note that its new lease of life was for its collective life as a City, the life of the Present, *i.e.*, of this World. It does not mean that individual sinners escaped the spiritual consequences of their sin, unless they individually repented and obtained God's mercy and forgiveness.

Against their will, to believe![1480]

حَتّٰى يَكُوْنُوْا مُؤْمِنِيْنَ ○

100. No soul can believe, except
By the Will of God,[1481]
And He will place Doubt[1482]
(Or obscurity) on those
Who will not understand.

١٠٠- وَمَا كَانَ لِنَفْسٍ اَنْ تُؤْمِنَ اِلَّا
بِاِذْنِ اللّٰهِ ؕ وَيَجْعَلُ الرِّجْسَ عَلَى الَّذِيْنَ
لَا يَعْقِلُوْنَ ○

101. Say: "Behold all that is
In the heavens and on earth";
But neither Signs nor Warners
Profit those who believe not.[1483]

١٠١- قُلِ انْظُرُوْا مَاذَا فِى السَّمٰوٰتِ وَ
الْاَرْضِ ؕ وَمَا تُغْنِى الْاٰيٰتُ وَالنُّذُرُ
عَنْ قَوْمٍ لَّا يُؤْمِنُوْنَ ○

102. Do they then expect
(Any thing) but (what happened
In) the days of the men
Who passed away before them?
Say: "Wait ye then:
For I, too, will wait with you."[1484]

١٠٢- فَهَلْ يَنْتَظِرُوْنَ اِلَّا مِثْلَ اَيَّامِ
الَّذِيْنَ خَلَوْا مِنْ قَبْلِهِمْ ؕ قُلْ فَانْتَظِرُوْٓا
اِنِّىْ مَعَكُمْ مِّنَ الْمُنْتَظِرِيْنَ ○

1480. If it had been God's Plan or Will not to grant the limited Free-will that He has granted to man, His omnipotence could have made all mankind alike: all would then have had Faith, but that Faith would have reflected no merit on them. In the actual world as it is, man has been endowed with various faculties and capacities, so that he should strive and explore, and bring himself into harmony with God's Will Hence Faith becomes a moral achievement, and to resist Faith becomes a sin. As a complementary proposition, men of Faith must not be impatient or angry if they have to contend against Unfaith, and most important of all, they must guard against the temptation of forcing Faith, *i.e.*, imposing it on others by physical compulsion, or any other forms of compulsion such as social pressure, or inducements held out by wealth or position, or other adventitious advantages. Forced faith is no faith. They should strive spiritually and let God's Plan work as He wills.

1481. To creatures endued with Will, Faith comes out of an active use of that Will. But we must not be so arrogant as to suppose that that is enough At best man is weak, and is in need of God's grace and help. If we sincerely wish to understand, He will help our Faith; but if not, our doubts and difficulties will only be increased. This follows as a necessary consequence, and in Quranic language all consequences are ascribed to God, the Cause of Causes.

1482. *Rijs* (from *rajisa, yarjasu*, or *rajusa, yarjusu*) has various meanings: *e.g.*, (1) filth, impurity, uncleanness, abomination, as in ix. 95; (2) hence, filthy deeds, foul conduct, crime, abomination, thus shading off into (1), as in v. 93; (3) hence punishment for crime, penalty, as in vi. 125; (4) a form of such punishment, *viz.*, doubt, obscurity, or unsettlement of mind, anger, indignation, as in ix. 125, and here, but perhaps the idea of punishment is also implied here.

1483. If Faith results from an active exertion of our spiritual faculties or understanding, it follows that if we let these die, God's Signs in His Creation or in the spoken Word which comes by inspiration through the mouths of His Messengers will not reach us any more than music reaches a deaf man.

1484. *Cf.* x. 20 and n. 1408. The argument about God's revelation of Himself to man was begun in those early sections of this Sūra and is being now rounded off towards the end of this Sūra with the same formula.

103. In the end We deliver
Our apostles and those who
believe:
Thus is it fitting on Our part
That We should deliver
Those who believe!

١٠٣- ثُمَّ نُنَجِّي رُسُلَنَا وَالَّذِينَ آمَنُوا
كَذَٰلِكَ
حَقًّا عَلَيْنَا نُنجِ الْمُؤْمِنِينَ ○

Section 11.

104. Say: "O ye men!
If ye are in doubt
As to my religion, (behold!)[1485]
I worship not what ye
Worship, other than God!
But I worship God—
Who will take your souls[1486]
(At death): I am commanded[1487]
To be (in the ranks)
Of the Believers,[1488]

١٠٤- قُلْ يَا أَيُّهَا النَّاسُ إِن كُنتُمْ فِي
شَكٍّ مِّن دِينِي فَلَا أَعْبُدُ الَّذِينَ
تَعْبُدُونَ مِن دُونِ اللَّهِ
وَلَٰكِنْ أَعْبُدُ اللَّهَ الَّذِي يَتَوَفَّاكُمْ
وَأُمِرْتُ أَنْ أَكُونَ مِنَ الْمُؤْمِنِينَ ○

105. "And further (thus): 'set thy face
Towards Religion with true piety,
And never in any wise
Be of the Unbelievers;

١٠٥- وَأَنْ أَقِمْ وَجْهَكَ لِلدِّينِ حَنِيفًا
وَلَا تَكُونَنَّ مِنَ الْمُشْرِكِينَ ○

106. "'Nor call on any,
Other than God;—
Such will neither profit thee
Nor hurt thee: if thou dost,
Behold! thou shalt certainly
Be of those who do wrong.'"

١٠٦- وَلَا تَدْعُ مِن دُونِ اللَّهِ
مَا لَا يَنفَعُكَ وَلَا يَضُرُّكَ
فَإِن فَعَلْتَ فَإِنَّكَ إِذًا مِّنَ الظَّالِمِينَ ○

107. If God do touch thee
With hurt, there is none
Can remove it but He:
If He do design some benefit

١٠٧- وَإِن يَمْسَسْكَ اللَّهُ بِضُرٍّ فَلَا كَاشِفَ
لَهُ إِلَّا هُوَ وَإِن يُرِدْكَ بِخَيْرٍ

1485. Other people may hesitate, or doubt, or wonder. But the righteous man has no doubt in his own mind, and he declares his Faith clearly and unambiguously to all, as did Mustafā.

1486. The worship of the One and True God is not a fancy worship, to be arrived at merely by reasoning and philosophy. It touches the vital issues of life and death—which are in His hands and His alone.

1487. Nor is the worship of One God an invention of the Prophet. It comes as a direct command, through him and to all.

1488. Individual Faith is good, but it is completed and strengthened by joining or forming a Righteous Society, in which the individual can develop and expand. Islam was never a religion of monks and anchorites. It laid great stress on social duties, which in many ways test and train the individual's character.

For thee, there is none
Can keep back His favour:
He causeth it to reach
Whomsoever of His servants
He pleaseth. And He is
The Oft-Forgiving, Most
Merciful.[1489]

فَلَا رَآدَّ لِفَضْلِهٖ ؕ يُصِيْبُ بِهٖ مَنْ يَّشَآءُ مِنْ عِبَادِهٖ ؕ وَهُوَ الْغَفُوْرُ الرَّحِيْمُ ۝

108. Say: "O ye men! Now
Truth hath reached you
From your Lord! Those who receive
Guidance, do so for the good
Of their own souls; those
Who stray, do so to their own loss:
And I am not (set) over you
To arrange your affairs."[1490]

١٠٨- قُلْ يٰۤاَيُّهَا النَّاسُ قَدْ جَآءَكُمُ الْحَقُّ مِنْ رَّبِّكُمْ ۚ فَمَنِ اهْتَدٰى فَاِنَّمَا يَهْتَدِيْ لِنَفْسِهٖ ۚ وَمَنْ ضَلَّ فَاِنَّمَا يَضِلُّ عَلَيْهَا ۚ وَمَآ اَنَا عَلَيْكُمْ بِوَكِيْلٍ ۝

109. Follow thou the inspiration
Sent unto thee, and be
Patient and constant, till God
Do decide: for He
Is the Best to decide.[1491]

١٠٩- وَاتَّبِعْ مَا يُوْحٰۤى اِلَيْكَ وَاصْبِرْ حَتّٰى يَحْكُمَ اللّٰهُ ۚ وَهُوَ خَيْرُ الْحٰكِمِيْنَ ۝ ع

1489. God is Oft-Forgiving, Most Merciful. Even when we suffer under trials and tribulations, it is for our good, and no one can remove them except He, when, in His Plan, he sees it to be best for all concerned. On the other hand, there is no power that can intercept His blessings and favours, and His bounty flows freely when we are worthy, and often when we are not worthy of it.

1490. The *Furqān*, the Criterion between right and wrong, has been sent to us from God. If we accept guidance, it is not as if we confer favours on those who bring us guidance. They suffer unselfishly for us, in order that we may be guided for our own good. On the other hand, if we reject it, it is our own loss. We have a certain amount of free-will, and the responsibility is ours and cannot be shifted to the Teachers sent by God.

1491. When, in spite of all the efforts of the men of God, people do not accept Truth, and evil seems to flourish for a time, we must wait and be patient, but at the same time we must not give up hope or persevering effort. For thus only can we carry out our part in the Plan of God.

INTRODUCTION TO SŪRA XI (*Hūd*).

For the chronological place of this Sūra and the general argument of Sūras x to xv, see Introduction to S. x.

In subject-matter this Sūra supplements the preceding one. In the last Sūra stress was laid on that side of God's dealings with man which leans to Mercy: here stress is laid on the side which deals with justice and the punishment of Sin when all Grace is resisted.

Summary.—God's revelation of mercy, His dealings with man, and His long-suffering patience are contrasted with man's ingratitude, his love of falsehood and vanity, and his crookedness (xi. 1-24, and C. 104).

Noah's unselfishness and humility in teaching his people the Truth of God were traduced by the ungodly, and his Message ridiculed and rejected. But he built his Ark under directions from God, and was saved, with peace and blessings, while his rejecters perished (xi. 25-49, and C. 105).

The prophet Hūd preached to his people 'Ad against false gods, and the prophet Ṣāliḥ to his people Thamūd against dishonouring the symbol of God's bounty. In both cases God's Signs were rejected, and the rejecters were blotted out (xi. 50-68, and C. 106).

Lot's people were given to abominations: Abraham pleaded for them, and Lot was sent out to them, but they went deeper and deeper into sin and suffered the Penalty. Shu'aib's people, the Midianites, were warned against fraud and mischief, but they reproached him with helplessness and were themselves destroyed (xi. 69-95, and C. 107).

It is arrogant leaders like Pharaoh who mislead men, and men bring ruin on themselves. But God is Just. The penalty for sin is real and abiding; therefore shun all wrong-doing, and serve God whole-heartedly (xi. 96-123, and C. 108).

C. 104.—God's Revelation teaches the Truth: it warns
(xi. 1-24.) Against wrong and gives glad tidings to the righteous:
Ungrateful man folds up his heart
And fails to see how all Nature points
To God and to the Hereafter: he but seeks
Petty issues, forgetting the Cause of Causes.
Not all the wisdom of man can produce
Aught like the Message which comes from God,
As the Light that leads and the Mercy
That forgives. Who then but will humble
Himself before God, seeking His light and His voice?

آياتها ١٢٣ (١١) سُورَةُ هُودٍ مَكِّيَّةٌ (٥٢) ركوعاتها ١٠

Sūra XI.

Hūd (The Prophet Hūd).

In the name of God, Most Gracious, Most Merciful.

1. A. L. R.[1492]
(This is) a Book,
With verses basic or fundamental[1493]
(Of established meaning),
Further explained in detail,—
From One Who is Wise
And Well-Acquainted (with all things):

2. (It teacheth) that ye should
Worship none but God.
(Say:) "Verily I am[1494]
(Sent) unto you from Him
To warn and to bring
Glad tidings:

3. "(And to preach thus), 'Seek ye
The forgiveness of your Lord,
And turn to Him in repentance;
That He may grant you
Enjoyment, good (and true),
For a term appointed,
And bestow His abounding grace
On all who abound in merit![1495]
But if ye turn away,
Then I fear for you
The Penalty of a Great Day:

4. "'To God is your return,
And He hath power
Over all things.'"

5. Behold! they fold up[1496]
Their hearts, that they may lie
Hid from Him! Ah! even
When they cover themselves
With their garments, He knoweth
What they conceal, and what
They reveal: for He knoweth
11 Well the (inmost secrets)
30 Of the hearts[1497]

بِسْمِ اللّٰهِ الرَّحْمٰنِ الرَّحِيْمِ ○

١- الٓرٰ كِتٰبٌ اُحْكِمَتْ اٰيٰتُهٗ
ثُمَّ فُصِّلَتْ مِنْ لَّدُنْ
حَكِيْمٍ خَبِيْرٍ ○

٢- اَلَّا تَعْبُدُوْٓا اِلَّا اللّٰهَ
اِنَّنِيْ لَكُمْ مِّنْهُ
نَذِيْرٌ وَّ بَشِيْرٌ ○

٣- وَّاَنِ اسْتَغْفِرُوْا رَبَّكُمْ ثُمَّ تُوْبُوْٓا اِلَيْهِ
يُمَتِّعْكُمْ مَّتَاعًا حَسَنًا اِلٰٓى اَجَلٍ مُّسَمًّى
وَّيُؤْتِ كُلَّ ذِيْ فَضْلٍ فَضْلَهٗ
وَاِنْ تَوَلَّوْا فَاِنِّيْٓ اَخَافُ عَلَيْكُمْ عَذَابَ
يَوْمٍ كَبِيْرٍ ○

٤- اِلَى اللّٰهِ مَرْجِعُكُمْ
وَهُوَ عَلٰى كُلِّ شَيْءٍ قَدِيْرٌ ○

٥- اَلَآ اِنَّهُمْ يَثْنُوْنَ صُدُوْرَهُمْ لِيَسْتَخْفُوْا
مِنْهُ اَلَا حِيْنَ يَسْتَغْشُوْنَ ثِيَابَهُمْ
يَعْلَمُ مَا يُسِرُّوْنَ وَمَا يُعْلِنُوْنَ
اِنَّهٗ عَلِيْمٌ بِذَاتِ الصُّدُوْرِ ○

1492. For the meaning of these mystic Letters, see Introduction to S. x.

1493. See n. 347 to iii. 7. Every basic principle is included in God's Revelation, and it is further illustrated and explained in detail.

1494. Muṣṭafā's Message—as was the Message of all apostles—was to warn against evil, and to bring the glad tidings of God's Mercy and Grace to all who would receive it in Faith and trust in God. This double Message is preached illustratively in this Sūra.

1495. The enjoyment of all good and true things in life refers, I think, to the present life with its limited term, and the abounding Grace refers to the higher spiritual reward, which begins here but is completed in the life to come.

1496. The heart (literally *breast* in Arabic) is already well guarded in the body; and secrets are supposed to be hidden in the heart or breast. Foolish persons might further cover up their hearts with cloaks, but even so, nothing can be hidden from God.

1497. *Cf.* iii. 119.

6. There is no moving creature
On earth but its sustenance[1498]
Dependeth on God : He knoweth
The time and place of its
Definite abode and its
Temporary deposit :[1499]
All is in a clear Record.[1500]

٦- وَمَا مِنْ دَآبَّةٍ فِى الْاَرْضِ اِلَّا
عَلَى اللّٰهِ رِزْقُهَا وَيَعْلَمُ مُسْتَقَرَّهَا وَ
مُسْتَوْدَعَهَا ؕ
كُلٌّ فِىْ كِتٰبٍ مُّبِيْنٍ ○

7. He it is Who created
The heavens and the earth
In six Days[1501]—and His Throne
Was over the Waters—[1502]
That He might try you,[1503]
Which of you is best
In conduct. But if
Thou wert to say to them,
"Ye shall indeed be raised up
After death", the Unbelievers
Would be sure to say,[1504]
"This is nothing but
Obvious sorcery!"

٧- وَهُوَ الَّذِىْ خَلَقَ السَّمٰوٰتِ وَالْاَرْضَ
فِىْ سِتَّةِ اَيَّامٍ وَّكَانَ عَرْشُهٗ عَلَى الْمَآءِ
لِيَبْلُوَكُمْ اَيُّكُمْ اَحْسَنُ عَمَلًا ؕ
وَلَئِنْ قُلْتَ اِنَّكُمْ مَّبْعُوْثُوْنَ مِنْۢ بَعْدِ
الْمَوْتِ
لَيَقُوْلَنَّ الَّذِيْنَ كَفَرُوْۤا
اِنْ هٰذَاۤ اِلَّا سِحْرٌ مُّبِيْنٌ ○

8. If We delay the penalty
For them for a definite term,
They are sure to say,
"What keeps it back?"[1505]

٨- وَلَئِنْ اَخَّرْنَا عَنْهُمُ الْعَذَابَ اِلٰٓى
اُمَّةٍ مَّعْدُوْدَةٍ لَّيَقُوْلُنَّ مَا يَحْبِسُهٗ ؕ

1498. *Cf.* vi. 59. Nothing happens in Creation except by the Word of God and with the knowledge of God. Not a leaf stirs but by His Will. Its maintenance in every sense is dependent on His Will.

1499. *Mustaqarr*=definite abode; where a thing stops or stays for some time, where it is established. *Mustauda'*=where a thing is laid up or deposited for a little while. Referring to animals, the former denotes its life on this earth; the latter its temporary pre-natal existence in the egg or the womb and its after-death existence in the tomb or whatever state it is in until its resurrection.

1500. *Cf.* vi. 59 and n. 880, and x. 61 and n. 1450.

1501. See n. 1031 to vii. 54.

1502. It is scientifically correct to say that all life was evolved out of the waters, and this statement also occurs in the Qur-ān, xxi. 30. The Throne of God's authority is metaphorically expressed as over the waters, *i.e.*, as regulating all life. Some such mystic meaning, I think, also attaches to the Gen. i. 2. The past sense "was" refers to the time before life developed in solid forms, on land and in air.

1503. The Creation we see around us is not idle sport or play (in Hindi, *Lila*) or whim on the part of God. It is the medium through which our spiritual life is to develop, with such free-will as we have. This life is our testing time.

1504. The Unbelievers, who do not believe in a Future life, think all talk of it is like a sorcerer's talk, empty of reality. But in this they show their ignorance, and they are begging the question.

1505. As much as to say: "Oh! all this talk of punishment is nonsense. There is no such thing!"

Ah ! On the day it (actually)
Reaches them, nothing will
Turn it away from them,
And they will be completely
Encircled by that which
They used to mock at !

أَلَا يَوْمَ يَأْتِيهِمْ لَيْسَ مَصْرُوفًا عَنْهُمْ
وَحَاقَ بِهِم
مَّا كَانُوا بِهِۦ يَسْتَهْزِءُونَ ۝ ع

SECTION 2.

9. If We give man a taste
Of Mercy from Ourselves,
And then withdraw it from him,
Behold ! he is in despair
And (falls into) blasphemy.[1506]

٩- وَلَئِنْ أَذَقْنَا ٱلْإِنسَٰنَ مِنَّا رَحْمَةً
ثُمَّ نَزَعْنَٰهَا مِنْهُ
إِنَّهُۥ لَيَـُٔوسٌ كَفُورٌ ۝

10. But if We give him a taste
Of (Our) favours after
Adversity hath touched him,
He is sure to say,
"All evil has departed from
me :"[1507]
Behold ! he falls into exultation
And pride.

١٠- وَلَئِنْ أَذَقْنَٰهُ نَعْمَآءَ
بَعْدَ ضَرَّآءَ مَسَّتْهُ
لَيَقُولَنَّ ذَهَبَ ٱلسَّيِّـَٔاتُ عَنِّيٓ
إِنَّهُۥ لَفَرِحٌ فَخُورٌ ۝

11. Not so do those who show
Patience and constancy, and
work[1508]
Righteousness ; for them
Is forgiveness (of sins)
And a great reward.

١١- إِلَّا ٱلَّذِينَ صَبَرُوا۟ وَعَمِلُوا۟ ٱلصَّٰلِحَٰتِ
أُو۟لَٰٓئِكَ لَهُم مَّغْفِرَةٌ
وَأَجْرٌ كَبِيرٌ ۝

12. Perchance thou mayest (feel
The inclination) to give up
A part of what is revealed[1509]
Unto thee, and thy heart

١٢- فَلَعَلَّكَ تَارِكٌۢ
بَعْضَ مَا يُوحَىٰٓ إِلَيْكَ

1506. He does not realise that some kinds of chastening are good for discipline and the training of our spiritual faculties.

1507. He takes it as a mattar of course, or as due to his own merit or cleverness! He does not realise that both in good and ill fortune there is a beneficent purpose in the Plan of God.

1508. Their attitude is the right one: to take ill-fortune with fortitude and good fortune with humility, and in either case go on persevering in good deeds to their fellow-creatures.

1509. Every man of God, when he not only encounters opposition, but is actually accused of falsehood and those very evils which he is protesting against, may feel inclined, in his human weakness, to ask himself the question, "Supposing I omit this little point, will God's Truth then be accepted more readily ?" Or he may think to himself, "If I had only more money to organise my campaign, or something which will draw people's attention, like the company of an angel, how much better can I push my Message ?" He is told that truth must be delivered as it is revealed, even though portions of it may be unpalatable, and that resources and other means to draw people to him are beside the point. He must use just such resources and opportunities as he has, and leave the rest to God.

Feeleth straitened lest they say,
" Why is not a treasure sent down
Unto him, or why does not
An angel come down with him ? "
But thou art there only to warn !
It is God that arrangeth
All affairs !

وَضَآئِقٌۢ بِهٖ صَدْرُكَ اَنْ يَّقُوْلُوْا
لَوْلَآ اُنْزِلَ عَلَيْهِ كَنْزٌ
اَوْ جَآءَ مَعَهٗ مَلَكٌ ؕ اِنَّمَآ اَنْتَ نَذِيْرٌ ؕ
وَاللّٰهُ عَلٰى كُلِّ شَىْءٍ وَّكِيْلٌ ○

13\. Or they may say, " He forged it."
Say, " Bring ye then ten Sūras
Forged, like unto it, and call
(To your aid) whomsoever
Ye can, other than God !—
If ye speak the truth ! [1510]

١٣- اَمْ يَقُوْلُوْنَ افْتَرٰىهُ ؕ قُلْ فَاْتُوْا بِعَشْرِ سُوَرٍ
مِّثْلِهٖ مُفْتَرَيٰتٍ وَّادْعُوْا مَنِ اسْتَطَعْتُمْ
مِّنْ دُوْنِ اللّٰهِ اِنْ كُنْتُمْ صٰدِقِيْنَ ○

14\. " If then they (your false gods)
Answer not your (call),
Know ye that this Revelation
Is sent down (replete) with the knowledge
Of God, and that there is
No god but He ! Will ye
Even then submit (to Islam) ? "

١٤- فَاِلَّمْ يَسْتَجِيْبُوْا لَكُمْ
فَاعْلَمُوْٓا اَنَّمَآ اُنْزِلَ بِعِلْمِ اللّٰهِ
وَاَنْ لَّآ اِلٰهَ اِلَّا هُوَ ۚ
فَهَلْ اَنْتُمْ مُّسْلِمُوْنَ ○

15\. Those who desire
The life of the Present
And its glitter,—to them
We shall pay (the price
Of) their deeds therein,—
Without diminution.[1511]

١٥- مَنْ كَانَ يُرِيْدُ الْحَيٰوةَ الدُّنْيَا
وَزِيْنَتَهَا نُوَفِّ اِلَيْهِمْ اَعْمَالَهُمْ فِيْهَا
وَهُمْ فِيْهَا لَا يُبْخَسُوْنَ ○

16\. They are those for whom
There is nothing in the Hereafter
But the Fire : vain
Are the designs they frame therein,
And of no effect
Are the deeds that they do !

١٦- اُولٰٓئِكَ الَّذِيْنَ لَيْسَ لَهُمْ فِى الْاٰخِرَةِ
اِلَّا النَّارُ ۖ وَحَبِطَ مَا صَنَعُوْا فِيْهَا
وَبٰطِلٌ مَّا كَانُوْا يَعْمَلُوْنَ ○

17\. Can they be (like) those
Who accept a Clear (Sign)
From their Lord, and whom
A witness from Himself [1512]

١٧- اَفَمَنْ كَانَ عَلٰى بَيِّنَةٍ
مِّنْ رَّبِّهٖ وَيَتْلُوْهُ شَاهِدٌ مِّنْهُ

1510\. *Cf.* ii. 23 and x. 38.

1511\. If worldly men desire the glitter of this world, they shall have it in full measure, but it is false glitter, and it involves the negation of that spiritual life which comes from the guidance of the inner light and from the revelation of God, as described in verse 17 below.

1512\. "*A witness from Himself*" : *i.e.*, the Book which was given to Muṣṭafā, the Holy Qur-ān, which is compared to the original Revelation given to Moses. We make no difference between one true and genuine Message and another, nor between one apostle and another,—for they all come from the One True God.

Doth teach, as did the Book
Of Moses before it,—a guide[1513]
And a mercy? They believe
Therein; but those of the Sects
That reject it,—the Fire
Will be their promised
Meeting-place. Be not then
In doubt thereon: for it is
The Truth from thy Lord:
Yet many among men
Do not believe!

وَمِن قَبْلِهِ كِتَٰبُ مُوسَىٰٓ إِمَامًا وَرَحْمَةً
أُولَٰٓئِكَ يُؤْمِنُونَ بِهِ وَمَن يَكْفُرْ بِهِ مِنَ
الْأَحْزَابِ فَالنَّارُ مَوْعِدُهُ
فَلَا تَكُ فِى مِرْيَةٍ مِّنْهُ
إِنَّهُ الْحَقُّ مِن رَّبِّكَ
وَلَٰكِنَّ أَكْثَرَ النَّاسِ لَا يُؤْمِنُونَ ○

18. Who doth more wrong
Than those who invent a lie
Against God? They will be
Turned back to the presence
Of their Lord, and the witnesses
Will say, "These are the ones
Who lied against their Lord!
Behold! the Curse of God
Is on those who do wrong!—

١٨- وَمَنْ أَظْلَمُ مِمَّنِ افْتَرَىٰ عَلَى اللَّهِ كَذِبًا
أُولَٰٓئِكَ يُعْرَضُونَ عَلَىٰ رَبِّهِمْ
وَيَقُولُ الْأَشْهَٰدُ
هَٰٓؤُلَآءِ الَّذِينَ كَذَبُوا عَلَىٰ رَبِّهِمْ
أَلَا لَعْنَةُ اللَّهِ عَلَى الظَّٰلِمِينَ ○

19. "Those who would hinder (men)
From the path of God
And would seek in it
Something crooked: these were
They who denied the
Hereafter!"[1514]

١٩- الَّذِينَ يَصُدُّونَ عَن سَبِيلِ اللَّهِ
وَيَبْغُونَهَا عِوَجًا
وَهُم بِالْآخِرَةِ هُمْ كَٰفِرُونَ ○

20. They will in no wise
Frustrate (His design) on earth,
Nor have they protectors
Besides God! Their penalty[1515]
Will be doubled! They lost
The power to hear,
And they did not see!

٢٠- أُولَٰٓئِكَ لَمْ يَكُونُوا مُعْجِزِينَ فِى الْأَرْضِ
وَمَا كَانَ لَهُم مِّن دُونِ اللَّهِ مِنْ أَوْلِيَآءَ وقف لازم
يُضَٰعَفُ لَهُمُ الْعَذَابُ مَا كَانُوا يَسْتَطِيعُونَ
السَّمْعَ وَمَا كَانُوا يُبْصِرُونَ ○

21. They are the ones who
Have lost their own souls:

٢١- أُولَٰٓئِكَ الَّذِينَ خَسِرُوٓا أَنفُسَهُمْ

1513. "Guide": the Arabic word here is *Imām*, a leader, a guide, one that directs to the true Path. Such a direction is an instance of the Mercy and Goodness of God to man. The Qur-ān and the Apostle Muḥammad are also called, each, a Guide and a Mercy, and so are these epithets applicable to previous Books and Apostles.

1514. *Cf.* vii. 45.

1515. *Cf.* vii. 38. In this context, it is implied that they committed a two-fold wrong: (1) in inventing falsehoods against God, which deadened their own soul, and (2) in leading others astray or hindering them from God's path. Thus they lost the faculty of hearing, which they might have used to hear the Word of God, and they blinded the faculty of sight by shutting out God's light.

And the (fancies) they invented
Have left them in the lurch!

وَضَلَّ عَنْهُم مَّا كَانُوا يَفْتَرُونَ ○

22. Without a doubt, these
Are the very ones who
Will lose most in the Hereafter!

٢٢- لَا جَرَمَ أَنَّهُمْ فِي الْآخِرَةِ هُمُ الْأَخْسَرُونَ ○

23. But those who believe
And work righteousness,
And humble themselves
Before their Lord,—[1516]
They will be Companions
Of the Garden, to dwell
Therein for aye!

٢٣- إِنَّ الَّذِينَ آمَنُوا وَعَمِلُوا الصَّالِحَاتِ
وَأَخْبَتُوا إِلَىٰ رَبِّهِمْ
أُولَٰئِكَ أَصْحَابُ الْجَنَّةِ
هُمْ فِيهَا خَالِدُونَ ○

24. These two kinds (of men)
May be compared to
The blind and deaf,
And those who can see
And hear well. Are they
Equal when compared?
Will ye not then take heed?

٢٤- مَثَلُ الْفَرِيقَيْنِ كَالْأَعْمَىٰ وَالْأَصَمِّ
وَالْبَصِيرِ وَالسَّمِيعِ
هَلْ يَسْتَوِيَانِ مَثَلًا أَفَلَا تَذَكَّرُونَ ○ ع

C. 105.—Noah walked righteously and humbly
(xi. 25-49.) As in the sight of God. With unselfish
Love for his people he warned them
And taught them. But they did flout
And reject his Message with scorn
And insults. God gave him directions
To build an Ark against the impending
Flood which was to purify the world
From Sin and Unrighteousness. In it
Were saved Noah and those who believed.
So were promised salvation and God's Peace.
And Blessings to the Righteous evermore.

Section 3.

25. We sent Noah to his People
(With a mission): "I have come
To you with a Clear Warning:

٢٥- وَلَقَدْ أَرْسَلْنَا نُوحًا إِلَىٰ قَوْمِهِ
إِنِّي لَكُمْ نَذِيرٌ مُّبِينٌ ○

26. "That ye serve none but God:
Verily I do fear for you

٢٦- أَن لَّا تَعْبُدُوا إِلَّا اللَّهَ إِنِّي أَخَافُ

1516. Note that the humility is to be "before their Lord," *i.e.*, in God's sight. There is no virtue, quite the contrary, in rubbing our noses to the ground before men. We are not to be arrogant even before men because we are humble as in God's sight. Nor does true humility lose self-confidence; for that self-confidence arises from confidence in the support and help of God.

The Penalty of a Grievous
Day."[1517]

عَلَيْكُمْ عَذَابَ يَوْمٍ أَلِيمٍ ○

27. But the Chiefs of the Unbelievers
Among his People said:
"We see (in) thee nothing
But a man like ourselves:
Nor do we see that any
Follow thee but the meanest
Among us, in judgment immature:
Nor do we see in you (all)
Any merit above us:
In fact we think ye are liars!"[1518]

٢٧- فَقَالَ الْمَلَأُ الَّذِينَ كَفَرُوا مِنْ قَوْمِهِ
مَا نَرٰىكَ إِلَّا بَشَرًا مِّثْلَنَا
وَمَا نَرٰىكَ اتَّبَعَكَ إِلَّا الَّذِينَ
هُمْ أَرَاذِلُنَا بَادِيَ الرَّأْيِ
وَمَا نَرٰى لَكُمْ عَلَيْنَا مِنْ فَضْلٍ
بَلْ نَظُنُّكُمْ كٰذِبِينَ ○

28. He said: "O my People!
See ye if (it be that)
I have a Clear Sign
From my Lord, and that He
Hath sent Mercy unto me
From His own Presence, but
That the Mercy hath been
Obscured from your sight?[1519]
Shall we compel you
To accept it when ye
Are averse to it?

٢٨- قَالَ يٰقَوْمِ أَرَءَيْتُمْ
إِنْ كُنْتُ عَلٰى بَيِّنَةٍ مِّنْ رَّبِّي
وَاٰتٰىنِي رَحْمَةً مِّنْ عِنْدِهِ
فَعُمِّيَتْ عَلَيْكُمْ
أَنُلْزِمُكُمُوهَا وَأَنْتُمْ لَهَا كٰرِهُونَ ○

29. "And O my People!
I ask you for no wealth

٢٩- وَيٰقَوْمِ لَا أَسْـَٔلُكُمْ عَلَيْهِ مَالًا

1517. Noah's mission was to a wicked world, plunged in sin. The mission had a double character, as in the mission of all men of God: it had to warn men against evil and call them to repentance, and it had to give them the glad tidings of God's Grace in case they turned back to God: it was a Guidance and Mercy.

1518. The Unbelievers were impelled by three powerful human motives of evil to resist Grace: (1) jealousy of other men; they said, "Why, you are no better than ourselves," half perceiving the Prophet's superiority, and half ignoring it; (2) contempt of the weak and lowly, who are often better intellectually, morally, and spiritually; they said, "We cannot believe or do what these fellows, our inferiors in social rank, believe or do!"; (3) arrogance and self-sufficiency, which is a vice cognate to (2), looked at from a different angle; they said, "We are really better than the lot of you!" Now the claim made on behalf of God's Message attacked all these three attitudes. And all they could say against it was to abuse it impatiently, and call it a lie.

1519. Noah's answer (like that of the Man of God who spoke in later ages in Mecca and Medina) is a pattern of humility, gentleness, firmness, persuasiveness, truth, and love for his own people. First, he meekly (not exultingly) informs them that he has got a Message from God. Secondly, he tells them that it is a Message of Mercy even in its warning, though in their arrogance the Mercy may be hidden from them. Thirdly, he tells them plainly that there can be no compulsion in Religion: but will they not accept with goodwill what is for their own benefit? He pleads with them as one of their own.

In return : my reward
Is from none but God : [1520]
But I will not drive away
(In contempt) those who believe :
For verily they are
To meet their Lord, and ye
I see are the ignorant ones !

إِنْ أَجْرِيَ إِلَّا عَلَى اللَّهِ
وَمَا أَنَا بِطَارِدِ الَّذِينَ آمَنُوا
إِنَّهُمْ مُلَاقُوا رَبِّهِمْ
وَلَٰكِنِّي أَرَاكُمْ قَوْمًا تَجْهَلُونَ ○

30. " And O my People !
Who would help me against God
If I drove them away ?
Will ye not then take heed ? [1521]

٣٠- وَيَا قَوْمِ مَنْ يَنْصُرُنِي مِنَ اللَّهِ
إِنْ طَرَدْتُهُمْ أَفَلَا تَذَكَّرُونَ ○

31. " I tell you not that [1522]
With me are the Treasures [1523]
Of God, nor do I know
What is hidden,
Nor claim I to be
An angel. Nor yet
Do I say, of those whom
Your eyes do despise [1524]
That God will not grant them
(All) that is good :
God knoweth best
What is in their souls :
I should, if I did,
Indeed be a wrong-doer."

٣١- وَلَا أَقُولُ لَكُمْ عِنْدِي خَزَائِنُ اللَّهِ
وَلَا أَعْلَمُ الْغَيْبَ
وَلَا أَقُولُ إِنِّي مَلَكٌ
وَلَا أَقُولُ لِلَّذِينَ تَزْدَرِي أَعْيُنُكُمْ
لَنْ يُؤْتِيَهُمُ اللَّهُ خَيْرًا
اللَّهُ أَعْلَمُ بِمَا فِي أَنْفُسِهِمْ
إِنِّي إِذًا لَمِنَ الظَّالِمِينَ ○

32. They said : " O Noah !
Thou hast disputed with us,

٣٢- قَالُوا يَا نُوحُ قَدْ جَادَلْتَنَا

1520. The fourth point in Noah's address meets their accusation that he was a liar, implying that he was serving some selfish end of his own : on the contrary, he says, he seeks no reward from them but will bear any insults they heap on him, for he looks to God rather than men. But, fifthly, if they insult the poor and needy who come to him in Faith, and think that he would send them away in order to attract the great ones of the land, he tells them plainly that they are mistaken. In fact, (sixthly), he has no hesitation in telling the blunt truth that *they* are the ignorant ones, and not the poor who came to seek God's Truth !

1521. But (seventhly) again he pleads, with as much earnestness as ever, that he is one of themselves, and just doing his truest duty. Would they have him do less? Indeed, would they not themselves see the Truth and come into the goodly company of Believers?

1522. The eighth point that Noah urges is that he is not a mere vulgar soothsayer pretending to reveal secrets not worth knowing, nor an angel living in another world, with no ties to them. He is their real well-wisher, delivering a true Message from God.

1523. *Cf.* vi. 50 and n. 867.

1524. But Noah will not close his argument without defending the men of Faith, whom the Chiefs despise because they are lacking in worldly goods. He tells them plainly that God perhaps sees in them something in which they, the arrogant Chiefs, are lacking. Their spiritual faculties can only be appreciated truly by Him to Whom all the secrets of the spirit are open. But he, Noah, must declare boldly his own Faith, and this is the ninth point in his argument.

And (much) hast thou prolonged
The dispute with us: now
Bring upon us what thou
Threatenest us with, if thou
Speakest the truth!?"[1525]

فَأَكْثَرْتَ جِدَالَنَا
فَأْتِنَا بِمَا تَعِدُنَا
إِن كُنتَ مِنَ الصَّادِقِينَ ○

33. He said: "Truly, God
Will bring it on you
If He wills,—and then,
Ye will not be able
To frustrate it![1526]

٣٣-قَالَ إِنَّمَا يَأْتِيكُم بِهِ اللَّهُ
إِن شَاءَ
وَمَا أَنتُم بِمُعْجِزِينَ ○

34. "Of no profit will be
My counsel to you,
Much as I desire
To give you (good) counsel,
If it be that God
Willeth to leave you astray:[1527]
He is your Lord!
And to Him will ye return!"

٣٤-وَلَا يَنفَعُكُمْ نُصْحِي
إِنْ أَرَدتُّ أَنْ أَنصَحَ لَكُمْ
إِن كَانَ اللَّهُ يُرِيدُ أَن يُغْوِيَكُمْ
هُوَ رَبُّكُمْ وَإِلَيْهِ تُرْجَعُونَ ○

35. Or do they say,
"He has forged it"? Say:
"If I had forged it,
On me were my sin!
And I am free
Of the sins of which
Ye are guilty![1528]

٣٥-أَمْ يَقُولُونَ افْتَرَاهُ
قُلْ إِنِ افْتَرَيْتُهُ فَعَلَيَّ إِجْرَامِي
وَأَنَا بَرِيءٌ مِّمَّا تُجْرِمُونَ ○

1525. To Noah's address the worldly Chiefs give a characteristic reply. In its aggressive spirit it is the very antithesis of the gentle remonstrances of Noah. Because he had gently and patiently argued with them, they impatiently accuse him of "disputing with them" and "prolonging the dispute". They are unable to deal with his points. So they arrogantly throw out their challenge, which is a compound of hectoring insolence, unreasoning scepticism, and biting irony. "You foretell disaster to us if we don't mend our ways! Let us see you bring it on! Now, if you please! Or shall we have to call you a liar?"

1526. To the blasphemous challenge addressed to Noah his only answer could be: "I never claimed that I could punish you. All punishment is in the hands of God, and He knows best when His punishment will descend. But this I can tell you! His punishment is sure if you do not repent, and when it comes, you will not be able to ward it off!"

1527. But Noah's heart bleeds for his people. They are preparing their own undoing! All his efforts are to be vain! Obstinate as they are, God's grace must be withdrawn, and then who can help them, and what use is any counsel? But again he will try to remind them of their Lord, and turn their face to Him. For their ultimate return to His judgment-seat is certain, to answer for their conduct.

1528. The fine narrative of dramatic power is here interrupted by a verse which shows that the story of Noah is also a Parable for the time and the ministry of Muḥammad the Apostle. The wonderful force and aptness of the story cannot be denied. The enemy therefore turns and says, "Oh! but you invented it!" The answer is, "No! but it is God's own truth! You may be accustomed to dealing in falsehoods, but I protest that I am free from such sins." The place of this verse here corresponds to the place of verse 49 at the end of the next Section.

While understanding this verse to refer to Muṣṭafā, as most of the accepted Commentators understand it, it is possible also, I think, to read it into the story of Noah, for all Prophets have similar spiritual experiences.

SECTION 4.

36. It was revealed to Noah:
"None of thy People will believe [1529]
Except those who have believed
Already! So grieve no longer
Over their (evil) deeds.

٣٦- وَأُوحِيَ إِلَىٰ نُوحٍ أَنَّهُۥ لَن يُؤْمِنَ مِن
قَوْمِكَ إِلَّا مَن قَدْ ءَامَنَ
فَلَا تَبْتَئِسْ بِمَا كَانُوا۟ يَفْعَلُونَ ۝

37. "But construct an Ark
Under Our eyes and Our [1530]
Inspiration, and address Me
No (further) on behalf
Of those who are in sin:
For they are about to be
Overwhelmed (in the Flood)."

٣٧- وَٱصْنَعِ ٱلْفُلْكَ
بِأَعْيُنِنَا وَوَحْيِنَا
وَلَا تُخَٰطِبْنِى فِى ٱلَّذِينَ ظَلَمُوٓا۟ ۚ
إِنَّهُم مُّغْرَقُونَ ۝

38. Forthwith he (starts)
Constructing the Ark:
Every time that the Chiefs
Of his People passed by him,
They threw ridicule on him.[1531]
He said: "If ye ridicule
Us now, we (in our turn)
Can look down on you
With ridicule likewise! [1532]

٣٨- وَيَصْنَعُ ٱلْفُلْكَ
وَكُلَّمَا مَرَّ عَلَيْهِ مَلَأٌ مِّن قَوْمِهِۦ سَخِرُوا۟
مِنْهُ ۚ
قَالَ إِن تَسْخَرُوا۟ مِنَّا
فَإِنَّا نَسْخَرُ مِنكُمْ كَمَا تَسْخَرُونَ ۝

39. "But soon will ye know
Who it is on whom
Will descend a Penalty
That will cover them

٣٩- فَسَوْفَ تَعْلَمُونَ ۙ
مَن يَأْتِيهِ عَذَابٌ

1529. The story of Noah is resumed. A point was reached, when it was clear that there was no hope of saving the sinners, who were courting their own destruction. It was to be a great Flood. So Noah was ordered to construct a great Ark or Ship, not a sailing ship, but a heavy vessel to remain afloat in the Flood, so that the righteous could be saved in it.

1530. It was to be built under the special instructions of God, to serve the special purpose it was intended to serve.

1531. The ridicule of the sinners, from their own point of view, was natural. Here was a preacher turned carpenter! Here was a plain in the higher reaches of the Mesopotamian basin, drained by the majestic Tigris, over 800 to 900 miles from the sea (the Persian Gulf) in a straight line! Yet he talks of a flood like the Sea! All material civilisations pride themselves on their Public Works and their drainage schemes. And here was a fellow relying on God! But did not their narrow pride seem ridiculous also to the man of God? Here were men steeped in sin and insolence! And they pit themselves against the power and the promise of God! Truly a contemptible race is man!

1532. The Arabic Aorist may be construed either by the present tense or the future tense, and both make good sense here. Following Zamakhshari, I construe in the present tense, because the future is so tragic for the sinners. For the time being the worldly ones looked down on the Believers as they always do; but the Believers relied on God, and pitied their critics for knowing no better!—for their arrogance was really ridiculous.

With shame,—on whom will be
Unloosed a Penalty lasting:"

يُخْزِيهِ وَيَحِلُّ عَلَيْهِ عَذَابٌ مُّقِيمٌ ○

40. At length, behold!
There came Our Command,
And the fountains of the earth[1533]
Gushed forth! We said:
"Embark therein, of each kind
Two, male and female,[1534]
And your family—except
Those against whom the Word
Has already gone forth,—[1535]
And the Believers."
But only a few
Believed with him.

٤٠- حَتّٰىٓ إِذَا جَآءَ أَمْرُنَا
وَفَارَ التَّنُّورُ
قُلْنَا احْمِلْ فِيهَا مِن كُلٍّ زَوْجَيْنِ
اثْنَيْنِ وَأَهْلَكَ إِلَّا مَن سَبَقَ عَلَيْهِ
الْقَوْلُ وَمَنْ آمَنَ
وَمَآ آمَنَ مَعَهُۥٓ إِلَّا قَلِيلٌ ○

41. So he said: "Embark ye
On the Ark,
In the name of God,
Whether it move
Or be at rest!
For my Lord is, be sure,
Oft-Forgiving, Most Merciful!"

٤١- وَقَالَ ارْكَبُوا فِيهَا
بِسْمِ اللّٰهِ مَجْرٖىٰهَا وَمُرْسٰىهَا
إِنَّ رَبِّي لَغَفُورٌ رَّحِيمٌ ○

42. So the Ark floated
With them on the waves
(Towering) like mountains,[1536]
And Noah called out
To his son, who had
Separated himself (from the rest):
"O my son! embark
With us, and be not
With the Unbelievers!"

٤٢- وَهِيَ تَجْرِي بِهِمْ فِي مَوْجٍ كَالْجِبَالِ
وَنَادٰى نُوحٌ ابْنَهُ
وَكَانَ فِي مَعْزِلٍ
يٰبُنَيَّ ارْكَب مَّعَنَا
وَلَا تَكُن مَّعَ الْكٰفِرِينَ ○

1533. *Fār-at-tannūru.* Two interpretations have been given: (1) the fountains or the springs on the surface of the earth bubbled over or gushed forth; or (2) the oven (of God's Wrath) boiled over. The former has the weight of the best authority behind it and I prefer it. Moreover, the same phrase occurs in xxiii. 27, where it is a clause coordinated (as here) with the coming of God's Command. These two passages may be compared with liv. 11-12, where it is said that water poured forth from the skies and gushed forth from the springs. This double action is familiar to any one who has seen floods on a large scale. The rain from above would saturate the great Ararat Plateau, and give great force to the springs and fountains in the valley of the Tigris below.

1534. *Zaujaini*: the dual number refers to the two individuals in each pair of opposite sexes. Some of the most authoritative Commentators (*e.g.*, Imam Rāzi) construe in this sense, though others construe it to mean two pairs of each species.

1535. A disobedient and recalcitrant son (or step-son or grandson) of Noah is mentioned below (xi. 42-43, 45-46). A member of the family, who breaks away from the traditions of the family in things that matter, ceases to share in the privileges of the family.

1536. The simile of mountains applies to the waves, which were mountain high,—literally, for the peaks were being submerged.

43. The son replied: "I will
Betake myself to some mountain:[1537]
It will save me from
The water." Noah said:
"This day nothing can save,
From the Command of God,
Any but those on whom
He hath mercy!"—
And the waves came
Between them, and the son
Was among those
Overwhelmed in the Flood.

44. Then the word went forth:[1538]
"O earth! swallow up
Thy water, and O sky!
Withhold (thy rain)!"
And the water abated,
And the matter was ended.
The Ark rested on Mount[1539]
Jūdī, and the word
Went forth: "Away
With those who do wrong!"

٤٣- قَالَ سَاٰوِيٓ إِلَىٰ جَبَلٍ
يَّعْصِمُنِي مِنَ الْمَآءِ
قَالَ لَا عَاصِمَ الْيَوْمَ
مِنْ أَمْرِ اللّٰهِ إِلَّا مَنْ رَّحِمَ
وَحَالَ بَيْنَهُمَا الْمَوْجُ
فَكَانَ مِنَ الْمُغْرَقِينَ ○

٤٤- وَقِيلَ يٰٓأَرْضُ ابْلَعِي
مَآءَكِ وَيٰسَمَآءُ
أَقْلِعِي وَغِيضَ الْمَآءُ وَقُضِيَ الْأَمْرُ
وَاسْتَوَتْ عَلَى الْجُودِيِّ
وَقِيلَ بُعْدًا لِّلْقَوْمِ الظّٰلِمِينَ ○

1537. The Unbelievers refuse to believe in God, but have great faith in material things! This young man was going to save himself on mountain peaks, not knowing that the peaks were themselves being submerged.

1538. A wonderful passage. The whole picture is painted in just a few words. The chain of material facts are linked together, not only in their relations to each other, but also in their relation to the spiritual forces that control them, and the spiritual consequences of Sin and wrong-doing. The drowning in the material sense was the least part of the Penalty. A whole new world came into existence after the Deluge—as always happens after any great catastrophe, like the World War of 1914-18.

1539. Let us get a little idea of the geography of the place. The letters J, B, and K are philologically interchangeable, and Jūdī, Gūdī, Kūdī are sounds that can pass into each other. There is no doubt that the name is connected with the name "Kurd", in which the letter *r* is a later interpolation, for the oldest Sumerian records name a people called Kūtī or Gūtū as holding the middle Tigris region not later than 2000 B.C. (see E. B., Kurdistan). That region comprises the modern Turkish district of Bohtan, in which Jabal Jūdī is situated (near the frontiers of modern Turkey, modern 'Irāq, and modern Syria), and the town of Jazīrat ibn 'Umar, (on the present Turco-Syrian frontier), and it extends into 'Irāq and Persia. The great mountain mass of the Ararat plateau dominates this district. This mountain system "is unique in the Old World in containing great sheets of water that are bitter lakes without outlets, Lake Van and Lake Urumiya being the chief" (E. B., Asia). Such would be the very region for a stupendous Deluge if the usual scanty rainfall were to be changed into a very heavy downpour. A glacier damming of Lake Van in the Ice Age would have produced the same result. The region has many local traditions connected with Noah and the Flood. The Biblical legend of Mount Ararat being the resting place of Noah's Ark is hardly plausible, seeing that the highest peak of Ararat is over 16,000 feet high. If it means one of the lower peaks of the Ararat system, it agrees with the Muslim tradition about Mount Jūdī (or Gūdī), and this is in accordance with the oldest and best local traditions. These traditions are accepted by Josephus, by the Nestorian Christians, and indeed by all the Eastern Christians and Jews, and they are the best in touch with local traditions. See (Viscount) J. Bryce, "*Transcaucasia and Ararat*," 4th ed., 1896, p. 216.

45. And Noah called upon
His Lord, and said:
"O my Lord! surely
My son is of my family!
And Thy promise is true,
And Thou art
The Justest of Judges!"

٤٥- وَنَادٰى نُوْحٌ رَّبَّهٗ فَقَالَ
رَبِّ اِنَّ ابْنِیْ مِنْ اَهْلِیْ
وَاِنَّ وَعْدَكَ الْحَقُّ
وَاَنْتَ اَحْكَمُ الْحٰكِمِيْنَ ○

46. He said: "O Noah!
He is not of thy family: [1540]
For his conduct is unrighteous.
So ask not of Me
That of which thou
Hast no knowledge!
I give thee counsel, lest
Thou act like the ignorant!"

٤٦- قَالَ يٰنُوْحُ اِنَّهٗ لَيْسَ مِنْ اَهْلِكَ ۚ
اِنَّهٗ عَمَلٌ غَيْرُ صَالِحٍ ۖ
فَلَا تَسْـَٔلْنِ مَا لَيْسَ لَكَ بِهٖ عِلْمٌ ۭ
اِنِّیْۤ اَعِظُكَ اَنْ تَكُوْنَ مِنَ الْجٰهِلِيْنَ ○

47. Noah said: "O my Lord!
I do seek refuge with Thee,
Lest I ask Thee for that
Of which I have no knowledge.
And unless Thou forgive me
And have Mercy on me,
I should indeed be lost!" [1541]

٤٧- قَالَ رَبِّ اِنِّیْۤ اَعُوْذُ بِكَ
اَنْ اَسْـَٔلَكَ مَا لَيْسَ لِیْ بِهٖ عِلْمٌ ۭ
وَاِلَّا تَغْفِرْ لِیْ وَتَرْحَمْنِیْۤ
اَكُنْ مِّنَ الْخٰسِرِيْنَ ○

48. The word came: "O Noah!
Come down (from the Ark)
With Peace from Us,
And Blessing on thee
And on some of the Peoples
(Who will spring) from those
With thee: but (there will be
Other) Peoples to whom We
Shall grant their pleasures [1542]
(For a time), but in the end
Will a grievous Penalty
Reach them from Us." [1543]

٤٨- قِيْلَ يٰنُوْحُ اهْبِطْ
بِسَلٰمٍ مِّنَّا وَبَرَكٰتٍ عَلَيْكَ
وَعَلٰۤى اُمَمٍ مِّمَّنْ مَّعَكَ ۭ
وَاُمَمٌ سَنُمَتِّعُهُمْ
ثُمَّ يَمَسُّهُمْ مِّنَّا
عَذَابٌ اَلِيْمٌ ○

1540. See n. 1535 above. Like all men of God, Noah was kind-hearted, but he is told that there can be no compromise with evil. And Noah acknowledges the reproof. There was a wife of Noah, who was also an unbelieving woman (lxvi. 10), and she suffered the fate of Unbelievers.

1541. Noah, in his natural affection and respect for ties of relationship, was overcome with human weakness in wishing to reverse the law of spiritual Justice. It was not sin but ignorance. His ignorance was corrected by divine inspiration, and he immediately saw the full Truth, acknowledged his error, and asked for God's forgiveness and mercy. This is the standard set for us all.

1542. *Cf.* ii. 126.

1543. Those who truly seek God's light and guidance and sincerely bend their will to His Will are freely admitted to God's grace. Notwithstanding any human weaknesses in them, they are advanced higher in the spiritual stage on account of their Faith, Trust, and Striving after Right. They are given God's Peace, which gives the soul true calmness and strength, and all the blessings that flow from spiritual life. This was given not only to Noah and his family but to all the righteous people who were saved with him. And their descendants were also promised those blessings on condition of righteousness. But some of them fell from grace, as we know in history. God's grace is not a social or family privilege. Each people and each individual must earnestly strive for it and earn it.

49. Such are some of the stories
Of the Unseen, which We
Have revealed unto thee:
Before this, neither thou
Nor thy People knew them.
So persevere patiently:
For the End is for those
Who are righteous.[1544]

٤٩- تِلْكَ مِنْ اَنْۢبَآءِ الْغَيْبِ
نُوْحِيْهَآ اِلَيْكَ ۚ مَا كُنْتَ تَعْلَمُهَآ اَنْتَ
وَلَا قَوْمُكَ مِنْ قَبْلِ هٰذَا ۚ فَاصْبِرْ ۚ
اِنَّ الْعَاقِبَةَ لِلْمُتَّقِيْنَ ۝

C. 106.—Awful were the fates of the 'Ād
(xi. 50-68.) And the Thamūd, two mighty peoples
Of ancient Arabia. They rejected
God and His Message and went on
In their evil ways,—the 'Ād
In their superstitions and arrogance,
And the Thamūd in their entrenched
Selfishness, denying to others the gifts
Of God's spacious earth! How swiftly
Were they wiped out, as if they
Had never been? But wrong can never stand!

SECTION 5.

50. To the 'Ād People
(We sent) Hūd, one
Of their own brethren.
He said: "O my people!
Worship God! ye have
No other god but Him.[1545]
(Your other gods) ye do nothing
But invent!

٥٠- وَاِلٰى عَادٍ اَخَاهُمْ هُوْدًا ۭ
قَالَ يٰقَوْمِ اعْبُدُوا اللّٰهَ
مَا لَكُمْ مِّنْ اِلٰهٍ غَيْرُهٗ ۭ
اِنْ اَنْتُمْ اِلَّا مُفْتَرُوْنَ ۝

51. "O my people! I ask of you
No reward for this (Message).
My reward is from none
But Him who created me:
Will ye not then understand?

٥١- يٰقَوْمِ لَآ اَسْـَٔلُكُمْ عَلَيْهِ اَجْرًا ۭ
اِنْ اَجْرِيَ اِلَّا عَلَى الَّذِيْ فَطَرَنِيْ ۭ
اَفَلَا تَعْقِلُوْنَ ۝

52. "And O my people! Ask
Forgiveness of your Lord,

٥٢- وَيٰقَوْمِ اسْتَغْفِرُوْا رَبَّكُمْ

1544. *Cf.* n. 1528 to xi. 35. The sum of the whole matter is that the righteous, who work for God and their fellow-men, may be traduced, insulted, and persecuted. But they will be sustained by God's Mercy. They must go on working patiently, for the End will all be for them and their Cause.

1545. *Cf.* the story of Hūd the apostle of the 'Ād People, in vii. 65-72. There the argument was how other Peoples treated their apostles as the Meccans were treating Muṣṭafā. Here we see another point emphasized; the insolence of the 'Ad in obstinately adhering to false gods after the true God had been preached to them, God's long-suffering grace to them, and finally God's justice in bringing them to book while the righteous were saved.

The locality in which the 'Ād flourished is indicated in n. 1040 to vii. 65.

And turn to Him (in repentance):
He will send you the skies [1545]
Pouring abundant rain,
And add strength
To your strength: [1547]
So turn ye not back
In sin!"

ثُمَّ تُوبُوٓا إِلَيْهِ يُرْسِلِ السَّمَآءَ عَلَيْكُم
مِّدْرَارًا
وَيَزِدْكُمْ قُوَّةً إِلَىٰ قُوَّتِكُمْ
وَلَا تَتَوَلَّوْا مُجْرِمِينَ ○

53. They said: "O Hūd!
No Clear (Sign) hast thou
Brought us, and we are not
The ones to desert our gods
On thy word! Nor shall we
Believe in thee! [1548]

٥٣- قَالُوا يٰهُودُ مَا جِئْتَنَا بِبَيِّنَةٍ
وَمَا نَحْنُ بِتَارِكِىٓ ءَالِهَتِنَا عَن قَوْلِكَ
وَمَا نَحْنُ لَكَ بِمُؤْمِنِينَ ○

54. "We say nothing but that
(Perhaps) some of our gods
May have seized thee [1549]
With imbecility." He said:
"I call God to witness,
And do ye bear witness,
That I am free from the sin
Of ascribing, to Him,

٥٤- إِن نَّقُولُ إِلَّا
اعْتَرَىٰكَ بَعْضُ ءَالِهَتِنَا بِسُوٓءٍ
قَالَ إِنِّىٓ أُشْهِدُ اللَّهَ وَاشْهَدُوٓا
أَنِّى بَرِىٓءٌ مِّمَّا تُشْرِكُونَ ○

1546. The beautiful metaphor about the skies coming down with rain has been obscured unnecessarily in most translations. The country of the 'Ād was an arid country, and rain was the greatest blessing they could receive. We can imagine this being said in a time of famine, when the people performed all sorts of superstitious rites and invocations instead of turning to the true God in faith and repentance. Further, when we remember that there were, in this tract in ancient times, dams like that at Maārib, for the storage of rain water, the effect is still further heightened in pointing to God's care and mercy in His dealings with men.

1547. Adding strength to strength may refer to increase of population, as some Commentators think. While other parts of Arabia were sparsely populated, the irrigated lands of the 'Ād supported a comparatively dense population and added to their natural strength in the arts of peace and war. But the term used is perfectly general. They were a powerful people in their time. If they obeyed God and followed the law of righteousness, they would be still more powerful, for "righteousness exalteth a nation."

1548. The argument of the Unbelievers is practically this: "We are not convinced by you; we don't want to be convinced: we think you are a liar,—or perhaps a fool!" (See next verse.)

1549. See n. 1548 above. Continuing their argument, the Unbelievers make a show of making all charitable allowances for Hūd, but in reality cut him to the quick by bringing in their false gods. "To be quite polite," said they, "we will not say that you are exactly a liar! Perhaps you have been touched with imbecility! Ah yes! You rail against what you call our false gods! Some of them have paid you out, and made you a fool! Ha! ha!" This mockery is even worse than their other false accusations. For it sets up false gods against the One True God, even in dealing with Hūd. So Hūd replies, with spirit and indignation: "At least keep God's name out of your futile talk! You know as well as I do, that I worship the One True God! You pretend that your false gods can smite a true man of God! I accept the challenge. Scheme and plot against me as you may, all of you—you and your gods! See if you have any power! I ask for no quarter from you! My trust is in God!"

55. " Other gods as partners!
So scheme (your worst) against me,
All of you, and give me
No respite.[1550]

٥٥- مِن دُونِهٖ فَكِيدُونِى
جَمِيعًا ثُمَّ لَا تُنظِرُونِ ۝

56. " I put my trust in God,
My Lord and your Lord!
There is not a moving
Creature, but He hath
Grasp of its fore-lock.[1551]
Verily, it is my Lord
That is on a straight Path.[1552]

٥٦- إِنِّى تَوَكَّلْتُ عَلَى اللّٰهِ رَبِّى وَرَبِّكُمْ ۭ
مَا مِن دَآبَّةٍ اِلَّا هُوَ اٰخِذٌۢ بِنَاصِيَتِهَا ۭ
اِنَّ رَبِّى عَلٰى صِرَاطٍ مُّسْتَقِيمٍ ۝

57. " If ye turn away,—
I (at least) have conveyed
The Message with which I
Was sent to you. My Lord
Will make another People
To succeed you, and you
Will not harm Him[1553]
In the least. For my Lord
Hath care and watch
Over all things."

٥٧- فَاِن تَوَلَّوْا فَقَدْ اَبْلَغْتُكُمْ
مَّآ اُرْسِلْتُ بِهٖٓ اِلَيْكُمْ ۭ
وَيَسْتَخْلِفُ رَبِّى قَوْمًا غَيْرَكُمْ ۚ
وَلَا تَضُرُّوْنَهٗ شَيْــًٔا ۭ
اِنَّ رَبِّى عَلٰى كُلِّ شَىْءٍ حَفِيظٌ ۝

58. So when Our decree
Issued, We saved Hūd
And those who believed
With him, by (special) Grace[1554]
From Ourselves: We saved them
From a severe Penalty.

٥٨- وَلَمَّا جَآءَ اَمْرُنَا نَجَّيْنَا هُوْدًا
وَّالَّذِيْنَ اٰمَنُوْا مَعَهٗ بِرَحْمَةٍ مِّنَّا ۚ
وَنَجَّيْنٰهُمْ مِّنْ عَذَابٍ غَلِيْظٍ ۝

59. Such were the 'Ad People:
They rejected the Signs

٥٩- وَتِلْكَ عَادٌ ۟ جَحَدُوْا بِاٰيٰتِ

1550. *Cf.* vii. 195 and n. 1168.

1551. *Grasp of the fore-lock*: an Arabic idiom, referring to a horse's fore-lock. The man who grasps it has complete power over the horse, and for the horse the fore-lock is as it were the crown of his beauty, the sum of his power of self-assertion. So God's power over all creatures is unlimited and no one can withstand His decree. *Cf.* xcvi. 15-16.

1552. That is, the standard of all virtue and righteousness is in the Will of God, the Universal Will that controls all things in goodness and justice. You are on a crooked Path. God's Path is a straight Path.

1553. Hūd was dealing with a people of pride and obstinate rebellion. He tells them that their conduct will only recoil on themselves. It can do no harm to God or in any way frustrate the beneficent Plan of God. He will only put some other people in their place to carry out His Plan. That Plan is referred to in the next sentence as " care and watch " over all his Creation.

1554. A few just men might suffer for the iniquities of the many. But God's Plan is perfect and eventually saves His own people by special Grace, if they have Faith and Trust in Him.

Of their Lord and Cherisher;
Disobeyed His Apostles;
And followed the command
Of every powerful, obstinate
Transgressor.[1555]

رَبِّهِمْ وَعَصَوْا رُسُلَهُ
وَاتَّبَعُوْٓا اَمْرَ كُلِّ جَبَّارٍ عَنِيْدٍ ○

60. And they were pursued
By a Curse in this Life,—
And on the Day of Judgment.
Ah! Behold! For the 'Ād
Rejected their Lord and Cherisher!
Ah! Behold! Removed (from sight)
Were 'Ād the People of Hūd!

٦٠- وَاُتْبِعُوْا فِيْ هٰذِهِ الدُّنْيَا لَعْنَةً
وَّيَوْمَ الْقِيٰمَةِ ؕ
اَلَآ اِنَّ عَادًا كَفَرُوْا رَبَّهُمْ ؕ
اَلَا بُعْدًا لِّعَادٍ قَوْمِ هُوْدٍ ○

SECTION 6.

61. To the Thamūd People
(We sent) Ṣaliḥ, one
Of their own brethren.[1556]
He said: "O my People!
Worship God: ye have
No other God but Him.
It is He Who hath produced you[1557]
From the earth and settled you
Therein: then ask forgiveness
Of Him, and turn to Him
(In repentance): for my Lord
Is (always) near, ready
To answer."

٦١- وَاِلٰى ثَمُوْدَ اَخَاهُمْ صٰلِحًا ۘ
قَالَ يٰقَوْمِ اعْبُدُوا اللّٰهَ
مَا لَكُمْ مِّنْ اِلٰهٍ غَيْرُهٗ ؕ
هُوَ اَنْشَاَكُمْ مِّنَ الْاَرْضِ وَاسْتَعْمَرَكُمْ فِيْهَا
فَاسْتَغْفِرُوْهُ ثُمَّ تُوْبُوْٓا اِلَيْهِ ؕ
اِنَّ رَبِّيْ قَرِيْبٌ مُّجِيْبٌ ○

62. They said: "O Ṣaliḥ!
Thou hast been of us!—

٦٢- قَالُوْا يٰصٰلِحُ قَدْ كُنْتَ فِيْنَا

1555. Instead of following the beneficent Lord who cherished them, they followed every rebel against God's Law, if he only obtained a little power to dazzle them.

1556. The story of Ṣāliḥ and the Thamūd people has been told from another point of view in vii. 73-79. The difference in the point of view there and here is the same as in the story of Hūd: see n. 1545 to xi. 50. Note how the story now is the same, and yet new points and details are brought out to illustrate each new argument. Note, also, how the besetting sin of the 'Ād—pride and obstinacy—is distinguished from the besetting sin of the Thamūd—the oppression of the poor, as illustrated by the test case and symbol of the She-camel: see n. 1044 to vii. 73. All sin is in a sense pride and rebellion; yet sins take particular hues in different circumstances, and these colours are brought out as in a most artistically painted picture—with the greatest economy of words and the most piercing analysis of motives. For the locality and history of the Thamūd see n. 1043 to vii. 73.

1557. For *Anshaa* as a process of creation see n. 923 to vi. 98 and the further references given there. As to his body, man has been produced from earth or clay, and his settlement on earth is a fact of his material existence. Therefore we must conform to all the laws of our physical being, in order that through our life on this earth we may develop that higher Life which belongs to the other part of our being, our spiritual heritage. Through the use we make of our health, of our tilth, of our pastures, of material facts of all kinds, will develop our moral and spiritual nature.

A centre of our hopes[1558]
Hitherto! Dost thou (now)
Forbid us the worship
Of what our fathers worshipped?
But we are really
In suspicious (disquieting)
Doubt as to that to which
Thou invitest us."

مَرْجُوًّا قَبْلَ هٰذَآ أَتَنْهٰنَآ
أَنْ نَّعْبُدَ مَا يَعْبُدُ اٰبَآؤُنَا
وَإِنَّنَا لَفِىْ شَكٍّ
مِّمَّا تَدْعُوْنَآ إِلَيْهِ مُرِيْبٍ ○

63. He said: "O my people!
Do ye see?—If I have
A Clear (Sign) from my Lord
And He hath sent Mercy
Unto me from Himself,—who[1559]
Then can help me
Against God if I were
To disobey Him? What
Then would ye add
To my (portion) but perdition?

٦٣- قَالَ يٰقَوْمِ أَرَءَيْتُمْ إِنْ كُنْتُ
عَلٰى بَيِّنَةٍ مِّنْ رَّبِّىْ وَاٰتٰنِىْ مِنْهُ
رَحْمَةً
فَمَنْ يَّنْصُرُنِىْ مِنَ اللّٰهِ إِنْ عَصَيْتُهٗ
فَمَا تَزِيْدُوْنَنِىْ غَيْرَ تَخْسِيْرٍ ○

64. "And O my people!
This she-camel of God is
A symbol to you:[1560]
Leave her to feed
On God's (free) earth,
And inflict no harm
On her, or a swift Penalty
Will seize you!"

٦٤- وَيٰقَوْمِ هٰذِهٖ نَاقَةُ اللّٰهِ لَكُمْ
اٰيَةً فَذَرُوْهَا تَأْكُلْ فِىْ أَرْضِ اللّٰهِ
وَلَا تَمَسُّوْهَا بِسُوْٓءٍ
فَيَأْخُذَكُمْ عَذَابٌ قَرِيْبٌ ○

65. But they did ham-string her.
So he said: "Enjoy yourselves
In your homes for three days:[1561]
(Then will be your ruin):

٦٥- فَعَقَرُوْهَا فَقَالَ تَمَتَّعُوْا فِىْ
دَارِكُمْ ثَلٰثَةَ أَيَّامٍ ؕ

1558. Ṣāliḥ's life with his people had been so righteous (like that of al-Amīn in later times) that he might have been chosen leader or king if he had only conformed to their superstitions and supported their sins. But he was born for a higher mission—that of a preacher of truth and righteousness and an ardent opponent of selfish privilege and a champion of the rights of humanity on God's free earth by the symbol of the she-camel: see n. 1044 to vii. 73.

1559. "God has been good to me and bestowed on me His light and the inestimable privilege of carrying His mission to you. Don't you see that if I fail to carry out his mission, I shall have to answer before Him? Who can help me in that case? The only thing which you can add to my misfortunes would be total perdition in the spiritual world." *Cf.* xi. 28.

1560. Ṣālih does not merely take up a negative attitude. He puts forward the she-camel as a Symbol: see n. 1044 to vii. 73. "Give up your selfish monopoly. Make God's gifts on this free earth available to all. Give the poor their rights, including grazing rights on common lands. Show your penitence and your new attitude by leaving this she-camel to graze freely. She is a Symbol, and therefore sacred to you." But their only reply was to defy the appeal and ham-string the camel. And so they went the way of all sinners—to total perdition.

1561. Just three days' time for further thought and repentance! But they paid no heed. A terrible earthquake came by night, preceded by a mighty rumbling blast (probably volcanic), such as is well-known in earthquake areas. It came by night and buried them in their own fortress homes, which they thought such places of security! The morning found them lying on their faces hidden from the light. How the mighty were brought low!

(Behold) there a promise
Not to be belied!"

ذٰلِكَ وَعْدٌ غَيْرُ مَكْذُوْبٍ ○

66. When Our Decree issued,
We saved Ṣāliḥ and those
Who believed with him,
By (special) Grace from
Ourselves—[1562]
And from the Ignominy
Of that Day. For thy Lord—
He is the Strong One, and Able
To enforce His Will.

٦٦- فَلَمَّا جَآءَ اَمْرُنَا نَجَّيْنَا صٰلِحًا
وَّالَّذِيْنَ اٰمَنُوْا مَعَهٗ بِرَحْمَةٍ مِّنَّا
وَمِنْ خِزْيِ يَوْمِئِذٍ ۭ
اِنَّ رَبَّكَ هُوَ الْقَوِيُّ الْعَزِيْزُ ○

67. The (mighty) Blast [1563] overtook
The wrong-doers, and they
Lay prostrate in their homes
Before the morning,—

٦٧- وَاَخَذَ الَّذِيْنَ ظَلَمُوا الصَّيْحَةُ
فَاَصْبَحُوْا فِيْ دِيَارِهِمْ جٰثِمِيْنَ ○

68. As if they had never
Dwelt and flourished there.
Ah! Behold! For the Thamūd
Rejected their Lord and Cherisher!
Ah! Behold! Removed
(From sight) were the Thamūd! [1564]

٦٨- كَاَنْ لَّمْ يَغْنَوْا فِيْهَا ۭ
اَلَآ اِنَّ ثَمُوْدَا۟ كَفَرُوْا رَبَّهُمْ ۭ
اَلَا بُعْدًا لِّثَمُوْدَ ○ ع

C. 107.—When the angels, on a mission to Sodom
(xi. 69-95.) And Gomorrah, Cities of the Plain,
Passed by Abraham, he entertained them
And received from them the Good News
Of the line of Prophets to spring from his loins.
He tried, in his goodness of heart, to intercede
For the wicked Cities, but they were steeped
In Sin and past all hope of repentance.
Lūṭ preached to them, but they flouted him
And went to their fate, as also did Midian.
The People of Shu'aib destroyed their commerce
By fraudulent dealings and love of brute force.
Marvellous are God's Mercies, and strange
Are the ways of ungrateful man!

SECTION 7.

69. There came Our Messengers
To Abraham with glad tidings.

٦٩- وَلَقَدْ جَآءَتْ رُسُلُنَآ اِبْرٰهِيْمَ بِالْبُشْرٰى

1562. *Cf.* xi. 58 above and n. 1554. For *'Azīz*, see n. 2818 to xxi 40.
1563. *Cf.* vii. 78 and n. 1047,—also n. 1561 above.
1564. *Cf.* xi 60 above.

They said, "Peace!" He answered,
"Peace!" and hastened
To entertain them
With a roasted calf.[1565]

قَالُوا سَلٰمًا ۖ قَالَ سَلٰمٌ فَمَا لَبِثَ
أَنْ جَآءَ بِعِجْلٍ حَنِيذٍ ○

70. But when he saw
Their hands went not
Towards the (meal), he felt
Some mistrust of them,
And conceived a fear of them.[1565-A]
They said: "Fear not:
We have been sent
Against the people of Lūṭ."[1566]

٧٠- فَلَمَّا رَآ أَيْدِيَهُمْ لَا تَصِلُ إِلَيْهِ نَكِرَهُمْ
وَأَوْجَسَ مِنْهُمْ خِيفَةً ۚ
قَالُوا لَا تَخَفْ
إِنَّآ أُرْسِلْنَآ إِلٰى قَوْمِ لُوطٍ ○

71. And his wife was standing
(There), and she laughed:[1567]
But We gave her
Glad tidings of Isaac,
And after him, of Jacob.

٧١- وَامْرَأَتُهُ قَآئِمَةٌ فَضَحِكَتْ
فَبَشَّرْنٰهَا بِإِسْحٰقَ ۙ
وَمِنْ وَّرَآءِ إِسْحٰقَ يَعْقُوبَ ○

1565. According to the sequence of Sūra vii, the next reference should be to the story of Lūṭ, and that story commences at xi. 77 below, but it is introduced by a brief reference to an episode in the life of his uncle Abraham, from whose seed sprang the peoples to whom Moses, Jesus, and Muḥammad Muṣṭafā were sent with the major Revelations. Abraham had by this time passed through the fire of persecutions in the Mesopotamian valleys; he had left behind him the ancestral idolatry of Ur of the Chaldees; he had been tried and he had triumphed over the persecution of Nimrūd; he had now taken up his residence in Canaan, from which his nephew Lot (Lūṭ) was called to preach to the wicked Cities of the Plain east of the Dead Sea which is itself called Baḥr Lūṭ. Thus prepared and sanctified, he was now ready to receive the Message that he was chosen to be the progenitor of a great line of Prophets, and that Message is now referred to.

Can we localise Nimrūd? If local tradition in place-names can be relied upon, this king must have ruled over the tract which includes the modern Nimrūd, on the Tigris, about twenty miles south of Mosul. This is the site of Assyrian ruins of great interest, but the rise of Assyria as an Empire was of course much later than the time of Abraham. The Assyrian city was called Kalakh (or Calah), and archæological excavations carried out there have yielded valuable results, which are however irrelevant for our Commentary.

1565-A. With oriental hospitality Abraham received the strangers with a salutation of Peace, and immediately placed before them a sumptuous meal of roasted calf. The strangers were embarrassed. They were angels and did not eat. If hospitality is refused in the East, it means that those who refuse it meditate no good to the would-be host. Abraham therefore had a feeling of mistrust and fear in his mind, which the strangers at once set at rest by saying that their mission was in the first place to help Lūṭ as a warner to the Cities of the Plain. But in the second place they had good news for Abraham: he was to be the father of great peoples!

1566. *The people of Lūṭ* means the people to whom Lūṭ was sent on his mission of warning, the people of the wicked Cities of the Plain, Sodom and Gomorrah.

1567. The narrative is very concise, and most of the details are taken for granted. We may suppose that the angels gave the news first to Abraham, who was already, according to Gen. xxi. 5, a hundred years of age, and his wife Sarah was not far short of ninety (Gen. xvii. 7). She was probably screened according to oriental custom. She could hardly believe the news. In her scepticism (some say in her joy) she laughed. But the news was formally communicated to her that she was to be the mother of Isaac, and through Isaac, the grandmother of Jacob. Jacob was to be a fruitful tree, with his twelve sons. But hitherto Abraham had had no son by her, and Sarah was past the age of child-bearing. "How could it be?" she thought.

72. She said : "Alas for me![1568]
Shall I bear a chlid,
Seeing I am an old woman,
And my husband here
Is an old man?
That would indeed
Be a wonderful thing!"

٧٢-قَالَتْ يَٰوَيْلَتَىٰٓ ءَأَلِدُ وَأَنَا۠ عَجُوزٌ
وَهَٰذَا بَعْلِى شَيْخًا ۖ
إِنَّ هَٰذَا لَشَىْءٌ عَجِيبٌ ○

73. They said : "Dost thou
Wonder at God's decree?
The grace of God
And His blessings on you,
O ye people of the house![1569]
For He is indeed
Worthy of all praise,
Full of all glory!"[1570]

٧٣-قَالُوٓا۟ أَتَعْجَبِينَ مِنْ أَمْرِ ٱللَّهِ
رَحْمَتُ ٱللَّهِ وَبَرَكَٰتُهُۥ عَلَيْكُمْ
أَهْلَ ٱلْبَيْتِ ۚ
إِنَّهُۥ حَمِيدٌ مَّجِيدٌ ○

74. When fear had passed
From (the mind of) Abraham
And the glad tidings[1571]
Had reached him, he
Began to plead with Us
For Lūt's people.

٧٤-فَلَمَّا ذَهَبَ عَنْ إِبْرَٰهِيمَ ٱلرَّوْعُ
وَجَآءَتْهُ ٱلْبُشْرَىٰ
يُجَٰدِلُنَا فِى قَوْمِ لُوطٍ ○

75. For Abraham was,
Without doubt, forbearing
(Of faults), compassionate,
And given to look to God.[1572]

٧٥-إِنَّ إِبْرَٰهِيمَ لَحَلِيمٌ
أَوَّٰهٌ مُّنِيبٌ ○

76. O Abraham! Ṣeek not this.
The decree of thy Lord
Hath gone forth : for them
There cometh a Penalty

٧٦-يَٰٓإِبْرَٰهِيمُ أَعْرِضْ عَنْ هَٰذَآ ۖ إِنَّهُۥ قَدْ
جَآءَ أَمْرُ رَبِّكَ ۖ وَإِنَّهُمْ ءَاتِيهِمْ عَذَابٌ

1568. This is as much a sigh of past regrets as of future wistfulness!

1569. *Ahl-ul-bait* = people of the house, a polite form of addressing the wife and members of the family. Blessings are here invoked on the whole family.

1570. This little episode of Abraham's life comes in fitly as one of the illustrations of God's wonderful providence in His dealings with man. Abraham had had a tussle with his father on behalf of Truth and Unity (vi. 74); he had passed through the fire of temptation unscathed (xxi. 68-69,; he had travelled to far countries, and was now ready to receive his great mission as the fountain-head of apostles in his old age. Humanly speaking it seemed impossible that he should have a son at his age, and yet it came to pass and became a corner-stone of sacred history.

1571. *Glad tidings* : not only that he was to have a son, but that he was to be a fountain-head of apostles. So he now begins to plead at once for the sinful people to whom Lot was sent as a warner.

1572. Like Mustafā, Abraham had three qualities in a pre-eminent degree, which are here mentioned : (1) he was long-suffering with other people's faults ; (2) his sympathies and compassion were very wide ; and (3) for every difficulty or trouble he turned to God and sought Him in prayer.

That cannot be turned back![1573]

غَيْرُ مَرْدُودٍ ○

77. When Our Messengers
Came to Lūṭ, he was
Grieved on their account
And felt himself powerless
(To protect) them. He said:
"This is a distressful day."[1574]

٧٧- وَلَمَّا جَآءَتْ رُسُلُنَا لُوطًا
سِيٓءَ بِهِمْ وَضَاقَ بِهِمْ ذَرْعًا
وَّقَالَ هٰذَا يَوْمٌ عَصِيبٌ ○

78. And his people came
Rushing towards him,
And they had been long
In the habit of practising
Abominations. He said:
"O my people! Here are
My daughters: they are purer
For you (if ye marry)![1575]
Now fear God, and cover me not
With shame about my guests!
Is there not among you
A single right-minded man?"

٧٨- وَجَآءَهُ قَوْمُهُ يُهْرَعُونَ إِلَيْهِ
وَمِنْ قَبْلُ كَانُوا يَعْمَلُونَ السَّيِّـَٔاتِ
قَالَ يٰقَوْمِ هٰٓؤُلَآءِ بَنَاتِي هُنَّ أَطْهَرُ لَكُمْ
فَاتَّقُوا اللّٰهَ
وَلَا تُخْزُونِ فِي ضَيْفِي
أَلَيْسَ مِنْكُمْ رَجُلٌ رَّشِيدٌ ○

79. They said: "Well dost thou
Know we have no need
Of thy daughters: indeed
Thou knowest quite well
What we want!"

٧٩- قَالُوا لَقَدْ عَلِمْتَ مَا لَنَا
فِي بَنٰتِكَ مِنْ حَقٍّ
وَإِنَّكَ لَتَعْلَمُ مَا نُرِيدُ ○

80. He said: "Would that I
Had power to suppress you

٨٠- قَالَ لَوْ أَنَّ لِي بِكُمْ قُوَّةً

1573. This is a sort of prophetic apostrophe. 'All your care and sympathy are useless, O Abraham! All your warning, O Lūṭ, will be unheeded! Alas! they are so deep in sin that nothing will reclaim them!' This is illustrated in verse 79 below. And now we proceed to Lūṭ and how he was dealt with by the wicked.

1574. The story of Lot, as referred to in vii. 80-84, laid emphasis on the rejection of Lot's mission by men who practised unnatural abominations. See n. 1049 to vii. 80. Here the emphasis is laid on God's dealings with men—in mercy for true spiritual service and in righteous wrath and punishment for those who defy the laws of nature established by Him;—also on men's dealings with each other and the contrast between the righteous and the wicked who respect no laws human or divine.

1575. The Biblical narrative suggests that the daughters were married and their husbands were close by (Gen. xix. 14) and that these same daughters afterwards committed incest with their father and had children by him (Gen. xix. 31). The holy Qur-ān nowhere suggests such abominations. Some Commentators suggest that "my daughters" in the mouth of a venerable man like Lūṭ, the father of his people, may mean any young girls of those Towns. "My son" (*waladī*) is still a common mode of address in Arabic-speaking countries when an elderly man addresses a young man.

Or that I could betake
Myself to some powerful
support."[1576]

أَوْ آوِي إِلَىٰ رُكْنٍ شَدِيدٍ ۝

81. (The Messengers) said: "O Lūt!
We are Messengers from thy Lord!
By no means shall they
Reach thee! Now travel
With thy family while yet
A part of the night remains,
And let not any of you
Look back: but thy wife[1577]
(Will remain behind):
To her will happen
What happens to the people.
Morning is their time appointed:
Is not the morning nigh?"

٨١- قَالُوا يَا لُوطُ إِنَّا رُسُلُ رَبِّكَ
لَنْ يَصِلُوا إِلَيْكَ
فَأَسْرِ بِأَهْلِكَ بِقِطْعٍ مِّنَ اللَّيْلِ
وَلَا يَلْتَفِتْ مِنكُمْ أَحَدٌ إِلَّا امْرَأَتَكَ ۖ
إِنَّهُ مُصِيبُهَا مَا أَصَابَهُمْ ۚ
إِنَّ مَوْعِدَهُمُ الصُّبْحُ ۚ
أَلَيْسَ الصُّبْحُ بِقَرِيبٍ ۝

82. When Our decree issued,
We turned (the cities)
Upside down, and rained down
On them brimstones[1578]
Hard as baked clay,[1579]
Spread, layer on layer,—

٨٢- فَلَمَّا جَاءَ أَمْرُنَا
جَعَلْنَا عَالِيَهَا سَافِلَهَا وَأَمْطَرْنَا عَلَيْهَا
حِجَارَةً مِّن سِجِّيلٍ مَّنضُودٍ ۝

83. Marked as from thy Lord:[1580]

٨٣- مُّسَوَّمَةً عِندَ رَبِّكَ ۖ

1576. Lot seemed helpless in the situation in which he found himself,—alone against a rabble of people inflamed with evil passions. He wished he had had the strength to suppress them himself or had had some powerful support to lean on! But the powerful support was there, though he had not realised it till then. It was the support of God. His guests were not ordinary men, but Angels who had come to test the people before they inflicted the punishment. They now declared themselves, and gave him directions to get away before the morning, when the punishment would descend on the doomed Cities of the Plain.

1577. Even in Lot's household was one who detracted from the harmony of the family. She was disobedient to her husband, and he was here obeying God's Command. She looked back and shared the fate of the wicked inhabitants of the Cities of the Plain: see also lxvi. 10. The Biblical narrative suggests that she was turned into a pillar of salt (Gen. xix. 26).

1578. *Cf.* vii. 84 and n. 1052.

1579. *Sijjīl*, a Persian word Arabicised, from *Sang-o-gil*, or *Sang-i-gil*, stone and clay, or hard as baked clay, according to the Qāmūs. Sodom and Gomorrah were in a tract of hard, caky, sulphurous soil, to which this description well applies. *Cf.* li. 33, where the words are "stones of clay" (*ḥijārat min ṭīn*) in connection with the same incident. On the other hand, in cv. 4, the word *sijjīl* is used for pellets of hard-baked clay in connection with Abraha and the Companions of the Elephant.

1580. If we take the words literally, they would mean that the showers of brimstones were marked with the destiny of the wicked as decreed by God. But would it not be better to take them figuratively, to mean that the shower of brimstones was especially appointed in God's Decree or Plan to mark the punishment for the crimes of Sodom and Gomorrah?

Nor are they[1581] ever far
From those who do wrong!

وَمَا هِيَ مِنَ الظّٰلِمِيْنَ بِبَعِيْدٍ ○

SECTION 8.

84. To the Madyan people[1582]
(We sent) Shu'aib, one
Of their own brethren: he said:
"O my people! worship God:
Ye have no other god
But Him. And give not
Short measure or weight:
I see you in prosperity,[1583]
But I fear for you
The Penalty of a Day
That will compass (you) all round.

٨٤- وَإِلٰى مَدْيَنَ أَخَاهُمْ شُعَيْبًا
قَالَ يٰقَوْمِ اعْبُدُوا اللّٰهَ مَا لَكُمْ مِّنْ إِلٰهٍ
غَيْرُهٗ
وَلَا تَنْقُصُوا الْمِكْيَالَ وَالْمِيْزَانَ
إِنِّيْٓ أَرٰىكُمْ بِخَيْرٍ
وَّإِنِّيْٓ أَخَافُ عَلَيْكُمْ عَذَابَ يَوْمٍ مُّحِيْطٍ ○

85. "And O my people! give
Just measure and weight,
Nor withhold from the people
The things that are their due:[1584]
Commit not evil in the land
With intent to do mischief.

٨٥- وَيٰقَوْمِ أَوْفُوا الْمِكْيَالَ وَالْمِيْزَانَ
بِالْقِسْطِ وَلَا تَبْخَسُوا النَّاسَ أَشْيَآءَهُمْ
وَلَا تَعْثَوْا فِي الْأَرْضِ مُفْسِدِيْنَ ○

86. "That which is left you
By God is best for you,[1585]

٨٦- بَقِيَّتُ اللّٰهِ خَيْرٌ لَّكُمْ

1581. *They*: Arabic, *hiya*: some Commentators take the pronoun to refer to the wicked cities so destroyed: the meaning then would be: those wicked cities were not so different from other cities that do wrong, for they would all suffer similar punishment! Perhaps it would be better to refer "they" to the stones of punishment by a metonymy for "punishment": 'punishment would not be far from any people that did wrong.'

1582. *Cf.* vii. 85-93. The location of Madyan is explained in n. 1053 to vii. 85 and the chronological place of Shu'aib in n. 1064 to vii. 93. The point of the reference here is different from that in S. vii. Here the emphasis is on God's dealings with men and men's crooked and obstinate ways: there the emphasis was rather on their treatment of their Prophet, thus throwing light on some of the sins of the Meccans in later times.

1583. The Midianites were a commercial people, and their besetting sin was commercial selfishness and fraudulent dealings in weights and measures. Their Prophet tells them that that is the surest way to cut short their "prosperity," both in the material and the spiritual sense. When the Day of Judgment comes, it will search out their dealings through and through: "it will compass them all round," and they will not be able to escape then, however much they may conceal their frauds in this world.

1584. Both Plato and Aristotle define justice as the virtue which gives every one his due. From this point of view Justice becomes the master virtue, and includes most other virtues. It was the lack of this that ruined the Midianites. Their selfishness was "intent on mischief," *i e.*, spoiling other people's business by not giving them their just dues.

1585. God's Law does not require that a man should deprive himself of the things that are necessary for his own well-being and development. If he follows God's Law, what is left him after he renders to others their just dues will be not only enough, but will be the best possible provision for his own physical and spiritual growth. Even the kindness and consideration which God's Law inculcates are in the best interests of the man's own soul. But of course the kindness and consideration must be spontaneous. It must flow from the man's own will, and cannot be forced on him by the Teachers who come from God to show him the way.

If ye (but) believed! But I am not set Over you to keep watch!"	إِن كُنتُم مُّؤْمِنِينَ ۚ وَمَآ أَنَا۠ عَلَيْكُم بِحَفِيظٍ ○
87. They said: "O Shu'aib! Does thy (religion of) prayer Command thee that we Leave off the worship which Our fathers practised, or That we leave off doing What we like with our property?[1586] Truly, thou art the one That forbeareth with faults And is right-minded!"[1587]	٨٧- قَالُوا۟ يَٰشُعَيْبُ أَصَلَوٰتُكَ تَأْمُرُكَ أَن نَّتْرُكَ مَا يَعْبُدُ ءَابَآؤُنَآ أَوْ أَن نَّفْعَلَ فِىٓ أَمْوَٰلِنَا مَا نَشَٰٓؤُا۟ ۖ إِنَّكَ لَأَنتَ ٱلْحَلِيمُ ٱلرَّشِيدُ ○
88. He said: "O my people! See ye whether I have A Clear (Sign) from my Lord, And He hath given me Sustenance (pure and) good[1588] As from Himself? I wish not, In opposition to you, to do That which I forbid you to do. I only desire (your) betterment To the best of my power; And my success (in my task) Can only come from God. In Him I trust, And unto Him I look.	٨٨- قَالَ يَٰقَوْمِ أَرَءَيْتُمْ إِن كُنتُ عَلَىٰ بَيِّنَةٍ مِّن رَّبِّى وَرَزَقَنِى مِنْهُ رِزْقًا حَسَنًا ۚ وَمَآ أُرِيدُ أَنْ أُخَالِفَكُمْ إِلَىٰ مَآ أَنْهَىٰكُمْ عَنْهُ ۚ إِنْ أُرِيدُ إِلَّا ٱلْإِصْلَٰحَ مَا ٱسْتَطَعْتُ ۚ وَمَا تَوْفِيقِىٓ إِلَّا بِٱللَّهِ ۚ عَلَيْهِ تَوَكَّلْتُ وَإِلَيْهِ أُنِيبُ ○
89. "And O my people! Let not my dissent (from you)[1589]	٨٩- وَيَٰقَوْمِ لَا يَجْرِمَنَّكُمْ

1586. It is the way of selfish and material minded people (1) to scoff at spiritual things like prayer and worship and (2) to hug their own property rights as if there were not other rights even greater than those of property!

1587. They grow sarcastic against Shu'aib. In effect they say: "You are a fine man! You teach us that we must be kind and forbearing with other people's faults, and now get at what you call our sins! You think you are the only right-minded man!"

1588. Shu'aib's answer is gentle and persuasive. First, he would ask them not to fly into a passion but satisfy themselves that he had a mission from God, and was working in the discharge of his mission: he was not merely finding fault with them. Secondly, though he was a poor man, he asked them to note that he was happy and comfortable: God had given him good sustenance, material and spiritual, as from Himself, though he did not resort to the sort of tricks which they considered necessary for their prosperity. Thirdly, if he forbade them anything he wished to apply the same standards to himself. Fourthly, all the advice which he is giving them is for their own good, which he desires to advance to the utmost of his powers. Fifthly, he is humble for himself; he would not set himself up to be their teacher or guide, or expect to be obeyed; the success of any of his efforts on their behalf must come from God's grace; will they not therefore turn to God, so that God's grace can heal them?

1589. Finally, Shu'aib appeals to them as man to man. "Because I differ from you, do not think I do not love you or feel for you. Let it not drive you into obstinacy and sin. I see things that you do not. My vision takes in the fate of previous generations who sinned, and perished on account of their sins. Turn therefore to God in repentance."

Cause you to sin,
Lest ye suffer
A fate similar to that
Of the people of Noah
Or of Hūd or of Ṣaliḥ,
Nor are the people of Lūṭ
Far off from you![1590]

شِقَاقِيْٓ اَنْ يُّصِيْبَكُمْ
مِّثْلُ مَآ اَصَابَ قَوْمَ نُوْحٍ
اَوْ قَوْمَ هُوْدٍ اَوْ قَوْمَ صٰلِحٍ ؕ
وَمَا قَوْمُ لُوْطٍ مِّنْكُمْ بِبَعِيْدٍ ○

90. "But ask forgiveness
Of your Lord, and turn
Unto Him (in repentance):
For my Lord is indeed
Full of mercy and loving-kindness."

٩٠- وَاسْتَغْفِرُوْا رَبَّكُمْ
ثُمَّ تُوْبُوْٓا اِلَيْهِ ؕ
اِنَّ رَبِّيْ رَحِيْمٌ وَّدُوْدٌ ○

91. They said: "O Shu'aib!
Much of what thou sayest
We do not understand![1591]
In fact among us we see
That thou hast no strength!
Were it not for thy family,
We should certainly
Have stoned thee!
For thou hast among us
No great position!"[1592]

٩١- قَالُوْا يٰشُعَيْبُ مَا نَفْقَهُ
كَثِيْرًا مِّمَّا تَقُوْلُ
وَاِنَّا لَنَرٰىكَ فِيْنَا ضَعِيْفًا ۚ
وَلَوْلَا رَهْطُكَ لَرَجَمْنٰكَ ؗ
وَمَآ اَنْتَ عَلَيْنَا بِعَزِيْزٍ ○

92. He said: "O my people!
Is then my family
Of more consideration with you
Than God? For ye cast Him
Away behind your backs
(With contempt). But verily
My Lord encompasseth
On all sides
All that ye do![1593]

٩٢- قَالَ يٰقَوْمِ اَرَهْطِيْٓ
اَعَزُّ عَلَيْكُمْ مِّنَ اللّٰهِ ؕ
وَاتَّخَذْتُمُوْهُ وَرَآءَكُمْ ظِهْرِيًّا ؕ
اِنَّ رَبِّيْ بِمَا تَعْمَلُوْنَ مُحِيْطٌ ○

93. "And O my people!
Do whatever ye can:

٩٣- وَيٰقَوْمِ اعْمَلُوْا عَلٰى مَكَانَتِكُمْ

1590. The generation of Lūṭ was not far off from the generation of Shu'aib chronologically if Shu'aib was only in the fourth generation from Abraham (see n. 1064 to vii. 93). Nor was its habitat geographically far from that of Shu'aib, as the Midianites wandered about from Sinai Peninsula to the Jordan valley (see n. 1053 to vii. 85).

1591. Spiritual things are easy to understand if we bring the right mind to them. But those who are contemptuous of them deliberately shut their eyes to God's Signs, and then pretend in their superior arrogance that they are 'quite beyond them'!

1592. What they do understand is brute strength. They practically say: "Don't you see that we have all the power and influence, and you, Shu'aib, are only a poor Teacher? We could stone you or imprison you or do what we like with you! Thank us for our kindness that we spare you—, for the sake of your family. It is more than you yourself deserve!"

1593. *Cf.* viii. 47.

I will do (my part) :[1594]
Soon will ye know
Who it is on whom
Descends the Penalty
Of ignominy, and who
Is a liar!
And watch ye!
For I too am watching
With you!"[1595]

إِنِّي عَامِلٌ ۖ
سَوْفَ تَعْلَمُونَ مَن يَأْتِيهِ عَذَابٌ
يُخْزِيهِ وَمَنْ هُوَ كَاذِبٌ ۖ
وَارْتَقِبُوا إِنِّي مَعَكُمْ رَقِيبٌ ۝

94. When Our decree issued,
We saved Shu'aib and those
Who believed with him,
By (special) Mercy from
Ourselves :[1596]
But the (mighty) Blast did seize
The wrong-doers, and they
Lay prostrate in their homes
By the morning,—

٩٤- وَلَمَّا جَاءَ أَمْرُنَا نَجَّيْنَا شُعَيْبًا
وَالَّذِينَ آمَنُوا مَعَهُ
بِرَحْمَةٍ مِّنَّا
وَأَخَذَتِ الَّذِينَ ظَلَمُوا الصَّيْحَةُ
فَأَصْبَحُوا فِي دِيَارِهِمْ جَاثِمِينَ ۝

95. As if they had never
Dwelt and flourished there![1597]
Ah! Behold! How the Madyan
Were removed (from sight)
As were removed the Thamūd!

٩٥- كَأَن لَّمْ يَغْنَوْا فِيهَا ۗ
أَلَا بُعْدًا لِّمَدْيَنَ كَمَا بَعِدَتْ ثَمُودُ ۝

C. 108.—How the arrogant Pharaoh misled his people
(xi. 96-123.) In resisting God's Message through Moses!
Thus did they ruin themselves! It was they
Who wronged themselves : for God is ever kind
And His punishments are just. All men
Will be brought to His Judgment-seat, and the good
Will be rewarded with bliss, as the evil
Will be consigned to misery. Eschew evil;
Stand firm in righteousness; be not immersed
In the lusts of this world. Learn from the stories
Of the past, and seek the Lord's Mercy :
Trust Him and serve and praise Him for ever!

1594. *Cf.* vi. 135 and n. 957.

1595. If the wicked will continue to blaspheme and mock, what can the godly say but this?—"Watch and wait! God's Plan works without fail! I have faith, and I too will watch with you for its fulfilment." *Cf.* x. 102, and n. 1484.

1596. *Cf.* xi. 66 and xi. 58, n. 1554.

1597. *Cf.* xi. 67-68. The blast was probably the tremendous noise which accompanies volcanic eruptions.

SECTION 9.

96. And we sent Moses,[1598]
With our Clear (signs)
And an authority manifest,

٩٦- وَلَقَدْ أَرْسَلْنَا مُوسَىٰ بِآيَاتِنَا
وَسُلْطَانٍ مُّبِينٍ ۝

97. Unto Pharaoh and his Chiefs:
But they followed the command[1599]
Of Pharaoh, and the command
Of Pharaoh was no right (guide).

٩٧- إِلَىٰ فِرْعَوْنَ وَمَلَئِهِ فَاتَّبَعُوا أَمْرَ
فِرْعَوْنَ ۖ وَمَا أَمْرُ فِرْعَوْنَ بِرَشِيدٍ ۝

98. He will go before his people
On the Day of Judgment,
And lead them into the Fire
(As cattle are led to water):[1600]
But woeful indeed will be
The place to which they are led!

٩٨- يَقْدُمُ قَوْمَهُ يَوْمَ الْقِيَامَةِ
فَأَوْرَدَهُمُ النَّارَ ۖ
وَبِئْسَ الْوِرْدُ الْمَوْرُودُ ۝

99. And they are followed
By a curse in this (life)
And on the Day of Judgment:
And woeful is the gift
Which shall be given
(Unto them)!

٩٩- وَأُتْبِعُوا فِي هَٰذِهِ لَعْنَةً
وَيَوْمَ الْقِيَامَةِ ۚ
بِئْسَ الرِّفْدُ الْمَرْفُودُ ۝

100. These are some of the stories
Of communities which We
Relate unto thee: of them
Some are standing,[1601] and some

١٠٠- ذَٰلِكَ مِنْ أَنبَاءِ الْقُرَىٰ
نَقُصُّهُ عَلَيْكَ ۖ مِنْهَا قَائِمٌ

1598 The story of Moses and Pharaoh is referred to in many places in the Qur-ān, each in connection with some special point to be illustrated. Here the point is that God's dealings with man are in all things and at all times just. But man falls under false leadership by deliberate choice and perishes along with his false leaders accordingly. In exercise of the intelligence and choice given him, man should be particularly careful to understand his own responsibilities and to profit from God's Signs, so as to attain to God's Mercy and blessings.

1599. Pharaoh is the type of the arrogant, selfish, and false leader, who poses as a power in rivalry with that of God. Such an attitude seems to attract unregenerate humanity, which falls a willing victim, in spite of the teaching and warning given by the men of God and the many moral and spiritual forces that beckon man towards God's Grace.

1600. *Arwada* = to lead, as cattle, down to their watering place. The metaphor is apt. The true herdsman is trusted by his normal flock, and he leads them in the heat of the day down to pleasant and cool watering places in order that they may slake their thirst and be happy. The false leader does the opposite: he takes them down to the fire of eternal misery! And yet men sin against their own intelligence, and follow the false leader like cattle without intelligence!

1601. *Some are standing*: like corn, which is ready to be reaped. Among the communities which remained was, and is, Egypt, although the Pharaoh and his wicked people have been swept away. The simile of standing corn also suggests that at no time can any town or community expect permanency, except in the Law of the Lord.

Have been mown down
(By the sickle of time).[1602]

وَّحَصِيدٌ ○

101. It was not We that wronged them:
They wronged their own souls:
The deities, other than God,
Whom they invoked, profited them
No whit when there issued
The decree of thy Lord:[1603]
Nor did they add aught
(To their lot) but perdition!

١٠١- وَمَا ظَلَمْنٰهُمْ وَلٰكِنْ ظَلَمُوٓا أَنْفُسَهُمْ
فَمَآ أَغْنَتْ عَنْهُمْ اٰلِهَتُهُمُ الَّتِي
يَدْعُونَ مِنْ دُونِ اللّٰهِ مِنْ شَيْءٍ
لَّمَّا جَآءَ أَمْرُ رَبِّكَ ؕ
وَمَا زَادُوهُمْ غَيْرَ تَتْبِيبٍ ○

102. Such is the chastisement
Of thy Lord when He chastises
Communities in the midst of
Their wrong: grievous, indeed,
And severe is His chastisement.

١٠٢- وَكَذٰلِكَ أَخْذُ رَبِّكَ إِذَآ أَخَذَ الْقُرٰى
وَهِيَ ظٰلِمَةٌ ؕ
إِنَّ أَخْذَهُٓ أَلِيمٌ شَدِيدٌ ○

103. In that is a Sign
For those who fear
The Penalty of the Hereafter:
That is a Day for which mankind
Will be gathered together:
That will be a Day
Of Testimony.[1604]

١٠٣- إِنَّ فِي ذٰلِكَ لَاٰيَةً لِّمَنْ خَافَ
عَذَابَ الْاٰخِرَةِ ؕ
ذٰلِكَ يَوْمٌ مَّجْمُوعٌ لَّهُ النَّاسُ
وَذٰلِكَ يَوْمٌ مَّشْهُودٌ ○

104. Nor shall We delay it
But for a term appointed.

١٠٤- وَمَا نُؤَخِّرُهُٓ إِلَّا لِأَجَلٍ مَّعْدُودٍ ○

105. The day it arrives,
No soul shall speak[1605]

١٠٥- يَوْمَ يَأْتِ لَا تَكَلَّمُ نَفْسٌ

1602. Nations grow and ripen and are mown down. If they disobeyed God, their end is evil: if they were true and godly, their harvest was good.

1603. All false and fleeting shadows must vanish before the reality and permanence of the decree of God. If we worshipped the false, we earned nothing but perdition.

1604. *Yaumun mashhūd*: To suggest the comprehensive meaning of the Arabic I have translated, "a Day of Testimony". I proceed to explain the various shades of meaning implied: (1) a Day to which all testimony points from every quarter; (2) a Day when testimony will be given before God's Judgment-seat, by all who are relevant witnesses, *e.g.*, the Prophets that preached, the men or women we benefited or injured, the angels who recorded our thoughts and deeds, or our thoughts and deeds personified; (3) a Day which will be witnessed, *i.e.*, seen by all, no matter how or where they died.

1605. *Speak i.e.*, either in self-defence or in accusation of others or to intercede for others, or to enter into conversation or ask questions, one with another. It will be a solemn Day, before the Great Judge of all, to whom everything will be known and whose authority will be unquestioned. There will be no room for quibbling or equivocation or subterfuge of any kind, nor can any one lay the blame on another or take the responsibility of another. Personal responsibility will be enforced strictly.

Except by His leave:
Of those (gathered) some
Will be wretched and some
Will be blessed.[1606]

إِلَّا بِإِذْنِهِ ۚ فَمِنْهُمْ
شَقِيٌّ وَسَعِيدٌ ○

106. Those who are wretched
Shall be in the Fire:
There will be for them
Therein (nothing but) the heaving
Of sighs and sobs: [1607]

١٠٦- فَأَمَّا الَّذِينَ شَقُوا فَفِي النَّارِ
لَهُمْ فِيهَا زَفِيرٌ وَشَهِيقٌ ○

107. They will dwell therein [1608]
For all the time that
The heavens and the earth
Endure, except as thy Lord
Willeth: for thy Lord
Is the (sure) Accomplisher
Of what He planneth.

١٠٧- خَالِدِينَ فِيهَا مَا دَامَتِ
السَّمَاوَاتُ وَالْأَرْضُ إِلَّا مَا شَاءَ رَبُّكَ ۚ
إِنَّ رَبَّكَ فَعَّالٌ لِمَا يُرِيدُ ○

108. And those who are blessed
Shall be in the Garden:
They will dwell therein [1609]
For all the time that
The heavens and the earth
Endure, except as thy Lord
Willeth: a gift without break.[1610]

١٠٨- وَأَمَّا الَّذِينَ سُعِدُوا فَفِي الْجَنَّةِ
خَالِدِينَ فِيهَا مَا دَامَتِ
السَّمَاوَاتُ وَالْأَرْضُ إِلَّا مَا شَاءَ رَبُّكَ ۖ
عَطَاءً غَيْرَ مَجْذُوذٍ ○

1606. *Shaqī* (wretched) and *Sa'īd* (blessed) have become almost technical theological terms. They are explained in the four following verses.

1607. The first word, *Zafīr*, translated "sighs", is applied to one part in the process of the braying of an ass, when he emits a deep breath. The second, *Shahīq*, translated "sobs", is the other process in the braying of an ass, when he draws in a long breath. This suggestion of an animal proverbial for his folly implies that the wicked, in spite of their arrogance and insolence in this world below, will at last realise that they have been fools after all, throwing away their own chances whenever they got them. In lxvii. 7 the word *Shahīq* is applied to the tremendous roaring in-take or devouring of Hell-fire.

1608. *Khālidīn*: This is the word which is usually translated "dwell for ever" or "dwell for aye". Here it is definitely connected with two conditions, *viz*: (1) as long as the heavens and the earth endure, and (2) except as God wills. Some Muslim theologians deduce from this the conclusion that the penalties referred to are not eternal, because the heavens and the earth as we see them are not eternal, and the punishments for the deeds of a life that will end should not be such as will never end. The majority of Muslim theologians reject this view. They hold that the heavens and the earth here referred to are not those we see now, but others that will be eternal. They agree that God's Will is unlimited in scope and power, but that It has willed that the rewards and punishments of the Day of Judgment will be eternal. This is not the place to enter into this tremendous controversy.

1609. Exactly the same arguments apply as in the last note.

1610. The felicity will be uninterrupted, unlike any joy or happiness which we can imagine in this life and which is subject to chances and changes, as our daily experience shows.

109. Be not then in doubt
As to what these men
Worship. They worship nothing[1611]
But what their fathers worshipped
Before (them): but verily
We shall pay them back
(In full) their portion[1612]
Without (the least) abatement.

١٠٩- فَلَا تَكُ فِي مِرْيَةٍ مِّمَّا يَعْبُدُ هٰٓؤُلَآءِ ؕ
مَا يَعْبُدُونَ إِلَّا
كَمَا يَعْبُدُ آبَآؤُهُم مِّن قَبْلُ ؕ
وَإِنَّا لَمُوَفُّوهُمْ نَصِيبَهُمْ غَيْرَ مَنقُوصٍ ○ ع

SECTION 10.

110. We certainly gave the Book
To Moses, but differences
Arose therein: had it not been
That a Word had gone forth
Before from thy Lord, the matter
Would have been decided[1613]
Between them: but they
Are in suspicious doubt
Concerning it.[1614]

١١٠- وَلَقَدْ آتَيْنَا مُوسَى الْكِتٰبَ فَاخْتُلِفَ
فِيهِ ؕ
وَلَوْلَا كَلِمَةٌ
سَبَقَتْ مِن رَّبِّكَ لَقُضِيَ بَيْنَهُمْ ؕ
وَإِنَّهُمْ لَفِي شَكٍّ مِّنْهُ مُرِيبٍ ○

111. And, of a surety, to all
Will your Lord pay back
(In full the recompense)
Of their deeds: for He
Knoweth well all that they do.[1615]

١١١- وَإِنَّ كُلًّا لَّمَّا لَيُوَفِّيَنَّهُمْ رَبُّكَ أَعْمَالَهُمْ ؕ
إِنَّهُ بِمَا يَعْمَلُونَ خَبِيرٌ ○

112. Therefore stand firm (in the straight
Path) as thou art commanded,—

١١٢- فَاسْتَقِمْ كَمَا أُمِرْتَ

1611. Their worship is not based on any spiritual attitude of mind. They merely follow the ways of their fathers.

1612. God will take fully into account all their motives in such mummery as they call worship, and they will have their full spiritual consequences in the future.

1613. *Cf.* x. 19. Previous revelations are not to be denied or dishonoured because those who nominally go by them have corrupted and deprived them of spiritual value by their vain controversies and disputes. It was possible to settle such disputes under the flag, as it were, of the old Revelations, but God's Plan was to revive and rejuvenate His Message through Islam, amongst a newer and younger people, unhampered by the burden of age-long prejudices.

1614. *Cf.* xi. 62. There is always in human affairs the conflict between the old and the new,—the worn-out system of our ancestors, and the fresh living spring of God's inspiration fitting in with new times and new surroundings. The advocates of the former look upon this latter not only with intellectual doubt but with moral suspicion, as did the People of the Book upon Islam, with its fresh outlook and vigorous realistic way of looking at things.

1615. *Cf.* xi. 109 above, with which the argument is now connected up by recalling the characteristic word ("pay back") and leading to the exhortation (in the verses following) to stand firm in the right path freshly revealed.

Thou and those who with thee
Turn (unto God); and transgress not
(From the Path): for He seeth
Well all that ye do.

وَمَنْ تَابَ مَعَكَ وَلَا تَطْغَوْا ۚ إِنَّهُ بِمَا تَعْمَلُونَ بَصِيرٌ ۝

113. And incline not to those
Who do wrong, or the Fire
Will seize you; and ye have
No protectors other than God,
Nor shall ye be helped.

١١٣- وَلَا تَرْكَنُوا إِلَى الَّذِينَ ظَلَمُوا فَتَمَسَّكُمُ النَّارُ ۙ وَمَا لَكُمْ مِنْ دُونِ اللَّهِ مِنْ أَوْلِيَاءَ ثُمَّ لَا تُنْصَرُونَ ۝

114. And establish regular prayers
At the two ends of the day[1616]
And at the approaches of the night:[1617]
For those things that are good
Remove those that are evil:[1618]
Be that the word of remembrance
To those who remember (their Lord):

١١٤- وَأَقِمِ الصَّلَوٰةَ طَرَفَيِ النَّهَارِ وَزُلَفًا مِنَ اللَّيْلِ ۚ إِنَّ الْحَسَنَاتِ يُذْهِبْنَ السَّيِّئَاتِ ۚ ذَٰلِكَ ذِكْرَىٰ لِلذَّاكِرِينَ ۝

115. And be steadfast in patience;
For verily God will not suffer
The reward of the righteous
To perish.

١١٥- وَاصْبِرْ فَإِنَّ اللَّهَ لَا يُضِيعُ أَجْرَ الْمُحْسِنِينَ ۝

116. Why were there not,
Among the generations before you,
Persons possessed of balanced[1619]
Good sense, prohibiting (men)

١١٦- فَلَوْلَا كَانَ مِنَ الْقُرُونِ مِنْ قَبْلِكُمْ أُولُوا بَقِيَّةٍ يَنْهَوْنَ

1616. *The two ends of the day*: Morning and afternoon. The morning prayer is the *Fajr*, after the light is up but before sunrise: we thus get up betimes and begin the day with the remembrance of God and of our duty to Him, just as an ambassador might start on his journey after saluting his king and receiving his blessing. The early afternoon prayer, *Ẓuhr*, is immediately after noon: we are in the midst of our daily life, and again we remember God.

1617. *Approaches of the night*: *Zulafun*, plural of *Zulfatun*, an approach, something near at hand. As Arabic has, like Greek, a dual number distinct from the plural, and the plural number is used here, and not the dual, it is reasonable to argue that at least three "approaches of the night" are meant. The late afternoon prayer, *'Aṣr*, can be one of these three, and the evening prayer, *Magrib*, just after sunset, can be the second. The early night prayer, *'Ishā*, at supper time when the glow of sunset is disappearing, would be the third of the "approaches of the night", when we commit ourselves to God before sleep. These are the five canonical prayers of Islām.

1618. "*Those things that are good*": in this context the words refer primarily to prayers and sacred thoughts, but they include all good thoughts, good words, and good deeds. It is by them that we keep away everything that is evil, whether referring to the past, the present, or the future.

1619. *Baqīyat*: some virtue or faculty that stands assault and is lasting; balanced good sense that stands firm to virtue and is not dazzled by the lusts and pleasures of this world, and is not deterred by fear from boldly condemning wrong if it was fashionable or customary. It is leaders possessed of such character that can save a nation from disaster or perdition. The scarcity of such leaders—and the rejection of the few who stood out—brought ruin among the nations whose example has already been set out to us as a warning.

In xi, 86 the word has a more literal meaning.

From mischief in the earth—
Except a few among them
Whom We saved (from harm)? [1620]
But the wrong-doers pursued
The enjoyment of the good things
Of life which were given them,
And persisted in sin.

عَنِ الْفَسَادِ فِي الْأَرْضِ إِلَّا قَلِيلًا
مِّمَّنْ أَنجَيْنَا مِنْهُمْ ۚ
وَاتَّبَعَ الَّذِينَ ظَلَمُوا مَا أُتْرِفُوا فِيهِ
وَكَانُوا مُجْرِمِينَ ○

117. Nor would thy Lord be
The One to destroy
Communities for a single
wrong-doing, [1621]
If its members were likely
To mend.

١١٧- وَمَا كَانَ رَبُّكَ لِيُهْلِكَ
الْقُرَىٰ بِظُلْمٍ
وَأَهْلُهَا مُصْلِحُونَ ○

118. If thy Lord had so willed,
He could have made mankind [1622]
One People: but they
Will not cease to dispute,

١١٨- وَلَوْ شَاءَ رَبُّكَ لَجَعَلَ النَّاسَ أُمَّةً
وَاحِدَةً وَلَا يَزَالُونَ مُخْتَلِفِينَ ○

119. Except those on whom thy Lord
Hath bestowed His Mercy:
And for this did He create
Them: and the Word
Of thy Lord shall be fulfilled:
"I will fill Hell with jinns
And men all together." [1623]

١١٩- إِلَّا مَن رَّحِمَ رَبُّكَ ۚ
وَلِذَٰلِكَ خَلَقَهُمْ ۗ وَتَمَّتْ كَلِمَةُ رَبِّكَ
لَأَمْلَأَنَّ جَهَنَّمَ مِنَ الْجِنَّةِ
وَالنَّاسِ أَجْمَعِينَ ○

1620. The exceptional men of firm virtue would have been destroyed by the wicked to whom they were an offence, had they not been saved by the grace and mercy of God. Or perhaps, but for such grace, they might themselves have succumbed to the evil around them, or been overwhelmed in the general calamity.

1621. There are different shades of interpretation for this verse. I follow Baidhāwi in construing *ẓulmin* here as "a single wrong". He thinks that the wrong referred to is *shirk*, or polytheism: God will not destroy for mere wrong belief if the conduct is right. I incline to interpret in more general terms. God is Long-Suffering and Oft-Forgiving: He is too Merciful to destroy for a single wrong, if there is any hope of reclaiming the wrong-doers to repentance and amendment or right life. An alternative interpretation is: "to destroy communities unjustly"....

1622. *Cf.* x. 19. All mankind might have been one. But in God's Plan man was to have a certain measure of free-will, and this made differences inevitable. This would not have mattered if all had honestly sought God. But selfishness and moral wrong came in, and people's disputations became mixed up with hatred, jealousy, and sin, except in the case of those who accepted God's grace, which saved them. The object of their creation was to raise them up spiritually by God's grace. But if they will choose the path of evil and fall into sin, God's decree must be fulfilled, and His justice will take its course. In the course of that justice Hell will be filled with men and spirits, such is the number of those who go astray.

1623. *Cf.* vii. 18 and vii. 179. If Satan and his evil spirits tempt men from the path of rectitude, the responsibility of the tempted, who choose the path of evil, is no less than that of the tempters, and they will both be involved in punishment together.

120. All that we relate to thee
Of the stories of the apostles,—
With it We make firm
Thy heart: in them there cometh
To thee the Truth, as well as
An exhortation and a message
Of remembrance to those who
believe.[1624]

١٢٠- وَكُلًّا نَّقُصُّ عَلَيْكَ مِنْ أَنۢبَآءِ الرُّسُلِ
مَا نُثَبِّتُ بِهِۦ فُؤَادَكَ
وَجَآءَكَ فِى هَٰذِهِ الْحَقُّ
وَمَوْعِظَةٌ وَذِكْرَىٰ لِلْمُؤْمِنِينَ ۝

121. Say to those who do not
Believe: "Do whatever ye can:
We shall do our part;[1624-A]

١٢١- وَقُل لِّلَّذِينَ لَا يُؤْمِنُونَ اعْمَلُوا۟
عَلَىٰ مَكَانَتِكُمْ إِنَّا عَٰمِلُونَ ۝

122. "And wait ye!
We too shall wait."[1625]

١٢٢- وَانتَظِرُوٓا۟ إِنَّا مُنتَظِرُونَ ۝

123. To God do belong
The unseen (secrets)
Of the heavens and the earth,
And to Him goeth back
Every affair (for decision):[1626]
Then worship Him,
And put thy trust in Him:
And thy Lord is not
Unmindful of aught
That ye do.

١٢٣- وَلِلَّهِ غَيْبُ السَّمَٰوَٰتِ وَالْأَرْضِ
وَإِلَيْهِ يُرْجَعُ الْأَمْرُ
كُلُّهُۥ فَاعْبُدْهُ
وَتَوَكَّلْ عَلَيْهِ
وَمَا رَبُّكَ بِغَٰفِلٍ عَمَّا تَعْمَلُونَ ۝ ع

1624. The stories of the Prophets in the Qur-ān are not mere narratives or histories: they involve three things: (1) they teach the highest spiritual Truth; (2) they give advice, direction, and warning, as to how we should govern our lives, and (3) they awaken our conscience and recall to us the working of God's Law in human affairs. The story of Joseph in the next Sūra is an illustration in point.

1624-A. *Cf.* xi. 93 and vi. 135, n. 957. 'The worst that ye can do will not defeat God's Plan; and as for us who believe, our obvious duty is to do our part as taught to us by God's revelation.

1625. *Cf.* xi. 93, n. 1595, and x. 102, n. 1484. If the wicked only wait, they will see how God's Plan unfolds itself. As for those who believe, they are glad to wait in perfect confidence, because they know that God is good and merciful, as well as just and true.

1626. *Cf* ii 210. There is nothing, secret or open, in our world or in Creation, which does not depend ultimately on God's Will and Plan. Every affair goes back to Him for decision. Therefore we must worship Him and trust Him. Worship implies many things: *e.g.* (1) trying to understand His nature and His Will; (2) realising His goodness and glory, and His working in us; as a means to this end, (3) keeping Him in constant remembrance and celebrating His praise, to whom all praise is due; and (4) completely identifying our will with His, which means obedience to His Law, and service to Him and His creatures in all sincerity.

INTRODUCTION TO SŪRA XII (*Yūsuf*).

For the chronological place of this Sūra and the general argument of Sūras x. to xv. see Introduction to Sūra x.

In subject-matter this Sūra is entirely taken up with the story (recapitulated rather than told) of Joseph, the youngest (but one) of the twelve sons of the patriarch Jacob. The story is called the most beautiful of stories (xii. 3) for many reasons: (1) it is the most detailed of any in the Qur-ān; (2) it is full of human vicissitudes, and has therefore deservedly appealed to men and women of all classes; (3) it paints in vivid colours, with their spiritual implications, the most varied aspects of life—the patriarch's old age and the confidence between him and his little best-beloved son, the elder brothers' jealousy of this little son, their plot and their father's grief, the sale of the father's darling into slavery for a miserable little price, carnal love contrasted with purity and chastity, false charges, prison, the interpretation of dreams, low life and high life, Innocence raised to honour, the sweet "revenge" of Forgiveness and Benevolence, high matters of state and administration, humility in exaltation, filial love, and the beauty of Piety and Truth.

The story is similar to but not identical with the Biblical story; but the atmosphere is wholly different. The Biblical story is like a folk-tale in which morality has no place. Its tendency is to exalt the clever and financially-minded Jew against the Egyptian, and to explain certain ethnic and tribal peculiarities in later Jewish history. Joseph is shown as buying up all the cattle and the land of the poor Egyptians for the State under the stress of famine conditions, and making the Israelites "rulers" over Pharoah's cattle. The Quranic story, on the other hand, is less a narrative than a highly spiritual sermon or allegory explaining the seeming contradictions in life, the enduring nature of virtue in a world full of flux and change, and the marvellous working of God's eternal purpose in His Plan as unfolded to us on the wide canvas of history. This aspect of the matter has been a favourite with Muslim poets and Sūfi exegetists, and is further referred to in Appendix VI (at the end of this Sūra), in connection with Jāmi's great Persian masterpiece, *Yūsuf-o-Zulaikhā*.

Summary.—Life is a dream and a vision, to be explained by stories and parables, as in the perspicuous Arabic Qur-ān. The truth, which Joseph the man of God saw in his vision, was unpalatable to his ten half-brothers, who plotted against him and sold him into slavery to a merchant for a few pieces of silver. (xii. 1-20, and C. 109.)

Joseph was taken by the merchant into Egypt, was bought by a great Egyptian court dignitary ('Azīz), who adopted him. The dignitary's wife sought, but in vain, to attract Joseph to the delights of earthly love. His resistance brought him disgrace and imprisonment, but he taught the truth even in prison and was known for his kindness. One of his fellow prisoners, to whom he had interpreted a dream, was released and received into favour as the King's cup-bearer. (xii. 21-42, and C. 110.)

The King had a vision, which Joseph (through the cup-bearer) got an opportunity of explaining. Joseph insisted that all the scandal that had been raised about him should be publicly cleared. He was received into favour, and was appointed wazīr

by the King. His half-brothers (driven by famine) came to Egypt and were treated kindly by Joseph without their knowing his identity. He asks them to bring his full brother, the youngest son, Benjamin. (xii. 43-68, and C. 111.)

Joseph detains Benjamin and by a stratagem convicts his half-brothers of their hatred and crime against himself, forgives them, and sends them to bring Jacob and the whole family from Canaan to Egypt. (xii. 69-93, and C. 112.)

Israel (Jacob) comes, is comforted, and settles in Egypt. The name of God is glorified. The truth of God endures for ever, and God's purpose is fully revealed in the Hereafter. (xii. 94-111, and C. 113).

C. 109.—Life and Wisdom are explained by Signs,
(xii. 1-20.) Symbols, Parables, and moving Stories,
In the Holy Qur-ān. A beautiful story
Is that of Joseph, the best-beloved son
Of Jacob. His future greatness
Was pre-figured in a vision, but his brothers
Were filled with envy and hate: they plotted
To get rid of him and threw him down
Into a well. Some merchants found him,
Bound for Egypt. The brothers sold him
Into slavery for a few silver coins,—
Him the noblest man of his age,
Marked out by God for a destiny
Of greatness, righteousness, and benevolence.

Sūra XII.

Yūsuf, or Joseph.

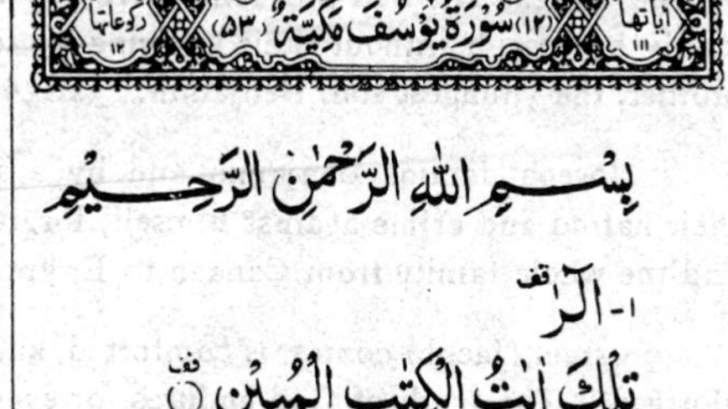

In the name of God, Most Gracious, Most Merciful.

بِسْمِ اللهِ الرَّحْمٰنِ الرَّحِيْمِ

1. A. L. R.[1627] These are
The Symbols[1628] (or Verses)
Of the Perspicuous Book.[1629]

١- الٓرٰ قف
تِلْكَ اٰيٰتُ الْكِتٰبِ الْمُبِيْنِ ۟

2. We have sent it down
As an Arabic Qur-ān,[1630]
In order that ye may
Learn wisdom.

٢- اِنَّآ اَنْزَلْنٰهُ قُرْءٰنًا عَرَبِيًّا
لَّعَلَّكُمْ تَعْقِلُوْنَ ۝

3. We do relate unto thee
The most beautiful of[1631] stories,
In that We reveal to thee
This (portion of the) Qur-ān:
Before this, thou too
Was among those
Who knew it not.

٣- نَحْنُ نَقُصُّ عَلَيْكَ اَحْسَنَ الْقَصَصِ
بِمَآ اَوْحَيْنَآ اِلَيْكَ هٰذَا الْقُرْاٰنَ ۖ
وَاِنْ كُنْتَ مِنْ قَبْلِهٖ لَمِنَ الْغٰفِلِيْنَ ۝

4. Behold, Joseph said
To his father: "O my father![1632]

٤- اِذْ قَالَ يُوْسُفُ لِاَبِيْهِ يٰٓاَبَتِ

1627. For the meaning of these mystic letters, see Introduction to S. x.

1628. *Āyāt*: Signs, Symbols, verses of the Qur-ān. The Symbolic meaning is particularly appropriate here, as the whole of Joseph's story is a Sign or a Miracle,—a wonder-working exposition of the Plan and Purpose of God.

1629. *Cf.* v. 17, n. 716. The predominant meaning of *Mubin* here is: one that explains or makes things clear.

1630. *Qur-ān* means: something (1) to be read, or (2) recited, or (3) proclaimed. It may apply to a verse, or a Sūra, or to the whole Book of Revelation.

1631. *Most beautiful of stories*: see Introduction to this Sūra. Eloquence consists in conveying by a word or hint many meanings for those who can understand and wish to learn wisdom. Not only is Joseph's story "beautiful" in that sense. Joseph himself was renowned for manly beauty: the women of Egypt, called him a noble angel (xii. 31), and the beauty of his exterior form was a symbol of the beauty of his soul. Moreover, the whole of the mystic meaning of Zulaikhā's love for him centres round the theme, how beauty can be falsely worshipped in a sort of disguised self-indulgence, contrasted with the growth of that true love of Beauty, which casts out Self and turns to the eternal Beauty of the Soul.

1632. For the Parable all that is necessary to know about Joseph is that he was one of the Chosen Ones of God. For the story it is necessary to set down a few more details. His father was Jacob, also called Israel the son of Isaac, the younger son of Abraham, (the elder son having been Ismā'il, whose story is told in ii. 124-129). Abraham may be called the Father of the line of Semitic prophecy. Jacob had four wives. From three of them he had ten sons. In his old age he had from Rachel (Arabic *Rāḥil*) a very beautiful woman, two sons Joseph and Benjamin (the youngest). At the time this story begins we may suppose that Joseph was about seventeen years of age. The place where Jacob and his family and his flocks were located was in Canaan, and is shown by tradition near modern Nāblūs (ancient Shechem), some thirty miles north of Jerusalem. The traditional site of the well into which Joseph was thrown by his brothers is still shown in the neighbourhood.

I did see eleven stars
And the sun and the moon :
I saw them prostrate themselves
To me!"[1633]

5. Said (the father) :
" My (dear) little son !
Relate not thy vision
To thy brothers, lest they
Concoct a plot against thee :[1634]
For Satan is to man
An avowed enemy ![1635]

6. " Thus will thy Lord
Choose thee and teach thee
The interpretation of stories[1636]
(and events)
And perfect His favour
To thee and to the posterity
Of Jacob—even as He
Perfected it to thy fathers
Abraham and Isaac aforetime !
For God is full of knowledge
And wisdom."[1637]

SECTION 2.

7. Verily in Joseph and his
brethren
Are Signs (or Symbols)

إِنِّي رَأَيْتُ أَحَدَ عَشَرَ كَوْكَبًا وَّالشَّمْسَ وَ
الْقَمَرَ رَأَيْتُهُمْ لِي سٰجِدِيْنَ ○

٥- قَالَ يٰبُنَيَّ
لَا تَقْصُصْ رُءْيَاكَ عَلٰٓى إِخْوَتِكَ
فَيَكِيْدُوْا لَكَ كَيْدًا ؕ
إِنَّ الشَّيْطٰنَ لِلْإِنْسَانِ عَدُوٌّ مُّبِيْنٌ ○

٦- وَكَذٰلِكَ يَجْتَبِيْكَ رَبُّكَ وَيُعَلِّمُكَ
مِنْ تَأْوِيْلِ الْأَحَادِيْثِ وَيُتِمُّ نِعْمَتَهٗ
عَلَيْكَ وَعَلٰٓى اٰلِ يَعْقُوْبَ كَمَآ
أَتَمَّهَا عَلٰٓى أَبَوَيْكَ مِنْ قَبْلُ إِبْرٰهِيْمَ وَ
إِسْحٰقَ ؕ
إِنَّ رَبَّكَ عَلِيْمٌ حَكِيْمٌ ○ ع

٧- لَقَدْ كَانَ فِيْ يُوْسُفَ وَإِخْوَتِهٖٓ اٰيٰتٌ

1633. Joseph was a mere lad of seventeen. But he was true and frank and righteous; he was a type of manly beauty and rectitude. His father loved him dearly. His half-brothers were jealous of him and hated him His destiny was pre-figured in the vision. He was to be exalted in rank above his eleven brothers (stars) and his father and mother (sun and moon), but as the subsequent story shows, he never lost his head, but always honoured his parents and repaid his brothers' craft and hatred with forgiveness and kindness.

1634. The young lad Yūsuf was innocent and did not even know of his brothers' guile and hatred, but the father knew and warned him.

1635. The story is brought up at once to its spiritual bearing. These wicked brothers were puppets in the hands of Evil. They allowed their manhood to be subjugated by Evil, not remembering that Evil was the declared opposite or enemy of the true nature and instincts of manhood.

1636. If Joseph was to be of the elect, he must understand and interpret Signs and events aright. The imagination of the pure sees truths, which those not so endowed cannot understand. The dreams of the righteous pre-figure great events, while the dreams of the futile are mere idle futilities. Even things that happen to us are often like dreams. The righteous man receives disasters and reverses, not with blasphemies against God, but with humble devotion, seeking to ascertain His Will. Nor does he receive good fortune with arrogance, but as an opportunity for doing good, to friends and foes alike. His attitude to histories and stories is the same : he seeks the edifying material which leads to God.

1637. Whatever happens is the result of God's Will and Plan. And He is good and wise, and He knows all things. Therefore we must trust Him. In Joseph's case he could look back to his fathers, and to Abraham, the True, the Righteous, who through all adversities kept his Faith pure and undefiled, and won through.

For Seekers (after Truth).[1638]

لِّلسَّآئِلِينَ ○

8. They said: "Truly Joseph
And his brother are loved
More by our father than we:
But we are a goodly body![1639]
Really our father is obviously
Wandering (in his mind)!

٨- إِذْ قَالُوا لَيُوسُفُ وَأَخُوهُ أَحَبُّ
إِلَىٰٓ أَبِينَا مِنَّا وَنَحْنُ عُصْبَةٌ
إِنَّ أَبَانَا لَفِي ضَلَٰلٍ مُّبِينٍ ○

9. "Slay ye Joseph or cast him out
To some (unknown) land,
That so the favour
Of your father may be
Given to you alone:
(There will be time enough)
For you to be righteous after
that!"[1640]

٩- اقْتُلُوا يُوسُفَ أَوِ اطْرَحُوهُ أَرْضًا
يَخْلُ لَكُمْ وَجْهُ أَبِيكُمْ
وَتَكُونُوا مِنۢ بَعْدِهِۦ
قَوْمًا صَٰلِحِينَ ○

10. Said one of them: "Slay not
Joseph, but if ye must
Do something, throw him down
To the bottom of the well:
He will be picked up
By some caravan of travellers."[1641]

١٠- قَالَ قَآئِلٌ مِّنْهُمْ لَا تَقْتُلُوا يُوسُفَ
وَأَلْقُوهُ فِي غَيَٰبَتِ الْجُبِّ يَلْتَقِطْهُ بَعْضُ
السَّيَّارَةِ إِن كُنتُمْ فَٰعِلِينَ ○

1638. In Joseph's story we have good and evil contrasted in so many different ways. Those in search of true spiritual knowledge can see it embodied in concrete events in this story of many facets, matching the colours of Joseph's many-coloured coat.

1639. The ten brothers not only envied and hated their innocent younger brothers Joseph and Benjamin. They despised and dishonoured their father as an ingnorant old fool,—in his dotage. In reality Jacob had the wisdom to see that his young and innocent sons wanted protection and to perceive Joseph's spiritual greatness. But his wisdom, to them, was folly or madness or imbecility, because it touched their self-love, as truth often does. And they relied on the brute strength of numbers – the ten hefty brethren against old Jacob, the lad Joseph, and the boy Benjamin!

1640. There seems to be some irony here, consistent with the cynical nature of these callous, worldly-wise brethren. The goodness of Joseph was a reproach to their own wickedness. Perhaps the grieved father contrasted Joseph against them, and sometimes spoke of it: "Why don't you be good like Joseph?" This was gall and wormwood to them. Real goodness was to them nothing but a name. Perhaps it only suggested hypocrisy to them. So they plotted to get rid of Joseph. In their mean hearts they thought that would bring back their father's love whole to them. But they valued that love only for what material good they could get out of it. On the other hand their father was neither foolish nor unjustly partial. He only knew the difference between gold and dross. They say in irony, "Let us first get rid of Joseph. It will be time enough then to pretend to be 'good' like him, or to repent of our crime after we have had all its benefits in material things!"

1641. One of the brethren, perhaps less cruel by nature, or perhaps more worldly-wise, said: "Why undertake the risk of blood-guiltiness? Throw him into the well you see there! Some travellers passing by will pick him up and remove him to a far country. If not, at least *we* shall not have killed him." This was false casuistry, but such casuistry appeals to sinners of a certain kind of temperament. The well was apparently a dry well, deep enough to prevent his coming out, but with no water in which he could be drowned. It was God's Plan to save him alive, but not to make Joseph indebted to any of his brethren for his life!

11. They said: "O our father!
Why dost thou not
Trust us with Joseph,—
Seeing we are indeed
His sincere well-wishers?[1642]

١١- قَالُوا يَٰٓأَبَانَا
مَا لَكَ لَا تَأْمَنَّا عَلَىٰ يُوسُفَ
وَإِنَّا لَهُۥ لَنَٰصِحُونَ ○

12. "Send him with us to-morrow
To enjoy himself and play,
And we shall take
Every care of him."[1643]

١٢- أَرْسِلْهُ مَعَنَا غَدًا يَرْتَعْ وَيَلْعَبْ
وَإِنَّا لَهُۥ لَحَٰفِظُونَ ○

13. (Jacob) said: "Really
It saddens me that ye
Should take him away:
I fear lest the wolf
Should devour him
While ye attend not[1644]
To him."

١٣- قَالَ إِنِّى لَيَحْزُنُنِىٓ أَن تَذْهَبُوا بِهِۦ
وَأَخَافُ أَن يَأْكُلَهُ ٱلذِّئْبُ
وَأَنتُمْ عَنْهُ غَٰفِلُونَ ○

14. They said: "If the wolf
Were to devour him
While we are (so large) a party,
Then should we indeed
(First) have perished
ourselves!"[1645]

١٤- قَالُوا لَئِنْ أَكَلَهُ ٱلذِّئْبُ
وَنَحْنُ عُصْبَةٌ
إِنَّآ إِذًا لَّخَٰسِرُونَ ○

15. So they did take him away,
And they all agreed

١٥- فَلَمَّا ذَهَبُوا بِهِۦ وَأَجْمَعُوٓا

1642. The plot having been formed, the brethren proceed to put it into execution. Jacob, knowing the situation, did not ordinarily trust his beloved Joseph with the brethren. The latter therefore remonstrate and feign brotherly affection.

1643. They did not expect their protestations to be believed in. But they added an argument that might appeal both to Jacob and Joseph. 'They were going to give their young brother a good time. Why not let him come out with them and play and enjoy himself to his heart's content?'

1644. Jacob did not know the precise plot, but he had strong misgivings But how could he put off these brethren? If they were driven to open hostility, they would be certain to cause him harm. He must deal with the brethren wisely and cautiously. He pleaded that he was an old man, and would miss Joseph and be sad without him. And after all, Joseph was not of an age to play with them. They would be attending to their own affairs, and a wolf might come and attack and kill Joseph. In saying this he was really unwittingly giving a cue to the wicked ones, for they use that very excuse in verse 17 below. Thus the wicked plot thickens, but there is a counter-plan also, which is drawing a noose of lies round the wicked ones, so that they are eventually driven into a corner, and have to confess their own guilt in verse 91 below, and through repentance obtain forgiveness.

1645. Jacob's objections as stated could be easily rebutted, and the brethren did so. They would be eleven in the party, and the ten strong and grown-up men would have to perish before the wolf could touch the young lad Joseph! So they prevailed, as verbal arguments are apt to prevail, when events are weaving their web on quite another Plan, which has nothing to do with verbal arguments. Presumably Benjamin was too young to go with them.

To throw him down
To the bottom of the well :
And We put into his heart [1646]
(This Message) : 'Of a surety
Thou shalt (one day)
Tell them the truth
Of this their affair
While they know (thee) not " [1647]

أَنْ يَّجْعَلُوْهُ فِيْ غَيٰبَتِ الْجُبِّ ۚ
وَاَوْحَيْنَآ اِلَيْهِ لَتُنَبِّئَنَّهُمْ
بِاَمْرِهِمْ هٰذَا
وَهُمْ لَا يَشْعُرُوْنَ ○

16. Then they came
To their father
In the early part
Of the night,
Weeping. [1648]

١٦- وَجَآءُوْٓ اَبَاهُمْ
عِشَآءً يَّبْكُوْنَ ○

17. They said : " O our father !
We went racing with one
another, [1649]
And left Joseph with our things ;
And the wolf devoured him....
But thou wilt never believe us
Even though we tell the truth." [1650]

١٧- قَالُوْا يٰٓاَبَانَآ اِنَّا ذَهَبْنَا نَسْتَبِقُ
وَتَرَكْنَا يُوْسُفَ عِنْدَ مَتَاعِنَا فَاَكَلَهُ
الذِّئْبُ ۚ وَمَآ اَنْتَ بِمُؤْمِنٍ لَّنَا
وَلَوْ كُنَّا صٰدِقِيْنَ ○ النصف

18. They stained his shirt [1651]
With false blood. He said :

١٨- وَجَآءُوْ عَلٰى قَمِيْصِهٖ بِدَمٍ كَذِبٍ ۗ

1646. God was with Joseph in all his difficulties, sorrows, and sufferings, as He is with all His servants who put their trust in Him. The poor lad was betrayed by his brothers, and left, perhaps to die or to be sold into slavery. But his heart was undaunted. His courage never failed him. On the contrary he had an inkling, a presentiment, of things that were to be—that his own rectitude and beauty of soul would land him on his feet, and perhaps some day, his brothers would stand in need of him, and he would be in a position to fulfil that need, and would do it gladly, putting them to shame for their present plotting and betrayal of him.

1647. This situation actually occurred when Joseph later on became the governor of Egypt and his brothers stood before him suing for his assistance although they did not know that he was their betrayed brother ; see xii. 89 below ; also xii. 58.

1648. The plotters were ready with their false tale for their father, but in order to make it appear plausible, they came some time after sundown, to show that they had made an effort to search for their brother and save him.

1649. They wanted to make out that they were not negligent of Joseph. They were naturally having games and exercise, while the boy was left with their belongings. It was the racing that prevented them from seeing the wolf. And Jacob's fears about the wolf (xii. 13 above) made them imagine that he would swallow the wolf story readily.

1650. They were surprised that Jacob received the story about the wolf with cold incredulity. So they grew petulant, put on an air of injured innocence, and bring out the blood-stained garment described in the next verse.

1651. Joseph wore a garment of many colours, described in Persian as a *qabā bū-qalamūn.* This was itself allegorical of the wonderful changes of fortune which Joseph underwent in his life. This was a special garment peculiar to Joseph. If the brethren could produce it blood-stained before their father, they thought he would be convinced that Joseph had been killed by a wild beast. But the stain on the garment was a stain of " false blood ",—not the blood of Joseph, but the blood of a goat which the brethren had killed expressly for this purpose.

" Nay, but your minds
Have made up a tale
(That may pass) with you.[1652]
(For me) patience is most fitting :
Against that which ye assert,
It is God (alone)
Whose help can be sought "...

قَالَ بَلْ سَوَّلَتْ لَكُمْ أَنفُسُكُمْ أَمْرًا ۖ
فَصَبْرٌ جَمِيلٌ ۖ
وَاللَّهُ الْمُسْتَعَانُ عَلَىٰ مَا تَصِفُونَ ○

19. Then there came a caravan[1653]
Of travellers: they sent
Their water-carrier (for water),
And he let down his bucket
(Into the well)...He said :
" Ah there! Good news![1654]
Here is a (fine) young man!"
So they concealed him[1655]
As a treasure! But God
Knoweth well all that they do![1656]

١٩-وَجَاءَتْ سَيَّارَةٌ
فَأَرْسَلُوا وَارِدَهُمْ فَأَدْلَىٰ دَلْوَهُ ۖ
قَالَ يَا بُشْرَىٰ هَٰذَا غُلَامٌ ۚ
وَأَسَرُّوهُ بِضَاعَةً ۚ
وَاللَّهُ عَلِيمٌ بِمَا يَعْمَلُونَ ○

20. The (Brethren) sold him
For a miserable price,—

٢٠-وَشَرَوْهُ بِثَمَنٍ

1652. Jacob saw that there had been some foul play, and he did not hesitate to say so. In effect he said: " Ah me! the tale you tell may be good enough for you, who invented it! But what about me, your aged father? What is there left in life for me now, with my beloved son gone? And yet what can I do but hold my heart in patience and implore God's assistance? I have faith, and I know that all that He does is for the best!"

1653. Then comes the caravan of unknown travellers--Midianite or Arab merchants travelling to Egypt with merchandise, such as the balm of Gilead in Trans-Jordania. In accordance with custom the caravan was preceded by advance parties to search out water and pitch a camp near. They naturally went to the well and let down their bucket. To their surprise the well was dry, but a handsome youth got into the bucket and came out in it when they hauled up the bucket!

1654. The water carrier is surprised and taken aback, when his bucket brings up, not water, but a youth of comely appearance, innocent like an angel, with a face as bright as the sun! What is he to make of it? Anyhow, to see him is a delight! And he shouts it out as a piece of good news. Some Commentators think that "*Bushrā*", the Arabic word for "Good news", is a proper noun, the name of the companion to whom he shouted.

1655. It was a caravan of merchants, and they think of everything in terms of the money to be made out of it! Here was an unknown, unclaimed youth, of surpassing beauty, with apparently a mind as refined as was his external beauty. If he could be sold in the opulent slave markets of Memphis or whatever was the capital of the Hyksos Dynasty then ruling in Egypt) see Appendix IV following S. vii.), what a price he would fetch! They had indeed lighted upon a treasure! And they wanted to conceal him lest he was another's slave and had run away from his master who might come and claim him! The circumstances were peculiar and the merchants were cautious. *Bidhā'at*=stock-in-trade; capital; money; wealth; treasure.

1656. To different minds the situation appeared different. Joseph must have felt keenly the edge of his brethren's treason. His father Jacob was lost in the sorrow of the loss of his best-beloved son. The brethren were exulting in their plan of getting rid of one whom they hated. The merchants were gloating over their gains. But the horizon of all was limited God knew their deeds and their feelings and motives, and He was working out His own Plan. Neither the best of us nor the worst of us know whither our Destiny is leading us—how evil plots are defeated and goodness comes to its own in marvellous ways!

For a few dirhams[1657] counted out:
In such low estimation
Did they hold him![1658]

بِثَمَنٍ بَخْسٍ دَرَاهِمَ مَعْدُودَةٍ ۚ
وَكَانُوا فِيهِ مِنَ الزَّاهِدِينَ ۝

C. 110.—Joseph was bought by a man high at Court
(xii. 21-42.) In Egypt, who asked his wife Zulaikhā
To treat him with honour, with a view
To his adoption as a son. But she burnt
With a passion of earthly love for him.
When Joseph refused to yield to her solicitations,
There was trouble and scandal, and Joseph
Had to go to prison. Here were shown
His greatness, and kindness, and wisdom.
The King's cup-bearer came in disgrace
To prison. Joseph instructed him and others
In the eternal Gospel of Unity. When released
And restored to favour, the cup-bearer
Forgot Joseph—for a time,—until
It pleased God to put into Joseph's hands
The keys of the prosperity of Egypt and the world.

Section 3.

21. The man in Egypt[1659]
Who bought him, said

٢١- وَقَالَ الَّذِي اشْتَرَاهُ مِنْ مِصْرَ

1657. *Dirham*; from Greek, *drachma*, a small silver coin, which varied in weight and value at different times and in different States. On the whole, it may be taken to have been of a value varying from about 6*d*. or 8*d*. to 10*d*. or 12*d*. in sterling, or say a quarter-rupee to a half-rupee.

1658. There was mutual deceit on both sides. The Brethren had evidently been watching to see what happened to Joseph: when they saw the merchants take him up and hide him, they came to claim his price as a run away slave, but dared not haggle over the price, lest their object, to get rid of him, should be defeated. The merchants were shrewed enough to doubt the claim in their own minds: but they dared not haggle lest they should lose a very valuable acquisition. And so the most precious of human lives in that age was sold into slavery for a few shillings!

1659. Joseph is now clear of his jealous brethren in the land of Canaan. The merchants take him to Egypt. In the city of Memphis (or whatever was the Egyptian capital then) he was exposed for sale by the merchants. The merchants had not miscalculated. There was a ready market for him: his handsome presence, his winning ways, his purity and innocence, his intelligence and integrity, combined with his courtesy and noble manliness, attracted all eyes to him. There was the keenest competition to purchase him, and in the highest Court circles Every competitor was outbid by a high court official, who is called in verse 30 below "the 'Azīz" (the Exalted in rank). Who was he? He was probably a eunuch. The highest court officials in ancient Egypt were eunuchs. So much was this the case that the term "court officer", and "eunuch" became practically synonymous (E. B., viii. 14). The 'Azīz, we may assume, was a eunuch, and childless. His wife, whom our tradition calls Zulaikhā, was only nominally a wife. She was a virgin. Our poetical tradition says that she was a princess of the West who saw Joseph in a dream first and fell in love with him. As her dream told her that her beloved was the wazīr of Egypt, her father arranged a match for her with the wazīr, neither of the parties having seen the other. While, therefore, she nominally passed as the 'Azīz's wife she secretly cherished her romantic unknown love until Joseph appeared on the scene. It was natural that the 'Azīz should want to adopt Joseph as his son, and he asked Zulaikhā to mother him and treat him as an honoured member of the household.

To his wife: "Make his stay
(Among us) honourable:[1660]
Maybe he will bring us
Much good, or we shall
Adopt him as a son."
Thus did We establish
Joseph in the land,[1661]
That We might teach him
The interpretation of stories[1662]
(And events). And God
Hath full power and control
Over His affairs; but most
Among mankind know it not.[1663]

22. When Joseph attained[1664]
His full manhood, We gave him

لِامْرَاَتِهٖٓ اَكْرِمِیْ
مَثْوٰىهُ عَسٰٓى اَنْ يَّنْفَعَنَآ
اَوْ نَتَّخِذَهٗ وَلَدًا
وَكَذٰلِكَ مَكَّنَّا لِيُوْسُفَ فِى الْاَرْضِ
وَلِنُعَلِّمَهٗ مِنْ تَاْوِيْلِ الْاَحَادِيْثِ
وَاللّٰهُ غَالِبٌ عَلٰٓى اَمْرِهٖ
وَلٰكِنَّ اَكْثَرَ النَّاسِ لَا يَعْلَمُوْنَ ○
٢٢- وَلَمَّا بَلَغَ اَشُدَّهٗٓ اٰتَيْنٰهُ

1660. See last note. The 'Aziz's motive was perhaps worldly. Such a handsome, attractive, intelligent son would get him more honour, dignity, power and wealth. But Zulaikhā had other feelings. Joseph was the man of her dreams! She had yet to purify her earthly passion, and to learn the true meaning of pure, spiritual love, before she could be worthy of Jeseph.

1661. How unerringly God's plan works! To teach Joseph wisdom and power, he had to be tested and proved in righteousness, and advanced and established in Egypt, so that Zulaikhā should be tested and purified of her dross, the women and men of Egypt should have a glimpse of God's Message, and the way prepared for Israel and his posterity to proclaim God's truth to the world and to make possible the subsequent missions of Moses and Muṣṭafā.

1662. *Aḥādīth* might be stories, things imagined or related, things that happened, in life or in true dreams. To suppose that phenomenal events are the only reality is a mark of one-sided materialism. As Hamlet said to Horatio, "there are more things in heaven and earth, Horatio, than are dreamt of in your philosophy." External events have their own limited reality, but there are bigger realities behind them, that sometimes appear darkly in the visions of ordinary men, but more clearly in the visions of poets, seers, sages, and prophets. Joseph had to be trained in seeing the realities behind events and visions. He was hated by his brothers and sold by them into slavery; they were sending him into the land of Egypt, where he was to rule men. He loved his father dearly and was separated from him, and his mother had died early: but his affection was not blunted, but drawn to a keener edge when his benevolent work benefited millions in Egypt, and in the world. His own vision of stars, sun, and moon prostrating themselves before him, was no idle dream of a selfish fool, but the prefigurement of a power, which, used rightly, was to make his own honour an instrument of service to millions he had not seen, through men and women whose own power and dignity were sanctified through him. He was to understand the hidden meaning of what seemed futilities, blunderings, snares, evil plottings, love gone wrong, and power used tyrannically. He was to interpret truth to those who would never have reached it otherwise.

1663. *Cf.*: "There is a divinity that shapes our ends, rough-hew them as we will." Only, in Shakespeare, (Hamlet, V. 2), we have a vague and distant ideal, an irresolute striving, an unsuccessful attempt at getting beyond "this too, too solid flesh"! In Joseph we have the man of God, sure in faith, above all carnal motives, and advancing the destiny of mankind with a conscious purpose, as the scroll of knowledge, wisdom, and power, unfolds itself before him by the grace of God, All-Good and All-Powerful.

1664. When Joseph left Canaan, he was a young and immature lad of seventeen or eighteen, but his nature was innocent and good. Through the vicissitudes of his fortune in Egypt, he grew in knowledge, judgment, and power.

Power and knowledge: thus do We
Reward those who do right.[1665]

حُكْمًا وَّعِلْمًا ۭ وَكَذٰلِكَ نَجْزِي الْمُحْسِنِيْنَ ۝

23. But she in whose house
He was, sought to seduce him[1666]
From his (true) self: she fastened
The doors, and said:
"Now come, thou (dear one)!"
He said: "God forbid!
Truly (thy husband) is
My lord! he made
My sojourn agreeable!
Truly to no good
Come those who do wrong!"[1667]

٢٣- وَرَاوَدَتْهُ الَّتِيْ هُوَ فِيْ بَيْتِهَا عَنْ نَّفْسِهٖ
وَغَلَّقَتِ الْاَبْوَابَ
وَقَالَتْ هَيْتَ لَكَ ۭ
قَالَ مَعَاذَ اللّٰهِ اِنَّهٗ رَبِّيْٓ اَحْسَنَ مَثْوَايَ ۭ
اِنَّهٗ لَا يُفْلِحُ الظّٰلِمُوْنَ ۝

24. And (with passion) did she
Desire him, and he would
Have desired her, but that
He saw the evidence[1668]
Of his Lord: thus
(Did We order) that We[1669]
Might turn away from him
(All) evil and shameful deeds:

٢٤- وَلَقَدْ هَمَّتْ بِهٖ ۚ وَهَمَّ بِهَا
لَوْلَآ اَنْ رَّاٰ بُرْهَانَ رَبِّهٖ ۭ
كَذٰلِكَ لِنَصْرِفَ عَنْهُ
السُّوْۗءَ وَالْفَحْشَاۗءَ ۭ

1665. *Muhsinīn*: those who do right, those who do good. Both ideas are implied. In following right conduct, you are necessarily doing good to yourself and to others. Joseph's resistance to Zulaikhā's carnal love advanced her herself to a glimpse of true spiritual love.

1666. Zulaikhā's true position is indicated in n. 1659 above. She loved much but her love was yet earthly, and was therefore unworthy of her and of Joseph. He had already been purified, but she was yet to be purified. Hence the conflict. However nominal her tie to her husband may have been, it was brought about by her own mistaken act, and she was bound to respect that tie and not to flout it, as her merely earthly passion impelled her to do. Not only in this was she guilty. The 'Azīz had treated Joseph with honour: he was more his guest and son than his slave. In trying to seduce Joseph in these circumstances, she was guilty of a crime against Joseph's own honour and dignity. And there was a third fault in her earthly love. True love blots Self out: it thinks more of the loved one than of the Self. Zulaikhā was seeking the satisfaction of her own selfish passion, and was in treason against Joseph's pure soul and his high destiny. It was inevitable that Joseph should repel her advances.

1667. Joseph's plea in rejecting Zulaikhā's love is threefold: '(1) I owe a duty, and so do you, to your husband, the 'Azīz: (2) the kindness, courtesy, and honour, with which he has treated me entitle him to more than mere gratitude from me; (3) in any case, do you not see that you are harbouring a guilty passion, and that no good can come out of guilt? We must all obey laws, human and divine.'

1668. She was blinded with passion, and his plea had no effect on her. He was human after all, and her passionate love and her beauty placed a great temptation in his path. But he had a sure refuge,—his faith in God. His spiritual eyes saw something that her eyes, blinded by passion, did not see. She thought no one saw when the doors were closed. He knew that God was there and everywhere. That made him strong, and proof against temptation.

1669. The credit of our being saved from sin is due, not to our weak earthly nature, but to God. We can only try, like Joseph, to be true and sincere; God will purify us and save us from all that is wrong. Tempted but true, we rise above ourselves.

For he was one of Our servants,
Sincere and purified.

إِنَّهُۥ مِنْ عِبَادِنَا ٱلْمُخْلَصِينَ ۝

25. So they both raced each other
To the door, and she
Tore his shirt from the back :[1670]
They both found her lord
Near the door. She said :
" What is the (fitting) punishment
For one who formed
An evil design against
Thy wife, but prison
Or a grievous chastisement ? "[1671]

٢٥- وَٱسْتَبَقَا ٱلْبَابَ
وَقَدَّتْ قَمِيصَهُۥ مِن دُبُرٍ
وَأَلْفَيَا سَيِّدَهَا لَدَا ٱلْبَابِ ۚ
قَالَتْ مَا جَزَآءُ مَنْ أَرَادَ بِأَهْلِكَ سُوٓءًا
إِلَّآ أَن يُسْجَنَ أَوْ عَذَابٌ أَلِيمٌ ۝

26. He said : " It was she
That sought to seduce me—[1672]
From my (true) self." And one
Of her household saw (this)
And bore witness, (thus) :—[1673]
" If it be that his shirt
Is rent from the front, then
Is her tale true,
And he is a liar !

٢٦- قَالَ هِىَ رَٰوَدَتْنِى عَن نَّفْسِى
وَشَهِدَ شَاهِدٌ مِّنْ أَهْلِهَآ
إِن كَانَ قَمِيصُهُۥ قُدَّ مِن قُبُلٍ
فَصَدَقَتْ
وَهُوَ مِنَ ٱلْكَٰذِبِينَ ۝

27. " But if it be that his shirt
Is torn from the back,

٢٧- وَإِن كَانَ قَمِيصُهُۥ قُدَّ مِن دُبُرٍ

1670. With Zulaikhā in her mad passion, the situation became intolerable, and Joseph made for the door. Zulaikhā ran after him to detain him. She tugged at his garment to detain him. As he was retreating, she could only catch hold of the back of his shirt, and in the struggle she tore it He was determined to open the door and leave the place, as it was useless to argue with her in her mad passion When the door was opened, it so happened, that the 'Azīz was not far off. We need not assume that he was spying, or had any suspicions either of Zulaikhā or Joseph. In his narrow limited way he was a just man. We can imagine Zulaikhā's consternation. One guilt leads to another. She had to resort to a lie, not only to justify herself but also to have her revenge on the man who had scorned her love. Slighted love (of the physical kind) made her ferocious, and she lost all sense of right and wrong.

1671. Her lie and her accusation were plausible. Joseph was found with his dress disarranged. She wanted the inference to be drawn that he had assaulted her and she had resisted. For one in his position it was a dreadful crime. Should he not be consigned to a dungeon or at least scourged? Perhaps she hoped that in either case he would be more pliable to her designs in the future.

1672. Joseph bore himself with dignity. He was too great and noble to indulge in angry recrimination. But he had to tell the truth. And he did it with quiet simplicity, without argument or bitterness,—and not caring whether he was believed or not. 'The love game was hers, not his, and it went too far in seeking to assault his person.'

1673. In the nature of things there was no eye-witness to what had happened between them. But as there was a scene and the whole household collected, wisdom came through one who was not immediately concerned. They say it was a child. If so, it illustrates the truth that the most obvious things are not noticed by people who are excited, but are plain to simple people who remain calm. Wisdom comes often through babes and sucklings.

Then is she the liar,
And he is telling the truth ! " [1674]

فَكَذَبَتْ وَهُوَ مِنَ الصّٰدِقِينَ ○

28. So when he saw his shirt,—
That it was torn at the back,—
(Her husband) said : " Behold !
It is a snare of you women ! [1675]
Truly, mighty is your snare !

٢٨- فَلَمَّا رَاٰ قَمِيصَهٗ قُدَّ مِنْ دُبُرٍ
قَالَ اِنَّهٗ مِنْ كَيْدِكُنَّ ط
اِنَّ كَيْدَكُنَّ عَظِيمٌ ○

29. " O Joseph, pass this over !
(O wife), ask forgiveness
For thy sin, for truly
Thou hast been at fault ! " [1676]

٢٩- يُوسُفُ اَعْرِضْ عَنْ هٰذَا وَاسْتَغْفِرِي
لِذَنْبِكِ اِنَّكِ كُنْتِ مِنَ الْخٰطِئِينَ ○

SECTION 4.

30. Ladies said in the City :
" The wife of the (great) 'Aziz [1677]
Is seeking to seduce her slave
From his (true) self :
Truly hath he inspired her
With violent love : we see
She is evidently going astray." [1678]

٣٠- وَقَالَ نِسْوَةٌ فِي الْمَدِينَةِ امْرَاَتُ الْعَزِيزِ
تُرَاوِدُ فَتٰهَا عَنْ نَفْسِهٖ قَدْ شَغَفَهَا
حُبًّا اِنَّا لَنَرٰهَا فِي ضَلٰلٍ مُّبِينٍ ○

1674. If Joseph's shirt was torn at the back, he must obviously have been retreating, and Zulaikhā must have been tugging from behind. No one could doubt who was the guilty party. Everybody saw it, and the 'Azīz was convinced.

1675. When the real fact became clear to every one, the Azīz as head of the household had to decide what to do. His own position was difficult, and it was made ridiculous. He was a high officer of state, say Grand Chamberlain. He was a eunuch. His dignity and rank were advanced by the so-called marriage with a high-born Princess. Was he going to proclaim to the world that Zulaikhā was running after a slave? He was probably fond of her, and he saw the innocence, loyalty, and sterling merit of Joseph. He must treat the whole affair as a woman's prank,—the madness of sex-love, and the tricks and snares connected with sex-love. He must take no further action but to rate his wife and do justice.

1676. As was only fair, he apologised to Joseph and begged him to give no further thought to the injury that had been done to him, first by the love-snare of one who was called his wife, secondly, by the utterly false charge made against him, and thirdly, by the scene, which must have been painful to a man of such spotless character as Joseph. That was not enough. He must ask Zulaikhā humbly to beg Joseph's pardon for the wrong that she had done him. And he must further ask Zulaikhā to consider her unbecoming conduct in itself, apart from any wrong done to Joseph. Probably Zulaikhā's thoughts about this must have been bitter. What did the Azīz know of the burning furnace of sex-hunger? "He jests at scars who never felt a wound!"

1677. '*Azīz*: title of a nobleman or officer of Court, of high rank. Considering all the circumstances, the office of Grand Chamberlain or minister may be indicated. But "'Azīz" I think is a title, not an office. I have not translated the title but left it as it is. "Excellency" or "Highness" would have specialised modern associations which I want to avoid.

1678. The 'Azīz's just, wise, and discreet conduct would have closed the particular episode of Zulaikhā's guilty conduct if only Mrs. Grundy had left her alone and she had not foolishly thought of justifying her conduct to Mrs. Grundy. The 'Azīz had reproved her, and he had the right and authority so to do. He also probably understood her. Joseph by his behaviour had upheld the highest standard both for himself and for her. Perhaps, her lower love having been foiled, she was trying to search within herself, and reach out after that higher love which does not indulge the Self, but suffers all things in silence, in order that constancy might make her worthy of even the thought of Joseph. But the tongues of the throng about her must wag, and she had not been sufficiently schooled to despise their malice and their invective. They knew nothing of the secret history of her heart or the true position and teaching of Joseph. Stung by their malevolent motives, she tried to justify herself to them by a stratagem, and she fell another stage below the self-sacrifice of true spiritual love!

31. When she heard
Of their malicious talk,
She sent for them
And prepared a banquet[1679]
For them: she gave
Each of them a knife:
And she said (to Joseph),
"Come out before them."
When they saw him,
Thy did extol him,
And (in their amazement)
Cut their hands: they said,
"God preserve us! no mortal
Is this! This is none other
Than a noble angel!"

٣١- فَلَمَّا سَمِعَتْ بِمَكْرِهِنَّ أَرْسَلَتْ إِلَيْهِنَّ
وَأَعْتَدَتْ لَهُنَّ مُتَّكَأً
وَآتَتْ كُلَّ وَاحِدَةٍ مِّنْهُنَّ سِكِّينًا
وَقَالَتِ اخْرُجْ عَلَيْهِنَّ فَلَمَّا رَأَيْنَهُ أَكْبَرْنَهُ
وَقَطَّعْنَ أَيْدِيَهُنَّ
وَقُلْنَ حَاشَ لِلَّهِ مَا هَٰذَا بَشَرًا
إِنْ هَٰذَا إِلَّا مَلَكٌ كَرِيمٌ ۝

32. She said: "There before you
Is the man about whom
Ye did blame me!
I did seek to seduce him from
His (true) self but he did
Firmly save himself guiltless!...[1680]
And now, if he doth not
My bidding, he shall certainly
Be cast into prison,
And (what is more)
Be of the company of the vilest!"

٣٢- قَالَتْ فَذَٰلِكُنَّ الَّذِي لُمْتُنَّنِي فِيهِ
وَلَقَدْ رَاوَدتُّهُ عَن نَّفْسِهِ
فَاسْتَعْصَمَ
وَلَئِن لَّمْ يَفْعَلْ مَا آمُرُهُ لَيُسْجَنَنَّ
وَلَيَكُونًا مِّنَ الصَّاغِرِينَ ۝

1679. When her reputation began to be pulled to pieces by Mrs. Grundy, with sundry exaggerations and distortions and malicious inuendos, Zulaik͟hā invited all ladies in society to a grand banquet. We can imagine them reclining at ease after the manner of fashionable banquets. When dessert was reached and the talk flowed freely about the gossip and scandal which made their hostess interesting, they were just about to cut the fruit with their knives, when, behold! Joseph was brought into their midst. Imagine the consternation which his beauty caused, and the havoc it played with their hearts! "Ah!", thought Zulaik͟hā, "now is your hypocrisy self-exposed! What about your reproaches to me? You have yourselves so lost your self-control that you have cut your own fingers!"

1680. Zulaik͟hā's speech is subtle, and shows that any repentance or compunction she may have felt is blotted out by the collective crowd mentality into which she has deliberately invited herself to fall. Her speech falls into two parts, with a hiatus between, which I have marked by the punctuation mark (...). In the first part there is a note of triumph, as much as to say, "Now you see! mine was no vulgar passion! you are just as susceptible! you would have done the same thing!" Finding encouragement from their passion and their fellow-feeling, she openly avows as a woman amongst women (by a sort of freemasonry) what she would have been ashamed to acknowledge to others before. She falls a step lower and boasts of it. A step lower still, and she sneers at Joseph's innocence, his firmness in saving himself guiltless! There is a pause. The tide of passion rises still higher, and the dreadful second part of her speech begins. It is a sort of joint consultation, though she speaks in monologue. The women all agree that no man has a right to resist their solicitations. Beauty spurned is the highest crime. And so now Zulaik͟hā rises to the height of tragic guilt and threatens Joseph. She forgets all her finer feeling, her real love, and is overpowered by brute passion. After all, he is a slave and must obey his mistress! Or, there is prison, and the company of the vilest, instead of the caresses of beauty and fashion in high places!" Poor, deluded, fallen Zulaik͟hā! She sank lower than herself, in seeking the support of the crowd around her! What pain and suffering and sorrow can expiate the depth of this crime?

33. He said: "O my Lord!
The prison is more
To my liking than that
To which they invite me:[1681]
Unless Thou turn away
Their snare from me,
I should (in my youthful folly)
Feel inclined towards them
And join the ranks of the
ignorant."[1682]

۳۳- قَالَ رَبِّ
السِّجْنُ أَحَبُّ إِلَيَّ مِمَّا يَدْعُونَنِيٓ إِلَيْهِ ۚ
وَإِلَّا تَصْرِفْ عَنِّي
كَيْدَهُنَّ أَصْبُ إِلَيْهِنَّ
وَأَكُن مِّنَ الْجٰهِلِينَ ۝

34. So his Lord hearkened to him
(In his prayer), and turned
Away from him their snare:[1683]
Verily He heareth and knoweth
(All things).

۳۴- فَاسْتَجَابَ لَهُ رَبُّهُ
فَصَرَفَ عَنْهُ كَيْدَهُنَّ ۚ
إِنَّهُ هُوَ السَّمِيعُ الْعَلِيمُ ۝

35. Then it occurred to the men,[1684]
After they had seen the Signs,
(That it was best)
To imprison him
For a time.

۳۵- ثُمَّ بَدَا لَهُم مِّنۢ بَعْدِ مَا رَأَوُا الْاٰيٰتِ
لَيَسْجُنُنَّهُ حَتّٰى حِينٍ ۝ ع ۱۴

1681. "*To which they invite me.*" Notice it is now "they" not "she". Where there was the snare of one woman before, it is now the collective snare of many women,—of womankind!

1682. Joseph's speech is characteristic. Like a true man of God, he takes refuge in God. He knows the weakness of human nature. He would not pit his own strength against the whole assault of evil. He will rely on God to turn evil away from him, and praise Him alone for any success he achieves in his fight. It is only the ignorant who do not know man's weakness and God's strength!

1683. Joseph was saved from the wiles of the women, which would have degraded him. But more, his truth and character were completely vindicated in the eyes of all concerned by the avowal of Zulaik͟hā.

1684. When Joseph's character was completely vindicated, there was no disgrace to him in being sent to prison after that. On the contrary the blame now would attach to those who for their own selfish motives restricted his liberty for a time. As a matter of fact various motives on the part of the many actors in this divine drama converged towards that end. For Joseph prison was better than the importunities of the women, and now, not one woman, but all society women were after him. To the women themselves it looked as if that was a lever which they could use to force his compliance. Vain, deluded creatures, to think that a man of God could be forced from the path of rectitude by threats or bribes. To the 'Azīz it appeared as if it might be in Zulaik͟hā's best interests that he should disappear from her view in prison. The decisive factor was the view of the men generally, who were alarmed at the consternation he had caused among the women. They knew that Joseph was righteous: they had seen the Signs of God in his wonderful personality and his calm and confident fortitude. But, it was argued, it was better that one man (even if righteous) should suffer in prison rather than that many should suffer from the extraordinary disturbance he was unwittingly causing in their social life. Not for the first nor for the last time did the righteous suffer plausibly for the guilt of the guilty. And so Joseph went to prison—for a time.

SECTION 5.

36. Now with him there came
Into the prison two young men.[1685]
Said one of them : " I see
Myself (in a dream)
Pressing wine." Said the other :
" I see myself (in a dream)
Carrying bread on my head,
And birds are eating thereof."[1686]
" Tell us" (they said) " the truth
And meaning thereof : for we
See thou art one
That doth good (to all)."[1687]

٣٦- وَدَخَلَ مَعَهُ السِّجْنَ فَتَيٰنِ ؕ
قَالَ اَحَدُهُمَآ اِنِّىْۤ اَرٰىنِىْۤ اَعْصِرُ خَمْرًا ۚ
وَقَالَ الْاٰخَرُ اِنِّىْۤ اَرٰىنِىْۤ اَحْمِلُ فَوْقَ
رَاْسِىْ خُبْزًا تَاْكُلُ الطَّيْرُ مِنْهُ ؕ
نَبِّئْنَا بِتَاْوِيْلِهٖ ۚ
اِنَّا نَرٰىكَ مِنَ الْمُحْسِنِيْنَ ○

37. He said : " Before any food
Comes (in due course)
To feed either of you,
I will surely reveal
To you the truth
And meaning of this
Ere it befall you .[1688]
That is part of the (Duty)
Which my Lord hath taught me.[1689]
I have (I assure you)

٣٧- قَالَ لَا يَاْتِيْكُمَا طَعَامٌ تُرْزَقٰنِهٖۤ
اِلَّا نَبَّاْتُكُمَا بِتَاْوِيْلِهٖ
قَبْلَ اَنْ يَّاْتِيَكُمَا ؕ
ذٰلِكُمَا مِمَّا عَلَّمَنِىْ رَبِّىْ ؕ اِنِّىْ

1685. Now opens another chapter in Joseph's life. The Plan of God develops. The wicked might plot; the weak might be swayed by specious arguments : but everything is used by the Universal Plan for its own beneficent purposes. Joseph must get into touch with the Pharaoh, in order to work out the salvation of Egypt, and yet it must be through no obligation to smaller men. And he must diffuse his personality and teach the truth to men of all sorts in prison.

1686. Two men came to the prison about the same time as Joseph. They were both apparently officers of the king (the Pharaoh), who had incurred his wrath. One was a cup-bearer (or butler or chief steward) whose duty was to prepare the king's wines and drinks. The other was the king's baker, whose duty was to prepare the king's bread. They were both in disgrace. The former dreamed that he was again carrying on his duties and pressing wine : the latter that he was carrying bread, but it did not reach his master, for the birds ate of it.

1687. Both these men saw the Signs of God about Joseph. They felt not only that he had wisdom, but that he was kind and benevolent, and would give of his wisdom even to strangers like themselves. They therefore told him their dreams and asked him to interpret them.

1688. The dream of one foreboded good to him, and of the other, evil to him. It was good that each should prepare for his fate. But Joseph's mission was far higher than that of merely foretelling events. He must teach the truth of God and thefaith in the Hereafter to both men. He does that first before he talks of the events of their phenomenal life. And yet he does it so tenderly. He does not tantalise them. In effect he says, " You shall learn everything before our next meal, but let me first teach you Faith ! "

1689. Joseph does not preach a pompous sermon, or claim any credit to himself for placing himself at their service. He is just doing his duty, and the highest good he can do to them is to teach them Faith.

Abandoned the ways
Of a people that believe not
In God and that (even)
Deny the Hereafter.[1690]

تَرَكْتُ مِلَّةَ قَوْمٍ لَّا يُؤْمِنُونَ بِاللَّهِ وَهُم بِالْآخِرَةِ هُمْ كَافِرُونَ ○

38. "And I follow the ways[1691]
Of my fathers,—Abraham,
Isaac, and Jacob; and never
Could we attribute any partners
Whatever to God: that (comes)
Of the grace of God to us
And to mankind: yet
Most men are not grateful

٣٨- وَاتَّبَعْتُ مِلَّةَ آبَاءِي إِبْرَاهِيمَ وَإِسْحَاقَ وَيَعْقُوبَ ۚ مَا كَانَ لَنَا أَن نُّشْرِكَ بِاللَّهِ مِن شَيْءٍ ۚ ذَٰلِكَ مِن فَضْلِ اللَّهِ عَلَيْنَا وَعَلَى النَّاسِ وَلَٰكِنَّ أَكْثَرَ النَّاسِ لَا يَشْكُرُونَ ○

39. "O my two companions.[1692]
Of the prison! (I ask you):
Are many lords differing
Among themselves better,
Or the One God,
Supreme and Irresistible?

٣٩- يَا صَاحِبَيِ السِّجْنِ أَأَرْبَابٌ مُّتَفَرِّقُونَ خَيْرٌ أَمِ اللَّهُ الْوَاحِدُ الْقَهَّارُ ○

40. "If not Him, ye worship nothing
But names which ye have
named,—[1693]
Ye and your fathers,—
For which God hath sent down
No authority: the Command
Is for none but God: He

٤٠- مَا تَعْبُدُونَ مِن دُونِهِ إِلَّا أَسْمَاءً سَمَّيْتُمُوهَا أَنتُمْ وَآبَاؤُكُم مَّا أَنزَلَ اللَّهُ بِهَا مِن سُلْطَانٍ ۚ إِنِ الْحُكْمُ إِلَّا لِلَّهِ ۚ

1690. These men were Egyptians, perhaps steeped in materialism, idolatry, and polytheism. He must teach them the Gospel of Unity. And he does it simply, by appealing to his own experience. 'I have found the Lord good: in prosperity and adversity I have been supported by Faith: in life no man can live by error or evil: perhaps one of you has done some wrong for which you find yourself here: perhaps one of you is innocent: in either case, will you not accept Faith and live for ever?'

1691. Again the same note of personal modesty. 'You may think I am as young as you, or younger. Yes, but I have the heritage of great men renowned for wisdom and truth, such as Abraham. Isaac, and Jacob. Surely what they knew is worthy of respect. Never did they swerve a hair's breadth from the Gospel of Unity. It is not that we boast. It was God's grace that taught us and God's grace is teaching all mankind. But men show their ingratitude by inventing other so-called gods.'

1692. Note the personal touch again. 'Are we not also companions in misfortune? And may I not speak to you on terms of perfect equality,—as one prisoner to another? Well then, do you really think a conflict of heterogeneous gods is better than the One True God, Whose power is supreme and irresistible?'

1693. 'If you name other gods, they are nothing but your inventions,—names which you and your fathers put forward without any reality behind them. Who gave you authority to do any such thing? The only reality is God. Authority can come from Him alone. It is only for Him to command. And He has distinctly commanded you to worship none other than Him. That is the only religion that is right,—that has stood and will stand and endure for ever. He has revealed it at all times by His Messengers and by His Signs. If men fail to understand, it is their own fault.

Hath commanded that ye worship
None but Him : that is
The right religion, but
Most men understand not...

أَمَرَ أَلَّا تَعْبُدُوٓا إِلَّآ إِيَّاهُ ۚ ذٰلِكَ الدِّينُ
الْقَيِّمُ وَلٰكِنَّ أَكْثَرَ النَّاسِ لَا يَعْلَمُونَ ۝

41\. " O my two companions[1694]
Of the prison ! As to one
Of you, he will pour out
The wine for his lord to drink :[1695]
As for the other, he will
Hang from the cross, and the birds
Will eat from off his head.[1696]
(So) hath been decreed
That matter whereof
Ye twain do enquire "...

٤١- يٰصَاحِبَيِ السِّجْنِ
أَمَّآ أَحَدُكُمَا فَيَسْقِي رَبَّهُ خَمْرًا ۚ
وَأَمَّا الْاٰخَرُ فَيُصْلَبُ فَتَأْكُلُ الطَّيْرُ مِنْ
رَّأْسِهٖ ۚ
قُضِيَ الْأَمْرُ الَّذِي
فِيهِ تَسْتَفْتِيَانِ ۝

42\. And of the two,
To that one whom he considered
About to be saved, he said :
" Mention me to thy lord." [1697]

٤٢- وَقَالَ لِلَّذِي ظَنَّ أَنَّهُ
نَاجٍ مِّنْهُمَا اذْكُرْنِي عِنْدَ رَبِّكَ

1694\. Having fulfilled his great duty, that touching the things of the spirit, Joseph now passes on, and comes to the things in which they were immediately interested,– the questions which they had asked him about their dreams and what they prognosticated of their immediate future. Notice how Joseph again puts himself into sympathy with them by repeating the phrase of *camaraderie*, " my two companions of the prison ! " For one he has good news, and for the other, bad news. He does not mince matters or waste words. He just barely tells the truth, hoping that the higher spiritual truths of which he has spoken will appear in their eyes, too, as of more importance than mere earthly triumphs or disasters,—(in Kipling's words) " both impostors all the same."

1695\. The cup-bearer had perhaps been proved innocent of the crime which had been charged against him, and was to be restored to the favour of the Pharaoh. He was to carry the cup and be the king's confidante again. How much more good he could do now, after the spiritual influence he had imbibed from Joseph the man of God ! He was more fortunate in having had Joseph's company than in being restored to his intimate position with the king ! Yet he was not a perfect man, as we shall see presently.

1696\. For the baker, alas ! he had bad news, and he tells it directly without tantalising him. Perhaps he had been found guilty—perhaps he had been really guilty—of some act of embezzlement or of joining in some palace intrigue, and he was to die a malefactor's death on the cross, followed by exposure to birds of the air—vultures pecking away at his eyes and cheeks, and all that had been his face and head ! Poor man ! If he was guilty, Joseph had taught him repentance, and we should like to think that he lost in this life but gained in the next. If he was innocent, the cruel death did not affect him. Joseph had shown him a higher and more lasting hope in the Hereafter.

1697\. Joseph never mentioned himself in interpreting the dream, nor ever thought of himself in his kindness to his fellow-sufferers in prison. It was afterwards, when the cup-bearer's dream came true, and he was being released on being restored to favour, that we can imagine him taking an affectionate leave of Joseph, and even asking him in his elation if he could do anything for Joseph. Joseph had no need of earthly favours,—least of all, from kings or their favourites. The divine grace was enough for him. But he had great work to do, which he could not do in prison–work for Egypt and her king, and the world at large. If the cup-bearer could mention him to the king, not by way of recommendation (*sifārish*), but because the king's own justice was being violated in keeping an innocent man in prison, perhaps that might help to advance the cause of the king and of Egypt. And so he said, " Mention me to Pharaoh."

But Satan made him forget[1698]
To mention him to his lord:
And (Joseph) lingered in prison
A few (more) years.[1699]

فَأَنسٰىهُ الشَّيْطٰنُ ذِكْرَ رَبِّهٖ
فَلَبِثَ فِي السِّجْنِ بِضْعَ سِنِينَ ۝ ع ٥

C. 111.—The king of Egypt saw a vision
(xii. 43-68) Which none of his grandees could explain.
The cup-bearer referred to Joseph,
Who was sent for by the king. But Joseph
Insisted that the voice of scandal,
Which had pointed to him, should be declared
In public to be false. After Zulaikha
Had paid a splendid ungrudging tribute
To his truth and righteousness, he came,
And was invested with supreme power
By the king. In times of plenty he organised
Great reserves to meet the needs
Of famine. When wide-spread famine at last
Prevailed, his brothers came from Canaan
In search of corn. He treated them kindly
And got them to bring his youngest brother
Benjamin: but they knew not that he was Joseph.

SECTION 6.

43. The king (of Egypt) said:[1700]
"I do see (in a vision)
Seven fat kine, whom seven
Lean ones devour,—and seven
Green ears of corn, and seven
(others)
Withered. O ye chiefs!
Expound to me my vision
If it be that ye can
Interpret visions."

٤٣- وَقَالَ الْمَلِكُ إِنِّيٓ أَرٰى سَبْعَ بَقَرٰتٍ
سِمَانٍ يَأْكُلُهُنَّ سَبْعٌ عِجَافٌ
وَّسَبْعَ سُنْبُلٰتٍ خُضْرٍ وَّأُخَرَ يٰبِسٰتٍ ؕ
يٰٓأَيُّهَا الْمَلَأُ أَفْتُونِي فِي رُءْيَايَ
إِنْ كُنْتُمْ لِلرُّءْيَا تَعْبُرُونَ ۝

1698. The eternal Plan does not put God's men under obligations to men commanding mere worldly favour or earthly power. If they are given a chance, the obligation is on the worldly men, however highly placed...In this case, the poor cup-bearer was but human. When he was in the midst of the Court, he forgot the poor fellow-prisoner languishing in prison. In this he yielded to the lower part of his nature, which is guided by Satan, the personification of evil,—a real force in our lives if we but knew it.

1699. *A few (more) years*: *bidh'* in Arabic signifies a small indefinite number, say up to 3, 5, 7, or 9 years.

1700. The Pharaoh is holding a Council. His confidential adviser the cup-bearer is present. The Pharaoh relates his double dream,—of seven fat kine being devoured by seven lean ones, and of seven fine full green ears of corn (presumably being devoured) by seven dry withered ears.

44. They said: "A confused medley
Of dreams: and we are not
Skilled in the interpretation
Of dreams."[1701]

٤٤- قَالُوٓا أَضْغَاثُ أَحْلَامٍ ۖ وَمَا نَحْنُ
بِتَأْوِيلِ الْأَحْلَامِ بِعٰلِمِينَ ○

45. But the man who had been
Released, one of the two
(Who had been in prison)
And who now bethought him
After (so long) a space of time,
Said: "I will tell you
The truth of its interpretation:
Send ye me (therefor)."[1702]

٤٥- وَقَالَ الَّذِى نَجَا مِنْهُمَا
وَادَّكَرَ بَعْدَ أُمَّةٍ
أَنَا أُنَبِّئُكُمْ
بِتَأْوِيلِهٖ فَأَرْسِلُونِ ○

46. "O Joseph!" (he said).
"O man of truth! Expound
To us (the dream)
Of seven fat kine
Whom seven lean ones
Devour, and of seven
Green ears of corn
And (seven) others withered:
That I may return
To the people, and that
They may understand."[1703]

٤٦- يُوسُفُ أَيُّهَا الصِّدِّيقُ
أَفْتِنَا فِى سَبْعِ بَقَرٰتٍ سِمَانٍ
يَأْكُلُهُنَّ سَبْعٌ عِجَافٌ
وَسَبْعِ سُنْبُلٰتٍ خُضْرٍ وَأُخَرَ يٰبِسٰتٍ ۙ
لَعَلِّىٓ أَرْجِعُ إِلَى النَّاسِ
لَعَلَّهُمْ يَعْلَمُونَ ○

47. (Joseph) said: "For seven years
Shall ye diligently sow

٤٧- قَالَ تَزْرَعُونَ سَبْعَ سِنِينَ

1701. No one in the Council apparently wanted to take the responsibility either of interpreting the dream, or of carrying out any measures consequent on the interpretation.

1702. At length the cup-bearer's conscience was awakened. He thought of Joseph. He (Joseph) was a truthful man, and the cup-bearer knew by personal experience how skilful he was in the interpretation of dreams. Perhaps he could get him released at this juncture by getting him to interpret the king's dream. If he had been frank, straight, and direct, he would have mentioned Joseph at once, and presented him to Pharaoh. But he had worldly subtlety. He wanted some credit for himself, at the same time that he fulfilled an old obligation. His petty conscience would be satisfied if he got Joseph's release, but meanwhile he wanted to see how much attention he could draw to himself in the court. So he just asked permission to withdraw in order to find the interpretation. He went straight to the prison, and addressed himself to Joseph, as in the following verse.

1703. The speech must have been longer, to explain the circumstances. We are just given the points From Joseph he conceals nothing. He knows that Joseph knows more than himself. He tells Joseph that if he got the meaning, he would go and tell the Council. It would be impertinent for the cup-bearer to hold out to Joseph, the man of God, the bribe of the hope of his release. Notice how blandly he avoids referring to his own lapse in having forgotten Joseph so long, and how the magnanimous Joseph has not a word of reproach, but gets straight on with the interpretation.

As is your wont :
And the harvests that ye reap,
Ye shall leave them in the ear,—[1704]
Except a little, of which
Ye shall eat.

دَاَبًا ۚ
فَمَا حَصَدْتُّمْ فَذَرُوْهُ فِيْ سُنْۢبُلِهٖٓ
اِلَّا قَلِيْلًا مِّمَّا تَاْكُلُوْنَ ○

48. " Then will come
After that (period)
Seven dreadful (years),
Which will devour
What ye shall have laid by
In advance for them,—
(All) except a little[1705]
Which ye shall have
(Specially) guarded.

٤٨- ثُمَّ يَاْتِيْ مِنْۢ بَعْدِ ذٰلِكَ
سَبْعٌ شِدَادٌ
يَّاْكُلْنَ مَا قَدَّمْتُمْ لَهُنَّ
اِلَّا قَلِيْلًا
مِّمَّا تُحْصِنُوْنَ ○

49. " Then will come
After that (period) a year
In which the people will have
Abundant water, and in which
They will press (wine and oil)."[1706]

٤٩- ثُمَّ يَاْتِيْ مِنْۢ بَعْدِ ذٰلِكَ عَامٌ
فِيْهِ يُغَاثُ النَّاسُ
وَفِيْهِ يَعْصِرُوْنَ ○ ع

1704. Joseph not only shows what will happen, but, unasked, suggests the measures to be taken for dealing with the calamity when it comes. There will be seven years of abundant harvest. With diligent cultivation they should get bumper crops. Of them they should take a little for their sustenance and store the rest in the ear, the better to preserve it from the pests that attack corn-heaps when they have passed through the threshing floor.

1705. There will follow seven years of dreadful famine, which will devour all the stores which they will have laid by in the good years. They must be careful, even during the famine, not to consume all the grain ; they must by special arrangement save a little for seed, lest they should be helpless even when the Nile brought down abundant waters from the rains at its sources.

1706. This is a symbol of a very abundant year, following the seven years of drought. The Nile must have brought abundant fertilising waters and silt from its upper reaches, and there was probably some rain also in Lower Egypt. The vine and the olive trees, which must have suffered in the drought, now revived, and yielded their juice and their oil ; among the annuals, also, the oil seeds, such as linseed, sesamum, and the castor oil plant, must have been grown, as there was irrigated land and to spare from the abundant grain crops. And the people's spirits revived, to enjoy the finer products of the earth, when their absolute necessities had been more than met in their grain crops.

SECTION 7.

50. So the king said:
"Bring ye him unto me."[1707]
But when the messenger
Came to him, (Joseph) said:
"Go thou back to thy lord,
And ask him, 'What is
The state of mind
Of the ladies
Who cut their hands'?[1708]
For my Lord is
Certainly well aware
Of their snare."[1709]

٥٠- وَقَالَ الْمَلِكُ ائْتُونِي بِهِ ۚ
فَلَمَّا جَاءَهُ الرَّسُولُ قَالَ
ارْجِعْ إِلَىٰ رَبِّكَ
فَاسْأَلْهُ مَا بَالُ النِّسْوَةِ اللَّاتِي
قَطَّعْنَ أَيْدِيَهُنَّ ۚ
إِنَّ رَبِّي بِكَيْدِهِنَّ عَلِيمٌ ○

51. (The king) said (to the ladies):
"What was your affair
When ye did seek to seduce
Joseph from his (true) self?"[1710]
The ladies said: "God
Preserve us! no evil

٥١- قَالَ مَا خَطْبُكُنَّ
إِذْ رَاوَدْتُنَّ يُوسُفَ عَنْ نَفْسِهِ ۚ
قُلْنَ حَاشَ لِلَّهِ مَا عَلِمْنَا عَلَيْهِ مِنْ سُوءٍ ۚ

1707. The cup-bearer must have reported Joseph's interpretation to the king, and the king naturally wanted to see Joseph himself. He sent a messenger to fetch him.

1708. The king's messenger must have expected that a prisoner would be only too overjoyed at the summons of the king. But Joseph, sure of himself, wanted some assurance that he would be safe from the sort of nagging and persecution to which he had been subjected by the ladies. We saw in verse 33 above that he preferred prison to their solicitations. He must therefore know what was in the mind of the women now. Note how discreetly he omits any particular mention of Zulaikhā, who after all had been kind to him, and whose unschooled love had been tested all these years and been nearly purified of its grosser elements by now. But Mrs. Grundy, who understood (and perhaps practised for herself) only the grosser side of her passion, must be put in her place, if Joseph was to have a chance of doing the great work for which he was marked out.

1709. If the king ("thy lord") did not know of all the snares which had been laid for Joseph by the ladies, God ("my Lord") knew all their secret motives and plots.

1710. Joseph's message was conveyed by the messenger to the king, who sent for the ladies concerned Among them came Zulaikhā. "What was this affair?" said the king: "tell me the whole truth."

Know we against him!"
Said the 'Azīz's wife:
" Now is the truth manifest
(To all): it was I
Who sought to seduce him
From his (true) self:
He is indeed of those
Who are (ever) true (and
virtuous).[1711]

قَالَتِ امْرَاَتُ الْعَزِيْزِ
الْـٰٔنَ حَصْحَصَ الْحَقُّ ز
اَنَا رَاوَدْتُّهٗ عَنْ نَّفْسِهٖ
وَاِنَّهٗ لَمِنَ الصّٰدِقِيْنَ ○

52. " This (say I), in order that
He may know that I
Have never been false
To him in his absence,
And that God will never
12 30 Guide the snare of the false ones."[1712]

٥٢- ذٰلِكَ لِيَعْلَمَ اَنِّيْ
لَمْ اَخُنْهُ بِالْغَيْبِ
وَاَنَّ اللّٰهَ لَا يَهْدِيْ كَيْدَ الْخَآئِنِيْنَ ○

1711. Zulaikhā stood by, while the other ladies answered. Their answer was the answer of Mrs. Grundy, grudgingly acknowledging the truth of Joseph's innocence and high principles, but holding a discreet silence about Mrs. Grundy's own part in egging on poor Zulaikhā to sin, wrong-doing, and revenge. When they had done, she began. She did not mince matters. She acknowledged her own guilt, freely and frankly. This was no time for her even to refer to other ladies,—their jealousy, their gross mindedness, their encouragement of all that was frail or evil in herself. These things she ignored. But to her awakened spiritual consciousness it was a triumph that Joseph, whom she adored, was true in every sense, in word and deed, and that that truth should be proclaimed in open Court before all, as was indeed already known to all concerned when she had taken the blame on herself before the assembly of ladies, and her own spirit had not yet been emancipated. What had happened to her since? She had learnt much in sorrow, pain, and humiliation. She had learnt the vanity of carnal love. But Joseph, true of heart, calm in every turn of fortune, had taught her to question herself whether, in spite of all her sin, she could not yet be worthy of him. Perhaps her husband was dead, and she a widow. But she must see whether she could understand love in the sense in which Joseph would have her understand it—that pure surrender of self, which has no earthy stain to it!

1712. I construe verses 52 and 53 to be a continuation of Zulaikhā's speech and have translated accordingly. There is both good reason and authority (*e.g.* Ibn Kathīr) for this. But the majority of Commentators construe verses 52-53 to be spoken by Joseph, in which case they would mean that Joseph was referring to his fidelity to the 'Azīz, that he had never taken advantage of his absence to play false with his wife, although he (Joseph) was human and liable to err. In my view Zulaikhā, while fully reprobating her own guilty conduct, claims that she has at least been constant, and that she hopes for mercy, forgiveness, and the capacity to understand at last what true love is. Whatever false charge she made, she made it in a moment of passion and to his face, never in cold blood, or behind his back.

Guide the snare of the false ones, *i.e.*, allow such snare to attain its goal.

53. " Nor do I absolve my own self
(Of blame) : the (human) soul
Is certainly prone to evil,[1712-A]
Unless my Lord do bestow
His Mercy : but surely
My Lord is Oft-Forgiving,
Most Merciful." [1713]

۵۳-وَمَآ أُبَرِّئُ نَفْسِيْ ۚ
إِنَّ النَّفْسَ لَأَمَّارَةٌ بِالسُّوْٓءِ
إِلَّا مَا رَحِمَ رَبِّيْ ۚ
إِنَّ رَبِّيْ غَفُوْرٌ رَّحِيْمٌ ○

54. So the king said :
" Bring him unto me ; [1714]
I will take him specially
To serve about my own person."
Therefore when he had spoken
To him, he said :
" Be assured this day,
Thou art, before our own Presence,
With rank firmly established,
And fidelity fully proved ! [1715]

۵۴-وَقَالَ الْمَلِكُ ائْتُوْنِيْ بِهٖٓ
أَسْتَخْلِصْهُ لِنَفْسِيْ ۚ
فَلَمَّا كَلَّمَهٗ قَالَ
إِنَّكَ الْيَوْمَ لَدَيْنَا
مَكِيْنٌ أَمِيْنٌ ○

55. (Joseph) said : " Set me
Over the store-houses [1716]
Of the land : I will
Indeed guard them,

۵۵-قَالَ اجْعَلْنِيْ عَلٰى خَزَآئِنِ الْأَرْضِ ۚ
إِنِّيْ حَفِيْظٌ

1712-A. *Ammāra* : prone, impelling, headstrong, passionate. See n. 5810 to lxxv. 2.

1713. See n. 1712. I construe this verse to be a continuation of Zulaikhā's speech. It is more appropriate to her than to Joseph. As I understand it, Zulaikhā has at last come to have a realisation of all that had been wrong in her conduct and a glimmering of the true meaning of spiritual love, which has something divine in it, and which cannot be attained except by the outpouring of all our soul to God.

1714. Joseph had not yet appeared before the king. The king's order in the same terms in verse 50 above had led to a message from Joseph and the subsequent public proceedings with the ladies. Now that Joseph's innocence, wisdom, truth, and trustworthiness had been proved, and confirmed by Zulaikhā's splendid tribute, and Joseph's own manly bearing before the king, the king was much impressed, and took him specially to serve about his own person as his trusty and confidential Wazīr. If, as is probable, the 'Azīz had by this time died (for he is never mentioned again) Joseph succeeded to his office, and he is addressed as 'Azīz in verse 78 below. But Joseph got more than his rank and powers, as specially selected to carry out a great emergency policy to meet the very difficult times of depression that were foretold. He was given plenary powers and the fullest confidence that a king could give to his most trusted and best-proved Wazīr or Prime Minister, with special access to his Person, like a Grand Chamberlain.

1715. Who was this Pharaoh, and what approximate date could we assign to him? He was probably a king of the Hyksos Dynasty, somewhere between the 19th and the 17th century B.C. See Appendix IV, on Egyptian Chronology and Israel (printed after S. vii).

1716. Joseph had been given plenary authority by the king. He could have enjoyed his dignity, drawn his emoluments, put the hard and perhaps unpopular work on the shoulders of others, and kept to himself the glitter and the kudos. But that was not his way, nor can it indeed be the way of any one who wants to do real service. He undertook the hardest and most unpopular task himself. Such a task was that of organising reserves in times of plenty, against the lean years to come. He deliberately asked to be put in charge of the granaries and store-houses, and the drudgery of establishing them and guarding them, for the simple reason that he understood that need better than any one else, and was prepared to take upon himself rather than throw on to another the obloquy of restricting supplies in times of plenty.

As one that knows
(Their importance)."

عَلِيۡمٌ ○

56. Thus did we give
Established power to Joseph
In the land, to take possession [1717]
Therein as, when, or where
He pleased. We bestow
Of Our mercy on whom
We please, and We suffer not,
To be lost, the reward
Of those who do good.

٥٦- وَكَذٰلِكَ مَكَّنَّا لِيُوسُفَ
فِى الۡاَرۡضِ يَتَبَوَّاُ مِنۡهَا حَيۡثُ يَشَآءُ
نُصِيۡبُ بِرَحۡمَتِنَا مَنۡ نَّشَآءُ
وَلَا نُضِيۡعُ اَجۡرَ الۡمُحۡسِنِيۡنَ ○

57. But verily the reward
Of the Hereafter
Is the best, for those
Who believe, and are constant
In righteousness.[1718]

٥٧- وَلَاَجۡرُ الۡاٰخِرَةِ خَيۡرٌ لِّلَّذِيۡنَ اٰمَنُوۡا
وَكَانُوۡا يَتَّقُوۡنَ ○ ع

SECTION 8.

58. Then came Joseph's
brethren: [1719]
They entered his presence,
And he knew them,
But they knew him not.

٥٨- وَجَآءَ اِخۡوَةُ يُوۡسُفَ فَدَخَلُوۡا عَلَيۡهِ
فَعَرَفَهُمۡ وَهُمۡ لَهٗ مُنۡكِرُوۡنَ ○

1717. What a wonderful example of the working of divine Providence! The boy whom his jealous brothers got rid of by selling him into slavery for a miserable price becomes the most trusted dignitary in a foreign land, chief minister in one of the greatest empires of the world of that day. And this not for himself only, but for his family, for the world at large, and for that noble example of righteousness and strenuous service, which he was to set for all time. According to tradition, Joseph's age was barely 30 at that time!

As, when, or where he pleased: *ḥaithu* refers to manner, time, or place. He had a Dictator's powers, but as his fidelity was fully proved (xii. 53) these powers were for service rather than for self.

1718. To the righteous, whatever rewards (if any) that come in this world are welcome for the opportunities of service which they open out. But the true and best reward is in the Hereafter.

1719. Years pass; the times of prosperity go by; famine holds the land in its grip; and it extends to neighbouring countries. Joseph's preparations are complete. His reserves are ample to meet the calamity. Not only does Egypt bless him, but neighbouring countries send to Egypt to purchase corn. All are received with hospitality, and corn is sold to them according to judicious measure.

Now there has been one sorrow gnawing at Joseph's heart. His poor father Jacob! How he must have wept, as indeed he did, at the loss of his beloved Joseph! And Joseph's little brother Benjamin, born of the same mother as himself; would the other ten brothers, not by the same mother, have any affection for him, or would they treat him, as they treated Joseph? How would the whole family be in these hard times? A sort of answer came when the ten selfish brothers, driven by famine, came from Canaan to buy corn. Joseph, though so great a man, kept the details of the famine department in his own hands: otherwise there might have been waste But to the public he was a mighty Egyptian administrator, probably in Egyptian dress, and with all the paraphernalia of his rank about him. When his brothers came, he knew them, but they did not know he was Joseph. In their thoughts Joseph was probably some menial slave in a remote household, perhaps already starved to death in these hard times!

59. And when he had furnished
Them forth with provisions
(Suitable) for them, he said :
" Bring unto me a brother
Ye have, of the same father
As yourselves, (but a different
mother) :
See ye not that I pay out
Full measure, and that I
Do provide the best hospitality ? [1720]

٥٩- وَلَمَّا جَهَّزَهُم بِجَهَازِهِمْ
قَالَ ائْتُونِي بِأَخٍ
لَّكُم مِّنْ أَبِيكُمْ
أَلَا تَرَوْنَ أَنِّي أُوفِي الْكَيْلَ
وَأَنَا خَيْرُ الْمُنزِلِينَ ○

60. " Now if ye bring him not
To me, ye shall have
No measure (of corn) from me,
Nor shall ye (even) come
Near me."

٦٠- فَإِن لَّمْ تَأْتُونِي بِهِ
فَلَا كَيْلَ لَكُمْ عِندِي
وَلَا تَقْرَبُونِ ○

61. They said : " We shall
Certainly seek to get
Our wish about him
From his father : [1721]
Indeed we shall do it."

٦١- قَالُوا سَنُرَاوِدُ عَنْهُ أَبَاهُ
وَإِنَّا لَفَاعِلُونَ ○

62. And (Joseph) told his servants
To put their stock-in-trade [1722]
(With which they had bartered)
Into their saddle-bags,
So they should know it only
When they returned to their
people,

٦٢- وَقَالَ لِفِتْيَانِهِ اجْعَلُوا بِضَاعَتَهُمْ فِي
رِحَالِهِمْ
لَعَلَّهُمْ يَعْرِفُونَهَا
إِذَا انقَلَبُوا إِلَىٰ أَهْلِهِمْ

1720. Joseph treated his brothers liberally. Perhaps he condescended to enter into conversation with these strangers, and enquired about their family. The ten brothers had come. Had they left a father behind them? What sort of a person was he? Very aged? Well, of course he could not come. Had they any other brothers? Doubtless the ten brothers said nothing about their lost Joseph, or told some lie about him But perhaps their host's kindly insistence brought Benjamin into the conversation. How old was he? Why had they not brought him? Would they bring him next time? Indeed they must, or they would get no more corn, and he—the great Egyptian Wazir—would not even see them.

1721. The brothers said: "Certainly, we shall try to beg him of our father, and bring him away with us: we shall certainly comply with your desire." In reality they probably loved Benjamin no more than they loved Joseph. But they must get food when the present supply was exhausted, and they must humour the great Egyptian Wazir. Note that they do not call Jacob "our father" but "his father": how little they loved their aged father, whom they identified with Joseph and Benjamin! Their trial and their instruction in their duties is now being undertaken by Joseph.

1722. *Bidhā'at*: stock in trade; capital with which business is carried on; money when it is used as capital for trade. It is better here to suppose that they were bartering goods for grain. *Cf.* xii. 19.

In order that they
Might come back.[1723]

لَعَلَّهُمْ يَرْجِعُونَ ○

63. Now when they returned
To their father, they said:
"O our father! No more
Measure of grain shall we get
(Unless we take our brother):
So send our brother with us,
That we may get our measure;
And we will indeed
Take every care of him."[1724]

٦٣- فَلَمَّا رَجَعُوٓا إِلَىٰٓ أَبِيهِمْ قَالُوا
يَٰٓأَبَانَا مُنِعَ مِنَّا ٱلْكَيْلُ
فَأَرْسِلْ مَعَنَآ أَخَانَا نَكْتَلْ
وَإِنَّا لَهُۥ لَحَٰفِظُونَ ○

64. He said: "Shall I trust you
With him with any result
Other than when I trusted you
With his brother aforetime?
But God is the best
To take care (of him),
And He is the Most Merciful
Of those who show mercy!"[1725]

٦٤- قَالَ هَلْ ءَامَنُكُمْ عَلَيْهِ إِلَّا
كَمَآ أَمِنتُكُمْ عَلَىٰٓ أَخِيهِ مِن قَبْلُ
فَٱللَّهُ خَيْرٌ حَٰفِظًا
وَهُوَ أَرْحَمُ ٱلرَّٰحِمِينَ ○

65. Then when they opened
Their baggage, they found
Their stock-in-trade had been
Returned to them. They said:
"O our father! What (more)
Can we desire? This our
Stock-in-trade has been returned[1726]
To us: so we shall get

٦٥- وَلَمَّا فَتَحُوا مَتَٰعَهُمْ وَجَدُوا
بِضَٰعَتَهُمْ رُدَّتْ إِلَيْهِمْ
قَالُوا يَٰٓأَبَانَا مَا نَبْغِى
هَٰذِهِۦ بِضَٰعَتُنَا رُدَّتْ إِلَيْنَا

1723. It was most important for Joseph's plan that they should come back. If they came back at all, they could not come without Benjamin after what he had told them. As an additional incentive to their coming back, he returns the price of the grain in such a way that they should find it in their saddle-bags when they reach home.

1724. On their return they no doubt told Jacob all that had transpired. But to beg Benjamin of him was no easy matter, as Jacob did not trust them and had no cause to trust them after their treatment of Joseph. So they use the argument of urgent necessity for all it is worth.

1725. I construe Jacob's answer to be a flat refusal to let Benjamin go with them. It would be like the former occasion when he trusted Joseph with them and they lost him. Did they talk of taking care of him? The only protection that he trusted was that of God. He at least showed mercy to old and young alike. Did man show such mercy? Witness his sad old age and his lost little Joseph! Would they bring down "his grey hairs with sorrow to the grave?"

1726. The ten brothers did not take their father's refusal as final. They opened their saddle-bags, and found that the price they had paid for their provisions had been returned to them. They had got the grain free! What more could they desire? The spell which Joseph had woven now worked. If they only went back, this kind Wazīr would give more grain if they pleased him. And the only way to please him was to take back their younger brother with them. It would cost them nothing. Judging by past experience they would get a whole camel's load of grain now. And so they stated their case to the aged father.

(More) food for our family ;
We shall take care of our brother ;
And add (at the same time)
A full camel's load (of grain
To our provisions).
This is but a small quantity.[1727]

وَنَمِيرُ أَهْلَنَا وَنَحْفَظُ أَخَانَا
وَنَزْدَادُ كَيْلَ بَعِيرٍ
ذَٰلِكَ كَيْلٌ يَسِيرٌ ○

66. (Jacob) said : " Never will I
Send him with you until
Ye swear a solemn oath to me,
In God's name, that ye
Will be sure to bring him back
To me unless ye are yourselves
Hemmed in (and made
powerless).[1728]
And when they had sworn
Their solemn oath,
He said : " Over all
That we say, be God
The Witness and Guardian ! "[1729]

٦٦- قَالَ لَنْ أُرْسِلَهُ مَعَكُمْ حَتَّىٰ
تُؤْتُونِ مَوْثِقًا مِّنَ اللَّهِ
لَتَأْتُنَّنِي بِهِ
إِلَّا أَن يُحَاطَ بِكُمْ
فَلَمَّا آتَوْهُ مَوْثِقَهُمْ
قَالَ اللَّهُ عَلَىٰ مَا نَقُولُ وَكِيلٌ ○

67. Further he said :
" O my sons ! enter not[1730]
All by one gate : enter ye
By different gates. Not that

٦٧- وَقَالَ يَٰبَنِيَّ لَا تَدْخُلُوا
مِن بَابٍ وَاحِدٍ وَادْخُلُوا مِنْ أَبْوَابٍ مُّتَفَرِّقَةٍ

1727. Two meanings are possible,—either or perhaps both. 'What we have brought now is nothing compared to what we shall get if we humour the whim of the Egyptian Wazir. And, moreover, Egypt seems to have plenty of grain stored up. What is a camel-load to her Wazir to give away ?'

1728. The appeal to the family's needs in the time of famine at length made Jacob relent, but he exacted a solemn promise from the brothers, under the most religious sanctions, that they would bring Benjamin back to him, unless they were themselves prevented, as the Insurance Policies say, "by an act of God," so that they became really powerless. To that promise Jacob called God to witness.

1729. This is more than a formula. God is invoked as present and witnessing the bargain, and to Him both parties make over the affair to arrange and fulfil.

1730. The Commentators refer to a Jewish or Eastern custom or superstition which forbade members of a numerous family to go together in a mass for fear of "the evil eye". But apart from East or West, or custom or superstition, it would be ridiculous for any large family of ten or eleven to parade together in a procession among strangers. But there was even a better reason in this particular case, which made Jacob's advice sound, and Jacob was, as stated in the next verse, a man of knowledge and experience. Here were eleven strangers dressed alike, in a dress not of the country, talking a strange language, coming in a time of stress, on an errand for which they had no credentials. Would they not attract undue attention and suspicion if they went together? Would they not be taken for spies?—or for men bent on some mischief, theft, or organised crime? Such a suspicion is referred to in verse 73 below. By entering separately they would attract little attention. Jacob very wisely tells them to take all human precautions. But like a man of God he warns them that human precautions would be no good if they neglect or run counter to far weightier matters—God's Will and Law. Above all, they must try to understand and obey this, and their trust should be on God rather than on human usages, institutions, or precautions, however good and reasonable these might be.

I can profit you aught
Against God (with my advice):
None can command except God:
On Him do I put my trust:
And let all that trust
Put their trust on Him."

وَمَآ أُغْنِى عَنكُم مِّنَ ٱللَّهِ مِن شَىْءٍ ۖ
إِنِ ٱلْحُكْمُ إِلَّا لِلَّهِ ۖ عَلَيْهِ تَوَكَّلْتُ ۖ وَعَلَيْهِ
فَلْيَتَوَكَّلِ ٱلْمُتَوَكِّلُونَ ○

68. And when they entered
In the manner their father
Had enjoined, it did not
Profit them in the least
Against (the Plan of) God:[1731]
It was but a necessity
Of Jacob's soul, which he[1732]
Discharged. For he was,
By Our instruction, full
Of knowledge (and experience):
But most men know not.[1733]

٦٨- وَلَمَّا دَخَلُوا۟ مِنْ حَيْثُ أَمَرَهُمْ أَبُوهُم
مَّا كَانَ يُغْنِى عَنْهُم مِّنَ ٱللَّهِ مِن شَىْءٍ
إِلَّا حَاجَةً فِى نَفْسِ يَعْقُوبَ قَضَىٰهَا ۚ
وَإِنَّهُۥ لَذُو عِلْمٍ لِّمَا عَلَّمْنَٰهُ
وَلَٰكِنَّ أَكْثَرَ ٱلنَّاسِ لَا يَعْلَمُونَ ○

C. 112.—When the brothers went back without Benjamin,
(xii. 69-93.) **Jacob was overwhelmed with grief, but he bore**
His affliction with patience and faith in God.
He refused to be comforted and sent his sons back,
To Egypt. At last Joseph revealed himself,
Forgave them, and sent his shirt by them
To Jacob, to tell him the good news
That Joseph lived and did great work
In Egypt, and had sent for his whole family
To come and rejoice and live in the land
Of Egypt, and be a blessing to all.

1731. See the last verse and n. 1730. Though they scrupulously observed their father's injunctions to the letter, their hearts were not yet pure, and they got into trouble, as the later story will show. They had the hardihood to cast aspersions on Joseph, not knowing that they were in Joseph's power. And Joseph took a noble revenge by planning a reunion of the whole family and shaming the ten brothers into repentance. He was the instrument for the fulfilment of God's Plan.

1732. It is a necessity of a Prophet's soul that he should speak out and teach all that he knows, to the worthy and unworthy alike. This Jacob did to his unworthy sons, as well as to his worthy sons whom he loved best. It was not for him as a Prophet to guarantee any results. In this case he could not save his sons from getting into trouble merely because they followed the letter of his advice in a small matter. Apply this to the teaching of a greater than Jacob. Men who literally observe some small injunctions of the Holy Prophet Muḥammad and neglect the greater principles which he taught cannot blame him for their troubles and difficulties. If they examined the matter, they would find that they brought the troubles on themselves.

1733. The men of God are full of knowledge,—not as men, but as taught by the grace of God. For men, as such, are (as Carlyle said) mostly fools,—devoid of knowledge and understanding.

Section 9.

69. Now when they came
Into Joseph's presence,[1734]
He received his (full) brother[1735]
To stay with him. He said
(To him): "Behold! I am thy (own)
Brother; so grieve not
At aught of their doings."[1736]

٦٩- وَلَمَّا دَخَلُوا عَلَىٰ يُوسُفَ
آوَىٰ إِلَيْهِ أَخَاهُ
قَالَ إِنِّي أَنَا أَخُوكَ
فَلَا تَبْتَئِسْ بِمَا كَانُوا يَعْمَلُونَ ○

70. At length when he had furnished
Them forth with provisions
(Suitable) for them, he put
The drinking cup into
His brother's saddle-bag.
Then shouted out a Crier:
"O ye (in) the Caravan!
Behold! ye are thieves,
Without doubt!"[1737]

٧٠- فَلَمَّا جَهَّزَهُم بِجَهَازِهِمْ
جَعَلَ السِّقَايَةَ فِي رَحْلِ أَخِيهِ
ثُمَّ أَذَّنَ مُؤَذِّنٌ
أَيَّتُهَا الْعِيرُ إِنَّكُمْ لَسَارِقُونَ ○

71. They said, turning towards them:
"What is it that ye miss?"

٧١- قَالُوا وَأَقْبَلُوا عَلَيْهِم مَّاذَا تَفْقِدُونَ ○

72. They said: "We miss
The great beaker of the king;

٧٢- قَالُوا نَفْقِدُ صُوَاعَ الْمَلِكِ

1734. The ten brothers, with Benjamin, arrived in Egypt, and waited on the great Wazir. Joseph again received them hospitably, even more so than before, as they had complied with his request to bring Benjamin. No doubt many shrewd and probing questions were asked by Joseph, and no doubt it was clear that Benjamin was one apart from the other ten. Bai<u>dh</u>āwi fills up the picture of the great feast for us. The guests were seated two by two. Benjamin was the odd one, and Joseph courteously took him to his own table.

1735. After the feast the question of lodgings arose. They were to be accommodated two by two. Again Benjamin was the odd one. What more natural than that the Wazir should take him to himself? He thus got a chance of privacy with him. He disclosed his identity to him, charging him to keep it a secret, and to take no notice of any strange doings that might occur. He must have learnt from Benjamin about his father and about the inner doings of the family. He must get them all together into Egypt under his own eye. He had a plan, and he proceeded to put it into execution.

1736. The past tense of *Kānū*, combined with the aorist of *Ya'malūn*, signifies that the reference is to their brother's doings, past, present, and future. Benjamin was not to mind what wrongs they had done in the past, or how they behaved in the present or the immediate future. Joseph had a plan that required Benjamin's silence in strange circumstances.

1737. Joseph's plan was to play a practical joke on them, which would achieve two objects. Immediately it would put them into some consternation, but nothing comparable to what he had suffered at their hands. When the plan was unravelled, it would make them thoroughly ashamed of themselves, and dramatically bring home their guilt to them. Secondly, it would give him an excuse to detain Benjamin and bring their aged father into Egypt. He contrived that a valuable drinking cup should be concealed in Benjamin's saddle-bag. When it was found after an ostentatious search, he would detain the supposed culprit, and attain his object, as the story relates further on.

For him who produces it,
Is (the reward of)
A camel load; I
Will be bound by it."

وَلِمَنْ جَآءَ بِهٖ حِمْلُ بَعِيْرٍ
وَّاَنَا بِهٖ زَعِيْمٌ ۝

73. (The brothers) said: "By God!
Well ye know that we
Came not to make mischief
In the land, and we are
No thieves!"[1738]

٧٣- قَالُوْا تَاللّٰهِ لَقَدْ عَلِمْتُمْ مَّا جِئْنَا
لِنُفْسِدَ فِي الْاَرْضِ
وَمَا كُنَّا سٰرِقِيْنَ ۝

74. (The Egyptians) said: "What then
Shall be the penalty of this,
If ye are (proved) to have
lied?"[1739]

٧٤- قَالُوْا فَمَا جَزَآؤُهٗ
اِنْ كُنْتُمْ كٰذِبِيْنَ ۝

75. They said: "The penalty
Should be that he
In whose saddle-bag
It is found, should be held
(As bondman) to atone[1740]
For the (crime). Thus it is
We punish the wrong-doers!"[1741]

٧٥- قَالُوْا جَزَآؤُهٗ مَنْ وُّجِدَ فِيْ رَحْلِهٖ
فَهُوَ جَزَآؤُهٗ
كَذٰلِكَ نَجْزِي الظّٰلِمِيْنَ ۝

76. So he[1742] began (the search)
With their baggage,

٧٦- فَبَدَاَ بِاَوْعِيَتِهِمْ

1738. As strangers in a strange land, they were liable to be suspected as spies or men who meditated some unlawful design, or some crime, such as theft, which would be common in a season of scarcity. The brothers protested against the absurdity of such a suspicion after they had been entertained so royally by the Wazīr.

1739. "That might be all very well," said the Egyptians, "but what if it is found by a search that you have in fact abused the Wazīr's hospitality by stealing a valuable cup?"

1740. We must try to picture to ourselves the mentality of the ten. They understood each other perfectly, in their sins as well as in other things. For themselves, the search held out no fears. Besides they had had no opportunity of stealing. But what of that young fellow Benjamin? They were ready to believe anything against him, the more so as the Wazīr's partiality for him had lent a keen edge to their jealousy. Judging by their own standards, they would not be surprised if he had stolen, seeing that he had had such opportunities—sitting at the High Table and staying with the Wazīr. They felt very self-righteous at the same time that they indulged in the luxury of accusing in their thoughts the most innocent of men! Supposing he had stolen, here would be a fine opportunity of getting rid of him. What about their solemn oath to their father? Oh! that was covered by the exception. He had done for himself. They had done all they could to protect him, but they were powerless. The old man could come and see for himself.

1741. This was their family custom. It was of course long anterior to the Mosaic Law, which laid down full restitution for theft, and if the culprit had nothing, he was to be sold for his theft (Exod. xxii. 3). But here the crime was more than theft. It was theft, lying, and the grossest abuse of confidence and hospitality. While the ten felt a secret satisfaction in suggesting the penalty, they were unconsciously carrying out Joseph's plan. Thus the vilest motives often help in carrying out the most beneficent plans.

1742. The pronoun "he" can only refer to Joseph. He may have been present all the time, or he may just have come up, as the supposed theft of the king's own cup (xii. 72 above) was a very serious and important affair, and the investigation required his personal supervision. All that his officers did by his orders was his own act. As the lawyers say: *Qui facit per alium, facit per se* (whoever does anything through another, does it himself).

Before (he came to) the baggage[1743]
Of his brother: at length
He brought it[1744] out of his
Brother's baggage. Thus did We
Plan for Joseph. He could not
Take his brother by the law
Of the king except that God[1745]
Willed it (so). We raise
To degrees (of wisdom) whom[1746]
We please: but over all
Endued with knowledge is One,
The All-Knowing.

77. They said: "If he steals,
There was a brother of his
Who did steal before (him)."[1747]
But these things did Joseph
Keep locked in his heart,
Revealing not the secrets to them.[1748]

قَبْلَ وِعَاءِ أَخِيهِ
ثُمَّ اسْتَخْرَجَهَا مِنْ وِعَاءِ أَخِيهِ ۚ
كَذَٰلِكَ كِدْنَا لِيُوسُفَ ۖ
مَا كَانَ لِيَأْخُذَ أَخَاهُ فِي دِينِ الْمَلِكِ
إِلَّا أَنْ يَشَاءَ اللَّهُ ۚ
نَرْفَعُ دَرَجَاتٍ مَنْ نَشَاءُ ۗ
وَفَوْقَ كُلِّ ذِي عِلْمٍ عَلِيمٌ ○

٧٧- قَالُوا إِنْ يَسْرِقْ فَقَدْ سَرَقَ أَخٌ
لَهُ مِنْ قَبْلُ ۚ
فَأَسَرَّهَا يُوسُفُ فِي نَفْسِهِ
وَلَمْ يُبْدِهَا لَهُمْ ۚ

1743. The Arabic word here used is *wi'āun*, plural *au'iya*, which includes bags, lockers, boxes, or any receptacles in which things are stored. Notice the appropriateness of the words used. The cup was concealed in a saddle-bag *(raḥl)*, verse 70 above. When it comes to searching, they must search *all* the baggage of every description if the search was to be convincing and effective.

1744. *It* refers to the drinking cup, the *siqāyat*, which is a feminine noun: hence the feminine pronoun *(hā)* in Arabic.

1745. Let no one suppose that it was a vulgar or wicked trick, such as we sometimes hear of in police courts, when property is planted on innocent men to get them into trouble. On the contrary it was a device or stratagem whose purpose was to show up wickedness in its true colours, to give it a chance of repentance, to bring about forgiveness and reconciliation, to give solace to the aged father who had suffered so much, and above all, to further that larger plan for the instruction of the world, which is unfolded in Israel's religious history. Joseph was a man of God, but he could not have carried out this plan or taken the first step, of detaining his brother, except with the will and permission of God, Whose Plan is universal and for all His creatures.

1746. If we examine this world's affairs, there are all sorts of plans, and all degrees of folly and wisdom. The wicked ones plan; the foolish ones plan; the simple ones plan; then there are men who think themselves wise and are perhaps thought to be wise, but who are foolish, and they have their plans: and there are degrees of real and beneficent wisdom among men. God, the Universal Planner, is above all. Anything good in our wisdom is but a reflection of His wisdom, and His wisdom can even turn folly and wickedness to good.

1747. The hatred of the Ten for Joseph and Benjamin comes out again. They are not only ready to believe evil of Benjamin, but they carry their thoughts back to Joseph and call him a thief as well. They had injured Joseph; and by a false charge of this kind they salve their conscience. Little did they suspect that Joseph was before them under another guise, and their falsehood and treachery would soon be exposed.

1748. There were many secrets: (1) that he was Joseph himself; (2) that his brother Benjamin knew him; (3) that there was no guilt in Benjamin, but the whole practical joke was in furtherance of a great plan (see n. 1745 above); (4) that they were giving themselves away, and were unconsciously facilitating the plan, though their motives were not above-board.

He (simply) said (to himself):
"Ye are the worse situated;[1749]
And God knoweth best
The truth of what ye assert!"

قَالَ اَنْتُمْ شَرٌّ مَّكَانًا ۚ وَاللّٰهُ اَعْلَمُ بِمَا تَصِفُوْنَ ○

78. They said: "O exalted one![1750]
Behold! he has a father,
Aged and venerable, (who will
Grieve for him); so take
One of us in his place;
For we see that thou art
(Gracious) in doing good."

٧٨- قَالُوْا يٰۤاَيُّهَا الْعَزِيْزُ اِنَّ لَهٗۤ اَبًا شَيْخًا كَبِيْرًا فَخُذْ اَحَدَنَا مَكَانَهٗ ۚ اِنَّا نَرٰىكَ مِنَ الْمُحْسِنِيْنَ ○

79. He said: "God forbid
That we take other than him
With whom we found
Our property: indeed
(If we did so), we should
Be acting wrongfully.[1751]

٧٩- قَالَ مَعَاذَ اللّٰهِ اَنْ نَّاْخُذَ اِلَّا مَنْ وَّجَدْنَا مَتَاعَنَا عِنْدَهٗۤ ۙ اِنَّاۤ اِذًا لَّظٰلِمُوْنَ ○

SECTION 10.

80. Now when they saw
No hope of his (yielding),
They held a conference in private.
The leader among them said:[1752]
"Know ye not that your father
Did take an oath from you
In God's name, and how,
Before this, ye did fail

٨٠- فَلَمَّا اسْتَيْـَٔسُوْا مِنْهُ خَلَصُوْا نَجِيًّا ؕ قَالَ كَبِيْرُهُمْ اَلَمْ تَعْلَمُوْۤا اَنَّ اَبَاكُمْ قَدْ اَخَذَ عَلَيْكُمْ مَّوْثِقًا مِّنَ اللّٰهِ وَمِنْ قَبْلُ مَا فَرَّطْتُّمْ

1749. "Ah!" thought Joseph, "you think that Benjamin is safely out of the way, and that Joseph was got rid of long since! Would you he surprised to know that you have given yourselves away, that you are now in the power of Joseph, and that Joseph is the very instrument of your exposure and (let us hope) of your repentance?"

1750. I have translated the title of *'Azīz* here as "the exalted one" when addressed to Joseph in order not to cause confusion with the other man, the 'Aziz to whom Zulaik͟hā was married, and who is apparently no longer now in the land of the living. See xii. 30 above, and notes 1677 and 1714.

1751. There is a little sparring now between the Ten and Joseph. They are afraid of meeting their father's wrath, and he holds them strictly to the bargain which they had themselves suggested.

1752. *Kabīr* may mean the eldest. But in xii. 78 above, *Kabīr* is distinguished from *Shaikh*, and I have translated the one as "venerable" and the other as "aged". In xx. 71, *Kabīr* obviously means "leader" or "chief", and has no reference to age. I therefore translate here by the word "leader", that brother among them who took the most active part in these transactions. His name is not given in the Qur-ān. The eldest brother was Reuben. But according to the biblical story the brother who had taken the most active part in this transaction was Judah, one of the elder brothers, being the fourth son, after Reuben, Simeon, and Levi, and of the same mother as these. It was Judah who stood surety to Jacob for Benjamin (Gen. xliii. 9). It is therefore natural that Judah should, as here, offer to stay behind.

In your duty with Joseph ?
Therefore will I not leave
This land until my father
Permits me, or God[1753]
Commands me ; and He
Is the best to command.

فِي يُوسُفَ فَلَنْ أَبْرَحَ الْأَرْضَ
حَتَّى يَأْذَنَ لِي أَبِي أَوْ يَحْكُمَ اللَّهُ لِي
وَهُوَ خَيْرُ الْحَاكِمِينَ ○

81. "Turn ye back to your father,
And say, 'O our father!
Behold! thy son committed theft!
We bear witness only to what
We know, and we could not
Well guard against the unseen!'[1754]

٨١- ارْجِعُوا إِلَى أَبِيكُمْ فَقُولُوا يَا أَبَانَا إِنَّ
ابْنَكَ سَرَقَ وَمَا شَهِدْنَا إِلَّا بِمَا عَلِمْنَا
وَمَا كُنَّا لِلْغَيْبِ حَافِظِينَ ○

82. "'Ask at the town where
We have been and the caravan
In which we returned,
And (you will find) we are
Indeed telling the truth.'"[1755]

٨٢- وَاسْأَلِ الْقَرْيَةَ الَّتِي كُنَّا فِيهَا
وَالْعِيرَ الَّتِي أَقْبَلْنَا فِيهَا
وَإِنَّا لَصَادِقُونَ ○

83. Jacob said: "Nay, but ye
Have yourselves contrived
A story (good enough) for you.[1756]
So patience is most fitting
(For me). Maybe God will
Bring them (back) all
To me (in the end).[1757]
For He is indeed full
Of knowledge and wisdom."

٨٣- قَالَ بَلْ سَوَّلَتْ لَكُمْ أَنْفُسُكُمْ أَمْرًا
فَصَبْرٌ جَمِيلٌ
عَسَى اللَّهُ أَنْ يَأْتِيَنِي بِهِمْ جَمِيعًا
إِنَّهُ هُوَ الْعَلِيمُ الْحَكِيمُ ○

1753. The pledge he had given was to his father, and in God's name. Therefore he was bound both to his father, and to God. He must await his father's orders and remain here as pledged, unless God opened out some other way. For example the Egyptian Wazir might relent : if so, he could go back with Benjamin to his father, and his pledge would be satisfied.

1754. 'He stole in secret and without our knowledge. How could we in the circumstances prevent it?' This may have been a good statement for the other nine brothers, but Judah was himself personally and specially pledged.

1755. To vouch for the truth of the story, the nine brothers are asked by Judah to appeal to their father to enquire at the place where they stayed and the caravan with which they came, and he would find that the facts were as they stated them. The nine brothers came back and told their father as they had been instructed by Judah.

1756. Jacob was absolutely stunned by the story. He knew his darling little Benjamin too well to believe that he had committed theft. He flatly refused to believe it, and called it a cock-and-bull story, which indeed it was, though not in the sense in which he reproached the nine brothers. With the eye of faith he saw clearly the innocence of Benjamin, though he did not see every detail of what had happened.

1757. With the eye of faith he clung to even a larger hope. Perhaps all three of his lost sons would come back,—Joseph, Benjamin, and Judah. His faith in God was unswerving, although alas! the present facts altogether unmanned him.

84. And he turned away from them,
And said: "How great
Is my grief for Joseph!"
And his eyes became white[1758]
With sorrow, and he fell
Into silent melancholy.

٨٤- وَتَوَلّٰى عَنْهُمْ وَقَالَ يٰٓاَسَفٰى عَلٰى يُوْسُفَ
وَابْيَضَّتْ عَيْنٰهُ مِنَ الْحُزْنِ
فَهُوَ كَظِيْمٌ ○

85. They said: "By God!
(Never) wilt thou cease
To remember Joseph
Until thou reach the last
Extremity of illness,
Or until thou die!"[1759]

٨٥- قَالُوْا تَاللّٰهِ تَفْتَؤُا
تَذْكُرُ يُوْسُفَ حَتّٰى تَكُوْنَ حَرَضًا اَوْ تَكُوْنَ
مِنَ الْهٰلِكِيْنَ ○

86. He said: "I only complain[1760]
Of my distraction and anguish
To God, and I know from God[1761]
That which ye know not ...

٨٦- قَالَ اِنَّمَآ اَشْكُوْا بَثِّيْ وَحُزْنِيْٓ اِلَى اللّٰهِ
وَاَعْلَمُ مِنَ اللّٰهِ مَا لَا تَعْلَمُوْنَ ○

87. "O my sons! go ye
And enquire about Joseph
And his brother, and never
Give up hope of God's
Soothing Mercy:[1762] truly
No one despairs of God's

٨٧- يٰبَنِيَّ اذْهَبُوْا فَتَحَسَّسُوْا مِنْ يُّوْسُفَ
وَاَخِيْهِ وَلَا تَايْـَٔسُوْا مِنْ رَّوْحِ اللّٰهِ
اِنَّهٗ لَا يَايْـَٔسُ مِنْ رَّوْحِ اللّٰهِ

1758. The old father's grief is indescribable. Yet with what master-strokes it is described here! One sorrow brings up the memory of another and a greater one. 'Benjamin is now gone! Oh but Joseph! his pretty dream of boyhood! his greatness foretold! and now how dark was the world! If he could but weep! Tears might give relief, and his red and swollen eyes might yet regain their light!' But his grief was too deep for tears. His eyes lost their colour, and became a dull white. The light became a mere blur, a white glimmer. Darkness seemed to cover everything. So it was in the outside world. So was it in his mind. His grief was unshared, unexpressed, and uncomplaining. Who could share it? Who could understand it? He bore his sorrow in silence. Yet his faith was undimmed, and he trimmed the lamp of patience, that sovereign virtue for those who have faith.

1759. A speech full of jealousy, taunting malice, and lack of understanding,—one that would have driven mad any one less endowed with patience and wisdom than was Jacob the man of God. It shows that the sons were still unregenerate, though the time of their repentance and reclamation was drawing nigh. The cruel heartlessness of their words is particularly out of place, as Jacob bore his sorrow in silence and complained to no mortal, but poured out his distraction and grief only to God, as stated in the next verse.

1760. Jacob's plaint to God is about himself, not about God's doings. He bewails the distraction of his mind and his occasional breaking out of those bounds of patience which he had set for himself.

1761. He knew of God's merciful and beneficent dealings with man in a way his shallow sons did not. And his perfect faith in God also told him that all would be well. He never gave up hope for Joseph, as his directions in the next verse show. They may be supposed to have been spoken after a little silence of grief and thought. That silence I have indicated in punctuation by three dots.

1762. The word is *rauḥ*, not *rūḥ*, as some translators have mistakenly construed it. *Rauḥ* includes the idea of a Mercy that stills or calms our distracted state, and is particularly appropriate here in the mouth of Jacob.

Soothing Mercy, except
Those who have no faith." [1763]

إِلَّا الْقَوْمُ الْكٰفِرُونَ ○

88. When, when they came
(Back) into (Joseph's) presence [1764]
They said: "O exalted one!
Distress has seized us
And our family: we have
(Now) brought but scanty capital:
So pay us full measure,
(We pray thee), and treat it
As charity to us: for God
Doth reward the charitable."

٨٨- فَلَمَّا دَخَلُوا عَلَيْهِ
قَالُوا يٰٓأَيُّهَا الْعَزِيزُ مَسَّنَا
وَأَهْلَنَا الضُّرُّ وَجِئْنَا بِبِضٰعَةٍ مُّزْجٰةٍ
فَأَوْفِ لَنَا الْكَيْلَ وَتَصَدَّقْ عَلَيْنَا
إِنَّ اللّٰهَ يَجْزِى الْمُتَصَدِّقِينَ ○

89. He said: "Know ye
How ye dealt with Joseph [1765]
And his brother, not knowing
(What ye were doing)?"

٨٩- قَالَ هَلْ عَلِمْتُمْ مَّا فَعَلْتُمْ بِيُوسُفَ
وَأَخِيهِ إِذْ أَنْتُمْ جٰهِلُونَ ○

90. They said: "Art thou indeed [1766]
Joseph?" He said. "I am
Joseph, and this is my brother:
God has indeed been gracious

٩٠- قَالُوٓا أَءِنَّكَ لَأَنْتَ يُوسُفُ قَالَ أَنَا
يُوسُفُ وَهٰذَآ أَخِى قَدْ مَنَّ اللّٰهُ عَلَيْنَا

1763. Jacob ignores and forgives the sting and malice in the speech of his sons, and like a true man of God, still wishes them well, gives them sound advice, and sends them on an errand which is to open their eyes to the wonderful ways of Providence as much as it will bring consolation to his own distressed soul. He asks them to go again in search of Joseph and Benjamin. Perhaps by now he had an idea that they might be together in Egypt. In any case their stock of grain is again low, and they must seek its replenishment in Egypt.

1764. The nine brothers come back to Egypt according to their father's direction. Their first care is to see the Wazir. They must tell him of all their father's distress and excite his pity, if perchance he might release Benjamin. They would describe the father's special mental distress as well as the distress which was the common lot of all in famine time. They had spent a great part of their capital and stock-in-trade. They would appeal to his charity. It might please so great a man, the absolute governor of a wealthy state. And they did so. Perhaps they mentioned their father's touching faith, and that brought Joseph out of his shell, as in the next verse.

1765. Joseph now wants to reveal himself and touch their conscience. He had but to remind them of the true facts as to their treatment of their brother Joseph, whom they pretended to have lost. He had by now also learnt from Benjamin what slights and injustice he too had suffered at their hands after Joseph's protection had been removed from him in their home. Had not Joseph himself seen them but too prone to believe the worst of Benjamin and to say the worst of Joseph? But Joseph would be charitable,—not only in the sense which they meant when they asked for a charitable grant of grain, but in a far higher sense. He would forgive them and put the most charitable construction on what they did,—that they knew not what they were doing!

1766. Their father's words the way events were shaping themselves, Joseph's questionings, perhaps Benjamin's manner now,—not a slave kept in subjection but one in perfect love and understanding with this great Wazir,—perhaps also a recollection of Joseph's boyish dream,—all these things had prepared their minds and they ask the direct question, "Art thou Joseph?" They get the direct reply, "Yes, I am Joseph; and if you have still any doubt of my identity, here is Benjamin: ask him. We have suffered much, but patience and right conduct are at last rewarded by God!"

To us (all): behold, he that is
Righteous and patient,—never
Will God suffer the reward
To be lost, of those
Who do right."

إِنَّهُۥ مَن يَتَّقِ وَيَصْبِرْ
فَإِنَّ ٱللَّهَ لَا يُضِيعُ أَجْرَ ٱلْمُحْسِنِينَ ○

91. They said: "By God! Indeed
Has God preferred thee
Above us, and we certainly
Have been guilty of sin!"[1767]

٩١- قَالُوا۟ تَٱللَّهِ لَقَدْ ءَاثَرَكَ ٱللَّهُ عَلَيْنَا
وَإِن كُنَّا لَخَٰطِـِٔينَ ○

92. He said: "This day
Let no reproach be (cast)[1768]
On you: God will forgive you,
And He is the Most Merciful
Of those who show mercy!

٩٢- قَالَ لَا تَثْرِيبَ عَلَيْكُمُ ٱلْيَوْمَ
يَغْفِرُ ٱللَّهُ لَكُمْ
وَهُوَ أَرْحَمُ ٱلرَّٰحِمِينَ ○

93. "Go with this my shirt,[1769]
And cast it over the face
Of my father: he will
Come to see (clearly). Then come
Ye (here) to me together
With all your family."

٩٣- ٱذْهَبُوا۟ بِقَمِيصِى هَٰذَا فَأَلْقُوهُ عَلَىٰ
وَجْهِ أَبِى يَأْتِ بَصِيرًا
وَأْتُونِى بِأَهْلِكُمْ أَجْمَعِينَ ○ ع

C. 113.—Jacob was comforted with the news.
(xii. 94-111.) The whole family moved to Egypt,
Where Joseph received them with honour.
He forgave his brothers, thanked and praised
God, and lived and died a righteous man.
So the story shows how the Plan of God
Doth work without fail: it defeats
The wiles of the wicked, turns evil to good,

1767. The scales fall from the eyes of the brothers. We may suppose that they had joined Judah at this interview, and perhaps what Judah had seen when he was alone helped in the process of their enlightenment. They are convicted of sin out of their own mouths, and now there is no *arrière pensée*, no reserve thought, in their minds. They freely confess their wrong-doing, and the justice of Joseph's preferment.

1768. Joseph is most generous. He is glad that they have at last seen the significance of what happened. But he will not allow them at this great moment of reconciliation to dwell on their conduct with reproaches against themselves. There is more urgent work to do. An aged and beloved father is eating out his heart in far Canaan in love and longing for his Joseph, and he must be told all immediately, and "comforted in body, mind, and estate," and so he tells the brothers to hurry back immediately with his shirt as a sign of recognition, as a proof of these wonderful happenings.

1769. It will be remembered that they had covered their crime by taking his shirt, putting on the stains of blood, and pretending that he had been killed by a wolf: see above, xii. 17-18. Now that they have confessed their crime and been forgiven, and they have joyful news to tell Jacob about Joseph. Joseph gives them another shirt of his to prove the truth of their story. It is a rich shirt, befitting a ruler of Egypt, to prove his good fortune, and yet perhaps its design and many colours (xii. 18, n. 1651) were reminiscent of the lost Joseph. The first shirt plunged Jacob into grief. This one will now restore him. See the verses following.

And ever leads those who are true
To beatitudes undreamt of. So
Did it happen in Muṣṭafa's life.
Will man not learn to rely on God
As the only Reality, turning away
From all that is fleeting or untrue?

SECTION 11.

94. When the Caravan left (Egypt),
Their father said: "I do indeed
Scent the presence of Joseph:[1770]
Nay, think me not a dotard."

٩٤- وَلَمَّا فَصَلَتِ الْعِيرُ قَالَ أَبُوهُمْ إِنِّي
لَأَجِدُ رِيحَ يُوسُفَ لَوْلَا أَن تُفَنِّدُونِ ○

95. They[1771] said: "By God!
Truly thou art in
Thine old wandering mind."

٩٥- قَالُوا تَاللَّهِ إِنَّكَ لَفِي ضَلَالِكَ الْقَدِيمِ ○

96. Then when the bearer[1772]
Of the good news came,
He cast (the shirt)
Over his face, and he
Forthwith[1773] regained clear sight.[1774]

He said: "Did I not say
To you, 'I know from God
That which ye know not?'"[1775]

٩٦- فَلَمَّا أَن جَاءَ الْبَشِيرُ أَلْقَاهُ عَلَىٰ وَجْهِهِ
فَارْتَدَّ بَصِيرًا ۚ
قَالَ أَلَمْ أَقُل لَّكُمْ ۚ
إِنِّي أَعْلَمُ مِنَ اللَّهِ
مَا لَا تَعْلَمُونَ ○

1770. Literally, 'I feel the scent, or the air, or the atmosphere or the breath of Joseph'; for *rīḥ* has all these significations. Or we might translate, 'I feel the presence of Joseph in the air'. When a long-lost friend is about to be found or heard of, many people have a sort of presentiment of it, which they call telepathy. In Jacob's case it was more definite. He had always had faith that Joseph was living and that his dream would be realised. Now that faith was proved true by his own sons; they had been undutiful, and hard, and ignorant; and circumstances had converged to prove it to them by ocular demonstration. Jacob's soul was more sensitive. No wonder he knew already before the news was actually brought to him.

1771. "They" must be the people around him, before the brothers actually arrived. These same brothers had sedulously cultivated the calumny that their father was an old dotard, and everybody around believed it, even after its authors had to give it up. Thus lies die hard, once they get a start.

1772. We may suppose this to have been Judah (see notes 1752 and 1753 above) who was pledged to his father for Benjamin, and who could now announce the good news not only of Benjamin but of Joseph. We can imagine him hurrying forward, to be the first to tell the news, though the plural pronoun for those whom Jacob addresses in this verse, and for those who reply in the next verse, shows that all the brothers practically arrived together.

1773. The particle *fa* ("then") has here the force of "forthwith".

1774. Jacob's sight had grown dim; his eyes had become white with much sorrow for Joseph (see xii. 84 above). His mind had also become dark and distracted (xii 85). Both his physical and mental vision now became clear and bright as before.

1775. He had said this (xii. 86) when everything was against him, and his sons were scoffers. Now they themselves have come to say that his faith was justified and his vision was true.

97. They said: "O our father! Ask for us forgiveness For our sins, for we Were truly at fault."	٩٧- قَالُوا يَٰٓأَبَانَا ٱسْتَغْفِرْ لَنَا ذُنُوبَنَآ إِنَّا كُنَّا خَٰطِـِٔينَ ۝
98. He said: "Soon[1776] will I Ask my Lord for forgiveness For you: for He is indeed Oft-Forgiving, Most Merciful."	٩٨- قَالَ سَوْفَ أَسْتَغْفِرُ لَكُمْ رَبِّىٓ ۖ إِنَّهُۥ هُوَ ٱلْغَفُورُ ٱلرَّحِيمُ ۝
99. Then when they entered[1777] The presence of Joseph, He provided a home For his parents with himself, And said: "Enter ye[1778] Egypt (all) in safety If it please God."	٩٩- فَلَمَّا دَخَلُوا عَلَىٰ يُوسُفَ ءَاوَىٰٓ إِلَيْهِ أَبَوَيْهِ وَقَالَ ٱدْخُلُوا مِصْرَ إِن شَآءَ ٱللَّهُ ءَامِنِينَ ۝
100. And he raised his parents High on the throne (of dignity),[1779] And they fell down in prostration, (All) before him. He said: "O my father! this is The fulfilment of my vision Of old! God hath made it Come true! He was indeed Good to me when He Took me out of prison	١٠٠- وَرَفَعَ أَبَوَيْهِ عَلَى ٱلْعَرْشِ وَخَرُّوا لَهُۥ سُجَّدًا ۖ وَقَالَ يَٰٓأَبَتِ هَٰذَا تَأْوِيلُ رُءْيَٰىَ مِن قَبْلُ قَدْ جَعَلَهَا رَبِّى حَقًّا ۖ وَقَدْ أَحْسَنَ بِىٓ إِذْ أَخْرَجَنِى مِنَ ٱلسِّجْنِ

1776. He fully intended to do this, but the most injured party was Joseph, and it was only fair that Joseph should be consulted. In fact Joseph had already forgiven his brothers all their past, and his father could confidently look forward to Joseph joining in the wish of the whole family to turn to God through their aged father Jacob in his prophetic office.

1777. At length the whole family arrived in Egypt and were re-united with Joseph. They were all entertained and provided with homes. But the parents were treated with special honour, as was becoming both to Joseph's character and ordinary family ethics. His mother Rachel had long been dead, but he had been brought up by his mother's sister Leah, whom his father had also married. Leah was now his mother. They were lodged with Joseph himself.

1778. This is in Arabic in the plural, not in the dual number. The welcome is for all to Egypt, and under the auspices of the Wazir of Egypt. They came, therefore, under God's will, to a double sense of security: Egypt was secure from the famine unlike the neighbouring countries; and they were to be cared for by the highest in the land.

1779. Certainly metaphorically: probably also literally. By Eastern custom the place of honour at a ceremonial reception is on a seat on a dais, with a special cushion of honour, such as is assigned to a bridegroom at his reception. To show his high respect for his parents, Joseph made them sit on a throne of dignity. On the other hand, his parents and his brothers,—all performed the ceremony of prostration before Joseph in recognition of his supreme rank in Egypt under the Pharaoh. And thus was fulfilled the dream or vision of his youth (xii. 4 above, and n. 1633).

And brought you (all here)[1780]
Out of the desert,
(Even) after Satan had sown
Enmity between me and my
brothers.
Verily my Lord understandeth
Best the mysteries of all
That He planneth to do.
For verily He is full
Of knowledge and wisdom.

101. " O my Lord! Thou hast
Indeed bestowed on me
Some power, and taught me
Something of the interpretation[1781]
Of dreams and events,—O Thou
Creator of the heavens[1782]
And the earth! Thou art
My Protector in this world
And in the Hereafter.
Take Thou my soul (at death)
As one submitting to Thy Will
(As a Muslim), and unite me
With the righteous."[1783]

وَجَآءَ بِكُم مِّنَ الْبَدْوِ
مِنۢ بَعْدِ أَن نَّزَغَ الشَّيْطٰنُ بَيْنِى وَبَيْنَ
إِخْوَتِىٓ
إِنَّ رَبِّى لَطِيفٌ لِّمَا يَشَآءُ
إِنَّهُۥ هُوَ الْعَلِيمُ الْحَكِيمُ ۝
١٠١- رَبِّ قَدْ ءَاتَيْتَنِى
مِنَ الْمُلْكِ وَعَلَّمْتَنِى مِن تَأْوِيلِ
الْأَحَادِيثِ
فَاطِرَ السَّمٰوٰتِ وَالْأَرْضِ
أَنتَ وَلِىِّۦ فِى الدُّنْيَا وَالْءَاخِرَةِ
تَوَفَّنِى مُسْلِمًا
وَأَلْحِقْنِى بِالصّٰلِحِينَ ۝

1780. Note how modest Joseph is throughout. The first things he thinks of among God's gracious favours to him are: (1) that he was brought out of prison and publicly proclaimed to be honest and virtuous; and (2) that his dear father was restored to him, as well as the brothers who had persecuted him all his life. He will say nothing against them personally. In his *ḥusn-i-ẓann* (habit of interpreting everyone and everything in the most favourable and charitable light), he looks upon them as having been misled. It was Satan (the power of Evil) that set them against him. But now all is rectified by the grace of God, to Whom he renders due praise.

Laṭīf : see n. 2844 to xxii. 63 ; the fourth meaning mentioned there applies here, with echoes of the other meanings.

1781. Then he turns to God in prayer, and again his modesty is predominant. He held supreme power under the king, but he calls it "some power" or authority. His reading of events and dreams had saved millions of lives in the great Egyptian famine; yet he refers to it as "something of the interpretation of dreams and events". And he takes no credit to himself. "All this," he says, "was Thy gift, O God! For such things can only come from the Creator of the heavens and the earth."

1782. Power in the doing of things as well as power in intelligent forecasts and plans,—both must look to God: otherwise the deed and the plan would be futile.

1783. Joseph's prayer may be analysed thus: (1) I am nothing; all power and knowledge are Thine; (2) such things can only come from Thee, for Thou art the Creator of all; (3) none can protect me from danger and wrong, but only Thou; (4) Thy protection I need both in this world and the next; (5) may I till death remain constant to Thee; (6) may I yield up my soul to Thee in cheerful submission to Thy will; (7) in this moment of union with my family after many partings let me think of the final union with the great spiritual family of the righteous. How marvellously apt to the occasion!

102. Such is one of the stories
Of what happened unseen,[1784]
Which We reveal by inspiration
Unto thee: nor wast thou[1785]
(Present) with them when they
Concerted their plans together
In the process of weaving their
plots.

١٠٢- ذلك من انباء الغيب
نوحيه اليك
وما كنت لديهم
اذ اجمعوا امرهم وهم يمكرون ○

103. Yet no faith will
The greater part of mankind
Have, however ardently
Thou dost desire it.[1786]

١٠٣- وما اكثر الناس
ولو حرصت بمؤمنين ○

104. And no reward dost thou ask
Of them for this: it is
No less than a Message
For all creatures.[1787]

١٠٤- وما تسئلهم عليه من اجر
ان هو الا ذكر للعلمين ○

[SECTION 12.

105. And how many Signs
In the heavens and the earth

١٠٥- وكاين من اية في السموت والارض

1784. The story is finished. But is it a story? It is rather a recital of forces and motives, thoughts and feelings, complications and results, ordinarily not seen by men. However much they concert their plans and unite their forces, whatever dark plots they back with all their resources,—the plan of God works irresistibly, and sweeps away all their machinations. The good win through in the end, but not always as they planned; the evil are foiled, and often their very plots help the good. What did the brothers desire in trying to get rid of Joseph, and what actually happened? How did Zulaik̲h̲ā form an image of her love, what false traps and sins did it not lead her into, and how, through it all, by her constancy and faith, did she see her way to a higher, nobler, and purer love? How wrong was it of the cup-bearer to forget Joseph, and yet how his very forgetfulness kept Joseph safe and undisturbed in prison until the day came when he should tackle the great problems of Pharaoh's kingdom? With every character in the story there are problems, and the whole is a beautifully balanced picture of the working of God's providence in man's chequered destiny.

1785. The holy Apostle was no actor in those scenes; yet by inspiration he was able to expound them in the divine light, as they had never been expounded before, whether in the Pentateuch or by any Seer before him. And allegorically they figured his own story,—how his own brethren sought to betray and kill him, how by God's providence he was not only saved but he won through, and how his own friends misconceived their love for him and had to be taught that true love which transcends sex and self. Of such a dream of love Plato had an inkling.

1786. In spite of such an exposition and such a convincing illustration, how few men really have true faith,—such a faith as Jacob had in the old story, or Muḥammad the Chosen One had, in the story which was actually unfolding itself on the world's stage when this Sūra was revealed, shortly before the Hijrat? Muṣṭafā's ardent wish and faith was to save his people and all mankind from the graceless condition of want of faith. But his efforts were flouted, and he had to leave his home and suffer all kinds of persecution; but, like Joseph, and more than Joseph, he was marked out for great work, which he finally achieved.

1787. The divine Message was priceless; it was not for the Messenger's personal profit, nor did he ask of men any reward for bringing it for their benefit. It was for all creatures,—literally, for all the worlds, as explained in i. 2, n. 20.

Do they pass by? Yet they
Turn (their faces) away from
them![1788]

يَمُرُّوْنَ عَلَيْهَا وَهُمْ عَنْهَا مُعْرِضُوْنَ ○

106. And most of them
Believe not in God
Without associating (others
As partners) with Him![1789]

١٠٦- وَمَا يُؤْمِنُ أَكْثَرُهُمْ بِاللّٰهِ
إِلَّا وَهُمْ مُّشْرِكُوْنَ ○

107. Do they then feel secure
From the coming against them
Of the covering veil[1790]
Of the wrath of God,—
Or of the coming against them
Of the (final) Hour
All of a sudden[1791]
While they perceive not?

١٠٧- أَفَأَمِنُوْٓا أَنْ تَأْتِيَهُمْ
غَاشِيَةٌ مِّنْ عَذَابِ اللّٰهِ
أَوْ تَأْتِيَهُمُ السَّاعَةُ بَغْتَةً
وَّهُمْ لَا يَشْعُرُوْنَ ○

108. Say thou: "This is my Way:
I do invite unto God,—
On evidence clear as
The seeing with one's eyes,—[1792]

١٠٨- قُلْ هٰذِهٖ سَبِيْلِيْٓ أَدْعُوْٓا إِلَى اللّٰهِ
عَلٰى بَصِيْرَةٍ

1788. Not only can we learn through Scripture of the working of God's providence in human history and the history of individual souls. His Signs are scattered literally throughout nature—throughout Creation—for all who have eyes to see. And yet man is so arrogant that he turns away his very eyes from them!

1789. Even if people profess a nominal faith in God, they corrupt it by believing in other things as if they were God's partners, or had some share in the shaping of the world's destinies! In some circles, it is idolatry, the worship of stocks and stones. In others, it is Christolatry and Mariolatry, or the deification of heroes and men of renown. In others it is the powers of Nature or of Life, or of the human intellect personified in Science or Art or invention, and this is the more common form of modern idolatry. Others again worship mystery, or imaginary powers of good or even evil: greed and fear are mixed up with these forms of worship. Islam calls us to worship the One True God, and Him only.

1790. *Gāshiyat* = covering veil, pall; used for the Judgment to come, which will be so dark and appalling as to hide up all other and petty things, and be the one great reality for the souls that were slaves to evil.

1791. The metaphor is changed, from intensity of darkness to suddenness of time. It will come before they are aware of it. Let them not feel any sense of safety in sin.

1792. Islam holds fast to the one central fact in the spiritual world,—the unity of God, and all Reality springing from Him and Him alone. There can be no one and nothing in competition with that one and only Reality. It is the essence of Truth. All other ideas or existences, including our perception of Self, are merely relative,—mere projections from the wonderful faculties which He has given to us. This is not, to us, mere hypothesis. It is in our inmost experience. In the physical world, they say that seeing is believing. In our inner world this sense of God is as clear as sight in the physical world. Therefore, Muṣṭafā and those who really follow him in the truest sense of the world, call all the world to see this Truth, feel this experience, follow this Way. They will never be distracted by metaphysical speculations, whose validity will always be doubtful, nor be deluded with phantoms which lead men astray.

I and whoever follows me.
Glory to God! and never
Will I join gods with God!"

أَنَا وَمَنِ اتَّبَعَنِي ۖ وَسُبْحَانَ اللَّهِ وَمَا أَنَا
مِنَ الْمُشْرِكِينَ ۝

109. Nor did We send before thee
(As apostles) any but men,[1793]
Whom We did inspire,—
(Men) living in human habitations.
Do they not travel
Through the earth, and see
What was the end
Of those before them?
But the home of the Hereafter[1794]
Is best, for those who do right.
Will ye not then understand?

١٠٩- وَمَا أَرْسَلْنَا مِن قَبْلِكَ إِلَّا رِجَالًا
نُوحِي إِلَيْهِم مِّنْ أَهْلِ الْقُرَىٰ ۗ
أَفَلَمْ يَسِيرُوا فِي الْأَرْضِ فَيَنظُرُوا كَيْفَ
كَانَ عَاقِبَةُ الَّذِينَ مِن قَبْلِهِمْ ۗ
وَلَدَارُ الْآخِرَةِ خَيْرٌ لِّلَّذِينَ اتَّقَوْا ۗ
أَفَلَا تَعْقِلُونَ ۝

110. (Respite will be granted)
Until, when the apostles
Give up hope (of their people)
And (come to) think that they
Were treated as liars,[1795]
There reaches them Our help,
And those whom We will
Are delivered into safety.
But never will be warded off
Our punishment from those
Who are in sin.

١١٠- حَتَّىٰ إِذَا اسْتَيْأَسَ الرُّسُلُ
وَظَنُّوا أَنَّهُمْ قَدْ كُذِبُوا
جَاءَهُمْ نَصْرُنَا فَنُجِّيَ مَن نَّشَاءُ ۖ
وَلَا يُرَدُّ بَأْسُنَا
عَنِ الْقَوْمِ الْمُجْرِمِينَ ۝

111. There is, in their stories,[1796]
Instruction for men endued

١١١- لَقَدْ كَانَ فِي قَصَصِهِمْ عِبْرَةٌ لِّأُولِي

1793. It was men that God sent as His Messengers to explain Him to men. He did not send angels or gods. Into His chosen men He breathed His inspiration, so that they could see truer than other men. But they were men living with men,—in men's habitations in town or country; not recluses or cenobites, who had no personal experience of men's affairs and could not be teachers of men in the fullest sense. Their deeds tell their own tale.

1794. The righteous, the men of God, had, as in Joseph's history, some evidence of God's providence in this very world with all its imperfections as reflecting our imperfections. But this world is of no real consequence to them. Their home is in the Hereafter. Joseph's earthly home was in Canaan: but he attained his glory elsewhere; and his spiritual Home is in the great Society of the Righteous (iii. 39).

1795. *Ẓannū* (come to think): I construe the nominative of this verb to be "the apostles" in agreement with the best authorities. *Kuẕibū* is the usual reading, though *Kuẕẕibū*, the alternative reading, also rests on good authority. I construe the meaning to be: that God gives plenty of rope to the wicked (as in Joseph's story) until His own Messengers feel almost that it will be hopeless to preach to them and come to consider themselves branded as liars by an unbelieving world; that the breaking-point is then reached; that God's help then comes swiftly to His men, and they are delivered from persecution and danger, while the wrath of God overtakes sinners, and nothing can then ward it off. This interpretation has good authority behind it, though there are differences of opinion.

1796. *Their stories, i.e.*, the stories of apostles or of the wicked; for the two threads inter-twine, as in Joseph's story.

With understanding. It is not
A tale invented, but a
confirmation
Of what went before it,—[1797]
A detailed exposition
Of all things, and a Guide
And a Mercy to any such
As believe.

الْأَلْبَابِ ۗ مَا كَانَ حَدِيثًا يُفْتَرَىٰ
وَلَٰكِن تَصْدِيقَ الَّذِي بَيْنَ يَدَيْهِ
وَتَفْصِيلَ كُلِّ شَيْءٍ
وَهُدًى وَرَحْمَةً لِّقَوْمٍ يُؤْمِنُونَ ۝

1797. A story like that of Joseph is not a purely imaginary fable. The People of the Book have it in their sacred literature. It is confirmed here in its main outline, but here there is a detailed spiritual exposition that will be found nowhere in earlier literature. The exposition covers all sides of human life. If properly understood it gives valuable lessons to guide our conduct,—an instance of God's grace and mercy to people who will go to Him in faith and put their affairs in His hands.

APPENDIX VI

Allegorical Interpretation of the Story of Joseph.

(Sūra xii.)

Spiritual things can only be understood by symbols taken from things which are familiar to us in this life. In a sense this fleeting life itself is a symbol. History is a symbol. The whole phenomenal world is a symbol. The reality lies behind it, like the real light behind the Cave, in Plato's Theory of Ideas. This is not to say that Islam agrees with the Vedantists in calling this whole visible world an illusion. It is an illusion to suppose that it is the only world. But it is equally an illusion to suppose that this world is of no consequence. It is of as much consequence as our thoughts, feelings, dreams, and Life. We have to make use of them, study and respect their laws, and obey the duties imposed on us by the spiritual part of us being entangled in their chain. But they are not eternal, and they will pass away. Our duty is to prepare ourselves for the truer life, the eternal life: we emancipate ourselves from them, not by fleeing them (for that is impossible), but by fulfilling our obligations in them, as an apprentice or probationer attains his real position by completing his apprenticeship or probation satisfactorily and so ceasing to be an apprentice or probationer.

From this point of view there is an allegorical meaning in all experience, history, and spiritual teaching. The temporary relationships, the fleeting events, our triumphs, defeats, and difficulties in this phenomenal world, are the bridges through which we pass to the higher world. Our temporal experiences are the foundation on which our greater and real Life is built up. This greater and real Life is not merely a thing of the future. It is within us all the time, if we only seek its truer light and try to fulfil our lower and temporal functions by the more stable principles with which it furnishes us.

The glimpses of the spiritual Joseph, as I understand them, in the Qur-ān, are afforded us "in order that we may learn wisdom" (xii. 2). Stories, events, visions, dreams, seem all to be assimilated under the Arabic word *Aḥādīth*. The real ones among them (as opposed to futile fancies) have all an inner meaning. It is only given to a few choicer spirits to understand and expound them. Joseph was one of these choicer spirits. From his boyhood he had an inner vision which he treasured up in his mind. Its meaning—or full meaning—only dawned on him afterwards. When it did, he was able to fulfil his mission in life.

This mission had many aspects. His father Jacob was also a Seer or Prophet, but Joseph in his maturity surpassed him in rank, and Joseph's life and filial love were as it were necessary to his father to complete and crown the full achievement of his life. Then Joseph, among his ten half-brothers and one full brother, had a protective and guiding mission. To Benjamin, his one full brother, and the youngest in the family, he was almost like a father when Jacob reached old age and resigned the headship of the family. The other brothers reflect all the pettiness, wickedness, jealousy, spite, hatred, injustice, and lower propensities of human life, combined with the latent reasonableness and the capacity to repent and turn over a new leaf, which it was Joseph's mission to awaken at the expense of much suffering to himself. The

ten brothers are shown to us collectively as acting as a human social group, with all their arrogance based on numbers and physical strength, and contempt of older and wiser experience. But we are also shown how the better side of human nature sometimes struggles to assert itself as against the baser and grosser standards of mass mentality, as when one of them advised them not to take Joseph's life (xii. 10), and again, later, when one of them felt ashamed to show himself before his father without Benjamin and offered to stay behind if perchance he could release Benjamin (xii. 78, 80). But it will be noticed that in both cases there was a good deal of alloy with the gold. The better nature of the individual has always a hard fight against the lower collective standards, which to unregenerate human nature seem to be the last word in morality, like the herd instinct in the lower animals. This is also shown in the actions and reactions between *Zulaikhā* and the Society women. Sometimes *Zulaikhā* was almost on the point of seeing the error of her ways, when her passion is inflamed and her higher nature suppressed by the bitter taste of what the world says and the discovery that those who cast the first stone at a delinquent would be the first to take all the so-called enjoyment of the sin which they are so prompt to reprobate in others.

To the merchants who found and purchased Joseph, the handsome young slave of winning ways was indeed "a treasure" (xii. 19). They understood that treasure in a material and grasping commercial spirit, but no doubt the road journey from Canaan to the Egyptian capital showed them the divinely-inspired virtuous side of Joseph, and it is impossible to suppose that they had not much spiritual profit out of it. The 'Azīz of Egypt, the high official who bought him, expected much good out of him, wanted to treat him with honour, and adopt him as a son (xii. 21). He no doubt saw (if but vaguely) the moral and spiritual grandeur of Joseph, but his highest privilege (though he may not have known it) was that he was able to be the instrument by which Joseph was "established in the land" (xii. 21); and that through him the strange, romantic, wholly feminine character of *Zulaikhā* was brought into touch with her ideal, and through sorrow, suffering, sin, and repentance, was at last able to catch a glimpse of that heavenly love of which she had dreamed and which she had so much misunderstood under the stress of human passion. On *Zulaikhā* our romantic Ṣūfī poetry has concentrated its attention in the story of Joseph, and of this we shall speak presently. In the 'Azīz's house Joseph attained his full manhood and endowment of Power and Knowledge from God (xii. 22). In her ardent way as a sinner *Zulaikhā* had a share in Joseph's development, for his virtue was tried through her beauty and passion and emerged triumphant.

The Society ladies who taunted *Zulaikhā* represent the prudish element in femininity. The contest between the jealous prude and the frank, impulsive victim of ardent love is well-figured in the relations between the ladies and *Zulaikhā* right to the end. Calculating hypocrisy and intolerant slander are farther from true love than a misconceived desire in earthly love, and this point is well brought out in Joseph's story. The ladies, when they cut their fingers at *Zulaikhā*'s feast, are the type of women who figuratively cut their souls in straining at a gnat and swallowing a camel.

Joseph's slavery and prison are the types of what a righteous man has to suffer through the sins and follies of others, in order (1) that he may bring some good to others, and (2) that he may develop his own character and high destiny. Without sorrow, suffering and striving—spiritual *Jihād*—even the best men cannot attain their full stature. Through them we are taught a true sense of values. The

slave must work, must labour, not for himself, but for others. If he does it in the right spirit, he exposes the hollowness of idleness, the ridiculous position of arrogance, and the futility of power which permits injustice. The prisoner who being innocent is put into a human prison enlarges his own spiritual liberty and opportunity, and perhaps shows up by contrast the darker and more impenetrable prison in whose grip his unjust incarcerators are held. The test is whether the innocent man who is put into prison or subjection is able to hold up his head. If so, he is able to achieve Burns's, ideal, "Preserve the dignity of man, with soul erect": for the *Tawakkul* of Islam will have made it a part of his nature to know for certain that "the Universal Plan will all protect."

The spiritual benefit which the two fellow-prisoners derived from Joseph's spiritual influence is explained in the notes to xii. 36-40. And then comes the period of Joseph's exaltation in worldly position, his strenuous administration of Egypt during fourteen eventful years, and perhaps to the end of his life, his opportunities to make the Pharaoh's power real and beneficent, instead of a mere simulacrum and a nervaless show, behind which lurked injustice and oppression. There is also the touching reunion of the family. The little artifice by which Joseph induces the brothers to confess their own hatred and spite (xii. 77) leads to their own self-exposure, preparatory to their repentance and forgiveness. On this and innumerable other points whole volumes could be written. But I will now pass on to *Z*ulaikhā and her treatment in our mystic-romantic poetry, for it forms an interesting commentary on what Islam has understood from one episode in Joseph's career.

In almost all Islamic languages the romance of Yūsuf and *Z*ulaikhā has justly attracted much attention in mystic poetry. Perhaps the order of the names should really be reversed and the romance should be called that of *Z*ulaikhā and Yūsuf. In Persian the great Firdausī tried his hand at it. But the great masterpiece is that of Jāmī whose dates fall between A.H. 817 and 898, equivalent to A.D. 1414-1492. I consider it one of the masterpieces of the world's literature. There is a good German translation by Rosenzweig and an English translation by R. T. H. Griffith. The translation by A. Rogers is not so good. The Urdu translations which I have seen are not worth mention. The original Persian is so grand and instructive that it is a pity that our Islamic students do not study it with the attention which it deserves. I shall give a very brief account of the version as developed by Jāmī: where I quote in English verse, I shall use Griffith's version (of 1881).

According to Jāmī, *Z*ulaikhā is a beautiful Princess, a daughter of a king of the West (*Magrib*). In her youth she dreamt a dream, in which she saw a handsome man, as noble and true as he was handsome, and she fell in love with him. So deep and constant was her love that she pined away for the love of the ideal man of her dream. She nursed her love and sorrow in secret, making only her nurse her confidante, in the hope that the nurse might by her secret arts procure a meeting with the dear love of her dreams. She had a second and a third dream, and in the third, she had the courage to ask the man in the vision his name and country. He did not tell her his name, but he said he was the Wazīr of Egypt.

Armed with this clue, *Z*ulaikhā refused all offers of marriage from kings and princes, cherishing in her heart only the image of the man she had seen in her dream, who she had learnt was the Wazīr of Egypt. At length her father is induced to send a wise man to Egypt, to arrange the marriage with the Wazīr, though he could not understand why the Princess should have refused the offers of kings and princes from

all over the world. The wise man interviews the Wazīr of Egypt, who is torn internally with many feelings. Here was a Princess who had refused the offers of great kings. His ambition was all aflame. How could he refuse ? Yet he knew his own condition. He was a eunuch. How could he accept ? He pleaded that the king of Egypt needed him so much that he could not be absent a single hour. But he would send 200 golden litters and 1000 slave-girls to wait on Zulaikhā and convey her with honour to Egypt. The agent of Zulaikhā's father knew that Zulaikhā's heart was so set upon the Wazīr of Egypt that it would be death to her if she could not get him. So he arranged the match and returned with what he supposed was good news. And Zulaikhā, too, was delighted. Her bliss knew no bounds. She now, she thought, had the prospect of union with the man of her dreams Thus, moralises the Poet, our joys and sorrows come from dreams and fancies !

Great preparations were made for Zulaikhā's bridai procession to Egypt. Zulaikhā's litter was carved with aloe and sandalwood ; its roof was resplendent with gems and gold like Jamshīd's tent : its curtains were hung with gold brocade. And in it was Zulaikhā, radiant and happy that she was now going to meet the lord of her love, whom she knew from her dreams, and to whom she would now be united for ever. When they approached the Egyptian capital, the Wazīr came out to meet his bride with a splendid equipage. Zulaikhā was all eagerness to feast her eyes with a sight of her beloved. She peeped through a hole in her curtain, when lo ! she was full of dismay. This Wazīr was not the man of her dreams !—not the man to whom she had plighted her troth, and to whom she would be faithful for life. She had in her dreams seen the image of Yūsuf, not of this 'Azīz. Never would she give her faith or her love or her virgin honour to another. She began to bemoan her fate "*Nishāndam nakhl-i-khurmā, khār bar-dād* (I planted a date-palm : what has come out but thorns ?) " She was in utter despair. What was to be done ? A voice came to her from the unseen world. It said : "True, this is not thy love ! But thy desire for thy true love will be satisfied through him. Fear him not. The jewel of thy virgin honour is safe with him. If a great sleeve is shown, but there is no hand within, what is there to hold a dagger ? " Zulaikhā had, of her own deliberate choice, had this marriage arranged. She mnst wed the eunuch. Whatever her grief, she must not complain. She went through the brilliant ceremony. But her heart was empty. It was given to the man of her dreams ! And it would never be another's ! And so she spent her days in outward splendour and inward grief, pining away in love unsatisfied.

At this time, perhaps, she had a glimpse of that true love in which self is blotted out. In her despair, in her anguish, she could see things which were later obscured to her in her pride and in the allurements of her sense. She poured out her soul in music. She had faith. "Surely," she thought, "thou gavest me no lying vision ! Why didst thou call thyself Wazīr of Egypt ? And I left my home and country to be with thee, to be thine ! I know I shall win thee in the end ! When that happy day comes, I shall be not I, but thou ! May I see thee soon ! "

"I shall roll up the carpet of life when I see
Thy dear face again, and shall cease to be ;
For self will be lost in that rapture, and all
The threads of my thought from my hand will fall ;
Not Me wilt thou find, for this Self will have fled ;
Thou wilt be my soul in mine own soul's stead.

All thought of Self will be swept from my mind,
And Thee, only, Thee, in my place shall it find ;
More precious than heaven, than earth more dear,
Myself were forgotten if Thou wert near."

She waited in faith and longing. At length came news of a great sensation in the market. A foreign merchant was bringing, they said, a slave the like of whom had never been seen, whether for looks, or wit, or integrity, or purity of word and mind. It was no slave, but a sun of splendour, a moon of goodness, a king in the realm of love ! The caravan had yet barely entered the city. But the king heard of it, and ordered the Wazīr (*Zulaikhā*'s nominal husband) to go and see and bring this new prodigy into the king's presence. When the Wazīr came to the caravan and saw Yūsuf, he found his beauty was even greater than rumour had described. He bowed down, with feelings akin to worship. But Yūsuf gently raised him and taught him the Gospel of Unity,—that worship was due to God alone. When the merchant was told of the king's order he pleaded delay on the ground that they were travel-stained and unfit to appear before the king until they had washed in the Nile and made themselves presentable.

Meanwhile the fame of Yūsuf's beauty, goodness, purity, and truth spread like wild-fire. Each one—man or woman—who possessed—or thought he or she possessed—any of these qualities even in a minute degree, grew jealous that another—a stranger and a slave—should draw away all hearts. To the merchant, the value of his " treasure " went up the more it was talked about. The king might perhaps pay the whole revenue of Egypt to purchase him. But there was one to whom Yūsuf's beauty was worth more than all the revenues of Egypt and who could outbid the king himself. This was *Zulaikhā*, the lovely Princess of the West, whose jewels were worth the revenues of twenty kingdoms, but who took no pleasure in them in pining for the love of her dreams. She, too, heard of this wonderful prodigy, and came to have a peep at it through the curtains of her litter. Behold ! when she saw Yūsuf, it was the very face she had seen in her dreams,—for which she had left home and people and country, and for which she had been praying and pining these many years ! She had no doubt about it whatever. She had found her love ! But to see is not to attain. The whole rabble saw Yūsuf, and he was to be presented to the king. She told her husband to present a humble petition to the king. The king knew that he, the Wazīr, had no son and could have none. The king knew the services which he as Wazīr had rendered to the king, his dynasty, and his country. Would the king permit him to bid for this wondrous slave with the Wazīr's own money ? If so, the king would get the slave just the same, but would afford his Wazīr the happiness of having a wonderful son in his house to carry on his name ? The king saw Yūsuf and accorded the Wazīr the very reasonable request which he had made. Perhaps, though the poet does not say so, the king wondered whether the Wazīr would be able to put up the whole of the money, and may have intended benevolently to supplement the good Wazīr's resources, should the need arise.

Then came a strange scene typical of Vanity Fair. Yūsuf was put up to auction. Every petty individual thought he or she could purchase Yūsuf ! One old woman had nothing but a little yarn she had spun. " Enough," she thought, " to give me the honour of standing in the market and boasting for ever that I had bid for Yūsuf." Some came from motives of curiosity : some from motives of jealousy.

Why should the world go mad after a beauty or a virtue of a kind different from what they themselves possessed, however homely? Some came with pride of purse. "A thousand gold pieces!" they shouted as if to stifle all competition. The bid went on to a hundred times as much. Nor did it stop there. "Of fragrant musk I will give to the full weight of Yūsuf!" said one who had travelled to the uttermost ends of the earth in search of costly perfumes. "No good!" said another: "I offer the same weight of the most costly rubies and diamonds!" Poor deluded mortals! "The heaven's glorious sun" was "not to be deep-searched with saucy looks!" The Wazīr's resources—and indeed the kingdom's revenues,—had been exceeded many times already in the bidding. But *Zulaikhā*, the Princess of the West, had untold wealth in her casket of gems. Yūsuf was more than life itself to her. She bade the Wazīr double the highest bid. This was conclusive. Yūsuf went to the Wazīr. And poor *Zulaikhā*! She knew that Yūsuf was worth more than the price she had paid for him! Yet, in her feminine weakness, she thought Yūsuf had a price! She thought that her beauty, her birth, her constancy, her unflinching gift of her person to him, would weigh in the scale. Alas! even these things were not enough for Yūsuf. The sale in the phenomenal world was all illusory in the real world. As *Zulaikhā* had not yet learnt this, she had yet to pass through many trials, temptations, sins, and sorrows, before her grosser self could be purged out and she could be fit to receive Yūsuf. Meanwhile, he who could talk to the lowest in prison on equal terms, was unattainable to *Zulaikhā*. The dust of his feet had made the merchant who had looked after him fabulously wealthy, but Yūsuf was still to be the prey to many prying glances, the mark of many poisoned arrows, the quarry of many cunning traps. But his soul was spotless, and his manhood remained unsullied.

At this point, about the middle of the story, we are introduced by the poet to a mysterious figure, the lovely Bāzīga, who is in some respects a foil to *Zulaikhā*. Bāzīga's speech is the key to the whole allegory. She is a princess of the 'Ād race, a people of Arabian antiquity referred to in many places in the Qur-ān, and described in n. 1040 to vii. 65. She had heard of Yūsuf, and had also come with great wealth to bid for him. She had had an interview and talk with Yūsuf, and he had turned her attention from himself to the Great Creator, and given her the precious Message of Unity and Truth. 'This world of visible beauty,' he had said, 'is but the screen of the invisible and ineffable beauty within. Any beauty or goodness that you see here is but a reflection or image of the perfect, real, and eternal Beauty, Goodness, and Truth, which you should seek.' Convinced by his teaching, she resigns all folly, and bursts into a splendid rhapsody, concluding with these words:—

> "Mine eyes have been touched by the Truth's pure ray,
> And the dream of folly has passed away.
> Mine eyes thou hast opened—God bless thee for it!—
> And mine heart to the Soul of the soul thou hast knit!
> From a fond strange love thou hast turned my feet,
> The Lord of all creatures to know and meet;
> If I bore a tongue in each single hair,
> Each and all should thy praises declare!"

She resigned her wealth and her pomp, attended to the needy, and spent her days in prayer and praise on the banks of the Nile.

Zulaikhā is not of that temperament, and she reaches Truth and Peace by a different and much more thorny path. She is still in the grip of the beauty of sense. She burns with the flame of animal love, and tempts Yūsuf He is above any passion inconsistent with truth and fidelity, but his heart is sore distressed to think that he should bring sorrow on those who loved him. His father loved him, and that caused his brothers the pain of jealousy and his father himself the pain of separation. He would gladly serve her and the Wazīr in all that was reasonable. But why seek to go beyond, on the road to evil ? Zulaikhā placed all sorts of temptations in his way, but he stood firm as a rock. At length she trapped him into a garden house and made overtures to him. But he fled. She pursued, and in the struggle, tore his shirt at the back. He made good his escape. Outside the house he met the Wazīr, but he was too kindly and forbearing, too solicitous of Zulaikhā's honour to betray her or say anything of what had happened. Nor did the Wazīr press him, but taking his hand in his own, entered the house with him. Zulaikhā, seeing them thus enter, linked in mutual confidence, had a cruel and baseless suspicion—that she had been humilitated and betrayed by Yūsuf. Her guilty conscience and injured pride spurred her on to impulsive lies and false accusations. Then was Yūsuf compelled, in a few simple words, to tell so much of the truth as would save the Wazīr from committing an act of injustice—an act inconsistent with his high office. The condition of the shirt decided the matter : the Wazīr asked Zulaikhā to seek God's pardon and charged Yūsuf to say nothing more of this affair, lest the Wazīr's own position should be compromised.

Yūsuf had no need of the Wazīr's words to make him discreet. But, says the poet, it suits not love to seek a corner of safety. Zulaikhā, roused by anger and revenge, threw prudence to the winds. Her conduct accused, rather than excused, her. Tongues wagged. Society exaggerated, or distorted, the voice of rumour, itself fed on exaggeration and distortion. Society pointed the finger of scorn at her. Good, bad, or hypocritical, the ladies all reviled her. 'Shameless woman, to throw herself on her slave ! And he to scorn her ! What was Egypt coming to ! If she had had their spirit or their charm, who could have resisted it ?' Stung by their insolence, Zulaikhā determined to have her revenge on the ladies. She invited them to a sumptuous banquet. At dessert, just as they were about to cut their oranges with their knives, Yūsuf was admitted to the assembly. The very sight of him dazzled the ladies. 'He is no man, but a noble angel !' they cried. In their extreme emotion they cut their fingers. Zulaikhā was more than justified in their eyes. But they had their own lower motives. Each lady thought in her heart that she could win his love where Zulaikhā had failed. Jealousy further inflamed Zulaikhā's passion. They advised her to soften the steel in the fire, to soften Yūsuf's heart in prison. Yūsuf was now beset with the persecution, not of one woman, but of many women, and he himself prayed for safety in prison. Many motives on the part of various people thus combined to send him to prison. They are analysed in my note 1684 to xii. 35. So to prison Yūsuf went, with all marks of disgrace and ignominy.

To the men in prison Yūsuf's advent was a blessing, for he taught them the Truth and showed them the Light. Such men as Yūsuf, says the poet, turn a hell into Paradise. To Zulaikhā's heart came new sorrow, new penitence, new tortures of conscience. Her heart was in prison with the prisoner. Her health gave way. In torturing and killing her false Self, she began almost to regain her true Self.

Meanwhile Yūsuf's goodness of heart made him a king among his fellow-prisoners. If any were ill, he tended them; if there was anything on their mind he sympathised with them and consoled them. They had unbounded faith in him, and they gladly took his teaching and profited by it. Two of them took their dreams to him and he interpreted them correctly. One of them was restored to the king's favour. When the king in his turn dreamed a dream, this man remembered Yūsuf and obtained the interpretation of the king's dream through him. Yūsuf was released from prison, raised to high honour, and given full authority in the land. The old Wazīr, Zulaikhā's husband, was dead, and Yūsuf was charged with the arrangements for meeting the great famine that was prognosticated. This part of the story is touched upon but lightly by the poet, as his theme is the love of Zulaikhā.

She, a widow, bereft of youth, honour, beauty, resources, health, even eye-sight, yet cherishes the memory of Yūsuf and waters it with her tears. He is now far above her in worldly station, as he always was above her in spiritual worth. Her humbled pride opens her spiritual eyes. She cries to him in her agony, and he listens. He knows the true from the false, and he is just. The woman whom he repelled when she was in the bloom of health, youth, and beauty, when she was rich, proud, and high in rank—now that she is meek, lowly, and sincere, finds favour in his sight. At his prayer her health, youth, and beauty are restored, and they are married in pure and true love. Even so, their love was not perfect until they united their hearts in pure worship to God.

The core of the allegory is in its definition of love,—the true and the eternal as distinguished from the false and the ephemeral. Life is subject to many changes, and so is what is ordinarily called Love among men.

" One is cast down to the earth, and one
Is lifted on high like the glorious sun.
Blessed is he who has wit to learn
How the favour of fortune may change and turn,
Whose head is not raised in his high estate,
Nor his heart in misfortune made desolate."

False love is only a toy for self-indulgence. Self, not the Other, is the governing motive.

" When love is not perfect, with one sole thought—
Himself – is the heart of the lover fraught.
He looks on his love as a charming toy,
The spring and source of his selfish joy.
One rose he would pluck from his love, and leave
A hundred thorns her lone heart to grieve."

Just as, in human affairs, there is true and false love, so in our inner and higher life, there is a divine love that transcends all human love. This is the contrast between the *'ishq ḥaqīqī* and the *'ishq majāzī*.

" How blest is he who can close his eye
And let the vain pageants of life pass by !—
Untouched by the magic of earth can keep
His soul awake while the senses sleep;
Scorn the false and the fleeting that meets the view,
And see what is hidden and firm and true !"

To the meek and lowly, who seek God's love in sincerity and are willing to sacrifice all that the external world holds dear, God grants His love in abundant measure. For every sin, followed by repentance and right will, there is forgiveness; but for persistent pride and hardness of heart there is nothing but the abyss.

This allegory has sometimes been compared to that of Cupid and Psyche in western literature. It goes back to Greek and Roman times. Cupid (or Eros) is Love (masculine): Psyche (feminine) is the human soul. The Platonic and Neoplatonic philosophy built up a doctrine of the human soul, caught in the snare of matter and sensuality, which must be raised up to its pristine purity by Love. The most picturesque form in which the allegory was worked up was by Apuleius (born about 125 A.D). It forms an episode in his Latin work ***The Metamorphoses*** or ***The Golden Ass.*** Here Psyche is the human soul whom Cupid (Love) carries off to a secluded spot. She is charged to check her curiosity and enjoy her bliss. Venus (earthly love) is jealous and makes Psyche break Love's condition, whereupon Love leaves her, and she falls into servitude to Venus (carnal love). After many adventures she is restored again by Cupid (true love) and they are re-united. The allegory has attracted many modern writers, including Robert Bridges (who has translated it) and Walter Pater who has adapted it in his ***Marius the Epicurean.*** William Morris has also introduced it in his ***Earthly Paradise.*** Among French writers whom it has attracted may be mentioned La Fontaine the fabulist, and Molière the dramatist. But the theme of that allegory is not as wide as the theme of the allegory of Yūsuf and Zulaik͟hā.

INTRODUCTION TO SŪRA XIII (*Ra'd*).

The chronological place of this Sūra and the general argument of Sūras x. to xv. has been described in the Introduction to S. x.

The special argument of this Sūra deals with that aspect of God's revelation of Himself to man and His dealings with him, which is concerned with certain contrasts which are here pointed out. There is the revelation to the Prophets, which comes in spoken words adapted to the language of the various men and groups of men to whom it comes; and there is the parallel revelation or Signs in the constant laws of external nature, on this earth and in the visible heavens. There is the contrast between recurring life and death already in the external world: why should men disbelieve in the life after death? They mock at the idea of punishment because it is deferred: but can they not see God's power and glory in thunder and the forces of nature? All creation praises Him: it is the good that endures and the evil that is swept away like froth or scum. Not only in miracles but in the normal working of the world, are shown God's power and mercy. What is Punishment in this world, compared to that in the life to come? Even here there are Signs of the working of his law: plot or plan as men will, it is God's Will that must prevail. This is illustrated in Joseph's story in the preceding Sūra.

Summary.—The Book of Revelation is true, and is confirmed by the Signs to be seen in visible nature. God Who created such mighty forces in outer nature can raise up man again after death. God's knowledge is all-compassing: so are His power and goodness (xiii. 1-18, and C. 114).

The righteous seek the pleasure of God and find Peace; the evil ones break His Law, cavil and dispute, and reject faith; the wrath of God will take them unawares, but in His own good time (xiii. 19-31, and C. 115).

So was it with apostles before: they were mocked, but the mockers were destroyed, while the righteous rejoiced and were established (xiii. 32-43, and C. 116.)

C. 114.—God's Truth comes to man in revelation
(xiii. 1-18.) And in nature. How noble are His works!
How sublime His government of the world!
They all declare forth His glory!
Yet man must strangely resist Faith,
And ask to see the Signs of His power
Rather than the Signs of His Mercy!
Doth not His knowledge search through
The most hidden things? Are not
Lightning and Thunder the Signs of His Might
As well as of His Mercy? He alone
Is Worthy of praise, and His Truth
Will stand when all vanities pass
Away like scum on the torrent of Time.

Sūra XIII.

Ra'd, *or* Thunder.

In the name of God, Most Gracious,
Most Merciful.

بِسْمِ اللّٰهِ الرَّحْمٰنِ الرَّحِيْمِ

1. A. L. M. R.[1798] These are
The Signs (or Verses)[1799]
Of the Book: that which
Hath been revealed unto thee
From thy Lord is the Truth;
But most men believe not.

١-الٓمّٓرٰ تِلْكَ اٰيٰتُ الْكِتٰبِ ۗ
وَالَّذِيْٓ اُنْزِلَ اِلَيْكَ مِنْ رَّبِّكَ الْحَقُّ
وَلٰكِنَّ اَكْثَرَ النَّاسِ لَا يُؤْمِنُوْنَ ○

2. God is He Who raised
The heavens without any pillars[1800]
That ye can see; is firmly
Established on the Throne
(of Authority);[1801]
He has subjected the sun
And the moon (to his Law)!
Each one runs (its course)
For a term appointed.
He doth regulate all affairs,[1802]
Explaining the Signs in detail,

٢-اَللّٰهُ الَّذِيْ رَفَعَ السَّمٰوٰتِ بِغَيْرِ عَمَدٍ
تَرَوْنَهَا ثُمَّ اسْتَوٰى عَلَى الْعَرْشِ
وَسَخَّرَ الشَّمْسَ وَالْقَمَرَ ۗ
كُلٌّ يَّجْرِيْ لِاَجَلٍ مُّسَمًّى ۗ
يُدَبِّرُ الْاَمْرَ يُفَصِّلُ الْاٰيٰتِ

1798. For A.L.M., see ii. 1, n. 25. For A.L.R., see Introduction to S. x. For abbreviated Letters generally see Appendix I. Here there seems to be a combination of the groups A.L.M. and A.L.R. We consider here not only the beginning (A.), the middle (L.), and the end (M.), of man's spiritual history, but also the immediate future of the interior of our organisation, such as it appeared to our Ummat towards the close of the Meccan period. But in trying to understand mystic symbolism, we must not be dogmatic. The befitting attitude is to say: God knows best.

1799. *Cf.* x. 1, n. 1382.

1800. Should we construe the clause "that ye can see" to refer to "pillars" or "to the heavens"? Either is admissible, but I prefer the former. Theheavens are supported on no pillars that we can see. What we see is the blue vault of heaven, but there are invisible forces or conditions created by God, which should impress us with His power and glory.

1801. *Cf.* x. 3, and n. 1386. We must not think that anything came into being by itself or carries out its functions by itself. God is the active Force through which everything has its life and being and through which everything is maintained and supported, even though fixed laws are established for its regulation and government. The "term appointed" limits the duration of their functioning: its ultimate return is to God, as its beginning proceeded from God.

1802. *Cf.* x. 31, n. 1425. Where the laws of nature are fixed, and everything runs according to its appointed course, the government and regulation behind it is still that of God. Where there is limited free-will as in man, yet the ultimate source of man's faculties is God. God cares for His creatures. He does not, as in the idea of polytheistic Greece, sit apart on Olympus, careless of His creatures.

That ye may believe with certainty
In the meeting with your Lord.[1803]

3. And it is He Who spread out
The earth, and set thereon
Mountains standing firm,
And (flowing) rivers: and fruit
Of every kind He made
In pairs, two and two:[1804]
He draweth the Night as a veil[1805]
O'er the Day. Behold, verily
In these things there are Signs
For those who consider!

4. And in the earth are tracts
(Diverse though) neighbouring,
And gardens of vines
And fields sown with corn,
And palm trees—growing[1806]
Out of single roots or otherwise:
Watered with the same water,
Yet some of them We make
More excellent than others to eat.[1807]
Behold, verily in these things

لَعَلَّكُمْ بِلِقَاۤءِ رَبِّكُمْ تُوْقِنُوْنَ ○

٣-وَهُوَ الَّذِيْ مَدَّ الْاَرْضَ وَجَعَلَ فِيْهَا
رَوَاسِيَ وَاَنْهٰرًا ۚ
وَمِنْ كُلِّ الثَّمَرٰتِ جَعَلَ فِيْهَا زَوْجَيْنِ
اثْنَيْنِ يُغْشِي الَّيْلَ النَّهَارَ ۚ
اِنَّ فِيْ ذٰلِكَ لَاٰيٰتٍ لِّقَوْمٍ يَّتَفَكَّرُوْنَ ○

٤-وَفِي الْاَرْضِ قِطَعٌ مُّتَجٰوِرٰتٌ وَّجَنّٰتٌ مِّنْ
اَعْنَابٍ وَّزَرْعٌ وَّنَخِيْلٌ صِنْوَانٌ وَّغَيْرُ
صِنْوَانٍ
يُّسْقٰى بِمَاۤءٍ وَّاحِدٍ ۗ
وَنُفَضِّلُ بَعْضَهَا عَلٰى بَعْضٍ فِي الْاُكُلِ

1803. One manifestation of His caring for His creatures, even where a limited amount of free-will is granted for their development, is that He is careful to explain His Signs both in nature and in express and detailed revelation through His Messengers, lest man should have any doubts whether he has to return ultimately to his Lord and account for all his actions during the "term appointed," when he was given some initiative by way of trial and preparation. If man attends carefully to the Signs, he should have no doubt whatever.

1804. I think that this refers to sex in plants, and I see M. P. has translated accordingly. Plants like animals have their reproductive apparatus,—male stamens and female pistils. In most cases the same flower combines both stamens and pistils, but in some cases these organs are specialised in separate flowers, and in some cases, even in separate trees. The date-palm of Arabia and the Papaiya of India, are instances of fruit trees which are uni-sexual.

1805 *Cf.* vii. 54 and n. 1032. The whole passage there may be compared with the whole passage here. Both their similarity and their variation show how closely reasoned each argument is, with expressions exactly appropriate to each occasion.

1806. Does "growing out of single roots or otherwise" qualify "palm trees" or "vines" and "corn" as well? The former construction is adopted by the classical Commentators: in which case the reference is to the fact either that two or more palm trees occasionally grow out of a single root, or that palm trees grow sometimes as odd trees and sometimes in great thick clusters. If the latter construction is adopted, the reference would be to the fact that date-palms (and palms generally) and some other plants arise out of a single tap-root, while the majority of trees arise out of a net-work of roots that spread out extensively. Here is adaptation to soil and water conditions,—another Sign or wonder of Creation.

1807. The date-palm, the crops of food-grains, and the grape-vine are all fed by the same kind of water. yet how different the harvests which they yield! And that applies to all vegetation. The fruit or eatable produce may vary in shape, size, colour, flavour, etc., in endless variety.

There are Signs for those
Who understand!

إِنَّ فِى ذَٰلِكَ لَءَايَٰتٍ لِّقَوْمٍ يَعْقِلُونَ ○

5. If thou dost marvel
(At their want of faith),
Strange is their saying:
"When we are (actually) dust,[1808]
Shall we indeed then be
In a creation renewed?" They are
Those who deny their Lord! They
Are those round whose necks
Will be yokes (of servitude):[1809]
They will be Companions
Of the Fire, to dwell therein
(For aye)!

٥- وَإِن تَعْجَبْ فَعَجَبٌ قَوْلُهُمْ
أَءِذَا كُنَّا تُرَٰبًا
أَءِنَّا لَفِى خَلْقٍ جَدِيدٍ ۗ
أُولَٰٓئِكَ ٱلَّذِينَ كَفَرُوا۟ بِرَبِّهِمْ ۖ
وَأُولَٰٓئِكَ ٱلْأَغْلَٰلُ فِىٓ أَعْنَاقِهِمْ ۖ وَأُولَٰٓئِكَ
أَصْحَٰبُ ٱلنَّارِ ۖ هُمْ فِيهَا خَٰلِدُونَ ○

6. They ask thee to hasten on
The evil in preference to the good:[1810]
Yet have come to pass,
Before them, (many) exemplary
Punishments! But verily
Thy Lord is full of forgiveness
For mankind for their wrong-doing,
And verily thy Lord
Is (also) strict in punishment.

٦- وَيَسْتَعْجِلُونَكَ بِٱلسَّيِّئَةِ قَبْلَ ٱلْحَسَنَةِ
وَقَدْ خَلَتْ مِن قَبْلِهِمُ ٱلْمَثُلَٰتُ ۗ
وَإِنَّ رَبَّكَ لَذُو مَغْفِرَةٍ
لِّلنَّاسِ عَلَىٰ ظُلْمِهِمْ ۖ
وَإِنَّ رَبَّكَ لَشَدِيدُ ٱلْعِقَابِ ○

7. And the Unbelievers say:
"Why is not a Sign sent down
To him from his Lord?"[1811]
But thou art truly

٧- وَيَقُولُ ٱلَّذِينَ كَفَرُوا۟ لَوْلَآ أُنزِلَ عَلَيْهِ
ءَايَةٌ مِّن رَّبِّهِۦٓ ۗ إِنَّمَآ أَنتَ

1808. After seeing the Signs in nature and the Signs in revelation, it is indeed strange that people should deny their Creator. But if they admit the Signs of the Creator, Who works marvels before their very eyes every day, why should they doubt that when they are reduced to dust, they can be raised up again? If one creation is possible, what difficulty can there be in accepting a renewed creation? It becomes then a question of an obstinate and rebellious will, for which the punishment is described.

1809. *Aglāl*: yokes (of servitude): *Cf.* vii. 157 and n. 1128. The punishment may be conceived of in two stages: immediately, yokes of servitude to superstition, falsehood, etc., as against the freedom in Faith; and finally, the Fire which burns the very soul.

1810. The Unbelievers by way of a taunt say: "If there is a punishment, let us see it come down now." The answer to it is threefold. (1) Why do you want to see the punishment rather than the mercy of God? Which is better? (2) Have you not heard in history of terrible punishments for evil? And have you not before your very eyes seen examples of wickedness brought to book? (3) God works not only in justice and punishment, but also in mercy and forgiveness, and mercy and forgiveness come first.

1811. After all the Signs that have just been mentioned it is mere fractiousness to say, "Bring down a Sign." Muṣṭafā brought Signs and credentials as other Prophets did, and, like them, refused to satisfy mere idle curiosity.

A warner, and to every people
A guide.[1812]

SECTION 2.

8. God doth know what
Every female (womb) doth bear,[1813]
By how much the wombs
Fall short (of their time
Or number) or do exceed.
Every single thing is before
His sight, in (due) proportion.

9. He knoweth the Unseen
And that which is open :
He is the Great,
The most High.[1814]

10. It is the same (to Him)
Whether any of you
Conceal his speech or
Declare it openly;
Whether he lie hid by night
Or walk forth freely by day.[1815]

11. For each (such person)[1816]
There are (angels) in succession,
Before and behind him :
They guard him by command

ع مُنْذِرٌ وَّلِكُلِّ قَوْمٍ هَادٍ ۝

٨- اَللّٰهُ يَعْلَمُ مَا تَحْمِلُ كُلُّ اُنْثٰى
وَمَا تَغِيْضُ الْاَرْحَامُ وَمَا تَزْدَادُ ؕ
وَكُلُّ شَيْءٍ عِنْدَهٗ بِمِقْدَارٍ ۝

٩- عٰلِمُ الْغَيْبِ وَالشَّهَادَةِ
الْكَبِيْرُ الْمُتَعَالِ ۝

١٠- سَوَآءٌ مِّنْكُمْ
مَّنْ اَسَرَّ الْقَوْلَ وَمَنْ جَهَرَ بِهٖ وَمَنْ
هُوَ مُسْتَخْفٍ بِالَّيْلِ وَسَارِبٌ بِالنَّهَارِ ۝

١١- لَهٗ مُعَقِّبٰتٌ مِّنْ بَيْنِ يَدَيْهِ وَمِنْ
خَلْفِهٖ يَحْفَظُوْنَهٗ مِنْ اَمْرِ اللّٰهِ ؕ

1812. The last sentence of this verse has usually been interpreted to mean that the Apostle's function was merely to warn, and that guidance was sent by God to every nation through its apostles. I think the following interpretation is equally possible: 'it is itself a Sign that Muṣṭafā should warn and preach and produce the Qur-ān, and the guidance which he brings is universal guidance, as from God.'

1813. The female womb is just an example, a type, of extreme secrecy. Not even the female herself knows what is in the womb,—whether it is a male young or a female young, whether it is one or more, whether it is to be born short of the standard time or to exceed the standard time. But the most hidden and apparently unknowable things are clear to God's knowledge: there is no mere chance: all things are regulated by God in just measure and proportion. The general proposition comes in the last sentence: "every single thing is before His sight, in (due) proportion."

1814. A verse of matchless rhythm in Arabic.

1815. Our most hidden thoughts and motives are known to Him at all times.

1816. See last verse. Every person, whether he conceals or reveals his thoughts, whether he skulks in darkness or goes about by day,—all are under God's watch and ward. His grace encompasses everyone, and again and again protects him, if he will only take the protection, from harm and evil. If in his folly he thinks he can secretly take some pleasure or profit, he is wrong, for recording angels record all his thoughts and deeds.

Of God. Verily never
Will God change the condition
Of a people until they
Change it themselves
(With their own souls).[1817]
But when (once) God willeth
A people's punishment,
There can be no
Turning it back, nor
Will they find, besides Him,
Any to protect

إِنَّ اللّٰهَ لَا يُغَيِّرُ مَا بِقَوْمٍ
حَتّٰى يُغَيِّرُوا مَا بِأَنْفُسِهِمْ ۗ
وَإِذَآ أَرَادَ اللّٰهُ بِقَوْمٍ سُوٓءًا
فَلَا مَرَدَّ لَهُ ۚ
وَمَا لَهُمْ مِّنْ دُونِهِ مِنْ وَّالٍ ۝

12. It is He Who doth show you
The lightning, by way
Both of fear and of hope:[1818]
It is He Who doth raise up
The clouds, heavy
With (fertilising) rain!

١٢- هُوَ الَّذِىْ يُرِيْكُمُ الْبَرْقَ
خَوْفًا وَّ طَمَعًا
وَّ يُنْشِئُ السَّحَابَ الثِّقَالَ ۝

13. Nay, thunder repeateth His praises,[1819]
And so do the angels, with awe:[1820]
He flingeth the loud-voiced
Thunder-bolts, and therewith
He striketh whomsoever He will...
Yet these (are the men)
Who (dare to) dispute
About God, with the strength
Of His power (supreme)![1821]

١٣- وَيُسَبِّحُ الرَّعْدُ بِحَمْدِهٖ
وَالْمَلٰٓئِكَةُ مِنْ خِيْفَتِهٖ ۚ
وَيُرْسِلُ الصَّوَاعِقَ
فَيُصِيْبُ بِهَا مَنْ يَّشَآءُ وَهُمْ يُجَادِلُوْنَ
فِى اللّٰهِ ۚ وَهُوَ شَدِيْدُ الْمِحَالِ ۝

1817. God is not intent on punishment. He created man virtuous and pure; he gave him intelligence and knowledge; he surrounded him with all sorts of instruments of His grace and mercy. If, in spite of all this, man distorts his own will and goes against God's Will, yet is God's forgiveness open to him if he will take it. It is only when he has made his own sight blind and changed his own nature or soul away from the beautiful mould in which God formed it, that God's Wrath will descend on him and the favourable position in which God placed him will be changed. When once the punishment comes, there is no turning it back. None of the things which he relied upon—other than God—can possibly protect him.

1818. Here then is the climax to the answer of the sarcastic challenge of the Unbelievers for punishment, in language of great sublimity. Why look to evil rather than to good?—to punishment rather than to mercy?—to the fear in the force and fire of the lightning rather than to the hope of good and abundant crops in the rain which will come behind the lightning clouds?

1819. Nay, thunder itself, which may frighten you, is but a tame and beneficent force before Him, declaring His praises, like the rest of creation. THUNDER thus aptly gives the name to this Sūra of contrasts, where what we may think terrible is shown to be really a submissive instrument of good in God's hands.

1820. And the angels, whom we think to be beautiful creatures of power and glory nearest to God, yet feel reverence and awe even as they praise His holy name.

1821. Who is puny man, to call God in question? *Cf.* some variations on this theme in the Book of Job, itself an Arabian book, *e.g.*, chapters 38 to 41.

14. For Him (alone) is prayer
In Truth:[1822] any others that they
Call upon besides Him hear them
No more than if they were
To stretch forth their hands
For water to reach their mouths
But it reaches them not:
For the prayer of those
Without Faith is nothing
But (futile) wandering
(in the mind).[1823]

١٤- لَهٗ دَعْوَةُ الْحَقِّ وَالَّذِيْنَ يَدْعُوْنَ
مِنْ دُوْنِهٖ
لَا يَسْتَجِيْبُوْنَ لَهُمْ بِشَيْءٍ
اِلَّا كَبَاسِطِ كَفَّيْهِ اِلَى الْمَآءِ لِيَبْلُغَ فَاهُ
وَمَا هُوَ بِبَالِغِهٖ
وَمَا دُعَآءُ الْكٰفِرِيْنَ اِلَّا فِيْ ضَلٰلٍ ○

15. Whatever beings[1824] there are
In the heavens and the earth
Do prostrate themselves to God[1825]
(Acknowledging subjection),— with
good-will
Or in spite of themselves:[1826]
So do their shadows[1827]
In the mornings and evenings.

١٥- وَلِلّٰهِ يَسْجُدُ
مَنْ فِي السَّمٰوٰتِ وَالْاَرْضِ
طَوْعًا وَّكَرْهًا
وَّظِلٰلُهُمْ بِالْغُدُوِّ وَالْاٰصَالِ ○ السجدة

1822. *Ḥaqq* = truth; right; what is due, befitting, proper. All these meanings are to be understood here. If we worship anything other than God (whether it is idols, stars, powers of nature, spirits, or deified men, or Self, or Power, or Wealth, Science or Art, Talent or Intellect), our worship is both foolish and futile.

1823. Without Faith, it is obvious that prayer or worship has no meaning whatever. It is but an aberration of the mind. But there is a deeper meaning. You may have false faith, as in superstitions or in worshipping things other than God, as explained in the last note. In that case, too, you are pursuing mere phantoms of the mind. When you come to examine it, it is mere imbecility or futility. Worship and prayer are justified only to the One True God.

1824. There is much mystic meaning here, and indeed in the whole of this highly poetical Sūra. Notice that the original of what I have translated "whatever being" is the personal pronoun *man*, not *mā*. This then refers to beings with a personality, *e g.*, angels, spirits, human beings, and possibly other things of objective (not necessarily material) existence, as contrasted with their Shadows or Simulacra or Appearances, or Phantasms, mentioned at the end of the verse. Both these Beings and their Shadows are subject to the Will of God. See notes 1825 and 1827.

1825. "Prostrate themselves": the posture means that they recognise their subjection to God's Will and Law, whether they wish it or not.

1826 "In spite of themselves": Satan and the Spirits of Evil. They would like to get away from the control of the All-good God, but they cannot, and they have to acknowledge His supremacy and lordship over them.

1827. Even the Shadows—creations of the Imagination, or projections from other things and dependent on the other things for their existence, as shadows are to substance—even such shadows are subject to God's Laws and Will, and cannot arise or have any effect on our minds except by His permission. The Shadows are longest and therefore most prominent when the sun is level, and tend to disappear as the sun approaches the zenith. But even when they are longest and most prominent, they are still subject to God's Will and Law. The sun itself in this connection has a mystic meaning, referring to Intelligence, true Insight, the divine Light.

16. Say: "Who is the Lord and Sustainer[1828]
Of the heavens and the earth?"
Say: "(It is) God."
Say: "Do ye then take
(For worship) protectors other
Than Him, such as have
No power either for good
Or for harm to themselves?"[1829]
Say: "Are the blind equal
With those who see?
Or the depths of darkness
Equal with Light?"
Or do they assign to God[1830]
Partners who have created
(Anything) as He has created,
So that the creation seemed
To them similar?
Say: "God is the Creator
Of all things: He is
The One, the Supreme and Irresistible."

١٦- قُلْ مَنْ رَّبُّ السَّمٰوٰتِ وَالْأَرْضِ
قُلِ اللّٰهُ
قُلْ أَفَاتَّخَذْتُمْ مِّنْ دُوْنِهٖٓ أَوْلِيَآءَ
لَا يَمْلِكُوْنَ لِأَنْفُسِهِمْ
نَفْعًا وَّلَا ضَرًّا
قُلْ هَلْ يَسْتَوِي الْأَعْمٰى وَالْبَصِيْرُ
أَمْ هَلْ تَسْتَوِي الظُّلُمٰتُ وَالنُّوْرُ
أَمْ جَعَلُوْا لِلّٰهِ شُرَكَآءَ خَلَقُوْا
كَخَلْقِهٖ فَتَشَابَهَ الْخَلْقُ عَلَيْهِمْ
قُلِ اللّٰهُ خَالِقُ كُلِّ شَيْءٍ
وَّهُوَ الْوَاحِدُ الْقَهَّارُ ۝

17. He sends down water[1831]
From the skies, and the channels
Flow, each according to its measure:
But the torrent bears away
The foam that mounts up
To the surface. Even so,

١٧- أَنْزَلَ مِنَ السَّمَآءِ مَآءً
فَسَالَتْ أَوْدِيَةٌۢ بِقَدَرِهَا
فَاحْتَمَلَ السَّيْلُ زَبَدًا رَّابِيًا

1828. The meaning of "*Rabb*" is explained in n. 20, to i. 2.

1829. *Cf.* v. 79.

1830. This verse may be analysed into six parts, each two parts going together like question and answer. Each except the fifth part is introduced by the word "Say", which is equivalent in old Arabic to inverted commas. The fifth part, "or do they assign......similar?" is not introduced by "Say", because it is in the indirect form.

(1) Who is the Lord and Sustainer of the Worlds? It is God. (2) And yet you worship other gods? No, no one can be equal to Him, any more than darkness is equal to light. (3) Your other gods have created nothing by which you can be misled? No indeed; He is the only Creator, the One and Supreme.

1831. This verse is full of parables. (1) It is God Who sends rain and He sends it to all. See how it flows in different channels according to their capacities. Some are sluggish; some have a swift current. Some form great rivers and irrigate wide tracts of country; some are clear crystal streams, perhaps in hilly tracts, with beds of clean pebbles which you can see through the water. Some produce delicious edible fish: and some are infested by crocodiles or injurious monsters. And there are degrees and degrees among brooks, streams, lakes, rivers, and seas. So with the rain of God's mercy and the knowledge and wisdom and guidance which He sends. All can receive it. Different ones will respond according to their capacities. (2) In the physical world, water is pure and beneficial. But froth and scum will gather according to local conditions. As the floods will carry off the scum and purify the water, so will the flood of God's spiritual mercy carry away our spiritual scum and purify the water. (3) The froth may make a great show on the surface, but it will not last. So will there be frothy knowledge, which will disappear, but God's Truth will endure.

Form that (ore) which they heat[1832]
In the fire, to make ornaments
Or utensils therewith,
There is a scum likewise.
Thus doth God (by parables)
Show forth Truth and Vanity.
For the scum disappears
Like froth cast out;
While that which is for the good
Of mankind remains
On the earth. Thus doth God
Set forth parables.

وَمِمَّا يُوقِدُونَ عَلَيْهِ فِي النَّارِ ابْتِغَاءَ
حِلْيَةٍ أَوْ مَتَاعٍ زَبَدٌ مِّثْلُهُ ۚ
كَذَٰلِكَ يَضْرِبُ اللَّهُ الْحَقَّ وَالْبَاطِلَ ۚ
فَأَمَّا الزَّبَدُ فَيَذْهَبُ جُفَاءً ۖ
وَأَمَّا مَا يَنفَعُ النَّاسَ فَيَمْكُثُ فِي الْأَرْضِ ۚ
كَذَٰلِكَ يَضْرِبُ اللَّهُ الْأَمْثَالَ ۝

18. For those who respond
To their Lord, are (all)
Good things. But those
Who respond not to Him,—
Even if they had all
That is in the heavens
And on earth, and as much more,
(In vain) would they offer it[1833]
For ransom. For them
Will the reckoning be terrible:
Their abode will be Hell,—
What a bed of misery!

١٨- لِلَّذِينَ اسْتَجَابُوا لِرَبِّهِمُ الْحُسْنَىٰ ۚ
وَالَّذِينَ لَمْ يَسْتَجِيبُوا لَهُ
لَوْ أَنَّ لَهُم مَّا فِي الْأَرْضِ جَمِيعًا
وَمِثْلَهُ مَعَهُ لَافْتَدَوْا بِهِ ۚ
أُولَٰئِكَ لَهُمْ سُوءُ الْحِسَابِ ۚ
وَمَأْوَاهُمْ جَهَنَّمُ ۖ وَبِئْسَ الْمِهَادُ ۝

وقف النبي عليه السلام

النصف ع

C. 115.—The seeing and the blind are not alike:
(xiii. 19-31.) **Nor are those blessed with Faith and those without.**
The former seek God, and attain
Peace and blessedness in their hearts,
And a final Home of rest: the latter
Are in a state of Curse, and their End
Is terrible. If God in His wisdom
Postpones retribution, it is for a time.
His promise never fails: it will come
To pass in His own good time.
In all things it is for Him to command.

SECTION 3.

19. Is then one who doth know
That that which hath been

١٩- أَفَمَن يَعْلَمُ أَنَّمَا

1832. In continuation of the last note, the fourth parable is that of metal ores: (4) the ore is full of baser admixture, but the fire will separate the gold from the dross for ornaments, or (5) some metal of household utility, with which you make every-day utensils, which the fire will separate from admixtures which you do not want. So the fire of God's test, either by adversity or by affluence, will search out the true metal in us and reject the dross. It will show us what is valuable or what is useful, from all sorts of scum and vanity which we collect and miscall knowledge.

1833. *Cf.* iii. 91 and x. 54.

Revealed unto thee
From thy Lord is the Truth,
Like one who is blind?[1834]
It is those who are
Endued with understanding
That receive admonition;—

أُنْزِلَ إِلَيْكَ مِنْ رَّبِّكَ الْحَقُّ
كَمَنْ هُوَ أَعْمٰى
إِنَّمَا يَتَذَكَّرُ أُولُوا الْأَلْبَابِ ۝

20. Those who fulfil the Covenant
Of God and fail not
In their plighted word;

٢٠- الَّذِيْنَ يُوْفُوْنَ بِعَهْدِ اللّٰهِ
وَلَا يَنْقُضُوْنَ الْمِيْثَاقَ ۝

21. Those who join together
Those things which God
Hath commanded to be joined,[1835]
Hold their Lord in awe,
And fear the terrible reckoning;

٢١- وَالَّذِيْنَ يَصِلُوْنَ مَآ أَمَرَ اللّٰهُ بِهٖٓ أَنْ
يُّوْصَلَ وَيَخْشَوْنَ رَبَّهُمْ وَيَخَافُوْنَ
سُوْٓءَ الْحِسَابِ ۝

22. Those who patiently persevere,
Seeking the countenance of their
Lord;
Establish regular prayers; spend,
Out of (the gifts) We have bestowed
For their sustenance, secretly
And openly; and turn off Evil
With good: for such there is
The final attainment
Of the (Eternal) Home,—[1836]

٢٢- وَالَّذِيْنَ صَبَرُوا ابْتِغَآءَ وَجْهِ رَبِّهِمْ
وَأَقَامُوا الصَّلٰوةَ وَأَنْفَقُوْا مِمَّا رَزَقْنٰهُمْ
سِرًّا وَّعَلَانِيَةً
وَّيَدْرَءُوْنَ بِالْحَسَنَةِ السَّيِّئَةَ
أُولٰٓئِكَ لَهُمْ عُقْبَى الدَّارِ ۝

23. Gardens of perpetual bliss:
They shall enter there,
As well as the righteous
Among their fathers, their spouses,

٢٣- جَنّٰتُ عَدْنٍ يَّدْخُلُوْنَهَا
وَمَنْ صَلَحَ مِنْ اٰبَآئِهِمْ وَأَزْوَاجِهِمْ

1834. In this section the contrast between Faith and Righteousness on the one hand and Infidelity and Evil on the other is set out. The righteous man is known as one who (1) receives admonition; (2) is true to his convenants; (3) follows the universal Religion of Faith and Practice joined together; (4) is patient and persevering in seeking God; and in practical matters he is known to be (5) regular in prayer; (6) generous in true charity, whether open or secret; and (7) not revengeful, but anxious to turn off evil with good, thus breaking the chain of evil which tends to perpetuate itself.

1835. That is, join faith with practice, love of God with love of man, and respect for all Prophets alike, *i.e.* follow the universal Religion, and not odd bits of it.

1836. Their journey in this life was at best a sojourn. The final Bliss is their eternal Home, which is further prefigured in the two following verses.

And their offspring:[1837] And angels shall enter unto them From every gate (with the salutation):	وَ ذُرِّيّٰتِهِمْ وَ الْمَلٰٓئِكَةُ يَدْخُلُوْنَ عَلَيْهِمْ مِّنْ كُلِّ بَابٍ ۝
24. "Peace unto you for that ye Persevered in patience! Now How excellent is the final Home!"	٢٤- سَلٰمٌ عَلَيْكُمْ بِمَا صَبَرْتُمْ فَنِعْمَ عُقْبَى الدَّارِ ۝
25. But those who break The Covenant of God, after Having plighted their word thereto, And cut asunder those things[1838] Which God has commanded To be joined, and work mischief In the land;—on them Is the Curse; for them Is the terrible Home![1839]	٢٥- وَالَّذِيْنَ يَنْقُضُوْنَ عَهْدَ اللّٰهِ مِنْۢ بَعْدِ مِيْثَاقِهٖ وَيَقْطَعُوْنَ مَآ اَمَرَ اللّٰهُ بِهٖٓ اَنْ يُّوْصَلَ وَ يُفْسِدُوْنَ فِي الْاَرْضِ ۙ اُولٰٓئِكَ لَهُمُ اللَّعْنَةُ وَ لَهُمْ سُوْٓءُ الدَّارِ ۝
26. God doth enlarge, or grant By (strict) measure, the Sustenance[1840] (Which He giveth) to whomso He pleaseth. (The worldly) rejoice In the life of this world: But the life of this world Is but little comfort In the Hereafter.[1841]	٢٦- اَللّٰهُ يَبْسُطُ الرِّزْقَ لِمَنْ يَّشَآءُ وَيَقْدِرُ ؕ وَ فَرِحُوْا بِالْحَيٰوةِ الدُّنْيَا ؕ وَ مَا الْحَيٰوةُ الدُّنْيَا فِي الْاٰخِرَةِ اِلَّا مَتَاعٌ ۝ ع

1837. The relationships of this life are temporal, but love in righteousness is eternal. In the eternal Gardens of Bliss the righteous will be re-united with all those near and dear ones whom they loved, provided only that they were righteous also; for in eternity nothing else counts. Blood-relationships and marriage relationships create certain physical bonds in this life, which may lead to much good, and possibly also to evil. All that is physical or evil will go. But the good will come forth with a new meaning in the final Reckoning. Thus ancestors and descendants, husbands and wives, brothers and sisters (for *Zurrīyat* includes them), whose love was pure and sanctified, will find new bliss in the perfecting of their love and will see a new and mystic meaning in the old and ephemeral bonds. Can we wonder at Jacob's re-union with Joseph, or that of Moses with Aaron, or of Muḥammad Muṣṭafā with the Lady Khadīja? In fact all the Righteous will be re-united in the Hereafter (xii. 101).

1838. This is the opposite of the things explained in xiii. 21 above, n. 1835.

1839. This is in contrast to the state of the blessed, described in xiii. 22-24 above. The Curse is the opposite of the Bliss, and the Terrible Home is the opposite of the Eternal Home, the Gardens of perpetual bliss.

1840. God, the Sustainer and Cherisher of all His creatures, gives sustenance to all,—the sustenance including all means for their physical, moral, intellectual and spiritual growth and development according to their needs and capacities. To some He grants it in abundance; to others He gives it in strict measure. No one can question Him, for His Will is supreme, and it is the measure of all good.

1841. *Cf.* ix. 38. The meaning here may also be: This present life is just a furniture, a convenience, a stepping stone, a probation, for the life to come. In itself it is less important than the Hereafter.

SECTION 4.

27. The Unbelievers say: "Why
Is not a Sign sent down
To him from his Lord?"[1842]
Say: "Truly God leaveth,
To stray, whom He will;
But He guideth to Himself
Those who turn to Him
In penitence,—

٢٧-وَيَقُولُ الَّذِينَ كَفَرُوا
لَوْلَآ أُنزِلَ عَلَيْهِ ءَايَةٌ مِّن رَّبِّهِۦ
قُلْ إِنَّ اللَّهَ يُضِلُّ مَن يَشَآءُ
وَيَهْدِىٓ إِلَيْهِ مَنْ أَنَابَ ۝

28. "Those who believe, and whose hearts
Find satisfaction in the remembrance
Of God: for without doubt
In the remembrance of God
Do hearts find satisfaction.[1843]

٢٨-الَّذِينَ ءَامَنُوا وَتَطْمَئِنُّ قُلُوبُهُم
بِذِكْرِ اللَّهِ
أَلَا بِذِكْرِ اللَّهِ تَطْمَئِنُّ الْقُلُوبُ ۝

29. "For those who believe
And work righteousness,
Is (every) blessedness,[1844]
And a beautiful place
Of (final) return."

٢٩-الَّذِينَ ءَامَنُوا وَعَمِلُوا الصَّلِحَتِ
طُوبَىٰ لَهُمْ وَحُسْنُ مَـَٔابٍ ۝

30. Thus have We sent thee
Amongst a People before whom
(Long since) have (other) Peoples
(Gone and) passed away;[1845]
In order that thou mightest
Rehearse unto them what We
Send down unto thee by inspiration;

٣٠-كَذَٰلِكَ أَرْسَلْنَٰكَ فِىٓ أُمَّةٍ
قَدْ خَلَتْ مِن قَبْلِهَآ أُمَمٌ
لِّتَتْلُوَا۟ عَلَيْهِمُ الَّذِىٓ أَوْحَيْنَآ إِلَيْكَ

1842. The question is repeated from xiii. 7 above: for the line of reasoning there suggested in answer is now completed, and another line of reasoning is now taken up. God provides every guidance for those who turn to Him in penitence, but He will leave those to wander astray who deliberately close their eyes and their hearts to His grace and the comfort that comes from remembering Him and celebrating His praises.

1843. The Sign or Miracle is not something external: it is something internal, something in your mind, heart, and soul. It depends on your inner spiritual experience. If you turn to God, that light, that experience, will come. If you do not, God will not force you.

1844. "Blessedness": *Ṭūbā*: an internal state of satisfaction, an inward joy which is difficult to describe in words, but which reflects itself in the life of the good man, through good and ill fortune, through good report and evil. And then, there is always the final goal to which his eyes are turned, the beautiful Home of rest in the Hereafter, after this life's struggles are over. That goal is God Himself.

1845. Our Prophet came later in time than other Prophets, to complete their Message and universalise Religion. And certainly it is after his age that the process of the unification of the world began. That process is not complete yet, but is proceeding apace.

Yet do they reject (Him),
The Most Gracious!
Say: "He is my Lord!
There is no god but He!
On Him is my trust,
And to Him do I turn!"[1846]

وَهُمْ يَكْفُرُوْنَ بِالرَّحْمٰنِ ؕ
قُلْ هُوَ رَبِّيْ لَآ اِلٰهَ اِلَّا هُوَ ۚ
عَلَيْهِ تَوَكَّلْتُ وَاِلَيْهِ مَتَابِ ○

31. If there were a Qur-ān
With which mountains were moved,
Or the earth were cloven asunder,
Or the dead were made to speak,
(This would be the one!)
But, truly, the Command is
With God in all things![1847]
Do not the Believers know,
That, had God (so) willed,
He could have guided
All mankind (to the Right)?

But the Unbelievers,—never
Will disaster cease to seize
Them for their (ill) deeds,
Or to settle close to their homes,
Until the promise of God
Come to pass, for, verily,
God will not fail
In His promise.[1848]

٣١- وَلَوْ اَنَّ قُرْاٰنًا سُيِّرَتْ بِهِ الْجِبَالُ
اَوْ قُطِّعَتْ بِهِ الْاَرْضُ
اَوْ كُلِّمَ بِهِ الْمَوْتٰى ؕ
بَلْ لِّلّٰهِ الْاَمْرُ جَمِيْعًا ؕ
اَفَلَمْ يَايْـَٔسِ الَّذِيْنَ اٰمَنُوْٓا
اَنْ لَّوْ يَشَآءُ اللّٰهُ لَهَدَى النَّاسَ جَمِيْعًا ؕ
وَلَا يَزَالُ الَّذِيْنَ كَفَرُوْا تُصِيْبُهُمْ
بِمَا صَنَعُوْا قَارِعَةٌ اَوْ تَحُلُّ قَرِيْبًا مِّنْ
دَارِهِمْ حَتّٰى يَاْتِيَ وَعْدُ اللّٰهِ ؕ
اِنَّ اللّٰهَ لَا يُخْلِفُ الْمِيْعَادَ ○ ع

C. 116.—The mockery of God's apostles is an old game
(xiii. 32-43.) Of the world. But God's Truth will come
To its own in good time. The End
Of the righteous is their Home of Bliss,
And they rejoice in the revelations
They receive. The Messengers of God
Take their due share in the life
Of the world; they win through by God's grace
Against all the plots of the world.
Their witness is from God, through His revelation.

1846. Faith tells us that no amount of opposition from Unbelievers can ever stop God's Plan.

1847. Everything is possible and in God's power. His Plan is beneficent and all-embracing. But it is not for His creatures to dictate to Him, or demand what He should do, or how He should do it. The Command is with God in all things. The Believers know His omnipotence, and they also know that He will order His world for the best.

1848. Let not the Unbelievers think that if they seem to prosper for a time, that is the end of the matter. They are warned about three things. (1) Their ill deeds must carry evil consequences for them all the time, though they may not perceive them for a certain time. (2) Their homes, their places of resort, the circles in which they move, will also be haunted by their ill deeds and their consequences. For evil makes a complex of its environment. The walls of Jericho, when they fall, must bring down all Jericho in its ruins. (3) The ultimate Disaster, the final Reckoning, must come, for God never fails in His promise. True values must eventually be restored: the good to the good, and the evil to the evil.

The Commentators draw illustrations from the life of the Apostle, his exile from Mecca, and his restoration. A similar miracle works in all history. But the Command is with God.

SECTION 5.

32. Mocked were (many) apostles[1849]
Before thee: but I granted
Respite to the Unbelievers,
And finally I punished them:
Then how (terrible) was My requital![1850]

٣٢- وَلَقَدِ اسْتُهْزِئَ بِرُسُلٍ مِّنْ قَبْلِكَ
فَأَمْلَيْتُ لِلَّذِينَ كَفَرُوا
ثُمَّ أَخَذْتُهُمْ فَكَيْفَ كَانَ عِقَابِ ○

33. Is then He Who standeth
Over every soul (and knoweth)
All that it doth,
(Like any others)? And yet
They ascribe partners to God.
Say: "But name them![1851]
Is it that ye will
Inform Him of something
He knoweth not on earth,
Or is it (just) a show
Of words?" Nay! to those
Who believe not, their pretence[1852]
Seems pleasing, but they are
Kept back (thereby) from the Path.
And those whom God leaves
To stray, no one can guide.

٣٣- أَفَمَنْ هُوَ قَائِمٌ عَلَىٰ كُلِّ نَفْسٍ بِمَا
كَسَبَتْ وَجَعَلُوا لِلَّهِ شُرَكَاءَ
قُلْ سَمُّوهُمْ
أَمْ تُنَبِّئُونَهُ بِمَا لَا يَعْلَمُ فِي الْأَرْضِ
أَم بِظَاهِرٍ مِّنَ الْقَوْلِ
بَلْ زُيِّنَ لِلَّذِينَ كَفَرُوا مَكْرُهُمْ
وَصُدُّوا عَنِ السَّبِيلِ
وَمَن يُضْلِلِ اللَّهُ فَمَا لَهُ مِنْ هَادٍ ○

34. For them is a Penalty
In the life of this world,[1853]
But harder, truly, is the Penalty
Of the Hereafter: and defender
Have they none against God.

٣٤- لَهُمْ عَذَابٌ فِي الْحَيٰوةِ الدُّنْيَا
وَلَعَذَابُ الْآخِرَةِ أَشَقُّ
وَمَا لَهُم مِّنَ اللَّهِ مِن وَاقٍ ○

35. The parable of the Garden
Which the righteous are promised!—

٣٥- مَثَلُ الْجَنَّةِ الَّتِي وُعِدَ الْمُتَّقُونَ

1849. *Cf.* vi. 10.

1850. The punishment was in many cases deferred. But when it did come, how terrible and exemplary it was!

1851. *Cf.* xii. 40. 'You have but to name your false gods, and you will see that they are nothing but names. There is no reality behind them, whereas God is the One great Reality. He penetrates everything through and through and knows all things. Do you dare to tell Him of something on earth that He does not know? Or is it just a trick or a show of words?

1852. All pretences and fancies seem attractive to their inventors, but alas! they are a great obstruction to the Path of Religion and Truth. However, if by their contumacy, they have cut themselves off from God's grace, who can guide them or reclaim them from their errors?

1853. The consequences of sin may be felt in this life itself, but they are nothing compared to the final penalties in the life to come.

Beneath it flow rivers :
Perpetual is the enjoyment
thereof[1854]
And the shade therein :[1855]
Such is the End
Of the Righteous ; and the End
Of Unbelievers is the Fire.[1856]

تَجْرِي مِن تَحْتِهَا الْأَنْهَٰرُ
أُكُلُهَا دَآئِمٌ وَظِلُّهَا
تِلْكَ عُقْبَى الَّذِينَ اتَّقَوا
وَّعُقْبَى الْكَٰفِرِينَ النَّارُ ○

36. Those to whom We have
Given the Book[1857] rejoice
At what hath been revealed
Unto thee : but there are
Among the clans[1858] those who
reject
A part thereof. Say:
" I am commanded to worship
God, and not to join partners
With Him. Unto him
Do I call, and
Unto Him is my return."

٣٦ - وَالَّذِينَ ءَاتَيْنَٰهُمُ الْكِتَٰبَ يَفْرَحُونَ
بِمَآ أُنزِلَ إِلَيْكَ وَمِنَ
الْأَحْزَابِ مَن يُنكِرُ بَعْضَهُ
قُلْ إِنَّمَآ أُمِرْتُ
أَنْ أَعْبُدَ اللَّهَ وَلَآ أُشْرِكَ بِهِ
إِلَيْهِ أَدْعُوا وَإِلَيْهِ مَـَٔابِ ○

37. Thus have We revealed it
To be a judgment of authority[1859]

٣٧ - وَكَذَٰلِكَ أَنزَلْنَٰهُ حُكْمًا

1854. For the comprehensive meaning of the root *akala* (literally " to eat "), see v. 69, n. 776. In its derived meaning it means fruit and enjoyment of all kinds, spiritual as well as other. The joys of heaven are not like the joys of the earth, which fade away or cloy. The joys of heaven are pure, lasting, and without any of the drawbacks which we associate with the joys of the sense.

1855. *Ẕillun* : literally shade ; hence, shelter, protection, security. All these meanings are implied. Shade is one of the delights of a garden. *Cf.* iv. 57, and n. 579.

1856. In this, as in other places, the Fire is contrasted with the Garden, as Misery is contrasted with Bliss. We can also imagine other incidents in contrast with those of the Garden ; *e.g.*, with the Fire will be drought, aridity, thirst, instead of beautiful rivers ; pain and suffering, instead of perpetual delight ; no protection against the fierceness of the heat, as contrasted with the cool shades ever deepening as you proceed in the Garden.

1857. *The Book* : in a general sense, Revelation. " Those to whom the Book hath been given " are both (1) the People of the Book of previous revelations, who study the new Revelation in Arabic without prejudice and find in it confirmation of what their ancestors had received ; and (2) the Muslims who receive the Qur-ān with such spiritual joy.

1858. *Aḥzāb* (plural of *ḥizb*)=parties, sects, troops, clans. The reference may be to the clans mentioned in xxx. 20 and 22 (that whole Sūra is called *Aḥzāb*). But we can understand it in a perfectly general sense. Among all sections of the people there are persons who would receive a portion of God's Truth but reject whatever does not suit them or fall in with their selfish aims or vain desires. The proper answer to them is: Surely, God's command is universal,—to worship and serve Him and refuse to bend the knee to any other ; the man of God finds his staff and support in it ; but he must invite all to share in its blessings ; it came from God, and to God shall we all return.

1859. The Qur-ān is in Arabic ; therefore the Arabs, among whom it was promulgated, could have no difficulty in understanding its precepts and using it in judging of right and wrong in all their affairs. But it is also universal ; therefore no one should give preference to his own vain fancies against this authoritative declaration.

In Arabic. Wert thou to follow
Their (vain) desires after the knowledge
Which hath reached thee,
Then wouldst thou find
Neither protector nor defender[1860]
Against God.

عَرَبِيًّا ۚ وَلَئِنِ اتَّبَعْتَ أَهْوَآءَهُم
بَعْدَ مَا جَآءَكَ مِنَ الْعِلْمِ ۙ
مَا لَكَ مِنَ اللَّهِ مِن وَلِيٍّ وَلَا وَاقٍ ○ ع

SECTION 6.

38. We did send apostles
Before thee, and appointed
For them wives and children:[1861]
And it was never the part
Of an apostle to bring a Sign
Except as God permitted[1862]
(Or commanded). For each period
Is a Book (revealed).[1863]

٣٨- وَلَقَدْ أَرْسَلْنَا رُسُلًا مِّن قَبْلِكَ وَ
جَعَلْنَا لَهُمْ أَزْوَاجًا وَذُرِّيَّةً ۚ
وَمَا كَانَ لِرَسُولٍ أَن يَأْتِيَ بِآيَةٍ
إِلَّا بِإِذْنِ اللَّهِ ۗ
لِكُلِّ أَجَلٍ كِتَابٌ ○

39. God doth blot out
Or confirm what He pleaseth:
With Him is
The Mother of the Book.[1864]

٣٩- يَمْحُوا اللَّهُ مَا يَشَآءُ وَيُثْبِتُ ۖ
وَعِندَهُۥٓ أُمُّ الْكِتَٰبِ ○

40. Whether We shall show thee
(Within thy life-time)
Part of what We promised them
Or take to ourselves thy soul

٤٠- وَإِن مَّا نُرِيَنَّكَ بَعْضَ الَّذِي نَعِدُهُمْ
أَوْ نَتَوَفَّيَنَّكَ

1860. *Cf.* ii. 120. The variation is in the single word "*Wāq*" here in place of "*Naṣīr*" in ii. 120. In each case the apt word is chosen not only for the rhythm in its own passage but for the general meaning in the Argument.

1861. All the apostles of whom we have any detailed knowledge, except one, had wives and children. The exception is Jesus the son of Mary. But his life was incomplete; his ministry barely lasted three years; his mission was limited; and he was not called upon to deal with the many-sided problems that arise in a highly organised society or State. We pay equal respect to him, because he was God's Messenger; but that is not to say that his Message covers the same universal ground as that of Muṣṭafā. There is no reproach for a normal human being if he lives a normal human life; there is glory if he beautifies it and sets a nobler example of virtue than other men, as did Muṣṭafā.

1862. No apostle performed any Miracle or showed forth any "Signs," except as God willed. God's Will (*Mashīyat*) is an all-wise, universal Plan, which is not formed for the benefit of one tribe or *millat* or of one age or country (see also next verse). The greatest Miracle in history was and is the Qur-ān. We can apprehend its beauty and grandeur to-day as much as did the people of Muṣṭafā's day,—even more, as our collective knowledge of nature and of God's creation has increased.

1863. *Kitāb*: I have translated "a Book (revealed)"; but it can aslo mean "a Law decreed" or "a Decree established." Ultimately the meaning is the same; for each age, according to God's wisdom, His Message is renewed.

1864. *Umm-ul-Kitāb*: Mother of the Book: the original foundation of all revelation; the Essence of God's Will and Law. *Cf.* iii. 7, and n. 347.

(Before it is all accomplished),—
Thy duty is to make
(The Message) reach them:
It is Our part
To call them to account.

فَإِنَّمَا عَلَيْكَ الْبَلٰغُ
وَعَلَيْنَا الْحِسَابُ ○

41. See they not that We
Gradually reduce the land
(In their control) from its
Outlying borders[1865]? (Where) God
Commands, there is none
To put back His command:
And He is Swift
In calling to account.

٤١- أَوَلَمْ يَرَوْا أَنَّا نَأْتِي الْأَرْضَ
نَنْقُصُهَا مِنْ أَطْرَافِهَا
وَاللّٰهُ يَحْكُمُ لَا مُعَقِّبَ لِحُكْمِهِ
وَهُوَ سَرِيعُ الْحِسَابِ ○

42. Those before them did (also)
Devise plots; but in all things
The master-planning is God's.[1866]
He knoweth the doings
Of every soul: and soon
Will the Unbelievers know
Who gets home in the End.

٤٢- وَقَدْ مَكَرَ الَّذِينَ مِنْ قَبْلِهِمْ
فَلِلّٰهِ الْمَكْرُ جَمِيعًا
يَعْلَمُ مَا تَكْسِبُ كُلُّ نَفْسٍ
وَسَيَعْلَمُ الْكُفّٰرُ لِمَنْ عُقْبَى الدَّارِ ○

43. The Unbelievers say: "No apostle[1867]
Art thou." Say: "Enough
For a witness between me
And you is God, and such
As have knowledge of the Book."[1868]

٤٣- وَيَقُولُ الَّذِينَ كَفَرُوا لَسْتَ مُرْسَلًا
قُلْ كَفٰى بِاللّٰهِ شَهِيدًا بَيْنِي وَبَيْنَكُمْ
وَمَنْ عِنْدَهُ عِلْمُ الْكِتٰبِ ○ ع

1865. In the Apostle's ministry at Mecca, the Most stiff-necked opposition came from the seat and centre of power in Mecca. The humbler people—the fringe of Meccan society—came in readily, as also did some tribes round about Mecca. After the Hijrat there was a hard struggle between Mecca and Medina, and at last the bloodless conquest of Mecca in A.H. 8 made the Pagan structure finally collapse, though it had already been sapped to its foundations. So, generally, Truth finds easiest entrance through the humble and lowly, and not in the beginning at the head-quarters of power, but in the fulness of time it makes its way everywhere with irresistible force.

1866. *Cf.* iii. 54 and n. 393.

1867. The enemies of Islam have to acknowledge that Muṣṭafā was a great and noble character, but they deny his apostleship. He could point to his credentials from God in the work which he achieved, and the Qur-ān which he brought.

1868. That is, those who have knowledge of revelation generally will recognise God's revelation in the holy Qur-ān. An alternative reading is "*min 'indi-hī*", which is written the same in Arabic, with only three vowel points different. If we adopt that, the last clause will be: "and from Him is (all) knowledge of the Book": *i.e.*, 'as all knowledge of the Book comes from God, the Qur-ān also bears witness to me'.

INTRODUCTION TO SŪRA XIV (*Ibrāhīm*).

For the chronology and the general argument of this Sūra in the series Sūras x. to xv., see Introduction to S. x.

The special subject-matter of this Sūra is a continuation of the concluding portion of the last Sūra, which explained how God's revelation gains ground in spite of selfish men's opposition. Here illustrations are given from the story of Moses and Abraham, and Abraham's Prayer for Mecca forms the core of the Sūra.

Summary.—Revelation leads man from darkness to light. It comes to each nation in its own language and for its own special circumstances. So was it with Moses and other apostles. There was a conflict of evil with good, but evil was destroyed. Parable of the Goodly Tree (xiv. 1-27, and C. 117).

Why will not men receive God's grace? Why will they choose to go astray? Abraham prayed to be saved from infidelity, himself and his posterity, and he prayed for Mecca, the city of the new revelation through Arabia. Good and Evil will find their proper retribution, and God's Plan of Unity will prevail (xiv. 28-52, and C. 118).

C. 117.—Revelation leads mankind from the depths
(xiv. 1-27.) Of darkness into light. It comes
To every age and nation in its own
Language. So was it before; so is it
Always. The apostles were doubted,
Insulted, threatened, and persecuted,
But their trust was sure in God.
It is Evil that will be wiped out.
God's Truth is as a goodly tree,
Firmly established on its roots,
Stretching its branches high and wide,
And bearing good fruit at all times.

Sūra XIV.

Ibrāhīm, or Abraham.

In the name of God, Most Gracious Most Merciful.

بِسْمِ اللّٰهِ الرَّحْمٰنِ الرَّحِيْمِ

1. A. L. R.[1869] A Book
Which We have revealed
Unto thee, in order that
Thou mightest lead mankind
Out of the depths of darkness
Into light—by the leave[1870]
Of their Lord—to the Way
Of (Him) the Exalted in Power,
Worthy of all Praise!—[1871]

١- الٓرٰ كِتٰبٌ اَنْزَلْنٰهُ
اِلَيْكَ لِتُخْرِجَ النَّاسَ
مِنَ الظُّلُمٰتِ اِلَى النُّوْرِ
بِاِذْنِ رَبِّهِمْ اِلٰى صِرَاطِ الْعَزِيْزِ الْحَمِيْدِ ۝

2. Of God, to Whom do belong
All things in the heavens
And on earth!
But alas for the Unbelievers[1872]
For a terrible Penalty
(Their Unfaith will bring them)!—

٢- اللّٰهِ الَّذِيْ
لَهٗ مَا فِي السَّمٰوٰتِ وَمَا فِي الْاَرْضِ
وَوَيْلٌ لِّلْكٰفِرِيْنَ مِنْ عَذَابٍ شَدِيْدِ ۝

3. Those who love the life[1873]
Of this world more than
The Hereafter, who hinder (men)
From the Path of God
And seek therein something crooked:
They are astray
By a long distance.

٣- الَّذِيْنَ يَسْتَحِبُّوْنَ الْحَيٰوةَ الدُّنْيَا عَلَى
الْاٰخِرَةِ وَيَصُدُّوْنَ عَنْ سَبِيْلِ اللّٰهِ
وَيَبْغُوْنَهَا عِوَجًا
اُولٰٓئِكَ فِيْ ضَلٰلٍ بَعِيْدٍ ۝

1869. For these Mystic Letters see Introduction to S. x.

1870. It is insisted on that every apostle speaks not from himself but from God. His leading into the light is but by the grace and mercy of God, not by any power of his own, or by any merit of those who hear him.

1871. In this and the next verse where the sentence is completed, three qualities of God are mentioned, *viz.*, (1) His exalted position above all Creation; (2) His goodness, which entitles Him, and Him alone, to Praise; and (3) His Power in all heaven and earth. Thus He stands in no need of man's worship; His goodness is all for the good of man (and His creatures); and His control over His creatures is complete; so He can carry out His Will and Plan.

1872. See the last note. That being the case, in what a sad plight are those who reject the Faith and Grace offered to them, and draw down on themselves all the terrible consequences of that rejection,—the Wrath to come!

1873. The Unbelievers are here characterised in three ways: (1) they love this ephemeral life and its vanities more than the true Life which goes into the Hereafter; (2) they not only harm themselves but mislead others; (3) their own crooked minds search for something crooked in God's straight Path (*Cf.* vii. 45). But in doing so, they go farther and farther from the Truth.

4. We sent not an apostle
Except (to teach) in the language[1874]
Of his (own) people, in order
To make (things) clear to them.
Now God leaves straying
Those whom He pleases
And guides whom He pleases:[1875]
And He is Exalted in Power,
Full of Wisdom.

۴- وَمَآ اَرْسَلْنَا مِنْ رَّسُوْلٍ
اِلَّا بِلِسَانِ قَوْمِهٖ لِيُبَيِّنَ لَهُمْ ؕ
فَيُضِلُّ اللّٰهُ مَنْ يَّشَآءُ
وَيَهْدِيْ مَنْ يَّشَآءُ ؕ
وَهُوَ الْعَزِيْزُ الْحَكِيْمُ ○

5. We sent Moses with Our Signs
(And the command). "Bring out
Thy people from the depths
Of darkness into light,
And teach them to remember
The Days of God."[1876] Verily
In this there are Signs
For such as are firmly patient
And constant,—grateful and
appreciative.[1877]

۵- وَلَقَدْ اَرْسَلْنَا مُوْسٰى بِاٰيٰتِنَآ
اَنْ اَخْرِجْ قَوْمَكَ مِنَ الظُّلُمٰتِ اِلَى النُّوْرِ ۙ
وَذَكِّرْهُمْ بِاَيّٰىمِ اللّٰهِ ؕ
اِنَّ فِيْ ذٰلِكَ لَاٰيٰتٍ
لِّكُلِّ صَبَّارٍ شَكُوْرٍ ○

6. Remember! Moses said
To his people: "Call to mind
The favour of God to you
When He delivered you[1878]

۶- وَاِذْ قَالَ مُوْسٰى لِقَوْمِهِ
اذْكُرُوْا نِعْمَةَ اللّٰهِ عَلَيْكُمْ اِذْ اَنْجٰىكُمْ

1874. If the object of a Message is to make things clear, it must be delivered in the language current among the people to whom the apostle is sent. Through them it can reach all mankind. There is even a wider meaning for "language." It is not merely a question of alphabets, letters, or words. Each age or people—or world in a psychological sense—casts its thoughts in a certain mould or form. God's Message—being universal—can be expressed in all moulds and forms, and is equally valid and necessary for all grades of humanity, and must therefore be explained to each according to his or her capacity or receptivity. In this respect the Qur-ān is marvellous. It is for the simplest as well as the most advanced.

1875. "*Whom He pleases*": the usual expression for *Mashiyat*, the universal Will and Plan, which is all-wise and on the highest plane of goodness and righteousness.

1876. "*The Days of God*": the days when God's mercy was specially shown to them. Every day and every hour and minute, God's grace flows to us abundantly, but there are special events in personal or national history which may be commemorated as Red-letter Days. Those to the Israelites were set out in great detail in ii. 30-61 and in other places.

1877. *Ṣabbār* is the intensive form, and includes all the ideas implied in *Ṣabr* (ii. 45 and n. 61, and ii. 153 n. 157) in an intensive degree. *Shakūr* and *Shākir* have in them the idea of appreciation, recognition, gratitude as shown in deeds of goodness and righteousness. Both terms are applied to God as well as to men. A slight distinction in shades of meaning may be noted. *Shakūr* implies that the appreciation is even for the smallest favours and response on the other side; it is a mental attitude independent of specific facts. *Shākir* implies bigger and more specific things.

1878. *Cf.* ii. 49. The reference back to Israel and Moses serves a double purpose—as an appeal to the People of the Book, and as a reminder to the Quraish of the favour now conferred on them by the coming among them of a greater Prophet than Moses.

From the people of Pharaoh:
They set you hard tasks
And punishments, slaughtered
Your sons, and let your women-folk
Live: therein was
A tremendous trial from your Lord."

مِّنْ اٰلِ فِرْعَوْنَ يَسُوْمُوْنَكُمْ سُوْٓءَ الْعَذَابِ
وَيُذَبِّحُوْنَ اَبْنَآءَكُمْ وَيَسْتَحْيُوْنَ نِسَآءَكُمْ
وَفِيْ ذٰلِكُمْ
بَلَآءٌ مِّنْ رَّبِّكُمْ عَظِيْمٌ ۝ ع

SECTION 2.

7. And remember! your Lord
Caused to be declared (publicly):
"If ye are grateful, I will
Add more (favours) unto you;
But if ye show ingratitude,[1879]
Truly my punishment
Is terrible indeed."

٧- وَاِذْ تَاَذَّنَ رَبُّكُمْ
لَئِنْ شَكَرْتُمْ لَاَزِيْدَنَّكُمْ
وَلَئِنْ كَفَرْتُمْ
اِنَّ عَذَابِيْ لَشَدِيْدٌ ۝

8. And Moses said: "If ye
Show ingratitude,[1880] ye and all
On earth together,—yet
Is God Free of all wants,[1881]
Worthy of all praise.

٨- وَقَالَ مُوْسٰى اِنْ تَكْفُرُوْا
اَنْتُمْ وَمَنْ فِي الْاَرْضِ جَمِيْعًا
فَاِنَّ اللّٰهَ لَغَنِيٌّ حَمِيْدٌ ۝

9. Has not the story
Reached you, (O people!), of those
Who (went) before you?—
Of the People of Noah,
And 'Ād, and Thamūd?—
And of those who (came)
After them? None knows them[1882]
But God. To them came

٩- اَلَمْ يَاْتِكُمْ نَبَؤُا الَّذِيْنَ مِنْ قَبْلِكُمْ
قَوْمِ نُوْحٍ وَّعَادٍ وَّثَمُوْدَ
وَالَّذِيْنَ مِنْۢ بَعْدِهِمْ
لَا يَعْلَمُهُمْ اِلَّا اللّٰهُ

1879. The various shades of meaning in *Shakara* are explained in n. 1877 above. *Kafara* implies: (1) to reject Faith, as in ii 6 and n. 30; (2) to be ungrateful for mercies and favours received, as here; (3) to resist God or Faith, as in iii. 13; (4) to deny (the Signs of God), as in iii. 21, or deny the mission of apostles, as in xiv. 9. *Kāfir* in the most general sense may be translated "Unbeliever"

1880. Ingratitude not only in feeling or words, but in disobedience, and wilful rejection and rebellion. If the whole of you band together against God, you do not detract from God's power one atom, because God does not depend upon you for anything, and His goodness and righteousness and praiseworthiness cannot be called in question by your contumacy.

1881. *Cf.* in Milton's sonnet On his Blindness: "God doth not need either man's work or His own gifts!"

1882. Even the names of all the Prophets are not known to men, much less the details of their story. If some "news" of them (for the word translated "story" may also be translated "news") reaches us, it is to give us spiritual instruction for our own lives.

Apostles with Clear (Signs);
But they put their hands[1883]
Up to their mouths, and said:
" We do deny (the mission)
On which ye have been sent,
And we are really
In suspicious (disquieting) doubt[1884]
As to that to which
Ye invite us."

جَاءَتْهُمْ رُسُلُهُمْ بِالْبَيِّنٰتِ
فَرَدُّوا أَيْدِيَهُمْ فِي أَفْوَاهِهِمْ
وَقَالُوا إِنَّا كَفَرْنَا بِمَا أُرْسِلْتُمْ بِهِ وَإِنَّا
لَفِي شَكٍّ مِمَّا تَدْعُونَنَا إِلَيْهِ مُرِيبٍ ○

10. Their apostles said: " Is there
A doubt about God,
The Creator of the heavens
And the earth? It is He[1885]
Who invites you, in order
That He may forgive you
Your sins and give you
Respite for a term appointed!"
They said: " Ah! ye are
No more than human,
Like ourselves! Ye wish
To turn us away from
The (gods) our fathers
Used to worship: then
Bring us some clear authority."[1886]

١٠- قَالَتْ رُسُلُهُمْ أَفِي اللّٰهِ شَكٌّ
فَاطِرِ السَّمٰوٰتِ وَالْأَرْضِ
يَدْعُوكُمْ لِيَغْفِرَ لَكُمْ مِنْ ذُنُوبِكُمْ
وَيُؤَخِّرَكُمْ إِلَى أَجَلٍ مُسَمًّى
قَالُوا إِنْ أَنْتُمْ إِلَّا بَشَرٌ مِثْلُنَا
تُرِيدُونَ أَنْ تَصُدُّونَا عَمَّا كَانَ يَعْبُدُ
آبَاؤُنَا فَأْتُونَا بِسُلْطٰنٍ مُبِينٍ ○

11. Their apostles said to them:
" True, we are human
Like yourselves, but God
Doth grant His grace

١١- قَالَتْ لَهُمْ رُسُلُهُمْ إِنْ نَحْنُ إِلَّا بَشَرٌ
مِثْلُكُمْ وَلٰكِنَّ اللّٰهَ يَمُنُّ عَلَى

1883. That is, either that the Unbelievers metaphorically put their hands up to the mouths of the Prophets to try to prevent them from proclaiming their Message, or that the Unbelievers put up their fingers to their own mouths, as much as to say "Don't listen to them," or bite their own fingers in token of incontinent rage. Whatever construction we adopt, the meaning is that they were intolerant of their apostles, even as the Quraish were intolerant of Muṣṭafā and did all they could to suppress God's Truth.

1884. *Cf.* xi. 62. The distinction between *Shakk* and *raib* may be noted. *Shakk* is intellectual doubt, a doubt as to fact: is it so, or is it not? *Raib* is something more than intellectual doubt; a suspicion that there is fraud or deception; something that upsets your moral belief, and causes a disquiet in your soul. In lii. 30, it is used as equivalent to "calamity" or "disaster", some punishment or evil. Both kinds of doubts and suspicions are hinted at against men of God.

1885. The apostles (generally) clear both kinds of doubt. "You cannot doubt the existence of God! Behold His works! We are not speaking for ourselves or deceiving you. We speak according to the Message of inspiration from God." Notice that the doubters had said to the Prophets, "Ye invite us." The Prophets say: "It is God Who invites you, and He does it to save you by His grace, and give you plenty of time (but not indefinite time) for penitence and amendment."

1886. Infidelity is illogical and argues in a circle. If the apostle speaks of God, the Unbeliever says, "You are only a man!" "But I speak from God!" "Oh well! our ancestral ways of worship are good enough for us!" "What if they are wrong?" "What authority have you for saying so?" "The highest authority, that from God!" And so we come back full circle! Then the wicked rely on violence, but it recoils on them, and they perish.

To such of His servants
As He pleases. It is not
For us to bring you
An authority except as God
Permits. And on God
Let all men of faith
Put their trust.

مَنْ يَّشَآءُ مِنْ عِبَادِهٖ
وَمَا كَانَ لَنَآ اَنْ نَّاْتِيَكُمْ بِسُلْطٰنٍ
اِلَّا بِاِذْنِ اللّٰهِ
وَعَلَى اللّٰهِ فَلْيَتَوَكَّلِ الْمُؤْمِنُوْنَ ○

12. "No reason have we why
We should not put our trust
On God. Indeed He
Has guided us to the Ways
We (follow). We shall certainly
Bear with patience all
The hurt you may cause us.
For those who put their trust
Should put their trust on God."

١٢- وَمَا لَنَآ اَلَّا نَتَوَكَّلَ عَلَى اللّٰهِ
وَقَدْ هَدٰىنَا سُبُلَنَا
وَلَنَصْبِرَنَّ عَلٰى مَآ اٰذَيْتُمُوْنَا
وَعَلَى اللّٰهِ فَلْيَتَوَكَّلِ الْمُتَوَكِّلُوْنَ ○ ع

SECTION 3.

13. And the Unbelievers said
To their apostles: "Be sure
We shall drive you out
Of our land, or ye shall
Return to our religion." [1887]
But their Lord inspired
(This Message) to them:
"Verily We shall cause
The wrong-doers to perish!

١٣- وَقَالَ الَّذِيْنَ كَفَرُوْا لِرُسُلِهِمْ
لَنُخْرِجَنَّكُمْ مِّنْ اَرْضِنَآ
اَوْ لَتَعُوْدُنَّ فِيْ مِلَّتِنَا
فَاَوْحٰٓى اِلَيْهِمْ رَبُّهُمْ لَنُهْلِكَنَّ
الظّٰلِمِيْنَ ○

14. "And verily We shall
Cause you to abide
In the land, and succeed them.
This for such as fear [1888]
The Time when they shall stand
Before My tribunal,—such
As fear the Punishment denounced."

١٤- وَلَنُسْكِنَنَّكُمُ الْاَرْضَ
مِنْ بَعْدِهِمْ
ذٰلِكَ لِمَنْ خَافَ مَقَامِيْ
وَخَافَ وَعِيْدِ ○

1887. The arguments in a circle were explained in the last note. But Infidelity looks upon argument merely as an amusement. Its chief weapon is physical force. As its only belief is in materialism, it thinks that threats of force will put down the righteous. It offers the choice between exile and violence against conformity to its own standards of evil, which it thinks to be good. But Faith is not to be cowed down by Force. Its source of strength is God, and it receives the assurance that violence will perish ultimately by violence, and that Faith and Good must stand and be established. In fact the good must inherit the earth and the evil ones be blotted out.

1888. "Fear" means here "have present before their minds something which should cause them fear, so that they should shape their conduct in order to avoid the ill consequences of wickedness."

15. But they sought victory and
decision[1889]
(There and then), and frustration
Was the lot of every
Powerful obstinate transgressor.[1890]

١٥- وَاسْتَفْتَحُوا وَخَابَ
كُلُّ جَبَّارٍ عَنِيدٍ ۝

16. In front of such a one
Is Hell, and he is given,
For drink, boiling fetid water.

١٦- مِّن وَرَآئِهِ جَهَنَّمُ وَيُسْقَىٰ مِن مَّآءٍ
صَدِيدٍ ۝

17. In gulps will he sip it,
But never will he be near
Swallowing it down his throat:
Death will come to him
From every quarter, yet
Will he not die: and
In front of him will be
A chastisement unrelenting.[1891]

١٧- يَتَجَرَّعُهُ وَلَا يَكَادُ يُسِيغُهُ
وَيَأْتِيهِ الْمَوْتُ مِن كُلِّ مَكَانٍ
وَمَا هُوَ بِمَيِّتٍ
وَمِن وَرَآئِهِ عَذَابٌ غَلِيظٌ ۝

18. The parable of those who
Reject their Lord is that
Their works are as ashes,[1892]
On which the wind blows
Furiously on a tempestuous day:
No power have they over
Aught that they have earned:
That is the straying
Far, far (from the goal).

١٨- مَّثَلُ الَّذِينَ كَفَرُوا بِرَبِّهِمْ أَعْمَالُهُمْ
كَرَمَادٍ
اشْتَدَّتْ بِهِ الرِّيحُ فِي يَوْمٍ عَاصِفٍ
لَّا يَقْدِرُونَ مِمَّا كَسَبُوا عَلَىٰ شَيْءٍ
ذَٰلِكَ هُوَ الضَّلَالُ الْبَعِيدُ ۝

1889. *Cf.* viii. 19. I have assumed that "they" in this verse is the same as "them" in the preceding verse, *i.e.*, the ungodly. Hoping for victory they forced a decision, and they got it—against themselves. Or they challenged a punishment, and it came in good time. Some Commentators construe "they" here to mean "the apostles": in that case the verse would mean: "The Apostles prayed for a victory and decision, and the ungodly were frustrated in their efforts to suppress the Truth."

1890. *Cf.* xi. 59.

1891. A graphic and deterrent picture, from the preaching of the earlier Prophets, of unrelieved horror of the torments of Hell. The door of escape by nihilation is also closed to them.

1892. Note the fulness of the parable. The works of the ungodly are in themselves light and unsubstantial like ashes: they are the useless rubbish that remains out of the faculties and opportunities which they have misused by burning them up. Further, the ashes are blown about hither and thither by the wind: the ungodly have no compass, direction, or purpose that can stand. The wind, too, which blows on them is no ordinary wind, nor the day on which they seek to enjoy the fruits of their labours an ordinary tranquil day: a furious gale is blowing, for such is the Wrath of God. They have neither internal peace nor external gain. In the scattering of the ashes they lose control even of such things as they might have earned but for their misdeeds. Their whole nature is contaminated. All their wishes go astray. They are carried so far, far away from what was in their minds. What did they aim at, and what did they achieve?

19. Seest thou not that God
Created the heavens and the earth
In Truth?[1893] If He so will,
He can remove you
And put (in your place)
A new Creation?

١٩- أَلَمْ تَرَ أَنَّ اللّٰهَ خَلَقَ السَّمٰوٰتِ وَالْأَرْضَ
بِالْحَقِّ ۚ إِنْ يَشَأْ يُذْهِبْكُمْ
وَيَأْتِ بِخَلْقٍ جَدِيدٍ ۝

20. Nor is that for God
Any great matter.[1894]

٢٠- وَمَا ذٰلِكَ عَلَى اللّٰهِ بِعَزِيزٍ ۝

21. They will all be marshalled
Before God together: then
Will the weak say to those[1895]
Who were arrogant, "For us,
We but followed you; can ye
Then avail us at all
Against the Wrath of God?"
They will reply, "If we
Had received the guidance[1896]
Of God, we should have
Given it to you: to us
It makes no difference (now)
Whether we rage, or bear
(These torments) with patience:
For ourselves there is no way
Of escape."

٢١- وَبَرَزُوا لِلّٰهِ جَمِيعًا
فَقَالَ الضُّعَفٰٓؤُا لِلَّذِينَ اسْتَكْبَرُوٓا
إِنَّا كُنَّا لَكُمْ تَبَعًا
فَهَلْ أَنْتُمْ مُّغْنُونَ عَنَّا مِنْ عَذَابِ
اللّٰهِ مِنْ شَيْءٍ ۚ
قَالُوا لَوْ هَدٰىنَا اللّٰهُ لَهَدَيْنٰكُمْ ۖ
سَوَآءٌ عَلَيْنَآ أَجَزِعْنَآ أَمْ صَبَرْنَا
مَا لَنَا مِنْ مَّحِيصٍ ۝

Section 4.

22. And Satan will say
When the matter is decided:[1897]
"It was God Who gave you
A promise of Truth: I too
Promised, but I failed
In my promise to you.

٢٢- وَقَالَ الشَّيْطٰنُ لَمَّا قُضِيَ الْأَمْرُ
إِنَّ اللّٰهَ وَعَدَكُمْ وَعْدَ الْحَقِّ
وَوَعَدْتُّكُمْ فَأَخْلَفْتُكُمْ ۖ

1893. *Haqq*: Truth, Right, Righteousness, True proportions, Reality. God's creation is not to be trifled with. It is built on righteousness, and those who do not obey its laws must give place to others who do. This warning is repeated again and again in history and in revelation. *Cf.* vi. 73.

1894. *'Azīz*: great, mighty, excellent, powerful, rare, precious.

1895. When the time for judgment comes, there are two kinds of disillusionment waiting for the ungodly. (1) Those who were misled and failed to see that each soul bears its own personal responsibility (ii. 134) and cannot shift it on to others, will turn to those who misled them, in the hope that they might intercede for them or do something to help them. They receive a plain answer as in the latter part of this verse. (2) Those who relied on Satan, the Power of Evil. His answer (in xiv. 22 below) is frank, cynical and brutal.

1896. Those whose power or specious intelligence or influence misled them—such as false priests or leaders—will find themselves in a parlous state. How can they help others? They themselves failed to profit from God's guidance, and they can with some justice retort that they put them in the wrong path as they followed it themselves!

1897. After the Judgment, Evil declares itself in its true colours. Frankly it says: 'I deceived you. The promise of God was true, but you believed me rather than God. I had no power to force you. I had but to call you, and you came running after me. You must blame yourselves. Did you think I was equal with God? I know too well that I was not and never could be. If you did wrong, you must suffer the Penalty.'

I had no authority over you
Except to call you, but ye
Listened to me: then
Reproach not me, but reproach
Your own souls. I cannot listen
To your cries, nor can ye
Listen to mine. I reject [1898]
Your former act in associating
Me with God.
For wrong-doers there must be
A grievous Penalty."

وَمَا كَانَ لِيَ عَلَيْكُم مِّن سُلْطٰنٍ
إِلَّآ أَن دَعَوْتُكُمْ فَاسْتَجَبْتُمْ لِي
فَلَا تَلُومُونِي وَلُومُوٓا أَنفُسَكُم
مَّآ أَنَا بِمُصْرِخِكُمْ وَمَآ أَنتُم بِمُصْرِخِيَّ
إِنِّي كَفَرْتُ بِمَآ أَشْرَكْتُمُونِ مِن قَبْلُ
إِنَّ الظّٰلِمِينَ لَهُمْ عَذَابٌ أَلِيمٌ ○

23. But those who believe
And work righteousness
Will be admitted to Gardens
Beneath which rivers flow,—
To dwell therein for aye
With the leave of their Lord.
Their greeting therein
Will be: "Peace!" [1899]

٢٣- وَأُدْخِلَ الَّذِينَ ءَامَنُوا وَعَمِلُوا الصّٰلِحٰتِ
جَنّٰتٍ تَجْرِي مِن تَحْتِهَا الْأَنْهٰرُ
خٰلِدِينَ فِيهَا بِإِذْنِ رَبِّهِمْ
تَحِيَّتُهُمْ فِيهَا سَلٰمٌ ○

24. Seest thou not how
God sets forth a parable?—
A goodly Word [1900]
Like a goodly tree,
Whose root is firmly fixed,
And its branches (reach)
To the heavens,—

٢٤- أَلَمْ تَرَ كَيْفَ ضَرَبَ اللّٰهُ مَثَلًا
كَلِمَةً طَيِّبَةً كَشَجَرَةٍ طَيِّبَةٍ
أَصْلُهَا ثَابِتٌ وَفَرْعُهَا فِي السَّمَآءِ ○

25. It brings forth its fruit [1901]
At all times, by the leave

٢٥- تُؤْتِيٓ أُكُلَهَا كُلَّ حِينٍ بِإِذْنِ

1898. See the last note. An alternative interpretation of this sentence may be: "I had already beforehand rebelled against God with Whom ye associated me."

1899. How this contrasts with the misery and the mutual self-recriminations of the ungodly!

1900. "Goodly word" is usually interpreted as the Divine Word, the Divine Message, the True Religion. It may also be interpreted in a more general sense as a word of truth, a word of goodness or kindness, which follows from a true appreciation of Religion. For Religion includes our duty to God and our duty to man. The "evil word" is opposite to this: false religion, blasphemy, false speech, or preaching or teaching unkindness and wrong-doing. The Word, in mystic language, is the root of the Deed, and is identified with the Deed.

1901. The goodly tree is known for: (1) its beauty: it gives pleasure to all who see it: (2) its stability; it remains firm and unshaken in storms, because its roots are firmly fixed in the earth; (3) its wide compass; its branches reach high, and it catches all the sunshine from heaven, and gives shade to countless birds in its branches and men and animals beneath it, and (4) its abundant fruit, which it yields at all times. So is the Good Word. It is as beautiful as it is true. It abides in all the changes and chances of this life, and even beyond (see verse 27 below): it is never shaken by sorrow or what seems to us calamity; its roots are deep down in the bed-rock facts of life. Its reach is universal, above, around, below: it is illuminated by the divine light from heaven, and its consolation reaches countless beings of all grades of life. Its fruit—the enjoyment of its blessings—is not confined to one season or one set of circumstances; furthermore the fortunate man who is the vehicle of that word has no self-pride; he attributes all its goodness, and his act in spreading it, to the Will and Leave of God. *Cf.* the New Testament Parable of the Sower (Matt. iv. 14-20) or of the Mustard-seed (Matt. iv. 30-32). In this Parable of the Qur-ān there are fewer words and more spiritual meaning, and the emphasis is on more essential things.

Of its Lord.
So God sets forth parables
For men, in order that
They may receive admonition.

رَبِّهَا ۗ وَيَضْرِبُ اللّٰهُ الْاَمْثَالَ
لِلنَّاسِ لَعَلَّهُمْ يَتَذَكَّرُوْنَ ○

26. And the parable
Of an evil Word
Is that of an evil tree:
It is torn up by the root
From the surface of the earth:
It has no stability.[1902]

٢٦- وَمَثَلُ كَلِمَةٍ خَبِيْثَةٍ كَشَجَرَةٍ خَبِيْثَةِ
اجْتُثَّتْ مِنْ فَوْقِ الْاَرْضِ مَا لَهَا مِنْ
قَرَارٍ ○

27. God will establish in strength
Those who believe, with the Word
That stands firm, in this world
And in the Hereafter; but God
Will leave, to stray, those
Who do wrong: God doeth
What He willeth.[1903]

٢٧- يُثَبِّتُ اللّٰهُ الَّذِيْنَ اٰمَنُوْا بِالْقَوْلِ
الثَّابِتِ فِى الْحَيٰوةِ الدُّنْيَا وَفِى الْاٰخِرَةِ ۚ
وَيُضِلُّ اللّٰهُ الظّٰلِمِيْنَ ۙ
وَيَفْعَلُ اللّٰهُ مَا يَشَآءُ ○ ع

C. 118.—But the evil not only choose evil
(xiv. 28-52.) For themselves but mislead others
To perdition. The godly should learn
From the Signs of God all around them,
And be on their guard against all
That is false. So Abraham prayed
Not only for his posterity, but for all:
For he foresaw the universality
Of God's Message in Islam.
That leads to the mystic doctrine
Of Oneness, which will be seen
In its fulness on the Great Day
When a new Earth and a new Heaven
Will proclaim the end of Evil
And the adjustment of all this life's accounts.

1902. The evil tree is the opposite of the goodly tree. The parallelism of contrast can be followed out in all the details of the last note.

1903. His Will and Plan may be above comprehension, but will prevail over all things. It is not like the will of man, who may plan good things but is not necessarily able to carry them out.

SECTION 5.

28. Hast thou not turned
Thy vision to those who[1904]
Have changed the favour of God.
Into blasphemy and caused
Their people to descend
To the House of Perdition?—

۲۸- أَلَمْ تَرَ إِلَى الَّذِينَ
بَدَّلُوا نِعْمَتَ اللَّهِ كُفْرًا
وَأَحَلُّوا قَوْمَهُمْ دَارَ الْبَوَارِ ○

29. Into Hell? They will burn
Therein,—an evil place
To stay in!

۲۹- جَهَنَّمَ يَصْلَوْنَهَا
وَبِئْسَ الْقَرَارُ ○

30. And they set up (idols)
As equal to God, to mislead
(Men) from the Path! Say:
"Enjoy (your brief power)!
But verily ye are making
Straightway for Hell!"

۳۰- وَجَعَلُوا لِلَّهِ أَندَادًا لِّيُضِلُّوا
عَن سَبِيلِهِ قُلْ تَمَتَّعُوا
فَإِنَّ مَصِيرَكُمْ إِلَى النَّارِ ○

31. Speak to my servants
Who have believed,[1905]
That they may establish
Regular prayers, and spend
(In charity) out of the Sustenance[1906]

۳۱- قُل لِّعِبَادِيَ الَّذِينَ آمَنُوا
يُقِيمُوا الصَّلَوٰةَ وَيُنفِقُوا مِمَّا

1904. There is a particular and a general meaning. The particular meaning is understood to be a reference to the Meccan Pagans who turned the House of God into a place for the worship of horrible idols and the practice of unseemly rites and cults. There is no real difficulty in accepting this as part of a late Meccan Sūra even without supposing it to be a prophecy. The Meccan Pagans had turned Religion into a blasphemous superstition, and were misguiding their people, persecuting the true Messenger of God and all who followed his teaching. Their cup of iniquity seemed about full, and they seemed to be heading to perdition, as later events indeed showed to be the case.

The general meaning is also clear. Selfish men, when they seize power, want worship for themselves or their Phantasies, in derogation of the true God. Power, which should have been an instrument of good, becomes in their hands an instrument of evil. They and their people rush headlong to perdition. "These be thy gods, O Israel!" has been a cry repeated again and again in history, in the face, or at the back, of men of God!

1905. Putting ourselves back in the position in which the Muslim community found themselves in Mecca just before the Hijrat, we can imagine how much encouragement and consolation they needed from the preaching, the Faith, and the steadfast character of Mustafa. Intolerant persecution was the order of the day; neither the life nor the property or reputation of the Muslims was safe. They are asked to find strength and tranquillity in prayer and in helping each other according to their needs and resources.

1906. Here, as elsewhere, "Sustenance" is to be taken in the literal as well as the metaphorical sense. There were many among the Muslims who were poor, or slaves, or depressed, because they were deprived of the means of livelihood on account of their Faith. They were to be fed, clothed, and sheltered, by those who had means. There were those who were ignorant and needed spiritual sustenance: they were to be taught and strengthened by those to whom God had given knowledge and firmness of character. Charity was to be ordinarily secret, so as to cut out all show or parade, and perhaps also lest the enemy should dry up those sources by unprincipled violence; but there must be much that had to be open and organised, so that all the needy could know where to go to be relieved.

We have given them,
Secretly and openly, before
The coming of a Day
In which there will be
Neither mutual bargaining[1907]
Nor befriending.

رَزَقْنٰهُمْ سِرًّا وَّعَلَانِيَةً
مِّنْ قَبْلِ اَنْ يَّاْتِيَ يَوْمٌ
لَّا بَيْعٌ فِيْهِ وَلَا خِلٰلٌ ○

32. It is God Who hath created
The heavens and the earth
And sendeth down rain
From the skies, and with it
Bringeth out fruits wherewith
To feed you; it is He
Who hath made the ships subject
To you, that they may sail
Through the sea by His Command;
And the rivers (also)
Hath He made subject to you.[1908]

٣٢- اَللّٰهُ الَّذِيْ خَلَقَ السَّمٰوٰتِ وَالْاَرْضَ
وَاَنْزَلَ مِنَ السَّمَآءِ مَآءً
فَاَخْرَجَ بِهٖ مِنَ الثَّمَرٰتِ رِزْقًا لَّكُمْ
وَسَخَّرَ لَكُمُ الْفُلْكَ
لِتَجْرِيَ فِي الْبَحْرِ بِاَمْرِهٖ
وَسَخَّرَ لَكُمُ الْاَنْهٰرَ ○

33. And He hath made subject
To you the sun and the moon,[1909]
Both diligently pursuing
Their courses; and the Night
And the Day hath He (also)
Made subject to you.

٣٣- وَسَخَّرَ لَكُمُ
الشَّمْسَ وَالْقَمَرَ دَآئِبَيْنِ
وَسَخَّرَ لَكُمُ الَّيْلَ وَالنَّهَارَ ○

1907. The great Day of Reckoning would be one on which all values would be changed. Wealth, as understood in this world, would no longer count. Should we not therefore use any wealth we have in this life, to give here and receive there? *Bai'* includes all bargaining,—barter, purchase and sale, etc. In this world, where wealth has some value, let us spend it and get for ourselves "treasures in heaven". In the next life each man will stand on his merits and personal responsibility. One man cannot help another. Let us here help each other to become true and righteous, so that our personal account may be favourable there.

1908. We must realise that behind all our strength, skill, and intelligence there is the power and goodness of God, Who gave us all these things. Man can understand and control the forces of nature so as to bring them to his own service: he can only do so, because (1) he has got these gifts from God, and (2) God has fixed definite laws in nature, of which he can take advantage by God's command and permission. He has been made Vicegerent on earth (ii. 30): God commanded the highest creatures to bow down to Adam (ii. 34). Man, by God's command, can use rain to produce food for himself; make ships to sail the seas; use rivers as highways, and cut canals for traffic and irrigation. Not only this, but even the heavenly bodies can (by God's command) contribute to his needs (see next verse).

1909. The sun gives out heat, which is the source of all life and energy on this planet, and produces the seasons of the year, by utilising which man can supply his needs, not only material, but immaterial in the shape of light, health, and other blessings. The sun and the moon together produce tides, and are responsible for atmospheric changes which are of the highest importance in the life of man. The succession of Day and Night is due to the apparent daily course of the sun through the skies; and the cool light of the moon performs other services different from those of warm day-light. Because there are laws here, which man can understand and calculate, he can use all such things for his own service, and in that sense the heavenly bodies are themselves made subject to him by God's command.

34. And He giveth you
Of all that ye ask for.[1910]
But if ye count the favours
Of God, never will ye
Be able to number them.
Verily, man is given up
To injustice and ingratitude.[1911]

٣٤- وَآتٰكُمْ مِّنْ كُلِّ مَا سَأَلْتُمُوْهُ ۚ
وَإِنْ تَعُدُّوْا نِعْمَتَ اللّٰهِ لَا تُحْصُوْهَا ۗ
إِنَّ الْإِنْسَانَ لَظَلُوْمٌ كَفَّارٌ ۝ ع

Section 6.

35. Remember Abraham said:[1912]
"O my Lord! make this city
One of peace and security:
And preserve me and my sons
From worshipping idols.[1913]

٣٥- وَإِذْ قَالَ إِبْرٰهِيْمُ رَبِّ اجْعَلْ هٰذَا
الْبَلَدَ اٰمِنًا وَّاجْنُبْنِيْ
وَبَنِيَّ أَنْ نَّعْبُدَ الْأَصْنَامَ ۝

36. "O my Lord! they have indeed
Led astray many among mankind;
He then who follows my (ways)
Is of me, and he that
Disobeys me,—but Thou
Art indeed Oft-Forgiving,
Most Merciful.

٣٦- رَبِّ إِنَّهُنَّ أَضْلَلْنَ كَثِيْرًا مِّنَ
النَّاسِ ۚ فَمَنْ تَبِعَنِيْ فَإِنَّهٗ مِنِّيْ ۚ
وَمَنْ عَصَانِيْ
فَإِنَّكَ غَفُوْرٌ رَّحِيْمٌ ۝

37. "O our Lord! I have made
Some of my offspring to dwell
In a valley without cultivation,[1914]
By Thy Sacred House;

٣٧- رَبَّنَا إِنِّيْ أَسْكَنْتُ مِنْ ذُرِّيَّتِيْ
بِوَادٍ غَيْرِ ذِيْ زَرْعٍ عِنْدَ بَيْتِكَ الْمُحَرَّمِ

1910. Sincere and true prayer in faith is answered by God. Thus He gives us everything which a wise and benevolent Providence can give.

1911. I have tried to render the intensive forms of the Arabic by what I consider their near equivalents here: the phrase "given up to injustice and ingratitude" suggests habitual ignoring of just values and ingratitude for the innumerable gifts and favours which God has showered on mankind.

1912. This Prayer of Abraham, the True in Faith, the progenitor of the Semitic peoples and the Prototype of their Religion, is introduced in this place, to illustrate the points referred to in the preceding section, xiv. 31-34, *viz.*, how the new Revelation through the Ka'ba bears out the universal Revelation of Prayer and Charity, Love of God and man, Recognition of God's handiwork in nature, and Insistence on man's turning away from false worship and ingratitude to God. Notice the four divisions into which it falls: (1) verses 35-36 are spoken by Abraham as on his own behalf ("O my Lord!"); (2) verse 37-38 are spoken on behalf of his progeny ("O our Lord!") but with special reference to the elder branch, the children of Ismā'īl; (3) verses 39-40 are again a personal appeal, but both branches of his family, *viz.*, the sons of Ismā'īl and Isaac, are expressly mentioned; (4) verse 41 is a Prayer for himself, his parents, and all Believers, typifying that in the universality of Islam all nations are to be blessed. Jerusalem, for the Mosaic Law and the Gospel of Jesus, was the centre and symbol for the Jewish race, though of course all God's Truth is universal; Mecca, the centre of the Arab race, was to throw off its tribal character and become universal, in spite of the Meccans themselves.

1913. *Cf.* ii. 125-129. Abraham (with Ismā'īl) built the Ka'ba, and Abraham asks a blessing on his handiwork and forgiveness for such lapses into idolatry as both branches of his family might fall into.

1914. The Meccan valley is enclosed by hills on all sides, unlike Medina, which has level cultivated plains. But just because of its natural isolation, it is fitted to be a centre for Prayer and Praise.

In order, O our Lord, that they
May establish regular Prayer :
So fill the hearts of some
Among men with love towards
them,
And feed them with Fruits :[1915]
So that they may give thanks.

رَبَّنَا لِيُقِيمُوا الصَّلٰوةَ
فَاجْعَلْ أَفْئِدَةً مِّنَ النَّاسِ تَهْوِيٓ
إِلَيْهِمْ
وَارْزُقْهُم مِّنَ الثَّمَرٰتِ لَعَلَّهُمْ يَشْكُرُونَ ○

38. " O our Lord ! truly Thou
Dost know what we conceal
And what we reveal :
For nothing whatever is hidden
From God, whether on earth
Or in heaven.[1916]

٣٨- رَبَّنَآ إِنَّكَ تَعْلَمُ مَا نُخْفِي
وَمَا نُعْلِنُ ۗ وَمَا يَخْفَىٰ عَلَى اللَّهِ مِن شَيْءٍ
فِي الْأَرْضِ وَلَا فِي السَّمَآءِ ○

39. " Praise be to God, Who hath
Granted unto me in old age
Ismā'īl and Isaac : for truly
My Lord is He, the Hearer
Of Prayer ![1917]

٣٩- الْحَمْدُ لِلَّهِ الَّذِي وَهَبَ لِي عَلَى الْكِبَرِ
إِسْمٰعِيلَ وَإِسْحٰقَ ۚ
إِنَّ رَبِّي لَسَمِيعُ الدُّعَآءِ ○

40. " O my Lord ! make me
One who establishes regular Prayer,
And also (raise such)
Among my offspring[1918]
O our Lord !
And accept Thou my Prayer.

٤٠- رَبِّ اجْعَلْنِي مُقِيمَ الصَّلٰوةِ
وَمِن ذُرِّيَّتِي ۚ
رَبَّنَا وَتَقَبَّلْ دُعَآءِ ○

41. " O our Lord ![1919] cover (us)[1920]
With Thy Forgiveness—me,

٤١- رَبَّنَا اغْفِرْ لِي

1915. *Cf.* ii. 126, and n. 128. (The " Fruits " are there explained.) The righteous, though they have to have sustenance, both in a literal and figurative sense, require also the love and sympathy of their fellow-men.

1916. In Abraham's prophetic mind was the secret and open enmity or contempt which the Children of Israel were to have for the Children of Ismā'īl (Arabs). He prays to God that they may be united in Islam, as indeed they were, except a small remnant.

1917. Abraham was 100 years old when Isaac was born (Gen. xxi. 5); and as Ismā'īl was 13 years old when Abraham was 99, (Gen. xvii. 24-25), Ismā'īl was also a son of his father's old age, having been born when Abraham was 86 years old. The younger son's progeny developed the Faith of Israel and that of Christ ; the elder son's progeny perfected the more universal Faith of Islam, the Faith of Abraham the True.

1918. Abraham prays for both branches of his family, having a wider vision than some of the later Children of Israel.

1919. Read again n. 1912 above. Having prayed for his progeny, Abraham now prays for God's grace on himself, his parents, and the whole Brotherhood of Faith, irrespective of family or race or time, to be perfected in the ideal of Islam.

1920. For the shades of meaning in the different words for Forgiveness, see n. 110 to ii. 109.

My parents,[1921] and (all) Believers,
On the Day that the Reckoning
Will be established ![1922]

وَلِوَالِدَيَّ وَلِلْمُؤْمِنِينَ يَوْمَ يَقُومُ
الْحِسَابُ ۝ ع

SECTION 7.

42. Think not that God
Doth not heed the deeds
Of those who do wrong.
He but giveth them respite
Against a Day when
The eyes will fixedly stare
In horror,—

۴۲- وَلَا تَحْسَبَنَّ اللّٰهَ غَافِلًا
عَمَّا يَعْمَلُ الظّٰلِمُوْنَ ۚ
إِنَّمَا يُؤَخِّرُهُمْ لِيَوْمٍ
تَشْخَصُ فِيْهِ الْأَبْصَارُ ۝

43. They running forward
With necks outstretched,
Their heads uplifted, their gaze
Returning not towards them,
And their hearts a (gaping) void ![1923]

۴۳- مُهْطِعِيْنَ مُقْنِعِيْ رُءُوْسِهِمْ
لَا يَرْتَدُّ إِلَيْهِمْ طَرْفُهُمْ ۚ
وَأَفْئِدَتُهُمْ هَوَاءٌ ۝

44. So warn mankind
Of the Day when the Wrath
Will reach them : then will
The wrong-doers say : "Our Lord !
Respite us (if only)
For a short Term : we will
Answer Thy Call, and follow
The apostles !"
"What! were ye not wont
To swear aforetime that ye
Should suffer no decline ?[1924]

۴۴- وَأَنْذِرِ النَّاسَ يَوْمَ يَأْتِيْهِمُ الْعَذَابُ
فَيَقُوْلُ الَّذِيْنَ ظَلَمُوْا رَبَّنَا
أَخِّرْنَا إِلَىٰ أَجَلٍ قَرِيْبٍ ۙ
نُّجِبْ دَعْوَتَكَ وَنَتَّبِعِ الرُّسُلَ ۗ
أَوَلَمْ تَكُوْنُوْا أَقْسَمْتُمْ مِّنْ قَبْلُ
مَا لَكُمْ مِّنْ زَوَالٍ ۝

1921. *My parents.* Abraham's father was an idolater (xliii. 26; vi. 74). Not only that, but he persecuted the Faith of Unity and threatened Abraham with stoning and exile (xix. 46); and he and his people cast him into the Fire to be burned (xxi. 52, 68). Yet Abraham's heart was tender, and he prayed for forgiveness for his father because of a promise which he had made (ix 114), though he renounced the land of his fathers (Chaldea).

1922. At the final Reckoning, all that may seem inequality or injustice in this world will be redressed. But the merits of the best of us will need God's Grace to establish us in that lasting Felicity which is promised to the righteous. And Abraham, as the father of Prophecy, prayed for all,—for the Universal Faith perfected in Islam.

1923. A picture of horror. The evil ones, when they realise the situation, will be dazed: their eyes will stare without expression, and never move back; their necks will be outstretched; their heads uplifted in terror of the Judgment from on High; and their hearts become empty of all hope or intelligence as the physical heart might become empty of blood when the circulation stops. In this state they will press forward to Judgment.

1924. *Zawāl,*=decline from the zenith, as that of the sun; decline from the highest point reached by a heavenly body in its course through the sky. The ungodly are apt to think that their power will remain in the ascendant, on account of some material advantages given them temporarily by God, but they are constantly receiving warnings in history and revelation and from the example of others before them. There is a warning to the contemporary Pagan Meccans here; but the warning is perfectly general, and for all time.

45. "And ye dwelt in the dwellings
Of men who wronged their own
Souls; ye were clearly shown
How We dealt with them;
And We put forth (many) Parables
In your behoof!"

۴۵- وَسَكَنْتُمْ فِي مَسٰكِنِ الَّذِيْنَ ظَلَمُوْٓا
اَنْفُسَهُمْ وَتَبَيَّنَ لَكُمْ كَيْفَ فَعَلْنَا بِهِمْ
وَضَرَبْنَا لَكُمُ الْاَمْثَالَ ۝

46. Mighty indeed were the plots
Which they made, but their plots
Were (well) within the sight
Of God, even though they were
Such as to shake the hills!

۴۶- وَقَدْ مَكَرُوْا مَكْرَهُمْ وَعِنْدَ اللّٰهِ
مَكْرُهُمْ ۭ وَاِنْ كَانَ مَكْرُهُمْ
لِتَزُوْلَ مِنْهُ الْجِبَالُ ۝

47. Never think that God would fail
His apostles in His promise:
For God is Exalted in Power,—
The Lord of Retribution.

۴۷- فَلَا تَحْسَبَنَّ اللّٰهَ مُخْلِفَ وَعْدِهٖ
رُسُلَهٗ ۭ اِنَّ اللّٰهَ عَزِيْزٌ ذُو انْتِقَامٍ ۝

48. One day the Earth will be
Changed to a different Earth,
And so will be the Heavens,[1925]
And (men) will be marshalled
Forth, before God, the One,
The Irresistible;

۴۸- يَوْمَ تُبَدَّلُ الْاَرْضُ غَيْرَ الْاَرْضِ
وَالسَّمٰوٰتُ وَبَرَزُوْا لِلّٰهِ
الْوَاحِدِ الْقَهَّارِ ۝

49. And thou wilt see
The Sinners that day
Bound together in fetters;—[1926]

۴۹- وَتَرَى الْمُجْرِمِيْنَ يَوْمَىِٕذٍ
مُّقَرَّنِيْنَ فِي الْاَصْفَادِ ۝

50. Their garments[1927] of liquid
pitch,[1928]
And their faces covered with Fire;

۵۰- سَرَابِيْلُهُمْ مِّنْ قَطِرَانٍ
وَّتَغْشٰى وُجُوْهَهُمُ النَّارُ ۝

1925. "A new earth and a new heaven" refers to (1) the entirely changed conditions at the end of things as we know them, so that we can only have the new world described to us by symbols and metaphors as in the following verses; and (2) to the spiritual world of changing values even as time goes on, so that the judgment on man begins gradually to take effect even while in externals he is in the phenomenal world, for in his inner being he is experiencing the effects, good or evil, of his conduct on earth. In the latter case, also, his mystic experience can only be described in symbols.

1926. The *fetters* will be their evil actions, thoughts, and motives, which they cannot shake off, as they could have shaken them off by repentance and amendment while there was yet time and opportunity to do so.

1927. *Sirbāl*; plural, *Sarābīl*: a garment or coat of mail, breast plate; something covering the most vital parts of the body, like the shirt or the Indian *kurtā*.

1928. *Qaṭirān*: black pitch, a resinous substance exuding from certain kinds of trees like the terebinth or the pines, or distilled from wood or coal. It catches fire readily. Issuing from the upper garments (*Sarābīl*) the flames soon cover the face, the most expressive part of man's essence or being. The metaphor of fetters (n. 1926) is now changed to that of pitch, which darkens and sets on fire the soul of man.

51. That God may requite
Each soul according
To its deserts;[1929]
And verily God is Swift
In calling to account.[1930]

٥١- لِيَجْزِيَ اللّٰهُ كُلَّ نَفْسٍ مَّا كَسَبَتْ ۚ
إِنَّ اللّٰهَ سَرِيعُ الْحِسَابِ ۝

52. Here is a Message for mankind:
Let them take warning therefrom,
And let them know that He
Is (no other than) One God:[1931]
Let men of understanding
Take heed.

٥٢- هٰذَا بَلٰغٌ لِّلنَّاسِ وَلِيُنْذَرُوا بِهٖ
وَلِيَعْلَمُوْٓا أَنَّمَا هُوَ إِلٰهٌ وَّاحِدٌ
وَّلِيَذَّكَّرَ أُولُوا الْأَلْبَابِ ۝

1929. *Its deserts*: *i.e.*, according to what it earned by its own acts, good or evil, in its life of probation.

1930. *Swift in calling to account*: We can understand this in two significations. (1) Let not the wicked think that because God, out of His infinite grace and mercy, grants respite, therefore the retribution will be slow in coming. When the time comes in accordance with God's Plan and Wisdom, the retribution will come so swiftly that the ungodly will be surprised and they will wish they could get more respite (xiv. 44). (2) On the great Day of Reckoning, let it not be supposed that, because there will be millions of souls to be judged, there will be any delay in judgment as in a human tribunal. It will be a new world and beyond the flight of Time. Or if a metaphor from time as we conceive it in this world can be taken, it will all be as it were in the twinkling of an eye (xvi. 77).

1931. Here is another aspect of the Truth of Unity. God being One, all justice is of one standard, for Truth is one, and we see it as one as soon as the scales of phenomenal diversity fall from our eyes. The one true Reality then emerges. Blessed are those who treasured this Truth in their souls already in their life of probation.

INTRODUCTION TO SŪRA XV (*Hijr*).

This is the last of the six Sūras of the A. L. M. series (x. to xv.). Its place in chronology is the late Meccan period, probably somewhere near the middle of that period. See Introduction to S. x., where will be found also an indication of the general subject-matter of the whole series in the gradation of Quranic teaching.

The special subject-matter of this Sūra is the protection of God's Revelation and God's Truth. Evil arose from Pride and the warping of man's will, but God's Mercy is the antidote, as was proved in the case of Abraham and Lot, and might have been proved by the people of the Aika and the Ḥijr if they had only attended to God's "Signs". The Qur-ān, beginning with the Seven Oft-repeated Verses, is the precious vehicle for the praises of God.

Summary.—God will guard His Revelation, in spite of the cavils of the Unbelievers; God is the source of all things; He knows His own people, whom He will gather to Himself (xv. 1-25, and C. 119).

How Evil arose through the pride of Iblīs, to whom a respite was granted for a period; but neither fear nor evil will affect those who receive God's Message. (xv. 26-50, and C. 120).

The Mercy of God to Abraham was conveyed by the same messengers that were sent to destroy the people of Lot for their unspeakable crimes; Evil brought its retribution also on the Companions of the Wood (*Aika*) and of the Rocky Tract *Ḥijr* (xv. 51-84, and C. 121).

The Qur-ān and its Sūras teach you to celebrate God's praises, learn humility in worship, and serve God all your life (xv. 85-99, and C. 122).

Sūra XV.

Al-Ḥijr, or The Rocky Tract.

In the name of God, Most Gracious, Most Merciful

1. A. L. R.[1932] These are
The Āyats[1933] of Revelation,—
13 Of a Qur-ān
30 That makes things clear.[1934]

C. 119.—God's Truth makes all things clear, and He
(xv. 1-25.)
Will guard it. But His Signs are not
For those who mock. Who fails to see
The majesty, beauty, order, and harmony
Blazoned in His Creation, and His goodness
To all His creatures, in the heavens
And on earth? With Him are the sources
Of all things, and He doth freely give
His gifts in due measure. He holds
The keys of Life and Death, and He will remain
When all else passes away.

1932. For these mystic letters, see Introduction to Sūra x.

1933. *Cf.* x. 1. and n. 1382.

1934. Note how appropriately the different phrases in which the Qur-ān is characterised, bring out its different aspects as a Revelation. Let us just consider the phrases used at the beginning of the six A. L. M. Sūras, of which this is the last in order of arrangement. In x. 1 we read, "Āyats (or verses or Signs) of the Book of Wisdom", the theme being the wonders of God's Creation, and its relation to His Revelation. In xi 1 we read, "a Book, with verses basic or fundamental, further explained in detail": the theme is God's Justice and punishment, to preserve the fundamental scheme of His Laws. In xii. 1 we read, "The Symbols (or verses) of the Perspicuous Book": the wonderful unfolding of God's Plan is explained in Joseph's story. In xiii. 1 we read, "The Signs (or verses) of the Book": the contrasts in the modes of God's Revelation and its reception by man are pointed out, but not illustrated by detailed examples as in Joseph's perspicuous story. In xiv. 1 we read, "A Book.........revealed......to lead......out of......darkness into light": the theme being Abraham's prayer for man to be rescued from the darkness of false worship into the light of Unity. Here, in xv, 1 we read, "Āyats (or verses) of Revelation,—of a Qur-ān that makes things clear (or perspicuous)": the theme being an explanation of evil, and how God's Truth is protected from it.

2. Again and again will those
Who disbelieve, wish that they
Had bowed (to God's Will)
In Islâm.[1935]

٢- رُبَمَا يَوَدُّ الَّذِينَ كَفَرُوا لَوْ كَانُوا مُسْلِمِينَ ○

3. Leave them alone, to enjoy[1936]
(The good things of this life)
And to please themselves:
Let (false) Hope amuse them: soon
Will knowledge (undeceive them).[1937]

٣- ذَرْهُمْ يَأْكُلُوا وَيَتَمَتَّعُوا وَيُلْهِهِمُ الْأَمَلُ فَسَوْفَ يَعْلَمُونَ ○

4. Never did We destroy
A population that had not
A term decreed and assigned
Beforehand.[1938]

٤- وَمَا أَهْلَكْنَا مِنْ قَرْيَةٍ إِلَّا وَلَهَا كِتَابٌ مَعْلُومٌ ○

5. Neither can a people anticipate
Its Term, nor delay it.[1939]

٥- مَا تَسْبِقُ مِنْ أُمَّةٍ أَجَلَهَا وَمَا يَسْتَأْخِرُونَ ○

6. They say: "O thou to whom
The Message is being revealed!
Truly thou art mad
(or possessed)![1940]

٦- وَقَالُوا يَا أَيُّهَا الَّذِي نُزِّلَ عَلَيْهِ الذِّكْرُ إِنَّكَ لَمَجْنُونٌ ○

1935. The time must inevitably come when those who allow themselves to be deceived by falsehood or deliberately break God's Law will find themselves in a terrible plight. They will then wish, ardently and again and again, that they had sought God's Will and walked in the light of Truth. That time may be early or late,—in this life, or at death, or at the Day of Judgment, but it must come. Man's own highest interest requires that he should awake to the Reality before it is too late for repentance.

1936. Literally, "to eat". *Cf.* v. 69 and n. 776.

1937. The foolish and the wicked set great store by the pleasures of this world. In their pride they think they have all knowledge. In the fulness of knowledge they will see how wrong they were. Meanwhile those who have received the Light should not for a single moment wonder at the apparent prosperity of the ungodly in this world. They should leave them alone, confident in the goodness and justice of God.

1938. *Kitābun ma'lūm*: literally, "a writing known". There are many shades of meaning implied. (1) For every people, as for every individual, there is a definite Term assigned: their faculty of choice gives them the opportunity of moulding their will according to God's Will, and thus identifying themselves with God's Universal Law. During that Term they will be given plenty of rope: after that Term is past, there will be no opportunity for repentance. (2) Neither the righteous nor the ungodly can hasten or delay the doom: God's Will must prevail, and He is All-Wise. (3) The destruction of a people is not an arbitrary punishment from God: the people bring it on themselves by their own choice; for the fixed Law or Decree of God is always made known to them beforehand, and in many ways.

1939. *Cf.* vii. 34. Also see the last note.

1940. Muṣṭafā was accused by the ungodly of being mad or possessed, because he spoke of higher things than they knew, and acted from motives purer and nobler than they could understand. So, in a minor degree, is the lot of all the righteous in the presence of an ungodly world. Their motives, actions, words, hopes, and aspirations are unintelligible to their fellows, and they are accused of being mad or out of their senses. But they know that they are on the right path, and it is the ungodly who are really acting against their own best interests.

7. "Why bringest thou not
Angels to us if it be
That thou hast the Truth?"[1941]

٧- لَوْ مَا تَأْتِينَا بِالْمَلَٰٓئِكَةِ إِن كُنتَ مِنَ الصَّٰدِقِينَ ۝

8. We send not the angels
Down except for just cause:[1942]
If they came (to the ungodly),
Behold! no respite would they
have![1943]

٨- مَا نُنَزِّلُ الْمَلَٰٓئِكَةَ إِلَّا بِالْحَقِّ وَمَا كَانُوٓا إِذًا مُّنظَرِينَ ۝

9. We have, without doubt,
Sent down the Message;
And We will assuredly
Guard it (from corruption).[1944]

٩- إِنَّا نَحْنُ نَزَّلْنَا الذِّكْرَ وَإِنَّا لَهُۥ لَحَٰفِظُونَ ۝

10. We did send apostles before thee
Amongst the religious sects[1945]
Of old:

١٠- وَلَقَدْ أَرْسَلْنَا مِن قَبْلِكَ فِى شِيَعِ الْأَوَّلِينَ ۝

11. But never came an apostle
To them but they mocked him.

١١- وَمَا يَأْتِيهِم مِّن رَّسُولٍ إِلَّا كَانُوا بِهِۦ يَسْتَهْزِءُونَ ۝

12. Even so do we let it creep
Into the hearts of the sinners—[1946]

١٢- كَذَٰلِكَ نَسْلُكُهُۥ فِى قُلُوبِ الْمُجْرِمِينَ ۝

13. That they should not believe
In the (Message); but the ways

١٣- لَا يُؤْمِنُونَ بِهِۦ ۖ وَقَدْ

1941. *Cf.* vi. 8-9, and notes 840, 841. On the part of the unbelievers, this is a mere taunt. They neither believe in God nor in angels nor in revelation nor in any but material things. It is ridiculous to suppose that they could be taken seriously.

1942. Angels are not sent down to satisfy the whim or curiosity of the unbelievers. They are sent to bring inspiration to God's messengers and to execute God's decrees.

1943. If the angels were to appear before the ungodly, it would mean that they came to execute just punishment, and then there would be no hope of respite possible for the ungodly.

1944. The purity of the text of the Qur-ān through thirteen centuries and a half is a foretaste of the eternal care with which God's Truth is guarded through all ages. All corruptions, inventions, and accretions pass away, but God's pure and holy Truth will never suffer eclipse even though the whole world mocked at it and were bent on destroying it.

1945. *Shiya un*, plural of *Shī'atun* = a sect, a religious division. Mankind sees fragments of Truth at a time, and is apt to fall into fragments and divisions. All true apostles of God come to reconcile these fragments or divisions, for they preach the true Gospel of Unity. So came Mustafā to bring back to Unity the many jarring sects among the Jews, Christians, and Pagans. His mission was held up to ridicule, but so was the mission of his predecessors. Mockery itself should not discourage the preachers of Truth.

1946. If evil and disbelief exist in the world, we must not be impatient or lose our own faith. We must recognise that if such things are permitted, they are part of the Universal Plan and purpose of God, Who is All-Wise and All-Good, but Whose wisdom and goodness we cannot fully fathom. One consolation we have, and that is stated in the next verse and the next note.

Of the ancients have passed
away.[1947]

خَلَتْ سُنَّةُ الْأَوَّلِينَ ○

14. Even if We opened out to them
A gate from heaven,[1948]
And they were to continue
(All day) ascending therein,

١٤- وَلَوْ فَتَحْنَا عَلَيْهِم بَابًا مِّنَ السَّمَاءِ
فَظَلُّوا فِيهِ يَعْرُجُونَ ○

15. They would only say:
" Our eyes have been intoxicated:
Nay, we have been bewitched
By sorcery."

١٥- لَقَالُوا إِنَّمَا سُكِّرَتْ أَبْصَارُنَا
بَلْ نَحْنُ قَوْمٌ مَّسْحُورُونَ ○ ع

SECTION 2.

16. It is We Who have set out[1949]
The Zodiacal Signs[1950] in the
heavens,
And made them fair-seeming
To (all) beholders;

١٦- وَلَقَدْ جَعَلْنَا فِي السَّمَاءِ بُرُوجًا
وَزَيَّنَّاهَا لِلنَّاظِرِينَ ○

17. And (moreover) We have guarded
them[1951]

١٧- وَحَفِظْنَاهَا

1947. Sects, divisions, and systems invented by men tend to pass away, but God's pure Truth of Unity endures for ever. This we see in history when we study it on a large scale. *Cf.* the parable in xiv. 24-26. *Khalat*: I have translated it here in the same sense as in xiii. 30, x. 102, and other places. Some Commentators give it a slightly different shade of meaning. The other meaning is seen in xlviii. 23.

1948. *Cf.* vi. 35. The spiritual kingdom is open to all to enter. But the entrance is not a mere matter of physical movement. It is a question of a total change of heart. Evil must cease to be evil, before it can see or enjoy Good. If we could suppose Evil, like Bottom the weaver, to be "translated" or in some way carried up to heaven, it would only think that the Truth was an illusion, and the reality was mere witchery. The taint is in its very nature, which must first be purified and rendered fit for the reception of light, truth, and bliss.

1949. Evil having been described, not as an external thing, but as a taint of the soul, we have in this section a glorious account of the purity and beauty of God's Creation. Evil is a blot on it, not a normal feature of it. Indeed, the normal feature is the guard which God has put on it, to protect it from evil.

1950. In the countless millions of stars in the universe which we see, the first step in our astronomical knowledge is to find marvellous order, beauty, and harmony, on a scale of grandeur which we appreciate more and more as our knowledge increases. The first broad belt that we distinguish is the Zodiac, which marks the sun's path through the heavens year after year and the limit of the wanderings of the moon and the planets. We make twelve divisions of it and call them Signs of the Zodiac. Each marks the solar path through the heavens as we see it, month after month. We can thus mark off the seasons in our solar year, and express in definite laws the most important facts in meteorology, agriculture, seasonal winds, and tides. Then there are the mansions of the moon, the mapping out of the Constellations, and the other marvellous facts of the heavens, some of which affect our physical life on this earth. But the highest lessons we can draw from them are spiritual. The author of this wonderful Order and Beauty is One, and He alone is entitled to our worship.

1951. Taking the physical heavens, we can imagine the supreme melody or harmony—the Music of the Spheres—guarded from every disturbing force. If by any chance any rebellious force of evil seeks to obtain, by stealth, a sound of that harmony to which all who make themselves consonant are freely invited, it is pursued by a shooting star, for there can be no consonance between evil and good.

From every evil spirit accursed :[1952]

مِنْ كُلِّ شَيْطٰنٍ رَّجِيْمٍ ۝

18. But any that gains a hearing[1953]
By stealth, is pursued
By a flaming fire, bright (to see).[1954]

١٨- اِلَّا مَنِ اسْتَرَقَ السَّمْعَ
فَاَتْبَعَهٗ شِهَابٌ مُّبِيْنٌ ۝

19. And the earth We have
spread out[1955]
(Like a carpet); set thereon
Mountains firm and immovable ;
And produced therein all kinds
Of things in due balance.[1956]

١٩- وَالْاَرْضَ مَدَدْنٰهَا
وَاَلْقَيْنَا فِيْهَا رَوَاسِيَ
وَاَنْۢبَتْنَا فِيْهَا مِنْ كُلِّ شَيْءٍ مَّوْزُوْنٍ ۝

20. And We have provided therein
Means of subsistence,—for you
And for those for whose sustenance
Ye are not responsible.[1957]

٢٠- وَجَعَلْنَا لَكُمْ فِيْهَا مَعَايِشَ
وَمَنْ لَّسْتُمْ لَهٗ بِرٰزِقِيْنَ ۝

21. And there is not a thing
But its (sources and) treasures[1958]

٢١- وَاِنْ مِّنْ شَيْءٍ اِلَّا عِنْدَنَا خَزَآئِنُهٗ

1952. *Rajīm*: driven away with stones, rejected, accursed. *Cf.* iii. 36.

1953. Spiritually speaking, order, beauty, harmony, light, and truth are repugnant to evil. It deliberately rejects them when offered freely as God's gifts. But its crooked nature loves to gain access by fraud or stealth. Its malevolent curiosity impels it to gain by stealth a sound of that harmony of which it is itself a negation. And its punishment is a flashing light, in itself most uncongenial to the powers of darkness, which are a negation of light. Notice that in the allegory the objective of Evil was to steal a hearing of Music: its punishment is therefore different—a flaming light which it did not seek. For both celestial harmony and celestial light are repugnant to the spirit of evil.

1954. A shooting star appears to be meant. *Cf.* xxxvii. 10.

1955. Majesty, order, beauty, and harmony are shown in all God's Creation, but especially in the heavens. Coming nearer to man God's care for man and His goodness are shown (besides His other qualities) in His creation of the earth. In highly poetical language, the earth is described as spread out like a carpet, on which the eternal hills act as weights to keep it steady.

1956 And every kind of thing is produced on the earth in due balance and measure. The mineral kingdom supports the vegetable, and they in their turn support the animal, and there is a link of mutual dependence between them. Excess is eliminated. The waste of one is made the food of another, and *vice versa*. And this in an infinite chain of gradation and inter-dependence.

1957. See last note. 'We provide sustenance of every kind, physical, mental, spiritual, etc., for you, (*i.e.*, for mankind). But We do more. We provide for everyone of Our creatures. And there are those of which mankind is not even cognisant. We provide for them also. There are those who may at first sight appear hostile to man, or whom man may consider hostile, such as wild and noxious animals. They are Our creatures, and We provide for them also, as they are Our creatures. But there is due order and balance in the economy of Our universal Plan.'

1958. *Khazāin*: treasures; store-houses; places where valuable things are accumulated, from which supplies are distributed from time to time as need arises.

(Inexhaustible) are with Us;
But We only send down
Thereof in due and ascertainable
measures.[1959]

وَمَا نُنَزِّلُهٗٓ
اِلَّا بِقَدَرٍ مَّعْلُوْمٍ ○

22. And We send the fecundating[1960]
winds,
Then cause the rain to descend
From the sky, therewith providing
You with water (in abundance),
Though ye are not the guardians[1961]
Of its stores.[1962]

٢٢- وَاَرْسَلْنَا الرِّيٰحَ لَوَاقِحَ
فَاَنْزَلْنَا مِنَ السَّمَآءِ مَآءً
فَاَسْقَيْنٰكُمُوْهُ
وَمَآ اَنْتُمْ لَهٗ بِخٰزِنِيْنَ ○

23. And verily, it is We
Who give life, and Who give[1963]
Death: it is We Who remain
Inheritors[1964]
(After all else passes away).

٢٣- وَاِنَّا لَنَحْنُ نُحْيٖ
وَنُمِيْتُ
وَنَحْنُ الْوٰرِثُوْنَ ○

1959. All the wonderful gifts and forces and energies which we see in the world around us have their sources and fountain-heads with God, the Creator and Sustainer of the Worlds. And what we see or perceive or imagine is just a small portion of what exists. That portion is sent out to us and to our world according to our needs or its needs from time to time as the occasion arises It is strictly limited according to rule and plan. Its source is unlimited and inexhaustible. In the same way the forces which we see operating around us, in nature or in the spiritual world, according to laws which we can grasp and ascertain, are mere derived forces, in the 2nd, 3rd, or *n*th degree. Their source and ultimate fountain head is with God.

1960. *Lawāqiḥ*, plural of *lāqiḥ*, from *laqaḥa*, to impregnate or fecundate the female date-palm by putting the pollen of the male tree on to the ovaries of the female tree. The date palm is uni sexual. The wind performs this office for many flowers. Here, by a bold metaphor, its fecundating quality is transferred to the clouds, which by means of rain produce all kinds of fruit, grain, and vegetation. The clouds as vapour are manipulated by the winds, which set up atmospheric currents resulting in condensation and the descent of rain. Note the appropriateness of the little particle "then", showing the connection of winds with rain.

1961. *Cf.* the previous verse, and n. 1958 Man may store water in cisterns, tanks, lakes, and head-waters of canals. But he has no control over its original sources, which are the clouds, which by the help of the winds, act as the grand distributors of water over wide spaces of the world's surface.

1962. This verse must be understood as furnishing an example of illustration of what is said in the last verse.

1963. Note how the argument has mounted up from xv. 16 onwards to xv. 23—from things most remote from man to things touching his inmost being, and each of them in its own way is a wonderful instance of God's glory and goodness, and the beauty, order, and harmony of His creation. First, the heavens, the zodiacal Signs, the stars, and the mysterious phenomena that we see above us; then the earth, and the perfect balance of life and forces therein, with man as an important factor, but not the only factor; then, the inexhaustible sources of energy, of which God alone is the fountain-head, but which come to us in measured proportions, as needed; and lastly, Life and Death itself, which will pass away but God will remain. A noble passage, and a fine vindication of God's wisdom and providence in dealing with His creatures.

1964. Literally, "We are the Heirs, or Inheritors." *Cf.* iii, 180: "To God belongs the heritage of the heavens and the earth." See also the latter part of n. 988 to vi. 165.

24. To Us are known those of you
Who hasten forward, and those
Who lag behind.[1965]

٢٤- وَلَقَدْ عَلِمْنَا الْمُسْتَقْدِمِينَ مِنكُمْ
وَلَقَدْ عَلِمْنَا الْمُسْتَأْخِرِينَ ۝

25. Assuredly it is thy Lord
Who will gather them together:
For He is Perfect in Wisdom
And Knowledge.

٢٥- وَإِنَّ رَبَّكَ هُوَ يَحْشُرُهُمْ
إِنَّهُ حَكِيمٌ عَلِيمٌ ۝

C. 120.—Man's origin was from dust, lowly;
(xv. 26-50.) But his rank was raised above that
Of other creatures because God breathed
Into him His spirit. Jealousy and arrogance
Caused the fall of Iblīs, the power of Evil:
But no power has Evil o'er those sincere
Souls who worship God and seek His Way.
Many are the gates of Evil, but Peace
And dignified joy will be the goal
Of those whom the Grace of God has made His own.

Section 3.

26. We created man from sounding clay,[1966]
From mud moulded into shape;

٢٦- وَلَقَدْ خَلَقْنَا الْإِنسَانَ مِن صَلْصَالٍ
مِّنْ حَمَإٍ مَّسْنُونٍ ۝

27. And the Jinn race, We had
Created before, from the fire
Of a scorching wind.[1967]

٢٧- وَالْجَانَّ خَلَقْنَاهُ مِن قَبْلُ مِن
نَّارِ السَّمُومِ ۝

28. Behold! thy Lord said
To the angels: "I am about
To create man, from sounding clay
From mud moulded into shape;

٢٨- وَإِذْ قَالَ رَبُّكَ لِلْمَلَٰئِكَةِ إِنِّي خَالِقٌ
بَشَرًا مِّن صَلْصَالٍ مِّنْ حَمَإٍ مَّسْنُونٍ ۝

1965. *Cf.* ix. 100, where the *Sābiqūn* may perhaps correspond to the *Mustaqdimīn* here. In that case the two classes are those who are the first to accept Faith and do deeds of righteousness and those who come later, but are still numbered with the righteous. A second alternative meaning may be: "those who preceded you in point of time and those who come after you in point of time; they are all known to God, and He will gather them all together on the Day of Judgment."

1966. *Ṣalṣāl*: dry clay which produces a sound, like pottery. *Cf.* lv. 14. Taking verses 26 and 29 together, I understand the meaning to be: that man's body was formed from wet clay moulded into shape and then dried until it could emit sound (perhaps referring to speech); that it was then further fashioned and completed; that into the animal form thus fashioned was breathed the spirit of God, which gave it a superiority over other Creation: and that the order for obeisance was then given.

1967. *Cf.* vi. 100, and n. 929. Hidden or invisible forces are aptly typified as arising "from the fire of scorching winds."

29. " When I have fashioned him
(In due proportion) and breathed
Into him of My spirit,
Fall ye down in obeisance
Unto him."[1968]

٢٩-فَإِذَا سَوَّيْتُهُ
وَنَفَخْتُ فِيهِ مِن رُّوحِي
فَقَعُوا لَهُ سَاجِدِينَ ۝

30. So the angels prostrated themselves,
All of them together :

٣٠-فَسَجَدَ الْمَلَائِكَةُ كُلُّهُمْ أَجْمَعُونَ ۝

31. Not so[1969] Iblis :[1970] he refused to be
Among those who prostrated
themselves.[1371]

٣١-إِلَّا إِبْلِيسَ
أَبَىٰ أَن يَكُونَ مَعَ السَّاجِدِينَ ۝

32. (God) said : " O Iblis !
What is your reason
For not being among those
Who prostrated themselves ? "

٣٢-قَالَ يَا إِبْلِيسُ مَا لَكَ
أَلَّا تَكُونَ مَعَ السَّاجِدِينَ ۝

33. (Iblis) said : " I am not one
To prostrate myself to man,
Whom Thou didst create
From sounding clay, from mud
Moulded into shape."

٣٣-قَالَ لَمْ أَكُن لِّأَسْجُدَ لِبَشَرٍ
خَلَقْتَهُ مِن صَلْصَالٍ
مِّنْ حَمَإٍ مَّسْنُونٍ ۝

34. (God) said : " Then get thee out
From here ; for thou art
Rejected, accursed.

٣٤-قَالَ فَاخْرُجْ مِنْهَا
فَإِنَّكَ رَجِيمٌ ۝

35. " And the Curse shall be
On thee till the Day of
Judgment."[1972]

٣٥-وَإِنَّ عَلَيْكَ اللَّعْنَةَ إِلَىٰ يَوْمِ الدِّينِ ۝

1968. Among other passages where the creation of Adam is referred to, *cf.* the following : ii 30-39 ; vii. 11-25. Note that here the emphasis is on three points : (1) the breathing of God's spirit into man *i.e.*, the faculty of God-like knowledge and will, which, if rightly used, would give man superiority over other creatures ; (2) the origin of evil in arrogance and jealousy on the part of Satan, who saw only the lower side of man (his clay) and failed to see the higher side, the faculty brought in by the spirit of God ; (3) that this evil only touches those who yield to it, and has no power over God's sincere servants, purified by His grace (xv. 40, 42). Adam is not here mentioned by name, but only Man, whose symbol is Adam.

1969 *Cf.* n. 49 to ii. 34.

1970. Iblis : the name has in it the root-idea of desperateness or rebellion. *Cf.* n. 52 to ii. 36.

1971. Apparently Iblis's arrogance had two grounds : (1) that man was made of clay while he was made of fire ; (2) that he did not wish to do what others did. Both grounds were false : (1) because man had the spirit of God breathed into him ; (2) because contempt of the angels who obeyed God's word showed not Iblis's superiority but his inferiority. The word "*boshar*" for man (verse 33) suggests a gross physical body.

1972. After the Day of Judgment the whole constitution of the universe will be different. There will be a new world altogether, on a wholly different plane. (*Cf.* xxi. 104.)

36. (Iblis) said: "O my Lord!
Give me then respite [1973]
Till the Day
The (dead) are raised."

٣٦- قَالَ رَبِّ فَأَنْظِرْنِيٓ
إِلَىٰ يَوْمِ يُبْعَثُونَ ۝

37. (God) said: "Respite
Is granted thee—

٣٧- قَالَ فَإِنَّكَ مِنَ الْمُنْظَرِينَ ۝

38. "Till the Day
Of the Time Appointed."

٣٨- إِلَىٰ يَوْمِ الْوَقْتِ الْمَعْلُومِ ۝

39. (Iblis) said: "O my Lord!
Because Thou hast put me [1974]
In the wrong, I will
Make (wrong) fair-seeming
To them on the earth,
And I will put them [1975]
All in the wrong,—

٣٩- قَالَ رَبِّ بِمَآ أَغْوَيْتَنِي
لَأُزَيِّنَنَّ لَهُمْ فِي الْأَرْضِ
وَلَأُغْوِيَنَّهُمْ أَجْمَعِينَ ۝

40. "Except Thy servants among them,
Sincere and purified
(By Thy grace)."

٤٠- إِلَّا عِبَادَكَ مِنْهُمُ الْمُخْلَصِينَ ۝

41. (God) said: "This (Way
Of My sincere servants) is
Indeed a Way that leads
Straight to Me.[1976]

٤١- قَالَ هَٰذَا
صِرَاطٌ عَلَيَّ مُسْتَقِيمٌ ۝

1973. What was this respite? The curse on Iblis remained, *i.e.*, he was deprived of God's grace and became in the spiritual world what an outlaw is in a political kingdom. An earthly kingdom may not be able to catch and destroy an outlaw. But God is Omnipotent, and such power as Iblis may have can only come through the respite granted by God. The respite then is what is expressed in xv. 39 below. In God's grant of limited free-will to man is implied the faculty of choosing between good and evil, and the faculty is exercised through the temptations and allurements put forward by Satan, "the open enemy" of man. This is for the period of man's probation on this earth. Even so, no temptations have power over the sincere worshippers of God, who are purified by His grace.

1974. *Agwaitanī*: 'thrown me out of the way, put me in the wrong': *Cf.* vii. 16. Satan as the Power of Evil cannot be straight or truthful even before God. By his own arrogance and rebellion he fell; he attributes this to God. Between God's righteous judgment and Satan's snares and temptations there cannot be the remotest comparison. Yet he presumes to put them on an equal footing. He is taking advantage of the respite.

1975. Iblis (the Rebellious) is powerless against God. He turns therefore against man and becomes Satan (the Enemy).

1976. To be sincere in the worship of God is to obtain purification from all stain of evil and exemption from all influence of evil. It changes the whole nature of man. After that, evil cannot touch him. Evil will acknowledge him to be beyond its power and will not even tempt him. Apart from such purified souls, everyone who worships God invites God's grace to protect him. But if he puts himself in the way of wrong and deliberately chooses evil, he must take the consequences. The blame is not even on Satan, the power of evil: it is on the sinner himself, who puts himself into his power; xiv. 22: xv. 42.

42. "For over My servants
No authority shalt thou
Have, except such as
Put themselves in the wrong
And follow thee."

۴۲-إِنَّ عِبَادِي لَيْسَ لَكَ عَلَيْهِمْ سُلْطَانٌ
إِلَّا مَنِ اتَّبَعَكَ مِنَ الْغَاوِينَ ○

43. And verily, Hell
Is the promised abode
For them all!

۴۳-وَإِنَّ جَهَنَّمَ
لَمَوْعِدُهُمْ أَجْمَعِينَ ○

44. To it are seven Gates:[1977]
For each of those Gates
Is a (special) class
(Of sinners) assigned.

۴۴-لَهَا سَبْعَةُ أَبْوَابٍ
لِكُلِّ بَابٍ مِنْهُمْ جُزْءٌ مَقْسُومٌ ○

SECTION 4.

45. The righteous (will be)
Amid Gardens
And fountains
(Of clear-flowing water).

۴۵-إِنَّ الْمُتَّقِينَ فِي جَنَّاتٍ
وَعُيُونٍ ○

46. (Their greeting will be):
"Enter ye here
In Peace and Security."

۴۶-ادْخُلُوهَا بِسَلَامٍ آمِنِينَ ○

47. And We shall remove
From their hearts any
Lurking sense of injury:[1978]
(They will be) brothers
(Joyfully) facing each other
On thrones (of dignity).

۴۷-وَنَزَعْنَا مَا فِي صُدُورِهِمْ
مِنْ غِلٍّ
إِخْوَانًا عَلَىٰ سُرُرٍ مُتَقَابِلِينَ ○

48. There no sense of fatigue
Shall touch them,
Nor shall they (ever)
Be asked to leave.

۴۸-لَا يَمَسُّهُمْ فِيهَا نَصَبٌ
وَمَا هُمْ مِنْهَا بِمُخْرَجِينَ ○

1977. Seven is a mystic number. The ways of sin are numerous, and if they are classified into seven, each of them points to a Gate that leads to Hell.

Apart from the literal meaning, which is itself based on metaphors, the whole of this section and indeed of this Sūra, is full of mystic meaning, which it is outside the power or scope or limits of a running Commentary to expound adequately.

1978. *Cf.* vii. 43, and n. 1021. The hearts and minds will be so purified that all past rancour, jealousy, or sense of injury will be obliterated. The true Brotherhood will be realised there, when each will have his own dignity; there will be no question of invidious comparisons; each will face the others with joy and confidence. There will be no sense of toil or fatigue, and the joy will last for ever.

49. Tell My servants[1979]
That I am indeed
The Oft-Forgiving,
Most Merciful;

٤٩- نَبِّئْ عِبَادِيٓ
أَنِّيٓ أَنَا الْغَفُورُ الرَّحِيمُ ○

50. And that My Penalty
Will be indeed
The most grievous Penalty.

٥٠- وَأَنَّ عَذَابِي هُوَ الْعَذَابُ الْأَلِيمُ ○

C. 121.—God's Grace and Mercy are always
(xv. 51-84.) First, but His Justice and Wrath will seize
Those who defy His Law. Even when
The unspeakable crimes of the Cities
Of the Plain made their destruction
Inevitable, God's message of Mercy
To mankind was sent to Abraham
And of safety to Lot. The last remnants
Of sin will be cut off, and the Signs
And Tokens thereof are plain for all
To see. The proud Companions of the Wood
And the builders of Rocky Fortresses
Were all swept away because of their sins.

51. Tell them about
The guests of Abraham.[1980]

٥١- وَنَبِّئْهُمْ عَن ضَيْفِ إِبْرٰهِيمَ ○ وقف لازم

52. When they entered his presence
And said, "Peace!"
He said, "We feel
Afraid of you!"[1981]

٥٢- إِذْ دَخَلُوا عَلَيْهِ فَقَالُوا سَلٰمًا ط
قَالَ إِنَّا مِنكُمْ وَجِلُونَ ○

53. They said: "Fear not!
We give thee glad tidings

٥٣- قَالُوا لَا تَوْجَلْ إِنَّا نُبَشِّرُكَ

1979. We must realise both sides of God's attributes: His mercy, grace, and forgiveness are unbounded; if we reject all this, His justice and punishment will also be beyond all that we can conceive.

1980. In illustration of the contrasts between Good and Evil, and the consequences that flow from them, we have now a reference to four incidents from the past, *viz.*: (1) an incident from the story of Abraham; (2) from that of Lot, nephew of Abraham, and the end of the Cities of the Plain, which he was sent to warn; (3) the People of the Wood; and (4) the People of the Rocky Tract (*Ḥijr*), after whom this Sūra is called. As usual, the recital of God's abounding grace comes first.

1981. For a full understanding of this reference to the angels who were Abraham's guests and came to announce the birth of a son to him in his old age, read xi. 69-73 and notes. The appearance of two strangers of uncommon appearance, who refused to partake of the host's sumptuous hospitality, made Abraham at first suspicious and afraid.

Of a son endowed
With wisdom."[1982]

بِغُلٰمٍ عَلِيْمٍ ○

54. He said: "Do ye give me
Glad tidings that old age
Has seized me? Of what,
Then, is your good news?"

٥٤- قَالَ اَبَشَّرْتُمُوْنِيْ عَلٰۤى اَنْ مَّسَّنِيَ الْكِبَرُ
فَبِمَ تُبَشِّرُوْنَ ○

55. They said: "We give thee
Glad tidings in truth:
Be not then in despair!"

٥٥- قَالُوْا بَشَّرْنٰكَ بِالْحَقِّ
فَلَا تَكُنْ مِّنَ الْقٰنِطِيْنَ ○

56. He said: "And who
Despairs of the mercy
Of his Lord, but such
As go astray?"[1983]

٥٦- قَالَ وَمَنْ يَّقْنَطُ مِنْ رَّحْمَةِ رَبِّهٖۤ
اِلَّا الضَّآلُّوْنَ ○

57. Abraham said:[1984] "What then
Is the business on which
Ye (have come), O ye
Messengers (of God)?"

٥٧- قَالَ فَمَا خَطْبُكُمْ
اَيُّهَا الْمُرْسَلُوْنَ ○

58. They said: "We have been
Sent to a people
(Deep) in sin,[1985]

٥٨- قَالُوْۤا اِنَّاۤ اُرْسِلْنَاۤ اِلٰى قَوْمٍ
مُّجْرِمِيْنَ ○

59. "Excepting the adherents
Of Lūṭ: them we are certainly

٥٩- اِلَّاۤ اٰلَ لُوْطٍ اِنَّا

1982. The birth of a son in old age to a sonless father was glad tidings to Abraham personally. The birth of a son endowed with wisdom promised something infinitely more. Considering that the angels were divine messengers, the wisdom referred to was divine wisdom, and the event became an event of prime importance in the world's religious history. For Abraham became, through his progeny, the root of the three great universal religions diffused throughout the world.

1983. Notice the gentle humour in the slight misunderstandings, which are no sooner expressed than they are removed.

1984. When cordial understanding was established between Abraham and his guests, and probably when the guests were about to depart, Abraham put a question to them: "What is the mission on which you are going?" It was further implied: "Is there anything I can do to help?" But no. The mission was one of Punishment for abominable sins. Note that the mention of God's Wrath is always linked with that of God's Mercy, and the Mercy comes first. The same angels that came to punish Sodom and Gomorrah were charged first to give the good news of God's Mercy to Abraham in the shape of a long line of Teachers of Righteousness.

1985. The Cities of the Plain round the Dead Sea, which to this day is called the Bahr Lūt. They were given to unspeakable abominations. Read in this connection xi. 77-83 and notes.

(Charged) to save (from harm),—[1986]
All—

لَمُنَجُّوهُمْ أَجْمَعِينَ ۝

60. " Except his wife, who,
We have ascertained,
Will be among those
Who will lag behind." [1987]

٦٠- إِلَّا امْرَأَتَهُ قَدَّرْنَا
إِنَّهَا لَمِنَ الْغَابِرِينَ ۝

ع

SECTION 5.

61. At length when the messengers
Arrived among the adherents [1988]
Of Lūt,

٦١- فَلَمَّا جَاءَ آلَ لُوطٍ الْمُرْسَلُونَ ۝

62. He said: " Ye appear
To be uncommon folk."

٦٢- قَالَ إِنَّكُمْ قَوْمٌ مُنْكَرُونَ ۝

63. They said: " Yea,
We have come to thee
To accomplish that
Of which they doubt.[1989]

٦٣- قَالُوا بَلْ جِئْنَاكَ
بِمَا كَانُوا فِيهِ يَمْتَرُونَ ۝

64. " We have brought to thee
That which is inevitably [1990]
Due, and assuredly
We tell the truth.

٦٤- وَأَتَيْنَاكَ بِالْحَقِّ
وَإِنَّا لَصَادِقُونَ ۝

65. " Then travel by night
With thy household,
When a portion of the night
(Yet remains), and do thou

٦٥- فَأَسْرِ بِأَهْلِكَ
بِقِطْعٍ مِنَ اللَّيْلِ

1986. Here, again, God's saving Grace is linked with His Wrath, and is mentioned first

1987. See xi. 81, and n. 1577.

1988. *Āl* means people who adhere to the ways and teaching of a great Teacher; *e.g.*, *Āl-i-Muhammadī*: it does not necessarily mean race or descendants. *Ahl* (xv. 65 below) usually implies "household" but may be taken in an extended sense to include People generally: see xv. 67. *Qaum* (xv. 62) may be any collection or aggregate of people. In xi. 70 the hostile inhabitants of the Cities of the Plain are called the *qaum-i-Lūṭ* (the People of Lūṭ). *Aṣḥāb* (companions) refers to a Group rather than to a People: *Cf.* xv. 78

1989. The unusual appearance of the angels struck Lot as it had struck Abraham. Knowing the abominable vices to which the Cities were addicted, he feared to entertain handsome young men They at once disclosed their mission to him in mystic language. In effect they said: "You, Lot, have been preaching in vain to these wicked Cities. When you warn them of their inevitable end, Destruction, they laugh and doubt. Now their doubt will be resolved. Their destruction will be accomplished before the morning."

1990. Another meaning of *Al-Ḥaqq*: the Punishment which is justly and inevitably due, which must certainly come to pass. *Cf.* xxii. 18.

Bring up the rear :
Let no one amongst you
Look back, but pass on
Whither ye are ordered."

وَاتَّبِعْ أَدْبَارَهُمْ وَلَا يَلْتَفِتْ مِنكُمْ أَحَدٌ
وَامْضُوا حَيْثُ تُؤْمَرُونَ ○

66. And We made known
This decree to him,
That the last remnants
Of those (sinners) should be
Cut off by the morning.[1991]

٦٦- وَقَضَيْنَآ إِلَيْهِ ذَٰلِكَ الْأَمْرَ
أَنَّ دَابِرَ هَٰٓؤُلَآءِ مَقْطُوعٌ مُّصْبِحِينَ ○

67. The inhabitants of the City
Came in (mad) joy
(At news of the young men).[1992]

٦٧- وَجَآءَ أَهْلُ الْمَدِينَةِ يَسْتَبْشِرُونَ ○

68. Lūṭ said : " These are
My guests : disgrace me not :

٦٨- قَالَ إِنَّ هَٰٓؤُلَآءِ ضَيْفِى فَلَا تَفْضَحُونِ ○

69. " But fear God,
And shame me not."

٦٩- وَاتَّقُوا اللَّهَ وَلَا تُخْزُونِ ○

70. They said : " Did we not
Forbid thee (to speak)
For all and sundry ? "[1993]

٧٠- قَالُوٓا أَوَلَمْ نَنْهَكَ عَنِ الْعَٰلَمِينَ ○

71. He said : " There are
My daughters (to marry),
If ye must act (so)."[1994]

٧١- قَالَ هَٰٓؤُلَآءِ بَنَاتِىٓ إِن كُنتُمْ فَٰعِلِينَ ○

72. Verily, by thy life (O Prophet),
In their wild intoxication,

٧٢- لَعَمْرُكَ إِنَّهُمْ لَفِى سَكْرَتِهِمْ

1991. As the last remnants of the wicked were to be cut off, and as the Mercy of God wished to save every true soul who might be with Lot, God's decree was made known to Lot, so that he might save his adherents.

1992. They were addicted to unnatural crime, and the news of the advent of handsome young men inflamed them. How true it is that at the very verge of destruction, men rush blindly to their fate, and cut off any last hope of repentance and mercy for themselves. *Cf.* xv. 72 below.

1993. I understand the meaning to be that Lot, the only righteous man in the City, had frequently remonstrated with the inhabitants against their unnatural crimes, and they had forbidden him to speak to them again on behalf of any one, "as if" (they might tauntingly say) "he was the protector of all and sundry".

Some Commentators understand the verse to mean : 'Did we not forbid thee to entertain any strangers ?'

1994. *Cf.* xi. 78, n. 1575. "My daughters" in the mouth of a venerable man may mean young girls of the City, which would be appropriate considering the large number of men who came to besiege Lot's house.

They wander in distraction,
To and fro.[1995]

يَعۡمَهُونَ ○

73. But the (mighty) Blast[1996]
Overtook them before morning;

٧٣- فَأَخَذَتۡهُمُ ٱلصَّيۡحَةُ مُشۡرِقِينَ ○

74. And We turned (the Cities)
Upside down, and rained down
On them brimstones
Hard as baked clay.[1997]

٧٤- فَجَعَلۡنَا عَٰلِيَهَا سَافِلَهَا وَأَمۡطَرۡنَا
عَلَيۡهِمۡ حِجَارَةً مِّن سِجِّيلٍ ○

75. Behold! in this are Signs
For those who by tokens
Do understand.

٧٥- إِنَّ فِي ذَٰلِكَ لَأٓيَٰتٖ لِّلۡمُتَوَسِّمِينَ ○

76. And the (Cities were)
Right on the high-road.[1998]

٧٦- وَإِنَّهَا لَبِسَبِيلٖ مُّقِيمٍ ○

77. Behold! in this
Is a Sign
For those who believe![1999]

٧٧- إِنَّ فِي ذَٰلِكَ لَأٓيَةٗ لِّلۡمُؤۡمِنِينَ ○

78. And the Companions of the Wood[2000]
Were also wrong-doers;

٧٨- وَإِن كَانَ أَصۡحَٰبُ ٱلۡأَيۡكَةِ لَظَٰلِمِينَ ○

1995. The wild, mad fury of passion and sin attains its own destruction and cuts off the last hope of repentance or mercy.

1996. *Aṣ-Ṣaiḥat*, the mighty Blast, is mentioned as accompanying earthquakes: *Cf.* xi. 67. 94. Here it was the violent wind and noise accompanying the shower of brimstones, possibly with some volcanic action.

1997. *Cf.* xi. 82 and notes, in which the word *Sijjīl* and its origin are explained.

1998. The Cities of Sodom and Gomorrah were utterly destroyed, and even their precise position cannot be identified. But the brimstone plain of the tract still exists, right on the highway between Arabia and Syria. To the traveller in the neighbourhood of the Dead Sea the whole locality presents a scene of dismal desolation which truly suggests the awful punishment for unspeakable crimes.

1999. Verse 75 refers to all who have the intelligence to grasp the Signs of God. Verses 76-77 specially refer to those who use the Arabia-Syria highroad. The desolation is specially brought home to them.

2000. "Companions of the Wood": *Aṣ-ḥāb ul Aikati.* Perhaps *Aika* is after all a proper noun, the name of a town or tract. Who were the Companions of the Aika? They are mentioned four times in the Qur-ān, *viz.*, here, and in xxvi. 176-191; xxxviii. 13; and *l.* 14. The only passage in which any details are given is xxvi. 176-191. There we are told that their Prophet was Shu'aib, and other details given correspond to those of the Madyan, to whom Shu'aib was sent as Apostle: see vii. 85-93. In my notes to that passage I have discussed the question of Shu'aib and the Madyan people. It is reasonable to suppose that the Companions of the Wood were either the same as the Madyan, or a Group among them or in their neighbourhood.

79. So We exacted retribution
From them. They were both[2001]
On an open highway,
Plain to see.

٧٩- فَانْتَقَمْنَا مِنْهُمْ ۘ
وَإِنَّهُمَا لَبِإِمَامٍ مُّبِينٍ ۝

SECTION 6.

80. The Companions of the Rocky
Tract[2002]
Also rejected the apostles:

٨٠- وَلَقَدْ كَذَّبَ أَصْحٰبُ الْحِجْرِ الْمُرْسَلِيْنَ ۝

81. We sent them Our Signs,
But they persisted
In turning away from them.

٨١- وَاٰتَيْنٰهُمْ اٰيٰتِنَا
فَكَانُوْا عَنْهَا مُعْرِضِيْنَ ۝

82. Out of the mountains[2003]
Did they hew (their) edifices,
(Feeling themselves) secure.

٨٢- وَكَانُوْا يَنْحِتُوْنَ مِنَ الْجِبَالِ بُيُوْتًا
اٰمِنِيْنَ ۝

83. But the (mighty) Blast[2004]
Seized them of a morning,

٨٣- فَاَخَذَتْهُمُ الصَّيْحَةُ مُصْبِحِيْنَ ۝

84. And of no avail to them
Was all that they did
(With such art and care)!

٨٤- فَمَآ اَغْنٰى عَنْهُمْ مَّا كَانُوْا يَكْسِبُوْنَ ۝

C. 122.—But God's Creation doth bear witness
(xv. 85-99.) To God's Design and Mercy. His Plan
Is sure. His gift of the glorious Qur-ān
Is more than any worldly goods can be.
So, while we denounce Sin openly,
Let us be gentle and kind, and adore
And serve our Lord all our lives

85. We created not the heavens,
The earth, and all between them,

٨٥- وَمَا خَلَقْنَا السَّمٰوٰتِ وَالْاَرْضَ وَمَا بَيْنَهُمَآ

2001. Both: *i.e.*, The Cities of the Plain and the Companions of the Aika.

2002. "The Rocky Tract" is undoubtedly a geographical name. On the maps of Arabia will be found a tract called the *Ḥijr*, north of Medina. Jabal *Ḥijr* is about 150 miles north of Medina. The tract would fall on the highway to Syria. This was the country of the Thamūd. For them and the country see vii. 73, n. 1043.

2003. Remains of these rock edifices in the *Ḥijr* are still found, and the City of Petra is not more than 380 miles from Jabal *Ḥijr*. See n. 1043 to vii. 73. "Petra" in Greek means "Rock". For the Inscriptions found there, and their significance, see Appendix IX to S. xxvi.

2004. The mighty rumbling noise and wind accompanying an earthquake. See vii. 78, n. 1047.

But for just ends.[2005]
And the Hour is surely
Coming (when this will be manifest).
So overlook (any human faults)
With gracious forgiveness.[2006]

إِلَّا بِالْحَقِّ
وَإِنَّ السَّاعَةَ لَآتِيَةٌ
فَاصْفَحِ الصَّفْحَ الْجَمِيلَ ○

86. For verily it is thy Lord
Who is the Master-Creator,[2007]
Knowing all things.

٨٦- إِنَّ رَبَّكَ هُوَ الْخَلَّاقُ الْعَلِيمُ ○

87. And We have bestowed
Upon thee the Seven
Oft-repeated (Verses)[2008]
And the Grand Qur-ān.

٨٧- وَلَقَدْ آتَيْنَاكَ سَبْعًا
مِّنَ الْمَثَانِي وَالْقُرْآنَ الْعَظِيمَ ○

88. Strain not thine eyes.
(Wistfully) at what We
Have bestowed on certain
classes[2009]
Of them, nor grieve over them:[2010]

٨٨- لَا تَمُدَّنَّ عَيْنَيْكَ
إِلَىٰ مَا مَتَّعْنَا بِهِ أَزْوَاجًا مِّنْهُمْ
وَلَا تَحْزَنْ عَلَيْهِمْ

2005. God's Creation is all for a true, just, and righteous purpose. *Cf.* x. 5. It is not for mere whim or sport: xxi. 16.

2006. The Hour will not be long delayed when the true Design and Pattern of Life will be manifest. We must not be impatient, if there appear to be, to our limited vision, apparent injustices. We must bear and forbear, and as far as our own personal feelings are concerned, we must overlook other people's faults with "a gracious forgiveness".

2007. *Khallāq*: the emphatic intensive form, as meaning the Creator, Who is perfect in His skill and knowledge, and Whose creation answers perfectly to His design. Therefore no one should think that anything has gone wrong in God's creation. What may seem out of joint is merely the result of our short-sighted standards. It often happens that what appears to us to be evil or imperfect or unjust is a reflection of our own imperfect minds. See the next two verses and notes.

2008. The Seven Oft-repeated Verses are usually understood to be the Opening Sūra, the *Fātiḥa*. They sum up the whole teaching of the Qur-an. What can be a more precious gift to a Muslim than the glorious Qur-ān or any Sūra of it? Worldly wealth, honour, possessions, or anything else, sinks into insignificance in comparison with it.

2009. It may be that other people have worldly goods which worldly men envy. Do they necessarily bring happiness? Even the temporary pleasure that they may give is not unmixed with spiritual poisons, and even so, will not last. The man of God looks with wistful eyes at other things,—the favour and countenance of God.

2010. The man of God, in his human love and sympathy, may grieve over certain classes of people who are puffed up with false notions and callous to the Message of God. But he should not make himself unhappy. There is no flaw in God's Plan, and it must prevail. This was addressed in the first instance to Mustafā, but in a minor degree, it applies to all righteous men.

But lower thy wing
(in gentleness)[2011]
To the Believers.

وَاخْفِضْ جَنَاحَكَ لِلْمُؤْمِنِينَ ○

89. And say : "I am indeed he
That warneth openly
And without ambiguity,"—[2012]

٨٩- وَقُلْ إِنِّيٓ أَنَا النَّذِيرُ الْمُبِينُ ○

90. (Of just such wrath)
As We sent down
On those who divided
(Scripture into arbitrary parts),—[2013]

٩٠- كَمَآ أَنزَلْنَا
عَلَى الْمُقْتَسِمِينَ ○

91. (So also on such)
As have made Qur-ān
Into shreds (as they please).[2014]

٩١- الَّذِينَ جَعَلُوا الْقُرْءَانَ عِضِينَ ○

92. Therefore, by the Lord,
We will, of a surety,
Call them to account,

٩٢- فَوَرَبِّكَ لَنَسْـَٔلَنَّهُمْ أَجْمَعِينَ ○

93. For all their deeds.[2015]

٩٣- عَمَّا كَانُوا يَعْمَلُونَ ○ ع

94. Therefore expound openly
What thou art commanded,
And turn away from those
Who join false gods with God.

٩٤- فَاصْدَعْ بِمَا تُؤْمَرُ
وَأَعْرِضْ عَنِ الْمُشْرِكِينَ ○

95. For sufficient are We
Unto thee against those

٩٥- إِنَّا كَفَيْنَٰكَ

2011. The metaphor is from a bird who lowers her wing in tender solicitude for her little ones. *Cf.* xvii. 24, where it is applied to "lowering the wing" to aged parents.

2012. In the ministry of Muṣṭafā there was no mincing of matters, no compromises with evil. Evil was denounced in unambiguous terms. *Mubīn* implies both openness and clearness, *i.e.*, freedom from ambiguity.

2013. The Commentators differ as to the precise signification of verses 90 and 91. Are the persons referred to in the two verses the same, or different? And who were they? I adopt the view, for which there is good authority, that the two classes of persons were different but similar. Verse 90, I think, refers to the Jews and Christians, who took out of Scripture what suited them, and ignored or rejected the rest : ii. 85, 101. For verse 91 see next note.

2014. The Meccan Pagans, in the early days of Islam, in order to dishonour and ridicule the Qur-ān, divided what was so far revealed, into bits, and apportioned them to people coming on pilgrimage to Mecca by different routes, slandering and abusing the Apostle of God.

2015. Those who ridicule Scripture in any form will all be called to account for their insolence, for they are all alike.

Who scoff,—[2016]

الْمُسْتَهْزِءِيْنَ ۝

96. Those who adopt, with God,
Another god : but soon
Will they come to know.

٩٦-الَّذِيْنَ يَجْعَلُوْنَ مَعَ اللّٰهِ اِلٰهًا اٰخَرَ
فَسَوْفَ يَعْلَمُوْنَ ۝

97. We do indeed know
How thy heart is distressed [2017]
At what they say.

٩٧-وَلَقَدْ نَعْلَمُ اَنَّكَ يَضِيْقُ صَدْرُكَ
بِمَا يَقُوْلُوْنَ ۝

98. But celebrate the praises
Of thy Lord, and be of those
Who prostrate themselves
In adoration.

٩٨-فَسَبِّحْ بِحَمْدِ رَبِّكَ
وَكُنْ مِّنَ السّٰجِدِيْنَ ۝

99. And serve thy Lord
Until there come unto thee
The Hour that is Certain.[2018]

٩٩-وَاعْبُدْ رَبَّكَ
حَتّٰى يَاْتِيَكَ الْيَقِيْنُ ۝ ع

2016. If the whole world is ranged against the man of God, as was at one time the case with the Apostle, and scoffs at all that is sacred, the sense of God's presence and protection outweighs all. And after all, the scoffers are creatures of a day. Soon will they find their level, and be undeceived as to all their falsehoods. But the Truth of God endures for ever.

2017. Literally, 'that thy breast is constrained'.

2018. *Yaqīn* : Certainty ; the Hour that is Certain ; death.

INTRODUCTION TO SŪRA XVI (*Naḥl*)

Chronologically this Sūra, like the six which preceded it, belongs to the late Meccan period, except perhaps verse 110 and some of the verses that follow. But the chronology has no significance In subject-matter it sums up, from a new point of view, the arguments on the great questions of God's dealings with man, His Self-revelation to man, and how the Messengers and the Message are writ large in every phase of God's Creation and the life of Man. The new point of view is that Nature points to Nature's God.

Summary.—Everything in Creation proclaims the glory of God. To man is given dominion over Nature, that man may recognise God's Unity and God's Truth (xvi. 1-25, and C. 123).

Man should never lose sight of his goal, which is the Good, or dispute with the great Teachers, who are sent to all Peoples, to bring about Unity : all creatures serve God (xvi. 26-50, and C. 124).

God's favours and man's ingratitude recounted. His Signs in the rain-bearing clouds, the cattle that give milk, the bee that produces honey, the wonderful relations of family and social life, and the refinements and comforts of civilization (xvi. 51-83, and C. 125).

The Messengers of Truth will bear witness against those who reject the Truth. God will judge us according to our faith and deeds (xvi. 84-100, and C. 126).

The Qur-ān is true : it guides and gives glad tidings Believe, and make the most of Life in all things good and lawful. Follow the example of Abraham : be true in Faith and righteous, and do good (xvi. 101-128, and C. 127).

C. 123.—God's Command must inevitably
(xvi. 1-25.) Come to pass. But all His Creation
Proclaims His glory, and leads to His Truth.
In all things has He furnished man
With favours innumerable,
To lead and guide him and bring him
To Himself. Why then does man
Refuse the Truth, except for arrogance ?
Why does he run after false gods,
Thus acting against his own lights
And misleading others less blest in knowledge ?

Sūra XVI.

Naḥl or The Bee.

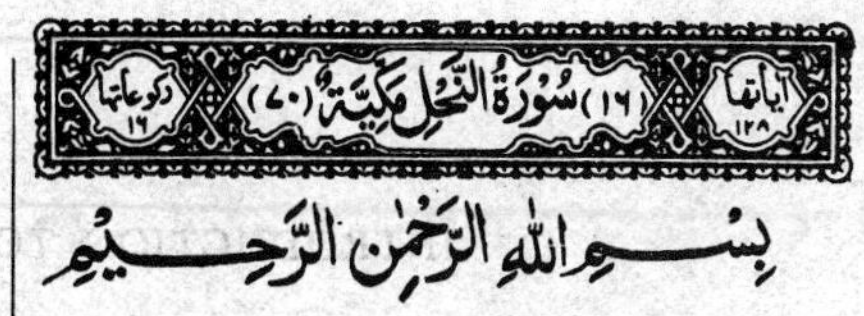

In the name of God Most Gracious, Most Merciful.

بِسْمِ اللّٰهِ الرَّحْمٰنِ الرَّحِيْمِ

1. (Inevitable) cometh (to pass)
The Command of God:[2019]
Seek ye not then
To hasten it: glory to Him,
And far is He above
Having the partners
They ascribe unto Him!

١- اَتٰۤى اَمْرُ اللّٰهِ
فَلَا تَسْتَعْجِلُوْهُ ؕ
سُبْحٰنَهٗ
وَتَعٰلٰى عَمَّا يُشْرِكُوْنَ ۝

2. He doth send down His angels
With inspiration of His Command,
To such of His servants
As He pleaseth, (saying):
"Warn (Man) that there is
No god but I: so do
Your duty unto Me."[2020]

٢- يُنَزِّلُ الْمَلٰۤئِكَةَ بِالرُّوْحِ مِنْ اَمْرِهٖ
عَلٰى مَنْ يَّشَآءُ مِنْ عِبَادِهٖۤ
اَنْ اَنْذِرُوْۤا اَنَّهٗ لَاۤ اِلٰهَ اِلَّاۤ
اَنَا فَاتَّقُوْنِ ۝

3. He has created the heavens
And the earth for just ends:[2021]
Far is He above having
The partners they ascribe to Him!

٣- خَلَقَ السَّمٰوٰتِ وَالْاَرْضَ بِالْحَقِّ ؕ
تَعٰلٰى عَمَّا يُشْرِكُوْنَ ۝

4. He has created man
From a sperm-drop;
And behold this same (man)
Becomes an open disputer![2022]

٤- خَلَقَ الْاِنْسَانَ مِنْ نُّطْفَةٍ
فَاِذَا هُوَ خَصِيْمٌ مُّبِيْنٌ ۝

2019. This is an answer to the taunt of the Pagans, who said: "If there is a god, the One True God, as you say, with unified control, why does He not punish the wrong-doers at once?" The answer is: "The decree of God will inevitably come to pass; it will come soon enough; when it comes, you will wish it were delayed; how foolish of you to wish even to cut off your last hope of forgiveness?"

2020. The Pagans, with their multiplicity of gods and goddesses, good and evil, could play one off against another. That is mere mockery of religion. With such conceptions, man cannot understand the Unity of Design in the Universe nor realise the Power and Glory of the One True God, to Whom alone worship and service are due.

2021. Not for sport, or fortuitously and without Design. *Cf.* xv. 85. Surely the Unity of Design in Creation also proves the Unity of God their Creator.

2022. Man's physical origin is lowly. Yet do men go back to material things, and neglect or dispute about the highest things in Life.

5. And cattle He has created[2023]
For you (men) : from them
Ye derive warmth,
And numerous benefits,[2024]
And of their (meat) ye eat.

٥- وَالْأَنْعَامَ خَلَقَهَا ۚ
لَكُمْ فِيهَا دِفْءٌ
وَمَنَافِعُ وَمِنْهَا تَأْكُلُونَ ۝

6. And ye have a sense
Of pride and beauty in them
As ye drive them home
In the evening, and as ye
Lead them forth to pasture
In the morning.[2025]

٦- وَلَكُمْ فِيهَا جَمَالٌ
حِينَ تُرِيحُونَ
وَحِينَ تَسْرَحُونَ ۝

7. And they carry your heavy loads
To lands that ye could not
(Otherwise) reach except with[2026]
Souls distressed : for your Lord
Is indeed Most Kind, Most Merciful

٧- وَتَحْمِلُ أَثْقَالَكُمْ إِلَىٰ بَلَدٍ لَّمْ تَكُونُوا
بَالِغِيهِ إِلَّا بِشِقِّ الْأَنفُسِ ۚ
إِنَّ رَبَّكُمْ لَرَءُوفٌ رَّحِيمٌ ۝

8. And (He has created) horses,
Mules, and donkeys, for you
To ride and use for show ;[2027]
And He has created (other) things
Of which ye have no knowledge.[2028]

٨- وَالْخَيْلَ وَالْبِغَالَ وَالْحَمِيرَ
لِتَرْكَبُوهَا وَزِينَةً ۚ
وَيَخْلُقُ مَا لَا تَعْلَمُونَ ۝

2023. Why will you go back to material things, considering that material things are made subservient to your use and enjoyment in various ways as suggested in the clauses that follow.

2024. From wool, and hair, and skins, and milk. Camel's hair makes warm robes and blankets ; and certain kinds of goats yield hair which makes similar fabrics. Sheep yield wool, and Llamas alpaca for similar uses. The skins and furs of many animals yield warm raiment or make warm rugs or bedding. The females of many of these animals yield good warm milk, a nourishing and wholesome diet. Then the flesh of many of these animals is good to eat. There are other uses, which the animals serve, and which are referred to later.

2025. The good man is proud of his cattle and is good to them. As they go to, and return from, pasture, morning and evening, he has a sense of his power and wealth and their beauty and docility. Will not man turn from these material facts to the great spiritual truths and purpose behind them ?

2026. The cattle and animals also carry loads, and thus make inter-communication between different lands easy. But for them there would have been many difficulties, not only physical, but psychological. Weary men carrying loads are in no mood for social and spiritual intercourse. This intercourse is made possible by the kindness and mercy of God.

2027. Horses, mules, and donkeys as well as other animals may be beasts of burden, but they may also be pedigree animals bred for beauty and for all those more refined uses, such as processions, in which grace and elegance is the predominant feature.

2028. If we examine the history of transport, there have been vast changes through the ages, from rude pack animals to fine equipages, and then through mechanical contrivances, such means of transport as elegant coaches, tramways and railways, useful motor lorries and Rolls-Royce cars, and air-ships and aeroplanes of all descriptions. At any given point of time, many of these were yet unknown to man. Nor can we suppose the limit to have been reached now or that it will ever be reached at any future time. Through the mind and ingenuity of man it is God that creates new things hitherto unknown to man.

9. And unto God leads straight[2029]
The Way, but there are ways
That turn aside : if God
Had willed, He could have
Guided all of you.

٩- وَعَلَى اللّٰهِ قَصْدُ السَّبِيْلِ
وَمِنْهَا جَآئِرٌ
وَلَوْ شَآءَ لَهَدٰىكُمْ اَجْمَعِيْنَ ○ ع

SECTION 2.

10. It is He Who sends down
Rain from the sky :
From it ye drink,
And out of it (grows)
The vegetation on which
Ye feed your cattle.

١٠- هُوَ الَّذِيْٓ اَنْزَلَ مِنَ السَّمَآءِ مَآءً
لَّكُمْ مِّنْهُ شَرَابٌ
وَّمِنْهُ شَجَرٌ فِيْهِ تُسِيْمُوْنَ ○

11. With it He produces
For you corn, olives,
Date-palms, grapes,
And every kind of fruit :
Verily in this is a Sign
For those who give thought.[2030]

١١- يُنْۢبِتُ لَكُمْ بِهِ الزَّرْعَ وَالزَّيْتُوْنَ وَ
النَّخِيْلَ وَالْاَعْنَابَ وَمِنْ كُلِّ الثَّمَرٰتِ
اِنَّ فِيْ ذٰلِكَ لَاٰيَةً لِّقَوْمٍ يَّتَفَكَّرُوْنَ ○

12. He has made subject to you
The Night and the Day ;[2031]
The Sun and the Moon ;
And the Stars are in subjection
By His Command : verily
In this are Signs
For men who are wise.

١٢- وَسَخَّرَ لَكُمُ الَّيْلَ وَالنَّهَارَ
وَالشَّمْسَ وَالْقَمَرَ وَالنُّجُوْمُ مُسَخَّرٰتٌۢ
بِاَمْرِهٖ
اِنَّ فِيْ ذٰلِكَ لَاٰيٰتٍ لِّقَوْمٍ يَّعْقِلُوْنَ ○

2029. Through material things "the Way" does always lead to God. But some minds are so obsessed with material things that they miss the pointers to the spiritual. God could have forced all to the true Way, but in His Will and Plan is the training of man's will, and that is done by the Signs in nature and in Revelation.

2030. The least thought and study of nature will show you God's wise and benign Providence in making the processes of nature subserve man's use and refined life. A higher degree of intelligence and study is required ("men who are wise") to understand God's Signs to man in the processes connected with the heavenly bodies (verse 12). And a still higher spiritual understanding ("men who celebrate His praises" with gratitude) to realise the marvellous gradations, colours, and nuances in the creatures on this little globe of ours (verse 13). Reason this out carefully.

2031. The Night and the Day are caused by astronomical rotations. What is important for man to note is how God has given intelligence to man to make use of this alternation for work and rest ; how man can, as soon as he rises from the primitive stage, get over their inequalities by artificial illuminants, such as vegetable or mineral oils, coal, gas, or electricity, which ultimately are derived from the stored-up energy of the sun ; how the sun's heat can be tempered by various artificial means and can be stored up for use by man as required ; how man can be independent of the tides caused by the moon and the sun, which formerly controlled navigation, but which no longer stand in man's way, with his artificial harbours and great sea-going ships ; how navigation was formerly subject to direct observation of the Polar Star and other stars, but how the magnetic needle and charts have now completely altered the position, and man can calculate and to a certain extent control magnetic variations, etc. In such ways the sun, the moon, and the stars themselves become useful servants to him, all by God's gift and His Command, without which there would have been no laws governing them and no intelligence to make use of them.

13. And the things on this earth
Which He has multiplied
In varying colours
(and qualities): [2032]
Verily in this is a Sign
For men who celebrate
The praises of God
(in gratitude). [2033]

١٣- وَمَا ذَرَأَ لَكُمْ فِي الْأَرْضِ
مُخْتَلِفًا أَلْوَانُهُ
إِنَّ فِي ذَٰلِكَ لَآيَةً
لِقَوْمٍ يَذَّكَّرُونَ

14. It is He Who has made [2034]
The sea subject, that ye
May eat thereof flesh
That is fresh and tender, [2035]
And that ye may extract
Therefrom ornaments to wear; [2036]
And thou seest the ships
Therein that plough the waves,
That ye may seek (thus)
Of the bounty of God [2037]
And that ye may be grateful.

١٤- وَهُوَ الَّذِي سَخَّرَ الْبَحْرَ
لِتَأْكُلُوا مِنْهُ لَحْمًا طَرِيًّا
وَتَسْتَخْرِجُوا مِنْهُ حِلْيَةً تَلْبَسُونَهَا
وَتَرَى الْفُلْكَ مَوَاخِرَ فِيهِ
وَلِتَبْتَغُوا مِنْ فَضْلِهِ
وَلَعَلَّكُمْ تَشْكُرُونَ

2032. Whose heart has not been moved by the glorious gradation of colours in the sunset clouds? The gradations are infinite, and it is only the eye of an artist that can express their collective beauty. They are but a type of the infinite variety and gradation of qualities in the spiritual sphere even in the little space of our own globe. The big things that can be measured and defined have been spoken of before. Here we have mention of the subtle nuances in the spiritual world which can only be perceived by men who are so high in spiritual insight that their only reaction is to "celebrate the praises of God" in gratitude for His infinite Mercies.

2033 Read again n. 2030 above, and see how subtly we are led up from the perception of the big to the perception of the subtle and delicate colours and qualities in the spiritual world.

2034. We have gone up in a climax of material things from the big to the subtle in the sky and the earth. Here we have another climax as regards the things of the sea. We get the delicate flesh of fishes and marine creatures of all kinds; we get the treasures of the deep: pearls, coral, amber, and things of that kind; and we have the stately ships ploughing the waves, for maritime commerce and intercourse, for unifying mankind, and for realising the spiritual bounty of God which can best be expressed by the boundless ocean.

2035. Connoisseurs know the delicate flavours of sea fish, such as the pomfret of the Indian Ocean, the herring of the North Atlantic, the mullet of Marseilles, and many another kind. *Ṭarī*, translated "fresh and tender," also refers to the soft moist nature of fresh fish. It is another wonder of God that salt water should produce flesh of such fresh, tender, and delicate flavour.

2036. Diving for pearls—in both the primitive and the more advanced form—is another instance of man's power over apparently inaccessible depths of the sea.

2037. After the material benefits which we get from the sea, we are asked to consider things of higher import to the spirit of man. There is the beautiful ship which stands as the symbol of international commerce and intercourse, things that may be of material benefit, but which have a higher aspect in unifying man and making his civilisation more universal. These are first steps in seeking of the "bounty of God" through the sea. But there are higher aspects. Navigation and international intercourse increase knowledge, which in its higher aspects should clean the mind and make it fitter to approach God. The salt water, which covers nearly 72 per cent. of the surface of the Globe, is itself a purifying and sanitary agent, and is a good symbol of the higher bounties of God, which are as boundless as the Ocean.

15. And He has set up
On the earth mountains [2038]
Standing firm, lest it should
Shake with you ; and rivers
And roads ; that ye
May guide yourselves ; [2039]

١٥- وَأَلْقَىٰ فِى الْأَرْضِ رَوَاسِىَ
أَن تَمِيدَ بِكُمْ وَأَنْهَٰرًا
وَسُبُلًا لَّعَلَّكُمْ تَهْتَدُونَ ○

16. And marks and sign-posts ;
And by the stars
(Men) guide themselves. [2040]

١٦- وَعَلَٰمَٰتٍ ۚ وَبِالنَّجْمِ
هُمْ يَهْتَدُونَ ○

17. Is then He Who creates
Like one that creates not ?
Will ye not receive admonition ? [2041]

١٧- أَفَمَن يَخْلُقُ كَمَن لَّا يَخْلُقُ ۗ
أَفَلَا تَذَكَّرُونَ ○

18. If ye would count up
The favours of God,
Never would ye be able
To number them : for God
Is Oft-Forgiving, Most Merciful. [2042]

١٨- وَإِن تَعُدُّوا نِعْمَةَ اللَّهِ
لَا تُحْصُوهَا ۗ
إِنَّ اللَّهَ لَغَفُورٌ رَّحِيمٌ ○

2038. *Cf.* xiii. 3 and xv. 19. It is a favourite figure of speech to speak of the earth as a spacious carpet spread beneath our feet and the eternal hills as a steadying agent to keep the carpet from rolling or shaking about. In lxxviii. 7 they are spoken of as pegs or stakes.

2039. In this passage (xvi. 15-16) we have the metaphor of the fixed mountains further allegorised. In these verses the key-words are indicated by the symbols for man's Guidance (*tahtadūn*). First, the physical symbols are indicated : the mountains that stand firm and do not change from day to day in the landscape, unlike shifting sand-dunes, or the coast line of the sea, or rivers and streams, which frequently change their courses ; then we have rivers and roads, which are more precise and therefore more useful, though less permanent ; then we have *'alāmāt* (sign-posts), any kinds of signs erected by man, like direction posts, light-houses or beacons, or provided in nature, as tall trees, etc. ; and finally, we have the pole-star, and now the magnetic needle, with its variations marked on navigation charts. All these are symbols for the higher Guidance which God provides for the spirit of man. See next note.

2040. See last note. Let us examine the completed allegory. As there are beacons, landmarks, and signs to show the way to men on the earth, so in the spiritual world. And it is ultimately God Who provides them, and this is His crowning Mercy. Like the mountains there are spiritual Landmarks in the missions of the Great Teachers : they should guide us, or teach us, to guide ourselves, and not shake hither and thither like a ship without a rudder or people without Faith. As rivers and streams mark out their channels, smoothing out levels so we have wholesome Laws and Customs established, to help us in our lives. Then we have the examples of Great Men as further sign-posts : "Lives of great men all remind us, We can make our lives sublime." In long-distance travel, the pole-star and the magnetic needle are our guides : so in our long-distance journey to the other world, we have ultimately to look to heavenly guidance or its reflection in God's Revelation.

2041 The supreme majesty of God having been set out in His favours of all kinds, it will be seen at once that the worship of any other than God is meaningless and ridiculous. Shall we not take the hint and understand ?

2042. Of all God's favours innumerable, His Mercy and Forgiveness in the spiritual plane is the greatest, and of eternal value to us in our future Lives.

19. And God doth know
What ye conceal,
And what ye reveal.

١٩- وَاللّٰهُ يَعْلَمُ مَا تُسِرُّوْنَ
وَمَا تُعْلِنُوْنَ ○

20. Those whom they invoke
Besides God create nothing
And are themselves created.[2043]

٢٠- وَالَّذِيْنَ يَدْعُوْنَ مِنْ دُوْنِ اللّٰهِ لَا
يَخْلُقُوْنَ شَيْـًٔا وَّهُمْ يُخْلَقُوْنَ ○ؕ

21. (They are things) dead,
Lifeless : nor do they know
When they will be raised up.[2044]

٢١- اَمْوَاتٌ غَيْرُ اَحْيَآءٍ ۚ
وَمَا يَشْعُرُوْنَ ۙ اَيَّانَ يُبْعَثُوْنَ ○ ع

SECTION 3.

22. Your God is One God:
As to those who believe not
In the Hereafter, their hearts
Refuse to know, and they
Are arrogant.[2045]

٢٢- اِلٰهُكُمْ اِلٰهٌ وَّاحِدٌ ۚ
فَالَّذِيْنَ لَا يُؤْمِنُوْنَ بِالْاٰخِرَةِ قُلُوْبُهُمْ
مُّنْكِرَةٌ وَّهُمْ مُّسْتَكْبِرُوْنَ ○

23. Undoubtedly God doth know
What they conceal,
And what they reveal:[2046]
Verily He loveth not the arrogant.

٢٣- لَا جَرَمَ اَنَّ اللّٰهَ يَعْلَمُ مَا يُسِرُّوْنَ
وَمَا يُعْلِنُوْنَ ؕ اِنَّهٗ لَا يُحِبُّ الْمُسْتَكْبِرِيْنَ ○

24. When it is said to them,
"What is it that your Lord[2047]

٢٤- وَاِذَا قِيْلَ لَهُمْ مَّاذَآ اَنْزَلَ رَبُّكُمْ ۙ

2043. God is the only Creator and the Ultimate Reality. Everything else is created by Him, and reflects His glory. How foolish then to worship any other than God!

2044. Idols are dead wood or stone. If men worship stars, or heroes, or prophets, or great men, they too have no life except that which was given by God. In themselves they are lifeless. If they worship figments of the imagination, they are reflections in a double degree, and have no life in themselves. All these things will be raised up on the Last Day, in order that false worshippers may be confronted with them. But they themselves cannot tell when that Day will be.

2045. Everything points to the One True Eternal God. If so, there is a Hereafter, for He has declared it. In so far as people do not believe this, the fault is in their Will: they do not wish to believe, and the motive behind is arrogance, the sin which brought about the fall of Iblis: ii. 34.

2046. *Cf.* xvi. 19, where the same words refer to man generally. Whether he conceals or reveals what is in his heart, God knows it, and as God is Oft-Forgiving, Most Merciful, His grace is available as His highest favour if man will take it. Here the reference is to those who "refuse to know", who reject God's guidance out of arrogance. God "loveth not the arrogant". Such men deprive themselves of God's grace.

2047. When the arrogant Unbelievers are referred to some definite argument or illustration from Scripture, they dismiss it contemptuously with the remark, "Tales of the ancients!" In this, they are not only playing with their own conscience, but misleading others, with perhaps less knowledge than themselves.

Has revealed?" they say,
"Tales of the ancients!"

قَالُوٓا۟ أَسَٰطِيرُ ٱلْأَوَّلِينَ ۝

25. Let them bear, on the Day
Of Judgment, their own burdens
In full, and also (something)
Of the burdens of those
Without knowledge, whom they
Misled. Alas, how grievous
The burdens they will bear![2048]

٢٥- لِيَحْمِلُوٓا۟ أَوْزَارَهُمْ كَامِلَةً يَوْمَ ٱلْقِيَٰمَةِ
وَمِنْ أَوْزَارِ ٱلَّذِينَ يُضِلُّونَهُم بِغَيْرِ عِلْمٍ
أَلَا سَآءَ مَا يَزِرُونَ ۝

C. 124.—In all ages wicked men tried to plot
(xvi. 26-50.) Against God's Way, but they never
Succeeded, and were covered with shame
In ways unexpected. The righteous
See good in God's Word, and their goal
Is the Good. Great Teachers were sent
To all nations, to warn against Evil
And guide to the Right. The penalty
For evil comes in many unexpected
Ways, for Evil is against Nature.
And all Nature proclaims God's Glory
And humbly serves Him, the Lord Supreme.

SECTION 4.

26. Those before them did also
Plot (against God's Way):
But God took their structures
From their foundations, and the
roof
Fell down on them from above;
And the Wrath seized them
From directions they did not
perceive.[2049]

٢٦- قَدْ مَكَرَ ٱلَّذِينَ مِن قَبْلِهِمْ
فَأَتَى ٱللَّهُ بُنْيَٰنَهُم مِّنَ ٱلْقَوَاعِدِ
فَخَرَّ عَلَيْهِمُ ٱلسَّقْفُ مِن فَوْقِهِمْ
وَأَتَىٰهُمُ ٱلْعَذَابُ مِنْ حَيْثُ لَا
يَشْعُرُونَ ۝

27. Then, on the Day of Judgment,
He will cover them

٢٧- ثُمَّ يَوْمَ ٱلْقِيَٰمَةِ يُخْزِيهِمْ

2048. Their responsibility or crime is twofold: (1) that they rejected God's Message, and (2) that they misled others. Their Penalty will also be double. In vi. 164, we are told that "no bearer of burdens can bear the burden of another". This is against the doctrine of vicarious atonement. Every man is responsible for his own sins: but the sin of misleading others is a sin of the misleader himself, and he must suffer the penalty for that also, without relieving those misled, of their responsibility.

2049. Evil will always devise plots against the men of God. So was it with Mustafa, and so was it with the apostles before him. But the imposing structures which the ungodly build up (metaphorically) collapse at the Command of God, and they are often punished from quarters from which they least expected punishment. For example, the Quraish were confident in their numbers, their organisation, and their superior equipment. But on the field of Badr they collapsed where they expected victory.

With shame, and say :
" Where are My 'partners'
Concerning whom ye used
To dispute (with the godly) ? "
Those endued with knowledge[2050]
Will say : " This Day, indeed,
Are the Unbelievers covered
With Shame and Misery,—

وَيَقُولُ أَيْنَ شُرَكَآءِيَ الَّذِينَ
كُنتُمْ تُشَٰٓقُّونَ فِيهِمْ ۚ
قَالَ الَّذِينَ أُوتُوا الْعِلْمَ إِنَّ الْخِزْيَ الْيَوْمَ
وَالسُّوٓءَ عَلَى الْكَٰفِرِينَ ۝

28. " (Namely) those whose lives the angels
Take in a state of wrong-doing
To their own souls."[2051]
Then would they offer submission
(With the pretence), " We did[2052]
No evil (knowingly)." (The angels
Will reply), " Nay, but verily
God knoweth all that ye did ;

٢٨- الَّذِينَ تَتَوَفَّىٰهُمُ الْمَلَٰٓئِكَةُ
ظَالِمِىٓ أَنفُسِهِمْ ۖ
فَأَلْقَوُا السَّلَمَ مَا كُنَّا نَعْمَلُ مِن سُوٓءٍ ۚ
بَلَىٰٓ إِنَّ اللَّهَ عَلِيمٌۢ
بِمَا كُنتُمْ تَعْمَلُونَ ۝

29. " So enter the gates of Hell,
To dwell therein.
Thus evil indeed
Is the abode of the arrogant."

٢٩- فَادْخُلُوٓا أَبْوَٰبَ جَهَنَّمَ خَٰلِدِينَ فِيهَا ۖ
فَلَبِئْسَ مَثْوَى الْمُتَكَبِّرِينَ ۝

30. To the righteous
(When) it is said, " What
Is it that your Lord[2053]
Has revealed ? " they say,
"All that is good." To those
Who do good, there is good
In this world, and the Home
Of the Hereafter is even better[2054]

٣٠- وَقِيلَ لِلَّذِينَ اتَّقَوْا مَاذَآ أَنزَلَ رَبُّكُمْ ۚ
قَالُوا خَيْرًا ۗ
لِّلَّذِينَ أَحْسَنُوا فِى هَٰذِهِ الدُّنْيَا حَسَنَةٌ ۚ
وَلَدَارُ الْءَاخِرَةِ خَيْرٌ ۚ

2050. The worshippers of false gods (the ungodly, the Unbelievers) will be unable to reply when brought before the Judgment Seat. The comment of those " endued with knowledge "—the Prophets and Teachers whom they had rejected—will be by way of indictment and explanation of the position of those before the Judgment Seat.

2051. That is, those who died in a state of *kufr*, or rebellion against God, which was really wrong-doing against their own souls.

2052. The excuse is a mere pretence. At first they were too dazed to reply. When they reply, they cannot deny the facts, but resort to the sinner's excuse of saying that they sinned through ignorance, and that their motives were not wrong. Such a plea raises a question of hidden thoughts which are difficult to appraise before a human tribunal. But here they are before their Divine Author, Who knows every secret of their souls, and before Whom no false plea can be of any value. So they are condemned.

2053. The contrast and parallelism is with xvi. 24, where the ungodly in their levity and their deliberate rejection of guidance find no profit from God's revelation.

2054. Unlike the ungodly, the good find good everywhere,—in this world and in the Hereafter ; because they understand and are in accord with the truths around them.

And excellent indeed is the Home
Of the righteous,—

وَلَنِعْمَ دَارُ الْمُتَّقِيْنَ ۝

31. Gardens of Eternity which they
Will enter : beneath them
Flow (pleasant) rivers : they
Will have therein all
That they wish : thus doth
God reward the righteous,—

٣١- جَنّٰتُ عَدْنٍ يَّدْخُلُوْنَهَا تَجْرِيْ مِنْ
تَحْتِهَا الْاَنْهٰرُ لَهُمْ فِيْهَا مَا يَشَآءُوْنَ ؕ
كَذٰلِكَ يَجْزِي اللّٰهُ الْمُتَّقِيْنَ ۝

32. (Namely) those whose lives
The angels take in a state [2055]
Of purity, saying (to them),
" Peace be on you ; enter ye
The Garden, because of (the good)
Which ye did (in the world)."

٣٢- الَّذِيْنَ تَتَوَفّٰىهُمُ الْمَلٰٓئِكَةُ طَيِّبِيْنَ ۙ
يَقُوْلُوْنَ سَلٰمٌ عَلَيْكُمُ ادْخُلُوا الْجَنَّةَ
بِمَا كُنْتُمْ تَعْمَلُوْنَ ۝

33. Do the (ungodly) wait until
The angels come to them,
Or there comes the Command
Of thy Lord (for their doom) ? [2056]
So did those who went
Before them. But God
Wronged them not : nay,
They wronged their own souls.

٣٣- هَلْ يَنْظُرُوْنَ اِلَّآ اَنْ تَاْتِيَهُمُ
الْمَلٰٓئِكَةُ اَوْ يَاْتِيَ اَمْرُ رَبِّكَ ؕ
كَذٰلِكَ فَعَلَ الَّذِيْنَ مِنْ قَبْلِهِمْ ؕ وَمَا ظَلَمَهُمُ
اللّٰهُ وَلٰكِنْ كَانُوْٓا اَنْفُسَهُمْ يَظْلِمُوْنَ ۝

34. But the evil results
Of their deeds overtook them,
And that very (Wrath)
At which they had scoffed
Hemmed them in.

٣٤- فَاَصَابَهُمْ سَيِّاٰتُ مَا عَمِلُوْا
وَحَاقَ بِهِمْ
مَّا كَانُوْا بِهٖ يَسْتَهْزِءُوْنَ ۝ ع

SECTION 5.

35. The worshippers of false gods
Say : " If God had so willed,
We should not have worshipped
Aught but Him—neither we [2057]

٣٥- وَقَالَ الَّذِيْنَ اَشْرَكُوْا لَوْ شَآءَ اللّٰهُ
مَا عَبَدْنَا مِنْ دُوْنِهٖ مِنْ شَيْءٍ نَّحْنُ

2055. *In a state of purity* : from the evils of this world, from want of faith and want of grace. Purity from such evil is the mark of true Islam, and those who die in such purity will be received into Felicity with a salutation of Peace.

2056. That is, until death comes to them, or some Punishment in this life itself, which precludes them from repentance and the Mercy of God.

2057. The old, old argument : if God is All-Powerful, why did He not force all persons to His Will ? This ignores the limited Free-will granted to man, which is the whole basis of Ethics. God gives man every opportunity of knowing and understanding things, but He does not force him, for that would be against the whole Plan on which our present Life is constituted.

Nor our fathers,—nor should
We have prescribed prohibitions[2058]
Other than His." So did those
Who went before them.
But what is the mission
Of apostles but to preach
The Clear Message?[2059]

وَلَآ اٰبَآؤُنَا وَلَا
حَرَّمْنَا مِنْ دُوْنِهٖ مِنْ شَيْءٍ
كَذٰلِكَ فَعَلَ الَّذِيْنَ مِنْ قَبْلِهِمْ
فَهَلْ عَلَى الرُّسُلِ اِلَّا الْبَلٰغُ الْمُبِيْنُ ○

36. For We assuredly sent
Amongst every People an apostle,[2060]
(With the Command), "Serve
God, and eschew Evil":
Of the people were some whom
God guided, and some
On whom Error became[2061]
Inevitably (established). So travel
Through the earth, and see
What was the end of those
Who denied (the Truth).

٣٦- وَلَقَدْ بَعَثْنَا فِيْ كُلِّ اُمَّةٍ رَّسُوْلًا
اَنِ اعْبُدُوا اللّٰهَ وَاجْتَنِبُوا الطَّاغُوْتَ
فَمِنْهُمْ مَّنْ هَدَى اللّٰهُ
وَمِنْهُمْ مَّنْ حَقَّتْ عَلَيْهِ الضَّلٰلَةُ
فَسِيْرُوْا فِي الْاَرْضِ
فَانْظُرُوْا كَيْفَ كَانَ عَاقِبَةُ الْمُكَذِّبِيْنَ ○

37. If thou art anxious
For their guidance, yet
God guideth not such
As He leaves to stray,[2062]
And there is none
To help them.

٣٧- اِنْ تَحْرِصْ عَلٰى هُدٰىهُمْ
فَاِنَّ اللّٰهَ لَا يَهْدِيْ مَنْ يُّضِلُّ
وَمَا لَهُمْ مِّنْ نّٰصِرِيْنَ ○

38. They swear their strongest oaths[2063]
By God, that God will not

٣٨- وَاَقْسَمُوْا بِاللّٰهِ جَهْدَ اَيْمَانِهِمْ لَا

2058. The Pagan Arabs prescribed various arbitrary prohibitions in the matter of meat: see vi. 143-145. These, of course, are not recognised by Islam, which also removed some of the restrictions of the Jewish Law: vi. 146. The general meaning, however, is far wider. Men erect their own taboos and prohibitions, barriers and restrictions, and ascribe them to Religion. This is wrong, and more consonant with Pagan practice than with Islam.

2059. *Clear Message: Mubīn*: in three senses: (1) a Message clear and unambiguous; (2) one that makes all things clear to those who try to understand, because it accords with their own nature as created by God; (3) one preached openly and to everyone.

2060. Even though God's Signs are everywhere in Nature and in men's own conscience, yet in addition God has sent human Messengers to every People to call their attention to the Good and turn them from Evil. So they cannot pretend that God has abandoned them or that He does not care what they do. His divine Grace always invites their will to choose the right.

2061. While some people accept the guidance of the divine Grace, others so surrender themselves to Evil that it must necessarily follow that Evil obtains a grip over them. They have only to travel through Time or Space to see the end of those who abandoned their lights and surrendered to Evil and Error. For *ḥaqqat* and the meaning of *ḥaqq* in this connection *cf.* xv. 64.

2062. When once God's Grace is rejected by any one, such a person loses all help and guidance. Such persons are then outside God's Grace, and therefore they are outside guidance.

2063. The strongest oath of the Pagan Arabs would be by the Supreme God: less strong oaths would be by their subordinate deities, or their ancestors, or other things they valued or held sacred.

Raise up those who die :[2064]
Nay, but it is a promise
(Binding) on Him in truth :
But most among mankind
Realise it not.

يَبْعَثُ اللّٰهُ مَنْ يَّمُوْتُ ط
بَلٰى وَعْدًا عَلَيْهِ حَقًّا
وَّلٰكِنَّ اَكْثَرَ النَّاسِ لَا يَعْلَمُوْنَ ۝

39. (They must be raised up),
In order that He may manifest
To them the truth of that
Wherein they differ, and that
The rejecters of Truth
May realise that they had
Indeed (surrendered to)
Falsehood.[2065]

٣٩-لِيُبَيِّنَ لَهُمُ الَّذِىْ
يَخْتَلِفُوْنَ فِيْهِ
وَلِيَعْلَمَ الَّذِيْنَ كَفَرُوْٓا
اَنَّهُمْ كَانُوْا كٰذِبِيْنَ ۝

40. For to anything which We
Have willed, We but say
The Word, " Be ", and it is.[2066]

٤٠-اِنَّمَا قَوْلُنَا لِشَىْءٍ اِذَآ اَرَدْنٰهُ اَنْ
نَّقُوْلَ لَهٗ كُنْ فَيَكُوْنُ ۝ ع

SECTION 6.

41. To those who leave
Their homes in the cause
Of God, after suffering
oppression,—[2067]
We will assuredly give
A goodly home in this world ;
But truly the reward
Of the Hereafter will be greater.
If they only realised (this) !

٤١-وَالَّذِيْنَ هَاجَرُوْا فِى اللّٰهِ
مِنْۢ بَعْدِ مَا ظُلِمُوْا
لَنُبَوِّئَنَّهُمْ فِى الدُّنْيَا حَسَنَةً ط
وَلَاَجْرُ الْاٰخِرَةِ اَكْبَرُ م
لَوْ كَانُوْا يَعْلَمُوْنَ ۝

42. (They are) those who persevere
In patience, and put
Their trust on their Lord.

٤٢-الَّذِيْنَ صَبَرُوْا وَعَلٰى رَبِّهِمْ يَتَوَكَّلُوْنَ ۝

2064. The usual Pagan creed is : 'If there is a God, it does not follow that He will raise us up : why should He?' The answer is twofold : (1) God has promised it, and God's promise is true ; (2) He must finally manifest the Truth to them, convict them of their falsehood, and enforce their personal responsibility (xvi. 39).

2065. See the last note.

2066. God's "Word" is in itself the Deed. God's Promise is in itself the Truth. There is no interposition of Time or Condition between His Will and its consequences, for He is the Ultimate Reality. He is independent of the proximate or material causes, for He Himself creates them and establishes their Laws as He pleases.

2067. There is no merit in suffering exile (*hijrat*) in itself. To have any merit, it must be : (1) in the cause of God, and (2) after such an oppression as forces the sufferer to choose between God and man. When these conditions are fulfilled, the exiles are entitled to the highest honour, as having made a great sacrifice in the cause of God. Such were the early Muslim exiles to Abyssinia ; such were the later exiles to Medina, before the Apostle himself left his home in Mecca and went to Medina ; and such were the exiles who went with the Prophet or followed him. , At all these stages, his approval or advice was always obtained, either specifically or generally.

43. And before thee also
The apostles We sent
Were but men,[2068] to whom
We granted inspiration : if ye
Realise this not, ask of those
Who possess the Message.[2069]

٤٣- وَمَآ أَرْسَلْنَا مِن قَبْلِكَ
إِلَّا رِجَالًا نُّوحِىٓ إِلَيْهِمْ فَسْـَٔلُوٓا أَهْلَ
الذِّكْرِ إِن كُنتُمْ لَا تَعْلَمُونَ ۝

44. (We sent them) with Clear Signs
And Books of dark prophecies ;[2070]
And We have sent down
Unto thee (also) the Message ;
That thou mayest explain clearly
To men what is sent
For them, and that they
May give thought.

٤٤- بِالْبَيِّنٰتِ وَالزُّبُرِ
وَأَنزَلْنَآ إِلَيْكَ الذِّكْرَ لِتُبَيِّنَ لِلنَّاسِ
مَا نُزِّلَ إِلَيْهِمْ
وَلَعَلَّهُمْ يَتَفَكَّرُونَ ۝

النصف

45. Do then those who devise
Evil (plots) feel secure
That God will not cause
The earth to swallow them up,
Or that the Wrath will not
Seize them from directions
They little perceive ?—[2071]

٤٥- أَفَأَمِنَ الَّذِينَ مَكَرُوا السَّيِّـَٔاتِ
أَن يَخْسِفَ اللّٰهُ بِهِمُ الْأَرْضَ
أَوْ يَأْتِيَهُمُ الْعَذَابُ
مِنْ حَيْثُ لَا يَشْعُرُونَ ۝

46. Or that He may not
Call them to account

٤٦- أَوْ يَأْخُذَهُمْ

2068. God's apostles were always men, not angels ; and their distinction was the inspiration they received.

2069. If the Pagan Arabs, who were ignorant of religious and other history, wondered how a man from among themselves could receive inspiration and bring a Message from God, let them ask the Jews, who had also received God's Message earlier through Moses, whether Moses was a man, or an angel, or a god. They would learn that Moses was a man like themselves, but inspired by God. "Those who possess the Message" may also mean any men of Wisdom, who were qualified to have an opinion in such matters.

2070. For "*Clear Signs*" see n. 401 to iii. 62. For *Zubur* (Books of dark prophecies), see iii. 184, and n. 490). As the People of the Book had received "Clear Signs" and inspired Books before, so also God's Message came to the Prophet Muḥammad through the Qur-ān, which superseded the earlier revelations, already corrupted in the hands of their followers.

2071. *Cf.* xvi. 26. The wicked plot against men of God in secret, forgetting that every hidden thought of theirs is known to God, and that for every thought and action of theirs they will have to account to God. And God's punishment can seize them in various ways. Four are enumerated here. (1) They may be swallowed up in the earth like Qārūn, whose story is told in xxviii. 76-81. He was swallowed up in the earth while he was arrogantly exulting on the score of his wealth. (2) It may be that, like Hāmān, the prime minister of Pharaoh, they are plotting against God, when they are themselves overwhelmed by some dreadful calamity : xl. 36-38 ; xxix. 39-40. The case of Pharaoh is also in point. He was drowned while he was arrogantly hoping to frustrate God's plans for Israel : x. 90-92. For (3) and (4) see the next two notes.

In the midst of their goings[2072]
To and fro, without a chance
Of their frustrating Him ?—

فِي تَقَلُّبِهِمْ فَمَا هُمْ بِمُعْجِزِينَ ○

47. Or that He may not
Call them to account
By a process of slow wastage—[2073]
For thy Lord is indeed
Full of kindness and mercy.

٤٧- أَوْ يَأْخُذَهُمْ عَلَىٰ تَخَوُّفٍ
فَإِنَّ رَبَّكُمْ لَرَءُوفٌ رَّحِيمٌ ○

48. Do they not look
At God's creation, (even)
Among (inanimate) things,—[2074]
How their (very) shadows
Turn round, from the right
And the left, prostrating
Themselves to God, and that
In the humblest manner ?

٤٨- أَوَلَمْ يَرَوْا إِلَىٰ مَا خَلَقَ اللّٰهُ مِنْ شَيْءٍ
يَتَفَيَّؤُا ظِلٰلُهُ
عَنِ الْيَمِينِ وَالشَّمَآئِلِ سُجَّدًا لِلّٰهِ
وَهُمْ دٰخِرُونَ ○

49. And to God doth obeisance
All that is in the heavens
And on earth, whether
Moving (living) creatures[2075]
Or the angels: for none
Are arrogant (before their Lord).

٤٩- وَلِلّٰهِ يَسْجُدُ مَا فِي السَّمٰوٰتِ وَمَا فِي
الْأَرْضِ مِنْ دَآبَّةٍ وَّالْمَلٰٓئِكَةُ
وَهُمْ لَا يَسْتَكْبِرُونَ ○

2072. (3) Or the punishment may come to people away from their homes and humble them in their pride. It so happened to Abū Jahl, who came exulting in his pride to the Battle of Badr (A.H. 2). His army was three times the size of the Muslim army from Medina. But it suffered a crushing defeat, and he himself was ignominiously slain.

2073. (4) Or, as often happens, the punishment comes slowly and imperceptibly, the power of the enemies of God being wasted gradually, until it is extinguished. This happened to the Meccans during the eight years of the Prophet's exile. The re-conquest of Mecca was bloodless, because the power of the enemy had gradually vanished. The Prophet was thus able to show the unexampled generosity and clemency which he showed on that occasion, for two of God's attributes are expressed in the titles "Full of kindness" (*Ra-ūf*) and "Full of mercy" (*Raḥim*).

2074. I take "*things*" here to be inanimate things, for the next verse speaks of living "moving creatures" and angels. By a metaphor even such inanimate things are spoken of as recognising God and humbly worshipping Him. Even their shadows turn round from right and left according to the light from above, and they humbly prostrate themselves on the ground to celebrate the praises of God. The "shadows" suggest how all things in this life are mere shadows of the true Reality in heaven; and they should turn and move in accordance with the divine light, as the shadows of trees and buildings move in one direction or another, and lengthen or shorten according to the light from heaven.

2075. *Moving creatures, i.e.*, living creatures. "All that is in the heavens or earth," includes every created thing. And created things are mentioned in three classes : inanimate things, ordinary living things, and angels. Even the highest angels are not arrogant : they bow down and serve their Lord, and so does all Creation.

50. They all revere their Lord,[2076]
High above them, and they do
All that they are commanded.

٥٠- يَخَافُونَ رَبَّهُمْ مِّنْ فَوْقِهِمْ
وَيَفْعَلُونَ مَا يُؤْمَرُونَ ۩ ○

C. 125.—There is but One God, He Who gives
(xvi. 51-83.) All blessings to man and other creatures.
His greatest gift is that He reveals
Himself. But in many tangible ways
He cares for man and provides for his growth
And sustenance. In rain, in milk,
In fruits and honey, and in Nature and the life
Of man, with his opportunities
Of social, moral, and spiritual growth,
Are Signs for those who understand.
Why then does man show ingratitude
By going after false gods and forgetting God?

Section 7.

51. God has said: "Take not
(For worship) two gods:[2077]
For He is just One God:
Then fear Me (and Me alone)."

٥١- وَقَالَ اللّٰهُ لَا تَتَّخِذُوْٓا اِلٰهَيْنِ اثْنَيْنِ
اِنَّمَا هُوَ اِلٰهٌ وَّاحِدٌ فَاِيَّايَ فَارْهَبُوْنِ ○

52. To Him belongs whatever
Is in the heavens and on earth,
And to Him is duty due always:
Then will ye fear other[2078]
Than God?

٥٢- وَلَهٗ مَا فِي السَّمٰوٰتِ وَالْاَرْضِ
وَلَهُ الدِّيْنُ وَاصِبًا
اَفَغَيْرَ اللّٰهِ تَتَّقُوْنَ ○

53. And ye have no good thing
But is from God: and moreover,
When ye are touched by distress,
Unto Him ye cry with groans;[2079]

٥٣- وَمَا بِكُمْ مِّنْ نِّعْمَةٍ فَمِنَ اللّٰهِ ثُمَّ
اِذَا مَسَّكُمُ الضُّرُّ فَاِلَيْهِ تَجْـَٔرُوْنَ ○

2076. God is so high above the highest of His creatures, that they all look up to him in awe and reverence. And they joyfully do their duty in serving Him. This is the meaning of the "fear of the Lord."

2077. The ancient Persians believed in two powers in the Universe, one good and the other evil. The Pagan Arabs also had pairs of deities: *e.g.*, *Jibt* (Sorcery) and *Ṭāgūt* (Evil), referred to in iv. 51, n. 573, or the idols on Safā and Marwa referred to in n. 160 to ii. 158: their names were Isāf and Nāila.

2078. The Pagans might have a glimmering of the One True God, but they had also a haunting fear of malevolent Powers of Evil. They are told that such fears are groundless. Evil has no power over those who trust in God: xv. 42. The only fear they should have is that of the Wrath of God. To the righteous all good things come from God, and they have no fear in their hearts.

2079. Which shows that the natural tendency of man is to seek God, the only Power which can truly relieve distress.

54. Yet, when He removes
The distress from you, behold!
Some of you turn to other gods
To join with their Lord—

٥٤- ثُمَّ إِذَا كَشَفَ الضُّرَّ عَنكُمْ
إِذَا فَرِيقٌ مِّنكُم بِرَبِّهِمْ يُشْرِكُونَ ○

55. (As if) to show their ingratitude
For the favours We have
Bestowed on them! Then enjoy
(Your brief day); but soon
Will ye know (your folly)!

٥٥- لِيَكْفُرُوا بِمَا آتَيْنَاهُمْ
فَتَمَتَّعُوا فَسَوْفَ تَعْلَمُونَ ○

56. And they (even) assign,
To things they do not know,[2080]
A portion out of that
Which We have bestowed
For their sustenance![2081]
By God, ye shall certainly
Be called to account
For your false inventions.

٥٦- وَيَجْعَلُونَ لِمَا لَا يَعْلَمُونَ
نَصِيبًا مِّمَّا رَزَقْنَاهُمْ
تَاللَّهِ لَتُسْأَلُنَّ
عَمَّا كُنتُمْ تَفْتَرُونَ ○

57. And they assign daughters[2082]
For God! - Glory be to Him!—
And for themselves (sons,—
The issue) they desire!

٥٧- وَيَجْعَلُونَ لِلَّهِ الْبَنَاتِ سُبْحَانَهُ
وَلَهُم مَّا يَشْتَهُونَ ○

58. When news is brought
To one of them, of (the birth
Of) a female (child), his face
Darkens, and he is filled
With inward grief!

٥٨- وَإِذَا بُشِّرَ أَحَدُهُم بِالْأُنثَىٰ
ظَلَّ وَجْهُهُ مُسْوَدًّا وَهُوَ كَظِيمٌ ○

59. With shame does he hide
Himself from his people,

٥٩- يَتَوَارَىٰ مِنَ الْقَوْمِ مِن سُوءِ

2080. Idols and fictitious gods are certainly things of which they have no knowledge, idols being lifeless things of whose life or doings no knowledge is possible, and fictitious gods being but figments of their imagination.

2081. *Cf.* vi. 136—140, 142-144, and v. 106. The Pagans, in assigning and dedicating some of their children, or some of their cattle, or some of the produce of their fields, to their false gods as sharers with the true Supreme God, made themselves doubly ridiculous; first, because every good thing that they valued was given to them by God, and how could they patronisingly assign to Him a share of His own gifts?—and secondly, because they brought in other gods as sharers, who had no existence whatever! Besides, the cattle and produce was given for their physical sustenance and the children for their social and spiritual sustenance, and how can they, poor creatures, give sustenance to God?

2082. Some of the Pagan Arabs called angels the daughters of God. In their own life they hated to have daughters, as explained in the next two verses. They practised female infanticide. In their state of perpetual war sons were a source of strength to them; daughters only made them subject to humiliating raids!

Because of the bad news
He has had!
Shall he retain it [2083]
On (sufferance and) contempt,
Or bury it in the dust? [2084]
Ah! what an evil (choice)
They decide on? [2085]

مَا بُشِّرَ بِهٖ ۚ
اَيُمْسِكُهٗ عَلٰى هُوْنٍ
اَمْ يَدُسُّهٗ فِى التُّرَابِ ۗ
اَلَا سَآءَ مَا يَحْكُمُوْنَ ○

60. To those who believe not
In the Hereafter, applies
The similitude of evil:
To God applies the highest [2086]
Similitude: for He is
The Exalted in Power,
Full of Wisdom.

٦٠- لِلَّذِيْنَ لَا يُؤْمِنُوْنَ بِالْاٰخِرَةِ
مَثَلُ السَّوْءِ ۚ وَلِلّٰهِ الْمَثَلُ الْاَعْلٰى ۗ
وَهُوَ الْعَزِيْزُ الْحَكِيْمُ ○ ع

Section 8.

61. If God were to punish
Men for their wrong-doing,
He would not leave, on the (earth),
A single living creature:
But He gives them respite
For a stated Term:
When their Term expires,
They would not be able
To delay (the punishment)
For a single hour, just as
They would not be able
To anticipate it (for a single
hour). [2087]

٦١- وَلَوْ يُؤَاخِذُ اللّٰهُ النَّاسَ بِظُلْمِهِمْ
مَّا تَرَكَ عَلَيْهَا مِنْ دَآبَّةٍ
وَّلٰكِنْ يُّؤَخِّرُهُمْ اِلٰٓى اَجَلٍ مُّسَمًّى ۚ
فَاِذَا جَآءَ اَجَلُهُمْ لَا يَسْتَاْخِرُوْنَ
سَاعَةً وَّ
لَا يَسْتَقْدِمُوْنَ ○

2083. "It," in this and the following clause, refers grammatically to the "news" (*mā bushshira bihi*). In meaning it refers to the "female child"—by the figure of speech known as metonymy.

2084. *Cf.* lxxxi. 8-9. The practice of female infanticide is condemned in scathing terms. Female children used to be buried alive by the Pagan Arabs

2085. It was an evil choice to decide on. Either alternative—to keep the poor girl as a thing of sufferance and contempt, bringing disgrace on the family, or to get rid of it by burying it alive—was cruel and indefensible.

2086. *Cf.* xxx. 27. God is above all comparison. But if, for our own understanding, we use any similitudes at all, the highest and noblest would be for God, and the vilest for the Unbelievers, for they deny their own nature. The Pagans reversed this process, and attributed daughters to God, when they considered daughters a sign of shame and ignominy to themselves!

2087. God's decree works without fail. If He were to punish for every wrong or shortcoming, not a single living creature on earth would escape punishment. But in His infinite mercy and forgiveness, He gives respite: He provides time for repentance. If the repentance is forthcoming, God's Mercy is forthcoming without fail. If not, the punishment comes inevitably on the expiry of the Term. The sinner cannot anticipate it by an insolent challenge, nor can he delay it when the time arrives. Let him not think that the respite given him may mean that he can do what he likes, and that he can escape scot-free from the consequences.

62. They attribute to God
What they hate (for themselves),[2088]
And their tongues assert
The falsehood that all good
things[2089]
Are for themselves: without doubt
For them is the Fire, and they
Will be the first to be
Hastened on into it!

٦٢- وَيَجْعَلُونَ لِلّٰهِ مَا يَكْرَهُونَ
وَتَصِفُ أَلْسِنَتُهُمُ الْكَذِبَ أَنَّ لَهُمُ
الْحُسْنٰى
لَا جَرَمَ أَنَّ لَهُمُ النَّارَ
وَأَنَّهُمْ مُّفْرَطُونَ ○

63. By God, We (also) sent
(Our apostles) to Peoples
Before thee; but Satan
Made, (to the wicked),
Their own acts seem alluring:
He is also their patron to-day,[2090]
But they shall have
A most grievous penalty.

٦٣- تَاللّٰهِ لَقَدْ أَرْسَلْنَا إِلٰى أُمَمٍ
مِّنْ قَبْلِكَ فَزَيَّنَ لَهُمُ الشَّيْطٰنُ أَعْمَالَهُمْ
فَهُوَ وَلِيُّهُمُ الْيَوْمَ
وَلَهُمْ عَذَابٌ أَلِيمٌ ○

64. And We sent down the Book
To thee for the express purpose,
That thou shouldst make clear
To them those things in which[2091]
They differ, and that it should be
A guide and a mercy
To those who believe.

٦٤- وَمَا أَنْزَلْنَا عَلَيْكَ الْكِتٰبَ
إِلَّا لِتُبَيِّنَ لَهُمُ الَّذِي اخْتَلَفُوا فِيهِ
وَهُدًى وَّرَحْمَةً
لِّقَوْمٍ يُّؤْمِنُونَ ○

65. And God sends down rain
From the skies, and gives therewith
Life to the earth after its death:
Verily in this is a Sign

٦٥- وَاللّٰهُ أَنْزَلَ مِنَ السَّمَآءِ مَآءً فَأَحْيَا بِهِ
الْأَرْضَ بَعْدَ مَوْتِهَا إِنَّ فِي ذٰلِكَ لَآيَةً

2088. See above. xvi 57-58 and notes.

2089. The philosophy of Pleasure (Hedonism) assumes that worldly enjoyment is good in itself and that there is nothing beyond. But it can be shown, even on its own ground, that every act has its inevitable consequences. No Good can spring out of Evil. For falsehood and wrong the agony of the Fire is waiting, and the boastful votaries of Falsehood will be the first to fall into it.

2090. In all ages and among all Peoples God sent His Messengers to teach the Truth and point the way to righteousness. But the allurements of Evil seemed always attractive, and many men preferred their own ways and the ways of their ancestors to the more difficult path of rectitude. This happened again in the time of Muṣṭafā, and will always happen as long as men succumb to Evil.

2091. But the path of duty before God's Messenger is clear. He is sent with the Revelation (the Qur-ān) for three express purposes: (1) that he should bring about unity among the jarring sects, for the Gospel of Unity, while preaching the One True God, leads also to the unity of mankind; (2) that the revelation should be a guide to right conduct; and (3) that it should show the path of repentance and salvation, and thus be the highest mercy to erring sinners.

For those who listen.[2092]

لِّقَوْمٍ يَّسْمَعُوْنَ ○

SECTION 9.

66. And verily in cattle (too)
Will ye find an instructive Sign.[2093]
From what is within their bodies,[2094]
Between excretions and blood,[2095]
We produce, for your drink,
Milk, pure and agreeable
To those who drink it.

٦٦- وَإِنَّ لَكُمْ فِي الْأَنْعَامِ لَعِبْرَةً ۚ
نُسْقِيكُمْ مِّمَّا فِي بُطُوْنِهٖ مِنْ بَيْنِ فَرْثٍ
وَّدَمٍ
لَّبَنًا خَالِصًا سَآئِغًا
لِّلشّٰرِبِيْنَ ○

67. And from the fruit
Of the date-palm and the vine,
Ye get out wholesome drink[2096]
And food : behold, in this
Also is a Sign
For those who are wise.

٦٧- وَمِنْ ثَمَرٰتِ النَّخِيْلِ وَالْأَعْنَابِ
تَتَّخِذُوْنَ مِنْهُ سَكَرًا وَّرِزْقًا حَسَنًا ۚ
إِنَّ فِي ذٰلِكَ لَاٰيَةً لِّقَوْمٍ يَّعْقِلُوْنَ ○

2092. When the earth with all its vegetation is well-nigh dead, parched and shrivelled up, a vivifying shower of rain from above gives it new life. This is a Sign or Emblem of spiritual life. When sin well-nigh kills the soul, the fertilising shower of God's Revelation from above puts new life into it.

2093. The spiritual sustenance which God gives is typified by the wonderful ways of sustenance in the physical world, which figure forth God's providence and loving care for His creation. And the wonderful transformations in the physical world, which all tend to the benefit of man, are also Signs of His supreme wisdom. In the previous verse rain was mentioned, which gives new life to dead nature. In this and the following two verses our attention is drawn to milk, the products of the date and the vine, and honey.

2094. *Their* : in the Arabic, it is "its", in the singular number, for two reasons : (1) cattle is the generic plural, and may be treated as a singular noun ; (2) the instructive Sign is in cattle collectively, but the milk is the product of each single individual.

2095. Milk is a secretion in the female body, like other secretions, but more specialised. Is it not wonderful that the same food, eaten by males and females, produces in the latter, when they have young, the wholesome and complete food, known as milk ? Then, when cattle are tamed and specially bred for milk, the supply of milk is vastly greater than is necessary for their young and lasts for a longer time than during the period they give suck to their young. And it is a wholesome and agreeable diet for man. It is pure, as typified by its whiteness. Yet it is a secretion like other secretions, between the excretions which the body rejects as worthless and the precious blood-stream which circulates within the body and is the symbol of life itself to the animal which produces it.

2096. There are wholesome drinks and foods that can be got out of the date-palm and the vine : *e.g.*, non-alcoholic drinks from the date and the grape, vinegar, date-sugar, grape-sugar, and dates and grapes themselves for eating. If *sakar* must be taken in the sense of fermented wine, it refers to the time before intoxicants were prohibited : this is a Meccan Sūra and the prohibition came in Medina

68. And thy Lord taught the Bee[2097]
To build its cells in hills,
On trees, and in (men's) habitations;

٦٨- وَاَوْحٰى رَبُّكَ اِلَى النَّحْلِ اَنِ اتَّخِذِيْ
مِنَ الْجِبَالِ بُيُوْتًا وَّمِنَ الشَّجَرِ وَمِمَّا يَعْرِشُوْنَ ۝

69. Then to eat of all
The produce (of the earth),[2098]
And find with skill the spacious[2099]
Paths of its Lord: there issues
From within their bodies
A drink of varying colours,
Wherein is healing for men:
Verily in this is a Sign
For those who give thought.

٦٩- ثُمَّ كُلِيْ مِنْ كُلِّ الثَّمَرٰتِ
فَاسْلُكِيْ سُبُلَ رَبِّكِ ذُلُلًا ؕ
يَخْرُجُ مِنْۢ بُطُوْنِهَا شَرَابٌ
مُّخْتَلِفٌ اَلْوَانُهٗ فِيْهِ شِفَآءٌ لِّلنَّاسِ ؕ
اِنَّ فِيْ ذٰلِكَ لَاٰيَةً لِّقَوْمٍ يَّتَفَكَّرُوْنَ ۝

70. It is God Who creates you
And takes your souls at death;
And of you there are
Some who are sent back
To a feeble age, so that[2100]
They know nothing after
Having known (much):
For God is All-Knowing,[2101]
All-Powerful.

٧٠- وَاللّٰهُ خَلَقَكُمْ ثُمَّ يَتَوَفّٰىكُمْ
وَمِنْكُمْ مَّنْ يُّرَدُّ اِلٰٓى اَرْذَلِ الْعُمُرِ
لِكَيْ لَا يَعْلَمَ بَعْدَ عِلْمٍ شَيْـًٔا ؕ
اِنَّ اللّٰهَ عَلِيْمٌ قَدِيْرٌ ۝ ع

2097. *Auḥā*: *waḥyun* ordinarily means inspiration, the Message put into the mind or heart by God. Here the Bee's instinct is referred to God's teaching, which it undoubtedly is. In xcix, 5, it is applied to the earth: we shall discuss the precise meaning when we come to that passage. The honey-comb, itself, with its hexagonal cells, geometrically perfect, is a wonderful structure, and is well called *buyūt*, homes. And the way the bee finds out inaccessible places, in the hills, in the trees, and even among the habitations of men, is one of the marvels of nature, *i.e.*, of God's working in His Creation.

2098. The bee assimilates the juice of various kinds of flowers and fruit, and forms within its body the honey which it stores in its cells of wax. The different kinds of food from which it makes its honey give different colours to the honey, *e.g.*, it is dark-brown, light-brown, yellow, white, and so on. The taste and flavour also varies, as in the case of heather honey, the honey formed from scented flowers, and so on. As food it is sweet and wholesome, and it is used in medicine. Note that while the instinctive individual acts are described in the singular number, the produce of "*their* bodies" is described in the plural, as the result of their collective effort.

2099. *Ẕululan*: two meanings are possible: (1) ways easy and spacious, referring to the unerring way in which bees find their way from long distances to their combs; and (2) the idea of humility and obedience in them. From both we can derive a metaphorical and spiritual meaning.

2100. Besides the mystery and beauty of the many processes going on in the working of God's Creation, there is the wonderful life of man himself on this earth: how he is created as a child; how he grows in intelligence and knowledge; and how his soul is taken back and his body suffers dissolution. In some cases he lives so long that he falls into a feeble old age like a second childhood: he forgets what he learnt and seems almost to go back in Time. Is not all this wonderful, and evidence of the Knowledge and Power of God?

2101. Our attention having been called to the remarkable transformations in life and nature, by which the Knowledge and Power of God work out His beneficent Plan for His creatures, we are reminded that man at best is but a feeble creature, but for the grace of God. We then pass on in the next Section to the differences in the gifts which men themselves enjoy, distinguishing them into so many categories. How much greater is the difference between the created things and their Creator?

Section 10.

71. God has bestowed His gifts
Of sustenance more freely on some
Of you than on others : those
More favoured are not going
To throw back their gifts
To those whom their right hands
Possess, so as to be equal
In that respect. Will they then
Deny the favours of God ?[2102]

٧١- وَاللّٰهُ فَضَّلَ بَعْضَكُمْ عَلٰى بَعْضٍ فِى
الرِّزْقِ ۚ فَمَا الَّذِيْنَ فُضِّلُوْا بِرَآدِّىْ رِزْقِهِمْ
عَلٰى مَا مَلَكَتْ اَيْمَانُهُمْ
فَهُمْ فِيْهِ سَوَآءٌ ۗ
اَفَبِنِعْمَةِ اللّٰهِ يَجْحَدُوْنَ ○

72. And God has made for you
Mates (and Companions) of your
own nature,[2103]
And made for you, out of them,
Sons and daughters and
grandchildren,[2104]
And provided for you sustenance
Of the best : will they
Then believe in vain things,
And be ungrateful for God's
favours ?—

٧٢- وَاللّٰهُ جَعَلَ لَكُمْ مِّنْ اَنْفُسِكُمْ اَزْوَاجًا
وَّجَعَلَ لَكُمْ مِّنْ اَزْوَاجِكُمْ بَنِيْنَ وَحَفَدَةً
وَّرَزَقَكُمْ مِّنَ الطَّيِّبٰتِ ۗ
اَفَبِالْبَاطِلِ يُؤْمِنُوْنَ
وَبِنِعْمَتِ اللّٰهِ هُمْ يَكْفُرُوْنَ ○

73. And worship others than God,—
Such as have no power
Of providing them, for
sustenance,[2105]

٧٣- وَيَعْبُدُوْنَ مِنْ دُوْنِ اللّٰهِ
مَا لَا يَمْلِكُ لَهُمْ رِزْقًا

2102. Even in the little differences in gifts, which men enjoy from God, men with superior gifts are not going to abandon them so as to be equal with men of inferior gifts, whom, perhaps, they hold in subjection. They will never deny their own superiority. How then (as the argument is pursued in the two following verses), can they ignore the immense difference between the Creator and created things, and make the latter, in their thoughts, partners with God?

2103. *Of your nature* : or of yourselves. *Cf.* iv. 1 and n. 504. Self, or Personality, or Soul, all imply a bundle of attributes, capacities, predilections, and dispositions, which we may sum up in the word *Nafs*, or nature. Woman was made to be (1) a mate or companion for man ; (2) except for sex, of the same nature as man, and therefore, with the same moral and religious rights and duties ; and (3) she is not to be considered a source of all evil or sin, as the Christian monks characterised her but rather as a blessing, one of the favours (*Ni'mat*) of God.

2104. *Ḥafadat* : collective plural, daughters, grandchildren, and descendants. The root *ḥafada* also implies obedient service and ministration. Just as the sons (first mentioned) should be a source of strength, so daughters and grandchildren should serve and contribute to the happiness of fathers and grandparents, and are to be looked upon as further blessings.

2105. "Sustenance" (*rizq*) in all this passage (xvi. 65-74), as elsewhere, implies all that is necessary for man's life and growth, physical, mental, moral, and spiritual. Milk, fruit, and honey are examples of physical gifts, with a metaphorical reference to mental and moral health ; family life is an example of moral and social and (ultimately) spiritual opportunities in the life of man ; and in xvi. 65 is an example of rain in the physical world as a type of God's revelation in the spiritual world.

With anything in heavens or earth,
And cannot possibly have
Such power?

مِّنَ السَّمٰوٰتِ وَالْاَرْضِ شَيْـًٔا
وَّلَا يَسْتَطِيْعُوْنَ ۝

74. Invent not similitudes[2106]
For God: for God knoweth,
And ye know not.

٧٤- فَلَا تَضْرِبُوْا لِلّٰهِ الْاَمْثَالَ ؕ
اِنَّ اللّٰهَ يَعْلَمُ وَاَنْتُمْ لَا تَعْلَمُوْنَ ۝

75. God sets forth the Parable
(Of two men: one) a slave
Under the dominion of
another;[2107]
He has no power of any sort;
And (the other) a man
On whom We have bestowed
Goodly favours from Ourselves,
And he spends thereof (freely),
Privately and publicly:
Are the two equal?
(By no means;)
Praise be to God. But
Most of them understand not.

٧٥- ضَرَبَ اللّٰهُ مَثَلًا عَبْدًا
مَّمْلُوْكًا لَّا يَقْدِرُ عَلٰى شَيْءٍ
وَّمَنْ رَّزَقْنٰهُ مِنَّا رِزْقًا حَسَنًا
فَهُوَ يُنْفِقُ مِنْهُ سِرًّا وَّجَهْرًا ؕ
هَلْ يَسْتَوٗنَ ؕ
اَلْحَمْدُ لِلّٰهِ ؕ
بَلْ اَكْثَرُهُمْ لَا يَعْلَمُوْنَ ۝

76. God sets forth (another) Parable
Of two men: one of them
Dumb, with no power
Of any sort; a wearisome burden
Is he to his master;
Whichever way he directs him,
He brings no good:[2108]
Is such a man equal
With one who commands

٧٦- وَضَرَبَ اللّٰهُ مَثَلًا رَّجُلَيْنِ اَحَدُهُمَآ
اَبْكَمُ لَا يَقْدِرُ عَلٰى شَيْءٍ وَّهُوَ كَلٌّ عَلٰى
مَوْلٰىهُ ۙ
اَيْنَمَا يُوَجِّهْهُّ لَا يَاْتِ بِخَيْرٍ ؕ
هَلْ يَسْتَوِيْ هُوَ ۙ وَمَنْ يَّاْمُرُ

2106. *Cf.* xvi. 60 above, and n. 2086. One instance of false similitudes is where Pagans say their gods are mere types or symbols, or where men pray to men as Intercessors.

2107. The first parable is of two men, one of whom is a slave completely under the dominion of another, with no powers of any sort, and another a free man, who is gifted in every way, and is most generous in bestowing out of his opulent wealth (material as well as intangible), privately and publicly, without let or hindrance; for he is his own master and owes no account to any one. The first is like the imaginary gods which men set up,—whether powers of nature, which have no independent existence but are manifestations of God, or deified heroes or men, who can do nothing of their own authority but are subject to the Will and Power of God; the second describes in a faint way the position of God, the Self-Subsistent, to Whom belongs the dominion of all hat is in heaven and earth, and Who bestows freely of His gifts on all His creatures.

2108. In the second Parable, one man is dumb; he can explain nothing, and he can certainly do nothing; he is only a wearisome burden to his master, no matter what his master asks him to do; or perhaps he is really harmful instead of bringing any good; such are idols (literal and metaphorical) when taken as false gods. The other man is in a position to command, and he commands what is just and righteous; not only his commands but his doings also are on the path of righteousness. Such are the qualities of God.

Justice, and is on
A Straight Way? [2109]

بِالْعَدْلِ وَهُوَ عَلٰى صِرَاطٍ مُّسْتَقِيْمٍ ○ ع

Section 11.

77. To God belongeth the
Mystery [2110]
Of the heavens and the earth.
And the Decision of the Hour [2111]
(Of Judgment) is as
The twinkling of an eye,
Or even quicker:
For God hath power
Over all things.

٧٧- وَلِلّٰهِ غَيْبُ السَّمٰوٰتِ وَالْاَرْضِ ؕ
وَمَآ اَمْرُ السَّاعَةِ اِلَّا كَلَمْحِ الْبَصَرِ
اَوْ هُوَ اَقْرَبُ ؕ
اِنَّ اللّٰهَ عَلٰى كُلِّ شَیْءٍ قَدِيْرٌ ○

78. It is He Who brought you
Forth from the wombs
Of your mothers when
Ye knew nothing; and He
Gave you hearing and sight
And intelligence and affections: [2112]
That ye may give thanks
(To God).

٧٨- وَاللّٰهُ اَخْرَجَكُمْ مِّنْۢ بُطُوْنِ
اُمَّهٰتِكُمْ لَا تَعْلَمُوْنَ شَيْـًٔا ۙ
وَّجَعَلَ لَكُمُ السَّمْعَ وَالْاَبْصَارَ وَالْاَفْـِٕدَةَ ۙ
لَعَلَّكُمْ تَشْكُرُوْنَ ○

79. Do they not look at
The birds, held poised
In the midst of (the air
And) the sky? Nothing
Holds them up but (the power [2113]
Of) God. Verily in this
Are Signs for those who believe.

٧٩- اَلَمْ يَرَوْا اِلَى الطَّيْرِ مُسَخَّرٰتٍ فِیْ جَوِّ
السَّمَآءِ ؕ مَا يُمْسِكُهُنَّ اِلَّا اللّٰهُ ؕ
اِنَّ فِیْ ذٰلِكَ لَاٰيٰتٍ لِّقَوْمٍ يُّؤْمِنُوْنَ ○

2109. The gist of the argument is that those who deviate from the worship of the true God commit twofold treason. (1) They do not recognise the immense difference between the Creator and created things, although, in their own little selfish lives, they are tenacious of any little differences there may be between themselves and other fellow-creatures not so gifted. (2) They are guilty of gross ingratitude in forgetting that the source of all goodness and power is God, to Whom alone they owe all the gifts they enjoy in life.

2110. The key to all things—not only those which we see and understand, but those which we do not see or of which we have no idea—is with God, Whose knowledge and power are supreme.

2111. We must not imagine the Day (or Hour or Moment) of Judgment like a prolonged trial in an open court. It is independent of Time. Even "the twinkling of an eye" is not an adequate figure of speech.

2112. Literally, 'hearts,' which are considered the centres of the affections, and in Arabic idiom, of intelligence also. We should therefore give thanks to God, not to imaginary deities or powers or forces.

2113. All the wonderful things in creation are due to the artistry, power, and wisdom of God. Such is the flight of birds in mid-air. So also are the inventions and discoveries, due to man's intelligence, in the next verse; for man's intelligence is a gift direct from God.

80. It is God Who made your
habitations
Homes of rest and quiet[2114]
For you; and made for you,
Out of the skins of animals,
(Tents for) dwellings, which
Ye find so light (and handy)
When ye travel and when
Ye stop (in your travels);[2115]
And out of their wool,
And their soft fibres[2116]
(Between wool and hair),
And their hair, rich stuff
And articles of convenience
(To serve you) for a time.[2117]

٨٠- وَاللّٰهُ جَعَلَ لَكُمْ مِّنْ بُيُوْتِكُمْ سَكَنًا
وَّجَعَلَ لَكُمْ مِّنْ جُلُوْدِ الْاَنْعَامِ
بُيُوْتًا تَسْتَخِفُّوْنَهَا يَوْمَ ظَعْنِكُمْ
وَيَوْمَ اِقَامَتِكُمْ
وَمِنْ اَصْوَافِهَا وَاَوْبَارِهَا
وَاَشْعَارِهَآ اَثَاثًا
وَّمَتَاعًا اِلٰى حِيْنٍ ○

81. It is God Who made.
Out of the things He created,
Some things to give you shade;[2118]
Of the hills He made some
For your shelter; He made you
Garments to protect you
From heat, and coats of mail
To protect you from
Your (mutual) violence.[2119]
Thus does He complete
His favours on you, that
Ye may bow to His Will[2120]
(In Islām).

٨١- وَاللّٰهُ جَعَلَ لَكُمْ مِّمَّا خَلَقَ
ظِلٰلًا وَّجَعَلَ لَكُمْ مِّنَ الْجِبَالِ
اَكْنَانًا وَّجَعَلَ لَكُمْ سَرَابِيْلَ
تَقِيْكُمُ الْحَرَّ
وَسَرَابِيْلَ تَقِيْكُمْ بَاْسَكُمْ كَذٰلِكَ يُتِمُّ
نِعْمَتَهٗ عَلَيْكُمْ لَعَلَّكُمْ تُسْلِمُوْنَ ○

2114. Man's social, intellectual, and spiritual gifts make, of his permanent dwellings, homes of rest and quiet, of refinement and the purer affections, which are the types, in this earthly life, of the highest spiritual Good, the love of God. The pure Home thus becomes the type of the highest spiritual Destiny of man. And these capacities in man are the gifts of God.

2115. When man travels, he wants temporary dwellings, tents, which he can make of the skins of animals, or of the fabrics of vegetable fibres, similar to the skins of animals. These tents are easy to carry when moving, and easy to pitch during halts.

2116. *Ṣūf*, wool, is what we get from sheep. *Sha'r*, hair, is what we get from goats or similar animals, for weaving into fabrics. *Wabar* is the soft camel's hair of which, also, fabrics are woven: they may be considered intermediate between the other two: by extension and analogy the term may be applied to furs and such things, by way of illustration.

2117. All such articles of refined luxury, and useful articles of comfort and convenience only last for a while, but they must be considered as God's gifts.

2118. For example, trees, gardens, the roofs of houses; also from another point of view, the fact that the sun's rays at various times and in various parts of the earth, come obliquely, thus causing shadow along with sunshine. In the hills there are caves and grottoes.

2119. Our clothes protect us from heat and cold, just as our armour protects us from the hurt which we might otherwise receive in battle.

2120. All these blessings, which have both a physical and (by promoting the good of man) a spiritual purpose, should teach us to rally to God and tune our will with His Universal Will, which is another name for Islam.

82. But if they turn away,
Thy duty is only to preach
The Clear Message.

٨٢- فَإِن تَوَلَّوْا
فَإِنَّمَا عَلَيْكَ الْبَلَٰغُ الْمُبِينُ ۝

83. They recognise the favours [2121]
Of God; then they deny them;
And most of them
Are (creatures) ungrateful.

٨٣- يَعْرِفُونَ نِعْمَتَ اللَّهِ ثُمَّ يُنكِرُونَهَا
وَأَكْثَرُهُمُ الْكَٰفِرُونَ ۝ ع

C. 126.—God's apostles, if rejected, will be witnesses
(xvi. 84-100.) Against those who reject God's Truth!
And all false gods will disappear.
A life of justice and righteousness is enjoined
By God, and the strictest fidelity, in intent
And action. For God will judge us
By our faith and deeds, and no evil
Shall have power over those who believe
And put their trust in God their Lord.

SECTION 12.

84. One Day We shall raise
From all Peoples a Witness: [2122]
Then will no excuse be accepted
From Unbelievers, nor will they
Receive any favours.

٨٤- وَيَوْمَ نَبْعَثُ مِن كُلِّ أُمَّةٍ شَهِيدًا
ثُمَّ لَا يُؤْذَنُ لِلَّذِينَ كَفَرُوا وَلَا هُمْ
يُسْتَعْتَبُونَ ۝

85. When the wrong-doers
(Actually) see the Penalty, [2123]
Then will it in no way
Be mitigated, nor will they
Then receive respite.

٨٥- وَإِذَا رَأَى الَّذِينَ ظَلَمُوا الْعَذَابَ
فَلَا يُخَفَّفُ عَنْهُمْ وَلَا هُمْ
يُنظَرُونَ ۝

86. When those who gave partners
To God will see their "partners",

٨٦- وَإِذَا رَأَى الَّذِينَ أَشْرَكُوا شُرَكَاءَهُمْ

2121. *'Arafa* is distinguished from *'alima* in implying a specific discernment (or recognition) of various qualities and uses. All mankind recognises the value of the blessings they enjoy, but in forgetting or disobeying their Author, the wicked show gross ingratitude; for in practice they deny their obligation to Him for those blessings.

2122. To each People is sent God's Messenger or Teacher, to point out the right way. There may be one, or there may be many. Such a Messenger (*Rasūl*) will be a witness that God's Truth was preached to all peoples in express terms, in addition to the Signs of God everywhere in nature. There will then be no room for excuses of any kind. Those who rejected God after repeated warnings cannot reasonably ask for more respite, as they have had every kind of respite during their life of probation; nor can they now take refuge behind God's Grace, which they had repeatedly rejected

2123. When the terrible Penalty is actually on them, it is too late for repentance and for asking for Mercy. Justice must take its course

They will say: "Our Lord!
These are our 'partners,' those
Whom we used to invoke [2124]
Besides Thee." But they will
Throw back their word at them
(And say): "Indeed ye are liars!"

قَالُوْا رَبَّنَا هٰٓؤُلَآءِ شُرَكَآؤُنَا الَّذِيْنَ
كُنَّا نَدْعُوْا مِنْ دُوْنِكَ ۚ
فَاَلْقَوْا اِلَيْهِمُ الْقَوْلَ اِنَّكُمْ لَكٰذِبُوْنَ ۝

87. That day shall they (openly) show [2125]
(Their) submission to God; and all
Their inventions shall leave
Them in the lurch.

٨٧- وَاَلْقَوْا اِلَى اللّٰهِ يَوْمَئِذِ ِالسَّلَمَ
وَضَلَّ عَنْهُمْ
مَّا كَانُوْا يَفْتَرُوْنَ ۝

88. Those who reject God
And hinder (men) from the Path
Of God—for them
Will We add Penalty
To Penalty; for that they
Used to spread mischief.

٨٨- اَلَّذِيْنَ كَفَرُوْا وَصَدُّوْا عَنْ سَبِيْلِ
اللّٰهِ زِدْنٰهُمْ عَذَابًا
فَوْقَ الْعَذَابِ بِمَا كَانُوْا يُفْسِدُوْنَ ۝

89. One day We shall raise
From all Peoples a witness
Against them, from amongst themselves: [2126]
And We shall bring thee
As a witness against these
(Thy people): and We have sent down
To thee the Book explaining
All things, a Guide, a Mercy,
And Glad Tidings to Muslims.

٨٩- وَيَوْمَ نَبْعَثُ فِيْ كُلِّ اُمَّةٍ شَهِيْدًا
عَلَيْهِمْ مِّنْ اَنْفُسِهِمْ
وَجِئْنَا بِكَ شَهِيْدًا عَلٰى هٰٓؤُلَآءِ ؕ
وَنَزَّلْنَا عَلَيْكَ الْكِتٰبَ تِبْيَانًا لِّكُلِّ شَيْءٍ
وَّهُدًى وَّرَحْمَةً وَّبُشْرٰى لِلْمُسْلِمِيْنَ ۝

SECTION 13.

90. God commands justice, the doing
Of good, and liberality to kith

٩٠- اِنَّ اللّٰهَ يَاْمُرُ بِالْعَدْلِ وَالْاِحْسَانِ وَ

2124. The worshippers of false gods will try to shift the responsibility from their own shoulders to that of the false gods. They will suggest (though they will not have the courage for such a bare-faced lie) that they were misled by the false gods. But their lying suggestion will be contradicted and thrown back at them as explained in the next note.

2125. In so far as the false gods were real things, such as deified men or forces of nature, they will openly disclaim them and then (as always) show their submission to God. In so far as the false gods were the inventions of the fancy of the idolaters, they will leave their worshippers in the lurch, for they will be shown as non-existent.

2126. To the thought expressed in xvi. 84 above, is added another detail here. Not only will there be witnesses from Peoples, but the witnesses will be men from amongst the Peoples themselves, men of their own kith and kin, who understood them and explained God's Message in their own language. The Apostle Muḥammad will be witness against the Arabs who rejected him. For those who believe in him (of all races and peoples), the Book which he brought will be an Explanation, a Guide, a Mercy and a Gospel.

And kin, and He forbids
All shameful deeds, and injustice
And rebellion : He instructs you,
That ye may receive admonition.[2127]

91. Fulfil the Covenant of God
When ye have entered into it,
And break not your oaths
After ye have confirmed them;
Indeed ye have made[2128]
God your surety; for God
Knoweth all that ye do.

92. And be not like a woman
Who breaks into untwisted strands
The yarn which she has spun,
After it has become strong.[2129]
Nor[2130] take your oaths to practise
Deception between yourselves,
Lest one party should be
More numerous than another :[2131]
For God will test you by this;
And on the Day of Judgment

إِيتَآئِ ذِي الْقُرْبَىٰ وَيَنْهَىٰ عَنِ الْفَحْشَآءِ
وَالْمُنكَرِ وَالْبَغْيِ يَعِظُكُمْ لَعَلَّكُمْ تَذَكَّرُونَ ○

٩١- وَأَوْفُوا بِعَهْدِ اللَّهِ إِذَا عَاهَدتُّمْ
وَلَا تَنقُضُوا الْأَيْمَانَ بَعْدَ تَوْكِيدِهَا
وَقَدْ جَعَلْتُمُ اللَّهَ عَلَيْكُمْ كَفِيلًا
إِنَّ اللَّهَ يَعْلَمُ مَا تَفْعَلُونَ ○

٩٢- وَلَا تَكُونُوا كَالَّتِي نَقَضَتْ
غَزْلَهَا مِن بَعْدِ قُوَّةٍ أَنكَاثًا
تَتَّخِذُونَ أَيْمَانَكُمْ دَخَلًا بَيْنَكُمْ
أَن تَكُونَ أُمَّةٌ هِيَ أَرْبَىٰ مِنْ أُمَّةٍ
إِنَّمَا يَبْلُوكُمُ اللَّهُ بِهِ وَلَيُبَيِّنَنَّ لَكُمْ يَوْمَ

2127. Justice is a comprehensive term, and may include all the virtues of cold philosophy. But religion asks for something warmer and more human, the doing of good deeds even where perhaps they are not strictly demanded by justice, such as returning good for ill, or obliging those who in worldly language "have no claim" on you; and of course *à fortiori* the fulfilling of the claims of those whose claims are recognised in social life. Similarly the opposites are to be avoided: everything that is recognised as shameful, and everything that is really unjust, and any inward rebellion against God's Law or our own conscience in its most sensitive form.

2128. The immediate reference may or may not be to the oath of fidelity to the Prophet taken at 'Aqaba fourteen months before the Hijra and repeated a little later: see v. 8, and n. 705. But the general meaning is much wider. And this may be viewed in two aspects (1) Every oath taken, or covenant made, is a Covenant before God, and should be faithfully observed. In this it approaches in meaning to v. 1. (2) In particular, every Muslim makes, by the profession, of his Faith, a Covenant with God, and he confirms that Covenant every time he repeats that profession. He should therefore faithfully observe the duties taught to him by Islam.

2129. The Covenant which binds us in the spiritual world makes us strong, like strands of fluffy cotton spun into a strong thread. It also gives us a sense of security against much evil in this world. It costs a woman much labour and skill to spin good strong yarn. She would be foolish indeed, after she has spun such yarn, to untwist its constituent strands and break them into flimsy pieces.

2130. *Nor*: I construe *tattakhizūna* with *lā takūnū* in the previous clause.

2131. Do not make your religion merely a game of making your own party numerically strong by alliances cemented by oaths, which you readily break when a more numerous party offers you its alliance. The Quraish were addicted to this vice, and in international politics at the present day, this seems to be almost a standard of national self-respect and international skill. Islam teaches nobler ethics for individuals and nations. A Covenant should be looked upon as a solemn thing, not to be entered into except with the sincerest intention of carrying it out; and it is binding even if large numbers are ranged against it.

He will certainly make clear
To you (the truth of) that
Wherein ye disagree.[2132]

الْقِيٰمَةِ
مَا كُنْتُمْ فِيهِ تَخْتَلِفُونَ ○

93. If God so willed, He
Could make you all one People :
But He leaves straying[2133]
Whom He pleases, and He guides
Whom He pleases : but ye
Shall certainly be called to account
For all your actions.

٩٣- وَلَوْ شَآءَ اللّٰهُ لَجَعَلَكُمْ أُمَّةً وَّاحِدَةً
وَّلٰكِنْ يُّضِلُّ مَنْ يَّشَآءُ وَيَهْدِي
مَنْ يَّشَآءُ ۖ وَلَتُسْـَٔلُنَّ
عَمَّا كُنْتُمْ تَعْمَلُونَ ○

94. And take not your oaths,
To practise deception between yourselves,[2134]
With the result that someone's foot
May slip after it was
Firmly planted, and ye may
Have to taste the evil (consequences)
Of having hindered (men)
From the Path of God,
And a mighty Wrath
Descend on you.

٩٤- وَلَا تَتَّخِذُوْٓا أَيْمَانَكُمْ
دَخَلًا بَيْنَكُمْ
فَتَزِلَّ قَدَمٌۢ بَعْدَ ثُبُوتِهَا
وَتَذُوقُوا السُّوْٓءَ
بِمَا صَدَدْتُّمْ عَنْ سَبِيلِ اللّٰهِ
وَلَكُمْ عَذَابٌ عَظِيمٌ ○

95. Nor sell the Covenant of God
For a miserable price :[2135]
For with God is (a prize)
Far better for you,
If ye only knew.

٩٥- وَلَا تَشْتَرُوا بِعَهْدِ اللّٰهِ ثَمَنًا قَلِيلًا ۚ
إِنَّمَا عِنْدَ اللّٰهِ هُوَ خَيْرٌ لَّكُمْ
إِنْ كُنْتُمْ تَعْلَمُونَ ○

2132. Disagreements need not necessarily cause conflict where the parties are sincere and honest and do not wish to take advantage of one another. In such cases they do not go by numbers, groupings, and alliances, but by just conduct as in the sight of God. Honest differences will be removed when all things are made clear in the Hereafter.

2133. *Cf.* xiv. 4 and n. 1875. God's Will and Plan, in allowing limited free-will to man, is, not to force man's will, but to give all guidance, and leave alone those who reject that guidance, in case they should repent and come back into Grace. But in all cases, in so far as we are given the choice, we shall be called to account for all our actions. "Leaving to stray" does not mean that we can do what we please. Our personal responsibility remains.

2134. In xvi. 92 above, the motive for false and fraudulent covenants was pointed out with reprobation. Now are pointed out the consequences, *viz.*, (1) to others; if they had not been deceived, they might have walked firmly on the Path, but now they lose faith and perhaps commit like frauds for which you will be responsible; (2) to yourselves; you have not only gone wrong yourselves; but have set others on the wrong path; and you deserve a double Penalty. Perhaps the "evil consequences" refer to this world, and the "Wrath" to the Hereafter.

2135. Any possible gain that you can make by breaking your Covenant and thus breaking God's Law must necessarily be miserable; while your own benefit is far greater in obeying God's Will and doing right.

96. What is with you must vanish:
What is with God will endure.
And We will certainly bestow,
On those who patiently persevere,
Their reward according to
The best of their actions.[2136]

٩٦- مَا عِنْدَكُمْ يَنْفَدُ وَمَا عِنْدَ اللّٰهِ بَاقٍ
وَلَنَجْزِيَنَّ الَّذِينَ صَبَرُوٓا
أَجْرَهُمْ بِأَحْسَنِ مَا كَانُوا يَعْمَلُونَ ○

97. Whoever works righteousness,
Man or woman, and has Faith,
Verily, to him will We give
A new Life, a life[2137]
That is good and pure, and We
Will bestow on such their reward
According to the best
Of their actions.[2138]

٩٧- مَنْ عَمِلَ صَالِحًا مِّنْ ذَكَرٍ أَوْ أُنْثٰى
وَهُوَ مُؤْمِنٌ فَلَنُحْيِيَنَّهٗ حَيٰوةً طَيِّبَةً ۚ
وَلَنَجْزِيَنَّهُمْ أَجْرَهُمْ بِأَحْسَنِ
مَا كَانُوا يَعْمَلُونَ ○

98. When thou dost read[2139]
The Qur-ān, seek God's protection
From Satan the Rejected One.

٩٨- فَإِذَا قَرَأْتَ الْقُرْاٰنَ فَاسْتَعِذْ بِاللّٰهِ
مِنَ الشَّيْطٰنِ الرَّجِيمِ ○

99. No authority has he over those
Who believe and put their trust
In their Lord.

٩٩- إِنَّهٗ لَيْسَ لَهٗ سُلْطٰنٌ عَلَى الَّذِينَ
اٰمَنُوا وَعَلٰى رَبِّهِمْ يَتَوَكَّلُونَ ○

100. His authority is over those
Only, who take him as patron
And who join partners with God.

١٠٠- إِنَّمَا سُلْطٰنُهٗ عَلَى الَّذِينَ يَتَوَلَّوْنَهٗ
وَالَّذِينَ هُمْ بِهٖ مُشْرِكُونَ ○

C. 127.—God's Truth may come in stages, but it gives
(xvi. 101-128.) Strength, guidance, and glad tidings, and should
Be held fast when once received. Be not
Like those who get puffed up with pride

2136. What comparison can there possibly be between spiritual Good, which will endure for ever, and any temporal advantage which you may snatch in this world, which will fade and vanish in no time? And then, God's generosity is unbounded. He rewards you, not according to your merits, but according to the very best of your actions.

2137. Faith, if sincere, means right conduct. When these two confirm each other, God's grace transforms our life. Instead of being troubled and worried, we have peace and contentment: instead of being assailed at every turn by false alarms and the assaults of evil, we enjoy calm and attain purity. The transformation is visible in this life itself, but the "reward" in terms of the Hereafter will be far beyond our deserts.

2138. The same ending as in the previous verse has the same effect as rhyme or a refrain in poetry, or the repetition of a leading *motif* in music. The argument is completed and rounded off.

2139. Evil has no authority or influence on those who put their trust in God. It is good to express that trust in outward actions, and a formal expression of it—as in the formula, "I seek God's protection from Evil"—helps us. Reading or reciting the Qur-ān should be understood both literally and figuratively, as the symbol of the earnest desire of the soul to know and understand God's Will and act in accordance therewith. Man is weak at best, and he should seek strength for his will in God's help and protection.

In worldly good, and scorn the Truth.
Enjoy the good things of life, but render
Thanks to God and obey His Law.
Be true in faith, and proclaim His Word
With gentle, patient wisdom : for God
Is with those who live in self-restraint
A pure, good, and righteous Life.

SECTION 14.

101. When We substitute one revelation[2140]
For another,—and God knows best
What He reveals (in stages),—
They say, "Thou art but a forger":
But most of them understand not.

١٠١- وَإِذَا بَدَّلْنَآ ءَايَةً مَّكَانَ ءَايَةٍ ۙ وَّاللّٰهُ
أَعْلَمُ
بِمَا يُنَزِّلُ قَالُوٓا إِنَّمَآ أَنْتَ مُفْتَرٍۭ ۚ
بَلْ أَكْثَرُهُمْ لَا يَعْلَمُونَ ○

102. Say, the Holy Spirit[2141] has brought
The revelation from thy Lord
In Truth, in order to strengthen
Those who believe,[2142] and as a Guide
And Glad Tidings to Muslims.

١٠٢- قُلْ نَزَّلَهُۥ رُوحُ الْقُدُسِ مِنْ رَّبِّكَ
بِالْحَقِّ لِيُثَبِّتَ الَّذِينَ ءَامَنُوا وَهُدًى
وَّبُشْرٰى لِلْمُسْلِمِينَ ○

103. We know indeed that they
Say, "It is a man that
Teaches him." The tongue
Of him they wickedly point to
Is notably foreign, while this
Is Arabic, pure and clear.[2143]

١٠٣- وَلَقَدْ نَعْلَمُ أَنَّهُمْ يَقُولُونَ إِنَّمَا يُعَلِّمُهُۥ
بَشَرٌ ۗ لِّسَانُ الَّذِى يُلْحِدُونَ إِلَيْهِ أَعْجَمِىٌّ
وَّهٰذَا لِسَانٌ عَرَبِىٌّ مُّبِينٌ ○

2140. See ii. 106, and n. 107. The doctrine of progressive revelation from age to age and time to time does not mean that God's fundamental Law changes. It is not fair to charge a man of God with forgery because the Message as revealed to him is in a different form from that revealed before, when the core of the Truth is the same, for it comes from God.

2141. The title of the Angel Gabriel, through whom the revelations came down.

2142. The People of the Book, if they had true faith, were themselves strengthened in their faith and cleared of their doubts and difficulties by the revelations brought by Muṣṭafā ; and all—whether People of the Book or not—who came within the fold of Islam, found the Qur-ān a Guide and a Gospel, *i.e.*, a substitute for the Mosaic Law and for the Christian Gospel, which had both been corrupted.

2143. The wicked attribute to men of God just such motives and springs of action as they themselves would be guilty of in such circumstances. The Pagans and those who were hostile to the revelation of God in Islam could not and cannot understand how such wonderful words could flow from the tongue of the Holy Prophet. They must needs postulate some human teacher. Unfortunately for their postulate, any possible human teacher they could think of would be poor in Arabic speech if he had all the knowledge that the Qur-ān reveals of previous revelations. Apart from that, even the most eloquent Arab could not, and cannot, produce anything of the eloquence, width, and depth of Quranic teaching, as is evident from every verse of the Book.

104. Those who believe not
In the Signs of God,—
God will not guide them,
And theirs will be
A grievous Penalty.

١٠٤- إِنَّ الَّذِينَ لَا يُؤْمِنُونَ بِآيٰتِ اللّٰهِ
لَا يَهْدِيهِمُ اللّٰهُ وَلَهُمْ عَذَابٌ أَلِيمٌ ○

105. It is those who believe not
In the Signs of God,
That forge falsehood:
It is they who lie![2144]

١٠٥- إِنَّمَا يَفْتَرِي الْكَذِبَ الَّذِينَ لَا يُؤْمِنُونَ
بِآيٰتِ اللّٰهِ ۚ وَأُولٰٓئِكَ هُمُ الْكٰذِبُونَ ○

106. Any one who, after accepting
Faith in God, utters Unbelief,—[2145]
Except under compulsion,
His heart remaining firm
In Faith—but such as
Open their breast to Unbelief,—
On them is Wrath from God,
And theirs will be
A dreadful Penalty.

١٠٦- مَنْ كَفَرَ بِاللّٰهِ مِنْ بَعْدِ إِيمٰنِهِ
إِلَّا مَنْ أُكْرِهَ وَقَلْبُهُ مُطْمَئِنٌّ بِالْإِيمٰنِ
وَلٰكِنْ مَنْ شَرَحَ بِالْكُفْرِ صَدْرًا
فَعَلَيْهِمْ غَضَبٌ مِنَ اللّٰهِ ۚ
وَلَهُمْ عَذَابٌ عَظِيمٌ ○

107. This because they love
The life of this world
Better than the Hereafter:
And God will not guide
Those who reject Faith.

١٠٧- ذٰلِكَ بِأَنَّهُمُ اسْتَحَبُّوا الْحَيٰوةَ الدُّنْيَا
عَلَى الْآخِرَةِ ۙ
وَأَنَّ اللّٰهَ لَا يَهْدِي الْقَوْمَ الْكٰفِرِينَ ○

108. Those are they whose hearts,
Ears, and eyes God has sealed
up,[2146]
And they take no heed.

١٠٨- أُولٰٓئِكَ الَّذِينَ طَبَعَ اللّٰهُ عَلَىٰ قُلُوبِهِمْ وَ
سَمْعِهِمْ وَأَبْصٰرِهِمْ ۖ وَأُولٰٓئِكَ هُمُ الْغٰفِلُونَ ○

109. Without doubt, in the Hereafter
They will perish.

١٠٩- لَا جَرَمَ أَنَّهُمْ فِي الْآخِرَةِ هُمُ الْخٰسِرُونَ ○

2144. It is clearly those who raise the cry of forgery that are guilty of falsehood, as there is not the least basis or even plausibility in their suggestion.

2145. The exception refers to a case like that of 'Ammār, whose father Yāsir and mother Sumayya, were subjected to unspeakable tortures for their belief in Islam, but never recanted. 'Ammār himself was of less mature age and faith, and in a weak moment, suffering under tortures himself and his mind acted on by the sufferings of his parents, uttered a word construed as recantation, though his heart never wavered and he came back at once to the Prophet, who consoled him for his pain and confirmed his faith. There is no permission in this for weakness or dissembling under torture or persecution.

2146. *Cf.* ii. 7. On account of their iniquities and their want of Faith their hearts and their senses become impervious to God's grace, and they run headlong to perdition.

110. But verily thy Lord,— To those who leave their homes After trials and persecutions,—[2147] And who thereafter strive And fight for the Faith And patiently persevere,— Thy Lord, after all this Is Oft-Forgiving, Most Merciful.	١١٠- ثُمَّ إِنَّ رَبَّكَ لِلَّذِينَ هَاجَرُوا مِنۢ بَعْدِ مَا فُتِنُوا ثُمَّ جَٰهَدُوا وَصَبَرُوٓا إِنَّ رَبَّكَ مِنۢ بَعْدِهَا لَغَفُورٌ رَّحِيمٌ ۝

Section 15.

111. One Day every soul Will come up struggling[2148] For itself, and every soul Will be recompensed (fully) For all its actions, and none Will be unjustly dealt with.	١١١- يَوْمَ تَأْتِى كُلُّ نَفْسٍ تُجَٰدِلُ عَن نَّفْسِهَا وَتُوَفَّىٰ كُلُّ نَفْسٍ مَّا عَمِلَتْ وَهُمْ لَا يُظْلَمُونَ ۝
112. God sets forth a Parable: A city enjoying security[2149] And quiet, abundantly supplied With sustenance from every place: Yet was it ungrateful For the favours of God: So God made it taste Of hunger and terror (in extremes) (Closing in on it) like a garment[2150] (From every side), because	١١٢- وَضَرَبَ ٱللَّهُ مَثَلًا قَرْيَةً كَانَتْ ءَامِنَةً مُّطْمَئِنَّةً يَأْتِيهَا رِزْقُهَا رَغَدًا مِّن كُلِّ مَكَانٍ فَكَفَرَتْ بِأَنْعُمِ ٱللَّهِ فَأَذَٰقَهَا ٱللَّهُ لِبَاسَ ٱلْجُوعِ وَٱلْخَوْفِ

2147. I take this verse to refer to such men as were originally with the Pagans but afterwards joined Islam, suffered hardships and exile, and fought and struggled in the Cause, with patience and constancy. Their past would be blotted out and forgiven. Men like Khālid ibn Walīd were numbered with the foremost heroes of Islam. In that case this verse would be a Medina verse, though the Sūra as a whole is Meccan. Perhaps it would he better to read, with some Commentators, *fatanū* in the active voice rather than *futinū* in the passive voice, and translate "after inflicting trials and persecutions (on Muslims)." Notice the parallelism in construction between this verse and verse 119 below.

2148. When the Reckoning comes, each soul will stand on its own personal responsibility. No one else can help it. Full justice will be done, and all the seeming inequalities of this world will be redressed.

2149. The reference may be to any of the cities or populations in ancient or modern times, which were favoured with security and other blessings from God, but which rebelled from God's Law and tasted the inevitable penalty, even in the midst of their iniquities. Some Commentators see here a reference to the city of Mecca under Pagan control. See next note.

2150. There is a double metaphor: (1) the *tasting* of hunger and terror after the abundant supplies and the full security which it had enjoyed; and (2) the complete *enfolding* of the City as with a *garment*, by these two scourges, hunger and a state of subjective alarm. If the reference is to Mecca shortly before its fall to the Muslims, the "hunger" was the seven years' severe famine which afflicted it, and the alarm was the constant fear in the minds of the Pagans that their day was done. Peace and prosperity were restored after the re-entry of the Apostle.

Of the (evil) which
(Its people) wrought.

بما كانوا يصنعون ○

113. And there came to them
An Apostle from among
themselves,
But they falsely rejected him;
So the Wrath seized them
Even in the midst
Of their iniquities.

١١٣- ولقد جاءهم رسول منهم
فكذبوه فأخذهم العذاب
وهم ظلمون ○

114. So eat of the sustenance
Which God has provided
For you, lawful and good;
And be grateful for the favours [2151]
Of God, if it is He
Whom ye serve.

١١٤- فكلوا مما رزقكم الله
حللا طيبا واشكروا نعمت الله
إن كنتم إياه تعبدون ○

115. He has only forbidden you [2152]
Dead meat, and blood,
And the flesh of swine,
And any (food) over which
The name of other than God
Has been invoked.
But if one is forced by necessity,
Without wilful disobedience,
Nor transgressing due limits,—
Then God is Oft-Forgiving,
Most Merciful.

١١٥- إنما حرم عليكم الميتة والدم
ولحم الخنزير وما أهل لغير الله به
فمن اضطر غير باغ
ولا عاد
فإن الله غفور رحيم ○

116. But say not—for any false
thing [2153]
That your tongues may put
forth,—
"This is lawful, and this
Is forbidden," so as to ascribe
False things to God. For those
Who ascribe false things
To God, will never prosper.

١١٦- ولا تقولوا لما تصف ألسنتكم
الكذب هذا حلل وهذا حرام
لتفتروا على الله الكذب
إن الذين يفترون على الله الكذب
لا يفلحون ○

2151. Ingratitude for God's sustenance (in the literal and figurative senses) may be shown in various ways: *e.g.* (1) by forgetting or refusing to acknowledge the true source of the bounty, *viz.*, God, (2) by misusing or misapplying the bounty, as by committing excesses in things lawful, or refusing to share them with others of God's creatures when the need arises, or (3) by falsely ascribing to God any prohibitions we may set up for ourselves for special reasons or because of our special idiosyncrasies.

2152. *Cf.* ii. 173 and notes, v. 4-5, and vi. 121 and 138-146.

2153. Men are apt to create taboos for themselves, out of superstition, and often for selfish ends, and enforce them in the name of religion. Nothing can be more reprehensible.

117. (In such falsehood)
Is but a paltry profit;
But they will have
A most grievous Penalty.

١١٧- مَتَاعٌ قَلِيلٌ
وَلَهُمْ عَذَابٌ أَلِيمٌ ○

118. To the Jews We prohibited
Such things as We have
Mentioned to thee before:[2154]
We did them no wrong,
But they were used to
Doing wrong to themselves.

١١٨- وَعَلَى الَّذِينَ هَادُوا حَرَّمْنَا
مَا قَصَصْنَا عَلَيْكَ مِن قَبْلُ ۚ وَمَا ظَلَمْنَاهُمْ
وَلَٰكِن كَانُوا أَنفُسَهُمْ يَظْلِمُونَ ○

119. But verily thy Lord,—
To those who do wrong
In ignorance, but who
Thereafter repent and make
amends,—
Thy Lord, after all this,
Is Oft-Forgiving, Most
Merciful.[2155]

١١٩- ثُمَّ إِنَّ رَبَّكَ لِلَّذِينَ عَمِلُوا السُّوءَ
بِجَهَالَةٍ ثُمَّ تَابُوا مِن بَعْدِ ذَٰلِكَ وَأَصْلَحُوا
إِنَّ رَبَّكَ مِن بَعْدِهَا
لَغَفُورٌ رَّحِيمٌ ○

Section 16.

120. Abraham was indeed a
model,[2156]
Devoutly obedient to God,
(And) true in faith, and he
Joined not gods with God:[2157]

١٢٠- إِنَّ إِبْرَاهِيمَ كَانَ أُمَّةً قَانِتًا لِّلَّهِ
حَنِيفًا ۖ وَلَمْ يَكُ مِنَ الْمُشْرِكِينَ ○

121. He showed his gratitude
For the favours of God,
Who chose him, and guided him
To a Straight Way.

١٢١- شَاكِرًا لِّأَنْعُمِهِ ۚ
اجْتَبَاهُ وَهَدَاهُ إِلَىٰ صِرَاطٍ مُّسْتَقِيمٍ ○

122. And We gave him Good
In this world, and he will be,

١٢٢- وَآتَيْنَاهُ فِي الدُّنْيَا حَسَنَةً ۖ وَإِنَّهُ

2154. See vi. 146 and n. The further prohibitions to them were a punishment for their hardness of hearts, and not a favour.

2155. See above, xvi. 110, and n. 2147. The parallelism in construction confirms the suggestion of the alternative reading which is made in that note. The similarity of expressions also rounds off the argument, as by a refrain in poetry. What follows now in this Sūra is an exhortation to right conduct.

2156. *Ummat*: a model, pattern, example for imitation: but the idea that he was an Ummat in himself, standing alone against his world, should not be lost sight of. See next note.

2157. The Gospel of Unity has been the corner-stone of spiritual Truth for all time. In this respect Abraham is the model and fountain-head for the world of western Asia and its spiritual descendants all over the world. Abraham was among a people (the Chaldæans) who worshipped stars and had forsaken the Gospel of Unity. He was among them but not of them. He suffered persecution, and left his home and his people, and settled in the land of Canaan.

In the Hereafter, in the ranks
Of the Righteous.[2158]

فِي الْآخِرَةِ لَمِنَ الصَّالِحِينَ ۝

123. So We have taught thee
The inspired (message),
"Follow the ways of Abraham
The True in Faith, and he
Joined not gods with God."

۱۲۳- ثُمَّ أَوْحَيْنَا إِلَيْكَ
أَنِ اتَّبِعْ مِلَّةَ إِبْرَاهِيمَ حَنِيفًا
وَمَا كَانَ مِنَ الْمُشْرِكِينَ ۝

124. The Sabbath was only made[2159]
(Strict) for those who disagreed
(As to its observance);
But God will judge between them
On the Day of Judgment,
As to their differences.[2160]

۱۲۴- إِنَّمَا جُعِلَ السَّبْتُ عَلَى الَّذِينَ اخْتَلَفُوا
فِيهِ وَإِنَّ رَبَّكَ لَيَحْكُمُ بَيْنَهُمْ يَوْمَ الْقِيَامَةِ
فِيمَا كَانُوا فِيهِ يَخْتَلِفُونَ ۝

125. Invite (all) to the Way
Of thy Lord with wisdom
And beautiful preaching;
And argue with them
In ways that are best
And most gracious:[2161]
For thy Lord knoweth best,
Who have strayed from His Path,

۱۲۵- ادْعُ إِلَى سَبِيلِ رَبِّكَ بِالْحِكْمَةِ
وَالْمَوْعِظَةِ الْحَسَنَةِ
وَجَادِلْهُمْ بِالَّتِي هِيَ أَحْسَنُ إِنَّ رَبَّكَ
هُوَ أَعْلَمُ بِمَنْ ضَلَّ عَنْ سَبِيلِهِ

2158 *Cf.* ii. 130.

2159. If Abraham's Way was the right way, the Jews were ready with the taunt, "Why don't you then observe the Sabbath?" The answer is twofold. (1) The Sabbath has nothing to do with Abraham. It was instituted with the Law of Moses because of Israel's hardness of heart (ii. 74); for they constantly disputed with their Prophet Moses (ii. 108), and there were constantly among them afterwards men who broke the Sabbath (ii. 65, and n. 79). (2) Which was the true Sabbath Day? The Jews observe Saturday. The Christians, who include the Old Testament in their inspired Scripture, observe Sunday, and a sect among them (the Seventh Day Adventists) disagree, and observe Saturday. So there is disagreement among the People of the Book. Let them dispute among themselves. Their dispute will not be settled till the Day of Judgment. Meanwhile, Muslims are emancipated from such stringent restrictions. For them there is certainly the Day of United Prayer on Friday, but it is in no sense like the Jewish or the Scotch Sabbath!

2160. *Cf.* ii. 113.

2161. In this wonderful passage are laid down principles of religious teaching, which are good for all time. But where are the Teachers with such qualifications? We must invite all to the Way of God, and expound His Universal Will; we must do it with wisdom and discretion, meeting people on their own ground and convincing them with illustrations from their own knowledge and experience, which may be very narrow, or very wide. Our preaching must be, not dogmatic not self-regarding, not offensive, but gentle, cosniderate, and such as would attract their attention. Our manner and our arguments should not be acrimonious, but modelled on the most courteous and the most gracious example, so that the hearer may say to himself, "This man is not dealing merely with dialectics; he is not trying to get a rise out of me; he is sincerely expounding the faith that is in him, and his motive is the love of man and the love of God."

And who receive guidance.[2162]

وَهُوَ اَعْلَمُ بِالْمُهْتَدِيْنَ ○

126. And if ye do catch them out,
Catch them out no worse
Than they catch you out:
But if ye show patience,
That is indeed the best (course)[2163]
For those who are patient.

١٢٦- وَاِنْ عَاقَبْتُمْ فَعَاقِبُوْا
بِمِثْلِ مَا عُوْقِبْتُمْ بِهٖ
وَلَئِنْ صَبَرْتُمْ لَهُوَ خَيْرٌ لِّلصّٰبِرِيْنَ ○

127. And do thou be patient,[2164]
For thy patience is but
From God; nor grieve over them:
And distress not thyself
Because of their plots.

١٢٧- وَاصْبِرْ وَمَا صَبْرُكَ
اِلَّا بِاللّٰهِ وَلَا تَحْزَنْ عَلَيْهِمْ
وَلَا تَكُ فِيْ ضَيْقٍ مِّمَّا يَمْكُرُوْنَ ○

128. For God is with those[2165]
14 Who restrain themselves,
30 And those who do good.

١٢٨- اِنَّ اللّٰهَ مَعَ الَّذِيْنَ اتَّقَوْا
وَّالَّذِيْنَ هُمْ مُّحْسِنُوْنَ ○ ع

2162. It may be that the Preacher sometimes says to himself "What is the use of teaching these people? they have made up their minds, or they are obstinate, or they are only trying to catch me out." Let him not yield to such a thought. Who knows how the seed of the Word of God may germinate in people's minds? It is not for man to look for results. Man's inner thoughts are known best to God.

2163. In the context this passage refers to controversies and discussions, but the words are wide enough to cover all human struggles, disputes, and fights. In strictest equity you are not entitled to give a worse blow than is given to you. But those who have reached a higher spiritual standard do not even do that. They restrain themselves, and are patient. Lest you should think that such patience only gives an advantage to the adversary, you are told that the contrary is the case: the advantage is with the patient, the self-possessed, those who do not lose their temper or forget their own principles of conduct.

2164. In the previous verse are laid down the principles of conduct in controversy for all Muslims: 'if you catch them out, you are not entitled to strike a heavier blow than you received, but it is better to restrain yourself and be patient.' There patience was *recommended*. In this verse a command is directly addressed to the Prophet, 'Do thou be patient.' It is a *command*: his standard as the Great Teacher is much higher: and he carried it out in his life. His patience and self-restraint were under circumstances of extraordinary provocation. In his human wisdom it may sometimes have seemed questionable whether forbearance and self-restraint might not be human weaknesses: he had to defend his people as well as himself against the enemy's persecutions. He is told here that he need not entertain any such fears. Patience (with constancy) in those circumstances was in accordance with God's own command. Nor was he to grieve if they rejected God's Message: the Prophet had done his duty when he boldly and openly proclaimed it. Nor was his heart to be troubled if they hatched secret plots against himself and his people. God would protect them.

2165. And the Sūra ends with the highest consolation which the righteous can receive: the assurance that God is with them. A double qualification is indicated for so high an honour,—(1) that they should not yield to human passion or anger or impatience, and (2) that they should go on with constancy doing good all around them. To attain to the Presence of God in the sense of "I am with you" is the culmination of the righteous man's aspiration.

INTRODUCTION TO SŪRA XVII (*Banī Isrā-īl*).

In the gradation of spiritual teaching (see Introduction to Sūra viii), we saw that the first seven Sūras sketched the early spiritual history of man, and led up to the formation of the new Ummat of Islam. Sūras viii to xvi formed another series dealing with the formation of the new Ummat and its consolidation, and God's dealing with man taken as an Ummat and considered in his social relations in organised communities (see Introduction to Sūras viii, x, and xvi). We now come to a fresh series, (Sūras xvii-xxix), which may be considered in three parts. Sūras xvii-xxi begin with an allusion to the *Mi'rāj* (of which more later), and proceed to spiritual history as touching individuals rather than nations. The old prophets and stories of the past are now referred to from this point of view. Sūras xxii-xxv refer to Hajj (pilgrimage), worship and prayer, chastity, privacy, etc., as related to a man's individual spiritual growth. Sūras xxvi-xxix go back to the old prophets and stories of the past, as illustrating the growth of the individual soul in its reactions against the lives of the communities and the reactions of the communities to the lives of its great individual souls.

Let us now consider S. xvii. by itself. It opens with the mystic Vision of the Ascension of the Holy Prophet : he was transported from the Sacred Mosque (of Mecca) to the Farthest Mosque (of Jerusalem) in a night and shown some of the Signs of God. The majority of Commentators take this Night Journey literally, but allow that there were other occasions on which a spiritual Journey or Vision occurred. Even on the supposition of a miraculous bodily Journey, it is conceded that the body was almost transformed into a spiritual fineness. The Hadīth literature gives details of this Journey and its study helps to elucidate its mystic meaning. The holy Prophet was first transported to the seat of the earlier revelations in Jerusalem, and then taken through the seven heavens, even to the Sublime Throne, and initiated into the spiritual mysteries of the human soul struggling in Space and Time. The Spaniard, Miguel Asin, Arabic Professor in the University of Madrid, has shown that this Mi'rāj literatue had a great influence on the Mediæval literature of Europe, and especially on the great Italian poem, the *Divine Comedy* (or Drama) of Dante, which towers like a landmark in mediæval European literature.

The reference to this great mystic story of the Mi'rāj is a fitting prelude to the journey of the human soul in its spiritual growth in life. The first steps in such growth must be through moral conduct—the reciprocal rights of parents and children, kindness to our fellow-men, courage and firmness in the hour of danger, a sense of personal responsibility, and a sense of God's Presence through prayer and praise.

The Mi'rāj is usually dated to the 27th night of the month of Rajab (though other dates, *e.g.*, 17th of Rabī' I, are also given) in the year before the Hijra. This fixes the date of the opening verse of the Sūra, though portions of the Sūra may have been a little earlier.

Summary.—The spiritual experiences of the men of God are given in order that God's Signs may be made clear to men : man is misled into evil, and must be guided to a sense of personal responsibility (xvii. 1-22, and C. 128).

Our service to God is shown also in our human relations, goodness to parents and kinsmen and strangers in want, as well as kindness to children, purity in sex relations, justice and respect for human life, protection of orphans, probity in all dealings, and avoidance of arrogance (xvii. 23-40, and C. 129).

God's glory is above all comparison, and the reception of His revelation marks off the man of faith from those who do not believe. But the Believers should speak fair and avoid dissensions, for God doth encompass all men (xvii 41-60, and C. 130).

Pride caused the fall of Iblīs, but the children of Adam have been raised in excellence above other Creation. They will be judged by their deeds. Prayer is good at stated times and at night, and the Qur-ān is offered as healing and mercy (xvii. 61-84, and C. 131).

Inspiration (the Qur-ān) is a Sign of God's grace, and men should accept it without making carping excuses. Be humble in prayer and praise (xvii. 85-111, and C. 132).

C. 128.—It is the privilege of the men of God
(xvii. 1-22.) To see the sublimest mysteries
Of the spiritual world and instruct men
In Righteousness; they warn and shield men
Against Evil. But nothing can lessen
Each soul's personal responsibility
For its own deeds. It carries its fate
Round its own neck. God's gifts
Are for all, but not all receive
The same gifts, nor are all gifts
Of equal dignity or excellence.

Sūra XVII.

Bani Isrā-il, or the Children of Israel.

In the name of God, Most Gracious, Most Merciful.

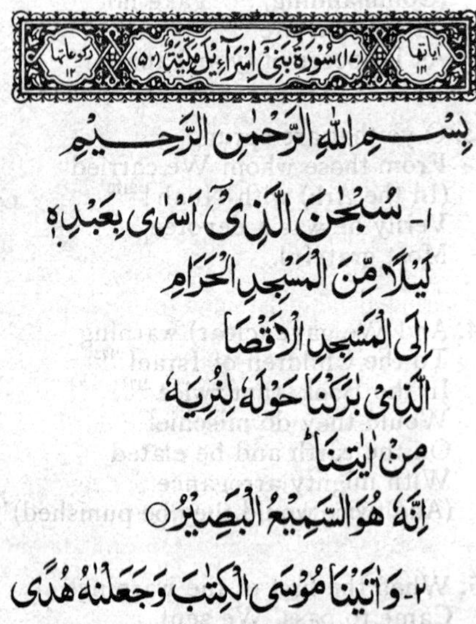

1. Glory to (God)
Who did take His Servant
For a Journey by night [2166]
From the Sacred Mosque [2167]
To the Farthest Mosque, [2168]
Whose precincts We did
Bless,—in order that We
Might show him some
Of Our Signs: for He
Is the One Who heareth
And seeth (all things). [2169]

2. We gave Moses the Book, [2170]
And made it a Guide

2166. The reference is to the *Mi'rāj*, for which see the Introduction to this Sūra.

2167. *Masjid* is a place of prayer: here it refers to the Ka'ba at Mecca. It had not yet been cleared of its idols and rededicated exclusively to the One True God. It was symbolical of the new Message which was being given to mankind.

2168. *The Farthest Mosque* must refer to the site of the Temple of Solomon in Jerusalem on the hill of Moriah, at or near which stands the Dome of the Rock, called also the Mosque of Ḥadhrat 'Umar. This and the Mosque known as the Farthest Mosque (*Masjid-ul-Aqṣā*) were completed by the Amīr 'Abd-ul-Malik in A.H. 68. *Farthest*, because it was the place of worship farthest west which was known to the Arabs in the time of the holy Prophet: it was a sacred place to both Jews and Christians, but the Christians then had the upper hand, as it was included in the Byzantine (Roman) Empire, which maintained a Patriarch at Jerusalem. The chief dates in connection with the Temple are: it was finished by Solomon about B.C. 1004; destroyed by the Babylonians under Nebuchadnezzar about 586 B.C.; rebuilt under Ezra and Nehemiah about 515 B.C.; turned into a heathen idol-temple by one of Alexander's successors, Antiochus Epiphanes, 167 B.C.; restored by Herod, B.C. 17 to A.D. 29; and completely razed to the ground by the Emperor Titus in A.D. 70. These ups and downs are among the greater Signs in religious history.

2169. God's knowledge comprehends all things, without any curtain of Time or any separation of Space. He can therefore see and hear all things, and the *Mi'rāj* was a reflection of this knowledge without Time or Space.

In this and the subsequent verses, the reference to God is generally in the first person and plural. But in the first and the last clause of this verse it is in the third person singular: "Glory to God, Who did take *His* Servant......"; "He is the One......". In each of these two instances, the clause expresses the point of view of God's creatures, who glorify Him, and whose hearing and seeing are ordinarily so limited that they can do nothing but glorify Him when one of His creatures is raised up to hear and see the Mysteries. It is *they* who glorify Him.

2170. *The Book*: the revelation that was given to Moses. It was there clearly laid down that those who followed Moses must consider God as all-in-all. "Thou shalt have no other gods before me; thou shalt not make unto thee any graven image......; thou shalt not bow down thyself to them nor serve them: for I the Lord thy God am a jealous God......;" etc. (Exod. xx. 3-5). These are the words of the English Bible. As a matter of fact the spirit of the Mosaic teaching went further. It referred all things to the Providence of God: God is the Disposer of all affairs, and we are to look to none but Him. This is Islam, and the *Mi'rāj* showed that it was the teaching of God from the most ancient times, and yet it was violated by the very people who claimed to be its custodians.

To the Children of Israel,
(Commanding): "Take not
Other than Me[2171]
As Disposer of (your) affairs."

لِّبَنِيٓ إِسْرَآءِيلَ أَلَّا تَتَّخِذُوا
مِن دُونِي وَكِيلًا ○

3. O ye that are sprung
From those whom We carried
(In the Ark) with Noah![2172]
Verily he was a devotee
Most grateful.

٣- ذُرِّيَّةَ مَنْ حَمَلْنَا مَعَ نُوحٍ
إِنَّهُۥ كَانَ عَبْدًا شَكُورًا ○

4. And We gave (clear) warning
To the Children of Israel[2173]
In the Book, that twice[2174]
Would they do mischief
On the earth and be elated
With mighty arrogance
(And twice would they be punished)!

٤- وَقَضَيْنَآ إِلَىٰ بَنِيٓ إِسْرَآءِيلَ
فِي الْكِتٰبِ لَتُفْسِدُنَّ فِي الْأَرْضِ مَرَّتَيْنِ
وَلَتَعْلُنَّ عُلُوًّا كَبِيرًا ○

5. When the first of the warnings
Came to pass, We sent
Against you Our servants
Given to terrible warfare:[2175]
They entered the very inmost
Parts of your homes;
And it was a warning
(Completely) fulfilled.

٥- فَإِذَا جَآءَ وَعْدُ أُولٰىهُمَا بَعَثْنَا
عَلَيْكُمْ عِبَادًا لَّنَآ أُولِي بَأْسٍ شَدِيدٍ
فَجَاسُوا خِلٰلَ الدِّيَارِ
وَكَانَ وَعْدًا مَّفْعُولًا ○

2171. Note the transition from "We" in the first clause to "Me" in the second clause. The first clause refers to the majesty of God as the Heavenly King; the second clause refers to His personal interest in all our affairs.

2172. After the Deluge of the time of Noah the only descendants of Noah were those who were saved in the Ark with him. They had special reason to celebrate the praises of God. But they relapsed into idolatry, sin, and abominations. They are reminded of the true and sincere devotion of Noah himself, as contrasted with the unworthiness of Noah's descendants, especially the Children of Israel.

2173. The Book is the revelation given to the Children of Israel. Here it seems to refer to the burning words of Prophets like Isaiah. For example, see Isaiah, chap. xxiv. or Isaiah v. 20-30, or Isaiah iii. 16-26.

2174. What are the two occasions referred to? It may be that "twice" is a figure of speech for "more than once", "often". Or it may be that the two occasions refer to (1) the destruction of the Temple by the Babylonian Nebuchadnezzar in 586 B.C., when the Jews were carried off into captivity, and (2) the destruction of Jerusalem by Titus in A.D. 70, after which the Temple was never re-built. See n. 2168 above. On both occasions it was a judgment of God for the sins of the Jews, their back-slidings, and their arrogance.

2175. A good description of the war-like Nebuchadnezzar and his Babylonians. They were servants of God in the sense that they were instruments through which the wrath of God was poured out on the Jews, for they penetrated through their lands, their Temple, and their homes, and carried away the Jews, men and women, into captivity. As regards "the daughters of Zion" see the scathing condemnation in Isaiah, iii, 16-26.

6. Then did We grant you
The Return as against them :[2176]
We gave you increase
In resources and sons,
And made you
The more numerous
In man-power.

٦- ثُمَّ رَدَدْنَا لَكُمُ الْكَرَّةَ عَلَيْهِمْ
وَأَمْدَدْنٰكُمْ بِأَمْوَالٍ وَّبَنِيْنَ
وَجَعَلْنٰكُمْ أَكْثَرَ نَفِيْرًا ○

7. If ye did well,
Ye did well for yourselves ;
If ye did evil,
(Ye did it) against yourselves.[2177]
So when the second
Of the warnings came to pass,
(We permitted your enemies)
To disfigure your faces,[2178]
And to enter your Temple[2179]
As they had entered it before,
And to visit with destruction
All that fell into their power.[2180]

٧- إِنْ أَحْسَنْتُمْ أَحْسَنْتُمْ لِأَنْفُسِكُمْ
وَإِنْ أَسَأْتُمْ فَلَهَا
فَإِذَا جَاءَ وَعْدُ الْآخِرَةِ
لِيَسُوْءٗا وُجُوْهَكُمْ
وَلِيَدْخُلُوا الْمَسْجِدَ كَمَا دَخَلُوْهُ أَوَّلَ مَرَّةٍ
وَّلِيُتَبِّرُوْا مَا عَلَوْا تَتْبِيْرًا ○

8. It may be that your Lord
May (yet) show Mercy[2181]

٨- عَسٰى رَبُّكُمْ أَنْ يَّرْحَمَكُمْ

2176. The return of the Jews from the Captivity was about 520 B C. They started life afresh. They rebuilt their Temple. They carried out various reforms and built up a new Judaism in connection with Ezra. See appendix II following S. v. For a time they prospered. Meanwhile their old oppressors the Babylonians had been absorbed by Persia. Subsequently Persia was absorbed in Alexander's Empire. The whole of western Asia was Hellenized, and the new school of Jews was Hellenized also, and had a strong centre in Alexandria. But their footing in Palestine continued, and under the Asmonæan Dynasty (B.C. 167-63), they had a national revival, and the names of the Maccabees are remembered as those of heroes. Another dynasty, that of the Idumæans, (B.C. 63 to B.C. 4), to which Herod belonged, also enjoyed some semi-independent power. The sceptre of Syria (including Palestine) passed to the Romans in B.C. 65, and Jewish feudatory Kings held power under them. But the Jews again showed a stiff-necked resistance to God's Messenger in the time of Jesus, and the inevitable doom followed in the complete and final destruction of the Temple under Titus in 70 A.D.

2177. This is a parenthetical sentence. If anyone follows God's Law, the benefit goes to himself: he does not bestow a favour on anyone else. Similarly evil brings its own recompense on the doer of evil.

2178. The second doom was due to the rejection of the Message of Jesus. "To disfigure your faces" means to destroy any credit or power you may have got : the face shows the personality of the man.

2179. Titus's destruction of Jerusalem in 70 A.D. was complete. He was a son of the Roman Emperor Vespasian, and at the date of the destruction of Jerusalem, had the title of Cæsar as heir to throne. He ruled as Roman Emperor from 79 to 81 A.D.

2180. Merivale in his *Romans Under the Empire* gives a graphic account of the siege and final destruction (ed. 1890, vii. 221-255). The population of Jerusalem was then 200,000. According to the Latin historian Tacitus it was as much as 600,000. There was a famine and there were massacres. There was much fanaticism. The judgment of Merivale is : "They" (the Jews) "were judicially abandoned to their own passions and the punishment which naturally awaited them" (vii. 221).

2181. Now we come to the time of our holy Prophet. In spite of all the past, the Jews could still have obtained God's forgiveness if they had not obstinately rejected the greatest of the Prophets also. If they were to continue in their sins, God's punishment would also continue to visit them.

Unto you; but if ye
Revert (to your sins),
We shall revert
(To Our punishments):
And We have made Hell
A prison for those who
Reject (all Faith).[2182]

وَإِنْ عُدْتُمْ عُدْنَا ۘ وَجَعَلْنَا جَهَنَّمَ لِلْكَٰفِرِينَ حَصِيرًا ۝

9. Verily this Qur-ān
Doth guide to that
Which is most right (or stable),[2183]
And giveth the glad tidings
To the Believers who work
Deeds of righteousness,
That they shall have
A magnificent reward;

٩- إِنَّ هَٰذَا الْقُرْءَانَ يَهْدِى لِلَّتِى هِىَ أَقْوَمُ وَيُبَشِّرُ الْمُؤْمِنِينَ الَّذِينَ يَعْمَلُونَ الصَّٰلِحَٰتِ أَنَّ لَهُمْ أَجْرًا كَبِيرًا ۝

10. And to those who believe not
In the Hereafter, (it announceth)
That We have prepared
For them a Penalty
Grievous (indeed).

١٠- وَأَنَّ الَّذِينَ لَا يُؤْمِنُونَ بِالْءَاخِرَةِ أَعْتَدْنَا لَهُمْ عَذَابًا أَلِيمًا ۝

SECTION 2.

11. The prayer that man
Should make for good,
He maketh for evil;[2184]
For man is given to
Hasty (deeds).

١١- وَيَدْعُ الْإِنسَٰنُ بِالشَّرِّ دُعَآءَهُۥ بِالْخَيْرِ ۖ وَكَانَ الْإِنسَٰنُ عَجُولًا ۝

12. We have made the Night
And the Day as two[2185]

١٢- وَجَعَلْنَا الَّيْلَ وَالنَّهَارَ ءَايَتَيْنِ

2182. There is such a thing as disgrace in this life, but the final disgrace is in the Hereafter, and that will be irretrievable.

Notice that the allegorical reference to Jewish history, when brought into relation with the mystic meaning of Mi'rāj, refers to the constant struggle of the individual soul against evil. It has its setbacks and its punishments. But if it is true to itself and is true to the Faith in God, God will give it strength and make it successful in its fight against evil. For God's Mercy is unbounded and comes to suffering humanity again and again.

2183. The instability and crookedness of the Jewish soul having been mentioned, the healing balm which should have cured it is now pointed out. The Message of the Qur-ān is for all. Those who have Faith and show that Faith in their conduct must reap their spiritual reward. But those who reject Faith cannot escape punishment. Apart from what is past, apart from questions of national or racial history, there is a spiritual Hope–and a spiritual Danger—for every soul.

2184. Man in his ignorance or haste mistakes evil for good, and desires what he should not have. The wise and instructed soul has patience and does not put its own desires above the wisdom of God. He receives with contentment the favours of God, and prays to be rightly guided in his desires and petitions.

2185. If we were to cry when it is night, we shall look foolish when it is day; for the night is but a preparation for the day: perhaps, as the last verse says, we pray for the day when we want rest for the night. Both are Signs from God. Darknes and light stand for ignorance and knowledge. "Where ingnorance is bliss, 'tis folly to be wise." Darkness and light may also stand for shadow and sunshine, sorrow and joy: both may be necessary for our development.

(Of Our) Signs: the Sign
Of the Night have We obscured,
While the Sign of the Day
We have made to enlighten
You; that ye may seek
Bounty from your Lord,[2186]
And that ye may know
The number and count
Of the years: all things
Have We explained in detail.

فَمَحَوْنَآ ءَايَةَ الَّيْلِ
وَجَعَلْنَآ ءَايَةَ النَّهَارِ مُبْصِرَةً
لِّتَبْتَغُوا فَضْلًا مِّن رَّبِّكُمْ
وَلِتَعْلَمُوا عَدَدَ السِّنِينَ وَالْحِسَابَ
وَكُلَّ شَىْءٍ فَصَّلْنَٰهُ تَفْصِيلًا ○

13. Every man's fate[2187]
We have fastened
On his own neck:
On the Day of Judgment
We shall bring out
For him a scroll,
Which he will see
Spread open.[2188]

١٣- وَكُلَّ إِنسَٰنٍ أَلْزَمْنَٰهُ
طَٰٓئِرَهُۥ فِى عُنُقِهِۦ
وَنُخْرِجُ لَهُۥ يَوْمَ الْقِيَٰمَةِ كِتَٰبًا
يَلْقَىٰهُ مَنشُورًا ○

14. (It will be said to him:)
"Read thine (own) record:
Sufficient is thy soul
This day to make out
An account against thee."[2189]

١٤- اقْرَأْ كِتَٰبَكَ
كَفَىٰ بِنَفْسِكَ الْيَوْمَ عَلَيْكَ حَسِيبًا ○

2186. By the physical light we see physical facts. And this physical gift of God is good for us in two ways: (1) we can arrange for our livelihood, or we can attain the knowledge of the physical sciences and gain some control over the physical forces of nature; and (2) the daily rising and setting of the sun gives us the computation of days and years, for the physical natural year is the solar year. But there is a spiritual light even more precious: by it we can similarly attain two objects, *viz*: (1) our spiritual livelihood and knowledge, and (2) our computation of the stages we reach in our spiritual years. Let us be patient and seek everything as from God,—in joy and in sorrow, in knowledge and in want of knowledge of those things which are above us. Let us rejoice in what God has given us, and not be impatient about those things which He in His wisdom has thought fit to withhold from us. But all things should be sought and striven for under the guidance of the All-Knowing God.

2187. *Fate*: *Ṭāir*, literally a bird, hence an omen, an evil omen, fate. *Cf.* xxxvi. 19. The Arabs, like the ancient Romans, sought to read the mysteries of human fate from the flight of birds. And many of us in our own day seek to read our future fortunes by similar superstitions. We read in the previous verse that there are Signs of God, but they are not meant to subserve the vulgar purpose of disclosing our future destiny in a worldly sense. They are meant for quite other purposes, as we have explained. Our real fate does not depend upon birds or omens or stars. It depends on our deeds, good or evil, and they hang round our necks. Man is the maker of his own fortune.

2188. These deeds, good or evil, will be embodied in a scroll which will be quite open to us in the light of the Day of Judgment, however much we may affect to be ignorant of it now or waste our energies in prying into mysteries that do not concern us.

2189. Our true accusers are our own deeds. Why not look to them instead of vainly prying into something superstitious which we call a book of fortune or a book of omens?

15. Who receiveth guidance,
Receiveth it for his own
Benefit: who goeth astray
Doth so to his own loss:[2190]
No bearer of burdens
Can bear the burden[2191]
Of another: nor would We
Visit with Our Wrath
Until We had sent
An apostle (to give warning).

١٥- مَنِ اهْتَدَىٰ فَإِنَّمَا يَهْتَدِي لِنَفْسِهِ ۖ
وَمَن ضَلَّ فَإِنَّمَا يَضِلُّ عَلَيْهَا ۚ
وَلَا تَزِرُ وَازِرَةٌ وِزْرَ أُخْرَىٰ ۗ
وَمَا كُنَّا مُعَذِّبِينَ
حَتَّىٰ نَبْعَثَ رَسُولًا ○

16. When We decide to destroy
A population, We (first) send
A definite order to those
Among them who are given
The good things of this life[2192]
And yet transgress; so that
The word is proved true[2193]
Against them: then (it is)
We destroy them utterly.

١٦- وَإِذَا أَرَدْنَا أَن نُّهْلِكَ قَرْيَةً أَمَرْنَا
مُتْرَفِيهَا فَفَسَقُوا فِيهَا
فَحَقَّ عَلَيْهَا الْقَوْلُ
فَدَمَّرْنَاهَا تَدْمِيرًا ○

17. How many generations
Have We destroyed after Noah?[2194]
And enough is thy Lord
To note and see
The sins of His servants.[2195]

١٧- وَكَمْ أَهْلَكْنَا مِنَ الْقُرُونِ مِن بَعْدِ
نُوحٍ ۗ وَكَفَىٰ بِرَبِّكَ بِذُنُوبِ عِبَادِهِ
خَبِيرًا بَصِيرًا ○

2190. The doctrine of personal responsibility is insisted on, and the basis of ethics is shown to be our own good or evil as furthering or obstructing our highest development.

2191. The doctrine of vicarious atonement is condemned. Salvation for the wicked cannot be attained by the punishment of the innocent. One man cannot bear the burden of another: that would be unjust. Every man must bear his own personal responsibility. *Cf.* vi. 164. But God never visits His wrath on anyone until due warning is conveyed to him through an accredited apostle.

2192. God's Mercy gives every chance to the wicked to repent. When wickedness gets so rampant that punishment becomes inevitable, even then God's Mercy and Justice act together. Those who are highly gifted from God—it may be with wealth or position, or it may be with talents and opportunities—are expected to understand and obey. They are given a definite order and warning. If they still transgress there is no further room for argument. They cannot plead that they were ignorant. The command of the Lord is proved against them, and its application is called for beyond doubt. Then it is that their punishment is completed.

2193. *Qaul* here has the sense of word, order, law, charge framed against one under a definite law.

2194. Noah's Flood is taken as a new starting point in history. But even after that hundreds of empires, towns, and generations have perished for their wickedness.

2195. Let not the wicked think, because they are given a lease of life and luxury for a time, that their wickedness has escaped notice. God notes and sees all things, both open and secret. He knows the hidden motives and thoughts of men, and He has no need of any other evidence. His knowledge and sight are all-sufficient.

18. If any do wish For the transitory things (Of this life), We readily[2196] Grant them—such things As We will, to such persons As We will: in the end Have We provided Hell For them: they will burn Therein, disgraced and rejected.[2197]	١٨- مَن كَانَ يُرِيدُ الْعَاجِلَةَ عَجَّلْنَا لَهُ فِيهَا مَا نَشَاءُ لِمَن نُّرِيدُ ثُمَّ جَعَلْنَا لَهُ جَهَنَّمَ يَصْلَاهَا مَذْمُومًا مَّدْحُورًا ○
19. Those who do wish For the (things of) the Hereafter,[2198] And strive therefor With all due striving, And have Faith,—[2199] They are the ones Whose striving is acceptable (To God).	١٩- وَمَنْ أَرَادَ الْآخِرَةَ وَسَعَىٰ لَهَا سَعْيَهَا وَهُوَ مُؤْمِنٌ فَأُولَٰئِكَ كَانَ سَعْيُهُم مَّشْكُورًا ○
20. Of the bounties of thy Lord We bestow freely on all— These as well as those: The bounties of thy Lord Are not closed (to anyone).[2200]	٢٠- كُلًّا نُّمِدُّ هَٰؤُلَاءِ وَهَٰؤُلَاءِ مِنْ عَطَاءِ رَبِّكَ وَمَا كَانَ عَطَاءُ رَبِّكَ مَحْظُورًا ○
21. See how We have bestowed More on some than on others; But verily the Hereafter Is more in rank and gradation	٢١- انظُرْ كَيْفَ فَضَّلْنَا بَعْضَهُمْ عَلَىٰ بَعْضٍ وَلَلْآخِرَةُ أَكْبَرُ دَرَجَاتٍ

2196. An explanation is now given of how it is that prosperity sometimes seems to attend the wicked. The explanation is threefold: (1) the transitory things of this life are worth little in the eternal scheme of things; (2) even they are provided, not just because their recipients wish for them, but according to a definite Plan of God; and (3) in the end there is for the wicked the eternal Misery and deprivation of grace,—the Hell which is worse than destruction in the terms of this world.

2197. All the pride and insolence will then be brought low. The disgrace and the exclusion from the "sight of the Face of God" will by themselves be punishments of which the magnitude cannot be measured in the terms of our present material life.

2198. This is in contrast to the last verse. Those who wish for mere earthly good sometimes get it and misuse it. Those whose eyes are fixed on the Hereafter, they too share in their Lord's bounty provided they fulfil the conditions explained in the next note; but their wishes and endeavours are more acceptable in the sight of God.

2199. A mere wish for moral and spiritual good is not enough. It must be backed up by hard endeavour and supported by a lively Faith. On those conditions the wishes are accepted by God.

2200. God's favours are showered on all,—the just and the unjust, the deserving and the undeserving. But there is a difference as explained in the last two verses.

And more in excellence.[2201]

وَأَكْبَرُ تَفْضِيلًا ۝

22\. Take not with God
Another object of worship ;[2202]
Or thou (O man !) wilt sit
In disgrace and destitution.[2203]

٢٢- لَا تَجْعَلْ مَعَ اللَّهِ إِلَٰهًا آخَرَ
فَتَقْعُدَ مَذْمُومًا مَخْذُولًا ۝ ع

C. 129.—To be worthy of the service of the One True God,
(xvii. 23-40.) We must love and serve His Creatures.
The parents who cherished us in childhood
Deserve our humble reverence and service : next
Come the rights of kinsmen, those in want,
And wayfaring strangers : to each
According to his need, not in spendthrift show.
And gentleness is needed to those whom we
Cannot help. God will provide. He has made
Life sacred and pure. Fulfil your trusts
For orphans and deal with all in strictest
Probity. Pry not into evil from curiosity,
And shun insolence : for God hates evil,—
The One, the Good, the Universal Lord !

SECTION 3.

23\. Thy Lord hath decreed
That ye worship none but Him,
And that ye be kind
To parents. Whether one
Or both of them attain
Old age in thy life,[2204]
Say not to them a word
Of contempt, nor repel them,
But address them
In terms of honour.

٢٣- وَقَضَىٰ رَبُّكَ أَلَّا تَعْبُدُوا إِلَّا إِيَّاهُ
وَبِالْوَالِدَيْنِ إِحْسَانًا
إِمَّا يَبْلُغَنَّ عِندَكَ الْكِبَرَ أَحَدُهُمَا
أَوْ كِلَاهُمَا فَلَا تَقُل لَّهُمَا أُفٍّ وَلَا تَنْهَرْهُمَا
وَقُل لَّهُمَا قَوْلًا كَرِيمًا ۝

2201\. Nor should man suppose that all gifts are of equal value. The spiritual ones rank far higher in dignity and real worth than the transitory ones. Therefore it is altogether wrong to compare the worldly prosperity of a wicked man with the apparent want of it to a man of spiritual worth. There is no comparison between them when measured by right standards.

2202\. The seeming inequality of gifts to men might make short-sighted men impugn the impartiality of God. But the fault lies with such men's own want of knowledge and want of Faith. There is no excuse for them to seek other objects of worship than God. For there is none worthy of worship except God.

2203\. If foolish men turn to false objects of worship, they will not only be disappointed, but they will lose the respect of their own fellow-men, and spiritually they will be reduced to destitution. All their talents and their works will be of no avail.

2204\. The spiritual and moral duties are now brought into juxtaposition. We are to worship none but God, because none but God is worthy of worship, not because "the Lord thy God is a jealous God, visiting the iniquity of the fathers upon the children unto the third and fourth generation of them that hate Me" (Exod. xx. 5).

Note that the act of worship may be collective as well as individual; hence the plural *ta'budū*. The kindness to parents is an individual act of piety; hence the singular *taqul*, *qul*, etc.

24. And, out of kindness,
Lower to them the wing[2205]
Of humility, and say:
" My Lord! bestow on them
Thy Mercy even as they
Cherished me in childhood."[2206]

٢٤-وَاخْفِضْ لَهُمَا جَنَاحَ الذُّلِّ مِنَ
الرَّحْمَةِ وَقُلْ رَّبِّ ارْحَمْهُمَا
كَمَا رَبَّيٰنِي صَغِيرًا ۝

25. Your Lord knoweth best
What is in your hearts:
If ye do deeds of righteousness,
Verily He is Most Forgiving
To those who turn to Him
Again and again
(in true penitence).[2207]

٢٥-رَبُّكُمْ أَعْلَمُ بِمَا فِي نُفُوسِكُمْ
إِنْ تَكُونُوا صٰلِحِينَ
فَإِنَّهُ كَانَ لِلْأَوَّابِينَ غَفُورًا ۝

26. And render to the kindred
Their due rights, as (also)
To those in want,
And to the wayfarer:[2208]
But squander not (your wealth)
In the manner of a spendthrift.[2209]

٢٦-وَاٰتِ ذَا الْقُرْبٰى حَقَّهُ
وَالْمِسْكِينَ وَابْنَ السَّبِيلِ
وَلَا تُبَذِّرْ تَبْذِيرًا ۝

2205. *Cf.* xv. 88 and n. 2011. The metaphor is that of a high-flying bird which lowers her wing out of tenderness to her offspring. There is a double aptness. (1) When the parent was strong and the child was helpless, parental affection was showered on the child: when the child grows up and is strong, and the parent is helpless, can he do less than bestow similar tender care on the parent? (2) But more: he must approach the matter with gentle humility: for does not parental love remind him of the great love with which God cherishes His creatures? There is something here more than simple human gratitude: it goes up into the highest spiritual region.

2206. Note that we are asked to honour our father and mother, not "that thy days may be long upon the land which the Lord thy God giveth thee" (Exod. xx. 12), but upon much higher and more universal grounds, such as befit a perfected revelation. In the first place, not merely respect, but cherishing kindness, and humility to parents, are commanded. In the second place, this command is bracketed with the command to worship the One True God: parental love should be to us a type of divine love: nothing that we can do can ever really compensate for that which we have received. In the third place (see next verse) our spiritual advancement is tested by this: we cannot expect God's forgiveness if we are rude or unkind to those who unselfishly brought us up.

2207. It is the heart, and its hidden and secret motives, by which we are judged: for God knows them all.

2208. In the Jewish Decalogue, which was given to a primitive and hard-hearted people, this refinement of kindness,—to those in want and to wayfarers (*i.e.* total strangers whom you come across) finds no place. Nor was there much danger of their wasting their substance out of exuberance. Even the command "to honour thy father and mother" comes after the ceremonial observance of the Sabbath. With us, the worship of God is linked up with kindness—to parents, kindred, those in want, those who are far from their homes though they may be total strangers to us. It is not mere verbal kindness. They have certain rights which must be fulfilled.

2209. All charity, kindness, and help are conditioned by our own resources. There is no merit if we merely spend out of bravado or for idle show. How many families are ruined by extravagant expenses at weddings, funerals, etc., or (as they may call it) to "oblige friends or relatives", or to give to able-bodied beggars? To no one was this command more necessary than it is to Muslims of the present day.

27. Verily spendthrifts are brothers
Of the Evil Ones;
And the Evil One
Is to his Lord (Himself)
Ungrateful.[2210]

٢٧- إِنَّ الْمُبَذِّرِيْنَ كَانُوْٓا إِخْوَانَ الشَّيٰطِيْنِ ط
وَكَانَ الشَّيْطٰنُ لِرَبِّهٖ كَفُوْرًا ○

28. And even if thou hast
To turn away from them
In pursuit of the Mercy
From thy Lord which thou
Dost expect, yet speak
To them a word
Of easy kindness.[2211]

٢٨- وَإِمَّا تُعْرِضَنَّ عَنْهُمُ
ابْتِغَآءَ رَحْمَةٍ مِّنْ رَّبِّكَ تَرْجُوْهَا
فَقُلْ لَّهُمْ قَوْلًا مَّيْسُوْرًا ○

29. Make not thy hand tied[2212]
(Like a niggard's) to thy neck,
Nor stretch it forth
To its utmost reach,
So that thou become
Blameworthy and destitute.

٢٩- وَلَا تَجْعَلْ يَدَكَ مَغْلُوْلَةً إِلٰى عُنُقِكَ
وَلَا تَبْسُطْهَا كُلَّ الْبَسْطِ
فَتَقْعُدَ مَلُوْمًا مَّحْسُوْرًا ○

30. Verily thy Lord doth provide
Sustenance in abundance
For whom He pleaseth, and He
Provideth in a just measure.[2213]
For He doth know
And regard all His servants.

٣٠- إِنَّ رَبَّكَ يَبْسُطُ الرِّزْقَ
لِمَنْ يَّشَآءُ وَيَقْدِرُ ط
إِنَّهٗ كَانَ بِعِبَادِهٖ خَبِيْرًا بَصِيْرًا ع ○

2210. Spendthrifts are not merely fools. They are of the same family as the Evil Ones. And the chief of the Evil Ones (notice the transition from the plural to the singular)—Satan himself—fell by his ingratitude to God. So those who misuse or squander God's gifts are also ungrateful to God.

2211. You may have to "turn away" from people for two reasons. (1) You may not have the wherewithal with which to entertain them and give them their rights; or (2) you may have to give them a wide berth because their thoughts are not as your thoughts. In either case there is no need to speak harshly to them. Your words should be those of "easy kindness", *i e*, the sort of kindness (not merely frigid politeness) which flows from pity and understanding and smooths over unnecessary difficulties in human intercourse.

2212. *Cf.* the phrase for niggardliness in v. 67. We are not to be so lavish as to make ourselves destitute and incur the just censure of wise men, nor is it becoming to keep back our resources from the just needs of those who have a right to our help. Even strangers have such a right, as we saw in xvii. 26 above. But we must keep a just measure between our capacity and other people's needs.

2213. If a foolish spendthrift pretends that his generosity, even if it ruins himself, is good for other people, he is reminded that God will take care of all. He knows every one's true needs and cares for them. He gives in abundance to some, but in all cases He gives in just measure. Who are we to pretend to greater generosity? A foolish Hindi saying was current in Oudh: *jis ko nā de Maulā, tis ko de Āṣaf-ud-daula*: "To those to whom the Lord gives not, Āṣaf-ud-daula gives." It was extravagance that ruined his family and wiped his kingdom of Oudh off the map.

Section 4.

31. Kill not your children [2214]
For fear of want : We shall
Provide sustenance for them
As well as for you.
Verily the killing of them
Is a great sin.

٣١-وَلَا تَقْتُلُوٓا أَوْلَٰدَكُمْ خَشْيَةَ إِمْلَٰقٍ ۖ
نَّحْنُ نَرْزُقُهُمْ وَإِيَّاكُمْ ۚ
إِنَّ قَتْلَهُمْ كَانَ خِطْـًٔا كَبِيرًا ○

32. Nor come nigh to adultery :
For it is a shameful (deed)
And an evil, opening the road [2215]
(To other evils).

٣٢-وَلَا تَقْرَبُوا۟ ٱلزِّنَىٰٓ ۖ إِنَّهُۥ كَانَ فَٰحِشَةً
وَسَآءَ سَبِيلًا ○

33. Nor take life—which God
Has made sacred—except
For just cause. And if
Anyone is slain wrongfully,
We have given his heir
Authority (to demand Qiṣāṣ [2216]
Or to forgive) : but let him
Not exceed bounds in the matter
Of taking life ; for he
Is helped (by the Law).

٣٣-وَلَا تَقْتُلُوا۟ ٱلنَّفْسَ ٱلَّتِى حَرَّمَ ٱللَّهُ
إِلَّا بِٱلْحَقِّ ۗ وَمَن قُتِلَ مَظْلُومًا
فَقَدْ جَعَلْنَا لِوَلِيِّهِۦ سُلْطَٰنًا
فَلَا يُسْرِف فِّى ٱلْقَتْلِ ۖ
إِنَّهُۥ كَانَ مَنصُورًا ○

34. Come not nigh
To the orphan's property
Except to improve it, [2217]

٣٤-وَلَا تَقْرَبُوا۟ مَالَ ٱلْيَتِيمِ إِلَّا بِٱلَّتِى
هِىَ أَحْسَنُ

2214 The Arabs were addicted to female infanticide. In a society perpetually at war a son was a source of strength whereas a daughter was a source of weakness. Even now infanticide is not unknown in other countries for economic reasons. This crime against children's lives is here characterised as one of the greatest of sins.

2215. Literally, "it is evil as a road (or a way)". Adultery is not only shameful in itself and inconsistent with any self-respect or respect for others, but it opens the road to many evils. It destroys the basis of the family ; it works against the interests of children born or to be born ; it may cause murders and feuds and loss of reputation and property, and also loosen permanently the bonds of society. Not only should it be avoided as a sin, but any approach or temptation to it should be avoided.

2216. On the subject of Qiṣāṣ see ii. 178 and the notes thereto. Under the strict limitations there laid down, a life may be taken for a life. The heir is given the right to demand the life ; but he must not exceed due bounds, because he is helped by the Law. Some Commentators understand "he" in "he is helped (by the Law)" to refer to the heir of the person against whom Qiṣāṣ is sought. He too will be helped by the Law, if the heir of the first slain exceeds the bounds of Law.

2217. *Cf.* vi. 152, and other passages relating to orphans, *e.g.*, ii. 220. If an orphan's property is touched at all, it should be to improve it, or to give him something better than he had before,—never to take a personal advantage for the benefit of the guardian. A bargain that may be quite fair as between two independent persons would be, under this verse, unfair as between a guardian and his orphan ward until the latter attains the full age of understanding.

Until he attains the age[2218]
Of full strength; and fulfil
(Every)[2219] engagement,
For (every) engagement
Will be enquired into
(On the Day of Reckoning).[2220]

حَتّٰى يَبْلُغَ اَشُدَّهٗ
وَاَوْفُوْا بِالْعَهْدِ
اِنَّ الْعَهْدَ كَانَ مَسْـُٔوْلًا ۝

35. Give full measure when ye
Measure, and weigh
With a balance that is straight:
That is the most fitting
And the most advantageous
In the final determination.[2221]

٣٥- وَاَوْفُوا الْكَيْلَ اِذَا كِلْتُمْ
وَزِنُوْا بِالْقِسْطَاسِ الْمُسْتَقِيْمِ
ذٰلِكَ خَيْرٌ وَّاَحْسَنُ تَاْوِيْلًا ۝

36. And pursue not that
Of which thou hast[2222]
No knowledge; for
Every act of hearing,
Or of seeing
Or of (feeling in) the heart
Will be enquired into
(On the Day of Reckoning).

٣٦- وَلَا تَقْفُ مَا لَيْسَ لَكَ بِهٖ عِلْمٌ
اِنَّ السَّمْعَ وَالْبَصَرَ
وَالْفُؤَادَ كُلُّ
اُولٰٓئِكَ كَانَ عَنْهُ مَسْـُٔوْلًا ۝

37. Nor walk on the earth[2223]
With insolence: for thou

٣٧- وَلَا تَمْشِ فِي الْاَرْضِ مَرَحًا اِنَّكَ

2218. *Ashuddun* means the age when the orphan reaches his full maturity of strength and understanding, say between the ages of 18 and 30. The age of legal majority may be 18 (as for certain purposes in India) or 21 (as in England). For certain purposes in Muslim law it may be less than 18. In the orphan's interest a much stricter standard is required in his case.

2219. The definite article *al* has here a generic meaning, and is best translated by "every".

2220. From the context the engagements referred to would relate to beneficial contracts connected with the orphan's property or promises or undertakings given by the guardian or implied in the terms of his appointment. But the words are general and may be interpreted in the general sense. Note that this sentence does not occur in the similar passage in vi. 152, where there was a discussion of social laws: it is appropriate here, where the discussion is about the guardian's personal and individual responsibility in a spiritual sense.

2221. Giving just measure and weight is not only right in itself but is ultimately to the best spiritual and material advantage of the person who gives it.

2222. Idle curiosity may lead us to nose into evil, through our ignorance that it is evil. We must guard against every such danger. We must only hear the things that are known to us to be of good report, and see things that are good and instructive, and entertain in our hearts feelings or in our minds ideas that we have reason to expect will be spiritually profitable to us. We shall be called to account for the exercise of every faculty that has been given to us. This goes a little farther than a famous sculpture on a Japanese temple in which three monkeys are shown as putting their hands to their ears, eyes, and mouths, respectively, to show that they were not prepared to hear any evil, or see any evil, or speak any evil. Here idle curiosity is condemned. Futility is to be avoided even if it does not reach the degree of positive evil.

2223. Insolence, or arrogance, or undue elation at our powers or capacities, is the first step to many evils. Besides, it is unjustified. All our gifts are from God.

Canst not rend the earth
Asunder, nor reach
The mountains in height.

لَنْ تَخْرِقَ الْاَرْضَ
وَلَنْ تَبْلُغَ الْجِبَالَ طُوْلًا ۝

38. Of all such things
The evil is hateful
In the sight of thy Lord.

٣٨- كُلُّ ذٰلِكَ كَانَ سَيِّئُهٗ
عِنْدَ رَبِّكَ مَكْرُوْهًا ۝

39. These are among the (precepts
Of) wisdom, which thy Lord
Has revealed to thee.[2224]
Take not, with God,
Another object of worship,
Lest thou shouldst be thrown
Into Hell, blameworthy and
rejected.[2225]

٣٩- ذٰلِكَ مِمَّآ اَوْحٰٓى اِلَيْكَ
رَبُّكَ مِنَ الْحِكْمَةِ ؕ
وَلَا تَجْعَلْ مَعَ اللّٰهِ اِلٰهًا اٰخَرَ
فَتُلْقٰى فِيْ جَهَنَّمَ مَلُوْمًا مَّدْحُوْرًا ۝

40. Has then your Lord,
(O Pagans!) preferred for you
Sons, and taken for Himself
Daughters among the angels ?[2226]
Truly ye utter
A most dreadful saying !

٤٠- اَفَاَصْفٰكُمْ رَبُّكُمْ بِالْبَنِيْنَ
وَاتَّخَذَ مِنَ الْمَلٰٓئِكَةِ اِنَاثًا ؕ
اِنَّكُمْ لَتَقُوْلُوْنَ قَوْلًا عَظِيْمًا ۝ ع

C. 130.—There is none like unto God. Exalted
(xvii. 41-60.) **Beyond measure is He. All Creation**
Declares His glory. His revelation
Is Truth, but is beyond comprehension
To those who believe not in the Hereafter.
Those who serve Him should beware
Lest words unseemly should escape them,
Whether to friend or foe. Avoid
Dissensions, and know tnat God's Wrath
When kindled is a terrible thing,
But we rejoice that He forbears and forgives.

2224. The moral law, as expounded in xvii. 23-39 is far in advance of the bare Decalogue in that it searches out motives, and draws pointed attention to the weak and helpless if we are to reach any spiritual understanding of God. It begins with a mention of the worship of the One True God and ends with a similar mention to close the argument, thus emphasizing the fact that the love of God embraces the love of man and practical help to our fellow-creatures.

2225. "Blameworthy" carries us back by reminiscence to xvii 29, between which and this verse there is mention of crimes committed out of covetousness and a selfish disregard of other people's rights. "Rejected" carries back our reminiscence to xvii. 18, from which to here we have a reference to crimes that lead to deprivation of God's grace. The latter is of course wider than the former. Note how subtly the two streams of thought are here conjoined.

2226. *Cf.* xvi. 57-59. Insistence on true worship means also exclusion of false worship or worship derogatory to God. In circles where daughters were despised and even their lives had to be protected by special legislation, what could have been more dreadful than ascribing daughters to god ?

SECTION 5.

41. We have explained (things)
In various (ways) in this Qur-ān,
In order that they may receive[2227]
Admonition, but it only increases
Their flight (from the Truth)!

٤١- وَلَقَدْ صَرَّفْنَا فِي هٰذَا الْقُرْاٰنِ لِيَذَّكَّرُوْا ۖ
وَمَا يَزِيْدُهُمْ اِلَّا نُفُوْرًا ۝

42. Say: if there had been
(Other) gods with Him,—
As they say,—behold,
They would certainly have
Sought out a way
To the Lord of the Throne![2228]

٤٢- قُلْ لَّوْ كَانَ مَعَهٗۤ اٰلِهَةٌ
كَمَا يَقُوْلُوْنَ اِذًا لَّابْتَغَوْا
اِلٰى ذِي الْعَرْشِ سَبِيْلًا ۝

43. Glory to Him! He is high
Above all that they say!—
Exalted and Great (beyond
measure)!

٤٣- سُبْحٰنَهٗ وَتَعٰلٰى عَمَّا يَقُوْلُوْنَ
عُلُوًّا كَبِيْرًا ۝

44. The seven heavens and the earth,
And all beings therein,
Declare His glory:
There is not a thing
But celebrates His praise;
And yet ye understand not
How they declare His glory![2229]
Verily He is Oft-Forbearing,
Most Forgiving!

٤٤- تُسَبِّحُ لَهُ السَّمٰوٰتُ السَّبْعُ وَالْاَرْضُ
وَمَنْ فِيْهِنَّ ۚ
وَاِنْ مِّنْ شَيْءٍ اِلَّا يُسَبِّحُ بِحَمْدِهٖ
وَلٰكِنْ لَّا تَفْقَهُوْنَ تَسْبِيْحَهُمْ ۗ
اِنَّهٗ كَانَ حَلِيْمًا غَفُوْرًا ۝

45. When thou dost recite
The Qur-ān, We put,

٤٥- وَاِذَا قَرَاْتَ الْقُرْاٰنَ جَعَلْنَا

2227. Things are explained in the Qur-ān from all points of view, individual and national, by means of stories, parables, and figures of speech, and by way of categorical commands. But those who are evil, instead of profiting by such instruction, often go farther and farther away from the Truth.

2228. There is only One True God. But if, as polytheists say, there had been subsidiary gods, they would yet have had to go to the Throne of the Supreme God, for they could have done nothing without Him. Thus the Islamic idea of the unity of the Godhead is quite different from polytheistic ideas of a supreme god, as in the Greek Pantheon, where Jupiter was often defied by the minor deities! But such ideas are absurd, as stated in the next verse.

2229. All Creation, animate and inanimate, sings God's praises and celebrates His glory,—animate, with consciousness, and inanimate, in the evidence which it furnishes of the unity and glory of God. The mystics believe that there is a soul in inanimate things also, which declares forth the glory of God. For all Nature bears witness to His power, wisdom, and goodness. It is only "ye", *i.e.*, those who reject the whole trend of your nature and deny Faith simply because ye have been given a limited amount of choice and free-will,—it is only such as "ye" that understand not what every other creature understands and proclaims with joy and pride. What must be your degradation! And yet God bears with you and forgives you! Such is His goodness!

Between thee and those who
Believe not in the Hereafter,
A veil invisible :[2230]

بَيْنَكَ وَبَيْنَ الَّذِينَ لَا يُؤْمِنُونَ بِالْآخِرَةِ
حِجَابًا مَّسْتُورًا ○

46. And We put coverings
Over their hearts (and minds)
Lest they should understand
The Qur-ān, and deafness[2231]
Into their ears : when thou
Dost commemorate thy Lord—
And Him alone—in the Qur-ān,
They turn on their backs,
Fleeing (from the Truth).

٤٦- وَّجَعَلْنَا عَلَىٰ قُلُوبِهِمْ
أَكِنَّةً أَن يَفْقَهُوهُ وَفِي آذَانِهِمْ وَقْرًا
وَإِذَا ذَكَرْتَ رَبَّكَ فِي الْقُرْآنِ وَحْدَهُ
وَلَّوْا عَلَىٰ أَدْبَارِهِمْ نُفُورًا ○

47. We know best why it is
They listen, when they listen[2232]
To thee ; and when they
Meet in private conference,
Behold, the wicked say,
"Ye follow none other than
A man bewitched !"

٤٧- نَّحْنُ أَعْلَمُ بِمَا يَسْتَمِعُونَ بِهِ إِذْ
يَسْتَمِعُونَ إِلَيْكَ وَإِذْ هُمْ نَجْوَىٰ
إِذْ يَقُولُ الظَّالِمُونَ
إِن تَتَّبِعُونَ إِلَّا رَجُلًا مَّسْحُورًا ○

48. See what similes they strike
For thee : but they have gone
Astray, and never can they
Find a way.[2233]

٤٨- انظُرْ كَيْفَ ضَرَبُوا لَكَ الْأَمْثَالَ
فَضَلُّوا فَلَا يَسْتَطِيعُونَ سَبِيلًا ○

49. They say : "What !
When we are reduced

٤٩- وَقَالُوا أَإِذَا كُنَّا

2230. *Veil invisible* : Some Commentators understand *mastūr* here as equivalent to *sātir* : a veil that makes invisible, a thick or dark veil. But I think that the meaning of *mastūr* (in the passive voice) as "hidden or invisible" is more consonant with the mystic meaning of the whole passage. If all nature, external and within ourselves, declares God's glory, those unfortunates who cut themselves off from their better nature are isolated from the men of God and the revelation of God, because (1) they are unfit for being in their company, and (2) because the men of God and the revelation of God must be protected from the pain which blasphemy or rebellion must cause to their unsullied nature. The veil is none the less real because it is invisible.

2231. The invisible veil being put against the ungodly on account of their deliberate rejection of Truth, the result is that their minds are fogged so that they cannot understand and their ears are clogged so that they cannot hear. In other words the effects of Evil become cumulative in shutting out God's grace.

2232. See last note. That being so, the only motive for the ungodly to listen to God's Truth is to scoff at it instead of to be instructed by it. They may make a show of listening, but when they meet together in private, they show themselves in their true colours. *Cf.* ii. 14. They cannot help seeing that there is singular charm and attractiveness in God's Word, and that it consoles, helps, and elevates many people who receive it in the right spirit. So they pretend that they are superior to such people and laugh at them for listening to some one who is only under the influence of something which they call magic !

2233. Note that the word used is "Sabīlan" "*a* way", not "*the* way". In going astray they have lost the way ; but never can they find *any* means of getting back to that way, or of justifying themselves or making good their wicked similes.

To bones and dust,
Should we really be raised up
(To be) a new creation?"[2234]

50. Say: "(Nay!) be ye
Stones or iron,

51. "Or created matter
Which, in your minds,
Is hardest (to be raised up),—
(Yet shall ye be raised up)!"
Then will they say:
"Who will cause us
To return?" Say: "He
Who created you first!"
Then will they wag
Their heads towards thee,[2235]
And say, "When will
That be?" Say, "May be
It will be quite soon!

52. "It will be on a Day
When He will call you,
And ye will answer
(His call) with (words
Of) His praise, and ye[2236]
Will think that ye tarried
But a little while!"[2237]

عِظَامًا وَّرُفَاتًا
ءَاِنَّا لَمَبْعُوثُونَ خَلْقًا جَدِيدًا ○

٥٠- قُلْ كُونُوا حِجَارَةً اَوْ حَدِيدًا ○

٥١- اَوْ خَلْقًا مِّمَّا يَكْبُرُ فِي صُدُورِكُمْ
فَسَيَقُولُونَ مَنْ يُّعِيدُنَا
قُلِ الَّذِي فَطَرَكُمْ اَوَّلَ مَرَّةٍ
فَسَيُنْغِضُونَ اِلَيْكَ رُءُوسَهُمْ
وَيَقُولُونَ مَتٰى هُوَ
قُلْ عَسٰى اَنْ يَّكُونَ قَرِيبًا ○

٥٢- يَوْمَ يَدْعُوكُمْ
فَتَسْتَجِيبُونَ بِحَمْدِهٖ
وَتَظُنُّونَ اِنْ لَّبِثْتُمْ اِلَّا قَلِيلًا ○

2234. They do not realise that God Who created them once out of nothing can create them again and again, with memories of their past, and in order to render to Him an account of how they used or misused the talents and opportunities which they were given. If it is to be a new Creation, what then? Bones and dust or ashes may yet retain something of the personality which was enshrined in them. But even if they were reduced to stones or iron or anything which their minds can conceive of as being most unlike them, yet there is nothing impossible to God! He has clearly sent a Message that we shall have to render an account of ourselves, and His Message is necessarily true.

2235. The sceptic shifts his ground when he is cornered in argument. It is no longer tenable for him to say that it cannot happen or that there is no one who can bring him back to life and memory. He now gets shaky, and says, "Well, when is that going to happen?" The actual time no man can tell. Indeed that event will be on a plane in which there will be no Time. Our relative ideas of time and place will have been completely overthrown, and it will appear to us then, not that it has been postponed too long, but that it has come too soon! See the next verse and note.

2236. It may be that this verse should not be in the inverted commas governed by the verb "say", in the last clause of the last verse. In that case, the answer to the sceptic would be finished in the last verse, and this verse would be a general statement applying also to the righteous, who will rise up celebrating the praises of God. But on the whole, I think it is better to take this verse as part of the answer to the sceptic referred to in the last verse.

2237. Whatever may have been your spiritual blindness in this life, the "new creation" will have opened your eyes to the Truth. No one will any longer be in any delusion as regards the Reality of God, and all will be forced, by their new circumstances, to recognise the Truth and sing God's praises. And all will be surprised at the seemingly short flight of time since they had their little ephemeral life on this earth. They will now appraise its true worth.

SECTION 6.

53. Say to My servants
That they should (only) say
Those things that are best :[2238]
For Satan doth sow
Dissensions among them :
For Satan is to man
An avowed enemy.

54. It is your Lord
That knoweth you best :
If He please, He granteth[2239]
You mercy, or if He please,
Punishment : We have not sent
Thee to be a disposer
Of their affairs for them.

55. And it is your Lord
That knoweth best all beings
That are in the heavens[2240]
And on earth : We
Did bestow on some Prophets
More (and other) gifts
Than on others : and We gave
To David (the gift
Of) the Psalms.[2241]

٥٣- وَقُل لِّعِبَادِي يَقُولُوا الَّتِي هِيَ
أَحْسَنُ ۚ إِنَّ الشَّيْطَٰنَ يَنزَغُ بَيْنَهُمْ ۚ
إِنَّ الشَّيْطَٰنَ كَانَ لِلْإِنسَٰنِ عَدُوًّا
مُّبِينًا ○

٥٤- رَّبُّكُمْ أَعْلَمُ بِكُمْ ۖ
إِن يَشَأْ يَرْحَمْكُمْ
أَوْ إِن يَشَأْ يُعَذِّبْكُمْ ۚ
وَمَا أَرْسَلْنَٰكَ عَلَيْهِمْ وَكِيلًا ○

٥٥- وَرَبُّكَ أَعْلَمُ
بِمَن فِي السَّمَٰوَٰتِ وَالْأَرْضِ ۗ
وَلَقَدْ فَضَّلْنَا بَعْضَ النَّبِيِّـۧنَ عَلَىٰ بَعْضٍ
وَآتَيْنَا دَاوُودَ زَبُورًا ○

2238. This command refers to two situations. (1) Even to your enemies and the enemies of God you should speak fair : who are you to judge others ? Judgment belongs to God alone, for He knows you (*i.e.* all mankind) best, and your personal knowledge is at best imperfect. And Satan is always trying to divide mankind. (2) Amongst yourselves, also, you should not entertain suspicions, but speak politely according to the best standards of human speech. A false or unkind word may destroy all your efforts at building up unity, because the forces of disruption are more numerous than the forces of unity.

2239. Man should never for a single moment entertain a thought that would imply that he was wiser than God. God's knowledge is all-embracing. If He grants mercy to some that you consider wicked or punishment to some that you consider righteous, it is your knowledge or your deductions that are at fault, not God's righteous Plan. Even men of God are not sent to arrange or dispose of men's affairs. but only to teach God's Message. How much less can ordinary men presume to judge other men ? The *Mashīyat*—Will and Plan of God—is above all human wisdom.

2240. Not only are we not to judge other ordinary men and carp at them. We are not to set up false standards for judging the men of God. If one was born of the unlearned Arab race, he yet was a mercy to all the worlds. If one spoke to God as *Kalīmullah* or another's life as *Rūḥ-ullah* began with a spiritual miracle ; it does not imply superiority. It only means that God's wisdom is more profound than we can fathom.

2241. The spiritual gifts with which the prophets came may themselves take different forms, according to the needs of the world and the times in which they lived, as judged by the wisdom of God. A striking example here given is the gift of song and music as given to David, but it implies no superiority of David over others. David was given the *Zabūr*, the Psalter or Psalms, intended to be sung for the worship of God and the celebration of God's praise. For the Book of Psalms, see the last part of n. 669 to iv. 163, where exactly the same words are used about David.

56. Say : " Call on those—
Besides Him—whom ye fancy :
They have neither the power
To remove your troubles
From you nor to change them." [2242]

٥٦- قُلِ ادْعُوا الَّذِينَ زَعَمْتُم مِّن دُونِهِ
فَلَا يَمْلِكُونَ كَشْفَ الضُّرِّ عَنكُمْ
وَلَا تَحْوِيلًا ۝

57. Those whom they call upon
Do desire (for themselves) means
Of access to their Lord,—
Even those who are nearest: [2243]
They hope for His Mercy
And fear His Wrath :
For the Wrath of thy Lord
Is something to take heed of

٥٧- أُولَٰئِكَ الَّذِينَ يَدْعُونَ يَبْتَغُونَ
إِلَىٰ رَبِّهِمُ الْوَسِيلَةَ أَيُّهُمْ أَقْرَبُ
وَيَرْجُونَ رَحْمَتَهُ وَيَخَافُونَ عَذَابَهُ ۚ
إِنَّ عَذَابَ رَبِّكَ كَانَ مَحْذُورًا ۝

58. There is not a population
But We shall destroy it
Before the Day of Judgment
Or punish it with
A dreadful Penalty : [2244]
That is written
In the (eternal) Record.

٥٨- وَإِن مِّن قَرْيَةٍ إِلَّا نَحْنُ مُهْلِكُوهَا
قَبْلَ يَوْمِ الْقِيَامَةِ أَوْ مُعَذِّبُوهَا عَذَابًا
شَدِيدًا ۚ
كَانَ ذَٰلِكَ فِي الْكِتَابِ مَسْطُورًا ۝

59. And We refrain from sending
The Signs, only because
The men of former generations
Treated them as false : [2245]

٥٩- وَمَا مَنَعَنَا أَن نُّرْسِلَ بِالْآيَاتِ إِلَّا
أَن كَذَّبَ بِهَا الْأَوَّلُونَ ۚ

2242. Men's suspicions of each other or of the prophets have been condemned in the previous verses. We now have the strongest condemnation of all, that of imagining any other being as being equal or in the same category with the One True God. God has all power : they have no power. They cannot remove men's troubles. They cannot even mitigate or change them so as to afford the least relief. Why indulge in false worship?

2243. Where men or heroes, or prophets or angels are worshipped, the worship is futile ; because (1) even if they are good and holy, and ever so near to God, yet the nearest of them have need to seek means of access to God, and they do seek such means, *viz.* : the hope of God's Grace ; (2) though by their very nature it is impossible for us to suppose that they will incur the Wrath of God, yet they are but creatures and are subject to the law of personal responsibility.

2244. These verses are a commentary on the last clause of the last verse. "The Wrath of thy Lord is something to take heed of." The godless thoughtlessly challenge God's Wrath, but do they realise its nature? Even the best of us must be moved with terror when we think of its consequences, were it not for His unbounded Mercy. Those who deny the Hereafter fail to realise its terrible Portents. They ask for Portents and Miracles now, but do they realise that their coming means destruction and misery to those who reject faith? They will come soon enough. The whole world will be convulsed before the Day of Judgment. The part of the wise is to prepare for it.

2245. Past generations treated Signs and Portents with contempt or rebellion, and brought about their own undoing. It is only God's Mercy that gives them Grace for a time and prevents the coming of those Portents and Punishments which would overwhelm them if they were put to their trial at once.

We sent the She-camel[2246]
To the Thamūd to open
Their eyes, but they
Treated her wrongfully:
We only send the Signs
By way of terror
(And warning from evil).[2247]

وَآتَيْنَا ثَمُودَ النَّاقَةَ
مُبْصِرَةً فَظَلَمُوا بِهَا
وَمَا نُرْسِلُ بِالْآيَاتِ إِلَّا تَخْوِيفًا ۝

60. Behold! We told thee
That thy Lord doth encompass
Mankind round about:[2248]
We granted the Vision
Which We showed thee,[2249]
But as a trial for men,—
As also the Cursed Tree[2250]
(Mentioned) in the Qur-ān:
We put terror (and warning)
Into them, but it only
Increases their inordinate
transgression!

٦٠- وَإِذْ قُلْنَا لَكَ إِنَّ رَبَّكَ أَحَاطَ بِالنَّاسِ
وَمَا جَعَلْنَا الرُّؤْيَا الَّتِي أَرَيْنَاكَ
إِلَّا فِتْنَةً لِلنَّاسِ
وَالشَّجَرَةَ الْمَلْعُونَةَ فِي الْقُرْآنِ
وَنُخَوِّفُهُمْ فَمَا يَزِيدُهُمْ
إِلَّا طُغْيَانًا كَبِيرًا ۝ ع

2246. An example is cited from the story of the Thamūd. A wonderful She-camel was sent among them as a Portent and a Symbol. In their wickedness they ham-strung her. So instead of her reclaiming them she was a cause of their destruction, as their sin and rebellion were laid bare. For the story of the She-camel and the references to the passages in which she is mentioned, see n. 1044 to vii. 73.

2247. Signs, Miracles, and Portents are sent by God as a warning, to strike terror into the hearts of evil-doers and reclaim them to the right path. I have discussed Fear as a motive for reclaiming certain kinds of hard hearts, in my note 82 to ii. 74. But some hearts are so hard that even this motive does not work. As they have a limited free-will given by God, they are to that extent free to choose. But when they actually choose evil, God in His infinite Mercy delays their punishment and removes the occasion for their immediate self-destruction by withholding the Signs which might make them transgress all the more and compass their total destruction.

2248. The reference may be to lxxii. 28, probably an earlier Meccan revelation. But the argument is independent of time. This verse falls naturally into three divisions. Warnings and Portents and Signs are sent or not sent according to God's All-Wise Plan of Mercy and Justice: this is in no wise inconsistent with the apparent freedom given to the wicked: because (1) in any case God is all round all His creatures, and His delay as a Sign of Mercy in no way diminishes His power; (2) the Visions of Truth vouchsafed to men of God are themselves Signs by which they can warn the ungodly; and (3) sometimes it is more merciful to give them time by not immediately bringing the matter to judgment.

2249. Some Commentators take this as referring to the Mi'rāj (xvii. 1) and others to other spiritual visions. Such visions are miracles, and become a stumbling block to unbelievers. They are an encouragement to men of faith. Thus they are "a trial for men".

2250. The tree *Zaqqūm*, a bitter and pungent tree described as growing at the bottom of Hell, a type of all that is disagreeable. See xxxvii. 62-65; xliv. 43-46; and lvi. 52. All these are Sūras chronologically earlier than this Sūra. The application of the name to a tree of the myrobalan kind in the region of Jericho is, I think, of post-Quranic date.

It is a trial for wrong-doers. See xxxvii. 63 and n. 4073.

C. 131.—Arrogance, jealousy, spite, and hatred
(xvii. 61-84.) Were the cause of the fall of Iblīs. Man
Was given pre-eminence above
Much of God's Creation, and owes
Higher responsibilities. He should give thanks
For God's mercies, and remember
The Day of Account. Not all the scheming
Of Evil will deflect God's righteous Plan
To protect His chosen ones. They should pray
Without ceasing, and seek His true Guidance;
For Truth will last, but Falsehood will perish.

SECTION 7.

61. Behold! We said to the
angels:[2251]
"Bow down unto Adam":
They bowed down except Iblīs:
He said, "Shall I bow down
To one whom Thou didst create
From clay?"

٦١- وَإِذْ قُلْنَا لِلْمَلَٰٓئِكَةِ اسْجُدُوا لِءَادَمَ
فَسَجَدُوٓا إِلَّآ إِبْلِيسَ
قَالَ ءَأَسْجُدُ لِمَنْ خَلَقْتَ طِينًا ○

62. He said, "Seest Thou? This is
The one whom Thou hast honoured
Above me! If Thou wilt but
Respite me to the Day
Of Judgment, I will surely
Bring his descendants
Under my sway—
All but a few!"[2252]

٦٢- قَالَ أَرَءَيْتَكَ هَٰذَا الَّذِى كَرَّمْتَ
عَلَىَّ لَئِنْ أَخَّرْتَنِ إِلَىٰ يَوْمِ
الْقِيَٰمَةِ لَأَحْتَنِكَنَّ ذُرِّيَّتَهُۥٓ
إِلَّا قَلِيلًا ○

63. (God) said: "Go thy way;[2253]
If any of them follow thee,
Verily Hell will be
The recompense of you (all)—
An ample recompense.

٦٣- قَالَ اذْهَبْ فَمَن تَبِعَكَ مِنْهُمْ
فَإِنَّ جَهَنَّمَ جَزَآؤُكُمْ جَزَآءً
مَّوْفُورًا ○

2251. *Cf.* vii. 11-18, which deals, as is the case here, with the temptation of the individual human soul, while ii. 30-38 deals with the collective race of man through Adam. Arrogance, jealousy, spite, and hatred are the ingredients in the story of Iblīs.

2252. The power of Evil over man is due to man's limited free-will. In other words man hands himself to Evil. As to those who loyally worship and serve God, Evil has no power over them. This is expressly mentioned in verse 65 below, and in other places.

2253. The power of Evil is summarily dismissed, but not without a clear warning. "Do thy worst; if any of them misuse their limited free-will and deliberately follow thee, they must take the consequences with thee; all of you must answer according to your personal responsibility."

64. "Lead to destruction those
Whom thou canst among them,[2254]
With thy (seductive) voice ;[2255]
Make assaults on them[2256]
With thy cavalry and thy
Infantry ; mutually share
With them wealth and children ;[2257]
And make promises to them."
But Satan promises them
Nothing but deceit.[2258]

٦٤- وَاسْتَفْزِزْ مَنِ اسْتَطَعْتَ مِنْهُمْ
بِصَوْتِكَ وَأَجْلِبْ عَلَيْهِمْ
بِخَيْلِكَ وَرَجِلِكَ وَشَارِكْهُمْ
فِي الْأَمْوَالِ وَالْأَوْلَادِ وَعِدْهُمْ ۚ
وَمَا يَعِدُهُمُ الشَّيْطَانُ إِلَّا غُرُورًا ○

65. "As for My servants,[2259]
No authority shalt thou
Have over them :"
Enough is thy Lord
For a Disposer of affairs.[2260]

٦٥- إِنَّ عِبَادِي لَيْسَ لَكَ عَلَيْهِمْ
سُلْطَانٌ ۚ وَكَفَىٰ بِرَبِّكَ وَكِيلًا ○

66. Your Lord is He
That maketh the Ship
Go smoothly for you
Through the sea, in order that
Ye may seek of His Bounty.[2261]
For He is unto you
Most Merciful.

٦٦- رَبُّكُمُ الَّذِي يُزْجِي لَكُمُ الْفُلْكَ
فِي الْبَحْرِ لِتَبْتَغُوا مِنْ فَضْلِهِ ۚ
إِنَّهُ كَانَ بِكُمْ رَحِيمًا ○

67. When distress seizes you
At sea, those that ye
Call upon—besides Himself—
Leave you in the lurch !
But when He brings you back
Safe to land, ye turn

٦٧- وَإِذَا مَسَّكُمُ الضُّرُّ فِي الْبَحْرِ ضَلَّ
مَنْ تَدْعُونَ إِلَّا إِيَّاهُ ۖ
فَلَمَّا نَجَّاكُمْ إِلَى الْبَرِّ أَعْرَضْتُمْ ۚ

2254. "Do thy worst ; but ye are both warned that that path leads to destruction."

2255. Evil has many snares for mankind. The one that is put in the foreground is the voice,—the seductive personal appeal, that "makes the worse appear the better part".

2256. The forcible assault of Evil is next mentioned under the metaphor of cavalry and infantry. It is when cajolery and tempting fair-seeming seem to fail that an attack is made in force with weapons of violence, of all kinds, like the different arms in an organised army.

2257. If the first assaults are resisted, Evil has other weapons in its armoury. Tangible fruits are dangled before the eyes, ill-gotten gains and children of sin, that follow from certain very alluring methods of indulgence in passions. Or it may be children dedicated to sin or worldly gains, etc. And then there are all kinds of promises for the future.

2258. This is a parenthetical clause inserted to show up what the promises of the Evil One are worth.

2259. This verse should be read along with the two preceding ones to complete their meaning. Evil has no power except over those who yield to its solicitations.

2260. As Evil has no authority over the sincere servants of God, they should put their trust completely in Him. For He is All-Sufficient to carry out their affairs, and by His grace, to save them from all harm and danger.

2261. This illustration of the sea, and the skill with which, by God's grace, men pass through it with ease in order to earn material gains by commerce, social gains by human intercourse, and spiritual gains by knowledge, is frequently used to enforce God's goodness to man. *Cf.* ii. 164.

Away (from Him). Most
ungrateful[2262]
Is man!

وَكَانَ الْإِنْسَانُ كَفُورًا ۝

68. Do ye then feel secure
That He will not cause you
To be swallowed up
Beneath the earth[2263]
When ye are on land,
Or that He will not send
Against you a violent tornado
(With showers of stones)
So that ye shall find
No one to carry out
Your affairs for you?

٦٨- أَفَأَمِنْتُمْ أَنْ يَخْسِفَ بِكُمْ
جَانِبَ الْبَرِّ
أَوْ يُرْسِلَ عَلَيْكُمْ حَاصِبًا
ثُمَّ لَا تَجِدُوا
لَكُمْ وَكِيلًا ۝

69. Or do ye feel secure
That He will not send you
Back a second time
To sea and send against you
A heavy gale to drown you
Because of your ingratitude,[2264]
So that ye find no helper
Therein against Us?

٦٩- أَمْ أَمِنْتُمْ أَنْ يُعِيدَكُمْ فِيهِ تَارَةً
أُخْرَىٰ فَيُرْسِلَ عَلَيْكُمْ قَاصِفًا مِنَ الرِّيحِ
فَيُغْرِقَكُمْ بِمَا كَفَرْتُمْ
ثُمَّ لَا تَجِدُوا لَكُمْ عَلَيْنَا بِهِ تَبِيعًا ۝

70. We have honoured the sons
Of Adam; provided them
With transport on land and sea;
Given them for sustenance things
Good and pure; and conferred
On them special favours,
Above a great part
Of Our Creation.[2265]

٧٠- وَلَقَدْ كَرَّمْنَا بَنِي آدَمَ
وَحَمَلْنَاهُمْ فِي الْبَرِّ وَالْبَحْرِ
وَرَزَقْنَاهُمْ مِنَ الطَّيِّبَاتِ وَفَضَّلْنَاهُمْ
عَلَىٰ كَثِيرٍ مِمَّنْ خَلَقْنَا تَفْضِيلًا ۝ ع

2262. Against God's gracious gifts and mercies is contrasted man's ingratitude. In danger he remembers the One True God, but relapses into his own fancies when the danger is past. *Cf.* also x. 22-23.

2263. Man is safe neither on land nor at sea except by the grace and mercy of God. How forcibly this is brought home to us by the Quetta earthquake of 31st May 1935, when tens of thousands of men, women, and children, perished in a few moments, by night, buried in debris! The stories of violent destructive tornadoes in such areas as the southern United States are equally impressive. The destruction is so sudden that the victims have no time to arrange anything. They are simply wiped out.

2264. If a man flees from the Wrath of God, there is no place secure for him. He may flee from sea to land, and back again from land to sea. But his life depends on the Disposer of all affairs. He may go again and again to sea, and perhaps finally end by being drowned.

2265. The distinction and honour conferred by God on man are recounted in order to enforce the corresponding duties and responsibilities of man. He is raised to a position of honour above the brute creation; he has been granted talents by which he can transport himself from place to place by land, sea, and now by air; all the means for the sustenance and growth of every part of his nature are provided by God; and his spiritual faculties (the greatest gift of God) raise him above the greater part of God's Creation. Should he not then realise his noble destiny and prepare for his real life in the Hereafter?

SECTION 8.

71. One day We shall call
Together all human beings
With their (respective) Imāms:[2266]
Those who are given their record
In their right hand
Will read it (with pleasure),
And they will not be
Dealt with unjustly
In the least.[2267]

٧١- يَوْمَ نَدْعُوا كُلَّ أُنَاسٍۭ بِإِمَامِهِمْ ۖ
فَمَنْ أُوتِيَ كِتَٰبَهُۥ بِيَمِينِهِۦ
فَأُو۟لَٰٓئِكَ يَقْرَءُونَ كِتَٰبَهُمْ
وَلَا يُظْلَمُونَ فَتِيلًا ○

72. But those who were blind
In this world, will be
Blind in the Hereafter,[2268]
And most astray
From the Path.

٧٢- وَمَن كَانَ فِى هَٰذِهِۦٓ أَعْمَىٰ
فَهُوَ فِى ٱلْءَاخِرَةِ أَعْمَىٰ
وَأَضَلُّ سَبِيلًا ○

73. And their purpose was
To tempt thee away
From that which We
Had revealed unto thee,
To substitute in Our name
Something quite different:[2269]
(In that case), behold!
They would certainly have
Made thee (their) friend!

٧٣- وَإِن كَادُوا۟ لَيَفْتِنُونَكَ عَنِ ٱلَّذِىٓ
أَوْحَيْنَآ إِلَيْكَ
لِتَفْتَرِىَ عَلَيْنَا غَيْرَهُۥ ۖ
وَإِذًا لَّٱتَّخَذُوكَ خَلِيلًا ○

74. And had We not
Given thee strength,

٧٤- وَلَوْلَآ أَن ثَبَّتْنَٰكَ

2266. I have discussed the various meanings of *Imām* in ii. 124, n. 124. What is the meaning here? The Commentators are divided. Some understand the meaning to be that each People or Group will appear with its Leader, who will bear witness to its virtues or sins: *Cf.* xvi. 84. Another view is that the Imām is their revelation, their Book. A third is that the Imām is the record of deeds spoken of in the next clause. I prefer the first.

2267. Literally, by the value of a *fatīl*, a small skin in the cleft of a date-stone: this has no value.

2268. On the Judgment Day the children of light will receive and peruse their record, and will render joyful thanks to God for His Mercies. What of the children of darkness? They had already been blind in this world's life, and they will not receive the light of God's Countenance then. On the contrary they will find that the longer the time they have travelled, the farther away they have gone from the Path. Notice the association of ideas—blindness, not seeing the light, going farther and farther away from the true Path.

2269. It happens with men of God, and it happened with the holy Prophet, that they are tempted by the world with many things which appeal to the world generally, if they would make some small concession in their favour. The "small concession" may hold the key of the position, and neutralise the whole teaching sent by God. If the Prophet had accepted wealth and position among the Quraish and "only respected" their idols! The Quraish would have taken him into their inner circle! A dishonest liar like Musailama would have jumped at the opportunity and been hailed as a friend and associate and made much of. But men of God are made of sterner stuff. They are given special strength to resist all plausible deception.

Thou wouldst nearly
Have inclined to them[2270]
A little.

لقد كدت تركن إليهم شيئا قليلا ۝

75. In that case We should
Have made thee taste
An equal portion (of punishment)
In this life, and an equal portion[2271]
In death : and moreover
Thou wouldst have found
None to help thee against Us ![2272]

٧٥- إذا لأذقنٰك
ضعف الحيوٰة وضعف الممات
ثم لا تجد لك علينا نصيرا ۝

76. Their purpose was to scare
Thee off the land,[2273]
In order to expel thee ;
But in that case they
Would not have stayed
(Therein) after thee,
Except for a little while.

٧٦- وإن كادوا ليستفزونك من الأرض
ليخرجوك منها وإذا لا يلبثون
خلفك إلا قليلا ۝

77. (This was Our) way
With the apostles We sent
Before thee : thou wilt find
No change in Our ways.[2274]

٧٧- سنة من قد أرسلنا قبلك من
رسلنا ولا تجد لسنتنا تحويلا ۝ ع

SECTION 9.

78. Establish regular prayers—[2275]
At the sun's decline

٧٨- أقم الصلوٰة لدلوك الشمس

2270. From a purely human point of view it may seem policy to make a small "concession" to men's weakness in order to fulfil a divine mission. But the divine Messenger is given special strength to resist such temptations.

2271. If such a thing was possible for a true Apostle of God, *viz.* : a compromise with evil and a dereliction of his mission, he would be no exception to the law of personal responsibility. Indeed, as the power and the responsibility were greater, the punishment would have been greater too. It would have been double,—an exposure in this life and the usual punishment in or after death for a desertion of the Truth.

2272. The motive held out by the world for a compromise with Truth is itself fallacious. The motive is that the compromise may bring influence, position, and opportunity, if not wealth and the other good things of life. But these themselves (if attained) would be of no use or help if pitted against the command of God.

2273. As happened in the case of the holy Prophet, the enemies try to frighten the man of God away from their midst, so that, once away, they could expel him and keep him out. But they are counting without the Plan of God. If they persecute the righteous, they dig their own graves!

2274. This was no new thing in history. God protects His own, and the ungodly cannot long enjoy the fruits of their unrighteousness even if their punishment be delayed a little while.

2275. The Commentators understand here the command for the five daily canonical prayers, *viz.* : the four from the declination of the sun from the zenith to the fullest darkness of the night, and the early morning prayer, Fajr, which is usually accompanied by a reading of the holy Qur-ān. The four afternoon prayers are : Ẕuhr, immediately after the sun begins to decline in the afternoon ; 'Aṣr, in the late afternoon ; Magrib, immediately after sunset ; and Ishā, after the glow of sunset has disappeared and the full darkness of the night has set in. There is difference of opinion as to the meaning of particular words and phrases, but none as to the general effect of the passage.

Till the darkness of the night,
And the morning prayer
And reading : for the prayer
And reading in the morning
Carry their testimony.[2276]

إِلَىٰ غَسَقِ اللَّيْلِ وَقُرْآنَ الْفَجْرِ ۖ
إِنَّ قُرْآنَ الْفَجْرِ كَانَ مَشْهُودًا ○

79. And pray in the small watches[2277]
Of the morning : (it would be)
An additional prayer
(Or spiritual profit)
For thee : soon will thy Lord
Raise thee to a Station
Of Praise and Glory ![2278]

٧٩- وَمِنَ اللَّيْلِ فَتَهَجَّدْ بِهِ
نَافِلَةً لَّكَ ۖ
عَسَىٰٓ أَن يَبْعَثَكَ رَبُّكَ مَقَامًا
مَّحْمُودًا ○

80. Say : " O my Lord !
Let my entry be[2279]
By the Gate of Truth
And Honour, and likewise
My exit by the Gate
Of Truth and Honour ;
And grant me
From Thy Presence
An authority to aid (me)."[2280]

٨٠- وَقُل رَّبِّ أَدْخِلْنِي
مُدْخَلَ صِدْقٍ
وَأَخْرِجْنِي مُخْرَجَ صِدْقٍ
وَاجْعَل لِّي مِن لَّدُنكَ سُلْطَٰنًا
نَّصِيرًا ○

2276. The morning prayer is specially singled out for separate mention, because the morning is a "holy hour" and special spiritual influences act on the soul awaking from the night's rest. Special testimony is borne to the prayers of this hour by the angelic host.

2277. This is held to be addressed specially to the holy Prophet who usually prayed more than the five canonical prayers. The *Tahajjud* was a prayer after midnight, in the small watches of the morning.

2278. To the Prophet was to be assigned in the Hereafter the highest Post of Honour and Glory —the *Maqām Maḥmūd.* There is much mystic meaning in this, implying his excellence above all other Prophets. The immediate reference may be to the hope that the Meccan persecution will soon be over and the glorious work in Medina will begin.

2279. The entry and exit here referred to may be interpreted in four senses : (1) entry into death and exit at the resurrection : for the righteous, who have purified their souls by prayer (last verse) and spiritual teaching from the Qur-ān (next verse), there is on each occasion a fuller and fuller realisation and enjoyment of truth and honour : for those who are estranged from God, the effect is the opposite : the truth becomes bitter and there is ignominy and exposure instead of honour : (2) entry for the holy Prophet into the new life at Medina, which was still in the womb of futurity, and exit from the life of persecution and the milieu of falsehood, which surrounded him in his native city of Mecca still given up to idolatry : (3) referring to the impending Hijrat again, the prayer may mean, "Let it be from pure motives of truth and spiritual honour, and not from motives of anger against the city of Mecca or its persecutors, or of ambition or worldly power from the city of Medina, which was ready to lay everything at the Apostle's feet" ; (4) generally, entry and exit at every stage of life.

2280. All prayer must be for God's aid and authority. However much we may plan, our success must depend on His aid. However nobler our motives, we have no right to imperil any lives unless there is authority in the Word of God. The Apostle only acts on God's commission and inspiration.

81. And say: "Truth has (now)
Arrived, and Falsehood perished:
For Falsehood is (by its nature)
Bound to perish."[2281]

٨١- وَقُلْ جَاءَ الْحَقُّ وَزَهَقَ الْبَاطِلُ
إِنَّ الْبَاطِلَ كَانَ زَهُوقًا ۝

82. We send down (stage by stage)
In the Qur-ān that which
Is a healing and a mercy
To those who believe:
To the unjust it causes
Nothing but loss after loss.[2282]

٨٢- وَنُنَزِّلُ مِنَ الْقُرْآنِ
مَا هُوَ شِفَاءٌ وَرَحْمَةٌ لِلْمُؤْمِنِينَ
وَلَا يَزِيدُ الظَّالِمِينَ إِلَّا خَسَارًا ۝

83. Yet when We bestow
Our favours on man,
He turns away and becomes
Remote on his side (instead
Of coming to Us), and when
Evil seizes him he
Gives himself up to despair![2283]

٨٣- وَإِذَا أَنْعَمْنَا عَلَى الْإِنْسَانِ
أَعْرَضَ وَنَأَىٰ بِجَانِبِهِ
وَإِذَا مَسَّهُ الشَّرُّ كَانَ يَئُوسًا ۝

84. Say: "Everyone acts
According to his own disposition:
But your Lord knows best
Who it is that is
Best guided on the Way."[2284]

٨٤- قُلْ كُلٌّ يَعْمَلُ عَلَىٰ شَاكِلَتِهِ
فَرَبُّكُمْ أَعْلَمُ بِمَنْ هُوَ أَهْدَىٰ سَبِيلًا ۝

C. 132.—Who can define the Spirit of Inspiration?
(xvii. 85-111.)
Its gift is the highest of God's Mercies
To man. The Qur-ān is divine, and no carpings
Can affect its greatness or the greatness
Of the Messenger who brought it to men.
Those who reject it will be called
To account on the Day of Judgment. Let not
Pride and Ignorance rush, like Pharaoh,
To the Punishment of the Hereafter.
The Qur-ān as revealed by stages teaches
The Truth: learn it and chant it, and praise
The Beautiful Names of God for ever!

2281. From its nature falsehood must perish, for it is the opposite of Truth, and Truth must ever prevail.

2282. In God's revelation there is healing for our broken spirits, hope for our spiritual future, and joy in the forgiveness of our sins. All who work in faith will share in these privileges. It is only the rebels against God's Law who will suffer loss. The more they will oppose Truth, the deeper down will they go into the mire—the state of sin and Wrath, which is worse than destruction.

2283. Truth saves us from two extremes: when we are happy, we are saved from being puffed up, for we realise that everything comes from God; and when we suffer misfortunes, we are not in despair, for we know that God is our sure refuge and help.

2284. If the wicked go their own ways, there is noting to discourage us. It is their nature. We must seek and hold fast to true guidance.

Section 10.

85. They ask thee concerning
The Spirit (of inspiration).[2285]
Say: "The Spirit (cometh)
By command of my Lord:
Of knowledge it is only
A little that is communicated
To you, (O men!)"

٨٥- وَيَسْـَٔلُونَكَ عَنِ الرُّوحِ
قُلِ الرُّوحُ مِنْ أَمْرِ رَبِّي
وَمَا أُوتِيتُم مِّنَ الْعِلْمِ إِلَّا قَلِيلًا

86 If it were Our Will,
We could take away
That which We have
Sent thee by inspiration:[2286]
Then wouldst thou find
None to plead thy affair
In that matter as against Us,—

٨٦- وَلَئِن شِئْنَا لَنَذْهَبَنَّ بِالَّذِي
أَوْحَيْنَا إِلَيْكَ
ثُمَّ لَا تَجِدُ لَكَ بِهِۦ عَلَيْنَا وَكِيلًا

87. Except for Mercy from thy
Lord:[2287]
For His Bounty is
To thee (indeed) great.

٨٧- إِلَّا رَحْمَةً مِّن رَّبِّكَ
إِنَّ فَضْلَهُۥ كَانَ عَلَيْكَ كَبِيرًا

88. Say: "If the whole
Of mankind and Jinns[2288]
Were to gather together
To produce the like
Of this Qur-ān, they
Could not produce
The like thereof, even if
They backed up each other

٨٨- قُل لَّئِنِ اجْتَمَعَتِ الْإِنسُ وَالْجِنُّ
عَلَىٰٓ أَن يَأْتُوا بِمِثْلِ
هَٰذَا الْقُرْءَانِ لَا يَأْتُونَ بِمِثْلِهِۦ
وَلَوْ كَانَ بَعْضُهُمْ لِبَعْضٍ

2285. What is the nature of inspiration? Who brings it? Can it ask its Bringer questions? Can we ask anything which we wish? These are the sort of questions always asked when inspiration is called in question. The answer is given here. Inspiration is one of those high spiritual mysteries which cannot be explained in the terms of our every-day human experience. It is spiritual. The Spirit (Gabriel) does not come of his own will. He comes by the command of God, and reveals what God commands him to reveal. Of the sum-total of true spiritual knowledge what a small part it is that ordinary mortals can understand! They can be only given that which they can understand, however dimly. We are not in a position to ask anything that we wish. If we did so, it would only make us look foolish, for the guidance comes from God's Wisdom, not from our worldly knowledge.

2286. Even the spiritual knowledge that comes to us comes because of the favour and mercy of God. If He were to withhold it, who can call Him in question?

2287. In that case the only one who can plead for us is the Mercy of God. We can interpret the phrase in its widest abstract sense, as well as in the concrete sense of the title which is applied to the holy Prophet Muḥammad, the Mercy of God. Thus we come from the abstract question to the concrete question of the Qur-ān, which is referred to by name in the verses that follow.

2288. For the meaning of "Jinns", see n. 929 to vi. 100.

With help and support.[2289]

89. And We have explained
To man, in this Qur-ān,
Every kind of similitude:[2290]
Yet the greater part of men
Refuse (to receive it)
Except with ingratitude![2291]

90. They say: "We shall not
Believe in thee, until thou
Cause a spring to gush
Forth for us from the earth,[2292]

91. "Or (until) thou have
A garden of date trees
And vines, and cause rivers
To gush forth in their midst,
Carrying abundant water;[2293]

92. "Or thou cause the sky
To fall in pieces, as thou
Sayest (will happen), against
us;[2294]

ظَهِيرًا ○

٨٩- وَلَقَدْ صَرَّفْنَا لِلنَّاسِ فِي هَٰذَا
الْقُرْآنِ مِن كُلِّ مَثَلٍ فَأَبَىٰ أَكْثَرُ
النَّاسِ إِلَّا كُفُورًا ○

٩٠- وَقَالُوا لَن نُّؤْمِنَ لَكَ حَتَّىٰ
تَفْجُرَ لَنَا مِنَ الْأَرْضِ يَنبُوعًا ○

٩١- أَوْ تَكُونَ لَكَ جَنَّةٌ مِّن نَّخِيلٍ
وَعِنَبٍ فَتُفَجِّرَ الْأَنْهَارَ خِلَالَهَا تَفْجِيرًا ○

٩٢- أَوْ تُسْقِطَ السَّمَاءَ
كَمَا زَعَمْتَ عَلَيْنَا كِسَفًا

2289. The proof of the Qur-ān is in its own beauty and nature, and the circumstances in which it was promulgated. The world is challenged to produce a Book like it and has not produced one. It is the only revealed Book whose text stands pure and uncorrupted to-day. *Cf.*, for a similar challenge, ii. 23, x. 38, and xi. 13.

2290. In the Qur-ān everything is explained in detail from various points of view, by commands, similitudes, examples, stories, parables, etc. It does not merely narrate stories or lay down vague abstract propositions. It gives every detailed help in outward and inner life.

2291. One form in which it can be received with ingratitude is to pay verbal tributes to it but not study it as it ought to be studied (ii. 121, *ḥaqqa tilāwatihi*), or to disobey its precepts or standards.

2292. *Cf.* ii. 60.

2293. This ill-assorted and crude jumble of the sort of miracles which the Unbelievers wanted is in very appropriate contrast to the sober and reasoned argument which is begun in the last sentence of verse 93 and continued in sections 11 and 12, which close this Sūra. It is throughout reminiscent of the materialistic imagination of Jewish sceptics, which was mainly responsible for the fall of the Jewish nation (see verse 104 below). For a thirsty people sojourning in a dry land, the finding of a spring of water as in the story of Moses or of the well of Zamzam is an appropriate miracle. But miracles are not for faithless crowds to gape at. A beautiful well-watered Garden is a symbol of Felicity; but a sceptic cannot order God to produce it for his pleasure. The same may be said about a house adorned with gold, except that its symbolism is even more materialistic. The fall of the sky or producing God face to face or cilmbing to the skies by a ladder, or bringing down a book of parchment which men could handle, are all irreverent suggestions that make no distinction between spiritual and material things.

2294. Contrast the sublime passages like that beginning with lxxxii. 1, or that in xxv. 25, where the final breaking up of the firmaments as we know them is referred to in the world's catastrophe, with the ridiculous demand that it should be done for the sport of the sceptics!

Or thou bring God
And the angels before (us)
Face to face;[2295]

أَوْ تَأْتِيَ بِاللّٰهِ وَالْمَلٰٓئِكَةِ قَبِيْلًا ۝

93. "Or thou have a house
Adorned with gold,
Or thou mount a ladder
Right into the skies.[2296]
No, we shall not even believe
In thy mounting until thou
Send down to us a book
That we could read."[2297]
Say: "Glory to my Lord!
Am I aught but a man,—
An apostle?"[2298]

٩٣- أَوْ يَكُوْنَ لَكَ بَيْتٌ مِّنْ زُخْرُفٍ
أَوْ تَرْقٰى فِي السَّمَآءِ ۚ
وَلَنْ نُّؤْمِنَ لِرُقِيِّكَ حَتّٰى
تُنَزِّلَ عَلَيْنَا كِتٰبًا نَّقْرَؤُهٗ ۗ
قُلْ سُبْحَانَ رَبِّيْ
هَلْ كُنْتُ إِلَّا بَشَرًا رَّسُوْلًا ۝

Section 11.

94. What kept men back
From Belief when Guidance
Came to them, was nothing
But this: they said,
"Has God sent a man[2299]
(Like us) to be (His) Apostle?"

٩٤- وَمَا مَنَعَ النَّاسَ أَنْ يُّؤْمِنُوْٓا إِذْ جَآءَهُمُ
الْهُدٰٓى إِلَّآ أَنْ قَالُوْٓا
أَبَعَثَ اللّٰهُ بَشَرًا رَّسُوْلًا ۝

95. Say, "If there were settled,
On earth, angels walking about[2300]

٩٥- قُلْ لَّوْ كَانَ فِي الْأَرْضِ مَلٰٓئِكَةٌ

2295. *Cf.* ii. 55 and iv. 153 about the desire of the Israelites to see God face to face; and vi. 8-9, about angels coming down to convince men.

2296. *Cf.* vi. 35 about a ladder to the skies.

2297. *Cf.* vi. 7 for the foolish idea of materialistic sceptics that a spiritual revelation could come down from the heavens on a piece of parchment that they can touch.

2298. An apostle of God is a man at the command of God, and not to satisfy the disingenuous whims and fancies of Unbelievers. Miracles greater than any that their foolish fancies could devise were before them. The Qur-ān was such a miracle, and it is a standing miracle that lasts through the ages. Why did they not believe? The real reason was spite and jealousy like that of Iblīs. See next verse.

2299. When a man is raised to honour and dignity, his sincere brothers rejoice, for it is an honour that reflects its glory on them. But those with evil in their hearts are jealous like their prototype Iblīs, (xvii. 61, n. 2251). To such men the mere fact that their own brother receives the grace of God is enough to turn them against that brother. Any other reasons they may devise are mere make-believe.

2300. The argument is that if angels inhabited this earth, an angel from heaven could be sent down as an apostle to them, as they could mutually understand each other, and the Message of God could be explained without difficulty. But the earth is inhabited by men, and the men themselves are divided into races, or groups, or nations. To each Group is sent an apostle from among their brethren: to 'Ād, *their brother* Hūd (xi. 50); to Thamūd, *their brother* Ṣāliḥ (xi. 61): and so on. As a matter of fact, with wicked men, constituted as they are, the appearance of an angel causes disturbance and an unseemly riot, as in the case of the angels that came to Lot (xi. 77-80). In any case they cannot carry out an effective mission among men (vi. 8-9).

In peace and quiet, We should
Certainly have sent them
Down from the heavens
An angel for an apostle."

يَمْشُوْنَ مُطْمَئِنِّيْنَ لَنَزَّلْنَا عَلَيْهِمْ
مِّنَ السَّمَآءِ مَلَكًا رَّسُوْلًا ۝

96. Say: "Enough is God
For a witness between me[2301]
And you: for He is
Well acquainted with His servants,
And He sees (all things).

٩٦- قُلْ كَفٰى بِاللّٰهِ شَهِيْدًا بَيْنِيْ وَبَيْنَكُمْ
اِنَّهٗ كَانَ بِعِبَادِهٖ خَبِيْرًا بَصِيْرًا ۝

97. It is he whom God guides,
That is on true guidance;
But he whom He leaves
Astray—for such wilt thou
Find no protector besides Him.[2302]
On the Day of Judgment
We shall gather them together,
Prone on their faces,
Blind, dumb, and deaf:
Their abode will be Hell:
Every time it shows abatement,
We shall increase for them
The fierceness of the Fire.[2303]

٩٧- وَمَنْ يَّهْدِ اللّٰهُ فَهُوَ الْمُهْتَدِ
وَمَنْ يُّضْلِلْ فَلَنْ تَجِدَ لَهُمْ اَوْلِيَآءَ
مِنْ دُوْنِهٖ
وَنَحْشُرُهُمْ يَوْمَ الْقِيٰمَةِ عَلٰى وُجُوْهِهِمْ
عُمْيًا وَّبُكْمًا وَّصُمًّا
مَاْوٰىهُمْ جَهَنَّمُ
كُلَّمَا خَبَتْ زِدْنٰهُمْ سَعِيْرًا ۝

98. That is their recompense,
Because they rejected Our Signs,
And said, "When we are reduced
To bones and broken dust,
Should we really be raised up
(To be) a new Creation?"[2304]

٩٨- ذٰلِكَ جَزَآؤُهُمْ بِاَنَّهُمْ كَفَرُوْا بِاٰيٰتِنَا
وَقَالُوْٓا ءَاِذَا كُنَّا عِظَامًا وَّرُفَاتًا
ءَاِنَّا لَمَبْعُوْثُوْنَ خَلْقًا جَدِيْدًا ۝

2301. 'If you want a real witness, it is not these sorts of fancy miracles, but the witness of the true ever-living God. God is always everywhere—and with you. Purify your hearts, and ask Him in true contrition and repentance, and He will guide you and show you the Way.'

2302. 'All your insincere subtleties are of no use. The only real guidance is the guidance of God. If you do not seek His grace, you will be lost. Besides Him, there is no true friend or protector.'

2303. 'If you still persist in your evil ways, what is to be your evil end? You will become more and more identified with the Company of Evil. You will come to shame and ignominy, like men thrown down prone on their faces. You will lose the use of all the faculties of judgment with which God has endowed you. Instead of seeing, you will be blind to God's Signs. Instead of having the power of seeking Him in prayer and rejoicing in His grace, you will be dumb. Instead of hearing the harmony and music of the spheres, as typified in the pure and harmonious lives of men, you will hear nothing or only hear dull or confused sounds like deaf men. The scorching fire of your punishment will not grow less, but grow more fierce as you go deeper into Hell.'

2304. This phrase is repeated from xvii. 49. The reminiscence rounds off the argument. After certain moral precepts to which Faith was linked, we have had a discussion of Unfaith. Its various motives have been analysed, and its penalties have been allegorically shadowed forth. After this, the example of Pharaoh is held as a type of Unfaith in the next section, and the Sūra closed with an exhortation to faith and a declaration of the glory of God.

99. See they not that God,
Who created the heavens
And the earth, has power
To create the like of them [2305]
(Anew)? Only He has
Decreed a term appointed,
Of which there is no doubt.
But the unjust refuse
(To receive it) except
With ingratitude.[2306]

٩٩- أَوَلَمْ يَرَوْا أَنَّ اللّٰهَ الَّذِي خَلَقَ السَّمٰوٰتِ
وَالْأَرْضَ قَادِرٌ عَلٰى أَنْ يَخْلُقَ مِثْلَهُمْ
وَجَعَلَ لَهُمْ أَجَلًا
لَا رَيْبَ فِيهِ ۚ
فَأَبَى الظّٰلِمُونَ إِلَّا كُفُورًا ۝

100. Say: "If ye had
Control of the Treasures
Of the Mercy of my Lord,
Behold, ye would keep them
Back, for fear of spending
Them: for man
Is (ever) niggardly!"[2307]

١٠٠- قُلْ لَوْ أَنْتُمْ تَمْلِكُونَ خَزَائِنَ
رَحْمَةِ رَبِّي
إِذًا لَأَمْسَكْتُمْ خَشْيَةَ الْإِنْفَاقِ ۚ
وَكَانَ الْإِنْسَانُ قَتُورًا ۝ ع

SECTION 12

101. To Moses We did give
Nine Clear Signs: [2308]
Ask the Children of Israel:
When he came to them,[2309]
Pharaoh said to him:
"O Moses! I consider thee,

١٠١- وَلَقَدْ آتَيْنَا مُوسٰى تِسْعَ آيٰتٍ
بَيِّنٰتٍ فَسْئَلْ بَنِي إِسْرَائِيلَ إِذْ جَاءَهُمْ
فَقَالَ لَهُ فِرْعَوْنُ

2305. God, Who created all that is in the heavens and on earth, has surely the power to revive the life of individual souls after their bodies have perished,—and revive them with memories of their past life and for a continuation of their spiritual history. Only He has fixed a term for each stage of our existence, which we can neither prolong nor shorten.

2306. This phrase carries us back to xvii. 89, after we began the argument about the real motives for the rejection of the Qur-ān by sceptics. That argument is now closed in a sort of minor circle within the major circle sketched in n. 2304 above.

2307. A fresh argument is now addressed to those who would confine God's revelations to a limited circle of men, such as they themselves belonged to. The immediate reference was to the Jews, who could not understand how any Gentiles could receive revelations and guidance even superior to what they considered their own birth-right. But the tendency is widespread in the human race. A particular race, or caste, or a particular kind of culture, claims to be the custodian of God's Message, whereas it is universal. God's Mercy is universal, and He scatters the priceless Treasures of His Mercy broadcast among His creatures. They are not exhausted by spending. It is only the misers who hoard their wealth for fear it should be used up by spending. 'Are you spiritual misers going to keep back God's holy Message from the multitude? Is that the reason why you deny the advent of the new Teacher, who comes as a Mercy to all men—to all Creation?'

2308. *Nine Clear Signs*: see vii. 133, n. 1091. The story of Pharaoh (or a phase of it) is here told with a view to exhibiting the decline of a soul on account of pride in outward power and dignity.

2309. *To them*: *i.e.* to Pharaoh, as sitting in his Council, with the Chiefs of his People. *Cf.* vii. 103. The whole scene is described in some detail from the point of view of nations or Ummats in vii. 103-133.

Indeed, to have been
Worked upon by sorcery ![2310]

إِنِّي لَأَظُنُّكَ يَٰمُوسَىٰ مَسْحُورًا ۝

102. Moses said, "Thou knowest
Well that these things
Have been sent down by none
But the Lord of the heavens
And the earth as eye-opening[2311]
Evidence : and I consider thee
Indeed, O Pharaoh, to be
One doomed to destruction !"

١٠٢- قَالَ لَقَدْ عَلِمْتَ مَآ أَنزَلَ
هَٰٓؤُلَآءِ إِلَّا رَبُّ ٱلسَّمَٰوَٰتِ
وَٱلْأَرْضِ بَصَآئِرَ
وَإِنِّي لَأَظُنُّكَ يَٰفِرْعَوْنُ مَثْبُورًا ۝

103. So he resolved to remove them[2312]
From the face of the earth :
But We did drown him
And all who were with him.

١٠٣- فَأَرَادَ أَن يَسْتَفِزَّهُم مِّنَ ٱلْأَرْضِ
فَأَغْرَقْنَٰهُ وَمَن مَّعَهُۥ جَمِيعًا ۝

104. And We said thereafter
To the Children of Israel,
"Dwell securely in the land[2313]
(Of promise)" : but when
The second of the warnings came
To pass, We gathered you
Together in a mingled crowd[2314]

١٠٤- وَقُلْنَا مِنۢ بَعْدِهِۦ لِبَنِيٓ إِسْرَٰٓءِيلَ
ٱسْكُنُوا۟ ٱلْأَرْضَ فَإِذَا جَآءَ وَعْدُ ٱلْـَٔاخِرَةِ
جِئْنَا بِكُمْ لَفِيفًا ۝

2310. At a different and later stage in the scene, Pharaoh's Chiefs call Moses a "sorcerer well-versed" (vii. 109). Here Moses, who had come with the Nine Signs but had not yet shown them, is reproached with being the object of sorcery ; he is practically told that he is mad !

2311. We can well suppose Moses to ask Pharaoh to recall all the past history of Moses, for Moses had been brought up in Pharaoh's palace in all the learning of the Egyptians. He could not therefore be mad, or a simpleton worked on by Egyptian magic. What he was going to show was something far greater : it was not the deceptive magic of Pharaoh's sorcerers, but true Signs that came from the God of all power. They were to open the eyes of his people, and if Pharaoh resisted faith, Moses warns him that Pharaoh in that case was doomed to destruction. This is the course of the soul that sinks down by Pride !

2312. Pharaoh on this tries various subterfuges and plans for removing not only Moses but all his people by doing away with them. The detailed story is not told here but may be read in S. vii. But God's Wrath descended on Pharaoh and those who were with him in body and mind. The Egyptians who repented were subject to Pharaoh's wrath but were saved from the Wrath of God (vii. 121-126).

2313. The Israelites were taken to the Promised Land in Palestine, and they established their own kingdom there, but they forfeited God's favour by their sins and backslidings and will have to answer like all souls by the law of personal responsibility at the Day of Judgment.

2314. The *second of the warnings* : the first was probably that mentioned above, in xvii. 5, and the second that mentioned in xvii. 7 (middle). When this second warning due to the rejection of Jesus came to pass, the Jews were gathered together in a mingled crowd, and they have never had a Jewish nationality since. Some Commentators understand the second warning to be the Day of Judgment, the Promise of the Hereafter.

105. We sent down the (Qur-ān)
In Truth, and in Truth[2315]
Has it descended: and We sent
Thee but to give Glad
Tidings and to warn (sinners).[2316]

١٠٥- وَبِالْحَقِّ أَنْزَلْنٰهُ وَبِالْحَقِّ نَزَلَ ۗ
وَمَآ أَرْسَلْنٰكَ إِلَّا مُبَشِّرًا وَّنَذِيرًا ○

106. (It is) a Qur-ān
Which We have divided
(Into parts from time to time),
In order that thou mightest
Recite it to men
At intervals: We have
Revealed it by stages.[2317]

١٠٦- وَقُرْاٰنًا فَرَقْنٰهُ لِتَقْرَاَهٗ عَلَى النَّاسِ
عَلٰى مُكْثٍ
وَّنَزَّلْنٰهُ تَنْزِيلًا ○

107. Say: "Whether ye believe
In it or not, it is true
That those who were given[2318]
Knowledge beforehand, when
It it recited to them,
Fall down on their faces
In humble prostration,

١٠٧- قُلْ اٰمِنُوْا بِهٖٓ اَوْ لَا تُؤْمِنُوْا ۗ
اِنَّ الَّذِيْنَ اُوْتُوا الْعِلْمَ مِنْ قَبْلِهٖٓ اِذَا
يُتْلٰى عَلَيْهِمْ
يَخِرُّوْنَ لِلْاَذْقَانِ سُجَّدًا ○

108. "And they say: 'Glory
To our Lord! Truly
Has the promise of our Lord
Been fulfilled!'"[2319]

١٠٨- وَّيَقُوْلُوْنَ سُبْحٰنَ رَبِّنَآ اِنْ
كَانَ وَعْدُ رَبِّنَا لَمَفْعُوْلًا ○

2315. The Qur-ān was sent down by God in Truth: it was not forged by any mortal. It has descended in Truth: it was not and has not been falsified or corrupted in the process of being communicated to mankind.

2316 The part of the Prophet was that of a Messenger: he was not responsible if the ungodly rejected it. He fulfilled his mission in promulgating and explaining it and leaving it as a legacy to the world.

2317. The marvel is that these parts, revealed at different times and in different circumstances, should fit together so closely and consistently as they do. All revelation is progressive. The previous revelations were also progressive. Each of them marked a stage in the world's spiritual history. Man's mind does not take in more than his spiritual state will have prepared him for. God's revelation comes as a light to illuminate our difficulties and show us the way in actual situations that arise.

2318. No one's belief or unbelief affects the beauty or grandeur of God's revelation. But those endowed with spiritual knowledge or insight know at once when they hear God's holy Word, and fall down and adore God. Those endowed with knowledge include those who had received previous revelations and had kept themselves free from corrupt ideas.

2319. Those who had received previous revelations find in the Qur-ān and in the Apostle who brought it, the promise of God fulfilled. Those who were spiritually prepared for it found in the same way the satisfaction of their spiritual yearnings: to them, also, God's promise was sent to be fulfilled.

109. They fall down on their faces
In tears, and it increases
Their (earnest) humility.[2320]

١٠٩- وَيَخِرُّونَ لِلْأَذْقَانِ يَبْكُونَ وَيَزِيدُهُمْ
خُشُوعًا ۩

110. Say: "Call upon God, or
Call upon Raḥmān:[2321]
By whatever name ye call
Upon Him, (it is well):
For to Him belong
The Most Beautiful Names.[2322]
Neither speak thy Prayer aloud,
Nor speak it in a low tone,[2323]
But seek a middle course
Between."

١١٠- قُلِ ادْعُوا اللَّهَ أَوِ ادْعُوا الرَّحْمَٰنَ
أَيًّا مَّا تَدْعُوا
فَلَهُ الْأَسْمَاءُ الْحُسْنَىٰ
وَلَا تَجْهَرْ بِصَلَاتِكَ وَلَا تُخَافِتْ بِهَا
وَابْتَغِ بَيْنَ ذَٰلِكَ سَبِيلًا

111. Say: "Praise be to God,
Who begets no son,
And has no partner
In (His) dominion:
Nor (needs) He any
To protect Him from
humiliation:[2324]
Yea, magnify Him
For His greatness and glory!"

١١١- وَقُلِ الْحَمْدُ لِلَّهِ الَّذِي لَمْ يَتَّخِذْ
وَلَدًا وَلَمْ يَكُن لَّهُ شَرِيكٌ فِي الْمُلْكِ
وَلَمْ يَكُن لَّهُ وَلِيٌّ مِّنَ الذُّلِّ
وَكَبِّرْهُ تَكْبِيرًا

2320. A feeling of earnest humility comes to the man who realises how, in spite of his own unworthiness, he is brought, by God's Mercy, into touch with the most sublime Truths. Such a man is touched with the deepest emotion, which finds its outlet in tears.

2321. *Cf.* vii. 180. *Raḥmān* describes one of the attributes of God,—His Grace and Mercy which come to the sinner even before he feels conscious of the need of it,—the preventive Grace which saves God's servants from sin. See n. 19 to i. 1. God can be invoked, either by His simple name, which includes all attributes, or in the highest Sūfi philosophy, rises above all attributes, or by one of the names implying the attributes by which we try to explain His nature to our limited understanding. The attribute of Mercy in *Raḥmān* was particularly repugnant to the Pagan Arabs (see xxv. 60, and xxi. 36): that is why special stress is laid on it in the Qur-ān.

2322. These Beautiful Names of God are many. For *tasbīḥ* purposes a list of 99 is made out in Ḥadīth literature: that in Tirmiẓi is considered authoritative. Qādhi Muḥammad Sulaimān has published an Urdu monograph on the subject, published by the Daftar Raḥmatun-lil-'Ālamīn, Patiala, 1930. Those who wish to see a poetic Commentary on the names in the form of stories in English may consult Sir Edwin Arnold's *Pearls of the Faith.* Sir Edwin's stories are of unequal merit, but a fine example is furnished by No. 4, *al-Malik*, "The King".

2323. *Cf.* vii, 205. All prayer should be pronounced with earnestness and humility, whether it is congregational prayer or the private outpouring of one's own soul. Such an attitude is not consistent with an over-loud pronunciation of the words, though in public prayers the standard of permissible loudness is naturally higher than in the case of private prayer. In public prayers, of course, the aẓān or call to prayer will be in a loud voice to be heard near and far, but the chants from the Sacred Book should be neither so loud as to attract the hostile notice of those who do not believe nor so low in tone as not to be heard by the whole congregation.

2324. A first step towards the understanding of God's nature is to clear our mind from superstitions, such as that God begot a son, or that He has partners, or that He is dependent upon other beings to protect Him from harm and humiliation. We must realise that He is the One and Only Reality: His greatness and glory are above anything we can conceive: but using our highest spiritual ideas, we must declare forth His greatness and glory.

The Sūra began with singing the glory and praises of God: it ends on the same note, concluding the argument. The next Sūra takes up the same theme from another point of view, and opens with the same note, "Praise be to God".

INTRODUCTION TO SŪRA XVIII (*Kahf*).

It has been explained in the Introduction to S. xvii how the five Sūras xvii to xxi develop the theme of the individual soul's spiritual history, and how they fit into the general scheme of exposition.

This particular Meccan Sūra may be called a lesson on the brevity and mystery of Life. First there is the story of the Companions of the Cave who slept therein for a long period, and yet thought they had been there only a day or less. Then there is the story of the mysterious Teacher who shows Moses how Life itself is a parable. And further there is the story of Ẓul-qarnain, the two-horned one, the powerful ruler of west and east, who made an iron wall to protect the weak against the strong. The parables refer to the brevity, uncertainty, and vanity of this life; to the many paradoxes in it, which can only be understood by patience and the fulness of knowledge; and to the need of guarding our spiritual gains against the incursions of evil.

Summary.—The Qur-ān is a direction and a warning. This life is brief and subject to vicissitudes. Our ideas of Time are defective, as shown in the story of the Companions of the Cave, who had faith, truth, patience, and other virtues. But their life was a mystery that can be fathomed but by few (xviii. 1-22, and C. 133).

Knowledge is for God: be on your guard against idle conjectures and cock-sure hopes. Learn from the Qur-ān Parable of the man who is puffed up with this world's goods and is brought to nought (xviii. 23-44, and C. 134).

This life is uncertain and variable: goodness and virtue are better and more durable. For the Day of Reckoning will come, with its Mercy and its Wrath (xviii. 45-59, and C. 135).

Moses in his thirst for knowledge forgot his limitations. Patience and faith were enjoined on him, and he understood when the paradoxes of Life were explained (xviii. 60-82, and C. 136).

Ẓul-qarnain had a wide dominion: he punished the guilty and rewarded the good: he protected the weak from the lawless: but he had faith, and valued the guidance of God. God is One, and His service is righteousness (xviii. 83-110, and C. 137).

C. 133.—The Book of Revelation gives straight
(xviii. 1-22.) Directions to make our lives straight,—
To warn us against Evil and guide us
To the Good everlasting. Teach the Truth,
But fret not about men rejecting it.
The Parable of the Companions of the Cave
Shows how God works wonders beyond
Our fathoming: how Faith is a sure
Refuge in ways we know not; how
Time itself works God's Plan
Before we know how it passes;
How He can give us rest, and raise
Us back to life against all odds;
And how futile it is to engage
In controversies about matters we know not.

Sūra XVIII.

Kahf, or the Cave.

In the name of God, Most Gracious,
Most Merciful.

بِسْمِ اللّٰهِ الرَّحْمٰنِ الرَّحِيْمِ

1. Praise be to God,[2325]
Who hath sent to His Servant
The Book, and hath allowed
Therein no Crookedness :[2326]

١- اَلْحَمْدُ لِلّٰهِ الَّذِیْۤ اَنْزَلَ عَلٰی عَبْدِهِ
الْكِتٰبَ وَلَمْ يَجْعَلْ لَّهٗ عِوَجًا ۜ

2. (He hath made it) Straight[2327]
(And Clear) in order that
He may warn (the godless)
Of a terrible Punishment
From Him, and that He
May give Glad Tidings
To the Believers who work
Righteous deeds, that they
Shall have a goodly Reward,

٢- قَيِّمًا لِّيُنْذِرَ
بَاْسًا شَدِيْدًا مِّنْ لَّدُنْهُ
وَيُبَشِّرَ الْمُؤْمِنِيْنَ الَّذِيْنَ يَعْمَلُوْنَ
الصّٰلِحٰتِ اَنَّ لَهُمْ اَجْرًا حَسَنًا ۙ

3. Wherein they shall
Remain for ever :[2328]

٣- مّٰكِثِيْنَ فِيْهِ اَبَدًا ۙ

4. Further, that He may warn
Those (also) who say,

٤- وَّيُنْذِرَ الَّذِيْنَ قَالُوا

2325. See n. 2324 to xvii. 111. The theme of the last Sūra, that God is good and worthy of all praise from His creatures, to whom He has granted a clear revelation, is continued in this Sūra. The spirit of man makes gradual progress upwards, through the grace and mercy of God.

2326. Some people's idea of a Sacred Book is that it should be full of mysteries—dark corners, ambiguous expressions, words so far removed from human speech that they cover anything or nothing. Pagan oracles were couched in language which suggested one meaning to the hearer and claimed to have the very opposite meaning in the light of events which actually happened subsequently. They were distinctly crooked, not straight. In the next verse the word "Straight" (*qaiyim*) is used to characterize the Qur-ān, in contrast to this word "crooked" (*'iwaj*). See also xix. 36, n. 2488.

2327. *Qaiyim* : straight, that which has no bends and no corners to mystify people, that which speaks clearly and unambiguously, that which guides to the right path. *Cf.* ix. 36, where the adjective is used for a straight usage, in contrast to usages, which tend to mystify and deceive people. The Qur-ān is above all things straight, clear, and perspicuous Its directions are plain for everyone to understand. Any book that deals with the highest mysteries of spiritual life must necessarily have portions whose full meaning is clearer to some minds than to others not so well prepared. But here there is nowhere any mystification, any desire to wrap up things in dark sayings repugnant to human reason. God's purpose is to give clear warning of spiritual dangers and lead up to the highest bliss.

2328. The "Reward" is not a material thing, or limited by time or space. It is a state of bliss. *Cf.* Milton's "The mind is its own place, and in itself can make a Heaven of Hell, a Hell of Heaven" (P. L. i. 254-55).

"God hath begotten a son": [2329]

اتَّخَذَ اللّٰهُ وَلَدًا ۝

5. No knowledge have they
Of such a thing, nor
Had their fathers. It is
A grievous thing that issues
From their mouths as a saying.[2330]
What they say is nothing
But falsehood!

٥- مَا لَهُمْ بِهٖ مِنْ عِلْمٍ وَّلَا لِاٰبَآئِهِمْ
كَبُرَتْ كَلِمَةً تَخْرُجُ مِنْ اَفْوَاهِهِمْ
اِنْ يَّقُوْلُوْنَ اِلَّا كَذِبًا ۝

6. Thou wouldst only, perchance,
Fret thyself to death,
Following after them, in grief,[2331]
If they believe not
In this Message.

٦- فَلَعَلَّكَ بَاخِعٌ نَّفْسَكَ عَلٰٓى اٰثَارِهِمْ
اِنْ لَّمْ يُؤْمِنُوْا بِهٰذَا الْحَدِيْثِ اَسَفًا ۝

7. That which is on earth
We have made but as
A glittering show for the earth,[2332]
In order that We may test
Them—as to which of them
Are best in conduct.

٧- اِنَّا جَعَلْنَا مَا عَلَى الْاَرْضِ
زِيْنَةً لَّهَا لِنَبْلُوَهُمْ
اَيُّهُمْ اَحْسَنُ عَمَلًا ۝

8. Verily what is on earth
We shall make but as

٨- وَاِنَّا لَجٰعِلُوْنَ مَا عَلَيْهَا

2329. The warning is not only needed for those who deny God or deny His Message, but also for those whose false ideas of God degrade religion in supposing that God begot a son, for God is One and is High above any ideas of physical reproduction.

2330. The attribution of a son "begotten" to God has no basis in fact or in reason. It is only a "word" or "saying" that issues out of their mouths. It is not even a dogma that is reasoned out or can be explained in any way that is consistent with the spiritual nature of God.

2331. In a reasonable world the preaching of a reasonable Faith like that of Islam would win universal acceptance. But the world is not altogether reasonable It caused great distress to the unselfish Preacher of Islam that his Message met with so much opposition. He wanted to point the way to salvation. He only got, in the Meccan period, abuse from the chiefs of the Meccans—abuse and persecution, not only for himself but for the Truth which he was preaching. A heart less stout than his might have been appalled at what seemed the hopeless task of reclaiming the world from falsehood, superstition, selfishness, wrong, and oppression. He is here consoled, and told that he was not to fret himself to death: he was nobly doing his duty, and, as after-events showed, the seed of Truth was already germinating, although this was not visible at the time. Besides, these "chiefs" and "leaders" were only strutting in false plumes: their glory was soon to fade for ever.

2332. This world's goods—, worldly power, glory, wealth, position, and all that men scramble for,—are but a fleeting show. The possession or want of them does not betoken a man's real value or position in the spiritual world, the world which is to endure. Yet they have their uses. They test a man's sterling quality. He who becomes their slave loses rank in the spiritual world. He who uses them if he gets them, and does not fall into despair if he does not get them, shows his true mettle and quality. His conduct proclaims him.

Dust and dry soil
(Without growth or herbage).[2333]

صَعِيدًا جُرُزًا ۝

9. Or dost thou reflect[2334]
That the Companions of the
Cave[2335]
And of the Inscription[2336]
Were wonders among Our Signs?

٩- أَمْ حَسِبْتَ أَنَّ أَصْحَٰبَ الْكَهْفِ
وَالرَّقِيمِ كَانُوا مِنْ ءَايَٰتِنَا عَجَبًا ۝

10. Behold, the youths betook
themselves[2337]

١٠- إِذْ أَوَى الْفِتْيَةُ

2333. The fairest sights on the earth will become as dust and waste when this earth vanishes, and true spiritual values are restored.

2334 A wonderful story or allegory is now referred to. Its lessons are : (1) the relativity of Time, (2) the unreality of the position of oppressor and oppressed, persecutor and presecuted, on this earth, (3) the truth of the final Resurrection, when true values will be restored, and (4) the potency of Faith and Prayer to lead to the Right. Wonderful though such things may seem to be, they happen every day on God's earth !

2335. The unbelieving Quraish were in the habit of putting posers to the holy Prophet—questions which they got from Christians and Jews, which they thought the Prophet would be unable to answer. In this way they hoped to discredit him. One of these questions was about the floating Christian legend of the Seven Sleepers of Ephesus. The Prophet not only told them the main story but pointed out the variations that were current, and rebuked men for disputing about such details (xviii. 22). Most important of all, he treated the story (under inspiration) as a parable, pointing to spiritual lessons of the highest value. This is Revelation in the highest sense of the term. The story is recapitulated in n. 2337 below.

2336. *Raqīm*=Inscription. So interpreted by the Jalālain, and the majority of Commentators agree. See n. 2337, below. Others think it was the name of the dog: see xviii. 18, and n. 2350 below.

2337. The bare Christian story (without the spiritual lessons taught in the Qur-ān) is told in Gibbon's *Decline and Fall of the Roman Empire* (end of chapter 33). In the reign of a Roman Emperor who persecuted the Christians, seven Christian youths of Ephesus left the town and hid themselves in a cave in a mountain near by. They fell asleep, and remained asleep for some generations or centuries. When the wall which sealed up the cave was being demolished, the youths awoke. They still thought of the world in which they had previously lived. They had no idea of the duration of time. But when one of them went to the town to purchase provisions, he found that the whole world had changed. The Christian religion, instead of being persecuted was fashionable : in fact it was now the State religion. His dress and speech, and the money which he brought, seemed to belong to another world. This attracted attention. The great ones of the land visited the Cave, and verified the tale by questioning the man's Companions

When the story became very popular and circulated throughout the Roman Empire, we may well suppose that an Inscription was put up at the mouth of the Cave. See verse 9 and n 2336. This inscription was probably to be seen for many years afterwards, as Ephesus was a famous city on the west coast of Asia Minor, about forty to fifty miles south of Smyrna. Later on, the K͟halīfa Wāt͟hiq (842-846 A D.) sent an expedition to examine and identify the locality, as he did about the Ẕul-Qarnain barrier in Central Asia (Appendix VII at the end of this Sūra).

A popular story circulating from mouth to mouth would necessarily be vague as to dates and vary very much in details. Somewhere about the 6th century A D. a Syriac writer reduced it to writing. He suggested that the youths were seven in number ; that they went to sleep in the reign of the Emperor Decius (who reigned from 249 to 151 A D, and who was a violent persecutor of Christianity) ; and that they awoke in the reign of Theodosius II, who reigned from 408 to 450 A.D. In our literature Decius is known as Daqyānūs (from the adjectival Latin from Decianus), and the name stands as a symbol of injustice and oppression, and also of things old fashioned and out-of-date, as *res Decianæ* must have been two or three centuries after Decius.

To the Cave : they said,
"Our Lord ! bestow on us
Mercy from Thyself,
And dispose of our affair
For us in the right way !"[2338]

إِلَى الْكَهْفِ فَقَالُوا رَبَّنَا آتِنَا
مِن لَّدُنكَ رَحْمَةً
وَهَيِّئْ لَنَا مِنْ أَمْرِنَا رَشَدًا ○

11. Then We draw (a veil)[2339]
Over their ears, for a number
Of years, in the Cave,
(So that they heard not) :

١١- فَضَرَبْنَا عَلَىٰ آذَانِهِمْ
فِي الْكَهْفِ سِنِينَ عَدَدًا ○

12. Then We roused them,[2340]
In order to test which
Of the two parties was best[2341]
At calculating the term
Of years they had tarried !

١٢- ثُمَّ بَعَثْنَاهُمْ لِنَعْلَمَ
أَيُّ الْحِزْبَيْنِ أَحْصَىٰ لِمَا لَبِثُوا أَمَدًا ○

SECTION 2.

13. We relate to thee their story
In truth : they were youths
Who believed in their Lord,
And We advanced them
In guidance :[2342]

١٣- نَحْنُ نَقُصُّ عَلَيْكَ نَبَأَهُم بِالْحَقِّ
إِنَّهُمْ فِتْيَةٌ آمَنُوا بِرَبِّهِمْ وَزِدْنَاهُمْ
هُدًى ○

14. We gave strength to their
hearts :[2343]

١٤- وَرَبَطْنَا عَلَىٰ قُلُوبِهِمْ

2338. The youths hid in the cave, but they trusted in God, and made over their whole case to Him in prayer. Then they apparently fell asleep, and knew nothing of what was happening in the world outside.

2339. *Drew (a veil) over their ears :* i.e. sealed their ears, so that they heard nothing. As they were in the Cave they saw nothing. So they were completely cut off from the outer world. It was as if they had died, with their knowledge and ideas remaining at the point of time when they had entered the Cave. It is as if a watch stops at the exact moment of some accident, and any one taking it up afterwards can precisely fix the time of the accident.

2340. *Roused them* : or raised them up from their sleep or whatever condition they had fallen into (xviii. 18), so that they began to perceive the things around them, but only with the memories of the time at which they had ceased to be in touch with the world.

2341. When they awoke to consciousness, they had lost all count of time. Though they had all entered together, and lain together in the same place for the same length of time, their impressions of the time they had passed were quite different. Time is thus related to our own internal experiences. We have to learn the lesson that men as good as ourselves may yet differ as to their reactions to certain facts, and that in such matters disputes are unseemly. It is best to say, "God knows best" (xviii. 19).

2342. Their Faith carried them higher and higher on the road to Truth. Faith is cumulative. Each step leads higher and higher, by the grace and mercy of God.

2343. So that they were not afraid to speak out openly, and protest the truth of the Unity which they clearly saw in their own minds and hearts.

Behold, they stood up[2344]
And said: "Our Lord is
The Lord of the heavens
And of the earth: never
Shall we call upon any god
Other than Him: if we
Did, we should indeed
Have uttered an enormity!

إذ قاموا فقالوا ربنا
رب السموت والارض لن
ندعوا من دونه الها لقد
قلنا اذا شططا ○

15. "These our people have taken[2345]
For worship gods other
Than Him: why do they
Not bring forward an authority
Clear (and convincing)
For what they do?
Who doth more wrong
Than such as invent
A falsehood against God?

١٥- هؤلاء قومنا اتخذوا من دونه
الهة ؕ
لولا يأتون عليهم بسلطن بين ؕ
فمن اظلم ممن افترى
على الله كذبا ○

16. "When ye turn away
From them and the things
They worship other than God,
Betake yourselves to the Cave:
Your Lord will shower
His mercies on you
And dispose of your affair
Towards comfort and ease."[2346]

١٦- وإذ اعتزلتموهم وما يعبدون إلا
الله فأووا الى الكهف
ينشر لكم ربكم من رحمته
ويهيئ لكم من امركم مرفقا ○

17. Thou wouldst have seen
The sun, when it rose,
Declining to the right[2347]
From their Cave, and when

١٧- وترى الشمس إذا طلعت
تزور عن كهفهم ذات اليمين وإذا

2344. We may suppose them to have taken their stand and made a public protest before they betook themselves to the Cave (xviii. 16). The story really begins at xviii. 13, and the verses xviii. 9-12 may be considered as introductory. As the emphasis is on spiritual lessons, the facts stated in the introductory part are passed over lightly in the story.

2345. Besides the heathen gods, the cult of the Emperors also became fashionable in the Roman Empire in the first three centuries of the Christian Era. The statue of Diana (Artemis) at Ephesus had been one of the wonders of the ancient world. The city was a great seaport and the capital of Roman Asia. We may therefore imagine how the heathen cults must have flourished there. St. Paul spent three years preaching there, and was mobbed and assaulted, and compelled to leave (Acts, xix. 1-41).

2346. That is, 'do not be afraid of anything: put your whole case in the hands of God: at present you are being persecuted; he will solve your difficulties and give you ease and comfort'. The public protest ends at verse 15. In verse 16 they are taking counsel among themselves. After they go into the Cave, verse 17 introduces us to the scene where they are lying in the midst of the Cave in tranquil confidence in God.

2347. In the latitude of Ephesus, 38° north, *i.e.* well above the sun's northern declination, a cave opening to north, would never have the heat of the sun within it, as the sunny side would be the south. If the youths lay on their backs with their faces looking to the north, *i.e.* towards the entrance of the Cave, the sun would rise on their right side, declining to the south, and set on their left side, leaving them cool and comfortable.

It set, turning away
From them to the left,
While they lay in the open
Space in the midst
Of the Cave. Such are
Among the Signs of God:
He whom God guides[2348]
Is rightly guided; but he
Whom God leaves to stray,—
For him wilt thou find
No protector to lead him
To the Right Way.

غَرَبَت تَّقْرِضُهُمْ ذَاتَ الشِّمَالِ
وَهُمْ فِي فَجْوَةٍ مِّنْهُ
ذَٰلِكَ مِنْ آيَاتِ اللَّهِ
مَن يَهْدِ اللَّهُ فَهُوَ الْمُهْتَدِ
وَمَن يُضْلِلْ فَلَن تَجِدَ
لَهُ وَلِيًّا مُّرْشِدًا ○

Section 3.

18. Thou wouldst have deemed them[2349]
Awake, whilst they were asleep,
And We turned them
On their right and on
Their left sides: their dog[2350]
Stretching forth his two fore-legs
On the threshold: if thou
Hadst come up on to them,
Thou wouldst have certainly
Turned back from them in flight,
And wouldst certainly have been
Filled with terror of them.[2351]

١٨- وَتَحْسَبُهُمْ أَيْقَاظًا وَهُمْ رُقُودٌ
وَنُقَلِّبُهُمْ ذَاتَ الْيَمِينِ وَذَاتَ الشِّمَالِ
وَكَلْبُهُم بَاسِطٌ ذِرَاعَيْهِ بِالْوَصِيدِ
لَوِ اطَّلَعْتَ عَلَيْهِمْ
لَوَلَّيْتَ مِنْهُمْ فِرَارًا
وَلَمُلِئْتَ مِنْهُمْ رُعْبًا ○

19. Such (being their state),
We raised them up (from sleep),
That they might question[2352]
Each other. Said one of them,

١٩- وَكَذَٰلِكَ بَعَثْنَاهُمْ لِيَتَسَاءَلُوا بَيْنَهُمْ
قَالَ قَائِلٌ مِّنْهُمْ

2348. The youths, having faith and trust in God, found safety and refuge in the Cave. They were protected from the persecution and violence of the heathen. Their prayer (xviii 16) was heard.

2349. Perhaps their eyes were open, even though their senses were sealed in sleep. They turned about on their sides as men do in sleep.

2350 The name of their dog is traditionally known as Qiṭmīr, but see n 2336 above.

2351. This graphic picture of the sleepers explains the human mechanism by which their safety was ensured by God from their Pagan enemies.

2352. This is the point of the story. Their own human impressions were to be compared, each with the other. They were to be made to see that with the best goodwill and the most honest enquiry they might reach different conclusions; that they were not to waste their time in vain controversies, but to get on to the main business of life; and that God alone had full knowledge of the things that seem to us so strange, or inconsistent, or inexplicable, or that produce different impressions on different minds. If they entered the Cave in the morning and woke up in the afternoon, one of them might well think they had been there only a few hours—only part of a day. This relative or fallacious impression of Time also gives us an inkling of the state when there will be no Time, of the Resurrection when all our little impressions of this life will be corrected by the final Reality. This mystery of time has puzzled many contemplative minds. *Cf.* "Dark time that haunts us with the briefness of our days" (Thomas Wolfe in "Of Time and the River").

"How long have ye stayed (here)?"
They said, "We have stayed
(Perhaps) a day, or part
Of a day." (At length)
They (all) said, "God (alone)
Knows best how long
Ye have stayed here...
Now send ye then one of you
With this money of yours[2353]
To the town: let him
Find out which is the best[2354]
Food (to be had) and bring some
To you, that (ye may)
Satisfy your hunger therewith:
And let him behave
With care and courtesy,
And let him not inform
Any one about you.

كَمْ لَبِثْتُمْ ۖ
قَالُوا لَبِثْنَا يَوْمًا أَوْ بَعْضَ يَوْمٍ ۚ
قَالُوا رَبُّكُمْ أَعْلَمُ بِمَا لَبِثْتُمْ
فَابْعَثُوا أَحَدَكُمْ بِوَرِقِكُمْ هَٰذِهِ
إِلَى الْمَدِينَةِ فَلْيَنْظُرْ أَيُّهَا أَزْكَىٰ
طَعَامًا فَلْيَأْتِكُمْ بِرِزْقٍ مِنْهُ
وَلْيَتَلَطَّفْ
وَلَا يُشْعِرَنَّ بِكُمْ أَحَدًا ○

نصف القرآن

20. "For if they should
Come upon you, they would
Stone you or force you[2355]
To return to their cult,
And in that case ye would
Never attain prosperity."[2356]

٢٠- إِنَّهُمْ إِنْ يَظْهَرُوا عَلَيْكُمْ
يَرْجُمُوكُمْ أَوْ يُعِيدُوكُمْ فِي مِلَّتِهِمْ
وَلَنْ تُفْلِحُوا إِذًا أَبَدًا ○

21. Thus[2357] did We make
Their case known to the people,

٢١- وَكَذَٰلِكَ أَعْثَرْنَا عَلَيْهِمْ

2353. They now give up barren controversy and come to the practical business of life. But their thoughts are conditioned by the state of things that existed when they entered the Cave. The money they carried was the money coined in the reign of the monarch who persecuted the Religion of Unity and favoured the false cults of Paganism.

2354. *Best food*: *i.e.*, purest, most wholesome, perhaps also most suitable for those who rejected idol worship, *i.e.*, not dedicated to idols. For they still imagined the world in the same state in which they had known it before they entered the Cave.

2355. They think that the world had not changed, and that the fierce persecution they knew was still raging, under which a man had to pay by his life for his religious faith, if he could not conform to Pagan worship.

2356. That is, never reap the spiritual good which your knowledge, instruction, and experience entitle you to attain. To become a renegade, to give up the Truth which you have won, simply on account of the fear of men, is the most despicable form of cowardice, and would rightly close the door of salvation if strict justice were to be done. But even then God's Mercy comes to the coward's aid so long as the door of repentance is open.

2357. *Thus*: in this way, by these means, *i.e.*, by the sending out of one of the Sleepers with the old money to the town to buy provisions. His old-fashioned dress, appearance, and speech, and the old uncurrent money which he brought, at once drew the attention of people to him. When they learnt his story, they realised that God, Who can protect His servants thus and raise them up from sleep after such a long time, has power to raise up men for the Resurrection, and that His promise of goodness and mercy to those who serve Him is true and was exemplified in this striking way. On the other hand, to the men of the Cave themselves, it became clear that God can change the situation before we are aware, and our hope in Him is not futile, and that even when we are on the brink of despair, a revolution is surely working in the world before the world itself realises it.

That they might know
That the promise of God
Is true, and that there can
Be no doubt about the Hour
Of Judgment. Behold,
They dispute among
themselves[2358]
As to their affair. (Some) said,
"Construct a building over them":
Their Lord knows best
About them: those who prevailed
Over their affair said,
"Let us surely build a place
Of worship over them."

لِيَعْلَمُوٓا أَنَّ وَعْدَ اللَّهِ
حَقٌّ وَأَنَّ السَّاعَةَ لَا رَيْبَ فِيهَا
إِذْ يَتَنَٰزَعُونَ بَيْنَهُمْ أَمْرَهُمْ فَقَالُوا
ابْنُوا عَلَيْهِم بُنْيَٰنًا
رَّبُّهُمْ أَعْلَمُ بِهِمْ قَالَ الَّذِينَ غَلَبُوا
عَلَىٰٓ أَمْرِهِمْ
لَنَتَّخِذَنَّ عَلَيْهِم مَّسْجِدًا ○

22. (Some) say they were three,
The dog being the fourth
Among them; (others) say
They were five, the dog
Being the sixth,—doubtfully
Guessing at the unknown;[2359]
(Yet others) say they were
Seven, the dog being the eighth.
Say thou: "My Lord
Knoweth best their number;
It is but few that know[2360]
Their (real case)." Enter not,
Therefore, into controversies
Concerning them, except
On a matter that is clear,[2361]
Nor consult any of them
About (the affair of) the
Sleepers.[2362]

٢٢- سَيَقُولُونَ ثَلَٰثَةٌ رَّابِعُهُمْ كَلْبُهُمْ
وَيَقُولُونَ خَمْسَةٌ سَادِسُهُمْ كَلْبُهُمْ
رَجْمًا بِالْغَيْبِ وَيَقُولُونَ سَبْعَةٌ
وَثَامِنُهُمْ كَلْبُهُمْ
قُل رَّبِّيٓ أَعْلَمُ بِعِدَّتِهِم
مَّا يَعْلَمُهُمْ إِلَّا قَلِيلٌ
فَلَا تُمَارِ فِيهِمْ
إِلَّا مِرَآءً ظَٰهِرًا
وَلَا تَسْتَفْتِ فِيهِم مِّنْهُمْ أَحَدًا ○

2358 The perversity of man is such that as soon as ever a glimpse of truth becomes manifest, men fall into controversies about it. The Sleepers could not judge about the duration of their stay in the Cave, but they wisely left the matter and attended to the urgent business of their lives. The townsfolk could not agree as to the significance of the event: they fell to discussing immaterial details. What sort of a memorial should they raise?—a house or a place of worship or a tablet? The place of worship was built. But the real significance of the spiritual meaning was missed until explained in the Qur-ān

2359. The controversy in after ages raged about the number of the Sleepers: were they three or five or seven? People answered, not from knowledge, but from conjecture. Gibbon's version, which has now become best known, makes the number of Sleepers seven. The point was immaterial: the real point was the spiritual lesson.

2360. The true significance of the story is known only to a few. Most men discuss futile details, which are not in their knowledge.

2361. It is unprofitable to enter such immaterial controversies and many others that have been waged about Religion by shallow men from time immemorial. Yet, if there is a matter of clear knowledge from experience that matters, we must openly proclaim it, that the world may be brought to listen to God's Truth.

2362. Vulgar story-mongers as such know little of the true significance of stories and parables. We have a clear exposition in the Qur-ān. What need is there to go into details of the number of men in the Cave, or of the time they remained there?

C. 134.—True knowledge is with God alone.
(xviii. 23-44.) We are not to dispute on matters
Of conjecture, but to rely on the Truth
That comes from God. As in the Parable.
The man who piles up wealth
And is puffed up with this world's goods,
Despising those otherwise endowed,
Will come to an evil end,
For his hopes were not built on God.

SECTION 4.

23. Nor say of anything,
"I shall be sure to do
So and so to-morrow"—

٢٣- وَلَا تَقُولَنَّ لِشَايْءٍ
إِنِّي فَاعِلٌ ذَٰلِكَ غَدًا ۝

24. Without adding, "So please
God!"[2363]
And call thy Lord to mind
When thou forgettest, and say,
"I hope that my Lord
Will guide me ever closer
(Even) than this
To the right road."[2364]

٢٤- إِلَّا أَن يَشَاءَ اللَّهُ ۚ وَاذْكُر رَّبَّكَ
إِذَا نَسِيتَ وَقُلْ عَسَىٰ أَن يَهْدِيَنِ رَبِّي
لِأَقْرَبَ مِنْ هَٰذَا رَشَدًا ۝

25. So they stayed in their Cave
Three hundred years, and (some)
Add nine (more)[2365]

٢٥- وَلَبِثُوا فِي كَهْفِهِمْ ثَلَاثَ مِائَةٍ
سِنِينَ وَازْدَادُوا تِسْعًا ۝

2363. Verses 23 and 24 are parenthetical. We must never rely upon our own resources so much as to forget God If by any chance we do forget. we must come back to Him and keep Him in remembrance, as did the Companions of the Cave.

2364. In geometry the perfect circle is an ideal. Any given circle that we draw is not so perfect that we cannot draw one closer to the ideal. So in our life, there is always the hope of drawing closer and closer to God.

2365. This verse should be read with the next verse. In the floating oral tradition the duration of time in the Cave was given differently in different versions. When the tradition was reduced to writing, some Christian writers (*e.g.*, Simeon Metaphrastes) named 372 years, some less. In round numbers 300 years in the solar Calendar would amount to 309 in the lunar Calendar. But the next verse points out that all these are mere conjectures : the number is known to God alone.

The authority on which Gibbon relies mentions two definite reigns, that of Decius (249-251 A.D.) and that of Theodosius II (408-450 A.D). Taking 250 and 450, we get an interval of 200 years. But the point of the story does not lie in the name of any given Emperor, but in the fact that the beginning of the period coincided with an Emperor who persecuted : the Emperor's name at the end of the period may be taken as approximately correct, because the story was recorded within two generations afterwards One of the worst Emperors to persecute the Christians was Nero who reigned from 54 to 68. If we took the end of his reign (A.D. 68) as the initial point, and (say) 440 A.D. as the final point, we get the 372 years of Simeon Metaphrastes. But none of these writers knew any more than we do. Our best course is to follow the Quranic injunction, "Say, God knows best how long they stayed" (xviii. 26). There is also a rebuke implied : 'do not imitate these men who love mischievous controversies!' After all, we are given the narrative more as a parable than as a story.

26. Say : " God knows best
How long they stayed :
With Him is (the knowledge
Of) the secrets of the heavens
And the earth : how clearly
He sees, how finely He hears
(Everything) ! They have no
protector[2366]
Other than Him ; nor does
He share His Command
With any person whatsoever.[2367]

٢٦- قُلِ اللّٰهُ اَعۡلَمُ بِمَا لَبِثُوۡا ۚ
لَهٗ غَيۡبُ السَّمٰوٰتِ وَالۡاَرۡضِ ؕ
اَبۡصِرۡ بِهٖ وَاَسۡمِعۡ ؕ
مَا لَهُمۡ مِّنۡ دُوۡنِهٖ مِنۡ وَّلِىٍّ
وَّلَا يُشۡرِكُ فِىۡ حُكۡمِهٖۤ اَحَدًا ○

27. And recite (and teach)
What has been revealed
To thee of the Book
Of thy Lord : none
Can change His Words,[2368]
And none wilt thou find
As a refuge other than Him.

٢٧- وَاتۡلُ مَاۤ اُوۡحِىَ
اِلَيۡكَ مِنۡ كِتَابِ رَبِّكَ ۚ
لَا مُبَدِّلَ لِكَلِمٰتِهٖ ۚ
وَلَنۡ تَجِدَ مِنۡ دُوۡنِهٖ مُلۡتَحَدًا ○

28. And keep thy soul content
With those who call
On their Lord morning
And evening, seeking[2369]
His Face ; and let not
Thine eyes pass beyond them,
Seeking the pomp and glitter
Of this Life ; nor obey
Any whose heart We
Have permitted to neglect
The remembrance of Us,
One who follows his own

٢٨- وَاصۡبِرۡ نَفۡسَكَ مَعَ الَّذِيۡنَ يَدۡعُوۡنَ
رَبَّهُمۡ بِالۡغَدٰوةِ وَالۡعَشِىِّ
يُرِيۡدُوۡنَ وَجۡهَهٗ وَلَا تَعۡدُ عَيۡنٰكَ عَنۡهُمۡ ۚ
تُرِيۡدُ زِيۡنَةَ الۡحَيٰوةِ الدُّنۡيَا ۚ
وَلَا تُطِعۡ مَنۡ اَغۡفَلۡنَا قَلۡبَهٗ
عَنۡ ذِكۡرِنَا وَاتَّبَعَ

2366. Who are "they" in this sentence? They may be the Companions of the Cave, for they put themselves under the protection of God, and disowned all attribution of partners to Him. Or "they" may refer to the people in general who go wrong and become "Mushriks", *i.e.*, attribute imaginary partners to God.

2367. *His Command* : *i.e.*, God's government of the world, or in His Judgment on the Day of Judgment.

2368. *His Words* : His Commands, Decrees, Orders.

2369. *Cf.* vi. 52, and n. 870. The true servants of God are those whose hearts are turned to Him morning, noon, and night, and who seek not worldly gain, but God's Grace, God's own Self, His Presence and nearness. "Face" is the symbol of Personality or Self. Even if they are poor in this world's goods, their society gives far more inward and spiritual satisfaction than worldly grandeur or worldly attractions.

Desires, whose case has
Gone beyond all bounds.[2370]

هَوٰىهُ وَكَانَ اَمْرُهٗ فُرُطًا ۝

29. Say, "The Truth is
From your Lord":
Let him who will,
Believe, and let him
Who will, reject (it):[2371]
For the wrong-doers We
Have prepared a Fire
Whose (smoke and flames),
Like the walls and roof
Of a tent, will hem
Them in: if they implore
Relief they will be granted
Water like melted brass,
That will scald their faces.
How dreadful the drink!
How uncomfortable a couch
To recline on!

٢٩- وَقُلِ الْحَقُّ مِنْ رَّبِّكُمْ
فَمَنْ شَآءَ فَلْيُؤْمِنْ
وَّمَنْ شَآءَ فَلْيَكْفُرْ
اِنَّآ اَعْتَدْنَا لِلظّٰلِمِيْنَ نَارًا
اَحَاطَ بِهِمْ سُرَادِقُهَا
وَاِنْ يَّسْتَغِيْثُوْا يُغَاثُوْا
بِمَآءٍ كَالْمُهْلِ يَشْوِى الْوُجُوْهَ
بِئْسَ الشَّرَابُ
وَسَآءَتْ مُرْتَفَقًا ۝

30. As to those who believe
And work righteousness,
Verily We shall not suffer
To perish the reward
Of any who do
A (single) righteous deed.[2372]

٣٠- اِنَّ الَّذِيْنَ اٰمَنُوْا وَعَمِلُوا الصّٰلِحٰتِ
اِنَّا لَا نُضِيْعُ اَجْرَ
مَنْ اَحْسَنَ عَمَلًا ۝

31. For them will be Gardens
Of Eternity; beneath them
Rivers will flow: they will
Be adorned therein
With bracelets of gold,
And they will wear

٣١- اُولٰٓئِكَ لَهُمْ جَنّٰتُ عَدْنٍ
تَجْرِىْ مِنْ تَحْتِهِمُ الْاَنْهٰرُ يُحَلَّوْنَ فِيْهَا
مِنْ اَسَاوِرَ مِنْ ذَهَبٍ وَّيَلْبَسُوْنَ

2370 For those who stray from God's path, God's Grace is ever anxious: it seeks to reclaim them and bring them back to the path. If such a one resists, and follows his own lusts, a point is reached when his case becomes hopeless. God's Grace does not then reach him, and he is abandoned to his pride and insolence. Beware of following the example or advice of such a one or seeking his society, or hankering after his wretched idols.

2371. Our choice in our limited Free-will involves a corresponding personal responsibility. We are offered the Truth: again and again is it pressed on our attention. If we reject it, we must take all the terrible consequences which are prefigured in the Fire of Hell. Its flames and roof will completely enclose us like a tent. Ordinarily there is water to quench the heat of thirst: here the only drink will be like molten brass, thick, heavy, burning, sizzling. Before it reaches the mouth of the unfortunates, drops of it will scald their faces as it is poured out

2372. The righteous will be rewarded, as has been said again and again, beyond their merits: xxviii. 84; xxx 39. Not a single good deed of theirs will lose its reward, and the mercy of God will blot out their sins.

Green garments[2373] of fine silk
And heavy brocade;
They will recline therein
On raised thrones.
How good the recompense!
How beautiful a couch
To recline on![2374]

ثِيَابًا خُضْرًا مِّنْ سُنْدُسٍ وَّإِسْتَبْرَقٍ
مُّتَّكِـِٔينَ فِيهَا عَلَى الْأَرَآئِكِ ۚ
نِعْمَ الثَّوَابُ ۚ
وَحَسُنَتْ مُرْتَفَقًا ۝ ع

SECTION 5.

32. Set forth to them
The parable of two men:
For one of them We provided
Two gardens of grape-vines
And surrounded them
With date palms;
In between the two
We placed corn-fields.[2375]

٣٢- وَاضْرِبْ لَهُمْ مَّثَلًا رَّجُلَيْنِ
جَعَلْنَا لِأَحَدِهِمَا جَنَّتَيْنِ مِنْ أَعْنَابٍ
وَّحَفَفْنٰهُمَا بِنَخْلٍ
وَّجَعَلْنَا بَيْنَهُمَا زَرْعًا ۝

33. Each of those gardens
Brought forth its produce,
And failed not in the least
Therein: in the midst
Of them We caused
A river to flow.

٣٣- كِلْتَا الْجَنَّتَيْنِ اٰتَتْ أُكُلَهَا
وَلَمْ تَظْلِمْ مِّنْهُ شَيْـًٔا ۙ
وَّفَجَّرْنَا خِلٰلَهُمَا نَهَرًا ۝

34. (Abundant) was the produce
This man had: he said
To his companion, in the course
Of a mutual argument:
"More wealth have I
Than you, and more honour
And power in (my following
Of) men."[2376]

٣٤- وَّكَانَ لَهٗ ثَمَرٌ ۚ فَقَالَ
لِصَاحِبِهٖ وَهُوَ يُحَاوِرُهٗٓ
أَنَا أَكْثَرُ مِنْكَ مَالًا
وَّأَعَزُّ نَفَرًا ۝

2373. Heaven is figured by all the pictures of ease and comfort which we can imagine in our present state: Gardens; perpetual springs of crystal water, which we can see as in a landscape from above; the finest and most costly ornaments; the most beautiful clothes to wear; green is the colour mentioned, because it is the most refreshing to the eye, and fits in well with the Garden; the wearer takes the choice of fine silk or heavy brocade; and for rest and comfort, high thrones of dignity on which the blessed ones recline.

2374. This picture is in parallel contrast to the picture of Misery in the last verse.

2375. Here is a simple parable of the contrast between two men. One was purse-proud, and forgot that what he had was from God, by way of a trust and a trial in this life. The other boasted of nothing: his trust was in God. The worldly wealth of the first was destroyed, and he had nothing left. The second was the happier in the end.

2376 The two men began to compare notes. The arrogant one was puffed up with his possessions, his income, and his large family and following, and thought in his self-complacency that it would last for ever. He was also wrong in looking down on his Companion, who, though less affluent, was the better man of the two.

35. He went into his garden
In a state (of mind)
Unjust to his soul:[2377]
He said, "I deem not
That this will ever perish,

٣٥- وَدَخَلَ جَنَّتَهُ وَهُوَ ظَالِمٌ لِّنَفْسِهِ ۚ
قَالَ مَآ أَظُنُّ أَن تَبِيدَ هَٰذِهِۦٓ أَبَدًا ۙ ○

36. "Nor do I deem
That the Hour (of Judgment)
Will (ever) come:
Even if I am brought back
To my Lord, I shall
Surely find (there)
Something better in exchange."[2378]

٣٦- وَمَآ أَظُنُّ ٱلسَّاعَةَ قَآئِمَةً ۙ
وَلَئِن رُّدِدتُّ إِلَىٰ رَبِّى
لَأَجِدَنَّ خَيْرًا مِّنْهَا مُنقَلَبًا ○

37. His companion said to him,
In the course of the argument
With him: "Dost thou deny
Him Who created thee
Out of dust, then out of
A sperm-drop, then fashioned
Thee into a man?[2379]

٣٧- قَالَ لَهُۥ صَاحِبُهُۥ وَهُوَ يُحَاوِرُهُۥٓ
أَكَفَرْتَ بِٱلَّذِى خَلَقَكَ مِن تُرَابٍ
ثُمَّ مِن
نُّطْفَةٍ ثُمَّ سَوَّىٰكَ رَجُلًا ○

38. "But (I think) for my part
That He is God,
My Lord, and none shall I
Associate with my Lord.

٣٨- لَّٰكِنَّا۠ هُوَ ٱللَّهُ
رَبِّى وَلَآ أُشْرِكُ بِرَبِّىٓ أَحَدًا ○

39. "Why didst thou not,
As thou wentest into
Thy garden, say: 'God's Will
(Be done)! There is no power
But with God!' If thou[2380]

٣٩- وَلَوْلَآ إِذْ دَخَلْتَ جَنَّتَكَ قُلْتَ مَا
شَآءَ ٱللَّهُ لَا قُوَّةَ إِلَّا بِٱللَّهِ ۚ إِن

2377. It was not wealth that ruined him, but the attitude of his mind. He was unjust, not so much to his neighbour, as to his own soul. In his love of the material, he forgot or openly defied the spiritual. As verse 37 shows, he took his companion with him, to impress him with his own importance, but the companion was unmoved.

2378. Here comes out the grasping spirit of the materialist. In his mind "better" means more wealth and more power, of the kind he was enjoying in this life, although in reality, even what he had, rested on hollow foundations and was doomed to perish and bring him down with it.

2379. The three stages of man's creation: first dust, or clay, itself created out of nothing, and forming the physical basis of his body; then, out of the produce of the earth as incorporated in the parents' body, the sperm drop (with the corresponding receptive element); and then when the different elements were mixed in due proportion, and the soul was breathed into him, the fashioned man. *Cf.* lxxxvii. 2, and xv. 28-29.

2380. The companion's argument divides itself into five parts. (1) He remonstrates against the proud man denying God. (2) He, from his own spiritual experience, proclaims that God is One and that He is good. (3) He points out to him the better way of enjoying God's gifts, with gratitude to Him. (4) He expresses contentment and satisfaction in God's dealings with him. (5) He gives a warning of the fleeting nature of this world's goods and the certainty of God's punishment for inordinate vanity.

Dost see me less than
Thee in wealth and sons,

تَرَنِ اَنَا اَقَلَّ مِنْكَ مَالًا وَّوَلَدًا ۝

40. " It may be that my Lord
Will give me something
Better than thy garden,
And that He will send
On thy garden thunderbolts
(By way of reckoning)
From heaven, making it
(But) slippery sand !—

٤٠- فَعَسٰى رَبِّيْٓ اَنْ يُّؤْتِيَنِ
خَيْرًا مِّنْ جَنَّتِكَ وَيُرْسِلَ
عَلَيْهَا حُسْبَانًا
مِّنَ السَّمَآءِ فَتُصْبِحَ صَعِيْدًا زَلَقًا ۝

41. " Or the water of the garden
Will run off underground
So that thou wilt never
Be able to find it." [2381]

٤١- اَوْ يُصْبِحَ مَآؤُهَا غَوْرًا
فَلَنْ تَسْتَطِيْعَ لَهٗ طَلَبًا ۝

42. So his fruits (and enjoyment)
Were encompassed (with ruin),
And he remained twisting
And turning his hands
Over what he had spent [2382]
On his property, which had
(Now) tumbled to pieces
To its very foundations,
And he could only say,
" Woe is me! Would I had
Never ascribed partners
To my Lord and Cherisher !" [2383]

٤٢- وَاُحِيْطَ بِثَمَرِهٖ
فَاَصْبَحَ يُقَلِّبُ كَفَّيْهِ
عَلٰى مَآ اَنْفَقَ فِيْهَا
وَهِيَ خَاوِيَةٌ عَلٰى عُرُوْشِهَا
وَيَقُوْلُ يٰلَيْتَنِيْ
لَمْ اُشْرِكْ بِرَبِّيْٓ اَحَدًا ۝

43. Nor had he numbers
To help him against God,
Nor was he able
To deliver himself. [2384]

٤٣- وَلَمْ تَكُنْ لَّهٗ فِئَةٌ يَّنْصُرُوْنَهٗ مِنْ
دُوْنِ اللّٰهِ وَمَا كَانَ مُنْتَصِرًا ۝

2381. The punishment was that of thunderbolts (*ḥusbānan*), but the general meaning of the word includes any punishment by way of a reckoning (*ḥisāb*), and I think that an earthquake is also implied, as it alters water-courses, diverts channels underground, throws up silt and sand, and covers large areas with ruin, as happened in the Bihar earthquake of 1934.

2382. " Fruits ", " spent ", " twisting of the hands ", should all be understood in a wide metaphorical sense, as well as the literal sense. He had great income and satisfaction, which were all gone. What resources he had lavished on his property ! His thoughts had been engrossed on it ; his hopes had been built on it ; it had become the absorbing passion of his life. If he had only looked to God, instead of to the ephemeral goods of this world !

2383. In this case, in his mind, there was his own Self and his Mammon as rivals to God !

2384. He had built up connections and obliged dependants, and was proud of having his " quiver full ". But where were all things when the reckoning came ? He could not help himself ; how could others be expected to help him !

44. There, the (only) protection comes
From God, the True One.
He is the Best to reward,
And the Best to give success.[2385]

٤٤- هُنَالِكَ الْوَلَايَةُ لِلّٰهِ الْحَقِّ ۭ
هُوَ خَيْرٌ ثَوَابًا وَّخَيْرٌ عُقْبًا ۝

C. 135.- (xviii. 45-59) The life of this world is ephemeral,
And its gains will not last. Good Deeds
Are the best of possessions in God's sight:
All will be levelled up on the Day
Of Judgment, and a new Order created
On the basis of Truth, according to the Book
Of Deeds. Pride is the root of Evil,
Rebellion, and wrong. Who will choose
Evil ones in preference to God? Let us accept
Truth, for though Falsehood may flourish
For a time, it must perish in the end.

Section 6.

45. Set forth to them
The similitude of the life
Of this world: it is like
The rain which We send
Down from the skies:
The earth's vegetation absorbs it,
But soon it becomes
Dry stubble, which the winds[2386]
Do scatter: it is (only) God
Who prevails over all things.

٤٥- وَاضْرِبْ لَهُمْ مَّثَلَ الْحَيٰوةِ
الدُّنْيَا كَمَاۗءٍ اَنْزَلْنٰهُ مِنَ السَّمَاۗءِ
فَاخْتَلَطَ بِهٖ نَبَاتُ الْاَرْضِ
فَاَصْبَحَ هَشِيْمًا تَذْرُوْهُ الرِّيٰحُ ۭ
وَكَانَ اللّٰهُ عَلٰي كُلِّ شَيْءٍ مُّقْتَدِرًا ۝

46. Wealth and sons are allurements
Of the life of this world:
But the things that endure,
Good Deeds, are best
In the sight of thy Lord,
As rewards, and best
As (the foundation for) hopes.[2387]

٤٦- اَلْمَالُ وَالْبَنُوْنَ زِيْنَةُ الْحَيٰوةِ الدُّنْيَا ۚ
وَالْبٰقِيٰتُ الصّٰلِحٰتُ خَيْرٌ
عِنْدَ رَبِّكَ ثَوَابًا وَّخَيْرٌ اَمَلًا ۝

2385. All else is vanity, uncertainty, the sport of Time. The only hope or truth is from God. Other rewards and other successes are illusory: the best Reward and the best Success come from God.

2386. Rain-water is a good thing in itself, but it does not last, and you can build no solid foundations on it. It is soon absorbed in the earth, and produces the flourishing appearance of grass and vegetation—for a time. Soon these decay, and become as dry stubble, which the least wind from any quarter will blow about like a thing of no importance. The water is gone, and so is the vegetation to which it lent a brave show of luxuriance temporarily. Such is the life of *this* world, contrasted with the inner and real Life, which looks to the Hereafter. God is the only enduring Power we can look to, supreme over all.

2387. Other things are fleeting: but Good Deeds have a lasting value in the sight of God. They are best as (or for) rewards in two ways: (1) they flow from us by the Grace of God, and are themselves rewards for our Faith; (2) they become the foundation of our hopes for the highest spiritual rewards in the Hereafter.

47. One Day We shall
Remove the mountains, and thou
Wilt see the earth
As a level stretch,[2388]
And We shall gather them,
All together, nor shall We
Leave out any one of them.

٤٧- وَيَوْمَ نُسَيِّرُ الْجِبَالَ وَ
تَرَى الْأَرْضَ بَارِزَةً ۙ
وَحَشَرْنٰهُمْ فَلَمْ نُغَادِرْ مِنْهُمْ أَحَدًا ۚ

48. And they will be marshalled
Before thy Lord in ranks,
(With the announcement),
"Now have ye come to Us
(Bare) as We created you[2389]
First: aye, ye thought
We shall not fulfil
The appointment made to you
To meet (Us)!": [2390]

٤٨- وَعُرِضُوا عَلٰى رَبِّكَ صَفًّا ۗ
لَقَدْ جِئْتُمُونَا كَمَا خَلَقْنٰكُمْ
أَوَّلَ مَرَّةٍ ۢ بَلْ زَعَمْتُمْ
أَلَّنْ نَّجْعَلَ لَكُمْ مَّوْعِدًا ۝

49. And the Book (of Deeds)
Will be placed (before you);
And thou wilt see
The sinful in great terror
Because of what is (recorded)
Therein; they will say,
"Ah! woe to us!
What a book is this!
It leaves out nothing
Small or great, but
Takes account thereof!"
They will find all that they
Did, placed before them:
And not one will thy Lord
Treat with injustice.[2391]

٤٩- وَوُضِعَ الْكِتٰبُ
فَتَرَى الْمُجْرِمِينَ مُشْفِقِينَ
مِمَّا فِيهِ وَيَقُولُونَ يٰوَيْلَتَنَا
مَالِ هٰذَا الْكِتٰبِ لَا يُغَادِرُ
صَغِيرَةً وَّلَا كَبِيرَةً
إِلَّا أَحْصٰهَا ۚ
وَوَجَدُوا مَا عَمِلُوا حَاضِرًا ۗ
وَلَا يَظْلِمُ رَبُّكَ أَحَدًا ۚ

2388. On the Day of Judgment none of our present landmarks will remain.

3389. We shall stand as we were created, with none of the adventitious possessions that we collected in this life, which will all have vanished.

2390. The sceptics will now at length be convinced of the Reality which will be upon them.

2391. Personal responsibility, for all deeds in this life will then be enforced. But it will be done with perfect justice. Expressed in the forms of this world, it will amount to a clear statement of all we did in this life: the record will be put before us to convince us. As it will be a perfect record, with no omissions and no wrong entries, it will be perfectly convincing. Where there is punishment, it has been earned by the wrong-doer's own deeds, not imposed on him unjustly.

Section 7.

50. Behold! We said
To the angels, "Bow down [2392]
To Adam": they bowed down
Except Iblīs. He was
One of the Jinns,[2393] and he
Broke the Command
Of his Lord.
Will ye then take him
And his progeny [2394] as protectors
Rather than Me? And they
Are enemies to you!
Evil would be the exchange [2395]
For the wrong-doers!

٥٠- وَاِذْ قُلْنَا لِلْمَلٰٓئِكَةِ اسْجُدُوْا
لِاٰدَمَ فَسَجَدُوْٓا اِلَّآ اِبْلِيْسَ ۭ كَانَ
مِنَ الْجِنِّ فَفَسَقَ عَنْ اَمْرِ رَبِّهٖ ۭ
اَفَتَتَّخِذُوْنَهٗ وَذُرِّيَّتَهٗٓ اَوْلِيَاۗءَ
مِنْ دُوْنِيْ وَهُمْ لَكُمْ عَدُوٌّ ۭ
بِئْسَ لِلظّٰلِمِيْنَ بَدَلًا ○

51. I called them not
To witness the creation
Of the heavens and the earth,
Nor (even) their own creation:
Nor is it for Me
To take as helpers
Such as lead (men) astray! [2396]

٥١- مَآ اَشْهَدْتُّهُمْ خَلْقَ
السَّمٰوٰتِ وَالْاَرْضِ وَلَا خَلْقَ اَنْفُسِهِمْ ۠
وَمَا كُنْتُ مُتَّخِذَ الْمُضِلِّيْنَ عَضُدًا ○

52. One Day He will say,
"Call on those whom ye
Thought to be My partners,"
And they will call on them,
But they will not listen
To them; and We shall
Make for them a place
Of common perdition.[2397]

٥٢- وَيَوْمَ يَقُوْلُ نَادُوْا
شُرَكَاۗءِيَ الَّذِيْنَ زَعَمْتُمْ فَدَعَوْهُمْ
فَلَمْ يَسْتَجِيْبُوْا لَهُمْ
وَجَعَلْنَا بَيْنَهُمْ مَّوْبِقًا ○

2392. *Cf.* ii. 34, where the story is told of the fall of mankind through Adam. Here the point is referred to in order to bring home the individual responsibility of the erring soul. 'Iblīs is your enemy; you have been told his history; will you prefer to go to him rather than to the merciful God, your Creator and Cherisher? What a false exchange you would make!'

2393. *Cf.* vi. 100, n. 929.

2394. *Satan's progeny*: we need not take the epithet literally. All his followers are his progeny: even the evil thoughts born in man out of Satan's influence are Satan's progeny.

2395. Out of the limited free-will that man has, if he were to choose Evil instead of Good, Satan instead of God, what a dreadful choice it would be! It would really be an evil exchange. For man is God's creature, cared for and cherished by Him. He abandons his Cherisher to become the slave of his enemy!

2396. God wants man's good: how can He take Evil for His partner?

2397. Some Commentators construe: "And We shall make a partition between them": *i.e.*, the Evil ones will not even be seen by their misguided followers, much as the latter may go on calling on them.

53. And the Sinful shall see
The Fire and apprehend
That they have to fall
Therein: no means will they
Find to turn away therefrom.

٥٣- وَرَاَ الْمُجْرِمُوْنَ النَّارَ فَظَنُّوْٓا اَنَّهُمْ
مُّوَاقِعُوْهَا
وَلَمْ يَجِدُوْا عَنْهَا مَصْرِفًا ۝ ع ١٩

SECTION 8.

54. We have explained
In detail in this Qur-ān,
For the benefit of mankind,
Every kind of similitude:
But man is, in most things,[2398]
Contentious.

٥٤- وَلَقَدْ صَرَّفْنَا فِيْ هٰذَا الْقُرْاٰنِ
لِلنَّاسِ مِنْ كُلِّ مَثَلٍ ۭ
وَكَانَ الْاِنْسَانُ اَكْثَرَ شَيْءٍ جَدَلًا ۝

55. And what is there
To keep back men
From believing, now that
Guidance has come to them,
Nor from praying for forgiveness
From their Lord, but that
(They ask that) the ways
Of the ancients be repeated[2399]
With them, or the Wrath
Be brought to them
Face to face?

٥٥- وَمَا مَنَعَ النَّاسَ اَنْ
يُّؤْمِنُوْٓا اِذْ جَاۗءَهُمُ الْهُدٰى
وَيَسْتَغْفِرُوْا رَبَّهُمْ اِلَّآ اَنْ
تَاْتِيَهُمْ سُنَّةُ الْاَوَّلِيْنَ
اَوْ يَاْتِيَهُمُ الْعَذَابُ قُبُلًا ۝

56. We only send the apostles
To give glad tidings
And to give warnings:[2400]
But the Unbelievers dispute
With vain argument, in order
Therewith to weaken the truth,
And they treat My Signs
As a jest, as also the fact
That they are warned!

٥٦- وَمَا نُرْسِلُ الْمُرْسَلِيْنَ اِلَّا مُبَشِّرِيْنَ
وَمُنْذِرِيْنَ ۚ وَيُجَادِلُ الَّذِيْنَ كَفَرُوْا
بِالْبَاطِلِ لِيُدْحِضُوْا بِهِ الْحَقَّ
وَاتَّخَذُوْٓا اٰيٰتِيْ
وَمَآ اُنْذِرُوْا هُزُوًا ۝

2398. If men had not cultivated the habit of contention and obstinacy, they would have found that the parables and similitudes of Scripture had fully met their difficulties, and they would gladly have obeyed the call of God.

2399. But man's obstinacy or contrariness asks or calls for a repetition of what happened to the wicked and those who rejected Faith in ancient times. Out of curiosity, or by way of challenge, they seem to court the Punishment and ask that it be brought to pass at once. But it will come soon enough, and then they will think it too early! *Cf.* xiii. 6 and n. 1810.

2400. The men of God are not sent to humour us with dialectics or satisfy the vulgar curiosity for miracles or dark unusual things. There is no "crookedness" (xviii. 1) in their preaching. They come to preach the Truth,—not in an abstract way, but with special reference to our conduct. They give us the good news of salvation lest we despair in the presence of Sin, and to warn us clearly of the dangers of Evil. Vain controversies about words only weaken their mission, or turn it into ridicule. The ungodly have a trick also of treating the earnest preaching to them itself as a jest and ridiculing it.

57. And who doth more wrong
Than one who is reminded
Of the Signs of his Lord,
But turns away from them,
Forgetting the (deeds) which his
hands[2401]
Have sent forth? Verily We
Have set veils over their hearts
Lest they should understand this,
And over their ears, deafness.
If thou callest them
To guidance, even then
Will they never accept guidance.

٥٧- وَمَنْ أَظْلَمُ مِمَّنْ ذُكِّرَ
بِآيَاتِ رَبِّهِ فَأَعْرَضَ عَنْهَا
وَنَسِيَ مَا قَدَّمَتْ يَدَاهُ
إِنَّا جَعَلْنَا عَلَىٰ قُلُوبِهِمْ
أَكِنَّةً أَنْ يَفْقَهُوهُ وَفِي آذَانِهِمْ وَقْرًا
وَإِنْ تَدْعُهُمْ إِلَى الْهُدَىٰ
فَلَنْ يَهْتَدُوا إِذًا أَبَدًا ○

58. But your Lord is Most Forgiving,
Full of Mercy. If He were
To call them (at once) to account
For what they have earned,
Then surely He would
Have hastened their Punishment:
But they have their appointed
Time, beyond which[2402] they
Will find no refuge.

٥٨- وَرَبُّكَ الْغَفُورُ ذُو الرَّحْمَةِ لَوْ
يُؤَاخِذُهُمْ بِمَا كَسَبُوا لَعَجَّلَ لَهُمُ الْعَذَابَ
بَلْ لَهُمْ مَوْعِدٌ لَنْ يَجِدُوا مِنْ دُونِهِ
مَوْئِلًا ○

59. Such were the populations
We destroyed when they
Committed iniquities; but
We fixed an appointed time
For their destruction.[2403]

٥٩- وَتِلْكَ الْقُرَىٰ أَهْلَكْنَاهُمْ لَمَّا
ظَلَمُوا وَجَعَلْنَا لِمَهْلِكِهِمْ مَوْعِدًا ○ ع

C. 136.—Moses was up against mysteries
(xviii. 60-82.) Which he wanted to explore. He searched
Out a man endued with knowledge
Derived from the divine springs from which
Flow the paradoxes of life. He is shown
Three such paradoxes and how human

2401. Considering the power of sin, and how it gets hold of the hearts of men, and considering all the wrongs that men have done, it is the height of folly and injustice on their part to turn away from warnings which are given expressly for their good. But a stage of callousness is reached, when, by their own choice, they have rendered themselves impervious to God's Grace. At that stage a veil is put over their hearts and they are left alone for a time, that they may commune with themselves and perhaps repent and seek God's Mercy again. If they do not, it is their own loss. See next verse.

2402. *Min dūni-hi*: should we take the pronoun to refer to "the appointed time," or to "your Lord," mentioned at the beginning of the verse? Most Commentators take the former view, and I have translated accordingly. But I agree with those who take the latter view, and the better translation would be: "But they have their appointed time, and except with God, they will find no refuge." That means that even during the period allowed them, when they are left to wander astray as they have rejected God's Grace. God's Mercy is open to them if they will repent and return; but nothing but God's Mercy can save them.

2403. The instances of exemplary Punishment in former times were also subject to this rule, that God gives plenty of rope to the wicked, in case they might turn, repent, and obtain His Mercy.

Impatience is inconsistent with their true
Understanding. The highest knowledge
Comes not except by divine gift,
And a constant, patient striving,
With Faith, to apprehend something
Of the purpose of the All-Wise God.

SECTION 9.

60. Behold, Moses said[2404]
To his attendant, "I will not
Give up until I reach
The junction of the two[2405]
Seas or (until) I spend
Years and years in travel."[2406]

٦٠- وَإِذْ قَالَ مُوسَىٰ لِفَتَىٰهُ لَآ أَبْرَحُ حَتَّىٰٓ أَبْلُغَ مَجْمَعَ ٱلْبَحْرَيْنِ أَوْ أَمْضِىَ حُقُبًا ۝

61. But when they reached
The Junction,[2407] they forgot
(About) their Fish,[2408] which took
Its course through the sea
(Straight) as in a tunnel.

٦١- فَلَمَّا بَلَغَا مَجْمَعَ بَيْنِهِمَا نَسِيَا حُوتَهُمَا فَٱتَّخَذَ سَبِيلَهُۥ فِى ٱلْبَحْرِ سَرَبًا ۝

2404. This episode in the story of Moses is meant to illustrate four points. (1) Moses was learned in all the wisdom of the Egyptians. Even so that wisdom did not comprehend everything, even as the whole stock of the knowledge of the present day, in the sciences and the arts, and in literature, (if it could be supposed to be gathered in one individual), does not include all knowledge. Divine knowledge, as far as man is concerned, is unlimited. Even after Moses received his divine mission of Apostleship, his knowledge was not so perfect that it could not receive further additions. (2) Constant effort is necessary to keep our knowledge square with the march of time, and such effort Moses is shown to be making. (3) The mysterious man he meets (xviii. 65 and n. 2411), to whom Tradition assigns the name of Khidhr (literally, Green), is the type of that knowledge which is ever green, fresh, and flourishing, ever in contact with life as it is actually lived, and not merely crystallised in books or second-hand sayings. The second kind of knowledge has its uses, but is only a stepping-stone to the first kind of knowledge, which is true knowledge and which is from God direct (xviii. 65). (4) There are paradoxes in life: apparent loss may be real gain; apparent cruelty may be real mercy; returning good for evil may really be justice and not generosity (xviii 79-82). God's wisdom transcends all human calculation.

2405. The most probable geographical location (if any is required in a story that is a parable) is where the two arms of the Red Sea join together, *viz.*, the Gulf of 'Aqaba and the Gulf of Suez. They enclose the Sinai Peninsula, in which Moses and the Israelites spent many years in their wanderings. There is also authority (see Baidhāwī's note) for interpreting the two seas as the two great streams of knowledge, which were to meet in the persons of Moses and Khidhr.

2406. *Huqub* means a long but indefinite space of time. Sometimes it is limited to 80 years.

2407. Literally, 'the Junction of (the space) between the two,' *i.e.*, the point at which the two seas were united.

2408. Moses was to go and find a servant of God, who would instruct him in such knowledge as he had not already got. He was to take a fish with him. The place where he was to meet his mysterious Teacher would be indicated by the fact that the fish would disappear when he got to that place. The fish is the emblem of the fruit of secular knowledge, which merges itself in divine knowledge at the point where human intelligence is ready for the junction of the two. But the mere merger of secular knowledge does not in itself produce divine knowledge. The latter has to be sought patiently.

62. When they had passed on
(Some distance), Moses said
To his attendant: "Bring us
Our early meal; truly
We have suffered much fatigue[2409]
At this (stage of) our journey."

٦٢- فَلَمَّا جَاوَزَا قَالَ
لِفَتٰىهُ اٰتِنَا غَدَآءَنَا لَقَدْ
لَقِيْنَا مِنْ سَفَرِنَا هٰذَا نَصَبًا ○

63. He replied: "Sawest thou
(What happened) when we
Betook ourselves to the rock?
I did indeed forget
(About) the Fish: none but
Satan made me forget
To tell (you) about it:[2410]
It took its course through
The sea in a marvellous way!"

٦٣- قَالَ اَرَءَيْتَ اِذْ اَوَيْنَآ
اِلَى الصَّخْرَةِ فَاِنِّيْ نَسِيْتُ الْحُوْتَ
وَمَآ اَنْسٰىنِيْهُ اِلَّا الشَّيْطٰنُ اَنْ اَذْكُرَهٗ
وَاتَّخَذَ سَبِيْلَهٗ فِي الْبَحْرِ عَجَبًا ○

64. Moses said: "That was what
We were seeking after:"
So they went back
On their footsteps, following
(The path they had come).

٦٤- قَالَ ذٰلِكَ مَا كُنَّا نَبْغِ
فَارْتَدَّا عَلٰٓى اٰثَارِهِمَا قَصَصًا ○

65. So they found one[2411]
Of Our servants,

٦٥- فَوَجَدَا عَبْدًا مِّنْ عِبَادِنَآ

2409. When they came to the Junction of the Seas, Moses forgot about the fish, and his attendant forgot to tell him of the fact that he had seen the fish escaping into the sea in a marvellous way. They passed on, but the stages now became heavier and heavier, and more fatiguing to Moses. So when our old knowledge is exhausted, and we come to the brink of new knowledge, we have a feeling of strangeness, heaviness, and difficulty, especially when we want to pass the new knowledge by and do not make it our own. Some refreshment, even if it be in our old traditional way, is required to sustain us. But we must retrace our steps, and seek the accredited repository of the knowledge which is our quest. It is our business to seek him out. We shall not find him without effort.

2410. The attendant actually saw the fish swimming away in the sea, and yet "forgot" to tell his master. In his case the "forgetting" was more than forgetting. Inertia had made him refrain from telling the important news. In such matters inertia is almost as bad as active spite, the suggestion of Satan. So new knowledge or spiritual knowledge is not only passed by in ignorance, but sometimes by culpable negligence.

2411. *One of Our servants*: his name is not mentioned in the Qur-ān, but Tradition gives it as Khidhr. Round him have gathered a number of picturesque folk tales, with which we are not here concerned. "*Khidhr*" means "Green": his knowledge is fresh and green, and drawn out of the living sources of life for it is drawn from God's own Presence. He is a mysterious being, who has to be sought out. He has the secrets of the paradoxes of Life, which ordinary people do not understand, or understand in a wrong sense, as we shall see further on. The nearest equivalent figure in the literature of the People of the Book is Melchizedek or Melchisedek (the Greek form in the New Testament). In Gen. xiv. 18-20, he appears as king of Salem, priest of the Most High God: he blesses Abraham, and Abraham gives him tithes. St. Paul allegorises him in his Epistle to the Hebrews (v. 6-10; vii. 1-10): "he was without father, without mother, without descent, having neither beginning of days nor end of life". That is to say, he appeared mysteriously: neither his parentage nor his pedigree is known, and he seems to live for all time. These qualities are also attributed to Khidhr in Muslim tradition.

On whom We had bestowed
Mercy from Ourselves
And whom We had taught
Knowledge from Our own [2412]
Presence.

اٰتَيْنٰهُ رَحْمَةً مِّنْ عِنْدِنَا
وَعَلَّمْنٰهُ مِنْ لَّدُنَّا عِلْمًا ○

66. Moses said to him:
"May I follow thee,
On the footing that
Thou teach me something
Of the (Higher) Truth
Which thou hast been taught?" [2413]

٦٦- قَالَ لَهٗ مُوْسٰى هَلْ اَتَّبِعُكَ
عَلٰٓى اَنْ تُعَلِّمَنِ
مِمَّا عُلِّمْتَ رُشْدًا ○

67. (The other) said: "Verily
Thou wilt not be able
To have patience with me! [2414]

٦٧- قَالَ اِنَّكَ لَنْ تَسْتَطِيْعَ مَعِيَ
صَبْرًا ○

68. "And how canst thou
Have patience about things
About which thy understanding
Is not complete?" [2415]

٦٨- وَكَيْفَ تَصْبِرُ عَلٰى
مَا لَمْ تُحِطْ بِهٖ خُبْرًا ○

69. Moses said: "Thou wilt
Find me, if God so will,
(Truly) patient: nor shall I
Disobey thee in aught." [2416]

٦٩- قَالَ سَتَجِدُنِيْٓ اِنْ شَآءَ اللّٰهُ
صَابِرًا وَّلَآ اَعْصِيْ لَكَ اَمْرًا ○

2412. Khidhr had two special gifts from God: (1) Mercy from His own Presence, and (2) Knowledge from His own Presence. The first freed him from the ordinary incidents of daily human life; and the second entitled him to interpret the inner meaning and mystery of events, as we shall see further on. Much could be and has been written about this from the mystic point of view.

2413. Moses, not understanding the full import of what he was asking, makes a simple request. He wants to learn something of the special Knowledge which God had bestowed on Khidhr.

2414. Khidhr smiles, and says that there will be many things which Moses will see with him, which Moses will not completey understand and which will make Moses impatient. The highest spiritual knowledge often seems paradoxical to those who have not the key to it.

2415. Khidhr does not blame Moses. Each one of us can only follow our own imperfect lights to the best of our judgment, but if we have Faith, we are saved many false steps.

2416. Moses has Faith. He adopts the true attitude of the learner to the Teacher, and promises to obey in all things, with the help of God. The Teacher is doubtful, but premits him to follow him on condition that he asks no questions about anything until the Teacher himself mentions it first.

70. The other said: "If then
Thou wouldst follow me,
Ask me no questions
About anything until I
Myself speak to thee
Concerning it."

٧٠- قَالَ فَإِنِ اتَّبَعْتَنِي
فَلَا تَسْأَلْنِي عَنْ شَيْءٍ حَتَّىٰ
أُحْدِثَ لَكَ مِنْهُ ذِكْرًا ۝

Section 10.

71. So they both proceeded:
Until, when they were
In the boat, he scuttled it.[2417]
Said Moses: "Hast thou
Scuttled it in order
To drown those in it?
Truly a strange thing
Hast thou done!"

٧١- فَانْطَلَقَا حَتَّىٰ إِذَا
رَكِبَا فِي السَّفِينَةِ خَرَقَهَا ۖ
قَالَ أَخَرَقْتَهَا لِتُغْرِقَ أَهْلَهَا ۚ
لَقَدْ جِئْتَ شَيْئًا إِمْرًا ۝

72. He answered: "Did I not
Tell thee that thou canst
Have no patience with me?"

٧٢- قَالَ أَلَمْ أَقُلْ إِنَّكَ لَنْ تَسْتَطِيعَ
مَعِيَ صَبْرًا ۝

73. Moses said: "Rebuke me not
For forgetting, nor grieve me
By raising difficulties
In my case."

٧٣- قَالَ لَا تُؤَاخِذْنِي بِمَا نَسِيتُ وَ
لَا تُرْهِقْنِي مِنْ أَمْرِي عُسْرًا ۝

74. Then they proceeded:
Until, when they met
A young man, he slew him.[2418]
Moses said: "Hast thou
Slain an innocent person
Who had slain none?
15 Truly a foul (unheard-of) thing
30 Hast thou done!"

٧٤- فَانْطَلَقَا حَتَّىٰ إِذَا لَقِيَا
غُلَامًا فَقَتَلَهُ ۙ قَالَ
أَقَتَلْتَ نَفْسًا زَكِيَّةً بِغَيْرِ نَفْسٍ ۖ
لَقَدْ جِئْتَ شَيْئًا نُكْرًا ۝

2417. The explanation follows in xviii. 79.

2418. The explanation follows in xviii. 80-81.

75. He answered: 'Did I not
Tell thee that thou canst
Have no patience with me?"

٧٥- قَالَ أَلَمْ أَقُل لَّكَ إِنَّكَ لَن
تَسْتَطِيعَ مَعِيَ صَبْرًا ○

76. (Moses) said: "If ever I
Ask thee about anything
After this, keep me not
In thy company: then wouldst
Thou have received (full) excuse
From my side.

٧٦- قَالَ إِن سَأَلْتُكَ عَن شَيْءٍ
بَعْدَهَا فَلَا تُصَٰحِبْنِي
قَدْ بَلَغْتَ مِن لَّدُنِّي عُذْرًا ○

77. Then they proceeded:
Until, when they came
To the inhabitants of a town,
They asked them for food,
But they refused them[2419]
Hospitality. They found there
A wall on the point of
Falling down, but he
Set it up straight.
(Moses) said: "If thou
Hadst wished, surely thou
Couldst have exacted some
Recompense for it!"[2420]

٧٧- فَانطَلَقَا حَتَّىٰٓ إِذَآ أَتَيَآ
أَهْلَ قَرْيَةٍ ٱسْتَطْعَمَآ أَهْلَهَا
فَأَبَوْا أَن يُضَيِّفُوهُمَا
فَوَجَدَا فِيهَا جِدَارًا
يُرِيدُ أَن يَنقَضَّ فَأَقَامَهُۥ
قَالَ لَوْ شِئْتَ لَتَّخَذْتَ عَلَيْهِ أَجْرًا ○

78. He answered: "This is
The parting between me
And thee: now will I
Tell thee the interpretation
Of (those things) over which
Thou wast unable
To hold patience.[2421]

٧٨- قَالَ هَٰذَا فِرَاقُ بَيْنِي وَبَيْنِكَ
سَأُنَبِّئُكَ بِتَأْوِيلِ
مَا لَمْ تَسْتَطِع عَّلَيْهِ صَبْرًا ○

79. "As for the boat,
It belonged to certain
Men in dire want:
They plied on the water:

٧٩- أَمَّا ٱلسَّفِينَةُ فَكَانَتْ لِمَسَٰكِينَ
يَعْمَلُونَ فِي ٱلْبَحْرِ

2419. The inhabitants were churlish. They broke the universal Eastern rule of hospitality to strangers, and thus showed themselves beyond the pale of ordinary human courtesies. Note that they would have been expected to *offer* hospitality of themselves, unasked. Here Moses and his companion actually had to ask for hospitality and were refused point-blank.

2420. As they were refused hospitality, they should, as self-respecting men, have shaken the dust of the town off their feet, or shown their indignation in some way. Instead of that, Khidhr actually goes and does a benevolent act. He rebuilds for them a falling wall, and never asks for any compensation for it. Perhaps he employed local workmen for it and paid them wages, thus actually benefiting a town which had treated him and his companion so shabbily! Moses is naturally surprised and asks, "Could you not at least have asked for the cost?"

2421. The story and the interpretation are given with the greatest economy of words. It would repay us to search for the meaning in terms of our own inner and outer experience.

I but wished to render it
Unserviceable, for there was
After them a certain king
Who seized on every boat
By force.[2422]

فَأَرَدْتُ أَنْ أَعِيبَهَا وَكَانَ وَرَآءَهُم مَّلِكٌ
يَأْخُذُ كُلَّ سَفِينَةٍ غَصْبًا ○

80. " As for the youth,
His parents were people
Of Faith, and we feared
That he would grieve them
By obstinate rebellion
And ingratitude (to God and
man).[2423]

٨٠- وَأَمَّا الْغُلٰمُ فَكَانَ أَبَوٰهُ
مُؤْمِنَيْنِ فَخَشِينَآ
أَنْ يُّرْهِقَهُمَا طُغْيَانًا وَّكُفْرًا ○

81." So we desired that
Their Lord would give them
In exchange (a son)
Better in purity (of conduct)
And closer in affection.[2424]

٨١- فَأَرَدْنَآ أَنْ يُّبْدِلَهُمَا رَبُّهُمَا
خَيْرًا مِّنْهُ زَكٰوةً وَّأَقْرَبَ رُحْمًا ○

82. " As for the wall,
It belonged to two youths,
Orphans, in the Town;
There was, beneath it,
A buried treasure, to which
They were entitled; their father

٨٢- وَأَمَّا الْجِدَارُ فَكَانَ لِغُلٰمَيْنِ
يَتِيمَيْنِ فِي الْمَدِينَةِ وَكَانَ تَحْتَهُ
كَنزٌ لَّهُمَا وَكَانَ أَبُوهُمَا

2422. They went on the boat, which was plying for hire. Its owners were not even ordinary men who plied for trade. They had been reduced to great poverty, perhaps from affluent circumstances, and deserved great commiseration, the more so as they preferred an honest calling to begging for charity. They did not know, but Khidhr did, that that boat, perhaps a new one, had been marked down to be commandeered by an unjust king who seized on every boat he could get—it may have been, for warlike purposes. If this boat had been taken away from these self-respecting men, they would have been reduced to beggary, with no resources left them. By a simple act of making it unseaworthy, the boat was saved from seizure. The owners could repair it as soon as the danger was past. Khidhr probably paid liberally in fares, and what seemed an unaccountably cruel act was the greatest act of kindness he could do in the circumstances.

2423. This seemed at first sight even a more cruel act than scuttling the boat. But the danger was also greater. Khidhr knew that the youth was a potential parricide. His parents were worthy, pious people, who had brought him up with love. He had apparently gone wrong. Perhaps he had already been guilty of murders and robberies and had escaped the law by subtleties and fraud. See next note.

2424. The son was practically an outlaw,—a danger to the public and a particular source of grief to his righteous parents. Even so, his summary capital punishment would have been unjustified if Khidhr had been acting on his own. But Khidhr was not acting on his own: see the latter part of the next verse. The plural " we " also implies that he was not acting on his own. He was acting on higher authority and removing a public scourge, who was also a source of extreme sorrow and humiliation to his parents. His parents are promised a better-behaved son who would love them and be a credit to them.

Had been a righteous man :[2425]
So thy Lord desired that
They should attain their age[2426]
Of full strength and get out
Their treasure—a mercy
(And favour) from thy Lord.
I did it not of my own[2427]
Accord. Such is the interpretation
Of (those things) over which
Thou wast unable
To hold patience."

صَالِحًا ۚ فَأَرَادَ رَبُّكَ
أَنْ يَّبْلُغَآ
أَشُدَّهُمَا وَيَسْتَخْرِجَا كَنْزَهُمَا ۖ
رَحْمَةً مِّنْ رَّبِّكَ ۚ
وَمَا فَعَلْتُهُ عَنْ أَمْرِي ۚ ذَٰلِكَ تَأْوِيلُ
مَا لَمْ تَسْطِعْ عَلَيْهِ صَبْرًا ۝ ع

C. 137.—Three episodes in the life of a great king.
(xviii. 83-110.) Ẓul-qarnain, illustrate how power
And opportunities should be used in the service
Of God: he punished the guilty indeed,
But was kind to the righteous; he left
Primitive people their freedom of life;
And he protected industrious people from grasping
Neighbours. But he relied upon God, and made them
Remember the Day of Judgment, when all
Will see the Truth and receive the Punishments
And Rewards earned in their present Life.

SECTION 11.

83. They ask thee concerning
Ẓul-qarnain.[2428] Say,

٨٣- وَيَسْـَٔلُونَكَ عَنْ ذِي الْقَرْنَيْنِ ۖ قُلْ

2425. The wall was in a ruinous state. If it had fallen, the treasure buried beneath it would have been exposed and would certainly have been looted, among so churlish and selfish a people. See n. 2419 above. The treasure had been collected and buried by a righteous man. It was not, in any sense of the word, ill-gotten gains: it was buried expressly in the interests of the orphans by their father before his death. It was intended that the orphans should grow up and safely take possession of their heritage. It was also expected that they would be righteous men like their father, and use the treasure in good works and in advancing righteousness among an otherwise wicked community. There was thus both public and private interests involved in all the three incidents. In the second incident Khidhr uses the word "we", showing that he was associating in his act the public authorities of the place, who had been eluded by the outlaw.

2426. *Age of full strength: Cf.* xvii. 34 and n. 2218.

2427. Those who act, not from a whim or a private impulse of their own, but from higher authority, have to bear the blame, with the vulgar crowd, for acts of the greatest wisdom and utility. In human affairs many things are inexplicable, which are things of the highest wisdom in the Universal Plan.

2428. Literally, "the Two-horned one", the King with the Two Horns, or the Lord of the Two Epochs. Who was he? In what age, and where did he live? The Qur-ān gives us no material on which we can base a positive answer. Nor is it necessary to find an answer, as the story is treated as a Parable. Popular opinion identifies Ẓul-qarnain with Alexander the Great. An alternative suggestion is an ancient Persian King, or a pre-historic Ḥimyarite King. See a brief account of the controversy in Appendix VII printed at the end of this Sūra.

Ẓul-qarnain was a most powerful king, but it was God, Who, in His universal Plan, gave him power and provided him with the ways and means for his great work. His sway extended over East and West, and over people of diverse civilisations. He was just and righteous, not selfish or grasping. He protected the weak and punished the unlawful and the turbulent. Three of his expeditions are described in the text, each embodying a great ethical idea involved in the possession of kingship or power.

"I will rehearse to you
Something of his story."

سَاَتْلُوْا عَلَيْكُمْ مِّنْهُ ذِكْرًا ۝

84. Verily We established his power
On earth, and We gave him
The ways and the means
To all ends.[2429]

۸۴- اِنَّا مَكَّنَّا لَهٗ فِى الْاَرْضِ وَاٰتَيْنٰهُ
مِنْ كُلِّ شَىْءٍ سَبَبًا ۝

85. One (such) way he followed,

۸۵- فَاَتْبَعَ سَبَبًا ۝

86. Until, when he reached
The setting of the sun,[2430]
He found it set
In a spring of murky water:
Near it he found a People:
We said: "O Ẕul-qarnain!
(Thou hast authority,) either
To punish them, or
To treat them with kindness."[2431]

۸۶- حَتّٰٓى اِذَا بَلَغَ مَغْرِبَ الشَّمْسِ
وَجَدَهَا تَغْرُبُ فِىْ عَيْنٍ حَمِئَةٍ
وَّوَجَدَ عِنْدَهَا قَوْمًا ۬ قُلْنَا يٰذَا الْقَرْنَيْنِ
اِمَّآ اَنْ تُعَذِّبَ وَاِمَّآ اَنْ تَتَّخِذَ فِيْهِمْ
حُسْنًا ۝

87. He said: "Whoever doth wrong,
Him shall we punish; then
Shall he be sent back[2432]
To his Lord; and He will
Punish him with a punishment
Unheard-of (before).

۸۷- قَالَ اَمَّا مَنْ ظَلَمَ فَسَوْفَ نُعَذِّبُهٗ
ثُمَّ يُرَدُّ اِلٰى رَبِّهٖ
فَيُعَذِّبُهٗ عَذَابًا نُّكْرًا ۝

88. "But whoever believes,
And works righteousness,—

۸۸- وَاَمَّا مَنْ اٰمَنَ وَعَمِلَ صَالِحًا

2429. Great was his power and great were his opportunities ("ways and means"), which he used for justice and righteousness. But he recognised that his power and opportunities were given to him as a trust by God. He had faith, and did not forget God.

2430. This is the first of the three episodes here mentioned, his expedition to the west. "Reaching the setting of the sun" does not mean the extreme west, for there is no such thing. West and East are relative terms. It means a western expedition terminated by a 'spring of murky water." This has puzzled Commentators, and they have understood this to mean the dark, tempestuous sea If Ẕul-qarnain is Alexander the Great, the reference is easily understood to be to Lychnitis (now Ochrida), west of Macedonia. It is fed entirely by underground springs in a limestone region, where the water is never very clear. (See Appendix VII at the end of this Sūra.)

2431. He had great power and a great opportunity. He got authority over a turbulent and unruly people. Was he going to be severe with them and chastise them, or was he going to seek peace at any price, *i.e.*, to wink at violence and injustice so long as it did not affect his power? He chose the better course, as described in the next verse. To protect the weak and the innocent, he punished the guilty and the headstrong, but he remembered always that the true Punishment would come in the Hereafter—the true and final justice before the throne of God.

2432. Though most powerful among kings, he remembered that his power was but human, and given by God. His punishments were but tentative, to preserve the balance of this life as he could appraise it. Even if his punishment was capital ("wrong doer sent back to his Lord") it was nothing compared to the spiritual consequences of sin, in the final Justice of God.

He shall have a goodly
Reward, and easy will be
His task as we order it
By our command."[2433]

فَلَهُۥ جَزَآءً ٱلْحُسْنَىٰ ۖ وَسَنَقُولُ لَهُۥ مِنْ أَمْرِنَا يُسْرًا

89. Then followed he (another) way,

٨٩- ثُمَّ أَتْبَعَ سَبَبًا

90. Until, when he came
To the rising of the sun,[2434]
He found it rising
On a people for whom
We had provided
No covering protection[2435]
Against the sun.

٩٠- حَتَّىٰٓ إِذَا بَلَغَ مَطْلِعَ ٱلشَّمْسِ وَجَدَهَا تَطْلُعُ عَلَىٰ قَوْمٍ لَّمْ نَجْعَل لَّهُم مِّن دُونِهَا سِتْرًا

91. (He left them) as they were:
We completely understood
What was before him.[2436]

٩١- كَذَٰلِكَ ۖ وَقَدْ أَحَطْنَا بِمَا لَدَيْهِ خُبْرًا

92. Then followed he (another) way,

٩٢- ثُمَّ أَتْبَعَ سَبَبًا

93. Until, when he reached
(A tract) between two mountains,[2437]
He found, beneath them, a people
Who scarcely understood a word.[2438]

٩٣- حَتَّىٰٓ إِذَا بَلَغَ بَيْنَ ٱلسَّدَّيْنِ وَجَدَ مِن دُونِهِمَا قَوْمًا لَّا يَكَادُونَ يَفْقَهُونَ قَوْلًا

2433. He never said like Pharaoh, "I am your Lord Most High!" (lxxix. 24). On the contrary his punishments were humbly regulated as not being final, and he laid more stress on the good he could do to those who lived normal lives in faith and righteousness. His rule was easy to them: he imposed no heavy tasks because of his power, but gave every opportunity to rich and poor for the exercise of virtue and goodness. Such is the spiritual lesson to be learned from the first episode.

2434. We now come to the second episode. This is an expedition to the east. "Rising of the sun" has a meaning corresponding to "setting of the sun" in xviii. 86, as explained in n. 2430.

2435. The people here lived very simple lives. Perhaps the climate was hot, and they required neither roofs over their heads, nor much clothing to protect them from the sun. What did he do with them? See next note.

2436. They were a primitive people. He did not fuss over their primitiveness, but left them in the enjoyment of peace and tranquillity in their own way. In this he was wise. Power is apt to be intolerant and arrogant, and to interfere in everything that does not accord with its own glorification. Not so Ẕul-qarnain. He recognised his own limitations in the sight of God: man never completely understands his own position, but if he devoutly looks to God, he will live and let live. This is the spiritual lesson from the second episode.

2437. The geography of the place (if geography is relevant in a parable story) is discussed in Appendix VII at the end of this Sūra

2438. It does not mean that they had no speech. It means that they did not understand the speech of the Conqueror. But they had parleys with him (through interpreters), as is evident from the verses following (xviii. 94-98).

94. They said: "O Zul-qarnain!
The Gog and Magog (people)[2439]
Do great mischief on earth:
Shall we then render thee
Tribute in order that
Thou mightest erect a barrier
Between us and them?

٩٤- قَالُوا يٰذَا الْقَرْنَيْنِ إِنَّ يَأْجُوجَ وَ
مَأْجُوجَ
مُفْسِدُونَ فِي الْأَرْضِ فَهَلْ نَجْعَلُ لَكَ
خَرْجًا عَلٰٓى أَنْ تَجْعَلَ بَيْنَنَا وَبَيْنَهُمْ سَدًّا ۝

95. He said: "(The power) in which
My Lord has established me
Is better (than tribute):[2440]
Help me therefore with strength
(And labour): I will
Erect a strong barrier
Between you and them:

٩٥- قَالَ مَا مَكَّنِّي فِيهِ رَبِّي
خَيْرٌ فَأَعِينُونِي بِقُوَّةٍ
أَجْعَلْ بَيْنَكُمْ وَبَيْنَهُمْ رَدْمًا ۝

96. "Bring me blocks of iron."[2441]
At length, when he had
Filled up the space between
The two steep mountain-sides,
He said, "Blow (with your
bellows)"
Then, when he had made[2442]
It (red) as fire, he said:
"Bring me, that I may
Pour over it, molten lead."

٩٦- اٰتُونِي زُبَرَ الْحَدِيدِ ط
حَتّٰى إِذَا سَاوٰى بَيْنَ الصَّدَفَيْنِ
قَالَ انْفُخُوا ط
حَتّٰى إِذَا جَعَلَهُ نَارًا لا
قَالَ اٰتُونِي أُفْرِغْ عَلَيْهِ قِطْرًا ط ۝

2439. Who were the Gog and Magog people? This question is connected with the question, Who was Zul-qarnain? Some discussion on the question will be found in Appendix VII at the end of this Sūra.

What we are mainly concerned with is the spiritual interpretation. The Conqueror had now arrived among a people who were different in speech and race from him, but not quite primitive, for they were skilled in the working of metals, and could furnish blocks (or bricks) of iron, melt metals with bellows or blow-pipes, and prepare molten lead (xviii. 96). Apparently they were a peaceable and industrious race, much subject to incursions from wild tribes who are called Gog and Magog. Against these tribes they were willing to purchase immunity by paying the Conqueror tribute in return for protection. The permanent protection they wanted was the closing of a mountain gap through which the incursions were made.

2440. Zul-qarnain was not greedy and did not want to impose a tribute to be carried away from an industrious population. He understood the power which God had given him, to involve duties and responsibilities on his part—the duty of protecting his subjects without imposing too heavy a taxation on them. He would provide the motive force and organising skill. Would they obey him and provide the material and labour, so that they could close the gap with a strong barrier, probably with well-secured gates? The word *radm*, translated "Barrier," does not necessarily mean a wall, but rather suggests a blocked door or entrance.

2441. I understand the defences erected to have been a strong barrier of iron, with iron Gates. The jambs of the Gates were constructed with blocks or bricks of iron, and the interstices filled up with molten lead, so as to form an impregnable mass of metal. It may be that there was a stone wall also, but that is not mentioned. There was none in the Iron Gate near Bukhārā; see Appendix VII at the end of this Sūra.

2442. *Made it (red) as fire*: what does "it" refer to? Probably to the iron, either in sheets or blocks, to be welded with the molten lead.

97. Thus were they made
Powerless to scale it
Or to dig through it.[2443]

٩٧- فَمَا اسْطَاعُوْٓا اَنْ يَّظْهَرُوْهُ
وَمَا اسْتَطَاعُوْا لَهٗ نَقْبًا ○

98. He said: "This is
A mercy from my Lord:[2444]
But when the promise
Of my Lord comes to pass,
He will make it into dust;
And the promise of
My Lord is true."

٩٨- قَالَ هٰذَا رَحْمَةٌ مِّنْ رَّبِّيْ ۚ
فَاِذَا جَآءَ وَعْدُ رَبِّيْ جَعَلَهٗ دَكَّآءَ ۚ
وَكَانَ وَعْدُ رَبِّيْ حَقًّا ○

99. On that day We shall
Leave them to surge
Like waves on one another:[2445]
The trumpet will be blown,
And We shall collect them
All together.

٩٩- وَتَرَكْنَا بَعْضَهُمْ يَوْمَئِذٍ
يَّمُوْجُ فِيْ بَعْضٍ وَّنُفِخَ فِي الصُّوْرِ
فَجَمَعْنٰهُمْ جَمْعًا ○

100. And We shall present
Hell that day for Unbelievers
To see, all spread out,—[2446]

١٠٠- وَّعَرَضْنَا جَهَنَّمَ يَوْمَئِذٍ لِّلْكٰفِرِيْنَ
عَرْضًا ○

101. (Unbelievers) whose eyes
Had been under a veil
From Remembrance of Me,
And who had been unable
Even to hear.[2447]

١٠١- الَّذِيْنَ كَانَتْ اَعْيُنُهُمْ فِيْ غِطَآءٍ
عَنْ ذِكْرِيْ وَكَانُوْا لَا يَسْتَطِيْعُوْنَ
سَمْعًا ○ ع

2443. The iron wall and gates and towers were sufficiently high to prevent their being scaled and sufficiently strong with welded metal to resist any attempt to dig through them.

2444. After all the effort which Ẓul-qarnain has made for their protection, he claims no credit for himself beyond that of discharging his duty as a ruler. He turns their attention to God, Who has provided the ways and means by which they can be helped and protected. But all such human precautions are apt to become futile. The time must come when they will crumble into dust. God has said so in His Revelation; and His Word is true.

And so the spiritual lesson from the third episode is: Take human precautions and do all in your power to protect yourselves from evil. But no protection is complete unless you seek the help and grace of God. The best of our precautions must crumble to dust when the appointed Day arrives.

2445. And so we pass on to the Last Days before the Great Summons comes from God. All human barriers will be swept away. There will be tumultuous rushes. The Trumpet will be blown, and the Judgment will be set on foot.

2446. If men had scoffed at Faith and the Hereafter, their eyes will be opened now, and they will see the terrible Reality.

2447. Those very men who refused to see the many Signs of God which in this world convey His Message and to hear the Word of the Lord when it came to them, will then see without any mistake the consequences fully brought up before them.

SECTION 12.

102. Do the Unbelievers think
That they can take
My servants as protectors
Besides Me? Verily We
Have prepared Hell
For the Unbelievers
For (their) entertainment.

١٠٢- أَفَحَسِبَ الَّذِينَ كَفَرُوا أَنْ يَتَّخِذُوا
عِبَادِي مِنْ دُونِي أَوْلِيَاءَ
إِنَّا أَعْتَدْنَا جَهَنَّمَ لِلْكٰفِرِينَ نُزُلًا ○

103. Say: "Shall we tell you
Of those who lose most
In respect of their deeds?—[2448]

١٠٣- قُلْ هَلْ نُنَبِّئُكُمْ بِالْأَخْسَرِينَ
أَعْمَالًا ○

104. "Those whose efforts have
Been wasted in this life,
While they thought that
They were acquiring good
By their works?"[2449]

١٠٤- الَّذِينَ ضَلَّ سَعْيُهُمْ فِي الْحَيٰوةِ
الدُّنْيَا وَهُمْ يَحْسَبُونَ أَنَّهُمْ يُحْسِنُونَ
صُنْعًا ○

105. They are those who deny
The Signs of their Lord
And the fact of their
Having to meet Him
(In the Hereafter): vain
Will be their works,
Nor shall We, on the Day
Of Judgment, give them
Any weight.[2450]

١٠٥- أُولٰٓئِكَ الَّذِينَ كَفَرُوا بِاٰيٰتِ رَبِّهِمْ
وَلِقَآئِهِ
فَحَبِطَتْ أَعْمَالُهُمْ
فَلَا نُقِيمُ لَهُمْ يَوْمَ الْقِيٰمَةِ وَزْنًا ○

106. That is their reward,
Hell; because they rejected
Faith, and took My Signs
And My Messengers
By way of jest.[2451]

١٠٦- ذٰلِكَ جَزَآؤُهُمْ جَهَنَّمُ بِمَا
كَفَرُوا وَاتَّخَذُوا اٰيٰتِي وَرُسُلِي هُزُوًا ○

2448. That is, those who prided themselves on their works in this life, and now find that those works are of no avail. Their loss is all the greater because they had a misplaced confidence in their own deeds or in the assistance of false "protectors". God is the only Protector: no one else's protection is of any use.

2449. Many people have such a smug sense of self-righteousness that while they go on doing wrong, they think that they are acquiring merit. So, in charity, all the elements that make for outward show or selfishness (as to get some worldly advantage) nullify the deed of charity. In the same way hypocrites sometimes affect to be surprised that their declared effort for somebody's good is not appreciated, when they are really seeking some hidden gain or false glory for themselves. The sincere are only those who believe in their spiritual responsibility and act as in God's sight.

2450. What weight can be attached to works behind which the motives are not pure, or are positively evil? They are either wasted or count against those who seek to pass them off as meritorious!

2451. False motives, pretence, deception, and hypocrisy, flourish because people do not take the higher life seriously. In effect they treat it as a jest. Signs and Messengers are sent as a special and personal Mercy from God, and for such things the first person singular is used as in this verse, even when it involves a sudden transition from the first person plural as in the last verse.

107. As to those who believe
And work righteous deeds,
They have, for their
entertainment,
The Gardens of Paradise,[2452]

١٠٧- إِنَّ الَّذِينَ آمَنُوا وَعَمِلُوا الصَّلِحَتِ
كَانَتْ لَهُمْ جَنَّتُ الْفِرْدَوْسِ نُزُلًا ۝

108. Wherein they shall dwell
(For aye): no change
Will they wish for from them.

١٠٨- خَلِدِينَ فِيهَا لَا يَبْغُونَ عَنْهَا
حِوَلًا ۝

109. Say: " If the ocean were
Ink (wherewith to write out)
The words of my Lord,[2453]
Sooner would the ocean be
Exhausted than would the words
Of my Lord, even if we
Added another ocean
Like it, for its aid."

١٠٩- قُلْ لَوْ كَانَ الْبَحْرُ مِدَادًا
لِكَلِمَتِ رَبِّي لَنَفِدَ الْبَحْرُ
قَبْلَ أَنْ تَنْفَدَ كَلِمَتُ رَبِّي
وَلَوْ جِئْنَا بِمِثْلِهِ مَدَدًا ۝

110. Say: " I am but a man
Like yourselves, (but)
The inspiration has come
To me, that your God is
One God: whoever expects
To meet his Lord, let him
Work righteousness, and,
In the worship of his Lord,
Admit no one as partner.[2454]

١١٠- قُلْ إِنَّمَا أَنَا بَشَرٌ مِّثْلُكُمْ
يُوحَى إِلَيَّ أَنَّمَا إِلَهُكُمْ إِلَهٌ
وَاحِدٌ فَمَنْ كَانَ يَرْجُوا لِقَاءَ رَبِّهِ
فَلْيَعْمَلْ عَمَلًا صَالِحًا
وَلَا يُشْرِكْ بِعِبَادَةِ رَبِّهِ أَحَدًا ۝

2452. *Firdaus* in Persian means an enclosed place, a park. In technical theological language the word is used for the inner circle of Heaven, or the highest Heaven, the destination of those who perfectly fulfil both requirements, *viz.*: a sound faith, and perfectly righteous conduct. Small faults in either respect are forgiven; the Mercy of God steps in Perhaps there is spiritual development and progress even after death.

2453. The Words and Signs and Mercies of God are in all Creation, and can never be rully set out in human language, however extended our means may be imagined to be.

2454. Righteousness and true respect for God—which excludes the worship of anything else, whether idols, or deified men, or forces of nature, or faculties of man, or Self—these are the criteria of true worship.

APPENDIX VII.

Who was Ẕul-qarnain?

(xviii. 83-98.)

As stated in my n. 2428 to xviii. 83, I do not consider that historical or geographical considerations have much bearing on a story treated as a Parable, as Ẕul-qarnain's story is. Indeed all stories or narrations are referred to in the Qur-ān as Parables, for their spiritual meaning. Heated controversies or dogmatic assertions as to precise dates, personalities, or localities, seem to me to be out of place. But a great deal of literature has been piled up among our writers on the subject, and it seems desirable to set down a few notes as to the different views that have been expressed.

What is the meaning of the name or title *Ẕul-qarnain*—"Lord of the two *Qarns*"? "*Qarn*" may mean: (1) a horn in the literal sense, as in the case of a ram or bull; (2) a horn in a metaphorical sense, as in English, the horns of a crescent, or by a further metaphor (not used in English), the horns of a kingdom or territory, two portions at opposite ends; (3) by another metaphor, a summit, a lock of hair, typifying strength, a crest such as Eastern kings wear on their diadems; (4) referring to time, an Epoch, an Age, a Generation. Meaning (1) is inapplicable to a man or a great King: but see the next paragraph about Alexander the Great. The other three meanings may be applicable, as implying: (2) Lord of East and West, Lord of wide territory or of two kingdoms; (3) Lord of two crests on his diadem, typifying two kingdoms, or a rank superior to that of an ordinary king; (4) Lord of more than one Epoch: one whose power and influence extend far beyond his lifetime.

If we accept the popular identification of Ẕul-qarnain with Alexander, all the three latter designations would be applicable to him, as he was Lord of the West and the East, Lord of the Greek States united for the first time (Hellenic Captain-General) and of the widely-extended Persian Dominion which included all Western Asia, Egypt, Central Asia, Afghanistán, and the Punjab (at least portions). He is represented on his coins with two horns on his head: he considered himself a son of Jupiter Ammon (who had the two horns of a ram), with a divine mission. He revolutionised the history of Europe, Asia, and Africa (Egypt), and his influence lasted for many generations after his death at the young age of 33. He lived from B.C. 356 to 323, but his name was one to conjure with for many centuries after him. It was not only on account of his political power, but his cultural influences. Through his conquests Greek art gave the impulse to Gandhara art in Central Asia and North-West India. The city of Alexandria which he founded in Egypt became the cultural centre, not only for Greece and Rome, but for Judaism and Christianity, and retained its supremacy till the sixth century of the Christian era. Justinian closed its schools of philosophy in 529. Its philosophic and scientific schools spread their influence over even a wider area than the Mediterranean basin.

Now the generality of the world of Islam have accepted Alexander the Great as the one meant by the epithet Ẕul-qarnain. But some of our 'Ulamā have raised doubts about it and made other suggestions. One is that it was not the Macedonian

Alexander the Great, but an earlier pre-historic king contemporary with Abraham; because, they say, Ẕul-qarnain was a man of Faith (xviii. 88, 98), while Alexander the Great was a Pagan and believed in Grecian gods. An identification with a supposed pre-historic king, about whom nothing is known, is no identification at all. On the other hand, all that is known about Alexander the Great shows that he was a man of lofty ideals. He died over three centuries before the time of Jesus, but that does not mean that he was not a man of Faith, for God revealed Himself to men of all nations in all ages. Alexander was a disciple of the philosopher Aristotle, noted for his pursuit of sound Truth in all departments of thought. Alexander's reference to Jupiter Ammon may have been no more than a playful reference to the superstitions of his time. Socrates spoke of the Grecian gods, and so did Aristotle and Plato; but it would be wrong to call them idolaters or men without Faith. In the Ethiopic traditional stories of Alexander the Great, he is represented as a great prophet.

Another suggestion made is that Ẕul-qarnain was an ancient king of Persia. A king of Persia is referred to as a Ram with two horns in the Book of Daniel (viii. 3) in the Old Testament. But in the same Book, the Ram with the two horns was smitten, cast down to the ground, and stamped upon by a he-goat with one horn (viii. 7-8). There is nothing in our literature to suggest that Ẕul-qarnain came to any such ignominious end. Nor is the Book of Daniel an authority worth consideration. Its authenticity is very doubtful. There is no question that it is a patch-work, as parts of it are in the Aramaic (or Chaldee) language and parts in Hebrew, and there are in it a number of Greek words. The Septuagint version contained large additions. "Daniel"—whoever the writer or writers were—refers to historical Persian kings. If it is argued that it was some old pre-historic Persian king who built the Iron Gates (xviii. 96) to keep out the Gog and Magog tribes (xviii. 94), this is no identification at all. There is no unanimity about the identity of the Iron Wall, or the Gog and Magog tribes. Both these subjects will be referred to presently.

Another suggestion made is that it was some old pre-historic Ḥimyarite king from Yemen, about whom nothing else is known. This, again, is no identification at all.

The question of Yājūj and Mājūj (Gog and Magog) and the iron Barrier built to keep them out is of some interest. It is practically agreed that they were the wild tribes of Central Asia which have made inroads on settled kingdoms and Empires at various stages of the world's history. The Chinese Empire suffered from their incursions and built the Great Wall of China to keep out the Manchus and Mongols. The Persian Empire suffered from them at various times and at various points. Their incursions into Europe in large hordes caused migrations and displacements of population on an enormous scale, and eventually broke up the Roman Empire. These tribes were known vaguely to the Greeks and Romans as "Scythians", but that term does not help us very much, either ethnically or geographically.

If we could locate the iron barrier or iron gates referred to in xviii. 96, we should have a closer idea of the tribes whom the barrier was meant to keep out. It is obvious that the Great Wall of China is out of the question. Begun in the third century B.C. and continued later, it covers the enormous length of 1,500 miles, and goes up the hills and down the valleys, with towers 40 feet high at intervals of 200 yards. Its average height is 20 to 30 feet. It is built of stone and earth. There is no particular

point in it which can be identified with the iron barrier in the text. No one has suggested that Zul-qarnain was a Chinese Emperor, and none of the great Conquerors of Western Asia can be credited with the building of the Chinese Wall.

The Barrier in the text must have been more in the nature of iron gates than an iron wall. Two Iron Gates, geographically far apart, have been suggested in the alternative. Sometimes they have been mixed up by writers not strong in geography. Both of them have local associations with the name of Alexander the Great. Both are near a town Derbend, and have borne the name of Bāb-ul-hadīd (Arabic for "Iron Gate"). Let us examine the case of each in turn.

The best known in modern times is at the town and seaport of Derbend in the middle of the western coast of the Caspian Sea. It is now in Soviet territory, in the district of Dāghistan. Before the southern expansion of Russia in 1813 it belonged to Persia. A spur of Mount Caucasus here comes up north, close to the sea. The Wall in question is 50 miles long, with an average height of 29 feet. As Āẕarbaijān (in Persia) is not far from this place, some writers have mixed up the Derbend Iron Gate with Āẕarbaijān, and some with the Caucasian town of K͟harz (Kars), which is to the south of the Caucasus. There are local traditions here, and in the Astrakhan region, at the mouth of the river Volga, higher up the Caspian, connecting this Caucasian Iron Gate with the name of Alexander, but there are good reasons why we should reject this as the site of the Iron Gate in the Quranic story. (1) This does not correspond exactly to the description in xviii. 96 ("the space between the two steep mountain sides"); the gap is between the mountain and the sea. (2) Alexander the Great (assuming that Ẕul-qarnain is Alexander), is not known to have crossed the Caucasus. (3) There is an Iron Gate which corresponds exactly to the description, in a locality which we know Alexander to have visited. (4) In the early days, when Muslims spread to all parts of the world, local legends were started by ignorant people connecting the places they knew with places referred to in the Qur-ān.

We now come to the Iron Gate which corresponds exactly to the Quranic description, and has the best claim to be connected with Alexander's story. It is near another Derbend in Central Asia, Hissar District, about 150 miles south-east of Buk͟hārā. A very narrow defile, with overhanging rocks, occurs on the main route between Turkestan and India: latitude 38°N; longitude 67°E. It is now called in Turki Buzghol-K͟hāna (Goat-house), but was formerly known as the Iron Gate (Arabic, *Bāb-ul-ḥadīd*; Persian, *Dar-i-āhanī*; Chinese *T'ie-men-kuan*). There is no iron gate there now, but there was one in the seventh century, when the Chinese traveller Hiouen Tsiang saw it on his journey to India. He saw two folding gates cased with iron and hung with bells. Near by is a lake named Iskandar Kul, connecting the locality with Alexander the Great. We know from history that Alexander, after his conquest of Persia and before his journey to India, visited Sogdiana (*Buk͟hārā*) and Maracanda (*Samarqand*). We also know from Muqaddasī, the Arab traveller and geographer, who wrote about A.H. 375 (A.D. 985-6) that the 'Abbāsī K͟halifa Wāthiq (842-846 A.D.) sent out a mission to Central Asia to report on this Iron Gate. They found the defile 150 yards wide: on two jambs made with bricks of iron welded together with molten lead, were hung two huge gates, which were kept closed. Nothing could correspond more exactly with the description in xviii. 95-96.

If, then, the Barrier in xviii. 95-98 refers to the Iron Gate near Bukhārā, we are able to proceed to a consideration of the Gog-Magog people with some confidence. They were the Mongol tribes on the other side of the Barrier, while the industrious men who did not understand Ẕul-qarnain's language were the Turks, with their agglutinative language, so different from the languages then spoken in Western Asia. The Barrier served its purpose for the time being. But the warning that the time must come when it must crumble to dust has also come true. It has crumbled to dust. Long since, the Mongols pushed through on their westward journey, pushing the Turks before them, and the Turks became a European Power and have still a footing in Europe. We need not bother about the legends of the Gog and Magog people. They were reputed to be giants, and two tiny hills in flat Cambridgeshire are derisively called the Gog-Magog hills! Similarly the statues of Gog and Magog in the Guildhall in London, which M.M.A. takes so seriously, only remind us how legends are apt to grow and get transported to strange places. In the Alexander legends of medieval Europe, Gog and Magog are said to have come with 400,000 men to the help of Porus whom Alexander defeated, and to have fled after that defeat. They fled to the mountains, and Alexander built a wall with brass gates to prevent their irruptions. See Paul Meyer, *Alexandre le Grand dans la litétrature française du Moyen Age*: Paris, 1886; Vol. 2, pp. 386-389.

Personally, I have not the least doubt that Zul-qarnain is meant to be Alexander the Great, the historic Alexander, and not the legendary Alexander, of whom more presently. My first appointment after graduation was that of Lecturer in Greek history. I have studied the details of Alexander's extraordinary personality in Greek historians as well as in modern writers, and have since visited most of the localities connected with his brief but brilliant career. Few readers of Quranic literature have had the same privilege of studying the details of his career. It is one of the wonders of the Qur-ān, that, spoken through an Ummī's mouth, it should contain so many incidental details which are absolutely true. The more our knowledge increases, the more we feel this. There are little touches which need not have been mentioned. They come in incidentally like the incidental remarks of a person full of knowledge, who does not intend to put forward those points but whose fulness of knowledge brings them in inevitably.

One such point occurs in the mention of Alexander's westward journey (xviii. 86). He saw the sun set in a piece of murky water which is described as a "Spring". Most Commentators have understood the "spring" to be the sea, and the "murky water" to be its dark-blue water. Niẕāmī, in his *Romance of Alexander*, takes Alexander right west along North Africa to Andalusia and the Atlantic Ocean. There is no historic proof that Alexander ever reached the Atlantic. But he was of course familiar with the deep-blue waters of the Mediterranean. The Mediterranean interpretation may pass if we had not a closer explanation. Alexander's first exploits were when he was a mere boy, in the reign of his father Philip. The region of Illyricum was due west of Macedonia, and Macedonia's first expansion was in that direction. The town of Lychnis was annexed to Macedonia and thus the western frontier of Macedonia was secured. The northern frontier towards the Danube had already been secured, and the lesson he subsequently gave to Thebes secured him against attack from the Greek States to the south, and prepared the way for his great march east against the Persian Empire. To the west of the town of Lychnis is a lake 170 square miles in area, fed by underground springs that issue through limestone rocks and give out murky water. Both town and lake are now called Ochrida, about 50 miles west of Monastir. The water is so dark that the river which forms the outlet of the lake to the north is called the Black Drin. Looking at the sunset from the town, the observer would see the sun set in a pool of murky water (xviii. 86). It was a question

before the boy Alexander—the dreamy, impulsive, fearless rider—whether he would put the barbarous Illyricans to the sword or show them mercy. He showed true discrimination and statesmanship. He punished the guilty but showed kindness to the innocent, and thus consolidated his power in the west. This I construe to be the meaning of xviii. 86-87; otherwise these verses do not seem to be perfectly clear.

Another point may be noted. The three episodes mentioned are the journey to the west, the journey to the east, and the journey to the Iron Gate. The journey to the west I have just explained. The journey to the east was to the Persian Empire. Here he found a people who lived in the open and wore little clothing. This might apply to people who live in an inland place in the latitude of Persepolis or Multan. He left them alone as they were (xviii. 91). He was not warring against populations: he was warring against the proud but effete Persian Empire. He left them as they were, with their local institutions, and under their local chiefs. In feeling he treated them as his own, not as aliens. In some things he himself adopted their ways. His followers misunderstood him. But God understood, for He approves of all things that lead to Unity among mankind.

The direction of the third journey is not mentioned. The Commentators suggest the north, but they might with better reason have suggested the south, as Alexander visited Egypt. But the visit to the Iron Gate was to the East—a continuation of his journey east. That is why the direction is not mentioned again. Here his mission was different. He had to protect a peaceful industrious population, whom perhaps the Persian Empire had failed to protect, against turbulent and restless invaders. He helped them to protect themselves, but warned them that all human precautions, though good and necessary, are vain without God's help.

Each of the episodes mentioned is historical. But the pomp and glitter of military conquest are not mentioned. On the contrary spiritual motives are revealed and commended. We need not know or learn any history or geography or science or psychology or ethics to understand them. But the more real knowledge we have, the more completely shall we understand them and the lessons to be drawn from them. The earthly journeys are treated as mere symbols to show us the evolution of a great and noble soul which achieved so much in a short earthly life.

His career was so extraordinary that it impressed his contemporaries as a world-event, as it undoubtedly was,—one of the greatest world-events in history. Legends began to grow up round his name. In many cases the legends overlaid the history. To-day the world is thrilled by Sir Aurel Stein's identification of Aornos, a very small geographical detail in a great career full of lessons, in political, ethical, and religious wisdom. But the generations immediately following Alexander's period wrote and transmitted all sorts of wonderful legends that passed current in East and West. The philosopher Kallisthenes had been with Alexander in Asia. Under his name was produced a Greek book in Alexandria some time before the second century of the Christian era. It was translated into Latin in the third century. Translations were subsequently made into most of the European languages. In Chaucer's time (1340-1400) these Alexander legends were known to every "wight that hath discrecion" (The Monk in *Canterbury Tales*).

Alexandria was a focus of Christian and Jewish learning for some centuries. The Christians also made Alexander a saint. The Jews carried the Alexander cycle into the East. Our Persian poet Jāmī (A.H. 535-599, A.D. 1141-1203) worked it up into his epic the *Iskandar-nāma.* He is careful to show the historical or semi-historical and the ethical parts separately. The one relates to action or exploits (*Iqbāl*) and the other to wisdom (*K͟hirad*). He had the advantage of the Qur-ān story before him. That story mentions three historical episodes incidentally, but draws our attention to matters of the weightiest spiritual significance, and that is the chief thing to note in the story.

INTRODUCTION TO SŪRA XIX (*Maryam*).

The spiritual growth of man as an individual soul having been explained in S. xvii. as beginning with the first principles of moral conduct and in S. xviii as being dependent upon our realisation of the brevity and mystery of this life and the true use of power as in the story of Ẓul-qarnain, we now pass on to the story of individual Messengers of God in their personal relations with their environment,—Yaḥyā with his father Zakarīya, Jesus with his mother Mary, Abraham with his unbelieving father, Moses with his brother Aaron, Ismā'īl with his family, and Idrīs in the high station to which he was called. Seeing how these great ones fitted into the scheme of life, man is condemned for his want of faith, or for degrading his faith to superstition, and warned of the Hereafter.

In chronology, it was revealed before the first resort of the batch of Muslims to Abyssinia, say seven years before the Hijrat.

Summary.—Zakarīya was anxious to have an heir to carry on God's work in a world of unrighteousness, and Yaḥyā was given to him (xix. 1-15, and C. 138).

Mary the mother of Jesus was maligned by her people, but Jesus comforted her and was good to her (xix. 16-40, and C. 139).

Abraham was persecuted for his Faith by his people, including his unbelieving father, but he withdrew from them, and was blessed ; Moses was helped by his brother Aaron ; Ismā'īl brought up his family in piety ; and Idrīs was truthful and pious in a high station : they showed the way ; yet men will not learn the good life (xix. 41-65, and C. 140).

Man should not disbelieve in the Hereafter, nor sully his faith by false notions about God (xix. 66-98, and C. 141).

C. 138.—Men of God show their qualities
(xix. 1-15.) In their private relationships as much
As in their public ministry. Zakarīya
Was anxious, in a world of unrighteousness,
To find a successor to continue his godly
Errand. He was given a son, Yaḥyā,
Who heralded Jesus, and lived a life
Of wisdom, gentle love, and purity.

Sūra XIX.

Maryam, or Mary.

In the name of God, Most Gracious, Most Merciful.

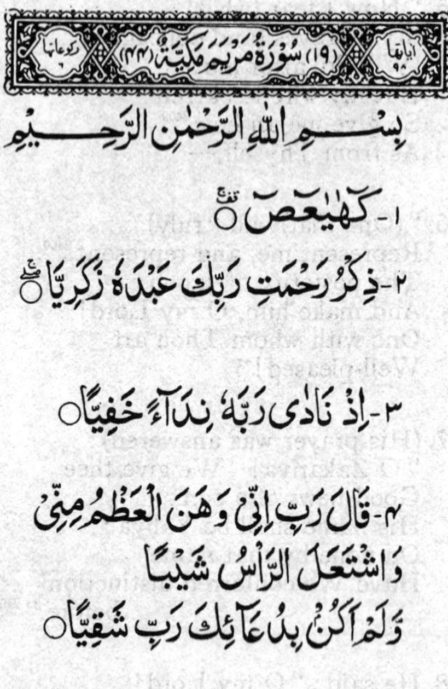

1. Kāf. Hā. Yā. 'Ain. Ṣād.[2455]

2. (This is) a recital[2456]
Of the Mercy of thy Lord
To His servant Zakarīya.

3. Behold! he cried
To his Lord in secret,[2457]

4. Praying: "O my Lord!
Infirm indeed are my bones,
And the hair of my head
Doth glisten with grey:
But never am I unblest,
O my Lord, in my prayer[2458]
To Thee!

2455. This is the only Sūra which begins with these five Abbreviated Letters, K., H., Y., 'A., Ṣ. For Abbreviated Letters generally, see Appendix I, pp. 118-120.

As stated in my note 25, such Letters are Symbols, of which the true meaning is known to God alone. We should not be dogmatic about any conjectures that we make. According to the interpretation of the last letter *Ṣād*, suggested in n. 989 to vii. 1. I should be disposed to accept Ṣād with the meaning of *Qiṣaṣ, i.e.*, stories of the Prophets. The main figures referred to here are: Zakarīya, Yaḥyā, Maryam, 'Isā, and Ibrāhīm: the others are mentioned but incidentally. The strong letter in ZaKarīya is K; in IbrāHīm, H; in YāḥYā and perhaps MarYam, Y; and in 'Isa,—'A (*Ain*). H also comes in Hārūn (Aaron), and the Arabic *Yā* comes in all the names including Ismā'īl and Idrīs.

I offer this suggestion with some diffidence. The suggestion of the *Tafsīr Kabīr* is that the letters stand for attributes of God: K. for *Kāfī* (the One sufficient in Himself): H. for *Hādī* (He who guides); Y. for *Yad* (Hand as a symbol of Power or Authority; *Cf.* xlviii. 10, "The Hand of God is above their hands"); 'A. for *'Alīm* (the All-Knowing); and Ṣ for *Ṣādiq* (The True One).

2456. The Mercy of God to Zakarīya was shown in many ways: (1) in the acceptance of his prayer; (2) in bestowing a son like Yaḥyā; and (3) in the love between father and son, in addition to the work which Yaḥyā did as God's Messenger for the world. *Cf.* iii. 38-41 and notes. There the public ministry was the point stressed; here the beautiful relations between the son and the father.

2457. *In secret*: because he feared that his own family and relatives were going wrong (xix. 5), and he wanted to keep the lamp of God burning bright. He could not very well mention the fear about his colleagues (who were his relations) in public.

2458. This preface shows the fervent faith of Zakarīya. Zakarīya was a priest of the Most High God. His office was in the Temple, and his relatives were his colleagues. But he found in them no true spirit of the service of God and man. He was filled with anxiety as to who would uphold the godly ideas he had in mind, which were strange to his worldly colleagues.

5. "Now I fear (what)
My relatives (and colleagues)
(Will do) after me:
But my wife is barren:
So give me an heir[2459]
As from Thyself,—

٥- وَإِنِّي خِفْتُ الْمَوَالِيَ مِن وَرَآءِي
وَكَانَتِ امْرَأَتِي عَاقِرًا
فَهَبْ لِي مِن لَّدُنكَ وَلِيًّا ۝

6. "(One that) will (truly)
Represent me, and represent[2460]
The posterity of Jacob;
And make him, O my Lord!
One with whom Thou art
Well-pleased!"

٦- يَرِثُنِي وَيَرِثُ
مِنْ آلِ يَعْقُوبَ ۖ
وَاجْعَلْهُ رَبِّ رَضِيًّا ۝

7. (His prayer was answered):
"O Zakarīya! We give thee
Good news of a son:
His name shall be Yaḥyā:
On none by that name
Have We conferred distinction
before."[2461]

٧- يَٰزَكَرِيَّا إِنَّا نُبَشِّرُكَ
بِغُلَٰمٍ اسْمُهُ يَحْيَىٰ
لَمْ نَجْعَل لَّهُ مِن قَبْلُ سَمِيًّا ۝

8. He said: "O my Lord!
How shall I have a son,
When my wife is barren
And I have grown quite decrepit
From old age?"

٨- قَالَ رَبِّ أَنَّىٰ يَكُونُ لِي غُلَٰمٌ
وَكَانَتِ امْرَأَتِي عَاقِرًا
وَقَدْ بَلَغْتُ مِنَ الْكِبَرِ عِتِيًّا ۝

2459. His was not merely a vulgar desire for a son. If it had been, he would have prayed much earlier in his life, when he was a young man. He was too full of true piety to put merely selfish things into his prayers. But here was a public need, in the service of the Lord. He was too old, but could he perhaps adopt a child—who would be an heir "as from God" (See n. 380 to iii. 38).

2460. It is true that an heir inherits property, but his higher duty is to represent in everything the personality of him from whom he inherits. It is doubtful whether Zakarīya had any worldly property. But he had character and virtue, as a man of God, and this he wanted to transmit to his heir as his most precious possession. It was almost the most precious possession of the posterity of Jacob. The people around him had fallen away from God's Message. Could his heir, like him, try and renew it?

2461. This was John the Baptist, the forerunner of Jesus. In accordance with his father's prayer he, and Jesus for whom he prepared the way, renewed the Message of God, which had been corrupted and lost among the Israelites. The Arabic form Yaḥyā suggests "Life". The Hebrew form is Johanan, which means "Jehovah has been Gracious". *Cf.* Ḥanānan in verse 13 below. It does not mean that the name was given for the first time, for we read of a Johanan the son of Careah in II Kings, xxv. 23, an otherwise obscure man. It means that God had, for the first time, called one of His elect by that name.

9. He said: "So (it will be):[2462]
Thy Lord saith, 'That is
Easy for Me: I did
Indeed create thee before,
When thou hadst been nothing!'"[2463]

٩- قَالَ كَذٰلِكَ ۚ قَالَ رَبُّكَ هُوَ عَلَيَّ هَيِّنٌ وَّقَدْ خَلَقْتُكَ مِنْ قَبْلُ وَلَمْ تَكُ شَيْئًا ○

10. (Zakarīya) said: "O my Lord!
Give me a Sign."[2464]
"Thy Sign," was the answer,
"Shall be that thou
Shalt speak to no man
For three nights,[2465]
Although thou art not dumb."

١٠- قَالَ رَبِّ اجْعَلْ لِّيْٓ اٰيَةً ؕ قَالَ اٰيَتُكَ اَلَّا تُكَلِّمَ النَّاسَ ثَلٰثَ لَيَالٍ سَوِيًّا ○

11. So Zakarīya came out
To his people
From his chamber:
He told them by signs
To celebrate God's praises
In the morning
And in the evening.

١١- فَخَرَجَ عَلٰى قَوْمِهٖ مِنَ الْمِحْرَابِ فَاَوْحٰٓى اِلَيْهِمْ اَنْ سَبِّحُوْا بُكْرَةً وَّعَشِيًّا ○

12. (To his son came the
command):[2466]
"O Yaḥyā! take hold

١٢- يٰيَحْيٰى خُذِ الْكِتٰبَ بِقُوَّةٍ ؕ

2462. Who is the "He" in this clause? As I have construed it, following the majority of Commentators, it means the angel who brought the message from God. *Cf.* xix. 21 below. But some Commentators construe it to refer to Zakarīya. In that case the meaning will be: Zakarīya after a little reflection said (in his wonder) "So!", *i.e*, "Can it really be so? Can I really have a son in my old age?" The speech following, "Thy Lord saith," etc., will then be that of the angel-messenger.

2463. Every man was nothing just before he was created, *i.e.*, his personality was called into being by God. Even if there are material processes in forming the body, in accordance with the laws of nature, the real creative force is in God. But here there is a subtler meaning. John was the harbinger of Jesus, preparing the way for him; and this sentence also prepares us for the more wonderful birth of Jesus himself: see verse 21 below. Everything is possible with God.

2464. The "Sign", I understand, was not in order to convince Zakarīya that the Lord's promise was true, for he had faith; but it was a symbol by which he was to show in his conduct that he was to conform to his new destiny as the father of Yaḥyā who was to come. Yaḥyā was to take up the work, and Zakarīya was to be silent, although the latter was sound in body and there was nothing to prevent him from speaking.

2465. Compare this verse with iii. 41. The variations are interesting. Here it is "for three nights": there it is "for three days". The meaning is the same, for a day is a period of 24 hours. But the point of view is different in each case. There it was from the point of view of the Ummat or Congregation, among whom he worked by day; here the point of view is that of his individual soul, which spent the nights in prayer and praise. Notice again that at the end of the next verse, we have here, "In the morning and in the evening", and at the end of iii. 41, "In the evening and in the morning"—showing again that the point of view is reversed.

2466. Time passes. The son is born. In this section of the Sūra the centre of interest is Yaḥyā, and the instruction is now given to him. 'Keep fast hold of God's revelation with all your might': for an unbelieving world had either corrupted or neglected it, and Yaḥyā (John the Baptist) was to prepare the way for Jesus, who was coming to renew and re-interpret it.

Of the Book with might":
And We gave him Wisdom[2467]
Even as a youth,

وَاٰتَيْنٰهُ الْحُكْمَ صَبِيًّا ۙ

13. And pity (for all creatures)
As from us, and purity:[2468]
He was devout,

١٣- وَّحَنَانًا مِّنْ لَّدُنَّا وَزَكٰوةً ۭ
وَكَانَ تَقِيًّا ۙ

14. And kind to his parents,
And he was not overbearing
Or rebellious.

١٤- وَّبَرًّا بِوَالِدَيْهِ
وَلَمْ يَكُنْ جَبَّارًا عَصِيًّا

15. So Peace on him
The day he was born,
The day that he dies,
And the day that he
Will be raised up
To life (again)![2469]

١٥- وَسَلٰمٌ عَلَيْهِ يَوْمَ وُلِدَ
وَيَوْمَ يَمُوْتُ
وَيَوْمَ يُبْعَثُ حَيًّا

C. 139.—Next comes the story of Jesus and his mother
(xix. 16-40.) Mary. She gave birth, as a virgin, to Jesus,
But her people slandered and abused her
As a disgrace to her lineage. Her son
Did defend her and was kind to her. He
Was a servant of God, a true Prophet,
Blessed in the gifts of Prayer and Charity,
But no more than a man: to call him
The son of God is to derogate from God's
Majesty, for God is High above all
His Creatures, the Judge of the Last Day.

2467. *Hukm*, translated Wisdom, implies something more than Wisdom; it is the Wisdom or Judgment that is entitled to judge and command, as in the matter of denouncing sin.

2468. John the Baptist did not live long. He was imprisoned by Herod, the tetrarch (provincial ruler under the Roman Empire), whom he had reproved for his sins, and eventually beheaded at the instigation of the woman with whom Herod was infatuated. But even in his young life, he was granted (1) wisdom by God, for he boldly denounced sin; (2) gentle pity and love for all God's creatures, for he moved among the humble and lowly, and despised "soft raiment"; and (3) purity of life, for he renounced the world and lived in the wilderness. All his work he did in his youth. These things showed themselves in his conduct, for he was devout, showing love to God and to God's creatures, and more particularly to his parents (for we are considering that aspect of his life): this was also shown by the fact that he never used violence, from an attitude of arrogance, nor entertained a spirit of rebellion against human or divine Law.

2469. This is spoken as in the life-time of Yaḥyā. Peace and God's Blessings were on him when he was born; they continue when he is about to die an unjust death at the hands of a tyrant; and they will be specially manifest at the Day of Judgment.

SECTION 2.

16. Relate in the Book
(The story of) Mary,[2470]
When she withdrew
From her family
To a place in the East.[2471]

١٦- وَاذْكُرْ فِي الْكِتٰبِ مَرْيَمَ
إِذِ انْتَبَذَتْ مِنْ أَهْلِهَا مَكَانًا شَرْقِيًّا ○

17. She placed a screen
(To screen herself) from them;
Then We sent to her
Our angel, and he appeared
Before her as a man
In all respects.

١٧- فَاتَّخَذَتْ مِنْ دُونِهِمْ حِجَابًا
فَأَرْسَلْنَا إِلَيْهَا رُوحَنَا
فَتَمَثَّلَ لَهَا بَشَرًا سَوِيًّا ○

18. She said: "I seek refuge
From thee to (God)
Most Gracious: (come not near)
If thou dost fear God."

١٨- قَالَتْ إِنِّي أَعُوذُ
بِالرَّحْمٰنِ مِنْكَ إِنْ كُنْتَ تَقِيًّا ○

19. He said: "Nay, I am only
A messenger from thy Lord,
(To announce) to thee
The gift of a holy son."[2472]

١٩- قَالَ إِنَّمَا أَنَا رَسُولُ رَبِّكِ
لِأَهَبَ لَكِ غُلٰمًا زَكِيًّا ○

20. She said: "How shall I
Have a son, seeing that
No man has touched me,
And I am not unchaste?"

٢٠- قَالَتْ أَنّٰى يَكُونُ لِي غُلٰمٌ
وَلَمْ يَمْسَسْنِي بَشَرٌ وَلَمْ أَكُ بَغِيًّا ○ الربع

21. He said: "So (it will be):
Thy Lord saith, 'That is
Easy for Me: and (We
Wish) to appoint him
As a Sign unto men
And a Mercy from Us':[2473]

٢١- قَالَ كَذٰلِكِ قَالَ رَبُّكِ
هُوَ عَلَيَّ هَيِّنٌ وَلِنَجْعَلَهُ
آيَةً لِلنَّاسِ وَرَحْمَةً مِنَّا

2470. *Cf.* the story of Mary as related in iii. 42-51. Here the whole theme is different: it is the personal side of the spiritual experiences of the worshippers of God in relation to their families or environment.

2471. To a private eastern chamber, perhaps in the Temple. She went into privacy, from her people and from people in general, for prayer and devotion. It was in this state of purity that the angel appeared to her in the shape of a man. She thought it *was* a man. She was frightened, and she adjured him not to invade her privacy.

2472. God had destined her to be the mother of the holy Prophet Jesus Christ, and now had come the time when this should be announced to her.

2473. The mission of Jesus is announced in two ways (1) he was to be a Sign to men; his wonderful birth and wonderful life were to turn an ungodly world back to God; and (2) his mission was to bring solace and salvation to the repentant. This, in some way or other, is the case with all apostles of God, and it was pre-eminently so in the case of the holy Apostle Muḥammad. But the point here is that the Israelites, to whom Jesus was sent, were a hardened race, for whom the message of Jesus was truly a gospel of Mercy.

It is a matter
(So) decreed."[2474]

وَكَانَ أَمْرًا مَّقْضِيًّا ○

22. So she conceived him,
And she retired with him
To a remote place.[2475]

٢٢- فَحَمَلَتْهُ فَانْتَبَذَتْ بِهٖ مَكَانًا قَصِيًّا ○

23. And the pains of childbirth
Drove her to the trunk
Of a palm-tree:
She cried (in her anguish):
"Ah! would that I had
Died before this! would that
I had been a thing
Forgotten and out of sight!"[2476]

٢٣- فَاَجَآءَهَا الْمَخَاضُ
اِلٰى جِذْعِ النَّخْلَةِ ۚ
قَالَتْ يٰلَيْتَنِىْ مِتُّ قَبْلَ هٰذَا
وَكُنْتُ نَسْيًا مَّنْسِيًّا ○

24. But (a voice) cried to her
From beneath the (palm-tree):
"Grieve not! for thy Lord
Hath provided a rivulet
Beneath thee;

٢٤- فَنَادٰىهَا مِنْ تَحْتِهَآ
اَلَّا تَحْزَنِىْ قَدْ جَعَلَ رَبُّكِ تَحْتَكِ سَرِيًّا ○

25. "And shake towards thyself
The trunk of the palm-tree:
It will let fall
Fresh ripe dates upon thee.[2477]

٢٥- وَهُزِّىْٓ اِلَيْكِ بِجِذْعِ النَّخْلَةِ
تُسٰقِطْ عَلَيْكِ رُطَبًا جَنِيًّا ○

26. "So eat and drink
And cool (thine) eye.[2478]
And if thou dost see
Any man, say, 'I have

٢٦- فَكُلِىْ وَاشْرَبِىْ وَقَرِّىْ عَيْنًا ۚ فَاِمَّا تَرَيِنَّ
مِنَ الْبَشَرِ اَحَدًا ۙ فَقُوْلِىْٓ اِنِّىْ

2474. For anything that God wishes to create, He says "Be", and it is (*Cf.* iii. 47). There is no interval between His decree and its accomplishment, except such as He imposes by His decree. Time may be only a projection of our own minds in this world of relativity.

2475. The annunciation and the conception, we may suppose, took place in Nazareth (of Galilee), say 65 miles north of Jerusalem. The delivery took place in Bethlehem about 6 miles south of Jerusalem. It was a remote place, not only with reference to the distance of 71 miles, but because in Bethlehem itself the birth was in an obscure corner under a palm-tree, from which perhaps the babe was afterwards removed to a manger in a stable.

2476. She was but human, and suffered the pangs of an expectant mother, with no one to attend on her. The circumstances being peculiar, she had got far away from her people.

2477. Unseen Providence had seen that she should not suffer from thirst or from hunger. The rivulet provided her with water also for ablutions.

2478. *Cool thine eye*: An idiom for "comfort thyself and be glad". The literal meaning should not, however, be lost sight of. She was to cool her eyes (perhaps full of tears), with the fresh water of the rivulet and take comfort that a remarkable babe had been born to her. She was also to look round, and if any one came near, she was to decline all conversation. It was quite true: she was under a vow, and could not talk to any one.

Vowed a fast to (God)
Most Gracious, and this day
Will I enter into no talk
With any human being' "[2479]

نذرت للرحمن صوما
فلن أكلم اليوم إنسيا ۝

27. At length she brought
The (babe) to her people,
Carrying him (in her arms).
They said: "O Mary!
Truly an amazing thing
Hast thou brought![2480]

٢٧- فأتت به قومها
تحمله
قالوا يمريم لقد جئت شيئا فريا ۝

28. "O sister of Aaron![2481]
Thy father was not
A man of evil, nor thy
Mother a woman unchaste!"

٢٨- يأخت هرون ما كان أبوك
امرأ سوء وما كانت أمك بغيا ۝

29. But she pointed to the babe.[2482]
They said: "How can we
Talk to one who is
A child in the cradle?"

٢٩- فأشارت إليه قالوا كيف
نكلم من كان في المهد صبيا ۝

30. He said: "I am indeed
A servant of God:
He hath given me
Revelation and made me
A prophet;

٣٠- قال إني عبد الله
اتني الكتب وجعلني نبيا ۝

31. "And He hath made me
Blessed wheresoever I be,

٣١- وجعلني مبركا أين ما كنت

2479. She was to decline all conversation with man or woman, on the plea of a vow to God. The "fast" here does not mean abstinence literally from eating and drinking. She has just been advised to eat the dates and drink of the stream. It means abstinence from the ordinary household meals, and indeed from human intercourse generally.

2480. The amazement of the people knew no bounds. In any case they were ready to think the worst of her, as she had disappeared from her kin for some time. But now she comes, shamelessly parading a babe in her arms! How she had disgraced the house of Aaron, the fountain of priesthood! We may suppose that the scene took place in the Temple in Jerusalem, or in Nazareth.

2481. Aaron the brother of Moses was the first in the line of Israelite priesthood. Mary and her cousin Elisabeth (mother of Yaḥyā) came of a priestly family, and were therefore "sisters of Aaron" or daughters of 'Imrān (who was Aaron's father). See n. 375 to iii. 35. Mary is reminded of her high lineage and the unexceptionable morals of her father and mother. How, they said, she had fallen, and disgraced the name of her progenitors!

2482. What could Mary do? How could she explain? Would they, in their censorious mood, accept her explanation? All she could do was to point to the child, who, she knew, was no ordinary child. And the child came to her rescue. By a miracle he spoke, defended his mother, and preached—to an unbelieving audience. See iii. 46, and n. 388.

And hath enjoined on me
Prayer and Charity as long
As I live;[2483]

وَاَوْصٰنِیْ بِالصَّلٰوةِ وَالزَّكٰوةِ مَا
دُمْتُ حَیًّا ۝

32. "(He) hath made me kind
To my mother, and not
Overbearing or miserable;[2484]

۳۲- وَّبَرًّا بِوَالِدَتِیْ وَلَمْ یَجْعَلْنِیْ جَبَّارًا
شَقِیًّا ۝

33. "So Peace is on me
The day I was born,
The day that I die,
And the day that I
Shall be raised up
To life (again)"![2485]

۳۳- وَالسَّلٰمُ عَلَیَّ یَوْمَ وُلِدْتُّ
وَیَوْمَ اَمُوْتُ
وَیَوْمَ اُبْعَثُ حَیًّا ۝

34. Such (was) Jesus the son
Of Mary: (it is) a statement
Of truth, about which
They (vainly) dispute.[2486]

۳۴- ذٰلِكَ عِیْسَى ابْنُ مَرْیَمَ
قَوْلَ الْحَقِّ الَّذِیْ فِیْهِ یَمْتَرُوْنَ ۝

35. It is not befitting
To (the majesty of) God
That He should beget
A son. Glory be to Him!
When He determines
A matter, He only says
To it, "Be", and it is.[2487]

۳۵- مَا كَانَ لِلّٰهِ اَنْ یَّتَّخِذَ مِنْ وَّلَدٍ
سُبْحٰنَهٗ اِذَا قَضٰٓى اَمْرًا
فَاِنَّمَا یَقُوْلُ لَهٗ كُنْ فَیَكُوْنُ ۝

36. Verily God is my Lord
And your Lord: Him

۳۶- وَاِنَّ اللّٰهَ رَبِّیْ وَرَبُّكُمْ

2483. There is a parallelism throughout the accounts of Jesus and Yaḥyā, with some variations. Both the parallelisms and the variations are interesting. For instance Jesus declares at the very outset that he is a servant of God, thus negativing the false notion that he was God or the son of God. The greatness of Yaḥyā is described in xix. 12-13 in terms that are not applied to Jesus, but the verses xix 14-15 as applied to Yaḥyā are in almost identical terms with those applied to Jesus here (xix. 32-33). Devotion in Prayer and Charity is a good description of the Church of Christ at its best, and pity, purity, and devotion in Yaḥyā are a good description of the ways leading to Prayer and Charity, just as John led to Jesus.

2484. Overbearing violence is not only unjust and harmful to those on whom it is practised; it is perhaps even more harmful to the person who practises it, for his soul becomes turbid, unsettled, and ultimately unhappy and wretched,—the state of those in Hell. Here the negative qualities are "not overbearing or miserable." As applied to John they were "not overbearing or rebellious." John bore his punishment from the State without any protest or drawing back.

2485. *Cf.* xix 15, and n. 2469. Christ was not crucified (iv. 157). But those who believe that he never died should ponder over this verse.

2486. The disputations about the nature of Jesus Christ were vain, but also persistent and sanguinary. The modern Christian churches have thrown them into the background, but they would do well to abandon irrational dogmas altogether.

2487. Begetting a son is a physical act depending on the needs of men's animal nature. God Most High is independent of all needs, and it is derogatory to Him to attribute such an act to Him. It is merely a relic of pagan and anthropomorphic materialist superstitions.

Therefore serve ye: this is
A Way that is straight.[2488]

فَاعْبُدُوهُ هَٰذَا صِرَاطٌ مُّسْتَقِيمٌ ○

37. But the sects differ
Among themselves: and woe
To the Unbelievers because
Of the (coming) Judgment[2489]
Of a momentous Day!

٣٧- فَاخْتَلَفَ الْأَحْزَابُ مِن بَيْنِهِمْ
فَوَيْلٌ لِّلَّذِينَ كَفَرُوا مِن مَّشْهَدِ
يَوْمٍ عَظِيمٍ ○

38. How plainly will they see
And hear, the Day that
They will appear before Us!
But the unjust to-day
Are in error manifest![2490]

٣٨- أَسْمِعْ بِهِمْ وَأَبْصِرْ يَوْمَ
يَأْتُونَنَا لَٰكِنِ الظَّالِمُونَ الْيَوْمَ فِي
ضَلَالٍ مُّبِينٍ ○

39. But warn them of the Day
Of Distress,[2491] when
The matter will be determined:
For (behold,) they are negligent
And they do not believe!

٣٩- وَأَنذِرْهُمْ يَوْمَ الْحَسْرَةِ إِذْ
قُضِيَ الْأَمْرُ وَهُمْ فِي غَفْلَةٍ وَهُمْ لَا
يُؤْمِنُونَ ○

40. It is We Who will inherit[2492]
The earth, and all beings
Thereon: to Us will they
All be returned.

٤٠- إِنَّا نَحْنُ نَرِثُ الْأَرْضَ وَمَنْ عَلَيْهَا
وَإِلَيْنَا يُرْجَعُونَ ○ ع

C. 140.—Abraham pleaded with loving earnestness
(xix. 41-65.) With his father to accept the truth of God:
He was turned out, but he retained
His gentleness and was blessed. Moses
Asked for the aid of his brother Aaron
And was true to his people. Ismā'īl
Was loyal to his father and his God, and was
A willing and accepted sacrifice to God.

2488. As opposed to the crooked superstitions which take refuge in all sorts of metaphysical sophistries to prove three in one and one in three. In the Qur-ān there is no crookedness (xviii. 1). Christ's teaching was simple, like his life, but the Christians have made it crooked.

2489. *Judgment*: the word in the original is *Mash-had*, which implies many things: (1) the time or place where evidence is taken, as in a Court of Judgment; (2) the time or place where people are produced (to be judged); and (3) the occasion for such production for the taking of evidence. A very expressive phrase for the Day of Judgment.

2490. *Cf.* l. 22, and that whole passage, where the Resurrection is described.

2491. *Ḥasrat*: Sighs, sighing, regrets, distress.

2492. *Cf.* iii. 180, n. 485; xv. 23 n. 1964. Material property passes from one to another: when one dies, another inherits it. God gives life and death, and all that survives after physical death goes back to God, the original source of all things.

Idrīs in his highest station held fast
To truth and integrity. Thus are the righteous
Shown true in their personal environment,
And inherit the Bliss in which the salutation
Is Peace—perfect Peace, the reward of the Constant.

SECTION 3.

41. (Also) mention in the Book
(The story of) Abraham:
He was a man of Truth,
A prophet.

٤١- وَاذْكُرْ فِي الْكِتٰبِ اِبْرٰهِيْمَ ۬ ؕ اِنَّهٗ كَانَ صِدِّيْقًا نَّبِيًّا ○

42. Behold, he said to his father:[2493]
"O my father! why
Worship that which heareth not
And seeth not, and can
Profit thee nothing?

٤٢- اِذْ قَالَ لِاَبِيْهِ يٰۤاَبَتِ لِمَ تَعْبُدُ مَا لَا يَسْمَعُ وَلَا يُبْصِرُ وَلَا يُغْنِيْ عَنْكَ شَيْئًا ○

43. "O my father! to me
Hath come knowledge which
Hath not reached thee:[2494]
So follow me: I will guide
Thee to a Way that
Is even and straight.[2495]

٤٣- يٰۤاَبَتِ اِنِّيْ قَدْ جَآءَنِيْ مِنَ الْعِلْمِ مَا لَمْ يَاْتِكَ فَاتَّبِعْنِيْۤ اَهْدِكَ صِرَاطًا سَوِيًّا ○

44. "O my father! serve not
Satan: for Satan is
A rebel against (God)
Most Gracious.[2496]

٤٤- يٰۤاَبَتِ لَا تَعْبُدِ الشَّيْطٰنَ ؕ اِنَّ الشَّيْطٰنَ كَانَ لِلرَّحْمٰنِ عَصِيًّا ○

45. "O my father! I fear
Lest a Penalty afflict thee[2497]
From (God) Most Gracious,
So that thou become
To Satan a friend."

٤٥- يٰۤاَبَتِ اِنِّيْۤ اَخَافُ اَنْ يَّمَسَّكَ عَذَابٌ مِّنَ الرَّحْمٰنِ فَتَكُوْنَ لِلشَّيْطٰنِ وَلِيًّا ○

2493. The reference to Abraham here is in relation to his tender solicitude for his father, who had not received the light of Unity, and to whom Abraham wanted to be a guide and friend.

2494. Some are more receptive of Light than others. It is their duty and privilege to guide and point to the right Way.

2495. *Sawīyan*—right, smooth, even; complete, perfect; hence the derived meanings: in xix. 10, 'in full possession of all the physical senses'; in that context, 'not dumb': in xix. 17, when the angel appears in the form of a man, 'completely like' a man, a man 'in all respects.'

2496. The rebellion is all the more heinous and inexcusable, considering that God is Most Just, Most Merciful, Most Gracious.

2497. To entertain a feeling of friendliness, instead of aversion, to Evil, is in itself a degradation of our nature, a Penalty which God imposes on our deliberate rejection of the Truth. And the friendliness to Evil also implies the sharing of the outlawry of Evil.

46. (The father) replied: "Dost thou
Hate my gods, O Abraham?
If thou forbear not, I will
Indeed stone thee:
Now get away from me
For a good long while!"[2498]

٤٦- قَالَ أَرَاغِبٌ أَنتَ عَنْ آلِهَتِي
يَا إِبْرَاهِيمُ ۖ لَئِن لَّمْ تَنتَهِ لَأَرْجُمَنَّكَ
وَاهْجُرْنِي مَلِيًّا ۝

47. Abraham said: "Peace be
On thee: I will pray
To my Lord for thy
forgiveness:[2499]
For He is to me
Most Gracious.

٤٧- قَالَ سَلَامٌ عَلَيْكَ ۖ
سَأَسْتَغْفِرُ لَكَ رَبِّي ۖ
إِنَّهُ كَانَ بِي حَفِيًّا ۝

48. "And I will turn away
From you (all) and from those
Whom ye invoke besides God:
I will call on my Lord:
Perhaps, by my prayer to my Lord,
I shall be not unblest."[2500]

٤٨- وَأَعْتَزِلُكُمْ وَمَا تَدْعُونَ
مِن دُونِ اللَّهِ وَأَدْعُو رَبِّي
عَسَىٰ أَلَّا أَكُونَ بِدُعَاءِ رَبِّي شَقِيًّا ۝

49. When he had turned away
From them and from those
Whom they worshipped besides
God, We bestowed on him
Isaac and Jacob, and each one
Of them We made a prophet.[2501]

٤٩- فَلَمَّا اعْتَزَلَهُمْ وَمَا يَعْبُدُونَ مِن دُونِ
اللَّهِ وَهَبْنَا لَهُ إِسْحَاقَ وَيَعْقُوبَ ۖ
وَكُلًّا جَعَلْنَا نَبِيًّا ۝

2498. Note the gentle persuasive tone of Abraham in his speeches in xix. 42-45 (for we may suppose those sentences to sum up a long course of arguments) and in xix. 47-48, contrasted with the brusque and repellent tone of the father's reply in this verse. The one was the outcome of the true Light which had come to Abraham from God, as the other was the outcome of Pagan arrogance and the worship of brute force. The spiritual lesson from this episode of Abraham's life may be stated in four propositions: (1) the pious son is dutiful to his father and wishes him well in all things, material and spiritual; (2) if the father refuses God's Light, the son will do his utmost to bring such Light to the father; (3) having received the Light, the son will never renounce that Light, even if he has to forfeit his father's love and renounce his home; (4) even if the father repels him and turns him out, his answer will be a soft answer, full of love and forgiveness on the one hand, but firmness on behalf of Truth on the other.

2499. *Cf.* ix. 114, where this promise of Abraham to pray for his father is referred to, and its limitations pointed out.

2500. Abraham left his father and the home of his fathers (Ur of the Chaldees) and never returned. He left because he was turned out, and because it was not possible for him to make any compromise with what was false in religion. In return for abuse, he spoke gentle words. And he expressed his fervent hope that at least he (Abraham) would have God's blessing in reply to his prayers. Here was a prefigurement of another Hijrat many centuries later! In both cases the prayer was abundantly fulfilled.

2501. Isaac and Isaac's son Jacob are mentioned here as carrying on one line of Abraham's traditions. The other line was carried on by Ismā'īl, who is mentioned independently five verses lower down, as his line got special honour in the Holy Prophet of Islam. That is why his mention comes after that of Moses *Cf.* xxi. 72.

50. And We bestowed
Of Our Mercy on them,
And We granted them
Lofty honour on the tongue[2502]
Of truth.

٥٠-وَوَهَبْنَا لَهُمْ مِّنْ رَّحْمَتِنَا
وَجَعَلْنَا لَهُمْ لِسَانَ صِدْقٍ عَلِيًّا ۝ ع

SECTION 4.

51. Also mention in the Book
(The story of) Moses:
For he was specially chosen,
And he was an apostle
(And) a prophet.[2503]

٥١-وَاذْكُرْ فِي الْكِتٰبِ مُوسٰى ز
إِنَّهُ كَانَ مُخْلَصًا
وَّكَانَ رَسُولًا نَّبِيًّا ۝

52. And We called him
From the right side[2504]
Of Mount (Sinai), and made
Him draw near to Us,
For mystic (converse).

٥٢-وَنَادَيْنٰهُ مِنْ جَانِبِ الطُّورِ الْأَيْمَنِ
وَقَرَّبْنٰهُ نَجِيًّا ۝

53. And, out of Our Mercy,[2505]
We gave him his brother
Aaron, (also) a prophet.

٥٣-وَوَهَبْنَا لَهُ مِنْ رَّحْمَتِنَا
أَخَاهُ هٰرُونَ نَبِيًّا ۝

2502. Abraham and his son and grandson Isaac and Jacob, and their line, maintained the banner of God's spiritual truth for many generations, and they won deservedly high praise—the praise of truth—on the tongues of men. Abraham prayed that he should be praised by the tongue of truth among men to come in later ages: xxvi. 84. Ordinary praise may mean nothing: it may be due to selfish flattery on the part of others or artful management by the person praised. Praise on the tongue of sincere truth is praise indeed!

2503. Moses was (1) especially chosen, and therefore prepared and instructed in all the wisdom of the Egyptians, in order that he might free his people from Egyptian bondage; there may also be a reference to Mose's title of Kalīmullāh, the one to whom God spoke without the intervention of angels but behind a cloud: see iv. 164, and n 670; (2) he was a prophet (*nabī*), in that he received inspiration; and (3) he was an apostle (*rasūl*) in that he had a Book of Revelation, and an Ummat or organised Community, for which he instituted laws.

2504. The incident here I think refers to the incidents described more fully in xx. 9-36; a reference may also be made to Exod. iii. 1-18 and iv. 1-17. There is a great deal of mystic meaning. The time is when Moses (with his family) was travelling and grazing the flocks of his father-in-law Jethro, just before he got his commission from God. The place is somewhere near Mount Sinai (*Jabal Mūsā*). Moses sees a Fire in the distance, but when he goes there, he hears a voice that tells him it is sacred ground. God asked him to put off his shoes and to draw near, and when he went near, great mysteries were revealed to him. He was given his commission, and his brother Aaron was given to him to go with him and aid him. It is after that that he and Aaron went and faced Pharaoh in Egypt, as narrated in vii. 103-144, etc. The *right side* of the mountain may mean that Moses heard the voice from the right side of the mountain as he faced it; or it may have the figurative meaning of "right" in Arabic, *i.e.*, the side which was blessed or sacred ground.

2505. Moses was diffident, and reluctant to go to Pharaoh as he had an impediment in his tongue, and he asked that his brother Aaron should be associated with him in his mission. God in His Mercy granted his request: xx. 25-36.

54. Also mention in the Book
(The story of) Ismā'īl:
He was (strictly) true
To what he promised,[2506]
And he was an apostle
(And) a prophet.

٥٤- وَاذْكُرْ فِي الْكِتٰبِ إِسْمٰعِيلَ
إِنَّهُ كَانَ صَادِقَ الْوَعْدِ
وَكَانَ رَسُولًا نَّبِيًّا ۝

55. He used to enjoin
On his people Prayer
And Charity, and he was
Most acceptable in the sight
Of his Lord.[2507]

٥٥- وَكَانَ يَأْمُرُ أَهْلَهُ بِالصَّلٰوةِ وَالزَّكٰوةِ
وَكَانَ عِنْدَ رَبِّهِ مَرْضِيًّا ۝

56. Also mention in the Book
The case of Idris:[2508]
He was a man of truth
(And sincerity), (and) a prophet:

٥٦- وَاذْكُرْ فِي الْكِتٰبِ إِدْرِيسَ
إِنَّهُ كَانَ صِدِّيقًا نَّبِيًّا ۝

57. And We raised him
To a lofty station.

٥٧- وَّرَفَعْنٰهُ مَكَانًا عَلِيًّا ۝

58. Those were some
Of the prophets on whom
God did bestow His Grace,—
Of the posterity of Adam,
And of those whom We
Carried (in the Ark)
With Noah, and of
The posterity of Abraham[2509]
And Israel—of those
Whom We guided and chose.

٥٨- أُولٰٓئِكَ الَّذِينَ أَنْعَمَ اللّٰهُ
عَلَيْهِم مِّنَ النَّبِيّٖنَ مِن ذُرِّيَّةِ ءَادَمَ
وَمِمَّنْ حَمَلْنَا مَعَ نُوحٍ
وَّمِن ذُرِّيَّةِ إِبْرٰهِيمَ
وَإِسْرٰٓءِيلَ وَمِمَّنْ هَدَيْنَا وَاجْتَبَيْنَآ

2506. Ismā'īl was *Zabīḥullah, i.e.*, the chosen sacrifice of God in Muslim tradition. When Abraham told him of the sacrifice, he voluntarily offered himself for it, and never flinched from his promise, until the sacrifice was redeemed by the substitution of a ram under God's commands. He was the fountain-head of the Arabian Ummat, and in his posterity came the Apostle of God. The Ummat and the Book of Islam reflect back the apostleship on Ismā'īl.

2507. An acceptable sacrifice: see last note.

2508. Idrīs is mentioned twice in the Qur-ān, *viz.*: here and in xxi 85, where he is mentioned among those who patiently persevered. His identification with the Biblical Enoch, who "walked with God" (Gen. v. 21-24), may or may not be correct. Nor are we justified in interpreting verse 57 here as meaning the same thing as in Gen. v. 24 ("God took him"), that he was taken up without passing through the portals of death. All we are told is that he was a man of truth and sincerity, and a prophet, and that he had a high position among his people. It is this point which brings him in the series of men just mentioned: he kept himself in touch with his people, and was honoured among them. Spiritual progress need not cut us off from our people, for we have to help and guide them. He kept to truth and piety in the highest station.

2509. The earlier generations are grouped into three epochs from a spiritual point of view: (1) from Adam to Noah, (2) from Noah to Abraham, and (3) from Abraham to an indefinite time, say to the time when the Message of God was corrupted and the need arose for the final Apostle of Unity and Truth. Israel is another name for Jacob.

Whenever the Signs
Of (God) Most Gracious
Were rehearsed to them,[2510]
They would fall down
In prostrate adoration
And in tears.

إذا تتلى عليهم
ءايت الرحمن
خروا سجدا وبكيا ○

59. But after them there followed
A posterity who missed
Prayers and followed after lusts
Soon, then, will they
Face Destruction,—[2511]

٥٩- فخلف من بعدهم خلف أضاعوا
الصلوة واتبعوا الشهوت فسوف يلقون
غيا ○

60. Except those who repent
And believe, and work
Righteousness : for these
Will enter the Garden
And will not be wronged
In the least,—

٦٠- إلا من تاب وءامن وعمل
صلحا فأولئك يدخلون الجنة
ولا يظلمون شيئا ○

61. Gardens of Eternity, those
Which (God) Most Gracious
Has promised to His servants
In the Unseen : for His promise
Must (necessarily) come to pass.

٦١- جنت عدن التي وعد الرحمن
عباده بالغيب
إنه كان وعده مأتيا ○

62. They will not there hear
Any vain discourse, but
Only salutations of Peace :[2512]
And they will have therein
Their sustenance,[2513] morning
And evening.

٦٢- لا يسمعون فيها لغوا إلا سلما
ولهم رزقهم فيها
بكرة وعشيا ○

2510. The original is in the Aorist tense, implying that the "Posterity" alluded to includes not only the apostles but their worthy followers who are true to God and uphold His standard.

2511. This selfish godless posterity gains the upper hand at certain times, but even then there is always a minority who see the error of their ways, repent and believe, and live righteous lives. They are not penalised in the Hereafter because they were associated with the ungodly in time. They reap the full reward of their faith and righteousness.

2512. *Salām*, translated "Peace", has a much wider signification. It includes (1) a sense of security and permanence, which is unknown in this life; (2) soundness, freedom from defects, perfection, as in the word *salīm* ; (3) preservation, salvation, deliverance, as in the word *sallama* ; (4) salutation, accord with those around us; (5) resignation, in the sense that we are satisfied and not discontented; besides (6) the ordinary meaning of Peace, *i.e.*, freedom from any jarring element. All these shades of meaning are implied in the word *Islām*. Heaven therefore is the perfection of Islām.

2513. *Sustenance* in the highest metaphorical sense, all the means of perfect satisfaction of the soul and its complete self-expression in the new conditions, which we can only imagine vaguely in our material life. *Morning and evening* : *i.e.*, early and late, all the time, always.

63. Such is the Garden which
We give as an inheritance
To those of Our servants
Who guard against evil.

٦٣- تِلْكَ الْجَنَّةُ الَّتِي نُورِثُ
مِنْ عِبَادِنَا مَنْ كَانَ تَقِيًّا ○

64. (The angels say :)[2514]
"We descend not but
By command of thy Lord :
To Him belongeth what is
Before us and what is
Behind us, and what is
Between : and thy Lord
Never doth forget,—

٦٤- وَمَا نَتَنَزَّلُ إِلَّا بِأَمْرِ رَبِّكَ
لَهُ مَا بَيْنَ أَيْدِينَا وَمَا
خَلْفَنَا وَمَا بَيْنَ ذَٰلِكَ
وَمَا كَانَ رَبُّكَ نَسِيًّا ○

65. "Lord of the heavens
And of the earth,
And of all that is
Between them : so worship Him,
And be constant and patient
In His worship : knowest thou
Of any who is worthy
Of the same Name as He ?"[2515]

٦٥- رَبُّ السَّمٰوٰتِ وَالْأَرْضِ
وَمَا بَيْنَهُمَا فَاعْبُدْهُ
وَاصْطَبِرْ لِعِبَادَتِهِ
هَلْ تَعْلَمُ لَهُ سَمِيًّا ○ ع

C. 141.—Why should man disbelieve in the Hereafter ?
(xix. 66-98.)
We all must pass through the fire of temptation,
But God Most Gracious will save us
If we accept Him and do right. Sin
May have its respite, but must run
To its own destruction. We must not
Dishonour God by holding false
And monstrous ideas of Him. Glory
To Him that He cares for all His creatures !

SECTION 5.

66. Man says : "What!
When I am dead, shall I
Then be raised up alive ?"

٦٦- وَيَقُولُ الْإِنْسَانُ
ءَإِذَا مَا مِتُّ لَسَوْفَ أُخْرَجُ حَيًّا ○

2514. We are apt to be impatient of the evils we see around us. We may give of our best service to God, and yet see no results. In our human short-sightedness we may complain within ourselves. We may address the Spirit of God, as Shelley addressed the Spirit of Poesy, "Rarely, rarely comest thou, Spirit of Delight!" But we must not be impatient. The angels of Grace come not haphazard, but by command of God according to His Universal Will and Purpose. God does not forget. If things are delayed, it is in accordance with a wise providence, which cares for all. Our plain duty is to be patient and constant in His service.

2515. The more we taste of the truth and mystery of life, the more do we realise that there is no one to be mentioned in the same breath as God. He is above all names. But when we think of His beautiful qualities, and picture them to ourselves by names which give us some idea of Him, we can search the whole wide world of our imagination, and we shall not find another to be compared with Him in name or quality. He is the One : praise be to Him!

67. But does not man
Call to mind that We
Created him before
Out of nothing?

٦٧- اَوَلَا يَذْكُرُ الْاِنْسَانُ اَنَّا
خَلَقْنٰهُ مِنْ قَبْلُ وَلَمْ يَكُ شَيْئًا ۝

68. So, by thy Lord,
Without doubt, We shall gather
Them together, and (also)
The Evil Ones (with them); [2516]
Then shall We bring them
Forth on their knees
Round about Hell; [2517]

٦٨- فَوَرَبِّكَ لَنَحْشُرَنَّهُمْ
وَالشَّيٰطِيْنَ ثُمَّ لَنُحْضِرَنَّهُمْ
حَوْلَ جَهَنَّمَ جِثِيًّا ۝

69. Then shall We certainly
Drag out from every sect
All those who were worst
In obstinate rebellion
Against (God) Most Gracious.

٦٩- ثُمَّ لَنَنْزِعَنَّ مِنْ كُلِّ شِيْعَةٍ
اَيُّهُمْ اَشَدُّ عَلَى الرَّحْمٰنِ عِتِيًّا ۝

70. And certainly We know best
Those who are most worthy
Of being burned therein.

٧٠- ثُمَّ لَنَحْنُ اَعْلَمُ بِالَّذِيْنَ
هُمْ اَوْلٰى بِهَا صِلِيًّا ۝

71. Not one of you but will [2518]
Pass over it: this is,
With thy Lord, a Decree
Which must be accomplished.

٧١- وَاِنْ مِّنْكُمْ اِلَّا وَارِدُهَا
كَانَ عَلٰى رَبِّكَ حَتْمًا مَّقْضِيًّا ۝

72. But We shall save those
Who guarded against evil,
And We shall leave
The wrong-doers therein,
(Humbled) to their knees.

٧٢- ثُمَّ نُنَجِّي الَّذِيْنَ اتَّقَوْا
وَّنَذَرُ الظّٰلِمِيْنَ فِيْهَا جِثِيًّا ۝

2516. The disbelief in a future state is not merely a philosophic doubt, but a warped will, a disingenuous obstinacy in face of our inner spiritual instincts and experiences. We were nothing before. Cannot the same God Who created us out of nothing also continue our personality? But if we refuse to accept His light and guidance, our state will grow worse and worse. We shall be deprived of His grace. We shall be herded with the Evil Ones. In utter humiliation we shall be faced with all the consequences of our refusal of Truth.

2517. *Round about Hell*: There are many ways leading to evil, and people get to it from all round. Hence the allegory of the seven Gates to Hell; see xv. 44, and n. 1977.

2518. Three interpretations are possible. (1) The general interpretation is that every soul must pass through or by or over the Fire. It may be the fire of temptation or anxiety or distress; but they must see Hell. Those who have had Taqwā (see n. 26 to ii. 2) will be saved by God's Mercy, while unrepentant sinners will suffer the torments in ignominy. (2) If we refer the pronoun "you" to those "in obstinate rebellion" in verse 69 above, both leaders and followers in sin, this verse only applies to the wicked. (3) Some refer this verse to the Bridge over Hell, the Bridge *Ṣirāṭ*, over which all must pass to their final Destiny. This Bridge s not mentioned in the Qur-ān.

73. When Our Clear Signs
Are rehearsed to them,
The Unbelievers say to those
Who believe, "Which of the two
Sides is best in point of
Position? which makes the best
Show in Council?"[2519]

٧٣- وَإِذَا تُتْلَىٰ عَلَيْهِمْ آيٰتُنَا بَيِّنٰتٍ
قَالَ الَّذِينَ كَفَرُوا لِلَّذِينَ آمَنُوٓا أَيُّ
الْفَرِيقَيْنِ خَيْرٌ مَّقَامًا وَّأَحْسَنُ
نَدِيًّا ۝

74. But how many (countless)
Generations before them
Have We destroyed,
Who were even better
In equipment and in glitter
To the eye?

٧٤- وَكَمْ أَهْلَكْنَا قَبْلَهُمْ
مِّنْ قَرْنٍ هُمْ أَحْسَنُ
أَثَاثًا وَّرِءْيًا ۝

75. Say: "If any men go
Astray, (God) Most Gracious
Extends (the rope) to them,
Until, when they see
The warning of God (being
Fulfilled)—either in punishment[2520]
Or in (the approach of)
The Hour,—they will
At length realise who is
Worst in position, and (who)
Weakest in forces!

٧٥- قُلْ مَنْ كَانَ فِي الضَّلٰلَةِ
فَلْيَمْدُدْ لَهُ الرَّحْمٰنُ مَدًّا ۚ
حَتّٰىٓ إِذَا رَأَوْا مَا يُوعَدُونَ إِمَّا الْعَذَابَ
وَإِمَّا السَّاعَةَ ۖ
فَسَيَعْلَمُونَ مَنْ هُوَ
شَرٌّ مَّكَانًا وَّأَضْعَفُ جُنْدًا ۝

76. "And God doth advance
In guidance those who seek
Guidance: and the things
That endure, Good Deeds,[2521]
Are best in the sight
Of thy Lord, as rewards,
And best in respect of
(Their) eventual returns."

٧٦- وَيَزِيدُ اللّٰهُ الَّذِينَ اهْتَدَوْا هُدًى ۗ
وَالْبٰقِيٰتُ الصّٰلِحٰتُ
خَيْرٌ عِنْدَ رَبِّكَ ثَوَابًا
وَّخَيْرٌ مَّرَدًّا ۝

2519. The Unbelievers may, for a time, make a better show in worldly position, or in people's assemblages where things are judged by the counting of heads. But Truth must prevail even in this world, and ultimately the positions must be reversed.

2520. God's warning is that every evil deed must have its punishment, and that there will be a Hereafter, the Day of Judgment, or the Hour, as it is frequently called. The punishment of evil often begins in this very life. For instance, over-indulgence and excesses of all kinds bring on their Nemesis quite soon in this very life. But some subtler forms of selfishness and sin will be punished—as every evil will be punished—in its own good time, as the Hour approaches. In either case, the arrogant boasting sinners will realise that their taunt—who is best in position and in forces? (xix. 73)—is turned against themselves.

2521. These lines are the same as in xviii. 46 (second clause), (where see n. 2387), except that the word *maradd* (eventual returns) is here substituted for *amal* (hope). The meaning is practically the same: but "hope" is more appropriate in the passage dealing generally with this world's goods, and "eventual returns" in the passage dealing with the sinner's specific investments and commitments in worldly position and organised cliques.

77. Hast thou then seen The (sort of) man who Rejects Our Signs, yet Says: "I shall certainly Be given wealth and children?"[2522]	٧٧- أَفَرَءَيْتَ ٱلَّذِى كَفَرَ بِـَٔايَـٰتِنَا وَقَالَ لَأُوتَيَنَّ مَالًا وَوَلَدًا ۝
78. Has he penetrated to The Unseen, or has he Taken a contract with (God) Most Gracious?	٧٨- أَطَّلَعَ ٱلْغَيْبَ أَمِ ٱتَّخَذَ عِندَ ٱلرَّحْمَـٰنِ عَهْدًا ۝
79. Nay! We shall record What he says, and We Shall add and add To his punishment.[2523]	٧٩- كَلَّا ۚ سَنَكْتُبُ مَا يَقُولُ وَ نَمُدُّ لَهُۥ مِنَ ٱلْعَذَابِ مَدًّا ۝
80. To Us shall return[2524] All that he talks of, And he shall appear Before Us bare and alone.	٨٠- وَنَرِثُهُۥ مَا يَقُولُ وَيَأْتِينَا فَرْدًا ۝
81. And they have taken (For worship) gods other than God, to give them Power and glory![2525]	٨١- وَٱتَّخَذُوا۟ مِن دُونِ ٱللَّهِ ءَالِهَةً لِّيَكُونُوا۟ لَهُمْ عِزًّا ۝
82. Instead, they shall reject Their worship, and become Adversaries against them.[2526]	٨٢- كَلَّا ۚ سَيَكْفُرُونَ بِعِبَادَتِهِمْ وَيَكُونُونَ عَلَيْهِمْ ضِدًّا ۝ ع

2522. Besides the man who boasts of wealth and power in actual possession, there is a type of man who boasts of getting them in the future and builds his worldly hopes thereon. Is he sure? He denies God, and His goodness and Mercy. But all good is in the hands of God. Can such a man then bind God to bless him when he rejects faith in God? Or does he pretend that he has penetrated to the mysteries of the future? For no man can tell what the future holds for him.

2523. Such a man deserves double punishment,—for rejecting God, and for his blasphemies with His holy name.

2524. Literally, "We shall inherit" *Cf.* xix. 40, and n. 2492. Even if the man had property and power, it must go back to the Source of all things, and the man must appear before the Judgment-seat, alone and unaccompanied, stripped of all the things from which he expected so much!

2525. *'Izz*=exalted rank, glory, power, might, the ability to impose one's will or to carry out one's will.

2526. *Cf.* x. 28-30, where the idols deny that they knew anything of their worship, and leave their worshippers in the lurch; and v. 119, where Jesus denies that he asked for worship, and leaves his false worshippers to the punishment or the mercy of God.

Section 6.

83. Seest thou not that We
Have set the Evil Ones on
Against the Unbelievers,
To incite them with fury ?[2527]

٨٣- أَلَمْ تَرَ أَنَّآ أَرْسَلْنَا الشَّيٰطِينَ
عَلَى الْكٰفِرِينَ تَؤُزُّهُمْ أَزًّا ۝

84. So make no haste
Against them, for We
But count out to them
A (limited) number (of days).

٨٤- فَلَا تَعْجَلْ عَلَيْهِمْ ۖ
إِنَّمَا نَعُدُّ لَهُمْ عَدًّا ۝

85. The day We shall gather
The righteous to (God)
Most Gracious, like a band
Presented before a king for honours,

٨٥- يَوْمَ نَحْشُرُ الْمُتَّقِينَ
إِلَى الرَّحْمٰنِ وَفْدًا ۝

86. And We shall drive
The sinners to hell,
Like thirsty cattle
Driven down to water,—[2528]

٨٦- وَّنَسُوقُ الْمُجْرِمِينَ إِلٰى جَهَنَّمَ
وِرْدًا ۝

87. None shall have the power
Of intercession, but such a one
As has received permission
(or promise)
From (God) Most Gracious.

٨٧- لَا يَمْلِكُونَ الشَّفٰعَةَ إِلَّا مَنِ
اتَّخَذَ عِنْدَ الرَّحْمٰنِ عَهْدًا ۝

88. They say: "(God) Most
Gracious
Has begotten a son!"

٨٨- وَقَالُوا اتَّخَذَ الرَّحْمٰنُ وَلَدًا ۝

89. Indeed ye have put forth
A thing most monstrous![2529]

٨٩- لَقَدْ جِئْتُمْ شَيْـًٔا إِدًّا ۝

2527. Under the laws instituted by God, when evil reaches a certain stage of rebellion and defiance, it is left to gather momentum and to rush with fury to its own destruction. It is given a certain amount of respite, as a last chance; but failing repentance, its days are numbered. The godly therefore should not worry themselves over the apparent worldly success of evil, but should get on with their own duties in a spirit of trust in God.

2528. Note the contrast between the saved and the doomed. The one march with dignity like honoured ones before a king, and the other rush in anguish to their punishment like a herd of cattle driven down by thirst to their watering place. Note the metaphor of the water. They rush madly for water but are plunged into the Fire!

2529. The belief in God begetting a son is not a question merely of words or of speculative thought. It is a stupendous blasphemy against God. It lowers God to the level of an animal. If combined with the doctrine of vicarious atonement, it amounts to a negation of God's justice and man's personal responsibility. It is destructive of all moral and spiritual order, and is condemned in the strongest possible terms.

90. At it the skies are ready
To burst, the earth
To split asunder, and
The mountains to fall down
In utter ruin,

٩٠- تَكَادُ السَّمٰوٰتُ يَتَفَطَّرْنَ مِنْهُ
وَتَنْشَقُّ الْاَرْضُ
وَتَخِرُّ الْجِبَالُ هَدًّا ۝

91. That they should invoke
A son for (God) Most Gracious.

٩١- اَنْ دَعَوْا لِلرَّحْمٰنِ وَلَدًا ۝

92. For it is not consonant
With the majesty of (God)
Most Gracious that He
Should beget a son.[2530]

٩٢- وَمَا يَنْۢبَغِيْ لِلرَّحْمٰنِ
اَنْ يَّتَّخِذَ وَلَدًا ۝

93. Not one of the beings
In the heavens and the earth
But must come to (God)
Most Gracious as a servant.

٩٣- اِنْ كُلُّ مَنْ فِي السَّمٰوٰتِ وَالْاَرْضِ
اِلَّآ اٰتِي الرَّحْمٰنِ عَبْدًا ۝

94. He does take an account
Of them (all), and hath
Numbered them (all) exactly.[2531]

٩٤- لَقَدْ اَحْصٰىهُمْ وَعَدَّهُمْ عَدًّا ۝

95. And everyone of them
Will come to Him singly
On the Day of Judgment.

٩٥- وَكُلُّهُمْ اٰتِيْهِ يَوْمَ الْقِيٰمَةِ فَرْدًا ۝

96. On those who believe
And work deeds of righteousness,
Will (God) Most Gracious
Bestow Love.[2532]

٩٦- اِنَّ الَّذِيْنَ اٰمَنُوْا وَعَمِلُوا الصّٰلِحٰتِ
سَيَجْعَلُ لَهُمُ الرَّحْمٰنُ وُدًّا ۝

97. So have We made
The (Qur-ān) easy
In thine own tongue,
That with it thou mayest give

٩٧- فَاِنَّمَا يَسَّرْنٰهُ بِلِسَانِكَ

2530. This basic principle was laid down early in the argument (xix. 35). It was illustrated by a reference to the personal history of many apostles, including Jesus himself, who behaved justly as men to their kith and kin and humbly served God. The evil results of such superstitions were pointed out in the case of many previous generations which went to their ruin by dishonouring God. And the argument is now rounded off towards the close of the Sūra.

2531. God has no sons or favourites or parasites, such as we associate with human beings. On the other hand every creature of His gets His love, and His cherishing care. Everyone of them, however humble, is individually marked before His Throne of Justice and Mercy, and will stand before Him on his own deserts.

2532. His own love, and the love of man's fellow-creatures, in this world and in the Hereafter. Goodness breeds love and peace, and sin breeds hatred and contention.

Glad tidings to the righteous,
And warnings to people
Given to contention.

لِتُبَشِّرَ بِهِ الْمُتَّقِينَ وَتُنْذِرَ بِهِ قَوْمًا لُّدًّا ○

98. But how many (countless)
Generations before them [2533]
Have We destroyed? Canst thou
Find a single one of them
(Now) or hear (so much
As) a whisper of them?

٩٨- وَكَمْ أَهْلَكْنَا قَبْلَهُمْ مِّنْ قَرْنٍ ۖ هَلْ تُحِسُّ مِنْهُمْ مِّنْ أَحَدٍ أَوْ تَسْمَعُ لَهُمْ رِكْزًا ○

2533. *Cf.* xix 74, from which this sentence is brought up as a reminiscence, showing the progress of sin, the Guidance which God gives to the good, the degradation of blasphemy, the respite granted, and the final End, when personal responsibility will be enforced.

INTRODUCTION TO SŪRA XX. (*Ṭā Hā*).

The chronology of this Sūra has some significance: it has some relation to the spiritual lessons which it teaches.

It was used with great effect in that remarkable scene which resulted in Ḥadhrat 'Umar's conversion, and which took place about the seventh year before the Hijrat.

The scene is described with dramatic details by Ibn Hishām. 'Umar had previously been one of the greatest enemies and persecutors of Islam. Like his blood-thirsty kinsmen the Quraish, he meditated slaying the Prophet, when it was suggested to him that there were near relations of his that had embraced Islam. His sister Fāṭima and her husband Sa'īd were Muslims, but in those days of persecution they had kept their faith secret. When 'Umar went to their house, he heard them reciting this Sūra from a written copy they had. For a while they concealed the copy. 'Umar attacked his sister and her husband, but they bore the attack with exemplary patience, and declared their faith. 'Umar was so struck with their sincerity and fortitude that he asked to see the leaf from which they had been reading. It was given to him: his soul was touched, and he not only came into the Faith but became one of its strongest supporters and champions.

The leaf contained some portion of this Sūra, perhaps the introductory portion. The mystic letters *Ṭā Hā* are prefixed to this Sūra. What do they mean? The earliest tradition is that they denote a dialectical interjection meaning "O man!" If so, the title is particularly appropriate in two ways. (1) It was a direct and personal address to a man in a high state of excitement, tempted by his temper to do grievous wrong, but called by God's Grace, as by a personal appeal, to face the realities, for God knew his inmost secret thoughts (xx. 7): the revelation was sent by God Most Gracious, out of His Grace and Mercy (xx. 5). (2) It takes up the story from the last Sūra, of man as a spiritual being and illustrates it in further details. It tells the story of Moses in the crisis of his life when he received God's Commission and in his personal relations with his mother, and how he came to be brought up in the Pharaoh's house, to learn all the wisdom of the Egyptians, for use in God's service, and in his personal relations with Pharaoh, whom we take to be his adoptive father (xxviii. 9). It further tells the story of a fallen soul who misled the Isrāelites into idolatry, and recalls how man's Arch-enemy Satan caused his fall. Prayer and praise are necessary to man to cure his spiritual blindness and enable him to appreciate God's revelation.

Summary.—The revelation of God (the Qur-ān) is not an occasion of distress, but is a gift of mercy from God Most Gracious (xx. 1-8, and C. 142).

How Moses was first chosen, and led to his mission to Pharaoh with his brother Aaron (xx. 9-36, and C. 143).

How the mother of Moses was directed to cast the infant Moses into the river, to be brought up in Pharaoh's house under God's own supervision, in order to preach to Pharaoh and declare God's glory (xx. 37-76, and C. 144).

How Moses was directed to lead his people and quell their rebellious spirit, and how that spirit was stirred up by Sāmirī (xx. 77-104, and C. 145).

On the Day of Judgment personal responsibility will be enforced, and God's Truth acknowledged: man should guard against Adam's enemy, Satan, and should renounce vanities, purify himself with prayer and praise, and await the call to God (xx. 105-135, and C. 146).

C. 142—God's revelation is not an occasion
(xx. 1-8.) For man's distress: it is a Message
To show that God All-Knowing sits
On the throne of Mercy and guides all affairs.
There is no god but He: to Him
Belong all the most beautiful Names.

Sūra XX.

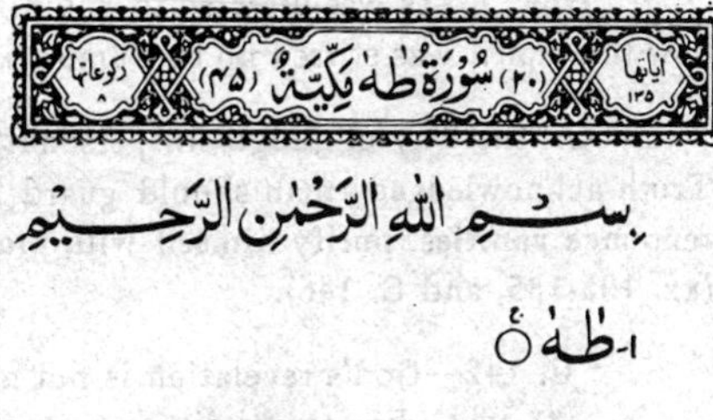

Ṭā-Hā. (Mystic Letters, Ṭ. H.)[2534]

In the name of God, Most Gracious, Most Merciful.

بِسْمِ اللّٰهِ الرَّحْمٰنِ الرَّحِيْمِ

1. *Ṭā-Hā.*[2534]

١- طٰهٰ ۚ

2. We have not sent down
The Qur-ān to thee to be
(An occasion) for thy distress,[2535]

٢- مَآ اَنْزَلْنَا عَلَيْكَ الْقُرْاٰنَ لِتَشْقٰٓى ۙ

3. But only as an admonition
To those who fear (God),—

٣- اِلَّا تَذْكِرَةً لِّمَنْ يَّخْشٰى ۙ

4. A revelation from Him
Who created the earth
And the heavens on high.

٤- تَنْزِيْلًا مِّمَّنْ خَلَقَ الْاَرْضَ
وَالسَّمٰوٰتِ الْعُلٰى ۗ

5. (God) Most Gracious[2536]
Is firmly established
On the throne (of authority).

٥- اَلرَّحْمٰنُ عَلَى الْعَرْشِ اسْتَوٰى

6. To Him belongs what is
In the heavens and on earth,
And all between them,
And all beneath the soil.[2537]

٦- لَهٗ مَا فِى السَّمٰوٰتِ وَمَا فِى الْاَرْضِ
وَمَا بَيْنَهُمَا وَمَا تَحْتَ الثَّرٰى

7. If thou pronounce the word
Aloud, (it is no matter):

٧- وَاِنْ تَجْهَرْ بِالْقَوْلِ فَاِنَّهٗ

2534. For an explanation see the Introduction to this Sūra. If the meaning is "O man!", that is itself a mystic meaning, as explained, but the letters form a word and would not be classified strictly as Abbreviated Letters: see n. 25 to ii. 1. This, however, is a question of classification and does not affect the meaning. That is conjectural, and no one can be dogmatic about it.

2535. God's revelation may cause some human trouble for two reasons: (1) it checks man's selfishness and narrowness of view, and (2) it annoys the wicked and causes them to jeer and persecute. These are mere incidental things, due to man's own shortcomings. As far as the trouble is concerned, the revelation is meant to give a warning, so that persecutors may be reclaimed, (and of course for men of faith it is a comfort and consolation, though that point does not arise in this context).

2536. *Cf.* x. 3 n. 1386. If things seem to be wrong in our imperfect vision on this earth, we must remember that God, Who encompasses all Creation and sits on the throne of Grace and Mercy, is in command, and our Faith tells us that all must be right. God's authority is not like an authority on earth, which may be questioned, or which may not last. His authority is "firmly established".

2537. An exhaustive definition of everything we can conceive of—what is in the heavens, on the earth, or between, or within the bowels of the earth.

For verily He knoweth
What is secret and what
Is yet more hidden.[2538]

يَعْلَمُ السِّرَّ وَأَخْفَى ۝

8. God! there is no god
But He! To Him belong
The Most Beautiful Names.[2539]

٨- اَللّٰهُ لَآ إِلٰهَ إِلَّا هُوَ ۚ
لَهُ الْأَسْمَآءُ الْحُسْنٰى ۝

C. 143.—The story of how Moses was chosen and told
(xx. 9-36.) Of his mission, has a high mystic meaning.
He was true to his family and solicitous
For their welfare. Encamped in the desert,
He saw a fire far off. Approaching,
He found it was holy ground. God
Did reveal Himself to him, so
That he saw life in things lifeless,
And light in his glorified Hand, that shone
White with light divine. Armed
With these Signs he was told to go forth
On his mission. But he thought of his brother
Aaron, and prayed that God might join him
In his mission, and his prayer was granted.

9. Has the story of Moses[2540]
Reached thee?

٩- وَهَلْ أَتٰىكَ حَدِيثُ مُوسٰى ۝

10. Behold, he saw a fire:[2541]
So he said to his family,

١٠- إِذْ رَاٰ نَارًا فَقَالَ لِأَهْلِهِ

2538. There are two or three implications. (1) Whatever you profess, or say aloud, gives no information to God: He knows not only what is secret and perhaps unknown to others, but what people take special care to conceal. (2) It does you no good to make insincere professions: your hidden motives are known to Him, Who alone matters. (3) If you read the Word of God, or if you pray to God, it is not necessary to raise your voice: in either case, God will judge you by your inner thoughts which are like an open book to Him.

2539. *Cf.* xvii. 110 and n. 2322. God is all in all, but the most beautiful things we can think of are referable to Him. A great deal is made, in our mystic philosophy, of the word "Name", which sums up attributes, and is almost equivalent to a Title of Honour.

2540. The story of Moses in its different incidents is told in many places in the Qur-ān, and in each case the phase most appropriate in the context is referred to or emphasised. In ii. 49-61, it was a phase from the religious history of mankind; in vii. 103-162, it was a phase from the story of the Ummat (or nation) of Israel, and the story was continued to the times after Moses; in xvii. 101-103, we have a picture of the decline of a soul in the arrogance of Pharaoh; here, in **xx.** 9-24, we have a picture of the rise of a soul in the commission given to Moses from God; in **xx.** 25-36, we have his spiritual relationship with his brother Aaron; in **xx.** 37-40, we have his spiritual relation with his mother and sister, and his upbringing; in **xx.** 41-76, we have his spiritual combat with Pharaoh; and in **xx.** 77-98, we have his spiritual combat with his own people, the Israelites. For other incidents, consult the Index.

2541. *A fire*: It appeared like an ordinary fire, which always betokens the presence of men in a desert or a lonely place. Moses made for it alone, to fetch the wherewithal for making a fire for his family, and perhaps to find some direction as to the way, from the people he should meet there. But it was not an ordinary fire. It was a Burning Bush: a Sign of the Glory of God.

"Tarry ye; I perceive
A fire; perhaps I can
Bring you some burning brand
Therefrom, or find some guidance
At the fire."[2542]

امكثوا إني آنست نارا
لعلي آتيكم منها بقبس
أو أجد على النار هدى ۝

11. But when he came
To the fire, a voice
Was heard: "O Moses!

١١- فلما أتاها نودي يموسى ۝

12. "Verily I am thy Lord!
Therefore (in My presence)[2543]
Put off thy shoes: thou art
In the sacred valley Ṭuwā.[2544]

١٢- إني أنا ربك فاخلع نعليك إنك
بالواد المقدس طوى ۝

13. "I have chosen thee:
Listen, then, to the inspiration
(Sent to thee).

١٣- وأنا اخترتك
فاستمع لما يوحى ۝

14. "Verily, I am God:
There is no god but I:
So serve thou Me (only),
And establish regular prayer
For celebrating My praise.

١٤- إنني أنا الله لا إله إلا
أنا فاعبدني
وأقم الصلوة لذكري ۝

15. "Verily the Hour is coming—[2545]
My design is to keep it

١٥- إن الساعة آتية أكاد

2542. The spiritual history of Moses begins here. It was his spiritual birth. His physical life, infancy, and upbringing are referred to later on, to illustrate another point. Moses, when he grew up, left the palace of Pharaoh and went to the Midianite people, in the Sinai peninsula. He married among them, and was now travelling with his family and his flocks, when he was called to his mission by God. He went to look for a fire for comfort and guidance. He found a higher and holier comfort and guidance. The whole passage is full of the highest mystic meaning, which is reflected in the short rhymed verses in the original. Both the rhythm and the meaning suggest the highest mystery.

2453. The shoes are to be put off as a mark of respect. In the parallel mystic meaning, Moses was now to put away his mere worldly interests, and anything of mere worldly utility, he having been chosen by the Most High God.

2544. This was the valley just below Mount Sinai, where subsequently he was to receive the Law. In the parallel mystic meaning, we are selected by trials in this humble life, whose valley is just as sacred and receives God's glory just as much as the heights of the Mount (*Ṭūr*) if we but have the insight to perceive it.

2545. The first need is to mend our lives and worship and serve God, as in the last verse. The next is to realise the meaning of the Hereafter, when every soul will get the meed of its conduct in this life.

Hidden—[2546] for every soul To receive its reward By the measure of Its Endeavour.	أُخۡفِيهَا لِتُجۡزَىٰ كُلُّ نَفۡسِۭ بِمَا تَسۡعَىٰ ۝
16. "Therefore let not such as Believe not therein But follow their own Lusts, divert thee therefrom,[2547] Lest thou perish!"...	١٦- فَلَا يَصُدَّنَّكَ عَنۡهَا مَن لَّا يُؤۡمِنُ بِهَا وَٱتَّبَعَ هَوَىٰهُ فَتَرۡدَىٰ ۝
17. "And what is that In thy right hand, O Moses?"	١٧- وَمَا تِلۡكَ بِيَمِينِكَ يَٰمُوسَىٰ ۝
18. He said, "It is[2548] My rod: on it I lean; with it I beat down fodder For my flocks; and In it I find Other uses."	١٨- قَالَ هِيَ عَصَايَ أَتَوَكَّؤُاْ عَلَيۡهَا وَأَهُشُّ بِهَا عَلَىٰ غَنَمِي وَلِيَ فِيهَا مَـَٔارِبُ أُخۡرَىٰ ۝
19. (God) said, "Throw it, O Moses!"	١٩- قَالَ أَلۡقِهَا يَٰمُوسَىٰ ۝
20. He threw it, and behold! It was a snake, Active in motion.[2549]	٢٠- فَأَلۡقَىٰهَا فَإِذَا هِيَ حَيَّةٞ تَسۡعَىٰ ۝

2546. *Ukhfī* may mean either "keep it hidden", or "make it manifest", and the Commentators have taken, some one meaning and some the other. If the first is taken, it means that the exact hour or day when the Judgment comes is hidden from man; if the second, it means that the fact of the Judgment to come is made known, that man may remember and take warning. I think that both meanings are implied, as is the case in mystic interpretation.

2547. Moses had yet to meet the formidable opposition of the arrogant Pharaoh and his proud Egyptians, and latter, the rebellion of his own people. In receiving his commission, he is warned of both dangers. The mystic meaning relates to man's own soul: when once the light reaches him let him hold fast to it, lest he perish. He will be beset with dangers of all kinds around him: the worst will be the danger of unbelieving people who seem to thrive on their selfishness and in following their own vain desires!

2548. Now comes the miracle of the rod. The rod itself has a manifold mystic meaning. First of all, the attention of Moses himself is drawn to it, and he thinks of the ordinary uses to which he puts it in his daily life.

2549. *Cf.* vii. 107, where a different word (*thu'bān* is used for "snake", and the qualifying adjective is "plain (for all to see)". The scene there is before Pharaoh and his magicians and people: the object is to show the hollowness of their magic by a miracle: the rod appears before them as a long and creeping, writhing serpent. Here there is a symbol to present God's Mystery to Moses's mind and understanding: the rod becomes a *Ḥaiy* (a *live* snake), and its *active* motion is what is most to be impressed on the mind of Moses, for there were no other spectators. So the highest spiritual mysteries can be grasped, with God's gift of insight, from the most ordinary things of daily use. Once they are grasped, there is no question of fear. They really are the virtues of this life lifted up to the glorious spiritual plane.

21. (God) said, " Seize it,
And fear not : We
Shall return it at once
To its former condition "...

٢١-قَالَ خُذْهَا وَلَا تَخَفْ ۖ
سَنُعِيدُهَا سِيرَتَهَا الْأُولَىٰ ○

22. " Now draw thy hand [2550]
Close to thy side :
It shall come forth white
(And shining), without harm
(Or stain),—as another Sign,—

٢٢-وَاضْمُمْ يَدَكَ إِلَىٰ جَنَاحِكَ تَخْرُجْ
بَيْضَاءَ مِنْ غَيْرِ سُوءٍ آيَةً أُخْرَىٰ ○

23. " In order that We
May show thee
(Two) of our Greater Signs.

٢٣-لِنُرِيَكَ مِنْ آيَاتِنَا الْكُبْرَى ○

24. " Go thou to Pharaoh, [2551]
For he has indeed
Transgressed all bounds."

٢٤-اذْهَبْ إِلَىٰ فِرْعَوْنَ إِنَّهُ طَغَىٰ ○ ع

SECTION 2.

25. (Moses) said : " O my Lord !
Expand me my breast ; [2552]

٢٥-قَالَ رَبِّ اشْرَحْ لِي صَدْرِي ○

26. " Ease my task for me ;

٢٦-وَيَسِّرْ لِي أَمْرِي ○

27. " And remove the impediment [2553]
From my speech,

٢٧-وَاحْلُلْ عُقْدَةً مِنْ لِسَانِي ○

28. " So they may understand
What I say :

٢٨-يَفْقَهُوا قَوْلِي ○

2550. The second of the greater Miracles shown to Moses was the " White (shining) Hand". Ordinarily, when the skin becomes white, it is a sign of disease, leprosy or something loathsome. Here there was no question of disease : on the contrary, the hand was glorified, and it shone as with a divine light. Such a miracle was beyond Egyptian or human magic. So, the instruments of our activity in daily life may be sanctified by being pressed close to that side of us which is spiritual : then they become bright and shining instruments for the carrying out of the divine Will. Or perhaps pressing the hand close to the side may be a metaphor for casting off fear : a bird when agitated shakes its wings about, but presses them close to its body when it sits composed. *Cf.* xxviii. 32.

2551. Moses, having been spiritually prepared now gets his definite commission to go to Pharaoh and point out the error of his ways. So inordinate was Pharaoh's vanity that he had it in his mind to say : " I am your Lord Most High ! " (lxxix. 24).

2552. The breast is reputed to be the seat of knowledge and affections. The gift of the highest spiritual insight is what he prays for first. *Cf.* xciv. 1. This was the most urgent in point of time There are three other things he also asks for : *viz.* (1) God's help in his task, which at first appears difficult to him ; (2) the gift of eloquence, and the removal of the impediment from his speech ; and (3) the counsel and constant attendance with him of his brother Aaron, whom he loved and trusted, for he would otherwise be alone among the Egyptians.

2553. Literally, " Loosen a knot from my tongue ".

29. "And give me a Minister
From my family,

٢٩- وَاجْعَلْ لِّيْ وَزِيْرًا مِّنْ اَهْلِيْ ○

30. "Aaron, my brother;

٣٠- هٰرُوْنَ اَخِي ○

31. "Add to my strength[2554]
Through him,

٣١- اشْدُدْ بِهٖٓ اَزْرِيْ ○

32. "And make him share
My task:

٣٢- وَاَشْرِكْهُ فِيْٓ اَمْرِيْ ○

33. "That we may celebrate[2555]
Thy praise without stint,

٣٣- كَيْ نُسَبِّحَكَ كَثِيْرًا ○

34. "And remember Thee
Without stint:

٣٤- وَّنَذْكُرَكَ كَثِيْرًا ○

35. "For Thou art He
That (ever) regardeth us."[2556]

٣٥- اِنَّكَ كُنْتَ بِنَا بَصِيْرًا ○

36. (God) said: "Granted
Is thy prayer, O Moses!"

٣٦- قَالَ قَدْ اُوْتِيْتَ سُؤْلَكَ يٰمُوْسٰى ○

C. 144.—From his birth was Moses prepared for his task.
(xx. 37-76.) His mother received guidance, so that
God's purpose might be fulfilled. Moses
Was brought up in Pharaoh's palace and trained
In all the learning of Egypt. Yet he drank
The love of his people in his mother's milk.
Adventures and trials he had, including
His stay with the Midianites—until
He was called to his double mission: to preach
To Pharaoh and the Egyptians, and to free
His own people. So he and Aaron went
To Pharaoh, who rejected God and His Signs,
But appointed a trial of strength between
His magicians and Moses. Moses won;
And the Truth of God was accepted
By some Egyptians, but not by Pharaoh.

2554. Literally, "Strengthen my back with him". A man's strength lies in his back and backbone so that he can stand erect and boldly face his tasks.

2555. The requests that Moses makes are inspired, not by earthly but by spiritual motives. The motive, expressed in the most general terms, is to glorify God, not in an occasional way, but systematically and continuously, "without stint." The clauses in this verse and the next, taken together, govern all the requests he makes, from verse 25 to verse 32.

2556. The celebration of God's praise and remembrance is one form of showing gratitude on the part of Moses for the Grace which God has bestowed upon him.

37. " And indeed We conferred A favour on thee Another time (before).	٣٧-وَلَقَدْ مَنَنَّا عَلَيْكَ مَرَّةً أُخْرَىٰ ۝
38. " Behold! We sent[2557] To thy mother, by inspiration, The message:	٣٨-إِذْ أَوْحَيْنَا إِلَىٰ أُمِّكَ مَا يُوحَىٰ ۝
39. " ' Throw (the child) Into the chest, and throw (The chest) into the river: The river will cast him Up on the bank, and he Will be taken up by one Who is an enemy to Me And an enemy to him ':[2558] But I cast (the garment Of) love over thee from Me:[2559] And (this) in order that Thou mayest be reared Under Mine eye.[2560]	٣٩-أَنِ اقْذِفِيهِ فِي التَّابُوتِ فَاقْذِفِيهِ فِي الْيَمِّ فَلْيُلْقِهِ الْيَمُّ بِالسَّاحِلِ يَأْخُذْهُ عَدُوٌّ لِّي وَعَدُوٌّ لَّهُ ۚ وَأَلْقَيْتُ عَلَيْكَ مَحَبَّةً مِّنِّي ۚ وَلِتُصْنَعَ عَلَىٰ عَيْنِي ۝
40. " Behold! thy sister goeth forth And saith, ' Shall I show you	٤٠-إِذْ تَمْشِي أُخْتُكَ فَتَقُولُ هَلْ أَدُلُّكُمْ

2557. The story is not told, but only those salient points recapitulated which bear on the spiritual upbringing and work of Moses. Long after the age of Joseph, who had been a Wazīr to one of the Pharaohs, there came on the throne of Egypt a Pharaoh who hated the Iraelites and wanted them annihilated. He ordered Israelite male children to be killed when they were born. Moses's mother hid him for a time, bụt when further concealment was impossible, a thought came into her mind that she should put her child into a chest and send the chest floating down the Nile. This was not merely a foolish fancy of hers. It was God's Plan to bring up Moses in all the learning of the Egyptians, in order that that learning itself should be used to expose what was wrong in it and to advance the glory of God. The chest was floated into the river Nile. It flowed on into a stream that passed through Pharaoh's Garden. It was picked up by Pharaoh's people and the child was adopted by Pharaoh's wife. See xxviii. 4-13.

2558. Pharaoh was an enemy to God, because he was puffed up and he blasphemed, claiming to be God himself. He was an enemy to the child Moses, because he hated the Israelites and wanted to have their male children killed; also because Moses stood for God's revelation to come.

2559. God made the child comely and lovable, and he attracted the love of the very people who, on general grounds, would have killed him.

2560. See n. 2558 above. By making the child Moses so attractive as to be adopted into Pharaoh's household, not only was Moses brought up in the best way possible from an earthly point of view, but God's special Providence looked after him in bringing his mother to him, as stated in the next verse, and thus nourishing him on his mother's milk and keeping him in touch, in his inner growth, with the feelings and sentiments of his people Israel.

One who will nurse
And rear the (child)?'[2561]
So We brought thee back
To thy mother, that her eye[2562]
Might be cooled and she
Should not grieve.
Then thou didst slay[2563]
A man, but We saved thee
From trouble, and We tried
Thee in various ways.
Then didst thou tarry
A number of years
With the people of Midian.[2564]
Then didst thou come hither
As ordained, O Moses!

عَلٰى مَنْ يَّكْفُلُهٗ ۭ
فَرَجَعْنٰكَ اِلٰٓى اُمِّكَ
كَيْ تَقَرَّ عَيْنُهَا وَلَا تَحْزَنَ ۥ
وَقَتَلْتَ نَفْسًا فَنَجَّيْنٰكَ
مِنَ الْغَمِّ وَفَتَنّٰكَ فُتُوْنًا ۥ
فَلَبِثْتَ سِنِيْنَ فِيْٓ اَهْلِ مَدْيَنَ ۥ
ثُمَّ جِئْتَ عَلٰى قَدَرٍ يّٰمُوْسٰى ○

41. "And I have prepared thee
For Myself (for service)"...

٤١- وَاصْطَنَعْتُكَ لِنَفْسِيْ ○

42. "Go, thou and thy brother,[2565]
With My Signs,

٤٢- اِذْهَبْ اَنْتَ وَاَخُوْكَ بِاٰيٰتِيْ

2561. We may suppose that the anxious mother, after the child was floated on the water, sent the child's sister to follow the chest from the bank and see where and by whom it was picked up. When it was picked up by Pharaoh's own family and they seemed to love the child, she appeared like a stranger before them, and said, "Shall I search out a good wet-nurse for the child, that she may rear the child you are going to adopt?" That was exactly what they wanted. She ran home and told her mother. The mother was delighted to come and fold the infant in her arms again and feed it at her own breast, and all openly and without any concealment.

2562. The mother's eyes had, we may imagine, been sore with scalding tears at the separation from her baby. Now they were cooled: a phrase meaning that her heart was comforted.

2563. Years passed. The child grew up. In outward learning he was of the house of Pharaoh. In his inner soul and sympathy he was of Israel. One day, he went to the Israelite colony and saw all the Egyptian oppression under which Israel laboured. He saw an Egyptian smiting an Israelite, apparently with impunity. Moses felt brotherly sympathy and smote the Egyptian. He did not intend to kill him, but in fact the Egyptian died of the blow. When this became known, his position in Pharaoh's household became impossible. So he fled out of Egypt, and was only saved by God's grace. He fled to the Sinai Peninsula, to the land of the Midianites, and had various adventures. He married one of the daughters of the Midianite chief, and lived with the Medianites for many years, as an Egyptian stranger. He had many trials and temptations, but he retained his integrity of character.

2564. See last note. After many years spent in a quiet life, grazing his father-in-law's flocks, he came one day to the valley of Ṭuwā underneath the great mountain mass of Sinai, called Ṭūr (in Arabic). The peak on the Arabian side (where Moses was) was called Horeb by the Hebrews. Then was fulfilled God's Plan: he saw the fire in the distance, and when he went up, he was addressed by God and chosen to be God's Messenger for that age.

2565. We may suppose that Moses had fled alone to the land of Midian, and that he had now come alone (with his family but not with his brother) to Ṭuwā, as described in n. 2542 above. When he was honoured with his mission, and was granted his request that his brother Aaron should accompany him, we may suppose that he took steps to get Aaron to come to him, and their meeting was in Ṭuwā. Some time may be supposed to have elapsed before they were in Egypt, and then they prayed, and received these directions in their Egyptian home.

Aaron was either an elder or a younger brother,—we are not told which. In either case he was born when the ban on Israelite new-born babes was not in operation. Moses had been out of touch with him, and it speaks greatly for his family affection that he remembered him and prayed for his comradeship in the most serious spiritual work of his life.

And slacken not,
Either of you, in keeping
Me in remembrance.

وَلَا تَنِيَا فِي ذِكْرِي ۝

43. "Go, both of you, to Pharaoh,[2566]
For he has indeed
Transgressed all bounds;[2567]

٤٣- اِذْهَبَآ اِلٰى فِرْعَوْنَ
اِنَّهٗ طَغٰى ۝

44. "But speak to him mildly;
Perchance he may take
Warning or fear (God)."[2568]

٤٤- فَقُوْلَا لَهٗ قَوْلًا لَّيِّنًا لَّعَلَّهٗ يَتَذَكَّرُ
اَوْ يَخْشٰى ۝

45. They (Moses and Aaron) said:
"Our Lord! We fear lest
He hasten with insolence[2569]
Against us, or lest he
Transgress all bounds."

٤٥- قَالَا رَبَّنَآ اِنَّنَا نَخَافُ
اَنْ يَّفْرُطَ عَلَيْنَآ اَوْ اَنْ يَّطْغٰى ۝

46. He said: "Fear not:
For I am with you:
I hear and see (everything).

٤٦- قَالَ لَا تَخَافَآ اِنَّنِيْ مَعَكُمَآ
اَسْمَعُ وَاَرٰى ۝

47. "So go ye both to him,
And say, 'Verily we are
Apostles sent by thy Lord:
Send forth, therefore, the Children
Of Israel with us, and
Afflict them not:[2570]
With a Sign, indeed,
Have we come from thy Lord!

٤٧- فَاْتِيٰهُ فَقُوْلَآ اِنَّا رَسُوْلَا رَبِّكَ
فَاَرْسِلْ مَعَنَا بَنِيْٓ اِسْرَآءِيْلَ ۥ
وَلَا تُعَذِّبْهُمْ ط
قَدْ جِئْنٰكَ بِاٰيَةٍ مِّنْ رَّبِّكَ ط

2566. Their mission was in the first instance to Pharaoh and to the Egyptians, and then to lead Israel out of Egypt.

2567. Compare the same phrase in **xx**. 24. Having glanced at the early life of Moses we come back now to the time when Moses's actual ministry begins. The earlier personal story of Moses is rounded off.

2568. So far Pharaoh in his inordinate vanity had forgotten himself and forgotten how small a creature he was before God. This was to be brought to his recollection, so that he might perhaps repent and believe, or at least be deterred by fear from "transgressing all bounds". Some men eschew wrong from sincere love of God and understanding of their fellow-men, and some (of coarser minds) from the fear of consequences. Even the latter conduct may be a step to the former.

2569. They were now in Egypt (see n. 2565 above) and therefore in the power of the Pharaoh. The local atmosphere called for the greatest courage and firmness on their part to carry out the dangerous mission which had been entrusted to them.

2570. The Children of Israel were subjected to all sorts of oppression and indignities. They were given hard tasks; their leaders were unjustly beaten; they were forced to make bricks without straw; and they "groaned in bondage" (Exod. v. 6-19, vi. 5).

And Peace to all
Who follow guidance ![2571]

وَالسَّلٰمُ عَلٰى مَنِ اتَّبَعَ الْهُدٰى ○

48. " ' Verily it has been revealed
To us that the Penalty
(Awaits) those who reject
And turn away.' "

٤٨- اِنَّا قَدْ اُوْحِيَ اِلَيْنَآ اَنَّ الْعَذَابَ
عَلٰى مَنْ كَذَّبَ وَتَوَلّٰى ○

49. (When this message was delivered),
(Pharaoh) said: " Who, then,
O Moses, is the Lord[2572]
Of you two? "

٤٩- قَالَ فَمَنْ
رَّبُّكُمَا يٰمُوْسٰى ○

50. He said: " Our Lord is
He Who gave to each
(Created) thing its form
And nature, and further,
Gave (it) guidance."[2573]

٥٠- قَالَ رَبُّنَا الَّذِيْٓ اَعْطٰى
كُلَّ شَيْءٍ خَلْقَهٗ ثُمَّ هَدٰى ○

51. (Pharaoh) said: " What then
Is the condition
Of previous generations? "[2574]

٥١- قَالَ فَمَا بَالُ الْقُرُوْنِ الْاُوْلٰى ○

2571. God, in His infinite Mercy, always offers Peace to the most hardened sinners, even those who are warring against Him. But, as stated in the next verse, their defiance cannot go on with impunity indefinitely. The punishment must inevitably come for sin, whether the sinner is great or small.

2572. Notice how subtly Pharaoh rejects the implication in Moses's speech, in which Moses had referred to "thy Lord" (verse 47). Pharaoh implicitly repudiates the suggestion that the God who had sent Moses and Aaron could possibly be Pharaoh's Lord. He asks insolently, " Who is this Lord of yours, of Whom ye speak as having sent you? "

2573. The answer of Moses is straightforward, dignified, and illuminating. He will not dispute about " my Lord " or " your Lord," the God of Israel, or the God of Egypt. He and his brother were proud to serve " our Lord," but He was the universal Lord and Cherisher, the One and Only God, Who had created all beings and all things. It was from Him that each created thing derived its form and nature, including such free-will and power as man had got. He, Pharaoh, was subject to the same condition. In order that the free-will should be rightly exercised, God had given guidance through His Messengers, and His Signs. Moses and Aaron stood as such Messengers, with such Signs. Will Pharaoh now understand and do right?

2574. But Pharaoh was not the man to accept teaching from the despised Israelite—one, too, who in his eyes was a renegade from the higher Egyptian civilisation. " If," he says in effect, " there is only one God, to Whom all things are referred, this is a new religion. What of the religion of our ancestors? Were they wrong in worshipping the Egyptian gods? And if they were wrong, are they in misery now? " He wanted to trap Moses into a scathing denunciation of his ancestors, which would at once have deprived him of the sympathy or the hearing of the Egyptian crowd.

52. He replied: "The knowledge
Of that is with my Lord,[2575]
Duly recorded: my Lord
Never errs, nor forgets,—

٥٢- قَالَ عِلْمُهَا عِندَ رَبِّي
فِي كِتَٰبٍ ۖ لَّا يَضِلُّ رَبِّي وَلَا يَنسَى ○

53. "He Who has made for you
The earth like a carpet
Spread out; has enabled you
To go about therein by roads[2576]
(And channels); and has sent
Down water from the sky."
With it have We produced[2577]
Divers pairs of plants[2578]
Each separate from the others.

٥٣- الَّذِي جَعَلَ لَكُمُ الْأَرْضَ مَهْدًا
وَسَلَكَ لَكُمْ فِيهَا سُبُلًا
وَأَنزَلَ مِنَ السَّمَاءِ مَاءً ۚ
فَأَخْرَجْنَا بِهِ أَزْوَاجًا مِّن نَّبَاتٍ شَتَّىٰ ○

54. Eat (for yourselves) and pasture
Your cattle: verily, in this
Are Signs for men
Endued with understanding.

٥٤- كُلُوا وَارْعَوْا أَنْعَامَكُمْ ۗ
إِنَّ فِي ذَٰلِكَ لَآيَاتٍ لِّأُولِي النُّهَىٰ ○ ع

SECTION 3.

55. From the (earth) did We
Create you, and into it
Shall We return you,
And from it shall We
Bring you out once again.[2579]

٥٥- مِنْهَا خَلَقْنَاكُمْ وَفِيهَا
نُعِيدُكُمْ وَمِنْهَا نُخْرِجُكُمْ تَارَةً أُخْرَىٰ ○

56. And We showed Pharaoh
All Our Signs, but he
Did reject and refuse.[2580]

٥٦- وَلَقَدْ أَرَيْنَاهُ آيَاتِنَا كُلَّهَا
فَكَذَّبَ وَأَبَىٰ ○

2575. Moses did not fall into the trap. He remembered the injunction given to him to speak mildly (xx. 44). He speaks mildly, but does not in any way whittle down the truth. He said in effect: 'God's knowledge is perfect, as if, with men, it were a record. For men may make mistakes or may not remember, but God never mistakes and never forgets. But God is not only All-Knowing: He is also All-Good. Look around you: the whole earth is spread out like a carpet. Men go to and fro in it freely. He sends abundance of water from the skies, which comes down in Nile floods and fertilises the whole soil of Egypt, and feeds men and animals.'

2576. *Sabīl* means not only a road, but would include water-roads or channels, and in modern conditions, airways—in fact all means of communication.

2577. This seems to be outside the speech of Moses, and connects itself with the following verses 54-56, as part of the Word of God, expanding the speech of Moses and explaining the working of God's Providence in nature.

2578. *Azwāj*: we might translate here (as in xv. 88) by "classes" instead of "pairs"; but as sex in plants seems to be referred to elsewhere (see xiii. 3, and n. 1804), I translate "pairs".

2579. This verse ought really to go into the last Section.

2580. This is a sort of general introduction to the spiritual combat between Moses and Pharaoh. The Signs are not only the countering of the fraudulent magic of Egypt with real miracles, but the subsequent Plagues (not mentioned here) and the Crossing of the Red Sea by Israel.

57. He said: "Hast thou come
To drive us out
Of our land with thy magic,[2581]
O Moses?

٥٧-قَالَ أَجِئْتَنَا لِتُخْرِجَنَا
مِنْ أَرْضِنَا بِسِحْرِكَ يٰمُوسٰى ۝

58. "But we can surely produce
Magic to match thine!
So make a tryst
Between us and thee,
Which we shall not fail
To keep—neither we nor thou—
In a place where both
Shall have even chances."[2582]

٥٨-فَلَنَأْتِيَنَّكَ بِسِحْرٍ مِّثْلِهِ
فَاجْعَلْ بَيْنَنَا وَبَيْنَكَ مَوْعِدًا
لَّا نُخْلِفُهُ نَحْنُ
وَلَآ أَنْتَ مَكَانًا سُوًى ۝

59. Moses said: "Your tryst
Is the Day of the Festival,[2583]
And let the people be assembled
When the sun is well up."

٥٩-قَالَ مَوْعِدُكُمْ يَوْمُ الزِّينَةِ
وَأَنْ يُحْشَرَ النَّاسُ ضُحًى ۝

60. So Pharaoh withdrew:
He concerted his plan,[2584]
And then came (back).

٦٠-فَتَوَلّٰى فِرْعَوْنُ فَجَمَعَ كَيْدَهُ
ثُمَّ أَتٰى ۝

61. Moses said to him:
Woe to you! Forge not
Ye a lie against God,
Lest He destroy you (at once)

٦١-قَالَ لَهُمْ مُوسٰى وَيْلَكُمْ لَا تَفْتَرُوا
عَلَى اللّٰهِ كَذِبًا فَيُسْحِتَكُمْ

2581. The Egyptians accused Moses of a design to deprive them of their land, and of exercising black magic. Both charges were palpably false. What Moses wanted to do was to free his people from bondage. The Egyptians had all the power in their possession; they wished to use the Israelites as untouchable helots; and any one who wanted to mitigate this injustice was branded as a dreadful person who wished to deprive them of their lawful rights. As to magic, the Egyptians judged Moses by themselves. They practised sorcery to deceive the people. They accused the man of God of doing the same, though both his outlook and the source of his strength were altogether different.

2582. *Suwan*: literally, 'equal, even'. It has been construed to mean: (1) a place equally distant for both sides, a central place, or (2) equally convenient to both sides, or (3) an open level plain, where the people can collect with ease. All these are possible meanings, but the one I have adopted is more comprehensive, and includes the others, *viz*: (4) a place where both sides shall have even chances, "a fair place," as Palmer laconically translates it.

2583 A great day of a Temple Festival, when the temples and streets were decorated, and people were on holiday, free from work. Moses makes this appointment in order to collect as large a number as possible, for his first duty is to preach the Truth. And he apparently did it with some effect with some Egyptians (xx. 70, 72-76), though the Pharaoh and his high and mighty officers rejected the Truth and afterwards paid the Penalty.

2584. Pharaoh was apparently taken aback at Moses appointing a solemn day of public Festival, when there would be a large concourse and there would be sure to be some people not in the Court clique, who might be critical of Pharaoh's own sorcerers. But probably there was something more in their dark counsels, something unfair and wicked, to which Moses refers in his speech in the next verse.

Utterly by chastisement: The forger must suffer[2585] Frustration!"	بِعَذَابٍ وَقَدْ خَابَ مَنِ افْتَرٰى ۝
62. So they disputed, one with Another, over their affair, But they kept their talk secret.[2586]	٦٢- فَتَنَازَعُوٓا أَمْرَهُم بَيْنَهُمْ وَأَسَرُّوا النَّجْوٰى ۝
63. They said: "These two Are certainly (expert) magicians: Their object is to drive you Out from your land With their magic, and To do away with your Most cherished institutions.[2587]	٦٣- قَالُوٓا إِنْ هٰذٰنِ لَسٰحِرٰنِ يُرِيدٰنِ أَن يُخْرِجٰكُم مِّنْ أَرْضِكُم بِسِحْرِهِمَا وَيَذْهَبَا بِطَرِيقَتِكُمُ الْمُثْلٰى ۝
64. "Therefore concert your plan, And then assemble In (serried) ranks: He wins (all along) to-day Who gains the upper hand"[2588]	٦٤- فَأَجْمِعُوا كَيْدَكُمْ ثُمَّ ائْتُوا صَفًّا ۚ وَقَدْ أَفْلَحَ الْيَوْمَ مَنِ اسْتَعْلٰى ۝
65. They said: "O Moses! Whether wilt thou That thou throw (first) Or that we be the first To throw?"	٦٥- قَالُوا يٰمُوسٰىٓ إِمَّآ أَن تُلْقِىَ وَإِمَّآ أَن نَّكُونَ أَوَّلَ مَنْ أَلْقٰى ۝
66. He said, "Nay, throw ye First!" Then behold	٦٦- قَالَ بَلْ أَلْقُوا ۖ فَإِذَا

2585. Moses had some idea of their trickery and deceit. They would palm off their fraudulent magic as coming from God or from their gods! He warns them that their tricks will stand exposed, and their hopes will be defeated.

2586. They knew that they had here to deal with no ordinary man, but a man with powers above what they could conceive of. But evil always thinks evil. Judging Moses and Aaron by their own standards, they thought that these two were also tricksters, with some tricks superior to their own. All they had to do was to stand together, and they must win. I construe xx. 63-64 to be their private talk among themselves, followed by their open challenge to Moses in xx 65.

2587. *Cf.* xx. 104. 'Your most cherished institutions,' *i.e.* 'your ancestral and time-honoured religion and magic'. *Muthlā*, feminine of *Amthal*, most distinguished, honoured, cherished. *Tarīqat*=way of life, institutions, conduct.

2588. Presumably Pharaoh was in this secret conference, and he promises the most lavish rewards to the magicians if they overcome Moses. See vii. 114. That—but I think more than that—is implied. That day was to be the crisis: if they won then, they would win all along, and Moses and his people would be crushed.

Their ropes and their rods—[2589]
So it seemed to him
On account of their magic—
Began to be in lively motion!

حِبَالُهُمْ وَعِصِيُّهُمْ يُخَيَّلُ إِلَيْهِ
مِنْ سِحْرِهِمْ أَنَّهَا تَسْعَىٰ ○

67. So Moses conceived
In his mind
A (sort of) fear.[2590]

٦٧- فَأَوْجَسَ فِي نَفْسِهِ خِيفَةً مُوسَىٰ ○

68. We said: "Fear not!
For thou hast indeed
The upper hand:

٦٨- قُلْنَا لَا تَخَفْ إِنَّكَ أَنْتَ الْأَعْلَىٰ ○

69. "Throw that which is
In thy right hand:
Quickly will it swallow up
That which they have faked
What they have faked
Is but a magician's trick:
And the magician thrives not,
(No matter) where he goes."[2591]

٦٩- وَأَلْقِ مَا فِي يَمِينِكَ
تَلْقَفْ مَا صَنَعُوا ۖ إِنَّمَا صَنَعُوا كَيْدُ سَاحِرٍ ۖ
وَلَا يُفْلِحُ السَّاحِرُ حَيْثُ أَتَىٰ ○

70. So the magicians were
Thrown down to prostration:
They said, "We believe
In the Lord of Aaron and Moses".[2592]

٧٠- فَأُلْقِيَ السَّحَرَةُ سُجَّدًا
قَالُوا آمَنَّا بِرَبِّ هَارُونَ وَمُوسَىٰ ○

71. (Pharaoh) said: "Believe ye
In Him before I give
You permission? Surely
This must be your leader,
Who has taught you magic![2593]
Be sure I will cut off

٧١- قَالَ آمَنْتُمْ لَهُ قَبْلَ أَنْ آذَنَ لَكُمْ ۖ
إِنَّهُ لَكَبِيرُكُمُ الَّذِي عَلَّمَكُمُ السِّحْرَ ۖ
فَلَأُقَطِّعَنَّ

2589. Their bag of tricks was so clever that it imposed upon all beholders. Their ropes and their rods were thrown, and seemed to move about like snakes. So realistic was the effect that even Moses felt the least bit of doubt in his own mind. He of course had no tricks, and he relied entirely on God.

2590. The concerted attack of evil is sometimes so well contrived from all points that falsehood appears and is acclaimed as the truth. The believer of truth is isolated, and a sort of moral dizziness creeps over his mind. But by God's grace Faith asserts itself, gives him confidence, and points out the specific truths which will dissipate and destroy the teeming brood of falsehood.

2591. The meaning may be either (1) that falsehood and trickery may have their day, but they cannot win everywhere, especially in the presence of Truth, or (2) that trickery and magic must come to an evil end.

2592. *Cf.* this passage with vii. 120-126 and the notes thereon.

2593. Pharaoh accuses his sorcerers who have been converted, of having been in league with Moses all the time, and in fact of having been led and taught by him! So arrogance and evil cannot conceive of God's worlds and worlds of beauty and truth beyond its own narrow vision! It is truly blind, and its very cleverness deludes it to wander far from the truth

Your hands and feet
On opposite sides, and I
Will have you crucified
On trunks of palm-trees:
So shall ye know for certain,
Which of us can give
The more severe and the more
Lasting Punishment!"

أَيْدِيَكُمْ وَ أَرْجُلَكُمْ مِّنْ خِلَافٍ
وَّلَأُوصَلِّبَنَّكُمْ فِي جُذُوعِ النَّخْلِ
وَلَتَعْلَمُنَّ أَيُّنَا أَشَدُّ
عَذَابًا وَّ أَبْقَى ۝

72. They said: "Never shall we
Regard thee as more than
The Clear Signs[2594] that have
Come to us, or than
Him Who created us!
So decree whatever thou
Desirest to decree: for thou
Canst only decree (touching)
The life of this world.[2595]

٧٢- قَالُوا لَن نُّؤْثِرَكَ عَلَىٰ
مَا جَاءَنَا مِنَ الْبَيِّنَٰتِ
وَالَّذِي فَطَرَنَا
فَاقْضِ مَا أَنتَ قَاضٍ
إِنَّمَا تَقْضِي هَٰذِهِ الْحَيَوٰةَ الدُّنْيَا ۝

73. "For us, we have believed
In our Lord: may He
Forgive us our faults,
And the magic to which
Thou didst compel us:[2596]
For God is Best
And Most Abiding."

٧٣- إِنَّا آمَنَّا بِرَبِّنَا
لِيَغْفِرَ لَنَا خَطَٰيَٰنَا وَمَا أَكْرَهْتَنَا عَلَيْهِ
مِنَ السِّحْرِ
وَاللَّهُ خَيْرٌ وَّ أَبْقَى ۝

74. Verily he who comes[2597]
To his Lord as a sinner
(At Judgment),—for him
Is Hell: therein shall he
Neither die nor live.

٧٤- إِنَّهُ مَن يَأْتِ رَبَّهُ مُجْرِمًا فَإِنَّ لَهُ
جَهَنَّمَ لَا يَمُوتُ فِيهَا وَلَا يَحْيَىٰ ۝

2594. *Clear Signs*: the miracles, the personality of the Messengers of God, the logic of events as they unfolded themselves, and the light of inner conviction in their own conscience. There are in addition the Signs and Proofs of God in nature, which are referred to in many places, *e.g.*, xx. 53-54.

2595. Thus was the first part of the mission of Moses—that to the Egyptians—fulfilled. See n. 1083 to vii. 126; also Appendix V, pp. 409-410.

2596. The magic, mummery, and deceptions which pertained to Egyptian Pagan religion became a creed, a State article of faith, to which all citizens were compelled to bow, and which its priests were compelled actively to practise. And Pharaoh was at the head of the whole system—the high priest or the supreme god. With justice, therefore, do the converted magicians lay the blame on Pharaoh, effectively negativing Pharaoh's disingenuous charge that they had been in league with Moses.

These falsehoods and deceptions—combined in many cases with horrid cruelties, open and secret,—were common to many Pagan systems. Some of them have been investigated in detail in Sir John G. Frazer's *Golden Bough*.

2597. The verses xx. 74-76 are best construed as comments on the story of the converted Egyptians who had "purified themselves (from evil)". But some construe them as a continuation of their speech.

75. But such as come
To Him as Believers
Who have worked righteous
deeds,—
For them are ranks exalted,—

٧٥- وَمَنْ يَّأْتِهٖ مُؤْمِنًا قَدْ عَمِلَ الصّٰلِحٰتِ
فَأُولٰٓئِكَ لَهُمُ الدَّرَجٰتُ الْعُلٰى ۝

76. Gardens of Eternity,
Beneath which flow rivers :
They will dwell therein
For aye : such is the reward
Of those who purify
Themselves (from evil).[2598]

٧٦- جَنّٰتُ عَدْنٍ تَجْرِيْ مِنْ تَحْتِهَا الْأَنْهٰرُ
خٰلِدِيْنَ فِيْهَا ۗ
وَذٰلِكَ جَزٰٓؤُا مَنْ تَزَكّٰى ۝

C. 145.—The people of Israel were rescued from bondage
(xx. 77-104.) And led on their way to the Promised Land.
God's Grace gave them light and guidance, but they
Rebelled under the leadership of one
Called the Sāmirī : he melted the gold
Of their jewels and made an idol—a calf
For their worship—a thing without life or power.
Moses destroyed the idol, and cursed
The man who led the people astray.

Section 4.

77. We sent an inspiration[2590]
To Moses : " Travel by night
With My servants, and strike
A dry path for them
Through the sea, without fear
Of being overtaken (by Pharaoh)
And without (any other) fear."

٧٧- وَلَقَدْ أَوْحَيْنَآ إِلٰى مُوْسٰٓى ۙ أَنْ أَسْرِ
بِعِبَادِيْ فَاضْرِبْ لَهُمْ طَرِيْقًا
فِي الْبَحْرِ يَبَسًا ۙ
لَّا تَخٰفُ دَرَكًا وَّلَا تَخْشٰى ۝

78. Then Pharaoh pursued them
With his forces, but
The waters completely
overwhelmed
Them and covered them up.

٧٨- فَأَتْبَعَهُمْ فِرْعَوْنُ بِجُنُوْدِهٖ
فَغَشِيَهُمْ مِّنَ الْيَمِّ مَا غَشِيَهُمْ ۝

79. Pharaoh led his people astray
Instead of leading them aright.[2600]

٧٩- وَأَضَلَّ فِرْعَوْنُ قَوْمَهٗ وَمَا هَدٰى ۝

2598. As the Egyptian magicians had done when they confessed the One True God.

2599. Time passes, and at last Moses is commanded to leave Egypt with his people by night. They were to cross the Red Sea into the Sinai Peninsula. They were told to have no fear of Pharaoh or of the sea or of the unknown desert country of Sinai into which they were going. They crossed dry-shod, while Pharaoh who came in pursuit with his troops was overwhelmed by the sea. He and his men all perished. There is no emphasis on this episode here. But the emphasis is laid on the hard task which Moses had with his own people after he had delivered them from the Egyptian bondage.

2600. It is the duty of kings and leaders to give the right lead to their people. Instead of that, the evil ones among them lead them astray and are the cause of the whole of the people perishing.

80. O ye Children of Israel! We delivered you from Your enemy, and We Made a Covenant with you On the right side of[2601] Mount (Sinai), and We sent Down to you Manna And quails :	٨٠- يٰبَنِىٓ إِسْرَآءِيلَ قَدْ أَنجَيْنَٰكُم مِّنْ عَدُوِّكُمْ وَوَٰعَدْنَٰكُمْ جَانِبَ ٱلطُّورِ ٱلْأَيْمَنَ وَنَزَّلْنَا عَلَيْكُمُ ٱلْمَنَّ وَٱلسَّلْوَىٰ ۝
81. (Saying): "Eat of the good[2602] Things We have provided For your sustenance, but Commit no excess therein, Lest My Wrath should justly Descend on you : and those On whom descends My Wrath Do perish indeed![2603]	٨١- كُلُوا۟ مِن طَيِّبَٰتِ مَا رَزَقْنَٰكُمْ وَلَا تَطْغَوْا۟ فِيهِ فَيَحِلَّ عَلَيْكُمْ غَضَبِى ۖ وَمَن يَحْلِلْ عَلَيْهِ غَضَبِى فَقَدْ هَوَىٰ ۝
82. "But, without doubt, I am (Also) He that forgives Again and again, to those Who repent, believe, And do right,—who, In fine, are ready to receive True guidance."	٨٢- وَإِنِّى لَغَفَّارٌ لِّمَن تَابَ وَءَامَنَ وَعَمِلَ صَٰلِحًا ثُمَّ ٱهْتَدَىٰ ۝
83. (When Moses was up on the Mount,[2604] God said:) "What made thee Hasten in advance of thy people, O Moses?"	٨٣- وَمَآ أَعْجَلَكَ عَن قَوْمِكَ يَٰمُوسَىٰ ۝
84. He replied : "Behold, they are Close on my footsteps :	٨٤- قَالَ هُمْ أُو۟لَآءِ عَلَىٰٓ أَثَرِى

2601. *Right side*: *Cf.* xix. 52, and n. 2504, towards the end. The Arabian side of Sinai (Jabal Mūsa) was the place where Moses first received his commission before going to Egypt, and also where he received the Law after the Exodus from Egypt.

2602. *Cf.* ii. 57 and n. 71; and vii. 160. I should like to construe this not only literally but also metaphorically. 'God has looked after you and saved you. He has given you ethical and spiritual guidance. Enjoy the fruits of all this, but do not become puffed up and rebellious (another meaning in the root *Ṭagā*); otherwise the Wrath of God is sure to descend on you.'

2603. This gives the key-note to Moses's constant tussle with his own people, and introduces immediately afterwards the incident of the golden calf.

2604. This was when Moses was up on the Mount for forty days and forty nights: ii. 51, and n. 66. Moses had left the elders of Israel with Aaron behind him: Exod. xxiv. 14. While he was in a state of ecstatic honour on the Mount, his people were enacting strange scenes down below. They were tested and tried, and they failed in the trial. They made a golden image of a calf for worship, as described below. See also vii. 148-150 and notes.

I hastened to Thee,
O my Lord,
To please Thee."

وَعَجِلْتُ إِلَيْكَ رَبِّ لِتَرْضَىٰ ○

85. (God) said: " We have tested
Thy people in thy absence:
The Sāmirī has led them[2605]
Astray."

٨٥-قَالَ فَإِنَّا قَدْ فَتَنَّا قَوْمَكَ مِنْ بَعْدِكَ
وَأَضَلَّهُمُ السَّامِرِيُّ ○

86. So Moses returned to his people
In a state of indignation
And sorrow. He said:
" O my people! did not
Your Lord make a handsome[2606]
Promise to you? Did then
The promise seem to you
Long (in coming)? Or did ye
Desire that Wrath should
Descend from your Lord on you,
And so ye broke your promise
To me?"

٨٦-فَرَجَعَ مُوسَىٰ إِلَىٰ قَوْمِهِ غَضْبَانَ
أَسِفًا ۚ قَالَ يَا قَوْمِ أَلَمْ
يَعِدْكُمْ رَبُّكُمْ وَعْدًا حَسَنًا ۚ
أَفَطَالَ عَلَيْكُمُ الْعَهْدُ أَمْ
أَرَدْتُمْ أَنْ يَحِلَّ عَلَيْكُمْ غَضَبٌ مِنْ
رَبِّكُمْ فَأَخْلَفْتُمْ مَوْعِدِي ○

87. They said: " We broke not
The promise to thee, as far
As lay in our power:
But we were made to carry
The weight of the ornaments[2607]
Of the (whole) people, and we

٨٧-قَالُوا مَا أَخْلَفْنَا مَوْعِدَكَ بِمَلْكِنَا
وَلَٰكِنَّا حُمِّلْنَا
أَوْزَارًا مِنْ زِينَةِ الْقَوْمِ

2605. Who was this Sāmirī? If it was his personal name, it was sufficiently near the meaning of the original root-word to have the definite article attached to it: *Cf.* the name of the Khalifa Mu'taṣim (*Al*-Mu'taṣim). What was the root for "Sāmirī"? If we look to old Egyptian, we have *Shemer*=A stranger, foreigner (Sir E. A. Wallis Budge's *Egyptian Hieroglyphic Dictionary*, 1920, p 815 *b*). As the Israelites had just left Egypt, they might quite well have among them an Egyptianised Hebrew bearing that nickname. That the name *Shemer* was subsequently not unknown among the Hebrews is clear from the Old Testament. In I Kings, xvi. 24 we read that Omri, king of Israel, the northern portion of the divided kingdom, who reigned about 903-896 B.C., built a new city, Samaria, on a hill which he bought from Shemer, the owner of the hill, for two talents of silver. See also Renan: *History of Israel*, ii. 210. For a further discussion of the word, see n. 2608 below.

2606. There are two promises referred to in this verse, the promise of God and the promise of the people of Israel. They form one Covenant, which was entered into through their leader Moses. See xx. 80, and ii. 63, n. 78. God's promise was to protect them and lead them to the Promised Land, and their promise was to obey God's Law and His commandments.

2607. *Cf.* Exod. xii. 35-36: the Israelites, before they left Egypt, borrowed from the Egyptians "jewels of silver and jewels of gold, and raiment"; and "they spoiled the Egyptians" *i.e.*, stripped them of all their valuable jewellery. Note that the answer of the backsliders is disingenuous in various ways. (1) The Sāmirī was no doubt responsible for suggesting the making of the golden calf, but they could not on that account disclaim responsibility for themselves: the burden of the sin is on him who commits it, and he cannot pretend that he was powerless to avoid it. (2) At most the weight of the gold they carried could not have been heavy even if one or two men carried it, but would have been negligible if distributed. (3) Gold is valuable, and it is not likely that if they wanted to disburde themselves of it, they had any need to light a furnace, melt it, and cast it into the shape of a calf.

Threw them (into the fire),
And that was what
The Sāmirī suggested.[2608]

فَقَذَفْنٰهَا فَكَذٰلِكَ اَلْقَى السَّامِرِيُّ ۝

88. "Then he brought out
(Of the fire) before the (people)
The image of a calf:[2609]
It seemed to low:[2610]
So they said: 'This is
Your god, and the god
Of Moses, but (Moses)
Has forgotten!'"[2611]

٨٨- فَاَخْرَجَ لَهُمْ
عِجْلًا جَسَدًا لَّهٗ خُوَارٌ
فَقَالُوْا هٰذَآ اِلٰهُكُمْ
وَاِلٰهُ مُوْسٰى ۥ فَنَسِيَ ۝

89. Could they not see that
It could not return them
A word (for answer), and that
It had no power either
To harm them or
To do them good?[2612]

٨٩- اَفَلَا يَرَوْنَ اَلَّا يَرْجِعُ اِلَيْهِمْ قَوْلًا ۥ
وَّلَا يَمْلِكُ لَهُمْ
ضَرًّا وَّلَا نَفْعًا ۝

SECTION 5.

90. Aaron had already, before this
Said to them: "O my people!
Ye are being tested in this:[2613]
For verily your Lord is (God)
Most Gracious: so follow me
And obey my command."[2614]

٩٠- وَلَقَدْ قَالَ لَهُمْ هٰرُوْنُ مِنْ قَبْلُ
يٰقَوْمِ اِنَّمَا فُتِنْتُمْ بِهٖ ۚ وَاِنَّ رَبَّكُمُ
الرَّحْمٰنُ فَاتَّبِعُوْنِيْ وَاَطِيْعُوْٓا اَمْرِيْ ۝

2608. See n. 2605 about the Sāmirī. If the Egyptian origin of the root is not accepted, we have a Hebrew origin in "Shomer" a guard, watchman, sentinel; allied to the Arabic *Samara, yasmuru*, to keep awake by night, to converse by night; *samīr*, one who keeps awake by night. The Sāmirī may have been a watchman, in fact or by nickname.

2609. See n. 1113 to vii. 148, where the same words are used and explained.

2610. See n. 1114 to vii. 148.

2611. *Moses has forgotten*: *i.e.*, 'forgotten both us and his god. He has been gone for so many days. He is searching for a god on the Mount when his god is really here!' This is spoken by the Sāmirī and his partisans, but the people as a whole accepted it, and it therefore becomes their speech.

2612. This is a parenthetical comment. How blind the people were! They had seen Signs of the true living God, and yet they were willing to worship this dead image! The true living God had spoken in definite words of command, while this calf could only emit some sounds of lowing, which were themselves contrived by the fraud of the priests. This image could do neither good nor harm, while God was the Cherisher and Sustainer of the Universe, Whose Mercy was unbounded and Whose Wrath was terrible.

2613. "Resist this temptation: you are being tested in this. Do not follow after the semi-Egyptian Sāmirī, but obey me."

2614. The Bible story makes Aaron the culprit, which is inconsistent with his office as the high priest of God and the right hand of Moses. See n. 1116 to vii. 150. Our version is more consistent, and explains in the Sāmirī the lingering influences of the Egyptian cult of Osiris the bull-god.

91. They had said: [2615] "We will not
Abandon this cult, but we
Will devote ourselves to it
Until Moses returns to us." [2616]

٩١-قَالُوا لَنْ نَّبْرَحَ عَلَيْهِ عٰكِفِيْنَ
حَتّٰى يَرْجِعَ اِلَيْنَا مُوْسٰى ○

92. (Moses) said: "O Aaron!
What kept thee back, when
Thou sawest them going wrong,

٩٢-قَالَ يٰهٰرُوْنُ مَا مَنَعَكَ
اِذْ رَاَيْتَهُمْ ضَلُّوْٓا ○

93. "From following me? Didst thou
Then disobey my order?" [2617]

٩٣-اَلَّا تَتَّبِعَنِ ؕ اَفَعَصَيْتَ اَمْرِيْ ○

94. (Aaron) replied: "O son
Of my mother! Seize (me) not
By my beard nor by
(The hair of) my head! [2618]
Truly I feared lest thou
Shouldst say, 'Thou hast caused
A division among the Children
Of Israel, and thou didst not
Respect my word!'" [2619]

٩٤-قَالَ يَبْنَؤُمَّ لَا تَاْخُذْ
بِلِحْيَتِيْ وَلَا بِرَاْسِيْ ۚ
اِنِّيْ خَشِيْتُ اَنْ تَقُوْلَ
فَرَّقْتَ بَيْنَ بَنِيْٓ اِسْرَآءِيْلَ
وَلَمْ تَرْقُبْ قَوْلِيْ ○

95. (Moses) said: "What then
Is thy case, O Sāmirī?" [2620]

٩٥-قَالَ فَمَا خَطْبُكَ يٰسَامِرِيُّ ○

96. He replied: "I saw what
They saw not: so I took

٩٦-قَالَ بَصُرْتُ بِمَا لَمْ يَبْصُرُوْا بِهٖ فَقَبَضْتُ

2615. Obviously Aaron's speech in the last verse, and the rebels' defiance in this verse, were spoken before the return of Moses from the Mount.

2616. The rebels had so little faith that they had given Moses up for lost, and never expected to see him again.

2617. Moses, when he came back, was full of anger and grief. His speech to Aaron is one of rebuke, and he was also inclined to handle him roughly: see next verse. The order he refers to is that stated in vii. 142, "Act for me amongst my people: do right, and follow not the way of those who do mischief".

2618. *Cf.* vii. 150.

2619. This reply of Aaron's is in no way inconsistent with the reply as noted in vii. 150. On the contrary there is a dramatic aptness in the different points emphasised on each occasion. In S. vii. we were discussing the Ummat of Israel, and Aaron rightly says, "The people did indeed reckon me as naught, and went near to slay me!" In adding, "Let not the enemies rejoice over my misfortune" he is referring by implication to his brother's wish to maintain unity among the people. Here the unity is the chief point to emphasise: we are dealing with the Sāmirī as mischief-monger, and he could best be dealt with by Moses, who proceeds to do so.

2620. Moses now turns to the Sāmirī, and the Sāmirī's reply in the next verse sums up his character in a few wonderful strokes of character-painting. The lesson of the whole of this episode is the fall of a human soul that nominally comes to God's Truth in a humble position but makes mischief when and as it finds occasion. It is no less dangerous and culpable than the arrogant soul, typified by Pharaoh, which gets into high places and makes its leadership the cause of ruin to a whole nation

A handful (of dust) from
The footprint of the Apostle,
And threw it (into the calf):
Thus did my soul suggest
To me." [2621]

قَبْضَةً مِّنْ اَثَرِ الرَّسُوْلِ
فَنَبَذْتُهَا وَكَذٰلِكَ سَوَّلَتْ لِيْ نَفْسِيْ ○

97. (Moses) said: "Get thee gone!
But thy (punishment) in this life
Will be that thou wilt say, [2622]
'Touch me not'; and moreover
(For a future penalty) thou hast
A promise that will not fail: [2623]
Now look at thy god,
Of whom thou hast become
A devoted worshipper:
We will certainly (melt) it
In a blazing fire and scatter
It broadcast in the sea!" [2624]

٩٧- قَالَ فَاذْهَبْ فَاِنَّ لَكَ فِي الْحَيٰوةِ
اَنْ تَقُوْلَ لَا مِسَاسَ
وَاِنَّ لَكَ مَوْعِدًا لَّنْ تُخْلَفَهٗ
وَانْظُرْ اِلٰٓى اِلٰهِكَ الَّذِيْ
ظَلْتَ عَلَيْهِ عَاكِفًا
لَنُحَرِّقَنَّهٗ ثُمَّ لَنَنْسِفَنَّهٗ فِي الْيَمِّ نَسْفًا ○

2621. This answer of the Sāmirī is a fine example of unblushing effrontery, careful evasion of issues, and invented falsehoods. He takes upon himself to pretend that he had far more insight than anybody else: he saw what the vulgar crowd did not see. He saw something supernatural. "The Apostle" is construed by many Commentators to mean the angel Gabriel. *Rasūl* (plural, *rusul*) is used in several places for "angels" *e.g.* in xi. 69, 77; xix. 19; and xxxv. 1. But if we take it to mean the Apostle Moses, it means that the Sāmirī saw something sacred or supernatural in his footprints; perhaps he thinks a little flattery would make Moses forgive him. The dust became sacred, and his throwing it into the calf's image made the claf.utter a lowing sound! As if that was the point at issue! He does not answer the charge of making an image for worship. But finally, with arrogant effrontery, he says, "Well, that is what my soul suggested to me, and that should be enough!"

2622. He and his kind were to become social lepers, untouchables; perhaps also sufficiently arrogant to hold others at arm's length, and say "*Noli me tangere*" (touch me not)

2623. Namely, the promised Wrath of God: see xx. 81; lxxxix. 25.

2624. The cast effigy was re-melted and destroyed. Thus ends the Sāmirī's story, of which the lessons are indicated in n. 2620 above. It may be interesting to pursue the transformations of the word Sāmirī in later times. For its origin see notes 2605 and 2608 above. Whether the root of Sāmirī was originally Egyptian or Hebrew does not affect the later history. Four facts may be noted. (1) There was a man bearing a name of that kind at the time of Moses, and he led a revolt against Moses and was cursed by Moses. (2) In the time of King Omri (903 896 B.C.) of the northern kingdom of Israel, there was a man called Shemer, from whom, according to the Bible, was bought a hill on which was built the new capital of the kingdom, the town of Samaria. (3) The name of the hill was *Shomer* (=watchman, vigilant guardian), and that form of the name also appears as the name of a man (see II Kings xii. 21); some authorities think the town was called after the hill and not after the man (Hastings's *Encyclopædia of Religion and Ethics*), but this is for our present purposes immaterial. (4) There was and is a dissenting community of Israelites called Samaritans, who have their own separate Pentateuch and Targum, who claim to be the true Children of Israel, and who hold the Orthodox Jews in contempt as the latter hold them in contempt; they claim to be the true guardians (*Shomerim*) of the Law, and that is probably the true origin of the name Samaritan, which may go further back in time than the foundation of the town of Samaria. I think it probable that the schism originated from the time of Moses, and that the curse of Moses on the Sāmirī explains the position.

98. But the God of you all
Is the One God: there is
No god but He: all things
He comprehends in His knowledge.

٩٨- اِنَّمَآ اِلٰهُكُمُ اللّٰهُ الَّذِیْ لَآ اِلٰهَ اِلَّا
هُوَ ؕ وَسِعَ كُلَّ شَیْءٍ عِلْمًا ۝

99. Thus do We relate to thee
Some stories of what happened
Before: for We have sent
Thee a Message from
Our own Presence.[2625]

٩٩- كَذٰلِكَ نَقُصُّ عَلَیْكَ مِنْ اَنْۢبَآءِ مَا
قَدْ سَبَقَ ۚ
وَقَدْ اٰتَیْنٰكَ مِنْ لَّدُنَّا ذِكْرًا ۝

100. If any do turn away
Therefrom, verily they will
Bear a burden
On the Day of Judgment;

١٠٠- مَنْ اَعْرَضَ عَنْهُ فَاِنَّهٗ
یَحْمِلُ یَوْمَ الْقِیٰمَةِ وِزْرًا ۝

101. They will abide in this (state):
And grievous will the burden[2626]
Be to them on that Day,—

١٠١- خٰلِدِیْنَ فِیْهِ ؕ
وَسَآءَ لَهُمْ یَوْمَ الْقِیٰمَةِ حِمْلًا ۝

102. The Day when the Trumpet
Will be sounded: that Day,
We shall gather the sinful,
Blear-eyed (with terror).[2627]

١٠٢- یَّوْمَ یُنْفَخُ فِی الصُّوْرِ
وَنَحْشُرُ الْمُجْرِمِیْنَ یَوْمَىِٕذٍ زُرْقًا ۝

103. In whispers will they consult
Each other: "Ye tarried not
Longer than ten (Days);"[2628]

١٠٣- یَّتَخَافَتُوْنَ بَیْنَهُمْ اِنْ لَّبِثْتُمْ
اِلَّا عَشْرًا ۝

104. We know best what they
Will say, when their leader[2629]

١٠٤- نَحْنُ اَعْلَمُ بِمَا یَقُوْلُوْنَ اِذْ یَقُوْلُ اَمْثَلُهُمْ

2625. Thus superseding previous revelations; for this (the Qur-ān) is direct from God, and is not a second-hand exposition on other men's authority.

2626. *Cf.* vi. 31. If people are so immersed in the evanescent falsehoods of this life as to turn away from the True and the Eternal, they will have a rude awakening when the Judgment comes. These very things that they thought so enjoyable here—taking advantage of others, material self-indulgence, nursing grievances instead of doing good, etc., etc.—will be a grievous burden to them that day, which they will not be able to escape or lighten.

2627. *Zurq*=having eyes different from the normal colour, which in the East is black and white; having blue eyes, or eyes afflicted with dimness or blindness, or squint; hence mataphorically, blear-eyed (with terror).

2628. Faced with eternity they will realise that their life on this earth, or the interval between their sin and their punishment, had a duration which practically amounted to nothing. They express this by the phrase "ten days", but their wiser heads think that even this is an over-estimate. It was but a brief day!

2629. *Cf.* xx. 63 and n. 2587. Note that it is the shrewdest and most versed in Life who will say this, because they will be the first to see the true situation.

Most eminent in Conduct
Will say: " Ye tarried not
Longer than a day!"

طَرِيقَةً إِن لَّبِثْتُمْ إِلَّا يَوْمًا ۝ ع

C. 14. —Such is the lure of Evil: but high
(xx. 105-135.) And low will be levelled on the Day
Of Judgment, before the Eternal, the Gracious,
The King, the Truth, who sends the Qur-ān
To teach and to warn. Will man remember
How Adam's arch-enemy, Satan, caused
His fall, and will he yet be blind
To the Signs of God? Nay,—but let
Not Evil make you impatient: the Prize
Of the Hereafter is better than aught
Of the glitter of this life: wait in Faith,
And the End will show the triumph
Of Truth, Goodness, and Righteousness.

SECTION 6.

105. They ask thee concerning[2630]
The Mountains: say, " My Lord
Will uproot them and scatter
Them as dust;[2631]

١٠٥- وَيَسْـَٔلُونَكَ عَنِ الْجِبَالِ فَقُلْ
يَنسِفُهَا رَبِّي نَسْفًا ۝

106. " He will leave them as plains
Smooth and level;

١٠٦- فَيَذَرُهَا قَاعًا صَفْصَفًا ۝

107. " Nothing crooked or curved
Wilt thou see in their place."

١٠٧- لَّا تَرَىٰ فِيهَا عِوَجًا وَلَا أَمْتًا ۝

108. On that Day will they follow
The Caller[2632] (straight): no
crookedness

١٠٨- يَوْمَئِذٍ يَتَّبِعُونَ الدَّاعِيَ لَا عِوَجَ لَهُ

2630. In the last verse, it was the deceptiveness and relativity of Time that was dealt with. Here we come to the question of space, solidity, bulk. The question was actually put to the holy Prophet: what will become of the solid Mountains, or in the English phrase, " the eternal hills"? They are no more substantial than anything else in this temporal world. When the " new wrold", (xiii. 5) of which Unbelievers doubted, is actually in being, the mountains will cease to exist. We can imagine the scene of judgment as a level plain, in which there are no ups and downs and no places of concealment. All is straight and level, without corners, mysteries, or lurking doubts.

2631. The one word *nasafa* carries the ideas of (1) tearing up by the roots, (2) scattering like chaff or dust, and (3) winnowing. Its twofold repetition here intensifies its meaning.

2632. *The Caller*: the angel whose voice will call and direct all souls. Gabriel will call, when Isrāfīl has sounded the Trumpet.

(Can they show) him: all
sounds[2633]
Shall humble themselves in
The Presence of (God) Most
Gracious:
Nothing shalt thou hear
But the tramp of their feet
(As they march).

وَخَشَعَتِ الْأَصْوَاتُ
لِلرَّحْمَٰنِ
فَلَا تَسْمَعُ
إِلَّا هَمْسًا ○

109. On that Day shall no
Intercession avail
Except for those for whom[2634]
Permission has been granted
By (God) Most Gracious
And whose word is
Acceptable to Him.

١٠٩- يَوْمَئِذٍ لَّا تَنفَعُ الشَّفَاعَةُ
إِلَّا مَنْ أَذِنَ لَهُ الرَّحْمَٰنُ
وَرَضِيَ لَهُ قَوْلًا ○

110. He knows what (appears
To His creatures as) before
Or after or behind them:[2635]
But they shall not compass it
With their knowledge.

١١٠- يَعْلَمُ مَا بَيْنَ أَيْدِيهِمْ
وَمَا خَلْفَهُمْ
وَلَا يُحِيطُونَ بِهِ عِلْمًا ○

111. (All) faces shall be humbled
Before (Him)—the Living,
The Self-Subsisting, Eternal:
Hopeless indeed will be
The man that carries
Iniquity (on his back).[2636]

١١١- وَعَنَتِ الْوُجُوهُ
لِلْحَيِّ الْقَيُّومِ ۖ
وَقَدْ خَابَ مَنْ حَمَلَ ظُلْمًا ○

2633. A beautiful personification of hushed Sound. First there is the loud blast of the Trumpet; then there is the soft angelic Voice calling "Arise". Then there is the stillness and hush of awe and reverence: only the tramp of the ranks marching along will be heard.

2634. *Cf.* ii. 255 in the Verse of the Throne. Here *man* is in the accusative case governed by *tanfa'u*, and it is better to construe as I have done. That is, intercession will benefit no one except those for whom God has granted permission, and whose word (of repentance) is true and sincere, and therefore acceptable to God. Others construe: no intercession will avail, except *by* those to whom God has granted permission, and whose word (of intercession) is acceptable to God. In that case the two distinct clauses have no distinct meanings.

2635. *Cf.* ii. 255 and n. 297. The slight difference in phraseology (which I have tried to preserve in the Translation) will be understood as a beauty when we reflect that here our attention is directed to the Day of Judgment, and in ii. 255 the wording is general, and applies to our present state also.

2636. The metaphor of the burden of sin which the unjust carry on their backs is referred to in **xx.** 100-101 (see n. 2626), in vi. 31, and in other passages. Note that *all* faces, those of the just as well as of the unjust, will be humble before God: the best of us can claim no merit equal to God's Grace. But the just will have Hope: while the unjust, now that the curtain of Reality has risen, will be in absolute Despair!

112. But he who works deeds
Of righteousness, and has faith,
Will have no fear of harm
Nor of any curtailment[2637]
(Of what is his due).

١١٢- وَمَن يَعْمَلْ مِنَ الصَّٰلِحَٰتِ وَهُوَ مُؤْمِنٌ فَلَا يَخَافُ ظُلْمًا وَلَا هَضْمًا ۝

113. Thus have We sent this
Down—an Arabic Qur-ān—
And explained therein in detail
Some of the warnings,
In order that they may
Fear God, or that it may
Cause their remembrance
(of Him).[2638]

١١٣- وَكَذَٰلِكَ أَنزَلْنَٰهُ قُرْءَانًا عَرَبِيًّا وَصَرَّفْنَا فِيهِ مِنَ الْوَعِيدِ لَعَلَّهُمْ يَتَّقُونَ أَوْ يُحْدِثُ لَهُمْ ذِكْرًا ۝

114. High above all is God,
The King, the Truth!
Be not in haste
With the Qur-ān before
Its revelation to thee[2639]
Is completed, but say,
"O my Lord! advance me
In knowledge."

١١٤- فَتَعَٰلَى اللَّهُ الْمَلِكُ الْحَقُّ ۗ وَلَا تَعْجَلْ بِالْقُرْءَانِ مِن قَبْلِ أَن يُقْضَىٰٓ إِلَيْكَ وَحْيُهُۥ ۖ وَقُل رَّبِّ زِدْنِي عِلْمًا ۝

115. We had already, beforehand,[2640]
Taken the covenant of Adam,

١١٥- وَلَقَدْ عَهِدْنَآ إِلَىٰٓ ءَادَمَ مِن قَبْلُ

2637. See the last note. Unlike the unjust, the righteous, who have come with Faith, will now find their Faith justified: not only will they be free from any fear of harm, but they will be rewarded to the full, or, as has been said in other passages, where His bounty rather than His justice is emphasised, they will get more than their due reward (iii. 27; xxxix. 10).

2638. The Qur-ān is in clear Arabic, so that even an unlearned people like the Arabs might understand and profit by its warnings, and the rest of the world may learn through them, as they did in the first few centuries of Islam and may do again when we Muslims show ourselves worthy to explain and exemplify its meaning. The evil are warned that they may repent; the good are confirmed in their Faith and strengthened by their remembrance of Him.

2639. God is above every human event or desire. His purpose is universal). But He is the Truth, the absolute Truth; and His kingdom is the true kingdom, that can carry out its will. That Truth unfolds itself gradually, as it did in the gradual revelation of the Qur-ān to the holy Apostle. But even after it was completed in a volume, its true meaning and purpose only gradually unfold themselves to any given individual or nation. No one should be impatient about it. On the contrary, we should always pray for increase in our own knowledge, which can never at any given moment be complete.

2640. The spiritual fall of two individual souls, Pharaoh and the Sāmirī, having been referred to, the one through overweening arrogance, and the other through a spirit of mischief and false harking back to the past, our attention is now called to the prototype of Evil who tempted Adam, the original Man, and to the fact that though man was clearly warned that Evil is his enemy and will only effect his ruin, he showed so little firmness that he succumbed to it at once at the first opportunity.

But he forgot: and We found On his part no firm resolve.	فَنَسِيَ وَلَمْ نَجِدْ لَهُ عَزْمًا ۝

SECTION 7.

116. When We said to the angels, "Prostrate yourselves to Adam", They prostrated themselves, but not Iblis: he refused.	١١٦- وَإِذْ قُلْنَا لِلْمَلٰٓئِكَةِ اسْجُدُوا لِاٰدَمَ فَسَجَدُوٓا اِلَّآ اِبْلِيْسَ ۖ اَبٰى ۝
117. Then We said: "O Adam! Verily, this is an enemy To thee and thy wife: So let him not get you Both out of the Garden, So that thou art landed In misery.[2641]	١١٧- فَقُلْنَا يٰٓاٰدَمُ اِنَّ هٰذَا عَدُوٌّ لَّكَ وَلِزَوْجِكَ فَلَا يُخْرِجَنَّكُمَا مِنَ الْجَنَّةِ فَتَشْقٰى ۝
118. "There is therein (enough provision) For thee not to go hungry [2642] Nor to go naked,	١١٨- اِنَّ لَكَ اَلَّا تَجُوْعَ فِيْهَا وَلَا تَعْرٰى ۝
119. "Nor to suffer from thirst, Nor from the sun's heat."	١١٩- وَاَنَّكَ لَا تَظْمَؤُا فِيْهَا وَلَا تَضْحٰى ۝
120. But Satan whispered evil To him: he said, "O Adam! Shall I lead thee to The Tree of Eternity [2643] And to a kingdom That never decays?"	١٢٠- فَوَسْوَسَ اِلَيْهِ الشَّيْطٰنُ قَالَ يٰٓاٰدَمُ هَلْ اَدُلُّكَ عَلٰى شَجَرَةِ الْخُلْدِ وَمُلْكٍ لَّا يَبْلٰى ۝

2641. See last note. The story is referred to, in order to draw attention to man's folly in rushing into the arms of Evil, though he had been clearly forewarned.

2642. Not only had the warning been given that Evil is an enemy to man and will effect his destruction, but it was clearly pointed out that all his needs were being met in the Garden of Happiness. Food and clothing, drink and shelter, were amply provided for. By these terms we must understand, if the Garden was a spiritual Garden, also spiritual good: the things that feed the soul and make it glad, that give it an æsthetic sense of beauty and afford it shelter from extremes of passion or emotion.

2643. The suggesion of the Evil One is clever, as it always is: it is false, and at the same time plausible. It is false, because (1) that felicity was not temporary, like the life of this world, and (2) they were supreme in the Garden, and a "kingdom" such as was dangled before them would only add to their sorrows. It was plausible, because (1) nothing had been said to them about Eternity, as the opposite of Eternity was not yet known, and (2) the sweets of Power arise from the savour of Self, and Self is an alluring (if false) attraction that misleads the Will.

121. In the result, they both
Ate of the tree, and so
Their nakedness appeared [2644]
To them: they began to sew
Together, for their covering,
Leaves from the Garden:
Thus did Adam disobey
His Lord, and allow himself [2645]
To be seduced.

١٢١-فَاَكَلَا مِنْهَا
فَبَدَتْ لَهُمَا سَوْاٰتُهُمَا
وَطَفِقَا يَخْصِفٰنِ عَلَيْهِمَا مِنْ وَّرَقِ
الْجَنَّةِ
وَعَصٰٓى اٰدَمُ رَبَّهٗ فَغَوٰى ○

122. But his Lord chose him
(For His Grace): He turned
To him, and gave him guidance.

١٢٢-ثُمَّ اجْتَبٰهُ رَبُّهٗ فَتَابَ
عَلَيْهِ وَهَدٰى ○

123. He said: "Get ye down,
Both of you,—all together, [2646]
From the Garden, with enmity
One to another: but if,
As is sure, there comes to you
Guidance from Me, whosoever
Follows My guidance, will not
Lose his way, nor fall [2647]
Into misery.

١٢٣-قَالَ اهْبِطَا مِنْهَا جَمِيْعًا
بَعْضُكُمْ لِبَعْضٍ عَدُوٌّ
فَاِمَّا يَاْتِيَنَّكُمْ مِّنِّيْ هُدًى
فَمَنِ اتَّبَعَ هُدَايَ
فَلَا يَضِلُّ وَلَا يَشْقٰى ○

124. "But whosoever turns away
From My Message, verily
For him is a life narrowed
Down, and We shall raise

١٢٤-وَمَنْ اَعْرَضَ عَنْ ذِكْرِيْ
فَاِنَّ لَهٗ مَعِيْشَةً ضَنْكًا وَّنَحْشُرُهٗ

2644. Hitherto they were clothed in the garb of Innocence and knew no evil. Now, when disobedience to God had sullied their soul and torn off the garment of their Innocence, their sullied Self appeared to themselves in all its nakedness and ugliness, and they had to resort to external things (leaves of the Garden) to cover the shame of their self-consciousness.

2645. Adam had been given the will to choose, and he chose wrong, and was about to be lost in the throng of the evil ones, when God's Grace came to his aid. His repentance was accepted, and God chose him for His Mercy, as stated in the next verse.

2646. The little variations between this passage and ii. 38 are instructive, as showing how clearly the particular argument is followed in each case. Here *ihbiṭā* ('get ye down') is in the dual number, and refers to the two individual souls, our common ancestors: in ii. 38 *ihbiṭū* is in the plural number, to include all mankind and Satan, for the argument is about the collective life of man. On the other hand, "all together" includes Satan, the spirit of evil, and the enmity "one to another" refers to the eternal feud between Man and Satan, between our better nature and Evil.

2647. For the same reason as in the last note, we have here the consequences of Guidance to the individual, *viz.*: being saved from going astray or from falling into misery and despair. In ii. 38, the consequences expressed, though they apply to the individual, are also appropriate taken collectively: "on them shall be no fear, nor shall they grieve."

Him up blind on the Day[2648]
Of Judgment."

يَوْمَ الْقِيٰمَةِ أَعْمٰى ○

125. He will say: "O my Lord!
Why hast thou raised me
Up blind, while I had
Sight (before)?"[2649]

١٢٥- قَالَ رَبِّ لِمَ حَشَرْتَنِيٓ
أَعْمٰى وَقَدْ كُنْتُ بَصِيرًا ○

126. (God) will say: "Thus
Didst thou, when Our Signs
Came unto thee, disregard
Them: so wilt thou,
This day, be disregarded."[2650]

١٢٦- قَالَ كَذٰلِكَ أَتَتْكَ اٰيٰتُنَا فَنَسِيتَهَا ۚ
وَكَذٰلِكَ الْيَوْمَ تُنْسٰى ○

127. And thus do We recompense
Him who transgresses beyond bounds
And believes not in the Signs
Of his Lord: and the Penalty
Of the Hereafter is far more
Grievous and more enduring.[2651]

١٢٧- وَكَذٰلِكَ نَجْزِي مَنْ أَسْرَفَ
وَلَمْ يُؤْمِنْ بِاٰيٰتِ رَبِّهٖ ۚ
وَلَعَذَابُ الْاٰخِرَةِ أَشَدُّ وَأَبْقٰى ○

128. Is it not a warning to such
Men (to call to mind)
How many generations before them
We destroyed, in whose haunts
They (now) move? Verily,
In this are Signs for men
Endued with understanding.[2652]

١٢٨- أَفَلَمْ يَهْدِ لَهُمْ
كَمْ أَهْلَكْنَا قَبْلَهُمْ مِنَ الْقُرُونِ
يَمْشُونَ فِي مَسٰكِنِهِمْ ۗ
إِنَّ فِي ذٰلِكَ لَاٰيٰتٍ لِأُولِي النُّهٰى ○ ع

2648. Again, as in the last two verses, there is a variation from the previous passage (ii. 39). The consequences of the rejection of God's guidance are here expressed more individually: a life narrowed down, and a blindness that will persist beyond this life. "A life narrowed down" has many implications: (1) it is a life from which all the beneficent influences of God's wide world are excluded; (2) it is a life for Self, not for all; (3) in looking exclusively to the "good things" of this life, it misses the true Reality.

2649. Because God gave him physical sight in this life for trial, he thinks he should be favoured in the real world, the world that matters! He misused his physical sight and made himself blind for the other world.

2650. 'You were deliberately blind to God's Signs: now you will not see God's favours, and will be excluded from His Grace.

2651. Blindness in the world of enduring Reality is far worse than physical blindness in the world of probation.

2652. *Cf.* xx. 54. This phrase concluded the argument of Moses with Pharaoh about Pharaoh's blindness to God and the Signs of God. Now it concludes the more general argument about men, concerning whom the saying arose: 'none are so blind as those who *will* not see.'

Section 8.

129. Had it not been
For a Word that went forth
Before from thy Lord,[2653]
(Their punishment) must necessarily
Have come; but there is
A term appointed (for respite).

١٢٩- وَلَوْلَا كَلِمَةٌ سَبَقَتْ
مِن رَّبِّكَ لَكَانَ لِزَامًا
وَأَجَلٌ مُّسَمًّى ۝

130. Therefore be patient with what
They say, and celebrate (constantly)[2654]
The praises of thy Lord,
Before the rising of the sun,
And before its setting;
Yea, celebrate them
For part of the hours
Of the night, and at the sides[2655]
Of the day: that thou
Mayest have (spiritual) joy.

١٣٠- فَاصْبِرْ عَلَىٰ مَا يَقُولُونَ وَسَبِّحْ
بِحَمْدِ رَبِّكَ قَبْلَ طُلُوعِ الشَّمْسِ
وَقَبْلَ غُرُوبِهَا ۖ
وَمِنْ آنَاءِ اللَّيْلِ فَسَبِّحْ وَأَطْرَافَ النَّهَارِ
لَعَلَّكَ تَرْضَىٰ ۝

131. Nor strain thine eyes in longing
For the things We have given
For enjoyment to parties
Of them, the splendour

١٣١- وَلَا تَمُدَّنَّ عَيْنَيْكَ إِلَىٰ مَا مَتَّعْنَا بِهِۦٓ
أَزْوَاجًا مِّنْهُمْ زَهْرَةَ

2653. *Cf.* x. 19 and n. 1407; also xi. 110. In God's holy Plan and Purpose, there is a wise adjustment of all interests, and a merciful chance and respite given to all, the unjust as well as the just, and His decree or word abides. The most wicked have a term appointed them for respite. Had it not been so, the punishment must necessarily have descended on them immediately for their evil deeds.

2654. All good men must be patient with what seems to them evil around them. That does not mean that they should sit still and do nothing to destroy evil; for the fight against evil is one of the cardinal points in Islam. What they are told is that they must not be impatient: they must pray to God and commune with Him, so that their patience and faith may be strengthened, and they may be able the better to grapple with evil. For they thus not only get strength but inward spiritual joy.

2655. *Ṭaraf*, plural *aṭrāf*, may mean sides, ends, extremities. If the day be compared to a tubular figure standing erect, the top and bottom are clearly marked, but the sides are not so clearly marked: they would be *aṭrāf* (plural), not *ṭarafain* (dual). Now the prayer before sunrise is clearly Fajr; that before sunset is 'Aṣr: "part of the hours of the night" would indicate Magrib (early night, just after sunset), and 'Ishā, before going to bed. There is left Ẓuhr, which is in the indefinite side or middle of the day: it may be soon after the sun's decline from noon, but there is considerable latitude about the precise hour. The majority of Commentators interpret in favour of the five Canonical prayers, and some include optional prayers. But I think the words are even more comprehensive. A good man's life is all one sweet Song of Praise to God.

Of the life of this world,
Through which We test them:
But the provision of thy Lord[2656]
Is better and more enduring.

الْحَيٰوةِ الدُّنْيَا ۙ لِنَفْتِنَهُمْ فِيْهِ ؕ
وَرِزْقُ رَبِّكَ خَيْرٌ وَّ اَبْقٰى ○

132. Enjoin prayer on thy people,
And be constant therein.
We ask thee not to provide[2657]
Sustenance: We provide it
For thee. But the (fruit of)
The Hereafter is for
Righteousness.

۱۳۲- وَاْمُرْ اَهْلَكَ بِالصَّلٰوةِ وَاصْطَبِرْ عَلَيْهَا ؕ
لَا نَسْــَٔلُكَ رِزْقًا ؕ نَحْنُ نَرْزُقُكَ ؕ
وَالْعَاقِبَةُ لِلتَّقْوٰى ○

133. They say: "Why does he
not[2658]
Bring us a Sign from
His Lord?" Has not
A Clear Sign come to them
Of all that was
In the former Books
Of revelation?

۱۳۳- وَقَالُوْا لَوْلَا
يَاْتِيْنَا بِاٰيَةٍ مِّنْ رَّبِّهٖ ؕ
اَوَلَمْ تَاْتِهِمْ بَيِّنَةُ
مَا فِى الصُّحُفِ الْاُوْلٰى ○

134. And if We had inflicted
On them a penalty before this,[2659]
They would have said:
"Our Lord! If only Thou
Hadst sent us an apostle,
We should certainly have followed

۱۳۴- وَلَوْ اَنَّاۤ اَهْلَكْنٰهُمْ بِعَذَابٍ مِّنْ
قَبْلِهٖ لَقَالُوْا رَبَّنَا لَوْلَاۤ اَرْسَلْتَ
اِلَيْنَا رَسُوْلًا فَنَتَّبِعَ

2656. The good things of this life may make a brave show, but they are as nothing compared with the good of the Hereafter. Both are provided by God. But the former are given to the just and the unjust as a test and trial, and in any case will pass away; while the latter come specially from God for His devoted servants, and are incomparably of more value and will last through eternity.

2657. Sustenance, in the sense of the ordinary needs of life, the man of God does not worry about. That is provided by God for all, the just and the unjust. But the special provision, the real Sustenance, the spiritual fruit, is for a righteous life in the service of God.

2658. The question or plea of the Unbelievers is disingenuous. Many Signs have come with this Revelation. But the one that should have appealed to those who believed in former revelations and should have convinced them was what was in their own books.

2659. If the Sign mentioned in the last note did not convince them, it would mean that they were not true to their own faith. They were not straight with themselves. In justice they should have been punished for their falsehood. But they were given further respite. Or they would again have argued in a circle, and said: "If only God had sent us a living apostle we should have believed!" The living apostle they flout because they want a Sign. The Sign they wish to ignore, because they want a living apostle!

Thy Signs before we were
Humbled and put to shame."

اٰيٰتِكَ مِنْ قَبْلِ اَنْ نَّذِلَّ وَنَخْزٰى ۝

135. Say: "Each one (of us)
Is waiting: wait ye, therefore,[2660]
And soon shall ye know
Who it is that is
On the straight and even[2661]
16 Way, and who it is
30 That has received guidance."

١٣٥- قُلْ كُلٌّ مُّتَرَبِّصٌ فَتَرَبَّصُوْا ۚ
فَسَتَعْلَمُوْنَ مَنْ
اَصْحٰبُ الصِّرَاطِ السَّوِيِّ
وَمَنِ اهْتَدٰى ۝ ع

2660. If people will not be true to their own lights, what further argument is left? The man of God can only say: "Let us wait the issue: my faith tells me that God's Truth must prevail." *Cf.* ix. 52.

2661. *Cf.* xix. 43. The straight and even Way must endure, and show that the man who follows it has received true guidance. All falsehood and crookedness must ultimately disappear.

INTRODUCTION TO SŪRA XXI (*Anbiyāa*).

The last Sūra dealt with the individual story (spiritual) of Moses and Aaron, and contrasted it with the growth of evil in individuals like Pharaoh and the Sāmirī, and ended with a warning against Evil, and an exhortation to the purification of the soul with prayer and praise. This Sūra begins with the external obstacles placed by Evil against such purification, and gives the assurance of God's power to defend men, illustrating this with reference to Abraham's fight against idolatry, Lot's fight against unnatural wickedness, Noah's against unbelief, that of David and Solomon against injustice and failure to proclaim God's glory by making full use of man's God-given faculties and powers, that of Job against impatience and want of self-confidence, that of Ismā'īl, Idrīs, and Zul-kifl against want of steady perseverance, that of Ẓun-nūn against hasty anger, that of Zakariya against spiritual isolation, and that of Mary against the lusts of this world. In each allusion there is a special point about the soul's purification. The common point is that the Prophets were not, as the vulgar suppose, just irresistible men. They had to win their ground inch by inch against all kinds of resistance from evil.

The chronology of this Sūra has no significance. It probably dates from the middle of the Meccan period of inspiration.

Summary.—Man treats, as he has always treated, the serious things of life with jest or contempt; but the Judgment must come, and Truth must triumph (xxi. 1-29, and C. 147).

Unity of Design, and certainty of God's Promise: God's protection and mercy, and His justice (xxi 30-50, and C. 148).

How Abraham triumphed over idols, as did others among God's chosen ones over various forms of evil (xxi. 51-93, and C. 149).

Work righteousness while it is yet time, for the Judgment will come, and only he righteous will inherit (xxi. 94-112, and C. 150).

C. 147.—Men may lightly treat God's Signs
(xxi. 1-29.) As jests, but the Judgment must come
Inevitably. His Message is true,
And delivered by God's Apostle, as from
Man to men. Truth must triumph,
And all false gods and false worship
Must come to naught: for God is One,
And His Truth has been one throughout the ages.

Sūra XXI.

Anbiyāa, or The Prophets

In the name of God, Most Gracious,
Most Merciful.

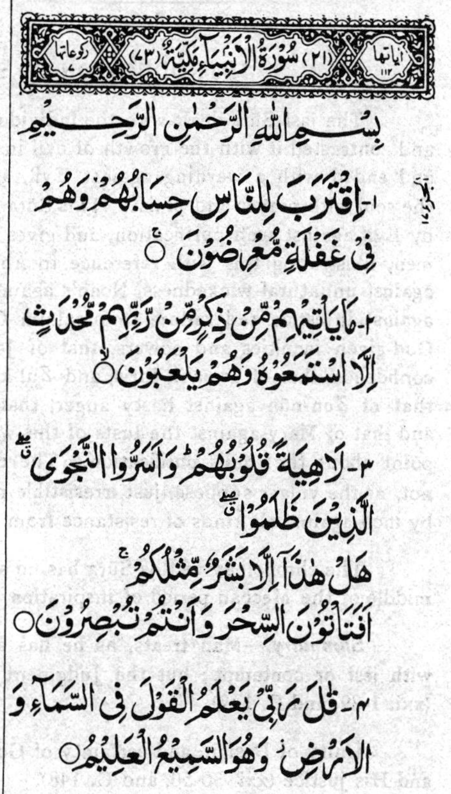

1. Closer and closer to mankind [2662]
Comes their Reckoning: yet they
Heed not and they turn away.

2. Never comes (aught) to them
Of a renewed Message [2663]
From their Lord, but they
Listen to it as in jest,—

3. Their hearts toying as with
Trifles. The wrong-doers
conceal [2664]
Their private counsels, (saying),
"Is this (one) more than
A man like yourselves?
Will ye go to witchcraft
With your eyes open?" [2665]

4. Say: [2666] "My Lord
Knoweth (every) word (spoken) [2667]
In the heavens and on earth:
He is the One that heareth
And knoweth (all things)."

2662. Every minute sees them nearer to their doom, and yet they are sadly heedless, and even actively turn away from the Message that would save them.

2663. In each age, when the Message of God is renewed, the very people who should have known better and welcomed the renewal and the sweeping away of human cobwebs, either receive it with amused self-superiority, which later turns to active hostility, or with careless indifference.

2664. God's Message is free and open, in the full light of day. His enemies plot against it in secrecy, lest their own false motives be exposed. Their jealousy prevents them from accepting a "man like themselves" as a teacher or warner or guide.

2665. Literally, "in a state in which you (actually) see (that it is witchcraft)". When God's Messenger is proved to be above them in moral worth, in true insight, in earnestness and power of eloquence, they accuse him of witchcraft, a word which may mean nothing, or perhaps some mysterious deceitful arts.

2666. Notice that in the usual Arabic texts printed in India the word *qāla* is here and in xxi. 112 below, as well as in xxiii. 112, spelt differently from the usual spelling of the word in other places (*e.g.*, in xx. 125-126). *Qul* is the reading of the Baṣra Qirāat, meaning, "Say thou" in the imperative. If we construe "he says", the pronoun refers to "this (one)" in the preceding verse, *viz.*: the Prophet. But more than one Commentator understands the meaning in the imperative, and I agree with them. The point is merely one of verbal construction. The meaning is the same in either case. See n. 2948 to xxiii. 112.

2667. Every word, whether whispered in secret (as in xxi. 3 above) or spoken openly, is known to God. Let not the wrong-doers imagine that their secret plots are secret to the Knower of all things.

5. "Nay," they say, "(these are)
Medleys of dreams!—Nay,
He forged it!—Nay,
He is (but) a poet![2668]
Let him then bring us
A Sign like the ones
That were sent to
(Prophets) of old!"

٥- بَلْ قَالُوٓا أَضْغَاثُ أَحْلَامٍ
بَلِ افْتَرٰىهُ بَلْ هُوَ شَاعِرٌ
فَلْيَأْتِنَا بِاٰيَةٍ كَمَآ
أُرْسِلَ الْاَوَّلُوْنَ ○

6. (As to those) before them,
Not one of the populations
Which We destroyed believed:
Will these believe?[2669]

٦- مَآ اٰمَنَتْ قَبْلَهُمْ مِّنْ قَرْيَةٍ
أَهْلَكْنٰهَا ۚ أَفَهُمْ يُؤْمِنُوْنَ ○

7. Before thee, also, the apostles
We sent were but men,
To whom We granted inspiration:
If ye realise this not, ask
Of those who possess the Message.[2670]

٧- وَمَآ أَرْسَلْنَا قَبْلَكَ إِلَّا رِجَالًا
نُّوْحِيٓ إِلَيْهِمْ فَسْئَلُوٓا أَهْلَ الذِّكْرِ إِنْ
كُنْتُمْ لَا تَعْلَمُوْنَ ○

8. Nor did We give them
Bodies that ate no food,
Nor were they exempt from death.[2671]

٨- وَمَا جَعَلْنٰهُمْ جَسَدًا لَّا يَأْكُلُوْنَ
الطَّعَامَ وَمَا كَانُوْا خٰلِدِيْنَ ○

9. In the end We fulfilled
To them Our promise,
And We saved them
And those whom We pleased,

٩- ثُمَّ صَدَقْنٰهُمُ الْوَعْدَ فَأَنْجَيْنٰهُمْ وَمَنْ
نَّشَآءُ

2668. The charges against God's inspired Apostle are heaped up. "Magic!" says one: that means, "We don't understand it!" Says another, "Oh! but we know! he is a mere dreamer of confused dreams!" If the "dreams" fit in with real things and vital experiences, another will suggest, "Oh yes! why drag in supernatural agencies? he is clever enough to forge it himself!" Or another suggests, "He is a poet! Poets can invent things and say them in beautiful words!" Another interposes, "What we should like to see is miracles, like those we read of in stories of the Prophets of old!"

2669. 'If such miracles as you read of failed to convince Unbelievers of old, what chance is there that these Unbelievers will believe? Miracles may come, but they are no cures for Unbelief.

2670. See xvi. 43 and n. 2069. This answers the Unbelievers' taunt, "he is just a man like ourselves!" True, but all apostles sent by God were men, not angels or another kind of beings, who could not understand men or whom men could not understand.

2671. As men they were subject to all the laws governing the physical bodies of men. They ate and drank, and their bodies perished in death.

But We destroyed those
Who transgressed beyond
bounds.[2672]

وَأَهْلَكْنَا الْمُسْرِفِينَ ○

10. We have revealed for you
(O men!) a book in which
Is a Message for you:
Will ye not then understand?

١٠- لَقَدْ أَنزَلْنَا إِلَيْكُمْ كِتَابًا فِيهِ
ذِكْرُكُمْ أَفَلَا تَعْقِلُونَ ○

SECTION 2.

11. How many were the populations
We utterly destroyed because
Of their iniquities, setting up
In their places other peoples?

١١- وَكَمْ قَصَمْنَا مِن قَرْيَةٍ كَانَتْ ظَالِمَةً وَ
أَنشَأْنَا بَعْدَهَا قَوْمًا آخَرِينَ ○

12. Yet, when they felt
Our Punishment (coming),
Behold, they (tried to) flee
From it.[2673]

١٢- فَلَمَّا أَحَسُّوا بَأْسَنَا
إِذَا هُم مِّنْهَا يَرْكُضُونَ ○

13. Flee not, but return to
The good things of this life
Which were given you,
And to your homes,
In order that ye may
Be called to account.[2674]

١٣- لَا تَرْكُضُوا وَارْجِعُوا إِلَىٰ مَا
أُتْرِفْتُمْ فِيهِ وَمَسَاكِنِكُمْ
لَعَلَّكُمْ تُسْأَلُونَ ○

14. They said: "Ah! woe to us!
We were indeed wrong-doers!"

١٤- قَالُوا يَا وَيْلَنَا إِنَّا كُنَّا ظَالِمِينَ ○

15. And that cry of theirs
Ceased not, till we made

١٥- فَمَا زَالَت تِّلْكَ دَعْوَاهُمْ حَتَّىٰ جَعَلْنَاهُمْ

2672. But, however difficult (or impossible) their mission may have appeared to them, or to the world at first, they won through eventually, even those who *seemed* to have been defeated. Examples are given in the latter part of this Sūra, especially in xxi. 51-93. They were delivered from the Wrath which overtook the Unbelievers, as were those with them who accepted God's Message and placed themselves in conformity with His Will and Plan. That is the meaning of "whom We pleased".

2673. When they had every chance of repentance and reform, they rejected God's Message, and perhaps even put up an open defiance. When they actually began to feel the Wrath coming, they began to flee, but it was too late! Besides, where could they flee to from the Wrath of God? Hence the ironical appeal to them in the next verse: better go back to your luxuries and what you thought were your permanent homes! *Cf.* Christ's saying in the present Gospel of St. Matthew (iii. 7): "O generation of vipers, who hath warned you to flee from the Wrath to come?"

2674. See last note. 'You thought your homes so comfortable: why don't you go back to them? You will be called to account. Perhaps there may be rewards to be given you, who knows?' This irony is itself the beginning of the Punishment. But the ungodly now see how wrong they had been. But their sighs and regrets now avail them nothing. It is too late. They are lost, and nothing can save them.

Them as a field
That is mown, as ashes
Silent and quenched.[2675]

حَصِيدًا خٰمِدِينَ ○

16. Not for (idle) sport did We[2676]
Create the heavens and the earth
And all that is between!

١٦- وَمَا خَلَقْنَا السَّمَآءَ وَالْأَرْضَ
وَمَا بَيْنَهُمَا لٰعِبِينَ ○

17. If it had been Our wish
To take (just) a pastime,
We should surely have taken
It from the things nearest
To Us, if We would
Do (such a thing)![2677]

١٧- لَوْ أَرَدْنَآ أَنْ نَّتَّخِذَ لَهْوًا
لَّاتَّخَذْنٰهُ مِنْ لَّدُنَّآ
إِنْ كُنَّا فٰعِلِينَ ○

18. Nay, We hurl the Truth
Against falsehood, and it knocks
Out its brain, and behold,
Falsehood doth perish!
Ah! woe be to you
For the (false) things
Ye ascribe (to Us).[2678]

١٨- بَلْ نَقْذِفُ بِالْحَقِّ عَلَى الْبٰطِلِ
فَيَدْمَغُهُ فَإِذَا هُوَ زَاهِقٌ
وَلَكُمُ الْوَيْلُ مِمَّا تَصِفُونَ ○

19. To Him belong all (creatures)
In the heavens and on earth:
Even those who are in His
(Very) Presence are not[2679]
Too proud to serve Him,
Nor are they (ever) weary
(Of His service):

١٩- وَلَهُ مَنْ فِي السَّمٰوٰتِ وَالْأَرْضِ
وَمَنْ عِنْدَهُ لَا يَسْتَكْبِرُونَ عَنْ عِبَادَتِهِ
وَلَا يَسْتَحْسِرُونَ ○

20. They celebrate His praises
Night and day, nor do they
Ever flag or intermit.

٢٠- يُسَبِّحُونَ الَّيْلَ وَالنَّهَارَ
لَا يَفْتُرُونَ ○

2675. The two similes present two different aspects of the lamentation of the ungodly. When they really see the Wrath to come, there is a stampede, but where can they go to? Their lamentation is now the only mark of their life. But it dies away, as corn vanishes from a field that is being mown, or as a dying fire is slowly extinguished! They do not die. They wish they were dead! (lxxviii. 40).

2676. The Hindu doctrine of *Lila*, that all things were created for sport, is here negatived. But more: with God we must not associate any ideas but those of Truth, Righteousness, Mercy, Justice, and the other attributes implied in His Beautiful Names. He does not jest nor play with His creatures.

2677. If such an idea as that of play or pastime had been possible with regard to God, and if He had wished really to indulge in pastime, He would have done it with creatures of Light nearest to Him, not with the lowly material creation that we see around us.

2678. Such as that (1) God has partners (xxi. 22), or (2) that He has begotten a son (xxi. 26), or (3) has daughters (xvi. 57), or any other superstitions derogatory to the dignity and glory of God.

2679. The pure angelic hosts, whom we imagine to be glorious creatures of light, high in the spiritual world, near the Throne of God Himself, are yet His creatures, and serve Him without ceasing, and are proud to do so. Such is the majesty of God Most High.

21. Or have they taken
(For worship) gods from the
earth[2680]
Who can raise (the dead)?[2681]

٢١- أَمِ اتَّخَذُوٓا ءَالِهَةً مِّنَ الْأَرْضِ
هُمْ يُنشِرُونَ ○

22. If there were, in the heavens
And the earth, other gods[2682]
Besides God, there would
Have been confusion in both!
But glory to God,
The Lord of the Throne:
(High is He) above
What they attribute to Him!

٢٢- لَوْ كَانَ فِيهِمَآ ءَالِهَةٌ إِلَّا اللَّهُ
لَفَسَدَتَا ۚ
فَسُبْحَٰنَ اللَّهِ رَبِّ الْعَرْشِ
عَمَّا يَصِفُونَ ○

23. He cannot be questioned
For His acts, but they[2683]
Will be questioned (for theirs).

٢٣- لَا يُسْـَٔلُ عَمَّا يَفْعَلُ وَهُمْ
يُسْـَٔلُونَ ○

24. Or have they taken
For worship (other) gods[2684]
Besides him? Say, "Bring
Your convincing proof: this
Is the Message of those
With me and the Message
Of those before me."[2685]
But most of them know not
The Truth, and so turn away.

٢٤- أَمِ اتَّخَذُوا مِن دُونِهِۦٓ ءَالِهَةً ۖ
قُلْ هَاتُوا بُرْهَٰنَكُمْ ۖ
هَٰذَا ذِكْرُ مَن مَّعِىَ وَذِكْرُ مَن قَبْلِى ۗ
بَلْ أَكْثَرُهُمْ لَا يَعْلَمُونَ
الْحَقَّ ۖ فَهُم مُّعْرِضُونَ ○

2680. The different kinds of false gods whom people raise from their imagination are now referred to. In verses 21-23, the reference is to the gods of the earth, whether idols or local godlings, or deified heroes, or animals or trees or forces of the nature around us, which men have from time to time worshipped. These, as deities, have no life except what their worshippers give to them.

2681. The answer of course is "no". No one but God can raise the dead to life. The miracle in the story of Jesus (iii. 49 and v. 113) was "by God's leave". It was a miracle of God, not one of Jesus by his own power or will.

2682. After the false gods of the earth (verse 21), are mentioned the false gods in the heavens and the earth, like those in the Greek Pantheon (verse 22), who quarrelled and fought and slandered each other and made their Olympus a perfect bear-garden!

2683. God is Self-Subsisting. All His creatures are responsible to Him and dependent on Him there is no other being to whom He can be responsible or on whom He can be dependent.

2684. See above, n. 2682, where two kinds of false worship are noted. Now we are warned against a third danger, the worship of false gods of any sort. Pagan man is prolific of creating abstract images for worship, including Self or abstract Intelligence or Power. In verse 26 below is mentioned a fourth kind of false worship, which imagines that God begets sons or daughters.

2685. This verse should be read with the next. All reason revolts against the idea of conflicting gods, and points to Unity in Creation and Unity in Godhead. This is not only the Message of Islam ("those with me") but the message of all prophets who came before the holy Prophet Muḥammad ("those before me"), and the line of prophets was closed with him. The Message given to every apostle in all ages was that of Unity as the fundamental basis of Order and Design in the world, material, moral, and spiritual.

25. Not an apostle did We
Send before thee without
This inspiration sent by Us
To him: that there is
No god but I; therefore
Worship and serve Me.

٢٥- وَمَآ اَرْسَلْنَا مِنْ قَبْلِكَ مِنْ رَّسُوْلٍ اِلَّا نُوْحِيْٓ اِلَيْهِ
اَنَّهٗ لَآ اِلٰهَ اِلَّآ اَنَا فَاعْبُدُوْنِ ۝

26. And they say: "(God)
Most Gracious has begotten[2686]
Offspring." Glory to Him!
They are (but) servants raised
To honour.

٢٦- وَقَالُوا اتَّخَذَ الرَّحْمٰنُ وَلَدًا سُبْحٰنَهٗ
بَلْ عِبَادٌ مُّكْرَمُوْنَ ۝

27. They speak not before[2687]
He speaks, and they act
(In all things) by His command.

٢٧- لَا يَسْبِقُوْنَهٗ بِالْقَوْلِ
وَهُمْ بِاَمْرِهٖ يَعْمَلُوْنَ ۝

28. He knows what is before them,
And what is behind them,
And they offer no intercession
Except for those who are
Acceptable,[2688] and they[2689] stand
In awe and reverence
Of His (glory).

٢٨- يَعْلَمُ مَا بَيْنَ اَيْدِيْهِمْ وَمَا خَلْفَهُمْ
وَلَا يَشْفَعُوْنَ اِلَّا لِمَنِ
ارْتَضٰى وَهُمْ مِّنْ خَشْيَتِهٖ مُشْفِقُوْنَ ۝

29. If any of them should say,
"I am a god besides Him",
Such a one We should
Reward with Hell: thus
Do We reward those
Who do wrong.

٢٩- وَمَنْ يَّقُلْ مِنْهُمْ اِنِّيْٓ اِلٰهٌ مِّنْ دُوْنِهٖ
فَذٰلِكَ نَجْزِيْهِ جَهَنَّمَ ۭ كَذٰلِكَ
نَجْزِي الظّٰلِمِيْنَ ۝ ع ٢

2686. This refers both to the Trinitarian superstition that God has begotten a son, and to the Arab superstition that the angels were daughters of God. All such superstitions are derogatory to the glory of God. The prophets and the angels are no more than servants of God: they are raised high in honour, and therefore they deserve our highest respect, but not our worship.

2687. They never say anything before they receive God's command to say it, and their acts are similarly conditioned. This is also the teaching of Jesus as reported in the Gospel of St John (xii. 49-50): "For I have not spoken of myself: but the Father which sent me, He gave me a commandment, what I should say, and what I should speak. And I know that His commandment is life everlasting: whatsoever I speak therefore, even as the Father said unto me, so I speak." If rightly understood, "Father" has the same meaning as our "Rabb", Sustainer and Cherisher, not Begetter or Progenitor.

2688. *Cf.* xx. 109. "Acceptable" means that they have conformed to the Will of God and obeyed His Law, thus winning the stamp of His approval.

2689. *They*: the usual interpretation refers the pronoun to the servants of God who intercede: it may also refer to those on whose behalf intercession is made: they do not take it as a matter of course, but stand in due awe and reverence of God's great glory and mercy.

C. 148.—Look at God's Creation: contemplate
(xxi. 30-50.) Its unity of Design and benevolence
Of Purpose. Death must come to all,
But life and faith are not objects of ridicule.
Truth will outlast all mockery: 'tis God
Who calls, because He cares for you,
And on His Judgment Seat will weigh
Each act, each thought, each motive, great
Or small, with perfect justice. Come,
Ye all, reject not His blessed Message.

SECTION 3.

30. Do not the Unbelievers see
That the heavens and the earth
Were joined together (as one[2690]
Unit of Creation), before
We clove them asunder?
We made from water[2691]
Every living thing. Will they
Not then believe?

٣٠- اَوَلَمْ يَرَ الَّذِيْنَ كَفَرُوْٓا اَنَّ السَّمٰوٰتِ
وَالْاَرْضَ كَانَتَا رَتْقًا فَفَتَقْنٰهُمَا ؕ
وَجَعَلْنَا مِنَ الْمَآءِ كُلَّ شَيْءٍ حَيٍّ ؕ
اَفَلَا يُؤْمِنُوْنَ ○

31. And We have set on the earth
Mountains standing firm,[2692]

٣١- وَجَعَلْنَا فِي الْاَرْضِ رَوَاسِيَ

2690. The evolution of the ordered worlds as we see them is hinted at. As man's intellectual gaze over the physical world expands, he sees more and more how Unity is the dominating note in God's wonderful Universe. Taking the solar system alone, we know that the maximum intensity of sun-spots corresponds with the maximum intensity of magnetic storms on this earth. The universal law of gravitation seems to bind all mass together. Physical facts point to the throwing off of planets from vast quantities of diffused nebular matter, of which the central condensed core is a sun.

2691. About 72 per cent. of the surface of our Globe is still covered with water, and it has been estimated that if the inequalities on the surface were all levelled, the whole surface would be under water, as the mean elevation of land sphere-level would be 7,000—10,000 feet below the surface of the ocean. This shows the predominance of water on our Globe. That all life began in the water is also a conclusion to which our latest knowledge in biological science points. Apart from the fact that protoplasm, the original basis of living matter, is liquid or semi-liquid and in a state of constant flux and instability, there is the fact that land animals, like the higher vertebrates, including man, show, in their embryological history, organs like those of fishes, indicating the watery origin of their original habitat. The constitution of protoplasm is about 80 to 85 per cent of water.

2692. *Cf.* xvi. 15 and n. 2038. *Lest it should shake with them*: here "them" refers back to "they" at the end of the preceding verse, meaning "Unbelievers". It might be mankind in general, but the pointed address to those who do not realise and understand God's mercies is appropriate, to drive home to them the fact that it is God's well-ordered providence that protects them normally from cataclysms like earthquakes, but that they could for their iniquities be destroyed in an instant, as the 'Ād and the Thamūd were destroyed before them. As pointed out in n. 2691 above, if the surface of the earth were levelled up, it would all be under water, and therefore the firm mountains are a further source of security to life which has evolved in terrestrial forms. Though the mountains may seem impassable barriers, yet God's providence has provided broad passes between them to afford highways for human communications.

Lest it should shake with them,
And We have made therein
Broad highways
(between mountains)
For them to pass through :
That they may receive guidance.[2693]

أَنْ تَمِيدَ بِهِمْ
وَجَعَلْنَا فِيهَا فِجَاجًا سُبُلًا
لَعَلَّهُمْ يَهْتَدُونَ ○

32. And We have made
The heavens as a canopy
Well guarded :[2694] yet do they
Turn away from the Signs
Which these things (point to)!

٣٢- وَجَعَلْنَا السَّمَاءَ سَقْفًا مَّحْفُوظًا ۚ
وَّهُمْ عَنْ اٰيٰتِهَا مُعْرِضُوْنَ ○

33. It is He Who created
The Night and the Day,
And the sun and the moon :
All (the celestial bodies)
Swim along, each in its[2695]
Rounded course.

٣٣- وَهُوَ الَّذِيْ خَلَقَ الَّيْلَ وَالنَّهَارَ
وَالشَّمْسَ وَالْقَمَرَ ۭ
كُلٌّ فِيْ فَلَكٍ يَّسْبَحُوْنَ ○

34. We granted not to any man
Before thee permanent life[2696]
(Here) : if then thou shouldst die,
Would they live permanently?

٣٤- وَمَا جَعَلْنَا لِبَشَرٍ مِّنْ قَبْلِكَ الْخُلْدَ ۭ
اَفَاۡىِٕنْ مِّتَّ فَهُمُ الْخٰلِدُوْنَ ○

35. Every soul shall have
A taste of death :[2697]
And We test you
By evil and by good

٣٥- كُلُّ نَفْسٍ ذَاۗىِٕقَةُ الْمَوْتِ ۭ
وَنَبْلُوْكُمْ بِالشَّرِّ وَالْخَيْرِ

2693. In both the literal and the figurative sense. Literally these natural mountain highways direct men in the way they should go. Figuratively, these wonderful instances of God's providence should turn men's thoughts to the true guidance of God in life and spiritual progress.

2694. *Canopy well guarded*: the heavens form a canopy that is secure from falling down : they also form a sublime spectacle and a Mystery that man can only faintly reach. Perhaps also the mystery of spiritual life is metaphorically hinted at. *Cf.* also xv. 17.

2695. I have indicated, unlike most translators, the metaphor of swimming implied in the original words : how beautiful it is to contemplate the heavenly bodies swimming through space (or ether) in their rounded courses before our gaze!

2696. Life on this planet without death has not been granted to any man. The Khidhr legends are popular tales. His life without death on this earth is nowhere mentioned in the Qur-ān. The taunt of the Unbelievers at the holy Prophet was therefore futile. Could any of them live without death at some time or other? Could they name any one who did?

2697. *Cf.* iii. 185, and n. 491. The soul does not die, but when it separates from the body at the death of the body, the soul gets a taste of death. In our life of probation on this earth, our virtue and faith are tested by many things : some are tested by calamities, and some by the good things of this life. If we prove our true mettle, we pass our probation with success. In any case all must return to God, and then will our life be appraised at its true value.

By way of trial.
To Us must ye return.

فتنة ۗ وإلينا ترجعون ○

36. When the Unbelievers see thee,
They treat thee not except
With ridicule. "Is this,"
(They say), "the one who talks [2698]
Of your gods?" And they
Blaspheme at the mention
Of (God) Most Gracious!

٣٦- وإذا راك الذين كفروا إن يتخذونك
إلا هزوا ۗ
أهذا الذي يذكر آلهتكم ۚ
وهم بذكر الرحمن هم كافرون ○

37. Man is a creature of haste: [2699]
Soon (enough) will I show
You My Signs; then
Ye will not ask Me
To hasten them!

٣٧- خلق الإنسان من عجل ۗ
سأريكم آياتي فلا تستعجلون ○

38. They say: "When will this
Promise come to pass,
If ye are telling the truth?"

٣٨- ويقولون متى هذا الوعد
إن كنتم صادقين ○

39. If only the Unbelievers [2700]
Knew (the time) when they
Will not be able
To ward off the Fire
From their faces, nor yet
From their backs, and (when)
No help can reach them!

٣٩- لو يعلم الذين كفروا حين
لا يكفون عن وجوههم النار
ولا عن ظهورهم ولا هم ينصرون ○

40. Nay, it may come to them
All of a sudden and confound
Them: no power will they
Have then to avert it,
Nor will they (then)
Get respite.

٤٠- بل تأتيهم بغتة فتبهتهم
فلا يستطيعون ردها
ولا هم ينظرون ○

2698. To the godly man the issue between false worship and true worship is a very serious matter. To the sceptics and unbelievers it is only a joke. They take it lightly, and laugh at the godly man. They not only laugh at him, but they blaspheme when the name of the One True God is mentioned. The reply to this is in the next verse.

2699. Haste is in the very bone and marrow of man. If he is granted respite for his own sake, in order that he may have a further chance of repentance and coming back to God, he says impatiently and incredulously: "Bring on the Punishment quickly, that I may see if what you say is true!" Alas, it is too true! When the Punishment actually comes near and he sees it, he will not want it hastened. He will want more time and further delay! Poor creature of haste!

2700. They would not be so unreasonable if they only realised the terrible future for them! The Fire will envelop them on all sides, and no help will then be possible. Is it not best for them now to turn and repent? The Punishment may come too suddenly, as is said in the next verse.

41. Mocked were (many)
Apostles before thee;
But their scoffers
Were hemmed in
By the thing that they mocked.[2701]

٤١- وَلَقَدِ اسْتُهْزِئَ بِرُسُلٍ مِّنْ قَبْلِكَ
فَحَاقَ بِالَّذِيْنَ سَخِرُوْا مِنْهُمْ
مَّا كَانُوْا بِهٖ يَسْتَهْزِءُوْنَ ۝

Section 4.

42. Say, "Who can keep
You safe by night and by day
From (the Wrath of) (God)
Most Gracious?"[2702] Yet they
Turn away from the mention
Of their Lord.

٤٢- قُلْ مَنْ يَّكْلَؤُكُمْ بِالَّيْلِ وَالنَّهَارِ
مِنَ الرَّحْمٰنِ ؕ
بَلْ هُمْ عَنْ ذِكْرِ رَبِّهِمْ مُّعْرِضُوْنَ ۝

43. Or have they gods that
Can guard them from Us?
They have no power to aid
Themselves, nor can they
Be defended from Us.[2703]

٤٣- اَمْ لَهُمْ اٰلِهَةٌ تَمْنَعُهُمْ مِّنْ دُوْنِنَا ؕ
لَا يَسْتَطِيْعُوْنَ نَصْرَ اَنْفُسِهِمْ
وَلَا هُمْ مِّنَّا يُصْحَبُوْنَ ۝

44. Nay, We gave the good things
Of this life to these men
And their fathers until
The period[2704] grew long for them;
See they not that We[2705]
Gradually reduce the land
(In their control) from
Its outlying borders? Is it
Then they who will win?

٤٤- بَلْ مَتَّعْنَا هٰۤؤُلَاۤءِ وَاٰبَاۤءَهُمْ
حَتّٰى طَالَ عَلَيْهِمُ الْعُمُرُ ؕ
اَفَلَا يَرَوْنَ اَنَّا نَاْتِى الْاَرْضَ
نَنْقُصُهَا مِنْ اَطْرَافِهَا ؕ
اَفَهُمُ الْغٰلِبُوْنَ ۝

2701. The same verse occurs at vi. 10, where see n. 843. 'What they are mocking at now will be in a position to mock them in due time.'

2702. 'God is most Gracious: if, in spite of His great mercy, you are so rebellious and depraved as to incur His Wrath, who is there who can save you? His Wrath can descend on you at any time, by night or by day.'

2703. *Aṣhaba*: to join as companion; with *'an* or *min* it has also the meaning of to defend or remove from someone. The full signification can only be got by a long paraphrase: 'they are not fit to be mentioned in the same breath with Us, nor can they be defended from Us.'

2704. *'Umr*, or *'Umur*: age, generation, period, time, life. Here "period" is most appropriate, as it covers many generations, "these men and their fathers."

2705. *Cf.* xiii. 41 and n. 1865. The particular signification is that Islam spread from the outer borders, social and geographical, gradually inwards. The social fringe was the humbler people, such as slaves and poor men. The geographical reference is to Medina and tribes away from the Mecca centre. The proud and unbelieving Quraish were the last to come in when the circle was gradually drawn tighter and tighter around them. The general signification applies to all times. God's Truth makes its way first among the poor and the lowly, those whose minds are unsoiled by prejudices of false pride or false knowledge, but it gradually hems in the obstinate, until it prevails in the end.

45. Say, "I do but warn you
According to revelation":
But the deaf will not hear
The call, (even) when
They are warned![2706]

٤٥- قُلْ إِنَّمَا أُنذِرُكُم بِالْوَحْيِ ۚ
وَلَا يَسْمَعُ الصُّمُّ الدُّعَاءَ
إِذَا مَا يُنذَرُونَ ○

46. If but a breath of the Wrath
Of thy Lord do touch them,
They will then say, "Woe
To us! we did wrong indeed!"

٤٦- وَلَئِن مَّسَّتْهُمْ نَفْحَةٌ مِّنْ عَذَابِ
رَبِّكَ لَيَقُولُنَّ يَا وَيْلَنَا إِنَّا كُنَّا ظَالِمِينَ ○

47. We shall set up scales
Of justice for the day
Of Judgment, so that
Not a soul will be dealt with
Unjustly in the least.
And if there be
(No more than) the weight
Of a mustard seed,[2707]
We will bring it (to account):
And enough are We
To take account.[2708]

٤٧- وَنَضَعُ الْمَوَازِينَ الْقِسْطَ لِيَوْمِ الْقِيَامَةِ
فَلَا تُظْلَمُ نَفْسٌ شَيْئًا ۖ
وَإِن كَانَ مِثْقَالَ حَبَّةٍ
مِّنْ خَرْدَلٍ أَتَيْنَا بِهَا ۗ
وَكَفَىٰ بِنَا حَاسِبِينَ ○

48. In the past We granted
To Moses and Aaron

٤٨- وَلَقَدْ آتَيْنَا مُوسَىٰ وَهَارُونَ

2706. According to the English saying, "none is so deaf as those who will not hear". When they deliberately shut their ears to warnings from the Merciful God, meant for their own good, the responsibility is their own. But their cowardice is shown in the next verse by their behaviour when the first breath of the Wrath reaches them.

2707. Not the smallest action, word, thought, motive, or predilection but must come into the account of God. *Cf.* Browning (in *Rabbi Ben Ezra*): "But all, the world's coarse thumb And finger failed to plumb, So passed in making up the main account; All instincts immature, All purposes unsure, That weighed not as his work, yet swelled the man's account; Thoughts hardly to be packed Into a narrow act, Fancies that broke through language and escaped; All I could never be, All, men ignored in me, This, I was worth to God, Whose wheel the pitcher shaped."

2708. The literalism of Sale has here excelled itself: he translates, "and there will be sufficient accountants with us"! What is meant is that when God takes account, His accounting will be perfect: there will be no flaw in it, as there may be in earthly accountants, who require other people's help in some matters of account which they do not understand for want of knowledge of that particular department they are dealing with. God's knowledge is perfect, and therefore His justice will be perfect also; for He will not fail to take into account all the most intangible things that determine conduct and character. See last note. There is no contradiction between this and xviii. 104-105, where it is said that men of vain works, *i.e.*, shallow hypocritical deeds, will have no weight attached to their deeds. In fact the two correspond.

The Criterion (for judgment),[2709]
And a Light and a Message
For those who would do right,—

الْفُرْقَانَ وَضِيَاءً وَذِكْرًا لِّلْمُتَّقِينَ ۝

49. Those who fear their Lord
In their most secret thoughts,
And who hold the Hour
(Of Judgment) in awe.[2710]

٤٩- الَّذِينَ يَخْشَوْنَ رَبَّهُم بِالْغَيْبِ وَهُم مِّنَ السَّاعَةِ مُشْفِقُونَ ۝

50. And this is a blessed
Message which We have
Sent down: will ye then
Reject it?[2711]

٥٠- وَهَٰذَا ذِكْرٌ مُّبَارَكٌ أَنزَلْنَاهُ ۚ أَفَأَنتُمْ لَهُ مُنكِرُونَ ۝

C. 149.—The great exemplars of virtue conquered
(xxi. 51-93.) Evil, each according to his circumstances:
Abraham stood staunch in the fire
Of persecution, unhurt; Lūṭ was bold
In reproving abominations; Noah survived
The Flood by his faith, in a world of Unbelief;
David sought justice, and sang God's praises;
Solomon by wisdom subdued the refractory;
Job was patient in suffering; Ismā'īl,
Idrīs, and Ẕul-kifl were true in constancy
Amid temptation; Jonah turned to God
After a short misunderstanding; Zakarīya
And his family were exemplars of devoutness;
And Mary of chastity. All men and women
Of God form one united Brotherhood.

2709. *Cf.* ii. 53 and n. 68, where the meaning of *Furqān* is discussed. Here three things are mentioned as given to Moses and Aaron: (1) The Criterion for judgment; this might well be the wonderful Proofs they saw of God's goodness and glory from which they could have no doubt as to God's will and command; (2) the Light; this was the inner enlightenment of their soul, such as comes from inspiration: and (3) the Message, the Book, the original Book of Moses, which Aaron as his lieutenant would also use as a guide for his people.

2710. Note the three kinds of fear mentioned in xxi. 48-49. *Taqwā* is the fear of running counter to the will of God; it is akin to the love of Him; for we fear to offend those we love: it results in right conduct, and those who entertain it are "those who would do right". Then there is *Khashyat*, the fear of God, lest the person who entertains it may be found, in his inmost thoughts, to be short of the standard which God wishes for him; this is also righteousness but in a less high degree than *Taqwā* which is akin to love. And thirdly, there is the fear of consequences on the Day of Judgment (*ishfāq*); this also may lead to righteousness, but is on a still lower plane. Perhaps the three correspond to the Criterion, the Light, and the Message (or Warning) of the last verse.

2711. Here is a man and a Book, greater than Moses and his Book. Are you going to reject him and it?

Section 5.

51. We bestowed aforetime
On Abraham his rectitude[2712]
Of conduct, and well were We
Acquainted with him.[2713]

٥١- وَلَقَدْ اٰتَيْنَآ اِبْرٰهِيْمَ رُشْدَهٗ مِنْ قَبْلُ
وَكُنَّا بِهٖ عٰلِمِيْنَ ۚ

52. Behold! he said
To his father and his people,[2714]
"What are these images,
To which ye are
(So assiduously) devoted?"

٥٢- اِذْ قَالَ لِاَبِيْهِ وَقَوْمِهٖ
مَا هٰذِهِ التَّمَاثِيْلُ الَّتِيْٓ
اَنْتُمْ لَهَا عٰكِفُوْنَ ۝

53. They said, "We found
Our fathers worshipping them."

٥٣- قَالُوْا وَجَدْنَآ اٰبَآءَنَا لَهَا عٰبِدِيْنَ ۝

54. He said, "Indeed ye
Have been in manifest
Error—ye and your fathers."

٥٤- قَالَ لَقَدْ كُنْتُمْ
اَنْتُمْ وَاٰبَآؤُكُمْ فِيْ ضَلٰلٍ مُّبِيْنٍ ۝

55. They said, "Have you
Brought us the Truth,
Or are you one
Of those who jest?"[2715]

٥٥- قَالُوْٓا اَجِئْتَنَا بِالْحَقِّ
اَمْ اَنْتَ مِنَ اللّٰعِبِيْنَ ۝

56. He said, "Nay, your Lord
Is the Lord of the heavens
And the earth, He Who
Created them (from nothing):[2716]
And I am a witness
To this (truth).

٥٦- قَالَ بَلْ رَّبُّكُمْ رَبُّ السَّمٰوٰتِ وَالْاَرْضِ
الَّذِيْ فَطَرَهُنَّ ۖ
وَاَنَا عَلٰى ذٰلِكُمْ مِّنَ الشّٰهِدِيْنَ ۝

2712. *Rushd*: right conduct, corresponding in action to the quality expressed in the epithet *Ḥanīf* (sound or true in Faith) applied to Abraham in ii. 135 and elsewhere.

2713. Hence Abraham's title "Friend of God" (*Khalīl-ullah*): iv. 125.

2714. Reference is made to Abraham in many places. In xix. 42-49 it was with reference to his relations to his father: the problem was how a righteous man should deal with his father, when his duty to his father conflicts with his duty to God. Here the problem is: how a righteous man should deal with evil and overcome it; how he should fight against evil, and if he is subjected to the fire of persecution, how his firmness draws God's Mercy, and the very troubles he is placed in become his comfort and joy.

2715. Abraham looked at life with a serious eye, and his people took it light-heartedly. He was devoted to Truth, and they cared more for ancestral custom. In the conflict he seemed to be in their power. But he was fearless, and he triumphed by God's Grace.

2716. For the various words for "creation" see n. 120 to ii. 117, where *faṭara* is explained and differentiated from other words of similar meaning.

57. "And by God, I have
A plan for your idols—
After ye go away
And turn your backs"...[2717]

٥٧- وَتَاللَّهِ لَأَكِيدَنَّ أَصْنَامَكُم
بَعْدَ أَن تُوَلُّوا مُدْبِرِينَ ○

58. So he broke them to pieces,
(All) but the biggest of them,
That they might turn
(And address themselves) to it.[2718]

٥٨- فَجَعَلَهُمْ جُذَاذًا إِلَّا كَبِيرًا لَّهُمْ
لَعَلَّهُمْ إِلَيْهِ يَرْجِعُونَ ○

59. They said, "Who has
Done this to our gods?
He must indeed be
Some man of impiety!"

٥٩- قَالُوا مَن فَعَلَ هَٰذَا بِآلِهَتِنَا
إِنَّهُ لَمِنَ الظَّالِمِينَ ○

60. They said, "We heard
A youth talk of them:[2719]
He is called Abraham."

٦٠- قَالُوا سَمِعْنَا فَتًى يَذْكُرُهُمْ
يُقَالُ لَهُ إِبْرَاهِيمُ ○

61. They said, "Then bring him
Before the eyes of the people,
That they may bear witness."

٦١- قَالُوا فَأْتُوا بِهِ عَلَىٰ أَعْيُنِ النَّاسِ
لَعَلَّهُمْ يَشْهَدُونَ ○

62. They said, "Art thou
The one that did this
With our gods, O Abraham?"[2720]

٦٢- قَالُوا أَأَنتَ فَعَلْتَ هَٰذَا
بِآلِهَتِنَا يَا إِبْرَاهِيمُ ○

2717. He wants to convince them of the powerlessness of their idols. But he does not do it underhand. He tells them that he is going to do something when once they are gone and their backs are turned to the idols,—as much as to say that the idols are dependent on their care and attention. Apparently the people are amused and want to see what he does. So they leave him to his own devices.

2718. He was enacting a scene, to make the people ashamed of worshipping senseless stocks and stones. He left the biggest idol untouched and broke the others to pieces, as if a fight had taken place between the idols, and the biggest had smashed the others. Would they turn to the surviving idol and ask him how it all happened?

2719. Different groups of people are speaking. Those who were not present at Abraham's speech in verse 57 ask, "who has done this?" Those who were, at once name him, whereupon a formal council of the people was held, and Abraham was arraigned.

2720. They asked him the formal question. There was no mystery about it. He had already openly threatened to do something to the idols, and people who had heard his threats were there. He now continues his ironic taunt to the idol-worshippers. 'You ask me! Why don't you ask the idols? Doesn't it look as if this big fellow has smashed the smaller ones in a quarrel?' If they do not ask the idols, they confess that the idols have not intelligence enough to answer! This argument is developed in verses 64-67. Note that while the false worshippers laughed at his earnestness, he pays them out by a grim practical joke, which at the same time advances the cause of Truth.

63. He said: " Nay, this Was done by— This is their biggest one! Ask them, if they Can speak intelligently!"	٦٣- قَالَ بَلْ فَعَلَهُ كَبِيرُهُمْ هٰذَا فَسْـَٔلُوهُمْ إِن كَانُوا يَنطِقُونَ ○
64. So they turned to themselves And said, " Surely ye Are the ones in the wrong!"[2721]	٦٤- فَرَجَعُوٓا إِلَىٰٓ أَنفُسِهِمْ فَقَالُوٓا إِنَّكُمْ أَنتُمُ ٱلظَّٰلِمُونَ ○
65. Then were they confounded[2722] With shame: (they said), " Thou knowest full well that These (idols) do not speak!"	٦٥- ثُمَّ نُكِسُوا عَلَىٰ رُءُوسِهِمْ لَقَدْ عَلِمْتَ مَا هٰٓؤُلَآءِ يَنطِقُونَ ○
66. (Abraham) said, " Do ye then Worship, besides God, Things that can neither Be of any good to you Nor do you harm?	٦٦- قَالَ أَفَتَعْبُدُونَ مِن دُونِ ٱللَّهِ مَا لَا يَنفَعُكُمْ شَيْـًٔا وَلَا يَضُرُّكُمْ ○
67. " Fie upon you, and upon[2723] The things that ye worship Besides God! Have ye No sense?"...	٦٧- أُفٍّ لَّكُمْ وَلِمَا تَعْبُدُونَ مِن دُونِ ٱللَّهِ أَفَلَا تَعْقِلُونَ ○
68. They said, " Burn him And protect your gods, If ye do (anything at all)!"	٦٨- قَالُوا حَرِّقُوهُ وَٱنصُرُوٓا ءَالِهَتَكُمْ إِن كُنتُمْ فَٰعِلِينَ ○

2721. Abraham's biting irony cut them to the quick. What could they say? They turned to each other. Some among them thought he had the best of the argument. They were not keen on idolatry, and they told their fellows that it was useless arguing with Abraham. They all hung their heads in shame. But presently they thought they would face out Abraham, and take his words literally. They said, " You know quite well that idols do not speak!" This was precisely what Abraham wanted them to say, and he delivered his final blow! See n. 2723 below.

2722. Literally, " they were turned down on their heads" which may suggest a metaphorical somersault, *i.e.*, that they recovered from their dawning shame for idolatry and were prepared to argue it out with the youth Abraham. But I think there is better authority for the interpretation I have adopted.

2723. As soon as they admitted in so many words that the idols could not speak, Abraham delivered his final attack: 'Then, why do you worship such useless impotent creatures?' After that, there remains nothing but the argument of violence, which they proceed to exercise, being the party in power. 'Burn him at the stake' is an easy cry! But it was not Abraham that suffered: it was his persecutors (xxi. 70).

69. We said, "O Fire![2724]
Be thou cool,
And (a means of) safety
For Abraham!"[2725]

٦٩- قُلْنَا يٰنَارُ كُونِي بَرْدًا
وَّسَلٰمًا عَلٰٓى إِبْرٰهِيمَ ۝

70. Then they sought a stratagem
Against him: but We
Made them the ones
That lost most![2726]

٧٠- وَأَرَادُوا بِهِۦ كَيْدًا
فَجَعَلْنٰهُمُ الْأَخْسَرِينَ ۝

71. But We delivered him
And (his nephew) Lūṭ
(And directed them) to the land[2727]
Which We have blessed
For the nations.

٧١- وَنَجَّيْنٰهُ وَلُوطًا إِلَى الْأَرْضِ
الَّتِي بٰرَكْنَا فِيهَا لِلْعٰلَمِينَ ۝

72. And We bestowed on him
Isaac

٧٢- وَوَهَبْنَا لَهُۥٓ إِسْحٰقَ

2724. The nature of fire, by all the physical laws of matter, is to be hot. The supremacy of mind over matter is a phrase much used, but the supremacy of the spiritual over the material is not so commonly understood. And yet it is the greatest factor in the estimate of Reality. The material is ephemeral and relative. The spiritual is eternal and absolute. Through all the fire of persecution and hatred Abraham remained unhurt. The fire became cool, and a means of safety for Abraham.

2725. Can we form any idea of the place where he passed through the furnace, and the stage in his career at which this happened? He was born in Ur of the Chaldees, a place on the lower reaches of the Euphrates, not a hundred miles from the Persian Gulf. This was the cradle, or one of the cradles, of human civilisation. Astronomy was studied here in very ancient times, and the worship of the sun, moon, and stars was the prevailing form of religion. Abraham revolted against this quite early in life, and his argument is referred to in vi. 74-82. They also had idols in their temples, probably idols representing heavenly bodies and celestial winged creatures. He was still a youth (xxi 60) when he broke the idols. This was stage No. 2. After this he was marked down as a rebel and persecuted. Perhaps some years passed before the incident of his being thrown into the Fire (xxi. 68-69) took place, or the incident may be only allegorical. Traditionally the Fire incident is referred to a king called Nimrūd, about whom see n. 1565 to xi. 69. If Nimrūd's capital was in Assyria, near Nineveh (site near modern Mosul), we may suppose either that the king's rule extended over the whole of Mesopotamia, or that Abraham wandered north through Babylonia to Assyria. Various stratagems were devised to get rid of him (xxi 70), but he was saved by the mercy of God. The final break came when he was probably a man of mature age and could speak to his father with some authority. This incident is referred to in xix. 41-48. He now left his ancestral lands, and avoiding the Syrian desert, came to the fertile lands of Aram or Syria, and so south to Canaan, when the incident of xi. 69-76 and the adventure of his nephew Lūṭ took place. It is some years after this that we may suppose he built the Ka'ba with Ismā'īl (ii. 124-29), and his prayer in xiv. 35-41 may be referred to the same time. His visit to Egypt (Gen. xii. 10) is not referred to in the Qur-ān.

2726. As they could not get rid of him by open punishment, they tried secret plans, but were foiled throughout. It was not he that lost, but they. On the contrary he left them and prospered and became the progenitor of great peoples.

2727. The land of Aram or Syria, which in its widest connotation includes Canaan or Palestine. Syria is a well-watered fertile land, with a Mediterranean sea-coast, on which the famous commerical cities of Tyre and Sidon were situated. Its population is very mixed, as it has been a bone of contention between all the great kingdoms and empires of Western Asia and Egypt, and European interest in it dates from the most ancient times and continues under the French Mandate to the present day.

And, as an additional gift,[2728]
(A grandson), Jacob, and We
Made righteous men of every one
(Of them).

وَيَعْقُوبَ نَافِلَةً ۗ
وَكُلًّا جَعَلْنَا صٰلِحِينَ ۝

73. And We made them
Leaders, guiding (men) by
Our Command, and We
Sent them inspiration
To do good deeds,
To establish regular prayers,
And to practise regular charity;
And they constantly served
Us (and Us only).[2729]

٧٣- وَجَعَلْنٰهُمْ أَئِمَّةً يَّهْدُوْنَ بِأَمْرِنَا
وَأَوْحَيْنَا إِلَيْهِمْ فِعْلَ الْخَيْرٰتِ
وَإِقَامَ الصَّلٰوةِ وَإِيْتَاءَ الزَّكٰوةِ ۚ
وَكَانُوْا لَنَا عٰبِدِيْنَ ۝

74. And to Lūṭ, too,
We gave Judgment and Knowledge,
And We saved him
From the town which practised
Abominations: truly they were
A people given to Evil,
A rebellious people.[2730]

٧٤- وَلُوْطًا اٰتَيْنٰهُ حُكْمًا وَّعِلْمًا
وَّنَجَّيْنٰهُ مِنَ الْقَرْيَةِ الَّتِيْ
كَانَتْ تَّعْمَلُ الْخَبٰٓئِثَ ۗ
إِنَّهُمْ كَانُوْا قَوْمَ سَوْءٍ فٰسِقِيْنَ ۝

75. And We admitted him
To Our Mercy: for he
Was one of the Righteous.

٧٥- وَأَدْخَلْنٰهُ فِيْ رَحْمَتِنَا ۗ
إِنَّهُ مِنَ الصّٰلِحِيْنَ ۝

SECTION 6.

76. (Remember) Noah, when
He cried (to Us) aforetime:[2730-A]
We listened to his (prayer)
And delivered him and his
Family from great distress.[2731]

٧٦- وَنُوْحًا إِذْ نَادٰى مِنْ قَبْلُ
فَاسْتَجَبْنَا لَهُ فَنَجَّيْنٰهُ وَأَهْلَهُ
مِنَ الْكَرْبِ الْعَظِيْمِ ۝

2728. *Nāfilat* has many meanings: (1) booty; (2) extra work or prayer; (3) extra or additional gift; (4) grandson. The two last significations are implied here. Not only was Abraham given a son in his old age; he was given not only Isaac, but several sons, the chief being Ismā'īl and Isaac, who both joined in burying him (Gen. xxv. 9); and he also saw grandsons. Ismā'īl is specially mentioned later (xxi. 85) apart from Isaac's line, on account of his special importance for Islam.

2729. The spiritual lesson from this passage may be recapitulated. The righteous man makes no compromise with evil. If the votaries of evil laugh at him he pays them in their own coin, but he stands firmly by his principles. His firmness causes some confusion among the followers of evil, and he openly declares the faith that is in him. They try, openly and secretly, to injure or kill him, but God protects him, while evil perishes from its own excesses.

2730. Lot's people were given to unspeakable abominations. His mission was to preach to them. He withstood Evil, but they rejected him. They were punished, but he and his followers were saved. See xv. 61-74; xi. 77-82; and vii. 80-84.

2730-A. The date of Noah was many centuries before that of Abraham.

2731. The contemporaries of Noah were given to Unbelief, oppression of the poor, and vain disputations. He carried God's Message to them, and standing fast in faith, built the Ark, in which he was saved with his followers from the Flood, while the wicked were drowned. See. xi. 25-48.

77. We helped him against
People who rejected Our Signs:
Truly they were a people
Given to Evil: so We
Drowned them (in the Flood)
All together.

٧٧- وَنَصَرْنَٰهُ مِنَ ٱلْقَوْمِ ٱلَّذِينَ كَذَّبُوا۟ بِـَٔايَٰتِنَآ
إِنَّهُمْ كَانُوا۟ قَوْمَ سَوْءٍ
فَأَغْرَقْنَٰهُمْ أَجْمَعِينَ ○

78. And remember David
And Solomon, when they
Gave judgment in the matter
Of the field into which
The sheep of certain people
Had strayed by night:
We did witness their judgment.

٧٨- وَدَاوُۥدَ وَسُلَيْمَٰنَ إِذْ
يَحْكُمَانِ فِى ٱلْحَرْثِ إِذْ نَفَشَتْ فِيهِ غَنَمُ
ٱلْقَوْمِ
وَكُنَّا لِحُكْمِهِمْ شَٰهِدِينَ ○

79. To Solomon We inspired[2732]
The (right) understanding
Of the matter: to each
(Of them) We gave Judgment
And Knowledge; it was
Our power that made
The hills and the birds
Celebrate Our praises,[2733]
With David: it was We
Who did (all these things).

٧٩- فَفَهَّمْنَٰهَا سُلَيْمَٰنَ
وَكُلًّا ءَاتَيْنَا حُكْمًا وَعِلْمًا
وَسَخَّرْنَا مَعَ دَاوُۥدَ ٱلْجِبَالَ
يُسَبِّحْنَ وَٱلطَّيْرَ
وَكُنَّا فَٰعِلِينَ ○

80. It was We Who taught him[2734]
The making of coats of mail

٨٠- وَعَلَّمْنَٰهُ صَنْعَةَ لَبُوسٍ

2732. The sheep, on account of the negligence of the shepherd, got into a cultivated field (or vineyard) by night and ate up the young plants or their tender shoots, causing damage, to the extent of perhaps a whole year's crop. David was king, and in his seat of judgment he considered the matter so serious that he awarded the owner of the field the sheep themselves in compensation for his damage. The Roman law of the Twelve Tables might have approved of this decision, and on the same principle was built up the Deodand doctrine of English Law, now obsolete. His son Solomon, a mere boy of eleven, thought of a better decision, where the penalty would better fit the offence. The loss was the loss of the fruits or produce of the field or vineyard: the *corpus* of the property was not lost. Solomon's suggestion was that the owner of the field or vineyard should not take the sheep altogether but only detain them long enough to recoup his actual damage, from the milk, wool, and possibly young of the sheep, and then return the sheep to the shepherd. David's merit was that he accepted the suggestion, even though it came from a little boy: Solomon's merit was that he distinguished between *corpus* and income, and though a boy, was not ashamed to put his case before his father. But in either case it was God Who inspired the true realisation of justice. He was present and witnessed the affair, as He is present everywhere.

2733. Whatever is in the heavens and the earth celebrates the praises of God: xvii. 44; lvii. 1; xvi. 48-50. Even the "thunder repeateth His praises": xiii. 13. All nature ever sings the praises of God. David sang in his Psalms, cxlviii. 7-10: "Praise the Lord from the earth, ye...mountains and all hills; ...creeping things and flying fowl!" All nature sings to God's glory, in unison with David, and angels, and men of God. If the Jewish Talmudists take this literally, there is no need for Muslims to do so. *Cf.* also xxxiv. 10 and xxxviii. 18-19.

2734. The making of coats of mail is attributed to David. It is defensive armour, and therefore its discovery and supply is associated with deeds of righteousness in xxxiv. 10-11, in contrast with the deadly weapons which man invents for offensive purposes. Indeed, all fighting, unless in defence of righteousness, is mere "violence."

For your benefit, to guard
You from each other's violence :
Will ye then be grateful ? [2735]

لَكُمْ لِتُحْصِنَكُمْ مِّنْ بَأْسِكُمْ ۚ فَهَلْ أَنتُمْ
شَٰكِرُونَ ○

81. (It was Our power that
Made) the violent (unruly)
Wind flow (tamely) for
Solomon, [2736]
To his order, to the land [2737]
Which We had blessed :
For We do know all things.

٨١- وَلِسُلَيْمَٰنَ الرِّيحَ عَاصِفَةً
تَجْرِي بِأَمْرِهِۦٓ إِلَى الْأَرْضِ الَّتِي بَٰرَكْنَا فِيهَا ۚ
وَكُنَّا بِكُلِّ شَيْءٍ عَٰلِمِينَ ○

82. And of the evil ones,
Were some who dived
For him, and did other work [2738]
Besides ; and it was We
Who guarded them.

٨٢- وَمِنَ الشَّيَٰطِينِ مَن يَغُوصُونَ لَهُۥ
وَيَعْمَلُونَ عَمَلًا دُونَ ذَٰلِكَ ۖ
وَكُنَّا لَهُمْ حَٰفِظِينَ ○

83. And (remember) Job, when
He cried to his Lord,
" Truly distress has seized me, [2739]
But Thou art the Most

٨٣- وَأَيُّوبَ إِذْ نَادَىٰ رَبَّهُۥٓ
أَنِّي مَسَّنِيَ الضُّرُّ وَأَنتَ

2735. David's good work then was : (1) he was open to learn wisdom wherever it came from ; (2) he sang the praises of God, in unison with all nature ; (3) he made defensive armour. But all these things he did, because of the faculties which God had given him, and we must be grateful for this and for all things to God.

2736. *Cf.* xxxiv. 12, and xxxviii. 36-38. This has been interpreted to mean that Solomon had miraculous power over the winds, and he could make them obey his orders. Rationalists say that he had naval power on the Mediterranean, and through the Gulf of 'Aqaba on the Red Sea, and that he therefore figuratively commanded the winds, and we may say the same of airmen at the present day. In any case the power behind was, and is, from God, Who has granted man intelligence and the faculties by which he can tame the more unruly forces of nature.

2737. Evidently Palestine, in which was Solomon's capital, though his influence extended far north in Syria, and perhaps far south in Arabia and Ethiopia. In the Roman ruins of Baalbek, fifty miles north of Damascus, is still shown a quarry of huge stones supposed to have been cut for Solomon. I have seen them with my own eyes. This local tradition is interesting, even if invented.

2738. As in n. 2736, the literalists and the rationalists take different views. The former say that Solomon had power over supernatural beings of evil, whom he compelled to dive for pearls and do other hard tasks. Rationalists refer this to hostile unruly races whom he subjected to his sway. It was God's power ultimately, Who granted him wisdom. Solomon tamed evil with Wisdom.

2739. Job (*Aiyūb*) was a prosperous man, with faith in God, living somewhere in the north-east corner of Arabia. He suffers from a number of calamities : his cattle are destroyed, his servants slain by the sword, and his family crushed under his roof. But he holds fast to his faith in God. As a further calamity he is covered with loathsome sores from head to foot. He loses his peace of mind, and he curses the day he was born. His false friends come and attribute his afflictions to sin. These "Job's comforters" are no comforters at all, and he further loses his balance of mind, but God recalls to him all His mercies, and he resumes his humility and give up self-justification. He is restored to prosperity, with twice as much as he had before ; his brethren and friends come back to him ; he had a new family of seven sons and three fair daughters. He lived to a good old age, and saw four generations of descendants. All this is recorded in the Book of Job in the Old Testament. Of all the Hebrew writings, the Hebrew of this Book comes nearest to Arabic.

Merciful of those that are
Merciful."

أَرْحَمُ الرَّٰحِمِينَ ۝

84. So We listened to him:
We removed the distress
That was on him,
And We restored his people
To him, and doubled
Their number,—as a Grace
From Ourselves, and a thing
For commemoration, for all
Who serve Us.[2740]

٨٤- فَاسْتَجَبْنَا لَهُ فَكَشَفْنَا مَا بِهِ مِن ضُرٍّ
وَءَاتَيْنَٰهُ أَهْلَهُ وَمِثْلَهُم مَّعَهُمْ
رَحْمَةً مِّنْ عِندِنَا
وَذِكْرَىٰ لِلْعَٰبِدِينَ ۝

85. And (remember) Ismā'īl,[2741]
Idrīs,[2742] and Ẓul-kifl,[2743] all
(Men) of constancy and patience;

٨٥- وَإِسْمَٰعِيلَ وَإِدْرِيسَ وَذَا الْكِفْلِ
كُلٌّ مِّنَ الصَّٰبِرِينَ ۝

86. We admitted them to
Our Mercy: for they
Were of the Righteous ones.

٨٦- وَأَدْخَلْنَٰهُمْ فِي رَحْمَتِنَا
إِنَّهُم مِّنَ الصَّٰلِحِينَ ۝

2740. Job is the pattern of humility, patience, and faith in God. It was with these weapons that he fought and conquered evil.

2741. Ismā'īl is mentioned specially, apart from the line which descended through Isaac (xxi. 72), as he was the founder of a separate and greater Ummat. His sufferings began in infancy (see n. 160 to ii. 158); but his steady constancy and submission to the will of God were specially shown when he earned the title of "Sacrifice to God" (see n. 2506 to xix. 54). That was the particular quality of his constancy and patience.

2742. For Idrīs see n. 2508 to xix. 56. He was in a high station in life, but that did not spoil him. He was sincere and true, and that was the particular quality of his constancy and patience.

2743 *Ẓul-kifl* would literally mean "possessor of, or giving, a double requital or portion"; or else, "one who used a cloak of double thickness," that being one of the meanings of *Kifl*. The Commentators differ in opinion as to who is meant, why the title is applied to him, and the point of his being grouped with Ismā'īl and Idrīs for constancy and patience. I think the best suggestion is that afforded by Karsten Niebuhr in his *Reisebeschreibung nach Arabien*, Copenhagen. 1778, ii. 264-266, as quoted in the *Encyclopædia of Islam* under "Dhul-Kifl". He visited Meshed 'Alī in 'Irāq, and also the little town called Kefil, midway between Najaf and Hilla (Babylon). Kefil, he says, is the Arabic form of Ezekiel. The shrine of Ezekiel was there, and the Jews came to it on pilgrimage.

If we accept "Ẓul-kifl" to be not an epithet, but an Arabicised form of "Ezekiel", it fits the context. Ezekiel was a prophet in Israel who was carried away to Babylon by Nebuchadnezzar after his second attack on Jerusalem (about B.C. 599). His Book is included in the English Bible (Old Testament). He was chained and bound, and put into prison, and for a time he was dumb (Ezekiel, iii. 25-26). He bore all with patience and constancy, and continued to reprove boldly the evils in Israel. In a burning passage he denounces false leaders in words which are eternally true: "Woe be to the shepherds of Israel that do feed themselves! Should not the shepherds feed the flocks? Ye eat the fat, and ye clothe you with the wool, ye kill them that are fed: but ye feed not the flock. The diseased have ye not strengthened, neither have ye healed that which was sick, neither have ye bound up that which was broken...", etc. (Ezekiel, xxxiv. 2-4).

Ẓul-kifl is again mentioned in xxxviii. 48 along with Ismā'īl and Elisha.

87. And remember Ẕun-nūn,[2744]
When he departed in wrath:
He imagined that We
Had no power over him!
But he cried through the depths
Of darkness, "There is
No god but Thou:
Glory to Thee: I was
Indeed wrong!"

٨٧- وَذَا النُّوْنِ اِذْ ذَّهَبَ مُغَاضِبًا
فَظَنَّ اَنْ لَّنْ نَّقْدِرَ عَلَيْهِ
فَنَادٰى فِى الظُّلُمٰتِ
اَنْ لَّآ اِلٰهَ اِلَّآ اَنْتَ سُبْحٰنَكَ
اِنِّىْ كُنْتُ مِنَ الظّٰلِمِيْنَ ۝

88. So We listened to him:
And delivered him from
Distress: and thus do We
Deliver those who have faith.

٨٨- فَاسْتَجَبْنَا لَهٗ وَنَجَّيْنٰهُ مِنَ الْغَمِّ
وَكَذٰلِكَ نُـْجِى الْمُؤْمِنِيْنَ ۝

89. And (remember) Zakarīyā,[2745]
When he cried to his Lord:
"O my Lord! leave me not
Without offspring, though Thou
Art the best of inheritors."[2746]

٨٩- وَزَكَرِيَّآ اِذْ نَادٰى رَبَّهٗ
رَبِّ لَا تَذَرْنِىْ فَرْدًا
وَّاَنْتَ خَيْرُ الْوٰرِثِيْنَ ۝

90. So We listened to him:
And We granted him

٩٠- فَاسْتَجَبْنَا لَهٗ وَوَهَبْنَا لَهٗ

2744. *Ẕun-nūn*, "the man of the Fish or the Whale", is the title of Jonah (Yūnus), because he was swallowed by a large Fish or Whale. He was the prophet raised to warn the Assyrian capital Nineveh. For Nineveh see n 1478 to x. 98. His story is told in xxxvii. 139-148. When his first warning was unheeded by the people, he denounced God's wrath on them. But they repented and God forgave them for the time being. Jonah, meanwhile, departed in wrath, discouraged at the apparent failure of his mission. He should have remained in the most discouraging circumstances, and relied on the power of God; for God had power both over Nineveh and over the Messenger He had sent to Nineveh. He went away to the sea and took a ship, but apparently the sailors threw him out as a man of bad omen in a storm. He was swallowed by a big Fish (or Whale), but in the depth of the darkness, he cried to God and confessed his weakness. The "darkness" may be interpreted both physically and spiritually: physically, as the darkness of the night and the storm and the Fish's body; spiritually as the darkness in his soul, his extreme distress in the situation which he had brought on himself. God Most Gracious forgave him. He was cast out ashore; he was given the shelter of a plant in his state of mental and physical lassitude. He was refreshed and strengthened, and the work of his mission prospered. Thus he overcame all his disappointment by repentance and Faith, and God accepted him.

2745. See xix. 2-15, and iii. 38-41. Zakariyā was a priest; both he and his wife were devout and punctilious in their duties. They were old, and they had no son. He was troubled in mind, not so much by the vulgar desire to have a son to carry on his line, but because he felt that his people were not unselfishly devout, and there would be no sincere work for God unless he could train up some one himself. He was given a son Yaḥyā (John the Baptist), who added to the devout reputation of the family, for he is called "noble, chaste, and a prophet," (iii. 39). All three, father, mother, and son, were made worthy of each other, and they repelled evil by their devout emulation in virtue.

2746. 'It is not that I crave a personal heir to myself: all things go back to Thee, and Thou art the best of inheritors: but I see no one around me sincere enough to carry on my work for Thee; wilt Thou give me one whom I can train?

Yaḥyā : We cured his wife's[2747]
(Barrenness) for him. These
(three)
Were ever quick in emulation
In good works : they used
To call on Us with love
And reverence, and humble
themselves
Before Us.

يَحْيٰى وَاَصْلَحْنَا لَهٗ زَوْجَهٗ ؕ
اِنَّهُمْ كَانُوْا يُسٰرِعُوْنَ فِى الْخَيْرٰتِ
وَيَدْعُوْنَنَا رَغَبًا وَّرَهَبًا ؕ
وَكَانُوْا لَنَا خٰشِعِيْنَ ۝

91. And (remember) her who[2748]
Guarded her chastity :
We breathed into her
Of Our Spirit, and We
Made her and her son
A Sign for all peoples.

٩١- وَالَّتِيْٓ اَحْصَنَتْ فَرْجَهَا
فَنَفَخْنَا فِيْهَا مِنْ رُّوْحِنَا
وَجَعَلْنٰهَا وَابْنَهَآ اٰيَةً لِّلْعٰلَمِيْنَ ۝

92. Verily, this Brotherhood
Of yours is a single Brotherhood,[2749]
And I am your Lord
And Cherisher : therefore
Serve Me (and no other).

٩٢- اِنَّ هٰذِهٖٓ اُمَّتُكُمْ اُمَّةً وَّاحِدَةً ۖ
وَّاَنَا رَبُّكُمْ فَاعْبُدُوْنِ ۝

93. But (later generations) cut off[2750]
Their affair (of unity),
One from another : (yet)
Will they all return to Us.

٩٣- وَتَقَطَّعُوْٓا اَمْرَهُمْ بَيْنَهُمْ ؕ
كُلٌّ اِلَيْنَا رٰجِعُوْنَ ۝ ع

C. 150.—No good deed is fruitless : work
(xxi. 94-112.) While yet there's time : for with Judgment
The door will be closed to repentance.
No false gods of fancy can help.

2747. Aṣlaḥa=to improve, to mend, to reform, to make better. Here, with reference to Zakariyā's wife, the signification is twofold : (1) that her barrenness would be removed, so that she could become a mother ; and (2) her spiritual dignity should be raised in becoming the mother of John the Baptist ; and by implication his also, in becoming the father of John.

2748. Mary the mother of Jesus. Chastity was her special virtue : with a son of virgin birth, she and Jesus became a miracle to all nations. That was the virtue with which they (both Mary and Jesus) resisted evil.

2749. *Ummat* : this is best translated by Brotherhood here. "Community", "race", and "nation," and "people" are words which import other ideas and do not quite correspond to "Ummat". "Religion" and "Way of Life" are derived meanings, which could be used in other passages, but are less appropriate here. Our attention has been drawn to people of very different temperaments and virtues, widely different in time, race, language, surroundings, history, and work to be performed, but forming the closest brotherhood as being men and women united in the highest service of God. They pre-figure the final and perfected Brotherhood of Islam.

2750. God's Message was and ever is one ; and His Messengers treated it as one. It is people of narrower views who come later and trade on the earlier names, that break up the Message and the Brotherhood into jarring camps and sects.

The Righteous will have no fear; for them
The angelic greetings will truly open
A new world, which they will inherit.
This was God's Message of old, and thesame
Is God's Message renewed: for God
Is one, and so is His Message, proclaimed
For all, freely and in loving Truth.

SECTION 7.

94. Whoever works any act
Of Righteousness and has Faith,—
His endeavour will not
Be rejected: We shall
Record it in his favour.[2751]

٩٤- فَمَن يَعْمَلْ مِنَ الصّٰلِحٰتِ وَهُوَ مُؤْمِنٌ
فَلَا كُفْرَانَ لِسَعْيِهِۦ
وَإِنَّا لَهُۥ كٰتِبُونَ ○

95. But there is a ban
On any population which
We have destroyed: that they[2752]
Shall not return,

٩٥- وَحَرٰمٌ عَلٰى قَرْيَةٍ
أَهْلَكْنٰهَآ أَنَّهُمْ لَا يَرْجِعُونَ ○

96. Until the Gog and Magog (people)[2753]
Are let through (their barrier),
And they swiftly swarm
From every hill.

٩٦- حَتّٰىٓ إِذَا فُتِحَتْ يَأْجُوجُ وَمَأْجُوجُ
وَهُم مِّن كُلِّ حَدَبٍ يَنسِلُونَ ○

97. Then will the True Promise
Draw nigh (of fulfilment):
Then behold! the eyes
Of the Unbelievers will[2754]
Fixedly stare in horror: "Ah!
Woe to us! we were indeed
Heedless of this; nay, we
Truly did wrong!"

٩٧- وَاقْتَرَبَ الْوَعْدُ الْحَقُّ
فَإِذَا هِىَ شٰخِصَةٌ أَبْصٰرُ الَّذِينَ كَفَرُوا۟
يٰوَيْلَنَا قَدْ كُنَّا فِى غَفْلَةٍ مِّنْ هٰذَا
بَلْ كُنَّا ظٰلِمِينَ ○

2751. God gives credit for every act of righteousness, however small: when combined with sincere Faith in God, it becomes the stepping stone to higher and higher things. It is never lost.

2752. But when wickedness comes to such a pass that the Wrath of God descends, as it did on Sodom, the case becomes hopeless. The righteous were warned and delivered before the Wrath descended. But those destroyed will not get another chance, as they flouted all previous chances. They will only be raised up at the approach of the Day of Judgment.

2753. For Gog and Magog see n. 2439 to xviii. 92. Their geographical position was discussed in Appendix VII, pp. 761-63. Here I do not think we are concerned with their geographical position. The name stands for wild and lawless tribes who will break their barriers and swarm through the earth. This will be one of the prognostications of the approaching Judgment.

2754. *Cf.* xiv. 42.

98. Verily ye, (Unbelievers),
And the (false) gods that
Ye worship besides God,
Are (but) fuel for Hell!
To it will ye (surely) come!

٩٨- إِنَّكُمْ وَمَا تَعْبُدُونَ مِن دُونِ ٱللَّهِ
حَصَبُ جَهَنَّمَ
أَنتُمْ لَهَا وَٰرِدُونَ ۝

99. If these had been gods,
They would not have got there![2755]
But each one will abide
Therein.

٩٩- لَوْ كَانَ هَٰٓؤُلَآءِ ءَالِهَةً مَّا وَرَدُوهَا
وَكُلٌّ فِيهَا خَٰلِدُونَ ۝

100. There, sobbing will be
Their lot, nor will they
There hear (aught else).

١٠٠- لَهُمْ فِيهَا زَفِيرٌ
وَهُمْ فِيهَا لَا يَسْمَعُونَ ۝

101. Those for whom
The Good (Record) from Us
Has gone before, will be
Removed far therefrom.[2756]

١٠١- إِنَّ ٱلَّذِينَ سَبَقَتْ لَهُم مِّنَّا ٱلْحُسْنَىٰٓ
أُو۟لَٰٓئِكَ عَنْهَا مُبْعَدُونَ ۝

102. Not the slightest sound
Will they hear of Hell:
What their souls desired,
In that will they dwell.

١٠٢- لَا يَسْمَعُونَ حَسِيسَهَا وَهُمْ فِى مَا
ٱشْتَهَتْ أَنفُسُهُمْ خَٰلِدُونَ ۝

103. The Great Terror will[2757]
Bring them no grief:
But the angels will meet them
(With mutual greetings):
"This is your Day,—
(The Day) that ye were promised."

١٠٣- لَا يَحْزُنُهُمُ ٱلْفَزَعُ ٱلْأَكْبَرُ
وَتَتَلَقَّىٰهُمُ ٱلْمَلَٰٓئِكَةُ
هَٰذَا يَوْمُكُمُ ٱلَّذِى كُنتُمْ تُوعَدُونَ ۝

2755. The ultimate proof of Truth and Falsehood will be that Truth will endure and come to its own, while Falsehood will be destroyed. And so the men who worshipped Truth will come to their own, while those who worshipped Falsehood will be in a Fire of Punishment they could scarcely have imagined before. In that state there will be nothing but regrets and sighs and groans, and these evil sounds will drown everything else.

2756. In contrast to the misery of those who rejected Truth and Right, will be the happiness of those who accepted it. Their record does not lag behind: in fact it goes before. Our Deeds go before our journey in this life is completed. What then is the Judgment? It is instantaneous: it will all be decided in the twinkling of an eye (xvi. 77). The good will not hear the least sound of the groans of evil. Their true soul's desires will be fulfilled—not temporarily as in this world, but in a permanent form.

2757. The Judgment and balancing of accounts will be a mighty Terror to the evil-doers. But it will cause, to the righteous, not grief or anxiety, but hope and happiness, for now they will be in a congenial atmosphere, and will see the fulfilment of their ideals in the meeting and greeting of the angels, preparatory to their enjoyment of the supreme Bliss—seeing the Face of God.

104. The Day that We roll up
The heavens like a scroll
Rolled up for books (completed),—
Even as We produced
The first Creation, so
Shall We produce [2758]
A new one: a promise
We have undertaken:
Truly shall We fulfil it.

١٠٤- يَوْمَ نَطْوِي السَّمَآءَ كَطَيِّ السِّجِلِّ لِلْكُتُبِ
كَمَا بَدَأْنَآ أَوَّلَ خَلْقٍ نُّعِيدُهُ
وَعْدًا عَلَيْنَآ
إِنَّا كُنَّا فَٰعِلِينَ ○

105. Before this We wrote
In the Psalms,[2759] after the Message
(Given to Moses):[2760] "My servants,
The righteous, shall inherit
The earth."

١٠٥- وَلَقَدْ كَتَبْنَا فِي الزَّبُورِ
مِنۢ بَعْدِ الذِّكْرِ
أَنَّ الْأَرْضَ يَرِثُهَا عِبَادِيَ الصَّٰلِحُونَ ○

106. Verily in this (Qur-ān)
Is a Message for people
Who would (truly) worship God.[2761]

١٠٦- إِنَّ فِي هَٰذَا لَبَلَٰغًا
لِّقَوْمٍ عَٰبِدِينَ ○

107. We sent thee not, but
As a Mercy for all creatures.[2762]

١٠٧- وَمَآ أَرْسَلْنَٰكَ إِلَّا رَحْمَةً لِّلْعَٰلَمِينَ ○

2758. The world—the universe—as we know it, will be folded up like a scroll of parchment, for it will have done its work. If God created all this world out of nothing, He can create an entirely new heaven and a new earth, on a plane of which we can form no conception in our present life. And He will do so, for that is His promise.

Some Commentators understand Sijill to be the name of the Recording Angel who closes the Book of a man's Deeds after the man's death.

2759. Zabūr: the Book of the Psalms of David. The name of David is expressly mentioned in connection with the Zabūr in iv. 163 and xvii. 55, although there the indefinite article is applied to the word as meaning a Book of Scripture. See Psalms xxv. 13, "his seed shall inherit the earth"; xxxvii. 11, "the meek shall inherit the earth" (quoted by Jesus in Matt. v. 3); and xxxvii. 29, "the righteous shall inherit the land." This may be understood both literally, as referring to power and authority on this earth, and figuratively, as referring to the new and real world of the spirit.

2760. The same promise occurs in the Pentateuch, Exod. xxxii. 13, "they shall inherit it (the land) for ever".

2761. The culmination of God's Revelation is in the Qur-ān, which confirms previous scriptures, corrects the errors which men introduced into them, and explains many points in detail for all who seek for right worship and service to God—whether they inherit the previous Books ("People of the Book") or not. It is a universal Message.

2762. There is no question now of race or nation, of a "chosen people" or the "seed of Abraham"; or the "seed of David"; or of Hindu Arya-varta; of Jew or Gentile, Arab or 'Ajam (Persian), Turk or Tājik, European or Asiatic, White or Coloured; Aryan, Semitic, Mongolian, or African; or American, Australian, or Polynesian. To all men and creatures other than men who have any spiritual responsibility, the principles universally apply.

108. Say: " What has come to me
By inspiration is that
Your God is One God:
Will ye therefore bow
To His Will (in Islām)? " [2763]

١٠٨- قُلْ إِنَّمَا يُوحَىٰٓ إِلَيَّ أَنَّمَآ
إِلَٰهُكُمْ إِلَٰهٌ وَاحِدٌ ۖ
فَهَلْ أَنتُم مُّسْلِمُونَ ○

109. But if they turn back,
Say: " I have proclaimed
The Message to you all alike
And in truth; but I
Know not whether that
Which ye are promised
Is near or far.[2764]

١٠٩- فَإِن تَوَلَّوْا فَقُلْ ءَاذَنتُكُمْ
عَلَىٰ سَوَآءٍ ۖ
وَإِنْ أَدْرِىٓ أَقَرِيبٌ
أَم بَعِيدٌ مَّا تُوعَدُونَ ○

110. " It is He Who knows
What is open in speech
And what ye hide
(In your hearts).[2765]

١١٠- إِنَّهُۥ يَعْلَمُ ٱلْجَهْرَ مِنَ ٱلْقَوْلِ
وَيَعْلَمُ مَا تَكْتُمُونَ ○

111. " I know not but that
It may be a trial
For you, and a grant
Of (worldly) livelihood
(To you) for a time." [2766]

١١١- وَإِنْ أَدْرِى لَعَلَّهُۥ فِتْنَةٌ
لَّكُمْ وَمَتَٰعٌ إِلَىٰ حِينٍ ○

2763. 'Not my God only, but also *your* God; for there is but One God, the Universal Lord, Who made and loves and cherishes all.'

2764. 'If you do not realise the significance of the Message, I at least have done my duty. I have given the Good News for the Righteous and the Warning for the Unjust, without favour or partiality, and without abating one jot of the truth, openly and squarely for all Do not ask me when the Good News and the Warning will be fulfilled. That is for God to decide, not for me or for you to know.'

2765. The Messenger of God freely and impartially teaches all how to carry out God's Will and live a good life. If some of them are hypocrites and come into the Ummat (Brotherhood) from baser motives and not the pure motives of the love of God, their motives and conduct will be judged by God and not by men.

2766. In the same way if men who come into the Brotherhood from pure motives and yet feel aggrieved that those outside are better off from a worldly point of view, they are wrong. It may be that the fleeting enjoyment of this world's goods is but a trial, and they should be grateful for being saved from temptation.

112. Say : [2767] " O my Lord !
Judge Thou in truth ! " [2768]
" Our Lord Most Gracious
Is the One Whose assistance
Should be sought against
The blasphemies ye utter ! " [2769]

١١٢- قُلَ رَبِّ احْكُمْ بِالْحَقِّ ؕ
وَرَبُّنَا الرَّحْمٰنُ الْمُسْتَعَانُ
عَلٰى مَا تَصِفُوْنَ ۝

2767. See above, n. 2666 to xxi. 4. The better reading is "Say" in the imperative, rather than "He (the Prophet) said (or says)" in the indicative mood. Note that, on that construction, there are three distinct things which the Prophet is asked to say : *viz.* : (1) the statement in verses 109-111, addressed to those who turn away from the Message ; (2) the prayer addressed to God in the first part of verse 112 ; and (3) the advice given indirectly to the Believers, in the second part of verse 112. I have marked these divisions by means of inverted commas.

768. That is, God's judgment as between the Teacher and those who refuse his Message, or between the righteous and those who taunt them for their poverty, will be the true one, and both the Teacher and the Ummat must leave the judgment to God.

2769. Blasphemy is a dreadful sin. We must guard ourselves from it. But as regards others, if we cannot prevent it, we must pray to God for assistance and not rely upon carnal weapons.

INTRODUCTION TO SŪRA XXII (*Hajj*).

We now come to a new series of four Sūras, dealing with the environments and methods contributing to our spiritual progress, as the last five Sūras dealt with the Messengers who came in various ways to proclaim the Truth and conquer evil. See Introduction to S. xvii.

The subject-matter of this particular Sūra is concerned mainly with the spiritual implications of the Sacred House, the Pilgrimage, the Sacrifices, Striving and Fighting in defence of Truth when attacked, and other acts that make for Unselfishness and uproot Falsehood.

On the chronology of this Sūra, opinion is divided. Some parts were probably revealed in the later Meccan period, and some in Medina. But the chronological question has no significance here.

Summary.—Importance of the spiritual Future, and need of firmness in Faith: help for Truth and punishment for Evil (xxii. 1-25, and C. 151).

Purity, Prayer, Humility, and Faith are implied in the Pilgrimage; in solemn Sacrifice we express our gratitude and reverence to God, and our desire to share food with our poorer brethren; Striving and Fighting in defence of Truth when attacked are necessary as tests of self-sacrifice (xxii. 26-48, and C. 152).

The promptings of Evil may hinder the work of God's Apostle, but that work must triumph, and the Mercy and Truth of God must be established; therefore serve God humbly, and He will protect and help you (xxii. 49-78, and C. 153).

C. 151.—Will not mankind take warning
(xxii. 1-25.) From the dreadful consequences of Evil
Clearly proclaimed to them? Will they
Dispute about God and the Life of the Future?
They have only to look around and within them,
And they will see vestiges of the Plan
And Purpose of God. Let them not halt
Between Good and Evil: God's Message as well
As His Messenger must win against all
Obstacles. Only the evil will be brought
To shame and agony. The good—whose speech
Is pure and conduct worthy of praise—
Will have a meed of refinement, beauty, and bliss.

Sūra XXII.

Hajj, or The Pilgrimage.

In the name of God, Most Gracious,
Most Merciful.

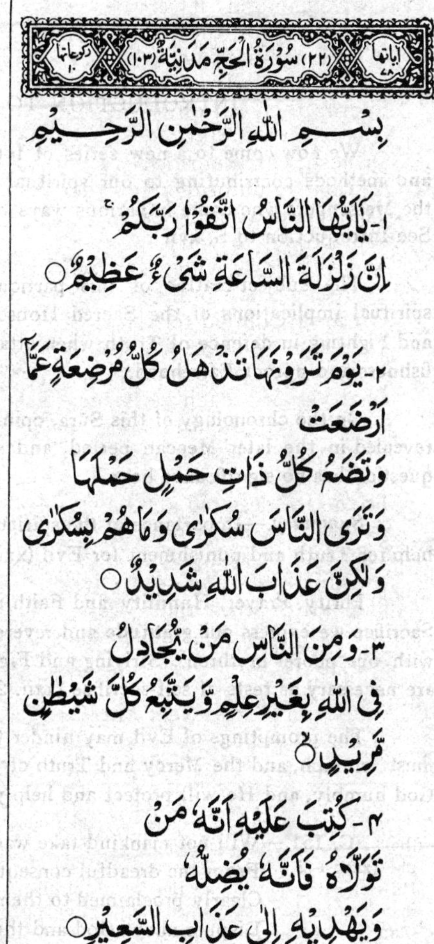

1. O mankind! Fear your Lord!
For the convulsion of the Hour
(Of Judgment) will be
A thing terrible![2770]

2. The Day ye shall see it,
Every mother giving suck
Shall forget her suckling-babe,
And every pregnant female
Shall drop her load (unformed):
Thou shalt see mankind
As in a drunken riot,[2771]
Yet not drunk: but dreadful
Will be the Wrath of God.

3. And yet among men
There are such as dispute
About God, without knowledge,
And follow every evil one
Obstinate in rebellion!

4. About the (Evil One)
It is decreed that whoever
Turns to him for friendship,
Him will he lead astray,
And he will guide him
To the Penalty of the Fire.[2772]

2770. As an introduction to the spiritual meaning of various symbolical acts in this life, the serious issues involved are indicated by showing how terrible the consequences will be for those who disobey God's Will. The terror will only be for those who rebel and disobey: the righteous will not suffer from it, but on the contrary will be greeted by angels with joy (xxi. 103)

2771. Three metaphors are used for the extreme terror which the Awful Day will inspire, (1) No mother abandons the baby at her breast in the greatest danger; yet that will happen in this Dreadful Hour. (2) An expectant mother carries the young life within her with great pride and hope: "hope" is the actual word used in Urdu for this physical state; yet the terror will overpower the hope at this "Hour", and nature's working will be reversed. (3) Men ordinarily retain their self-possession except under intoxication: here, without intoxication, they will be driven to frenzy with terror.

2772. Even after the warnings there are men who are such fools as to turn away from God Who created them and cherishes them with His love and care; they become outlaws in His Kingdom, making friends with Evil, which is a rebel in God's Kingdom.

5\. O mankind! if ye have
A doubt about the Resurrection,[2773]
(Consider) that We created you
Out of dust, then out of
Sperm, then out of a leech-like
Clot, then out of a morsel
Of flesh, partly formed[2774]
And partly unformed, in order
That We may manifest
(Our power) to you;
And We cause whom We will[2775]
To rest in the wombs
For an appointed term,
Then do We bring you out
As babes, then (foster you)
That ye may reach your age
Of full strength; and some
Of you are called to die,
And some are sent back
To the feeblest old age,
So that they know nothing
After having known (much).[2776]
And (further), thou seest
The earth barren and lifeless,
But when We pour down
Rain on it, it is stirred
(To life), it swells,
And it puts forth every kind
Of beautiful growth (in pairs).[2777]

٥- يٰٓأَيُّهَا النَّاسُ إِنْ كُنْتُمْ فِي رَيْبٍ مِّنَ الْبَعْثِ
فَإِنَّا خَلَقْنٰكُمْ مِّنْ تُرَابٍ
ثُمَّ مِنْ نُّطْفَةٍ ثُمَّ مِنْ عَلَقَةٍ
ثُمَّ مِنْ مُّضْغَةٍ مُّخَلَّقَةٍ
وَّغَيْرِ مُخَلَّقَةٍ لِّنُبَيِّنَ لَكُمْ ۭ
وَنُقِرُّ فِي الْأَرْحَامِ مَا نَشَآءُ إِلٰٓى أَجَلٍ مُّسَمًّى
ثُمَّ نُخْرِجُكُمْ طِفْلًا ثُمَّ لِتَبْلُغُوٓا أَشُدَّكُمْ
وَمِنْكُمْ مَّنْ يُّتَوَفّٰى
وَمِنْكُمْ مَّنْ يُّرَدُّ إِلٰٓى أَرْذَلِ الْعُمُرِ
لِكَيْلَا يَعْلَمَ مِنْ بَعْدِ عِلْمٍ شَيْـًٔا ۭ
وَتَرَى الْأَرْضَ هَامِدَةً
فَإِذَآ أَنْزَلْنَا عَلَيْهَا الْمَآءَ
اهْتَزَّتْ وَرَبَتْ
وَأَنْۢبَتَتْ مِنْ كُلِّ زَوْجٍ بَهِيجٍ ○

2773\. If they really have doubts in their minds about the life after death, they have only to turn their attention, either to their own nature, or to the nature around. How wonderful is their own physical growth, from lifeless matter, to seed, fertilised ovum, fœtus, child, youth, age, and death! How can they doubt that the Author of all these wonderful stages in their life here can also give them another kind of life after the end of this life? Or, if they look at external nature, they see the earth dead and barren, and God's fertilising showers bring it to life, growth, and beauty in various forms. The Creator of this great pageant of Beauty can surely create yet another and a newer world.

2774\. The stages of man's physical growth from nothing till he completes the cycle of this life are described in words whose accuracy, beauty, and comprehensiveness can only be fully understood by biologists. Parallel to the physical growth, may be understood man's inner growth, also by stages and by God's creative artistry.

2775\. That is, a male or a female child, a fair or an ugly child, a good or a rebellious child, etc., involving countless mysteries of genetics and heredity.

2776\. *Cf.* xvi. 70. In that passage the mystery of our life was used to illustrate God's abundant mercies and favours to us. Here it is used to illustrate God's power in giving us a future Life of even greater promise.

2777\. A beautiful nature passage so pregnant in meaning that the earnest student wonders what magic and truth have been conveyed in so few words. M. P.'s Egyptian colleague, Prof. Ghamrawi (see M. P.'s note on this passage) was but expressing the feelings of every careful student of the Qur-ān. The "subtlety and wealth of meaning" are indeed marvellous.

6. This is so, because God
Is the Reality : it is He
Who gives life to the dead,
And it is He Who has
Power over all things.[2778]

٦- ذٰلِكَ بِأَنَّ اللّٰهَ هُوَ الْحَقُّ
وَأَنَّهُ يُحْيِ الْمَوْتٰى
وَأَنَّهُ عَلٰى كُلِّ شَيْءٍ قَدِيْرٌ ۝

7. And verily the Hour will come:
There can be no doubt
About it, or about (the fact)
That God will raise up
All who are in the graves.

٧- وَّأَنَّ السَّاعَةَ اٰتِيَةٌ لَّا رَيْبَ فِيْهَا
وَأَنَّ اللّٰهَ يَبْعَثُ مَنْ فِي الْقُبُوْرِ ۝

8. Yet there is among men
Such a one as disputes
About God, without knowledge,
Without guidance, and without
A Book of Enlightenment,—[2779]

٨- وَمِنَ النَّاسِ مَنْ يُّجَادِلُ فِي اللّٰهِ بِغَيْرِ
عِلْمٍ
وَّلَا هُدًى وَّلَا كِتٰبٍ مُّنِيْرٍ ۝

9. (Disdainfully) bending his side,
In order to lead (men) astray
From the Path of God :
For him there is disgrace[2780]
In this life, and on the Day
Of Judgment We shall
Make him taste the Penalty
Of burning (Fire).

٩- ثَانِيَ عِطْفِهِ لِيُضِلَّ عَنْ سَبِيْلِ اللّٰهِ
لَهُ فِي الدُّنْيَا خِزْيٌ وَّنُذِيْقُهُ يَوْمَ
الْقِيٰمَةِ عَذَابَ الْحَرِيْقِ ۝

10. (It will be said) : "This is
Because of the deeds which
Thy hands sent forth,
For verily God is not
Unjust to His servants."[2781]

١٠- ذٰلِكَ بِمَا قَدَّمَتْ يَدٰكَ
وَأَنَّ اللّٰهَ لَيْسَ بِظَلَّامٍ لِّلْعَبِيْدِ ۝ ع

2778. All these beautiful and well-articulated pageants of life and nature point to the Reality behind them, *i.e.*, God. They will perish, but He is eternal. They are but shadows; the substance (if such a word may be used) is in Him. They are shifting and illusory, in the sense that they have neither permanency nor independent existence. But they have a sort of secondary reality in the sense in which a shadow is a real reflection from a substance. No Power or Existence has any meaning except as a reflection of God's ineffable Glory.

2779. For "Book of Enlightenment" see iii. 184 and n. 490. I understand "knowledge" to mean here their human knowledge or intelligence, "guidance" to mean divine guidance, such as comes from God or men of God or a revelation from God, and the "Book of Enlightenment" to mean the fundamental guide to good conduct, the clear rules laid down in all Dispensations to help men to lead good lives. The "Book of Enlightenment" may mean a revealed Book in which case "Guidance" would refer to divine guidance through a man of God.

2780. Some Commentators think this refers to Abū Jahl, but the words are perfectly general, and this type of man is common in all ages. The same may be said about verse 3 above : Commentators give the immediate reference to one Nadhar ibn Ḥārith.

2781. 'What you suffer is the consequence of your own sinful deeds; God is just; He is not unjust to the least of His creatures.'

SECTION 2.

11\. There are among men
Some who serve God,
As it were, on the verge :[2782]
If good befalls them, they are,
Therewith, well content ; but
If a trial comes to them,
They turn on their faces :
They lose both this world
And the Hereafter : that
Is loss for all to see !

١١- وَمِنَ النَّاسِ مَنْ يَّعْبُدُ اللّٰهَ عَلٰى حَرْفٍ ۚ
فَاِنْ اَصَابَهٗ خَيْرُ ٱطْمَاَنَّ بِهٖ ۚ
وَاِنْ اَصَابَتْهُ فِتْنَةُ ٱنْقَلَبَ عَلٰى وَجْهِهٖ ۚ
خَسِرَ الدُّنْيَا وَالْاٰخِرَةَ ۭ
ذٰلِكَ هُوَ الْخُسْرَانُ الْمُبِيْنُ ○

12\. They call on such deities,[2783]
Besides God, as can neither
Hurt nor profit them :
That is straying far indeed
(From the Way) !

١٢- يَدْعُوْا مِنْ دُوْنِ اللّٰهِ مَا لَا
يَضُرُّهٗ وَمَا لَا يَنْفَعُهٗ ۭ
ذٰلِكَ هُوَ الضَّلٰلُ الْبَعِيْدُ ○

13\. (Perhaps) they call on one
Whose hurt is nearer[2784]
Than his profit : evil, indeed,
Is the patron, and evil
The companion (for help) !

١٣- يَدْعُوْا لَمَنْ ضَرُّهٗٓ اَقْرَبُ مِنْ نَّفْعِهٖ ۭ
لَبِئْسَ الْمَوْلٰى وَلَبِئْسَ الْعَشِيْرُ ○

14\. Verily God will admit
Those who believe and work
Righteous deeds, to Gardens,
Beneath which rivers flow :
For God carries out
All that He plans.[2785]

١٤- اِنَّ اللّٰهَ يُدْخِلُ الَّذِيْنَ اٰمَنُوْا وَعَمِلُوا
الصّٰلِحٰتِ جَنّٰتٍ تَجْرِيْ مِنْ تَحْتِهَا الْاَنْهٰرُ ۭ
اِنَّ اللّٰهَ يَفْعَلُ مَا يُرِيْدُ ○

2782\. They are men whose minds are not firm : they will have faith, if all goes well with them, but as soon as they are tried, they are found wanting. They are a different kind from hypocrites. It is not fraud or double-dealing that is their sin : it is a weak mind, petty standards of judging right by success, a selfishness that gives nothing but asks for all, a narrow-mindedness that does not go beyond petty mundane calculations—a "nicely calculated less or more" of the good things of this world. They fail in both worlds, and their failure in this world is patent for every on-looker.

2783\. To such minds religion does not mean high endeavour, self-sacrifice for noble ends, the recognition of God's infinite world, but just a small concession to formalism, perhaps a present to an idol (literal or figurative), perhaps attendance at worship if it can be done without trouble ! It is false gods they worship, and the more they worship, the more they stray.

2784\. Such false worship is not always neutral, bringing neither harm nor good. Perhaps the harm comes first, and there is no help from God. Such minds are themselves demoralised, and render themselves unfit for help !

2785\. God is both true to His promise, and He has power to give full effect to His Will and Plan.

15. If any think that God
Will not help him
(His Apostle) in this world
And the Hereafter, let him
Stretch out a rope
To the ceiling and cut (himself)[2786]
Off: then let him see
Whether his plan will remove
That which enrages (him)!

١٥- مَنْ كَانَ يَظُنُّ اَنْ لَّنْ يَّنْصُرَهُ اللّٰهُ
فِى الدُّنْيَا وَالْاٰخِرَةِ
فَلْيَمْدُدْ بِسَبَبٍ اِلَى السَّمَآءِ ثُمَّ لْيَقْطَعْ
فَلْيَنْظُرْ هَلْ يُذْهِبَنَّ كَيْدُهٗ مَا يَغِيْظُ ○

16. Thus have We sent down[2787]
Clear Signs; and verily
God doth guide whom
He will!

١٦- وَكَذٰلِكَ اَنْزَلْنٰهُ اٰيٰتٍۢ بَيِّنٰتٍ
وَّاَنَّ اللّٰهَ يَهْدِىْ مَنْ يُّرِيْدُ ○

17. Those who believe (in the Qur-ān),
Those who follow the Jewish
(scriptures),
And the Sabians,[2788] Christians,
Magians,[2789] and Polytheists,—
God will judge between them

١٧- اِنَّ الَّذِيْنَ اٰمَنُوْا وَالَّذِيْنَ هَادُوْا
وَالصّٰبِـِٕيْنَ وَالنَّصٰرٰى وَالْمَجُوْسَ وَالَّذِيْنَ
اَشْرَكُوْٓا ۖ اِنَّ اللّٰهَ يَفْصِلُ بَيْنَهُمْ

2786. There is some difference of opinion as to the interpretation of this verse. Most Commentators are agreed that the pronoun "him" in the second line ("will not help him") refers to the holy Prophet, and that the "any" in the first line refers to his enemies, who wished to see him destroyed and removed from the scene of his labours. Ibn 'Abbās, whom I have followed here, and whom a great number of Commentators follow, construes the later clauses in the sense given in the text. Freely paraphrased, it means: if the enemies of God's Apostle are enraged at his successes, let them fix a rope to their ceiling and hang themselves. *Samāa* is thus rendered by the word "ceiling". If *Samāa* is rendered by the word "heaven" (the usual meaning), the paraphrase would be: if the enemies of God's Apostle are enraged at the help he gets from heaven, let them stretch a rope to heaven and see if they can cut off the help in that way!—in other words, they are fools if they think they can intercept God's help by their petty devices!

2787. Instead of plotting against God's Messenger, the Unbelievers should observe the Clear Signs which he has brought, and obey and follow the Guidance which comes from God according to the Laws which He has fixed by His holy Will and Plan.

2788. For Sabians, see n. 76 to ii. 62. They are also referred to in v. 72. In both those passages the Muslims are mentioned with the Jews, Christians, and Sabians, as receiving God's protection and mercy. Here, besides the four religions, there is further mention of Magians and Polytheists: it is not said that they would receive God's Mercy, but only that God will judge between the various forms of faith. The addition of Polytheists—those who join gods with God—may seem a little surprising. But the argument is that all forms of faith that are sincere (and not merely contumacious) are matters in which we as men cannot interfere. Our duty is to be tolerant within all the limits of tolerance—*i.e.*, so long as there is no oppression, injustice, and persecution. Where we can right an obvious wrong, it is our duty to do so; but it would be wrong on our part to rush in without power or authority simply because other people do not see our point of view.

2789. This is the only place where the Magians (*Majūs*) are mentioned in the Qur-ān. Their cult is a very ancient one. They consider Fire as the purest and noblest element, and worship it as a fit emblem of God. Their location was the Persian and Median uplands and the Mesopotamian valleys. Their religion was reformed by the Prophet Zardusht (date uncertain, about B.C. 600?). Their scripture is the Zend-Avesta, the bible of the Pārsis. They were "the Wise men of the East" mentioned in the Gospels.

On the Day of Judgment:
For God is witness
Of all things.

يَوْمَ الْقِيٰمَةِ ۗ اِنَّ اللّٰهَ عَلٰى كُلِّ شَیْءٍ
شَهِيْدٌ ○

18. Seest thou not that
To God bow down in worship
All things that are
In the heavens and on earth,—[2790]
The sun, the moon, the stars;
The hills, the trees, the animals;
And a great number among
Mankind? But a great number
Are (also) such as are
Fit for Punishment: and such
As God shall disgrace,—
None can raise to honour:
For God carries out
All that He wills.[2791]

۱۸- اَلَمْ تَرَ اَنَّ اللّٰهَ يَسْجُدُ لَهٗ
مَنْ فِى السَّمٰوٰتِ وَمَنْ فِى الْاَرْضِ
وَالشَّمْسُ وَالْقَمَرُ وَالنُّجُوْمُ وَالْجِبَالُ وَالشَّجَرُ
وَالدَّوَآبُّ وَكَثِيْرٌ مِّنَ النَّاسِ ۗ وَكَثِيْرٌ
حَقَّ عَلَيْهِ الْعَذَابُ ۗ
وَمَنْ يُّهِنِ اللّٰهُ فَمَا لَهٗ مِنْ مُّكْرِمٍ ۗ
اِنَّ اللّٰهَ يَفْعَلُ مَا يَشَآءُ ○ السجدة

19. These two antagonists dispute[2792]
With each other about their Lord:
But those who deny (their Lord),—
For them will be cut out
A garment of Fire:
Over their heads will be
Poured out boiling water.

۱۹- هٰذٰنِ خَصْمٰنِ اخْتَصَمُوْا فِىْ رَبِّهِمْ ۡ
فَالَّذِيْنَ كَفَرُوْا قُطِّعَتْ لَهُمْ
ثِيَابٌ مِّنْ نَّارٍ ۗ
يُصَبُّ مِنْ فَوْقِ رُءُوْسِهِمُ الْحَمِيْمُ ○

20. With it will be scalded
What is within their bodies,
As well as (their) skins.[2793]

۲۰- يُصْهَرُ بِهٖ مَا فِىْ بُطُوْنِهِمْ وَالْجُلُوْدُ ○

21. In addition there will be
Maces of iron (to punish) them.[2794]

۲۱- وَلَهُمْ مَّقَامِعُ مِنْ حَدِيْدٍ ○

2790. *Cf.* xxi. 79, and n. 2733. All created things, animate and inanimate, depend on God for their existence, and this dependence can be construed as their *Sajda* or bowing down in worship. Their very existence proclaims their dependence. How can they be objects of worship? For *haqqa* in this verse. *Cf.* xv. 64, n. 1990.

2791. *Cf.* xxii. 16. There the argument was that those who work in harmony with God's Law and Will will get their reward, for God always carries out His Plan. Here is the parallel argument: those who defy God's Will must suffer pain and disgrace, for God is well able to carry out His Will.

2792. *Two antagonists*: *i.e.*, parties of antagonists, *viz.*, Men of Faith, who confess their Lord and seek to carry out His Will, and Men who deny their Lord and defy His Will.

2793. The punishment, expressed in physical terms, will be all-pervading, not merely superficial.

2794. Read this with the next verse. There will be no escape from the final Punishment adjudged after the time of repentance is past.

22. Every time they wish
To get away therefrom,
From anguish, they will be
Forced back therein, and
(It will be said), "Taste ye
The Penalty of Burning!"

٢٢- كُلَّمَآ أَرَادُوٓا۟ أَن يَخْرُجُوا۟ مِنْهَا
مِنْ غَمٍّ أُعِيدُوا۟ فِيهَا
وَذُوقُوا۟ عَذَابَ ٱلْحَرِيقِ ۝

SECTION 3.

23. God will admit those
Who believe and work righteous
deeds,
To Gardens beneath which[2795]
Rivers flow: they shall be
Adorned therein with bracelets
Of gold and pearls; and
Their garments there
Will be of silk.

٢٣- إِنَّ ٱللَّهَ يُدْخِلُ ٱلَّذِينَ ءَامَنُوا۟ وَعَمِلُوا۟
ٱلصَّٰلِحَٰتِ
جَنَّٰتٍ تَجْرِى مِن تَحْتِهَا ٱلْأَنْهَٰرُ
يُحَلَّوْنَ فِيهَا مِنْ أَسَاوِرَ مِن ذَهَبٍ وَ
لُؤْلُؤًا ۖ وَلِبَاسُهُمْ فِيهَا حَرِيرٌ ۝

24. For they have been guided
(In this life) to the purest
Of speeches; they have been
Guided to the Path of Him
Who is Worthy of (all) Praise.

٢٤- وَهُدُوٓا۟ إِلَى ٱلطَّيِّبِ مِنَ ٱلْقَوْلِ
وَهُدُوٓا۟ إِلَىٰ صِرَٰطِ ٱلْحَمِيدِ ۝

25. As to those who have rejected
(God), and would keep back (men)
From the Way of God, and
From the Sacred Mosque, which
We have made (open) to (all) men—
Equal is the dweller there
And the visitor from the country—
And any whose purpose therein
Is profanity or wrong-doing—[2796]
Them will We cause to taste
Of a most grievous Penalty.

٢٥- إِنَّ ٱلَّذِينَ كَفَرُوا۟ وَيَصُدُّونَ عَن
سَبِيلِ ٱللَّهِ
وَٱلْمَسْجِدِ ٱلْحَرَامِ ٱلَّذِى جَعَلْنَٰهُ لِلنَّاسِ
سَوَآءً ٱلْعَٰكِفُ فِيهِ وَٱلْبَادِ ۚ
وَمَن يُرِدْ فِيهِ بِإِلْحَادٍۭ بِظُلْمٍ
نُّذِقْهُ مِنْ عَذَابٍ أَلِيمٍ ۝

C. 152.—For our spiritual growth are provided
(xxii. 26-48.) Symbols and means of expression in our ordinary
Lives. Such is the pilgrimage, meant
To gather men and women from far and near

2795. In xxii. 14 above, was described the meed of the Righteous as compared with the time-servers and those who worshipped false gods (*vv* 11-13): here we have the case of those who were persecuted, abused, prevented from entering the Ka'ba and deprived of all that makes life smooth, agreeable, and comfortable. For them the meed is described in metaphors that negative these afflictions: costly adornments (as against being stripped of home and property), purity of speech (as against the abuse they received), the Path of the Lord of Praise (as against the fierce and malignant persecution to which they were subjected).

2796. All these were enormities of which the Pagan clique in power in Mecca before and during the Hijrat were guilty.

To share in sacrifice, and prayer and praise,
In an age-old centre of worship. The sacrifices,
Too, are symbols of Piety of Heart,
A longing to share with fellow-men
In the bounties of God. In the Fight for Truth
Is tested our purity of motive, unselfishness
Of aim, and devotion to Right at the cost
Of Self. Fearless must we fight; for Truth
Has often been flouted, but must finally win.

SECTION 4.

26. Behold! We gave the site,[2797]
To Abraham, of the (Sacred)
House,
(Saying): "Associate not anything
(In worship) with Me;
And sanctify My House
For those who compass it round,[2798]
Or stand up,
Or bow, or prostrate themselves
(Therein in prayer).

٢٦- وَإِذْ بَوَّأْنَا لِإِبْرَٰهِيمَ مَكَانَ ٱلْبَيْتِ
أَن لَّا تُشْرِكْ بِى شَيْـًٔا
وَطَهِّرْ بَيْتِىَ لِلطَّآئِفِينَ
وَٱلْقَآئِمِينَ وَٱلرُّكَّعِ ٱلسُّجُودِ ○

27. "And proclaim the Pilgrimage
Among men: they will come
To thee on foot and (mounted)
On every kind of camel,
Lean on accout of journeys
Through deep and distant
Mountain highways;[2799]

٢٧- وَأَذِّن فِى ٱلنَّاسِ بِٱلْحَجِّ
يَأْتُوكَ رِجَالًا وَعَلَىٰ كُلِّ ضَامِرٍ
يَأْتِينَ مِن كُلِّ فَجٍّ عَمِيقٍ ○

28. "That they may witness
The benefits (provided) for them,[2800]

٢٨- لِّيَشْهَدُوا۟ مَنَٰفِعَ لَهُمْ

2797. The site of Mecca was granted to Abraham (and his son Ismā'il) for a place of worship that was to be pure (without idols, the worship being paid to the One True God) and universal, without being reserved (like Solomon's Temple of later times) to any one People or Race.

2798. *Cf.* ii. 125. Note that here the word *qāimīn* ('who stand up for prayer) occurs in place of *'ākifīn* (who use it as a retreat). In practice the meaning is the same. Those who go for a retreat to the Ka'ba stay there for the time being.

2799. When the Pilgrimage was proclaimed, people came to it from every quarter, near and far, on foot and mounted. The "lean camel" coming after a fatiguing journey through distant mountain roads typifies the difficulties of travel, which Pilgrims disregard on account of the temporal and spiritual benefits referred to in the next verse.

2800. There are benefits both for this our material life and for our spiritual life. Of the former kind are those associated with social intercourse which furthers trade and increases knowledge. Of the latter kind are the opportunities of realising some of our spiritual yearnings in sacred associations that go back to the most ancient times. Of both kinds may be considered the opportunities which the Pilgrimage provides for strengthening our international Brotherhood.

And celebrate the name
Of God, through the Days[2801]
Appointed, over the cattle[2802]
Which He has provided for them
(For sacrifice): then eat ye
Thereof and feed the distressed
Ones in want.

وَيَذْكُرُوا اسْمَ اللَّهِ فِي أَيَّامٍ مَّعْلُومَاتٍ
عَلَىٰ مَا رَزَقَهُم مِّن بَهِيمَةِ الْأَنْعَامِ
فَكُلُوا مِنْهَا وَأَطْعِمُوا الْبَائِسَ الْفَقِيرَ ○

29. "Then let them complete
The rites prescribed[2803]
For them, perform their vows,[2804]
And (again) circumambulate
The Ancient House."

٢٩- ثُمَّ لْيَقْضُوا تَفَثَهُمْ وَلْيُوفُوا نُذُورَهُمْ
وَلْيَطَّوَّفُوا بِالْبَيْتِ الْعَتِيقِ ○

30. Such (is the Pilgrimage):
Whoever honours the sacred
Rites of God, for him
It is good in the sight
Of his Lord. Lawful to you
(For food in Pilgrimage) are cattle,
Except those mentioned to you[2805]
(As exceptions): but shun
The abomination of idols,
And shun the word
That is false,—

٣٠- ذَٰلِكَ وَمَن يُعَظِّمْ حُرُمَاتِ اللَّهِ
فَهُوَ خَيْرٌ لَّهُ عِندَ رَبِّهِ
وَأُحِلَّتْ لَكُمُ الْأَنْعَامُ
إِلَّا مَا يُتْلَىٰ عَلَيْكُمْ
فَاجْتَنِبُوا الرِّجْسَ مِنَ الْأَوْثَانِ
وَاجْتَنِبُوا قَوْلَ الزُّورِ ○

31. Being true in faith to God,
And never assigning partners

٣١- حُنَفَاءَ لِلَّهِ غَيْرَ مُشْرِكِينَ

2801. The three special days of Ḥajj are the 8th, 9th, and 10th of the month of Ẓul-ḥajj, and the two or three subsequent days of *Tashrīq*: see the rites explained in n. 217 to ii. 197. But we may ordinarily include the first ten days of Ẓul-ḥajj in the term.

2802. The great day of commemorative Sacrifice ('Id-ul-Adhḥā) is the 10th of Ẓul-ḥajj: the meat then killed is meant to be eaten for food and distributed to the poor and needy. In present conditions, where much of it is wasted on the spot, it would be a good thing if the surplus meat were canned and utilised for export, or if the sacrifice were performed in some other form approved by due authority. *Bahīmat* means animal generally; *an'ām* means cattle specifically used for meat, and here for sacrifice.

2803. *Tafath*—the superfluous growth on one's body, such as nails, hair, etc., which it is not permitted to remove in *Iḥrām*. These may be removed on the 10th day, when the Ḥajj is completed: that is the rite of completion.

2804. The spirit of the Pilgrimage is not completed by the performance of the outward rites. The Pilgrim should carry in mind some vow of spiritual service and endeavour to perform it. Then comes the final *Ṭawāf*.

2805. The general food prohibitions will be found in ii. 173, v. 4-5, and vi. 121, 138-146. They are meant for health and cleanliness, but the worst abominations to shun are those of false worship and false speech. Here the question is about food during Pilgrimage. Lawful meat but not game is allowed.

To Him : if anyone assigns
Partners to God, he is
As if he had fallen
From heaven and been snatched up
By birds, or the wind
Had swooped (like a bird
On its prey) and thrown him
Into a far-distant place.[2806]

بِهٖ ۚ وَمَنْ يُّشْرِكْ بِاللّٰهِ
فَكَاَنَّمَا خَرَّ مِنَ السَّمَآءِ
فَتَخْطَفُهُ الطَّيْرُ
اَوْ تَهْوِيْ بِهِ الرِّيْحُ فِيْ مَكَانٍ سَحِيْقٍ ۝

32. Such (is his state) : and
Whoever holds in honour
The Symbols of God,[2807]
(In the sacrifice of animals),
Such (honour) should come truly
From piety of heart.

٣٢- ذٰلِكَ ۗ وَمَنْ يُّعَظِّمْ
شَعَآئِرَ اللّٰهِ
فَاِنَّهَا مِنْ تَقْوَى الْقُلُوْبِ ۝

33. In them [2808] ye have benefits
For a term appointed :
In the end their place
Of sacrifice is near [2809]
The Ancient House.

٣٣- لَكُمْ فِيْهَا مَنَافِعُ اِلٰٓى اَجَلٍ مُّسَمًّى
ثُمَّ مَحِلُّهَآ اِلَى الْبَيْتِ الْعَتِيْقِ ۝ ع

SECTION 5.

34. To every people did We
Appoint rites (of sacrifice),
That they might celebrate
The name of God over

٣٤- وَلِكُلِّ اُمَّةٍ جَعَلْنَا مَنْسَكًا
لِّيَذْكُرُوا اسْمَ اللّٰهِ عَلٰى مَا رَزَقَهُمْ

2806. A parable full of meaning. The man who falls from the worship of the One True God is like a man who falls from heaven. His being taken up with false objects of worship is like the falling man being picked up in the air by birds of prey. But the false objects of worship cannot hold him permanently in their grip. A fierce blast of wind—the Wrath of God—comes and snatches him away and throws him into a place far, far away from any place he could have imagined—into the hell of those who defied God.

2807. *Sha'āir*, symbols, signs, marks by which something is known to belong to some particular body of men, such as flags. In ii. 158 the word was applied to Ṣafā and Marwa : see n. 160 there. Here it seems to be applied to the rites of sacrifice. Such sacrifice is symbolical : it should betoken dedication and piety of heart. See below, xxii. 37.

2808. *In them* : in cattle, or animals offered for sacrifice. It is quite true that they are useful in many ways to man, *e.g.*, camels in desert countries are useful as mounts or for carrying burdens, or for giving milk, and so for horses and oxen ; and camels and oxen are also good for meat, and camel's hair can be woven into cloth ; goats and sheep also yield milk and meat, and hair or wool. But if they are used for sacrifice, they become symbols by which men show that they are willing to give up some of their own benefits for the sake of satisfying the needs of their poorer brethren.

2809. *Ilā*=towards, near. The actual sacrifice is not performed in the Ka'ba, but at Minā, five or six miles off, where the Pilgrims encamp : see n. 217 to ii. 197. *Thumma*=then, finally, in the end.; *i.e.*, after all the rites have been performed, Ṭawāf, Ṣafā and Marwa, and 'Arafāt.

The sustenance He gave them
From animals (fit for food).[2810]
But your God is One God :
Submit then your wills to Him
(In Islām) : and give thou
The good news [2811] to those
Who humble themselves, —

مِّنۢ بَهِيمَةِ الْأَنْعَٰمِ ۗ
فَإِلَٰهُكُمْ إِلَٰهٌ وَٰحِدٌ فَلَهُۥٓ أَسْلِمُوا۟ ۗ
وَبَشِّرِ الْمُخْبِتِينَ ○

35. To those whose hearts,
When God is mentioned,
Are filled with fear,
Who show patient perseverance
Over their afflictions, keep up
Regular prayer, and spend
(In charity) out of what
We have bestowed upon them.[2812]

٣٥- الَّذِينَ إِذَا ذُكِرَ اللَّهُ وَجِلَتْ قُلُوبُهُمْ
وَالصَّٰبِرِينَ عَلَىٰ مَآ أَصَابَهُمْ
وَالْمُقِيمِى الصَّلَوٰةِ ۙ
وَمِمَّا رَزَقْنَٰهُمْ يُنفِقُونَ ○

36. The sacrificial camels
We have made for you
As among the Symbols from
God : in them is (much)
Good for you : then pronounce
The name of God over them
As they line up (for sacrifice) :[2813]
When they are down
On their sides (after slaughter),
Eat ye thereof, and feed
Such as (beg not but)
Live in contentment,[2814]
And such as beg
With due humility : thus have

٣٦- وَالْبُدْنَ جَعَلْنَٰهَا لَكُم
مِّن شَعَٰٓئِرِ اللَّهِ
لَكُمْ فِيهَا خَيْرٌ ۖ
فَاذْكُرُوا۟ اسْمَ اللَّهِ عَلَيْهَا صَوَآفَّ ۖ
فَإِذَا وَجَبَتْ جُنُوبُهَا
فَكُلُوا۟ مِنْهَا وَأَطْعِمُوا۟
الْقَانِعَ وَالْمُعْتَرَّ ۚ كَذَٰلِكَ

2810. This is the true end of sacrifice, not propitiation of higher powers, for God is One, and He does not delight in flesh or blood (xxii. 37), but a symbol of thanksgiving to God by sharing meat with fellow-men. The solemn pronouncement of God's name over the sacrifice is an essential part of the rite.

2811. *The good news* : *i.e.* the Message of God, that He will accept in us the sacrifice of self for the benefit of our fellow-men.

2812. Some qualities of God's devotees are mentioned here, in ascending order : (1) Humility before God makes them receptive, and prepares them to listen to God's Message ; (2) fear of God, which is akin to love, touches their heart, and penetrates through their inmost being ; (3) they are not afraid of anything in mortal life ; they take their trials patiently, and they go on in a course of righteousness with constancy ; (4) their prayer now is not a matter of form, but a real communion with God, with a sense of confidence such as a faithful servant feels in the presence of a kind and loving master ; and (5) gratitude to God, as shown by practical acts of charity to all fellow-creatures.

2813. See n. 2808 to xxii. 33 above. What was expressed in general terms is applied here more particularly to camels, the most precious and useful animals of Arabia, whose mode of slaughter for sacrifice is different from that of smaller animals : the special word for such sacrifice is *Naḥr* (cviii. 2).

2814. There are ethics in begging, as in charity. No approval is given to arrogant and insolent begging, though the relief of distress of all kinds, deserved and undeserved, is included in charity. But those who beg with humility and those who receive gifts with gratitude and contentment are both mentioned for special attention. Charity should not be given for show, or to get rid of importunate demands. It should find out real needs and meet them.

We made animals subject
To you, that ye
May be grateful.

سَخَّرْنٰهَا لَكُمْ لَعَلَّكُمْ تَشْكُرُوْنَ ○

37. It is not their meat
Nor their blood, that reaches
God: it is your piety
Tnat reaches Him: He
Has thus made them subject
To you, that ye may glorify
God for His guidance to you:[2815]
And proclaim the Good News
To all who do right.

٣٧- لَنْ يَّنَالَ اللّٰهَ لُحُوْمُهَا وَلَا دِمَآؤُهَا
وَلٰكِنْ يَّنَالُهُ التَّقْوٰى مِنْكُمْ
كَذٰلِكَ سَخَّرَهَا لَكُمْ
لِتُكَبِّرُوا اللّٰهَ عَلٰى مَا هَدٰىكُمْ
وَبَشِّرِ الْمُحْسِنِيْنَ ○

38. Verily God will defend
(From ill) those who believe:
Verily, God loveth not
Any that is a traitor
To faith, or shows ingratitude.

٣٨- إِنَّ اللّٰهَ يُدٰفِعُ عَنِ الَّذِيْنَ اٰمَنُوْا
إِنَّ اللّٰهَ لَا يُحِبُّ كُلَّ خَوَّانٍ كَفُوْرٍ ○

SECTION 6.

39. To those against whom[2816]
War is made, permission
Is given (to fight), because
They are wronged;—and verily,
God is Most Powerful
For their aid;—

٣٩- أُذِنَ لِلَّذِيْنَ
يُقٰتَلُوْنَ بِأَنَّهُمْ ظُلِمُوْا
وَإِنَّ اللّٰهَ عَلٰى نَصْرِهِمْ لَقَدِيْرُ ○

40. (They are) those who have
Been expelled from their homes

٤٠- الَّذِيْنَ أُخْرِجُوْا مِنْ دِيَارِهِمْ

2815. The essence of sacrifice has been explained in n. 2810. No one should suppose that meat or blood is acceptable to the One True God. It was a Pagan fancy that God could be appeased by blood sacrifice. But God does accept the offering of our hearts, and as a symbol of such offer, some visible institution is necessary. He has given us power over the brute creation, and permitted us to eat meat, but only if we pronounce His name at the solemn act of taking life, for without this solemn invocation, we are apt to forget the sacredness of life. By the invocation we are reminded that wanton cruelty is not in our thoughts, but only the need of food. Now if we further deny ourselves the greater part of the food (some theologians fix the proportion at three-quarters or two-thirds) for the sake of our poorer brethren in solemn assembly in the precincts of the Ḥaram (sacred territory), our symbolic act finds practical expression in benevolence, and that is the virtue sought to be taught. We should be grateful to God for His guidance in this matter, in which many Peoples have gone wrong, and we should proclaim the true doctrine, so that virtue and charity may increase among men.

2816. Several translators have failed to notice that *yuqātalūna* (in the best-approved texts) is in the passive voice, "against whom war is made",—not "who take arms against the unbelievers" as Sale translates it. The clause "and verily...their aid" is parenthetical. Verse 40 connects on with "they are wronged". The wrong is indicated: 'driven by persecution from their home, for no other reason than that they worshipped the One True God.' This was the first occasion on which fighting—in self-defence—was permitted. This passage therefore undoubtedly dates from Medina.

In defiance of right,—
(For no cause) except
That they say, "Our Lord
Is God". Did not God
Check one set of people
By means of another,[2817]
There would surely have been
Pulled down monasteries, churches,
Synagogues, and mosques, in which
The name of God is
commemorated
In abundant measure. God will
Certainly aid those who
Aid His (cause);—for verily
God is Full of Strength,
Exalted in Might,[2818]
(Able to enforce His Will).

بِغَيْرِ حَقٍّ
إِلَّآ أَن يَقُولُوا رَبُّنَا
اللَّهُ ۗ وَلَوْلَا دَفْعُ اللَّهِ النَّاسَ
بَعْضَهُم بِبَعْضٍ
لَّهُدِّمَتْ صَوَامِعُ
وَبِيَعٌ وَصَلَوَٰتٌ وَمَسَٰجِدُ
يُذْكَرُ فِيهَا اسْمُ اللَّهِ كَثِيرًا ۗ
وَلَيَنصُرَنَّ اللَّهُ مَن يَنصُرُهُۥٓ ۗ
إِنَّ اللَّهَ لَقَوِىٌّ عَزِيزٌ ۝

41. (They are) those who,
If We establish them
In the land, establish
Regular prayer and give
Regular charity, enjoin
The right and forbid wrong:[2819]
With God rests the end
(And decision) of (all) affairs.

٤١- الَّذِينَ إِن مَّكَّنَّٰهُمْ فِى الْأَرْضِ
أَقَامُوا الصَّلَوٰةَ وَءَاتَوُا الزَّكَوٰةَ
وَأَمَرُوا بِالْمَعْرُوفِ وَنَهَوْا عَنِ الْمُنكَرِ ۗ
وَلِلَّهِ عَٰقِبَةُ الْأُمُورِ ۝

42. If they treat thy (mission)
As false, so did the Peoples

٤٢- وَإِن يُكَذِّبُوكَ فَقَدْ كَذَّبَتْ

2817. *Cf.* ii. 251, where the expression is used in connection with David's fight against the Philistines. To allow a righteous people to fight against a ferocious and mischief-loving people was fully justified. But the justification was far greater here, when the little Muslim community was not only fighting for its own existence against the Meccan Quraish, but for the very existence of the Faith in the One True God. They had as much right to be in Mecca and worship in the Ka'ba as the other Quraish; yet they were exiled for their Faith. It affected not the faith of one peculiar people. The principle involved was that of all worship, Jewish or Christian as well as Muslim, and of all foundations built for pious uses.

2818. *'Aziz* means Exalted in power, rank, dignity; Incomparable; Full of might and majesty; Able to enforce His Will. The last signification is the one that predominates here.

2819. The justification of the righteous in resisting oppression when not only they but their Faith is persecuted and when they are led by a righteous Imām, is that it is a form of self-sacrifice. They are not fighting for themselves, for land, power, or privilege. They are fighting for the right.

Before them (with their Prophets),—[2820] The People of Noah, And 'Ād and Thamūd;	قَبْلَهُمْ قَوْمُ نُوحٍ وَّعَادٌ وَّثَمُودُ ۝
43. Those of Abraham and Lūṭ;	٤٣- وَقَوْمُ إِبْرٰهِيمَ وَقَوْمُ لُوطٍ ۝
44. And the Companions[2821] Of the Madyan people; And Moses was rejected (In the same way). But I Granted respite to the Unbelievers, And (only) after that Did I punish them: But how (terrible) was My rejection (of them)![2822]	٤٤- وَّأَصْحٰبُ مَدْيَنَ وَكُذِّبَ مُوسٰى فَأَمْلَيْتُ لِلْكٰفِرِينَ ثُمَّ أَخَذْتُهُمْ فَكَيْفَ كَانَ نَكِيرِ ۝
45. How many populations have We Destroyed, which were given To wrong-doing? They tumbled down[2823] On their roofs. And how many Wells are lying idle and neglected,[2824] And castles lofty and well-built?	٤٥- فَكَأَيِّن مِّن قَرْيَةٍ أَهْلَكْنٰهَا وَهِيَ ظَالِمَةٌ فَهِيَ خَاوِيَةٌ عَلٰى عُرُوشِهَا وَبِئْرٍ مُّعَطَّلَةٍ وَقَصْرٍ مَّشِيدٍ ۝
46. Do they not travel Through the land, so that Their hearts (and minds)[2825] May thus learn wisdom	٤٦- أَفَلَمْ يَسِيرُوا فِي الْأَرْضِ فَتَكُونَ لَهُمْ قُلُوبٌ يَعْقِلُونَ بِهَا

2820. It is nothing new if the Prophet of God is accused of imposture. This was done in all ages; *e.g.*, Noah (vii. 64); Hūd the prophet of the *'Ād* people (vii. 66); Ṣāliḥ the prophet of the Thamūd (vii. 76); Abraham (xxi. 55); Lūṭ (vii. 82); Shu'aib the prophet of the Madyan people (vii. 85) and also of the Companions of the Wood (xv. 78). The case of Moses is mentioned apart, as his people survived to the time of our Prophet and survive to the present, and they frequently rebelled against Moses (ii. 49-61).

2821. Were they the same as the Companions of the Wood? See n. 2000 to xv. 78.

2822. My Wrath on them, and the complete reversal of their fortune in consequence.

2823. The roofs fell in first, and the whole structure, walls and all, came tumbling after, as happens in ruins. The place was turned upside down.

2824. In a dry country like Arabia, a well stands as a symbol for a living, flourishing population, and many place-names mean "the well of so-and-so" *e.g.*, Bīr 'Alī, a village just south of Medina, the quality of whose drinking water is famous, or Abyār Ibn Ḥassān, a noted stopping place on the road from Mecca to Medina, about 92 miles from Medina.

2825. The word for "heart" in Arabic speech imports both the seat of intelligent faculties and understanding as well as the seat of affections and emotions. Those who reject God's Message may have their physical eyes and ears, but their hearts are blind and deaf. If their faculties of understanding were active, would they not see the Signs of God's Providence and God's Wrath in nature around them and in the cities and ruins if they travel intelligently?

And their ears may
Thus learn to hear?
Truly it is not their eyes
That are blind, but their
Hearts which are
In their breasts.

أَوْ ءَاذَانٌ يَسْمَعُونَ بِهَا
فَإِنَّهَا لَا تَعْمَى الْأَبْصَٰرُ
وَلَٰكِن تَعْمَى الْقُلُوبُ الَّتِى فِى الصُّدُورِ ۝

47. Yet they ask thee
To hasten on the Punishment!
But God will not fail[2826]
In His promise. Verily
A Day in the sight of thy Lord
Is like a thousand years
Of your reckoning.

٤٧- وَيَسْتَعْجِلُونَكَ بِالْعَذَابِ
وَلَن يُخْلِفَ اللَّهُ وَعْدَهُۥ
وَإِنَّ يَوْمًا عِندَ رَبِّكَ كَأَلْفِ سَنَةٍ مِّمَّا
تَعُدُّونَ ۝

48. And to how many populations
Did I give respite, which[2827]
Were given to wrong-doing?
In the end I punished them.
To Me is the destination (of all).

٤٨- وَكَأَيِّن مِّن قَرْيَةٍ أَمْلَيْتُ لَهَا
وَهِىَ ظَالِمَةٌ ثُمَّ أَخَذْتُهَا
وَإِلَىَّ الْمَصِيرُ ۝ ع

C. 153.—The power of Evil is in insidious suggestions:
(xxii. 49-78.) They are only a trial to those whose hearts
Are inclined to evil, but Truth doth shine
The nobler for the Believers, by the grace
And guidance of God. Martyrs who give
Their all in the cause of God will find
A provision ample and eternal. The finest
And subtlest mysteries are but proofs of the goodness
Of God. Dispute not about rites and ceremonies:
Follow the Straight Way. Seek for worship
The Only True God, and strive in His service,
That ye may be witnesses among men
To God's Truth, as the Apostle is a witness to you.

SECTION 7.

49. Say: "O men! I am
(Sent) to you only to give

٤٩- قُلْ يَٰٓأَيُّهَا النَّاسُ إِنَّمَآ أَنَا۠ لَكُمْ

2826. If God gives respite, those to whom it is given have a real chance of repentance and amendment. He will not curtail His promise of respite. But on the other hand He has promised to call everyone to account for his deeds, and this involves justice and punishment for sin. This promise will also come true. It is foolish to try to hasten it. Time with Him is nothing. We keep count of time for our relative calculations. His existence is absolute, and not conditioned by Time or Place. What we call a thousand years may be nothing more than a day or a minute to Him.

2827. The argument begun in xxii. 45 is now rounded off and closed.

A clear warning:[2828]

نذير مبين ۝

50. "Those who believe and work
Righteousness, for them
Is forgiveness and a sustenance
Most generous.[2829]

٥٠- فالذين آمنوا وعملوا الصالحات
لهم مغفرة ورزق كريم ۝

51. "But those who strive
Against Our Signs, to frustrate[2830]
Them,—they will be
Companions of the Fire."

٥١- والذين سعوا في آياتنا معجزين
أولئك أصحاب الجحيم ۝

52. Never did We send
An apostle or a prophet
Before thee, but, when he
Framed a desire, Satan
Threw some (vanity)[2831]
Into his desire: but God
Will cancel anything (vain)
That Satan throws in,
And God will confirm
(And establish) His Signs:
For God is full of knowledge
And wisdom:[2832]

٥٢- وما أرسلنا من قبلك من رسول
ولا نبي إلا إذا تمنى
ألقى الشيطان في أمنيته
فينسخ الله ما يلقي الشيطان
ثم يحكم الله آياته
والله عليم حكيم ۝

53. That He may make
The suggestions thrown in
By Satan, but a trial[2833]
For those in whose hearts

٥٣- ليجعل ما يلقي
الشيطان فتنة للذين في قلوبهم

2828. It is the Apostle's duty to convey the warning in the clearest terms to the wicked. It is no part of his duty to coerce them or judge them, or bring on the Punishment for them. That only rests with God. But the warning itself is full of Mercy: for it gives the highest hope to the repentant sinner who turns and comes to God.

2829. The "sustenance" must be construed in the widest sense, spiritual as well as intellectual and physical. The reward of righteousness is far more generous than any merit there may be in the creature following the Will of his Creator.

2830. It will not be in their power to frustrate God's Plan; all they will do is to go further and further down in their spiritual state, deeper and deeper in their Hell.

2831. Prophets and apostles (the distinction is explained in n. 2503 to xix. 51) are but human. Their actions are righteous and their motives pure. But in judging things from a human point of view, the suggestion may come to their mind (from Satan) that it would be good to have power or wealth or influence for furthering God's cause, or that it may be good to conciliate some faction which may be irreconcilable. In fact, in God's Plan, it may be the opposite. God, in His mercy and inspiration, will cancel any false or vain suggestions of this kind, and confirm and strengthen His own Commands and make known His Will in His Signs or revelations.

2832. This clause and the similar clause at the end of the next verse are parenthetical.

2833. If any suggestion comes to the human mind that is not in accordance with God's Will and Plan, it has two opposite effects: to evil minds it is a trial and temptation from the Evil One, but to the mind well-instructed in Faith, it stands self-condemned at once, and becomes a means of strengthening the Faith and stimulating redoubled efforts to conform to the Will of God.

I a disease and who are[2834]
Hardened of heart: verily
The wrong-doers are in a schism
Far (from the Truth):

مَّرَضٌ وَّالْقَاسِيَةِ قُلُوبُهُمْ ۗ
وَإِنَّ الظّٰلِمِيْنَ لَفِيْ شِقَاقٍ بَعِيْدٍ ۝

54. And that those on whom[2835]
Knowledge has been bestowed
may learn
That the (Qur-ān) is the Truth
From thy Lord, and that they
May believe therein, and their hearts
May be made humbly (open)
To it: for verily God is
The Guide of those who believe,
To the Straight Way.

۵۴- وَّلِيَعْلَمَ الَّذِيْنَ أُوْتُوا الْعِلْمَ
أَنَّهُ الْحَقُّ مِنْ رَّبِّكَ
فَيُؤْمِنُوْا بِهٖ فَتُخْبِتَ لَهٗ قُلُوْبُهُمْ ۗ
وَإِنَّ اللّٰهَ لَهَادِ الَّذِيْنَ اٰمَنُوْا
إِلٰى صِرَاطٍ مُّسْتَقِيْمٍ ۝

55. Those who reject Faith
Will not cease to be[2836]
In doubt concerning (Revelation)
Until the Hour (of Judgment)
Comes suddenly upon them,
Or there comes to them
The Penalty of a Day of Disaster.

۵۵- وَلَا يَزَالُ الَّذِيْنَ كَفَرُوْا فِيْ مِرْيَةٍ مِّنْهُ
حَتّٰى تَأْتِيَهُمُ السَّاعَةُ بَغْتَةً
أَوْ يَأْتِيَهُمْ عَذَابُ يَوْمٍ عَقِيْمٍ ۝

56. On that Day the Dominion[2837]
Will be that of God:
He will judge between them:
So those who believe
And work righteous deeds will be
In Gardens of Delight.

۵۶- اَلْمُلْكُ يَوْمَئِذٍ لِّلّٰهِ ۗ يَحْكُمُ بَيْنَهُمْ ۗ
فَالَّذِيْنَ اٰمَنُوْا وَعَمِلُوا الصّٰلِحٰتِ فِيْ
جَنّٰتِ النَّعِيْمِ ۝

57. And for those who reject Faith
And deny Our Signs,
There will be a humiliating
Punishment.

۵۷- وَالَّذِيْنَ كَفَرُوْا وَكَذَّبُوْا بِاٰيٰتِنَا
فَأُولٰٓئِكَ لَهُمْ عَذَابٌ مُّهِيْنٌ ۝

2834. *Cf.* ii. 10. I understand the "disease in the heart" to be an earlier state of curse, which leads in an intensified form to a complete "hardening of the heart".

2835. The last clause in the last verse was parenthetical. Treat this clause as parallel with the first clause in verse 53, "that he may make", etc. Both will then connect with "God will confirm (and establish) His Signs" in verse 52. See n. 2833 above.

2836. The penalty of deliberately rejecting Faith is that the person doing so closes the channels of Mercy that flow from God. He will always be subject to doubts and superstitions, until the time comes when all earthly scales fall from his spiritual eyes. But then there will be no time for Repentance: it will be too late to profit by the guidance of God given through Revelation.

2837. Such power as Evil has over those who yield to it (xvii. 62-64) will then be gone, as the respite granted to Satan will be over, and God's Kingdom will be established.

SECTION 8.

58. Those who leave their homes
In the cause of God,
And are then slain or die,—
On them will God bestow verily
A goodly Provision:[2838]
Truly God is He Who
Bestows the best Provision.

٥٨- وَالَّذِينَ هَاجَرُوا فِي سَبِيلِ اللَّهِ
ثُمَّ قُتِلُوٓا أَوْ مَاتُوا
لَيَرْزُقَنَّهُمُ اللَّهُ رِزْقًا حَسَنًا ۚ
وَإِنَّ اللَّهَ لَهُوَ خَيْرُ الرَّٰزِقِينَ ○

59. Verily He will admit them
To a place with which
They shall be well pleased:
For God is All-Knowing,
Most Forbearing.[2839]

٥٩- لَيُدْخِلَنَّهُم مُّدْخَلًا يَرْضَوْنَهُ ۗ
وَإِنَّ اللَّهَ لَعَلِيمٌ حَلِيمٌ ○

60. That (is so). And if one
Has retaliated to no greater
Extent than the injury he received,
And is again set upon
Inordinately, God will help
Him: for God is One
That blots out (sins)
And forgives (again and again).[2840]

٦٠- ذَٰلِكَ ۖ وَمَنْ عَاقَبَ
بِمِثْلِ مَا عُوقِبَ بِهِ
ثُمَّ بُغِيَ عَلَيْهِ لَيَنصُرَنَّهُ اللَّهُ ۗ
إِنَّ اللَّهَ لَعَفُوٌّ غَفُورٌ ○

61. That is because God merges
Night into Day, and He
Merges Day into Night, and
Verily it is God Who hears

٦١- ذَٰلِكَ بِأَنَّ اللَّهَ يُولِجُ الَّيْلَ فِي النَّهَارِ
وَيُولِجُ النَّهَارَ فِي الَّيْلِ وَأَنَّ اللَّهَ سَمِيعٌ

2838. *Rizq*: sustenance, provision. I have preferred the latter word here, because after death we can only think of *rizq* in a large metaphorical sense, *i.e.*, all the provision necessary to equip the person for a full and happy Future Life, and also, I think, a provision for his dependants and near and dear ones in this life.

2839. Martyrdom is the sacrifice of life in the service of God. Its reward is therefore even greater than that of an ordinarily good life. The martyr's sins are forgiven by the very act of martyrdom, which implies service and self-surrender in the highest sense of the word. God knows all his past life but will forbear from calling him to account for things that should strictly come into his account.

2840. Ordinarily Muslims are enjoined to bear injuries with patience and return good for evil (xxiii. 96). But there are occasions when human feelings get the better of our wise resolutions, or when, in a state of conflict or war, we return "as good as we get". In that case our retaliation is permissible, provided the injury we inflict is not greater than that we receive. After such retaliation we are even, but if the other side again acts aggressively and goes beyond all bounds in attacking us, we are entitled to protection from God in spite of all our faults; for God is One that blots out our sins, and forgives again and again.

And sees (all things).[2841]	بَصِيْرٌ ○
62. That is because God—He[2842] Is the Reality; and those Besides Him whom they invoke,— They are but vain Falsehood: Verily God is He, Most High, Most Great.[2843]	٦٢- ذٰلِكَ بِأَنَّ اللّٰهَ هُوَ الْحَقُّ وَاَنَّ مَا يَدْعُوْنَ مِنْ دُوْنِهٖ هُوَ الْبَاطِلُ وَاَنَّ اللّٰهَ هُوَ الْعَلِيُّ الْكَبِيْرُ ○
63. Seest thou not that God Sends down rain from the sky, And forthwith the earth Becomes clothed with green? For God is He Who understands[2844] The finest mysteries, and Is well-acquainted (with them).	٦٣- اَلَمْ تَرَ اَنَّ اللّٰهَ اَنْزَلَ مِنَ السَّمَآءِ مَآءً فَتُصْبِحُ الْاَرْضُ مُخْضَرَّةً اِنَّ اللّٰهَ لَطِيْفٌ خَبِيْرٌ ○
64. To Him belongs all that is In the heavens and on earth: For verily God,—He is Free of all wants, Worthy of all praise.[2845]	٦٤- لَهٗ مَا فِي السَّمٰوٰتِ وَمَا فِي الْاَرْضِ وَاِنَّ اللّٰهَ لَهُوَ الْغَنِيُّ الْحَمِيْدُ ○ ع

2841. To some it may appear strange or even irreconcilable that God should be both Merciful and Just; that He should both protect His devotees and yet ask for their self-sacrifice: that He should command them to return good for evil, and yet permit retaliation under certain restrictions. But such thougnts are short-sighted. Do they not see many inconsistencies in all Life, all Nature, and all Creation? Why, even in such simple phenomena as Night and Day, the one merges into the other, and no one can tell when precisely the one begins and the other ends. Yet we can see in a rough sort of way that the one gives rest and the other activity, that the one reveals the beauties of the starry heavens and the other the splendour of the sun. In countless ways we can see there the wisdom and the fine artistry of God. And there are subtle nuances and mergings in nature that our intelligence can hardly penetrate. Now human life and human relations are far more complicated, and it is God alone Who can see all the subtle distinctions and hear the cries of *all* His creatures, in a world which Tennyson described as "red in tooth and claw".

2842. The emphatic construction calls attention to the fact that God is the only abiding Reality. All else is like shadows that will pass away.

2843. See n. 2841 above. Our vain imaginings, groundless doubts, foolish subtleties, and false worship should all give place to trust and faith in the one and only Reality.

2844. *Laṭīf*, as a name of God, is as difficult to define in words as the idea it seeks to represent is difficult to grasp in our minds. It implies: (1) fine, subtle (the basic meaning); (2) so fine and subtle as to be imperceptible to human sight; (3) so pure as to be incomprehensible; (4) with sight so perfect as to see and understand the finest subtleties and mysteries; (5) so kind and gracious as to bestow gifts of the most refined kind; extraordinarily gracious and understanding. No. 4 is the predominant meaning here and in xii. 100; Nos. 2 and 3 in vi. 103; and No. 5 in xlii. 19; but every shade of meaning must be borne in mind in each case, as a subsidiary factor in the spiritual melody.

2845. Each of the verses xxii. 61-63 mentioned two attributes of God with reference to the contents of that verse. This verse now sums up the whole argument, and the two attributes with which it closes sum up the idea by which we can understand God's goodness. God's loving kindness and mercies are not like those of human creatures who all depend upon one another, and often expect some kindness or recognition in return. God is above all wants and depends in no way whatever on His creatures. His mercies have therefore a special quality, which we cannot describe except by gratefully singing the praises of God. *Cf.* ii. 267.

SECTION 9.

65. Seest thou not that God
Has made subject to you (men)
All that is on the earth,
And the ships that sail[2846]
Through the sea by His command?
He withholds the sky (rain)[2847]
From falling on the earth
Except by His leave:
For God is Most Kind
And Most Merciful to man.

٦٥- أَلَمْ تَرَ أَنَّ اللّٰهَ سَخَّرَ لَكُمْ
مَّا فِي الْأَرْضِ وَالْفُلْكَ تَجْرِي فِي الْبَحْرِ
بِأَمْرِهٖ ۗ وَيُمْسِكُ السَّمَآءَ أَنْ تَقَعَ عَلَى
الْأَرْضِ إِلَّا بِإِذْنِهٖ ۗ
إِنَّ اللّٰهَ بِالنَّاسِ لَرَءُوفٌ رَّحِيمٌ ○

66. It is He Who gave you life,
Will cause you to die,
And will again give you
Life: truly man is
A most ungrateful creature!

٦٦- وَهُوَ الَّذِيٓ أَحْيَاكُمْ ثُمَّ يُمِيتُكُمْ
ثُمَّ يُحْيِيكُمْ ۗ
إِنَّ الْإِنْسَانَ لَكَفُورٌ ○

67. To every People have We
Appointed rites and ceremonies[2848]
Which they must follow:
Let them not then dispute
With thee on the matter,
But do thou invite (them)
To thy Lord: for thou art
Assuredly on the Right Way.

٦٧- لِكُلِّ أُمَّةٍ جَعَلْنَا مَنْسَكًا
هُمْ نَاسِكُوهُ فَلَا يُنَازِعُنَّكَ فِي الْأَمْرِ
وَادْعُ إِلَىٰ رَبِّكَ ۗ
إِنَّكَ لَعَلَىٰ هُدًى مُّسْتَقِيمٍ ○

68. If they do wrangle with thee,
Say, "God knows best
What it is ye are doing."[2849]

٦٨- وَإِنْ جٰدَلُوكَ
فَقُلِ اللّٰهُ أَعْلَمُ بِمَا تَعْمَلُونَ ○

2846. Land and sea have been made subject to man by God's command, so that man can develop his life freely on earth.

2847. *Samāa* means (1) something high, (2) a roof, a ceiling, (3) the sky, the canopy of heaven. (4) cloud or rain. I understand the last meaning here, though most authorities seem to render it by some such word as "sky". If we understand rain here, we have a complete picture of the three elements in which man lives—land, air and sea. Rain is also appropriate for mention with God's kindness and mercy. He regulates the rain for man's benefit.

2848. Rites and ceremonies may appear to be an unimportant matter compared with "weightier matters of the Law" and with the higher needs of man's spiritual nature. But they are necessary for social and religious organisation, and their effect on the individual himself is not to be despised. In any case, as they are visible external symbols, they give rise to the most heated controversies. Such controversies are to be deprecated. That does not mean that our rites and ceremonies are to be made light of. Those in Islam rest on the highest social and religious needs of man, and if we are convinced that we are on the Right Way, we should invite all to join us, without entering into controversies about such matters.

2849. 'You are only wrangling about matters about which you have no knowledge nor any deep religious feeling. The springs of your conduct are all open before God, and He will judge you.'

69. " God will judge between you
On the Day of Judgment
Concerning the matters in which
Ye differ."[2850]

٦٩- اَللّٰهُ يَحْكُمُ بَيْنَكُمْ يَوْمَ الْقِيٰمَةِ
فِيْمَا كُنْتُمْ فِيْهِ تَخْتَلِفُوْنَ ○

70. Knowest thou not that
God knows all that is
In heaven and on earth?
Indeed it is all
In a record, and that
Is easy for God.[2851]

٧٠- اَلَمْ تَعْلَمْ اَنَّ اللّٰهَ يَعْلَمُ مَا فِى السَّمَآءِ
وَالْاَرْضِ ؕ اِنَّ ذٰلِكَ فِىْ كِتٰبٍ ؕ
اِنَّ ذٰلِكَ عَلَى اللّٰهِ يَسِيْرٌ ○

71. Yet they worship, besides God,
Things for which no authority
Has been sent down to them,
And of which they have
(Really) no knowledge:
For those that do wrong
There is no helper.[2852]

٧١- وَيَعْبُدُوْنَ مِنْ دُوْنِ اللّٰهِ
مَا لَمْ يُنَزِّلْ بِهٖ سُلْطٰنًا
وَّمَا لَيْسَ لَهُمْ بِهٖ عِلْمٌ ؕ
وَمَا لِلظّٰلِمِيْنَ مِنْ نَّصِيْرٍ ○

72. When Our Clear Signs
Are rehearsed to them,
Thou wilt notice a denial[2853]
On the faces of the Unbelievers!
They nearly attack with violence
Those who rehearse Our Signs
To them. Say, "Shall I
Tell you of something
(Far) worse than these Signs?[2854]
It is the Fire (of Hell)!

٧٢- وَاِذَا تُتْلٰى عَلَيْهِمْ اٰيٰتُنَا بَيِّنٰتٍ
تَعْرِفُ فِىْ وُجُوْهِ الَّذِيْنَ كَفَرُوا الْمُنْكَرَ ؕ
يَكَادُوْنَ يَسْطُوْنَ بِالَّذِيْنَ
يَتْلُوْنَ عَلَيْهِمْ اٰيٰتِنَا ؕ
قُلْ اَفَاُنَبِّئُكُمْ بِشَرٍّ مِّنْ ذٰلِكُمْ ؕ اَلنَّارُ ؕ

2850. 'You not only find fault with the very few and simple rites and ceremonies in Islam: you, outside Islam, have no rites and ceremonies which you are yourselves agreed upon, either as Christians or as Jews, or one compared with the other.'

2851. We human beings can only think of knowledge being accurately and permanently preserved by means of a record. God's knowledge has all the qualities of a perfect record, and it is moreover complete and comprehensive. This is not difficult for Him from whom flow all knowledge and intelligence.

2852. When plain common-sense shows the absurdity of false worship, behind which there is neither knowledge, intelligence, nor authority (quite the contrary), who or what can help the false misguided creatures who dishonour God by false worship?

2853. *Munkar*: (1) a refusal to accept something offered; (2) a denial of something stated or pointed out; (3) a feeling of disapproval or active aversion, or disgust.

2854. There is irony here. 'You think God's revelations and Signs are distasteful to you! There will be something far more distasteful to you if you do not repent! What do you say to the inevitable Punishment.

God has promised it
To the Unbelievers!
And evil is that destination!"

وَعَدَهَا اللّٰهُ الَّذِيْنَ كَفَرُوْا ؕ
وَبِئْسَ الْمَصِيْرُ ۝

Section 10.

73. O men! Here is
A parable set forth!
Listen to it! Those
On whom, besides God,
Ye call, cannot create
(Even) a fly, if they all
Met together for the purpose!
And if the fly should snatch
Away anything from them,
They would have no power
To release it from the fly.
Feeble are those who petition[2855]
And those whom they petition!

٧٣- يٰۤاَيُّهَا النَّاسُ ضُرِبَ مَثَلٌ
فَاسْتَمِعُوْا لَهٗ ؕ اِنَّ الَّذِيْنَ تَدْعُوْنَ مِنْ
دُوْنِ اللّٰهِ
لَنْ يَّخْلُقُوْا ذُبَابًا وَّلَوِ اجْتَمَعُوْا لَهٗ ؕ
وَاِنْ يَّسْلُبْهُمُ الذُّبَابُ شَيْـًٔا
لَّا يَسْتَنْقِذُوْهُ مِنْهُ ؕ
ضَعُفَ الطَّالِبُ وَالْمَطْلُوْبُ ۝

74. No just estimate have they
Made of God: for God
Is He Who is strong
And able to carry out
His Will.[2856]

٧٤- مَا قَدَرُوا اللّٰهَ حَقَّ قَدْرِهٖ ؕ
اِنَّ اللّٰهَ لَقَوِيٌّ عَزِيْزٌ ۝

75. God chooses Messengers[2857]
From angels and from men
For God is He Who hears
And sees (all things).[2858]

٧٥- اَللّٰهُ يَصْطَفِيْ مِنَ الْمَلٰۤئِكَةِ رُسُلًا وَّ
مِنَ النَّاسِ ؕ اِنَّ اللّٰهَ سَمِيْعٌۢ بَصِيْرٌ ۝

76. He knows what is before them
And what is behind them:

٧٦- يَعْلَمُ مَا بَيْنَ اَيْدِيْهِمْ وَمَا خَلْفَهُمْ ؕ

2855. Both idols and their worshippers are poor, foolish, feeble creatures!

2856. No one can have a true idea of God, who descends to the base forms of false worship. God has all power, and He is fully able to carry out every part of His Will and Plan. He is exalted above all in power and dignity. *Cf.* xxii. 40 and n. 2818 for the full meaning of '*Azīz*.

2857. Men are chosen as Messengers to ordinary men; for ordinary men will not be able to understand and be in communion with beings so refined as angels. But angels are sent as Messengers to God's chosen apostles, to convey the Message from time to time. In either case they are chosen by God, are subject to God's Will, and should not be worshipped as gods.

2858. As God regards the humblest of His creatures and hears their prayer, He sends men apostles out of their own brethren (see last note), and to such apostles He communicates the highest spiritual Truths through His angels.

And to God go back
All questions (for decision).[2859]

77. O ye who believe!
Bow down, prostrate yourselves,
And adore your Lord;
And do good;
That ye may prosper.[2860]

78. And strive in His cause
As ye ought to strive,
(With sincerity and under
discipline).[2861]
He has chosen you, and has
Imposed no difficulties on you[2862]
In religion; it is the cult
Of your father Abraham.
It is He Who has named
You Muslims, both before[2863]
And in this (Revelation);
That the Apostle may be
A witness for you, and ye
Be witnesses for mankind![2864]
So establish regular Prayer,
Give regular Charity,
And hold fast to God!
He is your Protector—
17 The best to protect
30 And the Best to help!

وَإِلَى اللَّهِ تُرْجَعُ الْأُمُورُ ○

٧٧- يَٰٓأَيُّهَا الَّذِينَ آمَنُوا ارْكَعُوا وَاسْجُدُوا
وَاعْبُدُوا رَبَّكُمْ وَافْعَلُوا الْخَيْرَ
لَعَلَّكُمْ تُفْلِحُونَ ○ السجدة
عند الشافعي

٧٨- وَجَاهِدُوا فِي اللَّهِ حَقَّ جِهَادِهِ
هُوَ اجْتَبَاكُمْ وَمَا جَعَلَ عَلَيْكُمْ فِي
الدِّينِ مِنْ حَرَجٍ
مِلَّةَ أَبِيكُمْ إِبْرَاهِيمَ
هُوَ سَمَّاكُمُ الْمُسْلِمِينَ مِنْ قَبْلُ وَ
فِي هَٰذَا لِيَكُونَ الرَّسُولُ شَهِيدًا عَلَيْكُمْ
وَتَكُونُوا شُهَدَاءَ عَلَى النَّاسِ
فَأَقِيمُوا الصَّلَاةَ وَآتُوا الزَّكَاةَ
وَاعْتَصِمُوا بِاللَّهِ هُوَ مَوْلَاكُمْ
فَنِعْمَ الْمَوْلَىٰ وَنِعْمَ النَّصِيرُ ○

2859. Time, before or behind, may be of some importance to men. They may dispute as to what was the first Message, and what is the last Message. To God, this question of priority and posteriority is of no consequence. All questions go back ultimately to him and are judged on their merits.

2860. *Prosper*: in a spiritual sense, both in this life and the Hereafter.

2861. As far as the striving is concerned with Jihād in the narrow sense, see the limitations in n. 204 to ii. 190 and n. 205 to ii. 191. But the words are perfectly general and apply to all true and unselfish striving for spiritual good.

2862. The Jews were hampered by many restrictions, and their religion was racial. Christianity, as originally preached, was a hermit religion: "sell whatsoever thou hast" (Mark x. 21); "take no thought for the morrow" (Matt. vi. 34). Islam, as originally preached, gives freedom and full play to man's faculties of every kind. It is universal, and claims to date from Adam: father Abraham is mentioned as the great Ancestor of those among whom Islam was first preached (Jews, Christians, and Arab Quraish).

2863. *Before*: see Abraham's prayer in ii. 128. *In this Revelation*: in this very verse, as well as in other places.

2864. See ii. 143, and notes 143 and 144. As the Prophet is a guide and exemplar among us, so Muslims ought to be exemplars amongst mankind. The best witness to God's Truth are those who show its light in their lives.

INTRODUCTION TO SŪRA XXIII (*Mū-minūn*).

This Sūra deals with the virtues which are the seed-bed of Faith, especially in an environment in which Truth is denied and its votaries insulted and persecuted. But Truth is One and must prevail. Those who do wrong will be filled with vain regrets when it is too late for repentance.

It belongs to the late Meccan period.

Summary.—Faith, coupled with humility in prayer, charity, abstinence from vanity and from indulgence in appetites, and strict probity, must lead to final success, even though people mock and accuse the righteous of false motives, as did the contemporaries of Noah, of Moses, and of Jesus (xxiii. 1-50, and C. 154).

The apostles of God and the righteous form one Brotherhood, but those who make schisms and refuse to believe have ample evidence pointing to Truth and the goodness and greatness of God (xxiii. 51-92, and C. 155).

Evil must be repelled by goodness and faith in God; for the future life is sure, and those who disbelieve will wish for another chance when it is too late (xxiii. 93-118, and C. 156).

C. 154.—Faith leads to humility, avoidance
(xxiii. 1-50.) Of vanity in word and deed, charity,
Continence, faithful observance
Of trusts and covenants, and devout
Approach to God,—surest steps
To Bliss. Man carries in himself
Proofs of God's Providence; the same
Story is told if he looks at nature
Around him; and the long line of Teachers
Sent by God shows God's special care
Of humanity. What though they were
Rejected and scorned, maligned and persecuted?
God's Truth won through, as it always will.

Sūra XXIII.

Mū-minūn, or The Believers.

In the name of God, Most Gracious, Most Merciful.

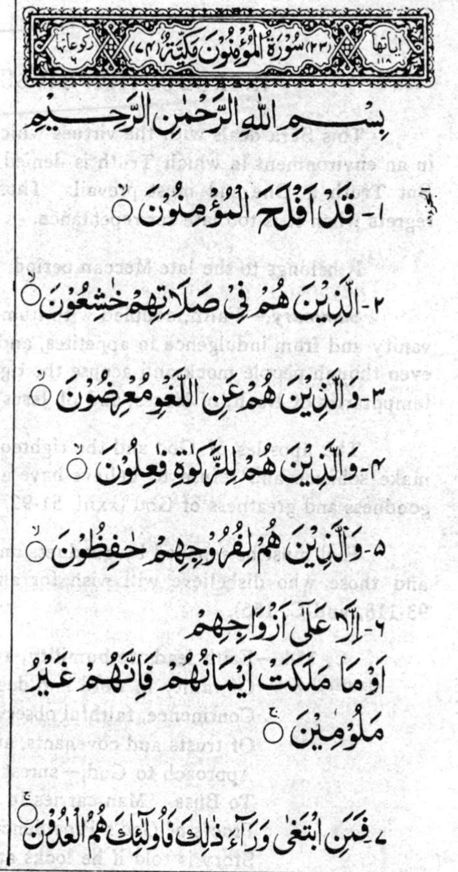

1. The Believers must
(Eventually) win through,—[2865]

2. Those who humble themselves[2866]
In their prayers;

3. Who avoid vain talk;

4. Who are active in deeds
Of charity;

5. Who abstain from sex,[2867]

6. Except with those joined
To them in the marriage bond,
Or (the captives) whom
Their right hands possess,—[2868]
For (in their case) they are
Free from blame,

7. But those whose desires exceed
Those limits are transgressors;—

2865. *Aflaḥa*: win through, prosper, succeed, achieve their aims or obtain salvation from sorrow and all evil. This verse connects on with verses 10 and 11 below. The success or victory may come in this world, but is certain and lasting in the world to come.

2866. Humility in prayer as regards (1) their estimate of their own worth in God's presence, (2) as regards their estimate of their own powers or strength unless they are helped by God, and (3) as regards the petitions they offer to God.

2867. The Muslim must guard himself against every kind of sex abuse or sex perversion. The new psychology associated with the name of Freud traces many of our hidden motives to sex, and it is common knowledge that our refinement or degradation may be measured by the hidden workings of our sex instincts. But even the natural and lawful exercise of sex is restricted to the marriage bond, under which the rights of both parties are duly regulated and maintained.

2868. This is further explained and amplified in iv. 25. It will be seen there that the status of a captive when raised to freedom by marriage is the same as that of a free woman as regards her rights, but more lenient as regards the punishment to be inflicted if she falls from virtue.

8. Those who faithfully observe
Their trusts and their covenants ;[2869]

٨- وَالَّذِينَ هُمْ لِأَمٰنٰتِهِمْ وَعَهْدِهِمْ رٰعُونَ

9. And who (strictly) guard[2870]
Their prayers ;—

٩- وَالَّذِينَ هُمْ عَلٰى صَلَوٰتِهِمْ يُحَافِظُونَ

10. These will be the heirs,[2871]

١٠- أُولٰٓئِكَ هُمُ الْوٰرِثُونَ

11. Who will inherit Paradise :
They will dwell therein
(For ever).

١١- الَّذِينَ يَرِثُونَ الْفِرْدَوْسَ هُمْ فِيهَا
خٰلِدُونَ

12. Man We did create
From a quintessence (of clay) ;[2872]

١٢- وَلَقَدْ خَلَقْنَا الْإِنْسَانَ مِنْ سُلٰلَةٍ
مِنْ طِينٍ

13. Then We placed him
As (a drop of) sperm

١٣- ثُمَّ جَعَلْنٰهُ نُطْفَةً

2869. Trusts may be express or implied. Express trusts are those where property is entrusted or duties are assigned by some one to some other whom he trusts, to carry out either immediately or in specified contingencies, such as death. Implied trusts arise out of power, or position, or opportunity ; *e.g.*, a king holds his kingdom on trust from God for his subjects : the Afghan official phrase for their kingdom used to be *Daulat-i-Khudā-dād* ('God-given kingdom'). The subject of covenants, express and implied, has been discussed in n. 682 to v. 1. Covenants create obligations, and express and implied trusts and covenants taken together cover the whole field of obligations.

2870. In verse 2 we were directed to the spirit of humility and earnestness in our prayers. Here we are told how necessary the habit of regular prayer is to our spiritual well-being and development, as it brings us closer to God, and thus sums up the light of the seven jewels of our Faith, *viz.*: (1) humility, (2) avoidance of vanity, (3) charity, (4) sex purity, (5) fidelity to trusts, and (6) to covenants, and (7) an earnest desire to get closer to God.

2871. *Cf.* xxi. 105, where it is said that the righteous will inherit the earth. In the first verse of this Sūra, the final success or victory is referred to. Truth will prevail even on this earth, but it may not be for any individual men of righteousness to see it : it may be in the time of their heirs and successors. But in the life to come, there is no doubt that every man will see the fruit of his life here, and the righteous will *inherit* heaven, in the sense that they will attain it after their death here.

2872. In this beautiful passage, God's creative work, as far as man is concerned, is recapitulated, in order to show man's real position in this life, and the certainty of the future : to which he was referred for his reward in verses 10-11 above. For the various stages of creation, see n. 120 to ii. 117. Here we are not concerned with the earliest stage, the creation of primeval matter out of nothing. It is also a process of creation when inorganic matter becomes living matter. Thus inorganic constituents of the earth are absorbed into living matter by way of food and living matter reproduces itself by means of sperm. This is deposited in the ovum and fertilises it and rests for a time in security in the mother's womb. The first change in the fertilised ovum is the conversion into a sort of clot of thickly congealed blood ; the zygote cells grow by segmentation ; then the mass gradually assumes shape in its growth as a fœtus. From the lump develop bones and flesh and organs and a nervous system. So far man's growth is like that of an animal, but a further process takes place which makes the infant animal into the infant man. This is the breathing of God's spirit into him (xv. 29) : that process need not be precisely at a given point of time. It may be a continuous process parallel to that of physical growth. The child is born ; it grows ; it decays and dies ; but after death another chapter opens for the individual, and it is to remind us of this most momentous chapter that the previous stages are recapitulated.

In a place of rest,[2873]
Firmly fixed ;

فِي قَرَارٍ مَّكِينٍ ۝

14. Then We made the sperm
Into a clot of congealed blood ;
Then of that clot We made
A (fœtus) lump ; then We
Made out of that lump
Bones and clothed the bones
With flesh ; then We developed
Out of it another creature.[2874]
So blessed be God,
The Best to create !

١٤- ثُمَّ خَلَقْنَا النُّطْفَةَ عَلَقَةً
فَخَلَقْنَا الْعَلَقَةَ مُضْغَةً فَخَلَقْنَا الْمُضْغَةَ
عِظَامًا فَكَسَوْنَا الْعِظَامَ لَحْمًا
ثُمَّ أَنشَأْنَاهُ خَلْقًا آخَرَ
فَتَبَارَكَ اللَّهُ أَحْسَنُ الْخَالِقِينَ ۝

15. After that, at length
Ye will die.[2875]

١٥- ثُمَّ إِنَّكُم بَعْدَ ذَٰلِكَ لَمَيِّتُونَ ۝

16. Again, on the Day
Of Judgment, will ye be
Raised up.

١٦- ثُمَّ إِنَّكُمْ يَوْمَ الْقِيَامَةِ تُبْعَثُونَ ۝

17. And We have made, above you,
Seven tracts ;[2876] and We
Are never unmindful
Of (Our) Creation.[2877]

١٧- وَلَقَدْ خَلَقْنَا فَوْقَكُمْ سَبْعَ طَرَائِقَ
وَمَا كُنَّا عَنِ الْخَلْقِ غَافِلِينَ ۝

2873. The growth in the fœtal stage is silent and unseen. The fœtus is protected in the mother's womb like a king in a castle ; it is firmly fixed, and gets the protection of the mother's body, on which it depends for its own growth until birth.

2874. From a mere animal, we now consider man as man. Is it not a Sign of wonder in itself that from dry dust (*turāb*, xxii. 5) or inorganic matter should be made protoplasm (moist clay or organic matter) ; from it should grow a new animal life ; and out of it should grow human life, with all its capacities and responsibilities ? Man carries within himself Signs of God's wisdom and power, and he can see them every day in the universe around him.

2875. Our physical death in this mortal life seems to make a break. But if it were the end of all, our life becomes meaningless. Our own instinct tells us that it cannot be so, and God assures us that there will be a resurrection for judgment.

2876. *Ṭarāiq* : tracts, roads, orbits, or paths of motion in the visible heavens. These seven are regular and clearly marked to our eyes, in the immense space that we see around us. We must go to astronomy to form any plausible theories of these motions. But their simplest observation gives us a sublime view of beauty, order, and grandeur in the universe. The assurance given in the next clause, that God cares for us and all His Creation, calls our attention to God's goodness, which is further illustrated in the subsequent verses.

2877. God's care for His Creation is ceaseless. A few examples of His care for our physical well-being are given in verses 18-22, and for our spiritual well-being, in Sections 2 to 5.

18. And We send down water From the sky according to[2878] (Due) measure, and We cause it To soak in the soil; And We certainly are able To drain it off (with ease).	١٨- وَأَنزَلْنَا مِنَ السَّمَاءِ مَاءً بِقَدَرٍ فَأَسْكَنَّاهُ فِي الْأَرْضِ وَإِنَّا عَلَىٰ ذَهَابٍ بِهِ لَقَادِرُونَ ○
19. With it We grow for you Gardens of date-palms And vines: in them have ye Abundant fruits: and of them Ye eat (and have enjoyment),—[2879]	١٩- فَأَنشَأْنَا لَكُم بِهِ جَنَّاتٍ مِّن نَّخِيلٍ وَأَعْنَابٍ لَّكُمْ فِيهَا فَوَاكِهُ كَثِيرَةٌ وَمِنْهَا تَأْكُلُونَ ○
20. Also a tree springing Out of Mount Sinai,[2880] Which produces oil, And relish for those Who use it for food.	٢٠- وَشَجَرَةً تَخْرُجُ مِن طُورِ سَيْنَاءَ تَنبُتُ بِالدُّهْنِ وَصِبْغٍ لِّلْآكِلِينَ ○
21. And in cattle (too) ye Have an instructive example:[2881] From within their bodies We produce (milk) for you	٢١- وَإِنَّ لَكُمْ فِي الْأَنْعَامِ لَعِبْرَةً نُّسْقِيكُم مِّمَّا فِي بُطُونِهَا

2878. Normally the rain comes well distributed; it soaks into the soil; the moisture is retained for a long time in all high grounds; it soaks and penetrates through many layers of soil and forms the architecture of physical geography; the retentive powers of higher soil enable rivers to flow perennially even where, as in India, the rainfall is seasonal and confined to a few months in the year. Another form in which water comes down from the sky according to due measure is in snow and hail: these also have their place in the economy of air and soil. Were it not for snow and glaciers in the higher mountain regions, some of the rivers would fail in their abundant flow. As wonderful as the supply of water and moisture is its drainage. It returns to the sea and air in all sorts of ways, and the formation of mist and clouds repeats the cycle. Were it not for the drainage and the clearance of the waters, we should have floods and waterlogging, as happens when the normal processes of nature are temporarily obstructed. The same thing happens when the rain comes down in other than due measure. These abnormal conditions also have their value. But how grateful should man be for God's gifts in the ceaseless processes of nature on such an enormous scale!

2879. *Cf.* vii. 19 and n. 776 to v. 69.

2880. For Arabia the best olives grow round about Mount Sinai. The fig, the olive, Mount Sinai, and the sacred city of Mecca are mentioned together in association in xcv. 1-3, where we shall consider the mystic meaning. Olive oil is an ingredient in medicinal ointments and in ointments used for religious ceremonies such as the consecration of kings. It has thus a symbolic meaning. If used for food, the olive has a delicious flavour. *Cf.* also xxiv. 35, where the olive is called a Blessed Tree, and n. 3000.

2881. *'Ibrat*: the root meaning of the verb is "to interpret, or expound, or instruct", as in xii. 43; the noun means, an interpretation, or example or Sign that instructs, as here and in xvi. 66, or gives warning, as in iii. 13. From cattle we get milk and meat; also from their skins we make leather for shoes, boots, straps, saddlery, and numerous other uses; from camel's hair and sheep's wool we weave cloth, hangings, carpets, etc.; from the horns of cattle we make cups and articles of ornament or use; and camels, horses, donkeys, mules, etc., are used for riding, carrying loads, or drawing vehicles.

To drink; there are, in them,
(Besides), numerous (other)
Benefits for you;
And of their (meat) ye eat;

وَلَكُمْ فِيهَا مَنَافِعُ كَثِيرَةٌ
وَّمِنْهَا تَأْكُلُونَ ۝

22. And on them, as well as
In ships, ye ride.

٢٢- وَعَلَيْهَا وَعَلَى الْفُلْكِ تُحْمَلُونَ ۝ ع

SECTION 2.

23. (Further, We sent a long line
Of prophets for your instruction).[2882]
We sent Noah to his people:[2883]
He said, "O my people!
Worship God! Ye have
No other god but Him.
Will ye not fear (Him)?"[2884]

٢٣- وَلَقَدْ أَرْسَلْنَا نُوحًا إِلَىٰ قَوْمِهِ
فَقَالَ يَٰقَوْمِ اعْبُدُوا اللَّهَ
مَا لَكُمْ مِّنْ إِلَٰهٍ غَيْرُهُ ۚ أَفَلَا تَتَّقُونَ ۝

24. The chiefs of the Unbelievers
Among his people said:
"He is no more than a man
Like yourselves: his wish is
To assert his superiority
Over you: if God had wished[2885]
(To send messengers),
He could have sent down
Angels: never did we hear
Such a thing (as he says),
Among our ancestors of old."

٢٤- فَقَالَ الْمَلَؤُا الَّذِينَ كَفَرُوا مِن قَوْمِهِ
مَا هَٰذَا إِلَّا بَشَرٌ مِّثْلُكُمْ يُرِيدُ
أَن يَتَفَضَّلَ عَلَيْكُمْ ۚ وَلَوْ شَاءَ اللَّهُ
لَأَنزَلَ مَلَٰئِكَةً
مَّا سَمِعْنَا بِهَٰذَا فِي آبَائِنَا الْأَوَّلِينَ ۝

25. (And some said): "He is[2886]
Only a man possessed:
Wait (and have patience)
With him for a time."

٢٥- إِنْ هُوَ إِلَّا رَجُلٌ بِهِ جِنَّةٌ
فَتَرَبَّصُوا بِهِ حَتَّىٰ حِينٍ ۝

2882. The material gifts having been mentioned, which we receive from a wise and kindly Providence, our attention is now directed to God's Providence in spiritual matters. He sent Teachers to instruct and guide us, and though they were mocked, rejected, and accused of falsehood and selfishness, they were protected by God, and God's Truth at length prevailed.

2883. "People" here is almost equivalent to "contemporaries".

2884. *Cf.* vii. 59. To fear God is to lead righteous lives and eschew evil.

2885. They attribute altogether wrong motives to him (such as would have actuated them themselves), in saying that he was trying to establish his own personal superiority over them by his preaching. Then they accuse him of falsehood in claiming to bring a message of God. "If", they say, "God had wished to send us messengers, He would have sent angels, not a man like ourselves and from among ourselves. Our ancestors did not worship One God: why should we?"

2886. I construe this to be a speech of another group among them. They thought he was mad, and best left alone. His madness would run out, or he would come to an evil end.

26. (Noah) said: "O my Lord!
Help me: for that they
Accuse me of falsehood!"

٢٦-قَالَ رَبِّ انْصُرْنِي بِمَا كَذَّبُوْنِ ○

27. So We inspired him
(With this message): "Construct
The Ark within Our sight [2887]
And under Our guidance: then
When comes Our command,
And the fountains of the earth [2888]
Gush forth, take thou on board
Pairs of every species, male [2889]
And female, and thy family—
Except those of them
Against whom the Word
Has already gone forth: [2890]
And address Me not
In favour of the wrong-doers;
For they shall be drowned
(In the Flood).

٢٧-فَأَوْحَيْنَآ إِلَيْهِ أَنِ اصْنَعِ
الْفُلْكَ بِأَعْيُنِنَا وَوَحْيِنَا
فَإِذَا جَآءَ أَمْرُنَا وَفَارَ التَّنُّوْرُ
فَاسْلُكْ فِيْهَا مِنْ كُلٍّ زَوْجَيْنِ اثْنَيْنِ
وَأَهْلَكَ إِلَّا مَنْ سَبَقَ عَلَيْهِ الْقَوْلُ
مِنْهُمْ
وَلَا تُخَاطِبْنِي فِي الَّذِيْنَ ظَلَمُوْا
إِنَّهُمْ مُّغْرَقُوْنَ ○

28. And when thou hast embarked [2891]
On the Ark—thou and those
With thee,—say: "Praise be
To God, Who has saved us
From the people who do wrong."

٢٨-فَإِذَا اسْتَوَيْتَ أَنْتَ وَمَنْ مَّعَكَ عَلَى
الْفُلْكِ فَقُلِ الْحَمْدُ لِلّٰهِ الَّذِي
نَجّٰنَا مِنَ الْقَوْمِ الظّٰلِمِيْنَ ○

29. And say: "O my Lord! [2892]
Enable me to disembark
With Thy blessing: for Thou
Art the Best to enable (us)
To disembark."

٢٩-وَقُلْ رَّبِّ أَنْزِلْنِي مُنْزَلًا مُّبٰرَكًا
وَّأَنْتَ خَيْرُ الْمُنْزِلِيْنَ ○

30. Verily in this there are
Signs (for men to understand);
(Thus) do We try (men). [2893]

٣٠-إِنَّ فِي ذٰلِكَ لَاٰيٰتٍ
وَّإِنْ كُنَّا لَمُبْتَلِيْنَ ○

2887. *Cf.* this whole passage with xi. 35-48, and notes thereon.

2888. See n. 1533 to xi. 40, where the word *Tannūr* is explained.

2889. See n. 1534 to xi. 40.

2890. See n. 1535 to xi. 40.

2891. For *istawā* see n. 1386 to x. 3. Here the meaning is: mounted on board, ascended, embarked.

2892. This second prayer was inspired when the Flood subsided, and the time came for disembarkation.

2893. Noah's contemporaries had all sorts of chances and warnings. But they refused to believe and perished. But God's Truth survived, and it went to the next and succeeding generations. Will not mankind understand?

31. Then We raised after them
Another generation.

۳۱- ثم انشانا من بعدهم قرنا اخرين ○

32. And We sent to them
An apostle from among
themselves,[2894]
(Saying), "Worship God!
Ye have no other god
But Him. Will ye not
Fear (Him)?"

۳۲- فارسلنا فيهم رسولا منهم
ان اعبدوا الله ما لكم من اله غيره
افلا تتقون ○

SECTION 3.

33. And the chiefs
Of his people, who disbelieved
And denied the Meeting
In the Hereafter, and on whom
We had bestowed the good things
Of this life, said: "He is
No more than a man
Like yourselves: he eats
Of that of which ye eat,
And drinks of what ye drink.

۳۳- وقال الملا من قومه الذين كفروا
وكذبوا بلقاء الاخرة واترفنهم في
الحيوة الدنيا ما هذا الا بشر مثلكم
ياكل مما تاكلون منه
ويشرب مما تشربون ○

34. "If ye obey a man
Like yourselves, behold,
It is certain ye will be lost.[2895]

۳۴- ولئن اطعتم بشرا مثلكم
انكم اذا لخسرون ○

35. "Does he promise that
When ye die and become dust
And bones, ye shall be
Brought forth (again)?

۳۵- ايعدكم انكم اذا متم وكنتم ترابا
وعظاما انكم مخرجون ○

36. "Far, very far is that
Which ye are promised!

۳۶- هيهات هيهات لما توعدون ○

2894. If this refers to any particular prophet, it must be Hūd whose mission was to the 'Ād people, or to Ṣāliḥ, whose mission was to the Thamūd people. That is the sequence after Noah in S. xi. 50-60 and 61-68. But I think that as the name is not mentioned, we are to understand in general the type of the post-Flood prophets until we come later on to Moses and Jesus. The object here is not to recount the stories, but to show that the resistance of the wicked made no difference to the triumph of God's holy Truth.

2895. The type of the narrow Sybarite, who enjoys the good things of this life, denies a future life, and is jealous of any one who presumes to widen his horizon, is here described in a few masterly strokes. He is bored by any mention of the serious things beyond his ken. What good is it, he says, to talk about the future? Enjoy the present. The gain is all in the present: the loss is all in the future.

37. "There is nothing but
Our life in this world!
We shall die and we live![2896]
But we shall never
Be raised up again!

٣٧- إِنْ هِيَ إِلَّا حَيَاتُنَا الدُّنْيَا
نَمُوتُ وَنَحْيَا
وَمَا نَحْنُ بِمَبْعُوثِينَ ۝

38. "He is only a man
Who invents a lie
Against God, but we
Are not the ones
To believe in him!"[2897]

٣٨- إِنْ هُوَ إِلَّا رَجُلٌ افْتَرَىٰ عَلَى اللَّهِ
كَذِبًا
وَمَا نَحْنُ لَهُ بِمُؤْمِنِينَ ۝

39. (The prophet) said:
"O my Lord! help me:
For that they accuse me
Of falsehood."[2898]

٣٩- قَالَ رَبِّ انْصُرْنِي بِمَا كَذَّبُونِ ۝

40. (God) said: "In but
A little while, they
Are sure to be sorry!"[2899]

٤٠- قَالَ عَمَّا قَلِيلٍ
لَيُصْبِحُنَّ نَادِمِينَ ۝

41. Then the Blast[2900] overtook them
With justice, and We made them
As rubbish of dead leaves[2901]
(Floating on the stream of Time)!
So away with the people
Who do wrong!

٤١- فَأَخَذَتْهُمُ الصَّيْحَةُ بِالْحَقِّ
فَجَعَلْنَاهُمْ غُثَاءً ۚ فَبُعْدًا لِلْقَوْمِ الظَّالِمِينَ ۝

42. Then We raised after them
Other generations.

٤٢- ثُمَّ أَنْشَأْنَا مِنْ بَعْدِهِمْ قُرُونًا آخَرِينَ ۝

43. No people can hasten
Their term, nor can they
Delay (it).

٤٣- مَا تَسْبِقُ مِنْ أُمَّةٍ أَجَلَهَا وَمَا
يَسْتَأْخِرُونَ ۝

2896. They seem to say: "There is no future life: that we shall die is certain; that we have this life is certain: some die, some are born, some live: and so the cycle continues: but how can dead men be raised to life?"

2897. "He is only a fool, and invents things, and attributes them to God's inspiration! We are too wise to believe such things!"

2898. See above, xxiii. 26. Every prophet is maligned and persecuted: it is always the same story with them, told in different ways.

2899. When the Punishment comes, they will be sorry for themselves, but it will be too late then.

2900. See xi. 66, and notes 1563 and 1561.

2901. *Guthā-un*: rubbish of dead leaves, or scum floating on a torrent.

44. Then sent We Our apostles
In succession: every time
There came to a people
Their apostle, they accused him
Of falsehood: so We made
Them follow each other
(In punishment): We made them
As a tale (that is told):[2902]
So away with a people
That will not believe!

٤٤- ثُمَّ أَرْسَلْنَا رُسُلَنَا تَتْرَا ۖ
كُلَّمَا جَاءَ أُمَّةً رَّسُولُهَا كَذَّبُوهُ
فَأَتْبَعْنَا بَعْضَهُم بَعْضًا
وَجَعَلْنَاهُمْ أَحَادِيثَ ۚ
فَبُعْدًا لِّقَوْمٍ لَّا يُؤْمِنُونَ ○

45. Then We sent Moses
And his brother Aaron,
With Our Signs and
Authority manifest,[2903]

٤٥- ثُمَّ أَرْسَلْنَا مُوسَىٰ وَأَخَاهُ هَارُونَ ۙ
بِآيَاتِنَا وَسُلْطَانٍ مُّبِينٍ ○

46. To Pharaoh and his Chiefs:
But these behaved insolently:
They were an arrogant people.

٤٦- إِلَىٰ فِرْعَوْنَ وَمَلَئِهِ
فَاسْتَكْبَرُوا وَكَانُوا قَوْمًا عَالِينَ ○

47. They said: "Shall we believe
In two men like ourselves?
And their people are subject[2904]
To us!"

٤٧- فَقَالُوا أَنُؤْمِنُ لِبَشَرَيْنِ مِثْلِنَا
وَقَوْمُهُمَا لَنَا عَابِدُونَ ○

48. So they accused them
Of falsehood, and they became
Of those who were destroyed.

٤٨- فَكَذَّبُوهُمَا فَكَانُوا مِنَ الْمُهْلَكِينَ ○

49. And We gave Moses
The Book, in order that
They might receive guidance.[2905]

٤٩- وَلَقَدْ آتَيْنَا مُوسَى الْكِتَابَ
لَعَلَّهُمْ يَهْتَدُونَ ○

2902. Their habitations and their organisation have been wiped out. What remains is merely a vague story of their existence, a tale that is told. Where their name remains, which is not always the case, it is only a by-word, suggesting all that is unstable and ephemeral,—"to point a moral and adorn a tale".

2903. Moses and Aaron had a twofold mission: (1) to Pharaoh and his Court, which failed because of Egyptian arrogance; (2) to the Israelites, for whom the Law was received on Mount Sinai, but they repeatedly rebelled against God. In both cases there were miracles ("Clear Signs") and other proofs which showed that they came at God's command and were inspired by His authority.

2904. Racial arrogance made the Egyptians say, 'These men belong to a race which we hold in subjection as our slaves: how can we accept them as messengers of God?'

2905. Here the reference is to the second part of the mission of Moses, that to the Israelites, which the Israelites rendered ineffective by their want of faith. See n. 2903 above.

50. And We made
The son of Mary
And his mother
As a Sign:[2906]
We gave them both
Shelter on high ground,
Affording rest and security
And furnished with springs.[2907]

٥٠- وَجَعَلْنَا ابْنَ مَرْيَمَ
وَأُمَّهُ آيَةً
وَآوَيْنَاهُمَا إِلَىٰ رَبْوَةٍ
ذَاتِ قَرَارٍ وَمَعِينٍ ۝

C. 155.—The Brotherhood of Truth is one in all ages:
(xxiii. 51-92.)
It is narrow men who create sects.
Let them not think that the goods
Of this world can shield them from evil
Or its consequences. God's Truth and His Messenger
Can be known to all: for He in His Mercy
Has given us faculties and judgment, if we
Would but use them. The Message is not
New: all Creation proclaims it: High
Above all is the Lord of Glory Supreme!

SECTION 4.

51. O ye apostles! enjoy[2908]
(All) things good and pure,
And work righteousness:
For I am well-acquainted
With (all) that ye do.

٥١- يَا أَيُّهَا الرُّسُلُ كُلُوا مِنَ الطَّيِّبَاتِ
وَاعْمَلُوا صَالِحًا
إِنِّي بِمَا تَعْمَلُونَ عَلِيمٌ ۝

52. And verily this Brotherhood
Of yours is a single Brotherhood,[2909]
And I am your Lord
And Cherisher: therefore
Fear Me (and no other).

٥٢- وَإِنَّ هَٰذِهِ أُمَّتُكُمْ أُمَّةً وَاحِدَةً
وَأَنَا رَبُّكُمْ فَاتَّقُونِ ۝

2906. The virgin birth of Jesus was a miracle both for him and his mother. She was falsely accused of unchastity, but the child Jesus triumphantly vindicated her by his own miracles (xix. 27-33), and showed by his life the meanness of the calumny against his mother.

2907. There is no need to look far for the place where mother and child were given secure shelter. It is described in xix. 22-26. It was the place to which she withdrew to be delivered when the time drew near. There was a fruitful palm-tree, evidently on high ground, for beneath it flowed a spring. She retired there in seclusion, and she and her child rested their until it was time for her to go to her people with her child.

2908. Literally, "eat". See n. 776 to v. 69. The men of God do not pose as ascetics, but receive gratefully all God's gifts, and show their gratitude by their righteous lives.

2909. *Cf.* xxi. 92-93. All prophets form one Brotherhood: their Message is one, and their religion and teaching are one; they serve the One True God, Who loves and cherishes them; and they owe their duty to Him and Him alone.

53. But people have cut off
Their affair (of unity),
Between them, into sects:
Each party rejoices in that
Which is with itself.[2910]

٥٣- فَتَقَطَّعُوٓا أَمْرَهُمْ بَيْنَهُمْ زُبُرًا ۖ
كُلُّ حِزْبٍ بِمَا لَدَيْهِمْ فَرِحُونَ ○

54. But leave them
In their confused ignorance
For a time.

٥٤- فَذَرْهُمْ فِى غَمْرَتِهِمْ حَتّٰى حِينٍ ○

55. Do they think that because
We have granted them abundance
Of wealth and sons,

٥٥- أَيَحْسَبُونَ أَنَّمَا نُمِدُّهُمْ بِهِ
مِنْ مَّالٍ وَّبَنِينَ ○

56. We would hasten them
On in every good? Nay,
They do not understand.[2911]

٥٦- نُسَارِعُ لَهُمْ فِى الْخَيْرٰتِ ۚ
بَلْ لَّا يَشْعُرُونَ ○

57. Verily those who live
In awe for fear of their Lord;

٥٧- إِنَّ الَّذِينَ هُمْ مِّنْ خَشْيَةِ رَبِّهِمْ مُّشْفِقُونَ ○

58. Those who believe
In the Signs of their Lord;

٥٨- وَالَّذِينَ هُمْ بِاٰيٰتِ رَبِّهِمْ يُؤْمِنُونَ ○

59. Those who join not (in worship)
Partners with their Lord;

٥٩- وَالَّذِينَ هُمْ بِرَبِّهِمْ لَا يُشْرِكُونَ ○

60. And those who dispense
Their charity with their hearts[2912]
Full of fear, because
They will return to their Lord;—

٦٠- وَالَّذِينَ يُؤْتُونَ مَآ اٰتَوْا وَّقُلُوبُهُمْ وَجِلَةٌ
أَنَّهُمْ إِلٰى رَبِّهِمْ رٰجِعُونَ ○

61. It is these who hasten
In every good work,
And these who are
Foremost in them.

٦١- أُولٰٓئِكَ يُسٰرِعُونَ فِى الْخَيْرٰتِ
وَهُمْ لَهَا سٰبِقُونَ ○

2910. The people who began to trade on the names of the prophets cut off that unity and made sects; and each sect rejoices in its own narrow doctrine, instead of taking the universal teaching of Unity from God. But this sectarian confusion is of man's making. It will last for a time, but the rays of Truth and Unity will finally dissipate it.

2911. Worldly wealth, power, and influence may be but trials. Let not their possessors think that they are in themselves things that will necessarily bring them happiness.

2912. Their hearts are full of reverence for God and fear lest their charity or their hearts be not good enough for acceptance before their Lord; for they have the certainty of a future life, in which they will stand before the Judgment Seat. They fear for their own worthiness, but they hope in Faith.

62. On no soul do We
Place a burden greater
Than it can bear:[2913]
Before Us is a record
Which clearly shows the truth:[2914]
They will never be wronged.

٦٢- وَلَا نُكَلِّفُ نَفْسًا إِلَّا وُسْعَهَا
وَلَدَيْنَا كِتٰبٌ يَنْطِقُ بِالْحَقِّ
وَهُمْ لَا يُظْلَمُونَ ۝

63. But their hearts are
In confused ignorance[2915]
Of this; and there are,
Besides that, deeds of theirs,[2916]
Which they will (continue)
To do,—

٦٣- بَلْ قُلُوبُهُمْ فِي غَمْرَةٍ مِّنْ هٰذَا
وَلَهُمْ أَعْمَالٌ مِّنْ دُونِ ذٰلِكَ
هُمْ لَهَا عٰمِلُونَ ۝

64. Until, when We seize
In Punishment those of them
Who received the good things
Of this world, behold,
They will groan in supplication!

٦٤- حَتّٰى إِذَا أَخَذْنَا مُتْرَفِيهِمْ بِالْعَذَابِ
إِذَا هُمْ يَجْـَٔرُونَ ۝

65. (It will be said):
"Groan not in supplication
This day; for ye shall
Certainly not be helped by Us.

٦٥- لَا تَجْـَٔرُوا الْيَوْمَ
إِنَّكُمْ مِّنَّا لَا تُنْصَرُونَ ۝

66. "My Signs used to be
Rehearsed to you, but ye
Used to turn back
On your heels—

٦٦- قَدْ كَانَتْ اٰيٰتِي تُتْلٰى عَلَيْكُمْ
فَكُنْتُمْ عَلٰى أَعْقَابِكُمْ تَنْكِصُونَ ۝

67. "In arrogance: talking nonsense
About the (Qur-ān), like one
Telling fables by night."[2917]

٦٧- مُسْتَكْبِرِينَ
بِهِ سٰمِرًا تَهْجُرُونَ ۝

2913. *Cf.* ii. 286 and n. 339.

2914. The record speaks clearly, and shows exactly what each soul has done and thought, and what is due to it in justice. The worst will receive full justice. The best will receive far more than their due: xxviii. 84.

2915. This is said of the Unbelievers who rejected Faith and rejoiced in the vanities of this world. In spite of the proclamation of Truth, they are doubtful of the future Life and Judgment.

2916. In addition to their rejection of Faith, they have against them positive deeds of wrong-doing, from which, on account of their contempt of the Light from God, they will not desist until they are sharply pulled up for punishment: and then repentance will be too late!

2917. *Sāmir*: one who remains awake by night, one who passes the night in talk or in the recital of stories or romances, a favourite amusement of the Days of Ignorance.

68. Do they not ponder over
The Word (of God), or
Has anything (new) come
To them that did not
Come to their fathers of old?[2918]

٦٨- أَفَلَمْ يَدَّبَّرُوا الْقَوْلَ
أَمْ جَاءَهُمْ مَا لَمْ يَأْتِ آبَاءَهُمُ الْأَوَّلِينَ ۝

69. Or do they not recognise
Their Apostle, that they
Deny him?

٦٩- أَمْ لَمْ يَعْرِفُوا رَسُولَهُمْ
فَهُمْ لَهُ مُنْكِرُونَ ۝

70. Or do they say, "he is
Possessed"? Nay, he has
Brought them the Truth,
But most of them
Hate the Truth.

٧٠- أَمْ يَقُولُونَ بِهِ جِنَّةٌ ۚ
بَلْ جَاءَهُمْ بِالْحَقِّ
وَأَكْثَرُهُمْ لِلْحَقِّ كَارِهُونَ ۝

71. If the Truth had been
In accord with their desires,
Truly the heavens and the earth,
And all beings therein
Would have been in confusion[2919]
And corruption! Nay, We
Have sent them their admonition,
But they turn away
From their admonition.

٧١- وَلَوِ اتَّبَعَ الْحَقُّ أَهْوَاءَهُمْ
لَفَسَدَتِ السَّمَاوَاتُ وَالْأَرْضُ وَمَنْ
فِيهِنَّ ۚ
بَلْ أَتَيْنَاهُمْ بِذِكْرِهِمْ
فَهُمْ عَنْ ذِكْرِهِمْ مُعْرِضُونَ ۝

72. Or is it that thou
Askest them for some[2920]
Recompense? But the recompense
Of thy Lord is best:
He is the Best of those
Who give sustenance.

٧٢- أَمْ تَسْأَلُهُمْ خَرْجًا
فَخَرَاجُ رَبِّكَ خَيْرٌ ۖ
وَهُوَ خَيْرُ الرَّازِقِينَ ۝

73. But verily thou callest them
To the Straight Way;

٧٣- وَإِنَّكَ لَتَدْعُوهُمْ إِلَىٰ صِرَاطٍ مُسْتَقِيمٍ ۝

2918. If they ponder over the matter, they will find that God's Message to humanity is as old as Adam. It is good for all ages. It never grows old, and it is never new.

2919. God is All-Wise and All-Good, and His architecture of the universe is on a perfect Plan. If these poor, low, selfish, ignorant creatures were to plan it according to their hearts' desires, it would be a dreadful world, full of confusion and corruption.

2920. This is the last of the questions, beginning with xxiii. 68 above, showing the absurdity of the position taken up by the Unbelievers. (1) The Message of God is as old as humanity: why do they fight shy of it? (2) They have known their Apostle to be true and righteous: why do they deny him? (3) Is it madness to bring the bitter Truth before them? (4) Does the Prophet ask any worldly reward from them? If not, why do they reject his unselfish efforts for their own good?

74. And verily those who
Believe not in the Hereafter
Are deviating from that Way.

٧٤- وَإِنَّ الَّذِينَ لَا يُؤْمِنُونَ بِالْآخِرَةِ
عَنِ الصِّرَاطِ لَنَاكِبُونَ ۝

75. If We had mercy on them
And removed the distress[2921]
Which is on them, they
Would obstinately persist
In their transgression,
Wandering in distraction
To and fro.

٧٥- وَلَوْ رَحِمْنَاهُمْ وَكَشَفْنَا مَا بِهِم مِّن
ضُرٍّ
لَّلَجُّوا فِي طُغْيَانِهِمْ
يَعْمَهُونَ ۝

76. We inflicted Punishment[2922]
On them, but they
Humbled not themselves
To their Lord, nor do they
Submissively entreat (Him)!—

٧٦- وَلَقَدْ أَخَذْنَاهُم بِالْعَذَابِ
فَمَا اسْتَكَانُوا لِرَبِّهِمْ
وَمَا يَتَضَرَّعُونَ ۝

77. Until We open on them
A gate leading to
A severe Punishment: then
Lo! they will be plunged
In despair therein![2923]

٧٧- حَتَّىٰ إِذَا فَتَحْنَا عَلَيْهِم بَابًا
ذَا عَذَابٍ شَدِيدٍ
إِذَا هُمْ فِيهِ مُبْلِسُونَ ۝ ع

SECTION 5.

78. It is He Who has created
For you (the faculties of)
Hearing, sight, feeling[2924]
And understanding: little thanks
It is ye give!

٧٨- وَهُوَ الَّذِي أَنشَأَ لَكُمُ
السَّمْعَ وَالْأَبْصَارَ وَالْأَفْئِدَةَ
قَلِيلًا مَّا تَشْكُرُونَ ۝

2921. The reference is to a very severe famine felt in Mecca, which was attributed by the Unbelievers to the presence of the holy Prophet among them and his preaching against their gods. As this is a Meccan Sūra, the famine referred to must be that described by Ibn Kat͟hīr as having occurred in the 8th year of the Mission, say about four years before the Hijra. There was also a post-Hijra famine, which is referred to by Buk͟hāri, but that was a later event.

2922. Some Commentators understand the battle of Badr to be meant here: if so, this particular verse would be of the Medina period. But it is better to understand it as referring to the same "distress" as in the preceding verse, or to punishments in general, which obstinate sinners refuse to take as warnings given to them to mend their ways and turn in repentance to God.

2923. *Cf.* vi. 44. If the little trials in the present life will not open their eyes, will great trials do so? Unfortunately they only cause in the wicked a feeling of despair. In the final Punishment after the Judgment, it will be too late for them to repent, and despair will be their only lot.

2924. As elsewhere, "heart" is to be understood as the seat both of feeling and intelligence. 'All the means by which knowledge can be gathered, judgment formed, and goodness cultivated, are provided for you by God. If you were grateful, you would use those in His service, which is expressed in your service to your fellow-men. But instead you ignore these gifts, question God's Providence, and blaspheme against Him!'

79. And He Has multiplied you
Through the earth, and to Him
Shall ye be gathered back.

٧٩- وَهُوَ الَّذِي ذَرَأَكُمْ فِي الْأَرْضِ
وَإِلَيْهِ تُحْشَرُونَ ○

80. It is He Who gives
Life and death, and to Him
(Is due) the alternation[2925]
Of Night and Day:
Will ye not then understand?

٨٠- وَهُوَ الَّذِي يُحْيِي وَيُمِيتُ
وَلَهُ اخْتِلَافُ الَّيْلِ وَالنَّهَارِ ۗ
أَفَلَا تَعْقِلُونَ ○

81. On the contrary they say
Things similar to what
The ancients said.[2926]

٨١- بَلْ قَالُوا مِثْلَ مَا قَالَ الْأَوَّلُونَ ○

82. They say: "What! When we
Die and become dust and bones,
Could we really be
Raised up again?

٨٢- قَالُوٓا ءَإِذَا مِتْنَا وَكُنَّا تُرَابًا وَعِظَامًا
ءَإِنَّا لَمَبْعُوثُونَ ○

83. "Such things have been promised
To us and to our fathers
Before! They are nothing
But tales of the ancients!"

٨٣- لَقَدْ وُعِدْنَا نَحْنُ وَآبَآؤُنَا هٰذَا مِنْ
قَبْلُ إِنْ هٰذَآ إِلَّآ أَسَاطِيرُ الْأَوَّلِينَ ○

84. Say: "To whom belong
The earth and all beings therein?
(Say) if ye know!"

٨٤- قُلْ لِّمَنِ الْأَرْضُ وَمَنْ فِيهَآ
إِنْ كُنْتُمْ تَعْلَمُونَ ○

85. They will say, "To God!"
Say: "Yet will ye not
Receive admonition?"[2927]

٨٥- سَيَقُولُونَ لِلّٰهِ ۗ
قُلْ أَفَلَا تَذَكَّرُونَ ○

86. Say: "Who is the Lord
Of the seven heavens,
And the Lord of the Throne
(Of Glory) Supreme?"[2928]

٨٦- قُلْ مَنْ رَّبُّ السَّمٰوٰتِ السَّبْعِ
وَرَبُّ الْعَرْشِ الْعَظِيمِ ○

2925. The alternation of Night and Day stands here as a symbol for all the beneficent processes of Nature provided by God for the comfort and growth of man's outer and inner life.

2926. And they are the more culpable, as they have received a later and completer revelation. Why should they now stand on the primitive ideas of their ancestors?

2927. If their argument is that such things about a future life cannot be known or proved, they are referred to the things which are actually before them. The tangible things of the earth—can they postulate their order or government except by a Power or Force or Energy outside them? They will admit that there is such a Power or Force or Energy. We call it God. Go a step further. We see a sublime Universe in the heavens above, stretching far, far beyond our ken. They will admit its existence and its grandeur. We ask them to entertain a feeling of reverence for the Power behind it, and to understand their own littleness and their dependence upon that Power.

2928. *Cf.* ix. 129.

87. They will say, "(They belong)
To God." Say: "Will ye not
Then be filled with awe?"[2929]

٨٧- سَيَقُولُونَ لِلَّهِ ۚ
قُلْ أَفَلَا تَتَّقُونَ ۝

88. Say: "Who is it in whose
Hands is the governance
Of all things,—who protects
(All), but is not protected
(Of any)? (Say) if ye know."

٨٨- قُلْ مَنْ بِيَدِهِ مَلَكُوتُ كُلِّ شَيْءٍ
وَهُوَ يُجِيرُ وَلَا يُجَارُ عَلَيْهِ
إِنْ كُنْتُمْ تَعْلَمُونَ ۝

89. They will say, "(It belongs)
To God." Say: "Then how
Are ye deluded?"[2930]

٨٩- سَيَقُولُونَ لِلَّهِ ۚ
قُلْ فَأَنَّىٰ تُسْحَرُونَ ۝

90. We have sent them the Truth:
But they indeed practise
Falsehood!

٩٠- بَلْ أَتَيْنَاهُمْ بِالْحَقِّ
وَإِنَّهُمْ لَكَاذِبُونَ ۝

91. No son did God beget,
Nor is there any god
Along with Him: (if there were
Many gods), behold, each god
Would have taken away
What he had created,
And some would have
Lorded it over others![2931]
Glory to God! (He is free)
From the (sort of) things
They attribute to Him!

٩١- مَا اتَّخَذَ اللَّهُ مِنْ وَلَدٍ
وَمَا كَانَ مَعَهُ مِنْ إِلَٰهٍ
إِذًا لَذَهَبَ كُلُّ إِلَٰهٍ بِمَا خَلَقَ
وَلَعَلَا بَعْضُهُمْ عَلَىٰ بَعْضٍ ۚ
سُبْحَانَ اللَّهِ عَمَّا يَصِفُونَ ۝

92. He knows what is hidden
And what is open: too high
Is He for the partners
They attribute to Him![2932]

٩٢- عَالِمِ الْغَيْبِ وَالشَّهَادَةِ
فَتَعَالَىٰ عَمَّا يُشْرِكُونَ ۝

2929. See n. 2927 above. 'If this great and glorious Universe inspires you with awe, surely the Power behind is more worthy of your awe, especially if you compare your dependence and its dependence upon Him.'

2930. 'The order and unity of purpose in the Universe argue unity of design and goodness in its Maker. Is it not then sheer madness for you to run after false fancies and fail to understand and obey His Will? It is delusion in you to seek other than God.'

2931. *Cf.* xvii. 42. The multiplicity of gods is intellectually indefensible, considering the unity of Design and Purpose in His wonderful Universe.

2932. To suppose that God has a son or family or partners or companions is to have a low idea of God, Who is high above all such relationships. He is the One True God, and there can be none to compare with Him.

C. 156.—Let us eschew evil, but not
(xxiii. 93-118.) Pay back evil in its own coin,
However great the temptation : no chance
Will there be to retrieve our conduct,
Once death cuts us off. Then we shall only
Have to wait for Judgment : none can pass
That Barrier : our deeds will be weighed,
And happy those whose good weighs more
In the scale than ill. Only Faith and Goodness
Will prevail in the end : so glory to the Lord
Of the Throne exalted, of Mercy and Honour !

SECTION 6.

93. Say : "O my Lord!
If Thou wilt show me
(In my lifetime) that which
They are warned against,—[2933]

٩٣- قُلْ رَّبِّ
إِمَّا تُرِيَنِّي مَا يُوعَدُونَ ۝

94. "Then, O my Lord! put me not
Amongst the people
Who do wrong!"

٩٤- رَبِّ فَلَا تَجْعَلْنِي فِي الْقَوْمِ
الظّٰلِمِينَ ۝

95. And We are certainly able
To show thee (in fulfilment)
That against which they are
warned.

٩٥- وَإِنَّا عَلَىٰ أَن نُّرِيَكَ
مَا نَعِدُهُمْ لَقٰدِرُونَ ۝

96. Repel evil with that[2934]
Which is best : We are
Well acquainted with
The things they say.

٩٦- اِدْفَعْ بِالَّتِي هِيَ أَحْسَنُ السَّيِّئَةَ
نَحْنُ أَعْلَمُ بِمَا يَصِفُونَ ۝

97. And say "O my Lord!
I seek refuge with Thee

٩٧- وَقُلْ رَّبِّ أَعُوذُ بِكَ

2933. In the first instance, this applied to the holy Apostle. His subsequent Hijrat from Mecca and the eventual overthrow of the Meccan oligarchy amply prove the fulfilment of the prophecy. But in general meaning it applies to all. We are taught that evil will be visited with a terrible punishment, not only in a future life, but in this very life when its cup is full and the time comes for punishment in God's Plan. If it has to come while we are still on the scene of this life, we are asked to pray that we may not be found in the company of those who draw such punishment on themselves. In other words we must eschew the society of evil ones.

2934. Whether people speak evil of you, in your presence or behind your back, or they do evil to you in either of those ways, all is known to God. It is not for you to punish. Your best course is not to do evil in your turn, but to do what will best repel the evil. Two evils do not make a good. *Cf.* xli. 34, n. 4504.

From the suggestions
Of the Evil Ones.[2935]

مِنْ هَمَزٰتِ الشَّيٰطِيْنِ ۝

98. "And I seek refuge with Thee
O my Lord! lest they
Should come near me."

٩٨-وَ اَعُوْذُ بِكَ رَبِّ اَنْ يَّحْضُرُوْنِ ۝

99. (In Falsehood will they be)[2936]
Until, when death comes
To one of them, he says:
"O my Lord! send me back[2937]
(To life),—

٩٩-حَتّٰٓى اِذَا جَآءَ اَحَدَهُمُ الْمَوْتُ
قَالَ رَبِّ ارْجِعُوْنِ ۝

100. "In order that I may
Work righteousness in the
things[2938]
I neglected."—"By no means!
It is but a word he says."—[2939]
Before them is a Partition[2940]
Till the Day they are
Raised up.

١٠٠-لَعَلِّيْٓ اَعْمَلُ صَالِحًا فِيْمَا تَرَكْتُ
كَلَّا ؕ اِنَّهَا كَلِمَةٌ هُوَ قَآئِلُهَا ؕ
وَمِنْ وَّرَآئِهِمْ بَرْزَخٌ
اِلٰى يَوْمِ يُبْعَثُوْنَ ۝

101. Then when the Trumpet
Is blown, there will be
No more relationships
Between them that day,
Nor will one ask after another![2941]

١٠١-فَاِذَا نُفِخَ فِى الصُّوْرِ
فَلَآ اَنْسَابَ بَيْنَهُمْ يَوْمَئِذٍ
وَّلَا يَتَسَآءَلُوْنَ ۝

2935. But in any case, shun evil for yourself, and you cannot do this without seeking the help and protection of God. Not only must you shun all promptings of evil, but you must shun its proximity. It may be that in retaliating on evil, or even in your curiosity to discover what evil is, you may fall into evil yourself. You should avoid going near it or anything which brings it near to you. And in this matter you should seek God's help.

2936. This verse I think connects on with xxiii. 90 above. Though God proclaims His Truth everywhere, the wicked cling to Falsehood until they face the reality of Death.

2937. The verb for "send me back" is in the plural in Arabic, which is construed either (1) as an emphatic form, as if the singular were repeated, or (2) as a plural of respect, though such a plural is not ordinarily used in addressing God, or (3) as a plural addressed to the angels, after the address to God in "O my Lord!"

2938. The unrighteous will ask for another chance. But it will be too late then. The time for repentance will then have passed.

2939. Their request will mean nothing. It will be treated merely as an empty word of excuse. They had plenty of chances in this life. Not only did they reject them, but they did not even believe in God or ask for His assistance.

2940. *Barzakh*: a partition, a bar or barrier; the place or state in which people will be after death and before Judgment. *Cf.* xxv. 53 and lv. 20. Behind them is the barrier of death, and in front of them is the Barzakh, partition, a quiescent state until the judgment comes.

2941. The old relationships of the world will then be dissolved. Each soul will stand on its merits.

102. Then those whose balance
(Of good deeds) is heavy,—
They will attain salvation : [2942]

١٠٢- فَمَن ثَقُلَتْ مَوَازِينُهُ
فَأُولَٰئِكَ هُمُ الْمُفْلِحُونَ ○

103. But those whose balance
Is light, will be those
Who have lost their souls ; [2943]
In Hell will they abide.

١٠٣- وَمَنْ خَفَّتْ مَوَازِينُهُ فَأُولَٰئِكَ الَّذِينَ
خَسِرُوا أَنفُسَهُمْ فِي جَهَنَّمَ خَالِدُونَ ○

104. The Fire will burn their faces,
And they will therein
Grin, with their lips displaced. [2944]

١٠٤- تَلْفَحُ وُجُوهَهُمُ النَّارُ
وَهُمْ فِيهَا كَالِحُونَ ○

105. " Were not My Signs rehearsed
To you, and ye did but
Treat them as falsehoods ? "

١٠٥- أَلَمْ تَكُنْ آيَاتِي تُتْلَىٰ عَلَيْكُمْ
فَكُنتُم بِهَا تُكَذِّبُونَ ○

106. They will say : " Our Lord !
Our misfortune overwhelmed us, [2945]
And we became a people
Astray !

١٠٦- قَالُوا رَبَّنَا غَلَبَتْ عَلَيْنَا شِقْوَتُنَا
وَكُنَّا قَوْمًا ضَالِّينَ ○

107. " Our Lord ! Bring us out
Of this : if ever we return
(To evil), then shall we be
Wrong-doers indeed ! "

١٠٧- رَبَّنَا أَخْرِجْنَا مِنْهَا
فَإِنْ عُدْنَا فَإِنَّا ظَالِمُونَ ○

108. He will say : " Be ye
Driven into it (with ignominy) !
And speak ye not to Me ! [2946]

١٠٨- قَالَ اخْسَئُوا فِيهَا
وَلَا تُكَلِّمُونِ ○

109. " A part of My servants
There was, who used to pray,

١٠٩- إِنَّهُ كَانَ فَرِيقٌ مِّنْ عِبَادِي يَقُولُونَ

2942. Good and evil deeds will be weighed against each other. If the good deeds prevail, the soul will attain *falāh, i.e.,* prosperity, well-being, bliss, or salvation ; if the contrary, there will be the misery and anguish of Hell.

2943. The loss or perdition will not mean that they will die and feel no more : xiv. 17. The punishment will mean nothing, if there was no sensibility, but total annihilation.

2944. That is to say, their faces will be disfigured with anguish, and their lips will quiver and fall out of place, exposing their teeth.

2945. 'The evil in us conquered us ; it was our misfortune that we surrendered to evil, and went astray.' They forget that it was by their own deliberate choice that they surrendered to evil, and they are reminded in verses 109-110 of the ridicule with which they covered godly men in their life on earth.

2946. After their flouting of God's Signs and their mockery of godly men on earth, they have forfeited their right to plead for mercy before God's Throne.

'Our Lord! we believe;
Then do Thou forgive us,
And have mercy upon us:
For Thou art the Best
Of those who show mercy!'

رَبَّنَآ اٰمَنَّا فَاغۡفِرۡ لَنَا
وَارۡحَمۡنَا وَاَنۡتَ خَيۡرُ الرّٰحِمِيۡنَ ○

110. "But ye treated them
With ridicule, so much so
That (ridicule of) them made you[2947]
Forget My Message while
Ye were laughing at them!

۱۱۰- فَاتَّخَذۡتُمُوۡهُمۡ سِخۡرِيًّا
حَتّٰٓى اَنۡسَوۡكُمۡ ذِكۡرِىۡ
وَكُنۡتُمۡ مِّنۡهُمۡ تَضۡحَكُوۡنَ ○

111. "I have rewarded them
This day for their patience
And constancy: they are indeed
The ones that have achieved
Bliss..."

۱۱۱- اِنِّىۡ جَزَيۡتُهُمُ الۡيَوۡمَ بِمَا صَبَرُوۡۤا ۙ
اَنَّهُمۡ هُمُ الۡفَآٮِٕزُوۡنَ ○

112. He will say:[2948] "What number
Of years did ye stay
On earth?"

۱۱۲- قٰلَ كَمۡ لَبِثۡتُمۡ فِى الۡاَرۡضِ عَدَدَ
سِنِيۡنَ ○

113. They will say: "We stayed
A day or part of a day:[2949]
But ask those who
Keep account."

۱۱۳- قَالُوۡا لَبِثۡنَا يَوۡمًا اَوۡ بَعۡضَ يَوۡمٍ
فَسۡـَٔلِ الۡعَآدِّيۡنَ ○

114. He will say: "Ye stayed
Not but a little,—
If ye had only known!

۱۱۴- قٰلَ اِنۡ لَّبِثۡتُمۡ اِلَّا قَلِيۡلًا
لَّوۡ اَنَّكُمۡ كُنۡتُمۡ تَعۡلَمُوۡنَ ○

115. "Did ye then think
That We had created you

۱۱۵- اَفَحَسِبۡتُمۡ اَنَّمَا خَلَقۡنٰكُمۡ

2947. Literally, 'they made you forget My Message'. The ungodly were so occupied in the backbiting and ridicule of the godly that the godly themselves became the unconscious cause of the ungodly forgetting the warnings declared by God against those who do not treat His Signs seriously. Thus evil often brings about its own ruin through the instrumentality of those whom it would make its victims.

2948. The usual Indian reading is "Qāla", "He will say". This follows the Kūfa Qirāat. The Baṣra Qirāat reads "*Qul*", "Say" (in the imperative). The point is only one of grammatical construction. See n. 2666 to xxi. 4.

2949. The question and answer about Time imply two things. (1) The attention of the ungodly is drawn to the extremely short time of the life in this world, compared to the eternity which they face: they are made to see this, and to realise how mistaken they were in their comparative valuation of things spiritual and things material. (2) Time, as we know it now, will have faded away and appear as almost nothing. It is just a matter relative to this life of temporary probation. *Cf.* the experience of the Companions of the Cave: xviii. 19.

In jest, and that ye Would not be brought back To Us (for account)?"[2950]	عَبَثًا وَّأَنَّكُمْ إِلَيْنَا لَا تُرْجَعُونَ ۝
116. Therefore exalted be God, The King, the Reality: There is no god but He, The Lord of the Throne Of Honour!	١١٦- فَتَعٰلَى اللّٰهُ الْمَلِكُ الْحَقُّ لَآ إِلٰهَ إِلَّا هُوَ رَبُّ الْعَرْشِ الْكَرِيمِ ۝
117. If anyone invokes, besides God, Any other god, he has No authority therefor; And his reckoning will be Only with his Lord![2951] And verily the Unbelievers Will fail to win through![2952]	١١٧- وَمَنْ يَّدْعُ مَعَ اللّٰهِ إِلٰهًا اٰخَرَ لَا بُرْهَانَ لَهٗ بِهٖ فَإِنَّمَا حِسَابُهٗ عِنْدَ رَبِّهٖ إِنَّهٗ لَا يُفْلِحُ الْكٰفِرُونَ ۝
118. So say: "O my Lord! Grant Thou forgiveness and mercy! For Thou art the Best Of those who show mercy!"	١١٨- وَقُلْ رَّبِّ اغْفِرْ وَارْحَمْ وَأَنْتَ خَيْرُ الرّٰحِمِينَ ۝

2950. God's Creation is not without a high serious purpose. It is not vain, or for mere play or sport. As far as man is concerned, the highest issues for him hang on his behaviour in this life. "Life is real, life is earnest, And the grave is not its goal", as Longfellow truly says. We must therefore earnestly search out God's Truth, encouraged by the fact that God's Truth is also, out of His unbounded mercy, searching us out and trying to reach us.

2951. Not with any one else whatever, as God is the only Reality. If men, out of the figments of their imagination, fancy other gods, they will be rudely undeceived. And God is Lord, *i.e.*, our Cherisher as well as our Creator. In spite of all our shortcomings and our rebellions, He will forgive us if we go to Him not on our merits but on His grace.

2952. See the same word used in describing the contrast with the Believers, in the first verse of this Sūra. Righteousness must win and all opposition to it must fail. Thus the circle of the argument is completed.

INTRODUCTION TO SŪRA XXIV (*Nūr*).

The environmental and social influences which most frequently wreck our spiritual ideals have to do with sex, and especially with its misuse, whether in the form of unregulated behaviour, of false charges or scandals, or breach of the refined conventions of personal or domestic privacy. Our complete conquest of all pitfalls in such matters enables us to rise to the higher regions of Light and of God-created Nature, about which a mystic doctrine is suggested. This subject is continued in the next Sūra.

As the reprobation of false slanders about women (xxiv. 11-20) is connected with an incident that happened to Hadhrat 'Āisha in A.H. 5-6. that fixes the chronological place of this Medina Sūra.

Summary.—Sex offences should be severely punished, but the strictest evidence should be required, and false slanderers are also worthy of punishment. Light talk about women reprobated (xxiv. 1-26, and C. 157).

Privacy should be respected, and the utmost decorum should be observed in dress and manners (xxiv. 27-34, and C. 158).

Parable of Light and Darkness : order and obedience in Nature point to the spiritual duty of man (xxiv. 35-57, and C. 159).

Domestic manners and manners in public or collective life all contribute to the highest virtues, and are part of our spiritual duties leading up to God (xxiv. 58-64, and C. 160).

C. 157.—Chastity is a virtue, for men and women,
(xxiv. 1-26.) Whether joined in marriage, or single,
Or widowed. The punishment for offences
In such matters should be public. No less
Grave is the launching of false charges
Or rumours against the fair reputation
Of women, or the spreading of such
Slanders, or the facile belief in them.
Evil is ever spreading its net:
Good men and women should ever be
On their guard, and pray for God's grace and mercy.

Sūra XXIV.

Nūr, or Light.

In the name of God, Most Gracious,
Most Merciful.

بِسۡمِ اللّٰهِ الرَّحۡمٰنِ الرَّحِيۡمِ

1. A Sūra which We
Have sent down and[2953]
Which We have ordained:
In it have We sent down
Clear Signs, in order that
Ye may receive admonition.

١- سُوۡرَةٌ اَنۡزَلۡنٰهَا وَفَرَضۡنٰهَا
وَاَنۡزَلۡنَا فِيۡهَاۤ اٰيٰتٍۭ بَيِّنٰتٍ
لَّعَلَّكُمۡ تَذَكَّرُوۡنَ ○

2. The woman and the man
Guilty of adultery or
fornication,—[2954]
Flog each of them
With a hundred stripes:[2955]
Let not compassion move you
In their case, in a matter
Prescribed by God, if ye believe
In God and the Last Day:
And let a party
Of the Believers
Witness their punishment.[2956]

٢- اَلزَّانِيَةُ وَالزَّانِىۡ
فَاجۡلِدُوۡا كُلَّ وَاحِدٍ مِّنۡهُمَا مِائَةَ جَلۡدَةٍ
وَّلَا تَاۡخُذۡكُمۡ بِهِمَا رَاۡفَةٌ
فِىۡ دِيۡنِ اللّٰهِ اِنۡ كُنۡتُمۡ
تُؤۡمِنُوۡنَ بِاللّٰهِ وَالۡيَوۡمِ الۡاٰخِرِ وَلۡيَشۡهَدۡ
عَذَابَهُمَا طَآئِفَةٌ مِّنَ الۡمُؤۡمِنِيۡنَ ○

3. Let no man guilty of
Adultery or fornication marry
Any but a woman
Similarly guilty, or an Unbeliever:
Nor let any but such a man
Or an Unbeliever
Marry such a woman:
To the Believers such a thing
Is forbidden.[2957]

٣- اَلزَّانِىۡ لَا يَنۡكِحُ اِلَّا زَانِيَةً اَوۡ مُشۡرِكَةً
وَّالزَّانِيَةُ لَا يَنۡكِحُهَاۤ اِلَّا زَانٍ اَوۡ مُشۡرِكٌ
وَحُرِّمَ ذٰلِكَ عَلَى الۡمُؤۡمِنِيۡنَ ○

2953. It must not be thought that the checking of sex offences or of minor improprieties, that relate to sex or privacy, are matters that do not affect spiritual life in the highest degree. These matters are intimately connected with spiritual teaching such as God has sent down in this Sūra. The emphasis is on "We": these things are not mere matters of convenience, but God has ordained them for our observance in life.

2954. *Zinā* includes sexual intercourse between a man and a woman not married to each other. It therefore applies both to adultery (which implies that one or both of the parties are married to a person or persons other than the ones concerned) and to fornication, which, in its strict signification, implies that both parties are unmarried. The law of marriage and divorce is made easy in Islam, so that there may be the less temptation for intercourse outside the well-defined incidents of marriage. This makes for greater self-respect for both man and woman. Other sex offences are also punishable, but this Section applies strictly to *Zinā* as above defined.

2955. *Cf.* iv. 15, and n. 523.

2956. The punishment should be open, in order to be deterrent.

2957. Islam commands sex purity, for men and for women, at all times,—before marriage, during marriage, and after the dissolution of marriage. Those guilty of illicit practices are shut out of the marriage circle of chaste men and women.

4. And those who launch
A charge against chaste women,
And produce not four witnesses
(To support their allegations),—
Flog them with eighty stripes;
And reject their evidence [2958]
Ever after: for such men
Are wicked transgressors;—

٤- وَالَّذِينَ يَرْمُونَ الْمُحْصَنٰتِ ثُمَّ لَمْ
يَأْتُوا بِأَرْبَعَةِ شُهَدَآءَ فَاجْلِدُوهُمْ ثَمٰنِينَ
جَلْدَةً وَّلَا تَقْبَلُوا لَهُمْ شَهٰدَةً أَبَدًا ۚ
وَأُولٰٓئِكَ هُمُ الْفٰسِقُونَ ○

5. Unless they repent thereafter [2959]
And mend (their conduct);
For God is Oft-Forgiving,
Most Merciful.

٥- إِلَّا الَّذِينَ تَابُوا مِنْ بَعْدِ ذٰلِكَ وَأَصْلَحُوا ۚ
فَإِنَّ اللّٰهَ غَفُورٌ رَّحِيمٌ ○

6. And for those who launch
A charge against their spouses,
And have (in support)
No evidence but their own,— [2960]

٦- وَالَّذِينَ يَرْمُونَ أَزْوٰجَهُمْ
وَلَمْ يَكُنْ لَّهُمْ شُهَدَآءُ إِلَّآ أَنْفُسُهُمْ

2958. The most serious notice is taken of people who put forward slanders or scandalous suggestions about women without adequate evidence. If anything is said against a woman's chastity, it should be supported by evidence twice as strong as would ordinarily be required for business transactions, or even in murder cases. That is, four witnesses would be required instead of two. Failing such preponderating evidence, the slanderer should himself be treated as a wicked transgressor and punished with eighty stripes. Not only would he be subjected to this disgraceful form of punishment, but he would be deprived of the citizen's right of giving evidence in all matters all his life, unless he repents and reforms, in which case he can be readmitted to be a competent witness.

2959. The punishment of stripes is inflicted in any case for unsupported slander. But the deprivation of the civic right of giving evidence can be cancelled by the man's subsequent conduct, if he repents, shows that he is sorry for what he did, and that he would not in future support by his statement anything for which he has not the fullest evidence. Secular courts do not enforce these principles, as their standards are lower than those which good Muslims set for themselves, but good Muslims must understand and act on the uuderlying principles, which protect the honour of womanhood. Abū Ḥanīfa considers that neither the stripes nor the incompetence for giving furture evidence is cancelled by repentance, but only the spiritual stigma of being "wicked transgressors". This of course is the more serious punishment, though it cannot be enforced in the Courts.

2960 The case of married persons is different from that of outsiders. If one of them accuses the other of unchastity, the accusation partly reflects on the accuser as well. Moreover, the link which unites married people, even where differences supervene, is sure to act as a steadying influence against the concoction of false charges of unchastity particularly where divorce is allowed (as in Islam) for reasons other than unchastity. Suppose a husband catches a wife in adultery. In the nature of things four witnesses—or even one outside witness—would be impossible. Yet after such an experience it is against human nature that he can live a normal married life. The matter is then left to the honour of the two spouses. If the husband can solemnly swear four times to the fact, and in addition invoke a curse on himself if he lies, that is *prima facie* evidence of the wife's guilt. But if the wife swears similarly four times and similarly invokes a curse on herself, she is in law acquitted of the guilt. If she does not take this step, the charge is held proved and the punishment follows. In either case the marriage is dissolved, as it is against human nature that the parties can live together happily after such an incident.

Their solitary evidence (Can be received) if they Bear witness four times (With an oath) by God That they are solemnly Telling the truth;	فَشَهَادَةُ أَحَدِهِمْ أَرْبَعُ شَهٰدٰتٍۭ بِاللّٰهِ إِنَّهُۥ لَمِنَ الصّٰدِقِينَ ○
7. And the fifth (oath) (Should be) that they solemnly Invoke the curse of God On themselves if they Tell a lie.	٧- وَالْخٰمِسَةُ أَنَّ لَعْنَتَ اللّٰهِ عَلَيْهِ إِنْ كَانَ مِنَ الْكٰذِبِينَ ○
8. But it would avert The punishment from the wife, If she bears witness Four times (with an oath) By God, that (her husband) Is telling a lie;	٨- وَيَدْرَؤُا عَنْهَا الْعَذَابَ أَنْ تَشْهَدَ أَرْبَعَ شَهٰدٰتٍۭ بِاللّٰهِ إِنَّهُۥ لَمِنَ الْكٰذِبِينَ ○
9. And the fifth (oath) Should be that she solemnly Invokes the wrath of God On herself if (her accuser) Is telling the truth.	٩- وَالْخٰمِسَةَ أَنَّ غَضَبَ اللّٰهِ عَلَيْهَآ إِنْ كَانَ مِنَ الصّٰدِقِينَ ○
10. If it were not For God's grace and mercy On you, and that God Is Oft-Returning, Full of wisdom,— (Ye would be ruined indeed).[2961]	١٠- وَلَوْلَا فَضْلُ اللّٰهِ عَلَيْكُمْ وَرَحْمَتُهُۥ وَأَنَّ اللّٰهَ تَوَّابٌ حَكِيمٌ ○ ع

SECTION 2.

11. Those who brought forward[2962] The lie are a body	١١- إِنَّ الَّذِينَ جَآءُو بِالْإِفْكِ عُصْبَةٌ

2961. *Cf.* xxiv. 11-14, and n. 2962, which illustrates the matter by a concrete instance.

2962. The particular incident here referred to occurred on the return from the expedition to the Banū Muṣṭaliq, A.H. 5-6. When the march was ordered, Ḥaḏhrat 'Āisha was not in her tent, having gone to search for a valuable necklace she had dropped. As her litter was veiled, it was not noticed that she was not in it, until the army reached the next halt. Meanwhile, finding the camp had gone, she sat down to rest, hoping that some one would come back to fetch her when her absence was noticed. It was night, and she fell asleep. Next morning she was found by Ṣafwān, a Muhājir, who had been left behind the camp expressly to pick up anything inadvertently left behind. He put her on his camel and brought her, leading the camel on foot. This gave occasion to enemies to raise a malicious scandal. The ringleader among them was the chief of the Medina Hypocrites, 'Abdullah ibn Ubai, who is referred to in the last clause of this verse. He had other sins and enormities to his debit, and he was left to the spiritual punishment of an unrepentant sinner, for he died in that state. The minor tools were given the legal punishment of the law, and after penitence mended their lives. They made good.

Among yourselves : think it not
To be an evil to you ;
On the contrary it is good [2963]
For you : to every man
Among them (will come
The punishment) of the sin
That he earned, and to him [2964]
Who took on himself the lead
Among them, will be
A Penalty grievous.

مِّنكُمْ لَا تَحْسَبُوهُ شَرًّا لَّكُمْ
بَلْ هُوَ خَيْرٌ لَّكُمْ
لِكُلِّ امْرِئٍ مِّنْهُم مَّا اكْتَسَبَ مِنَ الْإِثْمِ
وَالَّذِي تَوَلَّىٰ كِبْرَهُ مِنْهُمْ
لَهُ عَذَابٌ عَظِيمٌ ○

12. Why did not the Believers—
Men and women [2965]—when ye
Heard of the affair,—put
The best construction on it
In their own minds
And say, " This (charge)
Is an obvious lie " ?

١٢- لَوْلَا إِذْ سَمِعْتُمُوهُ
ظَنَّ الْمُؤْمِنُونَ وَالْمُؤْمِنَاتُ بِأَنفُسِهِمْ
خَيْرًا
وَقَالُوا هَٰذَا إِفْكٌ مُّبِينٌ ○

13. Why did they not bring
Four witnesses to prove it ? [2966]
When they have not brought
The witnesses, such men,
In the sight of God,
(Stand forth) themselves as liars !

١٣- لَوْلَا جَاءُو عَلَيْهِ بِأَرْبَعَةِ شُهَدَاءَ
فَإِذْ لَمْ يَأْتُوا بِالشُّهَدَاءِ
فَأُولَٰئِكَ عِندَ اللَّهِ هُمُ الْكَاذِبُونَ ○

14. Were it not for the grace
And mercy of God on you,
In this world and the Hereafter,
A grievous penalty would have
Seized you in that ye rushed
Glibly into this affair.[2967]

١٤- وَلَوْلَا فَضْلُ اللَّهِ عَلَيْكُمْ وَرَحْمَتُهُ
فِي الدُّنْيَا وَالْآخِرَةِ
لَمَسَّكُمْ فِي مَا أَفَضْتُمْ فِيهِ عَذَابٌ عَظِيمٌ ○

15. Behold, ye received it
On your tongues,

١٥- إِذْ تَلَقَّوْنَهُ بِأَلْسِنَتِكُمْ

2963. It is worse for a scandal to be whispered about with bated breath, than that it should be brought into the light of day and disproved.

2964. The ringleader : see n. 2962 above.

2965. Both men and women were involved in spreading the scandal. Their obvious duty was to put the best, not the worst, construction on the acts of one of the "mothers of the Believers".

2966. If any persons took it seriously, it was their duty to search for and produce the evidence, in the absence of which they themselves became guilty of slander.

2967. *Cf.* xxiv. 10 above. It was God's mercy that saved them from many evil consequences, both in this life and in the Hereafter,—in this life, because the Apostle's wise measures nipped in the bud any incipient estrangement between those nearest and dearest to him, and from a spiritual aspect in that the minor agents in spreading the scandal repented and were forgiven. No doubts and divisions, no mutual distrust, were allowed to remain in their hearts after the whole matter had been cleared up.

And said out of your mouths
Things of which ye had
No knowledge; and ye thought
It to be a light matter,
While it was most serious
In the sight of God.[2968]

وَتَقُولُونَ بِأَفْوَاهِكُمْ مَّا لَيْسَ لَكُمْ بِهٖ
عِلْمٌ وَّتَحْسَبُونَهٗ هَيِّنًا
وَّهُوَ عِنْدَ اللّٰهِ عَظِيمٌ ○

16. And why did ye not,
When ye heard it, say?—
"It is not right of us
To speak of this:
Glory to God! this is
A most serious slander!"[2969]

١٦- وَلَوْلَآ إِذْ سَمِعْتُمُوهُ قُلْتُمْ
مَّا يَكُونُ لَنَآ أَنْ نَّتَكَلَّمَ بِهٰذَا
سُبْحٰنَكَ هٰذَا بُهْتَانٌ عَظِيمٌ ○

17. God doth admonish you,
That ye may never repeat
Such (conduct), if ye
Are (true) Believers.

١٧- يَعِظُكُمُ اللّٰهُ أَنْ تَعُودُوا لِمِثْلِهٖٓ أَبَدًا
إِنْ كُنْتُمْ مُّؤْمِنِينَ ○

18. And God makes the Signs
Plain to you: for God
Is full of knowledge and wisdom.

١٨- وَيُبَيِّنُ اللّٰهُ لَكُمُ الْاٰيٰتِ
وَاللّٰهُ عَلِيمٌ حَكِيمٌ ○

19. Those who love (to see)
Scandal published broadcast
Among the Believers, will have
A grievous Penalty in this life
And in the Hereafter: God
Knows, and ye know not.[2970]

١٩- إِنَّ الَّذِينَ يُحِبُّونَ أَنْ تَشِيعَ الْفَاحِشَةُ
فِي الَّذِينَ اٰمَنُوا لَهُمْ عَذَابٌ أَلِيمٌ فِي
الدُّنْيَا وَالْاٰخِرَةِ وَاللّٰهُ يَعْلَمُ وَأَنْتُمْ لَا تَعْلَمُونَ ○

20. Were it not for the grace
And mercy of God on you,

٢٠- وَلَوْلَا فَضْلُ اللّٰهِ عَلَيْكُمْ وَرَحْمَتُهٗ

2968. There are three things here reprobated by way of spiritual teaching: (1) if others speak an evil word, that is no reason why you should allow it to defile your tongue; (2) if you get a thought or suspicion which is not based on your certain knowledge, do not give it currency by giving it expression; and (3) others may think it is a small matter to speak lightly of something which blasts a person's character or reputation: in the eyes of God it is a most serious matter in any case, but specially when it involves the honour and reputation of pious women.

2969. The right course would have been to stop any further currency of false slanders by ignoring them and at least refusing to help in their circulation. The exclamation "*Subḥānaka*", "Praise to Thee (O God!)", or "Glory to God!" is an exclamation of surprise and disavowal as much as to say, "We do not believe it! And we shall have nothing to do with you, O false slanderers!"

2970. What mischiefs can be planned by Evil to delude simple folk who mean no harm in their own minds but who by thoughtlessness are deluded step by step to become the instruments of Evil, may not be known to the most instructed of men, but it is all known to God. Man should therefore always be on his guard against the traps of Evil, and it is only God's grace that can save him.

And that God is
Full of kindness and mercy,
(Ye would be ruined indeed).[2971]

وَاَنَّ اللّٰهَ رَءُوْفٌ رَّحِيْمٌ ○ ع

SECTION 3.

21. O ye who believe!
Follow not Satan's footsteps:
If any will follow the footsteps
Of Satan, he will (but) command
What is shameful and wrong:
And were it not for the grace
And mercy of God on you,[2972]
Not one of you would ever
Have been pure: but God
Doth purify whom He pleases:[2973]
And God is One Who
Hears and knows (all things).

٢١- يٰۤاَيُّهَا الَّذِيْنَ اٰمَنُوْا لَا تَتَّبِعُوْا خُطُوٰتِ
الشَّيْطٰنِ ؕ وَمَنْ يَّتَّبِعْ خُطُوٰتِ الشَّيْطٰنِ
فَاِنَّهٗ يَاْمُرُ بِالْفَحْشَآءِ وَالْمُنْكَرِ ؕ وَلَوْلَا
فَضْلُ اللّٰهِ عَلَيْكُمْ وَرَحْمَتُهٗ مَا زَكٰى
مِنْكُمْ مِّنْ اَحَدٍ اَبَدًا ۙ وَّلٰكِنَّ اللّٰهَ
يُزَكِّيْ مَنْ يَّشَآءُ ؕ وَاللّٰهُ سَمِيْعٌ عَلِيْمٌ ○

22. Let not those among you
Who are endued with grace
And amplitude of means[2974]
Resolve by oath against helping
Their kinsmen, those in want,
And those who have left

٢٢- وَلَا يَاْتَلِ اُولُوا الْفَضْلِ مِنْكُمْ
وَالسَّعَةِ اَنْ يُّؤْتُوْٓا
اُولِي الْقُرْبٰى وَالْمَسٰكِيْنَ

2971. Note the refrain that comes four times in this passage, "Were it not for the grace and mercy of God,...". Each time it has a different application. (1) In xxiv. 10, it was in connection with the accusation of infidelity by one of the spouses against the other: they were both reminded of God's mercy and warned against suspicion and untruth. (2) In xxiv. 14, the Believers were told to be wary of false rumours lest they should cause pain and division among themselves: it is God's grace that keeps them united. (3) Here is an admonition for the future: there may be conspiracies and snares laid by Evil against simple people: it is God's grace that protects them. (4) In xxiv. 21, the general warning is directed to the observance of purity in act and in thought, concerning one's self and concerning others: it is only God's grace that can keep that purity spotless, for He hears prayers and knows of all the snares that are spread in the path of the good.

2972. See last note.

2973. Spotless purity in thought, word, and deed, includes the disposition to put the best construction on the motives of others, so that we ascribe no evil motive to the seeming indiscretions of virtuous people. Such a high standard can only come by the grace of God, Who hears all prayers and knows all the temptations to which human nature is subject. His Will and Plan make both for spiritual protection and spiritual peace, and we must place ourselves trustingly in his hands.

2974. The immediate reference was to Ḥadhrat Abū Bakr, the father of Ḥadhrat 'Āisha. He was blessed both with spiritual grace from God and with ample means, which he always used in the service of Islam and of Muslims. One of the slanderers of Ḥadhrat 'Āisha turned out to be Misṭaḥ, a cousin of Ḥadhrat Abū Bakr, whom he had been in the habit of supporting. Naturally Ḥadhrat Abū Bakr wished to stop that aid, but according to the highest standards of Muslim ethics he was asked to forgive and forget, which he did, with the happiest results to the peace and unity of the Muslim community. But the general application holds good for all time. A generous patron should not, in personal anger, withdraw his support even for serious faults if the delinquent repents and mends his ways. If God forgives us, who are we to refuse forgiveness to our fellows?

Their homes in God's cause:
Let them forgive and overlook.
Do you not wish
That God should forgive you?
For God is Oft-Forgiving,
Most Merciful.

وَالْمُهٰجِرِيْنَ فِيْ سَبِيْلِ اللّٰهِ ۖ وَلْيَعْفُوْا
وَلْيَصْفَحُوْا ۗ اَلَا تُحِبُّوْنَ اَنْ يَّغْفِرَ اللّٰهُ
لَكُمْ ۗ وَاللّٰهُ غَفُوْرٌ رَّحِيْمٌ ○

23. Those who slander chaste women,
Indiscreet but believing,[2975]
Are cursed in this life
And in the Hereafter:
For them is a grievous Penalty,—

٢٣- اِنَّ الَّذِيْنَ يَرْمُوْنَ الْمُحْصَنٰتِ
الْغٰفِلٰتِ الْمُؤْمِنٰتِ لُعِنُوْا فِي الدُّنْيَا وَ
الْاٰخِرَةِ ۖ وَلَهُمْ عَذَابٌ عَظِيْمٌ ○

24. On the Day when their tongues,
Their hands, and their feet
Will bear witness against them[2976]
As to their actions.

٢٤- يَّوْمَ تَشْهَدُ عَلَيْهِمْ اَلْسِنَتُهُمْ وَاَيْدِيْهِمْ
وَاَرْجُلُهُمْ بِمَا كَانُوْا يَعْمَلُوْنَ ○

25. On that Day God
Will pay them back
(All) their just dues,
And they will realise
That God is
The (very) Truth,
That makes all things manifest.[2977]

٢٥- يَوْمَئِذٍ يُّوَفِّيْهِمُ اللّٰهُ دِيْنَهُمُ الْحَقَّ
وَيَعْلَمُوْنَ اَنَّ اللّٰهَ
هُوَ الْحَقُّ الْمُبِيْنُ ○

26. Women impure are for men impure,
And men impure for women
impure
And women of purity
Are for men of purity,
And men of purity
Are for women of purity:
These are not affected

٢٦- اَلْخَبِيْثٰتُ لِلْخَبِيْثِيْنَ
وَالْخَبِيْثُوْنَ لِلْخَبِيْثٰتِ ۚ وَالطَّيِّبٰتُ
لِلطَّيِّبِيْنَ وَالطَّيِّبُوْنَ لِلطَّيِّبٰتِ ۚ
اُولٰٓئِكَ مُبَرَّءُوْنَ

2975. Good women are sometimes indiscreet because they think of no evil. But even such innocent indiscretion lands them, and those who hold them dear, in difficulties. Such was the case with Ḥadhrat 'Aisha, who was in extreme pain and anguish for a whole month because of the slanders spread about her. Her husband and her father were also placed in a most awkward predicament, considering their position and the great work in which they were engaged. But unprincipled people, who start false slanders, and their unthinking tools who help in spreading such slanders, are guilty of the gravest spiritual offence, and their worst punishment is the deprivation of God's grace, which is the meaning of a state of Curse.

2976. Our own limbs and faculties are the strongest witnesses against us if we misuse them for evil deeds instead of using them for the good deeds for which they were given to us.

2977. All that we thought of hiding will be clear as day before God's Judgment Seat, because He is the very essence of Truth and Reality. He is the true Light (xxiv. 35), of which all physical light is merely a type or reflection.

By what people say:[2978]
For them there is forgiveness,
And a provision honourable.[2979]

مِمَّا يَقُولُونَ ۖ
لَهُم مَّغْفِرَةٌ وَرِزْقٌ كَرِيمٌ ۝ ع

C. 158.—Privacy in the home is a nurse of virtue:
(xxiv. 27-34.) Respect it with dignity and decorum. Guard
Your eyes and thoughts with rules of modesty
In dress and manners: and learn from these
To keep your spiritual gaze from straying
To any but God. True marriage should teach
Us chastity and purity, and such
Are the virtues which lead us to the Light
Sublime which illuminates the world.

Section 4.

27. O ye who believe!
Enter not houses other than
Your own, until ye have
Asked permission and saluted
Those in them: that is
Best for you, in order that
Ye may heed (what is seemly).[2980]

28. If ye find no one[2981]
In the house, enter not
Until permission is given
To you: if ye are asked
To go back, go back:
That makes for greater purity

٢٧- يَا أَيُّهَا الَّذِينَ آمَنُوا لَا تَدْخُلُوا بُيُوتًا
غَيْرَ بُيُوتِكُمْ
حَتَّىٰ تَسْتَأْنِسُوا وَتُسَلِّمُوا عَلَىٰ أَهْلِهَا ۚ
ذَٰلِكُمْ خَيْرٌ لَّكُمْ لَعَلَّكُمْ تَذَكَّرُونَ ۝

٢٨- فَإِن لَّمْ تَجِدُوا فِيهَا أَحَدًا فَلَا تَدْخُلُوهَا
حَتَّىٰ يُؤْذَنَ لَكُمْ ۖ وَإِن قِيلَ لَكُمُ
ارْجِعُوا فَارْجِعُوا ۖ هُوَ أَزْكَىٰ

2978. The pure consort with the pure, and the impure with the impure. If the impure, out of the impurity of their thoughts, or imaginations, impute any evil to the pure, the pure are not affected by it, but they should avoid all occasions for random talk.

2979. *Forgiveness* for any indiscretion which they may have innocently committed, and spiritual provision or protection against the assaults of Evil. It is also meant that the more the evil ones attempt to defame or slander them, the more triumphantly will they be vindicated and provided with the physical and moral good which will advance their real life.

2980. The conventions of propriety and privacy are essential to a refined life of goodness and purity. The English saying that an Englishman's home is his castle, suggests a certain amount of exclusiveness and defiance. The Muslim principle of asking respectful permission and exchanging salutations ensures privacy without exclusiveness, and friendliness without undue familiarity.

2981. That is, if no one replies: there may be people in the house not in a presentable state. Or, even if the house is empty, you have no right to enter it until you obtain the owner's permission, wherever he may be. The fact of your not receiving a reply does not entitle you to enter without permission. You should wait, or knock twice or three times, and withdraw in case no permission is received. If you are actually asked to withdraw, as the inmates are not in a condition to receive you, you should *à fortiori* withdraw, either for a time, or altogether, as the inmates may wish you to do. Even if they are your friends, you have no right to take them by surprise or enter against their wishes. Your own purity of life and conduct as well as of motives is thus tested.

For yourselves: and God
Knows well all that ye do.

لَكُمْ وَاللّٰهُ بِمَا تَعْمَلُونَ عَلِيمٌ ○

29. It is no fault on your part
To enter houses not used
For living in, which serve
Some (other) use for you:[2982]
And God has knowledge
Of what ye reveal
And what ye conceal.

٢٩- لَيْسَ عَلَيْكُمْ جُنَاحٌ أَنْ تَدْخُلُوا بُيُوتًا
غَيْرَ مَسْكُونَةٍ فِيهَا مَتَاعٌ لَكُمْ
وَاللّٰهُ يَعْلَمُ مَا تُبْدُونَ وَمَا تَكْتُمُونَ ○

30. Say to the believing men
That they should lower
Their gaze and guard[2983]
Their modesty: that will make
For greater purity for them:
And God is well acquainted
With all that they do.

٣٠- قُلْ لِلْمُؤْمِنِينَ يَغُضُّوا مِنْ
أَبْصَارِهِمْ وَيَحْفَظُوا فُرُوجَهُمْ
ذٰلِكَ أَزْكَىٰ لَهُمْ
إِنَّ اللّٰهَ خَبِيرٌ بِمَا يَصْنَعُونَ ○

31. And say to the believing women
That they should lower
Their gaze and guard[2984]
Their modesty; that they
Should not display their
Beauty and ornaments[2985] except
What (must ordinarily) appear
Thereof; that they should

٣١- وَقُلْ لِلْمُؤْمِنَاتِ يَغْضُضْنَ
مِنْ أَبْصَارِهِنَّ وَيَحْفَظْنَ فُرُوجَهُنَّ
وَلَا يُبْدِينَ زِينَتَهُنَّ إِلَّا مَا ظَهَرَ
مِنْهَا وَلْيَضْرِبْنَ

2982 The rule about dwelling-houses is strict, because privacy is precious, and essential to a refined, decent, and well-ordered life. Such a rule of course does not apply to houses used for other useful purposes, such as an inn or caravanserai, or a shop, or a warehouse. But even here, of course, implied permission from the owner is necessary as a matter of common-sense. The question in this passage is that of refined privacy, not that of rights of ownership.

2983. The rule of modesty applies to men as well as women. A brazen stare by a man at a woman (or even at a man) is a breach of refined manners. Where sex is concerned, modesty is not only "good form": it is not only to guard the weaker sex, but also to guard the spiritual good of the stronger sex.

2984. The need for modesty is the same in both men and women. But on account of the differentiation of the sexes in nature, temperaments, and social life, a greater amount of privacy is required for women than for men, especially in the matter of dress and the uncovering of the bosom.

2985. *Zīnat* means both natural beauty and artificial ornaments. I think both are implied here, but chiefly the former. The woman is asked not to make a display of her figure or appear in undress except to the following classes of people: (1) her husband, (2) her near relatives who would be living in the same house, and with whom a certain amount of *negligé* is permissible; (3) her women, *i.e.*, her maid-servants, who would be constantly in attendance on her; some Commentators include all believing women; it is not good form in a Muslim household for women to meet other women, except when they are properly dressed; (4) slaves, male and female, as they would be in constant attendance; but this item would now be blank, with the abolition of slavery; (5) old or infirm men-servants; and (6) infants or small children before they get a sense of sex. *Cf.* also xxxiii, 59.

Draw their veils over
Their bosoms and not display
Their beauty except
To their husbands, their fathers,
Their husbands' fathers, their sons,
Their husbands' sons,
Their brothers or their brothers' sons,
Or their sisters' sons,
Or their women, or the slaves
Whom their right hands
Possess, or male servants
Free of physical needs,
Or small children who
Have no sense of the shame
Of sex; and that they
Should not strike their feet
In order to draw attention
To their hidden ornaments.[2986]
And O ye Believers!
Turn ye all together
Towards God, that ye
May attain Bliss.[2987]

بِخُمُرِهِنَّ عَلٰى جُيُوْبِهِنَّ
وَلَا يُبْدِيْنَ زِيْنَتَهُنَّ اِلَّا
لِبُعُوْلَتِهِنَّ اَوْ اٰبَآئِهِنَّ اَوْ اٰبَآءِ بُعُوْلَتِهِنَّ
اَوْ اَبْنَآئِهِنَّ اَوْ اَبْنَآءِ بُعُوْلَتِهِنَّ اَوْ اِخْوَانِهِنَّ
اَوْ بَنِيْٓ اِخْوَانِهِنَّ
اَوْ بَنِيْٓ اَخَوٰتِهِنَّ اَوْ نِسَآئِهِنَّ اَوْ مَا مَلَكَتْ
اَيْمَانُهُنَّ اَوِ التّٰبِعِيْنَ غَيْرِ اُولِي الْاِرْبَةِ
مِنَ الرِّجَالِ اَوِ الطِّفْلِ الَّذِيْنَ لَمْ يَظْهَرُوْا
عَلٰى عَوْرٰتِ النِّسَآءِ وَلَا يَضْرِبْنَ
بِاَرْجُلِهِنَّ لِيُعْلَمَ مَا يُخْفِيْنَ مِنْ زِيْنَتِهِنَّ
وَتُوْبُوْٓا اِلَى اللّٰهِ جَمِيْعًا اَيُّهَ الْمُؤْمِنُوْنَ
لَعَلَّكُمْ تُفْلِحُوْنَ ۝

32. Marry those among you
Who are single,[2988] or
The virtuous ones among
Your slaves, male or female:
If they are in poverty,
God will give them
Means out of His grace:
For God encompasseth all,[2989]
And He knoweth all things.

۳۲- وَاَنْكِحُوا الْاَيَامٰى مِنْكُمْ
وَالصّٰلِحِيْنَ مِنْ عِبَادِكُمْ وَاِمَآئِكُمْ
اِنْ يَّكُوْنُوْا فُقَرَآءَ يُغْنِهِمُ اللّٰهُ مِنْ فَضْلِهٖ
وَاللّٰهُ وَاسِعٌ عَلِيْمٌ ۝

2986. It is one of the tricks of showy or unchaste women to tinkle their ankle ornaments, to draw attention to themselves.

2987. While all these details of the purity and good form of domestic life are being brought to our attention, we are clearly reminded that the chief object we should hold in view is our spiritual welfare. All our brief life on this earth is a probation, and we must make our individual, domestic, and social life all contribute to our holiness, so that we can get the real success and bliss which is the aim of our spiritual endeavour. Mystics understand the rules of decorum themselves to typify spiritual truths. Our soul, like a modest maiden, allows not her eyes to stray from the One True God. And her beauty is not for vulgar show, but for God.

2988. The subject of sex ethics and manners brings us to the subject of marriage. "Single" (*ayāmā*, plural of *Aiyim*) here means any one not in the bond of wedlock, whether unmarried or lawfully divorced, or widowed. If we can, we must marry in our own circle, but if we have not the means, there is no harm if we choose from a lower circle, provided our choice is determined by virtue. Poverty in the other party does not matter if there is virtue and love. A happily married man has the best wealth in a virtuous wife, and his very happiness makes him a better potential earner of wealth. A slave becomes free by marriage.

2989. *Cf.* v. 57. God's mercy is for all: it is not confined to a class or grade of people.

33. Let those who find not
The wherewithal for marriage
Keep themselves chaste, until
God gives them means[2990]
Out of His grace.
And if any of your slaves
Ask for a deed in writing
(To enable them to earn
Their freedom for a certain sum),
Give them such a deed[2991]
If ye know any good
In them ; yea, give them
Something yourselves
Out of the means which
God has given to you.
But force not your maids[2992]
To prostitution when[2993] they desire
Chastity, in order that ye
May make a gain
In the goods of this life.
But if anyone compels them,
Yet, after such compulsion,
Is God Oft-Forgiving,
Most Merciful (to them).[2994]

٣٣- وَلْيَسْتَعْفِفِ الَّذِيْنَ لَا يَجِدُوْنَ نِكَاحًا
حَتّٰى يُغْنِيَهُمُ اللّٰهُ مِنْ فَضْلِهٖ ؕ
وَالَّذِيْنَ يَبْتَغُوْنَ الْكِتٰبَ
مِمَّا مَلَكَتْ اَيْمَانُكُمْ
فَكَاتِبُوْهُمْ اِنْ عَلِمْتُمْ فِيْهِمْ خَيْرًا ۖ
وَّاٰتُوْهُمْ مِّنْ مَّالِ اللّٰهِ الَّذِيْٓ اٰتٰىكُمْ ؕ
وَلَا تُكْرِهُوْا فَتَيٰتِكُمْ عَلَى الْبِغَآءِ
اِنْ اَرَدْنَ تَحَصُّنًا
لِّتَبْتَغُوْا عَرَضَ الْحَيٰوةِ الدُّنْيَا ؕ
وَمَنْ يُّكْرِهْهُّنَّ
فَاِنَّ اللّٰهَ مِنْ بَعْدِ اِكْرَاهِهِنَّ
غَفُوْرٌ رَّحِيْمٌ ۝

34. We have already sent down
To you verses making things
Clear, an illustration from (the story
Of) people who passed away
Before you, and an admonition
For those who fear (God).[2995]

٣٤- وَلَقَدْ اَنْزَلْنَآ اِلَيْكُمْ اٰيٰتٍ مُّبَيِّنٰتٍ
وَّمَثَلًا مِّنَ الَّذِيْنَ خَلَوْا مِنْ قَبْلِكُمْ
وَمَوْعِظَةً لِّلْمُتَّقِيْنَ ۝ ع

2990. A Muslim marriage requires some sort of a dower for the wife. If the man cannot afford that, he must wait and keep himself chaste. It is no excuse for him to say that he must satisfy his natural cravings within or outside marriage. It must be within marriage.

2991. The law of slavery in the legal sense of the term is now obsolete. While it had any meaning, Islam made the slave's lot as easy as possible. A slave, male or female, could ask for conditional manumission by a written deed fixing the amount required for manumission and allowing the slave meanwhile to earn money by lawful means and perhaps marry and bring up a family. Such a deed was not to be refused if the request was genuine and the slave had character. Not only that, but the master is directed to help with money out of his own resources in order to enable the slave to earn his or her own liberty.

2992. Where slavery was legal, what is now called the "white slave traffic" was carried on by wicked people like 'Abdullāh ibn Ubai, the Hypocrite leader at Medina. This is absolutely condemned. While modern nations have abolished ordinary slavery, the "White Slave Traffic" is still a big social problem in individual States and before the League of Nations. Here it is absolutely condemned. No more despicable trade can be imagined.

2993. I have translated "*in*" (literally, "if") by "when", because this is not a conditional clause but an explanatory clause, explaining the meaning of "force". "Forcing" a person necessarily means that it is against the wish or inclination of the person forced. Even if they were to give a formal consent, it is not valid because the persons concerned are in (legal, or now) economic slavery.

2994. The poor unfortunate girls, who are victims of such a nefarious trade, will yet find mercy from God, whose bounties extend to the lowest of His creatures.

2995. This prepares the way for the magnificent Verse of Light that follows, and its mystic meaning.

C. 159.—God is the Light of the heavens and the earth.
(xxiv. 35 57.) High above our petty evanescent lives,
He illumines our souls with means that reach
Our inmost being. Universal is
His light, so pure and so intense
That grosser beings need a veil
To take His rays: His elect are e'er
Absorbed in prayer and praise and deeds
Of love, unlike the children of Darkness,
Struggling in Depths profound of vanities
False. All Nature sings to the glory
Of God, and men of fraud and hypocrisy
Are but rebels in the Kingdom of God.

Section 5.

35. God is the Light[2996]
Of the heavens and the earth.[2997]
The parable of His Light
Is as if there were a Niche
And within it a Lamp:
The Lamp enclosed in Glass:[2998]

٣٥- اَللّٰهُ نُوْرُ السَّمٰوٰتِ وَالْاَرْضِ ؕ
مَثَلُ نُوْرِهٖ كَمِشْكٰوةٍ فِيْهَا مِصْبَاحٌ ؕ
اَلْمِصْبَاحُ فِىْ زُجَاجَةٍ ؕ

2996. Embedded within certain directions concerning a refined domestic and social life, comes this glorious parable of Light, which contains layer upon layer of allegorical truth about spiritual mysteries. No notes can do adequate justice to its full meaning. Volumes have been written on this subject, the most notable being Imām Gazālī's *Mishkāt-ul-Anwār*. In these notes I propose to explain the simplest meaning of this passage, reserving a brief account of Gazālī's exposition for Appendix VIII (printed at the end of this Sūra), pp. 920-924.

2997. The physical light is but a reflection of the true Light in the world of Reality, and that true Light is God. We can only think of God in terms of our phenomenal experience, and in the phenomenal world, light is the purest thing we know. But physical light has drawbacks incidental to its physical nature: *e.g.* (1) it is dependent upon some source external to itself; (2) it is a passing phenomenon; if we take it to be a form of motion or energy it is unstable, like all physical phenomena; (3) it is dependent on space and time; its speed is 186,000 miles per second, and there are stars whose light takes thousands of years before it reaches the earth. The perfect Light of God is free from any such defects.

2998. The first three points in the Parable centre round the symbols of the Niche, the Lamp, and the Glass. (1) The Niche (*Mishkāt*) is the little shallow recess in the wall of an Eastern house, fairly high from the ground, in which a light (before the days of electricity) was usually placed. Its height enabled it to diffuse the light in the room and minimised the shadows. The background of the wall and the sides of the niche helped to throw the light well into the room, and if the wall was white-washed, it also acted as a reflector: the opening in front made the way for the light. So with the spiritual Light: it is placed high, above worldly things; it has a niche or habitation of its own, in Revelation and other Signs of God; its access to men is by a special Way, open to all, yet closed to those who refuse its rays. (2) The Lamp is the core of the spiritual Truth, which is the real illumination; the Niche is nothing without it; the Niche is actually made for it. (3) The Glass is the transparent medium through which the Light passes. On the one hand, it protects the light from moths and other forms of low life (lower motives in man) and from gusts of wind (passions), and on the other, it transmits the light through a medium which is made up of and akin to the grosser substances of the earth (such as sand, soda, potash, etc.), so arranged as to admit the subtle to the gross by its transparency. So the spiritual Truth has to be filtered through human language or human intelligence to make it intelligible to mankind.

The glass as it were
A brilliant star:[2999]
Lit from a blessed Tree,[3000]
An Olive, neither of the East
Nor of the West,[3001]
Whose Oil is well-nigh
Luminous,
Though fire scarce touched it:[3002]
Light upon Light!
God doth guide
Whom He will
To His Light:[3003]
God doth set forth Parables
For men: and God
Doth know all things.

36. (Lit is such a Light)[3004]
In houses, which God
Hath permitted to be raised[3005]
To honour; for the celebration,

الزُّجَاجَةُ كَأَنَّهَا كَوْكَبٌ دُرِّيٌّ
يُوقَدُ مِنْ شَجَرَةٍ مُبَٰرَكَةٍ زَيْتُونَةٍ لَّا
شَرْقِيَّةٍ
وَلَا غَرْبِيَّةٍ يَكَادُ زَيْتُهَا يُضِيٓءُ
وَلَوْ لَمْ تَمْسَسْهُ نَارٌ
نُّورٌ عَلَىٰ نُورٍ يَهْدِي ٱللَّهُ لِنُورِهِۦ مَن يَشَآءُ
وَيَضْرِبُ ٱللَّهُ ٱلْأَمْثَٰلَ لِلنَّاسِ
وَٱللَّهُ بِكُلِّ شَيْءٍ عَلِيمٌ ۝
٣٦- فِي بُيُوتٍ أَذِنَ ٱللَّهُ
أَن تُرْفَعَ وَيُذْكَرَ

2999. The glass by itself does not shine. But when the light comes into it, it shines like a brilliant star. So men of God, who preach God's Truth, are themselves illuminated by God's Light and become the illuminating media through which that Light spreads and permeates human life.

3000. The olive tree is not a very impressive tree in its outward appearance. Its leaves have a dull greenish-brown colour, and in size it is inconspicuous. But its oil is used in sacred ceremonies and forms a wholesome ingredient of food. The fruit has a specially fine flavour. *Cf.* n. 2880 to xxiii. 20. For the illuminating quality of its oil, see n. 3002 below.

3001. This mystic Olive is not localised. It is neither of the East nor of the West. It is universal, for such is God's Light. As applied to the olive, there is also a more literal meaning, which can be allegorised in a different way. An olive tree with an eastern aspect gets only the rays of the morning sun; one with a western aspect, only the rays of the western sun. In the northern hemisphere the south aspect will give the sun's rays a great part of the day, while a north aspect will shut them out altogether, and *vice versa* in the southern hemisphere. But a tree in the open plain or on a hill will get perpetual sunshine by day: it will be more mature, and the fruit and oil will be of superior quality. So God's light is not localised or immature: it is perfect and universal.

3002. Pure olive oil is beautiful in colour, consistency, and illuminating power. The world has tried all kinds of illuminants, and for economic reasons or convenience, one replaces another. But for coolness, comfort to the eyes, and steadiness, vegetable oils are superior to electricity, mineral oils, and animal oils. And among vegetable oils, olive oil takes a high place and deserves its sacred associations. Its purity is almost like light itself: you may suppose it to be almost light before it is lit. So with spiritual Truth: it illuminates the mind and understanding imperceptibly, almost before the human mind and heart have been consciously touched by it.

3003. Glorious, illimitable Light, which cannot be described or measured. And there are grades and grades of it, passing transcendently into regions of spiritual height, which man's imagination can scarcely conceive of. The topmost pinnacle is the true prototypal Light, the real Light, of which all others were reflections, the Light of God. Hence the saying of the holy Prophet about God's "Seventy thousand veils of Light".

3004. The punctuation of the Arabic text makes it necessary to carry back the adverbial clause "in houses", to something in the last verse, say "Lit from a blessed Tree",—the intervening clauses being treated as parenthetical.

3005. That is, in all places of pure worship; but some Commentators understand special Mosques, such as the Ka'ba in Mecca, or the Mosques in Medina or Jerusalem; for these are specially held in honour.

In them, of His name:
In them is He glorified
In the mornings and
In the evenings, (again and
again),—[3006]

فِيهَا اسْمُهُ يُسَبِّحُ لَهُ فِيهَا
بِالْغُدُوِّ وَالْآصَالِ ○

37. By men whom neither
Traffic nor merchandise
Can divert from the Remembrance[3007]
Of God, nor from regular Prayer,
Nor from the practice
Of regular Charity:
Their (only) fear is
For the Day when
Hearts and eyes
Will be transformed[3008]
(In a world wholly new),—

٣٧- رِجَالٌ لَّا تُلْهِيهِمْ تِجَارَةٌ وَّلَا بَيْعٌ
عَن ذِكْرِ اللَّهِ وَإِقَامِ الصَّلَوٰةِ
وَإِيتَآءِ الزَّكَوٰةِ
يَخَافُونَ يَوْمًا تَتَقَلَّبُ
فِيهِ الْقُلُوبُ وَالْأَبْصَارُ ○

38. That God may reward them
According to the best[3009]
Of their deeds, and add
Even more for them
Out of His Grace:
For God doth provide
For those whom He will,
Without measure.

٣٨- لِيَجْزِيَهُمُ اللَّهُ أَحْسَنَ مَا عَمِلُوا
وَيَزِيدَهُم مِّن فَضْلِهِ
وَاللَّهُ يَرْزُقُ مَن يَشَآءُ
بِغَيْرِ حِسَابٍ ○

39. But the Unbelievers,—
Their deeds are like a mirage[3010]

٣٩- وَالَّذِينَ كَفَرُوا أَعْمَالُهُمْ كَسَرَابٍ

3006. *In the evenings*: the Arabic word is *Āṣāl*, a plural of a plural, to imply emphasis: I have rendered that shade of meaning by adding the words "again and again".

3007. "Remembrance of God" is wider than Prayer: it includes silent contemplation, and active service of God and His creatures. The regular Prayers and regular Charity are the social acts performed through the organised community.

3008 Some renderings suggest the effects of terror on the Day of Judgment. But here we are considering the case of the righteous, whose "fear" of God is akin to love and reverence and who (as the next verse shows) hope for the best reward from God. But the world they will meet will be a wholly changed world.

3009. The best of the righteous do not deserve the reward that they get: all their faults are forgiven, and only their best actions are considered in the reward that they get. Nay, more! Out of the unbounded Grace of God even more is added to them. For in giving rewards, God's bounty is boundless.

3010. We have had various metaphors to give us an idea of the beneficent Light of God in the spiritual world. Now we have contrasted metaphors to enable us to see those who deny or refuse that Light, and are overwhelmed in utter darkness. The Light (of God) is an absolute Reality, and is mentioned first, and the souls that follow that Light are a reflected reality and are mentioned after the Light. On the other hand the Darkness is not a reality in itself, but a negation of reality; the reflected existences that refuse the Light are mentioned, and then their state, which is Unreality. Two metaphors are given: a mirage, in this verse, and the depths of darkness in the sea, in the next.

In sandy deserts, which
The man parched with thirst
Mistakes for water ; until
When he comes up to it,
He finds it to be nothing :[3011]
But he finds God[3012]
(Ever) with him, and God
Will pay him his account :
And God is swift
In taking account.

بِقِيعَةٍ يَّحْسَبُهُ الظَّمْاٰنُ مَآءً ۗ
حَتّٰىٓ اِذَا جَآءَهٗ لَمْ يَجِدْهُ شَيْـًٔا
وَّوَجَدَ اللّٰهَ عِنْدَهٗ
فَوَفّٰىهُ حِسَابَهٗ ۗ
وَاللّٰهُ سَرِيْعُ الْحِسَابِ ۝

40\. Or (the Unbelievers' state)
Is like the depths of darkness
In a vast deep ocean,
Overwhelmed with billow
Topped by billow,
Topped by (dark) clouds :[3013]
Depths of darkness, one[3014]
Above another : if a man
Stretches out his hand,
He can hardly see it !
For any to whom God
Giveth not light,
There is no light ![3015]

٤٠- اَوْ كَظُلُمٰتٍ فِىْ بَحْرٍ
لُّجِّىٍّ يَّغْشٰىهُ مَوْجٌ مِّنْ فَوْقِهٖ
مَوْجٌ مِّنْ فَوْقِهٖ سَحَابٌ ۗ
ظُلُمٰتٌۢ بَعْضُهَا فَوْقَ بَعْضٍ ۗ
اِذَآ اَخْرَجَ يَدَهٗ لَمْ يَكَدْ يَرٰىهَا ۗ
وَمَنْ لَّمْ يَجْعَلِ اللّٰهُ لَهٗ نُوْرًا
فَمَا لَهٗ مِنْ نُّوْرٍ ۝ ع

Section 6.

41\. Seest thou not that it is
God Whose praises all beings
In the heavens and on earth[3016]
Do celebrate, and the birds

٤١- اَلَمْ تَرَ اَنَّ اللّٰهَ يُسَبِّحُ
لَهٗ مَنْ فِى السَّمٰوٰتِ وَالْاَرْضِ وَالطَّيْرُ

3011\. The mirage, of which I have seen several instances in the Arabian deserts and in Egypt, is a strange phenomenon of illusion. It is a trick of our vision. In the language of our Parable, it rejects the Light which shows us the Truth, and deceives us with Falsehood. A lonely traveller in a desert, nearly dying of thirst, sees a broad sheet of water. He goes in that direction, lured on and on, but finds nothing at all. He dies in protracted agony.

3012\. The rebel against God finds himself like the man deluded by a mirage. The Truth which he rejected is always with him. The mirage which he accepted leads to his destruction.

3013\. What a graphic picture of darkness in the depths of the Ocean, wave upon wave, and on top of all, dense dark clouds ! There is so little light even in ordinary depths of the Ocean that fishes which live there lose their eyes as useless organs. For lines 4-5 I am indebted to Gairdner's Translation of Gazālī's *Mishkāt*.

3014\. A contrast to "Light upon Light" in xxiv. 35 above.

3015\. The true source of Light in the world of Reality is God, and anyone who cuts himself off from that Light is in utter darkness indeed, for it is the negation of the only true Light, and not merely relative darkness, like that which we see, say, in the shadows of moonlight.

3016\. *Cf.* xxi. 19-20.

(Of the air) with wings [3017]
Outspread? Each one knows
Its own (mode of) prayer
And praise. And God
Knows well all that they do.

صَٰٓفَّٰتٍۖ كُلٌّ قَدۡ عَلِمَ صَلَاتَهُۥ وَتَسۡبِيحَهُۥۗ
وَٱللَّهُ عَلِيمُۢ بِمَا يَفۡعَلُونَ ○

42. Yea, to God belongs
The dominion of the heavens
And the earth; and to God
Is the final goal (of all).[3018]

٤٢- وَلِلَّهِ مُلۡكُ ٱلسَّمَٰوَٰتِ
وَٱلۡأَرۡضِۖ وَإِلَى ٱللَّهِ ٱلۡمَصِيرُ ○

43. Seest thou not that God
Makes the clouds move
Gently, then joins them
Together, then makes them
Into a heap?—then wilt thou
See rain issue forth [3019]
From their midst. And He
Sends down from the sky
Mountain masses (of clouds)
Wherein is hail: He strikes
Therewith whom He pleases
And He turns it away
From whom He pleases.
The vivid flash of His lightning
Well-nigh blinds the sight.

٤٣- أَلَمۡ تَرَ أَنَّ ٱللَّهَ يُزۡجِي سَحَابٗا
ثُمَّ يُؤَلِّفُ بَيۡنَهُۥ
ثُمَّ يَجۡعَلُهُۥ رُكَامٗا
فَتَرَى ٱلۡوَدۡقَ يَخۡرُجُ مِنۡ خِلَٰلِهِۦ وَيُنَزِّلُ
مِنَ ٱلسَّمَآءِ مِن جِبَالٖ فِيهَا مِنۢ بَرَدٖ
فَيُصِيبُ بِهِۦ مَن يَشَآءُ
وَيَصۡرِفُهُۥ عَن مَّن يَشَآءُۖ
يَكَادُ سَنَا بَرۡقِهِۦ يَذۡهَبُ بِٱلۡأَبۡصَٰرِ ○

44. It is God Who alternates
The Night and the Day: [3020]

٤٤- يُقَلِّبُ ٱللَّهُ ٱلَّيۡلَ وَٱلنَّهَارَۚ

3017. All denizens of the heavens, such as angels, all denizens of the earth (including the waters) such as man, animals, insects, fishes, etc., and all denizens of the air, such as birds, celebrate the praises of God. Each has his own mode of prayer and praise. It is not necessarily with words, for language (as we know it) is peculiar to man. But actions and other modes of self-expression recognise and declare the Glory of God.

3018. From Him we are; to Him we belong; and to Him we shall return. Not only we, but all Creation, proclaims this in the whole world.

3019. Artists, or lovers of nature, or observers of clouds will appreciate this description of cloud effects—thin clouds floating about in fantastic shapes, joining together and taking body and substance, then emerging as heavy clouds heaped up, which condense and pour forth their rain. Then the heavy dark clouds in the upper regions, that bring hail,—how distinct and yet how similar! They are truly like mountain masses! And when the hailstones fall, how local their area! It hits some localities and leaves free others almost interlaced! And the lightning—how blinding flashes come from thunderous clouds! In this Book of Nature can we not see the hand of the powerful and beneficent God?

3020. His power, wisdom, and goodness are shown no less in the regular phenomena of nature like the succession of Day and Night, than in the seasonal or seemingly irregular movements of clouds and rain and hail and lightning. Those who have the spiritual vision can read this Book of God with delight and instruction.

Verily in these things
Is an instructive example
For those who have vision!

إِنَّ فِي ذَٰلِكَ لَعِبْرَةً لِّأُولِي الْأَبْصَارِ ○

45. And God has created
Every animal from water:[3021]
Of them there are some
That creep on their bellies;
Some that walk on two legs;
And some that walk on four.[3022]
God creates what He wills;[3023]
For verily God has power
Over all things.

۴۵- وَاللَّهُ خَلَقَ كُلَّ دَابَّةٍ مِّن مَّاءٍ ۚ
فَمِنْهُم مَّن يَمْشِي عَلَىٰ بَطْنِهِ ۚ
وَمِنْهُم مَّن يَمْشِي عَلَىٰ رِجْلَيْنِ وَمِنْهُم
مَّن يَمْشِي عَلَىٰ أَرْبَعٍ ۚ يَخْلُقُ اللَّهُ مَا يَشَاءُ ۚ
إِنَّ اللَّهَ عَلَىٰ كُلِّ شَيْءٍ قَدِيرٌ ○

46. We have indeed sent down
Signs that make things manifest:
And God guides whom He wills
To a Way that is straight.

۴۶- لَّقَدْ أَنزَلْنَا آيَاتٍ مُّبَيِّنَاتٍ ۚ وَاللَّهُ
يَهْدِي مَن يَشَاءُ إِلَىٰ صِرَاطٍ مُّسْتَقِيمٍ ○

47. They[3024] say, "We believe
In God and in the Apostle,
And we obey": but
Even after that, some of them
Turn away: they are not
(Really) Believers.

۴۷- وَيَقُولُونَ آمَنَّا بِاللَّهِ وَبِالرَّسُولِ وَ
أَطَعْنَا ثُمَّ يَتَوَلَّىٰ فَرِيقٌ مِّنْهُم مِّن بَعْدِ
ذَٰلِكَ ۚ وَمَا أُولَٰئِكَ بِالْمُؤْمِنِينَ ○

48. When they are summoned
To God and His Apostle,
In order that he may judge
Between them, behold, some
Of them decline (to come).

۴۸- وَإِذَا دُعُوا إِلَى اللَّهِ وَرَسُولِهِ
لِيَحْكُمَ بَيْنَهُمْ إِذَا فَرِيقٌ مِّنْهُم
مُّعْرِضُونَ ○

3021. *Cf.* xxi. 30, n. 2691. Protoplasm is the basis of all living matter, and "the vital power of protoplasm seems to depend on the constant presence of water" (Lowson's Text-book of Botany, Indian Edition, London 1922, p. 23). Text books on Zoology are also clear on the point. For example, see T. J. Parker and W. A. Haswell, Text-book of Zoology, London 1910, vol. I, p. 15: "Living protoplasm always contains a large amount of water."

3022. The creeping things include worms and lowly forms of animal life as well as reptiles (like snakes), centipedes, spiders, and insects. Where these have legs they are small, and the description of creeping or crawling is more applicable to them than that of walking. Fishes and sea-animals generally cannot be said to walk: their swimming is like "creeping on their bellies". Two-legged animals include birds and man. Most of the mammals walk on four legs. This includes the whole of the animal world.

3023. In God's Will and Plan, the variety of forms and habits among animals is adapted to their various modes of life and stages of biological evolution.

3024. The Hypocrites, far from profiting from God's Light and Revelation, or declaring their open hostility, play fast and loose according to their selfish worldly aims.

49. But if the right is[3025]
On their side, they come
To him with all submission.

٤٩- وَإِنْ يَكُنْ لَّهُمُ الْحَقُّ
يَأْتُوٓا إِلَيْهِ مُذْعِنِينَ ۝

50. Is it that there is
A disease in their hearts?
Or do they doubt,
Or are they in fear,
That God and His Apostle
Will deal unjustly with them?
Nay, it is they themselves
Who do wrong.[3026]

٥٠- أَفِي قُلُوبِهِم مَّرَضٌ
أَمِ ارْتَابُوٓا أَمْ يَخَافُونَ
أَن يَحِيفَ اللَّهُ عَلَيْهِمْ وَرَسُولُهُۥ
بَلْ أُولَٰٓئِكَ هُمُ الظَّٰلِمُونَ ۝

Section 7.

51. The answer of the Believers,
When summoned to God
And His Apostle, in order
That he may judge between them,
Is no other than this:
They say, "We hear and we
obey": [3027]
It is such as these
That will attain felicity.[3028]

٥١- إِنَّمَا كَانَ قَوْلَ الْمُؤْمِنِينَ إِذَا دُعُوٓا
إِلَى اللَّهِ
وَرَسُولِهِۦ لِيَحْكُمَ بَيْنَهُمْ
أَن يَقُولُوا سَمِعْنَا وَأَطَعْنَا ۚ
وَأُولَٰٓئِكَ هُمُ الْمُفْلِحُونَ ۝

52. It is such as obey
God and His Apostle,
And fear God and do
Right, that will win
(In the end).

٥٢- وَمَن يُطِعِ اللَّهَ وَرَسُولَهُۥ
وَيَخْشَ اللَّهَ وَيَتَّقْهِ
فَأُولَٰٓئِكَ هُمُ الْفَآئِزُونَ ۝

53. They swear their strongest oaths
By God that, if only thou

٥٣- وَأَقْسَمُوا بِاللَّهِ جَهْدَ أَيْمَٰنِهِمْ لَئِنْ

3025. The Hypocrites only wanted to go to the judge who they thought was likely to give judgment in their favour. If their case was incontestable, and justice was on their side, they readily came to the Apostle, knowing that he was just and would judge in their favour, even against his own adherents. But if they had done wrong, an impartial judge was not to their taste. They would rather go to some one who would tip the balance in their favour! This form of selfishness and iniquity was not confined to the Hypocrites of Medina. It is common in all ages, and should be suppressed.

3026. The real fact is that their conscience smites them. They know their own iniquity, and do not wish to go before a just judge who would be open to no influence and would be sure to give a righteous decree.

3027. *Cf.* ii. 285. Contrast with it the attitude of the Unbelievers or Hypocrites, who say aloud, "we hear", but intend in their hearts to disobey (ii. 93).

3028. True happiness, whether here or in the Hereafter, is not to be attained by fraud or duplicity: it is the privilege of those who listen attentively to good counsel and carry it out in their lives.

Wouldst command them, they
Would leave (their homes).[3029]
Say : "Swear ye not;
Obedience is (more) reasonable ;
Verily, God is well acquainted
With all that ye do."

أَمَرْتَهُمْ لَيَخْرُجُنَّ
قُل لَّا تُقْسِمُوا طَاعَةٌ مَّعْرُوفَةٌ
إِنَّ اللَّهَ خَبِيرٌ بِمَا تَعْمَلُونَ ○

54. Say : "Obey God, and obey
The Apostle : but if ye turn
Away, he is only responsible
For the duty placed on him
And ye for that placed
On you. If ye obey him,
Ye shall be on right guidance.
The Apostle's duty is only
To preach the clear (Message).[3030]

٥٤- قُلْ أَطِيعُوا اللَّهَ وَأَطِيعُوا الرَّسُولَ
فَإِن تَوَلَّوْا فَإِنَّمَا عَلَيْهِ مَا حُمِّلَ
وَعَلَيْكُم مَّا حُمِّلْتُمْ
وَإِن تُطِيعُوهُ تَهْتَدُوا وَمَا عَلَى الرَّسُولِ
إِلَّا الْبَلَاغُ الْمُبِينُ ○

55. God has promised, to those
Among you who believe
And work righteous deeds, that He[3031]
Will, of a surety, grant them
In the land, inheritance
(Of power), as He granted it
To those before them ; that
He will establish in authority
Their religion—the one
Which He has chosen for them ;
And that He will change
(Their state), after the fear[3032]
In which they (lived), to one

٥٥- وَعَدَ اللَّهُ الَّذِينَ آمَنُوا مِنكُمْ
وَعَمِلُوا الصَّالِحَاتِ
لَيَسْتَخْلِفَنَّهُمْ فِي الْأَرْضِ
كَمَا اسْتَخْلَفَ الَّذِينَ مِن قَبْلِهِمْ
وَلَيُمَكِّنَنَّ لَهُمْ
دِينَهُمُ الَّذِي ارْتَضَىٰ لَهُمْ
وَلَيُبَدِّلَنَّهُم مِّن بَعْدِ خَوْفِهِمْ

3029. Some people, especially hypocrites, give hyperbolic assurances, as did the Medina Hypocrites to the holy Apostle, that they would do any bidding, even to the forsaking of their hearths and homes. To this they are ready to swear their strongest oaths, which mean nothing. They are asked to spare their oaths, and quietly do at least such unheroic duties as they are asked to do in every-day life. Idle words are not of the least value. God will judge by your actions, and He knows all, whether it is open or secret.

3030. 'If you disobey God's commands as explained by His Apostle, you are not going to be forced. The Apostle's mission is to train your will and explain clearly all the implications of your conduct. The responsibility for your conduct rests entirely on yourselves.'

3031. Three things are promised here, to those who have Faith and obey God's Law: (1) that they will inherit power and authority in the land, not for any selfish purposes of theirs nor by way of favouritism, but in order that they may maintain God's Law ; (2) that the Religion of Right, which God has chosen for them, will be openly established, and will suppress all wrong and oppression ; (3) that the righteous will live in peace and security, instead of having to suffer persecution, or leave their hearths and homes for the cause of God, or practise the rites of their Faith in secret.

3032. If this verse was revealed about the time of the Battle of the Ditch (*Khandaq*), also called the Battle of the Confederates (*Aḥzāb*), A.H. 4-5, we can imagine the comfort it gave to the Muslims who were besieged in Medina by a force ten times their number. The Muslims then lived in a state of great suspense and danger, and under arms for days on end. (See xxxiii. 9-20.) The security and authority they were promised came to them subsequently in abundant measure.

Of security and peace:
'They will worship Me (alone)
And not associate aught with Me.'
If any do reject Faith
After this, they are
Rebellious and wicked.

أَمْنًا ۚ يَعْبُدُونَنِي لَا يُشْرِكُونَ بِي شَيْئًا ۚ
وَمَنْ كَفَرَ بَعْدَ ذَٰلِكَ
فَأُولَٰئِكَ هُمُ الْفَاسِقُونَ ○

56. So establish regular Prayer
And give regular Charity;
And obey the Apostle;
That ye may receive mercy.

٥٦- وَأَقِيمُوا الصَّلَاةَ وَآتُوا الزَّكَاةَ
وَأَطِيعُوا الرَّسُولَ لَعَلَّكُمْ تُرْحَمُونَ ○

57. Never think thou
That the Unbelievers
Are going to frustrate
(God's Plan) on earth:
Their abode is the Fire,—
And it is indeed
An evil refuge!

٥٧- لَا تَحْسَبَنَّ الَّذِينَ كَفَرُوا
مُعْجِزِينَ فِي الْأَرْضِ ۚ
وَمَأْوَاهُمُ النَّارُ ۖ
وَلَبِئْسَ الْمَصِيرُ ○ ع

C. 160.—For a self-respecting life on earth, respect
(xxiv. 58-64.) For others' privacy is most essential,
In the home and abroad: but superstitions
Are not meet in intercourse amongst kin
Or true friends. In public council never
Fail to observe the most punctilious
Form and order: your self-respect
Demands that ye should give your Leader
Sincere respect and all obedience.
Ye may not know but God doth know
The inwardness of things both great and small.

Section 8.

58. O ye who believe![3033]
Let those whom your right
hands[3034]
Possess, and the (children) among
you

٥٨- يَا أَيُّهَا الَّذِينَ آمَنُوا لِيَسْتَأْذِنْكُمُ
الَّذِينَ مَلَكَتْ أَيْمَانُكُمْ وَالَّذِينَ

3033. We now come to rules of decorum within the family circle in refined society. Servants and children have rather more freedom of access, as they come and go at all hours, and there is less ceremony with them. But even in their case there are limitations. During the night, before morning prayer, *i.e.*, before dawn, they must discreetly ask for permission before they enter, partly because they must not unnecessarily disturb people asleep, and partly because the people are then undressed. The same applies to the time for the midday siesta, and again to the time after night prayers, when people usually undress and turn in to sleep. For grown-ups the rule is stricter: they must ask permission to come in at all times (xxiv. 59).

3034. This would mean slaves in a régime of slavery. But the principle applies to all personal servants, who have to render personal service to their masters or mistresses by day and by night.

Who have not come of age [3035]
Ask your permission (before
They come to your presence),
On three occasions : before
Morning prayer ; the while
Ye doff your clothes
For the noonday heat ;
And after the late-night prayer :
These are your three times [3036]
Of undress : outside those times
It is not wrong for you
Or for them to move about
Attending to each other :
Thus does God make clear
The Signs to you : for God
Is full of knowledge and wisdom.

لَمْ يَبْلُغُوا الْحُلُمَ مِنْكُمْ ثَلٰثَ مَرّٰتٍ ؕ
مِنْ قَبْلِ صَلٰوةِ الْفَجْرِ وَحِيْنَ تَضَعُوْنَ
ثِيَابَكُمْ مِّنَ الظَّهِيْرَةِ وَمِنْۢ بَعْدِ صَلٰوةِ
الْعِشَآءِ ؕ ثَلٰثُ عَوْرٰتٍ لَّكُمْ ؕ
لَيْسَ عَلَيْكُمْ وَلَا عَلَيْهِمْ جُنَاحٌۢ بَعْدَهُنَّ ؕ
طَوّٰفُوْنَ عَلَيْكُمْ بَعْضُكُمْ عَلٰى بَعْضٍ ؕ
كَذٰلِكَ يُبَيِّنُ اللّٰهُ لَكُمُ الْاٰيٰتِ ؕ
وَاللّٰهُ عَلِيْمٌ حَكِيْمٌ ○

59. But when the children among you [3037]
Come of age, let them (also)
Ask for permission, as do those
Senior to them (in age) : [3038]
Thus does God make clear
His Signs to you : for God
Is full of knowledge and wisdom. [3039]

٥٩- وَاِذَا بَلَغَ الْاَطْفَالُ مِنْكُمُ الْحُلُمَ
فَلْيَسْتَاْذِنُوْا كَمَا اسْتَاْذَنَ الَّذِيْنَ
مِنْ قَبْلِهِمْ ؕ كَذٰلِكَ يُبَيِّنُ اللّٰهُ لَكُمْ اٰيٰتِهٖ ؕ
وَاللّٰهُ عَلِيْمٌ حَكِيْمٌ ○

60. Such elderly women [3040] as are
Past the prospect of marriage,—
There is no blame on them
If they lay aside

٦٠- وَالْقَوَاعِدُ مِنَ النِّسَآءِ الّٰتِيْ لَا يَرْجُوْنَ
نِكَاحًا فَلَيْسَ عَلَيْهِنَّ جُنَاحٌ اَنْ يَّضَعْنَ

3035. I have translated "come of age" euphemistically for "attain the age of puberty".

3036. It is a mark of refinement for ladies and gentlemen not to be slipshod or vulgarly familiar, in dress, manners, or speech; and Islam aims at making every Muslim man or woman, however humble in station, a refined gentleman or lady, so that he or she can climb the ladder of spiritual development with humble confidence in God, and with the co-operation of his brothers and sisters in Islam. The principles here laid down apply, if they are interpreted with due elasticity, even if social and domestic habits change, with changes in climate or in racial and personal habits. Punctilious self-respect and respect for others, in small things as well as great, are the key-notes in these simple rules of etiquette.

3037. *Children among you*: *i.e.*, in your house, not necessarily your own children. All in the house, including the stranger within your gate, must conform to these wholesome rules.

3038. *Those senior to them*: literally, those before them, *i.e.*, those who have already become grown-up before these children attain their age. It is suggested that each generation as it grows up should follow the wholesome traditions of its predecessors. While they were children, they behaved like children : when they grow up, they must bahave like grown-ups.

3039. The refrain connects up this verse with the last verse, whose meaning is completed here. The slight variation ("*His* Signs" here, against "*the* Signs" there) shows that this verse is more personal, as referring to children who have now become responsible men and women.

3040. For elderly women in the home the rules of dress and decorum are not so exacting as for younger women, but they are also enjoined to study modesty, both because it is good in itself, and as an example to the younger people.

Their (outer) garments, provided
They make not a wanton display
Of their beauty: but
It is best for them
To be modest: and God
Is One Who sees and knows[3041]
All things.

ثِيَابَهُنَّ غَيْرَ مُتَبَرِّجٰتٍۭ بِزِينَةٍ ۖ
وَأَن يَسْتَعْفِفْنَ خَيْرٌ لَّهُنَّ ۗ
وَاللَّهُ سَمِيعٌ عَلِيمٌ ۝

61. It is no fault in the blind
Nor in one born lame, nor
In one afflicted with illness,[3042]
Nor in yourselves, that ye
Should eat in your own houses,
Or those of your fathers,
Or your mothers, or your brothers,
Or your sisters, or your father's brothers
Or your father's sisters,
Or your mother's brothers,
Or your mother's sisters,
Or in houses of which
The keys are in your possession,
Or in the house of a sincere
Friend of yours: there is
No blame on you, whether
Ye eat in company or
Separately. But if ye
Enter houses, salute each other—
A greeting of blessing
And purity as from God.[3043]

٦١- لَيْسَ عَلَى الْأَعْمَىٰ حَرَجٌ وَلَا عَلَى
الْأَعْرَجِ حَرَجٌ وَلَا عَلَى الْمَرِيضِ حَرَجٌ وَلَا
عَلَىٰ أَنفُسِكُمْ أَن تَأْكُلُوا مِن بُيُوتِكُمْ أَوْ
بُيُوتِ آبَائِكُمْ أَوْ بُيُوتِ أُمَّهٰتِكُمْ أَوْ بُيُوتِ
إِخْوٰنِكُمْ أَوْ بُيُوتِ أَخَوٰتِكُمْ أَوْ بُيُوتِ أَعْمٰمِكُمْ
أَوْ بُيُوتِ عَمّٰتِكُمْ أَوْ بُيُوتِ أَخْوٰلِكُمْ أَوْ بُيُوتِ
خٰلٰتِكُمْ أَوْ مَا مَلَكْتُم مَّفَاتِحَهُ أَوْ صَدِيقِكُمْ ۚ
لَيْسَ عَلَيْكُمْ جُنَاحٌ
أَن تَأْكُلُوا جَمِيعًا أَوْ أَشْتَاتًا ۚ
فَإِذَا دَخَلْتُم بُيُوتًا فَسَلِّمُوا عَلَىٰ أَنفُسِكُمْ
تَحِيَّةً مِّنْ عِندِ اللَّهِ مُبٰرَكَةً طَيِّبَةً ۚ

3041. Another example of a refrain: see n. 3039 above. Verses 58 and 59 were closer connected: their refrain was practically identical. This verse, though ancillary, is less closely connected: its refrain comes in like a half-note in a melody.

3042. There were various Arab superstitions and fancies which are combated and rejected here. (1) The blind, or the halt, or those afflicted with serious disease were supposed to be objects of divine displeasure, and as such not fit to be associated with us in meals in our houses: we are not to entertain such a thought, as we are no judges of the causes of people's misfortunes, which deserve our sympathy and kindness. (2) It was considered unbecoming to take meals in the houses of near relatives: this taboo is not approved. (3) A similar superstition about houses in our possession but not in our actual occupation is disapproved. (4) If people think they should not fall under obligation to casual friends, that does not apply to a sincere friend, in whose company a meal is not to be rejected, but welcomed. (5) If people make a superstition either that they should always eat separately, as in a *Chauka* in India, or that they must always eat in company, as some people weary of their own company think, either of them is wrong. Man is free and should regulate his life according to needs and circumstances.

3043. The shades of meaning in *Salām* are explained in n. 2512 to xix. 62. Here, we were first told that we might accept hospitality and good fellowship in each other's houses. Now we are told what spirit should animate us in doing so. It should not be a spirit only of self-satisfaction in a worldly sense. It should rather be a spirit of good-will in the highest spiritual sense of the term—purity of motives and purity of life, as in the sight of God. *Cf.* Dante in the *Paradiso* (iii. 85): "In His will is our Peace."

Thus does God make clear
The Signs to you: that ye
May understand.[3044]

كَذَٰلِكَ يُبَيِّنُ اللَّهُ لَكُمُ
الْآيَاتِ لَعَلَّكُمْ تَعْقِلُونَ ○

SECTION 9.

62. Only those are Believers,
Who believe in God and
His Apostle: when they are
With him on a matter
Requiring cellective action,[3045]
They do not depart until
They have asked for his leave;
Those who ask for thy leave
Are those who believe in God
And His Apostle; so when
They ask for thy leave,
For some business of theirs,
Give leave to those of them
Whom thou wilt,[3046] and ask
God for their forgiveness:[3047]
For God is Oft-Forgiving,
Most Merciful.

٦٢- إِنَّمَا الْمُؤْمِنُونَ الَّذِينَ آمَنُوا بِاللَّهِ
وَرَسُولِهِ وَإِذَا كَانُوا مَعَهُ عَلَىٰ أَمْرٍ جَامِعٍ
لَّمْ يَذْهَبُوا حَتَّىٰ يَسْتَأْذِنُوهُ
إِنَّ الَّذِينَ يَسْتَأْذِنُونَكَ
أُولَٰئِكَ الَّذِينَ يُؤْمِنُونَ بِاللَّهِ وَرَسُولِهِ
فَإِذَا اسْتَأْذَنُوكَ لِبَعْضِ شَأْنِهِمْ
فَأْذَن لِّمَن شِئْتَ مِنْهُمْ وَاسْتَغْفِرْ لَهُمُ
اللَّهَ
إِنَّ اللَّهَ غَفُورٌ رَّحِيمٌ ○

63. Deem not the summons
Of the Apostle among yourselves
Like the summons of one[3048]
Of you to another: God
Doth know those of you
Who slip away under shelter
Of some excuse: then
Let those beware who

٦٣- لَا تَجْعَلُوا دُعَاءَ الرَّسُولِ بَيْنَكُمْ
كَدُعَاءِ بَعْضِكُم بَعْضًا
قَدْ يَعْلَمُ اللَّهُ الَّذِينَ يَتَسَلَّلُونَ مِنكُمْ
لِوَاذًا ۚ فَلْيَحْذَرِ الَّذِينَ

3044. See notes 3039 and 3041 above. The refrain comes again, in a different form, closing the argument from a different point of view.

3045. *Matter requiring collective action*: anything that affects the Community as a whole: Jumu'a and 'Id prayers are periodical occasions of this kind, but what is meant here is, I think, joint consultations with a view to joint undertakings, such as a Jihād, or some kind of organisation in peace.

3046. That is, those to whom, in the exercise of your impartial discretion, you think it expedient to give leave. "Will", unless the context shows otherwise, means "right will", not a will without any definite principle behind it.

3047. In important matters of general consultation, even though leave of absence is given on sufficient excuse, it implies some defect in duty on the part of the person to whom the leave is given, and therefore the need of forgiveness from Him to Whom we owe duty in a perfect measure.

3048. Three significations are possible. One is that adopted in the Translation, which agrees with the view of most Commentators. Another would be: 'Do not think that the prayer of the Apostle of God is like your ordinary requests to another: the Apostle's prayer will be about serious matters and will be accepted by God.' A third interpretation would be: 'Do not address the Apostle familiarly as you would address one another: use proper terms of respect for him.'

Withstand the Apostle's order,
Lest some trial befall them,[3049]
Or a grievous Penalty
Be inflicted on them.

يُخَالِفُونَ عَنْ أَمْرِهِۦٓ أَن تُصِيبَهُمْ فِتْنَةٌ
أَوْ يُصِيبَهُمْ عَذَابٌ أَلِيمٌ ۝

64. Be quite sure that
To God doth belong
Whatever is in the heavens
And on earth. Well doth He
Know what ye are intent upon:[3050]
And one day they will be
Brought back to Him, and He
Will tell them the truth
Of what they did:[3051]
For God doth know
All things.

٦٤- أَلَآ إِنَّ لِلَّهِ
مَا فِى ٱلسَّمَٰوَٰتِ وَٱلْأَرْضِ ۖ
قَدْ يَعْلَمُ مَآ أَنتُمْ عَلَيْهِ
وَيَوْمَ يُرْجَعُونَ إِلَيْهِ فَيُنَبِّئُهُم بِمَا عَمِلُوا۟ ۗ
وَٱللَّهُ بِكُلِّ شَىْءٍ عَلِيمٌۢ ۝

3049. The "trial" is understood to be some misfortune in this life, and the "grievous Penalty" to be the punishment in the Hereafter.

3050. The condition or position you are in, the motives which actuate you, and the ends you have in view.

3051. Things misunderstood or maligned, falsely praised or held in honour, or fraudulently shown to be good when they are evil—everything will be revealed in its true light on the Day of final Judgment.

APPENDIX VIII.

Mystic Interpretation of the Verse of Light (xxiv. 35).

Among the beauties of the Qur-ān, not the least is that which sends its mystic interpreters into ecstasies of spiritual delight. While its plain meaning contains noble precepts of ordinary conduct, its mystic passages reveal spiritual mysteries which can only be expressed by the phrase "Light upon Light!" (xxiv. 35). It is an endless chain of illumination in which ordinary knowledge dissolves as if it were ignorance.

The highest place among the mystic interpreters should be assigned to Imām Gazālī, whose *Mishkāt-ul Anwār* deals with the verse of Light (xxiv. 35), the contrasted verse of Darkness (xxiv. 40), and the saying of the holy Prophet quoted by him from the Ḥadīth: "God has Seventy Thousand Veils of Light and Darkness: were He to withdraw their curtain, then would the splendours of His Aspect (or Countenance, or Face, *Wajh*) surely consume everyone who apprehended Him with his sight." In the *Mishkāt Sharīf* (Bāb-ul-Masājid, end of section 2) Jibrīl says: "*Ḳāna bainī wa bainahū sab'ūna alfa ḥijābin min nūrin*: Between me and Him are seventy thousand veils of Light."

English readers will thank me for drawing their attention to a meritorious English translation of Gazālī's interpretation of these sublime passages. It is in the Asiatic Society Monographs series, vol. xix: "Al-Ghazālī's *Mishkāt-ul-Anwār*, a Translation with Introduction, by W.H.T. Gairdner, published by the Royal Asiatic Society, London, 1924". They are asked to study this carefully, and better still (if they can), to study the original, and see for themselves how much spiritual wisdom is enshrined in just two verses of the holy Qur-ān, when interpreted by a learned Imām. And there are over 6,000 verses in the Qur-ān. In my Summary of Gazālī's argument I have used Gairdner's Translation throughout this Appendix.

Gazālī died in A.H. 505 (=1111 A.D.). He lived in an age when Greek philosophy and other philosophies had been studied by Muslims, many new arts and sciences had been added by them to the world's stock of knowledge, but the quest of the Timeless and the Universal was still urging thirsty enquirers on. It was his mission to expose the hollow pretensions of some superficial thinkers who pursued mirages. He turned Muslim thought in the direction of the subtler Realities of spiritual life. Within a century and a half of his death the Muslim world was engulfed in a mighty cataclysm which well-nigh wiped out its channels of culture and civilisation.

Now for Gazālī's argument.

If we take physical light as ordinarily understood, it is a phenomenon or appearance, and is therefore liable to pass away. For its illuminative power it has to depend upon the perceiving faculty or the perceiving instrument, the Eye. But

the Eye has many defects. It is only the perceiving faculty or intelligence which is properly entitled to the name of Light considered as a source of enlightenment.

The verses of the Qur-ān, in relation to Intelligence, have the value of sunlight in relation to eyesight The Qur-ān is therefore spoken of as the Light: "*For We have sent unto you a light* (*that is*) *manifest*": iv. 174.

Thus the physical eye sees by the sun; the spiritual eye sees by Revelation (the Qur-ān). There is a world invisible, with a Light of its own, quite different from the world visible, with its own physical light. The former, the spiritual world, is far above the physical world: not in space, for there is no question of space, but in grade. Yet the World of Sense is a type of the World of the Realm Celestial. All the Prophets are Lamps, and so are the Learned: but the difference between them is incalculable. If the Prophet of God is a Lamp Illuminant, that from which the Lamp is itself lit may fitly be symbolised by Fire. It is the Spirits Celestial, the angels, considered as the kindling-source of the Lamps Terrestrial, that can be compared alone with Fire: xxviii. 29-30. These Lamps Celestial have their own grades and orders, and the highest is the one nearest to the Ultimate Light.

That Ultimate Light is the final Fountain-head, Who is Light in and by Himself, not a light kindled from other lights. The term 'light' as applied to any other than this primary Light is purely metaphorical. But these metaphorical lights have various gradations. So are there gradations in their opposites. There is no darkness so intense as the darkness of Not-being. A dark thing is called "dark" simply because it cannot appear to anyone's vision; it never comes to exist for sight, though it may exist in itself. But that which has no existence for others *nor* for itself is assuredly the very extreme of darkness. In contrast with it is Being, which is therefore Light. Thus God Most High is the only Reality, as He is the only Light.

In the physical world Light is itself visible and makes other things visible. It lies behind all colour, and is apprehended with colour. Through its intense union with the colours, it may appear [under refraction] as colours and not as light at all. Its very intensity may cause its invisibility. So God is with all things, but some visions perceive Him not on account of His very brightness. [The absorption of some colours through the media through which they pass may result in the appearance of other colours. Some may consider it as a merit of the media. But it detracts from the appearance of the perfect colourless Light, which is the type for the perfection of God's Light.]

From the material world, the world of Sense, we rise through the world of Intelligence to the spiritual world, or the world of the Realm Supernal (or Celestial). This world of the Realm Supernal contains Light-substances, high and lofty, called "Angels", from which substances the various lights are effused upon the various mortal spirits.

The human soul has five faculties or spirits: (1) the sensory spirit which

takes in the information brought by the senses; (2) the imaginative spirit, which records the information conveyed by the senses and presents it to the intelligential spirit above it, when required; (3) the intelligential spirit, which apprehends ideas beyond the spheres of sense and imagination; these ideas are of universal application, and are symbolised by the particular things that are known by the senses; (4) the discursive [or ratiocinative] spirit, which takes the data of pure reason, combines them, and deduces from them abstract knowledge; (5) the transcendental prophetic spirit, which is possessed by prophets and some saints; by it the unseen tables and statutes of the Law are revealed from the other world, together with several of the sciences of the Realms Celestial and Terrestrial, and pre-eminently Theology, the science of Deity, which the intelligential and discursive spirits cannot compass. All of these are Lights, for it is through them that every kind of existing thing is manifested, including objects of sense or imagination.

These five faculties or spirits are symbolised by the Niche, Glass, Lamp, Tree, and Oil in the verse of Light. The Niche is the sensory spirit, whose lights come through the eyes, ears, nostrils, etc. The Glass is the Imagination; for it is made out of opaque substances [like sand, soda, potash, etc.], but is clarified and refined till it becomes transparent to the light of a lamp, and it also keeps the lamp from being put out by a draught or violent jerking. So Imagination, though its origin is from the ideas of grosser substances, becomes clarified and transparent to ideas of intelligence and to the light from them, as well as serves to hold knowledge together and prevents it from being disturbed, unsettled, and dissipated. The lamp is the intelligential spirit, which gives cognisance of divine ideas. The Tree is the ratiocinative spirit, which begins with a proposition, then branches into two, which become four, and so on. It leads to conclusions which in their turn become germs producing like conclusions, these latter being also susceptible of continuation, each with each. The Tree in the symbol is the Olive, which gives oil producing the most radiant illumination. So the ratiocinative spirit multiplies, establishes, and fixes all knowledge. Illumination can be infinitely multiplied; therefore a tree like the olive, whose oil can multiply light infinitely is entitled to be called "blessed" above other trees like fruit trees, whose fruit is consumed in use. Again, the ramifications of pure intelligential propositions do not admit of relation to direction or distance, and therefore the symbolical Tree may well be said to be "neither of the East nor of the West".

Finally, the Oil is the type of the transcendental prophetic spirit, which is absolutely luminous and clear. The thought-spirit is divided into that which needs to be instructed, advised, and supplied from without, if the acquisition of knowledge is to be continuous; while a portion of it is absolutely clear, as though it were self-luminous, and had no external source of supply. There are Saints whose light shines so bright that it is well-nigh independent of what the Angels supply. For the human soul there is a graded succession of Lights, and this explains the phrase "Light upon Light."

Now we come to the Darkness-verse (xxiv. 40). The man who has turned away from the path of guidance [light, truth],—he is false, he is darkness; nay,

he is darker than darkness. For darkness is neutral [or negative]; it leads one neither one way nor the other. But the minds of misbelievers, and the whole of their perceptions, are perverse, and support each other mutually in the actual deluding of their owners. That "vast deep ocean" is this world of mortal dangers, of evil chances, of blinding trouble. Wave upon wave of selfish passion darkens the man's soul. And the dark clouds above are rank beliefs and corrupt imaginings, which become so many veils veiling the misbeliever from the true faith, from knowledge of the Real, and from illumination by the sunligt of the Qur ān and human intelligence. As all our Lights have their source in the great Primary Light, the One Reality, there can be no light unless God gives the Light.

What is the meaning of the Prophet's saying that "God has Seventy Thousand Veils of Light and Darkness"? (*Inna lillāhi la-sab'īna alfa ḥijābin min nūrin wa ẓulmatin*). The number, 70,000, varies in different versions, and is not by way of definite enumeration, but rather to denote some indefinitely great quantity. There are three classes of men who are veiled from the ineffably glorious Light of God: (1) those veiled by Pure Darkness; (2) those veiled by mixed Light and Darkness; and (3) those veiled by Pure Light. In each class there are numerous sub-divisions. [When we take account of all these, we may well speak of 70,000 Veils.]

Those veiled by Pure Darkness are such as are atheists, or such as take something else, which is not God, for God. For example, they take Nature or Self for God. But there are numerous varieties of such men. One particularly mentioned by G̱azālī is the sort of men that confess with their tongues the Creed of Islam, but are probably urged to it by fear alone, or the desire to beg from Muslims, or to curry favour with them, or to get financial [or other] assistance out of them, or, by a merely fanatical zeal, to support the opinions of their fathers. If the Creed fails to impel them to good works, it will not secure their elevation from the dark sphere to light. Rather are their patron-saints devils, who lead them from the light into the darkness. But he whom the Creed so touches that evil disgusts him and good gives him pleasure, has passed from pure darkness even though he be a great sinner still.

Those veiled by mixed Light and Darkness may be: (1) those veiled by the darkness of the Senses; they are above those who worship Self, but they give God's attributes of Majesty and Beauty to sense-perceived bodies, or to Nature or the forces of nature; (2) those veiled by some light, mixed with the darkness of the Imagination; they have got above the senses, but they allow their Imagination to govern their ideas of God, Who is above anything that the imagination of man can conceive; and (3) those veiled by some Light divine, mixed with the darkness of Intelligence; they fall into anthropomorphism in their ideas of God [and fail to perceive that the Soul is above the Intellect].

Those veiled by Pure Light are those who have perceived spiritual truths up to a certain point, but whose eyes have been so dazzled by the Light itself that there is a Veil between them and the Light. But these are only the Few of the Few whom "the splendours of the Countenance sublime consume", and the majesty of

the Divine Glory obliterates ; so that they are themselves blotted out, annihilated. [That is the true meaning of the Buddha's *Nirvāna*.] For self-contemplation there is no more a place, because with the self they have no longer anything to do. Nothing then remain save the One, the Real : that becomes the experience of the soul. That is the true meaning of attainment or Salvation. And Gazālī concludes with the words : "Hard, hard it is to essay the discovery of the Lights Supernal that are beyond the Veil." How true, and how appropriate for all who seek to interpret the Light ! May God grant that their own feeble lights may not act as a veil between them and the Light Divine !

INTRODUCTION TO SŪRA XXV (*Furqān*).

This Sūra further develops the contrast between Light and Darkness, as symbolical of knowledge and ignorance, righteousness and sin, spiritual progress and degradation. It closes with a definition of the deeds by which the righteous are known in the environment of this world.

It is mainly an early Meccan Sūra, but its date has no significance.

Summary.—God's highest gift to man is that He has furnished a Criterion for judgment between right and wrong,—in His revelation, which teaches us the true significance of our eternal Future (xxv. 1-20, and C. 161).

Those who do not use that Criterion will be full of woe when the Judgment comes, for God gave full warning at all times (xxv. 21-44, and C. 162).

In the contrasts of shade and sun, night and day, death and life, and the whole ordering of God's Creation, men may learn of God Most Gracious; and the virtues of the righteous respond to God's care for them (xxv. 45-77, and C. 163).

C. 161.—Among the highest and greatest of the gifts of God
(xxv. 1-20.) Is His Revelation, which is the Criterion
By which we may judge between right
And wrong—between false and true worship,
Between the Message that comes from God
And the forgeries of men, between the Real
In our eternal Future and the Fancies
By which we are misled. The apostles of God
Come as men to live among men and guide them.

Sūra XXV.

Furqān, or The Criterion.

In the name of God, Most Gracious,
Most Merciful.

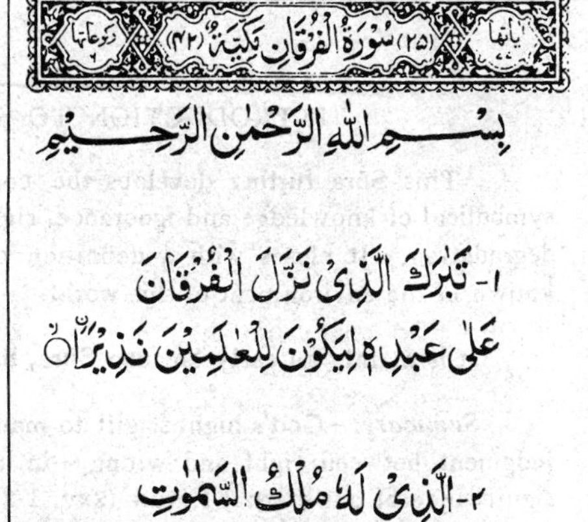

1. Blessed[3052] is He Who
Sent down the Criterion[3053]
To His Servant, that it[3054]
May be an admonition
To all creatures ;—

2. He to Whom belongs
The dominion of the heavens
And the earth : no son
Has He begotten, nor has He
A partner in His dominion :
It is He Who created
All things, and ordered them
In due proportions.[3055]

٢- الَّذِي لَهُ مُلْكُ السَّمٰوٰتِ
وَالْأَرْضِ وَلَمْ يَتَّخِذْ وَلَدًا وَّلَمْ يَكُنْ
لَّهُ شَرِيكٌ فِي الْمُلْكِ وَخَلَقَ
كُلَّ شَيْءٍ فَقَدَّرَهُ تَقْدِيرًا ۝

3. Yet have they taken,[3056]
Besides Him, gods that can
Create nothing but are themselves
Created ; that have no control
Of hurt or good to themselves ;
Nor can they control Death
Nor Life nor Resurrection.

٣- وَاتَّخَذُوا مِنْ دُونِهِ آلِهَةً
لَّا يَخْلُقُونَ شَيْئًا وَّهُمْ يُخْلَقُونَ وَلَا
يَمْلِكُونَ لِأَنْفُسِهِمْ ضَرًّا وَّلَا نَفْعًا وَّلَا
يَمْلِكُونَ مَوْتًا وَّلَا حَيٰوةً وَّلَا نُشُورًا ۝

3052. *Tabāraka*: the root meaning is "increase" or "abundance". Here that aspect of God's dealing with His creatures is emphasised, which shows His abundant goodness to all His creatures, in that He sent the Revelation of His Will, not only in the unlimited Book of Nature, but in a definite Book in human language, which gives clear directions and admonitions to all. The English word "blessed" hardly conveys that meaning, but I can find no other without departing far from established usage. To emphasise the meaning I have explained, I have translated "Blessed is...", but "Blessed be..." is also admissible, as it brings out another shade of meaning, that we praise and bless His holy name.

3053. That by which we can judge clearly between right and wrong. Here the reference is to the Qur-ān, which has already been symbolised by Light. This symbol is continued here, and many contrasts are shown, in the midst of which we can distinguish between the true and the false by God's Light, especially the contrast between righteousness and sin.

3054. The pronoun in *yakūna* may refer either to *Furqān* (the Criterion) or to *'Abd* (the holy Prophet). In either case the ultimate meaning is the same. The Qur-ān is the standing Criterion for judgment between right and wrong.

3055. The majesty of God and His independence of all wants or help are mentioned, to show how exceeding great is His goodness in revealing His Will to us.

3056. This is the first great distinction taught by the Criterion ; to know the nature of the true God, as against the false fancies of men.

4. But the Misbelievers say:
"Naught is this but a lie[3057]
Which he has forged,
And others have helped him
At it." In truth it is they
Who have put forward
An iniquity and a falsehood.

٤- وَقَالَ الَّذِيْنَ كَفَرُوْٓا اِنْ هٰذَآ اِلَّآ
اِفْكُ
اِفْتَرٰىهُ وَاَعَانَهٗ عَلَيْهِ قَوْمٌ اٰخَرُوْنَ ۚ
فَقَدْ جَآءُوْ ظُلْمًا وَّزُوْرًا ۞

5. And they say: "Tales of
The ancients, which he has caused
To be written: and they
Are dictated before him
Morning and evening."[3058]

٥- وَقَالُوْٓا اَسَاطِيْرُ الْاَوَّلِيْنَ اكْتَتَبَهَا
فَهِيَ تُمْلٰى عَلَيْهِ
بُكْرَةً وَّاَصِيْلًا ۞

6. Say: "The (Qur-ān) was sent down
By Him Who knows
The Mystery (that is) in the
heavens[3059]
And the earth: verily He
Is Oft-Forgiving, Most Merciful."

٦- قُلْ اَنْزَلَهُ الَّذِيْ يَعْلَمُ
السِّرَّ فِي السَّمٰوٰتِ وَالْاَرْضِ ۭ
اِنَّهٗ كَانَ غَفُوْرًا رَّحِيْمًا ۞

7. And they say: "What sort
Of an apostle is this,
Who eats food, and walks
Through the streets? Why
Has not an angel
Been sent down to him
To give admonition with him?[3060]

٧- وَقَالُوْا مَالِ هٰذَا الرَّسُوْلِ
يَاْكُلُ الطَّعَامَ وَيَمْشِيْ فِي الْاَسْوَاقِ ۭ
لَوْلَآ اُنْزِلَ اِلَيْهِ مَلَكٌ
فَيَكُوْنَ مَعَهٗ نَذِيْرًا ۞

3057. *Ifk*, which I have translated a "lie" may be distinguished from *zūr* at the end of this verse, translated "falsehood". The "lie" which the enemies attributed to the holy man of God was supposed to be something which did not exist in reality, but was invented by the Prophet with the aid of other people: the implication was that (1) the Revelation was not a revelation but a forgery, and that (2) the things revealed. *e g*, the news of the Hereafter, the Resurrection, the Judgment, the Bliss of the Righteous and the sufferings of the Evil, were fanciful and had no basis in fact. Delusion is also suggested. The reply is that, so far from that being the case, the facts were true and the charges were false (*zūr*),—the falsehood being due to the habits of iniquity for which the Misbelievers' whole mental and spiritual attitude was responsible.

3058. In their misguided arrogance they say: 'We have heard such things before; they are pretty tales which have come down from ancient times; they are good for amusement, but who takes them seriously?' When the beauty and power of the Revelation are pointed out, and its miracle as coming from an unlearned man, they again hint at other men who wrote them, though they could not produce any one who could write anything like it.

3059. The answer is that the Qur-ān teaches spiritual knowledge of what is ordinarily hidden from men's sight, and such knowledge can only come from God, to Whom alone is known the Mystery of the whole Creation. In spite of man's sin and shortcomings, He forgives, and He sends His most precious gift, *i e.*, the Revelation of His Will.

3060. This is another objection: 'He is only a man like us: why is not an angel sent down, if not by himself, at least with him?' The answer is: angels would be of no use to men as Messengers, as they and men would not understand each other, and if angels came, it might cause more confusion and wonder than understanding in men's minds. *Cf* xxi. 7-8; xxvii. 94-95. The office of an angel is different. A teacher for mankind is one who shares their nature, mingles in their life, is acquainted with their doings, and sympathises with their joys and sorrows.

"Or (why) has not a treasure
Been bestowed on him, or
Why has he (not) a garden
For enjoyment?"[3061] The wicked
Say: "Ye follow none other
Than a man bewitched."[3062]

٨- اَوْ يُلْقٰىٓ اِلَيْهِ كَنْزٌ اَوْ تَكُوْنُ لَهٗ جَنَّةٌ
يَّاْكُلُ مِنْهَا ۭ وَقَالَ الظّٰلِمُوْنَ اِنْ تَتَّبِعُوْنَ
اِلَّا رَجُلًا مَّسْحُوْرًا ○

9. See what kinds of comparisons
They make for thee!
But they have gone astray,
And never a way will they
Be able to find![3063]

٩- اُنْظُرْ كَيْفَ ضَرَبُوْا لَكَ الْاَمْثَالَ
فَضَلُّوْا فَلَا يَسْتَطِيْعُوْنَ سَبِيْلًا ○

SECTION 2.

10. Blessed is He Who,[3064]
If that were His Will,
Could give thee better (things)
Than those,—Gardens beneath
which[3065]
Rivers flow; and He could
Give thee Palaces (secure
To dwell in).

١٠- تَبٰرَكَ الَّذِيْٓ اِنْ شَاۗءَ
جَعَلَ لَكَ خَيْرًا
مِّنْ ذٰلِكَ جَنّٰتٍ تَجْرِيْ مِنْ تَحْتِهَا
الْاَنْهٰرُ ۙ وَيَجْعَلْ لَّكَ قُصُوْرًا ○

11. Nay, they deny the Hour
(Of the Judgment to come):[3066]
But We have prepared
A Blazing Fire for such
As deny the Hour:

١١- بَلْ كَذَّبُوْا بِالسَّاعَةِ ۣ
وَاَعْتَدْنَا لِمَنْ كَذَّبَ بِالسَّاعَةِ سَعِيْرًا ○

3061. Literally, 'that he may eat out of it'. As shown in n. 776 to v. 69, *akala* (to eat) has a comprehensive meaning, implying enjoyment of all kinds,—physical, social, mental and moral, and spiritual. Here, the garden itself stands for a type of the amenities of life: its fruits would be available for eating, its coolness for rest and refreshment, its waters and its landscape for æsthetic delight.

3062. *Cf.* xvii 47. This speech, of the wicked or the ungodly, is meant to be even more bitter than that of the Misbelievers. It makes out the Teacher to be a demented fool!

3063. The charges the enemies made against the Apostle of God recoiled on those who made them. The Apostle was vindicated, and went from strength to strength, for God's Truth will always prevail. The men who perversely leave the way of truth, righteousness, and sincerity, have not only missed *the* Way, but on account of their perversity they will never be able to find any way by which they can get back to Truth.

3064. *Cf.* above, xxv. 1. The reminiscent phrase shows that the first argument, about the Revelation and Prophethood, is completed, and we now pass on to the contrast, the fate of the rejecters of both.

3065. This phrase is usually symbolical of the Bliss in the Hereafter. If it were God's Plan, He could give his Messengers complete felicity and power in this life also. Instead of being persecuted, mocked, driven out of their homes, and having to exert their utmost powers of body, mind, and character to plant the flag of Truth in an unbelieving world, they could have lived in ease and security. But that would not have given the real lessons they came to teach struggling humanity by their example.

3066. Denying the Hour of Judgment means denying the power of Justice and Truth to triumph; it means asserting the dominion of Evil. But the Reality itself will punish them, as shown in the following verses.

12. When it sees them
From a place far off,
They will hear its fury
And its raging sigh.[3067]

١٢- إِذَا رَأَتْهُم مِّن مَّكَانٍۭ بَعِيدٍ
سَمِعُوا لَهَا تَغَيُّظًا وَزَفِيرًا ○

13. And when they are cast,
Bound together, into a
Constricted place therein, they
Will plead for destruction
There and then![3068]

١٣- وَإِذَآ أُلْقُوا مِنْهَا مَكَانًا ضَيِّقًا
مُّقَرَّنِينَ دَعَوْا هُنَالِكَ ثُبُورًا ○

14. "This day plead not
For a single destruction:
Plead for destruction oft-repeated!"

١٤- لَا تَدْعُوا الْيَوْمَ ثُبُورًا وَاحِدًا
وَادْعُوا ثُبُورًا كَثِيرًا ○

15. Say: "Is that best, or
The eternal Garden, promised[3069]
To the righteous? For them,
That is a reward as well
As a goal (of attainment).[3070]

١٥- قُلْ أَذَٰلِكَ خَيْرٌ أَمْ جَنَّةُ الْخُلْدِ
الَّتِي وُعِدَ الْمُتَّقُونَ ۚ كَانَتْ لَهُمْ جَزَآءً
وَمَصِيرًا ○

16. "For them there will be
Therein all that they wish for:
They will dwell (there) for aye:
A promise to be prayed for
From thy Lord."[3071]

١٦- لَهُمْ فِيهَا مَا يَشَآءُونَ خَٰلِدِينَ ۚ
كَانَ عَلَىٰ رَبِّكَ وَعْدًا مَّسْـُٔولًا ○

17. The Day He will gather
Them together as well as
Those whom they worship
Besides God, He will ask:[3072]

١٧- وَيَوْمَ يَحْشُرُهُمْ
وَمَا يَعْبُدُونَ مِن دُونِ اللَّهِ فَيَقُولُ

3067. For *zafīr*, a deep emission of breath or a sigh, see n. 1607 to xi. 106. Here the Fire is personified. It is raging with hunger and fury, and as soon as it sees them from ever so far, it emits a sigh of desire. Till then they had not realised their full danger. Now, just as their heart begins to tremble with terror, they are bound together—like with like,—and cast into the roaring flames!

3068. Anything—total annihilation—would be better than the anguish they will suffer. But no annihilation will be granted to them. One destruction will not be enough to wipe out the intensity of their anguish. They will have to ask for many destructions, but they will not get them!

3069. Shifting the scene back to this life, they may fairly be asked: "Here is the result of the two courses of conduct; which do you prefer?"

3070. To the righteous, the final Bliss will in one sense be a reward. But the word "reward" does not truly represent facts, for two reasons: (1) the Bliss will be greater than they deserved; and (2) righteousness is its own reward. The best way of expressing the result would be to say that their highest Wish will now have been attained; the goal will have been reached; they will be in God's Presence. That is salvation in the highest.

3071. That is the sort of thing—the Goal of God's Presence—to be prayed for from God, and not ephemeral things, even though they may be good. And that is the sort of thing that God has promised and undertaken to give.

3072. The question is as in a Court of Justice, to convince those who stand arraigned.

"Was it ye who led
These My servants astray,
Or did they stray
From the Path themselves?"

ءَاَنْتُمْ اَضْلَلْتُمْ عِبَادِيْ هٰٓؤُلَآءِ
اَمْ هُمْ ضَلُّوا السَّبِيْلَ ۝

18. They will say: "Glory to Thee!
Not meet was it for us
That we should take
For protectors others besides
Thee:[3073]
But Thou didst bestow,
On them and their fathers,
Good things (in life), until
They forgot the Message:
For they were a people
(Worthless and) lost."

١٨- قَالُوْا سُبْحٰنَكَ مَا كَانَ يَنْۢبَغِيْ لَنَآ
اَنْ نَّتَّخِذَ مِنْ دُوْنِكَ مِنْ اَوْلِيَآءَ
وَلٰكِنْ مَّتَّعْتَهُمْ وَاٰبَآءَهُمْ
حَتّٰى نَسُوا الذِّكْرَ ۚ
وَكَانُوْا قَوْمًۢا بُوْرًا ۝

19. (God will say): "Now
Have they proved you liars
In what ye say: so
Ye cannot avert (your penalty)[3074]
Nor (get) help." And whoever
Among you does wrong,
Him shall We cause to taste
Of a grievous Penalty.

١٩- فَقَدْ كَذَّبُوْكُمْ بِمَا تَقُوْلُوْنَ ۙ
فَمَا تَسْتَطِيْعُوْنَ صَرْفًا وَّلَا نَصْرًا ۚ
وَمَنْ يَّظْلِمْ مِّنْكُمْ
نُذِقْهُ عَذَابًا كَبِيْرًا ۝

20. And the apostles whom We
Sent before thee were all
(Men) who ate food
And walked through the streets:[3075]
We have made some of you
As a trial for others:[3076]
Will ye have patience?
18 For God is One Who
30 Sees (all things).

٢٠- وَمَآ اَرْسَلْنَا قَبْلَكَ مِنَ الْمُرْسَلِيْنَ
اِلَّآ اِنَّهُمْ لَيَاْكُلُوْنَ الطَّعَامَ وَيَمْشُوْنَ
فِي الْاَسْوَاقِ ۗ وَجَعَلْنَا بَعْضَكُمْ لِبَعْضٍ
فِتْنَةً ۗ اَتَصْبِرُوْنَ ۚ وَكَانَ رَبُّكَ بَصِيْرًا ۝ ع

3073. The creatures of God who were worshipped will prove that they never asked for worship: on the contrary they themselves worshipped God and sought the protection of God and of none but God. *Cf.* xlvi. 5-6. They will go further and show that the false worshippers added ingratitude to their other sins: for God bestowed abundance on them, and they blasphemed against God. They were indeed "worthless and lost", for the word *būr* bears both significations.

3074. The argument is as in a court of justice. If the false worshippers plead that they were misled by those whom they falsely worshipped, the latter will be confronted with them and will prove that plea to be false. No help can be got from them, and the penalty cannot then be averted. After all these things are thus explained in detail beforehand, all ungodly men should repent and turn to God. False worship is here indentified with sin, for sin is disobedience to God, and arises from a wrong appreciation of God's nature and His goodness to His creatures. The sinful man refuses, in his conduct, to serve God: he serves other things than God.

3075. *Cf.* above, xxv. 7.

3076. In God's universal Plan, each unit or thing serves a purpose. If some are rich, the poor should not envy them: it may be that the rich man's proximity is itself a trial of their virtue. If some are poor, the righteous rich should not despise or neglect them: it may be that their coming within their sight is a trial for the real feeling of charity or brotherly love in the rich. If *A* is bad-tempered or persecutes or ill-uses *B*, it may be an opportunity for *B* to show his patience or humility or his faith in the ultimate prevalence of justice and truth. Whatever our experiences with other human beings may be, we must make them subserve the ends of our spiritual improvement and perhaps theirs also.

C. 162.—Woe to the misbelievers who arrogantly
(xxv. 21-44.) Demand to see God, yet reject
His Signs! The Judgment will come,
And then they will see, too late, how evil
Casts nothing but treacherous snares for man.
Slowly comes God's Revelation, in ways
Most conducive to man's enlightenment.
Men in their folly reject the most obvious
Signs of God. Let them mock! Soon
Will they know! Alas! men ruled by self-impulse
Are worse than brute beasts to guide or control!

SECTION 3.

21. Such as fear not
The meeting with Us[3077]
(For Judgment) say:
"Why are not the angels
Sent down to us, or
(Why) do we not see[3078]
Our Lord?" Indeed they
Have an arrogant conceit
Of themselves, and mighty
Is the insolence of their impiety!

الجزء ١٩

٢١- وَقَالَ الَّذِينَ لَا يَرْجُونَ لِقَآءَنَا
لَوْلَآ أُنْزِلَ عَلَيْنَا الْمَلٰٓئِكَةُ
أَوْ نَرٰى رَبَّنَا ۗ
لَقَدِ اسْتَكْبَرُوْا فِيٓ أَنْفُسِهِمْ
وَعَتَوْ عُتُوًّا كَبِيْرًا ۝

22. The Day they see the angels,—
No joy will there be
To the sinners that Day:
The (angels) will say:
"There is a barrier
Forbidden (to you) altogether!"[3079]

٢٢- يَوْمَ يَرَوْنَ الْمَلٰٓئِكَةَ
لَا بُشْرٰى يَوْمَئِذٍ لِّلْمُجْرِمِيْنَ
وَيَقُوْلُوْنَ حِجْرًا مَّحْجُوْرًا ۝

23. And We shall turn
To whatever deeds they did
(In this life), and We shall
Make such deeds as floating dust
Scattered about.[3080]

٢٣- وَقَدِمْنَآ إِلٰى مَا عَمِلُوْا مِنْ عَمَلٍ
فَجَعَلْنٰهُ هَبَآءً مَّنْثُوْرًا ۝

3077. The blasphemers who have given up all Faith and laugh at the Hereafter: nothing is sacred to them: their arrogance and insolence are beyond all bounds.

3078. *Cf.* ii. 55. The Israelites in the time of Moses demanded to see God. But they were dazed with thunder and lightning even as they looked on. Indeed death would have been their fate, had it not been for the mercy of God.

3079. They will not be allowed to enjoy any of the felicity or peace which will be the normal state of the new world of Reality. Their own past will stand as a barrier to shut them off.

3080. The false hopes they built on in this life, and the deeds they did under the shadow of such false hopes will be dissipated as if they were dust flying about in the wind. They will have no value whatever.

24. The Companions of the Garden
Will be well, that Day,
In their abode, and have
The fairest of places for repose.[3081]

٢٤- أَصْحٰبُ الْجَنَّةِ يَوْمَئِذٍ خَيْرٌ مُّسْتَقَرًّا
وَّأَحْسَنُ مَقِيلًا ○

25. The Day the heaven shall be
Rent asunder with clouds,[3082]
And angels shall be sent down,
Descending (in ranks),—

٢٥- وَيَوْمَ تَشَقَّقُ السَّمَآءُ بِالْغَمٰمِ
وَنُزِّلَ الْمَلٰٓئِكَةُ تَنْزِيلًا ○

26. That Day, the dominion
As of right and truth,
Shall be (wholly) for (God)[3083]
Most Merciful: it will be
A Day of dire difficulty
For the Misbelievers.

٢٦- اَلْمُلْكُ يَوْمَئِذٍ
الْحَقُّ لِلرَّحْمٰنِ ؕ
وَكَانَ يَوْمًا عَلَى الْكٰفِرِينَ عَسِيرًا ○

27. The Day that the wrong-doer
Will bite at his hands,
He will say, "Oh! would that
I had taken a (straight) path
With the Apostle![3084]

٢٧- وَيَوْمَ يَعَضُّ الظَّالِمُ عَلٰى يَدَيْهِ
يَقُولُ يٰلَيْتَنِي اتَّخَذْتُ
مَعَ الرَّسُولِ سَبِيلًا ○

28. "Ah! woe is me!
Would that I had never
Taken such a one
For a friend!

٢٨- يٰوَيْلَتٰى لَيْتَنِي
لَمْ أَتَّخِذْ فُلَانًا خَلِيلًا ○

29. "He did lead me astray
From the Message (of God)
After it had come to me!
Ah! the Evil One is
But a traitor to man!"[3085]

٢٩- لَقَدْ أَضَلَّنِي عَنِ الذِّكْرِ بَعْدَ إِذْ
جَآءَنِي ؕ وَكَانَ الشَّيْطٰنُ لِلْإِنْسٰنِ
خَذُولًا ○

3081. The barrier which will shut out the evil ones will not exist for the righteous, who will have an abode of bliss and repose, for they will be in the Garden of God's Good Pleasure.

3082. It will be a new world, and the symbolism to describe it must necessarily draw upon our present experience of the finest things in nature. The sky, which now appears remote and unpeopled will be rent asunder. There will appear clouds of glory—angels and spiritual Lights of all grades and ranks (see Appendix VIII. p. 921),—and the true majesty and goodness of God will be visible as it should be in reality, and as it is not now, on account of "our muddy vesture of decay".

3083. See last note.

3084. The words are general, and for us the interest is in a general sense. A man who actually receives the Truth and is on the right path is all the more culpable if he is diverted from that path by the machinations of a worldly friend. The particular person whom some Commentators mention in this connection was one 'Uqba who received the light of Islam, but was misled afterwards by a worldly friend into apostasy and blasphemy. He came to an evil end afterwards.

3085. The seductive wiles of the Evil One are merely meant for snares. There is fraud and treachery in them. The deceived ones are left in the lurch after the way of escape is made impossible for them

Then the Apostle will say:
30 "O my Lord! Truly
My people took this Qur-ān
For just foolish nonsense."[3086]

٣٠- وَقَالَ الرَّسُوْلُ يٰرَبِّ إِنَّ
قَوْمِي اتَّخَذُوْا هٰذَا الْقُرْاٰنَ مَهْجُوْرًا ○

31. Thus have We made
For every prophet an enemy
Among the sinners: but enough
Is thy Lord to guide
And to help.[3087]

٣١- وَكَذٰلِكَ جَعَلْنَا لِكُلِّ نَبِيٍّ عَدُوًّا
مِّنَ الْمُجْرِمِيْنَ ۭ وَكَفٰى
بِرَبِّكَ هَادِيًا وَّنَصِيْرًا ○

32. Those who reject Faith
Say: "Why is not the Qur-ān
Revealed to him all at once?
Thus (is it revealed), that We
May strengthen thy heart[3088]
Thereby, and We have
Rehearsed it to thee in slow,
Well-arranged stages, gradually.

٣٢- وَقَالَ الَّذِيْنَ كَفَرُوْا
لَوْلَا نُزِّلَ عَلَيْهِ الْقُرْاٰنُ جُمْلَةً وَّاحِدَةً ۚ
كَذٰلِكَ ۚ لِنُثَبِّتَ بِهٖ فُؤَادَكَ ع
وَرَتَّلْنٰهُ تَرْتِيْلًا ○

33. And no question do they
Bring to thee but We
Reveal to thee the truth
And the best explanation
(thereof).[3089]

٣٣- وَلَا يَأْتُوْنَكَ بِمَثَلٍ
إِلَّا جِئْنٰكَ بِالْحَقِّ وَأَحْسَنَ تَفْسِيْرًا ○

3086. "*My people*" are of course the unbelieving Quraish. But they were only a handful of people whose vested interests were touched by the beneficent reforms initiated by Islam. They soon passed away, and all Arabic-speaking or Arabic-understanding people have considered the Qur-ān as a treasury of Truths expressed in the most beautiful possible language, with a meaning that grows deeper with research.

3087. It is the nature of sin to be hostile to truth and righteousness, but such hostility will not harm the righteous and need cause no misgiving, because God will guide and help those who work in His cause. And what could be better or more effective than His guidance and help?

3088. Three reasons are given for the gradual revelation of the Qur-ān. (1) "*To strengthen thy heart*": the tremendous task of winning the Arab nation, and, through them, the whole world, to Islam, required superhuman patience, constancy, and firmness, and these qualities were strengthened by the gradual promulgation of solutions to each difficulty as it arose. (2) "*Slow, well-arranged stages*": though the stages were gradual, as the occasion demanded from time to time, in the course of twenty-three years, the whole emerged, when completed, as a well-arranged scheme of spiritual instruction, as we have seen in following the arrangement of the Sūras. (3) *Questions put and answers given*: See next note.

3089. Divine knowledge is a fathomless ocean. But glimpses of it can be obtained by any individuals sincerely searching for the Truth. Their progress will be in grades. If they ask questions, and answers are then furnished to them, they are more likely to apprehend the Truth, as they have already explored the part of the territory in which they are interested. In the same way, when concrete questions arise by the logic of events, and they are answered not only for the occasion, but from a general stand-point, the teaching has a far greater chance of penetrating the human intelligence and taking shape in practical conduct. And this is the usual way of instruction in the Qur-ān.

34. Those who will be gathered
To Hell (prone) on their faces,—[3090]
They will be in an evil
Plight, and, as to Path,
Most astray.[3091]

٣٤- الَّذِينَ يُحْشَرُونَ عَلَىٰ وُجُوهِهِمْ إِلَىٰ
جَهَنَّمَ ۙ أُولَٰئِكَ شَرٌّ مَّكَانًا
وَأَضَلُّ سَبِيلًا ۝

SECTION 4.

35. (Before this,) We sent Moses
The Book, and appointed
His brother Aaron with him
As Minister;[3092]

٣٥- وَلَقَدْ آتَيْنَا مُوسَى الْكِتَٰبَ وَجَعَلْنَا
مَعَهُ أَخَاهُ هَٰرُونَ وَزِيرًا ۝

36. And We commanded: "Go ye
Both, to the people who
Have rejected our Signs:"
And those (people) We destroyed
With utter destruction.

٣٦- فَقُلْنَا اذْهَبَا إِلَى الْقَوْمِ
الَّذِينَ كَذَّبُوا بِآيَٰتِنَا ط
فَدَمَّرْنَٰهُمْ تَدْمِيرًا ۝

37. And the people of Noah,—
When they rejected the apostles,
We drowned them,
And We made them
As a Sign for mankind;[3093]
And We have prepared
For (all) wrong-doers
A grievous Penalty;—

٣٧- وَقَوْمَ نُوحٍ لَّمَّا كَذَّبُوا الرُّسُلَ
أَغْرَقْنَٰهُمْ وَجَعَلْنَٰهُمْ لِلنَّاسِ آيَةً ط
وَأَعْتَدْنَا لِلظَّٰلِمِينَ
عَذَابًا أَلِيمًا ۝

38. As also 'Ād and Thamūd,
And the Companions[3094]

٣٨- وَعَادًا وَثَمُودَا وَأَصْحَٰبَ

3090. That is, in ignominy.

3091. This verse may be compared and contrasted with xxv. 24 above. Here the argument is rounded off about the distinction between the Good and Evil in their final Destiny. The Good are to have "the fairest of places for repose", and in contrast, the Evil are, "as to Path, most astray" They have no repose, and their wanderings lead nowhere.

3092. *Cf.* xx. 29, and the whole passage there, which is merely referred to here, to show how previous apostles were treated, but how they stuck fast to the Criterion given, to distinguish between Good and Evil.

3093. The stories of Noah, of the prophets of 'Ād and Thamūd (and of other prophets), in the reactions of their communities to their teaching are told in xxvi. 105-159, below Here they are just mentioned to illustrate how little respect past ages had for their prophets and teachers of Truth. But God's Truth did not suffer: it was the blind rejecters of spiritual Truth who were wiped out.

3094. Commentators are not clear as to who the "*Companions of the Rass*" were. The root meaning of "*rass*" is an old well or shallow water-pit. Another root connects it with the burial of the dead. But it is probably the name of a town or place. The "Companions of the Rass" may well have been the people of Shu'aib, as they are here mentioned with the 'Ād, the Thamūd, and Lot's people, and the people of Shu'aib are mentioned in a similar connection in xxvi. 176-190 and in xi. 84-95. Shu'aib was the prophet of the Madyan people in the north-west of Arabia, where many old wells are found. There is however an oasis town *al-Rass* in the district of Qasīm in Middle Najd, about thirty-five miles south-west of the town of 'Unaiza, reputed to be the central point of the Arabian Peninsula, and situated midway between Mecca and Basra. See Doughty's *Arabia Deserta*, thin-paper one-volume edition, London 1926, II, 435, and Map, Lat. 26°N., and Long. 43°E.

Of the Rass, and many
A generation between them.

الرَّسِّ وَقُرُوْنًا بَيْنَ ذٰلِكَ كَثِيْرًا ○

39. To each one We set forth
Parables and examples;
And each one We broke
To utter annihilation
(For their sins).

٣٩- وَكُلًّا ضَرَبْنَا لَهُ الْاَمْثَالَ
وَكُلًّا تَبَّرْنَا تَتْبِيْرًا ○

40. And the (Unbelievers) must indeed
Have passed by the town
On which was rained[3095]
A shower of evil: did they not
Then see it (with their own
Eyes)? But they fear not
The Resurrection.

٤٠- وَلَقَدْ اَتَوْا عَلَى الْقَرْيَةِ الَّتِيْٓ
اُمْطِرَتْ مَطَرَ السَّوْءِ
اَفَلَمْ يَكُوْنُوْا يَرَوْنَهَا ۚ
بَلْ كَانُوْا لَا يَرْجُوْنَ نُشُوْرًا ○

41. When they see thee,
They treat thee no otherwise
Than in mockery: "Is this
The one whom God has sent
As an apostle?"

٤١- وَاِذَا رَاَوْكَ اِنْ يَّتَّخِذُوْنَكَ اِلَّا هُزُوًا
اَهٰذَا الَّذِيْ بَعَثَ اللّٰهُ رَسُوْلًا ○

42. "He indeed would well-nigh
Have misled us from
Our gods, had it not been
That we were constant
To them!"—Soon will they
Know, when they see
The Penalty, who it is
That is most misled
In Path![3096]

٤٢- اِنْ كَادَ لَيُضِلُّنَا عَنْ اٰلِهَتِنَا
لَوْلَآ اَنْ صَبَرْنَا عَلَيْهَا ۭ
وَسَوْفَ يَعْلَمُوْنَ حِيْنَ يَرَوْنَ الْعَذَابَ
مَنْ اَضَلُّ سَبِيْلًا ○

43. Seest thou such a one
As taketh for his god
His own passion (or impulse)?
Couldst thou be a disposer
Of affairs for him?[3097]

٤٣- اَرَءَيْتَ مَنِ اتَّخَذَ اِلٰهَهٗ هَوٰىهُ ۭ
اَفَاَنْتَ تَكُوْنُ عَلَيْهِ وَكِيْلًا ○

3095. This refers to Lūt's story and the destruction of Sodom and Gomorrah, the wicked cities of the plain near the Dead Sea, by a shower of brimstone. The site lies on the highway between Arabia and Syria. *Cf.* xv. 74, 76, and n. 1998.

3096. "*Path*" (*Sabīl*) is almost equivalent here to conduct, way of life.

3097. The man who worships his own passions or impulses or desires is the most hopeless to teach or lead or guide. If it were anything else the matter with him, the Teacher could argue with him. But Reason cannot prevail over blind passion. It is vain to hope that such a man could be led, until his mad desires are killed. No one could undertake any responsibility for him, for he obeys no law and follows no advice. He is worse than brute beasts, which may not understand, but at least follow the wholesome instincts implanted in them by God. The lawless man has killed his instincts and is unwilling to submit to guidance.

44. Or thinkest thou that most
Of them listen or understand?
They are only like cattle;—
Nay, they are worse astray
In Path.

٤٤- اَمْ تَحْسَبُ اَنَّ اَكْثَرَهُمْ يَسْمَعُوْنَ
اَوْ يَعْقِلُوْنَ ۭ اِنْ هُمْ اِلَّا كَالْاَنْعَامِ
بَلْ هُمْ اَضَلُّ سَبِيْلًا ۝ ع

C. 163.—But the Signs of God are everywhere
(xxv. 45-77.) In creation. The Sun and the Shadow,
The Day and the Night, the Wind and the Rain,—
All things in nature are symbols, and point
To the Law Divine, and the destiny, good
Or ill, of man. Will he not learn
And put his trust in Him, the Merciful?
His true servants ever adore him
In humility and fear of wrong, in faith
And just moderation in life, in respect
For duties owed to God and men
And self, in avoidance of all that is false
Or futile, in strict and grateful attention
To God's Message, and in the wish
To put themselves and their families
In the van of those who love and honour God.

SECTION 5.

45. Hast thou not turned[3098]
Thy vision to thy Lord?—
How He doth prolong[3099]
The Shadow! If He willed,
He could make it stationary!
Then do We make
The sun its guide;[3100]

٤٥- اَلَمْ تَرَ اِلٰى رَبِّكَ كَيْفَ مَدَّ الظِّلَّ ۚ
وَلَوْ شَاۗءَ لَجَعَلَهٗ سَاكِنًا ۚ
ثُمَّ جَعَلْنَا الشَّمْسَ عَلَيْهِ دَلِيْلًا ۝

3098. We saw in xxiv. 35 that God is the Light of the heavens and the earth, and we tried, in Appendix VIII, to catch a glimpse of the mystic meaning under the guidance of Imām Gazāli. We have now another sublime passage, in which we are asked to contemplate the Glory of God by a parable of the subtle play of Light and Shade in God's creation. Let us first understand the literal meaning as applied to the physical world, before attempting the spiritual interpretation, which takes us (if we are worthy) to the foot of the Throne of Glory.

3099. In our artificial life and surroundings we fail to see some of the finest mysteries of Light and Shade. We praise, and rightly, the wonderful colours of sunset. We see, particularly in climates more northerly than that of India, the subtle play of Light and Shade in the twilights succeeding sunsets. If we were as assiduous in seeing sunrises and the play of Light and Shade preceding them, we should see phenomena even more impressive, as the early morning seems to us more holy than any other time in the twenty-four hours of the sun's daily journey. There is first the false dawn, with its curious uncertain light and the curious long uncertain shadows which it casts. Then there are the streaks of black in the East, succeeded by the true dawn, with its delicate tones of colours and light and shade. The light of this true or false Dawn is not given by the direct rays of the sun. In a sense it is not light, but the shadows or reflections of light. And they gradually merge into actual sunrise, with its more substantial or more defined shadows, which we can definitely connect with the sun.

3100. The morning shadows are long but more definite, and their length and direction are seen to be guided by the sun. But they change insensibly every second or fraction of a second.

46. Then We draw it in[3101]
Towards Ourselves,—
A contraction by easy stages.[3102]

٤٦- ثُمَّ قَبَضْنٰهُ اِلَيْنَا قَبْضًا يَّسِيْرًا ○

47. And He it is Who makes
The Night as a Robe
For you, and Sleep as Repose,
And makes the Day
(As it were) a Resurrection.[3103]

٤٧- وَهُوَ الَّذِیْ جَعَلَ لَكُمُ الَّيْلَ لِبَاسًا
وَّالنَّوْمَ سُبَاتًا
وَّجَعَلَ النَّهَارَ نُشُوْرًا ○

48. And He it is Who sends
The Winds as heralds
Of glad tidings, going before[3104]
His Mercy, and We send down

٤٨- وَهُوَ الَّذِیْٓ اَرْسَلَ الرِّيٰحَ
بُشْرًاۢ بَيْنَ يَدَیْ رَحْمَتِهٖ ۚ وَاَنْزَلْنَا

3101. As the sun rises higher and higher, the shadows contract. In regions where the sun gets actually to the zenith at noon, there is no shadow left at that time. Where does it go to? It was but a shadow cast by a substance. and it gets absorbed by the substance which produced it. But all material substances are themselves but shadows (xvi. 48, and n. 1074), and the only true Reality is God, to Whom all things return. Thus are shadows absorbed in the self-subsisting Reality.

3102. Let us now reverently turn our vision (as far as we are able) to the symbolic meaning. God is the Light. All things in creation—whether concrete or abstract—are but shadows, depending on His Light. All shadows are not equal. He gives length or size of substance to such as He pleases. And some shadows almost become reflected lights, like the light of the false or the true Dawn. Such are holy men, in all kinds of gradations. The shadows are constantly in a state of flux; so are all things in Creation, all things we see or covet in this life. God, if He wills, can give some of them greater fixity or comparative stability. The sun is but a shadow of God's Light; yet it illuminates our whole world. So the great Prophet of the Age derives his light from God, and we can light our little spiritual candles from him. Or the Revelation is the sun's light, and we can light our life with it. As the light of the sun is identified with the sun, which is its living source, so is Revelation identified with the living Prophet through whom it comes.

3103. Here the symbolism presents a fresh point of view. It is still the contrast between Light and Shade; but the shade of Night is as a Robe to cover and screen us and give us Repose from activity; and the Light of Day is for striving, work, activity. Or again, the Night is like Death, our temporary Death before Judgment, the time during which our senses are as sealed in Sleep; and the Day is like the renewal of Life at the Resurrection.

3104. *Cf.* vii. 57. The Winds are heralds of Joy, ushering in Rain, which is one form of God's Mercy. Again, the symbolism presents a fresh point of view. Heat (which is connected with light) sets up currents in the atmosphere, besides sucking up moisture from the seas, and distributing it by means of Winds over wide surfaces of the earth. In the physical world we know the beneficent action of heat on life, and by contrast, we also know how intolerable high temperatures may become, and how the cloud-bearing Winds come as welcome heralds of rain. This is particularly true where there are marked contrasts of drought and rain as in India. The Monsoon winds and clouds are the Good Angels of Rain, as in Kalidas's "Megha-dūta". The symbolic meaning refers to God's Mercy, which to the ungodly may be as intolerable as extreme summer heat in the physical world, but which performs its beneficent mission of fostering care to all Creation. It may produce apparently unpleasant movements like Storms. But in reality they distribute God's Message, His greatest gift, among mankind, and are thus really heralds of joy to all who understand.

Pure water from the sky,—[3105]	مِنَ السَّمَاۤءِ مَاۤءً طَهُوۡرًا ۝
49. That with it We may give Life to a dead land, And slake the thirst Of things We have created,—[3106] Cattle and men in great numbers.	٤٩- لِّنُحۡیِۦَ بِهٖ بَلۡدَةً مَّیۡتًا وَّنُسۡقِیَهٗ مِمَّا خَلَقۡنَاۤ اَنۡعَامًا وَّاَنَاسِیَّ كَثِیۡرًا ۝
50. And We have distributed The (water) amongst them, in order[3107] That they may celebrate (Our) praises, but most men Are averse (to aught) but[3108] (Rank) ingratitude.	٥٠- وَلَقَدۡ صَرَّفۡنٰهُ بَیۡنَهُمۡ لِیَذَّكَّرُوۡا ۖ فَاَبٰۤی اَكۡثَرُ النَّاسِ اِلَّا كُفُوۡرًا ۝
51. Had it been Our Will, We could have sent A warner to every centre Of population.[3109]	٥١- وَلَوۡ شِئۡنَا لَبَعَثۡنَا فِیۡ كُلِّ قَرۡیَةٍ نَّذِیۡرًا ۝ ۖ
52. Therefore listen not To the Unbelievers, but strive	٥٢- فَلَا تُطِعِ الۡكٰفِرِیۡنَ وَجَاهِدۡهُمۡ

3105. Rain water (in pure air) is not only pure water distilled in air and sky, but it is the best purifying and sanitating agent on the largest scale known to us.

3106. The whole cycle of water,—sea, clouds, rain or hail or snow, rivers, and sea again,—is a remarkable illustration of the processes of nature making God's providence visible to us. The salts of the sea sanitate and purify all the filth that pours into it. Water action, in the form of rain, frost, glaciers, rivers, lakes, etc., is responsible for the building up and configuration of the crust of the earth, and is the chief agent in physical geography. A parched desert quickly comes to life under the action of water. All drinking water, whether derived from rivers, canals, lakes, reservoirs, springs, wells, or water-works of any kind, are ultimately traceable to rain. The connection of life with water is intimate. The physical basis of life itself, protoplasm, is in great part water: see xxv. 54 below.

3107. The water is distributed all over the world, in order that all life may receive its support according to its needs. In xxv. 48-50, we have the argument of contrasts stated in another way. Water is life, and is made available to sustain life all over the world: this is a physical fact which all can see. But water is also the symbol of spiritual life, whose sustaining principle is the Will of God as made known to us through Revelation. It sometimes comes to us in our inward or spiritual storms. Many violent unsettlements of the spirit are but heralds of the refreshing showers of spiritual understanding that come in their wake. They purify our souls, and produce spiritual Life even where there was a parched spiritual desert before. They continue to sustain us in our normal spiritual Life out of the reservoirs of God's Revelation, which are open to all, and well distributed in time and space. The universality of distribution is again referred to in the following verse.

3108. In contrast to God's abounding Mercy is man's base ingratitude: another symbolical contrast between Light and Darkness, or Water and Drought.

3109. God's Message has been distributed to all nations. If it had been necessary, a Prophet could have been sent to every town and village. But God's Plan is different. He has sent His Light to every heart, through His Signs in man's conscience, in Nature, and in Revelation.

Against them with the utmost Strenuousness, with the (Qur-ān).[3110]	بِهٖ جِهَادًا كَبِيرًا ۝
53. It is He Who has Let free the two bodies Of flowing water:[3111] One palatable and sweet, And the other salt And bitter; yet has He Made a barrier between them, A partition that is forbidden To be passed.[3112]	٥٣- وَهُوَ الَّذِي مَرَجَ الْبَحْرَيْنِ هٰذَا عَذْبٌ فُرَاتٌ وَّهٰذَا مِلْحٌ أُجَاجٌ ۚ وَجَعَلَ بَيْنَهُمَا بَرْزَخًا وَّحِجْرًا مَّحْجُورًا ۝
54. It is He Who has Created man from water:[3113] Then has He established Relationships of lineage[3114]	٥٤- وَهُوَ الَّذِي خَلَقَ مِنَ الْمَاءِ بَشَرًا فَجَعَلَهُ نَسَبًا

3110. The distribution of God's Signs being universal, the man of God pays no heed to carping critics who reject Faith. He wages the biggest Jihād of all, with the weapon of God's Revelation.

3111. *Maraja*: literally, let free or let loose cattle for grazing. *Baḥrain*: two seas, or two bodies of flowing water; for *baḥr* is applied both to the salt sea and to rivers. In the world taken as a whole, there are two bodies of water, *viz.*: (1) the great salt Ocean, and (2) the bodies of sweet water fed by rain, whether they are rivers, lakes, or underground springs: their source in rain makes them one, and their drainage, whether above-ground or underground, eventually to the Ocean, also makes them one. They are free to mingle, and in a sense they do mingle, for there is a regular water-cycle: see n. 3106 above: and the rivers flow constantly to the sea, and tidal rivers get sea-water for several miles up their estuaries at high tide. Yet in spite of all this, the laws of gravitation are like a barrier or partition set by God, by which the two bodies of water as a whole are always kept apart and distinct. In the case of rivers carrying large quantities of water to the sea, like the Mississippi or the Yangtse-Kiang, the river-water with its silt remains distinct from sea-water for a long distance out at sea. But the wonderful Sign is that the two bodies of water, though they pass through each other, remain distinct bodies, with their distinct functions.

3112. Again a new symbolic contrast; the two bodies of water, sweet and salt, free to intermingle, yet distinct as by an impassable barrier. Sweet water is the wholesome spiritual desires of man fed by the rain of God's Revelation; salt water is the bundle of worldly desires, ambitions, passions, and motives of man: the two may seem to mingle, yet they are always distinct, and there is an impassable barrier between them. The righteous judgment is the Criterion that distinguishes between them. Further, the two bodies of water, or the two seas, may mean the two kinds of knowledge, divine and human, as in the allegory in the story of Moses: see xviii. 60, and notes 2404 and 2405.

3113. The basis of all living matter in the physical world, protoplasm, is water: *Cf.* xxiv. 45 and xxi. 30, and notes thereon.

3114. Water is a fluid, unstable thing: yet from it arises the highest form of life known to us, in this world, man. And man has not only the functions and characteristics of the noblest animals, but his abstract relationships are also typical of his highest nature. He can trace lineage and pedigree, and thus remember and commemorate a long line of ancestors, to whom he is bound by ties of piety, which no mere animal can do. Further, there is the mystic union in marriage: it is not only like the physical union of animals, but it gives rise to relationships arising out of the sexes of individuals who were not otherwise related to each other. These are physical and social facts. But behind them, again, is the symbolical lesson of spiritual contrasts: as there is a long way to go between water and man, so there is a long way to go between an ordinary man and him who is lifted up to divine Light. As opposite sexes, though different in function, are one and contribute to each other's happiness, so persons of diverse talents may unite in the spiritual world for their own highest good and in the service of God.

And marriage: for thy Lord Has power (over all things).	وَّصِهْرًا ۗ وَكَانَ رَبُّكَ قَدِيْرًا ○
55. Yet do they worship, Besides God, things that can Neither profit them nor Harm them: and the Misbeliever Is a helper (of Evil), Against his own Lord![3115]	٥٥-وَيَعْبُدُوْنَ مِنْ دُوْنِ اللّٰهِ مَا لَا يَنْفَعُهُمْ وَلَا يَضُرُّهُمْ ۗ وَكَانَ الْكَافِرُ عَلٰى رَبِّهٖ ظَهِيْرًا ○
56. But thee We only sent To give glad tidings And admonition.	٥٦-وَمَآ اَرْسَلْنٰكَ اِلَّا مُبَشِّرًا وَّنَذِيْرًا ○
57. Say: "No reward do I Ask of you for it but this: That each one who will May take a (straight) Path To his Lord."	٥٧-قُلْ مَآ اَسْـَٔلُكُمْ عَلَيْهِ مِنْ اَجْرٍ اِلَّا مَنْ شَآءَ اَنْ يَّتَّخِذَ اِلٰى رَبِّهٖ سَبِيْلًا ○
58. And put thy trust In Him Who lives And dies not; and celebrate His praise; and enough is He To be acquainted with The faults of His servants;—[3116]	٥٨-وَتَوَكَّلْ عَلَى الْحَيِّ الَّذِيْ لَا يَمُوْتُ وَسَبِّحْ بِحَمْدِهٖ ۗ وَكَفٰى بِهٖ بِذُنُوْبِ عِبَادِهٖ خَبِيْرًا ○ ع
59. He Who created the heavens And the earth and all That is between, in six days,[3117] And is firmly established On the Throne (of authority):[3118] God Most Gracious: Ask thou, then, about Him Of any acquainted (with such things).[3119]	٥٩-الَّذِيْ خَلَقَ السَّمٰوٰتِ وَالْاَرْضَ وَمَا بَيْنَهُمَا فِيْ سِتَّةِ اَيَّامٍ ثُمَّ اسْتَوٰى عَلَى الْعَرْشِ ۚ اَلرَّحْمٰنُ فَسْـَٔلْ بِهٖ خَبِيْرًا ○

3115. Here is the highest contrast of all.—material things which are inert, and God, Whose goodness and power are supreme; Faith and Unfaith, meriting glad tidings and admonition; the selfish man who is self-centred, and the man of God, who works for others without reward.

3116. God knows our faults better than we or anyone else. It is no use hiding anything from Him. We must put our trust completely in Him. His care is for all, and He is God Most Gracious.

3117. *Cf.* vii. 54 and n. 1031.

3118. See n. 1386 to x. 3.

3119. The argument is about the question, in whom shall we put our trust? Worldly men put their trust in worldly things: the righteous man only in God. The true distinction will be quite clear from a ray of divine knowledge. If you do not see it all clearly, ask of those who possess such knowledge.

60. When it is said to them,
"Adore ye (God) Most Gracious!",
They say, "And what is (God)
Most Gracious? Shall we adore
That which thou commandest us?"
And it increases their flight
(From the Truth).[3120]

٦٠- وَإِذَا قِيلَ لَهُمُ اسْجُدُوا لِلرَّحْمٰنِ
قَالُوا وَمَا الرَّحْمٰنُ
أَنَسْجُدُ لِمَا تَأْمُرُنَا
وَزَادَهُمْ نُفُورًا ۩

SECTION 6

61. Blessed is He Who made
Constellations in the skies,
And placed therein a Lamp[3121]
And a Moon giving light;

٦١- تَبٰرَكَ الَّذِي جَعَلَ فِي السَّمَاءِ بُرُوجًا
وَّجَعَلَ فِيهَا سِرٰجًا وَّقَمَرًا مُّنِيرًا

62. And it is He Who made
The Night and the Day
To follow each other:
For such as have the will[3122]
To celebrate His praises
Or to show their gratitude.

٦٢- وَهُوَ الَّذِي جَعَلَ الَّيْلَ وَالنَّهَارَ خِلْفَةً
لِّمَنْ أَرَادَ أَنْ يَّذَّكَّرَ
أَوْ أَرَادَ شُكُورًا

63. And the servants of (God)
Most Gracious are those
Who walk on the earth
In humility, and when the
ignorant[3123]
Address them, they say,
"Peace!";

٦٣- وَعِبَادُ الرَّحْمٰنِ الَّذِينَ
يَمْشُونَ عَلَى الْأَرْضِ هَوْنًا
وَّإِذَا خَاطَبَهُمُ الْجٰهِلُونَ
قَالُوا سَلٰمًا

3120. Those who have no spiritual Light cannot understand this precept about putting all our trust in God. It seems to them foolish. They have no faith, or but a superficial faith. They may possibly take the name of God on their lips, but they cannot understand the full significance of His title of *Raḥmān* (Most Gracious). Perhaps they are afraid on account of their sins; perhaps they do not see how unbounded is the mercy of God. Such men are contrasted against the true servants of God, who are described below in xxv. 63-75.

3121. The glorious Lamp of the skies is the Sun; and next to him is the Moon, which gives borrowed light. The Constellations of course include the Signs of the Zodiac, which mark the path of the planets in the heavens.

3122. The scenes of the phenomenal world are Signs of the Self-Revelation of God, for those who understand and who have the will to merge their wills in His. This they do (1) by praising Him, which means understanding something of His nature, and (2) by gratitude to Him, which means carrying out His Will, and doing good to their fellow-creatures. These two attitudes of mind and heart give rise to various consequences in their lives, which are detailed in the following verses.

3123. *Ignorant*: in a spiritual sense. *Address*: in the aggressive sense. Their humility is shown in two ways: (1) to those in real search of knowledge, they give such knowledge as they have and as the recipients can assimilate; (2) to those who merely dispute, they do not speak harshly, but say "Peace!", as much as to say, "May it be well with you, may you repent and be better"; or "May God give me peace from such wrangling"; or "Peace, and Good-bye; let me leave you!"

64. Those who spend the night
In adoration of their Lord
Prostrate and standing ;[3124]

٦٤- وَالَّذِينَ يَبِيتُونَ لِرَبِّهِمْ سُجَّدًا وَّ
قِيَامًا ○

65. Those who say, "Our Lord!
Avert from us the Wrath
Of Hell, for its Wrath
Is indeed an affliction
grievous,—[3125]

٦٥- وَالَّذِينَ يَقُولُونَ رَبَّنَا
اصْرِفْ عَنَّا عَذَابَ جَهَنَّمَ ۖ
إِنَّ عَذَابَهَا كَانَ غَرَامًا ○

66. "Evil indeed is it
As an abode, and as
A place to rest in";[3126]

٦٦- إِنَّهَا سَاءَتْ مُسْتَقَرًّا وَّمُقَامًا ○

67. Those who, when they spend,
Are not extravagant and not
Niggardly, but hold a just (balance)
Between those (extremes);[3127]

٦٧- وَالَّذِينَ إِذَا أَنْفَقُوا لَمْ يُسْرِفُوا وَلَمْ
يَقْتُرُوا وَكَانَ بَيْنَ ذٰلِكَ قَوَامًا ○

68. Those who invoke not,
With God, any other god,
Nor slay such life as God
Has made sacred, except
For just cause, nor commit[3128]
Fornication;—and any that does
This (not only) meets punishment

٦٨- وَالَّذِينَ لَا يَدْعُونَ مَعَ اللّٰهِ إِلٰهًا اٰخَرَ
وَلَا يَقْتُلُونَ النَّفْسَ الَّتِي حَرَّمَ اللّٰهُ إِلَّا
بِالْحَقِّ وَلَا يَزْنُونَ ۚ
وَمَنْ يَّفْعَلْ ذٰلِكَ يَلْقَ أَثَامًا ○

3124. Humble prayer brings them nearer to God.

3125. This is a prayer of humility: such a person relies, not on any good works which he may have done, but on the Grace and Mercy of God; and he shows a lively sense of the Day of Judgment, when every action will weigh for or against a soul.

3126. The misery which results from sin is not only grievous to live in ("an abode") but also grievous "to rest in" or "to stand in", if it be only for a short time.

3127. In ordinary spending this is a wise rule. But even in charity, in which we give of our best, it is not expected that we should be extravagant, *i.e.*, that we should either do it for show, to impress other people, or do it thoughtlessly, which would be the case if we "rob Peter to pay Paul". We should certainly not be niggardly, but we should remember everyone's rights, including our own, and strike a perfectly just balance between them.

3128. Here three things are expressly condemned: (1) false worship, which is a crime against God; (2) the taking of life, which is a crime against our fellow-creatures; and (3) fornication, which is a crime against our self-respect, against ourselves. Every crime is against God, His creatures, and ourselves, but some may be viewed more in relation to one than to another. The prohibition against taking life is qualified: "except for just cause": *e.g.*, in judicial punishment for murder, or in self-preservation, which may include not only self-defence in the legal sense, but also the clearing out of pests, and the provision of meat under conditions of *Ḥalāl*: see n. 698 to v. 5. After this comes a long parenthesis, which ends with verse 71 below.

69. (But) the Penalty on the Day
Of Judgment will be doubled
To him, and he will dwell
Therein in ignominy,—[3129]

٦٩- يُضٰعَفْ لَهُ الْعَذَابُ يَوْمَ الْقِيٰمَةِ
وَيَخْلُدْ فِيهِ مُهَانًا ○

70. Unless he repents, believes,
And works righteous deeds,
For God will change
The evil of such persons
Into good, and God is
Oft-Forgiving, Most Merciful,[3130]

٧٠- إِلَّا مَنْ تَابَ وَاٰمَنَ وَعَمِلَ عَمَلًا
صَالِحًا فَأُولٰٓئِكَ يُبَدِّلُ اللّٰهُ سَيِّاٰتِهِمْ
حَسَنٰتٍ ۗ وَكَانَ اللّٰهُ غَفُورًا رَّحِيمًا ○

71. And whoever repents and does good
Has truly turned to God
With an (acceptable) conversion;—

٧١- وَمَنْ تَابَ وَعَمِلَ صَالِحًا
فَإِنَّهُ يَتُوبُ إِلَى اللّٰهِ مَتَابًا ○

72. Those who witness no falsehood,[3131]
And, if they pass by futility,[3132]
They pass by it
With honourable (avoidance);

٧٢- وَالَّذِينَ لَا يَشْهَدُونَ الزُّورَ ۙ
وَإِذَا مَرُّوا بِاللَّغْوِ مَرُّوا كِرَامًا ○

73. Those who, when they are
Admonished with the Signs
Of their Lord, droop not down[3133]
At them as if they were
Deaf or blind;

٧٣- وَالَّذِينَ إِذَا ذُكِّرُوا بِاٰيٰتِ رَبِّهِمْ
لَمْ يَخِرُّوا عَلَيْهَا صُمًّا وَّعُمْيَانًا ○

74. And theso who pray,
"Our Lord! Grant unto us
Wives and offspring who will be
The comfort of our eyes,[3134]

٧٤- وَالَّذِينَ يَقُولُونَ رَبَّنَا هَبْ لَنَا
مِنْ أَزْوَاجِنَا وَذُرِّيّٰتِنَا قُرَّةَ أَعْيُنٍ

3129. The three crimes just mentioned are specially detestable and infamous, and as ignominy will be added to other punishments, the penalty will be double that of ordinary punishment.

3130. But even in the case of great crimes, if there is true repentance as tested by a changed life in conduct, God's Mercy is available, and it will transform the repentant's nature from evil to good.

3131. *Witness no falsehood* has two significations, both implied in this passage: (1) those who give no evidence that is false; and (2) those who do not assist at anything which implies fraud or falsehood.

3132. There is not only condemnation of positive falsehood or of being mixed up with things implying falsehood; but futilities—vain random talk, unedifying jokes, useless show, etc.—are all condemned. If a good man finds himself in such an affair, he must withdraw from it in an honourable, dignified way, not in a fussy arrogant way.

3133. *Kharra* may mean: to fall down, to snore, to droop down as if the person were bored or inattentive, or did not wish to see or hear or pay attention.

3134. We must also pray for the maintenance of God's Law after us, through our wives and descendants: in our eyes they should not be mere accidents or play-things, but a real comfort and fulfilment of our spiritual longings. Perhaps, through them, as well through ourselves, we may, by God's grace, be able to give a lead for truth and righteousness.

And give us (the grace)
To lead the righteous."[3135]

وَّ اجْعَلْنَا لِلْمُتَّقِيْنَ اِمَامًا ۝

75. Those are the ones who
Will be rewarded with
The highest place in heaven,
Because of their patient constancy:
Therein shall they be met
With salutations and peace,

٧٥- اُولٰٓئِكَ يُجْزَوْنَ
الْغُرْفَةَ بِمَا صَبَرُوْا
وَيُلَقَّوْنَ فِيْهَا تَحِيَّةً وَّسَلٰمًا ۝

76. Dwelling therein;—how beautiful
An abode and place of rest!

٧٦- خٰلِدِيْنَ فِيْهَا ۭ حَسُنَتْ مُسْتَقَرًّا وَّمُقَامًا ۝

77. Say (to the Rejecters):
"My Lord is not uneasy
Because of you if ye call not on
Him:[3136]
But ye have indeed rejected
(Him), and soon will come
The inevitable (punishment)!"

٧٧- قُلْ مَا يَعْبَؤُا بِكُمْ رَبِّيْ
لَوْلَا دُعَاۗؤُكُمْ ۚ
فَقَدْ كَذَّبْتُمْ فَسَوْفَ يَكُوْنُ لِزَامًا ۝

3135. Let us recapitulate the virtues of the true servants of God: (1) they are humble and forbearing to those below them in spiritual worth; (2) they are constantly, by adoration, in touch with God; (3) they always remember the Judgment in the Hereafter; (4) they are moderate in all things; (5) they avoid treason to God, to their fellow-creatures, and to themselves; (6) they give a wide berth not only to falsehood but to futility; (7) they pay attention, both in mind and manner, to the Signs of their Lord; (8) their ambition is to bring up their families in righteousness and to lead in all good. A fine code of individual and social ethics, a ladder of spiritual development, open to all.

3136. Let not the wicked think that it causes God any annoyance or uneasiness if they do not serve or worship Him. He is high above all needs. But He turns in His Mercy to all who call on Him For those who arrogantly reject Him, the spiritual consequences (the Hell of spiritual misery and degradation) are inevitable, and must soon come to pass.

INTRODUCTION TO SŪRA XXVI (*Shu'arāa*).

This Sūra begins a new series of four Sūras (xxvi-xxix), which illustrate the contrast between the spirit of Prophecy and spiritual Light and the reactions to it in the communities among whom it appeared, by going back to old Prophets and the stories of the Past, as explained in the Introduction to S. xvii.

In this particular Sūra we have the story of Moses in his fight with Pharaoh and of Pharaoh's discomfiture. Other Prophets mentioned are Abraham, Noah, Hūd, Ṣāliḥ, Lūṭ, and Shu'aib. The lesson is drawn that the Qur ān is a continuation and fulfilment of previous Revelations, and is pure Truth, unlike the poetry of vain poets.

Chronologically the Sūra belongs to the middle Meccan period, when the contact of the Light of Prophecy with the milieu of Pagan Mecca was testing the Meccans in their most arrogant mood.

Summary.—The conflict of Unbelief with Truth is vain: so was the conflict of Pharaoh with Moses: Pharaoh's magicians bowed to the Truth, and Pharaoh and his hosts were drowned (xxvi. 1-69, and C. 164).

Nor did Abraham's people gain anything by their resisting the Truth he preached, and Noah's people perished by their Unbelief (xxvi. 70-122, and C. 165).

Hūd warned his people against reliance on their material strength, and Sālih against sacrilege, but in both cases the evil ones were brought low (xxvi. 123-159, and C. 166).

Lūṭ had to deal with unspeakable crimes, and Shu'aib against dishonest dealings and mischief; their teaching was rejected, but the rejecters were wiped out (xxvi. 160-191, and C. 167).

So, when the spirit of Prophecy came to Mecca, it was resisted by the votaries of Evil: but Truth is not like vain poetry, and must triumph at last (xxvi. 192-277, and C. 168).

C. 164.—God's Plan works unceasingly: His Light
(xxvi. 1-69.) Shines none the less brightly, because some
Reject it or mock at it. Moses was freed
From all fear when God gave him His Signs
And sent him to Pharaoh: he boldly
Proclaimed the Message, and won the wise ones
Of Egypt: the rejecters, with Pharaoh, perished,
And their heritage passed to worthier hands.

Sūra XXVI.

Shu'arāa, or The Poets.

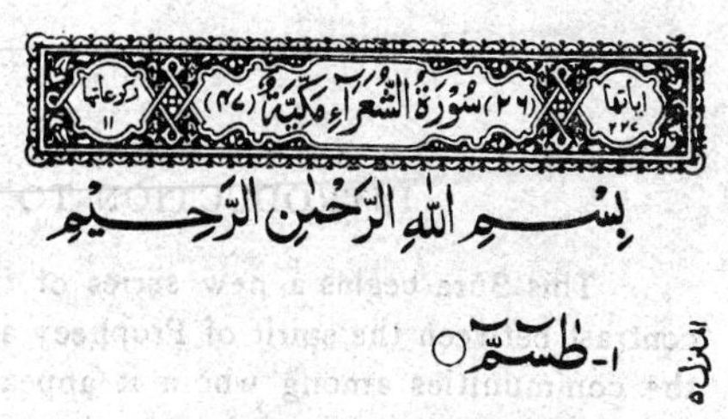

In the name of God, Most Gracious,
Most Merciful.

بِسْمِ اللّٰهِ الرَّحْمٰنِ الرَّحِيْمِ

1. *Ṭā. Sīn. Mīm.*[3137]

١- طٰسٓمٓ ○

2. These are Verses of the Book
That makes (things) clear.[3138]

٢- تِلْكَ اٰيٰتُ الْكِتٰبِ الْمُبِيْنِ ○

3. It may be thou frettest
Thy soul with grief, that they[3139]
Do not become Believers.

٣- لَعَلَّكَ بَاخِعٌ نَّفْسَكَ
اَلَّا يَكُوْنُوْا مُؤْمِنِيْنَ ○

4. If (such) were Our Will,[3140]
We could send down to them
From the sky a Sign,
To which they would bend
Their necks in humility.

٤- اِنْ نَّشَاْ نُنَزِّلْ عَلَيْهِمْ مِّنَ السَّمَآءِ اٰيَةً
فَظَلَّتْ اَعْنَاقُهُمْ لَهَا خٰضِعِيْنَ ○

5. But there comes not
To them a newly-revealed
Message from (God) Most Gracious,
But they turn away therefrom.

٥- وَمَا يَاْتِيْهِمْ مِّنْ ذِكْرٍ مِّنَ الرَّحْمٰنِ
مُحْدَثٍ اِلَّا كَانُوْا عَنْهُ مُعْرِضِيْنَ ○

3137. This is a combination of three Abbreviated Letters, as to which, generally, see Appendix I, printed at the end of S. ii. This particular combination occurs here and at the head of S. xxviii, while the intervening Sūra xxvii has it in the syncopated form *Ṭā. Sīn.* None of the explanatory conjectures which I have seen carries conviction to me. If the letters stand for *Ṭur-i-Sīnīn* (Mount Sinai) and *Mūsā* (Moses), whose story fills a large part of this Sūra, why is the letter *Mīm* omitted in S. xxvii, where the same meaning would apply? There is, however, one fact to which I should like to draw attention. There are eleven sections in this Sūra, and eight of them end with the word *Raḥīm* (with the final *Mīm*). The three exceptions are sections 2 and 3, and section 11. But sections 2 and 3 are part of the story of Moses, which is completed in section 4, and that ends with "*Raḥīm*". The main argument in section 11 ends at verse 217, which ends with *Raḥīm*. We can say that the whole Sūra is based on a refrain ending in the word "*Raḥīm*". Whether this has any bearing on our present enquiry I cannot say. My own position is that where we have material, we should pursue our researches, but we should never be dogmatic in such matters, as some Mysteries can never be solved by mere research.

3138. *Cf.* v. 17, and n. 716. The comparison of God's revelation with Light is continued.

3139. "They" are the Pagans of Mecca. From a human point of view it was a great disappointment to God's Apostle in the middle period of his Meccan ministry that the Meccans could not be brought to believe in the Truth.

3140. If it had been God's Will and Plan to force people's will, He could quite easily have forced the Meccans. But His Will and Plan work differently. His revelation is meant to train man's own will so that it conforms to God's beneficent purpose.

6. They have indeed rejected
(The Message): so they will
Know soon (enough) the truth
Of what they mocked at![3141]

٦- فَقَدْ كَذَّبُوا
فَسَيَأْتِيهِمْ أَنْبٰٓؤُا مَا كَانُوا بِهٖ يَسْتَهْزِءُوْنَ ○

7. Do they not look
At the earth,—how many
Noble things of all kinds
We have produced therein?[3142]

٧- أَوَلَمْ يَرَوْا إِلَى الْأَرْضِ
كَمْ أَنْبَتْنَا فِيهَا مِنْ كُلِّ زَوْجٍ كَرِيمٍ ○

8. Verily, in this is a Sign:
But most of them
Do not believe.

٨- إِنَّ فِي ذٰلِكَ لَاٰيَةً ط
وَمَا كَانَ أَكْثَرُهُمْ مُّؤْمِنِينَ ○

9. And verily, thy Lord
Is He, the Exalted in Might,[3143]
Most Merciful.

٩- وَإِنَّ رَبَّكَ
لَهُوَ الْعَزِيزُ الرَّحِيمُ ع ○

SECTION 2.

10. Behold, thy Lord called[3144]
Moses: "Go to the people
Of iniquity,—

١٠- وَإِذْ نَادٰى رَبُّكَ مُوسٰٓى
أَنِ ائْتِ الْقَوْمَ الظّٰلِمِينَ ○

11. "The people of Pharaoh:
Will they not fear God?"

١١- قَوْمَ فِرْعَوْنَ ط أَلَا يَتَّقُونَ ○

12. He said: "O my Lord!
I do fear that they
Will charge me with falsehood:

١٢- قَالَ رَبِّ
إِنِّيٓ أَخَافُ أَنْ يُّكَذِّبُونِ ○

3141. They may laugh at God's Message of righteousness. but they will soon see the power of Truth and realise the real significance of the movement which they opposed. Where were the Pagans of Mecca after Badr, and still more. after the bloodless surrender of Mecca? And the meaning may be applied universally in all history.

3142. If evil has a little run in this life, let them not run away with the notion that the world is for evil. They have only to look round at the physical and moral world around them, and they would be undeceived. But they are blind and without the Faith (the Light) which would open their eyes.

3143. One Who is able to carry out all His Will and Plans. See n. 2818 to xxii. 40.

3144. The part of the story of Moses told here is how Moses felt diffident about undertaking his commission; how God reassured him; how he went to Pharaoh with "the Signs"; how Pharaoh and his people rejected him; how their blasphemy recoiled on themselves, but the cause of God triumphed; in other words the point here is the reaction of a wicked people to the Light that was held up to them, considered in its relation to the mind of God's Messenger.

13. " My breast will be straitened.[3145]
And my speech may not go
(Smoothly): so send unto Aaron.

١٣- وَيَضِيقُ صَدْرِى وَلَا يَنطَلِقُ لِسَانِى
فَأَرْسِلْ إِلَىٰ هَٰرُونَ ۝

14. " And (further), they have
A charge of crime against me;[3146]
And I fear they may
Slay me."

١٤- وَلَهُمْ عَلَىَّ ذَنۢبٌ
فَأَخَافُ أَن يَقْتُلُونِ ۝

15. God said: " By no means!
Proceed then, both of you,
With Our Signs; We
Are with you, and will
Listen (to your call).

١٥- قَالَ كَلَّا ۖ فَٱذْهَبَا بِـَٔايَٰتِنَآ
إِنَّا مَعَكُم مُّسْتَمِعُونَ ۝

16. " So go forth, both of you,
To Pharaoh, and say:
'We have been sent
By the Lord and Cherisher
Of the Worlds;

١٦- فَأْتِيَا فِرْعَوْنَ فَقُولَآ
إِنَّا رَسُولُ رَبِّ ٱلْعَٰلَمِينَ ۝

17. " 'Send thou with us
The Children of Israel.' "

١٧- أَنْ أَرْسِلْ مَعَنَا بَنِىٓ إِسْرَٰٓءِيلَ ۝

18. (Pharaoh) said: " Did we not[3147]
Cherish thee as a child
Among us, and didst thou not
Stay in our midst
Many years of thy life?

١٨- قَالَ أَلَمْ نُرَبِّكَ فِينَا وَلِيدًا
وَلَبِثْتَ فِينَا مِنْ عُمُرِكَ سِنِينَ ۝

3145. As we should say in English, " My heart would fail me, and my tongue cleave to my mouth." Moses had an impediment in his speech, and his mission was risky: see next note. But God's Plan works in wondrous ways. Aaron was given to assist him in his mission, and Moses's shortcomings were transformed by God's grace into power, so that he became the most powerful leader of Israel.

3146. Moses was brought up in the palace of Pharaoh, as narrated in his personal story in **xx. 39-40** and n. 2563. When he was grown-up he saw an Egyptian smiting an Israelite, and as the Israelites were being generally oppressed by the Egyptians, Moses's anger was roused, and he slew the Egyptian. He then fled to the Midianite country in the Sinai peninsula, where he received the divine commission. But the charge of slaying the Egyptian was hanging against him. He was also apparently quick-tempered. But God's grace cured his temper and he became wise; his impediment in speech, for he stood up boldly to speak to Pharaoh; and his fear, for he dared the Egyptians with God's Signs, and they were afraid of him.

3147. There is here a little play of wit on the part of Pharaoh. When Moses speaks of the "Lord and Cherisher of the Worlds", Pharaoh says: " Who cherished you? Did we not bring you up as a child? Did you not grow up among us?" By implication Pharaoh suggests that he is the cherisher of Moses, and in any case Pharaoh laid claim to godhead himself.

19. "And thou didst a deed
Of thine which (thou knowest)[3148]
Thou didst, and thou art
An ungrateful (wretch)!"

١٩- وَفَعَلْتَ فَعْلَتَكَ الَّتِي فَعَلْتَ
وَأَنْتَ مِنَ الْكٰفِرِينَ ۝

20. Moses said: "I did it
Then, when I was
In error.[3149]

٢٠- قَالَ فَعَلْتُهَا
إِذًا وَّأَنَا مِنَ الضَّآلِّينَ ۝

21. "So I fled from you (all)
When I feared you;[3150]
But my Lord has (since)
Invested me with judgment
(And wisdom) and appointed me
As one of the apostles.

٢١- فَفَرَرْتُ مِنْكُمْ لَمَّا خِفْتُكُمْ
فَوَهَبَ لِي رَبِّي حُكْمًا
وَّجَعَلَنِي مِنَ الْمُرْسَلِينَ ۝

22. "And this is the favour[3151]
With which thou dost
Reproach me,—that thou
Hast enslaved the Children
Of Israel!"

٢٢- وَتِلْكَ نِعْمَةٌ تَمُنُّهَا عَلَيَّ
أَنْ عَبَّدْتَّ بَنِي إِسْرَآءِيلَ ۝

23. Pharaoh said: "And what
Is the 'Lord and Cherisher
Of the Worlds'?"[3152]

٢٣- قَالَ فِرْعَوْنُ وَمَا رَبُّ الْعٰلَمِينَ ۝

3148. Further, Pharaoh reminds Moses of his having slain the Egyptian, and taunts him: "You are not only a murderer: you are an ungrateful wretch" (using *kāfir* again in a double sense) "to have killed one of the race that brought you up!"

3149. What is Moses's reply? He is no longer afraid. He tells the whole truth, extenuating nothing in his own favour. "Yes I did it: but I did it under an error." There are three implications in this: "(1) I was wrong in doing it in a temper and in being hasty; (2) I was wrong in taking the law into my own hands, but I repented, and asked for God's pardon (xxviii. 15-16); (3) that was at a time when I was under your influence, but since then I am a changed man, as God has called me."

3150. He accounts for all his movements, much more than Pharaoh had asked for. He has nothing to hide. At that time he was under the influence of fear, and he had fled from him. Now he is serving God, the Lord of the Worlds. He has no fear: he is an apostle.

3151. Pharaoh had called Moses ungrateful and reproached him with all the favours which Moses had received from the Egyptians. "What favours?" he says; "Do you count it also as a favour to me that you have enslaved my brethren the Children of Israel?" Moses was now speaking as a man of God, not as an individual. Any individual favours he may have received were blotted out by the oppression of his people.

3152. Moses having eliminated all personalities, the argument now comes up to the highest plane of all,—the nature of God and His mercies. Moses had put forward this before, as implied in verse 16 above, but Pharaoh had twisted it into personalities. Now we come back to the real issue. It may have been in the same sitting, or it may have been in a later sitting.

24. (Moses) said: "The Lord
And Cherisher of the heavens
And the earth, and all between,—
If ye want to be
Quite sure."

٢٤- قَالَ رَبُّ السَّمٰوٰتِ وَالْأَرْضِ وَمَا
بَيْنَهُمَا ۖ
إِنْ كُنْتُمْ مُوقِنِينَ ○

25. (Pharaoh) said to those
Around: "Do ye not listen
(To what he says)?"[3153]

٢٥- قَالَ لِمَنْ حَوْلَهُ أَلَا تَسْتَمِعُونَ ○

26. (Moses) said: "Your Lord
And the Lord of your fathers
From the beginning!"

٢٦- قَالَ رَبُّكُمْ وَرَبُّ آبَائِكُمُ الْأَوَّلِينَ ○

27. (Pharaoh) said: "Truly
Your apostle who has been
Sent to you is
A veritable madman!"[3154]

٢٧- قَالَ إِنَّ رَسُولَكُمُ الَّذِي
أُرْسِلَ إِلَيْكُمْ لَمَجْنُونٌ ○

28. (Moses) said: "Lord of the East
And the West, and all between!
If ye only had sense!"

٢٨- قَالَ رَبُّ الْمَشْرِقِ وَالْمَغْرِبِ وَمَا
بَيْنَهُمَا ۖ إِنْ كُنْتُمْ تَعْقِلُونَ ○

29. (Pharaoh) said: "If thou
Dost put forward any god
Other than me, I will
Certainly put thee in prison!"[3155]

٢٩- قَالَ لَئِنِ اتَّخَذْتَ إِلٰهًا غَيْرِي
لَأَجْعَلَنَّكَ مِنَ الْمَسْجُونِينَ ○

30. (Moses) said: "Even if I
Showed you something
Clear (and) convincing?"[3156]

٣٠- قَالَ أَوَلَوْ جِئْتُكَ بِشَيْءٍ مُبِينٍ ○

3153. Moses had stirred up the wrath of Pharaoh both by putting forward the name of the One True God as against Pharaoh's pretended godhead, and by suggesting that any man of judgment would understand God's majesty. While Pharaoh turns to his people in indignation, Moses drives the nail in further: "He is the God of the heavens and the earth and all between: therefore He is also *your* God, and the God of your fathers from the beginning. Any other pretensions are false!"

3154. Pharaoh is further perturbed. In reply to Moses's statement that the One True God is also the God of the Egyptians and of Pharaoh also, Pharaoh says sarcastically to his Court: "Look at this 'apostle' of yours; he seems to be mad!" But Moses is not abashed. He boldly says what is the truth: "It is you who are mad! The God Whom I preach is the universal Lord,—of the East and of the West. He reigns wherever you go!"

3155. Now we come to the crisis. Pharaoh threatens Moses with prison for treason. Moses remains calm and still argues: "What if I show you a miracle? Will it convince you that I am not mad, and that I have behind me the Lord of all the Worlds?"

3156. The Egyptians were addicted to magic and sorcery, which was mostly false. If a true miracle were shown to them, would they believe? Perhaps they would see the hollowness of their own magic. In fact this actually happened with the Egyptian sorcerers themselves and perhaps with the commonalty. But Pharaoh and his Court were too arrogant, and battened too much on frauds to yield to Truth.

31. (Pharaoh) said: "Show it then,
If thou tellest the truth!"

٣١- قَالَ فَأْتِ بِهٖٓ اِنْ كُنْتَ مِنَ الصّٰدِقِيْنَ ۝

32. So (Moses) threw his rod,
And behold, it was
A serpent, plain (for all to see)!

٣٢- فَاَلْقٰى عَصَاهُ فَاِذَا هِىَ ثُعْبَانٌ مُّبِيْنٌ ۝

33. And he drew out his hand,
And behold, it was white
To all beholders! [3157]

٣٣- وَّنَزَعَ يَدَهٗ فَاِذَا هِىَ بَيْضَآءُ
لِلنّٰظِرِيْنَ ۝ ع

Section 3.

34. (Pharaoh) said to the Chiefs [3158]
Around him: "This is indeed
A sorcerer well-versed:

٣٤- قَالَ لِلْمَلَاِ حَوْلَهٗٓ
اِنَّ هٰذَا لَسٰحِرٌ عَلِيْمٌ ۝

35. "His plan is to get you out
Of your land by his sorcery;
Then what is it ye counsel?"

٣٥- يُّرِيْدُ اَنْ يُّخْرِجَكُمْ مِّنْ اَرْضِكُمْ
بِسِحْرِهٖ ۖ فَمَاذَا تَاْمُرُوْنَ ۝

36. They said: "Keep him
And his brother in suspense
(For a while), and dispatch
To the Cities heralds to collect—

٣٦- قَالُوْٓا اَرْجِهْ وَاَخَاهُ
وَابْعَثْ فِى الْمَدَآئِنِ حٰشِرِيْنَ ۝

37. "And bring up to thee
All (our) sorcerers well-versed."

٣٧- يَاْتُوْكَ بِكُلِّ سَحَّارٍ عَلِيْمٍ ۝

38. So the sorcerers were got
Together for the appointment
Of a day well-known, [3159]

٣٨- فَجُمِعَ السَّحَرَةُ لِمِيْقَاتِ يَوْمٍ مَّعْلُوْمٍ ۝

39. And the people were told:
"Are ye (now) assembled?—

٣٩- وَّقِيْلَ لِلنَّاسِ هَلْ اَنْتُمْ مُّجْتَمِعُوْنَ ۝

40. "That we may follow [3160]
The sorcerers (in religion)
If they win?"

٤٠- لَعَلَّنَا نَتَّبِعُ السَّحَرَةَ
اِنْ كَانُوْا هُمُ الْغٰلِبِيْنَ ۝

3157. *Cf.* vii. 107-8. See the whole passage there, and the notes thereon.

3158. In vii. 109 it is the Chiefs who say this. The fact is that it was a general consultation, and this was the general feeling, expressed in words by each to the others.

3159. *A day well-known*: a solemn day of festival: see xx. 59. The object was to get together as large a concourse of people as possible. It was confidently expected that the Egyptian sorcerers with all their organisation would win with their tricks against these amateur Israelites, and so the State cult of the worship of Pharaoh would be fastened on the necks of the people more firmly than ever.

3160. See the last note. The people are to come and witness the triumph of the State religion, so that they may become the more obedient to Pharaoh and more compliant with the demands of the priests. The State religion included magic and the worship of Pharaoh.

41. So when the sorcerers arrived,
They said to Pharaoh:
" Of course—shall we have
A (suitable) reward[3161]
If we win ?"

٤١- فَلَمَّا جَآءَ السَّحَرَةُ قَالُوا لِفِرْعَوْنَ
أَئِنَّ لَنَا لَأَجْرًا
إِن كُنَّا نَحْنُ الْغٰلِبِينَ ۝

42. He said: " Yea, (and more),—
For ye shall in that case
Be (raised to posts)
Nearest (to my person)."

٤٢- قَالَ نَعَمْ وَإِنَّكُمْ إِذًا
لَّمِنَ الْمُقَرَّبِينَ ۝

43. Moses said to them:
" Throw ye—that which
Ye are about to throw!"[3362]

٤٣- قَالَ لَهُم مُّوسَىٰٓ أَلْقُوا مَآ أَنتُم مُّلْقُونَ ۝

44. So they threw their ropes
And their rods, and said:
" By the might of Pharaoh,
It is we who will
Certainly win!"[3363]

٤٤- فَأَلْقَوْا حِبَالَهُمْ وَعِصِيَّهُمْ وَقَالُوا
بِعِزَّةِ فِرْعَوْنَ إِنَّا لَنَحْنُ الْغٰلِبُونَ ۝

45. Then Moses threw his rod,
When, behold, it straightway
Swallows up all
The falsehoods which they fake![3364]

٤٥- فَأَلْقَىٰ مُوسَىٰ عَصَاهُ
فَإِذَا هِيَ تَلْقَفُ مَا يَأْفِكُونَ ۝

46. Then did the sorcerers
Fall down, prostrate in adoration,

٤٦- فَأُلْقِيَ السَّحَرَةُ سٰجِدِينَ ۝

47. Saying: " We believe
In the Lord of the Worlds,

٤٧- قَالُوٓا ءَامَنَّا بِرَبِّ الْعٰلَمِينَ ۝

48. " The Lord of Moses and Aaron."

٤٨- رَبِّ مُوسَىٰ وَهٰرُونَ ۝

3161. There was no such thing as pure loyalty to an exploiting ruler like this Pharaoh. The sorcerers, who were probably also priests, were venal, and they hoped to establish their own hold on both king and people by the further enrichment of themselves and their order.

3162. The euphemism implies a taunt, as if Moses had said: " I know about your tricks! You pretend to throw ropes and rods, and make people believe they are snakes. But now come on!"

3163. Though Pharaoh claimed to be a god, it is not likely that those nearest to him—his priests and sorcerers—believed such a thing! But it was a game of mutual pretence before the world. And so they appeal to his " divine " power.

3164. The sorcerers' ropes and rods seemed to have become serpents, but the rod of Moses was mightier than all of them and quickly swallowed them up. So Truth is more powerful than tricks and will expose and destroy them.

49. Said (Pharaoh): "Believe ye
In Him before I give
You permission? Surely he
Is your leader, who has
Taught you sorcery!
But soon shall ye know![3165]

٤٩- قَالَ اٰمَنْتُمْ لَهٗ قَبْلَ اَنْ اٰذَنَ لَكُمْ
اِنَّهٗ لَكَبِيْرُكُمُ الَّذِىْ عَلَّمَكُمُ السِّحْرَ
فَلَسَوْفَ تَعْلَمُوْنَ ○

"Be sure I will cut off
Your hands and your feet
On opposite sides, and I
Will cause you all
To die on the cross!"

٥٠- لَاُقَطِّعَنَّ اَيْدِيَكُمْ وَ اَرْجُلَكُمْ
مِّنْ خِلَافٍ وَّ لَاُوصَلِّبَنَّكُمْ اَجْمَعِيْنَ ○

50. They said: "No matter!
For us, we shall but
Return to our Lord!

٥١- قَالُوْا لَا ضَيْرَ
اِنَّآ اِلٰى رَبِّنَا مُنْقَلِبُوْنَ ○

51. "Only, our desire is
That our Lord will
Forgive us our faults,
That we may become
Foremost among the Believers!"[3166]

٥٢- اِنَّا نَطْمَعُ اَنْ يَّغْفِرَ لَنَا رَبُّنَا خَطٰيٰنَآ
اَنْ كُنَّآ اَوَّلَ الْمُؤْمِنِيْنَ ○ ع

SECTION 4.

52. By inspiration We told Moses:
"Travel by night with
My servants; for surely
Ye shall be pursued."[3167]

٥٣- وَ اَوْحَيْنَآ اِلٰى مُوْسٰٓى اَنْ اَسْرِ
بِعِبَادِىْٓ اِنَّكُمْ مُّتَّبَعُوْنَ ○

53. Then Pharaoh sent heralds
To (all) the Cities,

3165. The sorcerers knew that they had met something very different from their tricks. God's spirit worked on them, and they professed the True God. As they represented the intelligence of the community, it may be presumed that they carried the intelligence of Egypt with them and perhaps some of the commonalty, who were impressed by the dramatic scene! Hence Pharaoh's anger, but it is the beginning of his decline!

3166. This is the core of the lesson enforced in this passage. What was the reaction of the environment to the Light or Message of God? (1) It transformed Moses so that he became a fearless leader, one of the foremost in faith. (2) From men like Pharaoh and his corrupt court, it called forth obstinacy, spite, and all the tricks and snares of Evil, but Evil was defeated on its own ground. (3) The very dupes of Evil were touched by the glorious Light of God, and they were ready to suffer tortures and death, their sole ambition (in their transformed state) being to be foremost in Faith!

3167. The rest of the story—of the plagues of Egypt—is passed over as not germane to the present argument. We come now to the story of Israel leaving Egypt, pursued by Pharaoh. Here again there are three contrasts: (1) the blind arrogance of the Egyptians, against the development of God's Plan; (2) the Faith of Moses, against the fears of his people; and (3) the final deliverance of the seed of righteousness, against the destruction of the hosts of brute force.

54. (Saying): "These (Israelites)
Are but a small band,

٥٤- فَأَرْسَلَ فِرْعَوْنُ فِي الْمَدَآئِنِ حٰشِرِيْنَ ۝

55. "And they are raging
Furiously against us;

٥٥- إِنَّ هٰٓؤُلَآءِ لَشِرْذِمَةٌ قَلِيْلُوْنَ ۝

56. "But we are a multitude
Amply fore-warned."

٥٦- وَإِنَّهُمْ لَنَا لَغَآئِظُوْنَ ۝

58. So We expelled them[3368]
From gardens, springs,

٥٨- فَأَخْرَجْنٰهُمْ مِّنْ جَنّٰتٍ وَّعُيُوْنٍ ۝

58. Treasures, and every kind
Of honourable position;

٥٨- وَّكُنُوْزٍ وَّمَقَامٍ كَرِيْمٍ ۝

59. Thus it was, but
We made the Children
Of Israel inheritors[3369]
Of such things.

٥٩- كَذٰلِكَ ۚ
وَأَوْرَثْنٰهَا بَنِيْٓ إِسْرَآءِيْلَ ۝

60. So they pursued them[3370]
At sunrise.

٦٠- فَأَتْبَعُوْهُمْ مُّشْرِقِيْنَ ۝

61. And when the two bodies
Saw each other, the people
Of Moses said: "We are
Sure to be overtaken."

٦١- فَلَمَّا تَرَآءَ الْجَمْعٰنِ
قَالَ أَصْحٰبُ مُوْسٰٓى إِنَّا لَمُدْرَكُوْنَ ۝

62. (Moses) said: "By no means!
My Lord is with me!
Soon will He guide me!"[3371]

٦٢- قَالَ كَلَّا ۚ إِنَّ مَعِيَ رَبِّيْ سَيَهْدِيْنِ ۝

3168. In deference to almost unanimous authority I have translated this passage (verses 58-60) as if it were a parenthetical statement of God's purpose. Personally I prefer another construction. According to that, verses 58-59 will be part of Pharaoh's proclamation: "We have dispossessed the Israelites from everything good in the land, and made them our slaves"; and verse 60 only will be parenthetical: "Poor ignorant men! you may oppress those who are helpless, but We (*i.e.*, God) have decreed that they shall inherit all these things", as they certainly did (for a time) in the Land of Promise, Palestine.

3169. The Children of Israel certainly inherited the gardens, springs, treasures, and honourable positions in Palestine after many years' wanderings in the wilderness. But when they were false to God, they lost them again, and another people (the Muslims) inherited them when they were true in Faith. These latter not only inherited Palestine but also Egypt, and the old Pharaonic power and institutions were lost for ever. "*Of such things*": literally, "of them".

3170. The story is here resumed after the parenthesis of verses 58-60.

3171. *Guide me*: *i.e.*, show me some way of escape from danger. This actually happened, for Pharaoh's host was drowned. The faith of Moses stands in strong contrast to the fears of his people,

63. Then We told Moses
By inspiration: "Strike
The sea with thy rod."
So it divided, and each
Separate part became
Like the huge, firm mass
Of a mountain.

٦٣- فَأَوْحَيْنَآ إِلَىٰ مُوسَىٰٓ أَنِ ٱضْرِب
بِّعَصَاكَ ٱلْبَحْرَ
فَٱنفَلَقَ فَكَانَ كُلُّ فِرْقٍ
كَٱلطَّوْدِ ٱلْعَظِيمِ ۝

64. And We made the other
Party approach thither.[3172]

٦٤- وَأَزْلَفْنَا ثَمَّ ٱلْءَاخَرِينَ ۝

65. We delivered Moses and all
Who were with him;

٦٥- وَأَنجَيْنَا مُوسَىٰ وَمَن مَّعَهُۥٓ أَجْمَعِينَ ۝

66. But We drowned the others.

٦٦- ثُمَّ أَغْرَقْنَا ٱلْءَاخَرِينَ ۝

67. Verily in this is a Sign:
But most of them
Do not believe.[3173]

٦٧- إِنَّ فِى ذَٰلِكَ لَءَايَةً ۖ
وَمَا كَانَ أَكْثَرُهُم مُّؤْمِنِينَ ۝

68. And verily thy Lord
Is He, the Exalted in Might,
Most Merciful.[3174]

٦٨- وَإِنَّ رَبَّكَ لَهُوَ ٱلْعَزِيزُ ٱلرَّحِيمُ ۝

C. 165.—Abraham patiently argued with his people
(xxvi. 70-122.) About God's Truth; prayed for wisdom
And righteousness, for himself, his father,
And future generations; and taught Truth
About the Hereafter. Noah preached
To a world of Unfaith, and would not reject
The humble and lowly: his arrogant rejecters
Were brought low: in him and his following
Were vindicated God's righteous Purpose and Mercy.

Section 5.

69. And rehearse to them
(Something of) Abraham's story.[3175]

٦٩- وَٱتْلُ عَلَيْهِمْ نَبَأَ إِبْرَٰهِيمَ ۝

3172. The miracle was twofold: (1) Moses with his people passed safely through the sea; and (2) Pharaoh and his great host were drowned in the sea.

3173. As it was then, so it is now. In spite of the obvious Signs of God, people who are blind in their obstinate resistance to Truth accomplish their own destruction, while humble, persecuted men of Faith are transformed by the Light of God, and obtain salvation.

3174. Nothing that the powers of Evil can do, will ever defeat the merciful Purpose of God. Evil, in resisting good, will effect its own destruction.

3175. For the argument of this Sūra the incidents in Abraham's life are not relevant and are not mentioned. What is mentioned is: (1) the steps by which he taught about the sin of false worship, in the form of a Dialogue; (2) the aims of a righteous man not only in his individual life, but for his ancestors and posterity, in the form of a Prayer; and (3) a picture of the Future Judgment, in the form of a vision. (1) is covered by verses 70-82; (2) by 83-87; and (3) by 88-102.

70. Behold, he said
To his father and his people:
"What worship ye?"

٧٠- إِذْ قَالَ لِأَبِيهِ وَقَوْمِهِ مَا تَعْبُدُونَ ○

71. They said: "We worship
Idols, and we remain constantly [3176]
In attendance on them."

٧١- قَالُوا نَعْبُدُ أَصْنَامًا فَنَظَلُّ لَهَا عَٰكِفِينَ ○

72. He said: "Do they listen
To you when ye call (on them),

٧٢- قَالَ هَلْ يَسْمَعُونَكُمْ إِذْ تَدْعُونَ

73. Or do you good or harm?"

٧٣- أَوْ يَنفَعُونَكُمْ أَوْ يَضُرُّونَ ○

74. They said: "Nay, but we
Found our fathers doing
Thus (what we do)."

٧٤- قَالُوا بَلْ وَجَدْنَا آبَاءَنَا كَذَٰلِكَ يَفْعَلُونَ ○

75. He said: "Do ye then
See whom ye have been
Worshipping,—

٧٥- قَالَ أَفَرَءَيْتُم مَّا كُنتُمْ تَعْبُدُونَ ○

76. "Ye and your fathers before you?—

٧٦- أَنتُمْ وَآبَاؤُكُمُ الْأَقْدَمُونَ ○

77. "For they are enemies to me; [3177]
Not so the Lord and Cherisher
Of the Worlds;

٧٧- فَإِنَّهُمْ عَدُوٌّ لِّي إِلَّا رَبَّ الْعَٰلَمِينَ ○

78. "Who created me, and
It is He who guides me;

٧٨- الَّذِي خَلَقَنِي فَهُوَ يَهْدِينِ ○

79. "Who gives me food and drink,

٧٩- وَالَّذِي هُوَ يُطْعِمُنِي وَيَسْقِينِ ○

80. "And when I am ill,
It is He who cures me;

٨٠- وَإِذَا مَرِضْتُ فَهُوَ يَشْفِينِ ○

81. "Who will cause me to die,
And then to live (again);

٨١- وَالَّذِي يُمِيتُنِي ثُمَّ يُحْيِينِ ○

3176. They want to show their true and assiduous devotion. But Abraham goes at once to the heart of the matter by asking: "To whom is your devotion paid? Is the object worthy of it?"

3177. 'The things that you worship are enemies to mankind; let me testify from my own personal experience: they are enemies to me: they can do me no good, but would lead me astray. Contrast with their impotence or their power of mischief the One True God Whom I worship: He created me and all the Worlds; He cherishes me and guides me; He takes care of me; and when I die, He will give me new life; He will forgive me and grant me final Salvation. Will you then come to this true worship? How can you doubt, after seeing the contrast of the one with the other? Is it not as the contrast between Light and Darkness?'

82. " And who, I hope,
Will forgive me my faults
On the Day of Judgment..

٨٢- وَالَّذِىٓ اَطْمَعُ اَنْ يَّغْفِرَ لِىْ خَطِيْٓـَٔتِىْ يَوْمَ الدِّيْنِ ۝

83. "O my Lord! bestow wisdom[3178]
On me, and join me
With the righteous;

٨٣- رَبِّ هَبْ لِىْ حُكْمًا وَّاَلْحِقْنِىْ بِالصّٰلِحِيْنَ ۝

84. " Grant me honourable mention
On the tongue of truth[3179]
Among the latest (generations);

٨٤- وَاجْعَلْ لِّىْ لِسَانَ صِدْقٍ فِى الْاٰخِرِيْنَ ۝

85. " Make me one of the inheritors
Of the Garden of Bliss;

٨٥- وَاجْعَلْنِىْ مِنْ وَّرَثَةِ جَنَّةِ النَّعِيْمِ ۝

86. " Forgive my father, for that
He is among those astray;

٨٦- وَاغْفِرْ لِاَبِىْٓ اِنَّهٗ كَانَ مِنَ الضَّآلِّيْنَ ۝

87. " And let me not be
In disgrace on the Day
When (men) will be raised up;—

٨٧- وَلَا تُخْزِنِىْ يَوْمَ يُبْعَثُوْنَ ۝

88. "The Day whereon neither[3180]
Wealth nor sons will avail,

٨٨- يَوْمَ لَا يَنْفَعُ مَالٌ وَّلَا بَنُوْنَ ۝

89. " But only he (will prosper)
That brings to God
A sound heart;

٨٩- اِلَّا مَنْ اَتَى اللّٰهَ بِقَلْبٍ سَلِيْمٍ ۝

90. " To the righteous, the Garden
Will be brought near,[3181]

٩٠- وَاُزْلِفَتِ الْجَنَّةُ لِلْمُتَّقِيْنَ ۝

3178. Having shown clearly the distinction between the False and the True, Abraham now shows in the form of a Prayer what his inmost wishes are. (1) He wants his own soul enlightened with divine wisdom, and (2) his heart and life filled with righteousness; (3) he will not be content with working for himself or his own generation; his view extends to all future generations; (4) and of course he wishes to attain the goal of the righteous, the Garden of the Bliss of the Divine Countenance; but he is not content with this; for (5) he wants his father and relatives to share in his spiritual joy, so that he can proudly see all whom he can reach, in an honourable station (contrasted with disgrace) on the Day of Judgment.

3179. *Cf.* xix. 50. The whole of the passage about Abraham there may be compared with this passage.

3180. Now we have a vision of the Day of Judgment. Nothing will then avail except a pure heart; all sorts of the so-called "good deeds" of this world, without the motive of purity, will be useless. The contrast of the Garden of Bliss with the Fire of Misery will be plainly visible. Evil will be shown in its true colours,—isolated, helpless, cursing and despairing; and all chances will then have been lost.

3181. The Good will only see good (the Garden of Bliss), and the Evil will only see evil (the Fire of Hell). The type of this contrast is shown to us in the world of our spiritual sense even in this life.

91. "And to those straying in Evil, The Fire will be placed In full view;	٩١- وَ بُرِّزَتِ الْجَحِيمُ لِلْغٰوِينَ ۝
92. "And it shall be said To them: 'Where are The (gods) ye worshipped—	٩٢- وَقِيلَ لَهُمْ أَيْنَمَا كُنْتُمْ تَعْبُدُونَ ۝
93. "'Besides God? Can they Help you or help themselves?'	٩٣- مِنْ دُونِ اللّٰهِ ۚ هَلْ يَنْصُرُونَكُمْ أَوْ يَنْتَصِرُونَ ۝
94. "Then they will be thrown Headlong into the (Fire),— They and those straying[3182] In Evil,	٩٤- فَكُبْكِبُوا فِيهَا هُمْ وَ الْغَاوٗنَ ۝
95. "And the whole hosts Of Iblīs together.	٩٥- وَجُنُودُ إِبْلِيسَ أَجْمَعُونَ ۝
96. "They will say there In their mutual bickerings:	٩٦- قَالُوا وَهُمْ فِيهَا يَخْتَصِمُونَ ۝
97. "'By God, we were truly In an error manifest,[3183]	٩٧- تَاللّٰهِ إِنْ كُنَّا لَفِي ضَلٰلٍ مُّبِينٍ ۝
98. "'When we held you as equals With the Lord of the Worlds;	٩٨- إِذْ نُسَوِّيكُمْ بِرَبِّ الْعٰلَمِينَ ۝
99. "'And our seducers were Only those who were Steeped in guilt.[3184]	٩٩- وَمَا أَضَلَّنَا إِلَّا الْمُجْرِمُونَ ۝
100. "'Now, then, we have none To intercede (for us),	١٠٠- فَمَا لَنَا مِنْ شَافِعِينَ ۝

3182. The false gods, being devils or personified false fancies, will be all involved in the punishment of Hell, together with their worshippers, and the ultimate sources of evil, the hosts of Iblīs or Satan.

3183. *Error manifest*: 'our error is now plainly manifest, but it should have been manifest to us before it was too late, because the Signs of God were always around us'. This will be said by the ungodly, whose eyes will then be fully opened.

3184. They now see that the people who seduced them were themselves evil and subject to the penalties of evil, and their seductions were frauds. They feel that they ought to have seen it before. For who would deliberately follow the paths of those condemned to misery and punishment? How simple they were not to see the true character of their seducers, though they had been warned again and again against them! It was their own folly that made them accept such obviously false guidance!

101. " 'Nor a single friend
To feel (for us).

١٠١- وَلَا صَدِيقٍ حَمِيمٍ ۝

102. " 'Now if we only had
A chance of return,
We shall truly be
Of those who believe!' "[3185]

١٠٢- فَلَوْ أَنَّ لَنَا كَرَّةً
فَنَكُونَ مِنَ الْمُؤْمِنِينَ ۝

103. Verily in this is a Sign
But most of them
Do not believe.

١٠٣- إِنَّ فِي ذَٰلِكَ لَآيَةً ۖ
وَمَا كَانَ أَكْثَرُهُم مُّؤْمِنِينَ ۝

104. And verily thy Lord
Is He, the Exalted in Might,
Most Merciful.

١٠٤- وَإِنَّ رَبَّكَ لَهُوَ الْعَزِيزُ الرَّحِيمُ ۝

SECTION 6.

105. The people of Noah rejected
The apostles.

١٠٥- كَذَّبَتْ قَوْمُ نُوحٍ الْمُرْسَلِينَ ۝

106. Behold, their brother Noah[3186]
Said to them: "Will ye not
Fear (God)?

١٠٦- إِذْ قَالَ لَهُمْ أَخُوهُمْ نُوحٌ أَلَا
تَتَّقُونَ ۝

107. "I am to you an apostle
Worthy of all trust:[3187]

١٠٧- إِنِّي لَكُمْ رَسُولٌ أَمِينٌ ۝

108. "So fear God, and obey me.

١٠٨- فَاتَّقُوا اللَّهَ وَأَطِيعُونِ ۝

109. "No reward do I ask
Of you for it: my reward
Is only from the Lord
Of the Worlds:

١٠٩- وَمَا أَسْأَلُكُمْ عَلَيْهِ مِنْ أَجْرٍ ۖ
إِنْ أَجْرِيَ إِلَّا عَلَىٰ رَبِّ الْعَالَمِينَ ۝

3185. This apparent longing for a chance of return is dishonest. If they were sent back, they would certainly return to their evil ways: vi. 27-28. Besides, they have had numerous chances already in this life, and they have used them for mischief or evil.

3186. Noah's generation had lost all faith and abandoned themselves to evil. They had rejected the Message of apostles previously sent to the world. Noah was sent to them as one of themselves (' their brother "). His life was open before them; he had proved himself pure in heart and conduct (like the holy Apostle of Arabia long after him), and worthy of every trust. Would they fear God and follow his advice? They could see that he had no ends of his own to serve. Would they not listen to him?

3187. *Amīn* = one to whom a trust has been given, with several shades of meaning implied: *e.g.*, (1) worthy of trust, (2) bound to deliver his trust, as a prophet is bound to deliver his Message, (3) bound to act entirely as directed by the trust, as a prophet is bound to give only the Message of God, and not add anything of his own, and (4) not seeking any interest of his own.

110. "So fear God, and obey me."[3188]

۱۱۰- فَاتَّقُوا اللّٰهَ وَاَطِيْعُوْنِ ۝

111. They said: "Shall we
Believe in thee when it is
The meanest that follow thee?"[3189]

۱۱۱- قَالُوْٓا اَنُؤْمِنُ لَكَ وَاتَّبَعَكَ الْاَرْذَلُوْنَ ۝

112. He said: "And what
Do I know as to
What they do?

۱۱۲- قَالَ وَمَا عِلْمِيْ بِمَا كَانُوْا يَعْمَلُوْنَ ۝

113. "Their account is only
With my Lord, if ye
Could (but) understand.

۱۱۳- اِنْ حِسَابُهُمْ اِلَّا عَلٰى رَبِّيْ لَوْ تَشْعُرُوْنَ ۝

114. "I am not one to drive away
Those who believe.[3190]

۱۱۴- وَمَآ اَنَا بِطَارِدِ الْمُؤْمِنِيْنَ ۝

115. "I am sent only
To warn plainly in public."

۱۱۵- اِنْ اَنَا اِلَّا نَذِيْرٌ مُّبِيْنٌ ۝

116. They said: "If thou
Desist not, O Noah!
Thou shalt be stoned
(to death)."[3191]

۱۱۶- قَالُوْا لَئِنْ لَّمْ تَنْتَهِ يٰنُوْحُ لَتَكُوْنَنَّ مِنَ الْمَرْجُوْمِيْنَ ۝

117. He said: "O my Lord!
Truly my people have
Rejected me.

۱۱۷- قَالَ رَبِّ اِنَّ قَوْمِيْ كَذَّبُوْنِ ۝

118. "Judge thou, then, between me
And them openly, and deliver

۱۱۸- فَافْتَحْ بَيْنِيْ وَبَيْنَهُمْ فَتْحًا وَّنَجِّنِيْ

3188. Note how the repetition rounds off the argument. See n. 3186 above.

3189. The leaders of the people are speaking, as the Quraish leaders spoke in the time of the holy Prophet. "We know that thou hast been trustworthy in thy life. But look at the 'tag rag and bob tail' that follow thee! Dost thou expect us to be like them or to be classed with them?" His answer was: "I know nothing against them; if they have done any wrong, or are only hypocrites, they are answerable to God; how can I drive them away from me, seeing that I am expressly sent to admonish all people?"

3190. *Cf.* xi. 29. All people who have faith have the right to come and listen to God's Word and receive God's Mercy, whether they are publicans and sinners, "Harijans" and low-caste men, men of "superior" or "inferior" races. The man of God welcomes them all, as His Message has to shine before the whole world.

3191. Two other cases occur to me where prophets of God were threatened with death by stoning: one was Abraham (xix. 46), and the other was Shu'aib (xi. 91). In neither case did the threats deter them from carrying out their mission. On the contrary the threats recoiled on those who threatened. So also did it happen in the case of Noah and the holy Prophet.

Me and those of the Believers
Who are with me."

وَمَنْ مَّعِىَ مِنَ الْمُؤْمِنِينَ ۝

119. So We delivered him
And those with him,
In the Ark filled
(With all creatures).[3192]

١١٩- فَأَنْجَيْنَٰهُ وَمَن مَّعَهُۥ
فِى الْفُلْكِ الْمَشْحُونِ ۝

120. Thereafter We drowned those
Who remained behind.

١٢٠- ثُمَّ أَغْرَقْنَا بَعْدُ الْبَاقِينَ ۝

121. Verily in this is a Sign:
But most of them
Do not believe.[3193]

١٢١- إِنَّ فِى ذَٰلِكَ لَءَايَةً ۖ
وَمَا كَانَ أَكْثَرُهُم مُّؤْمِنِينَ ۝

122. And verily thy Lord
Is He, the Exalted in Might,
Most Merciful.

١٢٢- وَإِنَّ رَبَّكَ لَهُوَ الْعَزِيزُ الرَّحِيمُ ۝

C. 166.—The 'Ād were addicted to arrogance;
(xxvi. 123-159.) They exulted in material strength
And possessions, and had no faith but in force:
They were brought low, as were the Thamūd,
Who gave way to extravagance, and were guilty
Of sacrilege in destroying a symbol
Of justice and fair-dealing: their repentance
Was too late: they were blotted out
Of the earth for the mischief they had made.

SECTION 7.

123. The 'Ād (people) rejected[3194]
The apostles.

١٢٣- كَذَّبَتْ عَادٌ الْمُرْسَلِينَ ۝

124. Behold, their brother Hūd
Said to them: "Will ye not
Fear (God)?

١٢٤- إِذْ قَالَ لَهُمْ أَخُوهُمْ هُودٌ
أَلَا تَتَّقُونَ ۝

3192. The story of Noah's Flood is told in xi. 36-48. Here the point emphasised is Noah's patience and constancy against threats, and the triumph and preservation of God's Truth even though the world was ranged against it.

3193. This and the following verse run like a refrain throughout this Sūra, and give the key-note to the subject-matter: how the Message of God is preached, how it is rejected in all ages, and how it triumphs at last, through the Mercy of God. See xxvi. 8-9, 68-69, 103-104, here (121-122), 139-140, 158-159, 174-175, and 190-191. There are minor refrains, like echoes in music, which will reveal themselves to the careful student.

3194. See n. 1040 to vii. 65 for the 'Ād people and their location. Here the emphasis is on the fact that they were materialists believing in brute force, and felt secure in their fortresses and resources, but were found quite helpless when God's Message came and they rejected it.

125. " I am to you an apostle
Worthy of all trust :[3195]

١٢٥-اِنِّىْ لَكُمْ رَسُوْلٌ اَمِيْنٌ ۙ

126. " So fear God and obey me.

١٢٦-فَاتَّقُوا اللّٰهَ وَاَطِيْعُوْنِ ۚ

127. " No reward do I ask
Of you for it : my reward
Is only from the Lord
Of the Worlds.

١٢٧-وَمَآ اَسْـَٔلُكُمْ عَلَيْهِ مِنْ اَجْرٍ ۚ
اِنْ اَجْرِيَ اِلَّا عَلٰى رَبِّ الْعٰلَمِيْنَ ۗ

128. " Do ye build a landmark
On every high place
To amuse yourselves ?[3196]

١٢٨-اَتَبْنُوْنَ بِكُلِّ رِيْعٍ اٰيَةً تَعْبَثُوْنَ ۙ

129. " And do ye get for yourselves
Fine buildings in the hope
Of living therein (for ever) ?

١٢٩-وَتَتَّخِذُوْنَ مَصَانِعَ لَعَلَّكُمْ
تَخْلُدُوْنَ ۚ

130. " And when ye exert
Your strong hand,
Do ye do it like men
Of absolute power ?[3197]

١٣٠-وَاِذَا بَطَشْتُمْ
بَطَشْتُمْ جَبَّارِيْنَ ۚ

131. " Now fear God, and obey me.[3198]

١٣١-فَاتَّقُوا اللّٰهَ وَاَطِيْعُوْنِ ۚ

132. " Yea, fear Him Who
Has bestowed on you
Freely all that ye know.[3199]

١٣٢-وَاتَّقُوا الَّذِيْٓ اَمَدَّكُمْ بِمَا
تَعْلَمُوْنَ ۚ

133. " Freely has He bestowed
On you cattle and sons,—

١٣٣-اَمَدَّكُمْ بِاَنْعَامٍ وَّبَنِيْنَ ۙ

3195. See n. 3187 to xxvi. 107 above.

3196. Any merely material civilisation prides itself on show and parade. Its votaries scatter monuments for all sorts of things in conspicuous places—monuments which commemorate deeds and events which are forgotten in a few generations ! *Cf.* Shelley's poem on Ozymandias: "I am Ozymandias, King of Kings ! Look on my works, ye mighty, and despair !......Boundless and bare the lonely and level sands stretch far away ! "

3197. " Without any responsibility or consideration for those who come within your power ? "

3198. See n. 3188 above.

3199. The gifts are described generally, immaterial and material. " All that ye know " includes not only material things, but knowledge and the faculties by which knowledge may be used for human well-being, all that makes life beautiful and refined. " Cattle " means wealth generally, and " sons " means population and man-power. " Gardens and Springs " are things that contribute to the delight and pleasure of man.

134. "And Gardens and Springs.

۱۳۴- وَجَنّٰتٍ وَّعُيُوْنٍ ۝

135. "Truly I fear for you
The Penalty of a Great Day."[3200]

۱۳۵- اِنِّيْٓ اَخَافُ عَلَيْكُمْ عَذَابَ يَوْمٍ عَظِيْمٍ ۝

136. They said: "It is the same
To us whether thou
Admonish us or be not
Among (our) admonishers![3201]

۱۳۶- قَالُوْا سَوَآءٌ عَلَيْنَآ اَوَعَظْتَ اَمْ لَمْ
تَكُنْ مِّنَ الْوٰعِظِيْنَ ۝

137. "This is no other than
A customary device
Of the ancients,[3202]

۱۳۷- اِنْ هٰذَآ اِلَّا خُلُقُ الْاَوَّلِيْنَ ۝

138. "And we are not the ones
To receive Pains and Penalties!"

۱۳۸- وَمَا نَحْنُ بِمُعَذَّبِيْنَ ۝

139. So they rejected him,
And We destroyed them.
Verily in this is a Sign:
But most of them
Do not believe.

۱۳۹- فَكَذَّبُوْهُ فَاَهْلَكْنٰهُمْ ۭ
اِنَّ فِيْ ذٰلِكَ لَاٰيَةً ۭ
وَمَا كَانَ اَكْثَرُهُمْ مُّؤْمِنِيْنَ ۝

140. And verily thy Lord
Is He, the Exalted in Might,
Most Merciful.

۱۴۰- وَاِنَّ رَبَّكَ لَهُوَ الْعَزِيْزُ الرَّحِيْمُ ۝ ع

SECTION 8.

141. The Thamūd (people) rejected[3203]
The apostles.

۱۴۱- كَذَّبَتْ ثَمُوْدُ الْمُرْسَلِيْنَ ۝

3200. "But you have misused all those gifts, and you will suffer the inevitable penalties for your misuse and for your ingratitude."

3201. "We are not going to attend to you whether you preach to us or not." The construction of the second clause, 'or be not among our admonishers" is a rapier cut at Hūd, as if they had said: "Oh yes! we have heard plenty of admonishers like you!" See the next verse.

3202. They said, as many of our modern enemies of religion say, "you are only reviving an ancient superstition, a dope of the crowd; there is no such thing as a Hereafter, or the sort of punishments you denounce!"

3203. For the Thamūd people see n. 1043 to vii. 73. They were great builders in stone and a people with agricultural wealth, but they were an exclusive people and oppressed the poor. The point emphasised here is: "How long will your wealth last, especially if you depress your own people and dishonour God's Signs by sacrilege?" The inscriptions on the Thamūd remains of rock-cut buildings in Al-Ḥijr are described in Appendix IX at the end of this Sūra.

142. Behold, their brother Ṣāliḥ
Said to them: "Will you not
Fear (God)?

١٤٢- إِذْ قَالَ لَهُمْ أَخُوهُمْ صَٰلِحٌ أَلَا تَتَّقُونَ ۝

143. "I am to you an apostle
Worthy of all trust.

١٤٣- إِنِّي لَكُمْ رَسُولٌ أَمِينٌ ۝

144. "So fear God, and obey me.

١٤٤- فَاتَّقُوا اللَّهَ وَأَطِيعُونِ ۝

145. "No reward do I ask
Of you for it: my reward
Is only from the Lord
Of the Worlds.

١٤٥- وَمَا أَسْأَلُكُمْ عَلَيْهِ مِنْ أَجْرٍ
إِنْ أَجْرِيَ إِلَّا عَلَىٰ رَبِّ الْعَٰلَمِينَ ۝

146. "Will ye be left secure,
In (the enjoyment of) all
That ye have here?—

١٤٦- أَتُتْرَكُونَ فِي مَا هَٰهُنَا آمِنِينَ ۝

147. "Gardens and Springs,

١٤٧- فِي جَنَّٰتٍ وَعُيُونٍ ۝

148. "And corn-fields and date palms
With spathes near breaking[3204]
(With the weight of fruit)?

١٤٨- وَزُرُوعٍ وَنَخْلٍ طَلْعُهَا هَضِيمٌ ۝

149. "And ye carve houses
Out of (rocky) mountains
With great skill.

١٤٩- وَتَنْحِتُونَ مِنَ الْجِبَالِ بُيُوتًا فَٰرِهِينَ ۝

150. "But fear God and obey me;

١٥٠- فَاتَّقُوا اللَّهَ وَأَطِيعُونِ ۝

151. "And follow not the bidding
Of those who are extravagant,—[3205]

١٥١- وَلَا تُطِيعُوا أَمْرَ الْمُسْرِفِينَ ۝

152. "Who make mischief in the land,
And mend not (their ways)."

١٥٢- الَّذِينَ يُفْسِدُونَ فِي الْأَرْضِ وَلَا
يُصْلِحُونَ ۝

153. They said: "Thou art only
One of those bewitched![3206]

١٥٣- قَالُوا إِنَّمَا أَنْتَ مِنَ الْمُسَحَّرِينَ ۝

3204. The date palm flowers on a long spathe: when the flowers develop into fruit, the heavy ones hang with the load of fruit. The Thamūd evidently were proud of their skill in producing corn and fruit and in hewing fine dwellings out of rocks, like the later dwellings of Roman times in the town of Petra.

3205. They are told: 'All your skill is very well; but cultivate virtue and do not follow the ways of those who put forward extravagant claims for men's powers and material resources, or who lead lives of extravagance in luxury and self-indulgence; that makes mischief: but the door of repentance is open: will you repent?'

3206. They think he is talking like a madman, and they say so.

154. " Thou art no more than
A mortal like us :
Then bring us a Sign,
If thou tellest the truth ! "

١٥٤- مَآ أَنتَ إِلَّا بَشَرٌ مِّثْلُنَا
فَأْتِ بِـَٔايَةٍ إِن كُنتَ مِنَ ٱلصَّٰدِقِينَ ۝

155. He said : " Here is
A she-camel : she has[3207]
A right of watering,
And ye have a right
Of watering, (severally)
On a day appointed.

١٥٥- قَالَ هَٰذِهِۦ نَاقَةٌ
لَّهَا شِرْبٌ وَلَكُمْ شِرْبُ
يَوْمٍ مَّعْلُومٍ ۝

156. " Touch her not with harm,
Lest the Penalty
Of a Great Day
Seize you."

١٥٦- وَلَا تَمَسُّوهَا بِسُوٓءٍ
فَيَأْخُذَكُمْ عَذَابُ يَوْمٍ عَظِيمٍ ۝

157. But they ham-strung her :
Then did they become
Full of regrets.[3208]

١٥٧- فَعَقَرُوهَا فَأَصْبَحُوا۟ نَٰدِمِينَ ۝

158. But the Penalty seized them.
Verily in this is a Sign :
But most of them
Do not believe.

١٥٨- فَأَخَذَهُمُ ٱلْعَذَابُ إِنَّ فِى ذَٰلِكَ لَءَايَةً
وَمَا كَانَ أَكْثَرُهُم مُّؤْمِنِينَ ۝

159. And verily thy Lord
Is He, the Exalted in Might,
Most Merciful.

١٥٩- وَإِنَّ رَبَّكَ لَهُوَ ٱلْعَزِيزُ ٱلرَّحِيمُ ۝

C. 167.—The task of Lot was a hard one : his mission
(xxvi. 160-191.) Was to people addicted to crimes abominable.
His reasoning with them was in vain : it only
Excited their wrath. They threatened to cast
Him out, but were themselves overwhelmed
In disaster. Shu'aib had to rebuke fraud
And commercial dishonesty : he met only
Ridicule, but the just and fair dealing
He preached was vindicated in the end.

3207. For this she-camel, see n. 1044 to vii. 73. The she-camel was to be a Sign and a test-case. Would they respect her rights of watering (and pasturage)?

3208. Their regrets were too late. They had themselves asked for a Sign. The Sign had been given them in the she-camel, which their prophet Ṣāliḥ had put forward as a test-case. Would they, through that symbol, respect the law of equity by which all people had rights in water and in the gifts of nature? They refused to respect that law, and committed sacrilege by deliberately killing the she-camel. They themselves came to an evil end.

SECTION 9

160. The people of Lūṭ rejected[3209] The apostles.	١٦٠- كَذَّبَتْ قَوْمُ لُوطٍ الْمُرْسَلِينَ ۝
161. Behold, their brother Lūṭ Said to them: "Will ye not Fear (God)?	١٦١- إِذْ قَالَ لَهُمْ أَخُوهُمْ لُوطٌ أَلَا تَتَّقُونَ ۝
162. "I am to you an apostle Worthy of all trust.	١٦٢- إِنِّي لَكُمْ رَسُولٌ أَمِينٌ ۝
163. "So fear God and obey me.	١٦٣- فَاتَّقُوا اللّٰهَ وَأَطِيعُونِ ۝
164. "No reward do I ask Of you for it: my reward Is only from the Lord Of the Worlds.	١٦٤- وَمَا أَسْأَلُكُمْ عَلَيْهِ مِنْ أَجْرٍ إِنْ أَجْرِيَ إِلَّا عَلَىٰ رَبِّ الْعٰلَمِينَ ۝
165. "Of all the creatures In the world, will ye Approach males,	١٦٥- أَتَأْتُونَ الذُّكْرَانَ مِنَ الْعٰلَمِينَ ۝
166. "And leave those whom God Has created for you To be your mates? Nay, ye are a people Transgressing (all limits)!"	١٦٦- وَتَذَرُونَ مَا خَلَقَ لَكُمْ رَبُّكُمْ مِّنْ أَزْوَاجِكُمْ بَلْ أَنْتُمْ قَوْمٌ عٰدُونَ ۝
167. They said: "If thou desist not, O Lūṭ! thou wilt assuredly Be cast out!"[3210]	١٦٧- قَالُوا لَئِنْ لَّمْ تَنْتَهِ يٰلُوطُ لَتَكُونَنَّ مِنَ الْمُخْرَجِينَ ۝
168. He said: "I do detest[3211] Your doings:"	١٦٨- قَالَ إِنِّي لِعَمَلِكُمْ مِّنَ الْقَالِينَ ۝

3209. The story of Lūṭ (Lot) will be found in vii 80-84: see n. 1049. Here the point is that the people of the Cities of the Plain were shamelessly addicted to vice against nature, and Lūṭ's warning only exasperated them, until they were destroyed by a shower of brimstone.

3210. Their threat to cast him out has a grim significance in what actually happened. They were destroyed where they were, and he was glad to escape the dreadful Punishment according to the warning he had received.

3211. He was only among them from a stern sense of duty. The whole atmosphere there was detestable to him, and he was glad to escape when duty no longer demanded his presence there. He prayed for deliverance from such surroundings.

169. "O my Lord! deliver me
And my family from
Such things as they do!"

١٦٩- رَبِّ نَجِّنِي وَأَهْلِي مِمَّا يَعْمَلُونَ ○

170. So We delivered him
And his family,—all

١٧٠- فَنَجَّيْنَهُ وَأَهْلَهُ أَجْمَعِينَ ○

171. Except an old woman[3212]
Who lingered behind.

١٧١- إِلَّا عَجُوزًا فِي الْغٰبِرِينَ ○

172. But the rest We destroyed
Utterly.

١٧٢- ثُمَّ دَمَّرْنَا الْاٰخَرِينَ ○

173. We rained down on them
A shower (of brimstone):[3213]
And evil was the shower
On those who were admonished
(But heeded not)!

١٧٣- وَأَمْطَرْنَا عَلَيْهِم مَّطَرًا
فَسَاءَ مَطَرُ الْمُنذَرِينَ ○

174. Verily in this is a Sign:
But most of them
Do not believe.

١٧٤- إِنَّ فِي ذٰلِكَ لَاٰيَةً
وَمَا كَانَ أَكْثَرُهُم مُّؤْمِنِينَ ○

175. And verily thy Lord
Is He, the Exalted in Might
Most Merciful.

١٧٥- وَإِنَّ رَبَّكَ لَهُوَ الْعَزِيزُ الرَّحِيمُ ○

SECTION 10.

176. The Companions of the
Wood[3214]
Rejected the apostles.

١٧٦- كَذَّبَ أَصْحٰبُ لْـَٔيْكَةِ الْمُرْسَلِينَ ○

177. Behold, Shu'aib[3215] said to them:
"Will ye not fear (God)?

١٧٧- إِذْ قَالَ لَهُمْ شُعَيْبٌ أَلَا تَتَّقُونَ ○

178. "I am to you an apostle
Worthy of all trust.

١٧٨- إِنِّي لَكُمْ رَسُولٌ أَمِينٌ ○

3212. This was Lūṭ's wife, who lingered behind and was among those who perished. See n. 1051 to vii. 83.

3213. See n. 1052 to vii. 84.

3214. See n. 2000 to xv. 78.

3215. For Shu'aib see n. 1054 to vii. 85.

179. " So fear God and obey me.

١٧٩- فاتقوا الله وأطيعون ○

180. " No reward do I ask
Of you for it : my reward
Is only from the Lord
Of the Worlds.

١٨٠- وما أسئلكم عليه من أجر
إن أجري إلا على رب العلمين ○

181. " Give just measure,[3216]
And cause no loss
(To others by fraud).

١٨١- أوفوا الكيل ولا تكونوا من
المخسرين ○

182. " And weigh with scales
True and upright.

١٨٢- وزنوا بالقسطاس المستقيم ○

183. " And withhold not things
Justly due to men,
Nor do evil in the land,
Working mischief.

١٨٣- ولا تبخسوا الناس أشياءهم
ولا تعثوا في الأرض مفسدين ○

184. " And fear Him Who created
You and (Who created)
The generations before (you)"

١٨٤- واتقوا الذي خلقكم
والجبلة الأولين ○

185. They said : " Thou art only
One of those bewitched !

١٨٥- قالوا إنما أنت من المسحرين ○

186. " Thou art no more than
A mortal like us,
And indeed we think
Thou art a liar ![3217]

١٨٦- وما أنت إلا بشر مثلنا
وإن نظنك لمن الكذبين ○

187. " Now cause a piece
Of the sky to fall on us,
If thou art truthful !"[3218]

١٨٧- فأسقط علينا كسفا من السماء
إن كنت من الصدقين ○

188. He said : " My Lord
Knows best what ye do."[3219]

١٨٨- قال ربي أعلم بما تعملون ○

3216. They were a commercial people, but they were given to fraud, injustice, and wrongful mischief (by intermeddling with others). They are asked to fear God and follow His ways : it is He Who also created their predecessors among mankind, who never prospered by fraud and violent wrong-doing, but only by justice and fair dealing.

3217. They deny that he is a prophet or that they are doing wrong, or that any former generations behaved differently. They think they are the true exponents of human nature, and that such as he —idealists—are mere madmen.

3218. 'If you really claim any real contact with God, let us see if you can bring down a piece of the sky to fall on us !'

3219. The challenge to bring down a piece of the sky was merely empty bravado, on the part of those who had called him a liar. But Shu'aib does not insult them. He merely says : "God is the best judge of your conduct : what more can I say ?" And God did punish them.

189. But they rejected him.
Then the punishment
Of a day of overshadowing
gloom[3220]
Seized them, and that was
The Penalty of a Great Day.[3221]

۱۸۹- فَكَذَّبُوهُ
فَأَخَذَهُمْ عَذَابُ يَوْمِ الظُّلَّةِ
إِنَّهُ كَانَ عَذَابَ يَوْمٍ عَظِيمٍ

190. Verily in that is a Sign:
But most of them
Do not believe.

۱۹۰- إِنَّ فِي ذَٰلِكَ لَآيَةً
وَمَا كَانَ أَكْثَرُهُمْ مُؤْمِنِينَ

191. And verily thy Lord
Is He, the Exalted in Might,
Most Merciful.[3222]

۱۹۱- وَإِنَّ رَبَّكَ لَهُوَ الْعَزِيزُ الرَّحِيمُ

C. 168.—Thus the Truth of God must win against folly
(xxvi. 192-227.) And falsehood. The Spirit of Inspiration
And Faith brought down the Qur-ān to the mind
Of the holy Prophet, that he might teach
In noble Arabic speech, and through it
Reach the world. If obstinate rebels
Do resist the Message, their day is brief:
With humble, gentle kindness it must make
Its way to all, nearest and farthest.
It is not like the vain words of poets false,
Wandering without a goal: it is Truth,
That fills the heart which trusts in God.

Section 11.

192. Verily this is a Revelation[3223]
From the Lord of the Worlds:

۱۹۲- وَإِنَّهُ لَتَنْزِيلُ رَبِّ الْعَالَمِينَ

193. With it came down
The Spirit of Faith and
Truth—[3224]

۱۹۳- نَزَلَ بِهِ الرُّوحُ الْأَمِينُ

3220. Perhaps a shower of ashes and cinders accompanying a volcanic eruption. If these people were the same as the Midianites, there was also an earthquake. See vii. 91 and n. 1063.

3221. It must have been a terrible day of wholesale destruction,—earthquake, volcanic eruption, lava, cinders and ashes and rumbling noises to frighten those whose death was not instantaneous.

3222. See above, n. 3193 to xxvi. 121.

3223. The hostile reception of some of the previous Messengers having been mentioned, the special characteristics of the Qur-ān are now referred to, to show (1) that it is true, and (2) that its rejection by the Meccan Pagans was of a piece with previous experience in the history of man: vested interests resist Truth, but it conquers.

3224. *Rūḥ-ul-amīn*, the epithet of Gabriel, who came with the inspired Messages to the holy Prophet, is difficult to render in a single epithet in translation. In n. 3187 to xxvi. 107 I have described some of the various shades of meaning attached to the adjective *Amīn* as applied to a Prophet. A further signification as attached to the Spirit of Inspiration is that it is the very quintessence of Faith and Truth, unlike the lying spirits which delude men with falsehood. On the whole, I think "the Spirit of Faith and Truth" will represent the original best here.

194. To thy heart and mind,[3225]
That thou mayest admonish

١٩٤- عَلٰى قَلْبِكَ لِتَكُوْنَ مِنَ الْمُنْذِرِيْنَ ۝

195. In the perspicuous
Arabic tongue.

١٩٥- بِلِسَانٍ عَرَبِيٍّ مُّبِيْنٍ ۝

196. Without doubt it is (announced)
In the mystic Books [3226]
Of former peoples.

١٩٦- وَاِنَّهٗ لَفِيْ زُبُرِ الْاَوَّلِيْنَ ۝

197. Is it not a Sign
To them that the Learned
Of the Children of Israel
Knew it (as true)? [3227]

١٩٧- اَوَلَمْ يَكُنْ لَّهُمْ اٰيَةً
اَنْ يَّعْلَمَهٗ عُلَمٰٓؤُا بَنِيْٓ اِسْرَآءِيْلَ ۝

198. Had We revealed it
To any of the non-Arabs,

١٩٨- وَلَوْ نَزَّلْنٰهُ عَلٰى بَعْضِ الْاَعْجَمِيْنَ ۝

199. And had he recited it
To them, they would not
Have believed in it.[3228]

١٩٩- فَقَرَاَهٗ عَلَيْهِمْ مَّا كَانُوْا بِهٖ
مُؤْمِنِيْنَ ۝

200. Thus have We caused it
To enter the hearts
Of the Sinners.[3229]

٢٠٠- كَذٰلِكَ سَلَكْنٰهُ فِيْ قُلُوْبِ الْمُجْرِمِيْنَ ۝

3225. *Qalb* (Heart) signifies not only the seat of the affections, but also the seat of the memory and understanding. The process of inspiration is indicated by the impression of the divine Message on the inspired one's heart, memory, and understanding, from which it was promulgated in human speech to the world. In this case the human speech was the perspicuous Arabic tongue, which would be plainly intelligible to the audience who would immediately hear it and be through them transmitted to all the world.

3226. In iii. 184 I have translated *Zubur* as Books of dark prophecies. See n. 490 there. Here perhaps mystic Scriptures of all kinds are meant, as the universal Message of Islam was adumbrated in all true Books of divine knowledge.

3227. Many of the Jewish Doctors recognised the holy Prophet's Message as a Message from God, *e.g.*, 'Abdullāh ibn Salām and Mukhairīq. The latter was a man of property, which he left for Islam. (There were also Christian monks and learned men who recognised the Prophet's mission.)

3228. The turn of Arabia having come for receiving God's Revelation, as was foretold in previous Revelations, it was inevitable that it should be in the Arab tongue through the mouth of an Arab. Otherwise it would have been unintelligible, and the Arabs could not have received the Faith and become the vehicles for its promulgation as actually happened in history.

3229. "Thus" I think means through the medium of the Arabic language and the Arab people. The Qur-ān penetrated through their language and their hearts. If the hard-hearted among them did not believe, they will see when the Penalty comes, how grievous a mistake they made. For the Penalty must come; even when they least expected it. They will be caught saying or thinking, "There is plenty of time; we can get another respite," when already it will have become too late for them to turn over a new leaf.

201. They will not believe In it until they see The grievous Penalty;	٢٠١- لَا يُؤْمِنُونَ بِهٖ حَتّٰى يَرَوُا الْعَذَابَ الْاَلِيْمَ ۝
202. But the (Penalty) will come To them of a sudden, While they preceive it not;	٢٠٢- فَيَأْتِيَهُمْ بَغْتَةً وَّ هُمْ لَا يَشْعُرُوْنَ ۝
203. Then they will say: "Shall we be respited?"	٢٠٣- فَيَقُوْلُوْا هَلْ نَحْنُ مُنْظَرُوْنَ ۝
204. Do they then ask For Our Penalty to be Hastened on? 3230	٢٠٤- اَفَبِعَذَابِنَا يَسْتَعْجِلُوْنَ ۝
205. Seest thou? If We do Let them enjoy (this life) For a few years,	٢٠٥- اَفَرَءَيْتَ اِنْ مَّتَّعْنٰهُمْ سِنِيْنَ ۝
206. Yet there comes to them At length the (Punishment) Which they were promised!	٢٠٦- ثُمَّ جَآءَهُمْ مَّا كَانُوْا يُوْعَدُوْنَ ۝
207. It will profit them not That they enjoyed (this life)!	٢٠٧- مَآ اَغْنٰى عَنْهُمْ مَّا كَانُوْا يُمَتَّعُوْنَ ۝
208. Never did We destroy A population, but had Its warners—	٢٠٨- وَمَآ اَهْلَكْنَا مِنْ قَرْيَةٍ اِلَّا لَهَا مُنْذِرُوْنَ ۝
209. By way of reminder; And We never are unjust.[3231]	٢٠٩- ذِكْرٰى ۛ وَمَا كُنَّا ظٰلِمِيْنَ ۝ ع
210. No evil ones have brought[3232] Down this (Revelation):	٢١٠- وَمَا تَنَزَّلَتْ بِهِ الشَّيٰطِيْنُ ۝

3230. While some sinners out of negligence postpone the day of repentance till it is too late, others more bold actually ask out of bravado that God's Punishment should be brought down on them at once, as they do not believe in God or His Punishment! The answer to them is: It will come soon enough—too soon, they will think, when it comes! *Cf.* xxii. 47 and notes.

3231. God will grant much respite to sinners, for He is Most Gracious and Merciful. But all this respite will profit them nothing if they are merely immersed in the vanities of this world. Again and again, in spite of their rebellion and their rejection, does God send warnings and warners before the final Punishment of Justice. For God knows human weakness, and He will never be unjust in the least.

3232. When anything extraordinary happens, there are always people desirous of putting the worst construction on it, and saying that it is the work of the evil ones, the devils. So when the Qur-ān came with its Message in wondrous Arabic, its enemies could only account for its power by attributing it to evil spirits! Such a beneficent message can never suit the purposes of the evil ones, nor would it be in their power to produce it. In fact Good and Evil are poles asunder, and Evil cannot even hear words of Good, of tender Pity for sinners and Forgiveness for the penitent!

211. It would neither suit them
Nor would they be able
(To produce it).

٢١١- وَمَا يَنۢبَغِي لَهُمْ وَمَا يَسْتَطِيعُونَ ۝

212. Indeed they have been removed
Far from even (a chance of)
Hearing it.

٢١٢- إِنَّهُمْ عَنِ السَّمْعِ لَمَعْزُولُونَ ۝

213. So call not on any
Other god with God,
Or thou wilt be among
Those under the Penalty.

٢١٣- فَلَا تَدْعُ مَعَ اللَّهِ إِلَٰهًا ءَاخَرَ
فَتَكُونَ مِنَ الْمُعَذَّبِينَ ۝

214. And admonish thy nearest
Kinsmen,

٢١٤- وَأَنذِرْ عَشِيرَتَكَ الْأَقْرَبِينَ ۝

215. And lower thy wing[3233]
To the Believers who
Follow thee.

٢١٥- وَاخْفِضْ جَنَاحَكَ لِمَنِ اتَّبَعَكَ
مِنَ الْمُؤْمِنِينَ ۝

216. Then if they disobey thee,
Say: "I am free (of responsibility)
For what ye do!"[3234]

٢١٦- فَإِنْ عَصَوْكَ
فَقُلْ إِنِّي بَرِيٓءٌ مِّمَّا تَعْمَلُونَ ۝

217. And put thy trust
On the Exalted in Might,
The Merciful,—

٢١٧- وَتَوَكَّلْ عَلَى الْعَزِيزِ الرَّحِيمِ ۝

218. Who seeth thee standing
Forth (in prayer),

٢١٨- الَّذِي يَرَىٰكَ حِينَ تَقُومُ ۝

219. And thy movements among
Those who prostrate themselves.[3235]

٢١٩- وَتَقَلُّبَكَ فِي السَّٰجِدِينَ ۝

3233. That is, be kind, gentle, and considerate with them, as a high flying bird is when she lowers her wing to her offspring. *Cf.* xvii. 24 and n. 2205, and xv. 88 and n. 2011.

3234. "Disobey thee" implied that they did something wrong, for the holy Prophet commanded what was right and forbade what was wrong. If, then, any of his flock did wrong, the responsibility was not his, for he, like a good shepherd, tried to keep them right. What was he then to do? He would continue his teaching. But if any of them went so far wrong as to try to injure their own Teacher, Leader, and Guide, there was nothing for him to fear. His trust was only in God, and God sees and appraises all men's actions at their true worth.

3235. Literally, the standing and prostration are postures in Muslim prayer: the holy Prophet was equally earnest, sincere, and zealous in prayer for himself and for all his people. But there is a wider meaning. The postures in prayer are symbolical of attitudes of mind, and behaviour in life generally, and the "movements" may refer also to various vicissitudes, in which a man's soul is tried and tested just as the body is exercised in standing, bowing, kneeling, and prostration in prayer. The Prophet's behaviour was exemplary in al the turns of fortune, and however foolish men may cavil, his purity and uprightness are fully known to God.

220. For it is He
Who heareth and knoweth
All things.

٢٢٠-إِنَّهُ هُوَ السَّمِيعُ الْعَلِيمُ ○

221. Shall I inform you,
(O people!), on whom it is
That the evil ones descend?[3236]

٢٢١-هَلْ أُنَبِّئُكُمْ عَلَىٰ مَنْ تَنَزَّلُ الشَّيٰطِينُ ○

222. They descend on every
Lying, wicked person,

٢٢٢-تَنَزَّلُ عَلَىٰ كُلِّ أَفَّاكٍ أَثِيمٍ ○

223. (Into whose ears) they pour
Hearsay vanities, and most
Of them are liars.

٢٢٣-يُلْقُونَ السَّمْعَ وَأَكْثَرُهُمْ كٰذِبُونَ ○

224. And the Poets,—[3237]
It is those straying in Evil,
Who follow them:

٢٢٤-وَالشُّعَرَاءُ يَتَّبِعُهُمُ الْغَاوُنَ ○

225. Seest thou not that they
Wander distracted in every
Valley?—

٢٢٥-أَلَمْ تَرَ أَنَّهُمْ فِي كُلِّ وَادٍ يَهِيمُونَ ○

226. And that they say
What they practise not?—

٢٢٦-وَأَنَّهُمْ يَقُولُونَ مَا لَا يَفْعَلُونَ ○

227. Except those who believe,[3238]
Work righteousness, engage much

٢٢٧-إِلَّا الَّذِينَ آمَنُوا وَعَمِلُوا الصّٰلِحٰتِ

3236. To people who maliciously suggested that the holy Prophet was possessed or inspired by evil spirits (xxvi. 210 above) the reply had already been made, but it is now declared that that suggestion is itself the work of Evil. Behind such suggestions are lying and wickedness, or at best some half-truths caught up in hearsay and twisted so as to show Good in an evil light.

3237. *The Poets*: to be read along with the exceptions mentioned in verse 227 below. Poetry and other arts are not in themselves evil, but may on the contrary be used in the service of religion and righteousness. But there is a danger that they may be prostituted for base purposes. If they are insincere ("they say what they do not") or are divorced from actual life or its goodness or its serious purpose, they may become instruments of evil or futility. They then wander about without any set purpose, and seek the depths (valleys) of human folly rather than the heights of divine light.

3238. Poetry and the fine arts which are to be commended are those which emanate from minds steeped in Faith, which try to carry out in life the fine sentiments they express in their artistic work, aim at the glory of God rather than at self-glorification or the fulsome praise of men with feet of clay, and do not (as in Jihād) attack anything except aggressive evil. In this sense a perfect artist should be a perfect man. Perfection may not be attainable in this life, but it should be the aim of every man, and especially of one who wishes to become a supreme artist, not only in technique but in spirit and essentials. Among the commendable poets contemporary with the holy Prophet may be mentioned Ḥassān and Labīd: the latter had the honour of being one of the seven whose poems were selected for "hanging" (the *Mu'allaqāt*) in the Days of Ignorance.

In the remembrance of God, And defend themselves only after They are unjustly attacked. And soon will the unjust[3239] Assailants know what vicissitudes Their affairs will take!	وَذَكَرُوا اللّٰهَ كَثِيْرًا وَّانْتَصَرُوْا مِنْ بَعْدِ مَا ظُلِمُوْا ۗ وَسَيَعْلَمُ الَّذِيْنَ ظَلَمُوْٓا اَيَّ مُنْقَلَبٍ يَّنْقَلِبُوْنَ ۝

3239. These were the scurrilous rhymesters, who were doomed to come to an evil end.

APPENDIX IX.

Thamūd Inscriptions at al-Hijr. (xxvi. 141-159; xv. 80-84; and vii. 73-79.)

Mr. C.M. Doughty travelled in North-Western Arabia and Najd in the 1880's, and his book *Arabia Deserta* forms one of the most notable of Arabian Travel-books. It was first published in two volumes by the Cambridge University Press in 1888, and has recently gone through several editions. The edition I have used is the unabridged one-volume edition printed in London in 1926. The references in this Appendix should be understood to refer to that edition.

Doughty travelled on the old Pilgrim Caravan route (*Darb-ul-Hajj*) with a Pilgrim Caravan from Damascus as far as Madāïn Ṣāliḥ, and then parted company with the Pilgrims and turned into Najd. Madāïn Ṣāliḥ (the Cities of Ṣāliḥ), is one of the stations on the Syrian Pilgrim route, about 180 miles north of Medina. Tabūk, to which the holy Prophet led an expedition in A.H. 9 (see Introduction to S. ix), is about 170 miles farther to the north-west, and Ma'an Junction about 150 miles still farther. Madāïn Ṣāliḥ was also an important station on the prehistoric gold and frankincense (*bakhūr*) route between Yemen and Egypt or Syria. In sacred history it marks the ruined site of the Thamūd people to whom the prophet Ṣāliḥ was sent, whose she-camel was a symbolic Sign and is connected with Ṣāliḥ's history. See n. 3208 to xxvi. 155-157. To the west and north-west of Madāïn Ṣāliḥ are three *Ḥarrats* or tracts of volcanic land covered with lava, stretching as far as Tabūk.

This is how Doughty describes his first view of Madāïn Ṣāliḥ, approaching from the north-west. "At length in the dim morning twilight, as we journeyed, we were come to a sandy brow and a straight descending-place betwixt cliffs of sandstones. There was some shouting in the forward, and Aswad bid me look up, 'this was a famous place, *Mabrak-an-Nāqa*'" (the kneeling place of the she-camel of Ṣāliḥ) "It is short, at first steep, and issues upon the plain of *al-Ḥijr*, which is Madāïn Ṣāliḥ; where the sun coming up showed the singular landscape of this valley-plain, encompassed with mighty sand-rock precipices (which here resemble ranges of city walls, fantastic towers, and castle buildings), and upon them lie high shouldering sand drifts. The bottom is sand, with much growth of desert bushes; and I perceived some thin sprinkled volcanic drift. Westward is seen the immense mountain blackness, terrible and lowering, of the Ḥarrat." (*Arabia Deserta*, p. 83, vol. I.)

Doughty took rubbings of some of the Inscriptions which were accessible to him and they were studied by the great Semitic scholar M. Ernest Renan and published by the Académie des Inscriptions et Belles-Lettres. Renan's Report in French is printed as an Appendix to Chapters IV, V and VI of *Arabia Deserta* (pp. 180-187, vol. I) and M. le Marquis de Vogüé's Note (also in French) on the Nabatæan sculptured Architecture at Madāïn Ṣāliḥ at pp. 620-623, vol. I.

The general result of these studies may be summarised. The sculpture and architecture are found to be of the same kind as in the Nabatæan monuments at Petra (for which see n. 1043 to vii. 73). At Petra there are no dated Inscriptions preserved, but at Madāïn Ṣāliḥ we have several. There are at Madāïn Ṣāliḥ perhaps 100 sepulchral rock-hewn chambers, in some of which are found human bones and remains, showing that the Nabatæans knew the art of embalming, and used linen of the same kind as was used in ancient Egypt. The tombs are dedicated in perpetuity to named families, and the named Nabatæan kings have, each, the epithet "loving his people". There are flat side-pilasters, and the figures of four-footed beasts, eagles, and other birds are discernible. Besides the sepulchral chambers, there is a great Hall or Council Chamber (*Līwān*), 25ft. × 27ft. × 13ft. This may have been a Temple. The gods worshipped were those whose names we know of from other Nabatæan sources,—Dusarés, Martaba, Allāt, Manā, Keïs, and Hubal. Allāt, Manāt, and Hubal are also known to us in connection with the idols of the Pagan Quraish of the Times of Ignorance. It is interesting to find the word *Mesjeda* (Arabic *Masjid*) already used here for a "place of worship". Triads of stones were worshipped as gods.

The Inscriptions have dates from 3 B.C. to 79 A.D. Within this short period of 82 years we can see something of the development of Semitic palæography. The writing becomes more and more cursive with the years. We have here a central point between Old Armenian, Square Hebrew, Palmyran, Sinaitic, Kūfī and Naskh.

We may treat the Nabatæans as historical, as we have established dates. The Thamūd were prehistoric, and occupied sites which were afterwards occupied by the Nabatæans and others. The kneeling place of Ṣāliḥ's she-camel *Mabrak-un-Nāqa*) and the well of the she-camel (*Bīr-un-Nāqa*), and a number of local names keep alive the race-memory of an ancient Arabian people and their prophet Ṣāliḥ.

INTRODUCTION TO SŪRA XXVII (*Naml*).

This Sūra is cognate in subject to the one preceding it and the two following it. Its chronological place is also in the same group of four, in the middle Meccan period.

Here there is much mystic symbolism. Wonders in the physical world are types of greater wonders in the spiritual world. The Fire, the White Hand, and the Rod, in the story of Moses; the speech of birds, the crowds of Jinns and men pitted against a humble ant, and the Hoopoe and the Queen of Sheba, in Solomon's story; the defeat of the plot of the nine wicked men in the story of Ṣāliḥ; and the crime of sin with open eyes in the story of Lot;—lead up to the lessons of true and false worship and the miracles of God's grace and revelation.

Summary.—Wonderful is Revelation, like the Fire which Moses saw, which was a glimpse of God's Glory, and His Miracles, which searched out those who refused Faith in spite of the light they had received (xxvii. 1-14, and C. 169).

Solomon knew the speech of Birds and had hosts of Jinns and men; yet the wise ant had ample defence against them: the Hoopoe who was absent at his muster, was yet serving him: the Queen of Sheba had a kingdom, but it submitted with conviction to the Wisdom of Solomon and the Kingdom of God (xxvii. 15-44, and C. 170).

Fools ascribe ill-luck to godliness as in Ṣāliḥ's story, or fall into their lusts with their eyes open, as in Lūṭs story; but their plots and their rage will be foiled by God (xxvii. 45-58, and C. 171).

God's glory and goodness are supreme over all Creation: Unfaith will yield to Faith in the final adjustment of values: so follow Revelation, serve God, and trust in Him (xxvii. 59-93, and C. 172).

C. 169.—Revelation shows us a glimpse of the spiritual
(xxvii. 1-14.) World, guides us in this life, and gives us
The Hope of eternal Bliss in the Hereafter.
It works a complete transformation in us,
As it did with Moses when he saw
The mystic Fire and was given the Signs
With which to reclaim a people lost
In superstition and sin, and proud of sin.

Sūra XXVII.

Naml, or the Ants.

سُوْرَةُ النَّمْلِ مَكِّيَّةٌ (٢٧) (٤٨) — اٰيَاتُهَا ٩٣ — رُكُوْعَاتُهَا ٧

In the name of God, Most Gracious,
Most Merciful.

بِسْمِ اللّٰهِ الرَّحْمٰنِ الرَّحِيْمِ

1. Ṭā. Sīn.[3240]
These are verses
Of the Qur-ān,—a Book
That makes (things) clear;

١- طٰسٓ
تِلْكَ اٰيٰتُ الْقُرْاٰنِ وَكِتَابٍ مُّبِيْنٍ ۙ

2. A Guide; and Glad Tidings
For the Believers,—[3241]

٢- هُدًى وَّبُشْرٰى لِلْمُؤْمِنِيْنَ ۙ

3. Those who establish regular prayers
And give in regular charity,
And also have (full) assurance
Of the Hereafter.

٣- الَّذِيْنَ يُقِيْمُوْنَ الصَّلٰوةَ وَيُؤْتُوْنَ الزَّكٰوةَ
وَهُمْ بِالْاٰخِرَةِ هُمْ يُوْقِنُوْنَ

4. As to those who believe not
In the Hereafter, We have
Made their deeds pleasing[3242]
In their eyes; and so they
Wander about in distraction.

٤- اِنَّ الَّذِيْنَ لَا يُؤْمِنُوْنَ بِالْاٰخِرَةِ
زَيَّنَّا لَهُمْ اَعْمَالَهُمْ فَهُمْ يَعْمَهُوْنَ ؕ

5. Such are they for whom
A grievous Penalty is (waiting):
And in the Hereafter theirs
Will be the greatest loss.[3243]

٥- اُولٰٓئِكَ الَّذِيْنَ لَهُمْ سُوْٓءُ الْعَذَابِ
وَهُمْ فِى الْاٰخِرَةِ هُمُ الْاَخْسَرُوْنَ

6. As to thee, the Qur-ān
Is bestowed upon thee
From the presence of One
Who is Wise and All-Knowing.

٦- وَاِنَّكَ لَتُلَقَّى الْقُرْاٰنَ
مِنْ لَّدُنْ حَكِيْمٍ عَلِيْمٍ

النصف

3240. See n. 3137 to xxvi. 1.

3241. Revelation is here presented in three aspects: (1) it explains things, the nature of God, our own position, and the spiritual world around; (2) it directs us to right conduct and keeps us from evil; and (3) to those who have Faith and accept its guidance, it gives the good news of forgiveness, purification, and the achievement of salvation.

3242. Those who reject God and follow Evil have a good conceit of themselves. Their deeds are pleasing to no one else. As they have rejected God's guidance, they are allowed to hug their own self-conceit, and given further respite for repentance. But they follow their own whims and wander about in distraction, as they have no standards such as guide the godly.

3243. The account will then be made up, and they will be found to be terribly in loss. They will be the worst in loss, for all their self-complacency.

7. Behold! Moses said[3244]
To his family. "I perceive
A fire; soon will I bring you
From there some information,
Or I will bring you
A burning brand to light
Our fuel, that ye may
Warm yourselves.

٧- إِذْ قَالَ مُوسَىٰ لِأَهْلِهِ إِنِّي آنَسْتُ نَارًا ۚ
سَآتِيكُم مِّنْهَا بِخَبَرٍ
أَوْ آتِيكُم بِشِهَابٍ قَبَسٍ
لَّعَلَّكُمْ تَصْطَلُونَ ۝

8. But when he came
To the (Fire), a voice
Was heard: "Blessed are those[3245]
In the Fire and those around:
And Glory to God,
The Lord of the Worlds.

٨- فَلَمَّا جَاءَهَا نُودِيَ أَن بُورِكَ
مَن فِي النَّارِ وَمَنْ حَوْلَهَا ۚ
وَسُبْحَانَ اللَّهِ رَبِّ الْعَالَمِينَ ۝

9. "O Moses! Verily,
I am God, the Exalted
In Might, the Wise!...

٩- يَا مُوسَىٰ إِنَّهُ أَنَا اللَّهُ الْعَزِيزُ الْحَكِيمُ ۝

10. "Now do thou throw thy rod!"[3246]
But when he saw it
Moving (of its own accord)
As if it had been a snake,
He turned back in retreat,
And retraced not his steps:
"O Moses!" (it was said),
"Fear not: truly, in My presence,
Those called as apostles
Have no fear,—[3247]

١٠- وَأَلْقِ عَصَاكَ ۚ
فَلَمَّا رَآهَا تَهْتَزُّ كَأَنَّهَا جَانٌّ
وَلَّىٰ مُدْبِرًا وَلَمْ يُعَقِّبْ ۚ
يَا مُوسَىٰ لَا تَخَفْ
إِنِّي لَا يَخَافُ لَدَيَّ الْمُرْسَلُونَ ۝

3244. *Cf.* xx. 9-24. Both there and here there is a reference to the dawn of Revelation in the heart of Moses. The points there emphasised will be found in the notes to that passage. Here the emphasis is on the wonderful nature of the Fire and the wonderful way in which Moses was transformed at the touch of spiritual Light. He was travelling in the Sinai desert with his family. Seeking ordinary light, he came upon a Light which took him to the highest mysteries of God. No doubt all his inner history had prepared him for his great destiny. It is the inner history that matters, and not the place or position of a man in the eyes of his ordinary fellows.

3245. *Those*: in the original the pronoun is in the singular, "*man*", which is often used with a plural meaning. The Commentators usually construe it to mean that it was not a physical fire, but it was the glory of the Angels, a reflection of the Glory of God. Hence the exclamation at the end of the verse.

3246. Moses was now transported into an entirely new world. What he had taken to be an ordinary fire was a gleam of the spiritual world,—rays from the angels of light. The desert in which he had been was the lower life stripped of its ornaments, leading to the divine light of Sinai. Through that Light he heard the Voice of the Source of Wisdom and Power. His own rod or staff was no longer the dead piece of wood that had hitherto supported him. It became instinct with life, a life that moved, and had the power of offence and defence in it, as all living Good must have in its fight with Evil. His own transformation is described in the next note.

3247. In this great, new, wonderful world, that was opening out to Moses, he had to get his vision adjusted to his new surroundings, as an ordinary man has to adjust his sight before he can see in any very strong light that is new to him. The staff which had become alive as a snake frightened him: yet it was to be his own instrument of work in his new mission. All fear was to be cast out of his mind, as befitted a man chosen by God.

11. " But if any have done wrong
And have thereafter substituted
Good to take the place of evil,[3248]
Truly, I am Oft-Forgiving,
Most Merciful.

١١- إِلَّا مَنْ ظَلَمَ ثُمَّ بَدَّلَ
حُسْنًا بَعْدَ سُوٓءٍ
فَإِنِّي غَفُورٌ رَّحِيمٌ ۝

12. " Now put thy hand into
Thy bosom, and it will
Come forth white without stain[3249]
(Or harm) : (these are) among
The nine Signs (thou wilt take)[3250]
To Pharaoh and his people :
For they are a people
Rebellious in transgression."

١٢- وَأَدْخِلْ يَدَكَ فِي جَيْبِكَ
تَخْرُجْ بَيْضَآءَ مِنْ غَيْرِ سُوٓءٍ
فِي تِسْعِ ءَايَٰتٍ إِلَىٰ فِرْعَوْنَ وَقَوْمِهِ
إِنَّهُمْ كَانُوا قَوْمًا فَٰسِقِينَ ۝

13. But when Our Signs came
To them, that should have[3251]
Opened their eyes, they said :
" This is sorcery manifest ! "

١٣- فَلَمَّا جَآءَتْهُمْ ءَايَٰتُنَا مُبْصِرَةً
قَالُوا هَٰذَا سِحْرٌ مُّبِينٌ ۝

14. And they rejected those Signs
In iniquity and arrogance,
Though their souls were convinced
Thereof : so see what was
The end of those
Who acted corruptly !

١٤- وَجَحَدُوا بِهَا
وَاسْتَيْقَنَتْهَآ أَنفُسُهُمْ ظُلْمًا وَعُلُوًّا
فَانظُرْ كَيْفَ كَانَ عَٰقِبَةُ الْمُفْسِدِينَ ۝

C. 170.—No less were David and Solomon versed
(xxvii. 15-44.) In knowledge and mystic wisdom. Even
Solomon could appreciate the wisdom
Of the humble Ant. He used all his power
And resources in extending the Kingdom

3248. His slaying the Egyptian (n. 3146 to xxvi. 14), however defensible from certain aspects, was yet something from his past that had to be washed off, and God, Oft-Forgiving, Most Merciful, did it out of His abounding Grace. Nay, more ; he was given a pure, Radiant Hand, as a Sign of his personal transformation, as stated in the next verse.

3249. *Cf.* xx. 22. There the expression is : " Draw thy hand close to thy side." As far as the physical act is concerned, the expressions there and here mean the same thing. Moses had a loose-fitting robe. If he put his hand within the folds of the robe, it would go to his bosom on the side of his body opposite to that from which his hand came ; *i.e.*, if it was his right hand it would go to the left side of his bosom. But the difference of expression has a little spiritual significance. The bosom here stands for his innermost being, which was being so transformed with divine light as to lend the radiance to his hand also, his instrument of action. The hand comes out white and radiant, without a stain. Ordinarily if the skin becomes white it is a sign of disease or leprosy. Here it was the opposite. It was a sign of radiance and glory from the higher Light.

3250. *The nine Signs* : see n. 1091 to vii. 133.

3251. The Signs should have clearly opened the eyes or any persons who honestly examined them and thought about them. Those who rejected them were perverse and were going against their own light and inner conviction. That was the aggravating feature of their sin.

Of God. In wonderful ways did He lead
The Queen of Sheba to the Light of the Faith
Of Unity, and confirmed her in pure
Worship, the worship of the Lord of the Worlds.

SECTION 2.

15. We gave (in the past)
Knowledge to David and
Solomon: [3252]
And they both said:
"Praise be to God, Who
Has favoured us above many
Of His servants who believe!" [3253]

١٥- وَلَقَدْ اٰتَيْنَا دَاوٗدَ وَسُلَيْمٰنَ عِلْمًا ۚ
وَقَالَا الْحَمْدُ لِلّٰهِ الَّذِىْ
فَضَّلَنَا عَلٰى كَثِيْرٍ مِّنْ عِبَادِهِ الْمُؤْمِنِيْنَ ○

16. And Solomon was David's heir. [3254]
He said: "O ye people!
We have been taught the speech [3255]
Of Birds, and on us
Has been bestowed (a little)
Of all things: this is
Indeed Grace manifest (from
God.)" [3256]

١٦- وَوَرِثَ سُلَيْمٰنُ دَاوٗدَ ،
وَقَالَ يٰۤاَيُّهَا النَّاسُ عُلِّمْنَا مَنْطِقَ الطَّيْرِ
وَاُوْتِيْنَا مِنْ كُلِّ شَىْءٍ ۚ
اِنَّ هٰذَا لَهُوَ الْفَضْلُ الْمُبِيْنُ ○

17. And before Solomon were
marshalled

١٧- وَحُشِرَ لِسُلَيْمٰنَ

3252. *Cf.* xxi 78-82. "Knowledge" means such knowledge as leads up to the higher things in life, the Wisdom that was shown in their decisions and judgments, and the understanding that enabled them to fulfil their mission in life. They were both just men and apostles of God. The Bible, as we have it, is inconsistent: on the one hand it calls David "a man after God's own heart" (1 Samuel, xiii. 14, and Acts xiii. 22); and the Christians acclaim Christ as a son of David; but on the other hand, horrible crimes are ascribed to him, which, if he had committed them, would make him a monster of cruelty and injustice. About Solomon, too, while he is described as a glorious king, there are stories of his lapses into sin and idolatry. The Muslim teaching considers them both to be men of piety and wisdom, and high in spiritual knowledge.

3253. They ascribed, as was proper, their knowledge, wisdom, and power to the only true Source of all good, God.

3254. The point is that Solomon not only inherited his father's kingdom but his spiritual insight and the prophetic office, which do not necessarily go from father to son.

3255. *Speech of Birds.* The spoken word in human speech is different from the means of communication which birds and animals have between each other. But no man can doubt that they have means of communication with each other, if he only observes the orderly flight of migratory birds or the regulated behaviour of ants, bees, and other creatures who live in communities. The wisdom of Solomon and others like him (he speaks of "we") consisted in understanding these things—in the animal world and in the lower fringes of human intelligence.

3256. "*A little of all things*": Solomon was a king of power and authority; outside his kingdom he had influence among many neighbouring peoples; he had knowledge of birds, and beasts and plants; he was just and wise, and understood men; and above all, he had spiritual insight, which brought him near to God. Thus he had something of all kinds of desirable gifts. And with true gratitude he referred them to God, the Giver of all gifts.

His hosts,—of Jinns and men
And birds, and they were all
Kept in order and ranks.[3257]

جُنُوْدُهٗ مِنَ الْجِنِّ وَالْاِنْسِ وَالطَّيْرِ
فَهُمْ يُوْزَعُوْنَ ○

18. At length, when they came
To a (lowly) valley of ants,
One of the ants said:
"O ye ants, get into
Your habitations, lest Solomon
And his hosts crush you
(Under foot) without knowing
it."[3258]

١٨- حَتّٰٓى اِذَآ اَتَوْا عَلٰى وَادِ النَّمْلِ
قَالَتْ نَمْلَةٌ يّٰٓاَيُّهَا النَّمْلُ ادْخُلُوْا
مَسٰكِنَكُمْ لَا يَحْطِمَنَّكُمْ سُلَيْمٰنُ وَجُنُوْدُهٗ
وَهُمْ لَا يَشْعُرُوْنَ ○

19. So he smiled, amused
At her speech; and he said:
"O my Lord! so order me
That I may be grateful
For Thy favours, which Thou
Hast bestowed on me and[3259]
On my parents, and that
I may work the righteousness
That will please Thee:[3260]
And admit me, by Thy Grace,
To the ranks of Thy
Righteous Servants."[3261]

١٩- فَتَبَسَّمَ ضَاحِكًا مِّنْ قَوْلِهَا وَقَالَ
رَبِّ اَوْزِعْنِيْٓ اَنْ اَشْكُرَ
نِعْمَتَكَ الَّتِيْٓ اَنْعَمْتَ عَلَيَّ
وَعَلٰى وَالِدَيَّ وَاَنْ اَعْمَلَ صَالِحًا
تَرْضٰىهُ وَاَدْخِلْنِيْ بِرَحْمَتِكَ
فِيْ عِبَادِكَ الصّٰلِحِيْنَ ○

3257. Besides the literal meaning, there are two symbolical meanings. (1) All his subjects of varying grades of intelligence, taste, and civilization, were kept in due order and co-operation, by his discipline, justice, and good government. (2) The gifts of various kinds, which he possessed (see last note), he used in proper order and co-ordination, as if they were a well disciplined army, thus getting the best possible results from them.

3258. This verse and the next, read together, suggest the symbolical meaning as predominant. The ant, to outward appearance, is a very small and humble creature. In the great pomp and circumstances of the world, she (generic feminine in Arabic) may be neglected or even trampled on by a people who mean her no harm. Yet, by her wisdom, she carries on her own life within her own sphere ("habitations") unmolested, and makes a useful contribution to the economy of the world. So there is room for the humblest people in the spiritual world.

3259. The counterpart to the position of the humble ant is the position of a great king like Solomon. He prays that his power and wisdom and all other gifts may be used for righteousness and for the benefit of all around him. The ant being in his thoughts, we may suppose that he means particularly in his prayer that he may not even unwittingly tread on humble beings in his pre-occupations with the great things of the world.

3260. The righteousness which pleases the world is often very different from the righteousness which pleases God. Solomon prays that he may always take God's Will as his standard, rather than the standards of men.

3261. In the Kingdom of God, righteousness is the badge of citizenship. And although there are great and noble grades (see n. 586 to iv. 69), the base of that citizenship is the universal brotherhood of righteousness. The greatest in that Kingdom are glad and proud to pray for that essential badge.

20. And he took a muster
Of the Birds; and he said:
" Why is it I see not
The Hoopoe? Or is he
Among the absentees? [3262]

٢٠-وَتَفَقَّدَ الطَّيْرَ فَقَالَ
مَا لِيَ لَآ أَرَى الْهُدْهُدَ
أَمْ كَانَ مِنَ الْغَآئِبِينَ ○

21. " I will certainly punish him
With a severe penalty,
Or execute him, unless he
Bring me a clear reason
(For absence)."

٢١-لَأُعَذِّبَنَّهُ عَذَابًا شَدِيدًا
أَوْ لَأَاذْبَحَنَّهُ أَوْ لَيَأْتِيَنِّي بِسُلْطٰنٍ مُّبِينٍ ○

22. But the Hoopoe tarried not
Far: he (came up and) said:
" I have compassed (territory)
Which thou hast not compassed,
And I have come to thee
From Saba [3263] with tidings true.

٢٢-فَمَكَثَ غَيْرَ بَعِيدٍ فَقَالَ
أَحَطْتُ بِمَا لَمْ تُحِطْ بِهِ
وَجِئْتُكَ مِنْ سَبَإٍ بِنَبَإٍ يَقِينٍ ○

23. " I found (there) a woman [3264]
Ruling over them and provided [3265]
With every requisite; and she
Has a magnificent throne.

٢٣-إِنِّي وَجَدْتُّ امْرَأَةً تَمْلِكُهُمْ وَأُوتِيَتْ
مِنْ كُلِّ شَيْءٍ وَّلَهَا عَرْشٌ عَظِيمٌ ○

3262. Solomon was no idle or easy-going king. He kept all his organisation strictly up to the mark, both his armies literally and his forces (metaphorically). His most mobile arm was the Birds, who were light on the wing and flew and saw everything like efficient scouts. One day he missed the Hoopoe in his muster. The hoopoe is a light, graceful creature, with elegant plumage of many colours, and a beautiful yellow crest on his head, which entitles him to be called a royal bird.

3263. Sabā may reasonably be identified with the Biblical Sheba (1 Kings x. 1-10). It is further referred to in the Sūra called after its name: xxxiv. 15-20. It was a city in Yemen, said to have been three days' journey (say 50 miles) from the city of Ṣan'ā. A recent German explorer, Dr. Hans Helfritz, claims to have located it in what is now Ḥadhramaut territory. The famous dam of Maārib made the country very prosperous, and enabled it to attain a high degree of civilization ("provided with every requisite" in the next verse). The Queen of Sheba therefore rightly held up her head high until she beheld the glories of Solomon.

3264. The Queen of Sheba (by name Bilqīs in Arabian tradition) came apparently from Yemen, but she had affinities with Abyssinia and possibly ruled over Abyssinia also. The Ḥabasha tribe (after whom Abyssinia was named) came from Yemen. Between the southern coast of Yemen and the north-eastern coast of Abyssinia (now occupied by Italy and France) there are only the Straits of Bāb-al-Mandab, barely twenty miles across. In the 10th or 11th century B.C. there were frequent invasions of Abyssinia from Arabia, and Solomon's reign of 40 years is usually synchronised with B.C. 992 to 952. The Sabæan and Ḥimyarite alphabets, in which we find the south Arabian pre-Islamic inscriptions, passed into Ethiopic, the language of Abyssinia. The Abyssinians possess a traditional history called "The Book of the Glory of Kings" (*Kebra Nagast*), which has been translated from Ethiopic into English by Sir E. A. Wallis Budge (Oxford, 1932). It gives an account of the Queen of Sheba and her only son Menyelek I, as founders of the Abyssinian dynasty.

3265. *Provided with every requisite*: I take this to refer not only to the abundance of spices and gems and gold in her country, but to sciences and arts, and perhaps the spiritual possibilities which made her accept the religion of Unity and Truth (xxvii. 44).

24. "I found her and her people
Worshipping the sun besides
God:[3266]
Satan has made their deeds
Seem pleasing in their eyes,
And has kept them away
From the Path,—so
They receive no guidance,—

٢٤- وَجَدْتُّهَا وَقَوْمَهَا يَسْجُدُونَ لِلشَّمْسِ
مِنْ دُونِ اللّٰهِ وَزَيَّنَ لَهُمُ الشَّيْطٰنُ
أَعْمَالَهُمْ فَصَدَّهُمْ عَنِ السَّبِيلِ
فَهُمْ لَا يَهْتَدُونَ ۙ

25. "(Kept them away from the Path),
That they should not worship
God, Who brings to light[3267]
What is hidden in the heavens
And the earth, and knows
What ye hide and what
Ye reveal.

٢٥- أَلَّا يَسْجُدُوا لِلّٰهِ الَّذِي
يُخْرِجُ الْخَبْءَ فِي السَّمٰوٰتِ وَالْأَرْضِ
وَيَعْلَمُ مَا تُخْفُونَ وَمَا تُعْلِنُونَ ۝

26. "God!—there is no god
But He!—Lord of the Throne[3268]
Supreme!"

٢٦- اَللّٰهُ لَا إِلٰهَ
إِلَّا هُوَ رَبُّ الْعَرْشِ الْعَظِيمِ ۝ السجدة

27. (Solomon) said: "Soon shall we
See whether thou hast told
The truth or lied![3269]

٢٧- قَالَ سَنَنْظُرُ أَصَدَقْتَ
أَمْ كُنْتَ مِنَ الْكٰذِبِينَ ۝

3266. The ancient religion of the people of Sabā (the Ḥimyar or Sabæans) consisted in the worship of the heavenly bodies, the sun, the planets, and the stars. Possibly the cult was connected with that of Chaldæa, the home-land of Abraham: see vi. 75-79 and notes thereon. Yemen had easy access to Mesopotamia and the Persian Gulf. by way of the sea, as well as with Abyssinia. That accounts for the Christians of Najrān and the Jewish dynasty of kings (*e.g.*, Ẕū-Nuwās, d. 525 A.D.) who persecuted them in the century before Islam,—also for the Christian Abyssinian Governor Abraha and his discomfiture in the year of the Prophet's birth (S. cv.), say 570 A.D. Jewish-Christian influences were powerful in Arabia in the sixth century of the Christian era.

The religion of these Sabæans (written in Arabic with a *Sīn*) should not be confounded with that of the Ṣabians (with a *Ṣād*), as to whom see n. 76 to ii. 62.

3267. The false worship of the Sabæans is here exposed in three ways: (1) that they were self-satisfied with their own human achievements, instead of looking up to God; and (2) that the light of the heavenly bodies which they worshipped was only dependent on the true Light of God, which extends over heaven and earth; the Creator should be worshipped rather than His Creation; and (3) God knows the hidden secrets of men's minds as well as the objects which they openly profess: are false worshippers really only worshipping their own selves, or the "sins they have a mind to" and are therefore afraid to go to God, Who knows all?

3268. The messenger (Hoopoe) is a pious bird, as befits a messenger of Solomon. After mentioning the false worship of the Sabæans, he pronounces the Creed of Unity, and emphasises God's attribute as Lord of the Throne of Glory supreme, in order to make it clear that whatever may be the magnificence of a human throne such as he has described (in verse 23), he is not in any way misled from his loyalty to Solomon, the exponent of the true Religion of Unity.

3269. Solomon does not doubt his messenger's plea that he has scouted a new country, but wants to test whether he has loosened the rein of his imagination in describing its splendours or its worship.

28. "Go thou, with this letter
Of mine, and deliver it
To them: then draw back
From them, and (wait to) see
What answer they return"...

٢٨- اِذْهَبْ بِّكِتٰبِىْ هٰذَا فَاَلْقِهْ اِلَيْهِمْ
ثُمَّ تَوَلَّ عَنْهُمْ فَانْظُرْ مَاذَا يَرْجِعُوْنَ ○

29. (The Queen) said: "Ye chiefs!
Here is—delivered to me—
A letter worthy of respect.

٢٩- قَالَتْ يٰۤاَيُّهَا الْمَلَؤُا
اِنِّىْۤ اُلْقِىَ اِلَىَّ كِتٰبٌ كَرِيْمٌ ○

30. "It is from Solomon, and is
(As follows): 'In the name [3270]
Of God, Most Gracious,
Most Merciful:

٣٠- اِنَّهٗ مِنْ سُلَيْمٰنَ وَاِنَّهٗ
بِسْمِ اللّٰهِ الرَّحْمٰنِ الرَّحِيْمِ ○

31. "'Be ye not arrogant
Against me, but come
To me in submission
(To the true Religion).'"

٣١- اَلَّا تَعْلُوْا عَلَىَّ
وَاْتُوْنِىْ مُسْلِمِيْنَ ○

ع

SECTION 3.

32. She said: "Ye chiefs!
Advise me in (this)
My affair: no affair
Have I decided
Except in your presence."

٣٢- قَالَتْ يٰۤاَيُّهَا الْمَلَؤُا اَفْتُوْنِىْ فِىْۤ اَمْرِىْ
مَا كُنْتُ قَاطِعَةً اَمْرًا
حَتّٰى تَشْهَدُوْنِ ○

33. They said: "We are endued
With strength, and given
To vehement war:
But the command is
With thee; so consider
What thou wilt command."

٣٣- قَالُوْا نَحْنُ اُولُوْا قُوَّةٍ
وَّاُولُوْا بَاْسٍ شَدِيْدٍ ۙ وَّالْاَمْرُ اِلَيْكِ
فَانْظُرِىْ مَاذَا تَاْمُرِيْنَ ○

34. She said: "Kings, when they [3271]
Enter a country, despoil it,

٣٤- قَالَتْ اِنَّ الْمُلُوْكَ اِذَا دَخَلُوْا قَرْيَةً

3270. Solomon expressly begins his letter with the formula of the true and universal Religion of Unity, and he invites to the true Faith the new people with whom he establishes honourable relations, not for worldly conquest but for the spreading of the Light of God.

3271. The character of Queen Bilqīs, as disclosed here, is that of a ruler enjoying great wealth and dignity, and the full confidence of her subjects. She does nothing without consulting her Council, and her Council are ready to carry out her commands in all things. Her people are manly, loyal, and contented, and ready to take the field against any enemy of their country. But their queen is prudent in policy, and is not willing to embroil her country in war. She has the discrimination to see that Solomon is not like ordinary kings who conquer by violence. Perhaps in her heart she has a ray of the divine light already, though her people are yet Pagans. She wishes to carry her people with her in whatever she does, because she is as loyal to them as they are to her. An exchange of presents would probably establish better relations between the two kingdoms. And perhaps she anticipates some spiritual understanding also, a hope which was afterwards realised. In Bilqīs we have a picture of womanhood, gentle, prudent, and able to tame the wilder passions of her subjects. She is like Una in Spenser's *Faërie Queene*.

And make the noblest
Of its people its meanest:
Thus do they behave.

اَفْسَدُوْهَا وَجَعَلُوْٓا اَعِزَّةَ اَهْلِهَآ اَذِلَّةً ۚ
وَكَذٰلِكَ يَفْعَلُوْنَ ○

35. "But I am going to send
Him a present, and (wait)
To see with what (answer)
Return (my) ambassadors."

٣٥- وَاِنِّيْ مُرْسِلَةٌ اِلَيْهِمْ بِهَدِيَّةٍ
فَنٰظِرَةٌۢ بِمَ يَرْجِعُ الْمُرْسَلُوْنَ ○

36. Now when (the embassy) came
To Solomon, he said:
"Will ye give me abundance
In wealth? But that which
God has given me is better
Than that which He has
Given you! Nay it is ye
Who rejoice in your gift![3272]

٣٦- فَلَمَّا جَآءَ سُلَيْمٰنَ قَالَ
اَتُمِدُّوْنَنِ بِمَالٍ فَمَآ
اٰتٰىنِۦَ اللّٰهُ خَيْرٌ مِّمَّآ اٰتٰىكُمْ ۚ
بَلْ اَنْتُمْ بِهَدِيَّتِكُمْ تَفْرَحُوْنَ ○

37. "Go back to them, and be sure
We shall come to them
With such hosts as they
Will never be able to meet:
We shall expel them
From there in disgrace,
And they will feel
Humbled (indeed)."

٣٧- اِرْجِعْ اِلَيْهِمْ فَلَنَاْتِيَنَّهُمْ
بِجُنُوْدٍ لَّا قِبَلَ لَهُمْ بِهَا
وَلَنُخْرِجَنَّهُمْ مِّنْهَآ اَذِلَّةً
وَّهُمْ صٰغِرُوْنَ ○

38. He said (to his own men):
"Ye Chiefs! which of you
Can bring me her throne[3273]
Before they come to me
In submission?"

٣٨- قَالَ يٰٓاَيُّهَا الْمَلَؤُا اَيُّكُمْ يَاْتِيْنِيْ
بِعَرْشِهَا قَبْلَ اَنْ يَّاْتُوْنِيْ مُسْلِمِيْنَ ○

39. Said an 'Ifrīt,[3274] of the Jinns:
"I will bring it to thee

٣٩- قَالَ عِفْرِيْتٌ مِّنَ الْجِنِّ اَنَا اٰتِيْكَ بِهٖ

3272. Poor Bilqīs! she thought she had arranged with womanly tact to conciliate Solomon, and at the same time pacify her warlike subjects! But the effect of the embassy with presents was the very opposite. Solomon took it as an insult that she should send her presents instead of her submission to the true Religion! He flung back the presents at her, as much as to say, "Let these baubles delight your own hearts! God has blessed me with plenty of worldly goods, and something infinitely better, *viz.*: His Light and Guidance! Why do you say nothing about that? Will you only understand the argument of armies and violence?" Or perhaps his speech was only meant for the Sabæan crowd. For when she actually came, he treated her kindly, and she accepted the religion of Unity.

3273. The throne is symbolical of power and dignity. So far her throne was based on material wealth: Solomon is going to alter it to a basis of Faith and the Religion of Unity.

3274. *'Ifrīt*: a large, powerful jinn, reputed to be wicked and crafty: hence he is anxious to be recognised as one that "could be trusted".

Before thou rise from thy
Council: indeed I have
Full strength for the purpose,
And may be trusted."

قَبْلَ اَنْ تَقُوْمَ مِنْ مَّقَامِكَ ۚ
وَاِنِّيْ عَلَيْهِ لَقَوِيٌّ اَمِيْنٌ ○

40. Said one who had knowledge[3275]
Of the Book: "I will
Bring it to thee within
The twinkling of an eye!"
Then when (Solomon) saw it
Placed firmly before him,
He said: "This is
By the grace of my Lord!—[3276]
To test me whether I am
Grateful or ungrateful!
And if any is grateful,
Truly his gratitude is (a gain)
For his own soul; but if
Any is ungrateful, truly
My Lord is Free of all Needs,
Supreme in Honour!"[3277]

٤٠- قَالَ الَّذِيْ عِنْدَهٗ عِلْمٌ مِّنَ الْكِتٰبِ
اَنَا اٰتِيْكَ بِهٖ قَبْلَ اَنْ يَّرْتَدَّ اِلَيْكَ طَرْفُكَ ؕ
فَلَمَّا رَاٰهُ مُسْتَقِرًّا عِنْدَهٗ
قَالَ هٰذَا مِنْ فَضْلِ رَبِّيْ
لِيَبْلُوَنِيْٓ ءَاَشْكُرُ اَمْ اَكْفُرُ ؕ
وَمَنْ شَكَرَ فَاِنَّمَا يَشْكُرُ لِنَفْسِهٖ ۚ
وَمَنْ كَفَرَ
فَاِنَّ رَبِّيْ غَنِيٌّ كَرِيْمٌ ○

41. He said: "Transform her throne
Out of all recognition by her:
Let us see whether she
Is guided (to the truth)[3278]

٤١- قَالَ نَكِّرُوْا لَهَا عَرْشَهَا
نَنْظُرْ اَتَهْتَدِيْٓ

3275. The symbolic meaning still continues. The big 'Ifrit had boasted of his brute strength, and his reliability. But this is not enough to transform a power (throne) based on materialism into one based on inward knowledge, knowledge of the heart and spirit, the sort of knowledge that comes from the Book of the Grace of God, the spirit of truth and benevolence which is the invisible magic of men of God. Even if worldly power and common honesty may be able to effect some good, it will take a comparatively long time, while the magic of spiritual love acts instantaneously. Solomon was thankful to God that he had men endowed with such power, and he had the throne of Bilqis transported to his Court and transformed as he desired, without Bilqis even knowing it.

3276. If Solomon had been ungrateful to God, *i.e.*, if he had worked for his own selfish or worldly ends, he could have used the brute strength of 'Ifrit to add to his worldly strength and glory. Instead of it he uses the higher magic of the Book,—of the Spirit—to transform the throne of Bilqis for her highest good, which means also the highest good of her subjects, by the divine Light. He had the two alternatives, and he chooses the better, and he thus shows his gratitude to God for the Grace He had given him.

3277. Man's gratitude to God is not a thing that benefits God, for God is high above all needs: it benefits a man's own soul and gives him higher rank in the spiritual world. *Per contra*, man's ingratitude will not detract from God's Glory and Honour or the value of God's generous gifts to man: for God is supreme in honour, glory, and generosity. *Karīm* in Arabic involves all three significations.

3278. The throne having been transformed, it will be a test to see whether Bilqis recognises it as her own and accepts it of her own free will as her own, or rejects it as something alien to her, something she will not accommodate herself to. So in our life. We get used to certain habits and customs and certain ways of thought. God's Message comes to transform us and set us on a different kind of throne, with our own active and willing consent. If we are wise, we feel honoured and grateful. If we are "obstinately rebellious", we reject it as not our own, and pine for the old slavery, as the Israelites pined for Egypt when they were under God's guidance in the wilderness.

Or is one of those who
Receive no guidance.'

أَمْ تَكُونُ مِنَ الَّذِينَ لَا يَهْتَدُونَ ○

42. So when she arrived,
She was asked, "Is this
Thy throne?" She said,
"It was just like this;[3279]
And knowledge was bestowed
On us in advance of this,
And we have submitted
To God (in Islām)."

٤٢- فَلَمَّا جَاءَتْ قِيلَ أَهٰكَذَا
عَرْشُكِ ۖ
قَالَتْ كَأَنَّهُ هُوَ ۚ
وَأُوتِينَا الْعِلْمَ مِنْ قَبْلِهَا
وَكُنَّا مُسْلِمِينَ ○

43. And he diverted her[3280]
From the worship of others
Besides God: for she was
(Sprung) of a people
That had no faith.

٤٣- وَصَدَّهَا مَا كَانَتْ تَعْبُدُ مِنْ
دُونِ اللَّهِ ۖ
إِنَّهَا كَانَتْ مِنْ قَوْمٍ كَافِرِينَ ○

44. She was asked to enter[3281]
The lofty Palace: but
When she saw it, she
Thought it was a lake
Of water, and she (tucked up
Her skirts), uncovering her legs.
He said: "This is
But a palace paved

٤٤- قِيلَ لَهَا ادْخُلِي الصَّرْحَ ۖ
فَلَمَّا رَأَتْهُ حَسِبَتْهُ لُجَّةً
وَكَشَفَتْ عَنْ سَاقَيْهَا ۚ
قَالَ إِنَّهُ صَرْحٌ

3279. Bilqis stands the test. She knows it was her throne, yet not exactly the same, for it was now much better. And she is proud of her good fortune, and acknowledges, for herself and her people, with gratitude, the light which was given to them by God, by which they recognised God's apostle in Solomon, and received the true Religion with all their will and heart and soul.

3280. Some Commentators and Translators adopt an alternative construction for the last clause of the last verse and the first clause of this verse. They understand the former to be spoken by Solomon and to mean, 'we had knowledge of God's Message and accepted it before her.' They understand the latter to mean, 'the worship of others besides God diverted her (from the true Religion).' If we accept the construction adopted in this Translation, the visit to Solomon confirmed the true Faith of Bilqis and prevented her from lapsing into her ancestral false worship.

3281. The symbolic meaning takes us a stage further. But first let us take the literal story. Bilqis, having been received with honour on her arrival, and having accepted the transformation of her throne, placed presumably in an outer building of the Palace, is asked to enter the great Palace itself. Its floor was made of slabs of smooth polished glass, that glistened like water. She thought it was water, and tucked up her clothes to pass through it, showing her bare feet and ankles. This was a very undignified position for a woman, especially one of the position of a Queen. Solomon immediately undeceived her, and told her the real facts, when she felt grateful, and joined herself with Solomon in praising God.

Smooth with slabs of glass."
She said: "O my Lord!
I have indeed wronged[3282]
My soul: I do (now)
Submit (in Islām), with Solomon,
To the Lord of the Worlds."

مُّمَرَّدٌ مِّنْ قَوَارِيرَ ۗ
قَالَتْ رَبِّ إِنِّي ظَلَمْتُ نَفْسِي
وَأَسْلَمْتُ مَعَ سُلَيْمَانَ لِلَّهِ رَبِّ الْعَالَمِينَ ۝

C. 171.—In Ṣaliḥ's pure preaching the evil Thamūd
(xxvii. 45-58.) Found omens of ill to themselves: in secret
They plotted to take his life, and like cowards
They made a league to cover their crime
With lies. Lo! on themselves recoiled
The plot: they perished in utter ruin.
The men admonished by Lot were false
To themselves: they insulted the nature given
Them by God, and mocked the Message of Purity.
Lo! they were buried in a shower of brimstone!

SECTION 4.

45. We sent (aforetime),
To the Thamūd, their brother[3283]
Ṣāliḥ, saying, "Serve God":
But behold, they became
Two factions quarrelling
With each other.

٤٥- وَلَقَدْ أَرْسَلْنَا إِلَىٰ ثَمُودَ أَخَاهُمْ
صَالِحًا أَنِ اعْبُدُوا اللَّهَ
فَإِذَا هُمْ فَرِيقَانِ يَخْتَصِمُونَ ۝

46. He said: "O my people!
Why ask ye to hasten on

٤٦- قَالَ يَا قَوْمِ لِمَ تَسْتَعْجِلُونَ

3282. In symbolic language, a new entrant into the Palace of divine knowledge, may yet carry in his mind many of the illusions of the lower world. The transparent crystal of Truth he may yet mistake for the unstable water of worldly vanity, which soils the vestments of those who paddle in it. This leads to many undignified positions and mistakes. But a gentle leader points out the truth. Instead of resenting it, the new entrant is grateful; acknowledges his own mistake freely and frankly; and heartily joins with the Teacher in the worship of God, the Source of all truth and knowledge.

3283. The main story of the Thamūd, who were broken up into two factions, the rich oppressing the poor and keeping them out of the good things of life and the test case of the She-camel, will be found in xxvi. 141-159 and the notes thereon. The point here is the secret plot of the nine men against the man of God, whose teaching, they thought, brought them ill-luck; but what they called ill-luck was the just punishment from God for their own ill-deeds. Their plot was foiled, and the whole community, which was involved in evil, was destroyed.

The evil in preference to the
good ?[3284]
If only ye ask God for forgiveness,
Ye may hope to receive mercy.

بِالسَّيِّئَةِ قَبْلَ الْحَسَنَةِ
لَوْلَا تَسْتَغْفِرُونَ اللَّهَ لَعَلَّكُمْ تُرْحَمُونَ ○

47. They said: "Ill omen
Do we augur from thee
And those that are with thee".
He said: "Your ill omen
Is with God; yea, ye are
A people under trial."[3285]

٤٧- قَالُوا اطَّيَّرْنَا بِكَ وَبِمَن مَّعَكَ
قَالَ طَائِرُكُمْ عِندَ اللَّهِ
بَلْ أَنتُمْ قَوْمٌ تُفْتَنُونَ ○

48. There were in the City
Nine men of a family,
Who made mischief in the land,
And would not reform.[3286]

٤٨- وَكَانَ فِي الْمَدِينَةِ تِسْعَةُ رَهْطٍ
يُفْسِدُونَ فِي الْأَرْضِ وَلَا يُصْلِحُونَ ○

49. They said: "Swear
A mutual oath by God
That we shall make
A secret night attack
On him and his people,[3287]
And that we shall then
Say to his heir (when he
Seeks vengeance): 'We were not
Present at the slaughter
Of his people, and we are
Positively telling the truth'."

٤٩- قَالُوا تَقَاسَمُوا بِاللَّهِ
لَنُبَيِّتَنَّهُ وَأَهْلَهُ
ثُمَّ لَنَقُولَنَّ لِوَلِيِّهِ مَا شَهِدْنَا مَهْلِكَ
أَهْلِهِ
وَإِنَّا لَصَادِقُونَ ○

3284. *Cf.* xiii. 6. The evil-doers were really hastening on their own punishment by their feuds against the poor. The advocates of justice were not bringing ill-luck to them. They were showing the way to ward it off. Their own injustice was bringing on their disaster.

3285. All evil unpunished is not evil condoned, but evil given a chance for reform. They are on trial, by the mercy of God. What they call "ill omen" is really the just punishment for their ill-deeds, and that punishment rests with God.

3286. They had made up their minds to wage a relentless war against justice. They did not destroy justice, but justice destroyed them.

3287. A most dastardly plot, because (1) it was to be secret, (2) by night, (3) taking their victims unawares, and (4) because careful provision was made that they should all tell lies together, saying that they knew nothing about it, in order to evade the vengeance which Ṣaliḥ's heirs (if any were left) or his tribe might want to exact! And yet such were exactly the plots laid against the holy Prophet himself.

50. They plotted and planned,[3288]
But We too planned,
Even while they perceived it not.

٥٠- وَمَكَرُوا مَكْرًا وَّمَكَرْنَا مَكْرًا
وَّهُمْ لَا يَشْعُرُونَ ○

51. Then see what was the end
Of their plot!—this,
That We destroyed them
And their people, all (of them).

٥١- فَانْظُرْ كَيْفَ كَانَ عَاقِبَةُ مَكْرِهِمْ ۙ
أَنَّا دَمَّرْنٰهُمْ وَقَوْمَهُمْ أَجْمَعِينَ ○

52. Now such were their houses,—
In utter ruin,—because
They practised wrong-doing.
Verily in this is a Sign
For people of knowledge.

٥٢- فَتِلْكَ بُيُوتُهُمْ خَاوِيَةً بِمَا ظَلَمُوا ۗ
إِنَّ فِي ذٰلِكَ لَاٰيَةً لِّقَوْمٍ يَّعْلَمُونَ ○

53. And We saved those
Who believed and practised
Righteousness.

٥٣- وَأَنْجَيْنَا الَّذِينَ اٰمَنُوا وَكَانُوا يَتَّقُونَ ○

54. (We also sent) Lūt[3289]
(As an apostle): behold,
He said to his people,
"Do ye do what is shameful
Though ye see (its iniquity)?

٥٤- وَلُوطًا إِذْ قَالَ لِقَوْمِهٖٓ
أَتَأْتُونَ الْفَاحِشَةَ
وَأَنْتُمْ تُبْصِرُونَ ○

55. Would ye really approach men
In your lusts rather than
Women? Nay, ye are
A people (grossly) ignorant![3290]

٥٥- أَئِنَّكُمْ لَتَأْتُونَ الرِّجَالَ شَهْوَةً مِّنْ
دُونِ النِّسَاءِ ۗ بَلْ أَنْتُمْ قَوْمٌ تَجْهَلُونَ ○

56. But his people gave
No other answer but this:
They said, "Drive out

٥٦- فَمَا كَانَ جَوَابَ قَوْمِهٖٓ إِلَّآ
أَنْ قَالُوٓا أَخْرِجُوٓا

3288. *Cf.* iii. 54. Their secret plotting is all known to God, but of God's just and beneficent plans they know nothing. And the wicked must come to an evil end.

3289. The story of Lūṭ is referred to elsewhere. The passages to which reference may be made here are: xxvi. 160-175, and vii. 80-84. But the point emphasised here is that the crime of the Cities of the Plain was against their own nature, and they saw its enormity, and yet they indulged in it. Can degradation go further? His wife was not apparently a Believer. Her previous sympathy with the sinful people "destined her" (verse 57 below) to a miserable end, as she lagged behind and shared in the destruction of her kinsfolk.

3290. The ignorance referred to here is the spiritual Ignorance, the Ignorance of how grossness and sins that bring shame on their own physical and moral nature are doomed to destroy them: it is their own loss. That they knew the iniquity of their sins has already been stated in the last verse. That knowledge makes their spiritual Ignorance all the more culpable, just as a man consciously deceiving people by half-truths is a greater liar than a man who tells lies inadvertently.

The followers of Lūt from
Your city: these are
Indeed men who want
To be clean and pure!" [3291]

آلَ لُوطٍ مِّن قَرۡيَتِكُمۡ
إِنَّهُمۡ أُنَاسٞ يَتَطَهَّرُونَ ○

57. But We saved him
And his family, except
His wife: her We destined
To be of those
Who lagged behind.

٥٧- فَأَنجَيۡنَٰهُ وَأَهۡلَهُۥٓ إِلَّا ٱمۡرَأَتَهُۥ
قَدَّرۡنَٰهَا مِنَ ٱلۡغَٰبِرِينَ ○

58. And We rained down on them
A shower (of brimstone):
And evil was the shower
On those who were admonished
(But heeded not)!

٥٨- وَأَمۡطَرۡنَا عَلَيۡهِم مَّطَرٗا
فَسَآءَ مَطَرُ ٱلۡمُنذَرِينَ ○

C. 172.—God's goodness and mercy are manifest
(xxvii. 59-93.)
Through all nature and in the heart and conscience
Of man. He alone knows all: our knowledge
Can at best be partial. Yet we can travel
Through space and time and see how Evil
Never prospered. God teaches us good,
But how can we see if we make ourselves blind?
At the end of all things shall we know how small
Is our state, but for God's Grace: let us bow
To His Will and accept His true guidance:
Let us praise Him and trust Him—now and for ever!

SECTION 5.

59. Say: Praise be to God,
And Peace on His servants [3292]
Whom He has chosen
(For His Message). (Who)
Is better?—God or
19 The false gods they associate
30 (With Him)?

٥٩- قُلِ ٱلۡحَمۡدُ لِلَّهِ وَسَلَٰمٌ عَلَىٰ عِبَادِهِ
ٱلَّذِينَ ٱصۡطَفَىٰٓ
ءَآللَّهُ خَيۡرٌ أَمَّا يُشۡرِكُونَ ○

3291. *Cf.* vii. 82-84. Instead of being ashamed on account of the consciousness of their own guilt, they attack the pure ones with their sarcasms, as if not they but the pure ones were in the wrong in trying to set them on the right way.

3292. God's revelation having been described as Light, Guidance, and Mercy, we ought all to be grateful to God for vouchsafing His revelation. We ought also to appreciate the services of God's Messengers, who are chosen to deliver His Message: we ought to send salutations of Peace on them, instead of plotting, as the wicked do, for their removal or persecution, or banishment or death. For these men of God undergo every kind of hardship and forego every kind of advantage or pleasure in life for serving mankind. And God is truth and goodness, and all our fancies of false worship are falsehoods and evils. Shall we prefer falsehood and evil to truth and goodness?

60. Or, who has created[3293]
The heavens and the earth,
And who sends you down
Rain from the sky?
Yea, with it We cause
To grow well-planted orchards
Full of beauty and delight:
It is not in your power
To cause the growth[3294]
Of the trees in them. (Can there be
Another) god besides God?
Nay, they are a people
Who swerve from justice.

٦٠- أَمَّنْ خَلَقَ السَّمٰوٰتِ وَالْأَرْضَ
وَأَنْزَلَ لَكُمْ مِّنَ السَّمَاءِ مَاءً
فَأَنْۢبَتْنَا بِهٖ حَدَآئِقَ ذَاتَ بَهْجَةٍ
مَا كَانَ لَكُمْ أَنْ تُنْۢبِتُوْا شَجَرَهَا
ءَاِلٰهٌ مَّعَ اللّٰهِ
بَلْ هُمْ قَوْمٌ يَّعْدِلُوْنَ ۝

61. Or, who has made the earth
Firm to live in; made
Rivers in its midst; set
Thereon mountains immovable;[3295]
And made a separating bar
Between the two bodies[3296]
Of flowing water?
(Can there be another) god
Besides God? Nay, most
Of them know not.

٦١- أَمَّنْ جَعَلَ الْأَرْضَ قَرَارًا
وَّجَعَلَ خِلٰلَهَآ أَنْهٰرًا وَّجَعَلَ لَهَا رَوَاسِيَ
وَجَعَلَ بَيْنَ الْبَحْرَيْنِ حَاجِزًا
ءَاِلٰهٌ مَّعَ اللّٰهِ
بَلْ أَكْثَرُهُمْ لَا يَعْلَمُوْنَ ۝

62. Or, who listens to the (soul)
Distressed when it calls
On Him, and who relieves[3297]
Its suffering, and makes you

٦٢- أَمَّنْ يُّجِيْبُ الْمُضْطَرَّ إِذَا دَعَاهُ
وَيَكْشِفُ السُّوْٓءَ وَيَجْعَلُكُمْ

3293. The order, beauty, and grandeur of the Universe are appealed to. They show unity of design and purpose. How can unjust, ignorant, foolish, heedless, false men think of a multiplicity of gods, or of any god besides the One True God?

3294. To make a single seed germinate and grow into a tree is beyond man's power. When it comes to a great well-laid-out garden of beauty and delight, no one would think it grew up of itself without a Gardener's consummate art. And the orchard is more than the trees in it: there is design and beauty in their arrangement: proper spaces have to be left between them for the growth of their roots, for the aeration of the soil beneath them, and for the penetration of air and sunlight between their branches. How can any one then think of the wonderful Universe as a whole, without thinking of the far higher Unity of Design, the evidence of the One True God?

3295. *Cf.* xvi. 15 and notes 2038 and 2039. The *terra firma*, the flowing water, and the cycle of water circulation—sea, vapour, clouds, rain, rivers, and sea again,—all one and yet all distinct, with a sort of wonderful barrier between salt water and fresh water: can man see all this and yet be ignorant of God?

3296. *Cf.* xxv. 53 and notes 3111 and 3112.

3297. Besides the evidence of external nature, there is the still more intimate evidence in man's inner conscience and heart. God listens to man's cry of agony and relieves his suffering, and He has given him superiority over other creation on this earth, through his mind and soul. Is man then going to run after inferior beings and forget God?

(Mankind) inheritors of the
earth? [3298]
(Can there be another) god
Besides God? Little it is
That ye heed!

خُلَفَآءَ الْاَرْضِ ؕ
ءَاِلٰهٌ مَّعَ اللّٰهِ ؕ
قَلِيْلًا مَّا تَذَكَّرُوْنَ ۝

63. Or, who guides you
Through the depths of darkness
On land and sea, and who
Sends the winds as heralds [3299]
Of glad tidings, going before
His Mercy? (Can there be
Another) god besides God?—
High is God above what
They associate with Him!

٦٣- اَمَّنْ يَّهْدِيْكُمْ فِىْ ظُلُمٰتِ الْبَرِّ وَالْبَحْرِ
وَمَنْ يُّرْسِلُ الرِّيٰحَ بُشْرًاۢ بَيْنَ يَدَىْ
رَحْمَتِهٖ ؕ
ءَاِلٰهٌ مَّعَ اللّٰهِ ؕ
تَعٰلَى اللّٰهُ عَمَّا يُشْرِكُوْنَ ۝

64. Or, who originates Creation,
Then repeats it, [3300]
And who gives you sustenance
From heaven and earth? [3301]
(Can there be another) god
Besides God? Say, "Bring forth
Your argument, if ye
Are telling the truth!" [3302]

٦٤- اَمَّنْ يَّبْدَؤُا الْخَلْقَ ثُمَّ يُعِيْدُهٗ
وَمَنْ يَّرْزُقُكُمْ مِّنَ السَّمَآءِ وَالْاَرْضِ ؕ
ءَاِلٰهٌ مَّعَ اللّٰهِ ؕ
قُلْ هَاتُوْا بُرْهَانَكُمْ اِنْ كُنْتُمْ صٰدِقِيْنَ ۝

65. Say: None in the heavens
Or on earth, except God,
Knows what is hidden: [3303]
Nor can they perceive
When they shall be raised
Up (for Judgment).

٦٥- قُلْ لَّا يَعْلَمُ مَنْ فِى السَّمٰوٰتِ
وَالْاَرْضِ الْغَيْبَ اِلَّا اللّٰهُ ؕ
وَمَا يَشْعُرُوْنَ اَيَّانَ يُبْعَثُوْنَ ۝

66. Still less can their knowledge
Comprehend the Hereafter: nay,

٦٦- بَلِ ادّٰرَكَ عِلْمُهُمْ فِى الْاٰخِرَةِ ۟ بَلْ

3298. *Cf.* vi. 165, n. 988.

3299. *Cf.* xxv. 48, n. 3104. After external nature, our attention was drawn to our inner consciousness; after that, it is drawn here to our social and collective life, in which we use the forces of nature for international intercourse, trade, agriculture, production, and economic well-being generally. In the next verse, we are asked to contemplate creation from its primeval stages, through its intermediate processes, to the final Destiny in a new Creation—a new heaven and a new earth.

3300. *Cf.* x. 34, and n. 1428.

3301. *Sustenance*: of course in the spiritual as well as the material sense.

3302. All the arguments point to the Unity of God: there is none whatever against it.

3303. The existence of God is certain. But nothing else can be known with certainty to our knowledge. He has told us of the Hereafter, and therefore we know it is true. But those who do not believe in God,—what knowledge or certainty can they have? Even when it is actually coming, they will not have the sense to perceive it.

They are in doubt and uncertainty
Thereanent; nay, they are blind
Thereunto![3304]

هُمْ فِي شَكٍّ مِّنْهَا
بَلْ هُم مِّنْهَا عَمُونَ ○ ع

Section 6.

67. The Unbelievers say: "What!
When we become dust,—
We and our fathers,—shall we
Really be raised (from the dead)?

٦٧- وَقَالَ الَّذِينَ كَفَرُوا أَءِذَا كُنَّا تُرَابًا
وَءَابَاؤُنَا أَئِنَّا لَمُخْرَجُونَ ○

68. "It is true we were promised
This,—we and our fathers
Before (us): these are nothing
But tales of the ancients."

٦٨- لَقَدْ وُعِدْنَا هَٰذَا نَحْنُ وَءَابَاؤُنَا
مِن قَبْلُ إِنْ هَٰذَا إِلَّا أَسَاطِيرُ الْأَوَّلِينَ ○

69. Say: "Go ye through the earth
And see what has been
The end of those guilty
(Of sin)."[3305]

٦٩- قُلْ سِيرُوا فِي الْأَرْضِ فَانظُرُوا كَيْفَ
كَانَ عَاقِبَةُ الْمُجْرِمِينَ ○

70. But grieve not over them,
Nor distress thyself
Because of their plots.[3306]

٧٠- وَلَا تَحْزَنْ عَلَيْهِمْ
وَلَا تَكُن فِي ضَيْقٍ مِّمَّا يَمْكُرُونَ ○

71. They also say: "When will
This promise (come to pass)?
(Say) if ye are truthful."

٧١- وَيَقُولُونَ مَتَىٰ هَٰذَا الْوَعْدُ
إِن كُنتُمْ صَادِقِينَ ○

72. Say: "It may be that
Some of the events which
Ye wish to hasten on
May be (close) in your pursuit!"[3307]

٧٢- قُلْ عَسَىٰ أَن يَكُونَ
رَدِفَ لَكُم بَعْضُ الَّذِي تَسْتَعْجِلُونَ ○

3304. The Unbelievers are generally materialists, who cannot go beyond the evidence of their physical senses. As to a spiritual vision of the future, their physical senses would only leave them in doubt and uncertainty, while their rejection of the spiritual Light makes them blind altogether to the spiritual world.

3305. Even if the Unbelievers are unwilling to take any mystic doctrine, they have only to observe what has actually happened on the earth, and they will see that evil always came to an evil end, and that Truth and righteousness ultimately won.

3306. *Cf.* xvi. 127, and n. 2164. The righteous need not worry over the unjust. The plots of the unjust can never defeat or deflect the purpose of God.

3307. The Unbelievers—or even men of half-hearted faith—may say, "Why worry over distant future events? Take the day as it comes!" But that is a fallacy. Judgment is certain, and it may be that this very hour may be the hour of doom for any given individual. This is the hour of repentance and amendment. For God wishes well to all mankind in spite of their ingratitude.

73. But verily thy Lord is Full of grace to mankind: Yet most of them are ungrateful.	٧٣- وَإِنَّ رَبَّكَ لَذُو فَضْلٍ عَلَى النَّاسِ وَلَٰكِنَّ أَكْثَرَهُمْ لَا يَشْكُرُونَ ○
74. And verily thy Lord knoweth All that their hearts do hide, As well as all that They reveal.	٧٤- وَإِنَّ رَبَّكَ لَيَعْلَمُ مَا تُكِنُّ صُدُورُهُمْ وَمَا يُعْلِنُونَ ○
75. Nor is there aught Of the Unseen, in heaven Or earth, but is (recorded)[3308] In a clear record.	٧٥- وَمَا مِنْ غَائِبَةٍ فِي السَّمَاءِ وَالْأَرْضِ إِلَّا فِي كِتَابٍ مُبِينٍ ○
76. Verily this Qur-ān doth explain To the Children of Israel Most of the matters In which they disagree.[3309]	٧٦- إِنَّ هَٰذَا الْقُرْآنَ يَقُصُّ عَلَىٰ بَنِي إِسْرَائِيلَ أَكْثَرَ الَّذِي هُمْ فِيهِ يَخْتَلِفُونَ ○
77. And it certainly is A Guide and a Mercy To those who believe.	٧٧- وَإِنَّهُ لَهُدًى وَرَحْمَةٌ لِلْمُؤْمِنِينَ ○
78. Verily thy Lord will decide Between them by His Decree:[3310] And He is Exalted in Might, All-Knowing.	٧٨- إِنَّ رَبَّكَ يَقْضِي بَيْنَهُمْ بِحُكْمِهِ وَهُوَ الْعَزِيزُ الْعَلِيمُ ○
79. So put thy trust in God: For thou art on (the Path Of) manifest Truth.	٧٩- فَتَوَكَّلْ عَلَى اللَّهِ إِنَّكَ عَلَى الْحَقِّ الْمُبِينِ ○

3308. The chain of cause and effect is certain and clear. We stand or fall by our record. In this sense the doctrine of "Karma" is true, but it needs to be modified by the doctrine of "Grace"; for man may repent and obtain God's Mercy, and God's Mercy is like a good angel always trying to reclaim man.

3309. The Jews had numerous sects. Some were altogether out of the pale, *e.g.*, the Samaritans, who had a separate *Taurāt* of their own: they hated the other Jews and were hated by them. But even in the orthodox body, there were several sects, of which the following may be mentioned: (1) the Pharisees, who were literalists, formalists, and fatalists, and had a large body of traditional literature, with which they overlaid the Law of Moses; (2) the Sadducees, who were rationalists, and seemed to have doubted the doctrine of the Resurrection or of a Hereafter; (3) the Essenes, who practised a sort of Communism and Asceticism and prohibited marriage. About many of their doctrines they had bitter disputes, which were settled by the Qur-ān, which supplemented and perfected the Law of Moses. It also explained clearly the nature of God and of Revelation, and the doctrine of the Hereafter.

3310. *Decree: ḥukm*: the disputes between rival sects can only be settled by the Decree of God,—(1) in the form of a Revelation, as was done by the Qur-ān, or (2) by the logic of events, for hundreds of sects have been extinguished and forgotten in the course of time, and (3) in the Decree of Judgment in the Hereafter, when all jarring sects will at length see their errors.

80. Truly thou canst not cause
The Dead to listen, nor
Canst thou cause the Deaf
To hear the call,
(Especially) when they
Turn back in retreat.[3311]

٨٠- إِنَّكَ لَا تُسْمِعُ الْمَوْتَىٰ
وَلَا تُسْمِعُ الصُّمَّ الدُّعَاءَ
إِذَا وَلَّوْا مُدْبِرِينَ ○

81. Nor canst thou be a guide
To the Blind, (to prevent them)
From straying : only those
Wilt thou get to listen
Who believe in Our Signs,
And they will bow in Islam.

٨١- وَمَا أَنْتَ بِهَادِي الْعُمْيِ عَنْ ضَلَالَتِهِمْ
إِنْ تُسْمِعُ إِلَّا
مَنْ يُؤْمِنُ بِآيَاتِنَا فَهُمْ مُسْلِمُونَ ○

82. And when the Word is[3312]
Fulfilled against them (the unjust),
We shall produce from the earth
A Beast to (face) them :[3313]
He will speak to them,
For that mankind did not
Believe with assurance
In Our Signs.

٨٢- وَإِذَا وَقَعَ الْقَوْلُ عَلَيْهِمْ
أَخْرَجْنَا لَهُمْ دَابَّةً مِنَ الْأَرْضِ
تُكَلِّمُهُمْ أَنَّ النَّاسَ
كَانُوا بِآيَاتِنَا لَا يُوقِنُونَ ○ ع

SECTION 7.

83. One Day We shall gather
Together from every people
A troop of those who reject
Our Signs, and they shall
Be kept in ranks,—

٨٣- وَيَوْمَ نَحْشُرُ مِنْ كُلِّ أُمَّةٍ
فَوْجًا مِمَّنْ يُكَذِّبُ بِآيَاتِنَا
فَهُمْ يُوزَعُونَ ○

84. Until, when they come
(Before the Judgment-seat),
(God) will say : "Did ye
Reject My Signs, though ye[3314]

٨٤- حَتَّىٰ إِذَا جَاءُو
قَالَ أَكَذَّبْتُمْ بِآيَاتِي وَلَمْ

3311. The Apostle's responsibility was to preach and show the way. Men and women of good-will had faith and accepted the Message. But he was not responsible for the obstinacy and perversity of men who turned away from God's Signs and rejected the Truth.

3312. *The Word* : the Decree or Sentence. the Decision to end the respite and restore the true values of right and wrong in a new world : their cup of iniquity will then have been full.

3313. The Beast will be one of the Signs of the Last Days to come, before the present World passes away and the new World is brought into being. In symbolic language it would represent gross Materialism. It will be the embodiment of fat worldly triumph, which will appeal to a misguided and degenerate world, because such a corrupt world will have no assured belief in the Signs of God or in spiritual Light. It will itself be a Sign or Portent, closing tne door of repentance. I do not know whether this Beast has any reference to the symbolism in chapter xii. of the Book of Revelation, which closes the New Testament. If *taklimuhum* is read instead of *tukallimuhum*, it would mean that the Beast would wound them ; symbolically, that Materialism would produce its own Nemesis.

3314. The charge against them will be : 'You had no knowledge, and yet you arrogantly rejected my Signs : is that true, or have you any plea in your defence ?'

Comprehended them not
In knowledge, or what
Was it ye did?"

تُحِيطُوا بِهَا عِلْمًا أَمَّاذَا كُنْتُمْ
تَعْمَلُونَ ○

85. And the Word will be[3315]
Fulfilled against them, because
Of their wrong-doing, and they
Will be unable to speak
(In plea).

٨٥- وَوَقَعَ الْقَوْلُ عَلَيْهِمْ بِمَا
ظَلَمُوا فَهُمْ لَا يَنْطِقُونَ ○

86. See they not that We
Have made the Night
For them to rest in
And the Day to give[3316]
Them light? Verily in this
Are Signs for any people
That believe!

٨٦- أَلَمْ يَرَوْا أَنَّا جَعَلْنَا الَّيْلَ
لِيَسْكُنُوا فِيهِ وَالنَّهَارَ مُبْصِرًا ط
إِنَّ فِي ذَٰلِكَ لَآيَاتٍ لِقَوْمٍ يُؤْمِنُونَ ○

87. And the Day that the Trumpet
Will be sounded—then will be
Smitten with terror those
Who are in the heavens,
And those who are on earth,
Except such as God will please
(To exempt): and all shall come
To His (Presence) as beings
Conscious of their lowliness.[3317]

٨٧- وَيَوْمَ يُنْفَخُ فِي الصُّورِ
فَفَزِعَ مَنْ فِي السَّمٰوٰتِ وَمَنْ فِي
الْأَرْضِ
إِلَّا مَنْ شَاءَ اللَّهُ ط
وَكُلٌّ أَتَوْهُ دٰخِرِينَ ○

88. Thou seest the mountains
And thinkest them firmly fixed:[3318]
But they shall pass away
As the clouds pass away:

٨٨- وَتَرَى الْجِبَالَ تَحْسَبُهَا جَامِدَةً
وَهِيَ تَمُرُّ مَرَّ السَّحَابِ ط

3315. There will be no plea, because the charge will be only too true. The Decree will be passed and executed.

3316. *Night, Day, Rest*, and *Light*: both in the literal and the symbolic sense. Any one with a scrap of faith or spiritual insight could see that the Night is a blessing when used for rest and a curse when used to cover ignorance or sin; and that the Day is for work and enlightenment, and its misuse is gross ingratitude to God. Or, understand Truth and practise Righteousness while it is yet Light and the Message of God is here to guide you: for there comes the Night when Endeavour will cease and there will be no room for Repentance.

3317. Arrogance will flee with Ignorance, and Self will see itself in its true place—that of humility and lowliness—when the scales of ignorance fall from its eyes.

3318. This is so in the present phase of phenomenal things, both literally and figuratively. There seems nothing more firm or fixed or permanent than the "eternal hills": yet when the new order of things comes and the new World is brought into being, they will be as flimsy and unsubstantial as clouds. So, in the revaluation of things in the spiritual World, persons or things or ideas that seem so great and so firmly established now will pass away like mere fancies and give way to the Reality of God.

(Such is) the artistry of God,
Who disposes of all things[3319]
In perfect order: for He is
Well acquainted with all that ye do.

صُنْعَ اللّٰهِ الَّذِىٓ اَتْقَنَ كُلَّ شَىْءٍ
اِنَّهٗ خَبِيْرٌۢ بِمَا تَفْعَلُوْنَ ○

89. If any do good, good will
(Accrue) to them therefrom;
And they will be secure
From terror that Day.

٨٩- مَنْ جَآءَ بِالْحَسَنَةِ فَلَهٗ خَيْرٌ مِّنْهَا
وَهُمْ مِّنْ فَزَعٍ يَّوْمَئِذٍ اٰمِنُوْنَ ○

90. And if any do evil,
Their faces will be thrown
Headlong into the Fire:[3320]
"Do ye receive a reward
Other than that which ye
Have earned by your deeds?"[3321]

٩٠- وَمَنْ جَآءَ بِالسَّيِّئَةِ فَكُبَّتْ وُجُوْهُهُمْ
فِى النَّارِ هَلْ تُجْزَوْنَ
اِلَّا مَا كُنْتُمْ تَعْمَلُوْنَ ○

91. For me, I have been
Commanded to serve the Lord[3322]
Of this City, Him Who has
Sanctified it and to Whom
(Belong) all things:
And I am commanded
To be of those who bow
In Islam to God's Will,—

٩١- اِنَّمَآ اُمِرْتُ اَنْ اَعْبُدَ رَبَّ
هٰذِهِ الْبَلْدَةِ الَّذِىْ حَرَّمَهَا
وَلَهٗ كُلُّ شَىْءٍ
وَّاُمِرْتُ اَنْ اَكُوْنَ مِنَ الْمُسْلِمِيْنَ ○

92. And to rehearse the Qur-ān:[3323]
And if any accept guidance,

٩٢- وَاَنْ اَتْلُوَا الْقُرْاٰنَ فَمَنِ اهْتَدٰى

3319. *Atqana*: to arrange or dispose of things with art, or so as to obtain the most perfect results. The present phenomenal world and the Future that is to be, all have a definite object and purpose in the Plan of God, Who knows perfectly what we are, what we do, what we think, and what we need. Who can praise His artistry enough?

3320. *Headlong*: it may be that the very things of which we were proudest, which we considered foremost in our present order of the world, will be the first to go into the Fire, as they are but the window-dressing (=faces) of Evil.

3321. There will be no punishment except such as has been deserved by actual conduct in the present life of probation.

3322. *The Lord of this City.* This was spoken in Mecca, say about the 5th year before the Hijrat, when the holy Prophet and his adherents were being persecuted as enemies to the cult of Mecca. So far from being against the true spirit of the holy City of Mecca, it was actually in furtherance of that spirit, which had been overlaid by the idolatries and abominations of the Pagan Quraish. They are told that the new Teaching is from the Lord of Mecca itself, the One True God, Who had sanctified it in the time of Abraham. Lest they should think that it was a local or tribal or narrow cult, it is added that He is not only Lord of this City, but Lord of the Worlds, "to Whom belong all things". It is a universal message; but how sad it would be if the Meccans, among whom it came first, were to reject it?

3323. The duty of the Apostle and his adherents was, first, to accept Islam and become themselves shining examples of God's grace and mercy, as they in fact were, and secondly, to preach that message and spread that Light to all around. It was not for them to force it on unwilling people: for any who rejected it would find their own spiritual loss in such rejection. But they must clearly warn them of the consequences.

They do it for the good
Of their own souls,
And if any stray, say:
"I am only a Warner".

فَإِنَّمَا يَهْتَدِي لِنَفْسِهِۦ ۖ وَمَن ضَلَّ فَقُلْ
إِنَّمَآ أَنَا۠ مِنَ ٱلْمُنذِرِينَ ○

93. And say: "Praise be to God,
Who will soon show you [3324]
His Signs, so that ye
Shall know them"; and thy Lord
Is not unmindful
Of all that ye do. [3325]

٩٣- وَقُلِ ٱلْحَمْدُ لِلَّهِ سَيُرِيكُمْ
ءَايَٰتِهِۦ فَتَعْرِفُونَهَا ۚ
وَمَا رَبُّكَ بِغَٰفِلٍ عَمَّا تَعْمَلُونَ ○

3324. In a few years after that, many wonderful things happened that removed the doubts of the doubters and confirmed the faith of the Believers. They showed how the logic of events proved the true mission of the holy Prophet. Other things some minds may not be able to grasp. But the logic of events is for all to see.

3325. Trials and tribulations, persecution and exile, and the patient endurance and constancy with which they were met by the Believers—all are known to God and will be credited to their spiritual account.

INTRODUCTION TO SŪRA XXVIII (*Qaṣaṣ*).

This Sūra continues the subject of Revelation and its reception by those to whom it is sent. But it emphasises new points: how the recipient of inspiration is prepared for his high destiny, even in the growth of his ordinary life, and how the rejection of God's Message by groups of men or by individuals is caused by overweening arrogance or avarice. The plight of those who reject the Truth is contrasted with the reward of the righteous.

With the possible exception of a few verses, it belongs to the late Meccan period, just preceding the Hijrat.

Summary.—Pharaoh was arrogant and unjust, but God's Plan was to strengthen the weak: in infancy Moses was prepared for his mission; in youth he trusted in the Lord and was guided; in his exile he found help and love; and when he was called, he was supported by God (xxviii. 1-42, and C. 173).

So was the holy Apostle Muḥammad fed spiritually by God's Grace, and his Revelation was recognised by those who knew the earlier Revelations: it came to an old and sacred Centre, to warn those seduced by this world's life (xxviii. 43-60, and C. 174).

The Future is with those who repent, have faith, and do good: for all Mercy and Truth are with God (xxviii. 61-75, and C. 175).

But men puffed up with wealth, like Qārūn, will come to an evil end, while the lowly and the righteous will attain God's Mercy (xxviii. 76-88, C. 176).

C. 173.—God's Apostles are men, and win through good life
(xxviii. 1-42.) By God's Grace and their Faith. So Moses
Was saved from the Tyrant's wrath in infancy,
And reared in the Tyrant's own den, but gently
In a mother's love. In youth was he endowed
With wisdom and knowledge, strength and the will
To do right. In sorrow or misfortune
He trusted in God and opened his heart
To Him. In self-imposed exile he won
Love by his chivalry and confidence by Truth.
In his mission he triumphed over arrogant
Wrong by his meekness, patience, and Faith.
So good follows good, and Evil must fall,
Cursed, loathed, disgraced, and despised.

Sūra XXVIII.

Qaṣaṣ, or the Narration.

In the name of God, Most Gracious, Most Merciful.

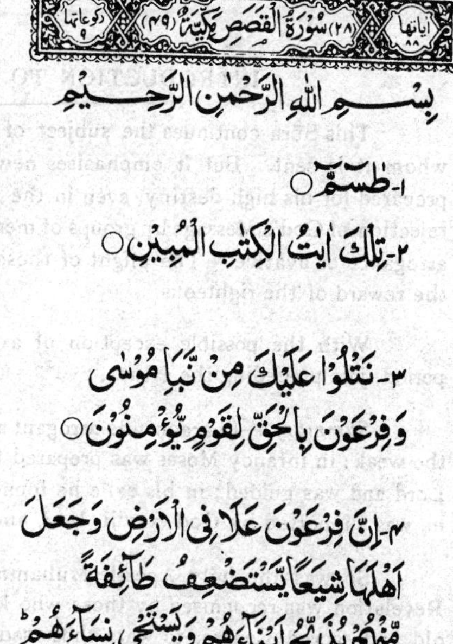

1. Ṭa. Sin. Mim.[3326]

2. These are Verses of the Book
That makes (things) clear.[3327]

3. We rehearse to thee some
Of the story of Moses
And Pharaoh in Truth,
For people who believe.[3328]

4. Truly Pharaoh elated himself
In the land and broke up
Its people into sections,[3329]
Depressing a small group
Among them: their sons he slew,
But he kept alive their females:
For he was indeed
A maker of mischief.

5. And We wished to be
Gracious to those who were
Being depressed in the land,[3330]
To make them leaders (in faith)
And make them heirs,

3326. See n. 3137 to xxvi. 1.

3327. See n. 3138 to xxvi. 2.

3328. The part of the story of Moses told here is how Moses and his mother were guided in the child's infancy, that even as he grew up, he might be prepared for his high destiny; how in youth he trusted God in the most awkward situations and sought His help; how he fled into exile, and yet found love and support because of his well-doing; and how, when he was called to his mission, he received God's favour, which defeated all the plots of his enemies. Thus God's Plan works continuously in the web of events which the Fates are supposed to be weaving. Those who have faith will thus see the hand of God in everything, and welcome the light that comes to them by Revelation. With such a Faith there is no room for Chance or blind Fate.

3329. For a king or ruler to make invidious distinctions between his subjects, and specially to depress or oppress any particular class of his subjects, is a dereliction of his kingly duties, for which he is responsible to God Pharaoh and his clique were intoxicated with pride of race and pride of material civilization, and grievously oppressed the Israelites. Pharaoh decreed that all male sons born to his Israelite subjects should be killed, and the females kept alive for the pleasure of the Egyptians. Moses was saved in a wonderful way, as related further.

3330. What Pharaoh wished was to crush them. But God's Plan was to protect them as they were weak, and indeed to make them custodians and leaders in His Faith, and to give them in inheritance a land "flowing with milk and honey". Here they were established in authority for such time as they followed God's Law. As regards Pharaoh and his ministers and hosts, they were to be shown that they would suffer, at the hands of the Israelites, the very calamities against which they were so confidently taking precautions for themselves.

6. To establish a firm place
For them in the land,
And to show Pharaoh, Hāmān,[3331]
And their hosts, at their hands,
The very things against which
They were taking precautions.[3332]

٦- وَنُمَكِّنَ لَهُمْ فِي الْأَرْضِ
وَنُرِيَ فِرْعَوْنَ وَهَامَانَ وَجُنُودَهُمَا
مِنْهُمْ مَّا كَانُوا يَحْذَرُونَ ○

7. So We sent this inspiration
To the mother of Moses:
"Suckle (thy child), but when
Thou hast fears about him,
Cast him into the river,[3333]
But fear not nor grieve:
For We shall restore him
To thee, and We shall make
Him one of Our apostles."

٧- وَأَوْحَيْنَا إِلَىٰ أُمِّ مُوسَىٰ
أَنْ أَرْضِعِيهِ ۚ فَإِذَا خِفْتِ عَلَيْهِ
فَأَلْقِيهِ فِي الْيَمِّ وَلَا تَخَافِي وَلَا تَحْزَنِي ۚ
إِنَّا رَادُّوهُ إِلَيْكِ وَجَاعِلُوهُ مِنَ
الْمُرْسَلِينَ ○

8. Then the people of Pharaoh
Picked him up (from the river):
(It was intended) that (Moses)
Should be to them an adversary
And a cause of sorrow:[3334]
For Pharaoh and Hāmān
And (all) their hosts were
Men of sin.

٨- فَالْتَقَطَهُ آلُ فِرْعَوْنَ
لِيَكُونَ لَهُمْ عَدُوًّا وَحَزَنًا ۗ
إِنَّ فِرْعَوْنَ وَهَامَانَ
وَجُنُودَهُمَا كَانُوا خَاطِئِينَ ○

9. The wife of Pharaoh said:
"(Here is) a joy of the eye,[3335]
For me and for thee:
Slay him not. It may be

٩- وَقَالَتِ امْرَأَتُ فِرْعَوْنَ قُرَّتُ عَيْنٍ
لِّي وَلَكَ ۖ لَا تَقْتُلُوهُ ۖ

3331. Hāmān was evidently Pharaoh's minister, not to be confounded with a Hāmān who is mentioned in the Old Testament (Esther iii. 1), as a minister of Ahasuerus (Xerxes) King of Persia, the same who invaded Greece, and ruled from B.C. 485 to 464.

3332. Pharaoh was trying to kill the Israelites. Instead, the Plagues of Egypt, invoked by Moses, killed thousands of Egyptians (vii. 133, and notes 1091-92), because "they were steeped in arrogance, —a people given to sin." In pursuing the Israelites in their flight, Pharaoh and his army were themselves overwhelmed in the sea.

3333. The Egyptian midwives had orders to kill Israelite babes. Moses was saved from them, and his mother nursed the infant at her breast herself. But when the danger of discovery was imminent, she put him into a chest or basket, and floated him on the river Nile. It flowed by the King's palace, and the chest with the baby was picked up, as related further on. The mother had no cause to fear or grieve afterwards, as the child grew up under her tender care and became afterwards one of the apostles of God.

3334. This was the Plan of Providence: that the wicked might cast a net round themselves by fostering the man who was to bring them to naught and be the instrument of their punishment,—or (looking at it from the other side) that Moses might learn all the wisdom of the Egyptians in order to expose all that was hollow and wicked in it.

3335. He was a darling to look at, and Pharaoh had apparently no son, but only a daughter, who afterwards shared his throne. This is on the supposition that the Pharaoh was Thothmes I (see Appendix IV, S. vii).

That he will be of use
To us, or we may adopt
Him as a son." And they
Perceived not (what they
Were doing)![3336]

عَسَىٰٓ أَن يَنفَعَنَآ أَوْ نَتَّخِذَهُۥ وَلَدًا
وَهُمْ لَا يَشْعُرُونَ ○

10. But there came to be
A void in the heart
Of the mother of Moses:
She was going almost to
Disclose his (case), had We
Not strengthened her heart
(With faith), so that she
Might remain a (firm) believer.[3337]

١٠- وَأَصْبَحَ فُؤَادُ أُمِّ مُوسَىٰ فَٰرِغًا
إِن كَادَتْ لَتُبْدِى بِهِۦ
لَوْلَآ أَن رَّبَطْنَا عَلَىٰ قَلْبِهَا
لِتَكُونَ مِنَ ٱلْمُؤْمِنِينَ ○

11. And she said to the sister
Of (Moses), "Follow him".
So she (the sister) watched him
In the character of a stranger.
And they knew not.

١١- وَقَالَتْ لِأُخْتِهِۦ قُصِّيهِ
فَبَصُرَتْ بِهِۦ عَن جُنُبٍ
وَهُمْ لَا يَشْعُرُونَ ○

12. And We ordained that he
Refused suck at first, until
(His sister came up
And) said: "Shall I
Point out to you the people
Of a house that will nourish
And bring him up for you[3338]
And be sincerely attached
To him?"...

١٢- وَحَرَّمْنَا عَلَيْهِ ٱلْمَرَاضِعَ مِن قَبْلُ
فَقَالَتْ هَلْ أَدُلُّكُمْ عَلَىٰٓ أَهْلِ بَيْتٍ
يَكْفُلُونَهُۥ لَكُمْ
وَهُمْ لَهُۥ نَٰصِحُونَ ○

13. Thus did We restore him
To his mother, that her eye
Might be comforted, that she
Might not grieve, and that
She might know that the promise
Of God is true: but
Most of them do not understand.[3339]

١٣- فَرَدَدْنَٰهُ إِلَىٰٓ أُمِّهِۦ كَىْ تَقَرَّ عَيْنُهَا وَ
لَا تَحْزَنَ وَلِتَعْلَمَ أَنَّ وَعْدَ ٱللَّهِ حَقٌّ
وَلَٰكِنَّ أَكْثَرَهُمْ لَا يَعْلَمُونَ ○

3336. In all life Providence so orders things that Evil is defeated by its own weapons. Not only is it defeated, but it actually, though unwittingly, advances the cause of Good! In non-religious language this is called the work of the Ironic Fates. If Thomas Hardy had not made Napoleon the Puppet of Fate in his "Dynasts", he could well have taken Pharaoh as an illustration of the Irony of Fate, or, as we should prefer to call it, the working of the Universal Plan.

3337. The mother's heart felt the gaping void at parting from her son; but her Faith in God's Providence kept her from betraying herself.

3338. *For you*: *i.e.* on your behalf. Thus Moses got the benefit of his mother's milk (symbolical of all the traditions and spiritual heritage of his ancestry and his people) as well as the prestige and the opportunities of being brought up in the royal family, with the best of teachers to teach him Egyptian wisdom. In addition, there was the comfort to his mother.

3339. God's promise is always true, but short-sighted people, if they are a little thwarted in their plan, do not understand that God's wisdom, power, and goodness are far more comprehensive than any little plans which they may form.

SECTION 2.

14. When he reached full age,
And was firmly established[3340]
(In life), We bestowed on him
Wisdom and knowledge: for thus
Do We reward those
Who do good.

١٤- ولما بلغ اشده
واستوى اتينه حكما وعلما ط
وكذلك نجزي المحسنين ○

15. And he entered the City
At a time when its people[3341]
Were not watching: and he
Found there two men fighting,—
One of his own religion,
And the other, of his foes.
Now the man of his own
Religion appealed to him
Against his foe, and Moses
Struck him with his fist[3342]
And made an end of him.
He said: "This is a work
Of Evil (Satan): for he is
An enemy that manifestly
Misleads!"

١٥- ودخل المدينة على حين غفلة
من اهلها فوجد فيها رجلين يقتتلن
هذا من شيعته وهذا من عدوه ج
فاستغاثه الذي من شيعته على الذي
من عدوه
فوكزه موسى فقضى عليه
قال هذا من عمل الشيطن ط
انه عدو مضل مبين ○

16. He prayed: "O my Lord!
I have indeed wronged my soul!
Do Thou then forgive me!"
So (God) forgave him: for He
Is the Oft-Forgiving, Most
Merciful.

١٦- قال رب اني ظلمت نفسي
فاغفر لي فغفر له ط
انه هو الغفور الرحيم ○

3340. *Full age* may be taken to be mature youth, say between 18 and 30 years of age. By that time a person is fully established in life: his physical build is completed, and his mental and moral habits are formed. In this case, as Moses was good at heart, true and loyal to his people, and obedient and just to those among whom he lived, he was granted wisdom and knowledge from on high, to be used for the times of conflict which were coming for him. His internal development being complete, he now goes out into the outer world, where he is again tried and proved, until he gets his divine commission.

3341. That may have been either the time of the noontide siesta, when all business is suspended even now in Egypt, or the time of night, when people are usually asleep. The latter is more probable, in view of verse 18 below. But there is also another suggestion. A guest in a Palace is not free to wander about at will in the plebeian quarters of the City at all sorts of hours, and this applies even more to an inmate of the Palace brought up as a son. Moses was therefore visiting the City privately and eluding the guards. His object may have been to see for himself how things were going on; perhaps he had heard that his people were being oppressed, as we may suppose that he had retained contact with his mother.

3342. His object was apparently to strike him so as to release the Israelite, not to kill the Egyptian. In fact he killed the Egyptian. This was unfortunate in more ways than one. His visit to the City was clandestine; he had taken the side of the weaker and despised party; and he had taken the life of an Egyptian. He was full of regrets and repentance, and he prayed to God, and obtained God's forgiveness.

17. He said: "O my Lord!
For that Thou hast bestowed
Thy Grace on me, never
Shall I be a help
To those who sin!"[3343]

١٧- قَالَ رَبِّ بِمَآ أَنْعَمْتَ عَلَىَّ
فَلَنْ أَكُونَ ظَهِيرًا لِّلْمُجْرِمِينَ ۝

18. So he saw the morning
In the City, looking about,
In a state of fear, when
Behold, the man who had,
The day before, sought his help
Called aloud for his help
(Again). Moses said to him:
"Thou art truly, it is clear,
A quarrelsome fellow!"[3344]

١٨- فَأَصْبَحَ فِى الْمَدِينَةِ خَآئِفًا يَتَرَقَّبُ
فَإِذَا الَّذِى اسْتَنصَرَهُۥ بِالْأَمْسِ
يَسْتَصْرِخُهُۥ
قَالَ لَهُۥ مُوسَىٰٓ
إِنَّكَ لَغَوِىٌّ مُّبِينٌ ۝

19. Then, when he decided to lay
Hold of the man who was[3345]
An enemy to both of them,
That man said: "O Moses!
Is it thy intention to slay me
As thou slewest a man
Yesterday? Thy intention is
None other than to become
A powerful violent man
In the land, and not to be
One who sets things right!"[3346]

١٩- فَلَمَّآ أَنْ أَرَادَ أَن يَبْطِشَ بِالَّذِى
هُوَ عَدُوٌّ لَّهُمَا
قَالَ يَٰمُوسَىٰٓ أَتُرِيدُ أَن تَقْتُلَنِى
كَمَا قَتَلْتَ نَفْسًۢا بِالْأَمْسِ ۖ إِن تُرِيدُ
إِلَّآ أَن تَكُونَ جَبَّارًا فِى الْأَرْضِ وَمَا
تُرِيدُ أَن تَكُونَ مِنَ الْمُصْلِحِينَ ۝

3343. He takes a conscious and solemn vow to dedicate himself to God, and to do nothing that may in any way assist those who were doing wrong. This was his general idea, but no plan had yet shaped itself in his mind, until a second catastrophe brought matters to a head, and he was plunged in adventure.

3344. The man was an Israelite. But Moses was himself in a distracted mood, for the reasons given in n. 3342 above, and he was exasperated at this public appeal to him again.

3345. When Moses considered further that the Egyptian was unjust and that the Egyptian was an enemy to Israel generally (including both Moses and the man assaulted), he was going to intervene again, when he received a double warning, one from the Egyptian who was fighting, and the other from some man (Israelite or Egyptian) who was friendly to him, as explained below. We may suppose that after the first day's fight, there had been a great deal of talk in the bazars, both among Israelites and Egyptians. Probably the Israelites were elated at finding a champion—perhaps more elated than they should have been, and in a provocative mood, which deserved Moses's rebuke. Probably the Egyptians had discussed who this new champion was, and had already apprised the Palace, to which Moses had not dared to return.

3346. The Egyptian saw the tactical advantage of his position. In effect he said: 'We have found out all about you. You live in the Palace, and yet you come clandestinely and kill our Egyptians. Are you going to do the same with me? You are nothing but a bully! And you talk of setting things right! That is what you should do if you were true to your salt!'

20. And there came a man,
Running, from the furthest end[3347]
Of the City. He said:
"O Moses! the Chiefs
Are taking counsel together
About thee, to slay thee:
So get thee away, for I
Do give thee sincere advice."

٢٠- وَجَاءَ رَجُلٌ مِّنْ أَقْصَا الْمَدِينَةِ يَسْعَىٰ
قَالَ يَٰمُوسَىٰٓ إِنَّ الْمَلَأَ يَأْتَمِرُونَ بِكَ
لِيَقْتُلُوكَ فَاخْرُجْ
إِنِّي لَكَ مِنَ النَّٰصِحِينَ ○

21. He therefore got away therefrom,[3348]
Looking about, in a state
Of fear. He prayed:
"O my Lord! save me
From people given to wrong-doing."

٢١- فَخَرَجَ مِنْهَا خَائِفًا يَتَرَقَّبُ
قَالَ رَبِّ نَجِّنِي
مِنَ الْقَوْمِ الظَّٰلِمِينَ ○ ع

SECTION 3.

22. When, when he turned his face
Towards (the land of) Madyan,[3349]
He said: "I do hope
That my Lord will show me
The smooth and straight Path."

٢٢- وَلَمَّا تَوَجَّهَ تِلْقَاءَ مَدْيَنَ
قَالَ عَسَىٰ رَبِّيٓ أَن يَهْدِيَنِي سَوَاءَ
السَّبِيلِ ○

23. And when he arrived at
The watering (place) in Madyan,[3350]
He found there a group
Of men watering (their flocks),
And besides them he found
Two women who were keeping

٢٣- وَلَمَّا وَرَدَ مَاءَ مَدْيَنَ
وَجَدَ عَلَيْهِ أُمَّةً مِّنَ النَّاسِ يَسْقُونَ
وَوَجَدَ مِن دُونِهِمُ امْرَأَتَيْنِ تَذُودَانِ

3347. Apparently rumours had reached the Palace, a Council had been held, and the death of Moses had been decreed!

3348. Moses saw that his position was now untenable, both in the Palace and in the City, and indeed anywhere in Pharaoh's territory. So he suffered voluntary exile. But he did not know where to go to. His mind was in a state of agitation. But he turned to God and prayed. He got consolation, and felt that after all it was no hardship to leave Egypt, where there was so much injustice and oppression.

3349. East of Lower Egypt, for about 300 miles, runs the Sinai Peninsula, bounded on the south by the Gulf of Suez, and on the north by what was the Isthmus of Suez, now cut by the Suez Canal. Over the Isthmus ran the highroad to Palestine and Syria, but a fugitive could not well take that road, as the Egyptians were after him. If he could, after crossing the Isthmus, plunge into the Sinai desert, east or south-east, he would be in the Midianite territory, where the people would be Arabs and not Egyptians. He turned thither, and again prayed to God for guidance.

3350. The first thing that a wanderer in a desert would make for would be an oasis where he could get water from a spring or well, the shade of trees against the scorching sun, and some human company. The Midianite watering place was probably a deep well, as surface springs are rare in sandy deserts, where the water level is low, unless there was a hill from which issued a spring.

Back (their flocks). He said:
"What is the matter with you?"
They said: "We cannot water
(Our flocks) until the shepherds
Take back (their flocks):
And our father is
A very old man."[3351]

قَالَ مَا خَطْبُكُمَا ۖ
قَالَتَا لَا نَسْقِي حَتَّىٰ يُصْدِرَ الرِّعَاءُ ۖ
وَأَبُونَا شَيْخٌ كَبِيرٌ ۝

24. So he watered (their flocks)
For them; then he turned back
To the shade, and said:
"O my Lord!
Truly am I
In (desperate) need
Of any good
That Thou dost send me!"...[3352]

٢٤- فَسَقَىٰ لَهُمَا
ثُمَّ تَوَلَّىٰ إِلَى الظِّلِّ فَقَالَ
رَبِّ إِنِّي لِمَا أَنزَلْتَ إِلَيَّ
مِنْ خَيْرٍ فَقِيرٌ ۝

25. Afterwards one of the (damsels)
Came (back) to him, walking
Bashfully. She said: "My father
Invites thee that he may
Reward thee for having watered[3353]
(Our flocks) for us." So when
He came to him and narrated
The story, he said:

٢٥- فَجَاءَتْهُ إِحْدَاهُمَا تَمْشِي عَلَى اسْتِحْيَاءٍ
قَالَتْ إِنَّ أَبِي يَدْعُوكَ لِيَجْزِيَكَ أَجْرَ
مَا سَقَيْتَ لَنَا ۚ
فَلَمَّا جَاءَهُ وَقَصَّ عَلَيْهِ الْقَصَصَ ۙ قَالَ

3351. Here is a pretty little idyll, told in the fewest and most beautiful words possible. Moses arrives at an oasis in the desert, weary and travel-worn, with his mind full of anxiety and uncertainty owing to his recent experiences in Egypt. He was thirsty and would naturally seek water. At the well or spring he found shepherds (or perhaps goat-herds) watering their flocks. As a stranger it was not for him to thrust himself among them. He waited under the shade of a tree until they should finish. He noticed two damsels, also waiting, with their flocks, which they had come to water. His chivalry was roused. He went at once among the goat-herds, made a place for the flocks of the damsels, gave them water, and then resumed his place in the shade. They were modest maidens, and had given him in three Arabic words the key of the whole situation. '*Abū-nā shaikhun kabīrun*: our father is a very old man, and therefore cannot come to water the flocks; we therefore do the work; we could not very well thrust ourselves among these men.'

3352. The maidens are gone, with smiles on their lips and gratitude in their hearts. What were the reflections of Moses as he returned to the shade of the tree? He returned thanks to God for the bright little vision which he had just seen. Had he done a good deed? Precious was the opportunity he had had. He had slaked his thirst. But he was a homeless wanderer and had a longing in his soul, which he dared not put into words. Those shepherds were no company for him. He was truly like a beggar in desperate need. For any little good that came his way, he was grateful. But what was this?—this vision of a comfortable household, presided over by an old man rich in flocks and herds, and richer still in two daughters, as modest as they were beautiful? Perhaps he would never see them again! But Providence was preparing another surprise for him

3353. Scarcely had he rested, when one of the damsels came back, walking with bashful grace! Modestly she gave her message. 'My father is grateful for what you did for us. He invites you, that he may thank you personally, and at least give some return for your kindness.

"Fear thou not: (well) hast thou
Escaped from unjust people."[3354]

لَا تَخَفْ نَجَوْتَ مِنَ الْقَوْمِ الظّٰلِمِيْنَ ○

26. Said one of the (damsels):
"O my (dear) father! engage[3355]
Him on wages: truly the best
Of men for thee to employ is
The (man) who is strong and
trusty"...[3356]

٢٦- قَالَتْ اِحْدٰىهُمَا يٰاَبَتِ اسْتَاْجِرْهُ
اِنَّ خَيْرَ مَنِ اسْتَاْجَرْتَ
الْقَوِيُّ الْاَمِيْنُ ○

27. He said: "I intend to wed
One of these my daughters
To thee, on condition that
Thou serve me for eight years;[3357]
But if thou complete ten years,
It will be (grace) from thee.
But I intend not to place
Thee under a difficulty:

٢٧- قَالَ اِنِّيْٓ اُرِيْدُ اَنْ اُنْكِحَكَ اِحْدَى ابْنَتَيَّ
هٰتَيْنِ عَلٰٓى اَنْ تَاْجُرَنِيْ ثَمٰنِيَ حِجَجٍ ۚ
فَاِنْ اَتْمَمْتَ عَشْرًا فَمِنْ عِنْدِكَ ۚ
وَمَآ اُرِيْدُ اَنْ اَشُقَّ عَلَيْكَ ۭ

3354. Nothing could have been more welcome than such a message, and through such a messenger. Moses went of course, and saw the old man. He found such a well-ordered patriarchal household. The old man was happy in his daughters and they in him. There was mutual confidence. They had evidently described the stranger to him in terms which made his welcome a foregone conclusion. On the other hand Moses had allowed his imagination to paint the father in something of the glorious colours in which his daughters had appeared to him like an angelic vision. The two men got to be friends at once. Moses told the old man his story,—who he was, how he was brought up, and what misfortunes had made him quit Egypt. Perhaps the whole household, including the daughters, listened breathlessly to his tale. Perhaps their wonder and admiration were mingled with a certain amount of pity—perhaps with some more tender feeling in the case of the girl who had been to fetch him. Perhaps the enchantment which Desdemona felt in Othello's story was working on her. In any case the stranger had won his place in their hearts. The old man, the head of the household, assured him of hospitality and safety under his roof. As one with a long experience of life he congratulated him on his escape. 'Who would live among unjust people? It is as well you are free of them!'

3355. A little time passes. A guest after all cannot stay for ever. They all feel that it would be good to have him with them permanently. The girl who had given her heart to him had spoken their unspoken thoughts. Why not employ him to tend the flocks? The father was old, and a young man was wanted to look after the flocks. And—there may be other possibilities.

3356. *Strong and trusty*: Moses had proved himself to be both, and these were the very qualities which a woman most admires in the man she loves.

3357. A little time passed, and at length the father broached the subject of marriage. It was not for the fugitive to suggest a permanent tie, especially when, in the wealth of this world, the girl's family was superior, and they had an established position, while he was a mere wanderer. The father asked if he would marry one of the daughters and stay with them for at least eight years, or if he liked, ten years, but the longer term was at his option. If he brought no dower, his service for that period was more than sufficient in lieu of dower. The particular girl intended was no doubt tacitly settled long before, by the mutual attraction of the young hearts themselves. Moses was glad of the proposal, and accepted it. They ratified it in the most solemn manner, by appealing to God. The old man, knowing the worth of his son-in-law, solemnly assured him that in any event he would not take advantage of his position to be a hard task-master or to insist on anything inconsistent with Moses's interests, should a new future open out to him. And a new and glorious future was awaiting him after his apprenticeship.

Thou wilt find me,
Indeed, if God wills,
One of the righteous."

سَتَجِدُنِیۡۤ اِنۡ شَآءَ اللّٰہُ مِنَ الصّٰلِحِیۡنَ ○

28. He said: "Be that (the agreement)
Between me and thee:
Whichever of the two terms
I fulfil, let there be
No ill-will to me.
Be God a witness
To what we say." [3358]

۲۸- قَالَ ذٰلِکَ بَیۡنِیۡ وَ بَیۡنَکَ ؕ
اَیَّمَا الۡاَجَلَیۡنِ قَضَیۡتُ فَلَا عُدۡوَانَ عَلَیَّ ؕ
وَ اللّٰہُ عَلٰی مَا نَقُوۡلُ وَکِیۡلٌ ○

Section 4.

29. Now when Moses had fulfilled
The term, and was travelling [3359]
With his family, he perceived
A fire in the direction
Of Mount Ṭūr. He said
To his family: "Tarry ye;
I perceive a fire; I hope
To bring you from there
Some information, or a burning
Firebrand, that ye may
Warm yourselves." [3360]

۲۹- فَلَمَّا قَضٰی مُوۡسَی الۡاَجَلَ وَ سَارَ بِاَہۡلِہٖۤ
اٰنَسَ مِنۡ جَانِبِ الطُّوۡرِ نَارًا ۚ
قَالَ لِاَہۡلِہِ امۡکُثُوۡۤا
اِنِّیۡۤ اٰنَسۡتُ نَارًا لَّعَلِّیۡۤ اٰتِیۡکُمۡ مِّنۡہَا بِخَبَرٍ
اَوۡ جَذۡوَۃٍ مِّنَ النَّارِ لَعَلَّکُمۡ تَصۡطَلُوۡنَ ○

30. But when he came
To the (Fire), a voice

۳۰- فَلَمَّاۤ اَتٰىہَا نُوۡدِیَ

3358. In patriarchal society it was not uncommon to have a marriage bargain of this kind conditional on a certain term of service. In this case the episode conveys two lessons. (1) A man destined to be an apostle of God is yet a man, and must pass through the ups and downs of life like any other man: only he will do it with more grace and distinction than other men. (2) The beautiful relations in love and marriage may themselves be a preparation for the highest spiritual destiny that may await a Messenger of God. A woman need not necessarily be a snare and a temptation: she may be the understanding help-mate that the Lady Khadija was to the holy Apostle

3359. The episode in the desert, full of human interest, now closes, and we come to the threshold of the sacred Call to the divine ministry of Moses. Here we may compare this passage with that in xxvii. 7-14 and previous passages. Note that a speech in such cases is not a literal report of spoken words, but a general rendering in human words of Commands, Events, and Thoughts, such as may be relevant in connection with any particular episode and its context. In this passage we are told, after reference to Moses's preparation for his high destiny, of the particular sin of Arrogance and Sacrilege of which Pharaoh was guilty (xxviii 38-39), how it was punished, and with what instruments in the hands of Moses and Pharaoh. The notes on the earlier passage should be read, as explanations already given need not now be repeated.

3360. Note how the transition is effected from the happy earthly life of Moses (with its previous earthly storm and stress) to the new spiritual storm and stress of his prophetic mission.

Was heard from the right bank
Of the valley, from a tree[3361]
In hallowed ground:
"O Moses! Verily
I am God, the Lord
Of the Worlds ...

مِن شَاطِئِ الْوَادِ الْأَيْمَنِ
فِي الْبُقْعَةِ الْمُبَارَكَةِ مِنَ الشَّجَرَةِ
أَن يَا مُوسَىٰ إِنِّي أَنَا اللَّهُ رَبُّ الْعَالَمِينَ ○

31. "Now do thou throw thy rod!"
But when he saw it
Moving (of its own accord)
As if it had been a snake,
He turned back in retreat,
And retraced not his steps:
"O Moses!" (it was said),
"Draw near, and fear not:
For thou art of those
Who are secure.[3362]

٣١- وَأَنْ أَلْقِ عَصَاكَ ۖ فَلَمَّا رَآهَا
تَهْتَزُّ كَأَنَّهَا جَانٌّ
وَلَّىٰ مُدْبِرًا وَلَمْ يُعَقِّبْ ۚ
يَا مُوسَىٰ أَقْبِلْ وَلَا تَخَفْ ۖ
إِنَّكَ مِنَ الْآمِنِينَ ○

32. "Move thy hand into
Thy bosom, and it will
Come forth white without stain
(Or harm), and draw thy hand
Close to thy side
(To guard) against fear.[3363]
Those are the two credentials
From thy Lord to Pharaoh
And his Chiefs: for truly
They are a people
Rebellious and wicked."

٣٢- اسْلُكْ يَدَكَ فِي جَيْبِكَ
تَخْرُجْ بَيْضَاءَ مِنْ غَيْرِ سُوءٍ
وَاضْمُمْ إِلَيْكَ جَنَاحَكَ مِنَ الرَّهْبِ ۖ
فَذَانِكَ بُرْهَانَانِ مِن رَّبِّكَ إِلَىٰ فِرْعَوْنَ وَ
مَلَئِهِ ۚ
إِنَّهُمْ كَانُوا قَوْمًا فَاسِقِينَ ○

33. He said: "O my Lord!
I have slain a man

٣٣- قَالَ رَبِّ إِنِّي قَتَلْتُ

3361. We are to suppose the appearance of a bush burning but not consumed (Exod, iii. 2), a device adopted by the Scottish Church in its armorial bearings. Scotland apparently took that emblem and motto (*Nec tamen consumebatur*, 'nevertheless it was not consumed') from the Synod of the Reformed Church of France, which had adopted it in 1583. (I am indebted for this information to the Rev. D.Y. Robertson, Chaplain of the Church of Scotland in Simla). The real explanation of the Burning Bush will be found in xxvii. 8, n. 3245: it was not a fire, but a reflection of the Glory of God.

3362. The verbal meaning is: 'you have nothing to fear from what appears to be a snake: it is a snake, not for you, but for Pharaoh.' But there is a deeper meaning besides. Moses had now been called to a higher and spiritual mission. He had to meet the hatred of the Egyptians and circumvent their trickery and magic. He had now the security of Faith: in all dangers and difficulties God would guide and protect him, for he was actually in God's service, one of the Elect.

3363. Literally, "draw thy wing close to thy side, (away) from fear". When a bird is frightened, it ruffles its wings and prepares to fly away, but when it is calm and composed, it sits with its wings drawn close to its sides, showing a mind secure from danger. *Cf.* also n. 2550 to xx. 22.

Among them, and I fear[3364]
Lest they slay me.

منهم نفسا فأخاف أن يقتلون ○

34. "And my brother Aaron—
He is more eloquent in speech
Than I: so send him
With me as a helper,
To confirm (and strengthen) me:
For I fear that they may
Accuse me of falsehood."

٣٤- وأخي هرون هو أفصح مني لسانا
فأرسله معي ردءا يصدقني ز
إني أخاف أن يكذبون ○

35. He said: "We will certainly
Strengthen thy arm through
Thy brother, and invest you both
With authority, so they
Shall not be able to[3365]
Touch you: with Our Signs
Shall ye triumph,—you two
As well as those
Who follow you."[3366]

٣٥- قال سنشد عضدك بأخيك
ونجعل لكما سلطانا
فلا يصلون إليكما ج بآيتنا ج
أنتما ومن اتبعكما الغلبون ○

36. When Moses came to them
With Our Clear Signs, they said:
"This is nothing but sorcery[3367]
Faked up: never did we
Hear the like among our fathers
Of old!"[3368]

٣٦- فلما جاءهم موسى بآيتنا بينت قالوا
ما هذا إلا سحر مفترى
وما سمعنا بهذا في آبائنا الأولين ○

3364. It is not that Moses is not reassured from all fear on account of the apparent snake which his rod had become, or from the sacred and unfamiliar surroundings in which he found himself. On this point his heart has been completely assured. But he is still new to his mission, and the future is obscure to his mind. Pharaoh was after him, to take his life, and apparently with good cause, because one of Pharaoh's men had been slain at his hands. And now he is commanded to go to Pharaoh and rebuke him and his Chiefs. The inner doubts and difficulties of his human mind he frankly lays before his Lord, and asks for a little human and visible support, which is granted him at once, *viz.*: the help of his brother Aaron.

3365 *To touch you*: to approach you anywhere near, in the wonders and Signs that you will show them under the divine authority with which you are invested.

3366 The potency of God's Light is such that its divine rays reach the humblest of those who seek after Him. The Prophets can certainly work wonders, but their sincere followers in Faith can do so also in their own spheres. Wonders may appeal to people, but they are not the highest signs of God's workings, and they are around us every day in our lives.

3367. This is what Moses was thinking of when he had said: "They may accuse me of falsehood". To accuse the purest Truth of lying is a favourite trick of those whose chief stock-in-trade is deception and sorcery and catching the attention of the vulgar by arts adapted to their ignorant minds!

3368. 'As to this higher talk of the worship of the One true God, why, our ancestors have worshipped power and patronage, as concentrated in Pharaoh, from the most ancient times!'

37. Moses said: "My Lord
Knows best who it is
That comes with guidance
From Him and whose End
Will be best in the Hereafter:
Certain it is that
The wrong-doers will not
prosper."[3369]

٣٧- وَقَالَ مُوسَىٰ رَبِّيٓ أَعْلَمُ
بِمَن جَآءَ بِالْهُدَىٰ مِنْ عِندِهِۦ
وَمَن تَكُونُ لَهُۥ عَاقِبَةُ الدَّارِ
إِنَّهُۥ لَا يُفْلِحُ الظَّٰلِمُونَ ○

38. Pharaoh said: "O Chiefs!
No god do I know for you[3370]
But myself: therefore,
O Hāmān! light me a (kiln
To bake bricks) out of clay,
And build me a lofty[3371]
Palace, that I may mount up
To the god of Moses:
But as far as I am concerned,
I think (Moses) is a liar!"

٣٨- وَقَالَ فِرْعَوْنُ يَٰٓأَيُّهَا الْمَلَأُ مَا عَلِمْتُ
لَكُم مِّنْ إِلَٰهٍ غَيْرِى
فَأَوْقِدْ لِى يَٰهَٰمَٰنُ عَلَى الطِّينِ
فَاجْعَل لِّى صَرْحًا لَّعَلِّىٓ أَطَّلِعُ إِلَىٰٓ إِلَٰهِ مُوسَىٰ
وَإِنِّى لَأَظُنُّهُۥ مِنَ الْكَٰذِبِينَ ○

39. And he was arrogant and insolent
In the land, beyond reason,—
He and his hosts: they thought
That they would not have
To return to Us!"[3372]

٣٩- وَاسْتَكْبَرَ هُوَ وَجُنُودُهُۥ فِى الْأَرْضِ
بِغَيْرِ الْحَقِّ
وَظَنُّوٓا أَنَّهُمْ إِلَيْنَا لَا يُرْجَعُونَ ○

40. So We seized him
And his hosts, and We
Flung them into the sea:[3373]
Now behold what was the End
Of those who did wrong!

٤٠- فَأَخَذْنَٰهُ وَجُنُودَهُۥ فَنَبَذْنَٰهُمْ فِى
الْيَمِّ
فَانظُرْ كَيْفَ كَانَ عَاقِبَةُ الظَّٰلِمِينَ ○

3369. *Cf.* vi. 135. The only argument in such a case is an appeal to God, and to the ultimate Future. Both of these appeals require Faith. But even if you do not rely on anything so high, you can see that Falsehood or evils crystallised in ancestral customs are not going to do any one any good.

3370. Pharaoh claimed, himself, to be God,—not only one god among many, but the only god: "I am your Lord Most High": lxxix. 24. At any rate he did not see why his people should worship any one but him

3371. I understand his speech to his minister Hāmān to be sarcastic. But some Commentators have taken it very seriously and imagined that he actually thought of reaching the heavens by building lofty towers.

3372. They did not believe in the Hereafter. They did not understand that every deed must have its inevitable consequence, good or evil, unless the Grace of God intervenes to save us from ourselves!

3373. Pharaoh and his hosts were drowned in the sea in their pursuit of the Israelites: see vii. 130-136. They are the type of men who lead—only to Destruction. They invite, not to Peace and Happiness, but to the Fire of Wrath, mutual Envy, and Hatred.

41. And We made them (but)
Leaders inviting to the Fire;
And on the Day of Judgment
No help shall they find.

٤١- وَجَعَلْنٰهُمْ اَئِمَّةً يَّدْعُوْنَ اِلَى النَّارِ ۚ وَيَوْمَ الْقِيٰمَةِ لَا يُنْصَرُوْنَ ○

42. In this world We made
A Curse to follow them: [3374]
And on the Day of Judgment
They will be among
The loathed (and despised).

٤٢- وَاَتْبَعْنٰهُمْ فِيْ هٰذِهِ الدُّنْيَا لَعْنَةً ۚ وَيَوْمَ الْقِيٰمَةِ هُمْ مِّنَ الْمَقْبُوْحِيْنَ ○ ع

C. 174.—As with Moses, so with the Apostle Muḥammad:
(xxviii. 43-60.) Revelation was given to him, by which
He knew and understood, and led men and was kind.
He was a Mercy to men, sent by God, to warn
Those in sin, and, by precept and example,
To bring the Light to their very doors.
Those who had spiritual eyes rejoiced,
And walked in God's ancient Way, now reopened,
Valuing the things of the Spirit as God's
Own gifts, to be their possession for ever!

Section 5.

43. We did reveal to Moses
The Book after We had
Destroyed the earlier generations,
(To give) Insight to men,
And Guidance and Mercy,
That they might receive
admonition. [3375]

٤٣- وَلَقَدْ اٰتَيْنَا مُوْسَى الْكِتٰبَ مِنْۢ بَعْدِ مَآ اَهْلَكْنَا الْقُرُوْنَ الْاُوْلٰى بَصَآئِرَ لِلنَّاسِ وَهُدًى وَّرَحْمَةً لَّعَلَّهُمْ يَتَذَكَّرُوْنَ ○

3374. Power and patronage may be lauded by sycophants and selfish place-hunters; but when they are misused, and when their exposure causes their fall, they suffer ignominy even in this life. If they manage to escape exposure while alive, it often happens that they are found out after their death, and the curses of many generations follow those whose oppressions and wrong-doing spoiled the fair face of God's earth. But even this is nothing to the true Punishment that will come in the Hereafter. There, true values will be restored, and some of the highest and mightiest will be in the lowest depths of degradation.

3375. After the destruction of the Pharaonic Tyranny and other similar Tyrannies before them, God began a new age of Revelation, the age of Moses and his Book. Humanity began as it were with a clean slate again. It was a full Revelation (or *Sharī'at*) which may be looked at from three points of view: (1) as Light or Insight for men, so that they should not grope in darkness; (2) as a Guide to show them the Way, so that they should not be misled into wrong Paths; and (3) as a Mercy from God, so that by following the Way they may receive God's Forgiveness and Grace. In vi. 91, we have a reference to Light and Guidance in connection with the Revelation of Moses, and in vi. 154 we have a reference to Guidance and Mercy in the same connection. Here all three are combined, with the substitution of *Baṣāir* for *Nūr*. *Baṣāir* is the plural of *Baṣīrat*, and may also be translated Proofs, as I have done in vi. 104. *Cf.* also vii. 203, n. 1175, where the word is translated "Lights"

44. Thou wast not on the Western[3376]
Side when We decreed
The Commission to Moses,
Nor wast thou a witness
(Of those events).

۴۴- وَمَا كُنتَ بِجَانِبِ الْغَرْبِيِّ إِذْ قَضَيْنَا
إِلَىٰ مُوسَى الْأَمْرَ وَمَا كُنتَ مِنَ
الشّٰهِدِينَ ○

45. But We raised up (new)
Generations, and long were the ages[3377]
That passed over them ;
But thou wast not a dweller
Among the people of Madyan,
Rehearsing Our Signs to them ;
But it is We Who send
Apostles (with inspiration).[3378]

۴۵- وَلٰكِنَّآ أَنْشَأْنَا قُرُونًا
فَتَطَاوَلَ عَلَيْهِمُ الْعُمُرُ ۚ
وَمَا كُنتَ ثَاوِيًا فِيٓ أَهْلِ مَدْيَنَ
تَتْلُوا عَلَيْهِمْ ءَايٰتِنَا
وَلٰكِنَّا كُنَّا مُرْسِلِينَ ○

46. Nor wast thou at the side
Of (the Mountain of) Ṭūr
When We called (to Moses).
Yet (art thou sent)
As a Mercy from thy Lord,
To give warning to a people[3379]
To whom no warner had come
Before thee : in order that
They may receive admonition.

۴۶- وَمَا كُنتَ بِجَانِبِ الطُّورِ
إِذْ نَادَيْنَا وَلٰكِن رَّحْمَةً مِّن رَّبِّكَ
لِتُنذِرَ قَوْمًا مَّآ أَتٰهُم مِّن نَّذِيرٍ
مِّن قَبْلِكَ لَعَلَّهُمْ يَتَذَكَّرُونَ ○

47. If (We had) not (sent thee
To the Quraish),— in case
A calamity should seize them
For (the deeds) that their hands
Have sent forth, they might say :
" Our Lord ! why didst Thou not[3380]

۴۷- وَلَوْلَآ أَن تُصِيبَهُم مُّصِيبَةٌۢ
بِمَا قَدَّمَتْ أَيْدِيهِمْ
فَيَقُولُوا رَبَّنَا لَوْلَآ

3376. The Sinai Peninsula is in the north-west corner of Arabia. But the reference here is, I think, to the western side of the valley of Ṭuwā. Mount Ṭur, where Moses received his prophetic commission, is on the western side of the valley.

3377. That is, there were many generations that passed between Moses and the holy Prophet. Yet he knew by inspiration of the events of those times. Even if he had lived then, he could not have known the events that took place among the Midianites, except by inspiration, as he did not dwell among them.

3378. 'Though thou wast not among the Midianites, Our inspiration has told thee of the momentous events that took place among them when Moses was with them This is itself a Sign that should make thy people understand.'

3379. This people was the Quraish. 'Though thou didst not see how Moses was invested with the prophetic office at Mount Ṭūr, thou hast had similar experience thyself and We have sent thee to the Quraish to warn them of all their sins, and to repent and come into the Faith.'

3380. Now that a warner has come among them with all the authority that previous apostles possessed and with all the knowledge which can only come by divine inspiration, they have no excuse left whatever. They cannot say, "No warner came to us." If any evil comes to them, as the inevitable result of their ill-deeds, they cannot blame God and say that they were not warned. *Cf.* xx. 134.

Send us an apostle? We
Should then have followed
Thy Signs and been amongst
Those who believe!"

أَرْسَلْتَ إِلَيْنَا رَسُولًا
فَنَتَّبِعَ آيَاتِكَ وَنَكُونَ مِنَ الْمُؤْمِنِينَ ○

48. But (now), when the Truth
Has come to them from Ourselves,
They say, "Why are not
(Signs) sent to him, like
Those which were sent to
Moses?"[3381]
Do they not then reject
(The Signs) which were formerly
Sent to Moses? They say:
"Two kinds of sorcery,
Each assisting the other!"[3382]
And they say: "For us,
We reject all (such things)!"

٤٨- فَلَمَّا جَاءَهُمُ الْحَقُّ مِنْ عِنْدِنَا
قَالُوا لَوْلَا أُوتِيَ مِثْلَ
مَا أُوتِيَ مُوسَىٰ
أَوَلَمْ يَكْفُرُوا بِمَا أُوتِيَ مُوسَىٰ مِنْ قَبْلُ
قَالُوا سِحْرَانِ تَظَاهَرَا
وَقَالُوا إِنَّا بِكُلٍّ كَافِرُونَ ○

49. Say: "Then bring ye
A Book from God,
Which is a better Guide
Than either of them,
That I may follow it!
(Do), if ye are truthful!"

٤٩- قُلْ فَأْتُوا بِكِتَابٍ مِنْ عِنْدِ اللَّهِ
هُوَ أَهْدَىٰ مِنْهُمَا
أَتَّبِعْهُ إِنْ كُنْتُمْ صَادِقِينَ ○

50. But if they hearken not[3383]
To thee, know that they
Only follow their own lusts:
And who is more astray
Than one who follows his own
Lusts, devoid of guidance
From God? For God guides not
People given to wrong-doing.

٥٠- فَإِنْ لَمْ يَسْتَجِيبُوا لَكَ فَاعْلَمْ أَنَّمَا
يَتَّبِعُونَ أَهْوَاءَهُمْ وَمَنْ أَضَلُّ مِمَّنِ
اتَّبَعَ هَوَاهُ بِغَيْرِ هُدًى مِنَ اللَّهِ
إِنَّ اللَّهَ لَا يَهْدِي الْقَوْمَ الظَّالِمِينَ ○ ع

3381. When a Revelation is sent to them, in the Qur-ān, adapted to all their needs and the needs of the time they live in, they hark back to antiquity. The holy Prophet was in many respects like Moses, but the times in which he lived were different from the times of Moses, and his age did not suffer from the deceptions of sorcery, like that of Moses. The remedies which his age and future ages required (for his Message was universal) were different. His miracle of the Qur-ān was different and more permanent than the Rod and the Radiant-White Hand of Moses. But supposing that the Quraish had been humoured in their insincere demands, would they have believed? Did they believe in Moses? They were only put up by the Jews to make objections which they themselves did not believe in.

3382. Moses was called a sorcerer by the Egyptians, and the wonderful words of the Qur-ān were called sorcery by the Quraish. As the Qur-ān confirmed the Message of Moses, the Quraish objectors said that they were in collusion. The Quraish did not believe in God's Revelation at all.

3383. They were challenged to produce something better, to be a guide in life. But as they could not, it was evident that their objections were fractious. They were only following their own selfish lusts of power, monopoly, and exploitation of the poor and ignorant. How can such people receive guidance?

SECTION 6.

51. Now have We caused
The Word to reach them
Themselves, in order that
They may receive admonition.[3384]

٥١- وَلَقَدْ وَصَّلْنَا لَهُمُ الْقَوْلَ
لَعَلَّهُمْ يَتَذَكَّرُونَ ○

52. Those to whom We sent
The Book before this,—they
Do believe in this (Revelation);

٥٢- الَّذِينَ آتَيْنَاهُمُ الْكِتَابَ مِنْ قَبْلِهِ
هُمْ بِهِ يُؤْمِنُونَ ○

53. And when it is recited
To them, they say: "We
Believe therein, for it is
The Truth from our Lord:
Indeed we have been Muslims
(Bowing to God's Will)
From before this.[3385]

٥٣- وَإِذَا يُتْلَىٰ عَلَيْهِمْ قَالُوا
آمَنَّا بِهِ إِنَّهُ الْحَقُّ مِنْ رَبِّنَا
إِنَّا كُنَّا مِنْ قَبْلِهِ مُسْلِمِينَ ○

54. Twice will they be given[3386]
Their reward, for that they
Have persevered, that they avert
Evil with Good, and that
They spend (in charity) out of
What We have given them.

٥٤- أُولَٰئِكَ يُؤْتَوْنَ أَجْرَهُمْ مَرَّتَيْنِ بِمَا
صَبَرُوا وَيَدْرَءُونَ بِالْحَسَنَةِ السَّيِّئَةَ
وَمِمَّا رَزَقْنَاهُمْ يُنْفِقُونَ ○

55. And when they hear vain talk,
They turn away therefrom
And say: "To us our deeds,
And to you yours;[3387]

٥٥- وَإِذَا سَمِعُوا اللَّغْوَ أَعْرَضُوا عَنْهُ
وَقَالُوا لَنَا أَعْمَالُنَا وَلَكُمْ أَعْمَالُكُمْ

3384. Before this the Quraish might have said that the Word of God had come to the Hebrews in their tongue or in Greek, which was used by the Hebrews in the time of Jesus. Now that Word is brought to their own doors, in their own Arabic tongue, by a man of their own race and family. Surely they have no excuse now for remaining strangers to the higher moral and spiritual law.

3385. There were Christians and Jews who recognised that Islam was a logical and natural development of God's revelations as given in earlier ages, and they not only welcomed and accepted Islam, but claimed, and rightly, that they had always been Muslims. In that sense Adam, Noah, Abraham, Moses, and Jesus had all been Muslims. There were Muslims who had been Christians or Jews, both in Mecca and Medina. But when some Commentators proceed to illustrate this Meccan verse by referring, for example, to the Christian converts who came from Abyssinia with Ja'far the brother of Ḥadhrat 'Alī, they make a historical slip. The verse is perfectly general. It applies even now. True adherents of the law of Moses and Jesus must be Muslims, and the converse is also true.

3386. Their credit is twofold, in that before they knew Islam, they followed the earlier Law in truth and sincerity, and when they were offered Islam, they readily recognised and accepted it, suffered in patient perseverance for its sake, and brought forth the fruits of righteousness.

3387. The righteous do not encourage idle talk or foolish arguments about things sacred. If they find themselves in some company in which such things are fashionable, they leave politely. Their only rejoinder is: "We are responsible for our deeds, and you for yours; we have no ill-will against you; we wish you well, and that is why we wish you to know of the knowledge we have received; after that knowledge you cannot expect us to go back to the Ignorance which we have left."

Peace be to you: we
Seek not the ignorant."

سَلٰمٌ عَلَيْكُمْ لَا نَبْتَغِي الْجٰهِلِينَ ○

56. It is true thou wilt not
Be able to guide every one,[3388]
Whom thou lovest; but God
Guides those whom He will.
And He knows best those
Who receive guidance.

٥٦- إِنَّكَ لَا تَهْدِي مَنْ أَحْبَبْتَ
وَلٰكِنَّ اللّٰهَ يَهْدِي مَنْ يَّشَآءُ ۚ
وَهُوَ أَعْلَمُ بِالْمُهْتَدِينَ ○

57. They say: "If we were
To follow the guidance with thee,
We should be snatched away[3389]
From our land." Have We not
Established for them a secure
Sanctuary, to which are brought
As tribute fruits of all kinds,—
A provision from Ourselves?
But most of them understand not.

٥٧- وَقَالُوٓا إِنْ نَّتَّبِعِ الْهُدٰى مَعَكَ
نُتَخَطَّفْ مِنْ أَرْضِنَا ۗ
أَوَلَمْ نُمَكِّنْ لَّهُمْ حَرَمًا آمِنًا
يُّجْبٰٓى إِلَيْهِ ثَمَرٰتُ كُلِّ شَيْءٍ رِّزْقًا مِّنْ
لَّدُنَّا وَلٰكِنَّ أَكْثَرَهُمْ لَا يَعْلَمُونَ ○

58. And how many populations
We destroyed, which exulted
In their life (of ease and plenty)!
Now those habitations of theirs,
After them, are deserted,—
All but a (miserable) few!
And We are their heirs![3390]

٥٨- وَكَمْ أَهْلَكْنَا مِنْ قَرْيَةٍۢ بَطِرَتْ
مَعِيشَتَهَا ۚ
فَتِلْكَ مَسٰكِنُهُمْ لَمْ تُسْكَنْ مِّنْۢ بَعْدِهِمْ
إِلَّا قَلِيلًا ۗ وَكُنَّا نَحْنُ الْوٰرِثِينَ ○

3388. The immediate occasion for this was the death of Abū Ṭalib, an uncle whom the holy Apostle loved dearly and who had befriended and protected him. The Apostle was naturally anxious that he should die in the profession of the true Faith, but the pagan Quraish leaders persuaded him to remain true to the faith of his fathers. This was an occasion of disappointment and grief to the Apostle. We are told that in such circumstances we should not grieve. All whom we love do not necessarily share our views or beliefs. We must not judge. God will guide whom He pleases and as He pleases. He alone knows the true inwardness of things.

3389. Some Quraish said: "We see the truth of Islam, but if we abandon our people, we shall lose our hold on the land, and other people will dispossess us." The answer is twofold, one literal and the other of deeper import. (1) 'Your land? Why, the sanctuary of Mecca is sacred and secure because God has made it so. If you obey God's Word, you will be strengthened, not weakened.' (2) 'Mecca is the symbol of the Fortress of Spiritual Well-being. The Fruit of every Deed comes or should come as a tribute to Spiritual Well-being. What are you afraid of? It is God's Fortress. The more you seek God, the stronger you are in the Fortress.'

3390. A life of ease and plenty is nothing to boast of. Yet peoples or cities or civilisations grow insolently proud of such things. There were many such in the past, which are now mere names! Their very sites are deserted in most cases, or buried in the *débris* of ages. India is full of such sites nearly everywhere. The sites of Harappa and Mohenjo Daro are the most ancient hitherto unearthed in India, and they are themselves in layers covering centuries of time! And how many more there may be, of which we do not know even names! Fatehpur-Sikri was a magnificent ruin within a single generation. And there are thousands of Qasbas once flourishing and now reduced to small villages or altogether deserted. But God is merciful and just. He does not destroy or degrade a people until they have had full opportunities of turning in repentance to Him and they have deliberately rejected His Law and continued in the practice of iniquity.

59. Nor was thy Lord the one
To destroy a population until
He had sent to its Centre
An apostle, rehearsing to them
Our Signs; nor are We
Going to destroy a population
Except when its members
Practise iniquity.

٥٩- وَمَا كَانَ رَبُّكَ مُهْلِكَ الْقُرٰى
حَتّٰى يَبْعَثَ فِىٓ أُمِّهَا رَسُولًا يَتْلُوا عَلَيْهِمْ
اٰيٰتِنَا ۚ وَمَا كُنَّا مُهْلِكِى الْقُرٰٓى
إِلَّا وَأَهْلُهَا ظٰلِمُونَ ۝

60. The (material) things which
Ye are given are but
The conveniences of this life
And the glitter thereof;[3391]
But that which is with God
Is better and more enduring:
Will ye not then be wise?

٦٠- وَمَآ أُوتِيتُم مِّن شَىْءٍ
فَمَتٰعُ الْحَيٰوةِ الدُّنْيَا وَزِينَتُهَا ۚ
وَمَا عِنْدَ اللّٰهِ خَيْرٌ وَّأَبْقٰىٓ ۚ
أَفَلَا تَعْقِلُونَ ۝

C. 175.—Material good is nothing compared
(xxviii. 61-75.) To the spiritual. In the Hereafter
No plea 'that others misled' will avail.
Each soul must answer for itself,
Whether it honoured God alone
Or worshipped something else,
And whether it received or rejected
The Teachers sent by God. The Wisdom
And Plan of God are beyond all praise:
All mercy and truth proceed from Him,
And there is no other—none—besides Him.

Section 7.

61. Are (these two) alike?—
One to whom We have made
A goodly promise, and who
Is going to reach its (fulfilment),[3392]
And one to whom We have
Given the good things of this
Life, but who, on the Day
Of Judgment, is to be among
Those brought up (for punishment)?

٦١- أَفَمَنْ وَّعَدْنٰهُ وَعْدًا حَسَنًا
فَهُوَ لَاقِيهِ كَمَنْ مَّتَّعْنٰهُ
مَتٰعَ الْحَيٰوةِ الدُّنْيَا
ثُمَّ هُوَ يَوْمَ الْقِيٰمَةِ مِنَ الْمُحْضَرِينَ ۝

3391. The good things of this life have their uses and serve their convenience. But they are fleeting and their value is infinitely lower than that of Truth and Justice and Spiritual Well-being, the gifts which come as it were from the very Presence of God. No wise soul will be absorbed in the one and neglect the other, or will hesitate for a moment if it comes to be a choice between them.

3392. The two classes of people are: (1) those who have faith in the goodly promise of God to the righteous, and who are doing everything in life to reach the fulfilment of that promise, *i.e.*, those who believe and work righteousness, and (2) those who are ungrateful for such good things in this life as God has bestowed on them, by worshipping wealth or power or other symbols or idols of their fancy, *i.e.*, those who reject Faith and lead evil lives, for which they will have to answer in the Hereafter. The two classes are poles asunder, and their future is described below.

62. That Day (God) will
Call to them, and say:
" Where are My 'partners'?—
Whom ye imagined (to be such)?."

٦٢- وَيَوْمَ يُنَادِيهِمْ فَيَقُولُ
أَيْنَ شُرَكَآءِيَ الَّذِينَ كُنتُمْ تَزْعُمُونَ ○

36. Those against whom the charge [3393]
Will be proved, will say:
" Our Lord! These are the ones
Whom we led astray:
We led them astray, as we
Were astray ourselves: we free
Ourselves (from them) in Thy
presence:
It was not us they worshipped." [3394]

٦٣- قَالَ الَّذِينَ حَقَّ عَلَيْهِمُ الْقَوْلُ
رَبَّنَا هٰٓؤُلَآءِ الَّذِينَ أَغْوَيْنَا ۚ
أَغْوَيْنٰهُمْ كَمَا غَوَيْنَا ۚ
تَبَرَّأْنَآ إِلَيْكَ ۖ مَا كَانُوٓا
إِيَّانَا يَعْبُدُونَ ○

64. It will be said (to them):
" Call upon your 'partners'
(For help)": they will call
Upon them, but they will not
Listen to them; and they
Will see the Penalty (before them);
(How they will wish)
'If only they had been
Open to guidance!'

٦٤- وَقِيلَ ادْعُوا شُرَكَآءَكُمْ
فَدَعَوْهُمْ فَلَمْ يَسْتَجِيبُوا لَهُمْ
وَرَأَوُا الْعَذَابَ ۚ
لَوْ أَنَّهُمْ كَانُوا يَهْتَدُونَ ○

65. That Day (God) will [3395]
Call to them, and say:
" What was the answer
Ye gave to the apostles?"

٦٥- وَيَوْمَ يُنَادِيهِمْ فَيَقُولُ
مَاذَآ أَجَبْتُمُ الْمُرْسَلِينَ ○

66. Then the (whole) story that day
Will seem obscure to them [3396]
(Like light to the blind)
And they will not be able
(Even) to question each other.

٦٦- فَعَمِيَتْ عَلَيْهِمُ الْأَنۢبَآءُ يَوْمَئِذٍ
فَهُمْ لَا يَتَسَآءَلُونَ ○

3393. This and the next verse are concerned with the examination of those who neglected truth and righteousness and went after the worship of false gods, *viz.*, their own lusts. These were the "partners" they associated with God. In so far as they were embodied in false or wicked leaders, the leaders will disown responsibility for them. 'We ourselves went wrong, and they followed our example, because it suited them: they worshipped, not us, but their own lusts.

3394. *Cf.* x. 28. False worship often names others, but really it is the worship of Self. The others whom they name will have nothing to do with them when the awful Penalty stands in the sight of both. Then each wrong-doer will have to look to his own case. The wicked will then realise the gravity of the situation and wish that they had accepted the true guidance of God's Messengers.

3395. Now we come to the examination of those who rejected or persecuted God's Messengers on the earth. It may be the same men as those mentioned in xxviii. 62-64, but this is a different count in the charge.

3396. In their utter confusion and despair their minds will be blank. The past will seem to them unreal, and the present unintelligible, and they will not even be able to consult each other, as every one's state will be the same.

67. But any that (in this life)
Had repented, believed, and worked
Righteousness, will have hopes
To be among those who
Achieve salvation.

٦٧- فَأَمَّا مَنْ تَابَ وَآمَنَ وَعَمِلَ صَالِحًا
فَعَسَىٰ أَنْ يَكُونَ مِنَ الْمُفْلِحِينَ ○

68. Thy Lord does create and choose
As He pleases:[3397] no choice
Have they (in the matter):
Glory to God! and far
Is He above the partners
They ascribe (to Him)!

٦٨- وَرَبُّكَ يَخْلُقُ مَا يَشَاءُ وَيَخْتَارُ ط
مَا كَانَ لَهُمُ الْخِيَرَةُ ط
سُبْحَٰنَ اللَّهِ وَتَعَٰلَىٰ عَمَّا يُشْرِكُونَ ○

69. And thy Lord knows all
That their hearts conceal
And all that they reveal.[3398]

٦٩- وَرَبُّكَ يَعْلَمُ مَا تُكِنُّ صُدُورُهُمْ
وَمَا يُعْلِنُونَ ○

70. And He is God: there is
No god but He. To Him
Be praise, at the first
And at the last:
For Him is the Command,
And to Him shall ye
(All) be brought back.

٧٠- وَهُوَ اللَّهُ لَا إِلَٰهَ إِلَّا هُوَ ط
لَهُ الْحَمْدُ فِي الْأُولَىٰ وَالْآخِرَةِ ز
وَلَهُ الْحُكْمُ وَإِلَيْهِ تُرْجَعُونَ ○

71. Say: See ye? If God
Were to make the Night[3399]

٧١- قُلْ أَرَءَيْتُمْ إِنْ جَعَلَ اللَّهُ عَلَيْكُمُ

3397. *As He pleases*: according to His own Will and Plan. God is not dependent on other people for advice or help. He has no partners. All creation is an act of His Will, and no one can direct Him how or why certain things should be, because He is supreme in wisdom and knowledge. He chooses His apostles also by His own unfettered choice. Inspiration or spiritual knowledge and dignity cannot be judged of by our relative or temporary standards. Worldly greatness or even wisdom do not necessarily go with spiritual insight.

3398. Men may form all sorts of vain wishes or conceal their designs. But God's Will is supreme, and nothing can withstand its fulfilment.

3399. In the physical world the Night and the Day are both blessings, the one for rest and the other for work, and the alternation itself is one of the mercies of God, and none but He can give us these blessings. If we were perpetually resting, or screened from the light, our faculties would be blunted and we should be worse than dead. If we were perpetually working, we should be tired, and we should also be dead in another way. This daily miracle keeps us alive and prepares us, in this our probationary life, for our final destiny in the Hereafter. So in the spiritual world. Some kinds of ignorance—such as ignorance of what is coming in the future—are necessary to conserve our powers and give rest to our minds and spirits, but if we were to remain ignorant perpetually, we should be spiritually dead. In the same way our spiritual strivings require periodical alternations of rest in the form of attention to our temporal concerns: hence the justification of a good and pure life on the plane of this earth also. Also, in the world's history, there are periods when a living apostle stimulates intense spiritual activity, and periods when it is comparatively quiescent (the so-called Dark Ages); but both are examples of the working of God's Plan of wisdom and mercy. But this applies only up to the Day of Judgment. After that we shall be on another plane altogether

Perpetual over you to the Day
Of Judgment, what god
Is there other than God,
Who can give you enlightenment?
Will ye not then hearken?

الَّيْلَ سَرْمَدًا إِلَىٰ يَوْمِ الْقِيٰمَةِ
مَنْ إِلٰهٌ غَيْرُ اللهِ يَأْتِيكُمْ بِضِيَآءٍ
أَفَلَا تَسْمَعُونَ ○

72. Say: See ye? If God
Were to make the Day
Perpetual over you to the Day
Of Judgment, what god
Is there other than God,
Who can give you a Night
In which ye can rest?
Will ye not then see?[3400]

٧٢- قُلْ أَرَءَيْتُمْ إِنْ جَعَلَ اللهُ عَلَيْكُمُ النَّهَارَ
سَرْمَدًا إِلَىٰ يَوْمِ الْقِيٰمَةِ
مَنْ إِلٰهٌ غَيْرُ اللهِ يَأْتِيكُمْ بِلَيْلٍ تَسْكُنُونَ
فِيهِ أَفَلَا تُبْصِرُونَ ○

73. It is out of His Mercy
That He has made for you
Night and Day,—that ye
May rest therein, and that
Ye may seek of His Grace;—
And in order that ye
May be grateful.

٧٣- وَمِنْ رَّحْمَتِهِ جَعَلَ لَكُمُ الَّيْلَ وَالنَّهَارَ
لِتَسْكُنُوا فِيهِ
وَلِتَبْتَغُوا مِنْ فَضْلِهِ
وَلَعَلَّكُمْ تَشْكُرُونَ ○

74. The Day that He will[3401]
Call on them, He will say:
"Where are My 'partners'?—
Whom ye imagined (to be such)?"

٧٤- وَيَوْمَ يُنَادِيهِمْ فَيَقُولُ أَيْنَ شُرَكَآءِيَ
الَّذِينَ كُنْتُمْ تَزْعُمُونَ ○

75. And from each people
Shall We draw a witness,[3402]
And We shall say: "Produce
Your Proof": then shall they
Know that the Truth is in
God (alone), and the (lies)
Which they invented will
Leave them in the lurch.[3403]

٧٥- وَنَزَعْنَا مِنْ كُلِّ أُمَّةٍ شَهِيدًا
فَقُلْنَا هَاتُوا بُرْهَانَكُمْ
فَعَلِمُوا أَنَّ الْحَقَّ لِلَّهِ
وَضَلَّ عَنْهُمْ مَّا كَانُوا يَفْتَرُونَ ○ ع

3400. In verse 71 was mentioned a "perpetual Night," for which the faculty of "hearkening" was appropriate, as all light was shut out. In this verse a perpetual Day is mentioned, for which the faculty of "seeing" is appropriate. Through many doors can the higher knowledge enter our souls. Shall we not use each of them as the occasion demands?

3401. *Cf.* xxviii. 62 above. The reminiscence of the words closes and rounds off the argument of this Section.

3402. *Cf.* iv. 41. The Prophet from each People or Nation will bear testimony that he preached the true gospel of Unity, and the People who rejected him will be asked to show the Proof or authority on which they rejected him: *Cf.* ii. 111.

3403. In that new world, God will be the only Truth or Reality, and all the fancies or lies, which had been invented in this world of reflected or relative truths mixed with illusions, will have vanished, and left those in the lurch who relied on them. *Cf.* vi. 24.

C. 176.—Men puffed up with wealth, like Qārūn,
(xxviii. 76-88.) Are not pleasing to God: for wealth
Is for service, not for hoarding or show
In the midst of his pride was Qārūn
Swallowed up in the earth, and the earth
Knew him no more! It is the righteous
That attain a happy End. Let nothing
Keep your eyes back from that End:
Then, and only then, shall ye reach
The only Reality, the glorious Reality,
Which is God, Who endureth for ever!

Section 8.

76. Qārūn was doubtless,[3404]
Of the people of Moses; but
He acted insolently towards them:
Such were the treasures We[3405]
Had bestowed on him, that
Their very keys would
Have been a burden to
A body of strong men.[3406]
Behold, his people said to him:
"Exult not, for God loveth not
Those who exult (in riches).

٧٦- إِنَّ قَارُونَ كَانَ مِنْ قَوْمِ مُوسَىٰ فَبَغَىٰ
عَلَيْهِمْ ۖ وَآتَيْنَاهُ مِنَ الْكُنُوزِ مَا
إِنَّ مَفَاتِحَهُ لَتَنُوأُ بِالْعُصْبَةِ أُولِي الْقُوَّةِ
إِذْ قَالَ لَهُ قَوْمُهُ
لَا تَفْرَحْ إِنَّ اللَّهَ لَا يُحِبُّ الْفَرِحِينَ ○

77. "But seek, with the (wealth)
Which God has bestowed on thee,
The Home of the Hereafter,[3407]
Nor forget thy portion in this

٧٧- وَابْتَغِ فِيمَا آتَاكَ اللَّهُ الدَّارَ الْآخِرَةَ
وَلَا تَنْسَ نَصِيبَكَ مِنَ

3404. Qārūn is identified with the Korah of the English Bible. His story is told in Num. xvi. 1-35. He and his followers, numbering 250 men, rose in rebellion against Moses and Aaron, on the ground that their position and fame in the congregation entitled them to equality in spiritual matters with the Priests,—that they were as holy as any, and they claimed to burn incense at the sacred Altar reserved for the Priests. They had an exemplary punishment: "the earth opened her mouth, and swallowed them up, and their houses, and all the men that appertained unto Korah, and all their goods: they, and all that appertained to them, went down alive into the pit, and the earth closed upon them: and they perished from among the congregation."

3405. Qārūn's boundless wealth is described in the Midrashim, or the Jewish compilations based on the oral teachings of the Synagogues, which however exaggerate the weight of the keys to be the equivalent of the load of 300 mules!

3406. *Uṣbat*: a body of men, here used indefinitely. It usually implies a body of 10 to 40 men. The old-fashioned keys were big and heavy, and if there were hundreds of treasure-chests, the keys must have been a great weight. As they were travelling in the desert, the treasures were presumably left behind in Egypt, and only the keys were carried. The disloyal Qārūn had left his heart in Egypt, with his treasures.

3407. That is, 'spend your wealth in charity and good works. It is God Who has given it to you, and you should spend it in God's cause. Nor should you forget the legitimate needs of this life, as misers do, and most people become misers who think too exclusively of their wealth. If wealth is not used properly, there are three evils that follow: (1) its possessor may be a miser and forget all claims due to himself and those about him; (2) he may forget the higher needs of the poor and needy, or the good causes which require support; and (3) he may even misspend on occasions and cause a great deal of harm and mischief." Apparently Qārūn had all three vices.

World: but do thou good,
As God has been good
To thee, and seek not
(Occasions for) mischief in the land:
For God loves not those
Who do mischief."

الدُّنْيَا وَأَحْسِن كَمَا أَحْسَنَ اللَّهُ إِلَيْكَ
وَلَا تَبْغِ الْفَسَادَ فِي الْأَرْضِ
إِنَّ اللَّهَ لَا يُحِبُّ الْمُفْسِدِينَ ○

78. He said: "This has been given
To me because of a certain
Knowledge which I have."[3408]
Did he not know that God
Had destroyed, before him,
(Whole) generations,—which were
Superior to him in strength
And greater in the amount
(Of riches) they had collected?
But the wicked are not
Called (immediately) to account[3409]
For their sins.

٧٨- قَالَ إِنَّمَا أُوتِيتُهُ عَلَىٰ عِلْمٍ عِندِي
أَوَلَمْ يَعْلَمْ أَنَّ اللَّهَ قَدْ أَهْلَكَ
مِن قَبْلِهِ مِنَ الْقُرُونِ
مَنْ هُوَ أَشَدُّ مِنْهُ قُوَّةً
وَأَكْثَرُ جَمْعًا
وَلَا يُسْأَلُ عَن ذُنُوبِهِمُ الْمُجْرِمُونَ ○

79. So he went forth among
His people in the (pride
Of his worldly) glitter.
Said those whose aim is
The Life of this World:
"Oh! that we had the like
Of what Qārūn has got!
For he is truly a lord
Of mighty good fortune!"[3410]

٧٩- فَخَرَجَ عَلَىٰ قَوْمِهِ فِي زِينَتِهِ
قَالَ الَّذِينَ يُرِيدُونَ الْحَيَوٰةَ الدُّنْيَا
يَٰلَيْتَ لَنَا مِثْلَ مَا أُوتِيَ قَٰرُونُ
إِنَّهُ لَذُو حَظٍّ عَظِيمٍ ○

80. But those who had been granted
(True) knowledge said: "Alas
For you! The reward of God
(In the Hereafter) is best
For those who believe
And work righteousness: but this

٨٠- وَقَالَ الَّذِينَ أُوتُوا الْعِلْمَ
وَيْلَكُمْ ثَوَابُ اللَّهِ خَيْرٌ
لِّمَنْ ءَامَنَ وَعَمِلَ صَٰلِحًا

3408. He was so blind and arrogant that he thought that his own merit, knowledge, and skill or cleverness had earned him his wealth, and that now, on account of it, he was superior to everybody else and was entitled to ride rough-shod over them. Fool!—he was soon pulled up by God.

3409. Even Qārūn was given a long run of enjoyment with his fabulous wealth before he had to be removed for the mischief he was doing.

3410. When he was in the hey-day of his glory, worldly people envied him and thought how happy they would be if they were in his place. Not so the people of wisdom and discernment. They knew of a more precious and lasting wealth, which is described in the next verse.

None shall attain, save those
Who steadfastly persevere
(in good)."

وَلَا يُلَقّٰهَآ اِلَّا الصّٰبِرُوْنَ ○

81. Then We caused the earth[3411]
To swallow up him and
His house; and he had not
(The least little) party
To help him against God,
Nor could he defend himself.

٨١- فَخَسَفْنَا بِهٖ وَبِدَارِهِ الْاَرْضَ ۗ
فَمَا كَانَ لَهٗ مِنْ فِئَةٍ يَّنْصُرُوْنَهٗ مِنْ دُوْنِ
اللّٰهِ ۗ وَمَا كَانَ مِنَ الْمُنْتَصِرِيْنَ ○

82. And those who had envied
His position the day before
Began to say on the morrow:
"Ah! It is indeed God
Who enlarges the provision[3412]
Or restricts it, to any
Of His servants He pleases!
Had it not been that God
Was gracious to us, He
Could have caused the earth
To swallow us up! Ah!
Those who reject God
Will assuredly never prosper."

٨٢- وَاَصْبَحَ الَّذِيْنَ تَمَنَّوْا مَكَانَهٗ
بِالْاَمْسِ يَقُوْلُوْنَ
وَيْكَاَنَّ اللّٰهَ يَبْسُطُ الرِّزْقَ لِمَنْ يَّشَآءُ
مِنْ عِبَادِهٖ وَيَقْدِرُ ۚ
لَوْلَآ اَنْ مَّنَّ اللّٰهُ عَلَيْنَا لَخَسَفَ بِنَا ۗ
ع وَيْكَاَنَّهٗ لَا يُفْلِحُ الْكٰفِرُوْنَ ○

Section 9.

83. That Home of the Hereafter
We shall give to those
Who intend not high-handedness
Or mischief on earth:[3413]

٨٣- تِلْكَ الدَّارُ الْاٰخِرَةُ نَجْعَلُهَا لِلَّذِيْنَ لَا
يُرِيْدُوْنَ عُلُوًّا فِى الْاَرْضِ وَلَا فَسَادًا ۗ

3411. See n 3404 above. *Cf.* also xvi. 45 and n. 2071. Besides the obvious moral in the literal interpretation of the story, that material wealth is fleeting and may be a temptation and a cause of fall, there are some metaphorical implications that occur to me. (1) Qārūn was with Israel in the wilderness: even his material wealth was of no use to him there; he had the mere empty keys; material wealth has no value in itself, but only a relative and local value. (2) In body he was with Israel in the wilderness, but his heart was in Egypt with its fertility and its slavery. Such is the case of many hypocrites, who like to be seen in righteous company but whose thoughts, longings, and doings are inconsistent with such company. (3) There is no good in this life but comes from God. To think otherwise is to set up a false god besides God. Our own merits are so small that they should never be the object of our idolatry. (4) If Qārūn on account of his wealth was setting himself up in rivalry with Moses and Aaron, he was blind to the fact that spiritual knowledge is far above any little cleverness in worldly affairs. Mob-leaders have no position before spiritual guides.

3412. *Provision* or Sustenance, both literally and figuratively: wealth and material things in life as well as the things that sustain our higher and spiritual faculties. The rabble, that admired Qārūn's wealth when he was in worldly prosperity, now sees the other side of the question and understands that there are other gifts more precious and desirable, and that these may actually be withheld from men who enjoy wealth and worldly prosperity. In fact it is false prosperity, or no prosperity in the real sense of the word, which is without spiritual well-being.

3413. *High-handedness* or arrogance, as opposed to submission to the Will of God, Islam. *Mischief*, as opposed to doing good, bringing forth fruits of righteousness. It is the righteous who will win in the end.

And the End is (best)
For the righteous.

وَالْعَاقِبَةُ لِلْمُتَّقِينَ ۝

84. If any does good, the reward
To him is better than
His deed; but if any
Does evil, the doers of evil
Are only punished (to the extent)
Of their deeds.[3414]

٨٤- مَنْ جَآءَ بِالْحَسَنَةِ فَلَهُ خَيْرٌ مِّنْهَا
وَمَنْ جَآءَ بِالسَّيِّئَةِ فَلَا يُجْزَى الَّذِينَ
عَمِلُوا السَّيِّاٰتِ اِلَّا مَا كَانُوا يَعْمَلُونَ ۝

85. Verily He Who ordained[3415]
The Qur-ān for thee, will bring
Thee back to the Place[3416]
Of Return. Say: "My Lord
Knows best who it is
That brings true guidance,
And who is in manifest error."[3417]

٨٥- اِنَّ الَّذِي فَرَضَ عَلَيْكَ الْقُرْاٰنَ
لَرَآدُّكَ اِلٰى مَعَادٍ
قُلْ رَّبِّيٓ اَعْلَمُ مَنْ جَآءَ
بِالْهُدٰى وَمَنْ هُوَ فِي ضَلٰلٍ مُّبِينٍ ۝

86 And thou hadst not expected
That the Book would be
Sent to thee except as
A Mercy from thy Lord:[3418]
Therefore lend not thou support
In any way to those

٨٦- وَمَا كُنْتَ تَرْجُوٓا اَنْ يُّلْقٰٓى
اِلَيْكَ الْكِتٰبُ اِلَّا رَحْمَةً مِّنْ رَّبِّكَ
فَلَا تَكُونَنَّ ظَهِيرًا

3414. A good deed has its sure reward, and that reward will be better than the merits of the doer. An evil deed may be forgiven by repentance, but in any case will not be punished with a severer penalty than justice demands.

3415. That is: ordered in His wisdom and mercy that the Qur-ān should be revealed, containing guidance for conduct in this life and the next, and further ordered that it should be read out and taught and its principles observed in practice. It is because of this teaching and preaching that the holy Prophet was persecuted, but as God sent the Qur-ān, He will see that those who follow it will not eventually suffer, but be restored to happiness in the Place of Return, for which see next note.

3416. *Place of Return*: (1) a title of Mecca; (2) the occasion when we shall be restored to the Presence of our Lord. It is said that this verse was revealed at *Juhfa*, on the road from Mecca to Medina, a short distance from Mecca, on the Hijrat journey. The Prophet was sad at heart, and this was given as consolation to him. If this was the particular occasion, the general meaning would refer the Place of Return to the occasion of the Resurrection, when all true values will be restored, however they may be disturbed by the temporary interference of Evil in this life.

3417. God knows the true from the false, and if we are persecuted for our Faith and attacked or spoken ill of because we dare to do right, our surest refuge is an appeal to God rather than to men.

3418. Revelation and the preaching of Truth may in the beginning bring persecution, conflict, and sorrow in its train; but in reality it is the truest mercy from God, which comes even without our expecting it, as it came to the apostles without their consciously asking for it. This is proved in the history of Moses related in this Sūra, and the history of the holy Prophet which it is meant to illustrate.

Who reject (God's Message).[3419]

87. And let nothing keep thee
Back from the Signs of God
After they have been revealed
To thee : and invite (men)
To thy Lord, and be not
Of the company of those
Who join gods with God.[3420]

بَعْدَ إِذْ أُنزِ[illegible] [illegible]اتُ اللّٰهِ
وَادْعُ إِلَىٰ رَبِّكَ
وَلَا تَكُونَنَّ مِنَ الْمُشْرِكِينَ ۝

88. And call not, besides God,
On another god. There is
No god but He. Everything
(That exists) will perish
Except His own Face.[3421]
To Him belongs the Command,
And to Him will ye
(All) be brought back.

٨٨- وَلَا تَدْعُ مَعَ اللّٰهِ إِلٰهًا اٰخَرَ
لَآ إِلٰهَ إِلَّا هُوَ
كُلُّ شَيْءٍ هَالِكٌ إِلَّا وَجْهَهُ
لَهُ الْحُكْمُ وَإِلَيْهِ تُرْجَعُونَ ۝

3419. If God's Message is unpalatable to Evil and is rejected by it, those who accept it may (in their natural human feelings) sometimes wonder that such should be the case, and whether it is really God's Will that the conflict which ensues should be pursued. Any such hesitation would lend unconscious support to the aggressions of evil and should be discarded. The servant of God stands forth boldly as His *Mujāhid* (fighter of the good fight), daring all, and knowing that God is behind him.

3420. The soldier of God, having taken up the fight against Evil, and knowing that he is in touch with the true Light, never yields an inch of ground. He is always to the fore in inviting others to his own ranks, but he himself refuses to be with those who worship anything else but God.

3421. This sums up the lesson of the whole Sūra. The only Reality is God. His "Face" or Self, Personality or Being is what we should seek, knowing that it is the only enduring thing of which we can have any conception. The whole phenomenal world is subject to flux and change and will pass away, but He will endure for ever. If we think of an impersonal God, an abstract force of good, we cannot reconcile it with the vital Self or Being, of which we have a faint echo or reflection in our intensest moments of spiritual exaltation. We know then that what we call our own Self has no meaning, for there is only one true Self, and that is God. This is also the Advaita doctrine of Shrī Shankara in his exposition of the *Brihad-aranyaka Upanishad* in Hindu philosophy.

INTRODUCTION TO SŪRA XXIX ('*Ankabūt*).

[illegible] Sūra is the last of the series begun with S. xvii, in which the growth [illegible] as an individual is considered, especially illustrated by the way [illegible] apostles were prepared for their work and received their mission, and th[illegible] in relation to the environments in which it was promulgated. (See [illegible] xvii.) It also closes the sub-series beginning with S. xxvi, which is [illegible] spiritual Light, and the reactions to it at certain periods of spiritual histo[ry]. (See [Intro]duction to S. xxvi.)

The last Sūra closed with [illegible] the doctrine of the *Ma'ād*, or final Return of man to God. This theme is [illegible]eloped here; and as it is continued in the subsequent three Sūras all bearing the [illegible]ted Letters A.L.M., it forms a connecting link between the present series and those Sūras.

In particular, emphasis is laid here on the necessity [illegible]nking actual conduct with the reception of God's revelation, and reference is again ma[de] to the stories of Noah, Abraham, and Lot among the apostles, and the stori[es of] Midian, 'Ād, Thamūd, and Pharaoh among the rejecters of God's Message. This world's life is contrasted with the real Life of the Hereafter.

Chronologically the main Sūra belongs to the late Middle Meccan period, but the chronology has no significance except as showing how clearly the vision of the Future was revealed long before the Hijrat, to the struggling Brotherhood of Islām.

Summary.—Belief is tested by trial in life and practical conduct : though Noah lived 950 years, his people refused Faith, and Abraham's generation threatened to burn Abraham (xxix. 1-27, and C. 177).

Lot's people not only rejected God's Message but publicly defied him in sin; the 'Ād and the Thamūd had intelligence but misused it, and Qārūn, Pharaoh, and Hāmān perished for their overweening arrogance : they found their worldly power as frail as a spider's web (xxix. 28-44, and C. 178).

The Qur-ān as a revelation stands on its own merits and is a Sign : it teaches the distinction between Right and Wrong, and shows the importance and excellence of the Hereafter (xxix. 45-69, and C. 179).

C. 177.—Faith must be tested in the conflicts
(xxix. 1-27.) Of practical life, but Good can never
Be submerged. On the contrary God
Will wash off all stains from those
Who strive, and admit them to the Fellowship
Of the Righteous. Not so are the hypocrites
And those who reject Faith. Their hearts
Are diseased, and they will not accept
The right though a Noah preached to them
For a thousand years, or an Abraham
Reasoned with them on God's most wonderful
Providence. But the true will ever search out
The Truth, and Truth will always prevail.

Sūra XXIX.

'*Ankabūt*, or the Spider.

In the name of God, Most Gracious, Most Merciful.

بِسْمِ اللَّهِ الرَّحْمَٰنِ الرَّحِيمِ

1. A. L. M.[3422]

١- الٓمٓ ۝

2. Do men think that
They will be left alone
On saying, "We believe",[3423]
And that they will not
Be tested?

٢- أَحَسِبَ النَّاسُ أَن يُتْرَكُوٓا
أَن يَقُولُوٓا ءَامَنَّا وَهُمْ لَا يُفْتَنُونَ ۝

3. We did test those
Before them, and God will
Certainly know[3424] those who are
True from those who are false.

٣- وَلَقَدْ فَتَنَّا الَّذِينَ مِن قَبْلِهِمْ فَلَيَعْلَمَنَّ
اللَّهُ الَّذِينَ صَدَقُوا وَلَيَعْلَمَنَّ الْكَٰذِبِينَ ۝

4. Do those who practise
Evil think that they
Will get the better of us?
Evil is their judgment![3425]

٤- أَمْ حَسِبَ الَّذِينَ يَعْمَلُونَ السَّيِّـَٔاتِ
أَن يَسْبِقُونَا ۚ سَآءَ مَا يَحْكُمُونَ ۝

5. For those whose hopes are
In the meeting with God[3426]
(In the Hereafter, let them strive);
For the Term (appointed)

٥- مَن كَانَ يَرْجُوا لِقَآءَ اللَّهِ
فَإِنَّ أَجَلَ

3422. For these Abbreviated Letters see n. 25 to ii. 1. We are asked to contrast, in our present life the real inner life against the outer life, and learn from the past about the struggles of the soul which upholds God's Truth, against the environment of evil, which resists it, and to turn our thoughts to the Ma'ād, or man's future destiny in the Hereafter.

3423. Mere lip profession of Faith is not enough. It must be tried and tested in the real turmoil of life. The test will be applied in all kinds of circumstances, in individual life and in relation to the environment around us, to see whether we can strive constantly and put God above Self. Much pain, sorrow, and self-sacrifice may be necessary, not because they are good in themselves, but because they will purify us, like fire applied to a goldsmith's crucible to burn out the dross.

3424. The word "know" is used here more in the sense of testing than of acquiring knowledge. God is All-Knowing: He needs no test to increase His own knowledge, but the test is to burn out the dross within ourselves, as explained in the last note.

3425. If the enemies of Truth imagine that they will "be first" by destroying Truth before it takes root, they are sadly at fault, for their own persecution may help to plant God's Truth more firmly in men's hearts.

3426. The men of Faith look forward to God. Their quest is God, and the object of their hopes is the meeting with God. They should strive with might and main to serve Him in this life, for this life is short, and the Term appointed for their probation will soon be over.

By God is surely coming:[3427]
And He hears and knows
(All things).

اللّٰهِ لَاٰتٍ ۗ وَهُوَ السَّمِيْعُ الْعَلِيْمُ ○

6. And if any strive (with might
And main), they do so
For their own souls:[3428]
For God is free of all
Needs from all creation.

٦- وَمَنْ جَاهَدَ فَاِنَّمَا يُجَاهِدُ لِنَفْسِهٖ ۗ
اِنَّ اللّٰهَ لَغَنِيٌّ عَنِ الْعٰلَمِيْنَ ○

7. Those who believe and work
Righteous deeds,—from them
Shall We blot out all evil
(That may be) in them,[3429]
And We shall reward
Them according to
The best of their deeds.

٧- وَالَّذِيْنَ اٰمَنُوْا وَعَمِلُوا الصّٰلِحٰتِ
لَنُكَفِّرَنَّ عَنْهُمْ سَيِّاٰتِهِمْ
وَلَنَجْزِيَنَّهُمْ اَحْسَنَ الَّذِيْ كَانُوْا
يَعْمَلُوْنَ ○

8. We have enjoined on man
Kindness to parents: but if
They (either of them) strive
(To force) thee to join
With Me (in worship)
Anything of which thou hast
No knowledge,[3430] obey them not.
Ye have (all) to return
To Me, and I will
Tell you (the truth)
Of all that ye did.[3431]

٨- وَوَصَّيْنَا الْاِنْسَانَ بِوَالِدَيْهِ حُسْنًا ۗ
وَاِنْ جَاهَدٰكَ لِتُشْرِكَ بِيْ
مَا لَيْسَ لَكَ بِهٖ عِلْمٌ فَلَا تُطِعْهُمَا ۗ
اِلَيَّ مَرْجِعُكُمْ
فَاُنَبِّئُكُمْ بِمَا كُنْتُمْ تَعْمَلُوْنَ ○

3427. The Term (*ajal*) may signify: (1) the time appointed for death, which ends the probation of this life; (2) the time appointed for this life, so that we can prepare for the Hereafter; the limit will soon expire. In either case the ultimate meaning is the same. We must strive *now*, and not postpone anything for the future. And we must realise and remember that every prayer we make to God is heard by Him, and that every unspoken wish or motive of our heart, good or bad, is known to Him, and goes to swell our spiritual account.

3428. All our striving enures to our own spiritual benefit. When we speak of serving God, it is not that we confer any benefit on Him. For He has no needs, and is independent of all His Creation. In conforming to His Will, we are seeking our own good, as in yielding to evil we are doing harm to ourselves.

3429. In striving to purify our Faith and our Life, we are enabled to rise above our own Karma, for God will forgive any evil in our past, purify any tendencies towards evil which we may have inherited from that past, and help to the attainment of a Future based on the best of what we have done rather than on the poor average of our own merits. The atonement or expiation is by God's Mercy, not by our merits or the merits or sacrifice of anyone else.

3430. That is, no certainty, in virtue of the spiritual light. In matters of faith and worship, even parents have no right to force their children. They cannot and must not hold up before them any worship but that of the One True God.

3431. Children and parents must all remember that they have all to go before God's tribunal, and answer, each for his own deeds. In cases where one set of people have lawful authority over another set of people (as in the case of parents and children), and the two differ in important matters like that of Faith, the latter are justified in rejecting authority: the apparent conflict will be solved when the whole truth is revealed to all eyes in the final Judgment.

9. And those who believe
And work righteous deeds,—
Them shall We admit
To the company of the
Righteous.[3432]

٩- وَالَّذِينَ اٰمَنُوا وَعَمِلُوا الصّٰلِحٰتِ
لَنُدْخِلَنَّهُمْ فِي الصّٰلِحِينَ ○

10. Then there are among men
Such as say, "We believe
In God"; but when they suffer
Affliction in (the cause of) God,
They treat men's oppression
As if it were the Wrath
Of God! And if help
Comes (to thee) from thy Lord,
They are sure to say,[3433]
"We have (always) been
With you!" Does not God
Know best all that is
In the hearts of all Creation?

١٠- وَمِنَ النَّاسِ مَنْ يَقُولُ اٰمَنَّا
بِاللّٰهِ فَإِذَآ أُوذِيَ فِي اللّٰهِ
جَعَلَ فِتْنَةَ النَّاسِ كَعَذَابِ اللّٰهِ ط
وَلَئِنْ جَآءَ نَصْرٌ مِّنْ رَّبِّكَ
لَيَقُولُنَّ إِنَّا كُنَّا مَعَكُمْ ط
أَوَلَيْسَ اللّٰهُ بِأَعْلَمَ بِمَا فِي صُدُورِ
الْعٰلَمِينَ ○

11. And God most certainly knows
Those who believe, and as certainly
Those who are Hypocrites.[3434]

١١- وَلَيَعْلَمَنَّ اللّٰهُ الَّذِينَ اٰمَنُوا
وَلَيَعْلَمَنَّ الْمُنٰفِقِينَ ○

12. And the Unbelievers say
To those who believe:
"Follow our path, and we
Will bear (the consequences)[3435]
Of your faults." Never
In the least will they
Bear their faults: in fact
They are liars!

١٢- وَقَالَ الَّذِينَ كَفَرُوا لِلَّذِينَ اٰمَنُوا
اتَّبِعُوا سَبِيلَنَا وَلْنَحْمِلْ خَطٰيٰكُمْ ط
وَمَا هُمْ بِحٰمِلِينَ مِنْ خَطٰيٰهُمْ مِّنْ شَيْءٍ ط
إِنَّهُمْ لَكٰذِبُونَ ○

3432. The picking up again of the words which began verse 7 above shows that the same subject is now pursued from another aspect. The expiation or reward which was first spoken of is not so much a tangible thing as a restoration of status The striving in righteous deeds will restore fallen man to the society of the Righteous,—the ideal Fellowship described in iv. 69 and n. 586.

3433. *Cf.* ix. 56. and other passages where the cunning of the Hypocrites is exposed. The man who turns away from Faith in adversity and only claims the friendship of the Faithful when there is something to be gained by it, is worthy of a double condemnation: first because he rejected Faith and Truth, and secondly because he falsely pretended to be of those whom he feared or hated in his heart. But nothing in all Creation is concealed from God.

3434. *Cf.* xxix. 3 above. The general opposition between Truth and Falsehood is now brought down to the specific case of the Hypocrites, who are against the Faith militant but swear friendship with it when it seems to be gaining ground. The argument is rounded off with the next two verses.

3435. Besides the hypocrite there is another type of man who openly scoffs at Faith. 'Take life as we take it,' he says; 'we shall bear your sins.' As if they could! Each soul bears its own burdens, and no one else can bear them. The principle also applies to the type of man who preaches vicarious atonement, for, if followed to its logical conclusion, it means both injustice and irresponsibility, and puts quite a different complexion on the nature of sin.

13. They will bear their own
Burdens, and (other) burdens
Along with their own,[3436]
And on the Day of Judgment
They will be called to account
For their falsehoods.

١٣- وَلَيَحْمِلُنَّ أَثْقَالَهُمْ
وَأَثْقَالًا مَّعَ أَثْقَالِهِمْ وَلَيُسْأَلُنَّ يَوْمَ
الْقِيَامَةِ عَمَّا كَانُوا يَفْتَرُونَ ۝

SECTION 2.

14. We (once) sent Noah
To his people, and he tarried
Among them a thousand years[3437]
Less fifty: but the Deluge
Overwhelmed them while they
(Persisted in) sin.

١٤- وَلَقَدْ أَرْسَلْنَا نُوحًا إِلَىٰ قَوْمِهِ فَلَبِثَ
فِيهِمْ أَلْفَ سَنَةٍ إِلَّا خَمْسِينَ عَامًا
فَأَخَذَهُمُ الطُّوفَانُ وَهُمْ ظَالِمُونَ ۝

15. But We saved him
And the Companions
Of the Ark, and We made
The (Ark) a Sign
For all Peoples!

١٥- فَأَنْجَيْنَاهُ وَأَصْحَابَ السَّفِينَةِ
وَجَعَلْنَاهَا آيَةً لِّلْعَالَمِينَ ۝

16. And (We also saved)
Abraham: behold, he said[3438]
To his people, "Serve God
And fear Him: that
Will be best for you—
If ye understand!

١٦- وَإِبْرَاهِيمَ إِذْ قَالَ
لِقَوْمِهِ اعْبُدُوا اللَّهَ وَاتَّقُوهُ
ذَٰلِكُمْ خَيْرٌ لَّكُمْ إِن كُنتُمْ تَعْلَمُونَ ۝

17. "For ye do worship idols
Besides God, and ye invent
Falsehood. The things that ye
Worship besides God have
No power to give you sustenance:

١٧- إِنَّمَا تَعْبُدُونَ مِن دُونِ اللَّهِ أَوْثَانًا وَ
تَخْلُقُونَ إِفْكًا إِنَّ الَّذِينَ تَعْبُدُونَ مِن
دُونِ اللَّهِ لَا يَمْلِكُونَ لَكُمْ رِزْقًا

3436. Besides the burden of their own infidelity, they will bear the burden of deluding others with falsehood.

3437. The story of Noah and his Flood is not told here. It is told in other places; *e.g.*, see xi. 25-48 or xxvi. 105-22. It is only referred to here to point out that Noah's period lasted a long time, 950 years. (*Cf.* Gen. ix. 28-29, where his whole age is declared to have been 950 years, of which 350 years were after the Flood). In spite of this long period, his contemporaries failed to listen, and they were destroyed. But the story of the Ark remains an everlasting Sign and Warning to mankind—a Sign of deliverance to the righteous and of destruction to the wicked.

3438. The story of Abraham has been told in various phases in different passages. The ones most germane to the present passage are: xxi. 51-72 (his being cast into the fire and being saved from it); and xix. 41-49 (his voluntary exile from the home of his fathers) Here the story is not told, but is referred to in order to stress the following points; (1) Abraham's people only responded to his preaching by threatening to burn him (xxix. 16-18, 24); (2) evil consorts with evil but will have a rude awakening (xxix. 25); (3) the good adhere to the good, and are blessed (xxix. 26-27). Note that the passage xxix. 19-23 is a parenthetical comment, though some Commentators treat a portion of it as part of Abraham's speech.

Then seek ye sustenance[3439]
From God, serve Him,
And be grateful to Him :
To Him will be your return.

فَابْتَغُوا عِنْدَ اللّٰهِ الرِّزْقَ وَاعْبُدُوهُ
وَاشْكُرُوا لَهٗ ؕ اِلَيْهِ تُرْجَعُونَ ۝

18. " And if ye reject (the Message),
So did generations before you :
And the duty of the apostle
Is only to preach publicly
(And clearly)."

١٨- وَاِنْ تُكَذِّبُوا فَقَدْ كَذَّبَ اُمَمٌ مِّنْ
قَبْلِكُمْ ؕ
وَمَا عَلَى الرَّسُولِ اِلَّا الْبَلٰغُ الْمُبِيْنُ ۝

19. See they not how God
Originates creation, then[3440]
Repeats it : truly that
Is easy for God.

١٩- اَوَلَمْ يَرَوْا كَيْفَ يُبْدِئُ اللّٰهُ الْخَلْقَ
ثُمَّ يُعِيْدُهٗ ؕ اِنَّ ذٰلِكَ عَلَى اللّٰهِ يَسِيْرٌ ۝

20. Say : " Travel through the earth[3441]
And see how God did
Originate creation ; so will
God produce a later creation :
For God has power
Over all things.

٢٠- قُلْ سِيْرُوْا فِى الْاَرْضِ فَانْظُرُوْا كَيْفَ
بَدَاَ الْخَلْقَ ثُمَّ اللّٰهُ يُنْشِئُ النَّشْاَةَ الْاٰخِرَةَ ؕ
اِنَّ اللّٰهَ عَلٰى كُلِّ شَىْءٍ قَدِيْرٌ ۝

21. " He punishes whom He pleases,
And He grants mercy to whom

٢١- يُعَذِّبُ مَنْ يَّشَآءُ وَيَرْحَمُ مَنْ

3439. *Sustenance* : in the symbolic as well as the literal sense. Seek from God all that is necessary for your upkeep and development, and for preparing you for your future Destiny. Lay all your hopes in Him and in no one else. Dedicate yourselves to His worship. He will give you all that is necessary for your growth and well being, and you should show your gratitude to Him by conforming your will entirely to His.

3440. The originating of creation is the creation of primeval matter. The repetition of the process of creation goes on constantly, for at every moment new processes are being called into being by the creative power of God, and according to His Laws. And the final creation as far as man is concerned will be in the Ma'ād, when the whole world as man sees it will be entirely newly created on a different plane. As far as God is concerned, there is nothing final,—no first and last, for He is infinite. He was before our First and will be after our Last, and if there is any meaning in these relative terms, He is the real First and the real Last.

3441. *Travel through the earth* : again, literally as well as symbolically. If we actually go through this wide earth, we shall see the wonderful things in His Creation—the Grand Canyon and the Niagaras in America, beautiful harbours like that at Sydney in Australia, mountains like Fujiyama, the Himalayas, and Elburz in Asia, the Nile with its wonderful cataracts in Africa, the Fiords of Norway, the Geysers of Iceland, the city of the midnight sun in Tromsoe, and innumerable wonders everywhere. But wonders upon wonders are disclosed in the constitution of matter itself, the atom, and the forces of energy, as also in the instincts of animals, and the minds and capacities of man. And there is no limit to these things. Worlds upon worlds are created and transformed every moment, within and presumably beyond man's vision. From what we know we can judge of the unknown.

He pleases, and towards Him
Are ye turned.[3442]

يَشَآءُ وَ اِلَيْهِ تُقْلَبُوْنَ ○

22. "Not on earth nor in heaven
Will ye be able (fleeing)
To frustrate (His Plan),
Nor have ye, besides God,
Any protector or helper."

٢٢- وَمَآ اَنْتُمْ بِمُعْجِزِيْنَ فِى الْاَرْضِ وَ
لَا فِى السَّمَآءِ وَ مَا لَكُمْ مِّنْ دُوْنِ اللّٰهِ مِنْ
وَّلِيٍّ وَّلَا نَصِيْرٍ ○ ع

SECTION 3.

23. Those who reject the Signs
Of God and the Meeting
With Him (in the Hereafter),—
It is they who shall despair
Of My mercy: it is they[3443]
Who will (suffer)
A most grievous Penalty.

٢٣- وَالَّذِيْنَ كَفَرُوْا بِاٰيٰتِ اللّٰهِ وَ لِقَآئِهٖٓ
اُولٰٓئِكَ يَئِسُوْا مِنْ رَّحْمَتِىْ
وَ اُولٰٓئِكَ لَهُمْ عَذَابٌ اَلِيْمٌ ○

24. So naught was the answer
Of (Abraham's) people except
That they said: "Slay him
Or burn him." But God
Did save him from the Fire.[3444]
Verily in this are Signs
For people who believe.

٢٤- فَمَا كَانَ جَوَابَ قَوْمِهٖٓ اِلَّآ
اَنْ قَالُوا اقْتُلُوْهُ اَوْ حَرِّقُوْهُ
فَاَنْجٰىهُ اللّٰهُ مِنَ النَّارِ
اِنَّ فِىْ ذٰلِكَ لَاٰيٰتٍ لِّقَوْمٍ يُّؤْمِنُوْنَ ○

25. And he said: "For you,
Ye have taken (for worship)
Idols besides God, out of
Mutual love and regard[3445]

٢٥- وَ قَالَ اِنَّمَا اتَّخَذْتُمْ
مِّنْ دُوْنِ اللّٰهِ اَوْثَانًا مَّوَدَّةَ

3442. I think *ilaihi tuqlabūn* is better translated "towards Him are ye turned" than "towards Him will be your return", as it implies not only the return of man to God in the Hereafter (*turja'ūn* in verse 17 above) but also the fact explained in verse 22 that man's needs are always to be obtained from God: man cannot frustrate God's designs, and can have no help or protection except from God: man has always to face God, whether man obeys God or tries to ignore God. Man will never be able to defeat God's Plan. According to His wise Will and Plan, He will grant His grace or withhold it from man.

3443. The emphasis is on "*they*" (*ulāika*). It is only the people who ignore or reject God's Signs and reject a Hereafter, that will find themselves in despair and suffering. God's Mercy is open to all, but if any reject His Mercy, they must suffer.

3444. See xxi. 66-70. Abraham was cast into the fire, but he was unhurt, by the grace of God. So righteous people suffer no harm from the plots of the wicked. But they must leave the environment of evil even if they have to forsake their ancestral home, as Abraham did.

3445. In sin and wickedness there is as much log-rolling as in politics. Evil men humour each other and support each other; they call each other's vices by high-sounding names. They call it mutual regard or friendship or love; at the lowest, they call it toleration. Perhaps they flourish in this life by such arts. But they deceive themselves, and they deceive each other. What will be their relations in the Hereafter? They will disown each other when each has to answer on the principle of personal responsibility. Each will accuse the others of misleading him, and they will curse each other. But there will then be no help, and they must suffer in the Fire.

Between yourselves in this life;
But on the Day of Judgment
Ye shall disown each other
And curse each other:
And your abode will be
The Fire, and ye shall have
None to help."

بَيْنِكُمْ فِي الْحَيٰوةِ الدُّنْيَا ۚ
ثُمَّ يَوْمَ الْقِيٰمَةِ يَكْفُرُ بَعْضُكُمْ بِبَعْضٍ
وَّيَلْعَنُ بَعْضُكُمْ بَعْضًا ۡ وَّمَاْوٰىكُمُ النَّارُ
وَمَا لَكُمْ مِّنْ نّٰصِرِيْنَ ۝

26\. But Lūṭ had faith in Him:[3446]
He said: "I will leave
Home for the sake of
My Lord: for He is
Exalted in Might, and Wise."

٢٦- فَاٰمَنَ لَهٗ لُوْطٌ ۘ وَقَالَ اِنِّيْ
مُهَاجِرٌ اِلٰى رَبِّيْ ؕ
اِنَّهٗ هُوَ الْعَزِيْزُ الْحَكِيْمُ ۝

وقف لازم

27\. And We gave (Abraham)
Isaac and Jacob, and ordained
Among his progeny Prophethood[3447]
And Revelation, and We
Granted him his reward
In this life; and he was
In the Hereafter (of the company)
Of the Righteous.[3448]

٢٧- وَوَهَبْنَا لَهٗٓ اِسْحٰقَ وَيَعْقُوْبَ وَجَعَلْنَا
فِيْ ذُرِّيَّتِهِ النُّبُوَّةَ وَالْكِتٰبَ
وَاٰتَيْنٰهُ اَجْرَهٗ فِي الدُّنْيَا ۚ
وَاِنَّهٗ فِي الْاٰخِرَةِ لَمِنَ الصّٰلِحِيْنَ ۝

C. 178.—Worldly power cannot through sin
(xxix. 28-44.) Defy the right, as was proved in the ministry
Of Lot; nor can Intelligence misused
Stand in the place of God's Light; nor
Can boastful insolence do aught
But dig its own grave. The strength
And skill, the beauty and power, of this world's
Life are no more than a Spider's Web,
Flimsy before the force of the eternal
Verities that flow from God Supreme!

28\. And (remember) Lūṭ: behold,
He said to his people:

٢٨- وَلُوْطًا اِذْ قَالَ لِقَوْمِهٖٓ

3446\. Lot was a nephew of Abraham. He adhered to Abraham's teaching and faith and accepted voluntary exile with him, for Abraham left the home of his fathers in Chaldæa and migrated to Syria and Palestine, where God gave him increase and prosperity, and a numerous family, who upheld the flag of Unity and the Light of God.

3447\. Isaac was Abraham's son and Jacob his grandson, and among his progeny was included Ismā'īl the eldest son of Abraham. Each of these became a fountain-head of Prophecy and Revelation, Isaac and Jacob through Moses, and Ismā'īl through the holy Apostle Muḥammad. Jacob got the name of "Israel" at Bethel: Gen. 32:28; 35:10, and his progeny got the title of "The Children of Israel".

3448\. *Cf.* xxix. 9, and iv. 69, n. 586.

" Ye do commit lewdness,
Such as no people in Creation[3449]
(Ever) committed before you.

إِنَّكُمْ لَتَأْتُونَ الْفَاحِشَةَ
مَا سَبَقَكُمْ بِهَا مِنْ أَحَدٍ مِّنَ الْعٰلَمِينَ ○

29. " Do ye indeed approach men,
And cut off the highway ?—[3450]
And practise wickedness
(Even) in your councils ? "
But his people gave no answer
But this : they said :
" Bring us the Wrath of God
If thou tellest the truth." [3451]

٢٩- أَئِنَّكُمْ لَتَأْتُونَ الرِّجَالَ وَتَقْطَعُونَ
السَّبِيلَ ۙ
وَتَأْتُونَ فِي نَادِيكُمُ الْمُنْكَرَ ۖ
فَمَا كَانَ جَوَابَ قَوْمِهِ إِلَّا أَنْ قَالُوا ائْتِنَا
بِعَذَابِ اللّٰهِ إِنْ كُنْتَ مِنَ الصّٰدِقِينَ ○

30. He said : " O my Lord !
Help Thou me against people
Who do mischief ! "

٣٠- قَالَ رَبِّ انْصُرْنِي
عَلَى الْقَوْمِ الْمُفْسِدِينَ ○

SECTION 4.

31. When Our Messengers came
To Abraham with the good news,[3452]
They said : " We are indeed
Going to destroy the people
Of this township :[3453] for truly
They are (addicted to) crime."

٣١- وَلَمَّا جَاءَتْ رُسُلُنَا إِبْرٰهِيمَ بِالْبُشْرٰى ۙ
قَالُوا إِنَّا مُهْلِكُوا أَهْلِ هٰذِهِ الْقَرْيَةِ ۚ إِنَّ
أَهْلَهَا كَانُوا ظٰلِمِينَ ○

3449. *Cf.* vii. 80. A discreet reference is made to their unspeakable crimes, which were against the laws of all nature.

3450. They infested highways and committed their horrible crimes not only secretly, but openly and publicly, even in their assemblies. Some Commentators understand "cutting off the highway" to refer to highway robberies : this is possible, and it is also possible that the crimes in their assemblies may have been injustice, rowdiness, etc. But the context seems to refer to their own special horrible crime, and the point here seems to be that they were not ashamed of it and that they practised it publicly. Degradation could go no further.

3451. This is another instance of their effrontery, in addition to that mentioned in vii. 82 : the two supplement each other. Here the point emphasised is that they did not believe in God or His Punishment, and dared God's Apostle Lot to bring about the Punishment if he could. And it did come and destroyed them.

3452. See xi. 69-76. The angels, who were coming on the mission to destroy the people who were polluting the earth with their crimes, called on their way on Abraham to give the good news of the birth of a son to him in his old age. When they told him their destination, he feared for his nephew who he knew was there. They reassured him and then came on to Lot.

3453. By translating "township" I imply the two neighbouring populations of Sodom and Gomorrah, who had already gone too far in their crime, their shamelessness, and their defiance, to profit by any mercy from God.

32. He said: "But there is
Lūṭ there." They said:
"Well do we know who
Is there: we will certainly
Save him and his following,—
Except his wife: she is
Of those who lag behind!"[3454]

٣٢- قَالَ إِنَّ فِيهَا لُوطًا ۚ قَالُوا
نَحْنُ أَعْلَمُ بِمَن فِيهَا ۖ
لَنُنَجِّيَنَّهُ وَأَهْلَهُ
إِلَّا امْرَأَتَهُ ۖ كَانَتْ مِنَ الْغٰبِرِينَ ○

33. And when Our Messengers
Came to Lūṭ, he was
Grieved on their account,
And felt himself powerless[3455]
(To protect) them: but they said:
"Fear thou not, nor grieve:
We are (here) to save thee
And thy following, except
Thy wife: she is
Of those who lag behind.

٣٣- وَلَمَّا أَن جَاءَتْ رُسُلُنَا لُوطًا
سِيءَ بِهِمْ وَضَاقَ بِهِمْ ذَرْعًا
وَقَالُوا لَا تَخَفْ وَلَا تَحْزَنْ ۖ
إِنَّا مُنَجُّوكَ وَأَهْلَكَ إِلَّا
امْرَأَتَكَ كَانَتْ مِنَ الْغٰبِرِينَ ○

34. "For we are going to
Bring down on the people
Of this township a Punishment[3456]
From heaven, because they
Have been wickedly rebellious."

٣٤- إِنَّا مُنزِلُونَ عَلَىٰ أَهْلِ
هٰذِهِ الْقَرْيَةِ رِجْزًا مِّنَ السَّمَاءِ
بِمَا كَانُوا يَفْسُقُونَ ○

35. And We have left thereof
An evident Sign,[3457]
For any people who
(Care to) understand.

٣٥- وَلَقَد تَّرَكْنَا مِنْهَا آيَةً بَيِّنَةً
لِّقَوْمٍ يَعْقِلُونَ ○

3454. She was not loyal to her husband. Tradition says that she belonged to the wicked people, and was not prepared to leave them. She had no faith in the mission either of her husband or of the angels who had come as his guests.

3455. This part of the story may be read in greater detail in xi. 77-83.

3456. The Punishment was a rain of brimstone, which completely overwhelmed the Cities, with possibly an earthquake and a volcanic eruption (see xi. 82).

3457. The whole tract on the east side of the Dead Sea (where the Cities were situated) is covered with sulphureous salts and is deadly to animal and plant life. The Dead Sea itself is called in Arabic the Baḥr Lūṭ (the sea of Lot). It is a scene of utter desolation, that should stand as a Symbol of the Destruction that awaits Sin.

36. To the Madyan (people)
(We sent) their brother Shu'aib.
Then he said: "O my people!
Serve God, and fear the Last
Day: nor commit evil
On the earth, with intent
To do mischief."

٣٦- وَإِلَىٰ مَدْيَنَ أَخَاهُمْ شُعَيْبًا
فَقَالَ يَٰقَوْمِ اعْبُدُوا اللَّهَ وَارْجُوا الْيَوْمَ
الْآخِرَ
وَلَا تَعْثَوْا فِي الْأَرْضِ مُفْسِدِينَ ۝

37. But they rejected him:
Then the mighty Blast [3458]
Seized them, and they lay
Prostrate in their homes
By the morning.

٣٧- فَكَذَّبُوهُ
فَأَخَذَتْهُمُ الرَّجْفَةُ
فَأَصْبَحُوا فِي دَارِهِمْ جَٰثِمِينَ ۝

38. (Remember also) the 'Ād
And the Thamūd (people): [3459]
Clearly will appear to you
From (the traces) of their buildings
(Their fate): the Evil One
Made their deeds alluring [3460]
To them, and kept them back
From the Path, though they
Were gifted with Intelligence
And Skill.

٣٨- وَعَادًا وَثَمُودَا۟
وَقَد تَّبَيَّنَ لَكُم مِّن مَّسَٰكِنِهِمْ
وَزَيَّنَ لَهُمُ الشَّيْطَٰنُ أَعْمَٰلَهُمْ
فَصَدَّهُمْ عَنِ السَّبِيلِ
وَكَانُوا مُسْتَبْصِرِينَ ۝

3458. The story of Shu'aib and the Madyan people is only referred to here. It is told in xi. 84-95. Their besetting sin was fraud and commercial immorality. Their punishment was a mighty Blast, such as accompanies volcanic eruptions. The point of the reference here is that they went about doing mischief on the earth, and never thought of the Ma'ād or the Hereafter, the particular theme of this Sūra. The same point is made by the brief references in the following two verses to the 'Ād and the Thamūd, and to Qārūn, Pharaoh, and Hāmān, though the besetting sin in each case was different. The Midianites were a commercial people and trafficked from land to land; their frauds are well described as spreading "mischief on the earth".

3459. For the 'Ād people see vii. 65-72, and n. 1040, and for the Thamūd, vii. 73-79, and n. 1043. The remains of their buildings show (1) that they were gifted with great intelligence and skill; (2) that they were proud of their material civilisation; and (3) their destruction argues how the greatest material civilisation and resources cannot save a People who disobey God's moral law.

3460. They were so arrogant and self-satisfied, that they missed the higher purpose of life, and strayed clean away from the Path of God. Though their intelligence should have kept them straight, Evil made them crooked and led them and kept them astray.

39. (Remember also) Qārūn,[3461]
Pharaoh, and Hāmān: there came
To them Moses with Clear Signs,
But they behaved with insolence
On the earth; yet they
Could not overreach (Us).

٣٩- وَقَارُونَ وَفِرْعَوْنَ وَهَامٰنَ
وَلَقَدْ جَآءَهُم مُّوسٰى بِالْبَيِّنٰتِ
فَاسْتَكْبَرُوا فِي الْأَرْضِ وَمَا كَانُوا سٰبِقِينَ

40. Each one of them We seized
For his crime: of them,
Against some We sent
A violent tornado (with showers[3462]
Of stones); some were caught
By a (mighty) Blast;[3463] some
We caused the earth[3464]
To swallow up; and some
We drowned (in the waters):[3465]
It was not God Who
Injured (or oppressed) them:
They injured (and oppressed)
Their own souls.

٤٠- فَكُلًّا أَخَذْنَا بِذَنْبِهِ
فَمِنْهُم مَّنْ أَرْسَلْنَا عَلَيْهِ حَاصِبًا
وَمِنْهُم مَّنْ أَخَذَتْهُ الصَّيْحَةُ
وَمِنْهُم مَّنْ خَسَفْنَا بِهِ الْأَرْضَ
وَمِنْهُم مَّنْ أَغْرَقْنَا
وَمَا كَانَ اللّٰهُ لِيَظْلِمَهُمْ
وَلٰكِن كَانُوٓا أَنفُسَهُمْ يَظْلِمُونَ

41. The parable of those who
Take protectors other than God
Is that of the Spider,
Who builds (to itself)

٤١- مَثَلُ الَّذِينَ اتَّخَذُوا مِن دُونِ اللّٰهِ
أَوْلِيَآءَ كَمَثَلِ الْعَنكَبُوتِ اتَّخَذَتْ

3461. For Qārūn see xxviii. 76-82; Pharaoh is mentioned frequently in the Qur-ān, but he is mentioned in association with Hāmān in xxviii. 6; for their blasphemous arrogance and defiance of God see xxviii. 38. They thought such a lot of themselves, but they came to an evil end.

3462. For *ḥāṣib* (violent tornado with showers of stones), see xvii. 68; this punishment was inflicted on the Cities of the Plain, to which Lot preached (liv. 34). Some Commentators think that this also applied to the 'Ad, but their punishment is described as by a violent and unseasonable cold wind (xli. 16; liv. 19 and lxix, 6), such as blows in sand-storms in the Aḥqāf, the region of shifting sands which was in their territory.

3463. For *ṣaiḥat* (Blast) see xi. 67 and n. 1561, as also n. 1047 to vii. 78 and n. 1996 to xv. 73. This word is used in describing the fate of (1) the Thamūd (xi, 67); Madyan (xi, 94); the population to which Lūṭ preached (xv. 73); and the Rocky Tract (Ḥijr, xv. 83), part of the territory of the Thamūd; also in the Parable of the City to which came three apostles, who found a single believer (xxxvi. 29).

3464. This was the fate of Qārūn: see xxviii. 81. *Cf.* also xvi. 45 and n. 2071.

3465. This was the fate of the hosts of Pharaoh and Hāmān (xxviii. 40) as well as the wicked generation of Noah (xxvi. 120).

A house; but truly
The flimsiest of houses[3466]
Is the Spider's house;—[3467]
If they but knew.

42. Verily God doth know
Of (every thing) whatever[3468]
That they call upon
Besides Him: and He is
Exalted (in power), Wise.

43. And such are the Parables
We set forth for mankind,
But only those understand them
Who have Knowledge.[3469]

44. God created the heavens
And the earth in true
(proportions):[3470]
20 Verily in that is a Sign
30 For those who believe.

بَيْتًا ۚ وَإِنَّ أَوْهَنَ الْبُيُوتِ
لَبَيْتُ الْعَنْكَبُوتِ ۘ لَوْ كَانُوا يَعْلَمُونَ ○

٤٢- إِنَّ اللَّهَ يَعْلَمُ
مَا يَدْعُونَ مِنْ دُونِهِ مِنْ شَيْءٍ ۚ
وَهُوَ الْعَزِيزُ الْحَكِيمُ ○

٤٣- وَتِلْكَ الْأَمْثَالُ نَضْرِبُهَا لِلنَّاسِ ۖ
وَمَا يَعْقِلُهَا إِلَّا الْعَالِمُونَ ○

٤٤- خَلَقَ اللَّهُ السَّمَاوَاتِ وَالْأَرْضَ بِالْحَقِّ ۚ
إِنَّ فِي ذَٰلِكَ لَآيَةً لِلْمُؤْمِنِينَ ○ ع

3466. The Spider's house is one of the wonderful Signs of God's creation. It is made up of fine silk threads spun out of silk glands in the spider's body. There are many kinds of spiders and many kinds of spider's houses. Two main types of houses may be mentioned. There is the tubular nest or web, a silk-lined house or burrow with one or two trap-doors. This may be called his residential or family mansion. Then there is what is ordinarily called a spider's web, consisting of a central point with radiating threads running in all directions and acting as tie-beams to the quasi-circular concentric threads that form the body of the web. This is his hunting box. The whole structure exemplifies economy in time, material, and strength. If an insect is caught in the net, the vibration set up in the radiating threads is at once communicated to the spider, who can come and kill his prey In case the prey is powerful, the spider is furnished with poison glands with which to kill his prey. The spider sits either in the centre of the web or hides on the under-side of a leaf or in some crevice, but he always has a single thread connecting him with his web, to keep him in telepnonic communication. The female spider is much bigger than the male, and in Arabic the generic gender of *'Ankabut* is feminine.

3467. Most of the facts in the last note can be read into the Parable. For their thickness the spider's threads are very strong from the point of view af relativity, but in our actual world they are flimsy, especially the threads of the gossamer spider floating in the air. So is the house and strength of the man who relies on material resources however fine or beautiful relatively; before the eternal Reality they are as nothing. The spider's most cunning architecture cannot stand against a wave of a man's hand. His poison glands are like the hidden poison in our beautiful worldly plans which may take various shapes but have seeds of death in them.

3468. The last verse told us that men, out of spiritual ignorance, build their hopes on flimsy unsubstantial things (like the spider's web) which are broken by a thousand chance attacks of wind and weather or the actions of animals or men. If they cannot fully grasp their own good, they should seek His Light. To Him everything is known,—men's frailty, their false hopes, their questionable motives, the false gods whom they enthrone in their midst, the mischief done by the neglect of Truth, and the way out for those who have entangled themselves in the snares of Evil. He is All-Wise and is able to carry out all He wills, and they should turn to Him.

3469. Parables seem simple things, but their profound meaning and application can only be understood by those who seek knowledge and by God's grace attain it.

3470. *Cf.* vi. 73 and n. 896. In all God's Creation, not only is there evidence of intelligent Purpose, fitting all parts together with wisdom, but also of supreme Goodness and cherishing Care, by which all needs are satisfied and all the highest and truest cravings fulfilled. These are like beckoning signals to lead on those who pray and search in Faith, those who with the intensest desire of their soul can pray, as in Cardinal Newman's Hymn, "Lead, kindly Light! Amid the encircling gloom, lead Thou me on!"

C. 179.—Proclaim the Message of God, and pray
(xxix. 45-69.) To Him for purity and guidance.
God's Revelation carries its own
Proofs and is recognised by men
Of wisdom. Its rejecters but lose
Their own chances of profiting
By the Truth, and attaining the Paths
That lead to God's own gracious Presence!

SECTION 5.

الجزء ٢١

45. Recite what is sent[3471]
Of the Book by inspiration
To thee, and establish
Regular Prayer: for Prayer
Restrains from shameful
And unjust deeds;
And remembrance of God
Is the greatest (thing in life)
Without doubt. And God knows
The (deeds) that ye do.

٤٥- اُتْلُ مَآ اُوْحِيَ اِلَيْكَ مِنَ الْكِتٰبِ
وَاَقِمِ الصَّلٰوةَ ط
اِنَّ الصَّلٰوةَ تَنْهٰى عَنِ الْفَحْشَآءِ وَالْمُنْكَرِ ط
وَلَذِكْرُ اللّٰهِ اَكْبَرُ ط
وَاللّٰهُ يَعْلَمُ مَا تَصْنَعُوْنَ ○

46. And dispute ye not
With the People of the Book,
Except with means better[3472]
(Than mere disputation), unless
It be with those of them
Who inflict wrong (and injury):[3473]
But say, "We believe
In the Revelation which has
Come down to us and in that
Which came down to you;

٤٦- وَلَا تُجَادِلُوْٓا اَهْلَ الْكِتٰبِ
اِلَّا بِالَّتِيْ هِيَ اَحْسَنُ ق
اِلَّا الَّذِيْنَ ظَلَمُوْا مِنْهُمْ
وَقُوْلُوْٓا اٰمَنَّا بِالَّذِيْٓ
اُنْزِلَ اِلَيْنَا وَاُنْزِلَ اِلَيْكُمْ

3471. The *tilāwat* of the Qur-ān implies: (1) rehearsing or reciting it, and publishing it abroad to the world; (2) reading it to ourselves; (3) studying it to understand it as it should be studied and understood (ii. 121); (4) meditating on it so as to accord our knowledge and life and desires with it. When this is done, it merges into real Prayer, and Prayer purges us of anything (act, plan, thought, motive, words) of which we should be ashamed or which would work injustice to others. Such Prayer passes into our inmost life and being, for then we realise the Presence of God, and that is true *ẓikr* (or remembrance), for remembrance is the bringing to mind of things as present to us which might otherwise be absent to us. And that is the greatest thing in life. It is subjective to us: it fills our consciousness with God. For God is in any case always present and knows all.

3472. Mere disputations are futile. In order to achieve our purpose as true standard-bearers for God, we shall have to find true common grounds of belief, as stated in the latter part of this verse, and also to show by our urbanity, kindness, sincerity, truth, and genuine anxiety for the good of others, that we are not cranks or merely seeking selfish or questionable aims.

3473. Of course those who are deliberately trying to wrong or injure others will have to be treated firmly, as we are guardians of each other. With them there is little question of finding common ground or exercising patience, until the injury is prevented or stopped.

Our God and your God Is One; and it is to Him We bow (in Islam)."[3474]	وَإِلَٰهُنَا وَإِلَٰهُكُمْ وَاحِدٌ وَنَحْنُ لَهُۥ مُسْلِمُونَ ○
47. And thus[3475] (it is) that We Have sent down the Book To thee. So the People Of the Book believe therein,[3476] As also do some of these[3477] (Pagan Arabs): and none But Unbelievers reject Our Signs.	٤٧- وَكَذَٰلِكَ أَنزَلْنَآ إِلَيْكَ ٱلْكِتَٰبَ فَٱلَّذِينَ ءَاتَيْنَٰهُمُ ٱلْكِتَٰبَ يُؤْمِنُونَ بِهِۦ وَمِنْ هَٰٓؤُلَآءِ مَن يُؤْمِنُ بِهِۦ وَمَا يَجْحَدُ بِـَٔايَٰتِنَآ إِلَّا ٱلْكَٰفِرُونَ ○
48. And thou wast not (able) To recite a Book before This (Book came), nor art thou (Able) to transcribe it With thy right hand:[3478] In that case, indeed, would	٤٨- وَمَا كُنتَ تَتْلُوا۟ مِن قَبْلِهِۦ مِن كِتَٰبٍ وَلَا تَخُطُّهُۥ بِيَمِينِكَ

3474. That is, the religion of all true and sincere men of Faith is, or should be, one; and that is the ideal of Islam.

3475. It is in this spirit that all true Revelation comes from God. God is One, and His Message cannot come in one place or at one time to contradict His Message in another place or at another time in spirit, though there may be local variations according to the needs or understanding of men at any given time or place.

3476. The sincere Jews and Christians found in the holy Prophet a fulfilment of their own religion. For the names of some Jews who recognised and embraced Islam, see n. 3227 to xxvi. 197. Among the Christians, too, the Faith slowly won ground. Embassies were sent by the holy Prophet in the 6th and 7th years of the Hijrat to all the principal countries round Arabia, *viz.*, the capital of the Byzantine Empire (Constantinople), the capital of the Persian Empire (Madâin), the Sāsānian capital known to the West by the Greek name of Ctesiphon, (about thirty miles south of modern Bagdād), Syria, Abyssinia, and Egypt. All these (except Persia) were Christian countries. In the same connection an embassy was also sent to Yamāma in Arabia itself (east of the Ḥijāz) where the Banū Ḥanīfa tribe was Christian, like the Ḥārith tribe of Najrān who voluntarily sent an embassy to Medina. All these countries except Abyssinia eventually became Muslim, and Abyssinia itself has a considerable Muslim population now and sent some Muslim converts to Medina in the time of the Prophet himself. As a generalisation it is true that the Jewish and the Christian peoples as they existed in the seventh century of the Christian era have been mainly absorbed by Islam, as well as the lands in which they predominated. Remnants of them built up new nuclei. The Roman Catholic Church conquered new lands among the northern (Germanic) Pagans and the Byzantine Church among the eastern (Slavonic) Pagans, and the Protestantism of the 16th century gave a fresh stimulus to the main ideas for which Islam stands, *viz.*, the abolition of priestcraft, the right of private judgment, the simplification of ritual, and the insistence upon the simple, practical, everyday duties of life.

3477. The Pagan Arabs also gradually came in until they were all absorbed in Islam.

3478. The holy Prophet was not a learned man. Before the Qur-ān was revealed to him, he never claimed to proclaim a Message from God. He was not in the habit of preaching eloquent truths as from a Book, before he received his Revelation, nor was he able to write or transcribe with his own hand. If he had had these worldly gifts, there would have been some plausibility in the charge of the talkers of vanities that he spoke not from inspiration but from other people's books, or that he composed the beautiful verses of the Qur-ān himself and committed them to memory in order to recite them to people. The circumstances in which the Qur-ān came bear their own testimony to its truth as from God.

The talkers of vanities
Have doubted.

إِذًا لَّارْتَابَ الْمُبْطِلُونَ ۝

49. Nay, here are Signs
Self-evident in the hearts
Of those endowed with
knowledge:[3479]
And none but the unjust
Reject Our Signs.[3480]

٤٩- بَلْ هُوَ ءَايَٰتٌۢ بَيِّنَٰتٌ فِى صُدُورِ
الَّذِينَ أُوتُوا الْعِلْمَ ۚ
وَمَا يَجْحَدُ بِـَٔايَٰتِنَآ إِلَّا الظَّٰلِمُونَ ۝

50. Yet they say: "Why
Are not Signs sent down
To him from his Lord?"
Say: "The Signs are indeed
With God: and I am
Indeed a clear Warner."[3481]

٥٠- وَقَالُوا لَوْلَآ أُنزِلَ عَلَيْهِ ءَايَٰتٌ مِّن
رَّبِّهِۦ ۖ قُلْ إِنَّمَا الْءَايَٰتُ عِندَ اللَّهِ
وَإِنَّمَآ أَنَا۠ نَذِيرٌ مُّبِينٌ ۝

51. And is it not enough
For them that We have
Sent down to thee
The Book which is rehearsed
To them? Verily, in it
Is Mercy and a Reminder
To those who believe.[3482]

٥١- أَوَلَمْ يَكْفِهِمْ أَنَّآ
أَنزَلْنَا عَلَيْكَ الْكِتَٰبَ يُتْلَىٰ عَلَيْهِمْ ۚ
إِنَّ فِى ذَٰلِكَ لَرَحْمَةً وَذِكْرَىٰ
لِقَوْمٍ يُؤْمِنُونَ ۝

SECTION 6.

52. Say: "Enough is God
For a Witness between me

٥٢- قُلْ كَفَىٰ بِاللَّهِ بَيْنِى

3479. "Knowledge" (*'ilm*) means both power of judgment in discerning the value of truth and acquaintance with previous revelations. It implies both literary and spiritual insight. To men so endowed, God's revelations and Signs are self-evident. They commend themselves to their hearts, minds, and understandings, which are typified in Arabic by the word *ṣadr*, "breast".

3480. *Cf.* the last clause of verse 47 above. There the argument was that the rejection of the Qur-ān was a mark of Unbelief. Now the argument is carried a stage farther. Such rejection is also a mark of injustice, a deliberate perversity in going against obvious Signs, which should convince all honest men.

3481. See last note. In the Qur-ān, as said in verse 49, are Signs which should carry conviction to all honest hearts. And yet the Unbelievers ask for Signs! They mean some special kinds of Signs or Miracles, such as their own foolish minds dictate. Everything is possible for God, but God is not going to humour the follies of men or listen to their disingenuous demands. He has sent an Apostle to explain His Signs clearly, and to warn them of the consequences of rejection. Is it not enough?

3482. The perspicuous Qur-ān, explained in detail by God's Messenger, in conjunction with God's Signs in nature and in the hearts of men, should be enough for all. It is mere fractious opposition to demand vaguely something more. *Cf.* also vi. 124, and n. 946.

And you: He knows
What is in the heavens[3483]
And on earth. And it is
Those who believe in vanities
And reject God, that
Will perish (in the end).[3484]

وَبَيْنَكُمْ شَهِيدًا ۚ يَعْلَمُ مَا فِي السَّمٰوٰتِ وَ
الْأَرْضِ ۗ وَالَّذِينَ آمَنُوا بِالْبَاطِلِ وَكَفَرُوا
بِاللَّهِ أُولٰٓئِكَ هُمُ الْخٰسِرُونَ ○

53. They ask thee
To hasten on the Punishment[3485]
(For them): had it not been
For a term (of respite)
Appointed, the Punishment
Would certainly have come
To them: and it will
Certainly reach them,—
Of a sudden, while they
Perceive not!

٥٣- وَيَسْتَعْجِلُونَكَ بِالْعَذَابِ ۚ
وَلَوْلَا أَجَلٌ مُسَمًّى
لَجَاءَهُمُ الْعَذَابُ ۚ
وَلَيَأْتِيَنَّهُمْ بَغْتَةً
وَهُمْ لَا يَشْعُرُونَ ○

54. They ask thee
To hasten on the Punishment:[3486]
But, of a surety,
Hell will encompass
The rejecters of Faith!—

٥٤- يَسْتَعْجِلُونَكَ بِالْعَذَابِ ۚ
وَإِنَّ جَهَنَّمَ لَمُحِيطَةٌ بِالْكٰفِرِينَ ○

55. On the Day that
The Punishment shall cover them
From above them and
From below them,[3487]
And (a Voice) shall say:
"Taste ye (the fruits)
Of your deeds!"[3488]

٥٥- يَوْمَ يَغْشٰهُمُ الْعَذَابُ
مِنْ فَوْقِهِمْ وَمِنْ تَحْتِ أَرْجُلِهِمْ
وَيَقُولُ ذُوقُوا مَا كُنْتُمْ تَعْمَلُونَ ○

3483. The test of a Revelation is whether it comes from God or not. This is made clear by the life and teachings of the Messenger who brings it. No fraud or falsehood can for a moment stand before God. All the most hidden things in heaven and earth are open before Him.

3484. If Truth is rejected, Truth does not suffer. It is the rejecters who suffer and perish in the end.

3485. *Cf.* xxii. 47 and n. 2826. The rejecters of Faith throw out a challenge out of bravado: 'Let us see if you can hasten the punishment on us!" This is a vain taunt. God's Plan will take its course, and can neither be delayed nor hastened. It is out of His Mercy that He gives respite to sinners,—in order that they may have a chance of repentance. If they do not repent, the Punishment must certainly come to them—and on a sudden, before they perceive that it is coming! And then it will be too late for repentance.

3486. The challenge of the wicked for Punishment was answered in the last verse by reference to God's merciful Respite, to give chances of repentance. It is answered in this verse by an assurance that if no repentance is forthcoming, the Punishment will be certain and of an all-pervasive kind. Hell will surround them on all sides, and above them and below them.

3487. *Cf.* a similar phrase in vi. 65.

3488. This is not merely a reproach, but a justification of the Punishment. "It is you who brought it on yourselves by your evil deeds: blame none but yourselves. God's Mercy gave you many chances: His Justice has now overtaken you!"

56. My servants who believe!
Truly, spacious is My Earth :[3489]
Therefore serve ye Me—
(And Me alone)!

٥٦- يٰعِبَادِيَ الَّذِينَ اٰمَنُوٓا اِنَّ اَرْضِي
وَاسِعَةٌ فَاِيَّايَ فَاعْبُدُونِ ○

57. Every soul shall have
A taste of death :[3490]
In the end to Us
Shall ye be brought back.

٥٧- كُلُّ نَفْسٍ ذَآئِقَةُ الْمَوْتِ
ثُمَّ اِلَيْنَا تُرْجَعُونَ ○

58. But those who believe
And work deeds of righteousness—
To them shall We give
A Home in Heaven,—[3491]
Lofty mansions beneath which
Flow rivers,—to dwell therein
For aye;—an excellent reward
For those who do (good)!—

٥٨- وَالَّذِينَ اٰمَنُوا وَعَمِلُوا الصّٰلِحٰتِ
لَنُبَوِّئَنَّهُمْ مِّنَ الْجَنَّةِ غُرَفًا
تَجْرِي مِنْ تَحْتِهَا الْاَنْهٰرُ خٰلِدِينَ فِيهَا
نِعْمَ اَجْرُ الْعٰمِلِينَ ○

59. Those who persevere in patience,
And put their trust
In their Lord and Cherisher.

٥٩- الَّذِينَ صَبَرُوا
وَعَلٰى رَبِّهِمْ يَتَوَكَّلُونَ ○

60. How many are the creatures
That carry not their own[3492]

٦٠- وَكَاَيِّنْ مِّنْ دَآبَّةٍ لَّا تَحْمِلُ

3489. There is no excuse for any one to plead that he could not do good or was forced to evil by his circumstances and surroundings, or by the fact that he lived in evil times. We must shun evil and seek good, and God's Creation is wide enough to enable us to do that, provided we have the will, the patience, and the constancy to do it. It may be that we have to change our village or city or country; or that we have to change our neighbours or associates; or to change our habits or our hours, our position in life or our human relationships, or our callings. Our integrity before God is more important than any of these things, and we must be prepared for exile (or *Hijrat*) in all these senses. For the means with which God provides us for His service are ample, and it is our own fault if we fail.

3490. *Cf.* iii. 185, n. 491, and xxi. 35 and n. 2697. Death is the separation of the soul from the body when the latter perishes. We should not be afraid of death, for it only brings us back to God. The various kinds of *hijrat* or exile, physical and spiritual, mentioned in the last note, are also modes of death in a sense: what is there to fear in them?

3491. The goodly homes mentioned in xvi. 41 referred to this life, but it was stated there that the reward of the Hereafter would be greater. Here the simile of the Home is referred to Heaven: it will be beautiful; it will be picturesque, with the sight and sound of softly-murmuring streams; it will be lofty or sublime; and it will be eternal.

3492. If we look at the animal creation, we see that many creatures seem almost helpless to find their own food or sustain their full life, being surrounded by many enemies. Yet in the Plan of God they find full sustenance and protection. So does man. Man's needs—as well as helplessness—are by many degrees greater. Yet God provides for him as for all His creatures. God listens to the wish and cry of all His creatures and He knows their needs and how to provide for them all. Man should not therefore hesitate to suffer exile or persecution in God's Cause.

Sustenance? It is God
Who feeds (both) them and you:
For He hears and knows
(All things).

رِزْقَهَا ۖ اللّٰهُ يَرْزُقُهَا وَإِيَّاكُمْ ۚ
وَهُوَ السَّمِيعُ الْعَلِيمُ ○

61. If indeed thou ask them[3493]
Who has created the heavens
And the earth and subjected[3494]
The sun and the moon
(To His Law), they will
Certainly reply, "God".
How are they then deluded
Away (from the truth)?

٦١- وَلَئِنْ سَأَلْتَهُمْ مَنْ خَلَقَ السَّمٰوٰتِ
وَالْأَرْضَ وَسَخَّرَ الشَّمْسَ وَالْقَمَرَ
لَيَقُولُنَّ اللّٰهُ ۚ
فَأَنّٰى يُؤْفَكُونَ ○

62. God enlarges the sustenance
(Which He gives) to whichever
Of His servants He pleases;[3495]
And He (similarly) grants
By (strict) measure, (as He pleases):
For God has full knowledge
Of all things.

٦٢- اَللّٰهُ يَبْسُطُ الرِّزْقَ
لِمَنْ يَشَاءُ مِنْ عِبَادِهِ
وَيَقْدِرُ لَهُ ۚ
إِنَّ اللّٰهَ بِكُلِّ شَيْءٍ عَلِيمٌ ○

63. And if indeed thou ask them[3496]
Who it is that sends down
Rain from the sky,
And gives life therewith
To the earth after its death,
They will certainly reply,
"God!" Say, "Praise be
To God!" But most
Of them understand not.

٦٣- وَلَئِنْ سَأَلْتَهُمْ مَنْ نَزَّلَ مِنَ السَّمَاءِ
مَاءً فَأَحْيَا بِهِ الْأَرْضَ مِنْ بَعْدِ مَوْتِهَا
لَيَقُولُنَّ اللّٰهُ ۚ قُلِ الْحَمْدُ لِلّٰهِ ۚ
بَلْ أَكْثَرُهُمْ لَا يَعْقِلُونَ ○

3493. *Cf.* xxiii. 84-89. "Them" in both passages refers to the sort of inconsistent men who acknowledge the power of God, but are deluded by false notions into disobedience of God's Law and disregard of God's Message.

3494. *Cf.* xiii. 2. and xxiii. 85. The perfect order and law in God's universe should be Signs to man's intelligence to get his own will into tune with God's Will; for only so can he hope to attain his full development.

3495. *Cf.* xiii. 26. Unequal gifts are not a sign of chaos in God's universe. God provides for all according to their real needs and their most suitable requirements, according to His perfect knowledge and understanding of His creatures.

3496. In xxix. 61 above, the point was that there is a certain type of man that realises the power of God, but yet goes after false ideas and false worship. Here the point is that there is another type of man to whom the goodness of God is made clear by rain and the gifts of nature and who realises the daily, seasonal, and secular changes which evidence God's goodness in giving us life (physical and spiritual) and reviving us after we seem to die,—and who yet fails to draw the right conclusion from it and to make his own life true and beautiful, so that, when his period of probation in this transitory life is ended, he can enter into his eternal heritage. Having come so far, such men fail at the crucial stage. At that stage they ought to have praised and glorified God and accepted His Grace and Light, but they show their want of true understanding by failing to profit by God's gifts.

Section 7.

64. What is the life of this world
But amusement and play?[3497]
But verily the Home
In the Hereafter,—that is
Life indeed, if they but knew.

٦٤- وَمَا هٰذِهِ الْحَيٰوةُ الدُّنْيَآ اِلَّا لَهْوٌ وَّ
لَعِبٌ ۚ وَاِنَّ الدَّارَ الْاٰخِرَةَ لَهِيَ الْحَيَوَانُ ۘ
لَوْ كَانُوْا يَعْلَمُوْنَ ○

65. Now, if they embark
On a boat, they call
On God, making their devotion
Sincerely (and exclusively) to
Him;[3498]
But when He has delivered
Them safely to (dry) land,
Behold, they give a share
(Of their worship to others)!—

٦٥- فَاِذَا رَكِبُوْا فِي الْفُلْكِ
دَعَوُا اللّٰهَ مُخْلِصِيْنَ لَهُ الدِّيْنَ ۚ
فَلَمَّا نَجّٰىهُمْ اِلَى الْبَرِّ
اِذَا هُمْ يُشْرِكُوْنَ ۙ

66. Disdaining ungratefully Our gifts,
And giving themselves up[3499]
To (worldly) enjoyment! But soon
Will they know.

٦٦- لِيَكْفُرُوْا بِمَآ اٰتَيْنٰهُمْ ۚ وَلِيَتَمَتَّعُوْا ۗ
فَسَوْفَ يَعْلَمُوْنَ ○

67. Do they not then see
That We have made
A Sanctuary secure, and that
Men are being snatched away
From all around them?[3500]
Then, do they believe in that

٦٧- اَوَلَمْ يَرَوْا اَنَّا جَعَلْنَا حَرَمًا اٰمِنًا
وَّيُتَخَطَّفُ النَّاسُ مِنْ حَوْلِهِمْ ۚ
اَفَبِالْبَاطِلِ يُؤْمِنُوْنَ

3497. *Cf.* vi. 32. Amusement and play have no lasting significance except as preparing us for the serious work of life. So this life is but an interlude, a preparation for the real Life, which is in the Hereafter. This world's vanities are therefore to be taken for what they are worth; but they are not to be allowed to deflect our minds from the requirements of the inner life that really matters.

3498. *Cf.* vii. 29, where I have slightly varied the English phrase according to the context.

It was shown in the last verse that the life of this world is fleeting, and that the true life—that which matters—is the Life of the Spirit. In contrast with this inner reality is now shown the short-sighted folly of man. When he faces the physical dangers of the sea, which are but an incident in the phenomenal world, he actually and sincerely seeks the help of God; but when he is safely back on land, he forgets the Realities, plunges into the pleasures and vanities of fleeting phenomena, and his devotion, which should be given exclusively to God, is shared by idols and vanities of his own imagination.

3499. Such folly results in the virtual rejection (even though it may not be express) of God and His Grace. It plunges man into the pleasures and vanities that merely delude and are bound to pass away. This delusion, however, will come to an end when the true Reality of the Hereafter will shine forth in all its splendour.

3500. If they want evidences of their folly in the phenomenal world itself, they will see sacred Sanctuaries where God's Truth abides safely in the midst of the Deluge of broken hopes, disappointed ambitions, and unfulfilled plans in the world around. The immediate reference was to the Sanctuary of Mecca and the gradual progress of Islam in the districts surrounding the Quraish in the midst of the trying Meccan period. But the general application holds good for all times and places.

Which is vain, and reject
The Grace of God?

وَبِنِعْمَةِ اللّٰهِ يَكْفُرُوْنَ ○

68. And who does more wrong[3501]
Than he who invents
A lie against God
Or rejects the Truth
When it reaches him?
Is there not a home
In Hell for those who
Reject Faith?

٦٨- وَمَنْ أَظْلَمُ مِمَّنِ افْتَرٰى عَلَى اللّٰهِ
كَذِبًا أَوْ كَذَّبَ بِالْحَقِّ لَمَّا جَآءَهٗ ۭ
أَلَيْسَ فِيْ جَهَنَّمَ مَثْوًى
لِّلْكٰفِرِيْنَ ○

69. And those who strive[3502]
In Our (Cause),—We will
Certainly guide them
To Our Paths:[3503]
For verily God
Is with those
Who do right.

٦٩- وَالَّذِيْنَ جَاهَدُوْا
فِيْنَا لَنَهْدِيَنَّهُمْ سُبُلَنَا ۭ
وَإِنَّ اللّٰهَ لَمَعَ الْمُحْسِنِيْنَ ○ ع

3501. *Cf.* vi. 21. Even from a worldly point of view those who reject God's Truth are at a disadvantage. But those who deliberately invent lies and set up false gods for worship,—what punishment can we imagine for them except a permanent deprivation of God's grace,—or in theological language, a home in Hell?

3502. "*Strive in Our Cause.*" All that man can do is to strive in God's Cause. As soon as he strives with might and main, with constancy and determination, the Light and Mercy of God come to meet him. They cure his defects and shortcomings. They provide him with the means by which he can raise himself above himself. They point out the Way, and all the Paths leading up to it. See next note.

3503. The Way of God (*ṣirāṭ-ul-Mustaqim*) is a Straight Way. But men have strayed from it in all directions. And there are numerous Paths by which they can get back to the Right Way, the Way in which the purity of their own nature, and the Will and Mercy of God, require them to walk. All these numerous Paths become open to them if once they give their hearts in keeping to God and work in right Endeavour (*Jihād*) with all their mind and soul and resources. Thus will they get out of the Spider's web of this frail world and attain to eternal Bliss in the fulfilment of their true Destiny.

INTRODUCTION TO SŪRA XXX (*Rūm*).

This Sūra, as remarked in the Introduction to the last Sūra, deals with the question of Ma'ād or the Final End of Things, from various points of view. In the last Sūra, we saw that Revelation was linked up with Life and Conduct, and Time (looking backwards and forwards) figured forth the frailty of this Life. In this Sūra the Time theme and its mystery are brought into relation with human history in the foreground and the evolution of the world in all its aspects in the background. The corruption introduced by man is cleared away by God, Whose Universal Plan points to the Hereafter. We shall see that the next two Sūras (xxxi. and xxxii.) present the theme in other aspects. All four are introduced with the Abbreviated Letters A. L. M., which (without being dogmatic) I have suggested as symbolical of the Past, Present and Future.

The chronology of this Sūra is significant. It was revealed about the 7th or the 6th year *before* the Hijrat, corresponding to 615-16 of the Christian era, when the tide of Persian conquest over the Roman Empire was running strong, as explained in Appendix X (to follow this Sūra).. The Christian Empire of Rome had lost Jerusalem to the Persians, and Christianity had been humbled in the dust. At that time it seemed outside the bounds of human possibility, even to one intimately acquainted with the inner resources and conditions of the Persian and Roman armies and empires, that the tables would be turned and the position reversed within the space of eight or nine years. The pro-Persian Pagan Quraish rejoiced exceedingly, and redoubled their taunts and persecution against the holy Prophet, whose Message was a renewal of the Message of Christ preached in Jerusalem. Then was this passage xxx. 1-6 revealed, clearly foreshadowing the final defeat of Persia (Appendix X. 14-16) as a prelude to the destruction of the Persian Empire. There is no doubt about the prophecy and its fulfilment. For the exulting Pagans of Mecca laid a heavy wager against the fulfilment of the prophecy with Ḥadhrat Abū Bakr, and they lost it on its fulfilment.

But the rise and fall even of such mighty empires as the Persian and Roman Empires, were but small events on the chequer-board of Time, compared to a mightier movement that was taking birth in the promulgation of Islam. In the seventh or sixth year *before* the Hijrat, and for a year or two after the Hijrat, Islam was struggling in the world like the still small voice in the conscience of humanity. It was scarcely heeded, and when it sought to insist upon its divine claim, it was insulted, assaulted, persecuted, boycotted, and (as it seemed) suppressed. The agony of Ṭāif (two years before the Hijrat) and the murder-plot on the eve of the Hijrat were yet to come. But the purpose of God is not to be thwarted. Badr (A.H. 2= A.D. 624), rightly called the critical Day of Decision, began to redress the balance of outward events in early Islam, in the same year in which Issus (Appendix X. 16) began to redress the balance of outward events in Perso-Roman relations. Mightier events were yet to come. A new inner World was being created through Islam.

This spiritual Revolution was of infinitely greater moment in world-history. The toppling down of priestcraft and false worship, the restoration of simplicity in faith and life, the rehabilitation of this life as the first step to the understanding of the Hereafter, the displacement of superstition and hair-splitting theology by a spirit of rational enquiry and knowledge, and the recognition of the divine as covering not merely an isolated thing called "Religion" but the whole way of Life, Thought, and Feeling,—this was and is the true Message of Islam and its mission. Its struggle—its fight—continues, but it is not without effect, as may be seen in the march of centuries in world-history.

Summary.—The ebb and flow of worldly power—as symbolised in the conflict of the Persian and Roman Empires—are but outward events: the deeper meaning is in the working of God's Universe—how Good and Evil reach their final End (xxx. 1-19, and C. 180).

The changes and changing variety in God's Creation, physical, moral, and spiritual, yet point to Unity in Nature and Religion: man should not break away from that Unity, but glorify Him, the One, for there is none like unto Him (xxx. 20-40, and C. 181).

The hands of men have wrought corruption and mischief: but God purifies the moral world as He does the world of physical nature, strengthening the weak and pulling down the mighty in due season: wait therefore in patience and constancy, and be not depressed (xxx. 41-60, and C. 182).

C. 180.—Great Empires rise and fall, conquer
(xxx. 1-19.) And are conquered, as happened
To Rome and Persia: but the true Decision
Is with God, Who will make the righteous
Rejoice. Men may see but the outward
Crust of things, but in truth the End
Of things is all-in-all. In His own
Good time He will separate good from evil:
Praise and glory to Him for ever!

Sūra XXX.

Rūm, or The Roman Empire.

In the name of God, Most Gracious, Most Merciful.

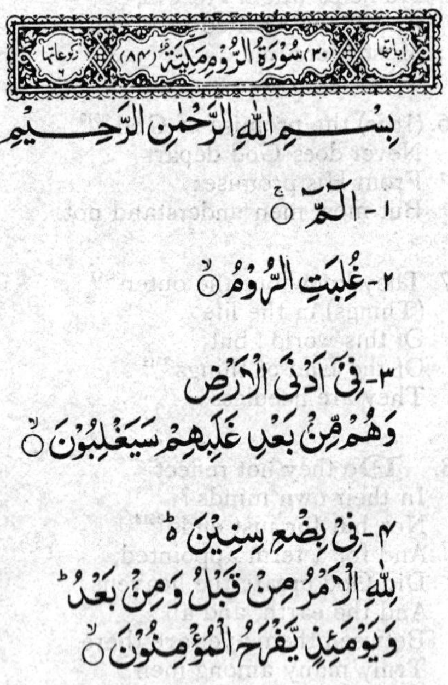

1. A. L. M.[3504]

2 The Roman Empire[3505]
Has been defeated—

3. In a land close by;
But they, (even) after
(This) defeat of theirs,
Will soon be victorious—[3506]

4. Within a few years.[3507]
With God is the Decision,
In the Past
And in the Future:
On that Day shall
The Believers rejoice—[3508]

3504. See n. 25 to ii. 1 and Introduction to this Sūra.

3505. The remarkable defeats of the Roman Empire under Heraclius and the straits to which it was reduced are reviewed in Appendix X (to follow this Sūra). It was not merely isolated defeats; the Roman Empire lost most of its Asiatic territory and was hemmed in on all sides at its capital, Constantinople. The defeat, "in a land close by" must refer to Syria and Palestine. Jerusalem was lost in 614-15 A.D., shortly before this Sūra was revealed.

3506. The Pagan Quraish of Mecca rejoiced at the overthrow of Rome by Persia. They were pro-Persian, and in their heart of hearts they hoped that the nascent movement of Islam, which at that time was, from a worldly point of view, very weak and helpless, would also collapse under their persecution. But they misread the true Signs of the times. They are told here that they would soon be disillusioned in both their calculations, and it actually so happened at the battle of Issus in 622 (the year of Hijrat) and in 624, when Heraclius carried his campaign into the heart of Persia (see Appendix X) and the Meccan Quraish were beaten off at Badr.

3507. *Bidh'un* in the text means a short period—a period of from three to nine years. The period between the loss of Jerusalem (614-15) by the Romans and their victory at Issus (622) was seven years, and that to the penetration of Persia by Heraclius was nine years. See last note.

3508. See n. 3506 and Appendix X, pp. 1072-74. The battle of Badr (2 A.H.=624 A.D.) was a real time of rejoicing for the Believers and a time of disillusionment for the arrogant Quraish, who thought that they could crush the whole movement of Islam in Medina as they had tried to do in Mecca, but they were signally repulsed. See n. 352 to iii. 13.

5. With the help of God.
He helps whom He will,[3509]
And He is Exalted in Might,
Most Merciful.

٥- بِنَصْرِ اللّٰهِ ۭ يَنْصُرُ مَنْ يَّشَاۗءُ ۭ
وَهُوَ الْعَزِيْزُ الرَّحِيْمُ ۝

6. (It is) the promise of God.[3510]
Never does God depart
From His promise:
But most men understand not.

٦- وَعْدَ اللّٰهِ ۭ لَا يُخْلِفُ اللّٰهُ وَعْدَهٗ
وَلٰكِنَّ اَكْثَرَ النَّاسِ لَا يَعْلَمُوْنَ ۝

7. They know but the outer[3511]
(Things) in the life
Of this world: but
Of the End of things[3512]
They are heedless.

٧- يَعْلَمُوْنَ ظَاهِرًا مِّنَ الْحَيٰوةِ الدُّنْيَا ښ
وَهُمْ عَنِ الْاٰخِرَةِ هُمْ غٰفِلُوْنَ ۝

8. Do they not reflect
In their own minds?
Not but for just ends[3513]
And for a term appointed,
Did God create the heavens
And the earth, and all
Between them: yet are there
Truly many among men
Who deny the meeting[3514]
With their Lord
(At the Resurrection)!

٨- اَوَلَمْ يَتَفَكَّرُوْا فِيْٓ اَنْفُسِهِمْ ۣ
مَا خَلَقَ اللّٰهُ السَّمٰوٰتِ وَالْاَرْضَ
وَمَا بَيْنَهُمَآ اِلَّا بِالْحَقِّ وَاَجَلٍ مُّسَمًّى ۭ
وَاِنَّ كَثِيْرًا مِّنَ النَّاسِ
بِلِقَاۗئِ رَبِّهِمْ لَكٰفِرُوْنَ ۝

3509. "*Whom He will.*" As explained elsewhere, God's Will or Plan is not arbitrary: it is full of the highest wisdom. His Plan is formed in mercy, so as to safeguard the interests of *all* his creatures, against the selfish aggrandizement of any section of them. And He is able to carry out His Plan in full, and there is no power that can stop or delay His Plan.

3510. The promise refers to the Decision of all things by the Command of God, Who will remove all troubles and difficulties from the path of His righteous Believers, and help them to rejoice over the success of their righteous Cause. This refers to all times and all situations. The righteous should not despair in their darkest moments, for God's help will come. Ordinarily men are puffed up if they score a seeming temporary success against the righteous, and do not realise that God's Will can never be thwarted.

3511. Men are misled by the outward show of things, though the inner reality may be quite different. Many seeming disasters are really godsends if we only understood.

3512. *Ākhirat*: I have usually translated "Hereafter". Here the context is perfectly general, and refers to the End of things or enterprises in history as well as the Hereafter in the technical theological sense.

3513. *Cf.* xv. 85. Here the argument is about the ebb and flow of worldly power, and the next clause is appropriately added, "and for a term appointed". Let not any one who is granted worldly power or advantage run away with the notion that it is permanent. It is definitely limited in the high Purpose of God, which is just and true. And an account will have to be given of it afterwards on a basis of strict personal responsibility.

3514. It is therefore all the more strange that there should be men who not only forget themselves but even deny that there is a return to God or an End or Hereafter, when a full reckoning will be due for this period of probation. They are asked to study past history, as in the next verse.

9. Do they not travel
Through the earth, and see
What was the End
Of those before them?
They were superior to them
In strength: they tilled
The soil and populated it
In greater numbers than these
Have done: there came to them
Their apostles with Clear (Signs),[3515]
(Which they rejected, to their
Own destruction): it was not
God who wronged them, but
They wronged their own souls.

٩- اَوَلَمْ يَسِيْرُوْا فِي الْاَرْضِ
فَيَنْظُرُوْا كَيْفَ كَانَ عَاقِبَةُ الَّذِيْنَ مِنْ
قَبْلِهِمْ كَانُوْٓا اَشَدَّ مِنْهُمْ قُوَّةً
وَّاَثَارُوا الْاَرْضَ وَعَمَرُوْهَآ اَكْثَرَ مِمَّا
عَمَرُوْهَا وَجَآءَتْهُمْ رُسُلُهُمْ بِالْبَيِّنٰتِ
فَمَا كَانَ اللّٰهُ لِيَظْلِمَهُمْ
وَلٰكِنْ كَانُوْٓا اَنْفُسَهُمْ يَظْلِمُوْنَ ۝

10. In the long run
Evil in the extreme[3516]
Will be the End of those
Who do evil; for that
They rejected the Signs
Of God, and held them up
To ridicule.

١٠- ثُمَّ كَانَ عَاقِبَةَ الَّذِيْنَ اَسَآءُوا السُّوْٓاٰى
اَنْ كَذَّبُوْا بِاٰيٰتِ اللّٰهِ
وَكَانُوْا بِهَا يَسْتَهْزِءُوْنَ ۝ ع

SECTION 2.

11. It is God Who begins
(The process of) creation;[3517]
Then repeats it; then
Shall ye be brought back
To Him.

١١- اَللّٰهُ يَبْدَؤُا الْخَلْقَ ثُمَّ يُعِيْدُهٗ
ثُمَّ اِلَيْهِ تُرْجَعُوْنَ ۝

3515. Let not any generation think that it is superior to all that went before it. We may be "heirs to all the ages, in the foremost files of time". That is no reason for arrogance, but on the contrary adds to our responsibility. When we realise what flourishing cities and kingdoms existed before, how they flourished in numbers and prosperity, what chances they were given, and how they perished when they disobeyed the law of God, we shall feel a sense of humility, and see that it was rebellion and self-will that brought them down. God was more than just. He was also merciful. But they brought about their own ruin.

3516. The Arabic superlative feminine, referring to the feminine noun *'Āqibat*, I have translated by "Evil in the extreme". In this life good and evil may seem to be mixed up, and it may be that some things or persons that are evil get what seem to be good rewards or blessings, while the opposite happens to the good. But this is only a temporary appearance. In the long run Evil will have its own evil consequences, multiplied cumulatively. And this, because Evil not only rejected God's Message of Good but laughed at Good and misled others.

3517. Nothing exists of its own accord or fortuitously. It is God Who originates all creation. What appears to be death may be only transformation; for God can and does recreate. And His creative activity is continuous. Our death is but a phenomenal event. What we become after death is the result of a process of recreation by God, Who is both the source and the goal of all things. When we are brought back to him, it will be as conscious and responsible beings, to receive the consequences of our brief life on this earth.

12. On the Day that
The Hour will be established,[3518]
The guilty will be
Struck dumb with despair.

١٢- وَيَوْمَ تَقُومُ السَّاعَةُ
يُبْلِسُ الْمُجْرِمُونَ ○

13. No intercessor will they have
Among their "Partners",[3519]
And they will (themselves)
Reject their "Partners".

١٣- وَلَمْ يَكُن لَّهُم مِّن شُرَكَآئِهِمْ شُفَعَٰٓؤُا۟
وَكَانُوا۟ بِشُرَكَآئِهِمْ كَٰفِرِينَ ○

14. On the Day that
The Hour will be established,—
That Day shall (all men)[3520]
Be sorted out.

١٤- وَيَوْمَ تَقُومُ السَّاعَةُ
يَوْمَئِذٍ يَتَفَرَّقُونَ ○

15. Then those who have believed
And worked righteous deeds,
Shall be made happy
In a Mead of Delight.

١٥- فَأَمَّا الَّذِينَ ءَامَنُوا۟ وَعَمِلُوا۟ الصَّٰلِحَٰتِ
فَهُمْ فِى رَوْضَةٍ يُحْبَرُونَ ○

16. And those who have rejected
Faith and falsely denied
Our Signs and the meeting
Of the Hereafter,—such
Shall be brought forth to
Punishment.

١٦- وَأَمَّا الَّذِينَ كَفَرُوا۟ وَكَذَّبُوا۟ بِـَٔايَٰتِنَا
وَلِقَآئِ الْأَخِرَةِ
فَأُو۟لَٰٓئِكَ فِى الْعَذَابِ مُحْضَرُونَ ○

17. So (give) glory to God,
When ye reach eventide[3521]

١٧- فَسُبْحَٰنَ اللَّهِ حِينَ تُمْسُونَ

3518. *The Hour will be established*: in due time the Hour will come when Judgment will be established, and the seeming disturbance of balance in this world will be redressed. Then the Good will rejoice, and the Guilty, faced with the Realities, will lose all their illusions and be struck dumb with despair.

3519. False worship will then appear in its true colours. Anything to which we offered the worship due to God alone, will vanish instead of being of any help. Indeed the deluded false worshippers, whose eyes will now be opened, will themselves reject their falsehoods, as the Truth will now shine with unquestioned splendour.

3520. In the fullness of time good and evil will all be sorted out and separated. The good will reach their destination of felicity in rich and luscious, well-watered meadows, which stand as the type of all that is fair to see and pleasant to feel. The evil will no longer imagine that they are enjoying good fortune, for the testing time will be over, and the grim reality will stare them in the face. That will be their Punishment.

3521. The special times for God's remembrance are so described as to include all our activities in life,—when we rise early in the morning, and when we go to rest in the evening: when we are in the midst of our work, at the decline of the sun, and in the late afternoon. It may be noted that these are all striking stages in the passage of the sun through our terrestrial day, as well as stages in our daily working lives. On this are based the hours of the five canonical prayers afterwards prescribed in Medina; *viz.* (1) early morning before sunrise (*Fajr*); (2) when the day begins to decline, just after noon (*Ẓuhr*); (3) in the late afternoon, say midway between noon and sunset (*'Aṣr*); and (4) and (5) the two evening prayers, one just after sunset (*Magrib*), and the other after the evening twilight has all faded from the horizon, the hour indicated for rest and sleep (*'Ishā*). *Cf.* xi. 114, nn. 1616-17; xvii. 78-79, n. 2275; xx. 130, n. 2655.

And when ye rise
In the morning;

وَحِيْنَ تُصْبِحُوْنَ ○

18. Yea, To Him be praise,
In the heavens and on earth;
And in the late afternoon
And when the day
Begins to decline.

١٨- وَلَهُ الْحَمْدُ فِى السَّمٰوٰتِ وَالْاَرْضِ
وَعَشِيًّا وَّحِيْنَ تُظْهِرُوْنَ ○

19. It is He Who brings out
The living from the dead,
And brings out the dead[3522]
From the living, and Who
Gives life to the earth[3523]
After it is dead:
And thus shall ye be
Brought out (from the dead).

١٩- يُخْرِجُ الْحَيَّ مِنَ الْمَيِّتِ
وَيُخْرِجُ الْمَيِّتَ مِنَ الْحَيِّ
وَيُحْيِ الْاَرْضَ بَعْدَ مَوْتِهَا ؕ
وَكَذٰلِكَ تُخْرَجُوْنَ ○ ع

C. 181.—God's Signs are many, and so are His mysteries:
(xxx. 20-40.) Yet each does point to His Unity, Goodness,
Power, and Mercy. There is none like
Unto Him. His teaching is one, and men
That split up His standard Religion
Are but following their own lusts. Ungrateful
Are they to give part-worship to others,
When all worship and praise and glory
Are due to Him and Him alone,
In Whom we have our life and being!

SECTION 3.

20. Among His Signs is this,
That He created you[3524]

٢٠- وَمِنْ اٰيٰتِهٖۤ اَنْ خَلَقَكُمْ

3522. *Cf.* x. 31. From dead matter God's creative act produces life and living matter, and even science has not yet been able to explain the mystery of life. Life and living matter again seem to reach maturity and again die, as we see every day. No material thing seems to have perpetual life. But again we see the creative process of God constantly at work, and the cycle of life and death seems to go on.

3523. *Cf.* ii. 164. The earth itself, seemingly so inert, produces vegetable life at once from a single shower of rain, and in various ways sustains animal life. Normally it seems to die in the winter in northern climates, and in a drought everywhere, and the spring revives it in all its glory. Metaphorically many movements, institutions, organisations, seem to die and then to live again, all under the wonderful dispensation of God. So will our personality be revived when we apparently die on this earth, in order to reap the fruit of this our probationary life.

3524. *Cf.* xviii. 37 and n. 2379. In spite of the lowly origin of man's body, God has given him a mind and soul by which he can almost compass the farthest reaches of Time and Space. Is this not enough for a miracle or Sign? From a physical point of view, see how man, a creature of dust, scatters himself over the farthest corners of the earth!

From dust; and then,—
Behold, ye are men
Scattered (far and wide)!

مِنْ تُرَابٍ
ثُمَّ إِذَآ أَنْتُمْ بَشَرٌ تَنْتَشِرُونَ ○

21. And among His Signs
Is this, that He created
For you mates from among [3525]
Yourselves, that ye may
Dwell in tranquillity with them, [3526]
And He has put love
And mercy between your (hearts):
Verily in that are Signs
For those who reflect.

٢١- وَمِنْ ءَايَٰتِهِۦٓ أَنْ خَلَقَ
لَكُمْ مِّنْ أَنْفُسِكُمْ أَزْوَاجًا
لِّتَسْكُنُوٓا إِلَيْهَا
وَجَعَلَ بَيْنَكُمْ مَّوَدَّةً وَّرَحْمَةً ۚ
إِنَّ فِي ذَٰلِكَ لَءَايَٰتٍ لِّقَوْمٍ يَتَفَكَّرُونَ ○

22. And among His Signs
Is the creation of the heavens
And the earth, and the variations [3527]
In your languages
And your colours: verily
In that are Signs
For those who know.

٢٢- وَمِنْ ءَايَٰتِهِۦ خَلْقُ السَّمَٰوَٰتِ
وَالْأَرْضِ وَاخْتِلَافُ أَلْسِنَتِكُمْ
وَأَلْوَانِكُمْ ۚ
إِنَّ فِي ذَٰلِكَ لَءَايَٰتٍ لِّلْعَٰلِمِينَ ○

23. And among His Signs
Is the sleep that ye take
By night and by day, [3528]
And the quest that ye

٢٣- وَمِنْ ءَايَٰتِهِۦ مَنَامُكُم بِالَّيْلِ وَالنَّهَارِ
وَابْتِغَآؤُكُم

3525. This refers to the wonderful mystery of sex. Children arise out of the union of the sexes. And it is always the female sex that brings forth the offspring, whether female or male. And the father is as necessary as the mother for bringing forth daughters.

3526. *Cf.* vii. 189. Unregenerate man is pugnacious in the male sex, but rest and tranquillity are found in the normal relations of a father and mother dwelling together and bringing up a family. A man's chivalry to the opposite sex is natural and God-given. The friendship of two men between each other is quite different in quality and temper from the feeling which unspoilt nature expects as between men and women. There is a special kind of love and tenderness between them. And as woman is the weaker vessel, that tenderness may from a certain aspect be likened to mercy, the protecting kindness which the strong should give to the weak.

3527. The variations in languages and colours may be viewed from the geographical aspect or from the aspect of periods of time. All mankind were created of a single pair of parents; yet they have spread to different countries and climates and developed different languages and different shades of complexions. And yet their basic unity remains unaltered. They feel in the same way, and are all equally under God's care. Then there are the variations in time. Old languages die out and new ones are evolved. New conditions of life and thought are constantly evolving new words and expressions, new syntactical structures, and new modes of pronunciation. Even old races die, and new races are born.

3528. If we consider deeply, sleep and dreams, the refreshment we get from sleep to wakefulness as well as from wakefulness to sleep, as also the state of our thoughts and feelings and sub-conscious self in these conditions, are both wonderful and mysterious. Normally we sleep by night and do our ordinary work "in quest of the Bounty of God" by day. But sleep and rest may come and be necessary by day, and we may have to work by night. And our work for our livelihood may pass by insensible transitions to our work or thought or service of a higher and spiritual kind. These processes suggest a background of things which we know but vaguely, but which are as much miracles as other Signs of God.

(Make for livelihood)
Out of His Bounty : verily
In that are Signs
For those who hearken.[3529]

مِّنْ فَضْلِهٖ
اِنَّ فِىْ ذٰلِكَ لَاٰيٰتٍ لِّقَوْمٍ يَّسْمَعُوْنَ ○

24. And among His Signs,
He shows you the lightning,
By way both of fear[3530]
And of hope, and He sends
Down rain from the sky
And with it gives life to
The earth after it is dead :
Verily in that are Signs
For those who are wise.

٢٤- وَمِنْ اٰيٰتِهٖ يُرِيْكُمُ الْبَرْقَ
خَوْفًا وَّطَمَعًا وَّيُنَزِّلُ
مِنَ السَّمَآءِ مَآءً فَيُحْىٖ بِهِ الْاَرْضَ بَعْدَ
مَوْتِهَا
اِنَّ فِىْ ذٰلِكَ لَاٰيٰتٍ لِّقَوْمٍ يَّعْقِلُوْنَ ○

25. And among His Signs is this,
That heaven and earth
Stand by His Command :[3531]
Then when He calls you,
By a single call, from the earth,
Behold, ye (straightway) come forth.

٢٥- وَمِنْ اٰيٰتِهٖٓ اَنْ تَقُوْمَ السَّمَآءُ وَالْاَرْضُ
بِاَمْرِهٖ ثُمَّ اِذَا دَعَاكُمْ دَعْوَةً مِّنَ الْاَرْضِ
اِذَآ اَنْتُمْ تَخْرُجُوْنَ ○

3529. From verse 20 to verse 25 are mentioned a series of Signs or Miracles, which should awaken our souls and lead us to true Reality if we try to understand God. (1) There is our own origin and destiny, which must necessarily be our subjective starting-point: "I think; therefore I am": no particular exertion of our being is here necessary (xxx. 20). (2) The first beginnings of social life arise through sex and love: see iv. 1, and n. 506; to understand this in all its bearings, we must "reflect" (xxx. 21). (3) The next point is to understand our diversities in speech, colour, etc., arising from differences of climate and external conditions; yet there is unity beneath that diversity, which we shall realise by extended knowledge (xxx. 22). (4) Next we turn to our psychological conditions, sleep, rest, visions, insight, etc.; here we want teaching and guidance, to which we must hearken (xxx. 23). (5) Next, we must approach the higher reaches of spiritual hopes and fears, as symbolised by such subtle forces of nature as lightning and electricity, which may kill the foolish or bring prosperity in its train by rain and abundant harvests; to understand the highest spiritual hopes and fears so symbolised, we want the highest wisdom (xxx. 24). (6) And lastly, we may become so transformed that we rise above all petty, worldly, ephemeral things: God calls to us and we rise, as from our dead selves to a Height which we can only describe as the Heaven of stability: here no human processes serve, for the Call of God Himself has come (xxx. 25-27).

3530. See last note, item (5) *Cf.* xiii. 12. To cowards lightning and thunder appear as terrible forces of nature: lightning seems to kill and destroy where its irresistible progress is not assisted by proper lightning-conductors. But lightning is also a herald of rain-bearing clouds and showers that bring fertility and prosperity in their train. This double aspect is also symbolical of spiritual fears and hopes,—fears lest we may not be found receptive or worthy of the irresistible perspicuous Message of God, and hopes that we may receive it in the right spirit and be blessed by its mighty power of transformation to achieve spiritual well-being. Note that the repetition of the phrase "gives life to the earth after it is dead" connects this verse with verse 19 above: in other words, the Revelation, which we must receive with wisdom and understanding, is a Sign of God's own power and mercy, and is vouchsafed in order to safeguard our own final Future.

3531. In the physical world, the sky and the earth, as we see them, stand unsupported, by the artistry of God. They bear witness to God, and in—that our physical life depends on them—the earth for its produce and the sky for rain, the heat of the sun, and other phenomena of nature—they call to our mind our relation to God Who made them and us. How can we then be so dense as not to realise that our higher Future—our Ma'ād—is bound up with the call and the mercy of God?

26. To Him belongs every being
That is in the heavens
And on earth: all are[3532]
Devoutly obedient to Him.

٢٦- وَلَهُ مَنْ فِي السَّمٰوٰتِ
وَالْأَرْضِ ۚ كُلٌّ لَّهُ قٰنِتُونَ ○

27. It is He Who begins
(The process of) creation;[3533]
Then repeats it; and
For Him it is most easy.
To Him belongs the loftiest[3534]
Similitude (we can think of)
In the heavens and the earth:
For He is Exalted in Might,
Full of wisdom.

٢٧- وَهُوَ الَّذِي يَبْدَؤُا الْخَلْقَ
ثُمَّ يُعِيدُهُ
وَهُوَ أَهْوَنُ عَلَيْهِ ۚ وَلَهُ الْمَثَلُ الْأَعْلٰى
فِي السَّمٰوٰتِ وَالْأَرْضِ ۚ
وَهُوَ الْعَزِيزُ الْحَكِيمُ ○ ع

SECTION 4.

28. He does propound
To you a similitude
From your own (experience):[3535]
Do ye have partners
Among those whom your right hands
Possess, to share as equals
In the wealth We have[3536]

٢٨- ضَرَبَ لَكُم مَّثَلًا مِّنْ أَنفُسِكُمْ ۚ
هَل لَّكُم مِّن مَّا مَلَكَتْ أَيْمَانُكُم
مِّن شُرَكَآءَ فِي مَا رَزَقْنٰكُمْ
فَأَنتُمْ فِيهِ سَوَآءٌ

3532. All nature in Creation not only obeys God, but devoutly obeys Him, *i.e.*, glories in its privilege of service and obedience. Why should we not do likewise? It is part of our original unspoilt nature, and we must respond to it, as all beings do, by their very nature.

3533. *Cf.* xxx. 11 above, where the same phrase began the argument about the beginning and end of all things being with God. This has been illustrated by reference to various Signs in Creation, and now the argument is rounded off with the same phrase.

3534. God's glory and God's attributes are above any names we can give to them. Human language is not adequate to express them. We can only form some idea of them at our present stage by means of Similitudes and Parables. But even so, the highest we can think of falls short of the true Reality. For God is higher and wiser than the highest and wisest we can think of.

3535. One way in which we can get some idea of the things higher than our own plane is to think of Parables and Similitudes drawn from our own lives and experience. And such a Similitude or Parable is offered to us now about false worship. See next note.

3536. God is far higher above His Creation than any, the highest, of His creatures can be above any, the lowest, of His creatures. And yet would a man share his wealth on equal terms with his dependants? Even what he calls his wealth is not really his own, but given by God. It is "his" in common speech by reason merely of certain accidental circumstances. How then can men raise God's creatures to equality with God in worship?

Bestowed on you? Do ye
Fear them as ye fear[3537]
Each other? Thus do We
Explain the Signs in detail
To a people that understand.[3538]

تَخَافُوْنَهُمْ كَخِيْفَتِكُمْ اَنْفُسَكُمْ ؕ
كَذٰلِكَ نُفَصِّلُ الْاٰيٰتِ لِقَوْمٍ يَّعْقِلُوْنَ ○

29. Nay, the wrong-doers (merely)
Follow their own lusts,
Being devoid of knowledge.
But who will guide those
Whom God leaves astray?[3539]
To them there will be
No helpers.

٢٩- بَلِ اتَّبَعَ الَّذِيْنَ ظَلَمُوْٓا اَهْوَآءَهُمْ
بِغَيْرِ عِلْمٍ ۚ
فَمَنْ يَّهْدِيْ مَنْ اَضَلَّ اللّٰهُ ؕ
وَمَا لَهُمْ مِّنْ نّٰصِرِيْنَ ○

30. So set thou thy face
Steadily and truly to the Faith:[3540]
(Establish) God's handiwork according
To the pattern on which
He has made mankind:
No change (let there be)
In the work (wrought)[3541]

٣٠- فَاَقِمْ وَجْهَكَ لِلدِّيْنِ حَنِيْفًا ؕ
فِطْرَتَ اللّٰهِ الَّتِيْ فَطَرَ النَّاسَ عَلَيْهَا ؕ
لَا تَبْدِيْلَ لِخَلْقِ

3537. Men fear each other as equals in a state of society at perpetual warfare. To remove this fear they appoint an authority among themselves—a King or sovereign authority whom they consider just—to preserve them from this fear and give them an established order. But they must obey and revere this authority and depend upon this authority for their own tranquillity and security. Even with their equals there is always the fear of public opinion. But men do not fear, or obey, or revere those who are their slaves or dependents. Man is dependent on God. And God is the Sovereign authority in an infinitely higher sense. He is in no sense dependent on us, but we must honour and revere Him and fear to disobey His Will or His Law. "The fear of God is the beginning of wisdom."

3538. *Cf.* vi. 55, and vii. 32, 174, etc.

3539. The wrong-doers—those who deliberately reject God's guidance and break God's Law—have put themselves out of the region of God's mercy. In this they have put themselves outside the pale of the knowledge of what is for their own good. In such a case they must suffer the consequences of the personal responsibility which flows from the grant of a limited free-will. Who can then guide them or help them?

3540. For *Hanīf* see n. 134 to ii. 135. Here "true" is used in the sense in which we say, "the magnetic needle is true to the north." Those who have been privileged to receive the Truth should never hesitate or swerve, but remain constant, as men who know.

3541. As turned out from the creative hand of God, man is innocent, pure, true, free, inclined to right and virtue, and endued with true understanding about his own position in the Universe and about God's goodness, wisdom, and power. That is his true nature, just as the nature of a lamb is to be gentle and of a horse is to be swift. But man is caught in the meshes of customs, superstitions, selfish desires, and false teaching. This may make him pugnacious, unclean, false, slavish, hankering after what is wrong or forbidden, and deflected from the love of his fellow-men and the pure worship of the One True God. The problem before spiritual Teachers is to cure this crookedness, and to restore human nature to what it should be under the Will of God.

By God : that is
The standard Religion :[3542]
But most among mankind
Understand not.

اللّٰهِ ذٰلِكَ الدِّيْنُ الْقَيِّمُ ۙ
وَلٰكِنَّ اَكْثَرَ النَّاسِ لَا يَعْلَمُوْنَ ۙ ○

31. Turn ye back in repentance[3543]
To Him, and fear Him :
Establish regular prayers,
And be not ye among those
Who join gods with God,—

٣١- مُنِيْبِيْنَ اِلَيْهِ وَاتَّقُوْهُ
وَاَقِيْمُوا الصَّلٰوةَ وَلَا تَكُوْنُوْا مِنَ
الْمُشْرِكِيْنَ ○

32. Those who split up
Their Religion, and become
(Mere) Sects,—each party
Rejoicing in that which[3544]
Is with itself !

٣٢- مِنَ الَّذِيْنَ فَرَّقُوْا دِيْنَهُمْ وَكَانُوْا
شِيَعًا ؕ
كُلُّ حِزْبٍ بِمَا لَدَيْهِمْ فَرِحُوْنَ ○

33. When trouble touches men,
They cry to their Lord,[3545]
Turning back to Him
In repentance : but when
He gives them a taste
Of Mercy as from Himself,
Behold, some of them
Pay part-worship to
Other god's besides their Lord,—

٣٣- وَاِذَا مَسَّ النَّاسَ ضُرٌّ دَعَوْا رَبَّهُمْ
مُنِيْبِيْنَ اِلَيْهِ
ثُمَّ اِذَآ اَذَاقَهُمْ مِّنْهُ رَحْمَةً
اِذَا فَرِيْقٌ مِّنْهُمْ بِرَبِّهِمْ يُشْرِكُوْنَ ۙ ○

34. (As if) to show their ingratitude
For the (favours) We have
Bestowed on them ! Then enjoy
(Your brief day) ; but soon

٣٤- لِيَكْفُرُوْا بِمَآ اٰتَيْنٰهُمْ ؕ
فَتَمَتَّعُوْا ۫ فَسَوْفَ

3542. In ix. 36 I translated *Dīn qaiyim* as "straight usage." Here the meaning is wider, as it includes the whole life, thoughts and desires of man. The "standard Religion," or the Straight Way is thus contrasted with the various human systems that conflict with each other and call themselves separate "religions" or "sects" (see verse 32 below). God's standard Religion is one, as God is One.

3543. "Repentance" does not mean sackcloth and ashes, or putting on a gloomy pessimism. It means giving up disease for health, crookedness (which is abnormal) for the Straight Way, the restoration of our nature as God created it from the falsity introduced by the enticements of Evil. To revert to the simile of the magnetic needle (n. 3540 above), if the needle is held back by obstructions, we must restore its freedom, so that it points true again to the magnetic pole.

3544. A good description of self-satisfied sectarianism as against real Religion. See n. 3542 above.

3545. *Cf.* x. 12. It is trouble, distress, or adversity that makes men realise their helplessness and turns their attention back to the true Source of all goodness and happiness. But when they are shown special Mercy—often more than they deserve—they forget themselves and attribute it to their own cleverness, or to the stars, or to some false ideas to which they pay court and worship, either to the exclusion of God or in addition to the lip-worship which they pay to God. Their action in any case amounts to gross ingratitude ; but in the circumstances it looks as if they had gone out of their way to show ingratitude.

Will ye know (your folly).[3546]

تعلمون ○

35. Or have We sent down
Authority to them, which
Points out to them[3547]
The things to which
They pay part-worship?

٣٥- ام انزلنا عليهم سلطنا
فهو يتكلم بما كانوا به يشركون ○

36. When We give men
A taste of Mercy,[3548]
They exult thereat:
And when some evil
Afflicts them because of
What their (own) hands
Have sent forth, behold,
They are in despair!

٣٦- واذا اذقنا الناس رحمة فرحوا بها
وان تصبهم سيئة
بما قدمت ايديهم
اذا هم يقنطون ○

37. See they not that God
Enlarges the provision and
Restricts it, to whomsoever[3549]
He pleases? Verily in that
Are Signs for those who believe.

٣٧- او لم يروا ان الله يبسط الرزق
لمن يشاء ويقدر
ان في ذلك لايت لقوم يؤمنون ○

38. So give what is due
To kindred, the needy,
And the wayfarer.
That is best for those

٣٨- فات ذا القربى حقه والمسكين و
ابن السبيل ذلك خير للذين

3546. *Cf.* xvi. 54. They are welcome to their fancies and false worship, and to the enjoyment of the pleasures of this Life, but they will soon be disillusioned. Then they will realise the true values of the things they neglected and the things they cultivated.

3547. Their behaviour is exactly as if they were satisfied within themselves that they were entitled or given a licence to worship God and Mammon. In fact the whole thing is their own invention or delusion.

3548. *Cf.* xxx. 33. In that passage the unreasonable behaviour of men in sorrow and in affluence is considered with reference to their attitude to God: in distress they turn to Him, but in prosperity they turn to other things. Here the contrast in the two situations is considered with reference to men's inner psychology: in affluence they are puffed up and unduly elated, and in adversity they lose all heart. Both attitudes are wrong. In prosperity men should realise that it is not their merits that deserve all the Bounty of God, but that it is given out of God's abundant generosity; in adversity they should remember that their suffering is brought on by their own folly and sin, and humbly pray for God's grace and mercy, in order that they may be set on their feet again. For, as the next verse points out, God gives opportunities, gifts, and the good things of life to every one, but in a greater or less measure, and at some time or other, according to His All-Wise Plan, which is the expression of His holy and benevolent Will.

3549. *Cf.* xxviii. 82 and n. 3412. Also see last note. God's grant of certain gifts to some, as well as His withholding of certain gifts from others, are themselves Signs (trials or warnings) to men of faith and understanding.

Who seek the Countenance,[3550]
Of God, and it is they
Who will prosper.[3551]

يُرِيدُونَ وَجْهَ اللَّهِ ۖ
وَأُولَٰئِكَ هُمُ الْمُفْلِحُونَ ○

39. That which ye lay out
For increase through the property
Of (other) people, will have[3552]
No increase with God:
But that which ye lay out
For charity, seeking
The Countenance of God,[3553]
(Will increase): it is
These who will get
A recompense multiplied.

٣٩- وَمَا آتَيْتُمْ مِنْ رِبًا لِيَرْبُوَ فِي أَمْوَالِ
النَّاسِ فَلَا يَرْبُو عِنْدَ اللَّهِ ۖ
وَمَا آتَيْتُمْ مِنْ زَكَاةٍ
تُرِيدُونَ وَجْهَ اللَّهِ
فَأُولَٰئِكَ هُمُ الْمُضْعِفُونَ ○

40. It is God Who has
Created you: further, He has
Provided for your sustenance;
Then He will cause you
To die; and again He will
Give you life. Are there
Any of your (false) "Partners"[3554]
Who can do any single
One of these things?
Glory to Him! and High
Is He above the partners[3555]
They attribute (to Him)!

٤٠- اللَّهُ الَّذِي خَلَقَكُمْ ثُمَّ رَزَقَكُمْ
ثُمَّ يُمِيتُكُمْ ثُمَّ يُحْيِيكُمْ ۖ
هَلْ مِنْ شُرَكَائِكُمْ
مَنْ يَفْعَلُ مِنْ ذَٰلِكُمْ مِنْ شَيْءٍ ۚ
ع سُبْحَانَهُ وَتَعَالَىٰ عَمَّا يُشْرِكُونَ ○

3550. For *Wajh* (Face, Countenance), see n. 114 to ii. 112. Also see vi. 52.

3551. In both this life and the next. See n. 29 to ii. 5.

3552. *Ribā* is any increase sought through illegal means, such as usury, bribery, profiteering, fraudulent trading, etc. See ii. 275-277 and notes 324-327. All unlawful grasping of wealth at other people's expense is condemned. Economic selfishness and many kinds of sharp practices, individual, national, and international, come under this ban. The principle is that any profit which we should seek should be through our own exertions and at our own expense, not through exploiting other people or at their expense, however we may wrap up the process in the spacious phraseology of high finance or City jargon. But we are asked to go beyond this negative precept of avoiding what is wrong. We should show our active love for our neighbour by spending of our own substance or resources or the utilisation of our own talents and opportunities in the service of those who need them. Then our reward or recompense will not be merely what we deserve. It will be multiplied to many times more than our strict account.

3553. Seeking the "Face" or "Countenance" of God, *i.e.*, out of our pure love for the *Dīdār-i-Ilāhi*, the true vision of God's own Self. See also n. 3550 above.

3554. The persons or things or ideas to which we give part-worship, while our whole and exclusive worship is due to God, are the "Partners" we set up. Do we owe our existence to them? Do they sustain our being? Can they take our life or give it back to us? Certainly not. Then how foolish of us to give them part-worship!

3555. *Cf.* x. 18 and similar passages.

C. 182.—The result of Evil is Evil. So
(xxx. 41-60.) Mischief spreads, but God will restore
The balance in the End. He did create
All things pure, and will purge and purify,
As He does the physical world with Winds.
Destruction awaits those that break
His Harmony and Law: it will come when least
Expected. Let the righteous wait and endure
With constancy, for Evil is shaky,
With no faith in itself and no roots,
And is doomed to perish utterly.

SECTION 5.

41. Mischief has appeared
On land and sea because
Of (the meed) that the hands
Of men have earned,[3556]
That (God) may give them
A taste of some of their
Deeds: in order that they[3557]
May turn back (from Evil).

٤١- ظَهَرَ الْفَسَادُ فِي الْبَرِّ وَالْبَحْرِ
بِمَا كَسَبَتْ أَيْدِي النَّاسِ
لِيُذِيقَهُمْ بَعْضَ الَّذِي عَمِلُوا
لَعَلَّهُمْ يَرْجِعُونَ ۝

42. Say: "Travel through the earth
And see what was the End
Of those before (you):
Most of them worshipped[3558]
Others besides God."

٤٢- قُلْ سِيرُوا فِي الْأَرْضِ
فَانْظُرُوا كَيْفَ كَانَ عَاقِبَةُ الَّذِينَ مِنْ
قَبْلُ ۚ كَانَ أَكْثَرُهُمْ مُشْرِكِينَ ۝

43. But set thou thy face
To the right Religion,
Before there come from God
The Day which there is[3559]

٤٣- فَأَقِمْ وَجْهَكَ لِلدِّينِ الْقَيِّمِ
مِنْ قَبْلِ أَنْ يَأْتِيَ يَوْمٌ لَا مَرَدَّ لَهُ

3556. God's Creation was pure and good in itself. All the mischief or corruption was introduced by Evil, *viz.*, arrogance, selfishness, etc. See n. 3541 to xxx. 30 above. As soon as the mischief has come in, God's mercy and goodness step in to stop it. The consequences of Evil must be evil, and this should be shown in such partial punishment as "the hands of men have earned," so that it may be a warning for the future and an invitation to enter the door of repentance.

3557. The ultimate object of God's justice and punishment is to reclaim man from Evil, and to restore him to the pristine purity and innocence in which he was created. The Evil introduced by his possession of a limited free-will should be eliminated by the education and purification of man's own will. For, with his will and motives purified, he is capable of much greater heights than a creature not endowed with any free-will.

3558. If you contemplate history and past experience (including spiritual experience), you will find that evil and corruption tended to destroy themselves, because they had false idols for worship, false standards of conduct, and false goals of desire.

3559. We should recover the balance that has been upset by Evil and Falsehood before it is too late. For a Day will surely come when true values will be restored and all falsehood and evil will be destroyed. Nothing but repentance and amendment can avert the consequences of Evil. When the Day actually comes, repentance will be too late: for the impassable barrier between Evil and Good will have been fixed, and the chance of return to God's pattern will have been lost.

No chance of averting :
On that Day shall men
Be divided (in two).[3560]

مِنَ اللّٰهِ يَوْمَئِذٍ يَّصَّدَّعُوْنَ ○

44. Those who reject Faith
Will suffer from that rejection :
And those who work righteousness
Will spread their couch
(Of repose) for themselves
(In heaven) :

٤٤- مَنْ كَفَرَ فَعَلَيْهِ كُفْرُهٗ ۚ
وَمَنْ عَمِلَ صَالِحًا
فَلِاَنْفُسِهِمْ يَمْهَدُوْنَ ○

45. That He may reward those
Who believe and work righteous
Deeds, out of His Bounty.[3561]
For He loves not those
Who reject Faith.[3562]

٤٥- لِيَجْزِيَ الَّذِيْنَ اٰمَنُوْا وَعَمِلُوا الصّٰلِحٰتِ
مِنْ فَضْلِهٖ ؕ
اِنَّهٗ لَا يُحِبُّ الْكٰفِرِيْنَ ○

46. Among His Signs is this,[3563]
That He sends the Winds,
As heralds of Glad Tidings,
Giving you a taste
Of His (Grace and) Mercy,—[3564]
That the ships may sail
(Majestically) by His Command
And that ye may seek[3565]

٤٦- وَمِنْ اٰيٰتِهٖٓ اَنْ يُّرْسِلَ الرِّيَاحَ
مُبَشِّرٰتٍ
وَّلِيُذِيْقَكُمْ مِّنْ رَّحْمَتِهٖ
وَلِتَجْرِيَ الْفُلْكُ بِاَمْرِهٖ وَلِتَبْتَغُوْا

3560. The sharp division will then have been accomplished between the unfortunate ones who rejected Truth and Faith and will suffer for their rejection, and the righteous who will attain Peace and Salvation: see next verse. Note that the state of the Blessed will not be merely a passive state. They will actively earn and contribute to their own happiness: "they will spread their couch of repose for themselves."

3561. Though the repose and bliss will have been won by the righteous by their own efforts, it must not be supposed that their own merits were equal to the reward they will earn. What they will get will be due to the infinite Grace and Bounty of God.

3562. In form this clause is (here as elsewhere) negative, but it has a positive meaning: God loves those who have faith and trust in Him, and will, out of His Grace and Bounty, reward them in abundant measure.

3563. The theme of God's artistry in the physical and the spiritual world was placed before us above in **xxx**. 20-27. Then, in verses 28-40, we were shown how man and nature were pure as they came out of the hand of God, and how we must restore this purity in order to fulfil the Will and Plan of God. Now we are told how the restorative and purifying agencies are sent by God Himself,—in both the physical and the spiritual world.

3564. *Cf.* vii 57 and n. 1036 and xxv. 48 and n. 3104.

3565. In the physical world, the winds not only cool and purify the air, and bring the blessings of rain, which fertilises the soil, but they help international commerce and intercourse among men through sea-ways and now by air-ways. Those who know how to take advantage of these blessings of God prosper and rejoice, while those who ignore or fail to understand these Signs perish in storms. So in the spiritual world: heralds of glad tidings were sent by God in the shape of apostles: those who profited by their Message prospered in spiritual gain, and those who ignored or opposed the Clear Signs perished spiritually: see next verse.

Of His Bounty : in order
That ye may be grateful.

مِنْ فَضْلِهٖ وَلَعَلَّكُمْ تَشْكُرُوْنَ ○

47. We did indeed send,
Before thee, apostles
To their (respective) peoples,
And they came to them
With Clear Signs : then,
To those who transgressed,
We meted out Retribution :
And it was due from us
To aid those who believed.

٤٧- وَلَقَدْ اَرْسَلْنَا مِنْ قَبْلِكَ رُسُلًا اِلٰى
قَوْمِهِمْ
فَجَآءُوْهُمْ بِالْبَيِّنٰتِ
فَانْتَقَمْنَا مِنَ الَّذِيْنَ اَجْرَمُوْا ؕ
وَكَانَ حَقًّا عَلَيْنَا نَصْرُ الْمُؤْمِنِيْنَ ○

48. It is God Who sends
The Winds, and they raise [3566]
The Clouds : then does He
Spread them in the sky
As He wills, and break them
Into fragments, until thou seest
Rain-drops issue from the midst
Thereof : then when He has
Made them reach such [3567]
Of His servants as He wills,
Behold, they do rejoice !—

٤٨- اَللّٰهُ الَّذِىْ يُرْسِلُ الرِّيٰحَ فَتُثِيْرُ سَحَابًا
فَيَبْسُطُهٗ فِى السَّمَآءِ
كَيْفَ يَشَآءُ وَيَجْعَلُهٗ كِسَفًا
فَتَرَى الْوَدْقَ يَخْرُجُ مِنْ خِلٰلِهٖ ۚ
فَاِذَآ اَصَابَ بِهٖ مَنْ يَّشَآءُ مِنْ عِبَادِهٖٓ
اِذَا هُمْ يَسْتَبْشِرُوْنَ ○

49. Even though, before they received
(The rain)—just before this—
They were dumb with despair !

٤٩- وَاِنْ كَانُوْا مِنْ قَبْلِ اَنْ يُّنَزَّلَ
عَلَيْهِمْ مِّنْ قَبْلِهٖ لَمُبْلِسِيْنَ ○

50. Then contemplate (O man !)
The memorials of God's Mercy !—
How He gives life [3568]
To the earth after
Its death : verily the Same
Will give life to the men

٥٠- فَانْظُرْ اِلٰٓى اٰثٰرِ رَحْمَتِ اللّٰهِ
كَيْفَ يُحْىِ الْاَرْضَ بَعْدَ مَوْتِهَا ؕ
اِنَّ ذٰلِكَ لَمُحْىِ

3566. Again the Parable of the Winds is presented from another aspect, both physical and spiritual. In the physical world, see their play with the Clouds ; how they suck up the moisture from terrestrial water, carry it about in dark clouds as needed, and break it up with rain as needed. So God's wonderful Grace draws up men's spiritual aspirations from the most unlikely places and suspends them as dark mysteries, according to His holy Will and Plan ; and when His Message reaches the hearts of men even in the smallest fragments, how its recipients rejoice, even though before it, they were in utter despair !

3567. See last note.

3568. After the two Parables about the purifying action of the Winds and their fertilising action, we now have the Parable of the earth that dies in winter or drought and lives again in spring or rain, by God's Grace : so in the spiritual sphere, man may be dead and may live again by the Breath of God and His Mercy if he will only place himself in God's hands.

Who are dead: for He
Has power over all things.

الْمَوْتَىٰ ۚ وَهُوَ عَلَىٰ كُلِّ شَيْءٍ قَدِيرٌ ○

51. And if We (but) send
A Wind from which [3569]
They see (their tilth)
Turn yellow,—behold,
They become, thereafter,
Ungrateful (Unbelievers)!

٥١- وَلَئِنْ أَرْسَلْنَا رِيحًا
فَرَأَوْهُ مُصْفَرًّا لَّظَلُّوا مِن بَعْدِهِ
يَكْفُرُونَ ○

52. So verily thou canst not
Make the dead to hear, [3570]
Nor canst thou make
The deaf to hear
The call, when they show
Their backs and turn away.

٥٢- فَإِنَّكَ لَا تُسْمِعُ الْمَوْتَىٰ
وَلَا تُسْمِعُ الصُّمَّ الدُّعَاءَ
إِذَا وَلَّوْا مُدْبِرِينَ ○

53. Nor canst thou lead back
The blind from their straying: [3571]
Only those wilt thou make
To hear, who believe
In Our Signs and submit
(Their wills in Islam).

٥٣- وَمَا أَنتَ بِهَادِ الْعُمْيِ عَن ضَلَالَتِهِمْ ۖ
إِن تُسْمِعُ إِلَّا مَن يُؤْمِنُ
بِآيَاتِنَا فَهُم مُّسْلِمُونَ ○ ع

SECTION 6.

54. It is God Who
Created you in a state
Of (helpless) weakness, then
Gave (you) strength after weakness,

٥٤- اللَّهُ الَّذِي خَلَقَكُم مِّن ضَعْفٍ
ثُمَّ جَعَلَ مِن بَعْدِ ضَعْفٍ قُوَّةً

3569. Another Parable from the forces of nature. We saw how the Winds gladdened, vivified, and enriched those who utilised them in the right spirit. But a wind might be destructive to tilth in certain circumstances: so the blessings of God may—by the wrong-doers resisting and blaspheming—bring punishment to the wrong-doers. Instead of taking the punishment in the right spirit - in the spirit in which Believers of God take their misfortunes,—the Unbelievers curse and deepen their sin!

3570. The marvels of God's creation can be realised in a general way by every one who has a disposition to allow such knowledge to penetrate his mind. But if men, out of perversity, kill the very faculties which God has given them, how can they then understand? Besides the men who deaden their spiritual sense, there are men who may be likened to the deaf, who lack one faculty but to whom an appeal can be made through other faculties, such as the sense of sight; but if they turn their backs and refuse to be instructed at all, how can the Truth reach them?

3571. See last note. Then there is the case of men about whom the saying holds true, that none are so blind as those who *will* not see. They *prefer* to stray in paths of wrong and of sense-pleasures. How can they be guided in any way? The only persons who gain by spiritual teaching are those who bring a mind to it—who believe and submit their wills to God's Will. This is the central doctrine of Islam.

Then, after strength, gave (you)
Weakness and a hoary head :[3572]
He creates as He wills,
And it is He Who has
All knowledge and power.

ثُمَّ جَعَلَ مِنْۢ بَعْدِ قُوَّةٍ ضُعْفًا وَّشَيْبَةً ۚ
يَخْلُقُ مَا يَشَآءُ ۚ وَهُوَ الْعَلِيْمُ الْقَدِيْرُ ○

55. On the Day that
The Hour (of reckoning)
Will be established,[3573]
The transgressors will swear
That they tarried not
But an hour : thus were
They used to being deluded !

٥٥ - وَيَوْمَ تَقُوْمُ السَّاعَةُ يُقْسِمُ الْمُجْرِمُوْنَ ۙ
مَا لَبِثُوْا غَيْرَ سَاعَةٍ ۚ
كَذٰلِكَ كَانُوْا يُؤْفَكُوْنَ ○

56. But those endued with knowledge
And faith will say :
" Indeed ye did tarry,
Within God's Decree,
To the Day of Resurrection,
And this is the Day[3574]
Of Resurrection : but ye—
Ye were not aware ! "

٥٦ - وَقَالَ الَّذِيْنَ اُوْتُوا الْعِلْمَ وَالْاِيْمَانَ
لَقَدْ لَبِثْتُمْ فِيْ كِتٰبِ اللّٰهِ اِلٰى يَوْمِ الْبَعْثِ ۫
فَهٰذَا يَوْمُ الْبَعْثِ
وَلٰكِنَّكُمْ كُنْتُمْ لَا تَعْلَمُوْنَ ○

57. So on that Day no excuse
Of theirs will
Avail the Transgressors,[3575]
Nor will they be invited (then)
To seek grace (by repentance).

٥٧ - فَيَوْمَئِذٍ لَّا يَنْفَعُ الَّذِيْنَ ظَلَمُوْا مَعْذِرَتُهُمْ
وَلَا هُمْ يُسْتَعْتَبُوْنَ ○

3572. What was said before about the people who make God's teaching "of none effect" does not mean that Evil will defeat Good. On the contrary we are asked to contemplate the mysteries of God's wisdom with another Parable. In our physical life we see how strength is evolved out of weakness and weakness out of strength. The helpless babe becomes a lusty man in the pride of his manhood, and then sinks to a feeble old age : and yet there is wisdom in all these stages in the Universal Plan. So God carries out His Plan in the spiritual world "as He wills", *i.e.*, according to His Will and Plan, and none can gainsay it. And His Plan is wise and can never be frustrated.

3573. Whatever the seeming inequalities may be now—when the good appear to be weak and the strong seem to oppress—will be removed when the balance will be finally redressed. That will happen in good time,—indeed so quickly that the Transgressors will be taken by surprise. They were deluded by the fact that what they took to be their triumph or their freedom to do what they liked was only a reprieve, a "Term Appointed", in which they could repent and amend and get God's Mercy. Failing this, they will then be up against the Penalties which they thought they had evaded or defied.

3574. The men of knowledge and faith knew all along of the true values—of the things of this ephemeral life and the things that will endure and face them at the End,—unlike the wrong-doers who were content with falsehoods and were taken by surprise, like ignorant men, when they faced the Realities.

3575. It will be no use for those who deliberately rejected the clearest warnings in God's Message to say : "Oh we did not realise this!" The excuse will be false, and it would be unreasonable to suppose that they would then be asked to seek Grace by repentance. It will then be too late.

58. Verily We have propounded
For men, in this Qur-ān
Every kind of Parable:
But if thou bring to them
Any Sign, the Unbelievers[3576]
Are sure to say, "Ye
Do nothing but talk vanities."

٥٨- وَلَقَدْ ضَرَبْنَا لِلنَّاسِ فِي هٰذَا
الْقُرْاٰنِ مِنْ كُلِّ مَثَلٍ ۭ
وَلَئِنْ جِئْتَهُمْ بِاٰيَةٍ لَّيَقُوْلَنَّ الَّذِيْنَ
كَفَرُوْٓا اِنْ اَنْتُمْ اِلَّا مُبْطِلُوْنَ ۝

59. Thus does God seal up[3577]
The hearts of those
Who understand not.

٥٩- كَذٰلِكَ يَطْبَعُ اللّٰهُ عَلٰي قُلُوْبِ الَّذِيْنَ
لَا يَعْلَمُوْنَ ۝

60. So patiently persevere: for
Verily the promise of God
Is true: nor let those[3578]
Shake thy firmness, who have
(Themselves) no certainty of faith.

٦٠- فَاصْبِرْ اِنَّ وَعْدَ اللّٰهِ حَقٌّ
وَّلَا يَسْتَخِفَّنَّكَ الَّذِيْنَ لَا يُوْقِنُوْنَ ۝ ع

3576. Things of the highest moment have been explained in the Qur-ān from various points of view, as in this Sūra itself, by means of parables and similitudes drawn from nature and from our ordinary daily life. But whatever the explanation, however convincing it may be to men who earnestly seek after Truth, those who deliberately turn their backs to Truth can find nothing convincing. In their eyes the explanations are mere "vain talk" or false arguments.

3577. When an attitude of obstinate resistance to Truth is adopted, the natural consequence (by God's Law) is that the heart and mind get more and more hardened with every act of deliberate rejection. It becomes more and more impervious to the reception of Truth, just as a sealed envelope is unable to receive any further letter or message after it is sealed. *Cf.* also ii. 7 and n. 31.

3578. The man of God does not slacken in his efforts or feel discouraged because the Unbelievers laugh at him or persecute him or even seem to succeed in blocking his Message. He has firm faith, and he knows that God will finally establish His Truth. He goes on in his divinely entrusted task, with patience and perseverance, which must win against the levity of his opponents, who have no faith or certainty at all to sustain them.

APPENDIX X.

First Contact of Islam with World Movements.

The contemporary Roman and Persian Empires (see xxx. 2-7 and notes).

The conflict between the Byzantine Emperor Heraclius and the Persian King Khusrau Parwīz (Chosroes II) is referred to in Sūra xxx. (*Rūm*). It will therefore be convenient now to review very briefly the relations of these two great empires and the way in which they gradually decayed before the rising sun of Islam. The story has not only a political significance, but a deep spiritual significance in world history.

2. If we take the Byzantine Empire as a continuation of the Empire that grew out of the Roman Republic, the first conflict took place in B.C. 53, when the Consul Crassus (famous for his riches) was defeated in his fight with the Parthians. If we go back further, to the time of the Greek City States, we can refer back to the invasion of Greece by Xerxes in B.C. 480-479 and the effective repulse of that invasion by sea and land by the united co-operation of the Greek States. The Persian Empire in those days extended to the western (Mediterranean) coast of Asia Minor. But as it included the Greek cities of Asia Minor, there was constant intercourse in war and peace between Persia and the Hellenic (Greek) world. The cities in Greece proper had their own rivalries and jealousies, and Greek cities or parties often invoked the aid of the Great King (Shahinshah of Persia) against their opponents. By the Peace of Antalcidas, B.C. 387, Persia became practically the suzerain power of Greece. This was under the Achæmenian Dynasty of Persia.

3. Then came the rise of Macedonia and Alexander's conquest of the Persian Empire (B.C. 330). This spread the Hellenic influence as far east as Central Asia, and as far south as Syria (including Palestine), Egypt, and Northern Africa generally. Rome in its expansion westwards reached the Atlantic, and in its expansion eastwards absorbed the territories of Alexander's successors, and became the mistress of all countries with a Mediterranean sea-coast. The nations of the Roman Empire "insensibly melted away into the Roman name and people" (Gibbon, chap. ii).

4. Meanwhile there were native forces in Persia which asserted themselves and established (A.D. 10) the Dynasty of the Arsacids (*Ashkāniān*). This was mainly the outcome of a revolt against Hellenism, and its spear-point was in Parthia. The Arsacids won back Persia proper, and established the western boundary of Persia in a line drawn roughly from the eastern end of the Black Sea southwards to the Euphrates at a point north-east of Palmyra. This would include the region of the Caucasus (excluding the Black Sea coast) and Armenia and Lower Mesopotamia, in the Persian Empire. And this was the normal boundary between Persia and the Roman Empire until the Islamic Empire wiped out the old Monarchy of Persia and

a great part of the Byzantine Empire, and annexed Egypt, Palestine, Syria, and gradually Asia Minor, finally extinguishing the whole of the Byzantine Empire.

5. Another stage in Persian history was reached when the Arsacids were overthrown and the Sāsānians came into power under Ardashīr I, A.D. 225. The Sāsānian Empire was in a sense a continuation of the Achæmenian Empire, and was a reaction against the corruptions of the Zoroastrian religion which had crept in under the Parthian Dynasty of the Arsacids. But the religious reforms were only partial. There was some interaction between Christianity and the Zoroastrian religion. For example, the great mystic Mānī, who was a painter as well as a religious leader, founded the sect of Manichæism. He flourished in the reign of Shāpūr I (A.D. 241-272) and seems to have preached a form of Gnostic faith, in which Alexandrian philosophy was mixed with Christian doctrine and the old Persian belief in the dual principle of Good and Evil. The Sāsānians failed to purify religion and only adhered to fire-worship as the chief feature of their cult. In manners and morals they succumbed to the vices of arrogance, luxury, sensuality, and monopoly of power and privilege, which it is the office of Religion to denounce and root out. That office was performed by Islam.

6. When the seat of the Roman Empire was transferred to Constantinople (Byzantium) in the time of Constantine (A.D. 330), the conflict between Rome and Persia became more and more frequent. The true Peninsula of Arabia was never conquered either by Rome or by Persia, although its outlying parts were absorbed in either the one or the other at various times. It is interesting to notice that the Roman Emperor Philip (A.D. 244-249) was a born Arab and that the architecture of the Nabatæans in the city of Petra and in Ḥijr shows a mixture of Roman, Greek, Egyptian, and indigenous Arab cultures.

7. Arabia received the cultural influences of Persia and the Byzantine Empire, but was a silent spectator of their conflicts until Islam was brought into the main currents of world politics.

8. The Yemen coast of Arabia, which was easily accessible by sea to Persia, was the battle-ground between the Persian Empire and the Abyssinian Empire just across the Red Sea. Abyssinia and Arabia had had cultural and political relations for many centuries. Amharic, the ruling language of Abyssinia, is closely allied to Arabic, and the Amharic people went as colonists and conquerors from Arabia through Yemen. Shortly before the birth of holy Prophet, Abyssinia had been in occupation of Yemen for some time, having displaced a Jewish dynasty. The Abyssinians professed the Christian religion, and although their Church was doctrinally separate from the Byzantine Church, there was a great deal of sympathy between the Byzantines and the Abyssinians on account of their common Christian religion. One of the Abyssinian viceroys in Yemen was Abraha, who conceived the design of destroying the Temple at Mecca. He led an expedition, in which elephants formed a conspicuous feature, to invade Mecca and destroy the Ka'ba. He met a disastrous repulse, which is referred to in the Qur-ān (Sūra cv.). This event was in the year of the Prophet's birth, and marks the beginning of the great conflict which enabled Arabia eventually to obtain a leading place among the nations of the

world. The year usually given for the Prophet's birth is 570 A.D., though the date must be taken as only approximate, being the middle figure between 569 and 571, the extreme possible limits. The Abyssinians having been overthrown, the Persians were established in Yemen, and their power lasted there until about the 7th year of the Hijra (approximately 628 A.D.), when Yemen accepted Islam.

9. The outstanding event in Byzantine history in the 6th century was the reign of Justinian (527-565) and in Persian history the reign of Anaushīrwān (531-579). Justinian is well-known for his great victories in Africa and for the great Digest he made of Roman Law and Jurisprudence. In spite of the scandalous life of his queen Theodora, he occupies an honourable place in the history of the Roman Empire. Anaushīrwān is known in Persian history as the "Just King". They were contemporary rulers for a period of 34 years. In their time the Roman and the Persian Empires were in close contact both in peace and war. Anaushīrwān just missed being adopted by the Roman Emperor. If the adoption had come off, he would have become one of the claimants to the Byzantine throne. He invaded Syria and destroyed the important Christian city of Antioch in 540-541. It was only the able defence of Belisarius, the Roman general, which saved the Roman Empire from further disasters in the east. On the other hand the Turanian Avars, driven in front of the Turks, had begun the invasion of Constantinople from the western side. Justinian also made an alliance with the Abyssinians as a Christian nation, and the Abyssinians and the Persians came into conflict in Yemen. Thus world conditions were hemming in Arabia on all sides. It was Islam that not only saved Arabia but enabled it to expand and to play a prominent part in world history after the annihilation of the Persian Empire and the partial destruction of the Byzantine Empire.

10. The sixth century of the Christian era and the first half of the seventh century were indeed a marvellous period in the world's history. Great events and transformations were taking place throughout the then known world. We have referred to the Roman Empire and the Persian Empire which dominated the civilised portions of Europe, Africa and Western Asia. The only two other countries of note in history in those days were India and China. In India there was the glorious period of Harsha Vardhana (606-647 A.D.), in which art, science, and literature flourished, political power was on a healthy basis, and religious enquiry was bringing India and China into close relationship. The famous Chinese Buddhist traveller Yuang-Chwang (or Yüang-Tsang or Hsüan-Tsang) perfomed his pious pilgrimage to India in 629-45. In China the glorious T'ang Dynasty was established in 618. The Chinese art of that Dynasty led the world. In political power Chinese extended from the Pacific in the east to the Persian Gulf on the west. There was unity and peace, and China—hitherto more or less isolated—received ambassadors from Persia, Constantinople, Magadha, and Nepal, in 643. But all this pomp and glitter had in it the seeds of decay. Persia and Byzantium collapsed in the next generation. India was in chaos after Harsha's death. The Chinese Empire could not long remain free from the "Barbarians": the Great Wall, begun in the third century B.C., was soon to be out of date. By about 683 the Khitans from the north-west and the Tibetans from the south were molesting China. The Germans, the Goths

and the Vandals were pressing further and further into the Roman Empire. From Asia the Avars and the Turks were pressing both on the Romans and the Persians, and sometimes playing off the one against the other. The simpler and less sophisticated nations, with their ruder but more genuine virtues, were gaining ground. Into all that welter came the Message of Islam, to show up, as by galvanic action, the false from the true, the empty from the eternal, the decrepit and corrupt from the vigorous and pure. The ground of History was being prepared for the New Birth in Religion.

11. Anaushīrwān was succeeded on the Persian throne by an unworthy son Hurmuz (579-590). Had it not been for the talents of his able General Bahrām, his Empire would have been ruined by the invasions of the Turks on one side and of the Romans on the other. Eventually Bahrām rebelled, and Hurmuz was deposed and killed. His son Khusrau Parwīz (Chosroes II) took refuge with the Byzantine Emperor Maurice, who practically adopted him as a son and restored him to the Persian throne with Roman arms. Khusrau reigned over Persia from 590 to 628. It was to him that the holy Prophet addressed one of his letters, inviting him to Islam towards the end of his life. It is not certain whether the letter was actually delivered to him or to his successor, as it is not easy to calculate precisely synchronous dates of the Christian era with those of the earliest years of the Hijrī era.

12. In Arabic and Persian records the term *Kisrā* refers usually to Khusrau Parwīz (Chosroes II) and sometimes to Khusrau Anaushīrwān (Chosroes I), while the term Khusrau is usually treated as generic,—as the title of the Kings of Persia generally. But this is by no means always the case. " Kisrā " is an Arabic form of " Khusrau ". The name of Anaushīrwān has been shortened from the time of Firdausī onwards to Nūshīrwān. The Pehlevi form is Anoshek-ruwān, " of immortal soul ".

13. The Roman Emperor Maurice (582-602) had a mutiny in his army, and his capital revolted against him. The army chose a simple centurion called Phocas as Emperor and executed Maurice himself. The usurper Phocas ruled from 602 to 610, but his tyranny soon disgusted the Empire. Heraclius, the governor (exarch) of a distant province in Africa, raised the standard of rebellion, and his young son, also called Heraclius, was sent to Constantinople to depose Phocas and assume the reins of power. It was this younger Heraclius, who ascended the throne of Constantinople in 610 and ruled till 642, who figures in Muslim history as *Hiraql*.

14. Khusrau Parwīz called himself the son of the Emperor Maurice. During his refuge at Constantinople he had married a Byzantine wife. In Nizāmī's Romance she is known as Maryam. According to some historians she was a daughter of the Emperor Maurice, but Gibbon throws doubt on that relationship. In any case he used the resources of the Persian Empire to fight the usurper Phocas. He invaded the Byzantine Empire in 603. The war between the Persians and the Romans became a national war and continued after the fall of Phocas in 610. The Persians had sweeping victories, and conquered Aleppo, Antioch, and the chief Syrian cities, including Damascus, in 611. Jerusalem fell to their arms in 614-15, just 8 to 7 years before the sacred Hijrat. The city was burnt and pillaged, the Christians were massacred, the churches were burnt, the burial-place of Christ was

itself insulted, and many relics, including the "true Cross" on which the Christians believed that Christ had been curcified, were carried away to Persia. The priests of the Persian religion celebrated an exultant triumph over the priests of Christ. In this pillage and massacre the Persians were assisted by crowds of Jews, who were discontented with the Christian domination, and the Pagan Arabs to whom any opportunity of plunder and destruction was in itself welcome. It is probably this striking event—this victory of the Persians over the Roman Empire—which is referred to in Sūra XXX (*Rūm*) of the Qur-ān. The Pagan Arabs naturally sided with the Persians in their destructive zeal, and thought that the destruction of the Christian power of Rome would also mean a setback to the Message of the Prophet, the true successor of Jesus. For our holy Prophet had already begun his mission and the promulgation of God's Revelation in A.D. 610. While the whole world believed that the Roman Empire was being killed by Persia, it was revealed to him that the Persian victory was short-lived and that within a period of a few years the Romans would conquer again and deal a deadly blow at the Persians. The Pagan Arabs, who were then persecuting the holy Prophet in Mecca, hoped that their persecution would destroy the holy Prophet's new Revelation. In fact both their persecution and the deadly blows aimed by the Persians and the Romans at each other were instruments in God's hands for producing those conditions which made Islam thrive and increase until it became the predominant power in the world.

15. The Persian flood of conquest did not stop with the conquest of Jerusalem. It went on to Egypt, which was also conquered and annexed to the Persian Empire in 616. The Persian occupation reached as far as Tripoli in North Africa. At the same time another Persian army ravaged Asia Minor and reached right up to the gates of Constantinople. Not only the Jews and Pagan Arabs, but the various Christian sects which had been persecuted as heretics by the Romans, joined in the fray and helped the Persians. The condition of Heraclius became indeed pitiable. With all these calamities, he had to deal with the Avars who were attacking from the other side of Constantinople, which was practically in a state of siege. Famine and pestilence added to the horrors of the situation.

16. In these desperate circumstances Heraclius conceived a brilliant plan. He knew that the Persians were weak in sea power. He used his sea power to attack them in the rear. In 622 (the year of the Hijra) he transported his army by sea through the Ægean Sea to the bay just south of the Taurus Mountains. He fought a decisive battle with the Persians at Issus, in the same plain in which Alexander the Great had defeated the Persians of his day in his famous march to Syria and Egypt. The Persians were taken by surprise and routed. But they had still a large force in Asia Minor, which they could have brought into play against the Romans if Heraclius had not made another and equally unexpected dash by sea from the north. He returned to Constantinople by sea, made a treaty with the Avars, and with their help kept the Persians at bay round the capital. Then he led three campaigns, in 623, 624 and 625, along the southern shore of the Black Sea and took the Persians again in the rear in the region round Trebizond and Kars. Through Armenia he penetrated into Persia and got into Mesopotamia. He was now in a position to strike at the very heart of the Persian Empire. A decisive battle was fought on the Tigris near the city of Mosul in December 627. Before this

battle, however, he had taken care to get the alliance of the Turks and with their help to relieve Constantinople in 626 against the Persians and the treacherous Avars who had then joined the Persians.

17. Heraclius celebrated his triumph in Constantinople in March 628. Peace was then made between the two Empires on the basis of the *status quo ante*. Heraclius, in pursuance of a vow he had made, went south in the autumn to Emessa (Ḥimṣ) and from there marched on foot to Jerusalem to celebrate his victories, and restore to its place the holy Cross which had been carried away by the Persians and was returned to the Emperor as a condition of peace. Heraclius's route was strewn with costly carpets, and he thought that the final deliverance had come for his people and his empire Either on the way, or in Jerusalem, he met a messenger from the holy Prophet, carrying a letter inviting him to the True Faith as renewed in the living Apostle of the age. He apparently received the messenger with courtesy. But he did not realise the full import of the new World which was being shaped according to God's plans, and the future that was opening out through the new Revelation. Perhaps in his heart he felt impressed by the story which he heard from the Arabs about the holy Prophet, but the apparent grandeur of his empire and the pride of his people prevented him from openly accepting the renewed Message of God. He caused a search to be made for any Arab who was sufficiently acquainted with the Prophet to tell him something about him. Abū Sufyān was then trading in a caravan in Syria. He was a cousin of the Prophet, and belonged to the Umaiya branch of the family. He was sent for to Jerusalem (Ælia Capitolina).

18. When Abū Sufyān was called to the presence of Heraclius, the Emperor questioned him closely about this new Prophet. Abū Sufyān himself was at that time outside Islam and really an enemy of the Prophet and of his Message. Yet the story he told—of the truth and the sincerity of the holy Apostle, of the way in which the poor and the lowly flocked to him, of the wonderful increase of his power and spiritual influence, and the way in which people who had once received the Light never got disillusioned or went back to their life of ignorance, and above all the integrity with which he kept all his covenants—made a favourable impression on the mind of Heraclius. That story is told in dramatic detail by Bukhārī and other Arabian writers.

19. The relations of the Persian Monarch with Islam were different. He—either Khusrau Parwīz or his successor—received the holy Apostle's messenger with contumely and tore up his letter. "So will his kingdom be torn up," said the holy Apostle when the news reached him. The Persian Monarch ordered his Governor in Yemen to go and arrest the man who had so far forgotten himself as to address the grandson of Anaushīrwān on equal terms. When the Persian Governor tried to carry out his Monarch's command, the result was quite different from what the great Persian King of Kings had expected. His agent accepted the truth of Islam, and Yemen was lost as a province to the Persian Empire and became a portion of the new Muslim State. Khusrau Parwīz died in February 628. He had been deposed and imprisoned by his own cruel and undutiful son, who reigned only for a year and a half. There were nine candidates for the Persian throne in the remaining four years. Anarchy reigned supreme in the Sāsānian Empire, until the dynasty

was extinguished by the Muslim victory at the battle of Madāin in 637. The great and glorious Persian monarchy, full of pride and ambition, came to an ignominious end, and a new chapter opened for Persia under the banner of Islam.

20. The Roman Empire itself began to shrink gradually, loosing its territory, not to Persia, but to the new Muslim Power which absorbed both the ancient Empires. This Power arose in its vigour to proclaim a new and purified creed to the whole world. Already in the last seven years of Heraclius's reign (635-642) several of the provinces nearest to Arabia had been annexed to the Muslim Empire. The Muslim Empire continued to spread on, in Asia Minor to the north and Egypt to the south. The Eastern Roman Empire became a mere shadow with a small bit of territory round its capital. Constantinople eventually surrendered to the Muslim arms in 1453.

21. That was the real end of the Roman Empire. But in the wonderful century in which the Prophet lived, another momentous Revolution was taking place. The Roman Pontificate of Gregory the Great (590-604) was creating a new Christianity as the old Christianity of the East was slowly dying out. The Patriarch of Constantinople had claimed to be the Universal Bishop, with jurisdiction over all the other bishops of Christendom. This had been silently but gradually questioned by the Popes of Rome. They had been building up a liturgy, a church organisation and a body of discipline for the clergy, different from those of the Holy Orthodox Church. They had been extending their spiritual authority in the Barbarian provinces of Gaul and Spain. They had been amassing estates and endowments. They had been accumulating secular authority in their own hands. Pope Gregory the Great converted the Anglo-Saxon invaders of Great Britain to his form of Christianity. He protected Italy from the ravages of the Franks and Lombards and raised the See of Rome to the position of a Power which exercised ample jurisdiction over the Western world. He was preparing the way for the time when one of his successors would crown under his authority the Frankish Charlemagne as Emperor of Rome and of the West (A.D. 800), and another of his successors would finally break away from the Orthodox Church of Constantinople in 1054 by the Pope's excommunication of the Patriarch of Constantinople and the Greeks. (See the last paragraph in Appendix V.)

References: - Among Western writers, the chief authority is Gibbon's *Decline and Fall of the Roman Empire*: mainly chapters 40-42, and 45-46: I have given references to other chapters in the body of this Appendix: his delineation of the characters of Heraclius and Chosroes II is brief but masterly. L. Drapeyron's French monograph, *L'Empereur Héraclius* (Paris, 1869) throws further light on an interesting personality. A. J. Butler's *Arab Conquest of Egypt* (Oxford, 1902) gives a good account of Heraclius. The famous French dramatist Corneille has left a Play on Heraclius, but it turns more on an intricate and imaginary plot in the early life of Heraclius than on the character of Heraclius as Emperor. Niẓāmī, in his *Khusrau-o-Sīhrīn* (571 H.=1175-66 A.D.) makes a reference at the end of his Romance to the holy Prophet's letter to the Persian King, and does attempt in the course of the Romance a picture of the King's character. He is a sort of wild Prince Hal before he comes to the throne. Shīrīn is an Armenian princess in love with Khusrau: she marries Khusrau after the death of his first wife Maryam, daughter of the Roman Emperor, and mother of the undutiful son who killed Khusrau and seized his throne. Among the other Eastern writers, we find a detailed description of the interview of Abū Sufyān in Bukhārī's *Ṣaḥīḥ* (Book on the beginning of Inspiration): the notes in the excellent English translation of Muḥammad Asad (Leopold Weiss) are helpful. Ṭabarī's History is as usual valuable. Mirkhond's (Khāwind-Shāh's) *Raudhat-uṣ-Ṣafā* (translated by Rehatsek) will give English readers a summary (at second hand) of the various Arabic authorities. Maulāna Shiblī's otherwise excellent *Sīrat-un-Nabī* is in this respect disappointing. Maulāna Ẓafar 'Alī's *Galaba-i-Rūm* (Urdu, Lahore; 1926) is interesting for its comments.

A note on the Persian capitals may be interesting. So long as Persia was under the influence of the Semitic Elamites, the chief residence of the rulers was at Sūsa, near the modern Dizful, about 50 miles north-east of Shustar. In the Medic or Median period (say B. C. 700 to 550) the capital was, as we should expect, in the highlands of Media, in Ecbatana, the site of the modern city of Hamadān, 180 miles west of modern Ṭihrān. Ecbatana remained even in Sāsānian times the summer capital of Persia. With the Achæmenians (B.C. 550 to 330) we come to a period of full national and imperial life. Sūsa was the chief Achæmenian capital from the time of Darius I onwards, though Persepolis (Istakhr) in the mountain region near modern Shīrāz, and about 40 miles north-east of Shīrāz, was used as the city of royal burial. Alexander himself, as Ruler in Persia, died in Babylon. Later, when the centre of gravity moved north and north-east, other sites were selected. The Arsacids (*Ashkānian*) or Parthians were a tribal power, fitly called in Arabic the *mulūk-uṭ-ṭawāif*, and had probably no fixed or centralised capital. The Sāsānians took over a site where there were a number of cities, among which were Ctesiphon and Seleucia on opposite banks of the river Tigris. This site is about 45 miles north of the old site of Babylon and 25 miles below the later city of Baghdād. Ctesiphon and Seleucia were Greek cities founded by one of Alexander's successors, Seleucia being named after Seleucus. This complex of seven cities was afterwards called by the Arabic name of Madāin ("the Cities"). The Takht-i-Kisrā (or Arch of Ctesiphon) still stands in a ruinous condition on this site. This seems to have been the chief capital of the Sāsānians at the Arab conquest, which may be dated either from the battle of Qādisīya or that of Madāin (both fought in 637 A D), after which Persia which then included 'Irāq came into the Muslim Empire. The 'Abbāsī Empire built Baghdād for its capital under Manṣūr in 762 A D. When that Empire was broken up in 1258 A.D. there was some confusion for two centuries. Then a national Persian Empire, the Ṣafawī (1499-1736) arose, and Shāh Salīm established his capital in the north-west corner in Ṭabrīz. Shāh 'Abbās the Great (1587-1628) had his capital at the more central city of Iṣpahān (or Iṣfahān). After the Ṣafawī dynasty confusion reigned again for about four decades, when the Afghans were in the ascendant. When the Qāchār (or Qājār) dynasty (1795-1925) was firmly establisbed under Aga Muḥammad Khān, Ṭihrān (Teheran), near the Caspian, where his family originated, became the capital, and it still remains the capital under the modern Pehlevi Dynasty.

APPENDIX XI.

Comparative Chronology of the Early Years of Islam

(See paras. 11 and 8 of Appendix X.)

The dates after the Hijrat, when given according to the Arabian Calendar, can usually be calculated exactly according to other Calendars, but it is not possible to synchronise exactly the earliest dates of the Arabian Calendar with the dates of the Christian Calendar, and for two reasons. In the first place, there seems to have been some discrepancy between the Calendars in Medina and in Mecca. In the second place, the Arabian Calendar was roughly luni-solar, before the years of the Farewell Pilgrimage (Ẕul-Ḥajj, 10 H.=March 632). The Pagan Arabs were in the habit of counting months by the appearance of the moon, but irregularly intercalating a month once in about three years to bring the calendar up into conformity with the seasons. They did not do it on any astronomical calculations or on any system, but just as it suited their own selfish purposes, thus often upsetting all the old-established conventions about the months of peace and security from war and thus getting an unfair advantage for the clique in power in Mecca over their enemies (see my n. 1295 to ix. 36). Unless exact mathematical calculations are applied and reduced to a well-established system, there is apt to be confusion, and this can well be taken advantage of by arbitrary cliques in power. After the holy Prophet's adoption of the purely lunar calendar for ecclesiastical purposes, there is no confusion. Every date after A.H. 10 is exactly convertible into a corresponding date in any other accurate calendar. Wüstenfeld's and other Comparative Tables of Muslim and Christian dates may therefore be relied upon for dates after A.H. 10, but much caution is necessary in synchronisation for earlier dates.

Maulānā Shiblī, in his *Sīrat-un-Nabī*, Vol. I, p. 124 (edition of 1335 H., 1918 C.), adopts for the Prophet's Birthday the date 20th April 571, following Maḥmūd Pāshā. They go on the basis of an astronomical event, the total eclipse of the sun that was visible in Medina on the day that the Prophet's son Ibrāhīm was taken to the mercy of God. But there is no agreement among the authorities as to the exact date *either* by the Christian or the Arabian Calendar. Shiblī, following Maḥmūd Pāshā, takes the date of the eclipse to be the 7th November 632. Muir (*Life*, ed. 1923, p. 429), assumes some date in June or July 631. L. Caetani (*Chronographia Islamica*, A.H. 10) gives the date of the eclipse as 4th or 5th July 631, which he synchronises with the 28th or 29th of Rabī' I, A.H. 10, but he quotes authorities for the death of Ibrāhīm as on the 16th June 631, synchronising it with the 10th of Rabī' I, A.H. 10. There is something wrong here, as the death and the eclipse occurred on the same day. Wāqidī gives the month as Rabī' I, A.H. 10, and gives Ibrāhīm a life of 15 months. But if Abū Dā-ūd and Baihaqī are correct, Ibrāhīm lived only 2 months and 10 days, and as his date of birth is given in Ẕul-Ḥajj A.H. 8, the date of death according to these authorities would be in

Rabī' I, A.H. 9. On a review of all the authorities I feel inclined to accept the date for the eclipse and the death of Ibrāhīm as 28th or 29th of Rabī' I, A.H. 10 = 4th or 5th July 631. But this cannot be asserted with certainty. The French work of reference, *L'art de vérifier les dates*, Paris 1818 (Vol. I, p. 310), gives the date of the solar eclipse as the 3rd of August 631, 2-30 P.M, and according to the system adopted in that book, the corresponding Hijra date would be the 28th Rabī' II, A.H. 10.

Even if this particular date was certain and exact, a certain amount of uncertainty remains in counting dates backwards. Most authorities assume a purely lunar year of 354 days for working backwards. Probably the Muslims in Medina counted in this way even before the lunar year was fixed exactly in A.H. 10. But the mass of Pagan Arabs in Mecca and elsewhere probably were all the time intercalating a month roughly once in three years, as has been stated before, until their power was utterly destroyed by the conquest of Mecca; and therefore precise exactitude in pre-Conquest dates or in the counting of people's ages in years before 8-10 A.H. is unattainable. See a note on this subject in Margoliouth's Life of the Prophet (p. xix. of the 3rd edition) and in Muir's Life (p. x. of the 1923 edition).

The date of the actual Hijrat as given in Caetani may be accepted as Sept.-Oct. 622, being in the month of Rabī' I. If the ninth of that month be accepted as the date of departure from the cave of Thaur, the best synchronised date would be 22nd September 622 C. But as the first month of the Arab year was (and is) Muḥarram, the Hijrī year I is counted as beginning on the 15th or 16th July 622(=1 Muḥarram A.H. 1). The formal adoption of the Hijrī era in official documents dates from the Khilāfat of Hadhrat 'Umar,—from the year 17-18 H. according to Ṭabarī.

Sir Wolseley Haig's *Comparative Tables of Muḥammadan and Christian Dates* (London, Luzac, 1932), gives in a handy form three comparative Tables which enable the synchronisation of Hijrī years from A.H. 1 to A H. 1421. The main Table for these years was printed earlier at the end of S. Haïm's *New English-Persian Dictionary*, Teheran, 1931. The exact title of Wüstenfeld's German Tables is: *Wüstenfeld-Mahler, Vergleichungs-Tabellen*, Leipzig, 1926 (2nd edition).

INTRODUCTION TO SŪRA XXXI (*Luqmān*).

The argument of the Final End of Things is here continued from another point of view. What is Wisdom? Where shall she be found? Will she solve the mysteries of Time and Nature, and that world higher than physical Nature, which brings us nearer to God? "Yes," is the answer; "if, as in the advice of Luqmān the Wise, human wisdom looks to God in true worship, ennobles every act of life with true kindness, but avoids the false indulgence that infringes the divine law,—and in short follows the golden mean of virtue." And this is indicated by every Sign in nature.

The chronology of this Sūra has no significance. In the main, it belongs to the late Meccan period.

Summary.—The earnest seekers after righteousness receive guidance, unlike the seekers after vanity, who perish : all Creation bears witness to this : Wisdom, as expounded by Luqmān the Wise, is true service to God, and consists in moderation (xxxi. 1-19, and C. 183).

True Wisdom is firm and enduring, and discerns God's Law in the working of His Creation : it looks to the Final End of Things, whose mystery is only known to God (xxxi. 20-34, and C. 184).

C. 183.—What is the Book of Wisdom? It is
(xxxi. 1-19.) A Guide and a Mercy to men, and teaches
Them how to attain Bliss. God's Mercies
Are infinite : how can men deny them?
Luqmān the Wise taught grateful worship
Of the One True God, and the service of men,
Beginning with Parents : every good deed
Is known to God and is brought to account.
So walk in the Golden Mean, and serve
Him with constancy and firmness of purpose.

Sūra XXXI, *Luqmān* (the Wise).

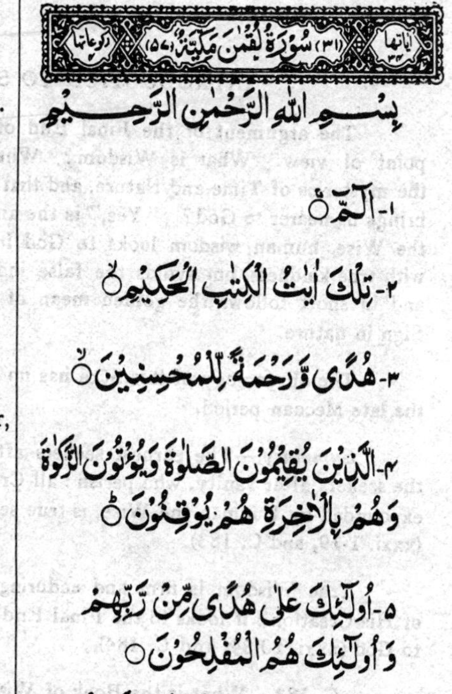

In the name of God, Most Gracious,
Most Merciful.

1. A. L. M.[3579]

2. These are Verses
Of the Wise Book,—[3580]

3. A Guide and a Mercy
To the Doers of Good,—[3581]

4. Those who establish regular Prayer,
And give regular Charity,
And have (in their hearts)
The assurance of the Hereafter.[3582]

5. These are on (true) guidance[3583]
From their Lord; and these
Are the ones who will prosper.

6. But there are, among men,
Those who purchase idle tales,[3584]

3579. See n. 25 to ii. 1 and Introduction to S. xxx.

3580. This Sūra relates to Wisdom, and the Qur-ān is appropriately called the Wise Book, or the Book of Wisdom. In verse 12 below there is a reference to Luqmān the Wise. "Wise" in this sense (*Ḥakīm*) means not only a man versed in knowledge human and divine, but one carrying out in practical conduct (*'amal*) the right course in life to the utmost of his power. His knowledge is correct and practical, but not necessarily complete: for no man is perfect. Such an ideal involves the conception of a man of heroic action as well as of deep and workman-like knowledge of nature and human nature,—not merely dreams or speculation. That ideal was fulfilled in a most remarkable degree in the holy Apostle, and in the sacred Book which was revealed through him. "The Wise Book" (*Kitāb-ul-ḥakīm*) is one of the titles of the Qur-ān.

3581. A guide to all, and, to those who accept its guidance, a source of mercy as leading them to Salvation.

3582. The righteous are distinguished here by three marks, which are summed up in the phrase "doers of good", *viz.*: (1) they yearn towards God in duty, love, and prayer, (2) they love and serve their fellow-men in charity, (3) they win peace and rest for themselves in the assured hope of the Future.

3583. They get these blessings because they submit their will to God's Will and receive His guidance. They will do well in this life (from the highest standpoint) and they will reach their true Goal in the Future.

3584. Life is taken seriously by men who realise the issues that hang upon it. But there are men of a frivolous turn of mind who prefer idle tales to true Realities and they are justly rebuked here. In the time of the holy Prophet there was a pagan Nadhr ibn al-Ḥārith who preferred Persian romances to the Message of God, and turned away ignorant men from the preaching of God's Word.

Without knowledge (or meaning),
To mislead (men) from the Path
Of God and throw ridicule
(On the Path): for such
There will be a humiliating
Penalty.

لِيُضِلَّ عَنْ سَبِيلِ اللّٰهِ بِغَيْرِ عِلْمٍ
وَّيَتَّخِذَهَا هُزُوًا
أُولٰٓئِكَ لَهُمْ عَذَابٌ مُّهِينٌ ○

7. When Our Signs are rehearsed
To such a one, he turns[3585]
Away in arrogance, as if
He heard them not, as if
There were deafness in both
His ears: announce to him
A grievous Penalty.

٧- وَإِذَا تُتْلٰى عَلَيْهِ اٰيٰتُنَا
وَلّٰى مُسْتَكْبِرًا
كَأَنْ لَّمْ يَسْمَعْهَا كَأَنَّ فِيٓ أُذُنَيْهِ وَقْرًا
فَبَشِّرْهُ بِعَذَابٍ أَلِيمٍ ○

8. For those who believe
And work righteous deeds,
There will be Gardens
Of Bliss,—

٨- إِنَّ الَّذِينَ اٰمَنُوا وَعَمِلُوا الصّٰلِحٰتِ
لَهُمْ جَنّٰتُ النَّعِيمِ ○

9. To dwell therein. The promise
Of God is true: and He
Is Exalted in power,[3586] Wise.

٩- خٰلِدِينَ فِيهَا وَعْدَ اللّٰهِ حَقًّا
وَهُوَ الْعَزِيزُ الْحَكِيمُ ○

10. He created the heavens
Without any pillars that ye[3587]
Can see; He set
On the earth mountains[3588]
Standing firm, lest it
Should shake with you;
And He scattered through it
Beasts of all kinds.[3589]
We send down rain[3590]
From the sky, and produce

١٠- خَلَقَ السَّمٰوٰتِ بِغَيْرِ عَمَدٍ تَرَوْنَهَا
وَأَلْقٰى فِي الْأَرْضِ رَوَاسِيَ
أَنْ تَمِيدَ بِكُمْ
وَبَثَّ فِيهَا مِنْ كُلِّ دَآبَّةٍ
وَأَنْزَلْنَا مِنَ السَّمَآءِ مَآءً فَأَنْبَتْنَا

3585. Such men behave as if they had heard nothing of serious import, or laugh at serious teaching. The loss will be their own. They will miss the higher things of life and be left out of God's blessings. Ignorance and arrogance are in most cases the causes of their fall.

3586. He is Exalted in power, and can carry out His Will, and nothing can stop the carrying out of His promise. He is also infinitely Wise: His promise is therefore full of meaning: it is not merely without purpose: it has a place in the Universal Plan.

3587. *Cf.* xiii. 2 and n. 1800.

3588. *Cf.* xvi. 15 and n. 2038.

3589. *Cf.* ii. 164 and n. 166.

3590. Note the change of the pronoun at this stage in the verse. Before this, God was spoken of in the third person, "He", and the acts of Creation referred to were acts that in the main were completed when the universe as we see it came into being, though its slow age-long evolution continues. After this, God speaks in the first person "We"—the plural of honour, as explained before (see n. 56 to ii. 38); and the processes spoken of are those that go on continually before us, as in the case of rain and the growth of the vegetable kingdom. In some way the creation of the heavens and the earth and animal life on it may be considered impersonal to man, while the processes of rain and vegetation may be considered in special personal relationship to him.

On the earth every kind
Of noble creature, in pairs.[3591]

فِيهَا مِن كُلِّ زَوْجٍ كَرِيمٍ ۝

11. Such is the Creation of God:
Now show Me[3592] what is there
That others besides Him
Have created: nay, but
The Transgressors are
In manifest error.

١١- هَٰذَا خَلْقُ اللَّهِ
فَأَرُونِي مَاذَا خَلَقَ الَّذِينَ مِن دُونِهِ
بَلِ الظَّالِمُونَ فِي ضَلَالٍ مُّبِينٍ ۝ ع

SECTION 2.

12. We bestowed (in the past)
Wisdom on Luqmān:[3593]
"Show (thy) gratitude to God."
Any who is (so) grateful
Does so to the profit
Of his own soul: but if
Any is ungrateful, verily[3594]
God is free of all wants,
Worthy of all praise.

١٢- وَلَقَدْ آتَيْنَا لُقْمَانَ الْحِكْمَةَ
أَنِ اشْكُرْ لِلَّهِ
وَمَن يَشْكُرْ فَإِنَّمَا يَشْكُرُ لِنَفْسِهِ
وَمَن كَفَرَ
فَإِنَّ اللَّهَ غَنِيٌّ حَمِيدٌ ۝

13. Behold, Luqmān said[3595]
To his son by way of

١٣- وَإِذْ قَالَ لُقْمَانُ لِابْنِهِ وَهُوَ

3591. I think that sex life in plants is referred to, as in xiii. 3, where see n. 1804, though the pairs here may refer to animals also. "Noble" (*karīm*) may refer to the more beneficent plants and trees (and animals), which God has created for man's use.

3592. The transition from "We" in the last verse to "Me" in this verse means a still more personal relation to God: (see n. 56 to ii. 38): as we are now asked about the true worship of God, as against the false worship of others besides God.

3593. The sage Luqmān, after whom this Sūra is called, belongs to Arab tradition. Very little is known of his life. He is usually associated with a long life, and his title is *Mu'ammar* (the long-lived). He is referred by some to the age of the 'Ād people, for whom see n. 1040 to vii. 65. He is the type of perfect wisdom. It is said that he belonged to a humble station in life, being a slave or a carpenter, and that he refused worldly power and a kingdom. Many instructive apologues are credited to him, similar to Æsop's Fables in Greek tradition. The identification of Luqmān and Æsop has no historical foundation, though it is true that the traditions about them have influenced each other.

3594. *Cf.* xiv. 8. The basis of the moral Law is man's own good, and not any benefit to God, for God is above all needs, and "worthy of all praise"; *i.e.* even in praising Him, we do not advance His glory. When we obey His Will, we bring our position into conformity with our own nature as made by Him.

3595. Luqmān is held up as a pattern of wisdom, because he realised the best in a wise life in this world, as based upon the highest Hope in the inner life. To him, as in Islam, true human wisdom is also divine wisdom: the two cannot be separated. The beginning of all wisdom, therefore, is conformity with the Will of God (xxxi. 12). That means that we must understand our relations to Him and worship Him aright (xxxi. 13). Then we must be good to mankind, beginning with our own parents (xxxi. 14). For the two duties are not diverse, but one. Where they appear to conflict, there is something wrong with the human will (see n. 3597).

Instruction: "O my son!
Join not in worship
(Others) with God: for
False worship is indeed
The highest wrong-doing."

يَعِظُهُ يٰبُنَيَّ لَا تُشْرِكْ بِاللّٰهِ ۗ
إِنَّ الشِّرْكَ لَظُلْمٌ عَظِيمٌ ۝

وقف النبي صلى الله عليه وسلم

14. And We have enjoined on man
(To be good) to his parents:
In travail upon travail
Did his mother bear him,
And in years twain[3596]
Was his weaning: (hear
The command), "Show gratitude
To Me and to thy parents:
To Me is (thy final) Goal.

١٤- وَوَصَّيْنَا الْإِنْسَانَ بِوَالِدَيْهِ ۚ
حَمَلَتْهُ أُمُّهُ وَهْنًا عَلَىٰ وَهْنٍ
وَفِصَالُهُ فِي عَامَيْنِ
أَنِ اشْكُرْ لِي وَلِوَالِدَيْكَ ۗ
إِلَيَّ الْمَصِيرُ ۝

نصف

15. "But if they strive[3597]
To make thee join
In worship with Me
Things of which thou hast
No knowledge, obey them not;
Yet bear them company
In this life with justice
(And consideration), and follow
The way of those who
Turn to Me (in love):[3598]
In the End the return
Of you all is to Me,
And I will tell you
The truth (and meaning)[3599]
Of all that ye did."

١٥- وَإِنْ جَاهَدَاكَ عَلَىٰ أَنْ تُشْرِكَ بِي
مَا لَيْسَ لَكَ بِهِ عِلْمٌ
فَلَا تُطِعْهُمَا
وَصَاحِبْهُمَا فِي الدُّنْيَا مَعْرُوفًا ۖ
وَاتَّبِعْ سَبِيلَ مَنْ أَنَابَ إِلَيَّ ۚ
ثُمَّ إِلَيَّ مَرْجِعُكُمْ
فَأُنَبِّئُكُمْ بِمَا كُنْتُمْ تَعْمَلُونَ ۝

3596. The set of milk teeth in a human child is completed at the age of two years, which is therefore the natural extreme limit for breast-feeding. In our artificial life the duration is much less.

3597. Where the duty to man conflicts with the duty to God, it means that there is something wrong with the human will, and we should obey God rather than man. But even here, it does not mean that we should be arrogant or insolent. To parents and those in authority, we must be kind, considerate, and courteous, even where they command things which we should not do and therefore disobedience becomes our highest duty.

The worship of things other than God is the worship of false things, things which are alien to our true knowledge, things that go against our own pure nature as created by God.

3598. In any apparent conflict of duties our standard should be God's Will, as declared to us by His command. That is the way of those who love God: and their motive in disobedience to parents or human authority where disobedience is necessary by God's Law, is not self-willed rebellion or defiance, but love of God, which means the true love of man in the highest sense of the word. And the reason we should give is: "Both you and I have to return to God; therefore not only must I follow God's Will, but you must command nothing against God's Will."

3599. These conflicts may appear to us strange and puzzling in this life. But in God's Presence we shall see their real meaning and significance. It may be that that was one way in which our true mettle could be tested: for it is not easy to disobey and love man at the same time.

16. " O my son ! " (said Luqmān),[3600]
" If there be (but) the weight
Of a mustard-seed and
It were (hidden) in a rock,[3601]
Or (anywhere) in the heavens or
On earth, God will bring it
Forth : for God understands[3602]
The finest mysteries, (and)
Is well-acquainted (with them).

١٦- يٰبُنَيَّ اِنَّهَآ اِنْ تَكُ مِثْقَالَ حَبَّةٍ
مِّنْ خَرْدَلٍ فَتَكُنْ فِىْ صَخْرَةٍ
اَوْ فِى السَّمٰوٰتِ اَوْ فِى الْاَرْضِ يَاْتِ بِهَا
اللّٰهُ ۗ
اِنَّ اللّٰهَ لَطِيْفٌ خَبِيْرٌ ۝

17. " O my son ! establish
Regular prayer, enjoin what is
Just, and forbid what is wrong :
And bear with patient constancy
Whate'er betide thee ; for this
Is firmness (of purpose)
In (the conduct of) affairs.

١٧- يٰبُنَيَّ اَقِمِ الصَّلٰوةَ
وَاْمُرْ بِالْمَعْرُوْفِ وَانْهَ عَنِ الْمُنْكَرِ
وَاصْبِرْ عَلٰى مَآ اَصَابَكَ ۗ
اِنَّ ذٰلِكَ مِنْ عَزْمِ الْاُمُوْرِ ۝

18. " And swell not thy cheek[1603]
(For pride) at men,
Nor walk in insolence
Through the earth ;
For God loveth not
Any arrogant boaster.

١٨- وَلَا تُصَعِّرْ خَدَّكَ لِلنَّاسِ
وَلَا تَمْشِ فِى الْاَرْضِ مَرَحًا ۗ
اِنَّ اللّٰهَ لَا يُحِبُّ كُلَّ مُخْتَالٍ فَخُوْرٍ ۝

19. "And be moderate
In thy pace, and lower[3604]

١٩- وَاقْصِدْ فِىْ مَشْيِكَ وَاغْضُضْ مِنْ

3600. Verses 14-15 are not the direct speech of Luqmān but flow by way of commentary on his teaching. He was speaking as a father to his son, and he could not very well urge respect for himself and draw the son's attention to the limitations of filial obedience. These verses may be supposed to be general directions flowing from Luqmān's teaching to men, and not directed to his son ; though in either case, as Luqmān got wisdom from God, it is divine principles that are enunciated.

3601. The mustard-seed is proverbially a small, minute thing, that people may ordinarily pass by. Not so God. Further emphasis is laid by supposing the mustard-seed to be hidden beneath a rock or in the cleft of a rock, or to be lost in the spacious expanse of the earth or of the heavens. To God everything is known, and He will bring it forth, *i.e.*, take account of it.

3602. For *Laṭīf* as a title applied to God, see n. 2844 to xxii. 63.

3603. The word " cheek " in English, too, means arrogance or effrontery, with a slightly different shade added, *viz.* : effrontery from one in an inferior position to one in a superior position. The Arabic usage is wider, and includes smug self-satisfaction and a sense of lofty superiority.

3604. The " Golden Mean " is the pivot of the philosophy of Luqmān as it is of the philosophy of Aristotle and indeed of Islam. And it flows naturally from a true understanding of our relation to God and His universe and to our fellow-creatures, especially man. In all things be moderate. Do not go the pace, and do not be stationary or slow. Do not be talkative and do not be silent. Do not be loud and do not be timid or half-hearted. Do not be too confident, and do not be cowed down. If you have patience, it is to give you constancy and determination, that you may bravely carry on the struggle of life. If you have humility, it is to save you from unseemly swagger, not to curb your right spirit and your reasoned determination.

Thy voice; for the harshest
Of sounds without doubt
Is the braying of the ass."

صَوْتِكَ ۭ اِنَّ اَنْكَرَ
الْاَصْوَاتِ لَصَوْتُ الْحَمِيْرِ ۝ ع

C. 184.—True Wisdom sees God's boundless Bounties
(xxxi. 20-34.) To man, and how all nature is made
To serve man's ends. It is due from us
To know our place, discern the limits
Of our knowledge, and see how far above us
Is God's Wisdom, and His Law. Let us not
Deceive ourselves. The end of all things
Will come, but the When and the How are known
To God alone, to Whom be all Praise!

SECTION 3.

20. Do ye not see
That God has subjected[3605]
To your (use) all things
In the heavens and on earth,
And has made His bounties
Flow to you in exceeding
Measure, (both) seen and
unseen?[3606]
Yet there are among men
Those who dispute about God,
Without knowledge and without
Guidance, and without a Book[3607]
To enlighten them!

٢٠- اَلَمْ تَرَوْا اَنَّ اللّٰهَ سَخَّرَ
لَكُمْ مَّا فِي السَّمٰوٰتِ وَمَا فِي الْاَرْضِ
وَاَسْبَغَ عَلَيْكُمْ نِعَمَهٗ ظَاهِرَةً وَّبَاطِنَةً ۭ
وَمِنَ النَّاسِ مَنْ يُّجَادِلُ فِي اللّٰهِ
بِغَيْرِ عِلْمٍ وَّلَا هُدًى
وَّلَا كِتٰبٍ مُّنِيْرٍ ۝

21. When they are told to follow
The (Revelation) that God
Has sent down, they say:
"Nay, we shall follow
The ways that we found
Our fathers (following)."[3608]

٢١- وَاِذَا قِيْلَ لَهُمُ اتَّبِعُوْا مَآ اَنْزَلَ اللّٰهُ
قَالُوْا بَلْ نَتَّبِعُ
مَا وَجَدْنَا عَلَيْهِ اٰبَاۗءَنَا ۭ

3605. God's Creation is independent of man. But God, in His infinite mercy, has given man the faculty to subdue the forces of nature and to penetrate through high mysteries with his powers of reason and insight. But this is not merely a question of power. For in His Universal Plan, all are safeguarded. But man's destiny, as far as we can see, is noble to the highest degree.

3606. God's grace and bounties work for us at all times. Sometimes we see them, and sometimes we do not. In things which we can apprehend with our senses, we can see God's grace, but even in them, sometimes it works beyond the sphere of our knowledge. In the inner or spiritual world, sometimes, when our vision is clear, we can see it working, and often we are not conscious of it. But it works all the same.

3607. Such men lack knowledge, as they make no use of their intellects but are swayed by their passions; they lack guidance, as they are impatient of control; and the fruits of revelation, or spiritual insight, do not reach them, as they reject Faith and Revelation.

3608. They do not realise that in the spiritual world, as in the physical world, there is constant progress for the live ones: they are spiritually dead, as they are content to stand on ancestral ways, many of them evil, and leading to perdition.

What! even if it is
Satan beckoning them
To the Penalty
Of the (Blazing) Fire?

أَوَلَوْ كَانَ الشَّيْطٰنُ يَدْعُوهُمْ
إِلٰى عَذَابِ السَّعِيرِ ○

22. Whoever submits
His whole self to God,
And is a doer of good,
Has grasped indeed
The most trustworthy
hand-hold:[3609]
And with God rests the End[3610]
And Decision of (all) affairs.

٢٢- وَمَنْ يُّسْلِمْ وَجْهَهٗٓ إِلَى اللّٰهِ
وَهُوَ مُحْسِنٌ
فَقَدِ اسْتَمْسَكَ بِالْعُرْوَةِ الْوُثْقٰى
وَإِلَى اللّٰهِ عَاقِبَةُ الْأُمُورِ ○

23. But if any reject Faith,
Let not his rejection
Grieve thee: to Us[3611]
Is their Return, and We
Shall tell them the truth
Of their deeds: for God
Knows well all that is
In (men's) hearts.

٢٣- وَمَنْ كَفَرَ فَلَا يَحْزُنْكَ كُفْرُهٗ
إِلَيْنَا مَرْجِعُهُمْ
فَنُنَبِّئُهُمْ بِمَا عَمِلُوا
إِنَّ اللّٰهَ عَلِيمٌۢ بِذَاتِ الصُّدُورِ ○

24. We grant them their pleasure
For a little while:[3612]
In the end shall We
Drive them to
A chastisement unrelenting.

٢٤- نُمَتِّعُهُمْ قَلِيلًا
ثُمَّ نَضْطَرُّهُمْ إِلٰى عَذَابٍ غَلِيظٍ ○

25. If thou ask them,
Who it is that created
The heavens and the earth.[3613]
They will certainly say,

٢٥- وَلَئِنْ سَأَلْتَهُمْ مَّنْ خَلَقَ
السَّمٰوٰتِ وَالْأَرْضَ لَيَقُولُنَّ

3609. *Cf.* ii. 256 and n. 301.

3610. *Cf.* xxii. 41. Everything goes back to God. He is our final Goal, as He is the final Goal of all things.

3611. The man of God should not grieve because people reject Faith. He should do his duty and leave the rest to God. Every soul must return to God for his reckoning. God knows everything, and His Universal Plan is full of wisdom.

3612. *Cf.* ii. 126. The respite in this life is of short duration. The ultimate Penalty of Evil is such as cannot be quenched. *Cf.* xiv. 17. It will be too late then to repent.

3613. *Cf.* xxiii. 84-89, and xxix. 61 and n. 3493. Men will acknowledge that God created the heavens and the earth, and yet fail to understand the love and goodness of God in continuing to cherish and maintain them with His gifts. Even if they allow this, they sometimes yet fall short of the corollary, that He is the only One to be worshipped, and run after their own false gods in the shapes of their fancies and lusts. They do not do the duties which, if they rightly understood their own nature and position, they should take a delight in doing.

"God". Say: "Praise be to God!"[3614]
But most of them
Understand not.

اللّٰهُ ۚ قُلِ الْحَمْدُ لِلّٰهِ ۚ
بَلْ اَكْثَرُهُمْ لَا يَعْلَمُوْنَ ○

26. To God belong all things
In heaven and earth: verily
God is He (that is)
Free of all wants,
Worthy of all praise.[3615]

٢٦- لِلّٰهِ مَا فِي السَّمٰوٰتِ وَالْاَرْضِ ۚ
اِنَّ اللّٰهَ هُوَ الْغَنِيُّ الْحَمِيْدُ ○

27. And if all the trees
On earth were pens
And the Ocean (were ink),
With seven Oceans behind it
To add to its (supply),
Yet would not the Words[3616]
Of God be exhausted
(In the writing): for God
Is Exalted in power,
Full of Wisdom.

٢٧- وَلَوْ اَنَّ مَا فِي الْاَرْضِ مِنْ شَجَرَةٍ
اَقْلَامٌ وَّالْبَحْرُ يَمُدُّهٗ
مِنْۢ بَعْدِهٖ سَبْعَةُ اَبْحُرٍ
مَّا نَفِدَتْ كَلِمٰتُ اللّٰهِ ۚ
اِنَّ اللّٰهَ عَزِيْزٌ حَكِيْمٌ ○

28. And your creation
Or your resurrection
Is in no wise but
As an individual soul:[3617]
For God is He Who
Hears and sees (all things).

٢٨- مَا خَلْقُكُمْ وَلَا بَعْثُكُمْ
اِلَّا كَنَفْسٍ وَّاحِدَةٍ ۚ
اِنَّ اللّٰهَ سَمِيْعٌۢ بَصِيْرٌ ○

3614. This ejaculation expresses our satisfaction that at least this is recognised,—that the Creator of the whole world is God. It is a pity that they do not go further and recognise other facts and duties (see the last note).

3615. *Cf.* above, xxxi. 12. There was begun the argument about showing gratitude to God, introducing Luqmān's teaching and philosophy. Such gratitude is shown by our understanding His love and doing our duty to Him by serving our fellow-men. For God Himself is Free from all wants and is in no way dependent on our service. That argument has been illustrated in various ways. But now we are told that it can never be completed, for no human tongue or human resources can be adequate either to praise him or to expound His Word.

3616. "*Words of God*": His wonderful Signs and Commandments are infinite and cannot be expressed if all the trees were made into pens, and all the wide Ocean, multiplied seven times, were made into ink. Any Book of His Revelation would deal with matters which man can understand and use in his life: there are mysteries beyond mysteries that man can never fathom. Nor would any praise that we could write with infinite resources be adequate to describe His power, glory, and wisdom.

3617. God's greatness and infinitude are such that He can create and cherish not only a whole mass, but each individual soul, and He can follow its history and doings until the final Judgment. This shows not only God's glory and omniscience and omnipotence: it also shows the value of each individual soul in His eyes, and lifts individual responsibility right up into relations with Him.

29. Seest thou not that
God merges Night into Day[3618]
And He merges Day into Night;
That He has subjected the sun,
And the moon (to His Law),
Each running its course
For a term appointed; and
That God is well acquainted
With all that ye do?

٢٩- أَلَمْ تَرَ أَنَّ اللَّهَ يُولِجُ الَّيْلَ فِي النَّهَارِ
وَيُولِجُ النَّهَارَ فِي الَّيْلِ
وَسَخَّرَ الشَّمْسَ وَالْقَمَرَ
كُلٌّ يَجْرِي إِلَى أَجَلٍ مُّسَمًّى
وَأَنَّ اللَّهَ بِمَا تَعْمَلُونَ خَبِيرٌ ○

30. That is because God is
The (only) Reality, and because
Whatever else they invoke[3619]
Besides Him is Falsehood;
And because God,—He is
The Most High, Most Great.

٣٠- ذَلِكَ بِأَنَّ اللَّهَ هُوَ الْحَقُّ وَأَنَّ
مَا يَدْعُونَ مِن دُونِهِ الْبَاطِلُ
وَأَنَّ اللَّهَ هُوَ الْعَلِيُّ الْكَبِيرُ ○ ع

SECTION 4.

31. Seest thou not that
The ships sail through
The Ocean by the grace
Of God?—that He may
Show you of His Signs?
Verily in this are Signs
For all who constantly persevere[3620]
And give thanks.

٣١- أَلَمْ تَرَ أَنَّ الْفُلْكَ تَجْرِي
فِي الْبَحْرِ بِنِعْمَتِ اللَّهِ
لِيُرِيَكُم مِّنْ آيَاتِهِ
إِنَّ فِي ذَلِكَ لَآيَاتٍ لِّكُلِّ صَبَّارٍ شَكُورٍ ○

32. When a wave covers them
Like the canopy (of clouds),
They call to God,
Offering Him sincere devotion.[3621]

٣٢- وَإِذَا غَشِيَهُم مَّوْجٌ كَالظُّلَلِ
دَعَوُا اللَّهَ مُخْلِصِينَ لَهُ الدِّينَ

3618 *Cf.* xxii. 61 and n. 2841 Even when we can form a conception of God's infinitude by His dealings with each individual in His Creation as in verse 28 above, it is still inadequate. What is an individual himself? What is his relation to the universal Laws of God? In outer nature we can see that there is no clear-cut line between night and day: each merges into the other. Yet the sun and moon obey definite laws. Though they seem to go on for ever, yet their existence and duration themselves are but an atom in God's great universe. How much more "merging" and imperceptible gradation there is in the inner and spiritual world? Our actions themselves cannot be classified and ticketed and labelled when examined in relation to motives and circumstances. Yet they are like an open book before God.

3619. *Cf.* xxii. 62 and notes 2842 and 2843. All the wonderful complexities, gradations, and nuances, that we find in Creation, are yet blended in one harmonious whole, that obeys Law and exemplifies Order. They therefore point to the One True God. He is the only Reality. All other things are but shadows, and if any of them is put up in competition or equality with Him, it can be only Falsehood. For He is higher and greater than anything we can imagine.

3620. Even the things that man makes are, as using the forces of Nature, evidence of the grace of God, Who has subdued these wonderful forces to the use of man. But this gift of mastery can only be understood and appreciated by constant perseverance, combined with a recognition of the divine gifts ("giving thanks"). *Ṣabbār* is an intensive form from *ṣabr* and I have indicated it by the adverb "constantly".

3621. *Cf.* vii. 29. Unlike the people mentioned in the last verse, who constantly seek God's help and give thanks for His mercies by using them aright and doing their duty, there is a class of men whose worship is merely inspired by terror. When they are in physical danger—the only kind of danger they appreciate,—*e.g.*, in a storm at sea, they genuinely think of God. But once the danger is past, they become indifferent or wish to appear good while dallying with evil. See next verse.

But when He has delivered them
Safely to land, there are
Among them those that halt[3622]
Between (right and wrong).
But none reject Our Signs
Except only a perfidious
Ungrateful (wretch)!

فَلَمَّا نَجّٰىهُمْ إِلَى الْبَرِّ فَمِنْهُمْ مُّقْتَصِدٌ
وَمَا يَجْحَدُ بِاٰيٰتِنَآ
إِلَّا كُلُّ خَتَّارٍ كَفُورٍ ○

33\. O mankind! do your duty
To your Lord, and fear
(The coming of) a Day
When no father can avail
Aught for his son, nor
A son avail aught
For his father.[3623]
Verily, the promise of God
Is true: let not then
This present life deceive you,
Nor let the Chief Deceiver[3624]
Deceive you about God.

٣٣- يٰٓأَيُّهَا النَّاسُ اتَّقُوْا رَبَّكُمْ وَاخْشَوْا
يَوْمًا لَّا يَجْزِيْ وَالِدٌ عَنْ وَّلَدِهٖ
وَلَا مَوْلُوْدٌ هُوَ جَازٍ عَنْ وَّالِدِهٖ شَيْـًٔا
إِنَّ وَعْدَ اللّٰهِ حَقٌّ
فَلَا تَغُرَّنَّكُمُ الْحَيٰوةُ الدُّنْيَا
وَلَا يَغُرَّنَّكُمْ بِاللّٰهِ الْغَرُوْرُ ○

34\. Verily the knowledge
Of the Hour is
With God (alone).
It is He Who sends down
Rain, and He Who knows
What is in the wombs.[3625]

٣٤- إِنَّ اللّٰهَ عِنْدَهٗ عِلْمُ السَّاعَةِ
وَيُنَزِّلُ الْغَيْثَ وَيَعْلَمُ مَا فِي الْأَرْحَامِ

3622\. They halt between two opinions. They are not against good, but they will not eschew evil. They are a contrast to those who "constantly persevere and give thanks". But such an attitude amounts really to "perfidious ingratitude".

3623\. On the Day of Reckoning no one can help another. The most loving father cannot help his son or be a substitute for him, and *vice versa*. Each will have his own personal responsibilities.

3624 The Chief Deceiver is the Power of Evil. It may make us forget that Time is fleeting and delude us by suggesting that the Reckoning may not come, whereas it is certain to come, because God's promise is true. We must not play with Time nor be deceived by appearances. The Day may come to-day or to-morrow or when we least expect it.

3625\. The question of Knowledge or Mystery governs both clauses here, *viz.*: Rain and Wombs. In fact it governs all the five things mentioned in this verse: *viz.* (1) the Hour; (2) Rain; (3) the Birth of a new Life (Wombs); (4) our Physical Life from day to day; (5) our Death. See n. 3627 below. As regards Rain we are asked to contemplate how and when it is sent down. The moisture may be sucked up by the sun's heat in the Arabian Sea or the Red Sea or the Indian Ocean near East Africa, or in the Lake Region in Central Africa. The winds drive it hither and thither across thousands of miles, or it may be, only short distances. "The wind bloweth where it listeth." No doubt it obeys certain physical Laws established by God, but how these Laws are interlocked, one with another! Meteorology, gravity, hydrostatics and dynamics, climatology, hygrometry, and a dozen other sciences are involved, end no man can completely master all of them, and yet this relates to only one of the millions of facts in physical nature, which are governed by God's Knowledge and Law. The whole vegetable kingdom is primarily affected by Rain. The mention of Wombs brings in the mystery of animal Life, Embryology, Sex, and a thousand other things. Who can tell—to take man alone—whether the child conceived is male or female, how long it will remain in the womb, whether it will be born alive, what sort of a new individual it will be,—a blessing or a curse to its parents, or to Society?

Nor does any one know
What it is that he will
Earn on the morrow:[3626]
Nor does any one know
In what land he is
To die. Verily with God
Is full knowledge and He
Is acquainted (with all things).[3627]

وَمَا تَدۡرِیۡ نَفۡسٌ
مَّاذَا تَكۡسِبُ غَدًا ؕ
وَمَا تَدۡرِیۡ نَفۡسٌۢ بِاَیِّ اَرۡضٍ تَمُوۡتُ ؕ
اِنَّ اللّٰهَ عَلِیۡمٌ خَبِیۡرٌ ٪

3626. "Earn" here, as elsewhere, means not only "earn one's livelihood" in a physical sense, but also to reap the consequences (good or ill) of one's conduct generally. The whole sentence practically means: "no man knows what the morrow may bring forth."

3627. See the five Mysteries summed up in n. 3625 above. The Argument is about the mystery of Time and Knowledge. We are supposed to know things in ordinary life. But what does that knowledge amount to in reality? Only a superficial acquaintance with things. And Time is even more uncertain. In the case of rain, which causes vegetable life to spring up, or in the case of new animal life, can we answer with precision questions as to When or How or Wherefore? So about questions of our life from day to day or of our death. These are great Mysteries, and full knowledge is with God only. How much more so in the case of the *Ma'ād*, the Final Hour, when all true values will be restored and the balance redressed? It is certain, but the When and the How are known to God alone.

INTRODUCTION TO SŪRA XXXII (*Sajda*).

This short Sūra closes the series of the four A. L. M. Sūras, which began with the 29th. Its theme is the mystery of Creation, the mystery of Time and the mystery of the *Ma'ād* (the Final End) as viewed through the light of God's revelation. The contemplation of these mysteries should lead to Faith and the adoration of God. In chronology it belongs to the middle Meccan period and is therefore a little earlier than the last, but its chronology has no significance.

Summary.—The mystery of Creation, the mystery of Time, and the mystery of the End of Things are but known by external symbols to man ; Revelation brings faith and humble adoration, and is a blessing like Rain, which brings life to dead soil (xxxii. 1-30, and C. 185).

C. 185.—How can Unbelievers realise the Mystery
(xxxii. 1-30.) Of Revelation ? They do not even
See the marvel and Mystery of Time
And God's Creation, and how they were themselves
Created ! If they could but see how the End
Will shape itself,—how the Good will be sorted out
From Evil ! The two are not equal in Goal.
Clear are the Signs and the Revelation of God—
In nature, history, and the Message of His living
Prophets. If they learn not now, alas !
It will be too late when Time's wings are furled.

Sūra XXXII

Sajda, or Adoration.

سُورَةُ السَّجْدَةِ مَكِّيَّةٌ (٣٢) (٧٥) — آياتها ٣٠ — ركوعاتها ٣

In the name of God, Most Gracious,
Most Merciful.

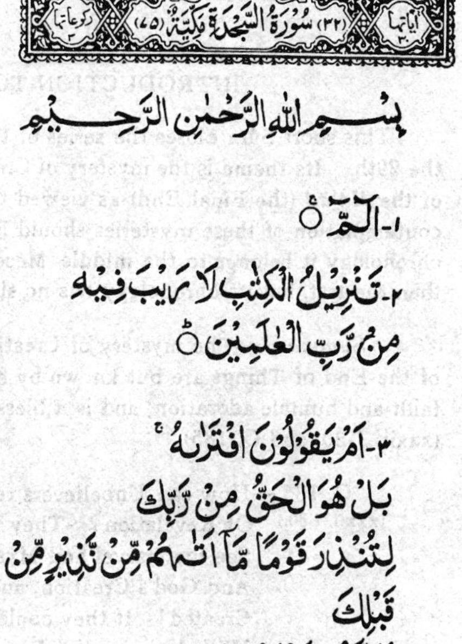

بِسْمِ اللَّهِ الرَّحْمٰنِ الرَّحِيمِ

1. A. L. M.[3628]

١- الٓمٓ ۝

2. (This is) the revelation
Of the Book in which
There is no doubt,—[3629]
From the Lord of the Worlds.

٢- تَنْزِيلُ الْكِتٰبِ لَا رَيْبَ فِيهِ
مِنْ رَّبِّ الْعٰلَمِينَ ۝

3. Or[3630] do they say,
"He has forged it"?
Nay, it is the Truth
From thy Lord, that thou
Mayest admonish a people
To whom no warner
Has come before thee:
In order that they
May receive guidance.[3631]

٣- أَمْ يَقُولُونَ افْتَرٰىهُ
بَلْ هُوَ الْحَقُّ مِنْ رَّبِّكَ
لِتُنْذِرَ قَوْمًا مَّآ أَتٰىهُمْ مِّنْ نَّذِيرٍ مِّنْ
قَبْلِكَ
لَعَلَّهُمْ يَهْتَدُونَ ۝

4. It is God Who has
Created the heavens
And the earth, and all
Between them, in six Days,[3632]

٤- اللَّهُ الَّذِي خَلَقَ السَّمٰوٰتِ
وَالْأَرْضَ وَمَا بَيْنَهُمَا فِي سِتَّةِ أَيَّامٍ

3628. See n. 25 to ii. 1, and Introduction to S. xxx.

3629. By the time of the holy Prophet the earlier Books of Revelation had been corrupted, by human ignorance or selfishness or fraud, or misinterpreted, or lost altogether. There were sects violently disputing with each other as to their true meaning. Such doubts had to be set at rest, and they were set at rest by the revelation of the Qur-ān. The Quranic inspiration came direct from God, the Lord of the Worlds, and did not consist merely of human conjectures or a reconstructed philosophy, in which there is always room for doubt or dispute. *Cf.* also ii. 2.

3630. The force of "or" (*am* in Arabic) is that the only alternative to the acceptance of the Book as a divine revelation is the supposition that it was a forgery by the holy Prophet. But the supposition is absurd on the face of it: because (1) the Quraish, his critics, knew him to be an honest and truthful man; (2) he was unlettered, and such a Book would have been beyond his powers as a simple unlettered Arab, unless God inspired it; and (3) there was a definite reason for its coming as it did, because the Arabs had received no Messenger before him, and God has sent Messengers to every nation.

3631. The Arabs very much needed guidance for themselves, and the advent of a World Prophet through them was what might have been expected in view of the past course of God's Revelations.

3632. *Six Days*: See n. 1031 to vii. 54. The "Day" does not mean a day as we reckon it, *viz.* one apparent course of the sun round the earth, for it refers to conditions which began before the earth and the sun were created. In verse 5 below, a Day is compared to a thousand years of our reckoning, and in lxx. 4 to 50,000 years. These figures "as we reckon" have no relation to "timeless Time", and must be taken to mean very long Periods, or Ages, or Æons. See further xli. 9-12, and notes.

And is firmly established
On the Throne (of authority):[3633]
Ye have none, besides Him,
To protect or intercede (for you):
Will ye not then
Receive admonition?

ثُمَّ اسْتَوٰى عَلَى الْعَرْشِ
مَا لَكُمْ مِّنْ دُوْنِهٖ مِنْ وَّلِيٍّ وَّلَا شَفِيْعٍ
اَفَلَا تَتَذَكَّرُوْنَ ۝

5. He rules (all) affairs
From the heavens
To the earth: in the end
Will (all affairs) go up[3634]
To Him, on a Day,
The space whereof will be
(As) a thousand years
Of your reckoning.

٥- يُدَبِّرُ الْاَمْرَ مِنَ السَّمَآءِ اِلَى الْاَرْضِ
ثُمَّ يَعْرُجُ اِلَيْهِ فِيْ يَوْمٍ
كَانَ مِقْدَارُهٗۤ اَلْفَ سَنَةٍ
مِّمَّا تَعُدُّوْنَ ۝

6. Such is He, the Knower
Of all things, hidden
And open, the Exalted
(In power), the Merciful;—[3635]

٦- ذٰلِكَ عٰلِمُ الْغَيْبِ وَالشَّهَادَةِ الْعَزِيْزُ
الرَّحِيْمُ ۝

7. He Who has made
Everything which He has created[3636]
Most Good: He began
The creation of man
With (nothing more than) clay,[3637]

٧- الَّذِيْۤ اَحْسَنَ كُلَّ شَيْءٍ خَلَقَهٗ
وَبَدَاَ خَلْقَ الْاِنْسَانِ مِنْ طِيْنٍ ۝

3633. *Cf.* x. 3. n. 1386. God created the World as we see it in six great Stages. But after the initial creation, He is still in authority and directs and controls all affairs. He has not delegated His powers to others, and Himself retired. Also see vii. 54.

3634. How could the immense mystery of Time behind our ideas of it be enforced on our minds better? Our Day may be a thousand or fifty thousand years, and our years in proportion. In the immense Past was God's act of creation: it still continues, for He guides, rules, and controls all affairs: and in the immense Future all affairs will go up to Him, for He will be the Judge, and His restoration of all values will be as in a Day or an Hour or the Twinkling of an eye; and yet to our ideas it will be as a thousand years!

3635. God's attributes, then, may be summed up with reference to Knowledge, Power, and Mercy. Where our knowledge is partial and uncertain, His is complete and certain. Where our power often falls short of the carrying out of our will, or needs the help of Time, His is complete and conterminous with His Will. Where our mercy seems to be bounded by or opposed to justice, His is absolute and unconditioned.

3636. God's creation in itself is good: it is beautiful, in proper proportions, and adapted for the functions it has to perform. There is no evil or disorder in it. Such evil or disorder as creeps in is due to man's will (as far as the world of man is concerned), and spiritual Teaching is directed to train and cure that will and bring it into conformity with the Universal Order and Plan.

3637. Man is asked to contemplate his own humble beginning. His material body (apart from life) is a piece of earth or clay, which is another term for primeval matter. Matter is therefore the first stage, but even matter was not self-created. It was created by God.

8. And made his progeny
From a quintessence
Of the nature of
A fluid despised :[3638]

٨- ثُمَّ جَعَلَ نَسْلَهُ مِنْ سُلٰلَةٍ
مِّنْ مَّآءٍ مَّهِيْنٍ ۚ

9. But He fashioned him
In due proportion, and breathed
Into him something of[3639]
His spirit. And He gave
You (the faculties of) hearing
And sight and feeling[3640]
(And understanding) :
Little thanks do ye give !

٩- ثُمَّ سَوّٰىهُ
وَنَفَخَ فِيْهِ مِنْ رُّوْحِهٖ
وَجَعَلَ لَكُمُ السَّمْعَ وَالْاَبْصَارَ وَالْاَفْـِٕدَةَ ؕ
قَلِيْلًا مَّا تَشْكُرُوْنَ ۝

10. And they say : "What !
When we lie, hidden
And lost, in the earth,
Shall we indeed be
In a Creation renewed ?[3641]
Nay, they deny the Meeting
With their Lord !"

١٠- وَقَالُوْٓا ءَاِذَا ضَلَلْنَا فِى الْاَرْضِ
ءَاِنَّا لَفِيْ خَلْقٍ جَدِيْدٍ ؕ
بَلْ هُمْ بِلِقَآئِ رَبِّهِمْ كٰفِرُوْنَ ۝

11. Say : "The Angel of Death,
Put in charge of you,
Will (duly) take your souls :[3642]
Then shall ye be brought
Back to your Lord."

١١- قُلْ يَتَوَفّٰىكُمْ مَّلَكُ الْمَوْتِ الَّذِيْ
وُكِّلَ بِكُمْ ثُمَّ اِلٰى رَبِّكُمْ تُرْجَعُوْنَ ۝ ع

3638. Then comes life and the reproduction of life. We are still looking at the purely physical aspect, but it is now a stage higher ; it is an animal. Its reproduction is through the sperm or semen, which is a quintessence of every part of the body of man. Yet it issues from the same part of his body as the urine, and is therefore despicable in man's sight. It is a living cell or cells, summing up so much ancestral life-history. *Cf.* xxiii. 12, and n 2872.

3639. The third stage is indicated by "fashioned him in due proportion". *Cf.* xv. 29. After fertilisation of ovum by the sperm, an individual life comes into existence, and it is gradually fashioned into shape ; its limbs are formed ; its animal life begins to function ; all the beautiful adaptations come into play. The fourth stage here mentioned is that of distinctive Man, into whom God's spirit is breathed. Then he rises higher than animals.

3640. As a complete man he gets the higher faculties. The five animal senses I understand to be included in the third stage. But in the fourth stage he rises higher, and is addressed in the second person, "you," instead of the third person "him". He has now the spiritual counterpart of hearing (*i.e.*, the capacity of hearing God's Message) and seeing (*i.e.*, the inner vision), and feeling the nobler heights of love and understanding the bearings of the inner life (both typified by the Heart). Yet with all these gifts, what thanks does unregenerate or corrupted man give to God ?

3641. *Cf.* xiii. 5. It has been the cry of Materialists and Sceptics through the ages not only to bound their horizon with this brief life, but to deny dogmatically that there can be a future life. Though this is against the professed principles of Sceptics, in practice they take up that attitude. Here "they" refers to those "who give little thanks" to God, mentioned in the last verse. The argument used against them is : if God can produce such a wonderful creation the first time, why can He not make it again ? That points to the possibility : our own general inner hope and expectation of a future life, coupled with Faith in God's work, is the ground of our certainty.

3642. If death is certain, as it is, and this life by itself in no way satisfies our instincts and expectations, we may be sure that the agency which separates our soul from our body will bring us into the new world. If we believe in a soul at all—the very foundation of Religion—we must believe in a Future, without which the soul has no meaning.

SECTION 2.

12. If only thou couldst see
When the guilty ones
Will bend low their heads
Before their Lord, (saying:)
"Our Lord! We have seen
And we have heard:[3643]
Now then send us back
(To the world): we will
Work righteousness: for we
Do indeed (now) believe."

١٢- وَلَوْ تَرَىٰٓ إِذِ الْمُجْرِمُونَ
نَاكِسُوا رُءُوسِهِمْ عِنْدَ رَبِّهِمْ
رَبَّنَآ أَبْصَرْنَا وَسَمِعْنَا
فَارْجِعْنَا
نَعْمَلْ صَالِحًا إِنَّا مُوقِنُونَ ○

13. If We had so willed,[3644]
We could certainly have brought
Every soul its true guidance:
But the Word from Me[3645]
Will come true, "I will
Fill Hell with Jinns
And men all together."

١٣- وَلَوْ شِئْنَا لَآتَيْنَا كُلَّ نَفْسٍ هُدٰهَا
وَلٰكِنْ حَقَّ الْقَوْلُ مِنِّي
لَأَمْلَأَنَّ جَهَنَّمَ مِنَ الْجِنَّةِ وَالنَّاسِ
أَجْمَعِينَ ○

14. "Taste ye then—for ye
Forgot the Meeting[3646]
Of this Day of yours,
And We too will
Forget you—taste ye
The Penalty of Eternity
For your (evil) deeds!"

١٤- فَذُوقُوا بِمَا نَسِيتُمْ لِقَآءَ يَوْمِكُمْ هٰذَا
إِنَّا نَسِينٰكُمْ
وَذُوقُوا عَذَابَ الْخُلْدِ
بِمَا كُنْتُمْ تَعْمَلُونَ ○

15. Only those believe
In Our Signs, who, when

١٥- إِنَّمَا يُؤْمِنُ بِاٰيٰتِنَا الَّذِينَ إِذَا

3643. In life on the new plane, there will be no room for deception or self-deception. The most hardened sinner will see the truth and the justice of the Day of Account. He will wish he could be sent back, but it will be too late. The world as we know it will have already passed away.

3644. Could evil have been avoided? Certainly everything is in God's power. If it had been His Will and Plan, He could have created a world in which there would have been no choice or will in any of His creatures. But that was not His Will and Plan. In the world as we see it, man has a certain amount of choice and free-will. That being so, He has provided Signs and means of instruction for man, in order that man's will may be straight and pure. A necessary corollary will be Punishment for the infraction of His Law. That Punishment must come to pass, for God's Word is true and must be fulfilled.

3645. *Cf.* xi. 119, n. 1623, and vii. 18, and see last note. Jinns are the evil spirits that tempt men, and the men who will suffer punishment will be those who have succumbed to their temptations.

3646. "*Forgot*": *Cf.* n. 1029 to vii. 51. "Forget" is here in the sense of "to ignore deliberately, to reject with scorn". In the sense of mistake or defect of knowledge it is inapplicable to the All-Perfect Being, for we are expressly told: "My Lord never errs, nor forgets": xx. 52.

They are recited to them,
Fall down in adoration,[3647]
And celebrate the praises
Of their Lord, nor are they
(Ever) puffed up with pride.

ذُكِّرُوا بِهَا خَرُّوا سُجَّدًا
وَسَبَّحُوا بِحَمْدِ رَبِّهِمْ
وَهُمْ لَا يَسْتَكْبِرُونَ ۩ السجدة

16. Their limbs do forsake[3648]
Their beds of sleep, the while
They call on their Lord,
In Fear and Hope:[3649]
And they spend (in charity)
Out of the sustenance which
We have bestowed on them.

١٦- تَتَجَافَىٰ جُنُوبُهُمْ عَنِ الْمَضَاجِعِ
يَدْعُونَ رَبَّهُمْ خَوْفًا وَطَمَعًا
وَمِمَّا رَزَقْنَاهُمْ يُنْفِقُونَ

17. Now no person knows
What delights of the eye[3650]
Are kept hidden (in reserve)
For them—as a reward
For their (good) Deeds.

١٧- فَلَا تَعْلَمُ نَفْسٌ
مَا أُخْفِيَ لَهُمْ مِنْ قُرَّةِ أَعْيُنٍ
جَزَاءً بِمَا كَانُوا يَعْمَلُونَ

18. Is then the man
Who believes no better
Than the man who is
Rebellious and wicked?[3651]
Not equal are they.

١٨- أَفَمَنْ كَانَ مُؤْمِنًا
كَمَنْ كَانَ فَاسِقًا
لَا يَسْتَوُونَ

19. For those who believe
And do righteous deeds,
Are Gardens as hospitable[3652]
Homes, for their (good) deeds.

١٩- أَمَّا الَّذِينَ آمَنُوا وَعَمِلُوا الصَّالِحَاتِ فَلَهُمْ
جَنَّاتُ الْمَأْوَىٰ نُزُلًا بِمَا كَانُوا يَعْمَلُونَ

3647. "*In adoration*": *Sujjadan*, or in a posture of prostration, expressive of deep humility and faith. This is the key-word of the Sūra, which bears the title of *Sajda*. All the Signs of God lead our thoughts upwards towards Him, and when they are expounded, our attitude should be one of humble gratitude to God. At this passage it is usual to bow in adoration.

3648. *Junūb*: sides, on which men sleep and turn in sleep: I have translated "limbs" for shortness. Holy men and women "breathless with adoration" shun soft, comfortable beds, and luxurious sleep. Their limbs are better exercised in offices of devotion and prayer, especially by night. Commentators specially refer this to Prayers called *Tahajjud*, which are offered after midnight in the small hours of the morning, in twelve *Rak'ats*.

3649. *In Fear and Hope*: in spiritual fear lest their dedication to God should not be sufficiently worthy to be accepted, and a spiritual longing or hope that their shortcomings will be overlooked by the Mercy of God. And their adoration is not shown only in Prayer, but also in practical Service and Charity, out of whatever gifts they may have received from God.

3650. *Delights of the eye*: an idiom for that which pleases most and gives most satisfaction. In our present state we can scarcely imagine the real Bliss that will come to us in the Future.

3651. The Future of the two classes—the Blessed and the Wicked—is described in verses 19-22.

3652. A home brings before our minds a picture of peace and happiness. When to it are added honour and hospitality, it adds further to the idea of happiness.

20. As to those who are
Rebellious and wicked, their abode
Will be the Fire: every time[3653]
They wish to get away
Therefrom, they will be forced
Thereinto, and it will be said
To them: "Taste ye
The Penalty of the Fire,
The which ye were wont
To reject as false."

٢٠- وَأَمَّا الَّذِينَ فَسَقُوا فَمَأْوٰىهُمُ النَّارُ
كُلَّمَآ أَرَادُوٓا أَنْ يَّخْرُجُوا مِنْهَآ
أُعِيدُوا فِيهَا
وَقِيلَ لَهُمْ ذُوقُوا عَذَابَ النَّارِ
الَّذِي كُنْتُمْ بِهٖ تُكَذِّبُونَ ○

21. And indeed We will make
Them taste of the Penalty
Of this (life) prior to[3654]
The supreme Penalty, in order
That they may (repent and) return.

٢١- وَلَنُذِيقَنَّهُمْ مِّنَ الْعَذَابِ الْأَدْنٰى
دُونَ الْعَذَابِ الْأَكْبَرِ
لَعَلَّهُمْ يَرْجِعُونَ ○

22. And who does more wrong
Than one to whom are recited
The Signs of his Lord,
And who then turns away[3655]
Therefrom? Verily from those
Who transgress We shall exact
(Due) Retribution.

٢٢- وَمَنْ أَظْلَمُ مِمَّنْ ذُكِّرَ
بِاٰيٰتِ رَبِّهٖ ثُمَّ أَعْرَضَ عَنْهَا
إِنَّا مِنَ الْمُجْرِمِينَ مُنْتَقِمُونَ ○

SECTION 3.

23. We did indeed aforetime
Give the Book to Moses:[3656]

٢٣- وَلَقَدْ اٰتَيْنَا مُوسَى الْكِتٰبَ

3653. *Cf.* xxii. 22. Just as the garden is the type of Bliss, so is the Fire the type of Penalty and suffering. There will be no getting away from it. What will be the thoughts of those who had earned it? "We used to reject the idea of the Consequences as a mere chimera: and now we find it to be true!" What will be their feelings then? How will they like it?

3654. The final Penalty is to come in the Hereafter. There is no doubt about it. But before it comes, a minor Penalty comes in this very life. It may be in some kind of misfortune, or it may be in the pangs of a tortured conscience or secret sorrow. But this minor Penalty may be really a mercy, as it gives them a chance of repentance and amendment.

3655. The worst and most hardened sinner is the man to whom God's Signs are actually brought home and who yet prefers Evil and turns away from the Light of God. The Signs may be in the words and guidance of a great Teacher or in some minor sorrow or warning, which he disregards with contumely. Or it may be in a catastrophic blow to his conscience, which should open his eyes, but from which he deliberately refuses to profit. The penalty—the Nemesis—must necessarily come eventually.

3656. "*The Book*" is not here co-extensive with Revelation. Moses had, revealed to him, a Law, a *sharī'at*, which was to guide his people in all the practical affairs of their life. Jesus, after him, was also inspired by God: but his *Injīl* or Gospel contained only general principles and not a Code or *sharī'at*. The holy Prophet was the next one to have a *sharī'at* or "Book" in that sense: for the Qur-ān contains both a Code and general principles. This Sūra is a Meccan Sūra. The Code came later in Medina. But he is given the assurance that he will also have a Code, to supersede the earlier Law, and complete the Revelation of God.

Be not then in doubt
Of its reaching (thee): [3657]
And We made it
A guide to the Children
Of Israel.

فلا تكن في مرية من لقائه
وجعلنه هدى لبني إسراءيل ○

24. And We appointed, from among
Them, Leaders, giving guidance [3658]
Under Our command, so long
As they persevered with patience
And continued to have faith
In Our Signs.

۲۴- وجعلنا منهم أئمة يهدون
بأمرنا لما صبروا
وكانوا بآيتنا يوقنون ○

25. Verily thy Lord will judge
Between them on the Day
Of Judgment, in the matters
Wherein they differ
(among themselves) [3659]

۲۵- إن ربك هو يفصل بينهم يوم
القيمة فيما كانوا فيه يختلفون ○

26. Does it not teach them
A lesson, how many generations
We destroyed before them,
In whose dwellings they
(Now) go to and fro? [3660]
Verily in that are Signs:
Do they not then listen? [3661]

۲۶- أولم يهد لهم كم أهلكنا من قبلهم
من القرون
يمشون في مسكنهم
إن في ذلك لآيت أفلا يسمعون ○

3657. "*Its reaching (thee)*": *liqā-i-hi.* Commentators differ as to the construction of the pronoun *hi*, which may be translated either "its" or "his". I construe it to refer to "the Book", as that gives the most natural meaning, as explained in the last note.

3658. The series of Judges, Prophets, and Kings in Israel continued to give good guidance, in accordance with God's Law, as long as the people continued in Faith and Constancy (persevering patience). When that condition ceased, God's grace was withdrawn, and the people broke up into wrangling sects and practically suffered national annihilation.

3659. These wrangles and disputes among them will continue until the Day of Judgment, but meantime a new *Ummat* (that of Islam) will arise and take its place, with a universal and unified Message for mankind.

3660. If a nation gone astray could only learn from the history of earlier nations that were destroyed for their evil! They could see vestiges of them in their daily goings to and fro: the Jews could see vestiges of the Philistines, Amalekites, etc., in Palestine, and the pagan Arabs, of the 'Ād and Thamūd in Arabia.

3661. "*Listen*"; *i.e.*, listen to the warnings conveyed in God's Signs. Notice how naturally the transition is effected from the physical to the spiritual,—from the ruined physical vestiges of ungodly nations on this earth to the more intangible Signs conveyed by History and Revelation. Here the sense of Hearing is mentioned, both in its physical and its metaphysical or spiritual aspect. In the next verse the sense of Sight is mentioned in both aspects.

27. And do they not see
That We do drive Rain[3662]
To parched soil (bare
Of herbage), and produce therewith
Crops, providing food
For their cattle and themselves?
Have they not the vision?[3663]

٢٧- أَوَلَمْ يَرَوْا أَنَّا نَسُوقُ الْمَآءَ
إِلَى الْأَرْضِ الْجُرُزِ
فَنُخْرِجُ بِهِ زَرْعًا تَأْكُلُ مِنْهُ أَنْعَامُهُمْ
وَأَنفُسُهُمْ أَفَلَا يُبْصِرُونَ ○

28. They say: "When will
This Decision be, if ye[3664]
Are telling the truth?"

٢٨- وَيَقُولُونَ مَتَىٰ هَٰذَا الْفَتْحُ
إِن كُنتُمْ صَٰدِقِينَ ○

29. Say: "On the Day
Of Decision, no profit
Will it be to Unbelievers
If they (then) believe!
Nor will they be granted
A respite."

٢٩- قُلْ يَوْمَ الْفَتْحِ لَا يَنفَعُ
الَّذِينَ كَفَرُوٓا إِيمَٰنُهُمْ
وَلَا هُمْ يُنظَرُونَ ○

30. So turn away from them,
And wait: they too[3665]
Are waiting.

٣٠- فَأَعْرِضْ عَنْهُمْ وَانتَظِرْ
إِنَّهُم مُّنتَظِرُونَ ○

3662. Again, as in the last verse, there is an easy transition from the physical to the spiritual. In physical nature there may be parched soil, which is to all intents and purposes dead. God sends rain, and the dead soil is converted into living land producing rich crops of fodder and corn, nuts and fruits, to satisfy the hunger of man and beast. So in the spiritual world. The dead man is revivified by God's grace and mercy, through His Revelation. He becomes not only an asset to himself but to his dependents and those around him.

3663. The verse begins with "do they not *see*?" (*a'wa lam yarau*), a physical act. It ends with "have they not the *vision*?" (*afa lā yubṣirūn*), a matter of spiritual insight. This is parallel to the two kinds of "hearing" or "listening", explained in n. 3661 above.

3664. The Unbelievers may say: "If all this which you say is true, tell us when this final restoration of Realities, Life, and true Values will come about." The answer is: "If you mean that you will postpone your repentance and reform till then, it will be no use: it will be too late for repentance, and no respite will be granted *then*: this is the Respite, and this is your chance."

3665. Read vi. 158 and n. 984 as a commentary on this. There it is said to the Unbelievers: "Wait ye: we too are waiting." Here the Righteous one is told: "Wait (thou): they too are waiting." The reversal of the order is appropriate: in each case the person (or persons) addressed is mentioned first. *Cf.* also vii. 71.

INTRODUCTION TO SŪRA XXXIII (*Aḥzāb*).

The series of mystic Sūras beginning with S. xxvi. having been closed with the last Sūra, we now come back to the hard facts of this life. Two questions are mainly considered here, *viz.*, (1) the attempt by violence and brute force to crush the truth, and (2) the attempt, by slander or unseemly conduct, to poison the relations of women with men.

As regards the first, the story of the Aḥzāb or Confederates, who tried to surround and annihilate the Muslim community in Medina, is full of underhand intrigues on the part of such diverse enemies as the Pagan Quraish, the Jews (Banū Nadhīr) who had been already expelled from Medina for their treachery, the Gaṭafān tribe of Bedouin Arabs from the interior, and the Jewish tribe of Banū Quraiẓa in Medina. This was the unholy Confederacy against Islam. But though they caused a great deal of anxiety and suffering to the beleaguered Muslims, Islam came triumphantly out of the trial and got more firmly established than ever.

The Quraish in Mecca had tried all sorts of persecution, boycott, insult, and bodily injuries to the Muslims, leading to their partial *hijrat* to Abyssinia and their Hijrat as a body to Medina. The first armed conflict between them and the Muslims took place at Badr in Ramadhān A.H. 2, when the Quraish were signally defeated. (See n. 352 to iii. 13). Next year (Shauwāl A.H. 3) they came to take revenge on Medina. The battle was fought at Uḥud, and though the Muslims suffered severely, Medina was saved and the Meccans had to return to Mecca with their object frustrated. Then they began to make a network of intrigues and alliances, and besieged Medina with a force of 10,000 men in Shauwāl and Ẓul-qa'd A.H. 5. This is the siege of the Confederates referred to in xxxiii. 9-27, which lasted over two weeks: some accounts give 27 days. It caused much suffering, from hunger, cold, an unceasing shower of arrows, and constant general or concentrated assaults. But it ended in the discomfiture of the Confederates, and established Islam firmer than ever. It was a well-organised and formidable attack, but the Muslims had made preparations to meet it. One of the preparations, which took the enemy by surprise, was the Trench (*Khandaq*) dug round Medina by the Prophet's order and under the supervision of Salmān the Persian. The siege and battle are therefore known as the Battle of the Trench or the Battle of the Confederates.

As regards the position and dignity of the ladies of the Prophet's Household and the Muslim women generally, salutary principles are laid down to safeguard their honour and protect them from slander and insult. The ladies of the Household interested themselves in social work and work of instruction for the Muslim women, and Muslim women were being trained more and more in community service. Two of them (the two Zainabs) devoted themselves to the poor. The nursing of the wounded on or by the battlefield was specially necessary in those days of warfare. The Prophet's daughter Fāṭima, then aged about 19 to 20, lovingly nursed her father's wounds at Uḥud (A.H. 3); Rufaida nursed Sa'd ibn Mu'āẓ's

wounds at the Siege of Medina by the Confederates (A.H. 5); and in the Khaibar expedition (A.H. 7) Muslim women went out from Medina for nursing service.

A portion of this Sūra sums up the lessons of the Battle of the Trench and must have been revealed some time after that Battle (Shauwāl A.H. 5). The marriage with *Zainab* referred to in verse 37 also took place in the same year. Some portions (*e.g.*, verse 27, see n. 3705) were probably revealed in A.H. 7 after the Khaibar settlement.

Summary.—The pagan customs in human relationships should be abandoned, and men and women should be held in honour according to natural relationships and spiritual position (xxxiii. 1-8, and C. 186).

The Battle of the Trench and its lessons: hypocrites and their fears: Truth and noble examples to be followed (xxxiii. 9-27, and C. 187).

High position and seemly conduct for the Apostle's wives: unhappy marriages (like *Zainab's*) not to be perpetuated on false scruples: Prophet's wives to be treated kindly and gently (xxxiii. 28-52, and C. 188).

Respect due to Apostle and his family: slander to be avoided and punished guard your words and your responsibilities (xxxiii. 53-73, and C. 189).

C. 186.—The issue of all things depends
(xxxiii. 1-8.) On God alone: we must put our trust
On Him as the Guardian of all affairs.
He loves truth in all things, both great
And small: call things by their right names.
If false relationships by custom or superstition
Do harm to men or women, shun them.
The spiritual Guide is more than Father:
The ladies of his household are Mothers
To the Believers—in rank, dignity, and duty.
The Guide will have to give an account,
In the Hereafter, of how the Truth was received
Which he was charged to proclaim to men.

Sūra XXXIII

Aḥzāb, or The Confederates.

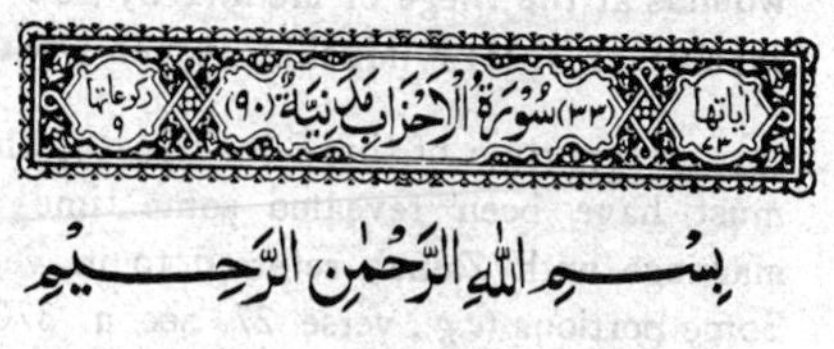

In the name of God, Most Gracious, Most Merciful.

بِسْمِ اللّٰهِ الرَّحْمٰنِ الرَّحِيْمِ

1. O Prophet! Fear God,
And hearken not
To the Unbelievers[3666]
And the Hypocrites:
Verily God is full
Of knowledge and wisdom.

١- يٰٓاَيُّهَا النَّبِيُّ اتَّقِ اللّٰهَ وَلَا تُطِعِ الْكٰفِرِيْنَ وَالْمُنٰفِقِيْنَ ۭ اِنَّ اللّٰهَ كَانَ عَلِيْمًا حَكِيْمًا ۝

2. But follow that which
Comes to thee by inspiration
From thy Lord: for God
Is well acquainted[3667]
With (all) that ye do.

٢- وَّاتَّبِعْ مَا يُوْحٰٓى اِلَيْكَ مِنْ رَّبِّكَ ۭ اِنَّ اللّٰهَ كَانَ بِمَا تَعْمَلُوْنَ خَبِيْرًا ۝

3. And put thy trust
In God, and enough is God[3668]
As a Disposer of affairs.

٣- وَّتَوَكَّلْ عَلَى اللّٰهِ ۭ وَكَفٰى بِاللّٰهِ وَكِيْلًا ۝

4. God has not made
For any man two hearts[3669]

٤- مَا جَعَلَ اللّٰهُ لِرَجُلٍ مِّنْ قَلْبَيْنِ

3666. The fifth year A.H. was a critical year in the external history of early Islam, and this Sūra must be read in the light of the events that then took place. As explained in the Introduction, the Grand Confederacy against Islam came and invested Medina and failed utterly. It consisted of the Meccan Unbelievers, the desert Arabs of Central Arabia, the Jews previously expelled for treachery from Medina, the Jews remaining in Medina, and the Hypocrites led by 'Abdullah ibn Ubai, who have already been described in ix. 43-110. Their bond of union was the common hatred of Islam, and it snapped under the reverses they met with. It is important to note three points. (1) The Jews as a body now lost their last chance of bearing the standard of Islam: the best of them had already accepted the renewal of God's Message. (2) A definite status was given to the Prophet's household, after the slanders on Ḥadhrat 'Āisha had been stilled (xxiv. 11-26, and the true position of the Mothers of the Believers had been cleared. (3) A further exposition of the purity of sex relation was given, based on the story of Ḥadhrat Zainab, the "Mother of the Poor". These points will be referred to in later notes.

3667. In the most adverse circumstances, in the midst of the assaults of Evil, the plots of treason and hypocrisy, the darts of slander and false charges, and stupid superstitions and taboos, the man of God should steer his course steadily according to God's Law and not fear human evil, in whatever form it appears. Men may misjudge, but God knows all. Men may try to overthrow Good, but Wisdom is with God.

3668. We must wholly trust God; He is the true and efficient Guardian of all interests. *Cf.* iv. 81, and n. 600.

3669. "*Two hearts in his (one) breast*": two inconsistent attitudes: such as serving God and Mammon; or subscribing to both Truth and Superstition; or hypocritically pretending one thing and intending another. Such a thing is against God's Law and Will. Apart from the condemnation of general hypocrisy, two pagan customs of the Times of Ignorance are mentioned, and their iniquity pointed out. See the notes 3670 and 3671. Nor can a man love two women with equal love; hence the injustice of marrying more than one wife; see the second clause in iv. 3.

In his (one) body : nor has
He made your wives whom
Ye divorce by Ẓihār [3670]
Your mothers : nor has He
Made your adopted sons [3671]
Your sons. Such is (only)
Your (manner of) speech
By your mouths. But God
Tells (you) the Truth, and He
Shows the (right) Way.

فِي جَوْفِهِ ۚ وَمَا جَعَلَ أَزْوَاجَكُمُ
اللَّائِي تُظَاهِرُونَ مِنْهُنَّ أُمَّهَاتِكُمْ ۚ
وَمَا جَعَلَ أَدْعِيَاءَكُمْ أَبْنَاءَكُمْ ۚ
ذَٰلِكُمْ قَوْلُكُم بِأَفْوَاهِكُمْ ۖ
وَاللَّهُ يَقُولُ الْحَقَّ وَهُوَ يَهْدِي السَّبِيلَ ○

5. Call them by (the names
Of) their fathers : that is
Juster in the sight of God.
But if ye know not [3672]
Their father's (names, call
Them) your Brothers in faith,
Or your *Maulās*.
But there is no blame
On you if ye make [3673]
A mistake therein :
(What counts is)
The intention of your hearts :
And God is Oft-Returning,
Most Merciful.

٥- ادْعُوهُمْ لِآبَائِهِمْ هُوَ أَقْسَطُ عِندَ
اللَّهِ ۚ فَإِن لَّمْ تَعْلَمُوا آبَاءَهُمْ
فَإِخْوَانُكُمْ فِي الدِّينِ
وَمَوَالِيكُمْ ۚ
وَلَيْسَ عَلَيْكُمْ جُنَاحٌ فِيمَا أَخْطَأْتُم بِهِ
وَلَٰكِن مَّا تَعَمَّدَتْ قُلُوبُكُمْ ۚ
وَكَانَ اللَّهُ غَفُورًا رَّحِيمًا ○

3670. This was an evil Arab custom, by which the husband selfishly deprived his wife of her conjugal rights and yet kept her tied to himself like a slave without her being free to remarry. He pronounced words importing that she was like his mother. After that she could not demand conjugal rights but was not free from his control and could not contract another marriage. See also lviii. 1-5, where this is condemned in the strongest terms and punishment is provided for it. A man sometimes said such words in a fit of anger : they did not affect him, but they degraded her position.

3671. If a man called another's son "his son", it might create complications with natural and normal relationships if taken too literally. It is pointed out that it is only a *façon de parler* in men's mouths, and should not be taken literally. The truth is the truth and cannot be altered by men's adopting "sons". "Adoption" in the technical sense is not allowed in Muslim Law. Those who have been "wives of your sons proceeding from your loins" are within the Prohibited Degrees of marriage; iv. 23 : but this does not apply to "adopted" sons.

3672. Freedmen were often called after their master's name as the "son of so and so". When they were slaves, perhaps their fathers' names were lost altogether. It is more correct to speak of them as the *Maulā* of so and so. But *Maulā* in Arabic might also imply a close relationship of friendship : in that case, too, it is better to use the right term instead of the term "son". "Brother" is not objectionable, because "Brotherhood" is used in a wider sense than "fatherhood" and is not likely to be misunderstood.

3673. What is aimed at is to destroy the superstition of erecting false relationships to the detriment or loss of true blood relations. It is not intended to penalise an unintentional slip in the matter, and indeed, even if a man deliberately calls another his son or father, who is not his son or father, out of politeness or affection. "God is Oft-Returning, Most Merciful". It is the action of mischievous parties which is chiefly reprehended, if they intend false insinuations. A mere mistake on their part does not matter.

6. The Prophet is closer
To the Believers than
Their own selves,[3674]
And his wives are [3675]
Their mothers. Blood-relations
Among each other have
Closer personal ties,
In the Decree of God.
Than (the Brotherhood of)
Believers and Muhājirs : [3676]
Nevertheless do ye
What is just to your
Closest friends : such is
The writing in the Decree
(Of God).

٦- اَلنَّبِيُّ اَوْلٰى بِالْمُؤْمِنِيْنَ مِنْ اَنْفُسِهِمْ
وَاَزْوَاجُهٗٓ اُمَّهٰتُهُمْ ۭ
وَاُولُوا الْاَرْحَامِ بَعْضُهُمْ
اَوْلٰى بِبَعْضٍ فِيْ كِتٰبِ اللّٰهِ
مِنَ الْمُؤْمِنِيْنَ وَالْمُهٰجِرِيْنَ
اِلَّآ اَنْ تَفْعَلُوْٓا اِلٰٓى اَوْلِيٰۗىِٕكُمْ مَّعْرُوْفًا ۭ
كَانَ ذٰلِكَ فِي الْكِتٰبِ مَسْطُوْرًا ○

7. And remember We took
From the Prophets their
Covenant : [3677]
As (We did) from thee :
From Noah, Abraham, Moses,
And Jesus the son of Mary :
We took from them
A solemn Covenant :

٧- وَاِذْ اَخَذْنَا مِنَ النَّبِيّٖنَ
مِيْثَاقَهُمْ وَمِنْكَ وَمِنْ نُّوْحٍ وَّاِبْرٰهِيْمَ
وَمُوْسٰى وَعِيْسَى ابْنِ مَرْيَمَ ۠
وَاَخَذْنَا مِنْهُمْ مِّيْثَاقًا غَلِيْظًا ○

3674. In spiritual relationship the Prophet is entitled to more respect and consideration than blood-relations. The Believers should follow him rather than their fathers or mothers or brothers, where there is conflict of duties. He is even nearer—closer to our real interests—than our own selves. In some Qirāats, like that of Ubai ibn Ka'b, occur also the words "and he is a father to them", which imply his spiritual relationship and connect on with the words "and his wives are their mothers". Thus his spiritual fatherhood would be contrasted pointedly with the repudiation of the vulgar superstition of calling any one like Zaid ibn Hāritha by the appellation Zaid ibn Muḥammad (xxxiii. 40): such an appellation is really disrespectful to the Prophet.

3675. See last note. This Sūra establishes the dignity and position of the Holy Prophet's wives, who had a special mission and responsibility as Mothers of the Believers They were not to be like ordinary women : they had to instruct women in spiritual matters visit and minister to those who were ill or in distress, and do other kindly offices in aid of the Prophet's mission.

3676 No man should deprive his blood-relations of such rights of maintenance and property as they might have. The community of Believers, inhabitants of Medina and those who had migrated to Medina from Mecca, also had their mutual rights, but they were not to be put forward as an excuse to defeat the prior rights of natural relationship. In the early Medina days, Anṣār were allowed to inherit from Muhājirs whose natural relations had not emigrated, but this practice was discontinued when normal relations were re-established between Mecca and Medina.

3677. *Cf.* iii 81. There is an implied covenant on all created things to follow God's Law, which is the law of their being : see v. 1. But there is a special implied covenant with all Prophets, strict and solemn, that they shall carry out their mission, proclaim God's Truth without fear or favour, and be ever ready in His service in all circumstances. That gives them their position and dignity as explained in the last verse, and their tremendous responsibility in respect of the people whom they come to instruct and lead to the right Path.

8. That (God) may question
The (Custodians) of Truth
concerning
The Truth they (were charged
with):[3678]
And He has prepared
For the Unbelievers
A grievous Penalty.

٨- لِّيَسْـَٔلَ الصّٰدِقِيْنَ
عَنْ صِدْقِهِمْ ۚ
وَاَعَدَّ لِلْكٰفِرِيْنَ
عَذَابًا اَلِيْمًا ۟ ع

C. 187.—When the formidable forces of a whole Confederacy
(xxxiii. 9-27.) Bent on destroying Islam burst
Upon Medina, it was God's grace that saved
The Muslims. The enemies and the Hypocrites
Did their best to defeat the purpose of God,
But they were foiled. In the Apostle was found
The ideal Leader for the men of God,
Who became heirs to the heritage misused
By enemies to Faith and the Laws of God.

SECTION 2.

9. O ye who believe!
Remember the Grace of God,
(Bestowed) on you, when
There came down on you
Hosts (to overwhelm you):[3679]
But We sent against them[3680]

٩- يٰۤاَيُّهَا الَّذِيْنَ اٰمَنُوا اذْكُرُوْا نِعْمَةَ اللّٰهِ
عَلَيْكُمْ اِذْ جَآءَتْكُمْ
جُنُوْدٌ فَاَرْسَلْنَا عَلَيْهِمْ

3678. The men to whom God's Truth has been committed for promulgation will be asked in the Hereafter as to how the Truth fared in the world—how it was received, who opposed it, and who assisted it. Like all trustees, they will have to give a full account of their trust. God knows all, and it will not add to His information. But it will be evidence for and against those to whom it was preached, so that the responsibility of those who dishonoured it may be duly enforced. The primary custodians of spiritual Truth are the Prophets, but in descending degrees all men to whom God's Message comes are included.

3679. In this verse is summed up the beginning and the end of the fateful struggle of the Siege of Medina in A H. 5. The composition of the unhallowed Confederacy that came to destroy Islam is referred to in the Introduction. They came with a force of ten to twelve thousand fighting men, an unprecedented army for that time and country. The battle is known as the Battle of the Trench.

3680. After a close investment of two to four weeks, during which the enemy were disheartened by their ill success, there was a piercing blast of the cold east wind. It was a severe winter, and February can be a very cold month in Medina, which is about 3,000 ft. above the sea-level. The enemy's tents were torn up, their fires were extinguished, the sand and rain beat in their faces, and they were terrified by the portents against them. They had already wellnigh fallen out amongst themselves, and beating a hasty retreat, they melted away. The Medina fighting strength was no more than 3,000, and the Jewish tribe of the Banū Quraiẓa who were in their midst was a source of weakness as they were treacherously intriguing with the enemy. And further there were the Hypocrites: see n. 3666 above. But there were hidden forces that helped the Muslims. Besides the forces of nature there were moral forces,—mutual distrust and bickerings in the enemy camp, and on the other side, perfect discipline among the real Muslims, and the superb leadership of the holy Prophet.

A hurricane and forces
That ye saw not:
But God sees (clearly)[3681]
All that ye do.

رِيحًا وَجُنُودًا لَّمْ تَرَوْهَا ۚ
وَكَانَ اللَّهُ بِمَا تَعْمَلُونَ بَصِيرًا ۝

10. Behold! they came on you
From above you and from
Below you, and behold,
The eyes became dim
And the hearts gaped[3682]
Up to the throats,
And ye imagined various
(Vain) thoughts about God!

١٠- إِذْ جَاءُوكُم مِّن فَوْقِكُمْ وَمِنْ أَسْفَلَ
مِنكُمْ وَإِذْ زَاغَتِ الْأَبْصَارُ
وَبَلَغَتِ الْقُلُوبُ الْحَنَاجِرَ
وَتَظُنُّونَ بِاللَّهِ الظُّنُونَا ۝

11. In that situation
Were the Believers tried:
They were shaken as by
A tremendous shaking.

١١- هُنَالِكَ ابْتُلِيَ الْمُؤْمِنُونَ
وَزُلْزِلُوا زِلْزَالًا شَدِيدًا ۝

12. And behold! The Hypocrites
And those in whose hearts
Is a disease (even) say: "God
And His Apostle promised us
Nothing but delusions!"[3683]

١٢- وَإِذْ يَقُولُ الْمُنَافِقُونَ وَالَّذِينَ فِي قُلُوبِهِم
مَّرَضٌ مَّا وَعَدَنَا اللَّهُ
وَرَسُولُهُ إِلَّا غُرُورًا ۝

13. Behold! A party among them
Said: "Ye men of Yathrib!
Ye cannot stand (the attack)!
Therefore go back!"
And a band of them
Ask for leave of the Prophet,

١٣- وَإِذْ قَالَت طَّائِفَةٌ مِّنْهُمْ يَا أَهْلَ يَثْرِبَ
لَا مُقَامَ لَكُمْ فَارْجِعُوا ۚ
وَيَسْتَأْذِنُ فَرِيقٌ مِّنْهُمُ النَّبِيَّ

3681. God sees everything. Therefore we may conclude that the discipline and moral fervour of the Muslims, as well as the enemy's insincerities, intrigues, and reliance on brute force, were all contributory causes to his repulse, under God's dispensation. There were many hidden causes which neither party saw clearly.

3682. The psychology of the combatants is described with matchless vigour in the holy Text. The onrush of the enemy was really tremendous. The Trench round Medina was between the defenders and the huge attacking force, which had some high ground behind them "above you": when any of them came through the valley or over the Trench, they seemed to come from below. The showers of arrows and stones on both sides must also have seemed to come from the air.

3683. Before this year's mass attack on Medina, the Muslims had successfully reached the Syrian border on the north, and there were hopes of reaching Yemen in the south. The holy Prophet had seen clear signs of expansion and victory for the Muslims. Now that they were shut in within the Trench on the defensive, the Hypocrites taunted them with having indulged in delusive hopes. But the event showed that the hopes were *not* delusive. They were realised beyond expectations in a few years.

Saying, "Truly our houses[3684]
Are bare and exposed," though
They were not exposed:
They intended nothing but
To run away.

يَقُولُونَ إِنَّ بُيُوتَنَا عَوْرَةٌ
وَمَا هِيَ بِعَوْرَةٍ
إِنْ يُرِيدُونَ إِلَّا فِرَارًا ○

14. And if an entry had
Been effected to them[3685]
From the sides of the (City),
And they had been
Incited to sedition,
They would certainly have
Brought it to pass, with
None but a brief delay!

۱۴- وَلَوْ دُخِلَتْ عَلَيْهِم
مِّنْ أَقْطَارِهَا
ثُمَّ سُئِلُوا الْفِتْنَةَ لَآتَوْهَا
وَمَا تَلَبَّثُوا بِهَا إِلَّا يَسِيرًا ○

15. And yet they had already
Covenanted with God not to turn
Their backs, and a covenant[3686]
With God must (surely)
Be answered for.

۱۵- وَلَقَدْ كَانُوا عَاهَدُوا اللَّهَ مِن قَبْلُ
لَا يُوَلُّونَ الْأَدْبَارَ ۚ
وَكَانَ عَهْدُ اللَّهِ مَسْئُولًا ○

16. Say: "Running away will not
Profit you if ye are
Running away from death[3687]
Or slaughter; and even if
(Ye do escape), no more
Than a brief (respite)
Will ye be allowed to enjoy!"

۱۶- قُل لَّن يَنفَعَكُمُ الْفِرَارُ إِن
فَرَرْتُم مِّنَ الْمَوْتِ
أَوِ الْقَتْلِ وَإِذًا لَّا
تُمَتَّعُونَ إِلَّا قَلِيلًا ○

3684. All the fighting men of Medina had come out of the City and camped in the open space between the City and the Trench that had been dug all round. The disaffected Hypocrites sowed defeatist rumours and pretended to withdraw for the defence of their homes, though their homes were not exposed, and were fully covered by the vigilant defensive force inside the Trench.

3685. The brunt of the fighting was on the north side, but the whole Trench was guarded. At one or two points enemy warriors did break in within the circuit of the Trench, but they were soon disposed of. Ḥadhrat 'Alī particularly distinguished himself in many fights, wearing the Prophet's own sword and armour. If any of the enemy had been able to penetrate into the City, the disaffected element, which was only sitting on the fence, would have risen against the Muslims at once—with no delay except what might have been necessary to put on their armour and arms.

3686. Apparently, after the battle of Uḥud, certain men who had then shown cowardice were forgiven on undertaking that they would behave better next time. A solemn promise made to the Apostle of God is a promise to God, and it cannot be broken with impunity.

3687. The coward in a fight does not usually save himself from death. He is subject, after desertion, to the fury both of the enemy and of his own side for cowardice and desertion. Assuming that he did escape with his life, where could he go to? The brand of cowardice will be on him, and he will be subject to the vengeance of his own people. In any case, his life would be in ignominy and would be brief, and he would have lost irretrievably the meed of valour.

17. Say: "Who is it that can
Screen you from God
If it be His wish
To give you Punishment
Or to give you Mercy?"[3688]
Nor will they find for themselves,
Besides God, any protector
Or helper.

18. Verily God knows those
Among you who keep back
(Men) and those who say
To their brethren, "Come along
To us", but come not
To the fight except
For just a little while,

19. Covetous over you.[3689]
Then when fear comes,
Thou wilt see them looking
To thee, their eyes revolving,
Like (those of) one over whom
Hovers death: but when
The fear is past,
They will smite you
With sharp tongues, covetous[3690]
Of goods. Such men have
No faith, and so God
Has made their deeds[3691]
Of none effect: and that
Is easy for God.[3692]

١٧- قُلْ مَنْ ذَا الَّذِي يَعْصِمُكُمْ مِّنَ اللَّهِ
إِنْ أَرَادَ بِكُمْ سُوٓءًا
أَوْ أَرَادَ بِكُمْ رَحْمَةً ۚ وَلَا يَجِدُونَ لَهُم مِّنْ
دُونِ اللَّهِ وَلِيًّا وَّلَا نَصِيرًا ○

١٨- قَدْ يَعْلَمُ اللَّهُ الْمُعَوِّقِينَ مِنكُمْ
وَالْقَآئِلِينَ لِإِخْوَانِهِمْ
هَلُمَّ إِلَيْنَا ۚ
وَلَا يَأْتُونَ الْبَأْسَ إِلَّا قَلِيلًا ○

١٩- أَشِحَّةً عَلَيْكُمْ ۚ فَإِذَا جَآءَ الْخَوْفُ
رَأَيْتَهُمْ يَنظُرُونَ إِلَيْكَ تَدُورُ أَعْيُنُهُمْ
كَالَّذِي يُغْشَىٰ عَلَيْهِ مِنَ الْمَوْتِ ۚ
فَإِذَا ذَهَبَ الْخَوْفُ سَلَقُوكُم بِأَلْسِنَةٍ
حِدَادٍ أَشِحَّةً عَلَى الْخَيْرِ ۚ
أُولَٰٓئِكَ لَمْ يُؤْمِنُوا فَأَحْبَطَ اللَّهُ أَعْمَالَهُمْ ۚ
وَكَانَ ذَٰلِكَ عَلَى اللَّهِ يَسِيرًا ○

3688. It is still worse if the cowardice or desertion is shown in a Cause, which, because of the high issues of truth and justice, may be called the Cause of God. How can any one escape God's Punishment? And in the same way, how can any one prevent another from obtaining God's Mercy by repentance and amendment? The better path, therefore, is to stand firm in God's Way, and if you fail through human weakness, to repent and seek God's Mercy. *Cf.* xxxiii. 24, and n. 3698 below.

3689. *Ashiḥḥatan*: covetous, grasping, niggardly. Here the meaning is towfold: (1) they spare themselves in the fight as compared with you; they are niggardly with themselves as against you; they contribute little either in personal effort or with their money and resources; and (2) they covet any gains made or booty won, on the part of the real fighters.

3690. In times of danger, they would look to the holy Prophet for protection, and keep themselves snugly from the fight. When the danger is past, they will come and brag and wrangle and show their covetousness or greed for gain though they gave of themselves but sparingly.

3691. Even any good they may have done becomes vain because of their motives of envy, greed, and covetousness, and their cowardice.

3692. It is not surprising that men's deeds fall as it were dead because there is no pure motive behind them. For men it may be difficult to probe motives, but it is easy for God, Whom hypocrisy or false show can never deceive.

20. They think that the Confederates
Have not withdrawn; and if
The Confederates should come
(again),
They would wish they were
In the deserts (wandering)
Among the Bedouins, and [3693]
Seeking news about you
(From a safe distance);
And if they were
In your midst, they
Would fight but little.

٢٠- يَحْسَبُونَ الْأَحْزَابَ لَمْ يَذْهَبُوا ۚ
وَإِن يَأْتِ الْأَحْزَابُ
يَوَدُّوا لَوْ أَنَّهُم بَادُونَ فِي الْأَعْرَابِ
يَسْأَلُونَ عَنْ أَنبَائِكُمْ ۖ
وَلَوْ كَانُوا فِيكُم
مَّا قَاتَلُوا إِلَّا قَلِيلًا ۝

SECTION 3.

21. We have indeed
In the Apostle of God
A beautiful pattern (of conduct)
For any one whose hope is [3694]
In God and the Final Day,
And who engages much [3695]
In the praise of God.

٢١- لَّقَدْ كَانَ لَكُمْ فِي رَسُولِ اللَّهِ
أُسْوَةٌ حَسَنَةٌ
لِّمَن كَانَ يَرْجُو اللَّهَ وَالْيَوْمَ الْآخِرَ
وَذَكَرَ اللَّهَ كَثِيرًا ۝

3693. This completes the picture of the psychology of the Hypocrites, begun at verse 12. Let us analyse it. (1) When they first saw the enemy they were already in a defeatist mood, and thought all was over (verse 12). (2) Not content with disloyalty themselves, they tried to infect others; who made paltry excuses to withdraw from the fight (verse 13). (3) They were ready to betray the City to the enemy if once the enemy had gained entrance (verse 14). (4) They forgot all the promises of fidelity which they had previously sworn (verse 15). (5) In their paltry calculations they forgot that cowardice in war does not pay (verses 16-17). (6) Without taking much part in the actual defence, they were ready to talk glibly and claim a lion's share in the fruits of the victory (verses 18-19). (7) Even when the enemy had withdrawn, their cowardly minds were still afraid that the enemy would return, and were already meditating what they would do in that case: perhaps they would dwell in the deserts and spy on Medina from a safe distance; and if caught in Medina they would fight little and intrigue much.

It was a miracle that with such men in their midst, the holy Prophet and his band won through.

3694. We now have the psychology of the Believers,—God-fearing men, led by that pattern of men and of leaders, Muḥammad Musṭafā.

3695. *Cf.* xxvi. 227: see especially the last clause of that verse in a Meccan Sūra, which was amply fulfilled in Medina.

22. When the Believers saw
The Confederate forces,
They said: "This is
What God and His Apostle [3696]
Had promised us, and God
And His Apostle told us
What was true." And it
Only added to their faith
And their zeal in obedience.

٢٢- وَلَمَّا رَاَ الْمُؤْمِنُوْنَ الْاَحْزَابَ
قَالُوْا هٰذَا مَا وَعَدَنَا اللّٰهُ وَرَسُوْلُهٗ
وَصَدَقَ اللّٰهُ وَرَسُوْلُهٗ
وَمَا زَادَهُمْ اِلَّآ اِيْمَانًا
وَّتَسْلِيْمًا ۝

23. Among the Believers are men
Who have been true to
Their Covenant with God:
Of them some have completed [3697]
Their vow (to the extreme),
And some (still) wait:
But they have never changed
(Their determination) in the least:

٢٣- مِنَ الْمُؤْمِنِيْنَ رِجَالٌ
صَدَقُوْا مَا عَاهَدُوا اللّٰهَ عَلَيْهِ
فَمِنْهُمْ مَّنْ قَضٰى نَحْبَهٗ وَمِنْهُمْ مَّنْ
يَّنْتَظِرُ
وَمَا بَدَّلُوْا تَبْدِيْلًا ۝

24. That God may reward
The men of Truth for
Their Truth, and punish
The Hypocrites if that be [3698]

٢٤- لِيَجْزِيَ اللّٰهُ الصّٰدِقِيْنَ بِصِدْقِهِمْ
وَيُعَذِّبَ الْمُنٰفِقِيْنَ اِنْ

3696. This is in contrast to what the Hypocrites said in verse 12 above. The divine promise of help and success is contingent upon our striving and faith. Nothing comes to the poltroon and the sceptical idler. Dangers and difficulties, and conflict with Evil, are foretold us, and we must meet them with fortitude and courage.

3697. In the fight for Truth were (and are) many who sacrificed their all—resources, knowledge, influence, life itself—in the Cause, and never wavered. If they won the crown of martyrdom, they were blessed. Such a one was Sa'd ibn Mu'āẓ, the chief of the Aus tribe, the intrepid standard-bearer of Islam, who died of a wound he had received in the Battle of the Trench. Other heroes fought valiantly and lived, always ready to lay down their lives. Both classes were staunch: they never changed or wavered.

3698. Before the Throne of God's Mercy there is always room for repentance and forgiveness, even after treason and crime: but the forgiveness will be according to God's Will and Plan, which will judge the penitent's sincerity and capacity for good to the nicest degree in his favour. *Cf.* also xxxiii. 17 above.

His Will, or turn to them
In Mercy: for God is
Oft-Forgiving, Most Merciful.

شَآءَ اَوۡ يَتُوۡبَ عَلَيۡهِمۡ‌ؕ
اِنَّ اللّٰهَ كَانَ غَفُوۡرًا رَّحِيۡمًا‌ ۚ‏

25. And God turned back
The Unbelievers for (all)
Their fury: no advantage[3699]
Did they gain; and enough
Is God for the Believers
In their fight. And God
Is full of Strength, Able
To enforce His Will.[3700]

٢٥-وَرَدَّ اللّٰهُ الَّذِيۡنَ كَفَرُوۡا بِغَيۡظِهِمۡ
لَمۡ يَنَالُوۡا خَيۡرًا‌ؕ
وَكَفَى اللّٰهُ الۡمُؤۡمِنِيۡنَ الۡقِتَالَ‌ؕ
وَكَانَ اللّٰهُ قَوِيًّا عَزِيۡزًا‌ ۚ‏

26. And those of the people[3701]
Of the Book who aided
Them—God did take them
Down from their strongholds[3702]

٢٦-وَاَنۡزَلَ الَّذِيۡنَ ظَاهَرُوۡهُمۡ مِّنۡ اَهۡلِ
الۡكِتٰبِ مِنۡ صَيَاصِيۡهِمۡ

3699. In spite of the mighty preparations and the great forces which the Meccans, in concert with the Central Arabian Bedouins, the discontented Jews, and the treacherous Hypocrites, brought to the siege of Medina, all their plans were frustrated. Their fury availed them nothing. They departed in hot haste. This was their last and dying effort. The initiative thererafter lay with the forces of Islam.

3700. For the meaning of *'Aziz*, see n. 2818 to xxii. 40.

3701. The reference is to the Jewish tribe of the Banū Quraiẓa. They counted among the citizens of Medina and were bound by solemn engagements to help in the defence of the City. But on the occasion of the Confederate siege by the Quraish and their allies they intrigued with the enemies and treacherously aided them. Immediately after the siege was raised and the Confederates had fled in hot haste, the Prophet turned his attention to these treacherous "friends" who had betrayed his City in the hour of danger.

3702. The Banū Quraiẓa (see last note) were filled with terror and dismay when Medina was free from the Quraish danger. They shut themselves up in their castles about three or four miles to the east (or north east) of Medina, and sustained a siege of 25 days, after which they surrendered, stipulating that they would abide by the decision of their fate at the hands of Sa'd ibn Mu'āẓ, chief of the Aus tribe, with which they had been in alliance.

And cast terror into
Their hearts, (so that)[3703]
Some ye slew, and some[3704]
Ye made prisoners.

وَقَذَفَ فِي قُلُوبِهِمُ الرُّعْبَ
فَرِيقًا تَقْتُلُونَ وَتَأْسِرُونَ فَرِيقًا ۝

27. And He made you heirs
Of their lands, their houses,
And their goods,
And of a land which[3705]

٢٧- وَأَوْرَثَكُمْ أَرْضَهُمْ وَدِيَارَهُمْ
وَأَمْوَالَهُمْ وَأَرْضًا لَّمْ

3703. Sa'd applied to them the Jewish Law of the Old Testament, not as strictly as the case warranted. In Deut. xx. 10-18, the treatment of a city "which is very far off from thee" is prescribed to be comparatively more lenient than the treatment of a city "of those people, which the Lord thy God does give thee for an inheritance," *i.e.*, which is near enough to corrupt the religion of the Jewish people. The punishment for these is total annihilation: "thou shalt save alive nothing that breatheth" (Deut. xx. 16). The more lenient treatment for far-off cities is described in the next note. According to the Jewish standard, then, the Quraiẓa deserved total extermination—of men, women, and children. They were in the territory of Medina itself, and further they had broken their engagements and helped the enemy.

3704. Sa'd adjudged them the milder treatment of the "far-off" cities which is thus described in the Jewish Law: "Thou shalt smite every male thereof with the edge of the sword: but the women and the little ones, and the cattle, and all that is in the city, even all the spoil thereof, shalt thou take unto thyself; and thou shalt eat the spoil of thine enemies, which the Lord thy God hath given thee" (Deut. xx. 13-14). The men of the Quraiẓa were slain: the women were sold as captives of war; and their lands and properties were divided among the Muhājirs.

3705. If this part of the Sūra was revealed after the autumn of the Hijra year 7, it refers to the result of the Khaibar expedition of that autumn. Khaibar is a Ḥarrat or volcanic tract, well-watered with many springs issuing from its basaltic rocks It has a good irrigation system and produces good harvests of grain and dates in its wet valleys, while the outcrop of rocks in the high ground affords sites for numerous fortresses. At present it is inhabited chiefly by men of the race of Bilāl (the Abyssinian) who played a prominent part in the expedition. It is a sort of island in the deserts on the outskirts of Najd. In the holy Prophet's time there were Jewish colonies settled here, but they were a source of constant trouble, especially after the Siege of Medina. It became a nest of all the hostile Jewish elements expelled for their treachery from elsewhere. Its capital, Khaibar, is about 90 miles due north of Medina. Its inhabitants offered some resistance, and Ḥadhrat 'Alī, though he had just risen from a bed of illness, performed prodigies of valour. After its surrender, a land settlement was made, which retained the cultivators of the soil on the land, but brought them under control, so that no further focus of active hostility should remain near Medina. The terms of the settlement will be found in Wāqidī.

Ye had not frequented
(Before). And God has
Power over all things.

تَطَـُٔوْهَا ۚ وَكَانَ اللّٰهُ عَلٰى كُلِّ شَىْءٍ قَدِيْرًا ۧ ع

C. 188 —The Prophet's household is not for worldly
(xxxiii. 28-52.) Ends : his consorts have a place
And dignity beyond ordinary women
They must recite and proclaim the Signs
Of God. For women have spiritual virtues
And duties like unto men. God decrees.
No unhappy wedlock: fear not
To dissolve such and provide what is right
And fitting for the service of God. High
Is the Prophet's position, and he must order
His household as best befits his work
And duties. God doth watch all things.

SECTION 4.

28. O Prophet! say
To thy Consorts:
" If it be that ye desire
The life of this world,
And its glitter,—then come![3706]
I will provide for your

٢٨- يٰٓاَيُّهَا النَّبِىُّ قُلْ لِّاَزْوَاجِكَ
اِنْ كُنْتُنَّ تُرِدْنَ الْحَيٰوةَ الدُّنْيَا
وَزِيْنَتَهَا فَتَعَالَيْنَ اُمَتِّعْكُنَّ

3706. We now come to the subject of the position of the Consorts of Purity (*azwāj muṭahharāt*), the wives of the holy Prophet. Their position was not like that of ordinary women or ordinary wives. They had special duties and responsibilities. The only youthful marriage of the holy Prophet was his first marriage—that with Ḥadhrat Khadija, the best of women and the best of wives. He married her fifteen years before he received his call to Apostleship ; their married life lasted for twenty-five years. and their mutual devotion was of the noblest, judged by spiritual as well as social standards. During her life he had no other wife, which was unusual for a man of his standing among his people. When she died, his age was 50, and but for two considerations, he would probably never have married again, as he was most abstemious in his physical life. The two considerations which governed his later marriages were : (1) compassion and clemency, as when he wanted to provide for suffering widows, who could not be provided for in any other way in that stage of society ; some of them, like Sauda, had issue by their former marriage, requiring protection ; (2) help in his duties of leadership, with women, who had to be instructed and kept together in the large Muslim family, where women and men had similar social rights. Ḥadhrat 'Āisha, daughter of Ḥadhrat Abū Bakr, was clever and learned, and in Ḥadith she is an important authority on the life of the Prophet. Ḥadhrat Zainab, daughter of Khuzaima, was specially devoted to the poor : she was called the "Mother of the Poor". The other Zainab, daughter of Jaḥsh, also worked for the poor, for whom she provided from the proceeds of her manual work, as she was skilful in leather work. But all the Consorts in their high position had to work and assist as Mothers of the Ummat. Theirs were not idle lives, like those of Odalisques, either for their own pleasure or the pleasure of their husband. They are told here that they had no place in the sacred Household if they merely wished for ease or worldly glitter. If such were the case, they could be divorced and amply provided for.

Enjoyment and set you free
In a handsome manner.

وَأُسَرِّحْكُنَّ سَرَاحًا جَمِيلًا ○

29. But if ye seek God
And His Apostle, and
The Home of the Hereafter,
Verily God has prepared
For the well-doers amongst you [3707]
A great reward.

٢٩- وَإِنْ كُنْتُنَّ تُرِدْنَ اللهَ وَرَسُولَهُ
وَالدَّارَ الْآخِرَةَ فَإِنَّ اللهَ أَعَدَّ
لِلْمُحْسِنٰتِ مِنْكُنَّ أَجْرًا عَظِيمًا ○

30. O Consorts of the Prophet
If any of you were guilty
Of evident unseemly conduct,[3708]
The Punishment would be
Doubled to her, and that
21/30 Is easy for God.[3709]

٣٠- يٰنِسَآءَ النَّبِيِّ مَنْ يَّأْتِ مِنْكُنَّ بِفَاحِشَةٍ
مُّبَيِّنَةٍ
يُّضٰعَفْ لَهَا الْعَذَابُ ضِعْفَيْنِ
وَكَانَ ذٰلِكَ عَلَى اللهِ يَسِيرًا ○

3707. They were all well-doers. But being in their exalted position, they had extra responsibility, and they had to be specially careful to discharge it. In the same way their reward would be "great", for higher services bring higher spiritual satisfaction, though they were asked to deny themselves some of the ordinary indulgences of this life.

3708. "*Evident unseemly conduct*": *i.e.*, proved misconduct, as opposed to false slanders from enemies. Such slanders were of no account, but if any of them had behaved in an unseemly manner, it would have been a worse offence than in the case of ordinary women, on account of their special position. Of course none of them were in the least guilty.

3709. *Cf.* xxxiii. 19 and n. 3692. The punishment in this life for a married woman's unchastity is very severe: for adultery, public flogging with a hundred stripes, under xxiv. 2; or for lewdness (see iv. 15) imprisonment; or stoning to death for adultery, according to certain precedents established in Canon Law. But here the question is not about this kind of punishment or this kind of offence. Even minor indiscretions, in the case of women who were patterns of decorum, would have been reprehensible: and the punishment in the Hereafter is on a higher plane, which we can scarcely understand. But God can appreciate every shade of motive in us. More or less is possible there, which might not be possible in the rough and ready law which we administer here.

31. But any of you that is
Devout in the service of
God and His Apostle,
And works righteousness,—
To her shall We grant
Her reward twice[3710]: and We
Have prepared for her
A generous Sustenance.[3711]

٣١- وَمَنْ يَّقْنُتْ مِنْكُنَّ لِلّٰهِ وَرَسُوْلِهٖ
وَتَعْمَلْ صَالِحًا
نُّؤْتِهَآ اَجْرَهَا مَرَّتَيْنِ
وَاَعْتَدْنَا لَهَا رِزْقًا كَرِيْمًا ۝

32. O Consorts of the Prophet!
Ye are not like any
Of the (other) women:[3712]
If ye do fear (God),
Be not too complaisant
Of speech, lest one
In whose heart is
A disease should be moved
With desire: but speak ye
A speech (that is) just.[3713]

٣٢- يٰنِسَآءَ النَّبِيِّ
لَسْتُنَّ كَاَحَدٍ مِّنَ النِّسَآءِ اِنِ اتَّقَيْتُنَّ
فَلَا تَخْضَعْنَ بِالْقَوْلِ
فَيَطْمَعَ الَّذِيْ فِيْ قَلْبِهٖ مَرَضٌ
وَّقُلْنَ قَوْلًا مَّعْرُوْفًا ۝

33. And stay quietly in
Your houses, and make not
A dazzling display, like
That of the former Times
Of Ignorance; and establish
Regular Prayer, and give
Regular Charity; and obey[3714]
God and His Apostle.
And God only wishes
To remove all abomination

٣٣- وَقَرْنَ فِيْ بُيُوْتِكُنَّ وَلَا تَبَرَّجْنَ
تَبَرُّجَ الْجَاهِلِيَّةِ الْاُوْلٰى
وَاَقِمْنَ الصَّلٰوةَ وَاٰتِيْنَ الزَّكٰوةَ وَاَطِعْنَ
اللّٰهَ وَرَسُوْلَهٗ
اِنَّمَا يُرِيْدُ اللّٰهُ لِيُذْهِبَ عَنْكُمُ الرِّجْسَ

3710. *Twice, i.e.* once as a righteous woman, and again as a Mother of the Believers, serving the believing women and thus showing her devotion to God and His Apostle.

3711. *Sustenance*: in the spiritual sense; all that is necessary to sustain her in happiness in her future life.

3712. This is the core of the whole passage. The Prophet's Consorts were not like ordinary women, nor was their marriage an ordinary marriage, in which only personal or social considerations enter. They had a special position and special responsibilities, in the matter of guiding and instructing women who came into the fold of Islam. Islam is a Way of Life, and the Muslims are a family: women have as much place in Islam as men, and their intimate instruction must obviously be through women.

3713. While they were to be kind and gentle to all, they were to be guarded on account of their special position, lest gross people might misunderstand or take advantage of their kindness. They were to make no vulgar worldly displays as in the times of Paganism.

3714. Obedience to God's Law sums up all duties. Regular Prayer (seeking nearness to God) and Regular Charity (doing good to fellow-creatures) are mentioned as specially symbolical of our Religion.

From you, ye Members[3715]
Of the Family, and to make
You pure and spotless.

أَهْلَ الْبَيْتِ وَيُطَهِّرَكُمْ تَطْهِيرًا ۝

34. And recite[3716] what is
Rehearsed to you in your
Homes, of the Signs of God
And His Wisdom:
For God understands
The finest mysteries and
Is well-acquainted (with them).[3717]

٣٤- وَاذْكُرْنَ مَا يُتْلَىٰ فِي
بُيُوتِكُنَّ مِنْ آيَاتِ اللَّهِ وَالْحِكْمَةِ ۚ
إِنَّ اللَّهَ كَانَ لَطِيفًا خَبِيرًا ۝ ع

SECTION 5.

35. For Muslim men and
women,—[3718]
For believing men and women,
For devout men and women,
For true men and women,
For men and women who are
Patient and constant, for men
And women who humble themselves,
For men and women who give[3719]
In charity, for men and women
Who fast (and deny themselves),
For men and women who
Guard their chastity, and
For men and women who

٣٥- إِنَّ الْمُسْلِمِينَ وَالْمُسْلِمَاتِ وَالْمُؤْمِنِينَ
وَالْمُؤْمِنَاتِ وَالْقَانِتِينَ وَالْقَانِتَاتِ وَ
الصَّادِقِينَ وَالصَّادِقَاتِ وَالصَّابِرِينَ وَ
الصَّابِرَاتِ وَالْخَاشِعِينَ وَالْخَاشِعَاتِ وَ
الْمُتَصَدِّقِينَ وَالْمُتَصَدِّقَاتِ وَالصَّائِمِينَ
وَالصَّائِمَاتِ وَالْحَافِظِينَ فُرُوجَهُمْ وَ
الْحَافِظَاتِ وَالذَّاكِرِينَ اللَّهَ كَثِيرًا وَالذَّاكِرَاتِ

3715. Notice the transition in this clause to the masculine gender, while before this the verbs and pronouns were in the feminine gender as referring to the consorts. The statement in this clause is now more general, including (besides the Consorts) the whole family, namely, Ḥaḏhrat Fāṭima the daughter, Ḥaḏhrat 'Alī the son-in-law, and their sons Ḥasan and Ḥusain, the beloved grandsons of the Prophet. The masculine gender is used generally, in speaking of a mixed assembly of men and women.

3716. The verb is *uẕkurna*, feminine gender, as referring to the *Azwāj* again. It means not only "remember", but "recite", "teach", "make known", "publish", the Message which ye learn at home from the holy Prophet, the fountain of spiritual knowledge. The "Signs of God" refer specially to the verses of the Qur-ān, and Wisdom to the resulting Instruction derived therefrom.

3717. *Cf.* xxii. 63, and n. 2844. God's understanding is perfect in every detail, however minute. Therefore use His Revelation for every phase of life.

3718. Islam, or submitting our will to God's Will, includes all the virtues, as particularly specified in this verse. See n. 3720.

3719. A number of Muslim virtues are specified here, but the chief stress is laid on the fact that these virtues are as necessary to women as to men. Both sexes have spiritual as well as human rights and duties in an equal degree, and the future "reward" of the Hereafter, *viz.*, Spiritual Bliss, is provided for the one as for the other.

Engage much in God's praise,—[3720]
For them has God prepared
Forgiveness and great reward.

أَعَدَّ اللَّهُ لَهُم مَّغْفِرَةً وَأَجْرًا عَظِيمًا

36. It is not fitting
For a Believer, man or woman,
When a matter has been decided
By God and His Apostle,
To have any option
About their decision:[3721]
If any one disobeys God
And His Apostle, he is indeed
On a clearly wrong Path.

٣٦- وَمَا كَانَ لِمُؤْمِنٍ وَلَا مُؤْمِنَةٍ
إِذَا قَضَى اللَّهُ وَرَسُولُهُ أَمْرًا
أَن يَكُونَ لَهُمُ الْخِيَرَةُ مِنْ أَمْرِهِمْ
وَمَن يَعْصِ اللَّهَ وَرَسُولَهُ
فَقَدْ ضَلَّ ضَلَالًا مُّبِينًا

37. Behold! thou didst say
To one who had received
The grace of God[3722]
And thy favour: "Retain thou
(In wedlock) thy wife,
And fear God." But thou
Didst hide in thy heart[3723]
That which God was about
To make manifest: thou didst
Fear the people, but it is

٣٧- وَإِذْ تَقُولُ لِلَّذِي
أَنْعَمَ اللَّهُ عَلَيْهِ وَأَنْعَمْتَ عَلَيْهِ
أَمْسِكْ عَلَيْكَ زَوْجَكَ وَاتَّقِ اللَّهَ
وَتُخْفِي فِي نَفْسِكَ مَا اللَّهُ مُبْدِيهِ
وَتَخْشَى النَّاسَ

3720. The virtues referred to are: (1) Faith, hope, and trust in God, and in His benevolent government of the world; (2) devotion and service in practical life; (3) love and practice of truth, in thought and intention, word and deed; (4) patience and constancy, in suffering and in right endeavour; (5) humility, the avoidance of an attitude of arrogance and superiority; (6) charity, *i.e.*, help to the poor and unfortunate ones in life, a special virtue arising out of the general duty of service (No. 2); (7) self-denial, typically in food, but generally in all appetites; (8) chastity, purity in sex life, purity in motive, thought, word, and deed; and (9) constant attention to God's Message, and cultivation of the desire to get nearer to God.

3721. We must not put our own wisdom in competition with God's wisdom. God's decree is often known to us by the logic of facts. We must accept it loyally, and do the best we can to help in our own way to carry it out. We must make our will consonant to the Universal Will.

3722. This was Zaid son of Ḥāritha, one of the first to accept the faith of Islam. He was a freedman of the holy Prophet, who loved him as a son and gave him in marriage his own cousin Zainab. The marriage however turned out to be unhappy. See next note.

3723. Zaid's marriage with the Prophet's cousin Zainab daughter of Jaḥsh was celebrated in Mecca eight years before the Hijrat, but it did not turn out happy. Zainab the high-born looked down upon Zaid the freedman who had been a slave. And he was not comely to look at. Both were good people in their own way, and both loved the Prophet, but there was mutual incompatibility and this is fatal to married life. Zaid wished to divorce her, but the Prophet asked him to hold his hand, and he obeyed. She was closely related to the Prophet; he had given a handsome marriage gift on her marriage to Zaid; and people would certainly talk if such a marriage was broken off, and poor Zainab's reputation would be ruined. This was the fear in the mind of the Prophet. But marriages are made on earth, not in heaven, and it is no part of God's Plan to torture people in a bond which should be a source of happiness but actually is a source of misery. Zaid's wish—indeed the mutual wish of the couple—was for the time being put away, but it became eventually an established fact, and everybody came to know of it.

More fitting that thou shouldst[3724]
Fear God. Then when Zaid
Had dissolved (his marriage)
With her, with the necessary[3725]
(Formality), We joined her
In marriage to thee:
In order that (in future)
There may be no difficulty
To the Believers in (the matter
Of) marriage with the wives[3726]
Of their adopted sons, when
The latter have dissolved
With the necessary (formality)
(Their marriage) with them.
And God's command must
Be fulfilled.

وَاللّٰهُ اَحَقُّ اَنْ تَخْشٰىهُ ؕ
فَلَمَّا قَضٰى زَيْدٌ مِّنْهَا وَطَرًا
زَوَّجْنٰكَهَا
لِكَيْ لَا
يَكُوْنَ عَلَى الْمُؤْمِنِيْنَ حَرَجٌ
فِيْۤ اَزْوَاجِ اَدْعِيَآئِهِمْ
اِذَا قَضَوْا مِنْهُنَّ وَطَرًا ؕ
وَكَانَ اَمْرُ اللّٰهِ مَفْعُوْلًا ۝

38. There can be no difficulty
To the Prophet in what
God has indicated to him[3727]
As a duty. It was
The practice (approved) of God
Amongst those of old
That have passed away.[3728]
And the command of God
Is a decree determined.[3729]

٣٨- مَا كَانَ عَلَى النَّبِيِّ مِنْ حَرَجٍ
فِيْمَا فَرَضَ اللّٰهُ لَهٗ ؕ
سُنَّةَ اللّٰهِ فِي الَّذِيْنَ خَلَوْا مِنْ قَبْلُ ؕ
وَكَانَ اَمْرُ اللّٰهِ قَدَرًا مَّقْدُوْرًا ۝

39. (It is the practice of those)
Who preach the Messages
Of God, and fear Him,
And fear none but God.

٣٩- الَّذِيْنَ يُبَلِّغُوْنَ رِسٰلٰتِ اللّٰهِ وَيَخْشَوْنَهٗ
وَلَا يَخْشَوْنَ اَحَدًا اِلَّا اللّٰهَ ؕ

3724. All actual facts are referred to God. When the marriage is unhappy, Islam permits and expects the bond to be dissolved, provided that all interests concerned are safeguarded. Apparently there was no issue here to be considered. Zainab had to be considered, and she obtained the dearest wish of her heart in being raised to be a Mother of the Believers, with all the dignity and responsibility of that position. See n. 3706 to xxxiii. 28 above.

3725. The 'Iddat or period of waiting after divorce (ii. 228, and n. 254) was duly completed.

3726. The Pagan superstition and taboo about adopted sons had to be destroyed. See xxxiii. 4-5 and notes 3671-3672 above.

3727. See n. 3724 above.

2728. The next clause is parenthetical. These words then connect on with verse 39. Among the people of the Book there was no taboo about adopted sons, as there was in Pagan Arabia.

3729. God's ordering of the world is always full of wisdom. Even our unhappiness and misery may actually have a great meaning for ourselves or others or both If our first Plan seems to fail, we must not murmur and repine, but retrieve the position by adopting a course which appears to be the best possible in the light of our duties as indicated by God. For God's Plan is framed on universal principles that cannot be altered by human action.

And enough is God
To call (men) to account.[3730]

وَكَفٰى بِاللّٰهِ حَسِيْبًا ○

40. Muḥammad is not
The father of any
Of your men, but (he is)
The Apostle of God,
And the Seal of the Prophets:[3731]
And God has full knowledge
Of all things.

٤٠- مَا كَانَ مُحَمَّدٌ اَبَآ اَحَدٍ مِّنْ رِّجَالِكُمْ
وَلٰكِنْ رَّسُوْلَ اللّٰهِ
وَخَاتَمَ النَّبِيّٖنَ ؕ
وَكَانَ اللّٰهُ بِكُلِّ شَيْءٍ عَلِيْمًا ○ ع

SECTION 6.

41. O ye who believe!
Celebrate the praises of God,
And do this often;

٤١- يٰاَيُّهَا الَّذِيْنَ اٰمَنُوا اذْكُرُوا اللّٰهَ ذِكْرًا
كَثِيْرًا ○

42. And glorify Him
Morning and evening.

٤٢- وَّسَبِّحُوْهُ بُكْرَةً وَّاَصِيْلًا ○

43. He it is Who sends[3732]
Blessings on you, as do
His angels, that He may
Bring you out from the depths
Of Darkness into Light:
And He is Full of Mercy
To the Believers.[3733]

٤٣- هُوَ الَّذِيْ يُصَلِّيْ عَلَيْكُمْ وَمَلٰٓئِكَتُهٗ
لِيُخْرِجَكُمْ مِّنَ الظُّلُمٰتِ اِلَى النُّوْرِ ؕ
وَكَانَ بِالْمُؤْمِنِيْنَ رَحِيْمًا ○

44. Their salutation on the Day
They meet Him will be
"Peace!"; and He has
Prepared for them
A generous Reward.

٤٤- تَحِيَّتُهُمْ يَوْمَ يَلْقَوْنَهٗ سَلٰمٌ ۚ
وَاَعَدَّ لَهُمْ اَجْرًا كَرِيْمًا ○

45. O Prophet! Truly We
Have sent thee as

٤٥- يٰاَيُّهَا النَّبِيُّ اِنَّآ اَرْسَلْنٰكَ

3730. Our responsibility is to God, not to men. Men's opinions may have a bearing on our own interpretation of duty, but when that duty is clear, our only course is to obey God rather than men.

3731. When a document is sealed, it is complete, and there can be no further addition. The holy Prophet Muḥammad closed the long line of Apostles. God's teaching is and will always be continuous, but there has been and will be no Prophet after Muḥammad. The later ages will want thinkers and reformers, not Prophets. This is not an arbitrary matter. It is a decree full of knowledge and wisdom: "for God has full knowledge of all things."

3732. *Blessings*: good wishes and mercies. God wishes well to all His creatures, and His angels carry out His work, for their will is in all things His Will. His chief and everlasting blessing is that He gives us a knowledge of the spiritual world, and helps us towards its attainment. For the symbolic meaning of Light and Darkness, see xxiv. 35-40 and notes.

3733. His Mercies are for all His creatures, but for those who believe and trust in Him, there are special mercies, "a generous Reward" as in the next verse.

A Witness, a Bearer[3734]
Of Glad Tidings,
And a Warner,—

شَاهِدًا وَمُبَشِّرًا وَنَذِيرًا ۝

46. And as one who invites
To God's (Grace) by His leave,[3735]
And as a Lamp
Spreading Light.

۴۶- وَدَاعِيًا إِلَى اللَّهِ بِإِذْنِهِ
وَسِرَاجًا مُنِيرًا ۝

47. Then give the glad tidings
To the Believers, that
They shall have from God
A very great Bounty.[3736]

۴۷- وَبَشِّرِ الْمُؤْمِنِينَ بِأَنَّ
لَهُمْ مِنَ اللَّهِ فَضْلًا كَبِيرًا ۝

48. And obey not (the behests)
Of the Unbelievers
And the Hypocrites,
And heed not their annoyances,[3737]
But put thy trust in God.
For enough is God
As a Disposer of affairs.

۴۸- وَلَا تُطِعِ الْكٰفِرِينَ وَالْمُنٰفِقِينَ
وَدَعْ أَذٰىهُمْ وَتَوَكَّلْ عَلَى اللَّهِ
وَكَفٰى بِاللَّهِ وَكِيلًا ۝

49. O ye who believe!
When ye marry believing women,
And then divorce them
Before ye have touched them,

۴۹- يٰٓأَيُّهَا الَّذِينَ اٰمَنُوٓا إِذَا نَكَحْتُمُ الْمُؤْمِنٰتِ
ثُمَّ طَلَّقْتُمُوهُنَّ مِنْ قَبْلِ أَنْ تَمَسُّوهُنَّ

3734. The Prophet was sent by God in five capacities. Three are mentioned in this verse, and the other two in the verse following. (1) He comes as a *Witness* to all men about the spiritual truths which had been obscured by ignorance or superstition, or by the dust of sectarian controversy. He did not come to establish a new religion or sect. He came to teach Religion. He is also a witness to God about men's doings and how they receive God's Message: see iv. 41 and n. 560. (2) He comes as a bearer of the *Glad Tidings* of the Mercy of God. No matter how far men may have transgressed, they have hope if they believe, repent, and live a good life. (3) He also comes as a *Warner* to those who are heedless. This life will not last. There is a Future Life, and that is all-important. See next note.

3735. See last note. The two other capacities in which the Prophet was sent are here specified. (4) He comes as one who has a right to *invite* all men to repentance and the forgiveness of sins; but he does this, not of his own authority, but by the permission and authority given to him by God. This is said lest people may deify the Prophet as they did with other Prophets before him. The personal responsibility of each individual remains, but the Prophet can lead him on to the Right and help him. (5) The Prophet also comes as a *Light* or a Lamp (*Sirāj*) to illuminate the whole world. In lxxi. 16 and elsewhere the same word (*Sirāj*) is used for the sun. The comparison is apt. When the sun appears, all the lesser lights pale before his light. And the Message of Islam, *i.e.*, of the Universal Religion, is to diffuse Light everywhere.

3736. The light of Islam is the Biggest Bounty possible and if they truly understand it, they should glory in it.

3737. Men of little or no Faith will often lay down the law and tell better men than themselves what to do. In case of refusal they shower insults and injuries. No attention is to be paid to them. It is their way. All will be right under the government of God.

No period of 'Iddat[3738]
Have ye to count
In respect of them:
So give them a present,[3739]
And set them free
In a handsome manner.[3740]

فَمَا لَكُمْ عَلَيْهِنَّ مِنْ عِدَّةٍ تَعْتَدُّونَهَا
فَمَتِّعُوهُنَّ
وَسَرِّحُوهُنَّ سَرَاحًا جَمِيلًا ۝

50. O Prophet! We have
Made lawful to thee[3741]
Thy wives to whom thou
Hast paid their dowers;[3742]
And those whom thy
Right hand possesses out of
The prisoners of war whom[3743]
God has assigned to thee;
And daughters of thy paternal
Uncles and aunts, and daughters
Of thy maternal uncles
And aunts, who migrated[3744]
(From Mecca) with thee;
And any believing woman
Who dedicates her soul

٥٠- يَا أَيُّهَا النَّبِيُّ إِنَّا أَحْلَلْنَا لَكَ
أَزْوَاجَكَ الَّتِي آتَيْتَ أُجُورَهُنَّ
وَمَا مَلَكَتْ يَمِينُكَ مِمَّا أَفَاءَ اللَّهُ عَلَيْكَ
وَبَنَاتِ عَمِّكَ وَبَنَاتِ عَمَّاتِكَ
وَبَنَاتِ خَالِكَ وَبَنَاتِ خَالَاتِكَ اللَّاتِي
هَاجَرْنَ مَعَكَ
وَامْرَأَةً مُؤْمِنَةً إِنْ وَهَبَتْ نَفْسَهَا

3738. See n. 254 to ii. 228. The 'Iddat counts for three monthly courses, or if there are no courses, for three months: see lxv. 4.

3739. This present is held, by some, to be in addition to the half dower due to them under ii. 237. If the dower had not yet been fixed, the gift would presumably be larger, and it would absorb the gift prescribed in ii. 236.

3740. The gift should be given with good grace, and the freedom of the woman should not be interfered with in any way. If she chooses to marry again immediately, no obstacle should be placed in her path. On no pretext should she be allowed to remain doubtful about her freedom.

3741. This introduces no new exemption or privilege. Verses 50-52 merely declare the points in which, on account of the special circumstances (see n. 3706 above), the Prophet's marriages differed from those of ordinary Muslims. This is considered under four heads, which we shall examine in the four notes following.

3742. Head 1. Marriage with dower (iv. 4): this is the universal Muslim marriage. The difference in the Prophet's case was that there was no limitation to the number of four (iv. 3), and women of the People of the Book (v. 6) were not among his wives, but only Believers. These points are not expressly mentioned here, but are inferred by his actual practice. Obviously women who are expected to instruct other women in Islam must be Muslims.

3743. Head 2. Women Prisoners of War: the same remark as in the last note. The point does not now arise, as the whole conditions and incidents of war have been altered and slavery has been abolished by international agreement.

3744. Head 3. These are first cousins, and not within the Prohibited Degrees of Marriage (see iv. 23-24). These are specially mentioned here by way of limitation. None of them could marry the Prophet unless she had performed the Hijrat with him. If she had not so performed it in spite of her close relationship, she could not be credited with any great fervour for Islam, or be considered suitable for instructing other women in Islam.

To the Prophet if the Prophet [3745] Wishes to wed her ;—this Only for thee, and not For the Believers (at large) ; We know what We have Appointed for them as to [3746] Their wives and the captives Whom their right hands Possess ;—in order that [3747] There should be no difficulty For thee. And God is Oft-Forgiving, Most Merciful.[3748]	لِلنَّبِيِّ إِنْ أَرَادَ النَّبِيُّ أَنْ يَسْتَنْكِحَهَا خَالِصَةً لَكَ مِنْ دُونِ الْمُؤْمِنِينَ قَدْ عَلِمْنَا مَا فَرَضْنَا عَلَيْهِمْ فِي أَزْوَاجِهِمْ وَمَا مَلَكَتْ أَيْمَانُهُمْ لِكَيْلَا يَكُونَ عَلَيْكَ حَرَجٌ وَكَانَ اللَّهُ غَفُورًا رَحِيمًا ○
51. Thou mayest defer (the turn [3749] Of) any of them that thou Pleasest, and thou mayest receive Any thou pleasest : and there Is no blame on thee if Thou invite one whose (turn) [3750]	٥١- تُرْجِي مَنْ تَشَاءُ مِنْهُنَّ وَتُؤْوِي إِلَيْكَ مَنْ تَشَاءُ وَمَنِ ابْتَغَيْتَ مِمَّنْ عَزَلْتَ فَلَا جُنَاحَ عَلَيْكَ

3745. Head 4. A believing woman who dedicates her soul to the Prophet: obviously this case, like the last, is only applicable to the Prophet, and it is hedged round with the limitation that the Prophet considers it a suitable and proper case of true service to the community and not merely a sentimental woman's freak. Some Commentators think there was no such case. But others, with whom I agree, think that this applies to *Zainab* bint Khuzaima, who had dedicated herself to the poor and was called the Mother of the Poor (*Umm-ul-masākīn*). Similarly the last head might possibly refer to Zainab bint Jaḥsh, who was a daughter of the Prophet's paternal aunt, herself a daughter of 'Abd-ul-Muṭṭalib.

3746. The ordinary law of Muslim marriage will be found chiefly in ii. 221-235, iv. 3-4, iv. 19-25, iv. 34-35, and v. 6.

3747. The words "this only for thee...right hands possess" are parenthetical, and the words "in order that..." connect on with the previous clauses beginning with "O Prophet, We have made lawful...wishes to wed her".

3748. Marriage is an important relationship not only in our physical life, but in our moral and spiritual life, and its effects extend not only to the parties themselves but to children and future generations. A number of special problems arise according to special circumstances. Every man and woman must seriously consider all sides of the question and must do the best in his or her power to temper instincts and inclinations with wisdom and guidance from God. God wishes to make every one's path easy, for He is indeed "Oft-Forgiving, Most Merciful".

3749. In iv. 3 it is laid down that more than one wife is not permissible "if ye fear that ye shall not be able to deal justly with them". In a Muslim household there is no room for a "favourite wife". In the special circumstances of the Prophet there were more than one, and he usually observed the rule of equality with them, in other things as well as in the rotation of conjugal rights. But considering that his marriages after he was invested with the Prophetic office were mainly dictated by other than conjugal or personal considerations (see n. 3706, xxxiii. 28), the rotation could not always be observed, though he observed it as much as possible. This verse absolves him from absolute adherence to a fixed rotation. There are other interpretations, but I agree with most of the Commentators in the view I have explained.

3750. Where the rotation was for some reason interfered with, it was permissible, by another interference with the usual rotation, to bring satisfaction to one who had been previously set aside. This was not only permitted, but commended, as tending to remove dissatisfaction and cheer and comfort the eyes and hearts of those who were disappointed in their turn.

Thou hadst set aside.
This were nigher to
The cooling of their eyes,[3751]
The prevention of their grief,
And their satisfaction—
That of all of them—
With that which thou
Hast to give them:[3752]
And God knows (all)
That is in your hearts:[3753]
And God is All-Knowing,
Most Forbearing.

ذٰلِكَ اَدْنٰىٓ اَنْ تَقَرَّ اَعْيُنُهُنَّ
وَلَا يَحْزَنَّ
وَيَرْضَيْنَ
بِمَآ اٰتَيْتَهُنَّ كُلُّهُنَّ ۭ
وَاللّٰهُ يَعْلَمُ مَا فِيْ قُلُوْبِكُمْ ۭ
وَكَانَ اللّٰهُ عَلِيْمًا حَلِيْمًا ۝

52. It is not lawful for thee
(To marry more) women[3754]
After this, nor to change
Them for (other) wives,
Even though their beauty
Attract thee, except any
Thy right hand should
Possess (as handmaidens):
And God doth watch
Over all things.

٥٢- لَا يَحِلُّ لَكَ النِّسَآءُ مِنْ بَعْدُ
وَلَآ اَنْ تَبَدَّلَ بِهِنَّ مِنْ اَزْوَاجٍ
وَّلَوْ اَعْجَبَكَ حُسْنُهُنَّ
اِلَّا مَا مَلَكَتْ يَمِيْنُكَ ۭ
وَكَانَ اللّٰهُ عَلٰي كُلِّ شَيْءٍ رَّقِيْبًا ۝

C. 189.—Believers should cultivate refined respect
(xxxiii. 53-73.) In social and spiritual life. As the Mothers
Of the Faithful have to uphold their dignity,
So should all women protect their honour
And uphold their dignity. The Hour
Will come when all Evil will be punished.

3751. *Cooling the eyes:* an Arabic idiom for cheering and comforting eyes which yearn to see those they love. A verse of Zeb-un-nisāa, daughter of the Mugal Emperor Aurangzeb, may be rendered thus:

"My heart is glad whenever lover-wise
I dwell upon thy beauties and thy grace!
But how can I content my hungry eyes,
That ask continually to see thy face?"

3752. There was not much in the way of worldly goods or satisfaction that the Prophet could give them: see xxxiii. 28 above. But he was kind, just, and true,—the best of men to his family, and they all clung to him.

3753. Our human hearts, however good on the whole, may yet, in their motives, have possibly some baser admixture. The feminine hearts are not more immune in this respect than the masculine. But everything is known and understood by God, Who will in His mercy make all allowance for our human weaknesses. His title of "Most Forbearing" (*Ḥalīm*) also gives His devoted worshippers the cue: why should we not also forbear with the faults and weaknesses of our neighbours and fellow-creatures?

3754. This was revealed in A.H. 7. After that the Prophet did not marry again, except the handmaiden Mary the Copt, who was sent as a present by the Christian Muqauqas of Egypt. She became the mother of Ibrāhīm, who died in his infancy.

Fear God, and always speak the word
That leads to Right. Arduous is the Quest
Of Mankind's high and noble Destiny,—
Beyond the reach of other creatures:
Let man but strive in Faith, and fulfil
God's Trust,—by the grace and mercy of God.

SECTION 7.

53. O ye who believe!
Enter not the Prophet's houses,—
Until leave is given you,—[3755]
For a meal, (and then)
Not (so early as) to wait
For its preparation: but when
Ye are invited, enter;
And when ye have taken
Your meal, disperse,
Without seeking familiar talk.
Such (behaviour) annoys
The Prophet: he is ashamed
To dismiss you, but
God is not ashamed
(To tell you) the truth.

And when ye
Ask (his ladies)[3756]
For anything ye want,
Ask them from before
A screen: that makes
For greater purity for
Your hearts and for theirs.

Nor is it right for you[3757]

٥٣- يَاأَيُّهَا الَّذِينَ آمَنُوا لَا تَدْخُلُوا
بُيُوتَ النَّبِيِّ إِلَّا أَنْ يُؤْذَنَ لَكُمْ إِلَىٰ
طَعَامٍ غَيْرَ نَاظِرِينَ إِنَاهُ
وَلَٰكِنْ إِذَا دُعِيتُمْ فَادْخُلُوا
فَإِذَا طَعِمْتُمْ فَانْتَشِرُوا
وَلَا مُسْتَأْنِسِينَ لِحَدِيثٍ ۚ
إِنَّ ذَٰلِكُمْ كَانَ يُؤْذِي النَّبِيَّ فَيَسْتَحْيِي
مِنْكُمْ ۖ
وَاللَّهُ لَا يَسْتَحْيِي مِنَ الْحَقِّ ۚ
وَإِذَا سَأَلْتُمُوهُنَّ مَتَاعًا
فَاسْأَلُوهُنَّ مِنْ وَرَاءِ حِجَابٍ ۚ
ذَٰلِكُمْ أَطْهَرُ لِقُلُوبِكُمْ وَقُلُوبِهِنَّ ۚ
وَمَا كَانَ لَكُمْ

3755. The rules of refined social ethics it is as necessary to teach to-day as it was with the rude Arabs whom the holy Prophet had to teach in his day. Those mentioned in this verse may be briefly recapitulated thus: (1) Enter not a friend's house without permission; (2) if invited to dine, don't go too early; you are asked to dine, not to wait for the preparation of the food; (3) be there at the time appointed, so that you enter when you are expected and invited; (4) after the meal, don't get familiar with your host, especially if there is a great distance between him and you; (5) don't waste time in tittle-tattle, causing inconvenience and perhaps annoyance to your host; (6) understand what is proper behaviour for you; he may be too polite to ask you to depart. All this has a spiritual as well as a social bearing: respect and delicate consideration for others are among the highest virtues.

3756. The actual manner of showing respect to ladies may be different in different circumstances. But it is an essential principle of good society to show the greatest deference to them. To the "Mothers of the Believers" this respect was due in an exceptional degree.

3757. Considering his position, the holy Prophet deserved to be respected before all other men and nothing should be done to cause him the least harm and annoyance. This applied not only during his life-time, but it applies now, because his teaching and personality are alive to us. It was not fitting that his widows, both for their own position and for the position of the Prophet, should be married by other men after him. And this mark of respect was duly observed in history.

That ye should annoy[3758]
God's Apostle, or that
Ye should marry his widows
After him at any time.
Truly such a thing is
In God's sight an enormity.

أَن تُؤْذُوا رَسُولَ اللَّهِ
وَلَا أَن تَنكِحُوا أَزْوَاجَهُ مِن بَعْدِهِ أَبَدًا
إِنَّ ذَٰلِكُمْ كَانَ عِندَ اللَّهِ عَظِيمًا ○

54. Whether ye reveal anything[3759]
Or conceal it, verily
God has full knowledge
Of all things.

٥٤- إِن تُبْدُوا شَيْئًا أَوْ تُخْفُوهُ
فَإِنَّ اللَّهَ كَانَ بِكُلِّ شَيْءٍ عَلِيمًا ○

55. There is no blame
(On these ladies if they
Appear) before their fathers[3760]
Or their sons, their brothers,
Or their brothers' sons,
Or their sisters' sons,
Or their women,
Or the (slaves) whom
Their right hands possess.
And, (ladies), fear God;
For God is Witness
To all things.

٥٥- لَا جُنَاحَ عَلَيْهِنَّ فِي آبَائِهِنَّ
وَلَا أَبْنَائِهِنَّ وَلَا إِخْوَانِهِنَّ
وَلَا أَبْنَاءِ إِخْوَانِهِنَّ وَلَا أَبْنَاءِ أَخَوَاتِهِنَّ
وَلَا نِسَائِهِنَّ وَلَا مَا مَلَكَتْ أَيْمَانُهُنَّ
وَاتَّقِينَ اللَّهَ
إِنَّ اللَّهَ كَانَ عَلَىٰ كُلِّ شَيْءٍ شَهِيدًا ○

56. God and His Angels
Send blessings on the Prophet:[3761]

٥٦- إِنَّ اللَّهَ وَمَلَائِكَتَهُ يُصَلُّونَ عَلَى النَّبِيِّ

3758. "*Annoy*": *Āḏā* (IV) may equally mean: to vex, to cause hurt or injury, to insult, to ill-treat by slander or unseemly conduct, or hurt the feelings of (some one). The Prophet came with a divine mission to teach and reclaim the world, and he is entitled to the respect of all, even of those who do not consciously acknowledge his mission, for his mission works constantly like the forces of nature. In a minor degree the "Mothers of the Believers" are also entitled to respect.

3759. Respect or opposition may be shown overtly or in devious hidden ways. All good and evil are open before God, and He will take due account of everything.

3760. This refers back to the Ḥijāb (screen) portion of verse 53 above. The list of those before whom the Prophet's wives could appear informally without a screen is their fathers, sons, brothers, brothers' or sisters' sons, serving women, and household slaves or servents. Commentators include uncles (paternal and maternal) under the heading "fathers". "*Their women*" is held to mean all women who belonged to the Muslim community: other women were in the position of strangers, whom they received not so intimately, but with the formality of a screen as in the case of men. Compare with this list and the wording here the list and the wording in xxiv. 31, which applies to all Muslim women. In the list here, husbands and husbands' relatives are not necessary to be mentioned, as we are speaking of a single household, that of the central figure in Islam; nor men-servants nor children, as there were none. In the wording, note that for Muslim women generally, no screen or *Ḥijāb* (Parda) is mentioned, but only a veil to cover the bosom, and modesty in dress. The screen was a special feature of honour for the Prophet's household, introduced about five or six years before his death.

3761. God and His angels honour and bless the holy Prophet as the greatest of men. We are asked to honour and bless him all the more because he took upon himself to suffer the sorrows and afflictions of this life in order to guide us to God's Mercy and the highest inner Life.

O ye that believe!
Send ye blessings on him,
And salute him
With all respect.

يَاَيُّهَا الَّذِيْنَ اٰمَنُوْا صَلُّوْا عَلَيْهِ
وَسَلِّمُوْا تَسْلِيْمًا ○

57. Those who annoy[3762]
God and His Apostle—
God has cursed them
In this world and
In the Hereafter,
And has prepared for them
A humiliating Punishment.

٥٧- اِنَّ الَّذِيْنَ يُؤْذُوْنَ اللّٰهَ وَرَسُوْلَهٗ
لَعَنَهُمُ اللّٰهُ فِى الدُّنْيَا وَالْاٰخِرَةِ
وَاَعَدَّ لَهُمْ عَذَابًا مُّهِيْنًا ○

58. And those who annoy
Believing men and women
Undeservedly, bear
(on themselves)[3763]
A calumny and a glaring sin.

٥٨- وَالَّذِيْنَ يُؤْذُوْنَ الْمُؤْمِنِيْنَ وَالْمُؤْمِنٰتِ
بِغَيْرِ مَا اكْتَسَبُوْا
فَقَدِ احْتَمَلُوْا بُهْتَانًا وَّاِثْمًا مُّبِيْنًا ○ ع

SECTION 8.

59. O Prophet! Tell
Thy wives and daughters,
And the believing women,[3764]
That they should cast
Their outer garments over[3765]
Their persons (when abroad):
That is most convenient,
That they should be known[3766]

٥٩- يٰاَيُّهَا النَّبِىُّ قُلْ لِّاَزْوَاجِكَ وَبَنٰتِكَ
وَنِسَآءِ الْمُؤْمِنِيْنَ
يُدْنِيْنَ عَلَيْهِنَّ مِنْ جَلَابِيْبِهِنَّ ط
ذٰلِكَ اَدْنٰٓى اَنْ يُّعْرَفْنَ

3762. *Cf.* n. 3758 above.

3763. *Cf.* iv. 112. In that passage we were told that any one who was himself guilty but accused an innocent man of his guilt, was obviously placing himself in double jeopardy; first, for his own original guilt, and secondly for the guilt of a false accusation. Here we take two classes of men instead of two individuals. The men and women of faith (if they deserve the name) and doing all they can to serve God and humanity. If they are insulted, hurt, or annoyed by those whose sins they denounce, the latter suffer the penalties of a double guilt, *viz.*, their sins to start with, and the insults or injuries they offer to those who correct them. Instead of resenting the preaching of Truth, they should welcome it and profit by it.

3764. This is for all Muslim women, those of the Prophet's household, as well as the others. The times were those of insecurity (see next verse) and they were asked to cover themselves with outer garments when walking abroad. It was never contemplated that they should be confined to their houses like prisoners.

3765. *Jilbāb*, plural *Jalābīb*: an outer garment; a long gown covering the whole body, or a cloak covering the neck and bosom.

3766. The object was not to restrict the liberty of women, but to protect them from harm and molestation under the conditions then existing in Medina. In the East and in the West a distinctive public dress of some sort or another has always been a badge of honour or distinction, both among men and women. This can be traced back to the earliest civilisations. Assyrian Law in its palmiest days (say, 7th century B.C.), enjoined the veiling of married women and forbade the veiling of slaves and women of ill fame: see *Cambridge Ancient History*, III. 107.

(As such) and not molested.
And God is Oft-Forgiving,[3767]
Most Merciful.

فَلَا يُؤْذَيْنَ ۗ وَكَانَ اللّٰهُ غَفُورًا رَّحِيمًا ۝

60. Truly, if the Hypocrites,
And those in whose hearts
Is a disease, and those who
Stir up sedition in the City,[3768]
Desist not, We shall certainly
Stir thee up against them:
Then will they not be
Able to stay in it
As thy neighbours
For any length of time:

٦٠- لَئِنْ لَّمْ يَنْتَهِ الْمُنٰفِقُونَ وَالَّذِيْنَ
فِيْ قُلُوبِهِمْ مَّرَضٌ
وَّالْمُرْجِفُونَ فِي الْمَدِيْنَةِ
لَنُغْرِيَنَّكَ بِهِمْ
ثُمَّ لَا يُجَاوِرُونَكَ فِيْهَآ اِلَّا قَلِيْلًا ۝

61. They shall have a curse[3769]
On them: wherever they
Are found, they shall be
Seized and slain
(Without mercy).

٦١- مَّلْعُونِيْنَ ۚ اَيْنَمَا ثُقِفُوْٓا
اُخِذُوْا وَقُتِّلُوْا تَقْتِيْلًا ۝

62. (Such was) the practice
(Approved) of God among those[3770]
Who lived aforetime:
No change wilt thou find
In the practice (approved)
Of God.

٦٢- سُنَّةَ اللّٰهِ فِي الَّذِيْنَ خَلَوْا مِنْ قَبْلُ ۚ
وَلَنْ تَجِدَ
لِسُنَّةِ اللّٰهِ تَبْدِيْلًا ۝

3767. This rule was not absolute: if for any reason it could not be observed, "God is Oft-Returning, Most Merciful".

3768. It was necessary to put down all kinds of unseemly conduct in the Prophet's City. And here is the warning in the plainest terms. And the warning had its effect. The "Hypocrites" were men who pretended to be in Islam but whose manners and morals were anti-Islamic. Those "with diseased hearts" may have been the ones that molested innocent women. "Those who stirred up sedition" put false rumours in circulation to excite the crowd. Alas! we must ask ourselves the question: "Are these conditions present among us to-day?"

3769. They will be deprived of the blessing and guidance of God. They sought to cause disorder in God's world—moral as well as material; but they will themselves be destroyed. Those who become outlaws, rebels against the Law, will themselves be destroyed by the Law. Capital punishment is the only adequate punishment for treason and crimes of sustained concerted violence—for the protection of the hearths and homes of innocent citizens and the honour of their women.

3770. The Jewish law was much more severe: see notes 3703 and 3704 to xxxiii. 26. That severity is mitigated in Islam. But it is a universal principle that any element which deliberately refuses to obey law and aggressively tries to subvert all order in society, secretly and openly, must be effectively suppressed, for the preservation of the life and health of the general community.

63. Men ask thee concerning
The Hour: say, "The knowledge[3771]
Thereof is with God (alone)":
And what will make thee
Understand?—perchance
The Hour is nigh!

٦٣- يَسْـَٔلُكَ النَّاسُ عَنِ السَّاعَةِ ۖ
قُلْ إِنَّمَا عِلْمُهَا عِندَ اللَّهِ ۚ
وَمَا يُدْرِيكَ لَعَلَّ السَّاعَةَ تَكُونُ
قَرِيبًا ۝

64. Verily God has cursed
The Unbelievers and prepared
For them a Blazing Fire,—

٦٤- إِنَّ اللَّهَ لَعَنَ الْكَافِرِينَ وَأَعَدَّ
لَهُمْ سَعِيرًا ۝

65. To dwell therein for ever:
No protector will they find,
Nor helper.

٦٥- خَالِدِينَ فِيهَا أَبَدًا ۖ
لَّا يَجِدُونَ وَلِيًّا وَلَا نَصِيرًا ۝

66. The Day that their faces
Will be turned upside down[3772]
In the Fire, they will say:
"Woe to us! would that
We had obeyed God
And obeyed the Apostle!"

٦٦- يَوْمَ تُقَلَّبُ وُجُوهُهُمْ فِي النَّارِ
يَقُولُونَ يَا لَيْتَنَا
أَطَعْنَا اللَّهَ وَأَطَعْنَا الرَّسُولَا ۝

67. And they would say:
"Our Lord! We obeyed
Our chiefs and our great ones,
And they misled us
As to the (right) path.

٦٧- وَقَالُوا رَبَّنَا إِنَّا أَطَعْنَا
سَادَتَنَا وَكُبَرَاءَنَا
فَأَضَلُّونَا السَّبِيلَا ۝

68. "Our Lord! Give them
Double Penalty[3773]
And curse them
With a very great Curse!"

٦٨- رَبَّنَا آتِهِمْ ضِعْفَيْنِ مِنَ الْعَذَابِ
وَالْعَنْهُمْ لَعْنًا كَبِيرًا ۝ ع

3771. *Cf.* vii. 187 and n. 1159, where the idea is further explained. The knowledge of the Final Hour is with God alone. The fact of its coming is certain; the exact time when it will come has not been revealed. If it were, it would disturb our thoughts and life. "Heavy were its burden through the heavens and the earth." But at any given moment it cannot be far distant. In theological language, each individual's death is a Final Hour, a *Qiyāmat Ṣugrā* (Lesser Day of Judgment). In that sense it is not the same for all individuals, and is certainly always near. "In the midst of life we are in death", as the Anglican Prayer-Book says in its Burial Service.

3772. The face is the expression of their Personality, their Self; and turning upside down is a sign of degradation and ignominy. When the Retribution comes, the evil ones will be humiliated, and they will wish that they had followed right guidance when they had the chance. They will then fall to accusing their leaders who misled them. But they forget their own personal responsibility.

3773. *Cf.* xxv. 69 and n. 3129, and xi. 20 and n. 1515. The double Penalty invoked will be because (1) they went wrong themselves and (2) they misled others.

SECTION 9.

69. O ye who believe!
Be ye not like those
Who vexed and insulted Moses,[3774]
But God cleared him
Of the (calumnies) they
Had uttered: and he
Was honourable in God's sight.

٦٩- يَـٰٓأَيُّهَا ٱلَّذِينَ ءَامَنُوا۟ لَا تَكُونُوا۟
كَٱلَّذِينَ ءَاذَوْا۟ مُوسَىٰ
فَبَرَّأَهُ ٱللَّهُ مِمَّا قَالُوا۟ ۚ
وَكَانَ عِندَ ٱللَّهِ وَجِيهًا ۝

70. O ye who believe!
Fear God, and (always) say
A word directed to the Right:[3775]

٧٠- يَـٰٓأَيُّهَا ٱلَّذِينَ ءَامَنُوا۟ ٱتَّقُوا۟ ٱللَّهَ
وَقُولُوا۟ قَوْلًا سَدِيدًا ۝

71. That He may make
Your conduct whole and sound
And forgive you your sins:
He that obeys God
And His Apostle, has already
Attained the highest
Achievement.[3776]

٧١- يُصْلِحْ لَكُمْ أَعْمَـٰلَكُمْ
وَيَغْفِرْ لَكُمْ ذُنُوبَكُمْ ۗ
وَمَن يُطِعِ ٱللَّهَ وَرَسُولَهُۥ فَقَدْ
فَازَ فَوْزًا عَظِيمًا ۝

72. We did indeed offer
The Trust[3777] to the Heavens

٧٢- إِنَّا عَرَضْنَا ٱلْأَمَانَةَ عَلَى ٱلسَّمَـٰوَٰتِ

3774. The people of Moses often vexed him and rebelled against him and against God's Law. Here the reference seems to be to Num. xii. 1-13. It is there said that Moses's own sister Miriam and his brother Aaron spoke against Moses because Moses had married an Ethiopian woman. God cleared Moses of the charge of having done anything wrong: "My servant Moses is not so, who is faithful in all mine house." Miriam was afflicted with leprosy for seven days as a punishment, after which she was forgiven, as also was Aaron. This is the Old Testament story. The holy Prophet was also attacked because of his marriage with Zainab bint Jaḥsh, but not by his own circle; his motives were of the highest and were completely vindicated as we have seen above.

3775. We must not only speak the truth as far as we know it, but we must always try to hit the right point; *i.e.*, we must not speak unseasonably, and when we do speak, we must not beat about the bush, but go straight to that which is right, in deed as well as in word. Then God will make our conduct right and cure any defects that there may be in our knowledge and character. With our endeavour directed straight to the goal, we shall be forgiven our errors, shortcomings, faults, and sins of the past.

3776. This is salvation, the attainment of our real spiritual desire or ambition, as we are on the highway to nearness to God.

3777. The Trust is something given to a person, over which he has a power of disposition; he is expected to use it as directed or expected, but he has the power to use it otherwise. There is no trust if the trustee has no power, and the trust implies that the giver of the trust believes and expects that the trustee would use it according to the wish of the creator of the trust, and not otherwise.

And the Earth
And the Mountains; [3778]
But they refused [3779]
To undertake it, [3780]
Being afraid thereof:
But man undertook it;— [3781]
He was indeed unjust [3782]
And foolish;—

وَالْأَرْضِ وَالْجِبَالِ
فَأَبَيْنَ أَنْ يَحْمِلْنَهَا
وَأَشْفَقْنَ مِنْهَا وَحَمَلَهَا الْإِنْسَانُ إِنَّهُ
كَانَ ظَلُومًا جَهُولًا ۝

3778. What is the meaning of the offer of the Trust to the Heavens, the Earth, and the Mountains? *Cf.* lix. 21, where the hypothetical sending down of the Qur-ān to the Mountains is mentioned, and it is mentioned that such Parables are put forth in order to aid men to reflection. We may therefore take the Mountains, the Earth, and the Heavens as symbolical. The mountains stand for firmness and stability: they have been created for this quality, and they are always true to that quality. An earthquake or a volcano has to do with movements within the earth's crust: it has nothing to do with the Mountain's will. In fact it has no free-will of any kind: there is no question of any Trust here. If we take the Earth as a whole, as a part of the solar system or a compendium of the terrestrial Nature we see around us, it obeys the fixed laws of God, and there is no Will or Trust. If we take the Heavens either as celestial space, or as symbolical of the Angels, they absolutely obey God's Will and law: they have no will of their own.

3779. The Heavens, the Earth, and the Mountains, *i.e.*, other creatures of God, besides man, refused to undertake a Trust or a responsibility, and may be imagined as happy without a choice of good or evil being given through their will. In saying that they refused, we imply a will, but we limit it by the statement that they did not undertake to be given a choice between good and evil. They preferred to submit their will entirely to God's Will, which is All-Wise and Perfect, and which would give them far more happiness than a faculty of choice, with their imperfect knowledge. Man was too audacious and ignorant to realise this, and the result has been that man as a race has been disrupted: the evil ones have betrayed the Trust and brought Punishment on themselves, though the good have been able to rise far above other Creation, to be the *muqarrabīn*, the nearest ones to God: lvi. 11 and lvi. 88. What can be higher than this for any creature?

It follows incidentally from this that the Heavens and the Earth were created before man was created, and this is in accordance with what we know of the physical world in science: man came on the scene at a comparatively late stage.

3780. *Ḥamala*: to undertake, bear, carry (the Trust or responsibility), to be equal to it. This is the ordinary meaning, and the majority of Commentators construe so. But some understand it to mean "to carry away, run away with, to embezzle (the thing entrusted); hence to be false to the Trust, to betray the Trust." In that case the sense of verses 72-73 would be: "God offered the Trust to other creatures, but they refused, lest they should betray it, being afraid from that point of view: but man was less fair to himself: in his ignorance he accepted and betrayed the Trust, with the result that some of his race became Hypocrites and Unbelievers and were punished, though others were faithful to the Trust and received God's Mercy." The resulting conclusion is the same under both interpretations.

3781. See ii. 30-34 and notes. God intended a very high destiny for man, and placed him in his uncorrupted state even above the angels, but in his corruption he made himself even lower than the beasts. What was it that made man so high and noble? The differentiating quality which God gave man was that God breathed something of His own spirit into man (xxxii. 9; xv. 29 and n. 1968; and other passages). This meant that man was given a limited choice of good and evil, and that he was made capable of Forbearance, Love, and Mercy. And in himself man summed up God's great world: man is in himself a microcosm.

3782. That man should undertake the God-like attributes (in however small a degree) of Will, Forbearance, Love, and Mercy, brought him nearer to God than was possible for any other creature of God. This was part of God's Will and Plan, but little did man realise then what a tremendous task he was undertaking or question himself whether he would be equal to it. *Ẓalūm* (translated "unjust") and *Jahūl* (ignorant) are both in the Arabic intensive form; as much as to say, 'man *signally* failed to measure his own powers or his own knowledge'. But God's Grace came to his assistance. Where man did his best, he won through by God's Grace, even though man's Best was but a poor Good.

How did man generically undertake this great Responsibility, which made him Vicegerent of God (ii. 30)? Here comes in the mystic doctrine of a Covenant, express or implied, between God and Humanity. See vii. 172-73 and notes 1146-48, also v. 1 and n. 682. A Covenant (*Mīthāq*) necessarily implies Trust, and its breach necessarily implies Punishment.

73. (With the result (that
God has to punish [3783]
The Hypocrites, men and women,
And the Unbelievers, men
And women, and God turns
In Mercy to the Believers, [3784]
Men and women: for God
Is Oft-Forgiving, Most Merciful.

٧٣- لِّيُعَذِّبَ اللَّهُ
الْمُنَٰفِقِينَ وَالْمُنَٰفِقَٰتِ وَالْمُشْرِكِينَ وَالْمُشْرِكَٰتِ
وَيَتُوبَ اللَّهُ عَلَى الْمُؤْمِنِينَ وَالْمُؤْمِنَٰتِ ۗ
وَكَانَ اللَّهُ غَفُورًا رَّحِيمًا ○ ع

3783. Man's generic Covenant, which flowed from his exercising the option given him, choosing Will, Forbearance, Love, and Mercy, made it necessary that breach of it should carry its own punishment. Breach of it is here classed under two heads: those who betray their Trust act either as Hypocrites or as Unbelievers. Hypocrites are those who profess Faith but bring not forth the fruits of Faith. Unbelievers are those who openly defy Faith, and from whom therefore no fruits of Faith are to be expected.

3784. Those who remain firm to their Faith and their Covenant (see notes 3781-82) will receive the aid of God's Grace; their faults and weaknesses will be cured; and they will be made worthy of their exalted Destiny. For God is Oft-Returning and Most Merciful.

So ends a Sūra which deals with the greatest complications and misunderstandings in our throbbing life here below, and points upwards to the Great Achievement, the highest Salvation.

INTRODUCTION TO SŪRA XXXIV (*Sabā*).

Now we begin a series of six Sūras, S. xxxiv. to S. xxxix, which recapitulate some of the features of the spiritual world. This Sūra leads off with emphasis on God's Mercy and Power and Turth. Then (in S. xxxv.) we are told how angels manifest the Power of God, and how different is Good from Evil and Truth from Falsehood. S. xxxvi. is devoted to the holy Prophet and the Qur-ān that came through him. In S. xxxvii. the emphasis is on the snares of the Evil One; in S. xxxviii., on the conquest of evil by wisdom and power as in the case of David and Solomon, and by Patience and Constancy as in the case of Job; and in S. xxxix. on the Final Judgment, which will sort out Faith from Unfaith and give to each its due.

The chronology has here no significance. This Sūra belongs to the early Meccan period.

Summary.—No Good or Truth is ever lost: Human Power and Prosperity are fleeting; but God's Power and Justice endure, and will enforce personal responsibility on man on the Last Day (xxxiv. 1-30, and C. 190).

Faith and Unfaith will eventually find their true places and truc values; Falsehood has no power: Truth is with God (xxxiv. 31-54, and C. 191).

C. 190.—God's Mercy and Power endure for ever:
(xxxiv. 1-30.) Man should understand and not resist
God's Revelation. Human wisdom and Power,
As given to David, were only for establishing
Righteousness. Human glory, like Solomon's,
Rested on slender foundations. Sabā
But enjoyed her fair and prosperous state
As long as she obeyed the Law
Of God, but perished for unrighteousness.
Learn, then, that the Mercy and Power, Wisdom
And Justice, of God are beyond all comparison.
Do right and prepare for the Final Day.

Sūra XXXIV.

Sabā, or the City of Sabā
(see verse 15).

In the name of God, Most Gracious, Most Merciful.

1. Praise be to God,[3785]
To Whom belong all things
In the heavens and on earth:
To Him be Praise
In the Hereafter:
And He is Full of Wisdom,
Acquainted with all things.

2. He knows all that goes[3786]
Into the earth, and all that
Comes out thereof; all that
Comes down from the sky[3787]
And all that ascends thereto·
And He is the Most Merciful,
The Oft-Forgiving.

3. The Unbelievers say,[3788]
"Never to us will come

3785. The declaration of God's Praise has much mystic meaning. All Creation declares His Praises, *i.e.*, manifests His Mercy and Power, Goodness and Truth—all the sublime attributes summed up in His Most Beautiful Names (vii. 180 and xvii 110 and notes). For man, to contemplate these is in itself a Revelation. This sentiment opens five Sūras of the Qur-ān evenly distributed, *viz.* i., vi., xviii., xxxiv., and xxxv. Here the point most emphasised is that His wisdom and mercy comprehend all things, extended in space or in time—here and everywhere, now and evermore.

3786. An ignorant man may think that water absorbed in the soil or seed sown beneath the sod is lost, but it replenishes numerous rills and streams, and feeds and sustains numerous roots and forms of life, and throws up all kinds of vegetable life. So with things that come out of the earth: who can count the myriad forms of herbs and trees that grow and perish, and yet sustain a continuous life for ages and ages? Yet these are symbolical of other things or entities beyond time or space, and beyond physical form. We see the birth and death of the animal part of man: when the is buried beneath the soil, the ignorant man thinks there is an end of him. But what countless stages still lie before him for his inner and spiritual life? And so with the Platonic Forms of Things: Goodness, Virtue, Mercy, and the various functions of the soul. They are never lost, but go up to God.

3787. The vapours that rise from the earth and ascend to the sky descend again as rain and snow and as symbols of God's Mercy. So are the prayers of the devout and the call of those in agony for help and light, answered by the descent of mercy and guidance, help and light from the Throne of Majesty. The imagery indicated in the last note can be worked out to moral and spiritual forces, and they all centre in God. Do not forget that, just as there is the element of Mercy, so there is an element of Justice and Punishment—in the physical forces as well as in the moral and spiritual forces, all centring in God.

3788. The last two verses prepared us to realise the position of Unbelievers in God's great Universe. They are the discord in the universal harmony of Prayer and Praise. Their existence is due to the grant of a limited free-will, the Trust which the Unbelievers have betrayed (see xxxiii. 72 and notes). But they must and will be eliminated: see verse 5 below. For there is nothing more certain in the world, physical, moral, and spiritual, than that every cause, great or small, must have its corresponding consequences.

The Hour": say, "Nay!
But most surely,
By my Lord,[3789] it will come
Upon you;—by Him
Who knows the unseen,—
From Whom is not hidden
The least little atom
In the Heavens or on earth:
Nor is there anything less
Than that, or greater, but
Is in the Record Perspicuous:[3790]

السَّاعَةُ ۖ قُلْ بَلَىٰ
وَرَبِّي لَتَأْتِيَنَّكُمْ
عَالِمِ الْغَيْبِ ۖ لَا يَعْزُبُ عَنْهُ مِثْقَالُ ذَرَّةٍ
فِي السَّمَاوَاتِ وَلَا فِي الْأَرْضِ
وَلَا أَصْغَرُ مِنْ ذَٰلِكَ وَلَا أَكْبَرُ
إِلَّا فِي كِتَابٍ مُبِينٍ ۝

4. That He may reward
Those who believe and work
Deeds of righteousness: for such
Is Forgiveness and a Sustenance[3791]
Most Generous."

٤- لِيَجْزِيَ الَّذِينَ آمَنُوا وَعَمِلُوا الصَّالِحَاتِ
أُولَٰئِكَ لَهُمْ مَغْفِرَةٌ وَرِزْقٌ كَرِيمٌ ۝

5. But those who strive
Against Our Signs, to frustrate[3792]
Them,—for such will be
A Penalty,—a Punishment
Most humiliating.

٥- وَالَّذِينَ سَعَوْا فِي آيَاتِنَا مُعَاجِزِينَ
أُولَٰئِكَ لَهُمْ عَذَابٌ
مِنْ رِجْزٍ أَلِيمٌ ۝

6. And those to whom[3793]
Knowledge has come see
That the (Revelation) sent down
To thee from thy Lord—
That is the Truth,
And that it guides

٦- وَيَرَى الَّذِينَ أُوتُوا الْعِلْمَ
الَّذِي أُنْزِلَ إِلَيْكَ مِنْ رَبِّكَ
هُوَ الْحَقَّ وَيَهْدِي

3789. The strongest emphasis and the most perfect assurance of certainty are indicated by reference to the authority of God Himself, the Ruler of the Day of Judgment.

3790. In the symbolical language of our own human experience, a record is more enduring than memory: in fact (if properly preserved) it is perpetual. If, further, it is expressed in clear language, without any obscurity, it can always be read with perfect precision and without any doubt whatever. Apply these qualities, free from human defects, to God's laws and decrees. They are unerring and enduring. Everything, great or small, will receive due recognition—a Reward for Good and a Punishment for Evil.

3791. "*Sustenance*": Spiritual in things spiritual, and physical in things physical. It implies not only the satisfaction of desire, but the provision of means for sustaining the ground won and for winning more ground in the march of progress.

3792. *Cf.* xxii. 51. God's Plan cannot be frustrated. It is those who work against it, who will be eliminated and destroyed.

3793. Against the doubts and vain imaginings of the Ignorant is the certainty of knowledge of the Enlightened: that God reveals Himself, and that His Revelation is true, and leads to the Path of true Guidance. That Path is the Path of God, Who, in His infinite Love and Mercy, is Worthy of all Praise.

It is possible to connect this with the "Record Perspicuous" in verse 3 above: 'it is perspicuous..., for the Enlightened do see...'

To the Path of the Exalted
(In Might), Worthy
Of all praise.

اِلٰى صِرَاطِ الْعَزِيْزِ الْحَمِيْدِ ○

7. The Unbelievers say
(In ridicule): "Shall we
Point out to you a man[3794]
That will tell you,
When ye are all scattered
To pieces in disintegration,
That ye shall (then be
Raised) in a New Creation?

٧- وَقَالَ الَّذِيْنَ كَفَرُوْا
هَلْ نَدُلُّكُمْ عَلٰى رَجُلٍ
يُّنَبِّئُكُمْ اِذَا مُزِّقْتُمْ كُلَّ مُمَزَّقٍ ۙ
اِنَّكُمْ لَفِيْ خَلْقٍ جَدِيْدٍ ○

8. "Has he invented a falsehood
Against God, or has
A spirit (seized) him?"—[3795]
Nay, it is those who
Believe not in the Hereafter,
That are in (real) Penalty,
And in farthest Error.

٨- اَفْتَرٰى عَلَى اللّٰهِ كَذِبًا اَمْ بِهٖ جِنَّةٌ ۭ
بَلِ الَّذِيْنَ لَا يُؤْمِنُوْنَ بِالْاٰخِرَةِ فِي
الْعَذَابِ
وَالضَّلٰلِ الْبَعِيْدِ ○

9. See they not what is
Before them and behind them,
Of the sky and the earth?[3796]
If We wished, We could
Cause the earth to swallow[3797]
Them up, or cause a piece
Of the sky to fall upon them.[3798]
Verily in this is a Sign
For every devotee that
Turns to God (in repentance).

٩- اَفَلَمْ يَرَوْا اِلٰى مَا بَيْنَ اَيْدِيْهِمْ وَمَا خَلْفَهُمْ
مِّنَ السَّمَاۗءِ وَالْاَرْضِ ۭ
اِنْ نَّشَاْ نَخْسِفْ بِهِمُ الْاَرْضَ
اَوْ نُسْقِطْ عَلَيْهِمْ كِسَفًا مِّنَ السَّمَاۗءِ ۭ
اِنَّ فِيْ ذٰلِكَ لَاٰيَةً لِّكُلِّ عَبْدٍ مُّنِيْبٍ ○ ع

3794. This is a taunt against the holy Prophet, and it is applicable to all who preach the doctrine of a Future Life. How is it possible, say the Unbelievers, that when a man's body is reduced to dust and scattered about, the man should rise again and become a new Creation? They add that such a preacher is inventing a deliberate falsehood or is demented.

3795. The answer is: the Future Life is the truest of all Truths; so far is the man who teaches it from being demented, that it is those who deny it, that lack knowledge and are in real jeopardy for their souls; for they persecute Truth and must not only suffer defeat, but go farther and farther from Realities and thus suffer the worst hallucination about the spiritual world.

3796. The men who walk in spiritual darkness and laugh at a Hereafter, have but to observe the Power of God in the nature around them. He Who created the heavens and the earth and sustains them can surely make a new Creation! And the cosmic Laws which are so just and inevitable should surely give them an idea of the inexorable Justice that must redress all balance.

3797. *Cf.* xvi. 45, and n. 2071. Who are these puny creatures—sceptics that question the might and majesty of God?

3798. *Cf.* xxvi. 187. This was actually a challenge hurled at Shu'aib and a shower of ashes and cinders came from above and overwhelmed the challengers!

SECTION 2.

10. We bestowed Grace aforetime
On David from Ourselves:[3799]
"O ye Mountains! sing ye
Back the Praises of God
With him! and ye birds
(Also)! And We made
The iron soft for him;—[3800]

١٠- وَلَقَدْ اٰتَيْنَا دَاوٗدَ مِنَّا فَضْلًا ؕ
يٰجِبَالُ اَوِّبِىْ
مَعَهٗ وَالطَّيْرَ ۚ
وَاَلَنَّا لَهُ الْحَدِيْدَ ۙ

11. (Commanding), "Make thou
Coats of mail, balancing well[3801]
The rings of chain armour,
And work ye righteousness;[3802]
For be sure I see
(Clearly) all that ye do."

١١- اَنِ اعْمَلْ سٰبِغٰتٍ وَّقَدِّرْ فِى السَّرْدِ
وَاعْمَلُوْا صَالِحًا ؕ
اِنِّىْ بِمَا تَعْمَلُوْنَ بَصِيْرٌ ۝

12. And to Solomon (We
Made) the Wind (obedient):[3803]
Its early morning (stride)
Was a month's (journey),
And its evening (stride)
Was a month's (journey);
And We made a Font[3804]
Of molten brass to flow

١٢- وَلِسُلَيْمٰنَ الرِّيْحَ
غُدُوُّهَا شَهْرٌ
وَّرَوَاحُهَا شَهْرٌ ۚ
وَاَسَلْنَا لَهٗ عَيْنَ الْقِطْرِ ؕ

3799. *Cf.* xxi. 79-80, and notes 2733-34. David had the gift of song and sacred music, and this is shown in his Psalms. All nature—hills and birds—sing and echo back the Praises of God.

3800. Iron or steel is hard stuff: but in the hands of a craftsman it becomes soft and pliable, and with it can be made instruments for the defence of righteousness. These, in the literal sense, are coats of mail, and defensive armour, and the manufacture of them is traditionally attributed to David. But, for warfare in the moral and spiritual world also, armour is required, and this can be made of some of the toughest and hardest facts of life.

3801. Coats of chain armour have to be made with cunning art, if the chains are to fit into each other and the whole garment is to be worn in comfort in fierce warfare.

3802. Note the transition from the singular, "make them coats of mail", to the plural, "and work ye righteousness". The first is addressed to David, who was the artificer of defensive armour; and the second is addressed to him and his whole people. He made the armour, but it was to be worn not only by him but all his warriors. But he and all his people were to be careful to see that they did not deviate from the paths of righteousness. Fighting is a dangerous weapon and may well degenerate (as it so often does) into mere violence. They were to see that this should not happen, and they were told that God was watching over them all with the personal solicitude implied in the singular pronoun "I".

3803. *Cf.* xxi. 81-82, n. 2736, and xxxviii. 36-38. See also xxvii 38-39. The winds are swift and can cover in a short morning's or evening's flight the distance which it takes a whole month to cover on foot or by bullock cart. In our own day, with air speeds of 400 miles and more per hour, this seems a moderate statement.

3804. In the Old Testament, II. Chronicles, Chapters iii., and iv., are described the various costly materials with which Solomon's Temple was built, and it was furnished with vessels, candle-sticks, lamps, censers, etc. "Solomon made all these vessels in great abundance: for the weight of the brass could not be found out" (II. Chronicles, iv. 18). "Also he made a molten sea of ten cubits from brim to brim, round in compass, and five cubits the height thereof; and a line of thirty cubits did compass it round about" (II. Chronicles, iv. 2). The receptacle or "sea" or Font was made of molten brass: presumably it contained flowing water for washing with.

For him; and there were
Jinns that worked in front[3805]
Of him, by the leave
Of his Lord, and if any
Of them turned aside
From Our command, We
Made him taste
Of the Penalty
Of the Blazing Fire.

ومن الجن من يعمل بين يديه
بإذن ربه
ومن يزغ منهم عن أمرنا
نذقه من عذاب السعير ○

13. They worked for him
As he desired, (making) Arches,[3806]
Images, Basons
As large as Reservoirs,
And (cooking) Cauldrons fixed
(In their places): "Work ye,[3807]
Sons of David, with thanks!
But few of My servants
Are grateful!"

١٣- يعملون له ما يشاء من محاريب
وتماثيل وجفان كالجواب
وقدور راسيات
اعملوا آل داود شكرا
وقليل من عبادي الشكور ○

14. Then, when We decreed
(Solomon's) death, nothing showed them
His death except a little[3808]
Worm of the earth, which

١٤- فلما قضينا عليه الموت
ما دلهم على موته
إلا دابة الأرض

3805. See xxvii. 17, and n. 3257. The workers who are called Jinns were only rough workers, working "in front of Solomon", *i.e.*, under his eyes and the supervision of his men. They should be distinguished from the skilled workers who worked heart and soul for the Temple, and who are addressed as the "Sons of David" in the next verse.

3806. *Miḥrāb* (Plural *Maḥārīb*), translated "arch", may be applied to any fine, elevated, spacious architectural structure. As the reference here is to the Temple of Solomon, the word "arches" is I think most appropriate. "Arches" would be structural Ornaments in the Temple. Images would be like the images of oxen and Cherubim mentioned in II. Chronicles, iv. 3 and iii. 14; the Basons (II. Chronicles iv. 22) were perhaps huge dishes round which many men could sit together and eat, according to ancient Eastern custom, while the cooking Cauldrons or Pots (II. Chronicles, iv. 16), were fixed in one place, being so large in capacity that they could not be moved about. Indian readers will get some idea of them from the huge cooking *Degs*, which they use in the 'Urs at Ajmīr Sharif.

3807. The building of the Temple was a great event in Israelite history. The motto here given is "Work!"; for only that would justify the maintenance of the Kingdom of David, which reached its zenith under Solomon. Without work, both literally, and figuratively for "righteous deeds", all that glory and power would be out of place, and it fell away in a few generations, with the decline of the moral spirit which was at its back.

3808. This allegory illustrates three points: (1) however great and glorious human power and grandeur may be, it is only for a time, and it may fade away even before people know of its decline; (2) the most remarkable events may be brought to light, not by a flourish of trumpets, but by a humble individual, unknown and unseen, who works imperceptibly and undermines even so strong a thing as staff, on which a great man may lean; (3) work done by men merely on the basis of brute strength or fear, as in the case of the Jinns, will not endure. This is brought up in strong contrast against the Power and Majesty of God, which will endure, which cannot be sapped, and which can only be fully appreciated by a training of the will and heart. In the same way, in David's story above, his mighty strength as a warrior (see ii. 251) and his skill in making armour are only to be valued when used, as it was used, in the service of God, in righteous works (xxxiv. 11).

Kept (slowly) gnawing away
At his staff : so when he
Fell down, the Jinns saw[3809]
Plainly that if they had
Known the unseen, they
Would not have tarried
In the humiliating Penalty
(Of their Task).

تَأْكُلُ مِنسَأَتَهُ
فَلَمَّا خَرَّ تَبَيَّنَتِ الْجِنُّ
أَن لَّوْ كَانُوا يَعْلَمُونَ الْغَيْبَ
مَا لَبِثُوا فِي الْعَذَابِ الْمُهِينِ ۝

15. There was, for Sabā,[3810]
Aforetime, a Sign in their
Home-land—two Gardens
To the right and to the left.
"Eat of the Sustenance (provided)
By your Lord, and be grateful
To Him : a territory fair and happy,
And a Lord Oft-Forgiving![3811]

١٥- لَقَدْ كَانَ لِسَبَإٍ فِي مَسْكَنِهِمْ آيَةٌ
جَنَّتَانِ عَن يَمِينٍ وَشِمَالٍ
كُلُوا مِن رِّزْقِ رَبِّكُمْ وَاشْكُرُوا لَهُ
بَلْدَةٌ طَيِّبَةٌ وَرَبٌّ غَفُورٌ ۝

16. But they turned away
(From God), and We sent
Against them the flood[3812]
(Released) from the Dams,[3813]

١٦- فَأَعْرَضُوا فَأَرْسَلْنَا
عَلَيْهِمْ سَيْلَ الْعَرِمِ

3809. The Jinns looked upon their work as a Penalty, and so it became to them. The people who worked at the Temple of Solomon as the People of David worked and gloried in their work as a thanksgiving to God, and their work became sanctified. The Jinns knew nothing of hidden secrets ; they only saw the obvious, and had not even the significance of the little worm that slowly gnawed away Solomon's staff.

3810. This is the same city and territory in Yemen as is mentioned in xxvii. 22 : see note there as to its location. There the period was the time of Solomon and Queen Bilqis. Here it is some centuries later. It was still a happy and prosperous country, amply irrigated from the Maārib dam. Its roads or perhaps its canals, were skirted by gardens on both sides, right and left : at any given point you always saw two gardens. It produced fruit, spices, and frankincense, and got the name of Araby the Blest for that part of the country.

3811. The land was fair to look upon ; the people happy and prosperous : and they enjoyed the blessings of God, Who is Gracious and does not punish small human faults or weaknesses.

3812. Into that happy Garden of Eden in Arabia Felix (Araby the Blest) came the insidious snake of Unfaith and Wrongdoing. Perhaps the people became arrogant of their prosperity, or of their science, or of their skill in irrigation engineering, in respect of the wonderful works of the Dam which their ancestors had constructed. Perhaps they got broken up into rich and poor, privileged and unprivileged, high-caste and low-caste, disregarding the gifts and closing the opportunities given by God to all His creatures. Perhaps they broke the laws of the very Nature which fed and sustained them. The Nemesis came. It may have come suddenly, or it may have come slowly. The pent-up waters of the eastern side of the Yemen highlands were collected in a high lake confined by the Dam of Maārib. A mighty flood came ; the dam burst ; and it has never been repaired since. This was a spectacular crisis : it may have been preceded and followed by slow desiccation of the country.

3813. "'*Arim*" (=Dams or Embankments) may have been a proper noun, or may simply mean the great earth-works lined with stone, which formed the Maārib dam, of which traces still exist. The French traveller T. J. Arnaud saw the town and ruins of the Dam of Maārib in 1843, and described its gigantic works and its inscriptions : See *Journal Asiatique* for January 1874 : the account is in French. For a secondary account in English, see W. B. Harris, *Journey Through Yemen*, Edinburgh, 1893. The dam as measured by Arnaud was two miles long and 120 ft. high. The date of its destruction was somewhere about 120 A.D., though some authorities put it much later.

And We converted their two
Garden (rows) into "gardens"
Producing bitter fruit,
And tamarisks, and some few
(Stunted) Lote-trees.[3814]

وَبَدَّلْنٰهُمْ بِجَنَّتَيْهِمْ جَنَّتَيْنِ
ذَوَاتَيْ اُكُلٍ خَمْطٍ
وَّاَثْلٍ وَّشَيْءٍ مِّنْ سِدْرٍ قَلِيْلٍ ○

17. That was the Requital
We gave them because
They ungratefully rejected
Faith:[3815]
And never do We give
(Such) requital except to such
As are ungrateful rejecters.

١٧- ذٰلِكَ جَزَيْنٰهُمْ
بِمَا كَفَرُوْا ؕ
وَهَلْ نُجٰزِيْٓ اِلَّا الْكَفُوْرَ ○

18. Between them and the Cities[3816]
On which We had poured
Our blessings, We had placed
Cities in prominent positions,
And between them We had
Appointed stages of journey
In due proportion: "Travel
therein,
Secure, by night and by day."

١٨- وَجَعَلْنَا بَيْنَهُمْ وَبَيْنَ الْقُرَى الَّتِيْ
بٰرَكْنَا فِيْهَا قُرًى ظَاهِرَةً
وَّقَدَّرْنَا فِيْهَا السَّيْرَ ؕ
سِيْرُوْا فِيْهَا لَيَالِيَ وَاَيَّامًا اٰمِنِيْنَ ○

19. But they said:[3817] "Our Lord!
Place longer distances

١٩- فَقَالُوْا رَبَّنَا بٰعِدْ بَيْنَ

3814. The flourishing "Garden of Arabia" was converted into a waste. The luscious fruit trees became wild, or gave place to wild plants with bitter fruit. The feathery leaved tamarisk, which is only good for twigs and wattle-work, replaced the fragrant plants and flowers. Wild and stunted kinds of thorny bushes, like the wild Lote-tree, which were good for neither fruit nor shade, grew in place of the pomegranates, the date-palms, and the grape-vines. The lote-tree belongs to the family Rhamnaceæ, *Zizyphus Spina Christi*, of which (it is supposed) Christ's crown of thorns was made, allied to the *Zizyphus Jujuba*, or *ber* tree of India. Wild, it is shrubby, thorny and useless. In cultivation it bears good fruit, and some shade, and can be thornless, thus becoming a symbol of heavenly bliss: lvi. 28.

3815. *Kafūr*: intensive form: "those who deliberately and continuously reject God and are ungrateful for His Mercies, as shown by their constant wrong-doing.

3816. An instance is now given of the sort of covetousness on the part of the people of Sabā, which ruined their prosperity and trade and cut their own throats. The old Frankincense route was the great Highway (*imām mubīn* xv. 79; *sabīl muqīm*, xv. 76) between Arabia and Syria. Through Syria it connected with the great and flourishing Kingdoms of the Euphrates and Tigris valleys on the one hand and Egypt on the other, and with the great Roman Empire round the Mediterranean. At the other end, through the Yemen Coast, the road connected, by sea transport, with India, Malaya, and China. The Yemen-Syria road was much frequented, and Madāin Ṣāliḥ was one of the stations on that route, and afterwards on the Pilgrim route: see Appendix IX to S. xxvi, p. 975. Syria was the land on which God "had poured His blessings", being a rich fertile country, where Abraham had lived: it includes the Holy Land of Palestine. The route was studded in the days of its prosperity with many stations (cities) close to each other, on which merchants could travel with ease and safety, "by night and by day". The close proximity of stations prevented the inroads of highwaymen.

3817. *Said*: in this and other places in the Qur-ān, "language" is used for thought or deed. The Commentators call it the "language of actual facts" (*zabān ḥāl*) as opposed to the "language of words" (*zabān qāl*).

Between our journey-stages": [3818]
But they wronged themselves
(therein).
At length We made them
As a tale (that is told), [3819]
And We dispersed them
All in scattered fragments.
Verily in this are Signs
For every (soul that is)
Patiently constant and grateful.

اَسۡفَارِنَا وَظَلَمُوۡۤا اَنۡفُسَهُمۡ
فَجَعَلۡنٰهُمۡ اَحَادِيۡثَ
وَمَزَّقۡنٰهُمۡ كُلَّ مُمَزَّقٍ ؕ
اِنَّ فِىۡ ذٰلِكَ لَاٰيٰتٍ
لِّـكُلِّ صَبَّارٍ شَكُوۡرٍ ○

20. And on them did Satan
Prove true his idea, [3820]
And they followed him, all
But a Party that believed.

٢٠- وَلَقَدۡ صَدَّقَ عَلَيۡهِمۡ اِبۡلِيۡسُ ظَنَّهٗ
فَاتَّبَعُوۡهُ اِلَّا فَرِيۡقًا مِّنَ الۡمُؤۡمِنِيۡنَ ○

21. But he had no authority
Over them,—except that We
Might test the man who [3821]
Believes in the Hereafter
From him who is in doubt
Concerning it: and thy Lord
Doth watch over all things.

٢١- وَمَا كَانَ لَهٗ عَلَيۡهِمۡ مِّنۡ سُلۡطٰنٍ
اِلَّا لِنَعۡلَمَ مَنۡ يُّؤۡمِنُ بِالۡاٰخِرَةِ
مِمَّنۡ هُوَ مِنۡهَا فِىۡ شَكٍّ ؕ
وَرَبُّكَ عَلٰى كُلِّ شَىۡءٍ حَفِيۡظٌ ○ ع

3818. The covetous Sabā people, in order to get more profit from travellers' supplies by concentrating them on a few stations which they could monopolise, tended to choke off traffic and ruin the big trade. Selfishness often runs counter to true self-interest. It is a historical fact that the great Yemen-Syria route in Arabia declined with the decline of Yemen. There were no doubt physical causes, but supreme above all were the moral causes, the grasping nature of the people, and their departure from the highest standards of righteousness.

3819. The people of Sabā were given every chance. They had prosperity, skill, trade and commerce, and a healthy and beautiful country. They also had, apparently, great virtues, and as long as they remained true to their virtues, *i.e.*, to the Law of God, they remained happy and contented. But when they became covetous and selfish, and became jealous of other people's prosperity instead of rejoicing in it, they fell from grace and declined. It may be that the climate changed, the rainfall became scantier, perhaps on account of the cutting down of hill forests; trade routes changed, on account of the people falling off in the virtues that make men popular: behind all the physical causes was the root-cause, that they began to worship mammon, self, greed, or materialism. They fell into the snare of Satan. They gradually passed out of history, and became only a name in a story. Moral: it is only God's Mercy that can give true happiness or prosperity, and happiness or prosperity is only a snare unless used for the highest service of God and man

3820. *Cf.* xvii. 62. Satan out of arrogance had said, when he asked for respite from the Most High: "I will bring (Adam's) descendants under my sway, all but a few." This was now proved true on the Sabā people. He had no power to force them. It was their own will that went wrong and put them into his power.

3821. *Might test*: the word in the original is *might know*. It is not that God does not know all. Why does He want to test? It is in order to help us subjectively, to train our will, to put us definitely the question, "Will you obey God or other than God?" *Cf.* n. 467 to iii. 154.

Section 3.

22. Say: "Call upon other (gods)[3822]
Whom ye fancy, besides God:
They have no power,—
Not the weight of an atom,—
In the heavens or on earth:[3823]
No (sort of) share have they
Therein, nor is any of them
A helper to God.

٢٢- قُلِ ادْعُوا الَّذِيْنَ زَعَمْتُمْ مِّنْ دُوْنِ
اللّٰهِ ۚ لَا يَمْلِكُوْنَ مِثْقَالَ ذَرَّةٍ
فِي السَّمٰوٰتِ وَلَا فِي الْاَرْضِ وَمَا لَهُمْ فِيْهِمَا
مِنْ شِرْكٍ وَّمَا لَهٗ مِنْهُمْ مِّنْ ظَهِيْرٍ ○

23. "No intercession can avail
In His Presence, except for those[3824]
For whom He has granted
Permission. So far (is this
The case) that, when terror
Is removed from their hearts[3825]
(At the Day of Judgment, then)
Will they say, 'What is it
That your Lord commanded?'[3826]
They will say, 'That which is
True and just; and He is
The Most High, Most Great'."

٢٣- وَلَا تَنْفَعُ الشَّفَاعَةُ عِنْدَهٗٓ
اِلَّا لِمَنْ اَذِنَ لَهٗ ۚ
حَتّٰٓى اِذَا فُزِّعَ عَنْ قُلُوْبِهِمْ
قَالُوْا مَاذَا ۙ قَالَ رَبُّكُمْ ۚ
قَالُوا الْحَقَّ ۚ
وَهُوَ الْعَلِيُّ الْكَبِيْرُ ○

24. Say: "Who gives you[3827]
Sustenance, from the heavens

٢٤- قُلْ مَنْ يَّرْزُقُكُمْ مِّنَ السَّمٰوٰتِ

3822. Other objects of worship, such as Self, or Money, or Power, or things we imagine will bring us luck or prosperity, though they can do nothing of the kind.

3823. The false gods have no power whatever either in heaven or on earth, either in influencing our spiritual life or our ordinary worldly life. To suppose that they have some share, or that they can give some help to God, even though God is Supreme, is both false and blasphemous. God is One and Supreme, without sharer, helper, or equal.

3824. *Cf.* xx. 109, n. 2634, where I have explained the two possible modes of interpretation. Each soul is individually and personally responsible. And if there is any intercession, it can only be by God's gracious permission. For the Day of Judgment will be a terrible Day, or Day of Wrath (*Dies Irae*) according to the Latin hymn, when the purest souls will be stupefied at the manifestation of God's Power. See next note.

3825. "Their hearts": the pronoun "their" is referred to the angels nearest to God. On the Day of Judgment there will be such an irresistible manifestation of Power that even they will be silent for a while, and will scarcely realise what is happening. They will question each other, and only thus will they regain their bearings. Or "their" may refer to those who seek intercession.

3826. In their mutual questionings they will realise that God's Judgment, as always, is right and just. Does this mean that no sort of intercession is required?

3827. There are six propositions introduced here with the word "Say", at verses 22, 24, 25, 26, 27, and 30. They clearly explain the doctrine of Unity (verse 22), the Mercy of God (verse 24), man's Personal Responsibility (verse 25), the Final Justice of God (verse 26), God's Power and Wisdom (verse 27), and the Inevitability of the Judgment, by which true values will be restored (verse 30).

And the earth?" Say:
"It is God; and certain it is
That either we or ye[3828]
Are on right guidance
Or in manifest error!"

وَالْأَرْضِ قُلِ اللَّهُ
وَإِنَّآ أَوْ إِيَّاكُمْ لَعَلَىٰ هُدًى
أَوْ فِي ضَلَـٰلٍ مُّبِينٍ ۝

25. Say: "Ye shall not be
Questioned as to our sins,[3829]
Nor shall we be questioned
As to what ye do."

٢٥- قُل لَّا تُسْـَٔلُونَ عَمَّآ أَجْرَمْنَا
وَلَا نُسْـَٔلُ عَمَّا تَعْمَلُونَ ۝

26. Say: "Our Lord will gather us
Together and will in the end
Decide the matter between us
(And you) in truth and justice:[3830]
And He is the One to decide,
The One Who knows all."

٢٦- قُلْ يَجْمَعُ بَيْنَنَا رَبُّنَا
ثُمَّ يَفْتَحُ بَيْنَنَا بِالْحَقِّ
وَهُوَ الْفَتَّاحُ الْعَلِيمُ ۝

27. Say: "Show me those whom
Ye have joined with Him
As partners: by no means
(Can ye). Nay, He is God,[3831]
The Exalted in Power,
The Wise."

٢٧- قُلْ أَرُونِيَ الَّذِينَ
أَلْحَقْتُم بِهِۦ شُرَكَآءَ كَلَّا
بَلْ هُوَ اللَّهُ الْعَزِيزُ الْحَكِيمُ ۝

28. We have not sent thee
But as a universal (Messenger)[3832]

٢٨- وَمَآ أَرْسَلْنَـٰكَ إِلَّا كَآفَّةً

3828. Right and Wrong, Good and Evil, are incompatible, one with another. In this matter we can make no compromise. It is true that in men there may be various degrees of good or evil mixed together, and we have to tolerate men as our fellow-creatures, with all their faults and shortcomings. But this does not mean that we can worship God and Mammon together. Wrong is the negation of Right as light is of darkness. Though there may be apparently varying depths of darkness, this is only due to the imperfection of our vision: it is varying strengths of light as perceived by our relative powers of sight. So we may perceive the Light of God in varying degrees according to our spiritual vision. But in simple questions of Right or Wrong, we are faced by the Categorical Imperative.

3829. Therefore do not persecute us, or bring personal animus to bear on us. We must do our duty in declaring the universal Message, which is for you as much as for us.

3830. Human controversies are vain and inconclusive. If you put your trust in God and we put our trust in God, we belong to one Brotherhood, and we shall see the perfect Truth finally when the Time comes.

3831. Wisdom and Power only belong to God. If you put your trust in other things, they will fail you, because they do not exist—as objects of worship. All else that you set your hearts upon will and must fail you, because they cannot in any wise be brought into rivalry with God.

3832. God's Revelation, through the holy Prophet, was not meant for one family or tribe, one race or set of people. It was meant for all mankind, to whom, if they turn to God, it is a Message of the glad tidings of His Mercy, and if they do not turn to him, it is a warning against sin and the inevitable Punishment. That the Punishment does not come immediately (as far as they perceive) is no reason for doubting it. It has been declared in clear and unequivocal terms, and nothing can be more certain. Why delay? Why ask carping questions? Why not profit by the Message, turn to God in repentance, and bring forth the fruits of righteousness?

To men, giving them
Glad tidings, and warning them
(Against sin), but most men
Understand not.

لِّلنَّاسِ بَشِيرًا وَّنَذِيرًا
وَّلٰكِنَّ اَكْثَرَ النَّاسِ لَا يَعْلَمُونَ ○

29. They say: "When will this
Promise (come to pass)
If ye are telling the truth?"

٢٩- وَيَقُولُونَ مَتٰى هٰذَا الْوَعْدُ
اِنْ كُنْتُمْ صٰدِقِيْنَ ○

30. Say: "The appointment to you
Is for a Day, which ye
Cannot put back for an hour[3833]
Nor put forward."

٣٠- قُلْ لَّكُمْ مِّيْعَادُ يَوْمٍ لَّا تَسْتَاْخِرُوْنَ
عَنْهُ سَاعَةً وَّلَا تَسْتَقْدِمُوْنَ ○

C. 191.—Unfaith has no stable foundations to rest on:
(xxxiv. 31-54) Misleaders and misled will all be responsible
For their deeds. True values are not to be judged
By the seeming good of this Life: true Good
Will come to its own in the End, however
Derided and scorned in the period of Trial.
Revelation and the Mission of the men of God
Will stand every test. God's Truth will endure,
While Falsehood will perish, and its votaries find
The doo of Repentance closed in the End.

SECTION 4.

31. The Unbelievers say:
"We shall neither believe
In this scripture nor in (any)
That (came) before it."[3834]
Couldst thou but see when
The wrong-doers will be made
To stand before their Lord,
Throwing back the word
(of blame)[3835]

٣١- وَقَالَ الَّذِيْنَ كَفَرُوْا لَنْ نُّؤْمِنَ
بِهٰذَا الْقُرْاٰنِ وَلَا بِالَّذِيْ بَيْنَ يَدَيْهِ
وَلَوْ تَرٰى اِذِ الظّٰلِمُوْنَ مَوْقُوْفُوْنَ عِنْدَ
رَبِّهِمْ ۚ
يَرْجِعُ

3833. When that Day actually arrives, your period of probation will have passed. It will be too late. Now is the time for action and spiritual profit.

3834. To the Pagans all scriptures are taboo, whether it be the Qur-ān or any Revelation that came before it. The people of the Book despised the Pagans, but in their arrogant assumption of superiority, prevented them, by their example, from accepting the latest and most universal Scripture when it came in the form of the Qur-ān. This relative position, of men who fancy themselves on their knowledge, and men whom they despise but exploit and mislead, always exists on this earth. I have mentioned the people of the Book and the Pagan Arabs merely by way of illustration.

3835. One disbelief is as bad as another. There is little to choose between them. But when the final account will be taken, there will be mutual recriminations between the one and the other.

On one another! Those who
Had been despised will say
To the arrogant ones:[3836]
"Had it not been for you,
We should certainly
Have been believers!"

بَعۡضُهُمۡ إِلَىٰ بَعۡضٍ ٱلۡقَوۡلَ
يَقُولُ ٱلَّذِينَ ٱسۡتُضۡعِفُواْ لِلَّذِينَ ٱسۡتَكۡبَرُواْ
لَوۡلَآ أَنتُمۡ لَكُنَّا مُؤۡمِنِينَ ○

32. The arrogant ones will say
To those who had been despised:
"Was it we who kept you
Back from Guidance after
It reached you? Nay, rather,
It was ye who transgressed."[3837]

٣٢- قَالَ ٱلَّذِينَ ٱسۡتَكۡبَرُواْ لِلَّذِينَ
ٱسۡتُضۡعِفُوٓاْ أَنَحۡنُ صَدَدۡنَٰكُمۡ عَنِ ٱلۡهُدَىٰ
بَعۡدَ إِذۡ جَآءَكُمۖ بَلۡ كُنتُم مُّجۡرِمِينَ ○

33. Those who had been despised
Will say to the arrogant ones:
"Nay! it was a plot
(Of yours) by day and by night:[3838]
Behold! ye (constantly) ordered us
To be ungrateful to God
And to attribute equals to
Him!"[3839]
They will declare (their)
repentance[3840]
When they see the Penalty:
We shall put yokes

٣٣- وَقَالَ ٱلَّذِينَ ٱسۡتُضۡعِفُواْ لِلَّذِينَ
ٱسۡتَكۡبَرُواْ بَلۡ مَكۡرُ ٱلَّيۡلِ وَٱلنَّهَارِ
إِذۡ تَأۡمُرُونَنَآ أَن نَّكۡفُرَ بِٱللَّهِ
وَنَجۡعَلَ لَهُۥٓ أَندَادٗاۚ
وَأَسَرُّواْ ٱلنَّدَامَةَ
لَمَّا رَأَوُاْ ٱلۡعَذَابَۚ
وَجَعَلۡنَا ٱلۡأَغۡلَٰلَ

3836. The Pagans will naturally say to the people of the Book: "You misled us; you had previous Revelations, and you should have known how God sent His Messengers; had it not been for your bad example, we should have received God's Revelation and become Believers." Or the humble followers will say this to their leaders, or those less gifted will say to those by whom they were misled and exploited. The dichotomy is between such as pretentiously held their heads high in the world and such as they profited by but held in contempt.

3837. In the mutual reproaches between the misleaders and the misled ones, there will be a grain of truth on both sides, and yet both were guilty in not realising their own personal responsibility.

3838. The more intelligent ones who exploit the weaker ones are constantly plotting night and day to keep the latter ignorant and under their thumb. They show them the ways of Evil, because by that means they are more in their power.

3839. If all men worshipped the true God, and none but Him, they could not on the one hand be trampled upon, and on the other hand they could not be unjust. It is in the worship of false ideals or false gods that alluring structures of fraud and injustice are built up.

3840. *Cf.* x. 54, and n. 1445. All these mutual recriminations would be swallowed up in the general realisation of the Truth by both sides in the Hereafter. They would be prepared openly to declare their repentance, but it would be too late. The yoke of slavery to Evil will be on their necks. God's justice put it there, but what else could it do? Their own sins will cry out against them and hold them under their yokes.

On the necks of the Unbelievers:
It would only be a requital
For their (ill) Deeds.

فِىٓ اَعْنَاقِ الَّذِيْنَ كَفَرُوْا ؕ
هَلْ يُجْزَوْنَ اِلَّا مَا كَانُوْا يَعْمَلُوْنَ ○

34. Never did We send
A Warner to a population,
But the wealthy ones among
them[3841]
Said: " We believe not
In the (Message) with which
Ye have been sent."

۳۴- وَمَآ اَرْسَلْنَا فِىْ قَرْيَةٍ مِّنْ نَّذِيْرٍ
اِلَّا قَالَ مُتْرَفُوْهَآ ۙ
اِنَّا بِمَآ اُرْسِلْتُمْ بِهٖ كٰفِرُوْنَ ○

35. They said: " We have more
In wealth and in sons,[3842]
And we cannot be punished."

۳۵- وَقَالُوْا نَحْنُ اَكْثَرُ اَمْوَالًا وَّاَوْلَادًا ۙ
وَّمَا نَحْنُ بِمُعَذَّبِيْنَ ○

36. Say: " Verily my Lord enlarges
And restricts the Provision[3843]
To whom He pleases, but
Most men understand not."

۳۶- قُلْ اِنَّ رَبِّىْ يَبْسُطُ الرِّزْقَ لِمَنْ يَّشَآءُ
وَيَقْدِرُ وَلٰكِنَّ اَكْثَرَ النَّاسِ لَا يَعْلَمُوْنَ ○ ع

SECTION 5.

37. It is not your wealth
Nor your sons, that will
Bring you nearer to Us[3844]
In degree: but only
Those who believe and work
Righteousness—these are
The ones for whom there is
A multiplied Reward[3845]

۳۷- وَمَآ اَمْوَالُكُمْ وَلَآ اَوْلَادُكُمْ
بِالَّتِىْ تُقَرِّبُكُمْ عِنْدَنَا زُلْفٰٓى
اِلَّا مَنْ اٰمَنَ وَعَمِلَ صَالِحًا ز
فَاُولٰٓئِكَ لَهُمْ جَزَآءُ الضِّعْفِ

3841. Whenever the Message of God comes, the vested interests range themselves against it. Worldly power has made them arrogant; worldly pleasures have deadened their sensibility to Truth. They reject the Message because it attacks their false position.

3842. Their arrogance is openly based on their worldly power and position, their family influence, and the strength of their man-power. Turn back again to the contrast drawn between the arrogant ones and those whom they despised, in verses 31-33.

3843. *Provision* (or Sustenance): good things of all kinds in this life, material goods as well as power, opportunities, influence, mental gifts, etc. These do not necessarily all go to the good, nor is their denial to be interpreted to mean that it is a withdrawal of God's favour. Very often the contrary is the case. Their distribution is in accordance with the Universal Plan and Purpose, which is all-wise and all-good. But ignorant people cannot understand this.

3844. The true test of progress in spiritual life is to be measured by other things than material wealth and influence. What we have to ask ourselves is: are we the least bit nearer to God?

3845. *Cf.* xxx. 39. All worldly good is but a shadow that will pass away. Its intrinsic and eternal value is small. But those who work righteousness in Faith are on the true path of self-development. The reward they will get will be infinitely more than their merits entitle them to. For they will partake of the boundless Bounties of God.

For their deeds, while
Secure they (reside)
In the dwellings on high! [3846]

بِمَا عَمِلُوْا وَهُمْ فِي الْغُرُفٰتِ اٰمِنُوْنَ ○

38. Those who strive against
Our Signs, to frustrate them, [3847]
Will be given over
Into Punishment.

٣٨- وَالَّذِيْنَ يَسْعَوْنَ فِيْٓ اٰيٰتِنَا مُعٰجِزِيْنَ
اُولٰٓئِكَ فِي الْعَذَابِ مُحْضَرُوْنَ ○

39. Say: " Verily my Lord enlarges
And restricts the Sustenance [3848]
To such of His servants
As He pleases: and nothing
Do ye spend in the least
(In His Cause) but He
Replaces it: for He is [3849]
The Best of those who
Grant Sustenance.

٣٩- قُلْ اِنَّ رَبِّيْ يَبْسُطُ الرِّزْقَ لِمَنْ يَّشَآءُ
مِنْ عِبَادِهٖ وَيَقْدِرُ لَهٗ
وَمَآ اَنْفَقْتُمْ مِّنْ شَيْءٍ فَهُوَ يُخْلِفُهٗ
وَهُوَ خَيْرُ الرّٰزِقِيْنَ ○

40. One Day He will
Gather them all together,
And say to the angels, [3850]
" Was it you that these
Men used to worship ? "

٤٠- وَيَوْمَ يَحْشُرُهُمْ جَمِيْعًا
ثُمَّ يَقُوْلُ لِلْمَلٰٓئِكَةِ
اَهٰٓؤُلَآءِ اِيَّاكُمْ كَانُوْا يَعْبُدُوْنَ ○

41. They will say, " Glory to Thee!
Our (tie) is with Thee—
As Protector [3851]—not with them.
Nay, but they worshipped

٤١- قَالُوْا سُبْحٰنَكَ اَنْتَ وَلِيُّنَا مِنْ دُوْنِهِمْ
بَلْ كَانُوْا يَعْبُدُوْنَ

3846. Their happiness will not only be great in quantity (" multiplied "), but it will be of a specially sublime quality (" dwellings on high "), and it will endure without any chance of its loss or diminution (" secure they reside ").

3847. *Cf.* xxxiv. 5, where the argument was urged that human efforts to defeat God's Plan will only bring humiliation to those who indulge in them. Here the argument is rounded off by the statement that such efforts, besides their failure, will land them in an abyss of punishment contrasted with the " dwellings on high " of the blessed ones.

3848. *Cf.* xxxiv. 36 above, and n. 3843.

3849. Even in the seeming inequality of distribution of the good things of life, God has a wise and merciful purpose; for nothing arises by chance. He is the best to give us, now and evermore, just those things which subserve our real needs and advance our inner development.

3850. Here we have the case of the worship of angels or supposed Powers of God, or supposed beneficent spirits that men turn to instead of worshipping the true God. In fact these are mere names to the false worshippers. It is not the Good that they worship but the Evil, which leads them astray.

3851. *Walī* in Arabic may mean Friend either in the sense of Protector and Benefactor or in the sense of the Beloved. The tie of benevolence, confidence, and friendship is implied, either active or passive. The angels first proclaim their dependence on God and their need of His protection, and then disclaim any idea of their having protected or encouraged the false worshippers to worship beings other than God. They go further, and suggest that when men pretended to worship angels, they worshipped, not angels, but Jinns. See next note.

The Jinns:[3852] most of them
Believed in them."

الْجِنَّ ۚ أَكْثَرُهُم بِهِم مُّؤْمِنُونَ ○

42. So on that Day
No power shall they have
Over each other, for profit
Or harm: and We shall
Say to the wrong-doers,
"Taste ye the Penalty[3853]
Of the Fire,—the which
Ye were wont to deny!"

٤٢- فَالْيَوْمَ لَا يَمْلِكُ بَعْضُكُمْ لِبَعْضٍ
نَّفْعًا وَلَا ضَرًّا ۖ
وَنَقُولُ لِلَّذِينَ ظَلَمُوا ذُوقُوا عَذَابَ
النَّارِ الَّتِي كُنتُم بِهَا تُكَذِّبُونَ ○

43. When Our Clear Signs
Are rehearsed to them,
They say, "This is only
A man who wishes
To hinder you from the (worship)[3854]
Which your fathers practised."
And they say, "This is
Only a falsehood invented!"
And the Unbelievers say
Of the Truth when it comes
To them, "This is nothing
But evident magic!"

٤٣- وَإِذَا تُتْلَىٰ عَلَيْهِمْ آيَاتُنَا بَيِّنَاتٍ
قَالُوا مَا هَٰذَا إِلَّا رَجُلٌ يُرِيدُ أَن يَصُدَّكُمْ
عَمَّا كَانَ يَعْبُدُ آبَاؤُكُمْ
وَقَالُوا مَا هَٰذَا إِلَّا إِفْكٌ مُّفْتَرًى ۚ
وَقَالَ الَّذِينَ كَفَرُوا لِلْحَقِّ لَمَّا جَاءَهُمْ
إِنْ هَٰذَا إِلَّا سِحْرٌ مُّبِينٌ ○

44. But We had not given
Them Books which they could
Study, nor sent apostles[3855]
To them before thee
As Warners.

٤٤- وَمَا آتَيْنَاهُم مِّن كُتُبٍ يَدْرُسُونَهَا ۖ
وَمَا أَرْسَلْنَا إِلَيْهِمْ قَبْلَكَ مِن نَّذِيرٍ ○

3852. *Jinns*: see vi. 100 and n. 929. The false worshippers pretended to worship the bright and radiant angels of good, but in reality worshipped the dark and hidden forces of evil,—the devils hidden within themselves or in the life around them. They trusted and believed in such forces of evil, although such forces of evil had really no power.

3853. The supposed "rivals" of God—the false things whereon men set their hopes and fears—will have no power whatever when true values are restored; and the Fire—the Penalty—which they doubted or derided, will become the dominating real thing in their experience.

3854. Apart from the worship of Evil in the guise of the Powers of Light, there is another form of false worship, which depends on ancestral tradition. "Why" it is said "should we not do as our fathers did?" They reject a new apostle of Truth simply because his teaching does not agree with the ways of their ancestors. The answer to this is given in verse 44 below. But meanwhile the rejecters' objection to new Truth is stated in three forms: (1) our ancestors knew nothing of this; (2) the story of inspiration is false; it is merely an invention; we do not believe in inspiration; (3) when in some particular points, the new Truth does work wonders in men's hearts, they account for it by saying it is magic. The third objection is merely traditional. What is magic? If it was merely deception, surely the Truth has proved itself to be above deception. The second objection is answered by the fact that the Apostle who comes with new spiritual Truth is acknowledged to be truthful in other relations of life: why should he be false where his preaching brings him no gain but much sorrow and persecution? For the ancestral objection see next note.

3855. The ancestors (as in the case of the Arabs of the Times of Ignorance) had received no revelation of the clear kind which an apostle and a Book bring them. This is a reason for welcoming, not for rejecting, new Truth.

45. And their predecessors rejected
(The Truth); these have
Not received a tenth
Of what We had granted[3856]
To those: yet when they rejected
My apostles, how (terrible)
Was My rejection (of them)!

٤٥- وَكَذَّبَ الَّذِينَ مِن قَبْلِهِمْ
وَمَا بَلَغُوا مِعْشَارَ مَا آتَيْنَاهُمْ
فَكَذَّبُوا رُسُلِي
فَكَيْفَ كَانَ نَكِيرِ ۝

SECTION 6.

46. Say: "I do admonish you
On one point: that ye
Do stand up before God,—
(It may be) in pairs,[3857]
Or (it may be) singly,—
And reflect (within yourselves):
Your Companion is not[3858]
Possessed: he is no less
Than a Warner to you,
In face of a terrible
Penalty."

٤٦- قُلْ إِنَّمَا أَعِظُكُم بِوَاحِدَةٍ
أَن تَقُومُوا لِلَّهِ مَثْنَىٰ وَفُرَادَىٰ
ثُمَّ تَتَفَكَّرُوا
مَا بِصَاحِبِكُم مِّن جِنَّةٍ
إِنْ هُوَ إِلَّا نَذِيرٌ لَّكُم
بَيْنَ يَدَيْ عَذَابٍ شَدِيدٍ ۝

47. Say: "No reward do I
Ask of you: it is (all)
In your interest: my reward[3859]
Is only due from God:
And He is Witness
To all things."

٤٧- قُلْ مَا سَأَلْتُكُم مِّنْ أَجْرٍ فَهُوَ لَكُمْ
إِنْ أَجْرِيَ إِلَّا عَلَى اللَّهِ
وَهُوَ عَلَىٰ كُلِّ شَيْءٍ شَهِيدٌ ۝

48. Say: "Verily my Lord
Doth cast the (mantle

٤٨- قُلْ إِنَّ رَبِّي يَقْذِفُ

3856. Passing to Peoples before the immediate ancestors, the People of the Book, or the People of Sabā and the 'Ād and Thamūd, had received favours and gifts, power and wealth, ten times more than were enjoyed by the Pagan Quraish. Yet when they turned away from God's Truth, God turned away from them, and what terrible consequences descended on them when they lost God's Grace! This should make everyone humble, not least the posterity of Muḥammad the Apostle if they forsake God's Truths! For they have received a higher Teaching!

3857. A crowd mentality is not the best for the perception of the final spiritual truths. For these, it is necessary that each soul should commune within itself with earnest sincerity as before God: if it requires a Teacher, let it seek out one, or it may be that it wants the strengthening of the inner convictions that dawn on it, by the support of a sympathiser or friend. But careful and heart-felt reflection is necessary to appraise the higher Truths.

3858. Note that in verses 46, 47, 48, 49, and 50, arguments are suggested to the Prophet, by which he can convince any right-thinking man of his sincerity and truth. Here the argument is that he is not possessed or out of his mind. If he is different from ordinary men, it is because he has to give a warning of a terrible spiritual danger to the men whom he loves but who will not understand his Message.

3859. *Cf.* x. 72. The second argument is that he has nothing to gain from them. His message is for their own good. He is willing to suffer persecution and insult, because he has to fulfil his mission from God.

Of) Truth (over His servants),—[3860]
He that has full knowledge
Of (all) that is hidden."

بِالْحَقِّ عَلَّامُ الْغُيُوبِ ○

49. Say: "The Truth has arrived,
And Falsehood neither creates[3861]
Anything new, nor restores
Anything."

٤٩- قُلْ جَاءَ الْحَقُّ
وَمَا يُبْدِئُ الْبَاطِلُ وَمَا يُعِيدُ ○

50. Say: "If I am astray,
I only stray to the loss
Of my own soul: but if
I receive guidance, it is[3862]
Because of the inspiration
Of my Lord to me:
It is He Who hears
All things, and is (ever) near."

٥٠- قُلْ إِنْ ضَلَلْتُ فَإِنَّمَا أَضِلُّ عَلَىٰ نَفْسِي
وَإِنِ اهْتَدَيْتُ فَبِمَا يُوحِي إِلَيَّ رَبِّي
إِنَّهُ سَمِيعٌ قَرِيبٌ ○

51. If thou couldst but see
When they will quake
With terror; but then
There will be no escape[3863]
(For them), and they will be
Seized from a position
(Quite) near.

٥١- وَلَوْ تَرَىٰ إِذْ فَزِعُوا
فَلَا فَوْتَ
وَأُخِذُوا مِنْ مَكَانٍ قَرِيبٍ ○

3860. God's Truth is so vast that no man in this life can compass the whole of it. But God in His mercy selects His servants on whom it is cast like a mantle. They see enough to be able to teach their fellow men. It is through that mantle—that mission received from God—that an apostle can speak with authority to men. He cannot explain the exact mystery of inspiration, but he *knows* it is from God, and this is his third argument.

3861. The fourth argument is that the Truth is final: it does not come and go: it creates new situations and new developments, and if by any chance it *seems* to be defeated for a time, it comes back and restores the true balance;—unlike Falsehood, which by its very nature is doomed to perish: xvii. 81. The Prophet's credentials are known by the test of Time. This was already becoming apparent to discerning eyes when this Sūra was revealed in Mecca, but it became clear to the whole world with the story of Islām's progress in Medina.

3862. If it could possibly be supposed that the Prophet was a self-deceived visionary, it would affect him only, and could not fail to appear in his personality. But in fact he was steady in his constancy and Faith, and he not only went from strength to strength, but won the enduring and whole-hearted love and devotion of his nearest and dearest and of those who most came into contact with him. How was this possible, unless he had the Truth and the inspiration of God behind him? This is the fifth and last argument in this passage.

3863. After the arguments for the reality and triumph of Truth, we are asked to contemplate the position of the opposers of Truth when Truth is established. They will be struck with terror; for Truth is all-compelling. They will wish they could get away from that position, but that would be impossible. They will not be able to move far; they will be held fast to the consequences of their own earlier conduct. They will be caught quite close to the point of their departure from Truth.

52. And they will say,
"We do believe (now)
In the (Truth)"; but how[3864]
Could they receive (Faith)
From a position (so) far off,—

٥٢- وَقَالُوٓا اٰمَنَّا بِهٖ ۚ
وَاَنّٰى لَهُمُ التَّنَاوُشُ مِنْ مَّكَانٍۢ بَعِيْدٍ ۝

53. Seeing that they did reject
Faith (entirely) before, and
That they (continually) cast[3865]
(Slanders) on the Unseen
From a position far off?

٥٣- وَّقَدْ كَفَرُوْا بِهٖ مِنْ قَبْلُ ۚ
وَيَقْذِفُوْنَ بِالْغَيْبِ مِنْ مَّكَانٍۢ بَعِيْدٍ ۝

54. And between them
And their desires,
Is placed a barrier,[3866]
As was done in the past
With their partisans:[3867]
For they were indeed
In suspicious (disquieting) doubt.[3868]

٥٤- وَحِيْلَ بَيْنَهُمْ وَبَيْنَ مَا يَشْتَهُوْنَ
كَمَا فُعِلَ بِاَشْيَاعِهِمْ مِّنْ قَبْلُ ۗ
اِنَّهُمْ كَانُوْا فِيْ شَكٍّ مُّرِيْبٍ ۝

3864. They will now profess their faith in Truth, but of what value will such profession be? Faith is a belief in things unseen: now everything is plain and open before them. The position in which they could have received Faith is left far off behind them, when Truth was struggling and asked for help or asylum, and they cruelly, arrogantly, insultingly repudiated Truth.

3865. Not only did they reject the Truth of the Unseen (the true Reality), but they spread all sorts of false and malicious insinuations at the preachers of Truth, calling them dishonest men, liars, hypocrites, and so on. They did it like a coward taking up a sneaking position far from the fight and speeding arrows at a distant target.

3866. What they desire is to suppress Truth and to indulge in the satisfaction of their own evil, selfish motives. They will be baulked in both, and that itself will be their anguish and punishment. That has always been the law in the eternal struggle between Right and Wrong. *Cf.* Shakespeare, (Troilus and Cressida, i. 3. 116), "Right and wrong, Between whose endless jar justice resides." All partisans of such narrow cliques have always suffered the same fate.

3867. Note that verses 51-54 are a powerful description of the conflict between right and wrong, and may be understood in many meanings. (1) The description applies to the position in the final Hereafter, as compared with the position in this Life. (2) It applies to the position of triumphant Islām in Medina and later, as compared with the position of persecuted Islām in its early days in Mecca. (3) It applies to the reversal of the position of right and wrong at various phases of the world's history, or of (4) individual history.

3868. *Cf.* xiv. 9, and see n. 1884.

INTRODUCTION TO SŪRA XXXV (*Fāṭir*).

See Introduction to the last Sūra.

This Sūra deals with the mystery of Creation and its maintenance, with various forces typified by the wings of Angels. Whether we look to outer nature or to man, God's Grace proclaims His Glory, and protects His votaries from Evil.

It is an early Meccan Sūra, but its chronology has no significance.

Summary.—The forces which maintain Creation, as typified by angels, were themselves created by God, to Whom alone all praise is due: all else is naught (xxxv. 1-26, and C. 192).

All good is from God: who then will choose Evil, and reach the doom that goes with Evil? (xxxv. 27-45, and C. 193).

C. 192.—God is the source of all things: all Power,
(xxxv. 1-26.) Wisdom, Beauty, and Truth flow from Him.
It is Evil that deceives and plots in the dark.
All knowledge is with God. The things
That are good and pure and true are not
As the things that are evil, deceitful, and false.
God is free of all needs: it is we
That need Him: let us seek His love and live.
His Message will save us from wrong, while dark
Is the fate of those who reject Him.
Praise and glory to Him, the Cherisher of all!

Sūra XXXV.

Fāṭir, or The Originator of Creation;
or *Malāika*, or The Angels.

In the name of God, Most Gracious,
Most Merciful.

بِسْمِ اللّٰهِ الرَّحْمٰنِ الرَّحِيْمِ

1. Praise be to God,[3869]
Who created (out of nothing)[3870]
The heavens and the earth,
Who made the angels[3871]
Messengers with wings,—
Two, or three, or four (Pairs):
He adds to Creation[3872]
As He pleases: for God
Has power over all things.

١-اَلْحَمْدُ لِلّٰهِ فَاطِرِ السَّمٰوٰتِ وَالْاَرْضِ
جَاعِلِ الْمَلٰٓئِكَةِ رُسُلًا اُولِيْٓ اَجْنِحَةٍ
مَّثْنٰى وَثُلٰثَ وَرُبٰعَ
يَزِيْدُ فِي الْخَلْقِ مَا يَشَآءُ
اِنَّ اللّٰهَ عَلٰى كُلِّ شَيْءٍ قَدِيْرٌ ۝

2. What God out of His Mercy
Doth bestow on mankind
There is none can withhold:
What He doth withhold,

٢-مَا يَفْتَحِ اللّٰهُ لِلنَّاسِ مِنْ رَّحْمَةٍ
فَلَا مُمْسِكَ لَهَا ۚ وَمَا يُمْسِكْ

3869. See n. 3785 to xxxiv. 1. When we praise God, it means that we understand and bring to mind that His glory and power are exercised for the good of His Creation, and this is the subject-matter of the Sūra.

3870. As man's knowledge of the processes of nature advances, he sees how complex is the evolution of matter itself, leaving out the question of the origin of Life and the spiritual forces, which are beyond the ken of experimental science. But this knowledge itself becomes a sort of "veil of Light" (see Appendix VIII, p. 923): man becomes so conscious of the proximate causes, that he is apt, in his pride, to forget the primal Cause, the Cause of Causes, the ultimate hand of God in Creation. And then, Creation is such a complex process: see some of the ideas involved explained by different words in n. 120 to ii. 117. The word *faṭara* here used means the creation of primeval matter, to which further creative processes have to be added by the hand of God, for God "adds to His Creation as He pleases", not only in quantity, but in qualities, functions, relations, and variations in infinite ways.

3871. The grosser ideas which men have of angels must be dismissed from our minds. They are beings expressive of qualities or powers, which may be typified by "wings". We need not suppose that angelic "wings" have muscles and feathers, like the wings of birds. If they had, how could there be three, or any odd number? We may suppose "two, three, or four" to refer to pairs of wings. But we must not suppose "two, three, or four" to express precise numbers, for in sacred literature we find mention of angels with six hundred wings. And we can imagine angels with just one pair of wings. They are Messengers or Instruments of God's Will, and may have a few or numerous Errands entrusted to them. *Cf.* the description of the Spirit of Inspiration in xxvi. 193, and of the spirits or angels for executing the Commands of God in lxxix. 1-5.

3872. See n. 3870 above, where the complexities of the creative processes is referred to. God's creation did not stop at some past time: it continues, for He has all power, and His mercies are ever poured forth without stint.

There is none can grant,[3873]
Apart from Him:
And He is the Exalted
In Power, Full of Wisdom.

فَلَا مُرْسِلَ لَهُ مِنْ بَعْدِهِ
وَهُوَ الْعَزِيزُ الْحَكِيمُ ○

3. O men! call to mind
The grace of God unto you!
Is there a Creator, other[3874]
Than God, to give you
Sustenance from heaven
Or earth? There is
No god but He: how
Then are ye deluded
Away from the Truth?

٣- يَا أَيُّهَا النَّاسُ اذْكُرُوا نِعْمَتَ اللَّهِ عَلَيْكُمْ
هَلْ مِنْ خَالِقٍ غَيْرُ اللَّهِ
يَرْزُقُكُمْ مِنَ السَّمَاءِ وَالْأَرْضِ
لَا إِلَٰهَ إِلَّا هُوَ
فَأَنَّىٰ تُؤْفَكُونَ ○

4. And if they reject thee,
So were apostles rejected[3875]
Before thee: to God
Go back for decision
All affairs.

٤- وَإِنْ يُكَذِّبُوكَ فَقَدْ كُذِّبَتْ رُسُلٌ مِنْ
قَبْلِكَ
وَإِلَى اللَّهِ تُرْجَعُ الْأُمُورُ ○

5. O men! certainly
The promise of God[3876]
Is true. Let not then
This present life deceive you,[3877]

٥- يَا أَيُّهَا النَّاسُ إِنَّ وَعْدَ اللَّهِ
حَقٌّ فَلَا تَغُرَّنَّكُمُ الْحَيَاةُ الدُّنْيَا

3873. As God is the Creator and Sustainer of all beings and things, so does His kindness extend to all Creatures. No one can intercept God's mercies and gifts. Whatever is His Will and Plan and Purpose He can and does carry out. And if from any creature He withholds any particular gifts, there is no other person or power that can give those gifts. But such withholding is not arbitrary. He is full of wisdom and goodness, and every act of His, whether He withholds or gives, is full of kindness and mercy to His creatures.

3874. As the primal Cause of all things is God, an appeal is made to man to turn to God instead of running after false fancies. God is not only the source, but the centre of all life and activity, and all affairs return to Him. The world is sustained, and human life is sustained, by God's grace and providence. "Sustenance" is to be taken, in Quranic language, for all that helps to maintain and develop every aspect of life, physical and spiritual. It would be the height of folly, then, for man to ignore God's gracious Message, as explained in His Revelation.

3875. And yet there will be human perversity which will reject the True and accept the False. The man of God is not discouraged by this, as everything ultimately returns to God, and we must trust to His Wisdom in His Universal Plan.

3876. In verse 3 above the appeal was on the basis of the Past and the Present: now the appeal is on the basis of the Future. Our origin is from God; we live, move, and have our being now in God; but remember also that there is a Future, in which we have to render an account of ourselves to God. God's grace has promised us the Garden of Bliss; His justice has promised us the Fire of Suffering. Both promises are certain to be fulfilled. On which side shall we range ourselves?

3877. *Cf.* xxxi. 33 and n. 3624. The deception of Evil takes two forms. (1) The seductive temptations of this world may deceive us into forgetting the Hereafter. (2) The Arch-Enemy himself may so blind our spiritual vision that we may say with him, "Evil! be thou my good!" We may be misled by easy stages. Are we on our guard?

Nor let the Chief Deceiver
Deceive you about God.

وَلَا يَغُرَّنَّكُم بِاللَّهِ الْغَرُورُ ○

6. Verily Satan is an enemy
To you: so treat him[3878]
As an enemy. He only
Invites his adherents,
That they may become
Companions of the Blazing Fire.

٦- إِنَّ الشَّيْطٰنَ لَكُمْ عَدُوٌّ فَاتَّخِذُوهُ عَدُوًّا
إِنَّمَا يَدْعُوا حِزْبَهُ
لِيَكُونُوا مِنْ أَصْحٰبِ السَّعِيرِ ○

7. For those who reject God,[3879]
Is a terrible Penalty: but
For those who believe
And work righteous deeds,
Is Forgiveness, and
A magnificent Reward.

٧- الَّذِينَ كَفَرُوا لَهُمْ عَذَابٌ شَدِيدٌ
وَالَّذِينَ آمَنُوا وَعَمِلُوا الصّٰلِحٰتِ
لَهُم مَّغْفِرَةٌ وَأَجْرٌ كَبِيرٌ ○

Section 2.

8. Is he, then, to whom
The evil of his conduct
Is made alluring, so
That he looks upon it[3880]
As good, (equal to one
Who is rightly guided)?
For God leaves to stray
Whom He wills, and guides
Whom He wills. So
Let not thy soul go out
In (vainly) sighing after them:
For God knows well
All that they do!

٨- أَفَمَن زُيِّنَ لَهُ سُوءُ عَمَلِهِ
فَرَآهُ حَسَنًا
فَإِنَّ اللَّهَ يُضِلُّ مَن يَشَاءُ
وَيَهْدِي مَن يَشَاءُ
فَلَا تَذْهَبْ نَفْسُكَ عَلَيْهِمْ حَسَرٰتٍ
إِنَّ اللَّهَ عَلِيمٌ بِمَا يَصْنَعُونَ ○

9. It is God Who sends
Forth the Winds, so that

٩- وَاللَّهُ الَّذِي أَرْسَلَ الرِّيٰحَ

3878. Evil is our enemy and should be treated as such. It is really foreign to our nature, however much it may disguise itself to deceive us as our friend, or a part of our own nature. Personifying the Spirit of Evil, we may say that he wants us to share in his own damnation. Shall we allow ourselves to fall into his snare?

3879. To reject God is to reject all the good which He has implanted in our nature. Are we going to be false to the true Pattern according to which He created us, and suffer the consequences? Or are we going to be true to that Pattern and achieve the high and noble Destiny intended for us?

3880. *Cf.* n. 3877 above. When a stage is reached at which a man accepts Evil as his Good, his case is hopeless. Can such a man profit by preaching or guidance? He has himself deliberately rejected all guidance. Such a man is best left to stray. Perhaps, even in the paths in which he is straying, some sudden flash of light may come to him! That may be as God wills in His holy and wise Purpose and Plan. But the man of God is not to worry or feel disheartened by such men's attitude. He must go on tilling the soil that is open to him. For God's Plan may work in all sorts of unexpected ways, as in the allegory in the next verse.

They raise up the Clouds,[3881]
And We drive them
To a land that is dead,
And revive the earth therewith
After its death: even so
(Will be) the Resurrection!

فَتُثِيرُ سَحَابًا
فَسُقْنٰهُ اِلٰى بَلَدٍ مَّيِّتٍ فَاَحْيَيْنَا بِهِ الْاَرْضَ
بَعْدَ مَوْتِهَا ؕ كَذٰلِكَ النُّشُوْرُ ○

10. If any do seek
For glory and power,—[3882]
To God belong
All glory and power.
To Him mount up
(All) Words of Purity:
It is He Who exalts
Each Deed of Righteousness.
Those that lay Plots[3883]
Of Evil,—for them
Is a Penalty terrible;
And the plotting of such
Will be void (of result).

١٠- مَنْ كَانَ يُرِيْدُ الْعِزَّةَ
فَلِلّٰهِ الْعِزَّةُ جَمِيْعًا ؕ
اِلَيْهِ يَصْعَدُ الْكَلِمُ الطَّيِّبُ
وَالْعَمَلُ الصَّالِحُ يَرْفَعُهٗ ؕ
وَالَّذِيْنَ يَمْكُرُوْنَ السَّيِّاٰتِ
لَهُمْ عَذَابٌ شَدِيْدٌ ؕ
وَمَكْرُ اُولٰٓئِكَ هُوَ يَبُوْرُ ○

11. And God did create[3884]
You from dust;
Then[3885] from a sperm-drop;
Then He made you
In pairs. And no female
Conceives, or lays down
(Her load), but with His
Knowledge. Nor is a man

١١- وَاللّٰهُ خَلَقَكُمْ مِّنْ تُرَابٍ
ثُمَّ مِنْ نُّطْفَةٍ ثُمَّ جَعَلَكُمْ اَزْوَاجًا ؕ
وَمَا تَحْمِلُ مِنْ اُنْثٰى وَلَا تَضَعُ
اِلَّا بِعِلْمِهٖ ؕ وَمَا

3881. The allegory here is double. (1) Dry, unpromising soil may seem to all intents and purposes dead; there is no source of water near; moisture is sucked up by the sun's heat in a far-off ocean, and clouds are formed; winds arise; it seems as if the wind "bloweth as it listeth", but it is really God's Providence that drives it to the dead land; the rain falls, and behold! there is life and motion and beauty everywhere! So in the spiritual world, God's Revelation is His Mercy and His Rain; there may be the individual resurrection (*Nushūr*) or unfolding of a soul. (2) So again, may be the general Resurrection (*Nushūr*), the unfolding of a new World in the Hereafter, out of an old World that is folded up and dead (*Takwīr*, S. lxxxi).

3882. Good and Evil are to be distinguished sharply. No good is ever lost: it goes up to the Throne of God. The humblest Good, in word or deed, is exalted to high rank. If man seeks for mere glory and power, there is no such thing apart from God. But seeking God, we attain to the highest glory and power.

3883. It is the nature of Evil to work underground, to hide from the Light, to plot against Righteousness; but Evil inevitably carries its own punishment. Its plots must fail miserably. And eventually Evil itself is to be blotted out.

3884. *Cf.* xviii. 37 and n. 2379; xxii. 5 and n. 2773; and xxx. 20, and n. 3524. Here the argument is that man's physical origin is lowly: his physical body is but dust; his life-sperm issues from a part of his body which he hides and considers as a place of shame; and the mystery of sex shows that no one individual among mankind is sufficient in himself. Glory and power and knowledge are not in him, but in God, from Whom alone he derives any glory, or power, or knowledge that he possesses.

3885. "Then" in this and the following clause refers, not to stages of time, but to stages in the argument. It is almost equivalent to "further", "also", "and in addition".

Long-lived granted length
Of days, nor is a part
Cut off from his life,
But is in a Decree[3886]
(Ordained). All this
Is easy to God.[3887]

يُعَمَّرُ مِنْ مُّعَمَّرٍ
وَّلَا يُنْقَصُ مِنْ عُمُرِهٖٓ اِلَّا فِيْ كِتٰبٍ ۭ
اِنَّ ذٰلِكَ عَلَى اللّٰهِ يَسِيْرٌ ○

12. Nor are the two bodies[3888]
Of flowing water alike,—
The one palatable, sweet,
And pleasant to drink,
And the other, salt
And bitter. Yet from each
(Kind of water) do ye
Eat flesh fresh and tender,[3889]
And ye extract ornaments[3890]
To wear; and thou seest
The ships therein that plough
The waves, that ye may
Seek (thus) of the Bounty
Of God that ye
May be grateful.

١٢- وَمَا يَسْتَوِي الْبَحْرٰنِ ۖ
هٰذَا عَذْبٌ فُرَاتٌ سَآئِغٌ شَرَابُهٗ
وَهٰذَا مِلْحٌ اُجَاجٌ ۭ
وَمِنْ كُلٍّ تَاْكُلُوْنَ لَحْمًا طَرِيًّا
وَّتَسْتَخْرِجُوْنَ حِلْيَةً تَلْبَسُوْنَهَا ۚ
وَتَرَى الْفُلْكَ فِيْهِ مَوَاخِرَ
لِتَبْتَغُوْا مِنْ فَضْلِهٖ
وَلَعَلَّكُمْ تَشْكُرُوْنَ ○

13. He merges Night into Day,[3891]
And He merges Day

١٣- يُوْلِجُ الَّيْلَ فِي النَّهَارِ وَيُوْلِجُ النَّهَارَ

3886. Things that appear most secret and mysterious to man are all known and ordained by God. They are all subject to God's Laws and Decrees. The mystery of human birth (see n. 3625 to xxxi, 34), the mystery of sex, the mystery of Life and Death and many other things, seem to man inexplicable. But they are all ordained by God, and their reasons are fully known to Him.

3887. Man's knowledge may be acquired laboriously and may be a burden to him. God's knowledge is different; it is no task or burden to Him. *Cf.* xxxiii. 19 and 30.

3888. See xxv. 53 and notes 3111 and 3112. The great salt Ocean with its seas and gulfs is all one: and the great masses of sweet water in rivers, lakes, ponds, and underground springs are also one: and each is connected with the other by the constant circulation going on, which sucks up vapours, carries them about in clouds or atmospheric moisture, and again brings them condensed into water or snow or hail to mingle with rivers and streams and get back into the Ocean.

3889. For this whole passage see xvi. 14 and notes 2034 and 2035. Both from the sea and from rivers and lakes we get fish, of which some kinds have a flesh particularly fresh and tender, and of a most delicate flavour.

3890. Such as pearls and coral from the sea, and such delicately tinted stones as the *'Aqīq* (carnelian), the agate, the goldstone, or other varieties of quartz pebbles found in river-beds, and considered as gems. Many such are found in the Ken river in Banda District (Bundelkhand). Some river sands also yield minute quantities of gold. In large navigable rivers and big Lakes like those of North America, as well as in the sea, there are highways for shipping and commerce.

3891. *Cf.* xxii. 61. The phases of Light in nature may have other uses. But for man they mark periods of rest and activity, and have great influence on his physical, moral, and spiritual life.

Into Night, and He has
Subjected the sun and
The moon (to His Law):[3892]
Each one runs its course
For a term appointed.
Such is God your Lord:[3893]
To Him belongs all Dominion.
And those whom ye invoke
Besides Him have not
The least power.[3894]

فِي الَّيْلِ وَسَخَّرَ الشَّمْسَ وَالْقَمَرَ
كُلٌّ يَجْرِي لِأَجَلٍ مُّسَمًّى
ذَٰلِكُمُ اللَّهُ رَبُّكُمْ لَهُ الْمُلْكُ
وَالَّذِينَ تَدْعُونَ مِن دُونِهِ
مَا يَمْلِكُونَ مِن قِطْمِيرٍ ۝

14. If ye invoke them,
They will not listen
To your call, and if[3895]
They were to listen,
They cannot answer
Your (prayer). On the Day
Of Judgment they will reject[3896]
Your "Partnership". And none,
(O man!) can tell thee[3897]
(The Truth) like the One
Who is acquainted with all things.

١٤- إِن تَدْعُوهُمْ لَا يَسْمَعُوا دُعَاءَكُمْ
وَلَوْ سَمِعُوا مَا اسْتَجَابُوا لَكُمْ
وَيَوْمَ الْقِيَامَةِ يَكْفُرُونَ بِشِرْكِكُمْ
وَلَا يُنَبِّئُكَ
مِثْلُ خَبِيرٍ ۝

SECTION 3.

15. O ye men! It is
Ye that have need

١٥- يَا أَيُّهَا النَّاسُ أَنتُمُ الْفُقَرَاءُ

3892. *Cf.* xiii. 2. The sun and the moon mark phases of light, and serve man during the periods of the day and the night. The sun marks the seasons, and is the source of heat and energy and physical life for the whole solar system. The sun and the moon run according to fixed laws, and they will continue to do so, not for ever, but for the period appointed for their duration by God.

3893. God's might and majesty, and God's goodness and wisdom, having been shown by a few examples, it follows that it is folly to seek or worship any other power but God. It only throws off man into false paths, and takes him farther and farther away from the Truth.

3894. *Qiṭmīr*: the thin, white skin that covers the date-stone. It has neither strength nor texture, and has no value whatever. Any one relying on any power other than that of God relies on nothing whatever. The *Qiṭmīr* is worse than the proverbial "broken reed". *Cf.* iv. 53 and iv. 124, where the word *naqīr*, 'the groove in a date-stone', is used similarly for a thing of no value or significance.

3895. False or imaginary objects of worship serve no purpose whatever. They cannot hear; if they could hear, they could not grant prayers or petitions. In fact, if they are real creatures, such as angels or deified human beings, they will very rightly repudiate any such worship as brings them into competition or "partnership" with God. See next note.

3896. *Cf.* x. 28 and n. 1418; also xxxiv. 40-41. No false ideas or false impressions will remain when true values are restored. Why not then accept the Truth now in this life, and get on to the true path of Grace?

3897. None can tell you the Truth better than He Who is All-Wise and All-Knowing. Why not accept His Message and receive His guidance?

Of God: but God is [3898]
The One Free of all wants,
Worthy of all praise.

إِلَى اللَّهِ
وَاللَّهُ هُوَ الْغَنِيُّ الْحَمِيدُ ○

16. If He so pleased, He
Could blot you out
And bring in
A New Creation

١٦- إِن يَشَأْ يُذْهِبْكُمْ
وَيَأْتِ بِخَلْقٍ جَدِيدٍ ○

17. Nor is that (at all)
Difficult for God.[3899]

١٧- وَمَا ذَٰلِكَ عَلَى اللَّهِ بِعَزِيزٍ ○

18. Nor can a bearer [3900] of burdens
Bear another's burden.
If one heavily laden should
Call another to (bear) his load,
Not the least portion of it
Can be carried (by the other),
Even though he be nearly [3901]
Related. Thou canst but
Admonish such as fear
Their Lord unseen [3902]
And establish regular Prayer.[3903]
And whoever purifies himself

١٨- وَلَا تَزِرُ وَازِرَةٌ وِزْرَ أُخْرَىٰ
وَإِن تَدْعُ مُثْقَلَةٌ إِلَىٰ حِمْلِهَا
لَا يُحْمَلْ مِنْهُ شَيْءٌ
وَلَوْ كَانَ ذَا قُرْبَىٰ
إِنَّمَا تُنذِرُ الَّذِينَ يَخْشَوْنَ رَبَّهُم
بِالْغَيْبِ وَأَقَامُوا الصَّلَاةَ وَمَن تَزَكَّىٰ

3898. What is man that God should care for him, instruct him, and send him special messengers to warn him of danger and harm? It is man that depends on God and has need of Him every moment of his life. God has no need of him, but He bestows His Grace on him as on all His creatures, out of His unbounded Mercy and loving-kindness. If it were God's Will, He could blot out man for his rebellion and create an entirely new world.

3899. There is no limit to God's creative power, nor is His creative energy anything rare or unusual. This is the force of the word *'Azīz* here. God's creative energy is exercised every moment, and it is the normal condition in the universe.

3900. Bearer: *ḥāmilatun*: feminine in Arabic, as referring to the soul (*nafs*), as in vi. 164.

3901. Natural relationship may be considered as a reasonable cause or opportunity for bearing each other's burdens. For example, a mother or a father might offer to die for her or his child, and *vice versa*. But this does not apply to spiritual matters. There the responsibility is strictly personal and cannot be transferred to another. In xxix. 13 we are told that the misleaders "will bear other burdens along with their own"; but the context shows that the "other" burdens are the burdens of deluding others with their falsehoods. Both sins are their own, *viz.*, their original sin, and the sin of deluding the others. But the responsibility will be doubled.

3902. *Bil-gaibi*: unseen in the adverbial sense. The man, who, though he does not see God, so realises God's Presence in himself as if he saw Him, is the man of genuine Faith, and for him God's Revelation comes through many channels and is always fruitful.

3903. Prayer is one of the means of purifying ourselves of lower motives in life, for in prayer we seek the Presence of God. But the purity which we seek is for our own souls: we confer no favour on God or on any Power in the spiritual world, as some imagine who make "gifts" to God. In any case the destination of all is to God.

Does so for the benefit Of his own soul; and The destination (of all) Is to God.	فَإِنَّمَا يَتَزَكّٰى لِنَفْسِهٖ ۚ وَإِلَى اللّٰهِ الْمَصِيْرُ ○
19. The blind and the seeing Are not alike;[3904]	١٩- وَمَا يَسْتَوِي الْأَعْمٰى وَالْبَصِيْرُ ○
20. Nor are the depths Of Darkness and the Light;	٢٠- وَلَا الظُّلُمٰتُ وَلَا النُّوْرُ ○
21. Nor are the (chilly) shade And the (genial) heat of the sun:	٢١- وَلَا الظِّلُّ وَلَا الْحَرُوْرُ ○
22. Nor are alike those[3905] That are living and those That are dead. God can Make any that He wills To hear; but thou Canst not make those To hear who are (Buried) in graves.	٢٢- وَمَا يَسْتَوِي الْأَحْيَآءُ وَلَا الْأَمْوَاتُ ۚ إِنَّ اللّٰهَ يُسْمِعُ مَنْ يَّشَآءُ ۚ وَمَآ أَنْتَ بِمُسْمِعٍ مَّنْ فِي الْقُبُوْرِ ○
23. Thou art no other Than a warner.[3906]	٢٣- إِنْ أَنْتَ إِلَّا نَذِيْرٌ ○
24. Verily We have sent thee In truth, as a bearer Of glad tidings,[3907] And as a warner:	٢٤- إِنَّآ أَرْسَلْنٰكَ بِالْحَقِّ بَشِيْرًا وَّنَذِيْرًا ۚ

3904. Now we are offered some contrasts between those who obey God's Law and are thus citizens of the Kingdom of Heaven and those who are rebels against God's Kingdom and are thus outlaws. How can they be considered alike? The godly are like those who see, as contrasted with those who are blind; and their motives and actions are like the purest and highest Light, contrasted with the depths of darkness; or, to take another metaphor, their lives are like the genial and warmth-giving heat of the sun, which benefits all who come within its influence, contrasted with the chilly shadows of gloom in which no vegetation flourishes.

3905. The final contrast is between the Living and the Dead; those whose future has in it the promise of growth and fulfilment, and those who are inert and on the road to perish. With God everything is possible: He can give Life to the Dead. But the human Teacher should not expect that people who are (spiritually) dead and buried will by any chance hear his call.

3906. The function of a Prophet is to preach God's Truth, to point out the right Way, to show men the need of repentance, and to warn them against the dangers which they incur by living a life of evil. He cannot compel them to accept the Truth or listen to the Message.

3907. It is God Who sends the Revelation. While there is warning in it for the heedless, there is good news (in Christian terms, the gospel) for those who listen and repent. The warning always came to all peoples before punishment.

And there never was
A people, without a warner
Having lived among them
(In the past).

وَإِنْ مِّنْ أُمَّةٍ
إِلَّا خَلَا فِيهَا نَذِيرٌ ○

25. And if they reject thee,
So did their predecessors,
To whom came their apostles
With Clear Signs, Books[3908]
Of dark prophecies,
And the Book
Of Enlightenment.

٢٥- وَإِنْ يُكَذِّبُوكَ فَقَدْ كَذَّبَ الَّذِينَ
مِنْ قَبْلِهِمْ ۚ
جَآءَتْهُمْ رُسُلُهُمْ بِالْبَيِّنٰتِ
وَبِالزُّبُرِ وَبِالْكِتٰبِ الْمُنِيرِ ○

26. In the end did I
Punish those who rejected
Faith: and how (terrible)[3909]
Was My rejection (of them)!

٢٦- ثُمَّ أَخَذْتُ الَّذِينَ كَفَرُوا
فَكَيْفَ كَانَ نَكِيرِ ○ ع

C. 193.—Man can see by his own experience
(xxxv. 27-45.) What infinite shades and grades of colour
There are in nature. So are there grades
In the spiritual world. The Good and the True
Understand God, Who knows and watches
Over all His creatures. The Good will reach
Eternal Bliss, while the Evil will find
No helper. Arrogance and plotting will be
The undoing of Evil: its doom
Is sure, if it fails to profit by the respite
Granted by the All-Merciful God.

Section 4.

27. Seest thou not that
God sends down rain
From the sky? With it
We then bring out produce
Of various colours.[3910]
And in the mountains

٢٧- أَلَمْ تَرَ أَنَّ اللّٰهَ أَنْزَلَ مِنَ السَّمَآءِ
مَآءً ۚ
فَأَخْرَجْنَا بِهِ ثَمَرٰتٍ مُّخْتَلِفًا أَلْوَانُهَا

3908. The three things here mentioned are also mentioned in iii. 184, where I have explained the meaning in n. 490. All spiritual teaching centres round the evidences of God in our lives, the mystic utterances of men of God, and the rules and laws which guide holy living.

3909. *Cf.* xxii. 44 and xxxiv. 45. The rejecters of God hardly realise the terrible consequences to them individually and collectively, if God's grace is withdrawn from them and they are left to perish in their own sins and wrong-doing.

3910. Everyone can see how God's artistry produces from rain the wonderful variety of crops and fruits—golden, green, red, yellow, and showing all the most beautiful tints we can think of. And each undergoes in nature the gradual shading off in its transformation from the raw stage to the stage of maturity.

Are tracts white and red,[3911]
Of various shades of colour,
And black intense in hue.

وَمِنَ الْجِبَالِ جُدَدٌ بِيضٌ وَحُمْرٌ
مُخْتَلِفٌ أَلْوَانُهَا وَغَرَابِيبُ سُودٌ ۝

28. And so amongst men
And crawling creatures and cattle,
Are they of various colours.[3912]
Those truly fear God,
Among His Servants,
Who have knowledge:[3913]
For God is Exalted in Might,
Oft-Forgiving.

٢٨- وَمِنَ النَّاسِ وَالدَّوَابِّ وَالْأَنْعَامِ
مُخْتَلِفٌ أَلْوَانُهُ كَذَٰلِكَ
إِنَّمَا يَخْشَى اللَّهَ مِنْ عِبَادِهِ الْعُلَمَاءُ
إِنَّ اللَّهَ عَزِيزٌ غَفُورٌ ۝

29. Those who rehearse the Book
Of God, establish regular Prayer,.
And spend (in Charity)[3914]
Out of what We have provided
For them, secretly and openly,
Hope for a Commerce[3915]
That will never fail:

٢٩- إِنَّ الَّذِينَ يَتْلُونَ كِتَابَ اللَّهِ وَأَقَامُوا
الصَّلَاةَ وَأَنْفَقُوا مِمَّا رَزَقْنَاهُمْ
سِرًّا وَعَلَانِيَةً يَرْجُونَ تِجَارَةً
لَنْ تَبُورَ

3911. These wonderful colours and shades of colours are to be found not only in vegetation but in rocks and mineral products. There are the white veins of marble and quartz or of chalk, the red laterite, the blue basaltic rocks, the ink-black flints, and all the variety, shade, and gradation of colours. Speaking of mountains, we think of their "azure hue" from a distance, due to atmospheric effects, and these atmospheric effects lead our thoughts to the glories of clouds, sunsets, the zodiacal light, the *aurora borealis*, and all kinds of Nature's gorgeous pageantry.

3912. In the physical shapes of human and animal life, also, we see variations in shades and gradations of colours of all kinds. But these variations and gradations, marvellous though they be, are as nothing compared with the variations and differences in the inner or spiritual world. See next note.

3913. In outer nature we can, through colours, understand and appreciate the finest shades and gradations. But in the spiritual world that variation or gradation is even more subtle and more comprehensive. Who can truly understand it? Only God's servants, who *know*, *i.e.*, who have the inner knowledge which comes through their acquaintance with the spiritual world,—it is such people who truly appreciate the inner world, and it is they who know that the fear of God is the beginning of wisdom. For such fear is akin to appreciation and love,—appreciation of all the marvellous beauties of God's outer and inner world ("God is Exalted in Might") and love because of His Grace and Kindness ("Oft-Forgiving"). But God's forgiveness extends to many who do not truly understand Him.

3914. The man of God takes God's Revelation ("the Book") to heart, ever seeks to get closer and closer to God ("regular Prayer"), and in doing so, is moved more and more to practical Charity for his fellow-creatures. He is not ashamed of his Charity ("openly"), but he does not do it to be seen of men ("secretly"): he just does what is necessary for his fellow-creatures, whether people talk about it or not.

3915. Here is a metaphor from commerce. The good man's Charity comes not merely out of superfluities, but out of "what God has provided" for him. He therefore recognises two things: (1) that his wealth (literal and metaphorical) is not his absolutely, but that it is given to him by God; and (2) that he must deny himself the use of some of it, as a merchant puts by some of his wealth to invest as capital. Only, the godly man's Commerce will never fail or fluctuate; because God guarantees him the return, and even adds something to the return out of His own Bounty. That is, God gives more than ever our merits deserve.

30. For He will pay them
Their meed, nay, He will
Give them (even) more
Out of His Bounty:
For He is Oft-Forgiving,[3916]
Most Ready to appreciate
(service).[3917]

٣٠- لِيُوَفِّيَهُمْ أُجُورَهُمْ
وَيَزِيدَهُم مِّن فَضْلِهِ ۚ
إِنَّهُ غَفُورٌ شَكُورٌ ○

31. What which We have revealed
To thee of the Book
Is the Truth,—confirming
What was (revealed) before it:
For God is assuredly—
With respect to His servants—
Well acquainted and[3918]
Fully Observant.

٣١- وَالَّذِي أَوْحَيْنَا إِلَيْكَ مِنَ الْكِتَٰبِ
هُوَ الْحَقُّ مُصَدِّقًا لِّمَا بَيْنَ يَدَيْهِ ۗ
إِنَّ اللَّهَ بِعِبَادِهِ
لَخَبِيرٌ بَصِيرٌ ○

32. Then[3919] We have given
The Book for inheritance
To such of Our servants
As We have chosen:
But there are among them[3920]
Some who wrong their own

٣٢- ثُمَّ أَوْرَثْنَا الْكِتَٰبَ الَّذِينَ
اصْطَفَيْنَا مِنْ عِبَادِنَا ۖ
فَمِنْهُمْ ظَالِمٌ لِّنَفْسِهِ ۚ

3916. No man is perfect. Everyone has his faults. But when a man tries his best in the service of God, his faults are blotted out, and he is treated as if he had committed no faults: "for God is Oft-Forgiving, and ready to appreciate service".

3917. *Cf.* xiv. 5, and n. 2877 for *shakūr*. God is ready to recognise, appreciate, and reward the smallest service, without regard to the defects in that service. His gracious acceptance is compared to "gratitude" among men.

3918. All Revelation is one. The Qur-ān therefore confirms the main and uncorrupted features of previous revelations. It must be so, because God is fully cognisant of the needs of every age and people; and therefore His Message, while it meets those needs, must in essence be the same. His Messengers did not meet each other as men; but their contact with God through inspiration unified their Message. And He cares for and watches over all men, and He knows fully what their needs are, even better than they know themselves.

3919. The force of "then" is that of finality. The Qur-ān is the last Book revealed. Or it may be here to point the contrast between "to thee" in the last verse, *i.e.*, the holy Apostle, in contradistinction to the People of Islam, who inherited the Book after him.

3920. The custodians of the Qur-ān after the holy Apostle were the People of Islam. They were chosen for the Book, not in any narrow sense, but in the sense that the Book was given for their age and they were charged to obey it and preserve and propagate it, so that all mankind should receive the Message. But it does not follow that they are all true and faithful to their charge, as indeed we see too painfully around us to-day. Just as mankind was chosen collectively to be Vicegerents for God, and yet some among mankind fell into evil,—even so, some in the house of Islam fail to follow the Light given to them, and thus "wrong their own souls". But some follow a middle course: in their case "the spirit indeed is willing, but the flesh is weak": their intentions are good, but they have much to learn yet of the true Muslim life and Muslim virtues. Then there is a third class: they may not indeed be perfect, but both their intentions and their conduct are sound, and they form an example to other men: they are "foremost" in every good deed. They are so, not by their own merits, but by the Grace of God. And they have reached the highest Achievement,—the salvation, which is typified by the various metaphors that follow.

Souls; some who follow
A middle course; and some
Who are, by God's leave,
Foremost in good deeds;
That is the highest Grace.

وَمِنْهُمْ مُّقْتَصِدٌ ۚ
وَمِنْهُمْ سَابِقٌۢ بِالْخَيْرٰتِ بِاِذْنِ اللّٰهِ ۗ
ذٰلِكَ هُوَ الْفَضْلُ الْكَبِيْرُ ۝

33. Gardens of Eternity will they [3921]
Enter: therein will they
Be adorned with bracelets [3922]
Of gold and pearls;
And their garments there
Will be of silk.

٣٣- جَنّٰتُ عَدْنٍ يَّدْخُلُوْنَهَا
يُحَلَّوْنَ فِيْهَا مِنْ اَسَاوِرَ مِنْ ذَهَبٍ وَّلُؤْلُؤًا ۚ
وَلِبَاسُهُمْ فِيْهَا حَرِيْرٌ ۝

34. And they will say:
"Praise be to God,
Who has removed from us
(All) sorrow: for our Lord
Is indeed Oft-Forgiving
Ready to appreciate (service): [3923]

٣٤- وَقَالُوا الْحَمْدُ لِلّٰهِ الَّذِيْٓ
اَذْهَبَ عَنَّا الْحَزَنَ ۭ
اِنَّ رَبَّنَا لَغَفُوْرٌ شَكُوْرُ ۝

35. "Who has, out of His Bounty,
Settled us in a Home
That will last: no toil
Nor sense of weariness [3924]
Shall touch us therein."

٣٥- الَّذِيْٓ اَحَلَّنَا دَارَ الْمُقَامَةِ مِنْ فَضْلِهٖ ۚ
لَا يَمَسُّنَا فِيْهَا نَصَبٌ
وَّلَا يَمَسُّنَا فِيْهَا لُغُوْبٌ ۝

36. But those who reject (God)—
For them will be
The Fire of Hell: [3925]
No term shall be determined

٣٦- وَالَّذِيْنَ كَفَرُوْا لَهُمْ نَارُ جَهَنَّمَ ۚ
لَا يُقْضٰى

3921. "The Garden" signifies their environment: all they see about them will give them comfort, rest, and satisfaction, and a feeling of beauty and dignity. The jewels and clothes signify their personal external state: here, again, everything will give them a sense of beauty and dignity, comfort, rest, and satisfaction. And finally, most important of all, comes their internal state, where again they will have the same sense of beauty, dignity, comfort, rest, and satisfaction: this is indicated by their words of Praise (verses 34-35).

3922. *Cf.* xviii. 31 and xxii. 23.

3923. *Cf.* above, xxxv. 30. Note how beautifully the argument is rounded off. In verse 30 they were told that "God is Oft-Forgiving, Most Ready to appreciate service". Now they have reached the Goal, and they have found the Promise profoundly true. All their hopes are fulfilled, and their sorrows ended.

3924. In case it should be thought that perpetual happiness might cloy or be dull, as would be the case in this life, it is added—as the experience of those who attain that state—that it is not so on that plane of existence. Not only is there Joy, but it remains fresh and leads to no weariness.

3925. The "Fire" is the opposite to the "Garden". Instead of there being comfort, rest, and satisfaction in their environment, there will be pain, suffering, and anguish. Instead of there being dignity there will be humiliation. And there will be no hope of its termination or abatement, not even a hope of annihilation.

For them, so they should die,
Nor shall its Penalty
Be lightened for them.
Thus do We reward
Every ungrateful one!

عَلَيْهِمْ فَيَمُوتُوا
وَلَا يُخَفَّفُ عَنْهُمْ مِّنْ عَذَابِهَا
كَذَٰلِكَ نَجْزِي كُلَّ كَفُورٍ

37. Therein will they cry
Aloud (for assistance):
"Our Lord! Bring us out:[3926]
We shall work righteousness,[3927]
Not the (deeds) we used
To do!"—"Did We not
Give you long enough life
So that he that would
Should receive admonition?
And (moreover) the warner
Came to you. So taste ye[3928]
(The fruits of your deeds):
For the Wrong-doers
There is no helper."

٣٧- وَهُمْ يَصْطَرِخُونَ فِيهَا
رَبَّنَا أَخْرِجْنَا نَعْمَلْ صَالِحًا
غَيْرَ الَّذِي كُنَّا نَعْمَلُ
أَوَلَمْ نُعَمِّرْكُم
مَّا يَتَذَكَّرُ فِيهِ مَن تَذَكَّرَ
وَجَاءَكُمُ النَّذِيرُ
فَذُوقُوا فَمَا لِلظَّالِمِينَ مِن نَّصِيرٍ

SECTION 5.

38. Verily God knows
(All) the hidden things
Of the heavens and the earth:[3929]
Verily He has full knowledge
Of all that is
In (men's) hearts.

٣٨- إِنَّ اللَّهَ عَالِمُ
غَيْبِ السَّمَاوَاتِ وَالْأَرْضِ
إِنَّهُ عَلِيمٌ بِذَاتِ الصُّدُورِ

39. He it is that has made
You inheritors in the earth:[3930]

٣٩- هُوَ الَّذِي جَعَلَكُمْ خَلَائِفَ فِي الْأَرْضِ

3926. *Cf.* xxiii. 107. Not only will their surroundings be the opposite of those in Heaven: their internal state will be one of humiliation, of piteous and fruitless appeals, of vain regrets for a past that cannot be recalled, and vain sighs for a future whose gates they have themselves barred. If they were sent back, they would relapse to their sins. *Cf.* vi. 28.

3927. *Cf.* vii. 53. Their hankering after another chance, after having deliberately rejected all chances, will have no basis of reason in it.

3928. They had a long enough respite for repentance and amendment. And moreover, besides all the other sources, in nature, history, and their own hearts, by which they could learn of the Right, they had the actual teaching and warning of an Apostle whose words spoke direct to them. In the circumstances the Penalty is only the fruit of their own conduct.

3929. Everything that exists is known to God: not only concrete things, but feelings, motives, plans, and acts of the will in the human breast.

3930. *Inheritors: khalāif.* In two senses: (1) as Vicegerents of God on earth, and (2) as successors to previous people who forfeited their rights by wrong-doing. The honour and dignity of (1) and the examples of the past in (2) should have kept them straight and made them truly grateful. See also vi. 165 and n. 988.

If, then, any do reject
(God), their rejection (works)
Against themselves : their
rejection[3931]
But adds to the odium
For the Unbelievers
In the sight of their Lord :
Their rejection but adds
To (their own) undoing.

40. Say : " Have ye seen[3932]
(These) 'Partners' of yours
Whom ye call upon
Besides God ? Show me
What it is they have created
In the (wide) earth.
Or have they a share
In the heavens ? Or
Have We given them a Book
From which they (can derive)
Clear (evidence) ?—Nay,
The wrong-doers promise
Each other nothing but delusions.

41. It is God Who sustains
The heavens and the earth,[3933]
Lest they cease (to function) :
And if they should fail,
There is none—not one—
Can sustain them thereafter :

فَمَنْ كَفَرَ فَعَلَيْهِ كُفْرُهُ ۖ
وَلَا يَزِيدُ الْكٰفِرِينَ كُفْرُهُمْ
عِنْدَ رَبِّهِمْ إِلَّا مَقْتًا ۖ
وَلَا يَزِيدُ الْكٰفِرِينَ كُفْرُهُمْ
إِلَّا خَسَارًا ○
٤٠- قُلْ أَرَءَيْتُمْ شُرَكَآءَكُمُ
الَّذِينَ تَدْعُونَ مِنْ دُونِ اللّٰهِ ۖ
أَرُونِي مَاذَا خَلَقُوا مِنَ الْأَرْضِ
أَمْ لَهُمْ شِرْكٌ فِي السَّمٰوٰتِ ۚ
أَمْ ءَاتَيْنٰهُمْ كِتٰبًا فَهُمْ عَلٰى بَيِّنَتٍ مِّنْهُ ۚ
بَلْ إِنْ يَعِدُ الظّٰلِمُونَ بَعْضُهُمْ بَعْضًا
إِلَّا غُرُورًا ○
٤١- إِنَّ اللّٰهَ يُمْسِكُ السَّمٰوٰتِ وَالْأَرْضَ
أَنْ تَزُولَا ۚ وَلَئِنْ زَالَتَآ
إِنْ أَمْسَكَهُمَا مِنْ أَحَدٍ مِّنْ بَعْدِهِ ۚ

3931. Their rejection and ingratitude only causes injury to themselves. They lose all honour and incur odium in the sight of God, and they complete their own undoing.

3932. The people who enthrone in their hearts for worship anything besides God may well be asked a few questions. Some of such questions are indicated in the text with terse precision : (1) Have you seen these gods of yours? Do they exist ? "Seeing" of course does not necessarily mean physical sight. We do not see the air, but no one doubts that it exists. And the air is a physical substance. There are forces that we know exist, but we do not see them. To us, who have Faith, God is a truer Reality than anything else that we know, including ourselves. Can the false worshippers say that of any of their false gods? (2) Have your gods created or originated anything on earth? You may worship power or wealth, but that is a scramble for things as between selfish men. Power or wealth does not create new men or new worlds. (3) Have they a share in the ordering of the heavens? "The heavens" may mean what you see in the physical universe of astronomy, or the still subtler inner life. Obviously your false gods fail there. (4) Or have these false gods a book or revelation from the Supreme God, with clear evidence, to give them authority to teach men ? The Prophets or Messengers of God have such authority, and they bring evidence of the One True God. The fact is that falsehood is falsehood, however much one form of it may support another by delusions.

3933. The universe, as we know it, shows not only evidence of initial design, but also the working of an intelligent Providence, which constantly sustains it. That is God. If you could imagine that removed, what is there to keep it going ? There would only be chaos.

Verily He is Most Forbearing,[3934]
Oft-Forgiving.

إِنَّهُۥ كَانَ حَلِيمًا غَفُورًا ۝

42. They swore their strongest oaths
By God that if a warner
Came to them, they would
Follow his guidance better[3935]
Than any (other) of the Peoples:
But when a warner came
To them, it has only
Increased their flight
(From righteousness),—

٤٢- وَأَقْسَمُوا بِٱللَّهِ جَهْدَ أَيْمَٰنِهِمْ
لَئِن جَآءَهُمْ نَذِيرٌ
لَّيَكُونُنَّ أَهْدَىٰ مِنْ إِحْدَى ٱلْأُمَمِ
فَلَمَّا جَآءَهُمْ نَذِيرٌ
مَّا زَادَهُمْ إِلَّا نُفُورًا ۝

43. On account of their arrogance
In the land and their
Plotting of Evil.[3936]
But the plotting of Evil
Will hem in only
The authors thereof. Now
Are they but looking for
The way the ancients[3937]
Were dealt with? But
No change wilt thou find
In God's way (of dealing):[3938]
No turning off wilt thou
Find in God's way (of dealing).

٤٣- ٱسْتِكْبَارًا فِى ٱلْأَرْضِ وَمَكْرَ ٱلسَّيِّئِ
وَلَا يَحِيقُ ٱلْمَكْرُ ٱلسَّيِّئُ
إِلَّا بِأَهْلِهِۦ
فَهَلْ يَنظُرُونَ إِلَّا سُنَّتَ ٱلْأَوَّلِينَ
فَلَن تَجِدَ لِسُنَّتِ ٱللَّهِ تَبْدِيلًا
وَلَن تَجِدَ لِسُنَّتِ ٱللَّهِ تَحْوِيلًا ۝

3934. God's world goes on according to the laws and decrees established by Him. There are occasional lapses and deviations on the part of His creatures. But He does not punish every petty fault. One of His merciful qualities is that of repeated forbearance and forgiveness.

3935. *Cf.* vi. 157. In the first instance this referred to the Quraish. Their attitude to the People of the Book had been one of lofty superiority or of insincere excuses. They twitted the Jews and Christians with deviating from their own lights and their own revelations; and for themselves, they said they had received no direct revelation from God, or they would have shown themselves the most amenable to discipline, the most ready to follow God's Law. This was before the holy Prophet received his mission from God. When he received it and announced it, they turned away from it. They fled from it and put a greater and greater distance between it and themselves. But this is the way of all sinners. They find much to carp at in others, and much to excuse in themselves. But when all grounds for excuse are removed, they will be found, not nearer, but farther and farther away, from truth and righteousness.

3936. Two causes are mentioned why the Truth is refused acceptance. (1) Unregenerate man is arrogant, and Truth and Righteousness expose all his pretences. (2) He hopes, by underhand plots, to undermine Truth and destroy it; but he is caught in his own snares, while Truth marches forward triumphant.

3937. In all history, men who followed evil were dealt with in three stages by God: (1) He was forbearing and merciful, and gave them respite; (2) He sent them admonition through His Messengers, or His Signs, or His revelation; (3) He dealt out justice and punishment. At any given moment, those given to iniquity may well be asked: "Are you going to wait through all these stages or are you going at once to repent, obtain forgiveness, and walk in the ways of righteousness?"

3938. God's Laws are fixed, and His ways of dealing with those who follow iniquity are the same in all ages. Our human will may falter or turn away from its course, but God's Will ever follows its course and cannot be turned away by any cause whatever.

44. Do they not travel
Through the earth, and see [3939]
What was the End
Of those before them,—
Though they were superior
To them in strength?
Nor is God to be frustrated
By anything whatever
In the heavens
Or on earth: for He
Is All-Knowing, All-Powerful.

۴۴- أَوَلَمْ يَسِيرُوا فِي الْأَرْضِ فَيَنظُرُوا
كَيْفَ كَانَ عَاقِبَةُ الَّذِينَ مِن قَبْلِهِمْ
وَكَانُوا أَشَدَّ مِنْهُمْ قُوَّةً
وَمَا كَانَ اللَّهُ لِيُعْجِزَهُ مِن شَيْءٍ
فِي السَّمَاوَاتِ وَلَا فِي الْأَرْضِ
إِنَّهُ كَانَ عَلِيمًا قَدِيرًا ○

45. If God were to punish [3940]
Men according to what
They deserve, He would not
Leave on the back
Of the (earth) a single [3941]
Living creature: but He
Gives them respite
For a stated Term:
When their Term expires,
Verily God has in His sight [3942]
All His servants.

۴۵- وَلَوْ يُؤَاخِذُ اللَّهُ النَّاسَ بِمَا كَسَبُوا
مَا تَرَكَ عَلَىٰ ظَهْرِهَا مِن دَابَّةٍ
وَلَٰكِن يُؤَخِّرُهُمْ إِلَىٰ أَجَلٍ مُّسَمًّى
فَإِذَا جَاءَ أَجَلُهُمْ
ع فَإِنَّ اللَّهَ كَانَ بِعِبَادِهِ بَصِيرًا ○

3939. *Cf.* xxx. 9. If no other argument will convince men who follow evil, let them travel through space or time, and learn from the experience of others. Evil always came to an evil end. Let not any one individual or generation think that it could escape by some special trick or power. Far wiser and more powerful men were personally brought to account for their iniquities.

3940. *Cf.* xvi. 61. There would be no salvation for any of us if we went merely on our deserts. It is God's mercy that saves us and helps us to a better and better life until we attain the goal of our existence.

3941. *A single living creature.* This may refer to man, the living crawling creature, with so many possibilities and yet so many weaknesses. But it may mean all creatures literally, as the life of this planet more or less centres round the life of man. He has been given dominion on this earth, and in his state of purity he is God's vicegerent.

3942. *Has in His sight all creatures: i.e.*, to deal with, accordingly to His laws of Forbearance, Mercy, and Justice: see n. 3937 above. The respite does not mean that any one escapes His vigilant eye. All will be dealt with according to their deeds, with justice tempered with Mercy.

INTRODUCTION TO SŪRA XXXVI (*Yā-Sīn*).

See Introduction to S. xxxiv. This particular Sūra is devoted to the holy Prophet and the Revelation which he brought. The Abbreviated Letters *Yā-Sīn* are usually construed as a title of the holy Prophet. But it is not permissible to be dogmatic about the meaning of Abbreviated Letters. See Appendix I after S. ii. This Sūra is considered to be "the heart of the Qur-ān", as it concerns the central figure in the teaching of Islam and the central doctrine of Revelation and the Hereafter. As referring to the Hereafter, it is appropriately read in solemn ceremonies after death.

In chronology it belongs to the middle or early Meccan period.

In S. xxxvii. 130 (a cognate Sūra) occurs the word *Il-yā-sīn* : See n. 4115-A.

Summary.—The Qur-ān is full of wisdom, and those are unfortunate who cannot profit by it : Parable of the City that defied—all but one—the Messengers of Grace and Mercy (xxxvi. 1-32, and C. 194).

Various Signs of God in nature and Revelation (xxxvi. 33-50, and C. 195).

The Resurrection and the Hereafter (xxxvi. 51-83, and C. 195).

C. 194.—The wisdom of Revelation—the Qur-ān received
(xxxvi. 1-32.) Through the holy Prophet—is a guide
To the Straight Path, and a warning against
The terrible state in which the yokes
Of Sin enslave us. The righteous receive it
With joy, for they believe in the Hereafter.
Behold, there was once a City, to which
Came two righteous men with the Gospel of Truth,
But they were rejected and persecuted : they were joined
By a third. But the City refused to believe
Or to turn from iniquity. Only one man was found
In its outskirts, to bear witness to Truth,
Faith, and Righteousness, and he did suffer
Martyrdom. He attained Peace, but mourned
For his people, in that they shut the gates
Of Salvation and God's Mercy on themselves.
Alas for man's short-sighted folly in defying
The Grace that would shield and deliver him!

Sūra XXXVI.

Yā-Sīn (being Abbreviated Letters).

In the name of God, Most Gracious, Most Merciful.

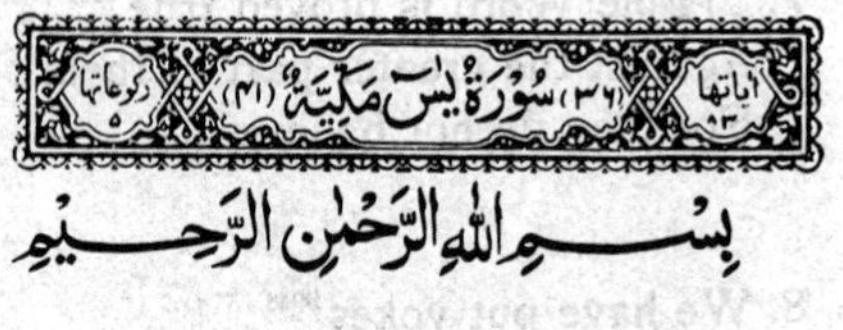

بِسْمِ اللّٰهِ الرَّحْمٰنِ الرَّحِيْمِ

1. Yā-Sīn.[3943]

١- يٰسٓ ۝

2. By the Qur-ān,[3944]
Full of Wisdom,—

٢- وَالْقُرْاٰنِ الْحَكِيْمِ ۝

3. Thou art indeed
One of the apostles,

٣- اِنَّكَ لَمِنَ الْمُرْسَلِيْنَ ۝

4. On a Straight Way.

٤- عَلٰى صِرَاطٍ مُّسْتَقِيْمٍ ۝

5. It is a Revelation[3945]
Sent down by (Him),
The Exalted in Might,
Most Merciful,

٥- تَنْزِيْلَ
الْعَزِيْزِ الرَّحِيْمِ ۝

6. In order that thou mayest
Admonish a people,
Whose fathers had received[3946]
No admonition, and who
Therefore remain heedless
(Of the Signs of God).

٦- لِتُنْذِرَ قَوْمًا
مَّآ اُنْذِرَ اٰبَآؤُهُمْ
فَهُمْ غٰفِلُوْنَ ۝

3943. Some Commentators take *Yā* to be the vocative particle, and *Sīn* to be the abbreviation of *Insān*, *Sīn* being the only "Firm Letter" in the word. In that case it would be an address to man, "O man!" But "man" in this connection is understood to mean the Leader of man, the noblest of mankind, Muḥammad the Prophet of God. For this Sūra deals mainly with the holy Prophet and his Message. But no dogmatic assertion can be made about the Abbreviated Letters, for which see Appendix I, following S. ii. *Yā-Sīn* is usually treated as a mystic title of the holy Prophet.

3944. The best credentials of the holy Prophet are: (1) the revelation which he brought ("the Qur-ān"), and the heroic unselfish life which he led ("on a Straight Way"). The appeal is therefore made on the testimony of these two facts.

3945. The Revelation again is characterised by two attributes which we find most helpful in contemplating the nature of God. It has force and power: for God is Exalted in Might and able to enforce His Will. And it brings a Message of hope and mercy: for God is Most Merciful. By its characteristics we know that the Qur-ān is from God.

3946. The Quraish had received no Prophet before, and therefore one of themselves was made the vehicle for the universal Message to the whole world. See C. 12-15.

7. The Word is proved true[3947]
Against the greater part of them:
For they do not believe.

٧- لَقَدْ حَقَّ الْقَوْلُ عَلَىٰٓ أَكْثَرِهِمْ
فَهُمْ لَا يُؤْمِنُونَ ○

8. We have put yokes[3948]
Round their necks
Right up to their chins,
So that their heads are
Forced up (and they cannot see).

٨- إِنَّا جَعَلْنَا فِىٓ أَعْنَاقِهِمْ أَغْلَالًا
فَهِىَ إِلَى الْأَذْقَانِ
فَهُمْ مُّقْمَحُونَ ○

9. And We have put
A bar in front of them[3949]
And a bar behind them,
And further, We have
Covered them up; so that
They cannot see.

٩- وَجَعَلْنَا مِنۢ بَيْنِ أَيْدِيهِمْ سَدًّا
وَمِنْ خَلْفِهِمْ سَدًّا
فَأَغْشَيْنَٰهُمْ
فَهُمْ لَا يُبْصِرُونَ ○

10. The same is it to them[3950]
Whether thou admonish them
Or thou do not admonish
Them: they will not believe.

١٠- وَسَوَآءٌ عَلَيْهِمْ ءَأَنذَرْتَهُمْ
أَمْ لَمْ تُنذِرْهُمْ لَا يُؤْمِنُونَ ○

3947. *Cf.* vii. 30, and n. 1012; also xvii. 16, and n. 2193. If people deliberately and obstinately refuse "to believe", *i.e.* to receive guidance and admonition, the result must be that God's grace and mercy are withdrawn from them. Their own perversity inevitably blocks up all channels for their correction.

3948. Man's misdeeds inevitably call forth the operation of God's Law, and therefore the result is in Quranic language attributed to God. The result of man's wilful disobedience is now described in a series of metaphors. (1) Refusal of God's Light means less and less freedom of action for man: the yoke of sin is fastened round man's neck, and it gets more and more tightened, right up to the chin. (2) The head is forced up and kept in a stiff position, so that the mind becomes befogged. Moral obliquity taints the intellect. According to the Sanskrit proverb, "When destruction comes near, understanding is turned upside down." According to the Latin proverb, "Whom God wishes to destroy, He first makes demented." In other words, iniquity not only *is* folly, but leads deeper and deeper into folly, narrowness of vision, and blindness to the finer things of life. (3) This state of deprivation of Grace leads to such a decline in spiritual vitality that the victim can neither progress nor turn back, as explained in the next verse.

3949. Their retreat is cut off, and their progress is impossible. Further, the Light that should come from above is cut off, so that they become totally devoid of any hope, and the last gleam of any spiritual understanding is extinguished in them.

3950. When the stage just described is reached, Revelation or spiritual teaching ceases to have any value for them. Why then preach? The answer is given in the verses following.

11. Thou canst but admonish[3951]
Such a one as follows
The Message and fears
The (Lord) Most Gracious,
unseen :[3952]
Give such a one, therefore,[3953]
Good tidings, of Forgiveness
And a Reward most generous.

١١- إِنَّمَا تُنذِرُ مَنِ اتَّبَعَ الذِّكْرَ
وَخَشِيَ الرَّحْمَٰنَ بِالْغَيْبِ
فَبَشِّرْهُ بِمَغْفِرَةٍ
وَأَجْرٍ كَرِيمٍ ۝

12. Verily We shall give life[3954]
To the dead, and We record
That which they send before
And that which they leave[3955]
Behind, and of all things
Have We taken account

١٢- إِنَّا نَحْنُ نُحْيِ الْمَوْتَىٰ
وَنَكْتُبُ مَا قَدَّمُوا وَآثَارَهُمْ
وَكُلَّ شَيْءٍ أَحْصَيْنَاهُ

3951. *Cf.* xxxv. 18. As far as those are concerned, who have obstinately delivered themselves to evil, the preaching of God's Message has no appeal, because their own will shuts them out. But there are others who are anxious to hear God's Message and receive God's grace. They love God and fear to offend against His holy Law, and their fear is not merely superficial but deep-seated: for while they do not yet see God, nor do other people see them, they have the same sense of God's presence as if they saw Him, and their religion is not a mere pose, "to be seen of men".

3952. See n. 3902 to xxxv. 18. *Unseen* is here adverbial : their reverence for God is unaffected by the fact that they do not see him, or that other people do not observe them, because their attitude arises out of a genuine love for God.

3953. To such persons the Message of God comes as a gospel or good news ; because it shows them the way of forgiveness for anything wrong in their past, and it gives them the promise of a full reward in the future,—generous beyond any deserts of their own, but arising out of God's unbounded Bounty.

3954. All this is possible, because there is the assurance of a Hereafter, in which God will be all-in-all, and evil will no longer bestride the world, as the term of its respite will have expired.

3955. Our deeds, good and bad, go to God's Judgment-seat before us. They will of course be brought to our account ; but our account will also be swelled by the example we left behind us and the consequences of our deeds, that will come into play or continue to operate after our earthly life has ceased. Our moral and spiritual responsibility is therefore much wider than as affects our own person.

In a clear Book[3956]
(Of evidence).

فِىٓ إِمَامٍ مُّبِينٍ ۝

SECTION 2.

13. Set forth to them,
By way of a parable,
The (story of) the Companions[3957]
Of the City. Behold,
There came apostles to it.

١٣- وَاضْرِبْ لَهُم مَّثَلًا
أَصْحٰبَ الْقَرْيَةِ ۘ
إِذْ جَآءَهَا الْمُرْسَلُونَ ۝

14. When We (first) sent
To them two apostles,
They rejected them:
But We strengthened them[3958]
With a third: they said,
"Truly, we have been sent
On a mission to you."

١٤- إِذْ أَرْسَلْنَآ إِلَيْهِمُ اثْنَيْنِ
فَكَذَّبُوهُمَا فَعَزَّزْنَا
بِثَالِثٍ فَقَالُوٓا
إِنَّآ إِلَيْكُم مُّرْسَلُونَ ۝

3956. *Cf.* ii. 124 and n. 124. All our account will be exactly preserved as in a book of record.

3957. Many of the classical Commentators have supposed that the City referred to was Antioch. Now Antioch was one of the most important cities in North Syria in the first century of the Christian era. It was a Greek city founded by Seleucus Nicator, one of the successors of Alexander, about 300 B.C. in memory of his father Antiochus. It was close to the sea, and had its sea-port at Seleucia. Soon after Christ his disciples successfully preached there, and they "were called Christians first in Antioch": Acts, xi. 26. It afterwards became the seat of a most important Bishopric of the Christian Church. In the story told here "by way of a parable", the City rejected the Message, and the City was destroyed: xxxvi. 29. Following Ibn Kathir, I reject the identification with Antioch decisively. No name, or period, or place is mentioned in the text. The significance of the story is in the lessons to be derived from it as a parable, for which see the next note. That is independent of name, time, or place.

3958. God sends His apostles or teachers of Truth by ones and twos, and where the opposition is great and He considers it necessary, he supports them with others. Their mission is divine, but they do not claim to be more than men. This is used by the unjust and the ungodly as if it were a reproach, whereas it should commend them to men, for mankind is glorified by such commission and by God's Self-revelation. The Message is clearly expressed in human language, but because it exposes all evil, men think it unlucky, as it checks their selfishness. It is often the poorest and most despised of mankind, from the outskirts or "farthest parts of the City", that accept the Message and are willing to work and die for it. The stiff-necked resist and accomplish their own destruction.

15. The (people) said: "Ye are
Only men like ourselves;[3959]
And (God) Most Gracious
Sends no sort of revelation:[3960]
Ye do nothing but lie."

١٥- قَالُوا مَآ أَنتُمْ إِلَّا بَشَرٌ مِّثْلُنَا
وَمَآ أَنزَلَ ٱلرَّحْمَٰنُ مِن شَىْءٍ
إِنْ أَنتُمْ إِلَّا تَكْذِبُونَ ○

16. They said: "Our Lord doth
Know that we have been sent
On a mission to you:[3961]

١٦- قَالُوا رَبُّنَا يَعْلَمُ
إِنَّآ إِلَيْكُمْ لَمُرْسَلُونَ ○

17. "And our duty is only
To proclaim the clear Message."[3962]

١٧- وَمَا عَلَيْنَآ إِلَّا ٱلْبَلَٰغُ ٱلْمُبِينُ ○

18. The (people) said: "For us,
We augur an evil omen[3963]

١٨- قَالُوٓا إِنَّا تَطَيَّرْنَا بِكُمْ

3959. *Cf.* Acts, xiv. 15, where Paul and Barnabas say, in the city of Lystra near the modern Konia: "We also are men with like passions with you, and preach unto you that ye should turn from these vanities..."

3960. They not only reject the mission of the particular apostles, but they deny the possibility of God's sending such mission. Note how they convict themselves of inconsistency by using God's name "Most Gracious", even though they may mean it ironically!

3961. Just as a Messenger whose credentials are doubted can refer to the authority granted by his Principal, as the highest proof of his mission, so these men of God invoke the authority of God in proof of their mission. In effect they say: "The knowledge of God is perfect, and He knows that our mission is from Him; if you do not, it is your own misfortune."

3962. Then they proceed to explain what their mission is. It is not to force them but to convince them. It is to proclaim openly and clearly God's Law, which they were breaking,—to denounce their sins and to show them the better path. If they were obstinate, it was their own loss. If they were rebellious against God, the punishment rested with God.

3963. *Ṭāir* means a bird. Like the Roman augurs, the Arabs had a superstition about deriving omens from birds. *Cf.* the English word "*auspicious*", from the Latin *avis*, a bird, and *specio*, I see. From *Ṭāir* (bird) came *ta-ṭaiyara*, or *iṭṭaiyara*, to draw evil omens. Because the men of God denounced evil, the evil-doers thought that they brought ill-luck to them. As a matter of fact any evil that happened to them was the result of their own ill-deeds. *Cf.* vii. 131, where the Egyptians ascribed their calamities to the ill-luck brought by Moses: and xxvii. 47, where the Thamūd ascribed ill-luck to the preaching of Ṣāliḥ.

From you : if ye desist not,
We will certainly stone you,
And a grievous punishment
Indeed will be inflicted
On you by us."

لَئِنْ لَّمْ تَنْتَهُوْا لَنَرْجُمَنَّكُمْ
وَلَيَمَسَّنَّكُمْ
مِّنَّا عَذَابٌ اَلِيْمٌ ○

19. They said : "Your evil omens
Are with yourselves :[3964]
(Deem ye this an evil omen),
If ye are admonished ?
Nay, but ye are a people
Transgressing all bounds !"[3965]

١٩- قَالُوْا طَآئِرُكُمْ مَّعَكُمْ
اَئِنْ ذُكِّرْتُمْ
بَلْ اَنْتُمْ
قَوْمٌ مُّسْرِفُوْنَ ○

20. Then there came running,
From the farthest part
Of the City, a man,[3966]
Saying, "O my People !
Obey the apostles :

٢٠- وَجَآءَ مِنْ اَقْصَا الْمَدِيْنَةِ
رَجُلٌ يَّسْعٰى قَالَ يٰقَوْمِ
اتَّبِعُوا الْمُرْسَلِيْنَ ○

21. "Obey those who ask
No reward of you
22 (For themselves), and who have
30 Themselves received Guidance.[3976]

٢١- اتَّبِعُوْا مَنْ لَّا يَسْـَٔلُكُمْ اَجْرًا
وَّهُمْ مُّهْتَدُوْنَ ○

3964. 'What ye call omens arise from your own ill-deeds. Do you suppose that a man who comes to warn you and teach you the better way brings you ill-luck ? Fie upon you !'

3965. To call Good evil and accuse of falsehood men of truth who come unselfishly to bring the message of the beneficent Mercy of God, is the very height of extravagance and transgression

3966. While the wealthy, influential, and fashionable men in the City were doubtful of God's providence and superstitiously believed in Chance and evil omens, the Truth was seen by a man in the outskirts of the City, a man held in low esteem by the arrogant. He had believed, and he wanted his City to believe. So, in Arabia, when the arrogant chiefs of the Quraish exiled the holy Prophet, it was men from Medina and from the outskirts, who welcomed him, believed in him, and supported his mission in every way.

3967. Prophets do not seek their own advantage. They serve God and humanity. Their hope lies in the good pleasure of God, to Whose service they are devoted. *Cf.* x. 72 ; xii. 104 ; etc

22. " It would not be reasonable
In me if I did not
Serve Him Who created me,[3968]
And to Whom ye shall
(All) be brought back.

٢٢- وَمَا لِيَ لَآ أَعْبُدُ الَّذِي
فَطَرَنِي
وَإِلَيْهِ تُرْجَعُونَ ○

23. " Shall I take (other) gods
Besides Him? If (God)
Most Gracious should
Intend some adversity for me,[3969]
Of no use whatever
Will be their intercession
For me, nor can they
Deliver me.

٢٣- ءَأَتَّخِذُ مِن دُونِهِۦٓ ءَالِهَةً
إِن يُرِدْنِ الرَّحْمَٰنُ بِضُرٍّ
لَّا تُغْنِ عَنِّي شَفَٰعَتُهُمْ شَيْـًٔا
وَلَا يُنقِذُونِ ○

24. " I would indeed,
If I were to do so,
Be in manifest Error.

٢٤- إِنِّيٓ
إِذًا لَّفِي ضَلَٰلٍ مُّبِينٍ ○

25. " For me, I have faith
In the Lord of you (all):[3970]
Listen, then, to me!"

٢٥- إِنِّيٓ ءَامَنتُ
بِرَبِّكُمْ فَاسْمَعُونِ ○

26. It was said: " Enter thou[3971]
The Garden." He said:
" Ah me! Would that
My People knew (what I know)!—

٢٦- قِيلَ ادْخُلِ الْجَنَّةَ قَالَ
يَٰلَيْتَ قَوْمِي يَعْلَمُونَ ○

3968. The argument throughout is that of intense personal conviction for the individual himself, coupled with an appeal to his people to follow that conviction and get the benefit of the spiritual satisfaction which he has himself achieved. He says in effect: 'how is it possible for me to do otherwise than to serve and adore my Maker? I shall return to Him, and so will you, and all this applies to you as much as to me.' Note how effective is the transition from the personal experience to the collective appeal.

3969. The next plea is that for exclusive service to God. 'Suppose it were proper to worship other gods—Mammon, Self, or imaginary deities set up as idols,—yet of what benefit would that be? All power is in God. In His universal Plan, He may think fit to give me some sorrow or punishment: would these subordinate deities be able to help me or intercede for me with Him? Not at all. What use would they be? In fact I should obviously be going astray,—wandering from the true Path.'

3970. Again a transition from the assured personal conviction to the appeal to all to profit by the speaker's experience. 'I have found the fullest satisfaction for my soul in God. He is my God, but He is your God also. My experience can be yours also. Will you not follow my advice, and prove for yourselves that the Lord is indeed good?'

3971. This godly and righteous man entered into the Peace of God, typified by the Garden of Rest and Beauty. Perhaps it is implied that he suffered martyrdom. But even then his thoughts were always with his People. He regretted their obstinacy and want of understanding, and wished even then that they might repent and obtain salvation, but they were obdurate and suffered for their sins as we learn from verses 28-29 below.

27. " For that my Lord [3972]
Has granted me Forgiveness
And has enrolled me
Among those held in honour ! "

٢٧- بِمَا غَفَرَ لِي رَبِّي
وَجَعَلَنِي مِنَ الْمُكْرَمِينَ ۝

28. And We sent not down
Against his People, after him,
Any hosts from heaven,
Nor was it needful
For Us so to do.

٢٨- وَمَا أَنْزَلْنَا عَلَىٰ قَوْمِهِ مِنْ بَعْدِهِ
مِنْ جُنْدٍ مِنَ السَّمَاءِ
وَمَا كُنَّا مُنْزِلِينَ ۝

29. It was no more than
A single mighty Blast, [3973]
And behold ! they were
(like ashes) [3974]
Quenched and silent.

٢٩- إِنْ كَانَتْ إِلَّا صَيْحَةً وَاحِدَةً
فَإِذَا هُمْ خَامِدُونَ ۝

30. Ah ! alas for (My) servants !
There comes not an apostle
To them but they mock him ! [3975]

٣٠- يَحَسْرَةً عَلَى الْعِبَادِ مَا يَأْتِيهِمْ مِنْ
رَسُولٍ إِلَّا كَانُوا بِهِ يَسْتَهْزِءُونَ ۝

31. See they not how many
Generations before them
We destroyed ? Not to them [3976]
Will they return :

٣١- أَلَمْ يَرَوْا كَمْ أَهْلَكْنَا قَبْلَهُمْ مِنَ
الْقُرُونِ أَنَّهُمْ إِلَيْهِمْ لَا يَرْجِعُونَ ۝

3972. This man was just a simple honest soul, but he heard and obeyed the call of the apostles and obtained his spiritual desire for himself and did his best to obtain salvation for his people. For he loved his people and respected his ancestral traditions as far as they were good, but had no hesitation in accepting the new Light when it came to him. All his past was forgiven him and he was raised to dignity and honour in the Kingdom of Heaven.

3973. God's Justice or Punishment does not necessarily come with pomp and circumstance, nor have the forces of human evil or wickedness the power to require the exertion of mighty spiritual forces to subdue them. A single mighty Blast—either the rumbling of an earthquake, or a great and violent wind—was sufficient in this case. *Cf.* xi 67 and n. 1561 (which describes the fate of the Thamūd ; also, n. 3463 to xxix. 40.

3974. *Cf.* xxi. 15. They had made a great deal of noise in their time, but they were reduced to silence, like spent ashes.

3975. *Cf.* vi. 10 and many other passages of similar import. Ignorant men mock at God's apostles, or any one who takes Religion seriously. But they do not reflect that such levity reacts on themselves. Their own lives are ruined and they cease to count. If they study history, they will see that countless generations were destroyed before them because they did not take Truth seriously and undermined the very basis of their individual and collective existence.

My servants is here equivalent to "men" God regrets the folly of men, especially as He cherishes them as His own servants.

3976 *Not to them will they return.* What do the two pronouns *them* and *they* refer to? Commentators and translators have construed them differently, and some of them evade the question. To my mind the best construction seems to be : the generations which we have destroyed before the people addressed ('do *they* not see?') will not be restored to the people addressed : *generations* (*qurūn*) standing for the periods of prosperity and good fortune enjoyed by the ancestors. They have all been wiped out : they will never be restored, but all people will be brought before the Judgment-seat for giving an account of their deeds.

32. But each one of them
All—will be brought
Before Us (for judgment).

ع ٣٢- وَإِنْ كُلٌّ لَّمَّا جَمِيعٌ لَّدَيْنَا مُحْضَرُونَ ۝

C. 195.—Are there not Signs enough around you
(xxxvi. 33-50.) To bear witness to God, and His saving Grace?
The earth dies and revives: there are mysteries
Of Life and Sex, of Light and the Stars
And Planets in heaven, that follow
Their orbits by Law and in harmony!
There are the ships and the modes of transport
By which man can conquer the forces
Around him with God-given Gifts!
Learn the Law of Goodness from them
And believe in the Hereafter: it will come
When least expected. Be prepared for God!

SECTION 3.

33. A Sign for them
Is the earth that is dead:[3977]
We do give it life,
And produce grain therefrom,
Of which ye do eat.

٣٣- وَآيَةٌ لَّهُمُ الْأَرْضُ الْمَيْتَةُ ۚ
أَحْيَيْنَاهَا وَأَخْرَجْنَا مِنْهَا حَبًّا
فَمِنْهُ يَأْكُلُونَ ۝

34. And We produce therein
Orchards with date-palms[3978]
And vines, and We cause
Springs to gush forth therein:

٣٤- وَجَعَلْنَا فِيهَا جَنَّاتٍ مِّن نَّخِيلٍ
وَأَعْنَابٍ وَفَجَّرْنَا فِيهَا مِنَ الْعُيُونِ ۝

35. That they may enjoy[3979]
The fruits of this (artistry):
It was not their hands[3980]
That made this:
Will they not then give thanks?

٣٥- لِيَأْكُلُوا مِن ثَمَرِهِ ۙ
وَمَا عَمِلَتْهُ أَيْدِيهِمْ ۖ
أَفَلَا يَشْكُرُونَ ۝

3977. Lest any one should say, 'if they are destroyed, how can they be brought before the Judgment-seat' a symbol is pointed to. The earth is to all intents and purposes dead in the winter, but God revives it in the spring *Cf.* ii. 164, xxx. 19, and many other passages to that effect.

3978. Date-palms and vines stand as symbols for fruit-trees of all kinds, these being the characteristic fruits of Arabia. Grain was mentioned in the last verse; fruit is mentioned now. All that is necessary for food and the satisfaction of the choicest palate is produced from what looks like inert soil, fertilised by rain and springs Here is wonderful evidence of the artistry and providence of God.

3979. Literally, *eat (akala)*. *Cf.* vii. 19, n. 1004 and v. 69, n. 776. The same wide meaning of profit, satisfaction, and enjoyment may be attached to the word "eat" in verse 33 above.

3980. Man may till the soil and sow the seed, but the productive forces of nature were not made by man's hands. They are the handiwork and artistry of God, and are evidence of God's providence for His creatures. See n. 3978 above.

36. Glory to God, Who created
In pairs all things that [3981]
The earth produces, as well as
Their own (human) kind
And (other) things of which
They have no knowledge.

۳۶- سُبْحٰنَ الَّذِیْ خَلَقَ الْاَزْوَاجَ كُلَّهَا
مِمَّا تُنْۢبِتُ الْاَرْضُ وَمِنْ اَنْفُسِهِمْ
وَمِمَّا لَا یَعْلَمُوْنَ ○

37. And a Sign for them
Is the Night: We withdraw [3982]
Therefrom the Day, and behold
They are plunged in darkness;

۳۷- وَاٰیَةٌ لَّهُمُ الَّیْلُ ۚۖ نَسْلَخُ مِنْهُ النَّهَارَ
فَاِذَا هُمْ مُّظْلِمُوْنَ ○

38. And the Sun
Runs his course
For a period determined [3983]
For him: that is
The decree of (Him),
The Exalted in Might,
The All-Knowing.

۳۸- وَالشَّمْسُ تَجْرِیْ
لِمُسْتَقَرٍّ لَّهَا ؕ
ذٰلِكَ تَقْدِیْرُ
الْعَزِیْزِ الْعَلِیْمِ ؕ○

39. And the Moon,—
We have measured for her [3984]
Mansions (to traverse)
Till she returns
Like the old (and withered)
Lower part of a date-stalk. [3985]

۳۹- وَالْقَمَرَ قَدَّرْنٰهُ مَنَازِلَ
حَتّٰی عَادَ
كَالْعُرْجُوْنِ الْقَدِیْمِ ○

3981. The mystery of sex runs through all creation,—in man, in animal life, in vegetable life, and possibly in other things of which we have no knowledge. Then there are pairs of opposite forces in nature, *e.g.*, positive and negative electricity, etc. The atom itself consists of a positively charged nucleus or proton, surrounded by negatively charged electrons. The constitution of matter itself is thus referred to pairs of opposite energies.

3982. "*Withdrawing the Day from the Night*" is a striking phrase, and very apt. The Day or the Light is the positive thing. The Night or Darkness is merely negative. We cannot withdraw the negative. But if we withdraw the real thing, the positive, which filled the void, nothing is left but the void. The whole of this section deals with Signs or Symbols,—things in the physical world around us, from which we can learn the deepest spiritual truths if we earnestly apply ourselves to them.

3983. *Mustaqarr* may mean: (1) a limit of time, a period determined, as in vi. 67, or (2) a place of rest or quiescence; or (3) a dwelling place, as in ii. 36. I think the first meaning is best applicable here; but some Commentators take the second meaning. In that case the simile would be that of the sun running a race while he is visible to us, and taking a rest during the night to prepare himself to renew his race the following day. His stay with the antipodes appears to us as his period of rest.

3984. The lunar mansions are the 28 divisions of the Zodiac, which are supposed to mark the daily course of the moon in the heavens from the time of the new moon to the time when the moon fades away in her "inter-lunar swoon", an expressive phrase coined by the poet Shelley.

3985. *'Urjūn*: a raceme of dates or of a date-palm; or the base or lower part of the raceme. When it becomes old, it becomes yellow, dry, and withered, and curves up like a sickle. Hence the comparison with the sickle-like appearance of the new moon. The moon runs through all her phases, increasing and decreasing, until she disappears, and then reappears as a little thin curve.

40. It is not permitted
To the Sun to catch up [3986]
The Moon, nor can
The Night outstrip the Day:
Each (just) swims along [3987]
In (its own) orbit
(According to Law).

٤٠- لَا الشَّمْسُ يَنۢبَغِي لَهَآ اَنْ تُدْرِكَ
الْقَمَرَ وَلَا الَّيْلُ سَابِقُ النَّهَارِ ؕ
وَكُلٌّ فِي فَلَكٍ يَّسْبَحُوْنَ ۝

41. And a Sign for them
Is that We bore [3988]
Their race (through the Flood)
In the loaded Ark;

٤١- وَاٰيَةٌ لَّهُمْ اَنَّا حَمَلْنَا
ذُرِّيَّتَهُمْ فِي الْفُلْكِ الْمَشْحُوْنِ ۝

42. And We have created
For them similar (vessels) [3989]
On which they ride.

٤٢- وَخَلَقْنَا
لَهُمْ مِّنْ مِّثْلِهٖ مَا يَرْكَبُوْنَ ۝

43. If it were Our Will, [3990]
We could drown them:
Then would there be
No helper (to hear
Their cry), nor could
They be delivered,

٤٣- وَاِنْ نَّشَاْ نُغْرِقْهُمْ
فَلَا صَرِيْخَ لَهُمْ
وَلَا هُمْ يُنْقَذُوْنَ ۝

3986. Though the sun and the moon both traverse the belt of the Zodiac, and their motions are different, they never catch up each other. When the sun and the moon are on the same side and on a line with the earth there is a solar eclipse, and when on opposite sides in a line, there is a lunar eclipse, but there is no clash. Their Laws are fixed by God, and form the subject of study in astronomy. Similarly Night and Day follow each other, but being opposites cannot coincide, a fit emblem of the opposition of Good and Evil, Truth and Falsehood: see also n. 3982 above.

3987. *Cf.* xxi. 33, and n. 2695. How beautifully the rounded courses of the planets and heavenly bodies are described, "swimming" through space, with perfectly smooth motion! As Shakespeare expresses it, each "in his motion like an angel sings, Still quiring to the young-eyed cherubims!"

3988. Besides the beauty of the Night, with the stars and the planets "swimming" in their rounded courses according to perfect Law, suggesting both symmetry and harmony, there are other Signs touching closely the life of man himself, projected through Time, in the past history of his race and in his own personal experience. The past history of his race takes us to the story of the Flood, which is symbolical of the deliverance of man from the forces of nature. Noah's Ark is the symbol of that deliverance. But the symbol still remains as a memorial: the Ark was a "Sign to all Peoples": xxix. 15. Man's own personal experience is appealed to in every ship afloat: see next note.

3989. The stately ships sailing through the seas, heavier than air, yet carrying man and his goods safely and smoothly across the waters, are another Sign for man. Ships are not mentioned, but (vessels) like the Ark: they would cover all kinds of sea-craft, but also the modern aircraft, which "swims" through air instead of through water.

3990. Were it not that God gives man the intelligence and ingenuity to construct and manage sea-craft and air-craft, the natural laws of gravity would lead to the destruction of any who attempted to pass through sea or air. It is the gift (mercy) of God that saves him.

44. Except by way of Mercy
From Us, and by way
Of (worldly) convenience
(To serve them) for a time.[3991]

۴۴- إِلَّا رَحْمَةً مِّنَّا وَ
مَتَاعًا إِلَىٰ حِينٍ ○

45. When they are told,
" Fear ye that which is [3992]
Before you and that which
Will be after you, in order
That ye may receive Mercy,"
(They turn back).

۴۵- وَإِذَا قِيلَ لَهُمُ اتَّقُوا مَا بَيْنَ
أَيْدِيكُمْ وَمَا خَلْفَكُمْ
لَعَلَّكُمْ تُرْحَمُونَ ○

46. Not a Sign comes to them
From among the Signs [3993]
Of their Lord, but they
Turn away therefrom.

۴۶- وَمَا تَأْتِيهِم مِّنْ آيَةٍ مِّنْ آيَاتِ
رَبِّهِمْ إِلَّا كَانُوا عَنْهَا مُعْرِضِينَ ○

47. And when they are told,
" Spend ye of (the bounties) [3994]
With which God
Has provided you," the Unbelievers
Say to those who believe:
" Shall we then feed those
Whom, if God had so willed,[3995]
He would have fed, (Himself) ?—

۴۷- وَإِذَا قِيلَ لَهُمْ أَنفِقُوا
مِمَّا رَزَقَكُمُ اللَّهُ ۙ
قَالَ الَّذِينَ كَفَرُوا لِلَّذِينَ آمَنُوا
أَنُطْعِمُ مَن لَّوْ يَشَاءُ اللَّهُ أَطْعَمَهُ ۖ

3991. *Cf.* xvi. 80. God has given man all these wonderful things in nature and utilities produced by the skill and intelligence which God has given to man. Had it not been for these gifts, man's life would have been precarious on sea or land or in the air. It is only God's Mercy that saves man from destruction for man's own follies, and that saving or the enjoyment of these utilities and conveniences he should not consider as eternal: they are only given for a time, in this life of probation.

3992. Man should consider and beware of the consequences of his past. and guard against the consequences in his future The present is only a fleeting moment poised between the past and the future. and gone even while it is being mentioned or thought about. Man should review his whole life and prepare for the Hereafter. If he does so, God is Merciful: He will forgive, and give strength for a better and higher life in the future. But this kind of teaching does not suit those steeped in this ephemeral life. They are bored, and turn away from it, to their own loss.

3993. The Signs of God are many, in His great world.—in nature, in the heart of man, and in the Revelation sent through His apostles. They turn away from all of them, as a man who has ruined his eyesight turns away from the light.

3994. To selfish men, the good may make an appeal, and say: "Look! God has given you wealth, or influence, or knowledge, or talent. Why not spend some of it in charity, *i.e.*, for the good of your fellow-creatures?" But the selfish only think of themselves and laugh such teaching to scorn.

3995. They are too full of themselves to have a corner in their hearts for others. "If," they say, "God gave them nothing, why should we?" There is arrogance in this as well as blasphemy: arrogance in thinking that they are favoured because of their merits, and blasphemy in laying the blame of other people's misfortunes on God. They further try to turn the tables on the Believers by pretending that the Believers are entirely on a wrong track. They forget that all men are on probation and trial: they hold their gifts on trust: those apparently less favoured, in that they have fewer of this world's goods, may be really more fortunate, because they are learning patience, self-reliance, and the true value of things ephemeral which is apt to be very much exaggerated in men's eyes.

Ye are in nothing
But manifest error."

إِنْ أَنتُمْ إِلَّا فِي ضَلَٰلٍ مُّبِينٍ ○

48. Further, they say, "When
Will this promise (come to pass),[3996]
If what ye say is true?"

٤٨- وَيَقُولُونَ مَتَىٰ هَٰذَا ٱلْوَعْدُ
إِن كُنتُمْ صَٰدِقِينَ ○

49. They will not (have
To) wait for aught
But a single Blast:
It will seize them while
They are yet disputing
Among themselves!

٤٩- مَا يَنظُرُونَ إِلَّا صَيْحَةً وَٰحِدَةً
تَأْخُذُهُمْ
وَهُمْ يَخِصِّمُونَ ○

50. No (chance) will they then
Have, by will, to dispose
(Of their affairs), nor
To return to their own people!

٥٠- فَلَا يَسْتَطِيعُونَ تَوْصِيَةً
وَلَآ إِلَىٰ أَهْلِهِمْ يَرْجِعُونَ ○ ع

C. 196.—When the Day comes, men will be taken
(xxxvi. 51-83.) Aback. The judgment-seat will be established.
Blessed will be those who attain Salvation:
Their Joy, Satisfaction, and Peace will be crowned
With nearness to their Lord!
Alas for the Sinful, who deliberately
Followed Evil: their own nature
And actions will speak against them:
They will face the realities of Punishment!
Both Revelation and Nature are eloquent
In instructing man for his own good
In the Hereafter, which will come
As a certainty. Praise and Glory to God!

SECTION 4.

51. The trumpet shall be[3997]
Sounded, when behold!
From the sepulchres (men)
Will rush forth
To their Lord!

٥١- وَنُفِخَ فِي ٱلصُّورِ
فَإِذَا هُم مِّنَ ٱلْأَجْدَاثِ
إِلَىٰ رَبِّهِمْ يَنسِلُونَ ○

3996. In addition to the arrogance and blasphemy referred to in the last note, they not only refuse Faith, but they taunt the men of Faith as if the men of Faith were dealing in falsehood: "If there is a Hereafter, tell us when it will be!" The answer is: "It will come sooner than you expect: you will yet be disputing about things of Faith and neglecting your opportunities in Life, when the Hour will sound, and you will have no time even to make your dispositions in this life: you will be cut off from everyone whom you thought to be near and dear to you, or able to help you!"

3997. Traditionally, the angel who will sound the Trumpet is Isrāfīl, but the name does not occur in the Qur-ān. The Trumpet is mentioned in many places: *e.g.*, vi. 73; lxxviii. 18, etc.

52. They will say: "Ah!
Woe unto us! Who
Hath raised us up
From our beds of repose?"...[3998]
(A voice will say:)
"This is what (God)
Most Gracious had promised,
And true was the word
Of the apostles!"

٥٢- قالوا يويلنا من
بعثنا من مرقدنا ۜ
هذا ما وعد الرحمن
وصدق المرسلون ○

53. It will be no more
Than a single Blast,[3999]
When lo! they will all
Be brought up before Us!

٥٣- إن كانت إلا صيحة واحدة
فإذا هم جميع لدينا محضرون ○

54. Then, on that Day,
Not a soul will be
Wronged in the least,[4000]
And ye shall but
Be repaid the meeds
Of your past Deeds.

٥٤- فاليوم لا تظلم نفس شيئا
ولا تجزون
إلا ما كنتم تعملون ○

55. Verily the Companions[4001]
Of the Garden shall
That Day have joy
In all that they do;

٥٥- إن أصحب الجنة
اليوم في شغل فكهون ○

3998. The dead will rise as in a stupor, and they will be confused in the new conditions! They will gradually regain their memory and their personality. They will be reminded that God in His grace and mercy had already announced the Hereafter in their probationary lives, and the word of God's apostles, which then seemed so strange and remote, was true and was now being fulfilled!

3999. Time and Space, as we know them here, will be no more. The whole gathering will be as in the twinkling of an eye. *Cf.* xxxvi. 49 above.

4000. The Judgment will be on the highest standard of Justice and Grace. Not the least merit will go unrewarded, though the reward will be for the righteous far more than their deserts. No penalty will be exacted but that which the doer himself by his past deeds brought on himself. *Cf.* xxviii. 84.

4001. We now have the symbolism for the indescribable Bliss of the Hereafter, in the four verses 55-58. Notice the subtle gradation in the description. First, in this verse, we have the nature of the *mise en scène* and the nature of the joy therein. It will be a Garden, *i.e.*, everything agreeable to see and hear and feel and taste and smell; our bodily senses will have been transformed, but we can imagine something corresponding to them in our spiritual being: delightfully green lawns and meadows, trees and shrubs; the murmur of streams and the songs of birds: the delicate texture of flowers and leaves and the shapes of beauty in clouds and mist; the flavours of fruits; and the perfumes of flowers and scents. The joy in the Garden will be an active joy, without fatigue: whatever we do in it, every employment in which we engage there, will be a source of joy without alloy.

56. They and their associates [4002]
Will be in groves
Of (cool) shade, reclining
On Thrones (of dignity);

٥٦- هُمْ وَأَزْوَاجُهُمْ فِي ظِلَٰلٍ
عَلَى الْأَرَائِكِ مُتَّكِئُونَ ۝

57. (Every) fruit (enjoyment) [4003]
Will be there for them;
They shall have whatever
They call for;

٥٧- لَهُمْ فِيهَا فَاكِهَةٌ
وَلَهُم مَّا يَدَّعُونَ ۝

58. "Peace!"—a Word [4004]
(Of salutation) from a Lord
Most Merciful!

٥٨- سَلَٰمٌ
قَوْلًا مِّن رَّبٍّ رَّحِيمٍ ۝

59. "And O ye in sin! [4005]
Get ye apart this Day!

٥٩- وَامْتَٰزُوا الْيَوْمَ أَيُّهَا الْمُجْرِمُونَ ۝

60. "Did I not enjoin [4006]
On you, O ye children

٦٠- أَلَمْ أَعْهَدْ إِلَيْكُمْ يَٰبَنِيٓ

4002. Secondly, the joy or happiness is figured to be, not solitary, but shared;—shared by associates like those we imagine in spiritual Love or Marriage; in whose fair faces "some ray divine reflected shines" (Jāmī); whose society is enjoyed in homes of happiness, situated in soothing shade, and furnished with thrones of dignity and peace.

4003. Thirdly, besides any external conditions of Bliss, the Bliss in the Hereafter has an inner quality, expressed by the word *fākihatun*. The root *fakiha* means 'to rejoice greatly,' 'to be full of merriment'. The ordinary meaning of 'fruit' attached to *fākihat* is derived from the idea that the flavour of choice, ripe fruit, delights the heart of man. Just as *akala* (to eat) is used for 'enjoyment', (v. 69, n. 776 and xiii. 35, n. 1854), so *fākihat*, 'fruit', stands here for that specially choice enjoyment, which goes with a fastidious and well-cultivated taste. In other words, it suggests that highest kind of joy which depends upon the inner faculty rather than any outward circumstance. This is further emphasised by the second clause, "they shall have whatever they call for". Again using the language of this life, the musician's heaven will be full of music; the mathematician's will be full of mathematical symmetry and perfection; the artist's will be full of beauty of form, and so on.

4004. Fourthly, we reach the highest grade of bliss, the mystic salutation "Peace!" from God Most Merciful. *Cf.* x. 10. That Word sums up the attainment of the final Goal. For it explains the nature of the Most High;—He is not only a Lord and Cherisher, but a Lord Whose supreme glory is Mercy, Peace, and Harmony!

4005. Notice how this finely balanced passage, after reaching the summit of sublimity in describing the state of the Blessed, in the word Salām, gradually takes us down to contemplate the state of the Sinners in a graduated descent.

In the first place, it refers to their negative state, their state of isolation. From this Day of Judgment, they will no longer have the chance of being with the Blessed and perhaps of profiting spiritually by that proximity. The first feature of the Day of Judgment is that it is a Day of Separation—of sorting out. Each soul now finds its own true level, as the period of probation is over.

4006. Secondly, there is a gentle reproach to the wrong-doers, more in sorrow than in anger. They are addressed as "children of Adam", to emphasise two facts, (1) that they have disgraced their ancestry, for Adam after his Fall repented and was forgiven, and the high Destiny of mankind has been the prize open to all his descendants, and (2) that God Most Merciful has throughout the ages continued to warn mankind against the snares laid by Satan, the avowed enemy of man, and that God's Grace was ever on the watch to help all to freedom from those snares,

Of Adam, that ye
Should not worship Satan;
For that he was to you
An enemy avowed?—

أَدَمَ أَنْ لَّا تَعْبُدُوا الشَّيْطٰنَ
إِنَّهُ لَكُمْ عَدُوٌّ مُّبِينٌ ۝

61\. "And that ye should [4007]
Worship Me, (for that) this
Was the Straight Way?

٦١- وَّأَنِ اعْبُدُونِي
هٰذَا صِرَاطٌ مُّسْتَقِيمٌ ۝

62\. "But he did lead astray
A great multitude of you.
Did ye not, then, understand? [4008]

٦٢- وَلَقَدْ أَضَلَّ مِنْكُمْ جِبِلًّا كَثِيرًا
أَفَلَمْ تَكُونُوا تَعْقِلُونَ ۝

63\. "This is the Hell [4009]
Of which ye were
(Repeatedly) warned!

٦٣- هٰذِهٖ جَهَنَّمُ
الَّتِي كُنْتُمْ تُوعَدُونَ ۝

64\. "Embrace ye the (Fire) [4010]
This Day, for that ye
(Persistently) rejected (Truth)."

٦٤- اِصْلَوْهَا الْيَوْمَ
بِمَا كُنْتُمْ تَكْفُرُونَ ۝

65\. That Day shall We set
A seal on their mouths.[4011]
But their hands will speak
To Us, and their feet
Bear witness, to all
That they did.

٦٥- اَلْيَوْمَ نَخْتِمُ عَلٰى أَفْوَاهِهِمْ
وَتُكَلِّمُنَا أَيْدِيهِمْ
وَتَشْهَدُ أَرْجُلُهُمْ بِمَا كَانُوا يَكْسِبُونَ ۝

4007\. Thirdly, besides the negative warning, a positive Way was shown to them—the Straight Way, the Way of those who receive God's Grace and attain to Bliss, the Rope which would save them from shipwreck, the Shield which would save them from assault, the key to the door of proximity to God.

4008\. Fourthly, it is pointed out that they were given Understanding (*'aql*), so that by their own faculties they could have judged their own best interests, and yet they betrayed or misused those faculties, and deliberately threw away their chances! And not only a few, but so many! They went gregariously to ruin in spite of the individual care which their Lord and Cherisher bestowed on them!

4009\. Fifthly, the naked fact is now placed before them,—the Hell,—the state of damnation, which they could so easily have avoided!

4010\. As they deliberately and persistently rejected all teaching, guidance, and warnings, they are now told to experience the Fire of Punishment, for it is but the consequence of their own acts.

4011\. The ungodly will now be dumbfounded. They will be unable to speak or offer any defence. (The consequences of all acts, which follow according to God's Law, are, in Quranic language, attributed to God). But their silence will not matter. Their own hands and feet will speak against them. "Hands and feet" in this connection are symbolical of all the instruments for action which they were given in this life, including their faculties and opportunities. The same extended meaning is to be understood for "eyes" in the following verse. *Cf.* also xli. 20-21, where eyes, ears, and skins are all mentioned as bearing witness against such as misused them.

66. If it had been Our Will,[4012]
We could surely have
Blotted out their eyes;
Then should they have
Run about groping for the Path,
But how could they have seen?

٦٦- وَلَوْ نَشَآءُ لَطَمَسْنَا عَلَىٰٓ أَعْيُنِهِمْ
فَٱسْتَبَقُوا ٱلصِّرَٰطَ
فَأَنَّىٰ يُبْصِرُونَ ۝

67. And if it had been
Our Will, We could
Have transformed them
(To remain) in their places;[4013]
Then should they have been
Unable to move about,
Nor could they have returned
(After error).

٦٧- وَلَوْ نَشَآءُ
لَمَسَخْنَٰهُمْ عَلَىٰ مَكَانَتِهِمْ
فَمَا ٱسْتَطَٰعُوا مُضِيًّا
وَلَا يَرْجِعُونَ ۝

SECTION 5.

68. If We grant long life
To any, We cause him
To be reversed in nature:[4014]
Will they not then understand?

٦٨- وَمَنْ نُعَمِّرْهُ نُنَكِّسْهُ فِى ٱلْخَلْقِ ۖ
أَفَلَا يَعْقِلُونَ ۝

69. We have not instructed
The (Prophet) in Poetry,[4015]
Nor is it meet for him:
This is no less than

٦٩- وَمَا عَلَّمْنَٰهُ ٱلشِّعْرَ
وَمَا يَنۢبَغِى لَهُۥٓ ۚ إِنْ هُوَ إِلَّا

4012. "*If it had been Our Will*": i.e., if such had been the Will and Plan of God. If God had not intended to give man his limited free-will, or power of choice, the case would have been different: there would have been no moral responsibility which could have been enforced. They could have had no sight or intelligence, and they could not have been blamed for not seeing or understanding. But such is not the case.

4013 If God's Plan had been to grant no limited freedom of choice or will to men, He could have created them quite different, or could have transformed them into stationary creatures, either in physical form as in the case of trees, or in moral or spiritual qualities, where there was no possibility either of progress or deterioration. Man would then have been unable to reach the heights of grandeur which are now open to him, or, if he goes wrong, to return through the door of repentance and mercy, and still pursue his path of ascent. But it was God's Plan to give man all these privileges, and man must shoulder all the responsibilities that go with them.

4014. This connects on with the last verse. Everything is possible with God. If you doubt how man can be transformed from his present nature, contemplate the transformations he already undergoes in his present nature at different ages. As a child his powers of mind and body are still undeveloped. As he grows, they grow, and certain moral qualities, such as courage, daring, the will to conquer, unfold themselves. In extreme old age these are again obscured, and a second childhood supervenes. The back of the man who walked proudly straight and erect is now bent. If these transformations take place even in his present nature and constitution, how much easier was it for God to cast him in an immobile mould? But God granted him instead the high possibilities and responsibilities referred to in the last note.

4015. *Cf.* xxvi. 224 and n. 3237. Here "Poetry" is used as connoting fairy tales, imaginary descriptions, things futile, false, or obscure, such as decadent Poetry is, whereas the Qur-ān is a practical guide, true and clear.

A Message and a Qur-ān
Making things clear:

ذِكْرٌ وَّقُرْاٰنٌ مُّبِيْنٌ ۝

70. That it may give admonition
To any (who are) alive,[4016]
And that the charge[4017]
May be proved against those
Who reject (Truth).

٧٠- لِّيُنْذِرَ مَنْ كَانَ حَيًّا
وَّيَحِقَّ الْقَوْلُ
عَلَى الْكٰفِرِيْنَ ۝

71. See they not that it is
We Who have created
For them—among the things
Which our hands have fashioned—
Cattle, which are under[4018]
Their dominion?—

٧١- اَوَلَمْ يَرَوْا اَنَّا خَلَقْنَا
لَهُمْ مِّمَّا عَمِلَتْ اَيْدِيْنَآ
اَنْعَامًا فَهُمْ لَهَا مٰلِكُوْنَ ۝

72. And that We have
Subjected them to their (use)?
Of them some do carry them
And some they eat:

٧٢- وَذَلَّلْنٰهَا لَهُمْ فَمِنْهَا
رَكُوْبُهُمْ وَمِنْهَا يَاْكُلُوْنَ ۝

73. And they have (other) profits[4019]
From them (besides), and they
Get (milk) to drink.
Will they not then
Be grateful?[4020]

٧٣- وَلَهُمْ فِيْهَا مَنَافِعُ
وَمَشَارِبُ
اَفَلَا يَشْكُرُوْنَ ۝

74. Yet they take (for worship)
Gods other than God,

٧٤- وَاتَّخَذُوْا مِنْ دُوْنِ اللّٰهِ اٰلِهَةً

4016. "Alive", both in English and Arabic, means not only "having physical life", but having all the active qualities which we associate with life. In religious language, those who are not responsive to the realities of the spiritual world are no better than those who are dead. The Message of God penetrates the hearts of those who are alive in the spiritual sense.

4017. *Cf.* xxviii. 63. If people reject Truth and Faith after they have been admonished and warned, the charge against them, of wilful rebellion, is proved. They cannot then plead either ignorance or inadvertence.

4018. If they are blind to other Signs of God, they can at least see the simple homely things of life in which they receive so many benefits from God's mercy. How is it that wild animals can be domesticated, and in domestication can be so useful to man? Man can use them for riding or for draught; he can use their flesh for food and drink their milk; he can use their hair or wool. *Cf.* xvi. 66, 80; and xxiii. 21-22.

4019. Such as skins for leather, furs for warmth, sheeo's wool or camel's hair for blankets or textiles, musk for perfume, and so on.

4020. The whole argument turns on this. 'Our teaching is for your own benefit. We confer all these blessings on you, and yet ye turn away from the Giver of all, and run after your own vain imaginations!

(Hoping) that they might
Be helped!

لَعَلَّهُمْ يُنصَرُونَ ۝

75. They have not the power
To help them: but they
Will be brought up
(Before Our Judgment-seat)
As a troop (to be condemned).[4021]

٧٥- لَا يَسْتَطِيعُونَ نَصْرَهُمْ
وَهُمْ لَهُمْ جُندٌ مُّحْضَرُونَ ۝

76. Let not their speech, then,[4022]
Grieve thee. Verily We know
What they hide as well as
What they disclose.

٧٦- فَلَا يَحْزُنكَ قَوْلُهُمْ إِنَّا نَعْلَمُ
مَا يُسِرُّونَ وَمَا يُعْلِنُونَ ۝

77. Doth not man see
That it is We Who
Created him from sperm?[4023]
Yet behold! he (stands forth)
As an open adversary!

٧٧- أَوَلَمْ يَرَ الْإِنسَانُ أَنَّا
خَلَقْنَاهُ مِن نُّطْفَةٍ
فَإِذَا هُوَ خَصِيمٌ مُّبِينٌ ۝

78. And he makes comparisons[4024]
For Us, and forgets his own
(Origin and) Creation:
He says, "Who can give
Life to (dry) bones
And decomposed ones (at that)?"

٧٨- وَضَرَبَ لَنَا مَثَلًا وَنَسِيَ خَلْقَهُ
قَالَ مَنْ يُحْيِ الْعِظَامَ
وَهِيَ رَمِيمٌ ۝

4021. There is some difference of opinion among Commentators as to the exact meaning to be attached to this clause. As I understand it, the meaning seems to be this. Man is apt to forget or turn away from the true God, the source of all the good which he enjoys, and to go after imaginary powers in the shape of gods, heroes, men, or abstract things like Science or Nature or Philosophy, or superstitious things like Magic, or Good-Fortune or Ill-Fortune, or embodiments of his own selfish desires. He thinks that they might help him in this Life or in the Hereafter (if he believes in a Hereafter). But they cannot help him: on the contrary all things that are false will be brought up and condemned before God's Judgment-seat, and the worshippers of the Falsehoods will also be treated as a troop favouring the Falsehoods and therefore worthy of condemnation. The Falsehoods, therefore, instead of helping them, will contribute to their condemnation.

4022. If men are so foolish as to reject God, let not the men of God grieve over it. They should do their duty, and leave the rest to God. God knows all the open and secret motives that sway the wicked, and His Plan must ultimately prevail, however much appearances may be against it at any given time.

4023. Man's disobedience and folly are all the more surprising, seeing that—apart from God's greatness and mercy—man is himself such a puny creature, created out of something that is less than a drop in the vast ocean of Existence. Yet man has the hardihood to stand out and dispute with his Maker, and institute idle comparisons as in the next verse!

4024. That is, man thinks that God is like His creatures, who at best have very limited powers, or man draws idle parallels like that mentioned at the end of this verse. 'Who can give life to dry bones, and decomposed ones at that?' Man certainly cannot, and no power in nature can do that. But why compare the powers and capacities of God's creatures with the powers and capacities of the Creator? The first creation—out of nothing—is far more difficult for us to imagine than a second or subsequent process for which there is already a basis. And God has power over all things.

79. Say, " He will give them
Life Who created them
For the first time ![4025]
For He is well-versed
In every kind of creation !—

٧٩- قُلْ يُحْيِيهَا الَّذِيٓ أَنْشَأَهَآ أَوَّلَ مَرَّةٍ
وَهُوَ بِكُلِّ خَلْقٍ عَلِيمٌ ۝

80. " The same Who produces
For you fire out of[4026]
The green tree, when behold !
Ye kindle therewith
(Your own fires) !

٨٠- الَّذِي جَعَلَ لَكُمْ مِّنَ الشَّجَرِ الْأَخْضَرِ
نَارًا
فَإِذَآ أَنْتُمْ مِّنْهُ تُوقِدُونَ ۝

81. " Is not He Who created
The heavens and the earth
Able to create the like[4027]
Thereof ? "—Yea, indeed !
For he is the Creator Supreme,
Of skill and knowledge (infinite) !

٨١- أَوَلَيْسَ الَّذِي خَلَقَ السَّمٰوٰتِ وَالْأَرْضَ
بِقٰدِرٍ عَلَىٰٓ أَنْ يَّخْلُقَ مِثْلَهُمْ
بَلٰى وَهُوَ الْخَلّٰقُ الْعَلِيمُ ۝

82. Verily, when He intends[4028]
A thing, His Command is,
" Be ", and it is !

٨٢- إِنَّمَآ أَمْرُهٗٓ إِذَآ أَرَادَ
شَيْئًا أَنْ يَّقُولَ لَهٗ كُنْ فَيَكُونُ ۝

83. So glory to Him
In Whose hands is
The dominion of all things :
And to Him will ye[4029]
Be all brought back.

٨٣- فَسُبْحٰنَ الَّذِي
بِيَدِهٖ مَلَكُوتُ كُلِّ شَيْءٍ
وَإِلَيْهِ تُرْجَعُونَ ۝

4025. God's creative artistry is evident in every phase of nature, and it works every minute or second. The more man understands himself and the things within his reach, the more he realises this. How foolish, then, for any one to set imaginary limits to God's powers ? There are more ways of creation than are dreamt of in man's imagination !

4026. Even older and more primitive than the method of striking fire against steel and flint is the method of using twigs of trees for the purpose. In the *E. B.*, 14th edition, ix. 262, will be found a picture of British Guiana boys making a fire by rotating a stick in a round hole in a piece of wood lying on the ground. The Arab method was to use a wooden instrument called the *Zinād*. It consisted of two pieces to be rubbed together. The upper one was called the *'Afār* or *Zand*, and the lower the *Markh*. The *markh* is a twig from a kind of spreading tree, the *Cynanchum viminale*, of which the branches are bare, without leaves or thorns. When they are tangled together, and a wind blows, they get ignited and strike fire (Lane's Arabic Lexicon). In modern Arabic *Zand* is by analogy applied to the flint piece used for striking fire with steel.

4027. *Cf.* lxxix. 27. Which is the more difficult to create,—man, or the heavens and the earth, with all creatures? God created the heavens and the earth, with all creatures, and He can create worlds and worlds like these in infinity To him it is a small matter to raise you up for the Hereafter.

4028. And His creation is not dependent on time, or instruments or means, or any conditions whatsoever. Existence waits on His Will, or Plan, or Intention. The moment He wills a thing, it becomes His Word or Command, and the thing forthwith comes into existence. *Cf.* ii. 117; xvi. 40, n. 2066; etc.

4029. All things were created by God ; are maintained by Him ; and will go back to Him. But the point of special interest to man is that man will also be brought back to God and is answerable to Him, and to Him alone. This Message is the core of Revelation ; it explains the meaning of the Hereafter ; and it fitly closes a Sūra specially connected with the name (*Yā-Sīn*) of the Holy Prophet.

INTRODUCTION TO SŪRA XXXVII (*Ṣāffāt*)

As explained in the Introduction to S. xxxiv, this is the fourth of a series of Sūras in which the mysteries of the spiritual world are manifested in different ways, tending to the defeat and final extirpation of Evil. The defeat of Evil is throughout connected with Revelation, and here the ranged fight is illustrated by a reference to the angels in heaven and to the earlier Prophets in our earthly history, from Noah to Jonah. In chronology this Sūra belongs to the early middle Meccan period.

Summary.—Through all the mysteries of the heavens and the earth, there is a sorting out of the evil against the good: their final destinations contrasted (xxxvii. 1-74, and C. 197).

Peace and victory came to Noah, Abraham, Moses and Aaron, Ilyās and Lūṭ, in their conflict with Evil (xxxvii. 75-138, and C. 198).

So was it with Jonah when he glorified God. But men will ascribe to God what is unworthy of Him: God's apostles strive for His glory, and shall be victorious (xxxvii. 139-182, and C. 199).

C. 197.—God is One, the Source and Centre
(xxxvii. 1-74.) Of all affairs, and we must work
In discipline, harmony, and unity
To put down Evil. The Hereafter
Is sure, when personal responsibility
Will be enforced. For the true
And sincere servants of God,
There will be the highest Bliss,
Unmixed and everlasting:
For those who defy God's Law
There will be the deepest enduring
Misery. Which will men choose?

Sūra XXXVII.

Ṣaffāt, or Those Ranged in Ranks.

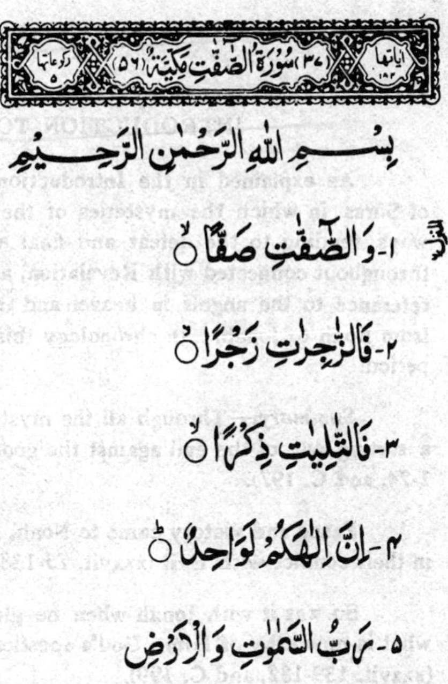

In the name of God, Most Gracious, Most Merciful.

1. By[4030] those who range
Themselves in ranks,[4031]

2. And so are strong
In repelling (evil),[4032]

3. And thus proclaim
The Message (of God)!

4. Verily, verily, your God
Is One!—[4033]

5. Lord of the heavens
And of the earth,

4030. At a later stage, we shall study the general meaning of the adjurations in the Qur-ān indicated by the particle *wa*. See App. xiv., p. 1786. Here we may note that the last Sūra (*Yā-Sīn*) practically began with the adjuration "by the Qur-ān, full of wisdom", emphasising the fact that Revelation was the evidence by which we could learn the highest wisdom of the spiritual world. Here our attention is called in three verses or clauses, to three definite attitudes which illustrate the triumph of Good and the frustration of Evil. See the notes following.

4031. Two questions arise: (1) are the doers of the three things noted in verses 1-3 the same persons, whose actions or qualities are differently described, or are they three distinct sets of persons? (2) in either case, who are they? As to (1) the most authoritative view is that the three clauses describe the same set of persons in different aspects. As to (2) some take them to refer to angels, and others understand by them the good men, the men of God, who strive and range themselves in God's service. The words are perfectly general, and I interpret them to refer to both classes. The feminine form is grammatically used in Arabic idiom for the indefinite plural. In xxxvii. 165 below, the word *ṣāffūn* is used in the definite plural, and seems to be spoken by these beings, angels or men of God or both, according to how we interpret this verse.

4032. The three acts in verses 1-3 are consecutive, as shown by the particle *fa*. I understand them to mean that angels and good men (1) are ever ready to range themselves in ranks in the service of God and work in perfect discipline and accord at all times; (2) that they check and frustrate evil wherever they find it and they are strengthened in doing so by their discipline and their ranging themselves in ranks; and (3) that this service furthers the Kingdom of God and proclaims His Message and His glory to all creation.

4033. That divine Message is summed up in the gospel of Divine Unity, on which the greatest emphasis is laid: "verily, verily your God is One". It is a fact intimately connected with our own life and destiny. '*Your* Lord is one Who cares for you and cherishes you; you are dear to Him. And He is *One*: it is only He that you have to look to, the source of all goodness, love, and power. You are not the sport of many contending forces or blind chances. There is complete harmony and unity in heaven and you have to put yourselves into unison with it—by discipline in ranks, by unity of plan and purpose in repelling evil, and by concerted action in promoting the Kingdom of God. Here is the mystery of the manifold variety of creation converging into the absolute Unity of the Creator.

And all between them,
And Lord of every point
At the rising of the sun ! [4034]

وَمَا بَيْنَهُمَا وَرَبُّ الْمَشَارِقِ ۝

6. We have indeed decked
The lower heaven [4035] with beauty
(In) the stars,—[4036]

٦- إِنَّا زَيَّنَّا السَّمَاءَ الدُّنْيَا
بِزِينَةٍ الْكَوَاكِبِ ۝

7. (For beauty) and for guard [4037]
Against all obstinate
Rebellious evil spirits,

٧- وَحِفْظًا مِّن كُلِّ شَيْطَٰنٍ مَّارِدٍ ۝

8. (So) they should not strain
Their ears in the direction
Of the Exalted Assembly [4038]

٨- لَّا يَسَّمَّعُونَ إِلَى الْمَلَإِ الْأَعْلَىٰ

4034. That Unity comprehends everything that exists—'the heavens and the earth, and all between them'. For He is their Lord. He is the Lord of the *Mashāriq*,—of every point at the rising of the sun. As the Commentators tell us, there are in the solar year only two equinoctial days, when the sun rises due east: on every other day the sun rises at a shifting point either north or south of due east. In vii. 137 we have *mashāriq al ar<u>dh</u>i wa magāribahā*, where the plural of the words for East and West is negligible, as the conjunction of the two embraces all points. The same may be said of lxx. 40, where God is called "Lord of all points in the East and the West". If we are speaking of longitudes, they may embrace all latitudes. In lv. 17 God is called "Lord of the *two* Easts and the *two* Wests", referring to the extreme points in either case. A cursory reader may ask, why is only the East referred to here? The reply is that it is not so much the East as the rising of the sun, on which stress is laid. The Arabic *mashriq* or *mashāriq* is close enough to the root-word *sharaqa*, to suggest, not so much the East as the rising of the sun, especially when the plural form is used. The glorious sun rises from different points, as seen by us, but it illuminates the whole heaven and earth. It is an emblem of Unity. We can see things from different points of view, but the centre of all things is God, and He is One.

4035. That is lower than the highest heaven, the Empyrean, the sphere of fire (*kurrat un nār*), the seat, we may suppose, of the Exalted Assembly (of angels) mentioned in verse 8 below. In the poetic imagery of the East as of the West, (*e.g.*, see Milton, *Paradise Lost*, III. 56, 481-3) there are the seven heavens of the planets of the solar system; above them is the sphere of the fixed stars; above them is the crystalline sphere balancing other motions; higher still is the *premum mobile* ('that first moved'), the source of heavenly motions; and above all, the Empyrean. The stars and planets thus come in the lower heavens. The same imagery will be found in Dante.

4036. 'Stars' may be taken here in the popular sense, as referring to fixed stars, planets, comets, shooting stars, etc. On a clear night the beauty of the starry heavens is proverbial. Here they are meant to illustrate two points: (1) their marvellous beauty and their groupings and motions (apparent or real) manifest and typify the Design and Harmony of the One true Creator; and (2) the power and glory behind them typify that there is a guard against the assaults of Evil (see verse 7 below).

4037. Verses 7-11 seem to refer to shooting stars. *Cf.* xv. 17-18, and notes 1951-53. The heavens typify not only beauty but power. The Good in God's world is guarded and protected against every assault of Evil. The Evil is not part of the heavenly system: it is a thing in outlawry, merely a self-willed rebellion,—"cast away on every side, repulsed under a perpetual penalty" (verses 8-9).

4038. We can form a mental picture of the Court of the Most High, in the highest heaven, conforming to the highest idea we can form of goodness, beauty, purity, and grandeur. The Exalted Assembly of angels is given some knowledge of the Plan and Will of God. Evil is altogether foreign to such an atmosphere, but is actuated by feelings of jealousy and curiosity. It tries to approach by stealth and overhear something from the august Assembly. It is repulsed and pursued by a flaming fire, of which we can form some idea in our physical world by the piercing trail of a shooting star.

But be cast away
From every side,

وَيُقْذَفُونَ مِنْ كُلِّ جَانِبٍ ○

9. Repulsed, for they are
Under a perpetual penalty,

٩- دُحُورًا وَلَهُمْ عَذَابٌ وَاصِبٌ ○

10. Except such as snatch away
Something by stealth, and they
Are pursued by a flaming[4039]
Fire, of piercing brightness.

١٠- إِلَّا مَنْ خَطِفَ الْخَطْفَةَ
فَأَتْبَعَهُ شِهَابٌ ثَاقِبٌ ○

11. Just ask their[4040] opinion:
Are they the more difficult
To create, or the (other) beings
We have created?
Them have We created
Out of a sticky clay![4041]

١١- فَاسْتَفْتِهِمْ أَهُمْ أَشَدُّ
خَلْقًا أَمْ مَنْ خَلَقْنَا
إِنَّا خَلَقْنَاهُمْ مِنْ طِينٍ لَازِبٍ ○

12. Truly dost thou marvel,[4042]
While they ridicule,

١٢- بَلْ عَجِبْتَ وَيَسْخَرُونَ ○

13. And, when they are
Admonished, pay no heed,—

١٣- وَإِذَا ذُكِّرُوا لَا يَذْكُرُونَ ○

14. And, when they see
A Sign, turn it
To mockery,

١٤- وَإِذَا رَأَوْا آيَةً يَسْتَسْخِرُونَ ○

15. And say, "This is nothing
But evident sorcery!

١٥- وَقَالُوا إِنْ هَٰذَا إِلَّا سِحْرٌ مُبِينٌ ○

16. "What! when we die,
And become dust and bones,

١٦- أَإِذَا مِتْنَا وَكُنَّا تُرَابًا وَعِظَامًا

4039. See last note and *Cf.* xv. 18 and notes 1953-54.

4040. "Their": "they" are the doubters, the evil ones, the deniers of God's grace and mercy, who laugh at Revelation and disbelieve in a Hereafter. Are they more important or more difficult to create than the wonderful variety of beings in God's spacious Creation? Do they forget their own lowly state, as having been created from muddy clay?

4041. *Cf.* vi. 2; vii. 12; xxxii. 7; etc.

4042. It is indeed strange that unregenerate man should forget, on the one hand, his lowly origin, and on the other hand, his high Destiny, as conferred upon him by the grace and mercy of God. The indictment of him here comprises four counts: (1) they ridicule the teaching of Truth; (2) instead of profiting by admonition, they pay no heed; (3) when God's Signs are brought home to them, they ridicule them as much as they ridiculed the teaching of Truth: and (4) when they have to acknowledge incontestable facts, they give them false names like "sorcery", which imply fraud or something which has no relation to their life, although the facts touch the inner springs of their life intimately.

Shall we (then) be
Raised up (again)?

ءَاِنَّا لَمَبْعُوْثُوْنَ ۝

17. "And also our fathers[4043]
Of old?"

١٧- اَوَ اٰبَآؤُنَا الْاَوَّلُوْنَ ۝

18. Say thou: "Yea, and ye shall
Then be humiliated
(On account of your evil)."[4044]

١٨- قُلْ نَعَمْ وَاَنْتُمْ دَاخِرُوْنَ ۝

19. Then it will be a single
(Compelling) cry;[4045]
And behold, they will
Begin to see![4046]

١٩- فَاِنَّمَا هِيَ زَجْرَةٌ وَّاحِدَةٌ
فَاِذَا هُمْ يَنْظُرُوْنَ ۝

20. They will say, "Ah!
Woe to us! this is
The Day of Judgment!"

٢٠- وَقَالُوْا يٰوَيْلَنَا
هٰذَا يَوْمُ الدِّيْنِ ۝

21. (A voice will say,)
"This is the Day[4047]
Of Sorting Out, whose
Truth ye (once) denied!"

٢١- هٰذَا يَوْمُ
الْفَصْلِ الَّذِيْ كُنْتُمْ بِهٖ تُكَذِّبُوْنَ ۝ ع

Section 2.

22. "Bring ye up",
It shall be said,

٢٢- اُحْشُرُوا الَّذِيْنَ

4043. Although the Hereafter, and the spiritual life of which it is a corollary, are the most solid facts in our intelligent existence, materialists deny them. They cannot believe that they could have any existence beyond the grave—still less their ancestors who died ages and ages ago: how could they ever come to life again?

4044. They are assured that the future life is a solid fact, but that it will be in very different conditions from those they know now. All their present arrogance will have been humbled in the dust. There will be another plane, in which souls will have experiences quite different from those in their probationary life here. In that life the virtues they lacked will count, and the arrogance they hugged will be brought low.

4045. *Cf.* xxxvi. 29, 49, and 53.

4046. Their spiritual blindness will then leave them. But they will be surprised at the suddenness of their disillusion.

4047. The Day of Judgment is the day of sorting out. *Cf.* xxxvi. 59. Good and evil will finally be separated, unlike the apparently inexplicable conditions in the present probationary life, when they seem to be mixed together.

"The wrong-doers
And their wives,[4048]
And the things they worshipped—

ظَلَمُوا
وَأَزْوَاجَهُمْ وَمَا كَانُوا يَعْبُدُونَ ○

23. "Besides God,
And lead them to the Way
To the (Fierce) Fire!

٢٣- مِن دُونِ اللَّهِ
فَاهْدُوهُمْ إِلَىٰ صِرَاطِ الْجَحِيمِ ○

24. "But stop them,[4049]
For they must be asked:

٢٤- وَقِفُوهُمْ إِنَّهُم مَّسْئُولُونَ ○

25. "'What is the matter
With you that ye
Help not each other?'"[4050]

٢٥- مَا لَكُمْ لَا تَنَاصَرُونَ ○

26. Nay, but that day they
Shall submit (to Judgment);[4051]

٢٦- بَلْ هُمُ الْيَوْمَ مُسْتَسْلِمُونَ ○

27. And they will turn to
One another, and question
One onother.

٢٧- وَأَقْبَلَ بَعْضُهُمْ عَلَىٰ بَعْضٍ
يَتَسَاءَلُونَ ○

28. They will say: "It was ye
Who used to come to us
From the right hand
(Of power and authority)!"[4052]

٢٨- قَالُوا إِنَّكُمْ
كُنتُمْ تَأْتُونَنَا عَنِ الْيَمِينِ ○

4048. That is, if their wives were also wrong-doers. They are separately mentioned, because the Arabic phrase for "wrong-doers" is of the masculine gender. All the associates in wrong-doing will be marshalled together. There will be personal responsibility: neither husband nor wife can lay the blame on the other.

4049. The scene here is after judgment. As, in an earthly tribunal, the prisoner or his advocate is asked why sentence should not be pronounced upon him, so here those who are proved to have been guilty of wrong are allowed to consider if anything or any one can help them. Then comes the exposure of the misleaders.

4050. Obviously no one can stand and intercede, for it is a question of personal responsibility for each soul. No one can help another.

4051. All the previous arrogance of this life will be gone, but they will face each other, and those who were given a false lead, as in the story of Pharaoh (*Cf.* xx. 79), will question their misleaders as in the following verses.

4052. This is the mutual recrimination of the sinners—those who sinned, against those whose instigation or evil example led them into sin. The misleaders in the life here below often used their power and influence to spread evil. The "right hand" is the hand of power and authority. Instead of using it for righteous purposes, they used it for evil,—selfishly for their own advantage, and mischievously for the degradation of others.

29. They will reply: "Nay, ye
Yourselves had no Faith![4053]

۲۹- قَالُوا بَلْ لَّمْ تَكُونُوا مُؤْمِنِينَ ۚ

30. "Nor had we any authority
Over you. Nay, it was
Ye who were a people
In obstinate rebellion!

۳۰- وَمَا كَانَ لَنَا عَلَيْكُم مِّن سُلْطَٰنٍ ۖ
بَلْ كُنتُمْ قَوْمًا طَٰغِينَ ۝

31. "So now has been proved true,[4054]
Against us, the Word
Of our Lord that we
Shall indeed (have to) taste
(The punishment of our sins).

۳۱- فَحَقَّ عَلَيْنَا قَوْلُ رَبِّنَآ ۖ
إِنَّا لَذَآئِقُونَ ۝

32. "We led you astray: for truly[4055]
We were ourselves astray."

۳۲- فَأَغْوَيْنَٰكُمْ إِنَّا كُنَّا غَٰوِينَ ۝

33. Truly, that Day, they will
(All) share in the Penalty.

۳۳- فَإِنَّهُمْ يَوْمَئِذٍ فِى ٱلْعَذَابِ مُشْتَرِكُونَ ۝

34. Verily that is how We
Shall deal with Sinners.

۳۴- إِنَّا كَذَٰلِكَ نَفْعَلُ بِٱلْمُجْرِمِينَ ۝

35. For they, when they were
Told that there is
No god except God, would
Puff themselves up with Pride,[4056]

۳۵- إِنَّهُمْ كَانُوٓا إِذَا قِيلَ لَهُمْ
لَآ إِلَٰهَ إِلَّا ٱللَّهُ يَسْتَكْبِرُونَ ۙ

4053. But the fact that others mislead, or that their evil example is before us, does not justify us in falling from right conduct. Faith should save us from the fall. But if we have ourselves no Faith—in righteousness, or a future life, or the reality of God's Law, how can we blame others? The misleaders can well say, "You will be judged according to your misdeeds!" The responsibility is personal, and cannot be shifted on to others. The others may get a double punishment,—for their own evil, and for misleading their weaker brethren. But the weaker brethren cannot go free from responsibility for their own deeds; for evil means a personal rebellion against God, if we believe in a personal God. Evil has no authority over us, except in so far as we deliberately choose it.

4054. God's decree of justice requires that every soul should taste the consequences of its own sins, and that decree must be fulfilled. No excuses can serve. It is only God's mercy that can save.

4055. Further, the misleaders can well urge against those who reproach them for misleading them: "How could you expect anything better from us? You were already warned by God's Message that we were astray."

4056. Selfish arrogance was the seed of sin and rebellion: ii. 34 (of Satan): xxviii. 39 (of Pharaoh); etc. It is that kind of arrogance which prevents man from mending his life and conduct. When he speaks of ancestral ways, or public opinion, or national honour, he is usually thinking of himself or of a small clique which thrives on injustice. The recognition of the true God, the one God, as the only standard of life and conduct, the only Reality, cuts out Self, and is therefore disagreeable to Sin. If false gods are imagined, who themselves would have weaknesses that fit in with sin, they give countenance to evils, and it becomes difficult to give them up, unless God's grace comes to our assistance.

36. And say: "What! Shall we
Give up our gods
For the sake of
A Poet possessed?"[4057]

٣٦- وَيَقُولُونَ أَئِنَّا لَتَارِكُوٓا۟ ءَالِهَتِنَا
لِشَاعِرٍ مَّجْنُونٍ ۝

37. Nay! he has come
With the (very) Truth,
And he confirms (the Message
Of) the apostles (before him).[4058]

٣٧- بَلْ جَآءَ بِٱلْحَقِّ
وَصَدَّقَ ٱلْمُرْسَلِينَ ۝

38. Ye shall indeed taste
Of the Grievous Penalty;—

٣٨- إِنَّكُمْ لَذَآئِقُوا۟ ٱلْعَذَابِ ٱلْأَلِيمِ ۝

39. But it will be no more
Than the retribution[4059]
Of (the Evil) that ye
Have wrought;—

٣٩- وَمَا تُجْزَوْنَ
إِلَّا مَا كُنتُمْ تَعْمَلُونَ ۝

40. But the sincere (and devoted)
Servants of God,—

٤٠- إِلَّا عِبَادَ ٱللَّهِ ٱلْمُخْلَصِينَ ۝

41. For them is a Sustenance[4060]
Determined,[4061]

٤١- أُو۟لَٰٓئِكَ لَهُمْ رِزْقٌ مَّعْلُومٌ ۝

42. Fruits (Delights);[4062] and they
(Shall enjoy) honour and dignity,

٤٢- فَوَٰكِهُ ۖ وَهُم مُّكْرَمُونَ ۝

43. In Gardens of Felicity,

٤٣- فِى جَنَّٰتِ ٱلنَّعِيمِ ۝

4057. Possessed of an evil spirit, or mad. Such was the charge which the Unbelievers sometimes levelled at the holy Prophet in the early stages of his preaching.

4058. The message of Islam, so far from being "mad" or in any way peculiar, is eminently conformable to reason and the true facts of nature as created by God. It is the Truth in the purest sense of the term, and confirms the Message of all true Messengers that ever lived.

4059. Justice demands that those who sow evil should reap the fruit, but the punishment is due to their own conduct and not to anything external to themselves.

4060. "*Sustenance*": metaphorical sense, correlated with the Fruits mentioned below: see next verse.

4061. "*Determined*": *Ma'lūm*: the reward of the Blessed will not be a chance or a fleeting thing. It will follow a firm Decree of God, on principles that can be known and understood.

4062. "*Fruits*": *Cf.* xxxvi 57, and n. 4003. The spiritual Delights are figured forth from parallel experiences in our present life, and follow an ascending order: Food and Fruits; Gardens of Bliss, (with all their charm, design, greenery, birds' songs, fountains, etc.); the Home of Happiness and Dignity, with congenial company seated on Thrones; Delicious Drinks from crystal Springs, for social pleasure; and the society of Companions of the opposite sex, with beauty and charm but none of the grossness too often incidental to such companionship in this life.

44. Facing each other
On Thrones (of dignity):

٤٤- عَلَىٰ سُرُرٍ مُّتَقَٰبِلِينَ ۝

45. Round will be passed
To them a Cup
From a clear-flowing fountain,

٤٥- يُطَافُ عَلَيْهِم بِكَأْسٍ
مِّن مَّعِينٍۭ ۝

46. Crystal-white, of a taste
Delicious to those
Who drink (thereof),

٤٦- بَيْضَآءَ لَذَّةٍ لِّلشَّٰرِبِينَ ۝

47. Free from headiness;[4063]
Nor will they suffer
Intoxication therefrom.

٤٧- لَا فِيهَا غَوْلٌ
وَلَا هُمْ عَنْهَا يُنزَفُونَ ۝

48. And besides them will be
Chaste women, restraining
Their glances, with big eyes[4064]
(Of wonder and beauty).

٤٨- وَعِندَهُمْ قَٰصِرَٰتُ
الطَّرْفِ عِينٌ ۝

49. As if they were[4065]
(Delicate) eggs closely guarded.

٤٩- كَأَنَّهُنَّ بَيْضٌ مَّكْنُونٌ ۝

50. Then they will turn to
One another and question
One another.[4066]

٥٠- فَأَقْبَلَ بَعْضُهُمْ عَلَىٰ بَعْضٍ
يَتَسَآءَلُونَ ۝

51. One of them will start
The talk and say:
"I had an intimate
Companion (on the earth),[4067]

٥١- قَالَ قَآئِلٌ مِّنْهُمْ
إِنِّي كَانَ لِي قَرِينٌ ۝

4063. The passing round of the social cup, as in the case of other pleasures, is without any of the drawbacks and evil accompaniments of the pleasures of this world, which are taken as types. In drink there is no intoxication: in fruit there is no satiety. *Cf.* Dante: "the bread of Angels upon which One liveth here and grows not sated by it." (*Paradiso*, Canto II., Longfellow's translation.)

4064. In the emblem used here, again, the pure type of chaste womanhood is figured. They are chaste, not bold with their glances: but their eyes are big with wonder and beauty, prefiguring grace, innocence, and a refined capacity of appreciation and admiration.

4065. This is usually understood to refer to the delicate complexion of a beautiful woman, which is compared to the transparent shell of eggs in the nest, closely guarded by the mother-bird; the shell is warm and free from stain In lv. 58 the phrase used is "like rubies and coral", referring to the red or pink of a beautiful complexion.

4066. *Cf.* above, xxxvii. 27, where the same phrase is used in the reverse conditions. In each case there is a going back to the earlier memories or experiences of this life.

4067. This companion was a sceptic, who laughed at Religion and a Hereafter. How the tables are now turned! The devout man backed up his Faith with a good life and is now in Bliss: the other was a cynic and made a mess of his life, and is now burning in the Fire of Regrets!

52. "Who used to say,
'What! art thou amongst those
Who bear witness to
The truth (of the Message)?

53. "'When we die and become
Dust and bones, shall we
Indeed receive rewards
And punishments?'"

54. (A voice) said: "Would ye
Like to look down?"

55. He looked down
And saw him
In the midst of the Fire.[4068]

56. He said: "By God!
Thou wast little short
Of bringing me to perdition!

57. "Had it not been for
The Grace of my Lord,[4069]
I should certainly have been
Among those brought (there)!

58. "Is it (the case) that
We shall not die,

59. "Except our first death,
And that *we*[4070]
Shall not be punished?"

60. Verily this is
The supreme achievement![4071]

٥٢- يَقُولُ أَئِنَّكَ
لَمِنَ الْمُصَدِّقِينَ ۝

٥٣- ءَإِذَا مِتْنَا وَكُنَّا تُرَابًا وَّعِظَامًا
ءَإِنَّا لَمَدِينُونَ ۝

٥٤- قَالَ هَلْ أَنْتُمْ مُّطَّلِعُونَ ۝

٥٥- فَاطَّلَعَ
فَرَاٰهُ فِي سَوَآءِ الْجَحِيمِ ۝

٥٦- قَالَ تَاللهِ
إِنْ كِدْتَّ لَتُرْدِينِ ۝

٥٧- وَلَوْلَا نِعْمَةُ رَبِّي
لَكُنْتُ مِنَ الْمُحْضَرِينَ ۝

٥٨- أَفَمَا نَحْنُ بِمَيِّتِينَ ۝

٥٩- إِلَّا مَوْتَتَنَا الْأُولَىٰ
وَمَا نَحْنُ بِمُعَذَّبِينَ ۝

٦٠- إِنَّ هٰذَا لَهُوَ الْفَوْزُ الْعَظِيمُ ۝

4068 He is allowed a peep into the state which he so narrowly escaped by the grace of God.

4069. And he gratefully acknowledges his short-comings: "I should have been a sinner just like this, but for the grace of God!" He sees that if he had erred it would have been no excuse to plead the other man's example He had Faith and was saved, to walk in the path of righteousness.

4070. After he realises the great danger from which he narrowly escaped, his joy is so great that he can hardly believe it! Is the danger altogether past now? Are the portals of death closed for ever? Is he safe now from the temptations which will bring him to ruin and punishment?

4071. The answer is: Yes. "Beyond the flight of Time, Beyond the realm of Death, There surely is some blessed clime, Where Life is not a breath!" In the words of Longfellow this was an aspiration on this earth. In the Hereafter it is a realisation!

Some interpret verses 60-62 as a continuation of the speech of the man in heaven. The meaning would in that case be the same.

61. For the like of this
Let all strive,
Who wish to strive.

٦١- لمثل هذا فليعمل العملون ○

62. Is that the better entertainment
Or the Tree of Zaqqūm?[4072]

٦٢- أذلك خير نزلا أم شجرة الزقوم ○

63. For We have truly
Made it (as) a trial[4073]
For the wrong-doers.

٦٣- إنا جعلنها فتنة للظلمين ○

64. For it is a tree
That springs out
Of the bottom of Hell-fire:

٦٤- إنها شجرة
تخرج في أصل الجحيم ○

65. The shoots of its fruit-stalks
Are like the heads
Of devils:

٦٥- طلعها
كأنه رءوس الشيطين ○

66. Truly they will eat thereof[4074]
And fill their bellies therewith.

٦٦- فإنهم لآكلون منها فمالئون منها البطون ○

67. Then on top of that
They will be given
A mixture made of
Boiling water.

٦٧- ثم إن لهم عليها
لشوبا من حميم ○

68. Then shall their return[4075]
Be to the (Blazing) Fire.

٦٨- ثم إن مرجعهم لإلى الجحيم ○

4072. *Cf.* xvii. 60, n. 2250. This bitter tree of Hell is a symbol of the contrast with the beautiful Garden of heaven with its delicious fruits.

4073. This dreadful bitter Tree of Hell is truly a trial to the wrong-doers. (1) It grows at the bottom of Hell; (2) even its fruit-stalks, which should have been tender, are like the heads of devils: (3) its produce is eaten voraciously; (4) on top of it is a boiling mixture to cut up their entrails (see next note); and (5) every time they complete this round of orgies they return to the same game. A truly lurid picture, but more lurid in reality are the stages in spiritual Evil. (1) It takes its rise in the lowest depths of corrupted human nature; (2) its tenderest affections are degraded to envy and hate; (3) the appetite for Evil grows with what it feeds on; (4) its "cures" serve but to aggravate the disease; and (5) the chain of evil is unending; one round is followed by another in interminable succession.

4074. The parable of fruits and drinks in the contrasted fortunes of the Good and the Evil is further elaborated in xlvii. 15, where the boiling water given to the evil ones cuts up their entrails.

4075. When they eat of the *zaqqūm* in the lowest depths of hell, they are apparently brought up to drink of the mixture as a further punishment, after which they go back to repeat the round.

69. **Truly they found their fathers**
On the wrong Path;

٦٩- إِنَّهُمْ أَلْفَوْا آبَاءَهُمْ ضَالِّينَ ۝

70. So they (too) were rushed[4076]
Down on their footsteps!

٧٠- فَهُمْ عَلَىٰٓ آثَارِهِمْ يُهْرَعُونَ ۝

71. And truly before them,
Many of the ancients
Went astray;—

٧١- وَلَقَدْ ضَلَّ قَبْلَهُمْ
أَكْثَرُ الْأَوَّلِينَ ۝

72. But We sent aforetime,[4077]
Among them, (apostles)
To admonish them;—

٧٢- وَلَقَدْ أَرْسَلْنَا فِيهِمْ مُّنذِرِينَ ۝

73. Then see what was
The End of those who[4078]
Were admonished
(but heeded not),—

٧٣- فَانظُرْ كَيْفَ
كَانَ عَاقِبَةُ الْمُنذَرِينَ ۝

74. Except the sincere (and devoted)[4079]
Servants of God.

٧٤- إِلَّا عِبَادَ اللَّهِ الْمُخْلَصِينَ ۝ ع

C. 198.—The Prophets of God formed a series
(xxxvii. 75-138.) That worked in God's service to instruct
Their fellow-men. In case of distress
God helped and delivered them. Men did flout
And persecute them, but they carried out
Their mission with constancy; and God's Purpose
Always won, to the destruction of Evil.
So was it in the story of Noah and the Flood,
Of Abraham the True, of Ismā'īl
Ready for self-sacrifice, of Isaac

4076. A grim reproach. 'You found your fathers doing wrong; and you must rush headlong in their footsteps to perdition!'

4077. It is human to err. The error is forgiven if there is repentance and amendment. The point is that God in His mercy at all times in history sent apostles and teachers to give His Message, and men deliberately rejected that Message.

4078. It is on the reception or rejection of God's teachings and guidance that judgment will come. In this world itself, see what is the teaching of history. Unrighteousness and wrong-doing never prosper in the long run.

4079. But there is always a band of sincere and devoted men who serve God, and the highest spiritual life is open to them.

Note that this verse occurs at xxxvii. 40 above, where the argument of the difference between the fates of the righteous and the unrighteous was begun. Here it is rounded off with the same phrase, and now we proceed to take illustrations from the early Prophets.

The righteous, of Moses and Aaron, of Elias
And Lot: all men of Faith, who receive
The blessings of posterity and Peace
And Salutation from God Most Gracious.

SECTION 3.

75. (In the days of old),
Noah cried to Us,[4080]
And We are the Best
To hear prayer.

٧٥- وَلَقَدْ نَادٰىنَا نُوحٌ فَلَنِعْمَ الْمُجِيبُونَ ۝

76. And We delivered him
And his people from
The Great Calamity,[4081]

٧٦- وَنَجَّيْنٰهُ وَأَهْلَهُۥ مِنَ الْكَرْبِ الْعَظِيمِ ۝

77. And made his progeny
To endure (on this earth);[4082]

٧٧- وَجَعَلْنَا ذُرِّيَّتَهُۥ هُمُ الْبَاقِينَ ۝

78. And We left (this blessing)
For him among generations[4083]
To come in later times:

٧٨- وَتَرَكْنَا عَلَيْهِ فِى الْاٰخِرِينَ ۝

79. "Peace and salutation to Noah
Among the nations!"[4084]

٧٩- سَلٰمٌ عَلٰى نُوحٍ فِى الْعٰلَمِينَ ۝

80. Thus indeed do We reward
Those who do right.

٨٠- إِنَّا كَذٰلِكَ نَجْزِى الْمُحْسِنِينَ ۝

81. For he was one
Of Our believing Servants.

٨١- إِنَّهُۥ مِنْ عِبَادِنَا الْمُؤْمِنِينَ ۝

4080. *Cf.* xxi. 76-77. The story of Noah occurs in many places: here the point is that when men gird themselves against evil, God protects them, and Evil cannot triumph against God's Plan.

4081. The Deluge, the Flood of Noah. The main story will be found in xi. 25-48.

4082. Noah's posterity survived the Flood in the Ark, while the rest perished.

4083. His name is remembered for ever, commencing a new era in religious history. Note that the words in verses 78-81, with slight modifications, form a sort of refrain to the following paragraphs about Abraham, Moses, and Elias, but not about Lot and Jonah. Lot was a nephew of Abraham, and may be supposed to belong to the story of Abraham. Jonah's career nearly ended in a tragedy for himself, and his people got a further lease of power "for a time" (xxxvii. 148). And both Lot and Jonah belong to a limited local tradition.

4084. The story of the Flood is found in some form or other among all nations, and not only among those who follow the Mosaic tradition. In Greek tradition the hero of the Flood is Deukalion, with his wife Pyrrha: in Indian tradition (*Shatapatha Brāhmana* and *Mahābhārata*) it is the sage Manū and the Fish. The Chinese tradition of a great Flood is recorded in *Shū-King*. Among American Indians the tradition was common to many tribes.

82. Then the rest We overwhelmed In the Flood.	٨٢- ثُمَّ أَغْرَقْنَا الْآخَرِينَ ۝
83. Verily among those Who followed his Way Was Abraham.[4085]	٨٣- وَإِنَّ مِن شِيعَتِهِ لَإِبْرَاهِيمَ ۝
84. Behold, he approached his Lord With a sound heart.[4086]	٨٤- إِذْ جَاءَ رَبَّهُ بِقَلْبٍ سَلِيمٍ ۝
85. Behold, he said to his father And to his people, "What Is that which ye worship?	٨٥- إِذْ قَالَ لِأَبِيهِ وَقَوْمِهِ مَاذَا تَعْبُدُونَ ۝
86. "Is it a Falsehood— Gods other than God— That ye desire? [4087]	٨٦- أَئِفْكًا آلِهَةً دُونَ اللَّهِ تُرِيدُونَ ۝
87. "Then what is your idea About the Lord of the Worlds?" [4088]	٨٧- فَمَا ظَنُّكُم بِرَبِّ الْعَالَمِينَ ۝
88. Then did he cast A glance at the Stars,	٨٨- فَنَظَرَ نَظْرَةً فِي النُّجُومِ ۝
89. And he said, "I am Indeed sick (at heart)!" [4089]	٨٩- فَقَالَ إِنِّي سَقِيمٌ ۝

4085. The main story will be found in xxi 51-73; but the episode about his readiness and that of his son to submit to the most extreme form of self-sacrifice under trial (in verses 102-107 below) is told here for the first time, as this Sūra deals with the theme, "Not my will, but Thine be done!" In "followed his way", the pronoun "his" refers to Noah, "he", of verse 81 above.

4086. *A sound heart: qalb salīm*: a heart that is pure, and unaffected by the diseases that afflict others. As the heart in Arabic is taken to be not only the seat of feelings and affections, but also of intelligence and resulting action, it implies the whole character. *Cf.* Abraham's title of *Ḥanīf* (the True): ii. 135 and n. 134. *Cf.* also xxvi. 89: "only he will prosper who brings to God a sound heart."

4087. False worship—worship of idols or stars or symbols, or Mammon or Self—is due either to false and degrading conceptions of God, or to a sort of make-believe, where practice is inconsistent with knowledge or ignores the inner promptings of Conscience. Abraham's challenge to his people is: 'Are you fools or hypocrites?'

4088. 'Do you not realise that the real Creator is One—above all the forms and superstitions that you associate with Him?'

4089. The grief was really preying on his mind and soul, that he should be associated with such falsehoods. His father himself was among the chief supporters of such falsehoods, and his people were given up wholly to them. He could not possibly share in their mummeries, and they left him in disgust. Then he made his practical protest in the manner narrated in xxi. 56-64.

90. So they turned away
From him, and departed.

٩٠- فَتَوَلَّوْا عَنْهُ مُدْبِرِينَ ۝

91. Then did he turn
To their gods and said,
"Will ye not eat
(Of the offerings before you)? . . .

٩١- فَرَاغَ إِلَىٰٓ ءَالِهَتِهِمْ فَقَالَ
أَلَا تَأْكُلُونَ ۝

92. "What is the matter
With you that ye
Speak not (intelligently)?"

٩٢- مَا لَكُمْ لَا تَنطِقُونَ ۝

93. Then did he turn
Upon them, striking (them)[4090]
With the right hand.[4091]

٩٣- فَرَاغَ عَلَيْهِمْ
ضَرْبًۢا بِٱلْيَمِينِ ۝

94. Then came (the worshippers)
With hurried steps,
And faced (him).

٩٤- فَأَقْبَلُوٓا۟ إِلَيْهِ يَزِفُّونَ ۝

95. He said: "Worship ye
That which ye have
(Yourselves) carved?[4092]

٩٥- قَالَ أَتَعْبُدُونَ مَا تَنْحِتُونَ ۝

96. "But God has created you
And your handiwork!"

٩٦- وَٱللَّهُ خَلَقَكُمْ وَمَا تَعْمَلُونَ ۝

97. They said, "Build him
A furnace, and throw him[4093]
Into the blazing fire!"

٩٧- قَالُوا۟ ٱبْنُوا۟ لَهُۥ بُنْيَـٰنًا
فَأَلْقُوهُ فِى ٱلْجَحِيمِ ۝

98. (This failing), they then
Sought a stratagem against him,[4094]

٩٨- فَأَرَادُوا۟ بِهِۦ كَيْدًا

4090. See the reference in the last note.

4091. *With the right hand*: as the right hand is the hand of power, the phrase means that he struck them with might and main and broke them.

4092. His action was a challenge, and he drives home the challenge now with argument. 'Do you worship your own handiwork? Surely worship is due to Him Who made you and made possible your handiwork!'

4093. The argument of Abraham was so sound that it could not be met by argument. In such cases Evil resorts to violence, or secret plotting. Here there was both violence and secret plotting. The violence consisted in throwing him into a blazing Furnace. But by the mercy of God the fire did not harm him (xxi. 69), and so they resorted to plotting. But the plotting, as the next verse (xxxvii. 98) shows, was a boomerang that recoiled on their own heads.

4094. *Cf.* xxi. 71. Their plot against the righteous Abraham failed. Abraham migrated from the country (Chaldea, Babylon, and Assyria) and prospered in Syria and Palestine. It was his persecutors that suffered humiliation.

But We made them the ones
Most humiliated!

فَجَعَلْنٰهُمُ الْاَسْفَلِيْنَ ○

99. He said: "I will go
To my Lord! He
Will surely guide me! [4095]

٩٩- وَقَالَ اِنِّيْ ذَاهِبٌ اِلٰى رَبِّيْ
سَيَهْدِيْنِ ○

100. "O my Lord! grant me
A righteous (son)!"

١٠٠- رَبِّ هَبْ لِيْ مِنَ الصّٰلِحِيْنَ ○

101. So We gave him
The good news [4096]
Of a boy ready
To suffer and forbear. [4097]

١٠١- فَبَشَّرْنٰهُ
بِغُلٰمٍ حَلِيْمٍ ○

102. Then, when (the son)
Reached (the age of)
(Serious) work with him,
He said: "O my son!
I see in vision [4098]
That I offer thee in sacrifice: [4099]
Now see what is
Thy view!" (The son) said:
"O my father! Do
As thou art commanded:

١٠٢- فَلَمَّا بَلَغَ مَعَهُ السَّعْيَ
قَالَ يٰبُنَيَّ اِنِّيْٓ اَرٰى فِى الْمَنَامِ
اَنِّيْٓ اَذْبَحُكَ
فَانْظُرْ مَاذَا تَرٰى
قَالَ يٰٓاَبَتِ افْعَلْ مَا تُؤْمَرُ

4095. This was the Hijrat of Abraham. He left his people and his land, because the Truth was dearer to him than the ancestral falsehoods of his people. He trusted himself to God, and under God's guidance he laid the foundations of great peoples. See n. 2725 to xxi. 69.

4096. This was in the fertile land of Syria and Palestine. The boy thus born was, according to Muslim tradition, (which however is not unanimous on this point), the first-born son of Abraham, *viz.* Ismā'īl. The name itself is from the root *Sami'a*, to hear, because God had heard Abraham's prayer (verse 100). Abraham's age when Ismā'īl was born was 86 (Gen. xvi. 16).

4097. The boy's character was to be *Ḥalīm*, which I have translated "ready to suffer and forbear". This title is also applied to Abraham (in ix. 114 and xi. 75). It refers to the patient way in which both father and son cheerfully offered to suffer any self-sacrifice in order to obey the Command of God. See next verse.

4098. Where did this vision occur? The Muslim view is that it was in or near Mecca. Some would identify it with the valley of Minā, six miles north of Mecca, where a commemoration sacrifice is annually celebrated as a rite of the Ḥajj on the tenth of Ẓul-Ḥijja, the 'Īd of Sacrifice, in memory of this Sacrifice of Abraham and Ismā'īl (see n. 217 to ii. 197). Others say that the original place of sacrifice was near the hill of Marwa (the companion hill to Ṣafā, ii. 158), which is associated with the infancy of Ismā'īl.

4099. At what stage in Abraham's history did this occur? See n. 2725 to xxi. 69. It was obviously after his arrival in the land of Cannan and after Ismā'īl had grown up to years of discretion. Was it before or after the building of the Ka'ba (ii. 127)? There are no data on which this question can be answered. But we may suppose it was before that event, and that event may itself have been commemorative.

Thou will find me,
If God so wills one
Practising Patience and
Constancy!"

سَتَجِدُنِيٓ إِن شَآءَ ٱللَّهُ
مِنَ ٱلصَّٰبِرِينَ ۝

103. So when they had both[4100]
Submitted their wills (to God),
And he had laid him
Prostrate on his forehead
(For sacrifice),[4101]

١٠٣- فَلَمَّآ أَسۡلَمَا
وَتَلَّهُۥ لِلۡجَبِينِ ۝

104. We called out to him,[4102]
"O Abraham!

١٠٤- وَنَٰدَيۡنَٰهُ أَن يَٰٓإِبۡرَٰهِيمُ ۝

105. "Thou hast already fulfilled
The vision!"—thus indeed
Do We reward
Those who do right.

١٠٥- قَدۡ صَدَّقۡتَ ٱلرُّءۡيَآۚ
إِنَّا كَذَٰلِكَ نَجۡزِي ٱلۡمُحۡسِنِينَ ۝

106. For this was obviously
A trial—

١٠٦- إِنَّ هَٰذَا لَهُوَ ٱلۡبَلَٰٓؤُاْ ٱلۡمُبِينُ ۝

4100. Note that the sacrifice was demanded of *both* Abraham and Ismā'īl. It was a trial of the will of the father and the son. By way of trial the father had the command conveyed to him in a vision. To make sure that it was not an idle dream, and, if it was a real order, to make sure that his son consented, he consulted the son. The son readily consented, and offered to stand true to his promise if his self-sacrifice was really required. The whole thing is symbolical. God does not require the flesh and blood of animals (xxii. 37), much less of human beings. But he does require the giving of our whole being to God, the symbol of which is that we should give up something very dear to us, if Duty requires that sacrifice.

4101. Our version may be compared with the Jewish-Christian version of the present Old Testament. The Jewish tradition, in order to glorify the younger branch of the family, descended from Isaac, ancestor of the Jews, as against the elder branch, descended from Ismā'īl, ancestor of the Arabs, refers this sacrifice to Isaac (Gen. xxii. 1-18). Now Isaac was born when Abraham was 100 years old (Gen. xxi. 5), while Ismā'īl was born to Abraham when Abraham was 86 years old (Gen. xvi. 16). Ismā'īl was therefore 14 years older than Isaac. During his first 14 years Ismā'īl was the *only* son of Abraham; at no time was Isaac the *only* son of Abraham. Yet, in speaking of the sacrifice, the Old Testament says (Gen. xxii. 2): "And He said, Take now thy son, thine *only* son Isaac, whom thou lovest, and get thee into the land of Moriah: and offer him there for a burnt offering..." This slip shows at any rate which was the older version, and how it was overlaid, like the present Jewish records, in the interests of a tribal religion. The "land of Moriah" is not clear: it was three days' journey from Abraham's place (Gen. xxii. 4). There is less warrant for identifying it with the hill of Moriah on which Jerusalem was afterwards built than with the hill of Marwa which is identified with the Arab tradition about Ismā'īl.

4102. In the Biblical version Isaac's consent is not taken; in fact Isaac asks, 'where is the lamb for sacrifice?' and is told that 'God would provide it'. It is a complete human sacrifice like those to Moloch. In our version it is as much a sacrifice by the will of Ismā'īl as by that of Abraham. And in any case it is symbolic: "this was obviously a trial"; "thou hast already fulfilled thy vision"; etc.

107. And We ransomed him
With a momentous sacrifice : [4103]

١٠٧- وَفَدَيْنٰهُ بِذِبْحٍ عَظِيمٍ ۝

108. And We left (this blessing) [4104]
For him among generations
(To come) in later times :

١٠٨- وَتَرَكْنَا عَلَيْهِ فِي الْاٰخِرِيْنَ ۝

109. " Peace and salutation
To Abraham ! "

١٠٩- سَلٰمٌ عَلٰٓى اِبْرٰهِيْمَ ۝

110. Thus indeed do We reward
Those who do right

١١٠- كَذٰلِكَ نَجْزِي الْمُحْسِنِيْنَ ۝

111. For he was one
Of Our believing Servants.

١١١- اِنَّهٗ مِنْ عِبَادِنَا الْمُؤْمِنِيْنَ ۝

112. And We gave him [4105]
The good news
Of Isaac—a prophet,—
One of the Righteous.

١١٢- وَبَشَّرْنٰهُ
بِاِسْحٰقَ نَبِيًّا مِّنَ الصّٰلِحِيْنَ ۝

113. We blessed him and Isaac :
But of their progeny
Are (some) that do right,
And (some) that obviously [4106]
Do wrong, to their own souls.

١١٣- وَبٰرَكْنَا عَلَيْهِ وَعَلٰٓى اِسْحٰقَ
وَمِنْ ذُرِّيَّتِهِمَا مُحْسِنٌ وَّظَالِمٌ
لِّنَفْسِهٖ مُبِيْنٌ ۝ ع

Section 4.

114. Again, (of old,)
We bestowed Our favour

١١٤- وَلَقَدْ مَنَنَّا

4103. The adjective qualifying " sacrifice " here, *'aẓīm*, (great, momentous) may be understood both in a literal and a figurative sense. In a literal sense it implies that a fine sheep or ram was substituted symbolically. The figurative sense is even more important. It was indeed a great and momentous occasion, when two men, with concerted will, " ranged themselves in the ranks " of those to whom self-sacrifice in the service of God was the supreme thing in life. This was a type of the service which Imām Ḥusain performed, many ages later, in 60 A.H., as I have explained in a separate pamphlet. But note that the ransom, *i.e.*, the commutation of sacrifice, was made not by the men, but by God. God wants our will and devotion, not necessarily our lives *in a physical sense.* He will find means, if we offer ourselves, to use us not for our destruction, but for our further advancement. In this sense, said Jesus, " he that loseth his life for my sake shall find it " (Matt. x. 39).

4104. *Cf.* above, xxxvii. 78-81 and n. 4083.

4105 Isaac was Abraham's second son, born of Sarah, when Abraham was 100 years of age. See n. 4101 above. He was also blessed and became the ancestor of the Jewish people. See next note.

4106. So long as the Children of Israel upheld the righteous banner of God, they enjoyed God's blessing, and their history is a portion of sacred history. When they fell from grace, they did not stop God's Plan : they injured their own souls.

On Moses and Aaron,[4107]

عَلٰى مُوسٰى وَهٰرُونَ ۝

115. And We delivered them
And their people from
(Their) Great Calamity ;[4108]

١١٥- وَنَجَّيْنٰهُمَا
وَقَوْمَهُمَا مِنَ الْكَرْبِ الْعَظِيمِ ۝

116. And We helped them,
So they overcame
(their troubles);[4109]

١١٦- وَنَصَرْنٰهُمْ فَكَانُوا هُمُ الْغٰلِبِينَ ۝

117. And We gave them
The Book which helps[4110]
To make things clear ;

١١٧- وَاٰتَيْنٰهُمَا الْكِتٰبَ الْمُسْتَبِينَ ۝

118. And We guided them
To the Straight Way.

١١٨- وَهَدَيْنٰهُمَا الصِّرَاطَ الْمُسْتَقِيمَ ۝

119. And We left (this blessing)[4111]
For them among generations
(To come) in later times:

١١٩- وَتَرَكْنَا عَلَيْهِمَا فِي الْاٰخِرِينَ ۝

120. "Peace and salutation
To Moses and Aaron!"

١٢٠- سَلٰمٌ عَلٰى مُوسٰى وَهٰرُونَ ۝

121. Thus indeed do We reward
Those who do right.

١٢١- اِنَّا كَذٰلِكَ نَجْزِي الْمُحْسِنِينَ ۝

122. For they were two
Of Our believing Servants.

١٢٢- اِنَّهُمَا مِنْ عِبَادِنَا الْمُؤْمِنِينَ ۝

4107. The story of Moses is told in numerous passages of the Qur-ān. The passages most illustrative of the present passage will be found in xxviii. 4 (oppression of the Israelites in Egypt) and xx. 77-79 (the Israelites triumphant over their enemies when the latter were drowned in the Red Sea).

4108. What could have been a greater calamity to them than that they should have been held in slavery by the Egyptians, that their male children should have been killed and their female children should have been saved alive for the Egyptians?

4109. The Israelites were delivered by three steps mentioned in verses 114, 115, and 116 respectively; but the consummation of God's favour on them was (verses 117-118) the Revelation given to them, which guided them on the Straight Way, so long as they preserved the Revelation intact and followed its precepts. The three steps were: (1) the divine commission to Moses and Aaron; (2) the deliverance from bondage; and (3) the triumphant crossing of the Red Sea and the destruction of Pharaoh's army.

4110. *Mustabīn* has a slightly different force from *Mubīn*. I have translated the former by "which *helps* to make things clear", and the latter by "which makes things clear",—apt descriptions as applied to the Taurāt and the Qur-ān.

4111. See above, xxxvii. 78-81 and n. 4083.

123. So also was Elias[4112]
Among those sent (by Us).

١٢٣- وَإِنَّ إِلْيَاسَ لَمِنَ الْمُرْسَلِينَ ۝

124. Behold, he said
To his people,
"Will ye not fear (God)?

١٢٤- إِذْ قَالَ لِقَوْمِهِ
أَلَا تَتَّقُونَ ۝

125. "Will ye call upon Baal[4113]
And forsake the Best
Of Creators,—

١٢٥- أَتَدْعُونَ بَعْلًا
وَتَذَرُونَ أَحْسَنَ الْخَالِقِينَ ۝

126. "God, your Lord and Cherisher
And the Lord and Cherisher
Of your fathers of old?"

١٢٦- اللَّهَ رَبَّكُمْ
وَرَبَّ آبَائِكُمُ الْأَوَّلِينَ ۝

127. But they rejected him,[4114]
And they will certainly
Be called up (for punishment),—

١٢٧- فَكَذَّبُوهُ فَإِنَّهُمْ لَمُحْضَرُونَ ۝

128. Except the sincere and devoted
Servants of God (among them).

١٢٨- إِلَّا عِبَادَ اللَّهِ الْمُخْلَصِينَ ۝

129. And We left (this blessing)[4115]
For him among generations
(To come) in later times:

١٢٩- وَتَرَكْنَا عَلَيْهِ فِي الْآخِرِينَ ۝

130. "Peace and salutation
To such as Elias!"[4115-A]

١٣٠- سَلَامٌ عَلَىٰ إِلْ يَاسِينَ ۝

4112. See n. 905 to vi. 85. Elias is the same as Elijah, whose story will be found in the Old Testament in 1 Kings xvii-xix, and 2 Kings i-ii. Elijah lived in the reign of Ahab (B.C. 896-874) and Ahaziah (B.C. 874-872), kings of the (northern) kingdom of Israel or Samaria. He was a prophet of the desert, like John the Baptist,—unlike our holy Prophet, who took part in, controlled, and guided all the affairs of his people. Both Ahab and Azariah were prone to lapse into the worship of Baal, the sun-god worshipped in Syria. That worship also included the worship of nature-powers and procreative powers, as in the Indian worship of the Lingam, and led to many abuses. King Ahab had married a princess of Sidon, Jezebel, a wicked woman who led her husband to forsake God and adopt Baal-worship. Elijah denounced all Ahab's sins as well as the sins of Ahaziah and had to flee for his life. Eventually, according to the Old Testament (2 Kings, ii-11) he was taken up in a whirlwind to heaven in a chariot of fire after he had left his mantle with Elisha the prophet.

4113. For Baal-worship see last note.

4114. They persecuted him and he had to flee for his life. Eventually he disappeared mysteriously: see n. 4112.

4115. See above, xxxvii. 78-81, and n. 4083.

4115-A. *Ilyāsīn* may be an alternative form of *Ilyās*: *Cf.* Sainâa (xxiii. 20) and *Sīnīn* (xcv. 2). Or it may be the plural of *Ilyās*, meaning "such people as Ilyās"

131. Thus indeed do We reward Those who do right.	١٣١- إِنَّا كَذَٰلِكَ نَجْزِي الْمُحْسِنِينَ ○
132. For he was one Of Our believing Servants.	١٣٢- إِنَّهُ مِنْ عِبَادِنَا الْمُؤْمِنِينَ ○
133. So also was Lūṭ[4116] Among those sent (by Us).	١٣٣- وَإِنَّ لُوطًا لَّمِنَ الْمُرْسَلِينَ ○
134. Behold, We delivered him And his adherents, all	١٣٤- إِذْ نَجَّيْنَٰهُ وَأَهْلَهُۥٓ أَجْمَعِينَ ○
135. Except an old woman Who was among those Who lagged behind:[4117]	١٣٥- إِلَّا عَجُوزًا فِي الْغَٰبِرِينَ ○
136. Then We destroyed The rest.	١٣٦- ثُمَّ دَمَّرْنَا الْآخَرِينَ ○
137. Verily, ye pass[4118] By their (sites), By day—	١٣٧- وَإِنَّكُمْ لَتَمُرُّونَ عَلَيْهِم مُّصْبِحِينَ ○
138. And by night: Will ye not understand?	١٣٨- وَبِالَّيْلِ ۗ أَفَلَا تَعْقِلُونَ ○ ع

C. 199.—So was it also with Jonah; he had
(xxxvii. 139-182.) His trials, but God had mercy on him,
And his mission was successful. How
Can men ascribe to God qualities
And relations derogatory to His nature?
High is He above all creatures.
The ranks of angels and apostles stand firm
In His service. Evil is sure to be overcome.
So Praise and Glory to God, the Lord
Of Honour and Power, and Peace to His apostles!

4116. The best illustration of this passage about Lūṭ will be found in vii. 80-84. He was an apostle sent to Sodom and Gomorrah, Cities of the Plain, by the Dead Sea. The inhabitants were given over to abominable crimes, against which he preached. They insulted him and threatened to expel him. But God in His mercy saved him and his family (with one exception, see the following note), and then destroyed the Cities.

4117. *Cf.* vii. 83, and n. 1051. Lot's wife had no faith: she lagged behind, and perished in the general ruin.

4118. *Cf.* xv. 76, and n. 1998. The tract where they lay is situated on the highway to Syria where the Arab caravans travelled regularly, "by day and by night". Could not future generations learn wisdom from the destruction of those who did wrong?

SECTION 5.

139. So also was Jonah[4119]
Among those sent (by Us).

١٣٩- وَإِنَّ يُونُسَ لَمِنَ الْمُرْسَلِينَ ۝

140. When he ran away
(Like a slave from captivity)[4120]
To the ship (fully) laden,

١٤٠- إِذْ أَبَقَ إِلَى الْفُلْكِ الْمَشْحُونِ ۝

141. He (agreed to) cast lots,[4121]
And he was condemned:

١٤١- فَسَاهَمَ فَكَانَ مِنَ الْمُدْحَضِينَ ۝

142. Then the big Fish[4122]
Did swallow him,
And he had done[4123]
Acts worthy of blame.

١٤٢- فَالْتَقَمَهُ الْحُوتُ
وَهُوَ مُلِيمٌ ۝

143. Had it not been
That he (repented and)
Glorified God,[4124]

١٤٣- فَلَوْلَا أَنَّهُ كَانَ مِنَ الْمُسَبِّحِينَ ۝

144. He would certainly have
Remained inside the Fish[4125]
Till the Day of Resurrection.

١٤٤- لَلَبِثَ فِي بَطْنِهِ إِلَى يَوْمِ يُبْعَثُونَ ۝

4119. For illustrative passages, see xxi. 87-88, n. 2744, and lxviii. 48-50. Jonah's mission was to the city of Nineveh, then steeped in wickedness. He was rejected and he denounced God's wrath on them, but they repented and obtained God's forgiveness. But Jonah "departed in wrath" (xxi. 87), forgetting that God has Mercy as well as forgiveness. See the notes following. *Cf.* x. 98, n. 1478.

4120. Jonah ran away from Nineveh like a slave from captivity. He should have stuck to his post and merged his own will in God's Will. He was hasty, and went off to take a ship. As if he could escape from God's Plan!

4121. The ship was fully laden and met foul weather. The sailors, according to their superstition, wanted to find out who was responsible for the ill-luck: a fugitive slave would cause such ill-luck. The lot fell on Jonah, and he was cast off.

4122. The rivers of Mesopotamia have some huge fishes. The word used here is *Ḥūt*, which may be a fish or perhaps a crocodile. If it were in an open northern sea, it might be a whale. The locality is not mentioned: in the Old Testament he is said to have taken ship in the port of Joppa (now Jaffa) in the Mediterranean (Jonah, i. 3), which would be not less than 600 miles from Nineveh. The Tigris river, mentioned by some of our Commentators, is more likely, and it contains some fishes of extraordinary size.

4123. See n. 4120.

4124. "But he cried through the depths of darkness, 'There is no god but Thee: glory to Thee! I was indeed wrong!'" (xxi. 87.)

4125. This is just the idiom. This was to be the burial and the grave of Jonah. If he had not repented, he could not have got out of the body of the creature that had swallowed him, until the Day of Resurrection, when all the dead would be raised up.

145. But We cast him forth
On the naked shore
In a state of sickness,[4126]

١٤٥- فَنَبَذْنَٰهُ بِٱلْعَرَآءِ وَهُوَ سَقِيمٌ ۝

146. And We caused to grow,
Over him, a spreading plant
Of the Gourd kind.

١٤٦- وَأَنۢبَتْنَا عَلَيْهِ شَجَرَةً مِّن يَقْطِينٍ ۝

147. And We sent him
(On a mission)
To a hundred thousand[4127]
(Men) or more.

١٤٧- وَأَرْسَلْنَٰهُ إِلَىٰ مِا۟ئَةِ أَلْفٍ أَوْ يَزِيدُونَ ۝

148. And they believed;
So We permitted them
To enjoy (their life)[4128]
For a while.

١٤٨- فَـَٔامَنُوا۟ فَمَتَّعْنَٰهُمْ إِلَىٰ حِينٍ ۝

149. Now ask them their opinion:[4129]
Is it that thy Lord
Has (only) daughters, and they
Have sons?—

١٤٩- فَٱسْتَفْتِهِمْ أَلِرَبِّكَ ٱلْبَنَاتُ وَلَهُمُ ٱلْبَنُونَ ۝

150. Or that We created
The angels female, and they
Are witnesses (thereto)?

١٥٠- أَمْ خَلَقْنَا ٱلْمَلَٰٓئِكَةَ إِنَٰثًا وَهُمْ شَٰهِدُونَ ۝

151. Is it not that they
Say, from their own invention,

١٥١- أَلَآ إِنَّهُم مِّنْ إِفْكِهِمْ لَيَقُولُونَ ۝

4126. *Cf.* xxxvii. 89 above. His strange situation might well have caused him to be ill. He wanted fresh air and solitude. He got both in the open plain, and the abundantly shady Gourd Plant or some fruitful tree like it gave him both shade and sustenance. The Gourd is a creeper that can spread over any roof or ruined structure.

4127. The city of Nineveh was a very large city. The Old Testament says: "Nineveh was an exceeding great city of three days' journey" (Jonah, iii. 3); "wherein are more than six score thousand persons" (Jonah, iv. 11). In other words its circuit was about 45 miles, and its population was over a hundred and twenty thousand inhabitants.

4128. They repented and believed, and Nineveh got a new lease of life. For the dates to which Jonah may be referred, and the vicissitudes of the City's history as the seat of the Assyrian Empire, see notes 1478-79 to x. 98.

The lessons from Jonah's story are: (1) that no man should take upon himself to judge of God's wrath or God's mercy; (2) that nevertheless God forgives true repentance, whether in a righteous man, or in a wicked city; and (3) that God's Plan will always prevail, and can never be defeated.

4129. We begin a new argument here. The Pagan Arabs called angels daughters of God. They themselves were ashamed of having daughters, and preferred to have sons, to add to their power and dignity. See xvi. 57-59, and n. 2082. Yet they invented daughters for God!

152. "God has begotten children"?[4130]
But they are liars!

١٥٢- وَلَدَ اللّٰهُ ۙ وَاِنَّهُمْ لَكٰذِبُوْنَ ○

153. Did He (then) choose[4131]
Daughters rather than sons?

١٥٣- اَصْطَفَى الْبَنَاتِ عَلَى الْبَنِيْنَ ؕ ○

154. What is the matter
With you? How judge ye?

١٥٤- مَا لَكُمْ ۟ كَيْفَ تَحْكُمُوْنَ ○

155. Will ye not then
Receive admonition?

١٥٥- اَفَلَا تَذَكَّرُوْنَ ۚ ○

156. Or have ye
An authority manifest?

١٥٦- اَمْ لَكُمْ سُلْطٰنٌ مُّبِيْنٌ ۙ ○

157. Then bring ye your Book
(Of authority) if ye be
Truthful!

١٥٧- فَاْتُوْا بِكِتٰبِكُمْ
اِنْ كُنْتُمْ صٰدِقِيْنَ ○

158. And they have invented
A blood-relationship[4132]
Between Him and the Jinns:
But the Jinns know
(Quite well) that they
Have indeed to appear
(Before His Judgment-seat)!

١٥٨- وَجَعَلُوْا بَيْنَهٗ وَبَيْنَ الْجِنَّةِ نَسَبًا ؕ
وَلَقَدْ عَلِمَتِ الْجِنَّةُ
اِنَّهُمْ لَمُحْضَرُوْنَ ○

159. Glory to God! (He is free)
From the things they ascribe
(To Him)!

١٥٩- سُبْحٰنَ اللّٰهِ
عَمَّا يَصِفُوْنَ ۙ ○

160. Not (so do) the Servants
Of God, sincere and devoted.[4133]

١٦٠- اِلَّا عِبَادَ اللّٰهِ الْمُخْلَصِيْنَ ○

4130. Any attribution to God of ideas derogatory to His Oneness and His supreme height above all creatures is likely to degrade our own conception of God's Universal plan, and is condemned in the strongest terms.

4131. There is the strongest irony in this passage.

4132. The angels are at least pure beings engaged in the service of God. But the Pagan superstitions not only connect them with God as daughters but even connect God by relationship with all kinds of spirits, good or evil! In some mythologies the most evil powers are gods or goddesses as if they belonged to the family of God the Creator and had some semblance of equality with Him! This, too, is repudiated in the strongest terms.

For Jinns see n. 929 to vi. 100.

4133. Those sincere in devotion to God never ascribe such degrading ideas to God.

161. For, verily, neither ye
Nor those ye worship—

١٦١- فَإِنَّكُمْ وَمَا تَعْبُدُونَ ۝

162. Can lead (any)[4134]
Into temptation
Concerning God,

١٦٢- مَا أَنتُمْ عَلَيْهِ بِفَاتِنِينَ ۝

163. Except such as are
(Themselves) going to
The blazing Fire!

١٦٣- إِلَّا مَنْ هُوَ صَالِ الْجَحِيمِ ۝

164. (Those ranged in ranks say):[4135]
" Not one of us but has
A place appointed ;

١٦٤- وَمَا مِنَّا إِلَّا لَهُ مَقَامٌ مَّعْلُومٌ ۝

165. " And we are verily
Ranged in ranks (for service);

١٦٥- وَإِنَّا لَنَحْنُ الصَّافُّونَ ۝

166. " And we are verily those
Who declare (God's) glory ! "

١٦٦- وَإِنَّا لَنَحْنُ الْمُسَبِّحُونَ ۝

167. And there were those[4136]
Who said,

١٦٧- وَإِن كَانُوا لَيَقُولُونَ ۝

168. " If only we had had
Before us a Message
From those of old,

١٦٨- لَوْ أَنَّ عِندَنَا
ذِكْرًا مِّنَ الْأَوَّلِينَ ۝

169. " We should certainly have
Been Servants of God,[4137]
Sincere (and devoted) ! "

١٦٩- لَكُنَّا عِبَادَ اللَّهِ الْمُخْلَصِينَ ۝

4134. Evil has no power over faith, truth, and sincerity. Such power as it has is over those who deliberately put themselves in the way of Destruction. It is their own will that leads them astray. If they were fortified against Evil by Faith, Patience, and Constancy, Evil would have no power to hurt them. God would protect them.

4135. To round off the argument of the Sūra we go back to the idea with which it began. Those who range themselves in ranks for the united service of God (see above, xxxvii. 1 and n. 4031)—whether angels or men of God—are content to keep their ranks and do whatever service is assigned to them. It is not for them to question God's Plan, because they know that it is good and that it will ultimately triumph. Any seeming delays or defeats do not worry them. Nor do they ever break their ranks.

4136. There were the sceptics or Unbelievers,—primarily the Pagan Arabs, but in a more extended sense, all who doubt God's providence or revelation.

4137. Such men take refuge in ancestral tradition. 'If our forefathers had had an inkling of Revelation or miracles, or had worshipped as we are now taught to worship, we should gladly have accepted. Or if they had had anything of the miracles which other nations of old are said to have received, we could then have accepted.' But now stronger and more convincing proofs have come to them in the Qur-ān in their own tongue, and they doubt and reject it.

170. But (now that the Qur-ān
Has come), they reject it :
But soon will they know ![4138]

١٧٠- فَكَفَرُوا بِهِ فَسَوْفَ يَعْلَمُونَ ○

171. Already has Our Word
Been passed before (this)
To Our Servants sent (by Us),

١٧١- وَلَقَدْ سَبَقَتْ كَلِمَتُنَا
لِعِبَادِنَا الْمُرْسَلِينَ ○

172. That they would certainly
Be assisted,

١٧٢- إِنَّهُمْ لَهُمُ الْمَنْصُورُونَ ○

173. And that Our forces,—[4139]
They surely must conquer.

١٧٣- وَإِنَّ جُنْدَنَا لَهُمُ الْغٰلِبُونَ ○

174. So turn thou away[4140]
From them for a little while,

١٧٤- فَتَوَلَّ عَنْهُمْ حَتّٰى حِينٍ ○

175. And watch them (how[4141]
They fare), and they soon
Shall see (how thou farest) !

١٧٥- وَأَبْصِرْهُمْ فَسَوْفَ يُبْصِرُونَ ○

176. Do they wish (indeed)[4142]
To hurry on our Punishment ?

١٧٦- أَفَبِعَذَابِنَا يَسْتَعْجِلُونَ ○

177. But when it descends
Into the open space[4143]
Before them, evil will be
The morning for those who
Were warned (and heeded not) !

١٧٧- فَإِذَا نَزَلَ بِسَاحَتِهِمْ
فَسَاءَ صَبَاحُ الْمُنْذَرِينَ ○

4138. God's Truth will manifest itself against all odds, and the whole world will see.

4139. The victory will be the victory of God's Truth by the forces of God, but every soldier in the army of Truth, who has done his duty, will be entitled to claim a share in the victory.

4140. Addressed in the first instance to the holy Prophet, but good for all time. He was not to be discouraged by his initial failures. Soon came victory to him from God. So is it always in the struggles of truth and righteousness. The righteous can afford to ignore opposition, confident in the strength which comes from the Grace of God.

4141. Watch and wait, for the Right must come to its own.

4142 The last verse enjoined Patience under the attacks of Evil, in the knowledge that evil must be conquered at last. Evil may perhaps turn back scoffingly and say, 'If a punishment is to come, why not bring it on now ?' Why indeed ? The answer is : when it comes, it will come like a rush by night when the enemy is overpowered, when he least expects it : when the day dawns, it is a sorry plight in which the enemy finds himself. *Cf.* xxii. 47, and n. 2826 ; and xxvi. 204, n. 3230.

4143. See last note. The parable is that of an enemy camp in a plain, which is surprised and destroyed by a night attack from the hills. Evil is the plight of any survivors in the morning. Their regrets will be all the more poignant if they had had some sort of a warning beforehand and had paid no heed to it !

178. So turn thou away [4144] From them for a little while,	١٧٨- وَتَوَلَّ عَنْهُمْ حَتّٰى حِيْنٍ ۝
179. And watch (how they fare) And they soon shall see (How thou farest)!	١٧٩- وَّاَبْصِرْ فَسَوْفَ يُبْصِرُوْنَ ۝
180. Glory to thy Lord, [4145] The Lord of Honour And Power! (He is free) From what they ascribe (To Him)!	١٨٠- سُبْحٰنَ رَبِّكَ رَبِّ الْعِزَّةِ عَمَّا يَصِفُوْنَ ۝
181. And Peace on the apostles!	١٨١- وَسَلٰمٌ عَلَى الْمُرْسَلِيْنَ ۝
182. And Praise to God, The Lord and Cherisher Of the Worlds.	١٨٢- وَالْحَمْدُ لِلّٰهِ رَبِّ الْعٰلَمِيْنَ ۝

4144. This and the following verse repeat verses 174-75 (with a slight verbal alteration). The argument in verses 176-77 brought in a new point. When that is finished, the repetition carries us back to the main argument, and rounds off the whole Sūra.

4145. This and the following two verses recapitulate: (1) Glory, Honour, and Power belong to God; (2) No one is equal to Him; (3) He sends apostles and revelations, and His aid will overcome all obstacles; for (4) He loves and cherishes all His Creation.

INTRODUCTION TO SŪRA XXXVIII (*Ṣād*).

For the place of this Sūra in the series of six, dealing with some of the mysteries of the spiritual world, see Introduction to S. xxxiv.

This Sūra, both in chronology and subject-matter, is cognate to S.xxxvii., and carries forward the same argument. But here the emphasis is laid on the working of earthly power when combined with spiritual power, and it is pointed out how much more significant (and real) spiritual power is. For this reason the illustrative stories are mainly those of David and Solomon who were kings as well as prophets, and a parallel is suggested with the unfolding public life of our holy Prophet.

Summary.—Worldly and evil men are surprised at the renewal of Truth and Righteousness; but righteousness has more power than worldly strength, as is seen in the story of kings like David, who had both (xxxviii. 1-26, and C. 200).

So also Solomon loved the Lord more than worldly power, which may be good but may be misused by evil men; so also Job and other men of power and insight, chose the path of final bliss rather than final misery (xxxviii. 27-64, and C. 201).

So also in the case of the final Messenger: his Gospel of Unity must triumph over all Jealousy and Arrogance in God's good time (xxxviii. 65-88, and C. 202).

C. 200.—Self-glory and Separatism, these
(xxxviii. 1-26.) Are among the roots of Evil, also Envy
And Suspicion. Not all the combinations
Of Evil can for a moment reverse
God's Purpose or His Justice. David,
Endowed with worldly Power and the Virtues,
Had yet to purge himself of the thought
Of Self-glory, which he did; and thus
He became one of those nearest to God.

Sūra XXXVIII.

Ṣād (being one of the Abbreviated Letters).

In the name of God, Most Gracious, Most Merciful.

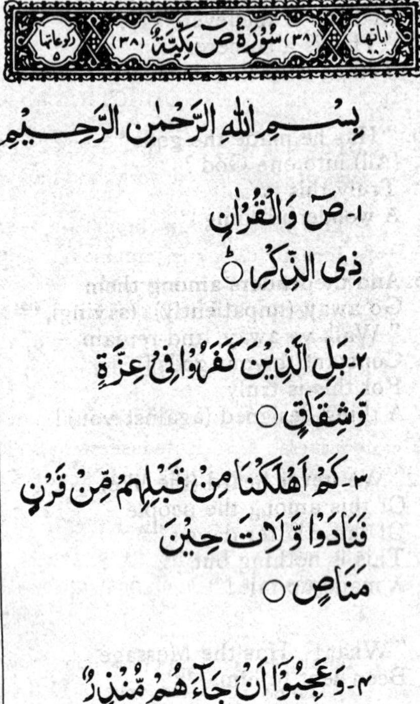

1. Ṣād:[4146]
By the Qur-ān,
Full of Admonition:[4147]
(This is the Truth).

2. But the Unbelievers
(Are steeped) in Self-glory[4148]
And Separatism.

3. How many generations
Before them did We destroy?
In the end they cried[4149]
(For mercy)—when
There was no longer time
For being saved!

4. So they wonder
That a Warner has come

4146. Ṣād is a letter of the Arabic alphabet. It is used here as an Abbreviated Letter, for which see Appendix I (at the end of Sūra ii.). See also the second para. of n. 989 to vii. 1 for this particular letter. No dogmatism is permissible in trying to interpret Abbreviated Letters. But it is suggested that it may stand for *Qiṣaṣ* ("Stories"), in which the dominant consonant is *ṣ*. For this Sūra is concerned mainly with the stories of David and Solomon as illustrative of the relative positions of spiritual and worldly power. Sale's note: "it may stand for Solomon": is a real howler: for in Arabic the letter Ṣād does not occur at all in the name of Solomon.

4147. *Full of admonition*: the word *ẓikr* is far more comprehensive than any single word or phrase that I can think of in English: it implies (1) remembrance in a spirit of reverence; (2) recital, celebrating the praises of God; (3) teaching, admonition, warning; (4) Message, Revelation, as in *Ah-luẓ-ẓikr*, "those who possess the Message" (xvi. 43, and n. 2069). In Ṣūfi phraseology it implies mystical enlightenment, both the aspiration and the attainment, for in the highest spiritual atmosphere, the two are one. Devotional exercises are also called *ẓikr*, with reference to meaning (2) above.

4148. The great root of Evil and Unbelief is Self-glory or Arrogance, as is pointed out in several places with regard to Satan: *cf.* below, xxxviii. 74-76. This leads to Envy and Separatism, or a desire to start a peculiar doctrine or sect of one's own, instead of a desire to find common grounds of belief and life, which lead to the Religion of Unity in God. This teaching of Unity was what the Pagans objected to in the holy Prophet (verse 5 below)!

4149. Teaching, Warning, Signs have been given by God to all nations and at all times, and yet nations have rebelled and gone wrong and suffered destruction. If only later generations could learn that wrong-doing results in self-destruction! For the justice of God merely carries out the result of their own choice and actions. At any time during their probation they could repent and obtain mercy, but their "Self-glory and Separatism" stand in the way. Ultimately they do cry for a way of escape, but it is then too late.

To them from among themselves ![4150]
And the Unbelievers say,
" This is a sorcerer
Telling lies !

مِّنْهُمْ ۖ وَقَالَ الْكَٰفِرُونَ
هَٰذَا سَٰحِرٌ كَذَّابٌ ۝

5. " Has he made the gods[4151]
(All) into one God ?
Truly this is
A wonderful thing ! "

٥- أَجَعَلَ الْآلِهَةَ إِلَٰهًا وَاحِدًا ۖ
إِنَّ هَٰذَا لَشَيْءٌ عُجَابٌ ۝

6. And the leaders among them
Go away (impatiently), (saying),[4152]
" Walk ye away, and remain
Constant to your gods !
For this is truly
A thing designed (against you) !

٦- وَانْطَلَقَ الْمَلَأُ مِنْهُمْ
أَنِ امْشُوا وَاصْبِرُوا عَلَىٰ آلِهَتِكُمْ ۖ
إِنَّ هَٰذَا لَشَيْءٌ يُرَادُ ۝

7. " We never heard (the like)
Of this among the people
Of these latter days :[4153]
This is nothing but
A made-up tale ! "

٧- مَا سَمِعْنَا بِهَٰذَا فِي الْمِلَّةِ الْآخِرَةِ ۖ
إِنْ هَٰذَا إِلَّا اخْتِلَاقٌ ۝

8. " What ! Has the Message
Been sent to him—[4154]

٨- أَأُنْزِلَ عَلَيْهِ الذِّكْرُ

4150. Their wonder is only stimulated. They are full of envy and spite against one of themselves who has been chosen by God to be His Messenger, and they vent their spite by making all sorts of false accusations. The man who was pre-eminent for truth and conscientious consideration, they call " a sorcerer and a liar " !

4151. And what is the offence of the Apostle of Unity ? That he has made all their fantastic gods disappear ; that in place of chaos he has brought harmony ; that in place of conflict he brings peace ! It *is* a wonderful thing, but not in the sarcastic sense in which the Unbelievers scoff at it !

4152. When the message of Islam was being preached in its infancy, and the Preacher and his followers were being persecuted by the Pagans, one of the devices adopted by the Pagan leaders was to get the Prophet's uncle Abū Ṭālib to denounce or renounce his beloved nephew. A conference was held with Abū Ṭālib for this purpose. On its failure the leaders walked away, and began to discredit the great movement by falsely giving out that it was designed against their personal influence, and to throw power into the hands of the Prophet. Ḥadhrat 'Umar's conversion occurred in the sixth year of the Mission (seventh year before the Hijrat). The circumstances connected with it (see Introduction to S. xx.) greatly alarmed the Quraish chiefs, who, greedy of autocracy themselves, confused the issue by accusing the righteous Preacher of plotting against their power.

4153. ' Whatever may have been the case in the past ', they said, ' our own immediate ancestors worshipped these idols in Mecca, and why should we give them up ? ' Self-complacency was stronger with them than Truth ; and so they call Truth " a made-up tale " ! Some Commentators interpret *millat ākhirat* to refer to the last religion preached before Islam, *viz.* Christianity, which had itself departed from Monotheism to Trinity, but the Pagan Arabs had little love for Christianity and could not have used these terms for it.

4154. Here comes in envy. ' If a Message had to come, why should it come to him, the orphan son of 'Abdullāh, and not to one of our own great men ? '

(Of all persons) among us?"... But they are in doubt Concerning My (own) Message![4155] Nay, they have not yet Tasted My Punishment!	مِنۢ بَيۡنِنَا ۚ بَلۡ هُمۡ فِي شَكّٖ مِّن ذِكۡرِيۚ بَل لَّمَّا يَذُوقُواْ عَذَابِ ۝
9. Or have they the Treasures Of the Mercy of thy Lord,—[4156] The Exalted in Power, The Grantor of Bounties Without measure?	٩- أَمۡ عِندَهُمۡ خَزَآئِنُ رَحۡمَةِ رَبِّكَ ٱلۡعَزِيزِ ٱلۡوَهَّابِ ۝
10. Or have they the dominion Of the heavens and the earth And all between? If so, Let them mount up[4157] With the ropes and means (To reach that end)!	١٠- أَمۡ لَهُم مُّلۡكُ ٱلسَّمَٰوَٰتِ وَٱلۡأَرۡضِ وَمَا بَيۡنَهُمَاۖ فَلۡيَرۡتَقُواْ فِي ٱلۡأَسۡبَٰبِ ۝
11. But there—will be[4158] Put to flight even a host Of confederates.	١١- جُندٞ مَّا هُنَالِكَ مَهۡزُومٞ مِّنَ ٱلۡأَحۡزَابِ ۝
12. Before them (were many Who) rejected apostles,—[4159] The People of Noah, And 'Ād, and Pharaoh The Lord of Stakes,[4160]	١٢- كَذَّبَتۡ قَبۡلَهُمۡ قَوۡمُ نُوحٖ وَعَادٞ وَفِرۡعَوۡنُ ذُو ٱلۡأَوۡتَادِ ۝

4155. They have no clear idea of how God's Message comes! It is not a worldly thing to be given to any one. It is a divine thing requiring spiritual preparation. If they close their eyes to it now, it will be brought home to them when they taste the consequences of their folly!

4156. If they set themselves to judge God, have they anything to show. comparable to God's Mercy and Power? He has both in infinite measure. Who are they to question the grant of His Mercy and Revelation to His own Chosen One?

4157. Weak and puny creatures though they are, they dare to raise their heads against the Omnipotent, as if they had dominion over Creation and not He! If they had any power, let them mount up to heaven and use all the means they have to that end, and see how they can frustrate God's Purpose!

4158. Of course they cannot frustrate God's Purpose. In that world—the spiritual world—they will be ignominiously routed, even if they form the strongest confederacy of the Powers of Evil that ever could combine. *Cf.* the last clause of verse 13 below.

4159. In their day, Noah's contemporaries, or the 'Ād and the Thamūd, so frequently mentioned, or Pharaoh the mighty king of Egypt, or the people to whom Lot was sent (*cf.* xxxvii. 75-82; vii. 65-73; vii. 103-137; vii. 80-84) were examples of arrogance and rebellion against God: they rejected the divine Message brought by their apostles, and they all came to an evil end. Will not their posterity learn their lesson?

4160. The title of Pharaoh, "Lord of the Stakes", denotes power and arrogance, in all or any of the following ways: (1) the stake makes a tent firm and stable, and is a symbol of firmness and stability; (2) many stakes mean a large camp and a numerous army to fight; (3) impaling with stakes was a cruel punishment resorted to by the Pharaohs in arrogant pride of power.

13. And <u>Th</u>amūd, and the People
Of Lūṭ, and the Companions [4161]
Of the Wood ;—such were
The Confederates.[4162]

١٣- وَثَمُودُ وَقَوْمُ لُوطٍ وَأَصْحٰبُ لْـَٔيْكَةِ
أُولٰٓئِكَ الْأَحْزَابُ ○

14. Not one (of them) but
Rejected the apostles,
But My Punishment
Came justly and inevitably [4163]
(On them).

١٤- إِنْ كُلٌّ إِلَّا كَذَّبَ الرُّسُلَ
فَحَقَّ عِقَابِ ○ ع

SECTION 2.

15. These (to-day) only wait
For a single mighty Blast,[4164]
Which (when it comes)
Will brook no delay.[4165]

١٥- وَمَا يَنْظُرُ هٰٓؤُلَآءِ إِلَّا صَيْحَةً وَاحِدَةً
مَّا لَهَا مِنْ فَوَاقٍ ○

16. They say : "Our Lord!
Hasten to us our sentence [4166]
(Even) before the Day
Of Account!"

١٦- وَقَالُوا رَبَّنَا عَجِّلْ لَّنَا قِطَّنَا
قَبْلَ يَوْمِ الْحِسَابِ ○

17. Have patience at what they
Say, and remember Our Servant
David, the man of strength : [4167]
For he ever turned (to God).

١٧- اِصْبِرْ عَلٰى مَا يَقُولُونَ وَاذْكُرْ عَبْدَنَا
دَاوٗدَ ذَا الْأَيْدِ إِنَّهٗٓ أَوَّابٌ ○

4161. *Companions of the Wood* : see xv. 78, and n. 2000.

4162. *Cf.* above, verse 11, and n. 4158.

4163. *Cf.* xv. 64, n. 1990 ; and xxii. 18.

4164. *Cf.* xxxvi. 29, and n. 3973.

4165. *Fawāq* : delay, the interval between one milking of a she-camel and another, either to give her a breathing space or to give her young time to suck,—or perhaps the milker to adjust his fingers. Such interval will be quite short. The derived meaning is that when the inevitable just punishment for sin arrives, it will not tarry, but do its work without delay.

4166. *Cf.* xxvi. 204 and n. 3230. Those who do not believe in the Hereafter say ironically : "Let us have our punishment and sentence now : why delay it ?" The last verse and the next verse supply the commentary. As to those who mock, they will find out the truth soon enough, when it is too late for repentance or mercy. As to the men of God, who are mocked, they must wait patiently for God to fulfil His Plan : even men who had worldly strength and power, like David, had to exercise infinite patience when mocked by their contemporaries.

4167. David was a man of exceptional strength, for even as a raw youth, he slew the Philistine giant Goliath. See ii. 249-252, and notes 286-87. Before that fight, he was mocked by his enemies and chidden even by his own elder brother. But he relied upon God, and won through, and afterwards became king.

18\. It was We that made
The hills declare,[4168]
In unison with him,
Our Praises, at eventide
And at break of day,

١٨- إِنَّا سَخَّرْنَا الْجِبَالَ
مَعَهُ يُسَبِّحْنَ
بِالْعَشِيِّ وَالْإِشْرَاقِ ○

19\. And the birds gathered
(In assemblies): all with him
Did turn (to God).[4169]

١٩- وَالطَّيْرَ مَحْشُورَةً ط
كُلٌّ لَهُ أَوَّابٌ ○

20\. We strengthened his kingdom,
And gave him wisdom
And sound judgment [4170]
In speech and decision.

٢٠- وَشَدَدْنَا مُلْكَهُ وَآتَيْنَاهُ الْحِكْمَةَ
وَفَصْلَ الْخِطَابِ ○

21\. Has the Story of
The Disputants reached thee ? [4171]
Behold, they climbed over
The wall of the private chamber ;

٢١- وَهَلْ أَتَاكَ نَبَأُ الْخَصْمِ
إِذْ تَسَوَّرُوا الْمِحْرَابَ ○

22\. When they entered
The presence of David,[4172]
And he was terrified
Of them, they said :
" Fear not : we are two
Disputants, one of whom
Has wronged the other :
Decide now between us
With truth, and treat us not
With unjustice, but guide us
To the even Path .

٢٢- إِذْ دَخَلُوا عَلَىٰ دَاوُدَ
فَفَزِعَ مِنْهُمْ قَالُوا لَا تَخَفْ ج
خَصْمَانِ بَغَىٰ بَعْضُنَا عَلَىٰ بَعْضٍ
فَاحْكُمْ بَيْنَنَا بِالْحَقِّ وَلَا تُشْطِطْ
وَاهْدِنَا إِلَىٰ سَوَاءِ الصِّرَاطِ ○

4168\. See n. 2733 to xxi. 79. All nature sings in unison and celebrates the praises of God. David was given the gift of music and psalmody, and therefore the hills and birds are expressed as singing God's praises in unison with him. The special hours when the hills and groves echo the songs of birds are in the evening and at dawn, when also the birds gather together, for those are respectively their roosting hours and the hours of their concerted flight for the day.

4169\. Note the mutual echo between this verse and verse 17 above. The Arabic *awwāb* is common to both, and it furnishes the rhyme or rhythm of the greater part of the Sūra, thus echoing the main theme: 'Turn to God in Prayer and Praise, for that is more than any worldly power or wisdom.'

4170\. *Cf.* n. 2732 to xxi. 79, for David's sound judgment in decisions ; he could also express himself aptly, as his Psalms bear witness.

4171\. This story or Parable is not found in the Bible, unless the vision here described be considered as equivalent to Nathan's parable in II Samuel, xi. and xii. Baidhāwi would seem to favour that view, but other Commentators reject it. David was a pious man, and he had a well-guarded private chamber (*miḥrāb*) for Prayer and Praise.

4172\. David used to retire to his private chamber at stated times for his devotions. One day, suddenly, his privacy was invaded by two men, who had obtained access by climbing over a wall. David was frightened at the apparition. But they said : " We have come to seek thy justice as king : we are brothers, and we have a quarrel, which we wish thee to decide."

23. "This man is my brother:[4173]
He has nine and ninety
Ewes, and I have (but) one:
Yet he says, 'Commit her
To my care,' and is (moreover)
Harsh to me in speech."

٢٣- إِنَّ هٰذَآ أَخِى
لَهُۥ تِسْعٌ وَّتِسْعُونَ نَعْجَةً وَّلِىَ نَعْجَةٌ وَّاحِدَةٌ
فَقَالَ أَكْفِلْنِيهَا وَعَزَّنِى فِى الْخِطَابِ ○

24. (David) said: "He has
Undoubtedly wronged thee[4174]
In demanding thy (single) ewe
To be added to his (flock
Of) ewes: truly many
Are the Partners (in business)[4175]
Who wrong each other:
Not so do those who believe
And work deeds of righteousness,
And how few are they?"...
And David gathered that we
Had tried him: he asked
Forgiveness of his Lord,[4176]
Fell down, bowing
(In prostration), and turned
(To God in repentance).

٢٤- قَالَ لَقَدْ ظَلَمَكَ
بِسُؤَالِ نَعْجَتِكَ إِلٰى نِعَاجِهٖ
وَإِنَّ كَثِيرًا مِّنَ الْخُلَطَآءِ لَيَبْغِى بَعْضُهُمْ
عَلٰى بَعْضٍ
إِلَّا الَّذِينَ اٰمَنُوا وَعَمِلُوا الصّٰلِحٰتِ
وَقَلِيلٌ مَّا هُمْ
وَظَنَّ دَاوٗدُ أَنَّمَا فَتَنّٰهُ
فَاسْتَغْفَرَ رَبَّهٗ وَخَرَّ رَاكِعًا وَّأَنَابَ ○ السجدة

25. So We forgave him
This (lapse): he enjoyed,
Indeed, a Near Approach to Us,
And a beautiful Place
Of (final) Return.

٢٥- فَغَفَرْنَا لَهٗ ذٰلِكَ
وَإِنَّ لَهٗ عِنْدَنَا لَزُلْفٰى
وَحُسْنَ مَاٰبٍ ○

4173. The brother who was most aggrieved said: "This my brother has a flock of ninety-nine sheep, and I have but one; yet he wants me to give up my one sheep to his keeping; and moreover he is not even fair-spoken. He talks like one meditating mischief, and he has not even the grace to ask as an equal, or one sharing in a business or an inheritance. What shall I do?"

4174. The circumstances were mysterious; the accusation was novel; it was not clear why the unjust brother should also have come with the complainant, risking his life in climbing the wall to evade the guard, and he certainly said nothing. But David was so full of self-complacence and kingly pride that he took them literally, and began to preach about the falsehood and the fraud of men, who should be content with what they have, but who always covet more.

4175. Especially, said David, is it wrong for brothers or men in partnership to take advantage of each other; but how few are the men who are righteous? He had in his mind his own devotion and justice. But lo and behold! the men disappeared as mysteriously as they had come. It was then that David realised that his vision had been a trial or temptation—a test of his moral or spiritual fibre! Great though he was as a king, and just though he was as a judge, the moment that he thought of these things in self-pride, his merit vanished. In himself he was as other men: it was God's grace that gave him wisdom and justice, and he should have been humble in the sight of God.

4176. Judged by ordinary standards, David had done no wrong; he was a good and just king. Judged by the highest standard of those nearest to God (*Muqarrabūn*, lvi. 11), the thought of self-pride and self-righteousness had to be washed off from him by his own act of self-realisation and repentance. This was freely accepted by God, as the next verse shows.

26. O David! We did indeed
Make thee a vicegerent[4177]
On earth : so judge thou
Between men in truth
(and justice):
Nor follow thou the lusts
(Of thy heart), for they will
Mislead thee from the Path[4178]
Of God : for those who
Wander astray from the Path
Of God, is a Penalty Grievous,
For that they forget
The Day of Accoutn.

٢٦- يٰدَاوٗدُ اِنَّا جَعَلْنٰكَ خَلِيْفَةً فِى الْاَرْضِ
فَاحْكُمْ بَيْنَ النَّاسِ بِالْحَقِّ
وَلَا تَتَّبِعِ الْهَوٰى
فَيُضِلَّكَ عَنْ سَبِيْلِ اللّٰهِ
اِنَّ الَّذِيْنَ يَضِلُّوْنَ عَنْ سَبِيْلِ اللّٰهِ
لَهُمْ عَذَابٌ شَدِيْدٌۢ
بِمَا نَسُوْا يَوْمَ الْحِسَابِ ۝

C. 201.—For just ends was the world created.
(xxxviii. 27-64.) Solomon, in the midst of his worldly power
And glory, never forgot God ; nor Job
In the midst of afflictions; nor other men
Of Power and Vision, whose patience and constancy
Brought them nearer to God. So should
All the righteous strive to win
The final Bliss, for truly grievous
Are the woes of Evil in the Final Account.

SECTION 3.

27. Not without purpose did We[4179]
Create heaven and earth
And all between! That
Were the thought of Unbelievers!
But woe to the Unbelievers
Because of the Fire (of Hell)!

٢٧- وَمَا خَلَقْنَا السَّمَآءَ وَالْاَرْضَ وَمَا بَيْنَهُمَا
بَاطِلًا ۭ ذٰلِكَ ظَنُّ الَّذِيْنَ كَفَرُوْا ۚ
فَوَيْلٌ لِّلَّذِيْنَ كَفَرُوْا مِنَ النَّارِ ۝

4177. *Cf.* ii. 30, and n. 47. David's kingly power, and the gifts of wisdom, justice, psalmody, and apostleship were bestowed on him as a trust. These great gifts were not to be a matter of self-glory.

4178. As stated in n. 4171 above, this vision and its moral are nownere to be found in the Bible. Those who think they see a resemblance to the Parable of the prophet Nathan (2 Samuel, xii. 1-12) have nothing to go upon but the mention of the "one ewe" here and the "one little ewe-lamb" in Nathan's Parable. The whole story is here different, and the whole atmosphere is different. The Biblical title given to David, "a man after God's own heart" is refuted by the Bible itself in the scandalous tale of heinous crimes attributed to David in chapters xi. and xii. of 2 Samuel, *viz.* adultery, fraudulent dealing with one of his own servants, and the contriving of his murder. Further, in chapter xiii., we have the story of rapes, incest, and fratricide in David's own household! The fact is that passages like those are mere *chroniques scandaleuses, i.e.*, narratives of scandalous crimes of the grossest character. The Muslim idea of David is that of a man just and upright, endowed with all the virtues, in whom even the least thought of self-elation has to be washed off by repentance and forgiveness. The spiritual lessons here taught soar into the highest regions of mysticism.

4179. *Cf.* iii. 191. Unbelief is the subjective negation of a belief in Order, Beauty, Purpose, and Eternal Life. Unbelief is to Faith as Chaos is to Cosmos, as the Fire of Misery is to the Garden of Bliss.

28. Shall We treat those
Who believe and work deeds[4180]
Of righteousness, the same
As those who do mischief
On earth? Shall We treat
Those who guard against evil,
The same as those who
Turn aside from the right?

٢٨- أَمْ نَجْعَلُ الَّذِينَ آمَنُوا وَعَمِلُوا الصّٰلِحٰتِ
كَالْمُفْسِدِينَ فِي الْأَرْضِ
أَمْ نَجْعَلُ الْمُتَّقِينَ
كَالْفُجَّارِ ○

29. (Here is) a Book which
We have sent down
Unto thee, full of blessings,[4181]
That they may meditate
On its Signs, and that
Men of understanding may
Receive admonition.

٢٩- كِتٰبٌ أَنْزَلْنٰهُ إِلَيْكَ
مُبٰرَكٌ لِيَدَّبَّرُوا آيٰتِهِ
وَلِيَتَذَكَّرَ أُولُوا الْأَلْبٰبِ ○

30. To David We gave
Solomon (for a son),—[4182]
How excellent in Our service!
Ever did he turn (to Us)!

٣٠- وَوَهَبْنَا لِدَاوٗدَ سُلَيْمٰنَ
نِعْمَ الْعَبْدُ إِنَّهٗ أَوَّابٌ ○

31. Behold, there were brought[4183]
Before him, at eventide,
Coursers of the highest breeding,[4184]
And swift of foot;

٣١- إِذْ عُرِضَ عَلَيْهِ بِالْعَشِيِّ
الصّٰفِنٰتُ الْجِيَادُ ○

4180. The reference to the Hereafter at the end of verse 26 above is of a piece with the whole tenor of this Sūra, which deals with the superiority of the spiritual kingdom and the Hereafter. If there were no Hereafter, how could you reconcile the inequalities of this world? Would not the Unbelievers be right in acting as if all Creation and all life were futile? But there *is* a Hereafter and God will not treat the Good and Evil alike. He is just and will fully restore the balance disturbed in this life.

4181. Revelation is not a mere chance or haphazard thing. It is a real blessing—among the greatest that God has bestowed on man. By meditation on it in an earnest spirit man may learn of himself, and his relation to nature around him and to God the Author of all. Men of understanding may, by its help, resolve all genuine doubts that there may be in their minds, and learn the true lessons of spiritual life.

4182. The greatest in this life have yet need of this spiritual blessing: without it all worldly good is futile. Referring back to the story of David, we are now introduced to Solomon, who was a great king but greater still because he served God and turned to Him. The Qur-ān, unlike the Old Testament, represents Solomon as a righteous king, not as an idolater, doing "evil in the sight of the Lord" (1 Kings, xi. 6).

4183. The passages about David and Solomon have been variously interpreted by the Commentators. The versions which I have suggested have good authority behind them, though I have followed my own judgment in filling in the details.

4184. *Ṣāfināt*: literally, horses that stand, when at ease, on three legs, firmly planted, with the hoof of the fourth leg resting lightly on the ground. This would imply breeding and a steady temper, to match with their quality of swiftness mentioned in the next clause.

32. And he said, "Truly
Do I love the love[4185]
Of Good, with a view
To the glory of my Lord,"—
Until (the sun) was hidden
In the veil (of Night): [4186]

٣٢- فَقَالَ إِنِّيٓ أَحْبَبْتُ حُبَّ الْخَيْرِ
عَن ذِكْرِ رَبِّي
حَتَّىٰ تَوَارَتْ بِالْحِجَابِ ○

33. "Bring them back to me."
Then began he to pass[4187]
His hand over (their) legs
And their necks.

٣٣- رُدُّوهَا عَلَيَّ فَطَفِقَ مَسْحًا بِالسُّوقِ
وَالْأَعْنَاقِ ○

34. And We did try[4188]
Solomon: We placed
On his throne a body[4189]
(Without life): but he did turn
(To Us in true devotion):

٣٤- وَلَقَدْ فَتَنَّا سُلَيْمَٰنَ
وَأَلْقَيْنَا عَلَىٰ كُرْسِيِّهِ جَسَدًا
ثُمَّ أَنَابَ ○

35. He said, "O my Lord!
Forgive me,[4190] and grant me[4191]

٣٥- قَالَ رَبِّ اغْفِرْ لِي وَهَبْ لِي

4185. The story is not found in the Old Testament. I interpret it to mean that, like his father David, Solomon was also most meticulous in not allowing the least motive of self to be mixed up with his spiritual virtues. He was fond of horses; he had great armies and wealth; but he used them all in God's service. *Cf.* xxvii. 19, n. 3259; xxvii. 40. n. 3276, etc. His battles were not fought for lust of blood, but as *Jihāds* in the cause of righteousness. His love of horses was not like that of a mere race-goer or of a warrior: there was a spiritual element in it. He loved by a kind of love which was spiritual,—the love of the highest Good.

4186. His review of his fine horses was interrupted by his evening devotions, but he resumed it after his devotions.

4187. Like all lovers of horses, he patted them on their necks and passed his hands over their fore-legs and was proud of having them—not as vanities but as a "lover of Good".

4188. What was the trial of Solomon? All the power, wealth, and glory, which were given to him were a spiritual trial to him. They might have turned another man's head, but he was staunch and true, and while he enjoyed and used all the power he had—over spirits, men, and the forces of nature, (see below), he kept his mind steady to the service of God. *Cf.* viii. 28, where "your possessions and your progeny" are declared to be "but a trial".

4189. "*The body without life*" *on his throne* has been variously interpreted. The interpretation that appeals to me most is that his earthly power, great as it was, was like a body without a soul, unless it was vivified by God's spirit. But Solomon did turn to God in true devotion, and his real power lay there. He did his best to root out idolatry, and he completed the Temple in Jerusalem for the worship of the One True God. *Cf.* his conversion of Bilqis the Queen of Sheba, xxvii. 40, n. 3276. See also vii. 148, where the same word *Jasad* is used in connection with the image of a calf which the Israelites had set up for worship in the absence of Moses. Men may worship worldly Power as they may worship an idol, and there is great temptation in such Power, though Solomon withstood such temptations.

I do not think that a reference to xxxiv. 14 (n. 3808) will fit the context here.

4190. The seeking of worldly Power, even if intended to be used for God's service, has a little of Self in it. It may be quite legitimate and even meritorious in ordinary men, but even the thought of it in a Prophet is to be apologised for. See a similar idea in the case of David explained in n. 4176 to xxxviii. 24 above.

4191. He asked for a Power that *he* would not misuse, though others might not be able to refrain from misusing it,—such as power over forces of nature or forces of violence (see the next three verses).

A Kingdom which,
(It may be), suits not
Another after me:
For Thou art the Grantor [4192]
Of Bounties (without measure).

مُلْكًا
لَّا يَنۢبَغِي لِأَحَدٍ مِّنۢ بَعْدِيٓ
إِنَّكَ أَنتَ ٱلْوَهَّابُ ۝

36. Then We subjected the Wind [4193]
To his power, to flow
Gently to his order,
Whithersoever he willed,—

٣٦- فَسَخَّرْنَا لَهُ ٱلرِّيحَ
تَجْرِي بِأَمْرِهِۦ رُخَآءً حَيْثُ أَصَابَ ۝

37. As also the evil ones, [4194]
(Including) every kind
Of builder and diver,—

٣٧- وَٱلشَّيَٰطِينَ كُلَّ بَنَّآءٍ وَغَوَّاصٍ ۝

38. As also others bound [4195]
Together in fetters.

٣٨- وَءَاخَرِينَ مُقَرَّنِينَ فِي ٱلْأَصْفَادِ ۝

39. "Such are Our Bounties:
Whether thou bestow them [4196]
(On others) or withhold them,
No account will be asked."

٣٩- هَٰذَا عَطَآؤُنَا
فَٱمْنُنْ أَوْ أَمْسِكْ
بِغَيْرِ حِسَابٍ ۝

40. And he enjoyed, indeed, [4197]
A Near Approach to Us,
And a beautiful Place
Of (final) Return.

٤٠- وَإِنَّ لَهُۥ عِندَنَا لَزُلْفَىٰ
وَحُسْنَ مَـَٔابٍ ۝

SECTION 4.

41. Commemorate Our Servant
Job. [4198]

٤١- وَٱذْكُرْ عَبْدَنَآ أَيُّوبَ إِذْ نَادَىٰ رَبَّهُۥٓ

4192. *Cf.* xxxviii. 9 above.

4193. *Cf.* xxi. 81, and n. 2736.

4194. *Cf.* xxi. 82, and n. 2738. *Cf.* also xxxiv. 12-13 and notes there: in the latter passage the spirits mentioned are called Jinns. The divers were probably those employed in pearl-fisheries.

4195. *Cf.* xiv. 49, where the same expression "bound together in fetters" is applied to Sinners on the Day of Judgment.

4196. God bestowed such abundant powers and bounties on Solomon that they could not be counted or measured; and he was free to give away anything he liked or keep anything he liked. In this was great temptation for an ordinary man. Solomon as a prophet withstood it and asked to be forgiven for power and such a kingdom as others might not be able to use lawfully. His earthly kingdom went to pieces after his death. But his name and fame endure. And what is more, he obtained a place among the Nearest Ones to God. See next verse.

4197. The same words are used of David in xxxviii. 25 above, thus symmetrically closing the argument about the two greatest kings in Israel.

4198. For this passage, verses 41-44, *cf.* xxi. 83-84.

Behold he cried to his Lord:
"The Evil One has afflicted
Me with distress[4199] and suffering!"

أَنِّي مَسَّنِيَ الشَّيْطٰنُ بِنُصْبٍ وَّعَذَابٍ ○

42. (The command was given:)
"Strike with thy foot:[4200]
Here is (water) wherein
To wash, cool and refreshing,
And (water) to drink."

٤٢- اُرْكُضْ بِرِجْلِكَ ۚ
هٰذَا مُغْتَسَلٌۢ
بَارِدٌ وَّشَرَابٌ ○

43. And We gave him (back)
His people, and doubled
Their number,—as a Grace[4201]
From Ourselves, and a thing
For commemoration, for all
Who have Understanding.

٤٣- وَوَهَبْنَا لَهٗۤ اَهْلَهٗ
وَمِثْلَهُمْ مَّعَهُمْ رَحْمَةً مِّنَّا
وَذِكْرٰى لِاُولِي الْاَلْبَابِ ○

44. "And take in thy hand
A little grass, and strike[4202]
Therewith: and break not
(Thy oath)." Truly We found
Him full of patience and constancy.
How excellent in Our service![4203]
Ever did he turn (to Us)!

٤٤- وَخُذْ بِيَدِكَ ضِغْثًا
فَاضْرِبْ بِّهٖ وَلَا تَحْنَثْ ۗ
اِنَّا وَجَدْنٰهُ صَابِرًا ۗ
نِعْمَ الْعَبْدُ ۗ اِنَّهٗۤ اَوَّابٌ ○

45. And commemorate Our Servants
Abraham, Isaac, and Jacob,
Possessors of Power and Vision.[4204]

٤٥- وَاذْكُرْ عِبٰدَنَآ اِبْرٰهِيْمَ وَاِسْحٰقَ وَ
يَعْقُوْبَ اُولِي الْاَيْدِيْ وَالْاَبْصَارِ ○

4199. The distress was of many kinds, physical, mental, and spiritual. See n. 2739 to xxi. 83. He suffered from loathsome sores; he lost his home, his possessions, and his family; and almost his balance of mind. But he did not lose Faith but turned to God (see verse 44 below), and the recuperative process began.

4200. The recuperative process having begun, he was commanded to strike the earth or a rock with his foot, and a fountain or fountains gushed forth,—to give him a bath and clean his body; to refresh his spirits; and to give him drink and rest. This is a fresh touch, not mentioned in S. xxi. or in the Book of Job, but adding beautifully to our realisation of the picture.

4201. *Cf.* xxi. 84, and notes 2739-2740.

4202. In his worst distress Job was patient and constant in faith, but apparently his wife was not. According to the Book of Job (ii. 9-10), "Then said his wife unto him, Dost thou still retain thine integrity? Curse God, and die. But he said unto her, Thou speakest as one of the foolish women speaketh. What? Shall we receive good at the hand of God, and shall we not receive evil? In all this did not Job sin with his lips." He must have said in his haste to the woman that he would beat her: he is asked now to correct her with only a wisp of grass, to show that he was gentle and humble as well as patient and constant.

4203. *Cf.* xxxviii. 30 above, where similar words are spoken of Solomon. Patience and constancy are also a form of service, if our attitude is due to an *active* faith in God, and not mere passivity. So Milton in his Sonnet: "They also serve who only stand and wait."

4204. In the last Sūra (xxxvii. 83-113) Abraham and Isaac (and by implication Jacob) were mentioned as resisting Evil and winning through. Here they are mentioned as men with spiritual power and vision, Israelite patriarchs, who bore witness to the Gospel of the Hereafter, and were therefore a blessing to their people, for they taught the Truth.

46. Verily We did choose them
For a special (purpose)—
Proclaiming the Message
Of the Hereafter.

۴۶- اِنَّآ اَخۡلَصۡنٰهُمۡ بِخَالِصَةٍ
ذِكۡرَى الدَّارِ ۝

47. They were, in Our sight,
Truly, of the company
Of the Elect and the Good.

۴۷- وَاِنَّهُمۡ عِنۡدَنَا لَمِنَ
الۡمُصۡطَفَيۡنَ الۡاَخۡيَارِ ۝

48. And commemorate Isma'il,[4205]
Elisha, and Zul-Kifl:
Each of them was
Of the company of the Good.

۴۸- وَاذۡكُرۡ اِسۡمٰعِيۡلَ وَالۡيَسَعَ وَ ذَا الۡكِفۡلِ
وَكُلٌّ مِّنَ الۡاَخۡيَارِ ۝

49. This is a Message
(Of admonition): and verily,
For the Righteous,[4206]
Is a beautiful place
Of (final) Return,—

۴۹- هٰذَا ذِكۡرٌ
وَاِنَّ لِلۡمُتَّقِيۡنَ لَحُسۡنَ مَاٰبٍ ۝

50. Gardens of Eternity,
Whose doors will (ever)
Be open to them;[4207]

۵۰- جَنّٰتِ عَدۡنٍ
مُّفَتَّحَةً لَّهُمُ الۡاَبۡوَابُ ۝

51. Therein will they
Recline (at ease);
Therein can they
Call (at pleasure)
For fruit in abundance,[4208]
And (delicious) drink;

۵۱- مُتَّكِـِٕيۡنَ فِيۡهَا
يَدۡعُوۡنَ فِيۡهَا بِفَاكِهَةٍ كَثِيۡرَةٍ
وَّشَرَابٍ ۝

4205. Ismā'īl, the Patriarch of the Arab race, was also mentioned (xxxvii. 101-107) as a pattern of self-sacrifice; now he is mentioned in the company of the Good, *i.e.*, of those who were a blessing to their people. Here he is bracketed with Elisha (for whom see n. 906 to vi 86), and Zul-Kifl (for whom see n. 2743 to xxi. 85). All these three were examples of constancy and patience under suffering.

4206. Some of the pre-eminent examples of the Elect and the Good having been mentioned, we have now a reference to the Righteous as a body (rank and file as well as leaders) and their future in the Hereafter as won by victory over Evil.

4207. The Final Bliss will not be a hole-and-corner thing, a pale reflection of some Palace or Retreat, where mystery reigns behind closed doors. Its doors will be open, and its inmates will be free to go in and out as they will, because their wills will be purified and brought into accord with the Universal Law.

4208. See n. 4003 to xxxvi. 57. The free Gardens are types of satisfaction in external surroundings; the comfortable reclining thrones, the fruit, and the drink are types of the soul's individual satisfaction; and the society of pure-minded companions, of equal ages, is the type of a soul's social satisfaction.

52. And beside them will be
Chaste women restraining[4209]
Their glances, (companions)
Of equal age.[4210]

٥٢- وَعِنْدَهُمْ قٰصِرٰتُ
الطَّرْفِ اَتْرَابٌ ۝

53. Such is the Promise
Made to you
For the Day of Account!

٥٣- هٰذَا مَا تُوْعَدُوْنَ
لِيَوْمِ الْحِسَابِ ۝

54. Truly such will be
Our Bounty (to you);
It will never fail;—

٥٤- اِنَّ هٰذَا لَرِزْقُنَا
مَا لَهٗ مِنْ نَّفَادٍ ۝

55. Yea, such! But—
For the wrong-doers
Will be an evil place[4211]
Of (final) Return!—

٥٥- هٰذَا ۚ وَاِنَّ لِلطّٰغِيْنَ
لَشَرَّ مَاٰبٍ ۝

56. Hell!—they will burn
Therein,—an evil bed
(Indeed, to lie on)!—[4212]

٥٦- جَهَنَّمَ ۚ يَصْلَوْنَهَا ۚ
فَبِئْسَ الْمِهَادُ ۝

57. Yea, such!—Then
Shall they taste it,—
A boiling fluid, and a fluid[4213]
Dark, murky, intensely cold!—

٥٧- هٰذَا ۙ فَلْيَذُوْقُوْهُ
حَمِيْمٌ وَّغَسَّاقٌ ۝

58. And other Penalties
Of a similar kind,
To match them!

٥٨- وَّاٰخَرُ مِنْ شَكْلِهٖٓ اَزْوَاجٌ ۝

4209. *Cf.* xxxvii. 48 and n. 4064, and xxxvi. 56, n. 4002. As we conceive happiness in this life, it is not complete if it is only solitary. How we hanker after some one who can share in our highest joy! That feeling is also figured here.

4210. To make the metaphor of social happiness complete, we want companionship of equal age. Age and youth cannot be happy together. It is not suggested that in the Timeless state figured here, there will be old age; but if it is possible to conceive of temperamental differences then, the company will be so arranged that it will be congenial. Or we can accept the type of youth and freshness as common to all in that happy state.

4211. This is in parallel contrast to the state of the Blessed in xxxviii. 49 above.

4212. *Cf.* xiv. 29. This continues the parallel contrast to the state of the Blessed already described.

4213. *Cf.* x. 4, and n. 1390. The conjunction of the boiling fluid with the dark, murky, intensely cold fluid heightens the effect of the Penalty. In place of harmony, there is the discord of extreme opposites. And the discord is not confined to this: it runs through the whole idea of Hell. See the next verse.

59. Here is a troop
Rushing headlong with you ![4214]
No welcome for them !
Truly, they shall burn
In the Fire !

٥٩- هٰذَا فَوْجٌ مُّقْتَحِمٌ مَّعَكُمْ ۚ
لَا مَرْحَبًا بِهِمْ ۚ
إِنَّهُمْ صَالُوا النَّارِ ○

60. (The followers shall cry
To the misleaders :)
" Nay, ye (too) ! No welcome
For you ! It is ye who
Have brought this upon us ![4215]
Now evil is (this) place
To stay in !"

٦٠- قَالُوا بَلْ أَنتُمْ ۖ
لَا مَرْحَبًا بِكُمْ ۖ
أَنتُمْ قَدَّمْتُمُوهُ لَنَا ۖ
فَبِئْسَ الْقَرَارُ ○

61. They will say : " Our Lord !
Whoever brought this upon us,—
Add to him a double[4216]
Penalty in the Fire ! "

٦١- قَالُوا رَبَّنَا مَن قَدَّمَ لَنَا هَٰذَا
فَزِدْهُ عَذَابًا ضِعْفًا فِي النَّارِ ○

62. And they will say :
" What has happened to us
That we see not men
Whom we used to number
Among the bad ones ?[4217]

٦٢- وَقَالُوا مَا لَنَا لَا نَرَىٰ رِجَالًا
كُنَّا نَعُدُّهُم مِّنَ الْأَشْرَارِ ○

63. " Did we treat them
(As such) in ridicule,
Or have (our) eyes
Failed to perceive them ? "

٦٣- أَتَّخَذْنَاهُمْ سِخْرِيًّا
أَمْ زَاغَتْ عَنْهُمُ الْأَبْصَارُ ○

64. Truly that is just and fitting,—[4218]
The mutual recriminations
Of the People of the Fire !

٦٤- إِنَّ ذَٰلِكَ لَحَقٌّ
تَخَاصُمُ أَهْلِ النَّارِ ○

4214. The wonder is that so many people should embrace Evil, and in so much hurry and eagerness ! Here they may be welcomed by the leaders of Evil, but in the final state it will be the opposite of welcome. They will be followed with reproaches and curses.

4215. It is the nature of Evil to shift the blame on to others. The followers will reproach the leaders, but none can escape personal responsibility for his own acts and deeds !

4216. *Cf.* vii. 38, and n. 1019. See also xi. 20. The evil ones now vent their spite on others. Here they ask for a double penalty for their misleaders, but they forget their own personal responsibility. In the next verse, they express their surprise that others have escaped the torments, which they themselves have earned !

4217. *The bad ones* : *i.e.*, the ones whom they (evil ones) ridiculed as fools sure to come to an evil end, because they refused to join in with the evil ones in their plots. The values are now reversed. The good ones are among the Blessed, and are not to be seen in the " Bed of Misery ". The ridicule is now against the evil ones.

4218. The mutual recriminations and spite are themselves a part of the Penalty, for such feelings increase their unhappiness.

C. 202.—The Gospel of Unity is the true Cure
(xxxviii. 65-88.) For Evil : for it gives the good news
Of God's Power Supreme, and His Mercy
And Forgiveness again and again. It warns
Us to avoid Evil, for Evil arose
From selfish Pride and Rebellion. No power
Has it over God's servants, sincere
And true : while Revelation comes
As a gift free to all God's Creation.

SECTION 5.

65. Say : " Truly am I
A Warner : no god
Is there but the One
God, Supreme and Irresistible,—[4219]

٦٥- قُلْ إِنَّمَآ أَنَا مُنذِرٌ ۖ وَمَا مِنْ إِلَٰهٍ إِلَّا ٱللَّهُ ٱلْوَٰحِدُ ٱلْقَهَّارُ ۝

66. " The Lord of the heavens
And the earth, and all
Between,—Exalted in Might,
Able to enforce His Will,[4220]
Forgiving again and again." [4221]

٦٦- رَبُّ ٱلسَّمَٰوَٰتِ وَٱلْأَرْضِ وَمَا بَيْنَهُمَا ٱلْعَزِيزُ ٱلْغَفَّٰرُ ۝

67. Say : " That is a Message
Supreme (above all),—

٦٧- قُلْ هُوَ نَبَؤٌا۟ عَظِيمٌ ۝

68. " From which ye
Do turn away ! [4222]

٦٨- أَنتُمْ عَنْهُ مُعْرِضُونَ ۝

69. " No knowledge have I
Of the Chiefs on high,
When they discuss
(Matters) among themselves.[4223]

٦٩- مَا كَانَ لِىَ مِنْ عِلْمٍۭ بِٱلْمَلَإِ ٱلْأَعْلَىٰٓ إِذْ يَخْتَصِمُونَ ۝

4219. *Cf.* xii. 39, where Joseph preaches to the men in prison. The one supreme Message of importance to mankind was (and is) the Unity of God : that He is the Creator and Sustainer of all ; that His Will is supreme ; that He can carry out His Will without question, and no powers of Evil can defeat it ; and that He forgives by His grace again and again. This Message the holy Prophet came to deliver, and he delivered it.

4220. In n. 2818 to xxii. 40, I have explained the full import of *'Azīz* as a title applied to God, and I have expressed two of the leading ideas involved, in the two lines here. The argument in this Sūra turns upon the contrast between earthly Power and the Divine Power : the one is impotent and the other is supreme.

4221. *Gaffār* is the emphatic intensive form, and I have accordingly translated it as " Forgiving again and again ". *Cf.* xx. 82.

4222. The Message which is of supreme import to mankind,—from that they turn away. Instead of profiting by it, they turn away to side issues, or unprofitable speculation : such as : what is the origin of Evil ; when will Judgment come ? etc.

4223. The hierarchy in Heaven, under God's command, discuss questions of high import in the Universe. Those are not necessarily revealed to men, except in so far as it is good for men to know, as in verses 71-85 below. But the chief thing for man is to know that God is Most Merciful, that He forgives again and again, and that Evil has no power over those who trust in God.

70. 'Only this has been revealed
To me: that I am
To give warning
Plainly and publicly."[4224]

٧٠- إِن يُوحَىٰ إِلَيَّ إِلَّا أَنَّمَا أَنَا
نَذِيرٌ مُّبِينٌ ○

71. Behold, thy Lord said[4225]
To the angels: "I am
About to create man
From clay:[4226]

٧١- إِذْ قَالَ رَبُّكَ لِلْمَلَٰٓئِكَةِ إِنِّي
خَٰلِقٌۢ بَشَرًا مِّن طِينٍ ○

72. "When I have fashioned him
(In due proportion) and breathed
Into him of My spirit,[4227]
Fall ye down in obeisance
Unto him."

٧٢- فَإِذَا سَوَّيْتُهُۥ وَنَفَخْتُ
فِيهِ مِن رُّوحِي
فَقَعُوا۟ لَهُۥ سَٰجِدِينَ ○

73. So the angels prostrated themselves,
All of them together:

٧٣- فَسَجَدَ ٱلْمَلَٰٓئِكَةُ كُلُّهُمْ أَجْمَعُونَ ○

74. Not so Iblīs: he
Was haughty, and became[4228]
One of those who reject Faith.

٧٤- إِلَّآ إِبْلِيسَ ٱسْتَكْبَرَ وَكَانَ
مِنَ ٱلْكَٰفِرِينَ ○

75. (God) said: "O Iblīs!
What prevents thee from
Prostrating thyself to one
Whom I have created
With My hands?[4229]
Art thou haughty?

٧٥- قَالَ يَٰٓإِبْلِيسُ مَا مَنَعَكَ
أَن تَسْجُدَ لِمَا خَلَقْتُ بِيَدَيَّ
أَسْتَكْبَرْتَ

4224. Two things are implied in *Mubīn*: (1) that the warning should be clear and perspicuous; there should be no mincing of matters, no ambiguity, no compromise with evil, vii. 184; (2) that the warning should be delivered publicly, before all people, in spite of opposition and persecution, xxvi. 115. Both these ideas I have tried to express in this passage.

4225. Two passages may be compared with this: *viz.*: (1) ii. 30-39, where merely the first stages of the Rebellion against God and its consequences to mankind are mentioned, and (2) xv. 29-40, where the further intrusion of evil in man's life here below is referred to, and an assurance is given that Evil will have no power except over those who yield to it. The latter is the passage most relevant here, as we are now dealing with the spiritual power of Revelation to defeat the machinations of Evil.

4226. This shows that the material world round us was created by God before God fashioned man and breathed of His soul into him. Geology also shows that man came on the scene at a very late stage in the history of this planet.

4227. See n. 1968 to xv. 29, where the spiritual significance of this is explained.

4228. Arrogance (self-love) is thus the root of Evil and of Unfaith.

4229. *With My hands*: *i.e.*, by My power and creative skill. This is the point. Man, as typified by Adam, is in himself nothing but frail clay. But as fashioned by God's creative power into something with God's spirit breathed into him, his dignity is raised above that of the highest creatures.

Or art thou one[4230]
Of the high (and mighty) ones?"

أَمْ كُنتَ مِنَ الْعَالِينَ ○

76. (Iblīs) said: "I am better
Than he: Thou createdst
Me from fire, and him
Thou createdst from clay."

٧٦- قَالَ أَنَا خَيْرٌ مِّنْهُ ۖ خَلَقْتَنِي
مِن نَّارٍ وَخَلَقْتَهُ مِن طِينٍ ○

77. (God) said: "Then get thee
Out from here: for thou
Art rejected, accursed.

٧٧- قَالَ فَاخْرُجْ مِنْهَا
فَإِنَّكَ رَجِيمٌ ○

78. "And My Curse shall be
On thee till the Day[4231]
Of Judgment."

٧٨- وَإِنَّ عَلَيْكَ لَعْنَتِي
إِلَىٰ يَوْمِ الدِّينِ ○

79. (Iblīs) said: "O my Lord!
Give me then respite[4232]
Till the Day
The (dead) are raised."

٧٩- قَالَ رَبِّ فَأَنظِرْنِي
إِلَىٰ يَوْمِ يُبْعَثُونَ ○

80. (God) said: "Respite then
Is granted thee—

٨٠- قَالَ فَإِنَّكَ مِنَ الْمُنظَرِينَ ○

81. "Till the Day
Of the Time Appointed."[4233]

٨١- إِلَىٰ يَوْمِ الْوَقْتِ الْمَعْلُومِ ○

82. (Iblīs) said: "Then,
By Thy Power,[4234] I will
Put them all in the wrong,—[4235]

٨٢- قَالَ فَبِعِزَّتِكَ
لَأُغْوِيَنَّهُمْ أَجْمَعِينَ ○

4230. If, then, Satan refuses, it is a rebellion against God. It arises from arrogance or haughtiness, an exaggerated idea of Self. Or, it is asked, are you really sufficiently high in rank to dispute with the Almighty? Of course he was not.

4231. See n. 1972 to xv. 35, where it is explained why the respite is to the Day of Judgment. The whole of that passage in S. xv. forms a good commentary on this.

4232. For the significance of the respite see n. 1973 to xv. 36.

4233. It is not an indefinite respite. It is for a period definitely limited, while this our Probation lasts in this world. It is part of the test as to how we use our limited free-will. After that, our whole existence will be on a different plane. The good will have been sorted out, the chain of consequences of the present world will be broken, and "a new Creation" will have taken the place of the present World.

4234. This phrase, this oath of Satan, is a fresh point introduced in this passage, because here we are dealing with Power—the Power of Good contrasted with Evil,—the spiritual Power of God as contrasted with the power that we see in our earthly affairs. Satan acknowledges that even his Power, such as it is, has no reality except in so far as it is permitted to operate by God in God's wise and universal Plan, and that it cannot harm the true and sincere worshippers of God.

4235. See n. 1974 to xv. 39.

83. " Except Thy Servants
Amongst them, sincere
And purified (by Thy grace)."

٨٣- إِلَّا عِبَادَكَ مِنْهُمُ الْمُخْلَصِينَ ○

84. (God) said: " Then
It is just and fitting—[4236]
And I say what is
Just and fitting—

٨٤- قَالَ فَالْحَقُّ
وَالْحَقَّ أَقُولُ ○

85. " That I will certainly fill[4237]
Hell with thee
And those that follow thee,—
Every one."

٨٥- لَأَمْلَأَنَّ جَهَنَّمَ مِنْكَ
وَمِمَّنْ تَبِعَكَ مِنْهُمْ أَجْمَعِينَ ○

86. Say: " No reward do I ask[4238]
Of you for this (Qur-ān),
Nor am I a pretender.[4239]

٨٦- قُلْ مَا أَسْأَلُكُمْ عَلَيْهِ مِنْ أَجْرٍ
وَمَا أَنَا مِنَ الْمُتَكَلِّفِينَ ○

87. " This is no less than
A Message to (all)[4240]
The Worlds.

٨٧- إِنْ هُوَ إِلَّا ذِكْرٌ لِلْعَالَمِينَ ○

88. " And ye shall certainly
Know the truth of it (all)[4241]
After a while."

٨٨- وَلَتَعْلَمُنَّ نَبَأَهُ بَعْدَ حِينٍ ○

4236. *Cf.* n. 1990 to xv. 64.

4237. *Cf.* vii. 18; vii. 179; and xi. 119, n. 1623. The punishment of defiance, disobedience, and rebellion is inevitable and just, and the followers who choose to identify themselves with the disobedience must suffer as well as the leaders. *Cf.* x. 33

4238. *Cf.* xxv. 57; xxvi. 109; and many other passages. The prophet of God neither seeks nor expects any reward from men. On the contrary he suffers much at their hands. He is unselfish and offers his services under God's inspiration. He is satisfied with the hope "that each one who will may take a straight Path to his Lord". That is his reward. And the reward he hopes for from God is similarly unselfish. He earnestly hopes to win His Good Pleasure—or, to use another metaphor, "to see His Face"

4239. *Mutakallif*: a man who pretends to things that are not true, or declares as facts things that do not exist, one who takes upon himself tasks to which he is not equal. True prophets are not people of that kind.

4240. So far from there being any false or selfish motive in the Message proclaimed in Revelation, it is a healing mercy to all mankind. More, it is in accord with all parts of God's Creation, and makes us kin with all Creation, the handiwork of the One True God.

4241. There may be many things which we in our "muddy vesture of decay" may not fully understand or take in. If we only follow the right Path, we shall arrive at the Goal in the Hereafter, and then everything will be clear to us.

INTRODUCTION TO SŪRA XXXIX (*Zumar*).

This is the last of the series of six Sūras beginning with S. xxxiv., which deal with the mysteries of the spiritual world, as leading up to the Ma'ād, or the Hereafter. See Introduction to S. xxxiv.

Its subject-matter is how Creation in its great variety is yet sorted out in Groups or Classes, all governed by one Plan, and created and sustained by One God, Who will separate Good from Evil at the last Day. The word *zumar* occurs in verses 71 and 73.

Its chronology has no significance. It belongs to the later Meccan period.

Summary.—The variety in Creation yet points to unity of Plan: there is only One God: to Him is due all worship and from Him flow all Justice and Grace (xxxix. 1-21, and C. 203).

There is unity in Revelation, and guidance comes from God alone: turn to Him only, for all else is false (xxxix. 22-52, and C. 204).

God's Mercy is all-embracing: despair not: seek it before it is too late: for Judgment and Justice will come for certain (xxxix. 53-75, and C. 205).

C. 203.—To God is due sincere devotion, and to Him
(xxxix. 1-21.) Alone: there is none like unto Him.
All nature obeys His laws, and our own
Growth and life proclaim Him Lord
And Cherisher. How can we blaspheme?
We must serve Him, the One, the True,
With sincere devotion, and follow His Law
In its highest meaning: or else the loss
Is our own. All nature proclaims
Aloud His Grace and Loving-kindness.

Sūra XXXIX.

Zumar, or the Crowds.

In the name of God, Most Gracious,
Most Merciful.

بِسْمِ اللّٰهِ الرَّحْمٰنِ الرَّحِيمِ

1. The revelation
Of this Book
Is from God,[4242]
The Exalted in Power,
Full of Wisdom.

١- تَنْزِيلُ الْكِتٰبِ مِنَ اللّٰهِ
الْعَزِيزِ الْحَكِيمِ ○

2. Verily it is We Who have
Revealed the Book to thee
In Truth: so serve God,
Offering Him sincere devotion.

٢- إِنَّآ أَنْزَلْنَآ إِلَيْكَ الْكِتٰبَ بِالْحَقِّ
فَاعْبُدِ اللّٰهَ مُخْلِصًا لَّهُ الدِّينَ ○

3. Is it not to God[4243]
That sincere devotion
Is due? But those who
Take for protectors others
Than God (say): "We only
Serve them in order that
They may bring us nearer[4244]
To God." Truly God
Will judge between them
In that wherein they differ.[4245]
But God guides not
Such as are false
And ungrateful.

٣- أَلَا لِلّٰهِ الدِّينُ الْخَالِصُ ۚ
وَالَّذِينَ اتَّخَذُوا مِنْ دُونِهِ أَوْلِيَآءَ ۘ
مَا نَعْبُدُهُمْ إِلَّا لِيُقَرِّبُونَآ إِلَى اللّٰهِ زُلْفٰى ۗ
إِنَّ اللّٰهَ يَحْكُمُ بَيْنَهُمْ
فِي مَا هُمْ فِيهِ يَخْتَلِفُونَ ۗ
إِنَّ اللّٰهَ لَا يَهْدِي
مَنْ هُوَ كٰذِبٌ كَفَّارٌ ○

4242. In connection with Revelation two qualities of God are mentioned: (1) that He is All-Powerful and can carry out His Will in spite of all opposition; and (2) that He is full of knowledge and wisdom. The first answers those who question how God can send Revelation to man; the second explains that true wisdom consists in carrying out God's Will as revealed to us.

4243. In the many Signs in Creation as described below, there yet is a clear indication of the unity of Plan, pointing to the Unity of the Creator. Worship or service is due to none but Him. And He wants exclusive and sincere devotion.

4244. Worshippers of Idols or of deities other than God, *e.g.*, saints or perhaps Wealth and Power, Science or Selfish Desire, may pretend that these are symbols that may get them nearer to their self-development, nearer to the goal of their life, nearer to God, but they are altogether on the wrong track.

4245. This departure of theirs from true worship, this divergence from the right way, produces endless disputations and sects. God will judge between them. But if they are determined to go after falsehoods and forget the gratitude and service which they owe to God, and God alone, they are putting themselves on a Path where they will get no guidance. They are cutting themselves off from revealed Truth.

4. Had God wished
To take to Himself
A son, He could have
Chosen whom He pleased
Out of those whom He [4246]
Doth create : but Glory
Be to Him! (He is above
Such things.) He is God,
The One, the Irresistible.

٤- لَوْ أَرَادَ اللَّهُ
أَن يَتَّخِذَ وَلَدًا
لَّاصْطَفَىٰ مِمَّا يَخْلُقُ مَا يَشَاءُ ۚ
سُبْحَانَهُ ۖ
هُوَ اللَّهُ الْوَاحِدُ الْقَهَّارُ ○

5. He created the heavens
And the earth
In true (proportions) : [4247]
He makes the Night
Overlap the Day, and the Day
Overlap the Night :
He has subjected
The sun and the moon
(To His law) :
Each one follows a course
For a time appointed.
Is not He the Exalted
In Power—He Who forgives [4248]
Again and again?

٥- خَلَقَ السَّمَاوَاتِ وَالْأَرْضَ بِالْحَقِّ ۖ
يُكَوِّرُ اللَّيْلَ عَلَى النَّهَارِ
وَيُكَوِّرُ النَّهَارَ عَلَى اللَّيْلِ
وَسَخَّرَ الشَّمْسَ وَالْقَمَرَ ۖ
كُلٌّ يَجْرِي لِأَجَلٍ مُّسَمًّى ۗ
أَلَا هُوَ
الْعَزِيزُ الْغَفَّارُ ○

6. He created you (all)
From a single Person : [4249]
Then created, of like nature,
His mate; and He
Sent down for you eight head [4250]
Of cattle in pairs :
He makes you,
In the wombs

٦- خَلَقَكُم مِّن نَّفْسٍ وَاحِدَةٍ
ثُمَّ جَعَلَ مِنْهَا زَوْجَهَا وَ
أَنزَلَ لَكُم مِّنَ الْأَنْعَامِ ثَمَانِيَةَ أَزْوَاجٍ ۚ
يَخْلُقُكُمْ فِي بُطُونِ

4246. It is blasphemy to say that God begot a son. If that were true, He should have had a wife (vi. 101), and His son would have been of the same kind as Himself; whereas God is one, with no one else like unto Him (cxii. 4). Begetting is an animal act which goes with sex. How can it be consistent with our conception of One Who is above all Creatures? If such a blasphemous thought were possible, as that God wanted some one else to help Him, He could have chosen the best of His creatures instead of lowering Himself to an animal act. But glory to God! He is above such things! His Unity is the first thing that we have to learn about Him. As He is Omnipotent, He requires no creatures to help Him or bring other creatures to Him.

4247. *Cf.* vi. 73, and n. 896.

4248. His Power is equalled by His Mercy. Who can there be like unto Him?

4249. *Cf.* iv. 1, and n. 504.

4250. See vi. 143-4, where four kinds of cattle are mentioned in pairs in connection with certain Arab superstitions which are there condemned. Here the same four kinds are mentioned as representative of domesticated cattle given by God as useful to man. These are sheep, goats, camels, and oxen. In Arab idiom the horse is not included among "cattle".

For the wisdom and goodness of God in granting man dominion over cattle, see xxxvi. 71-73.

Of your mothers,
In stages, one after another,[4251]
In three veils of darkness.[4252]
Such is God, your Lord
And Cherisher: to Him belongs
(All) dominion. There is
No god but He: then
How are ye turned away[4253]
(From your true Centre)?

أُمَّهٰتِكُمْ
خَلْقًا مِّنْ بَعْدِ خَلْقٍ فِي ظُلُمٰتٍ ثَلٰثٍ ۚ
ذٰلِكُمُ اللّٰهُ رَبُّكُمْ لَهُ الْمُلْكُ ۚ
لَآ إِلٰهَ إِلَّا هُوَ ۚ
فَأَنّٰى تُصْرَفُونَ ○

7. If ye reject (God),
Truly God hath no need
Of you; but He liketh not[4254]
Ingratitude from His servants:
If ye are grateful, He
Is pleased with you.
No bearer of burdens[4255]
Can bear the burden
Of another. In the End,
To your Lord is your Return,
When He will tell you
The truth of all
That ye did (in this life).
For He knoweth well
All that is in (men's) hearts.

٧- إِنْ تَكْفُرُوا فَإِنَّ اللّٰهَ غَنِيٌّ عَنْكُمْ ۖ
وَلَا يَرْضٰى لِعِبَادِهِ الْكُفْرَ ۚ
وَإِنْ تَشْكُرُوا يَرْضَهُ لَكُمْ ۗ
وَلَا تَزِرُ وَازِرَةٌ وِّزْرَ أُخْرٰى ۗ
ثُمَّ إِلٰى رَبِّكُمْ مَّرْجِعُكُمْ
فَيُنَبِّئُكُمْ بِمَا كُنْتُمْ تَعْمَلُونَ ۗ
إِنَّهُ عَلِيمٌ بِذَاتِ الصُّدُورِ ○

8. When some trouble toucheth man,[4256]
He crieth unto his Lord,

٨- وَإِذَا مَسَّ الْإِنْسَانَ ضُرٌّ دَعَا رَبَّهُ

4251. See xxii. 5, where the gradual physical growth of man in several successive stages is mentioned as one of the Signs of God's creative Power and cherishing care.

4252. The three veils of darkness which cover the unborn child are: the caul or membrane, the womb, and the hollow in which the womb is enclosed. But we might understand "three" in a cumulative rather than a numerical sense.

4253. It is clear that you owe your very existence and your maintenance, growth, and preservation, to God. He is the centre of your being: how is it that you are turned away by chance things from Him?

4254. God is independent of all wants, and therefore man's ingratitude does not affect God. But God cares for man, and therefore man's gratitude and service earn God's Good Pleasure, and man's ingratitude and rebellion are displeasing to God.

4255. *Cf.* vi. 164. The account is between you and God. No one else can take your burdens or carry your sins. Vicarious atonement would be unjust. You have to return to God in the Hereafter. You will find that He knows all that you did in this life, and its full significance. He will explain to you even better than you can understand yourself; because all your secret hidden motives, which you sometimes tried to ignore yourself, are fully known to Him.

4256. *Cf.* x. 12. Trouble and adversity often bring a man to his bearings. But if he is not firm and constant, he forgets the lessons which life is meant to teach him. As soon as he gets a little prosperity, he forgets that it is from God, and attributes it to something which may only be a secondary cause, *e.g.*, his own efforts or the Powers of Nature, or something which he has invented and made into a god, *e.g.*, idols or fate. God is the Ultimate Cause of all things. To set up rivals to Him in this way is not only wrong and degrading to the false worshipper himself, but misleads countless ignorant people, who may not be able to make allowances for the figures of speech or the symbolism by which subtler minds can explain away falsehoods.

Turning to Him in repentance:
But when He bestoweth
A favour upon him
As from Himself, (man)
Doth forget what he cried
And prayed for before,
And he doth set up
Rivals unto God,
Thus misleading others
From God's Path.
Say, "Enjoy thy blasphemy[4257]
For a little while:
Verily thou art (one)
Of the Companions of the Fire!"

9. As one who worships devoutly
During the hours of the night[4258]
Prostrating himself or standing
(In adoration), who takes heed
Of the Hereafter, and who
Places his hope in the Mercy
Of his Lord—(like one
Who does not)? Say:
"Are those equal, those who know
And those who do not know?
It is those who are
Endued with understanding
That receive admonition.[4259]

Section 2.

10 Say: "O ye
My servants who believe!
Fear your Lord.[4260]
Good is (the reward)
For those who do good
In this world.

مُنِيبًا إِلَيْهِ
ثُمَّ إِذَا خَوَّلَهُ نِعْمَةً مِّنْهُ
نَسِيَ مَا كَانَ يَدْعُوٓا إِلَيْهِ مِن قَبْلُ
وَجَعَلَ لِلَّهِ أَندَادًا
لِّيُضِلَّ عَن سَبِيلِهِۦ
قُلْ تَمَتَّعْ بِكُفْرِكَ قَلِيلًا
إِنَّكَ مِنْ أَصْحَٰبِ ٱلنَّارِ ۝

٩- أَمَّنْ هُوَ قَٰنِتٌ ءَانَآءَ ٱلَّيْلِ
سَاجِدًا وَقَآئِمًا يَحْذَرُ ٱلْءَاخِرَةَ
وَيَرْجُوا رَحْمَةَ رَبِّهِۦ
قُلْ هَلْ يَسْتَوِى ٱلَّذِينَ يَعْلَمُونَ
وَٱلَّذِينَ لَا يَعْلَمُونَ
إِنَّمَا يَتَذَكَّرُ أُوْلُوا ٱلْأَلْبَٰبِ ۝

١٠- قُلْ يَٰعِبَادِ ٱلَّذِينَ ءَامَنُوا ٱتَّقُوا رَبَّكُمْ
لِلَّذِينَ أَحْسَنُوا
فِى هَٰذِهِ ٱلدُّنْيَا حَسَنَةٌ

4257. Those who practise and those who teach evil and blasphemy may seem to flourish in this world. But their satisfaction will be of very short duration. They are treading all the while the Path that leads to the Fire of Perdition.

4258. *Cf.* iii. 113-117. It is a great thing when a man gets into the attitude of humble devotion to God. To him the hereafter is a real thing, and he prepares for it with good works. He does not build his hopes on the vanities of this world, but on God's Grace and Mercy. Such a man is "endued with understanding" and receives God's Message with fervour and alacrity. He is not to be compared with the cynic or the unbeliever, who knows nothing of the real value of the inner life.

4259. *Cf.* iii. 19.

4260. The "fear of God" (*Taqwā*) is explained in n. 26 to ii. 2. See also n. 2912 to xxiii. 60. The fear of God is akin to love, for it means that we are afraid to displease Him.

Spacious is God's earth ! [4261]
Those who patiently persevere
Will truly receive
A reward without measure ! "

وَ اَرْضُ اللّٰهِ وَاسِعَةٌ ؕ
اِنَّمَا يُوَفَّى الصّٰبِرُوْنَ اَجْرَهُمْ بِغَيْرِ حِسَابٍ ○

11. Say: "Verily, I am commanded
To serve God
With sincere devotion ;

١١- قُلْ اِنِّيْٓ اُمِرْتُ اَنْ اَعْبُدَ اللّٰهَ
مُخْلِصًا لَّهُ الدِّيْنَ ○

12. " And I am commanded
To be the first [4262]
Of those who bow
To God in Islam."

١٢- وَ اُمِرْتُ
لِاَنْ اَكُوْنَ اَوَّلَ الْمُسْلِمِيْنَ ○

13. Say : " I would, if I [4263]
Disobeyed my Lord,
Indeed have fear
Of the Penalty
Of a Mighty Day."

١٣- قُلْ اِنِّيْٓ اَخَافُ
اِنْ عَصَيْتُ رَبِّيْ
عَذَابَ يَوْمٍ عَظِيْمٍ ○

14. Say : " It is God I serve,
With my sincere
(And exclusive) devotion :

١٤- قُلِ اللّٰهَ اَعْبُدُ مُخْلِصًا لَّهٗ دِيْنِيْ ○

15. " Serve ye what ye will [4264]
Besides Him." Say :
" Truly, those in loss
Are those who lose
Their own souls
And their People [4265]
On the Day of Judgment :
Ah ! that is indeed
The (real and) evident Loss !

١٥- فَاعْبُدُوْا مَا شِئْتُمْ مِّنْ دُوْنِهٖ ؕ قُلْ
اِنَّ الْخٰسِرِيْنَ الَّذِيْنَ خَسِرُوْٓا اَنْفُسَهُمْ
وَ اَهْلِيْهِمْ يَوْمَ الْقِيٰمَةِ ؕ
اَلَا ذٰلِكَ هُوَ الْخُسْرَانُ الْمُبِيْنُ ○

4261. *Cf.* xxix. 56 and n. 3489. We must always do right. We cannot plead that the circumstances in which we find ourselves force our hands. If our home conditions do not allow us to act according to the Faith that is in us, we must be prepared to suffer ostracism or even exile.

4262. *Cf.* vi. 14. "The first" need not necessarily be chronological : it may also refer to the first rank in zeal, and in readiness to suffer for the Cause.

4263. *Cf.* vi. 15. The worst Penalty in a spiritual sense is the Displeasure of God, just as the highest achievement, the fulfilment of all desire, is the attainment of God's Good Pleasure : vi. 16.

4264. This is not a command or permission but a reproach and warning. The address of the man of God may be paraphrased thus : 'Whatever happens I will follow the command of God. He has revealed Himself, and I know that He is One, supreme over all creatures. Him alone will I serve. Is there any so ignorant as to seek anyone else ? Let him do so and see the result. The loss will be his own. For he falls from Grace into Evil.'

4265. The cult of Evil results in the destruction of all that is best and most valuable in us, as well as poisons all the affections which link us to our families, friends, and people, in the Final Adjustment, which we call the Day of Judgment.

16. They shall have Layers[4266]
Of Fire above them,
And Layers (of Fire)
Below them: with this
Doth God warn off[4267]
His Servants: "O My Servants!
Then fear ye Me!"

۱۶- لَهُمْ مِّنْ فَوْقِهِمْ ظُلَلٌ مِّنَ النَّارِ
وَمِنْ تَحْتِهِمْ ظُلَلٌ ۗ
ذٰلِكَ يُخَوِّفُ اللّٰهُ بِهٖ عِبَادَهٗ ۚ
يٰعِبَادِ فَاتَّقُوْنِ ○

17. Those who eschew Evil,—
And fall not into[4268]
Its worship,—and turn
To God (in repentance),—
For them is Good News:
So announce the Good News
To My Servants,—

۱۷- وَالَّذِيْنَ اجْتَنَبُوا الطَّاغُوْتَ اَنْ يَّعْبُدُوْهَا
وَاَنَابُوْۤا اِلَى اللّٰهِ لَهُمُ الْبُشْرٰى ۚ
فَبَشِّرْ عِبَادِ ○

18. Those who listen
To the Word,
And follow
The best (meaning) in it:[4269]
Those are the ones
Whom God has guided, and those
Are the ones endued
With understanding.

۱۸- الَّذِيْنَ يَسْتَمِعُوْنَ الْقَوْلَ
فَيَتَّبِعُوْنَ اَحْسَنَهٗ ۗ
اُولٰٓئِكَ الَّذِيْنَ هَدٰىهُمُ اللّٰهُ
وَاُولٰٓئِكَ هُمْ اُولُوا الْاَلْبَابِ ○

19. Is, then, one against whom
The decree of Punishment

۱۹- اَفَمَنْ حَقَّ عَلَيْهِ كَلِمَةُ الْعَذَابِ ۗ

4266. The consequences of Sin when Judgment comes are aptly figured by Layers upon Layers of Fire, which hem in the sinners above and below. It is also suggested that the Layers, though of Fire, have something dark in them—the scorching quality of Sin.

4267. But God does not leave mankind without warning. Man has been granted a limited amount of free-will, and in order to help him in its right use, all the consequences of his action are clearly explained to him. To those who will listen to Reason are given arguments which can be apprehended by their own intelligence; to those who are swayed by affections and emotion, an appeal is made in the name of the love of God; to those who understand nothing but fear, the warning is conveyed by a portrayal of the dreadful consequences of wrong-doing.

4268. There is always the danger that Evil may seize us even if we approach it out of mere curiosity. If we take an interest in it we may become its worshippers or slaves. The wise man eschews it altogether, and so he enrols among the Servants of God, and gets the good news of His Mercy and Good Pleasure.

4269. The Commentators construe this clause in two alternative ways. (1) If "word" be taken as any word, the clause would mean that good men listen to all that is said and choose the best of it. (2) If "word" be taken to mean God's Word, it would mean that they should listen reverently to it, and where permissive and alternative courses are allowed for those who are not strong enough to follow the higher course, those "endued with understanding" should prefer to attempt the higher course of conduct. For Example, it is permitted (within limits) to punish those who wrong us, but the nobler course is to repel evil with good (xxiii. 96); we should try to follow the nobler course. I prefer the latter construction: it accords better with my interpretation of the last verse: see n. 4268.

Is justly due (equal
To one who eschews evil)?[4270]
Wouldst thou, then, deliver
One (who is) in the Fire?

أَفَأَنتَ تُنقِذُ
مَن فِى النَّارِ ۝

20. But it is for those
Who fear their Lord,
That lofty mansions,[4271]
One above another,
Have been built:
Beneath them flow
Rivers (of delight): (such is)
The Promise of God:
Never doth God fail in
(His) promise.[4272]

٢٠- لَٰكِنِ الَّذِينَ اتَّقَوْا رَبَّهُمْ لَهُمْ
غُرَفٌ مِّن فَوْقِهَا غُرَفٌ مَّبْنِيَّةٌ
تَجْرِى مِن تَحْتِهَا الْأَنْهَٰرُ ۖ
وَعْدَ اللَّهِ ۖ
لَا يُخْلِفُ اللَّهُ الْمِيعَادَ ۝

21. Seest thou not that God
Sends down rain from
The sky, and leads it
Through springs in the earth?[4273]
Then He causes to grow,
Therewith, produce of various
Colours: then it withers;
Thou wilt see it grow yellow;
Then He makes it
Dry up and crumble away.
Truly, in this, is
A Message of remembrance to
Men of understanding.

٢١- أَلَمْ تَرَ أَنَّ اللَّهَ أَنزَلَ مِنَ السَّمَاءِ مَاءً
فَسَلَكَهُۥ يَنَٰبِيعَ فِى الْأَرْضِ
ثُمَّ يُخْرِجُ بِهِۦ زَرْعًا مُّخْتَلِفًا أَلْوَٰنُهُۥ
ثُمَّ يَهِيجُ فَتَرَىٰهُ مُصْفَرًّا
ثُمَّ يَجْعَلُهُۥ حُطَٰمًا ۚ
إِنَّ فِى ذَٰلِكَ
لَذِكْرَىٰ لِأُولِى الْأَلْبَٰبِ ۝

C. 204.—What distance separates the man
(xxxix. 22-52.) Whose heart is melted by the Message
Of God and enlightened by His Light,
And him who rejects Revelation! God

4270. If a man is already steeped in sin and has rejected God's Grace, how can we expect Revelation to work in his soul?

4271. *Cf.* xxix. 58, and xxxiv. 37. The idea of heaven here is that of a Home of sublimity and beauty, with a picturesque outlook, such as we would describe in this life by the type of a palace by gently-flowing streams. The mansions will also suggest generous space and architectural beauty, tiers upon tiers piled one upon another.

4272. *Mī'ād*: the time, place, and manner of the fulfilment of a Promise. God's promise will be fulfilled in all particulars better than we can possibly imagine.

4273. The circuit of water, by which the rain falls from the clouds, is absorbed through the earth, and flows through rivers or underground streams to the sea, where it again rises as vapour and forms clouds, was explained in notes 3111-12 to xxv. 53. Here our attention is drawn to one portion of the process. The rain fructifies the soil and the seeds. Produce of various kinds is raised. The harvest ripens and is gathered in. The plants wither, dry up, and crumble away. Men and animals are fed. And the circuit starts again in another season. Here is a Sign of the Grace and Goodness of God, clear to those who understand.

Teaches men by Parables : straight
Is His Word and clear. Any doubts in the minds
Of men will be resolved after Death:
Even now, God's Signs are enough : no other
Can guide. Death and his twin-brother,
Sleep, are in the hands of God : to Him
Is our Goal. He will judge in the End.
His Will is all-in-all. No other thing
Can be of any account before His Law.

SECTION 3.

22. Is one whose heart
God has opened to Islam,[4274]
So that he has received
Enlightenment from God,
(No better than one hard-hearted)?
Woe to those whose hearts
Are hardened against celebrating[4275]
The praises of God! They
Are manifestly wandering
(In error)!

٢٢- اَفَمَنْ شَرَحَ اللّٰهُ صَدْرَهٗ لِلْاِسْلَامِ
فَهُوَ عَلٰى نُوْرٍ مِّنْ رَّبِّهٖ ؕ
فَوَيْلٌ لِّلْقٰسِيَةِ
قُلُوْبُهُمْ مِّنْ ذِكْرِ اللّٰهِ ؕ
اُولٰٓئِكَ فِيْ ضَلٰلٍ مُّبِيْنٍ ۝

23. God has revealed
(From time to time)
The most beautiful Message
In the form of a Book,
Consistent with itself,[4276]
(Yet) repeating (its teaching

٢٣- اَللّٰهُ نَزَّلَ
اَحْسَنَ الْحَدِيْثِ كِتٰبًا
مُّتَشَابِهًا مَّثَانِيَ ۖ

4274. Those who listen to God's Message find at each stage God's Grace helping them more and more to expand their spiritual understanding and to receive God's light, so that they travel farther and farther to their Goal in the Path of Truth and Righteousness. They are not to be compared to those who shut out God's Light from their hearts. See next note.

4275. Just as there is spiritual progress for those who seek God, so there is more and more spiritual retrogression for those who close their hearts to God. Their hearts get hardened, and they allow less and less God's Grace to penetrate within. But it is obvious that they flounder on the Way, and cannot walk with the firm steps of those of assured Faith.

4276. Is *Mutashābih* here to be understood in the same sense as in iii. 7, where I have translated it as "allegorical"? See n. 347 to iii. 7. The better opinion is that there is a slightly different shade of meaning here, as suggested by the context. In the earlier passage, it was opposed to *Muḥ-kam* : here it is contrasted or compared to *Mat͟hānī*. The root meaning is : 'having something similar ; working by analogy or allegory, or parable ; having its parts consistent with each other'. The last meaning I adopt here. The Qur-ān was revealed in parts at different times. And yet its parts all conform to each other. There is no contradiction or inconsistency anywhere.

In various aspects): [4277]
The skins of those who
Fear their Lord tremble [4278]
Thereat; then their skins
And their hearts do soften
To the celebration of
God's praises. Such is
The guidance of God:
He guides therewith
Whom He pleases, [4279] but such
As God leaves to stray,
Can have none to guide.

تَقْشَعِرُّ مِنْهُ جُلُودُ الَّذِينَ
يَخْشَوْنَ رَبَّهُمْ
ثُمَّ تَلِينُ جُلُودُهُمْ وَقُلُوبُهُمْ
إِلَىٰ ذِكْرِ اللَّهِ ۚ ذَٰلِكَ هُدَى اللَّهِ
يَهْدِي بِهِ مَنْ يَشَاءُ ۚ
وَمَنْ يُضْلِلِ اللَّهُ
فَمَا لَهُ مِنْ هَادٍ ○

24. Is, then, one who
Has to fear the brunt
Of the Penalty on the Day
Of Judgment (and receive it)
On his face, [4280] (like one
Guarded therefrom)? It will

٢٤- أَفَمَنْ يَتَّقِي
بِوَجْهِهِ سُوءَ الْعَذَابِ
يَوْمَ الْقِيَامَةِ ۚ

4277. *Mathānī*: *Cf.* xv. 87, where we have translated "oft-repeated": "the seven *oft-repeated* (verses)". See n. 2008 to that passage. Here the meaning is similar, but the context gives a different colour to it, as is seen in the translation.

4278. The skin is the outer integument of the body. It receives the first shock from the impact of anything unusual, and it trembles and its hair stands on end under excitement. So in spiritual matters the first stimulation from God's Message is external. Those who receive Faith do it as it were with tremor and not with apathy But the next stage is that it penetrates their outer nature and goes right into their hearts. Their whole nature is "softened" to receive the beneficent Message, and it transforms them through and through.

4279. "Whom He pleases" and "leaves to stray" are explained fully in n. 2133 to xvi. 93. See also xiv. 4 and n. 1875.

4280. The unrepentant Sinners will receive the full Penalty on the Day of Judgment. They will receive it full in the face, *i.e.*, their whole being will be affected by it. Their hands (figuratively) will be tied, and they cannot therefore use their hands to ward off the Penalty of the Fire: in any case their hands will not have the power to ward it off. Are such helpless people to be compared for a moment with people who have received Grace and are therefore guarded from all harm and danger? Certainly not. To the evil the fruit of their deeds, and to the good the grace of their Lord!

Be said to the wrong-doers:
" Taste ye (the fruits
Of) what ye earned!"[4281]

وَقِيلَ لِلظَّٰلِمِينَ
ذُوقُوا مَا كُنتُمْ تَكْسِبُونَ ○

25. Those before them (also)
Rejected (revelation), and so
The Punishment came to them
From directions they did not
Perceive.[4282]

٢٥- كَذَّبَ الَّذِينَ مِن قَبْلِهِمْ
فَأَتٰهُمُ الْعَذَابُ
مِنْ حَيْثُ لَا يَشْعُرُونَ ○

26. So God gave them
A taste of humiliation
In the present life,[4283]
But greater is the Punishment
Of the Hereafter,
If they only knew!

٢٦- فَأَذَاقَهُمُ اللهُ الْخِزْيَ
فِي الْحَيٰوةِ الدُّنْيَا
وَلَعَذَابُ الْاٰخِرَةِ أَكْبَرُ لَوْ كَانُوا يَعْلَمُونَ ○

27. We have put forth
For men, in this Qur-ān
Every kind of Parable,[4384]
In order that they
May receive admonition.

٢٧- وَلَقَدْ ضَرَبْنَا لِلنَّاسِ فِي هٰذَا الْقُرْاٰنِ
مِنْ كُلِّ مَثَلٍ
لَّعَلَّهُمْ يَتَذَكَّرُونَ ○

28. (It is) a Qur-ān
In Arabic,[4285] without any

٢٨- قُرْاٰنًا عَرَبِيًّا غَيْرَ ذِي

4281. That is, of all their misdeeds, all the evil which they did in the world.

4282. *Cf.* xvi. 26. They will be punished from quarters or in ways they do not perceive. From their Unbelief and Rebellion they think they derive great advantages, but they suddenly find out, when too late, that that which they exulted in was the cause of their own undoing.

4283. *Cf.* ii. 114. Sin often brings disgrace and humiliation in this life, but the greater and truer punishment is in the Hereafter. But men often do not know the inwardness of this matter. If they flourish here for a time, they think they will escape the real consequences in the Hereafter. Or if they suffer a little harm here, they think that will make up the Penalty, and they will escape the Hereafter. Both ideas are wrong.

4284. Men can only understand high spiritual truths by parables and similitudes and these are given abundantly in the Qur-ān. The object is, not merely to tell stories, but to teach lessons of spiritual wisdom.

4285. Previous revelations had been in other languages. Now the revelation was given in Arabia in Arabic itself, the language of the country which all could understand. And it is a beautiful language, straight and flexible, and fit to be the vehicle of sublime truths. *Cf.* C. 12.

Crookedness (therein):[4286]
In order that they
May guard against Evil.

عِوَجٍ
لَّعَلَّهُمْ يَتَّقُوْنَ ○

29. God puts forth a Parable—
A man belonging to many[4287]
Partners at variance with each
other,
And a man belonging entirely
To one master: are those two
Equal in comparison?
Praise be to God![4288]
But most of them
Have no knowledge.

٢٩ - ضَرَبَ اللّٰهُ مَثَلًا
رَّجُلًا فِيْهِ شُرَكَآءُ مُتَشٰكِسُوْنَ
وَرَجُلًا سَلَمًا لِّرَجُلٍ ط
هَلْ يَسْتَوِيٰنِ مَثَلًا ط
اَلْحَمْدُ لِلّٰهِ ج
بَلْ اَكْثَرُهُمْ لَا يَعْلَمُوْنَ ○

30. Truly thou wilt die[4289]
(One day), and truly they
(Too) will die (one day).

٣٠ - اِنَّكَ مَيِّتٌ
وَّاِنَّهُمْ مَّيِّتُوْنَ ○

31. In the End will ye
(All), on the Day
23 Of Judgment, settle your disputes[4290]
30 In the presence of your Lord.

٣١ - ثُمَّ اِنَّكُمْ يَوْمَ الْقِيٰمَةِ
عِنْدَ رَبِّكُمْ تَخْتَصِمُوْنَ ○ ع

4286 See xviii. 1 and n. 2326. *Cf.* also vii. 45, n. 1024; and xix. 36, n. 2488.

4287. The difference between the creed of Polytheism and the Gospel of Unity is explained by the analogy of two men. One belongs to many masters; the masters disagree among themselves, and the poor man of many masters has to suffer from the quarrels of his many masters; it is an impossible and unnatural position. The other serves only one master; his master is good, and does all he can for his servant; the servant can concentrate his attention on his service; he is happy himself and his service is efficiently performed. Can there be any doubt as to (1) which of them is the happier, and (2) which of them is in a more natural position? No man can serve two, still less numerous, masters.

4288. God is praised that He has put us, not under gods many and lords many, but has, out of His infinite Mercy, allowed us direct approach to Him, the One, the True, the Eternal.

4289. Even the prophets are not exempt from bodily death, much less the righteous, but they live in their beneficent work and the memories they leave behind them. All men have to die, good and bad alike. But there is a life after death, and in that life all the unexplained things about which people dispute in this world will be made clear in the presence of God.

4290. See last note.

Section 4.

32. Who, then, doth more wrong
Than one who utters
A lie concerning God,[4291]
And rejects the Truth
When it comes to him!
Is there not in Hell[4292]
An abode for blasphemers?

٣٢- فَمَنْ أَظْلَمُ مِمَّنْ كَذَبَ عَلَى اللّٰهِ
وَكَذَّبَ بِالصِّدْقِ إِذْ جَآءَهُ ط
أَلَيْسَ فِي جَهَنَّمَ
مَثْوًى لِّلْكٰفِرِيْنَ ○

33. And he who brings the Truth
And he who confirms[4293]
(And supports) it—such are
The men who do right.

٣٣- وَالَّذِيْ جَآءَ بِالصِّدْقِ وَصَدَّقَ بِهٖٓ
أُولٰٓئِكَ هُمُ الْمُتَّقُوْنَ ○

34. They shall have all
That they wish for,[4294]
In the presence of their Lord:
Such is the reward
Of those who do good:

٣٤- لَهُمْ مَّا يَشَآءُوْنَ
عِنْدَ رَبِّهِمْ ط
ذٰلِكَ جَزٰٓؤُا الْمُحْسِنِيْنَ ○

35. So that God will
Turn off from them
(Even) the worst in their deeds[4295]
And give them their reward
According to the best
Of what they have done.

٣٥- لِيُكَفِّرَ اللّٰهُ عَنْهُمْ أَسْوَأَ الَّذِيْ عَمِلُوْا
وَيَجْزِيَهُمْ أَجْرَهُمْ بِأَحْسَنِ الَّذِيْ
كَانُوْا يَعْمَلُوْنَ ○

4291. When the creature deliberately adopts and utters falsehoods against his own Creator, in spite of the Truth being brought, as it were, to his very door by God's Signs, what offence can we imagine more heinous than this? In Christian theology this is the blasphemy "against the Holy Ghost" spoken of in Matt. xii. 31-32: "whosoever speaketh a word against the Son of man", (Christ)," it shall be forgiven him; but whosoever speaketh against the Holy Ghost, it shall not be forgiven him, neither in this world, neither in the world to come".

4292. Blasphemers have really no place to go to. The question form suggests that even Hell is not an *abode* for them; it is merely a place for punishment or a state of punishment.

4293. This is true of the Prophet, and all men of God and all righteous persons. Any one who preaches the Truth and brings home God's Signs to men is performing the duty of a right and noble life. In this he confirms the teaching of all previous men of God. Any one who supports and confirms such a teacher is also doing his duty and on the right way.

4294. At that stage their wills will have been purified, and they could wish for nothing that they could not or should not have. And it will be as "in the presence of their Lord". If an earthly king gives a decoration, how much greater is the honour when the investiture takes place by the king himself personally?

4295. The conjunction (*lām* in Arabic, translated "so that") indicates here the results, not the purpose. God's Reward is so bounteous, that if we truly and sincerely put our will into His keeping. He will remove the consequences not only of our minor faults but of the worst of our sins, and judge us according to the very best of our deeds.

36. Is not God enough[4296]
For His servant? But
They try to frighten thee
With other (gods) besides Him!
For such as God leaves
To stray, there can be
No guide.

٣٦- أَلَيْسَ اللَّهُ بِكَافٍ عَبْدَهُ ۖ
وَيُخَوِّفُونَكَ بِالَّذِينَ مِن دُونِهِ ۚ
وَمَن يُضْلِلِ اللَّهُ
فَمَا لَهُ مِنْ هَادٍ ○

37. And such as God doth[4297]
Guide there can be
None to lead astray.
Is not God Exalted
In Power, (Able to enforce
His Will), Lord of Retribution?[4298]

٣٧- وَمَن يَهْدِ اللَّهُ
فَمَا لَهُ مِن مُّضِلٍّ ۗ
أَلَيْسَ اللَّهُ بِعَزِيزٍ ذِي انتِقَامٍ ○

38. If indeed thou ask them
Who it is that created[4299]
The heavens and the earth,
They would be sure to say,
"God". Say: "See ye then?
The things that ye invoke
Besides God,—can they,
If God wills some Penalty
For me, remove His Penalty?—
Or if He wills some Grace
For me, can they keep back[4300]

٣٨- وَلَئِن سَأَلْتَهُم مَّنْ خَلَقَ السَّمَاوَاتِ وَ
الْأَرْضَ لَيَقُولُنَّ اللَّهُ ۚ قُلْ أَفَرَأَيْتُم
مَّا تَدْعُونَ مِن دُونِ اللَّهِ
إِنْ أَرَادَنِيَ اللَّهُ بِضُرٍّ
هَلْ هُنَّ كَاشِفَاتُ ضُرِّهِ
أَوْ أَرَادَنِي بِرَحْمَةٍ هَلْ هُنَّ مُمْسِكَاتُ

4296. The righteous man will find God enough for all the protection he needs, all the rest and peace he craves for, and all the happiness he can imagine. If the evil ones wish to frighten him with false gods, he knows that that is mere superstition. In the case of idols to whom worship is paid, this is easily intelligible. But there are other false gods which men worship,—wealth, position, power, science, selfish desire, and so on. The idea may occur to them: "this is the right course, but what will men say?" or "shall I lose my case if I tell the truth?" or "will it ruin my chances if I denounce sin in high places?" All such false gods will only mislead and leave their victims in the lurch. The worship of them will lose them the Grace of God, which wants to guide and comfort all who seek God.

4297. On the other hand if any one holds fast to God's Truth, nothing can mislead or betray him.

4298. God's Power can protect, and will defeat all plots against His Will, as well as punish Evil when it gets beyond bounds.

4299. *Cf.* xxix. 61; also n. 2927 to xxiii. 85. Most worshippers of false gods are not either atheists or sceptics. They admit the existence of God as an abstract proposition, but it has not come into their hearts and souls: it has not been translated into their lives. They run after false worship on account of ancestral custom or on account of their thoughtlessness or false environment, or on account of their own selfish desires or limited outlook. To them is addressed the argument: 'Ultimately your false gods can do nothing for you: why not turn to the One True God, on Whom you depend, and Who can give you Grace and Mercy, Justice and Punishment?'

4300. *Cf.* xxxiii. 17.

His Grace?" Say: "Sufficient
Is God for me!
In Him trust those
Who put their trust." [4301]

رَحْمَتِهٖ ۭ قُلْ حَسْبِيَ اللّٰهُ ۭ
عَلَيْهِ يَتَوَكَّلُ الْمُتَوَكِّلُوْنَ ○

39. Say: "O my people!
Do whatever ye can:
I will do (my part): [4302]
But soon will ye know—

۳۹- قُلْ يٰقَوْمِ اعْمَلُوْا عَلٰى مَكَانَتِكُمْ
اِنِّيْ عَامِلٌ ۚ فَسَوْفَ تَعْلَمُوْنَ ○

40. "Who it is to whom
Comes a Penalty [4303]
Of ignominy, and on whom
Descends a Penalty that abides."

۴۰- مَنْ يَّاْتِيْهِ عَذَابٌ يُّخْزِيْهِ
وَيَحِلُّ عَلَيْهِ عَذَابٌ مُّقِيْمٌ ○

41. Verily We have revealed
The Book to thee
In Truth, for (instructing)
mankind. [4304]
He, then, that receives guidance
Benefits his own soul:
But he that strays
Injures his own soul.
Nor art thou set [4305]
Over them to dispose
Of their affairs.

۴۱- اِنَّآ اَنْزَلْنَا عَلَيْكَ الْكِتٰبَ
لِلنَّاسِ بِالْحَقِّ ۚ
فَمَنِ اهْتَدٰى فَلِنَفْسِهٖ ۚ
وَمَنْ ضَلَّ فَاِنَّمَا يَضِلُّ عَلَيْهَا ۚ
وَمَآ اَنْتَ عَلَيْهِمْ بِوَكِيْلٍ ○ ع

Section 5.

42. It is God that takes
The souls (of men) at death; [4306]

۴۲- اَللّٰهُ يَتَوَفَّى الْاَنْفُسَ حِيْنَ مَوْتِهَا

4301. *Cf.* xii. 67 and xiv. 12. God alone is He Who will and can discharge any trust put in Him. All other things will fail. Therefore those who put their trust in anything should put their trust in God.

4302. *Cf.* xi. 121 and n. 1624-A.

4303. *Cf.* xi. 93. The two clauses, about those who suffer a Penalty of ignominy and those on whom descends a lasting Penalty, apparently refer to the same persons in two different aspects: (1) they suffer shame, and (2) their punishment endures.

4304. Revelation is sent by God through His messenger, but it is for all. It is given in order that men and women may be taught Righteousness. It is given in Truth: there is no pretence about it. It is for their own good. If they reject it and follow Evil, the loss is their own.

4305. God's apostles do all they can to teach mankind. But they cannot force men's wills. If men reject their teaching, the account of the rejecters is with God. *Cf.* vi. 107 and n. 935.

4306. The mystery of life and death, sleep and dreams, is a fascinating enigma, of which the solution is perhaps beyond the ken of man. A vast mass of superstition as well as imaginative and psychological literature has grown up about it. But the simplest and truest religious doctrine is laid down here in a few words. In death we surrender our physical life, but our soul does dot die; it goes back to a plane of existence in which it is more conscious of the realities of the spiritual world: "God takes the soul".

And those that die not
(He takes) during their sleep:[4307]
Those on whom He
Has passed the decree
Of death, He keeps back[4308]
(From returning to life),
But the rest He sends
(To their bodies)
For a term appointed.
Verily in this are Signs[4309]
For those who reflect.

وَالَّتِيْ لَمْ تَمُتْ فِيْ مَنَامِهَا ۚ
فَيُمْسِكُ الَّتِيْ قَضٰى عَلَيْهَا الْمَوْتَ
وَيُرْسِلُ الْاُخْرٰٓى
اِلٰٓى اَجَلٍ مُّسَمًّى ۭ
اِنَّ فِيْ ذٰلِكَ لَاٰيٰتٍ
لِّقَوْمٍ يَّتَفَكَّرُوْنَ ○

43. What! Do they take
For intercessors others[4310]
Besides God? Say: "Even if
They have no power whatever
And no intelligence?"

٤٣- اَمِ اتَّخَذُوْا مِنْ دُوْنِ اللّٰهِ شُفَعَاۗءَ ۭ
قُلْ اَوَلَوْ كَانُوْا لَا يَمْلِكُوْنَ شَيْـًٔا
وَّلَا يَعْقِلُوْنَ ○

44. Say: "To God belongs
Exclusively (the right

٤٤- قُلْ لِّلّٰهِ

4307. *Cf.* vi. 60. What is sleep? As far as animal life is concerned, it is the cessation of the working of the nervous system, though other animal functions, such as digestion, growth, and the circulation of the blood, continue, possibly at a different pace. It is the repose of the nervous system, and in this respect it is common to man and animals, and perhaps even to plants, if, as is probable, plants have a nervous system The mental processes (and certainly volition) are also suspended in sleep, except that in ordinary dreams there is a medley of recollections, which often present vividly to our consciousness things that do not or cannot happen in nature as we know it in our co-ordinated minds. But there is another kind of dream which is rarer—one in which the dreamer sees things as they actually happen, backwards or forwards in time, or in which gifted individuals see spiritual truths otherwise imperceptible to them. How can we explain this? It is suggested that our soul or personality,—that something which is above our animal life—is then in a plane of spiritual existence akin to physical death (see last note), when we are nearer to God. In poetic imagery, Sleep is "twin-brother to Death".

4308. Sleep being twin-brother to Death, our souls are for the time being released from the bondage of the flesh. God takes them for the time being. If, as some do, we are to die peacefully in sleep, our soul does not come back to the physical body, and the latter decays and dies. If we have still some period of life to fulfil according to God's decree, our soul comes back to the body, and we resume our functions in this life.

4309. If we contemplate these things, we can see more clearly many spiritual truths: *e.g.* (1) that our bodily life and death are not the whole story of our existence; (2) that in our bodily life we may be dead to the spiritual world, and in our bodily death, may be our awakening to the spiritual world; (3) that our nightly Sleep, besides performing the function of rest to our physical life, gives us a foretaste of what we call death, which does not end our personality; and (4) that the Resurrection is not more wonderful than our daily rising from Sleep, "twin-brother to Death".

4310. Let alone worship, men should not rely upon any power or person other than God to help them out or intercede for them. When it is idols, they are poor lifeless things which have obviously neither power nor intelligence. But even prophets or saints or heroes have no power to intercede except as God wills and permits. See next note.

To grant) Intercession:[4311]
To Him belongs the dominion
Of the heavens and the earth:
In the End, it is to Him[4312]
That ye shall be
Brought back."

الشَّفَاعَةُ جَمِيعًا ۖ
لَهُ مُلْكُ السَّمٰوٰتِ وَالْأَرْضِ ۖ
ثُمَّ إِلَيْهِ تُرْجَعُونَ ○

45. When God, the One and Only,
Is mentioned, the hearts
Of those who believe not
In the Hereafter are filled
With disgust and horror;[4313]
But when (gods) other than He
Are mentioned, behold,
They are filled with joy!

٤٥- وَإِذَا ذُكِرَ اللّٰهُ وَحْدَهُ اشْمَأَزَّتْ قُلُوبُ
الَّذِينَ لَا يُؤْمِنُونَ بِالْآخِرَةِ ۚ
وَإِذَا ذُكِرَ الَّذِينَ مِنْ دُونِهِ
إِذَا هُمْ يَسْتَبْشِرُونَ ○

46. Say: "O God!
Creator of the heavens
And the earth!
Knower of all that is
Hidden and open![4314]
It is Thou that wilt
Judge between Thy Servants
In those matters about which
They have differed."

٤٦- قُلِ اللّٰهُمَّ فَاطِرَ السَّمٰوٰتِ وَالْأَرْضِ
عٰلِمَ الْغَيْبِ وَالشَّهَادَةِ
أَنْتَ تَحْكُمُ بَيْنَ عِبَادِكَ
فِي مَا كَانُوا فِيهِ يَخْتَلِفُونَ ○

47. Even if the wrong-doers
Had all that there is
On earth, and as much more,[4315]
(In vain) would they offer it

٤٧- وَلَوْ أَنَّ لِلَّذِينَ ظَلَمُوا
مَا فِي الْأَرْضِ جَمِيعًا وَمِثْلَهُ مَعَهُ

4311. For *Shafā'at* (Intercession, Advocacy) see ii. 255; x. 3; xx. 109, n. 2634; and xxi. 28, n. 2688. It follows that no one can intercede with God, except (1) by God's permission, and (2) for those who have prepared themselves by penitence for God's acceptance. Even in earthly Courts, Advocacy is not permitted to any one: the Advocate must be granted the position of Advocate before he can plead before the judge. Nor can it be supposed that a plea for forgiveness or mercy can be put forward except on grounds recognised by equity and justice.

4312. At all times, including our present life, all dominion belongs to God. At the End of the present plane of existence, we shall be placed before God for Judgment. *Cf.* x. 4.

4313. To evil ones, the mention of the exclusive service of Good is hateful: they only rejoice when other motives are added, *e.g.*, personal indulgence, ancestral custom, and numerous things in life which compete with God's Law in this world.

4314. The mysteries of life and death, of worship and spiritual growth, are matters of high moment, which it may be difficult for us to apprehend in this present life. It is no use arguing about them and plunging in endless controversies. The proper attitude is to appeal to God humbly to accept our purified hearts and Faith, in the firm hope that everything which is now vague to us will be cleared up in the Hereafter, and to pray to Him for His guidance and mercy.

4315. *Cf.* xiii. 18. Those who reject God's Message must realise that the time will come when they will wish they had sacrificed everything in the cause of Truth and Righteousness. It will be too late then. Why not examine the matter seriously now and accept God's Grace and Light?

For ransom from the pain
Of the Penalty on the Day
Of Judgment : but something
Will confront them from God,
Which they could never
Have counted upon ![4316]

لَافْتَدَوْا بِهٖ مِنْ سُوْٓءِ الْعَذَابِ يَوْمَ الْقِيٰمَةِ ۭ
وَبَدَا لَهُمْ مِّنَ اللّٰهِ
مَا لَمْ يَكُوْنُوْا يَحْتَسِبُوْنَ ○

48. For the evils of their Deeds
Will confront them,
And they will be (completely)[4317]
Encircled by that which
They used to mock at !

٤٨- وَبَدَا لَهُمْ سَيِّاٰتُ مَا كَسَبُوْا
وَحَاقَ بِهِمْ
مَّا كَانُوْا بِهٖ يَسْتَهْزِءُوْنَ ○

49. Now, when trouble touches man,
He cries to Us :[4318]
But when We bestow
A favour upon him[4319]
As from Ourselves,
He says, " This has been
Given to me because of
A certain knowledge (I have) ! "[4320]
Nay, but this is
But a trial, but most
Of them understand not !

٤٩- فَاِذَا مَسَّ الْاِنْسَانَ ضُرٌّ دَعَانَا ۡ
ثُمَّ اِذَا خَوَّلْنٰهُ نِعْمَةً مِّنَّا ۙ
قَالَ اِنَّمَآ اُوْتِيْتُهٗ عَلٰى عِلْمٍ ۭ
بَلْ هِيَ فِتْنَةٌ
وَّلٰكِنَّ اَكْثَرَهُمْ لَا يَعْلَمُوْنَ ○

50. Thus did the (generations)
Before them say ! But
All that they did
Was of no profit to them.

٥٠- قَدْ قَالَهَا الَّذِيْنَ مِنْ قَبْلِهِمْ
فَمَآ اَغْنٰى عَنْهُمْ مَّا كَانُوْا يَكْسِبُوْنَ ○

51. Nay, the evil results
Of their deeds overtook them.[4321]
And the wrong-doers
Of this (generation)—
The evil results of their deeds
Will soon overtake them (too),[4322]

٥١- فَاَصَابَهُمْ سَيِّاٰتُ مَا كَسَبُوْا ۭ
وَالَّذِيْنَ ظَلَمُوْا مِنْ هٰٓؤُلَآءِ
سَيُصِيْبُهُمْ سَيِّاٰتُ مَا كَسَبُوْا ۙ

4316. This something wlll be beyond anything they can conceive of in this life. Just as the righteous will then attain a bliss which no human imagination can conceive of now, so the unrighteous will be in a misery of which they can form no conception now. See next note.

4317. How humiliating it will be for them to realise that the things they used to mock at are realities all around them, and the things they were so eager to pursue are mere falsehoods or vanities !

4318. *Cf.* xxx. 33 and n. 3545.

4319. *Cf.* xxxix. 8 above.

4320. *Cf.* xxviii 78, and n. 3408. Prosperity may be a trial as much as adversity.

4321. *Cf.* xvi. 34.

4322. It is the same story through the ages. People laugh at Truth, persecute Truth, and try to destroy Truth. But God's Plan is never to be frustrated. It will be carried out, and only the enemies of Truth will accomplish their own undoing. So it happened in Arabia : so will it happen always and everywhere.

And they will never be
Able to frustrate (Our Plan)!

وَمَا هُمْ بِمُعْجِزِينَ ۝

52. Know they not that
God enlarges the provision [4323]
Or restricts it, for any
He pleases? Verily, in this are
Signs for those who believe!

٥٢- أَوَلَمْ يَعْلَمُوا أَنَّ اللَّهَ يَبْسُطُ الرِّزْقَ
لِمَنْ يَشَاءُ وَيَقْدِرُ ۚ
إِنَّ فِي ذَٰلِكَ لَآيَاتٍ لِقَوْمٍ يُؤْمِنُونَ ۝

C. 205.—But no soul need be in despair because
(xxxix. 53-75.) Of its sin: God's Forgiveness and Mercy are
Unbounded Turn to God in repentance
Now, for at Judgment it will be too late.
Unity in worship and life is commanded
By God. Go not astray. When Judgment
Comes, it will be a new World.
In perfect justice will the followers
Of Evil be sorted out from the Good.
And the righteous will rejoice, singing
Praises to God with the angels on high.

Section 6.

53. Say: "O my Servants who
Have transgressed against their souls!
Despair not of the Mercy
Of God: for God forgives [4324]
All sins: for He is
Oft-Forgiving, Most Merciful.

٥٣- قُلْ يَا عِبَادِيَ الَّذِينَ أَسْرَفُوا عَلَىٰ أَنْفُسِهِمْ
لَا تَقْنَطُوا مِنْ رَحْمَةِ اللَّهِ ۚ إِنَّ اللَّهَ يَغْفِرُ
الذُّنُوبَ جَمِيعًا ۚ إِنَّهُ هُوَ الْغَفُورُ الرَّحِيمُ ۝

54. "Turn ye to your Lord
(In repentance) and bow
To His (Will), before [4325]
The Penalty comes on you:
After that ye shall not
Be helped.

٥٤- وَأَنِيبُوا إِلَىٰ رَبِّكُمْ وَأَسْلِمُوا لَهُ مِنْ قَبْلِ
أَنْ يَأْتِيَكُمُ الْعَذَابُ
ثُمَّ لَا تُنْصَرُونَ ۝

4323. *Cf.* xxviii. 82. God's gifts are given to all men—to some in a greater degree than to others. But it is all done according to His wise Plan, for His Will is just and looks to the good of all creatures. No one should therefore be puffed up in prosperity or cast down in adversity. Prosperity does not necessarily mean merit on man's part, nor adversity the reverse. Thinking men bear in mind the large Plan—which is visible in all God's Signs.

4324. *Forgives all sins: i.e.*, on sincere repentance and amendment of conduct.

4325. The exhortation in brief is: 'Repent and work righteousness, before it becomes too late'. No help will come to you when the Judgment is actually established and you stand before the Judgment-Seat.

55. "And follow the Best[4326]
Of (the courses) revealed
To you from your Lord,
Before the Penalty comes
On you—of a sudden,
While ye perceive not!—

٥٥-وَاتَّبِعُوٓا اَحْسَنَ مَآ اُنْزِلَ اِلَيْكُمْ مِّنْ
رَّبِّكُمْ مِّنْ قَبْلِ اَنْ يَّاْتِيَكُمُ الْعَذَابُ بَغْتَةً
وَّاَنْتُمْ لَا تَشْعُرُوْنَ ۝

56. "Lest the soul should (then)
Say: 'Ah! woe is me!—[4327]
In that I neglected
(My Duty) towards God,
And was but among those
Who mocked!'—

٥٦-اَنْ تَقُوْلَ نَفْسٌ يّٰحَسْرَتٰى
عَلٰى مَا فَرَّطْتُّ فِيْ جَنْۢبِ اللّٰهِ
وَاِنْ كُنْتُ لَمِنَ السّٰخِرِيْنَ ۝

57. "Or (lest) it should say:[4328]
'If only God had guided
Me, I should certainly
Have been among the righteous!'—

٥٧-اَوْ تَقُوْلَ لَوْ اَنَّ اللّٰهَ هَدٰىنِيْ
لَكُنْتُ مِنَ الْمُتَّقِيْنَ ۝

58. "Or (lest) it should say[4329]
When it (actually) sees
The Penalty: 'If only
I had another chance,
I should certainly be
Among those who do good!'

٥٨-اَوْ تَقُوْلَ حِيْنَ تَرَى الْعَذَابَ
لَوْ اَنَّ لِيْ كَرَّةً
فَاَكُوْنَ مِنَ الْمُحْسِنِيْنَ ۝

59. "(The reply will be:) 'Nay,[4330]
But there came to thee

٥٩-بَلٰى قَدْ جَآءَتْكَ

4326. *Cf.* xxxix. 18, and n. 4269. God's Command meets the weakness of His weakest servants, and only asks that His servants should surrender their selfish will to God's Will. In divine compassion, therefore, we are allowed to do just what we can, even though our standard should fall short of the highest standard. But our aim should be to follow the highest standard, and God's Grace will come to our assistance. But we must do so in this life,—and at once, as soon as the Word penetrates our mind or understanding. We must not delay a moment, for the Judgment may come at any time, suddenly, before we even perceive where we are.

4327. Many kinds of sighs and regrets will then assail us. In the first place, we shall see our shortcomings: we were negligent when we should have been serious: we mocked when we should have tried to learn and understand. But it will be too late then to retrieve our position.

4328. In the second place, we might be inclined to say, 'I wish I had received warning or guidance'. But this would not be true, because the warning and guidance are being conveyed in the clearest manner in God's Revelation. That is the force of 'lest it should say'. It could have said so, had it not seen that the objection is clearly anticipated in the call to repent and in the warning about the Hereafter.

4329. In the third place, when we stand face to face with the Penalty of our own deeds, we might say, 'I wish I had another chance'. But not one, but many, chances are being given, especially when we are told (verse 53 above): 'Despair not of the Mercy of God: for God forgives all sins: for He is Oft-Forgiving, Most Merciful'. The force of 'lest it should say' here is the same as explained in the last note.

4330. The reply explains how all such pleas have been anticipated and met It was deliberate rejection that will deserve and meet its consequences. It is further explained that the motive of sin, as with Satan, was haughtiness and Self. There is no room for Self when the only Reality is God.

My Signs, and thou didst
Reject them : thou wast [4331]
Haughty, and became one
Of those who reject Faith!'"

آيٰتِيْ فَكَذَّبْتَ بِهَا
وَاسْتَكْبَرْتَ وَكُنْتَ مِنَ الْكٰفِرِيْنَ ○

60. On the Day of Judgment
Wilt thou see those
Who told lies against God ;—
Their faces will be turned [4332]
Black ; is there not
In Hell an abode [4333]
For the Haughty ?

٦٠- وَيَوْمَ الْقِيٰمَةِ تَرَى
الَّذِيْنَ كَذَبُوْا عَلَى اللّٰهِ
وُجُوْهُهُمْ مُّسْوَدَّةٌ ط
اَلَيْسَ فِيْ جَهَنَّمَ مَثْوًى لِّلْمُتَكَبِّرِيْنَ ○

61. But God will deliver
The righteous to their place [4334]
Of salvation : no evil
Shall touch them,
Nor shall they grieve.

٦١- وَيُنَجِّي اللّٰهُ الَّذِيْنَ اتَّقَوْا بِمَفَازَتِهِمْ ز
لَا يَمَسُّهُمُ السُّوْٓءُ
وَلَا هُمْ يَحْزَنُوْنَ ○

62. God is the Creator
Of all things, and He
Is the Guardian and Disposer [4335]
Of all affairs.

٦٢- اَللّٰهُ خَالِقُ كُلِّ شَيْءٍ ز
وَّهُوَ عَلٰى كُلِّ شَيْءٍ وَّكِيْلٌ ○

63. To Him belong the keys
Of the heavens
And the earth :
And those who reject
The Signs of God,—
It is they who will [4336]
Be in loss.

٦٣- لَهٗ مَقَالِيْدُ السَّمٰوٰتِ وَالْاَرْضِ ط
وَالَّذِيْنَ كَفَرُوْا بِاٰيٰتِ اللّٰهِ
اُولٰٓئِكَ هُمُ الْخٰسِرُوْنَ ○ ع

4331. *Cf.* ii. 34. The example of the arch-sinner illustrates what happens in a minor degree in every kind of sinner.

4332. As spotless white is the symbol of purity, honour, and truth, so black is the symbol of evil, disgrace, and falsehood. Perhaps "black" in connection with Hell also refers to the scorching punishment of the Fire.

4333. *Cf.* above, xxxix. 32, and n. 4292, where the subtle implication of the interrogative form is explained.

4334. *Mafāzat* : place or state of safety or salvation, place or state of victory or achievement ; accomplishment of wish or desire. This is contrasted against the frustration, failure, and perdition of the children of evil,—what may be called damnation in theological phrase.

4335. God has not only created all the Worlds, but He maintains them and cares for them. He does not sit apart from His world. Everything depends upon Him.

4336. God has nothing to lose by the rebellion or disobedience of His creatures. It is they who lose, because they go counter to their own nature, the beautiful mould in which God created them.

Section 7.

64. Say : " Is it
Some one other than God
That ye order me [4337]
To worship, O ye
Ignorant ones ? "

٦٤- قُلْ أَفَغَيْرَ اللَّهِ
تَأْمُرُوٓنِّىٓ أَعْبُدُ
أَيُّهَا الْجَٰهِلُونَ ○

65. But it has already
Been revealed to thee,— [4338]
As it was to those
Before thee,—" If thou
Wert to join (gods
With God), truly fruitless [4339]
Will be thy work (in life),
And thou wilt surely
Be in the ranks of those
Who lose (all spiritual good) ".

٦٥- وَلَقَدْ أُوحِىَ إِلَيْكَ
وَإِلَى الَّذِينَ مِن قَبْلِكَ
لَئِنْ أَشْرَكْتَ
لَيَحْبَطَنَّ عَمَلُكَ
وَلَتَكُونَنَّ مِنَ الْخَٰسِرِينَ ○

66. Nay, but worship God,
And be of those who
Give thanks. [4340]

٦٦- بَلِ اللَّهَ فَاعْبُدْ
وَكُن مِّنَ الشَّٰكِرِينَ ○

67. No just estimate
Have they made of God, [4341]
Such as is due to Him :
On the Day of Judgment
The whole of the earth
Will be but His handful, [4342]
And the heavens will be

٦٧- وَمَا قَدَرُوا اللَّهَ
حَقَّ قَدْرِهِۦ
وَالْأَرْضُ جَمِيعًا قَبْضَتُهُۥ يَوْمَ الْقِيَٰمَةِ
وَالسَّمَٰوَٰتُ

4337. "*Order me*" : there is great irony here. The man of God turns to his critics and says: "You arrogate to yourselves the right to *order* me how to worship! But who are you? You are only ignorant men! My commission is from God. It is the same as came to men of God before me in all ages, *viz.* (1) that the only Truth is in the Gospel of Unity; and (2) that if you worship other things and turn away from God, your life will be wasted and all your probation will have been of no account.

4338. The Message of Unity, renewed in Islam, has been the Message of God since the world began.

4339. *Cf.* v. 6. False worship means that we run after fruitless things, and the main purpose of our spiritual lives is lost.

4340. To "give thanks" is to show by our conduct that we esteem the gifts of God and will use them in His service.

4341. *Cf.* vi. 91, and n. 909; and xxii. 74. In running after false gods or the powers of nature they have forgotten that all creatures are as nothing before God.

4342. See last note. The whole earth will be no more to God than a thing that a man might enclose in the hollow of his hand, nor will the heavens with their vast expanse be more than a scroll, which a man might roll up with his right hand, the hand of power and action. This is of course figurative. God is not a creature of flesh and blood, with hands or fingers. *Cf.* xxi. 104, and lxxxi. 1.

Rolled up in His right hand :
Glory to Him !
High is He above
The Partners they attribute
To Him !

مَطْوِيّٰتٌۢ بِيَمِيْنِهٖ
سُبْحٰنَهٗ
وَتَعٰلٰى عَمَّا يُشْرِكُوْنَ ۝

68. The Trumpet will (just)
Be sounded, when all
That are in the heavens
And on earth will swoon,[4343]
Except such as it will
Please God (to exempt).
Then will a second one
Be sounded, when, behold,
They will be standing
And looking on !

٦٨- وَنُفِخَ فِى الصُّوْرِ
فَصَعِقَ مَنْ فِى السَّمٰوٰتِ وَمَنْ فِى الْاَرْضِ
اِلَّا مَنْ شَآءَ اللّٰهُ
ثُمَّ نُفِخَ فِيْهِ اُخْرٰى
فَاِذَا هُمْ قِيَامٌ يَّنْظُرُوْنَ ۝

69. And the Earth will shine
With the glory of its Lord :[4344]
The Record (of Deeds)
Will be placed (open) ;
The prophets and the witnesses
Will be brought forward ;
And a just decision[4345]
Pronounced between them ;
And they will not
Be wronged (in the least).

٦٩- وَاَشْرَقَتِ الْاَرْضُ بِنُوْرِ رَبِّهَا
وَوُضِعَ الْكِتٰبُ
وَجِاىْٓءَ بِالنَّبِيّٖنَ وَالشُّهَدَآءِ
وَقُضِىَ بَيْنَهُمْ بِالْحَقِّ
وَهُمْ لَا يُظْلَمُوْنَ ۝

70. And to every soul will be
Paid in full (the fruit)

٧٠- وَوُفِّيَتْ كُلُّ نَفْسٍ

4343. *Ṣa'iqa* implied the idea of a swoon, or loss of all consciousness of being ; it implies a cessation of the normal functioning of the usual powers of life or feeling. The metaphor is that with the first Trumpet of the Resurrection, the whole world will cease to be in the form and the relations which we see now : there will be a new heaven and a new earth, see xiv. 48, n. 1925 ; human souls will for the time being be dazed and lose all memory or consciousness of time or place or personality. With the second one, they will stand in a new world ; they will see with clearer vision than ever before ; and judgment will proceed.

4344. It will be a new Earth. All traces of injustice or inequality, darkness or evil, will have gone. There will be the one universal Light, the Glory of God, which will now illuminate all. Falsehood, pretence, and illusion will have disappeared. Everything will be seen in its true light.

4345. It is in such a scene of Reality that Judgment will be held. Before the Throne of God (if we may use metaphors again to form some idea out of the things we know) the book of each man's deeds and motives will be placed wide open, which all may see ; the Prophets and Preachers of Truth, and the martyrs who gave their lives or made their real sacrifices in the cause of Truth, will be in the Court, to give evidence ; and the decision pronounced will be absolutely just, for the Judge will not only be just, but He will know every fact and circumstance, and His wisdom will give due weight to everything, great or small.

Of its deeds ; and (God)
Knoweth best all that [4346]
They do.

تَا عَمِلَتْ
وَهُوَ اَعْلَمُ بِمَا يَفْعَلُوْنَ ۝ ؏

SECTION 8.

71. The Unbelievers will be
Led to Hell in crowd : [4347]
Until, when they arrive there,
Its gates will be opened.
And its Keepers will say, [4348]
" Did not apostles come
To you from among yourselves,
Rehearsing to you the Signs
Of your Lord, and warning you
Of the Meeting of this Day
Of yours ?" The answer
Will be : " True : but
The Decree of Punishment
Has been proved true [4349]
Against the Unbelievers ! "

٧١- وَسِيْقَ الَّذِيْنَ كَفَرُوْا اِلٰى جَهَنَّمَ زُمَرًا ط
حَتّٰى اِذَا جَآءُوْهَا فُتِحَتْ اَبْوَابُهَا
وَقَالَ لَهُمْ خَزَنَتُهَا اَلَمْ يَاْتِكُمْ رُسُلٌ
مِّنْكُمْ
يَتْلُوْنَ عَلَيْكُمْ اٰيٰتِ رَبِّكُمْ وَيُنْذِرُوْنَكُمْ
لِقَآءَ يَوْمِكُمْ هٰذَا ط
قَالُوْا بَلٰى وَلٰكِنْ
حَقَّتْ كَلِمَةُ الْعَذَابِ عَلَى الْكٰفِرِيْنَ ۝

72. (To them) will be said :
" Enter ye the gates of Hell,
To dwell therein :
And evil is (this)
Abode of the arrogant ! " [4350]

٧٢- قِيْلَ ادْخُلُوْٓا اَبْوَابَ جَهَنَّمَ
خٰلِدِيْنَ فِيْهَا ج
فَبِئْسَ مَثْوَى الْمُتَكَبِّرِيْنَ ۝

73. And those who feared
Their Lord will be led
To the Garden in crowds : [4351]
Until behold, they arrive there ;

٧٣- وَسِيْقَ الَّذِيْنَ اتَّقَوْا رَبَّهُمْ اِلَى الْجَنَّةِ
زُمَرًا ط حَتّٰى اِذَا جَآءُوْهَا

4346. In an earthly court, a decision may possibly go wrong because the judge is deceived; here no deceit or mistake will be possible, for God knows all, and knows it better than any one else can.

4347. *Crowds* : this is the word which gives the key-note to the Sūra. If the soul does not stand to its own convictions or search out the Truth by itself, it will only be classed with the crowds that go to Perdition !

4348. The Keepers may be supposed to be angels, who know nothing of the conditions of evil on this earth, and are surprised at such crowds coming to the "Evil Abode". Their question is more like that of a remark or comment by the Chorus in a Greek Tragedy.

4349. *Cf.* x. 33. The answer is perhaps given by other angels : 'yes ; apostles were sent to them from among themselves, to warn them and to proclaim to them Mercy through repentance ; but the decree of God, which warned them of punishment, has now come true against them, for they rebelled and were haughty ; they rejected Truth, Faith, and Mercy !'

4350. As elsewhere, the root of Evil is pointed out to be in self-love and arrogance. *Cf.* ii. 34, etc.

4351. The righteous ones will also go in crowds, and not be alone. There is now a true sorting out. Verses 73-75 are parallel in contrast to verses 71-72 above.

Its gates will be opened;
And its Keepers will say:
"Peace be upon you!
Well have ye done![4352]
Enter ye here,
To dwell therein."

وَفُتِحَتْ أَبْوَابُهَا وَقَالَ لَهُمْ خَزَنَتُهَا
سَلَٰمٌ عَلَيْكُمْ طِبْتُمْ
فَادْخُلُوهَا خَٰلِدِينَ ۝

74. They will say: "Praise be[4353]
To God, Who has
Truly fulfilled His promise
To us, and has given us
(This) land in heritage:[4354]
We can dwell in the Garden
As we will: how excellent
A reward for those
Who work (righteousness)!"

٧٤- وَقَالُوا الْحَمْدُ لِلَّهِ الَّذِي
صَدَقَنَا وَعْدَهُ
وَأَوْرَثَنَا الْأَرْضَ
نَتَبَوَّأُ مِنَ الْجَنَّةِ حَيْثُ نَشَاءُ
فَنِعْمَ أَجْرُ الْعَٰمِلِينَ ۝

75. And thou wilt see
The angels surrounding
The Throne (Divine)
On all sides, singing Glory
And Praise to their Lord.
The Decision between them
(At Judgment) will be
In (perfect) justice,
And the cry (on all sides)
Will be, "Praise be to God,[4355]
The Lord of the Worlds!"

٧٥- وَتَرَى الْمَلَٰٓئِكَةَ حَآفِّينَ
مِنْ حَوْلِ الْعَرْشِ
يُسَبِّحُونَ بِحَمْدِ رَبِّهِمْ
وَقُضِيَ بَيْنَهُمْ بِالْحَقِّ
وَقِيلَ الْحَمْدُ لِلَّهِ
رَبِّ الْعَٰلَمِينَ ۝

4352. The angels in heaven are not surprised at the advent of the good and righteous souls. They are glad; they greet them with the salutation of Peace; they congratulate them; and they welcome them in.

4353. This is said by the new arrivals in heaven. As is right, they begin with the Praises of God, which shows at once their satisfaction and their gratitude.

4354. *In heritage: i.e.* as our Portion. *Cf.* iii. 180, and n. 485; vi. 165, and n. 988. There is no question here of their passing on any property to heirs. They are the final possessors of Heaven for eternity, by the grace of God.

4355. These are the opening words of the first Sūra, and they describe the atmosphere of the final Bliss in Heaven, in the light of the Countenance of their Lord, the Universal Lord of all!

INTRODUCTION TO SŪRA XL (*Mū-min*).

This Sūra is called "The Believer" (*Mū-min*) from the story of the individual Believer among the people of Pharaoh, who declares his faith and looks to the Future (verses 28-45). It is also called *Gāfir* (He who forgives, see verse 3). In S. xxiii, called *The Believers* (*Mū minūn*), the argument was about the collective force of Faith and Virtue. Here it is about the Individual's witness to Faith and Virtue, and his triumph in the End.

We now begin a series of seven Sūras (xl-xlvi) to which are affixed the Abbreviated Letters *Ḥā-Mīm*. Chronologically they all belong to the same period, the later Meccan Period, and they immediately follow the last Sūra in time. About the Abbreviated Letters generally, see Appendix I at the end of S. II. As to the precise meaning of *Ḥā-Mīm* no authoritative explanation is available. If *Mīm* here has a signification similar to *Mīm* in A.L M. (see n. 25 to ii), it means the End of things, the Last Day, and all these Sūras direct our special attention to that. *Ḥā*, the emphatic guttural, in contrast with the softer breathing of *Alif*, may be meant to suggest that the Beginning (see n. 25 to ii. 1, last paragraph) is only for the End, the Present for the Future, and to emphasize the eschatological element in Faith. But this is mere conjecture, and should be taken for no more than it is worth.

The general theme of the whole series is the relation of Faith to Unfaith, Revelation to Rejection, Goodness to Evil, Truth to Falsehood. It is shown that the first in each of these pairs is the real friend, helper, and protector of man, while the second is his enemy. The very word *Ḥamīm* in that sense is used in Sūras xl and xli (xl. 18 and xli. 34), while in the other Sūras we have words of equivalent import, *e.g. walī* or *naṣīr* (xlii. 8 and 31); *qarīn* (xliii. 36, 38); *maulā* (xliv. 41); *auliyāa* or *nāṣirīn* (xlv. 19, 34); and *auliyāa* (xlvi. 32). Is it permissible to connect the Abbreviated Letters *Ḥā-Mīm* with these ideas as expressed in the word *Ḥamīm*?

Another suggestion worthy of consideration is that *Ḥā* stands for *Ḥaiy*, and *Mīm* for Qaiyūm. These are two attributes of God, meaning, (1) the Living, and (2) the Self-Subsisting, Eternal. The one points to Life and Revelation, and the other to the Hereafter and Eternity; and both these matters are specially dealt with in the seven *Ḥā-Mīm* Sūras. The first letter of *Ḥaiy* (*Ḥā*) is appropriate for life, and the last letter of *Qaiyūm* is appropriate for the Last Days, the Ma'ād, the Hereafter. Again, this is mere conjecture, and should not be taken for more than it is worth.

Summary.—Faith is ever justified, for God forgives: but evil deeds must have evil fruits, for God knows and is just (xl. 1-20, and C. 206).

In all history Evil came to evil; the protest of Faith, in the midst of Evil, may be ignored; but Faith is protected by God, while Evil perishes (xl. 21-50, and C. 207).

No doubt is there of the Future Judgment; the Power, Goodness, and Justice of God are manifest; will man dispute, or will he accept the Signs before it is too late? (xl. 51-85, and C. 208).

C. 206.—Believe in God, For He is Perfect
(xl. 1-20.) In Knowledge and Power, forgives Sin
And accepts Repentance, and justly
Enforces His Law. Those who reject Him
Are but in deceit: His glory is sung
By the highest and purest. Give all devotion
To Him alone. The Day of Requital
Is ever drawing near, when Falsehood
Will vanish, and God's Truth and Justice
Will be established for all Eternity.

Sūra XL.

Mū-min, or The Believer.

In the name of God, Most Gracious,
Most Merciful.

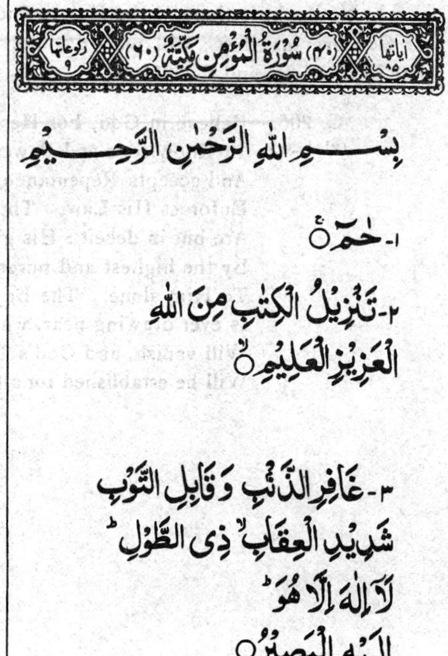

1. Ḥa-Mīm.[4356]

2. The revelation
Of this Book
Is from God,
Exalted in Power,
Full of Knowledge,—[4357]

3. Who forgiveth Sin,
Accepteth Repentance,[4358]
Is Strict in Punishment,
And hath a Long Reach
(In all things).
There is no god
But He: to Him
Is the Final Goal.

4. None can dispute
About the Signs of God[4359]
But the Unbelievers.
Let not, then,
Their strutting about[4360]
Through the land
Deceive thee!

4356. See paragraphs 2-4 of the Introduction to this Sūra.

4357. This verse is the same as xxxix: 1, except for the last words describing the attribute of God. In S. xxxix. 1, it was "Full of Wisdom", because stress was laid on the wisdom of God's Plan in ordering His World. In this Sūra the stress is laid on God's Knowledge, before which the shallow knowledge of men is vain (xl. 83).

4358. God's knowledge is supreme and all-reaching. But there are other attributes of His, which concern us even more intimately; *e g.*, He forgives sin and accepts our repentance when it is sincere and results in our change of heart and life: but He is also just, and strict in punishment; and so no loophole will be left for Evil except in repentance. And further, all His attributes reach forward to everything: His Mercy, as well as His Knowledge and Justice; His Bounties as well as His Punishments.

4359. God's knowledge and attributes are perfect, and everything around us proclaims this. We are surrounded by His Signs. It is only want of Faith that will make people dispute about them.

4360. *Cf.* iii. 196. Their strutting about shows how little they can read the Signs.

5. But (there were people) before them,
Who denied (the Signs),—
The People of Noah,
And the Confederates[4361]
(Of Evil) after them;
And every People plotted
Against their prophet,
To seize him, and disputed
By means of vanities,[4362]
Therewith to condemn
The Truth: but it was I
That seized them!
And how (terrible)[4363]
Was My Requital!

٥- كَذَّبَتْ قَبْلَهُمْ قَوْمُ نُوحٍ
وَّالْأَحْزَابُ مِنْ بَعْدِهِمْ
وَهَمَّتْ كُلُّ أُمَّةٍ بِرَسُولِهِمْ
لِيَأْخُذُوهُ وَجَادَلُوا بِالْبَاطِلِ
لِيُدْحِضُوا بِهِ الْحَقَّ
فَأَخَذْتُهُمْ
فَكَيْفَ كَانَ عِقَابِ ○

6. Thus was the Decree
Of thy Lord proved true
Against the Unbelievers;[4364]
That truly they are
Companions of the Fire!

٦- وَكَذَٰلِكَ حَقَّتْ كَلِمَتُ رَبِّكَ
عَلَى الَّذِينَ كَفَرُوا
أَنَّهُمْ أَصْحَابُ النَّارِ ○

7. Those who sustain[4365]
The Throne (of God)
And those around it
Sing Glory and Praise
To their Lord; believe
In Him; and implore Forgiveness
For those who believe:
"Our Lord! Thy Reach[4366]

٧- الَّذِينَ يَحْمِلُونَ الْعَرْشَ
وَمَنْ حَوْلَهُ يُسَبِّحُونَ بِحَمْدِ رَبِّهِمْ وَ
يُؤْمِنُونَ بِهِ وَيَسْتَغْفِرُونَ لِلَّذِينَ آمَنُوا
رَبَّنَا وَسِعْتَ

4361. *Cf.* xxxviii. 11-13, and n. 4158. All the hosts of wickedness collected together from history will have no power against God's Truth, or the Messenger of that Truth, or God's holy Plan for all His Creation.

4362. Whenever a great or vital Truth is proclaimed and renewed, there are always shallow minds that are ready to dispute about it! And what petty and vain arguments they advance! They think they can discredit or condemn the Truth in this way, or render "of none effect" God's Plan. But they are mistaken. If they seem to succeed for a time, that is merely their trial. They may try to plan and plot against God's men. But their plots will fail in the long run. They will themselves be caught in their own snares. And then, how terrible will be their Punishment!

4363. *Cf.* xiii. 32.

4364. *Cf.* xxxix. 71. The Decree, or Word, of God, by which Evil was to be judged and condemned, was proved true against these men. They are "Companions of the Fire": in other words, they are fit to live only in the environment of Evil!

4365. *Cf.* xxxix. 75. As the Throne of God is figurative, so is the act of sustaining or carrying it. Nor must we suppose that this is restricted to such ideas as we form of angels. All good men and women who rise to the spiritual dignity of carrying the throne of God, or being in the company of such as carry it, sing the praises and glory of God. They are a part of that environment, just as the evil ones are a part of the environment of the Blazing Fire. Their Faith is perfect, for they have seen the Glory with their own spiritual eyes; and they beg for forgiveness for their weaker brethren, who struggle in Faith and Repentance in God's Path

4366. *Cf.* verse 3 above.

Is over all things,
In Mercy and Knowledge.
Forgive, then, those who
Turn in Repentance, and follow
Thy Path; and preserve them
From the Penalty
Of the Blazing Fire!

كُلَّ شَيْءٍ رَّحْمَةً وَّعِلْمًا
فَاغْفِرْ لِلَّذِيْنَ تَابُوْا
وَاتَّبَعُوْا سَبِيْلَكَ
وَقِهِمْ عَذَابَ الْجَحِيْمِ ۝

8. "And grant, our Lord!
That they enter
The Gardens of Eternity,
Which Thou hast promised
To them, and to the righteous
Among their fathers,[4367]
Their wives, and their posterity!
For Thou art (He),
The Exalted in Might,
Full of Wisdom.

٨- رَبَّنَا وَاَدْخِلْهُمْ جَنّٰتِ عَدْنِ الَّتِيْ
وَعَدْتَّهُمْ
وَمَنْ صَلَحَ مِنْ اٰبَآئِهِمْ
وَاَزْوَاجِهِمْ وَذُرِّيّٰتِهِمْ ۭ
اِنَّكَ اَنْتَ الْعَزِيْزُ الْحَكِيْمُ ۝

9. "And preserve them
From (all) ills;
And any whom Thou
Dost preserve from ills[4368]
That Day,—on them
Wilt Thou have bestowed
Mercy indeed: and that
Will be truly (for them)
The highest Achievement".[4369]

٩- وَقِهِمُ السَّيِّاٰتِ ۭ
وَمَنْ تَقِ السَّيِّاٰتِ
يَوْمَئِذٍ فَقَدْ رَحِمْتَهٗ ۭ
وَذٰلِكَ هُوَ الْفَوْزُ الْعَظِيْمُ ۝ ع

SECTION 2.

10. The Unbelievers will be
Addressed: "Greater was
The aversion of God to you[4370]
Than (is) your aversion

١٠- اِنَّ الَّذِيْنَ كَفَرُوْا
يُنَادَوْنَ لَمَقْتُ اللّٰهِ اَكْبَرُ مِنْ مَّقْتِكُمْ

4367. There is nothing selfish in prayer. We pray for all who are true and sincere. But just as Evil is catching, so Goodness is catching in another sense. The associates of the Good and those near and dear to them also share in their goodness and happiness, if only they try to walk in the same Way. And the Grace of God is working for all, all the time.

4368. That is the final Judgment, and any who is saved from the evil consequences of their deeds in this life will truly have been saved by God's Mercy, and for them it is the highest achievement they could have, the attainment of all their wishes, the fulfilment of their destiny and the noblest purpose of their Life, the supreme Salvation and Felicity.

4369. Muslim Salvation, then, is more positive than mere safety from dangers or evils: it is the complete fulfilment of the noble destiny of man in the attainment of the fullest Grace.

4370. The Unbelievers having rejected God's Signs, they now see how they are shut out from Grace, and they feel disgusted with themselves. How much greater was God's displeasure with them, when He showered mercy upon mercy on them and they yet rebelled! How could they now hope for Grace!

To yourselves, seeing that ye
Were called to the Faith
And ye used to refuse."

11. They will say: "Our Lord!
Twice hast Thou made us[4371]
Without life, and twice
Hast Thou given us Life!
Now have we recognised
Our sins: is there
Any way out (of this)?"

12. (The answer will be:)
"This is because, when
God was invoked as
The Only (object of worship),[4372]
Ye did reject Faith,
But when partners were
Joined to Him, ye believed!
The Command is with God,[4373]
Most High, Most Great!"

13. He it is Who showeth
You His Signs, and sendeth
Down Sustenance for you[4374]
From the sky: but only
Those receive admonition
Who turn (to God).

14. Call ye, then, upon God
With sincere devotion to Him,

أَنفُسَكُمْ إِذْ تُدْعَوْنَ إِلَى الْإِيمَانِ
فَتَكْفُرُونَ ○

١١- قَالُوا رَبَّنَا أَمَتَّنَا اثْنَتَيْنِ
وَأَحْيَيْتَنَا اثْنَتَيْنِ
فَاعْتَرَفْنَا بِذُنُوبِنَا
فَهَلْ إِلَى خُرُوجٍ مِّن سَبِيلٍ ○

١٢- ذَٰلِكُم بِأَنَّهُ إِذَا دُعِيَ اللَّهُ
وَحْدَهُ كَفَرْتُمْ ج
وَإِن يُشْرَكْ بِهِ تُؤْمِنُوا ط
فَالْحُكْمُ لِلَّهِ الْعَلِيِّ الْكَبِيرِ ○

١٣- هُوَ الَّذِي يُرِيكُمْ آيَاتِهِ
وَيُنَزِّلُ لَكُم مِّنَ السَّمَاءِ رِزْقًا ط
وَمَا يَتَذَكَّرُ إِلَّا مَن يُنِيبُ ○

١٤- فَادْعُوا اللَّهَ مُخْلِصِينَ لَهُ الدِّينَ

4371. *Cf.* ii. 28: "How can ye reject the faith in God?—seeing that ye were without life, and He gave you life; then will He cause you to die, and will again bring you to life; and again to Him will ye return." Non-existence, or existence as clay without life was equiva'ent to death. Then came true Life on this earth; then came physical death or the cessation of our physical life; and now at the Resurrection, is the second life.

4372. *Cf.* xxxix. 45, and n. 4313. When exclusive devotion is not rendered to God, there is no true understanding, in the mind of a creature, of his own true position, or of the working of the Divine Will and Purpose. How can he then hope to achieve the purpose of his life, or obtain God's Mercy, which is the only way to obtain release from the consequences of Sin?

4373. At the Judgment, the matter will have passed out of the stage at which further chances could have been hoped for. But in any case God is High above all things, Great above all that we can conceive of, both in Mercy and in Justice. The Decision will be with Him, and Him alone.

4374. Lest it should be thought that God's Grace did not meet the Sinner again and again and offer God's Mercy again and again, it is pointed out that God's Signs were freely vouchsafed everywhere and continuously, and that every kind of means was provided for man's "Sustenance" or growth and development, physical, mental, and spiritual. But only those could take advantage of it who turned their attention to God, who submitted their will to Him.

Even though the Unbelievers [4375]
May detest it.

وَلَوْ كَرِهَ الْكٰفِرُوْنَ ○

15. Raised high above ranks
(Or degrees),[4376]
(He is) the Lord
Of the Throne (of authority):
By His Command doth He
Send the spirit (of inspiration)
To any of His servants [4377]
He pleases, that it may
Warn (men) of the Day
Of Mutual Meeting,—[4378]

١٥- رَفِيْعُ الدَّرَجٰتِ ذُو الْعَرْشِۚ
يُلْقِى الرُّوْحَ مِنْ اَمْرِهٖ
عَلٰى مَنْ يَّشَآءُ مِنْ عِبَادِهٖ
لِيُنْذِرَ يَوْمَ التَّلَاقِ ○

16. The Day whereon
They will (all) come forth:
Not a single thing
Concerning them is hidden
From God. Whose will be
The Dominion that Day? [4379]
That of God, the One,
The Irresistible!

١٦- يَوْمَ هُمْ بٰرِزُوْنَ ۚ
لَا يَخْفٰى عَلَى اللّٰهِ مِنْهُمْ شَىْءٌ ؕ
لِمَنِ الْمُلْكُ الْيَوْمَ ؕ
لِلّٰهِ الْوَاحِدِ الْقَهَّارِ ○

17. That Day will every soul
Be requited for what
It earned; no injustice
Will there be that Day,
For God is Swift [4380]
In taking account.

١٧- اَلْيَوْمَ تُجْزٰى كُلُّ نَفْسٍۢ بِمَا كَسَبَتْ ؕ
لَا ظُلْمَ الْيَوْمَ ؕ
اِنَّ اللّٰهَ سَرِيْعُ الْحِسَابِ ○

4375. *Cf.* ix. 33.

4376. He is raised far above any rank or degree which we can imagine. It is possible also to treat *Rafī'*, as equivalent to *Rāfi'*, meaning that He can raise His creatures to the highest ranks and degrees in His spiritual kingdom, for He is the fountain of all honour.

4377. The choosing of a man to be the recipient of inspiration—to be the standard-bearer of God's Truth—is the highest honour possible in the spiritual Kingdom. And God bestows that honour according to His own most perfect Will and Plan, which no one can question, for He is the fountain of all honour, dignity, and authority.

4378. All men will meet together and meet their Lord at the Resurrection, no matter how far scattered they may have been in life or in death.

4379. The Kingdom of God—of Justice, Truth, and Righteousness—will then be fully established. Evil can then no more come into competition with Good, even in the subjective consciousness of man.

4380. *Swift* in several senses: (1) the time of the present life or of the interval before Judgment, *i.e.*, before the restoration of true values, is so short as compared to Eternity, that it may be counted as negligible: in the next verse the Day is characterised as "(ever) drawing near"; (2) in spite of the great concourse of souls to be judged, the process of Judgment will be almost instantaneous, "in the twinkling of an eye" (xvi. 77), because everything is already known to God; and yet not the least injustice will be done.

18. Warn them of the Day
That is (ever) drawing near,
When the Hearts will
(Come) right up to the Throats[4381]
To choke (them);
No intimate friend[4382]
Nor intercessor will the
wrong-doers
Have, who could be
Listened to.

١٨- وَأَنذِرْهُمْ يَوْمَ الْآزِفَةِ
إِذِ الْقُلُوبُ لَدَى الْحَنَاجِرِ كَاظِمِينَ ۚ
مَا لِلظَّالِمِينَ مِنْ حَمِيمٍ
وَلَا شَفِيعٍ يُطَاعُ ۝

19. (God) knows of (the tricks)
That deceive with the eyes,[4383]
And all that the hearts
(Of men) conceal.[4384]

١٩- يَعْلَمُ خَائِنَةَ الْأَعْيُنِ
وَمَا تُخْفِي الصُّدُورُ ۝

20. And God will judge
With (Justice and) Truth:
But those whom (men)
Invoke besides Him, will
Not (be in a position)
To judge at all.
Verily it is God (alone)
Who hears and sees[4385]
(All things).

٢٠- وَاللَّهُ يَقْضِي بِالْحَقِّ ۖ
وَالَّذِينَ يَدْعُونَ مِن دُونِهِ
لَا يَقْضُونَ بِشَيْءٍ ۗ
إِنَّ اللَّهَ هُوَ السَّمِيعُ الْبَصِيرُ ۝

C. 207.—Travel in space and time, and you
(xl. 21-50.) Will see that Evil came to nothing

4381. *Hearts will come right up to the Throats to choke them*: an idiom implying that the whole of their life-functions will be choked up with terror. But a more subtle meaning emerges from further analysis. The heart (or the breast) is the seat of affection, emotion, and every kind of feeling, such as terror, pain, despair, etc. These things will as it were overflow right up to the throat and choke it. The throat is the vehicle for the voice; their voice will be choked, and they will be able to say nothing. The throat is the channel for food, which goes to the stomach and maintains a healthy functioning of life; the choking means that the healthy functioning will stop, and there will be nothing but woe.

4382. In that enforcement of personal responsibility, what sympathy or intercession can the wrong-doers get? *Is Ḥamīm* in any way connected with the Abbreviated Letters *Ḥā-Mīm* attached to this Sūra? See Introduction.

4383. Men may be taken in by tricks that deceive with the eyes, but God's perfect knowledge penetrates through all mysteries. "Deceive with the eyes" may mean several things: (1) a sleight of hand (literally or figuratively) may deceive in respect of the eyes of beholders, for the things that they see do not actually happen; (2) it may be the deceiver's own eyes that play false, because, for example, they show love when hatred is meant; or (3) it may be that the eyes of the beholder play him false, in that he sees things that he should not see, and thus sins with his eyes.

4384. Here we come into the region of evil motives and thoughts which may be concealed in the heart, breast, or mind, but which are all perfectly known to God.

4385. If men build their hopes or their faith in anything except the Divine Grace, they will find themselves deserted. Any pretences that they make will be known to God. On the other hand every single good act, or word, or motive, or aspiration of their will, will reach God's Throne of Mercy.

But evil. Mighty men of old
In arrogance plotted against God's Truth,
But were brought low. A humble Believer
In Pharaoh's Court stood up for Truth,
And counselled his People to obey the Right:
In earnest humility did he address them.
They heard him not. But he was saved,
And they were engulfed in the Wrath of God.

SECTION 3.

21. Do they not travel
Through the earth and see
What was the End
Of those before them?[4386]
They were even superior
To them in strength,
And in the traces (they[4387]
Have left) in the land:
But God did call them
To account for their sins,
And none had they
To defend them against God.

٢١- اَوَلَمْ يَسِيْرُوْا فِى الْاَرْضِ فَيَنْظُرُوْا
كَيْفَ كَانَ عَاقِبَةُ الَّذِيْنَ كَانُوْا مِنْ قَبْلِهِمْ ؕ
كَانُوْا هُمْ اَشَدَّ مِنْهُمْ قُوَّةً
وَّ اٰثَارًا فِى الْاَرْضِ
فَاَخَذَهُمُ اللّٰهُ بِذُنُوْبِهِمْ ؕ
وَمَا كَانَ لَهُمْ مِّنَ اللّٰهِ مِنْ وَّاقٍ ۝

22. That was because there came
To them their apostles[4388]
With Clear (Signs),
But they rejected them:
So God called them
To account: for He is
Full of Strength,
Strict in Punishment.

٢٢- ذٰلِكَ بِاَنَّهُمْ كَانَتْ تَّاْتِيْهِمْ رُسُلُهُمْ
بِالْبَيِّنٰتِ فَكَفَرُوْا
فَاَخَذَهُمُ اللّٰهُ ؕ
اِنَّهٗ قَوِيٌّ شَدِيْدُ الْعِقَابِ ۝

23. Of old We sent Moses,[4389]
With Our Signs
And an Authority manifest,

٢٣- وَلَقَدْ اَرْسَلْنَا مُوْسٰى بِاٰيٰتِنَا
وَسُلْطٰنٍ مُّبِيْنٍ ۝

4386. *Cf.* xxx. 9 and several other similar passages.

4387. See n. 3515 to xxx. 9. We can learn from the history of previous nations. Many of them were more powerful, or have left finer and more imposing monuments and made a deeper impression on the world around them than any particular generation addressed. "Traces" in the text may be taken in that extended sense. And yet all this did not save them from the consequences of their sins. They were called to account and punished. None of the power or pomp or skill of which they boasted could for a moment ward off the punishment when it came in God's good time.

4388. But God in His Mercy always sends a Message of warning and good news through his apostles, and He gives His apostles Clear Signs and an authority that can be recognised. Among the Clear Signs are. (1) the pure and unselfish lives of the apostles; (2) the revelation of truth which they bring; (3) their influence on the course of events in their own and succeeding generations; etc. Some of these may be so remarkable that they merit the name of Miracles.

4389. This is not the story of Moses himself, so much as an introduction to the story of the one just man who believed, in the court of Pharaoh: see verse 28 below. This Sūra (" The Believer ") is called after him.

24. To Pharaoh, Hāmān,[4390]
And Qārūn; but they
Called (him) "a sorcerer
Telling lies!"...

٢٤- إِلَىٰ فِرْعَوْنَ وَهَامَٰنَ وَقَٰرُونَ
فَقَالُوا۟ سَٰحِرٌ كَذَّابٌ ۝

25. Now, when he came to them[4391]
In Truth, from Us,
They said, "Slay the sons
Of those who believe[4392]
With him, and keep alive
Their females," but the plots
Of Unbelievers (end) in nothing
But errors (and delusions)!...

٢٥- فَلَمَّا جَآءَهُم بِٱلْحَقِّ مِنْ عِندِنَا
قَالُوا۟ ٱقْتُلُوٓا۟ أَبْنَآءَ ٱلَّذِينَ ءَامَنُوا۟
مَعَهُۥ وَٱسْتَحْيُوا۟ نِسَآءَهُمْ
وَمَا كَيْدُ ٱلْكَٰفِرِينَ إِلَّا فِى ضَلَٰلٍ ۝

26. Said Pharaoh: "Leave me
To slay Moses; and let him
Call on his Lord![4393]
What I fear is lest
He should change your religion,[4394]
Or lest he should cause
Mischief to appear
In the land!"

٢٦- وَقَالَ فِرْعَوْنُ ذَرُونِىٓ أَقْتُلْ مُوسَىٰ
وَلْيَدْعُ رَبَّهُۥٓ
إِنِّىٓ أَخَافُ أَن يُبَدِّلَ دِينَكُمْ
أَوْ أَن يُظْهِرَ فِى ٱلْأَرْضِ ٱلْفَسَادَ ۝

4390. Here are three types of Unfaith, each showing a different phase, and yet all united in opposition to the Truth and Mission of Moses. (1) Pharaoh is the type of arrogance, cruelty, and reliance on brute force; *Cf.* xxviii. 38-39. (2) Hāmān was Pharaoh's minister (n. 3331 to xxviii. 6; also xxviii. 38): he was the type of a sycophant who would pander to the vanity of any man in power. (3) Qārūn excelled in his wealth, was selfish in its use, and overbearing to the poor (xxviii. 76-81, and n. 3404). They all came to an evil end eventually.

4391. Verse 24 described the opposition of three types of Unfaith, which opposed Faith, in different ways, as described in the last note Qārūn, in his overweening insolence, may well have called Moses and Aaron "sorcerers telling lies" in the Sinai desert, as he despised priests and men of God, and might cast the Egyptian reproach in their teeth as a reminiscence. Here, in verse 25, we have an episode about the time of the birth of Moses: "them" and "they" refer to Pharaoh and his Court; the "coming" of Moses here refers to the time of his birth. On that construction, "with him", lower down in their speech would be elliptical, referring to "slay the sons", as if they had said, "Kill all Israelite male children: the unknown Prophet to be born would be amongst them: so kill them all with him." . In verse 26 we again skip some years and recall an episode when Moses, having got his mission, stood in Pharaoh's Court, and some of the Egyptian Commonalty were almost ready to believe in him.

4392. That is, the Israelites, for they were the custodians of God's Faith then. For the slaughter of Israelite children by Pharaoh, see xxviii. 4-6, and notes.

4393. This is an episode that occurs when Moses, invested with his mission, confronts Pharaoh in his Court and preaches to him: see xx. 49 and following verses; also xx. 57, 63.

4394. Some of Pharaoh's people did afterwards give up the worship of Pharaoh and of the Egyptian gods and believed "in the Lord of Aaron and Moses" and in fact suffered martyrdom for the Faith of Unity: xx. 70-73.

27. Moses said: "I have indeed
Called upon my Lord
And your Lord[4395]
(For protection) from every
Arrogant one who believes not
In the Day of Account!"

٢٧- وَقَالَ مُوسَىٰٓ إِنِّي عُذْتُ بِرَبِّي
وَرَبِّكُم مِّن كُلِّ مُتَكَبِّرٍ لَّا يُؤْمِنُ
بِيَوْمِ الْحِسَابِ ○ ع

SECTION 4.

28. A Believer, a man[4396]
From among the people
Of Pharaoh, who had concealed
His faith, said: "Will ye
Slay a man because he
Says, 'My Lord is God'?—
When he has indeed come
To you with Clear (Signs)
From your Lord? And if
He be a liar, on him
Is (the sin of) his lie;
But, if he is telling[4397]
The Truth, then will
Fall on you something
Of the (calamity) of which
He warns you: truly
God guides not one[4398]
Who transgresses and lies!

٢٨- وَقَالَ رَجُلٌ مُّؤْمِنٌ
مِّنْ ءَالِ فِرْعَوْنَ يَكْتُمُ إِيمَانَهُۥٓ
أَتَقْتُلُونَ رَجُلًا أَن يَقُولَ رَبِّيَ اللَّهُ
وَقَدْ جَآءَكُم بِالْبَيِّنَٰتِ مِن رَّبِّكُمْ
وَإِن يَكُ كَٰذِبًا فَعَلَيْهِ كَذِبُهُۥ
وَإِن يَكُ صَادِقًا
يُصِبْكُم بَعْضُ الَّذِي يَعِدُكُمْ
إِنَّ اللَّهَ لَا يَهْدِي مَنْ هُوَ
مُسْرِفٌ كَذَّابٌ ○

29. "O my People! yours
Is the dominion this day:

٢٩- يَٰقَوْمِ لَكُمُ الْمُلْكُ الْيَوْمَ

4395. The whole point of the Gospel of Unity which Moses preached was that the God of Moses and the God of Pharaoh, of Israel and of Egypt, the Lord of all the Worlds, was One,—the only True God. See xx. 49-50 and notes 2572 and 2573.

4396. There is nothing to justify the identification of this man with the man mentioned in xxviii. 20, who warned Moses long before Moses had received his mission. On the contrary, in this passage, the man is evidently speaking after Moses had received his mission, preached to Pharaoh, and got a certain amount of success, for which Pharaoh and his people were trying to seek his life. Moses had evidently already brought his Clear Signs.

4397. A commonsense view is put before them by an Egyptian who loves his own people and does not wish them to perish in sin. "Will you kill this man for calling on God? Have you not seen his character and behaviour? Do you not see the 'Clear Signs' about him that bespeak his credentials? Suppose for a moment that he is a liar and pretender: he will suffer for his falsehood, but why should you turn against God? But suppose that he is really inspired by God to tell you the truth and warn you against evil, what will be your fate when God's Wrath descends? For it must descend if he is a true Messenger sent by God."

4398. This is with reference to the "Clear signs". 'They are Signs of God's guidance, for God would never guide a man who exceeds the bounds of truth and tells you lies! Such a man is bound to be found out!'

Ye have the upper hand [4399]
In the land: but who
Will help us from
The Punishment of God,
Should it befall us?"
Pharaoh said: "I but
Point out to you that
Which I see (myself); [4400]
Nor do I guide you
But to the Path of Right!"

ظٰهِرِيْنَ فِي الْاَرْضِ
فَمَنْ يَّنْصُرُنَا مِنْ بَاْسِ اللّٰهِ اِنْ جَآءَنَا ۭ
قَالَ فِرْعَوْنُ مَآ اُرِيْكُمْ اِلَّا مَآ اَرٰى
وَمَآ اَهْدِيْكُمْ
اِلَّا سَبِيْلَ الرَّشَادِ ۝

30. Then said the man
Who believed: "O my People!
Truly I do fear
For you something like [4401]
The Day (of disaster)
Of the Confederates (in sin)!— [4402]

٣٠- وَقَالَ الَّذِيْٓ اٰمَنَ يٰقَوْمِ
اِنِّيْٓ اَخَافُ عَلَيْكُمْ مِّثْلَ
يَوْمِ الْاَحْزَابِ ۝

31. "Something like the fate
Of the People of Noah,
The 'Ād, and the Thamūd,
And those who came
After them: but God
Never wishes injustice [4403]
To His Servants.

٣١- مِثْلَ دَاْبِ قَوْمِ نُوْحٍ
وَّعَادٍ وَّثَمُوْدَ وَالَّذِيْنَ مِنْۢ بَعْدِهِمْ ۭ
وَمَا اللّٰهُ يُرِيْدُ ظُلْمًا لِّلْعِبَادِ ۝

32. "And O my People!
I fear for you a Day [4404]
When there will be
Mutual calling (and wailing),—

٣٢- وَيٰقَوْمِ اِنِّيْٓ اَخَافُ عَلَيْكُمْ
يَوْمَ التَّنَادِ ۝

4399. 'Do not be puffed up with arrogance because the power is in your hands at present! Do you deserve it? Will it last? If you are sinning and drawing upon yourselves God's Punishment, is there anything that can shield you from it?

4400. Pharaoh's egotism and arrogance come out. 'I can see and understand everything. As I see things, so do I direct you. The Path which I see must be right, and you must follow it.'

4401. He appeals to past history. 'Have you not heard of people who lived before you?—like the generations of Noah, the 'Ād, the Thamūd, and many more—who held together in sin against God's Preachers, but were wiped out for their sins?'

4402. *Cf.* xxxviii. 11-13, and n. 4158, also xl. 5, and n. 4361.

4403. 'All these disasters happened in history, and they will happen again to you if you do not give up evil. Do not for a moment think that God is unjust. It is you who are deliberately preparing the disasters by your conduct.'

4404. This Day may refer to the Day of Judgment, of which three features are here referred to. (1) People may wail and call to each other, but no one can help another: each one will have his own judgment to face; (2) the wicked will then be driven to Hell from the Judgment-Seat; and (3) there will be no one to help, guide, or intercede, because the grace and guidance of God had already been rejected. But the words are perfectly general, and are applicable to all stages at which the Wrath of God is manifest.

33. "A Day when ye
Shall turn your backs
And flee: no defender
Shall ye have from God:
Any whom God leaves
To stray, there is none
To guide ...

٣٣- يَوْمَ تُوَلُّونَ مُدْبِرِينَ
مَا لَكُم مِّنَ اللَّهِ مِنْ عَاصِمٍ
وَمَن يُضْلِلِ اللَّهُ
فَمَا لَهُ مِنْ هَادٍ ○

34. "And to you there came
Joseph in times gone by,[4405]
With Clear Signs, but
Ye ceased not to doubt
Of the (mission) for which
He had come: at length,
When he died, ye said:
'No apostle will God send[4406]
After him.' Thus doth God
Leave to stray such as
Transgress and live in doubt,—

٣٤- وَلَقَدْ جَاءَكُمْ يُوسُفُ مِن قَبْلُ بِالْبَيِّنَاتِ
فَمَا زِلْتُمْ فِي شَكٍّ
مِّمَّا جَاءَكُم بِهِ
حَتَّىٰ إِذَا هَلَكَ قُلْتُمْ
لَن يَبْعَثَ اللَّهُ مِن بَعْدِهِ رَسُولًا
كَذَٰلِكَ يُضِلُّ اللَّهُ مَنْ هُوَ مُسْرِفٌ مُّرْتَابٌ ○

35. "(Such) as dispute about
The Signs of God,
Without any authority
That hath reached them.
Grievous and odious
(Is such conduct)
In the sight of God
And of the Believers.
Thus doth God seal up[4407]
Every heart—of arrogant
And obstinate transgressors."

٣٥- الَّذِينَ يُجَادِلُونَ فِي آيَاتِ اللَّهِ
بِغَيْرِ سُلْطَانٍ أَتَاهُمْ
كَبُرَ مَقْتًا
عِندَ اللَّهِ وَعِندَ الَّذِينَ آمَنُوا
كَذَٰلِكَ يَطْبَعُ اللَّهُ عَلَىٰ كُلِّ قَلْبِ
مُتَكَبِّرٍ جَبَّارٍ ○

4405. So far he has been speaking of general religious tradition. Now, as an Egyptian, addressing Egyptians. he refers to the mission of Joseph in Egypt, for which see the whole of Sūra xii, and Appendix VI following it. Joseph was not born in Egypt, nor was he an Egyptian. With what wonderful incidents he came into Egypt! What difficulties did he not surmount among his own brothers first, and in the Egyptian family which afterwards adopted him! How injustice, spite, and forgetfulness on the part of others, yet wove a spell round him and made him a ruler and saviour of Egypt in times of famine! How he preached to prisoners in prison, to Zulaikhā in her household, to the Egyptian ladies in their banquet, and to the Court of Pharaoh generally! The Egyptians profited by the material gains which came to them through him, but as a nation remained sceptical of his spiritual truths for many generations after him.

4406. See Appendix IV, p. 406, for a discussion of the interval between Joseph and Moses. Perhaps the interval was about one to three centuries, a very short period for the memory of a learned nation like the Egyptians. And yet they as a nation ignored his spiritual work, and afterwards even persecuted Israel in Egypt until Moses delivered them. They actually saw the benefits conferred by Joseph, but did not realise that God's Kingdom works continuously even though men ignore it. See Appendix V, pp. 408-13, for a sketch of Religion in Egypt. For such men how could the Grace and Guidance of God be effective in their hearts?

4407. See the last note. The arrogant transgressors having closed their hearts to the Message of God and to every appeal made to them, it followed by God's Law that their hearts were sealed up to any fresh influences for good. *Cf.* vii. 100; also ii 7, and n. 31.

36. Pharaoh said: " O Hāmān!
Build me a lofty palace,[4408]
That I may attain
The ways and means—

٣٦- وَقَالَ فِرْعَوْنُ يٰهَامٰنُ ابْنِ لِي صَرْحًا
لَّعَلِّيٓ أَبْلُغُ الْأَسْبَابَ ۙ

37. " The ways and means
Of (reaching) the heavens,
And that I may mount up
To the God of Moses:
But as far as I am concerned,
I think (Moses) is a liar!"
Thus was made alluring,[4409]
In Pharaoh's eyes,
The evil of his deeds,
And he was hindered
From the Path; and the plot[4410]
Of Pharaoh led to nothing
But perdition (for him).

٣٧- أَسْبَابَ السَّمٰوٰتِ
فَأَطَّلِعَ إِلٰىٓ إِلٰهِ مُوسٰى
وَإِنِّي لَأَظُنُّهُ كَاذِبًا ۚ
وَكَذٰلِكَ زُيِّنَ لِفِرْعَوْنَ سُوٓءُ عَمَلِهِ
وَصُدَّ عَنِ السَّبِيلِ ۚ
وَمَا كَيْدُ فِرْعَوْنَ إِلَّا فِي تَبَابٍ ۝ ع

SECTION 5.

38. The man who believed said
Further: " O my People!
Follow me: I will lead
You to the Path of Right.[4411]

٣٨- وَقَالَ الَّذِيٓ اٰمَنَ يٰقَوْمِ
اتَّبِعُونِ أَهْدِكُمْ سَبِيلَ الرَّشَادِ ۚ

39. " O my People! This life
Of the present is nothing
But (temporary) convenience:
It is the Hereafter

٣٩- يٰقَوْمِ إِنَّمَا هٰذِهِ الْحَيٰوةُ الدُّنْيَا مَتَاعٌ ۡ
وَّإِنَّ الْاٰخِرَةَ

4408. *Cf.* xxviii. 38, and n. 3371. There are two points to be noted here. (1) Pharaoh, in the arrogance of his materialism, thinks of the Kingdom of Heaven like a kingdom on earth; he thinks of spiritual things in terms of palaces and ladders: notice that the word *asbāb* (ways and means) is emphasised by repetition. (2) His sarcasm turns Moses and God to ridicule. Really he does not believe in anything spiritual, and he frankly states that 'for his part he thinks Moses is a liar', though other men less lofty than he (Pharaoh) may be deceived by the Clear Signs of Moses.

4409. Pharaoh's speech shows how his own egotism and haughty arrogance brought him to this pass, that even the evil which he did seemed alluring in his own eyes! His heart was indeed sealed, and his arrogance prevented him from seeing the right path. (With the Kūfi Qirāat I read *sudda* in the passive voice.)

4410. Pharaoh had plotted to slay Moses (xl. 26) and to kill the Children of Israel (xl. 25). The plot recoiled on his own head and on the head of his people who joined in the plot; for they were all drowned in the Red Sea.

4411. Note the contrast between the earnest beseeching tone of the Believer here and the hectoring tone of Pharaoh in using similar words in xl. 29 above.

That is the Home
That will last.[4412]

هِيَ دَارُ الْقَرَارِ ○

40. "He that works evil
Will not be requited
But by the like thereof:
And he that works
A righteous deed—whether
Man or woman—and is
A Believer—such will enter
The Garden (of Bliss): therein
Will they have abundance[4413]
Without measure.

٤٠- مَنْ عَمِلَ سَيِّئَةً فَلَا يُجْزٰى إِلَّا مِثْلَهَا
وَمَنْ عَمِلَ صَالِحًا
مِّنْ ذَكَرٍ أَوْ أُنْثٰى وَهُوَ مُؤْمِنٌ
فَأُولٰئِكَ يَدْخُلُونَ الْجَنَّةَ
يُرْزَقُونَ فِيهَا بِغَيْرِ حِسَابٍ ○

41. "And O my People!
How (strange) it is[4414]
For me to call you
To Salvation while ye
Call me to the Fire!

٤١- وَيٰقَوْمِ
مَا لِيٓ أَدْعُوكُمْ إِلَى النَّجٰوةِ
وَتَدْعُونَنِيٓ إِلَى النَّارِ ○ نصف

42. "Ye do call upon me
To blaspheme against God,[4415]
And to join with Him
Partners of whom I have
No knowledge; and I
Call you to the Exalted
In Power, Who forgives
Again and again!"

٤٢- تَدْعُونَنِي لِأَكْفُرَ بِاللّٰهِ
وَأُشْرِكَ بِهِ مَا لَيْسَ لِي بِهِ عِلْمٌ
وَّأَنَا أَدْعُوكُمْ إِلَى
الْعَزِيزِ الْغَفَّارِ ○

43 "Without doubt ye do call
Me to one who is not
Fit to be called to,[4416]
Whether in this world,

٤٣- لَا جَرَمَ أَنَّمَا تَدْعُونَنِيٓ إِلَيْهِ
لَيْسَ لَهُ دَعْوَةٌ فِي الدُّنْيَا

4412. Faith makes him see the contrast between vanities, even though they may glitter temporarily, and the eternal Good that is destined for man.

4413. *Cf.* ii. 212. The spiritual Good will not only last. It will be a most liberal reward, far above any merits of the recipient.

4414. It may seem strange according to the laws of this world that he should be seeking their Good while they are seeking his damnation! But that is the merit of Faith. Its mission is to rescue its enemies and God's enemies, as far as their will will consent!

4415. The worship of Pharaoh was but typical of Egyptian blasphemy, but it had many sides, including the worship of heroes, animals, powers of good and evil in nature, and idols of all kinds. It is this comprehensive cult which required forgiveness again and again, but God is Exalted in Power, and gives such forgiveness on repentance.

4416. Faith is not content with its own inner vision and conviction. It can give ample arguments. Three are mentioned here: (1) nothing but God is worthy of worship, either in this world of sense or in the spiritual world; (2) our Return will be to God, the only Reality; and (3) the worship of Falsehood must necessarily lead to the Penalty of Falsehood, unless God's Mercy intervenes and forgives on our sincere repentance.

Or in the Hereafter;
Our Return will be
To God; and the Transgressors
Will be Companions
Of the Fire!

وَلَا فِي الْاٰخِرَةِ
وَاَنَّ مَرَدَّنَآ اِلَى اللّٰهِ
وَاَنَّ الْمُسْرِفِيْنَ هُمْ اَصْحٰبُ النَّارِ ○

44. "Soon will ye remember
What I say to you (now).[4417]
My (own) affair I commit
To God: for God (ever)
Watches over His Servants."

۴۴- فَسَتَذْكُرُوْنَ مَآ اَقُوْلُ لَكُمْ ؕ
وَاُفَوِّضُ اَمْرِيْٓ اِلَى اللّٰهِ ؕ
اِنَّ اللّٰهَ بَصِيْرٌۢ بِالْعِبَادِ ○

45. Then God saved him
From (every) ill that they
Plotted (against him),
But the brunt of the Penalty[4418]
Encompassed on all sides
The People of Pharaoh.

۴۵- فَوَقٰىهُ اللّٰهُ سَيِّاٰتِ مَا مَكَرُوْا
وَحَاقَ بِاٰلِ فِرْعَوْنَ
سُوْٓءُ الْعَذَابِ ○ۚ

46. In front of the Fire
Will they be brought,
Morning and evening:[4419]
And (the Sentence will be)
On the Day that
Judgment will be established:
"Cast ye the People
Of Pharaoh into
The severest Penalty!"

۴۶- اَلنَّارُ يُعْرَضُوْنَ عَلَيْهَا
غُدُوًّا وَّعَشِيًّا ۚ
وَيَوْمَ تَقُوْمُ السَّاعَةُ ۫
اَدْخِلُوْٓا اٰلَ فِرْعَوْنَ
اَشَدَّ الْعَذَابِ ○

47. Behold, they will dispute
With each other in the Fire![4420]
The weak ones (who followed)
Will say to those who
Had been arrogant, "We but
Followed you: can ye then

۴۷- وَاِذْ يَتَحَآجُّوْنَ فِي النَّارِ
فَيَقُوْلُ الضُّعَفٰٓؤُا لِلَّذِيْنَ اسْتَكْبَرُوْٓا
اِنَّا كُنَّا لَكُمْ تَبَعًا فَهَلْ اَنْتُمْ

4417. The wording suggests as if there was a plot to kill him, but he was saved, as the next verse shows. His thought to the last is with his People. 'No matter what you do to me: you will have cause to remember my admonition, when perhaps it is too late for you to repent. For my part I commit myself to the care of God, and my Faith tells me that all will be right.'

4418. The Pharaoh of the time of Moses, and his people, suffered many calamities in this world: vii. 130-136. But those were nothing to the spiritual Penalties mentioned in the next verse.

4419. When the Judgment really comes, it is not like an ordinary physical disaster. The Fire of Punishment is ever present—morning and evening—*i.e.*, at all times. The sentence becomes final and there is no mitigation.

4420. Just as Unity, Harmony, and Peace are symbols of Truth, Bliss, and Salvation, so Reproaches, Disputes, and Disorders are symbols of Hell.

Take (on yourselves) from us
Some share of the Fire?"

مُّغْنُونَ عَنَّا نَصِيبًا مِّنَ النَّارِ ○

48. Those who had been arrogant
Will say: "We are all [4421]
In this (Fire)! Truly,
God has judged
Between (His) Servants!"

٤٨- قَالَ الَّذِينَ اسْتَكْبَرُوٓا
إِنَّا كُلٌّ فِيهَآ
إِنَّ اللَّهَ قَدْ حَكَمَ بَيْنَ الْعِبَادِ ○

49. Those in the Fire will say
To the Keepers of Hell: [4422]
"Pray to your Lord
To lighten us the Penalty
For a Day (at least)!"

٤٩- وَقَالَ الَّذِينَ فِي النَّارِ لِخَزَنَةِ جَهَنَّمَ
ادْعُوا رَبَّكُمْ يُخَفِّفْ عَنَّا يَوْمًا
مِّنَ الْعَذَابِ ○

50. They will say: "Did there
Not come to you
Your apostles with Clear Signs?"
They will say, "Yes".
They will reply, "Then [4423]
Pray (as ye like)! But
The Prayer of those
Without Faith is nothing
But (futile wandering)
In (mazes of) error!"

٥٠- قَالُوٓا أَوَلَمْ تَكُ تَأْتِيكُمْ
رُسُلُكُم بِالْبَيِّنَٰتِ ط
قَالُوا بَلَىٰ ط
قَالُوا فَادْعُوا ج
وَمَا دُعَٰٓؤُا الْكَٰفِرِينَ إِلَّا فِي ضَلَٰلٍ ○ ع

C. 208.—God's grace and help are ever ready
(xl. 51-85.) For His servants who patiently persevere.
Let not arrogance blind the souls
Of men: the Hour of Judgment is bound
To come. The keys of Life and Death
Are in the hands of God. Dispute not
The Signs of God, but learn from History
And the world around you. Science and skill
Avail you not if the soul is dead.

4421. Note the evasion and cynicism of the answer, befitting the character of spiritual misleaders! 'What! are we not suffering with you in the same Fire! Pray to God if you like! He has pronounced His Judgment!' *Cf.* xiv. 21-22.

4422. *Cf.* xxxix. 71. The poor misguided ones will turn to the angels who are their Keepers, asking them to pray and intercede for them. But the angels are set there to watch over them, not to intercede for them. In their innocence they ask, 'Did you have no warnings from apostles, men like yourselves, in your past life?'

4423. The answer being in the affirmative, they will have to tell the dreadful truth: 'This is neither the time nor the place for prayer, for mercy! And in any case, Prayer without Faith is Delusion, and must miss its mark.' *Cf.* xiii. 14.

Section 6.

51. We will, without doubt,
Help Our apostles and those
Who believe, (both)
In this world's life
And on the Day
When the Witnesses[4424]
Will stand forth,—

٥١- اِنَّا لَنَنْصُرُ رُسُلَنَا وَالَّذِيْنَ
اٰمَنُوْا فِي الْحَيٰوةِ الدُّنْيَا
وَيَوْمَ يَقُوْمُ الْاَشْهَادُ ○

52. The Day when no profit
Will it be to Wrong-doers
To present their excuses,[4425]
But they will (only) have
The Curse and the Home
Of Misery.

٥٢- يَوْمَ لَا يَنْفَعُ الظّٰلِمِيْنَ مَعْذِرَتُهُمْ
وَلَهُمُ اللَّعْنَةُ
وَلَهُمْ سُوْٓءُ الدَّارِ ○

53. We did aforetime give Moses
The (Book of) Guidance,[4426]
And We gave the Book
In inheritance to the Children
Of Israel,—

٥٣- وَلَقَدْ اٰتَيْنَا مُوْسَى الْهُدٰى
وَاَوْرَثْنَا بَنِيْٓ اِسْرَآءِيْلَ الْكِتٰبَ ○

54. A Guide and a Message
To men of understanding.

٥٤- هُدًى وَّذِكْرٰى لِاُولِي الْاَلْبَابِ ○

55. Patiently, then, persevere :[4427]
For the Promise of God
Is true : and ask forgiveness[4428]
For thy fault, and celebrate

٥٥- فَاصْبِرْ اِنَّ وَعْدَ اللّٰهِ حَقٌّ
وَّاسْتَغْفِرْ لِذَنْۢبِكَ وَسَبِّحْ

4424. The Day of Judgment is described as "the Day when Witnesses will stand forth". This description implies two things: (1) that there man will be judged justly; his past actions and his faculties and opportunities will be witnesses as to the use he made of them (xxiv. 24); in fact he will himself be a witness against himself (vi. 130); and the prophets and just men will bear witness to the fact that they preached and warned men (xxxix 69; ii. 133).

4425. After the testimony mentioned in the last note, there will be no room for excuses, and if any were made, they could serve no purpose, unlike the state of matters in this world, where there is much make-believe, and Falsehood often masquerades as Truth and is accepted as such even by those who should know better.

4426. Moses was given a Revelation, and it was given in heritage to the Children of Israel, to preserve it, guide their conduct by it, and hold aloft its Message: but they failed in all these particulars.

4427. The Israelites corrupted or lost their Book; they disobeyed God's Law; and failed to proclaim and exemplify God's Message. That is why the new Revelation came to the holy Apostle. If, in the beginning, it was rejected and persecuted, there was no cause for discouragement; on the contrary, there was all the greater need for patience and perseverance.

4428. Every mortal according to his nature and degree of spiritual enlightenment falls short of the perfect standard of God (xvi. 61), and should therefore ask God for forgiveness. What is merit in an ordinary man may be a human shortcoming in one nearest to God: see xxxviii. 24-25, and notes 4175-76. Prophets have a further responsibility for their People or their Ummat, and they ask in a representative capacity.

The Praises of thy Lord
In the evening
And in the morning.[4429]

بِحَمْدِ رَبِّكَ
بِالْعَشِيِّ وَالْاِبْكَارِ ○

56. Those who dispute
About the Signs of God
Without any authority
Bestowed on them,—there is [4430]
Nothing in their breasts
But (the quest of) greatness,
Which they shall never
Attain to : seek refuge,
Then, in God : it is He
Who hears and sees (all things).

٥٦- اِنَّ الَّذِيْنَ يُجَادِلُوْنَ فِيْٓ اٰيٰتِ اللّٰهِ
بِغَيْرِ سُلْطٰنٍ اَتٰىهُمْ ۙ
اِنْ فِيْ صُدُوْرِهِمْ اِلَّا كِبْرٌ
مَّا هُمْ بِبَالِغِيْهِ ۚ فَاسْتَعِذْ بِاللّٰهِ ۭ
اِنَّهٗ هُوَ السَّمِيْعُ الْبَصِيْرُ ○

57. Assuredly the creation [4431]
Of the heavens
And the earth
Is a greater (matter)
Than the creation of men :
Yet most men understand not.

٥٧- لَخَلْقُ السَّمٰوٰتِ وَالْاَرْضِ
اَكْبَرُ مِنْ خَلْقِ النَّاسِ
وَلٰكِنَّ اَكْثَرَ النَّاسِ لَا يَعْلَمُوْنَ ○

58. Not equal are the blind
And those who (clearly) see : [4432]
Nor are (equal) those
Who believe and work
Deeds of righteousness, and
Those who do evil.
Little do ye learn
By admonition !

٥٨- وَمَا يَسْتَوِي الْاَعْمٰى وَالْبَصِيْرُ ۙ ۥ
وَالَّذِيْنَ اٰمَنُوْا وَعَمِلُوا الصّٰلِحٰتِ
وَلَا الْمُسِيْٓءُ ۭ
قَلِيْلًا مَّا تَتَذَكَّرُوْنَ ○

59. The Hour will certainly come : [4433]
Therein is no doubt :
Yet most men believe not.

٥٩- اِنَّ السَّاعَةَ لَاٰتِيَةٌ لَّا رَيْبَ فِيْهَا
وَلٰكِنَّ اَكْثَرَ النَّاسِ لَا يُؤْمِنُوْنَ ○

4429. *Cf.* iii. 41. Evening and morning are the best times for mystic contemplation and spiritual effort. But the phrase "evening and morning" may mean "at all times".

4430. The Disputers are actuated by nothing but the desire for self-glory and self-aggrandizement. Their desire is not likely to receive fruition, but others should take warning from it.

4431. The heavens and the earth include mankind and all other creatures and millions of stars. Man is himself but a tiny part of creation. Why should he be so ego-centric? The whole is greater than a tiny part of it. And God Who created the whole of the Worlds is able to do much more wonderful things than can enter the imagination of man. Why should man be arrogant and doubt the Resurrection, and take upon himself to doubt the possibility of God's Revelation? It is only because he has made himself blind. See next verse.

4432. The man of Faith who backs his faith by righteous conduct is like the man of clear vision, who sees things in their true perspective and walks with firm steps in the Way of God. The man who does evil is like a blind man : the Light of God is all around him, but the man has made himself blind, and he can see nothing. He has rejected Faith and cannot even learn by other people's admonition.

4433. "The Hour" is the crown and consummation of man's life on this earth,—the gateway to the Hereafter.

60. And your Lord says:
"Call on Me; I
Will answer your (Prayer): [4434]
But those who are
Too arrogant to serve Me
Will surely find themselves
In Hell—in humiliation!"

٦٠- وَقَالَ رَبُّكُمُ ادْعُونِيٓ
أَسْتَجِبْ لَكُمْ ط
إِنَّ الَّذِينَ يَسْتَكْبِرُونَ عَنْ عِبَادَتِي
سَيَدْخُلُونَ جَهَنَّمَ دَاخِرِينَ ○ ع

SECTION 7.

61. It is God Who has [4135]
Made the Night for you,
That ye may rest therein,
And the Day, as that
Which helps (you) to see.
Verily God is Full of
Grace and Bounty to men:
Yet most men give
No thanks.

٦١- اَللّٰهُ الَّذِي جَعَلَ لَكُمُ الَّيْلَ
لِتَسْكُنُوا فِيهِ
وَالنَّهَارَ مُبْصِرًا ط
إِنَّ اللّٰهَ لَذُو فَضْلٍ عَلَى النَّاسِ
وَلٰكِنَّ أَكْثَرَ النَّاسِ لَا يَشْكُرُونَ ○

62. Such is God, your Lord,
The Creator of all things.
There is no god but He:
Then how ye are deluded [4436]
Away from the Truth!

٦٢- ذٰلِكُمُ اللّٰهُ رَبُّكُمْ خَالِقُ كُلِّ شَيْءٍ م
لَآ إِلٰهَ إِلَّا هُوَ ز
فَأَنّٰى تُؤْفَكُونَ ○

63. Thus are deluded those [4137]
Who are wont to reject
The Signs of God.

٦٣- كَذٰلِكَ يُؤْفَكُ الَّذِينَ
كَانُوا بِاٰيٰتِ اللّٰهِ يَجْحَدُونَ ○

64. It is God Who has [4138]
Made for you the earth

٦٤- اَللّٰهُ الَّذِي جَعَلَ لَكُمُ الْأَرْضَ

4434. As this life is not the end of all things, and we are to have its fulfilment in the Hereafter: we have only to pray to the Lord of the Present and the Hereafter, and He will hear us, forgive us, guide us, and make our Path smooth. But Pride will have its fall,—and its humiliating Punishment: *Cf.* xxxvii. 18.

4435. The succession of Day and Night in our physical life is frequently appealed to, as a symbol to draw our attention to the Mercy and Bounty of God. If we viewed these things aright, we should serve God and seek Light from Him and Rest from Him, and celebrate His praises with gratitude.

4436. If we worship false gods, *i.e.,* go after vanities, what is it that deludes us and leads us astray? What could it be but our rank ingratitude and failure to use the understanding which God has given us?

4437. See the last two notes. If men are deluded by Falsehoods, it is because they reject Revelation and refuse to learn from the Signs of God all around them.

4438. The argument in the last two verses was from man's personal experiences of his physical life. In this and the next verse a parallel argument is addressed to man on a much higher plane: 'look at the spacious earth and the canopy of the sky; look at the special position you occupy above other animals that you know, in shape and form, and moral and spiritual capacities; consider your refinements in food and fruits and the higher spiritual Sustenance of which your physical food is a type; would you not indeed say that the Lord is good, and would you not glorify His holy name?'

As a resting place,[4439]
And the sky as a canopy,
And has given you shape—[4440]
And made your shapes
Beautiful,—and has provided
For you Sustenance,[4441]
Of things pure and good;—
Such is God your Lord.
So Glory to God,
The Lord of the Worlds!

65. He is the Living (One):[4442]
There is no god but He:
Call upon Him, giving Him
Sincere devotion. Praise be
To God, Lord of the Worlds!

66. Say: "I have been forbidden[4443]
To invoke those whom ye
Invoke besides God,—seeing that
The Clear Signs have come
To me from my Lord;
And I have been commanded
To bow (in Islām)
To the Lord of the Worlds."

67. It is He Who has[4444]
Created you from dust,

قَرَارًا وَّالسَّمَآءَ بِنَآءً
وَّصَوَّرَكُمْ فَأَحْسَنَ صُوَرَكُمْ
وَرَزَقَكُمْ مِّنَ الطَّيِّبٰتِ
ذٰلِكُمُ اللّٰهُ رَبُّكُمْ
فَتَبٰرَكَ اللّٰهُ رَبُّ الْعٰلَمِينَ ○

٦٥- هُوَ الْحَيُّ لَآ إِلٰهَ إِلَّا هُوَ
فَادْعُوهُ مُخْلِصِينَ لَهُ الدِّينَ
اَلْحَمْدُ لِلّٰهِ رَبِّ الْعٰلَمِينَ ○

٦٦- قُلْ إِنِّي نُهِيتُ أَنْ أَعْبُدَ الَّذِينَ
تَدْعُونَ مِنْ دُونِ اللّٰهِ
لَمَّا جَآءَنِيَ الْبَيِّنٰتُ مِنْ رَّبِّي
وَأُمِرْتُ أَنْ أُسْلِمَ لِرَبِّ الْعٰلَمِينَ ○

٦٧- هُوَ الَّذِي خَلَقَكُمْ مِّنْ تُرَابٍ

4439. *A resting place*: I understand this to imply a temporary place of rest or sojourn, a period of probation, to be followed by the eternal Home.

4440. *Cf.* vii. 11 and n. 996. The shape and form refer to the physical form as well as to the inborn moral and spiritual capacities of man. As regards physical form, *Cf.* Milton's description of Adam and Eve, "Two of far noble shape, erect and tall" (*Paradise Lost*, iv. 288). As regards moral and spiritual capacities, they are typified by the breathing of God's spirit into man: xv. 29.

4441. "*Sustenance*": all that is necessary for growth and development, physical, moral, and spiritual. *Cf.* n. 2105 to xvi. 73.

4442. The real, self-subsisting Life is only in Him: *Cf.* ii. 255, and n. 296. All other forms of life are but shadows compared to His perfect Light.

4443. If God, when we truly apprehend Him, is the only Reality, we must take our standard and inspiration from Him. All other objects of worship are mere delusions. To any one who sees this clearly, through God's Self revelations, the only possible course is to give up everything else, which his own inner experience as well as outer Revelation tell him is false or of a temporary nature, and to bring his own will and actions into complete unison with the only Reality: for that is the meaning of Islām, bowing to the Will of God. When we bow to the Real and Everlasting, we are automatically saved from falling victims to the False and Evanescent.

4444. *Cf.* this passage with xxii. 5 and notes 2773 and 2774. The various stages of man's physical life are: (1) first, simple matter (dust); (2) the sperm-drop in the father; (3) the fertilised ovum in the mother's womb; (4) out into the light, as a human child; (5) youth and full maturity; (6) decay; and (7) death. In some cases the later stages are curtailed or cut off; but in any case, a Term appointed is reached, so that the higher purpose of God's Will and Plan may be fulfilled in each given case, that man "may learn wisdom".

Then from a sperm-drop,
Then from a leech-like clot;
Then does He get you
Out (into the light)
As a child; then lets you
(Grow and) reach your age
Of full strength; then
Lets you become old,—
Though of you there are
Some who die before;—
And lets you reach
A Term appointed;
In order that ye
May learn wisdom.

ثُمَّ مِنْ نُّطْفَةٍ ثُمَّ مِنْ عَلَقَةٍ
ثُمَّ يُخْرِجُكُمْ طِفْلًا
ثُمَّ لِتَبْلُغُوْٓا اَشُدَّكُمْ
ثُمَّ لِتَكُوْنُوْا شُيُوْخًا ۚ
وَمِنْكُمْ مَّنْ يُّتَوَفّٰى مِنْ قَبْلُ
وَلِتَبْلُغُوْٓا اَجَلًا مُّسَمًّى
وَّلَعَلَّكُمْ تَعْقِلُوْنَ ○

68. It is He Who gives Life [4445]
And Death; and when He
Decides upon an affair,
He says to it, "Be",
And it is.

٦٨- هُوَ الَّذِيْ يُحْيٖ وَيُمِيْتُ ۚ
فَاِذَا قَضٰٓى اَمْرًا
فَاِنَّمَا يَقُوْلُ لَهٗ كُنْ فَيَكُوْنُ ○

Section 8.

69. Seest thou not those
That dispute concerning
The Signs of God?
How are they turned away [4446]
(From Reality)?—

٦٩- اَلَمْ تَرَ اِلَى الَّذِيْنَ يُجَادِلُوْنَ
فِيْٓ اٰيٰتِ اللّٰهِ ۭ
اَنّٰى يُصْرَفُوْنَ ○

70. Those who reject the Book [4447]
And the (revelations) with which
We sent Our apostles:
But soon shall they know,—

٧٠- اَلَّذِيْنَ كَذَّبُوْا بِالْكِتٰبِ وَبِمَآ اَرْسَلْنَا
بِهٖ رُسُلَنَا ۫ فَسَوْفَ يَعْلَمُوْنَ ○

4445. The keys of life and death are in God's hands. But He is not dependent on time or place or instruments or materials. All that He has to do is to say "Be", and it comes into existence. *Cf.* xvi. 40, and n. 2066; xxxvi. 82, and n. 4029. Conversely, His Will or Command is sufficient to annihilate Existence into Non-Existence (Life into Death) or determine the limits or conditions of Existence or Non-Existence.

4446. Those who dispute about the Signs of God which are clear to all who care to see, are merely in the mists of Unreality; *Cf.* x. 32.

4447. "The Book" may refer to the Holy Qur-ān or to the fundamental Revelation, the "Mother of the Book" (xiii. 39), while the Books revealed to the apostles are the definite Revelations that came down to men from time to time.

71. When the yokes (shall be) [4448]
Round their necks,
And the chains;
They shall be dragged along—

٧١- إِذِ الْأَغْلٰلُ فِىٓ أَعْنٰقِهِمْ وَالسَّلٰسِلُ ۚ
يُسْحَبُونَ ○

72. In the boiling fetid fluid; [4449]
Then in the Fire
Shall they be burned;

٧٢- فِى الْحَمِيمِ ۙ
ثُمَّ فِى النَّارِ يُسْجَرُونَ ○

73. Then shall it be said
To them: "Where are
The (deities) to which
Ye gave part-worship—

٧٣- ثُمَّ قِيلَ لَهُمْ
أَيْنَ مَا كُنتُمْ تُشْرِكُونَ ○

74. "In derogation of God?"
They will reply: "They have [4450]
Left us in the lurch:
Nay, we invoked not,
Of old, anything (that had
Real existence)." Thus
Does God leave
The Unbelievers to stray.

٧٤- مِن دُونِ اللَّهِ ۖ
قَالُوا ضَلُّوا عَنَّا
بَل لَّمْ نَكُن نَّدْعُوا مِن قَبْلُ شَيْـًٔا ۚ
كَذٰلِكَ يُضِلُّ اللَّهُ الْكٰفِرِينَ ○

75. "That was because [4451]
Ye were wont to rejoice
On the earth in things
Other than the Truth,
And that ye were wont
To be insolent.

٧٥- ذٰلِكُم بِمَا كُنتُمْ تَفْرَحُونَ
فِى الْأَرْضِ بِغَيْرِ الْحَقِّ
وَبِمَا كُنتُمْ تَمْرَحُونَ ○

76. "Enter ye the gates [4452]
Of Hell, to dwell therein:
And evil is (this) abode
Of the arrogant!"

٧٦- ادْخُلُوٓا أَبْوٰبَ جَهَنَّمَ خٰلِدِينَ فِيهَا ۖ
فَبِئْسَ مَثْوَى الْمُتَكَبِّرِينَ ○

4448. The rejection of God's Message, however brought, carries its own penalty. The yoke of spiritual slavery to Sin and Evil is fastened more and more firmly round the rejecter's neck, because there is no one to safeguard his freedom, and the chains of superstitions and the ugly consequences of evil restrict his freedom and the limited faculty of choice which was given by God to man. This process receives its climax at the Hour of Judgment.

4449. The sinner gets dragged further and further in the disgusting consequences of his evil actions, until the fire of destruction closes in upon him.

4450. All falsehoods will vanish: *Cf.* vii. 36. The only Reality will be fully manifest even to those to whom Evil was made to seem alluring in the lower life. They will feel in their inmost souls that they had been pursuing mere shadows, things of no real existence. This was the result of their rejecting the Light and the Grace of God: they got entangled in the mazes of error.

4451. God does not withdraw His grace from any unless (1) they actively and deliberately take a delight in things that are vain or false, and (2) they insolently reject the things that are true,—in other words, unless men are deliberately false to their own lights, as illuminated by the Light of God.

4452. *Cf.* xxxix. 72.

77. So persevere in patience;
For the Promise of God
Is true: and whether[4453]
We show thee (in this life)
Some part of what We
Promise them,—or We
Take thy soul (to Our Mercy)
(Before that),—(in any case)
It is to Us that
They shall (all) return.

78. We did aforetime send
Apostles before thee: of them[4454]
There are some whose story
We have related to thee,
And some whose story
We have not related
To thee. It was not
(Possible) for any apostle
To bring a Sign except
By the leave of God:
But when the Command[4455]
Of God issued,
The matter was decided
In truth and justice,
And there perished,
There and then, those
Who stood on Falsehoods.

SECTION 9.

79. It is God who made[4456]
Cattle for you, that ye

٧٧- فَاصْبِرْ إِنَّ وَعْدَ اللّٰهِ حَقٌّ ۚ
فَإِمَّا نُرِيَنَّكَ
بَعْضَ الَّذِي نَعِدُهُمْ
أَوْ نَتَوَفَّيَنَّكَ
فَإِلَيْنَا يُرْجَعُونَ ○

٧٨- وَلَقَدْ أَرْسَلْنَا رُسُلًا مِّن قَبْلِكَ مِنْهُم
مَّن قَصَصْنَا عَلَيْكَ
وَمِنْهُم مَّن لَّمْ نَقْصُصْ عَلَيْكَ ۗ
وَمَا كَانَ لِرَسُولٍ
أَن يَأْتِيَ بِآيَةٍ
إِلَّا بِإِذْنِ اللّٰهِ ۚ
فَإِذَا جَاءَ أَمْرُ اللّٰهِ
قُضِيَ بِالْحَقِّ
وَخَسِرَ هُنَالِكَ الْمُبْطِلُونَ ○

٧٩- اللّٰهُ الَّذِي جَعَلَ لَكُمُ الْأَنْعَامَ

4453. *Cf.* x. 46, and n. 1438. As the eventual justice and readjustment of values must take place, when every soul returns to the Judgment-seat of God, it makes no difference if good and evil meet their deserts in this very life or not. *Cf.* also xiii. 40.

4454. *Cf.* iv. 164. God sent Messengers of His Truth to every people. There are some whose names are known to us through the holy Qur-ān, but there are a large number whose names are not made known to us through that medium. We must recognise the Truth wherever we find it.

4455. The Signs of God are everywhere, and can be seen by the discerning eye at all times. But if any extraordinary Signs are demanded by cynics or Unbelievers, they will not be granted merely because they are demanded. It is God's Will that issues them, not merely the desire of human beings, even if he be a Messenger of God. But when an extraordinary Sign does issue by the Command of God, it means that the cup of the iniquitous is full; that their case is decided, and their time of respite is past; and that Justice takes the place of Mercy, and evil is blotted out.

4456. *Cf.* xvi. 5-8. The fact that beasts, which in their wild state are so noxious, are, when domesticated, so useful to man, is itself one of the great and standing Signs of God's care for man. The great usefulness of cattle is very instructive. They serve for riding, and many of them for food; further, they are used for the plough, and they produce milk, or wool, or hair; and from their carcases man derives bones and horns for many industrial uses; but passing on to higher aspects of life, they further social, moral, and spiritual uses as draught-animals, in that transport serves one of the fundamental purposes of civilisation, being in this respect like ships for international commerce: xxx 46, and n. 3565. It is by means of human intercourse through transport that we can carry out the highest needs of our culture, "any need there may be in our hearts", *i.e.*, in our inner being.

May use some for riding
And some for food;

لِتَرْكَبُوا مِنْهَا وَمِنْهَا تَأْكُلُونَ ۝

80. And there are (other) advantages
In them for you (besides);
That ye may through them
Attain to any need
(There may be) in your hearts;
And on them and on ships
Ye are carried.

٨٠- وَلَكُمْ فِيهَا مَنَافِعُ
وَلِتَبْلُغُوا عَلَيْهَا حَاجَةً
فِي صُدُورِكُمْ
وَعَلَيْهَا وَعَلَى الْفُلْكِ تُحْمَلُونَ ۝

81. And He shows you (always)[4457]
His Signs: then which
Of the Signs of God
Will ye deny?

٨١- وَيُرِيكُمْ آيَاتِهِ فَأَيَّ
آيَاتِ اللَّهِ تُنْكِرُونَ ۝

82. Do they not travel through
The earth and see what
Was the End of those
Before them? They were
More numerous than these
And superior in strength[4458]
And in the traces
(They have left) in the land:
Yet all that they accomplished
Was of no profit to them.

٨٢- أَفَلَمْ يَسِيرُوا فِي الْأَرْضِ فَيَنْظُرُوا
كَيْفَ كَانَ عَاقِبَةُ الَّذِينَ مِنْ قَبْلِهِمْ
كَانُوا أَكْثَرَ مِنْهُمْ وَأَشَدَّ قُوَّةً
وَآثَارًا فِي الْأَرْضِ
فَمَا أَغْنَى عَنْهُمْ مَا كَانُوا يَكْسِبُونَ ۝

83. For when their apostles
Came to them
With Clear Signs, they exulted[4459]
In such knowledge (and skill)

٨٣- فَلَمَّا جَاءَتْهُمْ رُسُلُهُمْ بِالْبَيِّنَاتِ
فَرِحُوا بِمَا عِنْدَهُمْ مِنَ الْعِلْمِ

4457. The Signs of God's goodness and mercy are so numerous that it is impossible to enumerate them. Which of them can any mortal deny? This is the theme of that highly poetical Sūra, *Raḥmān* (S. lv.).

4458. *Cf.* ix. 69. For any generation to take inordinate pride in its own single achievements in science or skill becomes ridiculous if we consider the broad stream of history. In the first place, men will find that a great deal of what they attribute to their own merits only became possible owing to the earlier work of their predecessors. Secondly, many of their predecessors were more numerous and mightier in power than they, although the perspective of time may have reduced the apparent depth of their influence, and the monuments which they have left behind may have suffered from the destroying hand of Time. Thirdly, and most important of all, when they forgot God and His inexorable Law, nothing of their own handiwork profited them: they perished in the common ruin as all vanities must perish. *Cf.* also xl. 21 above, and n. 4387. See how the recapitulation rounds off the argument.

4459. Arrogance and an exaggerated idea of Self were at the bottom of the Evil to which they succumbed.

As they had; but That very (Wrath) at which [4460] They were wont to scoff Hemmed them in.	وَحَاقَ بِهِمْ مَّا كَانُوا بِهِ يَسْتَهْزِءُونَ ○
84. But when they saw Our Punishment, they said: "We believe in God,— The One God – and we Reject the partners we used To join with Him."	٨٤- فَلَمَّا رَاَوْا بَاْسَنَا قَالُوٓا اٰمَنَّا بِاللّٰهِ وَحْدَهٗ وَكَفَرْنَا بِمَا كُنَّا بِهٖ مُشْرِكِيْنَ ○
85. But their professing the Faith [4461] When they (actually) saw Our Punishment was not going To profit them. (Such has been) God's way Of dealing with His servants (From the most ancient times). And even thus did The rejecters of God Perish (utterly)!	٨٥- فَلَمْ يَكُ يَنْفَعُهُمْ اِيْمَانُهُمْ لَمَّا رَاَوْا بَاْسَنَا سُنَّتَ اللّٰهِ الَّتِيْ قَدْ خَلَتْ فِيْ عِبَادِهٖ وَخَسِرَ هُنَالِكَ الْكٰفِرُوْنَ ○ ع ١٤

4460. *Cf.* xvi. 34. Nothing could stop the Justice of God punishing Evil. What they had ridiculed came as an inexorable fact. None of their grandeur or art or science or skill was of any use when they lost their souls!

4461. Again and again were they given chances, and again and again did they reject them. When it was too late, and in fact when it had no meaning, they offered to profess Faith. That was of no use. God does not accept unmeaning things of that kind. He wants to train and purify our will. For their disobedience and rebellion they perished utterly.

INTRODUCTION TO SŪRA XLI (*Ḥā-Mīm*).

This is the second of the series of seven Sūras bearing the Abbreviated Letters *Ḥā-Mīm*, as explained in the Introduction to S. xl. To prevent confusion with other Sūras of the *Ḥā-Mīm* series, the word *Sajda* is sometimes added to the title, making it *Ḥā-Mīm as-Sajda*, the double title being necessary as there is another Sūra called *Sajda* (S. xxxii). To avoid the double title, it is sometimes called *Fuṣṣilat*, from the occurrence of the word in verse 3.

The meaning of *Ḥā-Mīm* has been explained in the Introduction to S. xl, where will also be found a note on the chronology and general theme of the seven *Ḥā-Mīm* Sūras.

For this particular Sūra the theme is that the basis of Faith and Revelation is God's Power and Goodness, and the fruit of both is man's righteousness and healing.

Summary.—What is Revelation and Faith, and what is man's attitude to both, and what are its consequences? (xli. 1-32, and C. 209).

The fruits of Faith and Unfaith, Truth and Falsehood (xli. 33-54, and C. 210).

C. 209.—Revelation explains, and makes things clear;
(xli. 1-32.) It gives the message of hope and mercy,
And it warns men against the snares
Of Evil. Deny not God, the Lord
Of the Worlds, Whose glory and power
Are shown in Creation, and His Mercy
In Revelation. Learn from the fate
Of the Peoples of old! Learn from the warnings
Of your own nature : your very limbs
And faculties, if misused, bear witness
Against you. Repent ere it be too late.

Sūra XLI.
Ḥā-Mīm (Abbreviated Letters),
Or *Ḥā-Mīm Sajda*, or *Fuṣṣilat*
(See Introduction)

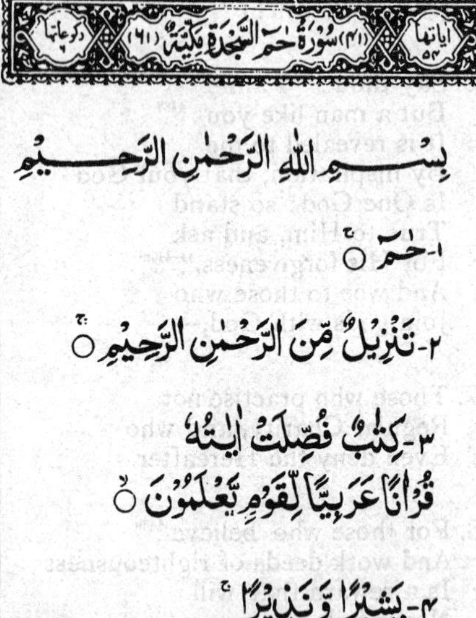

In the name of God, Most Gracious,
Most Merciful.

بِسْمِ اللّٰهِ الرَّحْمٰنِ الرَّحِيْمِ

1. Ḥā-Mīm:[4462]

١- حٰمٓ ۝

2. A revelation from (God),[4463]
Most Gracious, Most Merciful;—

٢- تَنْزِيْلٌ مِّنَ الرَّحْمٰنِ الرَّحِيْمِ ۝

3. A Book, whereof the verses
Are explained in detail;—
A Qur-ān in Arabic,
For people who understand;—

٣- كِتٰبٌ فُصِّلَتْ اٰيٰتُهٗ
قُرْاٰنًا عَرَبِيًّا لِّقَوْمٍ يَّعْلَمُوْنَ ۝

4. Giving Good News
And Admonition: yet most[4464]
Of them turn away,
And so they hear not.

٤- بَشِيْرًا وَّنَذِيْرًا ۚ
فَاَعْرَضَ اَكْثَرُهُمْ فَهُمْ لَا يَسْمَعُوْنَ ۝

5. They say: "Our hearts are[4465]
Under veils, (concealed)
From that to which thou
Dost invite us, and
In our ears is a deafness,
And between us and thee
Is a screen: so do[4466]
Thou (what thou wilt);

٥- وَقَالُوْا قُلُوْبُنَا فِيْٓ اَكِنَّةٍ
مِّمَّا تَدْعُوْنَآ اِلَيْهِ
وَفِيْٓ اٰذَانِنَا وَقْرٌ وَّمِنْۢ بَيْنِنَا وَبَيْنِكَ حِجَابٌ
فَاعْمَلْ

4462. Abbreviated Letters: see Introduction to S. xl. See also n. 4382 to xl. 18, and n. 4505 to xli. 34.

4463. In the last Sūra (xl. 2-3) the revelation was described with reference to some of the qualities of God, from Whom it came. Here it is described mainly with reference to its subject-matter. (1) It brings the Message of Grace and Mercy; (2) it is not merely a book of Dark Sayings, but everything is explained clearly and from various points of view; (3) it is in Arabic, the language of the people among whom it was first promulgated, and therefore easily intelligible to them if they take the trouble to understand; and (4) it opens the way to Forgiveness through Repentance and gives warning of all spiritual Dangers.

4464. With all the qualities mentioned in the last note, if men do not profit by its blessings, the fault lies in their will: they turn away, and thus fail to hear the voice that calls to them.

4465. The consequence of their wilful rejection is that a distance is created between Revelation and those for whom it is meant; their ears become deaf, so that the voice falls fainter and fainteron their ears: they feel a bar between themselves and the Messenger who comes to teach them. *Cf.* vii. 25.

4466. This is either a superiority complex adopting the sarcastic tone of an inferiority complex, or it expresses calculated indifference to spiritual teaching. In effect it says: 'Our hearts and minds are not intelligent enough to understand your noble ideas, nor our ears sufficiently acute to hear their exposition; you and we are quite different; there is a gulf between us. Why worry about us? You go your way, and we shall go ours!'

For us, we shall do
(What we will !) "

إِنَّنَا عٰمِلُونَ ○

6. Say thou : " I am
But a man like you :[4467]
It is revealed to me
By inspiration, that your God
Is One God : so stand
True to Him, and ask
For His forgiveness."[4468]
And woe to those who
Join gods with God,—

٦- قُلْ إِنَّمَآ أَنَا بَشَرٌ مِّثْلُكُمْ
يُوحٰىٓ إِلَىَّ أَنَّمَآ إِلٰهُكُمْ إِلٰهٌ وَّاحِدٌ
فَاسْتَقِيمُوٓا إِلَيْهِ
وَاسْتَغْفِرُوهُ ط
وَوَيْلٌ لِّلْمُشْرِكِينَ ○

7. Those who practise not
Regular Charity, and who
Even deny the Hereafter.

٧- الَّذِينَ لَا يُؤْتُونَ الزَّكٰوةَ
وَهُم بِالْاٰخِرَةِ هُمْ كٰفِرُونَ ○

8. For those who believe[4469]
And work deeds of righteousness
Is a reward that will
Never fail.

٨- إِنَّ الَّذِينَ اٰمَنُوا وَعَمِلُوا الصّٰلِحٰتِ
لَهُمْ أَجْرٌ غَيْرُ مَمْنُونٍ ○

SECTION 2.

9. Say : Is it that ye
Deny Him Who created
The earth in two Days ?[4470]
And do ye join equals
With Him ? He is
The Lord of (all)
The Worlds.

٩- قُلْ أَئِنَّكُمْ لَتَكْفُرُونَ بِالَّذِى
خَلَقَ الْأَرْضَ فِى يَوْمَيْنِ
وَتَجْعَلُونَ لَهُۥٓ أَندَادًا ط
ذٰلِكَ رَبُّ الْعٰلَمِينَ ○

4467. The reply is in effect : that the bringer of the Message is not an angel nor a god, and so there can and ought to be no barrier between him and his hearers ; but he has been chosen to bring a Message of Truth and Hope to them ; they should accept the Gospel of Unity, and by Repentance obtain God's Grace and Forgiveness.

4468. There is nothing but pity for those who reject Truth, run after false worship, have no sympathy or charity for their fellow-men, and even deny that there is any future Life.

4469. But blessed are those who have Faith. They will have a Future and a Bliss that will never fail.

4470. This is a difficult passage, describing the primal creation of our physical earth and the physical heavens around us. If we count the two Days mentioned in this verse, the four Days mentioned in verse 10, and the two Days mentioned in verse 12, we get a total of eight Days, while in many passages the creation is stated to have taken place in six Days : see vii. 54, n. 1031 ; and xxxii. 4, n. 3632. The Commentators understand the "four Days" in verse 10 to include the two Days in verse 9, so that the total for the universe comes to six Days. This is reasonable, because the processes described in verses 9 and 10 form really one series. In the one case it is the creation of the formless matter of the earth ; in the other case it is the gradual evolution of the form of the earth, its mountains and seas, and its animal and vegetable life, with the "nourishment in due proportion", proper to each. *Cf.* also xv. 19-20.

10. He set on the (earth),
Mountains standing firm,[4471]
High above it,
And bestowed blessings on
The earth, and measured therein
All things to give them
Nourishment in due proportion,
In four Days,[4472] in accordance
With (the needs of)
Those who seek (sustenance).[4473]

١٠- وَجَعَلَ فِيهَا رَوَاسِيَ مِن فَوْقِهَا
وَبٰرَكَ فِيهَا
وَقَدَّرَ فِيهَآ أَقْوَاتَهَا
فِيٓ أَرْبَعَةِ أَيَّامٍ
سَوَآءً لِّلسَّآئِلِينَ ○

11. Moreover He comprehended[4474]
In His design the sky,[4475]
And it had been (as) smoke:
He said to it
And to the earth:
"Come ye together,[4476]
Willingly or unwillingly."
They said: "We do come
(Together), in willing obedience."

١١- ثُمَّ اسْتَوَىٰٓ إِلَى السَّمَآءِ
وَهِيَ دُخَانٌ
فَقَالَ لَهَا وَلِلْأَرْضِ
ائْتِيَا طَوْعًا أَوْ كَرْهًا
قَالَتَآ أَتَيْنَا طَآئِعِينَ ○

12. So he completed them
As seven firmaments

١٢- فَقَضٰهُنَّ سَبْعَ سَمٰوَاتٍ

4471. *Cf.* xiii. 3 and xvi. 15, n. 2038. *High above it*: the highest mountains are 29,000 feet above sea-level, and the lowest depths of the bottom of the ocean are 31,600 feet below sea-level, so that the vertical difference between the highest and lowest points on the solid crust of the earth is about 11½ miles. The highland areas are the main sources of the water-supply in all the regions of the earth, and vegetable and animal life depends on water-supply.

4472. See n. 4470 above.

4473 *Sā-ilīn* may mean either (1) those who seek, or (2) those who ask or enquire. If the former meaning is adopted, the clause means that everything is apportioned to the needs and appetites of God's creatures. If the latter, it means that the needs of enquirers are sufficiently met by what is stated here.

4474. For *istawā* see n. 1386 to x. 3. *Cf.* also ii. 29.

4475. From lxxix. 30 it would appear as if the earth was spread out after the sky was made. In the present passage the creation of the earth and the evolution of life on our globe are mentioned first; and the making of the sky into the seven firmaments is mentioned last. The two statements are not inconsistent. It is stated here that when the sky was made into seven firmaments, it had existed previously as smoke, or vapour, or steam. The idea I derive from a collation of the relevant Quranic passages is that God first created primeval matter, which was as yet without order, shape, or symmetry. This state is called Chaos as opposed to Cosmos in Greek Cosmogony. The next stage would be the condensation of this primeval matter, into gases, liquids, or solids: on this subject no precise information is given us: it belongs to the realm of Physics. About the earth we are told of four stages or Days, and about the heavens, of two stages or Days. For Days seen n. 4477 below. If these stages proceeded or proceed together in time, it is obvious that each stage as we know it on earth is half as long as each stage in the heavens. But these are questions of Physics, Astronomy, or Geology, not questions of Religion.

4476. I take this to mean that God's design in creation was not to keep heaven and earth separate, but together, as we indeed are, being part of the solar system, and travellers through space, crossing the path of several comets. And all matter created by God willingly obeys the laws laid down for it.

In two Days,[4477] and He Assigned to each heaven Its duty and command. And We adorned The lower heaven With lights, and (provided it)[4478] With guard. Such Is the Decree of (Him) The Exalted in Might, Full of knowledge.	فِىْ يَوْمَيْنِ وَاَوْحٰى فِىْ كُلِّ سَمَآءٍ اَمْرَهَا ؕ وَزَيَّنَّا السَّمَآءَ الدُّنْيَا بِمَصَابِيْحَ ۖ وَحِفْظًا ؕ ذٰلِكَ تَقْدِيْرُ الْعَزِيْزِ الْعَلِيْمِ ۝
13. But if they turn away, Say thou: "I have warned You of a stunning Punishment (As of thunder and lightning)[4479] Like that which (overtook) The 'Ād and the Thamūd!"	١٣- فَاِنْ اَعْرَضُوْا فَقُلْ اَنْذَرْتُكُمْ صٰعِقَةً مِّثْلَ صٰعِقَةِ عَادٍ وَّثَمُوْدَ ۝ؕ
14. Behold, the apostles came To them, from before them[4480] And behind them, (preaching): "Serve none but God." They said, "If our Lord Had so pleased, He would	١٤- اِذْ جَآءَتْهُمُ الرُّسُلُ مِنْ بَيْنِ اَيْدِيْهِمْ وَمِنْ خَلْفِهِمْ اَلَّا تَعْبُدُوْٓا اِلَّا اللّٰهَ ؕ قَالُوْا لَوْ شَآءَ رَبُّنَا

4477. For "*Days*", which may include thousands of years, see vii 54, and n. 1031. They refer to stages in the evolution of physical nature. In the Biblical cosmogony, (Gen. i, and ii. 1-7), which reflects old Babylonian cosmogony, the scheme is apparently to be taken literally as to days and is as follows. The first day God created light; the second, the firmament; the third, the earth and vegetation; the fourth, the stars and planets; the fifth, fish and fowl from the sea; and the sixth, cattle, creeping things, beasts on land, and man; on the seventh day He ended His work and rested. Our scheme is wholly different. (1) God did not rest, and never rests. "His Throne doth extend over the heavens and the earth, and He feeleth no fatigue in guarding and preserving them"; (2) God's work has not ended; His activity still goes on: xxxii. 5; vii. 54; (3) man in our scheme does not come in with land animals; his advent is much later; (4) our stages are not sharply divided from each other, as in the above scheme, where the stars and planets having been created on the fourth day, it is not intelligible how the first three days were counted, nor how vegetation grew on the third day. Our stages for earth and heaven are not in sequence of time for the heavens and the earth. Our six stages are broadly speaking, (1) the throwing off of our planet from cosmic matter; (2) its cooling and condensing; (3) and (4) the growth of vegetable and animal life; (5) and (6) the parallel growth of the starry realm and our solar system.

4478. *Cf.* xv. 17, and n. 1951; also xxxvii. 6-9. The transition from the third person ("He completed," etc.) to the first person ("We adorned," etc.) may be noted. The act of creation is an impersonal act: the act of adornment and guarding is a personal favour to God's creatures.

4479. See verse 17 below.

4480. "*From before them and behind them*": *i.e.*, from every side. They were warned from every point of view.

Certainly have sent down angels[4481]
(To preach) : now we reject
Your mission (altogether)."

لَاَنْزَلَ مَلٰٓئِكَةً
فَاِنَّا بِمَآ اُرْسِلْتُمْ بِهٖ كٰفِرُوْنَ ○

15. Now the 'Ad behaved
Arrogantly through the land,
Against (all) truth and reason,[4482]
And said : "Who is superior
To us in strength ?" What !
Did they not see that
God, Who created them,
Was superior to them
In strength ? But they
Continued to reject Our Signs !

١٥- فَاَمَّا عَادٌ فَاسْتَكْبَرُوْا فِى الْاَرْضِ
بِغَيْرِ الْحَقِّ وَقَالُوْا مَنْ اَشَدُّ مِنَّا قُوَّةً ط
اَوَلَمْ يَرَوْا اَنَّ اللّٰهَ الَّذِىْ خَلَقَهُمْ
هُوَ اَشَدُّ مِنْهُمْ قُوَّةً ط
وَكَانُوْا بِاٰيٰتِنَا يَجْحَدُوْنَ ○

16. So We sent against them
A furious Wind through days[4483]
Of disaster, that We might
Give them a taste
Of a Penalty of humiliation
In this Life ; but the Penalty
Of a Hereafter will be
More humiliating still :
And they will find
No help.

١٦- فَاَرْسَلْنَا عَلَيْهِمْ رِيْحًا
صَرْصَرًا فِىْٓ اَيَّامٍ نَّحِسَاتٍ
لِّنُذِيْقَهُمْ عَذَابَ الْخِزْىِ فِى الْحَيٰوةِ الدُّنْيَا ط
وَلَعَذَابُ الْاٰخِرَةِ اَخْزٰى
وَهُمْ لَا يُنْصَرُوْنَ ○

17. As to the Thamūd,[4484]
We gave them guidance,
But they preferred blindness
(Of heart) to Guidance :
So the stunning Punishment[4485]
Of humiliation seized them,
Because of what they had earned.

١٧- وَاَمَّا ثَمُوْدُ فَهَدَيْنٰهُمْ
فَاسْتَحَبُّوا الْعَمٰى عَلَى الْهُدٰى
فَاَخَذَتْهُمْ صٰعِقَةُ الْعَذَابِ الْهُوْنِ
بِمَا كَانُوْا يَكْسِبُوْنَ ○

4481. *Cf.* xv. 7, n. 1941 ; vi. 8-9, n. 841-42. The 'Ād had more power and material civilisation than the Pagan Arabs contemporary with the holy Prophet. But the greater the material civilisation, the greater the arrogance as the besetting sin.

4482. *Against (all) truth and reason* : *Cf.* vii. 33. Their estimate of their own strength was greater than was justified by facts, but if they had all the strength which they arrogated to themselves, yet how could they stand before God ?

4483. The detailed story of the 'Ād and their besetting sin, and the preaching of their apostle Hūd to them will be found in xxvi. 123-140 ; also vii. 65-72, and n. 1040. For the furious Wind, *Cf.* liv. 19.

4484. The story of the Thamūd usually goes with that of the 'Ād. *Cf.* xxvi. 140-59 ; also vii. 73-79, and n. 1043.

4485. "*The stunning Punishment*" : *i.e.* deafening noises like those of thunder and lightning ; or the rumbling of a terrible earthquake. In vii. 78, an earthquake is suggested : see n. 1047 to that verse. *Cf.* also above, xli. 13.

18. But We delivered those
Who believed and practised
righteousness.

١٨- وَنَجَّيْنَا الَّذِينَ
آمَنُوا وَكَانُوا يَتَّقُونَ ۝

SECTION 3.

19. On the Day that
The enemies of God
Will be gathered together
To the Fire, they will
Be marched in ranks.[4486]

١٩- وَيَوْمَ
يُحْشَرُ أَعْدَاءُ اللَّهِ إِلَى النَّارِ
فَهُمْ يُوزَعُونَ ۝

20. At length, when they reach
The (Fire), their hearing,
Their sight, and their skins[4487]
Will bear witness against them,
As to (all) their deeds.

٢٠- حَتَّىٰ إِذَا مَا جَاءُوهَا
شَهِدَ عَلَيْهِمْ سَمْعُهُمْ وَأَبْصَارُهُمْ وَجُلُودُهُمْ
بِمَا كَانُوا يَعْمَلُونَ ۝

21. They will say to their skins:[4488]
"Why bear ye witness
Against us?" They will say:
"God hath given us speech,—
(He) Who giveth speech
To everything: He created
You for the first time,
And unto Him were ye
To return.

٢١- وَقَالُوا لِجُلُودِهِمْ لِمَ شَهِدْتُمْ عَلَيْنَا ۖ
قَالُوا أَنْطَقَنَا اللَّهُ الَّذِي
أَنْطَقَ كُلَّ شَيْءٍ
وَهُوَ خَلَقَكُمْ أَوَّلَ مَرَّةٍ
وَإِلَيْهِ تُرْجَعُونَ ۝

22. "Ye did not seek[4489]
To hide yourselves, lest

٢٢- وَمَا كُنْتُمْ تَسْتَتِرُونَ أَنْ يَشْهَدَ عَلَيْكُمْ

4486. "*Marched in ranks*": to show their further humiliation; for they will be like prisoners going to Punishment.

4487. All the members of their bodies and the faculties of their minds, which they misused, will bear witness against them. Similarly, in xxxvi. 65, their hands and their feet bear witness against them. The "skin" not only includes the sense of touch (which is so often misused in sex), but also the sense of taste and the sense of smell, which are specialised forms of the organ of touch. All the sensory organs, and all their intellectual and emotional counterparts advance us by their use and pull us down by their misuse. They become tell-tale witnesses against us if abused.

4488. A new phase of their existence will now dawn on them. They used to think that if they concealed their evil deeds from the rest of the world, nothing would happen to them! But God can give "tongues to trees", and can make every fact in life, known and unknown to the world, contribute to the elucidation of truth and justice. "Speech" on behalf of their senses and faculties should of course be understood figuratively. When we succumb to evil, our limbs and faculties themselves betray us.

4489. The limbs and faculties will say: "You did not seek to hide your evil from us: in fact you used us for your evil, because we were in your power. Did you not know that God knew everything, and that our knowledge would be evidence against you?"

Your hearing, your sight,
And your skins should bear
Witness against you! But
Ye did think that God
Knew not many of the the things
That ye used to do!

سَمْعُكُمْ وَلَآ أَبْصَٰرُكُمْ وَلَا جُلُودُكُمْ
وَلَٰكِن ظَنَنتُمْ أَنَّ ٱللَّهَ
لَا يَعْلَمُ كَثِيرًا مِّمَّا تَعْمَلُونَ ○

23. " But this thought of yours [4490]
Which ye did entertain
Concerning your Lord, hath
Brought you to destruction,
And (now) have ye become
Of those utterly lost!"

٢٣- وَذَٰلِكُمْ ظَنُّكُمُ ٱلَّذِى
ظَنَنتُم بِرَبِّكُمْ أَرْدَىٰكُمْ
فَأَصْبَحْتُم مِّنَ ٱلْخَٰسِرِينَ ○

24. If, then, they have patience, [4491]
The Fire will be
A Home for them!
And if they beg
To be received into favour,
Into favour will they not
(Then) be received.

٢٤- فَإِن يَصْبِرُوا۟
فَٱلنَّارُ مَثْوًى لَّهُمْ ۖ
وَإِن يَسْتَعْتِبُوا۟
فَمَا هُم مِّنَ ٱلْمُعْتَبِينَ ○

25. And We have destined
For them intimate companions [4492]
(Of like nature), who made
Alluring to them what was
Before them and behind them; [4493]
And the sentence among
The previous generations of Jinns [4494]
And men, who have passed away,

٢٥- وَقَيَّضْنَا لَهُمْ قُرَنَآءَ
فَزَيَّنُوا۟ لَهُم مَّا بَيْنَ أَيْدِيهِمْ وَمَا خَلْفَهُمْ
وَحَقَّ عَلَيْهِمُ ٱلْقَوْلُ فِىٓ أُمَمٍ
قَدْ خَلَتْ مِن قَبْلِهِم مِّنَ ٱلْجِنِّ وَٱلْإِنسِ ۖ

4490. " You now see the situation! We were given for your use and service. You misused us, to your own utter and irretrievable destruction!"

4491. *If they have patience*: there is sarcasm in the meaning. "Let them not be impatient: they will soon find a home in the Fire of Hell! If they ask for grace and forgiveness then, it will be too late."

4492. Just as the idea of happiness in heaven is expressed, not only by individual satisfaction, but by congenial society, so the idea of Punishment in hell is deepened by the fact that Evil will be made to meet evil: those who made sin fair-seeming in this life will be there to share in the regrets and mutual recriminations which will make life a burden. In fact, in these *Ḥā-Mīm* verses, the idea of fit companionship for the Good and uncongenial company for the Evil, runs like a thread throughout. See Introduction to S. xl.

4493. They painted in glowing colours the pleasures of sin in the past and the pleasures of sin in the future, thus practising a double deception, which will now be found out.

4494. *Jinns*: see n. 929 to vi. 100. All spirits of wickedness and all men who submitted to them, in the past, were under one common sentence; and future generations who embrace evil will also join them. *Cf.* vi. 128.

Is proved against them;
For they are utterly lost.[4495]

إِنَّهُمْ كَانُوا خَاسِرِينَ ۝ ع

SECTION 4.

26. The Unbelievers say:
"Listen not to this Qur-ān,[4496]
But talk at random
In the midst
Of its (reading), that ye
May gain the upper hand!"

٢٦- وَقَالَ الَّذِينَ كَفَرُوا لَا تَسْمَعُوا لِهَٰذَا
الْقُرْآنِ وَالْغَوْا فِيهِ
لَعَلَّكُمْ تَغْلِبُونَ ۝

27. But We will certainly
Give the Unbelievers a taste
Of a severe Penalty,
And We will requite them
For the worst of their deeds.[4497]

٢٧- فَلَنُذِيقَنَّ الَّذِينَ كَفَرُوا
عَذَابًا شَدِيدًا ۙ
وَلَنَجْزِيَنَّهُمْ أَسْوَأَ الَّذِي كَانُوا يَعْمَلُونَ ۝

28. Such is the requital
Of the enemies of God,—
The Fire: therein will be
For them the Eternal Home:
A (fit) requital, for
That they were wont
To reject Our Signs.

٢٨- ذَٰلِكَ جَزَاءُ أَعْدَاءِ اللَّهِ النَّارُ ۖ
لَهُمْ فِيهَا دَارُ الْخُلْدِ ۖ
جَزَاءً بِمَا كَانُوا بِآيَاتِنَا يَجْحَدُونَ ۝

29. And the Unbelievers will say:
"Our Lord! Show us those,[4498]
Among Jinns and men,
Who misled us: we shall
Crush them beneath our feet,
So that they become
The vilest (before all)."

٢٩- وَقَالَ الَّذِينَ كَفَرُوا رَبَّنَا أَرِنَا الَّذَيْنِ
أَضَلَّانَا مِنَ الْجِنِّ وَالْإِنْسِ
نَجْعَلْهُمَا تَحْتَ أَقْدَامِنَا
لِيَكُونَا مِنَ الْأَسْفَلِينَ ۝

30. In the case of those
Who say, "Our Lord

٣٠- إِنَّ الَّذِينَ قَالُوا رَبُّنَا

4495. The echo here of verse 23 above completes the argument from another point of view.

4496. A favourite trick of those who wish to dishonour Revelation is. not only not to listen to it themselves, but to talk loudly and insolently when it is being read, so that even the true listeners may not be able to perform their devotions. They think that they are drowning the voice of God: in fact they are piling up misery for themselves in the future. For God's voice can never be silenced.

4497. Nothing that they can do, however outrageous, will escape its fit punishment. And to reject God's Signs is to shut the very door to His Grace and Mercy.

4498. It is one of the qualities of sin and all evil, that it wishes to drag down others in its own camp, and rejoices to see them humiliated and disgraced, just as, in the opposite case, the good rejoice to help and honour others and make them happy wherever they can. *Cf.* vi. 12-113.

Is God ", and, further,[4499]
Stand straight and steadfast,
The angels descend on them
(From time to time):
" Fear ye not!" (they suggest),
" Nor grieve! But receive
The Glad Tidings
Of the Garden (of Bliss),
The which ye were promised!

اللّٰهُ ثُمَّ اسْتَقَامُوا
تَتَنَزَّلُ عَلَيْهِمُ الْمَلٰٓئِكَةُ
أَلَّا تَخَافُوا وَلَا تَحْزَنُوا
وَأَبْشِرُوا بِالْجَنَّةِ الَّتِي
كُنْتُمْ تُوعَدُونَ ○

31. " We are your protectors [4500]
In this life and
In the Hereafter:
Therein shall ye have
All that your souls[4501]
Shall desire; therein
Shall ye have all
That ye ask for!—

٣١ - نَحْنُ أَوْلِيَآؤُكُمْ
فِي الْحَيٰوةِ الدُّنْيَا وَفِي الْآخِرَةِ ج
وَلَكُمْ فِيهَا مَا تَشْتَهِيٓ أَنْفُسُكُمْ
وَلَكُمْ فِيهَا مَا تَدَّعُونَ ○

32. "A hospitable gift from One [4502]
Oft-Forgiving, Most Merciful!"

٣٢ - نُزُلًا مِّنْ غَفُورٍ رَّحِيمٍ ○ ع

C. 210.—The best of men is the man of Faith,
(xli. 33-54.) Who calls all men to share his Faith,
Whose life is pure, and whose law of life
Is the Will of God. Eschew all evil,
And adore God, and Him alone.
His Signs are everywhere, and His Message
Is the same through all the ages, a guide
And a healing to those who believe.
Dispute not, but live righteousness.
Knowledge belongs to God, but Falsehood
Deprives man of hope, humility,
And clear sight, and drives him to
Hypocrisy. So turn to Truth, and live.

4499. The people who succeed in eternal Life are those who recognise and understand the one and only Reality, that is God, and further shape their probationary Life firmly and steadfastly on the principles of that Truth and Reality. They will have their friends and protectors in the good angels, in contrast to the evil ones, who will have no friendship or protection, but only the reproaches of the Evil Ones.

4500. "*Protectors*": a key-thought for the *Ḥā-Mīm* Sūras. *Cf.* n. 4492 to xli. 25 above, and n. 4505 to xli. 34 below.

4501. Their desires will by then be so purified that desire, the expression of that desire, and the satisfaction of that desire will be practically synonymous for them: for they will be in complete accord with the true and only Reality.

4502. *Cf.* iii. 198. Through God's infinite Mercy and Forgiveness, they will now be in the position of guests to Host, and will receive unnumbered gifts out of all proportion to their own merits.

SECTION 5.

33. Who is better in speech[4503]
Than one who calls (men)
To God, works righteousness,
And says, "I am of those
Who bow in Islam"?

٣٣- وَمَنْ أَحْسَنُ قَوْلًا مِّمَّنْ دَعَآ إِلَى اللّٰهِ
وَعَمِلَ صَالِحًا
وَّ قَالَ إِنَّنِيْ مِنَ الْمُسْلِمِيْنَ ۝

34. Nor can Goodness and Evil[4504]
Be equal. Repel (Evil)
With what is better:
Then will he between whom
And thee was hatred
Become as it were
Thy friend and intimate![4505]

٣٤- وَلَا تَسْتَوِى الْحَسَنَةُ وَلَا السَّيِّئَةُ ۭ
اِدْفَعْ بِالَّتِيْ هِيَ أَحْسَنُ
فَإِذَا الَّذِيْ بَيْنَكَ وَبَيْنَهٗ عَدَاوَةٌ
كَأَنَّهٗ وَلِيٌّ حَمِيْمٌ ۝

35. And no one will be[4506]
Granted such goodness
Except those who exercise
Patience and self-restraint,—
None but persons of
The greatest good fortune.

٣٥- وَمَا يُلَقّٰهَآ
إِلَّا الَّذِيْنَ صَبَرُوْا ۚ
وَمَا يُلَقّٰهَآ إِلَّا ذُوْ حَظٍّ عَظِيْمٍ ۝

4503. *Better in speech*: *i.e.*, speaks better counsel; or is more worthy of being listened to. That his word reaches the highest mark of human speech is evidenced by three facts: (1) that he calls all to the Truth of God, showing that his thoughts are not centred on himself; (2) every deed of his is righteousness, showing that there is no divergence between his preaching and his conduct; and (3) he completely associates himself with the Will of God, showing that he is the full embodiment of Islam. What a fine description of the holy Prophet!

4504. You do not *return* good for evil, for there is no equality or comparison between the two. You repel or destroy evil with something which is far better, just as an antidote is better than poison. You foil hatred with love. You repel ignorance with knowledge, folly and wickedness with the friendly message of Revelation. The man who was in the bondage of sin, you not only liberate from sin, but make him your greatest friend and helper in the cause of God! Such is the alchemy of the Word of God! *Cf.* xxiii 96; xxviii. 54.

4505. *Hamim*: the key-word of the *Hā-Mīm* Sūras. See n. 4500 above, and Introduction to S. xl.

4506. The moral standard referred to in the last verse can only be reached by the exercise of the highest patience and self-restraint. All sorts of human weaknesses and counsels of pseudo-wisdom and "self-respect" will keep breaking in, but resist them as suggestions of Evil (see next verse). If you can reach anywhere near that high standard, you will be indeed most fortunate in a spiritual sense, for God's Revelation will have made you great and free.

36. And if (at any time)
An incitement to discord [4507]
Is made to thee
By the Evil One,
Seek refuge in God.
He is the One
Who hears and knows
All things.

٣٦- وَإِمَّا يَنْزَغَنَّكَ
مِنَ الشَّيْطٰنِ نَزْغٌ
فَاسْتَعِذْ بِاللّٰهِ ۚ
إِنَّهُ هُوَ السَّمِيعُ الْعَلِيمُ ○

37. Among His Signs are [4508]
The Night and the Day,
And the Sun and the Moon.
Adore not the sun
And the moon, but adore
God, Who created them,
If it is Him ye wish
To serve.

٣٧- وَمِنْ اٰيٰتِهِ الَّيْلُ وَالنَّهَارُ وَالشَّمْسُ وَ
الْقَمَرُ ۚ لَا تَسْجُدُوا لِلشَّمْسِ وَلَا لِلْقَمَرِ
وَاسْجُدُوا لِلّٰهِ الَّذِي خَلَقَهُنَّ
إِنْ كُنْتُمْ إِيَّاهُ تَعْبُدُونَ ○

38. But if the (Unbelievers)
Are arrogant, (no matter): [4509]
For in the presence
Of thy Lord are those
Who celebrate His praises
By night and by day.
And they never flag
(Nor feel themselves
Above it).

٣٨- فَإِنِ اسْتَكْبَرُوا
فَالَّذِينَ عِنْدَ رَبِّكَ
يُسَبِّحُونَ لَهُ بِالَّيْلِ وَالنَّهَارِ
وَهُمْ لَا يَسْـَٔمُونَ ○ السجدة

4507. *Nazaga* has in it the idea of discord, slander, disharmony, as well as incitements to such disturbances in the soul. They can only proceed from evil, and should be resisted with the help of God. See also last note.

4508. Night and Day are opposites, and yet, by the alchemy of God, they can both subserve the purpose of human good, because the Night can give rest while the Day can promote activity. The Sun and the Moon are similarly complementary. So, in moral and spiritual affairs, seeming opposites may by God's alchemy be made to subserve the purposes of Good. They are but instruments: God is the Cause. Adore God, and not the things which He has created. Use the things which He has created, but do not adore them.

4509. It does not in any way affect God if men rebel against Him. It is men's own loss. God's glory is being celebrated night and day by angels and men who receive the privilege of approaching His presence. To them it is a delight and an honour to be in the sunshine of Truth and Happiness.

39. And among His Signs
In this : thou seest
The earth barren and desolate ;[4510]
But when We send down
Rain to it, it is stirred
To life and yields increase.
Truly, He Who gives life[4511]
To the (dead) earth
Can surely give life
To (men) who are dead.
For He has power
Over all things.

٣٩- وَمِنْ اٰيٰتِهٖٓ اَنَّكَ تَرَى الْاَرْضَ خَاشِعَةً
فَاِذَآ اَنْزَلْنَا عَلَيْهَا الْمَآءَ
اهْتَزَّتْ وَرَبَتْ ؕ
اِنَّ الَّذِيْٓ اَحْيَاهَا
لَمُحْيِ الْمَوْتٰى ؕ
اِنَّهٗ عَلٰى كُلِّ شَيْءٍ قَدِيْرٌ ○

40. Those who pervert[4512]
The Truth in Our Signs
Are not hidden from Us.
Which is better?—he that
Is cast into the Fire,
Or he that comes safe through,
On the Day of Judgment?
Do what ye will :
Verily He seeth (clearly)
All that ye do.

٤٠- اِنَّ الَّذِيْنَ يُلْحِدُوْنَ فِيْٓ اٰيٰتِنَا لَا
يَخْفَوْنَ عَلَيْنَا ؕ
اَفَمَنْ يُّلْقٰى فِي النَّارِ خَيْرٌ
اَمْ مَّنْ يَّاْتِيْٓ اٰمِنًا يَّوْمَ الْقِيٰمَةِ ؕ
اِعْمَلُوْا مَا شِئْتُمْ ۙ
اِنَّهٗ بِمَا تَعْمَلُوْنَ بَصِيْرٌ ○

41. Those who reject the Message[4513]
When it comes to them

٤١- اِنَّ الَّذِيْنَ كَفَرُوْا بِالذِّكْرِ لَمَّا جَآءَهُمْ

4510. Evil makes of the souls of men what drought makes of land : it kills life, beauty, and fruitfulness. God's Word in the spiritual world has the same wonderful effect as rain has on barren land : it gives life, beauty, and fruitfulness. And the effect of God's Word is also seen through the lives of men who repel evil with what is better. They also convert dead souls (which harbour spite and hatred) into living souls, which come into the main current of spiritual life, and help in carrying out God's beneficent Purpose.

4511. Why should we wonder then at the potency of God's Word, whether in our probationary lives here, or in the eternal life of the Hereafter.

4512. *Pervert the Truth in Our Signs* : either by corrupting the scriptures or turning them to false and selfish uses ; or by neglecting the Signs of God in nature around them, or silencing His voice in their own conscience. Everything is known to God. Why not work for true salvation at the final Judgment?

4513. Mere rejection by men will not silence the Signs of God, which will work unintermittently and with the fullest potency.

(Are not hidden from Us).
And indeed it is a Book
Of exalted power.

وَاِنَّهٗ لَكِتٰبٌ عَزِيْزٌ ۙ○

42. No falsehood can approach it
From before or behind it :[4514]
It is sent down
By One Full of Wisdom,
Worthy of all Praise.

۴۲- لَا يَاْتِيْهِ الْبَاطِلُ مِنْۢ بَيْنِ يَدَيْهِ
وَلَا مِنْ خَلْفِهٖ ؕ
تَنْزِيْلٌ مِّنْ حَكِيْمٍ حَمِيْدٍ ○

43. Nothing is said to thee
That was not said
To the apostles before thee :[4515]
That thy Lord has
At His command (all) Forgiveness
As well as a most
Grievous Penalty.

۴۳- مَا يُقَالُ لَكَ اِلَّا مَا قَدْ قِيْلَ
لِلرُّسُلِ مِنْ قَبْلِكَ ؕ
اِنَّ رَبَّكَ لَذُوْ مَغْفِرَةٍ
وَّذُوْ عِقَابٍ اَلِيْمٍ ○

44. Had We sent this as
A Qur-ān (in a language)[4516]
Other than Arabic, they would
Have said : " Why are not
Its verses explained in detail ?
What ! (a Book) not in Arabic
And (a Messenger) an Arab ? "
Say : " It is a guide

۴۴- وَلَوْ جَعَلْنٰهُ قُرْاٰنًا اَعْجَمِيًّا
لَّقَالُوْا لَوْلَا فُصِّلَتْ اٰيٰتُهٗ ؕ
ءَاَعْجَمِيٌّ وَّعَرَبِيٌّ ؕ
قُلْ هُوَ

4514. God's Truth is fully guarded on all sides. No one can get the better of it by attacking it from before or behind it, openly or secretly, or in any way whatever.

4515. The gist of God's Message, now, before, and for ever, is the same : Mercy to the erring and repentant ; just punishment to those who wilfully rebel against God.

4516. *Cf.* xvi. 103-105 ; xii. 2 ; etc. It was most natural and reasonable that the Messenger being Arab, the Message should be in his own tongue, that he might explain it in every detail, with the greatest power and eloquence. Even though it was to be for the whole world, its initial exposition was thus to be in Arabic. But if people had no faith and were spiritually deaf or blind, it wou not matter in what language it came.

And a healing to those
Who believe ; and for those
Who believe not, there is
A deafness in their ears,[4517]
And it is blindness in their (eyes) :
They are (as it were)
Being called from a place
Far distant ! "

لِلَّذِينَ آمَنُوا هُدًى وَشِفَاءٌ ۖ
وَالَّذِينَ لَا يُؤْمِنُونَ
فِي آذَانِهِمْ وَقْرٌ وَهُوَ عَلَيْهِمْ عَمًى ۚ
ع ١٩ أُولَٰئِكَ يُنَادَوْنَ مِنْ مَكَانٍ بَعِيدٍ ○

SECTION 6.

45. We certainly gave Moses
The Book aforetime : but disputes
Arose therein. Had it not
Been for a Word[4518]
That went forth before
From thy Lord, (their differences)
Would have been settled
Between them : but they
Remained in suspicious
Disquieting doubt thereon.

٤٥- وَلَقَدْ آتَيْنَا مُوسَى الْكِتَابَ فَاخْتُلِفَ فِيهِ ۗ
وَلَوْلَا كَلِمَةٌ
سَبَقَتْ مِنْ رَبِّكَ
لَقُضِيَ بَيْنَهُمْ ۚ
وَإِنَّهُمْ لَفِي شَكٍّ مِنْهُ مُرِيبٍ ○

46. Whoever works righteousness
Benefits his own soul ;
Whoever works evil, it is
Against his own soul :
Nor is thy Lord ever
24 Unjust (in the least)
30 To His servants.

٤٦- مَنْ عَمِلَ صَالِحًا فَلِنَفْسِهِ ۖ
وَمَنْ أَسَاءَ فَعَلَيْهَا ۗ
وَمَا رَبُّكَ بِظَلَّامٍ لِلْعَبِيدِ ○

4517. *Cf.* xli. 5, and vi. 25. They pretended that it was too deep for them, when they meant that they were superior to it ! The fact was that by putting themselves in an artificially false position, they rendered themselves impervious to the Message. The voice of Revelation or the voice of conscience sounded to them as if it came from a far-off place ! They themselves made themselves strangers to it.

4518. Callousness and self-sufficiency in religion are often illustrated by sects like the Pharisees and Sadducees among the Jews. Where there are honest differences of opinion, they can, in God's Plan, lead to greater enquiry and emulation. Where the differences are fractious, there is often even then time left for repentance. In any case the Word or Decree of God is for the best good of all, and should not disturb Faith. *Cf.* x. 19. A good life, of faith and truth, is in our own interests, and the opposite against our own interests. God is never unjust.

47. To Him is referred[4519]
The Knowledge of the Hour
(Of Judgment : He knows all) :
No date-fruit comes out
Of its sheath, nor does
A female conceive (within
Her womb) nor bring forth
(Young), but by His Knowledge.
The Day that (God) will propound
To them the (question),[4520]
" Where are the Partners
(Ye attributed) to Me ? "
They will say, " We do
Assure Thee not one
Of us can bear witness ! "

٤٧- إِلَيْهِ يُرَدُّ عِلْمُ السَّاعَةِ ۚ
وَمَا تَخْرُجُ مِنْ ثَمَرٰتٍ مِّنْ أَكْمَامِهَا
وَمَا تَحْمِلُ مِنْ أُنْثٰى
وَلَا تَضَعُ إِلَّا بِعِلْمِهِ ۚ
وَيَوْمَ يُنَادِيهِمْ أَيْنَ شُرَكَاءِي
قَالُوٓا ءَاذَنّٰكَ
مَا مِنَّا مِنْ شَهِيدٍ ۝

48. The (deities) they used to invoke
Aforetime will leave them
In the lurch, and they
Will perceive that they
Have no way of escape.

٤٨- وَضَلَّ عَنْهُمْ مَّا كَانُوا يَدْعُونَ
مِنْ قَبْلُ
وَظَنُّوا مَا لَهُمْ مِّنْ مَّحِيصٍ ۝

49. Man does not weary[4521]
Of asking for good (things),
But if ill touches him,
He gives up all hope
(And) is lost in despair.

٤٩- لَا يَسْـَٔمُ الْإِنْسَانُ مِنْ دُعَاءِ الْخَيْرِ
وَإِنْ مَّسَّهُ الشَّرُّ
فَيَـُٔوسٌ قَنُوطٌ ۝

50. When We give him a taste[4522]
Of some mercy from Ourselves,

٥٠- وَلَئِنْ أَذَقْنٰهُ رَحْمَةً مِّنَّا

4519. There are profound mysteries which the knowledge of man cannot fathom but which are all open knowledge to God, because He plans, guides and controls all things. The precise time of the Hour of Judgment is one of these. We are not to dispute about matters like these, which are matters of speculation as far as human intelligence is concerned. Such speculations ruined the Ummat of Moses, and set them on the arid path of doubts and controversies. Our task is to do our duty and love God and man (see the last two verses). *Cf.* also xxi. 4.

4520. When the final restoration of true values comes, all falsehood will be exposed openly and publicly. The false gods will vanish, and their falsehood will be acknowledged by those who had lapsed from true worship. But it will be too late then for repentance.

4521. Not only is man prone to doubts and speculations in matters beyond his ken, thus disturbing the even tenor of his spiritual life : he is apt to run into opposite extremes in his daily experiences in this life. He is always hankering after the good things of this life. They are not all good for him. If he receives a little check, even though it may be to bring him to his bearings and turn his thoughts to higher things, he is apt to fall into despair.

4522. When men entertain false ideas of values in life, there are two or three possible attitudes they may adopt in reaction to their experiences. In the first place, their desire may be inordinate for the good things of this life, and any little check brings them into a mood of despair. See last note. In the second place, if their desire is granted, they are puffed up, and think that everything is due to their own cleverness or merit, and they forget God. Not only that, but they go a step further, and begin to doubt a Hereafter at all ! If by chance they have a faint glimmering of the Hereafter, which they cannot help recognising, they think themselves " favoured of Heaven ", because of some small favours given to them in this life by way of trial. Thus they turn all things, good or evil, away from their real purpose, because they are devoted to falsehood.

After some adversity has
Touched him, he is sure
To say, "This is due
To my (merit): I think not
That the Hour (of Judgment)
Will (ever) be established;
But if I am brought back
To my Lord, I have
(Much) good (stored) in His sight!"
But We will show
The Unbelievers the truth
Of all that they did,
And We shall give them
The taste of a severe
Penalty.

مِنۢ بَعۡدِ ضَرَّآءَ مَسَّتۡهُ
لَيَقُولَنَّ هٰذَا لِيۡ
وَمَآ اَظُنُّ السَّاعَةَ قَآئِمَةً
وَّلَئِنۡ رُّجِعۡتُ اِلٰى رَبِّيۡۤ
اِنَّ لِيۡ عِنۡدَهٗ لَلۡحُسۡنٰى
فَلَنُنَبِّئَنَّ الَّذِيۡنَ كَفَرُوۡا بِمَا عَمِلُوۡا
وَلَنُذِيۡقَنَّهُمۡ مِّنۡ عَذَابٍ غَلِيۡظٍ ○

51. When We bestow favours[4523]
On man, he turns away,
And gets himself remote
On his side (instead of[4524]
Coming to Us); and when
Evil seizes him, (he comes)
Full of prolonged prayer!

٥١- وَاِذَآ اَنۡعَمۡنَا عَلَى الۡاِنۡسَانِ
اَعۡرَضَ وَنَاٰ بِجَانِبِهٖ
وَاِذَا مَسَّهُ الشَّرُّ
فَذُوۡ دُعَآءٍ عَرِيۡضٍ ○

52. Say: "See ye if[4524-A]
The (Revelation) is (really)
From God, and yet do ye
Reject it? Who is more
Astray than one who
Is in a schism[4524-B]
Far (from any purpose)?"

٥٢- قُلۡ اَرَءَيۡتُمۡ اِنۡ كَانَ مِنۡ عِنۡدِ اللّٰهِ
ثُمَّ كَفَرۡتُمۡ بِهٖ
مَنۡ اَضَلُّ مِمَّنۡ
هُوَ فِيۡ شِقَاقٍۢ بَعِيۡدٍ ○

53. Soon will We show them
Our Signs in the (furthest)

٥٣- سَنُرِيۡهِمۡ اٰيٰتِنَا فِي

4523. The last verse and note dealt with men's distortion of the values of life. Here we come to men's ingratitude and hypocrisy. If they receive good, they go farther away from God, instead of coming nearer to him. If they suffer ill, they call on God and offer prolonged prayers, but it is not sincere devotion and therefore worthless.

4524. *Cf.* xvii. 83.

4524-A. An argument is now addressed, of a most searching nature. Examine your own souls. See if you do not really find something unusual in God's Revelation! If you do, and yet you reject it, what a terrible responsibility fastens itself on you? Could anything be more foolish or more misguided than to reject a Message which is transforming the whole world?

4524-B. 'If you resist the convictions of the whole world, you are only forming a Cave or a narrow obscure sect or schism, which serves no purpose, and is unfit to live in the broad light of Universal Religion.' *Cf.* ii. 176, n. 176.

Regions (of the earth), and [4524-C] In their own souls, until It becomes manifest to them That this is the Truth. Is it not enough that Thy Lord doth witness All things?	الْاٰفَاقِ وَفِیْٓ اَنْفُسِهِمْ حَتّٰی یَتَبَیَّنَ لَهُمْ اَنَّهُ الْحَقُّ ؕ اَوَلَمْ یَکْفِ بِرَبِّکَ اَنَّهٗ عَلٰی کُلِّ شَیْءٍ شَهِیْدٌ ○
54. Ah indeed! are they In doubt concerning The Meeting with their Lord? [4525] Ah indeed! it is He That doth encompass All things!	۵۴- اَلَآ اِنَّهُمْ فِیْ مِرْیَةٍ مِّنْ لِّقَآءِ رَبِّهِمْ ؕ اَلَآ اِنَّهٗ بِکُلِّ شَیْءٍ مُّحِیْطٌ ○ ع

4524-C. God's Truth always spreads, in its own good time, across to the uttermost ends of the earth, as it did in the case of Islam. But its intensive spread in the hearts and souls of people is even more remarkable than its extensive spread over large areas. Men like the four Companions of the Prophet—and many more—became leaders of men and arbiters of the world's fate. Medina, from being a focus of jarring tribes and factions that hated each other, became the seat of heroic actions and plans and the nursery of great and noble heroic deeds that resounded throughout the world. It makes no difference what men may say or do. God's Truth must prevail, and He knows who obstruct and who help.

4525. Short-sighted people may like to think that there may be no Judgment. But Judgment is inevitable and cannot be escaped, for God "doth encompass all things"

INTRODUCTION TO SŪRA XLII (*Shūrā*).

This is the third Sūra of the *Hā-Mīm* series of seven Sūras, for which see the Introduction to S. xl.

The theme is how evil and blasphemy can be cured by the Mercy and Guidance of God, which come through His Revelation. Men are asked to settle their differences in patience by mutual Consultation (xlii. 38); which explains the title of the Sūra.

Summary.—The Contrast of blasphemy and disputation against Revelation, Unity, and Faith, as relying on the Signs and the Mercy of God (xlii. 1-29, and C. 211).

Evil comes through men's own deeds, of which they cannot avoid the consequences, but Guidance comes through God's Mercy and Revelation (xlii. 30-53, and C. 212).

C. 211.—Inspiration is part of the Glory and Goodness
(xlii. 1-29.) Of God. His Unity is shown
In His Creation; yet man will turn
To false gods, and dispute about Religion.
Faith has been one at all times,
But sects and divisions rose through selfish
Contumacy. Let all contention cease,
And conduct weighed by the just balance
Of God's Word. The just and the unjust
Will all be brought before God, Whose Mercy
And Bounty are writ large in the Signs
In His marvellous Creation,—one, yet diverse!

Sūra XLII.

Shūrā, or Consultation.

In the name of God, Most Gracious, Most Merciful.

1. *Hā-Mīm*;[4526]

2. '*Ain. Sīn. Kāf.*[4527]

3. Thus doth (He) send
Inspiration to thee
As (He did) to those before thee,—[4528]
God, Exalted in Power,
Full of Wisdom.

4. To Him belongs all
That is in the heavens
And on earth : and He
Is Most High, Most Great.[4529]

5. The heavens are almost
Rent asunder from above them[4530]
(By His Glory) :
And the angels celebrate
The Praises of their Lord,
And pray for forgiveness
For (all) beings on earth :[4531]
Behold! Verily God is He,

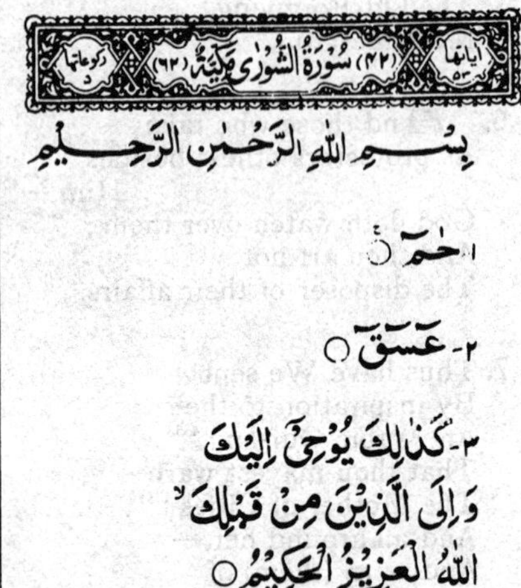

٤- لَهٗ مَا فِي السَّمٰوٰتِ وَمَا فِي الْاَرْضِ ؕ
وَهُوَ الْعَلِيُّ الْعَظِيْمُ ○

٥- تَكَادُ السَّمٰوٰتُ يَتَفَطَّرْنَ مِنْ فَوْقِهِنَّ
وَالْمَلٰٓئِكَةُ يُسَبِّحُوْنَ بِحَمْدِ رَبِّهِمْ
وَيَسْتَغْفِرُوْنَ لِمَنْ فِي الْاَرْضِ ؕ
اَلَآ اِنَّ اللّٰهَ هُوَ

4526. See Introduction to S. xl. paragraphs 2-4.

4527. This Sūra has a double set of Abbreviated Letters, one in the first verse, and one in this second verse. No authoritative explanation of this second set is available, and I refrain from speculation. See Appendix I.

4528. Inspiration is full of Power and Wisdom, and both these qualities are derived from the Power and Wisdom of God. Unlike human power, this Power is necessarily good and merciful; unlike human wisdom, this Wisdom is necessarily complete and indisputable.

4529. We cannot conceive the distance which separates the Most High from the highest of His creatures, God Most Great from the greatest of the beings that we can imagine. The highest heavens are mentioned in the next verse, as well as the noblest creatures that we can imagine, the angels.

4530. How can we conceive of sublimity and greatness in a higher degree than this, that the highest heavens are almost ready to burst asunder by His Glory, which is higher than all?

4531. The angels are the noblest and purest beings of whom we can conceive. They reflect on the one side God's Glory and Praise, and on the other, two other attributes of God, that look towards His erring creatures, *viz.*: Forgiveness and Mercy. The two sets of attributes are complementary. Believers and unbelievers alike are included in their solicitude and prayer. They thus proclaim in their own being and in their prayers the Greatness and unbounded Goodness of God.

The Oft-Forgiving,
Most Merciful.

الْغَفُورُ الرَّحِيمُ ۝

6. And those who take
As protectors others besides
Him,—[4532]
God doth watch over them;
And thou art not
The disposer of their affairs.

٦- وَالَّذِينَ اتَّخَذُوا مِن دُونِهِ أَوْلِيَاءَ
اللَّهُ حَفِيظٌ عَلَيْهِمْ
وَمَا أَنتَ عَلَيْهِم بِوَكِيلٍ ۝

7. Thus have We sent
By inspiration to thee
An Arabic Qur-ān:[4533]
That thou mayest warn
The Mother of Cities[4534]
And all around her,—
And warn (them) of
The Day of Assembly,
Of which there is no doubt:
(When) some will be[4535]
In the Garden, and some
In the Blazing Fire.

٧- وَكَذَٰلِكَ أَوْحَيْنَا إِلَيْكَ قُرْآنًا عَرَبِيًّا
لِّتُنذِرَ أُمَّ الْقُرَىٰ
وَمَنْ حَوْلَهَا
وَتُنذِرَ يَوْمَ الْجَمْعِ لَا رَيْبَ فِيهِ
فَرِيقٌ فِي الْجَنَّةِ
وَفَرِيقٌ فِي السَّعِيرِ ۝

8. If God had so willed,[4536]
He could have made them
A single people; but He
Admits whom He will
To His Mercy;
And the wrong-doers
Will have no protector
Nor helper.

٨- وَلَوْ شَاءَ اللَّهُ لَجَعَلَهُمْ
أُمَّةً وَاحِدَةً
وَلَٰكِن يُدْخِلُ مَن يَشَاءُ فِي رَحْمَتِهِ
وَالظَّالِمُونَ مَا لَهُم مِّن وَلِيٍّ وَلَا نَصِيرٍ ۝

9. What! Have they taken
(For worship) protectors

٩- أَمِ اتَّخَذُوا مِن دُونِهِ أَوْلِيَاءَ

4532. We now come to the contrast, the folly and ingratitude of man. But that cannot escape its final doom in the Universal Plan of God. Only Judgment rests with God. A Prophet is not responsible for the conduct of men, in a system which permits some limited free-will and personal responsibility.

4533. The point of the Qur-ān being in Arabic is that it is plain and intelligible to the people through whom and among whom it was promulgated; see next clause.

4534. The City of Mecca. See n. 913 to vi. 92. This is undoubtedly a Meccan verse. Even apart from the Qibla, Mecca is the centre of Islam, and "all around her" is the whole world.

4535. The contrast is again emphasised, as explained in the Summary.

4536. *Cf.* v. 51, and n. 761. It is one of the Signs of God that He has made us different, that we may be tried in the exercise of our will, and that we may reach, through righteousness and Faith, our highest development, and enjoy His gifts of Mercy and Grace. But we must not become contentious, and fall into evil: we must understand our own limitations. Otherwise we shall lose His grace and protection.

Besides Him? But it is
God,—He is the Protector,[4537]
And it is He Who
Gives life to the dead:
It is He Who has power
Over all things.

فَاللّٰهُ هُوَ الْوَلِيُّ
وَهُوَ يُحْيِ الْمَوْتٰى
وَهُوَ عَلٰى كُلِّ شَيْءٍ قَدِيْرٌ ۝

SECTION 2.

10. Whatever it be wherein
Ye differ, the decision
Thereof is with God:[4538]
Such is God my Lord:
In Him I trust,
And to Him I turn.

١٠- وَمَا اخْتَلَفْتُمْ فِيْهِ مِنْ شَيْءٍ فَحُكْمُهٗ
اِلَى اللّٰهِ ۭ ذٰلِكُمُ اللّٰهُ رَبِّيْ عَلَيْهِ تَوَكَّلْتُ ۖ
وَاِلَيْهِ اُنِيْبُ ۝

11. (He is) the Creator
Of the heavens and
The earth: He has made
For you pairs
From among yourselves,[4539]
And pairs among cattle:
By this means does He
Multiply you: there is nothing
Whatever like unto Him,
And He is the One
That hears and sees (all things).

١١- فَاطِرُ السَّمٰوٰتِ وَ الْاَرْضِ ۭ
جَعَلَ لَكُمْ مِّنْ اَنْفُسِكُمْ اَزْوَاجًا
وَّمِنَ الْاَنْعَامِ اَزْوَاجًا ۚ
يَذْرَؤُكُمْ فِيْهِ ۭ
لَيْسَ كَمِثْلِهٖ شَيْءٌ ۚ
وَهُوَ السَّمِيْعُ الْبَصِيْرُ ۝

12. To Him belong the keys
Of the heavens and the earth:

١٢- لَهٗ مَقَالِيْدُ السَّمٰوٰتِ وَ الْاَرْضِ ۚ

4537. There can be no greater ingratitude or blasphemy than to worship false gods, or to seek protection from things that have no power, when God—Who has power over all things—is always seeking to protect and cherish His creatures, and placing in their way all the means for attaining the best in them.

4538. In the highest issues of life men may see things differently. If their differences arise merely from selfish motives, or narrowness of vision, they are sinning against their own souls. If their differences arise from sincere but mistaken notions, their proper course is not to form divisions and sects, or to increase contention and hatred among men, but to leave all things to God, trusting in Him and turning to Him in all difficulties. The final decision in all things is with Him.

4539. The mystery of sex has not only its physical aspects, but its moral and spiritual aspects, and therefore mankind is in this respect differentiated from the lower animals, and among mankind the grades and qualities are suggested by the phrase "*from among yourselves*". As regards cattle, they are specially mentioned among the animals, as having special relations with man and specially subserving his needs, not only in the physical sphere, but also in the matter of transport, which is the key to all civilization and culture: *Cf.* xxxvi. 71-73; also xxiii. 21-22, where they are compared to ships, the symbol of international intercourse.

He enlarges and restricts.[4540]
The Sustenance to whom
He will: for He knows
Full well all things.

يَبْسُطُ الرِّزْقَ لِمَنْ يَّشَآءُ وَيَقْدِرُ ۚ
اِنَّهٗ بِكُلِّ شَيْءٍ عَلِيْمٌ ○

13. The same religion has He
Established for you as that
Which He enjoined on Noah—[4541]
The which We have sent
By inspiration to thee—
And that which We enjoined
On Abraham, Moses, and Jesus:
Namely, that ye should remain
Steadfast in Religion, and make
No divisions therein:[4542]
To those who worship
Other things than God,
Hard is the (way)
To which thou callest them.[4543]
God chooses to Himself
Those whom He pleases,
And guides to Himself
Those who turn (to Him).

١٣- شَرَعَ لَكُمْ مِّنَ الدِّيْنِ
مَا وَصّٰى بِهٖ نُوْحًا
وَّالَّذِيْٓ اَوْحَيْنَآ اِلَيْكَ
وَمَا وَصَّيْنَا بِهٖٓ اِبْرٰهِيْمَ وَمُوْسٰى وَعِيْسٰٓى
اَنْ اَقِيْمُوا الدِّيْنَ وَلَا تَتَفَرَّقُوْا فِيْهِ ۭ
كَبُرَ عَلَى الْمُشْرِكِيْنَ
مَا تَدْعُوْهُمْ اِلَيْهِ ۭ
اَللّٰهُ يَجْتَبِيْٓ اِلَيْهِ مَنْ يَّشَآءُ
وَيَهْدِيْٓ اِلَيْهِ مَنْ يُّنِيْبُ ○

14. And they became divided[4544]
Only after knowledge
Reached them,—through selfish
Envy as between themselves.
Had it not been
For a Word that

١٤- وَمَا تَفَرَّقُوْٓا اِلَّا مِنْۢ بَعْدِ مَا جَآءَهُمُ
الْعِلْمُ بَغْيًاۢ بَيْنَهُمْ ۭ
وَلَوْلَا كَلِمَةٌ

4540. "Sustenance", here as elsewhere, stands for all things that support every phase of life, physical, social, intellectual, or spiritual. *Cf.* x. 59, n. 1447. The source of all gifts is God; His bounty is inexhaustible, and He gives to all; but He does not give to all in the same measure, because, out of the fullness of His knowledge and wisdom, He can judge best what is best for any of His creatures.

4541. God's Religion is the same in essence, whether given, for example, to Noah, Abraham, Moses, or Jesus, or to our holy Prophet. The source of unity is the revelation from God. In Islam it is "established" as an institution, and does not remain merely a vague suggestion.

4542. Faith, Duty, or Religion, is not a matter to dispute about. The formation of sects is against the very principle of Religion and Unity. What we should strive for is steadfastness in duty and faith, and unity among mankind.

4543. Unity, unselfishness, love for God and man,—these things are inconsistent with selfish aggrandizement, unjust suppression of our fellow-creatures, false worship, and false conduct to our brethren. Hence the Gospel of Unity, though it is in complete accord with the pure pattern after which God made us, is yet hard to those who love self and falsehood. But Grace is free to all, and in His wise Plan, He will specially select Teachers to show the Way to humanity, and no one who turns to Him will lack guidance.

4544. *Cf.* ii. 213. If you reject Truth after it has reached you, it can only be through selfish contumacy or envy.

Went forth before [4545]
From thy Lord,
(Tending) to a Term appointed,
The matter would have
Been settled between them:
But truly those who have
Inherited the Book after them
Are in suspicious (disquieting) [4546]
Doubt concerning it.

سَبَقَتْ مِن رَّبِّكَ
إِلَىٰٓ أَجَلٍ مُّسَمًّى لَّقُضِيَ بَيْنَهُمْ ۚ
وَإِنَّ الَّذِينَ أُورِثُوا الْكِتَٰبَ مِنۢ بَعْدِهِمْ
لَفِي شَكٍّ مِّنْهُ مُرِيبٍ ○

15. Now then, for that (reason), [4547]
Call (them to the Faith),
And stand steadfast
As thou art commanded,
Nor follow thou their vain
Desires; but say: "I believe
In the Book which
God has sent down;
And I am commanded
To judge justly between you.
God is our Lord [4548]
And your Lord: For us
(Is the responsibility for)
Our deeds, and for you
For your deeds. There is
No contention between us
And you. God will
Bring us together,
And to Him is
(Our) final goal.

١٥- فَلِذَٰلِكَ فَادْعُ ۖ وَاسْتَقِمْ كَمَآ أُمِرْتَ ۖ
وَلَا تَتَّبِعْ أَهْوَآءَهُمْ ۖ
وَقُلْ ءَامَنتُ بِمَآ أَنزَلَ اللَّهُ مِن كِتَٰبٍ ۖ
وَأُمِرْتُ لِأَعْدِلَ بَيْنَكُمُ ۖ
اللَّهُ رَبُّنَا وَرَبُّكُمْ ۖ
لَنَآ أَعْمَٰلُنَا وَلَكُمْ أَعْمَٰلُكُمْ ۖ
لَا حُجَّةَ بَيْنَنَا وَبَيْنَكُمُ ۖ
اللَّهُ يَجْمَعُ بَيْنَنَا ۖ
وَإِلَيْهِ الْمَصِيرُ ○

4545. *Cf.* x. 19, and n. 1407. God's decree has allowed a certain Term during which a sinner has the chance of repentance and forgiveness. Were it not so, sin would be punished at once, and the matter would be decided straightway. So also, when people reject Truth from selfish or contumacious motives, they get rope: perchance they may repent.

4546. *Cf.* xiv. 9 and n. 1884. "Those who have inherited the Book" are the People of the Book, of the ages since the Book or Revelation came to them. Referring to the Jews and Christians contemporary with our Prophet, how true it is that they were broken up into hostile sects which hated and persecuted each other! Islam came to unite them, and it did. For the present phases of Christianity and Judaism are of later growth.

4547. How beautifully the mission of Islam is commended in this verse! (1) The more sectarianism and division there is in the world, the more need is there for the Gospel of Unity. (2) It must steadfastly pursue its way. (3) It must not be deflected by worldly or political motives. (4) Its faith must be directly in God and in God's Revelation. (5) It must judge justly between warring factions, as the Religion of Peace and Unity.

4548. The mission of Islam is further described. (6) The God whom it preaches is not an exclusive God: He is the Lord of the Worlds: to any given person, of whatever faith, 'He is your God, as well as mine.' (7) Our Faith is not a question of words; it is deeds which decide; each one of us has personal responsibility for his own conduct. (8) There is no cause of contention whatever, when we preach Unity, Truth, and the Hereafter. (9) If you have doubts, the final arbiter is God, and His Throne is our Goal.

16. But those who dispute
Concerning God after He
Has been accepted,—[4549]
Futile is their dispute
In the sight of
Their Lord: on them
Is Wrath, and for them
Will be a Penalty
Terrible.

١٦- وَالَّذِينَ يُحَاجُّونَ فِي اللَّهِ
مِنْ بَعْدِ مَا اسْتُجِيبَ لَهُ حُجَّتُهُمْ
دَاحِضَةٌ عِنْدَ رَبِّهِمْ
وَعَلَيْهِمْ غَضَبٌ
وَلَهُمْ عَذَابٌ شَدِيدٌ ○

17. It is God Who has
Sent down the Book in truth,
And the Balance[4550]
(By which to weigh conduct).
And what will make thee
Realise that perhaps the Hour
Is close at hand?

١٧- اللَّهُ الَّذِي أَنْزَلَ الْكِتٰبَ بِالْحَقِّ
وَالْمِيزَانَ
وَمَا يُدْرِيكَ
لَعَلَّ السَّاعَةَ قَرِيبٌ ○

18. Only those wish to[4551]
Hasten it who believe not
In it: those who believe
Hold it in awe,
And know that it is
The Truth. Behold, verily
Those that dispute concerning
The Hour are far astray.

١٨- يَسْتَعْجِلُ بِهَا الَّذِينَ لَا يُؤْمِنُونَ بِهَا
وَالَّذِينَ اٰمَنُوا مُشْفِقُونَ مِنْهَا وَيَعْلَمُونَ
أَنَّهَا الْحَقُّ أَلَا إِنَّ الَّذِينَ يُمَارُونَ فِي
السَّاعَةِ لَفِي ضَلٰلٍ بَعِيدٍ ○

19. Gracious is God[4552]
To His servants:[4553]

١٩- اللَّهُ لَطِيفٌ بِعِبَادِهِ

4549. *After He has been accepted.* The disputants are the Unbelievers who pugnaciously assault the minds of Believers after the Believers have by conviction accepted Faith in God as leading to spiritual Light. Such disputation is futile. An inner spiritual experience can never be shaken by dialectical assaults. On the contrary such disputations recoil on the heads of those who indulge in them. God's Wrath is on them in this life, and the terrible Penalty of the Hereafter must inevitably follow their evil plots against Truth.

4550. Revelation is like a balance, an instrument placed by God in our hands, by which we can weigh all moral issues, all questions of right and wrong in conduct. We must do so constantly. For the Judgment in any given case may come at any time: it may be quite near, and we must always be prepared. The Balance may also refer to the God-given faculty by which man can judge between right and wrong.

4551. The Unbelievers do not believe in Judgment and laugh at it. They say defiantly, "If there is to be a punishment, let it come at once!" The threefold answer to this will be found in n. 1810 to xiii. 6. With those who believe, the case is different. They know that the Hereafter is an awful Reality, and prepare for it. They see clearly on what a wrong track the scoffers are!

4552. *Laṭīf*: so kind, gracious, and understanding, as to bestow gifts finely suited to the needs of the recipients. For the various meanings of *Laṭīf*, see n. 2844 to xxii. 63. *Cf.* also xii. 100

4553. "Servants" here seems to include all men, just and unjust, for God provides for them all.

He gives Sustenance[4554]
To whom He pleases:
And He has Power
And can carry out
His Will.

يَرْزُقُ مَنْ يَّشَاۤءُ ۚ
وَهُوَ الْقَوِيُّ الْعَزِيْزُ ۝ ع

SECTION 3.

20. To any that desires
The tilth of the Hereafter,
We give increase
In his tilth; and to any
That desires the tilth
Of this world, We grant
Somewhat thereof, but he[4555]
Has no share or lot
In the Hereafter.

٢٠- مَنْ كَانَ يُرِيْدُ حَرْثَ الْاٰخِرَةِ
نَزِدْ لَهٗ فِيْ حَرْثِهٖ ۚ
وَمَنْ كَانَ يُرِيْدُ حَرْثَ الدُّنْيَا
نُؤْتِهٖ مِنْهَا
وَمَا لَهٗ فِي الْاٰخِرَةِ مِنْ نَّصِيْبٍ ۝

21. What! Have they partners[4556]
(In godhead), who have
Established for them some
Religion without the permission
Of God? Had it not
Been for the Decree
Of Judgment, the matter
Would have been decided
Between them (at once).
But verily the wrong-doers
Will have a grievous Penalty.

٢١- اَمْ لَهُمْ شُرَكٰۤؤُا شَرَعُوْا لَهُمْ مِّنَ الدِّيْنِ
مَا لَمْ يَاْذَنْ بِهِ اللّٰهُ ۚ
وَلَوْلَا كَلِمَةُ الْفَصْلِ
لَقُضِيَ بَيْنَهُمْ ۚ
وَاِنَّ الظّٰلِمِيْنَ
لَهُمْ عَذَابٌ اَلِيْمٌ ۝

22. Thou wilt see the wrong-doers[4557]
In fear on account of what

٢٢- تَرَى الظّٰلِمِيْنَ مُشْفِقِيْنَ مِمَّا

4554. *Sustenance, i.e.*, provision for all needs, physical, moral, spiritual, etc. "*To whom He pleases*" is not restrictive, but modal. 'God provides for all, but His provision is according to His wise Will and Plan, and not according to people's extravagant demands.' He can provide for all, because He has complete power and can carry out His Will. A further comment will be found in the next verse.

4555. The parable is from the efforts of the husbandman, who ploughs and prepares the soil, sows the seed, weeds in due season, and reaps the harvest. You reap as you sow. But God will add manifold advantages for spiritual tilth. To those who are only engrossed in the vanities of this world, something may accrue in this world, but the spiritual world is closed to them.

4556. Nothing can exist without the permission of God. Can people, who indulge in false worship say: "Why does God permit it?" The answer is: "a certain latitude is allowed with the grant of a limited form of free-will. When the time for Judgment comes, the Punishment is sure." See n. 1810 to xiii 6. *Decree (or Word) of Judgment*: See n. 1407 to x. 19.

4557. The chief feature of the punishment of wrong-doing is that the minds of the wrong-doers are haunted with terror on account of their own guilty conscience. They cannot possibly escape the weight of that terror.

They have earned, and (the burden
Of) that must (necessarily)
Fall on them. But those
Who believe and work
Righteous deeds will be
In the luxuriant meads[4558]
Of the Gardens: they shall
Have, before their Lord,
All that they wish for.
That will indeed be
The magnificent Bounty
(Of God).

كَسَبُوْا
وَهُوَ وَاقِعٌۢ بِهِمْ ؕ
وَالَّذِيْنَ اٰمَنُوْا وَعَمِلُوا الصّٰلِحٰتِ
فِيْ رَوْضٰتِ الْجَنّٰتِ ۚ
لَهُمْ مَّا يَشَآءُوْنَ عِنْدَ رَبِّهِمْ ؕ
ذٰلِكَ هُوَ الْفَضْلُ الْكَبِيْرُ ○

23. That is (the Bounty) whereof[4559]
God gives Glad Tidings
To His Servants who
Believe and do righteous deeds.
Say: "No reward do I
Ask of you for this
Except the love
Of those near of kin."[4560]
And if any one earns
Any good, We shall give
Him an increase of good
In respect thereof: for God
Is Oft-Forgiving, Most Ready[4561]
To appreciate (service).

٢٣- ذٰلِكَ الَّذِيْ يُبَشِّرُ اللّٰهُ عِبَادَهُ
الَّذِيْنَ اٰمَنُوْا وَعَمِلُوا الصّٰلِحٰتِ ؕ
قُلْ لَّآ اَسْـَٔلُكُمْ عَلَيْهِ اَجْرًا
اِلَّا الْمَوَدَّةَ فِي الْقُرْبٰى ؕ
وَمَنْ يَّقْتَرِفْ حَسَنَةً
نَّزِدْ لَهٗ فِيْهَا حُسْنًا ؕ
اِنَّ اللّٰهَ غَفُوْرٌ شَكُوْرٌ ○

24. What! Do they say,
"He has forged a falsehood
Against God"? But if God
Willed, He could seal up[4562]

٢٤- اَمْ يَقُوْلُوْنَ افْتَرٰى عَلَى اللّٰهِ كَذِبًا ۚ
فَاِنْ يَّشَاِ اللّٰهُ يَخْتِمْ

4558. In contrast with the withering terror of the wrong-doers is the ease and rational happiness of those who do good "On them shall be no fear, nor shall they grieve" (ii. 38). Their wills will have been purified, and they shall have all that they shall desire, "before their Lord". That is, their highest Bliss will be the sight of their Lord. No higher Bounty can they wish for.

4559. Heaven may be pictured to our minds in various forms. This is one of the highest, and God announces it freely to the righteous.

4560. No sort of tangible reward does the man of God ask for proclaiming the Glad Tidings of God. But at least he has the right to ask that his kith and kin should not persecute him and put all sorts of obstacles in his way, as did the Quraish against the holy Prophet. The love of kindred may be extended to mean the love of our common humanity, for all mankind are brothers descended from Adam. Everyone can understand the ordinary love of kindred. Can we not extend the idea to a mystical meaning of Love for all mankind, thus proving kinship with the divine Love, which in the story of Joseph is figured by the earthly love between the sexes?

4561. *Cf.* xxxv. 29-30, and notes 3915 (for increase) and 3917 (for God's appreciation of service).

4562. If any one has a doubt about a prophet's mission, let him look at the prophet's life, at his work, at his character. God loves Truth, not Falsehood. God's aid goes with Truth, not with Falsehood. The beauty and power of God's Word cannot be found in Falsehood. The false man's heart would be sealed, not expanded to new heights, as is that of the Message-bearer of God.

Thy heart. And God
Blots out Vanity, and proves
The Truth by His Words.
For He knows well
The secrets of all hearts.

عَلٰى قَلْبِكَ ۗ
وَيَمْحُ اللّٰهُ الْبَاطِلَ وَيُحِقُّ الْحَقَّ بِكَلِمٰتِهٖ ۗ
إِنَّهٗ عَلِيْمٌۢ بِذَاتِ الصُّدُوْرِ ○

25. He is the One that accepts[4563]
Repentance from His Servants
And forgives sins:
And He knows all
That ye do.

٢٥- وَهُوَ الَّذِىْ يَقْبَلُ التَّوْبَةَ عَنْ عِبَادِهٖ
وَيَعْفُوْا عَنِ السَّيِّاٰتِ
وَيَعْلَمُ مَا تَفْعَلُوْنَ ○

26. And He listens to[4564]
Those who believe and
Do deeds of righteousness,
And gives them increase
Of His Bounty: but
For the Unbelievers there is
A terrible Penalty.

٢٦- وَيَسْتَجِيْبُ الَّذِيْنَ اٰمَنُوْا
وَعَمِلُوا الصّٰلِحٰتِ وَيَزِيْدُهُمْ مِّنْ
فَضْلِهٖ ۗ
وَالْكٰفِرُوْنَ لَهُمْ عَذَابٌ شَدِيْدٌ ○

27. If God were to enlarge[4565]
The provision for His Servants,
They would indeed transgress
Beyond all bounds
Through the earth;
But He sends (it) down
In due measure
As He pleases.[4566]
For He is with His Servants
Well-acquainted, Watchful.

٢٧- وَلَوْ بَسَطَ اللّٰهُ الرِّزْقَ لِعِبَادِهٖ
لَبَغَوْا فِى الْاَرْضِ
وَلٰكِنْ يُّنَزِّلُ بِقَدَرٍ
مَّا يَشَآءُ ۗ
إِنَّهٗ بِعِبَادِهٖ خَبِيْرٌۢ بَصِيْرٌ ○

28. He is the One that sends down
Rain (even) after (men) have

٢٨- وَهُوَ الَّذِىْ يُنَزِّلُ الْغَيْثَ مِنْۢ بَعْدِ

4563. Whatever the sin, God's Mercy is open to sincere Repentance, at all times, until the decree of condemnation issues.

4564. To the prayers of the righteous He listens, and He gives them of His Bounty beyond their deserts. Every time they do a little good, they are increased in their goodness. Every right impulse or aspiration is strengthened and leads to progressive spiritual advancement.

4565. It may be objected that all prayers, even of good people, are not answered. The reply is: (1) that even everyone who is good does not necessarily know what is best for him, for the values in this life are curiously distorted; and (2) on account of their want of knowledge, if everyone got all he asked for, there would be chaos and confusion, and "transgression beyond bounds through the earth", for the different interests are so intermingled and balanced that some measure must be observed in granting people's wishes. This measure is best supplied by the watchful care of God and His perfect knowledge of all our real needs.

4566. "*As He pleases*" is here almost equivalent to "*as He thinks best*".

Given up all hope,[4567]
And scatters His Mercy
(Far and wide). And He
Is the Protector, Worthy
Of all Praise.

مَا قَنَطُوا
وَيَنْشُرُ رَحْمَتَهٗ ؕ
وَهُوَ الْوَلِيُّ الْحَمِيْدُ ۝

29. And among His Signs
Is the creation of
The heavens and the earth,
And the living creatures[4568]
That He has scattered
Through them:[4569] and He
Has power to gather them
Together when He wills.

٢٩- وَمِنْ اٰيٰتِهٖ خَلْقُ السَّمٰوٰتِ وَالْاَرْضِ
وَمَا بَثَّ فِيْهِمَا مِنْ دَآبَّةٍ ؕ
وَهُوَ عَلٰى جَمْعِهِمْ
اِذَا يَشَآءُ قَدِيْرٌ ۝

C. 212.—What we call the ills of life is due
(xlii. 30-53.) To our own ill-deeds, and many of them
Are forgiven by God. His Plan can never
Be frustrated. This Life is but a stage
Of convenience: live true and resist
All wrong, but learn the best way to do so.
On God rely; else no protector
Will you find. God's Revelation
Comes as a Guide and Mercy: it shows
The Straight Way, the Way of God All-Wise.

Section 4.

30. Whatever misfortune
Happens to you, is because

٣٠- وَمَآ اَصَابَكُمْ مِّنْ مُّصِيْبَةٍ فَبِمَا

4567. That men should get such a blessing as rain when they expect it according to ordinary calculations of probabilities does not impress them, as it is a daily occurrence. But God's mercy is more than this. It comes to our aid even when all hope is lost, and gives us new chances and new openings where we least expect them. His quality of cherishing and protecting His creatures is always active, and what higher praise can we give?

4568. *Dābbatun*: beasts, living, crawling creatures of all kinds: see n 166 to ii. 164. Similarly in xxiv. 45, and other passages, the word is used for living creatures of all kinds, life generally, whose material basis is the mysterious thing which science calls protoplasm. The more our biological knowledge increases, the more do we marvel at the unity of Life on the one hand, and its diversity on the other.

4569. Life is not confined to our one little Planet. It is a very old speculation to imagine some life like human life on the planet Mars. Though no scientific demonstration is possible, it is reasonable to suppose that Life in some form or other is scattered through some of the millions of heavenly bodies scattered through space. What a wonderful Sign of God! The Almighty Who created such countless beings has surely the power to bring them together.

Of the things your hands[4570]
Have wrought, and for many
(Of them) He grants forgiveness.

كَسَبَتْ اَيْدِيْكُمْ
وَيَعْفُوْا عَنْ كَثِيْرٍ ۝

31. Nor can ye frustrate (aught),
(Fleeing) through the earth;[4571]
Nor have ye, besides God,
Any one to protect
Or to help.

٣١- وَمَآ اَنْتُمْ بِمُعْجِزِيْنَ فِي الْاَرْضِ ۚ
وَمَا لَكُمْ مِّنْ دُوْنِ اللّٰهِ
مِنْ وَّلِيٍّ وَّلَا نَصِيْرٍ ۝

32. And among His Signs
Are the ships, smooth-running[4572]
Through the ocean, (tall)
As mountains.

٣٢- وَمِنْ اٰيٰتِهِ الْجَوَارِ
فِي الْبَحْرِ كَالْاَعْلَامِ ۝

33. If it be His Will,
He can still the Wind:
Then would they become
Motionless on the back
Of the (ocean). Verily
In this are Signs
For everyone who patiently[4573]
Perseveres and is grateful.

٣٣- اِنْ يَّشَاْ يُسْكِنِ الرِّيْحَ
فَيَظْلَلْنَ رَوَاكِدَ عَلٰى ظَهْرِهٖ ۭ
اِنَّ فِيْ ذٰلِكَ لَاٰيٰتٍ
لِّكُلِّ صَبَّارٍ شَكُوْرٍ ۝

34. Or He can cause them
To perish because of
The (evil) which (the men)
Have earned; but much
Doth He forgive.

٣٤- اَوْ يُوْبِقْهُنَّ بِمَا كَسَبُوْا
وَيَعْفُ عَنْ كَثِيْرٍ ۝

4570. All evil, all sorrow, all pain and affliction, are things not normal, things twisted from the pure and holy nature as created by God's hands. As far as man is concerned, his misfortunes are but the consequences of the things he has done. He must bear personal responsibility for them and not throw the blame on others.

4571. Every evil deed or word or thought must have its evil consequences: but if God forgives anything,—and He forgives much,—let no one imagine that he has defeated—or can defeat—God's Will or Plan. The only help or protection that is possible is from God. *Cf.* xxix. 22.

4572. The great and stately ships are appealed to again and again as being among the Signs of God, from many aspects. The aspect referred to here is how the great sailing ship runs prosperously as long as "the breath of heaven fills the sail", and what a miserable helpless creature she becomes when she once becomes becalmed. Students of English literature will remember the striking picture which Coleridge draws in his "Rime of the Ancient Mariner." The becalmed ship is as it were in the grip of Death because of the crime which the sailor had committed, and his mind feels psychologically the full force of the Sign. By analogy we can apply this to other craft: the steamer is not free from other dangers of the sea, nor air-craft from numerous dangers of the air.

4573. If we study such Signs in the right spirit, we learn the highest lessons for our spiritual life: on the one hand, patient perseverance with reliance on God, and on the other, a feeling or attitude of grateful thanks to God, that he enables us to achieve so much in spite of our shortcomings, and forgives in us so much that deserves punishment and disaster.

35. But let those know, who [4574]
Dispute about Our Signs,
That there is for them
No way of escape.

٣٥- وَّيَعْلَمَ الَّذِيْنَ يُجَادِلُوْنَ فِيْۤ اٰيٰتِنَاؕ
مَا لَهُمْ مِّنْ مَّحِيْصٍ ۝

36. Whatever ye are given (here)
Is (but) a convenience [4575]
Of this Life : but that
Which is with God
Is better and more lasting :
(It is) for those who believe [4576]
And put their trust
In their Lord ;

٣٦- فَمَاۤ اُوْتِيْتُمْ مِّنْ شَيْءٍ فَمَتَاعُ الْحَيٰوةِ
الدُّنْيَاۚ وَمَا عِنْدَ اللّٰهِ خَيْرٌ وَّاَبْقٰى
لِلَّذِيْنَ اٰمَنُوْا
وَعَلٰى رَبِّهِمْ يَتَوَكَّلُوْنَ ۝

37. Those who avoid the greater [4577]
Crimes and shameful deeds,
And, when they are angry
Even then forgive ;

٣٧- وَالَّذِيْنَ يَجْتَنِبُوْنَ كَبٰٓئِرَ الْاِثْمِ وَ
الْفَوَاحِشَ وَاِذَا مَا غَضِبُوْا هُمْ يَغْفِرُوْنَ ۝

38. Those who hearken [4578]
To their Lord, and establish

٣٨- وَالَّذِيْنَ اسْتَجَابُوْا لِرَبِّهِمْ وَاَقَامُوا

4574. If we treat God's Signs in the wrong spirit, *i.e.*, contumaciously reject them or constantly dispute about them instead of trying to understand them, we are told that such tactics will avail us nothing : we cannot escape the consequences of our sins. The only way to escape is by repentance on our part and the grant of mercy by God.

4575. Any good (or ill) which is our lot is only a temporary phase to serve the convenience of this life. But there is a higher good, which comes from God's own Presence. Such good is both superior in quality, and more permanent. In the same way, any ills that we may suffer in this life, have reference only to the conditions of this our life of probation. The ills that we "earn" in our spiritual Life—such as deprivation of God's Grace—are far more momentous and permanent.

4576. The higher and more permanent gifts which come from God's Presence are for those who truly worship and serve God. These are described by nine of their characteristics : *viz.* (1) they have Faith: and it follows that (2) they trust in God, instead of running after false standards or values: (3) they eschew the more serious offences against God's Law, and of course keep clear of any offences against sex ("shameful deeds"); (4) while knowing that they are not themselves perfect, they are ready to forgive others, even though they are sorely tried with anger and provocation; for the rest see n. 4578

4577. Here we are speaking of the ordinary man or woman who tries to follow God's Law: he or she is not perfect, but at least eschews the major breaches of conduct. For those higher in spiritual degree there is of course a stricter standard. But all are entitled to the blessing of Islam, whatever their degree.

4578. Continuing the enumeration of the characteristics described in n. 4576 above, we have the following further qualities in those who wish to serve God. (5) They are ready at all times to hearken to God's Signs, or to listen to the admonitions of men of God, and to follow the true Path, as they understand it; (6) they keep personal contact with God, by habits of Prayer and Praise; (7) their conduct in life is open and determined by mutual Consultation between those who are entitled to a voice, *e.g.*, in private domestic affairs, as between husband and wife, or other responsible members of the household; in affairs of business, as between partners or parties interested; and in State affairs, as between rulers and ruled, or as between different departments of administration, to preserve the unity of administration : (8) they do not forget Charity, or the help due to their weaker brethren, out of the wealth or gifts or talents or opportunities, which God has provided for themselves; and (9) when other people use them despitefully, they are not cowed down or terrorised into submission and acceptance of evil, but stand up for their rights within the limits mentioned in verse 40.

Regular prayer; who (conduct)
Their affairs by mutual
Consultation;[4579]
Who spend out of what
We bestow on them
For Sustenance;

الصَّلٰوةَ ص
وَ اَمۡرُهُمۡ شُوۡرٰى بَيۡنَهُمۡ ص
وَمِمَّا رَزَقۡنٰهُمۡ يُنۡفِقُوۡنَ ۝

39. And those who, when
An oppressive wrong is inflicted
On them, (are not cowed
But) help and defend themselves.[4580]

٣٩- وَالَّذِيۡنَ اِذَاۤ اَصَابَهُمُ الۡبَغۡىُ
هُمۡ يَنۡتَصِرُوۡنَ ۝

40. The recompense for an injury
Is an injury equal thereto[4581]
(In degree): but if a person
Forgives and makes reconciliation,

٤٠- وَجَزٰٓؤُا سَيِّئَةٍ سَيِّئَةٌ مِّثۡلُهَا ج
فَمَنۡ عَفَا وَاَصۡلَحَ

4579. "*Consultation.*" This is the key-word of the Sūra, and suggests the ideal way in which a good man should conduct his affairs, so that, on the one hand, he may not become too egotistical, and, on the other, he may not lightly abandon the responsibilities which devolve on him as a Personality whose development counts in the sight of God. See the points in head (7) under n. 4578 above. This principle was applied to its fullest extent by the holy Prophet in his private and public life, and was fully acted upon by the early rulers of Islam. Modern representative government is an attempt—by no means perfect—to apply this principle in State affairs. See my *Religious Polity of Islam.*

4580. This follows from the high value attached to an individual soul's Personality in Islam. *Cf.* last note. There are four possible situations that may arise: an individual may have to stand up against an oppressor (1) for his own trampled rights, or (2) for the rights of others within his ken; or (3) a community may have similarly to stand up for its own rights collectively; or (4) for the rights of others. Nos. 2, 3, and 4 are considered highly meritorious for all, though few have the courage or the spirit to rise to so high a standard. No. 1 is specially liable to abuse on account of man's selfishness; Nos. 2, 3, and 4 are also abused by men pretending to motives of public good when they are serving their own personal interests or idiosyncracies; hence the qualifications mentioned in the next four verses and the notes thereto.

4581. See last note. When you stand up for rights, either on private or public grounds, it may be through processes of law, or by way of private defence in so far as the law permits private action. But in all cases you must not seek a compensation greater than the injury suffered. The most you can do is to demand equal redress, *i.e.*, a harm equivalent to the harm done to you. Even this may serve to curb your unregenerate soul, or a community bent on revenge. But the ideal mode is not to slake your thirst for vengeance, but to follow better ways leading to the reform of the offender or his reconciliation. See xli. 34. and xxiii. 96. You can take steps to prevent repetition, by physical or moral means; the best moral means would be to turn hatred into friendship by forgiveness and love. In that case the compensation or reward (if we must use such terms) is infinitely greater, for it wins the good pleasure of God.

But this active righting of wrongs, whether by physical or by moral or spiritual means, which are commended as better, is an antithesis to the monkish doctrine, when you are smitten on one cheek, to turn the other also. This would not suppress, but encourage wrong-doing. It is practised by none but poltroons, and is preached only by hypocrites, or men who want to make slaves of others by depriving them of the power of self-defence. It occurs in two of the four canonical Gospels (Matt. v. 39, and Luke vi. 29), but we need not therefore assume that it was preached by Jesus.

His reward is due[4582]
From God : for (God)
Loveth not those who
Do wrong.[4583]

فَأَجْرُهُ عَلَى اللّٰهِ ۚ
إِنَّهُ لَا يُحِبُّ الظّٰلِمِينَ ۝

41. But indeed if any do help
And defend themselves
After a wrong (done)
To them, against such[4584]
There is no cause
Of blame.

٤١- وَلَمَنِ انْتَصَرَ بَعْدَ ظُلْمِهِ
فَأُولٰٓئِكَ مَا عَلَيْهِمْ مِّنْ سَبِيلٍ ۝

42. The blame is only[4585]
Against those who oppress
Men with wrong-doing
And insolently transgress
Beyond bounds through the land,
Defying right and justice:
For such there will be
A Penalty grievous.

٤٢- إِنَّمَا السَّبِيلُ عَلَى الَّذِينَ
يَظْلِمُونَ النَّاسَ
وَيَبْغُونَ فِي الْأَرْضِ بِغَيْرِ الْحَقِّ ۚ
أُولٰٓئِكَ لَهُمْ عَذَابٌ أَلِيمٌ ۝

43. But indeed if any
Show patience and forgive,[4586]
That would truly be
An exercise of courageous will
And resolution in the conduct
Of affairs.

٤٣- وَلَمَنْ صَبَرَ وَغَفَرَ
إِنَّ ذٰلِكَ لَمِنْ
عَزْمِ الْأُمُورِ ۝ ع

4582. To love God is the highest motive of our conduct, for it leads to the love of God's creatures; to win the approbation and love of God, is the highest reward, far transcending any compensation or satisfaction we can obtain in this life.

4583. God does not love those who do wrong. If, therefore, we tolerate wrong, or encourage wrong by allowing it to run rampant when we can prevent it, we fail in our duty to God.

4584. Such people are not to be blamed, though they are following the lower law. The blame is on those who arrogantly ride rough-shod over the land, oppressing people with grievous wrong. See next verse.

4585. The fact that men seek the lower rather than the higher Law is itself a result of arrogant wrong-doing, of which the type was the Pharaoh who claimed to be "your Lord Most High" and oppressed the Israelites, and kept his own people under slavery and subjection, and the false glamour of magic and deception.

4586. It is harder to be patient and forgive, and yet to get wrongs righted, as was done by the holy Prophet, than to bluster about and "punish the guilty" or "teach them lessons". It may look like futility or lack of purpose, but in reality it is the highest and noblest form of courage and resolution. And it may carry out the purpose of reform and the suppression of evil even better than stern punishment. The gentleness of innocence often "persuades where stronger measures fail." But of course circumstances alter cases, and there is some allowance also to be made for the personal equation of the men you have to deal with : in some cases severity may be called for, but it should be from a strict judicial motive, and not merely from personal anger or spite or any lower motive in disguise

SECTION 5.

44. For any whom God
Leaves astray, there is
No protector thereafter.
And thou wilt see
The wrong-doers, when
In sight of the Penalty,
Say : "Is there any way[4587]
(To effect) a return ?"

٤٤- وَمَن يُضْلِلِ اللَّهُ فَمَا لَهُ
مِن وَلِيٍّ مِّن بَعْدِهِ
وَتَرَى الظَّٰلِمِينَ لَمَّا رَأَوُا الْعَذَابَ
يَقُولُونَ هَلْ إِلَىٰ مَرَدٍّ مِّن سَبِيلٍ

45. And thou wilt see them
Brought forward to the (Penalty),
In a humble frame of mind
Because of (their) disgrace,[4588]
(And) looking with a stealthy
Glance. And the Believers
Will say : "Those are indeed[4589]
In loss, who have given
To perdition their own selves
And those belonging to them
On the Day of Judgment.
Behold ! Truly the wrong-doers
Are in a lasting Penalty !"

٤٥- وَتَرَىٰهُمْ يُعْرَضُونَ عَلَيْهَا خَٰشِعِينَ
مِنَ الذُّلِّ
يَنظُرُونَ مِن طَرْفٍ خَفِيٍّ
وَقَالَ الَّذِينَ ءَامَنُوٓا۟ إِنَّ
الْخَٰسِرِينَ الَّذِينَ خَسِرُوٓا۟ أَنفُسَهُمْ
وَأَهْلِيهِمْ يَوْمَ الْقِيَٰمَةِ
أَلَآ إِنَّ الظَّٰلِمِينَ فِى عَذَابٍ مُّقِيمٍ

46. And no protectors have they[4590]
To help them,
Other than God.
And for any whom God
Leaves to stray, there is
No way (to the Goal).

٤٦- وَمَا كَانَ لَهُم مِّنْ أَوْلِيَآءَ يَنصُرُونَهُم
مِّن دُونِ اللَّهِ
وَمَن يُضْلِلِ اللَّهُ فَمَا لَهُ مِن سَبِيلٍ

4587. When the actual consequences of evil are in sight, the foolish sinner wishes that it were possible to get back to the life of probation. But he neglected or abused it and rejected God's Grace all the time. How can he then be restored to a closed chapter of his life?

4588. They were very arrogant in their probationary life. Now will they be humbled to the dust. And they will be in utter despair and misery. They will not be able to see the favours and good things of the other life (*Cf.* xx. 124-126). Even their misery, which will face them as a terrible Reality, they will only be able to look at askance, so thoroughly cowed will be their spirit.

4589. This will be their thought, and their realised experience: 'after all, any troubles and sorrows, any persecutions and taunts which they suffered in the life of probation from the enemies of truth, were of no consequence; the real loss was that revealed at the Judgment at the restoration of true values; the wicked and the arrogant, have lost their own souls, and have brought to perdition all who attached themselves to them and followed their evil ways; and this Penalty is one that will endure! How much more real it is!'

4590. The argument begun in verse 44 above is here rounded off. 'If once men finally cut themselves off from God's guidance and care, they will have no protection whatever. All their false objects of worship will only mislead them further and further. How they will wish the fact blotted out when they are in sight of Judgment, and vainly wish for time to be reversed! They will be in the Fire, while the men whom they despised and rejected will have reached the final Goal! For them there will be no such way!'

47. Hearken ye to your Lord,
Before there come a Day
Which there will be
No putting back, because[4591]
Of (the ordainment of) God!
That Day there will be
For you no place of refuge
Nor will there be for you
Any room for denial[4592]
(Of your sins)!

٤٧- اِسْتَجِيْبُوْا لِرَبِّكُمْ مِّنْ قَبْلِ
اَنْ يَّاْتِيَ يَوْمٌ
لَّا مَرَدَّ لَهٗ مِنَ اللّٰهِ
مَا لَكُمْ مِّنْ مَّلْجَاٍ يَّوْمَئِذٍ
وَّمَا لَكُمْ مِّنْ نَّكِيْرٍ ○

48. If then they turn away,
We have not sent thee
As a guard over them.[4593]
Thy duty is but to convey
(The Message). And truly,
When We give man
A taste of a Mercy[4594]
From ourselves, he doth
Exult thereat, but
When some ill happens
To him, on account
Of the deeds which
His hands have sent forth,
Truly then is man ungrateful!

٤٨- فَاِنْ اَعْرَضُوْا فَمَآ اَرْسَلْنٰكَ عَلَيْهِمْ
حَفِيْظًا ۭ اِنْ عَلَيْكَ اِلَّا الْبَلٰغُ ۭ
وَاِنَّآ اِذَآ اَذَقْنَا الْاِنْسَانَ مِنَّا رَحْمَةً
فَرِحَ بِهَا ۚ
وَاِنْ تُصِبْهُمْ سَيِّئَةٌۢ
بِمَا قَدَّمَتْ اَيْدِيْهِمْ
فَاِنَّ الْاِنْسَانَ كَفُوْرٌ ○

49. To God belongs the dominion
Of the heavens and the earth.
He creates what He wills[4595]
(And plans). He bestows

٤٩- لِلّٰهِ مُلْكُ السَّمٰوٰتِ وَالْاَرْضِ ۭ
يَخْلُقُ مَا يَشَاۗءُ ۭ يَهَبُ لِمَنْ يَّشَاۗءُ اِنَاثًا

4591. The Day of Judgment is inevitable. God has ordained it, and it cannot in any way be put back.

4592. At Judgment no one can escape the consequences of his crimes or deeds. And no one can disavow them or deny them, or by any chance pretend that they do not apply to him.

4593. The warning is now given, that men may repent and do good, and pray for God's Mercy and Grace. If the warning is not heeded or is rejected, the man of God is not responsible for bringing about the Penalty or for forcing people to come to the right Path. He is not a guard set over them to free them from the need of exercising their limited free-will.

4594. *Cf.* xxx. 36. It is a sad reflection that men, when they receive some gift out of God's Mercy, exult in their good fortune and attribute it to some merit in themselves, instead of to the Grace and Mercy of God, thus missing the real lesson of Life. On the other hand, when they are in trouble, due to their own errors and shortcomings, they fall into despair and blame God, instead of blaming themselves. This is rank ingratitude. So they miss the true lesson of Life in that case also.

4595. Verses 49-50 deal, in their ordinary meaning, with God's creative power, replete with knowledge and continued purpose, contrasted with man's instincts and gropings after knowledge. The mystery of sex and parenthood is referred to in a new light. With reference to children, a parent is often spoken of as the "author" of their being. The growth of population and the proportion of males and females in it have various sociological and psychological implications; yet how little do parents really know about them? The knowledge of science as regards the determination of sex in the embryo is practically nothing. Even if advancing knowledge threw light on what may be called the mechanical aspects of the question, the profounder problems touched by it are beyond the reach of man. Yet they are not governed by chance. God has a meaning and purpose in all things, and His power is complete to carry out His purpose.

(Children) male or female
According to His Will (and Plan),

50. Or He bestows both males[4596]
And females, and He leaves
Barren whom He will:
For He is full
Of knowledge and power.

51. It is not fitting[4597]
For a man that God
Should speak to him
Except by inspiration,[4598]
Or from behind a veil,[4599]
Or by the sending
Of a Messenger[4600]
To reveal, with God's permission,
What God wills: for He
Is Most High, Most Wise.

52. And thus have We,
By Our command, sent

وَيَهَبُ لِمَن يَشَآءُ الذُّكُورَ ۝

٥٠- أَوْ يُزَوِّجُهُمْ ذُكْرَانًا وَإِنَاثًا
وَيَجْعَلُ مَن يَشَآءُ عَقِيمًا ط
إِنَّهُۥ عَلِيمٌ قَدِيرٌ ۝

٥١- وَمَا كَانَ لِبَشَرٍ
أَن يُكَلِّمَهُ اللَّهُ إِلَّا وَحْيًا
أَوْ مِن وَرَآئِ حِجَابٍ أَوْ يُرْسِلَ رَسُولًا
فَيُوحِيَ بِإِذْنِهِۦ مَا يَشَآءُ ط
إِنَّهُۥ عَلِىٌّ حَكِيمٌ ۝

٥٢- وَكَذَٰلِكَ أَوْحَيْنَآ إِلَيْكَ

4596. To parents themselves it is a mystery why a male or female child is given at any birth, or how the balance of the two sexes is made up in a family or in large groups of mankind, or why in some cases the womb is barren and the would-be parents are denied the joys and responsibilities of parenthood. But each individual human soul is precious in the Plan of God, and all these variations, besides their reactions on parents and on society, have a purpose to fulfil in the large Plan of God.

4597. This leads us on to the higher spiritual meaning of verses 49-50, as leading up to verses 51-53. Man is but a speck in God's creation. His growth and family relationships are not by any means comparable to God's creative acts, whose various stages are referred to in n. 120 to ii. 117, n. 916 to vi. 94, and n. 923 to vi. 98. That being so in the mysteries of man's daily life, how much more profound is the contrast between man and God in the apprehension of the higher spiritual problems concerned with Revelation? How can man be fit to speak to God? He is not fit. But there are three ways in which God, in His infinite Mercy, communicates with man, as described in verses 51-53.

4598. God is Most High, Most Wise; man is, in spite of his high destiny, often the lowest of the low (xcv. 5). Yet God, out of His infinite Mercy and Grace, has bestowed His revelation on man. How does it come about? Three ways are mentioned: (1) *Waḥyun*, Inspiration; (2) from behind a veil; and (3) by the sending of a Messenger: see the notes following.

Waḥyun, Inspiration, is interpreted to be of two kinds: (1) a suggestion thrown by God into the heart or mind of man, by which man understands the substance of the Message, whether it is a command or prohibition, or an explanation of a great truth; and (2) verbal or literal inspiration, by which the actual words of God are conveyed in human language. Orthodox opinion admits the existence of both kinds, though the latter ("recited", *matlū*) is held to be of a superior degree, only vouchsafed to the greater Prophets, while the former ("other than recited", *gair-matlū*) may be given not only to the greater Prophets but to other men of spiritual insight who have not attained the degree of Prophethood. If we accept the theory of verbal inspiration, it would also cover the Messages brought by the angel Gabriel: see n. 4600 below.

4599. *Behind a veil*: not of course a material veil, or screen, or Purdah, but the mystic Veil of Light, or 70,000 Veils of Light, for which see Appendix VIII to S. xxiv.

4600. *Messenger*: *Rasūl*: the angel Gabriel, through whom the revelations were given to the holy Prophet. These spiritual visions, conveying the message of Revelation, are the basis of the Qur-ān.

Inspiration to thee:
Thou knewest not (before)[4601]
What was Revelation, and
What was Faith; but We
Have made the (Qur-ān)
A Light, wherewith We
Guide such of Our servants
As We will; and verily
Thou dost guide (men)[4602]
To the Straight Way,—

رُوْحًا مِّنْ اَمْرِنَا ؕ
مَا كُنْتَ تَدْرِىْ مَا الْكِتٰبُ وَلَا الْاِيْمَانُ
وَلٰكِنْ جَعَلْنٰهُ نُوْرًا
نَّهْدِىْ بِهٖ مَنْ نَّشَآءُ مِنْ عِبَادِنَا ؕ
وَاِنَّكَ لَتَهْدِىْٓ اِلٰى صِرَاطٍ مُّسْتَقِيْمٍ ۙ

53. The Way of God,[4603]
To Whom belongs
Whatever is in the heavens
And whatever is on earth.
Behold (how) all affairs
Tend towards God!

٥٣- صِرَاطِ اللّٰهِ الَّذِىْ
لَهٗ مَا فِى السَّمٰوٰتِ وَمَا فِى الْاَرْضِ ؕ
اَلَآ اِلَى اللّٰهِ تَصِيْرُ الْاُمُوْرُ ؑ

4601. Before the receipt of his mission in his fortieth year, the holy Prophet, though a man of steadfast virtue and purity and unflinching in his search for Truth (see C. 22-23), was yet unacquainted with Revelation in the highest sense of the term, and with the certainty that comes from perfected Faith, or realised nearness to God. *Rūḥ*, which I have here translated Inspiration has also been understood by some Commentators to refer to the angel Gabriel, the vehicle of Revelation. The Light of the Qur-ān made all things clear to man, and to the world.

4602. The Qur-ān and the inspired Prophet who proclaimed it, are here identified. They were a Guide to men, showing the Straight Way. This Way is described in various ways: for example, see i. 6, and n. 22; xviii. 1-2, and notes 2326-27; and xc. 11-18.

4603. The most comprehensive description of the Straight Way is that it is the Way of God, the Way of the Universal Law; for God is the source, centre, and goal of all things in heaven and earth. Everything goes back to Him. According to our own understanding we make our own laws, our own standards, and our own institutions. But the ultimate test of their validity or authority is God's Will, as revealed to us by His Revelation.

INTRODUCTION TO SŪRA XLIII (*Zukhruf*)

This is the fourth Sūra of the *Ḥā-Mīm* series of seven Sūras. For their chronology and general theme see the Introduction to S. xl.

This Sūra deals with the contrasts between the real glory of Truth and Revelation and the false glitter of what people like to believe and worship. It cites the examples of Abraham, Moses, and Jesus, as exposing the False and holding up the Truth. The key-word (*Zukhruf*, Gold Adornments) occurs in verse 38, but the idea occurs all through the Sūra.

Summary.—The Book of Revelation makes things clear, even though the ignorant and foolish mock at it and ignore God's Signs : it will last, while its rejecters will perish (xliii. 1-25, and C. 213).

Abraham exposed the falsehood of traditional worship : the glitter and adornments of this world will not last : what was the end of Pharaoh in his arrogant fight with Moses? (xliii. 26-56, and C. 214).

Jesus was a servant of God, but his sectarian followers raised false disputations about him: all is known to God, Whose Truth will shine, in spite of unfaith (xliii. 57-89, and C. 215).

C. 213.—Revelation makes ever-lasting Truths
(xliii. 1-25.) Clear : those who mock merely undo themselves.
Consider the Signs of God's gracious kindness
Around you, and glorify Him : attribute not
Unworthy qualities nor any companions
To the One True God. Seek Truth in worship
More than mere ancestral ways,
And shut not out Revelation's Light.

Sūra XLIII.

Zukhruf, or Gold Adornments.

In the name of God, Most Gracious,
Most Merciful.

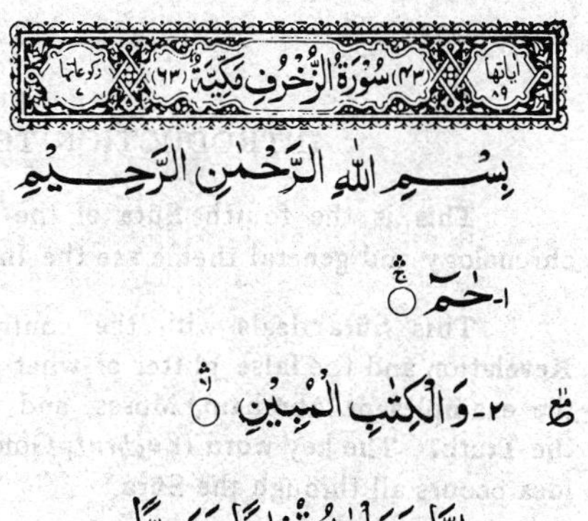

1. Ḥa-Mim.[4604]

2. By the Book that
Makes things clear,—

3. We have made it
A Qur-ān in Arabic,[4605]
That ye may be able
To understand (and learn wisdom).

٣-إِنَّا جَعَلْنَٰهُ قُرْءَٰنًا عَرَبِيًّا
لَّعَلَّكُمْ تَعْقِلُونَ ۝

4. And verily, it is
In the Mother of the Book,[4606]
In Our Presence, high
(In dignity), full of wisdom.

٤-وَإِنَّهُۥ فِىٓ أُمِّ ٱلْكِتَٰبِ
لَدَيْنَا لَعَلِىٌّ حَكِيمٌ ۝

5. Shall We then[4607]
Take away the Message
From you and repel (you),
For that ye are a people
Transgressing beyond bounds?

٥-أَفَنَضْرِبُ عَنكُمُ ٱلذِّكْرَ صَفْحًا
أَن كُنتُمْ قَوْمًا مُّسْرِفِينَ ۝

6. But how many were[4608]
The prophets We sent
Amongst the peoples of old?

٦-وَكَمْ أَرْسَلْنَا مِن نَّبِىٍّ فِى ٱلْأَوَّلِينَ ۝

4604. Abbreviated Letters: see Introduction to S. xl. paragraphs 2-4.

4605. *Cf.* xlii. 7, n. 4533.

4606. *Cf.* iii. 7, n. 347; and xiii. 39, n. 1864. The Mother of the Book, the Foundation of Revelation, the Preserved Tablet (*Lauḥ Maḥfūẓ*, lxxxv. 22), is the core or essence of revelation, the original principle or fountain-head of God's Eternal and Universal Law. From this fountain-head are derived all streams of knowledge and wisdom, that flow through Time and feed the intelligence of created minds. The Mother of the Book is in God's own Presence, and its dignity and wisdom are more than all we can think of in the spiritual world.

4607. In vouchsafing Revelation, what an inestimable Mercy has God conferred on mankind! Yet so many deluded souls are ungrateful, and ignore or oppose its teaching. If it were not for His attributes of Forgiveness and Forbearing He would be justified in withdrawing that Light, but He continues to shed it, that all who will may come and be blessed by it.

4608. In spite of, or because of, man's obstinate and rebellious nature, God sent prophet after prophet to the peoples of old, but there was among them always a party that ridiculed them and treated God's Signs as naught.

7. And never came there
A prophet to them
But they mocked him.

٧- وَمَا يَأْتِيهِم مِّن نَّبِيٍّ
إِلَّا كَانُوا بِهِ يَسْتَهْزِءُونَ ○

8. So We destroyed (them)—
Stronger in power than these;—
And (thus) has passed on [4609]
The Parable of the peoples
Of old.

٨- فَأَهْلَكْنَا أَشَدَّ مِنْهُم بَطْشًا
وَمَضَىٰ مَثَلُ الْأَوَّلِينَ ○

9. If thou wert
To question them, 'Who created
The heavens and the earth?' [4610]
They would be sure to reply,
'They were created by (Him),
The Exalted in Power,
Full of Knowledge';— [4611]

٩- وَلَئِن سَأَلْتَهُم مَّنْ
خَلَقَ السَّمَاوَاتِ وَالْأَرْضَ
لَيَقُولُنَّ خَلَقَهُنَّ
الْعَزِيزُ الْعَلِيمُ ○

10. (Yea, the same that) [4612]
Has made for you
The earth (like a carpet) [4613]
Spread out, and has made
For you roads (and channels)
Therein, in order that ye
May find guidance (on the way);

١٠- الَّذِي جَعَلَ لَكُمُ الْأَرْضَ مَهْدًا
وَجَعَلَ لَكُمْ فِيهَا سُبُلًا
لَّعَلَّكُمْ تَهْتَدُونَ ○

11. That sends down
(From time to time)

١١- وَالَّذِي نَزَّلَ

4609. The result of rebellion was destruction. And the pagan Meccan generation contemporary with the Prophet are reminded that the peoples of old who were destroyed were, many of them, more powerful than they, and that they, in disobeying God's Law, were inviting the same fate for themselves. The events of the past have become Parables for the present and the future.

4610. *Cf.* xxix. 61 and n. 3493; and xxxi. 25 and n. 3613. This class of men acknowledge God's Power and God's Knowledge or Wisdom, but do not realise God's infinite Mercy and care for His creatures.

4611. Note the beautiful rhetorical figure of speech here. The reply of the inconsistent men who do not follow God's Law is turned against themselves. When they acknowledge God's Power and Knowledge, their speech is interrupted, and the concomitant qualities of God's Mercy and care of His creatures, with pointed reference to the inconsistent ones themselves, is set out in eloquent terms, as completing what they themselves had said, and the right course of conduct is pointed out to them (verses 10-14).

4612. See last note.

4613. *Cf.* xx. 53 and n. 2576. *Mihād*, a carpet or bed spread out, implies not only freedom of movement but rest also. The 'roads and channels' carry out the idea of communications and include land routes, sea routes, and airways.

Rain from the sky
In due measure;—[4614]
And We raise to life
Therewith a land that is
Dead; even so will ye
Be raised (from the dead);—[4615]

مِنَ السَّمَآءِ مَآءًۢ بِقَدَرٍۚ
فَاَنْشَرْنَا بِهٖ بَلْدَةً مَّيْتًاۚ
كَذٰلِكَ تُخْرَجُوْنَ ○

12 That has created pairs[4616]
In all things, and has made
For you ships and cattle[4617]
On which ye ride,

١٢- وَالَّذِيْ خَلَقَ الْاَزْوَاجَ كُلَّهَا وَجَعَلَ
لَكُمْ مِّنَ الْفُلْكِ وَالْاَنْعَامِ مَا تَرْكَبُوْنَ ○

13. In order that ye may
Sit firm and square
On their backs, and when
So seated, ye may
Celebrate the (kind) favour[4618]
Of your Lord, and say,
"Glory to Him Who
Has subjected these
To our (use), for we
Could never have accomplished
This (by-ourselves),

١٣- لِتَسْتَوٗا عَلٰى ظُهُوْرِهٖ
ثُمَّ تَذْكُرُوْا نِعْمَةَ رَبِّكُمْ
اِذَا اسْتَوَيْتُمْ عَلَيْهِ وَتَقُوْلُوْا
سُبْحٰنَ الَّذِيْ سَخَّرَ لَنَا هٰذَا
وَمَا كُنَّا لَهٗ مُقْرِنِيْنَ ○

14. "And to our Lord, surely,[4619]
Must we turn back!"

١٤- وَاِنَّآ اِلٰى رَبِّنَا لَمُنْقَلِبُوْنَ ○

4614. *In due measure*: *i.e.*, according to needs, as measured by local as well as universal considerations. This applies to normal rainfall: floods and droughts are abnormal conditions, and may be called unusual manifestations of His power, fulfilling some special purpose that we may or may not understand.

4615. The clause 'And We raise...(from the dead)' is parenthetical. *Cf.* xxxv. 9, n. 3881. Note the transition from the third to the first person, to mark the Resurrection as a special act of God as distinguished from the ordinary processes of nature ordained by God.

4616. *Cf.* n. 2578 to xx. 53. Also see xxxvi. 36, n. 3981.

4617. By analogy all means of transport, including horses, camels, ships, steamers, railways, aeroplanes, airships, etc. The domestication of animals as well as the invention of mechanical means of transport require a skill and ingenuity in man, which are referred to God as His gifts or endowments to man.

4618. See last note. People of understanding attribute all good to its true and original source *viz.*: God.

4619. Men of understanding, every time they take a journey on earth, are reminded of that more momentous journey which they are taking on the back of Time to Eternity. Have they tamed Time to their lawful use, or do they allow Time to run away with them wildly to where they know not? Their goal is God, and their thoughts are ever with God.

15\. Yet they attribute[4620]
To some of His servants
A share with Him
(In His godhead)!
Truly is man a blasphemous
Ingrate avowed!

١٥- وَجَعَلُوا لَهُ مِنْ عِبَادِهِ جُزْءًا ۚ
إِنَّ الْإِنْسَانَ
لَكَفُورٌ مُبِينٌ ○ ع

SECTION 2.

16\. What! Has He taken[4621]
Daughters out of what He
Himself creates, and granted
To you sons for choice?

١٦- أَمِ اتَّخَذَ مِمَّا يَخْلُقُ بَنَاتٍ
وَأَصْفَاكُمْ بِالْبَنِينَ ○

17\. When news is brought[4622]
To one of them of (the birth
Of) what he sets up
As a likeness to (God)
Most Gracious, his face
Darkens, and he is filled
With inward grief!

١٧- وَإِذَا بُشِّرَ أَحَدُهُمْ
بِمَا ضَرَبَ لِلرَّحْمَٰنِ مَثَلًا
ظَلَّ وَجْهُهُ مُسْوَدًّا
وَهُوَ كَظِيمٌ ○

18\. Is then one brought up[4623]
Among trinkets, and unable
To give a clear account
In a dispute (to be
Associated with God)?

١٨- أَوَمَنْ يُنَشَّأُ فِي الْحِلْيَةِ
وَهُوَ فِي الْخِصَامِ
غَيْرُ مُبِينٍ ○

19\. And they make into females
Angels who themselves serve[4624]

١٩- وَجَعَلُوا الْمَلَائِكَةَ الَّذِينَ هُمْ عِبَادُ الرَّحْمَٰنِ

4620\. As a contrast to the men of true understanding are the ungrateful blasphemous creatures, who offer a share in godhead to others besides God! They imagine sons and daughters to God, and forget the true lesson of the whole of Creation, which points to the Unity of God. This theme is further developed in the following Section.

4621\. To imagine goddesses (female gods) or mothers or daughters to God was particularly blasphemous in the mouths of people who held the female sex in contempt. Such were the pagan Arabs, and such (it is to be feared) are some of the moderns. They wince when a daughter is born to them and hanker after sons. With that mentality, how can they attribute daughters to God?

4622\. *Cf.* xvi. 57-59 and notes. With scathing irony it is pointed out that what they hate and are ashamed of for themselves they attribute to God!

4623\. The softer sex is usually brought up among trinkets and ornaments, and, on account of the retiring modesty which for the sex is a virtue, is unable to stand up boldly in a fight and give clear indications of the will to win. Is that sort of quality to be associated with God?

4624\. Angels for grace and purity may be compared to the most graceful and the purest forms we know. But it is wrong to attribute sex to them. They are servants and messengers of God and so far from being rivals seeking worship, are always engaged in devotion and service. If any persons invent blasphemies about God, such blasphemies will form a big blot in their Book of Deeds, and they will be called to account for them.

God. Did they witness
Their creation ? Their evidence
Will be recorded, and they
Will be called to account !

إِنَاثًا ۚ أَشَهِدُوا خَلْقَهُمْ ۚ
سَتُكْتَبُ شَهَادَتُهُمْ وَيُسْأَلُونَ ○

20. (" Ah !") they say, " If
It had been the Will[4625]
Of (God) Most Gracious,
We should not have
Worshipped such (deities) ! "
Of that they have
No knowledge ! They
Do nothing but lie ![4626]

٢٠- وَقَالُوا لَوْ شَاءَ الرَّحْمَٰنُ
مَا عَبَدْنَاهُمْ ۗ
مَا لَهُمْ بِذَٰلِكَ مِنْ عِلْمٍ ۖ
إِنْ هُمْ إِلَّا يَخْرُصُونَ ○

21. What ! have We given them
A Book before this,
To which they are
Holding fast ?

٢١- أَمْ آتَيْنَاهُمْ كِتَابًا مِنْ قَبْلِهِ
فَهُمْ بِهِ مُسْتَمْسِكُونَ ○

22. Nay ! they say : " We found[4627]
Our fathers following
A certain religion,
And we do guide ourselves
By their footsteps."

٢٢- بَلْ قَالُوا إِنَّا وَجَدْنَا آبَاءَنَا
عَلَىٰ أُمَّةٍ
وَإِنَّا عَلَىٰ آثَارِهِمْ مُهْتَدُونَ ○

23. Just in the same way,
Whenever We sent a Warner
Before thee to any people,
The wealthy ones among them[4628]
Said : " We found our fathers
Following a certain religion,
And we will certainly
Follow in their footsteps."

٢٣- وَكَذَٰلِكَ مَا أَرْسَلْنَا مِنْ قَبْلِكَ فِي
قَرْيَةٍ مِنْ نَذِيرٍ إِلَّا قَالَ مُتْرَفُوهَا
إِنَّا وَجَدْنَا آبَاءَنَا عَلَىٰ أُمَّةٍ
وَإِنَّا عَلَىٰ آثَارِهِمْ مُقْتَدُونَ ○

4625. Worsted in argument they resort to a dishonest sarcasm. 'We worship these deities: if God does not wish us to do so, why does He not prevent us?' In throwing the responsibility on God, they ignore the limited free-will on which their whole life is based. They are really playing with truth. They are arguing against their own knowledge. They have no authority in any scripture, and indeed they are so slippery that they hold fast to no scripture at all.

4626. *Cf.* vi. 116.

4627. Then comes the argument about ancestral custom, which was repudiated by Abraham (see verses 26-28 below). Indeed a good reply to ancestral custom in the case of the Arabs was the example of Abraham, the True in Faith, for Abraham was the common ancestor of the Arabs and the Israelites.

4628. It is some privileged position, and not ancestral custom, which is really at the bottom of much falsehood and hypocrisy in the world. This has been seen again and again in religious history.

24. He said: "What![4629]
Even if I brought you
Better guidance than that
Which ye found
Your fathers following?"
They said: "For us,
We deny that ye (prophets)
Are sent (on a mission
At all)."

٢٤-قٰلَ اَوَلَوْ جِئْتُكُمْ بِاَهْدٰى
مِمَّا وَجَدْتُّمْ عَلَيْهِ اٰبَآءَكُمْ
قَالُوْٓا اِنَّا
بِمَآ اُرْسِلْتُمْ بِهٖ
كٰفِرُوْنَ ○

25. So We exacted retribution
From them: now see
What was the end
Of those who rejected (Truth)!

٢٥-فَانْتَقَمْنَا مِنْهُمْ فَانْظُرْ
كَيْفَ كَانَ عَاقِبَةُ الْمُكَذِّبِيْنَ ○

C. 214.—If the Arabs hark back to ancestry, why not
(xliii. 26-56.) Accept the Faith of Abraham the True?
He joined not gods with God. Spiritual
Worth is measured by other things
Than gold or silver or the adornments
Of this world. These are but things of the hour.
The lasting gifts are those of the Hereafter.
If Israel goes back to Moses, how he
Was mocked by Pharaoh in his pride
Of power! Yet Pharaoh and his deluded
People perished: so ends the pomp
And power and vanity of this world!

SECTION 3.

26. Behold! Abraham said[4630]
To his father and his people:
"I do indeed clear myself
Of what ye worship:

٢٦-وَاِذْ قَالَ اِبْرٰهِيْمُ لِاَبِيْهِ وَقَوْمِهٖٓ
اِنَّنِيْ بَرَآءٌ مِّمَّا تَعْبُدُوْنَ ○

27. "(I worship) only Him
Who made me, and He
Will certainly guide me."

٢٧-اِلَّا الَّذِيْ فَطَرَنِيْ
فَاِنَّهٗ سَيَهْدِيْنِ ○

4629. The Warner or apostle pointed out the merits and the truth of his teaching, and how superior it was to what they called their ancestral customs. But they denied his mission itself or the validity of any such mission. In other words they did not believe in inspiration or revelation, and went on in their evil ways, with the inevitable result that they brought themselves to destruction.

4630. The plea of ancestral ways is refuted by the example of Abraham, in two ways: (1) he gave up the ancestral cults followed by his father and his people, and followed the true Way, even at some sacrifice to himself; and (2) he was an ancestor of the Arabs, and if the Arabs stood on ancestral ways, why should they not follow their good ancestor Abraham, rather than their bad ancestors who fell into evil? See n. 4627 above. The incident in Abraham's story referred to here will be found in xxi. 51-70.

28. And he left it
As a Word [4631]
To endure among those
Who came after him,
That they may turn back
(To God).

٢٨- وَجَعَلَهَا كَلِمَةً
بَاقِيَةً فِي عَقِبِهِ
لَعَلَّهُمْ يَرْجِعُونَ ○

29. Yea, I have given [4632]
The good things of this life
To these (men) and
Their fathers, until the Truth
Has come to them,
And an Apostle
Making things clear.

٢٩- بَلْ مَتَّعْتُ هٰٓؤُلَآءِ وَاٰبَآءَهُمْ
حَتّٰى جَآءَهُمُ الْحَقُّ
وَرَسُولٌ مُّبِينٌ ○

30. But when the Truth came
To them, they said:
"This is sorcery, and we [4633]
Do reject it."

٣٠- وَلَمَّا جَآءَهُمُ الْحَقُّ قَالُوا
هٰذَا سِحْرٌ وَّإِنَّا بِهِ كٰفِرُونَ ○

31. Also, they say: "Why
Is not this Qur-ān sent
Down to some leading man
In either of the two [4634]
(Chief) cities?"

٣١- وَقَالُوا لَوْلَا نُزِّلَ هٰذَا الْقُرْاٰنُ
عَلٰى رَجُلٍ مِّنَ الْقَرْيَتَيْنِ
عَظِيمٍ ○

32. Is it they who would portion out
The Mercy of thy Lord? [4635]
It is We Who portion out
Between them their livelihood

٣٢- أَهُمْ يَقْسِمُونَ رَحْمَتَ رَبِّكَ ؕ
نَحْنُ قَسَمْنَا بَيْنَهُمْ مَّعِيشَتَهُمْ

4631. *A Word*: *i.e.*, the Gospel of Unity, *viz.*: "I worship only Him Who made me", as in verse 27. This was his teaching, and this was his legacy to those who followed him. He hoped that they would keep it sacred, and uphold the standard of Unity. *Cf.* C. 7-8. *Cf.* also xxxvii, 108-111.

4632. Note the first person singular, as showing God's personal solicitude and care for the descendants of Abraham in both branches. The context here refers to the prosperity enjoyed by Mecca and the Meccans until they rejected the truth of Islam when it was preached in their midst by an apostle whose Message was as clear as the light of the sun.

4633. When the pagan Meccans could not understand the wonderful power and authority with which the holy Prophet preached, they called his God-given influence sorcery!

4634. The world judges by its own low standards. From a worldly point of view, the holy Prophet was poor and an orphan. Why, they thought, should he be so richly endowed in spiritual knowledge and power? If such a gift had to come to a man among them, it was the right (they foolishly said) of one of the chiefs in either the sacred city of Mecca, or the fertile garden-city of Ṭāif!

4635. That is, spiritual gifts, those connected with Revelation. What audacity or folly in them to claim to divide or distribute them among themselves? They may think they are distributing the good things of this world among themselves. In a sense that may be true, but even here, their own power and initiative are very limited. Even here it is God's Will on which all depends. In His wisdom God allows some to grow in power or riches, and command work from others, and various relative gradations are established. Men scramble for these good things of this world, but they are of no value compared to the spiritual gifts.

In the life of this world:
And We raise some of them
Above others in ranks,
So that some may command
Work from others.
But the Mercy of thy Lord
Is better than the (wealth)
Which they amass.

فِي الْحَيٰوةِ الدُّنْيَا
وَرَفَعْنَا بَعْضَهُمْ فَوْقَ بَعْضٍ دَرَجٰتٍ
لِّيَتَّخِذَ بَعْضُهُمْ بَعْضًا سُخْرِيًّا ط
وَرَحْمَتُ رَبِّكَ خَيْرٌ مِّمَّا يَجْمَعُوْنَ ○

33. And were it not that [4636]
(All) men might become
Of one (evil) way of life,
We would provide,
For everyone that blasphemes
Against (God) Most Gracious,
Silver roofs for their houses,
And (silver) stair-ways
On which to go up,

٣٣- وَلَوْلَآ اَنْ يَّكُوْنَ النَّاسُ اُمَّةً وَّاحِدَةً
لَّجَعَلْنَا لِمَنْ يَّكْفُرُ بِالرَّحْمٰنِ
لِبُيُوْتِهِمْ سُقُفًا مِّنْ فِضَّةٍ
وَّمَعَارِجَ عَلَيْهَا يَظْهَرُوْنَ ○

34. And (silver) doors
To their houses, and thrones
(Of silver) on which
They could recline,

٣٤- وَلِبُيُوْتِهِمْ اَبْوَابًا وَّسُرُرًا
عَلَيْهَا يَتَّكِئُوْنَ ○

35. And also adornments [4637]
Of gold. But all this
Were nothing but conveniences
Of the present life:
The Hereafter, in the sight
Of thy Lord, is
For the Righteous.

٣٥- وَزُخْرُفًا ط
وَاِنْ كُلُّ ذٰلِكَ
لَمَّا مَتَاعُ الْحَيٰوةِ الدُّنْيَا ط
وَالْاٰخِرَةُ عِنْدَ رَبِّكَ لِلْمُتَّقِيْنَ ○ ع

SECTION 4.

36. If anyone withdraws himself [4638]
From remembrance

٣٦- وَمَنْ يَّعْشُ عَنْ ذِكْرِ

4636. So little value is attached in the spiritual world to silver or gold, or worldly ranks or adornments, that they would freely be at the disposal of everyone who denied or blasphemed God. were it not that in that case there would be too great temptation placed in the way of men, for they might all scramble to sell their spiritual life for wealth! They might have silver roofs and stair-ways, silver doors and thrones, and all kinds of adornments of gold. But God does not allow too great a temptation to be placed in the path of men. He distributes these things differently, some to unjust men, and some to just men, in various degrees, so that the possession of these is no test either of an unjust or a just life. His wisdom searches out motives far more subtle and delicate than any we are even aware of.

4637. *Adornments of gold*: the keyword to this Sūra. All false glitter and adornments of this world are as naught. They more often hinder than help.

4638. If men deliberately put away the remembrance of God from their minds, the natural consequence, under God's decree, is that they join on with evil. Like consorts with like. We can generalise evil in the abstract, but it takes concrete shape in our life-companions.

Of (God) Most Gracious,
We appoint for him
An evil one, to be
An intimate companion to him.

الرَّحْمٰنِ نُقَيِّضْ لَهٗ
شَيْطٰنًا فَهُوَ لَهٗ قَرِيْنٌ ○

37. Such (evil ones) really
Hinder them from the Path,[4639]
But they think that they
Are being guided aright!

٣٧- وَاِنَّهُمْ لَيَصُدُّوْنَهُمْ عَنِ السَّبِيْلِ
وَيَحْسَبُوْنَ اَنَّهُمْ مُّهْتَدُوْنَ ○

38. At length, when (such a one)[4640]
Comes to Us, he says
(To his evil companion):
"Would that between me
And thee were the distance
Of East and West!"[4641] Ah!
Evil is the companion (indeed)!

٣٨- حَتّٰٓى اِذَا جَآءَنَا قَالَ
يٰلَيْتَ بَيْنِيْ وَبَيْنَكَ بُعْدَ الْمَشْرِقَيْنِ
فَبِئْسَ الْقَرِيْنُ ○

39. When ye have done wrong,[4642]
It will avail you nothing,
That day, that ye shall be
Partners in punishment!

٣٩- وَلَنْ يَّنْفَعَكُمُ الْيَوْمَ اِذْ ظَّلَمْتُمْ
اَنَّكُمْ فِي الْعَذَابِ مُشْتَرِكُوْنَ ○

40. Canst thou then make[4643]
The deaf to hear, or give
Direction to the blind
Or to such as (wander)
In manifest error?[4644]

٤٠- اَفَاَنْتَ تُسْمِعُ الصُّمَّ
اَوْ تَهْدِي الْعُمْيَ
وَمَنْ كَانَ فِيْ ضَلٰلٍ مُّبِيْنٍ ○

4639. The downward course in evil is rapid. But the most tragic consequence is that evil persuades its victims to believe that they are pursuing good. They think evil to be their good. They go deeper and deeper into the mire, and become more and more callous. "*Them*" and "*they*" represent the generic plural of anyone who "withdraws himself from...God" (see last verse).

4640. If ever the presence of God is felt, or at the time of Judgment, a glimmering of truth comes to the deceived soul, and it cries to its evil companion in its agony, "Would that I had never come across thee! Would that we were separated poles apart!" But it cannot shake off evil. By deliberate choice it had put itself in its snare.

4641. *Distance of East and West*: literally, 'distance of the two Easts'. Most Commentators understand in this sense, but some construe the phrase as meaning the distance of the extreme points of the rising of the sun, between the summer solstice and the winter solstice. *Cf.* n. 4034 to xxxvii. 5. A good equivalent idiom in English would be "poles apart", for they could never meet.

4642. All partners in evil will certainly share in the punishment, but that is no consolation to any individual soul. Evil desires the evil of others, but that does not diminish its own torment, or get rid of the personal responsibility of each individual soul.

4643. *Cf.* xxx. 52-53. The evil go headlong into sin, and sink deeper and deeper until their spiritual faculties are deadened, and no outside help can bring them back. God's grace they have rejected.

4644. There is hope for a person who wanders in quest of truth, and even for one who wanders through mistake or by weakness of will. But there is none for one who, by deliberate choice, plunges into "manifest error", *i.e.* error which any one can see.

41. Even if We take thee [4645]
Away, We shall be sure
To exact retribution from them,

٤١- فَإِمَّا نَذْهَبَنَّ بِكَ
فَإِنَّا مِنْهُمْ مُّنْتَقِمُونَ ۝

42. Or We shall show thee
That (accomplished) which We
Have promised them :
For verily We shall
Prevail over them.

٤٢- أَوْ نُرِيَنَّكَ الَّذِي وَعَدْنَٰهُمْ
فَإِنَّا عَلَيْهِم مُّقْتَدِرُونَ ۝

43. So hold thou fast [4646]
To the Revelation sent down
To thee : verily thou
Art on a Straight Way.

٤٣- فَاسْتَمْسِكْ بِالَّذِي أُوحِيَ إِلَيْكَ
إِنَّكَ عَلَىٰ صِرَٰطٍ مُّسْتَقِيمٍ ۝

44. The (Qur-ān) is indeed
The Message, [4647] for thee
And for thy people ;
And soon shall ye
(All) be brought to account.

٤٤- وَإِنَّهُۥ لَذِكْرٌ لَّكَ وَلِقَوْمِكَ
وَسَوْفَ تُسْـَٔلُونَ ۝

45. And question thou our apostles [4648]
Whom We sent before thee ;
Did We appoint any deities
Other than (God) Most Gracious,
To be worshipped ?

٤٥- وَسْـَٔلْ مَنْ أَرْسَلْنَا مِن قَبْلِكَ مِن
رُّسُلِنَا أَجَعَلْنَا مِن دُونِ الرَّحْمَٰنِ ءَالِهَةً
يُعْبَدُونَ ۝

SECTION 5.

46. We did send Moses [4649]
Aforetime, with Our Signs,

٤٦- وَلَقَدْ أَرْسَلْنَا مُوسَىٰ بِـَٔايَٰتِنَا

4645. *Cf.* viii. 30 : "how the Unbelievers plotted against thee, to keep thee in bonds, or slay thee, or get thee out (of thy home)." They were always plotting against the holy Prophet in his Meccan period. But even if their plots had succeeded against human beings, they could not defeat God's Plan, nor escape the just punishment of their deeds. *Cf.* also x. 46, and n. 1438.

4646. Let the wicked rage, say what they like, or do their worst : the man of God is encouraged to go forward steadfastly in the Light given him, for he is on a Path that leads straight to God.

4647. *Ẕikrun*: Message, Remembrance, Cause of remembrance, Memorial, Title for remembrance to posterity. Thus two meanings emerge, not necessarily mutually exclusive. (1) The Qur-ān brings a Message of Truth and Guidance to the Apostle, and his people ; (2) the revelation of the Qur-ān raises the rank of the Apostle, and the people among whom, and in whose language, it was promulgated, making them worthy of remembrance in the world's history for all time. But the honour also carried its responsibilities. All who hear it must give an account of how far they profit by it spiritually.

4648. That is, by examining their Message, and asking the learned among their real followers. It will be found that no Religion really teaches the worship of other than God.

4649. For the story of Moses in detail, see vii. 103-137, but especially vii. 104, 130-136.

To Pharaoh and his Chiefs:
He said, "I am an apostle
Of the Lord of the Worlds."

إِلَىٰ فِرْعَوْنَ وَمَلَإِيْهٖ
فَقَالَ إِنِّي رَسُولُ رَبِّ الْعٰلَمِينَ ○

47. But when he came to them
With Our Signs, behold,
They ridiculed them.[4650]

٤٧- فَلَمَّا جَاءَهُمْ
بِاٰيٰتِنَآ إِذَا هُمْ مِّنْهَا يَضْحَكُونَ ○

48. We showed them Sign[4651]
After Sign, each greater
Than its fellow, and We
Seized them with Punishment,
In order that they
Might turn (to Us).

٤٨- وَمَا نُرِيهِمْ مِّنْ اٰيَةٍ
إِلَّا هِيَ أَكْبَرُ مِنْ أُخْتِهَا ۫
وَأَخَذْنٰهُمْ بِالْعَذَابِ لَعَلَّهُمْ يَرْجِعُونَ ○

49. And they said, "O thou[4652]
Sorcerer! Invoke thy Lord
For us according to
His covenant with thee;
For we shall truly
Accept guidance."

٤٩- وَقَالُوا يٰٓأَيُّهَ السّٰحِرُ ادْعُ لَنَا رَبَّكَ
بِمَا عَهِدَ عِنْدَكَ ۚ
إِنَّنَا لَمُهْتَدُونَ ○

50. But when We removed
The Penalty from them,
Behold, they broke their word.

٥٠- فَلَمَّا كَشَفْنَا عَنْهُمُ الْعَذَابَ
إِذَا هُمْ يَنْكُثُونَ ○

51. And Pharaoh proclaimed
Among his people, saying:
"O my people! Does not
The dominion of Egypt
Belong to me, (witness)[4653]
These streams flowing
Underneath my (palace)? What!
See ye not then?

٥١- وَنَادٰى فِرْعَوْنُ فِي قَوْمِهٖ قَالَ
يٰقَوْمِ أَلَيْسَ لِي مُلْكُ مِصْرَ
وَهٰذِهِ الْأَنْهٰرُ تَجْرِي مِنْ تَحْتِي ۚ
أَفَلَا تُبْصِرُونَ ○

4650. For the mockery of Moses and his Signs see xvii. 101; also below, xliii. 49, 52-53.

4651. Moses showed them nine Clear Signs: see n. 1091 to vii. 133; also xvii. 101. Each one of them in its own setting and circumstances was greater than any of its "sister" Signs. The object was if possible to reclaim as many Egyptians as possible from their defiance of God.

4652. This speech is half a mockery, and half a ruse. In spite of their unbelief, they had fear in their minds, and in order to stop the plagues, one after another, they promised to obey God, and when the particular plague was removed, they again became obdurate. See vii. 133-135.

4653. The *wāw* here in Arabic is the *Wāw ḥāliya*: the abundant streams from the Nile flowing beneath his palace being evidence of his power, prosperity, and sovereignty. The Nile made (and makes) Egypt, and the myth of the god Osiris was a compound of the myths of the Nile and the sun. The Pharaoh, therefore, as commanding the Nile, commanded the gods who personified Egypt. He boasted of water, and he perished in water,—a fitting punishment!

52\. "Am I not better
Than this (Moses), who
Is a contemptible wretch [4654]
And can scarcely
Express himself clearly?

٥٢- أَمْ أَنَا خَيْرٌ مِّنْ هَٰذَا الَّذِي
هُوَ مَهِينٌ ۙ
وَلَا يَكَادُ يُبِينُ ○

53\. "Then why are not [4655]
Gold bracelets bestowed
On him, or (why)
Come (not) with him
Angels accompanying him
In procession?"

٥٣- فَلَوْلَا أُلْقِيَ عَلَيْهِ أَسْوِرَةٌ مِّن ذَهَبٍ
أَوْ جَاءَ مَعَهُ الْمَلَائِكَةُ
مُقْتَرِنِينَ ○

54\. Thus did he make
Fools of his people,
And they obeyed him:
Truly were they a people
Rebellious (against God).

٥٤- فَاسْتَخَفَّ قَوْمَهُ
فَأَطَاعُوهُ ۚ
إِنَّهُمْ كَانُوا قَوْمًا فَاسِقِينَ ○

55\. When at length they [4656]
Provoked Us, We exacted
Retribution from them, and
We drowned them all.[4657]

٥٥- فَلَمَّا آسَفُونَا انتَقَمْنَا مِنْهُمْ
فَأَغْرَقْنَاهُمْ أَجْمَعِينَ ۙ

56\. And We made them
(A people) of the Past [4658]
And an Example
To later ages.

٥٦- فَجَعَلْنَاهُمْ سَلَفًا
وَمَثَلًا لِّلْآخِرِينَ ○ ع

4654\. Being a despised Israelite in any case, and having further an impediment in his speech. See xx. 27, and notes 2552-53.

4655\. Gold bracelets and gold chains were possibly among the insignia of royalty. In any case they betokened wealth, and the materialists judge a man's worth by his wealth and his following and equipage. So Pharaoh wanted to see Moses, if he had any position in the spiritual kingdom, invested with gold bracelets, and followed by a great train of angels as his Knight-companions! The same kind of proofs were demanded by the materialist Quraish of our holy Prophet. These were puerilities, but such puerilities go down with the crowd. Barring a few Egyptians who believed in God and in the Message of Moses, the rest of Pharaoh's entourage followed Pharaoh in his pursuit of revenge, and were drowned in the Red Sea.

4656\. God is long-suffering, and gives many and many opportunities to the most hardened sinners for repentance. But at length comes a time when His justice is provoked, and the inevitable punishment follows.

4657\. *Cf.* vii. 136.

4658\. Pharaoh and his hosts were blotted out, and became as a tale of the past. Their story is an instructive warning and example to future generations. The later course of Egyptian religion after the Exodus is referred to in Appendix V, pp. 408-413.

C. 215.—If Christians go back to Jesus, he
(xliii. 57-89.) Was but a man and a servant of God:
He came to still the jarring sects,
Not to create a new one: he preached
The One True God, his Lord. So give up
Disputing, and join in devotion to God.
That is the Way to the Garden of Bliss,
But the opposite leads to the Fire. Beware!
The Truth has come, and God knows how you
Receive it. He is the Lord of power and mercy.
The Truth must prevail: resist it not.

SECTION 6.

57. When (Jesus) the son[4659]
Of Mary is held up
As an example, behold,
Thy people raise a clamour
Thereat (in ridicule)!

٥٧- وَلَمَّا ضُرِبَ ابْنُ مَرْيَمَ مَثَلًا
إِذَا قَوْمُكَ مِنْهُ يَصِدُّونَ ○

58. And they say, "Are
Our gods best, or he?"
This they set forth
To thee, only by way
Of disputation: yea, they
Are a contentious people.

٥٨- وَقَالُوٓا ءَأٰلِهَتُنَا خَيْرٌ أَمْ هُوَ ۚ
مَا ضَرَبُوهُ لَكَ إِلَّا جَدَلًا ۚ
بَلْ هُمْ قَوْمٌ خَصِمُونَ ○

59. He was no more than
A servant: We granted
Our favour to him,
And We made him
An example to the Children[4660]
Of Israel.

٥٩- إِنْ هُوَ إِلَّا عَبْدٌ
أَنْعَمْنَا عَلَيْهِ
وَجَعَلْنٰهُ مَثَلًا لِّبَنِىٓ إِسْرَآءِيلَ ○

4659. Jesus was a man, and a prophet to the Children of Israel, "though his own received him not." Some of the churches that were founded after him worshipped him as "God" and as "the son of God", as do the Trinitarian churches to the present day. The orthodox churches did so in the time of the holy Prophet. When the doctrine of Unity was renewed, and the false worship of others besides God was strictly prohibited, all false gods were condemned, *e.g.*, at xxi. 98. The pagan Arabs looked upon Jesus as being in the same category as their false gods, and could not see why a foreign cult, or a foreign god, as they viewed him, should be considered better than their own gods or idols. There was no substance in this, but mere mockery, and verbal quibbling. Jesus was one of the greater prophets: he was not a god, nor was he responsible for the quibbling subtleties of the Athanasian Creed.

4660. A reference to the limited mission of the prophet Jesus, whose Gospel to the Jews only survives in uncertain fragmentary forms.

60. And if it were Our Will,[4661]
We could make angels
From amongst you, succeeding
Each other on the earth.

٦٠- وَلَوْ نَشَآءُ لَجَعَلْنَا مِنكُم مَّلَٰٓئِكَةً
فِى الْأَرْضِ يَخْلُفُونَ ○

61. And (Jesus) shall be[4662]
A Sign (for the coming
Of) the Hour (of Judgment):
Therefore have no doubt
About the (Hour), but
Follow ye Me : this
Is a Straight Way.

٦١- وَإِنَّهُۥ لَعِلْمٌ لِّلسَّاعَةِ
فَلَا تَمْتَرُنَّ بِهَا وَاتَّبِعُونِ ۚ
هَٰذَا صِرَٰطٌ مُّسْتَقِيمٌ ○

62. Let not the Evil One
Hinder you : for he is
To you an enemy avowed.

٦٢- وَلَا يَصُدَّنَّكُمُ الشَّيْطَٰنُ ۖ
إِنَّهُۥ لَكُمْ عَدُوٌّ مُّبِينٌ ○

63. When Jesus came
With Clear Signs, he said:
"Now have I come
To you with Wisdom,[4663]
And in order to make
Clear to you some
Of the (points) on which
Ye dispute : therefore fear God
And obey me.

٦٣- وَلَمَّا جَآءَ عِيسَىٰ بِالْبَيِّنَٰتِ قَالَ
قَدْ جِئْتُكُم بِالْحِكْمَةِ
وَلِأُبَيِّنَ لَكُم بَعْضَ الَّذِى تَخْتَلِفُونَ
فِيهِ ۖ
فَاتَّقُوا اللَّهَ وَأَطِيعُونِ ○

64. "For God, He is my Lord[4664]
And your Lord : so worship
Ye Him : this is
A Straight Way."

٦٤- إِنَّ اللَّهَ هُوَ رَبِّى وَرَبُّكُمْ فَاعْبُدُوهُ ۚ
هَٰذَا صِرَٰطٌ مُّسْتَقِيمٌ ○

4661. If it were said that the birth of Jesus without a father sets him above other prophets, the creation of angels without either father or mother would set them still higher, especially as angels do not eat and drink and are not subject to physical laws. But angels are not higher.

4662. This is understood to refer to the second coming of Jesus in the Last Days just before the Resurrection, when he will destroy the false doctrines that pass under his name, and prepare the way for the universal acceptance of Islam, the Gospel of Unity and Peace, the Straight Way of the Qur-ān.

4663. True wisdom consists in understanding the unity of the Divine purpose and the Unity of the Divine Personality. The man Jesus came to reconcile the jarring sects in Israel, and his true teaching was just the same as that which was expounded in a wider form by Islam. He did not claim to be God : why should not the Christians follow the doctrine of Unity rather than what has become their ancestral and traditional custom?

4664. In verses 26-28 an appeal is made to the pagan Arabs, that Islam is their own religion, the religion of Abraham their ancestor; in verses 46-54, an appeal is made to the Jews that Islam is the same religion as was taught by Moses, and that they should not allow their leaders to make fools of them; in verses 57-65 an appeal is made to the Christians that Islam is the same religion as was taught by Jesus, and that they should give up their sectarian attitude and follow the universal religion, which shows the Straight Way.

65. But sects from among
Themselves fell into disagreement:
Then woe to the wrong-doers,
From the Penalty
Of a Grievous Day!

٦٥- فَاخْتَلَفَ الْأَحْزَابُ مِنْ بَيْنِهِمْ ۚ
فَوَيْلٌ لِّلَّذِينَ ظَلَمُوا
مِنْ عَذَابِ يَوْمٍ أَلِيمٍ ۝

66. Do they only wait[4665]
For the Hour—that it
Should come on them
All of a sudden,
While they perceive not?

٦٦- هَلْ يَنظُرُونَ إِلَّا السَّاعَةَ
أَن تَأْتِيَهُم بَغْتَةً
وَهُمْ لَا يَشْعُرُونَ ۝

67. Friends on that Day[4666]
Will be foes, one
To another,—except
The Righteous.

٦٧- الْأَخِلَّاءُ يَوْمَئِذٍ بَعْضُهُمْ لِبَعْضٍ
عَدُوٌّ إِلَّا الْمُتَّقِينَ ۝

SECTION 7.

68. My devotees![4667]
No fear shall be
On you that Day,
Nor shall ye grieve,—

٦٨- يَا عِبَادِ لَا خَوْفٌ عَلَيْكُمُ الْيَوْمَ
وَلَا أَنتُمْ تَحْزَنُونَ ۝

69. (Being) those who have believed
In Our Signs and bowed
(Their wills to Ours) in Islām.

٦٩- الَّذِينَ آمَنُوا بِآيَاتِنَا وَكَانُوا مُسْلِمِينَ ۝

70. Enter ye the Garden,[4668]
Ye and your wives,
In (beauty and) rejoicing.

٧٠- ادْخُلُوا الْجَنَّةَ أَنتُمْ وَأَزْوَاجُكُمْ
تُحْبَرُونَ ۝

4665. *Cf.* xii. 107. What is there to wait for? The Hour of Judgment may come at any moment. It will come all of a sudden before they realise that it is on them. They should make up their minds to give up misleading disputations and come to the Straight Path.

4666. The hatred and spite, which are associated with evil, will be felt with peculiar intensity in that period of agony. That itself would be a punishment, from which the righteous will be free. The righteous will have passed all perils of falling into wrong frames of mind.

4667. The devotion and service to God result in the soul being made free from all fear and sorrow, as regards the past, present, and future, if we may take an analogy from Time for a timeless state. Such devotion and service are shown by (1) believing in God's Signs, which means understanding and accepting His Will, and (2) by merging our will completely in His universal Will, which means being in tune with the Infinite, and acting in all things to further His Kingdom.

4668. The Garden is the type of all that is beautiful to eye, mind, and soul, all that is restful and in tune, a complete state of bliss, such as we can scarcely conceive of in this troubled world. Several metaphors indicate how we can try to picture that bliss to ourselves in "this muddy vesture of decay."

71. To them will be passed[4669]
Round, dishes and goblets
Of gold : there will be
There all that the souls
Could desire, all that
The eyes could delight in :
And ye shall abide
Therein (for aye).

٧١- يُطَافُ عَلَيْهِم بِصِحَافٍ مِّن ذَهَبٍ
وَأَكْوَابٍ ۖ وَفِيهَا مَا تَشْتَهِيهِ الْأَنفُسُ
وَتَلَذُّ الْأَعْيُنُ ۖ
وَأَنتُمْ فِيهَا خَالِدُونَ ۝

72. Such will be the Garden
Of which ye are made[4670]
Heirs for your (good) deeds
(In life).

٧٢- وَتِلْكَ الْجَنَّةُ الَّتِي
أُورِثْتُمُوهَا بِمَا كُنتُمْ تَعْمَلُونَ ۝

73. Ye shall have therein
Abundance of fruit,[4671] from which
Ye shall have satisfaction.[4672]

٧٣- لَكُمْ فِيهَا فَاكِهَةٌ كَثِيرَةٌ
مِّنْهَا تَأْكُلُونَ ۝

74. The Sinners will be
In the Punishment of Hell,
To dwell therein (for aye):

٧٤- إِنَّ الْمُجْرِمِينَ فِي عَذَابِ جَهَنَّمَ
خَالِدُونَ ۝

75. Nowise will the (punishment)
Be lightened for them,
And in despair will they
Be there overwhelmed.

٧٥- لَا يُفَتَّرُ عَنْهُمْ
وَهُمْ فِيهِ مُبْلِسُونَ ۝

76. Nowise shall We[4673]
Be unjust to them :

٧٦- وَمَا ظَلَمْنَاهُمْ

4669. We shall have all our near and dear ones ("wives") with us : perfected Love will not be content with Self, but like a note of music will find its melody in communion with the others. The richest and most beautiful vessels will minister to our purified desires, and give complete and eternal satisfaction to our souls in every way.

4670. We shall be there, not as strangers, or temporary guests, but as heirs,—made heirs in eternity because of the good lives we had led on earth.

4671. "Fruit" and "eating" are metaphorical. Even as types or emblems, eating and drinking were suggested by "dishes and goblets of gold" in verse 71 above. The "fruit" here links on with the last words in the last verse (72), "ye are made heirs for your (good) deeds (in life)". It is not a doctrine of "rewards", strictly so called. A reward is measured by merit, but here the bliss is beyond all merits or deserts. It is a doctrine of works and their fruits : every deed must have its inevitable consequences. At first sight it may be compared to the doctrine of "Karma", but it differs from it in postulating God's unbounded Mercy, and the efficacy of Repentance.

4672. Literally, "shall eat". But the word *akala* is used in many places in the comprehensive sense of "enjoy", "have satisfaction". For example, see n. 776 to v. 69. *Cf.* also vii. 19 and n. 1004.

4673. The wrong-doers suffer not because God is unjust or cruel, nor as a deterrent to others, for the probationary period will then have passed, but because their evil deeds must bear their inevitable fruit. God's Grace was ever ready to offer opportunities for Repentance and Forgiveness. But they rejected them. They were unjust to themselves. This is complementary to the doctrine of works and their fruits, as explained in n. 4671 above.

But it is they who
Have been unjust themselves.

وَلٰكِنْ كَانُوْا هُمُ الظّٰلِمِيْنَ ۝

77. They will cry: "O Malik![4674]
Would that thy Lord
Put an end to us!"
He will say, "Nay, but
Ye shall abide!"[4675]

٧٧- وَ نَادَوْا يٰمٰلِكُ
لِيَقْضِ عَلَيْنَا رَبُّكَ ؕ
قَالَ اِنَّكُمْ مّٰكِثُوْنَ ۝

78. Verily We have brought[4676]
The Truth to you:
But most of you
Have a hatred for Truth.

٧٨- لَقَدْ جِئْنٰكُمْ بِالْحَقِّ
وَلٰكِنَّ اَكْثَرَكُمْ لِلْحَقِّ كٰرِهُوْنَ ۝

79. What! Have they settled[4677]
Some Plan (among themselves)?
But it is We Who
Settle things.

٧٩- اَمْ اَبْرَمُوْٓا اَمْرًا
فَاِنَّا مُبْرِمُوْنَ ۝

80. Or do they think[4678]
That We hear not
Their secrets and their
Private counsels? Indeed
(We do), and Our Messengers
Are by them, to record.

٨٠- اَمْ يَحْسَبُوْنَ اَنَّا لَا نَسْمَعُ
سِرَّهُمْ وَ نَجْوٰىهُمْ ؕ
بَلٰى وَ رُسُلُنَا لَدَيْهِمْ يَكْتُبُوْنَ ۝

81. Say: "If (God) Most Gracious
Had a son, I would[4679]
Be the first to worship."

٨١- قُلْ اِنْ كَانَ لِلرَّحْمٰنِ وَلَدٌ ۖ
فَاَنَا اَوَّلُ الْعٰبِدِيْنَ ۝

82. Glory to the Lord
Of the heavens and the earth,

٨٢- سُبْحٰنَ رَبِّ السَّمٰوٰتِ وَالْاَرْضِ

4674. *Mālik*: one who is lord or possessor; one who is in charge; applied to the Angel in charge of Hell.

4675. *Cf.* xx. 74. Annihilation is better than agony. But wrong-doers cannot destroy the "fruits" of their actions, by asking for annihilation.

4676. We come back now to the Present,—primarily to the time when Islam was being preached in Mecca, but by analogy the present time or any time. Truth is often bitter to the taste of those who live on Falsehoods and Shams and profit by them. They hate the Truth, and plot against it. But will they succeed? See next verse and note.

4677. Men cannot settle the high affairs of the universe. If they plot against the Truth, the Truth will destroy them, just as, if they accept the Truth, the Truth will make them free. It is God Who disposes of affairs.

4678. However secretly men may plot, everything is known to God. His Recording Angels are by, at all times and in all places, to prepare a Record of their Deeds for their own conviction when the time comes for Judgment.

4679. The man of God does not object to true worship in any form. But it must be true: it must not superstitiously attribute derogatory things to God, or foster false ideas.

The Lord of the Throne[4680]
(Of Authority)! (He is
Free) from the things
They attribute (to Him)!

رَبِّ الْعَرْشِ
عَمَّا يَصِفُوْنَ ۝

83. So leave them to babble
And play (with vanities)
Until they meet that Day[4681]
Of theirs, which they
Have been promised.

٨٣- فَذَرْهُمْ يَخُوْضُوْا وَيَلْعَبُوْا
حَتّٰى يُلٰقُوْا يَوْمَهُمُ الَّذِيْ
يُوْعَدُوْنَ ۝

84. It is He Who is God
In heaven and God on earth;
And He is Full
Of Wisdom and Knowledge.

٨٤- وَهُوَ الَّذِيْ فِي السَّمَآءِ اِلٰهٌ وَّفِي الْاَرْضِ
اِلٰهٌ ۭ وَهُوَ الْحَكِيْمُ الْعَلِيْمُ ۝

85. And blessed is He[4682]
To Whom belongs the dominion
Of the heavens and the earth,
And all between them:
With Him is the knowledge
Of the Hour (of Judgment):
And to Him shall ye
Be brought back.

٨٥- وَتَبٰرَكَ الَّذِيْ لَهٗ مُلْكُ
السَّمٰوٰتِ وَالْاَرْضِ وَمَا بَيْنَهُمَا ۚ
وَعِنْدَهٗ عِلْمُ السَّاعَةِ ۚ
وَاِلَيْهِ تُرْجَعُوْنَ ۝

86. And those whom they invoke
Besides God have no power
Of intercession;—only he[4683]
Who bears witness to the Truth,
And they know (him).

٨٦- وَلَا يَمْلِكُ الَّذِيْنَ يَدْعُوْنَ مِنْ دُوْنِهِ
الشَّفَاعَةَ
اِلَّا مَنْ شَهِدَ بِالْحَقِّ وَهُمْ يَعْلَمُوْنَ ۝

4680. *Cf.* vii. 54 and n. 1032. All Power, Authority, Knowledge, and Truth are with God. He neither begets nor is begotten. Glory to Him!

4681. *That Day of theirs*: they had their Day on earth; they will have a different sort of Day in the Hereafter, according to the promise of God about the Resurrection and Judgment, or perhaps about Retribution in this very life! So leave them to play about with their fancies and vanities. Truth must eventually prevail!

4682. We glorify God, and we call His name blessed, because He has not only supreme power and authority, but because we shall return to Him and see "the Light of His Countenance" (xxx. 38).

4683. The classical Commentators construe this clause differently. According to their construction, the clause would be translated, "except those who bear witness to the Truth, and with full knowledge." "Truth" they would construe to be the Gospel of Unity. According to them, while idols and false gods have no power of intercession, persons like Jesus, who is falsely worshipped by his misguided followers, but who himself preached the Gospel of Unity with full understanding, will have the power of intercession. This implies that we construe the singular *man shahida* to refer to the same person or persons as the plural *hum ya'lamūn*. This difficulty is removed if we construe as I have translated it. In that case "he who bears witness to the Truth" is the holy Prophet, who came to renew the Gospel of Unity, and "they know (him)" would refer to the Quraish, amongst whom he was brought up and among whom he earned the reputation of being a man of probity (*Amīn*).

87. If thou ask them, Who [4684]
Created them, they will
Certainly say, God : how
Then are they deluded
Away (from the Truth) ?

٨٧- وَلَئِن سَأَلْتَهُم مَّنْ خَلَقَهُمْ
لَيَقُولُنَّ اللَّهُ
فَأَنَّىٰ يُؤْفَكُونَ ۝

88. (God has knowledge) [4685]
Of the (Prophet's) cry,
"O my Lord! Truly
These are a people
Who will not believe!" [4686]

٨٨- وَقِيلِهِ يَٰرَبِّ
إِنَّ هَٰٓؤُلَآءِ قَوْمٌ لَّا يُؤْمِنُونَ ۝ وقف لازم

89. But turn away from them,
And say "Peace!" [4687]
But soon shall they know!

٨٩- فَاصْفَحْ عَنْهُمْ وَقُلْ سَلَٰمٌ ۚ
فَسَوْفَ يَعْلَمُونَ ۝ ع

4684. *Cf.* xxxi. 25, and n. 3613; and xxxix. 38, and n. 4299.

4685. Commentators are divided in opinion as to the construction. The best opinion is that which I have adopted, referring back *qīlihī* as a genitive governed by *'ilm* in verse 85. An alternative construction is to construe the *wāw* here as the *wāw qasamiya*: in that case we should have to suppose some other clause as understood, in order to complete the sense.

4686. The Prophet was much troubled in mind by the Unfaith of the Quraish: xviii. 6. He is here told to leave them alone for a time, for the Truth must soon prevail.

4687. *Cf.* xxv. 63, and n. 3123.

INTRODUCTION TO SŪRA XLIV (*Dukhān*).

For the chronology and the general theme of the Sūras of the ***Ḥā-Mīm*** series, of which this is the fifth, see the Introduction to S. xl.

The theme of this particular Sūra is how worldly pride and power are humbled in the dust if they resist spiritual forces, and how Evil and Good find their true setting in the Hereafter.

The title-word *Dukhān* occurs in verse 10. It means smoke or mist, and may refer to a drought or famine, as explained in the notes to that verse.

Summary.—Revelation explains clearly how worldly pride and arrogance may come to naught, even at long odds, against spiritual truths (xliv. 1-29, and C. 216).

A people may be given all blessings and may fail in its trust, as did Israel: will the Quraish learn the lesson of Good and Evil? (xliv. 30-59, and C. 217).

C. 216.—Blest is the night in which God's Message
(xliv. 1-29.) Comes down, as a Mercy to men, to warn them
Against Evil. How fractious of men to ignore
Or suppress such warnings? Proud Pharaoh
And his Chiefs did resist God's authority,
But their sins rebounded on themselves:
They were swallowed up by the sea; and their tilth,
Their gardens, their noble fanes and buildings,
And all the advantages of which they boasted
Passed to other hands. Not a tear
Was shed over them in heaven or earth.
Thus ends the tale of power misused.

Sūra XLIV.

Dukhān, or Smoke (or Mist).

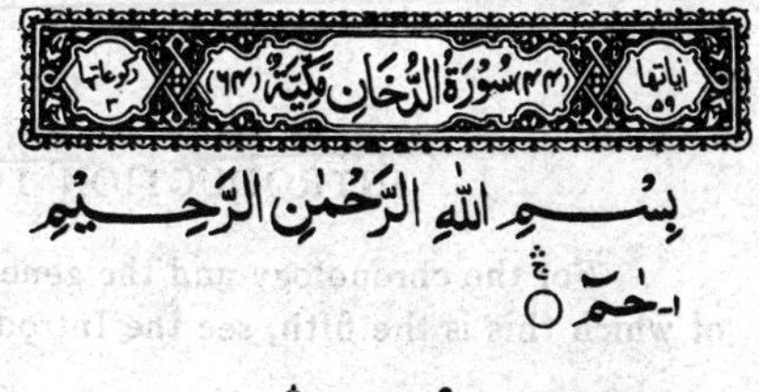

In the name of God, Most Gracious, Most Merciful.

بِسۡمِ اللّٰهِ الرَّحۡمٰنِ الرَّحِيۡمِ

1. Ḥa-*Mim.*[4688]

١- حٰمٓ

2. By the Book that[4689]
Makes things clear ;—

٢- وَالۡكِتٰبِ الۡمُبِيۡنِ

3. We sent it down
During a blessed night :[4690]
For We (ever) wish
To warn (against Evil).

٣- اِنَّاۤ اَنۡزَلۡنٰهُ فِىۡ لَيۡلَةٍ مُّبٰرَكَةٍ
اِنَّا كُنَّا مُنۡذِرِيۡنَ

4. In that (night) is made
Distinct every affair
Of wisdom,[4691]

٤- فِيۡهَا يُفۡرَقُ كُلُّ اَمۡرٍ حَكِيۡمٍ

5. By command, from Our
Presence. For We (ever)
Send (revelations),

٥- اَمۡرًا مِّنۡ عِنۡدِنَا
اِنَّا كُنَّا مُرۡسِلِيۡنَ

6. As a Mercy
From thy Lord :
For He hears and knows[4692]
(All things) ;

٦- رَحۡمَةً مِّنۡ رَّبِّكَ
اِنَّهٗ هُوَ السَّمِيۡعُ الۡعَلِيۡمُ

7. The Lord of the heavens
And the earth and all

٧- رَبِّ السَّمٰوٰتِ وَالۡاَرۡضِ وَمَا

4688. These Abbreviated Letters are discussed in the Introduction to S. xl. paragraphs 2-4.

4689. The Qur-ān is its own evidence. In the last Sūra (xliii. 3) stress was laid on the fact that everyone could understand it. Here the stress is on the fact that it is a Message of Mercy from God in that it warns mankind against evil.

4690. Usually taken to be a night in the month of Ramadhān, say the 23rd, 25th, or 27th night of that month. It is referred to as the Night of Power in xcvii. 1-2. See also ii. 185. But perhaps we need not fix it literally by the calendar. The night that a Message descends from God is indeed a blessed night, like a day of rain for a parched land.

4691. Such an occasion is one on which divine Wisdom places before us through Revelation the solution of spiritual problems of the highest import to mankind.

4692. It is because God is the friend of the friendless and the help of the helpless that He hears all sincere prayers, and as His knowledge embraces all things, He grants to us whatever is best for us, not as we see it, but as He knows it in His perfect knowledge.

Between them, if ye (but)
Have an assured faith.[4693]

بَيْنَهُمَا إِن كُنتُم مُّوقِنِينَ ○

8. There is no god but He:
It is He Who gives life
And gives death,—
The Lord and Cherisher
To you and your earliest
Ancestors.

٨- لَآ إِلَٰهَ إِلَّا هُوَ
يُحْيِ وَيُمِيتُ ۖ
رَبُّكُمْ وَرَبُّ ءَابَآئِكُمُ ٱلْأَوَّلِينَ ○

9. Yet they play about[4694]
In doubt.

٩- بَلْ هُمْ فِى شَكٍّ يَلْعَبُونَ ○

10. Then watch thou
For the Day[4695]
That the sky will
Bring forth a kind
Of smoke (or mist)[4696]
Plainly visible,

١٠- فَٱرْتَقِبْ
يَوْمَ تَأْتِى ٱلسَّمَآءُ بِدُخَانٍ
مُّبِينٍ ○

11. Enveloping the people:
This will be a Penalty
Grievous.

١١- يَغْشَى ٱلنَّاسَ ۖ
هَٰذَا عَذَابٌ أَلِيمٌ ○

4693. *Cf.* ii. 4. They cannot fully realise what a tremendous thing it is that God is their own Lord and Cherisher (next verse), as He is the Lord and Cherisher of the whole Universe, until they firmly believe,—until their Faith amounts to a certainty, secure and unshakable.

4694. The story is mainly about the Quraish. But there is a wider meaning behind it, applicable to men generally, and at all times. As a body the Quraish, especially in the earlier stages of the preaching of Islam, before they started persecution, received the Message with more amusement than hatred. They played about with it, and expressed doubts about it, whereas the Preacher was most earnest about it, with all his heart and soul in it, as he loved his people and wished to save them from their wickedness and folly.

4695. What Day is this? It obviously refers to a great calamity, and from the wording it is to be a great calamity in the future, seen with the prophetic eye. The word *yagshā* in verse 11 may be compared to *gāshiya* in lxxxviii. 1, which obviously refers to the final Day of Judgment. But verse 15 below ("We shall remove the Penalty for a while") shows that it is not the final Judgment referred to here, but some calamity that was to happen soon afterwards. Perhaps it was a famine, about which see the next note.

4696. The "smoke" or "mist" is interpreted on good authority to refer to a severe famine in Mecca, in which men were so pinched with hunger that they saw mist before their eyes when they looked at the sky. Ibn Kathīr in his *Tārīkh* mentions two famines in Mecca, one in the 8th year of the Mission, say the fourth year before the Hijra, and another about the 8th year after the Hijra. But as either or both of these famines lasted as many as seven years, the dates are to be taken very roughly. It is even possible that the two famines were continuous, of varying severity from year to year. Bukhārī mentions only the post-Hijrat famine, which was apparently so severe that men began to eat bones and carrion. Abū Sufyān (about 8 A.H.) approached the holy Prophet to intercede and pray for the removal of the famine, as the Pagans attributed it to the curse of the Prophet. Sūra xxiii., which is also Meccan, but of later date than the present Sūra, also refers to a famine: see xxiii 75, and n. 2921. As Sūras were not all revealed entire, but many came piecemeal, it is possible that particular verses in a given Sūra may be of different dates from the Sūra as a whole.

12. (They will say:)
"Our Lord! Remove
The Penalty from us,
For we do really believe!"

١٢- رَبَّنَا اكْشِفْ عَنَّا الْعَذَابَ
إِنَّا مُؤْمِنُونَ ○

13. How shall the Message
Be (effectual) for them,[4697]
Seeing that an Apostle
Explaining things clearly
Has (already) come to them,—

١٣- أَنَّىٰ لَهُمُ الذِّكْرَىٰ
وَقَدْ جَاءَهُمْ رَسُولٌ مُّبِينٌ ○

14. Yet they turn away
From him and say: "Tutored
(By others), a man possessed!"[4698]

١٤- ثُمَّ تَوَلَّوْا عَنْهُ
وَقَالُوا مُعَلَّمٌ مَّجْنُونٌ ○

15. We shall indeed remove[4699]
The Penalty for a while,
(But) truly ye will revert
(To your ways).

١٥- إِنَّا كَاشِفُوا الْعَذَابِ قَلِيلًا
إِنَّكُمْ عَائِدُونَ ○

16. One day We shall seize
You with a mighty onslaught:
We will indeed (then)
Exact Retribution!

١٦- يَوْمَ نَبْطِشُ الْبَطْشَةَ الْكُبْرَىٰ
إِنَّا مُنتَقِمُونَ ○

17. We did, before them,
Try the people of Pharaoh:[4700]

١٧- وَلَقَدْ فَتَنَّا قَبْلَهُمْ قَوْمَ فِرْعَوْنَ

4697. The Quraish had before them an Apostle whose purity of life was openly known to them; they themselves called him *al-Amīn* (worthy of all trust); he preached in their own language in words of burning eloquence and transparent clearness; yet they turned away from him and called him a madman, or one whose Message was not inspired by God, but written by some hidden hand (see next note)! How will the teaching of spiritual Truth make way among such unreasonable people?

4698. *Tutored*: see xvi. 103, and n. 2143.

Possessed: see xv. 6, and n. 1940.

4699. God gives every chance to all His creatures, however rebellious. He gives them a little trial, perhaps personal, perhaps economic, to see if that would bring them to their bearings, and train their will in the right direction. Some are thus reclaimed, and some do not learn. Perhaps, for the latter, he gives them a chance by removing the trial; some are reclaimed, and some still remain obdurate. And so, in His wisdom, He allows His grace to work, again and again, until, at the last, Judgment must seize the last and irreclaimable remnant "with a mighty onslaught".

Such working of God's Providence is clearly visible in the story of the Quraish. It is a pity that the economic conditions of Mecca have not been studied in detail in any of the standard biographies of the Prophet. The so-called biographies by non-Muslims, *e.g.*, Muir's *Life*, do not even mention any Meccan famine or its reactions on the Quraish mind!

4700. This reference is to the pride of Pharaoh and his Egyptians, and their fall, rather than to the story of Moses himself; just as in xliv. 30-33 the reference is to the blessings bestowed on Israel, contrasted with their pride, unbelief, and fall; and in xliv. 37, to the ancient Ḥimyar kingdom in Yaman, which similarly fell for its sins.

There came to them
An apostle most honourable,[4701]

وَجَآءَهُمْ رَسُولٌ كَرِيمٌ ۝

18. Saying : " Restore to me[4702]
The servants of God :
I am to you an apostle
Worthy of all trust ;[4703]

١٨- أَنْ أَدُّوٓا إِلَىَّ عِبَادَ اللّٰهِ ۖ
إِنِّى لَكُمْ رَسُولٌ أَمِينٌ ۝

19. " And be not arrogant
As against God :
For I come to you
With authority manifest.

١٩- وَأَنْ لَّا تَعْلُوا عَلَى اللّٰهِ ۚ
إِنِّىٓ اٰتِيكُمْ بِسُلْطٰنٍ مُّبِينٍ ۝

20. " For me, I have sought[4704]
Safety with my Lord
And your Lord, against
Your injuring me.[4705]

٢٠- وَإِنِّى عُذْتُ بِرَبِّى
وَرَبِّكُمْ أَنْ تَرْجُمُونِ ۝

21. " If ye believe me not,[4706]
At least keep yourselves
Away from me."

٢١- وَإِنْ لَّمْ تُؤْمِنُوا لِى
فَاعْتَزِلُونِ ۝

22. (But they were aggressive :)[4707]
Then he cried

٢٢- فَدَعَا

4701. *Most honourable* : this epithet is specially applied to Moses here, as expressing the truth, in contrast to the Pharaoh's false characterisation of him as " a contemptible wretch " (xliii. 52).

4702. The argument of Moses and his "authority manifest" will be found at vii. 104-108, 120-126, 130-137. Notice how fully he assumes the authority of his office here. He claims all " servants of God ", *i.e.*, true worshippers, as under his protection, for his mission was both to the Egyptians and the Israelites; he asks that they should be restored to *him* ; and he boldly denounces the Pharaoh's arrogance " as against God ".

4703. " Worthy of all trust " : *Amīn*, a title applied to prophets in S. xxvi. : *e.g.*, see xxvi. 107. As the holy Prophet had historically earned that title among his own people, the reminiscences of the story of Moses apply to him in his relations with the arrogant Quraish.

4704. It is no use their plotting his death or his vilification ; for his safety is in God. As he truly says, " God is not only *my* Lord, but *your* Lord also ; your responsibility arises apart from my preaching, but I preach in order to remind you of it."

4705. " *Injuring me* " : literally " stoning me ". " Stoning " may be here symbolical of any injury or vilification.

4706. If you do not believe me, at least go your ways : do not add to your sins by trying to suppress me and the Message of Truth which I bring : keep out of my way.

4707. They would not even leave him alone to do his duty. So he cried to God, not indeed to destroy them, for a Prophet does not judge, but only God judges ; he justified himself in prayer, that he had done his best, but they were obdurate in sin, and they were trying to oppress and injure the believers. Then came the order to march. They were to march under the cover of night, because the enemy was sure to pursue. They were to march with all believers, presumably believing Egyptians (such as were not martyred) as well as Israelites, for some Egyptians had believed : vii. 121.

To his Lord:
"These are indeed
A people given to sin."

رَبَّهٗٓ
اَنَّ هٰٓؤُلَآءِ قَوْمٌ مُّجْرِمُوْنَ ۝

23. (The reply came:)
"March forth with my servants
By night: for ye are
Sure to be pursued.

٢٣- فَاَسْرِ بِعِبَادِيْ لَيْلًا
اِنَّكُمْ مُّتَّبَعُوْنَ ۝

24. "And leave the sea
As a furrow (divided):[4708]
For they are a host
(Destined) to be drowned."

٢٤- وَاتْرُكِ الْبَحْرَ رَهْوًا ؕ
اِنَّهُمْ جُنْدٌ مُّغْرَقُوْنَ ۝

25. How many were the gardens[4709]
And springs they left behind,

٢٥- كَمْ تَرَكُوْا مِنْ جَنّٰتٍ وَّعُيُوْنٍ ۝

26. And corn-fields
And noble buildings,

٢٦- وَّزُرُوْعٍ وَّمَقَامٍ كَرِيْمٍ ۝

27. And wealth (and conveniences
Of life), wherein they
Had taken such delight!

٢٧- وَّنَعْمَةٍ كَانُوْا فِيْهَا فٰكِهِيْنَ ۝

28. Thus (was their end)!
And We made other people
Inherit (those things)!

٢٨- كَذٰلِكَ ۫
وَاَوْرَثْنٰهَا قَوْمًا اٰخَرِيْنَ ۝

29. And neither heaven[4710]
Nor earth shed a tear
Over them: nor were
They given a respite (again).

٢٩- فَمَا بَكَتْ عَلَيْهِمُ السَّمَآءُ وَالْاَرْضُ
وَمَا كَانُوْا مُنْظَرِيْنَ ۝

4708. For the passage of Moses and his following, the sea had divided: they were to pass through the gap or furrow and leave it alone, to lure on the Egyptian host, on which the sea afterwards closed in, totally destroying them.

4709. There follows a word-picture of all the fine and enjoyable things which the ruling caste had monopolised. Now these proud monopolists were drowned in the sea, and the inheritance went to other hands.

4710. They died, "unwept, unhonoured, and unsung". They were too inordinate to be given another chance. Pharaoh had claimed to be their supreme god, and they had followed him!

C. 217.—So with the Children of Israel:
(xliv. 30-59.) Granted gifts and favours, they became
Arrogant and fell. Can the Quraish
Escape the doom for sin? We created
The world for just ends. The Day
Will come when good and evil will be
Sorted out: each will meet
The fruits of its own deeds. Give good heed
To the Message revealed, and wait and watch.

SECTION 2.

30. We did deliver aforetime
The Children of Israel
From humiliating Punishment,[4711]

٣٠- وَلَقَدْ نَجَّيْنَا بَنِىٓ إِسْرَآءِيلَ
مِنَ الْعَذَابِ الْمُهِينِ ۝

31. Inflicted by Pharaoh, for he
Was arrogant (even) among
Inordinate transgressors.

٣١- مِنْ فِرْعَوْنَ ۚ
إِنَّهُۥ كَانَ عَالِيًا مِّنَ الْمُسْرِفِينَ ۝

32. And We chose them aforetime
Above the nations, knowingly,[4712]

٣٢- وَلَقَدِ اخْتَرْنَٰهُمْ عَلَىٰ عِلْمٍ عَلَى الْعَٰلَمِينَ ۝

33. And granted them Signs[4713]
In which there was
A manifest trial.

٣٣- وَءَاتَيْنَٰهُم مِّنَ الْءَايَٰتِ
مَا فِيهِ بَلَٰٓؤٌا مُّبِينٌ ۝

34. As to these (Quraish),[4714]
They say forsooth:

٣٤- إِنَّ هَٰٓؤُلَآءِ لَيَقُولُونَ ۝

4711. The Israelites were held in bondage prior to the Exodus. Their hard taskmaster placed every indignity on them, and by Pharaoh's decree their male children were to be killed, and their females were to be kept alive for the Egyptians.

4712. From degrading servitude, Israel was delivered, and taken, in spite of many rebellions and backslidings on the way, to "a land flowing with milk and honey", where later they established the glorious kingdom of David and Solomon. This was not merely fortuitous. In God's prescience it was to be a link in furthering the great universal Plan. But their being chosen did not mean that they could do what they liked. In that sense there is no "chosen race" before God. But God gives every race and every individual a chance, and when the race or individual fails to live up to it, he or it must fall and give place to others.

4713. Among the "Signs" given to Israel were their own Revelation under Moses, their prosperous land of Canaan, their flourishing Kingdom under David and Solomon, their prophets and teachers of Truth, and the advent of Jesus to reclaim the lost ones among them. All these were trials. When they failed in the trials, they were left to wander desolate and suffer.

4714. The cases of the Egyptians and the Israelites having been cited as great nations which fell through inordinate vanity and wrong-doing, the case is now pressed home against the Quraish leaders in their arrogance to the holy Prophet himself. They deny Revelation; they deny a future life, as the Sadducees did among the Jews before them; they persecute the man of God, and those who believe in him: and they mockingly demand that their ancestors should be brought back to life, if it is true that there is a future life. They are reminded that better men than they lived in their own country of Arabia, men who had knowledge of God's revelation under the earliest Dispensation. See next note. They perished because of their unbelief and wrong-doing. What chance have they unless they turn and repent?

35. "There is nothing beyond
Our first death,
And we shall not
Be raised again.

٣٥- إِنْ هِيَ إِلَّا مَوْتَتُنَا الْأُولَىٰ
وَمَا نَحْنُ بِمُنْشَرِينَ ○

36. "Then bring (back)
Our forefathers, if what
Ye say is true!"

٣٦- فَأْتُوا
بِآبَائِنَا إِنْ كُنْتُمْ صَادِقِينَ ○

37. What! are they better
Than the people of Tubba'[4715]
And those who were
Before them? We destroyed
Them because they were
Guilty of sin.[4716]

٣٧- أَهُمْ خَيْرٌ أَمْ قَوْمُ تُبَّعٍ
وَالَّذِينَ مِنْ قَبْلِهِمْ أَهْلَكْنَاهُمْ
إِنَّهُمْ كَانُوا مُجْرِمِينَ ○

38. We created not
The heavens, the earth,
And all between them,
Merely in (idle) sport:[4717]

٣٨- وَمَا خَلَقْنَا السَّمٰوٰتِ وَالْأَرْضَ
وَمَا بَيْنَهُمَا لَاعِبِينَ ○

39. We created them not
Except for just ends:
But most of them
Do not understand.

٣٩- مَا خَلَقْنٰهُمَآ إِلَّا بِالْحَقِّ
وَلٰكِنَّ أَكْثَرَهُمْ لَا يَعْلَمُونَ ○

40. Verily the Day of[4718]
Sorting Out is the time
Appointed for all of them,—

٤٠- إِنَّ يَوْمَ الْفَصْلِ
مِيقَاتُهُمْ أَجْمَعِينَ ○

4715. *Tubba'* is understood to be a title or family name of Ḥimyar kings in Yaman, of the tribe of Hamdān. The Ḥimyar were an ancient race. At one time they seem to have extended their hegemony over all Arabia and perhaps beyond, to the East African Coast. Their earliest religion seems to have been Sabianism, or the worship of the heavenly bodies. They seem at different times, later on, to have professed the Jewish and the Christian religion. Among the Embassies sent by the holy Prophet in A.H. 9-10 was one to the Ḥimyar of Yaman, which led to their coming into Islam. This was of course much later than the date of this Sūra.

4716. In prehistoric times the Ḥimyar and Yaman seem to have played a large part in Arabia and even beyond: see last note. But when they were intoxicated with power, they fell into sin, and gradually they ceased to count, not only in Arabia but even in Yaman.

4717. *Cf.* xxi. 16, and n. 2676. All creation is for a wise and just purpose. But men usually do not realise or understand it, because they are steeped in their own ignorance, folly, or passions.

4718. Day of Sorting Out, or the Day of Decision. *Cf.* xxxvii. 21, and n. 4047. Ignorance, prejudice, passion, spite, and selfishness, seem sometimes to flourish in this probationary life. In any case they are mixed up with knowledge, justice, commonsense, love and regard for others. But the good and the evil will be sorted out and separated at the Day of Judgment. There is a time appointed for it. In God's good time all will come right.

41. The Day when no protector [4719]
Can avail his client
In aught, and no help
Can they receive,

٤١- يَوْمَ لَا يُغْنِي مَوْلًى عَن مَّوْلًى شَيْئًا وَلَا هُمْ يُنصَرُونَ ۝

42. Except such as receive [4720]
God's Mercy : for He is
Exalted in Might, Most Merciful.

٤٢- إِلَّا مَن رَّحِمَ اللَّهُ ۚ إِنَّهُ هُوَ الْعَزِيزُ الرَّحِيمُ ۝

Section 3.

43. Verily the tree [4721]
Of Zaqqūm [4722]

٤٣- إِنَّ شَجَرَتَ الزَّقُّومِ ۝

44. Will be the food
Of the Sinful,—

٤٤- طَعَامُ الْأَثِيمِ ۝

45. Like molten brass ;
It will boil
In their insides,

٤٥- كَالْمُهْلِ يَغْلِي فِي الْبُطُونِ ۝

46. Like the boiling
Of scalding water.

٤٦- كَغَلْيِ الْحَمِيمِ ۝

47. (A voice will cry :
" Seize ye him
And drag him
Into the midst
Of the Blazing Fire !

٤٧- خُذُوهُ فَاعْتِلُوهُ إِلَىٰ سَوَاءِ الْجَحِيمِ ۝

48. " Then pour over his head
The Penalty of Boiling Water

٤٨- ثُمَّ صُبُّوا فَوْقَ رَأْسِهِ مِنْ عَذَابِ الْحَمِيمِ ۝

4719. When that Day comes, the strictest justice will prevail. No man, however prominently he may have walked on the world's stage, can help another. He himself will need help, not the sort of log-rolling help which high and low render to each other in this life, but which in the conditions of reality will be of no avail. The only things which will help will be the Mercy of God.

4720. God's Mercy will be the only thing of any efficacy : for He is both *able* to help (" Exalted in Might ") and *willing* to forgive (" Most Merciful ").

4721. Now follows a word-picture of the horrors to which Evil must lead us. What human language and what figures of speech can adequately describe them ?

4722. The opposite of " delicious Fruits " is the terrible tree of *Zaqqūm*, which is further described in xxxvii. 62-68, where see n. 4073. Also see xvii. 60, n. 2250.

49. " Taste thou (this) ! Truly wast thou Mighty, full of honour ! [4723]	۴۹- ذُقْ ۚ اِنَّكَ اَنْتَ الْعَزِيْزُ الْكَرِيْمُ ○
50. " Truly this is what Ye used to doubt ! " [4724]	۵۰- اِنَّ هٰذَا مَا كُنْتُمْ بِهٖ تَمْتَرُوْنَ ○
51. As to the Righteous (They will be) in A position of Security, [4725]	۵۱- اِنَّ الْمُتَّقِيْنَ فِيْ مَقَامٍ اَمِيْنٍ ○
52. Among Gardens and Springs ;	۵۲- فِيْ جَنّٰتٍ وَّعُيُوْنٍ ○
53. Dressed in fine silk [4726] And in rich brocade, They will face each other ; [4727]	۵۳- يَّلْبَسُوْنَ مِنْ سُنْدُسٍ وَّاِسْتَبْرَقٍ مُّتَقٰبِلِيْنَ ○
54. So ; and We shall Join them to Companions [4728] With beautiful, big, And lustrous eyes. [4729]	۵۴- كَذٰلِكَ وَزَوَّجْنٰهُمْ بِحُوْرٍ عِيْنٍ ○
55. There can they call For every kind of fruit [4730] In peace and security ;	۵۵- يَدْعُوْنَ فِيْهَا بِكُلِّ فَاكِهَةٍ اٰمِنِيْنَ ○

4723. In this particular Sūra the besetting sin we are considering is the arrogance born of place or power, wealth or honour, as understood in this world. The punishment of ignominy looks back to the kind of sin which is to be punished.

4724. When the Punishment becomes a realised fact, how foolish will those look who doubted whether there would be a Hereafter?

4725. There will be no uncertainty, as on this earth; no danger of discontinuance; no possibility of their satisfaction being terminated.

4726. *Cf.* xviii. 31, and n. 2373.

4727. Everything will be open and in social companionship: for all the petty feelings of jealousy or exclusiveness will have passed away.

4728. The Companions, like the scene, the dress, the outlook, and the fruit, will be beautiful. These symbolic words need not be taken to mean that there will be eating and drinking, or dressing, or marriage, or any physical things of that kind. There will be life, but free from all earthly grossness. The women as well as the men of this life will attain to this indescribable bliss: ix. 72; and objects of beauty, grace, and satisfaction, described symbolically, must apply to both.

4729. *Ḥūr* implies the following ideas: (1) purity; possibly the word *Ḥawwāriyūn*, as applied to the first Disciples of Jesus, is connected with this root; (2) beauty, especially of eyes, where the intense white of the eye-balls stands out against the intense black of the pupil, thus giving the appearance of lustre, and intense feeling, as opposed to dullness or want of expression; and (3) truth and good-will.

4730. The metaphorical signification is explained in n. 4671 to xliii. 73.

56. Nor will they there
Taste Death, except the first[4731]
Death ; and He will preserve
Them from the Penalty
Of the Blazing Fire,—[4732]

٥٦- لَا يَذُوقُونَ فِيهَا الْمَوْتَ إِلَّا الْمَوْتَةَ الْأُولَىٰ ۖ
وَوَقَاهُمْ عَذَابَ الْجَحِيمِ ۝

57. As a Bounty from thy Lord!
That will be
The supreme achievement![4733]

٥٧- فَضْلًا مِّن رَّبِّكَ ۚ
ذَٰلِكَ هُوَ الْفَوْزُ الْعَظِيمُ ۝

58. Verily, We have made
This (Qur-ān) easy,[4734]
In thy tongue,
In order that they
May give heed.

٥٨- فَإِنَّمَا يَسَّرْنَاهُ بِلِسَانِكَ
لَعَلَّهُمْ يَتَذَكَّرُونَ ۝

59. So wait thou and watch;
For they (too) are waiting.

٥٩- فَارْتَقِبْ إِنَّهُم مُّرْتَقِبُونَ ۝

4731. *First Death*: the ordinary natural death from this life, which brought them to the Garden of Felicity: there will be no further death after that. *Cf.* xxxvii. 59, and n. 4071.

4732. As in the Buddha's doctrine, the higher object of this our life is to obtain salvation from sorrow, pain, and the other incidents which make of it a constant struggle. In Islam we are taught that this is not possible by our unaided efforts. Certainly, striving on our part is an indispensable condition; but it is the Mercy of God which comes to our help and keeps us from the Fire of final Punishment. This is mentioned last as the foundation on which is built our eternal felicity and our positive spiritual joys.

4733. This is our idea of Salvation: the negative avoidance of all the consequences of evil, and the positive attainment of all—and more than all—that our hearts could possibly desire. For God's Bounty outstrips anything that our eyes have seen, or our ears have heard of, or our imagination can conceive.

4734. *Easy*: not only to understand, being in the Arabic tongue; but mellifluous, whose rhythm carries off our spirits to a higher spiritual plane. In another sense, it is difficult; for to get to its deepest meaning, we shall have to strive hard, as the contents of this Sūra alone will show.

INTRODUCTION TO SŪRA XLV (*Jāthiya*).

This is the sixth Sūra of the *Hā-Mīm* series : for their general theme and chronology, see the Introduction to S. xl.

Summary.—The title, "Bowing the knee", taken from verse 28, expresses the leading idea in the Sūra. In this life, in spite of the Signs of God, and the evidences of His goodness all around, men go about in Unfaith, and mocking at Faith ; but the End will bring them all to their knees.

C. 218.—The Signs of God are everywhere :
(xlv. 1-37.) His power, wisdom, and goodness are shown
Through all Creation and in Revelation.
How can man be so ungrateful
As to reject true Guidance, reaping thus
The fruits of Evil ? But men of Faith
Have patience and forgive their weaker
Brethren, and trust in the final justice
Of God. Form no sects, as was done
Aforetime, nor make your lusts your gods :
The Future is sure, and in the hands
Of God, to Whom all will bend the knee,
When Truth will shine in all its glory.
So praise and glory to God, the Lord
And Cherisher of all the worlds !

Sūra XLV.

Jathiya, or Bowing the Knee.

In the name of God, Most Gracious, Most Merciful.

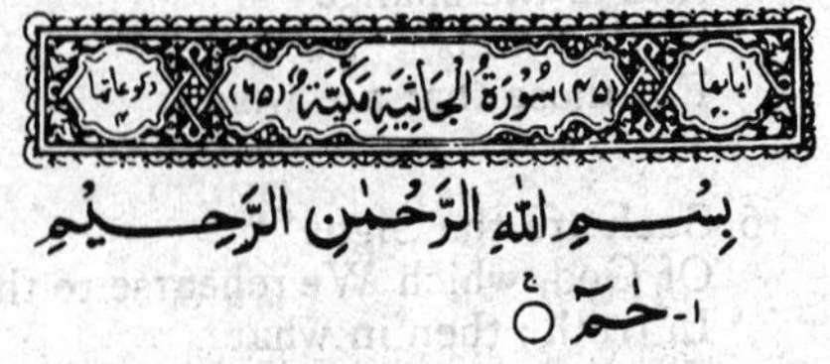

بِسْمِ اللّٰهِ الرَّحْمٰنِ الرَّحِيْمِ

1. *Ḥā-Mīm.*[4735]

١- حٰمٓ ۝

2. The revelation[4736]
Of the Book
Is from God
The Exalted in Power,
Full of Wisdom.

٢- تَنْزِيْلُ الْكِتٰبِ مِنَ اللّٰهِ الْعَزِيْزِ الْحَكِيْمِ ۝

3. Verily in the heavens[4737]
And the earth, are Signs
For those who believe.

٣- اِنَّ فِي السَّمٰوٰتِ وَالْاَرْضِ لَاٰيٰتٍ لِّلْمُؤْمِنِيْنَ ۝

4. And in the creation[4738]
Of yourselves and the fact
That animals are scattered
(Through the earth), are Signs
For those of assured Faith.

٤- وَفِيْ خَلْقِكُمْ وَمَا يَبُثُّ مِنْ دَآبَّةٍ اٰيٰتٌ لِّقَوْمٍ يُّوْقِنُوْنَ ۝

5. And in the alternation[4739]
Of Night and Day,
And the fact that God
Sends down Sustenance[4740] from
The sky, and revives therewith
The earth after its death,

٥- وَاخْتِلَافِ الَّيْلِ وَالنَّهَارِ وَمَآ اَنْزَلَ اللّٰهُ مِنَ السَّمَآءِ مِنْ رِّزْقٍ فَاَحْيَا بِهِ الْاَرْضَ بَعْدَ مَوْتِهَا

4735. See Introduction to S. xl. paragraphs 2-4.

4736. This verse is the same as xl. 2, except that "wisdom" is here substituted in the last line for "knowledge". This is appropriate, as in this Sūra we are dealing with the folly of those who reject God and His Signs, while S. xl. dealt with the individual soul's witness to Faith and Virtue.

4737. Verses 3-5 deal with some of the points in the noble argument in ii. 164, but again there are differences on account of the different context. Note that here the argument is divided into three parts, one in each verse. (1) In verse 3 we are dealing with big Signs external to ourselves, some of which are far beyond our personal experiences: for them we require Faith: they are Signs "for those who believe." For the other two see the next two notes.

4738. (2) These Signs are in our own nature and in the animals we meet with every day: here we have certainty within human limits: these are "for those of assured Faith."

4739. (3) These are our daily experiences from external things, but they affect us and our lives intimately: here are questions of deductions "for those that are wise."

4740. "Sustenance" is almost equivalent here to "rain". And "rain" itself, and its revival of a dead earth, refer symbolically to Revelation and its putting new life into a dead soul. Similarly the alternation of Night and Day, and the change of the winds, besides being Signs as wonderful phenomena of Nature, refer to spiritual ignorance and knowledge, rest and activity, and the constant beneficent changes that are going on in the world, making for the spread of the blessing of God's Revelation.

And in the change
Of the winds,—are Signs
For those that are wise.

وَتَصْرِيفِ الرِّيٰحِ اٰيٰتٌ
لِّقَوْمٍ يَّعْقِلُوْنَ ○

6. Such are the Signs[4741]
Of God, which We rehearse to thee
In truth: then in what
Exposition will they believe
After (rejecting) God
And His Signs?

٦- تِلْكَ اٰيٰتُ اللّٰهِ نَتْلُوْهَا عَلَيْكَ بِالْحَقِّ ۚ
فَبِاَيِّ حَدِيْثٍۢ بَعْدَ اللّٰهِ
وَاٰيٰتِهٖ يُؤْمِنُوْنَ ○

7. Woe to each sinful
Dealer in Falsehoods:[4742]

٧- وَيْلٌ لِّكُلِّ اَفَّاكٍ اَثِيْمٍ ○

8. He hears the Signs
Of God rehearsed to him,
Yet is obstinate and lofty,
As if he had not
Heard them: then announce
To him a Penalty Grievous!

٨- يَّسْمَعُ اٰيٰتِ اللّٰهِ تُتْلٰى عَلَيْهِ
ثُمَّ يُصِرُّ مُسْتَكْبِرًا كَاَنْ لَّمْ يَسْمَعْهَا ۚ
فَبَشِّرْهُ بِعَذَابٍ اَلِيْمٍ ○

9. And when he learns
Something of Our Signs,
He takes them in jest:
For such there will be
A humiliating Penalty.[4743]

٩- وَاِذَا عَلِمَ مِنْ اٰيٰتِنَا شَيْـًٔا
اتَّخَذَهَا هُزُوًا ؕ
اُولٰٓئِكَ لَهُمْ عَذَابٌ مُّهِيْنٌ ○

10. In front of them is
Hell: and of no profit
To them is anything
They may have earned,
Nor any protectors they
May have taken to themselves
Besides God: for them
Is a tremendous Penalty.[4744]

١٠- مِنْ وَّرَآئِهِمْ جَهَنَّمُ ۚ
وَلَا يُغْنِيْ عَنْهُمْ مَّا كَسَبُوْا شَيْـًٔا
وَّلَا مَا اتَّخَذُوْا مِنْ دُوْنِ اللّٰهِ اَوْلِيَآءَ ۚ
وَلَهُمْ عَذَابٌ عَظِيْمٌ ؕ ○

4741. If there are any to whom the Signs from Nature, from within their own heart and conscience, and from the voice of Revelation, are not enough to convince them, what possible kind of exposition will they accept?

4742. A soul so dead, as described in the last note, is indeed wretched. It will resort to falsehoods, in worship, in conduct, and in its attitude towards God. It will be obstinate, and pretend to be 'above such things'. It will hear the most beautiful Message but not profit by it. The loss or punishment is its own, and grievous it is!

4743. Note that in each of the verses 8-11 the Penalty is characterised by a certain description, which accords with the crime. (1) In verse 8, the man is arrogant about the Signs of God's love and care all around him, and his Penalty is "grievous". (2) In verse 9, he ridicules God's Signs, and his Penalty is "humiliating": he makes himself a ridiculous fool. (3) and (4) are described in the two following notes.

4744. (3) In verse 10 the sinner has piled up the good things of this life, and thinks he has got plenty of helpers and protectors, but all these things are of no use. On the contrary, his Penalty will be "tremendous", to correspond with the great pains which he has taken to multiply the gods of his worship.

11. This is (true) Guidance:
And for those who reject
The Signs of their Lord,
Is a grievous Penalty
Of abomination.[4745]

١١- هٰذَا هُدًى ۚ
وَالَّذِينَ كَفَرُوا بِآيَاتِ رَبِّهِمْ
لَهُمْ عَذَابٌ مِنْ رِجْزٍ أَلِيمٌ ۝

SECTION 2.

12. It is God Who has
Subjected the sea to you,[4746]
That ships may sail
Through it by His command,
That ye may seek
Of His Bounty, and that
Ye may be grateful.

١٢- اللَّهُ الَّذِي سَخَّرَ لَكُمُ الْبَحْرَ
لِتَجْرِيَ الْفُلْكُ فِيهِ بِأَمْرِهِ
وَلِتَبْتَغُوا مِنْ فَضْلِهِ
وَلَعَلَّكُمْ تَشْكُرُونَ ۝

13. And He has subjected
To you, as from Him,
All that is in the heavens[4747]
And on earth: behold,
In that are Signs indeed
For those who reflect.

١٣- وَسَخَّرَ لَكُمْ
مَا فِي السَّمَاوَاتِ وَمَا فِي الْأَرْضِ جَمِيعًا مِنْهُ ۚ
إِنَّ فِي ذَٰلِكَ لَآيَاتٍ لِقَوْمٍ يَتَفَكَّرُونَ ۝

14. Tell those who believe,
To forgive those who
Do not look forward
To the Days of God:[4748]

١٤- قُلْ لِلَّذِينَ آمَنُوا يَغْفِرُوا لِلَّذِينَ
لَا يَرْجُونَ أَيَّامَ اللَّهِ

4745. (4) In verse 11, he has flouted and rejected the specific guidance that came to him from the Word of God, or from the admonition of a man of God. His Penalty is a penalty of abomination: he earns unspeakable horror and abomination from all the Righteous, and is an unclean object in the Kingdom of Heaven.

4746. *Cf.* xvi. 14 and notes thereon, especially n. 2037. The one encircling ocean of our globe is one of the most significant facts in our physical geography. Its salt water is an agent of global sanitation. The salubrious effects of sea-air, with its ozone, are well known to everyone who has recouped his health by its means. Thanks to ships, the sea unites rather than divides: communications are, and have always been, more active between sea-coast towns than further inland. They thus further human intercourse, and help us to seek the "Bounty of God", not only in a commercial but in an intellectual and spiritual sense. All this is through "God's command" *i.e.* by His beneficent ordering of the universe, and we should be grateful.

4747. *Cf.* xxxi. 20, and n. 3605. The sea was only one example of God's cherishing care in making all things in nature available for the use of man, through the genius and faculties which He has given to man. Man should never forget that it is all "as from Him", *i.e.* from God. For is not man God's vicegerent on earth (ii. 30)?

4748. *Cf.* vii. 54, n. 1031. The "*Days of God*" I interpret to mean not periods of twenty-four hours, but the stages through which God's Purpose works in us, in bringing home to us a sense of sin and a sense of God's Mercy. We must be patient with those who have not yet acquired that sense. "Days of God" may also mean the Days of the Kingdom of God, when evil will be destroyed and God's authority will reign unquestioned.

It is for Him to recompense[4749]
(For good or ill) each People[4750]
According to what
They have earned.

لِيَجْزِيَ قَوْمًا
بِمَا كَانُوا يَكْسِبُونَ ○

15. If any one does[4751]
A righteous deed,
It enures to the benefit
Of his own soul;
If he does evil,
It works against
(His own soul).
In the end will ye
(All) be brought back
To your Lord.

١٥- مَنْ عَمِلَ صَالِحًا
فَلِنَفْسِهِ ۚ
وَمَنْ أَسَاءَ
فَعَلَيْهَا ۖ
ثُمَّ إِلَىٰ رَبِّكُمْ تُرْجَعُونَ ○

16. We did aforetime
Grant to the Children[4752]
Of Israel the Book,
The Power of Command,
And Prophethood; We gave
Them, for Sustenance, things[4753]
Good and pure; and We
Favoured them above the nations.

١٦- وَلَقَدْ آتَيْنَا بَنِي إِسْرَاءِيلَ الْكِتَابَ
وَالْحُكْمَ وَالنُّبُوَّةَ
وَرَزَقْنَاهُمْ مِنَ الطَّيِّبَاتِ
وَفَضَّلْنَاهُمْ عَلَى الْعَالَمِينَ ○

17. And We granted them
Clear Signs in affairs

١٧- وَآتَيْنَاهُمْ بَيِّنَاتٍ مِنَ الْأَمْرِ ۖ

4749. It is not for private persons to take vengeance even for the cause of right and justice. God will give due recompense for good or evil according to His own full Knowledge and righteous Plan, and in His own good time. Nor is it permissible even to a group of persons to arrogate to themselves the championship of the right. There are always apt to be private motives of hatred or enmity or mixed motives of that kind. These are, and must necessarily be absent in the case of a Jihād under a *righteous Imām*; for, by the very definition of the term, a righteous Imām is swayed by no feelings of a private nature and is guided by nothing but divine Light. It is private *vengeance* that is forbidden, not help, or striving, wherever possible, against evil.

4750. "People" here may be taken to be a group of common characteristics, *e.g.* the righteous in contrast with the unrighteous, the oppressed in contrast with the oppressors, and so on.

4751. Ordinarily good and evil come to their own even in this world; but in any case there is the final Judgment before God.

4752. The argument here is similar to that in xliv. 32-33, but it is more particularised here. Israel had the Revelation given through Moses, the power of judgment and command through the Kingdom of David and Solomon, and numerous prophetic warnings through such men as Isaiah and Jeremiah.

4753. "Sustenance", here as elsewhere, is to be understood both in a physical and metaphorical sense. The Mosaic Law laid down rules of diet, excluding things unclean, and it laid down rules for a pure and honourable life. In this way Israel became the standard-bearer of God's law, thus "favoured above the nations".

(Of Religion): it was only [4754]
After knowledge had been
Granted to them that they
Fell into schisms, through
Insolent envy [4755] among themselves.
Verily thy Lord will judge
Between them on the Day
Of Judgment as to those
Matters in which they
Set up differences.

فَمَا اخْتَلَفُوٓا اِلَّا مِنۢ بَعْدِ
مَا جَآءَهُمُ الْعِلْمُ
بَغْيًا بَيْنَهُمْ
اِنَّ رَبَّكَ يَقْضِىْ بَيْنَهُمْ يَوْمَ الْقِيٰمَةِ
فِيْمَا كَانُوْا فِيْهِ يَخْتَلِفُوْنَ ○

18. Then we put thee
On the (right) Way [4756]
Of Religion: so follow
Thou that (Way),
And follow not the desires
Of those who know not.

١٨- ثُمَّ جَعَلْنٰكَ عَلٰى شَرِيْعَةٍ مِّنَ الْاَمْرِ
فَاتَّبِعْهَا
وَلَا تَتَّبِعْ اَهْوَآءَ الَّذِيْنَ لَا يَعْلَمُوْنَ ○

19. They will be of no
Use to thee in the sight [4757]
Of God: it is only
Wrong-doers (that stand as)
Protectors, one to another:
But God is the Protector
Of the Righteous.

١٩- اِنَّهُمْ لَنْ يُّغْنُوْا عَنْكَ مِنَ اللّٰهِ شَيْـًٔا
وَاِنَّ الظّٰلِمِيْنَ بَعْضُهُمْ اَوْلِيَآءُ بَعْضٍ
وَاللّٰهُ وَلِيُّ الْمُتَّقِيْنَ ○

20. These are clear evidences [4758]
To men, and a Guidance
And Mercy to those
Of assured Faith.

٢٠- هٰذَا بَصَآئِرُ لِلنَّاسِ وَهُدًى
وَّرَحْمَةٌ لِّقَوْمٍ يُّوْقِنُوْنَ ○

4754. *Cf.* x. 93. The Jews were the more to blame that they fell from Grace after all the divine favours which they had enjoyed. Their schisms and differences arose from mutual envy, which was rebellious insolence against God. As the next verse shows, some of them (not all) rejected the mission of the holy Prophet, also through envy that a Prophet had come among the Arabians.

4755. *Cf.* ii. 90, and that whole passage, with its notes.

4756 *Sharī'at* is best translated the "right Way of Religion", which is wider than the mere formal rites and legal provisions, which mostly came in the Medina period, long after this Meccan verse had been revealed.

4757. That is, in thy service of God. Ignorant and contentious men are of no use or service to any Cause. The more you seek their help, the more do their ignorance and their contentiousness increase their own importance in their own eyes. Evil protects (or thinks it protects) evil: it has really no power of protection at all, for itself or for others. The righteous seek the protection of God, Who can and will protect them.

4758. The evidences of God's Signs should be clear to all men: to men of Faith, who accept God's Grace, they are a Guide and a Mercy.

21. What ! do those who
Seek after evil ways
Think that We shall
Hold them equal with [4759]
Those who believe and
Do righteous deeds,—that
Equal will be their
Life and their death ?
Ill is the judgment
That they make.

٢١- اَمْ حَسِبَ الَّذِيْنَ اجْتَرَحُوا السَّيِّاٰتِ
اَنْ نَّجْعَلَهُمْ
كَالَّذِيْنَ اٰمَنُوْا وَعَمِلُوا الصّٰلِحٰتِ ۙ سَوَآءً
مَّحْيَاهُمْ وَمَمَاتُهُمْ ط
سَآءَ مَا يَحْكُمُوْنَ ۝ ع

SECTION 3.

22. God created the heavens [4760]
And the earth for
Just ends, and in order
That each soul may find
The recompense of what
It has earned, and none
Of them be wronged.

٢٢- وَخَلَقَ اللّٰهُ السَّمٰوٰتِ وَالْاَرْضَ بِالْحَقِّ
وَلِتُجْزٰى كُلُّ نَفْسٍۢ
بِمَا كَسَبَتْ وَهُمْ لَا يُظْلَمُوْنَ ۝

23. Then seest thou such [4761]
A one as takes
As his god his own
Vain desire ? God has,
Knowing (him as such),
Left him astray, and sealed [4762]
His hearing and his heart
(And understanding), and put

٢٣- اَفَرَءَيْتَ مَنِ اتَّخَذَ اِلٰهَهٗ هَوٰىهُ
وَاَضَلَّهُ اللّٰهُ
عَلٰى عِلْمٍ وَّخَتَمَ عَلٰى سَمْعِهٖ وَقَلْبِهٖ

4759. Three meanings can be deduced. (1) The evil ones are not in God's sight like the righteous ones ; neither in life nor in death are they equal ; in life the righteous are guided by God and receive His Grace, and after death His Mercy, while the others reject His Grace, and after death receive condemnation. (2) Neither are the two the same in this life and in the after-life : if the wicked flourish here, they will be condemned in the Hereafter ; if the good are in suffering or sorrow here, they will receive comfort and consolation in the Hereafter. (3) The real life of the righteous—for they have received spiritual life—is not like the nominal life of the wicked, which is really death ; nor is the physical death of the righteous, which will bring them into eternal life, like the terrible death of the wicked, which will bring them to eternal misery.

4760. *Cf.* xliv. 38-39, and n. 4717. The government of the world is so ordered that each soul gets every chance for its full development, and it reaps the fruit of all its activities. If it breaks away from God's Grace, it suffers, but no injustice is done to anyone : on the contrary God's Bounty is always beyond man's deserts.

4761. If a man follows, not the laws of God, which are also the laws of his own pure nature as made by God, but the desires of his own distorted self, as shaped by the rebellion of his will, the inevitable consequence will be the withdrawal of God's grace and guidance. All his faculties will then be debased, and there will be nothing to guide him, unless he turns in repentance again to God.

4762. *Cf.* ii. 7 and notes.

A cover on his sight.
Who, then, will guide him
After God (has withdrawn
Guidance)? Will ye not
Then receive admonition?

وَجَعَلَ عَلٰى بَصَرِهٖ غِشٰوَةً
فَمَنْ يَّهْدِيْهِ مِنْۢ بَعْدِ اللّٰهِ
اَفَلَا تَذَكَّرُوْنَ ○

24. And they say: "What is
There but our life
In this world?
We shall die and we live,[4763]
And nothing but Time
Can destroy us." But
Of that they have no
Knowledge: they merely
conjecture:

٢٤- وَقَالُوْا مَا هِيَ اِلَّا حَيَاتُنَا الدُّنْيَا
نَمُوْتُ وَنَحْيَا وَمَا يُهْلِكُنَآ اِلَّا الدَّهْرُ
وَمَا لَهُمْ بِذٰلِكَ مِنْ عِلْمٍ
اِنْ هُمْ اِلَّا يَظُنُّوْنَ ○

25. And when Our Clear
Signs are rehearsed to them,
Their argument is nothing
But this: they say, "Bring[4764]
(Back) our forefathers, if
What ye say is true!"

٢٥- وَاِذَا تُتْلٰى عَلَيْهِمْ اٰيٰتُنَا بَيِّنٰتٍ
مَّا كَانَ حُجَّتَهُمْ اِلَّآ اَنْ قَالُوا
ائْتُوْا بِاٰبَآئِنَآ اِنْ كُنْتُمْ صٰدِقِيْنَ ○

26. Say: "It is God Who
Gives you life, then
Gives you death; then
He will gather you together
For the Day of Judgment
About which there is
No doubt": but most
Men do not understand.

٢٦- قُلِ اللّٰهُ يُحْيِيْكُمْ
ثُمَّ يُمِيْتُكُمْ ثُمَّ يَجْمَعُكُمْ اِلٰى يَوْمِ الْقِيٰمَةِ
لَا رَيْبَ فِيْهِ
وَلٰكِنَّ اَكْثَرَ النَّاسِ لَا يَعْلَمُوْنَ ○

SECTION 4.

27. To God belongs
The dominion of the heavens
And the earth, and
The Day that the Hour

٢٧- وَلِلّٰهِ مُلْكُ السَّمٰوٰتِ وَالْاَرْضِ
وَيَوْمَ تَقُوْمُ السَّاعَةُ

4763. *Cf.* xxiii. 37, and n. 2896. The additional touch here, "And nothing but Time can destroy us", suggests the materialist philosophy that Matter and Time are eternal backwards and forwards; and possibly also that though each individual perishes, the race lasts till Time destroys it. This is not knowledge but conjecture. Why not accept light from Him Who knows all?

4764. *Cf.* xliv. 36. It is no argument to say, "If there is a future life, bring back our forefathers and let us see them here and now!" It is not for a man to raise the dead when and where he pleases. It is for God to command. And His promise is about the general Resurrection for the Day of Judgment. In His hands are the keys of life and death.

Of Judgment is established,—
That Day will the dealers[4765]
In Falsehood perish!

يَوْمَئِذٍ يَّخْسَرُ الْمُبْطِلُوْنَ ○

28. And thou wilt see
Every sect bowing the knee:[4766]
Every sect will be called
To its Record: "This Day
Shall ye be recompensed
For all that ye did!

٢٨- وَتَرٰى كُلَّ اُمَّةٍ جَاثِيَةً
كُلُّ اُمَّةٍ تُدْعٰٓى اِلٰى كِتٰبِهَا
اَلْيَوْمَ تُجْزَوْنَ مَا كُنْتُمْ تَعْمَلُوْنَ ○

29. "This Our Record speaks
About you with truth:
For We were wont[4767]
To put on record
All that ye did."

٢٩- هٰذَا كِتٰبُنَا يَنْطِقُ عَلَيْكُمْ بِالْحَقِّ
اِنَّا كُنَّا نَسْتَنْسِخُ مَا كُنْتُمْ تَعْمَلُوْنَ ○

30. Then, as to those who
Believed and did righteous
Deeds, their Lord will
Admit them to His Mercy:
That will be the Achievement[4768]
For all to see.

٣٠- فَاَمَّا الَّذِيْنَ اٰمَنُوْا وَعَمِلُوا الصّٰلِحٰتِ
فَيُدْخِلُهُمْ رَبُّهُمْ فِيْ رَحْمَتِهٖ
ذٰلِكَ هُوَ الْفَوْزُ الْمُبِيْنُ ○

31. But as to those who
Rejected God, (to them
Will be said): "Were not
Our Signs rehearsed to you?
But ye were arrogant,
And were a people
Given to sin!

٣١- وَاَمَّا الَّذِيْنَ كَفَرُوْا
اَفَلَمْ تَكُنْ اٰيٰتِيْ تُتْلٰى عَلَيْكُمْ
فَاسْتَكْبَرْتُمْ
وَكُنْتُمْ قَوْمًا مُّجْرِمِيْنَ ○

4765. These vain wranglers about the future life and deniers of the Truth may have a run in this fleeting world; but the moment the world of Reality is established, they will see what they now deny. The facts will destroy their fancies, and they themselves will find themselves humiliated and lost, for having deliberately ignored God's Signs and acted in opposition to His holy Will.

4766. *Bowing the knee*: the key-phrase of the Sūra, and its title. *Cf.* xix. 72. Whatever the arrogance of the wicked may be in this life, whatever exclusive sects and divisions they may form, in this life, the time will come when they will humbly submit and bow the knee to the Truth. Before the Judgment-seat, when their Record is produced, they must necessarily be dumb.

4767. *Cf.* xliii. 80. Nothing misses the Recording Angel, and whatever is said in the Record is true.

4768. The attainment and satisfaction of all hopes and desires; the reaching of the final goal of Bliss. *Cf.* xliv. 57, and n. 4733.

32. "And when it was said
That the promise of God
Was true, and that the Hour—
There was no doubt
About its (coming), ye
Used to say, 'We
Know not what is[4769]
The Hour: we only think
It is an idea, and we
Have no firm assurance.'"

٣٢- وَإِذَا قِيلَ إِنَّ وَعْدَ اللَّهِ حَقٌّ
وَالسَّاعَةُ لَا رَيْبَ فِيهَا
قُلْتُم مَّا نَدْرِي مَا السَّاعَةُ
إِن نَّظُنُّ إِلَّا ظَنًّا
وَمَا نَحْنُ بِمُسْتَيْقِنِينَ ○

33. Then will appear to them
The evil (fruits) of what
They did, and they will be[4770]
Completely encircled by that
Which they used to mock at!

٣٣- وَبَدَا لَهُمْ سَيِّئَاتُ مَا
عَمِلُوا وَحَاقَ بِهِم
مَّا كَانُوا بِهِ يَسْتَهْزِءُونَ ○

34. It will also be said:
"This Day We will forget[4771]
You as ye forgot
The meeting of this Day
Of yours! And your
Abode is the Fire, and
No helpers have ye!

٣٤- وَقِيلَ الْيَوْمَ نَنسَاكُمْ
كَمَا نَسِيتُمْ لِقَاءَ يَوْمِكُمْ هَٰذَا
وَمَأْوَاكُمُ النَّارُ
وَمَا لَكُم مِّن نَّاصِرِينَ ○

35. "This, because ye used
To take the Signs of God
In jest, and the life
Of the world deceived you:"[4772]
(From) that Day, therefore,
They shall not be taken out
Thence, nor shall they be
Received into Grace.

٣٥- ذَٰلِكُم بِأَنَّكُمُ اتَّخَذْتُمْ آيَاتِ اللَّهِ
هُزُوًا وَغَرَّتْكُمُ الْحَيَاةُ الدُّنْيَا
فَالْيَوْمَ لَا يُخْرَجُونَ مِنْهَا
وَلَا هُمْ يُسْتَعْتَبُونَ ○

4769. There is arrogance as well as untruth in this pretence. The coming of Judgment has been proclaimed times out of number by every man of God. They cannot dismiss it as a mere idea or superstition. Their object is merely an ostentatious and lofty rejection of Faith.

4770. *Cf.* xi 8. Their mockery will be turned against themselves, for they will be hemmed in by the very Realities which they had ignored or doubted or laughed at.

4771. *Cf.* vii. 51 and n. 1029. "Forget" is of course metaphorical for "deliberately to ignore"

4772. It is implied that 'you deliberately allowed yourselves to be deceived by the vanities of this world', or 'that you put yourselves into a position where you were deceived, for you were expressly warned against Evil'.

36. Then Praise be to God,[4773]
Lord of the heavens
And Lord of the earth,—
Lord and Cherisher
Of all the worlds!

37. To Him be Glory
Throughout the heavens
And the earth: and He
25 Is Exalted in Power,
30 Full of Wisdom!

٣٦- فَلِلّٰهِ الْحَمْدُ رَبِّ السَّمٰوٰتِ
وَرَبِّ الْاَرْضِ
رَبِّ الْعٰلَمِيْنَ ۝

٣٧- وَلَهُ الْكِبْرِيَآءُ فِي السَّمٰوٰتِ وَالْاَرْضِ
وَهُوَ الْعَزِيْزُ الْحَكِيْمُ ۝ ع

4773. The argument having been completed about the fruits of this life being reaped in the *Ma'ād*, or the Hereafter, when perfect balance will be restored and perfect Justice will reign supreme, the Sūra closes with praise and glory to God, Who is not only Omnipotent but is full of Wisdom, and cherishes and cares for all His creation. We began with the remembrance of His Revelation and Mercy, and we close with the celebration of His goodness, power, and wisdom. Note how the argument is rounded off by the reminiscence of the last clause of the second verse of this Sūra.

INTRODUCTION TO SŪRA XLVI (*Aḥqāf*).

This is the seventh and last Sūra of the *Ḥā-Mīm* series. For the general theme and chronological place of these Sūras see the Introduction to S. xl.

The *Aḥqāf* (mentioned in verse 21) are the long and winding crooked tracts of sand-hills, characteristic of the country of the 'Ād people, adjoining Ḥadhramaut and Yaman : see vii. 65, n. 1040. These people had, at that time, probably a fertile irrigated country, but their sins brought on the calamity mentioned in xlvi. 24-25. The lesson of this Sūra is that if the Truth is challenged, the challenge will be duly answered, and Truth vindicated.

Summary.—All Creation has a Purpose behind it : Truth and Revelation will be vindicated, and those who question it will be undone by the very means by which they set such store : the righteous should wait in patience and constancy (xlvi. 1-35, and C. 219).

C. 219.—Creation is for just ends, and Falsehood
(xlvi. 1-35.) Is but straying from the Path :
Say what people may
Truth carries its own vindication :
Follow it firmly. Let age think of youth,
And youth not turn rebellious. There are fine
Gradations in the kingdom of God : then strive
For the best. Let not pride and arrogance
Undo you : the humble are often the best
Recipients of Truth. All will come right
In good time : so persevere with patient firmness
Of purpose. Justice that seems to tarry
Comes really on swiftest foot but sure.

Sūra XLVI.

Aḥqāf, or Winding Sand-tracts.

In the name of God, Most Gracious,
Most Merciful.

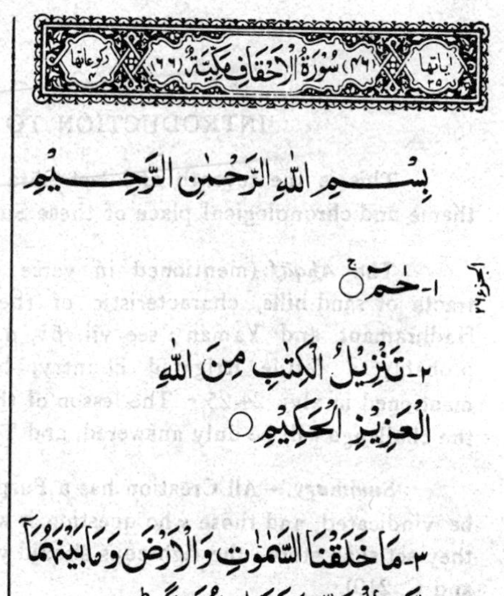

1. Ḥā-Mīm.[4774]

2. The revelation [4775]
Of the Book
Is from God
The Exalted in Power,
Full of Wisdom.

3. We created not [4776]
The heavens and the earth
And all between them
But for just ends, and
For a term appointed :
But those who reject Faith
Turn away from that
Whereof they are warned.

4. Say : "Do ye see [4777]
What it is ye invoke
Besides God ? Show me
What it is they
Have created on earth,
Or have they a share
In the heavens ?
Bring me a Book [4778]

١- حٰمٓ ○

٢- تَنْزِيْلُ الْكِتٰبِ مِنَ اللهِ
الْعَزِيْزِ الْحَكِيْمِ ○

٣- مَا خَلَقْنَا السَّمٰوٰتِ وَالْاَرْضَ وَمَا بَيْنَهُمَآ
اِلَّا بِالْحَقِّ وَاَجَلٍ مُّسَمًّى ط
وَالَّذِيْنَ كَفَرُوْا
عَمَّآ اُنْذِرُوْا مُعْرِضُوْنَ ○

٤- قُلْ اَرَءَيْتُمْ مَّا تَدْعُوْنَ مِنْ دُوْنِ
اللهِ اَرُوْنِيْ مَاذَا خَلَقُوْا مِنَ الْاَرْضِ
اَمْ لَهُمْ شِرْكٌ فِي السَّمٰوٰتِ ط
اِيْتُوْنِيْ بِكِتٰبٍ

4774. See Introduction to S. xl., paragraphs 2-4.

4775. This verse is the same as the second verse of the last Sūra, but the theme is worked out differently in the two Sūras. In S. xlv. was shown how deniers of Revelation will at last be humbled until they can no longer deny its truth and power. In this Sūra is shown how Truth and Revelation will be vindicated by patience and constancy (xlvi. 35).

4776. *Cf.* xlv. 22. Many things may appear to us in the present world as strange and inexplicable. But everything made by God has a just purpose which must be fulfilled. Nothing in this world is permanent : everything is for an appointed term. The Word of God alone abides. All else will pass away after it has fulfilled its purpose. But Unbelievers refuse to face the danger of which they are warned.

4777. Some people may rush thoughtlessly into false worship, because it is the fashion or an ancestral custom, etc. They are asked to pause and see for themselves. Have the false gods or falsehood created anything ? (They destroy much.) Or have they any share or lot in the things we associate with the heavens,—spiritual well-being, etc. ?

4778. 'Or is there any warrant for you from any earlier revelation, assuming that you do not believe in this Revelation ? Or can you point to the least scrap or remnant of real knowledge on which you can base what we condemn as your false life ? No, you cannot.

(Revealed) before this,
Or any remnant of knowledge
(Ye may have), if ye
Are telling the truth!

مِّن قَبْلِ هَٰذَآ أَوْ أَثَٰرَةٍ مِّنْ عِلْمٍ
إِن كُنتُمْ صَٰدِقِينَ ۝

5. And who is more astray[4779]
Than one who invokes,
Besides God, such as will
Not answer him to the Day
Of Judgment, and who
(In fact) are unconscious
Of their call (to them)?

٥- وَمَنْ أَضَلُّ
مِمَّن يَدْعُوا مِن دُونِ اللَّهِ
مَن لَّا يَسْتَجِيبُ لَهُ إِلَىٰ يَوْمِ الْقِيَٰمَةِ
وَهُمْ عَن دُعَآئِهِمْ غَٰفِلُونَ ۝

6. And when mankind
Are gathered together
(At the Resurrection),
They will be hostile
To them and reject
Their worship (altogether)!

٦- وَإِذَا حُشِرَ النَّاسُ
كَانُوا لَهُمْ أَعْدَآءً
وَكَانُوا بِعِبَادَتِهِمْ كَٰفِرِينَ ۝

7. When Our Clear Signs
Are rehearsed to them,
The Unbelievers say,
Of the Truth
When it comes to them:[4780]
"This is evident sorcery!"

٧- وَإِذَا تُتْلَىٰ عَلَيْهِمْ ءَايَٰتُنَا بَيِّنَٰتٍ
قَالَ الَّذِينَ كَفَرُوا لِلْحَقِّ
لَمَّا جَآءَهُمْ هَٰذَا سِحْرٌ مُّبِينٌ ۝

8. Or do they say,
"He has forged it"?
Say: "Had I forged it,
Then can ye obtain[4781]
No single (blessing) for me
From God. He knows best
Of that whereof ye talk
(So glibly)! Enough is He

٨- أَمْ يَقُولُونَ افْتَرَىٰهُ
قُلْ إِنِ افْتَرَيْتُهُ فَلَا تَمْلِكُونَ لِي مِنَ
اللَّهِ شَيْـًٔا
هُوَ أَعْلَمُ بِمَا تُفِيضُونَ فِيهِ كَفَىٰ بِهِ

4779. As there is no argument at all in favour of your sham worship, what sense is there in it? Either your false gods are senseless stocks and stones which will never answer you to the end of Time, being themselves devoid of understanding, or they are real objects which will disown you at the last. If you worshipped Self, your own misused faculties will witness against you at the last (xli. 20-23). If you worshipped good men or prophets, like Jesus, they will disown you (v. 119). Similarly, if you worshipped angels, they will disown you (xxxiv. 40-41).

4780. When the truth is actually brought to their doors, they call it sorcery! *Cf.* xxxvii. 12-15, and n. 4042.

4781. 'If I forged a message from myself as one purporting to come from God, you would not be able to see me enjoy any of the blessings from God which I enjoy: you would not see me calm and relying on God, nor would you see me bear the reputation of being a trustworthy man. A liar comes to an evil end. But what about those who talk so glibly and freely about things which they know not? God knows all, and He is my witness! But even against your false accusations, I pray for His forgiveness and mercy to you, for He is Oft-Forgiving, Most Merciful!'

For a witness between me
And you! And He is
Oft-Forgiving, Most Merciful."

شَهِيدًا بَيْنِي وَبَيْنَكُمْ ۖ
وَهُوَ الْغَفُورُ الرَّحِيمُ ○

9. Say: "I am no bringer[4782]
Of new-fangled doctrine
Among the apostles, nor
Do I know what will
Be done with me or
With you. I follow
But that which is revealed
To me by inspiration;
I am but a Warner
Open and clear."

٩- قُلْ مَا كُنْتُ بِدْعًا
مِّنَ الرُّسُلِ
وَمَا أَدْرِي مَا يُفْعَلُ بِي وَلَا بِكُمْ ۖ
إِنْ أَتَّبِعُ إِلَّا مَا يُوحَىٰ إِلَيَّ
وَمَا أَنَا إِلَّا نَذِيرٌ مُّبِينٌ ○

10. Say: "See ye?[4783]
If (this teaching) be
From God, and ye reject it,
And a witness from among
The Children of Israel testifies
To its similarity[4784]
(With earlier scripture),
And has believed
While ye are arrogant,
(How unjust ye are!)
Truly, God guides not
A people unjust."

١٠- قُلْ أَرَءَيْتُمْ إِنْ كَانَ مِنْ عِنْدِ اللَّهِ
وَكَفَرْتُمْ بِهِ
وَشَهِدَ شَاهِدٌ مِّنْ
بَنِي إِسْرَاءِيلَ عَلَىٰ مِثْلِهِ
فَآمَنَ وَاسْتَكْبَرْتُمْ ۖ
ع إِنَّ اللَّهَ لَا يَهْدِي الْقَوْمَ الظَّالِمِينَ ○

SECTION 2.

11. The Unbelievers say
Of those who believe:

١١- وَقَالَ الَّذِينَ كَفَرُوا لِلَّذِينَ آمَنُوا

4782. 'What is there to forge? All prophets have taught the Unity of God and our duty to mankind. I bring no new-fangled doctrine, but eternal truths that have been known to good men through the ages. It is to reclaim you that I have come. I do not know what will be your fate for all this callousness, nor what you will do to me. But this I know, that I am preaching truth and righteousness as inspired by God. My duty is only to proclaim aloud and clearly the Message entrusted to me by God. The rest I leave to God.'

4783. Another side of the argument is now presented. 'You pagan Arabs! You are puffed up with pride, though you are an ignorant nation. Among Israel there are men who understand the previous scriptures, and who find in the Qur-ān and its Preacher a true confirmation of the previous scriptures. They accept Islam as a fulfilment of the revelation of Moses himself! (See Deut. xviii. 18-19). And yet you hold back, though the Qur-ān has come in your own language, in order to help you to understand. How unjust and how shameful! In that case, with what face can you seek guidance from God?'

4784. There were learned Jews (and Christians) who saw in the holy Prophet the Messenger of God foreshadowed in previous Revelations, and accepted Islam. As this is a Meccan Sūra we need not construe this as a reference to 'Abdullāh ibn Salām, whose conversion was in Medina only two years before the Prophet's death, unless we accept this particular verse to be so late in date. The sincere Jews were in a position to understand how this Revelation fitted in with all they had learnt about Revelation.

"If (this Message) were[4785]
A good thing, (such men)
Would not have gone
To it first, before us!"
And seeing that they
Guide not themselves thereby,
They will say, "This is
An (old,) old falsehood!"

لَوْ كَانَ خَيْرًا
مَّا سَبَقُونَآ إِلَيْهِ
وَإِذْ لَمْ يَهْتَدُوا بِهِ
فَسَيَقُولُونَ هَٰذَآ إِفْكٌ قَدِيمٌ ۝

12. And before this, was[4786]
The Book of Moses
As a guide and a mercy:
And this Book confirms (it)
In the Arabic tongue;
To admonish the unjust,
And as Glad Tidings
To those who do right.

١٢- وَمِن قَبْلِهِۦ كِتَٰبُ مُوسَىٰٓ إِمَامًا وَرَحْمَةً
وَهَٰذَا كِتَٰبٌ مُّصَدِّقٌ لِّسَانًا عَرَبِيًّا
لِّيُنذِرَ ٱلَّذِينَ ظَلَمُوا
وَبُشْرَىٰ لِلْمُحْسِنِينَ ۝

13. Verily those who say,[4787]
"Our Lord is God,"
And remain firm
(On that Path),—
On them shall be no fear,[4788]
Nor shall they grieve.

١٣- إِنَّ ٱلَّذِينَ قَالُوا رَبُّنَا ٱللَّهُ
ثُمَّ ٱسْتَقَٰمُوا
فَلَا خَوْفٌ عَلَيْهِمْ وَلَا هُمْ يَحْزَنُونَ ۝

14. Such shall be Companions
Of the Garden, dwelling
Therein (for aye): a recompense
For their (good) deeds.

١٤- أُولَٰٓئِكَ أَصْحَٰبُ ٱلْجَنَّةِ خَٰلِدِينَ فِيهَا
جَزَآءًۢ بِمَا كَانُوا يَعْمَلُونَ ۝

4785. A great many of the early Muslims were in humble positions, and were despised by the Quraish leaders. 'If such men could see any good in Islam,' they said, 'there could be no good in it: if there had been any good in it, we should have been the first to see it!' The spiritually blind have such a good conceit of themselves! As they reject it, and as the Revelation is proved to have historic foundations, they can only call it "an old, old falsehood"!

4786. The last revealed Book which was a Code of Life (*Sharī'at*) was the Book of Moses: for that of Jesus was not such a Code, but merely moral precepts to sweep away the corruptions that had crept in. The Qur-ān has the same attitude to it as the teaching of Jesus had to the Law. Jesus said (Matt. v. 17): "Think not that I am come to destroy the Law or the prophets: I am not come to destroy, but to fulfil." But the corruptions took new forms in Christian Churches: an entirely new *Sharī'at* became necessary, and this was provided in Islam.

4787. To say, "Our Lord is God" is to acknowledge that we owe no service to any creature, and shall render none: God shall have our exclusive devotion. "To remain firm on that Path" is shown by our conduct: we prove that we love God and all His creatures, and will unflinchingly do our duty in all circumstances.

4788. *Cf.* ii. 38. The phrase occurs in numerous other places, with a new application on each occasion. Here, if our claim is true that 'our Lord is God', what fear can possibly come on us, or what calamity can there be to cause us grief? For our Lord is our Cherisher, Defender, and Helper, our Hope and our Comfort, which can never fail.

15. We have enjoined on man[4789]
Kindness to his parents:
In pain did his mother
Bear him, and in pain
Did she give him birth.
The carrying of the (child)
To his weaning is
(A period of) thirty months.[4790]
At length, when he reaches
The age of full strength[4791]
And attains forty years,
He says, "O my Lord!
Grant me that I may be
Grateful for Thy favour
Which Thou hast bestowed
Upon me, and upon both
My parents, and that I
May work righteousness
Such as Thou mayest approve;
And be gracious to me
In my issue. Truly
Have I turned to Thee
And truly do I bow
(To Thee) in Islām."

١٥- وَوَصَّيْنَا الْإِنْسَانَ بِوَالِدَيْهِ إِحْسَانًا ۖ
حَمَلَتْهُ أُمُّهُ كُرْهًا وَوَضَعَتْهُ كُرْهًا ۖ
وَحَمْلُهُ وَفِصَالُهُ ثَلَاثُونَ شَهْرًا ۚ
حَتَّىٰ إِذَا بَلَغَ أَشُدَّهُ
وَبَلَغَ أَرْبَعِينَ سَنَةً ۙ
قَالَ رَبِّ أَوْزِعْنِي
أَنْ أَشْكُرَ نِعْمَتَكَ الَّتِي
أَنْعَمْتَ عَلَيَّ وَعَلَىٰ وَالِدَيَّ
وَأَنْ أَعْمَلَ صَالِحًا تَرْضَاهُ
وَأَصْلِحْ لِي فِي ذُرِّيَّتِي ۖ
إِنِّي تُبْتُ إِلَيْكَ
وَإِنِّي مِنَ الْمُسْلِمِينَ ○

16. Such are they from whom
We shall accept the best[4792]
Of their deeds and pass by
Their ill deeds: (they shall

١٦- أُولَٰئِكَ الَّذِينَ نَتَقَبَّلُ عَنْهُمْ أَحْسَنَ
مَا عَمِلُوا وَنَتَجَاوَزُ عَنْ سَيِّئَاتِهِمْ

4789. *Cf.* xxix. 8 and xxxi. 14.

4790. In xxxi 14 the time of weaning was stated to be at the age of two years, *i.e.*, 24 months. See also ii. 233. That leaves six months as the *minimum* period of human gestation after which the child is known to be viable. This is in accordance with the latest ascertained scientific facts. The *average* period is 280 days, or ten times the inter-menstrual period, and of course the average period of weaning is much less than 24 months.

The maximum period of breast-feeding (2 years) is again in accordance with the time that the first dentition is ordinarily completed in a human child. The lower milk incisors in the centre come out between the 6th and 9th month; then come out the milk teeth at intervals, until the canines appear. The second molars come out at about 24 months, and with them the child has a complete apparatus of milk teeth. Nature now expects him to chew and masticate and be independent of his mother's milk completely. On the other hand it hurts the mother to feed from the breast after the child has a complete set of milk teeth. The permanent teeth begin at the sixth year, and the second molars come at 12 years. The third molars are the wisdom teeth, which may appear at 18 to 20 years, or not at all.

4791. The age of full strength (*as͟hudd*) is held to be between 18 and 30 or 32. Between 30 and 40 the man is in his best manhood. After that he begins to look to his growing issue, and rightly commends the new generation to God. Perhaps his spiritual faculties also gain the upper hand after 40.

4792. *Cf.* xxix. 7 and n. 3429.

Be) among the Companions
Of the Garden : a promise]
Of truth, which was
Made to them
(In this life).

فِیۡۤ اَصۡحٰبِ الۡجَنَّۃِ ؕ
وَعۡدَ الصِّدۡقِ الَّذِیۡ
کَانُوۡا یُوۡعَدُوۡنَ ○

17. But (there is one)[4793]
Who says to his parents,
"Fie on you! Do ye
Hold out the promise
To me that I
Shall be raised up,
Even though generations
Have passed before me
(Without rising again)?"
And they two seek
God's aid, (and rebuke
The son): "Woe to thee!
Have Faith! For the promise
Of God is true."
But he says, "This is
Nothing but tales
Of the ancients!"

١٧- وَالَّذِیۡ قَالَ لِوَالِدَیۡہِ
اُفٍّ لَّکُمَاۤ اَتَعِدٰنِنِیۡۤ اَنۡ اُخۡرَجَ
وَقَدۡ خَلَتِ الۡقُرُوۡنُ مِنۡ قَبۡلِیۡ ۚ
وَہُمَا یَسۡتَغِیۡثٰنِ اللّٰہَ
وَیۡلَکَ اٰمِنۡ ٭ۖ
اِنَّ وَعۡدَ اللّٰہِ حَقٌّ ۚۖ
فَیَقُوۡلُ مَا ہٰذَاۤ
اِلَّاۤ اَسَاطِیۡرُ الۡاَوَّلِیۡنَ ○

18. Such are they against whom[4794]
Is proved the Sentence
Among the previous generations
Of Jinns and men, that have
Passed away; for they will
Be (utterly) lost.

١٨- اُولٰٓئِکَ الَّذِیۡنَ حَقَّ عَلَیۡہِمُ الۡقَوۡلُ
فِیۡۤ اُمَمٍ قَدۡ خَلَتۡ مِنۡ قَبۡلِہِمۡ مِّنَ الۡجِنِّ
وَالۡاِنۡسِ ؕ اِنَّہُمۡ کَانُوۡا خٰسِرِیۡنَ ○

19. And to all[4795]
Are (assigned) degrees

١٩- وَلِکُلٍّ دَرَجٰتٌ

4793. A godly man often has an ungodly son, who flouts all that the father held sacred, and looks upon his father himself as old-fashioned and unworthy of respect or regard. The contrast in an individual family may be matched by the contrast in the passing and the rising generations of mankind. All this happens as a passing phase in the normal evolution of mankind, and there is nothing in this to be despondent about. What we have to do is for the maturer generations to bring up their successors in godly ways, and for the younger generations to realise that age and experience count for something, especially in the understanding of spiritual matters and other matters of the highest moment to man.

4794. *Cf.* xli. 25 and n. 4494. Each individual, each generation, and each people is responsible for its own good deeds or misdeeds. The law of actions and their fruits applies: you cannot blame one for another. The only remedy lies in seeking for God's Grace and Mercy, not only for ourselves but for others in brotherly or fatherly love.

This verse is in balanced contrast to verse 16 above.

4795. There is fine grading in the spiritual Kingdom. Every deed, good or bad, is judged and weighed to the minutest degree, with its motives, intentions, results, and relevant circumstances. It is not a mere rough classification. The fruits of evil will be exactly according to the degree of evil. But, as stated in other passages (*e.g.*, xxviii. 84), the reward of good deeds will be far beyond their merits, on account of the Mercy and unbounded Bounty of God.

According to the deeds
Which they (have done),
And in order that (God)
May recompense their deeds,
And no injustice be done
To them.

مِّمَّا عَمِلُوا ۚ
وَلِيُوَفِّيَهُمْ أَعْمَالَهُمْ
وَهُمْ لَا يُظْلَمُونَ ۝

20. And on the Day that
The Unbelievers will be
Placed before the Fire,
(It will be said to them):
"Ye received your good things [4796]
In the life of the world,
And ye took your pleasure
Out of them: but to-day
Shall ye be recompensed [4797]
With a Penalty of humiliation:
For that ye were arrogant
On earth without just cause,
And that ye (ever) transgressed."

٢٠- وَيَوْمَ يُعْرَضُ الَّذِينَ كَفَرُوا عَلَى النَّارِ ۖ
أَذْهَبْتُمْ طَيِّبَاتِكُمْ فِي حَيَاتِكُمُ الدُّنْيَا
وَاسْتَمْتَعْتُمْ بِهَا ۚ
فَالْيَوْمَ تُجْزَوْنَ عَذَابَ الْهُونِ
بِمَا كُنْتُمْ تَسْتَكْبِرُونَ فِي الْأَرْضِ بِغَيْرِ
الْحَقِّ
وَبِمَا كُنْتُمْ تَفْسُقُونَ ۝ ع

SECTION 3.

21. Mention (Hūd)
One of 'Ād's (own) brethren: [4798]
Behold, he warned his people
About the winding Sand-tracts: [4799]
But there have been Warners
Before him and after him:
"Worship ye none other
Than God: truly I fear
For you the Penalty
Of a Mighty Day."

٢١- وَاذْكُرْ أَخَا عَادٍ ۖ
إِذْ أَنْذَرَ قَوْمَهُ بِالْأَحْقَافِ
وَقَدْ خَلَتِ النُّذُرُ مِنْ بَيْنِ يَدَيْهِ وَمِنْ
خَلْفِهِ أَلَّا تَعْبُدُوا إِلَّا اللَّهَ ۖ
إِنِّي أَخَافُ عَلَيْكُمْ عَذَابَ يَوْمٍ عَظِيمٍ ۝

22. They said: "Hast thou come [4800]
In order to turn us aside

٢٢- قَالُوا أَجِئْتَنَا لِتَأْفِكَنَا عَنْ

4796. "*Received your good things*" implies (in Arabic) grabbing at them, being greedy of them, seeking them as fleeting pleasures rather than the more serious things of life, sacrificing the spiritual for the material.

4797. They will be told: 'You took your choice, and you must pay the price. You did wrong in a rebellious spirit, and prided yourselves on your wrong-doing, not occasionally, but of set purpose and constantly. Now will you be humbled in the dust, as a fitting punishment.'

4798. *Cf.* vii. 65, and note 1040. The point is that the Warner who was raised among the 'Ād people—as among other peoples—was not a stranger, but one of their own brethren, even as the holy Prophet began his preaching with a call to his own brethren the Quraish.

4799. *Winding Sand-tracts*: *Aḥqāf*: see Introduction to this Sūra. The very things, which, under irrigation and with God's Grace, gave them prosperity and power, were to be their undoing when they broke God's Law and defied His Grace. See verses 24-26 below.

4800. They were too much wedded to their evil ways—to the false gods that they worshipped—to appreciate the sincere advice of the man of God. They defied him and defied God Who had sent him. Mockingly they challenged him to bring on the threatened punishment! For they did not believe a word of what he said.

From our gods? Then bring
Upon us the (calamity)
With which thou dost
Threaten us, if thou
Art telling the truth!"

23. He said: "The Knowledge[4801]
(Of when it will come)
Is only with God: I
Proclaim to you the mission
On which I have been sent:
But I see that ye
Are a people in ignorance!"...

24. Then, when they saw[4802]
The (Penalty in the shape of)
A cloud traversing the sky,
Coming to meet their valleys,
They said, "This cloud
Will give us rain!"
"Nay, it is the (calamity)
Ye were asking to be
Hastened!—a wind
Wherein is a Grievous Penalty!

25. "Everything will it destroy
By the command of its Lord!"
Then by the morning they—[4803]
Nothing was to be seen
But (the ruins of) their houses!
Thus do We recompense
Those given to sin!

أٰلِهَتِنَا ۚ
فَأْتِنَا بِمَا تَعِدُنَآ
إِنْ كُنْتَ مِنَ الصّٰدِقِيْنَ ○
٢٣- قَالَ إِنَّمَا الْعِلْمُ عِنْدَ اللهِ ۖ
وَأُبَلِّغُكُمْ مَّآ أُرْسِلْتُ بِهٖ
وَلٰكِنِّيْٓ أَرٰىكُمْ قَوْمًا تَجْهَلُوْنَ ○
٢٤- فَلَمَّا رَأَوْهُ
عَارِضًا مُّسْتَقْبِلَ أَوْدِيَتِهِمْ ۙ
قَالُوْا هٰذَا عَارِضٌ مُّمْطِرُنَا ۚ
بَلْ هُوَ مَا اسْتَعْجَلْتُمْ بِهٖ ۚ
رِيْحٌ فِيْهَا عَذَابٌ أَلِيْمٌ ۙ ○
٢٥- تُدَمِّرُ كُلَّ شَيْءٍۢ بِأَمْرِ رَبِّهَا
فَأَصْبَحُوْا لَا يُرٰٓى إِلَّا مَسٰكِنُهُمْ ۚ
كَذٰلِكَ نَجْزِي الْقَوْمَ الْمُجْرِمِيْنَ ○

4801. The coming of the Punishment for evil was (and is always) certain. At what particular time it would come he could not tell. It is not for the prophet, but for God, to bring on the Penalty. But he saw that it was useless to appeal to them on account of the ignorance in which they were content to dwell.

4802. The Punishment came suddenly, and when they least expected it. They wanted rain, and they saw a cloud and rejoiced. Behold, it was coming towards their own tracts, winding through the hills. Their irrigation channels would be full, their fields would be green, and their season would be fruitful. But no! What is this? It is a tremendous hurricane, carrying destruction on its wings! A violent blast, with dust and sand! Its fury destroys everything in its wake! Lives lost! Fields covered with sand-hills! The morning dawns on a scene of desolation! Where were the men who boasted and defied their Lord! There are only the ruins of their houses to witness to the past!

4803. Here is the figure of speech known in rhetoric as aposiopesis, to heighten the effect of the suddenness and completeness of the calamity. In the Arabic text, the verb *aṣbaḥū*, in the third person plural, leads us to expect that we shall be told what they were doing in the morning. But no! They had been wiped out, and any small remnant had fled (see n. 1040 to vii. 65). Nothing was to be seen but the ruins of their houses.

26. And We had firmly established
Them in a (prosperity and) power
Which We have not given
To you (ye Quraish!)
And We had endowed them
With (faculties of)[4804]
Hearing, seeing, heart and intellect:
But of no profit to them
Were their (faculties of)
Hearing, sight, and heart
And intellect, when they
Went on rejecting the Signs[4805]
Of God; and they were
(Completely) encircled[4806]
By that which they
Used to mock at!

٢٦- وَلَقَدْ مَكَّنّٰهُمْ
فِيمَآ إِن مَّكَّنّٰكُمْ فِيهِ
وَجَعَلْنَا لَهُمْ سَمْعًا وَّأَبْصٰرًا وَّأَفْـِٔدَةً
فَمَآ أَغْنٰى عَنْهُمْ
سَمْعُهُمْ وَلَآ أَبْصٰرُهُمْ وَلَآ أَفْـِٔدَتُهُم
مِّن شَىْءٍ إِذْ كَانُوا۟ يَجْحَدُونَ بِـَٔايٰتِ اللَّهِ
وَحَاقَ بِهِم
مَّا كَانُوا۟ بِهِۦ يَسْتَهْزِءُونَ ۝

SECTION 4.

27. We destroyed aforetime
Populations round about you;[4807]
And We have shown
The Signs in various ways,
That they may turn (to Us).

٢٧- وَلَقَدْ أَهْلَكْنَا مَا حَوْلَكُم مِّنَ الْقُرٰى
وَصَرَّفْنَا الْءَايٰتِ لَعَلَّهُمْ يَرْجِعُونَ ۝

28. Why then was no help
Forthcoming to them from those
Whom they worshipped as gods,
Besides God, as a means
Of access (to God)? Nay,
They left them in the lurch:
But that was their
Falsehood and their invention.[4808]

٢٨- فَلَوْلَا نَصَرَهُمُ الَّذِينَ اتَّخَذُوا۟ مِن
دُونِ اللَّهِ قُرْبَانًا ءَالِهَةًۢ
بَلْ ضَلُّوا۟ عَنْهُمْ
وَذٰلِكَ إِفْكُهُمْ وَمَا كَانُوا۟ يَفْتَرُونَ ۝

4804. The 'Ād and their successors the Thamūd were more richly endowed with the faculties of the arts, sciences, and culture than ever were the Quraish before Islam. "Hearing and seeing" refer to the experimental faculties; the word "heart" in Arabic includes intellect, or the rational faculties, as well as the instruments of feeling and emotion, the æsthetic faculties. The Second 'Ād, or the Thamūd, have left interesting traces of their architecture in the country round the Ḥijr: see n. 1043 to vii. 73, and notes 2002-2003 to xv. 80-82.

4805. The highest talents and faculties of this world are useless in the spiritual world if we reject the laws of the spiritual world and thus become outlaws there.

4806. See n. 4770 to xlv. 33. They used to mock at God's Signs, but those were the very things which hemmed them in, and showed that they had more power and effectiveness than anything else.

4807. In Arabian history and tradition alone, to say nothing of God's Signs elsewhere, sin inevitably suffered its Punishment, and in various ways. Would not the later people take warning?

4808. The false things that they worshipped were figments of their imagination. If they had had any existence in fact, it was not of the kind they imagined.

29. Behold, We turned
Towards thee a company[4809]
Of Jinns (quietly) listening
To the Qur-ān: when they
Stood in the presence
Thereof, they said, "Listen
In silence!" When the (reading)
Was finished, they returned
To their people, to warn
(Them of their sins).

٢٩- وَإِذْ صَرَفْنَآ إِلَيْكَ نَفَرًا
مِّنَ الْجِنِّ يَسْتَمِعُونَ الْقُرْآنَ ج
فَلَمَّا حَضَرُوهُ قَالُوٓا أَنصِتُوا ج
فَلَمَّا قُضِيَ
وَلَّوْا إِلَىٰ قَوْمِهِم مُّنذِرِينَ ○

30. They said, "O our people!
We have heard a Book
Revealed after Moses,
Confirming what came
Before it: it guides (men)
To the Truth and
To a Straight Path.

٣٠- قَالُوا يَٰقَوْمَنَآ إِنَّا سَمِعْنَا كِتَٰبًا
أُنزِلَ مِنۢ بَعْدِ مُوسَىٰ
مُصَدِّقًا لِّمَا بَيْنَ يَدَيْهِ
يَهْدِيٓ إِلَى الْحَقِّ وَإِلَىٰ طَرِيقٍ مُّسْتَقِيمٍ ○

31. "O our people, hearken
To the one who invites[4810]
(You) to God, and believe
In him: He will forgive
You your faults,
And deliver you from
A Penalty Grievous.

٣١- يَٰقَوْمَنَآ أَجِيبُوا دَاعِيَ اللَّهِ
وَءَامِنُوا بِهِۦ
يَغْفِرْ لَكُم مِّن ذُنُوبِكُمْ
وَيُجِرْكُم مِّنْ عَذَابٍ أَلِيمٍ ○

32. "If any does not hearken
To the one who invites
(Us) to God, he cannot[4811]
Frustrate (God's Plan) on earth,
And no protectors can he have
Besides God: such men
(Wander) in manifest error."

٣٢- وَمَن لَّا يُجِبْ دَاعِيَ اللَّهِ
فَلَيْسَ بِمُعْجِزٍ فِي الْأَرْضِ
وَلَيْسَ لَهُۥ مِن دُونِهِۦٓ أَوْلِيَآءُ ط
أُولَٰٓئِكَ فِي ضَلَٰلٍ مُّبِينٍ ○

4809. *A company of Jinns.* *Nafar* (company) may mean a group of from three to ten persons. For *Jinns*, see n. 929 to vi. 100. I have usually translated "spirits", but here some unfamiliar class of men or beings seems to be meant. They listened to the reading of the Qur-ān with great respect. The next verse shows that they had heard of the Jewish religion, but they were impressed with the Message of Islam, and they seem to have gone back to their people to share the Good News with them.

4810. The one who invites all to God is the holy Prophet. He invites us to God: if we believe in God and His Apostle, God will forgive us our sins on our repentance and amendment of our lives, and save us the Penalty of the future life.

4811. If a person refuses to believe the Truth, or opposes it, it has not the least effect on God's holy Plan, which will go on to its completion; but it will deprive him of Grace and of any protection whatever; he will wander about as an outlaw in manifest helplessness.

33. See they not that
God, Who created the heavens
And the earth, and never
Wearied with their creation,[4812]
Is able to give life
To the dead? Yea, verily
He has power over all things.

٣٣- أَوَلَمْ يَرَوْا أَنَّ اللّٰهَ الَّذِي
خَلَقَ السَّمٰوٰتِ وَالْأَرْضَ
وَلَمْ يَعْيَ بِخَلْقِهِنَّ بِقٰدِرٍ عَلٰٓى أَنْ يُّحْيِيَ
الْمَوْتٰى ۭ بَلٰٓى إِنَّهٗ عَلٰى كُلِّ شَيْءٍ قَدِيْرٌ ۝

34. And on the Day that[4813]
The Unbelievers will be
Placed before the Fire,
(They will be asked,)
"Is this not the Truth?"
They will say, "Yea,
By our Lord!"
(One will say:)
"Then taste ye[4814]
The Penalty, for that ye
Were wont to deny (Truth)!"

٣٤- وَيَوْمَ يُعْرَضُ الَّذِيْنَ كَفَرُوْا عَلَى النَّارِ ۭ
أَلَيْسَ هٰذَا بِالْحَقِّ ۭ
قَالُوْا بَلٰى وَرَبِّنَا ۭ
قَالَ فَذُوْقُوا الْعَذَابَ
بِمَا كُنْتُمْ تَكْفُرُوْنَ ۝

35. Therefore patiently persevere,
As did (all) apostles
Of inflexible purpose;
And be in no haste
About the (Unbelievers). On the
Day
That they see the (Punishment)[4815]
Promised them, (it will be)
As if they had not
Tarried more than an hour
In a single day. (Thine
But) to proclaim the Message:[4816]
But shall any be destroyed
Except those who transgress?

٣٥- فَاصْبِرْ كَمَا صَبَرَ
أُولُوا الْعَزْمِ مِنَ الرُّسُلِ
وَلَا تَسْتَعْجِلْ لَّهُمْ ۭ
كَأَنَّهُمْ يَوْمَ يَرَوْنَ مَا يُوْعَدُوْنَ ۙ
لَمْ يَلْبَثُوْٓا إِلَّا سَاعَةً مِّنْ نَّهَارٍ ۭ
بَلٰغٌ ۚ
فَهَلْ يُهْلَكُ إِلَّا الْقَوْمُ الْفٰسِقُوْنَ ۝

4812. *Cf.* ii. 255 (Verse of the Throne): "His Throne doth extend over the heavens and the earth, and He feeleth no fatigue in guarding and preserving them." He Whose power is constant and unwearied in creating and preserving all things in heaven and earth can surely give life to the dead at the Resurrection.

4813. *Cf.* xlvi. 20, where the argument was closed about the undutiful son of a good father. After that the example of the 'Ād and of the believing Jinns was cited, and now is closed that argument in similar terms.

4814. The Truth which they denied is now all too clear to them. They are out of the Light of Truth, out of the Light of God's Countenance. And that in itself is a terrible Penalty.

4815. All spiritual work proceeds in its own good time. We should never be impatient either about its success or about the punishment which is bound to come for those who oppose it or wish to suppress it. The inevitable punishment is spoken of as the *Punishment promised*. It will come so soon and so suddenly that it will appear as if there was not the delay of a single hour in a single day! Time is a great factor in our affairs in this world, but it hardly counts in the spiritual Kingdom.

4816. The Preacher's duty is to proclaim the Message in unmistakable terms. If any human beings come in the way, it will be to their own destruction; but none but rebellious transgressor will be punished. There is always hope and forgiveness for repentance and amendment.

INTRODUCTION TO SŪRA XLVII (*Muhammad*).

We have examined and followed the current arrangement of the Sūras according to subject-matter and independently of chronology, and we have found that a logical thread runs through them. We have now finished more than five-sixths of the Qur-ān. The remaining sixth consists of short Sūras, but these are again grouped according to subject-matter.

We begin the first of such groups with a group of three Sūras (xlvii. to xlix.), which deal with the organisation of the Muslim Ummat or community both for external defence and in internal relations. The present Sūra deals with the necessity of defence against external foes by courage and strenuous fighting, and dates from about the first year of the Hijra, when the Muslims were under threat of extinction by invasion from Mecca.

Summary.—Aggressive hostility to Faith and Truth should be fought firmly, and God will guide (xlvii. 1-19, and C. 220).

Faint-heartedness condemned; those who strive and those who turn away will be sorted out (xlvii. 20-38, and C. 221).

C. 220.—No plots against Truth or Faith will succeed:
(xlvii. 1-19.) But those who follow both will be strengthened.
Be firm in the fight, and God will guide.
Rebellion against God is destruction: fidelity
Will cool the mind and feed the heart;
It will warm the affections and sweeten life.
Hypocrisy carries its own doom.

Sūra XLVII.

Muḥammad (the Prophet).

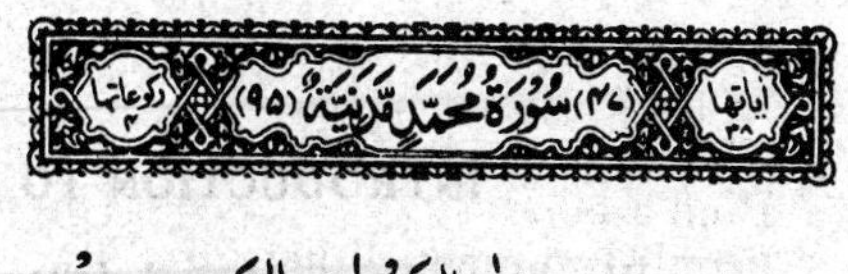

In the name of God, Most Gracious, Most Merciful.

بِسۡمِ اللّٰہِ الرَّحۡمٰنِ الرَّحِیۡمِ

1. Those who reject God
And hinder (men) from
The Path of God,—
Their deeds will God
Render astray[4817]
(From their mark).

۱-اَلَّذِیۡنَ کَفَرُوۡا
وَ صَدُّوۡا عَنۡ سَبِیۡلِ اللّٰہِ
اَضَلَّ اَعۡمَالَہُمۡ ○

2. But those who believe
And work deeds of
Righteousness, and believe
In the (Revelation) sent down
To Muḥammad—for it is
The Truth from their Lord,—
He will remove from them
Their ills and improve
Their condition.[4818]

۲-وَ الَّذِیۡنَ اٰمَنُوۡا وَ عَمِلُوا الصّٰلِحٰتِ
وَ اٰمَنُوۡا بِمَا نُزِّلَ عَلٰی مُحَمَّدٍ
وَّ ہُوَ الۡحَقُّ مِنۡ رَّبِّہِمۡ
کَفَّرَ عَنۡہُمۡ سَیِّاٰتِہِمۡ
وَ اَصۡلَحَ بَالَہُمۡ ○

3. This because those who
Reject God follow vanities,
While those who believe follow
The Truth from their Lord:
Thus does God set forth[4819]
For men their lessons
By similitudes.

۳-ذٰلِکَ بِاَنَّ الَّذِیۡنَ کَفَرُوا اتَّبَعُوا الۡبَاطِلَ
وَ اَنَّ الَّذِیۡنَ اٰمَنُوا اتَّبَعُوا الۡحَقَّ مِنۡ رَّبِّہِمۡ
کَذٰلِکَ یَضۡرِبُ اللّٰہُ لِلنَّاسِ اَمۡثَالَہُمۡ

4. Therefore, when ye meet[4820]
The Unbelievers (in fight),

۴-فَاِذَا لَقِیۡتُمُ الَّذِیۡنَ کَفَرُوۡا

4817. Whatever they do will miss its mark, because God is the source of all energy and life. If the wicked try to persecute men or seduce them from the Truth, the result will be the opposite of what they intend.

4818. *Bāl* means state or condition, whether external, or of the heart and mind. Both meanings apply here. The more the wicked rage, the better will be the position of the righteous, and God will make it easier and easier for the righteous to love and follow the Truth.

4819. We learn the greatest spiritual lessons by parables and similitudes from things that happen in the outer world. If a man goes after a mirage or a thing that has no real existence, he can never reach his goal, while the man that follows the kindly Light from God that leads him on must be happier in mind, sounder in heart, and firmer in life, generally for every moment that he lives.

4820. When once the fight (*Jihād*) is entered upon, carry it out with the utmost vigour, and strike home your blows at the most vital points (*smite at their necks*), both literally and figuratively. You cannot wage war with kid gloves.

Smite at their necks;
At length, when ye have
Thoroughly subdued them,
Bind a bond[4821]
Firmly (on them): thereafter
(Is the time for) either
Generosity or ransom:[4822]
Until the war lays down
Its burdens. Thus (are ye
Commanded): but if it
Had been God's Will,
He could certainly have exacted
Retribution from them (Himself);
But (He lets you fight)
In order to test you,[4823]
Some with others.
But those who are slain[4824]
In the way of God,—
He will never let
Their deeds be lost.

فَضَرْبَ الرِّقَابِ ۖ
حَتَّىٰٓ إِذَآ أَثْخَنتُمُوهُمْ
فَشُدُّوا۟ ٱلْوَثَاقَ
فَإِمَّا مَنًّۢا بَعْدُ
وَإِمَّا فِدَآءً
حَتَّىٰ تَضَعَ ٱلْحَرْبُ أَوْزَارَهَا ۚ ذَٰلِكَ ۛ
وَلَوْ يَشَآءُ ٱللَّهُ لَٱنتَصَرَ مِنْهُمْ
وَلَٰكِن لِّيَبْلُوَا۟ بَعْضَكُم بِبَعْضٍ ۗ
وَٱلَّذِينَ قُتِلُوا۟ فِى سَبِيلِ ٱللَّهِ
فَلَن يُضِلَّ أَعْمَٰلَهُمْ ۝

5. Soon will He guide them[4825]
And improve their condition,

٥- سَيَهْدِيهِمْ وَيُصْلِحُ بَالَهُمْ ۝

6. And admit them to
The Garden which He[4826]
Has announced for them.

٦- وَيُدْخِلُهُمُ ٱلْجَنَّةَ
عَرَّفَهَا لَهُمْ ۝

4821. In the first onset there must necessarily be great loss of life; but when the enemy is fairly beaten, which means, in a Jihād, that he is not likely to seek again the persecution of Truth, firm arrangements should be made to bring him under control. I thus construe the words "bind a bond firmly (on them)", but others have construed the words to mean, "after the enemy's numbers are fairly thinned down, prisoners may be taken". With this passage may be compared viii. 67, and n. 1234.

4822. When once the enemy is brought under control, generosity (*i.e.*, the release of prisoners without ransom) or ransom is recommended.

4823. The Believers are tested in Faith by the extent to which they are willing to make sacrifices, even to the laying down of their lives; and the enemies are tested as to whether they would repent and let the righteous live in freedom and security.

4824. There are two alternative readings, (1) *qātalū*, "those who fight", and (2) *qutilū*, "those who are slain". The meaning under the first reading is wider, and includes that under the second. I have translated on the basis of the second reading, which is in accordance with the text of the Royal Egyptian edition.

4825. If we read "who are slain" in the last clause but one of verse 4, (see last note), "guide" would mean "guide them in their spiritual journey after death". *Improve their condition*: see n. 4818 above. If after death, their minds and hearts will be more and more settled and at rest, and their spiritual satisfaction greater.

4826. "*The Garden which He has announced for them*": the state of Bliss which is declared in Revelation to be destined for those who serve God.

7. O ye who believe!
If ye will aid
(The cause of) God,
He will aid you,
And plant your feet firmly.

٧- يٰۤاَيُّهَا الَّذِيْنَ اٰمَنُوْۤا
اِنْ تَنْصُرُوا اللّٰهَ
يَنْصُرْكُمْ وَيُثَبِّتْ اَقْدَامَكُمْ ○

8. But those who reject (God),—
For them is destruction,
And (God) will render
Their deeds astray[4827]
(From their mark).

٨- وَالَّذِيْنَ كَفَرُوْا فَتَعْسًا لَّهُمْ
وَاَضَلَّ اَعْمَالَهُمْ ○

9. That is because they
Hate the Revelation of God;
So He has made
Their deeds fruitless.[4828]

٩- ذٰلِكَ بِاَنَّهُمْ كَرِهُوْا مَاۤ اَنْزَلَ اللّٰهُ
فَاَحْبَطَ اَعْمَالَهُمْ ○

10. Do they not travel[4829]
Through the earth, and see
What was the End
Of those before them
(Who did evil)?
God brought utter destruction
On them, and similar
(Fates await) those who
Reject God.

١٠- اَفَلَمْ يَسِيْرُوْا فِى الْاَرْضِ فَيَنْظُرُوْا
كَيْفَ كَانَ عَاقِبَةُ الَّذِيْنَ مِنْ قَبْلِهِمْ ؕ
دَمَّرَ اللّٰهُ عَلَيْهِمْ ۫
وَلِلْكٰفِرِيْنَ اَمْثَالُهَا ○

11. That is because God
Is the Protector of those
Who believe, but
Those who reject God
Have no protector.

١١- ذٰلِكَ بِاَنَّ اللّٰهَ مَوْلَى الَّذِيْنَ اٰمَنُوْا
وَاَنَّ الْكٰفِرِيْنَ لَا مَوْلٰى لَهُمْ ○ ع ٥

SECTION 2.

12. Verily God will admit
Those who believe and do
Righteous deeds, to Gardens
Beneath which rivers flow;

١٢- اِنَّ اللّٰهَ يُدْخِلُ الَّذِيْنَ اٰمَنُوْا وَعَمِلُوا
الصّٰلِحٰتِ جَنّٰتٍ تَجْرِىْ مِنْ تَحْتِهَا الْاَنْهٰرُ ؕ

4827. See above, xlvii. 1 and n. 4817.

4828. Their deeds are "*fruitless*" in the sense that they are vain; they do not produce the results intended by their doers. But they will not be exempt from producing the natural consequences of evil, *viz.*, further degradation and misery for the soul.

4829. The end of evil is evil. All past history and tradition shows that. Will not men of every generation learn that lesson? God helps His servants, but those who rebel against God have no one to help them.

While those who reject God
Will enjoy (this world)[4830]
And eat as cattle eat;
And the Fire will
Be their abode.

وَالَّذِينَ كَفَرُوا
يَتَمَتَّعُونَ وَيَأْكُلُونَ كَمَا تَأْكُلُ الْأَنْعَامُ
وَالنَّارُ مَثْوًى لَهُمْ ○

13. And how many cities,
With more power than
Thy city which has
Driven thee out,[4831]
Have We destroyed
(For their sins)?
And there was none
To aid them.

١٣- وَكَأَيِّنْ مِنْ قَرْيَةٍ هِيَ أَشَدُّ قُوَّةً
مِنْ قَرْيَتِكَ الَّتِي أَخْرَجَتْكَ
أَهْلَكْنَاهُمْ
فَلَا نَاصِرَ لَهُمْ ○

14. Is then one who is
On a clear[4832] (Path)
From his Lord,
No better than one
To whom the evil
Of his conduct seems pleasing,
And such as follow
Their own lusts?

١٤- أَفَمَنْ كَانَ عَلَىٰ بَيِّنَةٍ
مِنْ رَبِّهِ
كَمَنْ زُيِّنَ لَهُ سُوءُ عَمَلِهِ
وَاتَّبَعُوا أَهْوَاءَهُمْ ○

15. (Here is) a Parable
Of the Garden which
The righteous are promised:
In it are rivers
Of water incorruptible;[4833]
Rivers of milk
Of which the taste
Never changes; rivers

١٥- مَثَلُ الْجَنَّةِ الَّتِي وُعِدَ الْمُتَّقُونَ
فِيهَا أَنْهَارٌ مِنْ مَاءٍ غَيْرِ آسِنٍ
وَأَنْهَارٌ مِنْ لَبَنٍ
لَمْ يَتَغَيَّرْ طَعْمُهُ وَأَنْهَارٌ

4830. An apt simile. Beasts of the field eat their fill, but have no higher interests. Men who worship the world exclusively are no better: their pleasures and enjoyments rise no higher than those of the beasts of the field. They have no inkling of spiritual happiness. On the contrary, as they were endowed with spiritual faculties which they misused, they will not escape the Fire of Punishment, the Penalty of Sin.

4831. A reference to Pagan Mecca, which drove out the holy Prophet because of his righteousness and because he preached Repentance. The date of this Sūra must therefore be after the Hijrat.

4832. *Clear*, or enlightened; a Path on which shines the Light of God.

4833. In this symbolism there are four kinds of drinks and all kinds of fruits; and the summing up of all spiritual delights in the "Grace from their Lord". The four kinds of drinks are: (1) delicious, cool, pure water, not like earthly water, for it never suffers corruption; (2) milk which never turns sour, whose taste is like that of fresh warm milk drawn from the udder; (3) wine, not like any wine on earth, for it leaves no headaches behind, and causes no intoxication, which is a kind of madness or poison, but is ever a joy to drink; and (4) honey, pure and clear, with no admixture of wax or any foreign substance. These drinks, again speaking metaphorically, will cool the spirit, feed the heart, warm the affections, and sweeten life.

Of wine, a joy
To those who drink;
And rivers of honey
Pure and clear. In it
There are for them
All kinds of fruits;[4834]
And Grace from their Lord.[4835]
(Can those in such Bliss)
Be compared to such as
Shall dwell for ever
In the Fire, and be given,
To drink, boiling water,
So that it cuts up[4836]
Their bowels (to pieces)?

مِّنْ خَمْرٍ لَّذَّةٍ لِّلشّٰرِبِيْنَ ۚ
وَ اَنْهٰرٌ مِّنْ عَسَلٍ مُّصَفًّى ؕ
وَ لَهُمْ فِيْهَا مِنْ كُلِّ الثَّمَرٰتِ
وَ مَغْفِرَةٌ مِّنْ رَّبِّهِمْ ؕ
كَمَنْ هُوَ خَالِدٌ فِى النَّارِ
وَ سُقُوْا مَآءً حَمِيْمًا
فَقَطَّعَ اَمْعَآءَهُمْ ○

16. And among them are men
Who listen to thee,
But in the end, when they
Go out from thee,[4837]
They say to those who
Have received Knowledge,
"What is it he said
Just then?" Such are
Men whose hearts God
Has sealed, and who
Follow their own lusts.

١٦- وَ مِنْهُمْ مَّنْ يَّسْتَمِعُ اِلَيْكَ ۚ
حَتّٰۤى اِذَا خَرَجُوْا مِنْ عِنْدِكَ
قَالُوْا لِلَّذِيْنَ اُوْتُوا الْعِلْمَ
مَاذَا قَالَ اٰنِفًا ۫
اُولٰٓئِكَ الَّذِيْنَ طَبَعَ اللّٰهُ عَلٰى قُلُوْبِهِمْ
وَ اتَّبَعُوْۤا اَهْوَآءَهُمْ ○

17. But to those who receive[4838]
Guidance, He increases
The (light of) Guidance,
And bestows on them
Their Piety and Restraint
(From evil).

١٧- وَ الَّذِيْنَ اهْتَدَوْا
زَادَهُمْ هُدًى
وَّ اٰتٰىهُمْ تَقْوٰىهُمْ ○

4834. The signification of Fruits in their metaphorical sense has been already explained: see n. 4671 to xliii. 73. In the setting of the present verse, note that it implies a second degree of totality of Bliss, the third or highest and final degree being the Grace or Mercy of God.

4835. *Grace from their Lord*: that is the covering up or blotting out of sin and all that was sad or unsatisfactory in the lower life; the pure Light from the Countenance of God Most High: xcii. 20.

4836. *Cf.* xxxvii. 66-67, and n. 4074. Just as the Bliss of the Blessed will penetrate their being through and through, so the agony of the condemned ones will penetrate their being through and through. "Bowels" besides meaning their inmost being, also suggests the seat of their feelings and affections.

4837. *Cf.* x 42, and n. 1434; also vi. 25, 36, and n. 857. The case here referred to is that of the Hypocrites who came to the assemblies of Islam in Medina and pretended to listen to the Prophet's teaching and preaching. But their heart and mind were not in learning righteousness, but in carping at things they saw and heard. When they got out, they knew nothing of the teaching, but on the contrary asked foolish and ignorant questions, such as might raise doubts.

4838. Spiritual advancement is progressive: each step makes the next ones easier and more complete.

18. Do they then only wait [4839]
For the Hour,—that it
Should come on them
Of a sudden? But already
Have come some tokens [4840]
Thereof, and when it
(Actually) is on them,
How can they benefit
Then by their admonition?

١٨- فَهَلْ يَنْظُرُونَ إِلَّا السَّاعَةَ
أَنْ تَأْتِيَهُمْ بَغْتَةً
فَقَدْ جَاءَ أَشْرَاطُهَا ۚ
فَأَنَّىٰ لَهُمْ إِذَا جَاءَتْهُمْ
ذِكْرَاهُمْ ○

19. Know, therefore, that
There is no god
But God, and ask
Forgiveness for thy fault, [4841]
And for the men
And women who believe:
For God knows how ye [4842]
Move about and how
Ye dwell in your homes.

١٩- فَاعْلَمْ أَنَّهُ لَا إِلَٰهَ إِلَّا اللَّهُ
وَاسْتَغْفِرْ لِذَنْبِكَ
وَلِلْمُؤْمِنِينَ وَالْمُؤْمِنَاتِ ۗ
وَاللَّهُ يَعْلَمُ مُتَقَلَّبَكُمْ
وَمَثْوَاكُمْ ○ ع

C. 221.—Those eager for service want the call for service;
(xlvii. 20-38.) But the hypocrites blench at such call.
If it were not obeyed, and evil should get
The upper hand, will it not stalk arrogant
Over the land, and trample under foot
All claims of right and kinship? Fight it,
And fail not in the test of your mettle. Be bold
And establish the Flag of Righteousness
In the highest places. Thus comes Peace,
For which due sacrifice must be made.

4839. *Cf.* xliii. 66, and n. 4665.

4840. The sands of time are always running, and when a wrong is done, the time for its punishment is approaching every moment. No one should therefore wait. The time for repentance is *Now* at any given time. When the punishment comes, it is too late for repentance, and all admonition would be useless.

Looking to the particular time when this Sūra was revealed, *viz.*, about a year after the Hijrat, already there were Signs that the plans of the Pagans to crush Islam were crumbling to pieces. The Hijrat showed how much good-will there was in Medina for the holy man of God, and how many people from Mecca adhered to him. The battle of Badr showed that they could hold their own against odds of three to one.

4841. *Cf.* xl. 55, and n. 4428.

4842. The time and manner of our conducting ourselves at home and when we move about on our business are all material to the judgment of our conduct, and for every nuance in our moral and spiritual progress, we must seek God's help and guidance.

SECTION 3.

20. Those who believe say,[4843]
"Why is not a Sūra
Sent down (for us)?"
But when a Sūra
Of basic or categorical[4844]
Meaning is revealed,
And fighting is mentioned
Therein, thou wilt see those
In whose hearts is a disease[4845]
Looking at thee with a look
Of one in swoon at
The approach of death.
But more fitting for them—

٢٠- وَيَقُولُ الَّذِينَ آمَنُوا لَوْلَا نُزِّلَتْ سُورَةٌ
فَإِذَا أُنزِلَتْ سُورَةٌ مُّحْكَمَةٌ
وَذُكِرَ فِيهَا الْقِتَالُ
رَأَيْتَ الَّذِينَ فِي قُلُوبِهِم مَّرَضٌ
يَنظُرُونَ إِلَيْكَ نَظَرَ
الْمَغْشِيِّ عَلَيْهِ مِنَ الْمَوْتِ
فَأَوْلَىٰ لَهُمْ ۝

21. Were it to obey
And say what is just,
And when a matter[4846]
Is resolved on, it were
Best for them if they
Were true to God.

٢١- طَاعَةٌ وَقَوْلٌ مَّعْرُوفٌ
فَإِذَا عَزَمَ الْأَمْرُ
فَلَوْ صَدَقُوا اللَّهَ لَكَانَ خَيْرًا لَّهُمْ ۝

22. Then, is it[4847]
To be expected of you,
If ye were put in authority,
That ye will do mischief
In the land, and break
Your ties of kith and kin?

٢٢- فَهَلْ عَسَيْتُمْ إِن تَوَلَّيْتُمْ
أَن تُفْسِدُوا فِي الْأَرْضِ
وَتُقَطِّعُوا أَرْحَامَكُمْ ۝

4843. The men of faith and loyalty are eager and anxious to get a command to serve the Cause even if it be at the sacrifice of their lives. Not so the Hypocrites, "those in whose hearts is a disease". They are mortally afraid as mentioned below.

4844. *Cf.* iii. 7, and n. 347. The defence of truth and righteousness at all sacrifice, when a definite and categorical command issues from the righteous Imām under inspiration from God, is a fundamental condition of enlistment in the cause of God. It is true that Punishment and Judgment belong to God alone; but our mettle and fidelity have to be tested, (see verse 4 above), and God uses human agency in human affairs.

4845. *Cf.* ii. 10. The disease is hypocrisy, disloyalty to the Cause, want of courage and of the spirit of self-sacrifice, want of true understanding.

4846. The resolution is not taken except under guidance from God. Those, therefore, who fail to implement it by their own effort and sacrifice, are not true to God. And such disloyalty or cowardice is not even good for them from a worldly point of view. With what face can they meet their friends after their disgraceful conduct?

4847. It is no use to say, as the Quraish said, that it is not seemly to fight against kith and kin. From one point of view the stand against sin brings "not peace, but a sword". It is a case of either subduing evil or being subdued by evil. If evil gets the upper hand, it is not likely to respect ties of kith and kin. It did not in the case of the holy Prophet and his adherents, and had to be suppressed, to bring about the conditions necessary for peace.

23. Such are the men
Whom God has cursed[4848]
For He has made them
Deaf and blinded their sight.

٢٣- أُولَٰئِكَ الَّذِينَ لَعَنَهُمُ اللَّهُ
فَأَصَمَّهُمْ وَأَعْمَىٰ أَبْصَارَهُمْ ○

24. Do they not then
Earnestly seek to understand
The Qur-ān, or are
Their hearts locked up
By them?

٢٤- أَفَلَا يَتَدَبَّرُونَ الْقُرْآنَ
أَمْ عَلَىٰ قُلُوبٍ أَقْفَالُهَا ○

25. Those who turn back[4849]
As apostates after Guidance
Was clearly shown to them,—
The Evil One has instigated
Them and buoyed them up
With false hopes.

٢٥- إِنَّ الَّذِينَ ارْتَدُّوا عَلَىٰ أَدْبَارِهِم
مِّن بَعْدِ مَا تَبَيَّنَ لَهُمُ الْهُدَى ۙ
الشَّيْطَانُ سَوَّلَ لَهُمْ وَأَمْلَىٰ لَهُمْ ○

26. This, because they said[4850]
To those who hate what
God has revealed, "We
Will obey you in part
Of (this) matter"; but God
Knows their (inner) secrets.

٢٦- ذَٰلِكَ بِأَنَّهُمْ قَالُوا لِلَّذِينَ كَرِهُوا مَا
نَزَّلَ اللَّهُ سَنُطِيعُكُمْ فِي بَعْضِ الْأَمْرِ ۖ
وَاللَّهُ يَعْلَمُ إِسْرَارَهُمْ ○

27. But how (will it be)[4851]
When the angels take
Their souls at death,
And smite their faces[4852]
And their backs?

٢٧- فَكَيْفَ إِذَا تَوَفَّتْهُمُ الْمَلَائِكَةُ
يَضْرِبُونَ وُجُوهَهُمْ وَأَدْبَارَهُمْ ○

4848. *Cursed*: *i.e.*, deprived of His Grace: left them straying, because they deliberately rejected His guidance. The result is that what they hear is as if they had not heard, and what they see is as if they had not seen. They have no desire to understand God's Will or God's Revelation;—or is it that they have themselves locked and bolted their hearts and minds, so that nothing can penetrate them?

4849. Such men are entirely in the hands of Evil. They follow its suggestions, and their hopes are built on its deceptions.

4850. They have become so impervious to facts and truths, because, without the courage to oppose God's Cause openly, they secretly intrigue with God's enemies, and say that they will follow them part of the way, and by remaining partly in the other camp, they will be far more useful as spies and half-hearted doubters than by going over altogether. If they think that this game will be successful, they are mistaken. All the inner secrets and motives of their hearts are known to God. *Cf.* lix. 11.

4851. It is all very well for them to practise hypocrisy in this life. How will they feel at death, when they find that the angels know all, and touch the very spots they had taken such care to conceal?

4852. *Their faces and their backs*: there is a subtle metaphor. The *face* is what looks to the front, the side you present to the outer world; the *back* is what is not shown, what is hidden from the world. The hypocrites will be hit at both points. Or, the *face* is what they boast of, what they are proud of; the back is the skeleton in the cupboard, the things they dare not utter, but which yet haunt them. The hypocrites are hit on every side. *Cf.* viii. 50.

28. This because they followed
That which called forth
The Wrath of God, and
They hated God's good pleasure;
So He made their deeds
Of no effect.

٢٨- ذٰلِكَ بِاَنَّهُمُ اتَّبَعُوْا مَآ اَسْخَطَ اللّٰهَ
وَكَرِهُوْا رِضْوَانَهٗ
فَاَحْبَطَ اَعْمَالَهُمْ ○

SECTION 4.

29. Or do those in whose[4853]
Hearts is a disease, think
That God will not bring
To light all their rancour?

٢٩- اَمْ حَسِبَ الَّذِيْنَ فِيْ قُلُوْبِهِمْ مَّرَضٌ
اَنْ لَّنْ يُّخْرِجَ اللّٰهُ اَضْغَانَهُمْ ○

30. Had We so willed,
We could have shown them
Up to thee, and thou
Shouldst have known them[4854]
By their marks: but surely
Thou wilt know them
By the tone of their speech!
And God knows
All that ye do.

٣٠- وَلَوْ نَشَآءُ لَاَرَيْنٰكَهُمْ
فَلَعَرَفْتَهُمْ بِسِيْمٰهُمْ ؕ
وَلَتَعْرِفَنَّهُمْ فِيْ لَحْنِ الْقَوْلِ ؕ
وَاللّٰهُ يَعْلَمُ اَعْمَالَكُمْ ○

31. And We shall try you[4855]
Until We test those
Among you who strive
Their utmost and persevere
In patience; and We shall
Try your reported (mettle).[4856]

٣١- وَلَنَبْلُوَنَّكُمْ حَتّٰى نَعْلَمَ
الْمُجٰهِدِيْنَ مِنْكُمْ وَالصّٰبِرِيْنَ ۙ
وَنَبْلُوَا۟ اَخْبَارَكُمْ ○

32. Those who reject God,
Hinder (men) from
The Path of God, and resist
The Apostle, after Guidance

٣٢- اِنَّ الَّذِيْنَ كَفَرُوْا وَصَدُّوْا عَنْ سَبِيْلِ
اللّٰهِ وَشَآقُّوا الرَّسُوْلَ مِنْۢ بَعْدِ مَا تَبَيَّنَ لَهُمُ

4853. *Cf.* verse 20 above, and n. 4845. Being diseased at the very core of their being, they do not understand the simplest facts of spiritual life.

4854. Evil is not always necessarily branded in this life with a distinguishing mark or brand. But the discerning ones know. Evil is betrayed by its speech and behaviour.

4855. *Cf.* xxxiv. 21. and n. 3821. The test and trial is for our own psychological development, to help in the exercise of such choice as has been given to us in our free-will. *Cf.* also iii. 154, and n. 467.

4856. *Akhbār*: the things reported of you; reputation for courage and constancy, which has to be brought to the test of facts and experience In an epigram of Tacitus we are told of a Roman Emperor that he would have been considered in every way to have been worthy of being a ruler if only he had never ruled! So in life people may think us courageous, true, noble, and self-sacrificing; and we may consider ourselves as possessing all such virtues; but it is actual experience that will bring them to the test.

Has been clearly shown to them,[4857] Will not injure God In the least, but He Will make their deeds Of no effect.	الْهُدٰى لَنْ يَّضُرُّوا اللّٰهَ شَيْـًٔا ؕ وَسَيُحْبِطُ اَعْمَالَهُمْ ○
33. O ye who believe! Obey God, and obey The Apostle, and make Not vain your deeds!	٣٣- يٰۤاَيُّهَا الَّذِيْنَ اٰمَنُوْۤا اَطِيْعُوا اللّٰهَ وَاَطِيْعُوا الرَّسُوْلَ وَلَا تُبْطِلُوْۤا اَعْمَالَكُمْ ○
34. Those who reject God,[4858] And hinder (men) from the Path Of God, then die rejecting God,— God will not forgive them.	٣٤- اِنَّ الَّذِيْنَ كَفَرُوْا وَصَدُّوْا عَنْ سَبِيْلِ اللّٰهِ ثُمَّ مَاتُوْا وَهُمْ كُفَّارٌ فَلَنْ يَّغْفِرَ اللّٰهُ لَهُمْ ○
35. Be not weary and Faint-hearted, crying for peace, When ye should be[4859] Uppermost: for God is With you, and will never Put you in loss For your (good) deeds.	٣٥- فَلَا تَهِنُوْا وَتَدْعُوْۤا اِلَى السَّلْمِ ۖۗ وَاَنْتُمُ الْاَعْلَوْنَ ۖۗ وَاللّٰهُ مَعَكُمْ وَلَنْ يَّتِرَكُمْ اَعْمَالَكُمْ ○
36. The life of this world Is but play and amusement:[4860] And if ye believe And guard against evil, He will grant you Your recompense, and will not	٣٦- اِنَّمَا الْحَيٰوةُ الدُّنْيَا لَعِبٌ وَّلَهْوٌ ؕ وَاِنْ تُؤْمِنُوْا وَتَتَّقُوْا يُؤْتِكُمْ اُجُوْرَكُمْ وَلَا

4857. *Cf.* verse 25 above, and verse 34 below: in verse 25 was shown the source of the evil, *viz*, yielding to the deceptions of the Evil One; in this verse are shown the proximate consequences of such yielding to evil, *viz.*, failure of all we do; and in verse 34 below are shown the eternal consequences, *viz.*, our deprivation of God's Grace and Mercy.

4858. See last note.

4859. To those who are trying to root out evil, and *have authority* to do so, the question is not of peace or conflict, but of whether Good or Evil is to prevail. They must remember that Good must ultimately prevail, and God's help is with those who, as far as men can, are trying to further the universal Plan. *Cf.* n. 4847 to verse 22 above.

4860. *Cf.* vi. 32, and n. 855; and xxix. 64, and n. 3497. Amusement and play are not bad things in themselves. As preparations for the more serious life, they have their value. But if we concentrate on them, and neglect the business of life, we cannot prosper. So we must use our life in this world as a preparation for our spiritual or inner life.

Ask you (to give up)
Your possessions.[4861]

يَسْـَٔلْكُمْ أَمْوَالَكُمْ ۝

37. If He were to ask you
For all of them, and
Press you, ye would
Covetously withhold, and He
would[4862]
Bring out all your ill-feeling.[4863]

٣٧- إِن يَسْـَٔلْكُمُوهَا
فَيُحْفِكُمْ تَبْخَلُوا
وَيُخْرِجْ أَضْغَانَكُمْ ۝

38. Behold, ye are those[4864]
Invited to spend
(Of your substance)
In the Way of God:
But among you are some
That are niggardly. But any
Who are niggardly are so
At the expense of
Their own souls.
But God is free
Of all wants,
And it is ye that are needy.
If ye turn back[4865]
(From the Path), He will
Substitute in your stead
Another people; then they
Would not be like you!

٣٨- هَٰٓأَنتُمْ هَٰٓؤُلَآءِ
تُدْعَوْنَ لِتُنفِقُوا فِي سَبِيلِ اللَّهِ
فَمِنكُم مَّن يَبْخَلُ
وَمَن يَبْخَلْ فَإِنَّمَا يَبْخَلُ عَن نَّفْسِهِ
وَاللَّهُ الْغَنِيُّ
وَأَنتُمُ الْفُقَرَآءُ
وَإِن تَتَوَلَّوْا يَسْتَبْدِلْ قَوْمًا غَيْرَكُمْ
ثُمَّ لَا يَكُونُوٓا أَمْثَالَكُم ۝

4861. Complete self-sacrifice, if voluntarily offered, has a meaning: it means that the person's devotion is exclusively and completely for the Cause. But no law or rule can *demand* it. And a mere offer to kill yourself has no meaning. You should be ready to take risks to your life in fighting for the Cause, but you should aim at life, not death. If you live, you should be ready to place your substance and your acquisitions at the disposal of the Cause. But it is not reasonable to pauperise yourself and become a hanger-on for the Cause. Moreover, the inborn tendency to self-preservation in an average man would lead to concealment and niggardliness if *all* were asked for the Cause, by Law, and there would further be a feeling of bitterness and rebellion.

4862. *Cf.* iii. 180.

4863. *Cf.* above, verse 29. Rancour or ill-feeling, or any desire but that of devotion, should never be given a handle in a wise Law.

4864. Here the cases of the special devotee and of the average man with his human foibles are distinguished. Stinginess is not a virtue: it hurts more the finer nature of the individual practising it than it hurts the Cause. God is free of all wants and independent of any need that we can meet. His Cause is similarly independent of human aid. But it uses human agency for our own human advancement. The need to be able to serve in the Kingdom of Heaven is ours. We are the needy beggars who should claim the privilege before the Lord of Bounties unbounded.

4865. If we desert the Cause, the Cause will not fail. Better men than we will uphold the flag. But we should fall, and others will take our place, who are not so timid, half-hearted, or stingy. In Wordsworth's words, "High Heaven rejects the lore of nicely calculated less or more."

INTRODUCTION TO SŪRA XLVIII (*Fat-ḥ*).

1. This is the second of the group of three Medina Sūras described in the Introduction to S. xlvii. Its date is fixed by the mention of the Treaty of Ḥudaibīya, Ẓul-qa'd A.H. 6=Feb. 628 (see n. 1261 to ix. 13).

2. Ḥudaibīya is a plain, a short day's march to the north of Mecca, a little to the west of the Medina-Mecca road, as used in the Prophet's time. Six years had passed since the Prophet had left his beloved City, and it had been in the hands of the Pagan autocracy. But Islam had grown during these six years. Its Qibla was towards the Ka'ba. The Pagans had tried to attack Islam at various times and had been foiled. By Arab custom every Arab was entitled to visit the Sacred Enclosure unarmed, and fighting of any kind was prohibited during the Sacred Months (see n. 209 to ii. 194), which included the month of Ẓul-qa'd. In Ẓul-qa'd A.H. 6, therefore, the Prophet desired to perform the 'Umra or lesser pilgrimage (n. 212 to ii. 196), unarmed, but accompanied with his followers. A large following joined him, to the number of fourteen to fifteen hundred.

3. This was not to the liking of the Pagan autocracy at Mecca, which took alarm, and in breach of all Arab tradition and usage, prepared to prevent the peaceful party from performing the rites of pilgrimage. They marched out to fight the unarmed party. The Prophet turned a little to the west of the road, and encamped at Ḥudaibīya, where negotiations took place. On the one hand the Prophet was unwilling to give the Quraish any pretended excuse for violence in the Sacred Territory; on the other, the Quraish had learnt, by six years' bitter experience, that their power was crumbling on all sides, and Islam was growing with its moral and spiritual forces, which were also reflected in its powers of organisation and resistance. The enthusiasm with which the Covenant of Fealty was entered into under a tree in Ḥudaibīya (xlviii. 18) by that great multitude united in devotion to their great leader, was evidence of the great power which he commanded even in a worldly sense if the Quraish had chosen to try conclusions with him.

4. A peaceful Treaty was therefore concluded, known as the Treaty of Ḥudaibīya. It stipulated: (1) that there was to be peace between the parties for ten years; (2) that any tribe or person was free to join either party or make an alliance with it; (3) that if a Quraish person from Mecca, under guardianship, should join the Prophet without the guardian's permission, he (or she) should be sent back to the guardian, but in the contrary case, they should not be sent back; and (4) that the Prophet and his party were not to enter Mecca that year, but that they could enter unarmed the following year.

5. Item 3, not being reciprocal, was objected to in the Muslim camp, but it really was of little importance. Muslims under guardianship, sent back to Mecca, were not likely to renounce the blessings of Islam; on the other hand Muslims going to Mecca would be centres of influence for Islam, and it was more important that they should be allowed to remain there than that they should be sent back to Medina.

It was impossible to think that there would be apostates or renegades to Paganism! "Look on this picture, and on that!"

6. The Muslims faithfully observed the terms of the Treaty. The following year (A.H. 7) they performed the lesser Pilgrimage in great state for three days. It is true that the Meccans later on broke the Peace in the attack which one of their allied tribes (the Banū Bakr) made on the Muslim Banū K͟huzā'a (who were in alliance with the Prophet), but this led to the conquest of Mecca and the sweeping away of the autocracy. Meanwhile Ḥudaibīya was a great victory, moral and social, as well as political, and its lessons are expounded in this Sūra, as the lessons of Badr were expounded in viii. 42-48, and of Uḥud in iii. 121-129, 149-180.

Summary.—Victory comes from cool courage, devotion, faith, and patience, as shown at Ḥudaibīya; therefore remember God, and follow His Apostle (xlviii. 1-29, and C. *222*).

C. *222*.—Victory and Help go with calmness of mind,
(xlviii. 1-29.) Faith, fidelity, zeal, and earnestness,
Not with greed, lukewarmness, or timidity.
Discipline and obedience are essential
For service. The rewards for service are not
To be measured by immediate results,
But accrue in countless hidden ways
For Patience and Restraint. Be strong
Against Evil, but kind and gentle amongst
Yourselves: the seed will grow and become
Strong, to your wonder and delight.

Sūra XLVIII.

Fat-ḥ or Victory.

In the name of God, Most Gracious, Most Merciful.

1. Verily We have granted
Thee a manifest Victory:[4866]

2. That God may forgive thee[4867]
Thy faults of the past
And those to follow;
Fulfil His favour to thee;
And guide thee
On the Straight Way;

3. And that God may help[4868]
Thee with powerful help.

4. It is He Who sent
Down Tranquillity[4869]
Into the hearts of
The Believers, that they may
Add Faith to their Faith;—[4870]
For to God belong

4866. This is best referred to the Treaty of Ḥudaibīya, for which see the Introduction to this Sūra. By this Treaty the Meccan Quraish, after many years of unrelenting conflict with Islam, at length recognised Islam as (what they thought) an equal power with themselves. In reality the door was then opened for the free spread of Islam throughout Arabia and thence through the world.

4867. See n. 4428 to xl. 55, and *Cf.* xlvii. 19. Any mistakes of the past were now rectified, and any future ones prevented by the free scope now offered, by the act of the Quraish Pagans themselves, to the recognition and free promulgation of Islam.

4868. Three objects or results of the Treaty are mentioned: (1) forgiveness, which is equivalent to Mercy, (2) fulfilment of the dignity of Prophethood with the dignity of an effective and recognised position in Arabia; (3) opening up a straight way leading to Islam, by access to Mecca from next year, Mecca being the symbolic centre of Islam. These three are summed up in the comprehensive phrase "powerful (or effective) help".

4869. The results were achieved by tranquillity, calmness, and cool courage among the 1400 to 1500 unarmed men who accompanied the Prophet to Ḥudaibīya and who were threatened with violence by the excited Quraish leaders of Mecca.

4870. It is a casuistical question to ask, Are there degrees in Faith? The plain meaning is that Believers will see one Sign of God after another, and with each their Faith is confirmed. During all the long years of persecution and conflict they had Faith, but when they see their old enemies actually coming out to negotiate with them, their Faith is justified, fulfilled, and confirmed: and they turn in gratitude to God.

The Forces of the heavens[4871]
And the earth; and God is
Full of Knowledge and Wisdom;—

جُنُودُ السَّمٰوٰتِ وَالْأَرْضِ ۚ
وَكَانَ اللّٰهُ عَلِيمًا حَكِيمًا ۝

5. That He may admit[4872]
The men and women
Who believe, to Gardens
Beneath which rivers flow,
To dwell therein for aye,
And remove their ills
From them;—and that is,
In the sight of God,
The highest achievement
(For man),—

٥- لِيُدْخِلَ الْمُؤْمِنِينَ وَالْمُؤْمِنٰتِ
جَنّٰتٍ تَجْرِي مِنْ تَحْتِهَا الْأَنْهٰرُ
خٰلِدِينَ فِيهَا
وَيُكَفِّرَ عَنْهُمْ سَيِّاٰتِهِمْ ۚ
وَكَانَ ذٰلِكَ عِنْدَ اللّٰهِ فَوْزًا عَظِيمًا ۝

6. And that He may punish
The Hypocrites, men and
Women, and the Polytheists,
Men and women, who imagine
An evil opinion of God.
On them is a round[4873]
Of Evil: the Wrath of God
Is on them: He has cursed[4874]
Them and got Hell ready
For them: and evil
Is it for a destination.

٦- وَيُعَذِّبَ الْمُنٰفِقِينَ وَالْمُنٰفِقٰتِ
وَالْمُشْرِكِينَ وَالْمُشْرِكٰتِ
الظَّآنِّينَ بِاللّٰهِ ظَنَّ السَّوْءِ ۚ
عَلَيْهِمْ دَآئِرَةُ السَّوْءِ ۚ وَغَضِبَ اللّٰهُ عَلَيْهِمْ
وَلَعَنَهُمْ وَأَعَدَّ لَهُمْ جَهَنَّمَ ۖ
وَسَآءَتْ مَصِيرًا ۝

7. For to God belong[4875]
The Forces of the heavens
And the earth; and God is
Exalted in Power,
Full of Wisdom.

٧- وَلِلّٰهِ جُنُودُ السَّمٰوٰتِ وَالْأَرْضِ ۚ
وَكَانَ اللّٰهُ عَزِيزًا حَكِيمًا ۝

4871. There are visible forces which you see in the physical world. Men fight with armed forces, and the Muslims had to defend themselves with arms also, and not without success. But social, moral, and spiritual forces were fighting for them under God's command, and they were the real forces that established the Message of Islam and the position of its Leader and Preacher.

4872. This clause is co-ordinated to the previous clause, "That they may add Faith to their Faith". The intervening words, "For to God...and Wisdom" are parenthetical. The third co-ordinate clause comes in the next verse, "And that He may punish...". The skeleton construction will be, "God sends down calm courage to Believers, in order that they may be confirmed in their Faith; that they may qualify for the Bliss of Heaven; and that the evil ones may receive the punishment they deserve."

4873. They will be encircled (or hemmed in) by Evil.

4874. That is, deprived them of His Grace, on account of their continued rejection of it.

4875. These words are repeated (with a slight change) from the parenthetical clause in verse 4, to emphasize the assertion as a substantive proposition, that fighting and visible forces in the physical world are not the only forces with which God works out His Plan. The invisible forces are more important as they were at Ḥudaibiya. The slight difference is instructive; in the parenthetical clause, God's Knowledge was emphasized, and in the substantive clause it is God's Power. Knowledge plans, and Power executes.

8. We have truly sent thee [4876]
As a witness, as a
Bringer of Glad Tidings,
And as a Warner:

٨- إِنَّآ أَرْسَلْنٰكَ شَاهِدًا
وَّمُبَشِّرًا وَّنَذِيرًا ۝

9. In order that ye
(O men) may believe
In God and His Apostle,
That ye may assist
And honour Him,
And celebrate His praises
Morning and evening.

٩- لِّتُؤْمِنُوا بِاللّٰهِ وَرَسُولِهٖ
وَتُعَزِّرُوهُ وَتُوَقِّرُوهُ ۚ
وَتُسَبِّحُوهُ بُكْرَةً وَّأَصِيلًا ۝

10. Verily those who plight [4877]
Their fealty to thee
Do no less than plight
Their fealty to God:
The Hand of God is
Over their hands:
Then any one who violates
His oath, does so
To the harm of his own
Soul, and any one who
Fulfils what he has
Covenanted with God,—
God will soon grant him
A great Reward.

١٠- إِنَّ الَّذِينَ يُبَايِعُونَكَ
إِنَّمَا يُبَايِعُونَ اللّٰهَ ۚ
يَدُ اللّٰهِ فَوْقَ أَيْدِيهِمْ ۚ
فَمَنْ نَّكَثَ
فَإِنَّمَا يَنْكُثُ عَلٰى نَفْسِهٖ ۚ
وَمَنْ أَوْفٰى بِمَا عٰهَدَ عَلَيْهُ اللّٰهَ
فَسَيُؤْتِيهِ أَجْرًا عَظِيمًا ۝ ع

SECTION 2.

11. The desert Arabs who [4878]
Lagged behind will

١١- سَيَقُولُ لَكَ الْمُخَلَّفُونَ مِنَ الْأَعْرَابِ

4876. The Apostle came in order to establish Faith in God and true worship. We can view him in three capacities: (1) as a witness to help the weak if they were oppressed and check the strong if they did wrong; (2) as a giver of the Glad Tidings of God's Grace and Mercy to those who repented and lived good lives; and (3) as one who warned sinners of the consequences of their sin.

4877. In the Ḥudaibīya negotiations, when it was uncertain whether the Quraish would treat well or ill the Prophet's delegate to Mecca, there was a great wave of feeling in the Muslim camp of 1400 to 1500 men. They came with great enthusiasm and swore their fealty to the Prophet, by placing hand on hand according to the Arab custom; see paragraph 3 of the Introduction to this Sūra. This in itself was a wonderful demonstration of moral and material strength, a true Victory: it is called *Bai'at ur Ridhwān* (Fealty of God's Good Pleasure) in Islamic History. They placed their hands on the Prophet's hand, but the Hand of God was above them, and He accepted their Fealty.

'Alaihu is an archaic form for *'Alaihi*.

4878. When the Prophet started from Medina on the Mecca journey which ended in Ḥudaibīya, he asked all Muslims to join him in the pious undertaking, and he had a splendid response. But some of the desert tribes hung back and made excuses. Their faith was but lukewarm, and they did not want to share in any trouble which the Meccans might give to the unarmed Muslims on pilgrimage. Their excuse that they were engaged in looking after their flocks and herds and their families was an after-thought, and in any case made after the return of the Prophet and his party with enhanced prestige to Medina.

Say to thee:
"We were engaged in
(Looking after) our flocks
And herds, and our families:
Do thou then ask
Forgiveness for us." [4879]
They say with their tongues
What is not in their hearts.
Say: "Who then has
Any power at all
(To intervene) on your behalf
With God, if His Will
Is to give you some loss [4880]
Or to give you some profit?
But God is well acquainted
With all that ye do.

شَغَلَتْنَآ أَمْوَالُنَا وَأَهْلُونَا
فَاسْتَغْفِرْ لَنَا ۚ
يَقُولُونَ بِأَلْسِنَتِهِم
مَّا لَيْسَ فِي قُلُوبِهِمْ ۚ
قُلْ فَمَن يَمْلِكُ لَكُم مِّنَ اللَّهِ شَيْئًا
إِنْ أَرَادَ بِكُمْ ضَرًّا
أَوْ أَرَادَ بِكُمْ نَفْعًا ۚ
بَلْ كَانَ اللَّهُ بِمَا تَعْمَلُونَ خَبِيرًا ۝

12. "Nay, ye thought that
The Apostle and the Believers
Would never return to
Their families; this seemed
Pleasing in your hearts, [4881] and
Ye conceived an evil thought,
For ye are a people
Lost (in wickedness)."

١٢- بَلْ ظَنَنتُمْ أَن لَّن يَنقَلِبَ الرَّسُولُ
وَالْمُؤْمِنُونَ إِلَىٰ أَهْلِيهِمْ أَبَدًا
وَزُيِّنَ ذَٰلِكَ فِي قُلُوبِكُمْ وَظَنَنتُمْ ظَنَّ
السَّوْءِ وَكُنتُمْ قَوْمًا بُورًا ۝

13. And if any believe not
In God and His Apostle,
We have prepared,
For those who reject God,
A Blazing Fire!

١٣- وَمَن لَّمْ يُؤْمِن بِاللَّهِ وَرَسُولِهِ
فَإِنَّآ أَعْتَدْنَا لِلْكَافِرِينَ سَعِيرًا ۝

14. To God belongs the dominion
Of the heavens and the earth:
He forgives whom He wills, [4882]
And He punishes whom He

١٤- وَلِلَّهِ مُلْكُ السَّمَاوَاتِ وَالْأَرْضِ ۚ
يَغْفِرُ لِمَن يَشَآءُ وَيُعَذِّبُ مَن يَشَآءُ ۚ

4879. They said this with their tongues, but no thought of piety was in their hearts.

4880. Their false excuse was based on a calculation of worldly profit and loss. But what about the spiritual loss in detaching themselves from the holy Prophet or spiritual profit in joining in the splendidly loyal feelings of service and obedience which were demonstrated at Ḥudaibīya? And in any case they need not think that all their real and secret motives were not known to God.

4881. Their faith was so shaky that they thought the worst would happen, and that the Meccan Quraish would destroy the unarmed band. In their heart of hearts they would not have been sorry, because they were steeped in wickedness and rejoiced in the sufferings of others. But such persons will burn in the fire of their own disappointment.

4882. Evil must inevitably have its punishment, but there is one way of escape, *viz.*, through repentance and the Mercy of God. God's Justice will punish, but God's Mercy will forgive; and the Mercy is the predominant feature in God's universe: "He is Oft-Forgiving, Most Merciful."

Wills : but God is
Oft-Forgiving, Most Merciful.

وَكَانَ اللّٰهُ غَفُوْرًا رَّحِيْمًا ۝

15. Those who lagged behind[4883]
(Will say), when ye (are
Free to) march and take
Booty (in war) : "Permit us
To follow you." They wish
To change God's decree :
Say : "Not thus[4884]
Will ye follow us :
God has already declared[4885]
(This) beforehand" : then they
Will say, "But ye are[4886]
Jealous of us." Nay,
But little do they understand
(Such things).

١٥- سَيَقُوْلُ الْمُخَلَّفُوْنَ اِذَا انْطَلَقْتُمْ اِلٰى
مَغَانِمَ لِتَاْخُذُوْهَا ذَرُوْنَا نَتَّبِعْكُمْ ۚ
يُرِيْدُوْنَ اَنْ يُّبَدِّلُوْا كَلٰمَ اللّٰهِ ۗ
قُلْ لَّنْ تَتَّبِعُوْنَا كَذٰلِكُمْ
قَالَ اللّٰهُ مِنْ قَبْلُ ۚ
فَسَيَقُوْلُوْنَ بَلْ تَحْسُدُوْنَنَا ۗ
بَلْ كَانُوْا لَا يَفْقَهُوْنَ اِلَّا قَلِيْلًا ۝

16. Say to the desert Arabs[4887]
Who lagged behind : "Ye
Shall be summoned (to fight)
Against a people given to[4888]
Vehement war : then shall ye
Fight, or they shall submit.[4889]
Then if ye show obedience,
God will grant you
A goodly reward, but if
Ye turn back as ye

١٦- قُلْ لِّلْمُخَلَّفِيْنَ مِنَ الْاَعْرَابِ
سَتُدْعَوْنَ اِلٰى قَوْمٍ اُولِيْ بَاْسٍ شَدِيْدٍ
تُقَاتِلُوْنَهُمْ اَوْ يُسْلِمُوْنَ ۚ
فَاِنْ تُطِيْعُوْا يُؤْتِكُمُ اللّٰهُ اَجْرًا حَسَنًا ۚ
وَاِنْ تَتَوَلَّوْا كَمَا تَوَلَّيْتُمْ

4883. Now comes out another motive behind the minds of the laggards. The journey for pilgrimage had no promise of war booty. If at any future time there should be a promise of booty they would come ! But that is to reverse God's law and decree. Jihād is not for personal gain or booty : see S. viii. and Introduction to S. viii., paragraph 2. On the contrary Jihād is hard striving, in war and peace, in the Cause of God.

4884. *Not thus* : *i.e.* not on those terms ; not if your object is only to gain booty.

4885. See viii. 1, and n. 1179.

4886. The desert Arabs loved fighting and plunder, and understood such motives for war. The higher motives seemed to be beyond them. Like ignorant men they attributed petty motives or motives of jealousy if they were kept out of the vulgar circle of fighting for plunder. But they had to be schooled, and they were schooled to higher ideas of discipline, self-sacrifice, and striving hard for a Cause.

4887. While they are reproached for their supineness in the march which led to Ḥudaibīya, where there was danger but no prospect of booty, they are promised, if they learn discipline, to be allowed to follow the Banner of Islam where (as happened later in the Persian and Byzantine Wars) there was real fighting with formidable and well-organised armies.

4888. *Cf.* xxvii. 33.

4889. That is, you shall go forth to war if you learn discipline, not for booty, but for a great and noble Cause. For if your opponents submit to the Cause, there will be no fighting and no booty.

Did before, He will punish
You with a grievous Penalty."

مِّنْ قَبْلُ يُعَذِّبْكُمْ عَذَابًا أَلِيمًا ۝

17. No blame is there
On the blind, nor is
There blame on the lame,
Nor on one ill (if he
Joins not the war):
But he that obeys God [4890]
And His Apostle,—(God)
Will admit him to Gardens
Beneath which rivers flow;
And he who turns back,
(God) will punish him
With a grievous Penalty.

١٧- لَيْسَ عَلَى الْأَعْمَىٰ حَرَجٌ
وَلَا عَلَى الْأَعْرَجِ حَرَجٌ
وَلَا عَلَى الْمَرِيضِ حَرَجٌ ۗ
وَمَن يُطِعِ اللَّهَ وَرَسُولَهُ
يُدْخِلْهُ جَنَّاتٍ تَجْرِي مِن تَحْتِهَا الْأَنْهَارُ ۖ
وَمَن يَتَوَلَّ يُعَذِّبْهُ عَذَابًا أَلِيمًا ۝

SECTION 3.

18. God's Good Pleasure [4891]
Was on the Believers
When they swore Fealty
To thee under the Tree: [4892]
He knew [4893] what was
In their hearts, and He
Sent down Tranquillity [4894]
To them; and He rewarded
Them with a speedy Victory; [4895]

١٨- لَقَدْ رَضِيَ اللَّهُ عَنِ الْمُؤْمِنِينَ
إِذْ يُبَايِعُونَكَ تَحْتَ الشَّجَرَةِ
فَعَلِمَ مَا فِي قُلُوبِهِمْ
فَأَنزَلَ السَّكِينَةَ عَلَيْهِمْ
وَأَثَابَهُمْ فَتْحًا قَرِيبًا ۝

19. And many gains will they
Acquire (besides): and God
Is Exalted in Power,
Full of Wisdom.

١٩- وَمَغَانِمَ كَثِيرَةً يَأْخُذُونَهَا ۗ
وَكَانَ اللَّهُ عَزِيزًا حَكِيمًا ۝

4890. There may be neither fighting nor booty. But all who obey the righteous Imām's call to Jihād with perfect discipline will get the spiritual Rewards of the Hereafter. The blind, the maimed, and the infirm will of course be exempted from active compliance with the Call, but they can render such services as are within their power, and then they will not be excluded from the reward.

4891. The noun from the verb *radhiya* is *ridhwān* (Good Pleasure); hence the name of this *Bai'at*, *Bai'at ur Ridhwān*, the Fealty of God's Good Pleasure: see n. 4877 to xlviii. 10.

4892. The great ceremony of the Fealty of God's Good Pleasure took place while the holy Apostle sat under a tree in the plain of Ḥudaibīya. This Tree became very famous, and so much superstitious veneration was attached to it by later generations that it had to be cut down.

4893 Or tested: see n. 4855 to xlvii. 31.

4894. *Sakīna*=Peace, calm, sense of security and confidence, tranquillity. *Cf.* above xlviii. 4, and n. 4869. The same word is used in connection with the battle of Ḥunain in ix. 26, and in connection with the Cave of Thaur at an early stage in the Hijrat: ix. 40.

4895. The Treaty of Ḥudaibīya itself was a "speedy Victory": it followed immediately after the *Bai'at*

20. God has promised you
Many gains that ye shall [4896]
Acquire, and He has given [4897]
You these beforehand; and
He has restrained the hands
Of men from you; that it
May be a Sign for [4898]
The Believers, and that
He may guide you
To a Straight Path;

٢٠- وَعَدَكُمُ اللّٰهُ مَغَانِمَ كَثِيرَةً تَأْخُذُونَهَا
فَعَجَّلَ لَكُمْ هٰذِهِۦ
وَكَفَّ أَيْدِيَ النَّاسِ عَنكُمْ
وَلِتَكُونَ ءَايَةً لِّلْمُؤْمِنِينَ
وَيَهْدِيَكُمْ صِرَٰطًا مُّسْتَقِيمًا ○

21. And other gains (there are),
Which are not within [4899]
Your power, but which
God has compassed: and God
Has power over all things.

٢١- وَأُخْرَىٰ لَمْ تَقْدِرُوا عَلَيْهَا
قَدْ أَحَاطَ اللّٰهُ بِهَا
وَكَانَ اللّٰهُ عَلَىٰ كُلِّ شَيْءٍ قَدِيرًا ○

22. If the Unbelievers
Should fight you, they would [4900]
Certainly turn their backs;
Then would they find
Neither protector nor helper.

٢٢- وَلَوْ قَٰتَلَكُمُ الَّذِينَ كَفَرُوا
لَوَلَّوُا الْأَدْبَٰرَ
ثُمَّ لَا يَجِدُونَ وَلِيًّا وَلَا نَصِيرًا ○

23. (Such has been) the practice [4901]
(Approved) of God already
In the past: no change
Wilt thou find in
The practice (approved) of God.

٢٣- سُنَّةَ اللّٰهِ الَّتِي
قَدْ خَلَتْ مِن قَبْلُ
وَلَن تَجِدَ لِسُنَّةِ اللّٰهِ تَبْدِيلًا ○

24. And it is He Who
Has restrained their hands

٢٤- وَهُوَ الَّذِي كَفَّ أَيْدِيَهُمْ

4896. The gains so far seen from the *Bai'at* and their calm and disciplined behaviour were certainly great; but greater still were to follow in the spiritual sense, in the rapid spread of Islam, in the clearance from the Sacred House of the idolatrous autocracy, and in the universal acceptance of the Message of God in Arabia.

4897. The first fruits of the *Bai'at* were the victory or treaty of Ḥudaibiya, the cessation for the time being of the hostility of the Meccan Quraish, and the opening out of the way to Mecca. These things are implied in the phrase, "He has restrained the hands of men from you."

4898. Ḥudaibiya (in both the Bai'at and the Treaty) was truly a sign-post for the Believers: it showed the solidarity of Islam, and the position which the Muslims had won in the Arab world.

4899. *Other gains*: these are usually referred to the later victories of Islam, but we must view them not merely in their political or material aspect, but chiefly in the rise of Islam as a world power morally and spiritually.

4900. Their morale was now truly broken.

4901. *Cf.* xxxiii. 62.

From you and your hands
From them in the midst[4902]
Of Mecca, after that He
Gave you the victory
Over them. And God sees
Well all that ye do.

25. They are the ones who
Denied revelation and hindered you
From the Sacred Mosque
And the sacrificial animals,[4903]
Detained from reaching their
Place of sacrifice. Had there
Not been believing men
And believing women whom
Ye did not know that[4904]
Ye were trampling down
And on whose account
A crime would have accrued
To you without (your) knowledge,
(God would have allowed you
To force your way, but
He held back your hands)
That He may admit
To His Mercy whom He will.[4905]
If they had been[4906]
Apart, We should

عَنكُمْ وَأَيْدِيَكُمْ عَنْهُم بِبَطْنِ مَكَّةَ
مِنۢ بَعْدِ أَنْ أَظْفَرَكُمْ عَلَيْهِمْ ۚ
وَكَانَ ٱللَّهُ بِمَا تَعْمَلُونَ بَصِيرًا ۝
٢٥- هُمُ ٱلَّذِينَ كَفَرُوا
وَصَدُّوكُمْ عَنِ ٱلْمَسْجِدِ ٱلْحَرَامِ
وَٱلْهَدْىَ مَعْكُوفًا
أَن يَبْلُغَ مَحِلَّهُۥ ۚ
وَلَوْلَا رِجَالٌ مُّؤْمِنُونَ وَنِسَآءٌ مُّؤْمِنَٰتٌ
لَّمْ تَعْلَمُوهُمْ أَن تَطَـُٔوهُمْ
فَتُصِيبَكُم مِّنْهُم مَّعَرَّةٌۢ
بِغَيْرِ عِلْمٍ ۖ
لِّيُدْخِلَ ٱللَّهُ فِى رَحْمَتِهِۦ
مَن يَشَآءُ ۚ
لَوْ تَزَيَّلُوا

4902. Little incidents had taken place that might have plunged the Quraish and the Muslims from Medina into a fight. On the one hand, the Quraish were determined to keep out the Muslims, which they had no right to do: and on the other hand, the Muslims, though unarmed, had sworn to stand together, and if they had counter-attacked they could have forced their entrance to the Ka'ba, the centre of Mecca. But God restrained both sides from anything that would have violated the Peace of the Sanctuary, and after the Treaty was signed, all danger was past.

4903. The Muslims from Medina had brought the animals for sacrifice with them, and had put on the Iḥrām or pilgrim's garb (see n. 217 to ii. 197), but they were not only prevented from entering Mecca, but were also prevented from sending the sacrificial animals to the place of sacrifice in Mecca, as they could have done under ii. 196. The sacrifice was therefore actually offered at Ḥudaibīya.

4904. There were at the time in Mecca believing Muslims, men and women, and the faith of some of them was unknown to their brethren from Medina. Had a fight taken place in Mecca, even though the Muslims had been successful, they would unwittingly have killed some of these unknown Muslims, and thus would unwittingly have been guilty of shedding Muslim blood. This was prevented by the Treaty.

4905. God works according to His wise and holy Will and Plan, and not according to what seems to us, in the excitement of human life, to be the obvious course of things. By preventing a fight He saved many valuable lives, not only of Muslims but also of some who became Muslims afterwards and served Islam. He grants His Mercy on far higher standards than man in his limited horizon can see.

4906. If the party from Medina could have distinguished Muslims from non-Muslims among the Meccans, they might have been allowed to enter and punish the pagan Quraish for their inordinate vanity and gross breach of the unwritten law of the land. But in the actual circumstances the best solution was the Treaty of Ḥudaibīya.

Certainly have punished
The Unbelievers among them
With a grievous punishment.

لَعَذَّبْنَا الَّذِيْنَ كَفَرُوْا مِنْهُمْ
عَذَابًا اَلِيْمًا ○

26. While the Unbelievers
Got up in their hearts
Heat and cant—the heat[4907]
And cant of Ignorance,—
God sent down His Tranquillity[4908]
To his Apostle and to
The Believers, and made them
Stick close to the command
Of self-restraint; and well
Were they entitled to it[4909]
And worthy of it.
And God has full knowledge
Of all things.

٢٦ - اِذْ جَعَلَ الَّذِيْنَ كَفَرُوْا فِيْ قُلُوْبِهِمُ
الْحَمِيَّةَ حَمِيَّةَ الْجَاهِلِيَّةِ
فَاَنْزَلَ اللّٰهُ سَكِيْنَتَهٗ
عَلٰى رَسُوْلِهٖ وَعَلَى الْمُؤْمِنِيْنَ
وَاَلْزَمَهُمْ كَلِمَةَ التَّقْوٰى
وَكَانُوْٓا اَحَقَّ بِهَا وَاَهْلَهَا ؕ
وَكَانَ اللّٰهُ بِكُلِّ شَيْءٍ عَلِيْمًا ○ ع

SECTION 4.

27. Truly did God fulfil
The vision for His Apostle:[4910]
Ye shall enter the Sacred
Mosque, if God wills,
With minds secure, heads shaved,
Hair cut short, and without fear.
For He knew what ye
Knew not, and He granted,
Besides this, a speedy victory.[4911]

٢٧ - لَقَدْ صَدَقَ اللّٰهُ رَسُوْلَهُ الرُّءْيَا بِالْحَقِّ ۚ
لَتَدْخُلُنَّ الْمَسْجِدَ الْحَرَامَ اِنْ شَآءَ اللّٰهُ
اٰمِنِيْنَ ۙ مُحَلِّقِيْنَ رُءُوْسَكُمْ وَمُقَصِّرِيْنَ ۙ لَا
تَخَافُوْنَ ؕ فَعَلِمَ مَا لَمْ تَعْلَمُوْا
فَجَعَلَ مِنْ دُوْنِ ذٰلِكَ فَتْحًا قَرِيْبًا ○

28. It is He Who has sent
His Apostle with Guidance
And the Religion of Truth,
To proclaim it over

٢٨ - هُوَ الَّذِيْٓ اَرْسَلَ رَسُوْلَهٗ بِالْهُدٰى
وَدِيْنِ الْحَقِّ لِيُظْهِرَهٗ عَلَى

4907. While the Unbelievers were blustering and excited, and meticulously objected to introductory words such as "In the name of God, *Most Gracious, Most Merciful* (they did not like the titles), the Muslims were calm and collected, and got the substance of their demands embodied in the Treaty without worrying about words. This was due to their unity and trust in their Leader.

4908. *Cf.* above xlviii. 18, and n. 4894.

4909. *It*=Tranquillity. Their calmness amid much provocation was a gift of God; they had earned a right to it by their obedience and discipline, and showed themselves well worthy of it.

4910. The Prophet had had a dream that he had entered the Sacred Mosque at Mecca, just before he decided on the journey which resulted in the Treaty of Ḥudaibiya. By it he and his people could enter next year without the least molestation and in the full customary garb, with head shaved or hair cut short, and all the customary minor rites of pilgrimage.

4911. See above, xlviii. 18, and n. 4895.

All religion: and enough
Is God for a Witness.[4912]

الدِّيْنِ كُلِّهٖ ۭ وَكَفٰى بِاللّٰهِ شَهِيْدًا ۝

29. Muḥammad is the Apostle
Of God; and those who are
With him are strong
Against Unbelievers, (but)
Compassionate amongst each
other.[4913]
Thou wilt see them bow
And prostrate themselves
(In prayer), seeking Grace
From God and (His) Good
Pleasure.[4914]
On their faces are their
Marks, (being) the traces[4915]
Of their prostration.
This is their similitude
In the Taurāt;[4916]
And their similitude
In the Gospel is:[4917]
Like a seed which sends
Forth its blade, then
Makes it strong; it then
Becomes thick, and it stands

٢٩- مُحَمَّدٌ رَّسُوْلُ اللّٰهِ ۭ
وَالَّذِيْنَ مَعَهٗٓ اَشِدَّاۗءُ عَلَى الْكُفَّارِ
رُحَمَاۗءُ بَيْنَهُمْ
تَرٰىهُمْ رُكَّعًا سُجَّدًا
يَّبْتَغُوْنَ فَضْلًا مِّنَ اللّٰهِ وَرِضْوَانًا ۡ
سِيْمَاهُمْ فِيْ وُجُوْهِهِمْ مِّنْ اَثَرِ السُّجُوْدِ ۭ
ذٰلِكَ مَثَلُهُمْ فِي التَّوْرٰىةِ ۚۛ
وَمَثَلُهُمْ فِي الْاِنْجِيْلِ ۚۛ
كَزَرْعٍ
اَخْرَجَ شَطْــَٔهٗ فَاٰزَرَهٗ
فَاسْتَغْلَظَ فَاسْتَوٰى

4912. The divine disposition of events in the coming of Islam and its promulgation by the holy Prophet are themselves evidence of the truth of Islam and its all-reaching character; for there is nothing which it has not influenced. See also lxi. 9, n. 5442.

4913. *Cf.* ix. 128. The devotees of God wage unceasing war against evil, for themselves, and for others; but to their own brethren in faith—especially the weaker ones—they are mild and compassionate: they seek out every opportunity to sympathise with them and help them.

4914. Their humility is before God and His Apostle and all who have authority from God, but they yield no power or pomp, nor do they worship worldly show or glitter. Nor is their humility before God a mere show for men.

4915. The traces of their earnestness and humility are engraved on their faces, *i.e.* penetrate their inmost being, the face being the outward sign of the inner man. If we take it in its literal sense, a good man's face alone shows in him the grace and light of God; he is gentle, kind and forbearing, ever helpful, relying on God, and possessing a blessed Peace and Calmness (*Sakīna*, xlviii. 26) that can come from no other source.

4916. In the Book of Moses, which is now found in a corrupt form in the Pentateuch, the posture of humility in prayer is indicated by prostration: *e.g.*, Moses and Aaron "fell upon their faces", Num. xvi. 22.

4917. The similitude in the Gospel is about how the good seed is sown and grows gradually, even beyond the expectation of the sower: "the seed should spring and grow up, he knoweth not how; for the earth bringeth forth fruit of herself; first the blade, then the ear, after that the full corn in the ear": Mark, iv. 27-28. Thus Islam was preached by the holy Prophet; the seed seemed to human eyes lost in the ground; but it put forth its shoot, and grew, and became strong, until it was able to stand on its own legs, and its worst enemies recognised its existence and its right to live. Note how much more complete the parable is in the Qur-ān. The mentality of the sowers of the seed is expressed in beautiful terms: its growth and strength filled them "with wonder and delight."

On its own stem, (filling) The sowers with wonder And delight. As a result,[4918] It fills the Unbelievers With rage at them. God has promised those Among them who believe And do righteous deeds Forgiveness, And a great Reward.	عَلٰى سُوْقِهٖ يُعْجِبُ الزُّرَّاعَ لِيَغِيْظَ بِهِمُ الْكُفَّارَ ؕ وَعَدَ اللّٰهُ الَّذِيْنَ اٰمَنُوْا وَعَمِلُوا الصّٰلِحٰتِ مِنْهُمْ مَّغْفِرَةً وَّ اَجْرًا عَظِيْمًا ۟ ع

4918. I construe the particle "*li*" as expressing not the object, but the result. The result of the wonderful growth of Islam in numbers and strength was that its enemies were confounded, and raged furiously within their own minds, a contrast to the satisfaction, wonder, and delight of the Prophet and his Companions. The pronoun in "rage at *them*" of course refers to the Prophet and his Companions, and goes back to the earlier words, "on *their* faces" etc.

INTRODUCTION TO SŪRA XLIX (*Ḥujurāt*).

This is the third of the group of three Medina Sūras, which began with S. xlvii. See the Introduction to that Sūra.

Its subject-matter is the manners to be observed by the members of the rapidly-growing Muslim community, among themselves and towards its Leader. The key-word "*Ḥujurāt*" (Inner Apartments) occurs in verse 4.

Its date is referred to the Year of Deputations, A.H. 9, when a large number of deputations of all kinds visited Medina to offer their allegiance to Islam.

Summary.—A community must show its respect to its Leader in all forms of behaviour; quarrels are unseemly and should be composed; manners spring from morals; and mutual respect and confidence are a duty and a privilege in Islam (xlix. 1-18, and C. 223).

C. 223.—Respectful behaviour to the Leader, in manner,
(xlix. 1-18.) Voice, and demeanour, are the bonds and cement
Of an organised community. The whispers
Of rumour should be tested, and selfish impatience
Should be curbed to discipline. All quarrels
Should be composed, if necessary by the force
Of the community, but with perfect
Fairness and justice. Ridicule, taunts,
And biting words, should be avoided,
In presence or in absence. Suspicion
And spying are unworthy of men who believe.
All men are descended from one pair:
Their honour depends, not on race, but
On righteousness. Faith is not a matter
Of words, but of accepting God's Will
And striving in His Cause. The coming
Into Islam confers no favour on others,
But is itself a favour and a privilege,
A guidance for those who are true and sincere.

Ḥujurāt, or the Inner Apartments.

In the name of God, Most Gracious, Most Merciful.

بِسْمِ اللّٰهِ الرَّحْمٰنِ الرَّحِيْمِ

1. O ye who believe!
Put not yourselves forward[4919]
Before God and His Apostle;
But fear God: for God
Is He Who hears
And knows all things.

١- يٰۤاَيُّهَا الَّذِيْنَ اٰمَنُوْا لَا تُقَدِّمُوْا
بَيْنَ يَدَيِ اللّٰهِ وَرَسُوْلِهٖ وَاتَّقُوا اللّٰهَ ؕ
اِنَّ اللّٰهَ سَمِيْعٌ عَلِيْمٌ ۝

2. O ye who believe!
Raise not your voices[4920]
Above the voice of the Prophet,
Nor speak aloud to him
In talk, as ye may
Speak aloud to one another,
Lest your deeds become[4921]
Vain and ye perceive not.

٢- يٰۤاَيُّهَا الَّذِيْنَ اٰمَنُوْا
لَا تَرْفَعُوْۤا اَصْوَاتَكُمْ فَوْقَ صَوْتِ النَّبِيِّ
وَلَا تَجْهَرُوْا لَهٗ بِالْقَوْلِ كَجَهْرِ بَعْضِكُمْ لِبَعْضٍ
اَنْ تَحْبَطَ اَعْمَالُكُمْ وَاَنْتُمْ لَا تَشْعُرُوْنَ ۝

3. Those that lower their voice
In the presence of
God's Apostle,—their hearts
Has God tested for piety:[4922]
For them is Forgiveness
And a great Reward.

٣- اِنَّ الَّذِيْنَ يَغُضُّوْنَ اَصْوَاتَهُمْ عِنْدَ
رَسُوْلِ اللّٰهِ اُولٰٓئِكَ الَّذِيْنَ امْتَحَنَ اللّٰهُ
قُلُوْبَهُمْ لِلتَّقْوٰى ؕ لَهُمْ مَّغْفِرَةٌ وَّاَجْرٌ عَظِيْمٌ ۝

4. Those who shout out[4923]
To thee from without

٤- اِنَّ الَّذِيْنَ يُنَادُوْنَكَ مِنْ وَّرَآءِ

4919. Three shades of meaning are implied: (1) do not make yourselves conspicuous in word or deed when in the presence of God (*e g.* in a Mosque, or at Prayers or religious assemblies); (2) do not anticipate in word or deed what your Leader (God's Apostle) may say or do; (3) do not be impatient, trying to hasten things before the time is ripe, of which the best Judge is God, Who speaks through His Apostle. Be reverent in all things, as in the presence of God: for He hears and sees all things.

4920. It is bad manners to talk loudly before your Leader. Some ill-mannered people so raise their voices as to drown the voice of their Leader, in conversation or in Council.

4921. Such rudeness may even destroy the value of such services as they may otherwise have been able to render, and all this without their even realising the harm they were doing to the Cause.

4922. The essence of good manners arises from the heart. The man who really and sincerely respects his Leader has true piety in his heart, just as the man who does the opposite may undo the work of years by weakening the Leader's authority.

4923. To shout aloud to your Leader from outside his Apartments shows disrespect both for his person, his time, and his engagements. Only ignorant fools would be guilty of such unseemly behaviour. It is more seemly for them to wait and bide their time until he is free to come out and attend to them. But, in the Court of a spiritual King, much is forgiven that is due to lack of knowledge and understanding. In an earthly Court, ignorance of the Law excuseth no man. If a man behaved in that way to the General of an army or the Governor of a Province, not to speak of an earthly King, he would be laid hands on by the Guard, and could never gain the access he desires.

The Inner Apartments—
Most of them lack understanding.

الْحُجُرٰتِ اَكْثَرُهُمْ لَا يَعْقِلُوْنَ ○

5. If only they had patience
Until thou couldst
Come out to them,
It would be best
For them: but God is
Oft-Forgiving, Most Merciful.

٥- وَلَوْ اَنَّهُمْ صَبَرُوْا حَتّٰى تَخْرُجَ اِلَيْهِمْ
لَكَانَ خَيْرًا لَّهُمْ ۭ
وَاللّٰهُ غَفُوْرٌ رَّحِيْمٌ ○

6. O ye who believe!
If a wicked person comes[4924]
To you with any news,
Ascertain the truth, lest
Ye harm people unwittingly,
And afterwards become
Full of repentance for
What ye have done.

٦- يٰٓاَيُّهَا الَّذِيْنَ اٰمَنُوْٓا
اِنْ جَاۗءَكُمْ فَاسِقٌۢ بِنَبَاٍ
فَتَبَيَّنُوْٓا اَنْ تُصِيْبُوْا قَوْمًۢا بِجَهَالَةٍ
فَتُصْبِحُوْا عَلٰي مَا فَعَلْتُمْ نٰدِمِيْنَ ○

7. And know that among you[4925]
Is God's Apostle: were he,
In many matters, to follow
Your (wishes), ye would
Certainly fall into misfortune:
But God has endeared[4926]
The Faith to you, and
Has made it beautiful
In your hearts, and He
Has made hateful to you
Unbelief, wickedness, and
Rebellion: such indeed are
Those who walk in righteousness;—

٧- وَاعْلَمُوْٓا اَنَّ فِيْكُمْ رَسُوْلَ اللّٰهِ ۭ
لَوْ يُطِيْعُكُمْ فِيْ كَثِيْرٍ مِّنَ الْاَمْرِ لَعَنِتُّمْ
وَلٰكِنَّ اللّٰهَ حَبَّبَ اِلَيْكُمُ الْاِيْمَانَ
وَزَيَّنَهٗ فِيْ قُلُوْبِكُمْ
وَكَرَّهَ اِلَيْكُمُ الْكُفْرَ وَالْفُسُوْقَ وَالْعِصْيَانَ ۭ
اُولٰۗىِٕكَ هُمُ الرّٰشِدُوْنَ ○

8. A grace and favour
From God; and God
Is full of Knowledge
And Wisdom.

٨- فَضْلًا مِّنَ اللّٰهِ وَنِعْمَةً ۭ
وَاللّٰهُ عَلِيْمٌ حَكِيْمٌ ○

4924. All tittle-tattle or reports—especially if emanating from persons you do not know—are to be tested, and the truth ascertained. If they were believed and passed on, much harm may be done, of which you may have cause afterwards to repent heartily. Scandal or slander of all kinds is here condemned. That about women is specially denounced: xxiv. 11-20; 23-26.

4925. The man of God, if he consults his friends and associates, should not be expected to follow their advice in all matters. The judgment and responsibility are his: he sees farther than the rest, and he is less swayed by personal feeling than any one else.

4926. Fortunate indeed was the generation among whom the Prophet of God walked in his daily life. His example was inspiring. Their inner Faith was dear to them; it was a thing to be proud of in their innermost hearts; and they loved discipline, obedience, and righteousness. No wonder all their other disadvantages were neutralised, and they went from strength to strength. Nothing but the Grace of God could have brought about such a result.

9. If two parties among[4927]
The Believers fall into
A quarrel, make ye peace
Between them: but if
One of them transgresses
Beyond bounds against the other,
Then fight ye (all) against
The one that transgresses
Until it complies with
The command of God;
But if it complies, then
Make peace between them
With justice, and be fair:
For God loves those
Who are fair (and just).

٩- وَإِن طَائِفَتَانِ مِنَ الْمُؤْمِنِينَ اقْتَتَلُوا
فَأَصْلِحُوا بَيْنَهُمَا
فَإِن بَغَتْ إِحْدَاهُمَا عَلَى الْأُخْرَى
فَقَاتِلُوا الَّتِي تَبْغِي
حَتَّى تَفِيءَ إِلَى أَمْرِ اللَّهِ
فَإِن فَاءَتْ
فَأَصْلِحُوا بَيْنَهُمَا بِالْعَدْلِ وَأَقْسِطُوا
إِنَّ اللَّهَ يُحِبُّ الْمُقْسِطِينَ ○

10. The Believers are but
A single Brotherhood:[4928]
So make peace and
Reconciliation between your
Two (contending) brothers;
And fear God, that ye
May receive Mercy.

١٠- إِنَّمَا الْمُؤْمِنُونَ إِخْوَةٌ
فَأَصْلِحُوا بَيْنَ أَخَوَيْكُمْ
وَاتَّقُوا اللَّهَ لَعَلَّكُمْ تُرْحَمُونَ ○

SECTION 2.

11. O ye who believe!
Let not some men
Among you laugh at others:[4929]
It may be that
The (latter) are better
Than the (former):
Nor let some women
Laugh at others:

١١- يَا أَيُّهَا الَّذِينَ آمَنُوا
لَا يَسْخَرْ قَوْمٌ مِّن قَوْمٍ
عَسَى أَن يَكُونُوا خَيْرًا مِّنْهُمْ
وَلَا نِسَاءٌ مِّن نِّسَاءٍ

4927. Individual quarrels are easier to compose than group quarrels, or, in the modern world, national quarrels. But the collective community of Islam should be supreme over groups or nations. It would be expected to act justly and try to compose the quarrel, for peace is better than fighting. But if one party is determined to be the aggressor, the whole force of the community is brought to bear on it. The essential condition of course is that there should be perfect fairness and justice and respect for the highest principles; for Islam takes account of every just and legitimate interest without separating spiritual from temporal matters. The League of Nations fails because these essentials are absent.

4928. The enforcement of the Muslim Brotherhood is the greatest social ideal of Islam. On it was based the Prophet's Sermon at his last pilgrimage, and Islam cannot be completely realised until this ideal is achieved.

4929. Mutual ridicule ceases to be fun when there is arrogance or selfishness or malice behind it. We may laugh *with* people, to share in the happiness of life: we must never laugh *at* people in contempt or ridicule. In many things they may be better than ourselves!

It may be that
The (latter) are better
Than the (former):
Nor defame nor be [4930]
Sarcastic to each other,
Nor call each other
By (offensive) nicknames:
Ill-seeming is a name
Connoting wickedness,
(To be used of one)
After he has believed:
And those who
Do not desist are
(Indeed) doing wrong.

12. O ye who believe!
Avoid suspicion as much [4931]
(As possible): for suspicion
In some cases is a sin:
And spy not on each other,
Nor speak ill of each other
Behind their backs. Would any
Of you like to eat
The flesh of his dead [4932]
Brother? Nay, ye would
Abhor it . . . But fear God:
For God is Oft-Returning,
Most Merciful.

عَسٰٓى اَنْ يَّكُنَّ خَيْرًا مِّنْهُنَّ ۚ
وَلَا تَلْمِزُوْٓا اَنْفُسَكُمْ
وَلَا تَنَابَزُوْا بِالْاَلْقَابِ ۭ
بِئْسَ الِاسْمُ الْفُسُوْقُ
بَعْدَ الْاِيْمَانِ ۚ
وَمَنْ لَّمْ يَتُبْ
فَاُولٰۗىِٕكَ هُمُ الظّٰلِمُوْنَ ۝

١٢- يٰٓاَيُّهَا الَّذِيْنَ اٰمَنُوا
اجْتَنِبُوْا كَثِيْرًا مِّنَ الظَّنِّ ۡ
اِنَّ بَعْضَ الظَّنِّ اِثْمٌ وَّلَا تَجَسَّسُوْا
وَلَا يَغْتَبْ بَّعْضُكُمْ بَعْضًا ۭ
اَيُحِبُّ اَحَدُكُمْ اَنْ يَّاْكُلَ لَحْمَ اَخِيْهِ مَيْتًا
فَكَرِهْتُمُوْهُ ۭ وَاتَّقُوا اللّٰهَ ۭ
اِنَّ اللّٰهَ تَوَّابٌ رَّحِيْمٌ ۝

4930. Defamation may consist in speaking ill of others by the spoken or written word, or in acting in such a way as to suggest a charge against some person whom we are not in a position to judge. A cutting, biting remark or taunt or sarcasm is included in the word *lamaza*. An offensive nickname may amount to defamation, but in any case there is no point in using offensive nicknames, or names that suggest some real or fancied defect. They ill accord with the serious purpose which Muslims should have in life. For example, even if a man is lame, it is wrong to address him as "O lame one!" It causes him pain, and it is bad manners. So in the case of the rude remark, "the black man".

4931. Most kinds of suspicion are baseless and to be avoided, and some are crimes in themselves: for they do cruel injustice to innocent men and women. Spying, or enquiring too curiously into other people's affairs, means either idle curiosity, and is therefore futile, or suspicion carried a stage further, which almost amounts to sin. Back-biting also is a brood of the same genus. It may be either futile but all the same mischievous, or it may be poisoned with malice, in which case it is a sin added to sin.

4932. No one would like even to think of such an abomination as eating the flesh of his brother. But when the brother is dead, and the flesh is carrion, abomination is added to abomination. In the same way we are asked to refrain from hurting people's feelings when they are present; how much worse is it when we say things, true or false, when they are absent!

13. O mankind! We created[4933]
You from a single (pair)
Of a male and a female,
And made you into
Nations and tribes, that
Ye may know each other
(Not that ye may despise
(Each other). Verily
The most honoured of you
In the sight of God
Is (he who is) the most
Righteous of you.
And God has full knowledge
And is well acquainted
(With all things).

١٣- يَٰٓأَيُّهَا ٱلنَّاسُ إِنَّا خَلَقْنَٰكُم
مِّن ذَكَرٍ وَأُنثَىٰ
وَجَعَلْنَٰكُمْ شُعُوبًا
وَقَبَآئِلَ لِتَعَارَفُوٓا۟ ۚ
إِنَّ أَكْرَمَكُمْ
عِندَ ٱللَّهِ أَتْقَىٰكُمْ ۚ
إِنَّ ٱللَّهَ عَلِيمٌ خَبِيرٌ ○

14. The desert Arabs say,[4934]
" We believe." Say, " Ye
Have no faith; but ye
(Only) say, ' We have submitted[4935]
Our wills to God,'
For not yet has Faith
Entered your hearts.
But if ye obey God
And His Apostle, He
Will not belittle aught
Of your deeds: for God
Is Oft-Forgiving, Most Merciful."

١٤- قَالَتِ ٱلْأَعْرَابُ ءَامَنَّا ۖ
قُل لَّمْ تُؤْمِنُوا۟ وَلَٰكِن قُولُوٓا۟ أَسْلَمْنَا
وَلَمَّا يَدْخُلِ ٱلْإِيمَٰنُ فِى قُلُوبِكُمْ ۖ
وَإِن تُطِيعُوا۟ ٱللَّهَ وَرَسُولَهُۥ
لَا يَلِتْكُم مِّنْ أَعْمَٰلِكُمْ شَيْـًٔا ۚ
إِنَّ ٱللَّهَ غَفُورٌ رَّحِيمٌ ○

15. Only those are Believers
Who have believed in God
And His Apostle, and have
Never since doubted, but
Have striven with their
Belongings and their persons
In the Cause of God:
Such are the sincere ones.

١٥- إِنَّمَا ٱلْمُؤْمِنُونَ ٱلَّذِينَ ءَامَنُوا۟ بِٱللَّهِ وَ
رَسُولِهِۦ ثُمَّ لَمْ يَرْتَابُوا۟
وَجَٰهَدُوا۟ بِأَمْوَٰلِهِمْ وَأَنفُسِهِمْ فِى
سَبِيلِ ٱللَّهِ ۚ أُو۟لَٰٓئِكَ هُمُ ٱلصَّٰدِقُونَ ○

4933. This is addressed to all mankind and not only to the Muslim brotherhood, though it is understood that in a perfected world the two would be synonymous. As it is, mankind is descended from one pair of parents. Their tribes, races, and nations are convenient labels by which we may know certain differing characteristics. Before God they are all one, and he gets most honour who is most righteous.

4934. The desert Arabs were somewhat shaky in their faith. Their hearts and minds were petty, and they thought of petty things, while Islam requires the complete submission of one's being to God. See next verse. Some of the failings of the desert Arabs are described in xlviii. 11-15. But the reference here is said to be to the Banū Asad, who came to profess Islam in order to get charity during a famine.

4935. 'This is what ye ought to prove if your faith has any meaning, but ye only say it with your tongues.'

16. Say: "What! Will ye [4936]
Instruct God about your
Religion? But God knows
All that is in the heavens
And on earth: He has
Full knowledge of all things.

١٦- قُلْ أَتُعَلِّمُونَ اللّٰهَ بِدِينِكُمْ ۚ
وَاللّٰهُ يَعْلَمُ مَا فِي السَّمٰوٰتِ وَمَا فِي الْأَرْضِ ۚ
وَاللّٰهُ بِكُلِّ شَيْءٍ عَلِيمٌ ○

17. They impress on thee [4937]
As a favour that they
Have embraced Islam.
Say, "Count not your Islam
As a favour upon me:
Nay, God has conferred
A favour upon you
That He has guided you
To the Faith, if ye
Be true and sincere.

١٧- يَمُنُّونَ عَلَيْكَ أَنْ أَسْلَمُوا ۖ
قُلْ لَا تَمُنُّوا عَلَيَّ إِسْلَامَكُمْ ۚ
بَلِ اللّٰهُ يَمُنُّ عَلَيْكُمْ
أَنْ هَدٰىكُمْ لِلْإِيمَانِ
إِنْ كُنْتُمْ صٰدِقِينَ ○

18. "Verily God knows [4938]
The secrets of the heavens
And the earth: and God
Sees well all
That ye do."

١٨- إِنَّ اللّٰهَ يَعْلَمُ غَيْبَ السَّمٰوٰتِ وَ
الْأَرْضِ ۚ وَاللّٰهُ بَصِيرٌ بِمَا تَعْمَلُونَ ○ ع

4936. 'You say (or perhaps even think) that you are Muslims, but where are the fruits of your Faith? God knows the innermost motives and secrets of your heart, and you cannot deceive Him by attaching a certain label to yourselves.' Alas! that this answer to the desert Arabs is true of so many others in our own times!

4937. Islam in itself is a precious privilege. By accepting it we confer no favour on its preacher or on any community. If the acceptance is from the heart, it is a great favour done to those who accept, that the Light of God has entered their hearts and they have received guidance.

4938. This does not mean that we should seek petty motives in newcomers into the House of Islam. That would indeed be harbouring suspicions or allowing curiosity to spy out motives, which would be a crime under xlix. 12. We should be true, sincere, and devoted ourselves, and leave the case of others to God, from Whose eyes nothing is hidden.

INTRODUCTION TO SŪRA L. (*Qāf*).

We now come to a group of seven Meccan Sūras (*l*-lvi), dealing with God's revelation through nature, through history, and through the mouths of the Prophets, and pointing to the Hereafter. We saw that the last group of three (xlvii.—xlix.) dealt with the external and internal relations of the Ummat when formed. In the present group our attention is more particularly directed to aspects eschatological,—the Future before us when this life is done.

This particular Sūra belongs to the early Meccan period. After an appeal to nature and to the fate of wicked peoples in history, it removes as it were the veil (verse 22) from the Future after death.

Summary.—Sceptics can look up to the heavens above and to Nature around them, as well as to the fate of sin in the history of the past: will they doubt God's Revelation when the veil is lifted? (*l*. 1-29, and C. 224.)

A vision of the Day of Recompense and the Day of Reality (*l*. 30-45, and C. 225).

C. 224.—The Apostle's credentials are the Revelation
(*l*. 1-29.) He brings. Let them not wonder at the Message
Or at the News of the Hereafter. They have but
To look at the starry heavens and at Nature
Around them to see God's goodness and His power
To bring life out of the dead, and to punish
All wrong. Every deed, word, and thought are in
The eternal Record. Death will open
Your eyes and make you see Realities.
Then will every action bear
Its due fruit, and no soul can shift
Its responsibility on to another.

Sūra L.
Qāf.[4939]

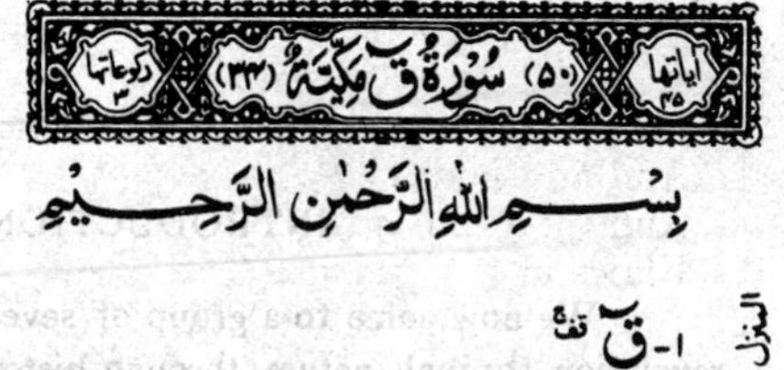

In the name of God, Most Gracious,
Most Merciful.

بِسْمِ اللّٰهِ الرَّحْمٰنِ الرَّحِيْمِ

1. *Qāf*:[4939]
By the Glorious[4940] Qur-ān
(Thou art God's Apostle).

١- قٓ
وَالْقُرْاٰنِ الْمَجِيْدِ

2. But they wonder that[4941]
There has come to them
A Warner from among
Themselves.
So the Unbelievers say:
"This is a wonderful thing!

٢- بَلْ عَجِبُوْٓا اَنْ جَآءَهُمْ
مُّنْذِرٌ مِّنْهُمْ
فَقَالَ الْكٰفِرُوْنَ هٰذَا شَيْءٌ عَجِيْبٌ

3. "What! When we die[4942]
And become dust, (shall we
Live again?) That is
A (sort of) Return
Far (from our understanding)."

٣- ءَاِذَا مِتْنَا
وَكُنَّا تُرَابًا
ذٰلِكَ رَجْعٌۢ بَعِيْدٌ

4. We already know
How much of them[4943]
The earth takes away:
With Us is a Record
Guarding (the full account).

٤- قَدْ عَلِمْنَا مَا تَنْقُصُ الْاَرْضُ مِنْهُمْ
وَعِنْدَنَا كِتٰبٌ حَفِيْظٌ

5. But they deny the truth
When it comes to them:
So they are in
A confused state.[4944]

٥- بَلْ كَذَّبُوْا بِالْحَقِّ لَمَّا جَآءَهُمْ
فَهُمْ فِيْٓ اَمْرٍ مَّرِيْجٍ

4939. This is an Abbreviated Letter. For Abbreviated Letters generally, see Appendix I (pp. 118-120). This particular Abbreviated Letter *Qāf* occurs only here as a single letter, and in combination at the beginning of S. xlii., where I was unable to explain the full combination. Here the Qāf is taken by several Commentators to represent "*Qudhiya-l-amru*", "the matter has been decreed," with reference to the eschatological trend of the Sūra. God knows best.

4940. *Majīd* (translated "Glorious") is one of the beautiful appellations of the Qur-ān. Its glory is that of the rising sun: the more it rises on your mental and spiritual horizon, the more you are lost in admiration of its glory. Its meanings are manifest and inexhaustible. The greater your experience, the more light is your spiritual eye able to bear. And in that glory is a beauty that none can tell who has not experienced it in his soul. It is in itself the proof of the mission of the holy Prophet.

4941. In a sense their wonder is natural: do we not wonder at the glorious sun? In another sense it is unnatural: what should we say of a man who fails to see in broad daylight?

4942. *Cf*. xxxvii. 16.

4943. The earth only corrupts and takes away the body when they are dead; it has no power over the soul. The full account of the soul's doings is in God's Record.

4944. If they deny what has been made clear to them, their minds must necessarily get into confusion. All nature declares the glory and goodness of God. Revelation explains the inequalities of this life and how they will be redressed in the Hereafter. If they do not accept this, they are not in a logical position. They cannot reconcile the known with the unknown.

6. Do they not look
At the sky above them ?—
How We have made it [4945]
And adorned it,
And there are no
Flaws in it ?

٦- أَفَلَمْ يَنظُرُوٓا إِلَى ٱلسَّمَآءِ فَوْقَهُمْ
كَيْفَ بَنَيْنَٰهَا وَزَيَّنَّٰهَا
وَمَا لَهَا مِن فُرُوجٍ ○

7. And the earth—
We have spread it out, [4946]
And set thereon mountains
Standing firm, and produced
Therein every kind of
Beautiful growth (in pairs)— [4947]

٧- وَٱلْأَرْضَ مَدَدْنَٰهَا
وَأَلْقَيْنَا فِيهَا رَوَٰسِىَ وَأَنۢبَتْنَا
فِيهَا مِن كُلِّ زَوْجٍۭ بَهِيجٍ ○

8. To be observed
And commemorated
By every devotee [4948]
Turning (to God).

٨- تَبْصِرَةً وَذِكْرَىٰ
لِكُلِّ عَبْدٍ مُّنِيبٍ ○

9. And We send down
From the sky Rain
Charged with blessing,
And We produce therewith
Gardens and Grain for harvests;

٩- وَنَزَّلْنَا مِنَ ٱلسَّمَآءِ مَآءً
مُّبَٰرَكًا
فَأَنۢبَتْنَا بِهِۦ جَنَّٰتٍ وَحَبَّ ٱلْحَصِيدِ ○

10. And tall (and stately) [4949]
Palm-trees, with shoots
Of fruit-stalks, piled
One over another;—

١٠- وَٱلنَّخْلَ بَاسِقَٰتٍ لَّهَا
طَلْعٌ نَّضِيدٌ ○

11. As sustenance for
(God's) Servants;—
And We give (new) life
Therewith to land that is
Dead: thus will be
The Resurrection.

١١- رِّزْقًا لِّلْعِبَادِ
وَأَحْيَيْنَا بِهِۦ بَلْدَةً مَّيْتًا
كَذَٰلِكَ ٱلْخُرُوجُ ○

4945. The greatest philosophers have found a difficulty in understanding the sceptical position when they contemplate the wonder and mystery of the skies with all the countless beautiful stars and planets and lights in them, and laws of order, motion, and symmetry, that respond to the highest mathematical abstractions without a flaw. Can blind Chance give rise to such conditions?

4946. *Cf.* xiii. 3; and xv. 19 and n. 1955. The earth is round, and yet it appears stretched out as a vast expanse, like a carpet kept steady with the weight of the mountains.

4947. *Cf.* xxii. 5, and n. 2777. Sex in plants may be hinted at: see n. 1804 to xiii. 3.

4948. For all these things go into his very heart and soul. He loves to contemplate them, to remember them for himself as evidence of God's goodness and glory, and to mention and proclaim them, in the form of Psalms, Hymns, or the Ẓikrs or Chants of the Ṣūfis and Saints.

4949. A beautiful nature passage. How graphic and unforgettable to any one who has seen a spring and summer in an Arabian oasis!

12. Before them was denied
(The Hereafter) by the People [4950]
Of Noah, the Companions
Of the Rass, the Thamūd,

١٢- كَذَّبَتْ قَبْلَهُمْ قَوْمُ
نُوحٍ وَّأَصْحٰبُ الرَّسِّ وَثَمُودُ ۝

13. The 'Ād, Pharaoh,
The Brethren of Lūṭ,

١٣- وَعَادٌ وَّفِرْعَوْنُ وَإِخْوَانُ لُوطٍ ۝

14. The Companions of the Wood,
And the People of Tubba';
Each one (of them) rejected
The apostles, and My warning
Was duly fulfilled (in them).

١٤- وَّأَصْحٰبُ الْأَيْكَةِ وَقَوْمُ تُبَّعٍ
كُلٌّ كَذَّبَ الرُّسُلَ
فَحَقَّ وَعِيدِ ۝

15. Were We then weary
With the first Creation,
That they should be
In confused doubt [4951]
About a new Creation?

١٥- أَفَعَيِينَا بِالْخَلْقِ الْأَوَّلِ
بَلْ هُمْ فِي لَبْسٍ
مِّنْ خَلْقٍ جَدِيدٍ ۝ ع

SECTION 2.

16. It was We Who
Created man, and We know
What dark suggestions his soul [4952]
Makes to him: for We
Are nearer to him
Than (his) jugular vein.

١٦- وَلَقَدْ خَلَقْنَا الْإِنسَانَ
وَنَعْلَمُ مَا تُوَسْوِسُ بِهِ نَفْسُهُ وَنَحْنُ
أَقْرَبُ إِلَيْهِ مِنْ حَبْلِ الْوَرِيدِ ۝

17. Behold, two (guardian angels) [4953]
Appointed to learn (his doings)
Learn (and note them),
One sitting on the right
And one on the left.

١٧- إِذْ يَتَلَقَّى الْمُتَلَقِّيَانِ
عَنِ الْيَمِينِ وَعَنِ الشِّمَالِ قَعِيدٌ ۝

4950. Just the names of the peoples of Arabian tradition who were punished for their sins are mentioned; their stories will be found elsewhere. For the *People of Noah*, see xi. 25-48 and other passages. For the *Companions of the Rass*, see xxv. 38 and n. 3094; for the *'Ād* and the *Thamūd*, see xxvi. 123-158, and other passages; for *Pharaoh* and his People, see ii. 49-50 and other passages; for the *Brethren of Lūṭ*, see vii. 80-84, and other passages; for the *Companions of the Wood*, see xv. 78-79, and n. 2000; and for the *People of Tubba'*, see xliv. 37 and n. 4715.

4951. *Cf.* xlvi. 33, and n. 4912.

4952. God created man, and gave him his limited free-will. God knows the inmost desires and motives of man even better than man does himself. He is nearer to a man than the man's own jugular vein. The jugular vein is the big trunk vein, one on each side of the neck, which brings the blood back from the head to the heart. The two jugular veins correspond to the two carotid arteries which carry the blood from the heart to the head. As the blood-stream is the vehicle of life and consciousness, the phrase "nearer than the jugular vein" implies that God knows more truly the innermost state of our feeling and consciousness than does our own ego.

4953. This must of course be taken figuratively. Two angels are constantly by him to note his thoughts, words, and actions. The allegory is further elaborated. One sits on the right side and notes his good deeds and the other on the left, to note his bad deeds; corresponding to the Companions of the Right and the Companions of the Left mentioned in lvi. 27 and 41.

18. Not a word does he[4954]
Utter but there is
A sentinel by him,
Ready (to note it).

١٨- مَا يَلْفِظُ مِنْ قَوْلٍ
إِلَّا لَدَيْهِ رَقِيبٌ عَتِيدٌ ○

19. And the stupor of death[4955]
Will bring truth (before
His eyes): "This was
The thing which thou
Wast trying to escape!"

١٩- وَجَاءَتْ سَكْرَةُ الْمَوْتِ بِالْحَقِّ ط
ذٰلِكَ مَا كُنْتَ مِنْهُ تَحِيدُ ○

20. And the Trumpet[4956]
Shall be blown:
That will be the Day
Whereof Warning (had been given).

٢٠- وَنُفِخَ فِي الصُّورِ ط
ذٰلِكَ يَوْمُ الْوَعِيدِ ○

21. And there will come forth
Every soul: with each
Will be an (angel) to drive,[4957]
And an (angel) to
Bear witness.

٢١- وَجَاءَتْ كُلُّ نَفْسٍ
مَّعَهَا سَائِقٌ وَّشَهِيدٌ ○

22. (It will be said:)
"Thou wast heedless
Of this; now have We
Removed thy veil,

٢٢- لَقَدْ كُنْتَ فِي غَفْلَةٍ مِّنْ هٰذَا
فَكَشَفْنَا عَنْكَ غِطَاءَكَ

4954. Then each "word" spoken is taken down by a "sentinel" (*raqīb*). This has been construed to mean that the sentinel only records words, not thoughts which are not uttered. Thoughts may be forgiven if not uttered, and still more if they do not issue in action. At the stage at which we clothe a thought in words, we have already done an action. The Recorders mentioned in the last verse make a complete Record, in order to supply motives and springs of action, which will affect the degrees or status in the spiritual Hereafter. The three together, individuals or kinds, make the honourable Recorders, *Kirāman Kātibīn*, (plural, not dual number) mentioned in lxxxii 11.

4955. What is stupor or unconsciousness to this probationary life will be the opening of the eyes to the spiritual world: for Death is the Gateway between the two. Once through that Gateway man will realise how the things which he neglected or looked upon as remote are the intimate Realities, and the things which seemed to loom large in his eyes in this world were shadows that have fled. The things he wanted to avoid are the things that have really come to pass. Both Good and Evil will realise the Truth now in its intensity.

4956. The next stage will be the Judgment, heralded with the blowing of the Trumpet. Every soul will then come forth.

4957. Several interpretations are possible, leading to the same allegorical truth, that the Judgment will be set up; the Record will be produced; the good and bad deeds will speak for and against; and complete justice will be done, each act leading to its own due fruit. (1) The (angel) to drive and the (angel) to bear witness may be the Recording Angels of the left and the right (verse 17); or (2) it may not be angels, but the evil deeds will drive like task-masters, and the good deeds will bear witness for the soul on trial; or (3) his misused limbs and faculties will drive him to his doom, while his well-used limbs and faculties will witness for him.

And sharp is thy sight[4958] This Day!"	فَبَصَرُكَ الْيَوْمَ حَدِيدٌ ۝
23. And his Companion[4959] will say: "Here is (his Record) ready With me!"	٢٣- وَقَالَ قَرِينُهُ هَٰذَا مَا لَدَيَّ عَتِيدٌ ۝
24. (The sentence will be:) "Throw, throw[4960] into Hell Every contumacious Rejecter (Of God)!—	٢٤- أَلْقِيَا فِي جَهَنَّمَ كُلَّ كَفَّارٍ عَنِيدٍ ۝
25. "Who forbade what was good, Transgressed all bounds, Cast doubts and suspicions;	٢٥- مَّنَّاعٍ لِّلْخَيْرِ مُعْتَدٍ مُّرِيبٍ ۝
26. "Who set up another god Beside God: throw him Into a severe Penalty."	٢٦- الَّذِي جَعَلَ مَعَ اللَّهِ إِلَٰهًا آخَرَ فَأَلْقِيَاهُ فِي الْعَذَابِ الشَّدِيدِ ۝
27. His Companion[4961] will say: "Our[4962] Lord! I did not Make him transgress,[4963] But he was (himself) Far astray."	٢٧- قَالَ قَرِينُهُ رَبَّنَا مَا أَطْغَيْتُهُ وَلَٰكِن كَانَ فِي ضَلَالٍ بَعِيدٍ ۝

4958. The clearness of vision will now be even greater: see n. 4955 above.

4959. *Qarīn*: Companion. If we take No. 1 of the constructions suggested in n. 4957, the Companion will be one of the Recording Angels mentioned above, in verse 21, perhaps the one that drives; or perhaps the third one mentioned in verse 18, for he has the Record ready with him. If we take any of the other constructions mentioned in n. 4957, it will be the evil deeds or the misused faculties. In any case it will be the factors on whose testimony his conviction will be based.

4960. The original for "throw", here and in verse 26 below, is in the dual number, which some Commentators explain by saying that the dual form is used for emphasis, as if the verb ("throw, throw") were twice repeated. Examples of this are found in Arabic. But is it possible that the dual refers to the two angels mentioned in verses 17 and 21? In that case the Companion in verse 27 will be the third one mentioned in verses 18 and 23. In any case the third one will be the one on whose Record the sentence will be passed.

4961. See last note. But some people understand by "Companion" here an evil associate in the world, an evil one who misled.

4962. *Our Lord.* One man speaks: "I did not", etc. Yet he uses the plural pronoun in saying, "Our Lord". This is beautifully appropriate, as he is speaking so as to include the person to be judged: as if he were to say, "Thou art my Lord, or the Lord of us angels or of all Creation, but Thou art his Lord also, for Thou didst cherish him and warn him, and he owed duties to Thee."

4963. Neither the Recording Angels nor the misused limbs and faculties, nor anything else whatever was responsible for the Evil: it was the personal responsibility of the Doer himself, with his free-will.

28. He will say: "Dispute not[4964]
With each other
In My Presence:
I had already in advance
Sent you[4965] Warning.

٢٨-قَالَ لَا تَخْتَصِمُوا لَدَيَّ
وَقَدْ قَدَّمْتُ إِلَيْكُمْ بِالْوَعِيدِ ۝

29. "The Word changes not
Before Me, and I do not
The least injustice
To My Servants."[4966]

٢٩-مَا يُبَدَّلُ الْقَوْلُ لَدَيَّ
وَمَا أَنَا بِظَلَّامٍ لِّلْعَبِيدِ ۝

C. 225.—As Goodness has possibilities unlimited,
(l. 30-45.) **So has Evil in the opposite direction.**
To those who bring a heart unsullied
And to God devoted, will be Peace,
Security, and Eternal Life—the Rays
From God's own Presence. Adore ye God
And pay no heed to whispers of Doubt
And Evil: these must vanish at Judgment,
When Truth and Justice reign supreme.

SECTION 3.

30. One Day We will
Ask Hell, "Art thou
Filled to the full?"[4967]
It will say, "Are there
Any more (to come)?"

٣٠-يَوْمَ نَقُولُ لِجَهَنَّمَ هَلِ
امْتَلَأْتِ
وَتَقُولُ هَلْ مِنْ مَّزِيدٍ ۝

31. And the Garden[4968]
Will be brought nigh

٣١-وَأُزْلِفَتِ الْجَنَّةُ

4964. It is suggested that sinners whose Record is black, driven into a corner, accuse others of misleading them: the others may be the Recorders, or their faculties or opportunities or surroundings or their associates in the world, or anything but themselves. Such recriminations are not allowed in the Court of Judgment.

4965. Besides, personal responsibility had already been clearly preached to them in God's Message, and they had been warned of the consequences. "You" is in the plural number: 'all of you who are before the Judgment-Seat had clear warning of the consequences of your conduct.'

4966. "*'Abd*" has two plurals: (1) *'Abīd*, as here, means all Servants of God, *i.e.* all his creatures; (2) *'Ibād* has the further connotation of Servants of God, devoted to his service; I have translated it in many cases by the word "devotees". The Sentence before the Judgment-Seat is pronounced with perfect justice; it does not change, and requires no change; the inevitable consequences of sin must follow; the time for Mercy is past.

4967 As the capacity of Good is unlimited, so is the capacity of Evil—unlimited. Hell is personified and asked, "Art thou sated to the full?" It replies, "If there are more to come, let them come." It is not satisfied.

4968. In this life, the ideals of the spirit, the accomplishment of the things in our hearts and our hopes, seem to be ever so far, seem even to recede as we think we come nearer. Not so in the Hereafter. The fruits of righteousness will no longer be in the distance. They will be realised. They will seem themselves to approach the Righteous.

To the Righteous,—no more A thing distant.	لِلْمُتَّقِينَ غَيْرَ بَعِيدٍ ۝
32. (A voice will say:) "This is what was Promised for you,— For every one who turned [4969] (To God) in sincere repentance, Who kept (His Law),	٣٢- هَٰذَا مَا تُوعَدُونَ لِكُلِّ أَوَّابٍ حَفِيظٍ ۝
33. "Who feared (God) Most Gracious unseen,[4970] And brought a heart Turned in devotion (to Him):	٣٣- مَّنْ خَشِيَ الرَّحْمَٰنَ بِالْغَيْبِ وَجَاءَ بِقَلْبٍ مُّنِيبٍ ۝
34. "Enter ye therein In Peace and Security;[4971] This is a Day Of Eternal Life!"	٣٤- ادْخُلُوهَا بِسَلَامٍ ذَٰلِكَ يَوْمُ الْخُلُودِ ۝
35. There will be for them Therein all that they wish,— And more besides In Our Presence.[4972]	٣٥- لَهُم مَّا يَشَاءُونَ فِيهَا وَلَدَيْنَا مَزِيدٌ ۝
36. But how many Generations before them Did We destroy (for their Sins),—stronger in power [4973] Than they? Then did they Wander through the land: Was there any place Of escape (for them)?	٣٦- وَكَمْ أَهْلَكْنَا قَبْلَهُم مِّن قَرْنٍ هُمْ أَشَدُّ مِنْهُم بَطْشًا فَنَقَّبُوا فِي الْبِلَادِ هَلْ مِن مَّحِيصٍ ۝

4969. The description of the Righteous is given in four masterly clauses: (1) those who turned away from Evil in sincere repentance; (2) those whose new life was good and righteous; (3) those who in their innermost hearts and in their most secret doings were actuated by God-fearing love, the fear that is akin to love in remembering God under His title of "Most Gracious"; and (4) who gave up their whole heart and being to Him.

4970. *Cf.* xxxvi. 11 and n. 3952; and xxxv. 18, and n. 3902.

4971. The true meaning of Islam: peace, security, salutation, and accord with God's Plan in all Eternity.

4972. To get all that our purified wishes and desires comprehend may seem to sum up final Bliss; but there is something still wanting, which is supplied by the Presence of God, the Light of His Countenance.

4973. While virtue and righteousness will accomplish their final goal, what will be the End of Sin? Let the past tell its story. Many powerful and arrogant generations were swept away, to stray in the paths of misery, without any way of escape from the consequences of their sin. This was already seen in the life of this world. In the world to come, it will be worse, as already stated in verses 24-26 above.

37. Verily in this[4974]
Is a Message
For any that has
A heart and understanding
Or who gives ear and
Earnestly witnesses (the truth).

٣٧- إِنَّ فِي ذَٰلِكَ لَذِكْرَىٰ
لِمَن كَانَ لَهُۥ قَلْبٌ
أَوْ أَلْقَى ٱلسَّمْعَ وَهُوَ شَهِيدٌ ○

38. We created the heavens[4975]
And the earth and all
Between them in Six Days,[4976]
Nor did any sense
Of weariness touch Us.[4977]

٣٨- وَلَقَدْ خَلَقْنَا ٱلسَّمَٰوَٰتِ وَٱلْأَرْضَ
وَمَا بَيْنَهُمَا فِي سِتَّةِ أَيَّامٍ
وَمَا مَسَّنَا مِن لُّغُوبٍ ○

39. Bear, then, with patience,
All that they say,
And celebrate the praises
Of thy Lord, before[4978]
The rising of the sun
And before (its) setting,

٣٩- فَٱصْبِرْ عَلَىٰ مَا يَقُولُونَ
وَسَبِّحْ بِحَمْدِ رَبِّكَ
قَبْلَ طُلُوعِ ٱلشَّمْسِ وَقَبْلَ ٱلْغُرُوبِ ○

40. And during part
Of the night, (also,)
Celebrate His praises,
And (so likewise)
After the postures[4979]
Of adoration.

٤٠- وَمِنَ ٱلَّيْلِ
فَسَبِّحْهُ وَ
أَدْبَٰرَ ٱلسُّجُودِ ○

4974. As Christ said (Matt. xi. 15), "he that hath ears to hear, let him hear". These are matters of high moment. Many spiritual lessons can be learnt from these things by any one who has the heart and understanding to apply to God's teaching and can give genuine thought to what he sees, as a witness does who has to swear to the facts on his oath.

4975. God's creation of the heavens and the earth in long stages or periods of time, as we count time, shows how things evolve in their own good time. We must therefore be patient if Good does not *seem* to come to its own according to *our* ideas. Our will should merge itself in God's Will, and we should praise Him, realising that He is All-Good, and that all adjustments will be in the Hereafter.

4976. *Cf.* vii. 54, n. 1031; and xli. 12, n. 4477.

4977. *Cf.* xxxv. 35.

4978. God should be remembered at all times. But the best time for individual adoration is early in the morning before sunrise, late in the day before sunset, and a portion of the night, when there is stillness in the air, and man's spirit loves to commune with things spiritual. Those who would connect this with the five canonical prayers, instituted at a later stage in Medina, would take the *Fajr* for the prayer before sunrise, the *Zuhr* and the *'Asr* for the afternoon prayers before sunset, and the *Magrib* and the *'Ishāa* for the night prayers.

4979. The general meaning of "*after the postures of adoration*" would be the contemplation and remembrance of God after prayers. Those who would connect this passage with the five canonical prayers understand these further prayers "following the *sujūd* or postures of adoration" to mean the extra or supernumerary prayers known as *nafl*, also the use of the Rosary in remembering the Names of God.

41. And listen for the Day [4980]
When the Caller will call
Out from a place
Quite near,—[4981]

۴۱- وَاسْتَمِعْ يَوْمَ يُنَادِ الْمُنَادِ
مِن مَّكَانٍ قَرِيبٍ ۝

42. The Day when they will
Hear a (mighty) Blast [4982]
In (very) truth: that
Will be the Day
Of Resurrection.

۴۲- يَوْمَ يَسْمَعُونَ الصَّيْحَةَ بِالْحَقِّ
ذَٰلِكَ يَوْمُ الْخُرُوجِ ۝

43. Verily it is We Who
Give Life and Death;
And to Us is
The Final Goal—

۴۳- إِنَّا نَحْنُ نُحْيِي وَنُمِيتُ
وَإِلَيْنَا الْمَصِيرُ ۝

44. The Day when
The Earth will be [4983]
Rent asunder, from (men)
Hurrying out: that will be
A gathering together,—
Quite easy for Us.[4984]

۴۴- يَوْمَ تَشَقَّقُ الْأَرْضُ عَنْهُمْ سِرَاعًا
ذَٰلِكَ حَشْرٌ
عَلَيْنَا يَسِيرٌ ۝

45. We know best what they [4985]
Say; and thou art not
One to overawe them
By force. So admonish
With the Qur-ān such
As fear My Warning!

۴۵- نَحْنُ أَعْلَمُ بِمَا يَقُولُونَ
وَمَا أَنتَ عَلَيْهِم بِجَبَّارٍ
فَذَكِّرْ بِالْقُرْآنِ مَن يَخَافُ وَعِيدِ ۝

4980. The Day of Resurrection, when the Call to the souls to arise and come to the Judgment-Seat will be immediately answered, and they will all arise and come forth. *Cf.* xxxvi. 49-53, and notes 3997 and 3999.

4981. In the life of this world it seemed all so remote. In the new life at the Resurrection it will all be so near; for there will be neither time nor space as we know them here.

4982. The word "*ṣaiḥatun*" (mighty Blast) is used for the Resurrection (as here) or for the sudden punishment of the guilty on this earth, as in xi. 67, where see further references.

4983. Men will hurry out from all corners of the earth to answer the call, and the earth itself will be rent asunder. In xxv. 25 the imagery used was the heaven being rent asunder, and angels coming out in ranks: see n. 3082. *Cf.* also lxxxiv. 1-4.

4984. It may seem to our material imaginations a difficult task to collect together the souls of all sorts of men, who died in all sorts of conditions at different times, but it will be a different kind of world and creation altogether, and to God all things are not only possible but easy.

4985. People may throw all sorts of doubts about the Judgment and the Hereafter. The Prophet's task is not to force them to accept anything. His task is to deliver the Message of the Qur-ān, and admonish those who are spiritually fit and ready to receive admonition and to prepare themselves for the new and higher life destined for man.

INTRODUCTION TO SŪRA LI. (*Ẕāriyāt*).

This is an early Meccan Sūra, with a highly mystic meaning. It is the second of the seven Sūras forming a group dealing with Revelation and the Hereafter. See Introduction to S. *l*. This Sūra deals with the varying ways in which Truth prevails irresistibly even against all human probabilities.

Summary.—The winds may blow and scatter, lift and rush, or divide in all directions; but the Truth and Promise of God are sure and stable, whereof you may see Signs both around and within you (li. 1-23, and C. 226).

Past events and what you see before you point to the unfailing consequences of all you do: God, of His Grace, sends you a Reminder: the loss is your own if you reject and deny (li. 24-60, and C. 227).

C. 226.—Various are the ways of working we see
(li. 1-23.) In God's world,—strong and gentle, scattering
And uniting: through it all runs a Purpose
True and stable, which we shall see fulfilled
On the Day of Judgment and Justice, which
Must inevitably come to pass: give up
False doctrines, which agree not among themselves
Or with facts. For evil must end in evil,
And good in joy and felicity. The good
Worship God and serve God's creatures:
Those needing help are ever in their thoughts.
They see Signs of God in all things in heaven
And earth, and in their own hearts and minds.

Sūra LI.

Zāriyāt, or the Winds That Scatter.

In the name of God, Most Gracious, Most Merciful.

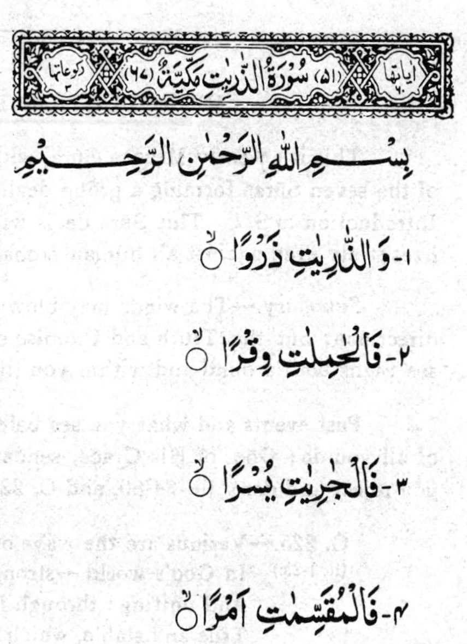

1. By the (Winds)[4986]
That scatter broadcast;[4987]

2. And those that[4988]
Lift and bear away
Heavy weights;

3. And those that[4989]
Flow with ease
And gentleness;

4. And those that[4990]
Distribute and apportion
By Command;—

4986. The atmosphere of mysticism starts from the beginning of the Sūra. Four agencies are mentioned in verses 1 to 4 as evidences or types or symbols of the certainty and unity of a Truth described in verses 5-6. What these agencies are is described by certain adjectival participles, the noun understood being usually taken to be "Winds": the word for Wind (*Rīh*) being feminine in Arabic. Some Commentators however understand other nouns as being implied, *e.g.* angels in all four verses, or different things in each of the four verses. I do not think that it is necessary to be precise about material things in spiritual parables. Whatever the agencies are, their different modes of working are evidence of the power and goodness of God, the Unity of His Plan, and the certainty of Good and Evil reaching their own destined ends, when Judgment and Justice will have given each one his due.

4987. Winds may blow strong, and scatter particles of dust far and wide; but they do not diminish by one jot the substance of God's material creation; on the contrary they help to readjust things. They reshape the configuration of the earth; in the vegetable kingdom they carry seeds about and plant new seeds in old soils; in the region of air they produce mighty changes in temperature and pressure that affect animal and vegetable life; they carry the moisture of equatorial Africa to the parched plains of India; and so on. Yet they are just one little agency showing God's working in the material world. So in the spiritual world. Revelation works mighty changes; it may be resisted, but the resistance will be swept away; it ever points to the one Great Final Event, "to which the whole Creation moves".

4988. The things that lift and bear away heavy weights may be the Winds that carry the heavy rain-clouds or that sweep off every resistance from their path, or it may be the heavy moisture-laden clouds themselves. So works Revelation: it lifts and sweeps away the burdens of custom, superstition, or man's inertia, and ever leads onwards to the destined End.

4989. These may be Winds that fill the sails of ships with gentle and favourable breezes, that carry men and merchandise to their destinations. Or they may be the ships themselves, whose smooth motion through the waters is described in many places by the verb *jarā*, "to flow", *e.g.* *cf.* ii. 164.

4990. These may be Winds (or other agencies) that distribute and apportion moisture or rain or atmospheric pressure or other blessings of God,—not haphazard but by fixed laws, *i.e.* according to the Command of their Lord. So with Revelation. Its blessings are distributed all round, and it produces its marvellous effects sometimes in the most unlikely places and ways.

5. Verily that which ye[4991]
Are promised is true;

٥- إِنَّمَا تُوعَدُونَ لَصَادِقٌ ۝

6. And verily Judgment[4992]
And Justice must
Indeed come to pass.

٦- وَإِنَّ الدِّينَ لَوَاقِعٌ ۝

7. By the Sky
With (its) numerous Paths,[4993]

٧- وَالسَّمَاءِ ذَاتِ الْحُبُكِ ۝

8. Truly ye are in
A doctrine discordant,[4994]

٨- إِنَّكُمْ لَفِي قَوْلٍ مُّخْتَلِفٍ ۝

9. Through which are deluded (away
From the Truth) such
As would be deluded.[4995]

٩- يُؤْفَكُ عَنْهُ مَنْ أُفِكَ ۝

10. Woe to the falsehood-mongers,—

١٠- قُتِلَ الْخَرَّاصُونَ ۝

11. Those who (flounder) heedless[4996]
In a flood of confusion:

١١- الَّذِينَ هُمْ فِي غَمْرَةٍ سَاهُونَ ۝

12. They ask, "When will be
The Day of Judgment
And Justice?"

١٢- يَسْأَلُونَ أَيَّانَ يَوْمُ الدِّينِ ۝

4991. *That which ye are promised*: the Promise of God about Mercy and Forgiveness to the Penitent, and Justice and Penalty to the Rebellious; the promise of the Hereafter; the promise that all does not end here, but that there is a truer and more lasting world to come, for which this is but a preparation.

4992. *Dīn*=the giving to each person his precise and just due; this is implied in Judgment and Justice. All the inequalities of this Life are to be redressed.

4993. The study of the numerous regular orbits of the planets and irregularly regular orbits of comets, and the various motions, visible or invisible, of the fixed stars or revolving stars, form in themselves a network of knowledge or science, of a highly technical nature; the highest astronomy or mathematics can only barely reach its fringe. But these have all a fixed Plan and Purpose under God's Dispensation. In them variety leads to Unity. In contrast look at the confused medley of doctrines, views, and dicta put forward by the Sceptics, as described in the next verse.

4994. *Qaul*=saying, word, theory, doctrine. *Mukhtalif*=differing, various, inconsistent with itself, discordant. No theory or doctrine based on a denial of a Hereafter can be consistent with spiritual facts as we know them, or with God's Goodness, Justice, and Mercy.

4995. Some Commentators draw from this a rigid doctrine of Calvinistic Predestination or Determinism, which I do not think is fairly deducible from the words. "*Ufika*" should I think be translated "*will* be or *would* be deluded", meaning "have the wish or desire to be", and not "must necessarily be deluded by eternal predestination". The word occurs in many places in the Qur-ān: *e.g. Cf.* v. 78, or ix. 30.

4996. They are in great spiritual danger: yet they care not.

13. (It will be) a Day
When they will be tried
(And tested) over the Fire!

١٣- يَوْمَ هُمْ عَلَى النَّارِ يُفْتَنُونَ ○

14. " Taste ye your trial!
This is what ye used
To ask to be hastened! " [4997]

١٤- ذُوقُوا فِتْنَتَكُمْ ۖ
هَٰذَا الَّذِي كُنتُم بِهِ تَسْتَعْجِلُونَ ○

15. As to the Righteous,
They will be in the midst
Of Gardens and Springs, [4998]

١٥- إِنَّ الْمُتَّقِينَ
فِي جَنَّاتٍ وَعُيُونٍ ○

16. Taking joy in the things
Which their Lord gives them,
Because, before then, they
Lived a good life.

١٦- آخِذِينَ مَا آتَاهُمْ رَبُّهُمْ ۚ
إِنَّهُمْ كَانُوا قَبْلَ ذَٰلِكَ مُحْسِنِينَ ○

17. They were in the habit [4999]
Of sleeping but little
By night,

١٧- كَانُوا قَلِيلًا مِّنَ اللَّيْلِ مَا
يَهْجَعُونَ ○

18. And in the hours
Of early dawn,
They (were found) praying
For Forgiveness; [5000]

١٨- وَبِالْأَسْحَارِ
هُمْ يَسْتَغْفِرُونَ ○

19. And in their wealth
And possessions (was remembered)
The right of the (needy,)
Him who asked, and him
Who (for some reason) was [5001]
Prevented (from asking).

١٩- وَفِي أَمْوَالِهِمْ
حَقٌّ لِّلسَّائِلِ
وَالْمَحْرُومِ ○

4997. They used to say scoffingly, "if there is to be punishment for our sins, let it come at once!" When it comes, they will know what a terrible thing it is! *Cf* xxvi. 204, n. 3230.

4998. Gardens and Springs are the two most frequent symbols for the highest satisfaction and bliss.

4999. They were engaged most of the night in worship and in the planning of good deeds. They preferred activity to idleness, the service of God and His creatures to the indulgence of Self.

5000. They were up early before dawn, ready for their devotions. The praying for Forgiveness and Mercy does not necessarily imply that they had committed fresh sins. Indeed they *began* the day with such devotions, showing their great humility before God and their anxious care for others, for whom they prayed as much as for themselves. See the last sentence of n. 21 to i. 5.

5001. True charity remembers not only those in need who ask, but also those who are prevented by some reason from asking. The man of true charity seeks out the latter. There may be various reasons which prevent a man from asking for help: (1) he may be ashamed to ask, or his sense of honour may prevent him from asking; (2) he may be so engrossed in some great ideal that he may not think of asking; (3) he may even not know that he is in need, especially when we think of wealth and possessions in a spiritual sense, as including spiritual gifts and talents; (4) he may not know that you possess the things that can supply his needs; and (5) he may be a dumb and helpless creature, whether a human being or a dumb animal, or any creature within your ken or power. Charity in the higher sense includes all help, from one better endowed to one less well endowed. *Cf.* n. 179 to ii. 177; also ii. 273-274, and notes 322 and 323.

20. On the earth
Are Signs for those
Of assured Faith,

٢٠- وَفِي الْأَرْضِ آيَاتٌ لِّلْمُوقِنِينَ ○

21. As also in your own [5002]
Selves: will ye not
Then see?

٢١- وَفِي أَنفُسِكُمْ ۚ أَفَلَا تُبْصِرُونَ ○

22. And in heaven is [5003]
Your Sustenance, as (also)
That which ye are promised.

٢٢- وَفِي السَّمَاءِ رِزْقُكُمْ وَمَا تُوعَدُونَ ○

23. Then, by the Lord [5004]
Of heaven and earth,
This is the very Truth,
As much as the fact
That ye can speak
Intelligently to each other.

٢٣- فَوَرَبِّ السَّمَاءِ وَالْأَرْضِ إِنَّهُ لَحَقٌّ مِّثْلَ مَا أَنَّكُمْ تَنطِقُونَ ○

C. 227.—Even Abraham the True had need to be told
(li. 24-60.) Before he could realise the purpose of God.
Clear Signs were sent for warning, as, of old,
To Pharaoh, the 'Ād, the Thamūd, and the people
Of Noah, and the warning inevitably came
To pass. Our Signs are for your instruction.
Heed them and learn by them. Those who believe
Find profit in their lives: those who reject
Or deny,—alas! they learn not from the past.
Woe unto them! The loss is their own!

SECTION 2.

24. Has the story [5005]
Reached thee, of the honoured
Guests of Abraham?

٢٤- هَلْ أَتَاكَ حَدِيثُ ضَيْفِ إِبْرَاهِيمَ الْمُكْرَمِينَ ○

5002. The Signs and Evidences of God are in all nature and within the body and soul of man, if man has but the spiritual eyes to see. *Cf.* xli. 53.

5003. "Sustenance", here as elsewhere, includes physical sustenance, as well as spiritual sustenance. Similarly heaven or sky has both the physical and the spiritual meaning. The physical sustenance grows from rain from the sky; the spiritual sustenance comes from divine aid, grace, and mercy, and includes the Good News and the Warning which come from Revelation about the Hereafter.

5004. Attention having been called to the Signs or Evidences of God's working on the earth, within ourselves, and in the heavens, in verses 20-22, an appeal is made to our own inner conscience, in the name of the Lord of heaven and earth, to acknowledge and act up to the truth of Revelation, and turn to the spiritual Realities. For they are as real as our own conscious and self-intelligent existence, on which is based all our knowledge. As a philosopher (Descartes) has said: "I think: therefore I am."

5005. *Cf.* xi. 69-73 and notes, where further details of the story will be found. *Cf.* also xv. 51-56.

25. Behold, they entered [5006]
His presence, and said:
"Peace!" He said, "Peace!"
(And thought, "These seem)
Unusual people." [5007]

٢٥- إِذْ دَخَلُوا عَلَيْهِ فَقَالُوا سَلٰمًا ط
قَالَ سَلٰمٌ ج
قَوْمٌ مُّنْكَرُوْنَ ○

26. Then he turned quickly [5008]
To his household, brought
Out a fatted calf,

٢٦- فَرَاغَ إِلَىٰ أَهْلِهِ
فَجَآءَ بِعِجْلٍ سَمِيْنٍ ○

27. And placed it before them...
He said, "Will ye not
Eat?"

٢٧- فَقَرَّبَهُ إِلَيْهِمْ
قَالَ أَلَا تَأْكُلُوْنَ ○

28. (When they did not eat),
He conceived a fear of them.
They said, "Fear not,"
And they gave him
Glad tidings of a son
Endowed with knowledge.

٢٨- فَأَوْجَسَ مِنْهُمْ خِيْفَةً ط
قَالُوا لَا تَخَفْ
وَبَشَّرُوْهُ بِغُلٰمٍ عَلِيْمٍ ○

29. But his wife came forward [5009]
(Laughing) aloud: she smote
Her forehead and said:
"A barren old woman!"

٢٩- فَأَقْبَلَتِ امْرَاَتُهُ فِيْ صَرَّةٍ
فَصَكَّتْ وَجْهَهَا وَقَالَتْ عَجُوْزٌ عَقِيْمٌ ○

30. They said, "Even so [5010]
Has thy Lord spoken:
26 And He is full
30 Of Wisdom and Knowledge."

٣٠- قَالُوا كَذٰلِكِ قَالَ رَبُّكِ ط
إِنَّهُ هُوَ الْحَكِيْمُ الْعَلِيْمُ ○

5006. They were angels, who appeared suddenly before him at his tent-door in the guise of men, and saluted him with the salutation of peace. He returned the salutation, but felt, from their appearance and their manner, that they were unusual, not ordinary, strangers.

5007. *Munkar*: unknown, uncommon, unusual, not customary, (hence by derived meaning, not applicable here, not fair or just); opposite in both primary and secondary meanings to *ma'rūf*, well-known, usual, customary, just. *Cf.* xv. 62.

5008. They seemed unusual strangers, but he said nothing and quietly proceeded to perform the rites of hospitality. He brought a roast fatted calf and placed it before them to eat. But the strangers did not eat (xi. 70). This disconcerted him. According to the laws of hospitality, a stranger under your roof is under your protection, but if he refuses to eat, he refuses your hospitality and keeps himself free from any ties of guest and host. "What were their designs?" thought Abraham, and he felt some distrust. But they were angels and could not eat. They declared themselves, and announced the birth to Abraham of a son endowed with wisdom,—in other words that Abraham was to be the head of a long line of Prophets! (xv. 53).

5009. Abraham's wife Sarah was old and barren. This news seemed to her too good to be true. She came forward, laughed aloud (xi. 71), struck her forehead with her hands, indicative of her amusement and incredulity as "a barren old woman": xi. 72.

5010. The angels said: "What may sound improbable to human beings will yet come to pass if God commands. And God thy Lord has spoken. So shall it be. For all His promises are full of wisdom and knowledge." So the angels on that occasion. But the application is for all time and to all human affairs. Never despair. However much Truth may be in the shade, it will shine with full splendour. And the Judgment will come, when good will come to its own!

31. (Abraham) said: "And what,
O ye Messengers,
Is your errand (now)?"

٣١- قَالَ فَمَا خَطْبُكُمْ
أَيُّهَا الْمُرْسَلُونَ ۝

32. They said, "We have
Been sent to a people
(Deep) in sin;—

٣٢- قَالُوٓا إِنَّآ أُرْسِلْنَآ إِلَىٰ قَوْمٍ
مُّجْرِمِينَ ۝

33. "To bring on, on them,
(A shower of) stones
Of clay (brimstone),[5011]

٣٣- لِنُرْسِلَ عَلَيْهِمْ
حِجَارَةً مِّن طِينٍ ۝

34. "Marked as from thy Lord[5012]
For those who trespass
Beyond bounds."

٣٤- مُّسَوَّمَةً عِندَ رَبِّكَ
لِلْمُسْرِفِينَ ۝

35. Then We evacuated[5013]
Those of the Believers
Who were there,

٣٥- فَأَخْرَجْنَا
مَن كَانَ فِيهَا مِنَ الْمُؤْمِنِينَ ۝

36. But We found not there
Any just (Muslim) persons
Except in one house:[5014]

٣٦- فَمَا وَجَدْنَا فِيهَا
غَيْرَ بَيْتٍ مِّنَ الْمُسْلِمِينَ ۝

37. And We left there
A Sign for such as
Fear the Grievous Penalty.[5015]

٣٧- وَتَرَكْنَا فِيهَآ ءَايَةً
لِّلَّذِينَ يَخَافُونَ الْعَذَابَ الْأَلِيمَ ۝

5011. *Cf.* xi. 82, and n. 1052 to vii. 84. The angels' errand of mercy to Abraham (to announce the succession of godly men in his line) was coupled with their errand of justice and punishment to the people of Lūṭ, the people of Sodom and Gomorrah, who were deep in the most abominable and unnatural sins. So God's Mercy and Justice go hand in hand in all human affairs. Faith has nothing to fear, and wickedness has only to turn and repent, to obtain God's Mercy.

5012. *Cf.* xi. 83, and n. 1580. Every crime has its due punishment, as marked out in the decrees of God.

5013. The only just or righteous persons found in Sodom and Gomorrah (Cities of the Plain by the Dead Sea) were in the house of Lūṭ, who was the apostle sent to call them to repentance. He and his believing family and adherents were told to leave in due time, and the wicked were destroyed in a shower of brimstone.

5014. That was the house of Lūṭ; and even there, his wife had no faith: she disobeyed the Command and perished: xi. 81, n. 1577.

5015. *The Grievous Penalty*: that is, the Final Judgment. The destruction of Sodom and Gomorrah in this life is taken as the type of the Final Judgment. The vestiges can be seen—as a Sign and a Warning—in ths sulphury plain round the Dead Sea: *Cf.* xv. 79.

38. And in Moses[5016]
(Was another Sign):
Behold, We sent him
To Pharaoh, with authority
Manifest.

٣٨- وَفِي مُوسَىٰٓ
إِذْ أَرْسَلْنَٰهُ إِلَىٰ فِرْعَوْنَ بِسُلْطَٰنٍ مُّبِينٍ ۝

39. But (Pharaoh) turned back
With his Chiefs, and said,
"A sorcerer, or
One possessed!"

٣٩- فَتَوَلَّىٰ بِرُكْنِهِۦ وَقَالَ
سَٰحِرٌ أَوْ مَجْنُونٌ ۝

40. So We took him
And his forces, and
Threw them into the sea;
And his was the blame.[5017]

٤٠- فَأَخَذْنَٰهُ وَجُنُودَهُۥ
فَنَبَذْنَٰهُمْ فِى ٱلْيَمِّ وَهُوَ مُلِيمٌ ۝

41. And in the 'Ād (people)[5018]
(Was another Sign):
Behold, We sent against them
The devastating Wind:

٤١- وَفِى عَادٍ
إِذْ أَرْسَلْنَا عَلَيْهِمُ ٱلرِّيحَ ٱلْعَقِيمَ ۝

42. It left nothing whatever
That it came up against,
But reduced it to ruin
And rottenness.

٤٢- مَا تَذَرُ مِن شَىْءٍ أَتَتْ عَلَيْهِ
إِلَّا جَعَلَتْهُ كَٱلرَّمِيمِ ۝

43. And in the Thamūd[5019]
(Was another Sign):
Behold, they were told,
"Enjoy (your brief day)[5020]
For a little while!"

٤٣- وَفِى ثَمُودَ
إِذْ قِيلَ لَهُمْ
تَمَتَّعُوا۟ حَتَّىٰ حِينٍ ۝

5016. *Cf.* xliv. 17-31. The story of Moses and Pharaoh is here just referred to. The points emphasized here are: (1) that Moses had manifest authority, yet Pharaoh doubted; (2) that Pharaoh's reliance was on his Chiefs and his forces, but they could not help when his doom came; and (3) that in the most extraordinary and incredible ways (judged by ordinary human standards), his arrogance and his reliance on his Chiefs and forces was his undoing.

5017. The ungodly Egyptians were all destroyed, but the chief blame lay on Pharaoh for misleading them. Pharaoh's punishment was just. He could not blame any one else. And certainly no one can blame the course of God's Justice, for God was long-suffering, and gave him many chances to repent.

5018. *Cf.* xlvi. 21-26. The point here is that the 'Ad were a gifted people: God had given them talents and material wealth: but when they defied God, they and all their belongings were destroyed in a night, by a hurricane which they thought was bringing them the rain to which they were looking forward. How marvellously God's Providence works, to help the good and destroy the wicked!

5019. See the story of the Thamūd and their prophet Ṣāliḥ in vii. 73-79. Here the point is the suddenness of their punishment and its unexpected nature.

5020. Ṣāliḥ their prophet gave them three days' clear warning for repentance (xi. 65). But they heeded him not. On the contrary they flouted him and continued in their evil courses.

44. But they insolently defied[5021]
The Command of their Lord:
So the stunning noise[5022]
(Of an earthquake) seized
Them, even while they
Were looking on.

٤٤- فَعَتَوْا عَنْ أَمْرِ رَبِّهِمْ فَأَخَذَتْهُمُ الصَّٰعِقَةُ وَهُمْ يَنظُرُونَ ○

45. Then they could not
Even stand (on their feet),[5023]
Nor could they help themselves.

٤٥- فَمَا اسْتَطَٰعُوا مِن قِيَامٍ وَمَا كَانُوا مُنتَصِرِينَ ○

46. So were the People[5024]
Of Noah before them:
For they wickedly transgressed.

٤٦- وَقَوْمَ نُوحٍ مِّن قَبْلُ إِنَّهُمْ كَانُوا قَوْمًا فَٰسِقِينَ ○ ع

SECTION 3.

47. With power and skill[5025]
Did We construct
The Firmament:
For it is We Who create
The vastness of Space.

٤٧- وَالسَّمَآءَ بَنَيْنَٰهَا بِأَيْي۟دٍ وَإِنَّا لَمُوسِعُونَ ○

5021. They had already defied the order to preserve the She-camel, which was symbolical of the grazing rights of the common people: see xi. 64-65 and n. 1560. They continued to flout the warnings of the prophet until the earthquake came on them with a stunning noise and buried them where they were: vii. 78; and xi. 67.

5022. *Ṣā'iqat*: a stunning sound like that of thunder and lightning (ii. 55); such a sound often accompanies an earthquake (see xli. 17, n. 4485, and vii. 78, and n. 1047).

5023. They were swept off in the earthquake.

5024. The generation of Noah was swept away in the Flood for their sins: vii. 59-64. The point is that such a Flood seemed so unlikely to them that they thought Noah was "wandering in his mind" when he delivered God's Message: vii. 60.

5025. If you do not wish to go back to the wonderful things in the past, which show the power and goodness of God, and His justice supreme over all wrong-doing, look at the wonderful things unfolding themselves before your very eyes! (1) The space in the heavens above! Who can comprehend it but He Who made it and sustains it? (2) The globe of the earth under your feet! How great its expanse seems over sea and land, and spread out for you like a wonderful carpet or bed of rest! (3) All things are in twos: sex in plants and animals, by which one individual is complementary to another; in the subtle forces of nature, Day and Night, positive and negative electricity, forces of attraction and repulsion: and numerous other opposites, each fulfilling its purpose, and contributing to the working of God's Universe: and in the moral and spiritual world, Love and Aversion, Mercy and Justice, Striving and Rest, and so on;—all fulfilling their functions according to the Artistry and wonderful Purpose of God. Everything has its counterpart, or pair, or complement. God alone is One, with none like Him, or needed to complement Him. These are noble things to contemplate. And they lead us to a true understanding of God's Purpose and Message.

48. And We have spread out
The (spacious) earth :
How excellently
We do spread out!

٤٨- وَالْأَرْضَ فَرَشْنٰهَا
فَنِعْمَ الْمٰهِدُوْنَ ○

49. And of every thing
We have created pairs :[5026]
That ye may receive
Instruction.

٤٩- وَمِنْ كُلِّ شَيْءٍ خَلَقْنَا زَوْجَيْنِ
لَعَلَّكُمْ تَذَكَّرُوْنَ ○

50. Hasten ye then (at once)[5027]
To God : I am from Him
A Warner to you,
Clear and open!

٥٠- فَفِرُّوْٓا اِلَى اللّٰهِ
اِنِّيْ لَكُمْ مِّنْهُ نَذِيْرٌ مُّبِيْنٌ ○

51. And make not another[5028]
An object of worship
With God :
I am from Him
A Warner to you,
Clear and open!

٥١- وَلَا تَجْعَلُوْا مَعَ اللّٰهِ اِلٰهًا اٰخَرَ
اِنِّيْ لَكُمْ مِّنْهُ
نَذِيْرٌ مُّبِيْنٌ ○

52. Similarly, no apostle came
To the Peoples before them,
But they said (of him)
In like manner,
"A sorcerer, or
One possessed"![5029]

٥٢- كَذٰلِكَ مَآ اَتَى الَّذِيْنَ مِنْ قَبْلِهِمْ مِّنْ
رَّسُوْلٍ اِلَّا قَالُوْا
سَاحِرٌ اَوْ مَجْنُوْنٌ ○

53. Is this the legacy[5030]
They have transmitted,

٥٣- اَتَوَاصَوْا

5026. See (3) in the last note. *Cf.* xxxvi. 36, n. 3981.

5027. If you understand Nature and yourselves aright, you will know that God is all in all, and you will fly at once to Him. This is the teaching which the Prophet of God has come to give you, in clear terms and openly to all.

5028. Verses 50 and 51, ending with the same clause to emphasize the connection between the two, should be read together. The Prophet's mission was (and is): (1) to show us the urgent need for repentance; and (2) to wean us from the precipice of false worship. The one convinces us of sin and opens the door to the Mercy of God; the other cures us of the madness of paying court to idle or worthless objects of desire; for in the worship of the One True God is included the best service to ourselves and our fellow-creatures. If fully understood, this sums up the whole duty of man: for it leads us by the right Path to the love of God and the love of man and of all creatures.

5029. They said this of Moses: li. 39. And they said this of the holy Prophet: xxxviii. 4; xliv. 14.

5030. There is a tradition of Evil as there is a tradition of Good. The ways of Evil in dealing with the teachers of Truth are similar in all ages. But such evil traditions would have no effect, were it not that the generation following them is itself ungodly, "transgressing beyond bounds"

One to another?
Nay, they are themselves
A people transgressing
Beyond bounds!

بِهٖ ۚ
بَلْ هُمْ قَوْمٌ طَاغُوْنَ ۝

54. So turn away[5031]
From them: not thine
Is the blame.

٥٤- فَتَوَلَّ عَنْهُمْ
فَمَآ اَنْتَ بِمَلُوْمٍ ۝

55. But teach (thy Message):
For teaching benefits
The Believers.

٥٥- وَّذَكِّرْ
فَاِنَّ الذِّكْرٰى تَنْفَعُ الْمُؤْمِنِيْنَ ۝

56. I have only created[5032]
Jinns and men, that
They may serve Me.

٥٦- وَمَا خَلَقْتُ الْجِنَّ وَالْاِنْسَ
اِلَّا لِيَعْبُدُوْنِ ۝

57. No Sustenance do I require[5033]
Of them, nor do I
Require that they should
Feed Me.

٥٧- مَآ اُرِيْدُ مِنْهُمْ مِّنْ رِّزْقٍ
وَّمَآ اُرِيْدُ اَنْ يُّطْعِمُوْنِ ۝

58. For God is He Who
Gives (all) Sustenance,—
Lord of Power,—[5034]
Steadfast (for ever).

٥٨- اِنَّ اللّٰهَ هُوَ الرَّزَّاقُ
ذُو الْقُوَّةِ الْمَتِيْنُ ۝

59. For the wrong-doers,
Their portion is like

٥٩- فَاِنَّ لِلَّذِيْنَ ظَلَمُوْا ذَنُوْبًا

5031. When the Prophet freely proclaims his Message, it is not his fault if obstinate wickedness refuses to listen. He can leave them alone, but he should continue to teach for the benefit of those who have Faith.

5032. Creation is not for idle sport or play: xxi. 16. God has a serious Purpose behind it, which, in our imperfect state, we can only express by saying that each creature is given the chance of development and progress towards the Goal, which is God. God is the source and centre of all power and all goodness, and our progress depends upon our putting ourselves into accord with His Will. This is His service. It is not of any benefit to Him: see the next two verses: it is for our own benefit.

5033. *Sustenance*: in both the literal and the figurative sense; so also "Feed Me" at the end of the verse. God is independent of all needs. It is therefore absurd to suppose that He should require *any* Sustenance, and still more absurd to suppose that we can feed Him! The gifts, the Sustenance, the goodness, all come from His side.

5034. God commands all power; therefore any power we seek must be from Him. And His power is steadfast, the same to-day as yesterday, and for ever. Therefore His help is always sure.

Unto the portion of their [5035]
Fellows (of earlier generations):
Then let them not ask Me
To hasten (that portion)!

مِثْلَ ذَنُوبِ أَصْحٰبِهِمْ
فَلَا يَسْتَعْجِلُونِ ○

60. Woe, then, to the Unbelievers,
On account of that Day [5036]
Of theirs which they
Have been promised!

٦٠- فَوَيْلٌ لِّلَّذِينَ كَفَرُوا مِن يَوْمِهِمُ
الَّذِي يُوعَدُونَ ○ ع

5035. Each generation, that acts like any of its predecessors, must meet a similar fate. If the wicked came to an evil end in the past, the same results will follow in the present and the future. The punishment will come suddenly enough: let them not in mockery ask that it should be hastened.

5036. That is, their eternal Punishment in the Hereafter, as well as any punishment that may come to them in this life.

INTRODUCTION TO SŪRA LII (*Ṭūr*).

This is the third of the group of seven Meccan Sūras described in the Introduction to S. *l*.

It is, like its predecessor, an early Meccan Sūra. The points here emphasized are : that Revelation is in accord with all God's Signs, including previous Revelations, and that the Hereafter is inevitable, and we must prepare for it.

Summary.—All Signs of God, including previous Revelations, point to the inevitable consequences of ill-deeds and good deeds: how can people deny or ignore the Message of Revelation? (lii. 1-49, and C. 228).

C. 228.—By the sacred Symbols—of the Mount
(lii. 1-49.) Sublime, the Eternal Record on an open
Scroll, the House of Worship thronged
With men, the Canopy blue of unfathomed
Heights, and the boundless Ocean with
Its resistless tidal Swell,—all acts
Of men must have their inevitable fruits.
New worlds will be born with the Day of Doom :
New values established by God's Decree.
Consumed will be Evil in the fire of Reality :
And Good will come to its own—in personal
And social Bliss, but most in the full
Realisation that God is good, the Beneficent,
The Merciful . . . Proclaim, then, the praises
Of the Lord, nor heed the slanders of Ignorance
Or Spite : for the Lord Who created will cherish ;
His Plan will overthrow the puny plots
Of men. Hold firm with patience in Faith
In the Hereafter, and sing His praises
Even in the busy marts of this world,
But chiefly in the stillness of the Night
And the holy hour of Dawn as the Stars
Retreat, singing glory to the Maker
Of their own most glorious Sun.

Sūra LII.

Ṭūr, or the Mount.

In the name of God, Most Gracious, Most Merciful.

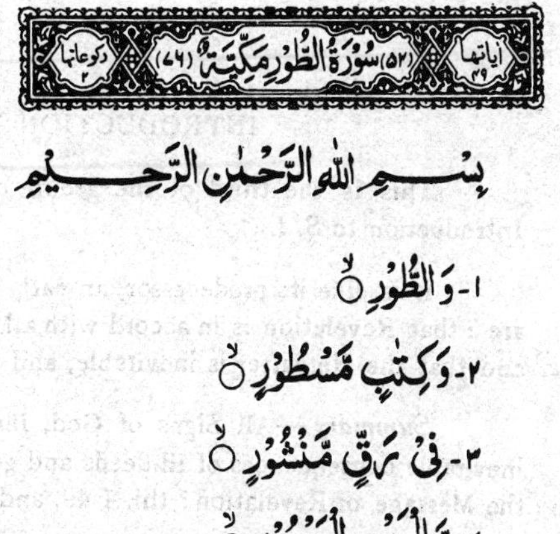

1. By the Mount (of Revelation);[5037]

2. By a Decree Inscribed[5038]

3. In a Scroll unfolded;

4. By the much-frequented Fane;[5039]

5. By the Canopy Raised High;[5040]

٥-وَالسَّقْفِ الْمَرْفُوْعِ ۝

5037. The adjuration is by five things which we shall presently explain. An appeal is made to these five Signs in verses 1 to 6, and the certainty of future events is asserted in the most emphatic terms in verses 7 to 28, in three parts, *viz.* the coming of Judgment and the passing away of this phenomenal world (verses 7-10); the future ill consequences of ill-deeds done (verses 11-16); and future attainment of bliss and complete realisation of God's love and mercy (verses 17-28).

5038. See last note. The five Signs to which appeal is made are: (1) the Mount (of Revelation), verse 1; (2) the Decree Inscribed, verses 2-3; (3) The Much-frequented Fane, verse 4; (4) the Canopy Raised High, verse 5; and (5) the Ocean filled with Swell, verse 6.

Let us examine these in detail. Each of them has a figurative and a mystic meaning. (1) The Mount is the sublime world of Revelation. In the case of Moses it is typified by Mount Sinai: *Cf.* xcv. 2, where it is mentioned in juxtaposition to the sacred territory of Mecca, xcv. 3. In the case of Jesus it is the Mount of Olives: *Cf.* xcv. 1, and also Matt. xxiv. 3-51, where Jesus made his striking pronouncement about the Judgment to come. In the case of Muḥammad it is the Mountain of Light, where the divine inspiration made him one with the spiritual world: *Cf* C. 31 and n. 11 (2). The Decree Inscribed is God's Eternal Decree. When it becomes Revelation to man, it is figured forth as something "inscribed", reduced to writing; and as it is made clear to the intelligence of man, it is further described as "in a scroll unfolded", that is, spread out so that everyone who has the will can seek its guidance.

5039. See the last two notes. (3) "The much-frequented Fane" (or House) is usually understood to mean the Ka'ba, but in view of the parallelism noted in the last note, it may be taken generally to mean any Temple or House of Worship dedicated to the true God. It would then include the Tabernacle of the Israelites in the wilderness, the Temple of Solomon, the Temple in which Jesus worshipped, and the Ka'ba which the holy Prophet purified and re-dedicated to true worship. These would be only illustrations. Other concrete places of worship would be included, and in a more abstract meaning, the heart of man, which craves, with burning desire, to find and worship God. The Fane is "much-frequented" as there is a universal desire in the heart of man to worship God, and his sacred Temples draw large crowds of devotees.

5040. (4) "The Canopy Raised High" is the canopy of heaven, to whose height or sublimity no limit can be assigned by the mind of man. It is Nature's Temple, in which all Creation worships God,—the Symbol in which the material and the visible merges into the spiritual and the intuitional.

6. And by the Ocean[5041] Filled with Swell;—[5042]	٦- وَالْبَحْرِ الْمَسْجُورِ ۝
7. Verily, the Doom of thy Lord Will indeed come to pass;—	٧- إِنَّ عَذَابَ رَبِّكَ لَوَاقِعٌ ۝
8. There is none Can avert it;—	٨- مَّا لَهُ مِن دَافِعٍ ۝
9. On the Day when[5043] The firmament will be In dreadful commotion.	٩- يَوْمَ تَمُورُ السَّمَآءُ مَوْرًا ۝
10. And the mountains will fly Hither and thither.[5044]	١٠- وَتَسِيرُ الْجِبَالُ سَيْرًا ۝
11. Then woe that Day To those that treat (Truth) as Falsehood;—[5045]	١١- فَوَيْلٌ يَوْمَئِذٍ لِّلْمُكَذِّبِينَ ۝

5041. (5) The Ocean—the vast, limitless, all encircling Ocean,—is the material symbol of the universal, unlimited, comprehensive nature of the invisible spiritual world. It is expressed to be *masjūr*, full of a mighty swell, boiling over, poured forth all over the earth, as if overwhelming all landmarks; *Cf.* lxxxi. 6:—a fitting description of the final disappearance of our temporal world in the supreme establishment of the Reality behind it.

5042. This completes the five Signs or Symbols by which man may know for certain of the Judgment to come. Note that they are in a descending order;—the highest, or most remote from man's consciousness, being mentioned first, and that nearest to man's consciousness being mentioned last. The truth of Revelation: its embodiment in a Prophet's Message given in human language; the universal appeal of divine worship; the starry world above; and the encircling Ocean, full of life and motion below,—all are evidences that the Day of God will finally come, and nothing can avert it.

In Ṣūfi interpretation each of these Symbols further typifies an aspect of the final Preacher of Unity: the Mount signifying his tremendous Personality; the Decree inscribed in a Scroll Unfolded, the perspicuous Qur-ān; the much-frequented Fane, his heart open to every living creature; the Canopy Raised on High, his spiritual eminence; and the Swelling Ocean, the vast sea of his living knowledge.

5043. The Day of Judgment is typified by two figures. (1) "The firmament will be in dreadful commotion." The heavens as we see them suggest to us peace and tranquillity, and the power of fixed laws which all the heavenly bodies obey. This will all be shaken in the rise of the new spiritual world. *Cf.* Matt. xxiv. 29: "Immediately after the tribulation of those days...the powers of the heavens shall be shaken." For (2) see next note.

5044. (2) The mountains are a type of firmness and stability. But things that we think of as firm and stable in this material life will be shaken to pieces, and will be no more substantial than a mirage in a desert. *Cf.* lxxviii. 20.

5045. That Day will be a Day of Woe to the wrong-doers described in two aspects, the rebels against God and God's Truth, just as it will be a Day of Joy and Thanksgiving to the Righteous, who are described in three aspects in verses 17 to 28. The rebels are here described as being those who openly defied Truth and plunged into wrong-doing, or who trifled with truth, who jested with serious matters, who had not the courage to plunge openly into wrong-doing but who secretly took profit out of it, who wasted their life in doubts and petty quibbles. It is difficult to say which attitude did more harm to themselves and to others. Both are aspects of deep-seated sin and rebellion. But the mercy of God was open to all if they had repented and amended their lives.

12. That play (and paddle)
In shallow trifles.

١٢- الَّذِينَ هُمْ فِي خَوْضٍ يَلْعَبُونَ ۝

13. That Day shall they be
Thrust down to the Fire
Of Hell, irresistibly.

١٣- يَوْمَ يُدَعُّونَ إِلَىٰ نَارِ جَهَنَّمَ دَعًّا ۝ ط

14. "This", it will be said,[5046]
"Is the Fire,—which ye
Were wont to deny!

١٤- هَٰذِهِ النَّارُ الَّتِي
كُنتُم بِهَا تُكَذِّبُونَ ۝

15. "Is this then a fake,[5047]
Or is it ye that
Do not see?

١٥- أَفَسِحْرٌ هَٰذَا
أَمْ أَنتُمْ لَا تُبْصِرُونَ ۝

16. "Burn ye therein:
The same is it to you
Whether ye bear it
With patience, or not:[5048]
Ye but receive the recompense
Of your (own) deeds."

١٦- اصْلَوْهَا
فَاصْبِرُوا أَوْ لَا تَصْبِرُوا سَوَاءٌ عَلَيْكُمْ ط
إِنَّمَا تُجْزَوْنَ مَا كُنتُمْ تَعْمَلُونَ ۝

17. As to the Righteous,[5049]
They will be in Gardens,
And in Happiness,—

١٧- إِنَّ الْمُتَّقِينَ
فِي جَنَّاتٍ وَنَعِيمٍ ۝

18. Enjoying the (Bliss) which
Their Lord hath bestowed
On them, and their Lord
Shall deliver them from
The Penalty of the Fire.

١٨- فَاكِهِينَ بِمَا آتَاهُمْ رَبُّهُمْ
وَوَقَاهُمْ رَبُّهُمْ عَذَابَ الْجَحِيمِ ۝

5046. In face of the Realities, it will be borne in on them how wrong it was for them in this life to deny or forget that every wicked thought or deed had its own retributive chain of consequences.

5047. Perhaps they had said that the Hereafter was a fake, mere old wives' tales! If they had given serious thought to the Signs of God, they would have been saved from that serious spiritual blindness: then they will see that the fault was their own, and that the warnings of the apostles of Truth were nothing but pure Truth.

5048. At that stage they will have no justification for anger or impatience: for their whole position will have been due to their own conduct and their rejection of God's Grace. Nor will there be time then for patience or repentance, for their period of probation will then have been over

5049. The Righteous will be in Bliss far beyond their merits: their sins and faults will be forgiven by the grace of God, which will save them from the penalties which they may have incurred from human frailty. It will be their own effort or striving which will win them God's grace: see verse 19 below. But the fruits will be greater than they could strictly have earned.

19. (To them will be said :)[5050]
"Eat and drink ye,
With profit and health,[5051]
Because of your (good) deeds."

١٩- كُلُوا وَاشْرَبُوا هَنِيْٓـًٔا
بِمَا كُنْتُمْ تَعْمَلُوْنَ ۝

20. They will recline (with ease)
On Thrones (of dignity)
Arranged in ranks;[5052]
And We shall join them
To Companions, with beautiful
Big and lustrous eyes.[5053]

٢٠- مُتَّكِـِٕيْنَ عَلٰى سُرُرٍ
مَّصْفُوْفَةٍ ۚ
وَ زَوَّجْنٰهُمْ بِحُوْرٍ عِيْنٍ ۝

21. And those who believe
And whose families[5054] follow
Them in Faith,—to them
Shall We join their families:
Nor shall We deprive them
(Of the fruit) of aught
Of their works:
(Yet) is each individual
In pledge for his deeds.[5055]

٢١- وَالَّذِيْنَ اٰمَنُوْا وَاتَّبَعَتْهُمْ ذُرِّيَّتُهُمْ
بِاِيْمَانٍ
اَلْحَقْنَا بِهِمْ ذُرِّيَّتَهُمْ
وَ مَآ اَلَتْنٰهُمْ مِّنْ عَمَلِهِمْ مِّنْ شَیْءٍ ؕ
كُلُّ امْرِیٍٕۢ بِمَا كَسَبَ رَهِيْنٌ ۝

5050. The bliss of the Righteous is described in three aspects: (1) their individual bliss, verses 17-20; (2) their social bliss, verses 21-24; and (3) their satisfaction in the dissipation of past shadows, and their full understanding of the goodness of God, verses 25-28.

5051. Individual satisfaction is expressed in three types or figures of speech, (1) eating and drinking, (2) thrones of dignity, and (3) the joy of individual companionship. But the eating and drinking will not be like the physical acts, which are subject to drawbacks, such as excess, after-effects and satiety: here there will be pure health, profit, and enjoyment. So about the other two: see the notes following.

Cf. with this the symbolical description of heaven in xxxvii. 40-49: while the general account is the same, special phases are brought out in the two passages to correspond with the context.

5052. Every one will have a Throne of dignity, but it does not follow that the dignity will be the same. Every one's Personality will be purified but it will not be merged into one general sameness.

5053. *Cf.* xliv. 54, and notes 4728 and 4729, where the meaning of Ḥūr is fully explained. This is the special sharing of individual Bliss, one with another. The next verse refers to the general social satisfaction shared with all whom we loved in this earthly life.

5054. *Zurrīyat*: literally, progeny, offspring, family; applied by extension to mean all near and dear ones whether related or not, ancestors and descendants, friends, a circle, a group, whether contemporaneous in time or not. Love is unselfish, and works not merely, or chiefly, for Self, but for others; provided the others have Faith and respond according to their capacities or degrees, they will be joined on to the Head of the Group, even though on individual merits their rank might be less. This applies specially to a Prophet and his *Ummat* (or following).

5055. As already explained in the last note, though the love poured out by Prophets, ancestors, descendants, friends, or good men and women, will secure for their loved ones the enjoyment of their society, it is an indispensable condition that the loved ones should also, according to their lights, have shown their faith and their goodness in deeds. Each individual is responsible for his conduct. In the kingdom of heaven there is no boasting of ancestors or friends. But it is part of the satisfaction of the good ones who poured out their love that those who were in any way worthy to receive their love should also be admitted to their society, and this satisfaction shall in no wise be diminished to them.

22. And We shall bestow On them, of fruit and meat,[5056] Anything they shall desire.	٢٢- وَأَمْدَدْنٰهُم بِفَاكِهَةٍ وَلَحْمٍ مِّمَّا يَشْتَهُونَ ○
23. They shall there exchange, One with another, A (loving) cup Free of frivolity,[5057] Free of all taint Of ill.	٢٣- يَتَنَازَعُونَ فِيهَا كَأْسًا لَّا لَغْوٌ فِيهَا وَلَا تَأْثِيمٌ ○
24. Round about them will serve, (Devoted) to them, Youths (handsome) as Pearls[5058] Well-guarded.	٢٤- وَيَطُوفُ عَلَيْهِمْ غِلْمَانٌ لَّهُمْ كَأَنَّهُمْ لُؤْلُؤٌ مَّكْنُونٌ ○
25. They will advance[5059] To each other, engaging In mutual enquiry.	٢٥- وَأَقْبَلَ بَعْضُهُمْ عَلَىٰ بَعْضٍ يَتَسَاءَلُونَ ○
26. They will say: "Aforetime, We were not without fear For the sake of our people.[5060]	٢٦- قَالُوا إِنَّا كُنَّا قَبْلُ فِي أَهْلِنَا مُشْفِقِينَ ○

5056. To be interpreted allegorically as the "feast of reason and the flow of soul." Note that this verse is embedded in the midst of the description of *social* bliss; the individual bliss figured by meat and drink has already been mentioned in verse 19 above. The social pleasures will be of any kind or quantity they shall desire. but their desires will then be purified, just as their pleasures will be on a different plane.

5057. Drinking or loving cups. in our life on this earth. are apt to be misused in two ways: (1) they may be occasions for mere frivolity or the wasting of time; (2) they may lead to evil thoughts, evil suggestions, evil talk. or evil deeds. To safeguard the allegory, it is added that the Cup in the final Bliss will be free from any taint of this kind. It will be pure love without any grossness whatever.

5058 The allegory is further continued. There is no question of sex in heaven. But the type of the grace and gentleness of womanhood having been implied in the word *Hūr* (verse 20 above), the type of the handsome and well-formed strength and splendour of manhood is mentioned here in the allegory of Pearls,—of the purest water, well-guarded from weathering and unsullied by rough usage. Their service will be the service of youth, whose glory is enthusiasm without self-interest.

Maknūn: well-guarded, kept close, concealed from exposure: the beautiful nacreous lustre of Pearls is disfigured by exposure to gases, vapours, or acids; when not actually in use they are best kept in closed caskets, guarded from deteriorating agencies.

5059. The third—and the highest—stage of Bliss, after individual Bliss and social Bliss, is the satisfaction of looking to the Past without its shadows and realising to the full in the Present the goodness of God. See n. 5050. This, again, is shared in mutual converse and confidence.

5060. A man may be good, and may within limits have found goodness in his own spiritual life, but may have anxieties about his family or friends whom he loves. All such shadows are removed in heaven by the Grace of God, and he is free to dwell on it in his confidential converse with other men similarly circumstanced.

27. "But God has been good
To us, and has delivered us
From the Penalty
Of the Scorching Wind.[5061]

٢٧- فَمَنَّ اللّٰهُ عَلَيْنَا
وَوَقٰىنَا عَذَابَ السَّمُوْمِ ۝

28. "Truly, we did call
Unto Him from of old:
Truly it is He,
The Beneficent, the Merciful!"[5062]

٢٨- اِنَّا كُنَّا مِنْ قَبْلُ نَدْعُوْهُ ۭ
اِنَّهٗ هُوَ الْبَرُّ الرَّحِيْمُ ۝ ع

SECTION 2.

29. Therefore proclaim thou[5063]
The praises (of thy Lord):
For by the Grace
Of thy Lord, thou art
No (vulgar) soothsayer, nor
Art thou one possessed.

٢٩- فَذَكِّرْ
فَمَآ اَنْتَ بِنِعْمَتِ رَبِّكَ
بِكَاهِنٍ وَّلَا مَجْنُوْنٍ ۝

30. Or do they say:—
"A Poet! we await
For him some calamity[5064]
(Hatched) by Time!"

٣٠- اَمْ يَقُوْلُوْنَ شَاعِرٌ
نَّتَرَبَّصُ بِهٖ رَيْبَ الْمَنُوْنِ ۝

31. Say thou: "Await ye!—
I too will wait[5065]
Along with you!"

٣١- قُلْ تَرَبَّصُوْا
فَاِنِّيْ مَعَكُمْ مِّنَ الْمُتَرَبِّصِيْنَ ۝

5061. "Us" includes the good man or woman and all whom he or she cared for. This would be an ever-expanding circle, until it includes all mankind through Teachers like the Chosen One. The "Scorching Wind" is the type of haste, arrogance, and fire, such as entered into the composition of Jinns: xv. 27. The destiny of man is to attain to calm, peace, security, the Garden of Bliss.

5062. 'Before this, we called upon Him, in faith that He is good: now we know in our inmost souls that He is indeed good,—the Beneficent, the Merciful.' This is the climax of the description of Heaven.

5063. The nature of the spiritual kingdom, with its apex in God, having been explained in the last section, the man of God is now exhorted to go on proclaiming the Message of God, despite all that the foolish, ignorant, or wicked men may say. The greatest of the Prophets was called a soothsayer, *i.e.*, one who tells fortunes by divination, or a madman possessed of some evil spirit, or a poet singing spiteful satires. Much more may lesser men be called by such names because they proclaim the Truth. They should go on in spite of it all.

5064. If a spiteful poet foretells evil calamities for men, men can afford to laugh at him, hoping that Time will bring about its revenge, and spite will come to an evil end. For the various meanings of *Raib*, see n. 1884 to xiv. 9. Some Commentators suggest Death as the Calamity hatched by Time.

5065. *Cf.* ix. 52. If the wicked wait or look for some calamity to befall the preacher of Truth, the preacher of Truth can with far more justice await the decision of the issue between him and his persecutors. For he stands for right, and God will support the right.

32. Is it that their faculties
Of understanding urge them[5066]
To this, or are they
But a people transgressing[5067]
Beyond bounds?

٣٢- أَمْ تَأْمُرُهُمْ أَحْلَامُهُم بِهَٰذَآ
أَمْ هُمْ قَوْمٌ طَاغُونَ ۝

33. Or do they say,
"He fabricated the (Message)"?[5068]
Nay, they have no faith!

٣٣- أَمْ يَقُولُونَ تَقَوَّلَهُۥ ۚ
بَل لَّا يُؤْمِنُونَ ۝

34. Let them then produce
A recital like unto it,—
If (it be) they speak
The Truth!

٣٤- فَلْيَأْتُوا۟ بِحَدِيثٍ مِّثْلِهِۦٓ
إِن كَانُوا۟ صَٰدِقِينَ ۝

35. Were they created of
nothing,[5069]
Or were they themselves
The creators?

٣٥- أَمْ خُلِقُوا۟ مِنْ غَيْرِ شَىْءٍ
أَمْ هُمُ ٱلْخَٰلِقُونَ ۝

36. Or did they create
The heavens and the earth?
Nay, they have
No firm belief.[5070]

٣٦- أَمْ خَلَقُوا۟ ٱلسَّمَٰوَٰتِ وَٱلْأَرْضَ ۚ
بَل لَّا يُوقِنُونَ ۝

5066. It may be that the persecutors of Truth are ignorant, and their deficient faculties of understanding mislead them, but it is more often the case that they are perverse rebels against the law of God, defending their own selfish interests, and preventing those whom they oppress, from getting justice.

5067. *Cf.* li. 53.

5068. As an alternative to the charges of being a soothsayer or a madman or a disgruntled poet, there is the charge of a forger or fabricator applied to the man of God when he produces his Message. This implies that there can be no Revelation or inspiration from God. Such an attitude negatives Faith altogether. But if this is so, can they produce a work of man that can compare with the inspired Word of God? They cannot. *Cf.* x. 37-39, and xvii. 88.

5069. "*Were they created of nothing?*" Three possible alternative meanings are suggested by the Commentators, according to the meaning we give to the Arabic preposition *min*=of, by, with, for. (1) 'Were they created by nothing? Did they come into existence of themselves? Was it a mere chance that they came into being? (2) Were they created as men out of nothing? Was there not a wonderful seed, from which their material growth can be traced, as the handiwork of a wise and wonderful Creator? Must they not then seek His Will? (3) Were they created for nothing, to no purpose? If they *were* created for a purpose, must they not try to learn that purpose by understanding God's Revelation?

5070. They obviously did not create the wonders of the starry heavens and the fruitful globe of the earth. But they can assign no definite cause to explain it, as they have no firm belief on the subject themselves.

37. Or are the Treasures
Of thy Lord with them,[5071]
Or are they the managers
(Of affairs)?

٣٧- أَمْ عِندَهُمْ خَزَآئِنُ رَبِّكَ
أَمْ هُمُ الْمُصَيْطِرُونَ ۝

38. Or have they a ladder,[5072]
By which they can (climb
Up to heaven and) listen
(To its secrets)? Then let
(Such a) listener of theirs
Produce a manifest proof.

٣٨- أَمْ لَهُمْ سُلَّمٌ
يَسْتَمِعُونَ فِيهِ ۚ
فَلْيَأْتِ مُسْتَمِعُهُم بِسُلْطَانٍ مُّبِينٍ ۝

39. Or has He only daughters[5073]
And ye have sons?

٣٩- أَمْ لَهُ الْبَنَاتُ وَلَكُمُ الْبَنُونَ ۝

40. Or is it that thou
Dost ask for a reward,[5074]
So that they are burdened
With a load of debt?—

٤٠- أَمْ تَسْأَلُهُمْ أَجْرًا
فَهُم مِّن مَّغْرَمٍ مُّثْقَلُونَ ۝

41. Or that the Unseen[5075]
Is in their hands,
And they write it down?

٤١- أَمْ عِندَهُمُ الْغَيْبُ
فَهُمْ يَكْتُبُونَ ۝

42. Or do they intend
A plot (against thee)?[5076]
But those who defy God
Are themselves involved
In a Plot!

٤٢- أَمْ يُرِيدُونَ كَيْدًا ۖ
فَالَّذِينَ كَفَرُوا
هُمُ الْمَكِيدُونَ ۝

5071. *Cf.* vi. 50, and n. 867. The Treasures of God's Knowledge are infinite. But the doubters and unbelievers have no access to them, much less can the doubters and unbelievers manage the wonders of this world. Must they not therefore seek grace and revelation from God?

5072. *Cf.* vi. 35: a reference to the Pagan belief that by means of a material ladder a man might climb up to heaven and learn its secrets!

5073. *Cf.* xvi. 57-59, and n. 2082. To the gospel of Unity it is repugnant to assign begotten sons or daughters to God. But the Arab superstition about angels being the daughters of God was particularly blasphemous as the Pagan Arabs hated to have daughters themselves and considered it a mark of humiliation!

5074. The men of God ask for no reward to preach the Message of God and direct men to the right Path. Why then do men shun them and persecute those who seek to bring blessings to them?

5075. The Unseen in the spiritual world is a subject of Revelation, though it works through the common everyday life of man. The men who reject Revelation simply because it is outside their own experience ought on the contrary to try to learn about it and seek to understand it.

5076. Shallow men who plot against Good are themselves the willing victims of insidious plots laid by Evil.

43. Or have they a god [5077]
Other than God?
Exalted is God
Far above the things
They associate with Him!

۴۳- اَمْ لَهُمْ اِلٰهٌ غَيْرُ اللّٰهِ ط
سُبْحٰنَ اللّٰهِ عَمَّا يُشْرِكُوْنَ ○

44. Were they to see
A piece of the sky [5078]
Falling (on them), they
Would (only) say: "Clouds
Gathered in heaps!"

۴۴- وَاِنْ يَّرَوْا كِسْفًا مِّنَ السَّمَآءِ سَاقِطًا
يَّقُوْلُوْا سَحَابٌ مَّرْكُوْمٌ ○

45. So leave them alone
Until they encounter
That Day of theirs,
Wherein they shall (perforce)
Swoon (with terror),— [5079]

۴۵- فَذَرْهُمْ حَتّٰى يُلٰقُوْا يَوْمَهُمُ الَّذِىْ
فِيْهِ يُصْعَقُوْنَ ○

46. The Day when their plotting
Will avail them nothing
And no help shall be
Given them.

۴۶- يَوْمَ لَا يُغْنِىْ عَنْهُمْ كَيْدُهُمْ شَيْـًٔا
وَّلَا هُمْ يُنْصَرُوْنَ ○

47. And verily, for those
Who do wrong, there is
Another punishment besides
this: [5080]
But most of them
Understand not.

۴۷- وَاِنَّ لِلَّذِيْنَ ظَلَمُوْا
عَذَابًا دُوْنَ ذٰلِكَ
وَلٰكِنَّ اَكْثَرَهُمْ لَا يَعْلَمُوْنَ ○

48. Now await in patience
The command of thy Lord:

۴۸- وَاصْبِرْ لِحُكْمِ رَبِّكَ

5077. This is the final and decisive question: Is there really any god other than the One True God? Every argument points to the negative. A series of questions has been asked above, pointing to the negative of the superstitions of the godless. The gospel of Unity, Revelation, and the Hereafter has thus been preached by a searching examination of the position of the Unbelievers. And the Sūra ends with an exhortation to leave alone those who will not believe because they wish not to believe, and to let Time work out the web and pattern of God's Plan.

5078. In xxvi. 187, Shu'aib, the man of God, is challenged by the Companions of the Wood "to cause a piece of the sky to fall on us, if thou art truthful." Such a challenge, in some form or other, is addressed to all men of God. It is mere defiance. It has no meaning. If a piece of the sky were to fall on them, it would not convince them, for they would only say: "These are only clouds gathered in heaps." They do not wish to believe. Otherwise there are ample Signs and Evidences of God's Plan in Creation and in man's own heart.

5079 That is, the Day of Judgment. *Cf.* xxxix. 68, and n. 4343.

5080 The final Judgment is for all. But in addition, wrong-doers have to fear a retribution or punishment in this very life, an open punishment through external events, or at least the bitter pangs of conscience within.

For verily thou art In Our eyes :[5081] And celebrate the praises Of thy Lord the while Thou standest forth,[5082]	فَإِنَّكَ بِأَعْيُنِنَا وَسَبِّحْ بِحَمْدِ رَبِّكَ حِينَ تَقُومُ ۝
49. And for part of the night[5083] Also praise thou Him,— And at the retreat[5084] Of the stars !	٤٩-وَمِنَ الَّيْلِ فَسَبِّحْهُ وَإِدْبَارَ النُّجُومِ ۝ ع

5081. The man of God must strive his utmost to proclaim the Message of God: as for results, it is not for him to command them. He must wait patiently, in the knowledge that he is not forgotten by God, but is constantly under God's eyes,—under His loving care and protection. And he must glorify God's name, as he is a standard-bearer of God's Truth.

5082. The translators and Commentators nearly all understand *taqūmu* in the sense of rising up from sleep. But the rendering I have given is consistent with Quranic usage. In xxvi. 218, we have the same two words *ḥīna taqūmu*, meaning "standing forth (in prayer)". In lvii. 25, we have "*li-yaqūm an-nāsu bil-qisṭi*", which obviously means "that men may stand forth in justice," *i.e.* do all their business in justice. In lxxviii 38, we have *yaqūmu* used for the angels standing forth in ranks.

On my rendering the meaning will be: 'celebrate God's praises when you stand forth in prayer, or at all times when you go about your business; but also for part of the night and at early dawn when worldly life is at a standstill.'

5083. It is not necessary to understand this for any particular canonical prayers It is good to spend a part of the night in prayer and praise: *Cf.* lxxiii. 6. And the Dawn is a daily recurring miracle of nature, full of spiritual influences and "testimony": *Cf.* xvii. 78-79.

5084. *Idbār-un-nujūm*: the retreat of the stars: the glorious hour of early dawn. In cxiii. 1. we seek God's protection as "Lord of the Dawn".

INTRODUCTION TO SŪRA LIII (*Najm*).

This is an early Meccan Sūra, and is the fourth of the series of seven which were described in the Introduction to S. *l*.

The particular theme of this Sūra is that Revelation is not an illusion: the illusion is in the minds of those who doubt and have false ideas of God: God is the source and goal of all things.

In some Sūras the consecutive arrangement is shown or suggested by a cue-word. Here the cue-word is "star", corresponding to "stars" in the last verse of the last Sūra. So in xlvi. 1, the words: "Exalted in Power, Full of Wisdom": are carried forward from the last verse of S. xlv, and indeed the same words occur in the first verse of S. xlv. So, again the words: "Most Merciful, Oft-Forgiving": in xxxiv. 2, refer back to the words: "Oft-Forgiving, Most Merciful": in the last line of S. xxxiii. In S. liv. 1, the nearness of Judgment recalls the same idea at the end of the previous Sūra (liii. 57). Other examples will also be found.

Summary.—The impression received by the Prophet in revelation is neither error on his part nor deception by others, nor does he speak from selfish motives: it comes clearly from God, Who is not what the vain imaginations of men conceive: He is all-in-all, First and Last, Lord of all, Ample in forgiveness (liii. 1-32, and C. 229).

Those who turn away are petty and ignorant, not knowing that God is the source and goal of all things—in men, in nature, and in the events of history: therefore serve ye Him (liii. 33-62, and C. 230).

C. 229.—True revelation is not a process
(liii. 1-32.) Either of error or deception, nor does
The Prophet speak from himself as he desires.
It is God's inspiration, true, without doubt.
It is reality,—the inner reality
Of heaven as far as knowledge can reach,
Not the false ideas and idols that men
Construct for themselves, names without truth
Behind them. The goal of all things is God,
As He is the One from Whom starts Reality.
No other can e'er intercede except
As He wills. He made us, and knows all
That we are. It is not for us to justify
Ourselves, but to offer ourselves as we are.

Sūra LIII.

Najm, or the Star.

In the name of God, Most Gracious, Most Merciful.

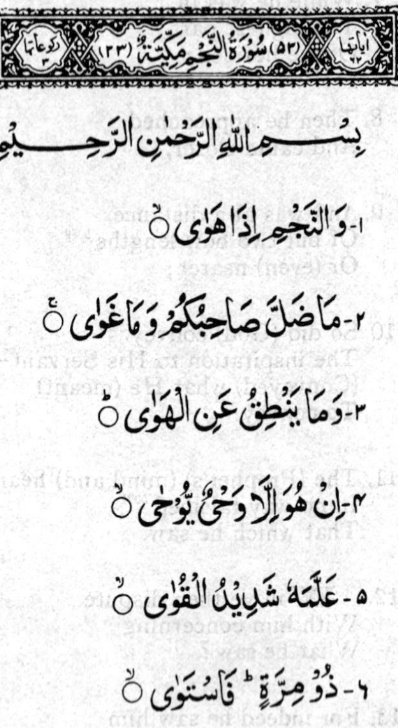

1. By the Star[5085]
When it goes down,—

2. Your Companion is neither[5086]
Astray nor being misled,

3. Nor does he say (aught)
Of (his own) Desire.

4. It is no less than
Inspiration sent down to him:

5. He was taught by one[5087]
Mighty in Power,

6. Endued with Wisdom:
For he appeared
(In stately form)

5085. *Najm* is interpreted in various ways. As most commonly accepted, it means either a Star generically, or the close cluster of seven stars known as the Pleiades in the Constellation Taurus, which the sun enters about the 21st of April every year. In mid-April, or a little later, the beautiful cluster would set just after the sun, after having gradually ascended the sky in the winter months. In late May, or a little later, it would rise just before the sun. In its western aspects, it might be considered a spring constellation. To open-air nations (including the Arabs) whose climate usually presents starry skies, this is an object of great interest, and many folklore tales gather round it. When so glorious a cluster is content to bow down in the horizon and merge its light in the greater light created by God (see the last three lines of C 228), it becomes a symbol of humility in beauty and power before the Most High, Whose revelation discloses the summit of beauty, power, and wisdom.

Hawā in the text may mean either "goes down (or sets)" or "rises". Whichever meaning we take, it makes no difference to the symbolic interpretation given above.

5086. "*Your Companion*" is the holy Prophet Muḥammad, who had lived among the Quraish all his life. He is defended from three kinds of charges that the Unbelievers brought against him: (1) that he was going astray, either through defect of intelligence or through carelessness; (2) that he was being misled or deceived by evil spirits; and (3) that he spoke out of a whim or impulse, or from a selfish desire to impress his own personality. None of these charges was true. On the contrary he had direct inspiration from God.

5087. This is referred by the Commentators to the angel Gabriel, through whom the inspiration came. *Cf.* lxxxi. 20.

7. While he was in
The highest part[5088]
Of the horizon:

٧- وَهُوَ بِالْاُفُقِ الْاَعْلٰى ۝

8. Then he approached
And came closer,

٨- ثُمَّ دَنَا فَتَدَلّٰى ۝

9. And was at a distance
Of but two bow-lengths[5089]
Or (even) nearer;

٩- فَكَانَ قَابَ قَوْسَيْنِ اَوْ اَدْنٰى ۝

10. So did (God) convey[5090]
The inspiration to His Servant—
(Conveyed) what He (meant)
To convey.

١٠- فَاَوْحٰى اِلٰى عَبْدِهٖ
مَآ اَوْحٰى ۝

11. The (Prophet's) (mind and) heart
In no way falsified[5091]
That which he saw.

١١- مَا كَذَبَ الْفُؤَادُ مَا رَاٰى ۝

12. Will ye then dispute
With him concerning
What he saw?

١٢- اَفَتُمٰرُوْنَهٗ عَلٰى مَا يَرٰى ۝

13. For indeed he saw him
At a second descent,[5092]

١٣- وَلَقَدْ رَاٰهُ نَزْلَةً اُخْرٰى ۝

14. Near the Lote-tree[5093]
Beyond which none may pass:

١٤- عِنْدَ سِدْرَةِ الْمُنْتَهٰى ۝

5088. Gabriel appeared in stately form, perhaps towering above the Mountain of Light (see C. 31). *Istawā* in verse 6, translated "appeared", means literally "mounted" or "ascended", or "set himself to execute a design": see n. 1386 to x. 3.

5089. Two bow-shots (counting 100 to 150 yards to a bow-shot) would be a clearly visible distance. But Ṣūfī mysticism would interpret: "two drawn bows, with their chords touching", making a complete circle of union. In this case the "one Mighty in Power" in verse 5 above would be not Gabriel, but the Supreme Being, Who Himself taught the Prophet.

5090. Gabriel would be just a messenger, to do no more than convey God's Message to God's Apostle.

5091. "Heart" in Arabic includes the faculty of intelligence as well as the faculty of feeling. The impression conveyed was pure truth; there was no illusion in it.

5092. The first occasion when Gabriel appeared in a visible form was at the Mountain of Light, when he brought his first revelation beginning with *Iqraa*: see C. 29-35. The second was at the Prophet's *Mi'rāj* or Ascension: see Introduction to S. xvii, paras 2-4. These were the only two occasions when Gabriel appeared in visible form. The Mi'rāj appearance was near the Lote-tree in the highest heaven, above which (figuratively) is the Throne of God.

5093. For the Lote-tree in its literal meaning, see n. 3814 to xxxiv. 16. The wild Lote is thorny; under cultivation it yields good fruit and shade, and is symbolic of heavenly bliss, as here and in lvi. 28. The symbolism here is that the farthest Lote-tree marked the bounds of heavenly knowledge as revealed to men, beyond which neither angels nor men could pass.

15. Near it is the Garden
Of Abode.[5094]

١٥- عِندَهَا جَنَّةُ الْمَأْوَىٰ ۝

16. Behold, the Lote-tree
Was shrouded
(In mystery unspeakable!)

١٦- إِذْ يَغْشَى السِّدْرَةَ مَا يَغْشَىٰ ۝

17. (His) sight never swerved,
Nor did it go wrong!

١٧- مَا زَاغَ الْبَصَرُ وَمَا طَغَىٰ ۝

18. For truly did he see,
Of the Signs of his Lord,
The Greatest!

١٨- لَقَدْ رَأَىٰ مِنْ آيَاتِ رَبِّهِ الْكُبْرَىٰ ۝

19. Have ye seen[5095]
Lat, and 'Uzza,

١٩- أَفَرَءَيْتُمُ اللَّٰتَ وَالْعُزَّىٰ ۝

20. And another,
The third (goddess), Manat?

٢٠- وَمَنَوٰةَ الثَّالِثَةَ الْأُخْرَىٰ ۝

21. What! For you[5096]
The male sex,
And for Him, the female?

٢١- أَلَكُمُ الذَّكَرُ وَلَهُ الْأُنثَىٰ ۝

22. Behold, such would be
Indeed a division
Most unfair!

٢٢- تِلْكَ إِذًا قِسْمَةٌ ضِيزَىٰ ۝

5094. The Mansion or Throne (figuratively) or Special Presence,—if the Throne or Presence could ever be localised in our thoughts: for God's "Throne doth extend over the heavens and the earth" (ii. 255). The point was reached when the spiritual knowledge of man could reach no higher. The Ṣūfis interpret the Lote-tree in Islam to be what the Burning Bush in the valley of Ṭuwā was to Moses: Q. xx. 10-13, and n. 2541; and Exod. iii. 1-6. Only, in the case of Moses it was but a prefigurement of the divine effulgence on this earth: in the case of Muḥammad it was the divine Glory in heaven itself, and it was "shrouded in mystery unspeakable". This was indeed "the Greatest of the Signs of the Lord" (liii. 18).

5095. From the heights of divine Glory, we come back again to this sorry earth, with its base idolatries. We are asked to "look at this picture, and at that!" The three principal idols of Pagan Arab Idolatry were the goddesses Lāt, Uzzā, and Man t. Opinions differ as to their exact forms: one version is that Lāt was in human shape, 'Uzzā had its origin in a sacred tree, and Manāt in a white stone. They all represented God in female form.

5096. To show God in human shape, or imagine sons or daughters of God, as if God were flesh, was in any case a derogation from the supreme glory of God, high above all creatures, even if the human shapes were invested with great beauty and majesty as in the Greek Pantheon. But when we consider in what low opinion Pagan Arabia held the female sex, it was particularly degrading to show God, or so-called daughters of God, in female shapes. Cf. xvi. 57-59, and n. 2082; also liii. 39, and n. 5073.

23. These are nothing but names
Which ye have devised,—[5097]
Ye and your fathers,—
For which God has sent
Down no authority (whatever).
They follow nothing but[5098]
Conjecture and what
Their own souls desire!—
Even though there has already
Come to them Guidance
From their Lord!

٢٣- إِنْ هِيَ إِلَّآ أَسْمَآءٌ
سَمَّيْتُمُوهَآ أَنتُمْ وَءَابَآؤُكُم
مَّآ أَنزَلَ ٱللَّهُ بِهَا مِن سُلْطَٰنٍ
إِن يَتَّبِعُونَ إِلَّا ٱلظَّنَّ وَمَا تَهْوَى ٱلْأَنفُسُ
وَلَقَدْ جَآءَهُم
مِّن رَّبِّهِمُ ٱلْهُدَىٰٓ ۝

24. Nay, shall man have (just)
Anything he hankers after?[5099]

٢٤- أَمْ لِلْإِنسَٰنِ مَا تَمَنَّىٰ ۝

25. But it is to God
That the End and
The Beginning (of all things)
Belong.

٢٥- فَلِلَّهِ
ٱلْءَاخِرَةُ وَٱلْأُولَىٰ ۝ ع

SECTION 2.

26. How many-so-ever be
The angels in the heavens,[5100]
Their intercession will avail
nothing
Except after God has given[5101]
Leave for whom He pleases
And that he is acceptable
To Him.

٢٦- وَكَم مِّن مَّلَكٍ فِى ٱلسَّمَٰوَٰتِ
لَا تُغْنِى شَفَٰعَتُهُمْ شَيْـًٔا
إِلَّا مِنۢ بَعْدِ أَن يَأْذَنَ ٱللَّهُ
لِمَن يَشَآءُ وَيَرْضَىٰٓ ۝

5097. *Cf.* vii. 71; xii. 40, n. 1693. The divine names which they give to stocks and stones, or to heroes living or dead, or even to prophets and men of God, are but the creations of their own fancy. Whatever they were, they were not gods.

5098. *Cf.* vi. 116. Conjecture is a dangerous thing in speaking of divine things. It follows lines which reflect the lusts of men's own hearts. Why not follow the divine guidance which comes through men of God?

5099. The unpurified desires of men's hearts often lead to destruction, for they are dictated by Evil. The true source of guidance and light is God, just as He is also the goal to which all persons and things—all existence—returns.

5100. We are apt to imagine the angelic host of heaven as beings of immense power. But their power is all derived from God. Men, when they attain to the highest spiritual dignities, may have even more power and position than angels in the sight of God, as is typified by angels being bidden to bow down to Adam: ii. 34. The Quraish superstition about angels being intermediaries and intercessors for man with God is condemned.

5101. *Cf.* xx. 109 and xxi. 28. No one can intercede except with the permission of God, and that permission will only be given for one who is acceptable to God. For a possible different shade of meaning, see n. 2634 to xx. 109.

27. Those who believe not
In the Hereafter, name
The angels with female names.[5102]

٢٧- إِنَّ الَّذِينَ لَا يُؤْمِنُونَ بِالْآخِرَةِ
لَيُسَمُّونَ الْمَلَٰٓئِكَةَ تَسْمِيَةَ الْأُنثَىٰ ○

28. But they have no knowledge
Therein. They follow nothing
But conjecture; and conjecture[5103]
Avails nothing against Truth.

٢٨- وَمَا لَهُم بِهِۦ مِنْ عِلْمٍ ۖ إِن يَتَّبِعُونَ إِلَّا
الظَّنَّ ۖ وَإِنَّ الظَّنَّ لَا يُغْنِى مِنَ الْحَقِّ شَيْـًٔا ○

29. Therefore shun those who
Turn away from Our Message
And desire nothing but
The life of this world.

٢٩- فَأَعْرِضْ عَن مَّن تَوَلَّىٰ عَن ذِكْرِنَا
وَلَمْ يُرِدْ إِلَّا الْحَيَوٰةَ الدُّنْيَا ○

30. That is as far as[5104]
Knowledge will reach them.
Verily thy Lord knoweth best
Those who stray from
His Path, and He knoweth
Best those who receive guidance.

٣٠- ذَٰلِكَ مَبْلَغُهُم مِّنَ الْعِلْمِ ۚ
إِنَّ رَبَّكَ هُوَ أَعْلَمُ بِمَن ضَلَّ
عَن سَبِيلِهِۦ وَهُوَ أَعْلَمُ بِمَنِ اهْتَدَىٰ ○

31. Yea, to God belongs all
That is in the heavens
And on earth: so that
He rewards those who do[5105]
Evil, according to their deeds,
And He rewards those who
Do good, with what is best.

٣١- وَلِلَّهِ مَا فِى السَّمَٰوَٰتِ وَمَا فِى الْأَرْضِ
لِيَجْزِىَ الَّذِينَ أَسَٰٓـُٔوا بِمَا عَمِلُوا
وَيَجْزِىَ الَّذِينَ أَحْسَنُوا بِالْحُسْنَى ○

32. Those who avoid
Great sins and shameful deeds,

٣٢- الَّذِينَ يَجْتَنِبُونَ كَبَٰٓئِرَ الْإِثْمِ وَالْفَوَٰحِشَ

5102. *Cf.* liii. 21 above, and n. 5096. The Pagan Quraish had no firm belief in the Hereafter. Their prayers for intercession to angels and deities was on account of their worldly affairs.

5103. *Cf.* liii 23 above, and n. 5098.

5104. Men with a materialist turn of mind, whose desires are bounded by sex and material things, will not go beyond those things. Their knowledge will be limited to the narrow circle in which their thoughts move. The spiritual world is beyond their ken. While persons with a spiritual outlook, even though they may fail again and again in attaining their full ideals, are on the right Path. They are willing to receive guidance, and God's Grace will find them out and help them.

5105. All deeds have their consequences, good or ill. But this is not an iron law, as the Determinists in philosophy, or the preachers of bare Karma, would have us believe. God does not sit apart. He governs the world. And Mercy as well as Justice are His attributes. In His Justice every deed or word or thought of evil has its consequence for the doer or speaker or thinker. But there is always in this life room for repentance and amendment. As soon as this is forthcoming, God's Mercy comes into action. It can blot out our evil, and the "reward" which it gives is nearly always greater than our merits

Only (falling into) small faults,—
Verily thy Lord is ample[5106]
In forgiveness. He knows
You well when He brings
You out of the earth,
And when ye are hidden
In your mothers' wombs.
Therefore justify not yourselves:[5107]
He knows best who it is
That guards against evil.

إِلَّا اللَّمَمَ ۚ إِنَّ رَبَّكَ وَاسِعُ الْمَغْفِرَةِ ۚ
هُوَ أَعْلَمُ بِكُمْ إِذْ أَنشَأَكُم مِّنَ الْأَرْضِ
وَإِذْ أَنتُمْ أَجِنَّةٌ فِي بُطُونِ أُمَّهَاتِكُمْ ۖ
فَلَا تُزَكُّوا أَنفُسَكُمْ ۖ
هُوَ أَعْلَمُ بِمَنِ اتَّقَىٰ ۝

C. 230.—When once in God's Way, turn not away,
(liii. 33-62.) Nor check your generous impulse to give
Your all to God. The spiritual world
Unseen is above all worldly bargains.
Each soul must bear its own responsibility.
It must strive its utmost and attain its end.
The final Goal of all is God:
In His hands are Laughter and Tears, Life
And Death, the mystery of Birth and Creation,
And the Hereafter. He controls our Bliss
And inner satisfaction. He is Lord
Of the highest and noblest in Nature. His hand
Traces the course of History. Learn,
Oh learn from His Revelation, and
Adore the Lord of your inmost Soul!

SECTION 3.

33. Seest thou one[5108]
Who turns back,

٣٣- أَفَرَأَيْتَ الَّذِي تَوَلَّىٰ ۝

34. Gives a little,
Then hardens (his heart)?

٣٤- وَأَعْطَىٰ قَلِيلًا وَأَكْدَىٰ ۝

5106. God's attributes of Mercy and Forgiveness are unlimited. They come into action without our asking, but on our bringing our wills as offerings to Him. Our asking or prayer helps us to bring our minds and wills as offerings to Him. That is necessary to frame our own psychological preparedness. It informs God of nothing, for He knows all.

5107. As God knows our inmost being, it is absurd for us to justify ourselves, either by pretending that we are better than we are, or by finding excuses for our conduct. We must offer ourselves unreservedly, such as we are: it is His Mercy and Grace that will cleanse us. If we try, out of love for Him, to guard against evil, our striving is all that He asks for.

5108. The particular reference in this passage, according to Baidhāwi, is to Walid ibn Mugaira, who bargained with a Quraish Pagan for a certain sum if the latter would take upon himself the sins of Walid. He paid a part of the sum but withheld the rest. The general application that concerns us is threefold: (1) if we accept Islam, we must accept it whole-heartedly and not look back to Pagan superstitions; (2) we cannot play fast and loose with our promises and (3) no man can bargain about spiritual matters, for he cannot see what his end will be, unless he follows the law of God, which is the law of righteousness.

35. What! Has he knowledge Of the unseen So that he can see?[5109]	۳۵-اَعِنْدَهٗ عِلْمُ الْغَيْبِ فَهُوَ يَرٰى ۝
36. Nay, is he not acquainted With what is in the books[5110] Of Moses—	۳۶-اَمْ لَمْ يُنَبَّاْ بِمَا فِيْ صُحُفِ مُوْسٰى ۝
37. And of Abraham[5111] Who fulfilled his engagements:—[5112]	۳۷-وَاِبْرٰهِيْمَ الَّذِيْ وَفّٰۤى ۝
38. Namely, that no bearer[5113] Of burdens can bear The burden of another;	۳۸-اَلَّا تَزِرُ وَازِرَةٌ وِّزْرَ اُخْرٰى ۝
39. That man can have nothing But what he strives for;	۳۹-وَاَنْ لَّيْسَ لِلْاِنْسَانِ اِلَّا مَا سَعٰى ۝
40. That (the fruit of) his striving[5114] Will soon come in sight;	۴۰-وَاَنَّ سَعْيَهٗ سَوْفَ يُرٰى ۝
41. Then will he be rewarded With a reward complete;	۴۱-ثُمَّ يُجْزٰىهُ الْجَزَآءَ الْاَوْفٰى ۝
42. That to thy Lord Is the final Goal;[5115]	۴۲-وَاَنَّ اِلٰى رَبِّكَ الْمُنْتَهٰى ۝

5109. 'So that he can see what will happen in the Hereafter': for no bargains can be struck about matters unknown.

5110. *Books of Moses*: apparently not the Pentateuch, the *Taurāt*, but some other book or books now lost. For example, the Book of the Wars of Jehovah is referred to in the Old Testament (Num. xxi. 14) but is now lost. The present Pentateuch has no clear message at all of a Life to come.

5111. No original *Book of Abraham* is now extant. But a book called "The Testament of Abraham" has come down to us, which seems to be a Greek translation of a Hebrew original. See n. 6094 to lxxxvii. 19, where the Books of Moses and Abraham are again mentioned together.

5112. One of the titles of Abraham is *Ḥanīf*, the True in Faith: *Cf.* xvi. 120, 123.

5113. Here follows a series of eleven aphorisms of ancient wisdom apparently incorporated in current Semitic folklore. The first is that a man's spiritual burden—the responsibility for his sin—must be borne by himself and not by another: *Cf.* vi. 164. There can be no vicarious atonement.

5114. The second and third aphorisms are that man must strive, or he will gain nothing; and that if he strives, the result must soon appear in sight and he will find his reward in full measure.

5115. The fourth, fifth, and sixth aphorisms are that all things return to God; that all our hope should be in Him, and we should fear none but Him; and that He alone can give Life and Death

43. That it is He Who
Granteth Laughter and Tears;

٤٣- وَأَنَّهُ هُوَ أَضْحَكَ وَأَبْكَىٰ ۝

44. That it is He Who
Granteth Death and Life;

٤٤- وَأَنَّهُ هُوَ أَمَاتَ وَأَحْيَا ۝

45. That He did create
In pairs,—male and female,[5116]

٤٥- وَأَنَّهُ خَلَقَ الزَّوْجَيْنِ الذَّكَرَ وَالْأُنثَىٰ ۝

46. From a seed when lodged
(In its place);

٤٦- مِن نُّطْفَةٍ إِذَا تُمْنَىٰ ۝

47. That He hath promised
A Second Creation
(Raising of the Dead);[5117]

٤٧- وَأَنَّ عَلَيْهِ النَّشْأَةَ الْأُخْرَىٰ ۝

48. That it is He Who
Giveth wealth and satisfaction;[5118]

٤٨- وَأَنَّهُ هُوَ أَغْنَىٰ وَأَقْنَىٰ ۝

49. That He is the Lord
Of Sirius (the Mighty Star);[5119]

٤٩- وَأَنَّهُ هُوَ رَبُّ الشِّعْرَىٰ ۝

50. And that it is He
Who destroyed the (powerful)
Ancient 'Ād (people),[5120]

٥٠- وَأَنَّهُ أَهْلَكَ عَادًا الْأُولَىٰ ۝

5116. The seventh aphorism relates to the mystery of sex: all things are created in pairs: each sex performs its proper function, and yet its wonderful working is part of the creative process of God: the living seed fructifies, but contains within itself all the factors disclosed in its later development and life.

5117. No less wonderful is the promise He has made about the raising of the dead, and a new life in the Hereafter, and this is the subject of the eighth aphorism.

5118. Wealth and material gain are sought by most men, in the hope that they will be a source of enjoyment and satisfaction. But this hope is not always fulfilled. There is a psychical and spiritual side to it. But both the material and the spiritual side depend upon the working of God's Plan. This is referred to in the ninth aphorism

5119. The tenth aphorism refers to a mighty phenomenon of nature, the magnificent star Sirius, which is such a prominent object in the skies, in the early part of the solar year, say, from January to April. It is the brightest star in the firmament. and its bluish light causes wonder and terror in Pagan minds. The Pagan Arabs worshipped it as a divinity. But God is the Lord, Creator and Cherisher, of the most magnificent part of Creation, and worship is due to Him alone.

5120. The eleventh and last aphorism refers to the punishment of the most powerful ancient peoples for their sins. For the 'Ād people, see n. 1040 to vii. 65, and for the Thamūd, see n. 1043 to vii. 73. They were strong; and they were talented: but their strength and their talents did not save them from being destroyed for their sins. The same may be said about the earlier generation of Noah, who were destroyed in the Flood: they "rejected Our Signs: they were indeed a blind people" (vii. 64); see also n. 1039 to vii 59; and xi. 25-49.

Ancient 'Ād (people): some Commentators construe, "*First 'Ād people*", distinguishing them from the later 'Ād people, a remnant that had their day and passed away.

51. And the Thamūd,
Nor gave them a lease
Of perpetual life.

٥١-وَثَمُودَا۟ فَمَآ أَبْقَىٰ ۙ

52. And before them,
The people of Noah,
For that they were (all)
Most unjust
And most insolent transgressors,

٥٢-وَقَوْمَ نُوحٍ مِّن قَبْلُ ۖ
إِنَّهُمْ كَانُوا۟ هُمْ أَظْلَمَ وَأَطْغَىٰ ۗ

53. And He destroyed
The Overthrown Cities [5121]
(Of Sodom and Gomorrah),

٥٣-وَالْمُؤْتَفِكَةَ أَهْوَىٰ ۙ

54. So that (ruins unknown)
Have covered them up.

٥٤-فَغَشَّىٰهَا مَا غَشَّىٰ ۚ

55. Then which of the gifts [5122]
Of thy Lord, (O man,)
Wilt thou dispute about?

٥٥-فَبِأَىِّ ءَالَآءِ رَبِّكَ تَتَمَارَىٰ

56. This is a Warner, [5123]
Of the (series of) Warners
Of old!

٥٦-هَٰذَا نَذِيرٌ مِّنَ النُّذُرِ الْأُولَىٰٓ

57. The (Judgment) ever approaching
Draws nigh:

٥٧-أَزِفَتِ الْـَٔازِفَةُ ۚ

58. No (soul) but God
Can lay it bare.

٥٨-لَيْسَ لَهَا مِن دُونِ اللَّهِ كَاشِفَةٌ ۗ

59. Do ye then wonder [5121]
At this recital?

٥٩-أَفَمِنْ هَٰذَا الْحَدِيثِ تَعْجَبُونَ ۙ

5121. Verses 53-60 may be construed as a commentary on the aphorisms. The story of the Overthrown Cities, to which Lot was sent for a warning, will be found in xi. 74-83 and the notes thereon. This story may well be treated as separate from the aphorisms as it refers to events that happened in the later life of Abraham.

5122. With a slight modification this forms the refrain of the next Sūra but one, the highly poetical Sūra of *Raḥmān*. In S. liv. 15, 17, etc., there is a similar refrain in different words. Every gift and benefit you have is from God, and to save you from the just punishment of your sins, God at all times sends revelations and Messengers to warn you. Why not accept God's Grace instead of disputing about it?

5123. The Prophet before the Quraish (and before us) continues the line of men of God who have come to teach mankind and lead men into unity and righteousness. Shall we not listen to his voice? Every day that passes, the Judgment approaches nearer and nearer. But God alone can say at what precise hour it will come to any of us. It is certain, and yet it is a mystery, which God alone can lay bare.

5124. Mere wondering will not do, even if it is the wonder of admiration. Each soul must strive and act, and God's Mercy will take it under its wings.

60. And will ye laugh[5125]
And not weep,—

٦٠- وَتَضْحَكُوْنَ وَلَا تَبْكُوْنَ ۝

61. Wasting your time
In vanities?

٦١- وَأَنْتُمْ سٰمِدُوْنَ ۝

62. But fall ye down in prostration
To God, and adore (Him)![5126]

٦٢- فَاسْجُدُوْا لِلّٰهِ وَاعْبُدُوْا ۝ السجدة

5125. The higher issues of Life and the Hereafter are serious, and therefore all that we do in this life is serious and important. We must shun inanities and frivolities. It is no laughing time. If we only realised our own shortcomings, we should weep, with our good angels who weep for us. But weeping by itself will not help. We must try and understand God and adore Him. Thus shall we be able to understand ourselves and our fellow-men.

5126. And so we are invited to prostrate ourselves and adore Him. For this is the true end of Revelation and the true attitude when we understand the world, Nature, History and the working of God's Plan.

INTRODUCTION TO SŪRA LIV (*Qamar*).

This is an early Meccan Sūra, the fifth in the series dealing with Judgment, and the truth of Revelation, as explained in the Introduction to S. *l*.

The theme of the Sūra is explained by the refrain: "Is there any that will receive admonition?" which occurs six times, at the end of each reference to a past story of sin and rejection of warnings and in the appeal to the simplicity of the Qur-ān (verses 15, 17, 22, 32, 40, and 51). There is an invitation to listen to the Message and turn to Truth and Righteousness.

Summary.—The Hour of Judgment is nigh, but men forget or reject the Message, as did the people of Noah, of 'Ād, of Thamūd, of Lot, and of Pharaoh. Is there any that will receive admonition? (liv. 1-55, and C. 231.)

C. 231.—With every breath of our life, comes nearer
(liv. 1-55.) And nearer the Hour of Judgment: the proud
Will be brought low: the lovers of ease
Will find themselves in hardship. Come!
Is there any that will truly receive admonition?
So said Noah, but his people rejected
The warning and perished. We have made
Our Revelation easy to understand and follow.
Is there any that will truly receive admonition?
So said the prophets of 'Ād and Thamūd;
So said the prophets deputed to the People
Of Lūṭ and of Pharaoh: but the wicked continued
In sin and defiance and perished. Will the present
Generation learn wisdom by warning? Alas!
Is there any that will truly receive admonition?
The Righteous will dwell in their Gardens of Bliss,—
In the joyful Assembly of realised Truth,
In the Presence of their Sovereign Most High!

Sūra LIV.

Qamar, or the Moon.

In the name of God, Most Gracious,
Most Merciful

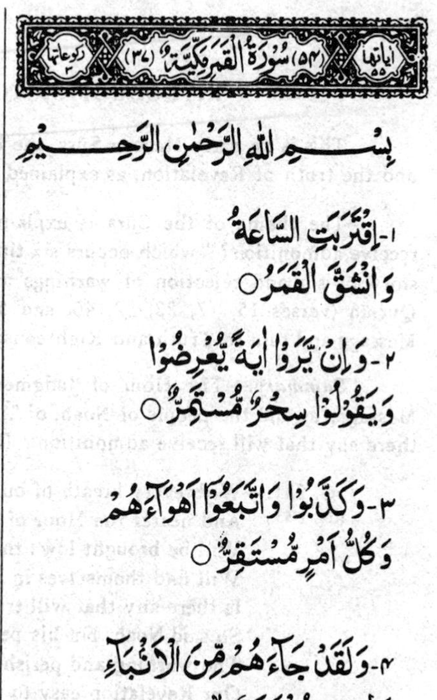

1. The Hour (of Judgment)[5127]
Is nigh, and the moon
Is cleft asunder.[5128]

2. But if they see
A Sign, they turn away,
And say, "This is
(But) transient magic."[5129]

3. They reject (the warning)
And follow their (own) lusts
But every matter has[5130]
Its appointed time.

4. There have already come
To them Recitals wherein[5131]
There is (enough) to check (them),

5. Mature wisdom ;—but
(The preaching of) Warners
Profits them not.

5127. See para. 2 of the Introduction to S. liii. The idea of the Judgment being nigh at the beginning of this Sūra connects it with the same idea at the end of the last Sūra (verse 57), though the actual words used in the two cases are different.

5128. Three explanations are given in the *Mufradāt*, and perhaps all three apply here : (1) that the moon once appeared cleft asunder in the valley of Mecca within sight of the Prophet, his Companions, and some Unbelievers ; (2) that the prophetic past tense indicates the future, the cleaving asunder of the moon being a Sign of the Judgment approaching ; and (3) that the phrase is metaphorical, meaning that the matter has become clear as the moon. That the first was noticed by contemporaries, including Unbelievers, is clear from verse 2. The second is an incident of the disruption of the solar system at the New Creation : *Cf.* lxxv. 8-9. And the third might well be implied as in eastern allegory, based on the other two.

5129. *Mustamirr* : transient, or powerful ; either meaning will apply. The Unbelievers acknowledge the unusual appearance, but call it magic. They do not therefore profit by the spiritual lesson.

5130. The prevalence of sin and the persecution of truth may have its day, but it must end at last.

5131. The stories of the sins of past generations having been visited with exemplary punishments were already in their possession, and should, if they had been wise, have opened their eyes and checked them in their mad career of sin. Five of these stories are again referred to later in this Sūra by way of illustration.

6. Therefore, (O Prophet,)[5132]
Turn away from them.
The Day that the Caller[5133]
Will call (them)
To a terrible affair,

٦- فَتَوَلَّ عَنْهُمْ ۘ
يَوْمَ يَدْعُ الدَّاعِ إِلَىٰ شَيْءٍ نُّكُرٍ ۝

7. They will come forth,—
Their eyes humbled—
From (their) graves, (torpid)[5134]
Like locusts scattered abroad,

٧- خُشَّعًا أَبْصَارُهُمْ يَخْرُجُونَ مِنَ الْأَجْدَاثِ
كَأَنَّهُمْ جَرَادٌ مُّنتَشِرٌ ۝

8. Hastening, with eyes transfixed,
Towards the Caller!—
"Hard is this Day!",
The Unbelievers will say.

٨- مُّهْطِعِينَ إِلَى الدَّاعِ ۖ
يَقُولُ الْكَافِرُونَ هَٰذَا يَوْمٌ عَسِرٌ ۝

9. Before them the People
Of Noah rejected (their apostle):
They rejected Our servant,[5135]
And said, "Here is
One possessed!", and he
Was driven out.

٩- كَذَّبَتْ قَبْلَهُمْ قَوْمُ نُوحٍ
فَكَذَّبُوا عَبْدَنَا وَقَالُوا مَجْنُونٌ وَازْدُجِرَ ۝

10. Then he called on his Lord:
"I am one overcome:
Do Thou then help (me)!"[5136]

١٠- فَدَعَا رَبَّهُ
أَنِّي مَغْلُوبٌ فَانتَصِرْ ۝

11. So We opened the gates
Of heaven, with water
Pouring forth.

١١- فَفَتَحْنَا أَبْوَابَ السَّمَاءِ بِمَاءٍ
مُّنْهَمِرٍ ۝

5132. For a time godlessness seems to triumph, but the triumph is short-lived. And in any case there is the great Reckoning of the Day of Judgment.

5133. The angel whose voice will call at the Resurrection and direct all souls. *Cf.* xx. 108-111.

5134. At one stage in the invasion of locust swarms, the locusts are torpid and are scattered abroad all over the ground. I have seen them on railway tracks in 'Irāq, crushed to death in hundreds by passing trains. The simile is apt for the stunned beings who will rise up in swarms from their graves and say, "Ah! woe unto us! who has raised us up?" (xxxvi. 52).

5135 The story of Noah and the Flood is frequently referred to in the Qur-ān. The passage which best illustrates this passage will be found in xi. 25-48 Note in that passage how they first insult and abuse him arrogantly; how he humbly argues with them; how they laugh him to scorn, as much as to say that he was a madman possessed of some evil spirit; and how the Flood comes and he is saved in the Ark, and the wicked are doomed to destruction.

5136. He did not call down punishment. He merely asked for help in his mission, as he felt himself overpowered by brute force and cast out, which prevented the fulfilment of his mission. But the wicked generation were past all repentance, and they were wiped out.

12. And We caused the earth
To gush forth with springs.
So the waters met (and rose)[5137]
To the extent decreed.

١٢- وَفَجَّرْنَا الْأَرْضَ عُيُونًا
فَالْتَقَى الْمَاءُ عَلَىٰ أَمْرٍ قَدْ قُدِرَ ۝

13. But We bore him
On an (Ark) made of
Broad planks and caulked[5138]
With palm-fibre :

١٣- وَحَمَلْنَاهُ عَلَىٰ
ذَاتِ أَلْوَاحٍ وَدُسُرٍ ۝

14. She floats under our eyes
(And care) : a recompense[5139]
To one who had been
Rejected (with scorn) !

١٤- تَجْرِي بِأَعْيُنِنَا
جَزَاءً لِمَنْ كَانَ كُفِرَ ۝

15. And We have left
This as a Sign[5140]
(For all time) : then
Is there any that will
Receive admonition ?[5141]

١٥- وَلَقَدْ تَرَكْنَاهَا آيَةً
فَهَلْ مِنْ مُدَّكِرٍ ۝

16. But how (terrible) was[5142]
My Penalty and My Warning ?

١٦- فَكَيْفَ كَانَ عَذَابِي وَنُذُرِ ۝

17. And We have indeed
Made the Qur-ān easy[5143]

١٧- وَلَقَدْ يَسَّرْنَا الْقُرْآنَ

5137. The torrents of rain from above combined with the gush of waters from underground springs, and caused a huge Flood which inundated the country.

5138 *Dusur*, plural of *disār*, which means the palm-fibre with which boats are caulked : from *dasara*, to ram in, to spear. A derived meaning is "nails", (which are driven into planks) : this latter meaning also applies, and is preferred by translators not familiar with the construction of simple boats.

5139. As usual, God's Mercy in saving His faithful servants takes precedence of His Wrath and Penalty. And He helps and rewards those whom the world rejects and despises !

5140. *Cf.* xxix 15, where the Ark (with the salvation it brought to the righteous) is mentioned as a Sign for all Peoples So also in xxv. 37 and xxvi. 121, it is a Sign for men. Similarly the saving of Lot, with the destruction of the wicked Cities of the Plain, is mentioned as a Sign left for those who would understand : xxix. 35, and li. 37.

5141. A refrain that occurs six times in this Sūra : see Introduction.

5142. While the Mercy of God is always prominently mentioned, we must not forget or minimise the existence of Evil, and the terrible Penalty it incurs if the Grace of God and His Warning are deliberately rejected.

5143. While the Qur-ān sums up the highest philosophy of the inner life, its simple directions for conduct are plain and easy to understand and act upon. Is this not in itself a part of the Grace of God ? And what excuse is there for any one to fail in receiving admonition ?

To understand and remember:
Then is there any that
Will receive admonition?

لِلذِّكْرِ
فَهَلْ مِنْ مُّدَّكِرٍ ○

18. The 'Ad (people) (too)
Rejected (Truth): then
How terrible was
My Penalty and My Warning?

١٨- كَذَّبَتْ عَادٌ
فَكَيْفَ كَانَ عَذَابِي وَنُذُرِ ○

19. For We sent against them[5144]
A furious wind, on a Day
Of violent Disaster,

١٩- إِنَّا أَرْسَلْنَا عَلَيْهِمْ رِيحًا صَرْصَرًا
فِي يَوْمِ نَحْسٍ مُّسْتَمِرٍّ ○

20. Plucking out men as if
They were roots of palm-trees
Torn up (from the ground).

٢٠- تَنْزِعُ النَّاسَ
كَأَنَّهُمْ أَعْجَازُ نَخْلٍ مُّنْقَعِرٍ ○

21. Yea, how (terrible) was
My Penalty and My Warning![5145]

٢١- فَكَيْفَ كَانَ عَذَابِي وَنُذُرِ ○

22. But We have indeed
Made the Qur-ān easy
To understand and remember:
Then is there any that
Will receive admonition?

٢٢- وَلَقَدْ يَسَّرْنَا الْقُرْآنَ لِلذِّكْرِ
فَهَلْ مِنْ مُّدَّكِرٍ ○ ع

Section 2.

23. The Thamūd (also)
Rejected (their) Warners.

٢٣- كَذَّبَتْ ثَمُودُ بِالنُّذُرِ ○

24. For they said: "What![5146]
A man! a solitary one

٢٤- فَقَالُوا أَبَشَرًا

5144. *Cf.* xli. 16. How graphic is the description of the tornado that uprooted them! It must indeed be a dreadful tornado that plucks up the palm-trees by their deep tap-roots. The "Day" is an indefinite period of time. The wind that destroyed the 'Ād people lasted seven nights and eight days: lxix. 7.

5145. Repeated from verse 18 to heighten the description of the sin, the penalty, and the criminal negligence of the sinners in refusing the warnings on account of their self-complacent confidence in their own strength and stability! It is repeated again as a secondary refrain in liv. 30 and (with slight modification) in liv. 32 and 39.

5146. The psychology of the Thamūd is more searchingly analysed here than in xli. 17, to show up the contrast between shallow men's ideas about Revelation, and the real sanity, humanism, social value, and truth of Revelation. To them the Revelation was brought by Ṣāliḥ.

From among ourselves!
Shall we follow such a one?[5147]
Truly should we then be
Straying in mind, and mad!

مِّنَّا وَاحِدًا نَّتَّبِعُهُۥٓ
إِنَّآ إِذًا لَّفِى ضَلَٰلٍ وَسُعُرٍ ۝

25. "Is it that the Message
Is sent to *him*,
Of all people amongst us?
Nay, he is a liar,
An insolent one!"[5148]

٢٥- ءَأُلْقِىَ الذِّكْرُ عَلَيْهِ مِنۢ بَيْنِنَا
بَلْ هُوَ كَذَّابٌ أَشِرٌ ۝

26. Ah! they will know
On the morrow, which is
The liar, the insolent one!

٢٦- سَيَعْلَمُونَ غَدًا
مَّنِ الْكَذَّابُ الْأَشِرُ ۝

27. For We will send
The she-camel[5149]
By way of trial for them.
So watch them, (O Ṣaliḥ),
And possess thyself in patience!

٢٧- إِنَّا مُرْسِلُوا النَّاقَةِ فِتْنَةً لَّهُمْ
فَارْتَقِبْهُمْ وَاصْطَبِرْ ۝

28. And tell them that
The water is to be
Divided between them:[5150]
Each one's right to drink
Being brought forward
(By suitable turns).

٢٨- وَنَبِّئْهُمْ أَنَّ الْمَآءَ
قِسْمَةٌۢ بَيْنَهُمْ
كُلُّ شِرْبٍ مُّحْتَضَرٌ ۝

29. But they called
To their companion,
And he took a sword
In hand, and hamstrung (her).

٢٩- فَنَادَوْا صَاحِبَهُمْ
فَتَعَاطَىٰ فَعَقَرَ ۝

30. Ah! how (terrible) was
My Penalty and My Warning!

٣٠- فَكَيْفَ كَانَ عَذَابِى وَنُذُرِ ۝

5147. Because the Preacher is one among so many, and different from them, although brought up among themselves, it is made a cause of reproach against him, when it should have been an index leading to a searching of their hearts and an examination of their ways.

5148. Pure abuse, as a contrast to Sāliḥ's expostulation! See xxvi. 141-158, and notes.

5149. See n. 1044 to vii. 73, for the she-camel as a trial or test case among selfish people who tried to monopolise water and pasture as against the poor.

5150. See xxvi. 155-56. All were to have water in due turn. It was to be no one's monopoly. And certainly the gates were not to be shut against the poor or their cattle.

31. For We sent against them[5151]
A single Mighty Blast,
And they became
Like the dry stubble used
By one who pens cattle.[5152]

٣١- إِنَّا أَرْسَلْنَا عَلَيْهِمْ صَيْحَةً وَاحِدَةً
فَكَانُوا كَهَشِيمِ الْمُحْتَظِرِ ۝

32. And we have indeed
Made the Qur-ān easy
To understand and remember:
Then is there any that
Will receive admonition?

٣٢- وَلَقَدْ يَسَّرْنَا الْقُرْآنَ لِلذِّكْرِ
فَهَلْ مِن مُّدَّكِرٍ ۝

33. The People of Lūṭ[5153]
Rejected (his) Warning.

٣٣- كَذَّبَتْ قَوْمُ لُوطٍ بِالنُّذُرِ ۝

34. We sent against them
A violent tornado
With showers of stones,[5154]
(Which destroyed them), except
Lūṭ's household: them We
Delivered by early Dawn,—

٣٤- إِنَّا أَرْسَلْنَا عَلَيْهِمْ حَاصِبًا
إِلَّا آلَ لُوطٍ ۖ
نَّجَّيْنَاهُم بِسَحَرٍ ۝

35. As a Grace from Us:
Thus do We reward
Those who give thanks.[5155]

٣٥- نِّعْمَةً مِّنْ عِندِنَا ۚ
كَذَٰلِكَ نَجْزِي مَن شَكَرَ ۝

36. And (Lūṭ) did warn them[5156]
Of Our Punishment, but
They disputed about the Warning.

٣٦- وَلَقَدْ أَنذَرَهُم بَطْشَتَنَا
فَتَمَارَوْا بِالنُّذُرِ ۝

5151. See n. 1047 to vii. 78, and *cf.* the same phrase "single Blast" used for the signal for the Resurrection in **xxxvi**. 53. In the case of the Thamūd, the destruction seems to have been by a severe earthquake accompanied with a terrible rumbling noise.

5152. They became like dry sticks such as are used by herdsmen in making pens or enclosures for their cattle.

5153. The story of Lot (Lūṭ) and the Cities of the Plain has been frequently referred to. See xi. 74-83.

5154. *Ḥāṣib*: a violent tornado bringing a shower of stones. The word occurs here; in xvii. 68 (without reference to any particular place); in **xxix**. 40 (where it seems to refer to Lot's Cities, see n. 3462); and in lxvii. 17 (where again there is no reference to a particular place). In Lot's Cities the shower was of brimstone: see xi. 82.

5155. "Giving thanks" to God in Quranic phrase is to obey God's Law, to do His Will, to practise righteousness, to use all gifts in His service.

5156. *Cf.* xi. 78-79.

37. And they even sought
To snatch away his guests[5157]
From him, but We blinded
Their eyes. (They heard:)
"Now taste ye My Wrath
And My Warning."

٣٧- وَلَقَدْ رَاوَدُوهُ عَن ضَيْفِهِ
فَطَمَسْنَآ أَعْيُنَهُمْ
فَذُوقُوا عَذَابِي وَنُذُرِ ○

38. Early on the morrow
An abiding Punishment
Seized them:

٣٨- وَلَقَدْ صَبَّحَهُم
بُكْرَةً عَذَابٌ مُّسْتَقِرٌّ ○

39. "So taste ye My Wrath
And My Warning."

٣٩- فَذُوقُوا عَذَابِي وَنُذُرِ ○

40. And We have indeed
Made the Qur-ān easy
To understand and remember:
Then is there any that
Will receive admonition?

٤٠- وَلَقَدْ يَسَّرْنَا الْقُرْآنَ لِلذِّكْرِ
فَهَلْ مِن مُّدَّكِرٍ ○ ع

SECTION 3.

41. To the People[5158]
Of Pharaoh, too, aforetime,
Came Warners (from God).

٤١- وَلَقَدْ جَآءَ آلَ فِرْعَوْنَ النُّذُرُ ○

42. The (people) rejected all
Our Signs; but We
Seized them with such Penalty
(As comes) from One
Exalted in Power,
Able to carry out His Will.

٤٢- كَذَّبُوا بِآيَاتِنَا كُلِّهَا
فَأَخَذْنَاهُمْ أَخْذَ
عَزِيزٍ مُّقْتَدِرٍ ○

5157. Lot had been preaching to them some time against their iniquities. The crisis of their fate came when the two angels came to Lot in the guise of handsome young men. The men of the whole City came in an uproar, assaulted his house, and tried to snatch away the two handsome men. Lot tried to prevent them, but was powerless. Darkness fell on their eyes, as the first stage in their punishment, and before next morning the wicked cities were buried under a shower of brimstone. Lot and his believing household were saved.

5158. The Egyptian people of old are the last people mentioned in this Sūra as an example of iniquity meeting with punishment. And the moral is driven home to the Pagan Quraish, to warn them of their fate if they persisted in their evil lives. The Egyptians had many Signs given them. They were a gifted people and had made much progress in the sciences and the arts. They could have learnt from history that when the highest virtues disappear, the nation must fall. Moses was brought up among them and commissioned to give God's Message to them. But they were arrogant; they were unjust to God's creatures; they followed debasing forms of worship; they mocked at Truth; and were at last punished with destruction in the Red Sea for their arrogant leaders and army. See x. 75-90 for a narrative.

43. Are your Unbelievers,
(O Quraish), better than they ?[5159]
Or have ye an immunity
In the Sacred Books ?

٤٣- أَكُفَّارُكُمْ خَيْرٌ مِّنْ أُولَٰئِكُمْ أَمْ لَكُم بَرَاءَةٌ فِي الزُّبُرِ ۝

44. Or do they say:
"We acting together
Can defend ourselves" ?

٤٤- أَمْ يَقُولُونَ نَحْنُ جَمِيعٌ مُّنتَصِرٌ ۝

45. Soon will their multitude
Be put to flight,
And they will show
Their backs.

٤٥- سَيُهْزَمُ الْجَمْعُ وَيُوَلُّونَ الدُّبُرَ ۝

46. Nay, the Hour (of Judgment)
Is the time promised them
(For their full recompense):[5160]
And that Hour will be
Most grievous and most bitter.

٤٦- بَلِ السَّاعَةُ مَوْعِدُهُمْ وَالسَّاعَةُ أَدْهَىٰ وَأَمَرُّ ۝

47. Truly those in sin
Are the ones
Straying in mind, and mad.[5161]

٤٧- إِنَّ الْمُجْرِمِينَ فِي ضَلَالٍ وَسُعُرٍ ۝

48. The Day they will be
Dragged through the Fire
On their faces,[5162] (they
Will hear:) "Taste ye
The touch of Hell!"

٤٨- يَوْمَ يُسْحَبُونَ فِي النَّارِ عَلَىٰ وُجُوهِهِمْ ذُوقُوا مَسَّ سَقَرَ ۝

5159. If the Egyptians with all their power and science were unable to resist the punishment of their sins, the Pagan Quraish are asked: how will you fare when you come to a trial of strength against God's Truth? You are not specially favoured so as to be immune from God's Law. And if you rely on your numbers, they will be a broken reed when the trial comes, as indeed happened at the Battle of Badr.

5160. The calculations of unjust men—on their science, their resources, their numbers, etc.—will in many cases be falsified even in this world, as stated in the last two verses, but their real Punishment will come with Judgment, *i.e.* when they find their real place in the spiritual world at the restoration of true values. It will then be a most grievous and bitter experience for them, throwing into the shade any calamities they may suffer in this life.

5161. *Cf.* liv. 24 above. Note how the tables are turned in the argument by the repetition. The unjust think that the godly are wandering in mind and mad. They will find that it is really they who were wandering in mind, and mad, even when they were in the plenitude of their power and in the enjoyment of all the good things of this life. These minor echoes heighten the effect of the major refrain mentioned in the Introduction.

5162. "*On their faces*": the Face is the symbol of Personality. Their whole Personality will be subverted and degraded—in the midst of the Fire of Suffering.

49. Verily, all things
Have We created
In proportion and measure.[5163]

٤٩- إِنَّا كُلَّ شَيْءٍ خَلَقْنَٰهُ بِقَدَرٍ ۝

50. And Our Command
Is but a single (Act),—[5164]
Like the twinkling
Of an eye.

٥٠- وَمَآ أَمْرُنَآ إِلَّا وَٰحِدَةٌ كَلَمْحٍۭ بِٱلْبَصَرِ ۝

51. And (oft) in the past,
Have We destroyed gangs[5165]
Like unto you: then
Is there any that
Will receive admonition?[5166]

٥١- وَلَقَدْ أَهْلَكْنَآ أَشْيَاعَكُمْ فَهَلْ مِن مُّدَّكِرٍ ۝

52. All that they do
Is noted in (their)
Books (of Deeds):[5167]

٥٢- وَكُلُّ شَيْءٍ فَعَلُوهُ فِى ٱلزُّبُرِ ۝

5163. God's Creation is not haphazard. Everything goes by law, proportion, and measure. Everything has its appointed time, place, and occasion, as also its definite limitation. Nothing happens but according to His Plan, and every deed, word, and thought of man has its fullest consequences, except in so far as the Grace or Mercy of God intervenes, and that is according to law and plan.

5164. While in the life of created things there is "proportion and measure", and a lag of time or distance or circumstance, in God's Command, the Design, the Word, the Execution, and the Consequences are but a single Act. The simile given is that of the twinkling of an eye, which is the shortest time that a simple man can think of: the cause which occasions the twinkling, the movement of the muscles connected with it, the closing of the eyelids, and their reopening, are all almost like a simultaneous act. By way of contrast take an illustration like that of a man writing a book. He must form the design in his mind; he must prepare himself by research, collection of knowledge, or of personal experience; he must use or acquire the art of writing; he must collect the materials for writing, *viz.*, paper, ink, pen, etc., and this will connect with a chain of manufacturing processes in which he is dependent upon other people's work and experience; then his book may have to be printed or lithographed or bound, and sold, or taken to a library, or presented to a friend, which will bring into play numerous other chains of processes, and dependence upon other people's work or skill; and the lag of Time, Space, and Circumstance will occur at numerous stages. In God's Command, the word "Be" (*kun*) includes everything, without the intervention of or dependence upon any other being or thing whatever. And this is also another phase of the philosophy of Unity.

5165. *Ashyā'akum*: 'gangs or parties or collections of men like you.'—addressed to wicked men who arrogantly rely upon their own strength or combination, neither of which can stand for a moment against the Will of God.

5166. The cases of Pharaoh's men of old and the Pagan Quraish are considered as parallel, and an appeal is addressed to the latter from the experience of the former: 'will ye not learn and repent?'

5167. The Book of Deeds is of course metaphorical. The point is that nothing which men do is lost—good or evil. Everything gives rise to an inevitable chain of consequences, from which a release is only obtained by the intervention of God's Grace acting on an act, a striving, of the human will to repent and turn to God.

53. Every matter, small and great,
Is on record.

٥٣- وَكُلُّ صَغِيرٍ وَكَبِيرٍ مُّسْتَطَرٌ ۝

54. As to the Righteous,
They will be in the midst
Of Gardens and Rivers,[5168]

٥٤- إِنَّ الْمُتَّقِينَ فِي جَنَّٰتٍ وَنَهَرٍ ۝

55. In an Assembly of Truth,[5169]
In the Presence of[5170]
A Sovereign Omnipotent.[5171]

٥٥- فِي مَقْعَدِ صِدْقٍ
عِندَ مَلِيكٍ مُّقْتَدِرٍ ۝

5168. The record, in the case of those who dishonoured and violated Truth, will lead to their undoing; but in the case of those who honoured the Truth and adopted it so as to shine in their righteous lives, the result is expressed by four metaphors, in an ascending degree of sublimity: (1) they will be in the midst of Gardens where rivers flow; (2) they will be in an Assembly of Truth; (3) in the Presence of God; (4) Whose sovereignty is omnipotent. See notes following, and Appendix XII, at the end of this Sūra.

(1) "*Gardens*" *with Rivers* (*flowing beneath*): this has been explained more than once already: *Cf.* n. 4668 to xliii. 70 The Garden suggests all the Bliss we can imagine through our senses. How the Garden ministers to the noblest functions of our senses is further explained in Appendix XII.

5169 (2) While we possess our bodily senses, the best conceptions we can form are through our sense-perceptions, and the Garden is a good symbol from that point of view. The next higher understanding of spiritual truth is through our intellect and our social satisfaction. This is best symbolised by the Assembly of Truth—the gathering in which we sit with our fellows and enjoy the realisation of Truth and the dissipation of falsehoods and half-truths.

5170. (3) But there is a higher conception still, something so intensely spiritual that it can only be expressed by reference to the Presence of God. God is present everywhere and at all times, but when His Presence becomes an actual realised experience to its fullest extent, then we have reached Heaven.

5171. (4) Such realisation of God, as is spoken of in the last note, can only be perfected when we know—it comes into our inmost being—that God is Sovereign, All-in-all, First and Last, not only for ourselves but for all persons and things and events. *Muqtadir*, which I have translated Omnipotent, implies something more: the eighth-declension form denotes not only complete mastery, but the further idea that the mastery arises from God's own nature, and depends on nothing else whatever.

APPENDIX XII

The Muslim Heaven (see liv. 54-55, and notes 5168-71)

To write about the Muslim Heaven adequately is to describe the spiritual ideals of Islam and its conception of the Hereafter for those who follow the true laws of their being as created by God and as explained in Revelation. Such a task would be beyond the scope of an Appendix. But I propose to collect here a few matters which have been referred to in scattered notes to the Quranic text, but which could not be fully explained in the space at the disposal of the notes. This is all the more necessary, as some ignorant critics of Islam imagine that Islam postulates a sensual heaven, and they press into service some garbled versions of what some of our own more material-minded brethren have said on the subject.

2. It is true that Islam uses the most varied imagery for describing spiritual matters which are really beyond description in words except by such imagery. But it carefully avoids using such imagery for God Himself, lest it should be misunderstood by shallow minds, and confines the use of such imagery to the description of human beings, who have, in their present life, some material forms of pleasure, satisfaction, and happiness, and some mental and social relations which conduce to such feelings, and which may therefore be used legitimately to typify the more spiritual joys and relationships of a spiritual Heaven. It knows nothing of the amours of gods and goddesses and the jealousies and bickerings that disfigure the Court of the Olympian Jove; and yet Greek Mythology was the most refined of all Pagan Mythologies. In spite of all Wagner's efforts to glorify the Valkyrian heaven, we have yet in that heaven high actions and high passions in an atmosphere of frustration and strife. The Christian imagery of the vision of God and God's Throne is that of " a jasper and a sardine stone," emeralds and crowns of gold, a sea of glass like unto crystal, and four and-twenty elders casting their crowns before the Throne, and glorifying God, but adding, " Thou hast created all things, and ***for thy pleasure*** they are and were created." (The concluding Book of the New Testament: The Revelation of St. John the Divine, Chapter iv). Our imagery never carries these metaphors to the Person of God, and we are not taught that the object of creation is God's pleasure; our teaching is that man was created for man's self-development and his attainment of his high destiny, which can be done by his understanding, obeying, and knowing God.

3. Our doctrine of the Hereafter is not strictly a doctrine of Rewards and Punishments. A promise of Rewards implies two things: (1) an inducement to a certain course of action by the motive of winning the reward; and (2) the apportionment of the reward to the merits and deserts of the receiver.

As to the motives, see iii. 31:—

Say: " If ye do love God,
Follow me: God will love you

And forgive you your sins :
For God is Oft-Forgiving,
Most Merciful.

Or again, in ii. 165 we have :—

But those of Faith
Are overflowing
In their love for God.

Certainly whatever good we do benefits our own souls, but the motive with which we should do it should be only as "seeking the glory (literally, Face, Countenance) of God" (ii. 272). The righteous persevere patiently in righteousness, seeking "the Countenance of their Lord" (xiii. 22).

4. Is the "Reward" apportioned to the merits or deserts of the receiver? Not at all. At best, our merits or deserts can amount to very little. But God's Mercy and Grace are vast and all-embracing (vi. 147). He has said: "My Mercy extendeth to all things" (vii. 156): His Grace is universal and all-pervasive; and "He is the Lord of Bounties unbounded" (iii. 74). If any man does good, "the reward to him is better than his deed: but if any does evil, the doers of evil are only punished to the extent of their deeds" (xxviii. 84). Thus His justice is strict but in favour of man; but his Grace is beyond calculation. "That which ye lay out for charity, seeking the Countenance of God, will increase: it is these who will get a recompense multiplied" (xxx. 39). See also n. 5909 to lxxviii. 36.

5. To be righteous merely for the hope of reward for one's self or for fear of punishment may be good at a certain elementary stage of spiritual progress when higher motives are yet unintelligible. But as the light of Islam illumines the soul more and more, it is seen that virtue is its own reward and evil is its own punishment: for the one accords with the Will of God, and the other is contrary to it—and therefore also contrary to the pure nature of man as made by God,—"God's handiwork according to the pattern on which He has made mankind: no change let there be in the work wrought by God: that is the standard Religion" (xxx. 30). "Is there any Reward for Good—other than Good?" (lv. 60). We are asked to "repent" when we have fallen into evil. But "repentance" does not mean sackcloth and ashes, or putting on a gloomy pessimism. It means giving up disease for health, crookedness (which is abnormal) for the Straight Way, the restoration of our nature as God created it from the falsity introduced by the enticements of Evil (n. 3543 to xxx. 31). The "fear of God" is the beginning of wisdom; but it is not fear in the ordinary sense of the term, for on the righteous "there shall be no fear, nor shall they grieve" (ii. 38). The fear of God is not a passive oppression by an outside feeling, but an active assertion of our own will not to offend our Lord and Cherisher. The fear is lest we lose His Good Pleasure. It is akin to love, and is a purification of our will. It is on our will that our future depends under the Grace and Mercy of God. We must strive to reach His Grace. Our strength is small, but He will accept the submission of our will (Islam), and His Grace will search us out; and our progress will proceed according to the Law which God in His wisdom has established.

6. Thus it becomes a doctrine of Law, or of "fruits of actions". Every deed must have its inevitable consequences (n. 4671 to xliii. 73). There is no vicarious atonement; for there is individual responsibility. And yet it is not a doctrine of "justification by deeds"; for the best of our actions fall short of the "heaven" which we hope for (see paragraph 4 above). Nor is it the same as the doctrine of *Karma*, which plays so prominent a part in Buddhist and Hindu philosophy. For we have a lively faith in God's Grace and Mercy: it can and does intervene for us and accepts our repentance and amendment, and gives us fresh chances at every stage of our probationary life. But our will is an important factor: we cannot accept a mechanical form of Determinism which eliminates the human will in the government of the microcosm within us, and even eliminates such a thing as the Divine Will in the government of the Macrocosm, or the great world without us.

7. Such being the fundamental aspects of our life and destiny, how can we best clothe our ideas of heaven in human language? Our Heaven is independent of Time, or Place, or fleeting Circumstance. No one can know precisely now the spiritual delights hidden in reserve for him (xxxii. 17). But we must necessarily use terms that imply all these three conditions. Therefore they can only be expressed by allegory or imagery. If we understand what the essence of the allegory or imagery is, we shall profit by it. If we branch out into fantastic applications that leave us in the material world, we shall never be able to get a glimpse of the spiritual world into which such allegory or imagery is intended to open a window for our spiritual eyes. Such allegory or imagery is supplied in abundance in the Qur-ān.

8. The simplest and yet the most far-reaching allegory that we can employ is that of the Garden—the Garden of Bliss (*Jannat* or *Jannat un Na'īm*, v. 68). In all Muslim languages, that word *Jannat* (Garden) is now specialised for Heaven. Let us analyse a few of the ideas which we can legitimately associate in this connection with the concrete word "Garden" and the abstract term "Bliss".

9. In this our life most of our sensations depend upon sense-perceptions, and we can reduce the highest and noblest of them to terms connected with the Garden. To each of our five senses, in their most refined form, does the Garden minister. For the eye there is the general green, with all the most delicate tints of green in the foliage, and the wonderful colours and shapes in flowers; the arrangement of paths and parterres; the various gradations of light and shade; the soft and melting beauty of clouds and mists; and the landscape views with cool rivers flowing underneath, or perhaps murmuring brooks. For the ear is the music of birds, the music of waterfalls, and the appropriate moonlight music of the human voice with or without the accompaniment of an instrument like a guitar. For the smell there is not only the perfume of flowers but the more subtle scents of foliage, moisture or morning dew, or even garden soil. For taste and touch the exquisite fruits, and for touch the soft rose petals and the carpet-like lawns, besides the gentle kiss of breezes, all minister to the highest bliss and fulfilment that we can imagine through our senses.

10. We picture not only a Garden, but a Garden with rivers or springs flowing beneath. This further enlarges our horizon. We can picture a landscape with banks, terraces, and sloping lawns, high ground, and valleys. What is the spiritual analogy for this? We must not imagine a dull place where all are engaged in perpetual psalm-singing. There will be differences in ranks, dignities, and tastes, according to each individual's growth and individuality: for that is the meaning of the persistence of Personality. And yet they will form one equal Brotherhood of Peace, one Society of Concord. There will be the four-fold classification according to the varying spiritual experiences gained in this life: (1) the Prophets who taught and led mankind; (2) the sincere Devotees of Truth, who supported the Cause in their person and with all their resources; (3) the Martyrs and Witnesses, who suffered and served; and (4) the righteous people generally, those who led ordinary lives, but always with righteous aims. All these are united in one beautiful Fellowship (see iv. 69, and n. 586). Or take that other classification indicated in lvi. 27 and 11: the righteous generally, the Companions of the Right Hand (as distinguished from the Companions of the Left Hand, who will not have reached Heaven), and those nearest to God in rank and dignity. The latter will have no interposing Veils of Light to obscure the pure Light of God from them (Appendix VIII, and xxiv. 35); for, in Ṣūfī language, they will have had the ineffable Bliss of seeing the "Divine Eyes". Possibly the Companions of the Garden and Those on the Heights (vii. 46) refer to the same two categories of souls. Whatever the precise interpretation of these mystic passages may be, there is no doubt that the retention of individual Personality in the Hereafter will mean Bliss of different kinds for each category.

11. How can we understand a psychological term like Bliss in general symbolical terms? If it is to convey the idea of satisfaction in any but abstract terms, we must have the symbolism of ordinary life, yet lifted up to ideas of refinement, delicacy, and satisfaction. The acts of eating and drinking are spiritualised and socialised. The choicest of meats, fruits, and drinks, which minister to the most sensitive taste, will be provided. Dress of most artistic taste will add dignity to social intercourse, and there will be thrones and symbols of honour. There will be companionship, individual companionship, companionship of equal age, as well as general companionship. And those whom we loved in this life—mothers, wives, sisters, relatives, children, friends – will all add to our joy by their company in a transformed Love as superior to earthly Love as in the Garden of Heaven to an earthly Garden. The condition of Faith and good Life is of course attached: for no disharmony can enter to mar the dignity of Heaven. (See xiii. 23 and n. 1837; xliii. 70-72, and n. 4668-70). Perfected Love will not be content with Self, but like a note of music will find its melody in communion with others.

12. Carnal sex has of course no place in Heaven, but sex in our constitution here has a mental and psychological value, which we can picture in our transformed and perfected Love above. The word Ḥūr, in such passages as xliv. 54, and lii. 20, has been much misunderstood and misrepresented. Grammatically it is not feminine in form, and the companionship of Ḥūrs will be for all in Heaven—men and women (as they were in this life), who will retain their personality but not their

carnal attributes. As in the word "angel" in English, (unlike its original Angelos in Greek or Angelus in Latin), there is with it an association of the specially feminine virtues of purity, grace, beauty, innocence, truth, and good-will (see n. 4729 to xliv. 54). In lxxviii. 33 are mentioned Maidens or Virgins of Equal Age, in a highly symbolical passage, where the notes may be consulted. But the masculine virtues of handsome and manly strength and the youthful enthusiasm for service are also mentioned in association with heaven (see lii. 24, and n. 5058). In other words the symbolism leads up from our ideas of beauty, grace, harmony, strength, youth, and service as we know these things in their most refined forms here, to something even nobler and purer which no language can adequately describe.

13. The symbolism of Springs or Fountains and Cups of Drink or Wine is also worked out in a beautiful way in S. lxxvi. (*Dahr*). Note that the Arabic word *Sharāb* means *either* Drink or Wine, and in Sūfī language, Wine or the Cup is the means of attaining spiritual Ecstasy. The Quranic language tempers Ecstasy with coolness, and associates a refreshing tonic, rather than an unbounded ecstasy, with spiritual fervour, especially in the earlier stages of spiritual Bliss, when the soul is yet new to its new world. Just after the Great Event of Judgment is passed, the righteous soul enters the regions of Bliss, and is given to drink of a Cup from the mystic fountain of Kāfūr (lxxvi. 5, n. 5835). *Kāfūr* literally means camphor: in symbolic language it stands for all that is wholesome, cooling and refreshing, soothing and agreeable. This is provided in unstinted measure. Then the yearning humility which filled the souls in the lower life gives place to a sense of possession: dignity and honour, typified by light silk garments, thrones, and the humility now shown to them by those around them (lxxvi.12-14). Then comes the setting of a Magnificent Realm, typifying Divine Glory. A drink of a Cup of Zanjabīl, typifying warmth and zest to the taste, from a fountain called *Sal-sabīl* ("Seek the Way"), festive clothes of ceremony, and rich setting of a Royal Banquet of beauty and splendour, stand as symbols to show the approach to the very Presence Ineffable. Further, there is a Spring or Fountain *Tasnīm*, which is only drunk neat by those Nearest to God: they alone can bear its fullest flavour, as they alone can bear the full effulgence of the Glory of God: but every righteous man will have a taste of this Fountain mixed with his heavenly Wine, to the extent that his spiritual advancement is capable of enjoying it (lxxxiii. 27-28).

14. For the highest Felicity in heaven is described to be in the nearness to God, in the Good Pleasure of God. See iii. 14-15:—

"Fair in the eyes of men
Is the love of things they covet:
Women and sons;
Heaped-up hoards of gold and silver;
Horses branded (for blood and excellence);
And wealth of cattle
And well-tilled land.

Such are the possessions

Of this world's life ;
But nearness to God
Is the best of the goals.

" Say : Shall I give you
Glad tidings of things
Far better than those ?
For the righteous are Gardens
In nearness to their Lord,
With rivers flowing beneath ;
Therein is their eternal home ;
With Companions pure and holy ;
And the Good Pleasure of God."

But the Good Pleasure of God has its counterpart in the Good Pleasure of man, raised to such eminence in Heaven.

" O thou soul !
In (complete) rest and satisfaction !
Come back thou
To thy Lord !—
Well pleased (thyself),
And well pleasing
Unto Him !

" Enter, thou, then,
Among My Devotees,—
Yea, enter thou
My Heaven ! "

(lxxxix. 27-30.)

15. This, then, is the Muslim idea of Salvation. It consists, not in being saved from the consequences of our sins by the sufferings or the merits of others, nor in *Nirvana*, or annihilation or absorption,—but in the achievement of a perfected Personality, a Bliss that grows up within us, and does not depend on external circumstances. It may require the utmost effort or striving (*Jihād*) of a lifetime or more. But it is the Supreme Achievement, the attainment of all desires, the Felicity *in excelsis* (xliv. 57, and n. 4733).

16. The several aspects of it are summed up in two passages of singular beauty, xxxvi. 55-58, and lii. 17-28, which should be studied along with the notes thereon. The first passage describes symbolically the *mise en scène* and the nature of the Bliss. It goes on to say that the happiness will not be solitary, but will be shared in association, on thrones of dignity and peace. It further figures the psychological inner satisfaction, unconnected with outer circumstances, but reflecting the inner tastes of Personalities : " they shall have whatever they call for " : the musician's heaven will be full of music ; the mathematician's will be full of mathematical symmetry and perfection ; the artist's will be full of beauty of form : the

Light will be one, but its rays will be many. And it winds up with the salutation of "Peace!" from God, Whose supreme glory is Mercy, Peace, and Harmony. In the second passage these points are again emphasised but from other points of view. Not only will there be individual satisfaction and social bliss, but it will be shared by families or friends whom we held dear in this life, provided their life made them worthy of that association. While the memory of love and all good in this life will endure, it will be purged of all old fears and anxieties in the supreme realisation—the crown and climax of the whole—that God is the One Reality—the Good, the Beneficent and the Merciful. The souls in Heaven will realise in the highest spiritual sense the Presence of God.

INTRODUCTION TO SŪRA LV (*Rahmān*).

The majority of Commentators consider this an early Meccan Sūra, though some consider at least a part of it as dating from Medina. The greater part of it is undoubtedly early Meccan.

It is highly poetical and mystical, and the refrain "Then which of the favours of your Lord will ye deny ?" is interspersed 31 times among its 78 verses.

It is the sixth of the series of seven dealing with Revelation, the favours of God, and the Hereafter : see Introduction to S. *l*.

Here the special theme is indicated by the refrain. The rhyme in most cases is in the Dual grammatical form, and the Argument implies that though things are created in pairs, there is an underlying Unity, through the Creator, in the favours which He bestows, and in the goal to which they are marching.

Summary.—God Most Gracious has sent Revelation, one of His greatest favours to man ; His creation is in pairs, well-balanced ; all created things receive His favours, but they will all pass away, and only God will endure through the ages (lv. 1-34, and C. 232).

Ultimately all evil shall return to its destination, as well as all Good, but ever blessed is the name of God, Lord of Glory, Honour and Bounty (lv. 35-78, and C. 233).

C. 232.—God's creatures! Which favours of God will ye deny ?
(lv 1-34) Most Gracious is God, Who reveals Himself
In the Qur-ān, in man's Intelligence,
And in the nature around man.
Balance and Justice, Goodness and Care,
Are the Laws of His Worlds. Created
From clay, man can yet comprehend
The Lord of the Easts and the Wests, Him
Who sustains all His creatures, Him
Who bestows the Jewels of Life and Faith,
Him Who abides when all else perisheth,
Him Whose Eternity is the Hope
Of man's Future, the Lord Everlasting
Of Justice and Glory and Bounty and Honour !
Which, then, of the favours of your Lord will ye deny ?

Sūra LV.

Raḥmān, or (God) Most Gracious.

In the name of God, Most Gracious,
Most Merciful.

1. (God) Most Gracious !

2. It is He Who has[5172]
Taught the Qur-ān.

3. He has created man :

4. He has taught him speech[5173]
(And Intelligence).

5. The sun and the moon
Follow courses (exactly)
computed ;[5174]

6. And the herbs[5175] and the trees—
Both (alike) bow in adoration.[5176]

7. And the Firmament has He
Raised high, and He has set up
The Balance (of Justice),[5177]

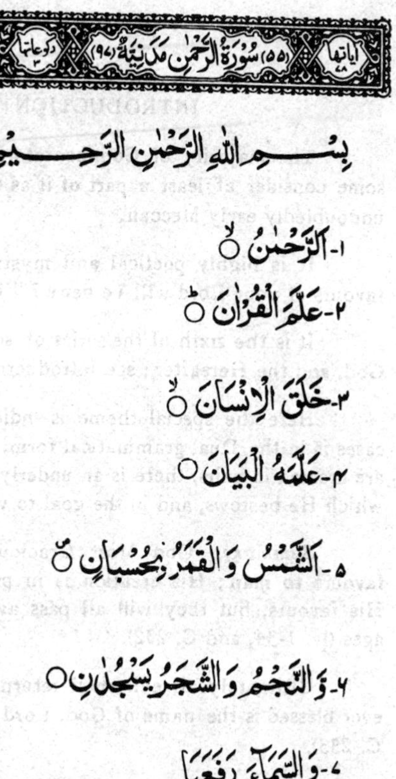

5172. The Revelation comes from God Most Gracious, and it is one of the greatest Signs of His grace and favour. He is the source of all Light, and His light is diffused throughout the universe.

5173. *Bayān* : intelligent speech ; power of expression : capacity to understand clearly the relations of things and to explain them. God has given this to man, and besides this revelation in man's own heart, has aided him with revelation in nature and revelation through prophets and apostles.

5174. In the great astronomical universe there are exact mathematical laws, which bear witness to God's Wisdom and also to His favours to His creatures ; for we all profit by the heat and light, the seasons, and the numerous changes in the tides and the atmosphere, on which the constitution of our globe and the maintenance of life depend.

5175. *Najm* : may mean stars collectively, or herbs collectively ; perhaps both meanings are implied.

5176. All nature adores God. *Cf.* xxii. 18, and n. 2790 ; xiii. 15 ; and xvi. 48-49.

5177. The "balance of justice" in this verse is connected with "the Balance" in the next two verses, that men may act justly to each other and observe due balance in all their actions, following the golden mean and not transgressing due bounds in anything. But the Balance is also connected figuratively with the heavens above in three symbols : (1) Justice is a heavenly virtue ; (2) the heavens themselves are sustained by mathematical balance ; and (3) the constellation Libra (the Balance) is entered by the sun at the middle of the zodiacal year.

8. In order that ye may
Not transgress (due) balance.

٨- اَلَّا تَطْغَوْا فِي الْمِيزَانِ ○

9. So establish weight with justice [5178]
And fall not short
In the balance.

٩- وَاَقِيمُوا الْوَزْنَ بِالْقِسْطِ
وَلَا تُخْسِرُوا الْمِيزَانَ ○

10. It is He Who has
Spread out the earth [5179]
For (His) creatures:

١٠- وَالْاَرْضَ وَضَعَهَا لِلْاَنَامِ ○

11. Therein is fruit
And date-palms, producing
Spathes (enclosing dates);

١١- فِيهَا فَاكِهَةٌ
وَالنَّخْلُ ذَاتُ الْاَكْمَامِ ○

12. Also corn, with (its)
Leaves and stalk for fodder,
And sweet-smelling plants.

١٢- وَالْحَبُّ ذُو الْعَصْفِ
وَالرَّيْحَانُ ○

13. Then which of the favours [5180]
Of your Lord will ye deny?

١٣- فَبِاَيِّ اٰلَاۤءِ رَبِّكُمَا تُكَذِّبٰنِ ○

5178. To be taken both literally and figuratively. A man should be honest and straight in every daily matter, such as weighing out things which he is selling: and he should be straight, just and honest, in all the highest dealings, not only with other people, but with himself and in his obedience to God's Law. Not many do either the one or the other when they have an opportunity of deceit. Justice is the central virtue, and the avoidance of both excess and defect in conduct keeps the human world balanced just as the heavenly world is kept balanced by mathematical order.

5179. How can God's favours be counted? Look at the earth alone. Life and the conditions here are mutually balanced for God's creatures. The vegetable world produces fruit of various kinds and corn or grain of various kinds for human food. The grain harvest yields with it fodder for animals in the shape of leaves and straw, as well as food for men in the shape of grain. The plants not only supply food but sweet-smelling herbs and flowers. *Raiḥān* is the sweet basil, but is here used in the generic sense, for agreeable produce in the vegetable world, to match the useful produce already mentioned.

5180. Both the pronoun "your" and the verb "will ye deny" are in the Arabic in the Dual Number. The whole Sūra is a symphony of Duality, which leads up to Unity, as explained in the Introduction. All creation is in pairs: li. 49, and notes 5025-26; xxxvi. 36, n. 3981. Justice is the conciliation of two opposites to unity, the settlement of the unending feud between Right and Wrong. The things and concepts mentioned in this Sūra are in pairs: man and outer nature; sun and moon; herbs and trees; heaven and earth; fruit and corn; human food and fodder for cattle; things nourishing and things sweet-smelling; and so on throughout the Sūra. Then there is man and Jinn, for which see n. 5182 below.

"*Will ye deny?*" that is, fail to acknowledge either in word or thought or in your conduct. If you misuse God's gifts or ignore them, that is equivalent to ingratitude or denial or refusal to profit by God's infinite Grace.

14. He created man
From sounding clay[5181]
Like unto pottery,

١٤- خَلَقَ الْإِنْسَانَ مِنْ صَلْصَالٍ كَالْفَخَّارِ ○

15. And He created Jinns[5182]
From fire free of smoke:

١٥- وَخَلَقَ الْجَانَّ مِنْ مَّارِجٍ مِّنْ نَّارٍ ○

16. Then which of the favours
Of your Lord will ye deny?[5183]

١٦- فَبِأَيِّ آلَاءِ رَبِّكُمَا تُكَذِّبَانِ ○

17. (He is) Lord
Of the two Easts[5184]
And Lord
Of the two Wests:

١٧- رَبُّ الْمَشْرِقَيْنِ وَرَبُّ الْمَغْرِبَيْنِ ○

18. Then which of the favours
Of your Lord will ye deny?

١٨- فَبِأَيِّ آلَاءِ رَبِّكُمَا تُكَذِّبَانِ ○

19. He has let free[5185]
The two bodies
Of flowing water,
Meeting together:

١٩- مَرَجَ الْبَحْرَيْنِ يَلْتَقِيَانِ ○

20. Between them is a Barrier
Which they do not transgress:

٢٠- بَيْنَهُمَا بَرْزَخٌ لَّا يَبْغِيَانِ ○

5181. See n. 1966 to xv. 26. The creation of men and Jinns is contrasted. Man was made of sounding clay, dry and brittle like pottery. The Jinn (see next note) was made from a clear flame of fire. Yet each has capacities and possibilities which only God's Grace bestows on them. How can they deny God's favours?

5182. For the meaning of Jinn, see n. 929 to vi. 100. They are spirits, and therefore subtle like a flame of fire. Their being free from smoke implies that they are free from grossness, for smoke is the grosser accompaniment of fire. If we take them to typify the hidden forces and capacities in man, created by God, both their potency and their value would be acknowledged. Then how can we deny the favours of God? Both the natural man with all his grossness and brittleness and the spiritual forces with all their fineness and clearness must join in the service of God.

5183. Part of the idea of this refrain will be found in xvi. 71, 72; xl. 81; and liii. 55 (where see n. 5122).

5184. *The two Easts* are the two extreme points where the sun rises during the year, and includes all the points between. Similarly the two Wests include the two extreme points of the sun's setting and all the points between. The Dual Number fits in with the general atmosphere of Duality in this Sūra. God is Lord of every region of the earth and sky, and He scatters His bounties everywhere. See also n. 4641 to xliii. 38, and n. 4034 to xxxvii. 5.

5185. See xxv. 53, and n. 3111, where it is explained how the two bodies of water, salt and sweet, meet together, yet keep separate, as if there was a barrier or partition between them. This is also one of the favours of God. Sea-water is a sanitating agent, while fresh water is sweet and palatable to drink. For the allegorical interpretation, see notes 2404-5 to xviii. 60; also n. 5186 (end) below.

21. Then which of the favours
Of your Lord will ye deny?

٢١- فَبِأَيِّ آلَآءِ رَبِّكُمَا تُكَذِّبٰنِ ○

22. Out of them come
Pearls and Coral:[5186]

٢٢- يَخْرُجُ مِنْهُمَا اللُّؤْلُؤُ وَالْمَرْجَانُ ○

23. Then which of the favours
Of your Lord will ye deny?

٢٣- فَبِأَيِّ آلَآءِ رَبِّكُمَا تُكَذِّبٰنِ ○

24. And His are the Ships[5187]
Sailing smoothly through the seas,
Lofty as mountains:[5188]

٢٤- وَلَهُ الْجَوَارِ الْمُنْشَئٰتُ فِي الْبَحْرِ كَالْأَعْلَامِ ○

25. Then which of the favours
Of your Lord will ye deny?

٢٥- فَبِأَيِّ آلَآءِ رَبِّكُمَا تُكَذِّبٰنِ ○

SECTION 2.

26. All that is on earth
Will perish:

٢٦- كُلُّ مَنْ عَلَيْهَا فَانٍ ○

27. But will abide (for ever)
The Face of thy Lord,—[5189]

٢٧- وَّيَبْقٰى وَجْهُ رَبِّكَ

5186. Pearls are produced by the oyster and coral by the polyp, a minute marine creature which, working in millions, has by its secretions produced the reefs, islands, and banks in and on both sides of the Red Sea and in other parts of the world. The pearl nas a translucent lustre, usually white, but sometimes pink or black. Coral is usually opaque, red or pink, but often white, and is seen in beautiful branching or cup-like shapes, as visitors to Port Sudan will recall. Both are used as gems, and stand here for gems generally. Mineral gems, such as agate and cornelian, are found in river-beds. Pearl oysters are also found in some rivers.

Taken allegorically, the two kinds of gems would denote the jewels of this life and the jewels of the spiritual world. The jewels of this world—like coral—are hard, widely spread over the world, comparatively cheap, and less absorptive of the light from above. The spiritual jewels—like pearls—are soft, rare, costly, and translucent, absorbent of light and showing the more lustre the more they are in light. The analogy can be carried further to the two seas—the two bodies of flowing water—mentioned in verses 19-20 above. They are the two kinds of knowledge—human and divine—referred to in the story of Moses and Khidhr: see notes 2404-5 to xviii. 60.

5187. The Ships—sailing ships and steamers, and by extension of analogy, aeroplanes and airships majestically navigating the air—are made by man, but the intelligence and science which made them possible are given by man's Creator; and therefore the Ships also are the gifts of God.

5188. *Lofty as mountains*: both in respect of the high sails, or masts, and in respect of the height to which the top of the ship towers above the surface of the sea. The 'Queen Mary'—the biggest ship afloat in 1936—has a height, from the keel to the top of the superstructure, of 135 ft, and from the keel to the mast-head, of 234 ft.

5189. The most magnificent works of man—such as they are—are but fleeting. Ships, Empires, the Wonders of Science and Art, the splendours of human glory or intellect, will all pass away. The most magnificent objects in outer Nature—the mountains and valleys, the sun and moon, the Constellation Orion and the star Sirius—will also pass away in their appointed time. But the only One that will endure for ever is the "Face" of God. "Face" expresses Personality, Glory, and Majesty, inner being, essence, self, all the noble qualities which we associate with the Beautiful Names of God. See n. 114 to ii. 112; also n. 1154 to vii. 180, and n. 2322 to xvii. 110.

Full of Majesty,
Bounty and Honour.[5190]

ذُو الْجَلٰلِ وَالْاِكْرَامِ ۝

28. Then which of the favours
Of your Lord will ye deny?

۲۸- فَبِاَيِّ اٰلَاۤءِ رَبِّكُمَا تُكَذِّبٰنِ ۝

29. Of Him seeks (its need)[5191]
Every creature in the heavens
And on earth:
Every day in (new) Splendour[5192]
Doth He (shine)!

۲۹- يَسْئَلُهٗ مَنْ فِي السَّمٰوٰتِ وَالْاَرْضِ ط
كُلَّ يَوْمٍ هُوَ فِيْ شَاْنٍ ۝

30. Then which of the favours
Of your Lord will ye deny?

۳۰- فَبِاَيِّ اٰلَاۤءِ رَبِّكُمَا تُكَذِّبٰنِ ۝

31. Soon shall We
Settle your affairs,
O both ye worlds![5193]

۳۱- سَنَفْرُغُ لَكُمْ اَيُّهَ الثَّقَلٰنِ ۝

32. Then which of the favours
Of your Lord will ye deny?

۳۲- فَبِاَيِّ اٰلَاۤءِ رَبِّكُمَا تُكَذِّبٰنِ ۝

33. O ye assembly of Jinns[5194]
And men! If it be

۳۳- يٰمَعْشَرَ الْجِنِّ وَالْاِنْسِ اِنِ اسْتَطَعْتُمْ

5190. *Ikrām*: two ideas are prominent in the word, (1) the idea of generosity, as proceeding from the person whose attribute it is, and (2) the idea of honour, as given by others to the person whose attribute it is. Both these ideas are summed up in "nobility" To make the meaning quite clear, I have employed in the translation the two words "Bounty and Honour" for the single word *Ikrām*. The same attributes recur in the last verse of this Sūra. In the Fact of God's Eternity is the Hope of our Future.

5191. Every single creature depends on God for its needs: of all of them the Cherisher and Sustainer is God. *Seek (its needs)*: does not necessarily mean 'seek them in words': what is meant is the dependence: the allusion is to the Source of supply.

5192. *Shān*: state, splendour; aim, work, business, momentous affair. God's is still the directing hand in all affairs: He does not sit apart, careless of mankind or of any of His creatures. But His working shows new Splendour every day, every hour, every moment.

5193 *Thaqal*: weight, something weighty, something weighed with something else. The two *thaqals* are the two worlds of Jinns and men,—the unseen world and the world before our eyes. They are both before God, and the affairs of both are conducted under His Command. If there are inequalities or apparent disturbances of balance, that is only for a season. God gives to both good and evil men a chance in this period of probation; but this period will soon be over, and Judgment will be established. To give you this chance, this probation, this warning, is itself a favour, by which you should profit, and for which you should be grateful.

5194. *Cf.* vi. 130, where the Jinns and men are addressed collectively. That whole passage, vi. 130-134, should be read as a commentary on this verse. 'If you think that because you do things in secret, or because some of your sins do not *seem* to meet their inevitable punishment or some of your good deeds seem to go unnoticed, do not be deceived. Judgment will soon come. You cannot possibly escape out of the zones in which your lives have been cast, without authority from God. Be grateful to God for the chances He has given you'. All that hath been promised unto you will come to pass: nor can ye frustrate it in the least bit" (vi. 134).

Ye can pass beyond
The zones of the heavens
And the earth, pass ye!
Not without authority
Shall ye be able to pass!

أَن تَنفُذُوا مِنْ أَقْطَارِ السَّمَٰوَٰتِ وَالْأَرْضِ فَانفُذُوا ۚ لَا تَنفُذُونَ إِلَّا بِسُلْطَٰنٍ ۝

34. Then which of the favours[5195]
Of your Lord will ye deny?

٣٤- فَبِأَيِّ آلَاءِ رَبِّكُمَا تُكَذِّبَانِ ۝

C. 233.—Let not Evil think that it will escape
(lv. 35-78.) Justice: its tell-tale Mark is on those
Who follow it, and it must meet its Reward
In the final adjustment. But the Good,
The Righteous, must reach their Fulfilment
In the Gardens of Bliss, where every Delight
Will be theirs in Beauty and Dignity.
How can such Delights be pictured in words?
In symbols subjective let each take his choice.
For Good can there ever be any Reward
Other than Good? Beautiful sights
And sounds, delicious fruits to nourish
The soul, and Companionship where Grace
Is mingled with Love, may figure forth our Bliss.
Blessed be God, full of Majesty and Bounty.
God's creatures! what favours of God will ye deny?

35. On you will be sent
(O ye evil ones twain!)[5196]
A flame of fire (to burn)
And a smoke (to choke):[5197]
No defence will ye have:

٣٥- يُرْسَلُ عَلَيْكُمَا شُوَاظٌ مِّن نَّارٍ ۙ وَنُحَاسٌ فَلَا تَنتَصِرَانِ ۝

36. Then which of the favours[5198]
Of your Lord will ye deny?

٣٦- فَبِأَيِّ آلَاءِ رَبِّكُمَا تُكَذِّبَانِ ۝

5195. Note how gradually we have been led up in the Argument. 'The Signs of God are all about you, in revelation, in your intelligence, and in nature around you. Your creation; the mystic light and heat typified by the sun in all directions; the cycle of waters in the physical earth and of Knowledge in the world of Intelligence; the help and cherishing care of God Himself;—all these things should teach you the Truth and warn you about the Future, which is more particularly referred to in the remainder of the Sūra.

5196. The Dual is with reference to the two worlds explained above in n. 5193.

5197. We now come to the terrors of the Judgment on the evil ones.

5198. Here and in some of the verses that follow, (verses 40, 42, and 45 below), the refrain applies with an ironical meaning. It is as if it was said: 'You used to laugh at Revelation, and at the warnings which were given for your own benefit in order to draw you to repentance and God's Mercy; what do you find now? Is not all that was said to you true?' To reject God's Law is in itself to deny God's Mercies.

37. When the sky is rent
Asunder, and it becomes red
Like ointment: [5199]

٣٧- فَإِذَا انْشَقَّتِ السَّمَاءُ
فَكَانَتْ وَرْدَةً كَالدِّهَانِ ۝

38. Then which of the favours
Of your Lord will ye deny?

٣٨- فَبِأَيِّ آلَاءِ رَبِّكُمَا تُكَذِّبَانِ ۝

39. On that Day
No question will be asked [5200]
Of man or Jinn
As to his sin,

٣٩- فَيَوْمَئِذٍ لَا يُسْأَلُ عَنْ ذَنْبِهِ
إِنْسٌ وَلَا جَانٌّ ۝

40. Then which of the favours
Of your Lord will ye deny?

٤٠- فَبِأَيِّ آلَاءِ رَبِّكُمَا تُكَذِّبَانِ ۝

41. (For) the sinners will be
Known by their Marks: [5201]
And they will be seized
By their forelocks and
Their feet.

٤١- يُعْرَفُ الْمُجْرِمُونَ بِسِيمَاهُمْ
فَيُؤْخَذُ بِالنَّوَاصِي وَالْأَقْدَامِ ۝

42. Then which of the favours
Of your Lord will ye deny?

٤٢- فَبِأَيِّ آلَاءِ رَبِّكُمَا تُكَذِّبَانِ ۝

43. This is the Hell which
The Sinners deny: [5202]

٤٣- هَٰذِهِ جَهَنَّمُ الَّتِي يُكَذِّبُ بِهَا الْمُجْرِمُونَ ۝

44. In its midst
And in the midst
Of boiling hot water
Will they wander round! [5203]

٤٤- يَطُوفُونَ بَيْنَهَا
وَبَيْنَ حَمِيمٍ آنٍ ۝

5199. Melting away like grease or ointment. The red colour will be due to the flames and the heat. The whole of the world as we know it now will dissolve.

5200. This does not of course mean that they will not be called to account for their sin. They will certainly be called to account for all their deeds: xv. 92 The meaning of this whole passage is that their personal responsibility will be enforced. But their own tongues and hands and feet will bear witness against them as to their actions: xxiv. 24. Every man will bear marks on his person, showing his classification in the Final Account: vii. 48. After these Marks are affixed, everyone's position and status in the Final Account will be known to everyone. As to the Judge on the Throne of Judgment, He will of course know all before Judgment is set up. But to give every chance to the accused, his record will be produced and shown to him (lxix. 19, 25; xviii. 49), and he will be given a chance to plead (vii. 53), but if a sinner, he will be in confusion (xxviii 66).

5201. *By their Marks*: see last note.

5202 It will then become too real to them. "Oh! that this too, too solid flesh would melt", as Hamlet said to his Queen-Mother (*Hamlet*, i. 2. 129).

5203. They will apparently have no rest. The fire will burn but not consume them, and their drink will be only boiling water.

45. Then which of the favours
Of your Lord will ye deny?

٤٥- فَبِأَيِّ آلَآءِ رَبِّكُمَا تُكَذِّبَانِ ۝

SECTION 3.

46. But for such as fear
The time when they will
Stand before (the Judgment Seat[5204]
Of) their Lord,
There will be two Gardens—[5205]

٤٦- وَلِمَنْ خَافَ
مَقَامَ رَبِّهِ
جَنَّتَانِ ۝

47. Then which of the favours
Of your Lord will ye deny?—

٤٧- فَبِأَيِّ آلَآءِ رَبِّكُمَا تُكَذِّبَانِ ۝

48. Containing all kinds
(Of trees and delights);—

٤٨- ذَوَاتَآ أَفْنَانٍ ۝

49. Then which of the favours
Of your Lord will ye deny?—

٤٩- فَبِأَيِّ آلَآءِ رَبِّكُمَا تُكَذِّبَانِ ۝

50. In them (each) will be
Two Springs flowing (free);[5206]

٥٠- فِيهِمَا عَيْنَانِ تَجْرِيَانِ ۝

51. Then which of the favours
Of your Lord will ye deny?—

٥١- فَبِأَيِّ آلَآءِ رَبِّكُمَا تُكَذِّبَانِ ۝

52. In them will be Fruits
Of every kind, two and two.[5207]

٥٢- فِيهِمَا مِن كُلِّ فَاكِهَةٍ زَوْجَانِ ۝

53. Then which of the favours
Of your Lord will ye deny?

٥٣- فَبِأَيِّ آلَآءِ رَبِّكُمَا تُكَذِّبَانِ ۝

5204. The reference to the Punishment of Sin having been dismissed in a few short lines, we now come to a description of the state of the Blessed in a number of spacious allegories. Their general nature has already been discussed in Appendiv XII at the end of the last Sūra, where see para. 9 for the significance of the allegory of the Garden.

5205. Here two Gardens are mentioned, and indeed four, counting the other two mentioned in lv. 62-76. Opinions are divided about this, but the best opinion is that the two mentioned in verses 46-61 are for the degree of those Nearest to God (*Muqarrabūn*), and those in verses 62-76 for the Companions of the Right Hand: see para 10 of Appendix XII, p. 1467 Why two for *each*? The Duality is to express variety, and the whole scheme of the Sūra runs in twos. There will be no dulness of uniformity: as our minds can conceive it now, there will be freshness in change, but it will be from Bliss to Bliss, and there will be Unity.

5206. *Two* Springs, for the same reasons as there will be two Gardens. See last note.

5207. The Duality of Fruits is for the same reason as the Duality of the Gardens. See n. 5205.

54. They will recline on Carpets,
Whose inner linings will be
Of rich brocade: the Fruit
Of the Gardens will be
Near (and easy of reach).[5208]

٥٤- مُتَّكِـِٔينَ عَلَىٰ فُرُشٍۭ
بَطَآئِنُهَا مِنْ إِسْتَبْرَقٍ ۚ
وَجَنَا ٱلْجَنَّتَيْنِ دَانٍ ۝

55. Then which of the favours
Of your Lord will ye deny?

٥٥- فَبِأَيِّ ءَالَآءِ رَبِّكُمَا تُكَذِّبَانِ ۝

56. In them will be (Maidens),[5209]
Chaste, restraining their glances,[5210]
Whom no man or Jinn
Before them has touched;—

٥٦- فِيهِنَّ قَٰصِرَٰتُ ٱلطَّرْفِ لَمْ يَطْمِثْهُنَّ
إِنسٌ قَبْلَهُمْ وَلَا جَآنٌّ ۝

57. Then which of the favours
Of your Lord will ye deny?—

٥٧- فَبِأَيِّ ءَالَآءِ رَبِّكُمَا تُكَذِّبَانِ ۝

58. Like unto rubies and coral.[5211]

٥٨- كَأَنَّهُنَّ ٱلْيَاقُوتُ وَٱلْمَرْجَانُ ۝

59. Then which of the favours
Of your Lord will ye deny?

٥٩- فَبِأَيِّ ءَالَآءِ رَبِّكُمَا تُكَذِّبَانِ ۝

60. Is there any Reward
For Good—other than Good?[5212]

٦٠- هَلْ جَزَآءُ ٱلْإِحْسَٰنِ إِلَّا ٱلْإِحْسَٰنُ ۝

61. Then which of the favours
Of your Lord will ye deny?

٦١- فَبِأَيِّ ءَالَآءِ رَبِّكُمَا تُكَذِّبَانِ ۝

62. And besides these two,
There are two other Gardens,—[5213]

٦٢- وَمِن دُونِهِمَا جَنَّتَانِ ۝

5208. The toil and fatigue of this life will be over: *Cf.* xxxv. 35.

5209. The symbolic meaning of female Companionship, in terms of grace, purity, innocence and beauty, is explained in para. 12 of Appendix XII. See also notes 4728-29 to xliv. 54.

5210. *Cf.* xxxvii. 48 and n. 4064. Their purity is the feature hereby chiefly symbolised.

5211. Delicate pink, with reference to their complexions and their beauty of form. The gems also indicate their worth and dignity.

5212. This is the summing up of all the symbolism used to express the Fruit of Goodness or Good. The symbolism must necessarily resort to comparative terms, to subjective ideas of Bliss. But the fullest expression can only be given in abstract terms: "Is there any reward for Good—other than Good?" Can anything express it better?

5213. See n. 5205 above.

63. Then which of the favours
Of your Lord will ye deny ?—

٦٣- فَبِأَيِّ آلَاءِ رَبِّكُمَا تُكَذِّبَانِ ○

64. Dark-green in colour [5214]
(From plentiful watering).

٦٤- مُدْهَامَّتَانِ ○

65. Then which of the favours
Of your Lord will ye deny ?

٦٥- فَبِأَيِّ آلَاءِ رَبِّكُمَا تُكَذِّبَانِ ○

66. In them (each) will be
Two Springs pouring forth water [5215]
In continuous abundance :

٦٦- فِيهِمَا عَيْنَانِ نَضَّاخَتَانِ ○

67. Then which of the favours
Of your Lord will ye deny ?

٦٧- فَبِأَيِّ آلَاءِ رَبِّكُمَا تُكَذِّبَانِ ○

68. In them will be Fruits,
And dates and pomegranates : [5216]

٦٨- فِيهِمَا فَاكِهَةٌ وَنَخْلٌ وَرُمَّانٌ ○

69. Then which of the favours
Of your Lord will ye deny ?

٦٩- فَبِأَيِّ آلَاءِ رَبِّكُمَا تُكَذِّبَانِ ○

70. In them will be
Fair (Companions), good,
beautiful ;— [5217]

٧٠- فِيهِنَّ خَيْرَاتٌ حِسَانٌ ○

71. Then which of the favours
Of your Lord will ye deny ?—

٧١- فَبِأَيِّ آلَاءِ رَبِّكُمَا تُكَذِّبَانِ ○

72. Companions restrained (as to [5218]
Their glances), in (goodly)
pavilions ;— [5219]

٧٢- حُورٌ مَقْصُورَاتٌ فِي الْخِيَامِ ○

5214. "*Dark-green in colour*" : these Gardens will also be fruitful and flourishing, and watered plentifully ; but their aspect and characteristics will be different, corresponding to the subjective differences in the ideas of Bliss among those who would respectively enjoy the two sets of Gardens.

5215. In comparison with the Springs in the other two Gardens, described in lv. 50 above, these Springs would seem to irrigate crops of vegetables and fruits requiring a constant supply of abundant water.

5216. See last note. *Cf.* also with lv. 52 above, where "fruits of every kind" are mentioned.

5217. See n 5209 above. Goodness and Beauty are specially feminine attributes.

5218. *Maqṣūrāt* here is the passive participle of the same verb as the active participle *Qāṣirāt* in lv. 56, xxxvii. 48 and xxxviii 52 As I have translated *Qāṣirāt* by the phrase "restraining (their glances)", I think I am right in translating the passive *Maqṣūrāt* by "restrained (as to their glances)". This is the only place in the Qur-ān where the passive form occurs.

5219. The Pavilions seem to add dignity to their status. In the other Gardens (lv. 58), the description "like rubies and corals" is perhaps an indication of higher dignity.

73. Then which of the favours Of your Lord will ye deny ?—	٧٣- فَبِأَيِّ آلَآءِ رَبِّكُمَا تُكَذِّبَانِ ۝
74. Whom no man or Jinn Before them has touched ; —	٧٤- لَمْ يَطْمِثْهُنَّ إِنْسٌ قَبْلَهُمْ وَلَا جَآنٌّ ۝
75. Then which of the favours Of your Lord will ye deny ?—	٧٥- فَبِأَيِّ آلَآءِ رَبِّكُمَا تُكَذِّبَانِ ۝
76. Reclining on green Cushions[5220] And rich Carpets of beauty.	٧٦- مُتَّكِـِٔينَ عَلَىٰ رَفْرَفٍ خُضْرٍ وَعَبْقَرِيٍّ حِسَانٍ ۝
77. Then which of the favours Of your Lord will ye deny ?	٧٧- فَبِأَيِّ آلَآءِ رَبِّكُمَا تُكَذِّبَانِ ۝
78. Blessed be the name Of thy Lord, Full of Majesty, Bounty and Honour.[5221]	٧٨- تَبَٰرَكَ ٱسْمُ رَبِّكَ ذِى ٱلْجَلَٰلِ وَٱلْإِكْرَامِ ۝

5220. *Cf.* the parallel words for the other two Gardens, in lv. 54 above, which suggest perhaps a higher dignity.

Rafraf is usually translated by Cushions or Pillows, and I have followed this meaning in view of the word "reclining". But another interpretation is "Meadows", in view of the adjective "green"— *'abqarī*: carpets richly figured and dyed, and skilfully worked.

5221. *Cf.* lv. 27 and n. 5190. This minor echo completes the symmetry of the two leading Ideas of this Sūra,—the Bounty and Majesty of God, and the Duty of man to make himself worthy of nearness to God.

INTRODUCTION TO SŪRA LVI (*Wāqi'a*).

This is the seventh and last Sūra of the series devoted to Revelation and the Hereafter, as explained in the Introduction to S. *l*.

It belongs to the early Meccan period, with the possible exception of one or two verses.

The theme is the certainty of the Day of Judgment and its adjustment of true Values (lvi. 1-56); God's Power, Goodness and Glory (lvi. 57-74); and the truth of Revelation (lvi. 75-96).

Summary.—When the Day of Judgment comes, the world as we know it will be shaken to its foundations, and men shall be sorted out into three sorts: Those nearest to God, in exalted Bliss; the Companions of the Right Hand, in Bliss; and the Companions of the Left Hand, in Misery (lvi. 1-56, and C. 234).

Surely the Power and Goodness of God, of which Revelation is a Sign, should lead man to accept the Message and glorify Him (lvi. 57-96, and C. 235).

C. 234.—The Event Inevitable is the Day
(lvi. 1-56.) Of Judgment: the world as we know it
Will be shaken to its depths, and its place
Will be taken by a world made new,
Where Good will be sorted out from Evil.
In Dignity and Bliss will the Good find Fulfilment:
Both those Nearest to the Throne of God,
And those who earned, by faith and good life,
The title, Companions of the Right Hand.
Who can tell of the Misery in which
The Companions of the Left Hand will live?
They will be as it were in a fierce blast
Of Fire; their drink but boiling water;
Their shade that of Black Smoke that chokes
Their lungs;—ever burning with hunger and thirst,
And never satisfied: fit emblems
Of the Life in Death to which Evil leads.

Sūra LVI.

Wāqi'a, or The Inevitable Event.

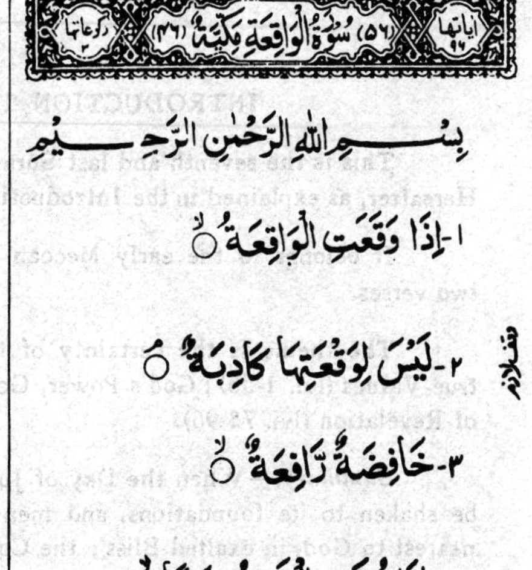

In the name of God, Most Gracious,
Most Merciful.

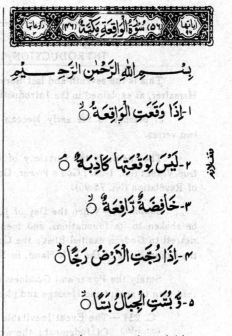

1. When the Event Inevitable[5222]
Cometh to pass,

2. Then will no (soul)
Entertain falsehood
Concerning its coming.

3. (Many) will it bring low;[5223]
(Many) will it exalt;

4. When the earth shall be
Shaken to its depths,

5. And the mountains shall
Be crumbled to atoms,[5224]

٥- وَّبُسَّتِ الْجِبَالُ بَسًّا ۝

6. Becoming dust scattered abroad,

٦- فَكَانَتْ هَبَآءً مُّنْبَثًّا ۝

7. And ye shall be sorted out
Into three classes.[5225]

٧- وَّكُنْتُمْ اَزْوَاجًا ثَلٰثَةً ۝

8. Then (there will be)
The Companions of
The Right Hand;—
What will be
The Companions of
The Right Hand?

٨- فَاَصْحٰبُ الْمَيْمَنَةِ
مَآ اَصْحٰبُ الْمَيْمَنَةِ

5222. The Event Inevitable is the Hour of Judgment. People may doubt now whether it will come. But when it comes, as it will come, suddenly upon them, it will come with such tremendous reality that it will be burnt deep into the experience of every soul. No one can then be deceived or entertain false notions about it.

5223. There will be a sorting out of Good and Evil. Or rather, (verse 7 below), there will be three main classes. Among the Good there will be the specially exalted class, those nearest to God (*muqarrabūn*, lvi. 11-26), and the righteous people generally, called the Companions of the Right Hand (*Aṣḥāb-ul-maimana*, lvi. 27-40). And there will be those in agony, the Companions of the Left Hand (*Aṣḥāb-ul-mash-ama*, lvi. 41-56). Many who were high and mighty in this life will be brought low for their sins, and many who were lowly but virtuous will be exalted to various ranks and degrees. The old landmarks will be lost in the inner world, as they will be in the outer world.

5224. The old physical world will disappear in the New Creation.

5225. See. n. 5223 above.

9. And the Companions of
The Left Hand,—
What will be
The Companions of
The Left Hand?

٩- وَأَصْحٰبُ الْمَشْـَٔمَةِ ۥ مَآ أَصْحٰبُ الْمَشْـَٔمَةِ ۝

10. And those Foremost
(In Faith) will be
Foremost (in the Hereafter).[5226]

١٠- وَالسّٰبِقُونَ السّٰبِقُونَ ۝

11. These will be
Those Nearest to God:[5227]

١١- أُولٰٓئِكَ الْمُقَرَّبُونَ ۝

12. In Gardens of Bliss:

١٢- فِى جَنّٰتِ النَّعِيمِ ۝

13. A number of people
From those of old,[5228]

١٣- ثُلَّةٌ مِّنَ الْأَوَّلِينَ ۝

14. And a few from those
Of later times.

١٤- وَقَلِيلٌ مِّنَ الْـَٔاخِرِينَ ۝

15. (They will be) on Thrones[5229]
Encrusted (with gold
And precious stones),

١٥- عَلٰى سُرُرٍ مَّوْضُونَةٍ ۝

16. Reclining on them,
Facing each other.[5230]

١٦- مُّتَّكِـِٔينَ عَلَيْهَا مُتَقٰبِلِينَ ۝

5226. "*Foremost (in Faith)*": there are two meanings, and both are implied. (1) Those who have reached the highest degree in spiritual understanding, such as the great prophets and teachers of mankind, will also take precedence in the Hereafter. (2) Those who are the first in time—the quickest and readiest—to accept God's Message—will have the first place in the Kingdom of Heaven. Verses 8, 9 and 10 mention the three main categories or classifications after Judgment. In the subsequent verses their happiness or misery are symbolised. This category, Foremost in Faith, is nearest to God.

5227. See n. 5223 above. Nearness to God is the test of the highest Bliss. The symbols that follow are mere reminiscences from our physical life.

5228. Of great Prophets and Teachers there were many before the time of the holy Prophet Muhammad. As he was the last of the Prophets, he and the great Teachers under his Dispensation will be comparatively fewer in number, but their teaching is the sum and flower of all mankind's spiritual experience.

5229. The costly Thrones will typify the high degree of their spiritual eminence.

5230. But they will not be separate each in his own corner. They will face each other. For they are all one, and their mutual society will be part of their Bliss.

17. Round about them will (serve)[5231]
Youths of perpetual (freshness),

١٧- يَطُوفُ عَلَيْهِمْ وِلْدَانٌ مُّخَلَّدُونَ ۝

18. With goblets, (shining) beakers,
And cups (filled) out of
Clear-flowing fountains:

١٨- بِأَكْوَابٍ وَأَبَارِيقَ ۙ
وَكَأْسٍ مِّن مَّعِينٍ ۝

19. No after-ache will they
Receive therefrom, nor will they
Suffer intoxication:[5232]

١٩- لَّا يُصَدَّعُونَ عَنْهَا
وَلَا يُنزِفُونَ ۝

20. And with fruits,
Any that they may select;

٢٠- وَفَاكِهَةٍ مِّمَّا يَتَخَيَّرُونَ ۝

21. And the flesh of fowls,
Any that they may desire.

٢١- وَلَحْمِ طَيْرٍ مِّمَّا يَشْتَهُونَ ۝

22. And (there will be) Companions
With beautiful, big,
And lustrous eyes,—[5233]

٢٢- وَحُورٌ عِينٌ ۝

23. Like unto Pearls[5234]
Well-guarded.

٢٣- كَأَمْثَالِ اللُّؤْلُؤِ الْمَكْنُونِ ۝

24. A Reward for the Deeds
Of their past (Life).

٢٤- جَزَاءً بِمَا كَانُوا يَعْمَلُونَ ۝

25. No frivolity will they[5235]
Hear therein, nor any
Taint of ill,—

٢٥- لَا يَسْمَعُونَ فِيهَا لَغْوًا
وَلَا تَأْثِيمًا ۝

5231. *Cf.* lii. 24. and n. 5058. The youth and freshness with which the attendants will serve is a symbol of true service such as we may expect in the spiritual world. That freshness will be perpetual, and not subject to any moods, or chances, or changes.

5232. The Feast of Reason and the Flow of Soul are typified by all that is best in the feasts in this imperfect world, but there will be none of the disadvantages incident to such feasts in this world, such as satiety, aches, excess, a sense of exhaustion, or loss of senses, etc. *Cf.* xxxvii. 47, and n. 4063. A goblet is a bowl without handles; a beaker has a "lip" and a stem; 'cup" is a general term.

5233. *Cf.* xliv. 54, and n. 4729. The companionship of Beauty and Grace is one of the highest pleasures of life. In this bodily life it takes bodily form. In the higher life it takes a higher form suitable to the spiritual world.

5234. *Cf.* lii. 24, where this description is applied to the youths who serve. See also n. 5058 there. In lvi. 78 below the adjective ***maknūn*** is applied to the Qur-ān, "the well-guarded Book".

5235. *Cf.* lii. 23. Apart from physical ills worldly feasts or delights are apt to suffer from vain or frivolous discourse, idle boasting, foolish flattery, or phrases pointed with secret venom or moral mischief. The negation of these from spiritual Bliss follows as a matter of course, but it is specially insisted on to guard against the perversities of human nature, which likes to read ill into the best that can be put in words.

26. Only the saying,[5236]
"Peace! Peace".

٢٦-اِلَّا قِيۡلًا سَلٰمًا سَلٰمًا ۝

27. The Companions of
The Right Hand,—
What will be
The Companions of
The Right Hand?

٢٧-وَ اَصۡحٰبُ الۡيَمِيۡنِ ۙ
مَاۤ اَصۡحٰبُ الۡيَمِيۡنِ ؕ ۝

28. (They will be) among[5237]
Lote-trees without thorns,

٢٨-فِىۡ سِدۡرٍ مَّخۡضُوۡدٍ ۙ ۝

29. Among Ṭalḥ trees[5238]
With flowers (or fruits)
Piled one above another,—

٢٩-وَّطَلۡحٍ مَّنۡضُوۡدٍ ۙ ۝

30. In shade long-extended,

٣٠-وَّ ظِلٍّ مَّمۡدُوۡدٍ ۙ ۝

31. By water flowing constantly,

٣١-وَّ مَآءٍ مَّسۡكُوۡبٍ ۙ ۝

32. And fruit in abundance,

٣٢-وَّ فَاكِهَةٍ كَثِيۡرَةٍ ۙ ۝

33. Whose season is not limited,
Nor (supply) forbidden,[5239]

٣٣-لَّا مَقۡطُوۡعَةٍ وَّلَا مَمۡنُوۡعَةٍ ۝

34. And on Thrones (of Dignity),
Raised high.

٣٤-وَّ فُرُشٍ مَّرۡفُوۡعَةٍ ؕ ۝

35. We have created
(their Companions)[5240]
Of special creation,

٣٥-اِنَّاۤ اَنۡشَاۡنٰهُنَّ اِنۡشَآءً ۙ ۝

5236. *Qīl* is best translated "saying", rather than "word". For the saying is an act, a thought, a fact, which may be embodied in a word, but which goes far beyond the word. The "Peace of God" is an atmosphere which sums up Heaven even better than "Bliss".

5237. *Lote-trees*: see xxxiv 16. n. 3814. The thornless lote-tree is a symbol of bliss and of high heaven: liii 14.

5238. *Ṭalḥ*: some understand by this the plantain or banana tree, of which the fruit is borne in bunches, one tier above another; but the banana tree does not grow in Arabia and its ordinary Arabic name is Mauz; perhaps it is better to understand a special kind of Acacia tree, which flowers profusely, the flowers appearing in tiers one above another.

5239. As it is not like earthly fruit, its season is not limited, nor is there any prohibition by law or custom or circumstance as to when or how it is to be consumed. The spiritual Fruit is free, unlimited, and inexhaustible.

5240. The pronoun in Arabic is in the feminine gender, but lest grosser ideas of sex should intrude, it is made clear that these Companions for heavenly society will be of special creation,—of virginal purity, grace, and beauty, inspiring and inspired by love, with the question of time and age eliminated. Thus every person among the Righteous will have the Bliss of Heaven and the Peace of God.

36. And made them
Virgin-pure (and undefiled),—

٣٦- فَجَعَلْنٰهُنَّ اَبْكَارًا ۝

37. Beloved (by nature),
Equal in age,—

٣٧- عُرُبًا اَتْرَابًا ۝

38. For the Companions
Of the Right Hand.

٣٨- لِّاَصْحٰبِ الْيَمِيْنِ ۝

SECTION 2.

39. A (goodly) number
From those of old,[5241]

٣٩- ثُلَّةٌ مِّنَ الْاَوَّلِيْنَ ۝

40. And a (goodly) number
From those of later times.

٤٠- وَ ثُلَّةٌ مِّنَ الْاٰخِرِيْنَ ۝

41. The Companions of
The Left Hand,—
What will be
The Companions of
The Left Hand?

٤١- وَ اَصْحٰبُ الشِّمَالِ ۚ۬
مَآ اَصْحٰبُ الشِّمَالِ ۝

42. (They will be) in the midst
Of a fierce Blast of Fire[5242]
And in Boiling Water,

٤٢- فِيْ سَمُوْمٍ وَّحَمِيْمٍ ۝

43. And in the shades
Of Black Smoke:[5243]

٤٣- وَّظِلٍّ مِّنْ يَّحْمُوْمٍ ۝

44. Nothing (will there be)
To refresh, nor to please:

٤٤- لَّا بَارِدٍ وَّلَا كَرِيْمٍ ۝

45. For that they were wont
To be indulged, before that,

٤٥- اِنَّهُمْ كَانُوْا قَبْلَ ذٰلِكَ

5241. This class—the righteous—will be a large company in Heaven, belonging to all the ages of the world. *Cf.* n. 5228 to lvi. 13 above. Such is the unbounded Bounty of God. These verses 39-40 should really be in the last Section.

5242. Notice the parallelism in the contrast between those in Bliss and those in Misery. The allegory in each case pursues the idea of contrast, and the allegories about Misery lose nothing by their terse brevity. The fierce Blast of Fire and the Boiling Water are in contrast to the happy Lote-tree and the flowers and fruits in verses 28-29 above.

5243. Even the Shades get a different quality in the Abode of Misery: shades of black smoke in contrast to the cool and refreshing long-extended shades of trees by brooks in verses 30-31 above.

In wealth (and luxury),[5244]

مُتْرَفِينَ ۝

46. And persisted obstinately
In wickedness supreme!

٤٦- وَكَانُوا يُصِرُّونَ عَلَى الْحِنْثِ الْعَظِيمِ ۝

47. And they used to say,
"What! when we die
And become dust and bones,[5245]
Shall we then indeed
Be raised up again?—

٤٧- وَكَانُوا يَقُولُونَ ۥ
أَئِذَا مِتْنَا وَكُنَّا تُرَابًا وَعِظَامًا
ءَإِنَّا لَمَبْعُوثُونَ ۝

48. "(We) and our fathers of old?"

٤٨- أَوَ آبَاؤُنَا الْأَوَّلُونَ ۝

49. Say: "Yea, those of old
And those of later times,

٤٩- قُلْ إِنَّ الْأَوَّلِينَ وَالْآخِرِينَ ۝

50. "All will certainly be
Gathered together for the meeting
Appointed for a Day
Well-known.[5246]

٥٠- لَمَجْمُوعُونَ ۥ إِلَىٰ مِيقَاتِ
يَوْمٍ مَّعْلُومٍ ۝

51. "Then will ye truly,—
O ye that go wrong,
And treat (Truth) as Falsehood!—

٥١- ثُمَّ إِنَّكُمْ أَيُّهَا الضَّالُّونَ
الْمُكَذِّبُونَ ۥ

52. "Ye will surely taste
Of the Tree of Zaqqūm.[5247]

٥٢- لَآكِلُونَ مِن شَجَرٍ مِّن زَقُّومٍ ۝

53. "Then will ye fill
Your insides therewith,

٥٣- فَمَالِئُونَ مِنْهَا الْبُطُونَ ۝

54. "And drink Boiling Water
On top of it:

٥٤- فَشَارِبُونَ عَلَيْهِ مِنَ الْحَمِيمِ ۝

5244. *Cf.* xxxiv. 34, and xliii. 23. We must read verses 45-46 together. They had wealth and the good things of life, but they used them in self-indulgence and shameless crime, and now they are in humiliation.

5245. Their want of belief and ridicule of God's Message contrasts with the stern reality which they see around them now.

5246. In xxvi. 38 (see n. 3159) the phrase "*a day well-known*" is used for a solemn day of festival, when the multitude of people gather together. The Day of Judgment is such a day in the supreme sense of the word.

5247. This is the Cursed Tree mentioned in xvii. 60, where see n. 2250. *Cf.* also xxxvii. 62, n. 4072; and xliv. 43-46 and n. 4722.

55. "Indeed ye shall drink
Like diseased camels
Raging with thirst!"[5248]

٥٥- فَشٰرِبُوْنَ شُرْبَ الْهِيْمِ ۝

56. Such will be their entertainment
On the Day of Requital!

٥٦- هٰذَا نُزُلُهُمْ يَوْمَ الدِّيْنِ ۝

C. 235.—Learn ye then to witness the Truth in your lives.
(lvi 57-96.) Your own creation and growth, the seeds
That ye sow in the ground, the Circuit of Water
Through streams, rivers, and seas, to vapour,
Clouds, and rain that feeds the streams,
The Fire that stands as an emblem of Life
And Light,—all point to your Lord Supreme.
His Revelation conveys the same Message
To the pure in heart. Will ye receive it
And live, assured of the truth of the Hereafter?
Glory and Praise to God the Beneficent,
Supreme in Justice, Mercy, and Truth!

57. It is We Who have
Created you: why will ye[5249]
Not witness the Truth?

٥٧- نَحْنُ خَلَقْنٰكُمْ
فَلَوْلَا تُصَدِّقُوْنَ ۝

58. Do ye then see?—
The (human Seed) that
Ye throw out,—

٥٨- اَفَرَءَيْتُمْ مَّا تُمْنُوْنَ ۝

59. Is it ye who create it,
Or are We the Creators?

٥٩- ءَاَنْتُمْ تَخْلُقُوْنَهٗۤ اَمْ نَحْنُ الْخٰلِقُوْنَ ۝

60. We have decreed Death
To be your common lot,[5250]
And We are not
To be frustrated

٦٠- نَحْنُ قَدَّرْنَا بَيْنَكُمُ الْمَوْتَ
وَمَا نَحْنُ بِمَسْبُوْقِيْنَ ۝

5248. A terrible picture of Misery in contrast to the Companionship of the Good, the True, and the Beautiful, on Thrones of Dignity, for the Companions of the Right Hand, in verses 34-38 above.

5249. Man is apt to forget his Creator, and even the fact that he, man, is a created being. The seed of his body, out of which his physical life starts, is not created by man, but by God in the process of the unfoldment of the world. Why will not man recognise and bear witness to this fact by a life of obedience to God's Law?

5250. Literally, 'to be in the midst of you'. Just as God has created this life that we see, so He has decreed that Death should be the common lot of all of us. Surely, if He can thus give life and death, as we see it, why should we refuse to believe that He can give us other Forms (in the Platonic sense) when this life is over? The Future Life, though indicated by what we know now, is to be on a wholly different plane.

61. From changing your Forms
And creating you (again)
In (Forms) that ye know not.

٦١- على ان نبدل امثالكم
وننشئكم في ما لا تعلمون ○

62. And ye certainly know already
The first form of creation :
Why then do ye not
Celebrate His praises ?

٦٢- ولقد علمتم النشاة الاولى
فلولا تذكرون ○

63. See ye the seed that [5251]
Ye sow in the ground ?

٦٣- افرءيتم ما تحرثون ○

64. Is it ye that cause it
To grow, or are We
The Cause ?

٦٤- ءانتم تزرعونه
ام نحن الزرعون ○

65. Were it Our Will,
We could crumble it
To dry powder, and ye would
Be left in wonderment,

٦٥- لو نشاء لجعلنه حطاما
فظلتم تفكهون ○

66. (Saying), " We are indeed
Left with debts (for nothing) : [5252]

٦٦- انا لمغرمون ○

67. " Indeed are we shut out
(Of the fruits of our labour) ".

٦٧- بل نحن محرومون ○

68. See ye the water
Which ye drink ?

٦٨- افرءيتم الماء الذي تشربون ○

69. Do ye bring it Down
(In rain) from the Cloud
Or do We ?

٦٩- ءانتم انزلتموه من المزن
ام نحن المنزلون ○

70. Were it Our Will,
We could make it

٧٠- لو نشاء جعلنه

5251. Having appealed to our own nature within us, He appeals now to the external nature around us, which should be evidence to us (1) of His loving care for us, and (2) of its being due to causes other than those which we produce and control. Three examples are given : (1) the seed which we sow in the soil ; it is God's processes in nature, which make it grow ; (2) the water which we drink ; it is God's processes in nature, that send it down from the clouds as rain, and distribute it through springs and rivers; (3) the fire which we strike ; it is again a proof of God's Plan and Wisdom in nature.

5252. The cultivator contracts debts for seed and gives labour for ploughing, sowing, watering, and weeding, in the hope of reaping a harvest. Should he not give thanks to God when his harvest is in ?

Salt (and unpalatable):[5253]
Then why do ye not
Give thanks?

اُجَاجًا
فَلَوْلَا تَشْكُرُوْنَ ۝

71. See ye the Fire
Which ye kindle?

٧١- اَفَرَءَيْتُمُ النَّارَ الَّتِىْ تُوْرُوْنَ ۝

72. Is it ye who grow
The tree which feeds[5254]
The fire, or do We
Grow it?

٧٢- ءَاَنْتُمْ اَنْشَاْتُمْ شَجَرَتَهَآ
اَمْ نَحْنُ الْمُنْشِـُٔوْنَ ۝

73. We have made it
A memorial (of Our handiwork),[5255]
And an article of comfort
And convenience for
The denizens of deserts.[5256]

٧٣- نَحْنُ جَعَلْنٰهَا تَذْكِرَةً
وَّمَتَاعًا لِّلْمُقْوِيْنَ ۝

74. Then celebrate with praises[5257]
The name of thy Lord,
The Supreme!

٧٤- فَسَبِّحْ بِاسْمِ رَبِّكَ
الْعَظِيْمِ ۝

5253. The mystery of the two streams of water, one sweet and the other salt, constantly mingling, and yet always separate, is referred to more than once. The never-ending circuit is established by streams and rivers mingling with the ocean, the ocean sending forth mists and steam through a process of evaporation which forms clouds, and the clouds by condensation pouring forth rain to feed the streams and rivers again: see notes 3111-2 to xxv. 53, and n. 5185 to lv. 19, and the further references given there.

5254. The relation of Fire to Trees is intimate. In nearly all the fire that we burn, the fuel is derived from the wood of trees. Even mineral coal is nothing but the wood of prehistoric forests petrified under the earth through geological ages. Fire produced out of green trees is referred to in xxxvi. 80; and n. 4026 there gives instances.

5255. Fire is a fit memorial of God's handiwork in nature. It is also an emblem of man's earliest civilisation. It can stand as a symbol of physical comfort and convenience to man, of the source of spiritual light, and also of the warning to Evil about its destruction. In the same way the sower's seed has a symbolical meaning in the preaching of the Message: see xlviii. 29, and n. 4917: and the Rain and the Streams of Water have a symbolical meaning: see notes 2404-5 to xviii. 60.

5256. *Cf.* xx. 10, and n. 2541, where the mystic meaning of the Fire which Moses saw in the desert is explained. Even ordinarily, a fire in a desert is a sign of human habitation; by following it you may get human society and human comfort. A fire, or light, or beacon in many places directs a traveller on the way Lighthouses at sea and beacons in modern aerodromes serve the same purpose for mariners and airmen.

Another parable about fire will be found in ii. 17-18, and n. 38.

5257. Seeing all these Signs in nature and their symbolical meaning in the spiritual world, man must turn to God and do His Will.

SECTION 3.

75. Furthermore I call
To witness the setting [5258]
Of the Stars,—

٧٥- فَلَآ أُقْسِمُ بِمَوٰقِعِ النُّجُومِ ۝

76. And that is indeed
A mighty adjuration [5259]
If ye but knew,—

٧٦- وَإِنَّهُ لَقَسَمٌ لَّوْ تَعْلَمُونَ عَظِيمٌ ۝

77. That this is indeed
A Qur-ān most honourable, [5260]

٧٧- إِنَّهُ لَقُرْءَانٌ كَرِيمٌ ۝

78. In a Book well-guarded,

٧٨- فِى كِتٰبٍ مَّكْنُونٍ ۝

79. Which none shall touch
But those who are clean:

٧٩- لَّا يَمَسُّهُ إِلَّا الْمُطَهَّرُونَ ۝

80. A Revelation from the Lord
Of the Worlds.

٨٠- تَنزِيلٌ مِّن رَّبِّ الْعٰلَمِينَ ۝

81. Is it such a Message
That ye would hold [5261]
In light esteem?

٨١- أَفَبِهٰذَا الْحَدِيثِ أَنتُم مُّدْهِنُونَ ۝

82. And have ye made it [5262]
Your livelihood that ye
Should declare it false?

٨٢- وَتَجْعَلُونَ رِزْقَكُمْ
أَنَّكُمْ تُكَذِّبُونَ ۝

5258. *The setting of the Stars*: a number of mystic meanings are attached. Here are three. (1) *Cf.* xliii. 1 and n. 5085: the setting of a glorious star is a symbol of humility before the power, beauty, and goodness of God. (2) It may refer to the extinction of the stars at the Day of Judgment, betokening the establishment of God's Justice and the Truth of His Revelation. (3) What is bright or beautiful to our senses may disappear from our ken within a few hours, even though its own existence may continue. All light is relative except the Light of God.

5259. The glory of the firmament as it exists, and the wonder of its passing away, are both evidence, to the discerning mind, of the Future which God has prepared, but this evidence can only be effective if men "but knew", *i.e.* turned their earnest attention to it.

5260. Your attention is drawn to the momentous issues of the Future by the Qur-ān. It is a Revelation described by four characteristics. (1) It is most honourable, *karim*, which implies, besides the fact that it is worthy of receiving honour, that it confers great favours on those who receive it. (2) It is well-guarded, *maknūn*; precious in itself, and well-preserved in its purity; see n. 5234 to lvi. 23; see also xv. 9, and n 1944. (3) None but the clean shall touch it,—clean in body, mind, thought, intention, and soul; only such can achieve real contact with its full meaning. (4) It is a Revelation from the Lord of the Worlds, and therefore universal for all.

5261. The Message being such as is described in the last note, how can any one ignore it or treat it with contempt or refuse to allow it to improve his life?

5262. The worst indictment of an enemy of Revelation would be that he should make Falsehood a source of filthy lucre for himself, or that he should let his precious life be corrupted by such unholy occupation.

83. Then why do ye not[5263]
(Intervene) when (the soul
Of the dying man)
Reaches the throat,—

٨٣- فَلَوْلَآ إِذَا
بَلَغَتِ الْحُلْقُومَ ۝

84. And ye the while
(Sit) looking on,—[5264]

٨٤- وَأَنْتُمْ حِينَئِذٍ تَنْظُرُونَ ۝

85. But We are nearer
To him than ye,
And yet see not,—

٨٥- وَنَحْنُ أَقْرَبُ إِلَيْهِ مِنْكُمْ
وَلٰكِنْ لَّا تُبْصِرُونَ ۝

86. Then why do ye not,—[5265]
If you are exempt
From (future) account,—

٨٦- فَلَوْلَآ إِنْ كُنْتُمْ غَيْرَ مَدِينِينَ ۝

87. Call back the soul,[5266]
If ye are true
(In your claim of Independence)?

٨٧- تَرْجِعُونَهَآ إِنْ كُنْتُمْ صٰدِقِينَ ۝

88. Thus, then, if he
Be of those Nearest to God,[5267]

٨٨- فَأَمَّآ إِنْ كَانَ مِنَ الْمُقَرَّبِينَ ۝

89. (There is for him) Rest
And Satisfaction,[5268] and
A Garden of Delights.

٨٩- فَرَوْحٌ وَّرَيْحَانٌ ۙ
وَّجَنَّتُ نَعِيمٍ ۝

5263. There is a hiatus after "*why do ye not?*"—and two parenthetical clauses,—after which the clause "*why do ye not?*" is resumed again in verse 86 below, with its complement in verse 87. It is permissible to the translator to add some such word as "*intervene*" here, to make the translation run smoothly.

5264. The dying man's friends, relatives, and companions may be sitting round him and quite close to him in his last moments, but God is nearer still at all times, for He is nearer than the man's own jugular vein (*l.* 16), and one of God's own titles is "Ever Near" (xxxiv. 50).

5265. These words resume the sentence begun at verse 83 above and interrupted by the two parenthetical clauses in verses 84 and 85. See n. 5263 above.

5266. The sentence may now be briefly paraphrased. 'If you disbelieve in Revelation and a future Judgment, and claim to do what you like and be independent of God, how is it you cannot call back a dying man's soul to his body when all of you congregate round him at his death-bed? But you are not independent of Judgment. There *is* a Day of Account, when you will have to be judged by your deeds in this life.'

5267. See above, lvi. 11-26 and notes.

5268. *Raiḥān*: sweet-smelling plants, as in lv. 12. Here used as symbolical of complete Satisfaction and Delight.

90. And if he be
Of the Companions of
The Right Hand,[5269]

٩٠- وَأَمَّآ إِن كَانَ مِنْ أَصْحَٰبِ ٱلْيَمِينِ ۝

91. (For him is the salutation),
"Peace be unto thee",[5270]
From the Companions
Of the Right Hand.

٩١- فَسَلَٰمٌ لَّكَ
مِنْ أَصْحَٰبِ ٱلْيَمِينِ ۝

92. And if he be
Of those who treat
(Truth) as Falsehood,[5271]
Who go wrong,

٩٢- وَأَمَّآ إِن كَانَ
مِنَ ٱلْمُكَذِّبِينَ ٱلضَّآلِّينَ ۝

93. For him is Entertainment
With Boiling Water,

٩٣- فَنُزُلٌ مِّنْ حَمِيمٍ ۝

94. And burning in Hell-Fire.

٩٤- وَتَصْلِيَةُ جَحِيمٍ ۝

95. Verily, this is
The Very Truth
And Certainty.[5272]

٩٥- إِنَّ هَٰذَا لَهُوَ حَقُّ ٱلْيَقِينِ ۝

96. So celebrate with praises[5273]
The name of thy Lord,
The Supreme.

٩٦- فَسَبِّحْ بِٱسْمِ رَبِّكَ ٱلْعَظِيمِ ۝ ع

5269. See above, lvi. 27-38 and notes.

5270. In lvi. 26 above the salutation of "Peace, Peace!" is addressed to those Nearest to God. Here we learn that it is also addressed to the Companions of the Right Hand. Both are in Gardens of Bliss: only the former have a higher Dignity than the latter.

5271. *Cf.* above, lvi. 51-55.

5272. "The assurance of the Hereafter" is one of the strongest features of Faith. For without it the apparent inequalities and injustices of this Life cannot be satisfactorily explained.

5273. *Cf.* lvi. 74 above. That was the conclusion of the argument about the Future from the examples of God's goodness in nature. Now we have the conclusion of the same argument from God's revelation through His inspired Messengers.

INTRODUCTION TO SŪRA LVII (*Ḥadīd*).

We have now studied the contents of nearly nine-tenths of the Qur-ān. We have found that the arrangement of the Sūras in the present Text is not haphazard, but that they follow a distinct logical order more helpful for study than the chronological order. The comprehensive scheme of building up the new *Ummat* or Brotherhood and its spiritual implications is now complete. The remaining tenth of the Qur-ān may be roughly considered in two parts. The first contains ten Sūras (S. lvii. to S. lxvi.), all revealed in Medina, and each dealing with some special point which needs emphasis in the social life of the Ummat. The second (S. lxvii. to cxiv.) contains short Meccan lyrics, each dealing with some aspect of spiritual life, expressed in language of great mystic beauty.

The present Medina Sūra is chiefly concerned with spiritual humility and the avoidance of arrogance, and a warning that retirement from the world may not be the best way of seeking the good pleasure of God. Its probable date is after the Conquest of Mecca, A.H. 8.

Summary.—God's Power and Knowledge extend to all things : follow His Light direct, without doubt or fear or half-heartedness, but with humility, generous charity, and faith, and not in a life of isolation from the world. (lvii 1-29, and C. 236.)

C. 236.—God is all-in-all : follow His Law
(lvii. 1-29.) And His Light, and obey His Apostle, who invites
You to deeds of goodness and charity.
Strive and spend your resources and yourselves
In the Cause of God : He will grant you a Light
To go before you and guide you to your Eternal
Goal, where no Evil can enter. When success
Crowns your efforts, even then is the time
To humble yourselves before God, in sincere
Witness to His Love. The pleasures here below
Are deceptive : be foremost in seeking God
And His Good Pleasure : trust Him : be not
Like those who mistook mere renunciation
Of the world for God's service. God's Grace
Is for all : be your love and your service for all.

Sûra LVII.

Ḥadid, or Iron.[5274]

*In the name of God, Most Gracious,
Most Merciful.*

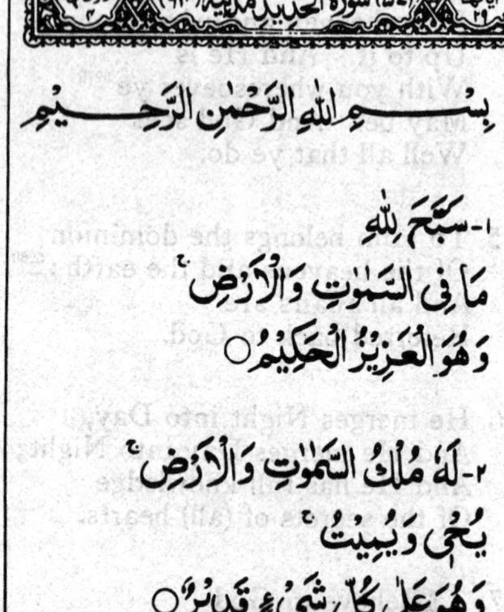

1. Whatever is in
The heavens and on earth,—
Let it declare
The Praises and Glory of God:[5275]
For He is the Exalted
In Might, the Wise.

2. To Him belongs the dominion
Of the heavens and the earth:
It is He Who gives
Life and Death; and He
Has Power over all things.

3. He is the First
And the Last,
The Evident
And the Immanent:[5276]
And He has full knowledge
Of all things.

٣- هُوَ الْاَوَّلُ وَالْاٰخِرُ
وَالظَّاهِرُ وَالْبَاطِنُ ۚ
وَهُوَ بِكُلِّ شَيْءٍ عَلِيْمٌ ۝

4. He it is Who created
The heavens and the earth
In six Days,[5277] and is moreover
Firmly established on the Throne
(Of authority).[5278] He knows
What enters within the earth

٤- هُوَ الَّذِيْ خَلَقَ السَّمٰوٰتِ وَالْاَرْضَ فِيْ
سِتَّةِ اَيَّامٍ ثُمَّ اسْتَوٰى عَلَى الْعَرْشِ ۚ
يَعْلَمُ مَا يَلِجُ فِي الْاَرْضِ

5274. Iron is the type and emblem of strength and reliability, on which depend the real virtues expounded in this Sûra, such as real humility, whole-heartedness, and charity, as opposed to Monasticism, Loadiceanism, and Niggardliness. See lvii 25 below.

5275. A connecting thought between this and the last Sûra, of which see verse 96 See also paragraph 3 of the Introduction to S. liii.

5276. *Bāṭin*: that which is within, as opposed to that which is evident in things outside. God has both these qualities. His Signs are everywhere evident in the whole universe. But He is also immanent within us and in the soul of all good things. The pair of seemingly opposite qualities, First and Last, Evident and Immanent, Power and Wisdom, Giving of Life and Death, etc., are referred to here, to point the contrast with our human frailty, in which monasticism may not be the same as humility, spending may not be the same as charity, and so on.

5277. "*In six Days*": see xli. 9-12, and notes; also more briefly, n. 1031 to vii. 54.

5278. *Cf.* x. 3, and n. 1386. It is not that God completed His Creation in six days and rested on the seventh day, or rests now. Certain external forms of the universe were by God's Command completed in six periods of evolution. But His creative process still goes on, and He is still, and will always be, on His Throne of authority, knowing all and guiding all affairs.

And what comes forth out
Of it, what comes down
From heaven and what mounts
Up to it. And He is
With you wheresoever ye [5279]
May be. And God sees
Well all that ye do.

وَمَا يَخْرُجُ مِنْهَا
وَمَا يَنْزِلُ مِنَ السَّمَاءِ وَمَا يَعْرُجُ فِيهَا ۖ
وَهُوَ مَعَكُمْ أَيْنَ مَا كُنْتُمْ ۚ
وَاللَّهُ بِمَا تَعْمَلُونَ بَصِيرٌ ○

5. To Him belongs the dominion
Of the heavens and the earth: [5280]
And all affairs are
Referred back to God.

٥- لَهُ مُلْكُ السَّمَاوَاتِ وَالْأَرْضِ ۚ
وَإِلَى اللَّهِ تُرْجَعُ الْأُمُورُ ○

6. He merges Night into Day,
And He merges Day into Night;
And He has full knowledge
Of the secrets of (all) hearts.

٦- يُولِجُ اللَّيْلَ فِي النَّهَارِ وَيُولِجُ النَّهَارَ
فِي اللَّيْلِ ۚ وَهُوَ عَلِيمٌ بِذَاتِ الصُّدُورِ ○

7. Believe in God
And His Apostle,
And spend (in charity)
Out of the (substance)
Whereof He has made you [5281]
Heirs. For, those of you
Who believe and spend
(In charity),—for them
Is a great Reward.

٧- آمِنُوا بِاللَّهِ وَرَسُولِهِ
وَأَنْفِقُوا مِمَّا جَعَلَكُمْ مُسْتَخْلَفِينَ فِيهِ ۖ
فَالَّذِينَ آمَنُوا مِنْكُمْ وَأَنْفَقُوا
لَهُمْ أَجْرٌ كَبِيرٌ ○

8. What cause have ye [5282]
Why ye should not believe
In God?—And the Apostle
Invites you to believe

٨- وَمَا لَكُمْ لَا تُؤْمِنُونَ بِاللَّهِ ۙ
وَالرَّسُولُ يَدْعُوكُمْ لِتُؤْمِنُوا

5279. He is everywhere. No Space or Time is without Him: yet He is independent of Space or Time. With reference to our own psychology, He is wherever we are, and He sees all that we do.

5280. See lvii. 2 above, where this phrase referred to God's complete authority over the whole of the external universe: the same phrase now refers to His complete authority over the abstract world—of thoughts and affairs. Every affair must finally go back to Him, whether it comes out here from Darkness into Light, or hides itself from Light into Darkness. God's knowledge penetrates into the inmost recesses of all Hearts.

5281. Whenever power or wealth or influence or any good thing is transferred from one person or group of persons to another, it involves added responsibilities to the persons receiving these advantages. They must be the more zealous in real charity and all good works, for that is a part of the evidence which they give of their faith and gratitude. And, besides, their good deeds, under the general law in the spiritual world, carry their own reward.

5282. "*What cause have ye why ye should not...?*" A figure of speech implying a far wider meaning than the words express. It is equivalent to saying: "There is every reason why ye *should* believe in God", etc. The same construction applies to verse 10 below.

In your Lord, and has
Indeed taken your Covenant,[5283]
If ye are men of faith.

بربكم
وقد أخذ ميثاقكم إن كنتم مؤمنين ○

9. He is the One Who
Sends to His Servant[5284]
Manifest Signs, that He
May lead you from
The depths of Darkness
Into the Light And verily,
God is to you
Most kind and Merciful.

٩- هو الذي ينزل على عبده آيات بينات
ليخرجكم من الظلمات إلى النور
وإن الله بكم
لرءوف رحيم ○

10. And what cause have ye
Why ye should not spend
In the cause of God?—
For to God belongs[5285]
The heritage of the heavens
And the earth.
Not equal among you
Are those who spent (freely)
And fought, before the Victory,[5286]
(With those who did so later).
Those are higher in rank
Than those who spent (freely)
And fought afterwards.
But to all has God promised
A goodly (reward). And God
Is well acquainted
With all that ye do.

١٠- وما لكم
ألا تنفقوا في سبيل الله
ولله ميراث السماوات والأرض
لا يستوي منكم
من أنفق من قبل الفتح وقاتل
أولئك أعظم درجة
من الذين أنفقوا من بعد وقاتلوا
وكلا وعد الله الحسنى
والله بما تعملون خبير ○ ع

5283. There are two shades of meaning. (1) There is the implied Covenant in a man who accepts the Gospel of Unity that he will bring forth all the fruits of that Gospel, *i.e.* believe in God, and serve God and humanity. See n. 682 to v. 1. (2) There were at various times express Covenants entered into by the Muslims to serve God and be true to the Prophet, comparable to the Covenants of the Jewish nation about the Message of Moses; *e.g.* the two Covenants of 'Aqaba (v. 8, and n. 705) and the Pledge of Ḥudaibiya (xlviii. 10, n. 4877). For the Covenant with Israel at Mount Sinai, see ii. 63, n. 78.

5284. The holy Prophet Muḥammad. The Signs sent to him were: (1) the Āyats of the Qur-ān, and (2) his life and work, in which God's Plan and Purpose were unfolded.

5285. "*To God belongs the heritage of...*": see n. 485 to iii. 180; also n. 988 to vi. 165; and n. 1964 to xv. 23.

5286. This is usually understood to refer to the Conquest of Mecca, after which the Muslims succeeded to the power and position which the Pagan Quraish had so misused at Mecca. Thereafter the Muslims had the hegemony of Arabia, and in a few centuries, for a time, the hegemony of the world. But the words are perfectly general, and we must understand the general meaning also: that the people who fight and struggle in God's Cause and give of their best to it at any time are worthy of praise: but those are worthy of special distinction who do it when the Cause is being persecuted and in most need of assistance, before victory comes.

SECTION 2.

11. Who is he that will
Loan to God a beautiful[5287]
Loan? For (God) will
Increase it manifold
To his credit,
And he will have (besides)
A liberal reward.

١١-مَنْ ذَا الَّذِي
يُقْرِضُ اللَّهَ قَرْضًا حَسَنًا
فَيُضٰعِفَهُ لَهُ
وَلَهُ أَجْرٌ كَرِيمٌ ۝

12. One Day shalt thou see
The believing men and
The believing women—
How their Light runs[5288]
Forward before them
And by their right hands:
(Their greeting will be):
"Good News for you this Day!
Gardens beneath which flow rivers!
To dwell therein for aye!
This is indeed
The highest Achievement!"[5289]

١٢-يَوْمَ تَرَى الْمُؤْمِنِينَ وَالْمُؤْمِنٰتِ
يَسْعٰى نُورُهُم بَيْنَ أَيْدِيهِمْ
وَبِأَيْمٰنِهِم بُشْرٰىكُمُ الْيَوْمَ
جَنّٰتٌ تَجْرِى مِن تَحْتِهَا الْأَنْهٰرُ
خٰلِدِينَ فِيهَا
ذٰلِكَ هُوَ الْفَوْزُ الْعَظِيمُ ۝

13. One Day will the Hypocrites—
Men and women—say
To the Believers: "Wait
For us! Let us borrow
(A light) from your Light!"[5290]
It will be said: "Turn
Ye back to your rear!
Then seek a light (where
Ye can)!" So a wall[5291]
Will be put up betwixt them,

١٣-يَوْمَ يَقُولُ الْمُنٰفِقُونَ وَالْمُنٰفِقٰتُ لِلَّذِينَ
ءَامَنُوا انظُرُونَا نَقْتَبِسْ مِن نُّورِكُمْ
قِيلَ ارْجِعُوا وَرَآءَكُمْ
فَالْتَمِسُوا نُورًا
فَضُرِبَ بَيْنَهُم بِسُورٍ لَّهُ

5287. *Cf.* ii. 245, n. 276.

5288. In the Darkness of the Day of Judgment there will be a Light to guide the righteous to their Destination. This will be the Light of their Faith and their Good Works. Perhaps the Light of the Right Hand mentioned here is the Light of their Good Works: for the Blessed will receive their Record in their right hand (lxix. 19-24).

5289. The highest Achievement, the highest felicity, the attainment of Salvation, the fulfilment of all desires. See n 4733 to xliv. 57.

5290. Watchful preparation in Life, and the light of Faith, which reflects the divine Light, are matters of personal Life, and cannot be borrowed from another. So, in Christ's parable of the Ten Virgins (Matt. xxv. 1-13), when the foolish ones had let their lamps go out for want of oil, they asked to borrow oil from the wise ones, but the wise ones answered and said, "Not so; ...but go ye rather to them that sell, and buy for yourselves"

5291. The wall of Personality, or Record of Deeds, will divide the Good from the Evil. But the Gateway in it will show that communication will not be cut off. Evil must realise that Good—*i.e.* Mercy and Felicity—had been within its reach, and that the Wrath which envelops it is due to its own rejection of Mercy.

With a gate therein.
Within it will be Mercy
Throughout, and without it,
All alongside, will be
(Wrath and) Punishment!

14. (Those without) will call out,
"Were we not with you?"[5292]
(The others) will reply, "True!
But ye led yourselves
Into temptation; ye looked forward
(To our ruin); ye doubted
(God's Promise); and (your false)
Desires deceived you; until
There issued the Command
Of God. And the Deceiver
Deceived you in respect of God.[5293]

15. "This Day shall no ransom
Be accepted of you, nor
Of those who rejected God.[5294]
Your abode is the Fire:
That is the proper place
To claim you: and an evil
Refuge it is!"

16. Has not the time arrived[5295]
For the Believers that
Their hearts in all humility
Should engage in the remembrance

بَابٌ ۭ
بَاطِنُهٗ فِيْهِ الرَّحْمَةُ
وَظَاهِرُهٗ مِنْ قِبَلِهِ الْعَذَابُ ۝

١٤- يُنَادُوْنَهُمْ اَلَمْ نَكُنْ مَّعَكُمْ ۭ
قَالُوْا بَلٰى وَلٰكِنَّكُمْ فَتَنْتُمْ اَنْفُسَكُمْ
وَتَرَبَّصْتُمْ وَارْتَبْتُمْ
وَغَرَّتْكُمُ الْاَمَانِيُّ
حَتّٰى جَاۗءَ اَمْرُ اللّٰهِ
وَغَرَّكُمْ بِاللّٰهِ الْغَرُوْرُ ۝

١٥- فَالْيَوْمَ لَا يُؤْخَذُ مِنْكُمْ فِدْيَةٌ
وَّلَا مِنَ الَّذِيْنَ كَفَرُوْا ۭ
مَاْوٰىكُمُ النَّارُ ۭ
هِيَ مَوْلٰىكُمْ ۭ وَبِئْسَ الْمَصِيْرُ ۝

١٦- اَلَمْ يَاْنِ لِلَّذِيْنَ اٰمَنُوْٓا
اَنْ تَخْشَعَ قُلُوْبُهُمْ لِذِكْرِ

5292. The evil will now claim some right of kinship or association or proximity with the good in earthly life; but in fact they had been arrogant and had selfishly despised them before. The reply will be: (1) you yourselves chose temptation and evil; (2) when you had power in your earthly life, you hoped for ruin to the good, and perhaps plotted for it; (3) you were warned by men of God, but you doubted God's very existence, and certainly His Mercy and Justice, and the Hereafter; (4) you followed your own lusts and neglected Reason and Truth; (5) you were given plenty of rope, but you followed your mad career, until Judgment came upon you, and now it is too late for repentance.

5293. The Arch-Deceiver (Satan) deceived you in respect of God in many ways: for example, he made you oblivious of God's Mercy and loving-kindness; he made you reject His Grace; he made you think that God's Justice may not overtake you; etc.

5294. In personal responsibility there is no room for vicarious ransom or for ransom by payments of gold or silver or by sacrifice of possessions. Nor can the crime be expiated for *after* Judgment. 'You' and 'those who rejected God' are two ways of looking at the same persons. 'You are rejected because you rejected God'.

5295. Humility and the remembrance of God and His Message are never more necessary than in the hour of victory and prosperity.

Of God and of the Truth
Which has been revealed (to them),
And that they should not
Become like those to whom
Was given Revelation aforetime,[5296]
But long ages passed over them
And their hearts grew hard?
For many among them
Are rebellious transgressors.

اللّٰهِ وَمَا نَزَلَ مِنَ الْحَقِّ ۙ
وَلَا يَكُونُوا كَالَّذِينَ
أُوتُوا الْكِتٰبَ مِنْ قَبْلُ
فَطَالَ عَلَيْهِمُ الْأَمَدُ فَقَسَتْ قُلُوبُهُمْ ۖ
وَكَثِيرٌ مِّنْهُمْ فٰسِقُونَ ○

17. Know ye (all) that
God giveth life
To the earth after its death![5297]
Already have We shown
The Signs plainly to you,
That ye may learn wisdom.

١٧- اِعْلَمُوٓا أَنَّ اللّٰهَ يُحْيِ الْأَرْضَ بَعْدَ
مَوْتِهَا ۚ قَدْ بَيَّنَّا لَكُمُ الْاٰيٰتِ
لَعَلَّكُمْ تَعْقِلُونَ ○

18. For those who give
In Charity, men and women,
And loan to God[5298]
A Beautiful Loan,
It shall be increased manifold
(To their credit),
And they shall have (besides)
A liberal reward.

١٨- إِنَّ الْمُصَّدِّقِينَ وَالْمُصَّدِّقٰتِ
وَأَقْرَضُوا اللّٰهَ قَرْضًا حَسَنًا
يُضٰعَفُ لَهُمْ
وَلَهُمْ أَجْرٌ كَرِيمٌ ○

19. And those who believe
In God and His apostles—
They are the Sincere[5299]
(Lovers of Truth), and

١٩- وَالَّذِينَ اٰمَنُوا بِاللّٰهِ وَرُسُلِهٖٓ
أُولٰٓئِكَ هُمُ الصِّدِّيقُونَ ۖ وَ

5296. The men immediately referred to are the contemporary Jews and Christians. To each of these Ummats was given God's Revelation, but as time passed, they corrupted it, became arrogant and hard-hearted, and subverted justice, truth, and the purity of Life. But the general lesson is far wider. No one is favoured of God except on the score of righteousness. Except on that score, there is no chosen individual or race. There is no blind good fortune or ill fortune. All happens according to the just laws and will of God. But at no time is humility or righteousness more necessary than in the hour of victory or triumph.

5297. As the dead earth is revived after the refreshing showers of rain, so is it with the spirit of man, whether as an individual or a race or Ummat. There is no cause for despair. God's Truth will revive the spiritual faculties if it is accepted with humility and zeal.

5298. *Cf.* lvii. 11; also see ii. 245, n. 276.

5299. *Cf.* iv. 69, and n. 586. The four categories there mentioned as constituting the beautiful Fellowship of Faith are: the Prophets who teach, the Sincere Lovers of Truth, the Witnesses who testify, and the Righteous who do good. Of these, the prophets or apostles have already been mentioned in this verse. The Righteous who do good are mentioned as the men and women given over to deeds of charity in verse 18.

The Witnesses (who testify),[5300]
In the eyes of their Lord:
They shall have their Reward
And their Light.[5301]
But those who reject God
And deny Our Signs,—
They are the Companions
Of Hell-Fire.

الشُّهَدَآءُ عِنْدَ رَبِّهِمْ ط
لَهُمْ اَجْرُهُمْ وَنُوْرُهُمْ ط
وَالَّذِيْنَ كَفَرُوْا وَكَذَّبُوْا بِاٰيٰتِنَآ
اُولٰٓئِكَ اَصْحٰبُ الْجَحِيْمِ ۝ ع

Section 3.

20. Know ye (all), that
The life of this world
Is but play and amusement,[5302]
Pomp and mutual boasting
And multiplying, (in rivalry)
Among yourselves, riches
And children.
Here is a similitude:[5303]
How rain and the growth
Which it brings forth, delight
(The hearts of) the tillers;[5304]
Soon it withers; thou
Wilt see it grow yellow;
Then it becomes dry
And crumbles away.
But in the Hereafter
Is a Penalty severe
(For the devotees of wrong).
And Forgiveness from God
And (His) Good Pleasure

٢٠- اِعْلَمُوْٓا اَنَّمَا الْحَيٰوةُ الدُّنْيَا
لَعِبٌ وَّلَهْوٌ
وَّزِيْنَةٌ وَّتَفَاخُرٌۢ بَيْنَكُمْ
وَتَكَاثُرٌ فِي الْاَمْوَالِ وَالْاَوْلَادِ ط
كَمَثَلِ غَيْثٍ اَعْجَبَ الْكُفَّارَ نَبَاتُهٗ
ثُمَّ يَهِيْجُ
فَتَرٰىهُ مُصْفَرًّا
ثُمَّ يَكُوْنُ حُطَامًا ط
وَفِي الْاٰخِرَةِ عَذَابٌ شَدِيْدٌ لا
وَّمَغْفِرَةٌ مِّنَ اللّٰهِ وَرِضْوَانٌ ط

5300. The Witnesses are not only Martyrs, but all those who carry the Banner of Truth against all odds and in all positions of danger, whether by pen or speech, or deed or counsel.

5301. Note that these two are specially high degrees in the spiritual kingdom, just short of Apostleship. For they have not only their reward in the spiritual Kingdom of God, like those who practise charity (verse 18 above), but they themselves become sources of light and leading.

5302. *Cf.* vi. 32, and n. 855. In the present passage the idea is further amplified. In this life people not only play and amuse themselves and each other, but they show off, and boast, and pile up riches and man-power and influence, in rivalry with each other.

5303. *Cf.* xxxix. 21, and n. 4273. Here the Parable is meant to teach a slightly different lesson. God's mercies are free and open to all, like His rain. But how do men make use of them? The good men take the real spiritual harvest and store the spiritual grain. The men who are in love with the ephemeral are delighted with the green of the tares and the grass; but such things give no real nourishment; they soon wither, become dry, and crumble to pieces, like the worldly pleasures and pomps, boastings and tumults, possessions and friends.

5304. *Kuffār* is here used in the unusual sense of 'tillers or husbandmen', because they sow the seed and cover it up with soil. But the ordinary meaning, 'Rejecters of Truth', is not absent. The allegory refers to such men.

(For the devotees of God).
And what is the life
Of this world, but
Goods and chattels
Of deception ?[5305]

وَمَا الْحَيٰوةُ الدُّنْيَآ
إِلَّا مَتَاعُ الْغُرُورِ ۝

21. Be ye foremost (in seeking)
Forgiveness from your Lord,
And a Garden (of Bliss),
The width whereof is
As the width of
Heaven and earth,[5306]
Prepared for those who believe
In God and His apostles:
That is the Grace of God,
Which He bestows on whom[5307]
He pleases: and God is
The Lord of Grace abounding.

٢١- سَابِقُوٓا إِلٰى مَغْفِرَةٍ مِّنْ رَّبِّكُمْ
وَجَنَّةٍ عَرْضُهَا
كَعَرْضِ السَّمَآءِ وَالْأَرْضِ ۙ
أُعِدَّتْ لِلَّذِينَ اٰمَنُوا بِاللّٰهِ وَرُسُلِهٖ ۭ
ذٰلِكَ فَضْلُ اللّٰهِ يُؤْتِيهِ مَنْ يَّشَآءُ ۭ
وَاللّٰهُ ذُو الْفَضْلِ الْعَظِيمِ ۝

22. No misfortune can happen
On earth or in your souls[5308]
But is recorded in
A decree before We bring[5309]
It into existence:
That is truly easy for God:

٢٢- مَآ أَصَابَ مِنْ مُّصِيبَةٍ فِي الْأَرْضِ وَ
لَا فِيٓ أَنْفُسِكُمْ إِلَّا فِي كِتٰبٍ مِّنْ قَبْلِ أَنْ
نَّبْرَأَهَا ۭ إِنَّ ذٰلِكَ عَلَى اللّٰهِ يَسِيرٌ ۝

23. In order that ye may
Not despair over matters
That pass you by,
Nor exult over favours
Bestowed upon you.
For God loveth not

٢٣- لِّكَيْلَا تَأْسَوْا عَلٰى مَا فَاتَكُمْ
وَلَا تَفْرَحُوا بِمَآ اٰتٰكُمْ ۭ
وَاللّٰهُ لَا يُحِبُّ

5305. *Cf.* iii. 185, and n. 492. Many of the attractive vanities of this world are but nets set by the Evil One to deceive man. The only thing real and lasting is the Good Life lived in the Light of God.

5306. *Cf.* iii. 133, and n. 452.

5307. "*Bestows on whom He pleases.*" That is, such grace and favour is beyond any one's own merits. It is bestowed by God according to His holy Will and Plan, which is just, merciful, and righteous.

5308 External disasters or misfortunes may strike people's eye or imagination, but there are worse crises and misfortunes in the spiritual world, which are of equal or greater importance to man's future. All this happens according to the Will and Plan of God. Even where we are allowed the exercise of our own wills, the consequences that follow are in accordance with the laws and Plan decreed by God beforehand.

5309. For *baraa*, 'to bring into existence', and other words denoting God's creative energy, see n. 120 to ii. 117; n. 916 to vi. 94; and n. 923 to vi. 98.

Any vainglorious boaster,—[5310]

24. Such persons as are[5311]
Covetous and commend
Covetousness to men.
And if any turn back[5312]
(From God's Way), verily
God is free of all needs,
Worthy of all praise.

25. We sent aforetime
Our apostles with Clear Signs
And sent down with them
The Book and the Balance[5313]
(Of Right and Wrong), that men
May stand forth in justice;
And We sent down[5314] Iron,[5315]
In which is (material for)
Mighty war, as well as
Many benefits for mankind,
That God may test who
It is that will help,

كُلَّ مُخْتَالٍ فَخُورٍ ۝
٢٤ - الَّذِينَ يَبْخَلُونَ
وَيَأْمُرُونَ النَّاسَ بِالْبُخْلِ ۗ
وَمَن يَتَوَلَّ
فَإِنَّ اللَّهَ هُوَ الْغَنِيُّ الْحَمِيدُ ۝
٢٥ - لَقَدْ أَرْسَلْنَا رُسُلَنَا بِالْبَيِّنَاتِ
وَأَنزَلْنَا مَعَهُمُ الْكِتَابَ وَالْمِيزَانَ
لِيَقُومَ النَّاسُ بِالْقِسْطِ ۖ
وَأَنزَلْنَا الْحَدِيدَ فِيهِ بَأْسٌ شَدِيدٌ
وَمَنَافِعُ لِلنَّاسِ
وَلِيَعْلَمَ اللَّهُ مَن يَنصُرُهُ

5310. In the external world, what people may consider misfortune or good fortune may both turn out to be illusory,—in Kipling's words, "both impostors just the same". The man of God does not grumble if some one else has possessions, nor exult if he has them. He does not covet and he does not boast. If he has any advantages, he shares them with other people, as he considers them not due to his own merits, but as gifts of God.

5311. Neither the Covetous nor the Boasters have any place in the Good Pleasure of God. The Covetous are particularly insidious, as their avarice and niggardliness not only keep back the gifts of God from men, but their pernicious example dries up the streams of Charity in others.

5312. It is Charity in God's Way that is specially in view here. If people are selfish and withhold their hand, they only injure themselves. They do not hurt God's Cause, for He is independent of all needs, and He will find other means of assisting His more meagrely-endowed servants; He is worthy of all praise in His care for His creatures.

5313. Three things are mentioned as gifts of God. In concrete terms they are the Book, the Balance, and Iron, which stand as emblems of three things which hold society together, *viz.* Revelation, which commands Good and forbids Evil; Justice, which gives to each person his due; and the strong arm of the Law, which maintains sanctions for evil-doers. For *Balance*, see also xlii. 17, and n. 4550.

5314. "*Sent down*": *anzala*: in the sense of revealed to man the use of certain things, created in him the capacity of understanding and using them: *cf.* xxxix. 6: "sent down for you eight head of cattle in pairs".

5315. *Iron*: the most useful metal known to man. Out of it is made steel, and from steel and iron are made implements of war, such as swords, spears, guns, etc., as well as instruments of peace, such as ploughshares, bricklayers' trowels, architects' and engineers' instruments, etc. Iron stands as the emblem of Strength, Power, Discipline, Law's sanctions, etc. Iron and steel industries have also been the foundation of the prosperity and power of modern manufacturing nations like England.

Unseen,[5316] Him and His apostles:[5317]
For God is Full of Strength,
Exalted in Might[5318]
(And able to enforce His Will).

وَرُسُلَهُۥ بِالْغَيْبِ ۚ
إِنَّ اللَّهَ قَوِيٌّ عَزِيزٌ ۝ ع

SECTION 4.

26. And We sent Noah
And Abraham, and established
In their line Prophethood
And Revelation: and some of
them[5319]
Were on right guidance,
But many of them
Became rebellious transgressors.

٢٦- وَلَقَدْ أَرْسَلْنَا نُوحًا وَإِبْرَٰهِيمَ
وَجَعَلْنَا فِي ذُرِّيَّتِهِمَا النُّبُوَّةَ وَالْكِتَٰبَ
فَمِنْهُم مُّهْتَدٍ ۖ
وَكَثِيرٌ مِّنْهُمْ فَٰسِقُونَ ۝

27. Then, in their wake,
We followed them up
With (others of) Our apostles:
We sent after them
Jesus the son of Mary,
And bestowed on him
The Gospel; and We ordained
In the hearts of those
Who followed him
Compassion and Mercy.[5320]

٢٧- ثُمَّ قَفَّيْنَا عَلَىٰٓ ءَاثَٰرِهِم بِرُسُلِنَا
وَقَفَّيْنَا بِعِيسَى ابْنِ مَرْيَمَ
وَءَاتَيْنَٰهُ الْإِنجِيلَ ۙ
وَجَعَلْنَا فِي قُلُوبِ الَّذِينَ اتَّبَعُوهُ
رَأْفَةً وَرَحْمَةً ۚ

5316. In xxi. 49, I have translated "in their most secret thoughts" for the more literal "unseen" (*bil-gaibi*). Perhaps the more literal "unseen" may do if understood in the adverbial sense as explained in xxxv. 18, n. 3902. The sincere man will help the Cause, whether he is seen or brought under notice or not.

5317. To help God and His apostles is to help their Cause. It is to give men an opportunity of striving and fighting for His Cause and proving their true mettle, for thus is their spirit tested. As explained in the next line, God in Himself is Full of Strength, Exalted in Power, and Able to enforce His Will, and He has no need of other assistance.

5318. *Cf.* xxii. 40 and n. 2818. "Strength" is specific; Power or Might is more abstract, the ability to enforce what is willed.

5319. *Some of them*: *i.e.*, of their line, or posterity, or Ummat. When the Book that was given to them became corrupted, many of them followed their own fancies and became transgressors.

5320. The chief characteristic of the teaching in the Gospels is humility and other-worldliness. The first blessings in the Sermon on the Mount are on "the poor in spirit", "they that mourn", and they that are "meek" (Matt. v. 3-5). Christ's disciples were enjoined to "take no thought for the morrow", and told: "Sufficient unto the day is the evil thereof" (Matt. vi. 34). They were also commanded "that ye resist not evil; but whosoever shall smite thee on thy right cheek, turn to him the other also" (Matt. v. 39). These are fragmentary presentments of an imperfect philosophy as seen through monastic eyes. In so far as they represent pity, sympathy with suffering, and deeds of mercy, they represent the spirit of Christ.

But the Monasticism
Which they invented
For themselves, We did not
Prescribe for them :[5321]
(We commanded) only
The seeking for the Good
Pleasure of God ; but that
They did not foster[5322]
As they should have done.
Yet We bestowed, on those
Among them who believed,[5323]
Their (due) reward, but
Many of them are
Rebellious transgressors.[5324]

وَرَهْبَانِيَّةً ابْتَدَعُوهَا
مَا كَتَبْنَاهَا عَلَيْهِمْ
إِلَّا ابْتِغَاءَ رِضْوَانِ اللّٰهِ
فَمَا رَعَوْهَا حَقَّ رِعَايَتِهَا
فَآتَيْنَا الَّذِينَ آمَنُوا مِنْهُمْ
أَجْرَهُمْ
وَكَثِيرٌ مِّنْهُمْ فٰسِقُونَ ○

28. O ye that believe![5325]
Fear God, and believe
In His Apostle, and He will
Bestow on you a double[5326]
Portion of His Mercy :
He will provide for you

٢٨- يٰٓأَيُّهَا الَّذِينَ آمَنُوا اتَّقُوا اللّٰهَ وَآمِنُوا
بِرَسُولِهِ يُؤْتِكُمْ
كِفْلَيْنِ مِن رَّحْمَتِهِ

5321. But God's Kingdom requires also courage, resistance to evil, the firmness, law, and discipline which will enforce justice among men. It requires men to mingle with men, so that they can uphold the standard of Truth, against odds if necessary. These were lost sight of in Monasticism, which was not prescribed by God.

5322. God certainly requires that men shall renounce the idle pleasures of this world, and turn to the Path which leads to God's Good Pleasure. But that does not mean gloomy lives, ("they that mourn"), nor perpetual and formal prayers in isolation. God's service is done through pure lives in the turmoil of this world. This spirit was lost, or at least not fostered by monastic institutions. On the contrary a great part of the "struggle and striving" for noble lives was suppressed.

5323. Many of them lost true Faith, or had their Faith corrupted by superstitions. But those who continued firm in Faith saw the natural development of Religion in Islam. Their previous belief was not a disadvantage to them, but helped them, because they kept it free from false and selfish prejudices. These are the ones who are further addressed at the beginning of verse 28 below.

5324. The corruptions in the Christian Church, the hair-splitting disputes, and mutual strife and hatred of sects had become a scandal by the time that the light of Islam came into the world. The pages of Gibbon's great History bear witness. Not only had the religion become void of grace, but the lives of the people, priests and laity, had fallen into great depths of degradation. See remarks in my Appendix V, pages 411-413, and the general picture in Kingsley's "*Hypatia*".

5325. From the context before (see n. 5323 above) and after (see next note), this is held to refer to the Christians and People of the Book who kept their Faith true and undefiled.

5326. The double portion refers to the past and the future. As noted in the last note, this passage is addressed to the Christians and the People of the Book, who, when honestly facing the question of the new Revelation in Islam, find in it the fulfilment of previous revelations, and therefore believe in God's Apostle Muḥammad, and walk by the new Light. Their previous merits will be duly recognised, and they will be treated on fully equal terms in the new Ummat. This is their double share, not necessarily more in quantity than that of their brethren in Islam who passed through no other gate, but having a twofold aspect.

A Light by which ye[5327]
Shall walk (straight
In your path), and He
Will forgive you (your past): [5328]
For God is Oft-Forgiving,
Most Merciful:

29. That the People of
The Book may know
That they have no power[5329]
Whatever over the Grace
Of God, that (His) Grace
Is (entirely) in his hand,
To bestow it on
Whomsoever He wills.
27 For God is the Lord
30 Of Grace abounding.

وَيَجْعَلْ لَّكُمْ نُوْرًا
تَمْشُوْنَ بِهٖ وَيَغْفِرْ لَكُمْ ؕ
وَاللّٰهُ غَفُوْرٌ رَّحِيْمٌ ۙ

٢٩- لِّئَلَّا يَعْلَمَ اَهْلُ الْكِتٰبِ
اَلَّا يَقْدِرُوْنَ عَلٰى شَىْءٍ مِّنْ فَضْلِ اللّٰهِ
وَاَنَّ الْفَضْلَ بِيَدِ اللّٰهِ
يُؤْتِيْهِ مَنْ يَّشَآءُ ؕ
ع وَاللّٰهُ ذُو الْفَضْلِ الْعَظِيْمِ ۝

5327. As this refers to the Christians and the People of the Book, the following saying of Christ in his last days may interest them: "'Yet a little while is the light with you. Walk while ye have the light, lest darkness come upon you... While ye have the light, believe in the light, that ye may be the children of light . These things spake Jesus, and departed, and did hide himself from them". (John, xii. 35-36). The light of Christ's Gospel soon departed; his Church was enveloped in darkness; then came the light again, in the fuller light of Islam. And they are asked to believe in the Light, and to walk in it. *Cf.* also lvii. 12, and n. 5288 above.

5328. Any wrongs they may have committed through ignorance or misconceptions in their previous religion will be forgiven them, as they have seen the new Light and walk by it.

5329. Let not any race, or people, or community, or group, believe that they have exclusive possession of God's Grace, or that they can influence its grant or its withholding. God's Grace is free, and entirely controlled by Him, independently of any priests and privileged people. He dispenses it according to His own wise and holy Will and Plan; and to His Grace there is no limit.

INTRODUCTION TO SŪRA LVIII (*Mujādila*).

This is the second of the ten Medina Sūras referred to in the Introduction to the last Sūra. Its subject-matter is the acceptance of a woman's Plea on behalf of herself and her children (see n. 5330 to lviii. 1 below), and a condemnation of all secret counsels and intrigues in the Muslim Brotherhood.

The date is somewhat close to that of S. xxxiii, say between A.H. 5 and A.H. 7.

Summary.—All false pretences, especially those that degrade a woman's position, are condemned,—as well as secret consultations between men and intrigues with falsehood, mischief, and sedition. (lviii. 1-22, and C. 237).

C. 237.—Let not false pretences or superstitions
(lviii. 1-22.) Degrade the position of woman. Eschew
Secret plottings and secret counsels.
Observe order and decorum in public assemblies,
And seek not in selfish pride to engage
Your Leader's private attention. It is wrong
To turn to the enemies of God for friendship:
They make their oaths a cloak for wrong-doing,
And keep back men from the Right. But none
Can resist the Power or the Judgment of God.
The righteous seek only His Good Pleasure,
And rejoice therein as their highest Achievement.

Sūra LVIII.

Mujādila, or The Woman who Pleads.

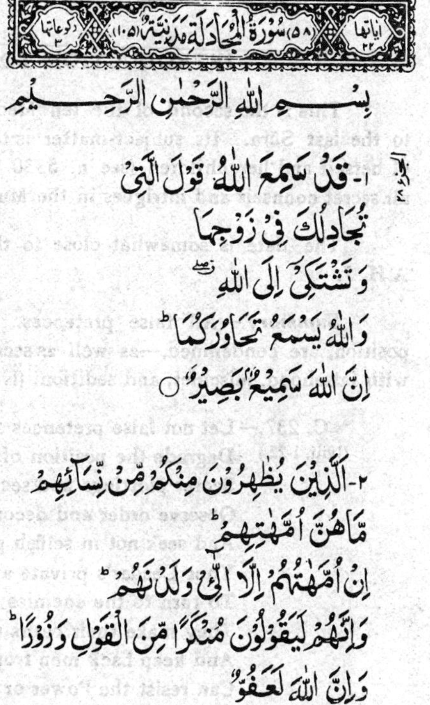

In the name of God, Most Gracious, Most Merciful.

1. God has indeed
Heard (and accepted) the statement
Of the woman who pleads[5330]
With thee concerning her husband
And carries her complaint
(In prayer) to God:
And God (always) hears
The arguments between both[5331]
Sides among you: for God
Hears and sees (all things).

2. If any men among you
Divorce their wives by *Zihār*[5332]
(Calling them mothers),
They cannot be their mothers:
None can be their mothers
Except those who gave them
Birth. And in fact
They use words (both) iniquitous[5333]
And false: but truly
God is One that blots out[5334]

5330. The immediate occasion was what happened to Khaula bint Tha'laba, wife of Aus son of Ṣāmit. Though in Islam, he divorced her by an old Pagan custom: the formula was known as *Ẓihār*, and consisted of the words "Thou art to me as the back of my mother". This was held by Pagan custom to imply a divorce and freed the husband from any responsibility for conjugal duties, but did not leave the wife free to leave the husband's home, or to contract a second marriage. Such a custom was in any case degrading to a woman. It was particularly hard on Khaula, for she loved her husband and pleaded that she had little children whom she had no resources herself to support and whom under *Ẓihār* her husband was not bound to support. She urged her plea to the Prophet and in prayer to God. Her just plea was accepted, and this iniquitous custom, based on false words, was abolished. See also n. 3670 to xxxiii. 4.

5331. For He is a just God, and will not allow human customs or pretences to trample on the just rights of the weakest of His creatures.

5332. See n. 5330 above.

5333. Such words are false in fact and iniquitous, inasmuch as they are unfair to the wife and unseemly in decent society.

5334. *Cf.* iv. 99 and xxii. 60. Were it not that God in His Mercy makes allowances for our weaknesses and the various grades of motives that actuate us, such conduct would be inexpiable. But He prescribes expiation as in the next verse, because He wishes to blot out what is wrong and give us a chance to reform by His forgiveness.

(Sins), and forgives
(Again and again).

غَفُورٌ ○

3. But those who divorce
Their wives by *Zihār*,
Then wish to go back[5335]
On the words they uttered,—
(It is ordained that
Such a one)
Should free a slave
Before they touch each other:
This are ye admonished
To perform: and God is
Well-acquainted with (all)
That ye do.

٣- وَالَّذِينَ يُظٰهِرُونَ مِن نِّسَآئِهِمْ
ثُمَّ يَعُودُونَ لِمَا قَالُوا
فَتَحْرِيرُ رَقَبَةٍ
مِّن قَبْلِ أَن يَتَمَآسَّا ط
ذٰلِكُمْ تُوعَظُونَ بِهِ ط
وَاللَّهُ بِمَا تَعْمَلُونَ خَبِيرٌ ○

4. And if any has not
(The wherewithal),[5336]
He should fast for
Two months consecutively
Before they touch each other.
But if any is unable
To do so, he should feed
Sixty indigent ones.[5337]
This, that ye may show
Your faith in God[5338]

٤- فَمَن لَّمْ يَجِدْ فَصِيَامُ شَهْرَيْنِ مُتَتَابِعَيْنِ
مِن قَبْلِ أَن يَتَمَآسَّا ج
فَمَن لَّمْ يَسْتَطِعْ
فَإِطْعَامُ سِتِّينَ مِسْكِينًا ط
ذٰلِكَ لِتُؤْمِنُوا بِاللَّهِ

5335. If *Zihār* were to be ignored as if the words were never uttered, it would mean that men may foolishly resort to it without penalty. It is therefore recognised in respect of the penalty which the man incurs, but safeguards the woman's rights. She can sue for maintenance for herself and her children, but her husband could not claim his conjugal rights. If it was a hasty act and he repented of it, he could not claim his conjugal rights until after the performance of his penalty as provided below. If she loved him, as in Khaula's case, she could also herself sue for conjugal rights in the legal sense of the term and compel her husband to perform the penalty and resume marital relations.

5336. *Cf.* iv. 92 The penalty is: to get a slave his freedom, whether it is your own slave or you purchase his freedom from another; if that is not possible, to fast for two months consecutively (in the manner of the Ramadhān fast); if that is not possible, to feed sixty poor. See next note.

5337. There is a great deal of learned argument among the jurists as to the precise requirements of Canon Law under the term "feeding" the indigent. For example, it is laid down that half a *Ṣā'* of wheat or a full *Ṣā'* of dates or their equivalent in money would fulfil the requirements, a *Ṣā'* being a measure corresponding roughly to about 9 lbs. of wheat in weight. Others hold that a *Mudd* measure equivalent to about 2¼ lbs. would be sufficient. This would certainly be nearer the daily ration of a man. It is better to take the spirit of the text in its plain simplicity, and say that an indigent man should be given enough to eat for two meals a day. The sixty indigent ones fed for a day would be equivalent to a single individual fed for sixty days, or two for thirty days, and so on. But there is no need to go into *minutiæ* in such matters.

5338. These penalties in the alternative are prescribed, that we may show our repentance and Faith and our renunciation of "iniquity and falsehood" (verse 2 above), whatever our circumstances may be.

And His Apostle.
Those are limits (set
By) God. For those who
Reject (Him), there is
A grievous Penalty.[5339]

وَرَسُوْلِهٖ ۭ
وَتِلْكَ حُدُوْدُ اللّٰهِ ۭ
وَلِلْكٰفِرِيْنَ عَذَابٌ اَلِيْمٌ ۝

5. Those who resist God
And His Apostle will be
Humbled to dust, as were
Those before them: for We
Have already sent down
Clear Signs. And the Unbelievers
(Will have) a humiliating Penalty,—

٥- اِنَّ الَّذِيْنَ يُحَاۗدُّوْنَ اللّٰهَ وَرَسُوْلَهٗ
كُبِتُوْا كَمَا كُبِتَ الَّذِيْنَ مِنْ قَبْلِهِمْ
وَقَدْ اَنْزَلْنَآ اٰيٰتٍۢ بَيِّنٰتٍ ۭ
وَلِلْكٰفِرِيْنَ عَذَابٌ مُّهِيْنٌ ۝

6. On the Day that
God will raise them
All up (again) and show
Them the truth (and meaning)[5340]
Of their conduct. God has
Reckoned its (value), though
They may have forgotten it,
For God is Witness
To all things.

٦- يَوْمَ يَبْعَثُهُمُ اللّٰهُ جَمِيْعًا
فَيُنَبِّئُهُمْ بِمَا عَمِلُوْا ۭ
اَحْصٰىهُ اللّٰهُ وَنَسُوْهُ ۭ
وَاللّٰهُ عَلٰي كُلِّ شَيْءٍ شَهِيْدٌ ۝ ع

SECTION 2.

7. Seest thou not that
God doth know (all) that is
In the heavens and
On earth? There is not
A secret consultation
Between three, but He
Makes the fourth among them,—[5341]
Nor between five but

٧- اَلَمْ تَرَ اَنَّ اللّٰهَ يَعْلَمُ
مَا فِي السَّمٰوٰتِ وَمَا فِي الْاَرْضِ ۭ
مَا يَكُوْنُ مِنْ نَّجْوٰى ثَلٰثَةٍ اِلَّا هُوَ
رَابِعُهُمْ وَلَا خَمْسَةٍ اِلَّا

5339. It would seem that this refers to the spiritual Penalty in the Hereafter for not complying with the small penalty here prescribed. The next verse would then refer to the bigger "humiliating Penalty" for "resistance" to God's Law generally.

5340. This phrase, "God will tell them the truth of their deeds (or their doings or their conduct)" occurs frequently. See v. 51, n. 762; v. 108, n. 811; vi. 60; ix. 94; etc. In this life there is a certain mist or illusion in our spiritual sight. We see things from different angles and dispute about them; we hide real motives, and pretend to virtues which we do not possess; others may attribute such virtues to us, and we may come to believe it ourselves; we conceive likes and hatreds on insufficient grounds; we forget what we should remember, and remember what we should forget. Our vision is narrow, and our values are false. On the Day of Account all this will be remedied. Not only will true values be restored, but we shall ourselves see the inwardness of things in our own lives, which we never saw before.

5341. Secrecy is a relative and limited term among ourselves. There is nothing hidden or unknown to God. Usually secrecy implies fear or distrust, plotting or wrong-doing. But all is open before God's sight.

He makes the sixth,—
Nor between fewer nor more,
But He is in their midst,
Wheresoever they be:
In the end will He
Tell them the truth
Of their conduct, on the Day
Of Judgment. For God
Has full knowledge
Of all things.

هُوَ سَادِسُهُمْ
وَلَآ أَدْنَىٰ مِن ذَٰلِكَ وَلَآ أَكْثَرَ
إِلَّا هُوَ مَعَهُمْ أَيْنَ مَا كَانُوا
ثُمَّ يُنَبِّئُهُم بِمَا عَمِلُوا يَوْمَ الْقِيَٰمَةِ
إِنَّ اللَّهَ بِكُلِّ شَيْءٍ عَلِيمٌ ○

8. Turnest thou not thy sight
Towards those who were
Forbidden secret counsels[5342]
Yet revert to that which
They were forbidden (to do)?
And they hold secret counsels
Among themselves for iniquity
And hostility, and disobedience
To the Apostle. And when
They come to thee,
They salute thee,[5343]
Not as God salutes thee,
(But in crooked ways):
And they say to themselves,
"Why does not God
Punish us for our words?"[5344]
Enough for them is Hell:
In it will they burn,
And evil is that destination!

٨- أَلَمْ تَرَ إِلَى الَّذِينَ نُهُوا عَنِ النَّجْوَىٰ
ثُمَّ يَعُودُونَ لِمَا نُهُوا عَنْهُ
وَيَتَنَٰجَوْنَ بِالْإِثْمِ وَالْعُدْوَٰنِ
وَمَعْصِيَتِ الرَّسُولِ
وَإِذَا جَاءُوكَ حَيَّوْكَ
بِمَا لَمْ يُحَيِّكَ بِهِ اللَّهُ
وَيَقُولُونَ فِي أَنفُسِهِمْ
لَوْلَا يُعَذِّبُنَا اللَّهُ بِمَا نَقُولُ
حَسْبُهُمْ جَهَنَّمُ يَصْلَوْنَهَا
فَبِئْسَ الْمَصِيرُ ○

9. O ye who believe!
When ye hold secret counsel,
Do it not for iniquity
And hostility, and disobedience

٩- يَٰٓأَيُّهَا الَّذِينَ ءَامَنُوٓا إِذَا تَنَٰجَيْتُمْ فَلَا
تَتَنَٰجَوْا بِالْإِثْمِ وَالْعُدْوَٰنِ وَمَعْصِيَتِ

5342. When the Muslim Brotherhood was acquiring strength in Medina, and the forces of disruption were being discomfited in open fight against the Messenger of Righteousness, the wicked resorted to duplicity and secret intrigues, in which the ringleaders were the disaffected Jews and the Hypocrites, whose machinations have been frequently referred to in the Qur-ān. *E.g.* see ii. 8-16; and iv. 142-145.

5343. The salutation of God was (and is) "Peace!" But the enemies, who had not the courage to fight openly, often twisted the words, and by using a word like "*Sām*", which meant "Death!" or "Destruction!" instead of "*Salām!*" (Peace!), they thought they were secretly venting their spite and yet apparently using a polite form of salutation. *Cf.* ii. 106, and n. 107, where another similar trick is exposed.

5344. The enemies derisively enjoyed their trick (see last note) according to their own perverted mentality. They asked blasphemously, "Why does not God punish us?" The answer is given: there *is* a Punishment, far greater than they imagine: it will come in good time: it will be the final Punishment after Judgment: it is delayed in order to give them a chance of repentance and reformation.

To the Prophet; but do it
For righteousness and self-restraint;[5345]
And fear God, to Whom
Ye shall be brought back.

الرَّسُولِ وَتَنَاجَوْا بِالْبِرِّ وَالتَّقْوٰى ؕ
وَاتَّقُوا اللّٰهَ الَّذِيْٓ اِلَيْهِ تُحْشَرُوْنَ ○

10. Secret counsels are only
(Inspired) by the Evil One,
In order that he may
Cause grief to the Believers;
But he cannot harm them
In the least, except as[5346]
God permits; and on God
Let the Believers
Put their trust.

١٠- اِنَّمَا النَّجْوٰى مِنَ الشَّيْطٰنِ
لِيَحْزُنَ الَّذِيْنَ اٰمَنُوْا
وَلَيْسَ بِضَآرِّهِمْ شَيْـًٔا اِلَّا بِاِذْنِ اللّٰهِ ؕ
وَعَلَى اللّٰهِ فَلْيَتَوَكَّلِ الْمُؤْمِنُوْنَ ○

11. O ye who believe!
When ye are told
To make room
In the assemblies,[5347]
(Spread out and) make room:
(Ample) room will God provide
For you. And when
Ye are told to rise up,[5348]
Rise up: God will
Raise up, to (suitable) ranks
(And degrees), those of you
Who believe and who have

١١- يٰٓاَيُّهَا الَّذِيْنَ اٰمَنُوْٓا اِذَا قِيْلَ لَكُمْ
تَفَسَّحُوْا فِي الْمَجٰلِسِ
فَافْسَحُوْا يَفْسَحِ اللّٰهُ لَكُمْ ۚ
وَاِذَا قِيْلَ انْشُزُوْا فَانْشُزُوْا
يَرْفَعِ اللّٰهُ
الَّذِيْنَ اٰمَنُوْا مِنْكُمْ ۙ وَالَّذِيْنَ

5345. Ordinarily secrecy implies deeds of darkness, something which men have to hide; see the next verse. But there are good deeds which may be concerted and done in secret: *e g.* charity, or the prevention of mischief, or the defeat of the dark plots of evil. The determining factor is the motive. Is the man doing some wrong or venting his spite, or trying to disobey a lawful command? Or is he doing some good, which out of modesty or self-renunciation he does not want known, or is he in a righteous cause defeating the machinations of Evil, which may involve great sacrifice of himself?

5346. Evil can harm no one who is good, except in so far as (1) there is some question of trial in God's Universal Plan, or (2) what appears to be harm may be real good. Nothing happens without God's will and permission. And we must always trust Him, and not our cleverness or any adventitious circumstances that draw us the least bit from the path of rectitude.

5347. Even when a great man or a Leader comes into an Assembly, we are not to press forward without discipline, as it causes inconvenience to him and detriment to public business. Nor are we to shut out other people who have equal rights to be in the Assembly. We must spread out, for God's earth is spacious, and so are our opportunities.

5348. Rising up is a mark of respect. Just as those who obey soon become worthy of command, so those who honour where honour is due, become themselves worthy of honour, in various degrees according to their capacities. "Rise up" may also here imply: 'when the Assembly is dismissed, do not loiter about'.

Been granted (mystic)
Knowledge.[5349]
And God is well-acquainted
With all ye do.

أُوتُوا الْعِلْمَ دَرَجَٰتٍ ط
وَاللَّهُ بِمَا تَعْمَلُونَ خَبِيرٌ ○

12. O ye who believe!
When ye consult
The Apostle in private,[5350]
Spend something in charity
Before your private consultation.
That will be best for you,
And most conducive
To purity (of conduct).[5351]
But if ye find not
(The wherewithal), God is
Oft-Forgiving, Most Merciful.

١٢- يَٰٓأَيُّهَا الَّذِينَ ءَامَنُوٓا إِذَا نَٰجَيْتُمُ الرَّسُولَ
فَقَدِّمُوا بَيْنَ يَدَىْ نَجْوَىٰكُمْ صَدَقَةً ط
ذَٰلِكَ خَيْرٌ لَّكُمْ وَأَطْهَرُ ط
فَإِن لَّمْ تَجِدُوا
فَإِنَّ اللَّهَ غَفُورٌ رَّحِيمٌ ○

13. Is it that ye are
Afraid of spending sums[5352]
In charity before your
Private consultation (with him)?

١٣- ءَأَشْفَقْتُمْ أَن تُقَدِّمُوا
بَيْنَ يَدَىْ نَجْوَىٰكُمْ صَدَقَٰتٍ ط

5349. Faith makes all people equal in the Kingdom of God, as regards the essentials of citizenship in the Kingdom. But there is leadership, and rank and degree, joined with greater or less responsibility, and that depends on Knowledge,—the true knowledge and insight which Mystics seek everywhere for advancing their service and responsibility in the Kingdom of God. Honour there comes with merit, and is not to be grabbed at.

5350. In the Kingdom of God all instruction or consultation is open and free. But human nature is weak. And people want special instruction or private consultation with the Teacher from one of several motives: (1) they may have, or think they have, a special case, which they are not willing to disclose to their brethren in general; (2) they may have some sense of delicacy or dignity, which can only be satisfied by a private interview; (3) they may even be selfish enough to want to monopolise the Teacher's time. These motives are, in an ascending order, worth discouraging; and yet, considering the weakness of human nature, they cannot be reprobated to the extent of shutting out their victims from chances of improvement. It is therefore recommended that they spend something in charity for the good of their poorer brethren before they indulge in such weaknesses.

5351. The charity is a sort of expiation for their pardonable weakness. Having made some monetary sacrifice for their poorer brethren they could face them with less shame, and the charity would direct their attention to the need for purifying their motives and conduct. At the same time, this special charity is not made obligatory, lest such persons should be shut out altogether from chances of the higher teaching on account of their pardonable foibles.

5352. Note the plural here, *Ṣadaqāt*, instead of the singular, *Ṣadaqat* in verse 12 above. While people with the foibles described in n. 5350 may be willing to spend "something" (small) in charity for a special consultation occasionally, they may be frightened of spending large sums when their needs for consultation may be numerous. What is to be done then? Are they to be shut out altogether? No. They are asked to be punctilious in the discharge of their normal duties of at least normal regular prayers and regular charity, "if God forgives you", *i.e.* if God's Messenger relieves them of further special contributions such as those noted in verse 12. This condition, "if God forgives you", provides the safeguard against the abuse of the privilege. The apostle would know in each case what is best for the individual and for the community.

If, then, ye do not so,
And God forgives you,
Then (at least) establish
Regular prayer; practise[5353]
Regular charity; and obey
God and His Apostle.
And God is well-acquainted
With all that ye do.

فَإِذْ لَمْ تَفْعَلُوا وَتَابَ اللَّهُ عَلَيْكُمْ
فَأَقِيمُوا الصَّلَوٰةَ وَآتُوا الزَّكَوٰةَ
وَأَطِيعُوا اللَّهَ وَرَسُولَهُ ۚ
وَاللَّهُ خَبِيرٌ بِمَا تَعْمَلُونَ ۝

SECTION 3.

14. Turnest thou not
Thy attention to those[5354]
Who turn (in friendship)
To such as have the Wrath
Of God upon them?[5355]
They are neither of you
Nor of them, and they
Swear to falsehood knowingly.[5356]

۱۴- أَلَمْ تَرَ إِلَى الَّذِينَ
تَوَلَّوْا قَوْمًا غَضِبَ اللَّهُ عَلَيْهِمْ ۖ
مَا هُمْ مِنْكُمْ وَلَا مِنْهُمْ
وَيَحْلِفُونَ عَلَى الْكَذِبِ وَهُمْ يَعْلَمُونَ ۝

15. God has prepared for them
A severe Penalty: evil
Indeed are their deeds.

۱۵- أَعَدَّ اللَّهُ لَهُمْ عَذَابًا شَدِيدًا ۖ
إِنَّهُمْ سَاءَ مَا كَانُوا يَعْمَلُونَ ۝

16. They have made their oaths
A screen (for their misdeeds):
Thus they obstruct (men)[5357]
From the Path of God:
Therefore shall they have
A humiliating Penalty.

۱۶- اتَّخَذُوا أَيْمَانَهُمْ جُنَّةً
فَصَدُّوا عَنْ سَبِيلِ اللَّهِ
فَلَهُمْ عَذَابٌ مُهِينٌ ۝

17. Of no profit whatever
To them, against God,
Will be their riches[5358]
Nor their sons:

۱۷- لَنْ تُغْنِيَ عَنْهُمْ
أَمْوَالُهُمْ وَلَا أَوْلَادُهُمْ مِنَ اللَّهِ شَيْئًا ۖ

5353. *Zakāt*, which I have translated "regular charity", was instituted about A.H. 2.

5354. This refers to the Hypocrites of Medina who pretended to be in Islam but intrigued with the Jews. See references as given in n. 5342 above.

5355. By this time the Jews of Medina and the Jewish tribes around had become actively hostile to Islam, and were being sharply called to account for their treachery.

5356. They knew that as Muslims their duty was to refrain from the intrigues of the enemies of Islam and to assist Islam against them.

5357. A false man, by swearing that he is true, makes his falsehood all the more heinous. He stands in the way of other people accepting Truth. He gives a handle to the cynics and the sceptics.

5358. They may arrogantly boast of riches and alliances and followers in man-power. But what are such worldly advantages before the Throne of the Disposer of all events? They must come to utter misery.

They will be Companions
Of the Fire, to dwell
Therein (for aye)!

أُولَٰئِكَ أَصْحَٰبُ ٱلنَّارِ ۖ هُمْ فِيهَا خَٰلِدُونَ ○

18. One Day will God
Raise them all up
(For Judgment): then
Will they swear to Him[5359]
As they swear to you:
And they think that they
Have something (to stand upon).
No, indeed! they are
But liars!

١٨- يَوْمَ يَبْعَثُهُمُ ٱللَّهُ جَمِيعًا فَيَحْلِفُونَ لَهُۥ كَمَا يَحْلِفُونَ لَكُمْ ۖ وَيَحْسَبُونَ أَنَّهُمْ عَلَىٰ شَىْءٍ ۚ أَلَآ إِنَّهُمْ هُمُ ٱلْكَٰذِبُونَ ○

19. The Evil One has
Got the better of them:[5360]
So he has made them
Lose the remembrance
Of God. They are the Party
Of the Evil One. Truly,
It is the Party
Of the Evil One
That will perish!

١٩- ٱسْتَحْوَذَ عَلَيْهِمُ ٱلشَّيْطَٰنُ فَأَنسَىٰهُمْ ذِكْرَ ٱللَّهِ ۚ أُولَٰئِكَ حِزْبُ ٱلشَّيْطَٰنِ ۚ أَلَآ إِنَّ حِزْبَ ٱلشَّيْطَٰنِ هُمُ ٱلْخَٰسِرُونَ ○

20. Those who resist
God and His Apostle
Will be among those
Most humiliated.[5361]

٢٠- إِنَّ ٱلَّذِينَ يُحَآدُّونَ ٱللَّهَ وَرَسُولَهُۥٓ أُولَٰئِكَ فِى ٱلْأَذَلِّينَ ○

21. God has decreed:
"It is I and My apostles
Who must prevail":
For God is One
Full of strength,
Able to enforce His Will.[5362]

٢١- كَتَبَ ٱللَّهُ لَأَغْلِبَنَّ أَنَا۠ وَرُسُلِىٓ ۚ إِنَّ ٱللَّهَ قَوِىٌّ عَزِيزٌ ○

5359. When Judgment is established, and before they realise the Truth, they may think (as now) that some oaths or excuses will save them. But they have not now—much less will they have then—any footing to stand upon. Falsehood is falsehood, and must perish. They must learn the worthlessness of their falsehood.

5360. Man's original nature as created by God is good (xxx. 30, and n. 3541). It is because man, in spite of the warnings he has received, allows Evil to get the mastery over him, that man forgets God and the divine qualities which God gave him. The result of the perversion is that man becomes a partisan of Evil, and as such dooms himself to perdition.

5361. There are various degrees of humiliation in the final state in the spiritual world. But the worst is the humiliation of being numbered among those who ignominiously attempted to resist the Irresistible.

5362. For the meaning of *'Azīz*, see n. 2818 to xxii. 40.

22. Thou wilt not find
Any people who believe
In God and the Last Day,
Loving those who resist
God and His Apostle,
Even though they were
Their fathers or their sons,[5363]
Or their brothers, or
Their kindred. For such
He has written Faith[5364]
In their hearts, and strengthened
Them with a spirit[5365]
From Himself. And He
Will admit them to Gardens
Beneath which Rivers flow,
To dwell therein (for ever).
God will be well pleased
With them, and they with Him.[5366]
They are the Party[5367]
Of God. Truly it is
The Party of God that
Will achieve Felicity.

٢٢- لا تجد قوما يؤمنون بالله واليوم الآخر
يوادون من حاد الله ورسوله
ولو كانوا آباءهم أو أبناءهم
أو إخوانهم أو عشيرتهم
أولئك كتب في قلوبهم الإيمان
وأيدهم بروح منه
ويدخلهم جنت
تجري من تحتها الأنهر خلدين فيها
رضي الله عنهم ورضوا عنه
أولئك حزب الله
ألا إن حزب الله هم المفلحون ○

5363. If any one believes in God and His goodness and justice, and in the Hereafter, in which all true values will be restored he will never love evil or wrong-doing or rebellion against God, even if these things are found in his nearest kith and kin.

5364. Faith in God is indelibly written on the tablets of their hearts, and they can never be false to God.

5365. *Cf.* ii. 87 and 253, where it is said that God strengthened the Prophet Jesus with the holy spirit. Here we learn that all good and righteous men are strengthened by God with the holy spirit. If anything, the phrase used here is stronger, " a spirit from Himself ". Whenever any one offers his heart in faith and purity to God, God accepts it, engraves that Faith on the seeker's heart, and further fortifies him with the divine spirit, which we can no more define adequately than we can define in human language the nature and attributes of God.

5366. Again we have the mystic doctrine of God's Good Pleasure as the highest goal of man, the spiritual heaven which he achieves by a life of purity and faith. He not only attains God's Good Pleasure as the crown of his felicity, but his own nature is so far transformed to the pattern of God's original creation that his own good pleasure is in nothing but in God's Good Pleasure. The mutual good pleasure shows the heights to which man can attain.

5367. This is in antithesis to the Party of the Evil One, mentioned in verse 19 above. That Party of Evil will perish, but while it has its run in the scheme of the present world, the Party of Truth and Reality may be figuratively called the Party of God, even though all Creation is God's in another sense.

INTRODUCTION TO SŪRA LIX (*Hashr*).

This is the third of the series of ten short Medina Sūras, dealing each with a special point in the life of the Ummat: see Introduction to S. lvii. The special theme here is how treachery to the Ummat on the part of its enemies recoils on the enemies themselves, while it strengthens the bond between the different sections of the Ummat itself, and this is illustrated by the story of the expulsion of the Jewish tribe of the Banū Nadhīr in Rabī' I, A.H. 4.

This fixes the date of the Sūra.

Summary.—The expulsion of the treacherous Jews from the neighbourhood of Medina was smoothly accomplished: their reliance on their fortified positions and on the faith of their allies in treachery proved futile. But the internal bonds in the Ummat were strengthened. Such is the wisdom of God, Lord of the Most Beautiful Names. (lix. 1-24, and C. 238).

C. 238.—God's wisdom foils the treachery of men,
(lix. 1-24.) And makes the path smooth for Believers who strive
Even against odds. Against God's decrees
All resistance is vain. In property taken
From the enemy, let those in need have a share,
And those who sacrifice their all for the Cause.
But those who lend a helping hand
In the hour of need do it for love
And crave no reward, nor feel the least
Envy or jealousy. They all rejoice
That the Brotherhood should thrive. Not so
The Hypocrites: they are false even among
Themselves. Perdition is the end
Of all evil. But the Good and Faithful
Will achieve felicity. Such is the power
Of Truth and God's Revelation. God!
There is no god but He!—the Good,
The Glorious, the Irresistible!
All Creation sings His praise,—
The Exalted in Might, the Wise!

Sūra LIX.

Ḥashr, or The Gathering (or Banishment, lix. 2-3).

In the name of God, Most Gracious, Most Merciful.

بِسْمِ اللّٰهِ الرَّحْمٰنِ الرَّحِيْمِ

1. Whatever is
In the heavens and
On earth, let it declare
The Praises and Glory [5368]
Of God: for He is
The Exalted in Might,
The Wise.

١- سَبَّحَ لِلّٰهِ
مَا فِي السَّمٰوٰتِ وَمَا فِي الْاَرْضِ ۚ
وَهُوَ الْعَزِيْزُ الْحَكِيْمُ ۝

2. It is He Who got out
The Unbelievers among
The People of the Book [5369]
From their homes
At the first gathering
(Of the forces).
Little did ye think
That they would get out: [5370]
And they thought
That their fortresses
Would defend them from God!
But the (Wrath of) God

٢- هُوَ الَّذِيْٓ اَخْرَجَ الَّذِيْنَ كَفَرُوْا مِنْ
اَهْلِ الْكِتٰبِ مِنْ دِيَارِهِمْ
لِاَوَّلِ الْحَشْرِ ؕ
مَا ظَنَنْتُمْ اَنْ يَّخْرُجُوْا
وَظَنُّوْٓا اَنَّهُمْ مَّانِعَتُهُمْ حُصُوْنُهُمْ مِّنَ اللّٰهِ
فَاَتٰىهُمُ اللّٰهُ

وقف النبي عليه الصلوة والسلام

5368. This verse, introducing the Sūra, is identical with lvii. 1, introducing S. lvii. The theme of both is the wonderful working of God's Plan and Providence. In the one case it referred to the conquest of Mecca and taught the lesson of humility. In this case it refers to the dislodgment of the treacherous Banū Nadhīr from their nest of intrigue in the neighbourhood of Medina, practically without a blow. See next note.

5369. This refers to the Jewish tribe of the Banū Nadhīr whose intrigues and treachery nearly undid the Muslim cause during the perilous days of the battle of Uḥud in Shawwāl, A.H. 3. Four months after, in Rabī' I, A.H. 4, steps were taken against them. They were asked to leave the strategic position which they occupied, about three miles south of Medina, endangering the very existence of the Ummat in Medina. At first they demurred, relying on their fortresses and on their secret alliances with the Pagans of Mecca and the Hypocrites of Medina. But when the Muslim army was gathered to punish them and actually besieged them for some days, their allies stirred not a finger in their aid, and they were wise enough to leave. Most of them joined their brethren in Syria, which they were permitted to do, after being disarmed. Some of them joined their brethren in Khaibar: see n. 3705 to xxxiii. 27. The Banū Nadhīr richly deserved punishment, but their lives were spared, and they were allowed to carry away their goods and chattels.

5370. That is, without actual hostilities, and the shedding of precious Muslim blood.

Came to them from quarters[5371]
From which they little
Expected (it), and cast
Terror into their hearts,
So that they destroyed
Their dwellings by their own[5372]
Hands and the hands
Of the Believers.
Take warning, then,
O ye with eyes (to see)!

مِنْ حَيْثُ لَمْ يَحْتَسِبُوْا ق
وَقَذَفَ فِيْ قُلُوْبِهِمُ الرُّعْبَ
يُخْرِبُوْنَ بُيُوْتَهُمْ بِأَيْدِيْهِمْ
وَأَيْدِي الْمُؤْمِنِيْنَ ق
فَاعْتَبِرُوْا يٰأُولِي الْأَبْصَارِ ○

3. And had it not been
That God had decreed
Banishment for them,[5373]
He would certainly have
Punished them in this world:
And in the Hereafter
They shall (certainly) have
The Punishment of the Fire.

٣- وَلَوْلَا أَنْ كَتَبَ اللّٰهُ عَلَيْهِمُ الْجَلَاءَ
لَعَذَّبَهُمْ فِي الدُّنْيَا ط
وَلَهُمْ فِي الْاٰخِرَةِ
عَذَابُ النَّارِ ○

4. That is because they
Resisted God and His Apostle:
And if any one resists God,[5374]
Verily God is severe
In Punishment.

٤- ذٰلِكَ بِأَنَّهُمْ شَاقُّوا اللّٰهَ وَرَسُوْلَهُ ج
وَمَنْ يُشَاقِّ اللّٰهَ
فَإِنَّ اللّٰهَ شَدِيْدُ الْعِقَابِ ○

5371. They had played a double game. Originally they were sworn allies of the Medina Muslims under the holy Prophet, but they secretly intrigued with the Mecca Pagans under Abū Sufyān and the Medina Hypocrites. They even tried treacherously to take the life of the Prophet while he was on a visit to them, breaking both the laws of hospitality and their own sworn alliance. They thought the Pagan Quraish of Mecca and the Hypocrites of Medina would help them, but they did not help them. On the contrary the eleven days' siege showed them their own helplessness. Their supplies were cut off; the exigencies of the siege necessitated the destruction of their outlying palm trees; and the unexpected turn in their fortunes disheartened them. Their hearts were struck with terror, and they capitulated. But they laid waste their homes before they left: see next note.

5372. Their lives were spared, and they were allowed ten days in which to remove themselves, their families, and such goods as they could carry. In order to leave no habitations for the Muslims they demolished their own houses and laid waste their property, to complete the destruction which the operations of war had already caused at the hands of the besieging force of the Muslims.

5373. Banishment was a comparatively mild punishment for them, but the Providence of God had decreed that a chance should be given to them even though they were a treacherous foe. Within two years, their brethren the Banū Quraiza showed that they had not profited by their example, and had to be dealt with in another way: see xxxiii. 26 and notes.

5374. The punishment of the Banū Nadhir was because in breaking their plighted word with the Apostle and in actively resisting God's Message and supporting the enemies of that Message, they rebelled against His holy Will. For such treason and rebellion the punishment is severe, and yet in this case it was seasoned with Mercy.

5. Whether ye cut down
(O ye Muslims !)
The tender palm-trees,
Or ye left them standing
On their roots, it was [5375]
By leave of God, and
In order that He might [5376]
Cover with shame
The rebellious transgressors.

٥- مَا قَطَعْتُم مِّن لِّينَةٍ
أَوْ تَرَكْتُمُوهَا قَائِمَةً عَلَىٰ أُصُولِهَا
فَبِإِذْنِ اللَّهِ
وَلِيُخْزِيَ الْفَاسِقِينَ ○

6. What God has bestowed
On His Apostle (and taken
Away) from them—for this
Ye made no expedition
With either cavalry or camelry : [5377]
But God gives power
To His apostles over
Any He pleases : and God [5378]
Has power over all things.

٦- وَمَا أَفَاءَ اللَّهُ عَلَىٰ رَسُولِهِ مِنْهُمْ
فَمَا أَوْجَفْتُمْ عَلَيْهِ مِنْ خَيْلٍ وَلَا رِكَابٍ
وَلَٰكِنَّ اللَّهَ يُسَلِّطُ رُسُلَهُ عَلَىٰ مَن يَشَاءُ
وَاللَّهُ عَلَىٰ كُلِّ شَيْءٍ قَدِيرٌ ○

7. What God has bestowed [5379]
On His Apostle (and taken
Away) from the people [5380]
Of the townships,—belongs

٧- مَّا أَفَاءَ اللَّهُ عَلَىٰ رَسُولِهِ
مِنْ أَهْلِ الْقُرَىٰ

5375. The unnecessary cutting down of fruit trees or destruction of crops, or any wanton destruction whatever in war, is forbidden by the law and practice of Islam. But some destruction may be necessary for putting pressure on the enemy, and to that extent it is allowed. But as far as possible, consistently with that objective of military operations, such trees should not be cut down. Both these principles are in accordance with the Divine Will, and were followed by the Muslims in their expedition.

5376. The arrogance of the Banū Nadhīr had to be humbled, and their power for mischief destroyed.

5377. Neither cavalry nor troops mounted on camels were employed in the siege. In fact the enemy surrendered at the first onset. See lix. 2, and n. 5369 above.

5378. God accomplishes His purpose in various ways, according to His wise and holy Will and Plan. In some cases a fight is necessary. In some cases the godly attain their objective and overawe the forces of evil without actual fighting.

5379. The Jews had originally come from outside Arabia, and seized on the land near Medina. They refused to adapt themselves to the people of Arabia, and were in fact a thorn in the side of the genuine Arabs of Medina. Their dispossession is therefore a restoration of the land to its original people. But the word "*Fai*" is here understood in a technical sense, as meaning property abandoned by the enemy or taken from him without a formal war. In that sense it is distinguished from "*Anfāl*", or spoils, taken after actual fighting, about which see viii 1 and 41.

5380. "*The people of the townships*" : the townships were the Jewish settlements round Medina, of the Banū Nadhīr, and possibly of other tribes. *Cf.* the "townships" mentioned in lix. 14 below. The reference cannot be to the Wādī-ul-Qurā (Valley of Towns), now Madāin Ṣāliḥ, which was subjugated after Khaibar and Fadak in A.H. 7, unless this verse is later than the rest of the Sūra.

To God,—to His Apostle[5381]
And to kindred and orphans,
The needy and the wayfarer;
In order that it may not
(Merely) make a circuit
Between the wealthy among you.
So take what the Apostle
Assigns to you, and deny
Yourselves that which he
Withholds from you.
And fear God; for God
Is strict in Punishment.

فَلِلّٰهِ وَلِلرَّسُوْلِ وَلِذِى الْقُرْبٰى وَالْيَتٰمٰى
وَالْمَسٰكِيْنِ وَابْنِ السَّبِيْلِ ۙ
كَىْ لَا يَكُوْنَ دُوْلَةً ۢ بَيْنَ الْاَغْنِيَآءِ مِنْكُمْ ؕ
وَمَآ اٰتٰىكُمُ الرَّسُوْلُ فَخُذُوْهُ ۚ
وَمَا نَهٰىكُمْ عَنْهُ فَانْتَهُوْا ۚ
وَاتَّقُوا اللّٰهَ ؕ اِنَّ اللّٰهَ شَدِيْدُ الْعِقَابِ ○

8. (Some part is due)
To the indigent Muhājirs,[5382]
Those who were expelled
From their homes and their
property,
While seeking Grace from God
And (His) Good Pleasure,
And aiding God and His Apostle:
Such are indeed
The sincere ones;—

٨- لِلْفُقَرَآءِ الْمُهٰجِرِيْنَ
الَّذِيْنَ اُخْرِجُوْا مِنْ دِيَارِهِمْ وَاَمْوَالِهِمْ
يَبْتَغُوْنَ فَضْلًا مِّنَ اللّٰهِ وَرِضْوَانًا
وَّيَنْصُرُوْنَ اللّٰهَ وَرَسُوْلَهٗ ؕ
اُولٰٓئِكَ هُمُ الصّٰدِقُوْنَ ○

9. But those who
Before them, had homes[5383]
(In Medina)
And had adopted the Faith,—
Show their affection to such
As came to them for refuge,
And entertain no desire
In their hearts for things

٩- وَالَّذِيْنَ تَبَوَّؤُ الدَّارَ
وَالْاِيْمَانَ مِنْ قَبْلِهِمْ
يُحِبُّوْنَ مَنْ هَاجَرَ اِلَيْهِمْ
وَلَا يَجِدُوْنَ فِىْ صُدُوْرِهِمْ حَاجَةً مِّمَّآ

5381. "*Belongs to God*": *i.e.*, to God's Cause; and the beneficiaries are further detailed. No shares are fixed; they depend upon circumstances, and are left to the judgment of the Leader. Compare a similar list of those entitled to Charity, in ii. 177, but the two lists refer to different circumstances and have different beneficiaries in addition to the portion common to both.

5382. The *Muhājirs* are those who forsook their homes and property in Mecca in order to assist the holy Prophet in his migration to Medina (*Hijrat*). Their devotion and sincerity were proved beyond doubt by their self-denial, and they were now to be rewarded.

5383. This refers to the *Anṣār* (the Helpers), the people of Medina, who accepted Islam when it was persecuted in Mecca, and who invited the holy Prophet to join them and become their Leader in Medina. The Hijrat was possible because of their goodwill and their generous hospitality. They entertained the Prophet and all the refugees (Muhājirs) who came with him. The most remarkable ties of full brotherhood were established between individual members of the one group and the other. Until the Ummat got its own resources, the Helpers regularly gave and the Refugees regularly received The Helpers counted it a privilege to entertain the Refugees, and even the poor vied with the rich in their spirit of self-sacrifice. When the confiscated land and property of the Banū Nadhir was divided, and the major portion was assigned to the Refugees, there was not the least jealousy on the part of the Helpers. They rejoiced in the good fortune of their brethren. And incidentally they were themselves relieved of anxiety and responsibility on their behalf.

Given to the (latter),
But give them preference
Over themselves, even though
Poverty was their (own lot).
And those saved from
The covetousness of their own
Souls,—they are the ones
That achieve prosperity.

أُوتُوا وَيُؤْثِرُونَ عَلَىٰٓ أَنْفُسِهِمْ
وَلَوْ كَانَ بِهِمْ خَصَاصَةٌ
وَمَنْ يُوقَ شُحَّ نَفْسِهِۦ
فَأُولَٰٓئِكَ هُمُ الْمُفْلِحُونَ

10. And those who came[5384]
After them say: "Our Lord!
Forgive us, and our brethren
Who came before us
Into the Faith,
And leave not,
In our hearts,
Rancour (or sense of injury)[5385]
Against those who have believed.
Our Lord! Thou art
Indeed Full of Kindness,
Most Merciful."

١٠- وَالَّذِينَ جَآءُو مِنْ بَعْدِهِمْ
يَقُولُونَ رَبَّنَا
اغْفِرْ لَنَا وَلِإِخْوَانِنَا الَّذِينَ سَبَقُونَا بِالْإِيمَانِ
وَلَا تَجْعَلْ فِي قُلُوبِنَا غِلًّا
لِلَّذِينَ آمَنُوا
رَبَّنَآ إِنَّكَ رَءُوفٌ رَحِيمٌ

SECTION 2.

11. Hast thou not observed
The Hypocrites say
To their misbelieving brethren
Among the People of the
Book?—[5386]
"If ye are expelled,
We too will go out
With you, and we will
Never hearken to any one
In your affair; and if
Ye are attacked (in fight)

١١- أَلَمْ تَرَ إِلَى الَّذِينَ نَافَقُوا يَقُولُونَ
لِإِخْوَانِهِمُ الَّذِينَ كَفَرُوا مِنْ أَهْلِ الْكِتَٰبِ
لَئِنْ أُخْرِجْتُمْ لَنَخْرُجَنَّ مَعَكُمْ
وَلَا نُطِيعُ فِيكُمْ أَحَدًا أَبَدًا
وَإِنْ قُوتِلْتُمْ

5384. *Those that came after them*: the immediate meaning would refer to later arrivals in Medina or later accessions to Islam, compared with the early Muhājirs. But the general meaning would include all future comers into the House of Islam. They pray, not only for themselves, but for all their brethren, and above all, they pray that their hearts may be purified of any desire or tendency to disparage the work or virtues of other Muslims or to feel any jealousy on account of their successes or good fortune.

5385. *Cf.* vii. 43, and n. 1021.

5386. The Jews of the Banū Nadhir had been assured by the Hypocrites of Medina of their support to their cause. They had thought that their defection from the Prophet's Cause would so weaken that cause that they would save their friends. But they never intended to undertake any act involving self-sacrifice on their part; if they had helped their Jewish friends, it was not likely that they would have succeeded; and if they had actually gone to the fight, they had neither valour nor fervour to support them, and they would have fled ignominiously before the discipline, earnestness, and Faith of the men of Islam.

We will help you ".
But God is witness [5387]
That they are indeed liars.

لَنَنْصُرَنَّكُمْ
وَاللّٰهُ يَشْهَدُ إِنَّهُمْ لَكٰذِبُوْنَ ○

12. If they are expelled,
Never will they go out
With them; and if they
Are attacked (in fight),
They will never help them;
And if they do help them,
They will turn their backs;
So they will receive no help. [5388]

١٢- لَئِنْ أُخْرِجُوْا لَا يَخْرُجُوْنَ مَعَهُمْ
وَلَئِنْ قُوْتِلُوْا لَا يَنْصُرُوْنَهُمْ
وَلَئِنْ نَّصَرُوْهُمْ لَيُوَلُّنَّ الْأَدْبَارَ
ثُمَّ لَا يُنْصَرُوْنَ ○

13. Of a truth ye are
Stronger (than they)
Because of the terror [5389]
In their hearts,
(Sent) by God.
This is because they are
Men devoid of understanding.

١٣- لَأَنْتُمْ أَشَدُّ
رَهْبَةً فِيْ صُدُوْرِهِمْ مِّنَ اللّٰهِ
ذٰلِكَ بِأَنَّهُمْ قَوْمٌ لَّا يَفْقَهُوْنَ ○

14. They will not fight you
(Even) together, except
In fortified townships,
Or from behind walls. [5390]
Strong is their fighting (spirit)
Amongst themselves:
Thou wouldst think
They were united,
But their hearts are divided: [5391]
That is because they

١٤- لَا يُقَاتِلُوْنَكُمْ جَمِيْعًا
إِلَّا فِيْ قُرًى مُّحَصَّنَةٍ أَوْ مِنْ وَّرَآءِ جُدُرٍ
بَأْسُهُمْ بَيْنَهُمْ شَدِيْدٌ
تَحْسَبُهُمْ جَمِيْعًا وَّقُلُوْبُهُمْ شَتّٰى
ذٰلِكَ بِأَنَّهُمْ

5387. For this actually happened. They never stirred a finger for the Jews, and they never intended to do so. And God knows all their motives and secrets: *cf.* xlvii. 26, n. 4850.

5388. All hopes founded on iniquity and treachery are vain and illusory. There may be honour among thieves. But there is no honour as between dishonest intriguers, and they are not likely to get any real help from any quarter.

5389. As construed here, the meaning is: 'Ye Muslims, even if ye are weak numerically, or they may have other seeming advantages, ye are really stronger than they are, because they have a wholesome fear in their minds, and God sends such fear into the hearts of wrong-doers! An alternative construction would yield the meaning: Being Unbelievers they fear you more than they fear God, because your valour they see, but in God they do not believe.

5390. They have not sufficient self-confidence or *élan* to sustain them in a fight except under material advantages or defences. Even if they join forces, they have not sufficient trust in each other to expose themselves to open fighting.

5391. 'It may be that they have a strong fighting spirit among themselves, but they have no Cause to fight for and no common objective to achieve. The Meccan Pagans want to keep their own unjust autocracy; the Medina Hypocrites wish for their own domination in Medina; and the Jews want their racial superiority established over the Arabs, of whose growing union and power they are jealous.' Their pretended alliance could not stand the strain of either a defeat or a victory. If they had been wise, they would have accepted the Cause of Unity, Faith, and Truth.

Are a people devoid
Of wisdom.

قَوْمٌ لَّا يَعْقِلُونَ ۝

15. Like those who lately[5392]
Preceded them, they have
Tasted the evil result
Of their conduct; and
(In the Hereafter there is)
For them a grievous Penalty;—

١٥- كَمَثَلِ الَّذِينَ مِن قَبْلِهِمْ قَرِيبًا
ذَاقُوا وَبَالَ أَمْرِهِمْ ۚ
وَلَهُمْ عَذَابٌ أَلِيمٌ ۝

16. (Their allies deceived them),
Like the Evil One,
When he says to man,
"Deny God": but when[5393]
(Man) denies God,
(The Evil One) says,
"I am free of thee:
I do fear God,
The Lord of the Worlds!"

١٦- كَمَثَلِ الشَّيْطَانِ
إِذْ قَالَ لِلْإِنسَانِ اكْفُرْ ۚ
فَلَمَّا كَفَرَ
قَالَ إِنِّي بَرِيءٌ مِّنكَ
إِنِّي أَخَافُ اللَّهَ رَبَّ الْعَالَمِينَ ۝

17. The end of both will be
That they will go
Into the Fire, dwelling
Therein for ever.
Such is the reward
Of the wrong-doers.

١٧- فَكَانَ عَاقِبَتَهُمَا أَنَّهُمَا فِي النَّارِ
خَالِدَيْنِ فِيهَا ۚ
وَذَٰلِكَ جَزَاءُ الظَّالِمِينَ ۝ ع

SECTION 3.

18. O ye who believe!
Fear God,[5394]

١٨- يَا أَيُّهَا الَّذِينَ آمَنُوا اتَّقُوا اللَّهَ ط

5392. The immediate reference was probably to the Jewish goldsmith tribe of the Qainuqā', who were also settled in a fortified township near Medina. They were also punished and banished for their treachery, about a month after the battle of Badr, in which the Meccan Pagans had suffered a signal defeat, in Shawwāl, A.H. 2. The Nadhir evidently did not take that lesson to heart. The general meaning is that we must learn to be on our guard against the consequences of treachery and sin. No fortuitous alliances with other men of iniquity will save us.

5393. An apt simile. Evil tempts man in all sorts of ways, and presents seductive promises and alliances to delude him into the belief that he will be saved from the consequences. The Evil One says, "Deny God": which means not merely denial in words, but denial in acts,—disobedience of God's Law, deviation from the path of rectitude. When the sinner gets well into the mire, the Evil One says cynically: "How can I help you against God? Don't you see I am afraid of Him? All our alliances and understandings were moonshine. You must bear the consequences of your own folly."

5394. The "fear of God" is akin to love; for it means the fear of offending Him or doing anything wrong that will forfeit His Good Pleasure. This is *Taqwā*, which implies self restraint, guarding ourselves from all sin, wrong, and injustice, and the positive doing of good. See ii. 2, and n. 26.

And let every soul look
To what (provision) he has[5394]
Sent forth for the morrow.
Yea, fear God :[5395-A]
For God is well-acquainted
With (all) that ye do.

وَلْتَنْظُرْ نَفْسٌ مَّا قَدَّمَتْ لِغَدٍ
وَاتَّقُوا اللّٰهَ
إِنَّ اللّٰهَ خَبِيرٌ بِمَا تَعْمَلُونَ ○

19. And be ye not like
Those who forgot God ;[5396]
And He made them forget
Their own souls ! Such
Are the rebellious transgressors !

١٩- وَلَا تَكُونُوا كَالَّذِينَ نَسُوا اللّٰهَ
فَأَنْسٰهُمْ أَنْفُسَهُمْ
أُولٰئِكَ هُمُ الْفٰسِقُونَ ○

20. Not equal are
The Companions of the Fire
And the Companions
Of the Garden :
It is the Companions
Of the Garden,
That will achieve Felicity.[5397]

٢٠- لَا يَسْتَوِي أَصْحٰبُ النَّارِ
وَأَصْحٰبُ الْجَنَّةِ
أَصْحٰبُ الْجَنَّةِ هُمُ الْفَآئِزُونَ ○

21. Had We sent down
This Qur-ān on a mountain,[5398]
Verily, thou wouldst have seen
It humble itself and cleave[5399]

٢١- لَوْ أَنْزَلْنَا هٰذَا الْقُرْاٰنَ عَلٰى جَبَلٍ
لَّرَأَيْتَهُ خٰشِعًا مُّتَصَدِّعًا

5395. The positive side of Taqwā or " fear of God " (see last note) is here emphasised. It is not merely a feeling or an emotion : it is an act, a doing of things which become a preparation and provision for the Hereafter,—the next life, which may be described as " the morrow " in relation to the present Life, which is " to-day ".

5395-A. The repetition emphasises both sides of *Taqwā* : " let your soul fear to do wrong, and let it do every act of righteousness ; for God observes both your inner motives and your acts, and in His scheme of things everything will have its due consequences "

5396. To forget God is to forget the only Reality. As we are only reflected realities, how can we understand or do justice to or remember ourselves, when we forget the very source of our being ?

5397. The others, the Companions of the Fire, will find their lives wasted and nullified. Their capacities will be rendered inert and their wishes will end in futility.

5398. There are two ideas associated in men's minds with a mountain : one is its height, and the other that it is rocky, stony, hard. Now comes the metaphor. The Revelation of God is so sublime that even the highest mountains humble themselves before it. The Revelation is so powerful and convincing that even the hard rock splits asunder under it. Will man then be so arrogant as to consider himself superior to it, or so hard-hearted as not to be affected by its powerful Message ? The answer is " No " for unspoilt man ; " Yes " for man when degraded by sin to be the vilest of creatures.

5399. *Cf.* vii. 143, and n. 1103, where, in the story of Moses, the Mount became as dust " when the Lord manifested His Glory ". Also *cf.* xxxiii. 72, and n. 3778, where the mountains are mentioned allegorically as an emblem of stability, but as refusing to accept the Trust (*Amānat*) because they felt themselves to be too humble to be equal to such a tremendous Trust.

Asunder for fear of God.
Such are the similitudes
Which We propound to men,
That they may reflect.

مِّنْ خَشْيَةِ اللّٰهِ ۚ وَتِلْكَ الْأَمْثَالُ نَضْرِبُهَا
لِلنَّاسِ لَعَلَّهُمْ يَتَفَكَّرُونَ ○

22. God is He, than Whom
There is no other god;—[5400]
Who knows (all things)
Both secret and open;
He, Most Gracious,
Most Merciful.

٢٢- هُوَ اللّٰهُ الَّذِي لَآ إِلٰهَ إِلَّا هُوَ ۚ
عٰلِمُ الْغَيْبِ وَالشَّهَادَةِ ۚ
هُوَ الرَّحْمٰنُ الرَّحِيمُ ○

23. God is He, than Whom
There is no other god;—[5401]
The Sovereign, the Holy One,
The Source of Peace
(and Perfection),
The Guardian of Faith,
The Preserver of Safety,[5402]
The Exalted in Might,
The Irresistible, the Supreme:[5403]

٢٣- هُوَ اللّٰهُ الَّذِي لَآ إِلٰهَ إِلَّا هُوَ ۚ
الْمَلِكُ الْقُدُّوسُ السَّلٰمُ
الْمُؤْمِنُ الْمُهَيْمِنُ
الْعَزِيزُ الْجَبَّارُ الْمُتَكَبِّرُ ۚ

5400. Here follows a passage of great sublimity, summing up the attributes of God. First, in this verse, we have the general attributes, which give us the fundamental basis on which we can form some idea of God. (1) We start with the proposition that no words are adequate to describe Him, and we can only call Him "He"; for there is nothing else like Him. (2) We think of His Unity; all the varying and conflicting forces in Creation are controlled by Him and look to Him, and we can never get a true idea of Him unless we understand the mystic meaning of Unity. (3) His knowledge extends to everything seen and unseen, present and future, near and far, in being and not in being: in fact these contrasts, which apply to our knowledge, do not apply to Him. (4) His Grace and (5) His Mercy are unbounded: see i. 1, and n. 19; and unless we realise these, we can have no true conception of our position in the working of His Will and Plan.

5401. This phrase is repeated from the last verse in order to lead us to the contemplation of some other attributes of God, after we have realised those which form our fundamental conceptions of God. See the preceding and the following note.

5402. How can a translator reproduce the sublimity and the comprehensiveness of the magnificent Arabic words, which mean so much in a single symbol? (1) "The Sovereign" in our human language implies the one undisputed authority which is entitled to give commands and to receive obedience, and which in fact receives obedience; the power which enforces law and justice. (2) Human authority may be misused, but in the title "the Holy One", we postulate a Being free from all stain or evil, and replete with the highest Purity. (3) "*Salām*" has not only the idea of Peace as opposed to Conflict, but wholeness as opposed to defects: hence our paraphrase "Source of Peace and Perfection". (4) *Mu-min*, one who entertains Faith, who gives Faith to others, who is never false to the Faith that others place in him: hence our paraphrase "Guardian of Faith". (5) "Preserver of Safety": guarding all from danger, corruption, loss, etc.: the word is used for the Qur-an in v. 51. These are the attributes of kindness and benevolence: in the next note are described the attributes of power.

5403. See last note. (6) God is not only good, but He can carry out His Will. (7) And if anything resists or opposes Him, His Will prevails. (8) For He is Supreme, above all things and creatures. Thus we come back to the Unity with which we began in verse 22.

Glory to God!
(High is He)
Above the partners[5404]
They attribute to Him.

سُبْحٰنَ اللّٰهِ
عَمَّا يُشْرِكُوْنَ ۝

24. He is God, the Creator,[5405]
The Evolver,
The Bestower of Forms[5406]
(Or Colours).
To Him belong[5407]
The Most Beautiful Names:
Whatever is in
The heavens and on earth,
Doth declare[5408]
His Praises and Glory:
And He is the Exalted
In Might, the Wise.

٢٤- هُوَ اللّٰهُ الْخَالِقُ
الْبَارِئُ الْمُصَوِّرُ
لَهُ الْاَسْمَآءُ الْحُسْنٰى ؕ
يُسَبِّحُ لَهٗ
مَا فِى السَّمٰوٰتِ وَالْاَرْضِ ۚ
وَهُوَ الْعَزِيْزُ الْحَكِيْمُ ۝ ع

5404. Such being God's attributes of Goodness and Power, how foolish is it of men to worship anything else but Him? Who can approach His glory and goodness?

5405. God's attributes of Goodness and Power having been referred to, we are now told of His creative energy, of which three aspects are here mentioned, as explained in the following note. The point is emphasised that He does not merely create and leave alone; He goes on fashioning, evolving new forms and colours, and sustaining all the energies and capacities which He has put into His Creation, according to various laws which He has established.

5406. The act or acts of creation have various aspects, and the various words used in this connection are summarised in n. 120 to ii. 117, as supplemented by n. 916 to vi. 94 and n. 923 to vi. 98. *Khalaqa* is the general term for creation, and the Author of all Creation is *Khāliq*. *Baraa* implies a process of evolving from previously created matter or state: the Author of this process is *Bāri-u*, the Evolver. *Ṣawwara* implies giving definite form or colour, so as to make a thing exactly suited to a given end or object: hence the title *Muṣawwir*, Bestower of Forms or Colours: for this shows the completion of the visible stage of creation.

5407. *Cf.* vii. 180, n. 1154; and xvii. 110, n. 2322.

5408. Thus the argument of the Sūra is rounded off on the same note as was struck at the beginning, lix. 1. The first verse and the last verse of the Sūra are the same, except as regards the tense of the verb *sabbaḥa*. In the first verse it is the optative form of the preterite *sabbaḥa*: 'let everything declare the Glory of God!' After the illustrations given, the declaratory form of the aorist is appropriate, *yusabbiḥu*: "everything doth declare the Glory of God'.

INTRODUCTION TO SŪRA LX (*Mumtaḥana*).

This is the fourth of the ten Medina Sūras, each dealing with a special point in the life of the Ummat.

Here the point is: what social relations are possible with the Unbelievers? A distinction is made between those who persecute you for your Faith and want to destroy you and your Faith, and those who have shown no such rancour. For the latter there is hope of mercy and forgiveness. The question of women and cross-marriages is equitably dealt with.

The date is after the Pagans had broken the treaty of Ḥudaibīya, for which see Introduction to S. xlviii,—say about A.H. 8, not long before the conquest of Mecca.

Summary.—The enemies of your Faith, who would exterminate you and your Faith, are not fit objects of your love: follow Abraham's example: but with those Unbelievers who show no rancour, you should deal with kindness and justice: marriages between Believers and Unbelievers. (lx. 1-13, and C. 239).

C. 239.—What social relations should you hold
(lx. 1-13.) With men whose hearts are filled with rancour,—
Who hate both God and men of God?
Surely you cannot offer love and friendship
To such as seek to destroy your Faith
And you. Seek protection for you and yours
From God and not from God's sworn enemies.
But deal kindly and justly with all: it may be
That those who hate you now may love you:
For God can order all things. But look not
For protection to those who are bent on driving
You out. Let not believing women
Be handed over to Unbelievers:
No marriage tie is lawful between them.
When women wish to join your society,
Take their assurance that they yield not
To sin or unbeseeming conduct.
Take every care to keep your society
Free and pure, and self-contained.

Sūra LX.

Mumtaḥana, or the Woman to be Examined. (lx. 10)

In the name of God, Most Gracious, Most Merciful.

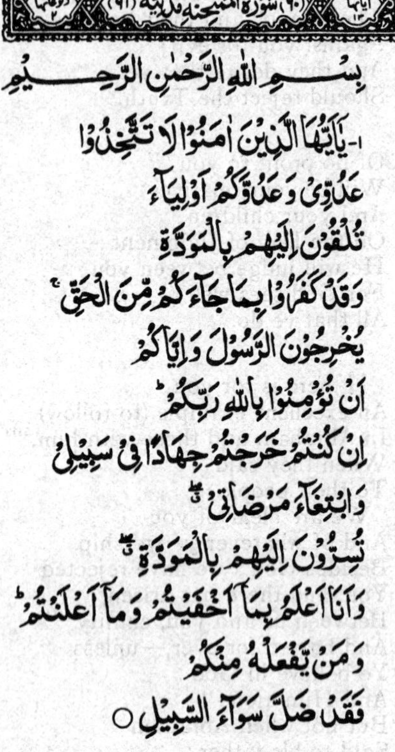

1. O ye who believe!
Take not My enemies
And yours as friends
(Or protectors),—offering them[5409]
(Your) love, even though
They have rejected the Truth
That has come to you,
And have (on the contrary)
Driven out the Prophet
And yourselves (from your homes),
(Simply) because ye believe
In God your Lord![5410]
If ye have come out
To strive in My Way
And to seek My Good Pleasure,
(Take them not as friends),
Holding secret converse
Of love (and friendship)
With them: for I know
Full well all that ye
Conceal and all that ye
Reveal. And any of you
That does this has strayed
From the Straight Path.

2. If they were to get[5411]
The better of you,

5409. The immediate occasion for this was a secret letter sent by one Ḥātib. a Muhājir, from Medina, to the Pagans at Mecca, in most friendly terms, seeking for their protection on behalf of his children and relatives left behind in Mecca. The letter was intercepted, and he confessed the truth. He was forgiven as he told the truth and his motive did not appear to be heinous, but this instruction was given for future guidance. This was shortly before the conquest of Mecca, but the principle is of universal application. You cannot be on terms of secret intimacy with the enemies of your Faith and people, who are persecuting your Faith and seeking to destroy your Faith and you. You may not do so even for the sake of your relatives, as it compromises the life and existence of your whole community.

5410. Such was the position of the Muslim community in Medina after the Hijrat and before the conquest of Mecca.

5411. Besides the question of your fidelity to your own people, even your own selfish interests require you to beware of secret intrigues with enemies. They will welcome you as cat's-paws. But what will happen when they have used you and got the better of you and your people? Then they will show you their hand. And a heavy hand it will be! Not only will they injure you with their hands but with their tongues! The only words they will use for you will be "Traitors to their own"! If they intrigue with you now, it is to pervert you from the Path of Truth and righteousness and win you over to their evil ways.

They would behave to you
As enemies, and stretch forth
Their hands and their tongues
Against you for evil;
And they desire that ye
Should reject the Truth.

يَكُونُوا لَكُمْ أَعْدَآءً
وَيَبْسُطُوٓا إِلَيْكُمْ أَيْدِيَهُمْ وَأَلْسِنَتَهُم بِالسُّوٓءِ
وَوَدُّوا لَوْ تَكْفُرُونَ ۝

3. Of no profit to you[5412]
Will be your relatives
And your children
On the Day of Judgment:
He will judge between you:
For God sees well
All that ye do.

٣- لَن تَنفَعَكُمْ أَرْحَامُكُمْ
وَلَآ أَوْلَادُكُمْ ۚ يَوْمَ الْقِيَامَةِ ۚ
يَفْصِلُ بَيْنَكُمْ ۚ
وَاللَّهُ بِمَا تَعْمَلُونَ بَصِيرٌ ۝

4. There is for you
An excellent example (to follow)
In Abraham and those with him,[5413]
When they said
To their people:
"We are clear of you
And of whatever ye worship
Besides God: we have rejected
You, and there has arisen,
Between us and you, enmity[5414]
And hatred for ever,—unless
Ye believe in God
And Him alone":
But not when Abraham
Said to his father:
"I will pray for forgiveness[5415]

٤- قَدْ كَانَتْ لَكُمْ أُسْوَةٌ حَسَنَةٌ
فِىٓ إِبْرَٰهِيمَ وَالَّذِينَ مَعَهُۥٓ
إِذْ قَالُوا لِقَوْمِهِمْ
إِنَّا بُرَءَٰٓؤُا مِنكُمْ وَمِمَّا تَعْبُدُونَ مِن دُونِ
اللَّهِ كَفَرْنَا بِكُمْ وَبَدَا
بَيْنَنَا وَبَيْنَكُمُ الْعَدَٰوَةُ وَالْبَغْضَآءُ أَبَدًا
حَتَّىٰ تُؤْمِنُوا بِاللَّهِ وَحْدَهُۥٓ
إِلَّا قَوْلَ إِبْرَٰهِيمَ لِأَبِيهِ لَأَسْتَغْفِرَنَّ

5412. The plea of children and relatives (see n. 5409 above) will be no excuse for treachery when the Day of Judgment comes. Your children and family will not save you. The Judgment will be in the hands of God, and He has full knowledge of all your overt and hidden acts and motives.

5413. See ix. 114. Abraham was tender-hearted, and loyal to his father and his people. He warned them against idolatry and sin, and prayed for his father, but when his father and his people became open enemies of God, Abraham entirely dissociated himself from them, and left his home, his father, his people, and his country. *Those with him* were his believing wife and nephew Lūt and any other Believers that went into exile with him.

5414. The enemies of God are enemies of the righteous, and they hate the righteous. Therefore the righteous must cut themselves off eternally from them, unless they repent and come back to God. In that case they receive God's mercy and are entitled to all the rights of love and brotherhood. This shows that our detestation is for evil, not for men as such, so long as there is a chance for repentance. See also verse 7 below. But we must give no chance to Evil for working evil on our Brotherhood at any time.

5415. Refer again to ix. 114, n. 1365: and n. 5413 above. Abraham's conduct is not condemned: it was a special case, and is not to be imitated by weaker men, who may fall into sin by thinking too much of sinners.

For thee, though I have
No power (to get) aught
On thy behalf from God."
(They prayed) : "Our Lord ![5416]
In Thee do we trust,
And to Thee do we turn
In repentance : to Thee
Is (our) final Goal.

لَكَ وَمَآ اَمۡلِكُ لَكَ مِنَ اللّٰهِ مِنۡ شَىۡءٍ ؕ
رَبَّنَا عَلَيۡكَ تَوَكَّلۡنَا
وَاِلَيۡكَ اَنَبۡنَا
وَاِلَيۡكَ الۡمَصِيۡرُ ۝

5. "Our Lord! Make us not
A (test and) trial[5417]
For the Unbelievers,
But forgive us, our Lord!
For Thou art the Exalted
In Might, the Wise."

٥- رَبَّنَا لَا تَجۡعَلۡنَا فِتۡنَةً لِّلَّذِيۡنَ كَفَرُوۡا
وَاغۡفِرۡ لَنَا رَبَّنَا ۚ
اِنَّكَ اَنۡتَ الۡعَزِيۡزُ الۡحَكِيۡمُ ۝

6. There was indeed in them[5418]
An excellent example for you
To follow,—for those
Whose hope is in God
And in the Last Day.
But if any turn away,
Truly God is Free of all[5419]
Wants, Worthy of all Praise.

٦- لَقَدۡ كَانَ لَكُمۡ فِيۡهِمۡ اُسۡوَةٌ حَسَنَةٌ
لِّمَنۡ كَانَ يَرۡجُوا اللّٰهَ وَالۡيَوۡمَ الۡاٰخِرَ ؕ
وَمَنۡ يَّتَوَلَّ
فَاِنَّ اللّٰهَ هُوَ الۡغَنِىُّ الۡحَمِيۡدُ ۝ ع

SECTION 2.

7. It may be that God
Will grant love (and friendship)[5420]
Between you and those whom
Ye (now) hold as enemies.
For God has power
(Over all things) ; And God is
Oft-Forgiving, Most Merciful.

٧- عَسَى اللّٰهُ اَنۡ يَّجۡعَلَ بَيۡنَكُمۡ
وَبَيۡنَ الَّذِيۡنَ عَادَيۡتُمۡ مِّنۡهُمۡ مَّوَدَّةً ؕ
وَاللّٰهُ قَدِيۡرٌ ؕ
وَاللّٰهُ غَفُوۡرٌ رَّحِيۡمٌ ۝

5416. This prayer indicates what our attitude should be. We must trust to God, and not to God's enemies to protect and befriend ourselves, our families, or those near and dear to us.

5417. In n. 1198 to viii. 25, I have explained the shades of meaning in the word *Fitnat*. In ii. 102 Hārūt and Mārūt were a trial to test the righteous who trusted in God from the unrighteous who resorted to evil and superstition. Here the prayer to God is that we should be saved from becoming so weak as to tempt the Unbelievers to try to attack and destroy us.

5418. *In them : i.e.*, in their attitude of prayer and reliance on God, and of dissociation from evil.

5419. If any one rejects God's Message or Law, the loss is his own. It is not God Who needs him or his worship or his sacrifice or his praise. God is independent of all wants, and His attributes are inherently deserving of all praise, whether the wicked give such praise or not, in word or deed.

5420. Apparent religious hatred or enmity or persecution may be due to ignorance or over-zeal in a soul, which God will forgive and use eventually in His service, as happened in the case of Ḥaḍhrat 'Umar, who was a different man before and after his conversion. As stated in n. 5414 above, we should hate evil, but not men as such.

8. God forbids you not,
With regard to those who
Fight you not for (your) Faith
Nor drive you out
Of your homes,
From dealing kindly and justly[5421]
With them: For God loveth
Those who are just.

٨- لَا يَنْهٰكُمُ اللّٰهُ عَنِ الَّذِيْنَ لَمْ يُقَاتِلُوْكُمْ فِي
الدِّيْنِ وَلَمْ يُخْرِجُوْكُمْ مِّنْ دِيَارِكُمْ
اَنْ تَبَرُّوْهُمْ وَتُقْسِطُوْٓا اِلَيْهِمْ ؕ
اِنَّ اللّٰهَ يُحِبُّ الْمُقْسِطِيْنَ ○

9. God only forbids you,
With regard to those who
Fight you for (your) Faith,
And drive you out
Of your homes, and support
(Others) in driving you out,
From turning to them
(For friendship and protection).
It is such as turn to them
(In these circumstances),
That do wrong.

٩- اِنَّمَا يَنْهٰكُمُ اللّٰهُ عَنِ الَّذِيْنَ قٰتَلُوْكُمْ
فِي الدِّيْنِ
وَاَخْرَجُوْكُمْ مِّنْ دِيَارِكُمْ
وَظٰهَرُوْا عَلٰٓى اِخْرَاجِكُمْ اَنْ تَوَلَّوْهُمْ ۚ
وَمَنْ يَّتَوَلَّهُمْ
فَاُولٰٓئِكَ هُمُ الظّٰلِمُوْنَ ○

10. O ye who believe!
When there come to you
Believing women refugees,[5422]
Examine (and test) them:
God knows best as to
Their Faith: if ye ascertain[5423]
That they are Believers,
Then send them not back
To the Unbelievers.
They are not lawful (wives)

١٠- يٰٓاَيُّهَا الَّذِيْنَ اٰمَنُوْٓا اِذَا جَآءَكُمُ الْمُؤْمِنٰتُ
مُهٰجِرٰتٍ فَامْتَحِنُوْهُنَّ ؕ
اَللّٰهُ اَعْلَمُ بِاِيْمَانِهِنَّ ۚ
فَاِنْ عَلِمْتُمُوْهُنَّ مُؤْمِنٰتٍ فَلَا تَرْجِعُوْهُنَّ
اِلَى الْكُفَّارِ ؕ لَا هُنَّ حِلٌّ

5421. Even with Unbelievers, unless they are rampant and out to destroy us and our Faith, we should deal kindly and equitably, as is shown by our holy Prophet's own example.

5422. Under the treaty of Ḥudaibīya [see Introduction to S. xlviii, paragraph 4, condition (3)], women under guardianship (including married women), who fled from the Quraish in Mecca to the Prophet's protection at Medina were to be sent back. But before this Āyat was issued, the Quraish had already broken the treaty, and some instruction was necessary as to what the Medina Muslims should do in those circumstances. Muslim women married to Pagan husbands in Mecca were oppressed for their Faith, and some of them came to Medina as refugees. After this, they were not to be returned to the custody of their Pagan husbands at Mecca, as the marriage of believing women with non-Muslims was held to be dissolved if the husbands did not accept Islam. But in order to give no suspicion to the Pagans that they were badly treated as they lost the dower they had given on marriage, that dower was to be repaid to the husbands. Thus helpless women refugees were to be protected at the cost of the Muslims.

5423. The condition was that they should be Muslim women. How were the Muslims to know? A non-Muslim woman, in order to escape from her lawful guardians in Mecca, might pretend that she was a Muslim. The true state of her mind and heart would be known to God alone. But if the Muslims, on an examination of the woman, found that she professed Islam, she was to have protection. The examination would be directed (among other things) to the points mentioned in verse 12 below.

For the Unbelievers, nor are
The (Unbelievers) lawful
(husbands)
For them. But pay
The Unbelievers what they
Have spent (on their dower).
And there will be no blame
On you if ye marry them[5424]
On payment of their dower
To them. But hold not
To the guardianship of[5425]
Unbelieving women : ask
For what ye have spent
On their dowers, and let
The (Unbelievers) ask for
What they have spent
(On the dowers of women
Who come over to you).
Such is the command
Of God : He judges
(With justice) between you.
And God is Full of
Knowledge and Wisdom.

لَهُمْ
وَلَا هُمْ يَحِلُّونَ لَهُنَّ ۖ
وَاٰتُوْهُمْ مَّآ اَنْفَقُوْا ۚ
وَلَا جُنَاحَ عَلَيْكُمْ اَنْ تَنْكِحُوْهُنَّ
اِذَآ اٰتَيْتُمُوْهُنَّ اُجُوْرَهُنَّ ۚ
وَلَا تُمْسِكُوْا بِعِصَمِ الْكَوَافِرِ
وَسْـَٔلُوْا مَآ اَنْفَقْتُمْ
وَلْيَسْـَٔلُوْا مَآ اَنْفَقُوْا ۚ
ذٰلِكُمْ حُكْمُ اللّٰهِ ۚ
يَحْكُمُ بَيْنَكُمْ ۚ
وَاللّٰهُ عَلِيْمٌ حَكِيْمٌ ○

11. And if any
Of your wives deserts you
To the Unbelievers,[5426]
And ye have an accession
(By the coming over of
A woman from the other side),
Then pay to those
Whose wives have deserted

١١- وَاِنْ فَاتَكُمْ شَيْءٌ مِّنْ اَزْوَاجِكُمْ
اِلَى الْكُفَّارِ
فَعَاقَبْتُمْ
فَاٰتُوا الَّذِيْنَ ذَهَبَتْ اَزْوَاجُهُمْ

5424. As the marriage was held to be dissolved (see n. 5422 above), there was no bar to the remarriage of the refugee Muslim woman with a Muslim man on the payment of the usual dower to her.

5425. Unbelieving women in a Muslim society would only be a clog and a handicap. There would be neither happiness for them, nor could they conduce in any way to a healthy life of the society in which they lived as aliens. They were to be sent away, as their marriage was held to be dissolved; and the dowers paid to them were to be demanded from the guardians to whom they were sent back, just as in the contrary case the dowers of believing women were to be paid back to their Pagan ex-husbands (n. 5422 above).

5426. A very unlikely contingency, considering how much better position the women occupied in Islam than under Pagan custom. But all contingencies have to be provided for equitably in legislation. If a woman went over to the Pagans, her dower would be recoverable from the Pagans and payable to the deserted husband. If a woman came over from the Pagans, her dower would be payable to the Pagans. Assuming that the two dowers were equal, the one would be set off against the other as between the two communities; but within the communities the deserted individual would be compensated by the individual who gains a wife. If the dowers were unequal, the balance would be recoverable as between the communities, and the adjustment would then be made as between the individuals. In practice the common Fund compensated the deserted husband in anticipation of any necessary adjustments.

The equivalent of what they
Had spent (on their dower).
And fear God,
In Whom ye believe.

مِّثْلَ مَآ أَنفَقُوا۟ۚ
وَاتَّقُوا اللَّهَ الَّذِىٓ أَنتُم بِهِۦ مُؤْمِنُونَ ○

12. O Prophet![5427]
When believing women come
To thee to take the oath
Of fealty to thee, that they
Will not associate in worship
Any other thing whatever
With God, that they
Will not steal, that they
Will not commit adultery
(Or fornication), that they
Will not kill their children,
That they will not utter
Slander, intentionally forging
Falsehood, and that they
Will not disobey thee
In any just matter,—
Then do thou receive
Their fealty, and pray to God[5428]
For the forgiveness (of
Their sins): for God is
Oft-Forgiving, Most Merciful.

١٢- يَٰٓأَيُّهَا النَّبِىُّ إِذَا جَآءَكَ الْمُؤْمِنَٰتُ
يُبَايِعْنَكَ عَلَىٰٓ
أَن لَّا يُشْرِكْنَ بِاللَّهِ شَيْـًٔا
وَلَا يَسْرِقْنَ وَلَا يَزْنِينَ
وَلَا يَقْتُلْنَ أَوْلَٰدَهُنَّ
وَلَا يَأْتِينَ بِبُهْتَٰنٍ
يَفْتَرِينَهُۥ بَيْنَ أَيْدِيهِنَّ وَأَرْجُلِهِنَّ
وَلَا يَعْصِينَكَ فِى مَعْرُوفٍ فَبَايِعْهُنَّ
وَاسْتَغْفِرْ لَهُنَّ اللَّهَۖ
إِنَّ اللَّهَ غَفُورٌ رَّحِيمٌ ○

13. O ye who believe!
Turn not (for friendship)
To people on whom
Is the Wrath of God.[5429]

١٣- يَٰٓأَيُّهَا الَّذِينَ ءَامَنُوا۟
لَا تَتَوَلَّوْا۟ قَوْمًا غَضِبَ اللَّهُ عَلَيْهِمْ

5427. Now come directions as to the points on which women entering Islam should pledge themselves. Similar points apply to men, but here the question is about women, and especially such as were likely, in those early days of Islam, to come from Pagan society into Muslim society in the conditions discussed in notes 5422 and 5423 above. A pledge on these points would search out their real motives: (1) to worship none but the One True God; (2) not to steal; (3) not to indulge sex outside the marriage tie; (4) not to commit infanticide; (the Pagan Arabs were prone to female infanticide); (5) not to indulge in slander or scandal; and (6) generally, to obey loyally the law and principles of Islam. The last was a comprehensive and sufficient phrase, but it was good to indicate also the special points to which attention was to be directed in those special circumstances. Obedience was of course to be in all things just and reasonable: Islam requires strict discipline but not slavishness.

5428. If pledges are sincerely given for future conduct, admission to Islam is open. If there is anything in the past, for which there is evidence of sincere repentance, forgiveness is to be prayed for. God forgives in such cases: how can man refuse to give such cases a real chance?

5429. So we come back to the theme with which we started in this Sūra: that we should not turn for friendship and intimacy to those who break God's Law and are outlaws in God's Kingdom. The various phases of this question, and the legitimate qualifications, have already been mentioned, and the argument is here rounded off. *Cf.* also lviii. 14.

Of the Hereafter they are
Already in despair, just as
The Unbelievers are
In despair about those
(Buried) in graves.[5430]

قَدْ يَئِسُوا مِنَ الْآخِرَةِ
كَمَا يَئِسَ الْكُفَّارُ مِنْ أَصْحٰبِ الْقُبُورِ

5430. The Unbelievers, who do not believe in a Future Life, can therefore have no hope beyond this life. Miserable indeed is this life to them; for the ills of this life are real to them, and they can have no hope of redress. But such is also the state of others—People of the Book or not—who wallow in sin and incur the divine Wrath. Even if they believe in a Future Life, it can only be to them a life of horror, punishment, and despair. For those of Faith the prospect is different. They may suffer in this life, but this life to them is only a fleeting shadow that will soon pass away. The Reality is beyond; there will be full redress in the Beyond, and Achievement and Felicity such as they can scarcely conceive of in the terms of this life.

INTRODUCTION TO SŪRA LXI (*Ṣaff*).

This is the fifth Sūra of the series of short Medina Sūras beginning with S. lvii. Its subject-matter is the need for discipline, practical work, and self-sacrifice in the cause of the Ummat. Its date is uncertain, but it was probably shortly after the battle of Uḥud, which was fought in Shawwāl, A.H. 3.

Summary.—God's Glory shines through all Creation: but what discipline can you show to back your words with action? What lessons can you learn from the stories of Moses and Jesus? Help the Cause, and God's help will come with glorious results (lxi. 1-14, and C. 240).

C. 240.—God's glory shines through all the universe.
(lxi. 1-14.) What deeds of unity and discipline,
Of love and righteousness, have *you*
To show in conduct? Or do you
Only mock and insult the apostles
As they did of old? Nay, trust in God
And strive your utmost in His Cause.
Little have you to give, but glorious
Is the reward that God will give you,—
Now and in the Eternal Life to come!

Sūra LXI.

Ṣaff, or Battle Array.

In the name of God, Most Gracious, Most Merciful.

1. Whatever is[5431]
In the heavens and
On earth, let it declare
The Praises and Glory
Of God: for He is
The Exalted in Might,
The Wise.

2. O ye who believe!
Why say ye that
Which ye do not?[5432]

3. Grievously odious is it
In the sight of God
That ye say that
Which ye do not.

4. Truly God loves those
Who fight in His Cause
In battle array, as if[5433]
They were a solid
Cemented structure.

5. And remember, Moses said[5434]
To his people: "O my people!

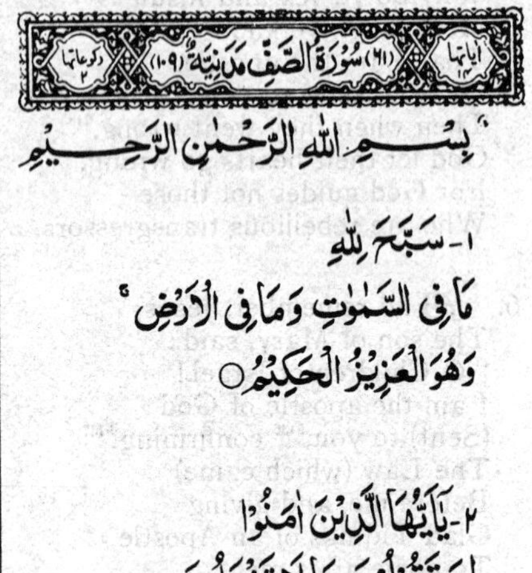

٣-كَبُرَ مَقْتًا عِنْدَ اللّٰهِ
اَنْ تَقُوْلُوْا مَا لَا تَفْعَلُوْنَ ○

٤-اِنَّ اللّٰهَ يُحِبُّ الَّذِيْنَ
يُقَاتِلُوْنَ فِيْ سَبِيْلِهٖ صَفًّا
كَاَنَّهُمْ بُنْيَانٌ مَّرْصُوْصٌ ○

٥-وَاِذْ قَالَ مُوْسٰى لِقَوْمِهٖ يٰقَوْمِ

5431. This verse is identical with lix. 1. The latter illustrated the theme of the wonderful working of God's providence in defeating the wiles of His enemies. Here the same theme is illustrated by showing the need for unshaken discipline if we are to receive the help of God.

5432. At Uḥud there was some disobedience and therefore breach of discipline. People had talked much, but had failed to back up their resolution in words with firmness in action. See n. 442 to iii. 121. But on all occasions when men's deeds are not commensurate with their words, their conduct is odious in the sight of God, and it is only due to God's Mercy if they are saved from disaster.

5433. A battle array, in which a large number of men stand, march, or hold together against assault as if they were a solid wall, is a striking example of order, discipline, cohesion, and courage. "*A solid cemented structure*" is even a better simile than the usual "solid wall", as the "structure" or building implies a more diversified organisation held together in unity and strength, each part contributing strength in its own way, and the whole held together not like a mass but like a living organism. *Cf.* also xxxvii. 1 and n. 4031.

5434. The people of Moses often rebelled against him, vexed his spirit, and insulted him. See xxxiii. 69, n. 3774, and (in the Old Testament) Num xii. 1-13. They did it, not through ignorance, but from a selfish, perverse, and rebellious spirit, for which they received punishment. The Ummat of Islam should remember and take note of it, and should avoid any deviation from the Law and Will of God.

Why do ye vex and insult
Me, though ye know
That I am the apostle
Of God (sent) to you?"
Then when they went wrong,[5435]
God let their hearts go wrong.
For God guides not those
Who are rebellious transgressors.

لِمَ تُؤْذُوْنَنِيْ
وَقَدْ تَّعْلَمُوْنَ اَنِّيْ رَسُوْلُ اللّٰهِ اِلَيْكُمْ ؕ
فَلَمَّا زَاغُوْٓا اَزَاغَ اللّٰهُ قُلُوْبَهُمْ ؕ
وَاللّٰهُ لَا يَهْدِي الْقَوْمَ الْفٰسِقِيْنَ ○

6. And remember, Jesus,
The son of Mary, said:
"O Children of Israel!
I am the apostle of God
(Sent) to you,[5436] confirming[5437]
The Law (which came)
Before me, and giving
Glad Tidings of an Apostle
To come after me,
Whose name shall be Aḥmad."[5438]
But when he came to them
With Clear Signs,[5439]
They said, "This is
Evident sorcery!"

٦- وَاِذْ قَالَ عِيْسَى ابْنُ مَرْيَمَ
يٰبَنِيْٓ اِسْرَآءِيْلَ اِنِّيْ رَسُوْلُ اللّٰهِ اِلَيْكُمْ
مُّصَدِّقًا لِّمَا بَيْنَ يَدَيَّ مِنَ التَّوْرٰىةِ
وَمُبَشِّرًا بِرَسُوْلٍ يَّاْتِيْ مِنْۢ بَعْدِي
اسْمُهٗٓ اَحْمَدُ ؕ
فَلَمَّا جَآءَهُمْ بِالْبَيِّنٰتِ
قَالُوْا هٰذَا سِحْرٌ مُّبِيْنٌ ○

7. Who doth greater wrong
Than one who invents

٧- وَمَنْ اَظْلَمُ مِمَّنِ افْتَرٰى

5435. The sinner's own will deviates, *i.e.* goes off from the right way, and he does wrong. That means that he shuts off God's grace. God then, after his repeated rebellion, withdraws the protecting Grace from him, and the sinner's heart is tainted: there is "a disease in his heart", which is the centre of his being: his spiritual state is ruined. God's guidance is withdrawn from him.

5436. The mission of Jesus was to his own people, the Jews. *Cf.* Matt. x. 5-6. See also Matt. xv. 24: "I am not sent but to the lost sheep of Israel;" also Matt. xv. 26: "It is not meet to take the children's bread, and to cast it to dogs."

5437. *Cf.* Matt. v. 17.

5438. "*Aḥmad*", or "*Muḥammad*", the Praised One, is almost a translation of the Greek word *Periclytos*. In the present Gospel of John, xiv. 16, xv. 26, and xvi. 7, the word "Comforter" in the English version is for the Greek word "*Paracletos*", which means "Advocate", "one called to the help of another, a kind friend", rather than "Comforter". Our doctors contend that Paracletos is a corrupt reading for Periclytos, and that in their original saying of Jesus there was a prophecy of our holy Prophet *Aḥmad* by name. Even if we read Paraclete, it would apply to the holy Prophet, who is "a Mercy for all creatures" (xxi. 107) and "most kind and merciful to the Believers" (ix. 128). See also n. 416 to iii. 81.

5439. Our holy Prophet was foretold in many ways; and when he came, he showed forth many Clear Signs, for his whole life from beginning to end was one vast miracle. He fought and won against odds. Without learning from men he taught the highest wisdom. He melted hearts that were hard, and he strengthened hearts that were tender and required support. In all his sayings and doings men of discernment could see the working of God's hand; yet the ignorant Unbelievers called it all Sorcery!—called that unreal which became the most solid fact of human history!

Falsehood against God,
Even as he is being invited[5440]
To Islām? And God
Guides not those
Who do wrong.

عَلَى اللّٰهِ الْكَذِبَ
وَهُوَ يُدْعٰىٓ إِلَى الْإِسْلَامِ
وَاللّٰهُ لَا يَهْدِي الْقَوْمَ الظّٰلِمِينَ ○

8. Their intention is
To extinguish God's Light
(By blowing) with their mouths:[5441]
But God will complete
(The revelation of) His Light,
Even though the Unbelievers
May detest (it).

٨- يُرِيدُونَ لِيُطْفِـُٔوا نُورَ اللّٰهِ بِأَفْوَاهِهِمْ
وَاللّٰهُ مُتِمُّ نُورِهِ
وَلَوْ كَرِهَ الْكٰفِرُونَ ○

9. It is He Who has sent
His Apostle with Guidance
And the Religion of Truth,
That he may proclaim it
Over all religion,[5442]
Even though the Pagans
May detest (it).

٩- هُوَ الَّذِيٓ أَرْسَلَ رَسُولَهُ بِالْهُدٰى
وَدِينِ الْحَقِّ
لِيُظْهِرَهُ عَلَى الدِّينِ كُلِّهِ
وَلَوْ كَرِهَ الْمُشْرِكُونَ ○ ع

Section 2.

10. O ye who believe!
Shall I lead you
To a bargain[5443] that will
Save you from
A grievous Penalty?—

١٠- يٰٓأَيُّهَا الَّذِينَ اٰمَنُوا
هَلْ أَدُلُّكُمْ عَلٰى تِجَارَةٍ
تُنْجِيكُمْ مِنْ عَذَابٍ أَلِيمٍ ○

5440. It is wrong in any case to uphold falsehoods and debasing superstitions, but it is doubly wrong when these are put forward in rivalry or opposition to the light of eternal Unity and Harmony which is Islam. See C. 7-11. God sends His guidance freely, but withdraws His Grace from those who wilfully do wrong.

5441. God's Light is unquenchable. A foolish, ignorant person who thinks of extinguishing it is like a rustic who wants to blow out electric light as he might blow out a rush candle! "*With their mouths*" also implies the babble and cackle of Ignorance against God's Truth. The more the foolish ones try to quench God's Light, the clearer it shines, to shame them!

5442. "*Over all religion*": in the singular: not over all other religions, in the plural. There is really only one true Religion, the Message of God, submission to the Will of God: this is called Islam. It was the religion preached by Moses and Jesus; it was the religion of Abraham, Noah, and all the prophets, by whatever name it may be called. If people corrupt that pure light, and call their religions by different names, we must bear with them, and we may allow the names for convenience. But Truth must prevail over all. See also ix. 33, n. 1290, and lxviii. 28, n. 4912.

5443. *Tijārat*: bargain, trade, traffic, transaction: something given or done, in return for something which we desire to get. What we give or do on our part is described in verse 11 below, and what we get is described in verse 12. It is truly a wonderful bargain: what we are asked to give is so little; what we are promised in return is so much. There comes God's unbounded Bounty and Munificence. *Cf.* also ix. 111, where the bargain is stated in another way.

11. That ye believe in God
And His Apostle, and that
Ye strive (your utmost)
In the Cause of God,
With your property
And your persons:
That will be best for you,
If ye but knew![5444]

١١- تُؤْمِنُونَ بِاللّٰهِ وَرَسُوْلِهٖ وَتُجَاهِدُوْنَ
فِيْ سَبِيْلِ اللّٰهِ بِأَمْوَالِكُمْ وَأَنْفُسِكُمْ ۭ
ذٰلِكُمْ خَيْرٌ لَّكُمْ
اِنْ كُنْتُمْ تَعْلَمُوْنَ ۝

12. He will forgive you
Your sins, and admit you
To Gardens beneath which
Rivers flow, and to beautiful
Mansions in Gardens
Of Eternity: that is indeed
The supreme Achievement.

١٢- يَغْفِرْ لَكُمْ ذُنُوْبَكُمْ
وَيُدْخِلْكُمْ جَنّٰتٍ تَجْرِيْ مِنْ تَحْتِهَا الْاَنْهٰرُ
وَمَسٰكِنَ طَيِّبَةً فِيْ جَنّٰتِ عَدْنٍ ۭ
ذٰلِكَ الْفَوْزُ الْعَظِيْمُ ۝

13. And another (favour
Will He bestow), which ye[5445]
Do love,—help from God
And a speedy victory.
So give the Glad Tidings
To the Believers.

١٣- وَاُخْرٰى تُحِبُّوْنَهَا ۭ
نَصْرٌ مِّنَ اللّٰهِ وَفَتْحٌ قَرِيْبٌ ۭ
وَبَشِّرِ الْمُؤْمِنِيْنَ ۝

14. O ye who believe!
Be ye helpers of God:[5446]
As said Jesus the son of Mary[5447]
To the Disciples, "Who will be
My helpers to (the work
Of) God?" Said the Disciples,

١٤- يٰٓاَيُّهَا الَّذِيْنَ اٰمَنُوْا كُوْنُوْٓا اَنْصَارَ اللّٰهِ
كَمَا قَالَ عِيْسَى ابْنُ مَرْيَمَ لِلْحَوَارِيّٖنَ
مَنْ اَنْصَارِيْٓ اِلَى اللّٰهِ ۭ قَالَ الْحَوَارِيُّوْنَ

5444. It would indeed be a great and wonderful bargain, to give so little and get so much, if we only knew and understood the comparative value of things,—the sacrifice of our fleeting advantages for forgiveness, the love of God, and eternal bliss.

5445. The supreme Achievement has already been mentioned, *viz.*: the Gardens of Eternity in the Presence of God. But lest that seem too remote or abstract for the understanding of men not spiritually advanced, another type or symbol or metaphor is mentioned which the men who first heard this Message could at once understand and appreciate—"which ye do love"; *viz.*: Help and Victory. For all striving in a righteous Cause we get God's help: and however much the odds against us may be, we are sure of victory with God's help. But all life is a striving or struggle,—the spiritual life even more than any other; and the final victory there is the same as the Garden of Eternity.

5446. If we seek God's help, we must first help God's Cause, *i.e.* dedicate ourselves to Him entirely and without reserve. This was also the teaching of Jesus, as mentioned in this verse. As found in the New Testament, the metaphor used is that of the Cross. "Then said Jesus to his disciples, if any man will come after me, let him deny himself, and take up his cross, and follow me." (Matt. xvi. 24).

5447. See iii. 52, and n. 392; and for the Biblical reference, see the last note. The names of the twelve Disciples will be found in Matt. x. 2-4.

<table>
<tr><td>"We are God's helpers!"
Then a portion of the Children
Of Israel believed, and
A portion disbelieved:
But We gave power
To those who believed,
Against their enemies,
And they became
The ones that prevailed.[5448]</td><td dir="rtl">نَحْنُ أَنصَارُ ٱللَّهِ
فَـَٔامَنَت طَّآئِفَةٌ مِّنۢ بَنِىٓ إِسْرَٰٓءِيلَ
وَكَفَرَت طَّآئِفَةٌ
فَأَيَّدْنَا ٱلَّذِينَ ءَامَنُوا۟ عَلَىٰ عَدُوِّهِمْ
فَأَصْبَحُوا۟ ظَٰهِرِينَ ۝</td></tr>
</table>

5448. A portion of the Children of Israel—the one that really cared for Truth—believed in Jesus and followed his guidance. But the greater portion of them were hard-hearted, and remained in their beaten track of formalism and false racial pride. The majority *seemed* at first to have the upper hand when they thought they had crucified Jesus and killed his Message. But they were soon brought to their senses. Jerusalem was destroyed by Titus in A.D. 70, and the Jews have been scattered ever since. "The Wandering Jew" has become a bye-word in many literatures. On the other hand, those who followed Jesus permeated the Roman Empire, brought many new races within their circle, and through the Roman Empire, Christianity became the predominant religion of the world until the advent of Islam. So is it promised to the people of Islām: they must prevail if they adhere to the Truth. Badr (A.H. 2) was a landmark against Pagan Arabia; Qādisīya (A.H. 14) and Madāin (A.H. 16) against the might of Persia: Yarmūk (A.H. 15) against the might of the Byzantine Empire in Christian Syria; and Heliopolis (A.H. 19) against the same Empire in Christian Egypt and Africa. These were symbols in external events. The moral and spiritual landmarks are less tangible, and more gradual, but none the less real. Mark how the arrogance and power of Priesthood have been quelled; how superstition and a belief in blind Fate have been checked; how the freedom of human individuals has been reconciled with the sanctity of marriage in the law of Divorce; how the civil position of women has been raised; how temperance and sobriety have been identified with religion; what impetus has been given to knowledge and experimental science; and how economic reconstruction has been pioneered by rational schemes for the expenditure and distribution of wealth.

INTRODUCTION TO SŪRA LXII (*Jumu'a*).

This is the sixth Sūra in the Medina series of short Sūras which began with S. lvii.

The special theme here is the need for mutual contact in the Community for worship and understanding: for the spirit of the Message is for all, ignorant and learned, in order that they may be purified and may learn wisdom.

The date has no special significance: it may be placed in the early Medina period, say between A.H. 2 and 5.

Summary.—The Revelation has come among unlearned men, to teach purity and wisdom not only to them but to others, including those who may have an older Message but do not understand it: meet solemnly for the Assembly (Friday) Prayer, and let not worldly interests deflect you therefrom. (lxii. 1-11, and C. 241).

C. 241.—God's care for His creatures is universal.
(lxii. 1-11.) His Revelation is for all—ignorant
And lowly as well as learned and high-placed,—
Now and for ever. None can arrogantly
Claim exclusive possession of God's gifts:
If they do, search their hearts within, and you
Will find them afraid of Death and Judgment.
Men of Faith! On the Day of Assembly,
When you hear the call, hasten earnestly
To answer it: leave off business, and join
In common worship and devotion. Then
You may disperse about your ordinary business,
But remember the Praises of God always:
It is He alone that can provide
For your every need, and *His* gifts are best.

Sūra LXII.

Jumu'a, or the Assembly (Friday)
Prayer.

*In the name of God, Most Gracious,
Most Merciful.*

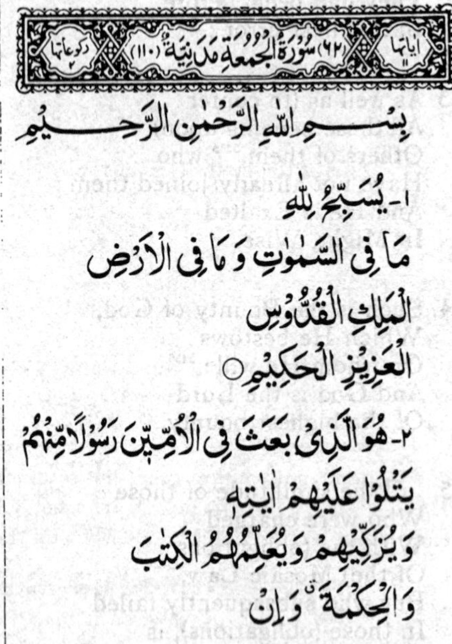

1. Whatever is
In the heavens and
On earth, doth declare[5449]
The Praises and Glory
Of God,—the Sovereign,[5450]
The Holy One, the Exalted
In Might, the Wise.

2. It is He Who has sent
Amongst the Unlettered[5451]
An apostle from among
Themselves, to rehearse
To them His Signs,[5452]
To sanctify them, and
To instruct them in Scripture[5453]
And Wisdom,—although[5454]

5449. See n. 5408 to lix. 24, where I have explained the difference in signification between *sabbaḥa* and *yusabbiḥu*. The latter form is used here, to express an actual fact. 'Everything declares the Praises and Glory of God, because God's mercies extend to all His creatures: He sends His Revelation for the benefit of the ignorant and unlettered as well as for those who have learning in their midst, especially as the latter are apt, by the very weight of their ponderous learning, to miss the real point and spirit of God's Message.'

5450. See lix. 23, and n. 5402. Here we have two of the divine attributes repeated from lix. 23 and two from the end of lix. 24, implying a reminiscence of all the beautiful divine attributes mentioned in that passage.

5451. *The Unlettered*: as applied to a people, it refers to the Arabs, in comparison with the People of the Book, who had a longer tradition of learning, but whose failure is referred to in verse 5 below. As applied to individuals, it means that God's Revelation is for the benefit of all men, whether they have worldly learning or not.

5452. *His Signs*: God's wonderful Signs in His Creation and in His ordering of the world. It may include the Verses of the Qur-ān, but they are more specifically referred to as "Scripture" in the next line but one.

5453. *Cf.* ii. 129, and n. 129. Read again the attributes in the last verse. God is full Sovereign, and therefore cares for all His subjects, including the meanest and most ignorant, and sends His apostles or messengers to them. He is the Holy One, and therefore purifies and sanctifies those who were steeped in superstition and wickedness. He is Exalted in Power, and therefore He can confer all these blessings on the most unlikely people (verse 3), and no one can stay His hand. He is wise, and therefore He instructs in wisdom, both through written Scriptures, and in other ways, *e.g.*, by means of a knowledge of life and its laws, and an understanding of His wonderful universe.

5454. Previous ignorance or error is no bar to a person or nation receiving the blessings of God's revelation, provided such person or nation has the will to come to God and the capacity to bear His Message. For an instance of incapacity through arrogance, see verse 6 below. For some remarks on the Arabs as vehicles of the new Light, see C. 12-15.

They had been, before,
In manifest error ;—

كَانُوا مِنْ قَبْلُ لَفِي ضَلٰلٍ مُّبِينٍ ۙ

3. As well as (to confer
All these benefits upon)
Others of them,[5455] who
Have not already joined them :
And He is Exalted
In Might, Wise.

٣- وَّاٰخَرِينَ مِنْهُمْ
لَمَّا يَلْحَقُوا بِهِمْ ۗ
وَهُوَ الْعَزِيزُ الْحَكِيمُ ۝

4. Such is the Bounty of God,
Which He bestows
On whom He will :[5456]
And God is the Lord
Of the highest bounty.

٤- ذٰلِكَ فَضْلُ اللّٰهِ
يُؤْتِيهِ مَنْ يَّشَآءُ ۗ
وَاللّٰهُ ذُو الْفَضْلِ الْعَظِيمِ ۝

5. The similitude of those
Who were charged
With the (obligations
Of the) Mosaic Law,
But who subsequently failed
In those (obligations), is
That of a donkey[5457]
Which carries huge tomes
(But understands them not).
Evil is the similitude
Of people who falsify
The Signs of God :
And God guides not
People who do wrong.

٥- مَثَلُ الَّذِينَ
حُمِّلُوا التَّوْرٰىةَ
ثُمَّ لَمْ يَحْمِلُوهَا كَمَثَلِ الْحِمَارِ
يَحْمِلُ اَسْفَارًا ۗ
بِئْسَ مَثَلُ الْقَوْمِ الَّذِينَ
كَذَّبُوا بِاٰيٰتِ اللّٰهِ ۗ
وَاللّٰهُ لَا يَهْدِي الْقَوْمَ الظّٰلِمِينَ ۝

6. Say: "O ye that
Stand on Judaism![5458]

٦- قُلْ يٰٓاَيُّهَا الَّذِينَ هَادُوٓا

5455 *Others of them*: refers to other persons or peoples who may be ignorant, *i.e.*, others than those among whom the holy Prophet came as an apostle. In other words his Message is for his Arab people and his non-Arab contemporaries as well as those who live in other ages, and have no personal contact with him or his Companions.

5456. That is, according to His wise Will and Plan, and also as a result of His unbounded generosity to all.

5457. The Children of Israel were chosen as special vehicles for God's Message early in history. When their descendants corrupted the Message and became guilty of all the abominations against which prophets like Isaiah inveighed with such zeal and fire, they merely became like beasts of burden that carry learning and wisdom on their backs but do not understand or profit by it.

5458 *Standing on Judaism* is a very different thing from following the Law and Will of God. An arrogant claim to be a chosen people, to be the exclusive possessors of divine teaching, to be exempt from any punishment for breaches of the divine law, (*cf.* ii. 88), is presumptuous blasphemy. It may be Judaism, but it is not in the spirit of Moses.

If ye think that ye
Are friends to God,
To the exclusion of
(Other) men, then express
Your desire for Death,
If ye are truthful!"[5459]

إن زعمتم أنكم أولياء لله من دون
الناس
فتمنوا الموت إن كنتم صدقين ○

7. But never will they
Express their desire
(For Death), because of
The (deeds) their hands
Have sent on before them!
And God knows well
Those that do wrong!

٧- ولا يتمنونه أبدا
بما قدمت أيديهم
والله عليم بالظلمين ○

8. Say: "The Death from which
Ye flee will truly
Overtake you: then will
Ye be sent back
To the Knower of things
Secret and open: and He
Will tell you (the truth[5460]
Of) the things that ye did!"

٨- قل إن الموت الذي تفرون منه
فإنه ملقيكم
ثم تردون إلى علم الغيب والشهادة
فينبئكم بما كنتم تعملون ○

SECTION 2.

9. O ye who believe!
When the call is proclaimed
To prayer on Friday[5461]
(The Day of Assembly),

٩- يأيها الذين آمنوا إذا نودي
للصلوة من يوم الجمعة

5459. *Cf.* ii. 94-96. If they claimed to be special friends of God, why do they not eagerly desire death, which would bring them nearer to God? But of all people they are the most tenacious of this life and the good things of this life! And they know that their grasping selfish lives have run up a score of sin against them, which will meet its recompense.

5460. Before God's Judgment-Seat, when Judgment is established, we shall see the full inwardness of all deeds in this world. The veil of illusion and delusion will be torn off. All our secret motives will be laid bare. The results of all our little plots and plans and their reactions on our spiritual and eternal welfare will be clearly visible to us. All make-believe will disappear.

5461. Friday, "the Muslim Sabbath", is primarily the Day of Assembly, the weekly meeting of the Congregation, when we show our unity by sharing in common public worship, preceded by a Khuṭba, in which the Imām (or Leader) reviews the week's spiritual life of the Community and offers advice and exhortation on holy living. Notice the gradations of social contact for Muslims if they followed the wise ordinances of their Faith. (1) Each individual remembers God for himself or herself five or more times every day, in the home or place of business, or local mosque, or open air, as the case may be. (2) On Friday in every week, there is a local meeting in the central mosque of each local centre,—it may be a village, or town, or ward of a big city. (3) At the two 'Ids every year, there is a larger local area meeting in one centre, the 'Id-gah. (4) Once at least in a lifetime, where possible, a Muslim shares in the vast international assemblage of the world, in the centre of Islam, at the Meccan Pilgrimage. A happy combination of decentralisation and centralisation, of individual liberty and collective meeting, and contact at various stages or grades. The mechanical part of this ordinance is easy to carry out. Are we carrying out the more difficult part?—the spirit of unity, brotherhood, mutual consultation, and collective understanding and action?

Hasten earnestly to the
Remembrance
Of God, and leave off
Business (and traffic):[5462]
That is best for you
If ye but knew![5463]

فَاسْعَوْا إِلَىٰ ذِكْرِ اللَّهِ
وَذَرُوا الْبَيْعَ
ذَٰلِكُمْ خَيْرٌ لَّكُمْ إِن كُنتُمْ تَعْلَمُونَ ○

10. And when the Prayer
Is finished, then may ye
Disperse through the land,
And seek of the Bounty
Of God: and celebrate
The Praises of God
Often (and without stint):
That ye may prosper.[5464]

١٠- فَإِذَا قُضِيَتِ الصَّلَوٰةُ فَانتَشِرُوا فِي الْأَرْضِ
وَابْتَغُوا مِن فَضْلِ اللَّهِ
وَاذْكُرُوا اللَّهَ كَثِيرًا
لَّعَلَّكُمْ تُفْلِحُونَ ○

11. But when they see
Some bargain or some
Amusement, they disperse
Headlong to it, and leave
Thee standing. Say:
"The (blessing) from the Presence
Of God is better than
Any amusement or bargain!
And God is the Best
To provide (for all needs)."[5465]

١١- وَإِذَا رَأَوْا تِجَٰرَةً أَوْ لَهْوًا
انفَضُّوا إِلَيْهَا وَتَرَكُوكَ قَائِمًا ط
قُلْ مَا عِندَ اللَّهِ خَيْرٌ
مِّنَ اللَّهْوِ وَمِنَ التِّجَٰرَةِ ط
وَاللَّهُ خَيْرُ الرَّٰزِقِينَ ○ ع

5462. The idea behind the Muslim weekly "Day of Assembly" is different from that behind the Jewish Sabbath (Saturday) or the Christian Sunday. The Jewish Sabbath is primarily a commemoration of God's ending His work and resting on the seventh day (Gen. ii. 2; Exod. xx. 11): we are taught that God needs no rest, nor does He feel fatigue (ii 255). The Jewish command forbids work on that day but says nothing about worship or prayer (Exod. xx. 10); our ordinance lays chief stress on the remembrance of God. Jewish formalism went so far as to kill the spirit of the sabbath, and call forth the protest of Jesus: "the sabbath was made for man, and not man for the sabbath" (Mark. ii. 27). But the Christian Church, although it has changed the day from Saturday to Sunday, has inherited the Jewish spirit: witness the Scottish Sabbath; except in so far as it has been secularised. Our teaching says: 'When the time for Jumu'a Prayer comes, close your business and answer the summons loyally and earnestly, meet earnestly, pray, consult and learn by social contact: when the meeting is over, scatter and go about your business'.

5463. The immediate and temporal worldly gain may be the ultimate and spiritual loss, and *vice versâ*.

5464. Prosperity is not to be measured by wealth or worldly gains. There is a higher prosperity,—the health of the mind and the spirit.

5465. Do not be distracted by the craze for amusement or gain. If you lead a righteous and sober life, God will provide for you in all senses, better than any provision you can possibly think of.

INTRODUCTION TO SŪRA LXIII (*Munāfiqūn*).

This is the seventh of the ten short Medina Sūras dealing with a special feature in the social life of the Brotherhood.

The special feature here dealt with is the wiles and mischief of the Hypocrite element in any community, and the need of guarding against it and against the temptation it throws in the way of the Believers.

The battle of Uḥud (Shawwāl A.H. 3) unmasked the Hypocrites in Medina: see iii. 167, and n. 476. This Sūra may be referred to some time after that event, say about 4 A.H. or possibly 5 A.H. if the words reported in verse 8 were uttered in the expedition against the Banū Musṭaliq, A.H. 5. (See n. 5475 below).

Summary.—False are the oaths of the Hypocrites: they only seek selfish ends: Believers should beware of their wiles and strive devotedly always for the Cause (lxiii. 1-11, and C. 242).

C. 242.—The oaths of Hypocrites are a screen
(lxiii. 1-11.) For their misdeeds. They think they deceive
With their fair exteriors and plausible talk,
But their minds are impervious to the real Truth.
They may plot to withhold from men of God
Such things of this world as they may command;
They may plot to expel and persecute the righteous;
They may call them ill names and slight them.
But to God belong the treasures of the heavens
And the earth, and He will bestow according
To His wise and universal Plan. Let not
The world's foolish craze divert the Believers
From the service of God—from good deeds and Charity.
Now is the time: all vain will be
Your pleas and your regrets when the shadow
Of Death cuts off your last chance of Repentance!

Sūra LXIII.

Munāfiqūn, or the Hypocrites.

In the name of God, Most Gracious, Most Merciful.

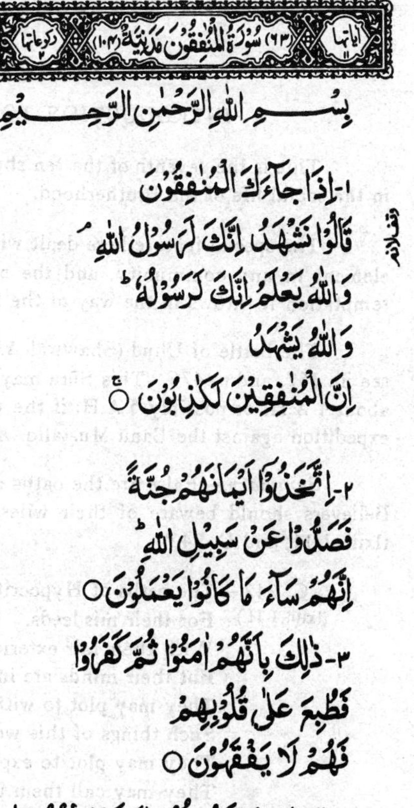

1\. When the Hypocrites [5466]
Come to thee, they say,
"We bear witness that thou
Art indeed the Apostle
Of God." Yea, God
Knoweth that thou art
Indeed His Apostle,
And God beareth witness
That the Hypocrites are
Indeed liars.

2\. They have made their oaths [5467]
A screen (for their misdeeds):
Thus they obstruct (men)
From the Path of God:
Truly evil are their deeds.

3\. That is because they believed,
Then they rejected Faith:
So a seal was set [5468]
On their hearts: therefore
They understand not.

4\. When thou lookest
At them, their exteriors [5469]

5466\. The hypocrite element, if one exists in any society, is a source of weakness and a danger to its health and its very existence. When the holy Prophet came to Medina in *Hijrat*, his arrival was welcome to all the patriotic citizens: it not only united them in common life and healed their old differences, but it brought honour and light to them in the person of the greatest living Teacher of Truth. But there were some baser elements filled with envy. Such hopes as they had entertained of attaining power and leadership by playing on the animosities of the factions were now dashed to the ground. They now began to work underground. For fear of the majority they dared not oppose the new growing Brotherhood of Righteousness They tried to undermine it by intriguing secretly with its enemies and swearing openly its loyalty to the holy Prophet. They were thoroughly unmasked and discredited at the battle of Uḥud. See iii. 167, and n. 476.

5467\. *Cf.* lviii. 16, and n. 5358. When they say that Muḥammad is the Apostle of God, it is God's own truth: but what is in their hearts? Nothing but falsehood.

5468\. *Cf.* ii. 7. Their double-dealing has fogged their understanding. In Arabic the heart is taken to be the seat of understanding as well as of affection.

5469\. The Hypocrites at all times are plausible people, and so were the Hypocrites of Medina. They present a fine exterior; they dress well; they can usually afford fine equipages; they try to win the confidence of every one, as they have no scruples in telling lies, and apparently expressing agreement with every one. Their words are fair-spoken, and as truth does not check their tongues, their flattery and deception know no bounds. But all this is on the outside. As they have no sincerity, nothing that they say or do is worth anything.

Please thee; and when
They speak, thou listenest
To their words. They are
As (worthless as hollow)
Pieces of timber propped up,[5470]
(Unable to stand on their own).
They think that every
Cry is against them.[5471]
They are the enemies;
So beware of them.
The curse of God be
On them! How are they
Deluded (away from the Truth)!

وَإِن يَقُولُوا تَسْمَعْ لِقَوْلِهِمْ
كَأَنَّهُمْ خُشُبٌ مُّسَنَّدَةٌ
يَحْسَبُونَ كُلَّ صَيْحَةٍ عَلَيْهِمْ
هُمُ الْعَدُوُّ فَاحْذَرْهُمْ
قَاتَلَهُمُ اللَّهُ
أَنَّىٰ يُؤْفَكُونَ ○

5. And when it is said
To them, "Come, the Apostle
Of God will pray for your[5472]
Forgiveness", they turn aside
Their heads, and thou wouldst
See them turning away
Their faces in arrogance.

٥- وَإِذَا قِيلَ لَهُمْ تَعَالَوْا
يَسْتَغْفِرْ لَكُمْ رَسُولُ اللَّهِ
لَوَّوْا رُءُوسَهُمْ وَرَأَيْتَهُمْ يَصُدُّونَ
وَهُم مُّسْتَكْبِرُونَ ○

6. It is equal to them
Whether thou pray for
Their forgiveness or not.[5473]
God will not forgive them.
Truly God guides not
Rebellious transgressors.

٦- سَوَاءٌ عَلَيْهِمْ أَسْتَغْفَرْتَ لَهُمْ أَمْ لَمْ
تَسْتَغْفِرْ لَهُمْ لَن يَغْفِرَ اللَّهُ لَهُمْ
إِنَّ اللَّهَ لَا يَهْدِي الْقَوْمَ الْفَاسِقِينَ ○

7. They are the ones who say,
"Spend nothing on those
Who are with God's Apostle,[5474]
To the end that they

٧- هُمُ الَّذِينَ يَقُولُونَ
لَا تُنفِقُوا عَلَىٰ مَنْ عِندَ رَسُولِ اللَّهِ حَتَّىٰ

5470. Good timber is strong in itself and can support roofs and buildings. Hollow timber is useless, and has to be propped up against other things. The Hypocrites are like rotten timber. They have no firm character themselves, and for others they are unsafe props to rely upon.

5471. Their conscience always troubles them. If any cry is raised, they immediately get alarmed, and think it is against themselves. Such men are worse than open enemies.

5472. Even hypocrisy like other sins can be forgiven by repentance and amendment, provided there is a will and earnest desire to turn from evil and seek the Grace of God. In this case there was none.

5473. The stiff-necked rejecters of God's Truth have made a wide gulf between themselves and God's Grace. No prayer for them will help them. In the attitude of rebellion and transgression they cannot obtain God's forgiveness.

5474. The *Muhājirūn*, who had come to be with the holy Prophet in Medina in exile, were received, helped, entertained by the *Anṣār* (Helpers). The Hypocrites in Medina did not like this, and tried in underhand ways to dissuade the good folk of Medina from doing all they could for the exiles. But their tricks did not succeed. The small Muslim community grew from strength to strength until they were able to stand on their own resources and greatly to augment the resources of their hosts as well. It is goodness that produces strength and prosperity, and God holds the keys of the treasures of man's well-being. It is not for God's enemies to dole out or withhold the unbounded treasures of God.

May disperse (and quit Medina)."
But to God belong
The treasures of the heavens
And the earth; but
The Hypocrites understand not.

8. They say, "If we[5475]
Return to Medina, surely
The more honourable (element)
Will expel therefrom the meaner".
But honour belongs to God
And His Apostle, and
To the Believers; but
The Hypocrites know not.

SECTION 2.

9. O ye who believe!
Let not your riches
Or your children divert you
From the remembrance of God.
If any act thus,
The loss is their own.[5476]

10. And spend something (in charity)
Out of the substance[5477]
Which We have bestowed
On you, before Death
Should come to any of you
And he should say,
"O my Lord! Why didst
Thou not give me
Respite for a little while?
I should then have given

يَنفَضُّوا
وَلِلَّهِ خَزَائِنُ السَّمٰوٰتِ وَالْأَرْضِ
وَلٰكِنَّ الْمُنٰفِقِينَ لَا يَفْقَهُونَ ○

٨- يَقُولُونَ لَئِن رَّجَعْنَا إِلَى الْمَدِينَةِ
لَيُخْرِجَنَّ الْأَعَزُّ مِنْهَا الْأَذَلَّ
وَلِلَّهِ الْعِزَّةُ وَلِرَسُولِهِ وَلِلْمُؤْمِنِينَ
وَلٰكِنَّ الْمُنٰفِقِينَ لَا يَعْلَمُونَ ○

٩- يٰأَيُّهَا الَّذِينَ آمَنُوا لَا تُلْهِكُمْ
أَمْوٰلُكُمْ وَلَا أَوْلٰدُكُمْ عَن ذِكْرِ اللَّهِ وَمَن
يَفْعَلْ ذٰلِكَ فَأُولٰئِكَ هُمُ الْخٰسِرُونَ ○

١٠- وَأَنفِقُوا مِن مَّا رَزَقْنٰكُم
مِّن قَبْلِ أَن يَأْتِيَ أَحَدَكُمُ الْمَوْتُ
فَيَقُولَ رَبِّ لَوْلَا أَخَّرْتَنِي
إِلَىٰ أَجَلٍ قَرِيبٍ
فَأَصَّدَّقَ

5475. Words of this import were spoken by 'Abdullāh ibn Ubai, the leader of the Medina Hypocrites, to or about the Exiles, in the course of the expedition against the Banū Muṣṭaliq in the fourth or fifth year of the Hijra. He had hopes of leadership which were disappointed by the coming to Medina of a man far greater than he. So he arrogated to himself and his clique the title of "the more honourable (element)" and slightingly spoke of the Emigrants as the "meaner" element that had intruded from outside.

5476. Riches and human resources of all kinds are but fleeting sources of enjoyment. They should not turn away the good man from his devotion to God. "Remembrance of God" includes every act of service and goodness, every kind thought and kind deed, for this is the service and sacrifice which God requires of us. If we fail in this, the loss is our own, not any one else's: for it stunts our own spiritual growth.

5477. "Substance" or "Sustenance", in every sense, literal and metaphorical. Whatever good we enjoy comes from God, and it is our duty to use some of it in the service of others, for that is Charity and the service of God. Every unselfish act is Charity. And we must not postpone our good resolutions to the future. Death may come suddenly on us, and we cannot *then* be allowed to plead for more time. Every present moment calls urgently for its good deed.

(Largely) in charity, and I Should have been one Of the doers of good".	وَأَكُنْ مِّنَ الصّٰلِحِينَ ○
11. But to no soul Will God grant respite [5478] When the time appointed (For it) has come; and God Is well acquainted With (all) that ye do.	١١- وَلَن يُؤَخِّرَ اللّٰهُ نَفْسًا إِذَا جَآءَ أَجَلُهَا ۚ وَاللّٰهُ خَبِيرٌۢ بِمَا تَعْمَلُونَ ○ ع

5478. When our limited period of probation is over, we cannot justly ask for more time, nor will more time be given to us then. Procrastination is itself a fault, and God knows every hidden thought and motive in our minds.

INTRODUCTION TO SŪRA LXIV (*Tagābun*).

This is the eighth of the short Medina Sūras, each dealing with a special aspect of the life of the Community.

The special aspect spoken of here is the mutual gain and loss of Good and Evil, contrasted in this life and in the Hereafter.

It is an early Medinā Sūra, of the year 1 of the Hijra or possibly even of the Meccan period just before the Hijrat. (See n. 5494 below).

Summary:—Both the Unbelievers and the Believers were created by the One True God, Who created all and knows all: why should Unbelief and Evil exult in worldly gain when their loss will be as manifest in the Hereafter as will be the gains of the Believers? (lxiv. 1-18, and C. 243).

C. 243.—The self-same God created all men.
(lxiv. 1-18.) If some do good and others evil,
And ye wonder how the good do suffer
And the evil thrive, remember the Final
Goal, when true adjustments will
Be made. The Gainers here will be
The Losers there, and the Losers Gainers.
Some of this exchange you will see
Even here, in this life, for Unbelievers
Who deny the Hereafter; but in the Hereafter,
Full account and true adjustment
Of good and ill will follow before
The Judgment-Seat: nay, Good will get
More than its full reward: for God
Is Bounteous, Merciful, Mighty, Wise.

Sūra LXIV.

Tagābun, or Mutual Loss and Gain.

سورة التغابن مدنية (٦٤) (١٠٨) — اٰياتها ١٨ — ركوعاتها ٢

In the name of God, Most Gracious,
Most Merciful.

بِسْمِ اللّٰهِ الرَّحْمٰنِ الرَّحِيْمِ

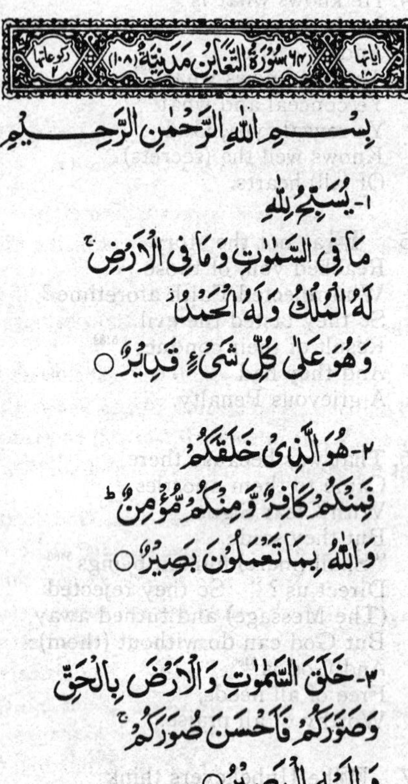

1. Whatever is
In the heavens and
On earth, doth declare[5479]
The Praises and Glory
Of God: to Him belongs
Dominion, and to Him belongs
Praise: and He has power
Over all things.

١- يُسَبِّحُ لِلّٰهِ
مَا فِي السَّمٰوٰتِ وَمَا فِي الْاَرْضِ ۚ
لَهُ الْمُلْكُ وَلَهُ الْحَمْدُ ۡ
وَهُوَ عَلٰى كُلِّ شَيْءٍ قَدِيْرٌ ○

2. It is He Who has
Created you; and of you
Are some that are
Unbelievers, and some[5480]
That are Believers:
And God sees well
All that ye do.

٢- هُوَ الَّذِيْ خَلَقَكُمْ
فَمِنْكُمْ كَافِرٌ وَّمِنْكُمْ مُّؤْمِنٌ ۭ
وَاللّٰهُ بِمَا تَعْمَلُوْنَ بَصِيْرٌ ○

3. He has created the heavens
And the earth
In just proportions,
And has given you shape,[5481]
And made your shapes
Beautiful: and to Him
Is the final Goal.[5482]

٣- خَلَقَ السَّمٰوٰتِ وَالْاَرْضَ بِالْحَقِّ
وَصَوَّرَكُمْ فَاَحْسَنَ صُوَرَكُمْ ۚ
وَاِلَيْهِ الْمَصِيْرُ ○

5479. *Cf.* lxii. 1, and n. 5449. All things by their very existence proclaim the Glory and the Praises of God. He has dominion over all things, but He uses His dominion for just and praiseworthy ends. He has power over all things; therefore He can combine justice with mercy, and His Plan and Purpose cannot be frustrated by the existence of Evil along with Good in His Kingdom.

5480. It is not that He does not see Rebellion and Evil, nor that He cannot punish them. He created all things pure and good, and if evil crept in by the grant of a limited free-will by Him, it is not unforeseen: it is in His wise and universal Plan, for giving man a chance of rising higher and ever higher.

5481. *Cf.* xl. 64, and n. 4440: also vii. 11 and n. 996. In addition to the beauty and grandeur of all God's Creation, He has endowed man with special aptitudes, faculties and capacities, and special excellencies which raise him at his best to the position of God's vicegerent on earth. "Beautiful" also includes the idea of "adapted to the ends for which they were created".

5482. "*The final Goal*": not only of mankind, but of all things created, whether material or in the realm of ideas and events. All things return to God: as they derive their origin from Him, so is the return or destination of all of them to God.

4. He knows what is
In the heavens
And on earth;
And He knows what[5483]
Ye conceal and what
Ye reveal: yea, God
Knows well the (secrets)
Of (all) hearts.

٤- يَعْلَمُ مَا فِى السَّمٰوٰتِ وَالْاَرْضِ
وَيَعْلَمُ مَا تُسِرُّوْنَ وَمَا تُعْلِنُوْنَ ۭ
وَاللّٰهُ عَلِيْمٌۢ
بِذَاتِ الصُّدُوْرِ ○

5. Has not the story
Reached you, of those
Who rejected Faith aforetime?
So they tasted the evil
Result of their conduct;[5484]
And they had
A grievous Penalty.

٥- اَلَمْ يَاْتِكُمْ نَبَؤُا الَّذِيْنَ كَفَرُوْا مِنْ قَبْلُ ۡ
فَذَاقُوْا وَبَالَ اَمْرِهِمْ
وَلَهُمْ عَذَابٌ اَلِيْمٌ ○

6. That was because there
Came to them apostles
With Clear Signs,
But they said:
"Shall (mere) human beings[5485]
Direct us?" So they rejected
(The Message) and turned away.
But God can do without (them):
And God is[5486]
Free of all needs,
Worthy of all praise.

٦- ذٰلِكَ بِاَنَّهٗ كَانَتْ تَّاْتِيْهِمْ رُسُلُهُمْ
بِالْبَيِّنٰتِ
فَقَالُوْٓا اَبَشَرٌ يَّهْدُوْنَنَا ۡ
فَكَفَرُوْا وَتَوَلَّوْا
وَّاسْتَغْنَى اللّٰهُ ۭ
وَاللّٰهُ غَنِيٌّ حَمِيْدٌ ○

7. The Unbelievers think
That they will not be

٧- زَعَمَ الَّذِيْنَ كَفَرُوْٓا اَنْ لَّنْ

5483. Not only does He create and develop and sustain all things; but all thoughts, motives, feelings, ideas, and events are known to Him. Therefore we must not imagine that, if some evil seems to go unpunished, it is not known to Him or has escaped His notice. His Plan is wise and good in its fullest compass: sometimes we do not see its wisdom and goodness because we see only a broken fragment of it, as our own intelligence is narrow.

5484. "The evil result of their conduct" begins to manifest itself in this very life, either in external events, or in internal restlessness and agonies of conscience. But its culminating force will be seen in the "grievous Penalty" of the Hereafter.

5485. This is referred to in a more expanded form in xiv. 9-11, which see.

5486. Their obedience is not necessary to God, nor will their rejection of Truth affect he validity of Truth or injure the progress of Truth. God is free of all needs or dependence on any circumstance whatever. He sends His Message for the good of mankind, and it is man who suffers by ignoring, rejecting, or opposing it.

Raised up (for Judgment).[5487]
Say : " Yea, by my Lord,
Ye shall surely be
Raised up : then shall ye
Be told (the truth) of
All that ye did.
And that is easy for God."

يُبْعَثُوا ۚ
قُلْ بَلَىٰ وَرَبِّي لَتُبْعَثُنَّ
ثُمَّ لَتُنَبَّؤُنَّ بِمَا عَمِلْتُمْ ۚ
وَذَٰلِكَ عَلَى اللَّهِ يَسِيرٌ ○

8. Believe, therefore, in God
And His Apostle, and
In the Light which We[5488]
Have sent down. And God
Is well acquainted
With all that ye do.

٨- فَآمِنُوا بِاللَّهِ وَرَسُولِهِ
وَالنُّورِ الَّذِي أَنْزَلْنَا ۚ
وَاللَّهُ بِمَا تَعْمَلُونَ خَبِيرٌ ○

9. The Day that He assembles
You (all) for a Day
Of Assembly,—that will be
A day of mutual loss[5489]
And gain (among you).
And those who believe
In God and work righteousness,—
He will remove from them[5490]
Their ills, and He will admit
Them to gardens beneath which[5491]

٩- يَوْمَ يَجْمَعُكُمْ لِيَوْمِ الْجَمْعِ
ذَٰلِكَ يَوْمُ التَّغَابُنِ ۗ
وَمَنْ يُؤْمِنْ بِاللَّهِ وَيَعْمَلْ صَالِحًا
يُكَفِّرْ عَنْهُ سَيِّئَاتِهِ
وَيُدْخِلْهُ جَنَّاتٍ تَجْرِي مِنْ تَحْتِهَا

5487. In other words, they think that there is no future life, and no responsibility for our actions beyond what we see in the present life. If that were true, all the profits of fraud and roguery, which remain unpunished in this world—and many do remain unpunished in this world—will remain with the wicked; and all the losses and pain suffered by integrity and righteousness, if they find no compensation in this life, will never find any compensation. This would be an odd result in a world of justice. We are taught that this is not true,—that it is certain that the balance will be redressed in a better future world; that there will be a resurrection of what we call the dead; and that on that occasion the full import of all we did will be made plain to us, and our moral and spiritual responsibility will be fully enforced.

5488. "*The Light which We have sent down*" : *i.e.*, the light of Revelation, the light of conscience, the light of reason, and every kind of true light by which we may know God and His Will. If we play false with any such lights, it is fully known to God.

5489. The Day of Judgment will truly be "a Day of Mutual Loss and Gain", as the title of this Sūra indicates. Men who thought they were laying up riches will find themselves paupers in the Kingdom of Heaven. Men who thought they were acquiring good by wrong-doing will find their efforts were wasted : xviii. 104. On the other hand the meek and lowly of this life will acquire great dignity and honour in the next; the despised ones doing good here will be the accepted ones there; the persecuted righteous will be in eternal happiness. The two classes will as it were change their relative positions.

5490. "*Remove from them their ills*". The ills may be sins, faults, mistakes, or evil tendencies; God will of His grace cover them up, and blot out the account against them; or they may be sorrows, sufferings, or disappointments: God may even change the evil of such persons into good, their apparent calamities into opportunities for spiritual advancement : xxv. 70. This is because of their sincere Faith as evidenced by their repentance and amendment.

5491. For "Gardens" as the symbol or type of the highest Bliss, see paragraphs 8-9 of Appendix XII, printed at the end of S. liv. ; pp. 1466-67.

Rivers flow, to dwell therein
For ever: that will be
The Supreme Achievement.

الْأَنْهٰرُ خٰلِدِيْنَ فِيْهَآ اَبَدًا ۭ
ذٰلِكَ الْفَوْزُ الْعَظِيْمُ ○

10. But those who reject Faith
And treat Our Signs
As falsehoods, they will be
Companions of the Fire,
To dwell therein for aye:
And evil is that Goal.

١٠- وَالَّذِيْنَ كَفَرُوْا وَكَذَّبُوْا بِاٰيٰتِنَآ
اُولٰۗىِٕكَ اَصْحٰبُ النَّارِ خٰلِدِيْنَ فِيْهَا ۭ
وَبِئْسَ الْمَصِيْرُ ○

SECTION 2.

11. No kind of calamity
Can occur, except
By the leave of God:
And if any one believes [5492]
In God, (God) guides his
Heart (aright): for God
Knows all things.

١١- مَآ اَصَابَ مِنْ مُّصِيْبَةٍ اِلَّا بِاِذْنِ اللّٰهِ ۭ
وَمَنْ يُّؤْمِنْۢ بِاللّٰهِ يَهْدِ قَلْبَهٗ ۭ
وَاللّٰهُ بِكُلِّ شَيْءٍ عَلِيْمٌ ○

12. So obey God, and obey
His Apostle: but if
Ye turn back, the duty
Of Our Apostle is but
To proclaim (the Message) [5493]
Clearly and openly.

١٢- وَاَطِيْعُوا اللّٰهَ وَاَطِيْعُوا الرَّسُوْلَ ۚ
فَاِنْ تَوَلَّيْتُمْ
فَاِنَّمَا عَلٰي رَسُوْلِنَا الْبَلٰغُ الْمُبِيْنُ ○

13. God! There is no god
But He: and on God,
Therefore, let the Believers
Put their trust.

١٣- اَللّٰهُ لَآ اِلٰهَ اِلَّا هُوَ ۭ
وَعَلَي اللّٰهِ فَلْيَتَوَكَّلِ الْمُؤْمِنُوْنَ ○

14. O ye who believe!
Truly, among your wives

١٤- يٰٓاَيُّهَا الَّذِيْنَ اٰمَنُوْٓا اِنَّ مِنْ اَزْوَاجِكُمْ

5492. What we consider calamities may be blessings in disguise. Pain in the body is often a signal of something wrong, which we can cure by remedial measures. So in the moral and spiritual world, we should in all circumstances hold firmly to the faith that nothing happens without God's knowledge and leave; and therefore there must be some justice and wisdom according to His great universal Plan. Our duty is to find out our own shortcomings and remedy them. If we try to do so in all sincerity of heart, God will give us guidance.

5493. The Apostle comes to guide and teach, not to force and compel. The Apostle's teaching is clear and unambiguous, and it is open and free to all. *Cf.* also v. 95.

And your children are (some
That are) enemies to[5494]
Yourselves: so beware
Of them! But if ye
Forgive and overlook,[5495]
And cover up (their faults),
Verily God is
Oft-Forgiving, Most Merciful.

وَأَوْلَادِكُمْ عَدُوًّا لَّكُمْ
فَاحْذَرُوهُمْ
وَإِن تَعْفُوا وَتَصْفَحُوا وَتَغْفِرُوا
فَإِنَّ اللَّهَ غَفُورٌ رَّحِيمٌ ۝

15. Your riches and your children
May be but a trial:[5496]
But in the Presence of God,
Is the highest Reward.

١٥- إِنَّمَا أَمْوَالُكُمْ وَأَوْلَادُكُمْ فِتْنَةٌ
وَاللَّهُ عِندَهُ أَجْرٌ عَظِيمٌ ۝

16. So fear God[5497]
As much as ye can;
Listen and obey;
And spend in charity
For the benefit of
Your own souls.[5498]
And those saved from
The covetousness of their own

١٦- فَاتَّقُوا اللَّهَ مَا اسْتَطَعْتُمْ
وَاسْمَعُوا وَأَطِيعُوا
وَأَنفِقُوا خَيْرًا لِّأَنفُسِكُمْ
وَمَن يُوقَ شُحَّ

5494. In some cases the demands of families, *i.e.*, wife and children may conflict with a man's moral and spiritual convictions and duties. In such cases he must guard against the abandonment of his convictions, duties, and ideals to their requests or desires. But he must not treat them harshly. He must make reasonable provision for them, and if they persist in opposing his clear duties and convictions, he must forgive them and not expose them to shame or ridicule, while at the same time holding on to his clear duty. Such cases occurred when godly men undertook exile from their native city of Mecca to follow the Faith in Medina. In some cases their families murmured, but all came right in the end.

5495. For the different words for "forgiveness" see n. 110 to ii. 109.

5496. Children may be a "*trial*" in many senses: (1) their different ways of looking at things may cause you to reflect, and to turn to the highest things of eternal importance; (2) their relationship with you and with each other may confront you with problems far more complicated than those in separate individual lives, and thus become a test of your own strength of character and sense of responsibility; (3) their conflict with your ideals (see n. 5494 above) may vex your spirit, but may at the same time search out your fidelity to God; and (4) their affection for you and your affection for them, may be a source of strength for you if it is pure, just as it may be a danger if it is based on selfish or unworthy motives. So also riches and worldly goods have their advantages as well as dangers.

5497. "*Fear God*" combined with "*as much as you can*" obviously means: "lead lives of self-restraint and righteousness": the usual meaning of *Taqwā*: see n. 26 to ii. 2.

5498. Charity is meant to help and do good to other people who need it. But it has the highest subjective value for the person who gives it. Like mercy "it blesseth him that gives and him that takes". It purifies the giver's soul: the affection that he pours out is for his own spiritual benefit and progress. *Cf.* Coleridge: "He prayeth best who loveth best all things both great and small, for the Great God Who loveth us, Who made and loveth all".

Souls,—they are the ones
That achieve prosperity.[5499]

نَفْسِهٖ فَاُولٰٓئِكَ هُمُ الْمُفْلِحُوْنَ ۝

17. If ye loan to God[5500]
A beautiful loan, He
Will double it to
Your (credit), and He
Will grant you Forgiveness:
For God is most Ready
To appreciate (service),[5501]
Most Forbearing,—

١٧- اِنْ تُقْرِضُوا اللّٰهَ قَرْضًا حَسَنًا
يُّضٰعِفْهُ لَكُمْ
وَيَغْفِرْ لَكُمْ ؕ
وَاللّٰهُ شَكُوْرٌ حَلِيْمٌ ۝ۙ

18. Knower of what is hidden
And what is open,
Exalted in Might,
Full of Wisdom.[5502]

١٨- عٰلِمُ الْغَيْبِ وَالشَّهَادَةِ
الْعَزِيْزُ الْحَكِيْمُ ۝ع

5499. *Cf* lix 9. Our worst enemy is within ourselves,—the grasping selfishness which would deprive others of their just rights or seize things which do not properly belong to it. If we can get over this covetous selfishness, we achieve real Prosperity in justice and truth.

5500. *Cf.* ii. 245 and n. 276. Our Charity or Love is called a loan to God, which not only increases our credit account manifold, but obtains for us the forgiveness of our sins, and the capacity for increased service in the future.

5501. *Cf.* xiv. 5, n. 1877; and xxxv. 30, n. 3917. God's appreciation of our service or our love goes far deeper than its intrinsic merits or its specific expression on our side. His reward is beyond our deserts, and passes over our defects. He judges by our motives, which He can read through and through: see next verse.

5502. God's Appreciation and Forbearing Kindness can reach so far beyond our merits, because (1) His universal knowledge comprehends hidden motives, which others cannot see in us; (2) His power is so great that He can afford to reward even the unworthy; and (3) His Wisdom is so great hat He can turn even our weakness into our strength.

INTRODUCTION TO SŪRA LXV (*Talāq*)

This is the ninth of the ten short Medina Sūras dealing with the social life of the Community. The aspect dealt with here is Divorce, and the necessity of precautions to guard against its abuse. The relations of the sexes are an important factor in the social life of the Commnuity, and this and the following Sūra deal with certain aspects of it. "Of all things permitted by Law", said the Prophet, "divorce is the most hateful in the sight of God". (Abū Dā-ūd, *Sunan*, xiii 3). While the sanctity of marriage is the essential basis of family life, the incompatibility of individuals and the weaknesses of human nature require certain outlets and safeguards if that sanctity is not to be made into a fetish at the expense of human life. That is why the question of Divorce is in this Sūra linked with the question of insolent impiety and its punishment.

The date is somewhere about A.H. 6, but the chronology has no significance.

Summary.—Provision to be made for women in case of Divorce; insolent impiety always leads to punishment (lxv. 1-12, and C. 244).

C. 244.—Guard well your truth and pure integrity
(lxv. 1-12.) In sex relations. Keep the tie
Of marriage sacred: but where it must
Be dissolved, use all precautions to ensure
Justice to the weaker party and protect
The interests of unborn or new-born lives
As well as social decency; and close not
To the last the door of reconciliation.
God's Laws must be obeyed: 'tis man's
Own loss if he is deaf to the Voice
Which teaches him, or blind to the Light
Which guides him. God's universe
Of beauty and wonder stands strong in wisdom:
Let man but tune himself thereto.

Sūra LXV.

Ṭalāq, or Divorce.

In the name of God, Most Gracious,
Most Merciful.

1. O Prophet![5503] When ye
Do divorce women,[5504]
Divorce them at their
Prescribed periods,[5505]
And count (accurately)
Their prescribed periods:
And fear God your Lord:[5506]
And turn them not out
Of their houses, nor shall
They (themselves) leave,[5507]
Except in case they are
Guilty of some open lewdness,
Those are limits
Set by God: and any
Who transgresses the limits
Of God, does verily
Wrong his (own) soul:
Thou knowest not if

5503. Note that in the first instance the Prophet is himself addressed individually, as the Teacher and representative of the Community. Then the actual directions: "when *ye*......": are addressed to the Community collectively.

5504. "Of all things permitted by law, Divorce is the most hateful in the sight of God": see Introduction to this Sūra. The general directions and limitations of Divorce may be studied in ii. 228-232, 236-237, 241, and notes; also iv. 35.

5505. *'Iddat*, as a technical term in divorce law, is explained in n. 254 to ii. 228. Its general meaning is "a prescribed period": in that general sense it is used in ii. 185 for a prescribed period for fasting.

5506. The prescribed period (see last note) is in the interests of the wife, of the husband, of an unborn child (if there is any), and of sex laws in nature, and therefore the elementary dictates of refined human society. In English Law the six months' interval between the decree *nisi* and the decree absolute in divorce attains the same purpose in a round-about way. The Commentators suggest that the divorce should not be pronounced during the courses. Read with ii. 222, this implies that any incipient differences between husband and wife should not be forced to an issue at a time when sex is least attractive and almost repulsive. Everything should be done to strengthen the social and spiritual aspects of marriage and keep down stray impulses of animal instinct. The parties are to think seriously in a mood of piety, keeping the fear of God in their minds.

5507. As Islam treats the married woman as a full juristic personality in every sense of the term a married woman has a right, in the married state, to a house or apartment of her own. And a house or apartment implies the reasonable expenses for its upkeep and for her own and her children's maintenance. And this is obligatory not only in the married state, but during the *'iddat*, which is necessarily a most trying period for the woman. During this period she must not only not be turned out, but it is not decent for her to leave of her own accord, lest the chances of reconciliation should be diminished: see the next note.

Perchance God will
Bring about thereafter
Some new situation.[5508]

لَعَلَّ اللّٰهَ يُحْدِثُ بَعْدَ ذٰلِكَ اَمْرًا ○

2. Thus when they fulfil
Their term appointed,
Either take them back
On equitable terms[5509]
Or part with them
On equitable terms;
And take for witness
Two persons from among you,
Endued with justice,
And establish the evidence[5510]
(As) before God. Such
Is the admonition given
To him who believes
In God and the Last Day.
And for those who fear
God, He (ever) prepares[5511]
A way out,

٢- فَاِذَا بَلَغْنَ اَجَلَهُنَّ
فَاَمْسِكُوْهُنَّ بِمَعْرُوْفٍ
اَوْ فَارِقُوْهُنَّ بِمَعْرُوْفٍ
وَّاَشْهِدُوْا ذَوَيْ عَدْلٍ مِّنْكُمْ وَاَقِيْمُوا
الشَّهَادَةَ لِلّٰهِ ۭ
ذٰلِكُمْ يُوْعَظُ بِهٖ
مَنْ كَانَ يُؤْمِنُ بِاللّٰهِ وَالْيَوْمِ الْاٰخِرِ ۥ
وَمَنْ يَّتَّقِ اللّٰهَ
يَجْعَلْ لَّهٗ مَخْرَجًا ○

3. And He provides for him
From (sources) he never
Could imagine. And if
Any one puts his trust
In God, sufficient is (God)
For him. For God will

٣- وَّيَرْزُقْهُ مِنْ حَيْثُ لَا يَحْتَسِبُ ۭ
وَمَنْ يَّتَوَكَّلْ عَلَى اللّٰهِ فَهُوَ حَسْبُهٗ ۭ
اِنَّ اللّٰهَ

5508. A reconciliation is possible, and is indeed recommended at every stage. The first serious differences between the parties are to be submitted to a family council on which both sides are represented (iv. 35); divorce is not to be pronounced when mutual physical attraction is at an ebb (n. 5506); when it is pronounced, there should be a period of probationary waiting: dower has to be paid and due provision has to be made for many things on equitable terms; every facility has to be given for reconciliation till the last moment, and impediments are provided against hasty impulses leading to rupture. "*Thou knowest not if perchance God will bring about thereafter some new situation.*"

5509. *Cf.* ii. 231. Everything should be done fairly and squarely, and all interests should be safeguarded.

5510. Publicity and the establishment of proper evidence ensure that no one will act unjustly or selfishly. All should remember that these are matters of serious import, affecting our most intimate lives, and therefore our position in the spiritual kingdom.

5511. In these very delicate and difficult matters, the wisdom of jurists provides a less satisfactory solution than a sincere desire to be just and true, which is described as the "fear of God". Where such a desire exists, God often provides a solution in the most unexpected ways or from the most unexpected quarters; *e.g.*, the worst enemies may be reconciled, or the cry or the smile of an infant baby may heal seemingly irreparable injuries or unite hearts seemingly alienated for ever. And Faith is followed at once by a psychological feeling of rest for the troubled spirit.

Surely accomplish His purpose:[5512]
Verily, for all things
Has God appointed
A due proportion.

بَالِغُ أَمْرِهٖ ؕ
قَدْ جَعَلَ اللّٰهُ لِكُلِّ شَيْءٍ قَدْرًا ○

4. Such of your women
As have passed the age
Of monthly courses, for them
The prescribed period, if ye
Have any doubts, is
Three months, and for those
Who have no courses
(It is the same):[5513]
For those who carry
(Life within their wombs),
Their period is until
They deliver their burdens:
And for those who
Fear God, He will
Make their path easy.[5514]

٤- وَالّٰٓـِٔيْ يَئِسْنَ مِنَ الْمَحِيْضِ مِنْ نِّسَآئِكُمْ
اِنِ ارْتَبْتُمْ
فَعِدَّتُهُنَّ ثَلٰثَةُ اَشْهُرٍ ۙ
وَّالّٰٓـِٔيْ لَمْ يَحِضْنَ ؕ
وَاُولَاتُ الْاَحْمَالِ
اَجَلُهُنَّ اَنْ يَّضَعْنَ حَمْلَهُنَّ ؕ
وَمَنْ يَّتَّقِ اللّٰهَ
يَجْعَلْ لَّهٗ مِنْ اَمْرِهٖ يُسْرًا ○

5. That is the Command
Of God, which He
Has sent down to you:
And if any one fears God,
He will remove his ills[5515]
From him, and will enlarge
His reward.

٥- ذٰلِكَ اَمْرُ اللّٰهِ اَنْزَلَهٗٓ اِلَيْكُمْ ؕ
وَمَنْ يَّتَّقِ اللّٰهَ يُكَفِّرْ عَنْهُ سَيِّاٰتِهٖ
وَيُعْظِمْ لَهٗٓ اَجْرًا ○

6. Let the women live
(In *'iddat*) in the same

٦- اَسْكِنُوْهُنَّ مِنْ حَيْثُ

5512. Our anger and our impatience have to be curbed. Our friends and our mates or associates may seem to us ever so weak and unreasonable, and the circumstances may be ever so disheartening: yet we must trust in God. How can we measure our own weakness or perhaps blindness? He knows all. His universal Purpose is always good. His Will must be accomplished, and we should wish for its accomplishment. His ordering of the universe observes a due, just, and perfect proportion.

5513. *Cf.* ii. 228. For normal women, the *'iddat* is the three monthly courses after separation: if there are no courses or if the courses are in doubt, it is three calendar months. By that time it will be clear whether there is pregnancy: if there is, the waiting period is till after delivery.

5514. *Cf.* n. 5511 above. If there is a true and sincere desire to obey the Will of God and do right, the difficulties will vanish, and these delicate matters will be settled for the greatest happiness of all.

5515. God's ordinance is nothing arbitrary. It is to help us, and to lead us on to our highest good, temporal and spiritual. If we obey God, His wisdom will not only solve our difficulties, but it will remove other ills that we may have, subjective and objective. Like a good shepherd, he will lead us on to more and more luscious pastures. With each step higher, our position becomes more and more sure and our reward more and more precious.

Style as ye live,
According to your means :
Annoy them not, so as
To restrict them.[5516]
And if they carry (life
In their wombs), then[5517]
Spend (your substance) on them
Until they deliver
Their burden: and if
They suckle your (offspring),
Give them their recompense :
And take mutual counsel
Together, according to
What is just and reasonable.
And if ye find yourselves[5518]
In difficulties, let another
Woman suckle (the child)
On the (father's) behalf.[5519]

سَكَنْتُمْ مِّنْ وُّجْدِكُمْ
وَلَا تُضَآرُّوْهُنَّ
لِتُضَيِّقُوْا عَلَيْهِنَّ ؕ
وَاِنْ كُنَّ اُولٰتِ حَمْلٍ
فَاَنْفِقُوْا عَلَيْهِنَّ حَتّٰى يَضَعْنَ حَمْلَهُنَّ ۚ
فَاِنْ اَرْضَعْنَ لَكُمْ فَاٰتُوْهُنَّ اُجُوْرَهُنَّ ۚ
وَاْتَمِرُوْا بَيْنَكُمْ بِمَعْرُوْفٍ ۚ
وَاِنْ تَعَاسَرْتُمْ
فَسَتُرْضِعُ لَهٗۤ اُخْرٰى ؕ

7. Let the man of means
Spend according to
His means : and the man
Whose resources are restricted,
Let him spend according
To what God has given him.
God puts no burden
On any person beyond
What He has given him.
After a difficulty, God
Will soon grant relief.[5520]

٧- لِيُنْفِقْ ذُوْ سَعَةٍ مِّنْ سَعَتِهٖ ؕ
وَمَنْ قُدِرَ عَلَيْهِ رِزْقُهٗ
فَلْيُنْفِقْ مِمَّاۤ اٰتٰىهُ اللّٰهُ ؕ
لَا يُكَلِّفُ اللّٰهُ نَفْسًا اِلَّا مَاۤ اٰتٰىهَا ؕ
سَيَجْعَلُ اللّٰهُ بَعْدَ عُسْرٍ يُّسْرًا ۟ ع

5516. *Cf.* n. 5507 above. A selfish man, because he has divorced his wife, may, in the probationary period before the divorce becomes absolute, treat her with contumely, and while giving her residence and maintenance, may so restrict it as to make her life miserable. This is forbidden. She must be provided on the same scale as he is, according to his status in life. There is still hope of reconciliation, and if not, yet the parting must be honourable.

5517 If there is pregnancy, a sacred third life comes on the scene, for which there is added responsibility (perhaps added hope of reconciliation) for both parents. In any case no separation is possible until after the child is born. Even after birth, if no reconciliation between parents is possible, yet for the nursing of the child and for its welfare the care of the mother remains the duty of the father, and there must be mutual counsel between him and the mother in all truth and sincerity.

5518. "*If ye find yourselves in difficulties*" : *e.g.*, if the mother's milk fails, or if her health fails, or if any circumstance arises which bars the natural course of the mother nursing her own child. There may be psychological difficulties also.

5519. That is, the father must stand all expenses, without cutting down the reasonable allowance to which the mother is entitled in the circumstances.

5520. We must trust in God, and do whatever is possible for us in the interests of the young life for which we are responsible. We must not be frightened by difficulties. God will give us relief and provide a solution if we act with honest integrity. *Cf.* xciv. 5-6.

Section 2.

8. How many populations
That insolently opposed[5521]
The command of their Lord
And of His apostles,
Did We not then
Call to account,—
To severe account ?—
And We imposed on them
An exemplary Punishment.[5522]

٨- وَكَأَيِّن مِّن قَرْيَةٍ عَتَتْ
عَنْ أَمْرِ رَبِّهَا وَرُسُلِهِ
فَحَاسَبْنَاهَا حِسَابًا شَدِيدًا
وَعَذَّبْنَاهَا عَذَابًا نُّكْرًا ○

9. Then did they taste
The evil result of
Their conduct, and the End
Of their conduct
Was Perdition.

٩- فَذَاقَتْ وَبَالَ أَمْرِهَا
وَكَانَ عَاقِبَةُ أَمْرِهَا خُسْرًا ○

10. God has prepared for them
A severe Punishment[5523]
(In the Hereafter).
Therefore fear God,
O ye men of understanding—
Who have believed !—
For God hath indeed
Sent down to you
A Message,—[5524]

١٠- أَعَدَّ اللَّهُ لَهُمْ عَذَابًا شَدِيدًا
فَاتَّقُوا اللَّهَ يَا أُولِي الْأَلْبَابِ
الَّذِينَ آمَنُوا
قَدْ أَنزَلَ اللَّهُ إِلَيْكُمْ ذِكْرًا ○

11. An Apostle, who rehearses
To you the Signs of God
Containing clear explanations,
That he may lead forth
Those who believe
And do righteous deeds

١١- رَّسُولًا يَتْلُو عَلَيْكُمْ آيَاتِ اللَّهِ
مُبَيِّنَاتٍ
لِّيُخْرِجَ الَّذِينَ آمَنُوا وَعَمِلُوا الصَّالِحَاتِ

5521. Insolent impiety consists not only in the breach of the rites of religion. Even more vital is the defiance of the laws of nature which God has made for us. These laws, for us human beings include those which relate to our fellow-beings in society, to whom kindness and consideration form the basis of our social duties. Our duties to our families and our children in intimate matters such as were spoken of in the last Section, are as important as any in our spiritual life. Peoples who forgot the moral law in marriage or family life perished in this world and will have no future in the Hereafter. The lessons apply not only to individuals but to whole nations or social groups.

5522. This refers to the present life : apparently the Hereafter is implied in verse 10 below.

5523. See last note.

5524. There is no excuse for us to go astray, seeing that God in His infinite Mercy has explained to us His Message by His many Signs around us and clearly by means of the human Teachers and Apostles whom He has sent for our instruction : see next verse.

From the depths of Darkness[5525]
Into Light. And those who
Believe in God and work
Righteousness, He will admit
To Gardens beneath which rivers
Flow, to dwell therein
For ever: God has indeed
Granted for them
A most excellent provision.

12. God is He Who
Created seven Firmaments[5526]
And of the earth
A similar number.[5527]
Through the midst
Of them (all) descends[5528]
His Command: that ye may
Know that God has power
Over all things, and that
God comprehends all things
In (His) Knowledge.

مِنَ الظُّلُمٰتِ اِلَى النُّوْرِ ؕ
وَمَنْ يُّؤْمِنْ بِاللّٰهِ وَيَعْمَلْ صَالِحًا
يُّدْخِلْهُ جَنّٰتٍ تَجْرِيْ مِنْ تَحْتِهَا الْاَنْهٰرُ
خٰلِدِيْنَ فِيْهَآ اَبَدًا ؕ
قَدْ اَحْسَنَ اللّٰهُ لَهٗ رِزْقًا ۝

١٢- اَللّٰهُ الَّذِيْ خَلَقَ سَبْعَ سَمٰوٰتٍ
وَّمِنَ الْاَرْضِ مِثْلَهُنَّ ؕ
يَتَنَزَّلُ الْاَمْرُ بَيْنَهُنَّ
لِتَعْلَمُوْٓا اَنَّ اللّٰهَ عَلٰى كُلِّ شَيْءٍ قَدِيْرٌ ۙ
وَّاَنَّ اللّٰهَ قَدْ اَحَاطَ بِكُلِّ شَيْءٍ عِلْمًا ۝ ع

5525 *Cf.* xxiv. 40: the unbelievers' state is "like the depths of darkness in a vast deep ocean, overwhelmed with billow topped by billow, topped by dark clouds; depths of darkness, one above another." *Cf.* ii 257: "God is the Protector of those who have Faith: from the depths of darkness He will lead them forth into light."

5526. "*Seven Firmaments.*" The literal meaning refers to the seven orbits or firmaments that we see clearly marked in the motions of the heavenly bodies in the space around us: see xxiii. 17. n. 2876. In poetical imagery there are the seven Planetary spheres, which form the lower heaven or heavens, with higher spheres culminating in the Empyrean, or God's Throne of Majesty: see notes 4035-36 to xxxvii. 6. The mystical meaning refers to the various grades in the spiritual or heavenly kingdom, the number seven being itself a mystical symbol, comprising many and yet forming an indivisible integer, the highest indivisible integer of one digit.

5527. See the last note, about the mystic number seven. As there are grades one above the other in the spiritual kingdom, there are similar grades in our life on this earth. If we take the literal meaning,—just as we see the heavenly spheres one above another, over our heads, so we can see that the crust of the earth is built up of geological strata one above another.

5528. But in all spheres of life and Creation, whatever conception we are able to form of them, it is certain that the Command or Law of God runs through them all, for His knowledge and power extend through all things.

INTRODUCTION TO SŪRA LXVI (*Tahrīm*).

This is the tenth and last of the series of short Medina Sūras which began with S. lvii: see Introduction to that Sūra. The point dealt with here is: how far the turning away from sex or the opposition of one sex against another or a want of harmony between the sexes may injure the higher interests of society.

The date may be taken to be somewhere about A.H. 7.

Summary.—The failings of the weaker sex should not turn away men from normal social life: harmony and mutual confidence should be taught and enforced, and God's blessing will descend on the virtuous even if their lot is cast with the wicked (lxvi. 1-12, and C. 245).

C. 245.—The relations between the sexes are embittered
(lxvi. 1-12.) By misunderstandings and conflicts that produce
Unhappiness and misery, personal and social.
Harmony and confidence are due between
The sexes, not disgust or isolation, which may
Please some but cause injustice to others.
Respect each other's confidence, and if
You fail, repent and make amends.
The good man seeks virtue for himself
And his family. If Evil is yoked to Good,
It must take the fruit of its own deeds;
The worldly tie will profit naught;
But Good should firmly make a stand
And will be saved, for God doth care
For all His true devoted Servants.

Sūra LXVI.

Taḥrīm, or Holding (something) to be Forbidden.

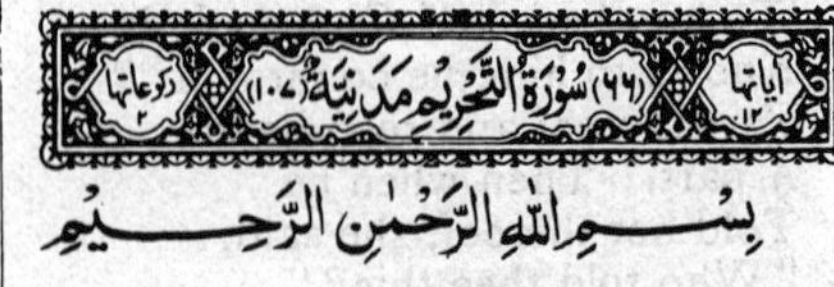

In the name of God, Most Gracious, Most Merciful.

بِسْمِ اللّٰهِ الرَّحْمٰنِ الرَّحِيْمِ

1. O Prophet! Why
Holdest thou to be forbidden
That which God has [5529]
Made lawful to thee?
Thou seekest to please [5530]
Thy consorts. But God
Is Oft-Forgiving, Most Merciful.

١-يٰٓاَيُّهَا النَّبِيُّ لِمَ تُحَرِّمُ
مَآ اَحَلَّ اللّٰهُ لَكَ ۚ
تَبْتَغِيْ مَرْضَاتَ اَزْوَاجِكَ ۭ
وَاللّٰهُ غَفُوْرٌ رَّحِيْمٌ ○

2. God has already ordained [5531]
For you, (O men),
The dissolution of your oaths
(In some cases): and God
Is your Protector, and He
Is Full of Knowledge
And Wisdom.

٢-قَدْ فَرَضَ اللّٰهُ لَكُمْ
تَحِلَّةَ اَيْمَانِكُمْ ۚ
وَاللّٰهُ مَوْلٰىكُمْ ۚ
وَهُوَ الْعَلِيْمُ الْحَكِيْمُ ○

3. When the Prophet disclosed
A matter in confidence [5532]

٣-وَاِذْ اَسَرَّ النَّبِيُّ

5529. The Prophet's household was not like other households. The Consorts of Purity were expected to hold a higher standard in behaviour and reticence than ordinary women, as they had higher work to perform. See n. 3706 to xxxiii. 28. But they were human beings after all, and were subject to the weaknesses of their sex, and they sometimes failed. The imprudence of Ḥadhrat 'Āisha (see n. 2962 to xxiv. 11) once caused serious difficulties: the holy Prophet's mind was sore distressed, and he renounced the society of his wives for some time. This renunciation seems to be referred to here. The situation was none the less difficult for him because she was a daughter of Ḥadhrat Abū Bakr, one of the truest and most intimate of his Companions and lieutenants. Ḥadhrat 'Umar's daughter Ḥafṣa was also sometimes apt to presume on her position, and when the two combined in secret counsel, and discussed matters and disclosed secrets to each other, they caused much sorrow to the holy Prophet, whose heart was tender and who treated all his family with exemplary patience and affection.

5530. The tender words of admonition addressed to the Consorts in xxxiii. 28-34 explain the situation far better than any comments can express. If the holy Prophet had been a mere husband in the ordinary sense of the term, he could not have held the balance even between his private feelings and his public duties. But he was not an ordinary husband, and he abandoned his renunciation on his realisation of the higher duties with which he was charged, and which required conciliation with firmness.

5531. *Cf.* ii. 224. If your vows prevent you from doing good, or acting rightly, or making peace between persons, you should expiate the vow, but not refrain from your good deed.

5532. Who these two consorts were, and what was the matter in confidence which was disclosed, we are not expressly told, but the facts mentioned in n. 5529 above will help us to understand this passage. It is needless to drag in all the petty womanish tittle-tattle which some Commentators have conjecturally collected, or the malicious insinuations of those who have not understood the saintly greatness of the holy Prophet. The sacred words imply that the matter was of great importance as to the principle involved, but that the details were not of sufficient importance for permanent record. For the lessons to be drawn, see the notes following.

To one of his consorts,
And she then divulged it
(To another), and God made it
Known to him, he confirmed[5533]
Part thereof and repudiated
A part. Then when he
Told her thereof, she said,
"Who told thee this?"
He said, "He told me
Who knows and is well-acquainted
(With all things)."

إِلَىٰ بَعْضِ أَزْوَٰجِهِۦ حَدِيثًا ۖ
فَلَمَّا نَبَّأَتْ بِهِۦ وَأَظْهَرَهُ ٱللَّهُ عَلَيْهِ
عَرَّفَ بَعْضَهُۥ وَأَعْرَضَ عَنۢ بَعْضٍ ۖ
فَلَمَّا نَبَّأَهَا بِهِۦ
قَالَتْ مَنْ أَنۢبَأَكَ هَٰذَا ۖ
قَالَ نَبَّأَنِىَ ٱلْعَلِيمُ ٱلْخَبِيرُ ○

4. If ye two turn in repentance[5534]
To Him, your hearts
Are indeed so inclined;
But if ye back up
Each other against him,
Truly God is his Protector,
And Gabriel, and (every)
Righteous one among those
Who believe,—and furthermore,[5535]
The angels—will back (him) up.

٤- إِن تَتُوبَآ إِلَى ٱللَّهِ
فَقَدْ صَغَتْ قُلُوبُكُمَا ۖ
وَإِن تَظَٰهَرَا عَلَيْهِ
فَإِنَّ ٱللَّهَ هُوَ مَوْلَىٰهُ وَجِبْرِيلُ وَصَٰلِحُ
ٱلْمُؤْمِنِينَ ۖ وَٱلْمَلَٰٓئِكَةُ بَعْدَ ذَٰلِكَ ظَهِيرٌ ○

5. It may be, if he
Divorced you (all),[5536]

٥- عَسَىٰ رَبُّهُۥٓ إِن طَلَّقَكُنَّ

5533. The moral we have to draw is manifold. (1) If anything is told us in confidence, especially by one at the head of affairs, we must not divulge it to our closest friend. (2) If such divulgence is made in the most secret whispers, God's Plan is such that it will come to light and expose those guilty of breach of confidence. (3) When the whispered version is compared with the true version and the actual facts, it will be found that the whispered version is in great part untrue, due to the misunderstanding and exaggeration inevitable in the circumstances. (4) The breach of confidence must inevitably redound to the shame of the guilty party, whose surprise only covers a sense of humiliation. See next note.

5534. There are further lessons. (5) Both the party betraying confidence and that encouraging the betrayal must purge their conduct by repentance. (6) Frank repentance would be what their hearts and conscience themselves would dictate, and they must not resist such amends on account of selfish obstinacy. (7) If they were to resist frank repentance and amends, they are only abetting each other's wrong, and they cannot prevail against all the spiritual forces which will be ranged on the side of the right.

5535. Do not forget the dual meaning: immediate, in application to the holy Prophet, and general, being the lesson which we ought all to learn. The holy Prophet could not be injured by any persons doing anything against him, even though they might unconsciously put him in great jeopardy: for God, the Angel Gabriel (who was the Messenger to him), and the whole Community, would protect him,—to say nothing of the army of angels or hidden spiritual forces that always guarded him. *Cf.* xxxiii. 56. The general lesson for us is that the good man's protection is that of the spiritual forces around him; it is divine protection, against which human weakness or folly will have no power.

5536. From the case of two in verse 4, we now come to the case of all the Consorts generally, in verse 5. *Cf.* xxxiii. 28-30. Their duties and responsibilities were higher than those of other women, and therefore their failure would also be more serious. This is only hypothetical, in order to show us the virtues expected of them: faith and devotion, worship and service, readiness for travel or *hijrat*, whether they were young or old, new to married life or otherwise. From them again the more general application follows—to all women in Islam.

That God will give him
In exchange Consorts
Better than you,—
Who submit (their wills),
Who believe, who are devout,
Who turn to God in repentance,
Who worship (in humility),
Who travel (for Faith) and fast,—[5537]
Previously married or virgins.

أَن يُبْدِلَهُۥٓ أَزْوَٰجًا خَيْرًا مِّنكُنَّ
مُسْلِمَٰتٍ مُّؤْمِنَٰتٍ
قَٰنِتَٰتٍ تَٰٓئِبَٰتٍ
عَٰبِدَٰتٍ سَٰٓئِحَٰتٍ
ثَيِّبَٰتٍ وَأَبْكَارًا ○

6. O ye who believe! [5538]
Save yourselves and your
Families from a Fire
Whose fuel is Men [5539]
And Stones, over which
Are (appointed) angels
Stern (and) severe,[5540]
Who flinch not (from
Executing) the Commands
They receive from God,
But do (precisely) what
They are commanded.

٦- يَٰٓأَيُّهَا ٱلَّذِينَ ءَامَنُوا۟ قُوٓا۟
أَنفُسَكُمْ وَأَهْلِيكُمْ نَارًا
وَقُودُهَا ٱلنَّاسُ وَٱلْحِجَارَةُ
عَلَيْهَا مَلَٰٓئِكَةٌ غِلَاظٌ شِدَادٌ
لَّا يَعْصُونَ ٱللَّهَ مَآ أَمَرَهُمْ
وَيَفْعَلُونَ مَا يُؤْمَرُونَ ○

7. (They will say),
"O ye Unbelievers!
Make no excuses
This Day! Ye are being [5541]

٧- يَٰٓأَيُّهَا ٱلَّذِينَ كَفَرُوا۟
لَا تَعْتَذِرُوا۟ ٱلْيَوْمَ ۖ إِنَّمَا

5537. *Sāiḥāt*: literally, those who travel about for the Faith, renouncing hearth and home; hence those who go on pilgrimage, who fast, who deny themselves the ordinary pleasures of life. Note that the spiritual virtues are named in the descending order: submitting their wills (Islam), faith and devotion, turning ever to worship and faith, and performing other rites, or perhaps being content with asceticism. And this applies to all women, maiden girls or women of mature experience who were widows or separated from previous husbands by divorce.

5538. Note how we have been gradually led up in admonition from two Consorts to all consorts, to all women, to all Believers, and to all men and women including Unbelievers. We must carefully guard not only our own conduct, but the conduct of our families, and of all who are near and dear to us. For the issues are most serious, and the consequences of a fall are most terrible.

5539. "*A Fire whose fuel is Men and Stones.*" *Cf.* ii. 24. This is a terrible Fire: not merely like the physical fire which burns wood or charcoal or substances like that, and consumes them. This spiritual Fire will have for its fuel men who do wrong and are as hard-hearted as stones, or stone Idols as symbolical of all the unbending Falsehoods in life.

5540. *Cf.* lxxiv. 31. We think of the angel nature as gentle and beautiful, but in another aspect perfection includes justice, fidelity, discipline, and the firm execution of duty according to lawful Commands. So, in the attributes of God Himself, Justice and Mercy, Kindness and Correction are not contradictory but complementary. An earthly ruler will be unkind to his loyal subjects if he does not punish evil-doers.

5541. 'This is no hardship or injustice imposed on you. It is all but the fruit of your own deeds; the result of your own deliberate choice.'

But requited for
All that ye did!"

تُجْزَوْنَ مَا كُنْتُمْ تَعْمَلُوْنَ ○ ع ١٩

SECTION 2.

8. O ye who believe![5542]
Turn to God
With sincere repentance:
In the hope that
Your Lord will remove[5543]
From you your ills
And admit you to Gardens
Beneath which Rivers flow,—
The Day that God
Will not permit
To be humiliated
The Prophet and those
Who believe with him.
Their Light will run[5544]
Forward before them
And by their right hands,
While they say, "Our Lord!
Perfect our Light for us,
And grant us Forgiveness:
For Thou hast power
Over all things."

٨- يٰٓاَيُّهَا الَّذِيْنَ اٰمَنُوْا
تُوْبُوْٓا اِلَى اللّٰهِ تَوْبَةً نَّصُوْحًا ط
عَسٰى رَبُّكُمْ
اَنْ يُّكَفِّرَ عَنْكُمْ سَيِّاٰتِكُمْ
وَيُدْخِلَكُمْ جَنّٰتٍ تَجْرِيْ مِنْ تَحْتِهَا الْاَنْهٰرُ لا
يَوْمَ لَا يُخْزِى اللّٰهُ النَّبِيَّ
وَالَّذِيْنَ اٰمَنُوْا مَعَهٗ ج
نُوْرُهُمْ يَسْعٰى بَيْنَ اَيْدِيْهِمْ وَبِاَيْمَانِهِمْ
يَقُوْلُوْنَ رَبَّنَآ اَتْمِمْ لَنَا نُوْرَنَا وَاغْفِرْ لَنَا ج
اِنَّكَ عَلٰى كُلِّ شَيْءٍ قَدِيْرٌ ○

9. O Prophet! Strive hard[5545]
Against the Unbelievers
And the Hypocrites,
And be firm against them.

٩- يٰٓاَيُّهَا النَّبِيُّ جَاهِدِ الْكُفَّارَ
وَالْمُنٰفِقِيْنَ وَاغْلُظْ عَلَيْهِمْ ط

5542. The opposition of sex against sex, individual or concerted, having been condemned, we are now exhorted to turn to the Light, and to realise that the good and righteous can retain their integrity even though their mates, in spite of all their example and precept, remain in evil and sin.

5543. Whatever may have been the faults of the past, unite in good deeds, and abandon petty sectional jealousies, and God will remove your difficulties and distresses, and all the evils from which you suffer. Indeed He will grant you the Bliss of Heaven, and save you from any humiliation which you may have brought on yourselves by your conduct and on the revered Prophet and Teacher whose name you professed to take.

5544. See lvii. 12, and n. 5288. The darkness of evil will be dispelled, and the Light of God will be realised by them more and more. But even so they will not be content: for they will pray for the least taint of evil to be removed from them, and perfection to be granted to them. In that exalted state they will be within reach of perfection,—not by their own merits, but by the infinite Mercy and Power of God.

5545. See ix. 73, where the same words introduce the argument against the Hypocrites. Here they introduce the argument against wickedness, which, though given the privilege of association with goodness and piety, persisted in wicked deeds, and in favour of those noble souls, which, though tied to wickedness, retained their purity and integrity. Two examples of each kind are given,—of women, as this Sūra is mainly concerned with women.

Their abode is Hell,—
An evil refuge (indeed).

وَمَاْوٰىهُمْ جَهَنَّمُ ۗ وَبِئْسَ الْمَصِيْرُ ○

10. God sets forth,
For an example
To the Unbelievers,
The wife of Noah[5546]
And the wife of Lūṭ:[5547]
They were (respectively)
Under two of our righteou
Servants, but they were
False to their (husbands),[5548]
And they profited nothing
Before God on their account,
But were told: "Enter ye
The Fire along with
(Others) that enter!"

١٠- ضَرَبَ اللّٰهُ مَثَلًا لِّلَّذِيْنَ كَفَرُوا
امْرَاَتَ نُوْحٍ وَّ امْرَاَتَ لُوْطٍ ۗ
كَانَتَا تَحْتَ عَبْدَيْنِ
مِنْ عِبَادِنَا صَالِحَيْنِ
فَخَانَتٰهُمَا
فَلَمْ يُغْنِيَا عَنْهُمَا مِنَ اللّٰهِ شَيْئًا
وَّقِيْلَ ادْخُلَا النَّارَ مَعَ الدّٰخِلِيْنَ ○

11. And God sets forth,
As an example
To those who believe,
The wife of Pharaoh:[5549]

١١- وَضَرَبَ اللّٰهُ مَثَلًا
لِّلَّذِيْنَ اٰمَنُوا امْرَاَتَ فِرْعَوْنَ ۘ

5546. Read Noah's story in xi. 36-48. Evidently his contemporary world had got so corrupt that it needed a great Flood to purge it. "None of thy people will believe except those who have believed already. So grieve no longer over their evil deeds." But there were evil ones in his own family. A foolish and undutiful son is mentioned in xi. 42-46. Poor Noah tried to save him and pray for him as one "of his family"; but the answer came: "he is not of thy family; for his conduct is unrighteous". We might expect such a son to have a mother like him, and here we are told that it was so. Noah's wife was also false to the standards of her husband, and perished in this world and in the Hereafter.

5547. The wife of Lūṭ has already been mentioned more than once. See xi. 81, and n. 1577; vii. 83, and n. 1051; etc. The world around her was wicked, and she sympathised with and followed that wicked world, rather than her righteous husband. She suffered the fate of her wicked world.

5548 "*False to their husbands*": not necessarily in sex, but in the vital spiritual matters of truth and conduct. They had the high privilege of the most intimate relationship with the noblest spirits of their age: but if they failed to rise to the height of their dignity, their relationship did not save them. They could not plead that they were the wives of pious husbands. They had to enter Hell like any other wicked women. There is personal responsibility before God. One soul cannot claim the merits of another, any more than one pure soul can be injured by association with a corrupt soul. The pure one should keep its purity intact. See the next two examples.

5549. Traditionally she is known as 'Āsiya, one of the four perfect women, the other three being Mary the mother of Jesus, Khadīja the wife of the holy Prophet, and Fāṭima his daughter. Pharaoh is the type of arrogance, godlessness, and wickedness. For his wife to have preserved her Faith, her humility, and her righteousness was indeed a great spiritual triumph. She was probably the same who saved the life of the infant Moses: xxviii. 9.

Behold she said:
"O my Lord! build
For me, in nearness[5550]
To Thee, a mansion
In the Garden,
And save me from Pharaoh
And his doings,
And save me from
Those that do wrong";

12. And Mary the daughter[5551]
Of 'Imrān, who guarded
Her chastity; and We
Breathed into (her body)[5552]
Of Our spirit; and she
Testified to the truth
Of the words of her Lord
And of his Revelations,
28 And was one of the
30 Devout (servants).[5553]

إِذْ قَالَتْ رَبِّ
ابْنِ لِي عِنْدَكَ بَيْتًا
فِي الْجَنَّةِ
وَنَجِّنِي مِنْ فِرْعَوْنَ وَعَمَلِهِ
وَنَجِّنِي مِنَ الْقَوْمِ الظّٰلِمِينَ ۝
١٢- وَمَرْيَمَ ابْنَتَ عِمْرٰنَ
الَّتِىٓ أَحْصَنَتْ فَرْجَهَا
فَنَفَخْنَا فِيهِ مِنْ رُّوحِنَا
وَصَدَّقَتْ بِكَلِمٰتِ رَبِّهَا
وَكُتُبِهِ وَكَانَتْ مِنَ الْقٰنِتِينَ ۝

5550. Her spiritual vision was directed to God, rather than to the worldly grandeur of Pharaoh's court. It is probable that her prayer implies a desire for martyrdom, and it may be that she attained her crown of martyrdom.

5551. 'Imrān was traditionally the name of the father of Mary the mother of Jesus: see n. 375 to iii. 35. She was herself one of the purest of women, though the Jews accused her falsely of unchastity: *cf.* xix. 27-28.

5552 *Cf.* xxi. 91. As a virgin she gave birth to Jesus: xix. 16 29. In xxxii. 9, it is said of Adam's progeny, man, that God "fashioned him in due proportion, and breathed into him something of His spirit". In xv. 29, similar words are used with reference to Adam. The virgin birth should not therefore be supposed to imply that God was the father of Jesus in the sense in which Greek mythology makes Zeus the father of Apollo by Latona or of Minos by Europa And yet that is the doctrine to which the Christian idea of "the only begotten Son of God" leads.

5553 Mary had true faith and testified her faith in the prophet Jesus and in his revelation as well as in the revelations which he came to confirm (and to foreshadow). She was of the company of the Devout of all ages. The fact that *Qānitīn* (devout) is not here in the feminine gender implies that the highest spiritual dignity is independent of sex. And so we close the lesson of this Sūra, that while sex is a fact of our physical existence, the sexes should act in harmony and co-operation, for in the highest spiritual matters we are all one. "We made her and her son a Sign for all peoples. Verily this Brotherhood of yours is a single Brotherhood, and I am your Lord and Cherisher: therefore serve Me and no other" (xxi. 91-92)

INTRODUCTION AND SUMMARY: SŪRA LXVII (*Mulk*).

We have now done fourteen-fifteenths of the Qur-ān, and have followed step by step the development of its argument establishing the Ummat or Brotherhood of Islam.

There is a logical break here. The remaining fifteenth consists of short spiritual Lyrics, mostly of the Meccan period, dealing mainly with the inner life of man, and in its individual aspects. They may be compared to Hymns or Psalms in other religious literature. But these short Quranic Sūras have a grandeur, a beauty, a mystic meaning, and a force of earnestness under persecution, all their own. With their sources in the sublimest regions of the Empyrean, their light penetrates into the darkest recesses of Life, into the concrete facts which are often mistaken for the whole of Reality, though they are but an insignificant portion and on the surface and fleeting. There is much symbolism in language and thought, in describing the spiritual in terms of the things we see and understand.

It is the contrast between the shadows of Reality here and the eternal Reality, between the surface world and the profound inner World, that is urged on our attention here.

This Sūra of 30 verses belongs to the Middle Meccan period, just before S. lxix. and S. lxx. God is mentioned here by the name *Raḥmān* (Most Gracious), as He is mentioned by the names of *Rabb* (Lord and Cherisher) and *Raḥmān* (Most Gracious) in S. xix.

C. 246.—Lordship in right and in fact belongs
(lxvii. 1-30.) To God Most Gracious, Whose Goodness
And Glory and Power are writ large
On all His Creation. The beauty and order
Of the Heavens above us proclaim Him.
Then who can reject His Call but those
In pitiful delusion? And who can fail
To accept, that truly knows himself
And the mighty Reality behind him?
The earth and the good things thereof are prepared
For man by his Gracious Lord, Who guards
Him from hourly dangers. Who sustains
The wonderful flight of the Birds in mid-air?
Above, and below, and in mid-air can we see
His boundless Signs. We know that His Promise
Of the Hereafter is true. The spring and source
Of the goodness of things is in Him, and will
Appear triumphant when the Hour is established.

Sūra LXVII.

Mulk, or Dominion.

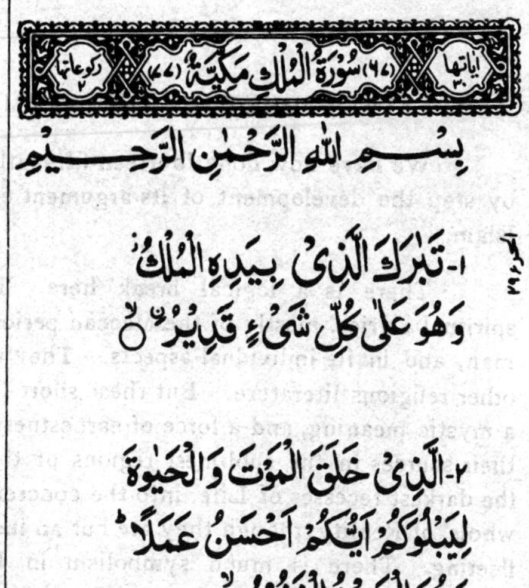

In the name of God, Most Gracious,
Most Merciful.

1. Blessed[5554] be He
In Whose hands
Is Dominion;[5555]
And He over all things
Hath Power;—

2. He Who created Death[5556]
And Life, that He
May try which of you
Is best in deed:[5557]
And He is the Exalted[5558]
In Might, Oft-Forgiving;—

5554. What do we mean when we bless the name of God, or proclaim (in the optative mood) that the whole Creation should bless the name of the Lord? We mean that we recognise and proclaim His beneficence to us; for all increase and happiness is through Him, "in His hands",—in the hands of Him Who also holds Dominion or Power. In our human affairs we sometimes see the separation of Dominion or Power from Goodness or Beneficence: in the divine nature we recognise that there is no separation or antithesis.

5555. *Mulk*: Dominion, Lordship, Sovereignty, the Right to carry out His Will, or to do all that He wills. *Power* (in the clause following) is the Capacity to carry out His Will, so that nothing can resist or neutralise it. Here is beneficence completely identified with Lordship and Power; and it is exemplified in the verses following. Note that "*Mulk*" here has a different shade of meaning from *Malakūt* in xxxvi. 83. Both words are from the same root, and I have translated both by the word "Dominion". But *Malakūt* refers to Lordship in the Invisible World, while *Mulk* to Lordship in the Visible World. God is Lord of both.

5556. "*Created Death and Life.*" Death is here put before Life, and it is created. Death is therefore not merely a negative state. In ii. 28 we read: "Seeing that ye were without life (literally, *dead*), and He gave you life; then will He cause you to die, and will again bring you to life; and again to Him will ye return." In liii. 44, again, Death is put before Life. Death, then, is: (1) the state before life began, which may be non-existence or existence in some other form; (2) the state in which Life as we know it ceases, but existence does not cease; a state of *Barzakh* (xxiii. 100), or Barrier or Partition, after our visible Death and before Judgment; after that will be the new Life, which we conceive of under the term Eternity.

5557. Creation, therefore, is not in mere sport, or without a purpose with reference to man. The state before our present Life, or the state after, we can scarcely understand. But our present Life is clearly given to enable us to strive by good deeds to reach a nobler state.

5558. All this is possible, because God is so Exalted in Might that He can perfectly carry out His Will and Purpose, and that Purpose is Love, Mercy, and Goodness to His creatures.

3. He Who created
The seven heavens [5559]
One above another:
No want of proportion
Wilt thou see
In the Creation
Of (God) Most Gracious.
So turn thy vision again:
Seest thou any flaw?

٣- الَّذِي خَلَقَ سَبْعَ سَمٰوٰتٍ طِبَاقًا
مَا تَرٰى فِي خَلْقِ الرَّحْمٰنِ مِنْ تَفٰوُتٍ
فَارْجِعِ الْبَصَرَ
هَلْ تَرٰى مِنْ فُطُورٍ ۝

4. Again turn thy vision [5560]
A second time: (thy) vision
Will come back to thee
Dull and discomfited,
In a state worn out.

٤- ثُمَّ ارْجِعِ الْبَصَرَ كَرَّتَيْنِ
يَنْقَلِبْ إِلَيْكَ الْبَصَرُ خَاسِئًا
وَّهُوَ حَسِيرٌ ۝

5. And We have,
(From of old),
Adorned the lowest heaven [5561]
With Lamps, and We
Have made such (Lamps)
(As) missiles to drive [5562]
Away the Evil Ones,
And have prepared for them
The Penalty
Of the Blazing Fire.

٥- وَلَقَدْ زَيَّنَّا السَّمَاءَ الدُّنْيَا
بِمَصَابِيحَ
وَجَعَلْنٰهَا رُجُومًا لِّلشَّيٰطِينِ
وَأَعْتَدْنَا لَهُمْ
عَذَابَ السَّعِيرِ ۝

6. For those who reject
Their Lord (and Cherisher) [5563]

٦- وَلِلَّذِينَ كَفَرُوا بِرَبِّهِمْ

5559. *Cf.* lxv. 12, and n. 5526-27. The heavens as they appear to our sight seem to be arranged in layers one above another, and ancient astronomy accounted for the motions of the heavenly bodies in an elaborate scheme of spheres. What we are concerned with here is the order and beauty of the vast spaces and the marvellous bodies that follow regular laws of motion in those enormous spaces in the visible world. From these we are to form some conception of the vastly greater Invisible World, for which we want special spiritual vision.

5560. Reverting to the symbolism of the external or visible world, we are asked to observe and study it again and again, and as minutely as our powers will allow. However closely we observe it, we shall find no flaw in it. Indeed the region of enquiry is so vast and stretches so far beyond our ken, that our eyes, aided with the most powerful telescopes, will confess themselves defeated in trying to penetrate to the ultimate mysteries. We shall find no defect in God's handiwork: it is our own powers that we shall find fail to go beyond a certain compass.

5561. "*Lowest* (or *nearest*) *heaven*": see n. 4035 to xxxvii. 6.

5562. The symbolic imagery of the shooting stars has been explained in xv. 16-18, notes 1951-54; and in xxxvii. 6-10, and notes thereon. The symbolism here takes us a step further. 'You find in the visible heavens perfection and beauty. The lights and the fires you see are holy and beneficent. But if you make fetishes of them, or hand yourselves to evil superstitions of your own imagination, are you not playing with Blazing Fire? Who can define the limits of your Penalty?'

5563. We have seen how the fire in the stars can suggest the beauty and order of the external world; and yet, when it meets with resistance and disharmony, it can burn and destroy. So in the moral and spiritual world. What can be a greater sign of evil, disharmony, and rebellion than to reject the Cherisher and Sustainer, on Whom our life depends, and from Whom we receive nothing but goodness? The Punishment, then, is Fire in its fiercest intensity, as typified in the next two verses.

Is the Penalty of Hell:
And evil is (such) destination.

عَذَابُ جَهَنَّمَ ۖ وَبِئْسَ الْمَصِيرُ ○

7. When they are cast therein,
They will hear
The (terrible) drawing in[5564]
Of its breath
Even as it blazes forth,

٧- إِذَا أُلْقُوا فِيهَا
سَمِعُوا لَهَا شَهِيقًا
وَهِيَ تَفُورُ ○

8. Almost bursting with fury:
Every time a Group
Is cast therein, its Keepers[5565]
Will ask, "Did no Warner
Come to you?"

٨- تَكَادُ تَمَيَّزُ مِنَ الْغَيْظِ ۖ
كُلَّمَا أُلْقِيَ فِيهَا فَوْجٌ سَأَلَهُمْ خَزَنَتُهَا
أَلَمْ يَأْتِكُمْ نَذِيرٌ ○

9. They will say: "Yes indeed;
A Warner did come to us,
But we rejected him
And said, 'God never
Sent down any (Message):
Ye are innothing but
An egregious delusion!'"[5566]

٩- قَالُوا بَلَىٰ قَدْ جَاءَنَا نَذِيرٌ ۙ
فَكَذَّبْنَا وَقُلْنَا مَا نَزَّلَ اللَّهُ مِنْ شَيْءٍ ۚ
إِنْ أَنْتُمْ إِلَّا فِي ضَلَالٍ كَبِيرٍ ○

10. They will further say:
"Had we but listened
Or used our intelligence,[5567]
We should not (now)

١٠- وَقَالُوا لَوْ كُنَّا نَسْمَعُ
أَوْ نَعْقِلُ مَا كُنَّا فِي

5564. For *shahīq* see n. 1607 to xi. 106. There *shahīq* (sobs) was contrasted with *zafīr* (sighs): in the one case it is the drawing in of breath, and in the other the emission of a deep breath. Here the latter process is represented by the verb *fāra*, to swell, to blaze forth, to gush forth. In xi. 40, the verb *fāra* was applied to the gushing forth of the waters of the Flood; here the verb is applied to the blazing forth of the Fire of Punishment. Fire is personified: in its in-take it has a fierce appetite; in the flames which it throws out, it has a fierce aggressiveness. And yet in ultimate result evil meets the same fate, whether typified by water or fire.

5565. *Cf.* xxxix. 71, n. 4348. "*Every time*": it may not be the same angels who are guarding the gates of Hell every time new inmates come in. The pure, innocent angel nature does not know the crookedness of human evil, and is surprised at so many human beings coming in for punishment: it wonders if no warning was conveyed to men, whereas in fact men have a warning in Clear Signs during all the period of their probation. The Clear Signs come from Revelation, from their own conscience, and from all nature around them.

5566. God's Signs were not only rejected or defied, but their very existence was denied. Nay, more, even their possibility was denied, and alas! righteous people and spiritual Teachers were persecuted or mocked (xxxvi. 30). They were called fools or madmen, or men under a delusion!

5567. Man has himself the power given to him to distinguish good from evil, and he is further helped by the teachings of the great Apostles or World Teachers. Where such Teachers do not come into personal contact with an individual or a generation, the true meaning of their teaching can be understood by means of the Reason which God has given to every human soul to judge by. It is failure to follow a man's own lights sincerely that leads to his degradation and destruction.

Be among the Companions
Of the Blazing Fire!"

أَصْحٰبِ السَّعِيرِ ۝

11. They will then confess[5568]
Their sins: but far
Will be (Forgiveness)
From the Companions
Of the Blazing Fire!

١١- فَاعْتَرَفُوا بِذَنْۢبِهِمْ
فَسُحْقًا لِّأَصْحٰبِ السَّعِيرِ ۝

12. As for those who
Fear their Lord unseen,[5569]
For them is Forgiveness
And a great Reward.

١٢- إِنَّ الَّذِينَ يَخْشَوْنَ رَبَّهُم بِالْغَيْبِ
لَهُم مَّغْفِرَةٌ وَأَجْرٌ كَبِيرٌ ۝

13. And whether ye hide
Your word or publish it,
He certainly has (full) knowledge,
Of the secrets of (all) hearts.

١٣- وَأَسِرُّوا قَوْلَكُمْ أَوِ اجْهَرُوا بِهِۦ ۖ
إِنَّهُۥ عَلِيمٌۢ بِذَاتِ الصُّدُورِ ۝

14. Should He not know,—
He that created?[5570]
And He is the One
That understands the finest
Mysteries (and) is
Well-acquainted (with them).

١٤- أَلَا يَعْلَمُ
مَنْ خَلَقَ
وَهُوَ اللَّطِيفُ الْخَبِيرُ ۝ ع

SECTION 2.

15. It is He Who has
Made the earth manageable[5571]

١٥- هُوَ الَّذِى جَعَلَ لَكُمُ الْأَرْضَ ذَلُولًا

5568. They will then have passed through the fire of Judgment and will now be in the fire of Punishment. The Reality will not only now be clear to them, but after the questionings of the angels they cannot even pretend to make any excuses. They will freely confess, but that is not repentance, for repentance implies amendment, and the time for repentance and amendment will have long been past.

5569. See n. 3902 to xxxv. 18. Read "unseen" adverbially. To fear the Lord is to love Him so intensely that you fear to do anything which is against His Will, and you do it because you realise Him intensely in your hearts, though you do not see Him with your bodily senses. Nor is it of any consequences whether other people see your love or the consequences that flow from your love, for your good deeds are for the love of God and not for show in the eyes of men. Such intensity of love obtains forgiveness for any past, and is indeed rewarded with God's love, which is immeasurably precious beyond any merits you may possess.

5570. He Who creates must necessarily know His own handiwork. But lest we should measure His knowledge by such imperfect knowledge as we possess. His knowledge is further characterised as understanding the finest mysteries and being well-acquainted with them (*Laṭīf* and *Khabīr*): see xxii. 63, n. 2844.

5571. *Ẓulūl* is used in ii. 71 for an animal trained and tractable; here it is used to qualify the earth, and I have translated 'manageable'. Man has managed to make paths through deserts and over mountains; through rivers and seas by means of ships; through the air by means of airways; he has made bridges and tunnels and other means of communication. But this he has only been able to do because God has given him the necessary intelligence and has made the earth tractable to that intelligence.

For you, so traverse
Ye through its tracts
And enjoy of the Sustenance
Which He furnishes: but
Unto Him is the Resurrection.[5572]

فَامْشُوا فِي مَنَاكِبِهَا
وَكُلُوا مِن رِّزْقِهِ ۖ
وَإِلَيْهِ النُّشُورُ ۝

16. Do ye feel secure that
He Who is in Heaven
Will not cause you
To be swallowed up[5573]
By the earth when it
Shakes (as in an earthquake)?

١٦- ءَأَمِنتُم مَّن فِي السَّمَاءِ
أَن يَخْسِفَ بِكُمُ الْأَرْضَ
فَإِذَا هِيَ تَمُورُ ۝

17. Or do ye feel secure
That He Who is in Heaven
Will not send against you
A violent tornado[5574]
(With showers of stones),
So that ye shall
Know how (terrible)
Was My warning?

١٧- أَمْ أَمِنتُم مَّن فِي السَّمَاءِ
أَن يُرْسِلَ عَلَيْكُمْ حَاصِبًا ۖ
فَسَتَعْلَمُونَ
كَيْفَ نَذِيرِ ۝

18. But indeed men before them
Rejected (My warning):
Then how (terrible) was
My rejection (of them)?[5575]

١٨- وَلَقَدْ كَذَّبَ الَّذِينَ مِن قَبْلِهِمْ
فَكَيْفَ كَانَ نَكِيرِ ۝

19. Do they not observe
The birds above them,[5576]

١٩- أَوَلَمْ يَرَوْا إِلَى الطَّيْرِ فَوْقَهُمْ

5572. In describing God's gifts and mercies and watchful care in this our temporary sojourn on this earth, it is made clear that the ultimate end is the Hereafter. The real Beyond, which is the goal, is the life after the Resurrection.

5573. *Cf.* xvii. 68, and n. 2263. Also *cf.* the story of Qārūn in xxviii. 76-82. If we feel safe on land, it is because God has made this earth amenable, manageable and serviceable to us (verse 15 above). But if we defy God and break His Law, have we any security, that even this comparatively unimportant safety in a fleeting world will last? Looking at it from a purely physical point of view, have there not been dreadful earthquakes, typhoons, and tornadoes?

5574. *Cf.* xvii. 68; and xxix. 40, n. 3462. Such a violent wind destroyed the wicked Cities which defied Lūṭ's warning.

5575. *Cf.* xxii. 42-44, and n. 2822.

5576. The flight of birds is one of the most beautiful and wonderful things in nature. The make and arrangement of their feathers and bones, and their stream-line shapes, from beak to tail, are instances of purposive adaptation. They soar with outstretched wings; they dart about with folded wings; their motions upwards and downwards, as well as their stabilisation in the air, and when they rest on their feet, have given many ideas to man in the science and art of aeronautics. But who taught or gave to birds this wonderful adaptation? None but God, Whose infinite Mercy provides for every creature just those conditions which are best adapted for its life.

Spreading their wings
And folding them in ?[5577]
None can uphold them
Except (God) Most Gracious :
Truly it is He
That watches over all things.

وقف لازم / وقف غفران / وقف منزل
صٰٓفّٰتٍ وَّيَقْبِضْنَ ؔ
مَا يُمْسِكُهُنَّ اِلَّا الرَّحْمٰنُ ؕ
اِنَّهٗ بِكُلِّ شَيْءٍۭ بَصِيْرٌ ○

20. Nay, who is there
That can help you,
(Even as) an army,[5578]
Besides (God) Most Merciful ?
In nothing but delusion
Are the Unbelievers.

٢٠- اَمَّنْ هٰذَا الَّذِيْ هُوَ جُنْدٌ لَّكُمْ
يَنْصُرُكُمْ مِّنْ دُوْنِ الرَّحْمٰنِ ؕ
اِنِ الْكٰفِرُوْنَ اِلَّا فِيْ غُرُوْرٍ ○

21. Or who is there
That can provide you[5579]
With Sustenance if He
Were to withhold His provision ?
Nay, they obstinately persist
In insolent impiety
And flight (from the Truth).

٢١- اَمَّنْ هٰذَا الَّذِيْ يَرْزُقُكُمْ
اِنْ اَمْسَكَ رِزْقَهٗ ۚ
بَلْ لَّجُّوْا فِيْ عُتُوٍّ وَّنُفُوْرٍ ○

22. Is then one who
Walks headlong, with his face[5580]
Grovelling, better guided,—
Or one who walks[5581]
Evenly on a Straight Way ?

٢٢- اَفَمَنْ يَّمْشِيْ مُكِبًّا عَلٰى وَجْهِهٖٓ
اَهْدٰٓى اَمَّنْ يَّمْشِيْ سَوِيًّا
عَلٰى صِرَاطٍ مُّسْتَقِيْمٍ ○

5577. In the Arabic, there is an artistic touch which it is not possible to reproduce in the translation. *Ṣāffāt* (spreading their wings) is in the form of the active participle, suggesting the continuous soaring on outspread wings; while *yaqbidhna* (folding them in) is in the Aorist form, suggesting the spasmodic flapping of wings.

5578. Not the greatest army that man can muster is of any use against the Wrath of God; while the constant watchful care of God is all-in-all to us, and we can never do without it. If the godless wander about in search for blessings otherwise than in the Mercy and Grace of God, they are wandering in vain delusions.

5579. "Sustenance" here, as elsewhere, (*e.g.*, in xvi. 73, n. 2105), refers to all that is necessary to sustain and develop life in all its phases, spiritual and mental, as well as physical. God Most Gracious is the Source of all our Sustenance, and if we persist in looking to Vanities for our Sustenance, we are pursuing a mirage, and, if we examine the matter, we are only following obstinate impulses of rebellion and impiety.

5580. *Cf.* xxvii. 90, and n. 3320. The man of probity is the man who walks evenly on a Straight Way, his feet guided by God's Light and his heart sustained by God's Mercy. The man who chooses evil grovels, with his face down, in paths of Darkness, stumbling on the way, and in constant distrust and fear, the fear of Evil. The two kinds of men are poles apart, although they live on the same earth, see the same Signs, and are fed with the same Mercies from God.

5581. Like Abraham trying to guide his unbelieving father : *Cf.* xix. 43.

23. Say: "It is He Who [5582]
Has created you (and made [5583]
You grow), and made
For you the faculties
Of hearing, seeing,
Feeling and understanding:
Little thanks it is ye give.

٢٣- قُلْ هُوَ الَّذِىٓ اَنْشَاَكُمْ
وَجَعَلَ لَكُمُ
السَّمْعَ وَالْاَبْصَارَ وَالْاَفْـِٕدَةَ ۭ
قَلِيْلًا مَّا تَشْكُرُوْنَ ○

24. Say: "It is He Who
Has multiplied you
Through the earth, [5584]
And to Him shall ye
Be gathered together."

٢٤- قُلْ هُوَ الَّذِىْ ذَرَاَكُمْ فِى الْاَرْضِ
وَاِلَيْهِ تُحْشَرُوْنَ ○

25. They ask: When will
This promise be (fulfilled)?—
If ye are telling [5585]
The truth.

٢٥- وَيَقُوْلُوْنَ مَتٰى هٰذَا الْوَعْدُ
اِنْ كُنْتُمْ صٰدِقِيْنَ ○

26. Say: "As to the knowledge
Of the time, it is
With God alone: [5586]
I am (sent) only
To warn plainly in public."

٢٦- قُلْ اِنَّمَا الْعِلْمُ عِنْدَ اللّٰهِ ۠
وَاِنَّمَآ اَنَا نَذِيْرٌ مُّبِيْنٌ ○

27. At length, when they
See it close at hand, [5587]
Grieved will be the faces
Of the Unbelievers,

٢٧- فَلَمَّا رَاَوْهُ زُلْفَةً
سِيْۤـَٔتْ وُجُوْهُ الَّذِيْنَ كَفَرُوْا

5582. The Teacher is asked to draw constant attention to God, the source of all growth and development, the Giver of the faculties by which we can judge and attain to higher and higher spiritual dignity. And yet, such is our self-will, we use our faculties for wrong purposes and thus show our ingratitude to God.

5583. For *anshaa* see n. 923 to vi. 98.

5584. Mankind, from one set of parents, has been multiplied and scattered through the earth. Men have not only multiplied in numbers, but they have developed different languages and characteristics, inner and outer. But they will all be gathered together at the End of Things, when the mischief created by the wrong exercise of man's will will be cancelled, and the Truth of God will reign universally.

5585. The Unbelievers are sceptical, but they are answered in the next two verses.

5586. The Judgment is certain to come. But when it will exactly come, is known to God alone. The Prophet's duty is to proclaim that fact openly and clearly. It is not for him to punish or to hasten the punishment of evil. *Cf.* xxii. 47-49.

5587. "*It*", *i.e.*, the fulfilment of the promise, the Day of Judgment. When it is actually in sight, then the Unbelievers realise that those whom they used to laugh at for their Faith were in the right, and that they themselves, the sceptics, were terribly in the wrong.

And it will be said
(To them): "This is
(The promise fulfilled),[5588]
Which ye were calling for!"

وَقِيلَ هٰذَا الَّذِي
كُنْتُمْ بِهٖ تَدَّعُونَ ۝

28. Say: "See ye?—
If God were
To destroy me,
And those with me,[5589]
Or if He bestows
His Mercy on us,—
Yet who can deliver
The Unbelievers from
A grievous Penalty?"

٢٨- قُلْ أَرَءَيْتُمْ
إِنْ أَهْلَكَنِيَ اللّٰهُ وَمَنْ مَّعِيَ
أَوْ رَحِمَنَا
فَمَنْ يُّجِيرُ الْكٰفِرِينَ مِنْ
عَذَابٍ أَلِيمٍ ۝

29. Say: "He is (God)
Most Gracious: we have
Believed in Him,
And on Him have we
Put our trust:
So, soon will ye know[5590]
Which (of us) it is
That is in manifest error."

٢٩- قُلْ هُوَ الرَّحْمٰنُ اٰمَنَّا بِهٖ
وَعَلَيْهِ تَوَكَّلْنَا
فَسَتَعْلَمُونَ
مَنْ هُوَ فِي ضَلٰلٍ مُّبِينٍ ۝

30. Say: "See ye?—
If your stream be
Some morning lost[5591]
(In the underground earth),
Who then can supply you
With clear-flowing water?"

٣٠- قُلْ أَرَءَيْتُمْ
إِنْ أَصْبَحَ مَاۤؤُكُمْ غَوْرًا
فَمَنْ يَّأْتِيكُمْ بِمَاۤءٍ مَّعِينٍ ۝ ع

5588. They had defiantly asked for it. Now that it has come near, and it is too late for repentance, there is "weeping and gnashing of teeth".

5589 The sceptics might say and do say to the righteous: "Ah well! if calamities come, they involve the good with the bad, just as you say that God showers His mercies on both good and evil!" The answer is: "Don't you worry about us; even supposing we are destroyed, with all who believe with us, is that any consolation to you? Your sins must bring on you suffering, and nothing can ward it off. If we get any sorrows or sufferings, we take them as a mere trial to make us better, for we believe in God's goodness and we put our trust in Him." See next verse.

5590. See the end of the last note. "Our Faith tells us that God will deliver us from all harm if we sincerely repent and lead righteous lives. You, Unbelievers, have no such hope. When the real adjustment of values is established, you will soon see whether we were in the wrong or you!"

5591. The Sūra is closed with a parable, taken from a vital fact of our physical life, and leading up to the understanding of our spiritual life. In our daily life, what would happen if we woke up some fine morning to find that the sources and springs of our water-supply had disappeared and gone down into the hollows of the earth? Nothing could save our life. Without water we cannot live, and water cannot rise above its level, but always seeks a lower level. So in spiritual life. Its sources and springs are in the divine wisdom that flows from on high. God is the real source of that life, as He is of all forms of life. We must seek His Grace and Mercy. We cannot find grace or mercy or blessing from anything lower. His Wisdom and Mercy are like fresh clear-flowing spring-water, not like the muddy murky wisdom and goodness of this lower world which is only relative, and which often hampers life rather than advances it.

INTRODUCTION AND SUMMARY: SŪRA LXVIII (*Qalam*).

This is a very early Meccan revelation. The general Muslim opinion is that a great part of it was second in order of revelation, the first being S. xcvi. (*Iqraa*), verses 1-5: see *Itqān*, Chapter 7.

The last Sūra having defined the true Reality in contrast with the false standards set up by men, this illustrates the theme by an actual historical example. Our holy Prophet was the sanest and wisest of men: those who could not understand him called him mad or possessed. So, in every age, it is the habit of the world to call Truth Falsehood and Wisdom Madness, and, on the other hand, to exalt Selfishness as Planning, and Arrogance as Power. The contrast is shown up between the two kinds of men and their real inner worth.

Summary.—Let the good carry on their work, in spite of the abuse of the Companions of Evil: let all remember God, before Whom all men are on trial (lxviii. 1-33, and C. 247).

True Judgment comes from God, and not from the false standards of men (lxviii. 34-52, and C. 248).

C. 247.—The Pen is the symbol of the permanent Record,
(lxviii. 1-33.) The written Decree, the perfect Order
In the government of the world. And by that token,
The man of God comes with a Plan
And Guidance that must win against
All detraction. Truth is high above Slander.
But men must be tried against selfishness
And overweening confidence in themselves
Such as would lead them to forget God
And His providence,—like the brothers who built
Castles in the air about their garden
And found it desolate in one night's storm.
But repentance brought them forgiveness:
Thus work the Wrath and the Mercy of God.

Sūra LXVIII.

Qalam, or the Pen, or *Nūn* (see n. 5592).

In the name of God, Most Gracious, Most Merciful.

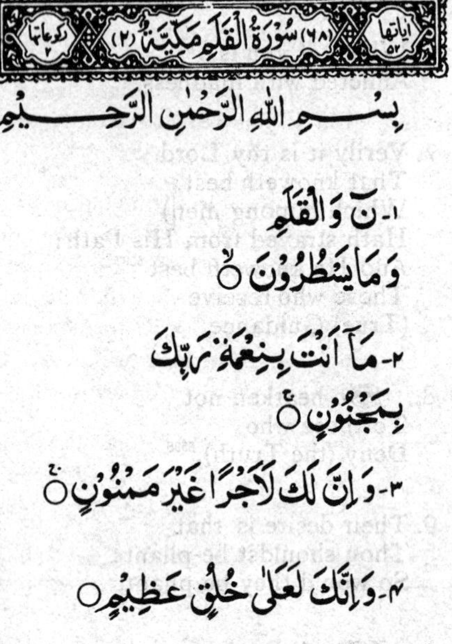

1. Nūn.[5592] By the Pen[5593]
And by the (Record)
Which (men) write,—

2. Thou art not,
By the grace of thy Lord,
Mad or possessed.[5594]

3. Nay, verily for thee
Is a Reward unfailing:[5595]

4. And thou (standest)
On an exalted standard
Of character.

5592. *Nūn* is an Abbreviated Letter: see Appendix I at the end of S. ii.

Nūn may mean a fish, or an ink-holder, or it may be just the Arabic letter of the alphabet, N. In the last case, it may refer to either or both of the other meanings. Note also that the Arabic rhyme in this Sūra ends in N. The reference to ink would be an appropriate link with the mystic Pen in verse 1. The reference to the fish would be appropriate with reference to the story of Jonah in verses 48-50. Jonah's title is "the Companion of the Fish", (Ẕun-Nūn, xxi. 87), as he was, in the story, swallowed by the Fish. The letter N could also symbolically represent Jonah in the Arabic form Yūnus, where the characteristic "Firm Letter" is N.

5593. The mystic Pen and the mystic Record are the symbolical foundations of the Revelation to man. The adjuration by the Pen disposes of the flippant charge that God's Messenger was mad or possessed. For he spoke words of power, not incoherent, but full of meaning, and through the Record of the Pen, that meaning unfolds itself, in innumerable aspects to countless generations. Muḥammad was the living Grace and Mercy of God, and his very nature exalted him above abuse and persecution.

5594. People usually call any one mad whose standards are different from their own. And madness is believed by superstitious people to be due to demoniacal possession, an idea distinctly in the minds of the New Testament writers: for Luke speaks of a man from whom the "devils" were cast out, as being then "clothed, and in his right mind" (Luke, viii. 35).

5595. Instead of being out of his right mind, the man of God had been raised to a great spiritual dignity, a reward that was not like an earthly reward that passes away, but one that was in the very core of his being, and would never fail him in any circumstances. He was really granted a nature and character far above the shafts of grief or suffering, slander or persecution.

5. Soon wilt thou see,[5596]
And they will see,

٥- فَسَتُبْصِرُ وَيُبْصِرُونَ ۝

6. Which of you is
Afflicted with madness.

٦- بِأَييِّكُمُ الْمَفْتُونُ ۝

7. Verily it is thy Lord
That knoweth best,
Which (among men)
Hath strayed from His Path:
And He knoweth best[5597]
Those who receive
(True) Guidance.

٧- إِنَّ رَبَّكَ هُوَ أَعْلَمُ
بِمَنْ ضَلَّ عَنْ سَبِيلِهِ ۖ
وَهُوَ أَعْلَمُ بِالْمُهْتَدِينَ ۝

8. So hearken not
To those who
Deny (the Truth).[5598]

٨- فَلَا تُطِعِ الْمُكَذِّبِينَ ۝

9. Their desire is that
Thou shouldst be pliant:
So would they be pliant.

٩- وَدُّوا لَوْ تُدْهِنُ فَيُدْهِنُونَ ۝

10. Heed not the type
Of despicable man,—[5599]
Ready with oaths,[5600]

١٠- وَلَا تُطِعْ كُلَّ حَلَّافٍ مَّهِينٍ ۝

5596. Though Mustafā's nature raised him above the petty spite of his contemporaries, an appeal is made to their reason and to the logic of events. Was it not his accusers that were really mad? What happened to Walīd ibn Mugaira, or Abū Jahl, or Abū Lahab?—and to God's Apostle and those who followed his guidance? The world's history gives the answer. And the appeal is not only to his contemporaries, but for all time.

5597. Men set up false standards of judgment. The right standard is that of God. For His knowledge is complete and all-embracing; He reads hidden motives as well as things that appear before men's sight; and He knows the past history in which the roots of present actions are embedded, as well as the future consequences of present actions.

5598. The enemies of God's truth are sometimes self-deceived. But quite often they have a glimmering of the truth in spite of their desire to shut their eyes. Then they compromise, and they would like the preachers of inconvenient truths to compromise with them. On those terms there would be mutual laudation. This easy path of making the best of both worlds is a real danger or temptation to the best of us, and we must be on our guard against it if we would really enter into the company of the Righteous who submit their wills to the Will of God. Abū Jahl freely offered impossible compromises to the holy Prophet.

5599. The type of each of these hateful qualities is not uncommon, though the combination of all in one man makes him peculiarly despicable, as was Walīd ibn Mugaira, who was a ringleader in calumniating our Prophet and who came to an evil end not long after the battle of Badr, in which he received injuries.

5600. It is only liars who swear on all occasions, small or great, because their ordinary word is not believed in. The true man's word, according to the proverb, is as good as his bond.

11. A slanderer, going about
With calumnies,

١١- هَمَّازٍ مَّشَّآءٍ بِنَمِيمٍ ۝

12. (Habitually) hindering (all) good,
Transgressing beyond bounds,
Deep in sin,

١٢- مَّنَّاعٍ لِّلْخَيْرِ مُعْتَدٍ أَثِيمٍ ۝

13. Violent (and cruel),—[5601]
With all that, base-born,—

١٣- عُتُلٍّ بَعْدَ ذَٰلِكَ زَنِيمٍ ۝

14. Because[5602] he possesses
Wealth and (numerous) sons.

١٤- أَن كَانَ ذَا مَالٍ وَبَنِينَ ۝

15. When to him are rehearsed
Our Signs,[5603]
"Tales of the Ancients",[5604]
He cries!

١٥- إِذَا تُتْلَىٰ عَلَيْهِ ءَايَٰتُنَا
قَالَ أَسَٰطِيرُ ٱلْأَوَّلِينَ ۝

16. Soon shall We brand
(The beast) on the snout![5605]

١٦- سَنَسِمُهُۥ عَلَى ٱلْخُرْطُومِ ۝

17. Verily We have tried them
As We tried the People

١٧- إِنَّا بَلَوْنَٰهُمْ كَمَا بَلَوْنَآ أَصْحَٰبَ

5601. Besides the self-deceiver and the easy-going man, there is a third type, even more degraded. He has no idea of truth or sincerity. He is ready to swear friendship with every one and fidelity to every cause. But at the same moment he will slander and backbite, and cause mischief even between good but credulous persons. Evil seems to be his good, and good his evil. He will not only pursue evil courses himself but prevent other people from doing right. When checked, he resorts to violence. In any case, he will intrude where he has no right, claiming relationship or power or consideration in circles which would gladly disown him. He is vain of his wealth or because he has a large following at his beck and call. Religion is to him merely old-fashioned superstition.

5602. "*Because*" may connect with "*heed not*" in verse 10, or with "*violent and cruel*" in verse 13. In the former case, we construe: 'Pay no attention to despicable men of the character described, simply because they happen to have wealth or influence, or much backing in man-power'. In the latter case, we construe: the fellow is violent and cruel, because he is puffed up with his wealth or riches or backing in man-power'. In the eyes of God such a man is in any case branded and marked out as a sinner.

5603. God's Signs, by which He calls us, are everywhere—in nature and in our very heart and soul. In Revelation, every verse is a Sign, for it stands symbolically for far more than it says. "Sign" (*Āyat*) thus becomes a technical term for a verse of the Qur-ān.

5604. *Cf.* vi. 25.

5605. Literally, proboscis, the most sensitive limb of the elephant. The sinner makes himself a beast and can only be controlled by his snout.

Of the Garden,[5606]
When they resolved to gather
The fruits of the (garden)
In the morning,

الْجَنَّةِ إِذْ أَقْسَمُوا لَيَصْرِمُنَّهَا مُصْبِحِينَ ۝

18. But made no reservation,
("If it be God's Will").[5607]

١٨- وَلَا يَسْتَثْنُونَ ۝

19. Then there came
On the (garden)
A visitation from thy Lord,[5608]
(Which swept away) all around,
While they were asleep.

١٩- فَطَافَ عَلَيْهَا طَائِفٌ مِّن رَّبِّكَ وَهُمْ نَائِمُونَ ۝

20. So the (garden) became,
By the morning, like
A dark and desolate spot,
(Whose fruit had been gathered).

٢٠- فَأَصْبَحَتْ كَالصَّرِيمِ ۝

21. As the morning broke,
They called out,
One to another,—

٢١- فَتَنَادَوْا مُصْبِحِينَ ۝

22. "Go ye to your tilth
(Betimes) in the morning,[5609]

٢٢- أَنِ اغْدُوا عَلَىٰ حَرْثِكُمْ

5606. "Why do the wicked flourish?" is a question asked in all ages. The answer is not simple. It must refer to (1) the choice left to man's will, (2) his moral responsibility, (3) the need of his tuning his will to God's Will, (4) the long-suffering quality of God, which allows the widest possible chance for the operation of (5) His Mercy, and (6) in the last resort, to the nature of spiritual Punishment, which is not a merely abrupt or arbitrary act, but a long, gradual process, in which there is room for repentance at every stage. All these points are illustrated in the remarkable Parable of the People of the Garden, which also illustrates the greed, selfishness, and heedlessness of man, as well as his tendency to throw the blame on others if he can but think of a scapegoat. All these foibles are shown, but the Mercy of God is boundless, and even after the worst sins and punishments, there may be hope of an even better orchard than the one lost, if only the repentance is true. and there is complete surrender to God's Will. But if, in spite of all this, there is no surrender of the will, then, indeed, the punishment in the Hereafter is something incomparably greater than the little calamities in the Parable.

5607. We must always remember, in all our plans, that they depend for their success on how far they accord with God's Will and Plan. His universal Will is supreme over all affairs. These foolish men had a secret plan to defraud the poor of their just rights, but they were put into a position where they could not do so. In trying to frustrate others, they were themselves frustrated.

5608. It was a terrible storm that blew down and destroyed the fruits and the trees. The whole place was changed out of all recognition

5609. Awaking from sleep, they were not aware that the garden had been destroyed by the storm overnight. They were in their own selfish dreams: by going very early, they thought they could cheat the poor of their share. See next note.

If ye would gather
The fruits."

إِن كُنتُمْ صَـٰرِمِينَ ۝

23. So they departed, conversing
In secret low tones, (saying)—

٢٣- فَٱنطَلَقُوا۟ وَهُمْ يَتَخَـٰفَتُونَ ۝

24. "Let not a single indigent[5610]
Person break in upon you
Into the (garden) this day."

٢٤- أَن لَّا يَدْخُلَنَّهَا ٱلْيَوْمَ عَلَيْكُم مِّسْكِينٌ ۝

25. And they opened the morning,
Strong in an (unjust) resolve.

٢٥- وَغَدَوْا۟ عَلَىٰ حَرْدٍ قَـٰدِرِينَ ۝

26. But when they saw
The (garden), they said:
"We have surely lost our way:[5611]

٢٦- فَلَمَّا رَأَوْهَا
قَالُوٓا۟ إِنَّا لَضَآلُّونَ ۝

27. "Indeed we are shut out
(Of the fruits of our labour)!"[5612]

٢٧- بَلْ نَحْنُ مَحْرُومُونَ ۝

28. Said one of them,
More just (than the rest):[5613]
"Did I not say to you,
'Why not glorify (God)?'"

٢٨- قَالَ أَوْسَطُهُمْ
أَلَمْ أَقُل لَّكُمْ لَوْلَا تُسَبِّحُونَ ۝

29. They said: "Glory
To our Lord! Verily we
Have been doing wrong!"

٢٩- قَالُوا۟ سُبْحَـٰنَ رَبِّنَآ إِنَّا كُنَّا ظَـٰلِمِينَ ۝

5610. The poor man has a right in the harvest—whether as a gleaner or as an artisan or a menial in an Eastern village. The rich owners of the orchard in the Parable wanted to steal a march at an early hour and defeat this right, but their greed was punished, so that it led to a greater loss to themselves. They wanted to cheat but had not the courage to face those they cheated, and by being in the field before any one was up they wanted to make it appear to the world that they were unconscious of any rights they were trampling on.

5611. Their fond dreams were dispelled when they found that the garden had been changed out of all recognition. It was as if they had come to some place other than their own smiling garden. Where they had expected to reap a rich harvest, there was only a howling wilderness. They reflected. Their first thought was of their own personal loss, the loss of their labour and the loss of their capital. They had plotted to keep out others from the fruits: now, as it happened, the loss was their own.

5612. *Cf.* lvi. 67. Also see last note.

5613. This was not necessarily a righteous man, but there are degrees in guilt. He had warned them, but he had joined in their unjust design.

30. Then they turned, one
Against another, in reproach.[5614]

٣٠- فَأَقْبَلَ بَعْضُهُمْ عَلٰى بَعْضٍ يَّتَلَاوَمُوْنَ ○

31. They said: "Alas for us!
We have indeed transgressed!

٣١- قَالُوْا يٰوَيْلَنَآ اِنَّا كُنَّا طٰغِيْنَ ○

32. "It may be that our Lord
Will give us in exchange
A better (garden) than this:
For we do turn to Him
(In repentance)!"[5615]

٣٢- عَسٰى رَبُّنَآ اَنْ يُّبْدِلَنَا خَيْرًا مِّنْهَآ
اِنَّآ اِلٰى رَبِّنَا رٰغِبُوْنَ ○

33. Such is the Punishment
(In this life); but greater
Is the Punishment[5616]
In the Hereafter,—
If only they knew!

٣٣- كَذٰلِكَ الْعَذَابُ ؕ
وَلَعَذَابُ الْاٰخِرَةِ اَكْبَرُ ۘ
لَوْ كَانُوْا يَعْلَمُوْنَ ○ ع

C. 248.—To evil and good there can never be the same
(lxviii. 34-52.) End: no authority can the unjust produce
For their false imaginings. In shame
Will they realise this on the Day when all
Illusions will vanish and they find that the time
For repentance is past. The good man should wait
And should never lose patience, even though
Things go dead against him. Jonah suffered
In agony, but his sincere repentance
Brought him the grace of his Lord, and he
Joined the company of the Righteous:
For Truth is firm and unshaken, is calm
And works good, through all God's Creation.

5614. When greed or injustice is punished, people are ready to throw the blame on others. In this case, one particular individual may have seen the moral guilt of defying the Will of God and the right of man, but if he shared in the enterprise in the hope of profit, he could not get out of all responsibility.

5615. If the repentance was true, there was hope. For God often turns a great evil to our good. If not true, they only added hypocrisy to their other sins.

The Parable presupposes that the garden came into the possession of selfish men, who were so puffed up with their good fortune that they forgot God. That meant that they also became harsh to their fellow-creatures. In their arrogance they plotted to get up early and defeat the claims of the poor at harvest time. They found their garden destroyed by a storm. Some reproached others, but those who sincerely repented obtained mercy. The "better garden" may have been the same garden, flourishing in a future season under God's gift of abundance.

5616. Even in this life the punishment for heedless or selfish arrogance and sin comes suddenly when we least expect it. But there is always room for God's Mercy if we sincerely repent. If the Punishment in this life seems to us so stupefying, how much worse will it be in the Hereafter, when the Punishment will not be only for a limited time, and the time for repentance will have passed?

SECTION 2.

34. Verily, for the Righteous,
Are Gardens of Delight,[5617]
In the Presence
Of their Lord.

٣٤- إِنَّ لِلْمُتَّقِينَ عِندَ رَبِّهِمْ جَنَّٰتِ ٱلنَّعِيمِ ○

35. Shall We then treat
The People of Faith
Like the People of Sin? [5618]

٣٥- أَفَنَجْعَلُ ٱلْمُسْلِمِينَ كَٱلْمُجْرِمِينَ ○

36. What is the matter
With you? How judge ye?

٣٦- مَا لَكُمْ كَيْفَ تَحْكُمُونَ ○

37. Or have ye a Book
Through which ye learn—

٣٧- أَمْ لَكُمْ كِتَٰبٌ فِيهِ تَدْرُسُونَ ○

38. That ye shall have,
Through it whatever
Ye choose? [5619]

٣٨- إِنَّ لَكُمْ فِيهِ لَمَا تَخَيَّرُونَ ○

39. Or have ye Covenants
With Us on oath,[5620]
Reaching to the Day
Of Judgment, (providing)
That ye shall have
Whatever ye shall demand?

٣٩- أَمْ لَكُمْ أَيْمَٰنٌ عَلَيْنَا بَٰلِغَةٌ إِلَىٰ يَوْمِ ٱلْقِيَٰمَةِ إِنَّ لَكُمْ لَمَا تَحْكُمُونَ ○

5617. All symbols of delight, expressed in terms of sense, are spiritualized by their being referred to the presence of God. The Garden is a joy, but the joy of this spiritual Garden is the sense of nearness to God. See also Appendix XII, paragraphs 8 to 10 (following S. liv), pp. 1466 67.

5618. The spiritual arrogance which rejects faith in God is perhaps the worst Sin, because it makes itself impervious to the Mercy of God, as a bed of clay is impervious to the absorption of water. It sets up its own standards and its own will, but how can it measure or bind the Will of God? It sets up its own fetishes,—idols, priests, gods, or godlings. The fetishes may be even God-given gifts or faculties, Intellect or Science, if pushed up to the position of idols. If they are made rivals to God, question them: Will they solve God's mysteries, or even the mysteries of Life and Soul?

5619. It is clearly against both logic and justice that men of righteousness should have the same End as men of sin. Even in this life, man cannot command whatever he chooses, though he is allowed a limited freedom of choice. How can he expect such a thing under a reign of perfect Justice and Truth?

5620. Nor can the Pagans plead that they have any special Covenants with God which give them a favoured position above other mortals. The "Chosen Race" idea of the Jews is also condemned. It is quite true that a certain race or group, on account of special aptitude may be chosen by God to uphold His truth and preach it. But this is conditional on their following God's Law. As soon as they become arrogant and selfish, they lose that position. They cannot have a perpetual and unconditional lease till the Day of Judgment.

40. Ask thou of them,
Which of them will stand
Surety for that!

٤٠- سَلْهُمْ اَيُّهُمْ بِذٰلِكَ زَعِيْمٌ ۚ

41. Or have they some
"Partners" (in Godhead)? [5621]
Then let them produce
Their "partners",
If they are truthful!

٤١- اَمْ لَهُمْ شُرَكَآءُ ۚ
فَلْيَاْتُوْا بِشُرَكَآئِهِمْ اِنْ كَانُوْا صٰدِقِيْنَ

42. The Day that the Shin [5622]
Shall be laid bare,
And they shall be summoned
To bow in adoration,
But they shall not be able,—

٤٢- يَوْمَ يُكْشَفُ عَنْ سَاقٍ
وَّيُدْعَوْنَ اِلَى السُّجُوْدِ
فَلَا يَسْتَطِيْعُوْنَ

43. Their eyes will be [5623]
Cast down,—ignominy will
Cover them; seeing that
They had been summoned
Aforetime to bow in adoration,
While they were whole, [5624]
(And had refused).

٤٣- خَاشِعَةً اَبْصَارُهُمْ تَرْهَقُهُمْ ذِلَّةٌ ۗ
وَقَدْ كَانُوْا يُدْعَوْنَ اِلَى السُّجُوْدِ
وَهُمْ سٰلِمُوْنَ

44. Then leave Me [5625] alone
With such as reject
This Message: by degrees
Shall We punish them

٤٤- فَذَرْنِيْ وَمَنْ يُّكَذِّبُ بِهٰذَا الْحَدِيْثِ ۗ
سَنَسْتَدْرِجُهُمْ

5621. "*Partners*" *in Godhead*: as in the doctrine of the Trinity, or indeed in any form of polytheism. Such a doctrine destroys the cardinal doctrine of the Unity of God.

5622. That is, when all mystery will vanish. The Shin is a Symbol for the most hidden mystery, as it is usually doubly covered, first by the skin, and secondly, by clothing. When it is laid bare, men will be summoned to adoration, not necessarily in words, but by the logic of facts, when the Reality will be fully manifest: the Glory will be too dazzling for the Unbelievers, whose past deliberate refusal, when they had freedom to choose, and yet rejected, will stand in their way.

5623. Their past memories, combined with their present position, will then fill them with a sense of the deepest dismay and humiliation. See last note.

5624. *Sālimūn*: whole, in full possession of the power of judgment and will; not constrained, as they now will be, by the Punishment staring them full in the face.

5625. Notice the transition between "Me" and "We" in this verse, and again to "I" and "My" in the next verse. The first person plural ordinarily used in the holy Qur-ān as God's Word, is the plural of respect. In Royal decrees the first person plural is similarly used. When the first person singular is used, it marks some special personal relation, either of Mercy or favours (as in ii. 38 or ii. 150) or of punishment, as here. (*Cf.* n. 56 to ii. 38).

From directions they perceive not.[5626]

مِّنۡ حَيۡثُ لَا يَعۡلَمُوۡنَ ۙ

45. A (long) respite will I
Grant them: truly
Powerful is My Plan.

٤٥- وَاُمۡلِىۡ لَهُمۡ ؕ
اِنَّ كَيۡدِىۡ مَتِيۡنٌ ۝

46. Or is it that thou dost
Ask them for a reward,[5627]
So that they are burdened
With a load of debt?—

٤٦- اَمۡ تَسۡـَٔـلُهُمۡ اَجۡرًا
فَهُمۡ مِّنۡ مَّغۡرَمٍ مُّثۡقَلُوۡنَ ۚ

47. Or that the Unseen[5628]
Is in their hands, so that
They can write it down?

٤٧- اَمۡ عِنۡدَهُمُ الۡغَيۡبُ فَهُمۡ يَكۡتُبُوۡنَ ۝

48. So wait with patience
For the Command
Of thy Lord, and be not
Like the Companion[5629]
Of the Fish,—when he
Cried out in agony.

٤٨- فَاصۡبِرۡ لِحُكۡمِ رَبِّكَ
وَلَا تَكُنۡ كَصَاحِبِ الۡحُوۡتِ ۘ
اِذۡ نَادٰى وَهُوَ مَكۡظُوۡمٌ ؕ

49. Had not Grace
From His Lord
Reached him, he
Would indeed have been

٤٩- لَوۡلَاۤ اَنۡ تَدٰرَكَهٗ
نِعۡمَةٌ مِّنۡ رَّبِّهٖ

5626. *Cf.* vii. 182. We must not be impatient if we see the wicked flourish. It may be that the very appearance of flourishing here may be a part of the Punishment. There may be an eventual punishment by a sort of Cataclysm; but evolutionary punishment is gradual and sure. In any case we cannot see God's Plan, as a whole, and it is not for us to question it.

5627. *Cf.* lii. 40. n. 5074. It costs the Unbelievers nothing to hear the Preacher, for the Preacher asks for no reward, and indeed suffers for their benefit. The Preacher need not look even for appreciation or conversions. Mustafā is addressed in the first instance, but there is always a universal interpretation. The righteous man asks for no reward for his preaching or example: if he did, the value would be too great for the world to pay for. The Unbelievers behave as if they had the secret of the Unseen, but they are empty triflers, for, if they only tried to formulate spiritual laws, they would fail.

5628. *Cf.* lii 41, n. 5075. The Unseen is certainly not within their knowledge or control. If it were, they could clearly write it down for their own guidance or the guidance of others. They should listen to the words of inspiration, sent by the Knower of all things.

5629. This was *Ẕun-Nūn*, or Jonah, for whom see n. 2744 to xxi. 87-88. *Cf.* also xxxvii. 139-148 and the notes there. Jonah was asked to preach to the people of Nineveh, a wicked city. He met with hostility and persecution, fled from his enemies, and took a boat. He was caught in a storm and thrown into the sea. He was swallowed by a fish or whale, but he repented in his living prison, and was forgiven. But the people of Nineveh were also forgiven, for they, too, repented. Here is a double allegory of God's mercy and forgiveness, and a command to patience, and complete and joyful submission to the Will of God.

Cast off on the naked[5630]
Shore, in disgrace.

لَنُبِذَ بِالْعَرَآءِ وَهُوَ مَذْمُومٌ ۝

50. Thus did his Lord[5631]
Choose him and make him
Of the company
Of the Righteous.[5632]

٥٠- فَاجْتَبٰهُ رَبُّهٗ
فَجَعَلَهٗ مِنَ الصّٰلِحِيْنَ ۝

51. And the Unbelievers
Would almost trip thee up[5633]
With their eyes when they
Hear the Message; and they
Say: "Surely he is possessed!"

٥١- وَاِنْ يَّكَادُ الَّذِيْنَ كَفَرُوْا لَيُزْلِقُوْنَكَ
بِاَبْصَارِهِمْ لَمَّا سَمِعُوا الذِّكْرَ
وَيَقُوْلُوْنَ اِنَّهٗ لَمَجْنُوْنٌ ۝

52. But it is nothing less
Than a Message[5634]
To all the worlds.

٥٢- وَمَا هُوَ اِلَّا ذِكْرٌ لِّلْعٰلَمِيْنَ ۝

5630. *Cf.* xxxvii. 145-146, and n. 4126.

5631. Jonah was chosen by God's Grace and Mercy to be God's Apostle to Nineveh. If in his human frailty he lost a little patience, he suffered his punishment, but his true and sincere repentance and recognition of God's goodness and mercy restored him from his physical and mental distress, and from the obscuration of the spiritual Light in him.

5632. *Cf.* iv. 69, n. 586. In the beautiful Fellowship of the Righteous there is room for all, of every grade of spiritual advancement, from the highest to the most ordinary. But, as in democratic politics every citizen's rights and status have complete recognition, so, in the spiritual Fellowship, the badge of Righteousness is the bond, even though there may be higher degrees of knowledge or experience.

5633. The eyes of evil men look at a good man as if they would "eat him up", or trip him up, or disturb him from his position of stability or firmness. They use all sorts of terms of abuse—"madman" or "one possessed by an evil spirit", and so on. *Cf.* lxviii. 2 above, and n. 5594. But the good man is unmoved, and takes his even course. The Message of God is true and will endure, and it is a Message to all Creation.

5634. This is the extreme antithesis to madness or demoniacal possession. So far from the holy Prophet uttering words disjointed or likely to harm people, he was bringing the Message of true Reality, which was to be the cure of all evil, evil in every kind of world. For the different kinds of worlds see n. 20 to i. 2.

INTRODUCTION AND SUMMARY: SŪRA LXIX (*Ḥāqqa*).

This Sūra belongs to the early middle period of Meccan Revelation. The eschatological argument is pressed home: 'the absolute Truth cannot fail; it must prevail; therefore be not lured by false appearances in this life; it is Revelation that points to the sure and certain Reality'.

C. 249.—In this fleeting world few things are what
(lxix. 1-52.) They seem. What then is sure Reality?
Nations and men in the past assumed
Arrogance and perished because they were unjust,
But that destruction was but a foretaste
Of the Doom to come in the Hereafter, when all
Creation will be on a new plane, and true values
Will be fully established: to the Righteous
Will be Bliss, and to Evil, Punishment.
The Word of Revelation is not a Poet's
Imagination or a Soothsayer's groping
Into the future. It is God's own Message,
Of Mercy to the Righteous, and warning
To those who reject the Truth. Praise
And Glory to the name of God Most High!

Sūra LXIX.

Ḥāqqa, or the Sure Reality.

In the name of God, Most Gracious, Most Merciful.

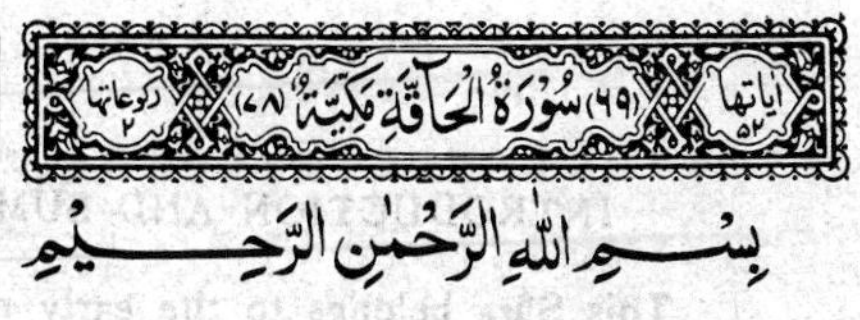

بِسْمِ اللّٰهِ الرَّحْمٰنِ الرَّحِيْمِ

1. The Sure Reality ! [5635]

١- اَلْحَآقَّةُ ۙ

2. What is the Sure Reality ?

٢- مَا الْحَآقَّةُ ۚ

3. And what will make
Thee realise what
The Sure Reality is ?

٣- وَمَآ اَدْرٰىكَ مَا الْحَآقَّةُ ۭ

4. The Thamūd [5636]
And the 'Ād people
(Branded) as false
The Stunning Calamity ! [5637]

٤- كَذَّبَتْ ثَمُوْدُ وَعَادٌۢ بِالْقَارِعَةِ ۙ

5. But the Thamūd,—
They were destroyed
By a terrible Storm [5638]
Of thunder and lightning !

٥- فَاَمَّا ثَمُوْدُ فَاُهْلِكُوْا بِالطَّاغِيَةِ ۙ

6. And the 'Ād,— [5639]
They were destroyed
By a furious Wind,
Exceedingly violent ;

٦- وَاَمَّا عَادٌ فَاُهْلِكُوْا بِرِيْحٍ صَرْصَرٍ عَاتِيَةٍ ۙ

5635. *Al-ḥāqqa*: the sure Truth: the Event that must inevitably come to pass; the state in which all falsehood and pretence will vanish, and the absolute Truth will be laid bare. The questions in the three verses raise an air of mystery. The solution is suggested in what happened to the Thamūd and the 'Ād, and other people of antiquity, who disregarded the Truth of God and came to a violent end, even in this life,—symbolically suggesting the great Cataclysm of the Hereafter, the Day of Doom.

5636. For these two peoples of antiquity, see n. 1043 to vii. 73, and n. 1040 to vii. 65.

5637. Another description of the terrible Day of Judgment. This word *Qāri'a* also occurs as the title of S. ci.

5638. The Thamūd were addicted to class arrogance. They oppressed the poor. The prophet Ṣāliḥ preached to them, and put forward a wonderful she-camel as a symbol of the rights of the poor, but they ham-strung her. See n. 1044 to vii. 73. They were destroyed in a mighty calamity, an earthquake accompanying a terrible thunderstorm.

5639. The 'Ād were an unjust people spoilt by their prosperity. The prophet Hūd preached to them in vain. They were apparently destroyed by a terrible blast of wind. See n. 1040 to vii. 65. See also xli. 15-16, n. 4483, and liv. 19, n. 5144.

7. He made it rage
Against them seven nights
And eight days in succession:
So that thou couldst see
The (whole) people lying
Prostrate in its (path),
As if they had been
Roots of hollow palm-trees [5640]
Tumbled down!

٧- سَخَّرَهَا عَلَيْهِمْ
سَبْعَ لَيَالٍ وَّثَمٰنِيَةَ أَيَّامٍ حُسُومًا
فَتَرَى الْقَوْمَ فِيهَا صَرْعٰى
كَأَنَّهُمْ أَعْجَازُ نَخْلٍ خَاوِيَةٍ ۝

8. Then seest thou any
Of them left surviving? [5641]

٨- فَهَلْ تَرٰى لَهُمْ مِّنْ بَاقِيَةٍ ۝

9. And Pharaoh, [5642]
And those before him, [5643]
And the Cities Overthrown, [5644]
Committed habitual Sin,

٩- وَجَآءَ فِرْعَوْنُ وَمَنْ قَبْلَهُ
وَالْمُؤْتَفِكٰتُ بِالْخَاطِئَةِ ۝

10. And disobeyed (each)
The apostle of their Lord;
So He punished them
With an abundant Penalty.

١٠- فَعَصَوْا رَسُولَ رَبِّهِمْ
فَأَخَذَهُمْ أَخْذَةً رَّابِيَةً ۝

11. We, when the water
(Of Noah's Flood) overflowed
Beyond its limits, [5645]
Carried you (mankind),
In the floating (Ark),

١١- إِنَّا لَمَّا طَغَا الْمَآءُ
حَمَلْنٰكُمْ فِي الْجَارِيَةِ ۝

5640. A graphic simile. Dead men all lying about like hollow trunks of palm-trees, with their roots exposed! The 'Ād were reputed to be of a tall stature.

5641. The calamity was thorough. The 'Ād were destroyed, and then the Thamūd, and only the tradition of them was left behind. See the references in n. 5636.

5642. Pharaoh's Apostle was Moses. See the story in vii. 103-137 and the notes there. Pharaoh was inordinately proud, and his fall was proportionately great: it gradually extended to his dynasty and his people: See Appendix V of S. vii, p. 410.

5643. If we follow the sequence of peoples whose sins destroyed them, as mentioned in vii. 59-158, we begin with Noah, then have the 'Ād and the Thamūd, then the Cities of the Plain, then Midian, then the people whose prophet was Moses (who occupies a central place in the canvas), and then the Pagan Quraish, to whom came the last and greatest of the prophets, our holy Prophet Muḥammad. This is the chronological sequence. Here there is no detail, nor even complete mention. But Noah is alluded to last, and the 'Ād and the Thamūd mentioned first, because the latter two belong to Arab tradition, and this is specially addressed to the Pagans of Mecca. Pharaoh is mentioned rather than Moses for the same reason, and any others are "those before Pharaoh".

5644. *The Cities Overthrown:* Sodom and Gomorrah, Cities of the Plain, to whom Lot preached: see ix. 70, n. 1330; and vii 80-84, n. 1049.

5645. It was a widespread Flood. *Cf.* vii. 59-64; also xi. 25-49. Noah was ridiculed for his preparations for the Flood: see xi. 38, n. 1531. But God had commanded him to build an Ark, in order that mankind in that region should be saved from perishing in the Flood. But only those of Faith got into the Ark and were saved. As the Ark was built to God's command, God "carried you (mankind) in the floating (Ark)".

12. That We might
Make it a Message[5646]
Unto you, and that ears
(That should hear the tale
And) retain its memory
Should bear its (lessons)
In remembrance.[5647]

١٢- لِنَجْعَلَهَا لَكُمْ تَذْكِرَةً
وَّتَعِيَهَآ أُذُنٌ
وَّاعِيَةٌ ○

13. Then, when one
Blast is sounded
On the Trumpet,[5648]

١٣- فَإِذَا نُفِخَ فِى الصُّورِ نَفْخَةٌ وَّاحِدَةٌ ○

14. And the earth is moved,
And its mountains,[5619]
And they are crushed to powder
At one stroke,—

١٤- وَّحُمِلَتِ الْأَرْضُ وَالْجِبَالُ
فَدُكَّتَا دَكَّةً وَّاحِدَةً ○

15. On that Day
Shall the (Great) Event
Come to pass,

١٥- فَيَوْمَئِذٍ وَّقَعَتِ الْوَاقِعَةُ ○

16. And the sky will be
Rent asunder, for it will
That Day be flimsy,

١٦- وَانْشَقَّتِ السَّمَآءُ فَهِيَ يَوْمَئِذٍ وَّاهِيَةٌ ○

17. And the angels will be
On its sides,[5650]

١٧- وَّالْمَلَكُ عَلٰٓى أَرْجَآئِهَا

5646. It was a memorial for all time, to show that evil meets with its punishment, but the good are saved by the mercy o God.

5647. *Cf.* the biblical phrase, "He that hath ears to hear, let him hear" (Matt. xi. 15). But the phrase used here has a more complicated import. An ear may hear, but for want of will in the hearer the hearer may not wish, for the future or for all time, to retain the memory of the lessons he has heard, even though for the time being he was impressed by it. The penetration of the truth has to be far deeper and subtler, and this is desired here.

5648. We now come to the Inevitable Event, the Day of Judgment, the theme of this Sūra. This is the first Blast referred to in **xxxix**. 68, n. 4343.

5649. The whole of our visible world, as we now know it, will pass away, and a new world will come into being. The mountains are specially mentioned, because they stand as the type of hardness, size, and durability. They will be "crushed to powder", *i.e.*, lose their form and being at one stroke.

5650. The whole picture is painted in graphic poetical images, to indicate that which cannot be adequately described in words, and which indeed our human faculties with their present limited powers are not ready to comprehend. The heavens will be rent asunder. We imagine the angels to live in the heavens. How shall we picture their state? They will gather round the sides, for the veils which hid the Glory of God will be gone, and that Glory will be the Throne, the symbol of His power and authority, of His justice and truth. *Cf.* also **xxxix**. 75.

And eight will, that Day,
Bear the Throne [5651]
Of thy Lord above them.

وَّيَحْمِلُ عَرْشَ رَبِّكَ فَوْقَهُمْ يَوْمَئِذٍ
ثَمٰنِيَةٌ ○

18. That Day shall ye be
Brought to Judgment:
Not an act of yours
That ye hide will be hidden.

١٨- يَوْمَئِذٍ تُعْرَضُوْنَ
لَا تَخْفٰى مِنْكُمْ خَافِيَةٌ ○

19. Then he that will be
Given his Record
In his right hand [5652]
Will say: "Ah here!
Read ye my Record!

١٩- فَاَمَّا مَنْ اُوْتِىَ كِتٰبَهٗ بِيَمِيْنِهٖ
فَيَقُوْلُ هَآؤُمُ اقْرَءُوْا كِتٰبِيَهْ ○

20. "I did really understand [5653]
That my Account would
(One Day) reach me!"

٢٠- اِنِّىْ ظَنَنْتُ اَنِّىْ مُلٰقٍ حِسَابِيَهْ ○

21. And he will be
In a life of Bliss,

٢١- فَهُوَ فِىْ عِيْشَةٍ رَّاضِيَةٍ ○

22. In a Garden on high,

٢٢- فِىْ جَنَّةٍ عَالِيَةٍ ○

23. The Fruits whereof [5654]
(Will hang in bunches)
Low and near.

٢٣- قُطُوْفُهَا دَانِيَةٌ ○

24. "Eat ye and drink ye,
With full satisfaction;

٢٤- كُلُوْا وَاشْرَبُوْا هَنِيْٓـًٔا

5651. See last note. Angels represent manifestations of divine glory. The number eight has perhaps no special significance, unless it be with reference to the shape of the "Throne". The Oriental Throne is often octagonal, and its bearers would be one at each corner. Or, if it is a square throne, there might be four bearers, and four in relief at any given time, making eight in all. The whole description is symbolical, as representing the majesty of God Most High.

5652. *Cf.* xvii. 71, where the righteous are described as those who are given their record in their right hand at Judgment. In lvi. 27, 38, and other passages, the righteous are called "Companions of the Right Hand".

5653. The righteous one rejoices that the faith he had during this world's life was fully justified, and is now actually realised before him. He quite understood and believed that good and evil must meet with their due consequences in the Hereafter, however much appearances may have been against it in the life in the lower world, "in the days that are gone."

5654. The symbolism is that of ripe, luscious grapes, hanging low in heavy bunches, so near that they could be gathered and enjoyed in dignified ease. *Cf.* also lv. 54; lxxvi. 14.

Because of the (good)
That ye sent before you,[5655]
In the days that are gone!"[5656]

بِمَآ أَسْلَفْتُمْ فِى ٱلْأَيَّامِ ٱلْخَالِيَةِ ۝

25. And he that will
Be given his Record
In his left hand,[5657]
Will say: "Ah! would
That my record had not
Been given to me!

٢٥- وَأَمَّا مَنْ أُوتِىَ كِتَٰبَهُۥ بِشِمَالِهِۦ
فَيَقُولُ يَٰلَيْتَنِى
لَمْ أُوتَ كِتَٰبِيَهْ ۝

26. "And that I had never
Realised how
My account (stood)!

٢٦- وَلَمْ أَدْرِ مَا حِسَابِيَهْ ۝

27. "Ah! would that (Death)[5658]
Had made an end of me!

٢٧- يَٰلَيْتَهَا كَانَتِ ٱلْقَاضِيَةَ ۝

28. "Of no profit to me
Has been my wealth!

٢٨- مَآ أَغْنَىٰ عَنِّى مَالِيَهْ ۝

29. "My power has
Perished from me!"...[5659]

٢٩- هَلَكَ عَنِّى سُلْطَٰنِيَهْ ۝

30. (The stern command will say):
"Seize ye him,
And bind ye him,[5660]

٣٠- خُذُوهُ فَغُلُّوهُ ۝

5655. *Cf.* ii. 110: "Whatever good ye send forth for your souls before you, ye shall find it with God: for God sees well all that ye do."

5656. It will be a wholly new world, a new earth and a new heaven, when the blessed might well think with calm relief of "the days that are gone". *Cf.* xiv. 48, and n. 1925. Even Time and Space will be no more, so that any ideas that we may form here will be found to have become wholly obsolete by them.

5657. This is in contrast to the righteous ones who will receive their record in their right hand. *Cf.* lxix. 19, n. 5652. The righteous are glad when they remember their past: their memory is itself a precious possession. The unjust are in agony when they remember their past. Their memory is itself a grievous punishment.

5658. The death as from this life was but a transition into a new world. They would wish that that death had been the end of all things, but it will not be.

5659. The intensest agony is when the soul loses power over itself, when the personality tries to realise itself in new conditions and cannot: this is life in death.

5660. Perhaps the word for 'bind' should be construed: 'bind his hands round his neck, to remind him that his hands when they were free were closed to all acts of charity and mercy': *Cf.* xvii. 29.

31. " And burn ye him
In the Blazing Fire.

٣١- ثُمَّ الْجَحِيمَ صَلُّوهُ ۝

32. " Further, make him march
In a chain, whereof[5661]
The length is seventy cubits!

٣٢- ثُمَّ فِي سِلْسِلَةٍ
ذَرْعُهَا سَبْعُونَ ذِرَاعًا فَاسْلُكُوهُ ۝

33. " This was he that
Would not believe[5662]
In God Most High,

٣٣- إِنَّهُ كَانَ لَا يُؤْمِنُ
بِاللَّهِ الْعَظِيمِ ۝

34. " And would not encourage[5663]
The feeding of the indigent!

٣٤- وَلَا يَحُضُّ عَلَىٰ طَعَامِ الْمِسْكِينِ ۝

35. " So no friend hath he
Here this Day.

٣٥- فَلَيْسَ لَهُ الْيَوْمَ هَاهُنَا حَمِيمٌ ۝

36. " Nor hath he any food
Except the corruption[5664]
From the washing of wounds,

٣٦- وَلَا طَعَامٌ
إِلَّا مِنْ غِسْلِينٍ ۝

37. " Which none do eat
But those in sin."

٣٧- لَّا يَأْكُلُهُ إِلَّا الْخَاطِئُونَ ۝ ع

5661. The effects of sin are described in words of glowing imagery. (1) "*Seize him*": the first step of the sinner is that he loses his spiritual liberty, and becomes a slave to passion, prejudice envy, hatred, and all the brood of evil. (2) "*Bind him*": his hands are bound round his neck; all his powers and generous impulses are checked and his sympathies are dried up. (3) "*Burn him in the Blazing Fire*": he is then consumed in the Flames of Destruction, for which he has made himself fit. (4) "*Make him march in a chain*": the consequences of sin ramify and extend, and it becomes a long chain, a chain seventy cubits long, that holds him in thrall from not one but many points of view. "Oh! what a tangled web we weave, when first we practise to deceive!" "Seventy" implies an indefinitely large number as in ix, 80.

5662. The grip of sin was fastened on sinners because they forsook God. They ran after their own lusts and worshipped them, or they ran after God's creatures, ignoring Him Who is the cause and source of all good.

5663. *Cf.* cvii. 3; lxxxix, 18. The practical result of their rebellion against the God of Mercy was that their sympathies dried up. Not only did they not help or feed those in need, but they hindered others from doing so. And they have neither friend nor sympathy (food) in the Hereafter.

5664. They wounded many people by their cruelty and injustice in this life. And the symbol of their reward is that they should feed on the corruption that issues from such wounds. Who but a sinner can contemplate such a thing?

SECTION 2.

38. So I do
Call to witness[5665]
What ye see

۳۸- فَلَآ أُقْسِمُ بِمَا تُبْصِرُونَ ۝

39. And what ye see not,

۳۹- وَمَا لَا تُبْصِرُونَ ۝

40. That this is
Verily the word
Of an honoured apostle;[5666]

۴۰- إِنَّهُۥ لَقَوْلُ رَسُولٍ كَرِيمٍ ۝

41. It is not the word
Of a poet:[5667]
Little it is
Ye believe!

۴۱- وَمَا هُوَ بِقَوْلِ شَاعِرٍ
قَلِيلًا مَّا تُؤْمِنُونَ ۝

42. Nor is it the word
Of a soothsayer:[5668]
Little admonition it is
Ye receive.

۴۲- وَلَا بِقَوْلِ كَاهِنٍ
قَلِيلًا مَّا تَذَكَّرُونَ ۝

43. (This is) a Message
Sent down from the Lord
Of the Worlds.

۴۳- تَنزِيلٌ مِّن رَّبِّ الْعَٰلَمِينَ ۝

44. And if the apostle
Were to invent
Any sayings in Our name,

۴۴- وَلَوْ تَقَوَّلَ عَلَيْنَا بَعْضَ الْأَقَاوِيلِ ۝

5665. This is an adjuration in the same form as that which occurs in lvi. 75, lxx. 40, xc. 1, and elsewhere. God's Word is the quintessence of Truth. But what if someone doubts whether a particular Message is God's Word communicated through His Apostle, or merely an imaginary tale presented by a poet, or a soothsayer's vain prophecy? Then we have to examine it in the light of our highest spiritual faculties. The witness to that Word is what we know in the visible world, in which falsehood in the long run gives place to truth, and what we know in the invisible world, through our highest spiritual faculties. We are asked to examine and test it in both these ways.

5666. *Honoured apostle*: one that is worthy of honour on account of the purity of his life, and may be relied upon not to invent things but to give the true inner experiences of his soul in Revelation.

5667. A poet draws upon his imagination, and the subjective factor is so strong that though we may learn much from him, we cannot believe as facts the wonderful tales he has to tell. And the poet who is not a Seer is merely a vulgar votary of exaggerations and falsehoods.

5668. A soothsayer merely pretends to foretell future events of no profound spiritual consequence. Most of his prophecies are frauds, and none of them is meant to teach lessons of real admonition. Such admonition is the work of an honoured apostle.

45. We should certainly seize him
By his right hand,[5669]

٤٥- لَأَخَذْنَا مِنْهُ بِالْيَمِينِ ۝

46. And We should certainly
Then cut off the artery
Of his heart:[5670]

٤٦- ثُمَّ لَقَطَعْنَا مِنْهُ الْوَتِينَ ۝

47. Nor could any of you
Withhold him[5671]
(From Our wrath).

٤٧- فَمَا مِنكُم مِّنْ أَحَدٍ عَنْهُ حَاجِزِينَ ۝

48. But verily this
Is a Message for
The God-fearing.

٤٨- وَإِنَّهُ لَتَذْكِرَةٌ لِّلْمُتَّقِينَ ۝

49. And We certainly know
That there are amongst you
Those that reject (it).

٤٩- وَإِنَّا لَنَعْلَمُ أَنَّ مِنكُم مُّكَذِّبِينَ ۝

50. But truly (Revelation)
Is a cause of sorrow[5672]
For the Unbelievers.

٥٠- وَإِنَّهُ لَحَسْرَةٌ عَلَى الْكَافِرِينَ ۝

51. But veri'y it is Truth[5673]
Of assured certainty.

٥١- وَإِنَّهُ لَحَقُّ الْيَقِينِ ۝

52. So glorify the name[5674]
Of thy Lord Most High.

٥٢- فَسَبِّحْ بِاسْمِ رَبِّكَ الْعَظِيمِ ۝ ع

5669. The right hand is the hand of power and action. Any one who is seized by his right hand is prevented from acting as he wishes or carrying out his purpose. The argument is that if an impostor were to arise, he would soon be found out. He could not carry out his fraud indefinitely. But the men of God, however much they are persecuted, gain more and more power every day, as did the holy Prophet, whose truth, earnestness, sincerity, and love for all, were recognised as his life unfolded itself.

5670. This would effectually stop the functioning of his life.

5671. The protection which the men of God enjoy in circumstances of danger and difficulty would not be available for impostors.

5672. The Message of God is glad tidings for those who believe in Him and follow His Law, for it is a message of Mercy and Forgiveness through repentance and amendment. But in the case of the wicked it is a cause of sorrow, for it denounces sin and proclaims the punishment of those who do not turn from evil.

5673. All Truth is in itself certain. But as received by men, and understood with reference to men's psychology, certainty may have certain degrees. There is the probability or certainty resulting from the application of man's power of judgment and his appraisement of evidence. This is '*ilm-ul-yaqīn*, certainty by reasoning or inference. Then there is the certainty of seeing something with our own eyes. "Seeing is believing." This is '*ain-ul-yaqīn*, certainty by personal inspection. See cii. 5, 7. Then, as here, there is the absolute Truth, with no possibility of error of judgment or error of the eye, (which stands for any instrument of sense-perception and any ancillary aids, such as microscopes, etc.). This absolute Truth is the *ḥaqq-ul-yaqīn* spoken of here.

5674. As God has given us this absolute Truth through His Revelation, it behoves us to understand it and be grateful to Him. We must celebrate His praises in thought, word and deed.

INTRODUCTION AND SUMMARY : SŪRA LXX (*Ma'ārij*).

This is another eschatological Sūra closely connected in subject-matter with the last one. Patience and the mystery of Time will show the ways that climb to Heaven. Sin and Goodness must each eventually come to its own.

Chronologically it belongs to the late early or early middle Meccan period, possibly soon after S. lxix.

C. 250.—Man can ascend to the Presence of God,
(lxx. 1-44.) But by gradual Ways and in process of Time.
But what is Time? A Day is as fifty
Thousand years, on two different planes.
What seems near is far, and what seems far is near.
So will be Judgment, when things as we know them
Will be transformed completely in a world
All new. Evil will come to its own,
Whatever its masks in this transitory world,
And good will surely reach its goal.
The good life is patient, in prayer
And well-doing, Faith and the earnest search
For the Good Pleasure of God, purity and probity.
These are the paths to the Heights and the Gardens
Of Bliss. No evil can enter there:
For the evil are other ways, leading
By steep descent to dark Ignominy!

Sūra LXX.

Ma'ārij, or the Ways of Ascent.

*In the name of God, Most Gracious,
Most Merciful.*

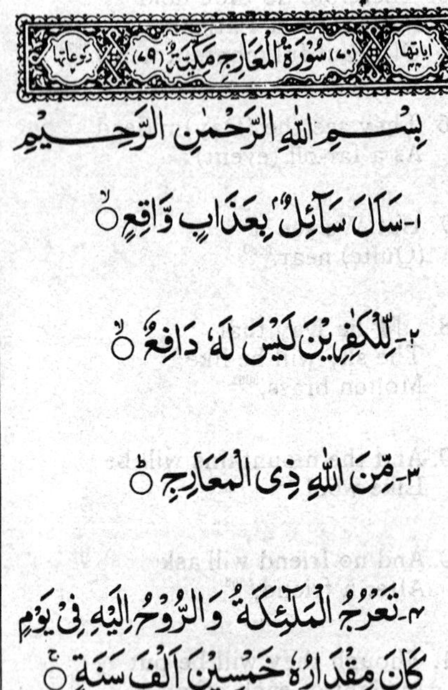

1. A questioner asked [5675]
About a Penalty
To befall—

2. The Unblievers,
The which there is none
To ward off,—

3. (A Penalty) from God,
Lord of the Ways
Of Ascent. [5676]

4. The angels and
The Spirit [5677] ascend
Unto Him in a Day [5678]
The measure whereof
Is (as) fifty thousand years :

5675. Any one might ask, When will Judgment come? That question usually implies doubt. The answer is: the mystery of Time is beyond man's comprehension. But there is something which touches him closely and concerns his conduct and his future welfare, and that is explained in four propositions. (1) Judgment is sure to come, and none can ward it off; (2) it will exact a dreadful Penalty from Unbelievers, but the righteous have nothing to fear; (3) it will be a Penalty from God, the Lord of both Justice and Mercy; it will not be merely a blind calamity of fate; and (4) further we are reminded of another title of God, "Lord of the Ways of Ascent"; which means that though He sits high on His Throne of Glory, He is not inaccessible, but in His infinite Mercy has provided ways of ascent to Him; see next note

5676. *Ma'ārij*: stair-ways, ways of ascent. In xliii. 33, the word is used in its literal sense: "silver stair-ways on which to go up". Here there is a profound spiritual meaning. Can we reach up to God Most High? In His infinite grace He gives that privilege to angels and spiritual beings, man being such in his highest aspect. But the way is not easy, nor can it be travelled in a day. See the next two notes.

5677. *Rūḥ*: "The Spirit". *Cf.* lxxviii. 38, "the Spirit and the angels"; and xcvii. 4, "the angels and the Spirit". In xvi. 2. we have translated *Rūḥ* by "*inspiration*". Some Commentators understand the angel Gabriel by "the Spirit". But I think a more general meaning is possible, and fits the context better. Man is gifted with the Spirit of God: xv. 29. In the spiritual kingdom we are all raised to the light of the Countenance of God, and His Glory transforms us.

5678. But such a glorious transformation is not to be attained without the highest spiritual exertion, and if we measure time as we measure it on the plane of this life, it may take thousands of years. In the spiritual plane it may be just a day or a moment. *Cf.* xxxii. 4-5, and notes 3632 and 3634.

5. Therefore do thou hold
Patience,—a Patience
Of beautiful (contentment).[5679]

٥- فَاصْبِرْ صَبْرًا جَمِيلًا ۝

6. They see the (Day) indeed
As a far-off (event):

٦- إِنَّهُمْ يَرَوْنَهُ بَعِيدًا ۝

7. But We see it
(Quite) near.[5680]

٧- وَنَرَاهُ قَرِيبًا ۝

8. The Day that
The sky will be like
Molten brass,[5681]

٨- يَوْمَ تَكُونُ السَّمَاءُ كَالْمُهْلِ ۝

9. And the mountains will be
Like wool,[5682]

٩- وَتَكُونُ الْجِبَالُ كَالْعِهْنِ ۝

10. And no friend will ask
After a friend,[5683]

١٠- وَلَا يَسْأَلُ حَمِيمٌ حَمِيمًا ۝

11. Though they will be put
In sight of each other,—
The sinner's desire will be:
Would that he could

١١- يُبَصَّرُونَهُمْ ۚ
يَوَدُّ الْمُجْرِمُ لَوْ

5679. The man of God, persecuted and in trouble with the world, should yet hold Patience—not the sort of patience which goes with complaints expressed or suppressed, as in the early history of Job, but the sort of patience that is *content* with the ordering of God's world, for he believes and knows it to be good, as did the holy Prophet Muḥammad. Such a patience is akin to Good Pleasure, for it arises from the purest faith and trust in God.

5680. The men of evil may see the just retribution for their sins so far off that they doubt whether it would ever come. But in God's sight, and on the scale of the Universal Plan, it is quite near; for time as we know it hardly exists in the spiritual world. It may come even in this life: but it is bound to come eventually.

5681. *Cf.* xviii. 29. (where the wrong-doer will have a drink like melted brass in Hell); and xliv. 45, (where his food will be like molten brass). Here the appearance of the sky is compared to molten brass, or, as some understand it, like the dregs of oil. What is conveyed by the metaphor is that the beautiful blue sky will melt away.

5682. *Cf.* ci. 5, where the metaphor of carded wool is used. The mountains which seem so solid will be like flakes of wool driven by the carder's hand.

5683. The world as we know it will have so completely passed away that the landmarks in the heavens and on earth will also have vanished. Not only that, but the human relationships of mind and heart will have been transformed by sin into something ugly and dreadful. The sinners will be so overcome with terror at the realisation of their personal responsibility that they will desert their most intimate friends, and indeed their very sight of each other will add to their agony.

Redeem himself from
The Penalty of that Day[5684]
By (sacrificing) his children,

يَفْتَدِي مِنْ عَذَابِ يَوْمِئِذٍ بِبَنِيهِ ۝

12. His wife and his brother,

١٢- وَصَاحِبَتِهِ وَأَخِيهِ ۝

13. His kindred who sheltered him,

١٣- وَفَصِيلَتِهِ الَّتِي تُؤْوِيهِ ۝

14. And all, all that is
On earth,—so it could
Deliver him:[5685]

١٤- وَمَن فِي الْأَرْضِ جَمِيعًا
ثُمَّ يُنجِيهِ ۝

15. By no means!
For it would be
The Fire of Hell!—

١٥- كَلَّا ۖ إِنَّهَا لَظَىٰ ۝

16. Plucking out (his being)
Right to the skull!—[5686]

١٦- نَزَّاعَةً لِّلشَّوَىٰ ۝

17. Inviting (all) such
As turn their backs[5687]
And turn away their faces
(From the Right),

١٧- تَدْعُو مَنْ أَدْبَرَ
وَتَوَلَّىٰ ۝

18. And collect (wealth)
And hide it (from use)!

١٨- وَجَمَعَ فَأَوْعَىٰ ۝

5684. The sinner will offer his children, his family, his kinsmen, who had sheltered and protected him,—in fact everything on earth that he could—as a ransom for himself. Such would be his selfishness and his agony.

5685. What would not the sinner give for his own deliverance! But nothing could save him. The Fire of Hell would be roaring for him!

5686. It would be a Fire not only burning his body, but reaching right up to his brains and his understanding, and—as is said in civ. 7—his heart and affections also. In other words the Penalty typified by the Fire will burn into his inmost being.

5687. The analysis of sin is given in four master-strokes, of which the first two refer to the will or psychology of the sinner, and the last two to the use he makes of the good things of this life. (1) Sin begins with turning your back to the Right, refusing to face it squarely, running away from it whether from cowardice or indifference. (2) But Conscience and the sense of Right will try to prevent the flight; the Grace of God will meet the sinner at all corners and try to reclaim him; the hardened sinner will deliberately turn away his face from it, insult it, and reject it. (3) The result of this psychology will be that he will abandon himself to greed, to the collection of riches, and the acquisition of material advantages to which he is not entitled; this may involve hypocrisy, fraud, and crime. (4) Having acquired the material advantages, the next step will be to keep others out of them, to prevent hoarded wealth from fructifying by circulation, to conceal it from envy or spite. This is the spiritual Rake's Progress.

19. Truly man was created Very impatient;—[5688]	١٩- إِنَّ الْإِنسَانَ خُلِقَ هَلُوعًا ۝
20. Fretful when evil Touches him;	٢٠- إِذَا مَسَّهُ الشَّرُّ جَزُوعًا ۝
21. And niggardly when Good reaches him;—[5689]	٢١- وَإِذَا مَسَّهُ الْخَيْرُ مَنُوعًا ۝
22. Not so those devoted To Prayer;—[5690]	٢٢- إِلَّا الْمُصَلِّينَ ۝
23. Those who remain steadfast To their prayer;	٢٣- الَّذِينَ هُمْ عَلَىٰ صَلَاتِهِمْ دَائِمُونَ ۝
24. And those in whose wealth Is a recognised right	٢٤- وَالَّذِينَ فِي أَمْوَالِهِمْ حَقٌّ مَّعْلُومٌ ۝
25. For the (needy) who asks And him who is prevented (For some reason from asking);[5691]	٢٥- لِّلسَّائِلِ وَالْمَحْرُومِ ۝
26. And those who hold To the truth of the Day Of Judgment;	٢٦- وَالَّذِينَ يُصَدِّقُونَ بِيَوْمِ الدِّينِ ۝

5688. Man, according to the Plan of God, was to be in the best of moulds (xcv. 4). But in order to fulfil his high destiny he was given free-will to a limited extent. The wrong use of this free-will makes his nature weak (iv. 28), or hasty (xvii. 11), or impatient, as here. That becomes his nature by his own act, but he is spoken of as so created because of the capacities given to him in his creation.

5689. In adversity he complains and gets into despair. In prosperity he becomes arrogant and forgets other people's rights and his own shortcomings. *Cf.*. xli. 49-50.

5690. The description of those devoted to Prayer is given in a number of clauses that follow, introduced by the words "Those who...". "Devoted to Prayer" is here but another aspect of what is described elsewhere as the Faithful and the Righteous. Devotion to prayer does not mean merely a certain number of formal rites or prostrations. It means a complete surrender of one's being to God. This means an earnest approach to and realisation of God's Presence ("steadfastness in Prayer"); acts of practical and real charity; an attempt to read this life in terms of the Hereafter; the seeking of the Peace of God and avoidance of His displeasure; chastity; probity true and firm witness; and guarding the sacredness of the Presence (verse 34).

5691. See n. 5001 to li. 19. True charity consists in finding out those in real need, whether they ask or not. Most frequently those who ask are idle men who insolently wish to live upon others. But all cases of those who ask should be duly investigated, in case a little timely help may set the erring on the way. But the man with wealth or talent or opportunity has the further responsibility of searching out those in need of his assistance, in order to show that he holds all gifts in trust for the service of his fellow-creatures.

27. And those who fear[5692]
The displeasure of their Lord,—

٢٧-وَالَّذِينَ هُمْ مِّنْ عَذَابِ رَبِّهِمْ مُّشْفِقُونَ ۝

28. For their Lord's displeasure
Is the opposite of Peace
And Tranquillity;—[5693]

٢٨-إِنَّ عَذَابَ رَبِّهِمْ غَيْرُ مَأْمُونٍ ۝

29. And those who guard
Their chastity,

٢٩-وَالَّذِينَ هُمْ لِفُرُوجِهِمْ حَافِظُونَ ۝

30. Except with their wives
And the (captives) whom[5694]
Their right hands possess,—
For (then) they are not
To be blamed,

٣٠-إِلَّا عَلَىٰ أَزْوَاجِهِمْ أَوْ مَا مَلَكَتْ
أَيْمَانُهُمْ
فَإِنَّهُمْ غَيْرُ مَلُومِينَ ۝

31. But those who trespass
Beyond this are transgressors;—

٣١-فَمَنِ ابْتَغَىٰ وَرَاءَ ذَٰلِكَ فَأُولَٰئِكَ هُمُ الْعَادُونَ ۝

32. And those who respect
Their trusts and covenants;[5695]

٣٢-وَالَّذِينَ هُمْ لِأَمَانَاتِهِمْ وَعَهْدِهِمْ رَاعُونَ ۝

33. And those who stand firm
In their testimonies;[5696]

٣٣-وَالَّذِينَ هُمْ بِشَهَادَاتِهِمْ قَائِمُونَ ۝

5692. A true fear of God is the fear of offending against His holy Will and Law, and is therefore akin to the love of God. It proceeds from the realisation that all true peace and tranquillity comes from attuning our will to the universal Will, and that sin causes discord, disharmony, and displeasure,—another name for the Wrath of God.

5693. Some would construe this verse: "And their Lord's displeasure is one against which there is no security"; meaning that the punishment of sin may come suddenly at any time, when you least expect it.

5694. Captives of war may be married as such: see iv. 25: but their status is inferior to that of free wives until they are free. This institution of the captives of war is now obsolete. Such inferiority of status as there was, was in the status of captivity, not in the status of marriage as such, in which there are no degrees, except by local customs, which Islam does not recognise.

5695. For obligations of trusts and covenants, express or implied, see n. 682 to v. 1. They are just as sacred in ordinary everyday life as they are in special spiritual relationships. In addition, our life itself, and such reason and talents as we possess, as well as our wealth and possessions are trusts, of which we must fulfil the duties punctiliously.

5696. If we know any truth of any kind, to that we must bear witness, as affecting the lives or interests of our fellow-beings,—firmly, not half-heartedly, without fear or favour, even if it causes loss or trouble to us, or if it loses us friends or associates.

34. And those who guard
(The sacredness) of their
worship;—[5697]

٣٤- وَالَّذِينَ هُمْ عَلَىٰ صَلَاتِهِمْ يُحَافِظُونَ ۝

35. Such will be
The honoured ones
In the Gardens (of Bliss).

٣٥- أُولَٰئِكَ فِي جَنَّاتٍ مُّكْرَمُونَ ۝ ع

SECTION 2.

36. Now what is
The matter with the Unbelievers
That they rush madly
Before thee—[5698]

٣٦- فَمَالِ الَّذِينَ كَفَرُوا
قِبَلَكَ مُهْطِعِينَ ۝

37. From the right
And from the left,
In crowds?

٣٧- عَنِ الْيَمِينِ وَعَنِ الشِّمَالِ عِزِينَ ۝

38. Does every man of them
Long to enter
The Garden of Bliss?

٣٨- أَيَطْمَعُ كُلُّ امْرِئٍ مِّنْهُمْ
أَن يُدْخَلَ جَنَّةَ نَعِيمٍ ۝

39. By no means!
For We have created them
Out of the (base matter)
They know![5699]

٣٩- كَلَّا إِنَّا خَلَقْنَاهُم مِّمَّا يَعْلَمُونَ ۝

40. Now I do
Call to witness[5700]

٤٠- فَلَا أُقْسِمُ

5697. Worship or prayer includes honest work, charity, and every good deed. To guard the sacredness of this ideal is to sum up the whole duty of man. We began with "steadfastness in prayer" in verse 23 above, and after a review of various aspects of the good man's life, close with the sacredness of worship, *i.e.* living as in the sight of God.

5698. *Before thee.* The Unbelievers did not believe in a Hereafter. When the Bliss of the Hereafter was described, as in the last verse, they ridiculed it and pretended to be running in for it as in a race. They are here rebuked in the same tone of sarcasm.

5699. The animal part of man is nothing to be proud of, and they know it. It is by spiritual effort, and long preparation through a good life that a man can rise above the mere animal part of him to his high dignity as a spiritual being, and his noble destiny in the Hereafter.

5700. For the form of adjuration, *cf.* lxix. 38, n. 5665; also lvi. 75. Here the witness placed before us by God is His own power and glory manifested in the splendour of sunrise and sunset at different points through the solar year.

The Lord of all points
In the East and the West[5701]
That We can certainly—[5702]

بِرَبِّ الْمَشْرِقِ وَالْمَغْرِبِ إِنَّا لَقَادِرُونَ ۝

41. Substitute for them
Better (men) than they;
And We are not
To be defeated
(In Our Plan).

٤١- عَلَىٰٓ أَنْ نُّبَدِّلَ خَيْرًا مِّنْهُمْ
وَمَا نَحْنُ بِمَسْبُوقِينَ ۝

42. So leave them
To plunge in vain talk
And play about,[5703]
Until they encounter
That Day of theirs which
They have been promised!—

٤٢- فَذَرْهُمْ يَخُوضُوا وَيَلْعَبُوا
حَتَّىٰ يُلَٰقُوا
يَوْمَهُمُ الَّذِي يُوعَدُونَ ۝

43. The Day whereon
They will issue
From their sepulchres
In sudden haste
As if they were
Rushing to a goal-post
(Fixed for them),—[5704]

٤٣- يَوْمَ يَخْرُجُونَ
مِنَ الْأَجْدَاثِ سِرَاعًا
كَأَنَّهُمْ إِلَىٰ نُصُبٍ يُوفِضُونَ ۝

44. Their eyes lowered
In dejection,—
Ignominy covering them
(All over)!
Such is the Day
The which they
Are promised!

٤٤- خَاشِعَةً أَبْصَارُهُمْ تَرْهَقُهُمْ ذِلَّةٌ
ذَٰلِكَ الْيَوْمُ الَّذِي
كَانُوا يُوعَدُونَ ۝ ع

5701. See n. 4034 to xxxvii. 5. If God has such power in the wonderful phenomena of the rising of the sun at varying points, repeated year after year, can you not see that He can easily substitute better men than you Unbelievers and blasphemers?

5702. The transition from the singular "I" to the plural "We" may be noted. See n. 56 to ii. 38.

5703. Their talk, their scepticism, is vain, because all spiritual evidence is against it; it is like the foolish play of people who do not think seriously. But the tremendous Day of Judgment and Reality will come, as described in the next two verses.

5704. Now there will be a definite Goal-post or Banner or Standard of Truth fixed, which all must acknowledge. But they will acknowledge it in shame and dejection. For the time for their repentance and amendment will then have passed.

INTRODUCTION AND SUMMARY : SŪRA LXXI (*Nūḥ*).

This is another early Meccan Sūra, of which the date has no significance. The theme is that while Good must uphold the standard of Truth and Righteousness, a stage is reached when it must definitely part company with Evil, lest Evil should spread its corruption abroad. This theme is embodied in the prayer of Noah just before the Flood. The story of Noah's agony is almost a Parable for the holy Prophet's persecution in the Meccan period.

C. 251.—The Prophet's Message, as was that of Noah,
(lxxi. 1-28.) Is a warning against sin, and the Good News of Mercy
Through the door of Repentance : for God is loving
And long-suffering, and His Signs are within us
And around us. But the sinners are obstinate :
They plot against Righteousness, and place their trust
In futile falsehoods. They will be swept away,
And the earth will be purged of Evil. Let us
Pray for Mercy and Grace for ourselves,
For those nearest and dearest to us,
And for all who turn in faith to God,
In all ages and all countries,
And amongst all Peoples.

Sūra LXXI.

Nūḥ, or Noah.

In the name of God, Most Gracious, Most Merciful.

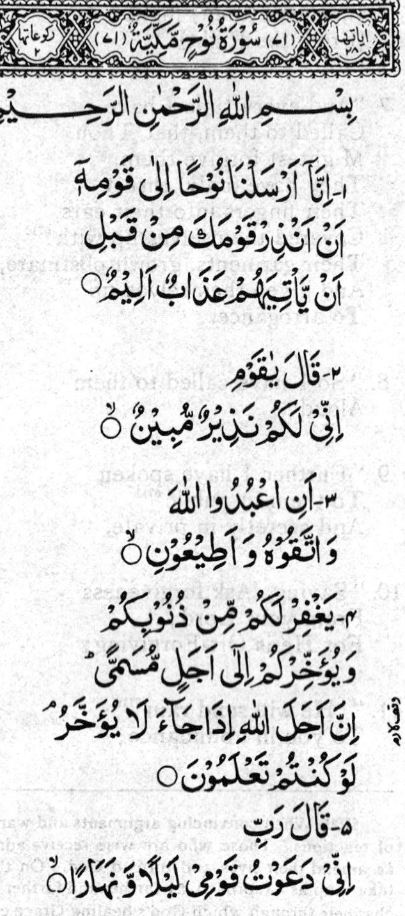

1. We sent Noah[5705]
To his People
(With the Command):
"Do thou warn thy People
Before there comes to them
A grievous Penalty."

2. He said: "O my People!
I am to you
A Warner, clear and open:[5706]

3. "That ye should worship
God, fear Him,
And obey me:[5707]

4. "So He may forgive you
Your sins and give you
Respite for a stated Term:
For when the Term given
By God is accomplished,
It cannot be put forward:[5708]
If ye only knew."

5. He said: "O my Lord!
I have called to my People
Night and day:

5705 Noah's mission is referred to in many places. See specially xi. 25-49 and notes. His contemporaries had completely abandoned the moral law. A purge had to be made, and the great Flood made it. This gives a new starting point in history for Noah's People,—*i.e.* for the remnant saved in the Ark.

5706. His Warning was to be both clear (*i.e.* unambiguous) and open (*i.e.* publicly proclaimed). Both these meanings are implied in *Mubīn*. *Cf.* lxvii. 26. The meaning of the Warning was obviously that if they had repented, they would have obtained mercy.

5707. Three aspects of man's duty are emphasized: (1) true worship with heart and soul; (2) God-fearing recognition that all evil must lead to self-deterioration and Judgment; (3) hence repentance and amendment of life, and obedience to good men's counsels.

5708. God gives respite freely; but it is for Him to give it. His command is definite and final; neither man nor any other authority can alter or in any way modify it. If we could only realise this to the full in our inmost soul, it would be best for us and lead to our happiness.

6. "But my call only
Increases (their) flight
(From the Right).[5709]

٦- فَلَمْ يَزِدْهُمْ دُعَاۤءِیْۤ اِلَّا فِرَارًا ۝

7. "And every time I have
Called to them, that Thou
Mightest forgive them,
They have (only) thrust
Their fingers into their ears,
Covered themselves up with[5710]
Their garments, grown obstinate,
And given themselves up
To arrogance.

٧- وَاِنِّیْ كُلَّمَا دَعَوْتُهُمْ لِتَغْفِرَ لَهُمْ
جَعَلُوْۤا اَصَابِعَهُمْ فِیْۤ اٰذَانِهِمْ
وَاسْتَغْشَوْا ثِيَابَهُمْ وَاَصَرُّوْا
وَاسْتَكْبَرُوا اسْتِكْبَارًا ۝

8. "So I have called to them
Aloud;

٨- ثُمَّ اِنِّیْ دَعَوْتُهُمْ جِهَارًا ۝

9. "Further I have spoken
To them in public[5711]
And secretly in private,

٩- ثُمَّ اِنِّیْۤ اَعْلَنْتُ لَهُمْ
وَاَسْرَرْتُ لَهُمْ اِسْرَارًا ۝

10. "Saying, 'Ask forgiveness
From your Lord;
For He is Oft-Forgiving;

١٠- فَقُلْتُ اسْتَغْفِرُوْا رَبَّكُمْ
اِنَّهٗ كَانَ غَفَّارًا ۝

11. "'He will send rain[5712]
To you in abundance;

١١- يُّرْسِلِ السَّمَاۤءَ عَلَيْكُمْ مِّدْرَارًا ۝

5709. When convincing arguments and warnings are placed before sinners, there are two kinds of reactions. Those who are wise receive admonition, repent, and bring forth fruits of repentance, *i.e.* amend their lives and turn to God. On the other hand, those who are callous to any advice take it up as a reproach, fly farther and farther from righteousness, and shut out more and more the channels through which God's healing Grace can reach them and work for them.

5710. The literal meaning would be that, just as they thrust their fingers into their ears to prevent the voice of the admonisher reaching them, so they covered their bodies with their garments that the light of truth should not penetrate to them, and that they should not even be seen by the Preacher. But there is a further symbolic meaning. "Their garments" are the adornments of vanities, their evil habits, customs, and traditions, and their ephemeral interests and standards. They drew them closer round them to prevent the higher Light reaching them. They grew obstinate and gave themselves up to the grossest form of selfish arrogance.

5711. Noah used all the resources of the earnest preacher: he dinned the Message of God into their ears; he spoke in public places; and he took individuals into his confidence, and appealed privately to them; but all in vain.

5712. They had perhaps been suffering from drought or famine. If they had taken the message in the right way, the rain would have been a blessing to them. They took it in the wrong way, and the rain was a curse to them, for it flooded the country and drowned the wicked generation. In the larger Plan, it was a blessing all the same; for it purged the world, and gave it a new start, morally and spiritually.

12 " ' Give you increase
In wealth and sons;
And bestow on you
Gardens and bestow on you
Rivers (of flowing water).[5713]

١٢- وَّيُمْدِدْكُمْ بِأَمْوَالٍ وَّبَنِيْنَ
وَيَجْعَلْ لَّكُمْ جَنّٰتٍ وَّيَجْعَلْ لَّكُمْ اَنْهٰرًا ۝

13. " ' What is the matter
With you, that ye
Place not your hope
For kindness and long-suffering
In God,—

١٣- مَا لَكُمْ
لَا تَرْجُوْنَ لِلّٰهِ وَقَارًا ۝

14. " ' Seeing that it is He
That has created you
In diverse stages ?[5714]

١٤- وَقَدْ خَلَقَكُمْ اَطْوَارًا ۝

15. " ' See ye not
How God has created
The seven heavens
One above another,[5715]

١٥- اَلَمْ تَرَوْا كَيْفَ خَلَقَ اللّٰهُ
سَبْعَ سَمٰوٰتٍ طِبَاقًا ۝

16. " ' And made the moon
A light in their midst,
And made the sun
As a (Glorious) Lamp ?[5716]

١٦- وَّجَعَلَ الْقَمَرَ فِيْهِنَّ نُوْرًا
وَّجَعَلَ الشَّمْسَ سِرَاجًا ۝

17. " ' And God has produced
You from the earth,
Growing (gradually),[5717]

١٧- وَاللّٰهُ اَنْۢبَتَكُمْ
مِّنَ الْاَرْضِ نَبَاتًا ۝

5713. Each of these blessings—rain and crops, wealth and man-power, flourishing gardens, and perennial streams—are indications of prosperity, and have not only a material but also a spiritual meaning. Note the last point, "rivers of flowing water". The perennial springs make the prosperity as it were permanent: they indicate a settled population, honest and contented, and enjoying their blessings here on earth as the foretaste of the eternal joys of heaven.

5714. *Cf.* xxii. 5, and notes 2773-2777; also xxiii. 12-17, and notes 2872-2875. The meaning here may be even wider. Man in his various states exhibits various wonderful qualities or capacities, mental and spiritual, that may be compared with the wonderful workings of nature on the earth and in the heavens. Will he not then be grateful for these Mercies and turn to God, Who created all these marvels?

5715. See n. 5559 to lxvii. 3.

5716. *Cf.* xxv. 61, where the sun is referred to as the glorious Lamp of the heavens: "Blessed is He Who made the Constellations in the skies, and placed therein a lamp, and a moon giving light."

5717. *Cf.* iii. 37, where the growth of the child Mary the Mother of Jesus is described by the same word *nabāt*, ordinarily denoting the growth of plants and trees. The simile is that of a seed sown, that germinates, grows, and dies, and goes back to the earth. In man, there is the further process of the Resurrection. *Cf.* also xx. 55.

18. " 'And in the End
He will return you
Into the (earth),
And raise you forth
(Again at the Resurrection)?

۱۸-ثُمَّ يُعِيدُكُمْ فِيهَا
وَيُخْرِجُكُمْ إِخْرَاجًا ○

19. " 'And God has made
The earth for you
As a carpet (spread out),[5718]

۱۹-وَاللَّهُ جَعَلَ لَكُمُ الْأَرْضَ بِسَاطًا ○

20. " 'That ye may go about
Therein, in spacious roads.' "[5719]

۲۰-لِتَسْلُكُوا مِنْهَا سُبُلًا فِجَاجًا ○

SECTION 2.

21. Noah said: "O my Lord!
They have disobeyed me,
But they follow (men)[5719-A]
Whose wealth and children
Give them no Increase
But only Loss.

۲۱-قَالَ نُوحٌ رَّبِّ إِنَّهُمْ عَصَوْنِي
وَاتَّبَعُوا مَن لَّمْ يَزِدْهُ مَالُهُ وَوَلَدُهُ
إِلَّا خَسَارًا ○

22. "And they have devised
A tremendous Plot.[5720]

۲۲-وَمَكَرُوا مَكْرًا كُبَّارًا ○

23. "And they have said
(To each other),
'Abandon not your gods:[5721]
Abandon neither Wadd
Nor Suwā', neither
Yagūth nor Ya'ūq,
Nor Nasr';—

۲۳-وَقَالُوا لَا تَذَرُنَّ آلِهَتَكُمْ
وَلَا تَذَرُنَّ وَدًّا وَلَا سُوَاعًا
وَلَا يَغُوثَ وَيَعُوقَ وَنَسْرًا ○

5718. *Cf.* xx. 53.

5719. *Fijāj* implies valley-roads or passes between mountains. Though there are mountain chains on the earth, God's artistry has provided even in such regions, valleys and channels by which men may go about. Mountain roads usually follow the valleys.

5719-A. Sinners always resent it as a reproach that righteous men should speak to them for their own good. They prefer smooth flatterers, and they worship power even though the depositaries of power are selfish men, who neither profit themselves nor profit others by the wealth and man-power that they collect round themselves. They forget that mere material things may be a delusion and a snare unless the moral and spiritual factor behind them sanctifies them.

5720. Having got material resources, the wicked devise plots to get rid of the righteous whose presence is a reproach to them. For a time their plots may seem tremendous and have the appearance of success, but they can never defeat God's Purpose.

5721. For an account of how these Pagan gods and superstitions connected with them originated, and how they became adopted into the Arabian Pagan Pantheon, see Appendix XIII at the end of this Sūra, pp. 1619-1623.

24. "They have already
Misled many; and
Grant Thou no increase
To the wrong-doers but in
Straying (from their mark)."[5722]

٢٤- وَقَدْ أَضَلُّوا كَثِيرًا ۚ
وَلَا تَزِدِ الظَّٰلِمِينَ إِلَّا ضَلَٰلًا ○

25. Because of their sins
They were drowned
(In the flood),[5723]
And were made to enter
The Fire (of Punishment):
And they found—
In lieu of God—
None to help them.

٢٥- مِمَّا خَطِيٓـَٰٔتِهِمْ أُغْرِقُوا
فَأُدْخِلُوا نَارًا ۚ
فَلَمْ يَجِدُوا لَهُم
مِّن دُونِ ٱللَّهِ أَنصَارًا ○

26. And Noah said:
"O my Lord! Leave not
Of the Unbelievers,
A single one on earth![5724]

٢٦- وَقَالَ نُوحٌ رَّبِّ لَا تَذَرْ
عَلَى ٱلْأَرْضِ مِنَ ٱلْكَٰفِرِينَ دَيَّارًا ○

27. "For, if Thou dost leave
(Any of) them, they will
But mislead Thy devotees,
And they will breed none
But wicked ungrateful ones.

٢٧- إِنَّكَ إِن تَذَرْهُمْ
يُضِلُّوا عِبَادَكَ
وَلَا يَلِدُوٓا إِلَّا فَاجِرًا كَفَّارًا ○

28. "O my Lord! Forgive me,
My parents, all who
Enter my house in Faith,
And (all) believing men

٢٨- رَّبِّ ٱغْفِرْ لِى وَلِوَٰلِدَىَّ
وَلِمَن دَخَلَ بَيْتِىَ مُؤْمِنًا

5722. Such Pagan superstitions and cults do not add to human knowledge or human well-being. They only increase error and wrong-doing. For example, how much lewdness resulted from the Greek and Roman Saturnalia! And how much lewdness results from ribald Holi songs! This is the natural result, and Noah in his bitterness of spirit prays that God's grace may be cut off from men who hug them to their hearts. They mislead others: let them miss their own mark! See also verse 28 below.

5723. The Punishment of sin seizes the soul from every side and in every form. Water (drowning) indicates death by suffocation, through the nose, ears, eyes, mouth, throat, and lungs. Fire has the opposite effects: it burns the skin, the limbs, the flesh, the brains, the bones, and every part of the body. So the destruction wrought by sin is complete from all points of view. And yet it is not death (xx. 74); for death would be a merciful release from the Penalty, and the soul steeped in sin has closed the gates of God's Mercy on itself. There they will abide, unless and "except as God willeth" (vi. 128). For time and eternity, as we conceive them now, have no meaning in the wholly new world which the soul enters after death or Judgment.

5724. The Flood was sent in order to purge all sin. The prayer of Noah is not vindictive. It simply means, "Cut off all the roots of sin". See next note.

And believing women :[5725]
And to the wrong-doers
Grant Thou no increase
But in Perdition ! "[5726]

وَلِلْمُؤْمِنِينَ وَالْمُؤْمِنٰتِ ۗ
وَلَا تَزِدِ الظّٰلِمِينَ إِلَّا تَبَارًا ۝

5725. Indeed he prays for himself, his parents, his guests, and all who in earnest faith turn to God, in all ages and in all places. Praying for their forgiveness is also praying for the destruction of sin.

5726. This is slightly different in form from verse 24 above, where see n. 5722. See also last note.

APPENDIX XIII.

Ancient Forms of Pagan Worship (see lxxi. 23, n. 5721).

From prehistoric times man has sought to worship powers of nature, or symbols representing those powers, or idols representing those symbols. In vulgar minds they become debased superstitions, and seem to come into competition with the worship of the one True God.

2. The five names mentioned in lxxi. 23 represent some of the oldest Pagan cults, before the Flood as well as after the Flood, though the names themselves are in the form in which they were worshipped by local Arab tribes. The names of the tribes have been preserved to us by the Commentators, but they are of no more than archæological interest to us now. But the names of the false gods are interesting to us from the point of view of comparative religion, as, under one form or another, such cults still exist in countries which have not accepted the Gospel of Unity, as they have always existed since man turned from his Maker and Sustainer to the worship of created things or invented fancies.

3. The names of the five false gods and the symbols under which they were represented were as follows :—

	Pagan god		*Shape*		*Quality represented*
1.	Wadd	...	Man	...	Manly Power.
2.	Suwā'	...	Woman	...	Mutability, Beauty.
3.	Yagūth	...	Lion (or Bull)	...	Brute Strength.
4.	Ya'ūq	...	Horse	...	Swiftness.
5.	Nasr	...	Eagle, or Vulture, or Falcon.	...	Sharp Sight, Insight.

It is not clear whether these names are to be connected with true Arabic verbal roots or are merely Arabicised forms of names derived from foreign cults, such as those of Babylonia or Assyria, the region of Noah's Flood. The latter supposition is probable. Even in the case of ***Wadd*** (Affection, Love) and ***Nasr*** (Eagle), which are good Arabic words, it is doubtful whether they are not, in this connection, translations or corruptions of words denoting foreign cults.

4. In studying ancient comparative mythologies we must never forget the following facts. (1) Men's ideas of God always tend to be anthropomorphic. The qualities which they admire they transfer to their godhead. (2) But fear in primitive man also leads to the transfer of anything mysterious or imagined to be injurious, to the Pantheon. Such things have to be placated in order that they may not injure man. Thus in popular Hinduism the goddess of small-pox, which causes terror over an ignorant countryside, has to be worshipped, placated, or appeased with sacrifice. (3) This leads to the worship of animals noxious to man, such as serpent-worship, which

has prevailed and still prevails in many primitive areas. In ancient Egyptian mythology the Crocodile (so common in the Nile), the Dog, the Bull, and the Ibis were worshipped both literally and symbolically. See Appendix V, p. 409. (4) But as men's knowledge grows, and they observe the wonderful heavenly bodies and their motions, they begin to feel their sublimity, beauty and mystery, and they transfer their worship to the heavenly bodies. The first great astronomers in the ancient world were the Babylonians and Chaldæans. Among them was Abraham's homeland. The allegory of Abraham (vi. 74-82 and notes) points to the importance of the cult of the worship of heavenly bodies and the fallacy in them. "It is those who believe, and confuse not their beliefs with wrong—that are truly in security, for they are on right guidance" (vi. 82). The Sabæan worship of heavenly bodies in Arabia had probably its source in Chaldæa (see last paragraph of n. 76 to ii. 62). (5) A further refined step in Paganism is to worship abstractions, to treat concrete things as symbols of abstract qualities which they represent. For example, the planet Saturn with its slow motion was treated as phlegmatic and evil. The planet Mars with its fiery red light was treated as betokening war and havoc and evil, and so on. Jupiter, with its magnificent golden light, was treated as lucky and benignant to any who came under its influence. Venus became the symbol and the goddess of carnal love. The Pagan Arabs erected Time (*Dahr*) into a deity, existing from eternity to eternity, and dispensing good and ill fortune to men. The ancient Ægean religion treated the vital principle in the same way, as spontaneous and eternal, and traces of this are found in many religions, ancient and modern. (6) The next step was to reincarnate as it were these qualities in beings of flesh and blood, with lives, feelings, and passions like those of ordinary men and women, and to fill up a confused Pantheon with gods and goddesses that quarrelled, hated, loved, were jealous, and suffered or enjoyed life like human beings. In such a Pantheon there was room for demi-gods and real human heroes that were worshipped as gods. The Greek poets and artists were past masters in carrying out this process, under cover of which they discussed profound human problems with great power. They made religion dramatic. While they gained in humanism, they lost the purer spiritual conceptions which lift the divine world far above the futilities and crimes of this life. Hierarchical Christianity has suffered from this inheritance of the Greek tradition. (7) Where there was a commingling of peoples and cultures, several of these ideas and processes got mixed up together. Gods and goddesses of different origins were identified one with another, *e.g.* Artemis, the chaste virgin huntress goddess of the Greek Pantheon, was identified with Diana of the Romans, Diana of the Ephesians (representing the teeming life of nature), and Selene the cold moon-goddess. Similarly Diana was identified with the Egyptian Isis, and Diana's twin-brother Apollo (the sun) with the Egyptian Osiris. Forces of nature, animals, trees, qualities, astronomical bodies, and various other factors got mixed up together, and formed a shapeless medley of superstitions, which are all condemned by Islam.

5. To revert to the worship of the heavenly bodies. The countless fixed stars in the firmament occupied always the same relative positions in the heavens, and did not impress the imagination of the ancients like the objects which stood out vividly with mysterious laws of relative motion. A few individual stars did attract the worshippers' attention; *e.g.* Sirius the Dog-star, the brightest fixed star in the heavens, with a bluish tinge in its light, and Algol the variable star, being Beta of the constellation

Perseus, whose variations can be perceived by the naked eye in two or three nights, became connected with many legends, myths, and superstitions. It is probably Sirius that is referred to as the fixed star in the Parable of Abraham (vi. 76). With regard to the fixed stars in their myriads, the astronomers turned their fancy to devising Groups or Constellations. But the moving "stars", or planets, each with its own individual laws of motion, stood out to them personified, each with a motion and therefore will or influence of its own. As they knew and understood them, they were seven in number, *viz.*: (1) and (2) the moon and the sun, the two objects which most closely and indubitably influence the tides, the temperatures, and the life on our planet; (3) and (4) the two inner planets, Mercury and Venus, which are morning and evening stars, and never travel far from the sun; and (5), (6), and (7) Mars, Jupiter, and Saturn, the outer planets, whose elongations from the sun on the ecliptic can be as wide as possible. The number seven became itself a mystic number, as explained in n. 5526 to lxv. 12.

6. It will be noticed that the sun and the moon and the five planets got identified each with a living deity, god or goddess, with characteristics and qualities of its own. The solar myth was a myth of very fruitful vitality, and got mixed up with many other myths and ideas. In late Roman religion it appears in the story of Apollo, the sun-god of light and learning and of manly beauty, twin brother to Diana the moon-goddess. In ancient Egypt it appears in the myth of Horus, the falcon-eyed, or of Ra or Rè, the Eye, which sees all things. Further, the eagle, or falcon, or hawk, became itself identified with the sun, with its piercing light. The sun myth mixes itself up with the myth of the Nile and with the cycle of legends connected with Isis and Osiris, who were subsequently identified with the moon and the sun divinities. In Babylon the name Shamash (Arabic, *Shams*) proclaims the glory of the sun-god corresponding to the old Sumerian Utu or Babbar, while the hymns to Sūrya (the sun) in the Rig-Veda and the cult of Mithra in Persia proclaim the dominance of sun-worship.

7. Moon-worship was equally popular in various forms. I have already referred to the classical legends of Apollo and Diana, twin brother and sister, representing the sun and the moon. The Egyptian Khonsu, traversing the sky in a boat, referred to the moon, and the moon legends also got mixed up with those about the god of magic, Thoth, and the Ibis. In the Vedic religion of India the moon-god was Soma, the lord of the planets, and the name was also applied to the juice which was the drink of the gods. It may be noted that the moon was a male divinity in ancient India; it was also a male divinity in ancient Semitic religion, and the Arabic word for the moon (*qamar*) is of the masculine gender. On the other hand, the Arabic word for the sun (*shams*) is of the feminine gender. The Pagan Arabs evidently looked upon the sun as a goddess and the moon as a god.

8. Of the five planets, perhaps Venus as the evening star and the morning star alternately impressed itself most on the imagination of astro-mythology. This planet was in different places considered both male and female. In the Bible (Isaiah, xiv. 12), the words "How art thou fallen, O Lucifer, son of the morning!" are understood to refer to the Morning Star in the first instance, and by analogy to the King of Babylon. The Fathers of tne Christian Church, on the other hand, transferred the name Lucifer to Satan, the power of evil. Mercury is a less conspicuous planet, and was looked upon as a child in the family, the father and mother being the moon and the sun, or the sun

and the moon (according to the sex attributed to these divinities), or else either the sun or the moon was the father and Venus the mother (the sexes being inter-changeable in the myths). Of the three outer planets, Jupiter is the most conspicuous: indeed, after the sun and the moon, it is the most conspicuous object in the heavens, and was reputed to be beneficent and to bestow good fortune. The sun and the moon being considered in a class apart, Jupiter was considered the father of the planets, and possibly his worship got occasionally mixed up with that of the sun. Mars and Saturn, as has already been stated, were considered malevolent planets, to be feared for the mischief that they might do; for the Pagan Pantheons worshipped powers both of good and evil.

9. It is remarkable that the days of the week are named after the seven planets of geocentric astronomy, and if we take them in alternate sequence they indicate the order in which their heavens were arranged with reference to proximity to the earth. The following table represents this grouping:—

Planet	*Presiding god or goddess*	*Day of the week in alternate sequence*
Moon	Diana	Sunday
Mercury	Mercury	Tuesday
Venus	Venus	Thursday
The Sun	Apollo	Saturday
Mars	Mars	Monday
Jupiter	Jupiter	Wednesday
Saturn	Saturn	Friday

This alternate sequence is carried into a circle, as the total number is seven, itself a mystic number.

10. These cross-currents and mixtures of nature-worship, astral-worship, hero-worship, worship of abstract qualities, etc., resulted in a medley of debasing superstitions which are summed up in the five names, Wadd, Suwā', Yagūth, Ya'ūq, and Nasr, as noted in paragraph 3 above. The time of Noah is taken to be the peak of superstition and false worship, and the most ancient cults may thus be symbolically brought under these heads. If Wadd and Suwā' represented Man and Woman, they might well represent the astral-worship of the moon and the sun, or the sun and the moon, or they might represent human self-glorification, the worship of Self as against God, or they might represent the worship of Manly Power and Female Beauty, or other abstract qualities of that kind. On the other hand, it is possible that the worship of Jupiter and Venus itself got mixed up with the worship of the sun-moon pair. One pair being identified with another pair in a Septet, the number seven was reduced to five, and the five (itself a mystic number) might itself represent the seven planets as then worshipped. Further, it may be that Nasr (the vulture, falcon, hawk, or eagle, the Egyptian Horus) also represents a solar myth, mixed up with the cult of the planets. These cross-currents of astro-mythological mixtures of cults are well-known to students of ancient popular religions. If the five names, from another angle of vision, represent qualities, the Wadd-Suwā' pair (Sun-Moon, Jupiter-Venus) would represent manly power and womanly beauty or mutability respectively, and the three remaining ones (paragraph 3) might represent Brute Strength, like that of a Bull or a Lion; Swiftness like that of a Horse or sharpness (of sight or intelligence) like that of a vulture, hawk, or eagle.

11. It may be noted that the five names of deities mentioned here to represent very ancient religious cults are well-chosen. They are not the names of the deities best known in Mecca, but rather those which survived as fragments of very ancient cults among the outlying tribes of Arabia, which were influenced by the cults of Mesopotamia (Noah's country). The Pagan deities best known in the Ka'ba and round about Mecca were Lāt, 'Uzzā, and Manāt. (Manāt was also known round Ya<u>th</u>rib, which afterwards became Medina.) See liii. 19-20. They were all female goddesses. Lāt almost certainly represents another wave of sun-worship : the sun being feminine in Arabic and in Semitic languages generally. "Lāt" may be the original of the Greek "Leto", the mother of Apollo the sun-god (*Encyclopædia of Islam*, I, p. 380). If so, the name was brought in prehistoric times from South Arabia by the great Incense Route (n. 3816 to xxxiv. 18) to the Mediterranean. 'Uzzā probably represents the planet Venus. The origin of Manāt is not quite clear, but it would not be surprising if it also turned out to be astral. The 360 idols established by the Pagans in the Ka'ba probably represented the 360 days of an inaccurate solar year. This was the actual "modern" Pagan worship as known to the Quraish contemporary with our Prophet. In sharp contrast to this is mentioned the ancient antediluvian worship under five heads, of which fragments persisted in outlying places, as they still persist in different forms and under different names in all parts of the world where the pure worship of God in unity and truth is not firmly established in the minds and hearts of men.

References: The classical work on Arabian idol-worship is Ibn al-Kalbi's *Kitāb-ul-aṣnām*, of the late second century of the Hijra. The book is not easily accessible. Our doctors of religion have evinced no interest in the study of ancient cults, or in comparative religion, and most of them had not before them the results of modern archæology. But a modern school of Egyptian archæologists is arising, which takes a great deal of interest in the antiquities of their own country. For astral worship consult Hastings' *Encyclopædia of Religion and Ethics*, articles on "Sun, Moon, and Stars," as worshipped in different countries. Consult also Sir E. A. Wallis Budge, *Gods of the Egyptians*, London 1904 ; A. H. Sayce, *Religions of Ancient Egypt and Babylonia*, Gifford Lectures, Edinburgh 1902 ; M. Jastrow, *Religion of Babylonia and Assyria*, Boston 1898 ; E. W. Hopkins, *Religions of India*, London 1896 ; G. A. Barton, *Sketches of Semitic Origins*, New York 1902. Any Classical Dictionary would give details of Greek and Roman Mythology. It is curious that the Indus Civilization, which resembles the Second Pre-diluvian Culture of Elam and Mesopotamia, does not clearly disclose any signs of astral worship. But this study is still in its tentative stage. There is tree and animal worship, phallic worship, and the worship of the great Mother-goddess. Animal worship regards strength, courage, virility, or swiftness, as in the Pagan Arabian deities we have been considering. See Sir John Marshall, *Mohenjo Daro and the Indus Civilization*, 3 vols. London 1931.

Sir J. G. Frazer, in his *Adonis, Attis, and Osiris* (4th ed, London 1914, Vol. I, pp. 8-9) refers to *Allatu* or Eresh-Kigal as "the stern queen of the infernal regions" in Babylonian religion: she was the goddess of the nether regions, of darkness and desolation, as her counterpart Ishtar was the chief goddess of the upper regions, of reproduction and fertility, associated with the planet Venus.

INTRODUCTION AND SUMMARY : SŪRA LXXII (*Jinn*).

This is a late Meccan Sūra, of which we can be tolerably certain of the date. It was two years before the Hijrat, when the Prophet, despised and rejected in his native city of Mecca, went to evangelise the lordly men of Ṭāif. They maltreated him and nearly killed him ; what caused him even greater pain was the maltreatment of the humble and lowly men who went with him. Ṭabarī has handed down that memorable Prayer of faith and humility which he offered in the midst of his suffering. On his return journey to Mecca, a glorious vision was revealed to him,—hidden spiritual forces working for him,—people not known to him accepting his mission while his own people were still rejecting him. Within two months some strangers from Medina had privately met him and laid the foundations of that Hijrat which was to change the fate of Arabia and the course of world-history.

C. 252.—Spiritual Truth finds its lodgment
(lxxii. 1-28.) In all sorts of unexpected places, and in all sorts
Of unexpected ways. The man of God,
When most depressed by the buffets of a world
Steeped in selfishness, sees a glorious vision :
Hidden spiritual forces work for him,
Make known the truth in marvellous ways,
And proclaim the Goodness and Judgment of God.
They reject all Error and lead others to purify
Their wills and come to God. Behold!
Every place and time, every gift
Is meet for the service of God, the One,
The True, Whose Word the righteous one
Proclaims and must proclaim at all cost.
Man's Duty is plain, but in the Kingdom
Of God, through God's chosen ones,
We rise to higher and higher Mysteries,
As may be expedient for us. Yet when
Or how our End may be, is not given
To man to know : let him but take
The Treasures well-guarded, that come to him,
And praise the Lord of all Knowledge and Wisdom !

Sūra LXXII.

Jinn, or the Spirits.

In the name of God, Most Gracious,
Most Merciful.

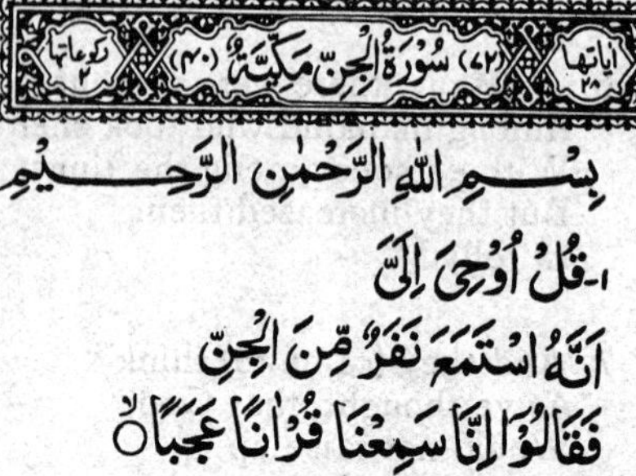

بِسْمِ اللَّهِ الرَّحْمَٰنِ الرَّحِيمِ

1. Say : It has been
Revealed[5727] to me that
A company of Jinns[5728]
Listened (to the Qur-ān).
They said, 'We have
Really heard a wonderful Recital![5729]

١- قُلْ أُوحِيَ إِلَيَّ
أَنَّهُ اسْتَمَعَ نَفَرٌ مِّنَ الْجِنِّ
فَقَالُوا إِنَّا سَمِعْنَا قُرْآنًا عَجَبًا ۝

2. 'It gives guidance
To the Right,
And we have believed therein:
We shall not join (in worship)
Any (gods) with our Lord.

٢- يَهْدِي إِلَى الرُّشْدِ
فَآمَنَّا بِهِ ۖ
وَلَن نُّشْرِكَ بِرَبِّنَا أَحَدًا ۝

3. 'And exalted is the Majesty
Of our Lord: He has
Taken neither a wife
Nor a son.[5730]

٣- وَأَنَّهُ تَعَالَىٰ جَدُّ رَبِّنَا
مَا اتَّخَذَ صَاحِبَةً وَلَا وَلَدًا ۝

4. 'There were some foolish ones
Among us, who used
To utter extravagant lies
Against God;

٤- وَأَنَّهُ كَانَ يَقُولُ سَفِيهُنَا
عَلَى اللَّهِ شَطَطًا ۝

5. 'But we do think
That no man or spirit

٥- وَأَنَّا ظَنَنَّا أَن لَّن تَقُولَ الْإِنسُ وَالْجِنُّ

5727. Revelation may be through various channels, and one of the channels may be a vision, by which the Prophet sees and hears events clearly passing before him. This particular vision may be the same as that referred to more briefly in xlvi. 29-32, where see n. 4809. The Jinns had evidently heard of previous revelations, that of Moses (xlvi. 30), and the error of Trinitarian Christianity (lxxii. 3). The people from whom they come have all sorts of good and bad persons, but they are determined to preach the good Message of Unity which they have heard and believed in.

5728. For Jinns, see n. 929 to vi. 100. We may take these to be spirits ordinarily unseen, or people who were strangers in Arabia, but had in their own private way heard and believed in the Gospel of Islam.

5729. The Holy Qur-ān would be to them a wonderful Recital—both in subject-matter and in the circumstance that it had come in Arabia among a pagan and ignorant nation.

5730. They abjure paganism and also the doctrine of a son begotten by God, which would also imply a wife of whom he was begotten. *Cf.* vi. 101.

Should say aught that is
Untrue against God.[5731]

عَلَى اللّٰهِ كَذِبًا ۝

6. 'True, there were persons
Among mankind who took shelter
With persons among the Jinns,
But they increased them
In folly.[5732]

٦- وَّ اَنَّهٗ كَانَ رِجَالٌ مِّنَ الْاِنْسِ
يَعُوْذُوْنَ بِرِجَالٍ مِّنَ الْجِنِّ
فَزَادُوْهُمْ رَهَقًا ۝

7. 'And they (came to) think
As ye thought, that God
Would not raise up
Any one (to Judgment).

٧- وَّ اَنَّهُمْ ظَنُّوْا كَمَا ظَنَنْتُمْ
اَنْ لَّنْ يَّبْعَثَ اللّٰهُ اَحَدًا ۝

8. 'And we pried into
The secrets of heaven;
But we found it filled
With stern guards
And flaming fires.[5733]

٨- وَّ اَنَّا لَمَسْنَا السَّمَآءَ
فَوَجَدْنٰهَا مُلِئَتْ حَرَسًا
شَدِيْدًا وَّ شُهُبًا ۝

9. 'We used, indeed, to sit there
In (hidden) stations, to (steal)
A hearing; but any
Who listens now[5734]
Will find a flaming fire
Watching him in ambush.

٩- وَّ اَنَّا كُنَّا نَقْعُدُ مِنْهَا مَقَاعِدَ لِلسَّمْعِ
فَمَنْ يَّسْتَمِعِ الْاٰنَ يَجِدْ لَهٗ
شِهَابًا رَّصَدًا ۝

5731. No one ought to entertain false notions about God. For by joining false gods in our ideas of worship, we degrade our conception of ourselves and the duty we owe to our Creator and Cherisher, to Whom we have to give a final account of life and conduct. If we worship idols or heavenly bodies, or human beings, or any creatures, or false fancies born of self or foolish abstractions, or the lusts and desires of our own hearts, we are not only doing violence to Truth, but we are causing discord in the harmony of the world.

5732. If human beings think that by a resort to some mysterious spirits they can shelter themselves from the struggles and actualities of their own lives, they are sadly mistaken. They must "dree their own weird", as the Scots would say. It is folly to try to escape from the duties which they can understand in their own natural surroundings, or to try to avoid the consequences of their own acts. Only such persons do so as do not realise that they will ultimately have to answer at the Judgment-seat of God, whose first outpost is in their own conscience.

5733. See notes 1951, 1953, and 1954 to xv. 17-18. See also n. 5562 to lxvii. 5. The speakers here have repented of sin and evil; but they recognise that there are evil ones among them, who love stealth and prying, but their dark plots will be defeated by vigilant guardians of the Right, whose repulse of the attacks of evil is figured by the shafts of meteoric light in the heavens.

5734. What is the force of "now"? It refers to the early Meccan period of Revelation. It means that whatever excuse there may have been before, for people to try to seek out the hidden truths of the Unseen World through spirits, there was none now, as the perspicuous Qur-ān had restored the Message of Unity and cleared religion of all the cobwebs, mysteries, and falsehoods with which priestcraft and pious fraud had overlaid it. The result is that such seekers after false hidden knowledge will find themselves confronted now by the flaming fire of the Qur-ān, which, like the shafts of meteoric light (see last note), will lie in wait for and nip such priestcraft and black magic in the bud,

10. 'And we understand not
Whether ill is intended
To those on earth,[5735]
Or whether their Lord
(Really) intends to guide
Them to right conduct.

١٠- وَّاَنَّا لَا نَدْرِیْۤ اَشَرٌّ
اُرِیْدَ بِمَنْ فِی الْاَرْضِ
اَمْ اَرَادَ بِهِمْ رَبُّهُمْ رَشَدًاۙ

11. 'There are among us
Some that are righteous,
And some the contrary:
We follow divergent paths.

١١- وَّاَنَّا مِنَّا الصّٰلِحُوْنَ وَمِنَّا دُوْنَ ذٰلِكَؕ
كُنَّا طَرَآئِقَ قِدَدًاۙ

12. 'But we think that we
Can by no means frustrate
God throughout the earth,
Nor can we frustrate Him
By flight.[5736]

١٢- وَّاَنَّا ظَنَنَّاۤ اَنْ لَّنْ نُّعْجِزَ اللّٰهَ فِی الْاَرْضِ
وَلَنْ نُّعْجِزَهٗ هَرَبًاۙ

13. 'And as for us,
Since we have listened
To the Guidance, we have
Accepted it: and any
Who believes in his Lord
Has no fear, either[5737]
Of a short (account)
Or of any injustice.

١٣- وَّاَنَّا لَمَّا سَمِعْنَا الْهُدٰۤى
اٰمَنَّا بِهٖؕ
فَمَنْ یُّؤْمِنْۢ بِرَبِّهٖ
فَلَا یَخَافُ بَخْسًا وَّلَا رَهَقًاۙ

14. 'Amongst us are some
That submit their wills
(To God), and some
That swerve from justice.
Now those who submit
Their wills—they have[5738]

١٤- وَّاَنَّا مِنَّا الْمُسْلِمُوْنَ
وَمِنَّا الْقٰسِطُوْنَؕ
فَمَنْ اَسْلَمَ فَاُولٰٓئِكَ

5735. To these spirits this revolutionary gospel is yet new, and appears like a flaming sword which destroys falsehood while it protects Truth. They frankly confess that they do not clearly understand whether on the whole it will be a mercy to mankind or a punishment for mankind forsaking the paths of God. But they rightly feel that it must be a blessing if all seek right Guidance.

5736. See last note. In any case, they know that God's Truth and God's Plan must prevail, and no one can frustrate God's purpose; or escape from it. Why not then bring the human will into conformity with it, and find Peace, as they have found, by the acceptance of Faith?

5737. Possibly, from this world's standards, it may be that a man suffers for his Faith. He may be laughed at, persecuted, and actually hurt, "in mind, body, or estate". But he is not perturbed. He takes it all cheerfully, because he knows that when his full account is made up—real gain against apparent loss,—he is a gainer rather than a loser. And his Faith tells him that God is a just God, and will never allow him to suffer any injustice, or permit the account of his merit to appear one whit shorter than it is.

5738. Any one who responds to true Guidance, and submits his will to God, finds that he makes rapid progress in the path of right conduct and right life. He gets more and more assurance that his destination is the Garden of Bliss.

Sought out (the path)
Of right conduct:

تَحَرَّوْا رَشَدًا ۝

15. 'But those who swerve,—
They are (but) fuel
For Hell-fire'—[5739]

١٥- وَأَمَّا الْقٰسِطُونَ فَكَانُوا لِجَهَنَّمَ حَطَبًا ۝

16. (And God's Message is):
"If they (the Pagans)
Had (only) remained
On the (right) Way,
We should certainly have
Bestowed on them Rain[5740]
In abundance.

١٦- وَأَنْ لَوِ اسْتَقَامُوا عَلَى الطَّرِيقَةِ لَأَسْقَيْنٰهُمْ مَّاءً غَدَقًا ۝

17. "That We might try them
By that (means).
But if any turns away
From the remembrance[5741]
Of his Lord, He will
Cause him to undergo
A severe Penalty.

١٧- لِّنَفْتِنَهُمْ فِيهِ ۚ وَمَنْ يُعْرِضْ عَنْ ذِكْرِ رَبِّهِ يَسْلُكْهُ عَذَابًا صَعَدًا ۝

18. "And the places of worship[5742]
Are for God (alone):
So invoke not any one
Along with God;

١٨- وَأَنَّ الْمَسٰجِدَ لِلّٰهِ فَلَا تَدْعُوا مَعَ اللّٰهِ أَحَدًا ۝

5739. An unjust life carries its own condemnation. It does no good to itself or to any one else. It bears no fruit. It becomes merely fuel for the Fire of Punishment.

5740. *Rain*: literally, water: stands for all kinds of blessings, material, moral, and spiritual. Among the spiritual blessings, is the insight into higher things, which results from our will and endeavour to stand firm on the right Way, the natural, moral, and spiritual Law established by God. All blessings come by way of trial: the more we have, the more is expected of us. A man of gifts, talents, or insight is expected to show a higher standard of love and unselfishness than one less gifted, just as a rich man is expected to give more in charity than a poor man.

5741. To remember God is to realise His presence, acknowledge His Goodness, and accept His guidance. If we fail to do so, by deliberately turning away, He will withdraw His Grace, and that will be a severe Penalty indeed.

5742. This is a Meccan Sūra, and *Masjid* must be understood, not in the later technical sense of a Mosque, but in the root meaning, of any place, or occasion of worship or humble prostration in the service of God, or any limbs or faculties or accessories used in such worship, *e.g.* hands and feet, lips and voice, understanding or organisation. A number of meanings therefore follow. (1) No place of worship whatever should be used for the worship of any other but the true God. The Ka'ba was then full of idols, but the idols and their votaries were usurpers. (2) Worship should not be mixed up with vain objects, but should be reserved for the sincere service of God. (3) All our gifts are for God's service, which includes the service of His creatures, and not for our vainglory.

19. "Yet when the Devotee[5743]
Of God stands forth
To invoke Him, they[5744] just
Make round him a dense crowd."

١٩- وَأَنَّهُ لَمَّا قَامَ عَبْدُ اللَّهِ يَدْعُوهُ كَادُوا
يَكُونُونَ عَلَيْهِ لِبَدًا ۞

Section 2.

20. Say : "I do
No more than invoke
My Lord, and I join not
With Him any (false god)."

٢٠- قُلْ إِنَّمَا أَدْعُوا رَبِّي
وَلَا أُشْرِكُ بِهِ أَحَدًا ۞

21. Say : "It is not
In my power to cause[5745]
You harm, or to bring
You to right conduct."

٢١- قُلْ إِنِّي لَا أَمْلِكُ
لَكُمْ ضَرًّا وَلَا رَشَدًا ۞

22. Say : "No one can
Deliver me from God[5746]
(If I were to disobey Him),
Nor should I find refuge
Except in Him,

٢٢- قُلْ إِنِّي لَنْ يُجِيرَنِي مِنَ اللَّهِ أَحَدٌ
وَلَنْ أَجِدَ مِنْ دُونِهِ مُلْتَحَدًا ۞

23. "Unless I proclaim what
I receive from God
And His Messages :
For any that disobey God
And His Apostle,—for them
Is Hell: they shall dwell
Therein for ever."

٢٣- إِلَّا بَلَاغًا مِنَ اللَّهِ وَرِسَالَاتِهِ
وَمَنْ يَعْصِ اللَّهَ وَرَسُولَهُ
فَإِنَّ لَهُ نَارَ جَهَنَّمَ
خَالِدِينَ فِيهَا أَبَدًا ۞

5743. *The Devotee of God* : the holy Apostle Muḥammad.

5744. *They.* The immediate reference was to the Pagan Quraish who were then in possession of the Ka'ba and who put all sorts of obstacles and indignities in the way of the holy Prophet for preaching the One True God and denouncing idol-worship. They used to surround him and mob him and to treat him as if he was guilty of some dreadful crime. But the wider application refers to the habit of the world to make a marked man of any who diverges from the beaten paths of their favourite sins and who pleads earnestly for the cause of Truth and righteousness. They ridicule him ; they surround him with jeers and obloquy ; and they try to make the physical condition of his life as difficult for him as possible.

5745. 'Do not suppose that I am going to harm you individually or socially ; the very opposite is my wish ; but I cannot force you to right conduct ; that must depend upon the purification of your own faith and will.'

5746. 'My mission is from God. I cannot choose but obey. He has charged me to deliver the Message, and if I were to disobey him, I would myself be worthy of His punishment, and no one can save me. From every kind of trouble and difficulty my only refuge is in Him. I must proclaim His Message : otherwise I am false to the mission He has entrusted to me.'

24. At length, when they
See (with their own eyes)
That which they are promised,—[5747]
Then will they know
Who it is that is
Weakest in (his) helper
And least important
In point of numbers.

٢٤- حَتّٰىٓ اِذَا رَاَوْا مَا يُوْعَدُوْنَ
فَسَيَعْلَمُوْنَ مَنْ اَضْعَفُ نَاصِرًا
وَّاَقَلُّ عَدَدًا ۝

25. Say : "I know not whether
The (Punishment) which ye
Are promised is near,[5748]
Or whether my Lord
Will appoint for it
A distant term.

٢٥- قُلْ اِنْ اَدْرِيْٓ
اَقَرِيْبٌ مَّا تُوْعَدُوْنَ
اَمْ يَجْعَلُ لَهٗ رَبِّيْٓ اَمَدًا ۝

26. "He (alone) knows the Unseen,
Nor does He make any one
Acquainted with his Mysteries,—[5749]

٢٦- عٰلِمُ الْغَيْبِ
فَلَا يُظْهِرُ عَلٰى غَيْبِهٖٓ اَحَدًا ۝

27. "Except an apostle[5750]
Whom He has chosen:

٢٧- اِلَّا مَنِ ارْتَضٰى مِنْ رَّسُوْلٍ

5747. When the Hereafter arrives, and true values are restored, they will see clearly that the Promise of God was true, and that death on this earth was not the end of all things. Then they will see that those who were accounted weak on this earth will, in the realm of Reality, be the strong ones; those who seemed to have no following here will have, there, all the great and true ones with them, to help them and welcome them to their own ranks.

5748. The coming of Judgment is certain. But the exact time, relatively to our standards on this earth, no one can tell. God alone knows it. Even a Prophet of God, as such, does not know the Mysteries of the Unseen World, except in so far as they have been revealed to him by God's Revelation. *Cf.* vi. 50, and notes 867-68.

5749. "Mystery", or the Unseen, has two aspects. The relative Unseen is so with reference to a particular person, because of the intervention of Time, Space, or particular circumstances. For example, I cannot see to-day a house which I saw last year, because it has since been pulled down. Or I cannot in Lahore see the "Gateway of India" in Bombay, although any one in Bombay can see it. Or I cannot see the satellites of Jupiter with the naked eye, though I can through a telescope. But the Absolute Unseen, the Absolute Mystery, or God's Mystery, is something which no creature can know or see, except in so far as God reveals it to him. And God reveals such things to the extent that is good for men, through His chosen apostles, among whom the greatest is Muḥammad, the personified Light of Unity. The exact time of the Hour of Judgment has not been so shown, because we must not wait for it, but live as if it is to be at this minute. See last note and next note, and the references there.

5750. *Cf.* iii. 179, and n. 482. See also last note.

And then He makes
A band of watchers[5751]
March before him
And behind him,

فَإِنَّهُ يَسْلُكُ
مِنْ بَيْنِ يَدَيْهِ وَمِنْ خَلْفِهِ رَصَدًا ۝

28. "That he may know
That they have (truly)[5751-A]
Brought and delivered
The Messages of their Lord:
And He surrounds[5752]
(All the mysteries) that are
With them, and takes account
Of every single thing."[5753]

٢٨- لِّيَعْلَمَ
أَن قَدْ أَبْلَغُوا رِسَالَاتِ رَبِّهِمْ
وَأَحَاطَ بِمَا لَدَيْهِمْ
وَأَحْصَىٰ كُلَّ شَيْءٍ عَدَدًا ۝ ع

5751. There is much mystic doctrine here. Revelation is not a mechanical or material thing. It has to be safeguarded from being distorted or corrupted by ignorance, selfishness, or the powers of evil. How can its precious and subtle worth and the spiritual safeguards against its misuse by human folly or the perversity of evil be expressed in plain human words? We can imagine a very great treasure, which has to be transmitted. To guard it against evilly-disposed persons, a strong escort is required, to march in front and behind, so as to protect it from all sides. When it reaches its destination, the escort presents its credentials and an Invoice showing the Treasure being transmitted. Then the destined receiver knows that it has come intact and feels satisfied. So about spiritual Revelation. The spiritual man recognises the credentials and checks the contents on the tablets of his own heart and insight. He has then no doubt that it is a true Message from God, and that those who bring it are the true messengers "of their Lord".

5751-A. *They*: the band of watchers. In "he may know" it is better to construe "he" to refer to the apostle who receives the Message from the "watchers".

5752. *Aḥāṭa*: surrounds, encompasses, encloses, guards on all sides, keeps under his own possession and control, and does not allow to be corrupted or debased. See last note but one.

5753. In the spiritual Kingdom,—as indeed, in all things,—God's knowledge, wisdom, and Plan comprehend all things, great and small. There is nothing which we do, nothing which happens that is outside His account.

INTRODUCTION AND SUMMARY: SŪRA LXXIII (*Muzzammil*).

This is one of the earliest Sūras to have been revealed. The first was S. xcvi. 1-5 (*Iqraa*), in the fortieth year of the Prophet's life, say about 12 years before the Hijra. Then there was an interruption (*Fatra*), of which the duration cannot be exactly ascertained, as there was no external history connected with it. The usual estimate puts it at about six months, but it may have been a year or two years. The years were then counted by the luni-solar calendar: see Appendix xi., p. 1077. The second Sūra in chronological order was probably a great portion of S. lxviii. (*Qalam*), which came after the *Fatra* was over. About the same time came this Sūra (say third) and S. lxxiv., which follows (say fourth), and the remainder of xcvi. We may roughly put the date of this Sūra at about 11 to 10 years before the Hijra.

The subject-matter is the significance of Prayer and Humility in spiritual life and the terrible fate of those who reject Faith and Revelation.

C. 253.—Devote yourself to the service of God
(lxxiii. 1-20.) In the stillness of the night, but not
All night. In the world's persecution rely
On God, Who will deal with His enemies fittingly.
Let not God's service be a matter
Of difficulty to you: do all your duties
In whole-hearted remembrance of God,
And ever seek His bountiful Grace.

Sūra LXXIII.

Muzzammil, or Folded in Garments.

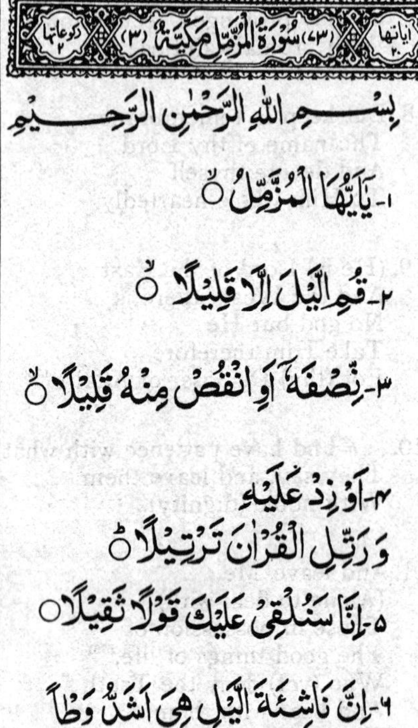

In the name of God, Most Gracious,
Most Merciful.

1. O thou folded
In garments ![5754]

2. Stand (to prayer) by night,
But not all night,—[5755]

3. Half of it,—
Or a little less,

4. Or a little more ;
And recite the Qur-ān[5756]
In slow, measured rhythmic tones.

5. Soon shall We send down
To thee a weighty Message.[5757]

6. Truly the rising by night
Is most potent for governing
(The soul), and most suitable
For (framing) the Word[5758]
(Of Prayer and Praise).

5754. *Muzzammil* : Some Commentators understand by this, "properly dressed for prayer", or "folded in a sheet, as one renouncing the vanities of this world". *Muzzammil* is one of the titles of our holy Prophet. But there is a deeper mystic meaning in this and the address "Thou wrapped up" of the next Sūra. Human nature requires warm garments and wrappings to protect the body from cold or heat or rain. But in the spiritual world these wrappings are useless : the soul must stand bare and open before God, in the silence of the night, but not too austerely, as the following verses show.

5755. The Prophet was prone to austerities in the cave of Hiraa, both before and after he received his mission, spending days and nights in prayer and contemplation. See C. 29. Midnight and after-midnight contemplation and prayers have technically received the name of *Tahajjud*. See also verse 20 below ; also xvii. 79.

5756. At this time there was only S. xcvi., S. lxviii, and possibly S. lxxiv, and the opening Sūra (*Al-Ḥamd*) ; but the heart of the Apostle had received enlightenment, and that Light was gradually finding expression in the verses of the Qur-ān. For us, now, with the whole of the Qur-ān before us, the injunction is specially necessary. The words of the Qur-ān must not be read hastily, merely to get through so much reading. They must be studied, and their deep meaning pondered over. They are themselves so beautiful that they must be lovingly pronounced in tones of rhythmic music.

5757. The Qur-ān as completed by degrees, after the *Fatra* (see Introduction to this Sūra).

5758. For contemplation, prayer, and praise, what time can be so suitable as the night, when calm and silence prevail, the voices of the market-place are still, and the silent stars pour forth their eloquence to the discerning soul.

7. True, there is for thee
By day prolonged occupation
With ordinary duties :[5759]

٧- إِنَّ لَكَ فِي ٱلنَّهَارِ سَبۡحًا طَوِيلٗا

8. But keep in remembrance
The name of thy Lord
And devote thyself
To Him whole-heartedly.

٨- وَٱذۡكُرِ ٱسۡمَ رَبِّكَ
وَتَبَتَّلۡ إِلَيۡهِ تَبۡتِيلٗا

9. (He is) Lord of the East
And the West : there is
No god but He :
Take Him therefore
For (thy) Disposer of Affairs.[5760]

٩- رَّبُّ ٱلۡمَشۡرِقِ وَٱلۡمَغۡرِبِ
لَآ إِلَٰهَ إِلَّا هُوَ
فَٱتَّخِذۡهُ وَكِيلٗا

10. And have patience with what
They say, and leave them
With noble (dignity).

١٠- وَٱصۡبِرۡ عَلَىٰ مَا يَقُولُونَ
وَٱهۡجُرۡهُمۡ هَجۡرٗا جَمِيلٗا

11. And leave Me
(Alone to deal with)
Those in possession of
The good things of life,[5761]
Who (yet) deny the Truth ;
And bear with them
For a little while.

١١- وَذَرۡنِي
وَٱلۡمُكَذِّبِينَ أُوْلِي ٱلنَّعۡمَةِ
وَمَهِّلۡهُمۡ قَلِيلًا

12. With Us are Fetters[5762]

١٢- إِنَّ لَدَيۡنَآ أَنكَالٗا

5759. A man of God, as a man, a member of a family, or a citizen, has many ordinary duties to perform ; and his work may be made difficult and irksome in protecting those who listen to his preaching and are therefore molested and persecuted by the world. But while discharging all his ordinary duties, he should work as in the presence of God, and in all matters and at all times retain the sense of God's nearness. His work may be on earth, but his heart is in Heaven.

5760. God is all-in-all. He is not in one place, but in all ; and He is Lord of all places. He rules the world. Therefore be not discouraged by the plots or enmity of wicked men. Leave all things to God ; trust Him ; He is just and will do justice. Only turn away from the unjust, but in a worthy and noble way ; *i.e.* to show them clearly that you do not fear them, but that you leave all affairs in God's hands. If we divide the world into hemispheres from north to south, "East and West" will cover all directions.

5761. Men who enjoy the good things of life have special cause for gratitude to God, Who bestowed them. When they are in the ranks of God's enemies, none but God can adequately deal with them.

5762. The result of sin is the loss of spiritual liberty ("fetters"). The limbs with which a man was intended to move freely about his business in the service of God are tied more and more closely, until they become paralysed, and his will itself becomes degraded.

(To bind them), and a Fire[5763]
(To burn them),

وَّجَحِيْمًا ۙ

13. And a Food that chokes,[5764]
And a Penalty Grievous.[5765]

١٣- وَّطَعَامًا ذَا غُصَّةٍ وَّعَذَابًا اَلِيْمًا ۙ

14. One Day the earth
And the mountains
Will be in violent commotion.
And the mountains will be
As a heap of sand
Poured out and flowing down.[5766]

١٤- يَوْمَ تَرْجُفُ الْاَرْضُ وَالْجِبَالُ
وَكَانَتِ الْجِبَالُ
كَثِيْبًا مَّهِيْلًا ۙ

15. We have sent to you,
(O men !) an apostle,
To be a witness concerning you,[5767]
Even as We sent
An apostle to Pharaoh.

١٥- اِنَّآ اَرْسَلْنَآ اِلَيْكُمْ رَسُوْلًا ۥ
شَاهِدًا عَلَيْكُمْ
كَمَآ اَرْسَلْنَآ اِلٰى فِرْعَوْنَ رَسُوْلًا ۗ

5763. Another effect of sin is the fire in his being, the conflagration in his soul. Evil passions seize him ; he loses his peace of mind ; and the fine talents and capacities in him fall off and are reduced to ashes like timber in a burning house.

5764. Furthermore, the appetite of sin grows with what it feeds on. Unlike a healthy man's food, which passes down his throat, gets assimilated, and yields him nourishment, the sinner's food gets choked in his throat : instead of nourishing him, it causes him pain : instead of satisfying him, it causes the sensation of baulked appetite and the desire for more and more infructuous food !

5765. In general terms, the Penalty of sin may be described as a Penalty Grievous, an Agony. It may come in this very life, but that in the Hereafter is certain ! See next verse.

We can also consider punishments from another aspect. The first object of punishment is to protect the innocent from the depredations of the criminal : we have to bind him. The next object is to produce in his heart the fire of repentance, to consume his evil proclivities and to light his conscience. Where that is not enough, a more drastic punishment for the callous is something which causes him pain in things which ordinarily cause him pleasure, such as food, drink, and the satisfaction of physical needs. People in whom the higher spiritual faculties are dead may perchance be awakened through the lower physical features of their life, which appeal to them. Where this also fails, there is finally the complete Agony, a type or symbol too terrible to contemplate.

5766. The Judgment is described as a violent commotion which will change the whole face of nature as we know it. Even the hard rock of mountains will be like loose sand running without any cohesion.

5767. Our holy Apostle has to warn his age, *i.e.* the present age, reclaim it from sin, and be a witness for the righteous and against evil, as Moses did his office in his age. For Pharaoh, his arrogance, and his punishment, see x. 75-92.

16. But Pharaoh disobeyed[5768]
The apostle ; so We
Seized him with
A heavy Punishment.

١٦- فَعَصٰى فِرْعَوْنُ الرَّسُوْلَ فَاَخَذْنٰهُ اَخْذًا وَّبِيْلًا ○

17. Then how shall ye,
If ye deny (God),
Guard yourselves against
A Day that will make
Children hoary-headed ?—[5769]

١٧- فَكَيْفَ تَتَّقُوْنَ اِنْ كَفَرْتُمْ يَوْمًا يَّجْعَلُ الْوِلْدَانَ شِيْبَا ○

18. Whereon the sky will be
Cleft asunder ?
His Promise needs must
Be accomplished.

١٨- السَّمَآءُ مُنْفَطِرٌۢ بِهٖ ۭ كَانَ وَعْدُهٗ مَفْعُوْلًا ○

19. Verily this is an Admonition :[5770]
Therefore, whoso will, let him
Take a (straight) path
To his Lord !

١٩- اِنَّ هٰذِهٖ تَذْكِرَةٌ ۚ فَمَنْ شَآءَ اتَّخَذَ اِلٰى رَبِّهٖ سَبِيْلًا ○

SECTION 2.

20. Thy Lord doth know
That thou standest forth
(To prayer) nigh two-thirds
Of the night, or half

٢٠- اِنَّ رَبَّكَ يَعْلَمُ اَنَّكَ تَقُوْمُ اَدْنٰى مِنْ ثُلُثَيِ الَّيْلِ وَنِصْفَهٗ

5768. Pharaoh the earthly king faces Moses the prophet of God. In earthly eyes it was Moses who disobeyed Pharaoh. In spiritual relations, it was Pharaoh who disobeyed Moses. Pharaoh represented an ancient and mighty kingdom, with a long history behind it, and a pride in its learning and science, art, organisation, and power. Moses led a depressed people, hewers of wood and drawers of water. But the might of God was behind him. What became of the wisdom, power, and armies of Pharaoh ? They were renr asunder when the day came, and the terror and surprise must have been the same as if the heavens had been rent asunder, and children's hair had turned grey ! But formidable revolutions turn children grey-haired in another way. Nations that were as children became wise before they in their turn decayed, and from similar disobedience to the laws of God. For God's law must stand and be fulfilled when all else is swept away.

5769. If already you deny and disobey God in this life of probation, how can you stand up to the Day of Judgment, the Day of the terrible Reality ? That Day is described in two metaphors : (1) It will be a time of such stress that even children will become like hoary-headed men ; (2) What we look upon as the eternal sky, ever the same, will be cleft asunder : *cf.* lxxxii. 1. In other words, the shape of things will be completely altered, both within man and in outer nature, and all true values will be restored. For the Promise of God, in this as in all other respects, cannot but be fulfilled.

5770. This is no empty threat. It is an admonition for your good. If you have the will, you can at once come for the Grace and Mercy of God, and obtain it. For Repentance and Amendment are the straight Way to the nearness of God.

The night, or a third[5771]
Of the night, and so doth
A party of those with thee.
But God doth appoint Night
And Day in due measure.
He knoweth that ye are
Unable to keep count thereof.[5772]
So He hath turned to you
(In mercy) : read ye,
Therefore, of the Qur-ān[5773]
As much as may be
Easy for you. He knoweth
That there may be (some)
Among you in ill-health ;
Others travelling through the land,
Seeking of God's bounty ;
Yet others fighting[5774]
In God's Cause. Read ye,
Therefore, as much of the Qur-ān
As may be easy (for you) ;
And establish regular Prayer
And give regular Charity ;
And loan to God
A Beautiful Loan.[5775]

وَثُلُثَهُ وَطَآئِفَةٌ مِّنَ الَّذِيْنَ مَعَكَ ط
وَاللّٰهُ يُقَدِّرُ الَّيْلَ وَالنَّهَارَ ط
عَلِمَ اَنْ لَّنْ تُحْصُوْهُ
فَتَابَ عَلَيْكُمْ
فَاقْرَءُوْا مَا تَيَسَّرَ مِنَ الْقُرْاٰنِ ط
عَلِمَ اَنْ سَيَكُوْنُ مِنْكُمْ مَّرْضٰى لا
وَاٰخَرُوْنَ يَضْرِبُوْنَ فِى الْاَرْضِ
يَبْتَغُوْنَ مِنْ فَضْلِ اللّٰهِ لا
وَاٰخَرُوْنَ يُقَاتِلُوْنَ فِىْ سَبِيْلِ اللّٰهِ صلے
فَاقْرَءُوْا مَا تَيَسَّرَ مِنْهُ لا
وَاَقِيْمُوا الصَّلٰوةَ وَاٰتُوا الزَّكٰوةَ
وَاَقْرِضُوا اللّٰهَ قَرْضًا حَسَنًا ط

5771. *Cf.*, above, lxxiii. 2-4. The Prophet, and a zealous band of his disciples, were often up, two-thirds of the night, or a half, or a third, rejecting sleep and giving themselves up to Prayer and Praise and the reading of the Qur-ān. They are told that this was too severe a tax on them, especially if their health was affected, or they were on a journey, or they were striving, with might and main, in other ways, for the cause of God. See the lines following.

5772. The usual meaning taken is that the counting of the exact hours of night and day may not be possible for ordinary people, in order to determine exactly the half, or the third, or the two-thirds of a night. The length of the night and the day varies every day of the solar year, and the precise hour of midnight can only be determined by exact observation in clear skies or by chronometers, which is not possible for everyone. But I understand it in a wider meaning. God fixes night and day in due proportions ; for rest and work, and according to seasonal variations. For prayer and praise no meticulous observations of that kind are necessary or possible. God's service can be done in many ways as detailed below. But we must give some time to devotion, as may be most easy and convenient to us, in various circumstances of health, travel, and the performance of various duties.

5773. The reading of the Qur-ān here is almost equivalent to Prayer and religious devotion. This is not to be made into an obsession or a burden. *Cf.* xx. 2 : "We have not sent down the Qur-ān to thee to be an occasion for thy distress." We must do it whole-mindedly, but not by formal mechanical computations.

5774. This refers to *Jihād*. The better opinion is that this particular verse was revealed in Medina, long after the greater part of the Sūra. The reference, further on, to canonical Prayers and regular Charity (*Zakāt*), points to the same conclusion.

5775. *Cf.* ii. 245, and n. 276, where the meaning of "a Beautiful Loan" is explained. See also lvii. 18. The "Beautiful Loan" should be that of our own souls. We should expect no returns in kind, for that is not possible. But the reward we shall find with God will be infinitely greater and nobler. *Cf.* the biblical phrase, "Lay up for yourselves treasures in heaven" (Matt. vi. 20).

And whatever good Ye send forth For your souls,[5776] Ye shall find it In God's Presence,— Yea, better and Greater, in Reward. And seek ye the Grace Of God: for God is[5777] Oft-Forgiving, Most Merciful.	وَمَا تُقَدِّمُوا لِأَنفُسِكُم مِّنْ خَيْرٍ تَجِدُوهُ عِندَ اللَّهِ هُوَ خَيْرًا وَأَعْظَمَ أَجْرًا وَاسْتَغْفِرُوا اللَّهَ إِنَّ اللَّهَ غَفُورٌ رَّحِيمٌ ۝ ع

5776. Any good that we do raises our own spiritual status and dignity. We must not think that when we speak of God's service or God's Cause, we are doing anything for His benefit: He is independent of all needs whatsoever.

5777. This emphasizes the need of God's Grace. Whatever good we do, our own merits are comparatively small. God's Grace must lift us up and blot out our shortcomings. Even in piety there may be an arrogance which may become a sin. We should always seek God's Mercy in all humility.

INTRODUCTION AND SUMMARY: SŪRA LXXIV (*Muddaththir*).

This Sūra dates from about the same time as the last one. Its subject-matter is also similar: Prayer and Praise, and the need of patience in a period of great spiritual stress: the unjust who cause sorrow and suffering now will themselves experience agony in the Hereafter.

C. 254.—The Seer, by devotion and contemplation,
(lxxiv. 1-56.) Prepares himself for the duties of Guide
And Leader to mankind: but when there comes
The clear Call, he must stand forth
And proclaim the Message,—in purity,
Unselfish devotion, and patience long-suffering;—
To save men from the Distress of the Final Day.
For many there be who glory in a life
Of ease and plenty, arrogant splendour,
And the applause of men, who scorn God's Truth
And reject the divine. How will they fare
When the Judgment comes, and the Penalty?
Every Fact in Life's grand Pageant
Is but a Portent for the Future.
Every soul is in pledge and must
Redeem itself by Faith and Prayer,
By Charity and earnest care for the Realities
Of Life. Bring but the will, and God
Will guide,—the Lord of Righteousness,
The Lord of Mercy and Forgiveness!

Sūra LXXIV.

Muddaththir, or One Wrapped Up.

In the name of God, Most Gracious, Most Merciful

1. O thou wrapped up[5778]
(In a mantle)!

2. Arise and deliver thy warning!

3. And thy Lord
Do thou magnify!

4. And thy garments[5779]
Keep free from stain!

5. And all abomination shun![5780]

6. Nor expect, in giving,
Any increase (for thyself)![5781]

5778. As usual, in these wonderful early mystic verses, there is a triple thread of thought: (1) A particular occasion or person is referred to; (2) a general spiritual lesson is taught; and (3) a more profound mystical reverie is suggested. As to (1), the Prophet was now past the stage of personal contemplation, lying down or sitting in his mantle; he was now to go forth boldly to deliver his Message and publicly proclaim the Lord; his heart had always been purified, but now all his outward doings must be dedicated to God, and conventional respect for ancestral customs or worship must be thrown aside; the work of his Apostleship was the most generous gift that could flow from his personality, but no reward or appreciation was to be expected from his people, but quite the contrary; there would be much call on his patience, but his contentment would arise from the good pleasure of God. As to (2), similar stages arise in a minor degree in the life of every good man, for which the Prophet's life is to be a universal pattern. As to (3), the Ṣufis understand, by the mantle and outward wrappings, the circumstances of our phenomenal existence, which are necessary to our physical comfort up to a certain stage; but we soon outgrow them, and our inner nature should then boldly proclaim itself; not that it brings any credit or reward with men; the very hope or expectation of such would be inconsistent with our higher nature, which should bear all checks and rejoice in the favour of God.

5779. Possibly, in its immediate application, there is a reference to the dirt and filth which the Pagans used to throw at the Prophet to insult and persecute him.

5780. *Rujz* or *Rijz*: abomination: usually understood to refer to idolatry. It is even possible that there was an idol called Rujz. But it has a wider signification, as including a mental state opposed to true worship, a state of doubt or indecision.

5781. The legal and commercial formula is that you give in order to receive. And usually you expect to receive what is worth *to you* a little more than you give. The spiritual consideration is that you give, but expect nothing from the receiver. You serve God and God's creatures.

7. But, for thy Lord's (Cause),[5782]
Be patient and constant!

٧- وَلِرَبِّكَ فَاصْبِرْ ۝

8. Finally, when the trumpet
Is sounded,

٨- فَإِذَا نُقِرَ فِي النَّاقُورِ ۝

9. That will be—that Day—
A Day of Distress,—[5783]

٩- فَذَٰلِكَ يَوْمَئِذٍ يَوْمٌ عَسِيرٌ ۝

10. Far from easy
For those without Faith.

١٠- عَلَى الْكَافِرِينَ غَيْرُ يَسِيرٍ ۝

11. Leave Me alone, (to deal)[5784]
With the (creature) whom
I created (bare and) alone!—[5785]

١١- ذَرْنِي وَمَنْ خَلَقْتُ وَحِيدًا ۝

12. To whom I granted
Resources in abundance,

١٢- وَجَعَلْتُ لَهُ مَالًا مَمْدُودًا ۝

13. And sons to be
By his side!—[5786]

١٣- وَبَنِينَ شُهُودًا ۝

14. To whom I made
(Life) smooth and comfortable!

١٤- وَمَهَّدْتُ لَهُ تَمْهِيدًا ۝

15. Yet is he greedy—
That I should add
(Yet more);—[5787]

١٥- ثُمَّ يَطْمَعُ أَنْ أَزِيدَ ۝

5782. Our zeal for God's Cause itself requires that we should not be impatient, and that we should show constancy in our efforts for His Cause. For we have faith, and we know that He is All-Good, All-Wise, and All-Powerful, and everything will ultimately be right.

5783 The Sinner's course is now shown in contrast to the Seeker's. The Sinner may be self-complacent now: but what will be his position when the Reckoning comes? Not easy; indeed a Day of Distress!

5784. The question of Justice and Punishment to men is for God alone. For man at his best can see only one side of truth, and only God is All-Knowing. He alone can judge the limits of Justice and Mercy.

5785. Man's adventitious advantages—wealth, power, position, talents—are not due to his own merits. They are gifts from God, Who created him. In himself he came bare and alone.

5786. The great ones of the earth may have wealth, a large following, sons by their side to defend them and do their bidding, and man-power to help them in their battles. Life may be smooth and agreeable to them. But their responsibility is to God.

5787. The Sinner takes God's gifts as if they were his right. The more he gets, the more is he greedy. Yet to God's Signs and revelations he is wilfully deaf or even openly rebellious. But he is only preparing the way for his own undoing.

16. By no means!
For to Our Signs
He has been refractory!

١٦- كَلَّا ۖ إِنَّهُۥ كَانَ لِـَٔايَٰتِنَا عَنِيدًا ۝

17. Soon will I visit him
With a mount of calamities![5788]

١٧- سَأُرْهِقُهُۥ صَعُودًا ۝

18. For he thought
And he plotted;—

١٨- إِنَّهُۥ فَكَّرَ وَقَدَّرَ ۝

19. And woe to him![5789]
How he plotted!—

١٩- فَقُتِلَ كَيْفَ قَدَّرَ ۝

20. Yea, woe to him:
How he plotted!—

٢٠- ثُمَّ قُتِلَ كَيْفَ قَدَّرَ ۝

21. Then he looked round;

٢١- ثُمَّ نَظَرَ ۝

22. Then he frowned
And he scowled;

٢٢- ثُمَّ عَبَسَ وَبَسَرَ ۝

23. Then he turned back
And was haughty;

٢٣- ثُمَّ أَدْبَرَ وَٱسْتَكْبَرَ ۝

24. Then said he:[5790]
"This is nothing but magic,
Derived from of old;

٢٤- فَقَالَ إِنْ هَٰذَآ إِلَّا سِحْرٌ يُؤْثَرُ ۝

25. "This is nothing but
The word of a mortal!"

٢٥- إِنْ هَٰذَآ إِلَّا قَوْلُ ٱلْبَشَرِ ۝

26. Soon will I
Cast him into Hell-Fire![5791]

٢٦- سَأُصْلِيهِ سَقَرَ ۝

5788 "A mount of calamities" or disasters: may be understood as a phrase for cumulative disasters in a spiritual sense.

5789. *Cf.* li 10: "Woe to the falsehood-mongers!"

5790. The Commentators understand the reference to be to Walid ibn Mugaira, who was a wealthy Sybarite, Pagan to the core, and an inveterate enemy to the holy Prophet. He and Abū Jahl did all they could, from the beginning of the preaching of Islam, to abuse and persecute the Preacher, to run down his doctrine, and to injure those who believed in it. But the meaning for us is much wider. There are Walids in all ages. They cannot understand divine inspiration, and seek to explain its wonderful influence over the lives of men by some such unmeaning formula as "magic". The eternal Hope is to them mere human delusion!

5791. The Sinner's perversity can only end in the Fire of Punishment. It enters his very being. See next note.

27. And what will explain To thee what Hell-Fire is?	٢٧- وَمَآ أَدْرٰىكَ مَا سَقَرُ ۝
28. Naught doth it permit To endure, and naught[5792] Doth it leave alone!—	٢٨- لَا تُبْقِى وَلَا تَذَرُ ۝
29. Darkening and changing The colour of man!	٢٩- لَوَّاحَةٌ لِّلْبَشَرِ ۝
30. Over it are Nineteen.[5793]	٣٠- عَلَيْهَا تِسْعَةَ عَشَرَ ۝
31. And We have set none[5794] But angels as guardians Of the Fire; and We Have fixed their number[5795]	٣١- وَمَا جَعَلْنَآ أَصْحٰبَ النَّارِ إِلَّا مَلٰٓئِكَةً وَّمَا جَعَلْنَا عِدَّتَهُمْ إِلَّا فِتْنَةً

5792 He is in a state in which he neither lives nor dies (lxxxvii. 13). Looked at in another way, the things that in a good man are meant to last and grow, are for the sinner destroyed, and no part of his nature is left untouched. The brightness of his very manhood is darkened and extinguished by sin.

5793. Who are the Nineteen? And why this number? The nineteen guardians of the Fire are understood symbolically to be angels or faculties of man. Imām Fakhruddin Rāzi refers to a classification of nineteen faculties or powers in man, which if used properly lead to his spiritual advancement, but if misused, lead to his perdition. These faculties or powers may well be compared to angels, for angels are the powers or instruments of action in the spiritual world. The rebellious angels are types of faculties put to wrong use.

5794. *Cf.* lxvi. 6, and n. 5540

There was a great volume of angelology in the religious literature of the People of the Book (*i.e.* the Jews and Christians) to whom (among others) an appeal is made in this verse. The Essenes, a Jewish brotherhood with highly spiritual ideas, to which perhaps the prophet Jesus himself belonged, had an extensive literature of angelology. In the Midrash also, which was a Jewish school of exegesis and mystical interpretation, there was much said about angels. The Eastern Christian sects contemporary with the birth of Islam had borrowed and developed many of these ideas, and their mystics owed much to the Gnostics and the Persian apocalyptic systems. In the New Testament the relation of the angels with Fire is referred to more than once. In Rev. ix 11 we have "the angel of the bottomless pit, whose name in the Hebrew tongue is Abaddon, but in the Greek tongue hath his name Apollyon". In Rev. xiv. 18 there is an "angel which had power over fire", and in Rev. xvi. 8 an angel has "power...given unto him to scorch men with fire". In the Old Testament (Daniel vii. 9-10) the essence of all angels is fire: thousand thousands of them issued as a fiery stream from before the Ancient of Days, whose "throne was like the fiery flame, and His wheels as burning fire".

5795. The mystic significance of numbers is a favourite theme with some writers, but I lay no stress on it. In Christian theology the number of the Beast, 666, in Rev. xiii. 18 has given rise to much controversy, and may refer only to the numerical value of the letters in the name of the Roman Emperor Nero. In our own literature I think that we ought to avoid too much insistence on speculative conjectures. But I will note one suggestion for what it is worth. The number is itself an indivisible number, and may be represented by the formula, twice seven plus five. Now seven is a mystic number: see lxv. 12, and n. 5526; there are seven heavens, seven gates of Hell (xv. 44), and so on. Five is also a mystic number: there are five senses in man, five canonical prayers, and so on. As there are seven heavens and a similar number of layers of the earth (lxv. 12), man's externally perceived world has fourteen layers, and if his subjective world can be counted in five units according to his five senses, the number of stages controlling his conduct may be counted as nineteen.

Only as a trial For Unbelievers,—in order That the People of the Book May arrive at certainty, And the Believers may increase In Faith,— and that no doubts May be left for the People Of the Book and the Believers, And that those in whose hearts Is a disease and the Unbelievers May say, "What symbol Doth God intend by this?" [5796] Thus doth God leave to stray Whom He pleaseth, and guide Whom He pleaseth: and none Can know the forces Of thy Lord, except He.[5797] And this is no other than A warning to mankind.	لِّلَّذِينَ كَفَرُوا لِيَسْتَيْقِنَ الَّذِينَ أُوتُوا الْكِتَٰبَ وَيَزْدَادَ الَّذِينَ ءَامَنُوٓا إِيمَٰنًا وَلَا يَرْتَابَ الَّذِينَ أُوتُوا الْكِتَٰبَ وَالْمُؤْمِنُونَ وَلِيَقُولَ الَّذِينَ فِى قُلُوبِهِم مَّرَضٌ وَالْكَٰفِرُونَ مَاذَآ أَرَادَ اللَّهُ بِهَٰذَا مَثَلًا كَذَٰلِكَ يُضِلُّ اللَّهُ مَن يَشَآءُ وَيَهْدِى مَن يَشَآءُ وَمَا يَعْلَمُ جُنُودَ رَبِّكَ إِلَّا هُوَ وَمَا هِىَ إِلَّا ذِكْرَىٰ لِلْبَشَرِ ع

SECTION 2.

32. Nay, verily: By the Moon,[5798]	٣٢- كَلَّا وَالْقَمَرِ

5796. There are four classes of people mentioned here. (1) The Muslims will have their faith increased, because they believe that all revelation, symbolic or otherwise, is from God Most Merciful, and all His forces will work in their favour. (2) The People of the Book, those who had received previous revelations of an analogous character, the Jews and Christians, had numerous sects disputing with each other on minute points of doctrine; but they will now, if they believe, find rest from controversies in a broad symbolical understanding of scripture. (3) Those in whose hearts is a disease (see ii. 8-10, notes 33-34), the insincere ones, the hypocrites, will only be mystified, because they believe nothing and have rejected the grace and mercy of God. (4) The Unbelievers have frankly done the same and must suffer similar consequences.

5797. It is a necessary consequence of moral responsibility and freedom of choice in man, that he should be left free to stray if he chooses to do so, in spite of all the warning and the instruction he receives. God's channels of warning and instruction—His spiritual forces—are infinite, as are His powers. No man can know them. But this warning or reminder is addressed to all mankind.

All things are referred to God. But we must not attribute evil to Him. In iv. 79 we are expressly told that the good comes from God, and the evil from ourselves.

5798. An oath in human speech cal in evidence something sacred in the heart of man. In God's Message, also, when delivered in human language, solemn emphasis is indicated by an appeal to something striking among the Signs of God, which will go straight to the human heart which is addressed. In each case the symbol of the appeal has reference to the particular point enforced in the argument. Here we are asked to contemplate three wonderful phenomena, and they lead up to the conclusion in verse 38. (1) The moon, next after the sun, is the most striking luminary to our sight. Its reflected light has for us even a greater mystery than the direct light of the sun, which looks to us like pure fire. The moon was worshipped as a deity in times of darkness. But in reality, though she rules the night, her rays are only reflections, and are wanting in warmth and vitality. So every soul which looks up to a mere creature of God for a sort of vicarious salvation is in spiritual darkness or error; for the true source of spiritual light and life is God, and God alone. For (2) the Night and (3) the Dawn, see the following note.

33. And by the Night[5799]
As it retreateth,

٣٣- وَالَّيْلِ إِذْ أَدْبَرَ ۙ

34. And by the Dawn
As it shineth forth,—

٣٤- وَالصُّبْحِ إِذَآ أَسْفَرَ ۙ

35. This is but one[5800]
Of the mighty (portents),

٣٥- إِنَّهَا لَإِحْدَى الْكُبَرِ ۙ

36. A warning to mankind,—

٣٦- نَذِيرًا لِّلْبَشَرِ ۙ

37. To any of you that
Chooses to press forward,
Or to follow behind;—[5801]

٣٧- لِمَن شَآءَ مِنكُمْ أَن يَتَقَدَّمَ أَوْ يَتَأَخَّرَ ۗ

38. Every soul will be (held)
In pledge for its deeds.[5802]

٣٨- كُلُّ نَفْسٍ بِمَا كَسَبَتْ رَهِينَةٌ ۙ

39. Except the Companions
Of the Right Hand,[5803]

٣٩- إِلَّآ أَصْحَٰبَ الْيَمِينِ ۛ ع

5799. (2) The Night when it is illuminated by the Moon is light in a sense, but it is really dark and must give place to (3) the Dawn when it comes, as the harbinger of the Sun. So in spiritual matters, when every soul realises its own responsibility, it will look less and less to reflected lights, and through the beauty of a dawn-like awakening, will be prepared more and more for the splendour of the light of God Himself, the goal of the Heaven of our dreams.

5800. "*This is but one,*" etc. There are numerous Signs of God, of which Judgment is one, and one of the mightiest portents. Or the reference may be to the waning of the Moon, the decline of the night, and the glorious sunrise, as tokens or symbols of the world renewed when the present transitory world passes away.

5801. Three interpretations are possible. (1) Those pressing forward may be the Righteous, and those following behind may be the laggards, the Unbelievers, who reject God's love, care, and mercy. (2) Men of two kinds of temperament may be referred to: those who are always in the van and those who are always in the rear. God's Message is open to both. But there may be a danger to both: in the one case, over-confidence, or hope in wrong things; in the other case, missing great opportunities so that their spiritual lives may be "bound in shallows and in miseries". Extremes should be avoided. (3) Or it may mean that the warning is effective only for those willing to move forwards or backwards, as the case may be, but is lost on the inert or the lethargic. For our moral and spiritual progress, we have in some cases to go forwards, but in some cases we have to retreat from false positions. The hopeless case is that of the obstinate man, whose heart is so dead that he dares not advance to the right or withdraw from the wrong.

5802. *Cf.* lii. 21. Man cannot shift his responsibility to vicarious saviours or saints. His redemption depends upon the grace of God, for which he should constantly and whole-heartedly strive by means of right conduct. If he does so he will be redeemed and he will join the Companions of the Right Hand.

5803. *Cf.* n. 5223 to lvi. 3, and see lvi. 27-38. The Companions of the Right Hand will be the Righteous or the Blessed in the Hereafter. Their grounds of merit will be Prayer, Charity, Earnestness, and Faith in God's just Judgment: all of which are within the reach of the humblest Seeker. They are not separate acts or virtues, but are all inter-connected. At Judgment, the pledge of their soul will be redeemed by God's Grace at the Taking of the Account.

40. (They will be) in Gardens
(Of Delight): they will
Question each other,

٤٠- فِي جَنَّٰتٖ يَتَسَآءَلُونَ ۝

41. And (ask) of the Sinners:

٤١- عَنِ ٱلۡمُجۡرِمِينَ ۝

42. "What led you
Into Hell-Fire?"

٤٢- مَا سَلَكَكُمۡ فِي سَقَرَ ۝

43. They will say:
"We were not of those
Who prayed;

٤٣- قَالُواْ لَمۡ نَكُ مِنَ ٱلۡمُصَلِّينَ ۝

44. "Nor were we of those
Who fed the indigent;

٤٤- وَلَمۡ نَكُ نُطۡعِمُ ٱلۡمِسۡكِينَ ۝

45. "But we used to talk
Vanities with vain talkers;

٤٥- وَكُنَّا نَخُوضُ مَعَ ٱلۡخَآئِضِينَ ۝

46. "And we used to deny
The Day of Judgment,

٤٦- وَكُنَّا نُكَذِّبُ بِيَوۡمِ ٱلدِّينِ ۝

47. "Until there came to us
(The Hour) that is certain."[5804]

٤٧- حَتَّىٰٓ أَتَىٰنَا ٱلۡيَقِينُ ۝

48. Then will no intercession
Of (any) intercessors
Profit them.

٤٨- فَمَا تَنفَعُهُمۡ شَفَٰعَةُ ٱلشَّٰفِعِينَ ۝

49. Then what is
The matter with them
That they turn away
From admonition?—[5805]

٤٩- فَمَا لَهُمۡ عَنِ ٱلتَّذۡكِرَةِ مُعۡرِضِينَ ۝

50. As if they were
Affrighted asses,

٥٠- كَأَنَّهُمۡ حُمُرٞ مُّسۡتَنفِرَةٞ ۝

5804. *Cf.* xv. 99, and n. 2018. The Hour that is Certain is usually taken to be Death. But it has also a more general meaning, referring to a state of mind in spiritual progress. If there is no faith, the light of Truth is shut out, or put off from time to time, until a crisis comes when the Truth becomes only too real, but the time for repentance is past, and there is only room for the agony of regrets.

5805. If the Day of Judgment is inevitable, it is strange that men should not heed a plain warning, but go on as if they were thoughtless and obstinate asses stampeding from a lion. Instead of heeding the warning, they try to avoid it. They are frightened at God's Word.

51. Fleeing from a lion!

٥١- فَرَّتْ مِنْ قَسْوَرَةٍ ۝

52. Forsooth, each one of them
Wants to be given[5806]
Scrolls (of revelation) spread out!

٥٢- بَلْ يُرِيدُ كُلُّ امْرِئٍ مِّنْهُمْ
أَنْ يُّؤْتٰى صُحُفًا مُّنَشَّرَةً ۝

53. By no means! But
They fear not the Hereafter.

٥٣- كَلَّا ۖ بَلْ لَّا يَخَافُونَ الْاٰخِرَةَ ۝

54. Nay, this surely
Is an admonition:

٥٤- كَلَّآ إِنَّهٗ تَذْكِرَةٌ ۝

55. Let any who will,[5807]
Keep it in remembrance!

٥٥- فَمَنْ شَآءَ ذَكَرَهٗ ۝

56. But none will keep it
In remembrance except
As God wills: He[5808]
Is the Lord of Righteousness,
And the Lord of Forgiveness.

٥٦- وَمَا يَذْكُرُوْنَ إِلَّآ أَنْ يَّشَآءَ اللّٰهُ ۗ
هُوَ أَهْلُ التَّقْوٰى
وَأَهْلُ الْمَغْفِرَةِ ۝

5806 *Cf.* xvii. 93: "Until thou send down to us a book that we could read." The Unbelievers pretend in ridicule that they would believe if a special message written on open scrolls and addressed to them severally were brought to them by a miracle! There is a disease in their hearts and understandings. The Teacher's warning is plain, and enough for any reasonable man who has the will to seek God.

5807. The Qur-ān itself is the admonition—the latest among the revealed Books of God. If man has the will to learn, he will keep the Message always before Him, and God's grace will help him to carry it out in his conduct.

5808. Righteousness as well as Forgiveness have their source in God's Will. Man's Righteousness has no meaning except in relation to the universal Will. For *Taqwā* see n. 26 to ii. 2. If we take the word here in the sense of "the fear of God", the translation would be: "He alone is worthy to be feared, and He alone is entitled to grant Forgiveness."

INTRODUCTION AND SUMMARY: SŪRA LXXV (*Qiyāmat*).

This Sūra belongs to the early Meccan period, but comes chronologically a good deal later than the last two Sūras.

Its subject-matter is the Resurrection, viewed from the point of view of Man, especially unregenerate Man, as he is now, and as he will be then,—his inner and psychological history.

C. 255.—Eschew all Evil: for man was not created
(lxxv. 1-40) Without purpose or without responsibility.
The Day of Account will come, and his own
Conscience bears witness that he
Must walk straight; for he must face
That Day's Realities. With patience await
The unfoldment of God's wise Purpose. Keep
The Hereafter ever in view. The faces
Of the Blest will beam with brightness and beauty.
For the others, Death will be a terror,—
For duties neglected and sins committed.
Woe unto man that he thinks not now
Of God's Purpose and the noble Destiny
For which God gave him Life and its Gifts.

Sūra LXXV.

Qiyāmat, or the Resurrection.

(٧٥) سُورَةُ الْقِيٰمَةِ مَكِّيَّةٌ (٣١)

In the name of God, Most Gracious, Most Merciful.

بِسْمِ اللّٰهِ الرَّحْمٰنِ الرَّحِيْمِ

1. I do call to witness[5809]
The Resurrection Day;

١- لَآ أُقْسِمُ بِيَوْمِ الْقِيٰمَةِ ۝

2. And I do call to witness
The self-reproaching spirit:[5810]
(Eschew Evil).

٢- وَلَآ أُقْسِمُ بِالنَّفْسِ اللَّوَّامَةِ ۝

3. Does man think that We
Cannot assemble his bones?[5811]

٣- أَيَحْسَبُ الْإِنْسَانُ أَلَّنْ نَّجْمَعَ عِظَامَهُ ۝

4. Nay, We are able to put
Together in perfect order
The very tips of his fingers.[5812]

٤- بَلٰى قٰدِرِيْنَ عَلٰٓى
أَنْ نُّسَوِّيَ بَنَانَهُ ۝

5. But man wishes to do
Wrong (even) in the time
In front of him.[5813]

٥- بَلْ يُرِيْدُ الْإِنْسَانُ
لِيَفْجُرَ أَمَامَهُ ۝

6. He questions: "When[5814]
Is the Day of Resurrection?"

٦- يَسْئَلُ أَيَّانَ يَوْمُ الْقِيٰمَةِ ۝

5809. *Cf.* lxx. 40, and n. 5700. Here the point to be enforced is understood: I have added it in brackets: "eschew Evil". The appeal is made to two considerations: (1) That every act has to be accounted for, and evil must have its recompense at the Resurrection; and (2) that man's own spirit has a conscience which would reproach him for sin, if he did not suppress that inner voice.

5810. Our doctors postulate three states or stages of the development of the human soul: (1) *Ammāra* (xii 53), which is prone to evil, and, if not checked and controlled, will lead to perdition; (2) *Lawwāma*, as here, which feels conscious of evil, and resists it, asks for God's grace and pardon after repentance and tries to amend; it hopes to reach salvation; (3) *Mutmainna* (lxxxix 27), the highest stage of all, when it achieves full rest and satisfaction. Our second stage may be compared to Conscience, except that in English usage Conscience is a faculty and not a stage in spiritual development.

5811. The Unbelievers' usual cry is: "What! when we are reduced to bones and dust, how can our personality be called to account?" (xvii. 49). The answer is: God has said so, and He will do it; for the death here is not the end of all things.

5812. An idiom for the most delicate parts of his body.

5813. It is bad enough not to repent of past sins. But the evil-doer who rejects a Day of Reckoning and has no conscience wants to go on in his career of sin and jeopardise his future also.

5814. The question is sceptical or derisive He does not believe that there is any chain of consequences in the Hereafter. He does not believe in a Hereafter.

7. At length, when
The Sight is dazed,[5815]

٧- فَإِذَا بَرِقَ الْبَصَرُ ۝

8. And the moon is
Buried in darkness.[5816]

٨- وَخَسَفَ الْقَمَرُ ۝

9. And the sun and moon
Are joined together,—[5817]

٩- وَجُمِعَ الشَّمْسُ وَالْقَمَرُ ۝

10. That Day will Man say:
"Where is the refuge ?"

١٠- يَقُولُ الْإِنْسَانُ يَوْمَئِذٍ أَيْنَ الْمَفَرُّ ۝

11. By no means!
No place of safety!

١١- كَلَّا لَا وَزَرَ ۝

12. Before thy Lord (alone),
That Day will be
The place of rest.

١٢- إِلَىٰ رَبِّكَ يَوْمَئِذٍ الْمُسْتَقَرُّ ۝

13. That Day will Man
Be told (all) that he
Put forward, and all
That he put back.[5818]

١٣- يُنَبَّؤُا الْإِنْسَانُ
يَوْمَئِذٍ بِمَا قَدَّمَ وَأَخَّرَ ۝

14. Nay, man will be
Evidence against himself,[5819]

١٤- بَلِ الْإِنْسَانُ عَلَىٰ نَفْسِهِ بَصِيرَةٌ ۝

15. Even though he were
To put up his excuses.

١٥- وَلَوْ أَلْقَىٰ مَعَاذِيرَهُ ۝

5815. At the Hour of Judgment the full light and glory of the Lord will shine, and the effulgence will daze man's eyes. For the world as we knew it will go to pieces and a new World will come into being.

5816 Not only will man's sight be dazed, but the great luminaries themselves will lose their light. The moon with its present reflected light will then cease to shine. All reflected or relative truth or goodness will sink into nothing before the true and only Reality.

5817. To the moon the sun is the original light, but the sun itself is a created light, and it will sink into nothingness along with the moon. Both will be like empty shells "whose lights are fled, whose glories dead", because the Prototype of all Light now shines in full splendour in a new World. See n. 4344 to **xxxix**. 69.

5818. All good and bad deeds, positive and negative, *i.e.* all sins of commission and omission, and all the good that a man did and all the evil that he omitted, all the influence that he radiated before him and all that he left behind him.

5819. *Cf.* **xxiv**. 24, and n. 2976: "On the Day when their tongues, their hands, and their feet will bear witness against them as to their actions." It is not what a man says about himself, or what others say of him, that determines judgment about him. It is what he is in himself. His own personality betrays him or commends him.

16. Move not thy tongue
Concerning the (Qur-ān)
To make haste therewith.[5820]

١٦- لَا تُحَرِّكْ بِهِ لِسَانَكَ لِتَعْجَلَ بِهِ ۝

17. It is for Us to collect it
And to promulgate it :

١٧- إِنَّ عَلَيْنَا جَمْعَهُ وَقُرْآنَهُ ۝

18. But when We have
Promulgated it, follow thou
Its recital (as promulgated) :

١٨- فَإِذَا قَرَأْنَاهُ فَاتَّبِعْ قُرْآنَهُ ۝

19. Nay more, it is
For us to explain it
(And make it clear) :

١٩- ثُمَّ إِنَّ عَلَيْنَا بَيَانَهُ ۝

20. Nay, (ye men !)
But ye love
The fleeting life,[5821]

٢٠- كَلَّا بَلْ تُحِبُّونَ الْعَاجِلَةَ ۝

21. And leave alone
The Hereafter.

٢١- وَتَذَرُونَ الْآخِرَةَ ۝

22. Some faces, that Day,[5822]
Will beam (in brightness
And beauty) ;—

٢٢- وُجُوهٌ يَوْمَئِذٍ نَّاضِرَةٌ ۝

23. Looking towards their Lord ;

٢٣- إِلَىٰ رَبِّهَا نَاظِرَةٌ ۝

5820 *Cf.* xx. 114, and n. 2639 : " Be not in haste with the Qur-ān before its revelation to thee is completed. " S lxxv. is an earlier revelation, and the shade of meaning is slightly different. The immediate meaning was that the holy Prophet was to allow the revelation conveyed to him to sink into his mind and heart and not to be impatient about it ; God would certainly complete it according to His Plan, and see that it was collected and preserved for men, and not lost ; that the inspired one was to follow it and recite it as the inspiration was conveyed to him ; and that it carries its own explanation according to the faculties bestowed by God on man. The general meaning follows the same lines : we must not be impatient about the inspired Word ; we must follow it as made clear to us by the faculties given to us by God.

5821 *Cf.* xxi. 37 Man loves haste and things of haste. For that reason he pins his faith on transitory things that come and go, and neglects the things of lasting moment, which come slowly, and whose true import will only be fully seen in the Hereafter.

5822. This passage (especially with reference to verses 26-28) would seem to refer to what our Doctors call the Lesser Judgment (*Qiyāmat-uṣ-Ṣugrā*), which takes place immediately after death, and not to the Greater or General Judgment, which may be supposed to be referred to in such passages as occur in S. lvi. There are other passages referring to the Lesser Judgment immediately after death ; *e.g.* vii 37. etc If I understand aright, the punishment of sin takes place in three ways : (1) it may take place in this very life, but this may be deferred, to give the sinner respite ; (2) it may be an agony immediately after death, with the Partition or *Barzakh* (xxiii. 100) separating the sinner from the final Resurrection ; and (3) in the final Resurrection, when the whole of the present order gives place to a wholly new World : xiv. 48.

24. And some faces, that Day,
Will be sad and dismal,

٢٤- وَوُجُوهٌ يَوْمَئِذٍ بَاسِرَةٌ ۝

25. In the thought that some
Back-breaking calamity was about
To be inflicted on them ;

٢٥- تَظُنُّ أَنْ يُفْعَلَ بِهَا فَاقِرَةٌ ۝

26. Yea, when (the soul)[5823]
Reaches to the collar-bone
(In its exit),

٢٦- كَلَّآ إِذَا بَلَغَتِ التَّرَاقِيَ ۝

27. And there will be a cry,
" Who is a magician
(To restore him) ? "

٢٧- وَقِيلَ مَنْ ۜ رَاقٍ ۝

28. And he[5824] will conclude
That it was (the Time)
Of Parting ;

٢٨- وَظَنَّ أَنَّهُ الْفِرَاقُ ۝

29. And one leg will be[5825]
Joined with another :

٢٩- وَالْتَفَّتِ السَّاقُ بِالسَّاقِ ۝

30. That Day the Drive
Will be (all) to thy Lord !

٣٠- إِلَىٰ رَبِّكَ يَوْمَئِذٍ الْمَسَاقُ ۝ ع

SECTION 2.

31. So he gave nothing
In charity, nor
Did he pray !—[5826]

٣١- فَلَا صَدَّقَ وَلَا صَلَّىٰ ۝

5823. A symbolic picture of the agony of death.

5824. He=the dying man, whose soul is referred to in verse 26 above.

5825. When the soul has departed, the legs of the dead body are placed together in position, in preparation for the rites preliminary to the burial. *Sāq* (literally, leg) may also be taken metaphorically to mean a calamity : calamity will be joined to calamity for the poor departed sinner's soul, as his life-story in this world is now done. Willy-nilly, he will now have to go before the Throne of Judgment.

5826. His indictment in this and the succeeding verse consists of four counts : (1) he neglected prayer ; (2) he neglected charity ; (3) he rejected Truth ; and (4) he turned away. In lxxiv. 43-46, the four counts are : (1) neglecting prayer ; (2) neglecting charity ; (3) talking vanities ; (4) denying the Day of Judgment ; see n. 5803. Nos. (1) and (2) are identical in both places, and Nos. (3) and (4) are analogous. Rejecting the truth is equivalent to talking vanities and making an alliance with falsehoods Denying the Day of Judgment means behaving as if no account was to be given of our actions, *i.e.* turning away from right conduct. An additional touch is found here in verse 33. See nevt note.

32. But on the contrary,
He rejected Truth
And turned away!

٣٢- وَلٰكِنْ كَذَّبَ وَتَوَلّٰى ۙ

33. Then did he stalk
To his family
In full conceit![5827]

٣٣- ثُمَّ ذَهَبَ اِلٰٓى اَهْلِهٖ يَتَمَطّٰى ۗ

34. Woe to thee,
(O man!), yea, woe!

٣٤- اَوْلٰى لَكَ فَاَوْلٰى ۙ

35. Again, woe to thee,
(O man!), yea, woe!

٣٥- ثُمَّ اَوْلٰى لَكَ فَاَوْلٰى ۗ

36. Does Man think
That he will be left
Uncontrolled, (without purpose)?[5828]

٣٦- اَيَحْسَبُ الْاِنْسَانُ اَنْ يُّتْرَكَ سُدًى ۗ

37. Was he not a drop
Of sperm emitted
(In lowly form)?[5829]

٣٧- اَلَمْ يَكُ نُطْفَةً
مِّنْ مَّنِيٍّ يُّمْنٰى ۙ

38. Then did he become
A leech-like clot;
Then did (God) make
And fashion (him)
In due proportion.

٣٨- ثُمَّ كَانَ عَلَقَةً
فَخَلَقَ فَسَوّٰى ۙ

39. And of him He made
Two sexes, male
And female.

٣٩- فَجَعَلَ مِنْهُ الزَّوْجَيْنِ
الذَّكَرَ وَالْاُنْثٰى ۗ

40. Has not He, (the same),
The power to give life
To the dead?

٤٠- اَلَيْسَ ذٰلِكَ بِقٰدِرٍ
عَلٰٓى اَنْ يُّحْـِۧيَ الْمَوْتٰى ۧ

5827. Conceit or arrogance is the root-cause of most Evil. By that cause fell Iblis: see ii. 34.

5828. *Sudan*: has many implications: (1) uncontrolled, free to do what he likes; (2) without any moral responsibility; not accountable for his actions; (3) without a purpose, useless; (4) forsaken.

5829. *Cf.* xxii. 5, where the argument is developed in greater detail. The briefer argument here may be stated thus. His lowly animal origin makes him no higher than a brute; his fœtal development is still that of a brute animal; then at some stage come human limbs and shape; the divine spirit is poured into him, and he is fashioned in due proportion for his higher destiny. In spite of that the mystery of sex remains in his nature: we are living souls, yet men and women. God Who creates these wonders,—has He not the power to bring the dead to life at the Resurrection?

INTRODUCTION AND SUMMARY : SŪRA LXXVI (*Dahr*).

The revelation of this Sūra was probably in the early Meccan period, with the possible exception of some verses, but its date has no significance.

Its theme is the contrast between the two classes of men, those who choose good and those who choose evil, with special reference to the former.

The title of the Sūra recalls a Pagan Arab idea, which personified Time as existing spontaneously from eternity to eternity and responsible for the misery or the happiness of mankind. In xlv. 24 we read : "They say,...'nothing but Time can destroy us'." This attitude is of course wrong. Time is a created thing : it has its mysteries, but it is no more eternal than matter. It is also relative to our conceptions and not absolute, as Einstein has proved. It is only God Who is Self Subsisting, Eternal from the beginning and Eternal to the end, the absolute Existence and Reality. We must not transfer His attributes to any figments of our imagination.

This deification of Time (*Dahr*) as against a living personal God has given rise to the term *dahrīya*, as applied to an atheist or a materialist.

The whole of the Sūra is full of the highest symbolism, as is generally the case with Meccan Sūras, and this should always be remembered in their interpretation.

C. 256.—Man was evolved out of nothing, and through low
(lxxvi. 1-31.) Beginnings; but he was given Insight
And Understanding. God showed him the Way;
And if man doth wilfully reject the Right,
Man but chooses Chains and Yokes and a Blazing
Fire within his own soul. Not so
The Devotees of Right: they attain
The Mystic Fountain of Kāfūr :
For, purely out of love for God,
They do good to God's Creatures, and serve them.
The Light of Beauty and Joy will be
On them. In full felicity and honour
Will they live in the garden of Delights, and share
In the Banquet—the Presence and Glory Divine !

* * * *

The Righteous are patient in Constant Devotion :
God's Way is open to all : whosoever
Has the Will, may attain to the Perfect Goal.

Sūra LXXVI.

Dahr, or Time.
or *Insān*, or Man.

In the name of God, Most Gracious, Most Merciful.

1. Has there not been[5830]
Over Man a long period
Of Time,[5831] when he was
Nothing—(not even) mentioned?

2. Verily We created
Man from a drop
Of mingled sperm,[5832]
In order to try him:
So We gave him (the gifts),
Of Hearing and Sight.

3. We showed him the Way:
Whether he be grateful
Or ungrateful (rests[5833]
On his will).

4. For the Rejecters
We have prepared

5830. The undoubted fact is mentioned in the form of a question, to get the assent of man. It is certain that the physical world existed long before man was ever heard of or mentioned, as geological records prove. It is also true that the spiritual world existed long before man came on the scene: see ii. 30-31. Man is here taken in a generic sense.

5831. *Dahr* is Time as a whole, or for a long period. Time used to be deified by the Pagan Arabs, as explained in the Introduction to this Sūra. An analogy can be found in the Greek ideas connected with Chronos or Kronos, themselves a blend of different myths. Kronos (or Time), they said, was the father of Zeus himself.

5832. *Mingled*: the female ovum has to be fertilised with the male sperm before a new animal can be born. Man as an animal has this humble origin. But he has been given the gift of certain faculties of receiving instruction (typified by Hearing) and of intellectual and spiritual insight (typified by Sight). His life has therefore a meaning: with a certain amount of free-will, he is to be God's vicegerent on earth (ii. 30). But he must be trained and tried, and that is the whole problem of human life.

5833. Besides the gift of the faculties, Man has been shown the Way by means of Revelation, through men of the highest spiritual standing. If he is grateful, he will accept Guidance, be of the Righteous, and join the company of the Blessed. If not, he rejects his destiny, puts chains round himself, thus losing his freedom, yokes round himself, thus burdening himself with sin, and gets into the Blazing Fire of Punishment, which scorches his inmost being. See next verse. His choice rests on his will.

Chains, Yokes, and
A Blazing Fire.[5834]

سَلٰسِلَاۡ وَ اَغۡلٰلًا وَّ سَعِیۡرًا ○

5. As to the Righteous,
They shall drink
Of a Cup (of Wine)
Mixed with *Kāfūr*,—[5835]

٥-اِنَّ الۡاَبۡرَارَ یَشۡرَبُوۡنَ مِنۡ كَاۡسٍ
كَانَ مِزَاجُهَا كَافُوۡرًا ○

6. A Fountain where
The Devotees of God
Do drink, making it
Flow in unstinted abundance.

٦-عَیۡنًا یَّشۡرَبُ بِهَا عِبَادُ اللّٰهِ
یُفَجِّرُوۡنَهَا تَفۡجِیۡرًا ○

7. They[5836] perform (their) vows,[5837]
And they fear a Day
Whose evil flies far and wide.[5838]

٧-یُوۡفُوۡنَ بِالنَّذۡرِ
وَ یَخَافُوۡنَ یَوۡمًا كَانَ شَرُّهٗ مُسۡتَطِیۡرًا ○

8. And they feed, for the love
Of God, the indigent,
The orphan, and the captive,—[5839]

٨-وَ یُطۡعِمُوۡنَ الطَّعَامَ عَلٰی حُبِّهٖ مِسۡكِیۡنًا
وَّ یَتِیۡمًا وَّ اَسِیۡرًا ○

5834. There is deep mystic symbolism here. All sin or wrong-doing binds the sinner in a chain of causes and effects, in which he loses his native liberty. It puts the yokes of custom, confirmed habits, and superstitions, which lie like a load on his spirit and choke his finer instincts. It lights the fire of passion, hate, spite, envy, and despair, from which it is difficult to escape to the refreshing waters of the Mercy of God. These refreshing waters come naturally to the Righteous: see next note.

5835. *Kāfūr* is literally Camphor. Symbolically it represents a fountain in the Realms of Bliss. It is a seasoning added to the Cup of pure, beatific Wine, which causes no intoxication (lvi. 18-19), but stands for all that is wholesome, agreeable, and refreshing. Camphor is cool and refreshing, and is given as a soothing tonic in Eastern medicine. In minute doses its odour and flavour are also agreeable.

5836. *They*: i.e. the Righteous: they are known in the present life by the virtues symbolically described in verses 7-10, and in the life of the Hereafter they will enjoy the Bliss symbolically described in verses 11-22.

5837. *Cf.* xxii. 29. The vows must be vows of spiritual service, which of course includes service to humanity, such as is mentioned in the next verse. They are Devotees of God, and they must perform all vows and contracts (v. 1 and n. 682). Vows of the Pagan sort, savouring of a sort of "bribe" to the Deity, are not approved.

5838. That is, they prepare for the Judgment to come, where the effects of Sin will not be transitory but far-reaching.

5839. *The captive*: when taken literally, it refers to the old state of things when captives of war had to earn their own food, or their own redemption; even ordinary prisoners in jail for criminal offences often starved unless food was provided for them by private friends or from their own earnings. But there is a further symbolic meaning, which applies to the indigent, the orphans, and the captives, *viz.*, those who are so in a spiritual sense: those who have no mental or moral resources, or have no one to look after them, or are held down in social or moral or economic captivity. They hunger for spiritual food, or perhaps their appetite is deadened, but the Righteous understand and supply their real needs. It has also been held that "captives" include dumb animals who are under subjection to man; they must be properly fed, housed, and looked after; and the righteous man does not forget them.

9. (Saying), "We feed you
For the sake of God alone:
No reward do we desire
From you, nor thanks.[5840]

٩- إِنَّمَا نُطْعِمُكُمْ لِوَجْهِ اللَّهِ
لَا نُرِيدُ مِنكُمْ جَزَاءً وَلَا شُكُورًا ○

10. "We only fear a Day
Of distressful Wrath
From the side of our Lord."[5841]

١٠- إِنَّا نَخَافُ مِن رَّبِّنَا
يَوْمًا عَبُوسًا قَمْطَرِيرًا ○

11. But God will deliver
Them from the evil
Of that Day, and will
Shed over them a Light[5842]
Of Beauty and
A (blissful) Joy.

١١- فَوَقَاهُمُ اللَّهُ شَرَّ ذَٰلِكَ الْيَوْمِ
وَلَقَّاهُمْ نَضْرَةً
وَسُرُورًا ○

12. And because they were
Patient and constant, He will
Reward them with a Garden
And (garments of) silk.[5843]

١٢- وَجَزَاهُم بِمَا صَبَرُوا
جَنَّةً وَحَرِيرًا ○

13. Reclining in the (Garden)
On raised thrones,[5844]
They will see there neither
The sun's (excessive heat)
Nor (the moon's) excessive cold.[5845]

١٣- مُّتَّكِئِينَ فِيهَا عَلَى الْأَرَائِكِ
لَا يَرَوْنَ فِيهَا شَمْسًا
وَلَا زَمْهَرِيرًا ○

14. And the shades of the (Garden)
Will come low over them,
And the bunches (of fruit),
There, will hang low
In humility.[5846]

١٤- وَدَانِيَةً عَلَيْهِمْ ظِلَالُهَا
وَذُلِّلَتْ قُطُوفُهَا تَذْلِيلًا ○

5840. These words need not be actually uttered. They express the true motives of pious and unpretentious Charity.

5841. It is a Day of Wrath for sin and evil. But the truly righteous are not self-righteous. They have the fear of God in their minds: they know they are human, and they fear lest they should be found wanting in the sight of God. But God in His Mercy gives them a bountiful Reward.

5842. *Cf.* lxxv. 22-23.

5843. *Cf.* xxii. 23.

5844. *Cf.* xviii. 31.

5845. The sun and the moon as we know them will be no longer there. It will be a new world on a different plane. But to give us an idea of comfort we recall the excessive heat of the sun especially in tropical climates, and the excessive cold of the moon especially in northern climates, and we negative them both. That is, the temperature metaphorically will be just that delightful one that is most agreeable to our sensations as we know them now. The moon is not mentioned, but *Zamharīr* (excessive cold) is sometimes used for the moon.

5846. Without sun and moon there will of course be no shade in the literal sense of the word. But for full comfort in the metaphor, there will be sheltering shade for rest and change from whatever light there be. But the whole idea in the metaphor here is that of humility. Even the shadows show humility: *cf.* xiii. 15. So does the fruit in hanging low for man. Man has now reached the height of his dignity.

15. And amongst them will be
Passed round vessels of silver[5847]
And goblets of crystal,—

١٥- وَيُطَافُ عَلَيْهِم بِآنِيَةٍ مِّن فِضَّةٍ
وَأَكْوَابٍ كَانَتْ قَوَارِيرَا۠ ۝

16. Crystal-clear, made of silver:[5848]
They will determine
The measure thereof
(According to their wishes).

١٦- قَوَارِيرَا۟ مِن فِضَّةٍ
قَدَّرُوهَا تَقْدِيرًا ۝

17. And they will be given
To drink there of a Cup
(Of Wine) mixed[5849]
With Zanjabīl,—

١٧- وَيُسْقَوْنَ فِيهَا كَأْسًا
كَانَ مِزَاجُهَا زَنجَبِيلًا ۝

18. A fountain there,
Called Salsabīl.[5850]

١٨- عَيْنًا فِيهَا تُسَمَّىٰ سَلْسَبِيلًا ۝

19. And round about them
Will (serve) youths
Of perpetual (freshness):[5851]
If thou seest them,
Thou wouldst think them
Scattered Pearls.[5852]

١٩- وَيَطُوفُ عَلَيْهِمْ وِلْدَانٌ مُّخَلَّدُونَ
إِذَا رَأَيْتَهُمْ
حَسِبْتَهُمْ لُؤْلُؤًا مَّنثُورًا ۝

20. And when thou lookest,
It is there thou wilt see

٢٠- وَإِذَا رَأَيْتَ ثَمَّ رَأَيْتَ

5847. *Cf.* xliii. 71, where "dishes and goblets of gold" are mentioned. As the whole thing is symbolical, gold or silver, or crystal does not matter. The idea conveyed is that of rarity, preciousness, and spotless splendour.

5848. That is, silver polished and white, and shining like crystal.

5849. *Cf.* above, lxxvi. 5-6, and n. 5835, where the Cup of *Kāfūr* (Camphor) was mentioned for coolness and refreshment to the Righteous, who had just passed the great Event of Judgment. The second stage is symbolised by verses 12-14, when they enter the Garden in Garments of Silk, and find that their former humility in the probationary life is rewarded with high honour in the new world they have entered. The third stage is in verses 15-21, where they settle down in Bliss, with Garments of fine silk and heavy brocades, with Ornaments and Jewels, with an ordered Feast of set service, and the Cup of *Zanjabīl*. This word literally means Ginger. In Eastern medicine Ginger is administered to give warmth to the body and zest to the taste. Metaphorically, this is appropriate for the Royal Feast which is now figured forth.

5850. This fountain *Salsabīl* brings us another metaphorical idea. The word literally means: "Seek the Way". The Way is now open to the presence of the Most High. The Banquet is spread. Get thyself ready. It is a "Realm Magnificent" (verse 20) in a new spiritual world.

5851. *Cf.* lvi. 17, and n. 5231.

5852. *Pearls* for beauty and splendour: *scattered*, because they are moving to and fro all round the Banquet.

A Bliss and
A Realm Magnificent.

نَعِيمًا وَّمُلْكًا كَبِيرًا ۝

21. Upon them will be
Green Garments of fine silk
And heavy brocade,
And they will be adorned
With Bracelets of silver ;[5853]
And their Lord will
Give to them to drink
Of a Wine
Pure and Holy.[5854]

٢١- عٰلِيَهُمْ ثِيَابُ سُنْدُسٍ خُضْرٌ وَّ
إِسْتَبْرَقٌ
وَّحُلُّوٓا أَسَاوِرَ مِن فِضَّةٍ
وَسَقٰهُمْ رَبُّهُمْ
شَرَابًا طَهُورًا ۝

22. " Verily this is a Reward
For you, and your Endeavour
Is accepted and recognised."

٢٢- إِنَّ هٰذَا كَانَ لَكُمْ جَزَآءً
وَّكَانَ سَعْيُكُم مَّشْكُورًا ۝ ع

SECTION 2.

23. It is We Who
Have sent down the Qur-ān
To thee by stages.[5855]

٢٣- إِنَّا نَحْنُ نَزَّلْنَا عَلَيْكَ الْقُرْاٰنَ
تَنْزِيلًا ۝

24. Therefore be patient
With constancy to the Command
Of thy Lord, and hearken not
To the sinner or the ingrate
Among them.

٢٤- فَاصْبِرْ لِحُكْمِ رَبِّكَ
وَلَا تُطِعْ مِنْهُمْ
اٰثِمًا أَوْ كَفُورًا ۝

25. And celebrate the name [5856]

٢٥- وَاذْكُرِ اسْمَ

5853. *Cf.* xviii. 31. The bracelets are there said to be of gold. But as the whole thing is symbolic to convey the idea of rarity and costliness, either gold or silver serves the purpose of symbolism. See n. 5847 above.

5854. This would seem to be the culmination of the honour which the Blessed receive at the Royal and Divine Banquet. The Wine Pure and Holy is the Sight, metaphorically, in Ṣūfī language, of the Face and Eyes of God. The words in the next verse express the sort of speech which will make the Guest a denizen of Heaven.

5855. The Qur-ān was being revealed stage by stage as the occasion demanded, and at the date of this Sūra it was still one of the earlier stages. Persecution, abuse, and false charges were being levelled against the man of God, but he is bidden to stand firm and do his duty. In a minor degree this applies to all of us who suffer in the cause of Truth.

5856. Three methods of Prayer and Devotion are mentioned : (1) to remember and celebrate the holy name of God always ; (2) to spend a part of the night in humble prostration ; and (3) to glorify Him in the long hours of a weary night of waiting and watching. As to (1), "morning and evening" means all the waking hours of our life, but in the special hours of morning and evening, the physical world without us, and the inner world within us, combine to make us specially receptive of spiritual influences. "*Name*" has a mystic meaning. The "name" of God includes His attributes, as a locked golden casket might include priceless jewels. Any one may carry the casket, even though he may not be worthy to handle the jewels. If he carries the casket, he is in potential possession of the jewels, and he hopes some time to get the key which opens the jewels to him. So the tyro, who celebrates the holy name of God, hopes some day to see the "Face" of God and be blessed with the privilege of proximity to His Person. For (2) and (3) see next note.

Of thy Lord morning
And evening,

رَبِّكَ بُكْرَةً وَّأَصِيلًا ۚ

26. And part of the night,
Prostrate thyself to Him;
And glorify Him[5857]
A long night through.

٢٦- وَمِنَ الَّيْلِ فَاسْجُدْ لَهُ
وَسَبِّحْهُ لَيْلًا طَوِيلًا ○

27. As to these, they love
The fleeting life,
And put away behind them[5858]
A Day (that will be) hard.

٢٧- إِنَّ هَٰؤُلَآءِ يُحِبُّونَ الْعَاجِلَةَ
وَيَذَرُونَ وَرَآءَهُمْ يَوْمًا ثَقِيلًا ○

28. It is We Who created
Them, and We have made
Their joints strong;[5859]
But, when We will,
We can substitute
The like of them[5860]
By a complete change.

٢٨- نَحْنُ خَلَقْنَٰهُمْ
وَشَدَدْنَآ أَسْرَهُمْ ج
وَإِذَا شِئْنَا
بَدَّلْنَآ أَمْثَٰلَهُمْ تَبْدِيلًا ○

29. This is an admonition:
Whosoever will, let him
Take a (straight) Path
To his Lord.

٢٩- إِنَّ هَٰذِهِۦ تَذْكِرَةٌ ج
فَمَن شَآءَ اتَّخَذَ إِلَىٰ رَبِّهِۦ سَبِيلًا ○

30. But ye will not,
Except as God wills;[5861]

٣٠- وَمَا تَشَآءُونَ إِلَّآ أَن يَشَآءَ اللَّهُ ط

5857. See last note. (2) Humble *prostration* to God means some visible mode or symbol of dedication. That is best done at night, when the soul, free from worldly occupations, is alone with its God. (3) The weary hours of a long night are no longer weary, but become full of meaning when we join in concert with the whole Creation, which glorifies God: lvii. 1.

5858. *Fleeting life*: *Cf.* lxxv. 20. *They*: the immediate reference was to the Pagan Quraish; the general reference is to the Unbelievers of all ages. They reject, or at least put away the thought of, a Hereafter, a Day that will be hard, for the easy pleasures of a fleeting life.

5859. God has not only created men, but "made their joints strong", *i.e.* given them the power and strength to withstand the temptations of Evil and stand firmly in the Path of Right.

5860. If, in spite of God's loving care, any particular men or group of men, misuse their powers or wilfully disobey God's Law, God will set them aside, and substitute others in their place, with like powers. God's gifts are free, but let no one think that he can monopolise them or misuse them without being called to answer for the trust. And the man of God must not be discouraged by the whole world being at some moment completely against him. God can in a moment make a complete change. Either the same men that fought against him will be his zealous adherents, or another generation will spring up, which will carry the flag of Righteousness to victory. God's Will and Plan work in their own good time.

5861. Man in himself is weak; he must seek God's Grace; without it he can do nothing; with it he can do all. For God knows all things, and His wisdom comprehends the good of all.

For God is full of
Knowledge and Wisdom.

إِنَّ اللَّهَ كَانَ عَلِيمًا حَكِيمًا ۝

31. He will admit
To His Mercy Whom He will;[5862]
But the wrong-doers,—
For them has He prepared
A grievous Penalty.

٣١- يُدْخِلُ مَن يَشَآءُ فِى رَحْمَتِهِۦ ۚ
وَٱلظَّٰلِمِينَ أَعَدَّ لَهُمْ عَذَابًا أَلِيمًۢا ۝

5862. That is, according to His just and wise Plan. If the will is right, it obtains God's Grace and Mercy. If the will of man rejects God, man must suffer the Penalty.

INTRODUCTION AND SUMMARY : SŪRA LXXVII (*Mursalāt*).

This Sūra belongs to the early Meccan period, somewhere near to S. lxxv. (*Qiyāmat*). The theme is somewhat similar. It denounces the horrors of the Hereafter, for those who rejected Truth. The refrain, "Ah woe, that Day, to the Rejecters of Truth!" which occurs ten times in its fifty verses, or, on an average, once in every five verses, indicates the *leitmotif*.

C. 257.—The winds in the world of nature are types
(lxxvii. 1-50.) Of God's Bounty and Power: they gently bring
The beneficent rain, and when roused to wrath,
They clean the world and wipe out Infection.
So works God's Revelation, in sunshine
And storm. It will root out Evil, and restore
True values at Judgment. Truly terrible
Will be that Day for the evil ones.
It will be a Day of Sorting out:
Ah woe, that Day, to the Rejecters of Truth!
Will man not learn from his own little story,
Or from nature around him? The Blazing Fire
Will be indeed an enveloping Punishment.
How dreadful the contrast with the Bliss of the Righteous!
Learn, ye, therefore, Humility, and approach
God's Throne in Repentance and Earnest Endeavour.

S ra LXXVII.

Mursalāt, or Those Sent Forth.

In the name of God, Most Gracious, Most Merciful.

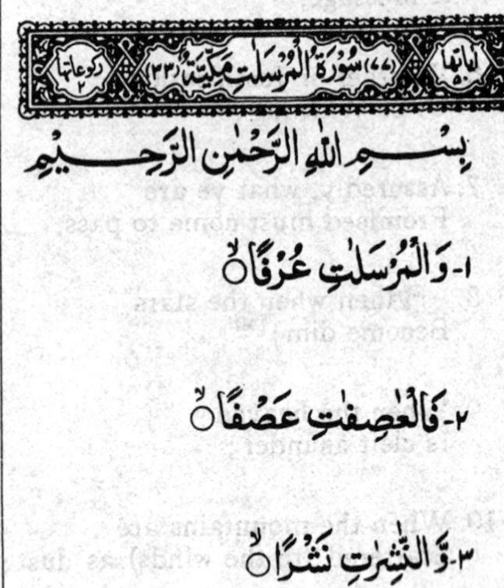

1. By the (Winds) Sent Forth[5863]
One after another
(To man's profit);[5864]

2. Which then blow violently
In tempestuous Gusts,[5865]

3. And scatter (things)
Far and wide;

4. Then separate them,
One from another,

٤- فَالْفٰرِقٰتِ فَرْقًا ۝

5863. This highly mystical Sūra begins with an appeal to five things, as pointing to the substantive statement in verse 7, that the Day of Justice and Judgment is bound to come, and we must prepare for it. It is difficult to translate, but easy to understand, if we remember that a triple thread of allegory runs through this passage (verses 1-7). The five things or phases, which will be presently considered in detail, refer to (*a*) Winds in the physical world, (*b*) Angels in the spiritual world, and (*c*) Prophets in the human world, connecting it with the spiritual world.

5864. Understanding the reference to Winds, we can see that they are powerful factors in the government of the physical world. (1) They come gently as harbingers of the blessings of rain and fertility (xv. 22; xxx. 48); but (2) they can come as violent tornadoes, uprooting and destroying (li. 41-42); (3) they can scatter seeds far and wide, and (4) they can separate chaff from grain, or clear the air from epidemics; and (5) they literally carry sound, and therefore Messages, and metaphorically they are instrumental in making God's Revelation accessible to hearers, whether by way of justification or repentance for the Penitent, or warning for unrepentant Sinners. All these things point to the power and goodness of God, and we are asked to believe that His promise of Mercy and Justice in the Hereafter is indeed true.

Cf. this passage with li. 1-6 (*Zāriyāt*) with which it has many affinities.

5865. If we understand the reference to be, not to Winds, but to Angels, they are agencies in the spiritual world, which carry out similar functions, changing and revolutionising the face of the world. (1) They come softly, on beneficent errands of Mercy; (2) they are charged with the mission of punishment and destruction for sin, as in the case of the two angels who came to Lūṭ (xv. 57-66); (3) they distribute God's Mercies as the Winds distribute good seeds; (4) they sort out the good from the evil among men; and (5) they are the agency through which God's Messages and Revelations are conveyed to the Prophets (see No. 5 in the last note).

5. Then spread abroad
A Message,[5866]

٥- فَالْمُلْقِيٰتِ ذِكْرًا ۙ

6. Whether of Justification
Or of Warning ;—

٦- عُذْرًا اَوْ نُذْرًا ۙ

7. Assuredly, what ye are
Promised must come to pass.

٧- اِنَّمَا تُوْعَدُوْنَ لَوَاقِعٌ ۗ

8. Then when the stars
Become dim ;[5867]

٨- فَاِذَا النُّجُوْمُ طُمِسَتْ ۙ

9. When the heaven
Is cleft asunder ;

٩- وَاِذَا السَّمَآءُ فُرِجَتْ ۙ

10. When the mountains are
Scattered (to the winds) as dust ;

١٠- وَاِذَا الْجِبَالُ نُسِفَتْ ۙ

11. And when the apostles
Are (all) appointed a time
(To collect) ;—[5868]

١١- وَاِذَا الرُّسُلُ اُقِّتَتْ ۗ

12. For what Day are these
(Portents) deferred ?

١٢- لِاَيِّ يَوْمٍ اُجِّلَتْ ۗ

5866. If we understand the reference to Prophets or Messengers of God, or the verses of Revelation which would be particularly appropriate for verses 5-6, we also get a satisfactory solution of the Allegory. (1) The Prophets have followed one another in a series : the verses of the Qur-ān came, one after another as needed ; in both cases it was for man's spiritual profit ; (2) they caused great disturbance in a spiritually decadent world ; they pulled down evil institutions root and branch, and substituted new ones ; (3) they proclaimed their truths far and wide, without fear and without favour ; (4) through them were sorted out men of Faith and rebels against God's Law ; and (5) they gave a Message, through which just men were justified through repentance, and evil men were warned of their sins.

Some Commentators take one or other of these allegories, and some apply one allegory to a few of these verses, and another to another few. In my opinion the Allegory is wide enough to comprehend all the meanings which I have sketched. I wish a translation could do justice to those marvellously terse sentences in the original.

5867. Now, in four verses (8-11), we are told, again allegorically, though we can take them literally if we like, the things that will happen in those last days. The lustre of the stars will become dim ; in fact they will disappear : *cf.* lxxxi. 2, and lxxxii. 2. The heaven's canopy will be torn asunder : *cf.* lxxxii. 1, and lxxiii. 18. The mountains will be uprooted and fly about like dust : *cf.* lxix. 14 ; lxxxi. 3 ; etc. All the old landmarks of the physical world as we know it will be swept away.

5868. The Resurrection will be established. In the world which will then have passed away, inspired Prophets had been sent in succession at different times to all nations. Now they will be gathered together in one place before the Judgment-seat to bear witness as to the righteous or the evil ones within their respective spheres of work. *Cf.* xxxix. 69.

13. For the Day of Sorting out.[5869]	١٣- لِيَوْمِ الْفَصْلِ ۝
14. And what will explain To thee what is The Day of Sorting out?	١٤- وَمَآ أَدْرٰىكَ مَا يَوْمُ الْفَصْلِ ۝
15. Ah woe, that Day, To the Rejecters of Truth!	١٥- وَيْلٌ يَوْمَئِذٍ لِّلْمُكَذِّبِينَ ۝
16. Did We not destroy The men of old[5870] (For their evil)?	١٦- أَلَمْ نُهْلِكِ الْأَوَّلِينَ ۝
17. So shall We make Later (generations) Follow them.	١٧- ثُمَّ نُتْبِعُهُمُ الْآخِرِينَ ۝
18. Thus do We deal With men of sin.	١٨- كَذٰلِكَ نَفْعَلُ بِالْمُجْرِمِينَ ۝
19. Ah woe, that Day, To the Rejecters of Truth!	١٩- وَيْلٌ يَوْمَئِذٍ لِّلْمُكَذِّبِينَ ۝
20. Have We not created You from a fluid (Held) despicable?—[5871]	٢٠- أَلَمْ نَخْلُقكُّم مِّن مَّآءٍ مَّهِينٍ ۝
21. The which We placed In a place of rest, Firmly fixed,[5872]	٢١- فَجَعَلْنٰهُ فِى قَرَارٍ مَّكِينٍ ۝

5869. *Cf.* xxxvii. 21. and n 4047; also xliv. 40, and n. 4718 That will be the Day of Judgment or Day of Decision. Good will then be completely separated from Evil. And the men who rejected Truth and flourished on Falsehood will find that in the world of Realities they will be absolutely nowhere. Hence the refrain of this Sūra, "Ah woe, that Day, to the Rejecters of Truth!" It sounds like a dirge on Sin.

5870. God's Law is always the same. Sin or corruption prepares its own destruction. It was so with the generation of Noah. In Arab tradition it was so with the 'Ad and the Thamūd. In our own day we see relics of prehistoric civilisations, in Egypt, Mesopotamia, the Indus Valley, and the Ægean: these were men of wonderful skill and resource, but they went under. If our generations, which pride themselves on their science and skill, desert God's Law, they will be certain to meet the same fate.

5871. *Cf.* xxxii. 8, n. 3638. Man is ashamed of the process of physical creation, by which he comes into being. Yet he is arrogant in life and neglectful of the Future.

5872. See n. 2873 to xxiii. 13. The silent growth in the mother's womb, and the protection and sustenance which the growing life receives from the life of the mother, are themselves wonders of creation.

22. For a period (of gestation),
Determined (according to need)?[5873]

٢٢- إِلَىٰ قَدَرٍ مَّعْلُومٍ ○

23. For We do determine
(According to need); for We[5874]
Are the Best to determine (things).

٢٣- فَقَدَرْنَا ۖ فَنِعْمَ الْقَادِرُونَ ○

24. Ah woe, that Day!
To the Rejecters of Truth!

٢٤- وَيْلٌ يَوْمَئِذٍ لِّلْمُكَذِّبِينَ ○

25. Have We not made
The earth (as a place)
To draw together

٢٥- أَلَمْ نَجْعَلِ الْأَرْضَ كِفَاتًا ○

26. The living and the dead,[5875]

٢٦- أَحْيَاءً وَأَمْوَاتًا ○

27. And made therein
Mountains standing firm,[5876]
Lofty (in stature);
And provided for you
Water sweet (and wholesome)?

٢٧- وَجَعَلْنَا فِيهَا رَوَاسِيَ شَامِخَاتٍ وَأَسْقَيْنَاكُم مَّاءً فُرَاتًا ○

28. Ah woe, that Day,
To the Rejecters of Truth!

٢٨- وَيْلٌ يَوْمَئِذٍ لِّلْمُكَذِّبِينَ ○

5873. The period roughly of nine months and ten days is subject to many adjustments. In fact throughout our pre-natal as well as post-natal life there are wonderful and nicely-balanced adjustments of which we are ourselves unconscious. Should we not turn in love and gratitude to God our Creator?

5874. Perhaps the life in the womb, in relation to the life after birth, is an allegory for our probationary life on earth in relation to the eternal Life to come. Perhaps, also, our state when we are buried in the tomb suggests an allegory to the life in the womb, in relation to the life in the Hereafter.

5875. What a wonderful parable! The earth is a place where death and life, decay and growth and decay, green grass, stubble, and fuel, corruption and purification jostle together,—one often leading to the other. The drama which we see with our own eyes in this world should enable us to appreciate the wonders in the spiritual world where the despised and rejected receive the highest honour, Lazarus rests in Abraham's bosom, and the Pharaoh is led in chains for his arrogance and his sin.

5876. See n. 2038 to xvi. 15. The solid mountains are frequently referred to: *cf.* xiii. 3. The parable here is that the mountains are of hard, solid rock, and yet they act as sponges to collect, store up, and filter sweet and wholesome water, which on account of their altitude they are able to distribute by gravity to the lower, dry land by means of rivers or springs. Any one who has seen the parched Meccan valleys and the delicious springs in the mountains around, or the *Zubaida Canal*, which is the main source of Mecca's water-supply, will appreciate the aptness of the metaphor, but it applies to any country, though not to so striking a degree. If the wisdom and power of God can do such things before your eyes, how can you reject His teaching of a still more wonderful future Life?

29. (It will be said :)
" Depart ye to that
Which ye used to reject
As false !

٢٩- اِنْطَلِقُوْٓا اِلٰى مَا كُنْتُمْ بِهٖ تُكَذِّبُوْنَ ۚ

30. " Depart ye to a Shadow[5877]
(Of smoke ascending)
In three columns,

٣٠- اِنْطَلِقُوْٓا اِلٰى ظِلٍّ ذِىْ ثَلٰثِ شُعَبٍ ۙ

31. " (Which yields) no shade
Of coolness, and is
Of no use against
The fierce Blaze.

٣١- لَّا ظَلِيْلٍ وَّلَا يُغْنِىْ مِنَ اللَّهَبِ ۗ

32. " Indeed it throws about
Sparks (huge) as Forts,[5878]

٣٢- اِنَّهَا تَرْمِىْ بِشَرَرٍ كَالْقَصْرِ ۚ

33. " As if there were
(A string of) yellow camels
(Marching swiftly)."[5879]

٣٣- كَاَنَّهٗ جِمٰلَتٌ صُفْرٌ ۗ

34. Ah woe, that Day,
To the Rejecters of Truth !

٣٤- وَيْلٌ يَّوْمَئِذٍ لِّلْمُكَذِّبِيْنَ ۞

35. That will be a Day
When they shall not

٣٥- هٰذَا يَوْمُ

5877. The Sinners, instead of reposing in cool shades, will only see the blazing Fire. The only shadow they will see will be that of Smoke, ascending in three columns, right, left, and above, *i.e.*, completely enveloping them. But it will give no comfort or coolness. On the contrary, it will contain huge sparks. The triple column may be explained in allegory by the black stain they threw on their life by the misuse of their faculties—converting Love into Hate, Understanding into Superstition and Folly, and Spiritual Insight into Worldly Greed. The Blaze of their Sins is cumulative: the columns of smoke show the kinds of sin, as, in the physical fire, different kinds of fuel give different kinds of smoke.

5878. *Qaṣr*: Fort, big building, palace. An alternative reading is *Qaṣar*, plural of *Qaṣarat (-un)*, meaning bundles of wood used for fuel: Ibn 'Abbās *apud* Bukhārī. I almost prefer this latter reading.

5879. The yellow sparks flying swiftly one after another suggest a string of camels marching swiftly, such as the Arabs of Nejd and central Arabia are so proud of. There is a double allegory. It refers not only to the colour and the rapid succession of sparks, but to the vanity of worldly pride, as much as to say: "your fine yellow camels in which you took such pride in the world are but sparks that fly away and even sting you in the Hereafter !" Smoke with sparks may also assume fantastic shapes like long-necked camels.

Be able to speak,[5880]

لَا يَنْطِقُونَ ۝

36. Nor will it be
Open to them
To put forth pleas.

٣٦- وَلَا يُؤْذَنُ لَهُمْ فَيَعْتَذِرُونَ ۝

37. Ah woe, that Day,
To the Rejecters of Truth!

٣٧- وَيْلٌ يَوْمَئِذٍ لِّلْمُكَذِّبِينَ ۝

38. That will be a Day
Of Sorting out! We shall
Gather you together
And those before (you)![5881]

٣٨- هَٰذَا يَوْمُ الْفَصْلِ ۚ
جَمَعْنَٰكُمْ وَالْأَوَّلِينَ ۝

39. Now, if ye have
A trick (or plot),
Use it against Me![5882]

٣٩- فَإِن كَانَ لَكُمْ كَيْدٌ فَكِيدُونِ ۝

40. Ah woe, that Day,
To the Rejecters of Truth!

٤٠- وَيْلٌ يَوْمَئِذٍ لِّلْمُكَذِّبِينَ ۝ ع

SECTION 2.

41. As to the Righteous,
They shall be amidst
(Cool) shades and springs
(Of water).[5883]

٤١- إِنَّ الْمُتَّقِينَ
فِي ظِلَٰلٍ وَعُيُونٍ ۝

5880. They will be dumbfounded; *i.e.* (when read with the next verse), they will not be in a position to put forward any valid defence or plea. Facts will speak too plainly against them. They might perversely try to deny false worship: vi. 23: but their own tongues and limbs will bear witness against them: xxiv. 24. Nor does the fighting out or settling of doctrinal disputes in the Hereafter (xxxix 31) amount to putting forward pleas in defence.

5881. We may suppose this as spoken primarily to the Quraish who were plotting against the Prophet. You may use all your wisdom and that of your ancestors, but you will not be able to defeat God or His Plan. See next verse.

5882. The plots against the holy Prophet were plots against God's Truth, and therefore against God. Can any one hope to profit by such plots? Can any one defeat God's Plan and Purpose? Let them try. They will only ruin themselves, as the Pagan leaders did. There can only be pity for such men. What will be their state in the Hereafter? "Ah woe, that Day, to the Rejecters of God's Truth!"

5883. This is in contrast to the triple shade of smoke and sin for the sinners, which neither gives them coolness nor protects them from the Blazing Fire. In mystic lore the Shades and Springs of Heaven are also interpreted allegorically. The Shade. *i.e.* Covering, of God's Good Pleasure, will be the greatest Boon of all, and the Spring of God's Love will be inexhaustible.

42. And (they shall have)
Fruits,—all they desire.[5884]

۴۲- وَفَوَاكِهَ مِمَّا يَشْتَهُونَ ۝

43. " Eat ye and drink ye
To your heart's content :
For that ye worked
(Righteousness).[5885]

۴۳- كُلُوا وَاشْرَبُوا هَنِيٓـًٔا
بِمَا كُنْتُمْ تَعْمَلُونَ ۝

44. Thus do We certainly
Reward the Doers of Good.

۴۴- إِنَّا كَذٰلِكَ نَجْزِي الْمُحْسِنِينَ ۝

45. Ah woe, that Day,
To the Rejecters of Truth !

۴۵- وَيْلٌ يَوْمَئِذٍ لِّلْمُكَذِّبِينَ ۝

46. (O ye Unjust !)
Eat ye and enjoy yourselves
(But) a little while,[5886]
For that ye are Sinners.

۴۶- كُلُوا وَتَمَتَّعُوا قَلِيلًا
إِنَّكُمْ مُّجْرِمُونَ ۝

47. Ah woe, that Day,
To the Rejecters of Truth !

۴۷- وَيْلٌ يَوْمَئِذٍ لِّلْمُكَذِّبِينَ ۝

48. And when it is said
To them, " Prostrate yourselves ! "
They do not so.[5887]

۴۸- وَإِذَا قِيلَ لَهُمُ ارْكَعُوا
لَا يَرْكَعُونَ ۝

5884. *Fruits*: see n. 4671 to xliii. 73. where the allegorical meaning of "fruit" and "eating" is explained.

5885. The fruits of righteousness are contentment in this life and the supreme Bliss in the next.

5886. "Eat" is of course symbolical of having the good things of life in this world. It may be that they are only given for a trial. Because their minds and wishes run to wrong things, the opportunities for wrong are multiplied, as the impetus for good or for evil increases progressively. They are asked to believe and repent. But if they do not, they are to be pitied, even for the good things of this life, for they will come to an evil End in the Hereafter.

5887. Prostration is a symbol of humility and a desire to get nearer to God by Prayer and a good life. Those who refuse to adopt this Path are to be pitied: how will they fare at Judgment ?

49. Ah woe, that Day,
To the Rejecters of Truth !

٤٩-وَيْلٌ يَّوْمَئِذٍ لِّلْمُكَذِّبِيْنَ ○

50. Then what Message,
29 After that,[5888]
30 Will they believe in ?

٥٠-فَبِاَيِّ حَدِيْثٍۭ بَعْدَهٗ
يُؤْمِنُوْنَ ○ ع

5888. "*That*" may refer to verse 48: they were given plain and clear Guidance, and they refused to accept it: after that what kind of Message will they accept? The Guidance referred to is obviously that of Islam or the Qur-ān.

INTRODUCTION AND SUMMARY : SŪRA LXXVIII (*Nabaa*).

This beautiful Meccan Sūra is not quite so early as the last (S. lxxvii) nor quite so late as S. lxxvi, but nearer in time to the latter.

It sets forth God's loving care in a fine nature-passage, and deduces from it the Promise of the Future, when Evil will be destroyed and Good will come to its own ; and invites all who have the will, to seek refuge with their Lord.

C. 258.—The Great News for man, in his spiritual Destiny,
(lxxviii. 1-40.) Is the Judgment to come, the Day of Sorting Out.
Do not the Power, the Goodness, and the Justice
Of God reveal themselves in all nature ?—
The Panorama around us, the voice in our souls,
And the harmony between heaven and earth ?
That Day is sure to arrive at its time
Appointed, when behold ! the present order
Will pass away. Then will the Fruits
Of Evil appear, and the Fruits of Righteousness.
God's blessings will be more than the merits of men ;
But who can argue with the Fountain of Grace ?
And who can prevent the course of Justice ?
Let us then, before it becomes too late,
Betake ourselves to our Lord Most Gracious !

Sūra LXXVIII.

Nabaa, or The (Great) News.

In the name of God, Most Gracious, Most Merciful.

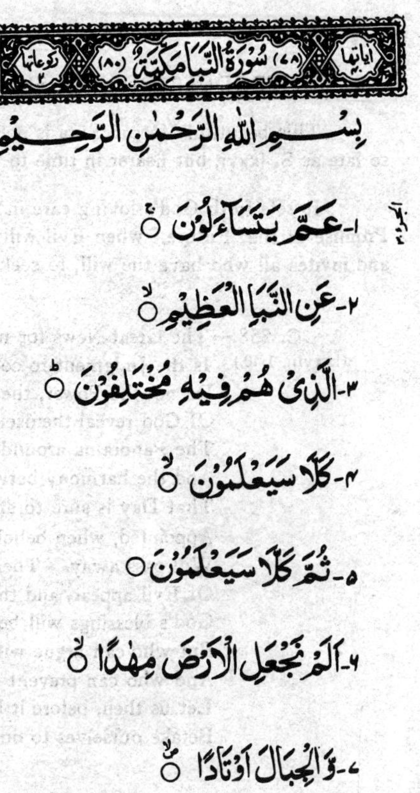

1. Concerning what
Are they disputing?

2. Concerning the Great News,[5889]

3. About which they
Cannot agree.

4. Verily, they shall soon
(Come to) know!

5. Verily, verily they shall
Soon (come to) know!

6. Have We not made
The earth as a wide[5890]
Expanse,

7. And the mountains as pegs?

5889. *Great News*: usually understood to mean the News or Message of the Resurrection or the Hereafter, about which there were various schools of thought among the Jews and Christians and other nations. There is practically nothing about the Resurrection in the Old Testament, and the Jewish sect of Sadducees even in the time of Christ denied the Resurrection altogether. The Pagan ideas of a future life—if any—varied from place to place and from time to time. Even in the early Christian Church, as we learn from Paul's First Epistle to the Corinthians, there were contentions in that little community (I. Corinthians, i. 11), and some definitely denied the resurrection of the dead (*ib.*, xv. 12).

Great News may also be translated *Great Message* or a *Message Supreme*, as I have translated at xxxviii. 67. In that case it would refer to the Qur-ān, or the Message of Revelation, or the Message of the Holy Prophet, about which there was great contention in those days. As this Message also lays great stress on the Day of Judgment and the Resurrection, the practical result by either mode of interpretation amounts to the same.

5890. See n. 2038 to xvi. 15. *Cf.* also xiii. 3 and xv. 19. The spacious expanse of the earth may be compared to a carpet, to which the mountains may metaphorically be supposed to act as pegs. The Signs of God are thus enumerated: the great panorama of outer nature (verses 6-7); the creation of Man in pairs, with the succession of rest and work fitting in with the succession of night and day (verses 8-11); the firmaments above, with their splendid lights (verses 12-13); and the clouds and rain and abundant harvests, which knit sky and earth and man together (verses 14-16). These point to God, and God's Message points to the Future Life.

8. And (have We not) created
You in pairs,

٨- وَّخَلَقْنٰكُمْ اَزْوَاجًا ۝

9. And made your sleep
For rest,

٩- وَّجَعَلْنَا نَوْمَكُمْ سُبَاتًا ۝

10. And made the night
As a covering,[5891]

١٠- وَّجَعَلْنَا الَّيْلَ لِبَاسًا ۝

11. And made the day
As a means of subsistence ?[5892]

١١- وَّجَعَلْنَا النَّهَارَ مَعَاشًا ۝

12. And (have We not)
Built over you
The seven firmaments,[5893]

١٢- وَبَنَيْنَا فَوْقَكُمْ
سَبْعًا شِدَادًا ۝

13. And placed (therein)
A Light of Splendour ?[5894]

١٣- وَّجَعَلْنَا سِرَاجًا وَّهَّاجًا ۝

14. And do We not send down
From the clouds water
In abundance,[5895]

١٤- وَّاَنْزَلْنَا مِنَ الْمُعْصِرٰتِ مَآءً
ثَجَّاجًا ۝

15. That We may produce
Therewith corn and vegetables,

١٥- لِّنُخْرِجَ بِهٖ حَبًّا وَّنَبَاتًا ۝

16. And gardens of luxurious growth ?

١٦- وَّجَنّٰتٍ اَلْفَافًا ۝

5891. The darkness of the night is as a covering. Just as a covering protects us from exposure to cold or heat, so this covering gives us spiritual respite from the buffets of the material world, and from the tiring activities of our own inner exertions. The rest in sleep (in verse 9) is supplemented by the covering of the night with which we are provided by God.

5892. "*Subsistence*" in English only partly covers the idea of *ma'āsh*, which includes every kind of life activity. The Day is specially illuminated, so runs the figure of speech, in order that these life-activities of all kinds may be fully exercised.

5893. See n. 5526 to lxv. 12 and n. 2876 to xxiii. 17, also xxxvii. 6 and notes there.

5894. That is, the sun. *Cf.* xxv. 61 ; xxxiii. 46 (where it is used metaphorically for the holy Prophet) ; and lxxi. 16.

5895. Note how the evidences of God and His beneficence are set out in four groups. (1) Look to external nature on the earth around you (verses 6-7) ; (2) your own nature, physical, mental and spiritual (verses 8-11) ; (3) the starry heavens, and the glory of the sun (verses 12-13); and (4) the interdependence of earth, air, and sky in the cycle of water, clouds, rain, corn and gardens, all serving in their several ways to further the whole plan of the World as it affects us. Can you not then believe that a Creator who does this will sort out Good and Evil on an appointed Day with real justice and power?

17. Verily the Day
Of Sorting Out[5896]
Is a thing appointed,—

١٧-إِنَّ يَوْمَ الْفَصْلِ كَانَ مِيقَاتًا ۝

18. The Day that the Trumpet[5897]
Shall be sounded, and ye
Shall come forth in crowds;

١٨-يَوْمَ يُنْفَخُ فِي الصُّورِ
فَتَأْتُونَ أَفْوَاجًا ۝

19. And the heavens
Shall be opened
As if there were doors,[5898]

١٩-وَفُتِحَتِ السَّمَاءُ
فَكَانَتْ أَبْوَابًا ۝

20. And the mountains
Shall vanish, as if
They were a mirage.

٢٠-وَسُيِّرَتِ الْجِبَالُ
فَكَانَتْ سَرَابًا ۝

21. Truly Hell is
As a place of ambush,—[5899]

٢١-إِنَّ جَهَنَّمَ كَانَتْ مِرْصَادًا ۝

22. For the transgressors
A place of destination:

٢٢-لِلطَّاغِينَ مَآبًا ۝

23. They will dwell therein
For ages.

٢٣-لَابِثِينَ فِيهَا أَحْقَابًا ۝

24. Nothing cool shall they taste
Therein, nor any drink,

٢٤-لَا يَذُوقُونَ فِيهَا بَرْدًا وَلَا شَرَابًا ۝

25. Save a boiling fluid
And a fluid, dark, murky,
Intensely cold,—[5900]

٢٥-إِلَّا حَمِيمًا
وَغَسَّاقًا ۝

5896. *Cf.* xxxvii. 21, n. 4047, and xxxvi. 59, n. 4005 (end). The Day of Judgment is the Day of Sorting Out, as between Good and Evil.

5897. The angel charged with the sounding of the Trumpet is Isrāfīl. It will herald Judgment. *Cf.* l. 20; also xxxix. 68, and n. 4343; and lxix. 13, n. 5648.

5898. A sign that the present order of things will have ceased to exist, and a new world will have come into being. Such a figure applies to the heavens in this verse and to the earth in the next verse. The mystery of what is beyond the heavens will have vanished through the doors which will then be opened. The solid mountains, as we suppose them to be, will have vanished like an unsubstantial mirage.

5899. Hell, the embodiment of evil, is lying in wait like an ambush for every one. We should be on our guard. For the transgressors, those who have wilfully rebelled against God, it will be a definite destination, from which there is no return, except, it may be, after ages, *i.e.* unless God so wills: *Cf.* vi. 128, and n. 951.

5900. *Cf.* x. 4, and n. 1390; also xxxviii. 57, and n. 4213.

26. A fitting recompense
(For them).[5901]

٢٦- جَزَآءً وِّفَاقًا ۝

27. For that they used not
To fear any account
(For their deeds),[5902]

٢٧- إِنَّهُمْ كَانُوا لَا يَرْجُونَ حِسَابًا ۝

28. But they (impudently) treated
Our Signs as false.

٢٨- وَكَذَّبُوا بِآيَاتِنَا كِذَّابًا ۝

29. And all things have We
Preserved on record.

٢٩- وَكُلَّ شَيْءٍ أَحْصَيْنَاهُ كِتَابًا ۝

30. "So taste ye (the fruits
Of your deeds);
For no increase[5903]
Shall We grant you,
Except in Punishment."

٣٠- فَذُوقُوا
فَلَن نَّزِيدَكُمْ إِلَّا عَذَابًا ۝ ع

SECTION 2.

31. Verily for the Righteous
There will be
A fulfilment of
(The Heart's) desires;[5904]

٣١- إِنَّ لِلْمُتَّقِينَ
مَفَازًا ۝

32. Gardens enclosed, and
Grapevines;[5905]

٣٢- حَدَآئِقَ وَأَعْنَابًا ۝

5901. Their transgressions go on progressively as they refuse to repent and turn to God. The fire of misery begins to blaze forth more and more fiercely, and there is nothing to cool that blaze; their food and drink themselves are tainted with the disorder of contradictory elements,—boiling hot drink, with intensely cold, murky, and disgusting fluids. These are fitting punishments for their crimes, which are inconsistent with the pure and gentle mould in which God had originally cast their nature.

5902. It was not isolated acts, but a continued course of evil conduct; they repudiated the moral and spiritual responsibility for their lives; and they impudently called Truth itself by false names and disdained God's Signs, which were vouchsafed for their instruction. These are not mere impressions; these are hard facts "preserved on record", so that every deed can have its due weight in making up the account.

5903. Just as there is a progressive deterioration in the sinner's soul when he surrenders himself to evil, so there is a progressive increase in the Penalty which he suffers.

5904. This is true Salvation. It is not only safety and felicity, but the attainment of the final Goal, the supreme Achievement, the Fulfilment of the highest in human nature, the satisfaction of the true and pure desires of the heart,—seeing the "Face of God". See n. 4733 to xliv. 57.

5905. The supreme Achievement, or the Fulfilment of the Heart's Desires, spoken of in the last verse, is now described in three symbols (verses 32-34), as further explained by two negatives (verse 35). The first symbol is the enclosed Fruit-Garden, and the symbol taken for the fruit is the Grape. As shown in paragraphs 8-10 of Appendix XII following S. liv, the Garden in its many aspects is the most frequent symbol adopted for Bliss. Here the symbolism is further particularised. The most carefully-tended Garden is a Fruit-Garden, with walls all round to protect it, and the most characteristic fruit mentioned here is the luscious Grape, both because it is a Fruit, and because it yields wine—the pure Wine of divine Love.

33. Companions of Equal Age;[5906]

٣٣- وَكَوَاعِبَ أَتْرَابًا ۝

34. And a Cup full
(To the Brim).[5907]

٣٤- وَكَأْسًا دِهَاقًا ۝

35. No Vanity shall they hear
Therein, nor Untruth;—[5908]

٣٥- لَا يَسْمَعُونَ فِيهَا لَغْوًا وَلَا كِذَّابًا ۝

36. Recompense from thy Lord,
A Gift, (amply) sufficient,[5909]—

٣٦- جَزَاءً مِّن رَّبِّكَ عَطَاءً حِسَابًا ۝

37. (From) the Lord
Of the heavens
And the earth,
And all between,—
(God) Most Gracious:
None shall have power
To argue with Him.[5910]

٣٧- رَّبِّ السَّمٰوٰتِ وَالْأَرْضِ
وَمَا بَيْنَهُمَا الرَّحْمٰنِ
لَا يَمْلِكُونَ مِنْهُ خِطَابًا ۝

5906. The second symbol is Companions of Equal Age, Maidens or Virgins, symbols of purity, grace, beauty, innocence, truth, and sympathy. See paragraph 12 of Appendix XII. The feminine itself here symbolises these qualities, and such will be the Companions for those who have been in this world either women or men, for there are no separate heavens for them. The stress here is laid on "Equal Age", for only by that symbol can complete sympathy and understanding be figured. As heaven will be "beyond the flight of Time, beyond the reign of Death", age or youth has no meaning there except as tokens of temperaments, tastes, and feelings, all of which will have their sacred Fulfilment.

5907. The third symbol, the Cup, takes us partly to the Grapes mentioned in verse 32 and partly to the Springs or Rivers mentioned with the Garden in so many places. See paragraphs 10 and 13 of Appendix XII. *Full to the Brim* brings to our mind the unbounded Bounty of God.

5908. The explanation of the three symbols is made further clear by the two negatives. (1) There will be no talk of vanities, such as are usually associated on this earth with pleasant Gardens Companions of equal age, or generous Cups flowing in Assemblies. (2) There will be no Untruth or Falsehood, Insincerity or Hollowness there. Everything will be on a plane of absolute Truth and Reality.

5909. The Recompense is not exactly a Reward in proportion to merit, but is rather a Gift or a Bounty from the Merciful,—a Gift most amply sufficient to satisfy all desire on that plane of purity. See paragraphs 3-6 of Appendix XII for a discussion of the doctrine of Rewards and Punishments. "*A Gift (amply) sufficient*" might almost be translated: a liberal and bountiful gift. *Cf.* the phrase, *A'ṭā fa aḥsaba*=he gave generously, or bountifully.

5910. No one has the right or the power to argue with God about the Gifts which He may bestow on His devotees beyond their deserts, (verse 36 above) or about the Penalty which His justice may inflict for sin or wrong-doing. He is high above all Creation. But He is also Most Gracious. Therefore He may permit special Dignitaries, of honour in His eyes, to plead for sinners, but they will only plead in truth and righteousness: see verse 38 below.

38. The Day that
The Spirit[5911] and the angels
Will stand forth in ranks,
None shall speak
Except any who is
Permitted by (God) Most Gracious,
And he will say
What is right.[5912]

39. That Day will be
The sure Reality:[5913]
Therefore, whoso will, let him
Take a (straight) Return
To his Lord!

40. Verily, We have warned you
Of a Penalty near,—[5914]
The Day when man will
See (the Deeds) which
His hands have sent forth,
And the Unbeliever will say,
"Woe unto me! Would that
I were (mere) dust!"[5915]

٣٨- يَوْمَ يَقُومُ الرُّوحُ وَالْمَلٰٓئِكَةُ صَفًّا ۖ
لَّا يَتَكَلَّمُونَ
إِلَّا مَنْ أَذِنَ لَهُ الرَّحْمٰنُ
وَقَالَ صَوَابًا ۝

٣٩- ذٰلِكَ الْيَوْمُ الْحَقُّ ۚ
فَمَن شَآءَ اتَّخَذَ إِلٰى رَبِّهِۦ مَـَٔابًا ۝

٤٠- إِنَّآ أَنذَرْنٰكُمْ عَذَابًا قَرِيبًا ۚ
يَوْمَ يَنظُرُ الْمَرْءُ مَا قَدَّمَتْ يَدَاهُ
وَيَقُولُ الْكَافِرُ
يٰلَيْتَنِى كُنتُ تُرٰبًۢا ۝ ع

5911. *The Spirit*: see n. 5677 to lxx. 4. Some Commentators understand by "the Spirit" the angel Gabriel as he is charged specially with bringing Messages to human apostles: see xxi. 193, n. 3224. Or perhaps he may be considered the chief of the angels. But it is better to take a wider meaning,—the souls of men collectively as they rise to the Judgment-Seat of God.

5912. See n. 5910 above. No one has the right to speak before the Judgment-Seat; but certain great Dignitaries may be given permission to plead for mercy for sinners, and they will only so plead if the mercy is not nugatory of God's universal justice.

5913. *Cf.* lxix. 1 and n. 5635. Judgment is sure to come, and Truth will then be free from all veils. Why should not man, therefore, now in this life of probation, turn back to God, and understand and do His Will?

5914. Is Judgment very near? Yes. There are three stages of Judgment. (1) Many of our sins and wrong-doings find their penalty in this very life. It may not be an open or striking event, but it corrodes the soul and conscience all the time. Let us therefore turn back to God in repentance and ask for forgiveness. (2) Where the Penalty is not actually perceived or is not visible in this life, Death is considered the Lesser Judgment for each individual soul: see n. 5822 to lxxv. 22. Death may come to anyone at any time, and we must all be ready for it. (3) Then there is the final Judgment, when the whole of the present order passes away, and there is a New World. Time as we know it will not exist. Fifty thousand years as we reckon now will be but as a Day: lxx. 4. According to those standards even this Final Judgment is quite near, and we must prepare for it. For it will be too late then for repentance.

5915. The Unbeliever, the Rejecter of God, will then find himself in a world of absolute Reality, in which there will be no place for him. He will neither live nor die: xx. 74. He will wish that he could be reduced to nothingness, but even that would not be possible.

INTRODUCTION AND SUMMARY: SŪRA LXXIX (*Nāzi'āt*).

This is also an early Meccan Sūra, of about the same date as the last, and deals with the mystic theme of Judgment from the point of view of Pride and its Fall. The parable of Pharaoh occupies a central place in the argument: for he said, "I am your Lord Most High", and perished with his followers.

C. 259.—Never can Evil escape God's order
(lxxix. 1-46.) And law: His angels are ever present
To bring the wicked to their bearings
And they ever strive and press forward to bring
Comfort, succour, and God's Mercy to those
Who seek it. Then will come the Day
When the proud shall be humbled, though they
Deny the coming Judgment. What happened
To Pharaoh? He flouted God's Message specially
Sent to him, and arrogantly proclaimed:
"I am your Lord Most High!" He perished
In this life and will answer for his deeds in the next.

* * *

But can ye not see, O men, the mighty
Works of God in the heavens and on earth?—
The darksome splendour of the Night with its Stars,
And the daylight splendour of the Sun?—
How the earth, with its spacious expanse and its mountains,
Yields moisture and pasture, and feeds and sustains
Men and cattle, through God's wise Providence?
Ah! transgress not all bounds and earn not the Fire
Of Punishment, but fear God and His Judgment,
And prepare for the Garden of Perpetual Bliss.
Delay not! The Judgment is sure, and it's nigh!

Sūra LXXIX.

Nāzi'āt, or Those Who Tear Out.

In the name of God, Most Gracious, Most Merciful

بِسْمِ اللّٰهِ الرَّحْمٰنِ الرَّحِيْمِ

1. By the (angels)[5916]
Who tear out
(The souls of the wicked)
With violence;[5917]

١- وَالنّٰزِعٰتِ غَرْقًا ۝

2. By those who gently
Draw out (the souls
Of the blessed);[5918]

٢- وَّالنّٰشِطٰتِ نَشْطًا ۝

3. And by those who glide
Along (on errands of mercy),[5919]

٣- وَّالسّٰبِحٰتِ سَبْحًا ۝

4. Then press forward
As in a race,

٤- فَالسّٰبِقٰتِ سَبْقًا ۝

5. Then arrange to do
(The Commands of their Lord),—

٥- فَالْمُدَبِّرٰتِ اَمْرًا ۝ وقف لازم

5916. The beginning of this Sūra may be compared with the beginning of S. lxxvii. A translator's task in such passages is extremely difficult. He has to do with highly mystical symbols expressed in elliptical language suitable for mysticism, and he has to render them in another language with words of precision intelligible to readers. It is therefore necessary for him to put in part of the Commentary in the Translation in such cases.

The evidence of five things is here invoked in verses 1—5, in order to lead to the conclusion in verse 6 and those following. Or, if we treat verses 3-5 as three stages of the same thing, there are three things to be considered in five stages. What are they? And what is the conclusion? See the following notes.

5917. There is much difference of opinion among the Commentators as to the five things or beings mentioned in these verses. I follow the general opinion in my interpretation, which is that angels are referred to as the agency which in their dealings with mankind show clearly God's Justice, Power, and Mercy, which again point to the Judgment to come, as a certainty which none can evade. The first point, referred to in this verse, is that the souls of the wicked are loath to part with their material body at death, but their will will not count: their souls will be wrenched out into another world. Who will then deny Resurrection and Judgment?

5918. The second point is that in contrast with the wicked, the souls of the blessed will be drawn out gently to their new life. They will be ready for it. In fact death for them will be a release from the grosser incidents of bodily sense. To them the approach of Judgment will be welcome.

5919. At all times there are errands of mercy and blessing and errands of justice, which the angels are prompt to execute by order of God. There are three features of this, thus giving the third, fourth, and fifth points. (3) Their movement is compared to that of gliding or swimming (*sabḥan*). In xxi. 33 this verb is applied to the motion of the celestial bodies: they all "swim along, each in its rounded course". *Cf.* Shakespeare, *Merchant of Venice*: "There's not an orb which thou behold'st, But in his motion like an angel sings, Still quiring to the young-eyed cherubims". (4) In hurrying on their errands the angels press forth as in a race. (5) And thus they promptly execute the orders of their Lord.

6. One Day everything that
Can be in commotion will
Be in violent commotion,[5920]

٦- يَوْمَ تَرْجُفُ الرَّاجِفَةُ ۝

7. Followed by oft-repeated
(Commotions):[5921]

٧- تَتْبَعُهَا الرَّادِفَةُ ۝

8. Hearts that Day[5922]
Will be in agitation;

٨- قُلُوبٌ يَوْمَئِذٍ وَاجِفَةٌ ۝

9. Cast down will be[5923]
(Their owners') eyes.

٩- أَبْصَارُهَا خَاشِعَةٌ ۝

10. They say (now): "What!
Shall we indeed be[5924]
Returned to (our) former state?—

١٠- يَقُولُونَ ءَإِنَّا
لَمَرْدُودُونَ فِي الْحَافِرَةِ ۝

11. "What!—when we shall
Have become rotten bones?"

١١- ءَإِذَا كُنَّا عِظَامًا نَّخِرَةً ۝

12. They say: "It would,
In that case, be
A return with loss!"

١٢- قَالُوا تِلْكَ إِذًا كَرَّةٌ خَاسِرَةٌ ۝

13. But verily, it will
Be but a single

١٣- فَإِنَّمَا هِيَ زَجْرَةٌ وَاحِدَةٌ ۝

5920. The evidence of the wonderful working of the spiritual world having been invoked in the first five verses, the conclusion is now drawn and stated. It is certain that one great Day (to be taken in a spiritual sense as the Day of Account), the whole world as we now see it in our lower life will be in violent revolution. It will be like an earthquake destroying all land-marks. But that will affect only things subject to change: they will suffer violent convulsions as a preliminary to their disappearance. But God and His divine order will not change: His "Face" abideth for ever, full of Majesty, Bounty, and Honour (lv. 27).

5921. The Commotion will be repeated again and again in the transitory world, to make way for the new world that will then come into being.

5922. All hearts will be in agitation: those of the blessed ones to see the beginning of the fulfilment of their Lord's Promise; those of the Rejecters of God for fear of His just Judgment.

5923. Similarly all eyes will be cast down: those of the blessed ones in humble modesty, and those of the Rejecters of God, in utter humiliation, sorrow, and shame, for their arrogance and insolence in their probationary life

5924. The Unbelievers say now, in their arrogance, insolence, and mocking defiance: "Surely death here is the end of all things! When we are dead and buried, and our bones are rotten, how can we be restored again?" They add, "If that were so, then we should indeed be in a turn of dreadful luck! Instead of gaining by the Resurrection, we should be in terrible loss (with our rotten bones)!" They mean this in biting mockery. But there will indeed be an Account taken, and they will indeed be in a terrible loss, for they will go to perdition!

(Compelling) Cry,[5925]

14. When, behold, they
Will be in the (full)
Awakening (to Judgment).[5926]

١٤- فَإِذَا هُمْ بِالسَّاهِرَةِ ۝

15. Has the story[5927]
Of Moses reached thee ?

١٥- هَلْ أَتٰىكَ حَدِيثُ مُوسٰى ۝

16. Behold, thy Lord did call
To him in the sacred valley
Of Ṭuwā :—[5928]

١٦- إِذْ نَادٰىهُ
رَبُّهُ بِالْوَادِ الْمُقَدَّسِ طُوًى ۝

17. " Go thou to Pharaoh,
For he has indeed
Transgressed all bounds :[5929]

١٧- اِذْهَبْ إِلٰى فِرْعَوْنَ
إِنَّهُ طَغٰى ۝

18. " And say to him,
' Wouldst thou that thou
Shouldst be purified
(From sin)?—

١٨- فَقُلْ هَلْ لَكَ إِلٰى
أَنْ تَزَكّٰى ۝

19. " ' And that I guide thee
To thy Lord, so thou[5930]
Shouldst fear Him ?' "

١٩- وَأَهْدِيَكَ إِلٰى رَبِّكَ
فَتَخْشٰى ۝

5925. Judgment will be inaugurated with a single compelling Cry. *Cf.* xxxvii 19. See also xxxvi. 29 and 49, where the single mighty Blast seems to refer to the sinners being cut off in this life and plunged into the other world where they will be further judged, and xxxvi. 53, where the final Judgment is referred to.

5926. They will have been more or less dormant before the Great Judgment, as contrasted with the Lesser Judgment (n. 5914 to lxxviii. 40, and n. 5822 to lxxv. 22). When the Resurrection comes, they will come fully into the new world, the old heaven and earth having then completely passed away, not only for them but absolutely.

5927. This is just a reference to the story of Moses told more fully in S. xx. 9-76. The lessons drawn are : (1) That even to an arrogant blasphemer and rebel against God's Law, like Pharaoh, God's grace was offered through a major Prophet Moses ; (2) that his rejection brought about his signal downfall even in this world ; and (3) that his humiliation and punishment will be completed in the Hereafter at Judgment.

5928. *Cf.* xx. 12.

5929. *Cf.* xx. 24.

5930. Even for such a one as Pharaoh, intoxicated with his own power and greatness, guidance and grace were offered through Moses.

20. Then did (Moses) show him
The Great Sign.[5931]

٢٠- فَأَرٰىهُ الْاٰيَةَ الْكُبْرٰى ۝

21. But (Pharaoh) rejected it
And disobeyed (guidance);

٢١- فَكَذَّبَ وَعَصٰى ۝

22. Further, he turned his back,
Striving hard (against God).

٢٢- ثُمَّ أَدْبَرَ يَسْعٰى ۝

23. Then he collected (his men)
And made a proclamation,

٢٣- فَحَشَرَ فَنَادٰى ۝

24. Saying, "I am your Lord,
Most High".

٢٤- فَقَالَ أَنَا رَبُّكُمُ الْأَعْلٰى ۝

25. But God did punish him,
(And made an) example
Of him,—in the Hereafter,
As in this life.[5932]

٢٥- فَأَخَذَهُ اللّٰهُ
نَكَالَ الْاٰخِرَةِ وَالْأُولٰى ۝

26. Verily in this is
An instructive warning[5933]
For whosoever feareth (God).

٢٦- إِنَّ فِي ذٰلِكَ لَعِبْرَةً
لِّمَنْ يَّخْشٰى ۝

SECTION 2.

27. What! Are ye the more
Difficult to create
Or the heaven (above)?[5934]
(God) hath constructed it:

٢٧- ءَأَنْتُمْ أَشَدُّ خَلْقًا
أَمِ السَّمَآءُ ۚ بَنٰهَا ۝

5931. What was the Great Sign? Some Commentators understand by it the "White Shining Hand": see n. 2550 to xx. 22-23. Others think it was the miracle of the rod that became a "snake active in motion": see xx. 20, n. 2549. These were among the Greater Signs: xx. 23. In xvii. 101 there is a reference to nine Clear Signs given to Moses, and these are specified in detail in n. 1091 to vii. 133. The fact is, there were many Signs given, "openly self-explained," but Pharaoh and his men "were steeped in arrogance,— a people given to sin" (vii. 133). The pre-eminently Great Sign was therefore the fact of Moses being sent to Pharaoh, which subsequently converted the magicians and the more learned Egyptians to the true God (xx. 70-73), though Pharaoh and his Chiefs resisted and suffered for their sins. The mystics understand by the "Great Sign" the Power of God as enshrined in His mystic Name, which none may know but the adepts in spiritual lore.

5932. See xx. 78-79, also vii. 135-137.

5933. *Cf.* xxiv. 44.

5934. If man grows arrogant or forgets his accountability to God, in his ignorance or thoughtlessness, he is reminded that he is only an insignificant speck in God's spacious Creation. All the excellence that man acquires is the gift of God, Who has bestowed on him a high Destiny if he fulfils the purpose of his creation: ii. 30-39. Then follows a nature passage, pointing to the glory of the heavens and the earth, and how they are both made to subserve the life of man.

28. On high hath He raised
Its canopy, and He hath
Given it order and perfection.[5935]

٢٨- رَفَعَ سَمْكَهَا فَسَوّٰىهَا ۝

29. Its night doth He
Endow with darkness,
And its splendour doth He
Bring out (with light).[5936]

٢٩- وَأَغْطَشَ لَيْلَهَا وَأَخْرَجَ ضُحٰىهَا ۝

30. And the earth, moreover,[5937]
Hath He extended
(To a wide expanse);

٣٠- وَالْأَرْضَ بَعْدَ ذٰلِكَ دَحٰىهَا ۝

31. He draweth out
Therefrom its moisture
And its pasture ;[5938]

٣١- أَخْرَجَ مِنْهَا مَآءَهَا وَمَرْعٰىهَا ۝

32. And the mountains
Hath He firmly fixed ; –[5939]

٣٢- وَالْجِبَالَ أَرْسٰىهَا ۝

33. For use and convenience[5940]
To you and your cattle.

٣٣- مَتَاعًا لَّكُمْ وَلِأَنْعَامِكُمْ ۝

5935. *Cf.* ii. 29. The mystery of the heavens with their countless stars and the planets obeying the laws of motion, and the sun and moon influencing the temperature and climates of the earth from thousands or millions of miles, illustrate the order and perfection which God has given to His Creation. Can man then remain exempt from his responsibility for his deeds, endowed as he is with a will, or deny the Day of Sorting Out, which is the Day of Judgment ?

5936. *Its* of course refers to the starry heaven. Both the Night and the Day have each its own beauty and its utility for man, as has been frequently pointed out in the Qur-ān. The night is a period of darkness, but it has also its splendours of light in the moon, or the planets Jupiter or Venus, or stars like Sirius or the Milky Way. These countless lights of night have their own beauty, and by day there is the splendour of the sun for us, which in Creation as a whole, is just one of countless stars.

5937. *Moreover* : or, more literally, *after that*. See n. 4475 to xli. 11.

5938. The underground springs and wells of water as well as rivers and glaciers in northern climates are due to the different levels of highlands and lowlands. They spread the moisture evenly as wanted, and give corn, fruits, and vegetables to man, and pastures and feeding grounds to beasts of the fields. For the wonderful circuit or cycle of water between heaven and earth, see notes 3106 (xxv. 49) and 3111 (xxv. 53).

5939. See n. 2038 to xvi. 15. The "eternal hills" are the main reservoirs for the storage and gradual distribution of water, the very basis for the life of man and beast.

5940. This clause I construe to apply to verses 30, 31, and 32 above. Everything on earth has, by God's bountiful providence, been arranged to subserve the use and convenience of man and the lower life which depends upon him. The intermediary between God's providence and the actual use made of God's other gifts is man's own intelligence and initiative, which are also gifts of God.

34. Therefore, when there comes
The great, overwhelming
(Event),—[5941]

٣٤- فَإِذَا جَآءَتِ الطَّآمَّةُ الْكُبْرٰى ۝

35. The Day when Man
Shall remember (all)
That he strove for,[5942]

٣٥- يَوْمَ يَتَذَكَّرُ الْإِنْسَانُ مَا سَعٰى ۝

36. And Hell-Fire shall be
Placed in full view[5943]
For (all) to see,—

٣٦- وَبُرِّزَتِ الْجَحِيْمُ
لِمَنْ يَّرٰى ۝

37. Then, for such as had
Transgressed all bounds,

٣٧- فَأَمَّا مَنْ طَغٰى ۝

38. And had preferred[5944]
The life of this world,

٣٨- وَاٰثَرَ الْحَيٰوةَ الدُّنْيَا ۝

39. The Abode will be
Hell-Fire;

٣٩- فَإِنَّ الْجَحِيْمَ هِيَ الْمَأْوٰى ۝

40. And for such as had
Entertained the fear
Of standing before[5945]
Their Lord's (tribunal)
And had restrained
(Their) soul from lower Desires,

٤٠- وَأَمَّا مَنْ خَافَ مَقَامَ رَبِّهٖ
وَنَهَى النَّفْسَ
عَنِ الْهَوٰى ۝

41. Their Abode will be
The Garden.

٤١- فَإِنَّ الْجَنَّةَ هِيَ الْمَأْوٰى ۝

5941. The Judgment, the time for sorting out all things according to their true, intrinsic, and eternal values.

5942. The Judgment will be not only for his acts but for his motives, "all he strove for". In this life he may forget his ill-deeds, but in the new conditions he will not only remember them, but the Fire of Punishment will be plainly visible to him, and not only to him, but it will be "for all to see". This will add to the sinner's humiliation.

5943. *Cf.* xxvi. 91.

5944. The abiding Punishment will be for those who had wilfully and persistently rebelled against God, "transgressing all bounds", and had given themselves up to the vanities and lusts of this lower life. This Punishment will not touch those who had repented and been forgiven, nor those guilty, through human frailty, of minor sins, whose deeds will be weighed in the balance against their good deeds: ci. 6-9.

5945. The contrast is complete and parallel: the persistent rebels against God's Law, who preferred the lower life, are to dwell in the Fire of Punishment, while those who humbly feared the punishment of sin and believing in their Lord's warnings, restrained their lower desires, will dwell in the Garden. See last note.

42. They ask thee[5946]
About the Hour,—' When
Will be its appointed time ? '

۴۲- يَسْـَٔلُوْنَكَ عَنِ السَّاعَةِ
اَيَّانَ مُرْسٰىهَا ۝

43. Wherein art thou (concerned)
With the declaration thereof ?

۴۳- فِيْمَ اَنْتَ مِنْ ذِكْرٰىهَا ۝

44. With thy Lord is
The Limit[5947] fixed therefor.

۴۴- اِلٰى رَبِّكَ مُنْتَهٰىهَا ۝

45. Thou art but a Warner
For such as fear it.[5948]

۴۵- اِنَّمَآ اَنْتَ مُنْذِرُ مَنْ يَّخْشٰىهَا ۝

46. The Day they see it,
(It will be) as if they
Had tarried but a single
Evening, or (at most till)
The following morn ![5949]

۴۶- كَاَنَّهُمْ يَوْمَ يَرَوْنَهَا
لَمْ يَلْبَثُوْٓا اِلَّا عَشِيَّةً
اَوْ ضُحٰىهَا ۝

5946 *Cf.* vii. 187 and n. 1159. Only God can reveal it. But were it known, "heavy were its burden through the heavens and the earth ".

5947. Our time has no sort of comparison with the timeless state in the new spiritual World in which the final Judgment will take place. Nor can its limits—how long it will last–be set except in the Will of Almighty God, Lord of Supreme Wisdom, Justice, and Goodness : xi 107-108. But it is near, in the sense explained in n. 5914 to lxxviii. 40.

5948. The warning is only effective for those who believe in God and in the Final Account. Such men immediately turn in repentance to God, and it is to lead such men and help them, that Prophets are sent.

5949. *Cf.* x. 45, where the expression used is : " it will be as if they had tarried but an hour of a day." Here the metaphor used is " a single evening, or, at most, till the following morn ". Death is like sleep, and may be compared to the evening of life. In sleep we do not know how the time passes. When we wake up from the sleep of Death at the Resurrection, we shall not know whether it was the following moment or the following hour after we slept, but we shall feel that it is morning, for we shall be conscious of all that goes on, as one awakened in the morning.

INTRODUCTION AND SUMMARY: SŪRA LXXX (*'Abasa*).

This is an early Meccan Sūra, and is connected with an incident which reflects the highest honour on the Prophet's sincerity in the Revelations that were vouchsafed to him even if they seemed to reprove him for some natural and human zeal that led him to a false step in his mission according to his own high standards.

He was once deeply and earnestly engaged in trying to explain the holy Qur-ān to Pagan Quraish leaders, when he was interrupted by a blind man, 'Abdullāh ibn Umm-i-Maktūm, one who was also poor, so that no one took any notice of him. He wanted to learn the Qur-ān. The holy Prophet naturally disliked the interruption and showed impatience. Perhaps the poor man's feelings were hurt. But he whose gentle heart ever sympathised with the poor and the afflicted, got new Light from above, and without the least hesitation published this revelation, which forms part of the sacred scripture of Islam, as described in verses 13-16. And the Prophet always afterwards held the man in high honour.

The incident was only a passing incident, but after explaining the eternal principles of revelation, the Sūra recapitulates the Mercies of God to man, and the consequences of a good or a wicked life here, as seen in the spiritual world to come, in the Hereafter.

C. 260.—Men not blest with the good things of this life
(lxxx. 1-42.) May yet be earnest seekers of Truth
And Purity, and deserve as much attention as those
Who seem to wield some influence, yet who
In their pride are self-sufficient. God's Message
Is universal: all have a right
To hear it. Held high in honour, kept
Pure and holy, it should be writ
By none but good and honourable men.

* * * *

God's Grace is showered on man not less
For his inner growth than in his outward
Life. There must be a final Reckoning,
When each soul must stand on its own past Record:
The faces, then, of the Blest will beam
With Joy and Light, while the Doers of Iniquity
Will hide in Dust and Shame and Darkness.

Sūra LXXX.

'Abasa, or He Frowned.

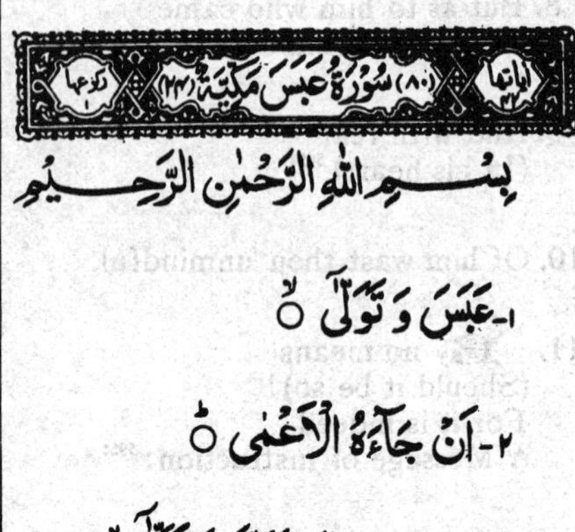

In the name of God, Most Gracious, Most Merciful.

1. (The Prophet) frowned
And turned away,[5950]

١- عَبَسَ وَتَوَلَّىٰٓ ۝

2. Because there came to him
The blind man (interrupting).

٢- أَن جَآءَهُ ٱلْأَعْمَىٰ ۝

3. But what could tell thee
But that perchance he might
Grow (in spiritual understanding)?—

٣- وَمَا يُدْرِيكَ لَعَلَّهُۥ يَزَّكَّىٰٓ ۝

4. Or that he might receive
Admonition, and the teaching
Might profit him?[5951]

٤- أَوْ يَذَّكَّرُ
فَتَنفَعَهُ ٱلذِّكْرَىٰٓ ۝

5. As to one who regards
Himself as self-sufficient,[5952]

٥- أَمَّا مَنِ ٱسْتَغْنَىٰ ۝

6. To him dost thou attend;

٦- فَأَنتَ لَهُۥ تَصَدَّىٰ ۝

7. Though it is no blame
To thee if he grow not[5953]
(In spiritual understanding).

٧- وَمَا عَلَيْكَ أَلَّا يَزَّكَّىٰ ۝

5950. See the Introduction to this Sūra for the incident to which this refers. The lesson is that neither spiritual worth nor the prospect of effective spiritual guidance is to be measured by a man's position in life. The poor, or the blind, the halt, or the maimed, may be more susceptible to the teaching of God's Word than men who are apparently gifted, but who suffer from arrogance and self-sufficiency.

5951. It may be that the poor blind man might, on account of his will to learn, be more likely to grow in his own spiritual development or to profit by any lessons taught to him even in reproof than a self-sufficient leader. In fact it was so. For the blind man became a true and sincere Muslim and lived to become a governor of Madīna.

5952. Such a one would be a Pagan Quraish leader, whom the holy Prophet was anxious to get into his fold, in order that the work of preaching God's Message might be facilitated. But such a Message works first amongst the simple and lowly, the poor and despised folk, and the mighty ones of the earth only come in when the stream rushes in with irresistible force.

5953. God's Message is for all, but if the great ones arrogantly keep back from it, it is no fault of the Preacher, so long as he has proclaimed the Message. He should attend to all, and specially to the humble and lowly.

8. But as to him who came
To thee striving earnestly,

٨- وَاَمَّا مَنْ جَآءَكَ يَسْعٰى ۝

9. And with fear
(In his heart),[5954]

٩- وَهُوَ يَخْشٰى ۝

10. Of him wast thou unmindful.

١٠- فَاَنْتَ عَنْهُ تَلَهّٰى ۝

11. By no means
(Should it be so)!
For it is indeed
A Message of instruction:[5955]

١١- كَلَّآ اِنَّهَا تَذْكِرَةٌ ۝

12. Therefore let whoso will,
Keep it in remembrance.

١٢- فَمَنْ شَآءَ ذَكَرَهٗ ۝

13. (It[5956] is) in Books
Held (greatly) in honour,

١٣- فِيْ صُحُفٍ مُّكَرَّمَةٍ ۝

14. Exalted (in dignity),
Kept pure and holy,

١٤- مَّرْفُوْعَةٍ مُّطَهَّرَةٍ ۝

15. (Written) by the hands
Of scribes—

١٥- بِاَيْدِيْ سَفَرَةٍ ۝

16. Honourable and
Pious and Just.

١٦- كِرَامٍ بَرَرَةٍ ۝

17. Woe to man!
What hath made him
Reject God?

١٧- قُتِلَ الْاِنْسَانُ مَآ اَكْفَرَهٗ ۝

5954. The fear in the blind man's heart may have been two-fold. (1) He was humble and God-fearing, not arrogant and self-sufficient; (2) being poor and blind, he feared to intrude; yet his earnest desire to learn the Qur-ān made him bold, and he came, perhaps unseasonably, but was yet worthy of encouragement, because of the purity of his heart.

5955. God's Message is a universal Message, from which no one is to be excluded,—rich or poor, old or young, great or lowly, learned or ignorant. If anyone had the spiritual craving that needed satisfaction, he was to be given precedence if there was to be any question of precedence at all.

5956. At the time this Sūra was revealed, there were perhaps only about 42 or 45 Sūras in the hands of the Muslims. But it was a sufficient body of Revelation of high spiritual value, to which the description given here could be applied. It was held in the highest honour; its place in the hearts of Muslims was more exalted than that of anything else; as God's Word, it was pure and sacred; and those who transcribed it were men who were honourable, just and pious. The legend that the early Sūras were not carefully written down and preserved in books is a pure invention. The recensions made later in the time of the first and the third Khalīfas were merely to preserve the purity and safeguard the arrangement of the text, at a time when the expansion of Islam among non-Arabic-speaking peoples made such precautions necessary.

18. From what stuff
Hath He created him?

۱۸- مِنْ اَيِّ شَيْءٍ خَلَقَهٗ ۝

19. From a sperm-drop:[5957]
He hath created him, and then
Mouldeth him in due proportions;

۱۹- مِنْ نُّطْفَةٍ ؕ خَلَقَهٗ فَقَدَّرَهٗ ۝

20. Then doth He make
His path smooth for him;

۲۰- ثُمَّ السَّبِيْلَ يَسَّرَهٗ ۝

21. Then He causeth him to die,
And putteth him in his Grave;[5958]

۲۱- ثُمَّ اَمَاتَهٗ فَاَقْبَرَهٗ ۝

22. Then, when it is
His Will, He will
Raise him up (again).

۲۲- ثُمَّ اِذَا شَآءَ اَنْشَرَهٗ ۝

23. By no means hath he
Fulfilled what God
Hath commanded him.[5959]

۲۳- كَلَّا لَمَّا يَقْضِ مَآ اَمَرَهٗ ۝

24. Then let man look
At his Food,[5960]
(And how We provide it):

۲۴- فَلْيَنْظُرِ الْاِنْسَانُ اِلٰى طَعَامِهٖٓ ۝

25. For that We pour forth
Water in abundance,

۲۵- اَنَّا صَبَبْنَا الْمَآءَ صَبًّا ۝

5957. *Cf.* lxxvi. 2. and n. 5832. The origin of man as an animal is lowly indeed. But what further faculties and capacities has not God granted to man? Besides his animal body, in which also he shares in all the blessings which God has bestowed on the rest of His Creation, man has been granted divine gifts which entitle him to be called the Vicegerent of God on earth : ii. 30. He has a will; he has spiritual perception; he is capable of divine love; he can control nature within certain limits, and subject nature's forces to his own use. And he has been given the power of judgment, so that he can avoid excess and defect, and follow the middle path. And that path, as well as all that is necessary for his life in its manifold aspects, has been made easy for him.

5958. *Cf.* xx. 55. Death is an inevitable event after the brief life on this earth, but it is also in a sense a blessing,—a release from the imperfections of this world, a close of the probationary period, after which will dawn the full Reality. "*The Grave*" may be understood to be the period between physical death and immortal Life, whatever may be the mode of disposal of the dead body. This intermediate period is the *Barzakh* or Partition : see n. 2940 to xxiii. 101.

5959. Though all these blessings and stages have been provided by God's Grace for the good of man, yet unregenerate man fails in carrying out the purpose of his creation and life.

5960. After a reference to man's inner history, there is now a reference to just one item in his daily outer life, his food : and it is shown how the forces of heaven and earth unite by God's Command to serve man and his dependants, "for use and convenience to you and your cattle" (verse 32 below). If that is the case with just one item, food, how much more comprehensive is God's beneficence when the whole of man's needs are considered!

26. And We split the earth
In fragments,[5961]

٢٦- ثم شققنا الأرض شقا ۝

27. And produce therein[5962] Corn,

٢٧- فأنبتنا فيها حبا ۝

28. And Grapes and nutritious Plants,

٢٨- وعنبا وقضبا ۝

29. And Olives and Dates,

٢٩- وزيتونا ونخلا ۝

30. And enclosed Gardens,[5963]
Dense with lofty trees,

٣٠- وحدائق غلبا ۝

31. And Fruits and Fodder,—

٣١- وفاكهة وأبا ۝

32. For use and convenience
To you and your cattle.[5964]

٣٢- متاعا لكم ولأنعامكم ۝

33. At length, when there
Comes the Deafening Noise,—[5965]

٣٣- فإذا جاءت الصاخة ۝

34. That Day shall a man
Flee from his own brother,

٣٤- يوم يفر المرء من أخيه ۝

35. And from his mother
And his father,

٣٥- وأمه وأبيه ۝

36. And from his wife
And his children.[5966]

٣٦- وصاحبته وبنيه ۝

5961. The water comes from the clouds in plentiful abundance; the earth is ploughed, and the soil is broken up in fragments, and yields an abundant harvest of cereals (Corn), trellised fruit (Grapes), and vegetable food (nutritious Plants), as well as fruit that can keep for long periods and serve many uses, like olives and dates.

5962. *Therein* : *i.e.* from within the earth or the soil.

5963. We not only get field crops such as were mentioned in n. 5961 above, but we have the more highly cultivated garden crops, both in the way of lofty trees, and in the way of carefully tended fruits like the fig; and then we have grass and all kinds of fodder.

5964. The same verse occurs at lxxix. 33, where n. 5940 explains the wider meaning in that context.

5965 Preliminary to the establishment of the Final Judgment.

5966. Even those who were nearest and dearest in this life will not be able or willing to help each other on that awful Day. On the contrary, if they have to receive a sentence for their sins, they will be anxious to avoid even sharing each other's sorrows or witnessing each other's humiliation; for each will have enough of his own troubles to occupy him. On the other hand, the Righteous will be united with their righteous families: lii. 21; and their faces will be "beaming, laughing, rejoicing" (lxxx. 38-39).

37. Each one of them,
That Day, will have
Enough concern (of his own)
To make him indifferent
To the others.[5967]

٣٧- لِكُلِّ امْرِئٍ مِّنْهُمْ
يَوْمَئِذٍ شَأْنٌ يُغْنِيهِ ۝

38. Some Faces that Day
Will be beaming,

٣٨- وُجُوهٌ يَوْمَئِذٍ مُّسْفِرَةٌ ۝

39. Laughing, rejoicing.

٣٩- ضَاحِكَةٌ مُّسْتَبْشِرَةٌ ۝

40. And other faces that Day
Will be dust-stained ;[5968]

٤٠- وَوُجُوهٌ يَوْمَئِذٍ عَلَيْهَا غَبَرَةٌ ۝

41. Blackness will cover them :

٤١- تَرْهَقُهَا قَتَرَةٌ ۝

42. Such will be
The Rejecters of God,
The Doers of Iniquity.

٤٢- أُولَٰئِكَ هُمُ الْكَفَرَةُ الْفَجَرَةُ ۝ ع

5967. *Cf.* lxx. 10-14. No friend will ask after a friend that Day. On the contrary the sinner will desire to save himself at the expense even of his own family and benefactors.

5968. The dust on the faces of the sinners will be in contrast to the beaming light on the faces of the righteous ; and the blackness in contrast to the "laughing, rejoicing" faces of the righteous. But the dust also suggests that being Rejecters of God, their faces and eyes and faculties were choked in dust, and the blackness suggests that being Doers of Iniquity they had no part or lot in Purity or Light. Another contrast may possibly be deduced : the humble and lowly may be "in the dust" in this life, and the arrogant sinners in sunshine, but the rôles will be reversed at Judgment.

INTRODUCTION TO SŪRA LXXXI (*Takwīr*).

This is quite an early Meccan Sūra, perhaps the sixth or seventh in chronological order. It opens with a series of highly mystical metaphors suggesting the break-up of the world as we know it (verses 1-13) and the enforcement of complete personal responsibility for each soul (verse 14). Then there is a mystical passage showing how the Quranic Revelation was true, and revealed through the angel Gabriel, and not merely a rhapsody from one possessed. Revelation is given for man's spiritual guidance (verses 14-29).

Comparable with this Sūra are the Sūras lxxxii and lxxxiv which may be read with this.

Summary

C. 261.—How can the soul's self-conviction be fitly
(lxxxi. 1-29.) Expressed, except by types of tremendous
Cataclysms in nature, and still more by tremendous
Searchings in the heart of man ? These want
Deep pondering. When once the spiritual Dawn
Has " breathed away " the Darkness of the Night,
The Vision Glorious clears all doubts,
And brings us face to face with Truth.
The highest Archangel in heaven is sent
By God to bring these truths to men
Through their Apostle. God's Grace flows freely :
We have but to tune our Will to His,—
The ever-loving Righteous God.

Sûra LXXXI.

Takwir, or the Folding Up.

In the name of God, Most Gracious, Most Merciful.

1. When the sun [5969]
(With its spacious light)
Is folded up ; [5970]

2. When the stars [5971]
Fall, losing their lustre ;

3. When the mountains vanish
(Like a mirage) ; [5972]

4. When the she-camels,
Ten months with young,
Are left untended ; [5973]

5. When the wild beasts
Are herded together

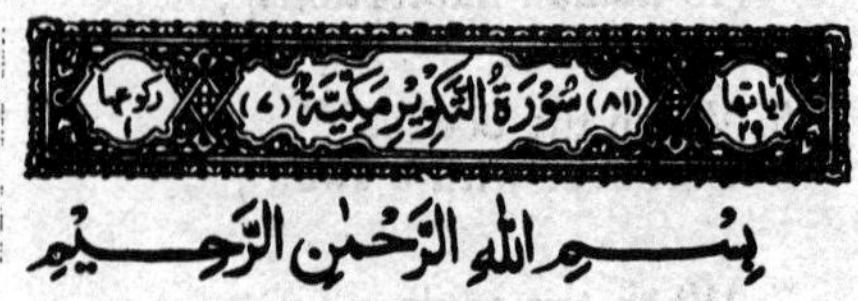

بِسْمِ اللّٰهِ الرَّحْمٰنِ الرَّحِيْمِ

١- اِذَا الشَّمْسُ كُوِّرَتْ

٢- وَاِذَا النُّجُوْمُ انْكَدَرَتْ

٣- وَاِذَا الْجِبَالُ سُيِّرَتْ

٤- وَاِذَا الْعِشَارُ عُطِّلَتْ

٥- وَاِذَا الْوُحُوْشُ حُشِرَتْ

5969. Verses 1 to 13 are conditional clauses, and the substantive clause is in verse 14. The time will come when nature's processes as we know them will cease to function, and the soul will only then know by self conviction the results of its actions. With reference to an individual soul, its resurrection is its supreme crisis : the whole world of sense, and even of imagination and reason, melts away, and its whole spiritual scroll is laid bare before it.

5970. The conditional clauses are twelve, in two groups of six. The first six affect the outer or physical life of man ; the last six, his inmost spiritual life. Let us take them one by one. (1) The biggest factor affecting us in the external physical World is the light, heat, and perhaps electric or magnetic energy of the sun. The sun is the source of all the light, heat, and energy, and indeed the source and support of all the physical life that we know. It is the biggest factor and yet most remote from us in our solar system. Yet the sources of our inner spiritual life will be greater and more lasting, for they will survive it. The sun as the centre of our solar system also stands as a symbol of the present order of things. The physical forces, as defined in Newton's laws of Matter and Attraction, will also break up with the break-up of the sun.

Is folded up : is folded up, or twisted up, like a sheet or a garment.

5971. (2) Next after the sun, we can derive faint lights from the innumerable stars in the firmament. For all the ages of which we have any record, these stars have remained fixed. Nothing can be more fixed ; yet they can and will fail.

5972. *Cf.* lxxviii. 20. (3) On our own earth the mountains—the " eternal hills "—seem the most striking examples of stability ; yet they will be swept away like a mirage, as if they had never existed.

5973. (4) The type of Arab property, as well as the type of the Arab pet, was the camel, and the most precious camel was the she-camel just about to be delivered of her young. She would in normal times be most sedulously cared for. But when all our landmarks of this life vanish, even she would be left untended. Nothing would then be as it is now.

(In human habitations);[5974]

6. When the oceans[5975]
Boil over with a swell;

٦- وَإِذَا الْبِحَارُ سُجِّرَتْ ۝

7. When the souls
Are sorted out,[5976]
(Being joined, like with like);

٧- وَإِذَا النُّفُوسُ زُوِّجَتْ ۝

8. When the female (infant),
Buried alive, is questioned—

٨- وَإِذَا الْمَوْءُدَةُ سُئِلَتْ ۝

9. For what crime
She was killed;[5977]

٩- بِأَيِّ ذَنْبٍ قُتِلَتْ ۝

10. When the Scrolls
Are laid open;[5978]

١٠- وَإِذَا الصُّحُفُ نُشِرَتْ ۝

5974. (5) In the present world, the wild animals fear each other, and they all fear man and normally keep away from human habitations. But when this order passes away, the lion will lie down with the lamb, and there will be scarcely any differentiation between human habitations and the wilds of the forests.

5975. See lii. 6 and n. 5041. (6) The oceans, which now keep their bounds, will surge and boil over, and overwhelm all landmarks. At present the waters seem to have reached their fixed and normal levels, but the whole equilibrium will then be disturbed. Such will be the complete wreck of this transitory world, at the approach of the dawn of the permanent Reality. But these are physical symbols, relating to the outer nature surrounding the physical nature of man. The remaining six, *viz.*: the 7th to the 12th, describe the ordering of the new spiritual World, from which all present seeming incongruities will be removed.

5976. *Cf.* lvi. 7, where the sorting out into three classes is mentioned, *viz.*: Those Nearest to God, the Companions of the Right Hand, and the Companions of the Left Hand. That was a sort of broad general division. The meaning in this passage is wider. (7) Whereas in this world of probation, good is mixed with evil, knowledge with ignorance, power with arrogance, and so on,—in the new world of Reality, all true values will be restored, and like will consort with like, for it will be a world of perfect Peace, Harmony, and Justice.

5977. (8) In this world of sin and sorrow, much unjust suffering is caused, and innocent lives sacrificed, without a trace being left, by which offenders can be brought to justice. A striking example before the Quraish was female infanticide: *cf.* xvi. 58-59, and n. 2084. The crime was committed in the guise of social plausibility in secret collusion, and no question was asked here But in the spiritual world of Justice, full questions will be asked, and the victim herself—dumb here—will be able to give evidence, for she had committed no crime herself. The proofs will be drawn from the very means used for concealment.

5978. (9) The Scrolls recording the deeds of men, good or bad, will then be laid open before all. *Cf.* l. 17-18, n. 4954; also lxxxii. 11-12. In the present phenomenal world, things may be concealed; but in the spiritual world of absolute Reality, every secret is opened out, good or bad. The whole tale of acts, omissions, motives, imponderable spiritual hurt, neglect, or help will be laid bare.

11. When the World on High[5979]
Is unveiled ;

١١- وَإِذَا السَّمَآءُ كُشِطَتْ ۝

12. When the Blazing Fire[5980]
Is kindled to fierce heat ;

١٢- وَإِذَا الْجَحِيمُ سُعِّرَتْ ۝

13. And when the Garden[5981]
Is brought near ;—[5982]

١٣- وَإِذَا الْجَنَّةُ أُزْلِفَتْ ۝

14. (Then) shall each soul know
What it has put forward.[5983]

١٤- عَلِمَتْ نَفْسٌ مَّآ أَحْضَرَتْ ۝

15. So verily I call[5984]
To witness the Planets—[5985]
That recede,

١٥- فَلَآ أُقْسِمُ بِالْخُنَّسِ ۝

5979. *The World on High* : literally, the Sky, or Heaven as standing for both the Blazing Fire and the Garden, the Home of the Hereafter. (10) The soul's spiritual Sky—the things it held high or sacred—will be stripped of the thin blue that gave rest—and partly illusion—to its spiritual eye in this world of illusions. Just as when an animal is skinned, its real flesh and blood and inner organs become visible, without any outer coating to hold them together, so the inmost state of the spiritual world will then become plain.

5980. (11) Then will burn the inner Hell,—an intense realisation of spiritual anguish, worse than the fiercest fire.

5981. (12) The last of the Metaphors, the Garden of Bliss—the Light of God's Face (xcii. 20)—will come in sight,—not yet attained, but visible, or "brought near". For the scales have fallen from the eyes, and the soul knows itself.

5982. In Eastern literature, especially in religious allegory, there are usually more meanings than one, enfolded in each other. They must be understood, if the reader wishes to get the full sense of the passage. This applies specially to the Qur-ān. The parallel meaning, favoured by the Ṣūfīs, take the first six physical facts (verses 1-6) also as allegorical. (1) As the sun is the centre of the solar system, so our lower self is the centre of our ordinary motives and desires ; the light of that self must be darkened to make room for the Reality. (2) The minor light of the stars is our ordinary human wisdom : this must be dropped before we get spiritual vision. (3) Our worldly ambitions are the mountains, which must vanish similarly. (4) Greed and love of gain are the camels big with young ; that must be left untended. (5) Our passions are the wild animals that must be tamed. (6) The oceans of divine grace must boil over and cover our whole being. All this must occur at any point of time, even to an individual in this life when God's Glory shines on him.

Another interpretation would be to apply it to the Lesser Judgment, when the soul passes out of this physical body , see lxxv. 22, n. 5822 ; lxxviii. 40, n. 5914 ; and lxxix. 14, n. 5926

5983. This is the conclusion. It is only on such conditions that the soul reaches its full realisation. *Put forward* : *cf.* "the Deeds which his hands have sent forth" in lxxviii. 40.

5984. *Cf.* lvi. 75, n 5258, for the witness that the heavenly bodies bear symbolically to the power, beauty, and goodness of God, in sending His Revelation. See n. 5798 to lxxiv. 32, for the significance of an adjuration in the Qur-ān.

5985. The appeal here is made to three things, the Planets, the Night, and the Dawn. (1) The Planets have a retrograde and a forward motion, and, during occultation, hide or disappear behind the sun or moon, or are otherwise invisible or appear stationary. They behave differently from the millions of stars around them. Yet they are not mere erratic bodies, but obey definite laws, and evidence the power and wisdom of God.

16. Go straight, or hide;

١٦- الْجَوَارِ الْكُنَّسِ ۝

17. And the Night
As it dissipates;[5986]

١٧- وَالَّيْلِ إِذَا عَسْعَسَ ۝

18. And the Dawn
As it breathes away
The darkness;—[5987]

١٨- وَالصُّبْحِ إِذَا تَنَفَّسَ ۝

19. Verily this is the word
Of a most honourable Messenger,[5988]

١٩- إِنَّهُ لَقَوْلُ رَسُولٍ كَرِيمٍ ۝

20. Endued with Power,
With rank before
The Lord of the Throne,[5989]

٢٠- ذِي قُوَّةٍ
عِندَ ذِي الْعَرْشِ مَكِينٍ ۝

21. With authority there,
(And) faithful to his trust.

٢١- مُطَاعٍ ثَمَّ أَمِينٍ ۝

22. And (O people!)
Your Companion is not
One possessed;[5990]

٢٢- وَمَا صَاحِبُكُم بِمَجْنُونٍ ۝

5986. How the Night gradually declines after its height at midnight! It seems gradually to steal away, and as Dawn approaches, to merge into Day. So a soul in spiritual darkness gradually awakes to its spiritual Dawn through Revelation.

5987. The slow "breathing out" of the darkness by the Dawn, shows us, by beautiful imagery, that these mysterious operations, of which people in their ignorance are frightened if they have to do with darkness, are really beneficent operations of God. They have nothing to do with evil spirits, or witches, or magic. For three questions were actually raised about the holy Prophet's Ministry by the ignorant. (1) Did his wonderful works come from himself and not from God? (2) Was he possessed of an evil spirit? In other words, was he mad? For that was the theory of madness then current. (3) Was he a soothsayer, or necromancer, or magician? For he had virtues, powers, and eloquence, so extraordinary that they could not understand him.

5988. They are told here that all their three theories were foolish. The Revelation was really from God. Their wonder should cease if they observe the daily miracles worked round them in nature. The bringer of God's Message was the angel Gabriel, and not an evil spirit.

5989. Not only was the bringer of the Revelation, Gabriel, an honourable Messenger, incapable of deceit, but he had, in the angelic kingdom, rank and authority before God's Throne, and he could convey an authoritative divine Message. He was, like the holy Apostle, faithful to his trust; and therefore there could be no question of the Message being delivered in any other way than exactly according to the divine Will and Purpose. These epithets could apply to the Prophet himself, but in view of verse 23 below, it is best to understand them of Gabriel.

5990. After describing the credentials of the Archangel Gabriel, the Text now appeals to the people to consider their own "Companion", the Prophet, who had been born among them and had lived with them, and was known to be an honourable, truthful, and trustworthy man. If Gabriel was the one who brought the Message to him, then there was no question of demoniacal possessoin. And the Prophet had seen him in his inspired vision "in the clear horizon".

23. And without doubt he saw him In the clear horizon.[5991]	٢٣- وَلَقَدْ رَاٰهُ بِالْاُفُقِ الْمُبِيْنِ ۝
24. Neither doth he withhold Grudgingly a knowledge Of the Unseen.[5992]	٢٤- وَمَا هُوَ عَلَى الْغَيْبِ بِضَنِيْنٍ ۝
25. Nor is it the word Of an evil spirit accursed.[5993]	٢٥- وَمَا هُوَ بِقَوْلِ شَيْطٰنٍ رَّجِيْمٍ ۝
26. Then whither go ye?[5994]	٢٦- فَاَيْنَ تَذْهَبُوْنَ ۝
27. Verily this is no less Than a Message To (all) the Worlds:[5995]	٢٧- اِنْ هُوَ اِلَّا ذِكْرٌ لِّلْعٰلَمِيْنَ ۝
28. (With profit) to whoever Among you wills To go straight:[5996]	٢٨- لِمَنْ شَآءَ مِنْكُمْ اَنْ يَّسْتَقِيْمَ ۝
29. But ye shall not will Except as God wills,— The Cherisher of the Worlds.	٢٩- وَمَا تَشَآءُوْنَ اِلَّآ اَنْ يَّشَآءَ اللّٰهُ رَبُّ الْعٰلَمِيْنَ ۝ ع

5991. Read along with this the whole passage in liii. 1-18 and notes there; specially n. 5092, where the two occasions are mentioned when there was a vision of inspiration: "For truly did he see, of the Signs of his Lord, the Greatest" (liii 18).

5992. Such would be the words of a soothsayer, guarded, ambiguous, and misleading. Here everything was clear, sane, true, and under divine inspiration.

5993. Such as evil suggestions of envy, spite, greed, selfishness, or other vices. On the contrary the teaching of the Qur-ān is beneficent, pointing to the Right Way, the Way of God. *Rajīm*: literally, driven away with stones, rejected with complete ignominy. *Cf.* xv. 17. The rite of throwing stones in the valley of Minā at the close of the Meccan Pilgrimage [see n. 217 (6) to ii. 197] suggests symbolically that the Pilgrim emphatically, definitely, and finally rejects all Evil.

5994. It has been shown that this is no word of a mortal, but that it is full of divine wisdom; that its teaching is not that of a madman, but sane to the core and in accordance with human needs; that it freely and clearly directs you to the right Path and forbids you the Path of evil. Why then hesitate? Accept the divine Grace; repent of your sins; and come to the higher Life.

5995. It is not meant for one class or race; it is universal, and is addressed to all the Worlds. For the meaning of "Worlds", see n. 20 to i. 2.

5996 *Cf.* lxxiv. 55-56. God is the Cherisher of the Worlds, Lord of Grace and Mercy, and His guidance is open to all who have the will to profit by it. But that will must be exercised in conformity with God's Will (verse 29). Such conformity is Islam. Verse 28 points to human free-will and responsibility; verse 29 to its limitations. Both extremes, *viz.*: cast-iron Determinism and an idea of Chaotic Free-will, are condemned.

INTRODUCTION AND SUMMARY: SŪRA LXXXII (*Infiṭār*).

In subject-matter this Sūra is cognate to the last, though the best authorities consider it a good deal later in chronology in the early Meccan Period.

Its argument is subject to the threefold interpretation mentioned in n. 5982 to lxxxi. 13, *viz.*, as referring (1) to the final Day of Judgment, (2) to the Lesser Judgment, on an individual's death, and (3) to the awakening of the Inner Light in the soul at any time, that being considered as Death to the Falsities of this life and a Re-birth to the true spiritual Reality.

C. 262.—(lxxxii. 1-19.)
How fixed is the order holding together
This material universe above and below us?
Yet it must give way before the vast
Unfathomed Truth in which man will see
His past and his future in true perspective.
To God he owes his life and all
Its blessings: will he not see
That the Future depends on Right and Justice?
Righteousness must come to its own,
And so must Discord and Rebellion.
The Day must come when Discord
Must finally cease, and the Peace of God
And His Command are all-in-all.

Sūra LXXXII.

Infiṭār, or The Cleaving Asunder.

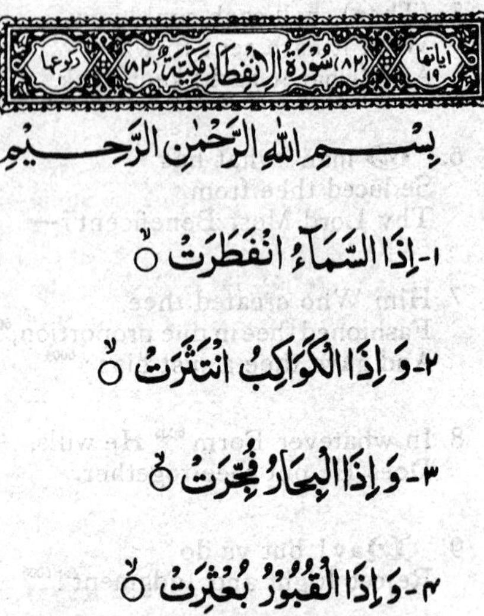

In the name of God, Most Gracious, Most Merciful.

بِسْمِ اللّٰهِ الرَّحْمٰنِ الرَّحِيْمِ

1. When [5997] the Sky
Is cleft asunder ; [5998]

١- إِذَا السَّمَآءُ انْفَطَرَتْ ۙ

2. When the Stars
Are scattered ; [5999]

٢- وَإِذَا الْكَوَاكِبُ انْتَثَرَتْ ۙ

3. When the Oceans
Are suffered to burst forth ; [6000]

٣- وَإِذَا الْبِحَارُ فُجِّرَتْ ۙ

4. And when the Graves
Are turned upside down ;— [6001]

٤- وَإِذَا الْقُبُوْرُ بُعْثِرَتْ ۙ

5997. *Cf.* the passage lxxxi. 1-14 and notes. For the three parallel interpretations, see the Introduction to this Sūra. There are four conditional clauses here, and the substantive clause is in verse 5. In S. lxxxi, there were 12 conditional clauses, and the conclusion was similar, but not expressed in precisely the same terms. See lxxxii. 5, n. 6002 below. The literal interpretation would be that the physical world as we see it now will be destroyed before the final Day of Judgment, establishing the true spiritual Reality. If the four clauses are interpreted metaphorically (see notes 5998-6001), we have a reference to the Lesser Judgment, the individual dawn of the true Reality at Death. If we interpret by the Ṣūfī method, the spiritual crisis may occur to any soul at any moment when these metaphorical events occur.

5998. *Cf.* lxxiii. 18, n. 5769. In the literal meaning, the beautiful blue sky overhead, which we take for granted in sunshine and storm, will be shattered to pieces before the new Spiritual World is established. Metaphorically, the partition which seems at present to divide things divine from this phenomenal world has to be shattered before each soul knows the inner Reality about itself.

5999. *Cf.* lxxxi. 2, where the word for "stars" (*Nujūm*) is different, and the verb is different. *Najm* has reference to brightness, and the verb "losing their lustre" was appropriate there, to show the opposite. *Kaukab* (used here) has more the meaning of a star as fixed in a constellation ; and the opposite of a fixed and definite order is "scattered", the verb used here. In fact, throughout this passage, the dominating idea is the disturbance of order and symmetry. The metaphor behind the scattering of the constellations is that in the present order of things we see many things associated together, *e.g.* rank with honour, wealth with comfort, etc. In the new Spiritual World this will be seen to have been merely fortuitous.

6000. *Cf.* lxxxi. 6, "when the oceans boil over with a swell". Here, "are suffered to burst forth" expresses the end of the present order of things. This may be in two ways, interpreted literally : (1) The barrier which keeps within their respective bounds the various streams of salt and fresh water (lv. 20, n. 5185) will be removed ; (2) the Ocean will overwhelm the whole Globe. Figuratively, the different streams of knowledge, great and small, will be levelled down : for only one Knowledge, the Light Divine, will hold the field.

6001. This item is not mentioned in lxxxi. 1-14. Here it is introduced to show that the whole order of things will be so reversed that even Death will not be Death. We think there is tranquillity in Death ; but there will be no tranquillity. Literally, and figuratively, Death will be the beginning of a new Life. What we think to be Death will bring forth Life.

5. (Then) shall each soul know
What it hath sent forward [6002]
And (what it hath) kept back.

٥- عَلِمَتْ نَفْسٌ مَّا قَدَّمَتْ
وَأَخَّرَتْ ۞

6. O man! what has
Seduced thee from
Thy Lord Most Beneficent?—

٦- يَٰٓأَيُّهَا ٱلْإِنسَٰنُ
مَا غَرَّكَ بِرَبِّكَ ٱلْكَرِيمِ ۞

7. Him Who created thee.
Fashioned thee in due proportion, [6003]
And gave thee a just bias; [6004]

٧- ٱلَّذِى خَلَقَكَ
فَسَوَّىٰكَ فَعَدَلَكَ ۞

8. In whatever Form [6005] He wills,
Does He put thee together.

٨- فِىٓ أَىِّ صُورَةٍ مَّا شَآءَ رَكَّبَكَ ۞

9. Nay! but ye do
Reject Right and Judgment! [6006]

٩- كَلَّا بَلْ تُكَذِّبُونَ بِٱلدِّينِ ۞

10. But verily over you
(Are appointed angels) [6007]
To protect you,—

١٠- وَإِنَّ عَلَيْكُمْ لَحَٰفِظِينَ ۞

11. Kind and honourable,—
Writing down (your deeds):

١١- كِرَامًا كَٰتِبِينَ ۞

6002. *Sent Forward* and *kept back*: may mean: the deeds of commission and omission in this life. Or the Arabic words may also be translated: *sent forward* and *left behind*; *i.e.*, the spiritual possibilities which it sent forward for its other life, and the physical things on which it prided itself in this life, but which it had to leave behind in this life. Or else, the things it put first and the things it put last in importance may change places in the new world of Reality. "The first shall be last and the last shall be first".

6003. *Cf.* xv. 29. God not only created man, but fashioned him in due proportions, giving him extraordinary capacities, and the means wherewith he can fulfil his high destiny.

6004. See n. 834 to vi. 1. Having given a limited free-will, He gave us a just bias through our reason and our spiritual faculties. If we err, it is our will that is at fault.

6005. By "Form" (*Ṣūrat*) here I understand the general shape of things in which any given personality is placed, including his physical and social environments, his gifts of mind and spirit, and all that goes to make up his outer and inner life. The Grace of God is shown in all these things, for His Will is formed from perfect knowledge, wisdom, and goodness.

6006. The goodness and mercies of God, and His constant watchful care of all His creatures should make men grateful, instead of which they turn away from the Right and deny the Day of Sorting Out, the Day when every action performed here will find its fulfilment in just reward or punishment.

6007. Besides the faculties given to man to guide him, and the Form and Personality through which he can rise by stages to the Presence of God, there are spiritual agencies around him to help and protect him, and to note down his Record, so that perfect justice may be done to him at the end. For these Guardian Angels, see *l.* 17-18, and n. 4954. The Record is of course figurative, for man's own good, so that perfect justice may be done. God's own knowledge is perfect, and independent of Records.

12. They know (and understand)
All that ye do.

١٢- يَعْلَمُونَ مَا تَفْعَلُونَ ○

13. As for the Righteous,
They will be in Bliss;

١٣- إِنَّ الْأَبْرَارَ لَفِي نَعِيمٍ ○

14 And the Wicked—
They will be in the Fire,

١٤- وَإِنَّ الْفُجَّارَ لَفِي جَحِيمٍ ○

15. Which they will enter [6008]
On the Day of Judgment,

١٥- يَصْلَوْنَهَا يَوْمَ الدِّينِ ○

16. And they will not be
Able to keep away therefrom.

١٦- وَمَا هُمْ عَنْهَا بِغَائِبِينَ ○

17. And what will explain
To thee what the Day
Of Judgment is?

١٧- وَمَا أَدْرَاكَ مَا يَوْمُ الدِّينِ ○

18. Again, what will explain
To thee what the Day
Of Judgment is? [6009]

١٨- ثُمَّ مَا أَدْرَاكَ مَا يَوْمُ الدِّينِ ○

19. (It will be) the Day
When no soul shall have
Power (to do) aught
For another: [6010]
For the Command, that Day,
Will be (wholly) with God.

١٩- يَوْمَ لَا تَمْلِكُ نَفْسٌ
لِنَفْسٍ شَيْئًا ۖ
وَالْأَمْرُ يَوْمَئِذٍ لِلَّهِ ○

6008. I understand this relative clause to govern "the Fire", *i.e.*, the Punishment. It will be postponed as long as possible, to give the Sinner every chance of repentance and amendment. But once the period of probation is past, it will be irrevocable. There will be no going back from it. By inference, the Righteous may individually reach some stage of Bliss at once, possibly in this life, possibly after death, though the Final Judgment will be the general and complete cessation of this fleeting world and the creation of the world of Eternity.

6009. From our ordinary experiences of this life, we can form no conception of the Final Judgment. We can speak of Rewards and Punishments, the Fruits of Actions, the Resurrection and the Tribunal, the Restoration of True Values, the Elimination of all Wrong, and a hundred other phrases. They might serve to introduce our minds vaguely to a new World, of which they cannot possibly form any adequate conception under present conditions. The question is repeated in verses 17-18 to emphasize this difficulty, and a simple answer is suggested, as explained in the next note.

6010. The answer is suggested by a negative proposition: 'No soul shall have power to do aught for another'. This is full of meaning. Personal responsibility will be fully enforced. In this world we all depend on one another proximately, though our ultimate dependence is always on God, now and for ever. But here a father helps a son forward; husband and wife influence each other's destinies; human laws and institutions may hold large masses of mankind under their grip; falsehood and evil may seem to flourish for a time, because a certain amount of limited free-will has been granted to man. This period will be all over then. The good and the pure will have been separated from the evil and the rebellious; the latter will have been rendered inert, and the former will have been so perfected that their wills will be in complete consonance with God's Universal Will. The Command, thenceforward, will be wholly with God.

INTRODUCTION AND SUMMARY: SŪRA LXXXIII (*Taṭfīf*).

This Sūra is close in time to the last one and the next one.

It condemns all fraud—in daily dealings, as well as and especially in matters of Religion and the higher spiritual Life.

C. 263.—Shun Fraud in all things : in little
(lxxxiii. 1-36.) Things of daily life, but specially
In those subtler forms of higher life,
Which will be exposed to view at Judgment,
However hidden they may be
In this life. Give every one his du
For the Record of ill deeds and good
Is fully kept, and the stains of sin
Corrupt the soul. Reject not the Real
Now, nor mock : for the time will come
When the True will come to its own, and then
The mighty arrogant will be abased !

Sūra LXXXIII.

Taṭfīf, or Dealing in Fraud.

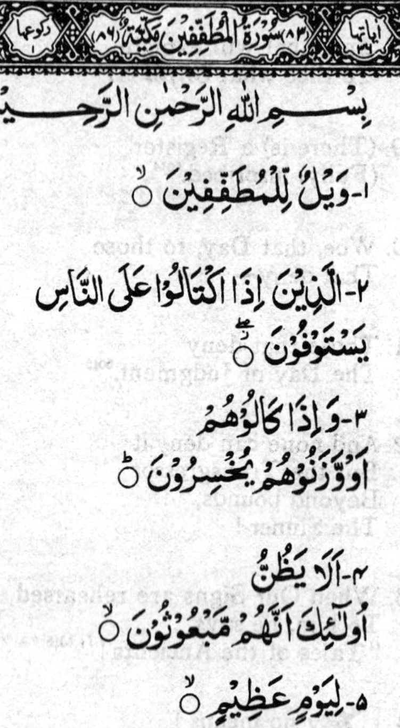

In the name of God, Most Gracious,
Most Merciful.

1. Woe to those
That deal in fraud,—[6011]

2. Those who, when they
Have to receive by measure
From men, exact full measure,

3. But when they have
To give by measure
Or weight to men,
Give less than due.

4. Do they not think
That they will be called
To account?—[6012]

5. On a Mighty Day,

٥-لِيَوْمٍ عَظِيمٍ

6. A Day when (all) mankind
Will stand before
The Lord of the Worlds?

٦-يَوْمَ يَقُومُ النَّاسُ
لِرَبِّ الْعٰلَمِينَ

7. Nay! Surely the Record
Of the Wicked is

٧-كَلَّآ إِنَّ كِتٰبَ الْفُجَّارِ

6011. "Fraud" must here be taken in a widely general sense. It covers giving short measure or short weight, but it covers much more than that. The next two verses make it clear that it is the spirit of injustice that is condemned,—giving too little and asking too much. This may be shown in commercial dealings, where a man exacts a higher standard in his own favour than he is willing to concede as against him. In domestic or social matters an individual or group may ask for honour, or respect, or services which he or they are not willing to give on their side in similar circumstances. It is worse than one-sided selfishness: for it is double injustice. But it is worst of all in religion or spiritual life: with what face can a man ask for Mercy or Love from God when he is unwilling to give it to his fellow-men? In one aspect this is a statement of the Golden Rule, 'Do as you would be done by'. But it is more completely expressed. You must give in full what is due from you, whether you expect or wish to receive full consideration from the other side or not.

6012. Legal and social sanctions against Fraud depend for their efficacy on whether there is a chance of being found out. Moral and religious sanctions are of a different kind. 'Do you wish to degrade your own nature?' 'Do you not consider that there is a Day of Account before a Judge Who knows all, and Who safeguards all interests, for He is the Lord and Cherisher of the Worlds? Whether other people know anything about your wrong or not, you are guilty before God'

(Preserved) in *Sijjīn*.[6013]

لَفِي سِجِّينٍ ۝

8. And what will explain
To thee what *Sijjīn* is?

٨- وَمَآ أَدْرٰىكَ مَا سِجِّينٌ ۝

9. (There is) a Register
(Fully) inscribed.[6014]

٩- كِتٰبٌ مَّرْقُومٌ ۝

10. Woe, that Day, to those
That deny—

١٠- وَيْلٌ يَّوْمَئِذٍ لِّلْمُكَذِّبِينَ ۝

11. Those that deny
The Day of Judgment.[6015]

١١- الَّذِينَ يُكَذِّبُونَ بِيَوْمِ الدِّينِ ۝

12. And none can deny it
But the Transgressor
Beyond bounds,
The Sinner!

١٢- وَمَا يُكَذِّبُ بِهٖٓ إِلَّا
كُلُّ مُعْتَدٍ أَثِيمٍ ۝

13. When Our Signs are rehearsed
To him, he says,
"Tales of the Ancients!"[6016]

١٣- إِذَا تُتْلٰى عَلَيْهِ اٰيٰتُنَا
قَالَ أَسَاطِيرُ الْأَوَّلِينَ ۝

14. By no means!
But on their hearts
Is the stain of the (ill)
Which they do![6017]

١٤- كَلَّا بَلْ ۜ
رَانَ عَلٰى قُلُوبِهِمْ مَّا كَانُوا يَكْسِبُونَ ۝

6013. This is a word from the same root as *Sijn*, a Prison. It rhymes with and is contrasted with *'Illīyīn* in verse 18 below. It is therefore understood by many Commentators to be a place, a Prison or a Dungeon in which the Wicked are confined pending their appearance before the Judgment-Seat. The mention of the Inscribed Register in verse 9 below may imply that *Sijjīn* is the name of the Register of Black Deeds, though verse 9 may be elliptical and may only describe the place by the significance of its contents.

6014. If we take *Sijjīn* to be the Register itself, and not the place where it is kept, the Register itself is a sort of Prison for those who do wrong. It is inscribed fully: *i.e.* no one is omitted who ought to be there, and for every entry there is a complete record, so that there is no escape for the sinner. Of course we must not understand a material Register, made up of paper or parchment and written with pen and ink. The whole description is figurative of the inescapable record which sin creates: every detail, of motive, manner, occasion, etc., contributes to the deterioration of the sinner.

6015. The fact of Personal Responsibility for each soul is so undoubted that people who deny it are to be pitied, and will indeed be in a most pitiable condition on the Day of Reckoning, and none but the most abandoned sinner can deny it, and he only denies it by playing with Falsehoods.

6016. *Cf.* vi. 25; lxviii. 15; etc. They scorn Truth and pretend that it is Falsehood.

6017. The heart of man, as created by God, is pure and unsullied. Every time that a man does an ill deed, it marks a stain or rust on his heart. But on repentance and forgiveness, such stain is washed off. If there is no repentance and forgiveness, the stains deepen and spread more and more, until the heart is sealed (ii. 7), and eventually the man dies a spiritual death. It is such stains that stand in the way of his perceiving Truths which are obvious to others. That is why he mocks at Truth and hugs Falsehood to his bosom.

31. And when they returned To their own people, They would return jesting;	٣١- وَإِذَا انْقَلَبُوٓا إِلَىٰٓ أَهْلِهِمُ انْقَلَبُوا فَكِهِينَ ۝
32. And whenever they saw them, They would say, "Behold! These are the people Truly astray!"[6027]	٣٢- وَإِذَا رَأَوْهُمْ قَالُوٓا إِنَّ هَٰٓؤُلَآءِ لَضَآلُّونَ ۝
33. But they had not been Sent as Keepers over them![6028]	٣٣- وَمَآ أُرْسِلُوا عَلَيْهِمْ حَٰفِظِينَ ۝
34. But on this Day The Believers will laugh At the Unbelievers:[6029]	٣٤- فَالْيَوْمَ الَّذِينَ ءَامَنُوا مِنَ الْكُفَّارِ يَضْحَكُونَ ۝
35. On Thrones (of Dignity) They will command (a sight) (Of all things).[6030]	٣٥- عَلَى الْأَرَآئِكِ يَنظُرُونَ ۝
36. Will not the Unbelievers Have been paid back For what they did?	٣٦- هَلْ ثُوِّبَ الْكُفَّارُ مَا كَانُوا يَفْعَلُونَ ۝ ع

6027. The wicked laugh at the righteous in this world in many ways: (1) They inwardly laugh at their Faith, because they feel themselves so superior. (2) In public places, when the righteous pass, they wink at each other and insult them. (3) In their own houses they run them down. (4) Whenever and wherever they see them, they reproach them with being fools who have lost their way, when the boot is really on the other leg. In the Hereafter all these tricks and falsehoods will be shown for what they are, and the tables will be reversed.

6028. But the wicked critics of the Righteous have no call in any case to sit in judgment over them. Who set them as Keepers or guardians over the Righteous? Let them look to their own condition and future first.

6029. The tables will then be reversed, and he laughs best who laughs last.

6030. A repetition of verse 23 above, but with a different shade of meaning. The Righteous on their Thrones of Dignity will be able to see all the true values restored in their own favour: but they will also see something else: they will also see the arrogant braggarts brought low, who brought about their own downfall by their own actions.

INTRODUCTION AND SUMMARY: SŪRA LXXXIV (*Inshiqāq*).

Chronologically this Sūra is closely connected with the last one. In subject-matter it resembles more S. lxxxii. and lxxxi., with which it may be compared.

By a number of mystic metaphors it is shown that the present phenomenal order will not last, and God's full Judgment will certainly be established: man should therefore strive for that World of Eternity and True Values.

C. 264.—All mysteries, fair or shrouded in gloom,
(lxxxiv. 1-25.) Will vanish when the full Reality
Stands revealed. If this Life is but Painful
Toil, there's the Hope of the Meeting with the Lord!
That will be Bliss indeed for the Righteous,
But woe to the arrogant dealers in sin!
Like the sunset Glow or the shades of Night,
Or the Moon's ever-changing light, man's life
Never rests here below, but travels ever onwards
Stage by stage. Grasp then God's Message
And reach the Heights, to reap a Reward
That will never fail through all eternity!

Sūra LXXXIV.

Inshiqāq, or The Rending Asunder.

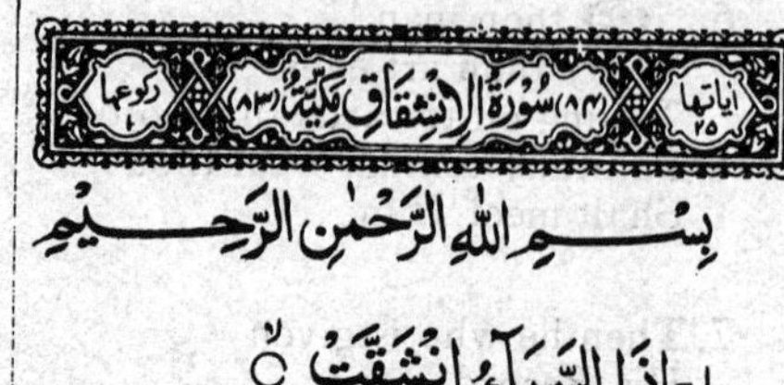

*In the name of God, Most Gracious,
Most Merciful.*

1. When the Sky is
Rent asunder,[6031]

١- إِذَا السَّمَآءُ انشَقَّتْ ۝

2. And hearkens to[6032]
(The Command of) its Lord,–
And it must needs
(Do so);—

٢- وَأَذِنَتْ لِرَبِّهَا
وَحُقَّتْ ۝

3. And when the Earth
Is flattened out,[6033]

٣- وَإِذَا الْأَرْضُ مُدَّتْ ۝

4. And casts forth
What is within it
And becomes (clean) empty,

٤- وَأَلْقَتْ مَا فِيهَا
وَتَخَلَّتْ ۝

5. And hearkens to[6034]
(The Command of) its Lord,—
And it must needs
(Do so);—(then will come
Home the full Reality).[6035]

٥- وَأَذِنَتْ لِرَبِّهَا
وَحُقَّتْ ۝

6031. The passing away of this world of sense to make way for a new World of Reality is here indicated by two Facts, which are themselves Symbols for a complete revolution in our whole knowledge and experience. At the beginning of S. lxxxii. and S. lxxxi, other Symbols were used, to lead up to the arguments there advanced. Here the two Symbols are: (1) the Sky being rent asunder and giving up its secrets, and (2) the Earth being flattened out from the globe it is, and giving up its secrets. See the following notes.

6032. We may think that the heavens we see above us,—high and sacred, seemingly vast and limitless, eternal and timeless—are not created matter. But they are. And they remain just so long as God wills it so, and not a moment longer. As soon as His Command issues for their dissolution, they will obey and vanish, and all their mystery will be emptied out. And it must necessarily be so; their very nature as created beings requires that they must hearken to the voice of their Creator, even to the extent of their own extinction.

6033. The Earth is a globe, enclosing within it many secrets and mysteries—gold and diamonds in its mines, heat and magnetic forces in its entrails, and the bodies of countless generations of men buried within its soil. At its dissolution all these contents will be disgorged: it will lose its shape as a globe, and cease to exist.

A more mystic meaning lies behind the ordinary meaning of the vanishing of the heavens and the earth as we see them. Our ideas of them—their subjective contents with reference to ourselves will also lose all shape and form and vanish before the eternal verities.

6034. See n. 6032. We think the earth so solid and real. All our perishable things dissolve into the earth. But the earth itself will dissolve into a truer Reality.

6035. The substantive clause, to follow the two conditional clauses preceding, may be filled up from the suggestion contained in lxxxii, 5.

6. O thou man!
Verily thou art ever
Toiling on towards thy Lord—[6036]
Painfully toiling,—but thou
Shalt meet Him.

٦- يَآيُّهَا الْإِنْسَانُ إِنَّكَ كَادِحٌ إِلَىٰ رَبِّكَ كَدْحًا فَمُلَٰقِيهِ ○

7. Then he who is given
His Record in his
Right hand,[6037]

٧- فَأَمَّا مَنْ أُوتِيَ كِتَٰبَهُۥ بِيَمِينِهِۦ ○

8. Soon will his account
Be taken by an easy reckoning,

٨- فَسَوْفَ يُحَاسَبُ حِسَابًا يَسِيرًا ○

9. And he will turn
To his people,[6038] rejoicing!

٩- وَيَنْقَلِبُ إِلَىٰٓ أَهْلِهِۦ مَسْرُورًا ○

10. But he who is given
His Record behind his back,—[6039]

١٠- وَأَمَّا مَنْ أُوتِيَ كِتَٰبَهُۥ وَرَآءَ ظَهْرِهِۦ ○

11. Soon will he cry
For Perdition,[6040]

١١- فَسَوْفَ يَدْعُوا ثُبُورًا ○

12. And he will enter
A Blazing Fire.

١٢- وَيَصْلَىٰ سَعِيرًا ○

13. Truly, did he go about
Among his people, rejoicing![6041]

١٣- إِنَّهُۥ كَانَ فِيٓ أَهْلِهِۦ مَسْرُورًا ○

6036. This life is ever full of toil and misery, if looked at as empty of the Eternal Hope which Revelation gives us. Hence the literature of pessimism in poetry and philosophy, which thinking minds have poured forth in all ages, when that Hope was obscured to them. "Our sweetest songs are those that tell of saddest thought." "To each his suffering; all are men condemned alike to groan!" It is the noblest men that have to "scorn delights and live laborious days" in this life. The good suffer on account of their very goodness: the evil on account of their Evil. But the balance will be set right in the end. Those that wept shall be made to rejoice, and those that went about thoughtlessly rejoicing, shall be made to weep for their folly. They will all go to their account with God and meet Him before His Throne of Judgment

6037. *Right Hand: Cf.* xvii. 71. These will be the fortunate ones, who spent their lives in goodness and truth: for them the account will be made easy; for even after the balancing, they will receive more than their merits deserve, on account of the infinite grace and mercy of God.

6038. *His people:* should be understood in a large sense, including all righteous persons of his category, (including of course all those nearest and dearest to him), who are spiritually of his family, whether before him or after him in time.

6039. In lxix. 24, the wicked are given their Record in their left hand. But their hands will not be free. Sin will have tied their hands behind their back: and thus they can only receive their Records in their left hand, behind their back.

6040. The wicked will cry for death and annihilation: but they will neither live nor die: xx. 74.

6041. The tables are now turned. His self-complacence and self-conceit in his lower life will now give place to weeping and gnashing of teeth! *Cf.* n. 6036 above.

14. Truly, did he think
That he would not
Have to return (to Us)! [6042]

15. Nay, nay! for his Lord
Was (ever) watchful of him!

16. So I do call [6043]
To witness the ruddy glow
Of Sunset; [6044]

17. The Night and its Homing; [6045]

18. And the Moon
In her Fulness: [6046]

19. Ye shall surely travel
From stage to stage. [6047]

١٤- إِنَّهُۥ ظَنَّ أَن لَّن يَحُورَ ۝

١٥- بَلَىٰٓ إِنَّ رَبَّهُۥ كَانَ بِهِۦ بَصِيرًا ۝

١٦- فَلَآ أُقْسِمُ بِالشَّفَقِ ۝

١٧- وَالَّيْلِ وَمَا وَسَقَ ۝

١٨- وَالْقَمَرِ إِذَا اتَّسَقَ ۝

١٩- لَتَرْكَبُنَّ طَبَقًا عَن طَبَقٍ ۝

6042. Most of the Evil in this world is due to the false idea that man is irresponsible, or to a mad and thoughtless indulgence of Self. Man is not irresponsible. He is responsible for every deed, word, and thought of his, to his Maker, to Whom he has to return, to give an account of himself. To remember this and act accordingly is to achieve salvation; to forget or flout that responsibility is to get into the Fire of self-deception and misery.

6043. The same form of adjuration as in lxix. 37. The substantive statement is in verse 19 below: "Ye shall surely travel from stage to stage". Nothing in this life is fixed, or will last. Three things are mentioned which on the one hand have remained from age to age for as far back as the memory of man can go, and yet each of them is but a short phase, gone as it were in the twinkling of an eye. See the following notes. So our life here is but a fleeting show. Its completion is to be looked for elsewhere.

6044. (1) The sun seems such a great reality that people worshipped him as a divinity. The beautiful glow it leaves when it sets is but momentary: it changes every moment and vanishes with the twilight

6045. (2) The Night is a phenomenon you see during almost half every twenty-four hours in ordinary latitudes. At nightfall, all the wandering flocks and herds come home. The men scattered abroad for their livelihood return home to rest and sleep. The Night collects them in their homes, and yet this phase of Homing lasts but a little while Presently all is silent and still. So will it be with our souls when this life is ended with our death. We shall be collected in a newer and larger Homing.

6046. (3) The astronomical Full Moon does not last a moment. The moment the moon is full, she begins to decline, and the moment she is in her "inter-lunar swoon", she begins her career anew as a growing New Moon. So is man's life here below. It is not fixed or permanent, either in its physical phases, or even more strikingly, in its finer phases, intellectual, emotional, or spiritual.

6047. Man travels and ascends stage by stage. In lxvii. 3 the same word in the form *ṭibāqan* was used of the heavens, as if they were in layers one above another. Man's spiritual life may similarly be compared to an ascent from one heaven to another.

20. What then is the matter
With them, that they
Believe not ?—[6048]

٢٠- فَمَا لَهُمْ لَا يُؤْمِنُونَ ۝

21. And when the Qur-ān
Is read to them, they
Fall not prostrate,[6049]

٢١- وَإِذَا قُرِئَ عَلَيْهِمُ الْقُرْآنُ لَا يَسْجُدُونَ ۝

22. But on the contrary
The Unbelievers reject (it).

٢٢- بَلِ الَّذِينَ كَفَرُوا يُكَذِّبُونَ ۝

23. But God has full Knowledge
Of what they secrete
(In their breasts).

٢٣- وَاللَّهُ أَعْلَمُ بِمَا يُوعُونَ ۝

24. So announce to them
A Penalty Grievous,

٢٤- فَبَشِّرْهُم بِعَذَابٍ أَلِيمٍ ۝

25. Except to those who believe
And work righteous deeds :
For them is a Reward
That will never fail.[6050]

٢٥- إِلَّا الَّذِينَ آمَنُوا وَعَمِلُوا الصَّالِحَاتِ لَهُمْ أَجْرٌ غَيْرُ مَمْنُونٍ ۝

6048. Considering man's high destiny, and the fact that this life is but a stage or a sojourn for him, it might be expected that he would eagerly embrace every opportunity of welcoming God's Revelation and ascending by Faith to heights of spiritual wisdom. There is something wrong with his will if he does not do so. Notice the transition from the second person in verse 19, where there is a direct appeal to God's votaries, to the third person in verses 20-21, where men who are rebels against God's Kingdom are spoken of as if they were aliens.

6049. *Prostrate* : out of eespect and humble gratitude to God.

6050. *Cf.* xli. 8.

INTRODUCTION AND SUMMARY : SŪRA LXXXV (*Burūj*).

This is one of the earlier Meccan Sūras, chronologically cognate with S. xci. The subject-matter is the persecution of God's votaries. God watches over His own, and will deal with the enemies of Truth as He dealt with them in the past.

C. 265.—Woe to those who persecute Truth !
(lxxxv. 1-22.) They are being watched by mighty Eyes ;
They will have to answer when the Judgment comes ;
And a clear Record will witness against them.
Are they cruel to men because of their Faith ?
The Fire they use will be turned against them.
For God is strong, and will subdue
The mightiest foes. Be warned, and learn
From His gracious Message, preserved through all Time !

Sūra LXXXV.

Burūj, or The Zodiacal Signs.

In the name of God, Most Gracious, Most Merciful.

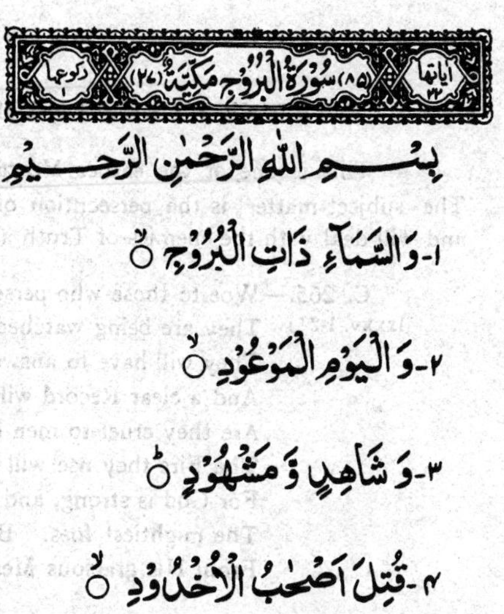

1. By the Sky, (displaying)[6051]
The Zodiacal Signs;[6052]

2. By the promised Day
(Of Judgment);[6053]

3. By one that witnesses,
And the subject of the witness;—[6054]

4. Woe to the makers
Of the pit (of fire),[6055]

6051. Here is an appeal to three mystic symbols in verses 1-3, and the substantive proposition is in verses 4-8, a denunciation of wicked persecutors of the votaries of God, persecutors who burnt righteous men at the stake for their Faith. The three mystic Symbols are: (1) the Glorious Sky, with the broad belt of the Constellations marking the twelve Signs of the Zodiac; (2) the Day of Judgment, when all evil will be punished; and (3) certain Persons that will be witnesses, and certain Persons or things that will be the subjects of the witness. See the notes following.

6052. See n. 1950 to xv. 16. The Stars of the Zodiac as well as of other Constellations are like the eyes of the Night. It may be that crimes are committed in the darkness of the night (literally or metaphorically). But countless eyes (metaphorically) are watching all the time, and every author of evil will be brought to book.

6053. The Day of Judgment, when the Sinner will have to give an account of every deed, open or hidden, is not merely a matter of speculation. It is definitely promised in revelation, and will inevitably come to pass. Woe then to the Sinners for their crimes.

6054. The literal meaning is clear, but its metaphorical application has been explained in a variety of ways by different Commentators. The words are fairly comprehensive, and should, I think, be understood in connection with Judgment. There the Witnesses may be: (1) the Prophets (iii. 81); God Himself (iii. 81, and x. 61); the Recording Angels (*l*. 21); the Sinner's own misused limbs (xxiv. 24); his record of deeds (xvii. 14); or the Sinner himself (xvii. 14). The subject of the witness may be the deed or crime, or the Sinner against whom the testimony cries out. The appeal to these things means that the Sinner cannot possibly escape the consequences of his crime. He should repent, seek God's Mercy, and amend his life.

6055. Who were the makers of the pit of fire in which they burnt people for their Faith? The words are perfectly general, and we need not search for particular names, except by way of illustration. In ancient history, and in Mediæval Europe, many lives were sacrificed at the stake because the victims did not conform to the established religion. In Arab tradition there is the story of Abraham: Nimrūd tries to burn him to death, but on account of Abraham's Faith, the fire became "a means of safety for Abraham": xxi. 69, and n. 2725. Another case cited is that of Ẕu-Nuwās, the last Ḥimyarite King of Yemen, by religion a Jew, who persecuted the Christians of Najrān and is said to have burnt them at the stake. He seems to have lived in the latter half of the sixth Christian century, in the generation immediately preceding the Prophet's birth in 570 A.D. While the words are perfectly general, a reference is suggested to the persecution to which the early Muslims were subjected by the Pagan Quraish. Among other cruelties, they were stripped, and their skins were exposed to the burning rays of the Arabian summer sun.

5. Fire supplied (abundantly)
With Fuel:

٥- النَّارِ ذَاتِ الْوَقُودِ ۝

6. Behold! they sat[6056]
Over against the (fire),

٦- إِذْ هُمْ عَلَيْهَا قُعُودٌ ۝

7. And they witnessed
(All) that they were doing
Against the Believers.

٧- وَهُمْ عَلَىٰ مَا يَفْعَلُونَ بِالْمُؤْمِنِينَ شُهُودٌ ۝

8. And they ill-treated them
For no other reason than
That they believed in God,
Exalted in Power,
Worthy of all Praise!—

٨- وَمَا نَقَمُوا مِنْهُمْ إِلَّا أَنْ يُؤْمِنُوا بِاللَّهِ الْعَزِيزِ الْحَمِيدِ ۝

9 Him to Whom belongs
The dominion of the heavens
And the earth!
And God is Witness
To all things.[6057]

٩- الَّذِي لَهُ مُلْكُ السَّمَاوَاتِ وَالْأَرْضِ ۚ وَاللَّهُ عَلَىٰ كُلِّ شَيْءٍ شَهِيدٌ ۝

10. Those who persecute (or draw
into temptation)
The Believers, men and women,
And do not turn
In repentance, will have
The Penalty of Hell:
They will have the Penalty
Of the Burning Fire.[6058]

١٠- إِنَّ الَّذِينَ فَتَنُوا الْمُؤْمِنِينَ وَالْمُؤْمِنَاتِ ثُمَّ لَمْ يَتُوبُوا فَلَهُمْ عَذَابُ جَهَنَّمَ وَلَهُمْ عَذَابُ الْحَرِيقِ ۝

11. For those who believe
And do righteous deeds,
Will be Gardens,[6059]
Beneath which Rivers flow:
That is the great Salvation,
(The fulfilment of all desires),[6060]

١١- إِنَّ الَّذِينَ آمَنُوا وَعَمِلُوا الصَّالِحَاتِ لَهُمْ جَنَّاتٌ تَجْرِي مِنْ تَحْتِهَا الْأَنْهَارُ ۚ ذَٰلِكَ الْفَوْزُ الْكَبِيرُ ۝

6056. The persecutors sat calmly to gloat over the agonies of their victims in the well-fed fire.

6057. It is suggested that the persecutors will richly deserve to be punished in the Fire of Hell. That Punishment will be far more real and lasting than the undeserved cruelty which they inflicted on men for their Faith in the One True God.

6058. If we distinguish the Penalty of Hell from that of the Burning Fire, we should take the latter metaphorically, as the Fire burning in their heart for their sins and ill deeds even in this life, the fire of hatred and greed, the fire of shame and sorrow, even in this life.

6059. The Garden as the type of Felicity is explained in Appendix xii., following S. liv.

6060. *Cf.* v. 122, n. 833.

12. Truly strong is the Grip
(And Power) of thy Lord.

١٢- إِنَّ بَطْشَ رَبِّكَ لَشَدِيدٌ ۝

13. It is He Who creates
From the very beginning,[6061]
And He can restore (life).

١٣- إِنَّهُ هُوَ يُبْدِئُ وَيُعِيدُ ۝

14. And He is the Oft-Forgiving,
Full of loving-kindness,

١٤- وَهُوَ الْغَفُورُ الْوَدُودُ ۝

15. Lord of the Throne of Glory,

١٥- ذُو الْعَرْشِ الْمَجِيدُ ۝

16. Doer (without let)[6062]
Of all that He intends.

١٦- فَعَّالٌ لِّمَا يُرِيدُ ۝

17. Has the story
Reached thee,
Of the Forces—[6063]

١٧- هَلْ أَتَاكَ حَدِيثُ الْجُنُودِ ۝

18. Of Pharaoh
And the Thamūd?

١٨- فِرْعَوْنَ وَثَمُودَ ۝

19. And yet the Unbelievers
(Persist) in rejecting
(The Truth)![6064]

١٩- بَلِ الَّذِينَ كَفَرُوا فِي تَكْذِيبٍ ۝

20. But God doth
Encompass them
From behind![6065]

٢٠- وَاللَّهُ مِن وَرَائِهِم مُّحِيطٌ ۝

6061. For the various words for "Creation" and the ideas implied in them, see n. 120 to ii. 117.

6062. God's Will is itself the Word and the Deed. There is no interval between them. He does not change His mind. No circumstance whatever can come between His Will and the execution thereof. Such are His Power and His Glory. Compare it with that of men, described in the next two verses.

6063. In contrast to the real, all-embracing, and eternal power of God, what are the forces of man at their best? Two examples are mentioned. (1) Pharaoh was a proud monarch of a powerful kingdom, with resources and organisation, material, moral, and intellectual, as good as any in the world. When he pitted himself against God's Prophet, he and his forces were destroyed. See lxxix. 15-26. (2) The Thamūd were great builders, and had a high standard of material civilization. But they defied the law of God and perished. See vii. 73-79, and n. 1043.

6064. In spite of the great examples of the past, by which human might and skill were shown to have availed nothing when the law of God was broken, the unbelievers persist (in all ages) in defying that law. But God will know how to deal with them.

6065. God encompasses every thing. But the wicked will find themselves defeated not only in conditions that they foresee, but from all sorts of unexpected directions, perhaps from behind them, *i.e.*, from the very people or circumstances which in their blindness they despised or thought of as helping them.

21. Nay, this is A Glorious Qur-ān,	٢١- بَلْ هُوَ قُرْاٰنٌ مَّجِيْدٌ ۙ
22. (Inscribed) in A Tablet Preserved![6066]	٢٢- فِىْ لَوْحٍ مَّحْفُوْظٍ ۧ

6066. God's Message is not ephemeral. It is eternal. The "Tablet" is not to be understood in a material sense, made of stone or metal. It is "preserved" or guarded from corruption: xv. 9: for God's Message must endure for ever. That Message is the "Mother of the book": see n. 347 to iii. 7.

INTRODUCTION AND SUMMARY : SŪRA LXXXVI (*Ṭāriq*).

This Sūra also belongs to the early Meccan period, perhaps not far removed from the last Sūra.

Its subject-matter is the protection afforded to every soul in the darkest period of its spiritual history. The physical nature of man may be insignificant, but the soul given to him by God must win a glorious Future in the end.

C. 266.—Through the darkest night comes the penetrating light
(lxxxvi. 1-17.) Of a glorious Star. Such is the power
Of Revelation : it protects and guides the erring.
For what is man ? But a creature of flesh
And bones ! But God by His Power doth raise
Man's state to a Life Beyond !—when lo !
All things hidden will be made plain.
Man's help will then be but the Word
Of God, which none can thwart. So wait
With gentle patience—for His Decision.

Sūra LXXXVI.

سُورَةُ الطَّارِقِ مَكِّيَّةٌ (٨٦)

Ṭariq, or The Night-Visitant.

In the name of God, Most Gracious, Most Merciful.

بِسْمِ اللّٰهِ الرَّحْمٰنِ الرَّحِيْمِ

1. By the Sky[6067]
And the Night-Visitant[6068]
(Therein);—

١- وَالسَّمَآءِ وَالطَّارِقِ ۝

2. And what will explain to thee
What the Night-Visitant is?—

٢- وَمَآ اَدْرٰىكَ مَا الطَّارِقُ ۝

3. (It is) the Star
Of piercing brightness;—

٣- النَّجْمُ الثَّاقِبُ ۝

4. There is no soul but has
A protector over it.[6069]

٤- اِنْ كُلُّ نَفْسٍ لَّمَّا عَلَيْهَا حَافِظٌ ۝

5. Now let man but think
From what he is created!

٥- فَلْيَنْظُرِ الْاِنْسَانُ مِمَّ خُلِقَ ۝

6. He is created from
A drop emitted—[6070]

٦- خُلِقَ مِنْ مَّآءٍ دَافِقٍ ۝

7. Proceeding from between
The backbone and the ribs:[6071]

٧- يَّخْرُجُ مِنْۢ بَيْنِ الصُّلْبِ وَالتَّرَآئِبِ ۝

6067. The appeal here is to a single mystic Symbol, *viz*: the Sky with its Night-Visitant; and the substantive proposition is in verse 4: "There is no soul but has a protector over it". In the last Sūra we considered the persecution of God's votaries, and how God protects them. Here the same theme is presented in another aspect. In the darkest sky shines out most brilliantly the light of the most brilliant star. So in the night of spiritual darkness—whether through ignorance or distress—shines the glorious star of God's Revelation. By the same token the man of Faith and Truth has nothing to fear. God will protect His own.

6068. This is explained in verse 3 below. The "Star of piercing brightness" is understood by some to be the Morning Star, by others to be the planet Saturn, by others again to be Sirius, or the Pleiads or shooting stars. I think it is best to take the "Star" in the collective or generic sense, for stars shine on every night in the year, and their piercing brightness is most noticeable on the darkest night.

6069. If man has a true spiritual understanding, he has nothing to be afraid of. He is protected by God in many ways that he does not even know. He may be an insignificant creature as a mere animal, but his soul raises him to a dignity above other creation. And all sorts of divine forces guard and protect him.

6070. See n 5832 to lxxvi. 2. See also last note.

6071. A man's seed is the quintessence of his body. It is therefore said metaphorically to proceed from his loins, *i.e.*, from his back between the hip-bones and his ribs. His back-bone is the source and symbol of his strength and personality. In the spinal cord and in the brain is the directive energy of the central nervous system, and this directs all action, organic and psychic. The spinal cord is continuous with the Medulla Oblongata in the brain.

8. Surely (God) is able
To bring him back
(To life)![6072]

٨- إِنَّهُ عَلَىٰ رَجْعِهِ لَقَادِرٌ ۝

9. The Day that
(All) things secret
Will be tested,

٩- يَوْمَ تُبْلَى السَّرَآئِرُ ۝

10. (Man) will have
No power,
And no helper.[6073]

١٠- فَمَا لَهُ مِنْ قُوَّةٍ
وَّلَا نَاصِرٍ ۝

11. By the Firmament[6074]
Which returns (in its round),

١١- وَالسَّمَآءِ ذَاتِ الرَّجْعِ ۝

12. And by the Earth
Which opens out[6075]
(For the gushing of springs
Or the sprouting of vegetation),—

١٢- وَالْأَرْضِ
ذَاتِ الصَّدْعِ ۝

13. Behold this is the Word
That distinguishes (Good
From Evil):[6076]

١٣- إِنَّهُ لَقَوْلٌ فَصْلٌ ۝

14. It is not a thing
For amusement.

١٤- وَّمَا هُوَ بِالْهَزْلِ ۝

6072. The Creator who can mingle the forces of psychic and physical muscular action in the creation of man, as explained in the last note, can surely give a new life after physical death here, and restore man's personality in the new world that will open out in the Hereafter.

6073. In that new world, all our actions, motives, thoughts, and imaginings of this life, however secret, will be brought into the open, and tested by the standards of absolute Truth, and not by false standards of custom, prejudice, or partiality. In that severe test, any adventitious advantages of this life will have no strength or force whatever, and cannot help in any way.

6074. The Firmament above is always the same, and yet it performs its diurnal round, smoothly and punctually. So does God's Revelation show forth the Truth, which like a circle is ever true to its centre,—which is ever the same, though it revolves through the changing circumstances of our present life.

6075. The earth seems hard, but springs can gush forth and vegetables sprout through it and make it green and soft. So is Truth: hard perhaps to mortals, but through the fertilising agency of Revelation, it allows our inner personality to sprout and blossom forth.

6076. See the last two notes. Revelation—God's Truth—can pierce through the hardest crusts, and ever lead us back to the centre and goal of our spiritual life: for it separates Good from Evil definitely. It is not mere play or amusement, any more than the Sky or the Earth is. It helps us in the highest issues of our life.

15. As for them,[6077] they
Are but plotting a scheme,

١٥- إِنَّهُمْ يَكِيدُونَ كَيْدًا ۝

16. And I am planning
A scheme.[6078]

١٦- وَأَكِيدُ كَيْدًا ۝

17. Therefore grant a delay
To the unbelievers:
Give respite to them
Gently (for awhile).[6079]

١٧- فَمَهِّلِ الْكَافِرِينَ أَمْهِلْهُمْ رُوَيْدًا ۝ ع

6977. Though God in His Mercy has provided a piercing light to penetrate our spiritual darkness, and made our beings responsive to the growth of spiritual understanding, just as the hard earth is responsive to the sprouting of a seed or the gushing of a stream, yet there are evil, unregenerate men who plot and scheme against the beneficent purpose of God. But their plots will be of no avail, and God's Purpose will prevail. It happened so with the Quraish who wanted to thwart the growth of Islam. It will be so in all ages.

6078. *Makara* is applied both to plotting with an evil purpose and planning with a good purpose. *Cf.* iii. 54, and n. "And the unbelievers plotted and planned, and God too planned, and the best of planners is God."

6079. Gentle forbearance with Evil shows our trust in God and God's Plan: for it can never be frustrated. This does not mean that we should assist or compromise with evil, or fail to put it down where we have the power. It means patience and humility where we have no visible power to prevent Evil.

INTRODUCTION AND SUMMARY : SŪRA LXXXVII (*A'lā*).

This is one of the earliest of the Meccan Sūras, being usually placed eighth in chronological order, and immediately after S. lxxxi.

The argument is that God has made man capable of progress by ordered steps, and by His Revelation will lead him still higher to purification and perfection.

C. 267.—Wonderful are the ways of God
(lxxxvii. 1-19.) In creation, and the love with which
He guides His creatures' destinies,
Gives them the means by which to ṣtrive
For maturity by ordered steps, and reach
The end most fitted for their natures.
His Law is just and easy, and His Grace
Iṣ ever ready to help: let us look
To the Eternal Goal, with hearts and souls
Of Purity, and glorify His name:
For in this changing, fleeting world,
His Word is always true, and will remain,
Through all the ages, ever the same.

Sūra LXXXVII.

A'la, or The Most High.

In the name of God, Most Gracious. Most Merciful.

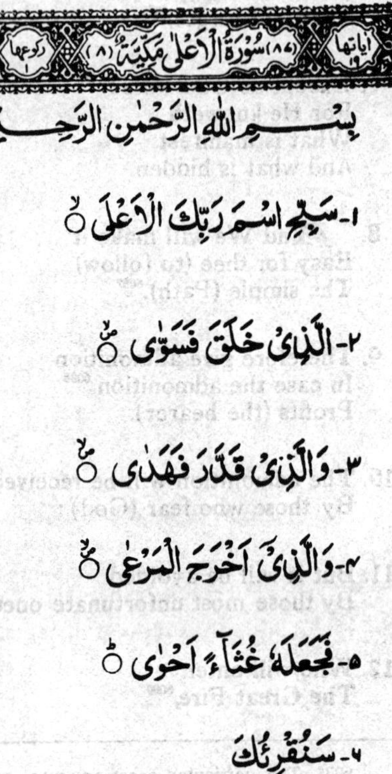

1. Glorify the name
Of thy Guardian-Lord [6080]
Most High,

2. Who hath created,[6081]
And further, given
Order and proportion ;

3. Who hath ordained laws.[6082]
And granted guidance ;

4. And Who bringeth out [6083]
The (green and luscious) pasture,

5. And then doth make it
(But) swarthy stubble.

6. By degrees shall We
Teach thee to declare [6084]

6080. The word "Lord" by itself is an inadequate rendering here for *Rabb.* For it implies cherishing, guarding from harm, sustaining, granting all the means and opportunities of development. See. n. 20 to i. 2. For shortness, perhaps "Guardian-Lord" will be sufficient in the Text.

6081. The story of Creation is wonderful and continuous. There are several processes which we contemplate in glorifying God's name. First, He brings us into being. Secondly, He endows us with forms and faculties exactly suited to what is expected of us, and to the environments in which our life will be cast, giving to everything due order and proportion.

6082. Thirdly, He has ordained laws and decrees, by which we can develop ourselves and fit ourselves into His whole scheme of evolution for all His Creation. He has measured exactly the needs of all, and given us instincts and physical and psychical predispositions which fit into His decrees. Fourthly, He gives us guidance, so that we are not the sport of mechanical laws. Our reason and our will are exercised, that we may reach the higher destiny of man.

6083. Fifthly, after maturity comes decay. But even in that decay, as when green pasture turns to stubble, we subserve other ends. In so far as we are animals, we share these processes with other forms of material Creation, animal, vegetable, and even mineral, which all have their appointed laws of growth and decay. But man's higher destiny is referred to in subsequent verses.

6084. The soul, as it reaches the Light of God, makes gradual progress, like a man going from darkness into light. So the Qur-ān was revealed by stages. So all revelation from God comes by stages.

As usual, there are two parallel meanings : (1) that connected with the occasion of direct inspiration to the holy Prophet ; and (2) the more general Message to mankind for all time. Everyone who understands the Message must declare it, in words, and still more, in his conduct.

(The Message), so thou
Shalt not forget,[6085]

فلا تنسى ○

7. Except as God wills:[6086]
For He knoweth
What is manifest
And what is hidden.

٧- إلا ما شاء الله ط
إنه يعلم الجهر وما يخفى ○

8. And We will make it
Easy for thee (to follow)
The simple (Path).[6087]

٨- ونيسرك لليسرى ○

9. Therefore give admonition
In case the admonition[6088]
Profits (the hearer).

٩- فذكر إن نفعت الذكرى ○

10. The admonition will be received
By those who fear (God):

١٠- سيذكر من يخشى ○

11. But it will be avoided
By those most unfortunate ones,

١١- ويتجنبها الأشقى ○

12. Who will enter
The Great Fire,[6089]

١٢- الذى يصلى النار الكبرى ○

6085. The particular occasion was an assurance to the Prophet, that though he was unlettered, the Message given to him would be preserved in his heart and in the hearts of men. The more general sense is that mankind, having once seized great spiritual truths, will hold fast to them, except as qualified in the following verse.

6086. There can be no question of this having any reference to the abrogation of any verses of the Qur-ān. For this Sūra is one of the earliest revealed, being placed about eighth according to the most accepted chronological order. While the basic principles of God's Law remain the same, its form, expression, and application have varied from time to time, *e.g.*, from Moses to Jesus, and from Jesus to Muḥammad. It is one of the beneficent mercies of God that we should forget some things of the past, lest our minds become confused and our development is retarded. Besides, God knows what is manifest and what is hidden, and His Will and Plan work with supreme wisdom and goodness.

6087. The Path of Islam is simple and easy. It depends on no abstruse mysteries or self-mortifications, but on straight and manly conduct in accordance with the laws of man's nature as implanted in him by God (xxx. 30). On the other hand, spiritual perfection may be most difficult, for it involves complete surrender on our part to God in all our affairs, thoughts, and desires: but after that surrender God's Grace will make our path easy.

6088. This is not so strong as the Biblical phrase, "Cast not pearls before swine" (Matt. vii. 6). The cases where admonition does produce spiritual profit and where it does not, are mentioned below in verses 10 and 11-13 respectively. God's Message should be proclaimed to all; but particular and personal admonitions are also due to those who attend and in whose hearts is the fear of God; in the case of those who run away from it and dishonour it, such particular and personal admonition is useless. They are the unfortunate ones who prepare their own ruin.

6089. The Great Fire is the final Penalty or Disaster in the Hereafter, as contrasted with the minor Penalties or Disasters from which all evil suffers from within in this very life.

13. In which they will then Neither die nor live.[6090]	١٣- ثُمَّ لَا يَمُوتُ فِيهَا وَلَا يَحْيٰى ۝
14. But those will prosper[6091] Who purify themselves,[6092]	١٤- قَدْ أَفْلَحَ مَنْ تَزَكّٰى ۝
15. And glorify the name Of their Guardian-Lord, And (lift their hearts) In Prayer.	١٥- وَذَكَرَ اسْمَ رَبِّهٖ فَصَلّٰى ۝
16. Nay (behold), ye prefer The life of this world ;	١٦- بَلْ تُؤْثِرُونَ الْحَيٰوةَ الدُّنْيَا ۝
17. But the Hereafter Is better and more enduring.	١٧- وَالْاٰخِرَةُ خَيْرٌ وَّاَبْقٰى ۝
18. And this is In the Books Of the earliest (Revelations),—[6093]	١٨- إِنَّ هٰذَا لَفِي الصُّحُفِ الْأُولٰى ۝
19. The Books of Abraham[6094] and Moses.[6095]	١٩- صُحُفِ إِبْرٰهِيمَ وَمُوسٰى ۝

6090. A terrible picture of those who ruin their whole future by evil lives here below. They introduce a discord into Creation, while life should be one great universal concord. And their past clings to them as part of their own will. They are not even like the dry swarthy stubble mentioned in verse 5 above, which grew naturally out of the luscious pasture, for they have grown harmful, in defiance of their own nature. "*Neither die nor live*" : *Cf.* xx. 74.

6091. *Prosper* : in the highest and spiritual sense ; attain to Bliss or Salvation : as opposed to "enter the Fire".

6092. The first process in godliness is to cleanse ourselves in body, mind, and soul. Then we shall be in a fit state to see and proclaim the Glory of God. That leads us to our actual absorption in Praise and Prayer.

6093. The law of righteousness and godliness is not a new law, nor are the vanity and short duration of this world preached here for the first time. But spiritual truths have to be renewed and reiterated again and again.

6094. No Book of Abraham has come down to us. But the Old Testament recognises that Abraham was a prophet (Gen: xx. 7). There is a book in Greek, which has been translated by Mr. G. H. Box, called the Testament of Abraham (published by the Society for the Promotion of Christian Knowledge, London, 1927). It seems to be a Greek translation of a Hebrew original. The Greek Text was probably written in the second Christian century, in Egypt, but in its present form it probably goes back only to the 9th or 10th Century. It was popular among the Christians. Perhaps the Jewish Midrash also refers to a Testament of Abraham.

6095. The original Revelation of Moses, of which the present Pentateuch is a surviving recension. See Appendix II., p. 282.

The present Gospels do not come under the definition of the "earliest" Books. Nor could they be called "Books of Jesus" : they were written not by him, but about him, and long after his death.

INTRODUCTION AND SUMMARY : SŪRA LXXXVIII (*Gāshiya*).

This is a late Sūra of the early Meccan period, perhaps close in date to S. lii. Its subject-matter is the contrast between the destinies of the Good and the Evil in the Hereafter,—on the Day when the true balance will be restored : the Signs of God even in this life should remind us of the Day of Account, for God is good and just, and His creation is for a just Purpose.

C. *268*.—Have you heard of that Tremendous Day
(lxxxviii. 1-26.) When the Good from the Evil will be separated ?

There will be Souls that Day will burn
And grovel in the blazing Fire of Wrath !
No Food can fill their Hunger : no Drink,
Alas, can slake their fierce Thirst !

There will be Souls that Day will shout
With Joy to the glory of their Lord !
Their past Endeavour will now be Achievement.
Raised high on Thrones of Dignity they
Will be Guests at the sumptuous Feast of Bliss.

Let man but look at his dominion o'er
The beasts of the field, or his glorious Canopy
Of stars, or the Eternal Hills that feed
His streams, or the wide expanse of Mother
Earth that nurtures him, and he
Will see the ordered Plan of God.
To Him must he return and give account !
Let him, then, learn his Lesson and live !

Sūra LXXXVIII.

G̲āshiya, or The Overwhelming Event.

In the name of God, Most Gracious, Most Merciful.

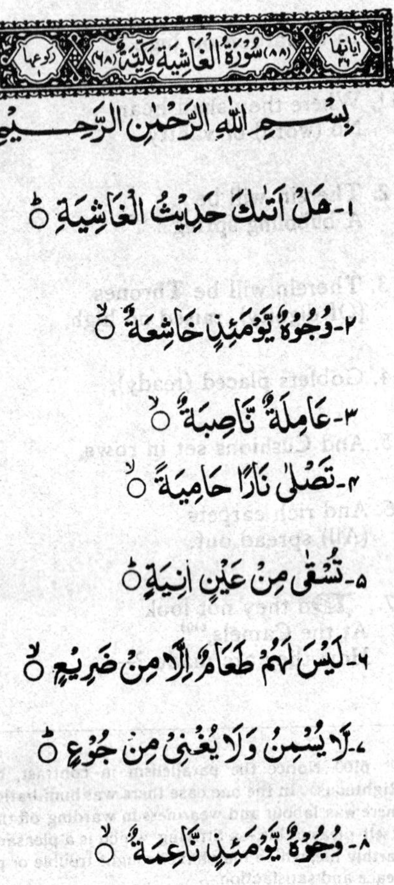

1. Has the story
Reached thee, of
The Overwhelming (Event)? [6096]

2. Some faces, that Day, [6097]
Will be humiliated,

3. Labouring (hard), weary,— [6098]

4. The while they enter
The Blazing Fire,—

5. The while they are given,
To drink, of a boiling hot spring,

6. No food will there be
For them but a bitter *Ḍharī'* [6099]

7. Which will neither nourish
Nor satisfy hunger.

8. (Other) faces that Day
Will be joyful,

6096. *G̲āshiya:* the thing or event that overshadows or overwhelms, that covers over or makes people lose their senses. In xii. 107, it is described as the "covering veil of the Wrath of God": where see n. 1790. The Day of Judgment is indicated, as the Event of overwhelming importance, in which all our petty differences of this imperfect world are covered over and overwhelmed in a new world of perfect justice and truth.

6097. *Cf.* lxxv. 22, 24.

6098. On the faces of the wicked will appear the hard labour and consequent fatigue of the task they will have in battling against the fierce Fire which their own Deeds will have kindled.

6099. The root-meaning implies again the idea of humiliation. Metaphorically, it is understood to be a plant, bitter and thorny, loathsome in smell and appearance, which will neither give fattening nourishment to the body nor in any way satisfy the burning pangs of hunger,—a fit plant for Hell, like *Zaqqūm* (lvi. 52; or xvii. 60, n. 2250).

9. Pleased with their Striving,—[6100]

10. In a Garden on high,[6101]

11. Where they shall hear
No (word) of vanity :

12. Therein will be
A bubbling spring : [6102]

13. Therein will be Thrones
(Of dignity), raised on high,

14. Goblets placed (ready),

15. And Cushions set in rows,

16. And rich carpets
(All) spread out.

17. Do they not look
At the Camels,[6103]
How they are made ?—

٩-لِّسَعْيِهَا رَاضِيَةٌ ○

١٠-فِي جَنَّةٍ عَالِيَةٍ ○

١١-لَّا تَسْمَعُ فِيهَا لَاغِيَةً ○

١٢-فِيهَا عَيْنٌ جَارِيَةٌ ○

١٣-فِيهَا سُرُرٌ مَّرْفُوعَةٌ ○

١٤-وَأَكْوَابٌ مَّوْضُوعَةٌ ○

١٥-وَنَمَارِقُ مَصْفُوفَةٌ ○

١٦-وَزَرَابِيُّ مَبْثُوثَةٌ ○

١٧-أَفَلَا يَنظُرُونَ
إِلَى الْإِبِلِ كَيْفَ خُلِقَتْ ○

6100. Notice the parallelism in contrast, between the fate of the Wicked and that of the Righteous. In the one case there was humiliation in their faces ; in the other, there is joy ; where there was labour and weariness in warding off the Fire, there is instead a healthy Striving, which is itself pleasurable,—a Striving which is a pleasant consequence of the spiritual Endeavour in the earthly life, which may have brought trouble or persecution from without, but which brought inward peace and satisfaction.

6101. The most important point is their inward state of joy and satisfaction, mentioned in verses 8-9. Now are mentioned metaphors of outer things of bliss, the chief of which is the Garden : see Appendix XII., following S. liv. The Garden is in contrast to the Fire. Its chief beauty will be that they will hear there nothing unbecoming, or foolish, or vain. It will be a Garden *on high*, in all senses,—fit for the best, highest, and noblest.

6102. Instead of the boiling hot spring (verse 5) there will be a bubbling spring of sparkling water. Instead of the grovelling and grumbling in the place of Wrath, there will be Thrones of Dignity, with all the accompaniments of a brilliant Assembly.

6103 In case men neglect the Hereafter as of no account, they are asked to contemplate four things, which they can see in every-day life, and which are full of meaning, high design, and the goodness of God to man. The first mentioned is the domesticated animal, which for Arab countries is *par excellence* the Camel What a wonderful structure has this Ship of the Desert ? He can store water in his stomach for days. He can live on dry and thorny desert shrubs His limbs are adapted to his life. He can carry men and goods. His flesh can be eaten Camel's hair can be used in weaving. And withal, he is so gentle ! Who can sing his praises enough ?

18. And at the Sky,[6104] How it is raised high ?—	١٨- وَإِلَى السَّمَآءِ كَيْفَ رُفِعَتْ ۝
19. And at the Mountains,[6105] How they are fixed firm ?—	١٩- وَإِلَى الْجِبَالِ كَيْفَ نُصِبَتْ ۝
20. And at the Earth,[6106] How it is spread out ?	٢٠- وَإِلَى الْأَرْضِ كَيْفَ سُطِحَتْ ۝
21. Therefore do thou give Admonition, for thou art One to admonish.	٢١- فَذَكِّرْ إِنَّمَآ أَنتَ مُذَكِّرٌ ۝
22. Thou art not one To manage (men's) affairs.[6107]	٢٢- لَّسْتَ عَلَيْهِم بِمُصَيْطِرٍ ۝
23. But if any turn away And reject God,—	٢٣- إِلَّا مَن تَوَلَّىٰ وَكَفَرَ ۝
24. God will punish him With a mighty Punishment.	٢٤- فَيُعَذِّبُهُ اللَّهُ الْعَذَابَ الْأَكْبَرَ ۝
25. For to Us will be Their Return ;	٢٥- إِنَّ إِلَيْنَآ إِيَابَهُمْ ۝
26. Then it will be for Us To call them to account.	٢٦- ثُمَّ إِنَّ عَلَيْنَا حِسَابَهُم ۝

6104. The second thing they should consider is the noble blue vault high above them,—with the sun and moon, the stars and planets, and other heavenly bodies. This scene is full of beauty and magnificence, design and order, plainness and mystery. And yet we receive our light and warmth from the sun, and what would our physical lives be without these influences that come from such enormous distances ?

6105. From every-day utility and affection in the Camel, to the utility in grandeur in the heavens above us, we had two instances touching our individual as well as our social lives. In the third instance, in the Mountains, we come to the utility to human kind generally in the services the Mountains perform in storing water, in moderating climate, and in various other ways which it is the business of Physical Geography to investigate and describe.

6106. The fourth and last instance given is that of the Earth as a whole, the habitation of mankind in our present phase of life. The Earth is a globe, and yet how marvellously it seems to be spread out before us in plains, valleys, hills, deserts, seas, etc. ! Can man, seeing these things, fail to see a Plan and Purpose in his life, or fail to turn to the great Creator before Whom he will have to give an account after this life is done ?

6107. The Prophet of God is sent to teach and direct people on the way. He is not sent to force their will, or to punish them, except in so far as he may receive authority to do so. Punishment belongs to God alone. And Punishment is certain in the Hereafter, when true values will be restored.

INTRODUCTION AND SUMMARY : SŪRA LXXXIX (*Fajr*).

This is one of the earliest of the Sūras to be revealed,—probably within the first ten in chronological order.

Its mystic meaning is suggested by contrasts,—contrasts in nature and in man's long history. Thus does it enforce the lesson of Faith in the Hereafter to "those who understand". Man's history and legendary lore show that greatness does not last and the proudest are brought low. For enforcing moral and spiritual truths, the strictest history is no better than legend. Indeed all artistic history is legend, for it is written from a special point of view.

Man is easily cowed by contrasts in his own fortunes, and yet he does not learn from them the lesson of forbearance and kindness to others, and the final elevation of goodness in the Hereafter. When all the things on which his mind and heart are set on this earth shall be crushed to nothingness, he will see the real glory and power, love and beauty, of God, for these are the light of the Garden of Paradise.

C. 269.—Man is apt to forget the contrasts
(lxxxix. 1-30.) In nature and life, and all that they mean
In his spiritual growth. Perchance his mind
Is so absorbed in what he sees,
That he doubts the vast Realities
He does not see. The Present makes
Him blind to the Past and to the Future.
Fooled by glory, he fears not a fall ;
And baulked in disaster, he gives up Hope
And sometimes Faith. Let him study
Nature and History, and restore his Faith :
Realising the Sure Event, the Hereafter,
Let him find his fullest fulfilment
In the service and the good-pleasure of God !

Sūra LXXXIX.

Fajr, or The Break of Day.

*In the name of God, Most Gracious,
Most Merciful.*

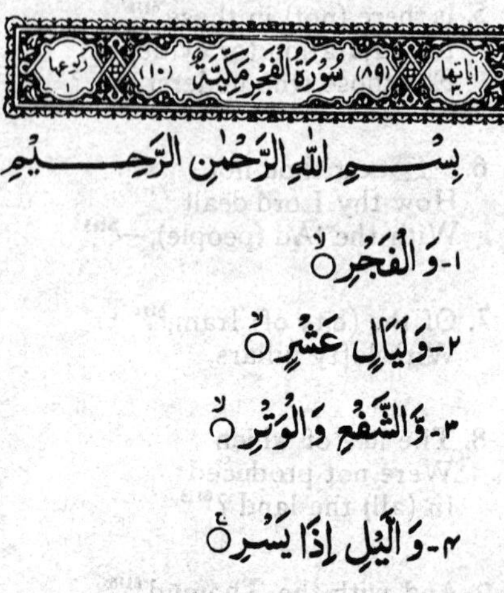

1. By the Break of Day ;[6108]

2. By the Nights twice five ;[6109]

3. By the Even
And Odd (contrasted) ;[6110]

4. And by the Night[6111]
When it passeth away ;—

6108. Four striking contrasts are mentioned, to show God's Power and Justice, and appeal to "those who understand". The first is the glory and mystery of the Break of Day. It just succeeds the deepest dark of the Night, when the first rays of light break through. Few people except those actually in personal touch with nature can feel its compelling power. In respect both of beauty and terror, of hope and inspiration, of suddenness and continuing increase of light and joy, this "holy time" of night may well stand as the type of spiritual awakening from darkness to Faith, from Death to Resurrection.

6109. By the Ten Nights are usually understood the first ten nights of *Zul-Ḥajj*, the sacred season of Pilgrimage. From the most ancient times Mecca was the centre of Arab pilgrimage. The story of Abraham is intimately connected with it : see ii. 125-127 and notes, also n. 217 to ii. 197. In times of Paganism various superstitions were introduced, which Islam swept away. Islam also purified the rites and ceremonies, giving them new meaning. The ten days specially devoted to the Ḥajj introduce a striking contrast in the life of Mecca and of the pilgrims. Mecca, from being a quiet secluded city, is then thronged with thousands of pilgrims from all parts of the world. They discard their ordinary dress—representing every kind of costume—to the simple and ordinary *Iḥrām* (n. 217); they refrain from every kind of fighting and quarrel ; they abstain from every kind of luxury and self-indulgence ; they hold all life sacred, however humble, except in the way of symbolical and carefully-regulated sacrifice ; and they spend their nights in prayer and meditation.

6110. The contrast between even and odd forms the subject of learned argument among those who deal with the mystic properties of numbers. In any case, even and odd follow each other in regular succession : each is independent, and yet neither is self-sufficient. In ultimate analysis every even number is a pair of odd ones. And all things go in pairs : see xxxvi. 36, and n. 3981. In the animal world pairs are but two individuals, and yet each is a complement of the other. Both abstract and concrete things are often understood in contrast with their opposites. Why should we not, in spiritual matters, understand this life better with reference to the Hereafter, and why should we disbelieve in the Hereafter simply because we cannot conceive of anything different from our present life ?

6111. That is, the last part of the night, just before full day-light. Note the gradations in spiritual awakening, and their symbols : first, the turn of the night, when just the first rays of day-light break through ; secondly, the social and institutional rites of religion, like those during the ten nights of Pilgrimage ; thirdly, when the usual contrast between the Here and Hereafter vanishes, and we can see heaven even here ; and lastly, when this world vanishes, the full light of Day arrives, and we see Reality face to face.

5. Is there (not) in these[6112]
An adjuration (or evidence)
For those who understand ?

٥- هَلْ فِي ذَٰلِكَ قَسَمٌ لِّذِي حِجْرٍ ۝

6. Seest thou not
How thy Lord dealt
With the 'Ād (people),—[6113]

٦- أَلَمْ تَرَ كَيْفَ
فَعَلَ رَبُّكَ بِعَادٍ ۝

7. Of the (city of) Iram,[6114]
With lofty pillars,

٧- إِرَمَ ذَاتِ الْعِمَادِ ۝

8. The like of which
Were not produced
In (all) the land ?[6115]

٨- الَّتِي لَمْ يُخْلَقْ مِثْلُهَا فِي الْبِلَادِ ۝

9. And with the Thamūd[6116]
(People), who cut out
(Huge) rocks in the valley ?—

٩- وَثَمُودَ الَّذِينَ
جَابُوا الصَّخْرَ بِالْوَادِ ۝

10. And with Pharaoh,
Lord of Stakes ?[6117]

١٠- وَفِرْعَوْنَ ذِي الْأَوْتَادِ ۝

6112. All these mystic Symbols draw our attention, like solemn adjurations in speech, to the profoundest mystery of our inner life, *viz.*: how from utter depths of darkness—ignorance or even degradation—God's wonderful Light or Revelation can lead us by contrast into the most beautiful sunshine of a glorious spiritual Day. But the contrast suggests also the opposite process as a corollary,—how resistance to God's light would destroy us utterly, converting our greatness or glory to perdition, as happened with the peoples of Arab antiquity, the 'Ād and the Thamūd, and the type of the powerful but arrogant and godless monarch, the Pharaoh of Egypt. Like a man with a bounded horizon, the average man does not understand these long-range mysteries of life, and we have need to pray that we may be of "those who understand".

6113. For the 'Ād see n. 1040 to vii 65. They seem to have possessed an ancient civilisation, which succumbed when they persistently broke God's law.

6114. Iram would seem to have been an ancient 'Ād capital, in southern Arabia. It boasted of lofty architecture ("lofty pillars"). Some Commentators understand Iram to be the name of an eponymous hero of the 'Ād, in which case the following line, "with lofty pillars", should be construed "of lofty stature". The 'Ād were a tall race.

6115. This tract of southern Arabia was once very prosperous (Arabia Felix) and contains ruins and inscriptions. It has always been an object of great interest to the Arabs. In the time of Mu'āwiya some precious stones were found among the ruins in this locality. Quite recently, a bronze lion's head and a bronze piece of gutter with a Sabæan inscription, found in Najrān, have been described in the *British Museum Quarterly*, vol. XI, No. 4, Sept. 1937.

6116. For the Thamūd see n. 1043 to vii. 73. Their civilisation shows traces of Egyptian, Syrian, and (later) Greek and Roman influences. They built fine temples, tombs, and buildings cut out of the solid rock. The cult of the goddess Lāt flourished among them.

6117. For "Lord of Stakes", see xxxviii 12, n. 4160 For Pharaoh's arrogance and his fall, see **xx.** 43, 78-79. The three examples given, the 'Ād, the Thamūd, and Pharaoh, show that neither nations nor individuals, however mighty, prosperous, or firmly established they may be, can live if they transgress the Law of God. The Law of God, which is also the law of the higher nature which He has bestowed on us, made them in the first place great and glorious: when they fell from it and "heaped mischief on mischief", they were swept away.

11. (All) these transgressed
Beyond bounds in the lands.

١١- الَّذِينَ طَغَوْا فِي الْبِلَادِ ۪ۙ

12. And heaped therein
Mischief (on mischief).

١٢- فَأَكْثَرُوا فِيهَا الْفَسَادَ ۪ۙ

13. Therefore did thy Lord
Pour on them a scourge
Of diverse chastisements :

١٣- فَصَبَّ عَلَيْهِمْ رَبُّكَ
سَوْطَ عَذَابٍ ۚ

14. For thy Lord is
(As a Guardian)
On a watch-tower.[6118]

١٤- إِنَّ رَبَّكَ لَبِالْمِرْصَادِ ۭ

15. Now, as for man,[6119]
When his Lord trieth him,
Giving him honour and gifts,
Then saith he, (puffed up),
"My Lord hath honoured me"

١٥- فَأَمَّا الْإِنْسَانُ إِذَا مَا ابْتَلَاهُ رَبُّهُ
فَأَكْرَمَهُ وَنَعَّمَهُ ۙ
فَيَقُولُ رَبِّي أَكْرَمَنِ ۭ

16. But when he trieth him,
Restricting his subsistence[6120]
For him, then saith he
(In despair), "My Lord
Hath humiliated me!"

١٦- وَأَمَّا إِذَا مَا ابْتَلَاهُ
فَقَدَرَ عَلَيْهِ رِزْقَهُ ۙ
فَيَقُولُ رَبِّي أَهَانَنِ ۚ

17. Nay, nay! But ye[6121]
Honour not the orphans!

١٧- كَلَّا بَل لَّا تُكْرِمُونَ الْيَتِيمَ ۙ

6118. Even though God's punishment is delayed, it is not to be supposed that He does not see all things. He is like a Guardian on a watch-tower defending His Law, and protecting the weak and innocent with His mighty arm. God's providence is ever vigilant : His punishment of evil-doers is a form of justice to the weak and the righteous whom they oppress. It is part of the signification of His title as *Rabb* (Cherisher).

6119. Contrast with God's justice and watchful care, man's selfishness and pettiness. God tries us both by prosperity and adversity : in the one we should show humility and kindness; and in the other, patience and faith. On the contrary, we get puffed up in prosperity and depressed in adversity, putting false values on this world's goods.

6120. *Subsistence*, in both the literal and the figurative sense. God provides for all, but people complain if the provision is measured and restricted to their needs, circumstances, and antecedents, and does not come up to their desires or expectations, or is different from that given to people in quite different circumstances.

6121. Even at our own valuation, if we are favoured with superfluities, do we think of the fatherless children, or the struggling poor? On the contrary, too many men are but ready to embezzle the helpless orphan's inheritance, and to waste their own substance in worthless riot instead of supplying the people's real needs.

18. Nor do ye encourage
One another[6122]
To feed the poor !—

١٨- وَلَا تَحَٰٓضُّونَ عَلَىٰ طَعَامِ ٱلْمِسْكِينِ ۝

19. And ye devour Inheritance—[6123]
All with greed,

١٩- وَتَأْكُلُونَ ٱلتُّرَاثَ أَكْلًا لَّمًّا ۝

20. And ye love wealth
With inordinate love !

٢٠- وَتُحِبُّونَ ٱلْمَالَ حُبًّا جَمًّا ۝

21. Nay ! When the earth
Is pounded to powder,[6124]

٢١- كَلَّآ إِذَا دُكَّتِ ٱلْأَرْضُ دَكًّا دَكًّا ۝

22. And thy Lord cometh,
And His angels,
Rank upon rank,

٢٢- وَجَآءَ رَبُّكَ
وَٱلْمَلَكُ صَفًّا صَفًّا ۝

23. And Hell, that Day,[6125]
Is brought (face to face),—
On that Day will man
Remember, but how will
That remembrance profit him ?

٢٣- وَجِاْىٓءَ يَوْمَئِذٍۭ بِجَهَنَّمَ ۚ
يَوْمَئِذٍ يَتَذَكَّرُ ٱلْإِنسَٰنُ
وَأَنَّىٰ لَهُ ٱلذِّكْرَىٰ ۝

24. He will say : "Ah !
Would that I had
Sent forth (Good Deeds)
For (this) my (Future) Life !"

٢٤- يَقُولُ يَٰلَيْتَنِى
قَدَّمْتُ لِحَيَاتِى ۝

25. For, that Day,
His Chastisement will be

٢٥- فَيَوْمَئِذٍ لَّا يُعَذِّبُ

6122. Kindness and generosity set up standards which even worldly men feel bound to follow out of social considerations even if they are not moved by higher motives. But the wicked find plausible excuses for their own hard-heartedness, and by their evil example choke up the springs of charity and kindness in others.

6123. Inheritance is abused in two ways. (1) Guardians and trustees for the inheritance of minors or women or persons unable to look after their own interests should fulfil their trusts with even more care than they devote to their own interests. Instead of that they selfishly "devour" the property. (2) Persons who inherit property in their own rights should remember that in that case, too, it is a sacred trust. They must use it for the purposes, objects, and duties which they also inherit. It gives them no licence to live in idleness or waste their days in riotous show.

6124. Our attention is now called to the Day of Reckoning. Whether we failed to respect the rights of the helpless here or actually suppressed those rights in our mad love for the good things of this life, we shall have to answer in the realm of Reality. This solid earth, which we imagine to be so real, will crumble to powder like dust before the real Presence, manifested in glory.

6125 The Retribution will at last come, and we shall realise it in our inmost being, all the illusions of this fleeting world having been swept away. Then we shall remember, and wish, too late, that we had repented Why not repent now ? Why not bring forth the fruits of repentance now, as a preparation for the Hereafter ?

Such as none (else)
Can inflict,[6126]

عَذَابَهُۥٓ أَحَدٌ ۝

26. And His bonds
Will be such as
None (other) can bind.

٢٦- وَلَا يُوثِقُ وَثَاقَهُۥٓ أَحَدٌ ۝

27. (To the righteous soul
Will be said :)
" O (thou) soul,[6127]
In (complete) rest
And satisfaction !

٢٧- يَٰٓأَيَّتُهَا ٱلنَّفْسُ
ٱلْمُطْمَئِنَّةُ ۝

28. " Come back thou
To thy Lord, —[6128]
Well pleased (thyself),
And well-pleasing
Unto Him !

٢٨- ٱرْجِعِىٓ إِلَىٰ رَبِّكِ
رَاضِيَةً مَّرْضِيَّةً ۝

29. " Enter thou, then,
Among my Devotees !

٢٩- فَٱدْخُلِى فِى عِبَٰدِى ۝

30. " Yea, enter thou
My Heaven ![6129]

٣٠- وَٱدْخُلِى جَنَّتِى ۝ ع

6126. " Chastisement " in this verse and the " binding in bonds " in the next verse are two distinct phases of the Penalty. " Chastisement " involves pain and agony, such as cannot be imagined anywhere else, or from any other source, for it touches our inmost soul and cannot be compared with anything our bodies may suffer or others may inflict. " Bonds " imply confinement, want of freedom, the closing of a door which was once open but which we deliberately passed by. We see that others accepted in faith and entered that door. This shutting out of what might have been is worse than any other bonds or confinement we can imagine, and may be worse than actual chastisement.

6127. The righteous enter into their inheritance and receive their welcome with a title that suggests freedom from all pain, sorrow, doubt, struggle, disappointment, passion, and even further desire : at rest, in peace ; in a state of complete satisfaction.

In Muslim theology, this stage of the soul is the final stage of bliss. The unregenerate human soul, that seeks its satisfaction in the lower earthly desires, is the *Ammāra* (xii. 53). The self-reproaching soul that feels conscious of sin and resists it is the *Lawwāma* (lxxv. 2, and n. 5810).

6128. Note that Evil finds itself isolated, and cries out in lonely agony (verse 24), while Good receives a warm welcome from the Lord of Goodness Himself.—also that it is the soul which enters heaven, and not the gross body which perishes.

6129. The climax of the whole is : " Enter My Heaven ! " Men may have imagined all kinds of heaven before, and many types and symbols are used in the sacred Word itself : see Appendix XII, after S. liv. But nothing can express the reality itself better than " My Heaven "—God's own Heaven ! May we reach it through God's grace !

INTRODUCTION AND SUMMARY : SŪRA XC (*Bulad*).

This is an early Meccan revelation, and refers to the mystic relation (by divine sanction) of the holy Prophet with the city of Mecca. He was born in that City, which had already been sacred for ages before. He was nurtured in that City and had (to use a modern phrase) the freedom of that City, belonging, as he did, to the noble family which held the government of its sacred percincts in its hands. But he was an orphan, and orphans in his day had a poor time. But his mind was turned to things divine. He protested against the prevailing idolatry and sin, and his parent City persecuted him and cast him out. He made another City, Yat͟hrib, his own : it became the *Madīnat-un-Nabī*, the City of the Prophet, and it has ever since been called Madīna. We can speak of Madīna as the Prophet's child. But the Prophet ever cherished in his heart the love of his parent City of Mecca, and in the fulness of time was received in triumph there. He purified it from all idols and abominations, re-established the worship of the One True God, overthrew the purse-proud selfish autocracy, restored the sway of the righteous (people of the Right Hand), the liberty of the slave, and the rights of the poor and downtrodden. What a wonderful career centring round a City? It becomes a symbol of the world's spiritual history.

C. 270.—The Prophet's own City persecuted him.

(XC. 1-20.) Honoured by his nativity, it sought to slay him :
Yet he loved it and purged it of all that was wrong.
What toil and struggle did it not involve?
Man is made for toil and struggle :
Let him not boast of ease and wealth.
He will be called to account for all his doings.
Let him use his God-given faculties, and tread
The steep path that leads to Heaven's Heights :
The steps thereto are Love, unselfish Love,
Given freely to God's creatures—all those
In need—and Faith in God, and Patience
Joined with self-restraint and kindness.
Thus only can we reach the ranks
Of the blest Companions of the Right Hand!

Sûra XC.

Balad, or The City.

In the name of God, Most Gracious, Most Merciful

1. I do call to witness[6130]
This City ;—

2. And thou art a freeman[6131]
Of this City ;—

3. And (the mystic ties
of) Parent and Child ;—[6132]

4. Verily We have created
Man into toil and struggle.[6133]

5. Thinketh he, that none
Hath power over him ?[6134]

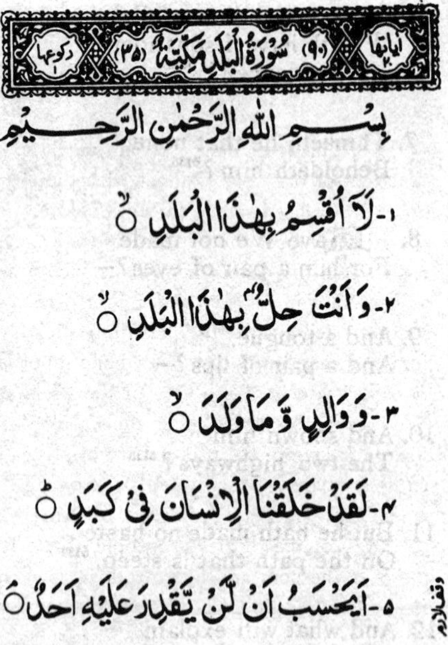
سورة البلد مكية (٩٠) (٣٥)
بسم الله الرحمن الرحيم
١- لا أقسم بهذا البلد ○
٢- وأنت حل بهذا البلد ○
٣- ووالد وما ولد ○
٤- لقد خلقنا الإنسان في كبد ○
٥- أيحسب أن لن يقدر عليه أحد ○

6130. The appeal to the mystic ties between the holy Prophet and his parent City of Mecca has been explained in the Introduction to this Sūra. It is a symbol of man's own history. Man is born for toil and struggle, and this is the substantive proposition in verse 4 below, which this appeal leads up to.

6131. *Ḥillun* : an inhabitant, a man with lawful rights, a man freed from such obligations as would attach to a stranger to the city, a freeman in a wider sense than the technical sense to which the word is restricted in modern usage. The Prophet should have been honoured in his native city. He was actually being persecuted. He should have been loved, as a parent loves a child. Actually his life was being sought, and those who believed in him were under a ban But time was to show that he was to come triumphant to his native city after having made Medina sacred by his life and work.

6132. A parent loves a child ordinarily : the father is proud and the mother, in spite of her birth-pains, experiences supreme joy when the child is born. But in abnormal circumstances there may be misunderstandings, even hatred between parent and child. So Mecca cast out her most glorious son, but it was only for a time. Mecca was sound at heart : only her power had been usurped by an ignorant autocracy which passed away, and Mecca was to receive back her glory at the hands of the son whom she had rejected but whom she welcomed back later. And Mecca retains for all time her sacred character as the centre of Islam.

6133. *Cf.* " Man is born unto trouble as the sparks fly upward " (Job, v. 7) ; " For all his days are sorrows, and his travail grief " (Ecclesiastes, ii. 23). Man's life is full of sorrow and vexation ; but our text has a different shade of meaning : man is born to strive and struggle ; and if he suffers from hardships, he must exercise patience, for God will make his way smooth for him (lxv. 7 ; xciv. 5-6). On the other hand no man should boast of worldly goods or worldly prosperity (see verses 5-7 below).

6134. See the end of last note. If a man has wealth, influence, or power, he should not behave as if it is to last for ever, or as if he has no responsibility for his acts and can do what he likes. All his gifts and advantages are given to him for trial. God, Who bestowed them on him, can take them away, and will do so if man fails in his trial.

6. He may say (boastfully) : Wealth have I squandered In abundance ! "[6135]	٦- يَقُوْلُ اَهْلَكْتُ مَالًا لُّبَدًا ۝
7. Thinketh he that none Beholdeth him ?[6136]	٧- اَيَحْسَبُ اَنْ لَّمْ يَرَهٗٓ اَحَدٌ ۝
8. Have We not made For him a pair of eyes ?—	٨- اَلَمْ نَجْعَلْ لَّهٗ عَيْنَيْنِ ۝
9. And a tongue,[6137] And a pair of lips ?—	٩- وَلِسَانًا وَّ شَفَتَيْنِ ۝
10. And shown him The two highways ?[6138]	١٠- وَهَدَيْنٰهُ النَّجْدَيْنِ ۝
11. But he hath made no haste On the path that is steep.[6139]	١١- فَلَا اقْتَحَمَ الْعَقَبَةَ ۝
12. And what will explain To thee the path that is steep ?—	١٢- وَمَآ اَدْرٰىكَ مَا الْعَقَبَةُ ۝

6135. The man who feels no responsibility and thinks that he can do what he likes in life forgets his responsibility to God. He boasts of his wealth and scatters it about, thinking that he can thus purchase the support of the world. For a time he may. But a rude awakening must come soon, for he bases his hopes on unsubstantial things. Or if he spends his substance on self-indulgence, he is weakening himself and putting himself into snares that must destroy him.

6136. God watches him, and sees all his acts and motives, and all the secret springs of his follies. But lest he should think the higher spiritual forces too remote for him, let him look within himself and use the faculties which God has given him. See the next verses following.

6137. The eyes give us the faculty of seeing, and may be taken in both the literal and the metaphorical sense. In the same way the tongue gives us the faculty of tasting in both senses. Along with the lips, it also enables us to speak, to ask for information and seek guidance, and to celebrate the praises of God.

6138. The two highways of life are : (1) the steep and difficult path of virtue, which is further described in the verses following, and (2) the easy path of vice and the rejection of God, referred to in verses 19-20 below. God has given us not only the faculties implied in the eyes, the tongue, and the lips, but also given us the judgment by which we can choose our way ; and He has sent us Teachers and Guides, with Revelation, to show us the right and difficult way.

6139. In spite of the faculties with which God has endowed man and the guidance which He has given him, man has been remiss. By no means has he been eager to follow the steep and difficult path which is for his own spiritual good. *Cf.* Matt. vii. 14 : "Strait is the gate, and narrow is the way, which leadeth unto life, and few there be that find it".

13. (It is :) freeing the bondman;[6140]

۱۳-فَكُّ رَقَبَةٍ ۝

14. Or the giving of food
In a day of privation[6141]

۱۴-أَوْ إِطْعَامٌ فِي يَوْمٍ ذِي مَسْغَبَةٍ ۝

15. To the orphan
With claims of relationship,[6142]

۱۵-يَتِيمًا ذَا مَقْرَبَةٍ ۝

16. Or to the indigent
(Down) in the dust.[6143]

۱۶-أَوْ مِسْكِينًا ذَا مَتْرَبَةٍ ۝

17. Then will he be[6144]
Of those who believe,
And enjoin patience, (constancy,
And self-restraint), and enjoin
Deeds of kindness and compassion.

۱۷-ثُمَّ كَانَ مِنَ الَّذِينَ آمَنُوا
وَتَوَاصَوْا بِالصَّبْرِ
وَتَوَاصَوْا بِالْمَرْحَمَةِ ۝

18. Such are the Companions
Of the Right Hand.[6145]

۱۸-أُولَٰئِكَ أَصْحَابُ الْمَيْمَنَةِ ۝

6140. The difficult path of virtue is defined as the path of charity or unselfish love, and three specific instances are given for our understanding : *viz.* (1) freeing the bondman, (2) feeding the orphan, and (3) feeding the indigent down in the dust. As regards the bondman, we are to understand not only a reference to legal slavery, which happily is extinct in all civilised lands, but many other kinds of slavery which flourish especially in advanced societies. There is political slavery, industrial slavery, and social slavery. There is the slavery of conventions, of ignorance, and of superstition. There is slavery to wealth or passions or power. The good man tries to liberate men and women from all kinds of slavery, often at great danger to himself. But he begins by first liberating himself.

6141. Feed those who need it, both literally and figuratively; but do so especially when there is privation or famine, literal or figurative, *i.e.*, when or where the sources of sustenance, physical, moral, or spiritual, are cut off.

6142. All orphans should be fed and helped. But ordinary orphans will come under the indigent in verse 16 below. The orphans related to us have a special claim on us. They should be near and dear to us, and if charity begins at home, they have the first claim on us.

6143. Persons down in the dust can only be helped from motives of pure charity, because nothing can be expected of them—neither praise nor advertisement nor any other advantage to the helper. Such help is help indeed. But there may be various degrees, and the help will be suited to the needs.

6144. Such practical charity and love will be the acid test of Faith and the teaching of all virtues. The virtues are summed up under the names of Patience (the Arabic word includes constancy and self-restraint) and compassionate kindness. Not only will they be the test by which the sincerity of their Faith will be judged : they will be the fruit which their Faith will constantly produce.

6145. *Cf.* lvi. 27-40, also n. 5223. They will be those who achieve salvation.

19. But those who reject
Our Signs, they are
The (unhappy) Companions
Of the Left Hand.[6146]

۱۹- وَالَّذِينَ كَفَرُوا بِآيَاتِنَا
هُمْ أَصْحَابُ الْمَشْأَمَةِ ۝

20. On them will be Fire
Vaulted over (all round).

۲۰- عَلَيْهِمْ نَارٌ مُّؤْصَدَةٌ ۝

6146. *Cf.* lvi. 41-56, also n. 5223. They will be the unfortunate ones enveloped in the Fire of lasting Penalty, heaped over them and all round them.

INTRODUCTION AND SUMMARY: SŪRA XCI (*Shams*).

This is one of the early Meccan revelations. Beginning with a fine nature passage, and leading up to man's need of realising his spiritual responsibility, it ends with a warning of the terrible consequences for those who fear not the Hereafter.

C. 271.—All nature around us and her pageants,
(xci. 1-15.) And the soul of man within, proclaim
The goodness of God. God gave the soul
The power of choice and the sense of Right
And Wrong. Let man keep it pure and attain
Salvation,—soil it with sin and reach
Perdition. Inordinate wrong-doing ruined
The Thamūd. They defied God's sacred Law
And His prophet, and went to Destruction for their crime.

Sūra XCI.

Shams, or The Sun.

In the name of God, Most Gracious, Most Merciful

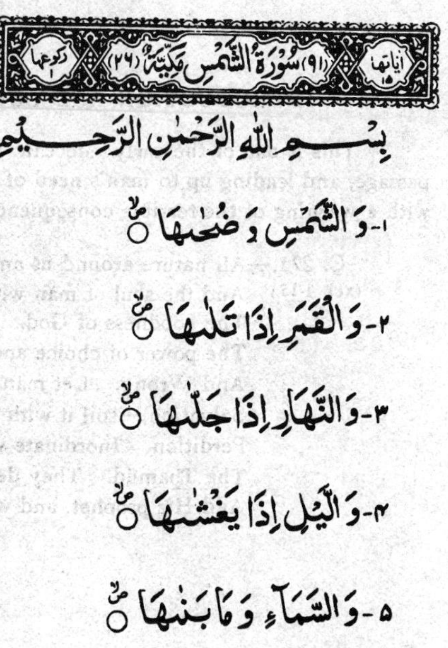

1. By the Sun[6147]
And his (glorious) splendour;

2. By the Moon[6148]
As she follows him;

3. By the Day as it[6149]
Shows up (the Sun's) glory;

4. By the Night as it
Conceals it;

5. By the Firmament[6150]
And its (wonderful) structure;[6151]

6147. Six types are taken in three pairs, from God's mighty works in nature, as tokens or evidence of God's providence and the contrasts in His sublime creation, which yet conduce to cosmic harmony (verses 1-6). Then (verses 7-8) the soul of man, with internal order and proportion in its capacities and faculties, as made by God, is appealed to as having been endowed with the power of discriminating between right and wrong. Then the conclusion is stated in verses 9-10, that man's success or failure, prosperity or bankruptcy, would depend upon his keeping that soul pure or his corrupting it.

6148. The first pair is the glorious sun, the source of our light and physical life, and the moon which follows or acts as second to the sun for illuminating our world. The moon, when she is in the sky with the sun, is pale and inconspicuous; in the sun's absence she shines with reflected light and may metaphorically be called the sun's vicegerent. So with Revelation and the great Prophets who brought it; and the minor Teachers who derive their light reflected, or perhaps doubly reflected, from the original source.

6149. The next contrasted pair consists, not of luminaries, but conditions, or periods of time, Day and Night. The Day reveals the sun's glory and the Night conceals it from our sight. So there may be contrasts in our subjective reception of divine light, but it is there, working all the time, and must reappear in its own good time.

6150. The next contrasted pair is the wonderful firmament on high, and the earth below our feet, stretching away to our wide horizons. The sky gives us rain, and the earth gives us food. Yet both work together: for the rain is moisture sucked up from the earth, and the food cannot grow without the heat and warmth of the sun. There are many other contrasts under this head; yet they all point to unity.

6151. The *mā maṣdariya* in Arabic, in this and the subsequent clauses, is best translated in English by nouns. Thus what would literally be "and the (wonderful) making or construction of it" or "the fact of its (wonderful) construction" is, idiomatically, "its (wonderful) structure." "The (wide) spreading out" of the earth is rendered "its (wide) expanse," and so on.

6. By the Earth
And its (wide) expanse;

٦- وَالْأَرْضِ وَمَا طَحٰهَا ۝

7. By the Soul,
And the proportion and order
Given to it; [6152]

٧- وَنَفْسٍ وَّمَا سَوّٰهَا ۝

8. And its enlightenment
As to its wrong
And its right;—

٨- فَأَلْهَمَهَا فُجُورَهَا
وَتَقْوٰهَا ۝

9. Truly he succeeds
That purifies it,

٩- قَدْ أَفْلَحَ مَنْ زَكّٰهَا ۝

10. And he fails
That corrupts it! [6153]

١٠- وَقَدْ خَابَ مَنْ دَسّٰهَا ۝

11. The Thamūd (people)
Rejected (their prophet)
Through their inordinate
Wrong-doing. [6154]

١١- كَذَّبَتْ ثَمُودُ
بِطَغْوٰهَا ۝

12. Behold, the most wicked
Man among them was
Deputed (for impiety). [6155]

١٢- إِذِ انْبَعَثَ أَشْقٰهَا ۝

13. But the apostle of God [6156]
Said to them: "It is

١٣- فَقَالَ لَهُمْ رَسُولُ اللهِ

6152. God makes the soul, and gives it order, proportion, and relative perfection, in order to adapt it for the particular circumstances in which it has to live its life. *Cf.* xxxii. 9. See also n. 120 to ii. 117. He breathes into it an understanding of what is sin, impiety, wrong-doing and what is piety and right conduct, in the special circumstances in which it may be placed. This is the most precious gift of all to man, the faculty of distinguishing between right and wrong. After the six external evidences mentioned in verses 1-6 above, this internal evidence of God's goodness is mentioned as the greatest of all. By these various tokens man should learn that his success, his prosperity, his salvation depends on himself,—on his keeping his soul pure as God made it; and his failure, his decline, his perdition depends on his soiling his soul by choosing evil.

6153. This is the core of the Sūra, and it is illustrated by a reference to the story of the Thamūd in the following verses.

6154. The allusion to the story of the Thamūd will be understood by a reference to vii 73-79; see specially n. 1044. Their prophet was Ṣāliḥ, but he had to deal with an arrogant people, who oppressed the poor and denied them their rights of watering and pasture for their cattle.

6155. The prophet Ṣāliḥ made a certain she-camel a Sign or Symbol, a test case "This she-camel of God is a Sign unto you: so leave her to graze in God's earth and let her come to no harm, or ye shall be seized with a grievous punishment" (vii. 73). But they plotted to kill her and sent the most wicked man among them to dare and do that deed of impiety It was probably when she came to drink at the stream that she was hamstrung and killed. See xxvi. 155, and liv. 27.

6156. That is, Ṣāliḥ: see last note.

A She-camel of God!
And (bar her not
From) having her drink!"

ناقَةَ اللهِ
وَسُقْيٰهَا ۝

14. Then they rejected him
(As a false prophet),
And they hamstrung her.[6157]
So their Lord, on account
Of their crime, obliterated
Their traces and made them
Equal (in destruction,
High and low)!

١٤- فَكَذَّبُوهُ
فَعَقَرُوهَا ۖ
فَدَمْدَمَ عَلَيْهِمْ رَبُّهُم بِذَنۢبِهِمْ
فَسَوّٰىهَا ۝

15. And for Him[6158]
Is no fear
Of its consequences.

١٥- وَلَا يَخَافُ عُقْبٰهَا ۝ ع

6157. The man who was deputed to do the impious deed of hamstringing the she-camel had of course the sympathy and co-operation of the whole people. Only he was more daring than the rest.

6158. This verse has been variously construed. I follow the general opinion in referring the pronoun "Him" to "their Lord" in the last verse and the pronoun "its" to the Punishment that was meted out to all, high and low, equally. In that case the meaning would be: God decreed the total destruction of the Thamūd; in the case of creatures any such destruction might cause a loss to them, and they might fear the consequences of such loss or destruction, but God has created and can create at will, and there can be no question of any such apprehension in His case. An alternative view is that "him" refers to the prophet Ṣāliḥ mentioned in verse 13. Then the interpretation would be: Ṣāliḥ had no fear of the consequences for himself; he had warned the wicked according to his commission; he was saved by God's mercy as a just and righteous man, and he left them with regrets (vii. 79). Yet another alternative refers "him" to the wicked man (mentioned in verse 12) who hamstrung the she-camel: he feared not the consequences of his deed.

INTRODUCTION AND SUMMARY : SŪRA XCII (*Lail*).

This was one of the first Sūras to be revealed,— within the first ten; and may be placed in date close to S. lxxxix and S. xciii. Note that in all these three Sūras the mystery and the contrast as between Night and Day are appealed to for the consolation of man in his spiritual yearning. Here we are told to strive our utmost towards God, and He will give us every help and satisfaction.

C. 272.—When we consider God's wonderful Creation,
(xcii. 1-21.) We see many mysteries—many opposites—
Many differences; the succession of nights
And days, the creation of male and female.
Can we wonder at the differences
In the nature and objectives of man?
He is endowed with Will, and he must strive
For the Right through all his diverse paths.
For the righteous the way is made the smoother
For bliss; for the arrogant crooked will,
The way is the smoother for Misery.
But God's guidance is always nigh,
If man will choose it. And what
Is the goal for those who choose aright?—
The sight of the Face of God Most High:
For that indeed is happiness supreme.

Sūra XCII.

Lail, or The Night.

In the name of God, Most Gracious, Most Merciful.

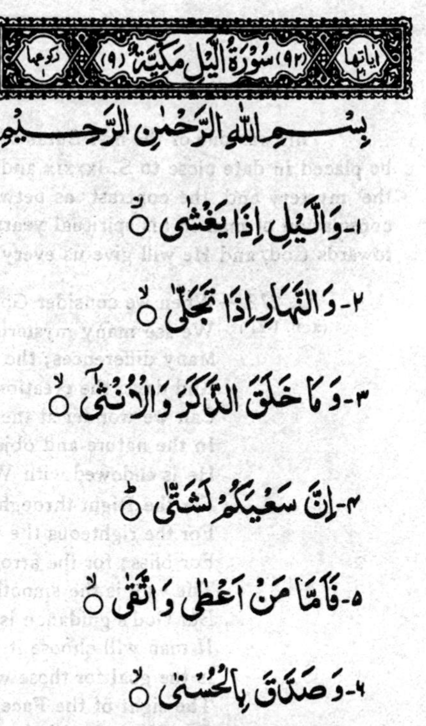

1. By the Night as it
Conceals (the light);[6159]

2. By the Day as it
Appears in glory;

3. By (the mystery of)[6160]
The creation of male
And female;—[6161]

4. Verily, (the ends) ye
Strive for are diverse.[6162]

5. So he who gives
(In charity) and fears (God),

6. And (in all sincerity)
Testifies to the Best,—[6163]

6159. The evidence of three things is invoked, *viz.* Night, Day, and the mystery of Sex, and the conclusion is stated in verse 4, that men's aims are diverse. But similarly there are contrasts in nature. What contrast can be greater than between Night and Day? When the Night spreads her veil, the sun's light is hidden, but not lost. The sun is in his place all the time, and will come forth in all his glory again in his own good time. *Cf.* xci 3 4, and n. 6149. Man pursuing diverse aims may find, owing to his own position, God's light obscured from him for a time, but he must strive hard to put himself in a position to reach it in all its glory.

6160. *Mā maṣdariya* as in xci. 5-7; see there n. 6151.

6161. The mystery of the sexes runs through all life. There is attraction between opposites; each performs its own functions, having special characters, primary and secondary, within limited spheres, and yet both have common characteristics in many other spheres. Each is indispensable to the other. Love in its noblest sense is the type of heavenly love and the highest good; in its debasement it leads to the lowest sins and the worst crimes. Here, then, striving is necessary for the highest good.

6162. There are wide contrasts in the nature and aims of men. These may be broadly divided into two classes, good and evil. As night replaces day on account of certain relative positions, but does not annihilate it, so evil may for a time obscure good but cannot blot it out. Again, night in certain circumstances (*e g.* for rest) is a blessing: so certain things, which may seem evils to us, may be really blessings in disguise Whatever our aims or positions, we must seek the highest truth from the light of God. Considering these contrasts, do not be surprised or depressed. Men's immediate aims may be different. The duty of all is to seek the one true Light.

6163. The good are distinguished here by three signs: (1) large-hearted sacrifices for God and men: (2) fear of God, which shows itself in righteous conduct, for *Taqwā* (see n. 26 to ii. 2) includes just action as well as a mental state: and (3) truth and sincerity in ever recognising and supporting all that is morally beautiful, for *Ḥusn* is the good as well as the beautiful.

7. We will indeed
Make smooth for him
The path to Bliss.[6164]

٧- فَسَنُيَسِّرُهُ لِلْيُسْرَىٰ ۝

8. But he who is
A greedy miser
And thinks himself
Self-sufficient,

٨- وَأَمَّا مَنْ بَخِلَ
وَاسْتَغْنَىٰ ۝

9. And gives the lie
To the Best,—[6165]

٩- وَكَذَّبَ بِالْحُسْنَىٰ ۝

10. We will indeed
Make smooth for him
The Path to Misery;

١٠- فَسَنُيَسِّرُهُ لِلْعُسْرَىٰ ۝

11. Nor will his wealth
Profit him when he
Falls headlong (into the Pit).[6166]

١١- وَمَا يُغْنِي عَنْهُ مَالُهُ
إِذَا تَرَدَّىٰ ۝

12. Verily We take[6167]
Upon Ourselves to guide,

١٢- إِنَّ عَلَيْنَا لَلْهُدَىٰ ۝

13. And verily unto Us
(Belong) the End
And the Beginning.[6168]

١٣- وَإِنَّ لَنَا لَلْآخِرَةَ وَالْأُولَىٰ ۝

6164. So far from there being any hardship in a good life, the righteous will enjoy their life more and more, and God will make their path smoother and smoother until they reach eventual Bliss.

6165. The evil are distinguished here by three signs: (1) selfish greed and denial of other people's rights; (2) arrogance and self-sufficiency (xcvi. 6-7); and (3) knowingly dishonouring Truth out of spite, or seeing ugliness where there is beauty. Such men's downward progress gathers momentum as they go, and their end can be nothing but Misery. Where will be their boasted wealth and possessions, or their self-confidence?

6166. Wealth amassed in this world will be of no use at the Day of Final Judgment, nor will any material advantages of this life bring profit by themselves in the spiritual world. What will count will be a life of truth and righteousness, and of goodness to all the creatures of God.

6167. God in His infinite mercy has provided full guidance to His creatures. All through His creation there are sign-posts indicating the right way. To man He has given the five senses of perception, with mental and spiritual faculties for co-ordinating his physical perceptions and leading him higher and higher in thought and feeling. He has besides sent inspired men for further teaching and guidance.

6168. In the End man will return to God, and even from the beginning of man's life God's mercies and loving care surround him. In the probationary period of man's life, he has a measure of free-will, and he is expected to use it in such a way as to bring his whole being into harmony with the universal Will and Law. For he will have to answer for the right use of his talents and opportunities. If man's will has any meaning, he has the choice of accepting God's guidance or rejecting it, and in the latter case he must take the consequences. Hence the warning of the future "Fire" in the next verse.

14. Therefore do I warn you
Of a Fire blazing fiercely ;

١٤- فَأَنذَرْتُكُمْ نَارًا تَلَظَّىٰ ۝

15. None shall reach it[6169]
But those most unfortunate ones

١٥- لَا يَصْلَىٰهَآ إِلَّا ٱلْأَشْقَى ۝

16. Who give the lie to Truth
And turn their backs.

١٦- ٱلَّذِى كَذَّبَ وَتَوَلَّىٰ ۝

17. But those most devoted
To God shall be[6170]
Removed far from it,—

١٧- وَسَيُجَنَّبُهَا ٱلْأَتْقَى ۝

18. Those who spend their wealth[6171]
For increase in self-purification,[6172]

١٨- ٱلَّذِى يُؤْتِى مَالَهُۥ يَتَزَكَّىٰ ۝

19. And have in their minds
No favour from anyone
For which a reward
Is expected in return,[6173]

١٩- وَمَا لِأَحَدٍ عِندَهُۥ
مِن نِّعْمَةٍ تُجْزَىٰٓ ۝

6169. The Fire of Punishment will not reach any except those who have deliberately sinned against their conscience and rejected God's Truth. The term used for them is "*Ashqā*" (superlative degree). *Cf.* lxxxvii. 11. The corresponding idea in Christian theology is expressed in the following sentence. "All manner of sin and blasphemy shall be forgiven unto men : but the blasphemy against the Holy Ghost shall not be forgiven unto men" (Matt. xii. 31).

"*None shall reach it but those.........*" : the sinners of a lesser degree than the *Ashqā*, though they may suffer a lighter punishment in Hell, will not suffer from the "Fire blazing fiercely".

6170. "Those most devoted to God" : the *Atqā*, the God-fearing men who live lives of purity, and seek only for the "Face of their Lord Most High." See the verses following.

6171. The spending may be for charity, or for good works, such as advancing the cause of knowledge or science, or supporting ideals, etc. "*Wealth*" must be understood not only for money or material goods, but also for any advantage or opportunity which a man happens to enjoy, and which he can place at the service of others.

6172. The Arabic root word *zakā* implies both increase and purification, and both meanings may be understood to be implied here. Wealth (understood both literally and metaphorically) is not for selfish enjoyment or idle show. It is held on trust. It may be a trial in itself, from which a man who emerges successfully is a man all the purer in his life ; and even if he was a good man before, his proper use of his wealth increases his position and dignity in the moral and spiritual world.

6173. The good man does not give in charity or do his good deeds with the motive that he is returning someone else's favour and compensating and rewarding someone for some service done to him or expecting some reward in return for his own good deed ; the sole motive in his mind is that he desires the Countenance or Good Pleasure of God Most High. This "Countenance" or "Face" (Arabic, *Wajh*) implies good pleasure or approval ; but it implies something more. It also means the Cause,—either the "final cause" or the "efficient cause" of Aristotelian philosophy. For the *Atqā* would refer everything, backwards in origin and forwards in destiny, to God. God is the source of their goodness, as well as its goal or purpose.

20. But only the desire
To seek for the Countenance
Of their Lord Most High;[6174]

٢٠- اِلَّا ابۡتِغَآءَ وَجۡهِ رَبِّهِ الۡاَعۡلٰى ۚ

21. And soon will they
Attain (complete) satisfaction.

٢١- وَلَسَوۡفَ يَرۡضٰى ۚ

6174. The definition of Righteousness, Charity, or Self-sacrifice, becomes thus highly spiritualised. The *Atqā* are so completely identified with God's Will that everything else is blotted out to them. What would seem to be sacrifice from other points of view, becomes their own highest pleasure and satisfaction—the "heaven" of the enlightened man. Every virtuous man will have his own bliss, for there are degrees in virtue and bliss. This supreme bliss is the portion—not the prize—of supreme virtue.

INTRODUCTION AND SUMMARY: SŪRA XCIII (*Dhuḥā*).

This Sūra is close in date to Sūras lxxxix and xcii, and the imagery drawn from the contrast of Night and Day is common to all three. In this Sūra the vicissitudes of human life are referred to, and a message of hope and consolation is given to man's soul from God's past mercies, and he is bidden to pursue the path of goodness and proclaim the bounties of God. This is the general meaning. In particular, the Sūra seems to have been revealed in a dark period in the outer life of the holy Prophet, when a man of less resolute will might have been discouraged. But the Prophet is told to hold the present of less account than the glorious Hereafter which awaited him like the glorious morning after a night of stillness and gloom. The Hereafter was, not only in the Future Life, but in his later life on this earth, full of victory and satisfaction.

C. 273.—What an example we have in the Prophet's life!
(xciii. 1-11.) When moments of inspiration were still,
His soul yet felt the power of that stillness,
Like one who prays by night and waits
For the dawn, knowing how the light grows brighter
Every hour till noon, and well content
That night and morn and the hours succeeding
Are but steps to the plenary splendour of noon.
He was content and consoled in the thought that God
Had bestowed His loving care on him
In the past, and so the future was sure.
He followed the Light Divine,—to help
The helpless, to attend with patience to the call
Of those in need, and to rehearse and proclaim
And share the boundless Bounties of God!

Sūra XCIII.

Dhuḥā, or The Glorious Morning Light.

In the name of God, Most Gracious, Most Merciful.

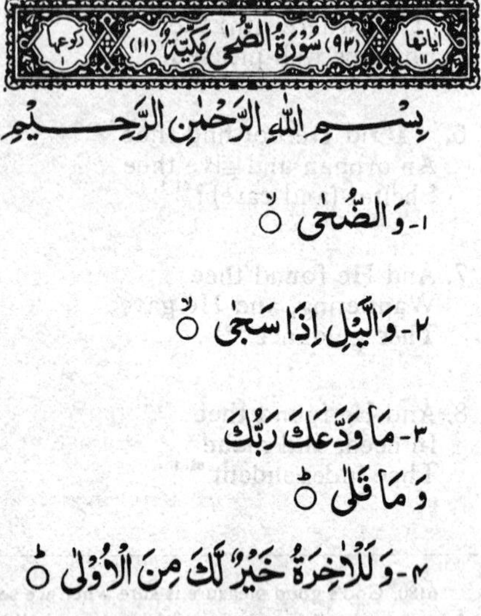

1. By the Glorious
Morning Light,[6175]

2. And by the Night[6176]
When it is still,—

3. Thy Guardian-Lord
Hath not forsaken thee,[6177]
Nor is He displeased.[6178]

4. And verily the hereafter
Will be better for thee
Than the present.[6179]

6175. The full morning light of the sun, when his splendour shines forth in contrast with the night which has passed. *Cf.* xci. 1. The growing hours of morning light, from sunrise to noon, are the true type of the growth of spiritual life and work, while the stillness of the night is, to those who know, only a preparation for it. We are not to imagine that the stillness or quiescence of the night is wasted, or means stagnation in our spiritual life. The stillness may seem lonely, but we are not alone, nor forsaken by God. Nor is such preparation, without immediate visible results, a sign of God's displeasure.

6176. *Cf.* xcii. 1-2. There Night is mentioned first, and Day second, to enforce the lesson of contrasts: the veil of the night naturally comes first before the splendour of daylight is revealed. Here the argument is different: the growing hours of morning light are the main thing and are mentioned first; while the hours of preparation and quiescence, which are subordinate, come second.

6177. As usual, there is the particular assurance to the holy Prophet, and the general assurance to mankind: see the Introduction to this Sūra. The early years of the Prophet's ministry might well have seemed blank. After inspiration there were days and periods of waiting. A sense of loneliness might well have weighed on his mind. His own tribe of the Quraish jeered at him, taunted and threatened him, and slandered and persecuted him as well as those who believed in him. But his faith was never shaken, not even to the extent of that cry of agony of Jesus: "My God! why hast Thou forsaken me?": (Mark, xvi. 34). Much less did it enter the Prophet's mind to think that God was angry with him, as the taunts of his enemies suggested.

6178. See last note. The more general meaning is similar. To the man who prepares for spiritual work and spiritual growth the chief thing is typified by the growing hours of the morning He should not be discouraged, nor overcome with a sense of loneliness in his early struggles or difficulties. The end will crown his work. God's care is always around him. If unsympathetic or hostile critics laugh at him or taunt him with being "mad" or "old-fashioned" or "ploughing his lonely furrow", his steady faith will uphold him. He will never believe that his earnest and sincere devotion to God, whatever be its results in this world, can be anything but pleasing to God.

6179. To the truly devout man, each succeeding moment is better than the one preceding it. In this sense the "hereafter" refers not only to the Future Life after death, but also to "the soul of goodness in things" in this very life. For even though some outward trappings of this shadow-world may be wanting, his soul is filled with more and more satisfaction as he goes on.

5. And soon will thy
Guardian-Lord give thee
(That wherewith) thou
Shalt be well-pleased.[6180]

٥- وَلَسَوْفَ يُعْطِيكَ رَبُّكَ فَتَرْضَىٰ ۝

6. Did He not find thee[6181]
An orphan and give thee
Shelter (and care)?[6182]

٦- أَلَمْ يَجِدْكَ يَتِيمًا فَآوَىٰ ۝

7. And He found thee
Wandering, and He gave
Thee guidance.[6183]

٧- وَوَجَدَكَ ضَالًّا فَهَدَىٰ ۝

8. And He found thee
In need, and made
Thee independent.[6184]

٨- وَوَجَدَكَ عَائِلًا فَأَغْنَىٰ ۝

6180. God's good pleasure is sure when we serve Him. But we are assured that even our feelings of doubt and suffering will vanish, and we shall have a sense of complete satisfaction, contentment, and active pleasure when our will is identified with the Will of God.

6181. Judge the future from the past. God has been good to you in your past experience: trust to His goodness in the future also. Again, there is a particular and a general meaning. Three facts are taken from the holy Prophet's outer life by way of illustration. Metaphorically they also apply to us. And further, the outer facts are themselves types for the spiritual life. See notes below.

6182. (1) There is the case of the orphan, literally and figuratively. Our holy Prophet was himself an orphan. His father 'Abdullāh died young before the child was born, leaving no property. The Prophet's mother Āmina was in ailing health, and he was chiefly brought up by his nurse Ḥalīma. His mother herself died when he was only six years old. His aged grandfather 'Abdul Muṭṭalib treated him as his own son, but died two years later. Thereafter his uncle Abū Ṭālib treated him as his own son. He was thus an orphan in more senses than one, and yet the love he received from each one of these persons was greater than ordinary parental love. Each one of us is an orphan in some sense or another, and yet someone's love and shelter come to us by the grace of God. In the spiritual world there is no father or mother: our very first sustenance and shelter must come from the grace of God.

6183. (2) The holy Prophet was born in the midst of the idolatry and polytheism of Mecca, in a family which was the custodian of this false worship. He wandered in quest of Unity and found it by the guidance of God. There is no implication whatever of sin or error on his part. But we may err and find ourselves wandering in mazes of error, in thought, motive, or understanding: we must pray for God's grace ever to give us guidance.

The Arabic root dhalla has various shades of meaning. In i. 7, I have translated it by the verb "stray". In liii. 2 the Prophet is defended from the charge of being "astray" or straying in mind. In xii. 8 and xii. 95 Jacob's sons use the word for their aged father, to suggest that he was senile and wandering in mind. In xxxii. 10 it is used of the dead, and I have translated "hidden and lost" (in the earth).

6184. (3) The holy Prophet inherited no wealth and was poor. The true, pure, and sincere love of Khadīja not only raised him above want, but made him independent of worldly needs in his later life, enabling him to devote his whole time to the service of God. So do we all find ourselves in some want or another, which, if we work whole-heartedly and sincerely is supplied to us by the grace of God. When we have found the Way, it is a laborious task to climb up in our poverty of spiritual equipment: God will give us spiritual riches in love and knowledge.

9. Therefore, treat not[6185]
The orphan with harshness,

10. Nor repulse the petitioner
(Unheard);[6186]

11. But the Bounty
Of thy Lord—
Rehearse and proclaim![6187]

٩- فَأَمَّا الْيَتِيمَ فَلَا تَقْهَرْ ۝

١٠- وَأَمَّا السَّائِلَ فَلَا تَنْهَرْ ۝

١١- وَأَمَّا بِنِعْمَةِ رَبِّكَ فَحَدِّثْ ۝ ع

6185. Verses 9-11 carry on, to a step further, the triple argument of verses 6-8, as explained in the preceding notes. The Prophet treated all orphans with tender affection and respect, setting an example to his contemporaries, who frequently took advantage of the helpless position of orphans, and in any case looked upon them as subordinate creatures to be repressed and kept in their place. Such an attitude is common in all ages. Helpless creatures ought, on the contrary, to be treated as sacred trusts, whether they are orphans, or dependants, or creatures of any kind unable to assert themselves, either through age, sex, social rank, artificial conditions, or any cause whatever.

6186. Then there are the people who come with petitions,—who have to ask for something. They may be genuine beggars asking for financial help, or ignorant people asking for knowledge, or timid people asking for some lead or encouragement. The common attitude is to scorn them or repulse them. The scorn may be shown even when alms or assistance is given to them. Such an attitude is wrong. Charity is of no moral value without sympathy and love. Nor is it charity to give to idle sturdy professional beggars, for show or to get rid of them. They are mere parasites on society. Every petition should be examined and judged on its merits.

6187. Besides the petitioners, who ask for help, there is the case of those who do not ask but are nevertheless poor—poor but contented in worldly goods, or poor in knowledge or resources and not even knowing that they are poor. If you are bountifully endowed by God, your duty is to make that Bounty spread far and wide. Proclaim it and share it, as the holy Prophet always did. Spiritually we all belong to one of these three classes in one sense or another,—orphans, petitioners, and victims of poverty. We all receive God's grace and guidance in some degree or other. We all owe it as a duty to our fellow-men to be kind and helpful to those less endowed in any respect than ourselves.

INTRODUCTION AND SUMMARY SŪRA XCIV (*Inshirāḥ*).

This short Sūra gives a message of hope and encouragement in a time of darkness and difficulty. It was revealed to the holy Prophet soon after the last Sūra (*Dhuḥā*), whose argument it supplements.

C. 274.—The Prophet's mind and heart had indeed
(xciv. 1-8.) Been expanded and purified ; the burden
Which pressed on his soul had been removed ;
And his name exalted in this world and the next.
For the righteous man there is no trouble
But is linked with ease and joy : he must strive
At every stage, and look to God
Alone as the goal of all his hopes.

Sūra XCIV.

Inshirāḥ, or The Expansion.

In the name of God, Most Gracious, Most Merciful.

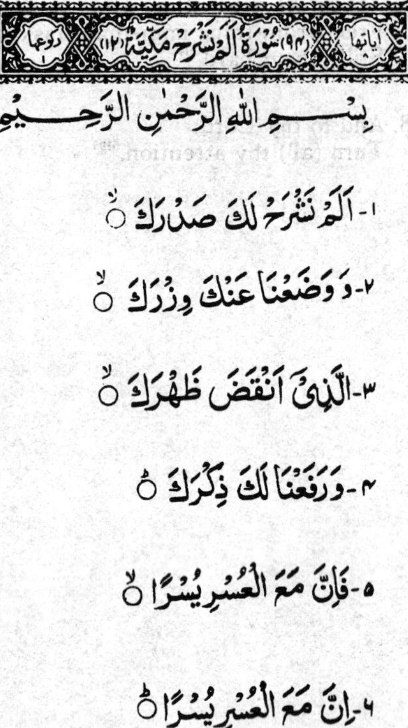

1. Have We not
Expanded thee thy breast ?—[6188]

2. And removed from thee
Thy burden[6189]

3. The which did gall
Thy back ?—

4. And raised high the esteem
(In which) thou (art held) ?[6190]

5. So, verily,
With every difficulty,
There is relief :[6191]

6. Verily, with every difficulty
There is relief.

6188. *Cf.* the prayer of Moses in xx. 25. The breast is symbolically the seat of knowledge and the highest feelings of love and affection, the treasure-house in which are stored the jewels of that quality of human character which approaches nearest to the divine. The holy Prophet's human nature had been purified, expanded, and elevated, so that he became a Mercy to all Creation. Such a nature could afford to ignore the lower motives of ordinary humanity which caused shameful attacks to be made on him. Its strength and courage could also bear the burden of the galling work which it had to do in denouncing sin, subduing it, and protecting God's creatures from its oppression.

6189. See last note. It is indeed a grievous and galling burden for a man to fight single-handed against sin. But God sends His grace and aid, and that burden is removed, or converted into joy and triumph in the service of the One True God.

6190. The Prophet's virtues, the magnanimity of his character, and his love for mankind were fully recognised even in his lifetime, and his name stands highest among the heroic leaders of mankind. The phrase used here is more comprehensive in meaning than that used for various prophets in xxxvii. 119 etc. : "We left this blessing for them among generations to come in later times".

6191. This verse is repeated for extra emphasis. Whatever difficulties or troubles are encountered by men, God always provides a solution, a way out, a relief, a way to lead to ease and happiness, if we only follow His Path and show our Faith by patience and well-doing. The solution or relief does not merely come *after* the Difficulty : it is provided *with* it. I understand the definite article in *al-'usr* in a generic sense, and translate : "every difficulty". In xcii. 7, I have translated *Yusr* as Bliss, and in xcii. 10, *'Usr* as Misery.

7. Therefore, when thou art
Free (from thine immediate task),
Still labour hard,[6192]

٧- فَإِذَا فَرَغْتَ فَانْصَبْ ۝

8. And to thy Lord
Turn (all) thy attention.[6193]

٨- وَإِلَىٰ رَبِّكَ فَارْغَبْ ۝

6192. *When thou art free* : or when thou art relieved. The words understood may be : from thy immediate task, that of preaching to men, denouncing sin, and encouraging righteousness ; or, from the difficulties that confronted thee. When that happens, that does not finish the labours of the man of God. It is only one step to them. He has constantly and insistently to go on. When there is rest from the task of instructing the world, the contact with the spiritual kingdom continues, and indeed it becomes more intimate and concentrated.

6193. The kingdom of God is everything. Other things are incidental, and really do not matter. Worldly greatness or success may be a means to an end, but it may also be a hindrance to true spiritual greatness. God is the goal of the righteous man's whole attention and desire.

INTRODUCTION AND SUMMARY : SŪRA XCV (*Tīn*).

This is also a very early Sūra. It appeals to the most sacred symbols to show that God created man in the best of moulds, but that man is capable of the utmost degradation unless he has Faith and leads a good life. In subject-matter this Sūra closely resembles S. ciii.

C. 275.—Nature and history and the Light of Revelation,
(xcv. 1-8.) Through the ages, show that man,
Created by God in the best of moulds,
Can yet fall to the lowest depths, unless
He lives a life of faith and righteousness.
Then will he reach his goal : if not,
He must stand his Judgment—none can doubt—
Before the wisest and justest of Judges.

Sūra XCV.

Tin, or The Fig.

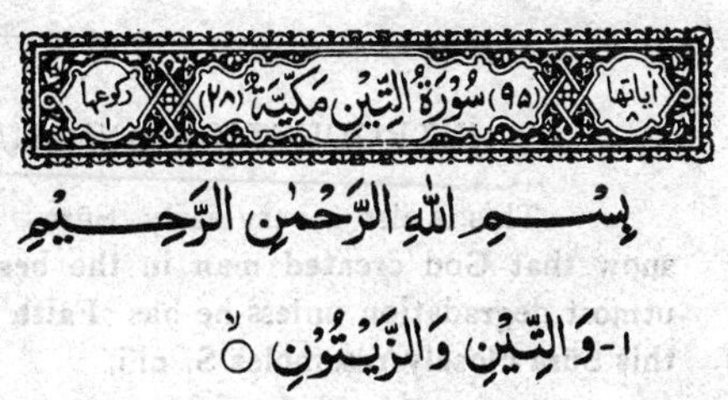

In the name of God, Most Gracious, Most Merciful.

بِسْمِ اللهِ الرَّحْمٰنِ الرَّحِيْمِ

1. By the Fig[6194]
And the Olive,[6195]

١-وَالتِّيْنِ وَالزَّيْتُوْنِ ۙ

2. And the Mount
Of Sinai,[6196]

٢-وَطُوْرِ سِيْنِيْنَ ۙ

3. And this City[6197]
Of security,—[6198]

٣-وَهٰذَا الْبَلَدِ الْاَمِيْنِ ۙ

6194. The substantive proposition is in verses 4-8, and it is clinched by an appeal to four sacred symbols, *viz.*, the Fig, the Olive, Mount Sinai, and the sacred City of Mecca. About the precise interpretation of the first two symbols, and especially of the symbol of the Fig, there is much difference of opinion. If we take the Fig literally to refer to the fruit or the tree, it can stand as a symbol of man's destiny in many ways. Under cultivation it can be one of the finest, most delicious, and most wholesome fruits in existence : in its wild state, it is nothing but tiny seeds, and is insipid. and often full of worms and maggots. So man at his best has a noble destiny : at his worst, he is "the lowest of the low". Christ is said to have cursed a fig tree for having only leaves, and not producing fruit (Matt. **xxi**. 18-20), enforcing the same lesson. There is also a parable of the fig tree in Matt. **xxiv**. 32-35. See also the parable of the good and evil figs in Jeremiah, xxiv. 1-10. But see n. 6198 below.

6195. For the sacred symbolism of the Olive, see n. 2880 to **xxiii**. 20, and notes 3000-3002 to **xxiv**. 35, where the parable of God's Light includes a reference to the Olive. But it is possible that the Olive here refers to the Mount of Olives, just outside the walls of the City of Jerusalem (see n. 5038 to lii. 2), for this is the scene in the Gospel story (Matt. **xxiv**. 3-4) of Christ's description of the Judgment to come.

6196. This was the Mountain on which the Law was given to Moses. See **xix**. 52, and n. 2504. The Law was given, and the glory of God was made visible. But did Israel faithfully obey the Law thereafter ?

6197. "This City of security" is undoubtedly Mecca. Even in Pagan times its sacred character was respected, and no fighting was allowed in its territory. But the same City, with all its sacred associations, persecuted the greatest of the Prophets and gave itself up for a time to idolatry and sin, thus presenting the contrast of the best and the worst.

6198. Having discussed the four symbols in detail, let us consider them together. It is clear that they refer to God's Light or Revelation, which offers man the highest destiny if he will follow the Way. Mecca stands for Islam, Sinai for Israel, and the Mount of Olives for Christ's original and pure Message. It has been suggested that the Fig stands for the *Ficus Indica*, the Bo-tree, under which Gautama Buddha obtained Nirvana. I hesitate to adopt the suggestion, but if accepted it would cover pristine Buddhism and the ancient Vedic religions from which it was an offshoot. In this way all the great religions of the world would be indicated. But even if we refer the Fig and the Olive to the symbolism in their fruit, and not to any particular religion, the contrast of Best and Worst in man's destiny remains, and that is the main thing.

4. We have inneed created man
In the best of moulds,[6199]

٤- لَقَدْ خَلَقْنَا الْإِنسَانَ فِي أَحْسَنِ تَقْوِيمٍ ۝

5. Then do We abase him
(To be) the lowest
Of the low,—[6200]

٥- ثُمَّ رَدَدْنَاهُ أَسْفَلَ سَافِلِينَ ۝

6. Except such as believe
And do righteous deeds :
For they shall have
A reward unfailing.

٦- إِلَّا الَّذِينَ آمَنُوا وَعَمِلُوا الصَّالِحَاتِ
فَلَهُمْ أَجْرٌ غَيْرُ مَمْنُونٍ ۝

7. Then what can,
After this, contradict thee,[6201]
As to the Judgment
(To come) ?

٧- فَمَا يُكَذِّبُكَ
بَعْدُ بِالدِّينِ ۝

8. Is not God
The wisest of Judges ?[6202]

٨- أَلَيْسَ اللَّهُ بِأَحْكَمِ الْحَاكِمِينَ ۝ ع

6199. *Taqwīm* : mould, symmetry, form, nature, constitution. There is no fault in God's creation. To man God gave the purest and best nature, and man's duty is to preserve the pattern on which God has made him : xxx. 30. But by making him His vicegerent, God exalted him *in posse* even higher than the angels, for the angels had to make obeisance to him (ii. 30-34, and n. 48). But man's position as vicegerent also gives him will and discretion, and if he uses them wrongly he falls even lower than the beasts. See next note.

6200 This verse should be read with the next. If man rebels against God, and follows after evil, he will be abased to the lowest possible position. For Judgment is sure. Those who use their faculties aright and follow God's Law will reach the high and noble destiny intended for them. That reward will not be temporary, but unfailing.

6201. *Thee* : may refer to the holy Prophet, or to man collectively. *After this* : i.e., when it is clearly shown to you that God created man true and pure, that He guides him, and that those who rebel and break His law will be punished and brought down in the Hereafter, who can doubt this, or contradict the Prophet when he gives warning ?

6202. God is wise and just Therefore the righteous have nothing to fear, but the evil ones cannot escape punishment.

INTRODUCTION AND SUMMARY : SŪRA XCVI (*Iqraa*, or *'Alaq*).

Verses 1-5 of this Sūra were the first direct Revelation to the holy Prophet. The circumstances, material and psychical, in which they came, are described in C. 28-30, which should be referred to.

After that there was an interval or break (*Fatra*), extending over some months or perhaps over a year. S. lxviii. is usually considered to have been the next revelation in point of time. But the remainder of this Sūra (xcvi. 6-19) came soon after the *Fatra*, and that portion is joined on to the first five verses containing the command to preach, because it explains the chief obstacle to the delivery of the message to man, *viz.* : man's own obstinacy, vanity, and insolence.

C. 276.—Noble is the mission of the Prophet, selected
(xcvi. 1-19.) To proclaim the Message of God, the Lord
And Cherisher of all His Creation, Whose measureless
Bounties include the instruction of man
In new and ever new knowledge. But alas
For man ! he fancies himself self-sufficient,
Turns away from the Path, and misleads others.
But nothing is hidden from God. He will bring
All untruth and sin and rebellion to Judgment,
And subdue all evil. The righteous bow
In adoration to God, and draw closer to Him.

Sūra XCVI.

Iqraa, or Read ! or Proclaim !

Or *'Alaq*, or The Clot of Congealed Blood.

In the name of God, Most Gracious, Most Merciful.

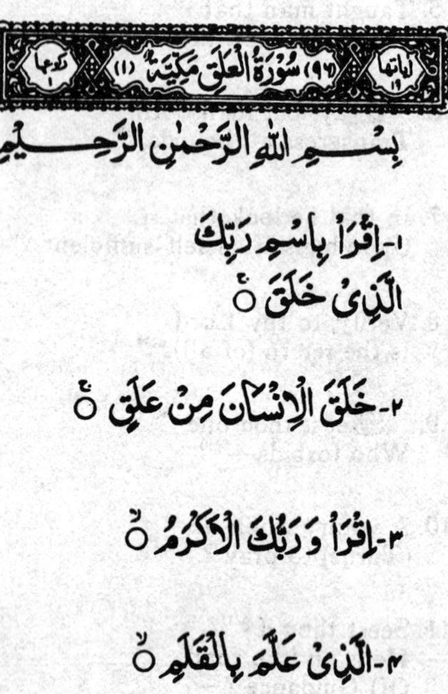

1. Proclaim ! (or Read !)[6203]
In the name[6204]
Of thy Lord and Cherisher,
Who created—

2. Created man, out of
A (mere) clot
Of congealed blood :[6205]

3. Proclaim ! And thy Lord
Is Most Bountiful,—

4. He Who taught
(The use of) the Pen,—[6206]

6203. *Iqraa* may mean "read", or "recite or rehearse", or "proclaim aloud", the object understood being God's Message. For an account of the circumstances in which this first revelation—the divine commission to preach and proclaim God's Message came to the holy Prophet, in the cave of Ḥiraa, see C. 27-31. In worldly letters he was unversed, but with spiritual knowledge his mind and soul were filled, and now had come the time when he must stand forth to the world and declare his mission.

6204. The declaration or proclamation was to be in the name of God the Creator. It was not for any personal benefit to the Prophet : to him there was to come bitter persecution, sorrow, and suffering. It was the call of God for the benefit of erring humanity. God is mentioned by his title of "thy Lord and Cherisher", to establish a direct nexus between the source of the Message and the one addressed. The Message was not merely an abstract proposition of philosophy, but the direct concrete message of a personal God to the creatures whom He loves and cherishes. "*Thy*" addressed to the Prophet is appropriate in two ways : (1) he was in direct contact with the divine Messenger (Gabriel) and Him Who sent the Messenger ; (2) he represented the whole of humanity, in a fuller sense than that in which Christ Jesus is the "Son of Man".

6205. *Cf.* xxiii. 14. The lowly origin of the animal in man is contrasted with the high destiny offered to him in his intellectual, moral, and spiritual nature by his "most bountiful" Creator. No knowledge is withheld from man, On the contrary, through the faculties freely given to him, he acquires it in such measure as outstrips his immediate understanding, and leads him ever to strive for newer and newer meaning.

6206. The symbol of a permanent revelation is the mystic Pen and the mystic Record. See n. 5593 to lxviii. 1.

The Arabic words for "teach" and "knowledge" are from the same root. It is impossible to produce in a Translation the complete orchestral harmony of the words for "read", "teach", "pen" (which implies reading, writing, books, study, research), "knowledge" (including science, self knowledge, spiritual understanding), and "proclaim", an alternative meaning of the word for "to read". This proclaiming or reading implies not only the duty of blazoning forth God's message, as going with the prophetic office, but also the duty of promulgation and wide dissemination of the Truth by all who read and understand it. The comprehensive meaning of *qaraa* refers not only to a particular person and occasion but also gives a universal direction. And this kind of comprehensive meaning, as we have seen, runs throughout the Qur-ān—for those who will understand.

5. Taught man that Which he knew not.[6207]	٥- عَلَّمَ الْإِنْسَانَ مَا لَمْ يَعْلَمْ ۝
6. Nay, but man doth Transgress all bounds,[6208]	٦- كَلَّآ إِنَّ الْإِنْسَانَ لَيَطْغَىٰٓ ۝
7. In that he looketh Upon himself as self-sufficient.	٧- أَنْ رَّاٰهُ اسْتَغْنَىٰ ۝
8. Verily, to thy Lord Is the return (of all).[6209]	٨- إِنَّ إِلَىٰ رَبِّكَ الرُّجْعَىٰ ۝
9. Seest thou one Who forbids—[6210]	٩- أَرَءَيْتَ الَّذِي يَنْهَىٰ ۝
10. A votary when he (Turns) to pray ?	١٠- عَبْدًا إِذَا صَلَّىٰ ۝
11. Seest thou if [6211] He is on (the road Of) Guidance ?—	١١- أَرَءَيْتَ إِنْ كَانَ عَلَى الْهُدَىٰٓ ۝
12. Or enjoins Righteousness ?	١٢- أَوْ أَمَرَ بِالتَّقْوَىٰ ۝

6207. God teaches us new knowledge at every given moment Individuals learn more and more day by day ; nations and humanity at large learn fresh knowledge at every stage. This is even more noticeable and important in the spiritual world.

6208. All our knowledge and capacities come as gifts from God. But man, in his inordinate vanity and insolence, mistakes God's gifts for his own achievements. The gifts may be strength or beauty, wealth, position, or power, or the more subtle gifts of knowledge or talents in individuals,—or Science, or Art, or Government, or Organisation for mankind in general.

6209. Man is not self-sufficient, either as an individual, or in his collective capacity. If he arrogates God's gifts to himself, he is reminded—backwards, of his lowly physical origin (from a drop of animal matter), and forwards, of his responsibility and final return to God.

6210. The words may be applied generally to perverse humanity, which seeks not only to rebel against God's Law, but also to prevent others from following it. There may however be a reference here to Abū Jahl, an inveterate enemy of Islam, who used in its early days to insult and persecute the holy Prophet and those who followed his teaching. He used, in particular, to use shameful methods to prevent the Prophet from going to the Ka'ba for devotions, and forbid any who came under his influence, from offering prayers or performing devotions. He was arrogant and purse-proud and met his end in the battle of Badr.

6211. Man's insolence leads to two results ; (1) self-destruction through self-misleading ; (2) a false example or false guidance to others. The righteous man must therefore test human example or human guidance by the question, "Is there God's guidance behind it ?" And visible light would be thrown on it by the question, "Does it lead to righteousness ?" A flouting of God and God's Truth answers the first question in the negative, and conduct which turns back from the eternal principles of Right answers the second

13. Seest thou if he[6212]
Denies (Truth) and turns away ?

١٣- أَرَءَيْتَ إِن كَذَّبَ وَتَوَلَّىٰٓ ۝

14. Knoweth he not
That God doth see ?

١٤- أَلَمْ يَعْلَم بِأَنَّ ٱللَّهَ يَرَىٰ ۝

15. Let him beware ! If he
Desist not, We will
Drag him by the forelock,—[6213]

١٥- كَلَّا لَئِن لَّمْ يَنتَهِ
لَنَسْفَعًۢا بِٱلنَّاصِيَةِ ۝

16. A lying, sinful forelock !

١٦- نَاصِيَةٍ كَـٰذِبَةٍ خَاطِئَةٍ ۝

17. Then, let him call
(For help) to his council[6214]
(Of comrades) :

١٧- فَلْيَدْعُ نَادِيَهُۥ ۝

18. We will call
On the angels of punishment
(To deal with him) ![6215]

١٨- سَنَدْعُ ٱلزَّبَانِيَةَ ۝

19. Nay, heed him not :
But bow down in adoration,
And bring thyself
The closer (to God) ![6216]

١٩- كَلَّا لَا تُطِعْهُ
وَٱسْجُدْ وَٱقْتَرِب ۝

6212. The usual trick of the ungodly is to refuse to face Truth. If they are placed in a corner, they deny what is obvious to reasonable men, and turn their backs.

6213. *Cf.* xi. 56, and n. 1551. The forelock is on the forehead, and is thus symbolical of the summit and crown of the man's power or dignity. To be dragged by it is to suffer the lowest dregs of humiliation. *Nasfa'an* is a syncopated form of the emphatic first person plural.

6214. The Pagan Quraish, who formed an oppressive junta or council to manage the Ka'ba were in sympathy with Abū Jahl, though they did not go to the unbridled lengths to which Abū Jahl went. But they could not, all combined, resist the onward march of the divine mission, though they did all they could to check it.

6215. All the combined forces of evil, though they may have worldly appearances in their favour, and though they may seem to be successful for a time, cannot stand against God. He has but to command His forces of punishment to exert themselves, and they will subdue evil, protect God's votaries and justify the faith for which the votaries suffer.

6216. The righteous man has no fear. He can disregard all the forces of evil that are brought against him. But he must learn humility : that is his defence. He will bow down in adoration to God. He must have the will to bring *himself* closer to God. For God is always close to him,—closer to him than his life blood in the jugular vein (*l.* 16). Man's humility and adoration remove him from being an insolent rebel on the one hand and, on the other, prepare his will to realise his nearness to God.

INTRODUCTION AND SUMMARY: SŪRA XCVII (*Qadr*).

The chronology of this Sūra has no significance. It is probably Meccan, though some hold that it was revealed in Medina.

The subject-matter is the mystic Night of Power (or Honour), in which Revelation comes down to a benighted world,—it may be to the wonderful Cosmos of an individual—and transforms the conflict of wrong-doing into Peace and Harmony —through the agency of the angelic host, representing the spiritual powers of the Mercy of God.

C. *277*.—Blessed indeed is the Night of Power!—
(xcvii. 1-5.) When the Mercy of God's Revelation breaks through
The darkness of the human soul!
All the Powers, of the world divine,
Speed on their mystic Message of Mercy,
By God's command, and bless every nook
And corner of the heart! All jars
Are stilled in the reign supreme of Peace,
Until this mortal night gives place
To the glorious day of an immortal world!

Sūra XCVII.

Qadr, or The Night of Power (or Honour).

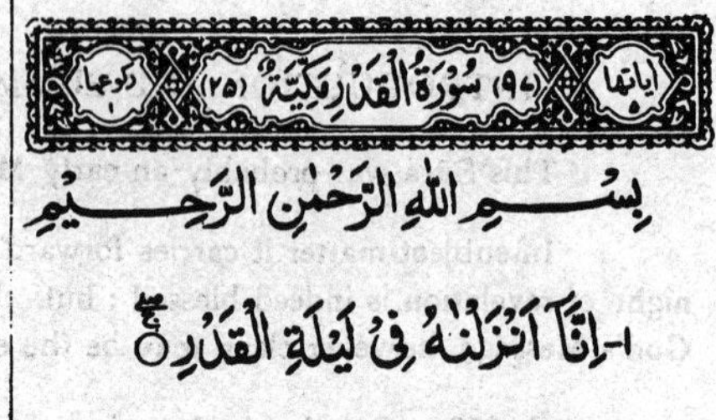

In the name of God, Most Gracious, Most Merciful.

بِسْمِ اللّٰهِ الرَّحْمٰنِ الرَّحِيْمِ

1. We have indeed revealed
This (Message)
In the Night of Power:[6217]

١- اِنَّآ اَنْزَلْنٰهُ فِيْ لَيْلَةِ الْقَدْرِ

2. And what will explain
To thee what the Night
Of Power is?

٢- وَمَآ اَدْرٰىكَ مَا لَيْلَةُ الْقَدْرِ

3. The Night of Power
Is better than
A thousand Months.[6218]

٣- لَيْلَةُ الْقَدْرِ خَيْرٌ مِّنْ اَلْفِ شَهْرٍ

4. Therein come down
The angels and the Spirit[6219]
By God's permission,
On every errand:

٤- تَنَزَّلُ الْمَلٰٓئِكَةُ وَالرُّوْحُ
فِيْهَا بِاِذْنِ رَبِّهِمْ مِنْ كُلِّ اَمْرٍ

5. Peace! . . . This
Until the rise of Morn![6220]

٥- سَلٰمٌ هِيَ حَتّٰى مَطْلَعِ الْفَجْرِ

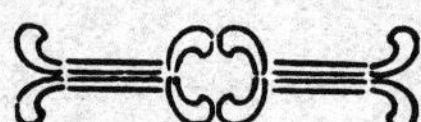

6217. *Cf.* xliv. 3 and n. 4690. Literalists refer to some particular night in the calendar, but there is no agreement as to which it is. The 23rd, 25th or 27th night of Ramadhān, as well as other nights, have been suggested. See, however, the Introduction to this Sūra. It is best to take this in the mystic sense, which also accords with verse 3 below, which says that the Night of Power is better than a thousand Months. It transcends Time: for it is God's Power dispelling the Darkness of Ignorance, by his Revelation, in every kind of affair.

6218. "A thousand" must be taken in an indefinite sense, as denoting a very long period of time. *Cf.* notes 3632 and 3634 to xxxii. 4-5, and n. 5678 to lxx. 4. This does not refer to our ideas of time, but to "timeless Time". One moment of enlightenment under God's Light is better than thousands of months or years of animal life, and such a moment converts the night of darkness into a period of spiritual glory.

6219. *The Spirit*: usually understood to be the angel Gabriel, the Spirit of Inspiration. But names are hardly necessary in the mystic world. See n. 5677 to lxx. 4.

6220. When the Night of spiritual darkness is dissipated by the glory of God, a wonderful Peace and a sense of Security arise in the soul. And this lasts on until this life closes, and the glorious Day of the new spiritual world dawns, when everything will be on a different plane, and the chequered nights and days of this world will be even less than a dream.

INTRODUCTION AND SUMMARY : SŪRA XCVIII (*Baiyina*).

This Sūra was probably an early Medina Sūra, or possibly a late Meccan Sūra.

In subject-matter it carries forward the argument of the last Sūra. The mystic night of revelation is indeed blessed : but those who reject Truth are impervious to God's Message, however clear may be the evidence in support of it.

C. 278.—But those who reject the light of Truth
xcviii. 1-8.) Are obstinate. Why should they persist
In evil ways when the Clear Evidence
Has come before them ? The straight Religion
Is simple : to adore with a pure heart
The God of Truth, to draw nigh to Him
In Prayer sincere, and to serve
Our fellow-creatures in charity and love.
To do aught else is to fall from Grace.
But Faith and Good Life lead straight to the Goal,—
The beauteous Gardens of Bliss Eternal,
And the mutual good pleasure of the Soul in her Lord.

Sūra XCVIII.

Baiyina, or The Clear Evidence.

In the name of God, Most Gracious,
Most Merciful

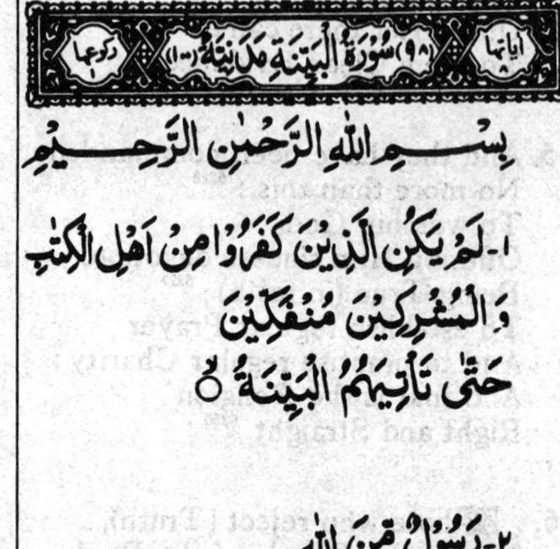

1. Those who reject (Truth),
Among the People of the Book[6221]
And among the Polytheists,[6222]
Were not going to depart
(From their ways) until
There should come to them
Clear Evidence,—[6223]

2. An apostle from God,
Rehearsing scriptures[6224]
Kept pure and holy:[6225]

3. Wherein are laws (or decrees)
Right and straight.[6226]

4. Nor did the People
Of the Book

6221. The People of the Book immediately referred to are the Jews and the Christians, who had received scriptures in the same line of prophecy in which came our holy Prophet. Their scriptures should have prepared them for the advent of the greatest and last of the Prophets. For the Jewish scriptures promised to the Jews, cousins or brethren to the Arabs, a prophet like Moses: "The Lord thy God will raise up unto thee a Prophet from the midst of thee, of thy brethren, like unto me; unto him ye shall hearken" (Deut. xviii. 15). And Christ promised a Comforter (John, xiv. 16; xv. 26; and xvi. 7; see my n. 5438 to lxi. 6) almost by name. The People of the Book fell from the true, straight, and standard religion, into devious ways, and would not come to the true Path until (they said) they were convinced by the arrival of the promised Prophet. But when the promised Prophet came in the person of Muḥammad, they rejected him, because they really did not seek for Truth but only followed their own fancies and desires.

6222. The Polytheists, the Pagans, had not previously believed in any scriptures. But yet, when clear evidence came to them, they should have believed. Yet they rejected the holy Prophet because they were not really searching for Truth, but were only following their own fancies and desires.

6223. The Clear Evidence was the holy Prophet himself, his life, his personality, and his teaching.

6224. *Cf.* ii. 151.

6225. *Cf.* lxxx. 13-16.

6226. *Qaiyim*: straight, as opposed to crooked; standard as opposed to irregular; definite and permanent, as opposed to casual or temporary. *Cf.* ix. 36; xii. 40; etc.

Make schisms,[6227]
Until after there came
To them Clear Evidence.

مِنۢ بَعۡدِ مَا جَآءَتۡهُمُ ٱلۡبَيِّنَةُ ۝

5. And they have been commanded
No more than this :[6228]
To worship God,
Offering Him sincere devotion,
Being True (in faith);[6229]
To establish regular Prayer;
And to practise regular Charity;
And that is the Religion
Right and Straight.[6230]

٥- وَمَآ أُمِرُوٓاْ إِلَّا
لِيَعۡبُدُواْ ٱللَّهَ مُخۡلِصِينَ لَهُ ٱلدِّينَ
حُنَفَآءَ وَيُقِيمُواْ ٱلصَّلَوٰةَ
وَيُؤۡتُواْ ٱلزَّكَوٰةَ
وَذَٰلِكَ دِينُ ٱلۡقَيِّمَةِ ۝

6. Those who reject (Truth),
Among the People of the Book
And among the Polytheists,
Will be in hell-fire,
To dwell therein (for aye).
They are the worst
Of creatures.[6231]

٦- إِنَّ ٱلَّذِينَ كَفَرُواْ
مِنۡ أَهۡلِ ٱلۡكِتَٰبِ وَٱلۡمُشۡرِكِينَ
فِي نَارِ جَهَنَّمَ خَٰلِدِينَ فِيهَآ
أُوْلَٰٓئِكَ هُمۡ شَرُّ ٱلۡبَرِيَّةِ ۝

7. Those who have faith
And do righteous deeds,—
They are the best
Of creatures.[6232]

٧- إِنَّ ٱلَّذِينَ ءَامَنُواْ وَعَمِلُواْ ٱلصَّٰلِحَٰتِ
أُوْلَٰٓئِكَ هُمۡ خَيۡرُ ٱلۡبَرِيَّةِ ۝

6227. The responsibility of the People of the Book is greater than that of Pagans, because the People of the Book had been prepared for the standard and straight Religion by the revelations which they had already received. Yet, when the clear evidence came in Islam, they resisted it, And what is this standard and straight Religion, free of all ambiguity, and free of all casual rights and ceremonies? They are summed up in three eternal principles, as explained in the next verse and the next note.

6228. The three eternal principles of Religion are: (1) sincere devotion to God; (2) Prayer and Praise as drawing man nearer to God and to the spiritual world; and (3) the service of God's creatures by deeds of practical charity.

6229. Ḥanif: see n. 134 to ii. 135.

6230. See n. 6226 above.

6231. To be given the faculty of discrimination between right and wrong, and then to reject truth and right, is the worst folly which a creature endowed with will can commit. It must necessarily bring its own punishment, whether the creature calls himself one of the children of Abraham or one of the redeemed of Christ, or whether he goes by the mere light of nature and reason as a Pagan. Honour in the sight of God is not due to race or professions of faith, but to sincere and righteous conduct (xlix. 13).

6232. Contrast this with the preceding verse. Human beings who live a life of faith and good deeds justify the purpose of their probation here. They attain the fulfilment of their highest hopes, which is their Heaven

8. Their reward is with God :
Gardens of Eternity,
Beneath which rivers flow;
They will dwell therein
For ever; God well pleased
With them, and they with Him :[6233]
All this for such as
Fear their Lord and Cherisher.[6234]

٨- جَزَآؤُهُمْ عِندَ رَبِّهِمْ جَنّٰتُ عَدْنٍ تَجْرِي مِن تَحْتِهَا الْأَنْهٰرُ خٰلِدِينَ فِيهَآ أَبَدًا ۖ رَّضِيَ اللَّهُ عَنْهُمْ وَرَضُوا۟ عَنْهُ ۚ ذٰلِكَ لِمَنْ خَشِيَ رَبَّهُۥ ۝

6233. The Good Pleasure of God is the final Bliss of Salvation. The good pleasure is mutual; the truly saved is he whose will has become completely identified with God's universal will. See Appendix XII. on the Muslim Heaven. *Cf.* lxxxix. 27-30.

6234. The fear of God is the fear to offend against His holy law, the fear to do anything which is against His holy Will. Such fear is akin to love; for with it dawns the consciousness of God's loving-care for all His creatures.

INTRODUCTION AND SUMMARY : SŪRA XCIX (*Zilzāl*).

This Sūra is close in date to the last : it is generally referred to the early Medina period, though it may possibly be of the late Meccan period.

It refers to the tremendous convulsion and uprooting which will take place when the present order of the world is dissolved and the new spiritual world of Justice and Truth takes its place. The symbol used is that of an earthquake which will shake our present material and phenomenal world to its very foundations. The mystic words in which the earthquake is described are remarkable for both power and graphic aptness. With that shaking all hidden mysteries will be brought to light.

C. 279.—The Hour of Judgment must needs be heralded
(xcix. 1-8.) By a mighty Convulsion : the Earth will give up
Her secrets and tell her tale of all
Man's doings : men will march in companies
And clearly see the inwardness
Of all their Deeds : not an atom of Good
Or Evil done, but will be shown
In the final Account of men convinced.

Sūra XCIX.

Zilzāl, or The Convulsion.

In the name of God, Most Gracious, Most Merciful.

1. When the Earth is
Shaken to her (utmost)
convulsion,[6235]

2. And the Earth throws up
Her burdens (from within),[6236]

3. And man cries (distressed):
'What is the matter with her?'—[6237]

4. On that Day will she
Declare her tidings:

5. For that thy Lord will
Have given her inspiration.[6238]

6. On that Day will men
Proceed in companies sorted out,[6239]

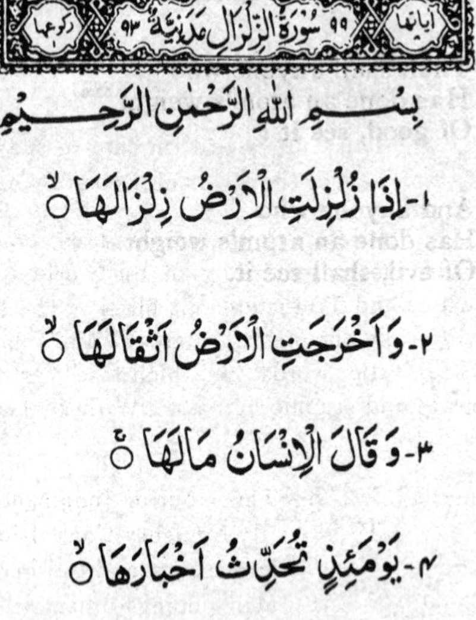

٦-يَوْمَئِذٍ يَّصْدُرُ النَّاسُ اَشْتَاتًا ۙ

6235. To the ordinary human observer a violent earthquake is a terrifying phenomenon, in its suddenness, in its mysterious origin, and in its power to destroy and uproot the strongest buildings and to bring up strange materials from the bowels of the earth. The Overwhelming Event (S. lxxxviii.) which ushers in the Judgment will be a bigger and more far-reaching convulsion than any earthquakes that we know. And yet the incidents of earthquakes may give us some idea of that supreme world-shaking Event.

6236. An earthquake, if accompanied by a volcanic eruption, throws up enormous boulders and lava from beneath the crust of the earth. They are thrown up as if they were a burden to the Earth personified. They may be all kinds of minerals, or treasures buried for secrecy. So in the great and final Convulsion, the dead who had been buried and forgotten will rise; matters and motives which had been secretly hidden and metaphorically buried will be brought to the light of day, and justice will be done in the full glare of absolute Truth.

6237. The puzzled agony suffered by the victims of a violent earthquake is as nothing compared to the experience of the new and wonderful world which will then open out to the gaze of man.

6238. The present order may be personified as the earth. It will pass away, but the Deeds done therein, even the most secret, will be brought to the full light of day. And this will be because God will give the Command, the inspiration or Word, by which alone all events do proceed. The "inspiration" is the Command or direction conveyed by instruction breathed into the Earth personified: she is directed to tell the whole story of what she knows. *Cf.* xvi. 68, n. 2097.

6239. In this world good and evil are mixed together. But then they will be sorted out, and each grade of good and evil will be sorted out. So they will proceed in companies to receive judgment. And they will be shown the exact import of everything that they had thought, said, or done, in this life of probation, however they may have concealed or misinterpreted it in this life. Everything will be considered in taking the account, and the account will convince the persons concerned themselves.

To be shown the Deeds That they (had done).	لِّيُرَوْا أَعْمَالَهُمْ ۝
7. Then shall anyone who Has done an atom's weight [6240] Of good, see it !	٧- فَمَن يَعْمَلْ مِثْقَالَ ذَرَّةٍ خَيْرًا يَرَهُ ۝
8. And anyone who Has done an atom's weight Of evil, shall see it.	٨- وَمَن يَعْمَلْ مِثْقَالَ ذَرَّةٍ شَرًّا يَرَهُ ۝ ع

6240. *Ẓarrāt*: the weight of an ant, the smallest living weight an odinary man can think of. Figuratively the subtlest form of good and evil will then be brought to account, and it will be done openly and convincingly: he "shall see it".

INTRODUCTION AND SUMMARY . SŪRA C ('*Ādiyāt*).

This is one of the earlier Meccan Sūras. In the depth of its mystery and the rhythm and sublimity of its language and symbolism, it may be compared with S. lxxix. Its subject-matter is the irresistible nature of spiritual power and knowledge, contrasted with unregenerate man's ingratitude, pettiness, helplessness, and ignorance.

C. 280.—There are those that fight, with eager charge,
(c. 1-11.) The hosts of evil, and storm its citadel.
But unregenerate Man shows less
Than gratitude for God's most gracious
Bounties : his life bears witness to his treason
And his greed. God's knowledge is all-embracing :
All things hidden will be laid bare at Judgment.

Sūra C.

'*Ādiyāt*, or Those that run.

In the name of God, Most Gracious, Most Merciful.

بِسْمِ اللّٰهِ الرَّحْمٰنِ الرَّحِيْمِ

1. By the (Steeds)[6241]
That run, with panting (breath),

١- وَالْعٰدِيٰتِ ضَبْحًا ۙ

2 And strike sparks of fire,[6242]

٢- فَالْمُوْرِيٰتِ قَدْحًا ۙ

3. And push home the charge
In the morning,[6243]

٣- فَالْمُغِيْرٰتِ صُبْحًا ۙ

4. And raise the dust
In clouds the while,[6244]

٤- فَاَثَرْنَ بِهٖ نَقْعًا ۙ

5. And penetrate forthwith
Into the midst (of the foe)
En masse;—[6245]

٥- فَوَسَطْنَ بِهٖ جَمْعًا ۙ

6241. The substantive proposition is in verses 6-8 below, and the metaphors and symbols enforcing the lesson are in verses 1-5 here. These symbols have at least three layers of mystic meaning: (1) Look at the chargers (mares or swift camels) panting for war on behalf of their masters. Off they go, striking fire with their hoofs by night at the behest of their riders; they push home the charge in the morning, chivalrously giving the enemy the benefit of daylight; and regardless of flashing steel or the weapons of their enemies they boldly penetrate into the midst of their foe, risking their lives for the Cause. Does unregenerate man show that fidelity to his Lord God? On the contrary he is ungrateful to God; he shows that by his deeds; he is violently in love with wealth and gain and things that perish. (2 By the figure of metonymy the brave fidelity of the war-horse may stand for that of the brave men and true who rally to the standard of God and carry it to victory, contrasted with the poltroonery and pettiness of unregenerate man. (3). The whole conflict, fighting, and victory, may be applied to spiritual warfare against those who are caught and overwhelmed in the camp of Evil.

6242. With their hoofs. If we suppose the march to be in the dead of night, the sparks of fire would be still more conspicuous.

6243. We may suppose a surprise attack, but yet a chivalrous attack by daylight. The foe is punished through his own lethargy and unpreparedness, apart from the strength, fire, and spirit of the forces of righteousness.

6244. The clouds of dust typify the ignorance and confusion in the minds of those who oppose Truth.

6245. The forces of evil mass themselves for strength, but their massing itself may become a means of their speedy undoing.

6. Truly Man is, To his Lord,[6246] Ungrateful ;	٦- إِنَّ الْإِنْسَانَ لِرَبِّهِ لَكَنُودٌ ۝
7. And to that (fact) He bears witness (By his deeds) ;[6247]	٧- وَإِنَّهُ عَلَىٰ ذَٰلِكَ لَشَهِيدٌ ۝
8. And violent is he In his love of wealth.[6248]	٨- وَإِنَّهُ لِحُبِّ الْخَيْرِ لَشَدِيدٌ ۝
9. Does he not know,— When that which is In the graves is Scattered abroad[6249]	٩- أَفَلَا يَعْلَمُ إِذَا بُعْثِرَ مَا فِي الْقُبُورِ ۝
10. And that which is (Locked up) in (human) breasts Is made manifest—	١٠- وَحُصِّلَ مَا فِي الصُّدُورِ ۝
11. That their Lord had been Well-acquainted with them, (Even to) that Day.?[6250]	١١- إِنَّ رَبَّهُمْ بِهِمْ يَوْمَئِذٍ لَخَبِيرٌ ۝

6246. Man, *i.e.*, unregenerate man, in contrast to those who receive guidance and wage unceasing war with Evil, is ungrateful to his Lord and Cherisher, Him Who created him and sustains him, and sends His blessings and favours at all times. The ingratitude may be shown by thoughts, words, and deeds,—by forgetting or denying God and His goodness, by misusing His gifts, or by injustice to His creatures. He is in this respect worse than the war-horse that risks his life in the service of his master.

6247. Man himself, by his conduct, proves the charge of treason against himself.

6248. What an evil choice he makes in committing treason against his own Benefactor by going after the petty baubles of this world's wealth of fleeting gains ?

6249. Dead bodies, secret plots, evil thoughts and imaginings, long since buried, will yet stand forth before the Judgment-seat of God. Instead of being closely hidden or blotted out—as they will have been from the consciousness of mankind,—they will stand out as from the consciousness of God, which is all-embracing and never suffers from sleep or fatigue.

6250. God's knowledge is full and vigilant at all times. But on that day it will reveal to men secrets which they had long forgotten ; for the Book of their Deeds will be made manifest at Judgment.

INTRODUCTION AND SUMMARY: SŪRA CI (*Al-Qāri'a*).

This Meccan Sūra describes the Judgment Day as the Day of Clamour, when men will be distracted and the landmarks of this world will be lost, but every deed will be weighed in a just balance, and find its real value and setting.

C. 281.—How will the senses of man stand the Noise
(ci. 1-11.) And Clamour of the great Day of Account,
Whereon this life's old landmarks will vanish,
And men will be helpless like scattered moths?
Nay, but a Balance of Justice will weigh
And appraise all Deeds: and those whose good
Will show substance and weight will achieve a Life
Of good pleasure and satisfaction, while those
Whose good will be light will find themselves,
Alas, in a blazing Pit of Punishment.

Sūra CI.

***Al-Qāri'a*, or The Day of Noise and Clamour.**

In the name of God, Most Gracious, Most Merciful.

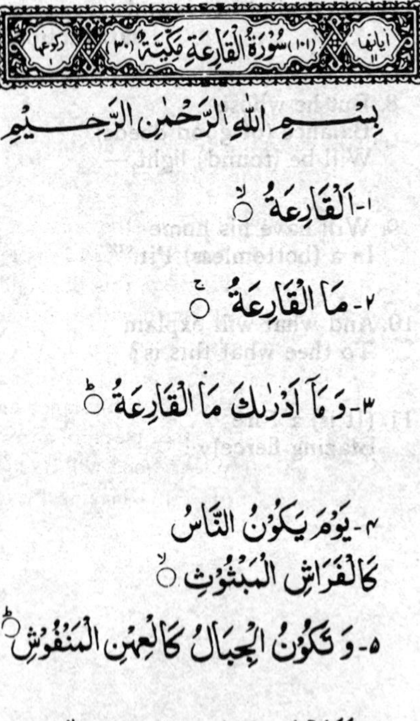

1. The (Day) of
Noise and Clamour:[6251]

2. What is the (Day)
Of Noise and Clamour?

3. And what will explain
To thee what the (Day)
Of Noise and Clamour is?

4. (It is) a Day whereon
Men will be like moths
Scattered about,[6252]

5. And the mountains
Will be like carded wool.[6253]

6. Then, he whose
Balance (of good deeds)[6254]
Will be (found) heavy,

6251. The Day of Noise and Clamour is the Day of Judgment, when the whole of the present order of things will be overthrown with a tremendous convulsion. *Cf.* n. 6235 to xcix. 1, and n. 6096 to lxxxviii. All our present landmarks will be lost. It will be a stunning experience to begin with, but it will inaugurate a new world of true and permanent values, in which every human deed will have its true and just consequences, as if weighed in the balance. See verses 6-11 below.

6252. Moths are frail light things. To see them scattered about in a violent storm gives some idea of the confusion, distress, and helplessness in which men will be at first overwhelmed on the Day of Account. Old memories will be like a book almost blotted out. New hopes will be vague in a new world just rising on the horizon. But it will be a perfectly just world, and no good action will be lost and no evil one but will have its compensating value estimated.

6253. *Cf.* n. 5682 to lxx. 9. The mountains are solid things, which seem as if nothing could move them. But in that tremendous cataclysm they will be scattered about like flakes of teased or carded wool. This is a metaphor to show that what we consider very substantial in this life will be as an airy nothing in the spiritual world.

6254. The Balance is of course figurative. The Good Deeds will be weighed and appraised. This appraisement will be of the nicest and justest kind: for it will take into account motives, temptations, provocations, surrounding conditions, antecedents, subsequent amends, and all possible connected circumstances. Against them, presumably, will be deeds of the opposite kind, appraised in the same way. If the good predominates, the judgment will be in the man's favour, and he will be ushered into a life of good pleasure and satisfaction. This will of course be on another plane.

7. Will be in a Life
Of good pleasure and
satisfaction.[6255]

٧- فَهُوَ فِي عِيشَةٍ رَّاضِيَةٍ ۝

8. But he whose
Balance (of good deeds)
Will be (found) light,—

٨- وَأَمَّا مَنْ خَفَّتْ مَوَازِينُهُ ۝

9. Will have his home
In a (bottomless) Pit.[6256]

٩- فَأُمُّهُ هَاوِيَةٌ ۝

10. And what will explain
To thee what this is?

١٠- وَمَا أَدْرَاكَ مَا هِيَهْ ۝

11. (It is) a Fire
Blazing fiercely!

١١- نَارٌ حَامِيَةٌ ۝ ع

6255. *Cf.* xcviii. 8, and n. 6233, but perhaps the Bliss is not of the same grade for all men. In every case it is bliss, but bliss suited to the particular nature of the individual concerned.

6256. Just as grades of bliss are indicated for the righteous, so apparently we are to understand grades of punishment suited to the sins of the individual sinners concerned.

INTRODUCTION AND SUMMARY: SŪRA CII (*Takā̲th̲ur*).

This probably early Meccan Sūra gives a warning against acquisitiveness, *i.e.* the passion for piling up quantities or numbers, whether in the good things of this world, or in man-power or in other forms of megalomania, which leave no time or opportunity for pursuing the higher things of life.

C. 282.—Be not engrossed in things ephemeral,
(cii 1-8.) To the neglect of higher things in life.
Life is but short, and Death will soon claim you.
Oh that men would only learn,
Before it is too late, the serious
Issues of the higher life! They must
Taste the consequences cf their neglect.
For every good enjoyed they must
In the Hereafter give a strict account.

Sūra CII.

Takathur **or Piling Up.**

In the name of God, Most Gracious, Most Merciful.

بِسْمِ اللّٰهِ الرَّحْمٰنِ الرَّحِيْمِ

1. The mutual rivalry
For piling up (the good things
Of this world) diverts you[6257]
(From the more serious things),

١- اَلْهٰكُمُ التَّكَاثُرُ ۙ

2. Until ye visit the graves.[6258]

٢- حَتّٰى زُرْتُمُ الْمَقَابِرَ ۗ

3. But nay, ye soon shall
Know (the reality).

٣- كَلَّا سَوْفَ تَعْلَمُوْنَ ۙ

4. Again, ye soon shall know !

٤- ثُمَّ كَلَّا سَوْفَ تَعْلَمُوْنَ ۗ

5. Nay, were ye to know
With certainty of mind,[6259]
(Ye would beware !)

٥- كَلَّا لَوْ تَعْلَمُوْنَ عِلْمَ الْيَقِيْنِ ۗ

6. Ye shall certainly see
Hell-fire ! [6260]

٦- لَتَرَوُنَّ الْجَحِيْمَ ۙ

7. Again, ye shall see it
With certainty of sight !

٧- ثُمَّ لَتَرَوُنَّهَا عَيْنَ الْيَقِيْنِ ۙ

6257. Acquisitiveness, that is, the passion for seeking an increase in wealth, position, the number of adherents or followers or supporters, mass production and mass organisation, may affect an individual as such, or it may affect whole societies or nations. Other people's example or rivalry in such things may aggravate the situation. Up to a certain point it may be good and necessary. But when it becomes inordinate and monopolises attention, it leaves no time for higher things in life, and a clear warning is here sounded from a spiritual point of view. Man may be engrossed in these things till death approaches, and he looks back on a wasted life, as far as the higher things are concerned.

6258. That is, until the time comes when you must lie down in the graves and leave the pomp and circumstance of an empty life. The true Reality will then appear before you. Why not try to strive for a little understanding of that Reality in this very life ?

6259. Three kinds of *yaqin* (certainty of knowledge) are described in n. 5673 to lxix. 51. The first is certainty of mind or inference mentioned here : we hear from someone, or we infer from something we know : this refers to our own state of mind. If we instruct our minds in this way, we should value the deeper things of life better, and not waste all our time in ephemeral things. But if we do not use our reasoning faculties now, we shall yet see with our own eyes the Penalty for our sins. It will be certainty of sight. We shall see Hell. See next verse. But the absolute certainty of assured Truth is that described in lxix. 51. That is not liable to any human error or psychological defect.

6260. See xix. 71-72, and n. 2518.

8. Then, shall ye be
Questioned that Day
About the joy [6261]
(Ye indulged in !)

ثُمَّ لَتُسْـَٔلُنَّ يَوْمَئِذٍ عَنِ النَّعِيمِ ۝ ٨

6261. We shall be questioned, *i.e.* we shall be held responsible for every kind of joy we indulge in —whether it was false pride or delight in things of no value, or things evil, or the enjoyment of things legitimate,—the last, to see whether we kept this within reasonable bounds.

INTRODUCTION AND SUMMARY: SŪRA CIII ('Aṣr).

This early Meccan Sūra refers to the testimony of Time through the Ages. All history shows that Evil came to an evil end. But Time is always in favour of those who have Faith, live clean and pure lives, and know how to wait, in patience and constancy. *Cf.* the theme of S. xcv.

C. 283.—Waste not, nor misuse, your life. Time
(ciii. 1-3.) Through the Ages bears witness that nothing remains
But Faith and Good Deeds, and the teaching of Truth
And the teaching of Patience and Constancy.
But for these, Man against Time is in loss!

Sūra CIII.

'*Aṣr*, or Time through the Ages.

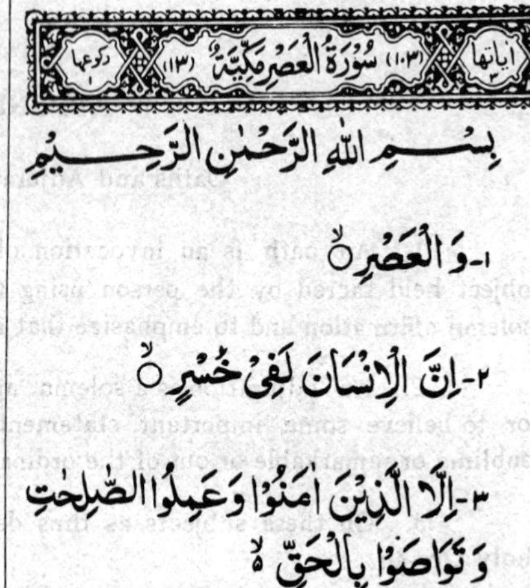

In the name of God, Most Gracious,
Most Merciful.

1. By (the Token of)
Time (through the Ages),[6262]

2. Verily Man
Is in loss,[6263]

3. Except such as have Faith,
And do righteous deeds,[6264]
And (join together)[6265]
In the mutual teaching
Of Truth, and of
Patience and Constancy.

6262. '*Aṣr* may mean: (1) Time through the Ages, or long periods, in which case it comes near to the abstract idea of Time, *Dahr*, which was sometimes deified by the Pagan Arabs (see Introduction to S. lxxvi.); (2) or the late afternoon, from which the '*Aṣr* canonical prayer takes its name (see n. 271 to ii. 238). A mystic use of both these ideas is understood here. An appeal is made to Time as one of the creations of God, of which everyone knows something but of which no one can fully explain the exact significance. Time searches out and destroys everything material. No one in secular literature has expressed the tyranny of "never-resting Time" better than Shakespeare in his Sonnets. For example, see Sonnets 5 ("never-resting Time"), 12 ("Nothing 'gainst Time's scythe can make defence"), and 64 ("When I have seen by Time's fell hand defaced The rich proud cost of outworn buried age"). If we merely run a race against Time, we shall lose. It is the spiritual part of us that conquers Time. See verse 3 below. For the "afternoon" idea see next note.

6263 If life be considered under the metaphor of a business bargain, man, by merely attending to his material gains, will lose. When he makes up his day's account in the afternoon, it will show a loss. It will only show profit if he has Faith, leads a good life, and contributes to social welfare by directing and encouraging other people on the Path of Truth and Constancy.

6264. Faith is his armour, which wards off the wounds of the material world; and his righteous life is his positive contribution to spiritual ascent.

6265. If he lived only for himself, he would not fulfil his whole duty. Whatever good he has, especially in moral and spiritual life, he must spread among his brethren, so that they may see the Truth and stand by it in patient hope and unshaken constancy amidst all the storm and stress of outer life. For he and they will then have attained Peace within.

APPENDIX XIV.

Oaths and Adjurations in the Qur-ān.

1. An oath is an invocation of the name of God or of some person or object held sacred by the person using the invocation, to witness the truth of a solemn affirmation and to emphasize that affirmation.

2. An adjuration is a solemn appeal to a person or persons to do some act or to believe some important statement by the evidence of something great or sublime or remarkable or out of the ordinary.

3. On these subjects as thus defined, let us review the teaching of the holy Qur-ān.

4. Among the Pagan Arabs the use of oaths became so common that it almost ceased to have any solemn meaning. On the other hand, when they wanted to suppress the rights of women or do some unjust acts, they would resort to an oath to do so, and then plead that they were bound by their oath when pressure was brought to bear on them to desist from their injustice. Thus, they doubly dishonoured oaths : they took the name of God lightly, and on the other hand, they made an oath an excuse for not doing what was right and just. It is much to be feared that our own contemporaries are not free from such forms of disrespect to God.

5. Such practices are condemned in the strongest terms in the Qur-ān. "Make not God's name an excuse in your oaths against doing good, or acting rightly, or making peace between persons" (ii. 224). Perjury is condemned as deception which hurts both the deceiver and the deceived. "Take not your oaths to practise deception between yourselves, with the result that someone's foot may slip after it was firmly planted, and ye may have to taste the evil consequences of having hindered men from the Path of God, and a mighty Wrath descend on you" (xvi. 94). See also iii. 77. You must not only fulfil your oaths, but you must fulfil all covenants, express or implied, and all your obligations of every kind, without reference to an oath : v. 1, n. 682.

6. Considering the harm caused by thoughtless oaths, in which there was no intention to deceive or to do wrong, it is provided that they may be expiated for. "God will not call you to account for what is futile in your oaths, but He will call you to account for your deliberate oaths : for expiation feed ten indigent persons...or clothe them, or give a slave his freedom. If that is beyond your means, fast for three days. That is the expiation for the oaths ye have sworn. But keep to your oaths" (v. 92). See also ii. 225 and lxvi. 2.

7. Some examples may be cited of the false oaths which were used for deception. The Hypocrites, "in whose hearts is a disease", "swore their strongest

oaths by God" that they would be with the Muslims, but treachery was in their hearts (v. 55-56). See also xxiv. 53. On the other hand, the oath of Joseph's wicked brethren, " By God ! ", in speaking to their father, (xii. 85), seems to be a mere expletive, used lightly, and therefore worthy of condemnation.

8. In passages like the following, the oath seems to be emphatic and solemn as in a court of law : –

xii 66 ... By Joseph's brethren, at Jacob's request.
xii. 73 ... By Joseph's brethren, to the Egyptians.
xxi. 57 ... By Abraham, to the Polytheists.
xxvi. 97 ... By the denizens of Hell, when they realise their wrong.
xxxvii. 56 ... By the righteous one in heaven, when he realises the great danger he escaped in life.
xxxviii. 82 ... By the Power of Evil, who solemnly swears by the power of God.
xlvi. 34 ... By the denizens of Hell, when they realise the Truth.

9. In the following passages addressed by God to men, an appeal is made to man's realisation of God's own greatness, goodness, and glory, or God's special relationship to man as Creator, Cherisher, and Protector, to teach him the lesson of truth and right conduct. In English phrase it might be rendered : " As I am thy Lord God, believe in Me and follow My Word."

iv. 65 ... " By thy Lord " (they can have no real faith until...).
xv. 92 ... " By thy Lord " (We will call them to account).
xvi. 56 ... " By God " (ye shall be called to account).
xvi. 63 ... " By God " (We sent apostles).
xix. 68 ... " By thy Lord " (We shall gather them together).
xxxiv. 3 ... " By my Lord " (said by the Prophet to assure men of the coming of the Hour of Judgment)
lxiv. 7 ... Do. Do.
li. 23 ... " By the Lord of heaven and earth " (this is the very Truth). See also lxx. 40 (paragraph 12 below).

10. Another way in which an appeal is made to men is by the evidence of the life of the holy Prophet, whose truth and purity were known to them, or by the holy Qur-ān, whose wonderful power over men's hearts was a miracle which they witnessed before their eyes :—

xv. 72 ... " By thy life " (to enforce the lesson of the unspeakable crime of Lot's people).

xxxvi. 2 ... " By the Qur-ān, Full of Wisdom " (to show the Prophet's inspiration).

xxxviii. 1 ... " By the Qur-ān, Full of admonition " (to show the error of the Unbelievers).

xliii. 2	...	" By the Book that Makes things clear "	(to show that Revelation is reasonable and conformable to truth).
xliv. 2		Do.	Do.
l. 1	...	" By the Glorious Qur-ān "	(to quell the wonder of the ignorant).

11. Now we come to the great mystic passages in the Meccan Sūras, in which men are adjured to turn to the wonders of the spiritual world by striking phrases full of sublimity, full of mystery, full of symbolism, and using the wonders of the heavens and the earth by way of illustration. They are the despair of the translator, because the words used are widely comprehensive, with little that is precise in them. There are layers upon layers of meaning, and only the profoundest spiritual experience can probe their depths. An attempt has been made in the notes to analyse and explain some of their meanings. All that we can do here is to bring them together into juxtaposition, to help the earnest student. They may be divided into three categories: (1) those introduced by the words " *Lā uqsimu* " (I do swear or I do call to witness), (2) those introduced by the particle *wa*, which is the general form of adjuration, and (3) those, mainly concerned with the Judgment to come, which are introduced by the adverb " *izā* " (when).

12. *Lā Uqsimu* (with the first person singular) implies that special attention is drawn to something by a personal and beneficent God, and an appeal is made to His creatures :—

lvi.	75		" The setting of the stars."	Other glories may set, but not the glory of Revelation.
lxix.	38	...	" What ye see and what ye see not."	Revelation is good for both outer and inner life.
lxx.	40	...	" The Lord of all points in the East and the West."	God's Kingdom extends everywhere.
lxxv.	1-2	...	" The Resurrection Day and the self-reproaching spirit."	Evil should be eschewed.
lxxxi.	15-18	...	" Planets, Night, and Dawn."	Nature may vary, but God's Light is ever the same.
lxxxiv.	16-18	...	" The ruddy glow of sunset, the Night, the Moon."	Man must travel from stage to stage.
xc.	1-3	...	" This City (of Mecca) and mystic ties."	Man is created for toil and struggle, but God has given him guidance.

13. The great mystic Symbols or Signs, introduced by the particle *wa*, by which man is adjured to turn to the higher life, are rich in suggestive imagery, which loses part of its charm by any attempt at precise definition :—

xxxvii.	1	...	" By those who range themselves in ranks ".
li.	1-4	...	" By the (Winds) that scatter broadcast " etc.
li.	7	...	" By the heaven with its numerous Paths " etc.
lii.	1-6	...	" By the Mount (of Revelation) " etc.

liii. 1	...	" By the Star when it goes down ".
lxviii. 1	...	" By the Pen and by the Record which men write ".
lxxiv. 32-34	...	" By the Moon, the Night, the Dawn ".
lxxvii. 1-5	...	" By the (Winds) sent forth . (to man's profit)" etc.
lxxix. 1-5	...	" By the (angels) who tear out " etc.
lxxxv. 1-3	...	" By the Sky (displaying) the Zodiacal Signs " etc.
lxxxvi. 1		" By the Sky and the Night-Visitant (therein) ".
lxxxvi. 11-12	...	" By the Firmament which returns (in its round), and by the Earth " etc.
lxxxix. 1-5	...	" By the Break of Day ", etc.
xci. 1-8	...	" By the Sun and its (glorious) splendour, By the Soul..." etc.
xcii. 1-3	...	" By the Night as it conceals (the light); By the Day as it appears in glory " etc.
xciii. 1-2	...	" By the Glorious morning Light " etc.
xcv. 1-3	...	" By the Fig and the Olive " etc.
c. 1-5	...	" By the (Steeds) that run with panting breath " etc.
ciii. 1	...	" By (the Token of) Time (through the Ages) ".

14. The great mystic Symbols introduced by the adverb " when" (*iẓā*) do not *in form* belong to the category of Adjurations, but their mystic meaning and imagery bring them within this category. They refer to the end of the present order of things, and the inauguration of the new world of perfect spiritual values, but they need not necessarily be understood in a definite sequence of time such as we know it, for the spiritual world overlaps the material :—

lxxvii. 8-11	...	" When the Stars become dim " etc.
lxxxi. 1-13	...	" When the Sun is folded up " etc.
lxxxii. 1-4	...	" When the Sky is cleft asunder " etc.
lxxxiv. 1-5	...	" When the Sky is rent asunder " etc.
xcix. 1-3	...	" When the Earth is shaken " etc.

15. Every Symbol is connected with the argument of the passage concerned, by way of metaphor or illustration. See n. 5798 to lxxiv. 32. The appropriate meaning suggested is explained in the notes to each passage as it occurs.

INTRODUCTION AND SUMMARY: SŪRA CIV (*Humaza*).

This Meccan Sūra condemns all sorts of scandal, backbiting, and selfish hoarding of wealth, as destroying the hearts and affections of men.

C. 284.—Woe to the man or woman who deals
(civ. 1-9.) In scandal, in word or act, or by insults
Or suggestions. Woe to the backbiter, e'en
If his tale is true, for the taint is in his motive.
Woe to the miser who blocks up the channels
Of use and service and dams up his wealth,
As if he could remain in possession
For all time! The Fire of Wrath will envelop them
And wither up their hearts and minds, and consume
That largeness of life which is the portion of mankind.

Sūra CIV.

Humaza, or the Scandal-monger.

In the name of God, Most Gracious,
Most Merciful.

1. Woe to every
(Kind of) scandal-monger
And backbiter,[6266]

2. Who pileth up wealth
And layeth it by,

3. Thinking that his wealth
Would make him last
For ever!

4. By no means! He will
Be sure to be thrown into
That which Breaks to Pieces.[6267]

5. And what will explain
To thee That which Breaks
To Pieces?

6. (It is) the Fire
Of (the Wrath of) God
Kindled (to a blaze),

7. The which doth mount
(Right) to the Hearts:[6268]

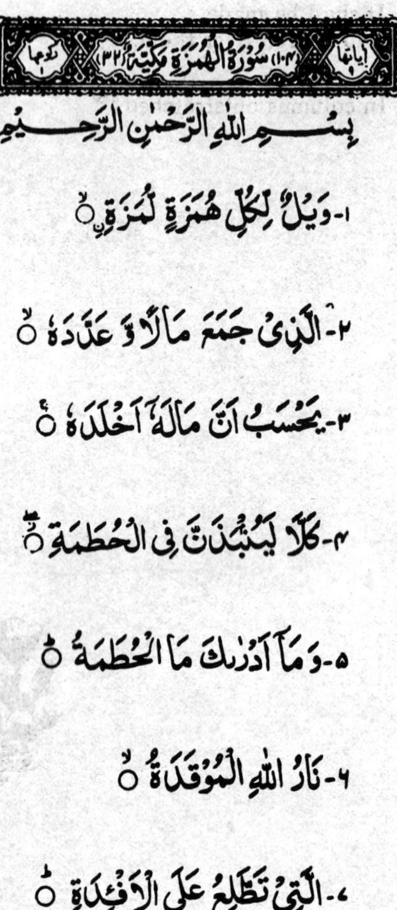

آياتها ٩ (١٠٤) سُورَةُ الْهُمَزَةِ مَكِّيَّةٌ (٣٢) ركوعها ١

بِسْمِ اللّٰهِ الرَّحْمٰنِ الرَّحِيمِ

١- وَيْلٌ لِّكُلِّ هُمَزَةٍ لُّمَزَةٍ ۝

٢- الَّذِي جَمَعَ مَالًا وَّعَدَّدَهُ ۝

٣- يَحْسَبُ أَنَّ مَالَهُ أَخْلَدَهُ ۝

٤- كَلَّا لَيُنْبَذَنَّ فِي الْحُطَمَةِ ۝

٥- وَمَا أَدْرٰىكَ مَا الْحُطَمَةُ ۝

٦- نَارُ اللّٰهِ الْمُوقَدَةُ ۝

٧- الَّتِي تَطَّلِعُ عَلَى الْأَفْئِدَةِ ۝

6266. Three vices are here condemned in the strongest terms: (1) scandal-mongering, talking or suggesting evil of men or women by word or innuendo, or behaviour, or mimicry, or sarcasm, or insult; (2) detracting from their character behind their backs, even if the things suggested are true, where the motive is evil; (3) piling up wealth, not for use and service to those who need it, but in miserly hoards, as if such hoards can prolong the miser's life or give him immortality: miserliness is itself a kind of scandal.

6267. *Ḥuṭama*: that which smashes or breaks to pieces: an apt description of the three anti-social vices condemned. For scandal-mongering and backbiting make any sort of cohesion or mutual confidence impossible; and the miser's hoards block up the channels of economic service and charity, and the circulation of good-will among men.

6268. This Fire of Punishment mounts right up to the hearts and minds of such men, and shuts them out of the love of their fellows. "Heart" in Arabic means not only the seat of affection, pity, charity, etc., but also of understanding and intelligent appreciation of things.

8. It shall be made
Into a vault over them,

٨- إِنَّهَا عَلَيْهِم مُّؤْصَدَةٌ ۝

9. In columns outstretched.[6269]

٩- فِي عَمَدٍ مُّمَدَّدَةٍ ۝

6269. Those guilty of these vices will be choked and suffocated, for this Vault of Fire will cover them all over, and its scorching columns will extend over a far wider area than they imagine.

INTRODUCTION AND SUMMARY: SŪRA CV (*Fīl*).

This early Meccan Sūra refers to an event that happened in the year of the birth of our holy Prophet, say about 570 A.D. Yaman was then under the rule of the Abyssinians (Christians), who had driven out the Jewish Himyar rulers. Abraha Ashram was the Abyssinian governor or viceroy. Intoxicated with power and fired by religious fanaticism, he led a big expedition against Mecca, intending to destroy the Ka'ba. He had an elephant or elephants in his train. But his sacrilegious intentions were defeated by a miracle. No defence was offered by the custodians of the Ka'ba as the army was too strong for them, but it was believed that a shower of stones, thrown by flocks of birds, destroyed the invading army almost to a man. The stones produced sores and pustules on the skin, which spread like a pestilence.

C. 285.—Let not man be intoxicated with power
(cv. 1-5.) Or material resources: they cannot defeat
The purpose of God. So Abraha Ashram
Found to his cost. His sacrilegious attack
On the holy Fane of God brought about
His own undoing: what seemed but frail
Destroyed his mighty hosts in a day!

Sūra CV.

Fīl, or The Elephant.

In the name of God, Most Gracious, Most Merciful.

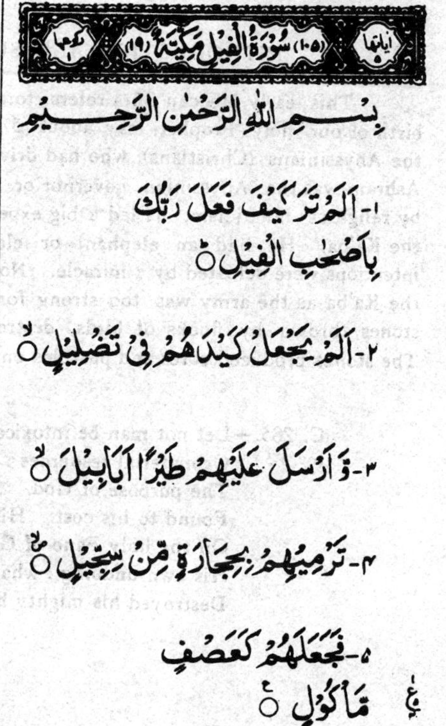

1. Seest[6270] thou not
How thy Lord dealt
With the Companions
Of the Elephant?[6271]

2. Did He not make
Their treacherous plan
Go astray?

3. And He sent against them
Flights of Birds,[6272]

4. Striking them with stones[6273]
Of baked clay.

5. Then did He make them
Like an empty field[6274]
Of stalks and straw,
(Of which the corn)
Has been eaten up.[6275]

6270. *Seest thou not?—i.e.* with thy mental vision. The incident happened in the very year of the holy Prophet's birth, barely two months before it.

6271. These were the troops of Abraha the Abyssinian, who invaded Mecca with a large army, in which were some elephants. See Introduction to this Sūra.

6272. The miracle consisted in the birds coming in large flights and flinging stones at the army which caused a great pestilence to arise and destroy the whole of Abraha's army.

6273. *Sijjīl*: see n. 1579 to xi. 82. The word also occurs at xv. 74. Stones of baked clay, or hard as baked clay, are part of the miracle in the story.

6274. A field, from which all the corn has been eaten up and only straw with stalks or stubble is left, is a field dead and useless. And such was the army of Abraha.—dead and useless. Another possible rendering would be: "like eaten straw and stubble found in the dung of animals". The meaning would be the same, but much more emphatic.

6275. The lesson to be drawn is twofold. For the Pagan Quraish of Mecca it was: 'God will protect His own; if you persecute the holy Prophet, he is greater than the mere building of the Ka'ba: will not God protect him?' For men in all ages it is: 'a man intoxicated with power can prepare armies and material resources against God's holy Plan; but such a man's plan will be his own undoing; he cannot prevail against God'.

INTRODUCTION AND SUMMARY: SŪRA CVI (*Quraish*).

This Meccan Sūra may well be considered as a pendant to the last. If the Quraish were fond of Mecca and proud of it, if they profited, by its central position and its guaranteed security, from their caravans of trade and commerce, let them be grateful, adore the One True God, and accept His Message.

C. 286.—Who gave the Quraish their talents for the arts
(cvi. 1-4) Of peace, for trade and commerce, and for journeys
South and north at proper seasons,
And made their home inviolable in Mecca?
Surely they, if any, should adore their Lord
And listen to His Message of Unity and Truth.

Sūra CVI.

Quraish or The Quraish, (Custodians of the Ka'ba).

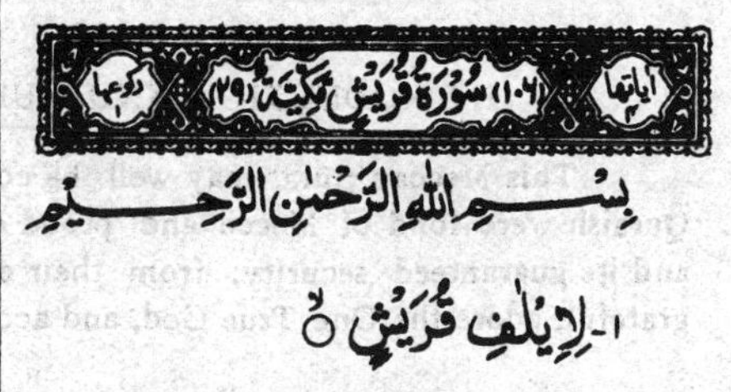

In the name of God, Most Gracious, Most Merciful.

1. For the covenants
(Of security and safeguard
Enjoyed) by the Quraish,[6276]

2. Their covenants (covering) journeys
By winter and summer,—[6277]

٢- إِلٰفِهِمْ رِحْلَةَ الشِّتَآءِ وَالصَّيْفِ ۝

3. Let them adore the Lord
Of this House,[6278]

٣- فَلْيَعْبُدُوا رَبَّ هٰذَا الْبَيْتِ ۝

4. Who provides them
With food against hunger,[6279]
And with security
Against fear (of danger).[6280]

٤- الَّذِىٓ أَطْعَمَهُم مِّن جُوعٍ ۬ وَّ ءَامَنَهُم مِّنْ خَوْفٍ ۝

6276. The Quraish were the noblest tribe of Arabia, the tribe to which belonged the holy Prophet himself. They had the custody of the Ka'ba, the central shrine of Arabia, and their possession of Mecca gave them a triple advantage: (1) they had a commanding influence over other tribes; (2) their central position facilitated trade and intercourse, which gave them both honour and profit; and (3) the Mecca territory being by Arabian custom inviolable from the ravages of war and private feuds, they had a secure position, free from fear of danger. This honour and advantage they owed to their position as servants of the sacred shrine of the Ka'ba. They owed it to God. Was it not therefore right and fitting that they should adore the One True God, and listen to His Message of Unity and Purity, brought by His Prophet?

In those days of general insecurity, their prestige as custodians of Mecca enabled them to obtain Covenants of security and safeguard from the rulers of neighbouring countries on all sides—Syria, Persia, Yaman, and Abyssinia—protecting their trade journeys in all seasons.

6277. See last note, especially section (2). On account of their trade journeys to the warmth of Yaman in the winter and the cooler regions of Syria and the north in the summer, the Quraish became practised travellers and merchants, acquired much knowledge of the world and many arts, and perfected their language as a polished medium of literary expression.

6278. The Ka'ba

6279. Their trade caravans enriched them, and drew people from distant parts to visit Mecca and bring their merchandise and gifts thither.

6280. Their territory being inviolable, they did not suffer from the dangers of constant warfare nor from private feuds of vengeance or breaches of the peace in their secure homes.

INTRODUCTION AND SUMMARY: SŪRA CVII (*Mā'ūn*).

This Sūra—at least the first half of it—belongs to the early Meccan period. The subject-matter is the meaning of true worship, which requires Faith, the practical and helpful love of those in need, and sincerity rather than show in devotion and charity.

C. 287.—What remains if you deny all Faith
(cvii 1-7) And personal Responsibility? Why then
Help the helpless or teach others
Deeds of Charity? Vain were worship
Without heart and soul. What think ye of men
Who make great show, but fail to meet
The simple needs of daily life?

Sūra CVII.

Mā'ūn. or Neighbourly Needs.

In the name of God, Most Gracious, Most Merciful

1. Seest thou one
Who denies the Judgment[6281]
(To come)?

2. Then such is the (man)
Who repulses the orphan
(With harshness),

3. And encourages not[6282]
The feeding of the indigent.

4. So woe to the worshippers

5. Who are neglectful
Of their Prayers,[6283]

6. Those who (want but)
To be seen (of men),[6284]

7. But refuse (to supply)
(Even) neighbourly needs.[6285]

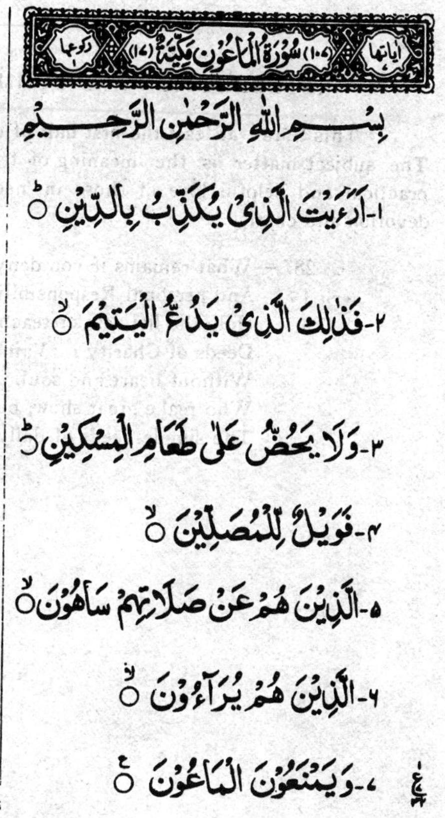

سُورَةُ الْمَاعُونِ مَكِّيَّةٌ

بِسْمِ اللَّهِ الرَّحْمَٰنِ الرَّحِيمِ

١- أَرَأَيْتَ الَّذِي يُكَذِّبُ بِالدِّينِ ○

٢- فَذَٰلِكَ الَّذِي يَدُعُّ الْيَتِيمَ ○

٣- وَلَا يَحُضُّ عَلَىٰ طَعَامِ الْمِسْكِينِ ○

٤- فَوَيْلٌ لِّلْمُصَلِّينَ ○

٥- الَّذِينَ هُمْ عَن صَلَاتِهِمْ سَاهُونَ ○

٦- الَّذِينَ هُمْ يُرَاءُونَ ○

٧- وَيَمْنَعُونَ الْمَاعُونَ ○

6281. *Din* may mean either (1) the Judgment to come, the responsibility in the moral and spiritual world, for all actions done by men, or (2) Faith, Religion, the principles of right and wrong in spiritual matters, which often conflict with selfish desires or predilections. It is men who deny Faith or future responsibility, that treat the helpless with contempt and lead arrogant selfish lives.

6282 The Charity or Love which feeds the indigent at the expense of Self is a noble form of virtue, which is beyond the reach of men who are so callous as even to discourage or forbid or look down upon the virtue of charity or kindness in others.

6283. True worship does not consist in the mere form of prayer, without the heart and mind being earnestly applied to seek the realisation of the presence of God, and to understand and do His holy Will.

6284. *Cf.* iv 142: "When they stand up to prayer, they stand without earnestness, to be seen of men, but little do they hold God in remembrance"

6285. Hypocrites make a great show of hollow acts of goodness, devotion, and charity. But they fail signally if you test them by little acts of neighbourly help or charity, the thousand little courtesies and kindnesses of daily life, the supply of needs which cost little but mean much.

INTRODUCTION AND SUMMARY: SŪRA CVIII (*Kauthar*).

This very brief early Meccan Sūra sums up in the single mystic word *Kauthar* (Abundance) the doctrine of spiritual Riches through devotion and sacrifice. The converse also follows: indulgence in hatred means the cutting off of all hope of this life and the Hereafter.

C. 288.—To the man of God, rich in divine
(cviii. 1-3.) Blessings, is granted a Fountain unfailing,
That will quench the spiritual thirst of millions.
Turn, then, in devotion and sacrifice to God,
Nor heed the venom of Hatred, which destroys
Its own hopes, alas, of the present and the future!

Sūra CVIII.

Kauthar, or Abundance.

In the name of God, Most Gracious, Most Merciful.

بِسۡمِ اللّٰهِ الرَّحۡمٰنِ الرَّحِيۡمِ

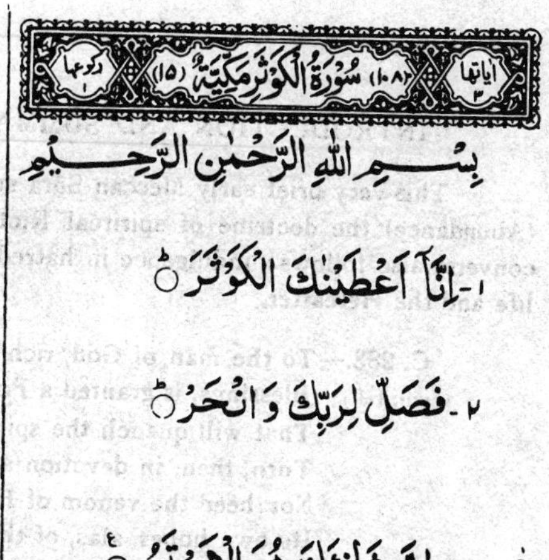

1. To thee have We
Granted the Fount
(of Abundance).[6286]

١- اِنَّاۤ اَعۡطَيۡنٰكَ الۡكَوۡثَرَ ؕ

2. Therefore to thy Lord
Turn in Prayer
And Sacrifice.[6287]

٢- فَصَلِّ لِرَبِّكَ وَانۡحَرۡ ؕ

3. For he who hateth thee,—[6288]
He will be cut off
(From Future Hope).

٣- اِنَّ شَانِئَكَ هُوَ الۡاَبۡتَرُ ۠

6286. *Kauthar*: the heavenly Fountain of unbounded grace and knowledge, mercy and goodness, truth and wisdom, spiritual power and insight, which was granted to the holy Prophet, the man of God, and in some degree or other, to all men and women who are sincere devotees of God. That Fountain quenches the highest spiritual thirst of man: it confers overflowing benefits of all kinds. *Cf.* ii. 269: "And he to whom wisdom is granted receiveth indeed a benefit overflowing". Such a person wants for nothing: worldly pomp and wealth are as dust beneath his feet.

6287. He who grants these blessings is God, and to God alone must we turn in adoration and thanksgiving, and in sacrifice. *Naḥr* = sacrifice: in a restricted ritual sense, the sacrifice of camels: see n. 2813 to xxii. 36. But the ritual is a mere Symbol. Behind it is a deep spiritual meaning: the meat slaughtered feeds the poor, and the slaughter is a symbol of the self-sacrifice in our hearts. "It is not their meat nor their blood, that reaches God: it is your piety that reaches Him" (xxii. 37).

6288. Hatred and spite are not constructive contributions to the work of this world, but its opposites. Abū Jahl and his Pagan confederates vented their personal spite and venom against the holy Prophet by taunting him with the loss of his two infant sons by Khadija, but where were these venomous detractors a few years afterwards, when the divine Light shone more brilliantly than ever? It was these that were cut off from all future hope, in this world and the next.

INTRODUCTION AND SUMMARY: SŪRA CIX (*Kāfirūn*).

This is another early Meccan Sūra. It defines the right attitude to those who reject Faith: in matters of Truth we can make no compromise, but there is no need to persecute or abuse anyone for his faith or belief.

C. 289.—The man of Faith holds fast to his faith,
(cix. 1-6.) Because he knows it is true. The man
Of the world, rejecting Faith, clings hard
To worldly interests. Let him mind
His worldly interests, but let him not
Force his interests on men sincere
And true, by favour, force, or fraud.

Sura CIX.

Kāfirūn, or Those who reject Faith.

In the name of God, Most Gracious, Most Merciful

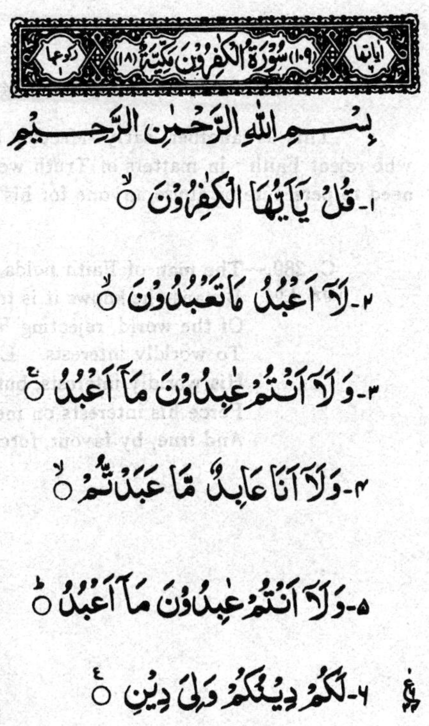

1. Say: O ye
That reject Faith![6289]

2. I worship not that
Which ye worship,

3. Nor will ye worship
That which I worship.[6290]

4. And I will not worship
That which ye have been
Wont to worship,

5. Nor will ye worship
That which I worship.

6. To you be your Way,
And to me mine.[6291]

6289. Faith is a matter of personal conviction, and does not depend on worldly motives. Worship should depend on pure and sincere Faith, but often does not: for motives of worldly gain, ancestral custom, social conventions or imitative instincts, or a lethargic instinct to shrink from enquiring into the real significance of solemn acts and the motives behind them, reduce a great deal of the world's worship to sin, selfishness, or futility. Symbolic idols may themselves be merely instruments for safeguarding the privileges of a selfish priestly class, or the ambitions, greed, or lust of private individuals. Hence the insistence of Islam and its Teacher on the pure worship of the One True God. The Prophet firmly resisted all appeals to worldly motives, and stood firm to his Message of eternal Unity.

6290. Verses 2-3 describe the conditions as they were at the time when this Sūra was revealed, and may be freely paraphrased: 'I am a worshipper of the One True God, the Lord of all, of you as well as of myself; but you on account of your vested interests have not the will to give up your false worship, of idols and self'. Verses 4-5 describe the psychological reasons: 'I, being a prophet of God, do not and cannot possibly desire to follow your false ancestral ways; and you, as custodians of the false worship, have not the will to give up your ways of worship, which are wrong'. The "will" in the translation represents less the future tense than the will, the desire, the psychological possibility: it tries to reproduce the Arabic noun-agent.

6291. 'I, having been given the Truth, cannot come to your false ways: you, having your vested interests, will not give them up. For your ways the responsibility is yours: I have shown you the Truth. For my ways the responsibility is mine: you have no right to ask me to abandon the Truth. Your persecutions will be vain: the Truth must prevail in the end'. This was the attitude of Faith then: but it is true for all time. Hold fast to Truth, "in scorn of consequence".

INTRODUCTION AND SUMMARY : SŪRA CX (*Naṣr*).

This beautiful Sūra was the last of the Sūras to be revealed *as a whole*, though the portion of the verse v. 4, " This day have I perfected your religion for you " etc., contains probably the last *words* of the Qur-ān to be revealed.

The date of this Sūra was only a few months before the passing away of the holy Prophet from this world, Rabi' I, A.H. 11. The place was either the precincts of Mecca at his Farewell Pilgrimage, Ẕulḥijja, A.H. 10, or Medina after his return from the Farewell Pilgrimage.

Victory is the crown of service, not an occasion for exultation. All victory comes from the help of God.

C. 290.—For that which is right the help of God
(cx. 1-3.) Is ever nigh, and victory !
When the spirit of men is stirred, they come
To the flag of faith in troops and battalions.
They are to be welcomed : but Praise and Glory
Belong to God : to Him we humbly
Turn and pray for Grace : for He
Is Oft-Returning in Grace and Mercy.

Sūra CX.

Naṣr, or Help.

In the name of God, Most Gracious, Most Merciful.

1. When comes the Help
Of God, and Victory,

2. And thou dost see
The People enter God's Religion
In crowds,[6292]

3. Celebrate the Praises
Of thy Lord, and pray
For His Forgiveness:[6293]
For He is Oft-Returning
(In Grace and Mercy).

6292. The Prophet migrated from Mecca to Medina, a hunted and persecuted man. In Medina all the forces of truth and righteousness rallied round him, and the efforts by the Meccans and their confederates to destroy him and his community recoiled on their own heads. Gradually all the outlying parts of Arabia ranged themselves round his standard, and the bloodless conquest of Mecca was the crown and prize of his patience and constant endeavour. After that, whole tribes and tracts of country gave their adhesion to him collectively, and before his earthly ministry was finished, the soil was prepared for the conquest of the wide world for Islam. What was the lesson to be learnt from this little epitome of the world's history ? Not man's self-glory, but humility ; not power but service ; not an appeal to man's selfishness or self-sufficiency, but a realisation of God's Grace and Mercy, and the abundant outpouring of God's Praises in word and conduct.

6293. Every man should humble himself before God, confess his human frailties, and seek God's grace ;—attributing any success that he gets in his work, not to his own merits, but to the goodness and mercy of God. But the Prophet of God had also another duty and privilege,—to pray for grace and forgiveness for his people in case any of them had exulted in their victory or done anything that they should not have done.

INTRODUCTION AND SUMMARY : SŪRA CXI (*Lahab*).

This very early Meccan Sūra, though it referred in the first instance to a particular incident in a cruel and relentless persecution, carries the general lesson that cruelty ultimately ruins itself. The man who rages against holy things is burnt up in his own rage. His hands, which are the instruments of his action, perish, and he perishes himself. No boasted wealth or position will save him. The women, who are made for nobler emotions, may, if they go wrong, feed unholy rage with fiercer fuel—to their own loss. For they may twist the torturing rope round their own neck. It is a common experience that people perish by the very means by which they seek to destroy others.

C. 291.—The Chosen One of God, in his earnest
(cxi. 1-5.) Desire to proclaim the Message, gathered
His kin together to hear and judge
With open minds between error and truth.
Behold, the fiery " Father of Flame "
Blazed up with foul abuse and curses,
And said to the holy one : " Perish thou ! "
With his hands he took stones and cast them
At the holy one's head. Purse-proud he headed
Relentless persecution. His wife
Laid snares, tied thorns with twisted ropes
Of prickly palm-leaf fibre, and strewed them
In the holy one's path on darkest nights,
For cruel sport ! But lo ! the curses,
Insults, spite, harmed not the Innocent,
But hit the wrong-doers themselves
And branded them with eternal infamy !

Sūra CXI.

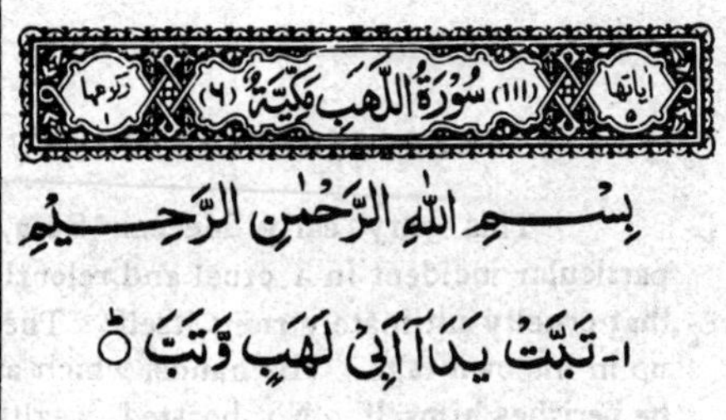

Lahab, or (the Father of) Flame.

In the name of God, Most Gracious, Most Merciful.

بِسْمِ اللهِ الرَّحْمٰنِ الرَّحِيْمِ

1. Perish the hands
Of the Father of Flame![6294]
Perish he!

١- تَبَّتْ يَدَآ اَبِيْ لَهَبٍ وَّتَبَّ ۝

2. No profit to him
From all his wealth,
And all his gains!

٢- مَآ اَغْنٰى عَنْهُ مَالُهٗ
وَمَا كَسَبَ ۝

3. Burnt soon will he be
In a Fire
Of blazing Flame!

٣- سَيَصْلٰى نَارًا ذَاتَ لَهَبٍ ۝

4. His wife shall carry
The (crackling) wood—
As fuel!—[6295]

٤- وَّامْرَاَتُهٗ ۭ حَمَّالَةَ الْحَطَبِ ۝

5. A twisted rope
Of palm-leaf fibre
Round her (own) neck!

٥- فِيْ جِيْدِهَا حَبْلٌ مِّنْ مَّسَدٍ ۝

6294. *Abū Lahab*, "Father of Flame", was the nick-name of an uncle of the holy Prophet, from his fiery hot temper and his ruddy complexion. He was one of the most inveterate enemies of early Islam. When the holy Prophet called together the Quraish and his own kith and kin to come and listen to his preaching and his warning against the sins of his people, the "Father of Flame" flared up and cursed the holy Prophet, saying "Perdition to thee!" According to the English saying, "the causeless curse will not come". His words were futile, but his power and strength were equally futile. The star of Islam rose higher and higher every day, and its persecutors dwindled in strength and power. Many of the leaders of persecution perished at Badr, and Abū Lahab himself perished a week after Badr, consumed with grief and his own fiery passions. Verse 3 was prophetic of his end in this very life, though it also refers to the Hereafter.

6295. Abū Lahab's wife was a woman of equally passionate spite and cruelty against the sacred person of the holy Prophet. She used to tie bundles of thorns with ropes of twisted palm-leaf fibre and carry them and strew them about on dark nights in the paths which the Prophet was expected to take, in order to cause him bodily injury. "To carry firewood" may also be symbolical for carrying tales between people to embroil them. This was also one of her vices. But she was laying up for herself another kind of Fire and another kind of Rope, the Fire of Punishment, and the Rope of Slavery to Evil. Thus does Evil prepare its own fate. This is the general lesson of sustained craft and cruel wrong-doing recoiling on the wrong-doer's head. See also Introduction to this Sūra.

INTRODUCTION AND SUMMARY : SŪRA CXII (*Ikhlāṣ*).

This early Meccan Sūra sums up in a few terse words the Unity of the Godhead—often professed, but frequently mixed up in the popular mind with debasing superstitions.

C. 292.—Keep Faith all pure and undefiled.
(cxii. 1-4.) There *is* God, the One and Only;
Eternal, Free of all needs; on Whom
Depend, to Whom go back, all things;
He hath no son nor father nor partner.
There is no person like unto Him.

Sūra CXII.

سُوْرَةُ الْاِخْلَاصِ مَكِّيَّةٌ (١١٢)

Ikhlāṣ, or Purity (of Faith).

In the name of God, Most Gracious, Most Merciful.

بِسْمِ اللّٰهِ الرَّحْمٰنِ الرَّحِيْمِ

1. Say: He is God,[6296]
The One and Only;[6297]

١- قُلْ هُوَ اللّٰهُ اَحَدٌ ۚ

2. God, the Eternal, Absolute;[6298]

٢- اَللّٰهُ الصَّمَدُ ۚ

3. He begetteth not,
Nor is He begotten;[6299]

٣- لَمْ يَلِدْ ۙ وَلَمْ يُوْلَدْ ۙ

4. And there is none
Like unto Him.[6300]

٤- وَلَمْ يَكُنْ لَّهٗ كُفُوًا اَحَدٌ ۧ

6296. The nature of God is here indicated to us in a few words, such as we can understand. The qualities of God are described in numerous places elsewhere, *e.g.*, in lix. 22-24, lxii. 1, and ii. 255. Here we are specially taught to avoid the pitfalls into which men and nations have fallen at various times in trying to understand God. The first thing we have to note is that His nature is so sublime, so far beyond our limited conceptions, that the best way in which we can realise Him is to feel that He is a Personality, "He", and not a mere abstract conception of philosophy. He is near us; He cares for us; we owe our existence to Him. Secondly, He is the One and Only God, the Only One to Whom worship is due; all other things or beings that we can think of are His creatures and in no way comparable to Him. Thirdly, He is Eternal, without beginning or end, Absolute, not limited by time or place or circumstance, the Reality before which all other things or places are mere shadows or reflections. Fourthly, we must not think of Him as having a son or a father, for that would be to import animal qualities into our conception of Him. Fifthly, He is not like any other person or thing that we know or can imagine: His qualities and nature are unique.

6297. This is to negative the idea of Polytheism, a system in which people believe in gods many and lords many. Such a system is opposed to our truest and profoundest conceptions of life. For Unity in Design, Unity in the fundamental facts of existence, proclaim the Unity of the Maker.

6298. *Ṣamad* is difficult to translate by one word. I have used two, "Eternal" and "Absolute". The latter implies: (1) that absolute existence can only be predicated of Him; all other existence is temporal or conditional; (2) that He is dependent on no person or things, but all persons or things are dependent on Him, thus negativing the idea of gods and goddesses who ate and drank, wrangled and plotted, depended on the gifts of worshippers, etc.

6299. This is to negative the Christian idea of the godhead, "the Father", "the only-begotten Son" etc.

6300. This sums up the whole argument and warns us specially against Anthropomorphism, the tendency to conceive of God after our own pattern, an insidious tendency that creeps in at all times and among all peoples.

INTRODUCTION AND SUMMARY: SŪRA CXIII (*Falaq*).

This early Meccan Sūra provides the antidote to superstition and fear by teaching us to seek refuge in God from every kind of ill arising from outer nature and from dark and evil plottings and envy on the part of others.

C. 293.—It is God Who brings forth light from darkness,
(cxiii. 1-5.) Life and activity from death, spiritual
Enlightenment from ignorance and superstition.
Banish fear, and trust His Providence.
No danger, then, from the outer world,
No secret plottings from perverted wills,
No disturbance of your happiness or good,
Can affect the fortress of your inmost soul.

Sûra CXIII.

Falaq, or The Dawn.

In the name of God, Most Gracious, Most Merciful

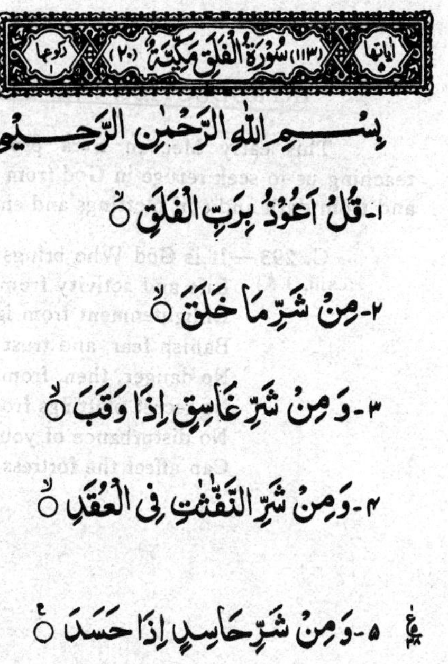

1. Say: I seek refuge[6301]
With the Lord of the Dawn,[6302]

2. From the mischief
Of created things;[6303]

3 From the mischief
Of Darkness as it overspreads;[6304]

4. From the mischief
Of those who practise
Secret Arts[6305]:

5. And from the mischief
Of the envious one
As he practises envy.[6306]

6301. In God's created world, there are all kinds of forces and counter-forces, especially those put in motion by beings who have been endowed with some sort of will. The forces of good may be compared to light, and those of evil to darkness. God can cleave the depths of darkness and produce light (vi. 96), and therefore we should cast off fear and take refuge in divine guidance and goodness.

6302. *Falaq* is the Dawn or Daybreak, the cleaving of darkness and the manifestation of light. This may be understood in various senses: (1) literally, when the darkness of the night is at its worst, rays of light pierce through and produce the dawn; (2) when the darkness of ignorance is at its worst, the light of God pierces through the soul and gives it enlightenment: xxiv. 35; (3) non-existence is darkness, and life and activity may be typified by light. The author and source of all true light is God, and if we seek Him, we are free from ignorance, superstition, fear, and every kind of evil.

6303. See n. 6301 above. Our trust in God is the refuge from every kind of fear and superstition, every kind of danger and evil. Three special kinds of mischief are specified in the next three verses, against which our best guard is our trust in God, the Light of the heavens and the earth. They are: (1) physical dangers, typified by darkness, (2) psychical dangers within us, typified by Secret Arts, and (3) psychical dangers from without us, resulting from a perverted will, which seeks to destroy any good that we enjoy.

6304. The darkness of the night, physical darkness, is a good type of physical dangers and difficulties. Many people are afraid of physical darkness, and all are afraid of physical injuries, accidents, and calamities. We should not fear, but having taken reasonable precautions, trust in God.

6305. *Those who practise Secret Arts*: literally, 'those (feminine) who blow on knots', this having been a favourite form of witchcraft practised by perverted women. Such secret arts cause psychological terror. They may be what is called black magic, or secret plottings, or the display of false and seductive charms (iii. 14), or the spreading of false and secret rumours or slanders to frighten men or deter them from right action. There is fraud in such things, but men are swayed by it. They should cast off fear and do their duty.

6306. Malignant envy, translated into action, seeks to destroy the happiness or the material or spiritual good enjoyed by other people. The best guard against it is trust in God with purity of heart.

INTRODUCTION AND SUMMARY: SŪRA CXIV (*Nās*).

This early Meccan Sūra is a pendant to the last Sūra, and concludes the Holy Qur-ān, with an appeal to us to trust in God, rather than man, as our sure shield and protection. It warns us specially against the secret whispers of evil within our own hearts.

C. 294.—Insidious Evil lies in wait
(cxiv. 1-6.) For man, and loves to whisper and withdraw,
Thus testing his will. But man can make
God his sure shield; for God doth care
For him and cherishes him: God is
The heavenly King who gives him laws:
And God is the Goal to which he will
Return and be judged. Let man but place
Himself in God's hands, and never can Evil
Touch him in his essential and inner life.

Sūra CXIV.

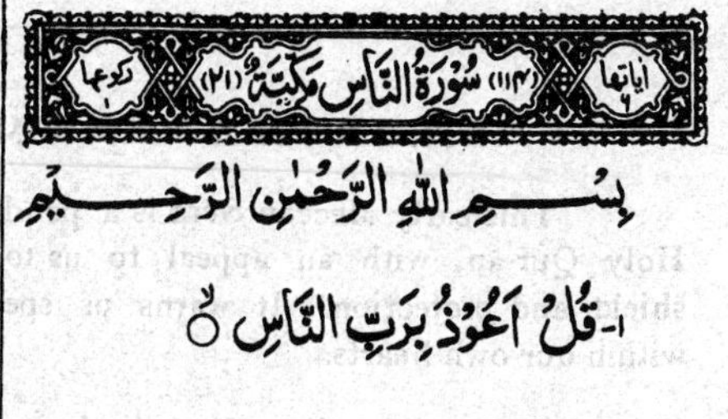

Nās, or Mankind.

In the name of God, Most Gracious, Most Merciful.

بِسْمِ اللّٰهِ الرَّحْمٰنِ الرَّحِيْمِ

1. Say: I seek refuge[6307]
With the Lord
And Cherisher of Mankind,[6308]

١- قُلْ اَعُوْذُ بِرَبِّ النَّاسِ ۙ

2. The King (or Ruler)
Of Mankind,

٢- مَلِكِ النَّاسِ ۙ

3. The God (or Judge)
Of Mankind,—

٣- اِلٰهِ النَّاسِ ۙ

4. From the mischief
Of the Whisperer[6309]
(Of Evil), who withdraws
(After his whisper),—

٤- مِنْ شَرِّ الْوَسْوَاسِ ۙ الْخَنَّاسِ ۙ

5. (The same) who whispers
Into the hearts of Mankind,—

٥- الَّذِيْ يُوَسْوِسُ فِيْ صُدُوْرِ النَّاسِ ۙ

6. Among Jinns
And among Men.[6310]

٦- مِنَ الْجِنَّةِ وَالنَّاسِ ۧ

6307. The previous Sūra pointed to the necessity of seeking God's protection against external factors which might affect an individual. Here the need of protection from internal factors, mankind being viewed as a whole, is pointed out. For this reason the threefold relation in which man stands to God is mentioned, as explained in the next note.

6308. Man's relation to God may be viewed in three aspects : (1) God is his Lord, Maker, and Cherisher ; God sustains him and cares for him ; He provides him with all the means for his growth and development, and for his proteciton against evil ; (2) God is his king or ruler ; more than any earthly king, God has authority to guide man's conduct, and lead him to ways which will make for his welfare ; and He has given him laws ; and (3) God is He to Whom mankind must return, to give an account of all their deeds in this life (ii. 156); God will be the Judge ; He is the goal of the Hereafter, and the only Being entitled to man's worship at any time. From all these aspects man could and should seek God's protection against evil.

6309. Evil insinuates itself in all sorts of insidious ways from within so as to sap man's will, which was given to man by God. This power of evil may be Satan or his host of evil ones, or evil men or the evil inclinations within man's own will : for there are "evil ones among men and Jinns, inspiring each other with flowery discourses by way of deception" (vi. 112). They secretly whisper evil and then withdraw, to make their net the more subtle and alluring.

6310. This last clause amplifies the description of the sources from which the whisper of evil may emanate : they may be men whom you may see or invisible spirits of evil working within. See last note. So long as we put ourselves in God's protection, and trust in God, evil cannot really touch us in our essential and inner life.

CONCLUSION

C. 295.—Thus spake, inspired, our holy Prophet,
Muḥammad, on whom we invoke God's blessings
For ever and ever ;—we who are heirs
To his teaching, his exemplary life,
And the golden thread which he inwove
Into the web of human history.
In pious retreats he prayed ; much thought
He gave to Life's most obstinate tangles ;
'Gainst odds he strove with might and main ;
Wisely he led ; gently he counselled ;
And firmly he subduéd Evil.

C. 296.—Mantle-clad,[6311] he solved the most baffling
Mysteries. His soul would scale
The heights of Heaven, yet showered its love
On the weak and lowly of this earth.
Like a cloud that catches the glory of the Sun,
He threw his protecting shade on all.
The widow's cry, and the orphan's, found
An answer in his heart, as did
The cry of Penury and Need.
He searched out those who felt no need,
Being by pride or ignorance blinded,
And he fulfilled their real wants.
His last great charge summed up the rule
Of spiritual life in linking Faith
With one universal Brotherhood.
Ah ! ne'er shall we see such life again !

C. 297.—But his clarion voice still speaks his message.
His love and wisdom still pour forth
Without stint the inexhaustible Treasures
Of God, for whosoe'er will bring
A purified heart to receive them.
And ne'er did the world, impoverishéd
By its own wayward lusts and greed,
Need those Treasures more than now !

6311. An epithet of mystic meaning, applied to the Prophet in the Qur-ān. See lxxiv. 1, n. 5778. I have in my mind a reminiscence of an Urdu Na't, or Song in praise of the holy Prophet.

C. 398.—There's still with us much sorrow and sin,
Injustice, oppression, wrong, and hate.
Still does Arrogance deaden Conscience,
Rob struggling souls of e'en the crumbs
Of Pity, and make, of loathsome flesh
And crumbling dust, fair-seeming Idols
For worship. Still does Ignorance blow
A mighty Horn and try to shame
True Wisdom. Still do men drive Slaves,—
Protesting smoothly the end of Slavery !
Still does Greed devour the substance
Of helpless ones within her power.
Nay, more,—the fine Individual Voice
Is smothered in the raucous din
Of Groups and Crowds that madly shout
What they call Slogans New,—
Old Falsehoods long discredited

C. 299.—What can we do to make God's Light
Shine forth through the Darkness around us ?
We must first let it shine in our own true Selves
With that Light in the niche of our inmost hearts
We can walk with steps both firm and sure :
We can humbly visit the comfortless
And guide their steps. Not we, but the Light
Will guide ! But oh ! the joy of being found
Worthy to bear the Torch, and to say
To our brethren : "I too was in Darkness,
Comfortless, and behold, I have found
Comfort and Joy in the Grace Divine !"

C. 300.—Thus should we pay the dues of Brotherhood,—
By walking humbly, side by side,
In the Ways of the Lord,
With mutual aid and comfort,
And heartfelt prayer,
Backed by action,
That God's good Purpose
May be accomplished
In us all together !

L'ENVOI.

Cowper wrote : " Oars alone can ne'er prevail To reach the distant coast ; The breath of heaven must swell the sail, Or all the toil is lost." I praise and glorify the name of God that He has enabled His humble servant to complete in manuscript the work of Interpretation at which he has systematically and unceasingly laboured for the last three years. My manuscript was completed in Lahore on the fourth of April 1937, my sixty-fifth birthday according to the solar calendar. My inner history during these three years has been one of joyful and concentrated exploration, undisturbed by the storms that vexed my outer life. I had not imagined that so much human jealousy, misunderstanding, and painful misrepresentation should pursue one who seeks no worldly gain and pretends to no dogmatic authority. But I have been much consoled by numerous appreciative letters from distant readers. I thank them and wish them to feel that they and I are fellow-riders (*Arabice, Zamīl*) on a steed of research in a field that is unlimited in scope and sublime compared to all ordinary knowledge. Such relationship is closer in spirit than ties of blood, or country, or any other joint enterprise whatsoever.

The printer and publisher hope now to bring out the whole completed volumes within two months. I have appended a short Index, which yet is fuller than is to be found in most Quranic Translations. A complete analytical Index, covering the text, notes, and commentary, such as I contemplated in my Preface, will take time to prepare, and will, if there is a demand, be issued as a separate volume at some future time.

And so I take leave of thee, Gentle Reader, and pray for thy spiritual advancement, as I wish thee to pray for mine.

WIMBLEDON :
November 14, 1937

'ABDULLĀH YŪSUF 'ALĪ

INDEX

Abbreviations used in the Index:
App.=Appendix;
C.=Rhythmic Commentary;
Intro.=Introduction to Sūra;
n.=note;
nn.=notes;
p.=page;
pp.=pages;
S.=Sūra.

W9-AIK-024